S0-BNS-509

AP* EDITION

The Earth and Its Peoples

FIFTH EDITION

A Global History

AP* EDITION

The Earth and Its Peoples

FIFTH EDITION

A Global History

Richard W. Bulliet
Columbia University

Pamela Kyle Crossley
Dartmouth College

Daniel R. Headrick
Roosevelt University

Steven W. Hirsch
Tufts University

Lyman L. Johnson
University of North Carolina—Charlotte

David Northrup
Boston College

Australia • Brazil • Japan • Korea • Mexico • Singapore • Spain • United Kingdom • United States

The Earth and Its Peoples, 5e
Richard W. Bulliet, Pamela Kyle Crossley, Daniel R. Headrick, Steven W. Hirsch, Lyman L. Johnson, David Northrup

Senior Publisher: Suzanne Jeans
Senior Acquisitions Editor: Nancy Blaine
Development Manager: Jeff Greene
Senior Development Editor: Tonya Lobato
Assistant Editor: Lauren Floyd
Editorial Assistant: Emma Goehring
Senior Media Editor: Lisa Ciccolo
Senior Marketing Manager: Katherine Bates
Marketing Coordinator: Lorreen Pelletier
Marketing Communications Manager: Christine Dobberpuhl
Senior Content Project Manager: Carol Newman
Senior Art Director: Cate Rickard Barr
Production Technology Analyst: Jeff Joubert
Print Buyer: Karen Hunt
Senior Rights Acquisition Account Manager: Katie Huha
Text Permissions Editor: Maria Maimone
Senior Photo Editor: Jennifer Meyer Dare
Photo Researcher: Carole Frohlich
Production Service: Lachina Publishing Services
Text Designer: Henry Rachlin
Cover Designer: Dutton & Sherman Design
Cover Image: Chinese painting, "Pounding the Clay" by Water-Driven Hammers, ca. 1800/ The Gallery Collection/Corbis
Compositor: Lachina Publishing Services

Vice President, Director of Advanced and Elective Products Program: Alison Zetterquist
Editorial Coordinator, Advanced and Elective Products Program: Jean L. Woy

Library of Congress Control Number: 2009940550

Student Edition:

ISBN-13: 978-1-439-0-8608-7

ISBN-10: 1-439-0-8608-7

Wadsworth
20 Channel Center Street
Boston, MA 02210
USA

Cengage Learning is a leading provider of customized learning solutions with office locations around the globe, including Singapore, the United Kingdom, Australia, Mexico, Brazil, and Japan. Locate your local office at **international.cengage.com/region**

Cengage Learning products are represented in Canada by Nelson Education, Ltd.

For your course and learning solutions, visit **www.cengage.com**

Printed in the United States of America
2 3 4 5 6 7 13 12 11

BRIEF CONTENTS

CONTENTS

MAPS

FEATURES

ENVIRONMENT + TECHNOLOGY

DIVERSITY + DOMINANCE

MATERIAL CULTURE

ISSUES IN WORLD HISTORY

PREFACE

When this textbook reached its fourth edition, the authors felt justified in assessing their work a success. The first edition contained a basic concept. The second used the myriad valuable comments made by teachers and reviewers to make major adjustments in the presentation of that concept. The third edition incorporated a further round of comments and suggestions aimed at filling lacunae and improving the flow of the exposition. In the fourth edition the authors focused on refining their work, updating bibliographies, and incorporating the most recent scholarship. As in each prior edition, expanded features and improved pedagogical aids played important roles in the revision process.

In the fifth edition it is the look and feel of the book that we have rethought in the interest of making the text more inviting and accessible to today's students of World History. The transition from a two-column to a one-column page layout was not easy. It entailed trimming words from the main narrative of the text without sacrificing significant content. Each author approached this task with a sigh, but with a realization that all written works, whether non-fiction or fiction, can benefit from yet one more revision concentrating on fluency and precision of expression. They also recognized that the resulting pages would be not only easier to read, but also graced with ample margins for auxiliary references, glossary definitions, and other pedagogical aids. Adding substantially to the book's new look is a completely redrawn set of maps that are both more vivid and more informative than the maps they replace.

Yet the overall goal of *The Earth and Its Peoples* remains unchanged: a textbook that speaks not only for the past but also to today's student and teacher. Students and teachers alike should take away from this text a broad vision of human societies beginning as sparse and disconnected communities reacting creatively to local circumstances; experiencing ever more intensive stages of contact, interpenetration, and cultural expansion and amalgamation; and arriving at a twenty-first-century world in which people increasingly visualize a single global community.

Process, not progress, is the keynote of this book. Students should come away from this book with a sense that the problems and promises of their world are rooted in a past in which people of every sort, in every part of the world, confronted problems of a similar character and coped with them as best they could. We believe that our efforts will help students see where their world has come from and learn thereby something useful for their own lives.

The primary differences between this AP* version of the fifth edition of *The Earth and Its Peoples* and the version aimed at college classrooms involve accommodating the World History course guidelines issued by The College Board. Since the course design begins with the Neolithic revolution, we have eliminated the substantial portion of the first chapter devoted to earlier phases of human development. This has allowed us to meld Chapter 1 and Chapter 2 of the comprehensive volume into a single, longer first chapter in this AP* version. A similar chronological problem involved The College Board's preference for the year 600 C.E. as the terminal point for the Foundations segments of the course. To accommodate this change from the year 1000 C.E., which we follow in our college version, we have relocated content in Chapters 6-9. However, no significant content has been discarded in this rearrangement.

A new feature has been added to help students practice for the AP* exam. At the end of each chapter they will find a set of multiple-choice questions in AP* format. These questions were written by Colin Ramsay, Lemon Bay High School, Englewood, Florida.

The "Document-Based Questions" section continues from the fourth edition; this appears at the end of the book. Written by Bill Strickland of East Grand Rapids High School, East Grand Rapids, Michigan, the document-based questions (DBQs) found at the end of the text are closely tied to the book's narrative structure. A total of ten DBQs are connected to various chapters of this book and are intended to help students learn how to analyze and assess the reliability of a variety of primary sources, photographs, charts, and maps in order to answer important historical questions.

COLLEGE BOARD AP* COURSE WORLD HISTORY COURSE REDESIGN

The College Board has redesigned the AP*World History course, beginning with the course starting in Fall 2011. The first exam of the redesigned course will be administered in May 2012. The redesign affects the structure of the course and the exam.

Accordingly, this reprint of *The Earth and Its Peoples*, Fifth Edition, incorporates many of the features of the redesigned course. First, the correlation chart (pp. xxx–xxiv) connecting the themes and concepts of the course to the pages of the text has been completely rewritten to reflect the new course design. The AP*-format multiple-choice questions found at the ends of the chapters now have four rather than five answer options. Some of the AP* Tips have been rewritten to conform to the new course structure. And finally, each of the end-of-chapter multiple-choice questions is classified according to the new periods, themes, and concepts of the course. This classification is posted on the teacher's website.

CENTRAL THEMES AND GOALS

We subtitled *The Earth and Its Peoples* "A Global History" because the book explores the common challenges and experiences that unite the human past. Although the dispersal of early humans to every livable environment resulted in a myriad of different economic, social, political, and cultural systems, all societies displayed analogous patterns in meeting their needs and exploiting their environments. Our challenge was to select the particular data and episodes that would best illuminate these global patterns of human experience.

To meet this challenge, we adopted two themes for our history: "technology and the environment" and "diversity and dominance." The first theme represents the commonplace material bases of all human societies at all times. It grants no special favor to any cultural group even as it embraces subjects of the broadest topical, chronological, and geographical range. The second theme expresses the reality that every human society has constructed or inherited structures of domination. We examine practices and institutions of many sorts: military, economic, social, political, religious, and cultural, as well as those based on kinship, gender, and literacy. Simultaneously we recognize that alternative ways of life and visions of societal organization continually manifest themselves both within and in dialogue with every structure of domination.

With respect to the first theme, it is vital for students to understand that technology, in the broad sense of experience-based knowledge of the physical world, underlies all human activity. Writing is a technology, but so is oral transmission from generation to generation of lore about medicinal or poisonous plants. The magnetic compass is a navigational technology, but so is Polynesian mariners' hard-won knowledge of winds, currents, and tides that made possible the settlement of the Pacific islands.

All technological development has come about in interaction with environments, both physical and human, and has, in turn, affected those environments. The story of how humanity has changed the face of the globe is an integral part of our first theme. Yet technology and the environment do not explain or underlie all important episodes of human experience. The theme of "diversity and dominance" informs all our discussions of politics, culture, and society. Thus when narrating the histories of empires, we describe a range of human experiences within and beyond the imperial frontiers without assuming that imperial institutions are a more fit topic for discussion than the economic and social organization of pastoral nomads or the lives of peasant women. When religion and culture occupy our narrative, we focus not only on the dominant tradition but also on the diversity of alternative beliefs and practices.

ORGANIZATION

The Earth and Its Peoples uses eight broad chronological divisions to define its conceptual scheme of global historical development.

In **Part One: The Emergence of Human Communities, to 500 B.C.E.,** we examine important patterns of human communal organization in both the Eastern and Western Hemispheres. Small, dispersed human communities living by foraging spread to most parts of the world over domestic animals. On the basis of these new modes of sustenance, population grew, permanent towns appeared, and political and religious authority, based on collection and control of agricultural surpluses, spread over extensive areas.

Part Two: The Formation of New Cultural Communities, 1000 B.C.E.–600 C.E., introduces the concept of a "cultural community," in the sense of a coherent pattern of activities and symbols pertaining to a specific human community. While all human communities develop distinctive cultures, including those discussed in Part One, historical development in this stage of global history prolonged and magnified the impact of some cultures more than others. In the geographically contiguous African-Eurasian landmass, the cultures that proved to have the most enduring influence traced their roots to the second and first millennia B.C.E.

Part Three: Growth and Interaction of Cultural Communities, 600–1200, deals with early episodes of technological, social, and cultural exchange and interaction on a continental scale both within and beyond the framework of imperial expansion. These are so different from earlier interactions arising from more limited conquests or extensions of political boundaries that they constitute a distinct era in world history, an era that set the world on the path of increasing global interaction and interdependence that it has been following ever since.

In **Part Four: Interregional Patterns of Culture and Contact, 1200–1550,** we look at the world during the three and a half centuries that saw both intensified cultural and commercial contact and increasingly confident self-definition of cultural communities in Europe, Asia, and Africa. The Mongol conquest of a vast empire extending from the Pacific Ocean to eastern Europe greatly stimulated trade and interaction. In the West, strengthened European kingdoms began maritime expansion in the Atlantic, forging direct ties with sub-Saharan Africa and beginning the conquest of the civilizations of the Western Hemisphere.

Part Five: The Globe Encompassed, 1500–1750, treats a period dominated by the global effects of European expansion and continued economic growth. European ships took over, expanded, and extended the maritime trade of the Indian Ocean, coastal Africa, and the Asian rim of the Pacific Ocean. This maritime commercial enterprise had its counterpart in European colonial empires in the Americas and a new Atlantic trading system. The contrasting capacities and fortunes of traditional land empires and new maritime empires, along with the exchange of domestic plants and animals between the hemispheres, underline the technological and environmental dimensions of this first era of complete global interaction.

In **Part Six: Revolutions Reshape the World, 1750–1870,** the word *revolution* is used in several senses: in the political sense of governmental overthrow, as in France and the Americas; in the metaphorical sense of radical transformative change, as in the Industrial Revolution; and in the broadest sense of a perception of a profound change in circumstances and world-view. Technology and environment lie at the core of these developments. With the rapid ascendancy of the Western belief that science and technology could overcome all challenges—environmental or otherwise—technology became an instrument not only of transformation but also of domination, to the point of threatening the integrity and autonomy of cultural traditions in nonindustrial lands.

Part Seven: Global Diversity and Dominance, 1850–1945, examines the development of a world arena in which people conceived of events on a global scale. Imperialism, world war, international economic connections, and world-encompassing ideological tendencies, such as nationalism and socialism, present the picture of a globe becoming increasingly interconnected. European dominance took on a worldwide dimension, seeming at times to threaten the diversity of human cultural experience with permanent subordination to European values and philosophies, while at other times triggering strong political or cultural resistance.

For **Part Eight: Perils and Promises of a Global Community, 1945 to the Present,** we divided the period since World War II into three time periods: 1945–1975, 1975–1991, and 1991 to the present. The challenges of the Cold War and postcolonial nation building dominated most of the period and unleashed global economic, technological, and political forces that became increasingly important in all aspects of human life. Technology is a key topic in Part Eight because of its integral role in the growth of a global community and because its many benefits in improving the quality of life seem clouded by real and potential negative impacts on the environment. Also highlighted are the harsh realities of war and economic disruption that have marked the first decade of the twenty-first century.

FEATURES AND NEW AP* PEDAGOGICAL AIDS

As with previous editions, the fifth edition offers a number of valuable features and pedagogical aids designed to pique student interest in specific World History topics and help them process and retain key information. Historical essays for each of the eight parts called *Issues in World History* were added in the previous edition and were specifically designed to alert students to broad and recurring conceptual issues that are of great interest to contemporary historians; this feature has proved to be an teacher and student favorite. Four in-chapter essays on *Material Culture,* also new in the previous edition, call particular attention to the many ways in which objects and processes of everyday life can play a role in understanding human history on a broad scale. Thus essays like "Wine and Beer in the Ancient World" and "Fast Food" are not only interesting in and of themselves but also suggestive of how today's world historians find meaning in the ordinary dimensions of human life. The *Environment and Technology* feature, which has been a valuable resource in all prior editions of *The Earth and its Peoples,* serves to illuminate the major theme of the text by demonstrating the shared material bases of all human societies across time. Finally, *Diversity and Dominance,* also core to the theme of the text, is the primary source feature that brings a myriad of real historical voices to life in a common struggle for power and autonomy.

Pedagogical aids include the following:

New AP* Tips In the margins of each chapter, AP* test-taking tips offer candid advice to students about information that commonly appears on the exam.

New AP* Review Questions At the end of each chapter, AP* review questions, formatted like the questions that appear on the real exam, offer additional practice for students and a useful means of evaluation for teachers.

Chapter Opening Focus Questions These questions are keyed to every major subdivision of the chapter and serve to help students focus on the core chapter concepts.

New Section Reviews Short bullet-point reviews have been added in this edition to summarize each major section in every chapter and remind students of key information.

New Chapter Conclusions Every chapter now ends with a comparative conclusion that replaces the old summaries and helps students better synthesize chapter material and understand how it fits into the larger picture.

New Section Headings Additional section headings have been added in every chapter to help organize the material into smaller digestible units and to help students and teachers locate key parts of the discussion.

New Marginal Key Term with Definitions Students will no longer have to flip to the back of the textbook to look up unfamiliar terms.

New eBook and Web Resource Boxes A complete list of website and eBook assets is provided at the end of every chapter.

CHANGES IN THIS EDITION

In addition to the many new pedagogical aids outlined above, numerous minor chapter-by-chapter changes have been made, including new illustrations, new maps, streamlining of the textual discussion, and updates to many of the boxed feature essays. Here are a few highlights:

- An expanded discussion of external influences on early Southeast Asian civilizations appears in Chapter 6.
- Chapter 9 updates include a revised discussion of the beleaguered Byzantine Empire and factors that contributed to its demise, including Arab invasions and religious schisms
- A new section heading in Chapter 9 called "The Time of Insecurity" discusses Muslim invasions and the rise of the Carolingian Empire in Medieval Europe.
- A revised discussion of Social Rebellion after the Black Death now appears in Chapter 14.
- A new heading in Chapter 16 "The Counter Reformation and the Politics of Religion" includes a discussion of religion and the ambition of kings.
- The introduction to Chapter 21 has been revised.

- Chapter 31 includes an updated discussion about the Cold War confrontation between West and East plus a revised discussion of apartheid and South Africa's struggle for independence
- The Environment and Technology feature in Chapter 32 has been thoroughly updated to include discussion and pictures of the latest technology.
- Chapter 33 features new material on the 2008 U.S. presidential election and the economic crisis. In addition, a new Diversity and Dominance feature called "Conflict and Civilization" now appears in this chapter.

ANCILLARIES

A wide array of supplements accompany this text to assist students with different learning needs and to help teachers master today's various classroom challenges.

Teacher Resources

*Teacher's Resource Guide for the Advanced Placement Program** Prepared by Sheila Phipps of Appalachian State University, Monty Armstrong of Cerritos High School in Cerritos, California, and Patrick Whelan of St. Stephen's Episcopal School in Bradenton, Florida. Based on the college Instructor's Manual, this manual is designed to help teachers make optimal use of *The Earth and Its Peoples* in preparing for the AP* exam, and includes a description of the exam, advice about how to prepare students, AP focus sections, instructional objectives, chapter outlines, lecture suggestions, suggested debate and research topics, cooperative learning activities, and suggested online resources.

PowerLecture CD-ROM with ExamView® and JoinIn® This dual platform, all-in-one multimedia resource includes the Instructor's Resource Manual; Test Bank (content developed by Kathleen Addison of California State University, Northridge, and includes key term identification, multiple-choice, short answer/essay, and map questions); Microsoft® PowerPoint® slides of both lecture outlines and images and maps from the text that can be used as offered, or customized by importing personal lecture slides or other material; and JoinIn® PowerPoint® slides with clicker content. Also included is ExamView, an easy-to-use assessment and tutorial system that allows teachers to create, deliver, and customize tests in minutes. Teachers can build tests with as many as 250 questions using up to 12 question types, and using ExamView's complete word-processing capabilities, they can enter an unlimited number of new questions or edit existing ones.

HistoryFinder This searchable online database allows teachers to quickly and easily download thousands of assets, including art, photographs, maps, primary sources, and audio/video clips. Each asset downloads directly into a Microsoft® PowerPoint® slide, allowing teachers to easily create PowerPoint presentations for their classrooms.

WebTutor™ on Blackboard® With WebTutor's text-specific, pre-formatted content and total flexibility, teachers can easily create and manage their own custom course website. WebTutor's course management tool gives teachers the ability to provide virtual office hours, post syllabi, set up threaded discussions, track student progress with the quizzing material, and much more. For students, WebTutor offers real-time access to a full array of study tools, including animations and videos that bring the book's topics to life, plus chapter outlines, summaries, learning objectives, glossary flashcards (with audio), practice quizzes, and weblinks. Ask your sales representative about available discounts.

WebTutor™ on WebCT® With WebTutor's text-specific, pre-formatted content and total flexibility, teachers can easily create and manage their own custom course website. WebTutor's course management tool gives teachers the ability to provide virtual office hours, post syllabi, set up threaded discussions, track student progress with the quizzing material, and much more. For students, WebTutor offers real-time access to a full array of study tools, including animations and videos that bring the book's topics to life, plus chapter outlines, summaries, learning objectives, glossary flashcards (with audio), practice quizzes, and weblinks.

WebTutor™ on Angel® With WebTutor's text-specific, pre-formatted content and total flexibility, teachers can easily create and manage their own custom course website. WebTutor's course management tool gives teachers the ability to provide virtual office hours, post syllabi, set up threaded discussions, track student progress with the quizzing material, and much more. For students, WebTutor offers real-time access to a full array of study tools, including animations and videos that bring the book's topics to life, plus chapter outlines, summaries, learning objectives, glossary flashcards (with audio), practice quizzes, and weblinks.

Student Resources

*Fast Track to a 5: Preparing for the AP**World History Examination.* This test-prep manual, written by Ty Healy, Walter Johnson High School, Bethesda, Maryland; Patrick Whelan, St Stephens Episcopal School, Bradenton, Florida; and Barbara Ozuna, Paschal High School, Fort Worth, Texas, includes an introduction for students on taking the AP* Exam, a diagnostic test to help students assess their level of preparedness, review chapters following the AP*topic list, with multiple-choice and free-response questions for each chapter, and two complete practice tests. *Fast Track to a 5* may be purchased either with the text or separately.

Book Companion Site A website for students that features a wide assortment of resources to help students master the subject matter. The website includes a glossary, flashcards, crossword puzzles, learning objectives, pre-class quizzes, essay questions, critical thinking exercises, and weblinks. Throughout the text, icons direct students to relevant exercises and self-testing material located on the student companion website.

CL eBook This interactive multimedia ebook links out to rich media assets such as video and MP3 chapter summaries. Through this ebook, students can also access self-test quizzes, chapter outlines, focus questions, fill-in-the-blank exercises, chronology puzzles, essay questions (for which the answers can be emailed to their teachers), primary source documents with critical thinking questions, and interactive (zoomable) maps. Ask your sales representative about available discounts.

*AP*Student Study Guide* Written by Bill Strickland of East Grand Rapids High School, East Grand Rapids, Michigan, and thoroughly revised by Angela Lee of Weston High School, Weston, Massachusetts, this guide contains learning objectives, key-term identifications, multiple-choice questions, short-answer and essay questions, and map exercises. The Study Guide is published in two volumes; Volume I contains Chapters 1-15; Volume II, Chapters 16-33. Ask your sales representative about available discounts.

Wadsworth World History Resource Center Wadsworth's World History Resource Center gives your students access to a "virtual reader" with hundreds of primary sources including speeches, letters, legal documents and transcripts, poems, maps, simulations, timelines, and additional images that bring history to life, along with interactive assignable exercises. A map feature including Google Earth™ coordinates and exercises will aid in student comprehension of geography and use of maps. Students can compare the traditional textbook map with an aerial view of the location today. Ask your sales representative about available discounts.

The History Handbook, 1e Prepared by Carol Berkin of Baruch College, City University of New York and Betty Anderson of Boston University. This book teaches students both basic and history-specific study skills such as how to read primary sources, research historical topics, and correctly cite sources. Substantially less expensive than comparable skill-building texts, *The History Handbook* also offers tips for Internet research and evaluating online sources.

Doing History: Research and Writing in the Digital Age, 1e Prepared by Michael J. Galgano, J. Chris Arndt, and Raymond M. Hyser of James Madison University. Whether you're starting down the path as a history major, or simply looking for a straightforward and systematic guide to writing a successful paper, you'll find this text to be an indispensible handbook to historical research. This text's "soup to nuts" approach to researching and writing about history addresses every step of the process, from locating your sources and gathering information, to writing clearly and making proper use of various citation styles to avoid plagiarism.

The Modern Researcher, 6e Prepared by Jacques Barzun and Henry F. Graff of Columbia University. This classic introduction to the techniques of research and the art of expression is used widely in history courses, but is also appropriate for writing and research methods courses in other departments. Barzun and Graff thoroughly cover every aspect of research, from the selection of a topic through the gathering, analysis, writing, revision, and publication of findings presenting the process not as a set of rules but through actual cases that put the subtleties of research in a useful context. Ask your sales representative about available discounts.

Reader Program Cengage Learning publishes a number of readers, some containing exclusively primary sources, others a combination of primary and secondary sources, and some designed to guide students through the process of historical inquiry. Visit Cengage.com/history for a complete list of readers.

Rand McNally Historical Atlas of the World, 1e This valuable resource features over 70 maps that portray the rich panoply of the world's history from preliterate times to the present. They show how cultures and civilization were linked and how they interacted. The maps show change by presenting the dynamics of expansion, cooperation, and conflict. This atlas includes maps that display the world from the beginning of civilization; the political development of all major areas of the world; expanded coverage of Africa, Latin America, and the Middle East; the current Islamic World; and the world population change in 1900 and 2000.

Document Exercise Workbook Prepared by Donna Van Raaphorst, Cuyahoga Community College. A collection of exercises based around primary sources. Available in two volumes.

ACKNOWLEDGMENTS

In preparing the fifth edition, we benefited from the critical readings of many colleagues. Our sincere thanks go in particular to the following instructors and teachers: Susan Autry, Central Piedmont Community College; Anna Collins, Arkansas Tech University; William Connell, Christopher Newport University; Gregory Crider, Winthrop University; Shawn Dry, Oakland Community College; Nancy Fitch, California State University, Fullerton; Christine Haynes, University of North Carolina at Charlotte; Mark Herman, Edison College; Bram Hubbell, Friends Seminary; Ellen J. Jenkins, Arkansas Tech University; Frank Karpiel, The Citadel; Ken Koons, Virginia Military Institute; David Longfellow, Baylor University; Heather Lucas, Georgia Perimeter College; John Maunu, Grosse Ile High School; Jeff Pardue, Gainesville State College; Craig Patton, Alabama A & M University; Paul Philp, John Paul II High School; Linda Scherr, Mercer County Community College; Robert Sherwood, Georgia Military College; Brett Shufelt, Copiah-Lincoln Community College; Kristen Walton, Salisbury University; Christopher Ward, Clayton State University; Kurt Waters, Centreville High School; William Wood, Point Loma Nazarene University.

Special thanks to Colin Ramsay of Lemon Bay High School in Englewood, Florida, who prepared the AP* Tips and the AP* Review Questions at the end of each chapter. Our thanks also go to Patrick Whelan, St. Stephen's Episcopal School, Bradenton, Florida, for his work updating the text for the redesigned world history course.

When textbook authors set out on a project, they are inclined to believe that 90 percent of the effort will be theirs and 10 percent that of various editors and production specialists employed by their publisher. How very naïve. This book would never have seen the light of day had it not been for the unstinting labors of the great team of professionals who turned the authors' words into beautifully presented print. Our debt to the staff of Wadsworth, Cengage Learning remains undiminished in the fifth edition. Nancy Blaine, Senior Sponsoring Editor, has offered us firm but sympathetic guidance throughout the revision process. Tonya Lobato offered astute and sympathetic assistance as the authors worked to incorporate many new ideas and subjects into the text. Carol Newman, Senior Project Editor, moved the work through the production stages to meet a challenging schedule. Carole Frohlich did an outstanding job of photo research. And Susan Zorn again lent her considerable copyediting skills to the text.

We thank also the many students whose questions and concerns, expressed directly or through their instructors and teachers, shaped much of this revision. We continue to welcome all readers' suggestions, queries, and criticisms. Please contact us at our respective institutions.

CORRELATION OF AP* WORLD HISTORY COURSE AND *THE EARTH AND ITS PEOPLES*, FIFTH EDITION

Topic	**Pages**
Period 1: Technological and Environmental Transformations, to c. 600 B.C.E.	
• **Key Concept 1.1. Big Geography and the Peopling of the Earth**	
I. Archeological evidence indicates that during the Paleolithic era, hunting-foraging bands of humans gradually migrated from their origin in East Africa to Eurasia, Australia, and the Americas, adapting their technology and cultures to new climate regions.	6-8
• **Key Concept 1.2. The Neolithic Revolution and Early Agricultural Societies**	
I. Beginning about 10,000 years ago, the Neolithic Revolution led to the development of new and more complex economic and social systems.	5, 9-12
II. Agriculture and pastoralism began to transform human societies.	12-16, 102-103
• **Key Concept 1.3. The Development and Interactions of Early Agricultural, Pastoral, and Urban Societies**	
I. Core and foundational civilizations developed in a variety of geographical and environmental settings where agriculture flourished.	16-17, 24-26, 31, 40-41, 58-63
II. The first states emerged within core civilizations.	17-20, 26-28, 31-33, 41-43, 51-54, 70-76
III. Culture played a significant role in unifying states through laws, language, literature, religion, myths, and monumental art.	20-24, 27-333, 42, 52-54, 84-86, 112-116
Period 2: Organization and Reorganization of Human Societies, c. 600 B.C.E. to 600 C.E.	
• **Key Concept 2.1. The Development and Codification of Religious and Cultural Traditions**	
I. Codifications and further developments of existing religious traditions provided a bond among the people and an ethical code to live by.	84-90, 119-120, 175-182
II. New belief systems and cultural traditions emerged and spread, often asserting universal truths.	47-50, 120-122, 152-153, 178-180, 183-184
III. Belief systems affected gender roles (such as Buddhism's encouragement of a monastic life or Confucianism's emphasis on filial piety).	164-179, 187-190
IV. Other religious and cultural traditions continued parallel to the codified, written belief systems in core civilizations.	145, 164, 167, 192
V. Artistic expressions, including literature and drama, architecture, and sculpture, show distinctive cultural developments.	121-122, 198-199, 218

Topic	Pages
• **Key Concept 2.2. The Development of States and Empires**	
I. The number and size of imperial societies grew dramatically by imposing political unity on areas where previously there had been competing states.	90-94, 108-111, 145-147, 157-162, 182-187, 325-326
II. Empires and states developed new techniques of imperial administration based, in part, on the success of earlier political forms.	111-112
III. Imperial societies displayed unique social and economic dimensions.	117-118, 126-127, 130-135, 142-152, 162-163, 187-190
IV. The Roman, Han, Maurya and Gupta empires created political, cultural, and administrative difficulties that they could not manage, which eventually led to their decline, collapse, and transformation into successor empires or states.	155-156, 164-165, 190
• **Key Concept 2.3. Emergence of Transregional Networks of Communication and Exchange**	
I. Land and water routes created transregional trade, communication, and exchange networks in the Eastern Hemisphere, while separate networks connected the peoples and societies of the Americas somewhat later.	201-212
II. New technologies facilitated long-distance communication and exchange.	206-207, 214
III. Alongside the trade in goods, the exchange of people, technology, religious and cultural beliefs, food crops, domesticated animals, and disease pathogens developed across far-flung networks of communication and exchange.	192-194, 204-206, 218-219
Period 3: Regional and Transregional Interactions, c. 600 C.E. to c. 1450	
• **Key Concept 3.1. Expansion and Intensification of Communication and Exchange Networks**	
I. Improved transportation technologies and commercial practices led to an increased volume of trade, and expanded the geographical range of existing and newly active trade networks.	214, 273-274, 323, 348, 357-358, 385-392, 404, 430-432
II. The movement of peoples caused environmental and linguistic effects.	228, 240, 259, 387-388, 428-430
III. Cross-cultural exchanges were fostered by the intensification of existing, or the creation of new, networks of trade and communication.	223, 287-288, 293-294, 348, 352-353, 380-381, 389
IV. There was continued diffusion of crops and pathogens throughout the Eastern Hemisphere along the trade routes.	302, 348, 401-402
• **Key Concept 3.2. Continuity and Innovation of State Forms and Their Interactions**	
I. Empires collapsed and were reconstituted; in some regions new state forms emerged.	232-239, 244, 254-256, 284-291, 299-301, 316-319, 328-331, 382-385
II. Interregional contacts and conflicts between states and empires encouraged significant technological and cultural transfers, for example between Tang China and the Abbasids, across the Mongol empires, and during the Crusades.	238-239, 286-287, 348

Topic	Pages
• **Key Concept 3.3. Increased Economic Productive Capacity and Its Consequences**	
I. Innovations stimulated agricultural and industrial production in many regions.	296, 361-362, 401, 551-552
II. The fate of cities varied greatly, with periods of significant decline, and with periods of increased urbanization buoyed by rising productivity and expanding trade networks.	348, 401-407, 470-471, 596
III. Despite significant continuities in social structures and in methods of production, there were also some important changes in labor management and in the effect of religious conversion on gender relations and family life.	241-244, 277, 296-297, 342, 392-393
Period 4: Global Interactions, c. 1450 to c. 1750	
• **Key Concept 4.1. Globalizing Networks of Communication and Exchange**	
I. In the context of the new global circulation of goods, there was an intensification of all existing regional trade networks that brought prosperity and economic disruption to the merchants and governments in the trading regions of the Indian Ocean, Mediterranean, Sahara, and overland Eurasia.	430-432, 442-445
II. European technological developments in cartography and navigation built on previous knowledge developed in the classical, Islamic, and Asian worlds, and included the production of new tools (such as the astrolabe or revised maps), innovations in ship designs (such as caravels), and an improved understanding of global wind and currents patterns—all of which made transoceanic travel and trade possible.	434-435
III. Remarkable new transoceanic maritime reconnaissance occurred in this period.	359-361, 430-439, 564-567
IV. The new global circulation of goods was facilitated by royal chartered European monopoly companies that took silver from Spanish colonies in the Americas to purchase Asian goods for the Atlantic markets, but regional markets continued to flourish in Afro-Eurasia by using established commercial practices and new transoceanic shipping services developed by European merchants.	468-470, 481-482, 520, 529-534, 563, 579-580
V. The new connections between the Eastern and Western hemispheres resulted in the Columbian Exchange.	490-492
VI. The increase in interactions between newly connected hemispheres and intensification of connections within hemispheres expanded the spread and reform of existing religions and created syncretic belief systems and practices.	460-463
VII. As merchants' profits increased and governments collected more taxes, funding for the visual and performing arts, even for popular audiences, increased.	378-379, 415-417, 459
• **Key Concept 4.2. New Forms of Social Organization and Modes of Production**	
I. Traditional peasant agriculture increased and changed, plantations expanded, and demand for labor increased. These changes both fed and responded to growing global demand for raw materials and finished products.	496-499, 504-506, 521-529, 538-539, 587-588

Topic	Pages
II. As new social and political elites changed, they also restructured new ethnic, racial, and gender hierarchies.	499-504, 578-579
• **Key Concept 4.3. State Consolidation and Imperial Expansion**	
I. Rulers used a variety of methods to legitimize and consolidate their power.	473-481, 537-538, 554
II. Imperial expansion relied on the increased use of gunpowder, cannons, and armed trade to establish large empires in both hemispheres.	504-513, 548-563, 572, 581-582
III. Competition over trade routes (such as Omani-European rivalry in the Indian Ocean or piracy in the Caribbean), state rivalries (such as the Thirty Years War or the Ottoman-Safavid conflict), and local resistance (such as bread riots) all provided significant challenges to state consolidation and expansion.	560, 564-565
Period 5: Industrialization and Global Interaction, c. 1750 to c. 1900	
• **Key Concept 5.1. Industrialization and Global Capitalism**	
I. Industrialization fundamentally changed how goods were produced.	630-640, 744-746
II. New patterns of global trade and production developed that further integrated the global economy as industrialists sought raw materials and new markets for the increasing amount of goods produced in their factories.	676-680, 704-708, 791-794
III. To facilitate investments at all levels of industrial production, financiers developed and expanded various financial institutions.	646-647, 747
IV. There were major developments in transportation and communication, including railroads, steamships, telegraphs, and canals.	638-640
V. The development and spread of global capitalism led to a variety of responses.	646-650, 688-692, 715-717
VI. The ways in which people organized themselves into societies also underwent significant transformations in industrialized states due to the fundamental restructuring of the global economy.	640-646
• **Key Concept 5.2. Imperialism and Nation-State Formation**	
I. Industrializing powers established transoceanic empires.	699-701, 704-708, 711-734, 764-766, 772-791
II. Imperialism influenced state formation and contraction around the world.	697-698, 743, 756, 761, 788-789
III. New racial ideologies, especially Social Darwinism, facilitated and justified imperialism.	761-762, 773-774
• **Key Concept 5.3. Nationalism, Revolution, and Reform**	
I. The rise and diffusion of Enlightenment thought that questioned established traditions in all areas of life often preceded the revolutions and rebellions against existing governments.	467, 602-606, 670-672
II. Beginning in the 18th century, peoples around the world developed a new sense of commonality based on language, religion, social customs, and territory. These newly imagined national communities linked this identity with the borders of the state, while governments used this idea to unite diverse populations.	622-623, 756-758

Topic	Pages
III. The spread of Enlightenment ideas and increasing discontent with imperial rule propelled reformist and revolutionary movements.	601, 606-621, 656-661, 694-696, 701-705, 764-766
IV. The global spread of Enlightenment thought and the increasing number of rebellions stimulated new transnational ideologies and solidarities.	622-623, 675-676, 750-755
• **Key Concept 5.4. Global Migration**	
I. Migration in many cases was influenced by changes in demography in both industrialized and unindustrialized societies that presented challenges to existing patterns of living.	672-675, 747-750
II. Migrants relocated for a variety of reasons.	672-675, 747-750
III. The large-scale nature of migration, especially in the 19th century, produced a variety of consequences and reactions to the increasingly diverse societies on the part of migrants and the existing populations.	672-675
Period 6: Accelerating Global Change and Realignments, c. 1900 to the Present	
• **Key Concept 6.1. Science and the Environment**	
I. Researchers made rapid advances in science that spread throughout the world, assisted by the development of new technology.	821-825, 935-936
II. Humans fundamentally changed their relationship with the environment.	822-825, 853-854, 926-941
III. Disease, scientific innovations, and conflict led to demographic shifts.	821-822, 850-852, 928
• **Key Concept 6.2. Global Conflicts and Their Consequences**	
I. Europe dominated the global political order at the beginning of the 20th century, but both land-based and transoceanic empires gave way to new forms of transregional political organization by the century's end.	858-870, 896-904
II. Emerging ideologies of anti-imperialism contributed to the dissolution of empires.	862-870, 916-919
III. Political changes were accompanied by major demographic and social consequences.	815-820, 852, 926
IV. Military conflicts occurred on an unprecedented global scale.	797-814, 838-850, 870-874, 886-896, 914-919, 924-926
V. Although conflict dominated much of the 20th century, many individuals and groups—including states—opposed this trend. Some individuals and groups, however, intensified the conflicts.	862-863, 904-905, 947-948, 954-961
• **Key Concept 6.3. New Conceptualizations of Global Economy, Society, and Culture**	
I. States, communities, and individuals became increasingly interdependent, a process facilitated by the growth of institutions of global governance.	808-811, 888-892, 909-910, 948-954
II. People conceptualized society and culture in new ways; some challenged old assumptions about race, class, gender, and religion, often using new technologies to spread reconfigured traditions.	820-821, 961-964
III. Popular and consumer culture became global.	964-967

ABOUT THE AUTHORS

RICHARD W. BULLIET Professor of Middle Eastern History at Columbia University, Richard W. Bulliet received his Ph.D. from Harvard University. He has written scholarly works on a number of topics: the social and economic history of medieval Iran *(The Patricians of Nishapur* and *Cotton, Climate, and Camels in Early Islamic Iran),* the history of human-animal relations *(The Camel and the Wheel* and *Hunters, Herders, and Hamburgers),* the process of conversion to Islam *(Conversion to Islam in the Medieval Period),* and the overall course of Islamic social history *(Islam: The View from the Edge* and *The Case for Islamo-Christian Civilization).* He is the editor of the *Columbia History of the Twentieth Century.* He has published four novels, coedited *The Encyclopedia of the Modern Middle East,* and hosted an educational television series on the Middle East. He was awarded a fellowship by the John Simon Guggenheim Memorial Foundation and was named a Carnegie Corporation Scholar.

PAMELA KYLE CROSSLEY Pamela Kyle Crossley received her Ph.D. in Modern Chinese History from Yale University. She is Professor of History and Rosenwald Research Professor in the Arts and Sciences at Dartmouth College. Her books include *A Translucent Mirror: History and Identity in Qing Imperial Ideology; The Manchus; Orphan Warriors: Three Manchu Generations and the End of the Qing World;* and (with Lynn Hollen Lees and John W. Servos) *Global Society: The World Since 1900.* Her research, which concentrates on the cultural history of China, Inner Asia, and Central Asia, has been supported by the John Simon Guggenheim Memorial Foundation and the National Endowment for the Humanities.

DANIEL R. HEADRICK Daniel R. Headrick received his Ph.D. in History from Princeton University. Professor of History and Social Science, Emeritus, at Roosevelt University in Chicago, he is the author of several books on the history of technology, imperialism, and international relations, including *The Tools of Empire: Technology and European Imperialism in the Nineteenth Century; The Tentacles of Progress: Technology Transfer in the Age of Imperialism; The Invisible Weapon: Telecommunications and International Politics; Technology: A World History, Power Over Peoples: Technology, Environments and Western Imperialism, 1400 to the Present,* and *When Information Came of Age: Technologies of Knowledge in the Age of Reason and Revolution, 1700–1850.* His articles have appeared in the *Journal of World History* and the *Journal of Modern History,* and he has been awarded fellowships by the National Endowment for the Humanities, the John Simon Guggenheim Memorial Foundation, and the Alfred P. Sloan Foundation.

STEVEN W. HIRSCH Steven W. Hirsch holds a Ph.D. in Classics from Stanford University and is currently Associate Professor of Classics and History at Tufts University. He has received grants from the National Endowment for the Humanities and the Massachusetts Foundation for Humanities and Public Policy. His research and publications include *The Friendship of the Barbarians: Xenophon and the Persian Empire,* as well as articles and reviews in the *Classical Journal,* the *American Journal of Philology,* and the *Journal of Interdisciplinary History.* He is currently working on a comparative study of ancient Mediterranean and Chinese civilizations.

LYMAN L. JOHNSON Professor of History at the University of North Carolina at Charlotte, Lyman L. Johnson earned his Ph.D. in Latin American History from the University of Connecticut. A two-time Senior Fulbright-Hays Lecturer, he also has received fellowships from the Tinker Foundation, the Social Science Research Council, the National Endowment for the Humanities, and the American Philosophical Society. His recent books include *Death, Dismemberment, and Memory; The Faces of Honor*(with Sonya Lipsett-Rivera); *The Problem of Order in Changing Societies; Essays on the Price History of Eighteenth-Century Latin America*(with Enrique Tandeter); and *Colonial Latin America*(with Mark A. Burkholder). He also has published in journals, including the *Hispanic American Historical Review,* the *Journal of Latin American Studies,* the *International Review of Social History, Social History,* and *Desarrollo Económico.* He recently served as president of the Conference on Latin American History.

DAVID NORTHRUP Professor of History at Boston College, David Northrup earned his Ph.D. in African and European History from the University of California at Los Angeles. He earlier taught in Nigeria with the Peace Corps and at Tuskegee Institute. Research supported by the Fulbright-Hays Commission, the National Endowment for the Humanities, and the Social Science Research Council led to publications concerning pre-colonial Nigeria, the Congo (1870–1940), the Atlantic slave trade, and Asian, African, and Pacific islander indentured labor in the nineteenth century. A contributor to the *Oxford History of the British Empire* and *Blacks in the British Empire,* his latest book is *Africa's Discovery of Europe, 1450–1850.* In 2004 and 2005 he served as president of the World History Association.

NOTE ON SPELLING AND USAGE

Where necessary for clarity, dates are followed by the letters C.E. or B.C.E. The abbreviation C.E. stands for "Common Era" and is equivalent to A.D. (*anno Domini,* Latin for "in the year of the Lord"). The abbreviation B.C.E. stands for "before the Common Era" and means the same as B.C. ("before Christ"). In keeping with our goal of approaching world history without special concentration on one culture or another, we chose these neutral abbreviations as appropriate to our enterprise. Because many readers will be more familiar with English than with metric measurements, however, units of measure are generally given in the English system, with metric equivalents following in parentheses.

In general, Chinese has been Romanized according to the *pinyin* method. Exceptions include proper names well established in English (e.g., *Canton, Chiang Kaishek*) and a few English words borrowed from Chinese (e.g., *kowtow*). Spellings of Arabic, Ottoman Turkish, Persian, Mongolian, Manchu, Japanese, and Korean names and terms avoid special diacritical marks for letters that are pronounced only slightly differently in English. An apostrophe is used to indicate when two Chinese syllables are pronounced separately (e.g., *Chang'an*).

For words transliterated from languages that use the Arabic script—Arabic, Ottoman Turkish, Persian, Urdu—the apostrophe indicating separately pronounced syllables may represent either of two special consonants, the *hamza* or the *ain.* Because most English-speakers do not hear the distinction between these two, they have not been distinguished in transliteration and are not indicated when they occur at the beginning or end of a word. As with Chinese, some words and commonly used place-names from these languages are given familiar English spellings (e.g., *Quran* instead of *Qur'an, Cairo* instead of *al-Qahira*). Arabic romanization has normally been used for terms relating to Islam, even where the context justifies slightly different Turkish or Persian forms, again for ease of comprehension.

Before 1492 the inhabitants of the Western Hemisphere had no single name for themselves. They had neither a racial consciousness nor a racial identity. Identity was derived from kin groups, language, cultural practices, and political structures. There was no sense that physical similarities created a shared identity. America's original inhabitants had racial consciousness and racial identity imposed on them by conquest and the occupation of their lands by Europeans after 1492. All of the collective terms for these first American peoples are tainted by this history. *Indians, Native Americans, Amerindians, First Peoples,* and *Indigenous Peoples* are among the terms in common usage. In this book the names of individual cultures and states are used wherever possible. *Amerindian* and other terms that suggest transcultural identity and experience are used most commonly for the period after 1492.

There is an ongoing debate about how best to render Amerindian words in English. It has been common for authors writing in English to follow Mexican usage for Nahuatl and Yucatec Maya words and place-names. In this style, for example, the capital of the Aztec state is spelled Tenochtitlán, and the important late Maya city-state is spelled Chichén Itzá. Although these forms are still common even in the specialist literature, we have chosen to follow the scholarship that sees these accents as unnecessary. The exceptions are modern place-names, such as Mérida and Yucatán, which are accented. A similar problem exists for the spelling of Quechua and Aymara words from the Andean region of South America. Although there is significant disagreement among scholars, we follow the emerging consensus and use the spellings *khipu* (not *quipu*), *Tiwanaku* (not *Tiahuanaco*), and *Wari* (not *Huari*). However, we keep *Inca* (not *Inka*) and *Cuzco* (not *Cusco*), since these spellings are expected by most of our potential readers and we hope to avoid confusion.

PREPARING FOR THE AP* WORLD HISTORY EXAM

Advanced Placement is a challenging yet stimulating experience. Whether you are taking an AP* course at your school or you are working on AP independently, the stage is set for a great intellectual journey. As the school year progresses and you burrow deeper and deeper into the coursework, you can see the broad concepts, events, conflicts, resolutions, and personalities that have shaped the history of our complex world. Examining the cultural, political, and economic developments that have brought great change while acknowledging the continuities that remain throughout world history is a thrilling task. Fleshing out those forces of change and continuity in world history is exciting. More exciting still is recognizing references to those forces in the media and how history has shaped current world events.

But as spring approaches and the College Board examination begins to loom on the horizon, Advanced Placement can seem quite intimidating, given the enormous scope and extent of the information you need to know. If you are intimidated by the College Board examination, you are certainly not alone.

The best way to approach an AP* examination is to master it, not let it master you. If you manage your time effectively, you will eliminate one major obstacle—learning a considerable amount of factual material along with the analytical skills needed to be a true world historian. In addition, if you can think of these tests as a way to show off how your mind works, you have a leg up: attitude *does* help. If you are not one of those students, there is still a lot you can do to sideline your anxiety. Focused review and practice time will help you master the examination so that you can walk in with confidence and get a 5.

BEFORE THE EXAM

By February, long before the exam, you need to make sure that you are registered to take the test. Many schools take care of the paperwork and handle the fees for their AP* students, but check with your teacher or the AP* coordinator to make sure that you are on the registration list. (This is especially important if you have a documented disability and need test accommodations.) If you are studying AP* independently, call AP* Services at the College Board for the name of the local AP* coordinator, who will help you through the registration process.

The evening before the exam is not a great time for partying. Nor is it a great time for cramming. If you like, look over class notes or drift through your textbook, but concentrate on the broad outlines, not the small details, of the course. Then relax. Get your things together for the next day. Sharpen a fistful of no. 2 pencils with good erasers for the multiple-choice section of the test; set out several black or dark-blue ballpoint pens for the free-response questions; get a watch and turn off the alarm if it has one; get a piece of fruit or a snack bar and a bottle of water for the break; make sure you have your Social Security number, photo identification, and admission ticket. After you have done all that, put your mind at ease, go to bed, and get a good night's sleep. An extra hour of sleep is more valuable than an extra hour of study.

On the day of the examination, make certain to eat breakfast—fuel for the brain. Studies show that students who eat a hot breakfast before testing get higher grades. You will be given a ten-minute break between Section I and Section II; the World History exam lasts for over three hours, so be prepared for a long morning. You do not want to be distracted by a growling stomach or hunger pangs. Be sure to wear comfortable clothes, taking along a sweater in case the heating or air-conditioning is erratic. When you get to the testing location, make certain to comply with all security procedures. Cell phones are not allowed, so leave yours at home or in your locker if at all possible. Be careful not to drink a lot of liquids, necessitating trips to the bathroom, which take up valuable test time.

Remember, preparation is key, even on the fast track! Best wishes on your journey to success—go out and get that 5.

TAKING THE AP* WORLD HISTORY EXAM

The AP* World History exam consists of two sections: Section I has seventy multiple-choice questions that make up half of your overall exam score. Section II has three parts. Section II, Part A, is the document-based question (DBQ); Section II, Part B, is the continuity and change over time question; Section II, Part C, is the comparative question. You will have 55 minutes for the multiple-choice portion of the test. Answer sheets for the multiple-choice questions are then collected, and you will be given a short break. You then have a total of 130 minutes for all three parts of Section II. There is a mandatory 10 minutes for reading the documents for the DBQ. The College Board recommends that you take 40 minutes to write the DBQ essay, then spend 40 minutes—5 minutes to plan and 35 minutes to write—on each of the two other essays. The essays are weighted equally, and together they make up the other half of your total exam score. Your proctor will monitor the time, but you need to keep an eye on your watch and pace yourself so you can do your best on all three essays. Remember that watch alarms are not allowed.

Here is a chart to help you visualize the breakdown of the exam:

Section	**Multiple-Choice**	**Free-Response (Essay)**		
Weight	50% of Exam	50% of Exam		
		16.7% of Exam	16.7% of Exam	16.7% of Exam
# of Questions	70	DBQ Document-Based Question	Continuity and Change over Time	Compare and Contrast
Time Allowed	55 minutes	10 minutes mandated for reading DBQ documents; 120 self-budgeted minutes to write 3 essays		
Suggested Pace	approx. 45 seconds per question	40 minutes to write	40 minutes to plan and write	40 minutes to plan and write

STRATEGIES FOR THE MULTIPLE-CHOICE SECTION

Here are some rules of thumb to help you work your way through the multiple-choice questions:

- **Answer every question.** There is no longer a penalty for wrong answers, so it is to your advantage to answer every question, even if you have to guess. Some students go through the exam and answer all the questions to which they know the answers and then go back to focus on the more difficult ones. If you do this, be sure to mark the correct lines on the answer sheet.
- **Read the question carefully** Pressured for time, many students make the mistake of reading the questions too quickly or merely skimming them. By reading a question carefully, you may already have some idea about the correct answer. You can then look for it in the responses. Careful reading is especially important in EXCEPT or NOT questions because, unlike the typical multiple-choice question, all the answers are right except for one.
- **Eliminate any answer you know is wrong** You can write on the multiple-choice questions in the test book. As you read through the responses, draw a line through any answer you know is wrong.
- **Read all of the possible answers, then choose the most accurate response** AP* exams are written to test your precise knowledge of a subject. Sometimes there are a few probable answers but one of them is more accurate. For example, a question dealing with the Berlin Conference of 1885 may have an answer that seems correct: "It was a conference of European nations." However, there may be an even better answer, one that is more specific to the topic: "It allowed European nations to carve up Africa for their economic gain."

- **Avoid absolute responses** These answers often include the words "always" or "never." For example, the statement "The Inca always practiced human sacrifice" is an overstatement because the Inca practiced animal and textile sacrifice and small amounts of human sacrifice.
- **Mark and skip tough questions** If you are hung up on a question, mark it in the margin of the question book. You can come back to it later if you have time. Make sure you skip that question on your answer sheet too.

TYPES OF MULTIPLE-CHOICE QUESTIONS

There are various kinds of multiple-choice questions. Here are some suggestions for how to approach each kind:

Classic/Best Answer Questions

This is the most common type of multiple-choice question. It simply requires you to read the question and select the most correct answer. For example:

1. Confucianism originated in
   (A) Japan
   (B) India
   (C) Russia
   (D) China

ANSWER: **D**. This is a question that has only one correct answer. Confucianism originated in China and nowhere else.

EXCEPT Questions

In the EXCEPT question, all of the answers are correct but one. The best way to approach these questions is as true/false. Mark a T or F in the margin next to each possible answer. There should be only one false answer, and that is the one you should select. For example:

1. All of the following were true about the Taiping Rebellion EXCEPT
   (A) it was a civil war that lasted over a decade
   (B) it stemmed partly from continuing tension over the opium trade
   (C) it occurred during the Mongol rule in China
   (D) it revealed the ethnic tensions in China in the mid-nineteenth century

ANSWER: **C**. The Taiping Rebellion occurred during the Qing Empire and revealed many of the difficult economic, social, and political issues of China in the nineteenth century.

Photograph/Illustration Questions

These questions require you to interpret a picture in order to gain information in a different way. A good approach is to examine the picture before you read the question and possible responses. Ask yourself what the artist or photographer is trying to convey. For example:

1. Which of the following statements is the most accurate description of the above illustration?
   (A) Japanese society rejecting Western technologies
   (B) Japanese society in the eighteenth century
   (C) an example of the type of influence the West had on Japan after the Meiji Restoration
   (D) a protest poster put out by women seeking more political rights for women in Japan

ANSWER: **C**. This poster shows the types of items the Japanese brought in from the West after the Meiji Restoration of the mid-nineteenth century. Western clothing and sewing machines were in high demand. The woman, in western dress, is shown contentedly sewing as the man looks on approvingly.

Chart/Graph Questions

These questions require you to examine the data on a chart or graph. While these questions are not difficult, spending too much time interpreting a chart or graph may slow you down. To avoid this, first read the question and all of the possible answers so that you know what you are looking for. Before you look at the chart, you may be able to eliminate some obviously incorrect responses. For example:

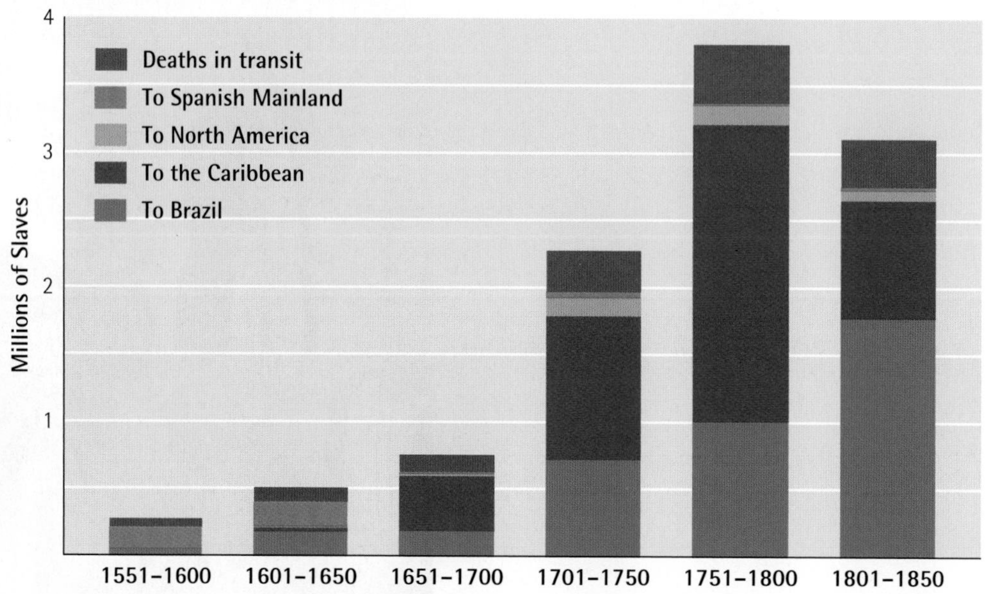

1. Which of the following statements does the above table best support?
   (A) The transatlantic slave trade remained at the same level from 1551 to 1850.
   (B) The period 1801–1850 witnessed the largest forced migration of African slaves.
   (C) Most slaves came from East Africa.
   (D) Beginning in 1651, the majority of slaves were brought to the Caribbean and Brazil.

ANSWER: **D**. After analyzing the table, option A can be eliminated because the measurement bars are not level in *any* period. Option B is incorrect because the total number of Africans in transit was highest in the period 1751–1800 and declined some in the period 1801–1850. Option C is incorrect in that there is no way to tell from the table what percentage of the slaves came from a specific region in Africa. Because the bars for transit of slaves to the Caribbean and Brazil are longest beginning in 1651, option D is the correct answer.

Political Cartoon Questions

These questions require you to interpret a political cartoon. Every political cartoon contains symbolism and a point of view. Examine the cartoon before you read the question and possible responses to determine what each part of the drawing represents and to identify the artist's viewpoint. For example:

1. What is the viewpoint expressed in the above cartoon?
   (A) The United States rejected the Roosevelt Corollary to the Monroe Doctrine.
   (B) Under Roosevelt the United States allowed European nations to take part in the colonization of South America.
   (C) Roosevelt brought the Caribbean under the control of the United States.
   (D) Roosevelt was protecting the Caribbean nations from U.S. intervention.

Answer: **C**. Roosevelt actually strengthened the Monroe Doctrine with his Roosevelt Corollary. Therefore A and B are incorrect because one of the primary purposes of the Monroe Doctrine and the Roosevelt Corollary was to prevent European intervention in the Western Hemisphere. Because the United States consistently intervened in South American affairs, answer D is incorrect.

Interpreting a Map

For history students, maps are used to describe not just geography but social and political organization as well. Asked to interpret a map, you can pick up a lot of information just by looking at the key.

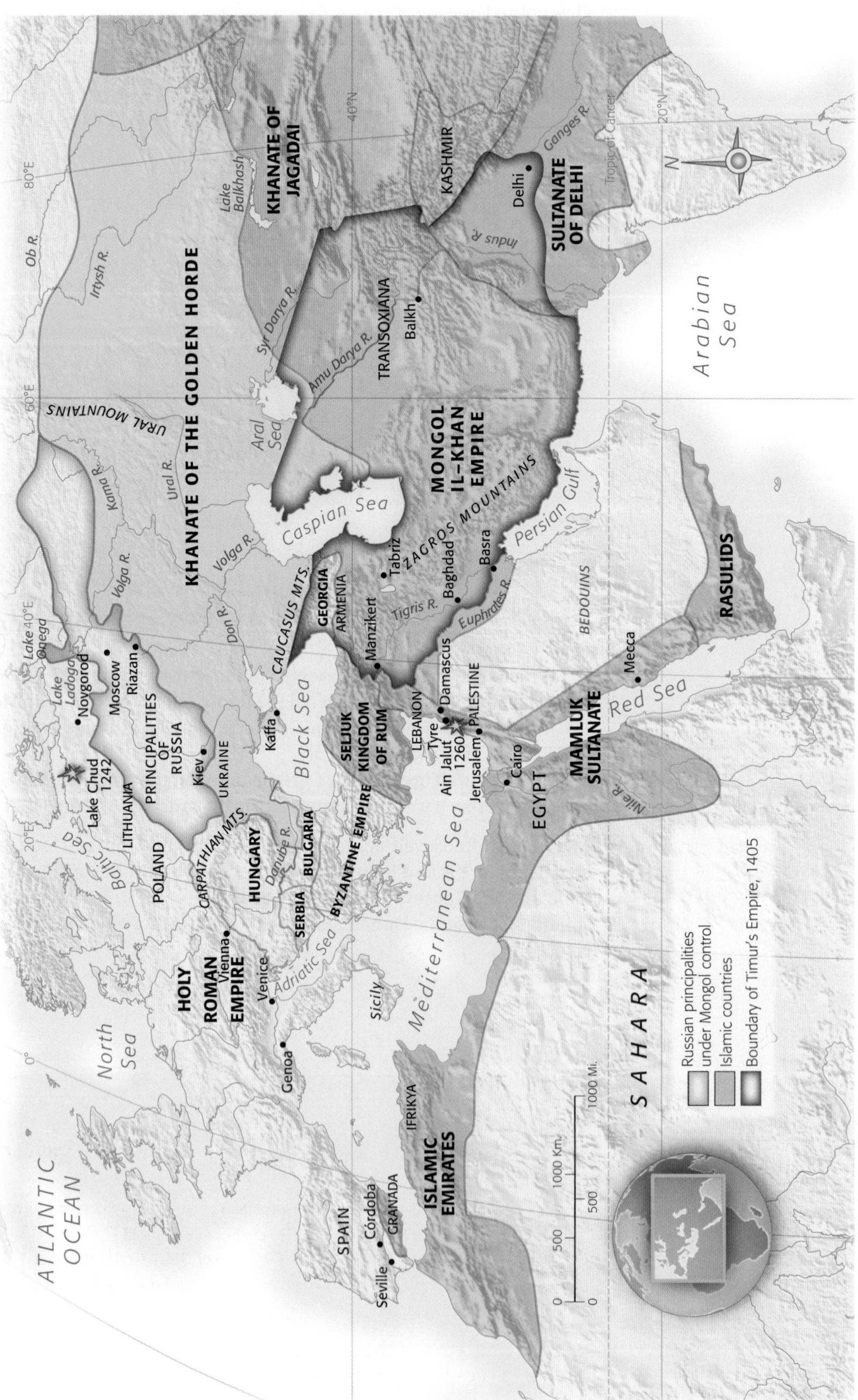

1. This map of western Eurasia in the 1300s shows
   (A) the coexistence of Mongol domains and Islamic sultanates
   (B) the khanate of the Great Khan, which Khubilai Khan ruled
   (C) the Mongol takeover of all of western Eurasia
   (D) the Mongol takeover of all of the Islamic world

ANSWER: **A**. The map shows both Mongol khanates and Islamic kingdoms. The answer cannot be B because the domains of the Great Khan were in Central and East Asia. It cannot be C or D because we see other kingdoms that the Mongols did not control, including those of western Europe.

FREE-RESPONSE QUESTIONS

In Section II of the AP World History exam, you are required to write essays for three free-response questions. Part A presents the document-based question (DBQ). For the DBQ, you are given 10 minutes for reading the documents and organizing and outlining your material, and 40 minutes for writing the essay. Part B is the continuity and change over time essay, and Part C is the comparative essay. For Part B and Part C, you should allow 40 minutes each, 5 minutes to plan and outline and 35 minutes to write.

Each of the three essays is scored on a scale of nine, with nine the highest score. Each essay has its own rubric, with specific requirements for meeting seven basic core points. If and only if those seven basic core points are met can your essay be considered for expanded core. Expanded core can earn you one or two more points. The key to success on each of these essays is understanding and internalizing each rubric's components. That is what we will focus on here.

AP Tip

For each essay in Section II, the AP examination has built in time for you to develop an outline. Time spent on an outline is important for a number of reasons:

- It prevents you from writing an essay that is unorganized because you begin writing whatever comes into your head at the moment.
- It allows you to determine your analytical thesis after seeing the evidence you can gather to support your argument.
- It provides you with an opportunity to brainstorm before writing the essay.

Once you have outlined your essay, it is time to put pen to paper. Remember that examination readers are looking for a clear thesis backed up with specifics. Concentrate on setting out accurate information in straightforward, concise prose. You cannot mask vague information with elegant prose.

The Document-Based Question

As its name implies, the DBQ presents you with a wide variety of information in the form of four to ten documents. Most of the documents come from primary sources. Primary sources are those that are contemporaneous with a time period or event, and they include everything from maps, political cartoons, photographs, and illustrations to speeches, essays, books, documentaries, and editorials.

All free-response essays require you to utilize your knowledge of the topic, but with the DBQ your essay needs to be based on the documents. Your goal is to demonstrate your ability to tease out the thrust and substance of each document, and then use that information in an analytical and evaluative essay. Thus the following are necessary for a quality DBQ essay according to the AP World History rubric:

- **Has an acceptable thesis (1 point)** An acceptable thesis is one that makes an analytical argument that responds specifically to what the prompt is calling for you to address in the DBQ.

- **Addresses all of the documents and demonstrates understanding of all or all but one (1 point)** You need to use *every document* and show that you get the essential idea(s) of each one. You may misunderstand one but still get the point because you addressed it. Remember that ignoring one document is NOT the same as misinterpreting it.
- **Supports thesis with appropriate evidence from all of the documents (2 points)** A thesis must be supported by good evidence drawn from each document to support the claims made in your thesis. (You can still get the two points if you misinterpret a document as long as you addressed all of the documents.) You need to demonstrate your ability to pull such evidence from each document and discuss the evidence in your own words in terms of how it relates to the thesis you have written in response to the DBQ prompt. *Do not just quote the documents or summarize them in a list!* You need to analyze them and show that you can make historical connections in your own words. You get only one point here if you support your thesis with evidence from all but two documents. But getting only one point here means you will not meet basic core, so make sure you use specific evidence from all of the documents!
- **Analyzes point of view in at least TWO documents (1 point)** This is one of the hardest tasks on the DBQ for students to remember to do. It is very important that historians consider the author of a document—how class, gender, nationality, profession, and the like shaped a person's experience or interpretation of a particular historical event. Background information can help us understand why an individual might have a particular point of view or opinion or why a document might have a particular tone to it—for example, a tone of anger or a tone of respect. You need to be able to show your ability to account for the point of view in at least two documents. It is not enough to just say what point of view you see presented in the documents; you must then account for why that point of view exists in the source. Ask yourself how the point of view affects the document's content. A good place to begin looking for clues to the point of view is the source line of the document. The source line gives the author or speaker in the document, the date of the document, which helps you place the document in a larger historical context, and it often has other important pieces of information about the document as well. *Always read the source line!*
- **Analyzes documents by grouping them in TWO or THREE ways, depending on the question (1 point)** Grouping documents is an important skill because it shows your ability to recognize the relationships that exist between documents. You can group documents several ways, but the answer to how you group them often lies in the prompt, which instructs you on how to approach the documents and analyze them. For example, if you are asked to analyze cause and impact, a reasonable way to organize the documents would be to group those that show causes and group those that show impact. You can also group documents by similarities and differences you see in them. Sometimes it is appropriate to group them chronologically. Again, the key is to look at what the prompt is telling you to do.
- **Identifies and explains the need for ONE type of appropriate additional document or source (1 point)** As world historians, we are always trying to get as complete a picture as possible regarding the different points of view and experiences of individuals and societies. Therefore, the documents you are given are often not enough to get the fullest picture of a historical experience. You are asked to think about what other documents would add to your analysis of a historical situation. You should be thinking, "Whose voices am I missing?" "What particular document would help me understand this historical moment better?" You are not asked to come up with an actual primary source document that you know exists; rather *you are asked to come up with a realistic hypothetical source that would provide further insight in addressing the prompt.* For example, perhaps you are doing a DBQ on the French Revolution and you have no documents from women. A diary entry from a woman of the Second Estate in prerevolutionary France would add to your analysis of the causes of the French Revolution. The DBQ prompt gives some specifications for your additional document, so always begin with the prompt. This is another element of the DBQ that students often forget to address, so remember that you must provide an additional document AND explain WHY you need it. Be sure, too, to tie it back to the prompt.

If you meet all seven of the basic core requirements, there are many ways that you can earn an additional two points—expanded core—on the DBQ. For example, you can offer additional groupings, analyze point of view in most or all documents, explain the need for more than just the one additional document, and bring in relevant outside historical content. You can also get expanded core if you do a particularly good job of shaping your thesis so that your argument is very clear, analyzing and covering all aspects of the prompt, analyzing the documents, or using the documents persuasively.

Take a look at this sample DBQ, one containing five documents.

1. Using the documents, analyze the role of ritual in Mesoamerican society during the period 600–1450. Identify an additional document and explain how it would help your analysis of the role of rituals in Mesoamerica.

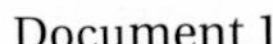

Document 1

Source: The Mesoamerican Ball Game

Document 2

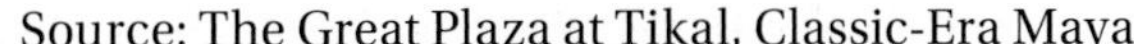

Source: The Great Plaza at Tikal, Classic-Era Maya

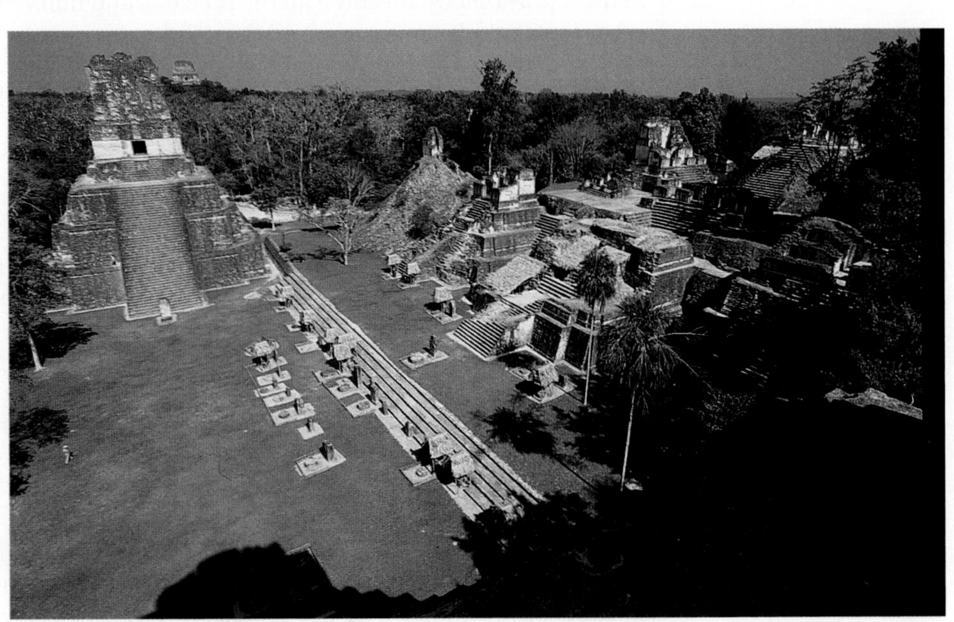

Document 3

Source: The Temple of the Sun, Tenochtitlan

Document 4

Source: An Aztec's assessment of Toltec accomplishments

In truth [the Toltecs] invented all the precious and marvelous things. . . . All that now exists was their discovery. . . . And these Toltecs were very wise; they were thinkers, for they originated the year count, the day count. All their discoveries formed the book for interpreting dreams. . . . And so wise were they [that] they understood the stars which were in the heavens.

Document 5

Source: Description of Moctezuma II by a Spaniard who participated in the conquest of the Aztec Empire

. . . Many great lords walked before the great Montezuma [Moctezuma II, r. 1502–1520], sweeping the ground on which he was to tread and laying down cloaks so that his feet should not touch the earth. Not one of these chieftains dared look him in the face.

The first step is an analysis of each document in order to come up with evidence in order to create your thesis. What is the meaning of the document? What or who is the source, and how does that affect their point of view? The source provides important clues in the position being put forth in the document. As you analyze the meaning or significance of the document, jot down margin notes—generalizations that relate to the document and the prompt. For example:

- **Margin note for Document 1** *An example of ritual permeating every area of life, including sport.*
- **Margin note for Document 2** Shows the sophisticated architecture used to perform public rituals. Shows the importance of publicizing ritual and the grandeur of ritual. Clearly important in the society by looking at the buildings indicative of this Mesoamerican culture.
- **Margin note for Document 3** Similar to document two in showing the grandeur of buildings dedicated to religious ritual; particular importance of the Sun, which is a central deity in Mesoamerican culture.
- **Margin note for Document 4** *Astronomy and calendar work were very important parts of ritual life in Mesoamerican society.* This document is especially valuable for its point of view; the Aztec is praising the earlier Toltecs for their relationship to the cosmos. Questions to consider for analysis of point of view: "What was the relationship between the Aztecs and Toltecs?" "Why would the tone of this document be one of great respect?"
- **Margin note for Document 5** One of the conquerors comments on the godlike way the Aztec king is treated by the common person. Because the source is a Spaniard, this document is interesting for its point of view. Think about why the Spaniard would comment on this.

Once you have done this, you should group the documents. One way to group them might be by documents specifically about the Aztecs versus those about other Mesoamerican societies. You could also group the documents that show architecture. Be thinking about whose voice(s) you are missing so you will begin to get some ides about what your additional document(s) should be and how they will help you answer the prompt. Also remember you need to do point of view for two, which in this case would be documents four and five. You want to account for the tone of respect that the Aztecs show the Toltecs in Document 4. You should also analyze why the Spaniard, a foreigner, has his point of view about the behavior of the people toward Moctezuma II. Give some thought to what you can add to reach expanded core. Finally, write your thesis, making sure it answers the prompt and shows your argument for how ritual was used in Mesoamerican society. *Make sure your thesis has an argument and does not just repeat the prompt.* With good planning at the beginning, your DBQ should be in great shape!

The Continuity and Change Over Time Essay

AP World History covers an enormous amount of time. The continuity and change over time essay is a unique essay because it asks you to step back and examine and analyze certain trends, characteristics, or patterns over a large span of time. You are often given a choice of region in which to discuss patterns of continuity and change.

One of the most challenging aspects of an essay like this is figuring out how to break down large time periods that might span hundreds or thousands of years. One effective approach is to break the period down into stages. If it is not possible or relevant to break the period down into stages, do not worry. The most important thing is to take the reader of your essay through the entire period using key events of change and continuity. You need to be able to address continuities in history that span large time periods and account for why those continuities persist through periods of change. The following is the AP World History rubric for the continuity and change over time essay:

- **Has an acceptable thesis (1 point)** To have an acceptable thesis for the continuity and change over time essay, you need to address the entire time period in question. Take the reader through the main stages of change you will address as they pertain to the issue (for example, trade or cultural identity) that you are asked to discuss. Your thesis must also include the continuity you see present in the entire period and an overall statement of analysis. Continuity and change over time thesis statements are often hard to do in one sentence, so you want to write a well organized, clear and comprehensive thesis; if you need more than one sentence, make sure they are consecutive, flow together to make a clear thesis paragraph, and be mindful of your length.
- **Addresses all parts of the question (2 points)** The most important thing to remember here is that in order to address all parts of the question, you must discuss both change and continuity in your essay. You will only get one point for addressing the question if you address change but not continuity or vice versa.

- **Substantiates thesis with appropriate historical evidence (2 points)** Again, a thesis with no evidence to support it is unacceptable to historians. You need to cite specific examples of both change and continuity. You will get only one point if you partially substantiate your thesis with appropriate evidence. This can happen if you do not provide enough specific, relevant examples of evidence or if you do not have evidence for both change and continuity.
- **Uses relevant world historical context effectively to explain continuity and change over time (1 point)** Change does not happen in a vacuum. In world history change occurs for both short- and long-term reasons that often involve more than just one region or country. It is essential for you to place change in the larger context and identify global processes that bring about change. You should also be able to discuss how continuities persist despite global forces that bring about change. For example, you could say, "Despite the changes in labor brought by the Industrial Revolution, slavery of Africans continued in certain parts of the Americas up through the end of the nineteenth century."
- **Analyzes the process of continuity and change over time (1 point)** It is not enough to just say that something changed; you must also account for WHY the change occurred and how it impacted those in a particular region or country. You also should account for WHY continuity persisted. Remember, you always want to show your ability to analyze and do higher-level critical thinking.
- If your essay meets these basic core requirements, it can be considered for an additional one or two points in expanded core. The continuity and change over time essay can receive those points for the following reasons: a clear thesis that is comprehensive while being analytical; addressing all parts of the question evenly - time periods, regions, and/or issues; providing ample evidence to support your argument; and analysis of all the issues that pertain to the time period. See the Diagnostic Test for a full sample continuity and change over time essay.

The Comparative Essay

The comparative essay is the third and final essay for the AP World History exam. Comparison is often thought to imply similarity, but for this essay you are expected to both compare and contrast particular characteristics in two regions. The AP World History rubric for the comparative essay is as follows:

- **Has an acceptable thesis (1 point)** Be sure your thesis makes a comparative argument that addresses the particular issues in the prompt. For example, if you are asked to compare the economic systems in China and Japan from 1450 to 1900, you need to be sure your thesis states how China and Japan were economically similar as well as different and why that was the case. Explaining why ensures that your thesis is analytical.
- **Addresses all parts of the question (2 points)** For the full two points, you need to address both similarities and differences. You get one point if you address only one or the other, which means you will not get basic core.
- **Substantiates thesis with appropriate historical evidence (2 points)** Appropriate means accurate. Be sure that the evidence you are using is accurate and works as a legitimate comparison. Appropriate also means that it addresses the characteristic or issue you are asked to compare. If you are asked to compare economic systems and you are providing evidence that compares social systems, that is not appropriate evidence for economic systems even if it is accurate. Work to have appropriate evidence for both similarities as well as differences. Minimal appropriate evidence will earn you one point, which means you will not get all seven basic core points.
- **Makes at least one relevant direct comparison between/among societies (1 point)** You are comparing two different regions and the societies among them. A direct comparison means that you are comparing those societies within the same sentence. For instance, if you are asked to compare the political systems of the Byzantine Empire and feudal Europe, you should not discuss the Byzantine Empire in one paragraph and feudal Europe in another. You need to decide during your planning time what specific political characteristics were similar and different about the two societies in terms of political structure and make sure that in each paragraph you discuss both regions. That makes for a direct comparison. For example, if they had similar laws but different roles for kings, then one paragraph should be about law,

in which you compare both societies, and one paragraph should be about the role of kings, in which you contrast both societies.

- **Analyzes at least one reason for a similarity or difference identified in a direct comparison (1 point)** It is not enough to list the political similarities and differences between the Byzantine Empire and feudal Europe. You must also explain WHY those similarities and differences existed.

If you meet these basic core requirements, you can earn an additional one or two points in expanded core. Comparative essays are given those points for the following reasons: a clear thesis that is comprehensive while being analytical; addressing all parts of the question evenly—time periods, regions, and/or issues; providing ample evidence to support your argument; making several direct comparisons rather than the one or two required for basic core; and consistent analysis of the causes and effects of these direct comparisons rather than the one piece of analysis required for basic core.

To conclude, here are some tips for writing AP World History essays:

- **Thesis** Be sure that your thesis statement is at the very beginning of your essay. You need to present your main argument right up front so it is clear what you are proving in your essay.
- **Grammar** You will not lose points for spelling or grammar errors, but it is important to write as coherently as possible. Remember, if the reader cannot understand what you are trying to say or cannot follow your arguments, it will be harder to get the necessary information across for points. It is also important to write as neatly and legibly as possible so all of your good ideas can be understood!
- **Dates** Do not panic if you cannot remember a specific date; try to use a broader description such as "early nineteenth century" or "by the end of the sixth century" if you cannot remember the exact date.
- **Quality over quantity** Remember: quality, not quantity. Writing a lot does not mean you are writing what needs to be in your essay. Focus on making sure you are hitting all the rubric points rather than writing long introductions and conclusions. Make your argument, prove it with evidence and wrap up. You want to have time to do all three essays well.

PART I

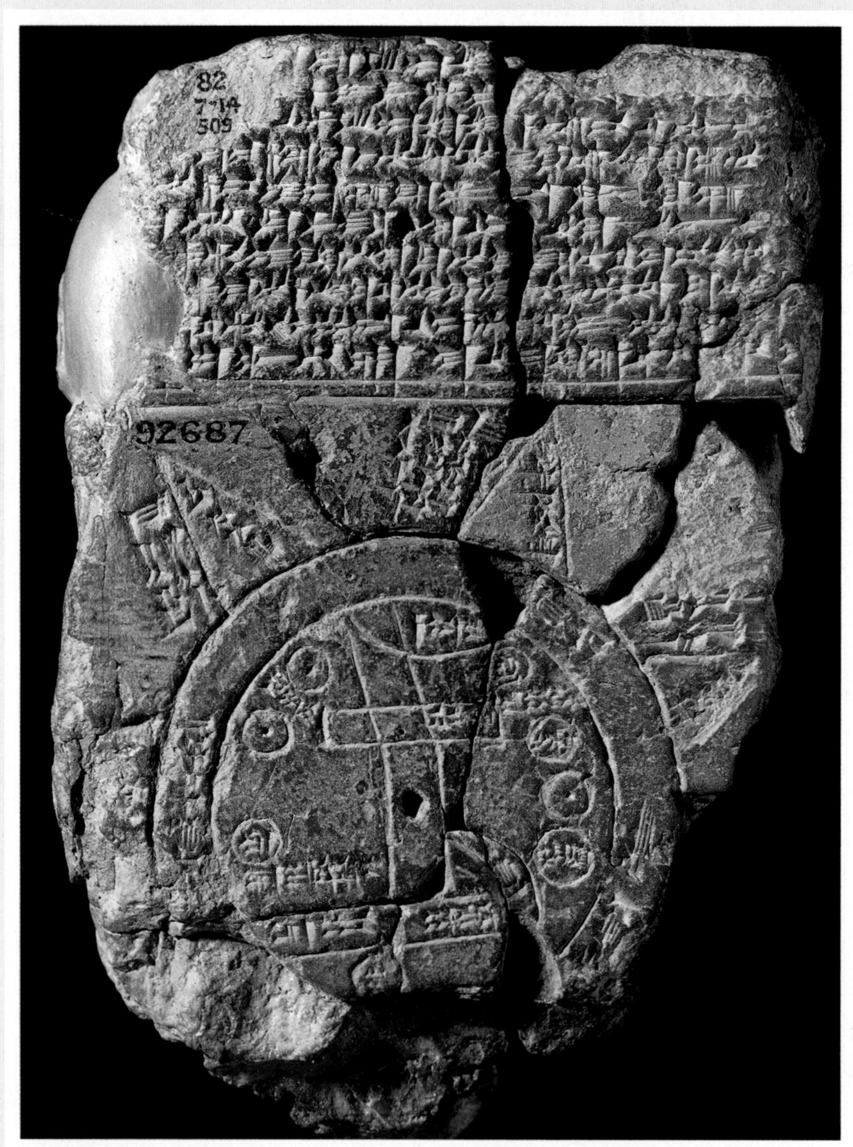

British Museum/HIP/Art Resource, NY

Babylonian Map of the World, ca. 600 B.C.E. This map on a clay tablet, with labels written in Akkadian cuneiform, shows a flat, round world with the city of Babylon at the center. Nearby features of the Mesopotamian landscape include the Euphrates River, mountains, marshes, and cities. Beyond the great encircling salt sea are seven islands. Like many ancient peoples, the Babylonians believed that distant lands were home to legendary beasts, strangely formed peoples, and mysterious natural phenomena.

The Emergence of Human Communities, to 500 B.C.E.

Human beings evolved over several million years from primates in Africa. Able to walk upright and possessing large brains, hands with opposable thumbs, and the capacity for speech, early humans used teamwork and created tools to survive in diverse environments. They spread relatively quickly to almost every habitable area of the world, hunting and gathering wild plant products. Around 10,000 years ago some groups began to cultivate plants, domesticate animals, and make pottery vessels for storage. This led to permanent settlements—at first small villages but eventually larger towns as well.

The earliest complex societies arose in the great river valleys of Mesopotamia, Egypt, Pakistan, and northern China. In these arid regions agriculture depended on river water, and centers of political power arose to organize the labor required to dig and maintain irrigation channels. Kings and priests dominated these early societies from the urban centers, helped by administrators, scribes, soldiers, merchants, craftsmen, and others with specialized skills. Surplus food grown in the countryside by a dependent peasantry sustained the activities of these groups.

Certain centers came to dominate broader expanses of territory, seeking access to raw materials, especially metals. This development also stimulated long-distance trade and diplomatic relations between major powers. Artisans made weapons, tools, and ritual objects from bronze. Culture and technology spread to neighboring regions, such as southern China, Nubia, Syria-Palestine, Anatolia, and the Aegean.

In the Western Hemisphere, different geographical circumstances called forth distinctive patterns of technological and cultural response in the early civilizations in southern Mexico and the Andean region of South America.

CHAPTER

1

CHAPTER OUTLINE

- **Before Civilization**
- **Mesopotamia**
- **Egypt**
- **The Indus Valley Civilization**
- **Conclusion**

DIVERSITY + DOMINANCE ***Violence and Order in the Babylonian New Year's Festival***

ENVIRONMENT + TECHNOLOGY ***The Iceman***

David Coulson/Robert Estall Photo Agency

Engraving of Two Cattle in the Sahara, ca. 5000 B.C.E. Around 10,000 B.C.E. people settled in the central Sahara and began to engrave rocks with pictures of animals. The engravings display an expert knowledge of animal stance, movement, and anatomy.

Visit the website and ebook for additional study materials and interactive tools: www.cengage.com/history/bullietearthpeople5e

From the Origins of Agriculture to the First River-Valley Civilizations

- What cultural achievements characterized life in the Neolithic period?
- How did Mesopotamian civilization emerge, and what technologies promoted its advancement?
- What role did the environment and religion play in the evolution of Egyptian civilization?
- What does the material evidence tell us about the nature of the Indus Valley civilization, and what is the most likely reason for its collapse?

The *Epic of Gilgamesh*, whose roots date to before 2000 B.C.E., defines *civilization* as the people of ancient Mesopotamia (present-day Iraq) understood it. Gilgamesh, an early king, sends a temple prostitute to tame Enkidu (EN-kee-doo), a wild man who lives like an animal in the grasslands, perhaps symbolizing the foraging lifestyle of the preagricultural populations of the Mesopotamian borderlands. Using her sexual charms to win Enkidu's trust, the temple prostitute tells him:

> Come with me to the city, to Uruk (OO-rook), to the temple of Anu and the goddess Ishtar . . . to Uruk, where the processions are and music, let us go together through the dancing to the palace hall where Gilgamesh presides.[1]

She clothes Enkidu and teaches him to eat cooked food, drink beer, and bathe and oil his body. Her words and actions signal some of the traits of civilized life in ancient Mesopotamia.

The Mesopotamians, like other peoples throughout history, equated civilization with their own way of life, but *civilization* is an ambiguous concept, and the charge that a particular group is "uncivilized" has been used throughout human history to justify many things. Thus, it is important to explain the common claim that the first advanced civilizations emerged in Mesopotamia and Egypt sometime before 3000 B.C.E.

PRIMARY SOURCE: The *Epic of Gilgamesh* Find out how Gilgamesh's friend Enkidu propels him on a quest for immortality, and whether or not that quest is successful.

Scholars agree that certain political, social, economic, and technological traits are indicators of **civilization**: (1) cities as administrative centers, (2) a political system based on control of a defined territory rather than kinship connections, (3) many people engaged in specialized, non-food-producing activities, (4) status distinctions based largely on accumulation of substantial wealth by some groups, (5) monumental building, (6) a system for keeping permanent records, (7) long-distance trade, and (8) major advances in science and the arts. The earliest societies exhibiting these traits developed in the floodplains of great rivers: the Tigris (TIE-gris) and Euphrates (you-FRAY-teez) in Iraq, the Indus in Pakistan, the Yellow (Huang He [hwang huh]) in China, and the Nile in Egypt (see Map 1.2 on page 14). The periodic flooding of the rivers deposited fertile silt and provided water for agriculture, but it also threatened lives and property. To protect themselves and channel the forces of nature, people living near the rivers created new technologies and forms of political and social organization.

civilization An ambiguous term often used to denote more complex societies but sometimes used by anthropologists to describe any group of people sharing a set of cultural traits.

AP* Exam Tip The interaction of geography and climate with the development of human society is tested on the exam.

In this chapter, we describe the origins of domestication among the scattered groups of foragers living at the end of the last Ice Age (a long period when glaciers covered much of North America, Europe, and Asia) and the rise of complex societies in Mesopotamia, Egypt, and the Indus River Valley from approximately 3500 to 1500 B.C.E. (China, developing slightly later, is discussed in Chapter 2).

BEFORE CIVILIZATION

culture Socially transmitted patterns of action and expression. *Material culture* refers to physical objects, such as dwellings, clothing, tools, and crafts. Culture also includes arts, beliefs, knowledge, and technology.

history The study of past events and changes in the development, transmission, and transformation of cultural practices.

Stone Age The historical period characterized by the production of tools from stone and other nonmetallic substances. It was followed in some places by the Bronze Age and more generally by the Iron Age.

Paleolithic The period of the Stone Age associated with the evolution of humans. It predates the Neolithic period.

Neolithic The period of the Stone Age associated with the ancient Agricultural Revolution(s). It follows the Paleolithic period.

Evidence of early humans' splendid creative abilities first came to light in 1940 near Lascaux in southern France. Youths who stumbled onto the entrance to a vast underground cavern found its walls covered with paintings of animals, including many that had been extinct for thousands of years. Other ancient cave paintings have been found in Spain, Africa, Australia, and elsewhere.

To even the most skeptical person, these artistic troves reveal rich imaginations and sophisticated skills, qualities also apparent in the stone tools and in the evidence of complex social relations uncovered from prehistoric sites. The production of such artworks and tools over wide areas and long periods of time demonstrates that skills and ideas were not simply individual expressions but were deliberately passed along within societies. These learned patterns of action and expression constitute **culture**. Culture includes material objects, such as dwellings, clothing, tools, and crafts, along with nonmaterial values, beliefs, and languages. Although it is true that some animals also learn new ways, their activities are determined primarily by inherited instincts. Only human communities trace profound cultural developments over time. The development, transmission, and transformation of cultural practices and events are the subject of **history**.

The first recognizable cultural activity, toolmaking, first appeared around 2 million years ago. The **Stone Age**, which lasted from then until around 4,000 years ago, can be a misleading label. Stone tools abound at archaeological sites, but not all tools were of stone. They were made as well of bone, skin, and wood, materials that survive poorly. In addition, the Stone Age encompasses many cultures and subperiods. Among the major subdivisions, the **Paleolithic** (Old Stone Age) lasted until 10,000 years ago, about 3,000 years after the end of the last Ice Age. The **Neolithic** (New Stone Age), which is associated with the origins of agriculture, followed.

Food Gathering and Stone Tools

Fossilized animal bones bearing the marks of butchering tools testify to the scavenging and hunting activities of Stone Age peoples, but anthropologists do not believe that early humans depended primarily on meat for their food. The few surviving present-day **foragers** (hunting and food-gathering peoples) in Africa derive the bulk of their day-to-day nourishment from wild vegetable foods, with meat reserved for feasts. The same was probably true for Stone Age peoples, even though tools for gathering and processing vegetable foods have left few traces because they were made of perishable materials. Ancient humans would have used skins and mats woven from leaves for collecting fruits, berries, and wild seeds. They would have dug edible roots out of the ground with wooden sticks.

Cooking, Traveling, and Shelter

foragers People who support themselves by hunting wild animals and gathering wild edible plants and insects.

Both meat and vegetables become tastier and easier to digest when they are cooked. The first cooked foods were probably found by accident after wildfires. Humans may have been setting fires deliberately as early as 1.5 million years ago, but only with the appearance of clay cooking pots some 12,500 years ago in East Asia is there hard evidence of cooking.

Researchers studying present-day foragers infer that Ice Age women would have done most of the gathering and cooking (which they could do while caring for small children). Older women past childbearing age would have been the most knowledgeable and productive food gatherers. Men, with stronger arms, would have been more suited than women to hunting, particularly for large animals.

All recent foragers have lived in small bands. The community has to have enough members to defend itself from predators and divide responsibility for collection and preparation of foods. However, too many members would exhaust the food available in the band's immediate vicin-

CHRONOLOGY

	Mesopotamia	Egypt	Indus Valley
8000 B.C.E.	8000–2000 B.C.E. Neolithic (New Stone Age); earliest agriculture		
3000 B.C.E.	3000–2350 B.C.E. Early Dynastic (Sumerian)	3100–2575 B.C.E. Early Dynastic	
2500 B.C.E.		2575–2134 B.C.E. Old Kingdom	2600 B.C.E. Beginning of Indus Valley civilization
	2350–2230 B.C.E. Akkadian (Semitic)	2134–2040 B.C.E. First Intermediate Period	
	2112–2004 B.C.E. Third Dynasty of Ur (Sumerian)	2040–1640 B.C.E. Middle Kingdom	
2000 B.C.E.			
	1900–1600 B.C.E. Old Babylonian (Semitic)	1640–1532 B.C.E. Second Intermediate Period	1900 B.C.E. End of Indus Valley civilization
		1532–1070 B.C.E. New Kingdom	
1500 B.C.E.	1500–1150 B.C.E. Kassite		

ity. The band has to move at regular intervals to follow migrating animals and take advantage of seasonally ripening plants in different places. Archaeological evidence from Ice Age campsites suggests that early humans, too, lived in highly mobile bands.

Because frequent moves were necessary, early hunter-gatherers did not lavish much time on housing. Natural shelters under overhanging rocks or in caves were favorite camping places to which bands returned at regular intervals. Where the climate was severe or where natural shelters did not exist, people erected huts of branches, stones, bones, skins, and leaves. Large, solid structures were common in fishing villages that grew up along riverbanks and lakeshores, where the abundance of fish permitted people to occupy the same site year-round.

Clothing and Lifestyle

Animal skin cloaks were probably an early form of clothing. While the oldest evidence of fibers woven into cloth dates from about 26,000 years ago, the appearance of the body louse around 70,000 years ago has been linked to people beginning to wear close-fitting garments. An "Iceman" from 5,300 years ago, whose frozen remains were found in the European Alps in 1991, was wearing many different garments made of animal skins sewn together with cord fashioned from vegetable fibers and rawhide (see Environment and Technology: The Iceman).

Although accidents, erratic weather, and disease might take a heavy toll on a foraging band, day-to-day existence was probably not particularly hard or unpleasant. Studies suggest that, in game-rich areas, obtaining necessary food, clothing, and shelter would have occupied only from three to five hours a day. This would have left a great deal of time for artistic endeavors, toolmaking, and social life.

Nonstone Technologies, Art, and Religion

The foundations of science, art, and religion were built during the Stone Age. Basic to human survival was extensive knowledge about the natural environment. Gatherers learned which local plants were best for food and when they were available. Successful hunting required intimate knowledge of the habits of game animals. People learned how to use plant and animal parts for clothing, twine, building materials, and dyes; minerals for paints and stones for tools; and various natural substances for medicine and consciousness altering. It is very likely that the transmission of such knowledge involved verbal communication, even though direct evidence for language appears only in later periods.

Early music and dance have left no traces, but there is abundant evidence of painting and drawing. Because many cave paintings feature wild animals that were hunted for food, some believe they were meant to record hunting scenes or formed part of magical and religious rites to ensure successful hunting. However, a newly discovered cave in southern France features rhinoceroses, panthers, bears, and other animals that probably were not hunted for food. Other drawings include people dressed in animal skins and smeared with paint. In many caves there

ENVIRONMENT + TECHNOLOGY

The Iceman

The discovery of the well-preserved remains of a man at the edge of a melting glacier in the European Alps in 1991 provided detailed information about everyday technologies of the fourth millennium B.C.E. Not just the body of this "Iceman" was well preserved. His clothing, his tools, and even the food in his stomach survived in remarkably good condition.

Dressed from head to toe for the cold weather of the mountains, the fifty-year-old man was wearing a fur hat fastened under the chin with a strap, a vest of different colored deerskins, leather leggings and loincloth, and a padded cloak made of grasses. His calfskin shoes also were padded with grass for warmth and comfort. The articles of clothing had been sewn together with fiber and leather cords. He carried a birch-bark drinking cup.

In a leather fanny pack he carried small flint tools for cutting, scraping, and punching holes, as well as some tinder for making a fire. He also carried a leather quiver with flint-tipped arrows, but his 6-foot (1.8-meter) bow was unfinished, lacking a bowstring. In addition, he had a flint knife and a tool for sharpening flints. His most sophisticated tool, indicating the dawning of the age of metals, was a copper-bladed ax with a wooden handle.

A small arrowhead lodged in his shoulder caused the Iceman's death. In his stomach, researchers found the remains of the meat-rich meal he had eaten not long before he died.

The Iceman This is an artist's rendition of what the Iceman might have looked like. Notice his tools, remarkable evidence of the technology of his day.

are stencils of human hands. Are these the signatures of the artists or the world's oldest graffiti? Some scholars suspect that other marks in cave paintings and on bones from this period may represent efforts at counting or writing. Other theories suggest that cave and rock art represent concerns with fertility, efforts to educate the young, or elaborate mechanisms for time reckoning.

Without written texts it is difficult to know about the religious beliefs of early humans. Sites of deliberate human burials from about 100,000 years ago give some hints. The fact that an adult was often buried with stone implements, food, clothing, and red-ochre powder suggests that early people revered their leaders enough to honor them after death and may imply a belief in an afterlife.

Today we recognize that the Stone Age, whose existence was scarcely dreamed of two centuries ago, was a formative period. Important in its own right, it also laid the foundation for major changes ahead as human communities passed from being food gatherers to food producers.

The Agricultural Revolutions

For most of human existence people ate only wild plants and animals. But around 10,000 years ago global climate changes seem to have induced some societies to enhance their food supplies with domesticated plants and animals. More and more people became food producers over the following millennia. Although hunting and gathering did not disappear, this transition from foraging to food production was one of the great turning points in history because it fostered a rapid increase in population and greatly altered humans' relationship to nature.

Agricultural Revolutions The change from food gathering to food production that occurred between ca. 8000 and 2000 B.C.E. Also known as the Neolithic Revolution.

Because agriculture arose in combination with new kinds of stone tools, archaeologists called this period of change the "Neolithic" and the rise of agriculture the "Neolithic Revolution." But that name can be misleading: first, stone tools were not its essential component, and second, it was not a single event but a series of separate transformations in different parts of the world. A better term is **Agricultural Revolutions**, which emphasizes that the central change was in food production and that agriculture arose independently in many places. In some cases agriculture included the domestication of animals for food as well as the cultivation of new food crops (see Map 1.1).

A Gradual Process

Food gathering gave way to food production in stages spread over hundreds of generations. The process may have begun when forager bands, returning year after year to the same seasonal camps, deliberately scattered the seeds of desirable plants in locations where they would thrive and discouraged the growth of competing plants by clearing them away. Such semicultivation could have supplemented food gathering for many generations. Eventually, families choosing to concentrate on food production would have settled permanently near their fields.

The presence of new, specialized tools for agriculture first alerted archaeologists to the beginning of a food production revolution. These included polished stone heads to work the soil, sharp stone chips embedded in bone or wooden handles to cut grain, and stone mortars to pulverize grain. Since stone axes were not very efficient for clearing away shrubs and trees, farmers used fire to get rid of unwanted undergrowth (the ashes were a natural fertilizer).

Middle East Wheat and Barley

The transition to agriculture occurred first in the Middle East. By 8000 B.C.E. humans, by selecting the highest-yielding strains, had transformed certain wild grasses into the domesticated grains now known as emmer wheat and barley. They had also discovered that alternating the cultivation of grains and pulses (plants yielding edible seeds such as lentils and peas) helped maintain soil fertility. Women, the principal gatherers of wild plant foods, probably played a major role in this transition to plant cultivation, but the heavy work of clearing the fields would have fallen to men.

 **AP* Exam Tip** It is important to understand agricultural, pastoral and foraging societies and their demographic characteristics.

Plants domesticated in the Middle East spread to Greece as early as 6000 B.C.E., to the light-soiled plains of central Europe and along the Danube River shortly after 4000 B.C.E., and then to other parts of Europe over the next millennium (see Map 1.1). Early farmers in Europe and elsewhere practiced shifting cultivation, also known as swidden agriculture. After a few growing seasons, the fields were left fallow (abandoned to natural vegetation) for a time to restore their fertility, and new fields were cleared nearby. From around 2600 B.C.E. people in central Europe began using ox-drawn wooden plows to till heavier and richer soils.

African, Asian, and American Crops

Wheat and barley could not spread farther south because the rainfall patterns in most of Africa were unsuited to their growth. Instead, separate Agricultural Revolutions took place in Saharan and sub-Saharan Africa, beginning almost as early as in the Middle East. During a particularly wet period after 8000 B.C.E. people in what is now the eastern Sahara began to cultivate sorghum, a grain derived from wild grasses they had previously gathered. Over the next three thousand years the Saharan farmers domesticated pearl millet, blackeyed peas, a kind of peanut, sesame, and gourds. In the Ethiopian highlands farmers domesticated finger millet and a grain called teff. The return of drier conditions about 5000 B.C.E. led many Saharan farmers to move to the Nile Valley, where the annual flooding of the river provided moisture for farming. People in the rain forests of equatorial West Africa domesticated yams and a variety of rice.

The kind of rice eaten in most places today, which thrives in warm and wet conditions, was first domesticated in southern China, the northern half of Southeast Asia, or northern India, possibly as early as 10,000 B.C.E. but more likely closer to 5000 B.C.E. In India several pulses (including hyacinth beans, green grams, and black grams) domesticated about 2000 B.C.E. were cultivated along with rice.

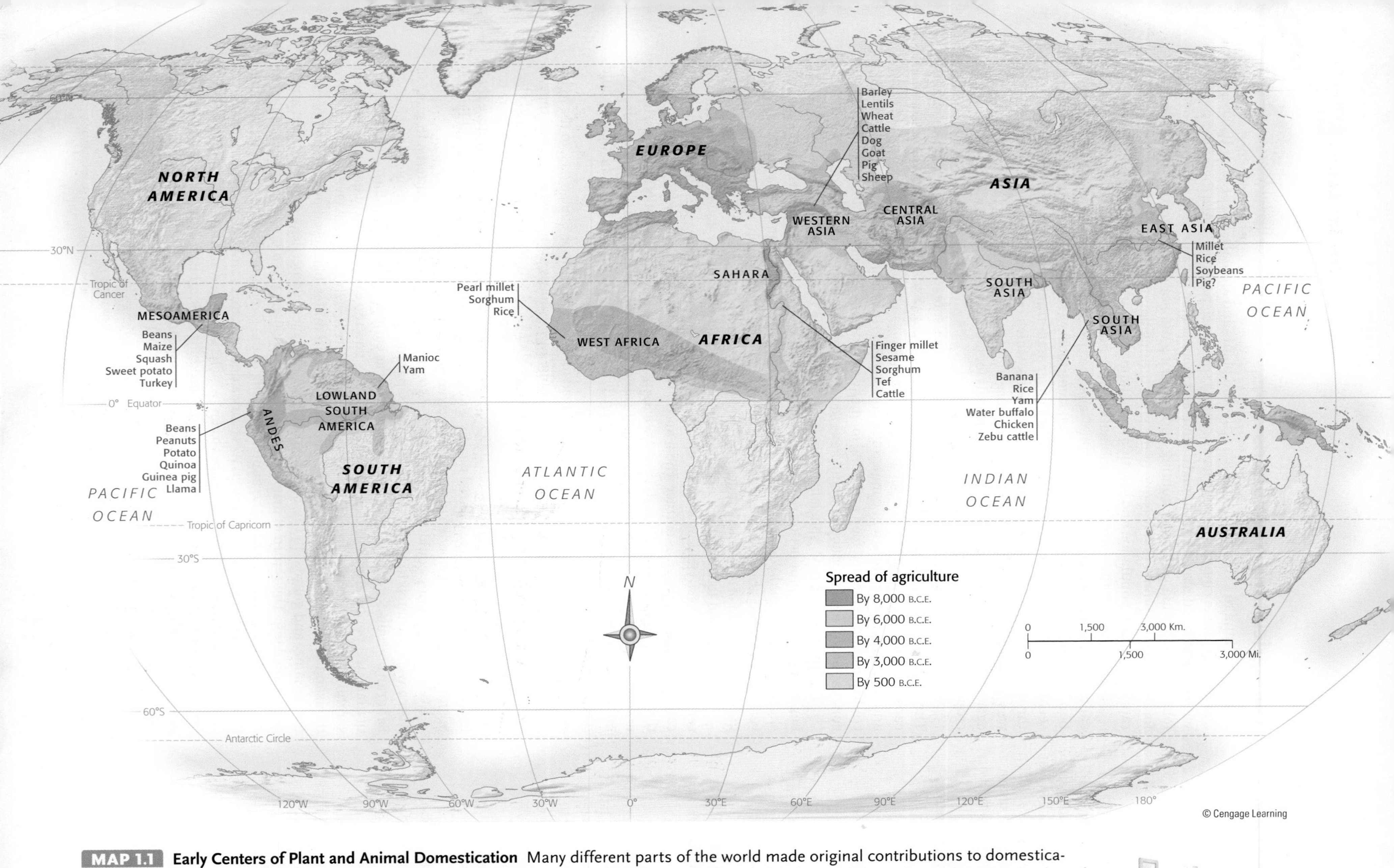

MAP 1.1 Early Centers of Plant and Animal Domestication Many different parts of the world made original contributions to domestication during the Agricultural Revolutions that began about 10,000 years ago. Later interactions helped spread these domesticated animals and plants to new locations. In lands less suitable for crop cultivation, pastoralism and hunting remained more important for supplying food.

Interactive Map

The inhabitants of the American continents were domesticating other crops by about 5000 B.C.E.: maize (mayz) (corn) in Mexico, manioc in Brazil and Panama, and beans and squash in Mesoamerica. By 4000 B.C.E., the inhabitants of Peru were developing potatoes and quinoa (kee-NOH-uh), a protein-rich seed grain. Insofar as their climates and soils permitted, other farming communities throughout the Americas adopted these crops, along with tomatoes and peppers.

Animal Domestication

The domestication of animals also expanded rapidly during these same millennia. The first domesticated animal was the dog, possibly tamed to help early hunters in Siberia track game. Later animals were initially domesticated to provide meat and were later exploited for milk, fiber, and energy.

Refuse heaps outside some Middle East villages during the centuries after 7000 B.C.E. show that sheep and goat bones gradually replaced gazelle bones. Since genetically inherited tameness is part of the definition of domestication, it is assumed that reproductive isolation of captive sheep and goats from their wild cousins was a necessary part of the process. How and why people isolated animals in this fashion is unclear and probably differs from one species to another. Selective breeding for desirable characteristics such as high milk production and long wooly coats eventually led to distinct breeds of sheep and goats. Domestic cattle and pigs are of similar antiquity to sheep and goats, though scholars debate the location of their first domestication.

Elsewhere, other animal species were domesticated during the centuries before 3000 B.C.E.: donkeys in northern Africa, camels in Arabia (one-humped) and Central Asia (two-humped), water buffalo in China, and humped-back Zebu (ZEE-boo) cattle in India. Varieties of domesticated animals spread from one region to another.

Once cattle became tame enough to be yoked to plows, which occurred long after their initial domestication, they became essential to grain production. In addition, animal droppings provided valuable fertilizer. However, there were two notable deviations from the pattern of complementary agriculture and animal husbandry. In the Americas comparatively few species of wild animals became domesticated, and domesticated species from the Eastern Hemisphere could not spread to the Americas because the land bridge to Asia had been submerged by raised sea levels. Domesticated llamas provided transport and wool, while guinea pigs, dogs, and turkeys furnished meat. Hunting remained the most important source of meat for Amerindians.

Pastoralism

In the more arid parts of Africa and Central Asia, pastoralism, a way of life dependent on large herds of small and large stock, predominated. As the Sahara approached its maximum dryness around 2500 B.C.E., pastoralists replaced farmers, who migrated southward (see Chapter 7). Moving their herds to new pastures and watering places throughout the year made pastoralists almost as mobile as foragers and discouraged accumulation of bulky possessions and construction of substantial dwellings. Early herders probably relied more heavily on milk than on meat, since killing animals reduced their herds. During wet seasons, they may also have done some hasty crop cultivation or bartered meat and skins for plant foods with nearby farming communities.

Agriculture and Ecological Crisis

Why did the Agricultural Revolutions occur? Some theories assume that people were drawn to food production by its obvious advantages. However, most experts believe that climate change drove people to abandon hunting and gathering in favor of agriculture or pastoralism. With the end of the Great Ice Age, the temperate lands became exceptionally warm between 6000 and 2000 B.C.E., the era when people in many parts of the world adopted agriculture. The precise nature of the crisis probably varied. Shortages of wild food in the Middle East caused by a dry spell or population growth may have prodded people to take up food production. Elsewhere, a warmer, wetter climate could turn grasslands into forest, reducing supplies of game and wild grains.

In many drier parts of the world, where wild food remained abundant, people did not take up agriculture. The inhabitants of Australia continued to rely exclusively on foraging until recent centuries. Many Amerindians in the arid grasslands from Alaska to the Gulf of Mexico hunted bison, while in the Pacific Northwest others took up salmon-fishing. Abundant supplies of fish, shellfish, and aquatic animals permitted food gatherers east of the Mississippi River to thrive, and conditions in the equatorial rain forest and the southern part of Africa also favored retention of the older ways. The reindeer-based societies of northern Eurasia were also unaffected by the spread of farming.

Whatever the causes, the gradual adoption of food production transformed most parts of the world. A hundred thousand years ago there were fewer than 2 million people, and their range was largely confined to the temperate and tropical regions of Africa and Eurasia. The population may have fallen even lower during the last glacial epoch, between 32,000 and 13,000 years ago. Then, as the glaciers retreated and people took up agriculture, their numbers rose. World population may have reached 10 million by 5000 B.C.E. and then mushroomed to between 50 million and 100 million by 1000 B.C.E.[2] This increase led to important changes in social and cultural life.

Life in Neolithic Communities

Evidence that an ecological crisis may have driven people to food production has prompted a reexamination of the assumption that farmers enjoyed better lives than foragers. Modern studies demonstrate that food producers have to work much harder and for much longer periods than do food gatherers, clearing and cultivating land, guiding herds to pastures, and guarding them from predators.

Early farmers were less likely to starve because they could store food between harvests, but their diet was less varied and nutritious than that of foragers. Skeletal remains show that Neolithic farmers were shorter on average than earlier food-gathering peoples. Farmers were also more likely to die at an earlier age because people in permanent settlements were more exposed to diseases. Their water was contaminated by human waste; disease-bearing vermin and insects infested their bodies and homes; and they could catch new diseases from their domesticated animals.

The Spread of Agriculture

So how did farmers displace foragers? Some researchers have envisioned a violent struggle between practitioners of the two ways of life; others have argued for a more peaceful transition. In most cases, farmers seem to have displaced foragers by gradual infiltration rather than by conquest.

The key to the food producers' expansion may have been the fact that their small surpluses gave them a long-term advantage in population growth by ensuring higher survival rates during times of drought or other crisis. Archaeologist Colin Renfrew argues that over a few centuries farming-population densities in Europe could have increased by a factor of fifty to one hundred. As population rose, individuals who had to farm far from their native village would have formed a new settlement close to their fields. A steady, nonviolent expansion of only 12 to 19 miles (20 to 30 kilometers) a generation could have repopulated the whole of Europe between 6500 and 3500 B.C.E.[3] So gradual a process need not have provoked sharp conflicts with existing foragers, who simply could have stayed clear of the agricultural frontier or gradually adopted agriculture themselves. New studies that map genetic changes also attest to a gradual spread of agricultural people across Europe from southeast to northwest.[4]

Society and Religion

The expanding farming communities were organized around kinship and marriage. Nuclear families (parents and their children) probably lived in separate households but felt solidarity with all those related to them by descent from common ancestors. These kinship units, known as lineages (LIN-ee-ij) or clans, acted together to defend their common interests and land. Some societies trace descent equally through both parents, but most give greater importance to descent through either the mother (matrilineal [mat-ruh-LIN-ee-uhl] societies) or the father (patrilineal [pat-ruh-LIN-ee-uhl] societies). It is important not to confuse tracing descent through women (matrilineality) with the rule of women (matriarchy [MAY-tree-ahr-key]).

Kinship systems influenced early agricultural people's outlook on the world. Burials of elders might be occasions for elaborate ceremonies expressing their descendants' group solidarity. Plastered skulls found in the ancient city of Jericho (JER-ih-koh) (see Map 1.2) may be evidence of such early ancestor reverence or worship.

A society's religious beliefs tend to reflect relations to nature. The religion of food gatherers tended to center on sacred groves, springs, and wild animals. Pastoralists worshiped the Sky God who controlled the rains and guided their migrations. In contrast, the religion of many farming communities centered on the Earth Mother, a female deity believed to be the source of all new life.

megaliths Structures and complexes of very large stones constructed for ceremonial and religious purposes in Neolithic times.

A recently discovered complex of stone structures in the Egyptian desert that was in use by 5000 B.C.E. includes burial chambers presumably for ancestors, a calendar circle, and pairs of upright stones that frame the rising sun on the summer solstice. The builders must have been deeply concerned with the cycle of the seasons and how they were linked to the movement of heavenly bodies. Other **megaliths** (meaning "big stones") were erected elsewhere. Observation

Megalithic Constructions

and worship of the sun are evident at the famous Stonehenge site in England, constructed about

G. Dagli Orti/The Art Archive

www.knoweth.com

Passage-Tomb at Newgrange, Ireland Dating to around 3200 B.C.E., Newgrange is one of the oldest and most impressive Neolithic stuctures. A wall of white quartz stones rises above a row of horizontal megaliths on either side of the entrance, from which a passage leads to a spacious interior chamber. For several minutes each year, at sunrise on the winter solstice, the chamber is illuminated by a shaft of light which passes through the "roof-box" above the entrance.

2000 B.C.E., and megalithic burial chambers dating from 4000 B.C.E. are evidence of ancestor rituals in western and southern Europe. The early ones appear to have been communal burial chambers, erected by descent groups to mark their claims to farmland. In the Middle East, the Americas, and other parts of the world, giant earth burial mounds may have served similar functions.

Most early farmers lived in small villages, but in some parts of the world a few villages grew into more densely populated towns that were centers of trade and specialized crafts. These towns had grander dwellings and ceremonial buildings, as well as large structures for storing surplus food until the next harvest. Farmers could make most buildings, tools, and containers in their spare time, but in large communities some craft specialists devoted their full time to making products of unusual complexity or beauty.

Jericho and Çatal Hüyük

Two early towns in the Middle East that have been extensively excavated are Jericho on the west bank of the Jordan River and Çatal Hüyük (cha-TAHL hoo-YOOK) in central Turkey. (Map 1.2 shows their locations.) Jericho, located near a natural spring, was an unusually large and elaborate agricultural settlement. Around 8000 B.C.E. it had round, mud-brick dwellings that may have been modeled on hunters' tents. A millennium later, rectangular buildings with finely plastered walls and floors and wide doorways opened onto central courtyards. A massive stone wall surrounding the 10-acre (4-hectare) settlement defended it against attacks.

The ruins of Çatal Hüyük, an even larger town, date to between 7000 and 5000 B.C.E. and cover 32 acres (13 hectares). Its residents also occupied plastered mud-brick rooms with elaborate decorations, but Çatal Hüyük had no defensive wall. Instead, the walls of the town's houses formed a continuous barrier without doors or large windows. Residents entered their house by means of ladders through holes in the roof.

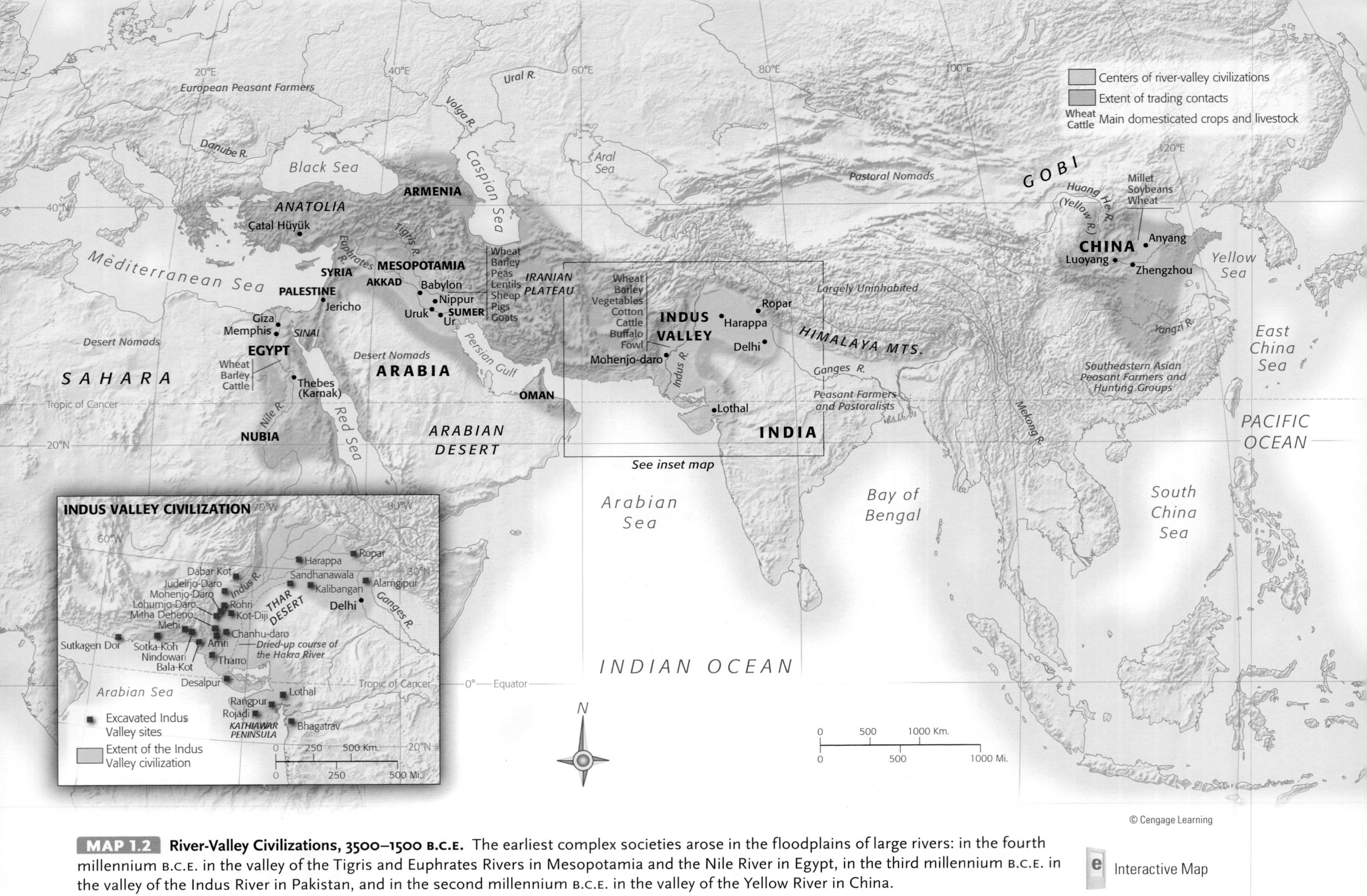

MAP 1.2 **River-Valley Civilizations, 3500–1500 B.C.E.** The earliest complex societies arose in the floodplains of large rivers: in the fourth millennium B.C.E. in the valley of the Tigris and Euphrates Rivers in Mesopotamia and the Nile River in Egypt, in the third millennium B.C.E. in the valley of the Indus River in Pakistan, and in the second millennium B.C.E. in the valley of the Yellow River in China.

Neolithic Goddess Many versions of a well-nourished and pregnant female figure were found at Çatal Hüyük. Here she is supported by twin leopards whose tails curve over her shoulders. To those who inhabited the city some 8,000 years ago, the figure likely represented fertility and power over nature.

Çatal Hüyük prospered from long-distance trade in obsidian, a hard volcanic rock that craftspeople made into tools, weapons, mirrors, and ornaments. Other residents made fine pottery, wove baskets and woolen cloth, made stone and shell beads, and worked leather and wood. House sizes varied, but there is no evidence of a dominant class or centralized political structure. Fields around the town produced crops of barley and emmer wheat, as well as vegetables. Pigs were kept along with goats and sheep. Yet wild foods—acorns, wild grains, and game animals—still featured prominently in the residents' diet.

Wall paintings, remarkably similar to earlier cave paintings, reveal the continuing importance of hunting. Scenes depict people adorned with the skins of wild leopards, and men were buried with weapons of war and hunting, not the tools of farming.

For every two houses in Çatal Hüyük, there is a religious shrine. Many rooms contain depictions of horned wild bulls, female breasts, goddesses, leopards, and handprints. Rituals involved burning grains, legumes, and meat as offerings, but there is no evidence of live animal sacrifice. Statues of plump female deities far outnumber statues of male deities, suggesting that the inhabitants primarily venerated a goddess. According to the site's principal excavator, "it seems extremely likely that the cult of the goddess was administered mainly by women."[5]

Metallurgy and Architecture

Metalworking became an important specialized occupation in the late Neolithic period. At Çatal Hüyük objects of copper and lead—metals that occur naturally in a fairly pure form—date to about 6400 B.C.E. In many parts of the world silver and gold were also worked at an early date. Because of their rarity and softness, those metals did not replace stone tools and weapons but were used primarily to make decorative or ceremonial objects. The discovery of many such objects in graves suggests they were symbols of status and power.

The emergence of towns and individuals engaged in crafts and other specialized occupations added to the workload of agriculturalists. Extra food had to be produced for nonfarmers such as priests and artisans. Added labor was needed to build permanent houses, town walls, and towers, not to mention religious structures and megalithic monuments. It is not known whether these tasks were performed freely or coerced.

SECTION REVIEW

- Around 10,000 years ago, during the Neolithic Age, humans began to cultivate plants and to domesticate animals in various parts of the world. Climate change is probably the major reason for the switch from food gathering to food production.
- Although farming is often harder than hunting and gathering, agriculturalists, because of their capacity to increase their population, expanded across much of the planet at the expense of hunter-gatherers. The process was gradual and largely peaceful. In some places pastoralism, the dependence on herd animals, prevailed.
- Megaliths and other monumental structures are products of the diverse religious beliefs and practices of Neolithic societies.
- In some places small agricultural villages developed into towns that were centers of trade and home to craftsmen and other specialized professions. Jericho and Çatal Hüyük are two excavated sites that give us vivid glimpses of early Neolithic towns.

MESOPOTAMIA

 **AP* Exam Tip** Be able to compare and contrast two of the early civilizations.

The name *Mesopotamia* means "land between the rivers" in Greek, reflecting the centrality of the Euphrates and Tigris Rivers to the way of life in this region (see Map 1.3). Mesopotamian civilization developed in the plain alongside and between the rivers, which originate in the mountains of eastern Anatolia (modern Turkey) and empty into the Persian Gulf. This is an alluvial plain—a flat, fertile expanse built up over many millennia by silt deposited by the rivers.

Mesopotamia lies mostly within modern Iraq. To the north and east, an arc of mountains extends from northern Syria and southeastern Anatolia to the Zagros (ZAG-ruhs) Mountains, which separate the plain from the Iranian Plateau. The Syrian and Arabian deserts lie to the west and southwest, the Persian Gulf to the southeast.

Settled Agriculture in an Unstable Landscape

Irrigation Agriculture

Although the first domestication of plants and animals took place in the "Fertile Crescent" region of northern Syria and southeastern Anatolia around 8000 B.C.E., agriculture did not come to Mesopotamia until approximately 5000 B.C.E. Since the region lacks adequate rainfall (at least 8 inches [20 centimeters] is needed annually), farming in hot, dry southern Mesopotamia depended on irrigation—the artificial provision of water to crops. Farmers did not use the natural spring floods because they could be sudden and violent and came at the wrong time when grain crops were ripening in the field. Moreover, the floods could cause the rivers to change course, cutting off fields and population centers from water and river communication. Shortly after 3000 B.C.E. the Mesopotamians learned to construct canals to carry water to their fields.

By 4000 B.C.E. farmers were using ox-drawn plows to turn over the earth. An attached funnel dropped a carefully measured amount of seed into the furrow. Barley was the main cereal crop because of its ability to tolerate hot, dry conditions and withstand the salt drawn to the surface by evaporation. To replenish the nutrients in the soil, fields were left fallow (unplanted) every other year. Date palms provided food, fiber, and wood, while garden plots produced vegetables. Reed plants, which grew on the riverbanks and in the marshy southern delta, could be woven into mats, baskets, huts, and boats. Fish was a dietary staple, and herds of sheep and goats, which grazed on fallow land or beyond the zone of cultivation, provided wool, milk, and meat. Donkeys, originally domesticated in Northeast Africa, carried burdens, while carts were pulled by cattle. In the second millennium B.C.E. they were joined by newly introduced camels from Arabia and horses from the mountains.

Sumerians The people who dominated southern Mesopotamia through the end of the third millennium B.C.E. They were responsible for the creation of many fundamental elements of Mesopotamian culture, such as irrigation technology, cuneiform, and religious conceptions, taken over by their Semitic successors.

Semitic Family of related languages long spoken across parts of western Asia and northern Africa. In antiquity these languages included Hebrew, Aramaic, and Phoenician. The most widespread modern member of the Semitic family is Arabic.

Sumerians and Semites

The people living in Mesopotamia at the start of the "historical period"—the period for which we have written evidence—were the **Sumerians**. Archaeological evidence places them in southern Mesopotamia by 5000 B.C.E. and perhaps even earlier. The Sumerians created the framework of civilization in Mesopotamia during a long period of dominance in the fourth and third millennia B.C.E. Other peoples lived in Mesopotamia as well. Personal names recorded in inscriptions from northerly cities from as early as 2900 B.C.E. reveal the presence of people who spoke a **Semitic** (suh-MIT-ik) language. (*Semitic* refers to a family of languages spoken in parts of western Asia and northern Africa, including ancient Hebrew, Aramaic [ar-uh-MAY-ik], Phoenician [fi-NEE-shuhn], and modern Arabic.) Possibly the descendants of nomads who had migrated into the Mesopotamian plain from the western desert, these Semites seem to have lived in peace with the Sumerians, adopting their culture and sometimes achieving positions of wealth and power.

By 2000 B.C.E. the Semitic peoples had become politically dominant, and from this time forward the Semitic language Akkadian (uh-KAY-dee-uhn) supplanted Sumerian, although the Sumerian cultural legacy was preserved. Sumerian-Akkadian dictionaries were compiled and Sumerian literature was translated. Other ethnic groups, including mountain peoples such as the Kassites (KAS-ite) as well as Elamites (EE-luh-mite) and Persians from Iran, also played a part in Mesopotamian history.

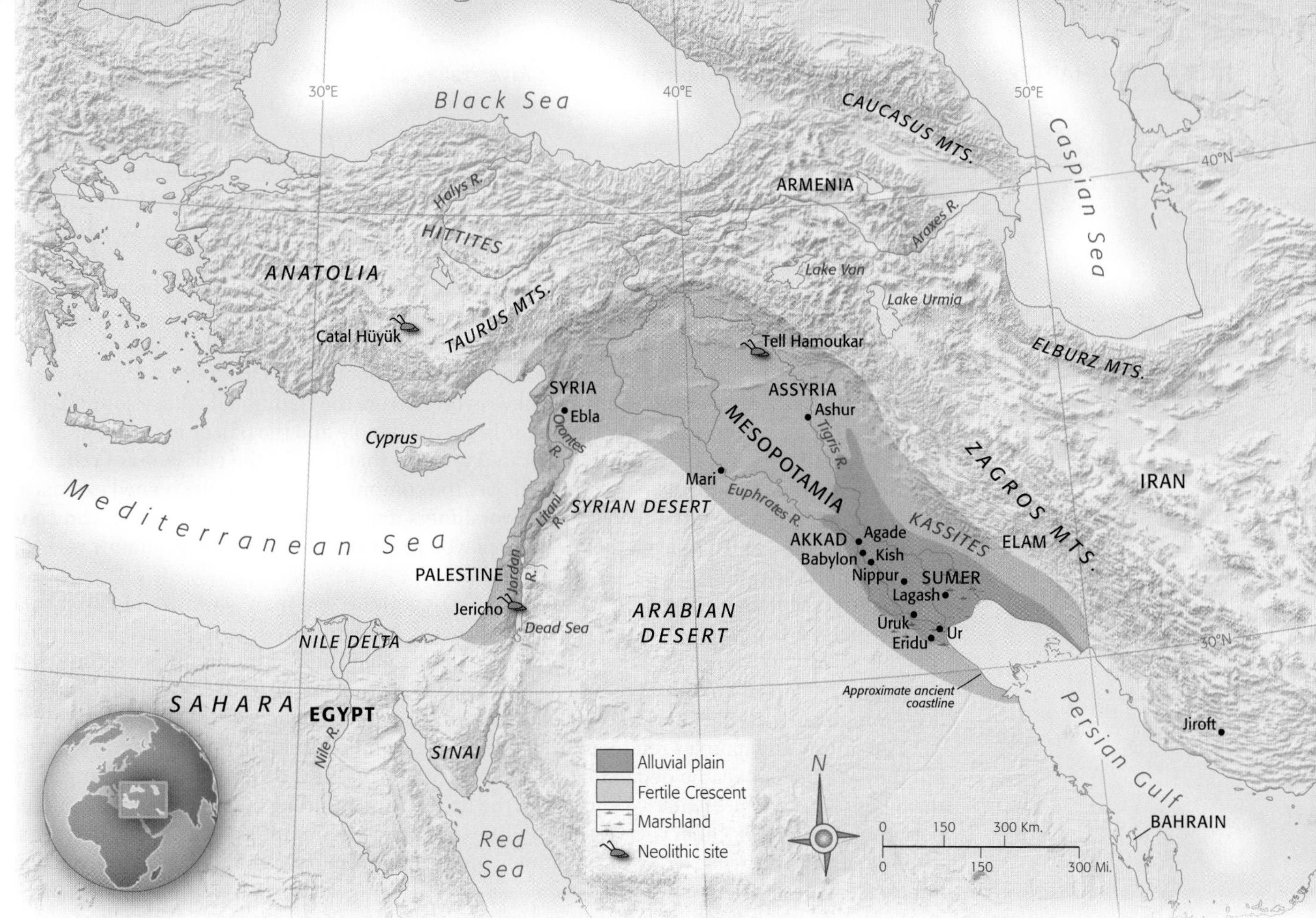

Interactive Map

MAP 1.3 **Mesopotamia** In order to organize labor resources to create and maintain an irrigation network in the Tigris-Euphrates Valley, a land of little rain, the Sumerians of southern Mesopotamia developed new technologies, complex political and social institutions, and distinctive cultural practices.

Cities, Kings, and Trade

Villages and Cities

Mesopotamia was a land of villages and cities. Groups of farming families banded together in villages to protect one another, work together at key times in the agricultural cycle, and share tools, barns and threshing floors. Village society also provided companionship and a pool of potential marriage partners.

Most cities evolved from villages. When a successful village grew, small satellite villages developed nearby and eventually merged with the main village to form an urban center. Historians use the term **city-state** to designate these self-governing urban centers and the agricultural territories they controlled. Cities needed food, and many Mesopotamian city dwellers went out each day to labor in nearby fields. However, some urban residents did not engage in food production but instead specialized in crafts, manufacturing pottery, artwork, clothing, and weapons, tools, and other objects forged out of metal. Others served the gods or carried out administrative duties. These specialists depended on the surplus food production of the countryside. Mesopotamian cities collected crop surpluses from the villages in their vicinity and in return provided rural districts with military protection against bandits and raiders and access to manufactured goods produced by urban specialists.

city-state A small independent state consisting of an urban center and the surrounding agricultural territory. A characteristic political form in early Mesopotamia, Archaic and Classical Greece, Phoenicia, and early Italy.

Stretches of uncultivated land, either desert or swamp, served as buffers between the many small city-states of early Mesopotamia. Nevertheless, disputes over land, water rights, and movable property often sparked hostilities between neighboring cities and prompted most to build protective walls of sun-dried mud bricks.

Religious and Political Leaders

Mesopotamians opened new land to agriculture by building and maintaining irrigation networks. Canals brought water to fields far from the rivers; dams raised the level of the river so that water could flow by gravity into the canals; and drainage ditches carried water away from flooded fields before evaporation could draw salt and minerals harmful to crops to the surface. Dikes protected fields near the riverbanks from floods. Because the rivers carried so much silt, clogged channels needed constant dredging.

Successful operation of these irrigation systems required leaders able to organize large numbers of people to work together. Other projects called for similar coordination: the harvest, sheep shearing, the construction of fortification walls and large public buildings, and warfare. Little is known about the political institutions of early Mesopotamian city-states, although there are traces of a citizens' assembly that may have evolved from the traditional village council. The two centers of power attested in written records are the temple and the palace of the king.

Each city had one or more centrally located temples that housed the cult (a set of religious practices) of the deity or deities who watched over the community. The temples owned extensive agricultural lands and stored the gifts that worshipers donated. The leading priests, who controlled the shrines and managed their wealth, played prominent political and economic roles in early communities.

In the third millennium B.C.E. the *lugal* (LOO-gahl), or "big man"—we would call him a king—emerged in Sumerian cities. A plausible theory maintains that certain men chosen by the community to lead the armies in time of war extended their authority in peacetime and assumed key judicial and ritual functions. The location of the temple in the city's heart and the less prominent location of the king's palace attest to the later emergence of royalty.

The priests and temples retained influence because of their wealth and religious mystique, but they gradually became dependent on the palace. Normally, the king portrayed himself as the deity's earthly representative and saw to the upkeep and building of temples and the proper performance of ritual. Other royal responsibilities included maintaining city walls and defenses, extending and repairing irrigation channels, guarding property rights, warding off outside attackers, and establishing justice.

Early Regional Empires

PRIMARY SOURCE: The State Regulates Health Care: Hammurabi's Code and Surgeons Consider the various rewards and punishments for surgeons who either succeed or fail at their job in 1800 B.C.E.

Babylon The largest and most important city in Mesopotamia. It achieved particular eminence as the capital of the Amorite king Hammurabi in the eighteenth century B.C.E. and the Neo-Babylonian king Nebuchadnezzar in the sixth century B.C.E.

Hammurabi Amorite ruler of Babylon (r. 1792–1750 B.C.E.). He conquered many city-states in southern and northern Mesopotamia and is best known for a code of laws, inscribed on a black stone pillar, illustrating the principles to be used in legal cases.

Some city-states became powerful enough to dominate others. Sargon (SAHR-gone), ruler of the city of Akkad (AH-kahd) around 2350 B.C.E., was the first to unite many cities under one king and capital. Sargon and the four family members who succeeded him over a period of 120 years secured their power in several ways. They razed the walls of conquered cities, installed governors backed by garrisons of Akkadian troops, and gave land to soldiers to ensure their loyalty. Being of Semitic stock, they adapted the cuneiform (kyoo-NEE-uh-form) system of writing used for Sumerian (discussed later in the chapter) to express their own language.

For reasons that remain obscure, the Akkadian state fell around 2230 B.C.E. The Sumerian language and culture became dominant again in the cities of the southern plain under the Third Dynasty of Ur (2112–2004 B.C.E.). Through campaigns of conquest and marriage alliances, this dynasty of five kings flourished for a century. While not controlling territories as extensive as those of the Akkadians, they maintained tight control by means of a rapidly expanding bureaucracy of administrators and obsessive recordkeeping. Messengers and well-maintained road stations enabled rapid communication, and an official calendar, standardized weights and measures, and uniform writing practices increased the efficiency of the central administration.

In the northwest the kings erected a great wall 125 miles (201 kilometers) in length to keep out the nomadic Amorites (AM-uh-rite), but in the end nomad incursions combined with an Elamite attack from the southeast toppled the Third Dynasty of Ur. The Semitic Amorites founded a new city at **Babylon**, not far from Akkad. Toward the end of a long reign, **Hammurabi** (HAM-uh-rah-bee) (r. 1792–1750 B.C.E.) launched a series of aggressive military campaigns, and Babylon became the capital of what historians have named the "Old Babylonian" state, which stretched beyond Sumer and Akkad into the north and northwest from 1900 to 1600 B.C.E. Hammurabi's famous Law Code, inscribed on a polished black stone pillar, provided judges with a lengthy set of examples illustrating principles to use in deciding cases. Many offenses were met with severe physical punishments and, not infrequently, the death penalty.

Trade

The far-reaching conquests of some states were motivated, at least in part, by the need to obtain vital resources. The alternative was to trade for raw materials, and long-distance commerce flourished in most periods. Evidence of boats used in river and sea trade appears as early as the fifth millennium B.C.E. Wool, barley, and vegetable oil were exported in exchange for wood from cedar forests in Lebanon and Syria, silver from Anatolia, gold from Egypt, copper from the eastern Mediterranean and Oman (on the Arabian peninsula), and tin from Afghanistan. Precious stones used for jewelry and carved figurines came from Iran, Afghanistan, and Pakistan.

AP* Exam Tip Social classes are a major comparison topic in the exam.

In the third millennium B.C.E. merchants were primarily employed by the palace or temple, the only two institutions with the financial resources and long-distance connections to organize the collection, transport, and protection of goods. Merchants exchanged surplus food from the estates of kings or temples for raw materials and luxury goods. In the second millennium B.C.E. more commerce came into the hands of independent merchants, and guilds (cooperative associations formed by merchants) became powerful forces in Mesopotamian society. Items could be bartered—traded for one another—or valued in relation to fixed weights of precious metal, primarily silver, or measures of grain.

Mesopotamian Society

Social Classes

Urbanized civilizations generate social divisions—variations in the status and legal and political privileges of certain groups of people. The rise of cities, specialization of labor, centralization of power, and the use of written records enabled some groups to amass unprecedented wealth. Temple leaders and kings controlled large agricultural estates, and the palace administration collected taxes from subjects. An elite class acquired large landholdings, and soldiers and religious officials received plots of land in return for their services.

The Law Code of Hammurabi in eighteenth-century B.C.E. Babylonia reflects three social divisions: (1) the free, landowning class, which included royalty, high-ranking officials, warriors, priests, merchants, and some artisans and shopkeepers; (2) the class of dependent farmers and artisans, whose legal attachment to royal, temple, or private estates made them the primary rural work force; and (3) the class of slaves, primarily employed in domestic service. Penalties for crimes prescribed in the Law Code depended on the class of the offender, with the most severe punishments reserved for the lower orders.

Slaves and Peasants

Slavery was not as prevalent and fundamental to the economy as it would be in the later societies of Greece and Rome (see Chapters 4 and 5). Many slaves came from mountain tribes, either captured in war or sold by slave traders. Others were people unable to pay their debts. Normally slaves were not chained, but they were identified by a distinctive hairstyle; if given their freedom, a barber shaved off the telltale mark. In the Old Babylonian period, as the class of people who were not dependent on the temple or palace grew in numbers and importance, the amount

Mesopotamian Cylinder Seal Seals indicated the identity of an individual and were impressed into wet clay or wax to "sign" legal documents or to mark ownership of an object. This seal, produced in the period of the Akkadian Empire, depicts Ea (second from right), the god of underground waters, symbolized by the stream with fish emanating from his shoulders; Ishtar, whose attributes of fertility and war are indicated by the date cluster in her hand and the pointed weapons showing above her wings; and the sun-god Shamash, cutting his way out of the mountains with a jagged knife, an evocation of sunrise.

of land and other property in private hands increased, and the hiring of free laborers became more common. Slaves, dependent workers, and hired laborers were all compensated with commodities such as food and oil in quantities proportional to their age, gender, and tasks.

scribe In the governments of many ancient societies, a professional position reserved for men who had undergone the lengthy training required to be able to read and write using cuneiforms, hieroglyphics, or other early, cumbersome writing systems.

The daily lives of ordinary Mesopotamians, especially those in villages or on large estates in the countryside, left few archaeological or written remains. Peasants built houses of mud brick and reed, which quickly disintegrate, and they had few metal possessions. Being illiterate, they left no written record of their lives. It is likewise difficult to discover much about the experiences of women. The written sources were produced by male **scribes**—trained professionals who applied their reading and writing skills to tasks of administration—and for the most part reflect elite male activities.

Women

Anthropologists theorize that women lost social standing and freedoms in societies where agriculture superseded hunting and gathering. In hunting-and-gathering societies women provided most of the community's food from their gathering activities, and this work was highly valued. But in Mesopotamia food production depended on the heavy physical labor of plowing, harvesting, and digging irrigation channels, jobs usually performed by men. Since food surpluses permitted families to have more children, bearing and rearing children became the primary occupation of many women, preventing them from acquiring the specialized skills of the scribe or artisan. However, women could own property, maintain control of their dowry (a sum of money given by the woman's father to support her in her husband's household), and even engage in trade. Some worked outside the household in textile factories and breweries or as prostitutes, tavern keepers, bakers, or fortunetellers. Nonelite women who stayed at home helped with farming, planted vegetable gardens, cooked, cleaned, fetched water, tended the household fire, and wove baskets and textiles.

The standing of women seems to have declined further in the second millennium B.C.E., perhaps because of the rise of an urbanized middle class and an increase in private wealth. The laws favored the rights of husbands. Although Mesopotamian society was generally monogamous, a man could take a second wife if the first gave him no children, and in later Mesopotamian history kings and wealthy men had several wives. Marriage alliances arranged between families made women into instruments for preserving and increasing family wealth. Alternatively, a family might decide to avoid a daughter's marriage—and the resulting loss of a dowry—by dedicating her to the service of a deity as "god's bride."

Gods, Priests, and Temples

Gods

The Sumerian gods embodied the forces of nature. When the Semitic peoples became dominant, they equated their deities with those of the Sumerians. Myths of the Sumerian gods were transferred to their Semitic counterparts, and many of the same rituals continued to be practiced. People imagined the gods as anthropomorphic (an-thruh-puh-MORE-fik)—like humans in form and conduct. They thought the gods had bodies and senses, sought nourishment from sacrifice, enjoyed the worship and obedience of humanity, and were driven by lust, love, hate, anger, and envy. The Mesopotamians feared their gods, believing them responsible for the natural disasters that occurred without warning in their environment, and sought to appease them.

State Religion

The public, state-organized religion is most visible in the archaeological record. Cities built temples and showed devotion to the divinities who protected the community. The temple precinct, encircled by a high wall, contained the shrine of the chief deity; open-air plazas; chapels for lesser gods; housing, dining facilities, and offices for priests and other temple staff; and craft shops, storerooms, and service buildings. The most visible part of the temple compound was the **ziggurat** (ZIG-uh-rat), a multistory, mud-brick, pyramid-shaped tower approached by ramps and stairs. Scholars are not certain of the ziggurat's function and symbolic meaning.

ziggurat A massive pyramidal stepped tower made of mud bricks. It is associated with religious complexes in ancient Mesopotamian cities, but its function is unknown.

A temple was considered the god's residence, and the cult statue in its interior shrine was believed to embody the deity's life force. Priests anticipated and met every need of the divine image in a daily cycle of waking, bathing, dressing, feeding, moving around, entertaining, soothing, and revering. These efforts reflected the claim of the Babylonian Creation Myth that humankind had been created from the blood of a vanquished rebel deity in order to serve the gods. Several thousand priests may have staffed a large temple like that of the chief god Marduk at Babylon.

Priests passed their hereditary office and sacred lore to their sons, and their families lived on rations of food from the deity's estates. The amount a priest received depended on his rank

D.Collon/Visual Connection Archive

Ziggurat of Ur-Nammu, ca. 2100 B.C.E. Built at Ur by King Ur-Nammu for the Sumerian moon-god, Nanna, an exterior made of fine bricks baked in a kiln encloses a sun-dried mud-brick core. Three ramps on the first level converge to form a stairway to the second level. The function of ziggurats is not known.

within a complicated hierarchy of status and specialized function. The high priest performed the central acts in the great rituals. Certain priests made music to please the gods, while others exorcised evil spirits. Still others interpreted dreams and divined the future by examining the organs of sacrificed animals, reading patterns in the rising incense smoke, or casting dice.

Private Religion

Harder to determine are the everyday beliefs and religious practices of the common people. Scholars do not know how much access the general public had to the temple buildings, although individuals did place votive statues in the sanctuaries, believing that these miniature replicas of themselves could continually seek the deity's favor. The survival of many **amulets** (small charms meant to protect the bearer from evil) and representations of a host of demons suggests widespread belief in magic—the use of special words and rituals to manipulate and control the forces of nature. For example, people believed that a headache was caused by a demon that could be driven out of the ailing body. In return for a gift or sacrifice, a god or goddess might reveal information about the future. Elite and common folk came together in great festivals such as the twelve-day New Year's Festival held each spring in Babylon to mark the beginning of a new agricultural cycle (see Diversity and Dominance: Violence and Order in the Babylonian New Year's Festival).

amulet Small charm meant to protect the bearer from evil. Found frequently in archaeological excavations in Mesopotamia and Egypt, amulets reflect the religious practices of the common people.

Technology and Science

The term *technology*, from the Greek word *techne*, meaning "skill" or "specialized knowledge," normally refers to the tools and machines that humans use to manipulate the physical world. Many scholars now use the term more broadly for any specialized knowledge used to transform the natural environment and human society.

Writing

An important example of the broader type of technology is writing, which first appeared in Mesopotamia before 3300 B.C.E. The earliest inscribed tablets, found in the chief temple at Uruk, date from a time when the temple was the most important economic institution in the community. According to a plausible recent theory, writing originated from a system of tokens used to keep track of property—such as sheep, cattle, or cart wheels—when increases in the amount of accumulated wealth and the complexity of commercial transactions strained people's memories. The tokens, made in the shape of the commodity, were sealed in clay balls, and pictures of the tokens were incised on the outside of the balls as a reminder of what was inside. Eventually, people realized that the incised pictures were an adequate record, making the tokens inside the ball redundant. These pictures were the first written symbols. Each symbol represented an object and could also stand for the sound of the word for that object if the sound was part of a longer word.

The usual method of writing involved pressing the point of a sharpened reed into a moist clay tablet. Because the reed made wedge-shaped impressions, the early realistic pictures were increasingly stylized into a combination of strokes and wedges, a system known as **cuneiform** (Latin for "wedge-shaped") writing. Mastering this system required years of training and practice. Several hundred signs were in use at any one time, as compared to the twenty-five or so signs in an alphabetic system. The prestige and regular employment that went with their position may have made scribes reluctant to simplify the cuneiform system. In the Old Babylonian

cuneiform A system of writing in which wedge-shaped symbols represented words or syllables. It originated in Mesopotamia and was used initially for Sumerian and Akkadian but later was adapted to represent other languages of western Asia. Because so many symbols had to be learned, literacy was confined to a relatively small group of administrators and scribes.

DIVERSITY + DOMINANCE

Violence and Order in the Babylonian New Year's Festival

The twelve-day Babylonian New Year's Festival was one of the most important religious celebrations in ancient Mesopotamia. Fragmentary documents of the third century B.C.E. *(fifteen hundred years after Hammurabi) provide most of our information, but because of the continuity of culture over several millennia, the later Babylonian New Year's Festival preserves many of the beliefs and practices of earlier epochs.*

In the first days of the festival, most activities took place in inner chambers of the temple of Marduk, patron deity of Babylon, attended only by high-ranking priests. A key ceremony was a ritualized humiliation of the king, followed by a renewal of the institution of divinely sanctioned kingship:

On the fifth day of the month Nisannu . . . they shall bring water for washing the king's hands and then shall accompany him to the temple Esagil. The *urigallu*-priest shall leave the sanctuary and take away the scepter, the circle, and the sword from the king. He shall bring them before the god Bel [Marduk] and place them on a chair. He shall leave the sanctuary and strike the king's cheek. He shall accompany the king into the presence of the god Bel. He shall drag him by the ears and make him bow to the ground. The king shall speak the following only once: "I did not sin, lord of the countries. I was not neglectful of the requirements of your godship. I did not destroy Babylon. The temple Esagil, I did not forget its rites. I did not rain blows on the cheek of a subordinate." . . . [The *urigallu*-priest responds:] "The god Bel will listen to your prayer. He will exalt your kingship. The god Bel will bless you forever. He will destroy your enemy, fell your adversary." After the *urigallu*-priest says this, the king shall regain his composure. The scepter, circle, and sword shall be restored to the king.

Also in the early days of the festival, a priest recited the entire Babylonian Creation Epic to the image of Marduk. After relating the origins of the gods from the mating of two primordial creatures, Tiamat, the female embodiment of the salt sea, and Apsu, the male embodiment of fresh water, the myth tells how Tiamat gathered an army of older gods and monsters to destroy the younger generation of gods.

All the Anunnaki [the younger gods], the host of gods gathered into that place tongue-tied; they sat with mouths shut for they thought, "What other god can make war on Tiamat? No one else can face her and come back." . . . Lord Marduk exulted, . . . with racing spirits he said to the father of gods, "Creator of the gods who decides their destiny, if I must be your avenger, defeating Tiamat, saving your lives, call the Assembly, give me precedence over all the rest; . . . now and for ever let my word be law; I, not you, will decide the world's nature, the things to come. My decrees shall never be altered, never be annulled, but my creation endures to the ends of the world." . . . He took his route towards the rising sound of Tiamat's rage, and all the gods besides, the fathers of the gods pressed in around him, and the lord approached Tiamat. . . . When Tiamat heard him her wits scattered, she was possessed and shrieked aloud, her legs shook from the crotch down, she gabbled spells, muttered maledictions, while the gods of war sharpened their weapons. . . . The lord shot his net to entangle Tiamat, and the pursuing tumid wind, Imhullu, came from behind and beat in her face. When the mouth gaped open to suck him down he drove Imhullu in, so that the mouth would not shut but wind raged through her belly; her carcass blown up, tumescent. She gaped. And now he shot the arrow that split the belly, that pierced the gut and cut the womb. . . .

He split it apart like a cockle-shell; with the upper half he constructed the arc of sky, he pulled down the bar and set a watch on the waters, so they should never escape. . . . He projected positions for the Great Gods conspicuous in the sky, he gave them a starry aspect as constellations; he measured the year, gave it a beginning and an end, and to each month of the twelve three rising stars. . . . Through her ribs he opened gates in the east and west, and gave them strong bolts on the right and left; and high in the belly of Tiamat he set the zenith. He gave the moon the luster of a jewel, he gave him all the night, to mark off days, to watch by night each month the circle of a waxing waning light. . . . When Marduk had sent out the moon, he took the sun and set him to complete the cycle from this one to the next New Year. . . .

Then Marduk considered Tiamat. He skimmed spume from the bitter sea, heaped up the clouds, spindrift of wet and wind

period, the growth of private commerce brought an increase in the number of people who could read and write, but only a small percentage of the population was literate.

The earliest Mesopotamian documents are economic, but cuneiform came to have wide-ranging uses. Written documents marked with the seal of the participants became the primary proof of legal actions. Texts were written about political, literary, religious, and scientific topics. Cuneiform is not a language but rather a system of writing. Developed originally for the Sumerian language, it was later adapted to the Akkadian language of the Mesopotamian Semites as well as to other languages of western Asia, such as Hittite, Elamite, and Persian.

Transportation, Metallurgy, and Engineering

Other technologies enabled the Mesopotamians to meet the challenges of their physical environment. Wheeled carts and sledlike platforms dragged by cattle were used to transport goods in some locations. In the south, where numerous water channels cut up the landscape, and cooling rain, the spittle of Tiamat. With his own hands from the steaming mist he spread the clouds. He pressed hard down the head of water, heaping mountains over it, opening springs to flow: Euphrates and Tigris rose from her eyes, but he closed the nostrils and held back their springhead. He piled huge mountains on her paps and through them drove water-holes to channel the deep sources; and high overhead he arched her tail, locked-in to the wheel of heaven; the pit was under his feet, between was the crotch, the sky's fulcrum. Now the earth had foundations and the sky its mantle. . . .

Marduk considered and began to speak to the gods assembled in his presence. This is what he said, "In the former time you inhabited the void above the abyss, but I have made Earth as the mirror of Heaven, I have consolidated the soil for the foundations, and there I will build my city, my beloved home. A holy precinct shall be established with sacred halls for the presence of the king. When you come up from the deep to join the Synod you will find lodging and sleep by night. When others from heaven descend to the Assembly, you too will find lodging and sleep by night. It shall be BABYLON the home of the gods. The masters of all crafts shall build it according to my plan." . . . Now that Marduk has heard what it is the gods are saying, he is moved with desire to create a work of consummate art. He told Ea the deep thought in his heart.

"Blood to blood
I join,
blood to bone
I form
an original thing,
its name is MAN,
aboriginal man
is mine in making.

"All his occupations
are faithful service . . ."

Ea answered with carefully chosen words, completing the plan for the gods' comfort. He said to Marduk, "Let one of the kindred be taken; only one need die for the new creation. Bring the gods together in the Great Assembly; there let the guilty die, so the rest may live."

Marduk called the Great Gods to the Synod. . . . The king speaks to the rebel gods, "Declare on your oath if ever before you spoke the truth, who instigated rebellion? Who stirred up Tiamat? Who led the battle? Let the instigator of war be handed over; guilt and retribution are on him, and peace will be yours for ever."

The great Gods answered the Lord of the Universe, the king and counselor of gods, "It was Kingu who instigated rebellion, he stirred up that sea of bitterness and led the battle for her." They declared him guilty, they bound and held him down in front of Ea, they cut his arteries and from his blood they created man; and Ea imposed his servitude. . . .

Much of the subsequent activity of the festival, which took place in the temple courtyard and streets, was a reenactment of the events of the Creation Myth. The festival occurred at the beginning of spring, when the grain shoots were beginning to emerge, and its essential symbolism concerns the return of natural life to the world. The Babylonians believed that the natural world had an annual life cycle consisting of birth, growth, maturity, and death. In winter the cycle drew to a close, and there was no guarantee that life would return to the world. Babylonians hoped proper performance of the New Year's Festival would encourage the gods to grant a renewal of time and life, in essence to re-create the world.

QUESTIONS FOR ANALYSIS

1. **According to the Creation Epic, how did the present order of the universe come into being? What does the violent nature of this creation tell us about the Mesopotamian view of the physical world and the gods?**
2. **How did the symbolism of the events of the New Year's Festival, with its ritual reading and reenactment of the story of the Creation Myth, validate such concepts as kingship, the primacy of Babylon, and mankind's relationship to the gods?**
3. **What is the significance of the distinction between the "private" ceremonies celebrated in the temple precincts and the "public" ceremonies that took place in the streets of the city? What does the festival tell us about the relationship of different social groups to the gods?**

Source: Adapted from James B. Pritchard, ed., *Ancient Near Eastern Texts Relating to the Old Testament*, 3d ed. with supplement (Princeton, NJ: Princeton University Press, 1969), 332–334.

bronze An alloy of copper with a small amount of tin (or sometimes arsenic), it is harder and more durable than copper alone. The term *Bronze Age* is applied to the era—the dates of which vary in different parts of the world—when bronze was the primary metal for tools and weapons. The demand for bronze helped create long-distance networks of trade.

boats and barges predominated. In northern Mesopotamia, donkeys were the chief pack animals for overland caravans before the advent of the camel around 1200 B.C.E. (see Chapter 7).

The Mesopotamians had to import metals, but they became skilled in metallurgy, refining ores containing copper and alloying them with arsenic or tin to make **bronze**. Craftsmen poured molten bronze into molds to produce tools and weapons. The cooled and hardened bronze took a sharper edge than stone, was less likely to break, and was more easily repaired. Stone implements remained in use among poor people, who could not afford bronze.

Widely available clay was used to make dishes and storage vessels. By 4000 B.C.E. the potter's wheel, a revolving platform spun by hands or feet, made possible the rapid production of vessels with precise and complex shapes. Mud bricks, dried in the sun or baked in an oven for greater durability, were the primary building material. Construction of city walls, temples, and palaces required practical knowledge of architecture and engineering. For example, the reed mats that Mesopotamian builders laid between the mud-brick layers of ziggurats served the same stabilizing purpose as girders in modern high-rise construction.

Warfare

Early military forces were nonprofessional militias of able-bodied men called up for short periods when needed. The powerful states of the later third and second millennia B.C.E. built up armies of well-trained and well-paid full-time soldiers. In the early second millennium B.C.E. horses appeared in western Asia, and the horse-drawn chariot came into vogue. Infantry found themselves at the mercy of swift chariots carrying a driver and an archer who could easily run them down. Using increasingly effective siege machinery, Mesopotamian soldiers could climb over, undermine, or knock down the walls protecting the cities of their enemies.

Mathematics and Science

Mesopotamians used a base-60 number system in which numbers were expressed as fractions or multiples of 60 (in contrast to our base-10 system; this is the origin of the seconds and minutes we use today). Advances in mathematics and careful observation of the skies made the Mesopotamians sophisticated practitioners of astronomy. Priests compiled lists of omens or unusual sightings on earth and in the heavens, together with a record of the events that coincided with them. They consulted these texts at critical times, for they believed that the recurrence of such phenomena could provide clues to future developments. The underlying premise was that the elements of the material universe, from the microscopic to the macrocosmic, were interconnected in mysterious but undeniable ways.

SECTION REVIEW

- Mesopotamia was home to a complex civilization that developed in the plain of the Tigris and Euphrates Rivers beginning in the fourth millennium B.C.E.
- The elements of civilization initially created by the Sumerians, the earliest known people to live in Mesopotamia, were later taken over and adapted by the Semitic peoples who became dominant in the region.
- The temples of the gods, the earliest centers of political and economic power, gradually became subordinate to kings.
- City-states, centered on cities that coalesced out of villages and controlled rural territory, were initially independent but later were united under various empires.
- Mesopotamian society was divided into three classes: free landowners and professionals in the cities, dependent peasants and artisans on rural estates, and slaves in domestic service.
- Mesopotamians feared their gods, who embodied the often-violent forces of nature.
- Cuneiform writing, which originally evolved from a system of tokens used for economic records, came to have a wide range of uses in several languages.
- A range of technologies (metallurgy, ceramics, transportation, and engineering) and sciences (mathematics and astronomy) enabled Mesopotamians to meet the challenges of their environment.

EGYPT

 **PRIMARY SOURCE: The Hymn to the Nile** Discover the degree to which the Nile River is viewed as godlike and the perceived power it has over the survival of the people of Egypt.

No place exhibits the impact of the natural environment on the history and culture of a society better than ancient Egypt. Located at the intersection of Asia and Africa, Egypt was protected by surrounding barriers of desert and a harborless, marshy seacoast. Whereas Mesopotamia was open to migration or invasion and was dependent on imported resources, Egypt's natural isolation and material self-sufficiency fostered a unique culture that for long periods had relatively little to do with other civilizations.

The Land of Egypt: "Gift of the Nile"

River and Desert

The fifth-century B.C.E. Greek traveler Herodotus (he-ROD-uh-tuhs) called Egypt the "gift of the Nile." The world's longest river, the Nile flows northward from Lake Victoria and several

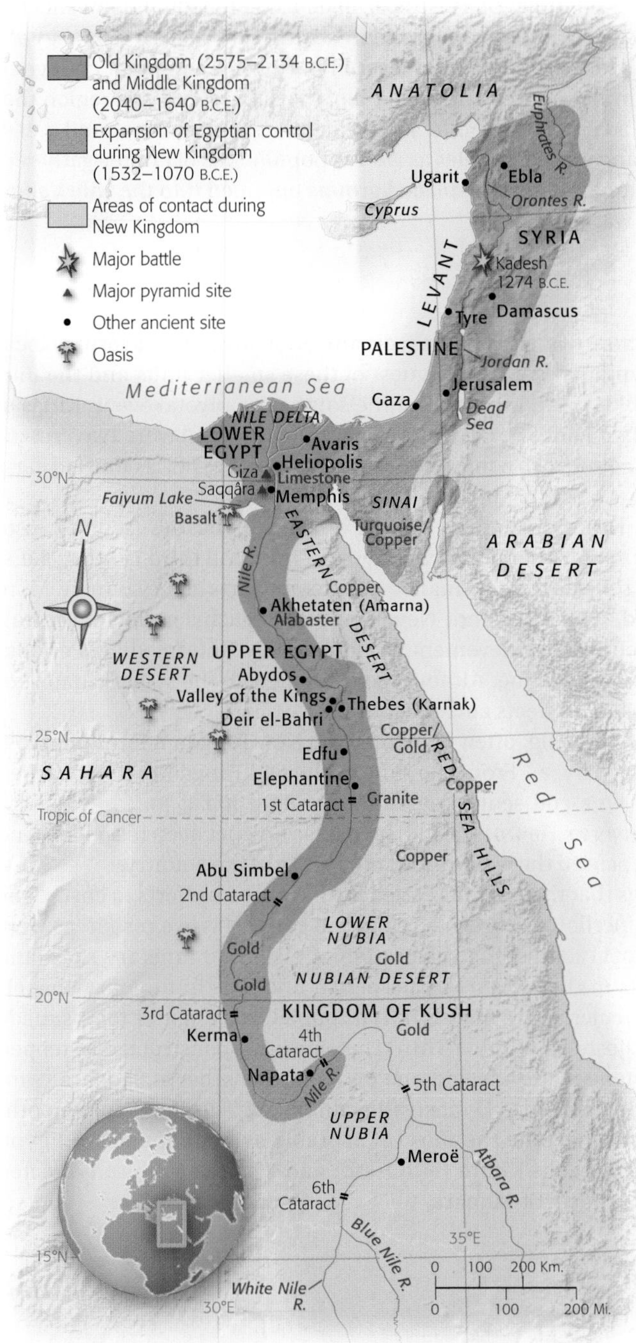

MAP 1.4 **Ancient Egypt** The Nile River, flowing south to north, carved out of the surrounding desert a narrow green valley that became heavily settled in antiquity.

Interactive Map

large tributaries in the highlands of tropical Africa, carving a narrow valley between a chain of hills on either side, until it reaches the Mediterranean Sea (see Map 1.4). Though bordered mostly by desert, the banks of the river support lush vegetation. About 100 miles (160 kilometers) from the Mediterranean the Nile divides into channels to form a triangular delta. Most of the population, then as now, lived on the twisting, green ribbon of land alongside the river or in the Nile Delta. The rest of the country, 90 percent or more, is a bleak and inhospitable desert of mountains, rocks, and dunes. The ancient Egyptians distinguished between the low-lying, life-sustaining dark soil of the "Black Land" along the river and the elevated, deadly "Red Land" of the desert.

The river was the main means of travel and communication, with the most important cities located upstream away from the Mediterranean. Because the river flows from south to north, the Egyptians called the southern part of the country "Upper Egypt" and the northern delta "Lower Egypt." In most periods the southern boundary of Egypt was the First Cataract of the Nile, the northernmost of a series of impassable rocks and rapids below Aswan (AS-wahn) (about 500 miles [800 kilometers] south of the Mediterranean). At times Egyptian control extended farther south into what they called "Kush" (later Nubia, today part of southern Egypt and northern Sudan). The Egyptians also settled a chain of large oases west of the river, green and habitable "islands" in the midst of the desert.

While the hot, sunny climate favored agriculture, rain rarely falls south of the delta, and agriculture was entirely dependent on river water. Each September the river overflowed its banks, spreading water into the bordering basins, and irrigation channels carried water farther out into the valley to increase the area suitable for planting. Unlike the Tigris and Euphrates, the Nile flooded at exactly the right time for grain agriculture. When the waters receded, they left behind a moist, fertile layer of mineral-rich silt, where farmers could easily plant their crops. Egyptian creation myths commonly featured the emergence of a life-supporting mound of earth from a primeval swamp.

The level of the flood's crest determined the abundance of the next harvest. "Nilometers," stone staircases with incised units of measure placed along the river's edge, gauged the flood surge. When the flood was too high, dikes protecting inhabited areas were washed out, and much damage resulted. When the floods were too low for several years, less land could be cultivated, and the country experienced famine and decline. The ebb and flow of successful and failed regimes seems to have been linked to the cycle of floods. Nevertheless, remarkable stability characterized most eras, and Egyptians viewed the universe as an orderly and beneficent place.

Natural Resources

Egypt was well endowed with natural resources and far more self-sufficient than Mesopotamia. Egyptians used papyrus reeds growing in marshy areas to make sails, ropes, and a kind of paper. Hunters pursued the abundant wild animals and birds in the marshes and on the edge of the desert, and fishermen netted fish from the river. Building stone was quarried and floated downstream from southern Egypt. Clay for mud bricks and pottery could be found almost everywhere. The state organized armed expeditions and forced labor to exploit copper and turquoise deposits in the Sinai desert to the east and gold from Nubia to the south.

The farming villages that appeared in Egypt as early as 5500 B.C.E. relied on domesticated plant and animal species that had originated several millennia earlier in western Asia. Egypt's emergence as a focal point of civilization stemmed, at least in part, from a gradual change in climate from the fifth to the third millennium B.C.E. Until then, the Sahara, the vast region that is now the world's largest desert, had a relatively mild and wet climate, and its lakes and grasslands supported a variety of plant and animal species as well as populations of hunter-gatherers (see Chapter 7). As the Sahara became a desert, displaced groups migrated into the Nile Valley, where they developed a sedentary way of life.

Divine Kingship

Unification

pharaoh The central figure in the ancient Egyptian state. Believed to be an earthly manifestation of the gods, he used his absolute power to maintain the safety and prosperity of Egypt.

ma'at Egyptian term for the concept of divinely created and maintained order in the universe. Reflecting the ancient Egyptians' belief in an essentially beneficent world, the divine ruler was the earthly guarantor of this order.

The increase in population led to more complex political organization, including a form of local kingship. Later generations of Egyptians saw the conquest of these smaller units and the unification of all Egypt by Menes (MEH-neez), a ruler from the south, as a pivotal event. Kings of Egypt bore the title "Ruler of the Two Lands"—Upper and Lower Egypt—and wore two crowns symbolizing the unification of the country. In contrast to Mesopotamia, Egypt was unified early in its history.

Historians organize Egyptian history using the system of thirty dynasties (sequences of kings from the same family) identified by Manetho, an Egyptian from the third century B.C.E. The rise and fall of dynasties often reflects the dominance of different parts of the country. More generally, scholars refer to the "Old," "Middle," and "New Kingdoms," each a period of centralized political power and brilliant cultural achievement, punctuated by "Intermediate Periods" of political fragmentation and cultural decline. Although experts debate the specific dates for these periods, the chronology on page 7 reflects current opinion.

The Egyptian state centered on the king, often known by the New Kingdom term **pharaoh**, from an Egyptian phrase meaning "palace." From the time of the Old Kingdom, if not earlier, Egyptians considered the king to be a god sent to earth to maintain **ma'at** (muh-AHT), the divinely authorized order of the universe. He was the indispensable link between his people and the gods, and his benevolent rule ensured the welfare and prosperity of the country.

Royal Tombs

pyramid A large, triangular stone monument, used in Egypt and Nubia as a burial place for the king. The largest pyramids, erected during the Old Kingdom near Memphis with stone tools and compulsory labor, reflect the Egyptian belief that the proper and spectacular burial of the divine ruler would guarantee the continued prosperity of the land.

So much depended on the kings that their deaths called forth elaborate efforts to ensure the well-being of their spirits on their perilous journey to rejoin the gods. Massive resources were poured into the construction of royal tombs, the celebration of elaborate funerary rites, and the sustenance of the kings' spirits in the afterlife by perpetual offerings in funerary chapels attached to the royal tombs. Early rulers were buried in flat-topped, rectangular tombs made of mud brick. Around 2630 B.C.E. Djoser (JO-sur), a Third Dynasty king, constructed a stepped **pyramid** consisting of a series of stone platforms laid one on top of the other at Saqqara (suh-KAHR-uh), near Memphis. Rulers in the Fourth Dynasty filled in the steps to create the smooth-sided, limestone pyramids that have become the most memorable symbol of ancient Egypt. Between 2550 and 2490 B.C.E. the pharaohs Khufu (KOO-foo) and Khefren (KEF-ren) erected huge pyramids at Giza, several miles north of Saqqara.

Model of Egyptian River Boat, ca. 1985 B.C.E. This model was buried in the tomb of a Middle Kingdom official, Meketre, who is shown in the cabin being entertained by musicians. The captain stands in front of the cabin, the helmsman on the left steers the boat with the rudder, while the lookout on the right lets out a weighted line to determine the river's depth. Lightweight ships equipped with sails and oars were well suited for travel on the peaceful Nile and sometimes were used for voyages on the Mediterranean and Red Seas.

Egyptians accomplished this construction with stone tools (bronze was still expensive and rare) and no machinery other than simple levers, pulleys, and rollers. What made it possible was almost unlimited human muscle power. Calculations of the human resources needed to build a pyramid within the lifetime of the ruler suggest that large numbers of people must have been pressed into service for part of each year, probably during the flood season when no agricultural work could be done. Although this labor was compulsory, the Egyptian masses probably regarded it as a kind of religious service that helped ensure prosperity. The age of the great pyramids lasted only about a century, although pyramids continued to be built on a smaller scale for two millennia.

Memphis The capital of Old Kingdom Egypt, near the head of the Nile Delta. Early rulers were interred in the nearby pyramids.

Administration and Communication

Centralized Administration

Ruling dynasties usually placed their capitals in the area of their original power base. **Memphis**, near the apex of the delta (close to Cairo, the modern capital), held this central position during the Old Kingdom. **Thebes**, far to the south, supplanted it during the Middle and New Kingdom periods (see Map 1.4).

Thebes Capital city of Egypt and home of the ruling dynasties during the Middle and New Kingdoms. Amon, patron deity of Thebes, became one of the chief gods of Egypt. Monarchs were buried across the river in the Valley of the Kings.

The administrative system began at the village level and progressed to the districts into which the country was divided and, finally, to the central government in the capital city. Bureaucrats kept track of land, products, and people, extracting as taxes a substantial portion of the country's annual revenues—at times as much as 50 percent. This income supported the palace, bureaucracy, and army, as well as the construction and maintenance of temples and great monuments celebrating the ruler's reign. The government maintained a monopoly over key sectors of the economy and controlled long-distance trade. This was different from Mesopotamia, where commerce increasingly fell into the hands of an acquisitive urban middle class.

Writing

The hallmark of the administrative class was literacy. A writing system had been developed by the beginning of the Early Dynastic period. **Hieroglyphics** (high-ruh-GLIF-iks), the earliest form of this system, were picture symbols standing for words, syllables, or individual sounds. Hieroglyphic writing long continued to be used on monuments and ornamental inscriptions. By 2500 B.C.E., however, a cursive script, in which the original pictorial nature of the symbol was less apparent, had been developed for the everyday needs of administrators and copyists. The Egyptians used writing for many purposes other than administrative recordkeeping. Their written literature included tales of adventure and magic, love poetry, religious hymns, and instruction manuals on technical subjects. Scribes in workshops attached to the temples made copies of traditional texts, working with ink on a writing material made from the **papyrus** (puh-PIE-ruhs) reed. The plant grew only in Egypt but was in demand throughout the ancient world and was exported in large quantities.

hieroglyphics A system of writing in which pictorial symbols represented sounds, syllables, or concepts. It was used for official and monumental inscriptions in ancient Egypt. Because of the long period of study required to master this system, literacy in hieroglyphics was confined to a relatively small group of scribes and administrators. Cursive symbol-forms were developed for rapid composition on other media, such as papyrus.

When the monarchy was strong, the king appointed officials, promoted them on the basis of ability and accomplishment, and gave them grants of land cultivated by dependent peasants. Low-level officials were assigned to villages and district capitals; high-ranking officials served in the royal capital. When Old Kingdom officials died, they were buried in tombs around the monumental tomb of the king so that they could serve him in death as they had in life.

Tensions Between Rulers and Officials

Throughout Egyptian history there was an underlying tension between the centralizing power of the monarchy and the decentralizing tendencies of the bureaucracy. One sign of the breakdown of royal power in the late Old Kingdom and First Intermediate Period was the placement of officials' tombs in their home districts, where they spent much of their time and exercised power more or less independently, rather than near the royal tomb. Another sign was the tendency of administrative posts to become hereditary. The early monarchs of the Middle Kingdom restored centralized control by reducing the power and prerogatives of the old elite and creating a new class of loyal administrators.

papyrus A reed that grows along the banks of the Nile River in Egypt. From it was produced a coarse, paperlike writing medium used by the Egyptians and many other peoples in the ancient Mediterranean and Middle East.

Cities

It has often been said that Egypt lacked real cities because the political capitals were primarily extensions of the palace and central administration. Compared to Mesopotamia, a far larger percentage of Egyptians lived in rural villages and engaged in agriculture, and Egypt's wealth derived to a higher degree from the land and its products. But there were towns and cities in ancient Egypt, although they were less crucial to the economic and cultural dynamism of the country than were Mesopotamian urban centers. Unfortunately, archaeologists have been unable to excavate many ancient urban sites in Egypt because they lie beneath modern communities.

Foreign Relations and Trade

During the Old and Middle Kingdoms, Egypt's foreign policy was essentially isolationist. All foreigners were considered enemies. When necessary, local militia units backed up a small standing army of professional soldiers. Nomadic groups in the eastern and western deserts and Libyans to the northwest were a nuisance rather than a real danger and were readily handled by the Egyptian military. Egypt's interests abroad focused on maintaining access to valuable resources rather than on acquiring territory. Trade with the coastal towns of the Levant (luh-VANT) (modern Israel, the Palestinian territories, Lebanon, and Syria) brought in cedar wood. In return, Egypt exported grain, papyrus, and gold.

In all periods the Egyptians had a particularly strong interest in goods from the south. Nubia had rich sources of gold (Chapter 2 examines the rise of a civilization in Nubia that, though considerably influenced by Egypt, created a vital and original culture that lasted for more than two thousand years), and the southern course of the Nile offered the easiest passage to sub-Saharan Africa. In the Old Kingdom, Egyptian noblemen led donkey caravans south to trade for gold, incense, and products of tropical Africa such as ivory, dark ebony wood, and exotic jungle animals. A line of forts along the southern border protected Egypt from attack. In the early second millennium B.C.E. Egyptian forces struck south into Nubia, extending the border to the Third Cataract of the Nile and taking possession of the gold fields. Still farther to the south, perhaps in the coastal region of present-day Sudan or Eritrea, lay the fabled land of Punt (poont), source of the fragrant myrrh resin burned on the altars of the Egyptian gods.

The People of Egypt

The million to million and a half inhabitants of Egypt included various physical types, ranging from dark-skinned people related to the populations of sub-Saharan Africa to lighter-skinned people akin to the populations of North Africa and western Asia. Although Egypt did not experience the large-scale migrations and invasions common in Mesopotamia, settlers periodically trickled into the Nile Valley and assimilated with the people already living there.

Although some Egyptians had higher status and more wealth and power than others, in contrast to Mesopotamia no formal class structure emerged. At the top of the social hierarchy were the king and high-ranking officials. In the middle were lower-level officials, local leaders, priests and other professionals, artisans, and well-to-do farmers. At the bottom were peasants, who made up the vast majority of the population.

Peasant Life

Any account of the lives of ordinary Egyptians is largely conjectural; the villages of ancient Egypt, like those of Mesopotamia, left few traces in the archaeological or literary record. In tomb paintings of the elite, artists indicated status by pictorial conventions, such as obesity for wealthy and comfortable patrons, baldness and deformity for the working classes. Egyptian poets frequently used metaphors of farming and hunting, and papyrus documents preserved in the hot, dry sands tell of property transactions and legal disputes among ordinary people.

Peasants living in rural villages engaged in the seasonally changing tasks of grain agriculture: plowing, sowing, reaping, and threshing. They also maintained and extended the irrigation network of channels, basins, and dikes. Meat from domesticated animals—cattle, sheep, goats, and poultry—and fish supplemented a diet based on wheat or barley, beer, and vegetables. Villagers shared implements, work animals, and storage facilities and helped one another at peak times in the agricultural cycle and in the construction of houses and other buildings. They prayed and feasted together at festivals to the local gods. Periodically they had to contribute labor to state projects. If taxation or compulsory service was too great a burden, flight into the desert was the only escape.

Women's Lives

Some information is available about the lives of women of the upper classes, but it is filtered through the brushes and pens of male artists and scribes. Tomb paintings show women of the royal family and elite classes accompanying their husbands and engaging in typical domestic activities. They are depicted with dignity and affection, though they are clearly subordinate to the men. The artistic convention of depicting men with a dark red and women with a yellow flesh tone implies that the elite woman's proper sphere was indoors, away from the searing sun. In the beautiful love poetry of the New Kingdom, lovers address each other in terms of apparent equality and express emotions of romantic love.

Legal documents show that Egyptian women could own property, inherit from their parents, and will their property to whomever they wished. Marriage, usually monogamous, was not confirmed by any legal or religious ceremony and essentially constituted a decision by a man and woman to establish a household together. Either party could dissolve the relationship, and the divorced woman retained rights over her dowry. At certain times queens and queen-mothers played significant behind-the-scenes roles in the politics of the court, and priestesses sometimes supervised the cults of female deities. In general, the limited evidence suggests that women in ancient Egypt were treated more respectfully and had more legal rights and social freedom than women in Mesopotamia.

Belief and Knowledge

Gods

Egyptian religion was rooted in the landscape of the Nile Valley and the vision of cosmic order that it evoked. The consistency of their environment—the sun rose every day in a clear and cloudless sky, and the river flooded on schedule every year, ensuring a bounteous harvest—persuaded the Egyptians that the natural world was a place of recurrent cycles and periodic renewal. The sky was imagined to be a great ocean surrounding the inhabited world. The sun-god Re (ray) traversed this blue waterway in a boat by day, then returned through the Underworld at night, fighting off the attacks of demonic serpents so that he could be born anew in the morning. In one especially popular story Osiris (oh-SIGH-ris), a god who once ruled Egypt, was slain by his jealous brother Seth, who then scattered the dismembered pieces. Isis, Osiris's devoted sister and wife, found and reconstructed the remnants, and Horus, his son, took revenge on Seth. Osiris was restored to life and installed as king of the Underworld, and his example gave people hope of a new life in a world beyond this one.

The king, who was seen as Horus and as the son of Re, was thus associated with both the return of the dead to life and the life-giving and self-renewing sun-god. He was the chief priest of Egypt, intervening with the gods on behalf of his land and people. Egyptian rulers zealously built new temples, refurbished old ones, and made lavish gifts to the gods. Much of the country's wealth was directed to religious activities in a ceaseless effort to win the gods' favor, maintain the continuity of divine kingship, and ensure the renewal of the life-giving forces that sustained the world.

The many gods of ancient Egypt were diverse in origin and nature. Some were normally depicted with animal heads; others were always given human form. Few myths about the origins and adventures of the gods have survived, but there must have been a rich oral tradition. Many towns had temples for locally prominent deities. When a town became the capital of a ruling dynasty, the chief god of that town became prominent across the land. Thus did Ptah (puh-TAH) of Memphis, Re of Heliopolis (he-lee-OP-uh-lis), and Amon (AH-muhn) of Thebes become gods of all Egypt, serving to unify the country and strengthen the monarchy. As in Mesopotamia, some temples possessed extensive landholdings worked by dependent peasants, and the priests who administered the deity's wealth were influential locally and sometimes even throughout the land.

Public and Private Cult

e PRIMARY SOURCE: The Egyptian Book of the Dead's Declaration of Innocence Read the number of potential sins that would likely tarnish a journeying spirit and prevent entrance into the realm of the blessed.

Cult activities were carried out in the inner reaches of the temples, off limits to all but the priests who served the needs of the deity by attending to his or her statue. During great festivals, the priests paraded a boat-shaped litter carrying the shrouded statue and cult items of the deity around the town. This brought large numbers of people into contact with the deity in an outpouring of devotion and celebration. But little is known about the day-to-day beliefs and practices of the common people. In the household family members made small offerings to Bes, the grotesque god of marriage and domestic happiness, to local deities, and to the family's ancestors. They relied on amulets and depictions of demonic figures to protect the bearer and ward off evil forces. In later times Greeks and Romans commented that the devotion to magic was especially strong in Egypt.

Burial and Afterlife

Egyptians believed in the afterlife and made extensive preparations for safe passage to the next world and a comfortable existence once they arrived there. A common belief was that death was a journey beset with hazards. The Egyptian Book of the Dead, present in many excavated tombs, contained rituals and spells to protect the journeying spirit. The final challenge was the weighing of the deceased's heart in the presence of the judges of the Underworld to determine whether the person had led a good life and deserved to reach the ultimate blessed destination.

Obsession with the afterlife led to great concern about the physical condition of the cadaver and to the perfection of mummification techniques to preserve the dead body. The idea probably grew out of the early practice of burying the dead in the hot, dry sand on the edge of the desert, where bodies decomposed slowly. The elite classes utilized the most expensive kind of

Scene from the Egyptian Book of the Dead, ca. 1300 B.C.E. The mummy of a royal scribe named Hunefar is approached by members of his household before being placed in the tomb. Behind Hunefar is jackal-headed Anubis, the god who will conduct the spirit of the deceased to the afterlife. The Book of the Dead provided Egyptians with the instructions they needed to complete this arduous journey and gain a blessed existence in the afterlife.

mummy A body preserved by chemical processes or special natural circumstances, often in the belief that the deceased will need it again in the afterlife. In ancient Egypt the bodies of people who could afford mummification underwent a complex process of removing organs, filling body cavities, dehydrating the corpse with natron, and then wrapping the body with linen bandages and enclosing it in a wooden sarcophagus.

mummification. Vital organs were removed, preserved, and stored in stone jars laid out around the corpse, and body cavities were filled with various packing materials. The cadaver, immersed for long periods in dehydrating and preserving chemicals, eventually was wrapped in linen. The **mummy** was then placed in one or more decorated wooden caskets and deposited in a tomb.

The form of the tomb reflected the wealth and status of the deceased. Common people made do with simple pit graves or small mud-brick chambers, while the privileged classes built larger tombs. Kings erected pyramids and other grand edifices, employing subterfuge to hide the sealed chamber containing the body and treasures, as well as curses and other magical precautions to foil tomb robbers. Rarely did they succeed, however, and archaeologists have seldom discovered an undisturbed royal tomb. The tombs, usually built at the edge of the desert so as not to tie up valuable farmland, were filled with pictures, food, and the objects of everyday life to provide whatever the deceased might need in the next life. Small figurines called shawabtis (shuh-WAB-tees) were included to play the part of servants and take the place of the deceased in case the afterlife required periodic compulsory labor. The elite classes attached chapels to their tombs and left endowments to subsidize the daily attendance of a priest and offerings of foodstuffs to sustain their spirits for all eternity.

The ancient Egyptians made remarkable advances in many areas of knowledge. The process of mummification taught them about human anatomy, and Egyptian doctors were in demand in the courts of western Asia. They developed mathematics to

SECTION REVIEW

- Most of the population of ancient Egypt lived alongside the Nile River or in the delta.
- Egypt was well-endowed with natural resources and largely self-sufficient.
- Because the king was the essential link between the people of Egypt and their gods, lavish resources were poured into the construction of pyramids and other royal tombs.
- Hieroglyphic and other systems of writing were used by administrators and also for many genres of literature.
- The population of Egypt was physically diverse, and there was no formal system of classes.
- The status and privileges of Egyptian women were superior to that of their Mesopotamian counterparts, and poetry reveals an ideal of romantic love.
- Obsessed with the afterlife, Egyptians used mummification to preserve dead bodies, constructed elaborate tombs, and employed the Book of the Dead to navigate the hazardous journey to a blessed final destination.
- Egyptians acquired substantial knowledge about medicine, mathematics, astronomy, and engineering.

Science and Technology

measure the dimensions of fields and to calculate the quantity of agricultural produce owed to the state. Through careful observation of the stars they constructed the most accurate calendar in the world, and they knew that the appearance of the star Sirius on the horizon shortly before sunrise meant that the Nile flood surge was imminent. Pyramids, temple complexes, and other monumental building projects called for great skill in engineering. Long underground passageways were excavated to connect mortuary temples by the river with tombs near the desert's edge. On several occasions Egyptian kings dredged out a canal more than 50 miles (80 kilometers) long in order to join the Nile Valley to the Red Sea and expedite the transport of goods.

THE INDUS VALLEY CIVILIZATION

Civilization arose almost as early in South Asia as in Mesopotamia and Egypt. In the fertile floodplain of the Indus River, farming created the food surplus essential to urbanized society.

Natural Environment

A plain of more than 1 million acres (400,000 hectares) stretches from the mountains of western Pakistan east to the Thar (tahr) Desert in the Sind (sinned) region of modern Pakistan (see Map 1.2). Over many centuries silt carried downstream and deposited by the Indus River has elevated the riverbed and its banks above the level of the plain. Twice a year the river overflows and inundates surrounding land as far as 10 miles (16 kilometers). In March and April melting snow from the Pamir (pah-MEER) and Himalaya (him-uh-LAY-uh) mountain ranges feeds the floods. In August, the great monsoon (seasonal wind) blowing off the ocean to the southwest brings rains that cause a second flood. Farmers in this region of little rainfall are thus able to plant and harvest two crops a year. In ancient times the Hakra (HAK-ruh) River (sometimes referred to as the Saraswati), which has since dried up, ran parallel to the Indus about 25 miles (40 kilometers) to the east and supplied water to a second cultivable area.

Adjacent regions shared many cultural traits with this core area. To the northeast is the Punjab, where five rivers converge to form the main course of the Indus. Lying beneath the towering Himalaya range, the Punjab receives considerably more rainfall than the central plain but is less prone to flooding. Settlements spread as far east as Delhi (DEL-ee) in northwest India. Settlement also extended south into the great delta where the Indus empties into the Arabian Sea, and southeast into India's hook-shaped Kathiawar (kah-tee-uh-WAHR) Peninsula, an area of alluvial plains and coastal marshes. The Indus Valley civilization covered an area much larger than the zone of Mesopotamian civilization.

Harappa Site of one of the great cities of the Indus Valley civilization of the third millennium B.C.E. It was located on the northwest frontier of the zone of cultivation (in modern Pakistan) and may have been a center for the acquisition of raw materials, such as metals and precious stones, from Afghanistan and Iran.

Material Culture

Urban Centers

Mohenjo-Daro Largest of the cities of the Indus Valley civilization. It was centrally located in the extensive floodplain of the Indus River in contemporary Pakistan. Little is known about the political institutions of Indus Valley communities, but the large scale of construction at Mohenjo-Daro, the orderly grid of streets, and the standardization of building materials are evidence of central planning.

The Indus Valley civilization flourished from approximately 2600 to 1900 B.C.E. Although archaeologists have located several hundred sites, the culture is best known from the remains of two great cities first discovered eighty years ago. Since the ancient names of these cities are unknown, they are referred to by modern names: **Harappa** and **Mohenjo-Daro** (moe-hen-joe–DAHR-oh). Unfortunately, the high water table at these sites makes excavation of the earliest levels of settlement nearly impossible.

Settled agriculture in this region dates back to at least 5000 B.C.E. The precise relationship between the Indus Valley civilization and earlier cultural complexes in the Indus Valley and in the hilly lands to the west is unclear. Also unclear are the forces that gave rise to urbanization, population increase, and technological advances in the mid-third millennium B.C.E. Nevertheless, the case for continuity with the earlier cultures seems stronger than the case for a sudden transformation due to the arrival of new peoples.

This society produced major urban centers. Harappa, 3.5 miles (5.6 kilometers) in circumference, may have housed a population of 35,000. Mohenjo-Daro was several times larger. High, thick brick walls surrounded each city. The streets were laid out in a rectangular grid, and covered drainpipes carried away waste. The consistent width of streets and length of city blocks and the uniformity of the mud bricks used in construction suggest a strong central authority. The seat of this authority may have been the citadel—an elevated, enclosed compound containing

Courtesy, National Museum, Karachi

Man from Mohenjo-Daro, ca. 2600–1900 B.C.E. This statue of a seated man wearing a cloak and headband was carved from a soft stone called steatite. It is often called the "Priest-King" because some scholars believe it may represent someone with religious and secular authority, but the true identity and status of this person are unknown.

large buildings. Scholars think the well-ventilated structures nearby were storehouses of grain for feeding the urban population and for export. The presence of barracks may point to some regimentation of skilled artisans.

Different centers may have had different functions. Mohenjo-Daro dominates the great floodplain of the Indus. Harappa, which is nearly 500 miles (805 kilometers) to the north, is on a frontier between farmland and herding land, and may have served as a "gateway" for procuring the copper, tin, and precious stones of the northwest. Coastal towns in the south gathered fish and highly prized seashells and engaged in seaborne trade with the Persian Gulf.

Mohenjo-Daro and Harappa have been extensively excavated, and published accounts of the Indus Valley civilization tend to treat them as the norm. Most people, however, lived in smaller settlements, which exhibit the same artifacts and the same standardization of styles and shapes as the large cities. Some scholars attribute this standardization to extensive exchange of goods within the zone of Indus Valley civilization, rather than to the urban centers' control of the smaller settlements.

Technology

There is a greater quantity of metal in the Indus Valley than in Mesopotamia and Egypt, and most metal objects are utilitarian tools and other everyday objects. In contrast, more jewelry and other decorative metal objects have been unearthed in Mesopotamia and Egypt. Apparently metals were available to a broad cross-section of the population in the Indus Valley, while primarily reserved for the elite in the Middle East.

Technologically, the Indus Valley people showed skill in irrigation, used the potter's wheel, and laid the foundations of large public buildings with mud bricks fired to rocky hardness in kilns (sun-dried bricks would have dissolved quickly in floodwaters). They also had a system of writing with more than four hundred signs. Archaeologists have recovered thousands of inscribed seal stones and copper tablets, but no one has been able to decipher these documents.

Trade and Culture

The people of the Indus Valley had widespread trading contacts. They had ready access to the metals and precious stones of eastern Iran and Afghanistan, as well as to ore deposits in western India, building stone, and timber. Goods were moved on rivers within the zone of Indus Valley culture. Indus Valley seal stones have also been found in the Tigris-Euphrates Valley, indicating that Indus Valley merchants served as middlemen in long-distance trade, obtaining raw materials from the northwest and shipping them to the Persian Gulf. The undeciphered writing on seal stones may represent the names of merchants who stamped their wares.

We know little about the political, social, economic, and religious institutions of Indus Valley society. Attempts to link artifacts and images to cultural features characteristic of later periods of Indian history (see Chapter 6)—including a system of hereditary occupational groups with priests predominating, bathing tanks like those later found in Hindu temples, depictions of gods and sacred animals on seal stones, a cult of the mother-goddess—are highly speculative. Further knowledge about this society awaits additional archaeological finds and the deciphering of the Indus Valley script.

Transformation of the Indus Valley Civilization

The Indus Valley cities were abandoned sometime after 1900 B.C.E. Archaeologists once thought that invaders destroyed them, but they now believe this civilization suffered "systems failure"—a breakdown of the fragile interrelationship of political, social, and economic systems that sustained order and prosperity. The cause may have been one or more natural disasters, such as an earthquake or massive flooding. Gradual ecological changes may also have played a role as the Hakra river system dried up and salinization (an increase in the amount of salt in the soil, inhibiting plant growth) and erosion increased.

Towns no longer on the river, ports separated from the sea by silt deposits in the deltas, and the loss of fertile soil and water would have necessitated the relocation of populations and a change in the livelihood of those who remained. The causes and pace of change probably varied in different areas. The urban centers eventually succumbed, however, and village-based farming and herding took their place. As the interaction between regions lessened, regional variation replaced the standardization of technology and style of the previous era. It is important to keep in mind that in most cases like this the majority of the population adjusts to the new circumstances. But members of the elite, who depend on the urban centers and complex political and economic structures, lose the source of their authority and are merged with the population as a whole.

SECTION REVIEW

- The Indus Valley civilization occupied a large territory, including the fertile Indus floodplain as well as adjacent regions.
- Both the major urban centers and smaller settlements exhibit a uniformity of techniques and styles that indicates a possible strong central control.
- The Indus Valley people were technologically advanced in irrigation, ceramics, and construction. Metals were more widely available than in Mesopotamia and Egypt. The writing system has not been deciphered.
- The Indus Valley had widespread trading contacts, reaching as far as Mesopotamia.
- Cities were abandoned and the civilization declined after 1900 B.C.E., probably as a result of natural disasters or environmental changes.

CONCLUSION

It is no accident that the first civilizations to develop high levels of political centralization, urbanization, and technology were situated in river valleys where rainfall was insufficient for reliable agriculture. Dependent on river water to irrigate the cultivated land that fed their populations, Mesopotamia, Egypt, and the Indus Valley civilization channeled considerable human resources into the construction and maintenance of canals, dams, and dikes. This required the formation of political centers that could organize the necessary labor force.

In both Egypt and Mesopotamia, kingship emerged as the dominant political form. The Egyptian king's divine origins and symbolic association with the forces of renewal made him central to the welfare of the entire country and gave him religious authority superseding the temples and priests. Egyptian monarchs lavished much of the country's wealth on their tombs, believing that a proper burial would ensure the continuity of kingship and the attendant blessings that it brought to the land and people. Mesopotamian rulers, who were not normally regarded as divine but still dominated the religious institutions, built new cities, towering walls, splendid palaces, and religious edifices as lasting testaments to their power.

The unpredictable and violent floods in the Tigris-Euphrates Basin were a constant source of alarm for the people of Mesopotamia. In contrast, the predictable, opportune, and gradual Nile floods were eagerly anticipated events in Egypt. The relationship with nature stamped the religious outlooks of both peoples, since their gods embodied the forces of the environment. Mesopotamians nervously tried to appease their harsh deities so as to survive in a dangerous world. Egyptians largely trusted in and nurtured the supernatural powers that, they believed, guaranteed orderliness and prosperity. The Egyptians also believed that, although the journey to the next world was beset with hazards, the righteous spirit that overcame them could look forward to a blessed existence. In contrast, Gilgamesh, the hero of the Mesopotamian epic, is tormented by terrifying visions of the afterlife: disembodied spirits of the dead stumbling around in the darkness of the Underworld for all eternity, eating dust and clay and slaving for the heartless gods of that realm.

Although the populations of Egypt and Mesopotamia were ethnically heterogeneous, both regions experienced a remarkable degree of cultural continuity. New immigrants readily assimilated to the dominant language, belief system, and lifestyles of the civilization. Mesopotamia developed sharp social divisions that were reflected in the class-based penalties set down in the Law Code of Hammurabi, whereas Egyptian society was less urban and less stratified. Mesopotamian women's apparent loss of freedom and legal privilege in the second millennium B.C.E. also may have been related to the higher degree of urbanization and class stratification in this society. In contrast, Egyptian pictorial documents, love poems, and legal records indicate respect and greater equality for women in the valley of the Nile.

Because of the lack of readable texts, we can say very little about the political institutions, social organization, and religious beliefs of the Indus Valley people. However, they clearly possessed technologies on a par with those found in Mesopotamia and Egypt. To transform the natural environment and human society, all three civilizations developed writing systems, irrigation, bronze casting, and techniques for producing monumental architecture. The striking uniformity in the planning and construction of cities and towns and in the shapes and styles of artifacts argues for easy communication and some kind of interdependence among the far-flung Indus Valley settlements, as does the relatively rapid collapse of this civilization as a result of ecological changes.

KEY TERMS

civilization p. 5
culture p. 6
history p. 6
Stone Age p. 6
Paleolithic p. 6
Neolithic p. 6
foragers p. 6
Agricultural Revolutions p. 9
megaliths p. 12
Sumerians p. 16
Semitic p. 16
city-state p. 17
Babylon p. 18
Hammurabi p. 18
scribe p. 20
ziggurat p. 20
amulet p. 21
cuneiform p. 21
bronze p. 23
pharaoh p. 26
ma'at p. 26
pyramid p. 26
Memphis p. 27
Thebes p. 27
hieroglyphics p. 27
papyrus p. 27
mummy p. 30
Harappa p. 31
Mohenjo-Daro p. 31

EBOOK AND WEBSITE RESOURCES

e Primary Sources

The *Epic of Gilgamesh*

The State Regulates Health Care: Hammurabi's Code and Surgeons

The Hymn to the Nile

The Egyptian Book of the Dead's Declaration of Innocence

e Interactive Maps

Map 1.1 Early Centers of Plant and Animal Domestication

Map 1.2 River-Valley Civilizations, 3500–1500 B.C.E.

Map 1.3 Mesopotamia

Map 1.4 Ancient Egypt

Plus flashcards, practice quizzes, and more. Go to: www.cengage.com/history/bullietearthpeople5e

SUGGESTED READING

Anthony, David W. *The Horse, the Wheel, and Language.* 2008. A solid discussion of the evidence and the interpretive problems relating to the origins and spread of Eurasian pastoralism.

Ehrenberg, Margaret. *Women in Prehistory.* 1989. Provides interesting, though necessarily speculative, discussions of women's history.

Fagan, Brian. *People of the Earth: An Introduction to World Prehistory,* 12th ed. 2006. A reliable textbook introduction to human prehistory.

Johnson, Allen W., and Timothy Earle. *The Evolution of Human Societies: From Foraging Group to Agrarian State.* 1987. Explores the transition from hunting and gathering to food production.

Kenoyer, Jonathan Mark. *Ancient Cities of the Indus Valley Civilization.* 1998. Up-to-date treatment by a leading specialist.

Kuhrt, Amelie. *The Ancient Near East, c. 3000–330 B.C.*, 2 vols. 1995. The best introduction to the historical development of western Asia and Egypt.

Mellaart, James. *Çatal Hüyük: A Neolithic Town in Anatolia.* 1967. An account of one of the first cities, written for the general reader by the principal excavator.

Mohen, Jean-Pierre. *The World of Megaliths.* 1990. Analyzes early monumental architecture.

Possehl, Gregory L. *The Indus Civilization: A Contemporary Perspective.* 2002. Another solid treatment of the Indus Valley civilization.

Postgate, J. N. *Early Mesopotamia: Society and Economy at the Dawn of History.* 1992. Presents deep insights into the political, social, and economic dynamics of Mesopotamian society.

Roaf, Michael. *Cultural Atlas of Mesopotamia and the Ancient Near East.* 1990. An excellent introduction to the geography, chronology, and basic institutions and cultural concepts of ancient western Asia.

Romer, John. *People of the Nile: Everyday Life in Ancient Egypt.* 1982. A highly readable treatment of social history.

Silverman, David P., ed. *Ancient Egypt.* 1997. A lavishly illustrated introduction to the many facets of ancient Egyptian civilization.

Snell, Daniel C. *Life in the Ancient Near East 3100–322 B.C.E.* 1997. A rich account of social and economic matters for those already familiar with the main outlines of ancient Near Eastern history.

Vivante, Bella, ed. *Women's Roles in Ancient Civilizations: A Reference Guide.* 1999. Contains articles by specialists on many ancient societies, including Mesopotamia and Egypt.

NOTES

1. David Ferry, *Gilgamesh: A New Rendering in English Verse* (New York: Noonday Press, 1992).
2. Colin McEvedy and Richard Jones, *Atlas of World Population History* (New York: Penguin Books, 1978), 13–15.
3. Colin Renfrew, *Archaeology and Language: The Puzzle of Indo-European Origins* (New York: Cambridge University Press, 1988), 125, 150.
4. Luigi Cavalli-Sforza, L. Luca, Paolo Menozzi, and Alberto Piazza, *The History and Geography of Human Genes* (Princeton, NJ: Princeton University Press, 1994).
5. James Mellaart, *Çatal Hüyük: A Neolithic Town in Anatolia* (New York: McGraw-Hill, 1967), 202.

AP* REVIEW QUESTIONS FOR CHAPTER 1

1. All of the following are indicators of a civilization EXCEPT
   (A) Monument buildings
   (B) Large, well-equipped armies
   (C) A system for keeping permanent records
   (D) Long-distance trade

2. The most important change that took place in the Neolithic Era was
   (A) the development of stone tools.
   (B) the cooking of food.
   (C) the development of agriculture.
   (D) ceremonial burial of the dead.

3. Archaeological evidence suggests that the Agricultural Revolutions began in
   (A) the Middle East.
   (B) East Africa.
   (C) Central Asia.
   (D) South Asia.

4. By the late Neolithic period, the people of Çatal Hüyük had developed the use of
   (A) step pyramids.
   (B) glassmaking.
   (C) sundials.
   (D) copper metallurgy.

5. One of the most important developments of the Sumerians was
   (A) dry farming.
   (B) woolen cloth.
   (C) a political hierarchy.
   (D) a written record.

6. Mesopotamian city-states flourished because
   (A) they developed long-distance trade.
   (B) they conquered an area large enough to make themselves self-sufficient.
   (C) they invented specialized labor.
   (D) they had powerful armies.

7. While it is likely that women lost power and freedom with the spread of agriculture, in Mesopotamia
   (A) they could hold political office.
   (B) they could reign.
   (C) they could own property.
   (D) many served as warriors.

8. The Sumerian gods were
   (A) anthropomorphic.
   (B) the same gods as the ancient Hebrew gods.
   (C) all female.
   (D) private gods that an individual chose to worship.

9. Which of the following is the best explanation of why Egypt was able to develop a unique culture?
   (A) It was the first real civilization to develop and had no enemies.
   (B) It had natural isolation and material self-sufficiency.
   (C) Its neighbors were all tribute states of Egypt.
   (D) Its armies were the most powerful in the region.

10. Following the practice of Manetho, an Egyptian priest from the third century B.C.E., historians divide Egyptian history into dynasties, which are
    (A) segments of time equaling 100 years.
    (B) times when a kingdom rose until it fell.
    (C) sequences of kings from the same family.
    (D) based on the religion of the Egyptians.

11. One of the hallmarks of the administrative class in Egypt was that

    (A) membership in it was inherited by the eldest son.
    (B) only lower nobility could work in it.
    (C) it included the priests.
    (D) bureaucrats were literate.

12. In the second millennium B.C.E., Egypt invaded Nubia because

    (A) Nubia had gold fields.
    (B) Nubia had a leader who claimed to be the pharaoh.
    (C) Nubia had access to goods from across the Sahara.
    (D) Nubia had allied with Mesopotamia.

13. One of the major difficulties in understanding the Indus Valley civilization is that

    (A) there is a lack of artifacts.
    (B) archaeologists are not sure of its exact location.
    (C) its written language cannot be read.
    (D) all of its cities have been destroyed.

CHAPTER

2

CHAPTER OUTLINE

- Early China, 2000–221 B.C.E.
- Nubia, 3100 B.C.E.–350 C.E.
- Celtic Europe, 1000–50 B.C.E.
- First Civilizations of the Americas: The Olmec and Chavín, 1200–250 B.C.E.
- Conclusion

ENVIRONMENT + TECHNOLOGY *Divination in Ancient Societies*

DIVERSITY + DOMINANCE *Human Nature and Good Government in the* Analects *of Confucius and the Legalist Writings of Han Fei*

Wall Painting of Nubians Arriving in Egypt with Rings and Bags of Gold, Fourteenth Century B.C.E. This image decorated the tomb of an Egyptian administrator in Nubia.

Visit the website and ebook for additional study materials and interactive tools: www.cengage.com/history/bullietearthpeople5e

New Civilizations in the Eastern and Western Hemispheres, 2200–250 B.C.E.

- How did early Chinese rulers use religion to justify and strengthen their power?
- How did the technological and cultural influences of Egypt affect the formation of Nubia?
- What were the causes behind the spread of Celtic peoples across much of continental Europe, and the later retreat of Celtic cultures to the western edge of the continent?
- What role did interaction between humans and the environment play in the development of early civilizations in the Americas?

Around 2200 B.C.E. an Egyptian official named Harkhuf (HAHR-koof) set out from Aswan (AS-wahn), on the southern boundary of Egypt, for a place called Yam, far to the south in the land that later came to be called Nubia. He brought gifts from the Egyptian pharaoh for the ruler of Yam, and he returned home with three hundred donkeys loaded with incense, ebony, ivory, and other exotic products from tropical Africa. Despite the diplomatic fiction of exchanging gifts, we should probably regard Harkhuf as a brave and enterprising merchant. He returned with something so special that the eight-year-old boy pharaoh, Pepi II, could not contain his excitement. He wrote:

> Come north to the residence at once! Hurry and bring with you this pygmy whom you brought from the land of the horizon-dwellers live, hale, and healthy, for the dances of the god, to gladden the heart, to delight the heart of king Neferkare [Pepi] who lives forever! When he goes down with you into the ship, get worthy men to be around him on deck, lest he fall into the water! When he lies down at night, get worthy men to lie around him in his tent. Inspect ten times at night! My majesty desires to see this pygmy more than the gifts of the mine-land and of Punt![1]

Scholars identify Yam with Kerma, later the capital of the kingdom of Nubia, on the upper Nile in modern Sudan. For Egyptians, Nubia was a wild and dangerous place. Yet it was developing a more complex political organization, and this illustration demonstrates how vibrant the commerce and cultural interaction between Nubia and Egypt would later become.

The complex societies examined in this chapter emerged later than those in Mesopotamia, Egypt, and the Indus Valley and in more varied ecological conditions, sometimes independently, sometimes under the influence of older centers. Whereas the older river-valley civilizations were largely self-sufficient, most of the new civilizations discussed in this chapter and the next were shaped by networks of long-distance trade.

In the second millennium B.C.E. a civilization based on irrigation agriculture arose in the valley of the Yellow River and its tributaries in northern China. In the same epoch, in Nubia (southern Egypt and northern Sudan), the first complex society in tropical Africa continued to develop from the roots observed earlier by Harkhuf. The first millennium B.C.E. witnessed the spread of Celtic peoples across much of continental Europe, as well as the flourishing of the earliest complex societies of the Western Hemisphere, the Olmec of Mesoamerica and the Chavín culture on the flanks of the Andes Mountains in South America. These societies had no contact with one another, and they represent a variety of responses to different environmental and historical circumstances. However, they have certain features in common and collectively point to a distinct stage in the development of human societies.

EARLY CHINA, 2000–221 B.C.E.

AP* Exam Tip Be prepared to compare at least two of the early civilizations discussed in Chapters 1 and 2: Mesopotamia, Egypt, Indus Valley, Shang, Olmec, and Chavin.

On the eastern edge of the vast Eurasian landmass, Neolithic cultures developed as early as 8000 B.C.E. A more complex civilization evolved in the second and first millennia B.C.E. Under the Shang and Zhou dynasties, many of the elements of classical Chinese civilization emerged and spread across East Asia. As in Mesopotamia, Egypt, and the Indus Valley, the rise of cities, specialization of labor, bureaucratic government, writing, and other advanced technologies depended on the exploitation of a great river system—the Yellow River (Huang He [hwahng-HUH]) and its tributaries—to support intensive agriculture.

Geography and Resources

China is isolated by formidable natural barriers: the Himalaya (him-uh-LAY-uh) mountain range on the southwest; the Pamir (pah-MEER) and Tian Mountains and the Takla Makan (TAH-kluh muh-KAHN) Desert on the west; and the Gobi (GO-bee) Desert and the treeless, grassy hills and plains of the Mongolian steppe to the northwest and north (see Map 2.1). To the east lies the Pacific Ocean. Although China's separation was not total—trade goods, people, and ideas moved back and forth between China, India, and Central Asia—in many respects its development was distinctive.

The East Asian Environment

Most of East Asia is covered with mountains, making overland travel and transport difficult. The great river systems of eastern China, however—the Yellow and the Yangzi (yang-zuh) Rivers and their tributaries—facilitate east-west movement. In the eastern river valleys dense populations practiced intensive agriculture; on the steppe lands of Mongolia, the deserts and oases of Xinjiang (shin-jyahng), and the high plateau of Tibet sparser populations lived largely by herding. The climate zones of East Asia range from the dry, subarctic reaches of Manchuria in the north to the lush, subtropical forests of the south, and a rich variety of plant and animal life are adapted to these zones.

Within the eastern agricultural zone, the north and the south have quite different environments. Each region developed distinctive patterns for land use, the kinds of crops grown, and the organization of agricultural labor. The monsoons that affect India and Southeast Asia (see Chapter 1) drench southern China with heavy rainfall in the summer, the most beneficial time for agriculture. In northern China rainfall is much more erratic. As in Mesopotamia and the Indus Valley, Chinese civilization developed in relatively adverse conditions on the northern plains, a demanding environment that stimulated important technologies and political traditions as well as the philosophical and religious views that became hallmarks of Chinese civilization. By the third century C.E., however, the gradual flow of population toward the warmer southern lands caused the political and intellectual center to move south.

loess A fine, light silt deposited by wind and water. It constitutes the fertile soil of the Yellow River Valley in northern China.

The eastern river valleys and North China Plain contained timber, stone, scattered deposits of metals, and, above all, potentially productive land. Winds blowing from Central Asia deposit a yellowish-brown dust called **loess** (less) (these particles suspended in the water give the Yellow River its distinctive hue and name). Over the ages a thick mantle of soil has accumulated that is extremely fertile and soft enough to be worked with wooden digging sticks.

Intensive Agriculture

In this landscape, agriculture required the coordinated efforts of large numbers of people. Forests had to be cleared. Earthen dikes were constructed to protect nearby fields from recurrent floods on the Yellow River. To cope with the periodic droughts, reservoirs were dug to store river water and rainfall. Retaining walls partitioned the hillsides into flat arable terraces.

The staple crops in the northern region were millet, a grain indigenous to China, and wheat, which had spread to East Asia from the Middle East. Rice, which requires a warmer climate,

CHRONOLOGY

	China	Nubia	Celtic Europe	Americas
	8000–2000 B.C.E. Neolithic cultures	4500 B.C.E. Early agriculture in Nubia		3500 B.C.E. Early agriculture in Mesoamerica and Andes
2500 B.C.E.				2600 B.C.E. Rise of Caral
2000 B.C.E.	2000 B.C.E. Bronze metallurgy	2200 B.C.E. Harkhuf's expeditions to Yam		
	1750–1045 B.C.E. Shang dynasty	1750 B.C.E. Rise of kingdom of Kush based on Kerma		
1500 B.C.E.		1500 B.C.E. Egyptian conquest of Nubia		1200–900 B.C.E. Rise of Olmec civilization, centered on San Lorenzo
1000 B.C.E.	1045–221 B.C.E. Zhou dynasty	1000 B.C.E. Decline of Egyptian control in Nubia	1000 B.C.E. Origin of Celtic culture in Central Europe	900–600 B.C.E. La Venta, the dominant Olmec center 900–250 B.C.E. Chavín civilization in the Andes
		750 B.C.E. Rise of kingdom based on Napata		
	600 B.C.E. Iron metallurgy	712–660 B.C.E. Nubian kings rule Egypt		600–400 B.C.E. Ascendancy of Tres Zapotes and Olmec decline
500 B.C.E.			500 B.C.E. Celtic elites trade for Mediterranean goods 500–300 B.C.E. Migrations across Europe	500 B.C.E. Early metallurgy in Andes
	551–479 B.C.E. Life of Confucius			
	356–338 B.C.E. Lord Shang brings Legalist reforms to Qin state		390 B.C.E. Celts sack Rome	
		300 B.C.E.–350 C.E. Kingdom of Meroë		

AP* Exam Tip The impact of agriculture on the local environment is an important point to understand.

prospered in the Yangzi River Valley. The cultivation of rice required a great outlay of labor. Rice paddies—the fields where rice is grown—must be flat and surrounded by water channels to bring and lead away water according to a precise schedule. Seedlings sprout in a nursery and are transplanted to the paddy, which is then flooded. Flooding eliminates weeds and rival plants and supports microscopic organisms that keep the soil fertile. When the crop is ripe, the paddy is drained; the rice stalks are harvested with a sickle; and the edible kernels are separated out. The reward for this effort is a harvest that can feed more people per cultivated acre than any other grain, which explains why the south eventually became more populous than the north.

The Shang Period, 1750–1045 B.C.E.

Early Societies

Archaeological evidence shows that the Neolithic population of China grew millet, raised pigs and chickens, and used stone tools. They made pottery on a wheel and fired it in high-temperature kilns. They pioneered the production of silk cloth, first raising silkworms on the leaves of mulberry trees, then carefully unraveling their cocoons to produce silk thread. They built walls of pounded earth by hammering the soil inside temporary wooden frames until it became hard as cement. By 2000 B.C.E. they had begun to make bronze (a thousand years after the beginnings of bronze-working in the Middle East).

In later times legends depicted the early rulers of China as ideal and benevolent masters in a tranquil Golden Age. They were followed by the first dynasty, called Xia (shah), who were in turn succeeded by the **Shang** (shahng) dynasty. Since scholars are uncertain about the historical reality of the Xia, Chinese history really begins with the rise of the Shang.

Shang The dominant people in the earliest Chinese dynasty for which we have written records (ca. 1750–1045 B.C.E.).

Little is known about how the Shang rose to dominance ca. 1750 B.C.E., since written documents only appear toward the end of Shang rule. These documents are the so-called oracle bones, the shoulder bones of cattle and the bottom shells of turtles employed by Shang rulers to obtain information from ancestral spirits and gods (see Environment and Technology: Divination in Ancient Societies). The writing on the oracle bones concerns the king, his court, and religious practices, with little about other aspects of Shang society. The same limitations apply to the archaeological record, primarily treasure-filled tombs of the Shang ruling class.

Oracle Bones and Shang Religion

The earliest known oracle bone inscriptions date to the thirteenth century B.C.E., but the system was already so sophisticated that some scholars believe writing in China could be considerably older. In the Shang writing system the several hundred characters (written symbols) were originally pictures of objects that become simplified over time, with each character representing a one-syllable word for an object or idea. It is likely that only a small number of people at court used this system. Nevertheless, the Shang writing system is the ancestor of the system still used in China and elsewhere in East Asia today. Later Chinese writing developed thousands of more complex characters that provide information about both the meaning of the word and its sound.

Scholars have reconstructed the major features of Shang religion from the oracle bones. The supreme god, Di (dee), who resides in the sky and unleashes the power of storms, is felt to be distant and unconcerned with the fate of humans, and cannot be approached directly. When people die, their spirits survive in the same supernatural sphere as Di and other gods of nature. These ancestral spirits, organized in a heavenly hierarchy that mirrors the social hierarchy on earth, can intervene in human affairs. The Shang ruler has direct access to his more recent ancestors, who have access to earlier generations, who can, in turn, intercede with Di. Thus the ruler is the crucial link between Heaven and earth, using his unrivaled access to higher powers to promote agricultural productivity and protect his people from natural disasters. This belief, which persisted throughout Chinese history, has been an extremely effective rationale for authoritarian rule.

The king was often on the road, traveling to the courts of his subordinates to reinforce their loyalty, but it is uncertain how much territory in the North China Plain was effectively controlled by the Shang. Excavations at sites elsewhere in China show artistic and technological traditions so different that they are probably the products of independent groups. Both the lack of writing elsewhere in early China

Arthur M. Sackler Museum, Harvard University Art Museums, USA/ Bequest of Grenville L. Winthrop/The Bridgeman Art Library

Shang Period Bronze Vessel Vessels such as this large wine jar were used in rituals by the Shang ruling class to make contact with their ancestors. As both the source and the proof of the elite's authority, these vessels were often buried in Shang tombs. The complex shapes and elaborate decorations testify to the artisans' skill.

King and Elite

AP* Exam Tip The political structure of each early civilization is an important comparison point to understand.

and the Han-era conception that China had always been unified obscure from us the probable ethnic, linguistic, and cultural diversity of early China.

The Shang elite were a warrior class reveling in warfare, hunting, exchanging gifts, feasting, and drinking. They fought with bronze weapons and rode into battle on horse-drawn chariots, a technology that originated in western Asia. Frequent military campaigns provided these warriors with a theater for brave achievements and yielded considerable plunder. Many prisoners of war were taken in these campaigns and made into slaves and sacrificial victims.

Excavated tombs of Shang royal and elite families, primarily from the vicinity of Anyang (ahn-yahng) (see Map 2.1), contain large quantities of valuable objects made of metal, jade, bone, ivory, shell, and stone, including musical instruments, jewelry, mirrors, weapons, and bronze vessels. These vessels, intricately decorated with stylized depictions of real and imaginary animals, were used to make offerings to ancestral spirits. Possession of bronze objects was a sign of status and authority. The tombs also contain the bodies of family members, servants, and prisoners of war who were killed at the time of the burial. It appears that the objects and people were intended to serve the main occupant of the tomb in the afterlife.

Cities

Shang cities are not well preserved in the archaeological record, partly because of the climate of northern China and partly because of the building materials used. With stone in short supply, cities were protected by massive walls of pounded earth, and buildings were constructed with wooden posts and dried mud. A number of sites appear to have served at different times as centers of political control and religion, with palaces, administrative buildings and storehouses, royal tombs, shrines of gods and ancestors, and houses of the nobility. The common people lived in agricultural villages outside these centers.

e Interactive Map

MAP 2.1 China in the Shang and Zhou Periods, 1750–221 B.C.E. The Shang dynasty arose in the second millennium B.C.E. in the floodplain of the Yellow River. While southern China benefits from the monsoon rains, northern China depends on irrigation. As population increased, the Han Chinese migrated from their eastern homeland to other parts of China, carrying with them their technologies and cultural practices. Other ethnic groups predominated in more outlying regions, and the nomadic peoples of the northwest constantly challenged Chinese authority.

Shang Dynasty
Early Zhou Dynasty
Late Zhou, Warring States Period
Excavated Zhou city site
Winter monsoon winds
Summer monsoon winds

Southern limit of wheat cultivation/northern limit of rice cultivation

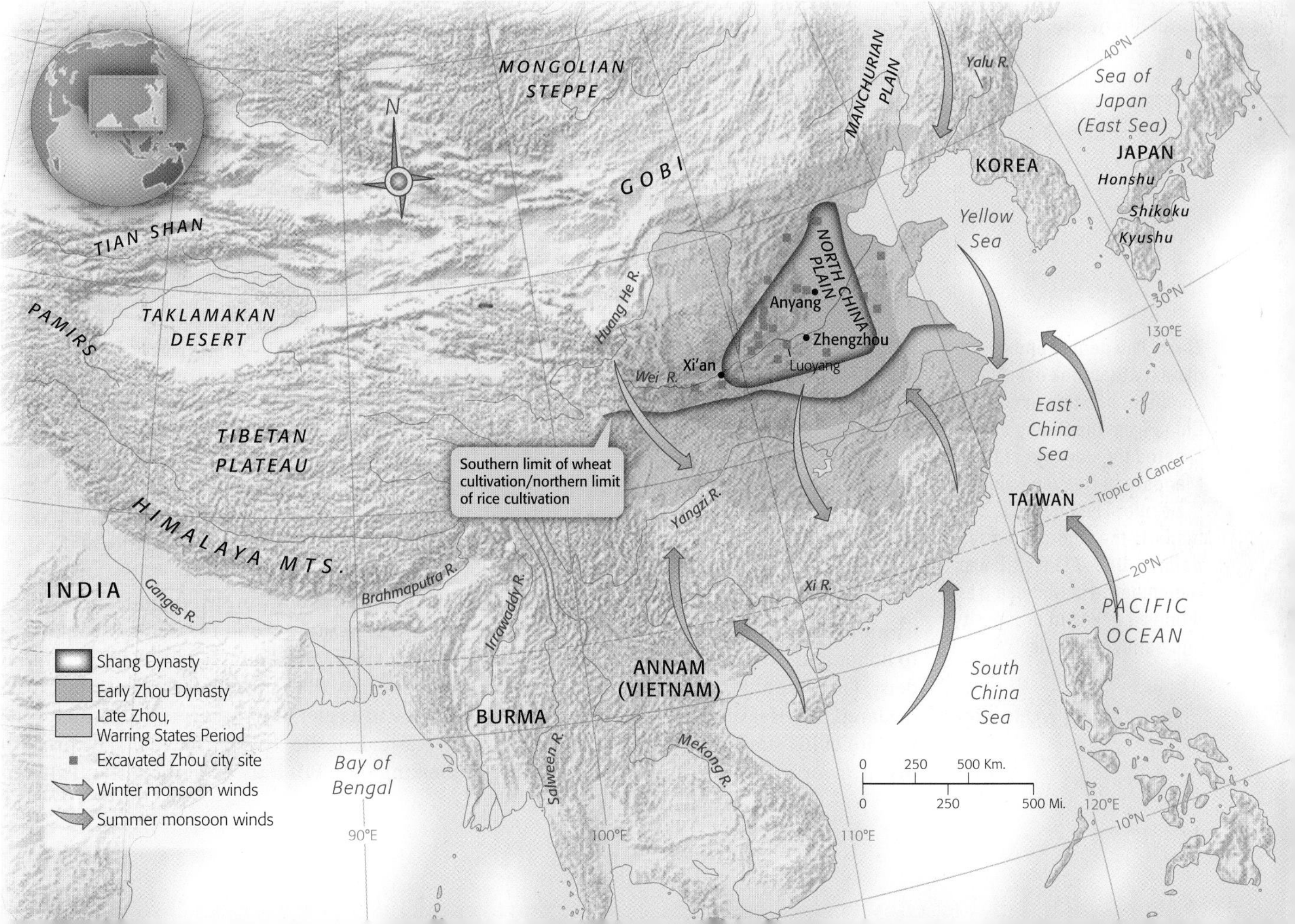

ENVIRONMENT + TECHNOLOGY

Divination in Ancient Societies

Many ancient peoples believed that the gods controlled the forces of nature and shaped destinies. Starting from this premise, they practiced various techniques of divination—the interpretation of phenomena in the natural world as signs of the gods' will and intentions. Through divination the ancients sought to communicate with the gods and thereby anticipate—even influence—the future.

The Shang ruling class in China frequently sought information from ancestors and other higher powers. The Shang monarch himself, with the help of religious experts, often functioned as the intermediary, since he had access to his own ancestors, who had a high ranking in the hierarchy of the spirit world. Chief among the tools of divination were oracle bones. Holes were first drilled in the shoulder bone of an ox or the bottom shell of a turtle to weaken it, and a red-hot pointed stick was applied, causing the bone or shell to crack. The cracks were then "read" by skilled interpreters as answers, on the part of the ancestor who was being consulted, to whatever questions had been asked. The questions, answers, and, often, confirmation of the accuracy of the prediction were subsequently incised on the shell or bone, providing a permanent record of matters of importance to the ruler, such as imminent weather, the yield of the upcoming harvest, the health of the king and his family, the proper performance of rituals, the prospects of military campaigns and hunting expeditions, and the mood of powerful royal ancestors and other divine forces. Tens of thousands of oracle bones survive as a major source of information about Shang life.

In Mesopotamia in the third and second millennia B.C.E. the most important type of divination involved close inspection of the form, size, and markings of the organs of sacrificed animals. Archaeologists have found models of sheeps' livers labeled with explanations of the meaning of various features. Two other techniques of divination were following the trail of smoke from burning incense and examining the patterns that resulted when oil was thrown on water.

From about 2000 B.C.E. Mesopotamian diviners also foretold the future from their observation of the movements of the sun, moon, planets, stars, and constellations. In the centuries after 1000 B.C.E. celestial omens were the most important source of predictions about the future, and specialists maintained precise records of astronomical events. Mesopotamian mathematics, essential for calculations of the movements of celestial bodies, was the most sophisticated in the ancient Middle East. Astrology, with its division of the sky into the twelve segments of the zodiac and its use of the position of the stars and planets to predict an individual's destiny, developed out of long-standing Mesopotamian attention to the movements of celestial objects. Horoscopes—charts with calculations and predictions based on an individual's date of birth—have been found from shortly before 400 B.C.E.

Greeks and Romans frequently used divination before making decisions. Most famous among the many oracle sites in Greece was Delphi, in a stunning location overlooking the Gulf of Corinth, where advice was sought from the god Apollo. A private individual or the official envoy from a Greek community, after leaving the customary gift for the god and entering the temple, had his question conveyed to the priestess, who fell into a trance (recent geological studies have discovered that the temple lay directly above a fissure, and scholars speculate that a gas rising up into the chamber may have put the priestess into an intoxicated state) and delivered a wild utterance that was then "translated" and written down by the priests who administered the shrine. Information and advice from

The Zhou Period, 1045–221 B.C.E.

Zhou The people and dynasty that took over the dominant position in north China from the Shang and created the concept of the Mandate of Heaven to justify their rule. The Zhou era, particularly the vigorous early period (1045–771 B.C.E.), was remembered in Chinese tradition as a time of prosperity and benevolent rule.

In the mid-eleventh century B.C.E. the Shang were overthrown by the **Zhou** (joe), whose homeland lay several hundred miles to the west, in the valley of the Wei (way) River. While the ethnic origin of the Zhou is unclear (their traditions acknowledged that their ancestors had lived for generations among the western "barbarians"), they took over many elements of Shang culture. The Zhou line of kings was the longest lasting and most revered of all dynasties in Chinese history. The two founders were Wen, a vassal ruler who, after being held prisoner for a time by his Shang overlord, initiated a rebellion of disaffected Shang subjects; and his son, Wu, who mounted a successful attack on the Shang capital and was enthroned as the first ruler of the new dynasty.

The Mandate of Heaven

Wu justified his achievement in a manner that became the norm throughout subsequent Chinese history. Claiming that the last Shang ruler was depraved and tyrannical, neglecting to honor gods and ancestors and killing and abusing his subjects, he invoked the highest Zhou deity, Tian (tyehn) ("Heaven"), who was more compassionate than the aloof Di of the Shang. Wu declared that Heaven granted authority and legitimacy to a ruler as long as he looked out for the welfare of his subjects; the monarch, accordingly, was called the "Son of Heaven." The proof of divine favor was the prosperity and stability of the kingdom. But if the ruler persistently failed

Chinese Divination Shell After inscribing questions on a bone or shell, the diviner applied a red-hot point and interpreted the resulting cracks as a divine response.

Courtesy of the Institute of History and Philology, Academia Sinica

the god at Delphi helped Greek communities choose where to place new settlements during the centuries of colonization throughout the Mediterranean and Black Seas, and Delphic priests may have collected information from the many travelers who came their way and then dispensed it by means of oracles.

Greek and Roman sources report on practices of divination among the Celts. Predicting the future is one of the many religious functions attributed to the Druids, as well as to a specialized group of "seers." Among their methods were careful observation of the flight patterns of birds and of the appearance of sacrificial offerings. In Ireland a ritual specialist ate the meat of a freshly killed bull, lay down to sleep on the bull's hide, and then had prophetic dreams. The most startling form of Celtic divination is described by the geographer Strabo:

> *The Romans put a stop to [the] customs . . . connected with sacrifice and divination, as they were in conflict with our own ways: for example, they would strike a man who had been consecrated for sacrifice in the back with a sword, and make prophecies based on his death-spasms.*

Such horrifying reports were used by the Romans to justify the conquest of Celtic peoples in order to "civilize" them.

Little is known about the divinatory practices of early American peoples. The Olmec produced polished stone mirrors whose concave surfaces gave off reflected images that were thought to emanate from a supernatural realm. Painted basins found in Olmec households have been compared to those attested for later Mesoamerican groups. In the latter, women threw maize kernels onto the surface of water-filled basins and noted the patterns by which they floated or sank. By this means they ascertained information useful to the family, such as the cause and cure of illness, the right time for agricultural tasks or marriage, and favorable names for newborn children.

It may seem surprising that divination is being treated here as a form of technology. Most modern people would regard such interpretations of patterns in everyday phenomena as mere superstition. However, for ancient peoples who believed that the gods directly controlled events in the natural world, divination amounted to the application of these principles of causation to the socially beneficial task of acquiring information about the future. These techniques were usually known only to a class of experts whose special training and knowledge gave them high status in their society.

Mandate of Heaven Chinese religious and political ideology developed by the Zhou, according to which it was the prerogative of Heaven, the chief deity, to grant power to the ruler of China and to take away that power if the ruler failed to conduct himself justly and in the best interests of his subjects.

in these duties and neglected the warning signs of flood, famine, invasion, or other disasters, Heaven could withdraw this "Mandate" and transfer it to another, more worthy ruler and family. This theory of the **Mandate of Heaven**, which validated the institution of monarchy by connecting the religious and political spheres, served as the foundation of Chinese political thought for three thousand years.

Much more is known about the early centuries of Zhou rule (the Western Zhou Period, 1045–771 B.C.E.) than the preceding Shang era because of the survival of written texts, above all the *Book of Documents*, a collection of decrees, letters, and other historical records, and the *Book of Songs*, an anthology of 305 poems, ballads, and folksongs that illuminate the lives of rulers, nobles, and peasants. Additionally, members of the Zhou elite recorded their careers and cited honors received from the rulers in bronze inscriptions.

Zhou Government

e PRIMARY SOURCE: The *Book of Documents* Read this Confucian classic to discover how rulers gain or lose the right to rule, an authority known as the Mandate of Heaven.

To consolidate his power, King Wu distributed territories to his relatives and allies, which they were to administer and profit from so long as they remained loyal to him. These regional rulers then apportioned pieces of their holdings to their supporters, creating a pyramidal structure of political, social, and economic relations often referred to as "feudal," borrowing terminology from the European Middle Ages.

When Wu died, his son and heir, Cheng (chung), was too young to assume full powers, and for a time the kingdom was run by his uncles, especially the Duke of Zhou. The Duke of Zhou is one of the most famous figures in early Chinese history, in large part because the philosopher Confucius later celebrated him as the ideal administrator who selflessly served as regent for his young nephew at a delicate time for the new dynasty, then dutifully returned power as soon as the lawful ruler came of age.

The early Zhou rulers constructed a new capital city in their homeland (near modern Xi'an), and other urban centers developed in succeeding centuries. Cities were laid out on a grid plan aligned with the north polar star, with gates in the fortification walls opening to the cardinal directions and major buildings facing south. This was in keeping with an already ancient concern, known as *feng shui* (fung shway) ("wind and water"), to orient structures so that they would be in a harmonious relationship with the terrain, the forces of wind, water, and sunlight, and the invisible energy perceived to be flowing through the natural world.

Religion and Daily Life

Alongside the new primacy of the Zhou deity Tian and continuation of religious practices inherited from the Shang era, new forms of divination developed. One increasingly popular method involved throwing down a handful of long and short stalks of the milfoil or yarrow plant and interpreting the patterns they formed. Over time a multilayered text was compiled, called the *Book of Changes*, that explained in detail the meanings of each of the sixty-four standard patterns formed by the stalks. In later ages this practice and the accompanying text also came to be used as a vehicle for self-examination and contemplation of the workings of the world.

The *Book of Songs* provides extraordinary glimpses into the lives, activities, and feelings of a diverse cross-section of early Chinese people—elite and common, male and female, urban and rural. We can glean much from these poems about the situation of women in early China. Some describe men and women choosing each other and engaging in sex outside of marriage. Other poems tell of arranged marriages in which the young woman anxiously leaves home and birth family behind and journeys to the household of an unknown husband and new family. One poem describes the different ways that infant boys and girls were welcomed into an aristocratic family. The male was received like a little prince: placed on a bed, swaddled in expensive robes, and given a jade scepter to play with as a symbol of his future authority; the female was placed on the floor and given the weight from a weaving loom to indicate her future obligations of subservience and household labor.

Fragmentation and Rivalry

Over the period from the eleventh to eighth centuries B.C.E. the power of the Zhou monarch gradually eroded, largely because of the feudal division of territory and power. In 771 B.C.E. the Zhou capital was attacked by a coalition of enemies, and the dynasty withdrew to a base farther east, at Luoyang (LWOE-yahng). This change ushers in the Eastern Zhou Period (771–221 B.C.E.), a long era in which the Zhou monarchs remained as figureheads, given only nominal allegiance by the rulers of many virtually independent states scattered across northern and central China.

The first part of the Eastern Zhou era is called the Spring and Autumn Period (771–481 B.C.E.) because of the survival of a text, the *Spring and Autumn Annals*, that provides a spare historical record of events in the small eastern state of Lu. Later writers added commentaries that fleshed out this skeletal record. The states of this era were frequently at odds with one another and employed various tactics to protect themselves and advance their interests, including diplomatic initiatives, shifting alliances, and coups and assassinations as well as conventional warfare. The overall trend was gradual consolidation into a smaller number of larger and more powerful kingdoms.

Warfare was a persistent feature of the period, and there were important transformations in the character and technology of war. In the Shang and early Zhou periods, warfare largely had been conducted by members of the elite, who rode in chariots, treated battle as an opportunity for displays of skill and courage, and adhered to a code of heroic conduct. But in the high-stakes conflicts of the Eastern Zhou era, there was a shift to much larger armies made up of conscripted farmers who fought bloody battles, unconstrained by noble etiquette, in which large numbers were slaughtered. Some men undertook the study of war and composed handbooks, such as Sunzi's *Art of War*. Sunzi (soon-zuh) approaches war as a chess game in which the successful general employs deception, intuits the energy potential inherent in the landscape, and psychologically manipulates both friend and foe. The best victories are achieved without fighting so that one can incorporate the unimpaired resources of the other side.

Technological advances also impacted warfare. In the last centuries of the Zhou, the Chinese learned from the nomadic peoples of the northern steppes to put fighters on horseback. By 600 B.C.E. iron began to replace bronze as the primary metal for tools and weapons. There is mounting evidence that ironworking also came to China from the nomadic peoples of the northwest. Metalworkers in China were the first in the world to forge steel by removing carbon during the iron-smelting process.

Another significant development was the increasing size and complexity of the governments that administered Chinese states. Rulers ordered the careful recording of the population, the land, and its agricultural products so that the government could compel peasants to donate labor for public works projects (digging and maintaining irrigation channels and building roads, defensive walls, and palaces), conscript them into the army, and collect taxes. Skilled officials supervised the expanding bureaucracies of scribes, accountants, and surveyors and advised the rulers on various matters. Thus there arose a class of educated and ambitious men who traveled from state to state offering their services to the rulers—and their theories of ideal government.

AP* Exam Tip Be prepared to identify and discuss the diffusion of the major religious systems of the classical civilizations.

Confucianism, Daoism, and Chinese Society

The Eastern Zhou era, despite being plagued by political fragmentation, frequent warfare, and anxious uncertainty, was also a time of great cultural development. The two most influential "philosophical" systems of Chinese civilization—Confucianism and Daoism—had their roots in this period, though they would be further developed and adapted to changing circumstances in later times.

Confucianism

Confucius Western name for the Chinese philosopher Kongzi (551–479 B.C.E.). His doctrine of duty and public service had a great influence on subsequent Chinese thought and served as a code of conduct for government officials.

Kongzi (kohng-zuh) (551–479 B.C.E.), known in the West by the Latin form of his name, **Confucius**, withdrew from public life after unsuccessful efforts to find employment as an official and adviser to a number of rulers of the day. He attracted a circle of students to whom he presented his wide-ranging ideas on morality, conduct, and government. His sayings were handed down orally by several generations of disciples before being compiled in written form as the *Analects* (see Diversity and Dominance: Human Nature and Good Government in the *Analects* of Confucius and the Legalist Writings of Han Fei). This work, along with a set of earlier texts that were believed (probably wrongly) to have been edited by Confucius—the *Book of Documents*, the *Book of Songs*, the *Book of Changes*, and the *Spring and Autumn Annals*—became the core texts of Confucianism.

Confucius drew upon traditional institutions and values but gave them new shape and meaning. He looked back to the early Zhou period as a Golden Age of wise rulers and benevolent government, models to which the people of his own "broken" society should return. He also placed great importance on the "rituals," or forms of behavior, that guide people in their daily interactions with one another, since these promote harmony in human relations.

For Confucius the family was the fundamental component of society, and the ways in which family members regulated their conduct in the home prepared them to serve as citizens of the state. Each person had his or her place and duties in a hierarchical order that was determined by age and gender. The "filiality" of children to parents, which included obedience, reverence, and love, had its analogue in the devotion of subjects to the ruler. Another fundamental virtue for Confucius was *ren* (ruhn), sometimes translated as "humaneness," which traditionally meant the feelings between family members and which was expanded into a universal ideal of benevolence and compassion that would, ideally, pervade every activity. Confucianism placed immense value on the practical task of making society function smoothly at every level. It provided a philosophical and ethical framework for conducting one's life and understanding one's place in the world. But it was not a religion. While Confucius urged respect for gods, ancestors, and religious traditions, he felt that such supernatural matters were unknowable.

Confucius's ideas were little known in his own time, but his teachings were preserved and gradually spread to a wider audience. Some disciples took Confucianism in new directions. Mengzi (muhng-zuh) (known in the West as Mencius, 371–289 B.C.E.), who did much to popularize Confucian ideas in his age, believed in the essential goodness of all human beings and argued that, if people were shown the right way by virtuous leaders, they would voluntarily do the right thing. Xunzi (shoon-zuh) (ca. 310–210 B.C.E.), on the other hand, concluded that people had to be compelled to make appropriate choices. (This approach led to the development of a school of thought called Legalism, discussed later in this chapter.) As we shall see in Chapter 5, in the era of the emperors a revised Confucianism became the dominant political philosophy and the core of the educational system for government officials.

Daoism Chinese school of thought, originating in the Warring States Period with Laozi. Daoism offered an alternative to the Confucian emphasis on hierarchy and duty.

If Confucianism emphasized social engagement, its great rival, **Daoism** (DOW-ism), urged withdrawal from the empty formalities, rigid hierarchy, and distractions of Chinese society. Laozi (low-zuh) is regarded as the originator of Daoism, although virtually nothing is known

DIVERSITY + DOMINANCE

Human Nature and Good Government

in the Analects of Confucius and the Legalist Writings of Han Fei

While monarchy (the rule of one man) was the standard form of government in ancient China and was rarely challenged, political theorists and philosophers thought a great deal about the qualities of the ideal ruler, his relationship to his subjects, and the means by which he controlled them. These considerations about how to govern people were inevitably molded by fundamental assumptions about the nature of human beings. In the Warring States Period, as the major states struggled desperately with one another for survival and expansion, such discussions took on a special urgency, and the Confucians and Legalists came to represent two powerful, and largely contradictory, points of view.

The Analects *are a collection of sayings of Confucius, probably compiled and written down several generations after he lived, though some elements may have been added even later. They cover a wide range of matters, including ethics, government, education, music, and rituals. Taken as a whole, they are a guide to living an honorable, virtuous, useful, and satisfying life. While subject to reinterpretation according to the circumstances of the times, Confucian principles have had a great influence on Chinese values and behavior ever since.*

Han Fei (280–233 B.C.E.*), who was, ironically, at one time the student of a Confucian teacher, became a Legalist writer and political adviser to the ruler of the ambitious state of Qin. Eventually he lost out in a power struggle at court and was forced to kill himself.*

The following selections illuminate the profound disagreements between Confucians and Legalists over the essential nature of human beings and how the ruler should conduct himself in order to most effectively govern his subjects and protect his kingdom.

Confucius

4:5 Confucius said: "Riches and honors are what all men desire. But if they cannot be attained in accordance with the *dao [the way]* they should not be kept. Poverty and low status are what all men hate. But if they cannot be avoided while staying in accordance with the *dao*, you should not avoid them. If a Superior Man departs from *ren* [humaneness], how can he be worthy of that name? A Superior Man never leaves *ren* for even the time of a single meal. In moments of haste he acts according to it. In times of difficulty or confusion he acts according to it."

16:8 Confucius said: "The Superior Man stands in awe of three things: (1) He is in awe of the decree of Heaven. (2) He is in awe of great men. (3) He is in awe of the words of the sages. The inferior man does not know the decree of Heaven; takes great men lightly and laughs at the words of the sages."

4:14 Confucius said: "I don't worry about not having a good position; I worry about the means I use to gain position. I don't worry about being unknown; I seek to be known in the right way."

7:15 Confucius said: "I can live with coarse rice to eat, water for drink and my arm as a pillow and still be happy. Wealth and honors that one possesses in the midst of injustice are like floating clouds."

13:6 Confucius said: "When you have gotten your own life straightened out, things will go well without your giving orders. But if your own life isn't straightened out, even if you give orders, no one will follow them."

12:2 Zhonggong asked about the meaning of *ren*. The Master said: "Go out of your home as if you were receiving an important guest. Employ the people as if you were assisting at a great ceremony. What you don't want done to yourself, don't do to others. Live in your town without stirring up resentments, and live in your household without stirring up resentments."

1:5 Confucius said: "If you would govern a state of a thousand chariots (a small-to-middle-size state), you must pay strict attention to business, be true to your word, be economical in expenditure and love the people. You should use them according to the seasons."

2:3 Confucius said: "If you govern the people legalistically and control them by punishment, they will avoid crime, but have no personal sense of shame. If you govern them by means of virtue and control them with propriety, they will gain their own sense of shame, and thus correct themselves."

12:7 Zigong asked about government. The Master said, "Enough food, enough weapons and the confidence of the people." Zigong said, "Suppose you had no alternative but to give up one of these three, which one would be let go of first?" The Master said, "Weapons." Zigong said, "What if you had to give up one of the remaining two, which one would it be?" The Master said, "Food. From ancient times, death has come to all men, but a people without confidence in its rulers will not stand."

12:19 Ji Kang Zi asked Confucius about government saying: "Suppose I were to kill the unjust, in order to advance the just. Would that be all right?"

Confucius replied: "In doing government, what is the need of killing? If you desire good, the people will be good. The nature of the Superior Man is like the wind, the nature of the inferior man is like the grass. When the wind blows over the grass, it always bends."

2:19 The Duke of Ai asked: "How can I make the people follow me?" Confucius replied: "Advance the upright and set aside the crooked, and the people will follow you. Advance the crooked and set aside the upright, and the people will not follow you."

2:20 Ji Kang Zi asked: "How can I make the people reverent and loyal, so they will work positively for me?" Confucius said, "Approach them with dignity, and they will be reverent. Be filial and compassionate and they will be loyal. Promote the able and teach the incompetent, and they will work positively for you."

Han Fei

Past and present have different customs; new and old adopt different measures. To try to use the ways of a generous and lenient government to rule the people of a critical age is like trying to drive a runaway horse without using reins or whips. This is the misfortune that ignorance invites. . . .

Humaneness *[ren]* may make one shed tears and be reluctant to apply penalties, but law makes it clear that such penalties must be applied. The ancient kings allowed law to be supreme and did not give in to their tearful longings. Hence it is obvious that humaneness cannot be used to achieve order in the state. . . .

The best rewards are those that are generous and predictable, so that the people may profit by them. The best penalties are those that are severe and inescapable, so that the people will fear them. The best laws are those that are uniform and inflexible, so that the people can understand them. . . .

Hardly ten men of true integrity and good faith can be found today, and yet the offices of the state number in the hundreds. . . . Therefore the way of the enlightened ruler is to unify the laws instead of seeking for wise men, to lay down firm policies instead of longing for men of good faith. . . .

When a sage rules the state, he does not depend on people's doing good of themselves; he sees to it that they are not allowed to do what is bad. If he depends on people's doing good of themselves, then within his borders he can count fewer than ten instances of success. But if he sees to it that they are not allowed to do what is bad, then the whole state can be brought to a uniform level of order. Those who rule must employ measures that will be effective with the majority and discard those that will be effective with only a few. Therefore they devote themselves not to virtue but to law. . . .

When the Confucians of the present time counsel rulers, they do not praise those measures that will bring order today, but talk only of the achievements of the men who brought order in the past. . . . No ruler with proper standards will tolerate them. Therefore the enlightened ruler works with facts and discards useless theories. He does not talk about deeds of humaneness and rightness, and he does not listen to the words of scholars. . . .

Nowadays, those who do not understand how to govern invariably say, "You must win the hearts of the people!". . . The reason you cannot rely on the wisdom of the people is that they have the minds of little children. If the child's head is not shaved, its sores will spread; and if its boil is not lanced, it will become sicker than ever . . . for it does not understand that the little pain it suffers now will bring great benefit later. . . .

Now, the ruler presses the people to till the land and open up new pastures so as to increase their means of livelihood, and yet they consider him harsh; he draws up a penal code and makes the punishments more severe in order to put a stop to evil, and yet the people consider him stern. . . . He makes certain that everyone within his borders understands warfare and sees to it that there are no private exemptions from military service; he unites the strength of the state and fights fiercely in order to take its enemies captive, and yet the people consider him violent. . . . [These] types of undertaking all ensure order and safety to the state, and yet the people do not have sense enough to rejoice in them.

QUESTIONS FOR ANALYSIS

1. **What do Confucius and Han Fei believe about the nature of human beings? Are they intrinsically good and well-behaved, or bad and prone to misbehave?**
2. **What are the qualities of an ideal ruler for Confucius and Han Fei?**
3. **By what means can the ruler influence his subjects in Confucian thought? How should the ruler compel obedience in the people in Legalist thought?**
4. **What do Confucians and Legalists think about the value of the past as a model for the present?**
5. **Why might Confucius's passionate concern for ethical behavior on the part of officials and rulers arise at a time when the size and power of governments were growing?**

Daoism

about him, and some scholars doubt his existence. Laozi is credited with the foundational text of Daoism, the *Classic of the Way of Virtue*, a difficult book full of ambiguity and paradox, beautiful poetic images, and tantalizing hints of "truths" that cannot be adequately explained with words. It raises questions about whether the material world in which we operate is real or a kind of dream that blocks us from perceiving a higher reality. It argues that education, knowledge, and rational analysis are obstacles to understanding and that we would be better off cultivating our senses and trusting our intuitions. The primal world of the distant past was happy and blessed before civilization and "knowledge" corrupted it. The Daoist sage strives to lead a tranquil existence by retreating from the stresses and obligations of a chaotic society. He avoids useless struggles, making himself soft and malleable so that the forces that buffet people can flow harmlessly around him. He chooses not to "act" because such action almost always leads to a different outcome from the one desired, whereas inaction may bring the desired outcome. And he has no fear of death because, for all we know, death may be merely a transformation to another plane of existence. In the end, in a world that is always changing and lacks any absolute morality or meaning, all that matters is the individual's fundamental understanding of, and accommodation to, the *Dao*, the "path" of nature.

yin/yang In Chinese belief, complementary factors that help to maintain the equilibrium of the world. Yang is associated with masculine, light, and active qualities; yin with feminine, dark, and passive qualities.

Daoism, like Confucianism, would continue to evolve for many centuries, adapting to changes in Chinese society and incorporating many elements of traditional religion, mysticism, and magic. Although Daoism and Confucianism may appear to be thoroughly at odds regarding the relationship of the individual and the larger society, many Chinese through the ages have drawn on both traditions, and it has been said that the typical Chinese scholar-official was a Confucian in his work and public life but a Daoist in the privacy of his study.

Male and Female Roles

The classical Chinese patterns of family and property took shape in the later Zhou period. The kinship structures of the Shang and early Zhou periods, based on the clan (a relatively large group of related families), gave way to the three-generation family of grandparents, parents, and children as the fundamental social unit. Fathers had absolute authority over women and children, arranged marriages for their offspring, and could sell the labor of family members. Only men could conduct rituals and make offerings to the ancestors, though women helped maintain the household's ancestral shrines. A man was limited to one wife but was permitted additional sexual partners, who had the lower status of concubines. A man whose wife died had a duty to remarry in order to produce male heirs to keep alive the cult of the ancestors, whereas women were discouraged from remarrying.

In Chinese tradition the concept of **yin/yang** represented the complementary nature of male and female roles in the natural order. The male principle (yang) was equated with the sun: active, bright, and shining; the female principle (yin) corresponded to the moon: passive, shaded, and reflective. Male toughness was balanced by female gentleness, male action and initiative by female endurance and need for completion, and male leadership by female supportiveness. In its earliest form, the theory considered yin and yang as equal and alternately dominant, like day and night, creating balance in the world. However, as a result of the changing role of women in the Zhou period and the pervasive influence of Confucian ideology, the male principle came to be seen as superior to the female.

The Warring States Period, 481–221 B.C.E.

The second half of the Eastern Zhou era is conventionally called the Warring States Period (481–221 B.C.E.) because the scale and intensity of rivalry and warfare between the states accelerated. More successful states conquered and absorbed less capable rivals, and by the beginning of the third century B.C.E. only seven major states remained. Each state sought security by any and all means: building

Warring States Period Bronze Figurine The figurine of a youth, made of bronze, was produced in the Warring States Period, but the jade birds perched atop the staffs were originally carved in the Shang era. The youth has braided hair and is wearing boots and an elaborately decorated robe. The chain may indicate that these were live birds rather than images.

walls to protect its borders; putting into the field the largest possible armies; experimenting with military organization, tactics, and technology; and devising new techniques of administration to produce the greatest revenues. Some wars were fought against non-Chinese peoples living on the margins of the states' territories or even in enclaves within the states. In addition to self-defense, the aim of these campaigns was often to increase the territory available for agriculture, since cultivated land was, ultimately, the source of wealth and manpower. The conquered peoples assimilated over time, becoming Chinese in language and culture.

The Qin and Legalism

The most innovative of all the states of this era was Qin (chin), on the western edge of "the Central States" (the term used for the Chinese lands of north and central China). Coming from the same Wei River Valley frontier region as the Zhou long before, and exposed to barbarian influences and attacks, the Qin rulers commanded a nation of hardy farmers and employed them in large, well-trained armies. The very vulnerability of their circumstances may have inspired the Qin rulers of the fourth and third centuries B.C.E. to take great risks, for they were the first to put into practice the philosophy and methods of the Legalist school of political theorists. In the mid-fourth century B.C.E. Lord Shang was put in charge of the Qin government. He maintained that the Confucians were mistaken in looking to an idealized past for solutions and naïve in thinking that the ruler should worry about his subjects' opinions. In Lord Shang's view, the ruler should trust his own judgment and employ whatever means are necessary to compel obedience and good behavior in his subjects. In the end, Legalists were willing to sacrifice individual freedom to guarantee the security and prosperity of the state. To strengthen the ruler, Lord Shang moved to weaken the Qin nobility, sending out centrally appointed district governors, abolishing many of the privileges of the nobility, and breaking up large estates by requiring property to be divided equally among the surviving sons. Although he eventually became entangled in bitter intrigue at court and was killed in 338 B.C.E., the Qin rulers of the third century B.C.E. continued to employ Legalist advisers and pursue Legalist policies, and, as we shall see in Chapter 5, they converted the advantages gained from this approach into a position of unprecedented power.

SECTION REVIEW

- The challenges of engaging in agriculture in the varied environments of East Asia led to the formation of complex, hierarchical societies.
- The Shang and Zhou rulers of early China developed religious ideologies (oracle bone divination, Mandate of Heaven theories) that justified monarchic systems of government.
- The feudal organization of the Zhou state led, over time, to the weakening of the monarch's authority and the rise of many essentially independent states.
- The rivalry and conflict of Chinese states in the later Zhou era led to the rise of bureaucracies, administrative experts, and more deadly forms of warfare.
- This era also saw the rise and rivalry of major philosophical systems: Confucianism, Daoism, and Legalism.
- Although yin/yang theory regarded the male and female principles as interdependent, men were dominant in the family, and the influence of Confucianism led to a reduction in women's status and rights.

NUBIA, 3100 B.C.E.–350 C.E.

Since the first century B.C.E. the name *Nubia* has been applied to a thousand-mile (1,600-kilometer) stretch of the Nile Valley lying between Aswan and Khartoum (kahr-TOOM) and straddling the southern part of the modern nation of Egypt and the northern part of Sudan (see Map 2.2). Nubia is the only continuously inhabited territory connecting sub-Saharan Africa (the lands south of the Sahara Desert) with North Africa. For thousands of years it has served as a corridor for trade between tropical Africa and the Mediterranean. Nubia was richly endowed with natural resources such as gold, copper, and semiprecious stones.

Nubia's location and natural wealth, along with Egypt's hunger for Nubian gold, explain the early rise of a civilization with a complex political organization, social stratification, metallurgy, monumental building, and writing. Scholars have moved away from the traditional view that Nubian civilization simply imitated Egypt, and they now emphasize the mutually beneficial interactions between Egypt and Nubia and the growing evidence that Nubian culture also drew on influences from sub-Saharan Africa.

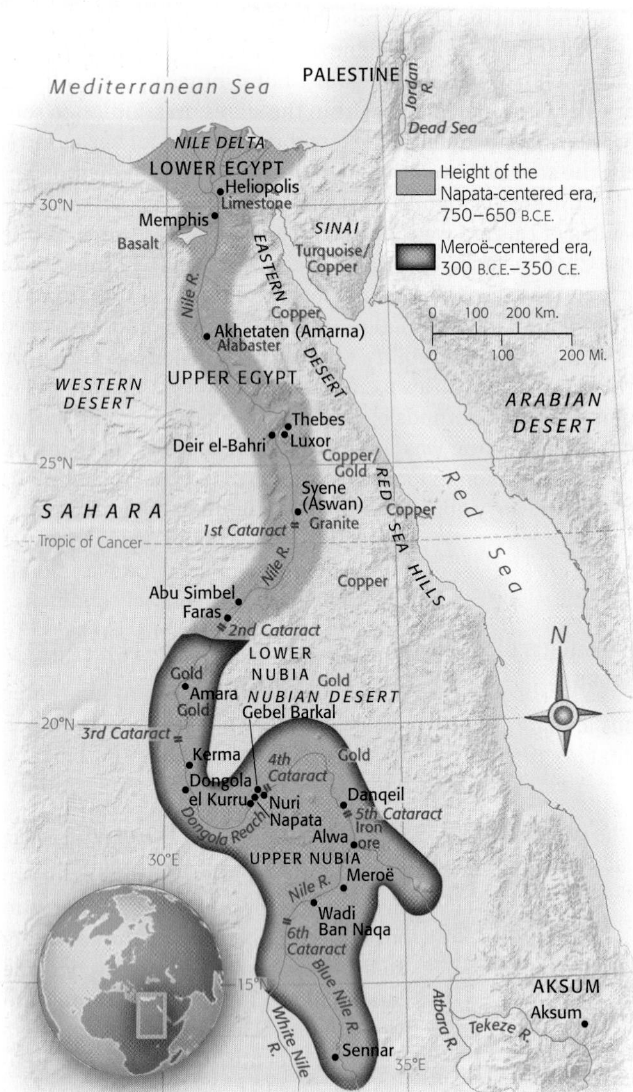

MAP 2.2 Ancient Nubia The land route alongside the Nile River as it flows through Nubia has long served as a corridor connecting sub-Saharan Africa with North Africa. Centuries of Egyptian occupation, as well as time spent in Egypt by Nubian hostages, mercenaries, and merchants, led to a marked Egyptian cultural influence in Nubia. (Based on Map 15 from *The Historical Atlas of Africa*, ed. by J. F. Ade Ajayi and Michael Crowder. Reprinted by permission of Addison Wesley Longman Ltd.)

Interactive Map

Early Cultures and Egyptian Domination 2300–1100 B.C.E.

The central geographical feature of Nubia, as of Egypt, is the Nile River. This part of the Nile flows through a landscape of rocky desert, grassland, and fertile plain. River irrigation was essential for agriculture in a climate that was severely hot and, in the north, nearly without rainfall. Six cataracts, barriers formed by large boulders and rapids, obstructed boat traffic. Boats operating between the cataracts and caravans skirting the river made travel and trade possible.

In the fifth millennium B.C.E. bands of people in northern Nubia made the transition from seminomadic hunting and gathering to a settled life based on grain agriculture and cattle herding. From this time on, the majority of the population lived in agricultural villages alongside the river. Even before 3000 B.C.E. Egyptian craftsmen worked in ivory and in ebony wood—products of tropical Africa that came through Nubia.

Nubia enters the historical record around 2300 B.C.E. in Old Kingdom Egyptian accounts of trade missions to southern lands. At that time Aswan, just north of the First Cataract, was the southern limit of Egyptian control. As we saw with the journey of Harkhuf at the beginning of this chapter, Egyptian officials stationed there led donkey caravans south in search of gold, incense, ebony, ivory, slaves, and exotic animals from tropical Africa. This was dangerous work, requiring delicate negotiations with local Nubian chiefs to secure protection, but it brought substantial rewards to those who succeeded.

Egyptian Domination

During the Middle Kingdom (ca. 2040–1640 B.C.E.), Egypt adopted a more aggressive stance toward Nubia. Egyptian rulers sought to control the gold mines in the desert east of the Nile and to cut out the Nubian middlemen who drove up the cost of luxury goods from the tropics. The Egyptians erected a string of mud-brick forts on islands and riverbanks south of the Second Cataract. The forts regulated the flow of trade goods and protected the southern frontier of Egypt against Nubians and nomadic raiders from the desert. There seem to have been peaceable relations but little interaction between the Egyptian garrisons and the indigenous population of northern Nubia, which continued to practice its age-old farming and herding ways.

Farther south, where the Nile makes a great U-shaped turn in the fertile plain of the Dongola Reach (see Map 2.2), a more complex political entity was evolving from the chiefdoms of the third millennium B.C.E. The Egyptians gave the name **Kush** to the kingdom whose capital was located at Kerma, one of the earliest urbanized centers in tropical Africa. Beginning around 1750 B.C.E. the kings of Kush built fortification walls and monumental structures of mud brick. The dozens or even hundreds of servants and wives sacrificed for burial with the kings, as well as the rich objects found in their tombs, testify to the wealth and power of the rulers of Kush and imply a belief in an afterlife in which attendants and possessions would be useful. Kushite craftsmen were skilled in metalworking, whether for weapons or jewelry, and produced high-quality pottery.

Kush An Egyptian name for Nubia, the region alongside the Nile River south of Egypt, where an indigenous kingdom with its own distinctive institutions and cultural traditions arose beginning in the early second millennium B.C.E.

Gebel Barkal This model of Gebel Barkal, the "Holy Mountain" of Nubia, made of sandstone and with traces of the original paint, was deposited in the Temple of Amon at Gebel Barkal by a Nubian king. The original door is missing, as well as a seated figurine inside, possibly an image of Amon. Resting on a band representing a swamp with papyrus reeds, the doorway is flanked on either side by relief images of a winged goddess and a king wearing a short kilt.

During the expansionist New Kingdom (ca. 1532–1070 B.C.E.) the Egyptians penetrated more deeply into Nubia (see Chapter 3). They destroyed Kush and its capital and extended their frontier to the Fourth Cataract. A high-ranking Egyptian official called "Overseer of Southern Lands" or "King's Son of Kush" ruled Nubia from a new administrative center at Napata (nah-PAH-tuh), near Gebel Barkal (JEB-uhl BAHR-kahl), the "Holy Mountain," believed to be the home of a local god. Exploiting the mines of Nubia, Egypt supplied gold to the states of the Middle East. Fatalities were high among native workers in the brutal desert climate, and the army had to ward off attacks from desert nomads.

Five hundred years of Egyptian domination in Nubia left many marks. The Egyptian government imposed Egyptian culture on the native population. Children from elite families were brought to the Egyptian royal court to guarantee the good behavior of their relatives in Nubia; they absorbed Egyptian language, culture, and religion, which they later carried home with them. Other Nubians served as archers in the Egyptian armed forces. The manufactured goods that they brought back to Nubia have been found in their graves. The Nubians built towns on the Egyptian model and erected stone temples to Egyptian gods, particularly Amon. The frequent depiction of Amon with the head of a ram may reflect a blending of the chief Egyptian god with a Nubian ram deity.

The Kingdom of Meroë, 800 B.C.E.–350 C.E.

Egypt's weakness after 1200 B.C.E. led to the collapse of its authority in Nubia. In the eighth century B.C.E. a powerful new native kingdom emerged in southern Nubia. Its history can be divided into two parts. During the early period, between the eighth and fourth centuries B.C.E., Napata, the former Egyptian headquarters, was the primary center. During the later period, from the fourth century B.C.E. to the fourth century C.E., the center was farther south, at **Meroë** (MER-oh-ee), near the Sixth Cataract.

Meroë Capital of a flourishing kingdom in southern Nubia from the fourth century B.C.E. to the fourth century C.E. In this period Nubian culture shows more independence from Egypt and the influence of sub-Saharan Africa.

For half a century, from around 712 to 660 B.C.E., the kings of Nubia ruled all of Egypt as the Twenty-fifth Dynasty. They conducted themselves in the age-old manner of Egyptian rulers. They were addressed by royal titles, depicted in traditional costume, and buried according to Egyptian custom. However, they kept their Nubian names and were depicted with the physical features of sub-Saharan Africans. They inaugurated an artistic and cultural renaissance, building on a monumental scale for the first time in centuries and reinvigorating Egyptian art, architecture, and religion. The Nubian kings resided at Memphis, the Old Kingdom capital, while Thebes, the New Kingdom capital, was the residence of a celibate female member of the king's family who was titled "God's Wife of Amon."

Nubian Domination of Egypt

The Nubian dynasty made a disastrous mistake in 701 B.C.E. when it offered help to local rulers in Palestine who were struggling against the Assyrian Empire. The Assyrians retaliated by invading Egypt and driving the Nubian monarchs back to their southern domain by 660 B.C.E.

Napata again became the chief royal residence and religious center of the kingdom. However, Egyptian cultural influences remained strong. Court documents continued to be written in Egyptian hieroglyphs, and the mummified remains of the rulers were buried in modestly-sized sandstone pyramids along with hundreds of shawabti (shuh-WAB-tee) figurines.

The Shift South to Meroë

By the fourth century B.C.E. the center of gravity had shifted south to Meroë, perhaps because Meroë was better situated for agriculture and trade, the economic mainstays of the Nubian kingdom. As a result, sub-Saharan cultural patterns gradually replaced Egyptian ones. Egyptian hieroglyphs gave way to a new set of symbols, still essentially undeciphered, for writing the Meroitic language. People continued to worship Amon as well as Isis, an Egyptian goddess connected to fertility and sexuality, but those deities had to share the stage with Nubian deities like the lion-god Apedemak. Meroitic art combined Egyptian, Greco-Roman, and indigenous traditions.

 **AP* Exam Tip** Gender roles in each of the classical civilizations are an important issue for the exam.

Women of the royal family played an important role in Meroitic politics, another reflection of the influence of sub-Saharan Africa. In their matrilineal system the king was succeeded by the son of his sister. Nubian queens sometimes ruled by themselves and sometimes in partnership with their husbands. They played a part in warfare, diplomacy, and the building of temples and pyramid tombs. They are depicted in scenes reserved for male rulers in Egyptian imagery, smiting enemies in battle and being suckled by the mother-goddess Isis.

Meroë was a huge city for its time, more than a square mile in area, dominating fertile grasslands and converging trade routes. Great reservoirs were dug to catch precious rainfall, and the city was a major center for iron smelting. Although much of the city is still buried under the sand, in 2002 archaeologists using a magnetometer to detect buried structures discovered a large palace. The Temple of Amon was approached by an avenue lined with stone rams, and the walled precinct of the "Royal City" was filled with palaces, temples, and administrative buildings. The ruler, who may have been regarded as divine, was assisted by a professional class of officials, priests, and army officers.

Meroë collapsed in the early fourth century C.E., overrun by nomads from the western desert who had become more mobile because of the arrival of the camel in North Africa. Already weakened when profitable commerce with the Roman Empire was diverted to the Red Sea and to the rising kingdom of Aksum (AHK-soom) (in present-day Ethiopia), the end of the Meroitic kingdom was as closely linked to Nubia's role in long-distance commerce as its beginning.

SECTION REVIEW

- Nubia's natural wealth and location on the trade route between Egypt and sub-Saharan Africa, along with Egypt's hunger for Nubian gold, explain the early rise of a complex civilization there.
- During long periods of Egyptian domination, as well as a period in which Nubian rulers controlled Egypt, Nubian culture and technology were strongly influenced by Egyptian practices.
- During the Meroitic period, Nubia came under stronger cultural influences stemming from sub-Saharan Africa, as seen in the prominent role of queens.
- The city of Meroë was large and impressive, with monumental palaces, temples, and boulevards. It controlled agriculture and trade and was a center of metallurgy.
- Nubia's collapse in the early fourth century C.E. was due to shifting trade routes and attacks by desert nomads.

CELTIC EUROPE, 1000–50 B.C.E.

Continental Europe

The southern peninsulas of Europe—present-day Spain, Italy, and Greece—share in the mild climate of all the Mediterranean lands and are separated from "continental" Europe to the north by high mountains (the Pyrenees and Alps). Consequently, the history of southern Europe in antiquity is primarily connected to that of the Mediterranean and Middle East, at least until the Roman conquests north of the Alps (see Chapters 3, 4, and 5).

Continental Europe (including the modern nations of France, Germany, Switzerland, Austria, the Czech Republic, Slovakia, Hungary, Poland, and Romania—see Map 2.3) was well suited to agriculture and herding. It contained broad plains with good soil and had a temperate climate with cold winters, warm summers, and ample rainfall. It was well endowed with natural resources such as timber and metals, and large, navigable rivers facilitated travel and trade.

MAP 2.3 **The Celtic Peoples** Celtic civilization originated in central Europe in the early part of the first millennium B.C.E. Around 500 B.C.E. Celtic peoples began to migrate, making Celtic civilization the dominant cultural style in Europe north of the Alps. The Celts' interactions with the peoples of the Mediterranean, including Greeks and Romans, involved both warfare and trade. (From *Atlas of Classical History*, Fifth Edition, by Michael Grant. Copyright © 1994 by Michael Grant. Used by permission of Oxford University Press, Inc.)

e Interactive Map

Humans had lived in this part of Europe for many thousands of years (see Chapter 1), but their lack of any system of writing severely limits our knowledge of the earliest inhabitants. Around 500 B.C.E., as Celtic peoples spread from their original homeland across a substantial portion of Europe, they came into contact with the literate societies of the Mediterranean and thereby entered the historical record. Information about the early **Celts** (kelts) comes from the archaeological record, the accounts of Greek and Roman travelers and conquerors, and the oral traditions of Celtic Wales and Ireland that were written down during the European Middle Ages.

Celts Peoples sharing common linguistic and cultural features that originated in Central Europe in the first half of the first millennium B.C.E.

The Spread of the Celts

The term *Celtic* refers to a branch of the large Indo-European family of languages found throughout Europe and in western and southern Asia. Scholars link the Celtic language group to archaeological remains first appearing in parts of present-day Germany, Austria, and the Czech Republic after 1000 B.C.E. (see Map 2.3). Many early Celts lived in or near hill-forts—lofty natural locations made more defensible by earthwork fortifications. By 500 B.C.E. Celtic elites were trading with Mediterranean societies for crafted goods and wine. This contact may have stimulated the new styles of Celtic manufacture and art that appeared at this time.

Homeland and Migrations

These new cultural features coincided with a period in which Celtic groups migrated to many parts of Europe. The motives behind these population movements, the precise timing, and the manner in which they were carried out are not well understood. Celts occupied nearly all of France and much of Britain and Ireland, and they merged with indigenous peoples to create

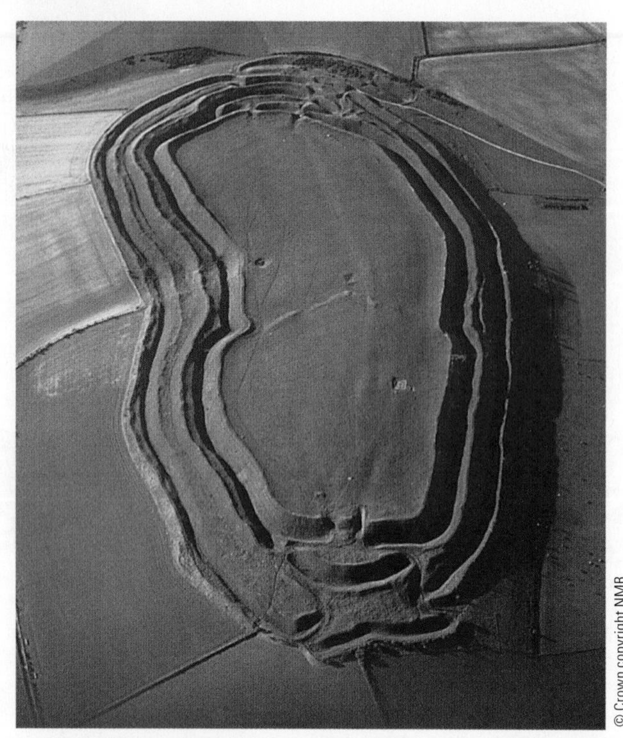

Celtic Hill-Fort in England Hundreds of these fortresses have been found across Europe. They served as centers of administration, gathering points for Celtic armies, manufacturing centers, storage depots for food and trade goods, and places of refuge. The natural defense offered by a hill could be improved, as here, by the construction of ditches and earthwork walls. Particularly effective was the so-called Gallic Wall, made of a combination of earth, stone, and timber to create both strength and enough flexibility to absorb the pounding from siege engines.

the Celtiberian culture of northern Spain. Other Celtic groups overran northern Italy (they sacked Rome in 490 B.C.E.), raided into central Greece, and settled in central Anatolia (modern Turkey). By 300 B.C.E. Celtic peoples were spread across Europe north of the Alps, from present-day Hungary to Spain and Ireland. Their traces remain in many place names in Europe today.

These widely diffused Celtic groups shared elements of language and culture, but there was no Celtic "nation," for they were divided into hundreds of small, loosely organized kinship groups. In the past scholars built up a generic picture of Celtic society derived largely from the observations of Greek and Roman writers. Current scholarship is focusing attention on the differences as much as the similarities among Celtic peoples. It is unlikely that the ancient Celts identified themselves as belonging to anything akin to our modern conception of "Celtic civilization."

Mediterranean Observers

Greek and Roman writers were struck by the appearance of male Celts—their burly size, long red hair, shaggy mustaches, and loud, deep voices—and by their strange apparel, trousers (usually an indication of horse-riding peoples) and twisted gold neck collars. Particularly terrifying were the warriors who fought naked and made trophies of the heads of defeated enemies. Surviving accounts describe the Celts as wildly fond of war, courageous, childishly impulsive and emotional, and fond of boasting and exaggeration, yet quick-witted and eager to learn.

Celtic Society

Warriors, Druids, and Commoners

One of the best sources of information about Celtic society is the account of the Roman general Gaius Julius Caesar, who conquered Gaul (present-day France) between 58 and 51 B.C.E. Many Celtic groups in Gaul had once been ruled by kings, but by the time of the Roman invasion they periodically chose public officials, perhaps under Greek and Roman influence.

Celtic society was divided into an elite class of warriors, professional groups of priests and bards (singers of poems about glorious deeds of the past), and commoners. The warriors owned land and flocks of cattle and sheep and monopolized both wealth and power. The common people labored on their land. The Celts built houses (usually round in Britain, rectangular in France) out of wattle and daub—a wooden framework filled in with clay and straw—with thatched straw roofs. Several such houses belonging to related families might be surrounded by a wooden fence for protection.

The warriors of Welsh and Irish legend reflect a stage of political and social development less complex than that of the Celts in Gaul. They raided one another's flocks, reveled in drunken feasts, and engaged in contests of strength and wit. At banquets warriors would fight to the death just to claim the choicest cut of the meat, the "hero's portion."

Druids The class of religious experts who conducted rituals and preserved sacred lore among some ancient Celtic peoples.

Druids, the Celtic priests in Gaul and Britain, formed a well-organized fraternity that performed religious, judicial, and educational functions. Trainees spent years memorizing prayers, secret rituals, legal precedents, and other traditions. The priesthood was the one Celtic institution that crossed tribal lines. The Druids sometimes headed off warfare between feuding groups and served as judges in cases involving Celts from different groups. In the first century C.E. the Roman government attempted to stamp out the Druids, probably because of concern that they

The Gundestrup Cauldron This silver vessel was found in a peat bog in Denmark, but it must have come from elsewhere. It is usually dated to the second or first century B.C.E. On the inside left are Celtic warriors on horse and on foot, with lozenge-shaped shields and long battle-horns. On the inside right is a horned deity, possibly Cernunnos.

The National Museum of Denmark

might serve as a rallying point for Celtic opposition to Roman rule and also because of their involvement in human sacrifices.

The Celts supported large populations by tilling the heavy but fertile soils of continental Europe. Their metallurgical skills probably surpassed those of the Mediterranean peoples. Celts on the Atlantic shore of France built sturdy ships that braved ocean conditions, and they developed extensive trade networks along Europe's large, navigable rivers. One lucrative commodity was tin, which Celtic traders from southwest England brought to Greek buyers in southern France. By the first century B.C.E. some hill-forts were evolving into urban centers.

Celtic Women

Women's lives were focused on child rearing, food production, and some crafts. Their situation was superior to that of women in the Middle East and in the Greek and Roman Mediterranean. Greek and Roman sources depict Celtic women as strong and proud. Welsh and Irish tales portray clever, self-assured women who sit at banquets with their husbands and engage in witty conversation. Marriage was a partnership to which both parties contributed property. Each had the right to inherit the estate if the other died. Celtic women also had greater freedom in their sexual relations than did their southern counterparts.

Tombs of elite women have yielded rich collections of clothing, jewelry, and furniture for use in the next world. Daughters of the elite were married to leading members of other tribes to create alliances. When the Romans invaded Celtic Britain in the first century C.E., they sometimes were opposed by Celtic tribes headed by queens, although some experts see this as an abnormal circumstance created by the Roman invasion itself.

Belief and Knowledge

Celtic Religion

Historians know the names of more than four hundred Celtic gods and goddesses, mostly associated with particular localities or kinship groups. More widely revered deities included Lug (loog), the god of light, crafts, and inventions; the horse-goddess Epona (eh-POH-nuh); and the horned god Cernunnos (KURN-you-nuhs). "The Mothers," three goddesses depicted together holding symbols of abundance, probably played a part in a fertility cult. Halloween and May Day preserve the ancient Celtic holidays of Samhain (SAH-win) and Beltaine (BEHL-tayn), respectively, which took place at key moments in the agricultural cycle.

The early Celts did not build temples but instead worshiped wherever they felt the presence of divinity—at springs, groves, and hilltops. At the sources of the Seine and Marne Rivers in France, archaeologists have found huge caches of wooden statues thrown into the water by worshipers.

The burial of elite members of early Celtic society in wagons filled with extensive grave goods suggests belief in some sort of afterlife. In Irish and Welsh legends, heroes and gods pass back and forth between the natural and supernatural worlds much more readily than in the mythology of other cultures, and magical occurrences are commonplace. Celtic priests set forth a doctrine of reincarnation—the rebirth of the soul in a new body.

Conquest and Assimilation

The Roman conquest from the second century B.C.E. to the first century C.E. of Spain, southern Britain, France, and parts of Central Europe curtailed the evolution of Celtic society. The peoples in these lands were largely assimilated to Roman ways (see Chapter 5). That is why the inhabitants of modern Spain and France speak languages that are descended from Latin. From the third century C.E. on, Germanic invaders weakened the Celts still further, and the English language has a Germanic base. Only on the western fringes of the European continent—in Brittany (northwest France), Wales, Scotland, and Ireland—did Celtic peoples maintain their language, art, and culture into modern times.

SECTION REVIEW

- Around 500 B.C.E. Celtic-speaking peoples from Central Europe began to spread across much of "continental" Europe.
- Most of what we know about the ancient Celts comes from archaeological discoveries and the written reports of Greek and Roman observers, who depict them as impulsive and fond of war.
- Celts lived in relatively small kinship (tribal) groups that were dominated by warrior elites. Hill-forts served as places of assembly and refuges.
- The Celts worshiped many gods in natural settings. The Druids, a priestly class in Gaul (France) and Britain, played a major role in religion, education, and intertribal legal matters.
- The Roman Empire's conquest of Celtic lands, followed later by Germanic invasions, pushed Celtic language and culture to the western edge of the European continent.

FIRST CIVILIZATIONS OF THE AMERICAS: THE OLMEC AND CHAVÍN, 1200–250 B.C.E.

New theories about the peopling of the Americas suggest that the process may have been more complex than previously suspected and may have involved people traveling by sea as well as trekking across a land bridge between Siberia and Alaska. It is generally held that humans reached the Western Hemisphere through a series of migrations from Asia (see Chapter 1). Some scholars believe that the first migrations occurred as early as 35,000 to 25,000 B.C.E., but most accept a later date of 18,000 to 14,000 B.C.E. Thus, the peoples in the Western Hemisphere were virtually isolated from the rest of the world for at least fifteen thousand years.

Over thousands of years the population of the Americas grew and spread throughout the hemisphere, adapting to environments that included polar extremes, tropical rain forests, and high mountain ranges as well as deserts, woodlands, and prairies. Well before 1000 B.C.E. the domestication of new plant varieties, the introduction of new technologies, and a limited development of trade led to greater social stratification and the beginnings of urbanization in several regions. By 1000 B.C.E. a number of centers had begun to project their political and cultural power over broad territories. Two of the hemisphere's most impressive cultural traditions developed in Mesoamerica (Mexico and northern Central America) and in the mountainous Andean region of South America. The cultural legacies of the Olmec and Chavín would persist for more than a thousand years.

The Mesoamerican Olmec, 1200–400 B.C.E.

Mesoamerica is a region of great geographic and climatic diversity. It is extremely active geologically, experiencing both earthquakes and volcanic eruptions. Mountain ranges break the region into microenvironments, including the temperate climates of the Valley of Mexico and the Guatemalan highlands, the tropical forests of the Peten and Gulf of Mexico coast, the rain forest of the southern Yucatán and Belize, and the drier scrub forest of the northern Yucatán (see Map 2.4).

Within these ecological niches, Amerindian peoples developed specialized technologies that exploited indigenous plants and animals, as well as minerals like obsidian, quartz, and jade. Early settlements depended on the region's rich plant diversity and on fishing. By 3500 B.C.E. the

MAP 2.4 Olmec and Chavín Civilizations The regions of Mesoamerica (most of modern Mexico and Central America) and the Andean highlands of South America have hosted impressive civilizations since early times. The civilizations of the Olmec and Chavín were the originating civilizations of these two regions, providing the foundations of architecture, city planning, and religion.

Interactive Map

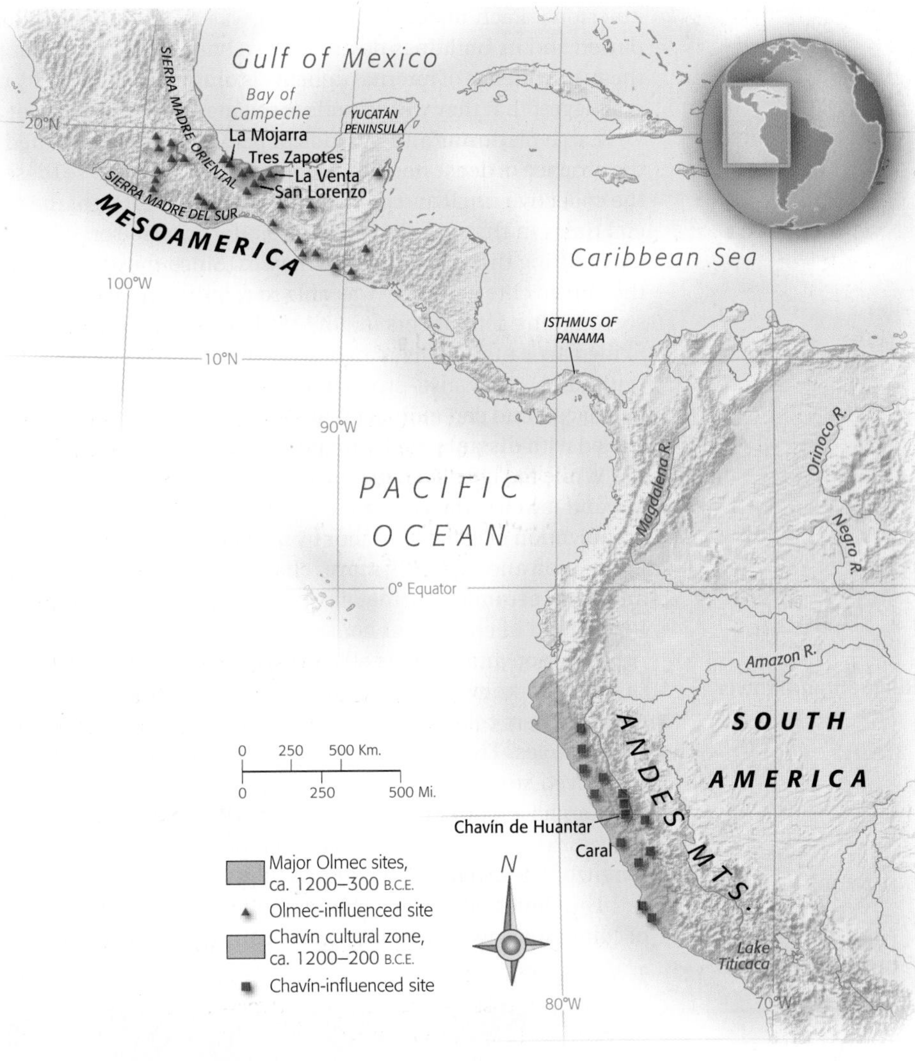

staples of the Mesoamerican diet—corn (maize), beans, and squash—had been domesticated. Manioc, a calorie-rich root crop, was also grown in the floodplains. The ability of farmers to produce dependable surpluses of these products permitted the first stages of craft specialization and social stratification. Eventually, contacts across environmental boundaries led to trade and cultural exchange. Enhanced trade, increasing agricultural productivity, and rising population led, in turn, to urbanization and the gradual appearance of powerful political and religious elites. As religious and political elites emerged, they used their prestige and authority to organize the population to dig irrigation and drainage canals, develop raised fields in wetlands that could be farmed more intensively, and construct monumental religious and civic buildings.

Origins of Olmec Civilization

Olmec The first Mesoamerican civilization. Between ca. 1200 and 400 B.C.E., the Olmec people of central Mexico created a vibrant civilization that included intensive agriculture, wide-ranging trade, ceremonial centers, and monumental construction.

The most influential early Mesoamerican civilization was the **Olmec**, flourishing between 1200 and 400 B.C.E. (see Map 2.4). The center of Olmec civilization was located near the tropical Atlantic coast of what are now the Mexican states of Veracruz and Tabasco. The earliest major center was located at San Lorenzo (1200–900 B.C.E.; the names of early American sites are modern, since, in the absence of written records, the ancient names are unknown). La Venta (LA BEN-tah), which developed at about the same time, became the most important Olmec center after 900 B.C.E., when San Lorenzo was abandoned or destroyed. Tres Zapotes (TRACE zah-POE-tace) was the last dominant center, rising to prominence after La Venta collapsed or was destroyed around 600 B.C.E. The relationship among these centers is unclear. Scholars have found little evidence to suggest that they were either rival city-states or dependent centers of a centralized political authority. It appears that each center developed independently to exploit and exchange specialized products like salt, cacao (chocolate beans), clay for ceramics, and limestone. Each major Olmec center was eventually abandoned, its monuments defaced and buried and its buildings destroyed. Archaeologists interpret these events differently; some see them as evidence of internal upheavals or military attacks by neighboring peoples, whereas others suggest that they were rituals associated with the death of a ruler.

Ceremonial Centers

Large platforms and mounds of packed earth dominated Olmec urban centers. Because of the absence of dense housing precincts, scholars believe these centers primarily accommodated the collective ritual and political activities that brought the rural population to the cities at special times in the year. Some of the platforms also served as foundations for elite residences, in effect lifting the elite above the masses. Since these centers had small permanent populations, the Olmec elite evidently was able to require and direct the labor of thousands of people from surrounding settlements for low-skill tasks like moving dirt and stone construction materials. Skilled artisans who lived in or near the urban core decorated the buildings with carvings and sculptures. They also produced high-quality crafts, such as exquisite carved jade figurines, necklaces, and ceremonial knives and axes. There is also evidence for a class of merchants who traded with distant peoples for obsidian, jade, and pottery.

While the elite lived in houses decorated with finely crafted objects and wore elegant clothing and jewelry, the commoners lived in small structures constructed of sticks and mud. The organization of collective labor by the Olmec elites benefited the commoners by increasing food production and making it more reliable. People also enjoyed a more diverse diet. Utilitarian pots and small ceramic figurines as well as small stone carvings associated with religious belief have been found in commoner households. This suggests that at least some advantages gained from urbanization and growing elite prosperity were shared broadly in the society.

Religion and Power

Little is known about Olmec political structure, but it seems likely that the rise of major urban centers coincided with the appearance of a form of kingship that combined religious and secular roles. The authority of the rulers and their kin groups is suggested by a series of colossal carved stone heads, some as large as 11 feet (3.4 meters) high. Since each head is unique, most archaeologists believe they were portraits carved to memorialize individual rulers. This theory is reinforced by the location of the heads close to the major urban centers, especially San Lorenzo. These remarkable stone sculptures are the best-known monuments of Olmec culture.

The Olmec elite used elaborate religious rituals to control this complex society. Thousands of commoners were drawn from the countryside to attend awe-inspiring ceremonies at the cen-

Olmec Head Giant heads sculpted from basalt are a widely recognized legacy of Olmec culture. Sixteen heads have been found, the largest approximately 11 feet (3.4 meters) tall. Experts in Olmec archaeology believe the heads are portraits of individual rulers, warriors, or ballplayers.

ters. The elevated platforms and mounds with carved stone veneers served as potent backdrops for these rituals. Rulers and their close kin came to be associated with the gods through bloodletting and human sacrifice, evidence of which is found in all the urban centers.

The Olmec were polytheistic, and most of their deities had both male and female natures. Human and animal characteristics were also blended. The ability of humans to transform themselves into powerful animals, such as jaguars, crocodiles, snakes, and sharks, is a common decorative motif. Rulers were especially associated with the jaguar.

Shamans (individuals who claimed the ability to make direct contact with supernatural powers) attached to the elite organized religious life and provided practical advice about the periodic rains essential to agricultural life. From their close observation of the stars, they produced a calendar that was used to organize ritual life and agriculture, and they laid out the ceremonial centers in alignment with the paths of certain stars. They probably were responsible for developing a form of writing (as yet undeciphered) that may have influenced later innovations among the Maya (see Chapter 11). The Olmec were also the likely originators of a ritual ball game that became an enduring part of Mesoamerican ceremonial life.

Cultural Legacy

There is little evidence for an Olmec empire. Given the limited technological and agricultural capacity of the society, it is unlikely that the power of the Olmec could have been projected militarily over significant distances. However, the discovery of Olmec products and images, such as jade carvings decorated with the jaguar-god, as far away as the Pacific coast of Central America and the Central Plateau of Mexico shows that the Olmec exercised cultural influence over a wide area. This influence would endure for centuries. All subsequent Mesoamerican civilizations shared fundamental elements of material culture, technology, religious belief and ritual, political organization, art, architecture, and sports.

Early South American Civilization: Chavín, 900–250 B.C.E.

Geography and environment played a critical role in the development of human society in the Andes. The region's diverse environments—a mountainous core, arid coastal plain, and dense interior jungles—challenged human populations, encouraging the development of specialized regional production as well as widespread social institutions and cultural values that facilitated interregional exchanges and shared labor responsibilities.

Trade and the Rise of Chavín

The earliest urban centers in the Andean region were villages of a few hundred people built along the coastal plain or in the foothills near the coast. The abundance of fish and mollusks along the coast of Peru provided a dependable food supply, while the introduction of corn (maize) cultivation from Mesoamerica increased the food supplies of the coast and interior foothills, allowing greater levels of urbanization. The coastal populations traded fish, shellfish, and decorative shells for corn, other foods, and eventually textiles produced in the foothills. The two regions also exchanged ceremonial practices, religious motifs, and aesthetic ideas.

Recent discoveries demonstrate that as early as 2600 B.C.E. the vast site called Caral in the Supe Valley had developed many of the characteristics now viewed as the hallmarks of later Andean civilization, including ceremonial plazas, pyramids, elevated platforms and mounds, and extensive irrigation works. The scale of the public works in Caral suggests a population of thousands and a political structure capable of organizing the production and distribution of maritime and agricultural products over a broad area.

Chavín The first major urban civilization in South America (900–250 B.C.E.).

Chavín (see Map 2.4) inherited many of the cultural and economic characteristics of Caral. Its capital, Chavín de Huantar (cha-BEAN day WAHN-tar), was located at 10,300 feet (3,139 meters) in the eastern range of the Andes north of the modern city of Lima. Between 900 and 250 B.C.E. Chavín dominated a densely populated region that included large areas of the Peruvian coastal plain and Andean foothills. Chavín de Huantar's location at the intersection of trade routes allowed the city's rulers to organize and prosper from trade among distinct ecological zones and gain an advantage over regional rivals. As Chavín grew, its trade linked the coastal economy with the inland producers of quinoa (a local grain), corn, and potatoes, with the herders of llamas in the high mountain valleys, and, to a lesser extent, with the producers of coca (the leaves were chewed, producing a mild narcotic effect) and fruits in the tropical lowlands on the eastern flank of the Andes.

The development of these trade networks led to reciprocal labor obligations that permitted the construction and maintenance of roads, bridges, temples, palaces, and large irrigation and drainage projects as well as textile production. The exact nature of these reciprocal labor obligations at Chavín is unknown. In later Andean civilizations groups of related families who held land communally and claimed descent from a common ancestor organized these labor obligations. Group members thought of themselves as brothers and sisters and were obligated to aid one another, providing a model for the organization of labor and the distribution of goods at every level of Andean society.

llama A hoofed animal indigenous to the Andes Mountains in South America. It was the only domesticated beast of burden in the Americas before the arrival of Europeans.

Llamas, first bred in the mountainous interior of Peru, were the only domesticated beasts of burden in the Americas, and they played an important role in the integration of the Andean region. Llamas provided meat and wool and decreased the labor needed to transport goods. A single driver could control ten to thirty animals, each carrying up to 70 pounds (32 kilograms); a human porter could carry only about 50 pounds (22.5 kilograms). By moving goods from one ecological zone to another, llamas promoted specialization of production and increased trade. Thus, they were crucial to Chavín's development, not unlike the camel in the evolution of trans-Saharan trade (see Chapter 7).

Society and Technology

Class distinctions appear to have increased in this period. Modern scholars see evidence that both local chiefs and a more powerful chief or king dominated Chavín's politics. A class of priests directed religious life. The most common decorative motif in sculpture, pottery, and textiles was a jaguar-man similar in conception to the Olmec symbol. In both civilizations and in many other cultures in the Americas, this powerful predator provided an enduring image of religious authority.

Chavín housed a large complex of multilevel platforms made of packed earth or rubble and faced with cut stone or adobe (sun-dried brick made of clay and straw). Small buildings used for ritual purposes or as elite residences were built on these platforms. Nearly all the buildings were decorated with relief carvings of serpents, condors, jaguars, or human forms. The largest building at Chavín de Huantar measured 250 feet (76 meters) on each side and rose to a height of 50 feet (15 meters). Its hollow interior contained narrow galleries and small rooms that may have housed the remains of royal ancestors.

Metallurgy in the Western Hemisphere was first developed in the Andean region ca. 500 B.C.E. The later introduction of metallurgy in Mesoamerica, like the appearance of maize agriculture in the Andes, suggests sustained trade and cultural contacts between the two regions. Archaeological investigations of Chavín de Huantar and smaller centers have uncovered remarkable silver, gold, and gold alloy ornaments that represent a clear advance over earlier technologies. Improvements in both the manufacture and decoration of textiles are also associated with the rise of Chavín. Excavations of graves reveal that superior-quality textiles as well as gold crowns, breastplates, and jewelry distinguished rulers from commoners. These rich objects, the quality and abundance of pottery, and the monumental architecture of the major centers all suggest the presence of highly skilled artisans as well. The sheer quality of Chavín's products contributed to the reputation and prestige of the culture.

SECTION REVIEW

- Well before 1000 B.C.E. newly domesticated plants, new technologies, and trade led to greater social stratification and the beginnings of urbanization in Mesoamerica and the Andean region of South America.
- The Olmec of Mesoamerica (1200–400 B.C.E.) and the Chavín civilization (900–250 B.C.E.) in the Andes coordinated exchanges of goods between different ecological zones. Their styles were widely emulated and persisted long afterward.
- Ruling elites residing in urban centers staged elaborate religious ceremonies designed to impress subjects and enhance their prestige.
- Olmec societies were probably ruled by kings, who were depicted by giant stone heads. Olmec shamans communicated with the spirit world, supervised the calendar, and may have created a system of writing.
- Chavín depended on llamas, the only domesticated beasts of burden in the hemisphere, to transport goods between regions.
- Metallurgy originated in the Andean region and later spread to Mesoamerica.

The enormous scale of the capital and the dispersal of Chavín's pottery styles, religious motifs, and architectural forms over a wide area have led some scholars to claim that Chavín imposed some form of political and economic control over its neighbors by military force. Most scholars believe, however, that, as in the case of the Olmec civilization, Chavín's influence depended more on the development of an attractive religious belief system and related rituals. Chavín's most potent religious symbol, a jaguar deity, was dispersed over a broad area, and archaeological evidence suggests that Chavín de Huantar served as a pilgrimage site.

Decline

There is no convincing evidence, like defaced buildings or broken images, that the eclipse of Chavín (unlike the Olmec centers) was associated with conquest or rebellion. However, recent investigations have suggested that increased warfare throughout the region around 200 B.C.E. disrupted Chavín's trade and undermined the authority of the governing elite. Regardless of what caused the collapse of this powerful culture, the technologies, material culture, statecraft, architecture, and urban planning associated with Chavín influenced the Andean region for centuries.

CONCLUSION

Environment and Organization

The civilizations of early China, Nubia, the Celts, the Olmec, and Chavín emerged in very different ecological contexts in widely separated parts of the globe, and the patterns of organization, technology, behavior, and belief that they developed were, in large part, responses to the challenges and opportunities of those environments.

In the North China Plain, as in the river-valley civilizations of Mesopotamia and Egypt, the presence of great, flood-prone rivers and the lack of dependable rainfall led to the formation of powerful institutions capable of organizing large numbers of people to dig and maintain irrigation channels and build dikes. An authoritarian central government has been a recurring feature of Chinese history from at least as early as the Shang monarchy.

In Nubia, the initial impetus for the formation of a strong state was the need for protection from desert nomads and from the Egyptian rulers who coveted Nubian gold and other resources. Control of these resources and of the trade route between sub-Saharan Africa and the north, as well as the agricultural surplus to feed administrators and specialists in the urban centers, made the rulers of Kerma, Napata, and Meroë wealthy and powerful.

The Celtic peoples of continental Europe never developed a strong state. They occupied fertile lands with adequate rainfall for agriculture, grazing territory for flocks, and timber for fuel and construction. Kinship groups dominated by warrior elites and controlling compact territories were the usual form of organization. The Celtic elites of Central Europe initially traded for luxury goods with the Mediterranean, and when they began to expand into lands to the west and south after 500 B.C.E. they came into even closer contact with Mediterranean peoples. Eventually many Celtic groups were incorporated into the Roman Empire.

Although the ecological zones in Mesoamerica and South America in which the Olmec and Chavín cultures emerged were quite different, both societies created networks that brought together the resources and products of disparate regions. Little is known about the political and social organization of these societies, but archaeological evidence makes clear the existence of ruling elites that gathered wealth and organized labor for the construction of monumental centers.

Religion and Power

In all these societies the elites used religion to bolster their position. The Shang rulers of China were indispensable intermediaries between their kingdom and powerful and protective ancestors and gods. Bronze vessels were used to make offerings to ancestral spirits, and divination by means of oracle bones delivered information of value to the ruler and kingdom. Their Zhou successors developed the concept of the ruler as divine Son of Heaven who ruled in accord with the Mandate of Heaven. In its religious practices, as in other spheres, the civilization that developed in Nubia was powerfully influenced by its interactions with the more complex and technologically advanced neighboring society in Egypt. Nubian rulers built temples and pyramid tombs on the Egyptian model, but they also synthesized Egyptian and indigenous gods, beliefs, and rituals. Olmec and Chavín urban centers were the sites of dazzling ritual displays that reinforced the authority of the elites who resided in them. Olmec shamans attached to the elite made contact with supernatural powers, organized religious life, and directed the planning of the ceremonial centers to be aligned with the stars. Among the Celtic peoples of Gaul and Britain, the Druids constituted an elite class of priests who performed vital religious, legal, and educational functions. However, unlike the other civilizations surveyed in this chapter, the Celts did not construct temples and ceremonial centers, and instead worshiped hundreds of gods and goddesses in natural surroundings, where they felt the presence of divinity.

A Tale of Two Hemispheres

Scholars have debated why powerful civilizations appeared many centuries later in the Western Hemisphere than in the Eastern Hemisphere. Recent theories have focused on environmental differences. The Eastern Hemisphere was home to a far larger number of wild plant and animal species that were particularly well suited to domestication. In addition, the natural east-west axis of the huge landmass of Europe and Asia allowed for the relatively rapid spread of domesticated plants and animals to climatically similar zones along the same latitudes. Settled agriculture led to population growth, more complex political and social organization, and increased technological sophistication. In the Americas, by contrast, there were fewer wild plant and animal species that could be domesticated, and the north-south axis of the continents made it more difficult for domesticated species to spread because of variations in climate at different latitudes. As a result, the processes that foster the development of complex societies evolved somewhat more slowly.

KEY TERMS

loess p. 40
Shang p. 42
Zhou p. 44
Mandate of Heaven p. 45
Confucius p. 47
Daoism p. 47
yin/yang p. 50
Kush p. 52
Meroë p. 53
Celts p. 55
Druids p. 56
Olmec p. 59
Chavín p. 61
llama p. 62

EBOOK AND WEBSITE RESOURCES

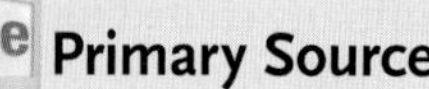

Primary Source

The *Book of Documents*

Interactive Maps

Map 2.1 China in the Shang and Zhou Periods, 1750–221 B.C.E.

Map 2.2 Ancient Nubia

Map 2.3 The Celtic Peoples

Map 2.4 Olmec and Chavín Civilizations

Plus flashcards, practice quizzes, and more. Go to: www.cengage.com/history/bullietearthpeople5e

SUGGESTED READING

Blunden, Caroline, and Mark Elvin. *Cultural Atlas of China.* 1983. Contains general geographic, ethnographic, and historical information about China through the ages, as well as many maps and illustrations.

Burger, Richard L. *Chavín and the Origins of Andean Civilization.* 1992. The most useful summary of recent research on Chavín.

Coe, Michael. *The Olmec World.* 1996. In-depth treatment of the earliest complex society in Mesoamerica.

Coe, Michael, Elizabeth P. Benson, and Dean R. Snow. *Atlas of Ancient America.* 1986. A compendium of maps and information on early societies in the Western Hemisphere.

de Bary, Wm Theodore, and Irene Bloom. *Sources of Chinese Tradition*, vol. 1 (2nd ed.). 1999. A superb collection of translated excerpts from a wide range of sources, accompanied by perceptive introductions.

Diamond, Jared. *Guns, Germs, and Steel: The Fates of Human Societies.* 1997. Tackles the difficult question of why technological development occurred at different times and took different paths in the Eastern and Western Hemispheres.

Di Cosmo, Nicola. *Ancient China and Its Enemies: The Rise of Nomadic Power in East Asian History.* 2002. Sets the development of Chinese civilization in the broader context of interactions with nomadic neighbors.

Fiedel, Stuart. *Prehistory of the Americas.* 1987. Provides an excellent summary of the early history of the Western Hemisphere.

Green, Miranda J. *The Celtic World*. 1995. A large and comprehensive collection of articles on many aspects of Celtic civilization.

Hansen, Valerie. *The Open Empire: A History of China to 1600*. 2000. Devotes substantial attention to ancient China and emphasizes China's connections with other cultures.

James, Simon. *The World of the Celts*. 1993. A concise, well-illustrated introduction to ancient Celtic civilization.

O'Connor, David. *Ancient Nubia: Egypt's Rival in Africa*. 1993. Informative, well-illustrated text based on a major exhibition of Nubian antiquities.

Schwartz, Benjamin I. *The World of Thought in Ancient China*. 1985. A broad introduction to early Chinese ethical and spiritual concepts.

Taylor, John H. *Egypt and Nubia*. 1991. Emphasizes the fruitful interaction of the Egyptian and Nubian cultures.

Temple, Robert. *The Genius of China: 3,000 Years of Science, Discovery, and Invention*. 1986. Explores many aspects of Chinese technology, using a division into general topics such as agriculture, engineering, and medicine.

NOTES

1. Quoted in Miriam Lichtheim, ed., *Ancient Egyptian Literature: A Book of Readings* (Berkeley: University of California Press, 1978).

AP* REVIEW QUESTIONS FOR CHAPTER 2

1. Shang cities served as
   (A) military and economic centers.
   (B) political and religious centers.
   (C) ceremonial centers and markets.
   (D) economic and ceremonial centers.

2. Shang China developed
   (A) the concept of an aristocracy.
   (B) the earliest known divination techniques.
   (C) the first known bureaucracy.
   (D) bronze metallurgy.

3. Early Zhou monarchs justified their rule by
   (A) claiming a direct lineage to Shang rulers.
   (B) enforcing rigid military rule over the people.
   (C) citing Confucian texts on governing.
   (D) claiming that they held the Mandate of Heaven.

4. Decentralization was a weakness in the Zhou state because
   (A) ambitious local rulers tended to operate on their own and become a threat to Zhou rule.
   (B) trade was fragmented under this system.
   (C) bureaucrats could not maintain accurate records of tribute payments.
   (D) the Zhou kings had to maintain several capital cities to enforce discipline on their subjects.

5. The idea that human beings are essentially evil and will behave in an orderly fashion only if compelled to by harsh laws and harsh punishments is most closely associated with the ideas of
   (A) Taoism.
   (B) Legalism.
   (C) Confucianism.
   (D) animism.

6. The idea that there is a hierarchy in life that includes family and society is a part of
   (A) Confucian teachings.
   (B) Shang culture.
   (C) customs of the Zhou people.
   (D) the teachings of Laozi.

7. Which of the following is an example of five centuries of Egyptian domination of Nubia?
   (A) Nubian towns built on the Egyptian model
   (B) Stone temples erected to Egyptian gods in Nubia
   (C) Nubian archers serving in Egypt's military
   (D) All of the above

8. After the collapse of Nubia, Meroë became the center of power in southern Egypt because
   (A) its armies defeated Nubia.
   (B) the Meroitic leaders allied with Egypt against Nubia.
   (C) it was at the conflux of several major trade routes.
   (D) it controlled Nubia's gold fields.

9. As in early Mesopotamia, Olmec leaders were able to control
   (A) construction of irrigation canals.
   (B) trade with the nearby Maya.
   (C) agricultural surpluses.
   (D) the religion.

10. One of the earliest South American civilizations, it is likely that the Chavín located their capital in the Andes north of the modern city of Lima to
    (A) avoid contact with other cultures.
    (B) gain control of key trade routes.
    (C) herd their animals on mountain plains.
    (D) control water for irrigation canals.

11. Unlike the civilizations of the Middle East, the Olmec and the Chavín
    (A) were polytheistic.
    (B) educated all of their citizens.
    (C) lived in virtual isolation from the rest of the world.
    (D) were a trade empire and did not grow their own food.

CHAPTER 3

CHAPTER OUTLINE

- **The Cosmopolitan Middle East, 1700–1100 B.C.E.**
- **The Aegean World, 2000–1100 B.C.E.**
- **The Assyrian Empire, 911–612 B.C.E.**
- **Israel, 2000–500 B.C.E.**
- **Phoenicia and the Mediterranean, 1200–500 B.C.E.**
- **Failure and Transformation, 750–550 B.C.E.**
- **Conclusion**

DIVERSITY + DOMINANCE *Protests Against the Ruling Class in Israel and Babylonia*

ENVIRONMENT + TECHNOLOGY *Ancient Textiles and Dyes*

Courtesy, Lorenzo Camillo

The Harbor Area of Ancient Carthage The military and civilian harbors, with their central location in the city, were at the heart of Carthage's naval and commercial power.

Visit the website and ebook for additional study materials and interactive tools: www.cengage.com/history/bullietearthpeople5e

The Mediterranean and Middle East, 2000–500 B.C.E.

- How did a cosmopolitan civilization develop in the Middle East during the Late Bronze Age, and what forms did it take?
- What civilizations emerged in the Aegean world, and what relationship did they have to the older civilizations to the east?
- How did the Assyrian Empire rise to power and eventually dominate most of the ancient Middle East?
- How did the civilization of Israel develop, following both cultural patterns typical of other societies and its own religious tradition?
- How did the Phoenicians use trade and commerce to gain an important place in the Mediterranean world?
- Between 750 and 550 B.C.E., how did changing political structures transform the ancient Middle East?

Ancient peoples' stories—even when not historically accurate—provide valuable insights into how they thought about their origins and identity. One famous story concerned the founding of the city of Carthage (KAHR-thuhj) in present-day Tunisia, which for centuries dominated the commerce of the western Mediterranean. Tradition held that Dido and her supporters fled the Phoenician city-state of Tyre (tire) in southern Lebanon after her husband was murdered by her brother, the king. Landing on the North African coast, they made contact with local people, who offered them as much land as a cow's hide could cover. Cleverly cutting the hide into narrow strips, they marked out a substantial territory for Kart Khadasht, the "New City" (called *Carthago* by their Roman enemies). The photo at the beginning of this chapter shows the harbor.

This story highlights the spread of cultural patterns from older centers to new regions, as well as the migration of Late Bronze Age and Early Iron Age peoples in the Mediterranean lands and western Asia. Trade, diplomatic contacts, military conquests, and the relocation of large numbers of people spread knowledge, beliefs, practices, and technologies.

By the early first millennium B.C.E. many societies of the Eastern Hemisphere were entering the **Iron Age**, using iron instead of bronze for tools and weapons. Iron offered several advantages. It was a single metal rather than an alloy, and there were many sources of iron ore. Once the technology had been mastered—iron has to be heated to a higher temperature than bronze, and its hardness depends on the amount of carbon added during the forging process—iron tools were found to have harder, sharper edges than bronze tools.

Iron Age Historians' term for the period during which iron was the primary metal for tools and weapons. The advent of iron technology began at different times in different parts of the world.

The first part of this chapter resumes the story of Mesopotamia and Egypt in the second millennium B.C.E.: their relations with neighboring peoples, the development of a prosperous, "cosmopolitan" network of states in the Middle East, and the period of destruction and decline that set in around 1200 B.C.E. We also look at how the Minoan and Mycenaean civilizations of the Aegean Sea were inspired by the technologies and cultural patterns of the older Middle Eastern centers and prospered from participation in long-distance trade networks. The remainder of the chapter examines the resurgence of this region in the Early Iron Age, from 1000 to

AP* Exam Tip The development of iron metallurgy is a highlight in the AP* Course Outline.

500 B.C.E. The focus is on three societies: the Assyrians of northern Mesopotamia; the Israelites of Israel; and the Phoenicians of Lebanon and their colonies in the western Mediterranean, mainly Carthage. After the decline of the ancient centers dominant throughout the third and second millennia B.C.E., these societies evolved into new political, cultural, and commercial centers.

THE COSMOPOLITAN MIDDLE EAST, 1700–1100 B.C.E.

Both Mesopotamia and Egypt succumbed to outside invaders in the seventeenth century B.C.E. Eventually the outsiders were either ejected or assimilated, and conditions of stability and prosperity were restored. Between 1500 and 1200 B.C.E. a number of large states dominated the Middle East (see Map 3.1), controlling the smaller states and kinship groups as they competed with, and sometimes fought against, one another for control of valuable commodities and trade routes.

The Late Bronze Age in the Middle East was a "cosmopolitan" era of widely shared cultures and lifestyles. Diplomatic relations and commercial contacts between states fostered the flow of goods and ideas, and elite groups shared similar values and enjoyed a relatively high standard of living. The peasants in the countryside, who constituted the majority of the population, saw some improvement in their standard of living but reaped fewer benefits from the increasing contacts and trade.

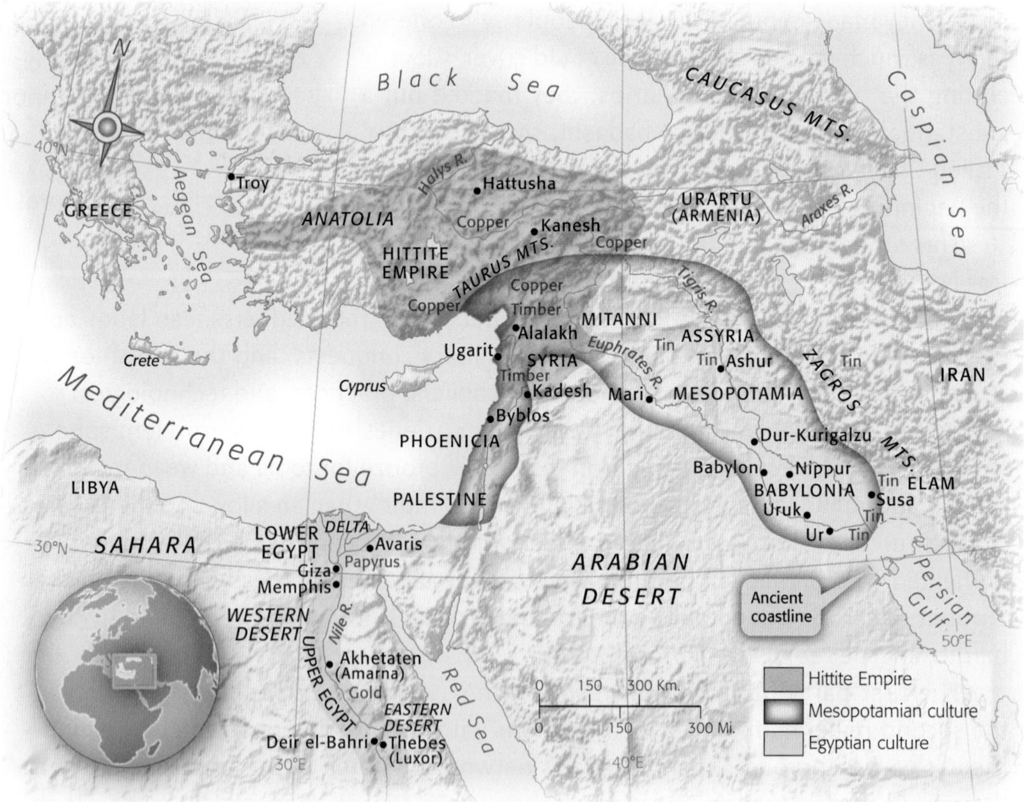

Interactive Map

MAP 3.1 The Middle East in the Second Millennium B.C.E. Although warfare was not uncommon, treaties, diplomatic missions, and correspondence in Akkadian cuneiform fostered cooperative relationships between states. All were tied together by extensive networks of exchange centering on the trade in metals, and peripheral regions, such as Nubia and the Aegean Sea, were drawn into the web of commerce.

CHRONOLOGY

	Western Asia	Egypt	Syria–Palestine	Mediterranean
2000 B.C.E.	2000 B.C.E. Horses in use 1700–1200 B.C.E. Hittites dominant in Anatolia	2040–1640 B.C.E. Middle Kingdom 1640–1532 B.C.E. Hyksos dominate northern Egypt 1532 B.C.E. Beginning of New Kingdom	1800 B.C.E. Abraham migrates to Canaan	2000 B.C.E. Rise of Minoan civilization on Crete; early Greeks arrive in Greece 1600 B.C.E. Rise of Mycenaean civilization in Greece
1500 B.C.E.	1500 B.C.E. Hittites develop iron metallurgy 1460 B.C.E. Kassites assume control of southern Mesopotamia 1200 B.C.E. Destruction of Hittite kingdom	1470 B.C.E. Queen Hatshepsut dispatches expedition to Punt 1353 B.C.E. Akhenaten launches reforms 1290–1224 B.C.E. Reign of Ramesses the Great 1200–1150 B.C.E. Sea Peoples attack Egypt 1070 B.C.E. End of New Kingdom	1500 B.C.E. Early "alphabetic" script developed at Ugarit 1250–1200 B.C.E. Israelite occupation of Canaan 1150 B.C.E. Philistines settle southern coast of Israel	1450 B.C.E. Destruction of Minoan palaces in Crete 1200–1150 B.C.E. Destruction of Mycenaean centers in Greece
1000 B.C.E.	1000 B.C.E. Iron metallurgy begins 911 B.C.E. Rise of Neo-Assyrian Empire 744–727 B.C.E. Reforms of Tiglathpileser 668–627 B.C.E. Reign of Ashurbanipal 626–539 B.C.E. Neo-Babylonian kingdom 612 B.C.E. Fall of Assyria	750 B.C.E. Kings of Kush control Egypt 671 B.C.E. Assyrian conquest of Egypt	1000 B.C.E. Jerusalem made Israelite capital 969 B.C.E. Hiram of Tyre comes to power 960 B.C.E. Solomon builds First Temple 920 B.C.E. Division into two kingdoms of Israel and Judah 721 B.C.E. Assyrian conquest of northern kingdom 701 B.C.E. Assyrian humiliation of Tyre	1000 B.C.E. Iron metallurgy 814 B.C.E. Foundation of Carthage
600 B.C.E.			587 B.C.E. Capture of Jerusalem 515 B.C.E. Deportees from Babylon return to Jerusalem 450 B.C.E. Completion of Hebrew Bible; Hanno the Phoenician explores West Africa	550–300 B.C.E. Rivalry of Carthaginians and Greeks in western Mediterranean

Western Asia

Babylonia and Assyria

By 1500 B.C.E. Mesopotamia was divided into two distinct political zones: Babylonia in the south and Assyria in the north (see Map 3.1). The city of Babylon had gained political and cultural ascendancy over the southern plain under the dynasty of Hammurabi in the eighteenth and seventeenth centuries B.C.E. (see Chapter 1). Subsequently Kassites (KAS-ite) from the Zagros (ZAH-groes) Mountains to the east migrated into southern Mesopotamia, and by 1460 B.C.E.

Remains of a Sunken Cargo Ship from the Late Bronze Age Underwater archaeologists excavate a merchant vessel that went down off the coast of southern Turkey ca. 1300 B.C.E. To the left of the wooden keel and planking is a stone anchor, to the right a row of copper ingots. The vessel was carrying a cargo of copper and tin ingots, as well as Canaanite pots that probably contained incense, fine pottery from Cyprus, sub-Saharan ebony wood and elephant tusks, and some Mycenaean Greek objects, illustrating the wide-ranging seaborne trade in the eastern Mediterranean in that era.

a Kassite dynasty ruled in Babylon. The Kassites retained names in their native language but otherwise embraced Babylonian language and culture and intermarried with the native population. During their 250 years in power, the Kassite rulers of Babylonia defended their core area and traded for raw materials, but they did not pursue territorial conquest.

The "Old Assyrian" kingdom in northern Mesopotamia was more ambitious. As early as the twentieth century B.C.E. the city of Ashur (AH-shoor) on the northern Tigris anchored a busy trade route stretching across the northern plain to the Anatolian Plateau. Assyrian merchant families settled outside the walls of Anatolian cities and exchanged textiles and tin (a component of bronze) for Anatolian silver. After 1400 B.C.E. a resurgent "Middle Assyrian" kingdom engaged in campaigns of conquest and expansion of its economic interests.

The Hittites of Anatolia

Hittites A people from central Anatolia who established an empire in Anatolia and Syria in the Late Bronze Age. With wealth from the trade in metals and military power based on chariot forces, the Hittites vied with New Kingdom Egypt for control of Syria-Palestine before falling to unidentified attackers ca. 1200 B.C.E.

Other dynamic states emerged on the periphery of the Mesopotamian heartland, including Elam in southwest Iran and Mitanni (mih-TAH-nee) in the broad plain between the upper Euphrates and Tigris Rivers. Most formidable of all were the **Hittites** (HIT-ite), who became the foremost power in Anatolia from around 1700 to 1200 B.C.E. From their capital at Hattusha (haht-tush-SHAH), near present-day Ankara (ANG-kuh-ruh) in central Turkey, they deployed the fearsome new technology of horse-drawn war chariots. The Hittites exploited Anatolia's rich metal deposits to play a key role in international commerce.

The Hittites also first developed a technique for making tools and weapons of iron. Heating the ore until it was soft enough to shape, they pounded it to remove impurities and then plunged it into cold water to harden. They kept knowledge of this process secret because it provided military and economic advantages. In the disrupted period after 1200 B.C.E., blacksmiths from the Hittite core area may have migrated and spread iron technology.

The Spread of Mesopotamian Culture

AP* Exam Tip Be prepared to compare how different political and cultural concepts spread.

During the second millennium B.C.E. Mesopotamian political and cultural concepts spread across western Asia. Akkadian (uh-KAY-dee-uhn) became the language of diplomacy and correspondence between governments. The Elamites (EE-luh-mite) and Hittites, among others, adapted the cuneiform system to write their own languages. In the Syrian coastal city-state of Ugarit (OO-guh-reet), thirty cuneiform symbols were used to write consonant sounds, an early use of the alphabetic principle and a considerable advance over the hundreds of signs required in conventional cuneiform and hieroglyphic writing. Mesopotamian myths, legends, and styles of art and architecture were widely imitated. Newcomers who had learned and improved on the lessons of Mesopotamian civilization often put pressure on the old core area. The small, fractious city-states of the third millennium B.C.E. had been concerned only with their immediate neighbors in southern Mesopotamia. In contrast, the larger states of the second millennium B.C.E. interacted politically, militarily, and economically in a geopolitical sphere encompassing all of western Asia.

New Kingdom Egypt

After flourishing for nearly four hundred years (see Chapter 1), the Egyptian Middle Kingdom declined in the seventeenth century B.C.E. As officials in the countryside became increasingly independent and new groups migrated into the Nile Delta, central authority broke down and Egypt entered a period of political fragmentation and economic decline. Around 1640 B.C.E. Egypt came under foreign rule for the first time, at the hands of the Hyksos (HICK-soes), or "Princes of Foreign Lands."

The Hyksos

Historians are uncertain who the Hyksos were and how they came to power. Semitic peoples had been migrating from the Syria-Palestine region (present-day Syria, Jordan, Lebanon, Israel, and the Palestinian territories) into the eastern Nile Delta for centuries. In the chaotic conditions of this time, various groups may have cooperated to establish control, first in the delta and then in the middle of the country. The Hyksos possessed advantageous military technologies, such as the horse-drawn war chariot and a composite bow, made of wood and horn, that had greater range and velocity than the simple wooden bow. The Hyksos intermarried with Egyptians, used the Egyptian language, and maintained Egyptian institutions and culture. Nevertheless, in contrast to the easy assimilation of outsiders such as the Kassites in Mesopotamia, the Egyptians, with their strong ethnic identity, continued to regard the Hyksos as "foreigners."

New Kingdom Expansion

As with the formation of the Middle Kingdom five hundred years earlier, the reunification of Egypt under a native dynasty was accomplished by princes from Thebes. After three decades of warfare, Kamose (KAH-mose) and Ahmose (AH-mose) expelled the Hyksos from Egypt and inaugurated the New Kingdom, which lasted from about 1532 to 1070 B.C.E.

A century of foreign domination had injured Egyptian pride and shattered the isolationist mindset of earlier eras. New Kingdom Egypt was an aggressive and expansionist state. By extending its territorial control north into Syria-Palestine and south into Nubia, Egypt won access to timber, gold, and copper (bronze metallurgy took hold in Egypt around 1500 B.C.E.), as well as taxes and tribute payments from the conquered peoples. The occupied territories provided a buffer zone, protecting Egypt from attack. In Nubia, Egypt imposed direct control and pressed the native population to adopt Egyptian language and culture. In the Syria-Palestine region, in contrast, the Egyptians stationed garrisons at strategically placed forts and supported cooperative local rulers.

Hatshepsut Queen of Egypt (r. 1473–1458 B.C.E.). She dispatched a naval expedition to Punt (possibly northeast Sudan or Eritrea), the faraway source of myrrh. There is evidence of opposition to a woman as ruler, and after her death her name and image were frequently defaced.

In this period of innovation, Egypt fully participated in the diplomatic and commercial networks linking the states of western Asia. Egyptian soldiers, administrators, diplomats, and merchants traveled widely, bringing back new fruits and vegetables, new musical instruments, and new technologies, such as an improved potter's wheel and weaver's loom.

One woman held the throne of New Kingdom Egypt. When her husband died, Queen **Hatshepsut** (hat-SHEP-soot) claimed the royal title for herself (r. 1473–1458 B.C.E.). In inscriptions she often used the male pronoun for herself, and drawings and sculptures show her wearing the long, conical beard of the Egyptian ruler.

Unconventional Rulers

Around 1470 B.C.E. Hatshepsut sent a naval expedition down the Red Sea to the fabled land of Punt (poont), probably near the coast of eastern Sudan or Eritrea. Hatshepsut was seeking the source of myrrh (murr), a reddish-brown resin from the hardened sap of a local tree, which the Egyptians burned on the altars of their gods and used in medicines and cosmetics. When the expedition returned with myrrh and sub-Saharan luxury goods—ebony, ivory, cosmetics, live monkeys, panther skins—Hatshepsut celebrated the achievement in a great public display and in words and pictures on the walls of her mortuary temple at Deir el-Bahri (DARE uhl–BAH-ree). She may have used the success of this expedition to bolster her claim to the throne. After her death, her image was defaced and her name blotted out wherever it appeared, presumably by officials opposed to a woman ruler.

Akhenaten Egyptian pharaoh (r. 1353–1335 B.C.E.). He built a new capital at Amarna, fostered a new style of naturalistic art, and created a religious revolution by imposing worship of the sun-disk.

Another untraditional ruler ascended the throne as Amenhotep (ah-muhn-HOE-tep) IV, but he soon began to refer to himself as **Akhenaten** (ah-ken-AHT-n) (r. 1353–1335 B.C.E.), meaning "beneficial to the Aten" (AHT-n) (the disk of the sun). Changing his name was one way to spread his belief in Aten as the supreme deity. He closed the temples of other gods, challenging

The Mortuary Temple of Queen Hatshepsut at Deir el-Bahri, Egypt, ca. 1460 B.C.E. This beautiful complex of terraces, ramps, and colonnades featured relief sculptures and texts commemorating the famous expedition to Punt. Hatshepsut, facing resistance from traditionalists opposed to a woman ruling Egypt, sought to prove her worth by publicizing the opening of direct contact with the source of highly prized myrrh.

the age-old supremacy of the chief god Amon (AH-muhn) and the power and influence of his priests. Some scholars have credited Akhenaten with the invention of monotheism—the belief in one exclusive god. It is likely, however, that Akhenaten was attempting to reassert the superiority of the king over the priests and to renew belief in the king's divinity. Worship of Aten was confined to the royal family: the people of Egypt were pressed to revere the divine ruler.

Akhenaten built a new capital at modern-day Amarna (uh-MAHR-nuh), halfway between Memphis and Thebes (see Map 3.1). He transplanted thousands of Egyptians to construct the site and serve the ruling elite. Akhenaten and his artists created a new style that broke with the conventions of earlier art: the king, his wife Nefertiti (nef-uhr-TEE-tee), and their daughters were depicted in fluid, natural poses with strangely elongated heads and limbs and swelling abdomens.

Akhenaten's reforms were strongly resented by government officials and priests whose privileges and wealth were linked to the traditional system. After his death the temples were reopened; Amon was reinstated as chief god; the capital was returned to Thebes; and the institution of kingship was weakened to the advantage of the priests. The boy-king Tutankhamun (tuht-uhnk-AH-muhn) (r. 1333–1323 B.C.E.), famous solely because his was the only royal tomb found by archaeologists that had not been pillaged by robbers, reveals both in his name (meaning "beautiful in life is Amon") and in his insignificant reign the ultimate failure of Akhenaten's revolution.

Ramesses II A long-lived ruler of New Kingdom Egypt (r. 1290–1224 B.C.E.). He reached an accommodation with the Hittites of Anatolia after a standoff in battle at Kadesh in Syria. He built on a grand scale throughout Egypt.

The rulers of a new dynasty, the Ramessides (RAM-ih-side), returned to the policy of conquest and expansion that Akhenaten had neglected. The greatest of these monarchs, **Ramesses II** (RAM-ih-seez), ruled for sixty-six years (r. 1290–1224 B.C.E.) and dominated his age. Ramesses undertook monumental building projects all over Egypt. Living into his nineties, he had many

Colossal Statues of Ramesses II at Abu Simbel Strategically placed at a bend in the Nile River so as to face the southern frontier, this monument was an advertisement of Egyptian power. A temple was carved into the cliff behind the gigantic statues of the pharaoh. Within the temple, a corridor decorated with reliefs of military victories leads to an inner shrine containing images of the divine ruler seated alongside three of the major gods. In a modern marvel of engineering, the monument was moved to higher ground in the 1960s C.E. to protect it from rising waters when a dam was constructed.

wives and may have fathered more than a hundred children. Since 1990 archaeologists have been excavating a network of corridors and chambers carved deep into a hillside near Thebes, where many sons of Ramesses were buried.

Commerce and Communication

International Trade

Early in his reign Ramesses II fought the Hittites to a draw in a major battle at Kadesh in northern Syria (1285 B.C.E.). Subsequently, diplomats negotiated a treaty, which was strengthened by Ramesses' marriage to a Hittite princess. At issue was control of Syria-Palestine, strategically located between the great powers of the Middle East and at the end of the east-west trade route across Asia. Inland cities—such as Mari (MAH-ree) on the upper Euphrates and Alalakh (UH-luh-luhk) in western Syria—received overland caravans. Coastal towns—particularly Ugarit and the Phoenician towns of the Lebanese seaboard—extended commerce to the lands ringing the Mediterranean Sea.

AP* Exam Tip The development of interregional trading systems is a major comparison point.

Any state seeking to project its power needed metals for tools, weapons, and ornamentation. Commerce in metals energized the long-distance trade of the time. We have seen the Assyrian traffic in silver from Anatolia (above) and the Egyptian passion for Nubian gold (see Chapter 2). Copper came from Anatolia and Cyprus, tin from Afghanistan and possibly the British Isles. Both ores had to be carried long distances and pass through a number of hands before reaching their final destinations.

New modes of transportation expedited communications and commerce across great distances and inhospitable landscapes. Horses, domesticated by nomadic peoples in Central Asia, were brought into Mesopotamia through the Zagros Mountains around 2000 B.C.E. and reached Egypt before 1600 B.C.E. The speed of travel and communication made possible by horses

Horses and Camels

SECTION REVIEW

- In the Late Bronze Age trade and diplomatic contacts between states fostered the flow of goods and ideas, and elite groups enjoyed similar lifestyles and a relatively high standard of living.
- Immigrant groups that came to power in Babylonia (Kassites) and Egypt (Hyksos) assimilated to Babylonian and Egyptian language and culture.
- New peoples in western Asia who learned and improved on the technologies and culture of Mesopotamian civilization challenged the old core area.
- The Hittites used the technologies of chariot warfare and iron metallurgy to dominate Anatolia.
- New Kingdom Egypt abandoned traditional isolationism and extended control over Syria-Palestine and Nubia. The era was marked by rulers who challenged tradition—Hatshepsut, Akhenaten, and Ramesses.
- Long-distance trade networks were based on metals and expedited by the advent of horses and camels.

contributed to the creation of large states and empires, enabling soldiers and government agents to cover great distances quickly. Swift, maneuverable horse-drawn chariots became the premier instrument of war. The team of driver and archer could run up and unleash a volley of arrows or trample terrified foot-soldiers.

Sometime after 1500 B.C.E. in western Asia, but not for another thousand years in Egypt, people began to make common use of camels, though the animal may have been domesticated a millennium earlier in southern Arabia. Thanks to their strength and ability to go long distances without water, camels were able to travel across barren terrain. Their physical qualities eventually led to the emergence of a new kind of desert nomad and the creation of cross-desert trade routes (see Chapter 7).

THE AEGEAN WORLD, 2000–1100 B.C.E.

The influence of Mesopotamia, Syria-Palestine, and Egypt was felt as far away as the Aegean Sea, a gulf of the eastern Mediterranean. The emergence of the Minoan (mih-NO-uhn) civilization on the island of Crete and the Mycenaean (my-suh-NEE-uhn) civilization of Greece is another manifestation of the fertilizing influence of older centers on outlying lands and peoples, who then struck out on their own unique paths of cultural evolution. With few deposits of metals and little timber, Aegean peoples had to import these commodities, as well as additional food supplies, from abroad. As a result, the rise, success, and eventual fall of the Minoan and Mycenaean societies were closely tied to their commercial and political relations with other peoples in the region.

Minoan Crete

Minoan Prosperous civilization on the Aegean island of Crete in the second millennium B.C.E. The Minoans engaged in far-flung commerce around the Mediterranean and exerted powerful cultural influences on the early Greeks.

By 2000 B.C.E. the island of Crete (see Map 3.2) was home to the first European civilization to have complex political and social structures and advanced technologies like those found in western Asia and northeastern Africa. Archaeologists named this civilization **Minoan** after King Minos, who, in Greek legend, ruled a naval empire in the Aegean and kept the monstrous Minotaur (MIN-uh-tor) (half-man, half-bull) in a mazelike labyrinth built by the ingenious inventor Daedalus (DED-ih-luhs). Thus later Greeks recollected a time when Crete had been home to many ships and skilled craftsmen.

The ethnicity of the Minoans is uncertain, and their writing has not been deciphered. But the distribution of Cretan pottery and other artifacts around the Mediterranean and Middle East testifies to widespread trading connections. Egyptian, Syrian, and Mesopotamian influences can be seen in the design of the Minoan palaces, centralized government, and system of writing. The absence of identifiable representations of Cretan rulers, however, contrasts sharply with the grandiose depictions of kings in the Middle East and suggests a different conception of authority. Also noteworthy is the absence of fortifications at the palace sites and the presence of high-quality indoor plumbing.

Statuettes of women with elaborate headdresses and serpents coiling around their limbs may represent fertility goddesses. Colorful frescoes (paintings done on the moist plaster sur-

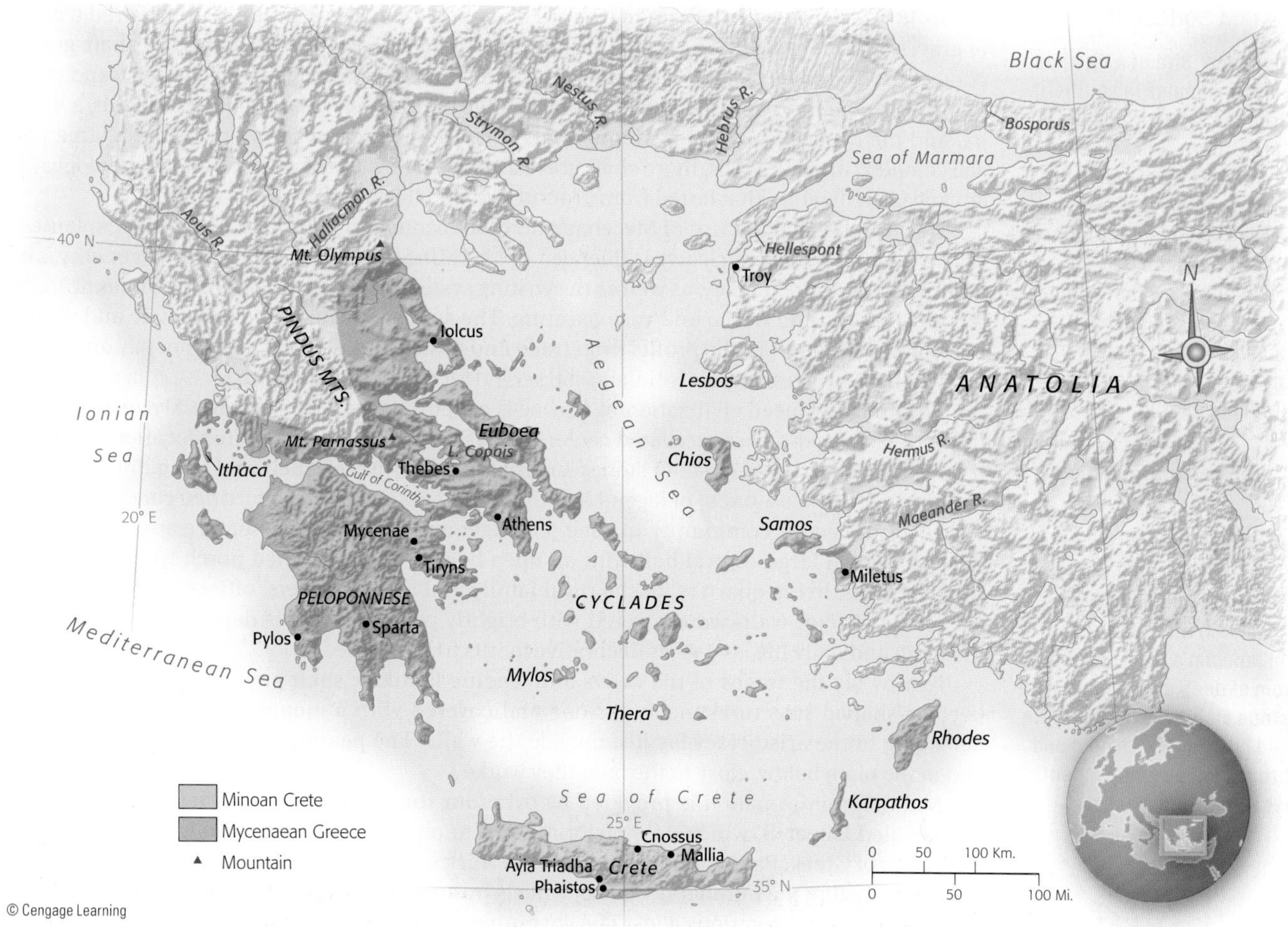

MAP 3.2 Minoan and Mycenaean Civilizations of the Aegean The earliest complex civilizations in Europe arose in the Aegean Sea. The Minoan civilization on the island of Crete evolved in the later third millennium B.C.E. and had a major cultural influence on the Mycenaean Greeks. Palaces decorated with fresco paintings, a centrally controlled economy, and the use of writing for recordkeeping are conspicuous features of these societies.

Interactive Map

faces of walls) in the palaces portray groups of women in frilly skirts conversing or watching performances. We do not know whether pictures of young acrobats vaulting over the horns and back of an onrushing bull show a religious activity or mere sport. The stylized depictions of scenes from nature on vases—plants with swaying leaves and playful octopuses winding their tentacles around the surface of the vase—communicate a delight in the beauty and order of the natural world.

All the Cretan palaces except at Cnossus (NOSS-suhs), along with the houses of the elite and peasants in the countryside, were deliberately destroyed around 1450 B.C.E. Because Mycenaean Greeks took over at Cnossus, most historians regard them as the culprits.

Mycenaean Greece

Speakers of an Indo-European language ancestral to Greek migrated into the Greek peninsula around 2000 B.C.E. Through intermarriage, blending of languages, and melding of cultural practices, the indigenous population and the newcomers created the first Greek culture. For centuries this society remained simple and static. Farmers and shepherds lived in Stone Age conditions, wringing a bare living from the land. Then, sometime around 1600 B.C.E., life changed relatively suddenly.

A Sudden Rise

Mycenae Site of a fortified palace complex in southern Greece that controlled a Late Bronze Age kingdom. In Homer's epic poems, Mycenae was the base of King Agamemnon, who commanded the Greeks besieging Troy. Contemporary archaeologists call the complex Greek society of the second millennium B.C.E. "Mycenaean."

In 1876 a German businessman, Heinrich Schliemann (SHLEE-muhn), discovered a circle of graves at **Mycenae** (my-SEE-nee), in southern Greece. These deep, rectangular **shaft graves** contained the bodies of men, women, and children and were filled with gold jewelry and ornaments, weapons, and utensils. Clearly, some people in this society had acquired wealth, authority, and the capacity to mobilize human labor. Subsequent excavation uncovered a large palace complex, massive walls, more shaft graves, and other evidence of a rich and technologically advanced civilization that lasted from around 1600 to 1150 B.C.E.

How can the sudden rise of Mycenae and other centers in mainland Greece be explained? These early Greeks were clearly influenced by the Minoan palaces, centralized economy, and administrative bureaucracy, as well as the writing system. They adopted Minoan styles of architecture, pottery, and fresco and vase painting. The sudden accumulation of power and wealth may have resulted from the profits from trade and piracy and perhaps also from pay and booty brought back by mercenaries (soldiers who served for pay in foreign lands).

Mycenaean Palaces

shaft graves A term used for the burial sites of elite members of Mycenaean Greek society in the mid-second millennium B.C.E. At the bottom of deep shafts lined with stone slabs, the bodies were laid out along with gold and bronze jewelry, implements, weapons, and masks.

This first advanced civilization in Greece is called "Mycenaean" because Mycenae was the first site excavated. Other excavated centers reveal similar features: a hilltop location and high, thick fortification walls made of stones so large that later Greeks believed the giant, one-eyed Cyclopes (SIGH-kloe-pees) of legend had lifted them into place. The fortified citadel provided refuge for the entire community in time of danger and contained the palace and administrative complex. A large central hall with an open hearth and columned porch was surrounded by courtyards, living quarters for the royal family and their retainers, offices, storerooms, and workshops. Palace walls were covered with brightly painted frescoes depicting scenes of war, the hunt, and daily life, as well as decorative motifs from nature.

Nearby lay the tombs of the rulers and leading families: shaft graves at first; later, grand beehive-shaped structures made of stone and covered with a mound of earth. Large houses belonging to the aristocracy lay just outside the walls. The peasants lived on the lower slopes and in the plain below, close to the land they worked.

Additional information is provided by over four thousand baked clay tablets written in a script called **Linear B**, which uses pictorial signs to represent syllables and is recognizably an early form of Greek. Palace administrators kept track of people, animals, and objects in exhaustive detail, listing the number of chariot wheels in storerooms, the rations paid to workers, and the gifts dedicated to various gods. The government exercised a high degree of control over the economy, organizing grain production and the wool industry from raw material to finished product. The tablets reveal little, however, about the political and legal system, social structure, gender relations, and religious beliefs. They tell nothing about historical figures (not even the name of a single Mycenaean king), particular historical events, or relations with other Mycenaean centers or foreign peoples.

International Commerce and Contacts

Linear B A set of syllabic symbols, derived from the writing system of Minoan Crete, used in the Mycenaean palaces of the Late Bronze Age to write an early form of Greek. It was used primarily for palace records, and the surviving Linear B tablets provide substantial information about the economic organization of Mycenaean society and tantalizing clues about political, social, and religious institutions.

Long-distance contact and trade were made possible by the seafaring skill of Minoans and Mycenaeans. Commercial vessels depended primarily on wind and sail. In general, ancient sailors preferred to sail in daylight hours and keep the land in sight. Their light, wooden vessels with low keels could run up onto the beach, allowing the crew to go ashore to eat and sleep at night.

Cretan and Greek pottery and crafted goods are found not only in the Aegean but also in other parts of the Mediterranean and Middle East. The oldest artifacts are Minoan; then Minoan and Mycenaean objects are found side by side; and eventually Greek wares replace Cretan goods altogether. Such evidence indicates that Cretan merchants pioneered trade routes and established trading posts and were later joined by Mycenaean traders, who supplanted them in the fifteenth century B.C.E.

The numerous Aegean pots found throughout the Mediterranean and Middle East once contained such products as wine and olive oil. Other possible exports include textiles, weapons, and other crafted goods, as well as slaves and mercenary soldiers. Aegean sailors also may have transported the trade goods of other peoples.

As for imports, amber (a translucent, yellowish-brown fossilized tree resin used for jewelry) from northern Europe and ivory carved in Syria have been discovered at Aegean sites, and the large population of southern Greece may have relied on imports of grain. Above all, the Aegean lands needed metals, both gold and the copper and tin needed to make bronze. Several sunken ships carrying copper ingots have been found on the floor of the Mediterranean. Only the elite classes owned metal goods, which may have been symbols of their superior status.

Mycenaeans were tough, warlike, and acquisitive. They traded with those who were strong and took from those who were weak. This led to conflict with the Hittite kings of Anatolia in the

Archaeological Receipts Fund, Athens

Fresco from the Aegean Island of Thera, ca. 1650 B.C.E. This picture shows the arrival of a fleet in a harbor as people watch from the walls of the town. The Minoan civilization of Crete was famous in legend for its naval power. The fresco reveals the appearance and design of ships in the Bronze Age Aegean. In the seventeenth century B.C.E., the island of Thera was devastated by a massive volcanic explosion, thought by many to be the origin of the myth of Atlantis sinking beneath the sea.

fourteenth and thirteenth centuries B.C.E. Documents in the archives at the Hittite capital refer to the king and land of Ahhijawa (uh-key-YAW-wuh), most likely a Hittite rendering of *Achaeans* (uh-KEY-uhns), a term used by Homer for the Greeks. They indicate that relations were sometimes friendly, sometimes strained, and that the people of Ahhijawa took advantage of Hittite preoccupation or weakness. The *Iliad*, Homer's tale of the Achaeans' ten-year siege and eventual destruction of Troy, a city on the fringes of Hittite territory controlling the sea route between the Mediterranean and Black Seas, should be seen against this backdrop of Mycenaean belligerence and opportunism. Archaeology has confirmed a destruction at Troy around 1200 B.C.E.

The Fall of Late Bronze Age Civilizations

Migration and Destruction

Hittite difficulties with Ahhijawa and the Greek attack on Troy foreshadowed the troubles that culminated in the destruction of many of the old centers of the Middle East and Mediterranean around 1200 B.C.E. In this period, for reasons not well understood, large numbers of people were on the move. As migrants swarmed into one region, they displaced other peoples, who then joined the tide of refugees.

Around 1200 B.C.E. unidentified invaders destroyed the Hittite capital, Hattusha, and the Hittite kingdom in Anatolia came crashing down. The tide of destruction moved south into Syria, and the great coastal city of Ugarit was swept away. Egypt managed to beat back two attacks: an assault on the Nile Delta around 1220 B.C.E. by "Libyans and Northerners coming from all lands," and a major invasion by the "Sea Peoples" about thirty years later. Although the Egyptian ruler claimed a great victory, the Philistines (FIH-luh-steen) occupied the coast of Palestine (this is the origin of the name subsequently used for this region). Egypt soon surrendered all its territory in Syria-Palestine and lost contact with the rest of western Asia. The Egyptians also lost their foothold in Nubia, opening the way for the emergence of the native kingdom centered on Napata (see Chapter 2).

The Mycenaean Fall and Consequences

Among the invaders listed in the Egyptian inscriptions are the Ekwesh (ECK-wesh), who could be Achaeans—that is, Greeks. In these troubled times it is easy to imagine the participation of opportunistic Mycenaeans. The Mycenaean centers also saw trouble coming; at some sites they began to build more extensive fortifications and took steps to guarantee the water supply of the citadels. But their efforts were in vain, and nearly all the palaces were destroyed in the first half of the twelfth century B.C.E.

How these events came about is unclear. The archaeological record contains no trace of foreign invaders. An attractive explanation combines external and internal factors, since it is likely to be more than coincidence that the demise of Mycenaean civilization occurred at roughly the same time as the fall of other great civilizations in the region. Since the Mycenaean ruling class depended on the import of vital commodities and the profits from trade, the destruction of major trading partners and disruption of trade routes would have weakened their position. Competition for limited resources may have led to internal unrest and, ultimately, political collapse.

The end of Mycenaean civilization illustrates the interdependence of the major centers of the Late Bronze Age. It also highlights the consequences of political and economic collapse. The destruction of the palaces ended the domination of the ruling class. The massive administrative apparatus revealed in the Linear B tablets disappeared. The technique of writing was forgotten, since it had been known only to a few palace officials and was no longer useful. Archaeological studies indicate the depopulation of some regions of Greece and an inflow of people to other regions that had escaped destruction. The Greek language persisted, and a thousand years later people were still worshiping gods mentioned in the Linear B tablets. People also continued to make the vessels and implements that they were familiar with, although with a marked decline in artistic and technical skill in a much poorer society. The cultural uniformity of the Mycenaean Age gave way to regional variations in shapes, styles, and techniques, reflecting increased isolation of different parts of Greece.

Thus perished the cosmopolitan world of the Late Bronze Age in the Mediterranean and Middle East. Societies that had long prospered through complex links of trade, diplomacy, and shared technologies now collapsed in the face of external violence and internal weakness, and the peoples of the region entered a centuries-long "Dark Age" of poverty, isolation, and loss of knowledge.

SECTION REVIEW

- The Minoan civilization on the island of Crete and the Mycenaean civilization of Greece were strongly influenced by the older centers in Egypt, Syria, and Mesopotamia, yet they followed unique paths of cultural evolution.
- By 2000 B.C.E. Crete was home to the first European civilization with complex political and social structures and advanced technologies.
- The sudden rise to wealth and power of Mycenae and other centers in mainland Greece ca. 1600 was due to the influence of Minoan Crete and the Mycenaeans' insertion into trade networks.
- The Linear B tablets reveal how the Mycenaean palaces exerted centralized control over the economy, and Hittite documents show the Mycenaeans to be aggressive and acquisitive.
- The economic interdependence of Late Bronze Age states increased their vulnerability to attacks by migrating peoples ca. 1200 B.C.E. The region descended into a centuries-long "Dark Age."

Neo-Assyrian Empire An empire extending from western Iran to Syria-Palestine, conquered by the Assyrians of northern Mesopotamia between the tenth and seventh centuries B.C.E. They used force and terror and exploited the wealth and labor of their subjects. They also preserved and continued the cultural and scientific developments of Mesopotamian civilization.

THE ASSYRIAN EMPIRE, 911–612 B.C.E.

A number of new centers emerged in western Asia and the eastern Mediterranean in the centuries after 1000 B.C.E. The most powerful and successful was the **Neo-Assyrian Empire** (911–612 B.C.E.). Compared to the flat expanse of Babylonia to the south, the Assyrian homeland in northern Mesopotamia is hillier and has a more temperate climate and greater rainfall.

Peasant farmers, accustomed to defending themselves against raiders from the mountains to the east and north and the arid plain to the west, provided the foot-soldiers for the revival of Assyrian power. The rulers of the Neo-Assyrian Empire led a ceaseless series of campaigns: westward across the plain and desert as far as the Mediterranean, north into mountainous Urartu (ur-RAHR-too) (modern Armenia), east across the Zagros range onto the Iranian Plateau,

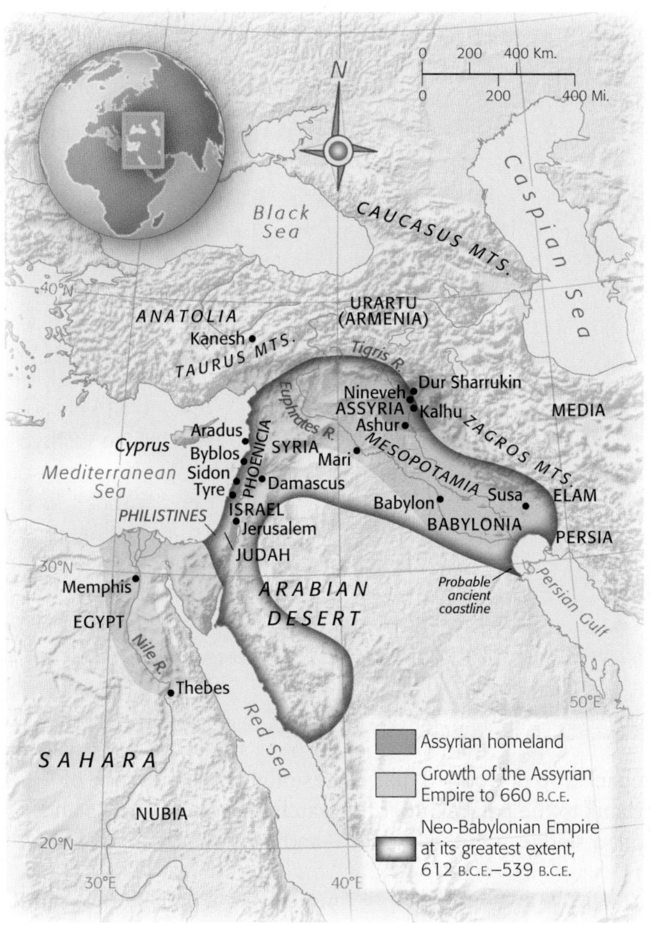

MAP 3.3 The Assyrian Empire From the tenth to the seventh century B.C.E. the Assyrians of northern Mesopotamia created the largest empire the world had yet seen, extending from the Iranian Plateau to the eastern shore of the Mediterranean and containing a diverse array of peoples.

e Interactive Map

and south along the Tigris River to Babylonia. These campaigns provided immediate booty and the prospect of tribute and taxes. They also secured access to vital resources such as iron and silver and gave the Assyrians control of international commerce. Driven by pride, greed, and religious conviction, the Assyrians defeated all the great kingdoms of the day. At its peak their empire stretched from Anatolia, Syria-Palestine, and Egypt in the west, across Armenia and Mesopotamia, and as far as western Iran. The Assyrians created a new kind of empire, larger in extent than anything seen before (see Map 3.3) and dedicated to the enrichment of the imperial center at the expense of the subjugated periphery.

God and King

The king was literally and symbolically the center of the Assyrian universe. All the land belonged to him, and all the people, even the highest-ranking officials, were his servants. Assyrians believed that the gods chose the king as their earthly representative. Normally the king selected one of his sons to succeed him, a choice confirmed by divine oracles and the Assyrian elite. In the revered ancient city of Ashur the high priest anointed the new king's head with oil and gave him the insignia of kingship: a crown and scepter. The kings also were buried in Ashur.

Messengers and spies brought the king information from every corner of the empire. The king appointed officials, heard complaints, dictated correspondence to an army of scribes, and received foreign envoys. He was the military leader, responsible for planning campaigns, and was often away from the capital commanding operations in the field.

Religion and Propaganda

The king devoted much of his time to supervising the state religion, attending elaborate public and private rituals, and overseeing the upkeep of the temples. He made no decisions of state without consulting the gods through rituals of divination. All actions were carried out in the name of Ashur, the chief god. Military victories were cited as proof of Ashur's superiority over the gods of the conquered peoples.

Relentless government propaganda secured popular support for military campaigns that mostly benefited the king and the nobility. Royal inscriptions posted throughout the empire catalogued recent victories, extolled the unshakeable determination of the king, and promised ruthless punishments to anyone who resisted. Relief sculptures depicting hunts, battles, sieges, executions, and deportations covered the walls of the royal palaces. Looming over most scenes was the king, larger than anyone else, muscular and fierce. Few visitors to the Assyrian court could fail to be awed—and intimidated.

Conquest and Control

Military Might and Terror Tactics

Superior military organization and technology lay behind Assyria's unprecedented conquests. Early armies consisted of men who served in return for grants of land and peasants and slaves contributed by large landowners. Later, King Tiglathpileser (TIG-lath-pih-LEE-zuhr) (r. 744–727 B.C.E.) created a core army of professional soldiers made up of Assyrians and the most formidable subject peoples. At its peak the Assyrian state could mobilize a half-million troops, including

Courtesy of the Trustees of the British Museum

Wall Relief from the Palace of Sennacherib at Nineveh Against a backdrop of wooded hills representing the landscape of Assyria, workers are hauling a huge stone sculpture from the riverbank to the palace under the watchful eyes of officials and soldiers. They accomplish this task with simple equipment—a lever, a sledge, and thick ropes—and a lot of human muscle power.

mass deportation The forcible removal and relocation of large numbers of people or entire populations. The mass deportations practiced by the Assyrian and Persian Empires were meant as a terrifying warning of the consequences of rebellion. They also brought skilled and unskilled labor to the imperial center.

light-armed bowmen and slingers who launched stone projectiles, armored spearmen, cavalry equipped with bows or spears, and four-man chariots.

Iron weapons gave Assyrian soldiers an advantage over many opponents, and cavalry provided speed and mobility. Assyrian engineers developed machinery and tactics for besieging fortified towns. They dug tunnels under the walls, built mobile towers for archers, and applied battering rams to weak points. Couriers and signal fires provided long-distance communication, while a network of spies gathered intelligence.

The Assyrians used terror tactics to discourage resistance and rebellion, inflicting harsh punishments and publicizing their brutality: civilians were thrown into fires, prisoners were skinned alive, and the severed heads of defeated rulers hung on city walls. **Mass deportation**—the forced uprooting of entire communities and resettlement elsewhere—broke the spirit of rebellious peoples. Although this tactic had a long history in the ancient Middle East, the Neo-Assyrian monarchs used it on an unprecedented scale, and up to 4 million people may have been relocated. Deportation also shifted human resources from the periphery to the center, where the deportees worked on royal and noble estates, opened new lands for agriculture, and built palaces and cities.

Administration and Exploitation

PRIMARY SOURCE: An Assyrian Emperor's Resume: Ferocious Conquests a Specialty Read the inscription left behind by Ashurnasirpal, in which he promotes himself as an especially effective—and brutal—military leader.

The Assyrians never discovered an effective method of governing an empire of such vast distances, varied landscapes, and diverse peoples. Control tended to be tight at the center and in lands closest to the core area, and less so farther away. The Assyrian kings waged many campaigns to reinstate control over territories subdued in previous wars. Provincial officials oversaw the collection of tribute and taxes, maintained law and order, raised troops, undertook public works, and provisioned armies and administrators passing through their territory. Provincial governors were subject to frequent inspections by royal overseers.

The Assyrians ruthlessly exploited the wealth and resources of their subjects. Military campaigns and administration were funded by plunder and tribute. Wealth from the periphery was funneled to the center, where the king and nobility grew rich. Triumphant kings expanded the ancestral capital and religious center at Ashur and built magnificent new royal cities encircled by high walls and containing ornate palaces and temples. Dur Sharrukin (DOOR SHAH-roo-keen), the "Fortress of Sargon," was completed in a mere ten years by a massive labor force composed of prisoners of war and Assyrian citizens who owed periodic service to the state.

Nevertheless, the Assyrian Empire was not simply parasitic. There is some evidence of royal investment in provincial infrastructure. The cities and merchant classes thrived on expanded long-distance commerce, and some subject populations were surprisingly loyal to their Assyrian rulers.

Assyrian Society and Culture

Elite and Common People

The elite class was bound to the monarch by oaths of obedience, fear of punishment, and the expectation of rewards, such as land grants or shares of booty and taxes. Skilled professionals—priests, diviners, scribes, doctors, and artisans—were similarly bound.

Surviving sources primarily shed light on the deeds of kings and elites. Only a little is known about the lives and activities of the millions of Assyrian subjects. The government did not distinguish between native Assyrians and the increasingly large number of immigrants and deportees in the Assyrian homeland. All were referred to as "human beings," entitled to the same legal protections and liable for the same labor and military service. Over time the inflow of outsiders changed the ethnic makeup of the core area.

The vast majority of subjects worked on the land. The agricultural surpluses they produced allowed substantial numbers of people—the standing army, government officials, religious experts, merchants, artisans, and other professionals in the towns and cities—to engage in specialized activities.

Individual artisans and small workshops in the towns manufactured pottery, tools, and clothing, and most trade took place at the local level. The state fostered long-distance trade, since imported luxury goods—metals, fine textiles, dyes, gems, and ivory—brought in substantial customs revenues and found their way to the royal family and elite classes. Silver was the basic medium of exchange, weighed out for each transaction in a time before the invention of coins.

Library of Ashurbanipal A large collection of writings drawn from the ancient literary, religious, and scientific traditions of Mesopotamia. It was assembled by the seventh-century B.C.E. Assyrian ruler Ashurbanipal. The many tablets unearthed by archaeologists constitute one of the most important sources of present-day knowledge of the long literary tradition of Mesopotamia.

Scholarship

Assyrian scholars preserved and built on the achievements of their Mesopotamian predecessors. When archaeologists excavated the palace of Ashurbanipal (ah-shur-BAH-nee-pahl) (r. 668–627 B.C.E.), one of the last Assyrian kings, at Nineveh (NIN-uh-vuh), they discovered more than twenty-five thousand tablets or fragments. The **Library of Ashurbanipal** contained official documents as well as literary and scientific texts. Some were originals that had been brought to the capital; others were copies made at the king's request. The "House of Knowledge" referred to in some documents may have been an academy that attracted learned men to the imperial center. Much of what we know about Mesopotamian art, literature, science, and earlier history comes from discoveries at Assyrian sites.

SECTION REVIEW

- Tough farmers in northern Mesopotamia provided the foot-soldiers for the rise of the Neo-Assyrian Empire, which dominated western Asia from the late tenth to seventh centuries B.C.E.
- Ceaseless campaigns of conquest brought booty, tribute and taxes, and control of international commerce and valuable resources.
- The all-powerful Assyrian king, claiming the support of the god Ashur, was at the center of government and the state religion.
- The Assyrians employed military might, propaganda, and state terrorism to intimidate their subjects, but they never developed an effective system of political control and frequently had to reconquer territory.
- The Assyrians ruthlessly funneled the wealth and resources of their subjects to the center, where the king and nobility grew rich. Frequent mass deportations provided manpower to build royal cities and work the lands of the elite.
- Assyrian scholars preserved and added to the long intellectual and scientific legacy of Mesopotamian civilization.

ISRAEL, 2000–500 B.C.E.

AP* Exam Tip Judaism is one of the major belief systems that it is important to understand for success on the exam.

The small land of Israel probably appeared insignificant to the Assyrian masters of western Asia, but it would play an important role in world history. Two interconnected dramas played out here between around 2000 and 500 B.C.E. First, a loose collection of nomadic groups engaged in herding and caravan traffic became a sedentary, agricultural people, developed complex political and social institutions, and became integrated into the commercial and diplomatic networks of the Middle East. Second, these people transformed the austere cult of a desert god into the concept of a single, all-powerful, and all-knowing deity, in the process creating ethical and intellectual traditions that underlie the beliefs and values of Judaism, Christianity, and Islam.

Land and People

Israel In antiquity, the land between the eastern shore of the Mediterranean and the Jordan River, occupied by the Israelites from the early second millennium B.C.E. The modern state of Israel was founded in 1948.

The land and people at the heart of this story have gone by various names: Canaan, Israel, Palestine; Hebrews, Israelites, Jews. For the sake of consistency, the people are referred to here as *Israelites*, the land they occupied in antiquity as **Israel**.

Israel is a crossroads, linking Anatolia, Egypt, Arabia, and Mesopotamia (see Map 3.4). Its natural resources are few. The Negev Desert and the vast wasteland of the Sinai (SIE-nie) lie to the south. The Mediterranean coastal plain was usually in the hands of others, particularly the Philistines, throughout much of this period. Galilee to the north, with its sea of the same name, was a relatively fertile land of grassy hills and small plains. The narrow ribbon of the Jordan River runs down the eastern side of the region into the Dead Sea, so named because its high salt content is toxic to life.

Origins, Exodus, and Settlement

The Hebrew Bible

Hebrew Bible A collection of sacred books containing diverse materials concerning the origins, experiences, beliefs, and practices of the Israelites. Most of the extant text was compiled by members of the priestly class in the fifth century B.C.E. and reflects the concerns and views of this group.

Information about ancient Israel comes partly from archaeological excavations and documents such as the royal annals of Egypt and Assyria. Fundamental, but also problematic, are the texts preserved in the **Hebrew Bible** (called the Old Testament by Christians), a compilation of several collections of materials that originated with different groups and advocated particular interpretations of past events. Traditions about the Israelites' early history were long transmitted orally. Not until the tenth century B.C.E. were they written down in a script borrowed from the Phoenicians. The text that we have today dates from the fifth century B.C.E., with a few later additions, and reflects the point of view of the priests who controlled the Temple in Jerusalem. The Hebrew language of the Bible reflects the speech of the Israelites until about 500 B.C.E., when it was supplanted by Aramaic. Historians disagree about how accurately this document represents Israelite history. However, it provides a foundation to be used critically and tested against archaeological discoveries.

Early Pastoralists

The history of ancient Israel follows a familiar pattern in the ancient Middle East: Nomadic pastoralists, occupying marginal land between the inhospitable desert and settled agricultural areas, sometimes engaged in trade and sometimes raided the farms and villages of settled peoples, but eventually they settled down to an agricultural way of life and later developed a unified state.

PRIMARY SOURCE: Moses Descends Mount Sinai with the Ten Commandments Find out why the god of the Old Testament issued the Ten Commandments and what he promised Moses's people in return for keeping—or violating—them.

The Hebrew Bible tells the story of Abraham and his descendants. Born in the city of Ur in southern Mesopotamia, Abraham rejected the idol worship of his homeland and migrated with his family and livestock across the Syrian desert. Eventually he arrived in the land of Israel, which had been promised to him and his descendants by the Israelite god, Yahweh.

These "recollections" of the journey of Abraham (who, if he was a real person, probably lived around 1800 B.C.E.) may compress the experiences of generations of pastoralists who migrated from the grazing lands between the upper reaches of the Tigris and Euphrates Rivers to the Mediterranean coastal plain. They camped by a permanent water source in the dry season, then drove herds of sheep, cattle, and donkeys to a well-established sequence of grazing areas during the rest of the year. The animals provided them with milk, cheese, meat, and cloth.

The nomadic Israelites and the settled peoples were suspicious of one another. This friction between herders and farmers permeates the story of the innocent shepherd Abel, who was killed by his farmer brother Cain, and the story of Sodom (SOE-duhm) and Gomorrah (guh-MORE-uh), two cities that Yahweh destroyed because of their wickedness.

Egypt and the Exodus

In the Hebrew Bible, Abraham's son Isaac and then his grandson Jacob became the leaders of this wandering group of herders. In the next generation the squabbling sons of Jacob's several wives sold their brother Joseph as a slave to passing merchants heading for Egypt. Through luck

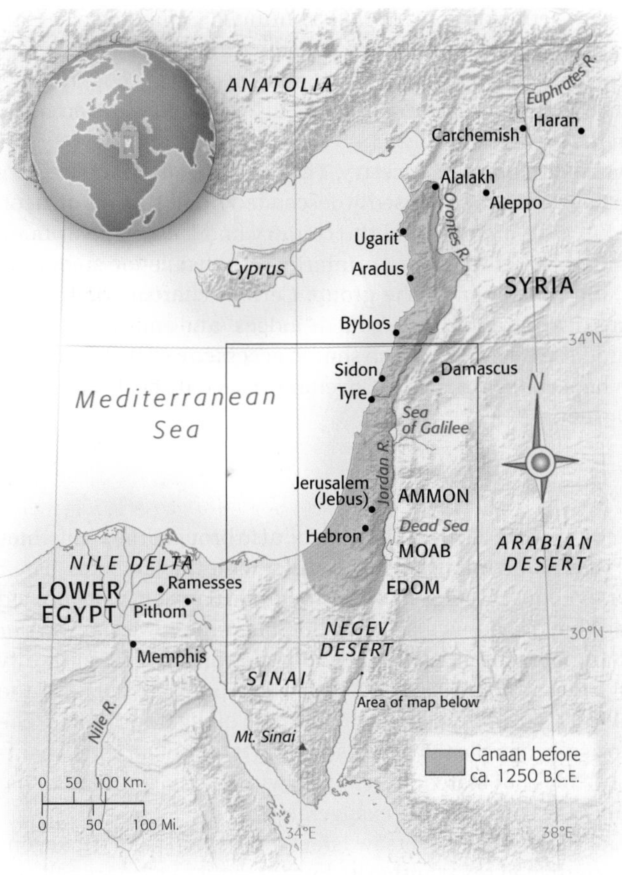

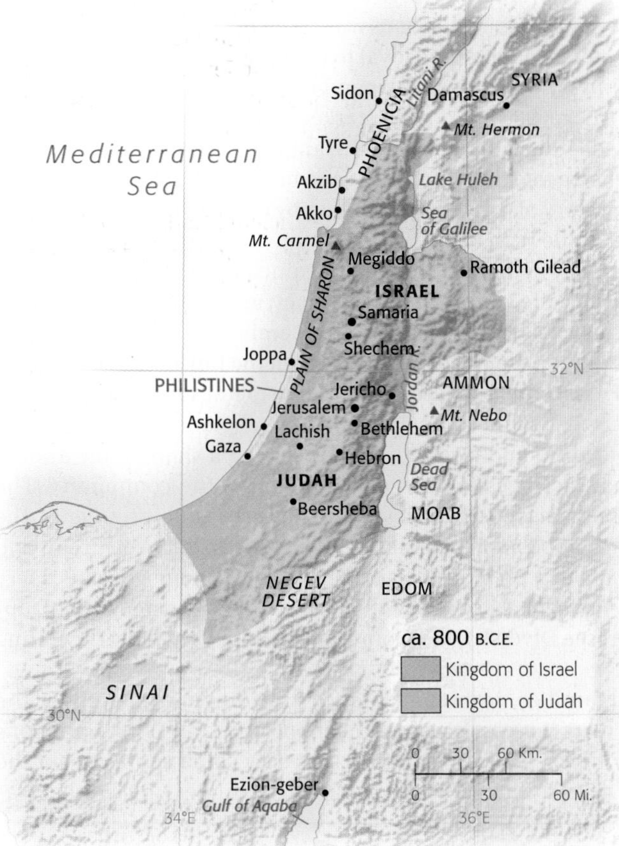

MAP 3.4 Phoenicia and Israel The lands along the eastern shore of the Mediterranean Sea—sometimes called the Levant or Syria-Palestine—have always been a crossroads, traversed by migrants, nomads, merchants, and armies moving between Egypt, Arabia, Mesopotamia, and Anatolia.

Interactive Map

and ability Joseph became a high official at the pharaoh's court. Thus he was in a position to help his people when drought struck and forced the Israelites to migrate to Egypt. The sophisticated Egyptians looked down on these rough herders and eventually enslaved them and put them to work on royal building projects.

Several points need to be made about this biblical account. First, the Israelite migration to Egypt and later enslavement may have been connected to the rise and fall of the Hyksos. Second, although surviving Egyptian sources do not refer to Israelite slaves, they do complain about Apiru (uh-PEE-roo), a derogatory term applied to caravan drivers, outcasts, bandits, and other marginal groups. Some scholars believe there may be a connection between the similar-sounding terms *Apiru* and *Hebrew*. Third, the period of alleged Israelite slavery coincided with the ambitious building programs launched by several New Kingdom pharaohs. However, there is little archaeological evidence of an Israelite presence in Egypt.

According to the Hebrew Bible, the Israelites were led out of captivity by Moses, an Israelite with connections to the Egyptian royal family. The narrative of their departure, the Exodus, is overlaid with folktale motifs, including the ten plagues that Yahweh inflicted on Egypt to persuade the pharaoh to release the Israelites, and the miraculous parting of the waters of the Red Sea that enabled the refugees to escape. Oral tradition may have embellished memories of a real emigration from Egypt followed by years of wandering in the wilderness of Sinai.

During their forty years in the desert, as reported in the Hebrew Bible, the Israelites entered into a "covenant" or pact with their god, Yahweh: They would be his "Chosen People" if they promised to worship him exclusively. This was confirmed by tablets that Moses brought down from the top of Mount Sinai, inscribed with the Ten Commandments that set out the basic tenets of Jewish belief and practice. The Commandments prohibited murder, adultery, theft, lying, and envy and demanded respect for parents and rest from work on the Sabbath, the seventh day of the week.

The biblical account proceeds to tell how Joshua, Moses's successor, led the Israelites from the east side of the Jordan River into the land of Canaan (KAY-nuhn) (modern Israel and the Palestinian territories), where they attacked and destroyed Canaanite (KAY-nuh-nite) cities. Archaeological evidence confirms the destruction of some Canaanite towns between 1250 and 1200 B.C.E., though not precisely the towns mentioned in the biblical account. Shortly thereafter, lowland sites were resettled and new sites were established in

Settlement in Canaan

the hills. The material culture of the new settlers was cruder but continued Canaanite patterns. Most scholars doubt that Canaan was conquered by a unified Israelite army. In a time of widespread disruption, movements of peoples, and decline and destruction of cities throughout this region, it is more likely that Israelite migrants took advantage of the disorder and were joined by other groups and even refugees from the Canaanite cities.

The new coalition of peoples invented a common ancestry. The "Children of Israel," as they called themselves, were divided into twelve tribes supposedly descended from the sons of Jacob and Joseph. Each tribe was installed in a different part of the country and led by one or more chiefs. Such leaders usually had limited power and were primarily responsible for mediating disputes and seeing to the welfare and protection of the group. Certain charismatic figures, famed for their daring in war or genius in arbitration, were called "Judges" and enjoyed a special standing that transcended tribal boundaries. The tribes also shared access to a shrine in the hill country at Shiloh (SHIE-loe), which housed the Ark of the Covenant, a sacred chest containing the tablets that Yahweh had given Moses.

Rise of the Monarchy

The troubles afflicting the eastern Mediterranean around 1200 B.C.E. also brought the Philistines to the coastal plain of Israel, where they came into frequent conflict with the Israelites. Their wars were memorialized in Bible stories about the long-haired strongman Samson, who toppled a Philistine temple, and the shepherd boy David, whose slingshot felled the towering warrior Goliath. A religious leader named Samuel recognized the need for a strong central authority and anointed Saul as the first king of Israel around 1020 B.C.E. When Saul perished in battle, the throne passed to David (r. ca. 1000–960 B.C.E.). Many scholars regard the biblical account for the period of the monarchy as more historically reliable than the earlier parts, although some maintain that the archaeological record still does not match up very well with that narrative and that the wealth and power of the early kings have been greatly exaggerated.

David and Solomon

A gifted musician, warrior, and politician, David oversaw Israel's transition from tribal confederacy to unified monarchy. He strengthened royal authority by making the captured hill city of Jerusalem his capital. Soon after, David brought the Ark to Jerusalem, making the city the religious as well as political center of the kingdom. A census was taken to facilitate the collection of taxes, and a standing army, with soldiers paid by and loyal to the king, was established. These innovations enabled David to win military victories and expand Israel's borders.

The reign of David's son Solomon (r. ca. 960–920 B.C.E.) marked the high point of the Israelite monarchy. Alliances and trade linked Israel with near and distant lands. Solomon and Hiram, the king of Phoenician Tyre, dispatched a fleet into the Red Sea to bring back gold, ivory, jewels, sandalwood, and exotic animals. The story of the visit to Solomon by the queen of Sheba may be mythical, but it reflects the reality of trade with Saba (SUH-buh) in south Arabia (present-day Yemen) or the Horn of Africa (present-day Somalia). The wealth gained from military and commercial ventures supported a lavish court life, a sizeable bureaucracy, and an intimidating chariot army that made Israel a regional power. Solomon undertook an ambitious building program employing slaves and the compulsory labor of citizens. To strengthen the link between religious and secular authority, he built the **First Temple** in Jerusalem. The Israelites now had a central shrine and an impressive set of rituals that could compete with other religions in the area.

First Temple A monumental sanctuary built in Jerusalem by King Solomon in the tenth century B.C.E. to be the religious center for the Israelite god Yahweh. The Temple priesthood conducted sacrifices, received a tithe or percentage of agricultural revenues, and became economically and politically powerful.

The Temple priests became a powerful and wealthy class, receiving a share of the annual harvest in return for making animal sacrifices to Yahweh on behalf of the community. The expansion of Jerusalem, new commercial opportunities, and the increasing prestige of the Temple hierarchy changed the social composition of Israelite society. A gap between urban and rural, rich and poor, polarized a people that previously had been relatively homogeneous. Fiery prophets, claiming revelation from Yahweh, accused the monarchs and aristocracy of corruption, impiety, and neglect of the poor (see Diversity and Dominance: Protests Against the Ruling Class in Israel and Babylonia).

Israelite Society

The Israelites lived in extended families, several generations residing together under the authority of the eldest male. Male heirs were of paramount importance, and first-born sons received a double share of the inheritance. If a couple had no son, they could adopt one, or the husband could have a child by the wife's slave attendant. If a man died childless, his brother was expected to marry his widow and sire an heir.

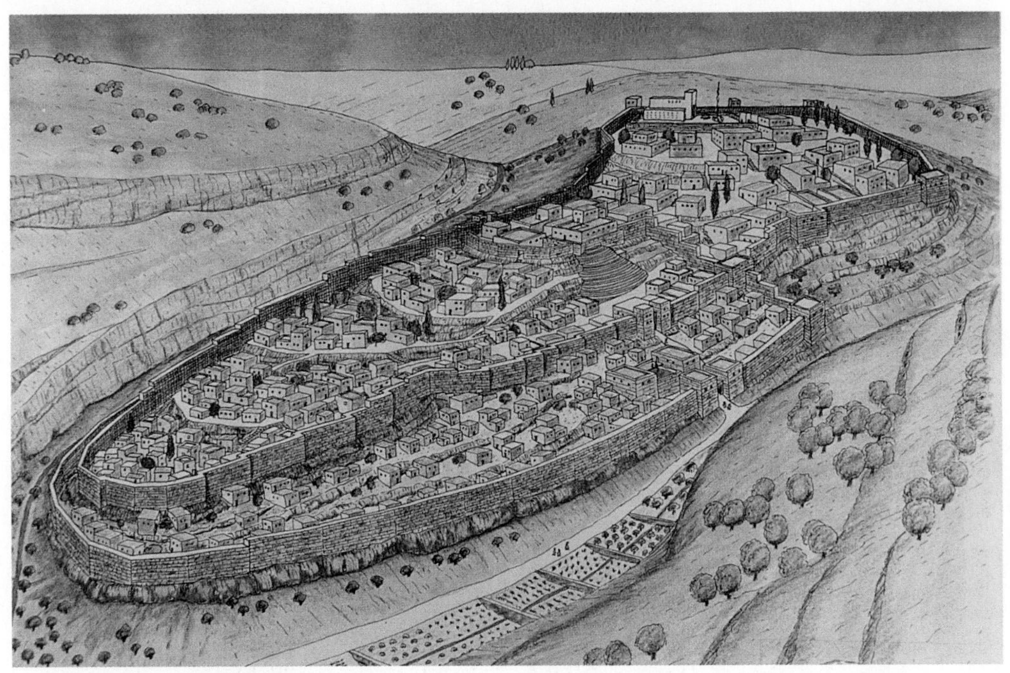

Ritmeyer Archaeological Design

Artist's Rendering of Solomon's Jerusalem Strategically located in the middle of lands occupied by the Israelite tribes and on a high plateau overlooking the central hills and the Judaean desert, Jerusalem was captured around 1000 B.C.E. by King David, who made it his capital (the City of David is at left, the citadel and palace complex at center). The next king, Solomon, built the First Temple to serve as the center of worship of the Israelite god, Yahweh. Solomon's Temple (at upper right) was destroyed during the Neo-Babylonian sack of the city in 587 B.C.E. The modest structure soon built to take its place was replaced by the magnificent Second Temple, erected by King Herod in the last decades of the first century B.C.E. and destroyed by the Romans in 70 C.E.

In early Israel, because women provided vital goods and services that sustained the family, they were respected and had some influence with their husbands. Unlike men, however, they could not inherit property or initiate divorce, and a woman caught in extramarital relations could be put to death. Peasant women labored with other family members in agriculture or herding in addition to caring for the house and children. As the society became urbanized, some women worked outside the home as cooks, perfumers, wet nurses, prostitutes, and singers of laments at funerals. A few women reached positions of power, such as Deborah the Judge, who led troops in battle against the Canaanites. "Wise women" composed sacred texts in poetry and prose. This reality has been obscured, in part by the male bias of the Hebrew Bible, in part because the status of women declined as Israelite society became more urbanized.

monotheism Belief in the existence of a single divine entity. Some scholars cite the devotion of the Egyptian pharaoh Akhenaten to Aten (sun-disk) and his suppression of traditional gods as the earliest instance. The Israelite worship of Yahweh developed into an exclusive belief in one god, and this concept passed into Christianity and Islam.

Fragmentation and Dispersal

After Solomon's death around 920 B.C.E., resentment over royal demands for money and labor and the neglect of tribal prerogatives split the monarchy into two kingdoms: Israel in the north, with its capital at Samaria (suh-MAH-ree-yuh); and Judah (JOO-duh) in the southern territory around Jerusalem (see Map 3.4). The two were sometimes at war, sometimes allied.

Division and Disaster

This period saw the final formulation of **monotheism**, the belief in Yahweh as the one and only god. Nevertheless, many Israelites were attracted to the ecstatic rituals of the Canaanite storm-god Baal (BAHL) and the fertility goddess Asherah (uh-SHARE-uh). Prophets condemned the adoption of foreign ritual and threatened that Yahweh would punish Israel severely.

The two Israelite kingdoms and other small states in the region laid aside their rivalries to mount a joint resistance to the Neo-Assyrian Empire, but to no avail. In 721 B.C.E. the Assyrians destroyed the northern kingdom of Israel and deported much of its population to the east.

Protests Against the Ruling Class in Israel and Babylonia

Israelite society underwent profound changes in the period of the monarchy, and the new opportunities for some to acquire considerable wealth led to greater disparities between rich and poor. A series of prophets publicly challenged the behavior of the Israelite ruling elite. They denounced the changes in Israelite society as corrupting people and separating them from the religious devotion and moral rectitude of an earlier, better time. The prophets often spoke out on behalf of the uneducated, inarticulate, illiterate, and powerless lower classes, and they thus provide valuable information about the experiences of different social groups. Theirs was not objective reporting, but rather the angry, anguished visions of unconventional individuals.

The following excerpt from the Hebrew Bible is taken from the book of Amos. A herdsman from the southern kingdom of Judah in the era of the divided monarchy, Amos was active in the northern kingdom of Israel in the mid-eighth century B.C.E., when Assyria threatened the Syria-Palestine region.

1:1 The following is a record of what Amos prophesied. He was one of the herdsmen from Tekoa. These prophecies about Israel were revealed to him during the time of King Uzziah of Judah and King Jeroboam son of Joash of Israel. . . .

3:1 Listen, you Israelites, to this message which the Lord is proclaiming against you. This message is for the entire clan I brought up from the land of Egypt:

3:2 "I have chosen you alone from all the clans of the earth. Therefore I will punish you for all your sins." . . .

3:9 Make this announcement in the fortresses of Ashdod and in the fortresses in the land of Egypt. Say this: "Gather on the hills around Samaria! [capital of the northern kingdom] Observe the many acts of violence taking place within the city, the oppressive deeds occurring in it." . . .

3:11 "Therefore," says the sovereign Lord, "an enemy will encircle the land. Your power, Samaria, will be taken away; your fortresses will be looted."

3:12 This is what the Lord says: "Just as a shepherd salvages from the lion's mouth a couple of leg bones or a piece of an ear, so the Israelites who live in Samaria will be salvaged. They will be left with just a corner of a bed, and a part of a couch." . . .

4:1 Listen to this message, you "cows of Bashan" who live on Mount Samaria! You oppress the poor; you crush the needy. You say to your husbands, "Bring us more to drink so we can party!"

4:2 The sovereign Lord confirms this oath by his own holy character: "Certainly the time is approaching! You will be carried away in baskets, every last one of you in fishermen's pots.

4:3 Each of you will go straight through the gaps in the walls; you will be thrown out toward Harmon." . . .

5:11 "Therefore, because you make the poor pay taxes on their crops and exact a grain tax from them, you will not live in the houses you built with chiseled stone, nor will you drink the wine from the fine vineyards you planted.

5:12 Certainly I am aware of your many rebellious acts and your numerous sins. You torment the innocent, you take bribes, and you deny justice to the needy at the city gate. . . .

5:21 I absolutely despise your festivals. I get no pleasure from your religious assemblies.

5:22 Even if you offer me burnt and grain offerings, I will not be satisfied; I will not look with favor on the fattened calves you offer in peace.

5:23 Take away from me your noisy songs; I don't want to hear the music of your stringed instruments." . . .

6:4 They lie around on beds decorated with ivory, and sprawl out on their couches. They eat lambs from the flock, and calves from the middle of the pen.

6:5 They sing to the tune of stringed instruments; like David they invent musical instruments.

6:6 They drink wine from sacrificial bowls, and pour the very best oils on themselves.

6:7 Therefore they will now be the first to go into exile, and the religious banquets where they sprawl out on couches will end.

7:10 Amaziah the priest of Bethel sent this message to King Jeroboam of Israel: "Amos is conspiring against you in the very heart of the kingdom of Israel! The land cannot endure all his prophecies.

7:11 As a matter of fact, Amos is saying this: 'Jeroboam will die by the sword and Israel will certainly be carried into exile away from its land.'"

7:12 Amaziah then said to Amos, "Leave, you visionary! Run away to the land of Judah! Earn money and prophesy there!

7:13 Don't prophesy at Bethel any longer, for a royal temple and palace are here!"

7:14 Amos replied to Amaziah, "I was not a prophet by profession. No, I was a herdsman who also took care of sycamore fig trees.

7:15 Then the Lord took me from tending flocks and gave me this commission, 'Go! Prophesy to my people Israel!'" . . .

8:8 "Because of this the earth will quake, and all who live in it will mourn. The whole earth will rise like the River Nile, it will surge upward and then grow calm, like the Nile in Egypt.

8:9 In that day," says the sovereign Lord, "I will make the sun set at noon, and make the earth dark in the middle of the day.

8:10 I will turn your festivals into funerals, and all your songs into funeral dirges. I will make everyone wear funeral clothes and cause every head to be shaved bald. I will make you mourn as if you had lost your only son; when it ends it will indeed have been a bitter day." . . .

9:8 "Look, the sovereign Lord is watching the sinful nation, and I will destroy it from the face of the earth. But I will not completely destroy the family of Jacob," says the Lord.

9:9 "For look, I am giving a command and I will shake the family of Israel together with all the nations. It will resemble a sieve being shaken, when not even a pebble falls to the ground. . . .

9:11 In that day I will rebuild the collapsing hut of David. I will seal its gaps, repair its ruins, and restore it to what it was like in days gone by."

A document from Babylon, which may have been composed around 1000 B.C.E., reveals the prevalence of similar inequities and abuses in that society. It is presented as a dialogue between a man in distress (who, despite his claim of low status, is literate and presumably comes from the urban middle class) and his compassionate friend.

Sufferer

I have looked around in the world, but things are turned around.
The god does not impede the way of even a demon.
A father tows a boat along the canal,
While his son lies in bed.
The eldest son makes his way like a lion,
The second son is happy to be a mule driver.
The heir goes about along the streets like a peddler,
The younger son (has enough) that he can give food to the destitute.
What has it profited me that I have bowed down to my god?
I must bow even to a person who is lower than I,
The rich and opulent treat me, as a younger brother, with contempt. . . .

Friend

O wise one, O savant, who masters knowledge,
Your heart has become hardened and you accuse the god wrongly.
The mind of the god, like the center of the heavens, is remote;
Knowledge of it is very difficult; people cannot know it.
Among all the creatures whom Aruru formed
Why should the oldest offspring be so . . . [text uncertain]?
In the case of a cow, the first calf is a runt,
The later offspring is twice as big.
A first child is born a weakling,
But the second is called a mighty warrior.
Though it is possible to find out what the will of the god is, people do not know how to do it.

Sufferer

Pay attention, my friend, understand my clever ideas,
Heed my carefully chosen words.
People extol the words of a strong man who has learned to kill
But bring down the powerless who has done no wrong.
They confirm (the position of) the wicked for whom what should be an abomination is considered right
Yet drive off the honest man who heeds the will of his god.
They fill the [storehouse] of the oppressor with gold,
But empty the larder of the beggar of its provisions.
They support the powerful, whose . . . [text uncertain] is guilt,
But destroy the weak and trample the powerless.
And, as for me, an insignificant person, a prominent person persecutes me.

Friend

Narru, king of the gods, who created mankind,
And majestic Zulummar, who pinched off the clay for them,
And goddess Mami, the queen who fashioned them,
Gave twisted speech to the human race.
With lies, and not truth, they endowed them forever.
Solemnly they speak favorably of a rich man,
"He is a king," they say, "riches should be his,"
But they treat a poor man like a thief,
They have only bad to say of him and plot his murder,
Making him suffer every evil like a criminal, because he has no . . . [text uncertain].
Terrifyingly they bring him to his end, and extinguish him like glowing coals.

Sufferer

You are kind, my friend; behold my trouble,
Help me; look on my distress; know it.
I, though humble, wise, and a suppliant,
Have not seen help or aid even for a moment.
I have gone about the square of my city unobtrusively,
My voice was not raised, my speech was kept low.
I did not raise my head, but looked at the ground,
I did not worship even as a slave in the company of my associates.
May the god who has abandoned me give help,
May the goddess who has [forsaken me] show mercy,
The shepherd, the sun of the people, pastures (his flock) as a god should.

QUESTIONS FOR ANALYSIS

1. **For whom is Amos's message primarily intended? How does the ruling class react to Amos's prophetic activity, and how does he respond to their tactics?**
2. **What does Amos see as wrong in Israelite society, and who is at fault? Why are even the religious practices of the elite criticized?**
3. **What will be the means by which God punishes Israel, and why does God punish it this way? What grounds for hope remain?**
4. **What are the main complaints of the Babylonian Sufferer, and where does he look for a solution? Do the Babylonian gods seem to be less directly involved in human affairs than the Israelite deity?**

New settlers were brought in from Syria, Babylon, and Iran, changing the area's ethnic, cultural, and religious character. The kingdom of Judah survived more than a century longer, sometimes rebelling, sometimes paying tribute to the Assyrians or the Neo-Babylonian kingdom (626–539 B.C.E.) that succeeded them. When the Neo-Babylonian monarch Nebuchadnezzar (NAB-oo-kuhd-nez-uhr) captured Jerusalem in 587 B.C.E., he destroyed the Temple and deported to Babylon the royal family, the aristocracy, and many skilled workers such as blacksmiths and scribes.

Diaspora Greek word meaning "dispersal," used to describe the communities of a given ethnic group living outside their homeland. Jews, for example, spread from Israel to western Asia and Mediterranean lands in antiquity and today can be found throughout the world.

The deportees prospered so well in their new home "by the waters of Babylon" that half a century later most of their descendants refused the offer of the Persian monarch Cyrus (see Chapter 4) to return to their homeland. This was the origin of the **Diaspora** (die-ASS-peh-rah)—a Greek word meaning "dispersion" or "scattering." This dispersion outside the homeland of many Jews—as we may now call these people, since an independent Israel no longer existed—continues to this day. To maintain their religion and culture, the Diaspora communities developed institutions like the synagogue (Greek for "bringing together"), a communal meeting place that served religious, educational, and social functions.

Diaspora and Identity

Several groups of Babylonian Jews did make the long trek back to Judah in the later sixth and fifth centuries B.C.E. They rebuilt the Temple in modest form and edited the Hebrew Bible into roughly its present form.

The loss of political autonomy and the experience of exile had sharpened Jewish identity. With an unyielding monotheism as their core belief, Jews lived by a rigid set of rules. Dietary restrictions forbade the eating of pork and shellfish and mandated that meat and dairy products not be consumed together. Ritual baths were used to achieve spiritual purity. The Jews venerated the Sabbath (Saturday, the seventh day of the week) by refraining from work and from fighting, following the example of Yahweh, who, according to the Bible, rested on the seventh day after creating the world (this is the origin of the concept of the week and the weekend). These strictures and others, including a ban on marrying non-Jews, tended to isolate the Jews from other peoples, but they also fostered a powerful sense of community and the belief that the Jews were protected by a watchful and beneficent deity.

SECTION REVIEW

- Because of its strategic location, the small, resource-poor land of Israel has played an important role in world history.
- The history of the ancient Israelites can be reconstructed by critically comparing information in the Hebrew Bible with archaeological discoveries.
- The early Israelites were nomadic pastoralists, but eventually they settled down as farmers and herders in Canaan.
- As a result of their rivalry with the coastal Philistines, the once loosely organized Israelite tribes united under a monarchy, with Jerusalem as the capital.
- Urbanization, wealth from trade, and the status of the Temple priesthood created divisions within Israelite society. Fiery prophets railed against the greed and corruption of the elite.
- Following conquests by the Assyrian Empire and Neo-Babylonian kingdom, many Israelites were taken from their homeland. Diaspora communities created new institutions, a distinctive way of life, and a strong Jewish identity.

PHOENICIA AND THE MEDITERRANEAN, 1200–500 B.C.E.

Phoenicians Semitic-speaking Canaanites living on the coast of modern Lebanon and Syria in the first millennium B.C.E. From major cities such as Tyre and Sidon, Phoenician merchants and sailors explored the Mediterranean, engaged in widespread commerce, and founded Carthage and other colonies in the western Mediterranean.

While the Israelite tribes were forging a united kingdom, the people who occupied the Mediterranean coast to the north were developing their own distinctive civilization. Historians follow the Greeks in calling them **Phoenicians** (fi-NEE-shun), though they referred to themselves as "Can'ani"—Canaanites. Despite few written records and archaeological remains disturbed by frequent migrations and invasions, some of their history can be reconstructed.

The Phoenician City-States

When the eastern Mediterranean was disturbed by violent upheavals and mass migrations around 1200 B.C.E., many Canaanite settlements in the Syria-Palestine region were destroyed. Aramaeans (ah-ruh-MAY-uhn)—nomadic pastoralists similar to the early Israelites—migrated into the interior portions of Syria. Farther south, Israelite herders and farmers settled in the interior of present-day Israel. The Philistines occupied the southern coast and introduced iron-based metallurgy to this part of the world.

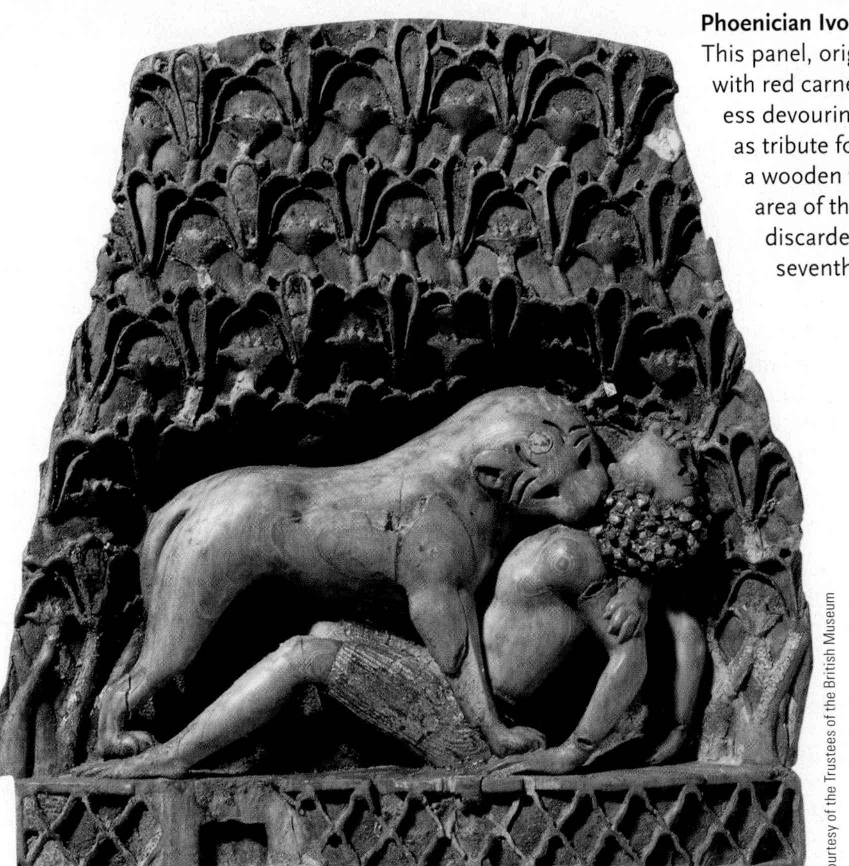

Phoenician Ivory Panel, Ninth to Eighth Century B.C.E. This panel, originally covered with gold leaf and inlaid with red carnelian and blue lapis lazuli, depicts a lioness devouring a boy. Produced in Phoenicia, perhaps as tribute for the Assyrian king, it was probably part of a wooden throne. It was found in a well in the palace area of the Assyrian capital Nimrud, where it was discarded when the city was destroyed in the late seventh century B.C.E.

Political and Economic Development

By 1100 B.C.E. Canaanite territory had shrunk to a narrow strip of present-day Lebanon between the mountains and the sea (see Map 3.4). Rivers and rocky spurs of Mount Lebanon sliced the coastal plain into a series of small city-states, chief among them Byblos (BIB-loss), Berytus (buh-RIE-tuhs), Sidon (SIE-duhn), and Tyre. The inhabitants of this densely populated area adopted new political forms and turned to seaborne commerce and new kinds of manufacture for their survival. A thriving trade in raw materials (cedar and pine, metals, incense, papyrus), foodstuffs (wine, spices, salted fish), and crafted luxury goods (carved ivory, glass, and textiles colored with a highly prized purple dye extracted from the murex snail) brought considerable wealth to the Phoenician city-states and gave them an important role in international politics (see Environment and Technology: Ancient Textiles and Dyes).

The Phoenicians developed earlier Canaanite models into an "alphabetic" system of writing with about two dozen symbols, in which each symbol represented a sound. (The Phoenicians represented only consonants, leaving the vowel sounds to be inferred by the reader. The Greeks later added symbols for vowel sounds, creating the first truly alphabetic system of writing—see Chapter 4.) Little Phoenician writing survives, however, probably because scribes used perishable papyrus.

The Ascendancy of Tyre

Before 1000 B.C.E. Byblos was the most important Phoenician city-state. It was a distribution center for cedar timber from the slopes of Mount Lebanon and for papyrus from Egypt. King Hiram, who came to power in 969 B.C.E., was responsible for Tyre's rise to prominence. According to the Hebrew Bible, he formed a close alliance with the Israelite king Solomon and provided skilled Phoenician craftsmen and cedar wood for building the Temple in Jerusalem. In return, Tyre gained access to silver, food, and trade routes to the east and south. In the 800s B.C.E. Tyre took control of nearby Sidon and dominated the Mediterranean coastal trade.

Located on an offshore island, Tyre was practically impregnable. It had two harbors connected by a canal, a large marketplace, a magnificent palace complex with treasury and archives, and temples to the gods Melqart (MEL-kahrt) and Astarte (uh-STAHR-tee). Some of its thirty

Ancient Textiles and Dyes

Throughout human history the production of textiles—cloth for clothing, blankets, carpets, and coverings of various sorts—required an expenditure of human labor second only to the work necessary to provide food. Nevertheless, textile production in antiquity has left few archaeological traces. The plant fibers and animal hair used for cloth quickly decompose except in rare circumstances. Some textile remains have been found in the hot, dry conditions of Egypt, the cool, arid Andes of South America, and the peat bogs of northern Europe. But most of our knowledge of ancient textiles depends on the discovery of equipment used in textile production—such as spindles, loom weights, and dyeing vats—and on pictorial representations and descriptions in texts.

Private collection

Ancient Peruvian Textiles The weaving of Chavín was famous for its color and symbolic imagery. Artisans both wove designs into the fabric and used paint or dyes to decorate plain fabric. This early Chavín painted fabric was used in a burial. Notice how the face suggests a jaguar and the headdress includes the image of a serpent.

Cloth production usually has been the work of women for a simple but important reason. Responsibility for child rearing limits women's ability to participate in other activities but does not consume all their time and energy. In many societies textile production has been complementary to child-rearing activities, for it can be done in the home, is relatively safe, does not require great concentration, and can be interrupted without consequence. The growing and harvesting of plants such as cotton or flax (from which linen is made) and the shearing of wool from sheep and, in the Andes, llamas are outdoor activities, but the subsequent stages of production can be carried out inside the home. The basic methods of textile production did not change much from early antiquity until the late eighteenth century C.E., when the fabrication of textiles was transferred to mills and mass production began.

When textile production has been considered "women's work," most of the output has been for household consumption. However, women weavers in Peru developed new raw materials, new techniques, and new decorative motifs around three thousand years ago. They began to use the wool of llamas and alpacas in addition to cotton. Three women worked side by side and passed the weft from hand to hand in order to produce a fabric of greater width. Women weavers also introduced embroidery and decorated garments with new religious motifs, such as the jaguar-god. Their high-quality textiles were given as tribute to the elite and were used to trade for luxury goods.

More typically, men dominated commercial production. In ancient Phoenicia, fine textiles with bright, permanent colors became a major export product. Most prized was the red-purple known as Tyrian purple because Tyre was the major source. Persian and Hellenistic kings wore robes dyed this color, and a white toga with a purple border was the sign of a Roman senator.

The production of Tyrian purple was an exceedingly laborious process. The spiny dye-murex snail lives on the sandy Mediterranean bottom at depths ranging from 30 to 500 feet (10 to 150 meters). Nine thousand snails were needed to produce 1 gram (0.035 ounce) of dye. The dye was made from a colorless liquid in the snail's hypobranchial gland. The gland sacs were removed, crushed, soaked with salt, and exposed to sunlight and air for some days; then they were subject to controlled boiling and heating.

Huge mounds of broken shells on the Phoenician coast are testimony to the ancient industry. The snail may have been rendered nearly extinct at many locations, and some scholars speculate that Phoenician colonization in the Mediterranean was motivated in part by the search for new sources of snails.

thousand inhabitants lived in suburbs on the mainland. Its one weakness was its dependence on the mainland for food and fresh water.

Little is known about the internal affairs of Tyre and other Phoenician cities. The names of a series of kings are preserved, and the scant evidence suggests that the political arena was dominated by leading merchant families. Between the ninth and seventh centuries B.C.E. the Phoenician city-states contended with Assyrian aggression, followed in the sixth century B.C.E. by the expansion of the Neo-Babylonian kingdom and later the Persian Empire (see Chapter 4). The Phoenician city-states preserved their autonomy by playing the great powers off against one another when possible and by accepting a subordinate relationship to a distant master when necessary.

Expansion into the Mediterranean

The Western Settlements

After 900 B.C.E. Tyre turned its attention westward, establishing colonies on Cyprus, a copper-rich island 100 miles (161 kilometers) from the Syrian coast (see Map 3.4). By 700 B.C.E. a string of settlements in the western Mediterranean formed a "Phoenician triangle" composed of the North African coast from western Libya to Morocco; the south and southeast coast of Spain, including Gades (GAH-days) (modern Cadiz [kuh-DEEZ]) on the Strait of Gibraltar, controlling passage between the Mediterranean and the Atlantic Ocean; and the islands of Sardinia, Sicily, and Malta off the coast of Italy (see Map 3.5). Many settlements were situated on promontories or offshore islands in imitation of Tyre. The Phoenician trading network spanned the entire Mediterranean.

Frequent and destructive Assyrian invasions of Syria-Palestine and the lack of arable land to feed a swelling population probably motivated Tyrian expansion. Overseas settlement provided an outlet for excess population, new sources of trade goods, and new trading partners. Tyre

e Interactive Map

MAP 3.5 Colonization of the Mediterranean In the ninth century B.C.E., the Phoenicians of Lebanon began to explore and colonize parts of the western Mediterranean, including the coast of North Africa, southern and eastern Spain, and the islands of Sicily and Sardinia. The Phoenicians were primarily interested in access to valuable raw materials and trading opportunities.

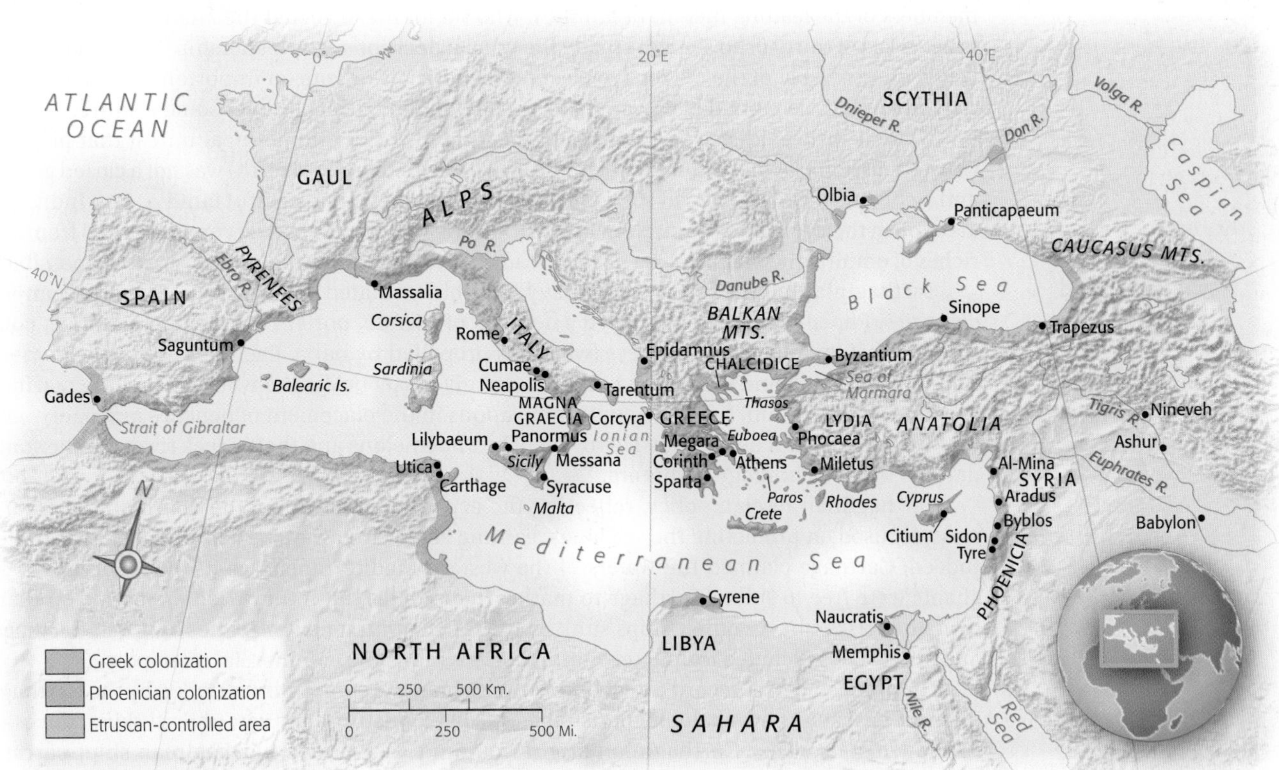

maintained its autonomy until 701 B.C.E. by paying tribute to the Assyrian kings. In that year it finally fell to an Assyrian army that stripped it of much of its territory and population, allowing Sidon to become the leading city in Phoenicia.

Carthage's Commercial Empire

The City of Carthage

Carthage City located in present-day Tunisia, founded by Phoenicians ca. 800 B.C.E. It became a major commercial center and naval power in the western Mediterranean until defeated by Rome in the third century B.C.E.

Historians know far more about **Carthage** and the other Phoenician colonies than they do about the Phoenician homeland. Much of this comes from Greek and Roman reports of their wars with the western Phoenician communities. For example, the account of the origins of Carthage that begins this chapter comes from Roman sources but probably is based on a Carthaginian original. Archaeological excavation has roughly confirmed the city's traditional foundation date of 814 B.C.E. The new settlement grew rapidly and soon dominated other Phoenician colonies in the west.

Located just outside the present-day city of Tunis in Tunisia, on a promontory jutting into the Mediterranean, Carthage stretched between the original hilltop citadel and a double harbor. The inner harbor could accommodate 220 warships. A watchtower allowed surveillance of the surrounding area, and high walls made it impossible to see in from the outside. The outer commercial harbor was filled with docks for merchant ships and shipyards. In case of attack, the harbor could be closed off by a huge iron chain.

Government offices ringed a large central square where magistrates heard legal cases outdoors. The inner city was a maze of narrow, winding streets, multistory apartment buildings, and sacred enclosures. Farther out was a sprawling suburban district where the wealthy built spacious villas amid fields and vegetable gardens. This entire urban complex was enclosed by a wall 22 miles (35 kilometers) in length. At the most critical point—the 2-1/2-mile-wide (4-kilometer) isthmus connecting the promontory to the mainland—the wall was over 40 feet (13 meters) high and 30 feet (10 meters) thick and had high watchtowers.

With a population of roughly 400,000, Carthage was one of the largest cities in the world by 500 B.C.E. The population was ethnically diverse, including people of Phoenician stock, indigenous peoples ancestral to modern-day Berbers, and immigrants from other Mediterranean lands as well as sub-Saharan Africa. The Phoenicians readily intermarried with other peoples.

Each year two "judges" were elected from upper-class families to serve as heads of state and carry out administrative and judicial functions. The real seat of power was the Senate, where members of the leading merchant families, who sat for life, directed the affairs of the state. An inner circle of thirty or so senators made the crucial decisions. The leadership occasionally convened an Assembly of the citizens to elect public officials or vote on important issues, particularly when they were divided or wanted to stir up popular enthusiasm for some venture.

There is little evidence at Carthage of the kind of social and political unrest that plagued Greece and Rome. A merchant aristocracy (unlike an aristocracy of birth) was not a closed group, and a climate of economic and social mobility allowed newly successful families and individuals to push their way into the circle of influential citizens. Insofar as everyone benefited from the riches of empire, the masses were usually ready to defer to those who made prosperity possible.

Naval Power and Commerce

Carthaginian power rested on its navy, which dominated the western Mediterranean for centuries. Phoenician towns provided a network of friendly ports. The Carthaginian fleet consisted of fast, maneuverable galleys (warships propelled by oars). Each bore a sturdy, pointed ram in front that could pierce the hull of an enemy vessel below the water line, while marines (soldiers aboard a ship) fired weapons. Innovations in the placement of benches and oars eventually made room for as many as 170 rowers. The Phoenicians and their Greek rivals set the standard for naval technology in this era.

Carthaginian foreign policy, reflecting the economic interests of the dominant merchant class, focused on protecting the sea lanes, gaining access to raw materials, and fostering trade. Indeed, Carthage claimed the waters of the western Mediterranean as its own. Foreign merchants were free to sail to Carthage to market their goods, but if they tried to operate on their own, they risked having their ships sunk by the Carthaginian navy. Treaties between Carthage and other states included formal recognition of this maritime commercial monopoly.

The archaeological record provides few clues about the commodities traded by the Carthaginians. These may have included perishable goods—foodstuffs, textiles, animal skins, slaves—and raw metals whose Carthaginian origin would not be evident. Carthaginian ships carried goods manufactured elsewhere, and products brought to Carthage by foreign traders were reexported.

There is also evidence for trade with sub-Saharan Africa. Hanno (HA-noe), a Carthaginian captain of the fifth century B.C.E., claimed to have sailed through the Strait of Gibraltar into the Atlantic Ocean and to have explored the West African coast (see Map 3.5). Other Carthaginians explored the Atlantic coast of Spain and France and secured control of an important source of tin in the "Tin Islands," probably Cornwall in southwestern England.

War and Religion

A Different Kind of Empire

The Carthaginian state did not directly rule a large territory. A belt of fertile land in northeastern Tunisia, owned by Carthaginians but worked by native peasants and imported slaves, provided a secure food supply. Beyond this core area the Carthaginians ruled most of their "empire" indirectly and allowed other Phoenician communities in the western Mediterranean to remain independent. These Phoenician communities looked to Carthage for military protection and followed its lead in foreign policy. Only Sardinia and southern Spain were put under the direct control of a Carthaginian governor and garrison, presumably to safeguard their agricultural, metal, and manpower resources.

Carthage's focus on trade may explain the unusual fact that citizens were not required to serve in the army: they were of more value in other capacities, such as trading activities and the navy. Since the indigenous North African population was not politically or militarily well organized, Carthage had little to fear close to home. When Carthage was drawn into a series of wars with the Greeks and Romans from the fifth through third centuries B.C.E., it relied on mercenaries from the most warlike peoples in its dominions or from neighboring areas. These well-paid mercenaries were under the command of Carthaginian officers. In contrast to most ancient states, the Carthaginians separated military command from civilian government. Generals were chosen by the Senate and kept in office for as long as they were needed.

Carthaginian Religion

Like the deities of Mesopotamia (see Chapter 1), the gods of the Carthaginians—chief among them Baal Hammon (BAHL ha-MOHN), a male storm-god, and Tanit (TAH-nit), a female fertility figure—were powerful and capricious entities who had to be appeased by anxious worshipers. Roman sources report that members of the Carthaginian elite would sacrifice their

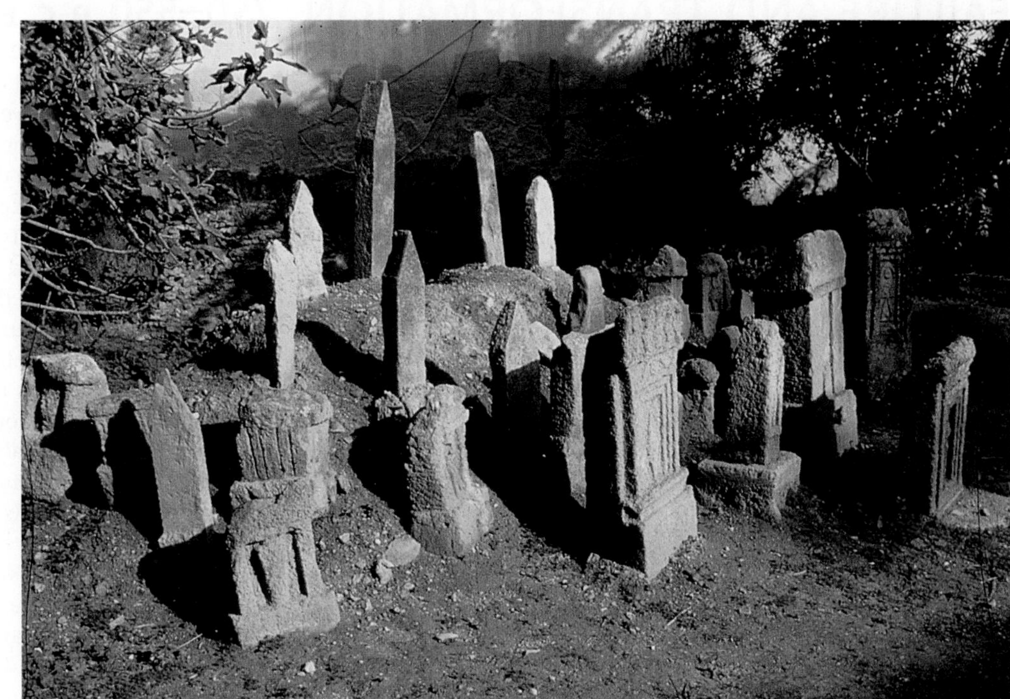

The Tophet of Carthage Here, from the seventh to second centuries B.C.E., the cremated bodies of sacrificed children were buried. Archaeological excavation has confirmed the claim in ancient sources that the Carthaginians sacrificed children to their gods at times of crisis. Stone markers, decorated with magical signs and symbols of divinities as well as family names, were placed over ceramic urns containing the ashes and charred bones of one or more infants or, occasionally, older children.

SECTION REVIEW

- Following the upheavals ca. 1200 B.C.E., Canaanite communities on the coast of Lebanon adopted the city-state political form and turned to seaborne commerce and new kinds of manufacture for their survival.
- In the tenth century B.C.E., Tyre, located on a practically impregnable offshore island and led by a king and merchant aristocracy, became the dominant Phoenician state.
- A string of settlements in the western Mediterranean formed a "Phoenician triangle" comprising the coasts of North Africa and Spain and islands off the coast of Italy.
- Carthage, founded in present-day Tunisia a little before 800 B.C.E., led the coalition of Phoenician communities in the western Mediterranean.
- Carthaginian power rested on its navy, which enforced a Carthaginian commercial monopoly in the western Mediterranean. For land warfare, Carthage relied on mercenaries from the most warlike peoples in the region, under the command of Carthaginian officers.
- The religion of the Carthaginians, which included the sacrifice of children in times of crisis, was perceived as different and despicable by their Greek and Roman rivals.

own male children in times of crisis. Excavations at Carthage and other western Phoenician towns have turned up *tophets* (TOE-fet)—walled enclosures where thousands of small, sealed urns containing the burned bones of children lay buried. Originally practiced by the upper classes, child sacrifice became more common and involved broader elements of the population after 400 B.C.E.

Plutarch (PLOO-tawrk), a Greek who lived around 100 C.E., long after the demise of Carthage, wrote the following on the basis of earlier sources:

> *The Carthaginians are a hard and gloomy people, submissive to their rulers and harsh to their subjects, running to extremes of cowardice in times of fear and of cruelty in times of anger; they keep obstinately to their decisions, are austere, and care little for amusement or the graces of life.*[1]

We should not take the hostile opinions of Greek and Roman sources at face value. Still, it is clear that the Carthaginians were perceived as different and that cultural barriers, leading to misunderstanding and prejudice, played a significant role in the conflicts among these peoples of the ancient Mediterranean. In Chapter 5 we follow the protracted and bloody struggle between Rome and Carthage for control of the western Mediterranean.

FAILURE AND TRANSFORMATION, 750–550 B.C.E.

Assyrian Pressure

The extension of Assyrian power over the entire Middle East had enormous consequences for all the peoples of the region. In 721 B.C.E. the Assyrians destroyed the northern kingdom of Israel and deported a substantial portion of the population, and for over a century the southern kingdom of Judah faced relentless pressure. Assyrian threats and demands for tribute spurred the Phoenicians to explore and colonize the western Mediterranean. Tyre's fall to the Assyrians in 701 B.C.E. accelerated the decline of the Phoenician homeland, but the western colonies, especially Carthage, flourished. Even Egypt, for so long impregnable behind its desert barriers, fell to Assyrian invaders in the mid-seventh century B.C.E. Southern Mesopotamia was reduced to a protectorate, with Babylon alternately razed and rebuilt by Assyrian kings of differing dispositions. Urartu and Elam, Assyria's nearby rivals, were destroyed.

By 650 B.C.E. Assyria stood unchallenged in western Asia. But the arms race with Urartu, the frequent expensive campaigns, and the protection of lengthy borders had sapped Assyrian resources. Assyrian brutality and exploitation aroused the hatred of conquered peoples. At the same time,

SECTION REVIEW

- The extension of Assyrian power over the entire Middle East had enormous consequences for all the peoples of the region.
- The costs of frequent military campaigns, the hatred of conquered peoples aroused by Assyrian brutality, and changes in the ethnic composition of the army and the population of the homeland weakened the Assyrian state.
- The Neo-Babylonians and the Medes of northwest Iran launched a series of attacks on the Assyrian homeland that destroyed the chief cities by 612 B.C.E. and led to the depopulation of northern Mesopotamia.
- The Neo-Babylonian kingdom took over much of the territory of the Assyrian Empire and fostered a cultural renaissance.

changes in the ethnic composition of the army and the population of the homeland had reduced popular support for the Assyrian state.

The Neo-Babylonian Kingdom

Neo-Babylonian kingdom Under the Chaldaeans (nomadic kinship groups that settled in southern Mesopotamia in the early first millennium B.C.E.), Babylon again became a major political and cultural center in the seventh and sixth centuries B.C.E. After participating in the destruction of Assyrian power, the monarchs Nabopolassar and Nebuchadnezzar took over the southern portion of the Assyrian domains.

Two new political entities spearheaded resistance to Assyria. First, Babylonia had been revived by the Neo-Babylonian, or Chaldaean (chal-DEE-uhn), dynasty (the Chaldaeans had infiltrated southern Mesopotamia around 1000 B.C.E.). Second, the Medes (MEED), an Iranian people, were extending their kingdom on the Iranian Plateau in the seventh century B.C.E. The two powers launched a series of attacks on the Assyrian homeland that destroyed the chief cities by 612 B.C.E. The destruction systematically carried out by the victorious attackers led to the depopulation of northern Mesopotamia.

The Medes took over the Assyrian homeland and the northern plain as far as eastern Anatolia, but most of the territory of the old empire fell to the **Neo-Babylonian kingdom** (626–539 B.C.E.), thanks to the energetic campaigns of kings Nabopolassar (NAB-oh-poe-lass-uhr) (r. 625–605 B.C.E.) and Nebuchadnezzar (r. 604–562 B.C.E.). Babylonia underwent a cultural renaissance. The city of Babylon was enlarged and adorned, becoming the greatest metropolis of the world in the sixth century B.C.E. Old cults were revived, temples rebuilt, festivals resurrected. The related pursuits of mathematics, astronomy, and astrology reached new heights.

CONCLUSION

The Late Bronze Age in the Middle East was a "cosmopolitan" era of shared lifestyles and technologies. Patterns of culture that had originated long before in Egypt and Mesopotamia persisted into this era. Peoples such as the Amorites, Kassites, and Chaldaeans, who migrated into the Tigris-Euphrates plain, were largely assimilated into the Sumerian-Semitic cultural tradition, adopting its language, religious beliefs, political and social institutions, and forms of artistic expression. Similarly, the Hyksos, who migrated into the Nile Delta and controlled much of Egypt for a time, adopted the ancient ways of Egypt. When the founders of the New Kingdom finally ended Hyksos domination, they reinstituted the united monarchy and the religious and cultural traditions of earlier eras.

The Late Bronze Age expansion of commerce and communication stimulated the emergence of new civilizations, including those of the Minoans and Mycenaean Greeks in the Aegean Sea. These new civilizations borrowed heavily from the technologies and cultural practices of Mesopotamia and Egypt, creating dynamic syntheses of imported and indigenous elements.

Ultimately, the very interdependence of the societies of the Middle East and eastern Mediterranean made them vulnerable to the destructions and disorder of the decades around 1200 B.C.E. The entire region slipped into a "Dark Age" of isolation, stagnation, and decline that lasted several centuries. The early centuries after 1000 B.C.E. saw a resurgence of political organization and international commerce, as well as the spread of technologies and ideas. The Assyrians created an empire of unprecedented size and diversity through superior organization and military technology, and they maintained it through terror and deportations of subject peoples.

The Israelites began as nomadic pastoralists, then settled permanently in Canaan. Conflict with the Philistines forced them to adopt a more complex political structure, and under the monarchy Israelite society grew more urban and economically stratified. While the long, slow evolution of the Israelites from wandering groups of herders to an agriculturally based monarchy followed a common pattern in ancient western Asia, the religious and ethical concepts that they formulated were unique and have had a powerful impact on world history.

After the upheavals of the Late Bronze Age, the Phoenician city-states along the coast of Lebanon flourished. Under pressure from the Neo-Assyrian Empire, the Phoenicians, with Tyre in the lead, began spreading westward into the Mediterranean. Carthage became the most important city outside the Phoenician homeland. Ruled by leading merchant families, it extended its commercial empire throughout the western Mediterranean, maintaining power through naval superiority.

The far-reaching expansion of the Assyrian Empire was the most important factor in the transformation of the ancient Middle East. The Assyrians destroyed many older states and, directly or indirectly, displaced large numbers of people. Their brutality, as well as the population shifts that resulted from their deportations, undercut support for their state. The Chaldaeans and Medes led resistance to Assyrian rule. After the swift collapse of Assyria, the Chaldaeans expanded the Neo-Babylonian kingdom, enlarged the city of Babylon, and presided over a cultural renaissance.

KEY TERMS

EBOOK AND WEBSITE RESOURCES

Primary Sources

An Assyrian Emperor's Resume: Ferocious Conquests a Specialty

Moses Descends Mount Sinai with the Ten Commandments

Interactive Maps

Map 3.1 The Middle East in the Second Millennium B.C.E.

Map 3.2 Minoan and Mycenaean Civilizations of the Aegean

Map 3.3 The Assyrian Empire

Map 3.4 Phoenicia and Israel

Map 3.5 Colonization of the Mediterranean

Plus flashcards, practice quizzes, and more. Go to: www.cengage.com/history/bullietearthpeople5e

SUGGESTED READING

Barber, Elizabeth Wayland. *Women's Work: The First 20,000 Years: Women, Cloth, and Society in Early Times.* 1994. An intriguing account of textile manufacture in antiquity, with emphasis on the social implications and primary role of women.

Bryce, Trevor. *The Kingdom of the Hittites*, new edition. 2005. The most up-to-date treatment of the history of the Hittites.

Chadwick, John. *The Mycenaean World.* 1976. A still valuable reconstruction of the earliest complex Greek society by a scholar who helped to decipher the Linear B tablets.

Curtis, J. E., and J. E. Reade, eds. *Art and Empire: Treasures from Assyria in the British Museum.* 1995. The catalogue for a museum exhibition, with chapters relating the art to many facets of Assyrian life.

Hornung, Erik. *Akhenaten and the Religion of Light.* 1999. Focused on religious innovations, but deals more broadly with many facets of the reign of Akhenaten.

Krzyszkowska, O., and L. Nixon. *Minoan Society.* 1983. Examines the archaeological evidence for the Minoan civilization of Crete.

Kuhrt, Amelie. *The Ancient Near East, c. 3000–300 B.C.*, 2 vols. 1995. The best introduction to the historical development of western Asia and Egypt.

Lancel, Serge. *Carthage: A History.* 1997. A wide-ranging treatment of Carthaginian history and civilization.

Lesko, Barbara, ed. *Women's Earliest Records: From Ancient Egypt and Western Asia.* 1989. A collection of papers on the experiences of women in the ancient Middle East.

Markoe, Glenn. *Phoenicians.* 2000. A general introduction to the Phoenicians in their homeland.

Pritchard, James B., ed. *Ancient Near Eastern Texts Relating to the Old Testament*, 3rd ed. 1969. A large collection of primary texts in translation from ancient western Asia and Egypt.

Saggs, H. F. W. *Babylonians*. 1995. Devotes several chapters to this more thinly documented epoch in the history of southern Mesopotamia.

Sandars, N. K. *The Sea Peoples: Warriors of the Ancient Mediterranean*. 1978. Explores the disruptions and destructions in the eastern Mediterranean in the Late Bronze Age.

Sasson, Jack M., ed. *Civilizations of the Ancient Near East*, 4 vols. 1995. Fundamental for all periods in the ancient Middle East, with nearly two hundred articles by contemporary experts and bibliography on a wide range of topics.

Shanks, Hershel, ed. *Ancient Israel: From Abraham to the Roman Destruction of the Temple* (revised and expanded edition). 1999. A general historical introduction to Israel throughout antiquity, with chapters written by leading experts.

NOTES

1. Plutarch, *Moralia*, 799 D, trans. B. H. Warmington, *Carthage* (Harmondsworth, England: Penguin, 1960), 163.

AP* REVIEW QUESTIONS FOR CHAPTER 3

1. Many historians believe that the Hittites were the first civilization to develop the use of
   (A) iron.
   (B) cuneiform.
   (C) step pyramids.
   (D) ceramics.

2. Akhenaten's attempts to reform Egypt and reaffirm the power of the king over the priests have led many historians to believe that he supported
   (A) exiling the priests.
   (B) making the king a divine being.
   (C) returning the capital to Thebes.
   (D) making a truce with the Hittites.

3. In Mycenaean society, the government bureaucracy
   (A) maintained a high degree of control over the economy.
   (B) recorded daily events.
   (C) maintained no financial records.
   (D) contained no scribes.

4. The Assyrian Empire is considered the first true empire because
   (A) it was one cohesive group of people.
   (B) it conquered Egypt, which had been the greatest civilization up to that time.
   (C) its use of iron technology was the most sophisticated for the time.
   (D) it was the first to rule over far-flung lands and diverse peoples.

5. As a way to break up rebellious communities, the Assyrians
   (A) encouraged defeated communities to intermarry with the Assyrians.
   (B) employed mass deportations from one portion of the empire to another.
   (C) allowed for significant amounts of self-determination among the conquered people.
   (D) traded them as slaves.

6. While ancient Israel was a crossroads of trade, it had an inherent weakness because
   (A) it was too close to Egypt.
   (B) it was located in Semitic lands.
   (C) it had few natural resources.
   (D) its people spoke a different language than those around it.

7. The Israelite monarchy reached its peak with the reign of
   (A) David.
   (B) Sargon.
   (C) Solomon.
   (D) Moses.

8. The capture of Jerusalem, the destruction of Solomon's temple, and the beginning of the Diaspora took place at the hands of the
   (A) Philistines.
   (B) Egyptians.
   (C) Carthaginians.
   (D) Babylonians.

9. The movement of the Phoenicians into the coastal region of the western Mediterranean Sea was likely caused by
   (A) Assyrian aggression and the growth of the Assyrian Empire.
   (B) good trade relations with Greece and Carthage.
   (C) access to water resources.
   (D) access to Egyptian trade routes.

10. Trade was such an important aspect of Carthaginian life that
    (A) it was not taxed.
    (B) the Carthaginians ruled their empire indirectly.
    (C) the Carthaginians did not require military service.
    (D) the Carthaginians did not conquer neighbors for fear of upsetting trade relationships.

11. Which of the following is an accurate assessment of the Assyrians?
    (A) While they were a large empire, they did not impact trade in the region.
    (B) They were the most important factor in the transformation of the ancient Middle East.
    (C) Their collapse was swift, indicating their weakness as a military power.
    (D) They conquered mainly pastoralist societies and were not able to defeat more advanced peoples.

ANIMAL DOMESTICATION

Because the earliest domestication of plants and animals took place long before the existence of written records, we cannot be sure how and when humans first learned to plant crops and make use of tamed animals. Historians usually link the two processes as part of a Neolithic Revolution, but they were not necessarily connected.

The domestication of plants is much better understood than the domestication of animals. Foraging bands of humans primarily lived on wild seeds, fruits, and tubers. Eventually some humans tried planting seeds and tubers, favoring varieties that they particularly liked, and a variety that may have been rare in the wild became more common. When such a variety suited human needs, usually by having more food value or being easier to grow or process, people stopped collecting the wild types and relied on farming and further developing their new domestic type.

In the case of animals, the basis of selection to suit human needs is less apparent. Experts looking at ancient bones and images interpret changes in hair color, horn shape, and other visible features as indicators of domestication. But these visible changes did not generally serve human purposes. It is usually assumed that animals were domesticated for their meat, but even this is questionable. Dogs, which may have become domestic tens of thousands of years before any other species, were not eaten in most cultures, and cats, which became domestic much later, were eaten even less often. As for the uses most commonly associated with domestic animals, some of the most important, such as milking cows, shearing sheep, and harnessing oxen and horses to pull plows and vehicles, first appeared hundreds and even thousands of years after domestication.

Cattle, sheep, and goats became domestic around ten thousand years ago in the Middle East and North Africa. Coincidentally, wheat and barley were being domesticated at roughly the same time in the same general area. This is the main reason historians generally conclude that plant and animal domestication are closely related. Yet other major meat animals, such as chickens, which originated as jungle fowl in Southeast Asia, and pigs, which probably became domestic separately in several parts of North Africa, Europe, and Asia, have no agreed-upon association with early plant domestication. Nor is plant domestication connected with the horses and camels that became domestic in western Asia and the donkeys that became domestic in the Sahara region around six thousand years ago. Moreover, though the wild forebears of these species were probably eaten, the domestic forms were usually not used for meat.

In the Middle East humans may have originally kept wild sheep, goats, and cattle for food, though wild cattle were large and dangerous and must have been hard to control. It is questionable whether, in the earliest stages, keeping these animals captive for food would have been more productive than hunting. It is even more questionable whether the humans who kept animals for this purpose had any reason to anticipate that life in captivity would cause them to become domestic.

Human motivations for domesticating animals can be better assessed after a consideration of the physical changes involved in going from wild to domestic. Genetically transmitted tameness, defined as the ability to live with and accept handling by humans, lies at the core of the domestication process. In separate experiments with wild rats and foxes in the twentieth century, scientists found that wild individuals with strong fight-or-flight tendencies reproduce poorly in captivity, whereas individuals with the lowest adrenaline levels have the most offspring in captivity. In the wild, the same low level of excitability would have made these individuals vulnerable to predators and kept their reproduction rate down. However, early humans probably preferred the animals that seemed the tamest and destroyed those that were most wild. In the rat and fox experiments, after twenty generations or so, the surviving animals were born with much smaller adrenal glands and greatly reduced fight-or-flight reactions. Since adrenaline production normally increases in the transition to adulthood, many of the low-adrenaline animals also retained juvenile characteristics, such as floppy ears and pushed-in snouts, both indicators of domestication.

Historians disagree about whether animal domestication was a deliberate process or the unanticipated outcome of keeping animals for other purposes. Some assume that domestication was an understood and reproducible process. Others argue that, since a twenty-generation time span for wild cattle and other large quadrupeds would have amounted to several human lifetimes, it is unlikely that the people who ended up with domestic cows had any recollection of how the process started. This would also rule out the possibility that people who had unwittingly domesticated one species would have attempted to repeat the process with other species, since they did not know what they and their ancestors had done to produce genetically transmitted tameness.

Historians who assume that domestication was an understood and reproducible process tend to conclude that humans domesticated every species that could be domesticated. This is unlikely. Twentieth-century efforts to domesticate bison, eland, and elk have not fully succeeded, but they have generally not been maintained for as long as twenty generations. Rats and foxes have more rapid reproduction rates, and the experiments with them succeeded.

Animal domestication is probably best studied on a case-by-case basis as an unintended result of other processes. In some instances, sacrifice probably played a key role. Religious traditions of animal sacrifice rarely utilize, and sometimes prohibit, the ritual killing of wild animals. It is reasonable to suppose that the practice of capturing wild animals and holding them for sacrifice eventually led to the appearance of genetically transmitted tameness as an unplanned result.

Horses and camels were domesticated relatively late, and most likely not for meat consumption. The societies within which these animals first appeared as domestic species already had domestic sheep, goats, and cattle for meat, and they used oxen to carry loads and pull plows and carts. Horses, camels, and later reindeer may represent successful experiments with substituting one draft animal for another, with genetically transmitted tameness an unexpected consequence of separating animals trained for riding or pulling carts from their wilder kin.

Once human societies had developed the full range of uses of domestic animals—meat, eggs, milk, fiber, labor, transport—the likelihood of domesticating more species diminished. In the absence of concrete knowledge of how domestication had occurred, it was usually easier for people to move domestic livestock to new locations than to attempt to develop new domestic species. Domestic animals accompanied human groups wherever they ventured, and this practice triggered enormous environmental changes as domestic animals, and their human keepers, competed with wild species for food and living space.

PART II

CHAPTER 4 **Greece and Iran, 1000–30 B.C.E.**

CHAPTER 5 **An Age of Empires: Rome and Han China, 753 B.C.E.–600 C.E.**

CHAPTER 6 **India and Southeast Asia, 1500 B.C.E.–600 C.E.**

Austrian National Library, picture archives, Vienna: Cod. 324, Segm. VII–VIII

Map of the Roman World, ca. 250 C.E. **The Peutinger Table, drawn on a 22-foot-long manuscript of the twelfth century C.E., is ultimately derived from a map of the world as known to inhabitants of the Roman Empire ca. 100 C.E. This portion depicts (from top to bottom) southern Russia, Greece on the left, Anatolia on the right, the island of Crete, and the north coast of Africa. The main purpose appears to have been to show roads and distances, and sizes and geographical relationships of places are often distorted.**

The Formation of New Cultural Communities, 1000 B.C.E.–600 C.E.

From 1000 B.C.E. to 600 C.E. important changes in the ways of life established in the river-valley civilizations in the two previous millennia occurred, and the scale of human institutions and activities increased. On the shores of the Mediterranean and in Iran, India, and Southeast Asia, new centers arose in lands watered by rainfall and worked by a free peasantry. These societies developed new patterns of political and social organization and economic activity, and they moved in new intellectual, artistic, and spiritual directions.

The rulers of the empires of this era constructed extensive networks of roads and promoted urbanization. These measures brought more rapid communication, trade over greater distances, and the broad diffusion of religious ideas, artistic styles, and technologies. Large cultural zones unified by common traditions emerged—Iranian, Hellenistic, Roman, Hindu, and Chinese—and exercised substantial influence on subsequent ages.

The expansion of agriculture and trade and improvements in technology led to population increases, the spread of cities, and the growth of a comfortable middle class. In many places iron replaced bronze as the preferred metal for weapons, tools, and utensils, and metals were available to more people than in the preceding age. People using iron tools cleared extensive forests around the Mediterranean, in India, and in eastern China. Iron weapons gave an advantage to the armies of Greece, Rome, and imperial China.

New systems of writing, more easily and rapidly learned, moved the preservation and transmission of knowledge out of the control of specialists and gave birth to new ways of thinking, new genres of literature, and new types of scientific endeavor.

CHAPTER

4

CHAPTER OUTLINE

- Ancient Iran, 1000–486 B.C.E.
- The Rise of the Greeks, 1000–500 B.C.E.
- The Struggle of Persia and Greece, 546–323 B.C.E.
- The Hellenistic Synthesis, 323–30 B.C.E.
- Conclusion

DIVERSITY + DOMINANCE *Persian and Greek Perceptions of Kingship*

MATERIAL CULTURE *Wine and Beer in the Ancient World*

ENVIRONMENT + TECHNOLOGY *Ancient Astronomy*

Bibliotheque nationale de France

Painted Cup of Arcesilas of Cyrene The ruler of this Greek community in North Africa supervises the weighing and export of silphium, a valuable medicinal plant.

Visit the website and ebook for additional study materials and interactive tools: www.cengage.com/history/bullietearthpeople5e

Greece and Iran, 1000–30 B.C.E.

- How did the Persian Empire rise from its Iranian homeland and succeed in controlling vast territories and diverse cultures?
- What were the distinctive beliefs, philosophies, and arts of Greek civilization and how and why did they evolve in the Archaic and Classical periods?
- How did the Persian Wars and their aftermath affect the politics and culture of ancient Greece and Iran?
- How did Greeks and non-Greeks interact and develop new cultural syntheses during the Hellenistic Age?

The Greek historian Herodotus (heh-ROD-uh-tuhs) (ca. 485–425 B.C.E.) describes a famine on the island of Thera in the Aegean Sea in the seventh century B.C.E. It caused the desperate inhabitants to send out a portion of the young men to found a new settlement on the coast of North Africa (modern Libya) called Cyrene. This is one of our best descriptions of the process by which Greeks spread from their homeland to many parts of the Mediterranean and Black Seas between the eighth and sixth centuries B.C.E., carrying their language, technology, and culture with them. Cyrene became a large and prosperous city-state, largely thanks to its exports of silphium—a plant valued for its medicinal properties—as seen on this painted cup with an image of Arcesilas, the ruler of Cyrene, supervising the weighing and transport of the product.

Greek Cyrene quietly submitted to the Persian king Cambyses (kam-BIE-sees) in the 520s B.C.E., in one of the more peaceful encounters of the city-states of Greece with the Persian Empire. This event reminds us that the Persian Empire (and the Hellenistic Greek kingdoms that succeeded it) brought together, in eastern Europe, western Asia, and northwest Africa, peoples and cultural systems that had little direct contact previously, thereby stimulating new cultural syntheses. The claim often has been made that the rivalry and wars of Greeks and Persians from the sixth to fourth centuries B.C.E. were the first act of a drama that has continued intermittently ever since: the clash of the civilizations of East and West, of two peoples and two ways of life that were fundamentally different and almost certain to come into conflict. Some see current tensions between the United States and Middle Eastern states such as Iran, Iraq, and Afghanistan as the latest manifestation of this age-old conflict.

Ironically, Greeks and Persians had more in common than they realized. Both spoke languages belonging to the same Indo-European language family found throughout Europe and western and southern Asia. Many scholars believe that all the ancient peoples who spoke languages belonging to this family inherited fundamental cultural traits, forms of social organization, and religious outlooks from their shared past.

ANCIENT IRAN, 1000–486 B.C.E.

Iran, the "land of the Aryans," links western Asia with southern and Central Asia, and its history has been marked by this mediating position (see Map 4.1). In the sixth century B.C.E. the vigorous Persians of southwest Iran created the largest empire the world had yet seen. Heirs to the long legacy of Mesopotamian culture, they introduced distinctly Iranian elements and developed new forms of political and economic organization in western Asia.

Relatively little written material from within the Persian Empire has survived, so we are forced to view it mostly through the eyes of the ancient Greeks—outsiders who were ignorant at best, often hostile, and interested primarily in events that affected themselves. (Iranian groups and individuals are known in the Western world by Greek approximations of their names; thus these familiar forms are used here, with the original Iranian names given in parentheses.) This Greek perspective leaves us less informed about developments in the central and eastern portions of the Persian Empire. Nevertheless, recent archaeological discoveries and close analysis of the limited written material from within the empire can supplement and correct the perspective of the Greek sources.

Geography and Resources

Iran is bounded by the Zagros (ZUHG-roes) Mountains to the west, the Caucasus (KAW-kuh-suhs) Mountains and Caspian Sea to the northwest and north, the mountains of Afghanistan and the desert of Baluchistan (buh-loo-chi-STAN) to the east and southeast, and the Persian Gulf to the southwest. The northeast is less protected by natural boundaries, and from that direction Iran was open to attacks by the nomads of Central Asia.

e Interactive Map

MAP 4.1 The Persian Empire Between 550 and 522 B.C.E., the Persians of southwest Iran, under their first two kings, Cyrus and Cambyses, conquered each of the major states of western Asia—Media, Babylonia, Lydia, and Egypt. The third king, Darius I, extended the boundaries as far as the Indus Valley to the east and the European shore of the Black Sea to the west. The first major setback came when the fourth king, Xerxes, failed in his invasion of Greece in 480 B.C.E. The Persian Empire was considerably larger than its predecessor, the Assyrian Empire. For their empire, the Persian rulers developed a system of provinces, governors, regular tribute, and communication by means of royal roads and couriers that allowed for efficient operations for two centuries.

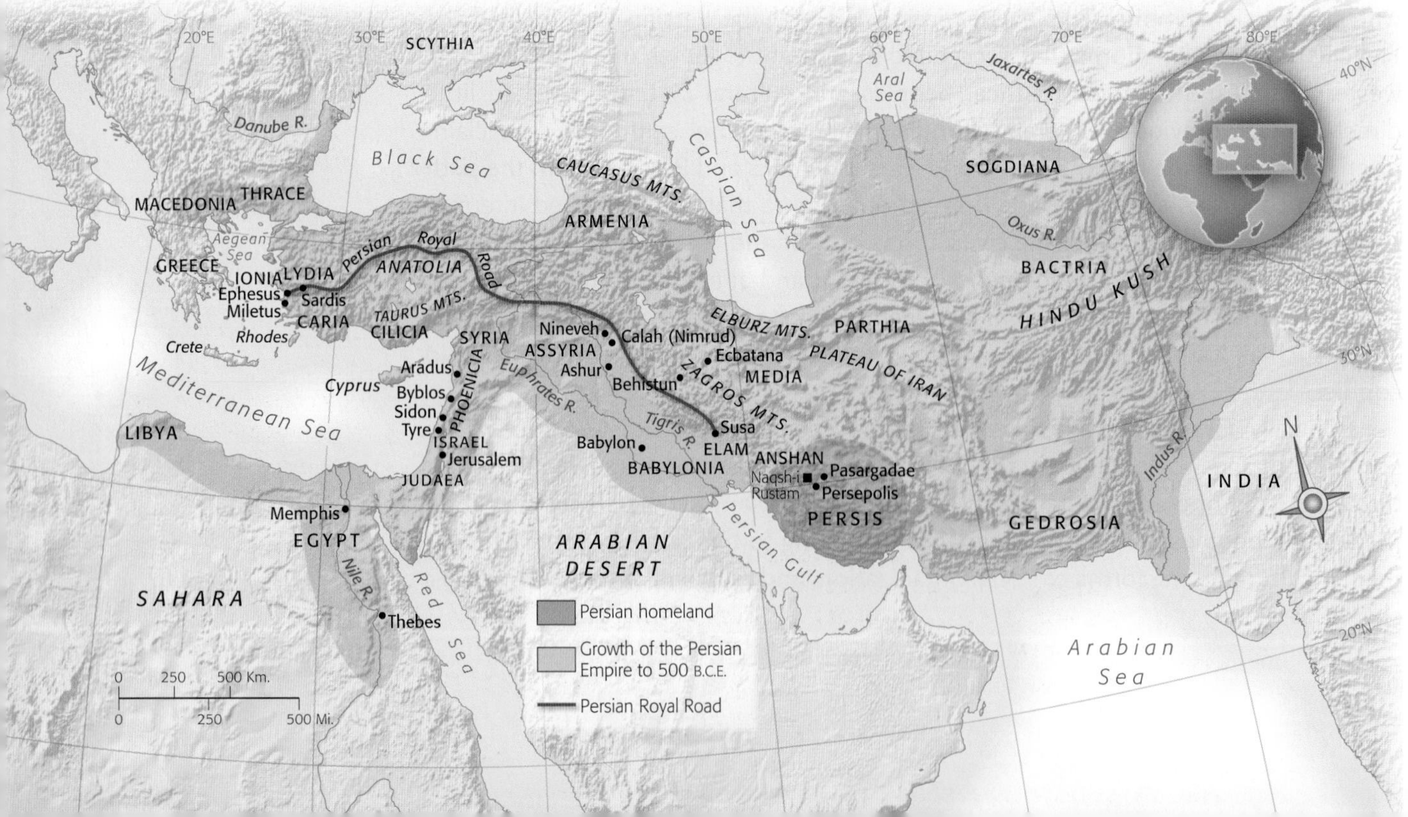

CHRONOLOGY

	Greece and the Hellenistic World	Persian Empire
1000 B.C.E.	1150–800 B.C.E. Greece's "Dark Age"	ca. 1000 B.C.E. Persians settle in southwest Iran
800 B.C.E.	ca. 800 B.C.E. Resumption of Greek contact with eastern Mediterranean	
	800–480 B.C.E. Greece's Archaic period	
	ca. 750–550 B.C.E. Era of colonization	
	ca. 700 B.C.E. Beginning of hoplite warfare	
600 B.C.E.	ca. 650–500 B.C.E. Era of tyrants	
	594 B.C.E. Solon reforms laws at Athens	
		550 B.C.E. Cyrus overthrows Medes
	546–510 B.C.E. Pisistratus and sons hold tyranny at Athens	550–530 B.C.E. Reign of Cyrus
		546 B.C.E. Cyrus conquers Lydia
		539 B.C.E. Cyrus takes control of Babylonia
		530–522 B.C.E. Reign of Cambyses; Conquest of Egypt
		522–486 B.C.E. Reign of Darius
500 B.C.E.	499–494 B.C.E. Ionian Greeks rebel against Persia	
	490 B.C.E. Athenians check Persian punitive expedition at Marathon	
	480–323 B.C.E. Greece's Classical period	480–479 B.C.E. Xerxes' invasion of Greece
	477 B.C.E. Athens becomes leader of Delian League	
	461–429 B.C.E. Pericles dominant at Athens; Athens completes evolution to democracy	
	431–404 B.C.E. Peloponnesian War	
400 B.C.E.	399 B.C.E. Trial and execution of Socrates	387 B.C.E. King's Peace makes Persia arbiter of Greek affairs
	359 B.C.E. Philip II becomes king of Macedonia	
	338 B.C.E. Philip takes control of Greece	334–323 B.C.E. Alexander the Great defeats Persia and creates huge empire
		323–30 B.C.E. Hellenistic period
300 B.C.E.	ca. 300 B.C.E. Foundation of the Museum in Alexandria	
	200 B.C.E. First Roman intervention in the Hellenistic East	
100 B.C.E.		
	30 B.C.E. Roman annexation of Egypt, the last Hellenistic kingdom	

The fundamental topographical features of Iran are high mountains at the edges, salt deserts in the interior depressions, and mountain streams draining into interior salt lakes and marshes. Ancient Iran never had a dense population. The best-watered and most populous parts of the country lie to the north and west; aridity increases and population decreases as one moves south and east. On the interior plateau, oasis settlements sprang up beside streams or springs. The Great Salt Desert, which covers most of eastern Iran, and Baluchistan in the southeast corner were extremely inhospitable. Scattered settlements in the narrow plains beside the Persian Gulf were cut off from the interior plateau by mountain barriers.

In the first millennium B.C.E. irrigation enabled people to move down from the mountain valleys and open the plains to agriculture. To prevent evaporation of precious water in the hot, dry climate, they devised underground irrigation channels. Constructing and maintaining these channels and the vertical shafts that provided access to them was labor-intensive. Normally, local leaders oversaw the expansion of the network in each district. Activity accelerated when a strong central authority organized large numbers of laborers. Even so, human survival depended on a delicate ecological balance, and a buildup of salt in the soil or a falling water table sometimes forced the abandonment of settlements.

Iran's mineral resources—copper, tin, iron, gold, and silver—were exploited on a limited scale in antiquity. Mountain slopes, more heavily wooded than they are now, provided fuel and materials for building and crafts. Because this austere land could not generate much of an agricultural surplus, objects of trade tended to be minerals and crafted goods such as textiles and carpets.

The Rise of the Persian Empire

Iranians, Medes, and Persians

In antiquity many groups of people, whom historians refer to collectively as "Iranians" because they spoke related languages and shared certain cultural features, spread across western and Central Asia—an area comprising not only the modern state of Iran but also Turkmenistan, Afghanistan, and Pakistan. Several of these groups arrived in western Iran near the end of the second millennium B.C.E. The first to achieve a complex level of political organization were the Medes (*Mada* in Iranian). They settled in the northwest and came under the influence of the ancient centers in Mesopotamia and Urartu (modern Armenia and northeast Turkey). The Medes played a major role in the destruction of the Assyrian Empire in the late seventh century B.C.E. According to Greek sources, Median kings extended their control westward across Assyria into Anatolia (modern Turkey) and also southeast toward the Persian Gulf, a region occupied by another Iranian people, the Persians (*Parsa*). However, some scholars doubt the Greek testimony about a well-organized Median kingdom controlling such extensive territories.

Cyrus Founder of the Achaemenid Persian Empire. Between 550 and 530 B.C.E. he conquered Media, Lydia, and Babylon. Revered in the traditions of both Iran and the subject peoples, he employed Persians and Medes in his administration and respected the institutions and beliefs of subject peoples.

The Persian rulers—called Achaemenids (a-KEY-muh-nid) because they traced their lineage back to an ancestor named Achaemenes—cemented their relationship with the Median court through marriage. **Cyrus** (*Kurush*), the son of a Persian chieftain and a Median princess, united the various Persian tribes and overthrew the Median monarch around 550 B.C.E. His victory should perhaps be seen less as a conquest than as an alteration of the relations between groups, for Cyrus placed both Medes and Persians in positions of responsibility and retained the framework of Median rule. The differences between these two Iranian peoples were not great, and the Greeks could not readily tell them apart.

The early inhabitants of western Iran had a patriarchal family organization: The male head of the household had nearly absolute authority over family members. Society was divided into three social and occupational classes: warriors, priests, and peasants. Warriors were the dominant element. A landowning aristocracy, they took pleasure in hunting, fighting, and gardening.

Gold Model of Four-Horse Chariot from the Eastern Achaemenid Empire This model is part of the Oxus Treasure, a cache of gold and silver objects discovered in Tajikistan. Seated on a bench next to the chariot driver, the main figure wears a long robe, a hood, and a torque around his neck, the garb of a Persian noble. It is uncertain whether this model was a child's toy or a votive offering to a deity.

The king was the most illustrious member of this group. The priests, or Magi (*magush*), were ritual specialists who supervised the proper performance of sacrifices. The common people—peasants—were primarily village-based farmers and shepherds.

Early Rulers and Conquests

Over the course of two decades the energetic Cyrus (r. 550–530 B.C.E.) redrew the map of western Asia. In 546 B.C.E. he defeated the kingdom of Lydia, and all Anatolia, including the Greek city-states on the western coast, came under Persian control. In 539 B.C.E. he swept into Mesopotamia and overthrew the Neo-Babylonian dynasty that had ruled since the decline of Assyrian power (see Chapter 3). A skillful propagandist, Cyrus showed respect to the Babylonian priesthood and native traditions.

After Cyrus lost his life in 530 B.C.E. while campaigning against nomadic Iranians in the northeast, his son Cambyses (*Kambujiya*, r. 530–522 B.C.E.) set his sights on Egypt, the last of the great ancient kingdoms of the Middle East. The Persians prevailed in a series of bloody battles, then sent exploratory expeditions south to Nubia and west to Libya. Greek sources depict Cambyses as a cruel and impious madman, but contemporary documents from Egypt show him operating in the same practical vein as his father, cultivating local priests and notables and respecting native traditions.

Darius I Third ruler of the Persian Empire (r. 521–486 B.C.E.). He crushed the widespread initial resistance to his rule and gave all major government posts to Persians rather than to Medes. He established a system of provinces and tribute, began construction of Persepolis, and expanded Persian control in the east (Pakistan) and west (northern Greece).

When Cambyses died in 522 B.C.E., a Persian nobleman distantly related to the royal family, **Darius I** (duh-RIE-uhs) (*Darayavaush*), seized the throne. His success in crushing many early challenges to his rule testifies to his skill, energy, and ruthlessness. From this reign forward, Medes played a lesser role, and the most important posts went to members of leading Persian families. Darius (r. 522–486 B.C.E.) extended Persian control eastward as far as the Indus Valley and westward into Europe, where he bridged the Danube River and chased the nomadic Scythian (SITH-ee-uhn) peoples north of the Black Sea. The Persians erected a string of forts in Thrace (modern-day northeast Greece and Bulgaria) and by 500 B.C.E. were on the doorstep of Greece. Darius also promoted the development of maritime routes. He dispatched a fleet to explore the waters from the Indus Delta to the Red Sea, and he completed a canal linking the Red Sea with the Nile.

Imperial Organization

Darius's Reorganization of the Empire

AP* Exam Tip The imperial organization of ancient Persia is important information to know.

The empire of Darius I was the largest the world had yet seen (see Map 4.1). Stretching from eastern Europe and Libya to Pakistan, from southern Russia to Sudan, it encompassed multiple ethnic groups and many forms of social and political organization. Darius can rightly be considered a second founder of the Persian Empire, after Cyrus, because he created a new organizational structure that was maintained throughout the remaining two centuries of the empire's existence.

satrap The governor of a province in the Achaemenid Persian Empire, often a relative of the king. He was responsible for protection of the province and for forwarding tribute to the central administration. Satraps in outlying provinces enjoyed considerable autonomy.

Darius divided the empire into about twenty provinces, each under the supervision of a Persian **satrap** (SAY-trap), or governor, who was often related or connected by marriage to the royal family. The satrap's court was a miniature version of the royal court. The tendency for the position of satrap to become hereditary meant that satraps' families lived in the province governed by their head, acquired knowledge about local conditions, and formed connections with the local elite. The farther a province was from the center of the empire, the more autonomy the satrap had, because slow communications made it impractical to refer most matters to the central administration.

One of the satrap's most important duties was to collect and send tribute to the king. Darius prescribed how much precious metal each province was to contribute annually. Some of it was disbursed for necessary expenditures, but most was hoarded. As precious metal was taken out of circulation, the price of gold and silver rose, and provinces found it increasingly difficult to meet their quotas. Evidence from Babylonia indicates a gradual economic decline setting in by the fourth century B.C.E. The increasing burden of taxation and official corruption may have inadvertently caused the economic downturn.

Well-maintained and patrolled royal roads connected the outlying provinces to the heart of the empire. Way stations were built at intervals to receive important travelers and couriers carrying official correspondence. Military garrisons controlled strategic points, such as mountain passes, river crossings, and important urban centers.

The Royal Court

The king had numerous wives and children. Women of the royal family could become pawns in the struggle for power, as when Darius strengthened his claim to the throne by marrying two daughters and a granddaughter of Cyrus. Greek sources portray Persian queens as vicious intriguers, poisoning rival wives and plotting to win the throne for their sons. However, a recent study suggests that the Greek stereotype misrepresents the important role played by Persian women in protecting family members and mediating conflicts.[1] Both Greek sources and documents within the empire reveal that Persian elite women were politically influential, possessed substantial property, traveled, and were prominent on public occasions.

The king and his court moved with the seasons, living in luxurious tents on the road and in palaces in the ancient capitals of Mesopotamia and Iran. Besides the royal family, the king's large entourage included several other groups: (1) the sons of Persian aristocrats, who were educated at court and also served as hostages for their parents' good behavior; (2) many noblemen, who were expected to attend the king when they were not otherwise engaged; (3) the central administration, including officials and employees of the treasury, secretariat, and archives; (4) the royal bodyguard; and (5) countless courtiers and slaves. Long gone were the simple days when the king hunted and caroused with his warrior companions. Inspired by Mesopotamian conceptions of monarchy, the king of Persia had become an aloof figure of majesty and splendor: "The Great King, King of Kings, King in Persia, King of countries." He referred to everyone, even the Persian nobility, as "my slaves," and anyone who approached him had to bow down before him.

The king owned vast tracts of land throughout the empire. Some of it he gave to his supporters. Donations called "bow land," "horse land," and "chariot land" in Babylonian documents obliged the recipient to provide the corresponding form of military service. Scattered around the empire were gardens, orchards, and hunting preserves belonging to the king and high nobility. The *paradayadam* (meaning "walled enclosure"—the term has come into English as *paradise*), a green oasis in an arid landscape, advertised the prosperity that the king could bring to those who loyally served him.

Administration

Surviving administrative records from the Persian homeland reveal how the complex tasks of administration were managed. Government officials distributed food and other essential commodities to large numbers of workers of many different nationalities. Some of these workers may have been prisoners of war brought to the center of the empire to work on construction projects, maintain and expand the irrigation network, and farm the royal estates. Workers were divided into groups of men, women, and children. Women received less than men of equivalent status, but pregnant women and women with babies received additional support. Men and women performing skilled jobs received more than their unskilled counterparts. Administrators were provided with authorizations to requisition food and other necessities while traveling on official business.

The central administration was not based in the Persian homeland but closer to the geographical center of the empire, in Elam and Mesopotamia, where it could employ the trained administrators and scribes of those ancient civilizations. The administrative center of the empire was Susa, the ancient capital of Elam, in southwest Iran near the present-day border with Iraq. It was to Susa that Greeks and others went with requests and messages for the king. A party of Greek ambassadors would need at least three months to make the journey. Additional time spent waiting for an audience with the Persian king, delays due to weather, and the duration of the return trip probably kept the ambassadors away from home a year or more.

Persepolis A complex of palaces, reception halls, and treasury buildings erected by the Persian kings Darius I and Xerxes in the Persian homeland. It is believed that the New Year's festival was celebrated here, as well as the coronations, weddings, and funerals of the Persian kings, who were buried in cliff-tombs nearby.

However, on certain occasions the kings returned to one special place back in the homeland. Darius began construction of a ceremonial capital at **Persepolis** (per-SEH-poe-lis) (*Parsa*). An artificial platform was erected, and on it were built a series of palaces, audience halls, treasury buildings, and barracks. Here, too, Darius and his son Xerxes (ZERK-sees), who completed the project, were inspired by Mesopotamian traditions, for the great Assyrian kings had created new fortress-cities as advertisements of their wealth and power.

Ideology and Religion

Persepolis and the Vision of Empire

Darius's approach to governing can be seen in the luxuriant relief sculpture that covers the foundations, walls, and stairwells of the buildings at Persepolis. Representatives of all the peoples of the empire—recognizable by their distinctive hair, beards, dress, hats, and footwear—are depicted bringing gifts to the king. In this exercise in what today we would call public relations or propaganda, Darius crafted a vision of an empire of vast extent and abundant resources in which all the subject peoples willingly cooperate. On his tomb Darius subtly contrasted the

Courtesy of the Oriental Institute, University of Chicago

View of the East Front of the Apadana (Audience Hall) at Persepolis, ca. 500 B.C.E. Persepolis, in the Persian homeland, was built by Darius I and his son Xerxes, and it was used for ceremonies of special importance to the Persian king and people—coronations, royal weddings, funerals, and the New Year's festival. The stone foundations, walls, and stairways of Persepolis are filled with sculpted images of members of the court and embassies bringing gifts, offering a vision of the grandeur and harmony of the Persian Empire.

character of his rule with that of the Assyrian Empire, the Persians' predecessors in these lands (see Chapter 3). Where Assyrian kings had gloried in their power and depicted subjects staggering under the weight of a giant platform that supported the throne, Darius's artists showed erect subjects shouldering the burden willingly and without strain.

What actually took place at Persepolis? This opulent retreat in the homeland was the scene of events of special significance for the king and his people: the New Year's Festival, coronation, marriage, death, and burial. The kings from Darius on were buried in elaborate tombs cut into the cliffs at nearby Naqsh-i Rustam (NUHK-shee ROOS-tuhm).

Another perspective on what the Persian monarchy claimed to stand for is provided by several dozen royal inscriptions that have survived (see Diversity and Dominance: Persian and Greek Perceptions of Kingship). At Naqsh-i Rustam, Darius makes the following claim:

> *Ahuramazda* (ah-HOOR-uh-MAZZ-duh) *[the chief deity], when he saw this earth in commotion, thereafter bestowed it upon me, made me king. . . . By the favor of Ahuramazda I put it down in its place. . . . I am of such a sort that I am a friend to right, I am not a friend to wrong. It is not my desire that the weak man should have wrong done to him by the mighty; nor is that my desire, that the mighty man should have wrong done to him by the weak.*[2]

SECTION REVIEW

- The Medes and the Persians of western Iran created complex societies in the seventh and sixth centuries B.C.E. under Mesopotamian influence.
- Cyrus, the founder of the Achaemenid Persian Empire, conquered most of western Asia, while his son Cambyses captured Egypt.
- Darius was a second founder of the empire, creating new systems for administration and collection of tribute.
- The king and his large entourage moved among several imperial centers: Susa was the administrative capital, and Persepolis in the homeland was the site of royal ceremonials.
- Darius was a brilliant propagandist, adapting Zoroastrian religious teachings to create an ideology justifying the empire.
- Zoroastrianism was one of the great religions of the ancient world, holding people to a high ethical standard, and may have influenced Judaism and Christianity.

DIVERSITY + DOMINANCE

Persian and Greek Perceptions of Kingship

An important internal source of information about the Persian Empire are the inscriptions commissioned by several kings. They provide valuable insights into how the kings conceived of the empire and their position as monarch, as well as the values they claimed to uphold. Darius carved the longest text into a cliff face at Behistun (beh-HISS-toon)*, high above the road leading from Mesopotamia to northwest Iran.*

I am Darius, the great king, king of kings, the king of Persia, the king of countries, the son of Hystaspes, the grandson of Arsames, the Achaemenid . . . from antiquity we have been noble; from antiquity has our dynasty been royal. . . .

King Darius says: By the grace of Ahuramazda am I king; Ahuramazda has granted me the kingdom.

King Darius says: These are the countries which are subject unto me, and by the grace of Ahuramazda I became king of them: Persia, Elam, Babylonia, Assyria, Arabia, Egypt, the countries by the Sea, Lydia, the Greeks, Media, Armenia, Cappadocia, Parthia, Drangiana, Aria, Chorasmia, Bactria, Sogdiana, Gandara, Scythia, Sattagydia, Arachosia and Maka; twenty-three lands in all.

King Darius says: These are the countries which are subject to me; by the grace of Ahuramazda they became subject to me; they brought tribute unto me. Whatsoever commands have been laid on them by me, by night or by day, have been performed by them.

King Darius says: Within these lands, whosoever was a friend, him have I surely protected; whosoever was hostile, him have I utterly destroyed. . . .

King Darius says: As to these provinces which revolted, lies made them revolt, so that they deceived the people. Then Ahuramazda delivered them into my hand; and I did unto them according to my will.

King Darius says: You who shall be king hereafter, protect yourself vigorously from lies; punish the liars well, if thus you shall think, "May my country be secure!" . . .

King Darius says: On this account Ahuramazda brought me help, and all the other gods, all that there are, because I was not wicked, nor was I a liar, nor was I a tyrant, neither I nor any of my family. I have ruled according to righteousness. . . .

Another document, found at Persepolis, expands on the qualities of an exemplary ruler. Although it purports to be the words of Xerxes, it is almost an exact copy of an inscription of Darius, illustrating the continuity of concepts through several reigns.

A great god is Ahuramazda, who created this excellent thing which is seen, who created happiness for man, who set wisdom and capability down upon King Xerxes. . . .

The right, that is my desire. To the man who is a follower of the lie I am no friend. I am not hot-tempered. Whatever befalls me in battle, I hold firmly. I am ruling firmly my own will.

The man who is cooperative, according to his cooperation thus I reward him. Who does harm, him according to the harm I punish. It is not my wish that a man should do harm; nor indeed is it my wish that if he does harm he should not be punished. . . .

What a man does or performs, according to his ability, by that I become satisfied with him, and it is much to my desire, and I am well pleased, and I give much to loyal men. . . .

The royal inscriptions are certainly propaganda, but that does not mean they lack validity. To be effective, propaganda must be predicated on the moral values, political principles, and religious beliefs that are familiar and acceptable in a society, and thus it can provide us with a window on those views. The inscriptions also allow us to glimpse the personalities of Darius and Xerxes and how they wished to be perceived.

The Greek historian Herodotus creates a vivid portrait of Xerxes in his account of Xerxes' invasion of Greece in 480 B.C.E. He is drawing on information derived from Greeks who served in the Persian army, as well as the proud popular traditions of the Greek states that successfully resisted the invasion.

In this city Pythius son of Atys, a Lydian, sat awaiting them; he entertained Xerxes himself and all the king's army with the greatest hospitality, and declared himself willing to provide money for the war. . . . Xerxes was pleased with what he said and replied: "My Lydian friend, since I came out of Persia I have so far met with no man who was willing to give hospitality to my army, nor who came into my presence unsummoned and

Zoroastrianism A religion originating in ancient Iran that became the official religion of the Achaemenids. It centered on a single benevolent deity, Ahuramazda, who engaged in a struggle with demonic forces before prevailing and restoring a pristine world. It emphasized truth-telling, purity, and reverence for nature.

As this inscription makes clear, behind Darius and the empire stands the will of god. Ahuramazda made Darius king, giving him a mandate to bring order to a world in turmoil and ensure that all people be treated justly. Ahuramazda is the great god of a religion called **Zoroastrianism** (zo-roe-ASS-tree-uh-niz-uhm), and it is probable that Darius and his successors were Zoroastrians.

The origins of this religion are shrouded in uncertainty. The *Gathas*, hymns in an archaic Iranian dialect, are said to be the work of Zoroaster (zo-roe-ASS-ter) (*Zarathushtra*), who probably lived in eastern Iran sometime between 1700 and 500 B.C.E. He revealed that the world had been created by Ahuramazda, "the wise lord," but its original state of perfection and unity had been badly damaged by the attacks of Angra Mainyu (ANG-ruh MINE-yoo), "the hostile spirit," backed by a host of demons. The struggle between good and evil plays out over offered to furnish money for the war, besides you. But you have entertained my army nobly and offer me great sums. In return for this I give you these privileges: I make you my friend. . . . Remain in possession of what you now possess, and be mindful to be always such as you are; neither for the present nor in time will you regret what you now do.". . .

[some time later] As Xerxes led his army away, Pythius the Lydian, . . . encouraged by the gifts that he had received, came to Xerxes and said, "Master, I have a favor to ask that I desire of you, easy for you to grant and precious for me to receive." Xerxes supposed that Pythius would demand anything rather than what he did ask and answered that he would grant the request, bidding him declare what he desired. When Pythius heard this, he took courage and said: "Master, I have five sons, and all of them are constrained to march with you against Hellas. I pray you, O king, take pity on me in my advanced age, and release one of my sons, the eldest, from service, so that he may take care of me and of my possessions; take the four others with you, and may you return back with all your plans accomplished." Xerxes became very angry and thus replied: "Villain, you see me marching against Hellas myself, and taking with me my sons and brothers and relations and friends; do you, my slave, who should have followed me with all your household and your very wife, speak to me of your son? Be well assured of this, that a man's spirit dwells in his ears; when it hears good words it fills the whole body with delight, but when it hears the opposite it swells with anger. When you did me good service and promised more, you will never boast that you outdid your king in the matter of benefits; and now that you have turned aside to the way of shamelessness, you will receive a lesser requital than you merit. You and four of your sons are saved by your hospitality; but you shall be punished by the life of that one you most desire to keep." With that reply, he immediately ordered those who were assigned to do these things to find the eldest of Pythius's sons and cut him in half, then to set one half of his body on the right side of the road and the other on the left, so that the army would pass between them.

Xerxes has ordered a bridge to be built to transport his troops over the Hellespont strait.

The men who had been given this assignment made bridges starting from Abydos across to that headland; the Phoenicians one of flaxen cables, and the Egyptians a papyrus one.

From Abydos to the opposite shore it is a distance of seven stadia. But no sooner had the strait been bridged than a great storm swept down, breaking and scattering everything. When Xerxes heard of this, he was very angry and commanded that the Hellespont be whipped with three hundred lashes, and a pair of fetters be thrown into the sea. I have even heard that he sent branders with them to brand the Hellespont. He commanded them while they whipped to utter words outlandish and presumptuous, "Bitter water, our master thus punishes you, because you did him wrong though he had done you none. Xerxes the king will pass over you, whether you want it or not; in accordance with justice no one offers you sacrifice, for you are a turbid and briny river." He commanded that the sea receive these punishments and that the overseers of the bridge over the Hellespont be beheaded.

QUESTIONS FOR ANALYSIS

1. **How does Darius justify his assumption of power in the Behistun inscription? What is his relationship to Ahuramazda, the Zoroastrian god, and what role does divinity play in human affairs?**
2. **How does Darius conceptualize his empire (look at a map and follow the order in which he lists the provinces), and what are the expectations and obligations that he places on his subjects? What does his characterization of his opponents as liars tell us about his view of human nature?**
3. **Looking at the document of Xerxes from Persepolis, what qualities (physical, mental, and moral) are desirable in a ruler? What is the Persian concept of justice?**
4. **How do the stories in Herodotus accord with the Persian conceptions of empire, kingship, and justice seen in the royal inscriptions? Where do we see gleeful Greek subversions of those ideals?**

Sources: First selection from Behistun inscription translated by L. W. King and R. C. Thompson, *The Sculptures and Inscription of Darius the Great on the Rock of Behistun in Persia* (London, 1907) (http://www.livius.org/be-bm/behistun03.html); second selection from Persepolis (http://www.livius.org); third selection reprinted by permission of the publishers and the Trustees of the Loeb Classical Library from *Herodotus*, Volume III, Loeb Classical Library Volume 119, translated by A. D. Godley, pp. 27–29, 34–35, 38–39, 44–46, Cambridge, Mass.: Harvard University Press, Copyright 1922 by the President and Fellows of Harvard College, The Loeb Classical Library® is a registered trademark of the President and Fellows of Harvard College.

Religious Ideology

thousands of years, with good ultimately destined to prevail. Humanity is a participant in this cosmic struggle, and individuals are rewarded or punished in the afterlife for their actions in life.

Darius has brilliantly joined the moral theology of Zoroastrianism to political ideology. In essence, he is claiming that the divinely ordained mission of the empire is to bring all the scattered peoples of the world back together again under a regime of justice and thereby to restore the perfection of creation.

In keeping with this Zoroastrian world-view, the Persians were sensitive to the beauties of nature and venerated beneficent elements, such as water, which was not to be polluted by human excretion, and fire, which was worshiped at fire altars. Corpses were exposed to wild beasts and the elements to prevent them from putrefying in the earth or tainting the sanctity of fire. Persians were also expected to keep promises and tell the truth. In his inscriptions Darius castigated evildoers as followers of "the Lie."

The Zoroastrian Legacy

Zoroastrianism was one of the great religions of the ancient world. It preached belief in one supreme deity, held humans to a high ethical standard, and promised salvation. It traveled across western Asia with the advance of the Persian Empire, and it may have exerted a major influence on Judaism and thus, indirectly, on Christianity. God and the Devil, Heaven and Hell, reward and punishment, and the Messiah and the End of Time all appear to be legacies of this profound belief system. Because of the accidents of history—the fall of the Achaemenid Persian Empire in the later fourth century B.C.E. and the Islamic conquest of Iran in the seventh century C.E. (see Chapter 8)—Zoroastrianism has all but disappeared, except among a relatively small number of Parsees, as Zoroastrians are now called, in Iran and India.

PRIMARY SOURCE: ***Gathas*** Gain a sense of the spiritual message and vision of Zarathushtra, the great Persian Prophet, through this devotional hymn.

THE RISE OF THE GREEKS, 1000–500 B.C.E.

Because Greece was a relatively resource-poor region, the cultural developments of the first millennium B.C.E. were only possible because the Greeks had access to raw materials and markets abroad. Greek merchants, mercenaries, and travelers were in contact with other peoples and brought home foreign goods and ideas. Under the pressure of population, poverty, war, or political crisis, Greeks settled in other parts of the Mediterranean and Black Sea, bringing their language and culture and influencing other societies. Encounters with the different practices and beliefs of other peoples stimulated the formation of a Greek identity and sparked interest in geography, ethnography, and history. A two-century-long rivalry with the Persian Empire helped shape the destinies of the Greek city-states.

Geography and Resources

Greece is part of an ecological zone encompassing the Mediterranean Sea and the lands surrounding it (see Map 3.5). This zone is bounded by the Atlantic Ocean to the west, the several ranges of the Alps to the north, the Syrian Desert to the east, and the Sahara to the south. The lands lying within this zone have a similar climate, a similar sequence of seasons, and similar plants and animals. In summer a weather front near the entrance of the Mediterranean impedes the passage of storms from the Atlantic, allowing hot, dry air from the Sahara to creep up over the region. In winter the front dissolves and ocean storms roll in, bringing waves, wind, and cold. It was relatively easy for people to migrate to new homes within this ecological zone without altering familiar cultural practices and means of livelihood.

Greek civilization arose in the lands bordering the Aegean Sea: the Greek mainland, the Aegean islands, and the western coast of Anatolia (see Map 4.2). Southern Greece is a dry and rocky land with small plains separated by low mountain ranges. No navigable rivers ease travel or the transport of commodities. The small islands dotting the Aegean were inhabited from early times. People could sail from Greece to Anatolia almost without losing sight of land. The sea was always a connector, not a barrier. From about 1000 B.C.E. Greeks began settling on the western edge of Anatolia. Broad and fertile river valleys near the coast made Ionia, as the ancient Greeks called this region, a comfortable place.

Greek farmers depended on rainfall to water their crops. The limited arable land, thin topsoil, and sparse rainfall in the south could not sustain large populations. Farmers planted grain (mostly barley, which was hardier than wheat) in the flat plain, olive trees at the edge of the plain, and grapevines on the terraced lower slopes of the foothills. Sheep and goats grazed in the hills during the growing season. In northern Greece, where the rainfall is greater and the land opens out into broad plains, cattle and horses were more abundant. These lands had few metal deposits and little timber, but both building stone, including fine marble, and clay for the potter were abundant.

The Greek mainland has a deeply pitted coastline with many natural harbors. A combination of circumstances—the difficulty of overland transport, the availability of good anchorages, and the need to import metals, timber, and grain—drew the Greeks to the sea. They obtained timber from the northern Aegean, gold and iron from Anatolia, copper from Cyprus, tin from the western Mediterranean, and grain from the Black Sea, Egypt, and Sicily. Sea transport was much

MAP 4.2 Ancient Greece By the early first millennium B.C.E. Greek-speaking peoples were dispersed throughout the Aegean region, occupying the Greek mainland, most of the islands, and the western coast of Anatolia. The rough landscape of central and southern Greece, with small plains separated by ranges of mountains, and the many islands in the Aegean favored the rise of hundreds of small, independent communities. The presence of adequate rainfall meant that agriculture was organized on the basis of self-sufficient family farms. As a result of the limited natural resources of this region, the Greeks had to resort to sea travel and trade with other lands in the Mediterranean to acquire metals and other vital raw materials.

cheaper and faster than overland transport. Thus, some Greeks reluctantly embarked upon the sea in their small, frail ships, hugging the coastline or island-hopping where possible.

The Emergence of the Polis

The Dark Age

The first flowering of Greek culture in the Mycenaean civilization of the second millennium B.C.E., described in Chapter 3, was largely an adaptation to the Greek terrain of the imported institutions of Middle Eastern palace-dominated states. For several centuries after the destruction of the Mycenaean palace-states, Greece lapsed into a "Dark Age" (ca. 1150–800 B.C.E.), a time of depopulation, poverty, and backwardness that left few traces in the archaeological record.

During the Dark Age, the Greeks were largely isolated from the rest of the world. The importation of raw materials, especially metals, had been the chief source of Mycenaean prosperity.

Lack of access to resources lay behind the poverty of the Dark Age. With fewer people to feed, the land was largely given over to grazing animals. Although there was continuity of language, religion, and other aspects of culture, there was a sharp break with the authoritarian Mycenaean political structure and centralized control of the economy. This opened the way for the development of new political, social, and economic forms rooted in the Greek environment.

New Ideas from the East

The isolation of Greece ended by 800 B.C.E. when Phoenician ships began to visit the Aegean (see Chapter 3), inaugurating what scholars term the "Archaic" period of Greek history (ca. 800–480 B.C.E.). Soon Greek ships were also plying the waters of the Mediterranean in search of raw materials, trade opportunities, and fertile farmland.

New ideas arrived from the east, such as the depiction of naturalistic human and animal figures and imaginative mythical beasts on painted pottery. The most auspicious gift of the Phoenicians was a writing system. The Phoenicians used twenty-two symbols to represent the consonants in their language, leaving the vowel sounds to be inferred by the reader. To represent Greek vowel sounds, the Greeks utilized some of the Phoenician symbols for which there were no equivalent sounds in the Greek language. This was the first true alphabet, a system of writing that fully represents the sounds of spoken language. An alphabet offers tremendous advantages over systems of writing such as cuneiform and hieroglyphics, whose signs represent entire words or syllables. Because cuneiform and hieroglyphics required years of training and the memorization of hundreds of signs, they were known only by a scribal class whose elevated social position stemmed from their mastery of the technology. With an alphabet only a few dozen signs are required, and people can learn to read and write in a relatively short period of time.

Some scholars maintain that the Greeks first used alphabetic writing for economic purposes, such as to keep inventories of a merchant's wares. Others propose that it was created to preserve the oral epics so important to the Greeks. Whatever its first use, the Greeks soon applied the new technology to new forms of literature, law codes, religious dedications, and epitaphs on gravestones. This does not mean, however, that Greek society immediately became literate in the modern sense. For many centuries, Greece remained a primarily oral culture: people used storytelling, rituals, and performances to preserve and transmit information. Many of the distinctive intellectual and artistic creations of Greek civilization, such as theatrical drama, philosophical dialogues, and political and courtroom oratory, resulted from the dynamic interaction of speaking and writing.

The Nature of the Polis

The early Archaic period saw a veritable explosion of population. Studies of cemeteries in the vicinity of Athens show a dramatic population increase (perhaps fivefold or more) during the eighth century B.C.E. This was probably due, in part, to more intensive use of the land, as farming replaced herding and families began to work previously unused land on the margins of the plains. The accompanying shift to a diet based on bread and vegetables rather than meat may have increased fertility and life span. Another factor was increasing prosperity based on the importation of food and raw materials. Rising population density caused villages to merge and become urban centers. Freed from agricultural tasks, some members of the society were able to develop specialized skills in other areas, such as crafts and commerce.

Greece at this time consisted of hundreds of independent political entities, reflecting the facts of Greek geography—small plains separated by mountain barriers. The Greek **polis** (POE-lis) (usually translated "city-state") consisted of an urban center and the rural territory it controlled. City-states came in various sizes, with populations as small as several thousand or as large as several hundred thousand in the case of Athens.

polis The Greek term for a city-state, an urban center and the agricultural territory under its control. It was the characteristic form of political organization in southern and central Greece in the Archaic and Classical periods. Of the hundreds of city-states in the Mediterranean and Black Sea regions settled by Greeks, some were oligarchic, others democratic, depending on the powers delegated to the Council and the Assembly.

Most urban centers had certain characteristic features. A hilltop *acropolis* (uh-KRAW-poe-lis) ("top of the city") offered refuge in an emergency. The town spread out around the base of this fortified high point. An *agora* (ah-go-RAH) ("gathering place") was an open area where citizens came together to ratify decisions of their leaders or to assemble with their weapons before military ventures. Government buildings were located there, but the agora developed into a marketplace as well, since vendors everywhere set out their wares wherever crowds gather. Fortified walls surrounded the urban center; but as the population expanded, new buildings went up beyond the perimeter.

City and country were not as sharply distinguished as they are today. The urban center depended on its agricultural hinterland to provide food, and many people living within the walls of the city worked on nearby farms during the day. Unlike the dependent workers on the estates of Mesopotamia, the rural populations of the Greek city-states were free members of the community.

Robert Harding World Imagery

The Acropolis at Athens This steep, defensible plateau jutting up from the Attic Plain served as a Mycenaean fortress in the second millennium B.C.E., and the site of Athens has been continuously occupied since that time. In the mid-sixth century B.C.E. the tyrant Pisistratus built a temple to Athena, the patron goddess of the community. It was destroyed by the Persians when they invaded Greece in 480 B.C.E. The Acropolis was left in ruins for three decades as a reminder of what the Athenians sacrificed in defense of Greek freedom, but in the 440s B.C.E. Pericles initiated a building program, using funds from the naval empire that Athens headed. These construction projects, including a new temple to Athena—the Parthenon—brought glory to the city and popularity to Pericles and to the new democracy that he championed.

Hoplite Warfare

hoplite A heavily armored Greek infantryman of the Archaic and Classical periods who fought in the close-packed phalanx formation. Hoplite armies—militias composed of middle- and upper-class citizens supplying their own equipment—were for centuries superior to all other military forces.

Each polis was fiercely jealous of its independence and suspicious of its neighbors, leading to frequent conflict. By the early seventh century B.C.E. the Greeks had developed a new kind of warfare, waged by **hoplites** (HAWP-lite)— heavily armored infantrymen who fought in close formation. Protected by a helmet, a breastplate, and leg guards, each hoplite held a round shield over his own left side and the right side of the man next to him and brandished a thrusting spear, keeping a sword in reserve. The key to victory was maintaining the cohesion of one's own formation while breaking open the enemy's line. Most of the casualties were suffered by the defeated army in flight.

There was a close relationship between hoplite warfare and agriculture. Greek states were defended by armies of private citizens—mostly farmers—called up for brief periods of crisis, rather than by a professional class of soldiers. Although this kind of fighting called for strength to bear the weapons and armor, as well as courage to stand one's ground in battle, no special training was needed. Campaigns took place when farmers were available, in the windows of time between major tasks in the agricultural cycle. When a hoplite army marched into the fields of another community, the enraged farmers of that community, who had toiled to develop their land and buildings, rarely refused the challenge. Though brutal and terrifying, the clash of two hoplite lines provided a quick decision. Battles rarely lasted more than a few hours, and the survivors could promptly return home to tend their farms.

Colonization

AP* Exam Tip For the exam, be prepared to explain why people moved and the impact that those moves had on the region.

The expanding population soon surpassed the capacity of the small plains, and many communities sent excess population abroad to establish independent "colonies" in distant lands (see the story at the beginning of this chapter). Not every colonist left willingly. Sources tell of people being chosen by lot and forbidden to return on pain of death. Others, seeing an opportunity to escape from poverty, avoid the constraints of family, or find adventure, voluntarily sought their fortunes on the frontier. After obtaining the approval of the god Apollo from his sanctuary at Delphi, the colonists departed, carrying fire from the communal hearth of the "mother-city," a symbol of the kinship and religious ties that would connect the two communities. They settled by the sea in the vicinity of a hill or other natural refuge. The "founder," a prominent member of the mother-city, allotted parcels of land and drafted laws for the new community. In some cases the indigenous population was driven away or reduced to semiservile status; in other cases there was intermarriage between colonists and natives.

A wave of colonization from the mid-eighth through mid-sixth centuries B.C.E. spread Greek culture far beyond the land of its origins. New settlements sprang up in the northern Aegean area, around the Black Sea, and on the Libyan coast of North Africa. In southern Italy and on the island of Sicily (see Map 3.5) another Greek core area was established. Greek colonists were able to transplant their entire way of life because of the general similarity in climate and ecology in the Mediterranean lands.

Greeks began to use the term *Hellenes* (HELL-leans) (*Graeci* is what the Romans later called them) to distinguish themselves from *barbaroi* (the root of the English word *barbarian*). Interaction with new peoples and exposure to their different practices made the Greeks aware of the factors that bound them together: their language, religion, and lifestyle. It also introduced them to new ideas and technologies. Developments first appearing in the colonial world traveled back to the Greek homeland—urban planning, new forms of political organization, and new intellectual currents.

tyrant The term the Greeks used to describe someone who seized and held power in violation of the normal procedures and traditions of the community. Tyrants appeared in many Greek city-states in the seventh and sixth centuries B.C.E., often taking advantage of the disaffection of the emerging middle class and, by weakening the old elite, unwittingly contributing to the evolution of democracy.

Coinage was invented in the early sixth century B.C.E., probably in Lydia (western Anatolia), and soon spread throughout the Greek world and beyond. A coin was a piece of metal whose weight and purity, and thus value, were guaranteed by the state. Silver, gold, bronze, and other metals were attractive choices for a medium of exchange: sufficiently rare to be valuable, relatively lightweight and portable, virtually indestructible, and therefore permanent. Prior to the invention of coinage, people weighed out quantities of metal in exchange for items they wanted to buy. Coinage allowed for more rapid exchanges of goods as well as for more efficient record-keeping and storage of wealth. It stimulated trade and increased the total wealth of the society. Even so, international commerce could still be confusing because different states used different weight standards that had to be reconciled, just as people have to exchange currencies when traveling today.

Political Evolution

e PRIMARY SOURCE: The Trojan Hero Hector Prepares to Meet His Destiny Read an excerpt from one of the most famous Greek epic poems, the *Iliad*, by Homer.

By reducing surplus population, colonization helped relieve pressures within Archaic Greek communities. Nevertheless, this was an era of political instability. Kings ruled the Dark Age societies depicted in Homer's *Iliad* and *Odyssey*, but at some point councils composed of the heads of noble families superseded the kings. This aristocracy derived its wealth and power from ownership of large tracts of land. Peasant families worked this land, occupying small plots and handing over a portion of the crop to the owner. Debt-slaves, who had borrowed money or seed from the lord and lost their freedom when unable to repay the loan, also worked the land. Also living in a typical community were free peasants, who owned small farms, and urban-based craftsmen and merchants, who began to constitute a "middle class."

In the mid-seventh and sixth centuries B.C.E. in one city-state after another, a **tyrant**—a person who seized and held power in violation of the normal political traditions of the community—gained control. Greek tyrants were often disgruntled or ambitious members of the aristocracy, backed by the emerging middle class. New opportunities for economic advancement and the declining cost of metals meant that more and more men could acquire arms and serve as hoplite soldiers in the local militias. These individuals must have demanded increased political rights as the price of their support for the tyrant.

democracy System of government in which all "citizens" (however defined) have equal political and legal rights, privileges, and protections, as in the Greek city-state of Athens in the fifth and fourth centuries B.C.E.

Ultimately, the tyrants were unwitting catalysts in an evolving political process. Some were able to pass their positions on to their sons, but eventually the tyrant-family was ejected. Authority in the community developed along one of two lines: toward oligarchy (OLL-ih-gahr-key), the exercise of political privilege by the wealthier members of society, or toward **democracy**, the exercise of political power by all free adult males.

Religion

Greek religion encompassed a wide range of cults and beliefs. The ancestors of the Greeks brought a collection of sky-gods with them when they entered the Greek peninsula at the end of the third millennium B.C.E. Male gods predominated, but several female deities had important roles. Some gods represented forces in nature: for example, Zeus sent storms and lightning, and Poseidon was master of the sea and earthquakes. The two great epic poems of Homer, the *Iliad* and *Odyssey*, which Greek schoolboys memorized and professional performers recited, put a distinctive stamp on the personalities of these deities. The Homeric gods were anthropomorphic (an-thruh-puh-MORE-fik)—that is, conceived as humanlike in appearance (though taller, more beautiful, and more powerful than mere mortals) and humanlike in their displays of emotion. Indeed, the chief difference between them and human beings was humans' mortality.

sacrifice A gift given to a deity, often with the aim of creating a relationship, gaining favor, and obligating the god to provide some benefit to the sacrificer, sometimes in order to sustain the deity and thereby guarantee the continuing vitality of the natural world.

Worship of the gods at state-sponsored festivals was as much an expression of civic identity as of personal piety. **Sacrifice**, the central ritual of Greek religion, was performed at altars in front of the temples that the Greeks built to be the gods' places of residence. Greeks gave their

Vase Painting Depicting a Sacrifice to the God Apollo, ca. 440 B.C.E. For the Greeks, who believed in a multitude of gods who looked and behaved like humans, the central act of worship was the sacrifice, the ritualized offering of a gift. Sacrifice created a relationship between the human worshiper and the deity and raised expectations that the god would bestow favors in return. Here we see a number of male devotees, wearing their finest clothing and garlands in their hair, near a sacred outdoor altar and statue of Apollo. The god is shown at the far right, standing on a pedestal and holding his characteristic bow and laurel branch. The first worshiper offers the god bones wrapped in fat. All of the worshipers will feast on the meat carried by the boy.

gods gifts, often as humble as a small cake or a cup of wine poured on the ground, in the hope that the gods would favor and protect them. In more spectacular forms of sacrifice, a group of people would kill one or more animals, spray the altar with the victim's blood, burn parts of its body so that the aroma would ascend to the gods on high, and enjoy a rare feast of meat.

Greek individuals and communities sought advice or predictions about the future from oracles—sacred sites where they believed the gods communicated with humans. Especially prestigious was the oracle of Apollo at Delphi in central Greece. Petitioners left gifts in the treasuries, and the god responded to their questions through his priestess, who gave forth obscure utterances. Because most Greeks were farmers, fertility cults, whose members worshiped and sought to enhance the productive forces in nature (usually conceived as female), were popular, though often hidden from modern view because of our dependence on literary texts expressing the values of an educated, urban elite.

New Intellectual Currents

The changes taking place in Greece in the Archaic period—new technologies, increasing prosperity, and social and political development—led to innovations in intellectual outlook and artistic expression. One distinctive feature of the period was a growing emphasis on the uniqueness and rights of the individual. We see clear signs of individualism in the new lyric poetry—short verses in which the subject matter is intensely personal, drawn from the experience of the poet and expressing his or her feelings. Archilochus (ahr-KIL-uh-kuhs), a soldier and poet living in the first half of the seventh century B.C.E., made a surprising admission:

Lyric Poetry

> *Some barbarian is waving my shield, since I was obliged to leave that perfectly good piece of equipment behind under a bush. But I got away, so what does it matter? Let the shield go; I can buy another one equally good.*[3]

Here Archilochus is poking fun at the heroic ideal that regarded dishonor as worse than death. In challenging traditional values and expressing personal views, lyric poets paved the way for the modern Western conception of poetry.

Science and History

In the sixth century B.C.E. Xenophanes (zeh-NOFF-uh-nees) called into question the kind of gods that Homer had popularized.

> *But if cattle and horses or lions had hands, or were able to draw with their hands and do the works that men can do, horses would draw the forms of the gods like horses, and cattle like cattle, and they would make their bodies such as they each had themselves.*[4]

e PRIMARY SOURCE: A Lyric Poem Laments an Absent Lover Read a poem by Sappho, a celebrated ancient Greek poet, known for her sensual language.

Early philosophers like Xenophanes rejected traditional religious conceptions and sought rational explanations. They were primarily concerned with how the world was created, what it is made of, and why changes occur. Some postulated various combinations of earth, air, fire, and water as the primal elements that combine or dissolve to form the numerous substances found in nature. One advanced the theory that the world is composed of microscopic atoms (from a Greek word meaning "indivisible") moving through the void of space, colliding randomly and combining in various ways to form many substances. This model, in some respects startlingly similar to modern atomic theory, was essentially a lucky intuition, but it attests to the sophistication of these thinkers. Most of these thinkers came from Ionia and southern Italy, where Greeks were in close contact with non-Greek peoples. The shock of encountering different ideas may have stimulated new lines of inquiry.

In Ionia in the sixth century B.C.E., a group of men referred to as logographers (loe-GOG-ruff-er) ("writers of prose accounts"), taking advantage of the nearly infinite capacity of writing to store information, gathered data on a wide range of topics, including ethnography (description of foreign people's physical characteristics and cultural practices), the geography of unfamiliar lands, foundation stories of important cities, and the origins of famous Greek families. They were the first to write in prose—the language of everyday speech—rather than poetry, which had long facilitated the memorization essential in an oral society. *Historia*, "investigation/research," was the Greek term for the method they used to collect, sort, and select information. In the later fifth century B.C.E. **Herodotus** (ca. 485–425 B.C.E.) published his *Histories*. Early parts of the work are filled with the geographic and ethnographic reports, legends, and marvels dear to the logographers, but in later sections Herodotus focuses on the great event of the previous generation: the wars between the Greeks and the Persian Empire.

Herodotus Heir to the technique of *historia* ("investigation/research") developed by Greeks in the late Archaic period. He came from a Greek community in Anatolia and traveled extensively, collecting information in western Asia and the Mediterranean lands. He traced the antecedents and chronicled the wars between the Greek city-states and the Persian Empire, thus originating the Western tradition of historical writing.

Herodotus declared his new conception of his mission in the first lines of the book:

> *I, Herodotus of Halicarnassus, am here setting forth my history, that time may not draw the color from what man has brought into being, nor those great and wonderful deeds, manifested by both Greeks and barbarians, fail of their report, and, together with all this, the reason why they fought one another.*[5]

In seeking to discover *why* Greeks and Persians came to blows, Herodotus became a historian, directing the all-purpose techniques of *historia* to the narrower service of *history* in the modern sense. For this achievement he is known as the "father of history."

Athens and Sparta

The two preeminent Greek city-states of the late Archaic and Classical periods were Athens and Sparta. The different character of these communities underscores the potential for diversity in human societies, even those arising in similar environmental and cultural contexts.

The Spartan Military State

The ancestors of the Spartans migrated into the Peloponnese (PELL-uh-puh-neze), the southernmost part of the Greek mainland, around 1000 B.C.E. For a time Sparta followed a typical path of development, participating in trade and fostering the arts. Then in the seventh century B.C.E. something altered the character of the Spartan state. Like many other parts of Greece, the Spartan community was feeling the effects of increasing population and a shortage of arable land. However, instead of sending out colonists, the Spartans invaded the fertile plain of neighboring Messenia (see Map 4.2). They took over Messenia and reduced the native population to the status of helots (HELL-ut), state-owned serfs, the most abused and exploited population on the Greek mainland.

Fear of a helot uprising led to the evolution of the unique Spartan way of life. The Spartan state became a military camp in a permanent state of preparedness. Territory in Messenia and Laconia (the Spartan homeland) was divided into several thousand lots and assigned to Spartan citizens. Helots worked the land and turned over a portion of what they grew to their Spartan

SECTION REVIEW

- In the resource-poor Greek Aegean, prosperity and advancement depended on seaborne trade for metals and other vital materials.
- Hundreds of independent city-states existed in the fragmented Greek landscape. Rainfall-based agriculture allowed the land to be worked by independent farmers who were free citizens of their communities.
- Rapidly expanding population led to urbanization and to colonization, the migration of Greeks to new settlements around the Mediterranean and Black Seas.
- The rise of a middle class and the dependence of communities on a hoplite militia led to political unrest and an extension of political rights to more people.
- The Greeks created the first true alphabetic writing system, but Greece long remained a primarily oral society. New ideas challenged traditional notions, leading to individualism, science, and history.
- Sparta and Athens, though part of the same Greek civilization, evolved politically in different directions: Sparta toward a military oligarchy, Athens to democracy.

masters, who were freed from food production and able to spend their lives in military training and service.

The Spartan soldier was the best in Greece, and the professional Spartan army was superior to the citizen militias of other Greek states. The Spartans, however, paid a huge personal price for their military readiness. At age seven, boys were taken from their families and put into barracks, where they were toughened by severe discipline, beatings, and deprivation. A Spartan male's whole life was subordinated to the needs of the state. Sparta essentially stopped the clock, declining to participate in the economic, political, and cultural renaissance taking place in the Archaic Greek world. There were no longer any poets or artists at Sparta. To maintain equality among citizens, precious metals and coinage were banned, and Spartans were forbidden to engage in commerce. The fifth-century B.C.E. Athenian historian Thucydides (thoo-SID-ih-dees) remarked that in his day Sparta appeared to be little more than a large village and that no future observer of the ruins of the site would be able to guess its power.

The Spartans, practicing a foreign policy that was cautious and isolationist, cultivated a mystique by rarely putting their reputation to the test. Reluctant to march far from home for fear of a helot uprising, the Spartans maintained regional peace through the Peloponnesian League, a system of alliances between Sparta and its neighbors.

Athens and Democracy

In comparison with other Greek city-states, Athens possessed an unusually large and populous territory: the entire region of Attica, containing a number of moderately fertile plains and well suited for cultivation of olive trees. In addition to the urban center of Athens, located 5 miles (8 kilometers) from the sea where the sheer-sided Acropolis towered above the plain, the peninsula was dotted with villages and a few larger towns.

In 594 B.C.E., however, Athens was on the verge of civil war, and a respected member of the elite class, Solon, was appointed lawgiver and granted extraordinary powers. He divided Athenian citizens into four classes based on the annual yield of their farms. Those in the top three classes could hold state offices. Members of the lowest class, with little or no property, could participate in meetings of the Assembly. This arrangement, which made political rights a function of wealth, was far from democratic, but it broke the monopoly on power of a small circle of aristocratic families. Solon also abolished the practice of enslaving individuals for failure to repay their debts, thereby guaranteeing the freedom of Athenian citizens.

Nevertheless, political turmoil continued until 546 B.C.E., when an aristocrat named Pisistratus (pie-SIS-truh-tuhs) seized power. To strengthen his position and weaken the aristocracy, the tyrant enticed the largely rural population to identify with the urban center of Athens, where he was the dominant figure. He undertook a number of monumental building projects, including a Temple of Athena on the Acropolis. He also instituted or expanded several major festivals that drew people to Athens for religious processions, performances of plays, and athletic and poetic competitions.

Pericles Aristocratic leader who guided the Athenian state through the transformation to full participatory democracy for all male citizens, supervised construction of the Acropolis, and pursued a policy of imperial expansion that led to the Peloponnesian War. He formulated a strategy of attrition but died from the plague early in the war.

Pisistratus passed the tyranny on to his sons, but with Spartan assistance the Athenians turned the tyrant-family out in the last decade of the sixth century B.C.E. In the 460s and 450s B.C.E. **Pericles** (PER-eh-kleez) and his political allies took the last steps in the evolution of Athenian democracy, transferring all power to popular organs of government: the Assembly, Council of 500, and People's Courts. Men of moderate or little means now could participate fully in the political process, being selected by lot to fill even the highest offices and being paid for public service so they could take time off from their work. The focal point of Athenian political life became the Assembly of all citizens. Several times a month proposals were debated; decisions were made openly, and any citizen could speak to the issues of the day.

During this century and a half of internal political evolution, Athens's economic clout and international reputation rose steadily. From the time of Pisistratus, Athenian exports, especially olive oil, became increasingly prominent all around the Mediterranean, crowding out the products of other Greek commercial powerhouses such as Corinth (see Map 4.2). Extensive trade increased the numbers and wealth of the middle class and helps explain why Athens took the path of increasing democratization.

THE STRUGGLE OF PERSIA AND GREECE, 546–323 B.C.E.

Persian Wars Conflicts between Greek city-states and the Persian Empire, ranging from the Ionian Revolt (499–494 B.C.E.) through Darius's punitive expedition that failed at Marathon (490 B.C.E.) and the defeat of Xerxes' massive invasion of Greece by the Spartan-led Hellenic League (480–479 B.C.E.). This first major setback for Persian arms launched the Greeks into their period of greatest cultural productivity. Herodotus chronicled these events in the first "history" in the Western tradition.

For many Greeks of the fifth and fourth centuries B.C.E., Persia was the great enemy and the wars with Persia were crucial events. The Persians probably were more concerned about threats farther east. Nevertheless, the encounters of Greeks and Persians over a period of two centuries were of profound importance for the history of the eastern Mediterranean and western Asia.

Early Encounters

Cyrus's conquest of Lydia in 546 B.C.E. led to the subjugation of the Greek cities on the Anatolian seacoast. In the years that followed, local groups or individuals who collaborated with the Persian government ruled their home cities with minimal Persian interference. All this changed when the Ionian Revolt, a great uprising of Greeks and other subject peoples on the western frontier, broke out in 499 B.C.E. The Persians needed five years and a massive infusion of troops and resources to stamp out the insurrection.

The failed revolt led to the **Persian Wars**—two Persian attacks on Greece in the early fifth century B.C.E. In 490 B.C.E. Darius dispatched a force to punish Eretria (er-EH-tree-uh) and Athens, two mainland states that had aided the Ionian rebels. Eretria was betrayed to the Persians, and the survivors were marched off to permanent exile in southwest Iran. The Athenians probably would have suffered a similar fate if their hoplites had not defeated the more numerous but lighter-armed Persian troops in a sharp engagement at Marathon, 26 miles (42 kilometers) from Athens.

Xerxes' Great Invasion

In 480 B.C.E. Darius's son and successor, Xerxes (*Khshayarsha*, r. 486–465 B.C.E.), set out with a huge invasionary force consisting of the Persian army, contingents from all the peoples of the empire, and a large fleet of ships drawn from maritime subjects. Crossing the narrow Hellespont strait, Persian forces descended into central and southern Greece (see Map 4.2). Xerxes sent messengers ahead to most Greek states, demanding "earth and water"—tokens of submission.

Many Greek communities acknowledged Persian overlordship. But an alliance of southern Greek states bent on resistance was formed under the leadership of the Spartans. This Hellenic League initially failed to halt the Persian advance. At the pass of Thermopylae (thuhr-MOP-uh-lee) in central Greece, three hundred Spartans and their king gave their lives to buy time for their allies to escape. However, after the city of Athens had been sacked, the Persian navy was lured into the narrow straits of nearby Salamis (SAH-lah-miss), sacrificing their advantage in numbers and maneuverability, and suffered a devastating defeat. The following spring (479 B.C.E.), the Persian land army was routed at Plataea (pluh-TEE-uh), and the immediate threat to Greece receded. A number of factors account for the outcome: the Persians' difficulty in supplying their very large army in a distant land; their tactical error at Salamis; the superiority of heavily armed Greek hoplite soldiers over lighter-armed Asiatic infantry; and the tenacity of people defending their homeland and liberty.

The Greeks then went on the offensive. Athens's stubborn refusal to submit and the vital role played by the Athenian navy, which made up half the allied fleet, had earned the city a large measure of respect. The next phase of the war—driving the Persians away from the Aegean and liberating Greek states still under Persian control—was naval. Thus Athens replaced land-based, isolationist Sparta as leader of the campaign against Persia. In 477 B.C.E. the Delian (DEE-lih-yuhn) League was formed. Initially a voluntary alliance of Greek states to prosecute the war against Persia, in less than twenty years Athenian-led League forces swept the Persians from the waters of the eastern Mediterranean and freed all Greek communities except those in distant Cyprus (see Map 3.5).

The Height of Athenian Power

Athens's Naval Empire

The Classical period of Greek history (480–323 B.C.E.) begins with the successful defense of the Greek homeland. Ironically, the Athenians, who had played such a crucial role, exploited these events to become an imperial power. A string of successful campaigns and the passage of time led many of their complacent Greek allies to contribute money instead of military forces. The Athenians used the money to build up and staff their navy. Eventually they saw the other members of the Delian League as their subjects and demanded annual contributions and other signs of submission. States that deserted the League were brought back by force, stripped of their defenses, and subordinated to Athens.

Athens's mastery of naval technology transformed Greek warfare and politics and brought great power and wealth to Athens itself. Unlike commercial ships, whose stable, round-bodied hulls were propelled by a single square sail, military vessels could not risk depending on the wind. By the late sixth century B.C.E. the **trireme** (TRY-reem), a sleek, fast vessel powered by 170 rowers, had become the premier warship. Athenian crews, by constant practice, became the best in the eastern Mediterranean, able to reach speeds of 7 knots and perform complex maneuvers.

trireme Greek and Phoenician warship of the fifth and fourth centuries B.C.E. It was sleek and light, powered by 170 oars arranged in three vertical tiers. Manned by skilled sailors, it was capable of short bursts of speed and complex maneuvers.

The effectiveness of the Athenian navy had significant consequences at home and abroad. The emergence at Athens of a democratic system in which each male citizen had an equal share is connected to the new primacy of the fleet. Hoplites, who had to provide their own armor and weapons, were members of the middle and upper classes. Rowers, in contrast, came from the lower classes, but because they were the source of Athens's power, they could insist on full rights.

The navy allowed Athens to project its power farther than would be possible with a hoplite militia, which could be kept in arms for only short periods of time. In previous Greek wars, the victorious state could not occupy a defeated neighbor permanently and was satisfied with booty and, perhaps, minor adjustments to boundary lines. Athens was able to continually dominate and exploit other, weaker communities in an unprecedented way.

The Benefits of Empire

Athens used its power to promote its economic interests. Athens's port, Piraeus (pih-RAY-uhs), became the most important commercial center in the eastern Mediterranean. The money collected from the subject states helped subsidize the increasingly expensive Athenian democracy as well as construction of beautiful buildings on the Acropolis, including the majestic new temple of Athena, the Parthenon. The Athenian leader Pericles redistributed the profits of empire to the many Athenians working on the construction and decoration of these monuments and gained extraordinary popularity.

Replica of Ancient Greek Trireme Greek warships had a metal-tipped ram in front to pierce the hulls of enemy vessels and a pair of steering rudders in the rear. Though equipped with masts and sails, in battle these warships were propelled by 170 rowers. This modern, full-size replica, manned by international volunteer crews, is helping scholars to determine attainable speeds and maneuvering techniques.

Paul Lipke/Trireme Trust USA

AP* Exam Tip It is important to understand the core ideas of Greek philosophy.

Other cultural achievements were supported indirectly by the profits of empire. Wealthy Athenians paid the production costs of the tragedies and comedies performed at state festivals. The most creative artists and thinkers in the Greek world were drawn to Athens. Traveling teachers called Sophists ("wise men") provided instruction in logic and public speaking to pupils who could afford their fees. The new discipline of rhetoric—the construction of attractive and persuasive arguments—gave those with training and quick wits a great advantage in politics and the courts.

Philosophy at Athens

Socrates Athenian philosopher (ca. 470–399 B.C.E.) who shifted the emphasis of philosophical investigation from questions of natural science to ethics and human behavior. He attracted young disciples from elite families but made enemies by revealing the ignorance and pretensions of others, culminating in his trial and execution by the Athenian state.

These new intellectual currents came together in 399 B.C.E. when the philosopher **Socrates** (ca. 470–399 B.C.E.) was brought to trial. A sculptor by trade, Socrates spent most of his time in the company of young men who enjoyed conversing with him and observing him deflate the pretensions of those who thought themselves wise. He wryly commented that he knew one more thing than everyone else: that he knew nothing. At his trial, Socrates easily disposed of the charges of corrupting the youth and not believing in the gods of the city. He argued that the real basis of the hostility he faced was twofold: (1) He was being held responsible for the actions of several of his aristocratic students who had tried to overthrow the Athenian democracy. (2) He was being blamed for the controversial teachings of the Sophists, which were widely believed to contradict traditional religious beliefs and undermine morality. In Athenian trials, juries of hundreds of citizens decided guilt and punishment, often motivated more by emotion than by legal principles. The vote that found Socrates guilty was close. But his lack of contrition in the penalty phase—he proposed that he be rewarded for his services to the state—led the jury to condemn him to death by drinking hemlock. Socrates's disciples regarded his execution as a martyrdom, and smart young men such as Plato withdrew from public life and dedicated themselves to the philosophical pursuit of knowledge and truth.

PRIMARY SOURCE: *Apologia* Learn why Socrates was condemned to death and why he refused to stop questioning the wisdom of his countrymen.

This period witnesses an important stage in the transition from orality to literacy. Socrates himself wrote nothing, preferring to converse with people. His student Plato (ca. 428–347 B.C.E.) may represent the first truly literate generation that gained much knowledge from books and habitually wrote down their thoughts. On the outskirts of Athens Plato founded the Academy, where young men could pursue a course of higher education. Yet even Plato retained traces of the orality of the world in which he had grown up. He wrote dialogues—an oral form—in which his protagonist, Socrates, uses the "Socratic method" of question and answer to reach a deeper understanding of values such as justice, excellence, and wisdom. Plato refused to write down the most advanced stages of the philosophical and spiritual training that took place at his Academy. He believed that full apprehension of a higher reality, of which our own sensible world is but a pale reflection, could be entrusted only to "initiates" who had completed the earlier stages.

PRIMARY SOURCE: Aristotle on Politics Discover the strengths and weaknesses, as Aristotle saw it, of kingdoms, aristocracies, and democracies.

The third of the great classical philosophers, Aristotle (384–322 B.C.E.), came from Stagira in the northern Aegean. After several decades of study at Plato's Academy, he was chosen by the king of Macedonia, Philip II, who had a high regard for Greek culture, to tutor his son Alexander. Later, Aristotle returned to Athens to found his own school, the Lyceum. Of a very different temperament than the mystical Plato, Aristotle collected and categorized a vast array of knowledge. He lectured and wrote about politics, philosophy, ethics, logic, poetry, rhetoric, physics, astronomy, meteorology, zoology, and psychology, laying the foundations for many modern disciplines.

Inequality in Classical Greece

AP* Exam Tip Social inequality and labor systems are major comparison topics.

Athens, the inspiration for the concept of democracy in the Western tradition, was a democracy only for the relatively small percentage of inhabitants who were citizens—free adult males of pure Athenian ancestry. Excluding women, children, slaves, and foreigners, this group amounted to 30,000 or 40,000 people out of a total population of approximately 300,000—only 10 or 15 percent.

Slavery

Slaves, mostly of foreign origin, constituted perhaps one-third of the population of Attica in the fifth and fourth centuries B.C.E., and the average Athenian family owned one or more. Slaves were needed to run the shop or work on the farm while the master attended meetings of the Assembly or served on one of the boards that oversaw the day-to-day activities of the state. The slave was a "living piece of property," required to do any work, submit to any sexual acts, and receive any punishments the owner ordained. Most Greek slaves were domestic servants, often working on the same tasks as the master or mistress. Close daily contact between owners and slaves meant that a relationship often developed, making it hard for slave owners to deny the

Scala/Art Resource, NY

Vase Painting Depicting Women at an Athenian Fountain House, ca. 520 B.C.E. Paintings on Greek vases provide the most vivid pictorial record of ancient Greek life. The subject matter usually reflects the interests of the aristocratic males who purchased the vases—warfare, athletics, mythology, drinking parties—but sometimes we are given glimpses into the lives of women and the working classes. These women are presumably domestic servants sent to fetch water for the household from the public fountain. The large water jars they are filling are like the one on which this scene is depicted.

essential humanity of their slaves. Still, Aristotle rationalized the institution of slavery by arguing that *barbaroi* (non-Greeks) lacked the capacity to reason and thus were better off under the direction of rational Greek owners.

Women

The position of women varied across Greek communities. The women of Sparta, who were expected to bear and raise strong children, were encouraged to exercise, and they enjoyed a level of public visibility and outspokenness that shocked other Greeks. Athens may have been at the opposite extreme as regards the confinement and suppression of women. Ironically, the exploitation of women in Athens, as of slaves, made possible the high degree of freedom enjoyed by men in the democratic state. Greek men justified the confinement of women by claiming that they were naturally promiscuous and likely to introduce other men's children into the household.

Athenian marriages were unequal affairs. A new husband might be thirty, reasonably well educated, a veteran of war, and experienced in business and politics. Under law he had nearly absolute authority over the members of his household. He arranged his marriage with the parents of his prospective wife, who was likely to be a teenager brought up with no formal education and only minimal training in weaving, cooking, and household management. Coming into the home of a husband she hardly knew, she had no political rights and limited legal protection. The primary function of marriage was to produce children, preferably male. It is likely that many more girls than boys were victims of infanticide—the killing through exposure of unwanted children.

Husbands and wives had limited contact. The man spent the day outdoors attending to work or political responsibilities; he dined with male friends at night; and usually he slept alone in the men's quarters (see Material Culture: Wine and Beer in the Ancient World). The woman stayed home to cook, clean, raise the children, and supervise the servants, going out only to attend funerals and religious rituals and to make discreet visits to female relatives. During the three-day Thesmophoria (thes-moe-FOE-ree-uh) festival, the women of Athens lived together and managed their own affairs in a great encampment, carrying out mysterious rituals to enhance the fertility of the land. The appearance of assertive women on the Athenian stage is also suggestive. Although the plays were written by men and probably reflect a male fear of strong women, the playwrights must have had models in their mothers, sisters, and wives.

The inequality of men and women posed obstacles to creating a "meaningful relationship" between the sexes. To find his intellectual and emotional equal, a man often looked to other men. Bisexuality was common in ancient Greece, as much a product of the social structure as of biological inclinations. A common pattern was that of an older man wooing a youth, in the process mentoring him and initiating him into the community of adult males.

Peloponnesian War A protracted (431–404 B.C.E.) and costly conflict between the Athenian and Spartan alliance systems that convulsed most of the Greek world. The war was largely a consequence of Athenian imperialism. Possession of a naval empire allowed Athens to fight a war of attrition. Ultimately, Sparta prevailed because of Athenian errors and Persian financial support.

Failure of the City-State and Triumph of the Macedonians

The Peloponnesian War

The emergence of Athens as an imperial power in the half-century after the Persian invasion aroused the suspicions of other Greek states and led to open hostilities between former allies. In 431 B.C.E. the **Peloponnesian War** broke out. This nightmarish struggle between the Athenian

MATERIAL CULTURE

Wine and Beer in the Ancient World

The most prized beverages of ancient peoples were wine and beer. Sediments found in jars excavated at a site in northwest Iran prove that techniques for the manufacture of wine were known as early as the sixth millennium B.C.E. Beer dates back at least as far as the fourth millennium B.C.E. Archaeological excavations have brought to light the equipment used in preparing, transporting, serving, and imbibing these beverages.

In Egypt and Mesopotamia, beer, made from wheat or barley by an elaborate process, was the staple drink of both the elite and the common people. Women prepared beer for the family in their homes, and breweries produced large quantities for sale. Because the production process left chaff floating on the surface of the liquid, various means were employed to filter this out. Sculptures on Mesopotamian stone reliefs and seals show several drinkers drawing on straws immersed in a large bowl. Archaeologists have found examples of the perforated metal cones that fit over the submerged ends of the straws and filtered the liquid beer drawn through them.

The sharing of beer from a common vessel by several people probably was seen as creating a bond of friendship among the participants. Archaeologists have also found individual beer "mugs" resembling a modern watering can: closed bowls with a perforated spout to filter the chaff and a semicircular channel carrying the liquid into the drinker's mouth.

Ephorate of Prehistoric and Classical Antiquities, Vergina

Silver and Bronze Wine Set These beautifully crafted vessels were found in northern Greece in a tomb believed to be that of King Philip of Macedonia, the father of Alexander the Great. They include an amphora for storing wine, a pitcher for pouring, and several two-handled bowls and cups for drinking.

In Greece, Rome, and other Mediterranean lands, where the climate was suitable for cultivating grape vines, wine was the preferred beverage. Vines were prepared in February and periodically pinched and pruned. The

and Spartan alliance systems involved most of the Greek world. It was a war unlike any previous Greek war because the Athenians used their naval power to insulate themselves from the dangers of a siege by land. In midcentury they had built three long walls connecting the city with the port of Piraeus and the adjacent shoreline. At the start of the war, Pericles formulated an unprecedented strategy, refusing to engage the Spartan-led armies that invaded Attica each year. Pericles knew that, as long as Athens controlled the sea lanes and was able to provision itself, the enemy hoplites must soon return to their farms and the city could not be starved into submission. The Peloponnesian War dragged on for nearly three decades with great loss of life and squandering of resources. It sapped the morale of all Greece and ended only with the surrender of Athens after defeat in a naval battle in 404 B.C.E. The Persian Empire had bankrolled the construction of ships by the Spartan alliance, so Sparta finally was able to take the conflict into Athens's own element, the sea.

The victorious Spartans, who had entered the war championing "the freedom of the Greeks," took over Athens's overseas empire until their own increasingly highhanded behavior aroused the opposition of other city-states. Indeed, the fourth century B.C.E. was a time of nearly continuous skirmishing among Greek states. The independent polis, from one point of view the glory of Greek culture, was also fundamentally flawed because it fostered rivalry, fear, and warfare among neighboring communities.

Internal conflict in the Greek world allowed the Persians to recoup old losses. By the terms of the King's Peace of 387 B.C.E., to which most of the states of war-weary Greece subscribed, full-grown grapes were picked in September, then crushed—with a winepress or by people trampling on them—to produce a liquid that was sealed in casks for fermentation. The new vintage was sampled the following February. Exuberant religious festivals marked key moments in the cycle. Initially expensive and therefore confined to the wealthy and for religious ceremonies, in later antiquity wine became available to a wider spectrum of people. Unlike beer, which requires refrigeration, wine can be stored for a long time in sealed containers and thus could be transported and traded across ancient lands. The usual containers for wine were long, conical pottery jars, which the Greeks called *amphoras*.

The Greeks, who normally mixed wine with water (and thought it scandalous that Persians drank undiluted wine), developed an elaborate array of vessels, made of pottery, metal, and glass, to facilitate mixing, serving, and drinking the precious liquid (see the photo on the facing page). *Kraters* were large mixing bowls into which the wine and water were poured. The *hydria* was used to carry water, and a heater could be used to warm the water when that was desired. Another special vessel could be used to chill the wine by immersion in cold water. Ladles and elegantly narrow vessels with spouts were used to pour the concoction into the drinkers' cups. The most popular shapes for individual drinking vessels were a shallow bowl with two handles, called a *kylix*, and the *kantharos*, a large, deep, two-handled cup. Another popular implement in Greece and western Asia was the *rhyton*, a horn-shaped vessel that tapered into the head and forepaws of an animal with a small hole at the base. The drinker would fill the horn, holding his thumb over the hole until he was ready to drink or pour, then move his thumb and release a thin stream of wine that appeared to be coming out of the animal's mouth.

The drinking equipment belonging to wealthy Greeks was often decorated with representations of the god of wine, Dionysus, holding a kantharos and surrounded by a dense tangle of vines and grape clusters. His entourage included the half-human, half-horse Centaurs; and the Maenads, literally "crazy women," female worshipers who drank wine and engaged in frenzied dancing until they achieved an ecstatic state and sensed the presence of the god.

Greeks, Romans, and other Mediterranean peoples used wine for more conventional religious ceremonies, pouring libations on the ground or on the altar as an offering to the gods. It was also used as a disinfectant and painkiller or as an ingredient in various medicines. Above all, wine was featured at the banquets and drinking parties that forged and deepened social bonds. In the Greek world, the *symposion* (meaning "drinking together") was held after the meal. The host presided over the affair, making the crucial decision about the proportion of water to wine, suggesting topics of conversation, and trying to keep some semblance of order. There might also be entertainment in the form of musicians, dancers, and acrobats.

In Shang China, magnificent bronze vessels whose surfaces were covered with abstract designs and representations of otherworldly animals were used in elaborate ceremonies at ancestral shrines (see photo on page 42). The vessels contained offerings of wine and food for the spirits of the family's ancestors, who were imagined to still need sustenance in the afterlife. The treasured bronze vessels were often buried with their owners so that they could continue to employ them after death. In later periods, as the ancestral sacrifices became less important, beautiful bronze vessels, as well as their ceramic counterparts, became part of the equipment at the banquets of the well-to-do.

all of western Asia, including the Greek communities of the Anatolian seacoast, were conceded to Persia. The Persian king became the guarantor of a status quo that kept the Greeks divided and weak. Luckily for the Greeks, rebellions in Egypt, Cyprus, and Phoenicia as well as intrigues among some of the satraps in the western provinces diverted Persian attention from thoughts of another Greek invasion.

Philip and the Rise of Macedonia

Meanwhile, in northern Greece developments were taking place that would irrevocably alter the balance of power. Philip II (r. 359–336 B.C.E.) transformed his previously backward kingdom of Macedonia into the premier military power in the Greek world. (Although southern Greeks had long doubted the "Greekness" of the rough and rowdy Macedonians, many modern scholars regard their language and culture as Greek at base, though much influenced by contact with non-Greek neighbors.) Philip made a number of improvements to the traditional hoplite formation. He increased the striking power and mobility of his force by equipping soldiers with longer thrusting spears and less armor. Because horses thrived in the broad plains of the north, he experimented with the coordinated use of infantry and cavalry. His engineers developed new kinds of siege equipment, including the first catapults—machines using the power of twisted cords to hurl arrows or stones great distances. For the first time it became possible to storm a fortified city rather than wait for starvation to take effect.

In 338 B.C.E. Philip defeated a coalition of southern states and established the Confederacy of Corinth as an instrument for controlling the Greek city-states. Philip had himself appointed military commander for a planned all-Greek campaign against Persia, and his generals established a bridgehead on the Asiatic side of the Hellespont. Philip apparently was following the advice of Greek thinkers who had pondered the lessons of the Persian Wars of the fifth century B.C.E. and urged a crusade against the national enemy as a means of unifying their quarrelsome countrymen.

Alexander's Conquest of Persia

Alexander King of Macedonia in northern Greece. Between 334 and 323 B.C.E. he conquered the Persian Empire, reached the Indus Valley, founded many Greek-style cities, and spread Greek culture across the Middle East. Later known as Alexander the Great.

We will never know how far Philip's ambitions extended, for an assassin killed him in 336 B.C.E. When **Alexander** (356–323 B.C.E.), his son and heir, crossed into Asia in 334 B.C.E., his avowed purpose was to exact revenge for Xerxes' invasion a century and half before. He defeated the Persian forces of King Darius III (r. 336–330 B.C.E.) in three pitched battles in Anatolia and Mesopotamia, and he ultimately campaigned as far as the Punjab region of modern Pakistan. After more than two centuries of domination in the Middle East, the Achaemenid Persian Empire had fallen.

Alexander the Great, as he came to be called, maintained the framework of Persian administration in the lands he conquered, recognizing that it was well adapted to local circumstances and familiar to the subject peoples. At first, he replaced Persian officials with his own Macedonian and Greek comrades. To control strategic points in his expanding empire, he established a series of Greek-style cities, beginning with Alexandria in Egypt, and settled wounded and aged former soldiers in them. After his decisive victory in northern Mesopotamia (331 B.C.E.), he began to experiment with leaving cooperative Persian officials in place. He also admitted some Persians and other Iranians into his army and the circle of his courtiers, and he adopted elements of Persian dress and court ceremonial. Finally, he married several Iranian women who had useful royal or aristocratic connections, and he pressed his leading subordinates to do the same.

Scholars have reached widely varying conclusions about why Alexander adopted these policies, which were fiercely resented by the Macedonian nobility. Alexander may have operated from a combination of pragmatic and idealistic motives. He set off on his Asian campaign with visions of glory, booty, and revenge. But the farther east he traveled, the more he began to see himself as the legitimate successor of the Persian king (a claim facilitated by the death of Darius III at the hands of subordinates). Besides recognizing that he had responsibilities to all the diverse peoples who fell under his control, he also may have realized the difficulty of holding down so vast an empire by brute force and without the cooperation of important elements among the conquered peoples. In this, he was following the example of the Achaemenids.

SECTION REVIEW

- The unsuccessful revolt of Greek city-states in western Anatolia led to two Persian attacks on Greece in the early fifth century B.C.E.
- An ambitious Athens took control of a naval empire in the Aegean. The wealth brought in by the empire subsidized Athenian democracy and culture.
- Ironically, Athenian male citizens were freed up to participate in government and politics by restricting the rights and exploiting the labor of slaves and women.
- The Spartans and their allies, frightened by the growing power of Athens, initiated the lengthy Peloponnesian War but were only able to win with Persian help.
- In the mid-fourth century B.C.E., Philip II made Macedonia into a military power and forcibly united the Greek city-states.
- His son Alexander the Great conquered and took over the Persian Empire.

THE HELLENISTIC SYNTHESIS, 323–30 B.C.E.

Hellenistic Age Historians' term for the era, usually dated 323–30 B.C.E., in which Greek culture spread across western Asia and northeastern Africa after the conquests of Alexander the Great. The period ended with the fall of the last major Hellenistic kingdom to Rome, but Greek cultural influence persisted until the spread of Islam in the seventh century C.E.

Alexander died suddenly in 323 B.C.E. at the age of thirty-two, with no clear plan for the succession. This event ushered in a half-century of chaos as the most ambitious and ruthless of his officers struggled for control of the vast empire. When the dust cleared, the empire had been broken up into three major kingdoms, each ruled by a Macedonian dynasty—the Seleucid (sih-LOO-sid), Ptolemaic (tawl-uh-MAY-ik), and Antigonid (an-TIG-uh-nid) kingdoms (see Map 4.3). Each kingdom faced a unique set of circumstances, and although they frequently were at odds with one another, a rough balance of power prevented any one from gaining the upper hand and enabled smaller states to survive by playing off the great powers.

Historians call the epoch ushered in by Alexander the "**Hellenistic Age**" (323–30 B.C.E.) because the lands in northeastern Africa and western Asia that came under Greek rule became "Hellenized"—that is, powerfully influenced by Greek culture. This was a period of large kingdoms with heterogeneous populations, great cities, powerful rulers, pervasive bureaucracies, and vast disparities in wealth—a far cry from the small, homogeneous, independent city-states of Archaic and Classical Greece. It was a cosmopolitan age of long-distance trade and communications, which saw the rise of new institutions like libraries and universities, new kinds of scholarship and science, and the cultivation of sophisticated tastes in art and literature.

The Three Kingdoms

Ptolemies The Macedonian dynasty, descended from one of Alexander the Great's officers, that ruled Egypt for three centuries (323–30 B.C.E.). From their magnificent capital at Alexandria on the Mediterranean coast, the Ptolemies largely took over the system created by Egyptian pharaohs to extract the wealth of the land, rewarding Greeks and Hellenized non-Greeks serving in the military and administration.

Alexandria City on the Mediterranean coast of Egypt founded by Alexander. It became the capital of the Hellenistic kingdom of the Ptolemies. It contained the famous Library and the Museum, a center for leading scientific and literary figures. Its merchants engaged in trade with areas bordering the Mediterranean and the Indian Ocean.

The Seleucids, who took over the bulk of Alexander's conquests, faced the greatest challenges. The Indus Valley and Afghanistan soon split off, and over the course of the third and second centuries B.C.E. Iran was lost to the Parthians. From their capital at Syrian Antioch (AN-tee-awk), the Seleucid monarchs controlled Mesopotamia, Syria, and parts of Anatolia. Their sprawling territories were open to attack from many directions, and, like the Persians before them, they had to deal with many ethnic groups organized under various political and social forms. In the countryside, where most of the native peoples resided, the Seleucids largely maintained the Persian administrative system. They also continued Alexander's policy of founding Greek-style cities throughout their domains. These cities served as administrative centers and were also used to attract colonists from Greece, since the Seleucids needed Greek soldiers, engineers, and administrators.

The dynasty of the **Ptolemies** (TAWL-uh-meze) ruled Egypt and sometimes laid claim to adjacent Syria-Palestine. The people of Egypt belonged to only one ethnic group and were easily controlled because the vast majority were farmers in villages alongside the Nile. The Ptolemies essentially perfected an administrative structure devised by the pharaohs to extract the surplus wealth of this populous and productive land. The Egyptian economy was centrally planned and highly controlled. Vast revenues poured into the royal treasury from rents (the king owned most of the land), taxes of all sorts, and royal monopolies on olive oil, salt, papyrus, and other key commodities.

The Ptolemies ruled from **Alexandria**, the first of the new cities laid out by Alexander himself. Whereas Memphis and Thebes, the capitals of ancient Egypt, had been located upriver, Alexandria was situated where the westernmost branch of the Nile runs into the Mediterranean Sea, linking Egypt and the Mediterranean world. In the language of the bureaucracy, Alexandria was technically "beside Egypt" rather than in it, as if to emphasize the gulf between rulers and subjects.

The Ptolemies also encouraged the immigration of Greeks from the homeland and, in return for their skills and collaboration in the military or civil administration, gave them land and a privileged position in the new society. But the Ptolemies did not plant Greek-style cities throughout the Egyptian countryside. Only the last Ptolemy, Queen Cleopatra (r. 51–30 B.C.E.), even bothered to learn the language of her Egyptian subjects. Periodic insurrections in the countryside were signs of the Egyptians' growing resentment of the Greeks' exploitation and arrogance.

The Antigonid dynasty ruled a compact and ethnically homogeneous kingdom in the Macedonian homeland and northern Greece. Garrisons at strong-points gave the Antigonids a toehold in

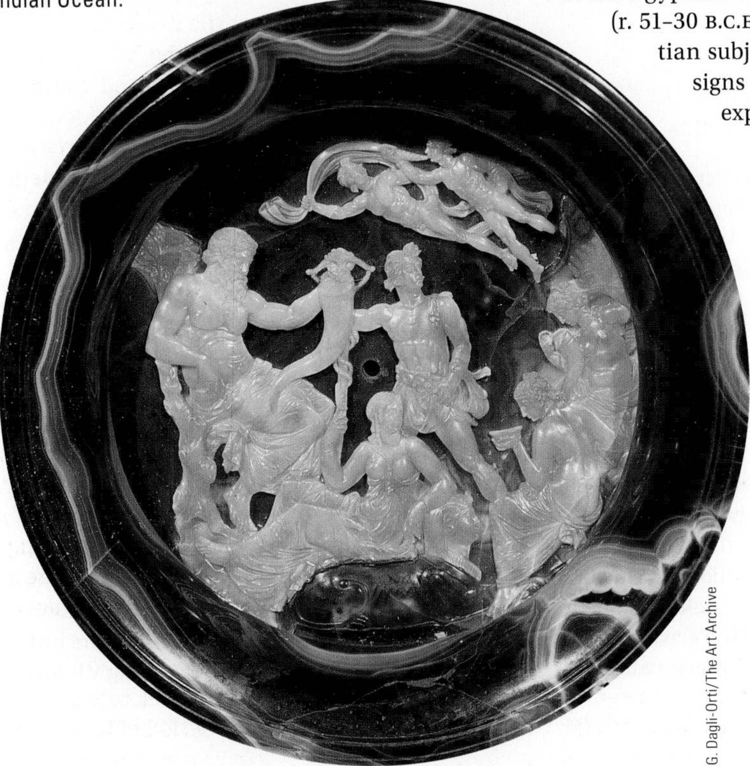

G. Dagli-Orti/The Art Archive

Hellenistic Cameo, Second Century B.C.E. This sardonyx cameo is an allegory of the prosperity of Ptolemaic Egypt. At left, the bearded river-god Nile holds a horn of plenty while his wife, seated on a sphinx and dressed like the Egyptian goddess Isis, raises a stalk of grain. Their son, at center, carries a seed bag and the shaft of a plow. The Seasons are seated at right. Two wind-gods float overhead. The style is entirely Greek, but the motifs are a blending of Greek and Egyptian elements.

ENVIRONMENT + TECHNOLOGY

Ancient Astronomy

Long before the advent of writing, people studied the appearance and movement of objects in the sky and used this information for a variety of purposes. Ancient hunters, herders, and farmers all coordinated their activities with the cycle of seasons during the year so that they could follow the migrations of prey, find appropriate pastures for domestic animals, and perform vital agricultural tasks.

Ancient farmers drew on an intimate knowledge of the night sky. Hesiod (HEE-see-uhd), who lived around 700 B.C.E., composed a poem called *Works and Days* describing the annual cycle of tasks on a Greek farm. How did the ancient Greeks, with no clocks, calendars, or newspapers, know where they were in the cycle of the year? They oriented themselves by close observation of natural phenomena such as the movements of planets, stars, and constellations in the night sky. Hesiod gives the following advice for determining the proper times for planting and harvesting grain:

Pleiades rising in the dawning sky, Harvest is nigh.
Pleiades setting in the waning night, Plowing is right.

The Pleiades (PLEE-uh-dees) are a cluster of seven stars visible to the naked eye. The ancient Greeks observed that individual stars, clusters, and constellations moved from east to west during the night and appeared in different parts of the sky at different times of the year. (In fact, the apparent movement of the stars is due to the earth's rotation on its axis and orbit around the sun against a background of unmoving stars.) Hesiod is telling his audience that, when the Pleiades appear above the eastern horizon just before the light of the rising sun makes all the other stars invisible (in May on the modern calendar), a sensible farmer will cut down his grain crop. Some months later (in our September), when the Pleiades dip below the western horizon just before sunrise, it is time to plow the fields and plant seeds for the next year's harvest.

Farmers such as Hesiod were primarily concerned with the seasons of the year. However, there was also a need to divide the year up into smaller units. The moon, so easily visible in the night sky and with clear phases, offered the unit of the month. Unfortunately, the lunar and solar cycles do not fit comfortably together, since twelve lunar months falls eleven days short of the solar cycle of a 365-day year. Ancient peoples wrestled with ways of reconciling the two cycles, and the months of varying lengths and leap years in our present-day calendar are the legacy of this dilemma.

The complex societies that arose from the fourth millennium B.C.E. onward had additional needs for information derived from astronomical observation, and these needs reflected the distinctive characteristics of those societies. In ancient Egypt an administrative calendar was essential for recordkeeping and the regular collection of taxes by the government. The Egyptians discovered that a calendar based on lunar months could be kept in harmony with the solar year by inserting an extra month five times over a nineteen-year cycle. They also learned from experience that the flooding of the Nile River—so vital for Egyptian agriculture—happened at the time when Sirius, the brightest star in the sky, rose above the eastern horizon just before the sun came up.

In the second millennium B.C.E., the Babylonians began to make and record very precise naked-eye observations of

central and southern Greece, and the shadow of Macedonian intervention always hung over the south. The southern states met the threat by banding together into confederations, such as the Achaean (uh-KEY-uhn) League in the Peloponnese, in which member-states maintained local autonomy but pooled resources and military power.

Athens and Sparta, the two leading cities of the Classical period, stood out from these confederations. The Spartans clung to the myth of their own invincibility and made a number of heroic but futile stands against Macedonian armies. Athens, which held a special place in the hearts of all Greeks because of the artistic and literary accomplishments of the fifth century B.C.E., pursued a policy of neutrality. The city became a large museum, filled with the relics and memories of a glorious past, as well as a university town that attracted the children of the well-to-do from all over the Mediterranean and western Asia.

Alexandria

In an age of cities, the greatest city of all was Alexandria, with a population of nearly half a million. At its heart was the royal compound, containing the palace and administrative buildings, as well as the magnificent Mausoleum of Alexander. The first Ptolemy had stolen the body of Alexander on its way back to Macedonia for burial, seeking legitimacy for his dynasty by claiming the blessing of the great conqueror, who was declared to be a god. Two harbors linked the commerce of the Mediterranean with the Red Sea and Indian Ocean. A great lighthouse—

the movements of the sun, the moon, and the visible planets, of occasional eclipses, and of other unusual celestial occurrences. Believing that the phenomena they saw in the sky sometimes contained messages and warnings of disaster, the rulers supported specialists who observed, recorded, and interpreted these "signs" from the gods. Using a sophisticated system of mathematical notation, they figured out the regularities of certain cycles and were able to predict future occurrences of eclipses and the movements of the planets.

Whereas Babylonian science observed and recorded data, Greek philosophers tried to figure out why the heavenly bodies moved as they did and what the actual structure of the *kosmos* (Greek for an "orderly arrangement") was. Aristotle pointed out that because the earth's shadow, as seen on the face of the moon during a lunar eclipse, was curved, the earth must be a sphere. Eratosthenes (eh-ruh-TOSS-thih-nees) made a surprisingly accurate calculation of the circumference of the earth. Aristarchus (ah-ris-TAWR-kiss) calculated the distances and relative sizes of the moon and sun. He also argued against the prevailing notion that the earth was the center of the universe, asserting that the earth and other planets revolved around the sun. Other Greek theorists pictured the earth as a sphere at the center of a set of concentric spheres that rotated, carrying along the seven visible "planets"—the moon, Mercury, Venus, the sun, Mars, Jupiter, Saturn—with the outermost ring containing the stars that maintain a fixed position relative to one another.

As a result of the conquests of Alexander the Great, Mesopotamia came under Greek control and Greek astronomers gained access to the many centuries of accumulated records of Babylonian observers. This more precise information allowed Greek thinkers to further refine their models for the structure and movement of celestial objects. The Greek conception of the universe, in the form set down by the second-century C.E. astronomer Claudius Ptolemy, became the basis of scientific thinking about these matters for the next 1,400 years in the Islamic Middle East and Christian Europe.

Ronald Sheridan/Ancient Art & Architecture Collection, Ltd.

Tower of the Winds, Athens, Second Century B.C.E. Designed in the Hellenistic period by the astronomer Andronicus of Cyrrhus, the eight sides are decorated with images of the eight directional winds. Sundials on the exterior showed the time of day, and a water-driven mechanism inside the tower revealed the hours, days, and phases of the moon.

the first of its kind, a multistory tower with a fiery beacon visible at a distance of 30 miles (48 kilometers)—was one of the wonders of the ancient world.

Alexandria gained further luster from its famous Library, with several hundred thousand volumes, and from its Museum, or "House of the Muses" (divinities who presided over the arts and sciences), a research institution supporting the work of the greatest poets, philosophers, doctors, and scientists of the day. These well-funded institutions made possible significant advances in sciences such as mathematics, medicine, and astronomy (see Environment and Technology: Ancient Astronomy).

Greek residents of Alexandria enjoyed citizenship in a Greek-style polis with an Assembly, a Council, and officials who dealt with local affairs. Public baths and shaded arcades offered places to relax and socialize with friends. Ancient plays were revived in the theaters, and musical performances and demonstrations of oratory took place in the concert halls. Gymnasia, besides providing facilities for exercise, were where young men of the privileged classes were schooled in athletics, music, and literature. Jews had their own civic government, officials, and law courts and predominated in two of the five main residential districts. Other quarters were filled with the sights, sounds, and smells of ethnic groups from Syria, Anatolia, and the Egyptian countryside.

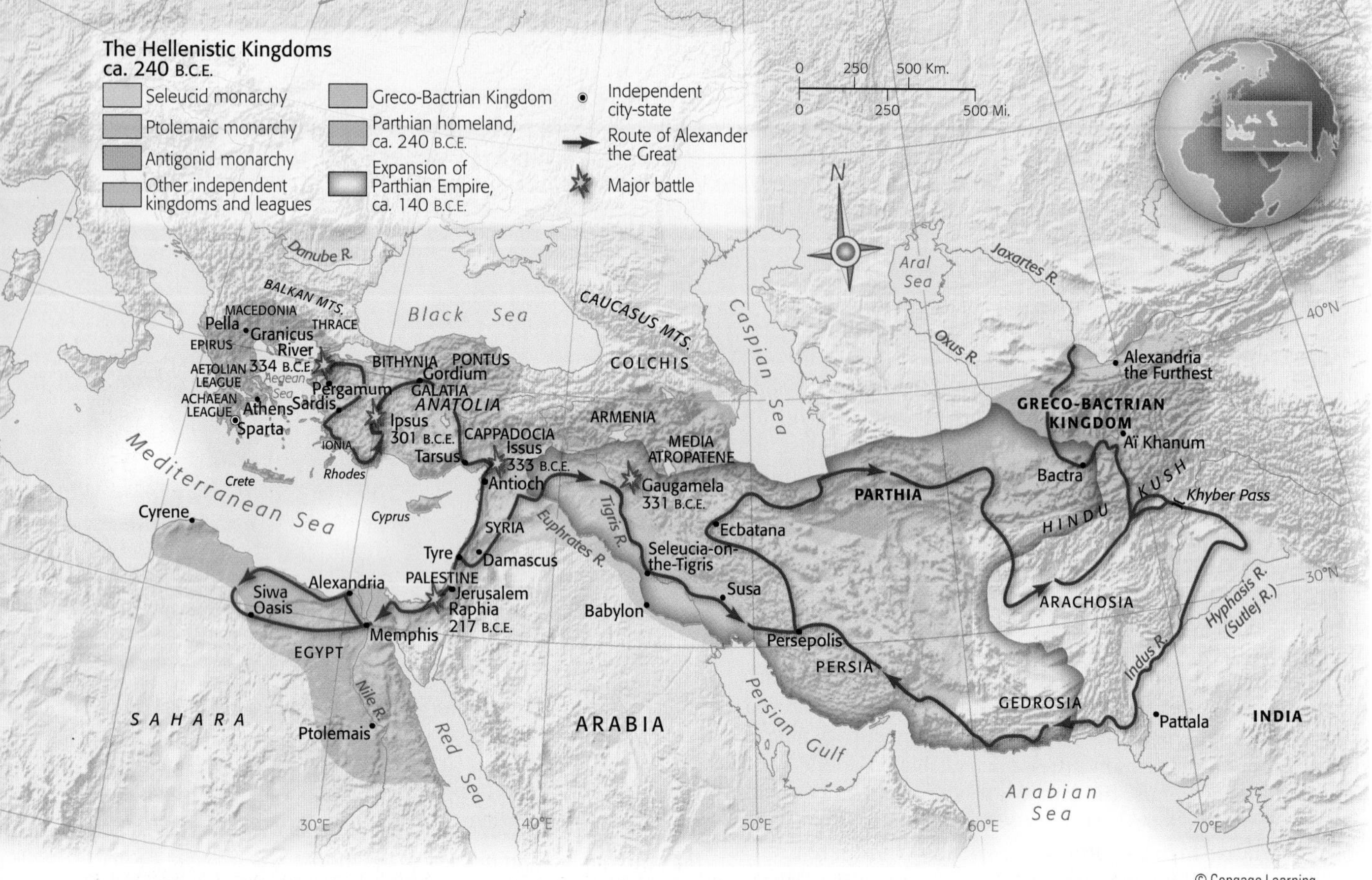

MAP 4.3 Hellenistic Civilization After the death of Alexander the Great in 323 B.C.E., his vast empire soon split apart into a number of large and small political entities. A Macedonian dynasty was established on each continent: the Antigonids ruled the Macedonian homeland and tried with varying success to extend their control over southern Greece; the Ptolemies ruled Egypt; and the Seleucids inherited the majority of Alexander's conquests in Asia, though they lost control of the eastern portions because of the rise of the Parthians of Iran in the second century B.C.E. This period saw Greeks migrating in large numbers from their overcrowded homeland to serve as a privileged class of soldiers and administrators on the new frontiers, where they replicated the lifestyle of the city-state.

e Interactive Map

In all the Hellenistic states, ambitious members of the indigenous populations learned the Greek language and adopted elements of Greek lifestyle, since this put them in a position to become part of the privileged and wealthy ruling class. For the ancient Greeks, to be Greek was primarily a matter of language and lifestyle rather than physical traits. In the Hellenistic Age there was a spontaneous synthesis of Greek and indigenous ways. Egyptians migrated to Alexandria, and Greeks and Egyptians intermarried in the villages of the countryside. Greeks living amid the monuments and descendants of the ancient civilizations of Egypt and western Asia were exposed to the mathematical and astronomical wisdom of Mesopotamia, the elaborate mortuary rituals of

SECTION REVIEW

- In the Hellenistic Age, Greeks controlled western Asia and northwest Africa. Greek culture would have a strong influence in this region for a thousand years.
- Alexander's empire was broken up into three major successor kingdoms in Europe, Asia, and Africa, each with its own unique challenges.
- Alexandria in Egypt, capital of the Ptolemies, was the greatest city in the world. It had a large and diverse population and was a center of commerce for the Mediterranean Sea and Indian Ocean.
- The Ptolemies created the greatest library of antiquity and the Museum, a center of research fostering advances in scholarship, science, technology, and medicine.
- Ambitious and elite members of indigenous peoples learned Greek and adopted a Greek lifestyle in order to be part of the privileged ruling class, while Greeks borrowed from the ancient heritages of Egypt and Mesopotamia.

Egypt, and the many attractions of foreign religious cults. With little official planning or blessing, stemming for the most part from the day-to-day experiences and actions of ordinary people, a great multicultural experiment unfolded as Greek and Middle Eastern cultural traits clashed and merged.

CONCLUSION

Profound changes took place in the lands of the eastern Mediterranean and western Asia in the first millennium B.C.E., with Persians and Greeks playing pivotal roles. Let us compare the impacts of these two peoples and assess the broad significance of these centuries.

The empire of the Achaemenid Persians was the largest empire yet to appear in the world, encompassing a wide variety of landscapes, peoples, and social, political, and economic systems. How did the Persians manage this diverse collection of lands for more than two centuries? The answer did not lie entirely in brute force. The Persian government demonstrated flexibility and tolerance in its handling of the laws, customs, and beliefs of subject peoples. Persian administration, superimposed on top of local structures, left a considerable role for native institutions.

The Persians also displayed a flair for public relations. Their brand of Zoroastrian religion underlined the authority of the king as the appointee of god, champion of justice, and defender of world order against evil and destructive forces. In their art and inscriptions, the Persian kings broadcast an image of a benevolent empire in which the dependent peoples gladly contributed to the welfare of the realm.

Western Asia underwent significant changes in the period of Persian supremacy. By imposing a uniform system of law and administration and by providing security and stability, the Persian government fostered prosperity, at least for some. It also organized labor on a large scale to construct an expanded water distribution network and work the extensive estates of the Persian royal family and nobility.

Most difficult to assess is the cultural impact of Persian rule. A new synthesis of the long-dominant culture of Mesopotamia with Iranian elements is most visible in the art, architecture, and inscriptions of the Persian monarchs. The Zoroastrian religion may have spread across the empire and influenced other religious traditions, such as Judaism, but Zoroastrianism does not appear to have had broad, popular appeal. The Persian administration relied heavily on the scribes and written languages of its Mesopotamian, Syrian, and Egyptian subjects, and literacy remained the preserve of a small, professional class. Thus the Persian language does not seem to have been widely adopted by inhabitants of the empire.

Nearly two centuries of trouble with the Greeks on their western frontier vexed the Persians, but they were primarily concerned with the security of their eastern and northeastern frontiers, where they were vulnerable to attack by the nomads of Central Asia. The technological differences between Greece and Persia were not great. The only significant difference was the hoplite arms and military formation used by the Greeks, which often allowed them to prevail over the Persians. The Persian king's response in the later fifth and fourth centuries B.C.E. was to hire Greek mercenaries to employ hoplite tactics for his benefit.

Alexander's conquests brought changes to the Greek world almost as radical as those experienced by the Persians. Greeks spilled out into the sprawling new frontiers in northeastern Africa and western Asia, and the independent city-state became inconsequential in a world of large kingdoms. The centuries of Greek domination had a far more pervasive cultural impact on the Middle East than did the Persian period. Whereas Alexander had been inclined to preserve the Persian administrative apparatus, leaving native institutions and personnel in place, his successors relied almost exclusively on a privileged class of Greek soldiers, officers, and administrators.

Equally significant were the foundation of Greek-style cities, which exerted a powerful cultural influence on important elements of the native populations, and a system of easily learned alphabetic Greek writing, which led to more widespread literacy and more effective dissemination of information. The result was that the Greeks had a profound impact on the peoples and lands of the Middle East, and Hellenism persisted as a cultural force for a thousand years.

KEY TERMS

Cyrus p. 110
Darius I p. 111
satrap p. 111
Persepolis p. 112
Zoroastrianism p. 114
polis p. 118
hoplite p. 119
tyrant p. 120
democracy p. 120
sacrifice p. 120
Herodotus p. 122
Pericles p. 123
Persian Wars p. 124
trireme p. 125
Socrates p. 126
Peloponnesian War p. 127
Alexander p. 130
Hellenistic Age p. 130
Ptolemies p. 131
Alexandria p. 131

EBOOK AND WEBSITE RESOURCES

Primary Sources

Gathas

The Trojan Hero Hector Prepares to Meet His Destiny

A Lyric Poem Laments an Absent Lover

Apologia

Aristotle on Politics

Interactive Maps

Map 4.1 The Persian Empire

Map 4.2 Ancient Greece

Map 4.3 Hellenistic Civilization

Plus flashcards, practice quizzes, and more. Go to: www.cengage.com/history/bullietearthpeople5e

SUGGESTED READING

Briant, Pierre. *From Cyrus to Alexander: A History of the Persian Empire.* 2002. The most up-to-date history of ancient Persia, by the leading scholar in this field.

Brosius, Maria. *Women in Ancient Persia, 559–331 B.C.* 1996. Gathers and evaluates the scattered evidence.

Bugh, Glenn R., ed. *The Cambridge Companion to the Hellenistic World.* 2006. Essays by leading authorities on many aspects of Hellenistic history and culture.

Cawkwell, George. *The Greek Wars: The Failure of Persia.* 2006. Examines the two-centuries-long encounter from a Persian perspective.

Curtis, John, and Nigel Tallis, eds. *Forgotten Empire: The World of Ancient Persia.* 2005. The catalogue of a major exhibition at the British Museum, containing both magnificent illustrations and scholarly essays on Persian history and culture.

Dillon, Matthew, ed. *Ancient Greece: Social and Historical Documents from Archaic Times to the Death of Socrates,* 2nd ed. 2000. A wide-ranging collection of documents in translation with explanatory notes.

Fantham, Elaine, Helene Peet Foley, Natalie Boymel Kampen, Sarah B. Pomeroy, and H. Alan Shapiro. *Women in the Classical World: Image and Text.* 1995. A strong exposition of the roles, experiences, and treatment of women in Greek and Roman society, combining texts and visual images with interpretation.

Grant, Michael, and Rachel Kitzinger, eds. *Civilization of the Ancient Mediterranean,* 3 vols. 1987. Essays by contemporary experts on nearly every aspect of ancient Greco-Roman civilization, with select bibliographies.

Hanson, Victor Davis. *The Other Greeks: The Family Farm and the Agrarian Roots of Western Civilization.* 1995. Emphasizes the centrality of farming to the development of Greek institutions and values.

Hanson, Victor Davis. *The Western Way of War: Infantry Battle in Classical Greece.* 1989. A clear and gripping description of every aspect of the most terrifying and effective form of combat in antiquity.

Havelock, Eric A. *The Muse Learns to Write: Reflections on Orality and Literacy from Antiquity to the Present.* 1986. Explores the profound effects of alphabetic literacy on the Greek mind.

Heckel, Waldemar, and Lawrence A. Trittle, eds. *Alexander the Great: A New History.* 2009. Essays by leading experts on Alexander's life, times, and legacy.

Kuhrt, Amelie. *The Persian Empire: A Corpus of Sources from the Achaemenid Period,* 2 vols. 2007. Makes available a wide range of documents in translation with explanatory notes.

Pomeroy, Sarah B., Stanley M. Burstein, Walter Donlan, and Jennifer Tolbert Roberts. *Ancient Greece: A Political, Social, and Cultural History,* 2nd ed. 2007. An up-to-date, well-written account of Greek history and culture.

The Perseus Project (*www.perseus.tufts.edu*). A remarkable Internet site containing hundreds of ancient texts, thousands of photographs of artifacts and sites, maps, encyclopedias, dictionaries, and other resources for the study of Greek (and Roman) civilization.

NOTES

1. Maria Brosius, *Women in Ancient Persia, 559–331 B.C.* (Oxford and New York: Oxford University Press, 1996).
2. Quoted in Roland G. Kent, *Old Persian: Grammar, Texts, Lexicon*, 2nd ed. (New Haven, CT: American Oriental Society, 1953), 138, 140.
3. Richmond Lattimore, *Greek Lyrics*, 2nd ed. (Chicago: University of Chicago Press, 1960), 2.
4. G. S. Kirk and J. E. Raven, *The Presocratic Philosophers: A Critical History with a Selection of Texts* (Cambridge, England: Cambridge University Press, 1957), 169.
5. Herodotus, *The History*, trans. David Grene (Chicago: University of Chicago Press, 1988), 33. (Herodotus 1.1)

AP* REVIEW QUESTIONS FOR CHAPTER 4

1. One of the major problems that historians face in studying ancient Persia is that
   (A) much of the source material was written from the point of view of the Greeks.
   (B) the written language is difficult to understand.
   (C) there is no archaeological evidence other than ruins.
   (D) much of the evidence remains submerged in the Tigris and Euphrates Rivers.

2. Darius may be considered the most important of the Persian kings because
   (A) he reigned for the longest time.
   (B) he began the empire.
   (C) of his conquests and his reorganization of the empire.
   (D) he controlled the Silk Road.

3. In the later Persian Empire, provinces, overseen by governors, were divided into
   (A) maji.
   (B) satraps.
   (C) Mujahedeen.
   (D) Elamites.

4. In construction projects, Darius and Xerxes were inspired by the traditions of
   (A) Egypt.
   (B) the Indus Valley.
   (C) Mesopotamia.
   (D) the Shang dynasty.

5. King Darius said: "By the grace of Ahuramazda am I king." This statement indicates that Darius likely worshiped as a(an)
   (A) Elamite.
   (B) Zoroastrian.
   (C) Nestorian.
   (D) Hebrew.

6. Which of the following is a true statement concerning Zoroastrianism?
   (A) It was a monotheistic polytheism.
   (B) It originated in Egypt or North Africa.
   (C) It had no creation story.
   (D) It is thought to have had a large impact on Judaism.

7. The Greeks were drawn to the sea because
   (A) overland travel was difficult.
   (B) they needed to import metals.
   (C) Greece had good anchorages.
   (D) All of the above

8. The first true alphabet emerged in Greece when the Greeks merged their vowel sounds with the symbols from
   (A) Romans.
   (B) Egyptians.
   (C) Phoenicians.
   (D) Persians.

9. Most Greek urban centers had a place of refuge in case of emergency known as a(an)
   (A) acropolis.
   (B) agora.
   (C) hoplite.
   (D) polis.

10. Greek colonization began as a way to
    (A) convert the *barbaroi* to Greek customs and culture.
    (B) relieve population pressures on the Greek world.
    (C) prevent the Persians from gaining control of the Mediterranean Sea.
    (D) control the growth of Rome.

11. In the sixth century B.C.E., Greeks began to record their stories, history, poetry, and other writings. The men who began this are called
    (A) scribes.
    (B) entrecotes.
    (C) logographers.
    (D) hoplites.

12. The Greeks city-states formed the _______ as a way to prosecute the war against the Persians.

    (A) Ionian Conference
    (B) Athenian League
    (C) Spartan Confederation
    (D) Delian League

13. In Athenian marriages, the duty of the women was to

    (A) produce male children.
    (B) serve as the equal partner of the male.
    (C) farm the land.
    (D) operate the family business.

14. The Ptolemies ruled from

    (A) Athens.
    (B) Sparta.
    (C) Persia.
    (D) Alexandria.

CHAPTER

5

CHAPTER OUTLINE

- Rome's Creation of a Mediterranean Empire, 753 B.C.E.–600 C.E.
- The Origins of Imperial China, 221 B.C.E.–220 C.E.
- Conclusion

DIVERSITY + DOMINANCE *The Treatment of Slaves in Rome and China*

ENVIRONMENT + TECHNOLOGY *Water Engineering in Rome and China*

Scala/Art Resource, NY

Dancing Girl Wearing Silk Garment, Second–Third Century C.E. This Roman mosaic depicts a musician accompanying a dancer who is wearing a sheer garment of silk imported from China.

Visit the website and ebook for additional study materials and interactive tools: www.cengage.com/history/bullietearthpeople5e

An Age of Empires: Rome and Han China, 753 B.C.E.–600 C.E.

- How did Rome create and maintain its vast Mediterranean empire?
- How did imperial China evolve under the Qin and Han dynasties?
- What were the most important similarities and differences between these two empires, and what do the similarities and differences tell us about the circumstances and the character of each?

According to Chinese sources, in the year 166 C.E. a group of travelers identifying themselves as envoys from Andun, the king of distant Da Qin, arrived at the court of the Chinese emperor Huan, one of the Han rulers. Andun was Marcus Aurelius Antoninus, the emperor of Rome. As far as we know, these travelers were the first "Romans" to reach China, although they probably were residents of one of the eastern provinces of the Roman Empire, and they probably stretched the truth in claiming to be official representatives of the Roman emperor. More likely they were merchants hoping to set up a profitable trading arrangement at the source of the silk so highly prized in the West. Chinese officials, however, were in no position to disprove their claim, since there was no direct contact between the Roman and Chinese Empires.

We do not know what became of these travelers, and their mission apparently did not lead to more regular contact between the empires. Even so, the episode raises some interesting points. First, the last centuries B.C.E. and the first centuries C.E. saw the emergence of two manifestations of a new kind of empire. Second, Rome and China were linked by far-flung international trading networks encompassing the entire Eastern Hemisphere, and they were dimly aware of each other's existence.

The Roman Empire encompassed all the lands surrounding the Mediterranean Sea as well as sizeable portions of continental Europe and the Middle East. The Han Empire stretched from the Pacific Ocean to the oases of Central Asia. The largest empires the world had yet seen, they succeeded in centralizing control to a greater degree than earlier empires; their cultural impact on the lands and peoples they dominated was more pervasive; and they were remarkably stable and lasted for many centuries.

Thousands of miles separated Rome and Han China; neither influenced the other. Why did two such unprecedented political entities flourish at the same time? And why did they develop roughly similar solutions to certain problems? Historians have put forth theories stressing supposedly common factors—such as climate change and the pressure of nomadic peoples from Central Asia on the Roman and Chinese frontiers—but no theory has won general support.

AP* Exam Tip The differences between empires like Rome and Han China are major comparison points on the exam. These types of comparisons make excellent essay topics.

ROME'S CREATION OF A MEDITERRANEAN EMPIRE, 753 B.C.E.–600 C.E.

Rome's central location contributed to its success in unifying Italy and then all the lands ringing the Mediterranean Sea (see Map 5.1). The middle of three peninsulas that jut from the European landmass into the Mediterranean, the boot-shaped Italian peninsula and the large island of Sicily constitute a natural bridge almost linking Europe and North Africa. Italy was a crossroads in the Mediterranean, and Rome was a crossroads within Italy. Rome lay at the midpoint of the peninsula, about 15 miles (24 kilometers) from the western coast, where a north-south road intersected an east-west river route. The Tiber River on one side and a double ring of seven hills on the other afforded natural protection to the site.

Italy is a land of hills and mountains. The Apennine range runs along its length like a spine, separating the eastern and western coastal plains, while the arc of the Alps shields it on the north. Many of Italy's rivers are navigable, and passes through the Apennines and through the snowcapped Alps allowed merchants and armies to travel overland. The mild Mediterranean climate affords a long growing season and conditions suitable for a wide variety of crops. The hillsides, largely denuded of cover today, were well forested in ancient times, providing timber for construction and fuel. The region of Etruria in the northwest was rich in iron and other metals.

Even though as much as 75 percent of the total area of the Italian peninsula is hilly, there is still ample arable land in the coastal plains and river valleys. Much of this land has extremely fertile volcanic soil and sustained a much larger population than was possible in Greece. While expanding within Italy, the Roman state created effective mechanisms for tapping the human resources of the countryside.

A Republic of Farmers, 753–31 B.C.E.

Origins

Republic The period from 507 to 31 B.C.E., during which Rome was largely governed by the aristocratic Roman Senate.

Senate A council whose members were the heads of wealthy, landowning families. Originally an advisory body to the early kings, in the era of the Roman Republic the Senate effectively governed the Roman state and the growing empire. Under Senate leadership, Rome conquered an empire of unprecedented extent in the lands surrounding the Mediterranean Sea.

Popular legend maintained that Romulus was cast adrift on the Tiber River as a baby, was nursed by a she-wolf, and founded the city of Rome in 753 B.C.E. Archaeological research, however, shows that the Palatine Hill was occupied as early as 1000 B.C.E. The merging of several hilltop communities to form an urban nucleus, made possible by the draining of a swamp on the site of the future Roman Forum (civic center), took place shortly before 600 B.C.E. The Latin speech and cultural patterns of the inhabitants of the site were typical of the indigenous population of most of the peninsula. However, tradition remembered Etruscan immigrants arriving in the seventh century B.C.E., and Rome came to pride itself on offering refuge to exiles and outcasts.

Agriculture was the essential economic activity in the early Roman state, and land was the basis of wealth. As a consequence, social status, political privilege, and fundamental values were related to land ownership. Most early Romans were self-sufficient farmers who owned small plots of land. A small number of families managed to acquire large tracts of land. The heads of these wealthy families were members of the Senate—a "Council of Elders" that played a dominant role in the politics of the Roman state. According to tradition, there were seven kings of Rome between 753 and 507 B.C.E. The first was Romulus; the last was the tyrannical Tarquinius Superbus. In 507 B.C.E. members of the senatorial class, led by Brutus "the Liberator," deposed Tarquinius Superbus and instituted a *res publica*, a "public possession," or republic.

The Republic

The **Republic**, which lasted from 507 to 31 B.C.E., was not a democracy in the modern sense. Sovereign power resided in an Assembly of the male citizens where the votes of the wealthy classes counted for more than the votes of poor citizens. Each year a slate of officials was chosen, with members of the elite competing vigorously to hold offices in a prescribed order. The culmination of a political career was to be selected as one of the two consuls who presided over meetings of the Senate and Assembly and commanded the army on military campaigns.

The real center of power was the **Senate**. Technically an advisory council, first to the kings and later to the annually changing Republican officials, the Senate increasingly made policy and governed. Senators nominated their sons for public offices and filled Senate vacancies from the ranks of former officials. This self-perpetuating body, whose members served for life, brought together the state's wealth, influence, and political and military experience.

CHRONOLOGY

	Rome	China
1000 B.C.E.	1000 B.C.E. First settlement on site of Rome	
500 B.C.E.	507 B.C.E. Establishment of the Republic	480–221 B.C.E. Warring States Period
300 B.C.E.	290 B.C.E. Defeat of tribes of Samnium gives Romans control of Italy 264–202 B.C.E. Wars against Carthage guarantee Roman control of western Mediterranean	221 B.C.E. Qin emperor unites eastern China
200 B.C.E.	200–146 B.C.E. Wars against Hellenistic kingdoms lead to control of eastern Mediterranean	202 B.C.E. Han dynasty succeeds Qin 140–87 B.C.E. Emperor Wu expands the Han Empire 109–91 B.C.E. Sima Qian writes history of China
100 B.C.E.	88–31 B.C.E. Civil wars and failure of the Republic 31 B.C.E.–14 C.E. Augustus establishes the Principate	9–23 C.E. Wang Mang usurps throne 25 C.E. Han capital transferred from Chang'an to Luoyang
50 C.E.	45–58 C.E. Paul spreads Christianity in the eastern Mediterranean	99 C.E. Ban Zhao composes "Lessons for Women"
200 C.E.	235–284 C.E. Third-Century Crisis	220 C.E. Fall of Han dynasty
300 C.E.	324 C.E. Constantine moves capital to Constantinople	

Class, Conflicts, and Social Relations

The inequalities in Roman society led to periodic conflict between the elite (called "patricians" [puh-TRISH-uhn]) and the majority of the population (called "plebeians" [pluh-BEE-uhn]), a struggle known as the Conflict of the Orders. On several occasions the plebeians refused to work or fight, and even physically withdrew from the city, in order to pressure the elite to make political concessions. One result was publication of the laws on twelve stone tablets ca. 450 B.C.E., which served as a check on arbitrary decisions by judicial officials. Another important reform was the creation of new officials, the tribunes (TRIH-byoon), who were drawn from the nonelite classes and who could veto, or block, actions of the Assembly or officials that threatened the interests of the lower orders. The elite, though forced to give in on key points, found ways to blunt the reforms, in large part by bringing the plebeian leadership into an expanded elite.

patron/client relationship In ancient Rome, a fundamental social relationship in which the patron—a wealthy and powerful individual—provided legal and economic protection and assistance to clients, men of lesser status and means, and in return the clients supported the political careers and economic interests of their patron.

The basic unit of Roman society was the family, made up of the several living generations of family members plus domestic slaves. The oldest living male, the *paterfamilias*, exercised absolute authority over other family members. More generally, important male members of the society possessed *auctoritas*, a quality that elicited obedience from their inferiors.

Complex ties of obligation, such as the **patron/client relationship**, bound together individuals of different classes. Clients sought the help and protection of patrons, men of wealth and influence. A patron provided legal advice and representation, physical protection, and loans of money in tough times. In turn, the client was expected to follow his patron into battle, work on his land, and support him in the political arena. Throngs of clients awaited their patrons in the morning and accompanied them to the Forum for the day's business. Especially large retinues brought great prestige. Middle-class clients of aristocrats might be patrons of poorer men. In Rome inequality was accepted, institutionalized, and turned into a system of mutual benefits and obligations.

MAP 5.1 **The Roman Empire** The Roman Empire came to encompass all the lands surrounding the Mediterranean Sea, as well as parts of continental Europe. When Augustus died in 14 C.E., he left instructions to his successors not to expand beyond the limits he had set, but Claudius invaded southern Britain in the mid-first century and the soldier-emperor Trajan added Romania early in the second century. Deserts and seas provided solid natural boundaries, but the long and vulnerable river border in central and eastern Europe would eventually prove expensive to defend and vulnerable to invasion by Germanic and Central Asian peoples.

Interactive Map

Alinari/Art Resource, NY

Statue of a Roman Carrying Busts of His Ancestors, First Century B.C.E. Roman society was extremely conscious of status, and the status of an elite Roman family was determined in large part by the public achievements of ancestors and living members. A visitor to a Roman home found portraits of distinguished ancestors in the entry hall, along with labels listing the offices they held. Portrait heads were carried in funeral processions.

Historical sources rarely report the activities of Roman women, largely because they played no public role, and nearly all our information pertains to the upper classes. In early Rome, a woman was like a child in the eyes of the law. She started out under the absolute authority of her paterfamilias. When she married, she came under the jurisdiction of the paterfamilias of her husband's family. Unable to own property or represent herself in legal proceedings, she depended on a male guardian to protect her interests.

Despite these limitations, Roman women were less constrained than their Greek counterparts (see Chapter 4). Over time they gained greater personal protection and economic freedom: for instance, some employed a form of marriage that left a woman under the jurisdiction of her father and independent after his death. There are many stories of strong women with great influence on their husbands or sons who helped shape Roman history. From the first century B.C.E. on, Roman poets confess their love for educated and outspoken women.

Religion

Early Romans believed in invisible forces known as *numina*. Vesta, the living, pulsating energy of fire, dwelled in the hearth. Janus guarded the door. The Penates watched over food stored in the cupboard. Other deities resided in nearby hills, caves, grottoes, and springs. Romans made small offerings of cakes and liquids to win the favor of these spirits. Certain gods had larger spheres of operation—for example, Jupiter was the god of the sky, and Mars initially was a god of agriculture as well as war.

The Romans labored to maintain the *pax deorum* ("peace of the gods"), a covenant between the gods and the Roman state. Boards of priests drawn from the aristocracy performed sacrifices and other rituals to win the gods' favor. In return, the gods were expected to favor the undertakings of the Roman state.

When the Romans came into contact with the Greeks of southern Italy (see Chapter 4), they equated their major deities with Greek gods—for example, Jupiter with Greek Zeus, Mars with Greek Ares—and they took over the myths attached to those gods.

Expansion in Italy and the Mediterranean

Causes and Instruments of Expansion

AP* Exam Tip It is important to understand the growth and expansion of classical empires.

Around 500 B.C.E. Rome was a relatively unimportant city-state in central Italy. Three and a half centuries later, Rome was the center of a huge empire encompassing virtually all the lands surrounding the Mediterranean Sea. Expansion began slowly, then picked up momentum, reaching a peak in the third and second centuries B.C.E. Some scholars attribute this expansion to the greed and aggressiveness of a people fond of war. Others observe that the structure of the Roman state encouraged war, because the two consuls had only one year in office in which to gain military glory. The Romans invariably claimed that they were only defending themselves. The pattern was that the Romans, feeling insecure, expanded the territory under their control in order to provide a buffer against attack. However, each new conquest became vulnerable and led to further expansion.

The chief instrument of Roman expansion was the army. All male citizens owning a specified amount of land were subject to service. The Roman soldiers' equipment—body armor, shield, spear, and sword—was not far different from that of Greek hoplites, but the Roman battle line was more flexible than the phalanx, being subdivided into units that could maneuver independently. Roman armies were famous for their training and discipline. One observer noted

Peter Rockwell, Rome

Scene from Trajan's Column, Rome, ca. 113 C.E. The Roman emperor Trajan erected a marble column 125 feet (38 meters) in height to commemorate his triumphant campaign in Dacia (modern Romania). The relief carving, which snakes around the column for 656 feet (200 meters), illustrates numerous episodes of the conquest and provides a detailed pictorial record of the equipment and practices of the Roman army in the field. This panel depicts soldiers building a fort.

that a Greek army would lazily seek a naturally defended hilltop to camp for the night, but a Roman army would always laboriously fortify an identical camp in the plain.

Rome's conquest of Italy was sparked by friction between the hill tribes of the Apennines, who drove their herds to seasonal grazing grounds, and the farmers of the coastal plains. In the fifth century B.C.E. Rome led a league of central Italian cities organized for defense against the hill tribes. On several occasions in the fourth century B.C.E. the Romans protected the wealthy and sophisticated cities of Campania, the region on the Bay of Naples possessing the richest farmland in Italy. By 290 B.C.E., in the course of three wars with the Samnite tribes of central Italy, the Romans had extended their "protection" over nearly the entire peninsula.

Unlike the Greeks, who were reluctant to share the privileges of citizenship with outsiders, the Romans often granted some or all of the political, legal, and economic privileges of Roman citizenship to conquered populations. They co-opted the most influential people in the conquered communities and made Rome's interests their interests. Rome demanded soldiers from its Italian subjects, and a seemingly inexhaustible reservoir of manpower was a key element of its military success. In a number of crucial wars, Rome was able to endure higher casualties than the enemy and to prevail by sheer numbers.

Overseas Provinces

Between 264 and 202 B.C.E. Rome fought two protracted and bloody wars against the Carthaginians, those energetic descendants of Phoenicians from Lebanon who had settled in present-day Tunisia and dominated the commerce of the western Mediterranean (see Chapter 3). The Roman state emerged as the unchallenged master of the western Mediterranean and acquired its first overseas provinces in Sicily, Sardinia, and Spain (see Map 5.1). Between 200 and 146 B.C.E. a series of wars pitted the Roman state against the major Hellenistic kingdoms in the eastern Mediterranean. The Romans were at first reluctant to occupy such distant territories and withdrew their troops at the conclusion of several wars. But when the settlements that they imposed failed to take root—often because Rome's "friends" in the Greek world did not understand that they were expected to be deferential and obedient clients to their Roman patron—the frustrated Roman government took over direct administration of these lands. The conquest of the Celtic peoples of Gaul (modern France; see Chapter 2) by Rome's most brilliant general, Gaius Julius Caesar, between 59 and 51 B.C.E. led to Rome's first territorial acquisitions in Europe's heartland.

At first the Romans resisted extending their system of governance and citizenship rights to the distant provinces. Indigenous elite groups willing to collaborate with the Romans were given considerable autonomy, including responsibility for local administration and tax collection. Every year a senator who recently had held a high office was dispatched to each province to serve as governor. Accompanied by a small retinue of friends and relations who served as advisers and deputies, he was responsible for defending the province against outside attack and internal disruption, overseeing the collection of taxes and other revenues due Rome, and deciding legal cases.

Over time, this system of provincial administration proved inadequate. Officials were chosen because of their political connections and often lacked competence. Yearly changes of governor meant that incumbents had little time to gain experience or make local contacts. Although many governors were honest, some unscrupulously extorted huge sums of money from the provincial populace. While governing an ever-larger Mediterranean empire, the Romans were still relying on the institutions and attitudes that developed when Rome was merely a city-state.

The Failure of the Republic

Economic and Social Changes in Italy

Rome's success in creating a vast empire unleashed forces that eventually destroyed the Republican system of government. The frequent wars and territorial expansion of the third and second centuries B.C.E. produced profound changes in the Italian landscape. Most of the wealth generated by the conquest and control of new provinces ended up in the hands of the upper classes. Italian farmers were away from home on military service for long periods of time, and while they were away, investors took over their farms by purchase, deception, or intimidation. The small, self-sufficient farms of the Italian countryside, whose peasant owners had been the backbone of the Roman legions, were replaced by *latifundia*, literally "broad estates," or ranches.

e **PRIMARY SOURCE: A Man of Unlimited Ambition: Julius Caesar** Find out how Roman attitudes toward kingship led to the assassination of Julius Caesar.

The owners of these large estates grazed herds of cattle or grew crops—such as grapes for wine—that brought in big profits, rather than growing wheat, the staple food of ancient Italy. As a result, the population in the burgeoning cities of Italy became dependent on expensive imported grain. Meanwhile, the cheap slave labor provided by prisoners of war (see Diversity and Dominance: The Treatment of Slaves in Rome and China) made it hard for peasants who had lost their farms to find work in the countryside. When they moved to Rome and other cities, they found no work there either, and they lived in dire poverty. The growing urban masses, idle and prone to riot, would play a major role in the political struggles of the late Republic.

The Civil Wars

Principate A term used to characterize Roman government in the first three centuries C.E., based on the ambiguous title princeps ("first citizen") adopted by Augustus to conceal his military dictatorship.

Augustus Honorific name of Octavian, founder of the Roman Principate, the military dictatorship that replaced the failing rule of the Roman Senate. After defeating all rivals, between 31 B.C.E. and 14 C.E. he laid the groundwork for several centuries of stability and prosperity in the Roman Empire.

equites In ancient Italy, prosperous landowners second in wealth and status to the senatorial aristocracy. The Roman emperors allied with this group to counterbalance the influence of the old aristocracy and used the equites to staff the imperial civil service.

One consequence of the decline of peasant farmers in Italy was a shortage of men who owned the property required for military service. At the end of the second century B.C.E. Gaius Marius—a "new man," as the Romans called politically active individuals who did not belong to the traditional ruling class—accepted into his legions poor, propertyless men, and promised them farms upon retirement from military service. These troops became devoted to Marius and helped him get elected to an unprecedented (and illegal) six consulships.

Between 88 and 31 B.C.E., a series of ambitious individuals—Sulla, Pompey, Julius Caesar, Mark Antony, and Octavian—commanded armies more loyal to them than to the state. Their use of Roman troops to increase their personal power led to bloody civil wars. The city of Rome was taken by force on several occasions, and victorious commanders executed opponents and controlled the state.

The Roman Principate, 31 B.C.E.–330 C.E.

Julius Caesar's grandnephew and heir, Octavian (63 B.C.E.–14 C.E.), eliminated all rivals by 31 B.C.E. and carefully set about refashioning the Roman system of government. He maintained the forms of the Republic—the offices, honors, and privileges of the senatorial class—but fundamentally altered the realities of power. A military dictator in fact, he never called himself king or emperor, claiming merely to be *princeps*, "first among equals," in a restored Republic. Thus, the period following the Republic is called the **Principate**.

Augustus, one of the many honorific titles that the Senate gave Octavian, connotes prosperity and piety, and it became the name by which he is best known to posterity. Augustus's patience and intuitive grasp of human nature enabled him to manipulate all the groups in Roman society. When he died in 14 C.E., after forty-five years of carefully veiled rule, few could remember the Republic. During his reign Egypt and parts of the Middle East and Central Europe were added to the empire, leaving only the southern half of Britain and modern Romania to be added later.

Augustus allied himself with the ***equites*** (EH-kwee-tays), the class of well-to-do Italian merchants and landowners second in wealth and social status to the senatorial class. This body of competent and self-assured individuals became the core of a new, paid civil service that helped run the Roman Empire. At last Rome had a governmental bureaucracy up to the task of managing a large empire with considerable honesty, consistency, and efficiency.

DIVERSITY + DOMINANCE

The Treatment of Slaves in Rome and China

Although slavery existed in most ancient societies, Rome was one of the few in which slave labor became the foundation of the economy. During the frequent wars of the second century B.C.E., large numbers of prisoners were enslaved. The prices of such slaves were low, and landowners and manufacturers found they could compel slaves to work longer and harder than hired laborers. Periodically, the harsh working and living conditions resulted in slave revolts.

The following excerpt, from one of several surviving manuals on agriculture, gives advice about controlling and efficiently exploiting slaves.

When the head of a household arrives at his estate, . . . he must go round his farm on a tour of inspection on the very same day, if that is possible, if not, then on the next day. When he has found out how his farm has been cultivated and which jobs have been done and which have not been done, then on the next day after that he must call in his manager and ask him which are the jobs that have been done and which remain, and whether they were done on time, and whether what still has to be done can be done, and how much wine and grain and anything else has been produced. When he has found this out, he must make a calculation of the labor and the time taken. If the work doesn't seem to him to be sufficient, and the manager starts to say how hard he tried, but the slaves weren't any good, and the weather was awful, and the slaves ran away, and he was required to carry out some public works, then when he has finished mentioning these and all sorts of other excuses, you must draw his attention to your calculation of the labor employed and time taken. If he claims that it rained all the time, there are all sorts of jobs that can be done in rainy weather—washing wine-jars, coating them with pitch, cleaning the house, storing grain, shifting muck, digging a manure pit, cleaning seed, mending ropes or making new ones; the slaves ought to have been mending their patchwork cloaks and their hoods. On festival days they would have been able to clean out old ditches, work on the public highway, prune back brambles, dig up the garden, clear a meadow, tie up bundles of sticks, remove thorns, grind barley and get on with cleaning. If he claims that the slaves have been ill, they needn't have been given such large rations. When you have found out about all these things to your satisfaction, make sure that all the work that remains to be done will be carried out. . . . The head of the household should examine his herds and arrange a sale; he should sell the oil if the price makes it worthwhile, and any wine and grain that is surplus to needs; he should sell any old oxen, cattle or sheep that are not up to standard, wool and hides, an old cart or old tools, an old slave, a sick slave—anything else that is surplus to requirements. The head of a household ought to sell, and not to buy. (Cato the Elder, *Concerning Agriculture*, bk. 2, second century B.C.E.)

Cato, the Roman author of that excerpt, was notorious for his stern manner and hard-edged traditionalism, and while he does not represent the approach of all Roman masters—in reality, the treatment of slaves varied widely—he expresses a point of view that Roman society found acceptable.

Slavery was far less prominent in ancient China. During the Warring States Period, dependent peasants as well as slaves worked the large holdings of the landowning aristocracy. The Qin government sought to abolish slavery, but the institution persisted into the Han period, although it involved only a small fraction of the population and was not a central component of the economy. The relatives of criminals could be seized and enslaved, and poor families sometimes sold unwanted children into slavery. In China, slaves, whether they belonged to the state or to individuals, generally performed domestic tasks, as can be seen in the following text.

Wang Ziyuan of Shu Commandery went to the Jian River on business, and went up to the home of the widow Yang Hui,

So popular was Augustus when he died that four members of his family succeeded to the position of "emperor" (as we call it) despite serious personal and political shortcomings. However, because of Augustus's calculated ambiguity about his role, the position of emperor was never automatically regarded as hereditary, and after the mid-first century C.E. other families obtained the post. In theory the early emperors were affirmed by the Senate; in reality they were chosen by the armies. By the second century C.E. a series of very capable emperors instituted a new mechanism of succession: each adopted a mature man of proven ability as his son and trained him as his successor.

While Augustus had felt it important to appeal to Republican traditions and conceal the source and extent of his power, this became less necessary over time, and later emperors exercised their authority more overtly. In imitation of Alexander the Great and the Hellenistic kings, who had a male slave named Bianliao. Wang Ziyuan requested him to go and buy some wine. Picking up a big stick, Bianliao climbed to the top of the grave mound and said: "When my master bought me, Bianliao, he only contracted for me to care for the grave and did not contract for me to buy wine for some other gentleman."

Wang Ziyuan was furious and said to the widow: "Wouldn't you prefer to sell this slave?"

Yang Hui said: "The slave's father offered him to people, but no one wanted him." Wang Ziyuan immediately settled on the sale contract.

The slave again said: "Enter in the contract everything you wish to order me to do. I, Bianliao, will not do anything not in the contract."

Wang Ziyuan said: "Agreed."

The text of the contract said:

The gentleman Wang Ziyuan, of Zizhong, purchases from the lady Yang Hui of Anzhi village in Zhengdu, the bearded male slave, Bianliao, of her husband's household. The fixed sale [price] is 15,000 [cash]. The slave shall obey orders about all kinds of work and may not argue.

He shall rise at dawn and do an early sweeping. After eating he shall wash up. Ordinarily he should pound the grain mortar, tie up broom straws, carve bowls and bore wells, scoop out ditches, tie up fallen fences, hoe the garden, trim up paths and dike up plots of land, cut big flails, bend bamboos to make rakes, and scrape and fix the well pulley. In going and coming he may not ride horseback or in the cart, [nor may he] sit crosslegged or make a hubbub. When he gets out of bed he shall shake his head [to wake up], fish, cut forage, plait reeds and card hemp, draw water for gruel, and help in making zumo [drink]. He shall weave shoes and make [other] coarse things. [The list of tasks continues for two-and-a-half pages.] . . .

He shall be industrious and quick-working, and he may not idle and loaf. When the slave is old and his strength spent, he shall plant marsh grass and weave mats. When his work is over and he wishes to rest he should pound a picul [of grain]. Late at night when there is no work he shall wash clothes really white. If he has private savings they shall be the master's gift, or from guests. The slave may not have evil secrets; affairs should be open and reported. If the slave does not heed instructions, he shall be whipped a hundred strokes.

The reading of the text of the contract came to an end. The slave was speechless and his lips were tied. Wildly he beat his head on the ground, and beat himself with his hands; from his eyes the tears streamed down, and the drivel from his nose hung a foot long.

He said: "If it is to be exactly as master Wang says, I would rather return soon along the yellow-soil road, with the grave worms boring through my head. Had I known before I would have bought the wine for master Wang, I would not have dared to do that wrong." (Wang Bao, first century B.C.E.)

This story was meant to be humorous and no doubt exaggerates the amount of work that could be demanded from a slave, but it shows that Chinese slaves could be forced to work hard and engaged in many of the same menial tasks as their Roman counterparts. It also appears that slaves in China were legally protected by contracts that specified and limited what could be demanded of them.

QUESTIONS FOR ANALYSIS

1. **Why might slavery have been less important in Han China than in the Roman Empire? Why would the treatment of slaves have been less harsh in China than in Rome?**
2. **In what ways were slaves treated like other forms of property, such as animals and tools? In what ways was a slave's "humanity" taken into account?**
3. **What are some of the passive-resistance tactics that slaves resorted to, and what did they achieve by these actions?**

Source: First selection from Thomas Wiedemann, *Greek and Roman Slavery*, pp. 183–184, published by Johns Hopkins University Press. Copyright © 1981. Reprinted by permission of Taylor and Francis Books UK. Second selection reprinted with the permission of Scribner, a Division of Simon & Schuster, Inc. from *Slavery in China During the Former Han Dynasty* by Clarence Martin Wilbur (Russell & Russell, New York), 1967.

many Roman emperors were officially deified (regarded as gods) after death. A cult of the living emperor developed as a way to increase the loyalty of subjects.

Roman Law

During the Republic a body of laws had developed, including decrees of the Senate, bills passed in the Assembly, and the practices of public officials who heard cases. In the later Republic legal experts began to analyze laws and legal procedures to determine the underlying principles, then applied these principles to the creation of new laws required by a changing society. These experts were less lawyers in the modern sense than teachers, though they were sometimes consulted by officials or the parties to legal actions.

During the Principate the emperor became a major source of new laws. Roman law was studied and codified with a new intensity by the class of legal experts, and their interpretations often had the force of law. The basic divisions of Roman law—persons, things, and actions—reveal the importance of property and the rights of individuals in Roman eyes. The culmination of this long process of development and interpretation of the law was the sixth-century C.E. Digest of Justinian. Roman law has remained the foundation of European law to this day.

An Urban Empire

Life in the Cities

The Roman Empire of the first three centuries C.E. was an "urban" empire. This does not mean that most people lived in cities. Perhaps 80 percent of the 50 to 60 million people in the empire engaged in agriculture and lived in villages or isolated farms. The empire, however, was administered through a network of towns and cities, and the urban populace benefited most.

Numerous towns had several thousand inhabitants, while a few major cities had several hundred thousand. Rome itself had approximately a million residents. The largest cities strained the technological capabilities of the ancients; providing adequate food and water and removing sewage were always problems.

In Rome the upper classes lived in elegant townhouses on one of the hills. The house was centered around an *atrium*, a rectangular courtyard with an open skylight that let in light and rainwater for drinking and washing. Surrounding the atrium were a large dining room for dinner and drinking parties, an interior garden, a kitchen, and possibly a private bath. Bedrooms were on the upper level. The floors were decorated with pebble mosaics, and the walls and ceilings were covered with frescoes (paintings done directly on wet plaster) of mythological scenes or outdoor vistas, giving a sense of openness in the absence of windows. The typical aristocrat

Courtesy, Leo C. Curran

Roman Shop Selling Food and Drink The bustling town of Pompeii on the Bay of Naples was buried in ash by the eruption of Mt. Vesuvius in 79 C.E. Archaeologists have unearthed the streets, stores, and houses of this typical Roman town. Shops such as this sold hot food and drink served from clay vessels set into the counter. Shelves and niches behind the counter contained other items. In the background can be seen a well-paved street and a public fountain where the inhabitants could fetch water.

also owned a number of villas in the Italian countryside to which the family could retreat to escape the pressures of city life.

The poor lived in crowded slums in the low-lying parts of the city. Damp, dark, and smelly, with few furnishings, these wooden tenements were susceptible to frequent fires. Fortunately, Romans could spend much of the day outdoors, working, shopping, eating, and socializing.

The cities, towns, and even the ramshackle settlements that sprang up on the edge of frontier forts were miniature replicas of the capital city in political organization and physical layout. A town council and two annually elected officials drawn from the local elite ran regional affairs with considerable autonomy. This "municipal aristocracy" imitated the manners and conduct of Roman senators, endowing their communities with attractive elements of Roman urban life—civic buildings, temples, gardens, baths, theaters, amphitheaters—and putting on games and public entertainments.

Life in the Countryside

In the countryside hard work and drudgery were relieved by occasional holidays and village festivals and by the everyday pleasures of sex, family, and conversation. Rural people had to fend for themselves in dealing with bandits, wild animals, and other hazards of country life. They had little direct contact with the Roman government other than occasional run-ins with bullying soldiers and the dreaded arrival of the tax collector.

pax romana Literally, "Roman peace," it connoted the stability and prosperity that Roman rule brought to the lands of the Roman Empire in the first two centuries C.E. The movement of people and trade goods along Roman roads and safe seas allowed for the spread of cultural practices, technologies, and religious ideas.

The concentration of land ownership in ever fewer hands was temporarily reversed by the distribution of farms to veteran soldiers during the civil wars of the late Republic, but it resumed in the era of the emperors. However, after the era of conquest ended in the early second century C.E., slaves were no longer plentiful or inexpensive, and landowners needed a new source of labor. "Tenant farmers" cultivated plots of land in return for a portion of their crops. The landowners lived in the cities and hired foremen to manage their estates. Thus wealth was concentrated in the cities but was based on the productivity of rural laborers.

Commerce

Some urban dwellers got rich from manufacture and trade. Commerce was greatly enhanced by the **pax romana** ("Roman peace"), the safety and stability guaranteed by Roman might. Grain, meat, vegetables, and other bulk foodstuffs usually were exchanged locally because transportation was expensive and many products spoiled quickly. However, the city of Rome imported massive quantities of grain from Sicily and Egypt to feed its huge population, and special naval squadrons performed this vital task.

Glass, metalwork, delicate pottery, and other fine manufactured products were exported throughout the empire. The centers of production, originally located in Italy, moved into the provinces as knowledge of the necessary skills spread. Other merchants traded in luxury items from far beyond the boundaries of the empire, especially silk from China and spices from India and Arabia.

Romanization The process by which the Latin language and Roman culture became dominant in the western provinces. Indigenous peoples in the provinces often chose to Romanize because of the political and economic advantages that it brought, as well as the allure of Roman success.

Roman armies stationed on the frontiers were a large market that promoted the prosperity of border provinces. The revenues collected by the central government transferred wealth from the rich interior provinces like Gaul (France) and Egypt, first to Rome to support the emperor and the central government, then to the frontier provinces to subsidize the armies.

Romanization and Citizenship

Romanization—the spread of the Latin language and Roman way of life—was strongest in the western provinces, whereas Greek language and culture, a legacy of the Hellenistic kingdoms, predominated in the eastern Mediterranean (see Chapter 4). Modern Portuguese, Spanish, French, Italian, and Romanian evolved from the Latin language. The Roman government did not force Romanization. Many provincials chose to adopt Latin and the cultural habits that went with it. There were advantages to speaking Latin and wearing a *toga* (the traditional cloak worn by Roman male citizens), just as people in today's developing nations see advantages in moving to the city, learning English, and wearing Western clothing. Latin facilitated dealings with the Roman administration and helped merchants get contracts to supply the military. Many also were drawn to the aura of success surrounding the language and culture of the dominant people.

The empire gradually granted Roman citizenship, with its privileges, legal protections, and exemptions from some types of taxation, to people living outside Italy. Men who completed a twenty-six-year term of service in the native military units that backed up the Roman legions were granted citizenship and could pass this coveted status on to their descendants. Emperors made grants of citizenship to individuals or entire communities as rewards for good service. Finally, in 212 C.E. the emperor Caracalla granted citizenship to all free, adult, male inhabitants of the empire.

The gradual extension of citizenship mirrored the empire's transformation from an Italian dominion into a commonwealth of peoples. As early as the first century C.E. some of the leading literary and intellectual figures came from the provinces. By the second century even the emperors hailed from Spain, Gaul, and North Africa.

The Rise of Christianity

AP* Exam Tip Be prepared to explain the formation of Christianity.

During this period of general peace and prosperity, events were taking place in the East that, though little noted at the moment, would be of great historical significance. The Jewish homeland of Judaea (see Chapter 3), roughly equivalent to present-day Israel, came under direct Roman rule in 6 C.E. Over the next half-century Roman governors insensitive to the Jewish belief in one god provoked opposition to Roman rule. Many waited for the arrival of the Messiah, the "Anointed One," a military leader who would drive out the Romans and liberate the Jewish people.

Jesus and Paul

Jesus A Jew from Galilee in northern Israel who sought to reform Jewish beliefs and practices. He was executed as a revolutionary by the Romans. Hailed as the Messiah and son of God by his followers, he became the central figure in Christianity, a belief system that developed in the centuries after his death.

Paul A Jew from the Greek city of Tarsus in Anatolia, he initially persecuted the followers of Jesus but, after receiving a revelation on the road to Syrian Damascus, became a Christian. Taking advantage of his Hellenized background and Roman citizenship, he traveled throughout Syria-Palestine, Anatolia, and Greece, preaching the new religion and establishing churches. Finding his greatest success among pagans ("gentiles"), he began the process by which Christianity separated from Judaism.

This is the context for the career of **Jesus**, a young Jewish carpenter from the Galilee region in northern Israel. Since the portrait of Jesus found in the New Testament largely reflects the viewpoint of followers a half-century after his death, it is difficult to determine the motives and teachings of the historical Jesus. Some experts believe that he was essentially a rabbi, or teacher. Offended by Jewish religious and political leaders' excessive concern with money and power and by the perfunctory nature of mainstream Jewish religious practice in his time, he prescribed a return to the personal faith and spirituality of an earlier age. Others stress his connections to the apocalyptic fervor found in certain circles of Judaism, such as John the Baptist and the community that authored the Dead Sea Scrolls. They view Jesus as a fiery prophet who urged people to prepare themselves for the imminent end of the world and God's ushering in of a blessed new age. Still others see him as a political revolutionary, upset by the downtrodden condition of the peasants in the countryside and the poor in the cities, who determined to drive out the Roman occupiers and their collaborators among the Jewish elite. Whatever the real nature of his mission, the charismatic Jesus eventually attracted the attention of the Jewish authorities in Jerusalem, who regarded popular reformers as potential troublemakers. They turned him over to the Roman governor, Pontius Pilate. Jesus was imprisoned, condemned, and executed by crucifixion, a punishment usually reserved for common criminals. After his death his followers, the Apostles, sought to spread his teachings among their fellow Jews and persuade them that he was the Messiah and had been resurrected (returned from death to life).

Paul, a Jew from the Greek city of Tarsus in southeast Anatolia, converted to the new creed. Between 45 and 58 C.E. he threw his enormous talent and energy into spreading the word. Traveling throughout Syria-Palestine, Anatolia, and Greece, he became increasingly frustrated with the refusal of most Jews to accept that Jesus was the Messiah and had ushered in a new age. Many Jews, on the other hand, were appalled by the failure of the followers of Jesus to maintain traditional Jewish practices. Discovering a spiritual hunger among many non-Jews, Paul redirected his efforts toward them and set up a string of Christian (from the Greek name *christos*, meaning "anointed one," given to Jesus by his followers) communities in the eastern Mediterranean. Paul's career exemplifies the cosmopolitan nature of the Roman Empire. Speaking both Greek and Aramaic, he moved comfortably between the Greco-Roman and Jewish worlds. He used Roman roads, depended on the peace guaranteed by Roman arms, called on his Roman citizenship to protect him from the arbitrary action of local authorities, and moved from city to city in his quest for converts. In 66 C.E. long-building tensions in Roman Judaea erupted into a full-scale revolt that lasted until 73. One of the casualties of the Roman reconquest of Judaea was the Jerusalem-based Christian community, which focused on converting the Jews. This left the field clear for Paul's non-Jewish converts, and Christianity began to diverge more and more from its Jewish roots.

Persecution and Growth of the Church

For more than two centuries, the sect grew slowly but steadily. Many of the first converts were from disenfranchised groups—women, slaves, the urban poor. They received respect not accorded them in the larger society and obtained positions of responsibility when the members of early Christian communities democratically elected their leaders. However, as the religious movement grew and prospered, it developed a hierarchy of priests and bishops and became subject to bitter disputes over theological doctrine (see Chapter 9).

As monotheists forbidden to worship other gods, early Christians were persecuted by Roman officials, who regarded their refusal to worship the emperor as a sign of disloyalty. Despite occasional government-sponsored persecution and spontaneous mob attacks, or perhaps because of them, the young Christian movement continued to gain strength and attract converts. By the late third century C.E. its adherents were a sizeable minority within the Roman Empire and included many educated and prosperous people with posts in the local and imperial governments.

The expansion of Christianity should be seen as part of a broader religious tendency. In the Hellenistic and Roman periods, a number of cults gained popularity by claiming to provide secret information about the nature of life and death and promising a blessed afterlife to their adherents. Arising in the eastern Mediterranean, they spread throughout the Greco-Roman lands in response to a growing spiritual and intellectual hunger not satisfied by traditional pagan practices. These included the worship of the mother-goddess Cybele in Anatolia, the Egyptian goddess Isis, and the Iranian sun-god Mithra. As we shall see, the ultimate victory of Christianity over these rivals had as much to do with historical circumstances as with its spiritual appeal.

aqueduct A conduit, either elevated or underground, that used gravity to carry water from a source to a location—usually a city—that needed it. The Romans built many aqueducts in a period of substantial urbanization.

Technology and Transformation

Engineering

AP* Exam Tip Be sure to understand the impact of technology on the growth of large state structures.

The relative safety and ease of travel brought by Roman arms and roads enabled merchants to sell their wares and early Christians to spread their faith. Surviving remnants of roads, fortification walls, aqueducts, and buildings testify to the engineering expertise of the ancient Romans. Some of the best engineers served with the army, building bridges, siege works, and ballistic weapons that hurled stones and shafts. **Aqueducts**—long elevated or underground conduits—carried water from a source to an urban center, using only the force of gravity (see Environment and

Roman Aqueduct Near Tarragona, Spain The growth of towns and cities challenged Roman officials to provide an adequate supply of water. Aqueducts channeled water from a source, sometimes many miles away, to an urban complex, using only the force of gravity. To bring an aqueduct from high ground into the city, Roman engineers designed long, continuous rows of arches that maintained a steady downhill slope. Scholars sometimes can roughly estimate the population of an ancient city by calculating the amount of water that was available to it.

Robert Freck/Woodfin Camp & Associates

Water Engineering in Rome and China

People needed water to drink; it was vital for agriculture; and it provided a rapid and economical means for transporting people and goods. Some of the most impressive technological achievements of ancient Rome and China involved hydraulic (water) engineering.

Roman cities, with their large populations, required abundant and reliable sources of water. One way to obtain it was to build aqueducts—stone channels to bring water from distant lakes and streams to the cities. The water flowing in these conduits was moved only by the force of gravity. Surveyors measured the land's elevation and plotted a course that very gradually moved downhill.

Aqueducts were well-built structures made of large cut stones closely fitted and held together by a cement-like mortar. Some were elevated atop walls or bridges, which made it difficult for unauthorized parties to tap the water line for their own use. Portions of some aqueducts were built underground. Construction was labor-intensive, and often both design and construction were carried out by military personnel. This was one of the ways in which the Roman government kept large numbers of soldiers busy in peacetime.

Sections of aqueduct that crossed rivers presented the same construction challenges as bridges. Roman engineers lowered prefabricated wooden cofferdams—large, hollow cylinders—into the riverbed and pumped out the water so workers could descend and construct cement piers to support the arched segments of the bridge. This technique is still used for construction in water.

When an aqueduct reached the outskirts of a city, the water flowed into a reservoir, where it was stored. Pipes connected the reservoir to different parts of the city. Even within the city, gravity provided the motive force until the water reached the public fountains used by the poor and the private storage tanks of individuals wealthy enough to have plumbing in their houses.

In ancient China, rivers running generally in an east-west direction were the main thoroughfares. The earliest development of complex societies centered on the Yellow River Valley, but by the beginning of the Qin Empire the Yangzi River Valley and regions farther south were becoming increasingly important to China's political and economic vitality. In this era the Chinese began to build canals connecting the northern and southern zones, at first for military purposes but eventually for transporting commercial goods as well. In later periods, with the acquisition of more advanced engineering skills, an extensive network of canals was built, including the 1,100-mile-long (1,771-kilometer-long) Grand Canal.

One of the earliest projects was the Magic Canal. A Chinese historian reports that the Qin emperor Shi Huangdi ordered his engineers to join two rivers by a 20-mile-long (32.2-kilometer-long) canal so that he could more easily supply his armies of conquest in the south. Construction of the canal posed a difficult engineering challenge because the rivers Hsiang and Li, though coming within 3 miles (4.8 kilometers) of one another, flowed in opposite directions and with a strong current.

The engineers took advantage of a low point in the chain of hills between the rivers to maintain a relatively level grade. The final element of the solution was to build a snout-shaped mound to divide the waters of the Hsiang, funneling part of that river into an artificial channel. Several spillways further reduced the volume of water flowing into the canal. The joining of the two rivers completed a network of waterways that permitted continuous inland water transport of goods between the latitudes of Beijing and Guangzhou (Canton), a distance of 1,250 miles (2,012 kilometers). Modifications were made in later centuries, but the Magic Canal is still in use.

Robert Temple, photographer

The Magic Canal Engineers of Shi Huangdi, "First Emperor" of China, exploited the contours of the landscape to connect the river systems of northern and southern China.

Technology: Water Engineering in Rome and China). The Romans pioneered the use of arches, which allow even distribution of great weights without thick supporting walls. The invention of concrete—a mixture of lime powder, sand, and water that could be poured into molds—allowed the Romans to create vast vaulted and domed interior spaces, unlike the rectilinear pillar-and-post construction of the Greeks.

Defense

Defending borders that stretched for thousands of miles was a major challenge. Augustus advised against further expanding the empire because the costs of administering and defending subsequent acquisitions would be greater than the revenues. The Roman army was reorganized and redeployed to reflect the shift from an offensive to a defensive strategy. At most points the empire was protected by mountains, deserts, and seas. But the lengthy Rhine and Danube river frontiers in Germany and Central Europe were vulnerable. They were guarded by a string of forts with small garrisons adequate for dealing with raiders. On particularly desolate frontiers, such as in Britain and North Africa, the Romans built long walls to keep out intruders.

Most of Rome's neighbors were less technologically advanced and more loosely organized and so did not pose a serious threat to the security of the empire. The one exception was the Parthian kingdom, heir to the Mesopotamian and Persian Empires, which controlled the lands on the eastern frontier (today's Iran and Iraq). For centuries Rome and Parthia engaged in a rivalry that sapped both sides without any significant territorial gain by either party.

The Third-Century Crisis

Third-Century Crisis Historians' term for the political, military, and economic turmoil that beset the Roman Empire during much of the third century C.E.: frequent changes of ruler, civil wars, barbarian invasions, decline of urban centers, and near-destruction of long-distance commerce and the monetary economy. After 284 C.E. Diocletian restored order by making fundamental changes.

The Roman state prospered for two and a half centuries after Augustus's reforms, but in the third century C.E. cracks in the edifice became visible. Historians use the expression "**Third-Century Crisis**" to refer to the period from 235 to 284 C.E., when political, military, and economic problems beset and nearly destroyed the Roman Empire. The most visible symptom of the crisis was the frequent change of rulers. Twenty or more men claimed the office of emperor during this period. Most reigned for only a few months or years before being overthrown by rivals or killed by their own troops. Germanic tribesmen on the Rhine/Danube frontier took advantage of the frequent civil wars and periods of anarchy to raid deep into the empire. For the first time in centuries, Roman cities began to erect walls for protection. Several regions, feeling that the central government was not adequately protecting them, broke away and turned power over to a leader who promised to put their interests first.

These crises had a devastating impact on the empire's economy. Buying the loyalty of the armies and defending the increasingly permeable frontiers drained the treasury. The unending demands of the central government for more tax revenues, as well as the interruption of commerce by fighting, eroded the towns' prosperity. Shortsighted emperors, desperate for cash, secretly reduced the amount of precious metal in coins and pocketed the excess. The public quickly caught on, and the devalued coinage became less and less acceptable in the marketplace. The empire reverted to a barter economy, a far less efficient system that further curtailed large-scale and long-distance commerce.

AP* Exam Tip Be able to explain the decline and collapse of empire in Rome, India, and China.

The municipal aristocracy, once the most vital and public-spirited class in the empire, was slowly crushed out of existence. As town councilors, its members were personally liable for shortfalls in taxes owed to the state. The decline in trade eroded their wealth, and many began to evade their civic duties and even went into hiding.

Population shifted out of the cities and into the countryside. Many sought employment and protection from both raiders and government officials on the estates of wealthy and powerful country landowners. The shrinking of cities and movement of the population to the country estates were the first steps in a demographic shift toward the social and economic structures of the European Middle Ages—roughly seven hundred years during which wealthy rural lords dominated a peasant population tied to the land (see Chapter 9).

Diocletian and Constantine

Just when things looked bleakest, one man pulled the empire back from the brink of disaster. Like many rulers of that age, Diocletian came from one of the eastern European provinces most vulnerable to invasion. A commoner by birth, he had risen through the ranks of the army and gained power in 284. The proof of his success is that he ruled for more than twenty years and died in bed.

Diocletian implemented radical reforms that saved the Roman state by transforming it. To halt inflation (the process by which prices rise as money becomes worth less), Diocletian issued an edict specifying the maximum prices for various commodities and services. He froze many people into professions regarded as essential and required them to train their sons to succeed them. This unprecedented government regulation of prices and vocations had unforeseen consequences. A "black market" arose among buyers and sellers who ignored the government's price controls (and threats to impose the death penalty on violators). Many inhabitants of the empire began to see the government as an oppressive entity that no longer deserved their loyalty.

Constantine Roman emperor (r. 312–337). After reuniting the Roman Empire, he moved the capital to Constantinople and made Christianity a favored religion.

When Diocletian resigned in 305, the old divisiveness reemerged as various claimants battled for the throne. The eventual winner was **Constantine** (r. 306–337), who reunited the entire empire under his sole rule by 324.

In 312 Constantine won a key battle at the Milvian Bridge near Rome. He later claimed that he had seen a cross—the sign of the Christian God—superimposed on the sun before the battle. Believing that the Christian God had helped him achieve the victory, in the following year Constantine issued the Edict of Milan, ending the persecution of Christianity and guaranteeing freedom of worship to Christians and all others. Throughout his reign he supported the Christian church, although he tolerated other beliefs as well. Historians disagree about whether Constantine was spiritually motivated or pragmatically seeking to unify the peoples of the empire under a single religion. In either case, his embrace of Christianity was of tremendous significance. Large numbers of people began to convert when they saw that Christians seeking political office or government favors had clear advantages over non-Christians.

In 324 Constantine transferred the imperial capital from Rome to Byzantium, an ancient Greek city on the Bosporus (BAHS-puhr-uhs) strait leading from the Mediterranean into the Black Sea. The city was renamed Constantinople (cahn-stan-tih-NO-pul), "City of Constantine." This move both reflected and accelerated changes already taking place. Constantinople was closer than Rome to the most-threatened borders in eastern Europe (see Map 5.1). The urban centers and middle class in the eastern half of the empire had better withstood the Third-Century Crisis than those in the western half. In addition, more educated people and more Christians were living in the eastern provinces (see Chapter 9).

The conversion of Constantine and the transfer of the imperial capital are often seen as the end of Roman history. Though many changes that culminated during Constantine's reign had their roots in the previous two centuries, the two halves of the empire followed different pathways thereafter. The Western Empire, increasingly overrun by migrating Germanic peoples, came to an end in 476 when the last emperor, Romulus Augustulus, abdicated. (The melding of the Germanic and Roman cultural traditions will be discussed in Chapter 9.)

However, the eastern, or Byzantine, portion of the empire continued to flourish. Several emperors ordered collections of laws and edicts to be made. The most famous and complete collection was the *Corpus Juris Civilis* (*Body of Civil Law*) compiled in Latin by seventeen legal scholars at the behest of the emperor Justinian (r. 527–565), whose armies also briefly reoccupied some old imperial territories in Italy and Tunisia. The greatest Byzantine architectural creation, Constantinople's Hagia Sophia ("Sacred Wisdom") cathedral, proved to be a more lasting monument to Justinian's reign. It represents a continuation of artistic creativity manifested in the design and ornamentation of churches and monasteries, and the painting of religious images known as icons. (The later centuries of Byzantine history are discussed in Chapter 9.)

SECTION REVIEW

- Rome's central location in Italy and the Mediterranean, and its ability to draw on the manpower resources of Italy, were important factors in its rise to empire.
- Early Rome was ruled by kings, but the Republic, inaugurated shortly before 500 B.C.E., was guided by the Senate, a council of the heads of wealthy families.
- Roman expansion, first in Italy, then throughout the Mediterranean, was due to several factors: the ambition and desire for glory of its leaders, weaker states appealing to Rome for protection, and Roman fear of others' aggression.
- Within Italy, and later in the overseas provinces, Rome co-opted the elites of subject peoples and extended its citizenship. Many subjects in the western provinces adopted the Latin language and Roman lifestyle.
- The civil wars that brought down the Republic were fought by armies more loyal to their leaders than to the state.
- Augustus developed a new system of government, the Principate, and while claiming to restore the Republic, he really created a military dictatorship.
- The Third-Century Crisis almost destroyed Rome, but Diocletian and Constantine saved the empire by transforming it.
- Christianity originated in the turbulent province of Judaea in the first century C.E., and despite official and spontaneous persecution, it grew steadily. Constantine's embrace of Christianity in the early fourth century C.E. made it virtually the official religion of the empire.

THE ORIGINS OF IMPERIAL CHINA, 221 B.C.E.–220 C.E.

The early history of China (described in Chapter 2) was characterized by the fragmentation that geography dictated. The Shang (ca. 1750–1045 B.C.E.) and Zhou (1045–221 B.C.E.) dynasties ruled over a compact zone in northeastern China. The last few centuries of nominal Zhou rule—the Warring States Period—saw frequent hostilities among a group of small states with somewhat different languages and cultures.

In the second half of the third century B.C.E. one of the warring states—the **Qin** (chin) state of the Wei (way) Valley—rapidly conquered its rivals and created China's first empire (221–206 B.C.E.). Built at great cost in human lives and labor, the Qin Empire barely survived the death of its founder, **Shi Huangdi** (shih wahng-dee). Power soon passed to a new dynasty, the **Han**, which ruled China from 202 B.C.E. to 220 C.E. (see Map 5.2). Thus began the long history of imperial China—a tradition of political and cultural unity and continuity that lasted into the early twentieth century and still has meaning for the very different China of our time.

Qin A people and state in the Wei Valley of eastern China that conquered rival states and created the first Chinese empire (221–206 B.C.E.). The Qin ruler, Shi Huangdi, standardized many features of Chinese society and ruthlessly marshaled subjects for military and construction projects, engendering hostility that led to the fall of his dynasty shortly after his death. The Qin framework was largely taken over by the succeeding Han Empire.

The Qin Unification of China, 221–206 B.C.E.

From the mid-third century B.C.E., Qin began to methodically conquer and incorporate the other Chinese states, and by 221 B.C.E. it had unified all northern and central China in the first Chinese "empire." The name *China*, by which this land is known in the Western world, is probably derived from *Qin*. Qin emerged as the ultimate winner because of a combination of factors: the toughness and military preparedness of a frontier state long accustomed to defending itself against "barbarian" neighbors, the wholehearted adoption of severe Legalist methods for exploiting the natural and human resources of the kingdom (see Chapter 2), and the surpassing ambition of a ruthless and energetic young king.

Shi Huangdi

The Qin monarch, Zheng (jahng), came to the throne at the age of thirteen in 246 B.C.E. Guided by a circle of Legalist advisers, he launched a series of wars of conquest. After defeating the last of his rivals in 221 B.C.E., he gave himself a title that symbolized the new state of affairs—Shi Huangdi, or "First Emperor"—and claimed that his dynasty would last ten thousand generations.

Shi Huangdi Founder of the short-lived Qin dynasty and creator of the Chinese Empire (r. 221–210 B.C.E.). He is remembered for his ruthless conquests of rival states, standardization of practices, and forcible organization of labor for military and engineering tasks. His tomb, with its army of life-size terracotta soldiers, has been partially excavated.

The new regime eliminated rival centers of authority. Its first target was the landowning aristocracy of the conquered states and the system on which aristocratic wealth and power had been based. The Qin government abolished primogeniture, the right of the eldest son to inherit all the landed property, requiring estates to be broken up and passed on to several heirs. A new, centrally controlled administrative structure was put in place, with district officials appointed by the king and watched over by his agents.

Han A term used to designate (1) the ethnic Chinese people who originated in the Yellow River Valley and spread throughout regions of China suitable for agriculture and (2) the dynasty of emperors who ruled from 202 B.C.E. to 220 C.E.

The Qin government's commitment to standardization helped create a unified Chinese civilization. A code of law, in force throughout the empire, applied punishments evenhandedly to all members of society. The Qin also imposed standardized weights and measures, a single coinage, a common system of writing, and even a specified axle-length for carts so that they would create a single set of ruts in the road.

Li Si (luh suh), the Legalist prime minister, persuaded Shi Huangdi that the scholars (primarily Confucian rivals of the Legalists; see Chapter 2) were subverting the goals of the regime. The Legalists viewed Confucian expectations of benevolent and nonviolent conduct from rulers as an intolerable check on the government's absolute power. Furthermore, the Confucians' appeal to the past impeded the new order being created by the Qin. A crackdown on the scholars ensued in which many Confucian books were publicly burned and many scholars brutally executed.

Clash with the Nomads

AP* Exam Tip Understand the role of legal systems in the development of the Chinese bureaucracy.

Shi Huangdi was determined to secure the northern border against nomadic raids on Chinese territory. Pastoralists and farmers had always exchanged goods on the frontier. Herders sought food and crafted goods produced by farmers and townsfolk, and farmers depended on the herders for animals and animal products. Sometimes, however, nomads raided the settled lands and took what they needed. For centuries the Chinese kingdoms had struggled with these tough, horse-riding warriors, building long walls along the frontier to keep them away from vulnerable farmlands. Shortly before the Qin unification of China, several states had begun to train soldiers on horseback to contend with the mobile nomads.

Xiongnu A confederation of nomadic peoples living beyond the northwest frontier of ancient China. Chinese rulers tried a variety of defenses and stratagems to ward off these "barbarians," as they called them, and finally succeeded in dispersing the Xiongnu in the first century C.E.

Shi Huangdi sent a large force to drive the nomads far north. His generals succeeded momentarily, extending Chinese territory beyond the great northern loop of the Yellow River. They also connected and extended earlier walls to create a continuous fortification, the ancestor of the Great Wall of China. A recent study concludes that, contrary to the common belief that the purpose of the wall was defensive—to keep the "barbarians" out of China—its primary function was offensive, to take in newly captured territory, to which large numbers of Chinese peasants were now dispatched and ordered to begin cultivation.[1]

Shi Huangdi's attack on the nomads had an unanticipated consequence. The threat to their way of life created by the Chinese invasion drove the normally fragmented and quarreling nomad groups to unite in a great confederacy under the dynamic leadership of Maodun (mow-doon). This **Xiongnu** (SHE-OONG-noo) Confederacy would pose a huge military threat to China for centuries, with frequent wars and high costs in lives and resources.

Needing many people to serve in the armies, construct roads and walls on the frontiers, and build new cities, palaces, and a monumental tomb for the ruler, the Qin government instituted an oppressive program of compulsory military and labor services and relocated large groups of people. The recent discovery of a manual of Qin laws used by an administrator, with prescriptions less extreme than expected, suggests that the sins of the Qin may have been exaggerated

 Interactive Map

MAP 5.2 **Han China** The Qin and Han rulers of northeast China extended their control over all of eastern China and extensive territories to the west. A series of walls in the north and northwest, built to check the incursions of nomadic peoples from the steppes, were joined together to form the ancestor of the present-day Great Wall of China. An extensive network of roads connecting towns, cities, and frontier forts promoted rapid communication and facilitated trade. The Silk Road carried China's most treasured products to Central, South, and West Asia and the Mediterranean lands.

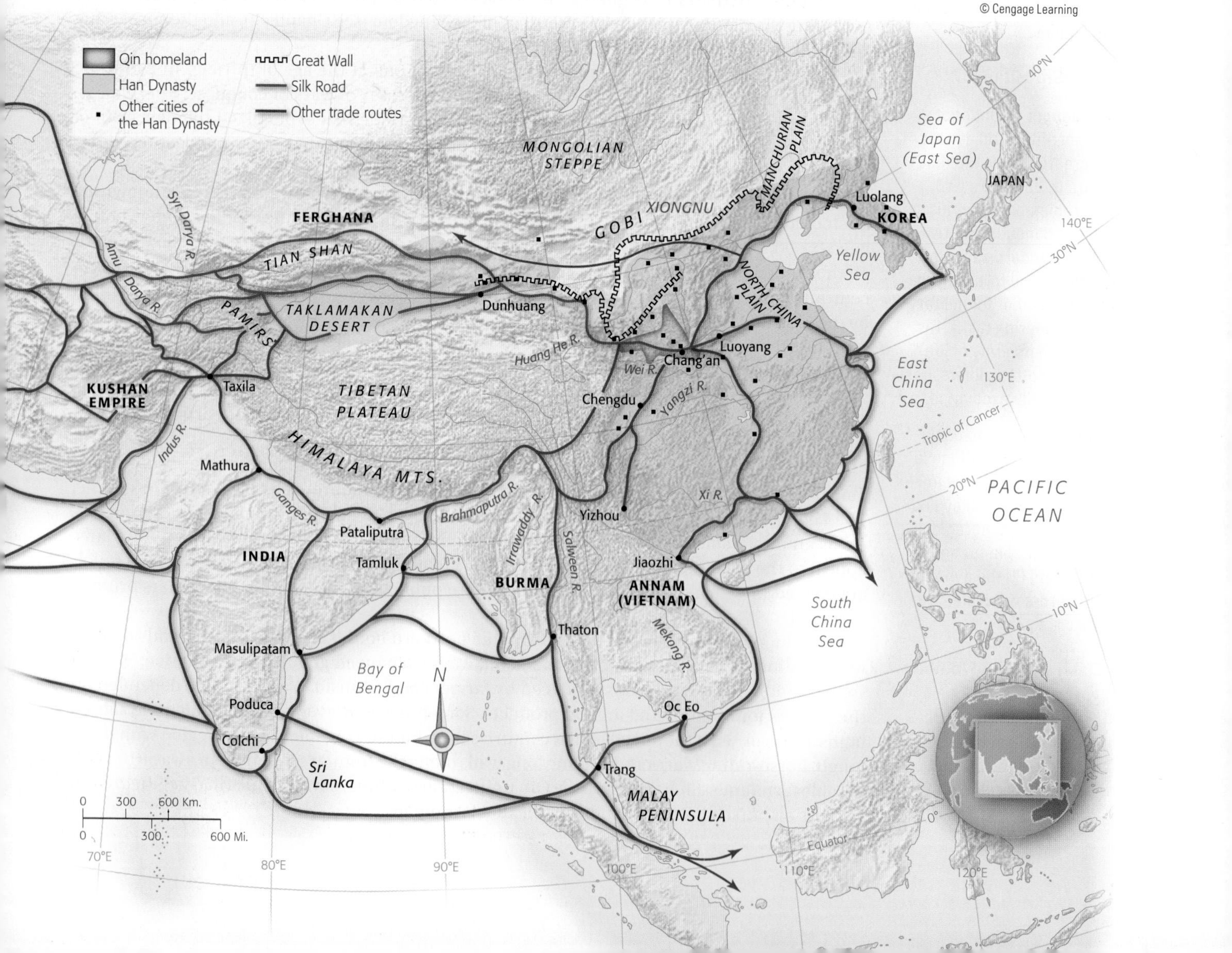

© Dennis Cox/ChinaStock

Terracotta Soldiers from the Tomb of Shi Huangdi, "First Emperor" of China, Late Third Century B.C.E. Near the monumental tomb that he built for himself, the First Emperor filled a huge underground chamber with more than seven thousand life-sized baked-clay statues of soldiers. The terracotta army was unearthed in the 1970s.

by later sources. Nevertheless, the widespread uprisings that broke out after the death of Shi Huangdi attest to the harsh nature of the Qin regime.

Fall of the Qin

When Shi Huangdi died in 210 B.C.E., several officials schemed with one of his sons to place him on the throne. The First Emperor was buried in a monumental tomb whose layout mirrored the geography of China, and the tomb was covered with a great mound of earth. Nearby were buried life-size sculptures of seven thousand soldiers to guard him in the afterlife, a more humane alternative to the human sacrifices of earlier eras. This terracotta (baked clay) army was discovered in the 1970s C.E., but the burial mound remains unexcavated.

AP* Exam Tip Be prepared to discuss the political structure of ancient China, but not specific dynastic transitions.

The new emperor proved to be weak. Uprisings broke out on many fronts, reflecting both the resentment of the old aristocracies that had been deprived of wealth and privilege, and the anger of the commoners against excessive compulsory labor, forced relocations, and heavy taxation. By 206 B.C.E. Qin rule had been broken—the "ten-thousand-generation dynasty" had lasted only fifteen years. Nevertheless, the most important achievements of the Qin, the unification of China and the creation of a single, widely dispersed Chinese style of civilization, would endure.

The Long Reign of the Han, 202 B.C.E.–220 C.E.

Gaozu

Despite the overthrow of the Qin, fighting continued among various rebel groups. In 202 B.C.E. Liu Bang (le-oo bahng) prevailed and inaugurated a new dynasty, the Han, that would govern China for more than four centuries (202 B.C.E.–220 C.E.). The Han created the machinery and ideology of imperial government that would prevail for two millennia, and Chinese people today refer to themselves ethnically as "Han."

Gaozu The throne name of Liu Bang, one of the rebel leaders who brought down the Qin and founded the Han dynasty in 202 B.C.E.

The new emperor, generally known by the throne name **Gaozu** (gow-zoo), came from a modest background. Stories stress his peasant qualities: fondness for drink, blunt speech, and easy manner. Gaozu and his successors courted popularity and consolidated their rule by denouncing the harshness of the Qin and renouncing many Qin laws. In reality, however, they

Gold Belt Buckle, Xiongnu, Second Century B.C.E. The Xiongnu, herders in the lands north of China, shared the artistic conventions of nomadic peoples across the steppes of Asia and eastern Europe, such as this fluid, twisting representation of the animals on which they depended for their livelihood. Shi Huangdi's military incursion into their pasturelands in the late third century B.C.E. catalyzed the formation of the Xiongnu Confederacy, whose horse-riding warriors challenged the Chinese for centuries.

maintained—with sensible modifications—many Legalist-inspired institutions of the Qin to control far-flung territories and diverse populations.

The early Han rulers faced tough challenges. China had been badly damaged by the harsh exactions of the Qin and the widespread fighting in the period of rebellions. Because the economy needed time to recover, Gaozu and his immediate successors had to be frugal, keeping costs down to reduce taxes and undertaking measures to improve the state of agriculture. For instance, during prosperous times the government collected and stored surplus grain that could be sold at reasonable prices in times of shortage.

Gaozu reverted to the traditional feudal grants the Qin had abolished. The eastern parts of China were parceled out to relatives and major supporters, while the rest was divided into "commanderies" directly controlled by the central government. Over the next few reigns, these fiefs were reabsorbed as rebellions or deaths of the rulers provided the opportunity.

When Gaozu marched north to confront a Xiongnu incursion, he and his troops were trapped, and he had to negotiate a safe passage home for his army. Realizing the inferiority of Han troops and the limited funds for a military buildup, he adopted a policy of appeasing the Xiongnu. This essentially meant buying them off by dispatching annual "gifts" of rice, silk, and wine, as well as marrying a Han princess to the Xiongnu ruler.

Wu

While the throne passed to a young child when Gaozu died in 195 B.C.E., real power lay with Gaozu's formidable wife, Empress Lü (lyew). Throughout the Han era, empresses played a key role in determining which of the many sons (the emperors had multiple wives and concubines) would succeed to the throne, and they often chose minors or weak figures whom they and their male relatives could control. Under such circumstances Wu came to the throne as a teenager in 141 B.C.E. The deaths of his grandmother and uncle soon opened the way for him to rule in his own right, and thus began one of the longest and most eventful reigns in the history of the dynasty (141–87 B.C.E.).

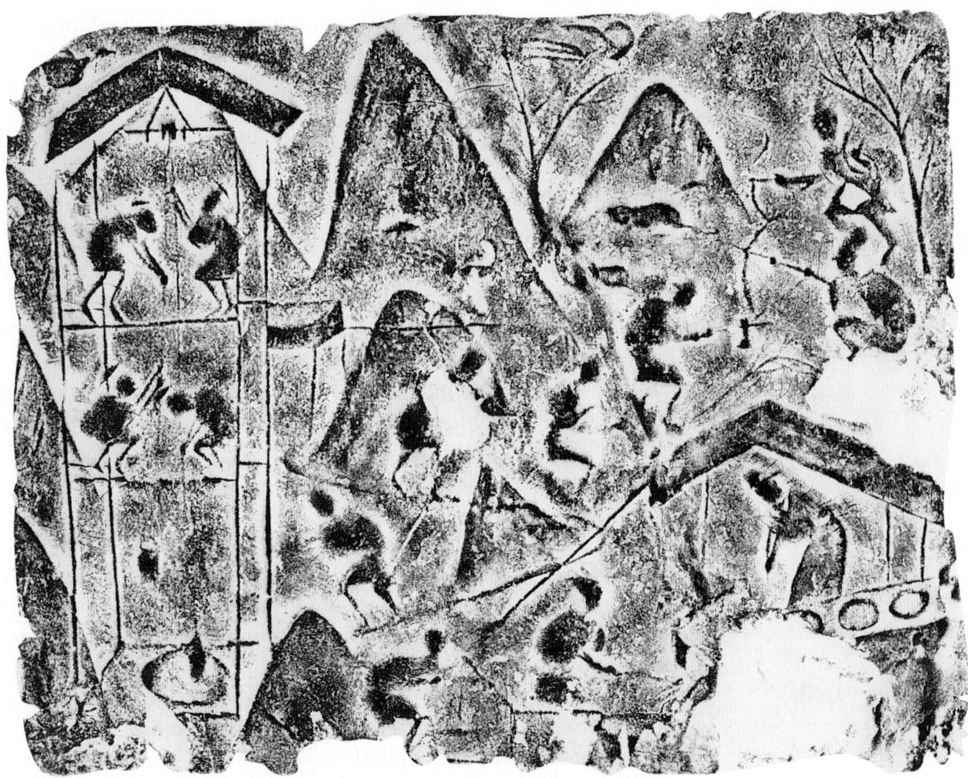

Rubbing of Salt Mining
Found in a Chinese tomb of the first century C.E., this rubbing illustrates a procedure for mining salt. The tower on the left originally served as a derrick for drilling a deep hole through dirt and rock. In this scene workers are hauling up buckets full of brine (saltwater) from underground deposits. In the background are hunters in the mountains.

Sima Qian Chief astrologer for the Han dynasty emperor Wu. He composed a monumental history of China from its legendary origins to his own time and is regarded as the Chinese "father of history."

We know much about the personality and policies of this emperor because of **Sima Qian** (sih-muh chyehn) (ca. 145–85 B.C.E.), whom scholars regard as the first true "historian" in China. Serving as "chief astrologer" at the Han court, Sima Qian was castrated by Wu for defending a disgraced general. He therefore presents a generally negative view, portraying Wu as being manipulated by religious charlatans promising him magical powers, immortality, and séances with the dead. Reading his account carefully, however, one could also conclude that Wu used religious pageantry to boost his own power.

Indeed, Wu did much to increase the power of the emperor. He launched military operations south into Fujian, Guangdong, and northern Vietnam, and north into Manchuria and North Korea. He abandoned the policy of appeasing the Xiongnu, concluding that this approach had failed since the nomads still made periodic attacks on the northern frontier. Wu built up his military, especially the cavalry, and went on the offensive. Thus began decades of bitter, costly fighting between China and the Xiongnu. In the long run Wu and his successors prevailed, and by the mid-first century C.E. the Xiongnu Confederacy disintegrated, though nomad groups still threatened Chinese lands.

Wu dispatched forces to explore and conquer territories northwest of the Chinese heartland, essentially modern Gansu and Xinjiang (SHIN-jyahng). His goals were to improve access to large numbers of horses for his expanding cavalry and to pressure the Xiongnu on their western flank. Thus began the incorporation of this region into greater China. This expansion also brought new economic opportunities, laying the foundations for the Silk Road over which silk and other lucrative trade goods would be carried to Central, southern, and western Asia (see Chapter 7).

The military buildup and frequent wars with the Xiongnu were expensive, forcing Wu to find new revenues. One solution was government monopolies on several high-profit commodities: salt, iron, and alcoholic beverages. These measures were highly controversial.

Another momentous development was the adoption of Confucianism—modified to meet the circumstances of the era—as the official ideology of the imperial system. A university was opened on the outskirts of the capital city, Chang'an (chahng-ahn), and local officials were ordered to send a certain number of promising students from their districts each year. For two thousand years Chinese government would depend on scholar-officials promoted for their performance on exams probing their knowledge of Confucian texts. This alliance of Confucians and the imperial government, fraught with tensions, required compromises on both sides. The Confucians gained access to employment and power but had to accommodate ethical principles to the reality of far-from-perfect rulers. The emperors won the backing and services of a class of competent, educated people but had to deal with the Confucians' expectation that rulers should model ethical behavior and their insistence on giving often unwelcome advice.

Chinese Society

The Chinese government periodically conducted a census of inhabitants, and the results for 2 C.E. revealed 12 million households and 60 million people. Then, as now, the vast majority lived in the eastern river-valley regions where intensive agriculture could support a dense population.

The Family

The fundamental unit was the family, including not only the living but all previous generations. The Chinese believed their ancestors maintained an interest in the fortunes of living family members, so they consulted, appeased, and venerated them. Each generation must produce sons to perpetuate the family and maintain the ancestor cult that provided a kind of immortality to the deceased. In earlier times multiple generations and groups of families lived together, but by the imperial era independent nuclear families were the norm.

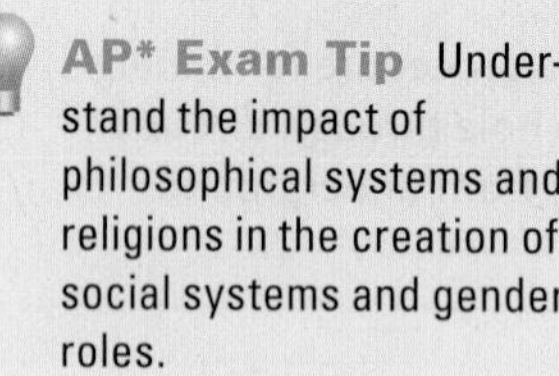
AP* Exam Tip Understand the impact of philosophical systems and religions in the creation of social systems and gender roles.

Within the family was a clear-cut hierarchy headed by the oldest male. Each person had a place and responsibilities, based on gender, age, and relationship to other family members, and people saw themselves as part of an interdependent unit rather than as individual agents. Parents' authority over children did not end with the passing of childhood, and parents occasionally took mature children to court for disobedience. The family inculcated the basic values of Chinese society: loyalty, obedience to authority, respect for elders and ancestors, and concern for honor and appropriate conduct. Because the hierarchy in the state mirrored the hierarchy in the family—peasants, soldiers, administrators, and rulers all made distinctive contributions to the welfare of society—these same attitudes carried over into the relationship between individuals and the state.

Women

Traditional beliefs about conduct appropriate for women are preserved in a biography of the mother of the Confucian philosopher Mencius (Mengzi):

> *A woman's duties are to cook the five grains, heat the wine, look after her parents-in-law, make clothes, and that is all! . . . [She] has no ambition to manage affairs outside the house. . . . She must follow the "three submissions." When she is young, she must submit to her parents. After her marriage, she must submit to her husband. When she is widowed, she must submit to her son.*[2]

In reality, a woman's status depended on her "location" within various social institutions. Women of the royal family, such as wives of the emperor or queen-mothers, could be influential political figures. A young bride, whose marriage had been arranged by her parents, would go to live with her husband's family, where she was, initially, a stranger who had to prove herself. Mothers-in-law had authority over their sons' wives, and mothers, sisters, and wives competed for influence with the men of the household and a larger share of the family's resources.

e PRIMARY SOURCE: Lessons for Women Discover what Ban Zhao, the foremost female writer in Han China, had to say about the proper behavior of women.

"Lessons for Women," written at the end of the first century C.E. by Ban Zhao (bahn jow), illuminates the unresolved tensions in Han society's attitudes toward women. Instructing her own daughters on how to conduct themselves as proper women, Zhao urges them to conform to traditional expectations by obeying males, maintaining their husbands' households, performing domestic chores, and raising the children. Yet she also makes an impassioned plea for the education of girls and urges husbands to respect and not beat their wives.

Chang'an

Chang'an City in the Wei Valley in eastern China. It became the capital of the Qin and early Han Empires. Its main features were imitated in the cities and towns that sprang up throughout the Han Empire.

People lived in various milieus—cities, rural villages and farms, or military camps on the frontiers—and their activities and the quality of their lives were shaped by these contexts. From 202 B.C.E. to 8 C.E.—the period of the Early, or Western, Han—the capital was at **Chang'an** (modern Xi'an [shee-ahn]), in the Wei Valley, an ancient seat of power from which the Zhou and Qin dynasties had emerged. Protected by a ring of hills but with ready access to the fertile plain, Chang'an was surrounded by a wall of pounded earth and brick 15 miles (24 kilometers) in circumference. In 2 C.E. its population was 246,000. Part of the city was carefully planned. Broad thoroughfares running north and south intersected with others running east and west. High walls protected the palaces, administrative offices, barracks, and storehouses of the imperial compound, to which access was restricted. Temples and marketplaces were scattered about the civic center. Chang'an became a model of urban planning, its main features imitated in cities and towns throughout China (it is estimated that between 10 and 30 percent of the population lived in urban centers). From 25 to 220 C.E. the Later, or Eastern, Han established its base farther east, in the more centrally located Luoyang (LWOE-yahng).

Han literature describes the appearance of the capitals and the activities taking place in the palace complexes, public areas, and residential streets. Moralizing writers criticized the excesses of the elite. Living in multistory houses, wearing fine silks, traveling in ornate horse-drawn carriages, well-to-do officials and merchants devoted their leisure time to art and literature, occult religious practices, elegant banquets, and various entertainments—music and dance, juggling and acrobatics, dog and horse races, and cock and tiger fights. In stark contrast, the common people inhabited a sprawling warren of alleys, living in dwellings packed "as closely as the teeth of a comb."

Scholars, Merchants, and Soldiers

gentry In China, the class of prosperous families, next in wealth below the rural aristocrats, from which the emperors drew their administrative personnel. Respected for their education and expertise, these officials became a privileged group and made the government more efficient and responsive than in the past. The term gentry also denotes the class of landholding families in England below the aristocracy.

While the upper echelons of scholar-officials resided in the capital, lower-level bureaucrats were scattered throughout smaller cities and towns serving as headquarters for regional governments. These scholar-officials, or **gentry** (JEHN-tree) as they are sometimes called, shared a common Confucian culture and ideology. Exempt from taxes and compulsory military or labor services, they led comfortable lives by the standards of the time. While the granting of government jobs on the basis of performance on the exams theoretically should have given everyone an equal chance, in reality the sons of the gentry had distinct advantages in obtaining the requisite education in classical texts. Thus the scholar-officials became a self-perpetuating, privileged class. The Han depended on local officials for day-to-day administration of their far-flung territories. They collected taxes, regulated conscription for the army and labor projects, provided protection, and settled disputes.

Merchant families also were based in the cities, and some became very wealthy. However, ancient Chinese society viewed merchants with suspicion, accusing them of greedily driving prices up through speculation and being parasites who lived off the work of others. Advisers to the emperors periodically blamed merchants for the economic ills of China and proposed harsh measures, such as banning them and their children from holding government posts.

The state required two years of military service, and large numbers of Chinese men spent long periods away from home as soldiers in distant frontier posts, building walls and forts, keeping an eye on barbarian neighbors, fighting when necessary, and growing crops to support themselves. Poems written by soldiers complain of rough conditions in the camps, tyrannical officers, and the dangers of confrontations with enemy forces, but above all they are homesick, missing and worrying about aged parents and vulnerable wives and children.

New Forms of Thought and Belief

The Han period was rich in intellectual developments, thanks to the relative prosperity of the era, the growth of urban centers, and state support of scholars. In their leisure time scholar-officials read and wrote in a range of genres, including poetry, philosophy, history, and technical subjects.

History

The Chinese had been preserving historical records since the early Zhou period. However, Sima Qian, the aforementioned "chief astrologer" of Emperor Wu, is "the father of history" in China, both because he created an organizational framework that became the standard for subsequent historical writing and because he sought the causes of events. Sima's monumental history, covering 2,500 years from legendary early emperors to his own time, was organized in a very different way from Western historical writing. It was divided into five parts: dynastic histories, accounts of noble families, biographies of important individuals and groups (such as Confucian scholars, assassins, barbarian peoples), a chart of historical events, and essays on special topics such as the calendar, astrology, and religious ceremonies. The same event may be narrated in more than one section, sometimes in a different way, inviting the reader to compare and interpret the differences. Sima may have utilized this approach to offer carefully veiled interpretations of past and present. Historians and other scholars in Han China had the advantage, as compared to their Western counterparts, of being employed by the government, but the disadvantage of having to limit their criticism of that government.

Technology

There were advances in science and technology. Widespread belief in astrology engendered astronomical observation of planets, stars, and other celestial objects. The watermill, which harnessed the power of running water to turn a grindstone, was used in China long before it appeared in Europe. The development of a horse collar that did not constrict breathing allowed Chinese horses to pull heavier loads than European horses. The Chinese first made paper, perhaps as early as the second century B.C.E., replacing the awkward bamboo strips of earlier eras. Improvements in military technology included horse breeding techniques to supply the cavalry and a reliable crossbow trigger. The Qin and Han built thousands of miles of roads—comparable in scale to the roads of the Roman Empire—to connect parts of the empire and move armies quickly. They also built a network of canals connecting the river systems of northern and southern China (see Environment and Technology: Water Engineering in Rome and China). One clever inventor even created an early seismometer to register earthquakes and indicate the direction where the event took place.

Religion

Chinese religion encompassed a wide spectrum of beliefs. Like the early Romans, the Chinese believed that divinity resided within nature. Most people believed in ghosts and spirits. The state maintained shrines to the lords of rain, winds, and soil, as well as to certain great rivers and high mountains. Sima Qian devoted an essay to the connection between religion and power, showing how emperors used ancient ceremonies and new-fangled cults to secure their authority. Daoism (see Chapter 2) became popular with the common people, incorporating an array of mystical and magical practices, including alchemy (the art of turning common materials into precious metals such as gold) and the search for potions that would impart immortality. Because Daoism questioned tradition and rejected the hierarchy and rules of the Confucian elite classes, charismatic Daoist teachers led several popular uprisings in the unsettled last decades of the Han dynasty.

Perhaps as early as the first century C.E. Buddhism (BOOD-izm) began to trickle into China. Originating in northern India in the fifth century B.C.E. (see Chapter 6), it slowly spread through South Asia and into Central Asia, carried by merchants on the Silk Road. Certain aspects of Buddhism fit comfortably with Chinese values: reverence for classic texts was also a feature of Confucianism, and the emphasis on severing attachments to material goods and pleasures found echoes in Daoism. But in other ways the Chinese were initially put off by Buddhist practices. The fact that Buddhist monks withdrew from their families to live in monasteries, shaved off their hair, and abstained from sex and procreation of children was repugnant to traditional Chinese values, which emphasized the importance of family ties, the body as an inviolable gift from parents, and the need to produce children to maintain the ancestor cult. Gradually Buddhism gained acceptance and was reshaped to fit the Chinese context, a process accelerated by the non-Chinese dynasties that dominated the north after the fall of the Han.

Decline of the Han

Wang Mang

A break in the long sequence of Han rulers occurred early in the first century C.E. when an ambitious official named Wang Mang (wahng mahng) seized power (9–23 C.E.). The new ruler implemented major reforms to address serious economic problems and to cement his popularity with the common people, including limiting the size of the estates of the rich and giving the surplus land to landless peasants. However, a cataclysmic flood that changed the course of the Yellow River caused large numbers of deaths and economic losses. Members of the Han family and other elements of the elite resisted their loss of status and property, and widespread poverty engendered a popular uprising of the "Red Eyebrows," as the insurgents were called. Wang Mang was besieged in his palace and killed, and a member of the Han royal family was soon installed as emperor. In 25 C.E., the capital was moved east to Luoyang.

The dynasty continued for another two centuries, but the imperial court was frequently plagued by weak leadership and court intrigue, with royal spouses and their families jockeying for power behind immature or ineffectual monarchs. Poems from this period complain of corrupt officials, unchecked attacks by barbarians, uprisings of desperate and hungry peasants, the spread of banditry, widespread poverty, and despair.

Fall of the Han

Several factors contributed to the fall of the Han. Continuous military vigilance along the frontier burdened Han finances and exacerbated the economic troubles of later Han times. Despite the earnest efforts of Qin and early Han emperors to reduce the power and wealth of the aristocracy and turn land over to a free peasantry, by the end of the first century B.C.E. nobles and successful merchants again controlled huge tracts of land. Many peasants sought their protection against the demands of the imperial government, which was thereby deprived of tax revenues and manpower. The system of military conscription broke down, forcing the government to hire more and more foreign soldiers and officers, men willing to serve for pay but not necessarily loyal to the Han state. By the end of the second century the empire was convulsed by civil wars, and in 220 C.E. a triumphant general named Cao Cao (tsow tsow) formally terminated the Han dynasty.

With the fall of the Han, China entered a period of political fragmentation that lasted until the rise of the Sui (sway) and Tang (tahng) dynasties in the late sixth and early seventh centuries C.E., a story we take up in Chapter 10. In this period the north was dominated by a series of barbarian peoples who combined elements of their own practices with the foundation of Chinese culture. Many ethnic Chinese migrated south into the Yangzi Valley, where Chinese rulers prevailed, and in this era the center of gravity of both the population and Chinese culture shifted to the south.

SECTION REVIEW

- The tough, disciplined frontier kingdom of Qin conquered all rival kingdoms and unified China by 221 B.C.E. The First Emperor and his Legalist advisers imposed standardization in many spheres and compelled the labor of many people.
- The Qin attack on the northern nomads led to the formation of the formidable Xiongnu Confederacy, which long posed a military threat to China.
- The Han dynasty added to the Qin foundation, creating fundamental patterns of imperial government that lasted for two millennia.
- Emperor Wu went on the offensive against the nomads, extended Chinese control in the northwest, and began to use Confucian scholars as government officials.
- The family, with its strict hierarchy, roles for each member, and values of deference and obedience, prepared citizens for their obligations to the state.
- The layout, buildings, and activities in the capital city, Chang'an, were replicated in cities and towns across China. Regional administration was based on this network of urban centers.
- The Han era saw major intellectual and technological developments, as well as the arrival of Buddhism in China.
- The fall of the Han dynasty early in the third century C.E. was followed by the takeover of the northern plain by barbarian peoples. Many Chinese fled south to the Yangzi River Valley, which became the new center of gravity for Chinese civilization.

CONCLUSION

Both the Roman Empire and the first Chinese empire arose from relatively small states that, because of their discipline and military toughness, were initially able to subdue their neighbors. Ultimately they unified widespread territories under strong central governments.

Agriculture was the fundamental economic activity and source of wealth. Government revenues primarily derived from a percentage of the annual harvest. Both empires depended initially on sturdy independent farmers pressed into military service or other forms of compulsory labor. Conflicts over who owned the land and how it was used were at the heart of political and social turmoil. The autocratic rulers of the Roman and Chinese states secured their positions by breaking the power of the old aristocratic families, seizing their excess land, and giving land to small farmers. The later reversal of this process, when wealthy noblemen again gained control of vast tracts of land and reduced the peasants to dependent tenant farmers, signaled the erosion of state authority.

Both empires spread out from an ethnically homogeneous core to encompass widespread territories containing diverse ecosystems, populations, and ways of life. Both brought those regions a cultural unity that has persisted, at least in part, to the present day. This development involved far more than military conquest and political domination. As the population of the core areas outstripped available resources, Italian and Han settlers moved into new regions, bringing their languages, beliefs, customs, and technologies. Many people in the conquered lands were attracted to the culture of the ruler nation and chose to adopt these practices and attach themselves to a "winning cause." Both empires found similar solutions to the problems of administering far-flung territories and large populations in an age when communication depended on men on horseback or on foot. The central government had to delegate considerable autonomy to local officials. These local elites identified their own interests with the central government they loyally served. In both empires a kind of civil service developed, staffed by educated and capable members of a prosperous middle class.

Technologies that facilitated imperial control also fostered cultural unification and improvements in the general standard of living. Roads built to expedite the movement of troops became the highways of commerce and the spread of imperial culture. A network of cities and towns linked the parts of the empire, providing local administrative bases, promoting commerce, and radiating imperial culture into the surrounding countryside. The majority of the population still resided in the countryside, but those living in urban centers enjoyed most of the advantages of empire. Cities and towns modeled themselves on the capital cities of Rome and Chang'an. Travelers found the same types of buildings and public spaces, and similar features of urban life, in outlying regions that they had seen in the capital.

The empires of Rome and Han China faced similar problems of defense: long borders located far from the administrative center and aggressive neighbors who coveted their prosperity. Both had to build walls and maintain chains of forts and garrisons to protect against incursions. The cost of frontier defense was staggering and eventually eroded the economic prosperity of the two empires. As imperial governments demanded more taxes and services from the hard-pressed civilian population, they lost the loyalty of their own people, many of whom sought protection on the estates of powerful rural landowners. Rough neighbors gradually learned the skills that had given the empires an initial advantage and were able to close the "technology gap." The Roman and Han governments eventually came to rely on soldiers hired from the same "barbarian" peoples who were pressing on the frontiers. Eventually, both empires were so weakened that their borders were overrun and their central governments collapsed. Ironically, the newly dominant immigrant groups were so deeply influenced by imperial culture that they maintained it to the best of their abilities.

In referring to the eventual failure of these two empires, we are brought up against important differences that led to different long-term outcomes. In China the imperial model was revived in subsequent eras, but the lands of the Roman Empire never again achieved the same level of unification. Several interrelated factors account for the different outcomes.

First, these cultures had different attitudes about the relationship of individuals to the state. In China the individual was more deeply embedded in the larger social group. The Chinese family, with its emphasis on a precisely defined hierarchy, unquestioning obedience, and solemn rituals of deference to elders and ancestors, served as the model for society and the state. Moreover, Confucianism, which sanctified hierarchy and provided a code of conduct for public officials, arose long before the imperial system and could be revived and tailored to fit changing political circumstances. Although the Roman family had its own hierarchy and traditions of obedience, the cult of ancestors was not as strong as among the Chinese, and the family was not the organizational model for Roman society and the Roman state. Also, there was no Roman equivalent of Confucianism—no ideology of political organization and social conduct that could survive the dissolution of the Roman state.

Opportunities for economic and social mobility were greater in the Roman Empire than in ancient China. Whereas the merchant class in China was frequently disparaged and constrained by the government, the absence of government interference in the Roman Empire resulted in greater economic mobility and a thriving and influential middle class in the towns and cities. The Roman army, because it was composed of professional soldiers in service for decades and constituting a distinct and increasingly privileged group, frequently played a decisive role in political conflict. In China, on the other hand, the army was drawn from draftees who served for two years and was much less likely to take the initiative in struggles for power.

Although Roman emperors tried to create an ideology to bolster their position, they were hampered by the persistence of Republican traditions and the ambiguities about the position of emperor deliberately cultivated by Augustus. As a result, Roman rulers were likely to be chosen by the army or by the Senate; the dynastic principle never took deep root; and the cult of the emperor had little spiritual content. This stands in sharp contrast to the unambiguous Chinese belief that the emperor was the divine Son of Heaven with privileged access to the beneficent power of the royal ancestors. Thus, in the lands that had once constituted the western part of the Roman Empire, there was no compelling basis for reviving the position of emperor and the territorial claims of empire in later ages.

Finally, Christianity, with its insistence on monotheism and one doctrine of truth, negated the Roman emperor's pretensions to divinity and was unwilling to compromise with pagan beliefs. The spread of Christianity through the provinces during the Late Roman Empire, and the decline of the western half of the empire in the fifth century C.E. (see Chapter 9), constituted an irreversible break with the past. On the other hand, Buddhism, which came to China in the early centuries C.E. and flourished in the post-Han era (see Chapter 10), was more easily reconciled with traditional Chinese values and beliefs.

KEY TERMS

Republic p. 142
Senate p. 142
patron/client relationship p. 143
Principate p. 147
Augustus p. 147
equites p. 147
pax romana p. 151
Romanization p. 151
Jesus p. 152
Paul p. 152
aqueduct p. 153
Third-Century Crisis p. 155
Constantine p. 156
Qin p. 157
Shi Huangdi p. 157
Han p. 157
Xiongnu p. 158
Gaozu p. 159
Sima Qian p. 161
Chang'an p. 163
gentry p. 163

EBOOK AND WEBSITE RESOURCES

Primary Sources

A Man of Unlimited Ambition: Julius Caesar

Lessons for Women

Interactive Maps

Map 5.1 The Roman Empire

Map 5.2 Han China

Plus flashcards, practice quizzes, and more. Go to: www.cengage.com/history/bullietearthpeople5e

SUGGESTED READING

Boatwright, Mary T., Daniel J. Gargola, and Richard J. A. Talbert. *The Romans: From Village to Empire*. 2004. A good new survey of Roman history.

Cherry, David, ed. *The Roman World: A Sourcebook*. 2001. A selection of thematically organized ancient sources in translation.

Clark, Gillian. *Christianity and Roman Society*. 2004. Investigates the rise of Christianity.

de Bary, Wm. Theodore, and Irene Bloom, eds. *Sources of Chinese Tradition*, vol. 1, 2nd ed. 2000. A broad selection of ancient sources in translation with explanatory notes.

Di Cosmo, Nicola. *Ancient China and Its Enemies: The Rise of Nomadic Power in East Asian History*. 2002. Explores the interactions of Chinese and nomads on the northern frontier.

Dyson, Stephen L. *The Creation of the Roman Frontier*. 1985. Examines Roman military expansion and defense of the frontiers.

Hinsch, Bret. *Women in Early Imperial China*. 2002. A stimulating analysis of women's many roles in the early imperial period.

Lewis, Mark Edward. *The Early Chinese Empires: Qin and Han*. 2007. A thorough, up-to-date account of the first imperial dynasties.

Loewe, Michael. *Everyday Life in Early Imperial China During the Han Period, 202 B.C.–A.D. 220*. 1988. Examines many typical facets of Chinese society in the Han era.

Matz, David. *Daily Life of the Ancient Romans*. 2002. Looks at the features that typified daily life.

Millar, Fergus. *The Emperor in the Roman World (31 B.C.–A.D. 337)*. 1977. A comprehensive study of the position of the princeps.

Scheidel, Walter, ed. *Rome and China: Comparative Perspectives on Ancient World Empires*. 2009. Leading scholars make illuminating comparisons of political, legal, military, social, and economic factors.

Stambaugh, John E. *The Ancient Roman City*. 1988. Highlights the characteristics of Roman urban centers.

Turcan, Robert. *The Gods of Ancient Rome: Religion in Everyday Life from Archaic to Imperial Times*. 2000. An accessible introduction to Roman religion in its public and private manifestations.

Ward-Perkins, Bryan. *The Fall of Rome and the End of Civilization*. 2005. Examines the momentous changes occurring in Rome's last centuries.

NOTES

1. Nicola Di Cosmo, *Ancient China and Its Enemies: The Rise of Nomadic Power in East Asian History* (Cambridge: Cambridge University Press, 2002), 155–158.
2. Patricia Buckley Ebrey, ed., *Chinese Civilization and Society: A Sourcebook* (New York: Free Press, 1981), 33–34.

AP* REVIEW QUESTIONS FOR CHAPTER 5

1. The most essential activity in early Rome was
   (A) trade.
   (B) farming.
   (C) fishing.
   (D) military conquest.

2. In Roman families, the authority figure was the oldest male. This situation is known as
   (A) patronage.
   (B) rule by the paterfamilias.
   (C) primogeniture.
   (D) the patron relationship.

3. Unlike the Greeks, the Romans
   (A) were a peaceful people who practiced diplomacy over farming.
   (B) were a naval power.
   (C) granted Roman citizenship to conquered people.
   (D) forced conversion to the Roman state religion.

4. One of the major impacts of the pax romana was
   (A) the facilitation of trade.
   (B) major wars against Persia.
   (C) the conquest of Arabia.
   (D) the rise of tenant farming.

5. One of the most enduring consequences of the Roman Empire was
   (A) the expansion of the Roman tax system.
   (B) the idea of electing officials.
   (C) the spread of the Latin language.
   (D) Roman military arts.

6. The Romans originally viewed Christians negatively because
   (A) they were not Roman in origin.
   (B) Jesus had offended the Roman government.
   (C) Judaism was a banned religion.
   (D) their monotheism kept them from worshiping the Roman emperor.

7. As the Western Roman Empire collapsed in the 500s, Rome
   (A) remained the locus of the Christian church.
   (B) was abandoned by all of the wealthy citizens.
   (C) lost its trade centers to Naples.
   (D) became the capital of the Franks.

8. By the early Han dynasty, China's population had
   (A) stabilized and stopped growing due to the warfare of the time.
   (B) shifted away from the river valleys.
   (C) become centered on Beijing.
   (D) grown because of intensive agricultural practices.

9. Like Rome, the Qin and Han
   (A) faced similar problems with defense of the empire.
   (B) had to delegate autonomy to local officials.
   (C) built thousands of miles of roads to facilitate trade.
   (D) All of the above

10. Qin and Han emperors had to ally themselves with the gentry as one strategy to weaken the rural aristocrats. In China, the gentry were
    (A) similar to peasant farmers in Europe.
    (B) the class of prosperous and educated families just below the aristocrats.
    (C) the traditional warrior class of China.
    (D) the lower class of priests.

11. Which of the following is true of the Han collapse?
    (A) Nomadic bands raided.
    (B) Official corruption spread.
    (C) Peasant uprisings increased.
    (D) All of the above

12. Which of the following is true of Rome and the Han dynasty?
    (A) Buddhism was more easily reconciled with the Han than Christianity was with Rome.
    (B) Both Rome and the Han were governed by ethnic minorities.
    (C) Rome and Han armies were made up of mercenary soldiers.
    (D) Both Rome and the Han used the idea of the Mandate of Heaven.

CHAPTER 6

CHAPTER OUTLINE

- Foundations of Indian Civilization, 1500 B.C.E.–300 C.E.
- Imperial Expansion and Collapse, 324 B.C.E.–550 C.E.
- Southeast Asia, 50–600 C.E.
- Conclusion

ENVIRONMENT + TECHNOLOGY *Indian Mathematics*

DIVERSITY + DOMINANCE *Relations Between Women and Men in the* Kama Sutra *and the* Arthashastra

Dinodia Photo Library

The Thousand Pillared Hall in the Temple of Minakshi at Madurai At the annual Chittarai Festival, the citizens of this city in south India celebrate the wedding of their patron goddess, Minakshi, to Shiva.

Visit the website and ebook for additional study materials and interactive tools: www.cengage.com/history/bullietearthpeople5e

India and Southeast Asia, 1500 B.C.E.–600 C.E.

- What historical forces led to the development of complex social groupings in ancient India?
- How, in the face of powerful forces that tended to keep India fragmented, did two great empires—the Mauryan Empire of the fourth to second centuries B.C.E. and the Gupta Empire of the fourth to sixth centuries C.E.—succeed in unifying much of India?
- How did a number of states in Southeast Asia become wealthy and powerful by exploiting their position on the trade routes between China and India?

In the Bhagavad-Gita (BUH-guh-vahd GEE-tuh), the most renowned Indian sacred text, the legendary warrior Arjuna (AHR-joo-nuh) rides out in his chariot to the open space between two armies preparing for battle. Torn between his social duty to fight for his family's claim to the throne and his conscience, which balks at the prospect of killing relatives, friends, and former teachers in the enemy camp, Arjuna slumps down in his chariot and refuses to fight. But his driver, the god Krishna (KRISH-nuh) in disguise, persuades him, in a carefully structured dialogue, both of the necessity to fulfill his duty as a warrior and of the proper frame of mind for performing these acts. In the climactic moment of the dialogue Krishna endows Arjuna with a "divine eye" and permits him to see the true appearance of God:

> It was a multiform, wondrous vision,
> with countless mouths and eyes
> and celestial ornaments,
>
> Everywhere was boundless divinity
> containing all astonishing things,
> wearing divine garlands and garments,
> anointed with divine perfume.
>
> If the light of a thousand suns
> were to rise in the sky at once,
> it would be like the light
> of that great spirit.
>
> Arjuna saw all the universe
> in its many ways and parts,
> standing as one in the body
> of the god of gods.[1]

In all of world literature, this is one of the most compelling attempts to depict the nature of deity. Graphic images emphasize the vastness, diversity, and multiplicity of the god, but in the end we learn that Krishna is the organizing principle behind all creation, that behind diversity and multiplicity lies a higher unity.

This is an apt metaphor for Indian civilization. The enormous variety of the Indian landscape is mirrored in the patchwork of ethnic and linguistic groups that

---

[1]From Bhagavad-Gita, translated by Barbara Stoler Miller, translation copyright © 1986 by Barbara Stoler Miller. Used by permission of Bantam Books, a division of Random House, Inc.

occupy it, the political fragmentation that has marked most of Indian history, the elaborate hierarchy of social groups into which the Indian population is divided, and the thousands of deities who are worshiped at innumerable holy places that dot the subcontinent. Yet, in the end, one can speak of an Indian civilization united by shared views and values. The photograph shows the interior of a temple in the city of Madurai in southern India. Here the ten-day Chittarai Festival, the most important religious event of the year, celebrates the wedding of a local goddess, Minakshi, and the great Hindu god Shiva, symbolizing the reconciliation of local and national deities, southern and northern cultural practices, and male and female potentialities.

This chapter surveys the history of South and Southeast Asia from approximately 1500 B.C.E. to 600 C.E., highlighting the evolution of defining features of Indian civilization. Considerable attention is given to Indian religious conceptions, due both to religion's profound role in shaping Indian society and the sources of information available to historians. For reasons that will be explained below, writing came late to India, and ancient Indians did not develop a historical consciousness like other peoples of antiquity and took little interest in recording specific historical events.

FOUNDATIONS OF INDIAN CIVILIZATION, 1500 B.C.E.–300 C.E.

India is called a *subcontinent* because it is a large—roughly 2,000 miles (3,200 kilometers) in both length and breadth—and physically isolated landmass. It is set off from the rest of Asia to the north by the Himalayas (him-uh-LAY-uhs), the highest mountains on the planet, and by the Indian Ocean on its eastern, southern, and western sides (see Map 6.1). The most permeable frontier, used by invaders and migrating peoples, lies to the northwest, but people using this corridor must cross the mountain barrier of the Hindu Kush (HIHN-doo KOOSH) (via the Khyber [KIE-ber] Pass) and the Thar (tahr) Desert east of the Indus River.

AP* Exam Tip The Indian subcontinent is called South Asia on the AP* World History exam.

monsoon Seasonal winds in the Indian Ocean caused by the differences in temperature between the rapidly heating and cooling landmasses of Africa and Asia and the slowly changing ocean waters. These strong and predictable winds have long been ridden across the open sea by sailors, and the large amounts of rainfall that they deposit on parts of India, Southeast Asia, and China allow for the cultivation of several crops a year.

The Indian Subcontinent

The subcontinent—which encompasses the modern nations of Pakistan, Nepal, Bhutan, Bangladesh, India, and the adjacent island of Sri Lanka—divides into three distinct topographical zones. The mountainous northern zone contains the heavily forested foothills and high meadows on the edge of the Hindu Kush and Himalaya ranges. Next come the great basins of the Indus and Ganges (GAHN-jeez) Rivers. Originating in the snow-clad Tibetan mountains to the north, these rivers have repeatedly overflowed their banks and deposited layer on layer of silt, creating large alluvial plains. Northern India is divided from the third zone, the peninsula proper, by the Vindhya range and the Deccan (de-KAN), an arid, rocky plateau. The tropical coastal strip of Kerala (Malabar) in the west, the Coromandel Coast in the east with its web of rivers descending from the central plateau, the flatlands of Tamil Nadu on the southern tip of the peninsula, and the island of Sri Lanka often have followed paths of political and cultural development separate from those of northern India.

The northern rim of mountains shelters the subcontinent from cold Arctic winds and gives it a subtropical climate. The most dramatic source of moisture is the **monsoon** (seasonal wind). The Indian Ocean is slow to warm or cool, while the vast landmass of Asia swings between seasonal extremes of heat and cold. The temperature difference between water and land acts like a bellows, producing a great wind. The southwest monsoon begins in June, absorbing huge amounts of moisture from the Indian Ocean and dropping it over a swath of India that encompasses the rain forest belt on the western coast and the Ganges Basin. Three harvests a year are possible in some places. Rice is grown in the moist, flat Ganges Delta (modern Bengal). Else-

CHRONOLOGY

	India	Southeast Asia
2000 B.C.E.		ca. 2000 B.C.E. Swidden agriculture ca. 1600 B.C.E. Beginning of migrations from mainland Southeast Asia to islands in Pacific and Indian Oceans
1500 B.C.E.	ca. 1500 B.C.E. Migration of Indo-European peoples into northwest India	
1000 B.C.E.	ca. 1000 B.C.E. Indo-European groups move into the Ganges Plain	
500 B.C.E.	ca. 500 B.C.E. Siddhartha Gautama founds Buddhism; Mahavira founds Jainism 324 B.C.E. Chandragupta Maurya becomes king of Magadha and lays foundation for Mauryan Empire 273–232 B.C.E. Reign of Ashoka 184 B.C.E. Fall of Mauryan Empire	
1 C.E.	320 C.E. Chandra Gupta establishes Gupta Empire	ca. 50–560 C.E. Funan dominates southern Indochina and the Isthmus of Kra
500 C.E.	550 C.E. Collapse of Gupta Empire	ca. 500 C.E. Trade route develops through Strait of Malacca

where the staples are wheat, barley, and millet. The Indus Valley, in contrast, gets little precipitation (see Chapter 1), and agriculture requires extensive irrigation.

Although invasions and migrations usually came by land through the northwest corridor, the ocean has not been a barrier to travel and trade. Mariners learned to ride the monsoon winds across open waters from northeast to southwest in January and to make the return voyage in July. Ships sailed west across the Arabian Sea to the Persian Gulf, the southern coast of Arabia, and East Africa, and east across the Bay of Bengal to Indochina and Indonesia (see Chapter 7).

Many characteristic features of later Indian civilization may derive from the Indus Valley civilization of the third and early second millennia B.C.E., but proof is hard to come by because writing from that period has not yet been deciphered. That society, with its advanced social organization and technology, succumbed around 1900 B.C.E. to some kind of environmental crisis (see Chapter 1).

Vedas Early Indian sacred "knowledge"—the literal meaning of the term—long preserved and communicated orally by Brahmin priests and eventually written down. These religious texts, including the thousand poetic hymns to various deities contained in the Rig Veda, are our main source of information about the Vedic period (ca. 1500–500 B.C.E.).

The Vedic Age

Arya Migrations

Historians call the period from 1500 to 500 B.C.E. the Vedic Age, after the **Vedas** (VAY-duhs), religious texts that are our main source of information about the period. The foundations for Indian civilization were laid in the Vedic Age. Most historians believe that new groups of people—animal-herding warriors speaking Indo-European languages—migrated into northwest India around 1500 B.C.E. Some argue for a much earlier Indo-European presence in this region in conjunction with the spread of agriculture. In any case, in the mid-second millennium B.C.E. northern India entered a new historical period associated with the dominance of Indo-European groups.

After the collapse of the Indus Valley civilization there was no central authority to direct irrigation efforts. The region became home to kinship groups that depended mostly on their herds of cattle for sustenance. These societies were patriarchal, with the father dominating the family as the king ruled the tribe. Members of the warrior class boasted of their martial skill and courage, relished combat, celebrated with lavish feasts of beef and rounds of heavy drinking, and filled their leisure time with chariot racing and gambling.

AP* Exam Tip It is best to focus on the impact of a technology, here iron metallurgy, rather than on the specific time in which it was developed.

After 1000 B.C.E. some groups migrated east into the Ganges Plain. New technologies made this advance possible. Iron tools—harder than bronze and able to hold a sharper edge—allowed settlers to fell trees and work the newly cleared land with plows pulled by oxen. The soil of the Ganges Plain was fertile, well watered by the annual monsoon, and able to sustain two or three crops a year. As in Greece at roughly the same time (see Chapter 4), the use of iron tools to open new land for agriculture must have led to a significant increase in population.

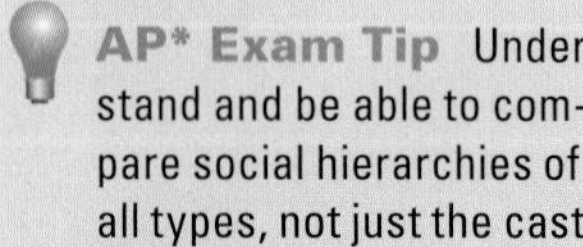

AP* Exam Tip Understand and be able to compare social hierarchies of all types, not just the caste system in India.

Stories about this era, not written down until much later but long preserved by memorization and oral recitation, speak of bitter warfare between two groups of people: the Aryas, relatively light-skinned speakers of Indo-European languages, and the Dasas, dark-skinned speakers of Dravidian languages. It is possible that some Dasas were absorbed into Arya populations and that elites from both groups merged. For the most part, however, Aryas pushed the Dasas south into central and southern India, where their descendants still live. Today Indo-European languages are primarily spoken in northern India, while Dravidian speech prevails in the south.

Class and Caste

varna/jati Two categories of social identity of great importance in Indian history. Varna are the four major social divisions: the Brahmin priest class, the Kshatriya warrior/administrator class, the Vaishya merchant/farmer class, and the Shudra laborer class. Within the system of varna are many jati, regional groups of people who have a common occupational sphere and who marry, eat, and generally interact with other members of their group.

karma In Indian tradition, the residue of deeds performed in past and present lives that adheres to a "spirit" and determines what form it will assume in its next life cycle. The doctrines of karma and reincarnation were used by the elite in ancient India to encourage people to accept their social position and do their duty.

Skin color has been a persistent concern of Indian society and is one of the bases for its historically sharp internal divisions. Over time there evolved a system of ***varna***—literally "color," though the word came to indicate something akin to "class." Individuals were born into one of four classes: *Brahmin*, comprising priests and scholars; *Kshatriya* (kshuh-TREE-yuh), warriors and officials; *Vaishya* (VIESH-yuh), merchants, artisans, and landowners; or *Shudra* (SHOOD-ra), peasants and laborers. The designation *Shudra* originally may have been reserved for Dasas, who were given the menial jobs in society. Indeed, the very term *dasa* came to mean "slave." Eventually a fifth group was marked off: the Untouchables. They were excluded from the class system, and members of the other groups literally avoided them because of the demeaning or polluting work to which they were relegated—such as leather tanning, which involved touching dead animals, and sweeping away ashes of the dead after cremations.

People at the top of the social pyramid could explain why this hierarchy existed. According to one creation myth, a primordial creature named Purusha allowed itself to be sacrificed. From its mouth sprang the class of Brahmin priests, the embodiment of intellect and knowledge. From its arms came the Kshatriya warrior class, from its thighs the Vaishya landowners and merchants, and from its feet the Shudra workers.

The varna system was just one of the mechanisms developed to regulate relations between different groups. Within the broad class divisions, the population was further subdivided into numerous ***jati***, or birth groups (sometimes called *castes*, from a Portuguese term meaning "breed"). Each jati had its proper occupation, duties, and rituals. Individuals who belonged to a given jati lived with members of their group, married within the group, and ate only with members of the group. Elaborate rules governed their interactions with members of other groups. Members of higher-status groups feared pollution from contact with lower-caste individuals and had to undergo elaborate rituals of purification to remove any taint.

The class and caste systems came to be connected to a widespread belief in reincarnation. The Brahmin priests taught that every living creature had an immortal essence: the *atman*, or "breath." Separated from the body at death, the atman was later reborn in another body. Whether the new body was that of an insect, an animal, or a human depended on the **karma**, or deeds, of the atman in its previous incarnations. People who lived exemplary lives would be reborn into the higher classes. Those who misbehaved would be punished in the next life by being relegated to a lower class or even a lower life form. The underlying message was: You are where you deserve to be, and the only way to improve your lot in the next cycle of existence is to accept your current station and its attendant duties.

Vedic Religion

The dominant deities in Vedic religion were male and associated with the heavens. To release the dawn, Indra, god of war and master of the thunderbolt, daily slew the demon encasing the universe. Varuna, lord of the sky, maintained universal order and dispensed justice. Agni, the force of fire, consumed the sacrifice and bridged the spheres of gods and humans.

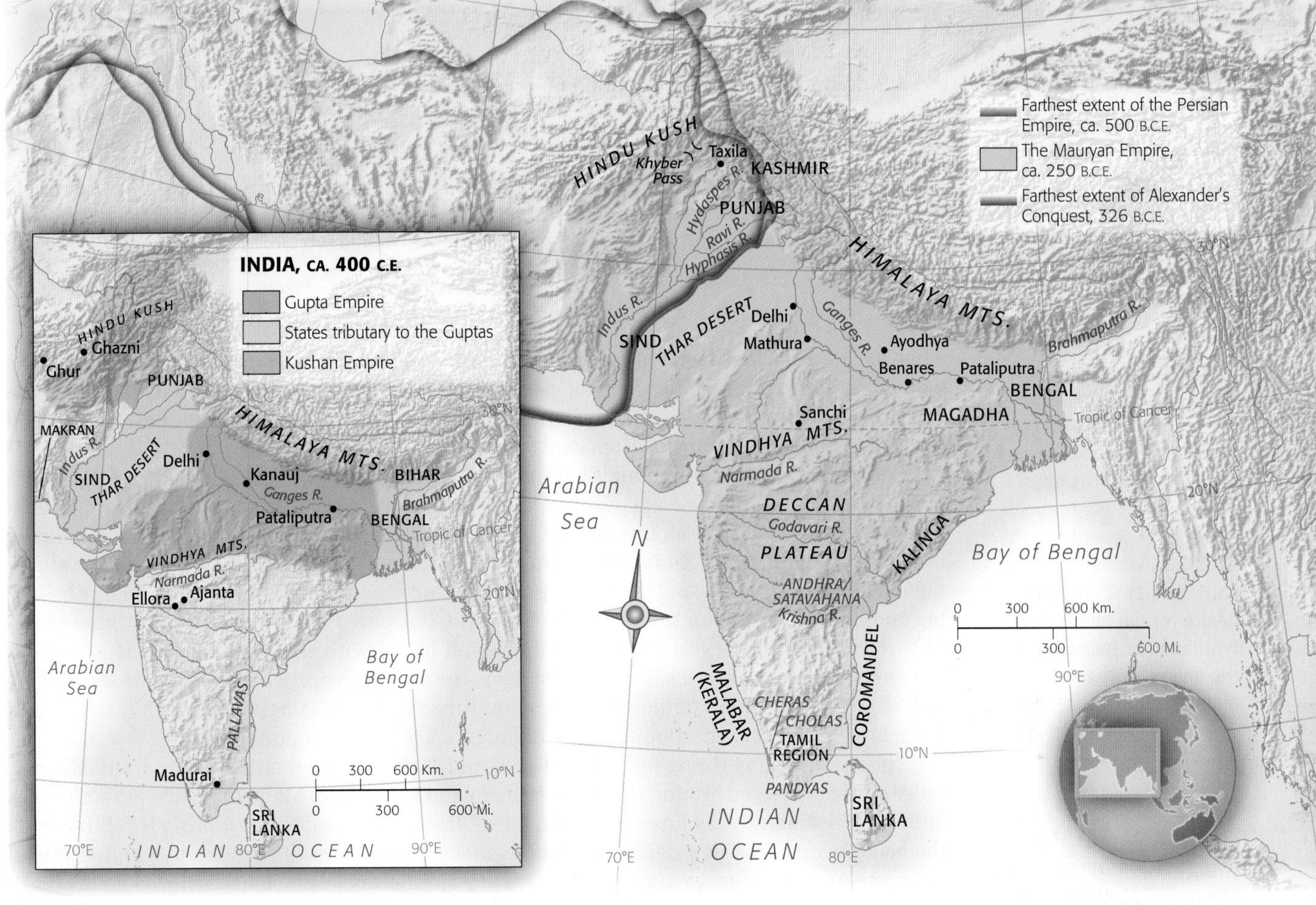

MAP 6.1 **Ancient India** Mountains and ocean largely separate the Indian subcontinent from the rest of Asia. Migrations and invasions usually came through the Khyber Pass in the northwest. Seaborne commerce with western Asia, Southeast Asia, and East Asia often flourished. Peoples speaking Indo-European languages migrated into the broad valleys of the Indus and Ganges Rivers in the north. Dravidian-speaking peoples remained the dominant population in the south. The diversity of the Indian landscape, the multiplicity of ethnic groups, and the primary identification of people with their class and caste lie behind the division into many small states that has characterized much of Indian political history.

e Interactive Map

Sacrifice—the dedication to a god of a valued possession, often a living creature—was the essential ritual. The purpose of these offerings was to invigorate the gods and thereby sustain their creative powers and promote stability in the world.

Brahmin priests controlled the sacrifices, for only they knew the rituals and prayers. The *Rig Veda*, a collection of more than a thousand poetic hymns to various deities, and the *Brahmanas*, detailed prose descriptions of procedures for ritual and sacrifice, were collections of priestly lore couched in the Sanskrit language of the Arya upper classes. This information was handed down orally from one generation of priests to the next. The priests' "knowledge" (the term *veda* means just that) was the basis of their economic well-being. They were amply rewarded for officiating at sacrifices, and their knowledge gave them social and political power because they were the indispensable intermediaries between gods and humans. Some scholars hypothesize that the Brahmins resisted the introduction of writing in order to preserve their control of sacred knowledge. This might explain why writing came into widespread use in India later than in other societies of equivalent complexity. However, we may be unaware of earlier uses of writing because it involved perishable materials that have not survived in the archaeological record.

e **PRIMARY SOURCE: The *Rig Veda*** Read how Indra, "the thunder-wielder," slew Vritra, "firstborn of dragons," and how Purusha created the universe through an act of ritual sacrifice.

It is difficult to uncover the experiences of women in early India. Limited evidence indicates that women in the Vedic period studied sacred lore, composed religious hymns, and participated in the sacrificial ritual. They could own property and usually did not marry until reaching their middle or late teens. Several strong and resourceful women appear in the Indian epic poems originating in this era.

The sharp internal divisions and complex hierarchy of Indian society served important social functions. They provided each individual with a clear identity and role and offered the benefits of group solidarity and support. However, there is evidence that groups sometimes were able to upgrade their status. Thus the elaborate system of divisions was not static and provided a mechanism for working out social tensions. Many of these features have persisted into modern times.

Challenges to the Old Order: Jainism and Buddhism

moksha The Hindu concept of the spirit's "liberation" from the endless cycle of rebirths. There are various avenues—such as physical discipline, meditation, and acts of devotion to the gods—by which the spirit can distance itself from desire for the things of this world and be merged with the divine force that animates the universe.

After 700 B.C.E. various forms of reaction against Brahmin power and privilege emerged. People who objected to the rigid hierarchy of classes and castes or the community's demands on the individual could retreat to the nearby forest that still covered much of ancient India. These wild places symbolized freedom from societal constraints.

Certain charismatic individuals who abandoned their town or village and moved to the forest attracted bands of followers. Calling into question the priests' exclusive claims to wisdom and the necessity of Vedic chants and sacrifices, they offered an alternate path to salvation: the individual pursuit of insight into the nature of the self and the universe through physical and mental discipline (*yoga*), special dietary practices, and meditation. They taught that by distancing oneself from desire for the things of this world, one could achieve **moksha**, or "liberation." This release from the cycle of reincarnations and union with the divine force that animates the universe sometimes was likened to "a deep, dreamless sleep." The *Upanishads* (ooh-PAH-nee-shad)—a collection of more than one hundred mystical dialogues between teachers and disciples—reflect this questioning of the foundations of Vedic religion.

Jainism

AP* Exam Tip The details of Jainism are less emphasized than the major teachings of Hinduism and Buddhism on the AP* exam.

The most serious threat to Vedic religion and Brahmin prerogatives came from two new religions that emerged around this time: Jainism and Buddhism. Mahavira (540–468 B.C.E.) was known to his followers as Jina, "the Conqueror," from which is derived *Jainism* (JINE-iz-uhm), the belief system that he established. Emphasizing the holiness of the life force animating all living creatures, Mahavira and his followers practiced strict nonviolence. They wore masks to prevent accidentally inhaling small insects, and they carefully brushed off a seat before sitting down. Those who gave themselves over completely to Jainism practiced extreme asceticism and

Dinodia Photo Library

Carved Stone Gateway Leading to the Great Stupa at Sanchi Pilgrims traveled long distances to visit stupas, mounds containing relics of the Buddha. The complex at Sanchi, in central India, was begun by Ashoka in the third century B.C.E., though the gates probably date to the first century C.E. This relief shows a royal procession bringing the remains of the Buddha to the city of Kushinagara.

Robert Fisher

Sculpture of the Buddha, Second or Third Century C.E. This depiction of the Buddha, showing the effects of a protracted fast before he abandoned asceticism for the path of moderation, is from Gandhara in the northwest. It displays the influence of Greek artistic styles emanating from Greek settlements established in that region by Alexander the Great in the late fourth century B.C.E.

nudity, ate only what they were given by others, and eventually starved themselves to death. Less zealous Jainists, restricted from agricultural work by the injunction against killing, were city dwellers engaged in commerce and banking.

Far more significant for Indian and world history was the rise of Buddhism. So many stories were told about Siddhartha Gautama (563–483 B.C.E.), known as the **Buddha**, "the Enlightened One," that it is difficult to separate fact from legend. He came from a Kshatriya family of the Sakyas, a people in the foothills of the Himalayas. As a young man he enjoyed the princely lifestyle to which he had been born, but at some point he abandoned family and privilege to become a wandering ascetic. After six years of self-deprivation, he came to regard asceticism as no more likely to produce spiritual insight than the luxury of his previous life, and he decided to adhere to a "Middle Path" of moderation. Sitting under a tree in a deer park near Benares on the Ganges River, he gained a sudden and profound insight into the true nature of reality, which he set forth as "Four Noble Truths": (1) life is suffering; (2) suffering arises from desire; (3) the solution to suffering lies in curbing desire; and (4) desire can be curbed if a person follows the "Eightfold Path" of right views, aspirations, speech, conduct, livelihood, effort, mindfulness, and meditation. Rising up, the Buddha preached his First Sermon, a central text of Buddhism, and set into motion the "Wheel of the Law." He soon attracted followers, some of whom took vows of celibacy, nonviolence, and poverty.

Buddha An Indian prince named Siddhartha Gautama, who renounced his wealth and social position. After becoming "enlightened" (the meaning of *Buddha*), he enunciated the principles of Buddhism. This doctrine evolved and spread throughout India and to Southeast, East, and Central Asia.

Buddhism

In its original form, Buddhism centered on the individual. Although not quite rejecting the existence of gods, it denied their usefulness to a person seeking enlightenment. What mattered was living one's life with moderation, in order to minimize desire and suffering, and searching for spiritual truth through self-discipline and meditation. The ultimate reward was *nirvana*, literally "snuffing out the flame." With nirvana came release from the cycle of reincarnations and achievement of a state of perpetual tranquility. The Vedic tradition emphasized the eternal survival of the atman, the "breath" or nonmaterial essence of the individual. In contrast, Buddhism regarded the individual as a composite without any soul-like component that survived upon entering nirvana.

When the Buddha died, he left no final instructions, instead urging his disciples to "be their own lamp." As the Buddha's message—contained in philosophical discourses memorized by his followers—spread throughout India and into Central, Southeast, and East Asia, its very success began to subvert the individualistic and essentially atheistic tenets of the founder. Buddhist monasteries were established, and a hierarchy of Buddhist monks and nuns came into being. Worshipers erected *stupas* (STOO-puh) (large earthen mounds symbolizing the universe) over relics of the cremated founder. Believers began to worship the Buddha himself as a god. Many Buddhists also revered *bodhisattvas* (boe-dih-SUT-vuh), men and women who had achieved enlightenment and were on the threshold of nirvana but chose to be reborn into mortal bodies to help others along the path to salvation.

e **PRIMARY SOURCE: Setting in Motion the Wheel of Law** Siddhartha's first sermon contains the core teaching of Buddhism: to escape, by following the Middle Path, the suffering caused by desire.

The makers of early pictorial images refused to show the Buddha as a living person and represented him only indirectly, through symbols such as his footprints, his begging bowl, or the tree under which he achieved enlightenment, as if to emphasize his achievement of a state of nonexistence. From the second century C.E., however, statues of the Buddha and bodhisattvas began to proliferate, done in native sculptural styles and in a style that showed the influence

Mahayana Buddhism "Great Vehicle" branch of Buddhism followed in China, Japan, and Central Asia. The focus is on reverence for Buddha and for bodhisattvas, enlightened persons who have postponed nirvana to help others attain enlightenment.

Theravada Buddhism "Way of the Elders" branch of Buddhism followed in Sri Lanka and much of Southeast Asia. Theravada remains close to the original principles set forth by the Buddha; it downplays the importance of gods and emphasizes austerity and the individual's search for enlightenment.

of the Greek settlements established in Bactria (modern Afghanistan) by Alexander the Great (see Chapter 4). A schism emerged within Buddhism. Devotees of **Mahayana** (mah-huh-YAH-nuh) ("Great Vehicle") **Buddhism** embraced the popular new features, while practitioners of **Theravada** (there-uh-VAH-duh) ("Teachings of the Elders") **Buddhism** followed most of the original teachings of the founder.

The Evolution of Hinduism

Challenged by new, spiritually satisfying, and egalitarian movements, Vedic religion made important adjustments, evolving into **Hinduism**, the religion of hundreds of millions of people in South Asia today. The foundation of Hinduism is the Vedic religion of the Arya peoples of northern India. But Hinduism also incorporated elements drawn from the Dravidian cultures of the south, such as an emphasis on intense devotion to the deity and the prominence of fertility rituals. Also present are elements of Buddhism.

The process by which Vedic religion was transformed into Hinduism by the fourth century C.E. is largely hidden from us. The Brahmin priests maintained their high social status and influence. But sacrifice, though still part of traditional worship, was less central, and there was more opportunity for direct contact between gods and individual worshipers.

The Hindu Gods

Hinduism A general term for a wide variety of beliefs and ritual practices that have developed in the Indian subcontinent since antiquity. Hinduism has roots in ancient Vedic, Buddhist, and south Indian religious concepts and practices. It spread along the trade routes to Southeast Asia.

The gods were altered, both in identity and in their relationships with humanity. Two formerly minor deities, Vishnu (VIHSH-noo) and Shiva (SHEE-vuh), became preeminent. Hinduism emphasized the worshiper's personal devotion to a particular deity, usually Vishnu, Shiva, or Devi (DEH-vee) ("the Goddess"). Both Shiva and Devi appear to be derived from the Dravidian tradition, in which fertility cult and female deities played a prominent role. Vishnu, who has a clear Arya pedigree, remains more popular in northern India, while Shiva is dominant in the Dravidian south. These gods can appear in many guises. They are identified by various cult names and are represented by a complex symbolism of stories, companion animals, birds, and objects.

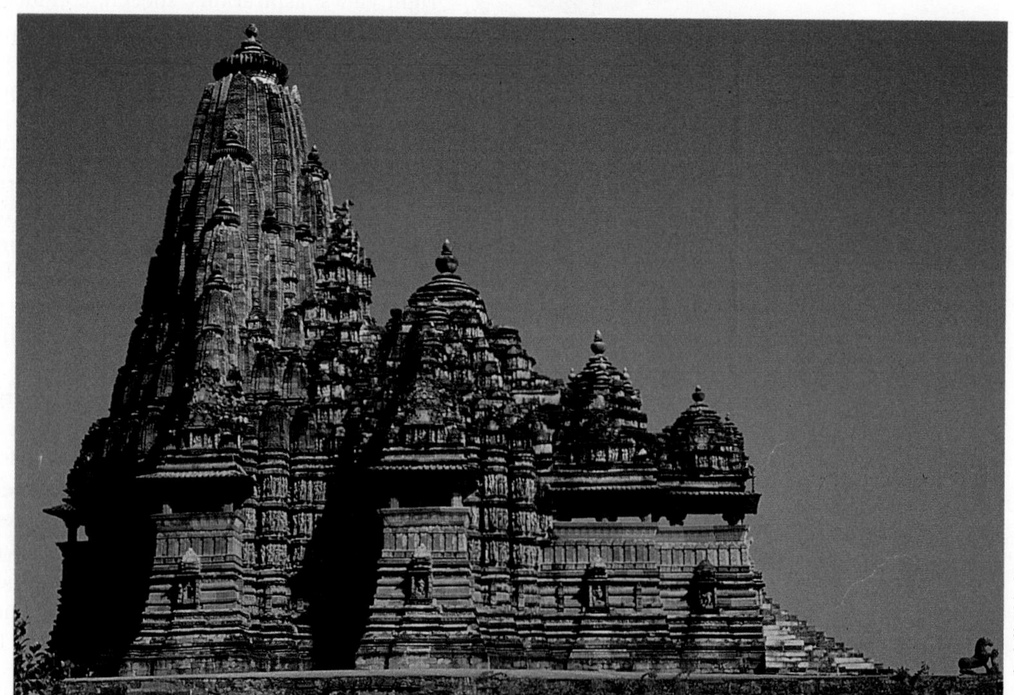

Jean-Louis Nou/aka-images

Hindu Temple at Khajuraho This sandstone temple of the Hindu deity Shiva, representing the celestial mountain of the gods, was erected at Khajuraho, in central India, around 1000 C.E., but it reflects the architectural symbolism of Hindu temples developed in the Gupta period. Worshipers made their way through several rooms to the image of the deity, located in the innermost "womb-chamber" directly beneath the tallest tower.

Borromeo/Art Resource, NY

Vishnu Rescuing the Earth Goddess, Fifth Century C.E. This sculpture, carved into the rock wall of a cave at Udayagiri in eastern India, depicts Vishnu in his incarnation as a boar rescuing the Earth Goddess from the vast ocean. As the god treads triumphantly on a subdued snake demon and the joyful goddess clings to his snout, a chorus of gods and sages applaud the miracle.

Vishnu, the preserver, is a benevolent deity who helps his devotees in time of need. Hindus believe that whenever demonic forces threaten the cosmic order, Vishnu appears on earth in one of a series of *avataras*, or incarnations. Among his incarnations are the legendary hero Rama, the popular cowherd-god Krishna, and the Buddha (a clear attempt to co-opt the rival religion's founder). Shiva, who lives in ascetic isolation on Mount Kailasa in the Himalayas, is a more ambivalent figure. He represents both creation and destruction, for both are part of a single, cyclical process. He often is represented performing dance steps that symbolize the acts of creation and destruction. Devi manifests herself in various ways—as a full-bodied mother-goddess who promotes fertility and procreation, as the docile and loving wife Parvati, and as the frightening deity who, under the name Kali or Durga, lets loose a torrent of violence and destruction.

The multiplicity of gods (330 million according to one tradition), sects, and local practices within Hinduism is dazzling, reflecting the ethnic, linguistic, and cultural diversity of India. Yet within this variety there is unity. Ultimately, all the gods and spirits are seen as manifestations of a single divine force that pervades the universe. This sense of underlying unity is expressed in texts, such as the passage from the Bhagavad-Gita quoted at the beginning of this chapter; in the different potentials of women represented in the various manifestations of Devi; and in composite statues that are split down the middle—half Shiva, half Vishnu—as if to say that they are complementary aspects of one cosmic principle.

Forms of Worship

Hinduism offers the worshiper a variety of ways to approach god and obtain divine favor—through special knowledge of sacred truths, mental and physical discipline, or extraordinary devotion to the deity. Worship centers on the temples, which range from humble village shrines to magnificent, richly decorated stone edifices built under royal patronage. Beautifully proportioned statues in which the deity may take up temporary residence are adored and beseeched by eager worshipers. A common form of worship is *puja*, service to the deity, which can take the form of bathing, clothing, or feeding the statue. Potent blessings are conferred on the man or woman who glimpses the divine image.

Pilgrimage to famous shrines and attendance at festivals offer worshipers additional opportunities to show devotion. The entire Indian subcontinent is dotted with sacred places where worshipers can directly sense and benefit from the inherent power of divinity. Mountains, caves, and certain trees, plants, and rocks are enveloped in an aura of mystery and sanctity. Hindus consider the Ganges River especially sacred, and each year millions of devoted worshipers bathe in its waters and receive their restorative and purifying power. The habit of pilgrimage has promoted contact and the exchange of ideas among people from different parts of India and has helped create a broad Hindu identity and the concept of India as a single civilization, despite enduring political fragmentation.

Religious duties may vary, depending not only on the worshiper's social standing and gender but also his or her stage of life. A young man from one of the three highest classes undergoes a ritual rebirth through the ceremony of the sacred thread, marking the attainment of manhood and readiness to receive religious knowledge. From this point, the ideal life cycle passes through four stages: (1) the young man becomes a student and studies the sacred texts; (2) he then becomes a householder, marries, has children, and acquires material wealth; (3) when his grandchildren are born, he gives up home and family and becomes a forest dweller, meditating on the nature and meaning of existence; (4) he abandons his personal identity altogether and becomes a wandering ascetic awaiting death. In the course of a virtuous life he has fulfilled first his duties to society and then his duties to himself, so that by the end he is so disconnected from the world that he can achieve moksha (liberation).

The successful transformation of a religion based on Vedic antecedents and the ultimate victory of Hinduism over Buddhism—Buddhism was driven from the land of its birth, though it maintains deep roots in Central, East, and Southeast Asia (see Chapters 7 and 10)—are remarkable phenomena. Hinduism responded to the needs of people for personal deities with whom they could establish direct connections. The austerity of Buddhism in its most authentic form, its denial of the importance of gods, and its expectation that individuals find their own path to enlightenment may have demanded too much of ordinary people. The very features that made Mahayana Buddhism more accessible to the populace—gods, saints, and myths—also made it more easily absorbed into the vast social and cultural fabric of Hinduism.

SECTION REVIEW

- The Aryas, pastoralist warriors, migrated into the Indus River Valley ca. 1500 B.C.E. and the Ganges plain after 1000 B.C.E., driving the Dasas into the southern part of the peninsula.
- The system of classes and castes, a mechanism for regulating the interactions of different groups, was linked to the concept of reincarnation and used to justify the power of the higher classes.
- Brahmin domination was challenged by new religions—Jainism and Buddhism.
- Theravada Buddhism remained close to the ideas of the founder, but Mahayana Buddhism developed gods, saints, monasteries, and shrines.
- Hinduism, created from a Vedic base but including Dravidian and Buddhist elements, preserved Brahmin status and privilege but allowed worshipers to make direct contact with the supernatural.
- Behind the diversity and multiplicity of Indian religion lies an ultimate unity.

IMPERIAL EXPANSION AND COLLAPSE, 324 B.C.E.–550 C.E.

Political unity in India, on those rare occasions when it has been achieved, has not lasted long. A number of factors have contributed to India's habitual political fragmentation. Different terrains called forth varied forms of organization and economic activity, and peoples occupying diverse zones differed in language and cultural practices. Perhaps the most significant barrier to political unity lay in the complex social hierarchy. Individuals identified themselves primarily in terms of their class and caste; allegiance to a higher political authority was secondary.

Despite these divisive factors, two empires arose in the Ganges Plain: the Mauryan (MORE-yuhn) Empire of the fourth to second centuries B.C.E. and the Gupta (GOOP-tuh) Empire of the fourth to sixth centuries C.E. Each extended political control over much of the subcontinent and fostered the formation of a common Indian civilization.

The Mauryan Empire, 324–184 B.C.E.

Origins of the Mauryan Empire

Around 600 B.C.E. independent kinship groups and states dotted the landscape of north India. The kingdom of Magadha, in eastern India south of the Ganges (see Map 6.1), began to play an increasingly influential role, however, thanks to wealth based on agriculture, iron mines, and its strategic location astride the trade routes of the eastern Ganges Basin. In the late fourth century B.C.E. Chandragupta Maurya (MORE-yuh), a young man from the Vaishya or Shudra class, gained control of Magadha and expanded it into the **Mauryan Empire**—India's first centralized empire. He may have been inspired by the example of Alexander the Great, who had followed up his conquest of the Persian Empire with a foray into the Punjab (northern Pakistan) in 326 B.C.E. (see Chapter 4). Chandragupta (r. 324–301 B.C.E.) and his successors Bindusara (r. 301–273 B.C.E.) and Ashoka (r. 273–232 B.C.E.) extended Mauryan control over the entire subcontinent except the southern tip. Not until the height of the Mughal Empire of the seventeenth century C.E. was so much of India again under the control of a single government.

Mauryan Empire The first state to unify most of the Indian subcontinent. It was founded by Chandragupta Maurya in 324 B.C.E. and survived until 184 B.C.E. From its capital at Pataliputra in the Ganges Valley it grew wealthy from taxes on agriculture, iron mining, and control of trade routes.

Tradition holds that Kautilya, a crafty elderly Brahmin, guided Chandragupta in his conquests and consolidation of power. Kautilya is said to have written a surviving treatise on government, the *Arthashastra* (ahr-thuh-SHAHS-truh). Although recent studies have shown that the *Arthashastra* in its present form is a product of the third century C.E., its core text may well go back to Kautilya. This coldly pragmatic guide to political success and survival advocates the so-called *mandala* (man-DAH-luh) (circle) theory of foreign policy: "My enemy's enemy is my friend." It also presents schemes for enforcing and increasing the collection of tax revenues, and it prescribes the use of spies to keep watch on everyone in the kingdom.

A tax equivalent to as much as one-fourth the value of the harvest supported the Mauryan kings and government. Other revenues came from tolls on trade; government monopolies on mining, liquor sales, and the manufacture of weapons; and fees charged to those using the irrigation network. Close relatives and associates of the king governed administrative districts based on traditional ethnic boundaries. A large imperial army—with infantry, cavalry, and chariot divisions and the fearsome new element of war elephants—further secured power. Standard coinage issued throughout the empire was used to pay government and military personnel and promoted trade.

The Mauryan capital was at Pataliputra (modern Patna), where five tributaries join the Ganges. Surrounded by rivers and further protected by a timber wall and moat, the city extended along the riverbank for 8 miles (13 kilometers). Busy and crowded (the population has been estimated at 270,000), it was governed by six committees with responsibility for manufacturing, trade, sales, taxes, the welfare of foreigners, and the registration of births and deaths.

Ashoka

Ashoka, Chandragupta's grandson, is an outstanding figure in early Indian history. At the beginning of his reign he engaged in military campaigns that extended the boundaries of the empire. During his conquest of Kalinga, a coastal region southeast of Magadha, hundreds of thousands of people were killed, wounded, or deported. Overwhelmed by the brutality of this victory, the young monarch became a convert to Buddhism and preached nonviolence, morality, moderation, and religious tolerance in both government and private life.

Ashoka Third ruler of the Mauryan Empire in India (r. 273–232 B.C.E.). He converted to Buddhism and broadcast his precepts on inscribed stones and pillars, the earliest surviving Indian writing.

Ashoka publicized this program by inscribing edicts on great rocks and polished pillars of sandstone scattered throughout his enormous empire. Among the inscriptions that have survived—they constitute the earliest decipherable Indian writing—is the following:

> *For a long time in the past, for many hundreds of years have increased the sacrificial slaughter of animals, violence toward creatures, unfilial conduct toward kinsmen, improper conduct toward Brahmins and ascetics. Now with the practice of morality by King [Ashoka], the sound of war drums has become the call to morality. . . . You [government officials] are appointed to rule over thousands of human beings in the expectation that you will win the affection of all men. All men are my children. Just as I desire that my children will fare well and be happy in this world and the next, I desire the same for all men. . . . King [Ashoka] . . . desires that there should be the growth of the essential spirit of morality or holiness among all sects. . . . There should not be glorification of one's own sect and denunciation of the sect of others for little or no reason. For all the sects are worthy of reverence for one reason or another.*[2]

Ashoka, however, was not naive. Despite his commitment to peaceful means, he reminded potential transgressors that "the king, remorseful as he is, has the strength to punish the wrong-doers who do not repent."

Commerce and Culture in an Era of Political Fragmentation

The Mauryan Empire prospered for a time after Ashoka's death in 232 B.C.E. Then, weakened by dynastic disputes and the expense of maintaining a large army and administrative bureaucracy, it collapsed from the pressure of attacks in the northwest in 184 B.C.E. Five hundred years passed before another indigenous state exercised control over northern India.

Foreign Powers in the Northwest

In the meantime, a series of foreign powers dominated the northwest, present-day Afghanistan and Pakistan, and extended their influence east and south. The first was the Greco-Bactrian kingdom (180–50 B.C.E.), descended from troops and settlers left in Afghanistan by Alexander the Great. Greek influence is evident in the art of this period and in the designs of coins. Occupation by two nomadic groups from Central Asia followed, resulting from large-scale movements of peoples set off by the pressure of Han Chinese forces on the Xiongnu (see Chapter 5). The Shakas, an Iranian people driven southwest along the mountain barrier of the Pamirs and Himalayas, were dominant from 50 B.C.E. to 50 C.E. They were followed by the Kushans (KOO-shahn), originally from Xinjiang in northwest China, who were preeminent from 50 to 240 C.E. At its height the Kushan kingdom controlled much of present-day Uzbekistan, Afghanistan, Pakistan, and northwest India, fostering trade and prosperity by connecting to both the overland Silk Road and Arabian seaports (see Chapter 7). The eastern Ganges region reverted to a patchwork of small principalities, as it had been before the Mauryan era.

Economic and Cultural Vitality

Despite political fragmentation in the five centuries after the Mauryan collapse, there were many signs of economic, cultural, and intellectual vitality. The network of roads and towns that had sprung up under the Mauryans fostered lively commerce within the subcontinent, and India was at the heart of international land and sea trade routes that linked China, Southeast Asia, Central Asia, the Middle East, East Africa, and the lands of the Mediterranean. The growth of crafts (metalwork, cloth making and dying, jewelry, perfume, glass, stone and terracotta sculpture), the increasing use of coins, and the development of local and long-distance commerce fostered the expansion and prosperity of urban centers. In the absence of a strong central authority, guilds of merchants and artisans became politically powerful in the towns. They were wealthy patrons of culture and endowed the religious sects to which they adhered—particularly Buddhism and Jainism—with richly decorated temples and monuments.

During the last centuries B.C.E. and first centuries C.E. the two greatest Indian epics, the *Ramayana* (ruh-muh-YAH-nuh) and the *Mahabharata* (muh-huh-BAH-ruh-tuh), based on oral predecessors dating back many centuries, achieved their final form. The events that both epics describe are said to have occurred several million years in the past, but the political forms, social organization, and other elements of cultural context—proud kings, beautiful queens, wars among kinship groups, heroic conduct, and chivalric values—seem to reflect the conditions of the early Vedic period, when Arya warrior societies were moving onto the Ganges Plain.

Mahabharata A vast epic chronicling the events leading up to a cataclysmic battle between related kinship groups in early India. It includes the Bhagavad-Gita.

Bhagavad-Gita The most important work of Indian sacred literature, a dialogue between the great warrior Arjuna and the god Krishna on duty and the fate of the spirit.

The vast pageant of the ***Mahabharata*** (it is eight times the length of the Greek *Iliad* and *Odyssey* combined) tells the story of two sets of cousins, the Pandavas and Kauravas, whose quarrel over succession to the throne leads them to a cataclysmic battle at the field of Kurukshetra. The battle is so destructive on all sides that the eventual winner, Yudhishthira, is reluctant to accept the fruits of so tragic a victory.

The **Bhagavad-Gita**, quoted at the beginning of this chapter, is a self-contained (and perhaps originally separate) episode set in the midst of those events. The great hero Arjuna, at first reluctant to fight his own kinsmen, is tutored by the god Krishna and learns the necessity of fulfilling his duty as a warrior. Death means nothing in a universe in which souls will be reborn again and again. The climactic moment comes when Krishna reveals his true appearance—awesome and overwhelmingly powerful—and his identity as time itself, the force behind all creation and destruction. The Bhagavad-Gita offers an attractive resolution to the tension in Indian civilization between duty to society and duty to one's own soul. Disciplined action—that is, action taken without regard for any personal benefits that might derive the gods and will be rewarded by release from the cycle of rebirt

This era also saw significant advances in science and techno knowledge of herbal remedies. Panini (late fourth century B.C.E of Sanskrit word forms and grammar. His work led to the star ing its natural development and turning it into a formal, litera Prakrits—popular dialects—emerged to become the ancesto languages of northern and central India.

Central and Southern India

This period of political fragmentation in the north also saw the rise dynasty (also called Andhra) in the Deccan Plateau from the second century B.C.E. to the early third century C.E. (see Map 6.1). Elements of north Indian technology and culture—including iron metallurgy, rice-paddy agriculture, urbanization, writing, coinage, and Brahmin religious authority—spread throughout central India, and indigenous kinship groups were absorbed into the Hindu system of class and caste.

Tamil kingdoms The kingdoms of southern India, inhabited primarily by speakers of Dravidian languages, which developed in partial isolation, and somewhat differently, from the Arya north. They produced epics, poetry, and performance arts. Elements of Tamil religious beliefs were merged into the Hindu synthesis.

The three **Tamil kingdoms** of Cholas, Pandyas, and Cheras in the southernmost parts of the peninsula were in frequent conflict with one another and experienced periods of ascendancy and decline, but they persisted in one form or another for over two thousand years. The period from the third century B.C.E. to the third century C.E. was a "classical" period of great literary and artistic productivity. Under the patronage of the Pandya kings and the intellectual leadership of an academy of five hundred authors, works of literature on a wide range of topics—grammatical treatises, collections of ethical proverbs, epics, and short poems about love, war, wealth, and the beauty of nature—were produced, and music, dance, and drama were performed.

The Gupta Empire, 320–550 C.E.

Rise of the Gupta Empire

In the early fourth century C.E., following the decline of the Kushan and Satavahana regimes in northern and central India, a new imperial entity took shape in the north. Like its Mauryan predecessor, the **Gupta Empire** emerged from the Ganges Plain and had its capital at Pataliputra. The founder, consciously modeling himself on the first Mauryan king, called himself Chandra Gupta (r. 320–335). The monarchs of this dynasty never controlled territories as extensive as those of the Mauryans. Nevertheless, over the fifteen-year reign of Chandra Gupta and the forty-year reigns of his three successors—the war-loving Samudra Gupta, Chandra Gupta II, a famed patron of artists and scholars, and Kumara Gupta—Gupta power and influence reached across northern and central India, west to Punjab and east to Bengal, north to Kashmir, and south into the Deccan Plateau (see Map 6.1).

Gupta Empire A powerful Indian state based, like its Mauryan predecessor, on a capital at Pataliputra in the Ganges Valley. It controlled most of the Indian subcontinent through a combination of military force and its prestige as a center of sophisticated culture.

Political Organization

This new empire enjoyed the same strategic advantages as its Mauryan predecessor, sitting astride important trade routes, exploiting the agricultural productivity of the Ganges Plain, and controlling nearby iron deposits. Although similar methods for raising revenue and administering broad territories were adopted, Gupta control was never as effectively centralized as Mauryan authority. The Gupta administrative bureaucracy and intelligence network were smaller and less pervasive. A standing army, whose strength lay in the excellent horsemanship (learned from the nomadic Kushans) and skill with bow and arrow of its cavalry, maintained tight control and taxation in the core of the empire. Governors, whose position often passed from father to son, had a freer hand in the more outlying areas. Distant subordinate kingdoms and areas inhabited by kinship groups made annual donations of tribute, and garrisons were stationed at key frontier points. At the local level, villages were managed by a headman and council of elders, while the guilds of artisans and merchants had important administrative roles in the cities.

theater-state Historians' term for a state that acquires prestige and power by developing attractive cultural forms and staging elaborate public ceremonies (as well as redistributing valuable resources) to attract and bind subjects to the center. Examples include the Gupta Empire in India and Srivijaya in Southeast Asia.

Limited in its ability to enforce its will on outlying areas, the empire found ways to "persuade" others to follow its lead. One medium of persuasion was the splendor, beauty, and orderliness of life at the capital and royal court. The Gupta Empire is a good example of a "**theater-state**." A constant round of solemn rituals, dramatic ceremonies, and exciting cultural events was a potent advertisement for the benefits of association with the empire. The center collected luxury goods and profits from trade and redistributed them to dependents through the exchange of gifts and other means. Subordinate princes gained prestige by emulating the Gupta center

NMENT + TECHNOLOGY

...ian Mathematics

The so-called Arabic numerals used in most parts of the world today were developed in India. The Indian system of place-value notation was far more efficient than the unwieldy numerical systems of Egyptians, Greeks, and Romans, and the invention of zero was a profound intellectual achievement. This system is used even more widely than the alphabet derived from the Phoenicians (see Chapter 3) and is, in one sense, the only truly global language.

In its fully developed form the Indian method of arithmetic notation employed a base-ten system. It had separate columns for ones, tens, hundreds, and so forth, as well as a zero sign to indicate the absence of units in a given column. This system makes possible the economical expression of even very large numbers. It also allows for the performance of calculations not possible in a system like the numerals of the Romans, where any real calculation had to be done mentally or on a counting board.

A series of early Indian inscriptions using the numerals from 1 to 9 are deeds of property given to religious institutions by kings or other wealthy individuals. They were incised in the Sanskrit language on copper plates. The earliest known example has a date equivalent to 595 C.E. A sign for zero is attested by the eighth century, but textual evidence leads to the inference that a place-value system and the zero concept were already known in the fifth century.

This Indian system spread to the Middle East, Southeast Asia, and East Asia by the seventh century. Other peoples quickly recognized its capabilities and adopted it, sometimes using indigenous symbols. Europe received the new technology somewhat later. Gerbert of Aurillac, a French Christian monk, spent time in Spain between 967 and 970, where he was exposed to the mathematics of the Arabs. A great scholar and teacher who eventually became Pope Sylvester II (r. 999–1003), he spread word of the "Arabic" system in the Christian West.

Knowledge of the Indian system of mathematical notation eventually spread throughout Europe, partly through the use of a mechanical calculating device—an improved version of the Roman counting board, with counters inscribed with variants of the Indian numeral forms. Because the counters could be turned sideways or upside down, at first there was considerable variation in the forms. But by the twelfth century they had become standardized into forms close to those in use today. As the capabilities of the place-value system for calculations became clear, the counting board fell into disuse. This led to the adoption of the zero sign—not necessary on the counting board, where a column could be left empty—by the twelfth century. Leonardo Fibonacci, a thirteenth-century C.E. Italian who learned algebra in Muslim North Africa and employed the Arabic numeral system in his mathematical treatise, gave additional impetus to the movement to discard the traditional system of Roman numerals.

Why was this marvelous system of mathematical notation invented in ancient India? The answer may lie in the way its range and versatility correspond to elements of Indian cosmology. The Indians conceived of immense spans of time—trillions of years (far exceeding current scientific estimates of the age of the universe as approximately 14 billion years)—during which innumerable universes like our own were created, existed for a finite time, then were destroyed. In one popular creation myth, Vishnu is slumbering on the coils of a giant serpent at the bottom of the ocean, and worlds are being created and destroyed as he exhales and inhales. In Indian thought our world, like others, has existed for a series of epochs lasting more than 4 million years, yet the period of its existence is but a brief and insignificant moment in the vast sweep of time. The Indians developed a number system that allowed them to express concepts of this magnitude.

Facsimile by Georges Ifrah. Reproduced by permission of Georges Ifrah.

Copper Plate with Indian Numerals This property deed from western India shows an early form of the symbol system for numbers that spread to the Middle East and Europe and today is used all over the world.

on whatever scale they could manage, and they maintained close ties through visits, gifts, and marriages to the Gupta royal family.

Astronomers, mathematicians, and other scientists received royal support. Indian mathematicians invented the concept of zero and developed the "Arabic" numerals and system of place-value notation used in most parts of the world today (see Environment and Technology: Indian Mathematics). The Gupta monarchs also supported poets and dramatists and the compilation of law codes and grammatical texts.

Benoy K. Behl

Wall Painting from the Caves at Ajanta, Fifth or Sixth Century C.E. During and after the Gupta period, natural caves in the Deccan were turned into shrines decorated with sculpture and painting. This painting depicts one of the earlier lives of the Buddha, a king named Mahajanaka who lost and regained his kingdom, here listening to his queen, Sivali. While representing scenes from the earlier lives of the Buddha, the artists also give us glimpses of life at the royal court in their own times.

Because of the moist climate of the Ganges Plain, few archaeological remains from the Gupta era have survived. An eyewitness account, however, provides valuable information about Pataliputra, the capital city. A Chinese Buddhist monk named Faxian (fah-shee-en) made a pilgrimage to the homeland of his faith around 400 C.E. and left a record of his journey:

> *The royal palace and halls in the midst of the city, which exist now as of old, were all made by spirits which [King Ashoka] employed, and which piled up the stones, reared the walls and gates, and executed the elegant carving and inlaid sculpture-work—in a way which no human hands of this world could accomplish. . . . By the side of the stupa of Ashoka, there has been made a Mahayana [Buddhist] monastery, very grand and beautiful; there is also a Hinayana [Theravada] one; the two together containing six hundred or seven hundred monks. The rules of demeanor and the scholastic arrangements in them are worthy of observation.*[3]

Women

There was a decline in the status of women in this period (see Diversity and Dominance: Relations Between Women and Men in the *Kama Sutra* and the *Arthashastra*). As in Mesopotamia, Greece, and China, several factors—urbanization, increasingly complex political and social structures, and the emergence of a nonagricultural middle class that placed high value on the acquisition and inheritance of property—led to a loss of women's rights and an increase in male control over women's behavior.

Relations Between Women and Men in the Kama Sutra *and the* Arthashastra

The ancient Indians articulated three broad areas of human concern: dharma—the realm of religious and moral behavior; artha—the acquisition of wealth and property; and kama—the pursuit of pleasure. The Kama Sutra, *which means "Treatise on Pleasure," while best known in the West for its detailed descriptions of erotic activities, is actually far more than a sex manual. It addresses, in a very broad sense, the relations between women and men in ancient Indian society, providing valuable information about the activities of men and women, the psychology of relationships, the forms of courtship and marriage, the household responsibilities of married women, appropriate behavior, and much more. The author of this text, Vatsyayana, lived in the third century* C.E.

When a girl of the same caste, and a virgin, is married in accordance with the precepts of Holy Writ, the results of such a union are the acquisition of Dharma and Artha, offspring, affinity, increase of friends, and untarnished love. For this reason a man should fix his affections upon a girl who is of good family, whose parents are alive, and who is three years or more younger than himself. She should be born of a highly respectable family, possessed of wealth, well connected, and with many relations and friends. She should also be beautiful, of a good disposition, with lucky marks on her body, and with good hair, nails, teeth, ears, eyes and breasts, neither more nor less than they ought to be, and no one of them entirely wanting, and not troubled with a sickly body. . . . But at all events, says Ghotakamukha [an earlier writer], a girl who has been already joined with others (i.e., no longer a maiden) should never be loved, for it would be reproachable to do such a thing.

Now in order to bring about a marriage with such a girl as described above, the parents and relations of the man should exert themselves, as also such friends on both sides as may be desired to assist in the matter. These friends should bring to the notice of the girl's parents the faults, both present and future, of all the other men that may wish to marry her, and should at the same time extol even to exaggeration all the excellencies, ancestral and paternal, of their friend, so as to endear him to them. . . . Others again should rouse the jealousy of the girl's mother by telling her that their friend has a chance of getting from some other quarter even a better girl than hers.

A girl should be taken as a wife, as also given in marriage, when fortune, signs, omens, and the words of others are favourable, for, says Ghotakamukha, a man should not marry at any time he likes. A girl who is asleep, crying, or gone out of the house when sought in marriage, or who is betrothed to another, should not be married. The following also should be avoided:

- One who is kept concealed
- One who has an ill-sounding name
- One who has her nose depressed
- One who has her nostril turned up
- One who is formed like a male
- One who is bent down
- One who has crooked thighs
- One who has a projecting forehead
- One who has a bald head
- One who does not like purity
- One who has been polluted by another
- One who is disfigured in any way
- One who has fully arrived at puberty
- One who is a friend
- One who is a younger sister
- One who is a Varshakari [prone to extreme perspiration]

But some authors say that prosperity is gained only by marrying that girl to whom one becomes attached, and that therefore no other girl but the one who is loved should be married by anyone. . . .

A virtuous woman, who has affection for her husband, should act in conformity with his wishes as if he were a divine being, and with his consent should take upon herself the whole care of his family. She should keep the whole house well cleaned, and arrange flowers of various kinds in different parts of it, and make the floor smooth and polished so as to give the whole a neat and becoming appearance. She should surround the house with a garden, and place ready in it all the materials required for the morning, noon and evening sacrifices. Moreover she should herself revere the sanctuary of the Household Gods. . . .

As regards meals, she should always consider what her husband likes and dislikes and what things are good for him, and what are injurious to him. When she hears the sounds of his footsteps coming home she should at once get up and be ready to do whatever he may command her, and either order her female servant to wash his feet, or wash them herself. When

Women in India lost the right to own or inherit property. They were barred from studying sacred texts and participating in sacrificial rituals. In many respects, they were treated as equivalent to the lowest class, the Shudra. A woman was expected to obey first her father, then her husband, and finally her sons. Girls were married at an increasingly early age, sometimes as young as six or seven. This practice meant that the prospective husband could be sure of his going anywhere with her husband, she should put on her ornaments, and without his consent she should not either give or accept invitations, or attend marriages and sacrifices, or sit in the company of female friends, or visit the temples of the Gods. And if she wants to engage in any kind of games or sports, she should not do it against his will. In the same way she should always sit down after him, and get up before him, and should never awaken him when he is asleep.

The core of the Arthashastra, *which means "Science of Wealth," may have been composed in the later third century* B.C.E. *by Kautilya, an adviser to the first Mauryan ruler, Chandragupta, but the text as we have it includes later additions. While the Arthashastra is primarily concerned with how the ruler may gain and keep power, it includes prescriptions on other aspects of life, including the kinds of problems that may threaten or destroy marriages.*

If a woman either brings forth no live children, or has no male issue, or is barren, her husband shall wait for eight years before marrying another. If she bears only a dead child, he has to wait for ten years. If she brings forth only females, he has to wait for twelve years. Then, if he is desirous to have sons, he may marry another. . . . If a husband either is of bad character, or is long gone abroad, or has become a traitor to his king, or is likely to endanger the life of his wife, or has fallen from his caste, or has lost virility, he may be abandoned by his wife. . . .

Women of refractive natures shall not be taught manners by using such expressions as "You, half-naked!; you, fully-naked; you, cripple; you, fatherless; you, motherless." Nor shall she be given more than three beats, either with a bamboo bark or with a rope or with the palm of the hand, on her hips. . . .

A woman who hates her husband, who has passed the period of seven turns of her menses, and who loves another, shall immediately return to her husband both the endowment and jewelry she has received from him, and allow him to lie down with another woman. A man, hating his wife, shall allow her to take shelter in the house of a beggar woman, or of her lawful guardians or of her kinsmen. . . . A woman, hating her husband, cannot divorce her husband against his will. Nor can a man divorce his wife against her will. But from mutual enmity divorce may be obtained. . . .

If a woman engages herself in amorous sports, or drinking in the face of an order to the contrary, she shall be fined three panas. She shall pay a fine of six panas for going out at daytime to sports or to see a woman or spectacles. She shall pay a fine of twelve panas if she goes out to see another man or for sports. For the same offences committed at night the fines shall be doubled. If a woman goes out while the husband is asleep or intoxicated, or if she shuts the door of the house against her husband, she shall be fined twelve panas. If a woman keeps him out of the house at night, she shall pay double the above fine. If a man and a woman make signs to each other with a view to sensual enjoyment, or carry on secret conversation for the same purpose, the woman shall pay a fine of twenty-four panas and the man double that amount. . . . For holding conversation in suspicious places, whips may be substituted for fines. In the center of the village, an outcaste person may whip such women five times on each of the sides of their body. . . .

A Kshatriya who commits adultery with an unguarded Brahman woman shall be punished with the highest amercement; a Vaishya doing the same shall be deprived of the whole of his property; and a Shudra shall be burnt alive wound round in mats. . . . A man who commits adultery with a woman of low caste shall be banished, with prescribed marks branded on his forehead, or shall be degraded to the same caste. A Shudra or an outcaste who commits adultery with a woman of low caste shall be put to death, while the woman shall have her ears and nose cut off.

QUESTIONS FOR ANALYSIS

1. **In what ways are women given essentially equal treatment to men in these excerpts? In what ways are they treated unequally?**
2. **On what bases do men and women choose spouses and lovers? How does the class status of the two individuals play a part in these choices?**
3. **What were the most important household responsibilities of ancient Indian women? What social, intellectual, and cultural activities did they engage in?**
4. **In light of the prescriptions for how a married woman should treat her husband, what do you think was the nature of the emotional relationship of husband and wife? How might this differ from marriages in our society? Why did some marriages fail in ancient India?**

Sources: First selection from Sir Richard Burton and F. F. Arbuthnot, *The Kama Sutra of Vatsyayana* (1883), sections III.1, III.4, III.5, IV.1, found at http://www.sacredtexts.com/sex/kama/index.htm. Second selection from R. Shamasastry, *Kautilya's Arthashastra*, 2nd ed. (1923), sections III.2, III.3, IV.13, from Internet Indian History Sourcebook at http://www.fordham.edu/halsall/india/kautilya2.html.

wife's virginity and, by bringing her up in his own household, could train her to suit his purposes. The most extreme form of control took place in parts of India where a widow was expected to cremate herself on her husband's funeral pyre. This ritual, called *sati* (suh-TEE), was seen as a way of keeping a woman "pure." Women who declined to make this ultimate gesture of devotion were forbidden to remarry, shunned socially, and given little opportunity to earn a living.

Some women escaped male control by entering a Jainist or Buddhist religious community. Status also gave women more freedom. Women who belonged to powerful families and courtesans trained in poetry and music as well as ways of providing sexual pleasure had high social standing and sometimes gave money for the erection of religious shrines.

Religion in the Gupta Period

The Mauryans had been Buddhists, but the Gupta monarchs were Hindus. They revived ancient Vedic practices to bring an aura of sanctity to their position. This period also saw a reassertion of the importance of class and caste and the influence of Brahmin priests. In return for the religious validation of their rule given by the Brahmins, the Guptas gave the priests extensive grants of land. The Brahmins became wealthy from the revenues, which they collected directly from the peasants, and they even exercised administrative and judicial authority over the villages in their domains. Nevertheless, it was an era of religious tolerance. The Gupta kings were patrons for Hindu, Buddhist, and Jain endeavors. Buddhist monasteries with hundreds or even thousands of monks and nuns in residence flourished in the cities, and a Buddhist university was established at Nalanda. Northern India was the destination of Buddhist pilgrims from Southeast and East Asia, traveling to visit the birthplace of their faith.

PRIMARY SOURCE: The *Laws of Manu* See how the principle of dharma justifies the traditional roles of men and women and of priests, warriors, merchants, and servants in Hindu society.

The classic form of the Hindu temple evolved during the Gupta era. Sitting atop a raised platform surmounted by high towers, the temple was patterned on the sacred mountain or palace in which the gods of mythology resided, and it represented the inherent order of the universe. From an exterior courtyard worshipers approached the central shrine, where the statue of the deity stood. Paintings or sculptured depictions of gods and mythical events covered the walls of the best-endowed sanctuaries. Cave-temples carved out of rock were also richly adorned with frescoes or sculpture.

The vibrant commerce of the previous era continued into the Gupta period. Artisan guilds played an influential role in the economic, political, and religious life of the towns. The Guptas sought control of the ports on the Arabian Sea but saw a decline in trade with the weakened Roman Empire. In compensation, trade with Southeast and East Asia was on the rise. Adventurous merchants from the ports of eastern and southern India made the sea voyage to the Malay (muh-LAY) Peninsula and islands of Indonesia in order to exchange Indian cotton cloth, ivory, metalwork, and animals for Chinese silk or Indonesian spices. The overland Silk Road from China was also in operation but was vulnerable to disruption by Central Asian nomads (see Chapter 7).

Decline and Transformation

By the later fifth century C.E. the Gupta Empire was coming under pressure from the Huns. These nomadic invaders from the steppes of Central Asia poured into the northwest corridor. Defense of this distant frontier region eventually exhausted the imperial treasury, and the empire collapsed by 550.

During and after the centuries of Gupta ascendancy and decline in the north, the Deccan Plateau and the southern part of the peninsula followed an independent path. In this region, where the landscape is segmented by mountains, rocky plateaus, tropical forests, and sharply cut river courses, there were many small centers of power. From the sixth to twelfth centuries, the Pallavas, Chalukyas, and other warrior dynasties collected tribute and plundered as far as their strength permitted, storing their wealth in urban fortresses. These rulers sought legitimacy and fame as patrons of religion and culture, and much of the distinguished art and architecture of the period were produced in the kingdoms of the south. Many elements of northern Indian religion and culture spread in the south, including the class and caste system, Brahmin religious authority, and worship of Vishnu and Shiva. These kingdoms also served as the conduit through which Indian religion and culture reached Southeast Asia.

SECTION REVIEW

- The Mauryan Empire, founded in the late fourth century B.C.E. by Chandragupta Maurya, eventually controlled most of the subcontinent.
- King Ashoka, a convert to Buddhism, inscribed stones and pillars with a call to nonviolence, moderation, and religious toleration.
- After the Mauryan fall in 184 B.C.E., foreign occupiers—Indo-Greeks, Shakas, and Kushans—controlled the northwest.
- Despite political fragmentation, commerce and culture thrived.
- A renaissance of art and literature occurred in the Tamil kingdoms of south India between the third century B.C.E. and the third century C.E.
- The Gupta Empire, while not as extensive as the Mauryan Empire, fostered scholarship, science, and the arts from the fourth to sixth centuries C.E.

MAP 6.2 **Southeast Asia** Southeast Asia's position between the ancient centers of civilization in India and China had a major impact on its history. In the first millennium C.E. a series of powerful and wealthy states arose in the region by gaining control of major trade routes: first Funan, based in southern Vietnam, Cambodia, and the Malay Peninsula, then Srivijaya on the island of Sumatra, then smaller states on the island of Java. Shifting trade routes led to the demise of one and the rise of others.

SOUTHEAST ASIA, 50–600 C.E.

Southeast Asia consists of three geographical zones: the Indochina mainland, the Malay Peninsula, and thousands of islands extending on an east-west axis far out into the Pacific Ocean (see Map 6.2). Encompassing a vast area of land and water, this region is now occupied by the countries of Myanmar (myahn-MAH) (Burma), Thailand, Laos, Cambodia, Vietnam, Malaysia, Singapore, Indonesia, Brunei (broo-NIE), and the Philippines. Poised between the ancient centers of China and India, Southeast Asia has been influenced by the cultures of both civilizations. The region first rose to prominence and prosperity because of its intermediate role in the trade exchanges between southern and eastern Asia.

The strategic importance of Southeast Asia is enhanced by the region's natural resources. This is a geologically active zone; the islands are the tops of a chain of volcanoes. Lying along the equator, Southeast Asia has a tropical climate. The temperature hovers around 80 degrees Fahrenheit (30 degrees Celsius), and the monsoon winds provide dependable rainfall throughout the year. Thanks to several growing cycles each year, the region is capable of supporting a large human population. The most fertile agricultural lands lie along the floodplains of the largest silt-bearing rivers or contain rich volcanic soil deposited by ancient eruptions.

Early Civilization

Rain forest covers much of Southeast Asia. As early as 2000 B.C.E. people in this region practiced swidden agriculture, clearing land for farming by cutting and burning the vegetation. The

Ecology and Population

cleared land was farmed for several growing seasons. When the soil was exhausted, the farmers abandoned the patch, allowing the forest to reclaim it, while they cleared and cultivated other nearby fields in similar fashion. Rice was the staple food—labor-intensive (see Chapter 2), but able to support a large population. A number of plant and animal species spread from Southeast Asia to other regions, including rice, soybeans, sugar cane, yams, bananas, coconuts, chickens, and pigs.

The Malay peoples who became the dominant population in this region were the product of several waves of migration from southern China beginning around 3000 B.C.E. Some indigenous peoples merged with the Malay newcomers; others retreated to remote mountain and forest zones. Subsequently (beginning, perhaps, around 1600 B.C.E.), rising population and disputes within communities prompted streams of people to leave the Southeast Asian mainland for the islands. By the first millennium B.C.E. Southeast Asians had developed impressive navigational skills. They knew how to ride the monsoon winds and interpret the patterns of swells, winds, clouds, and bird and sea life. Over a period of several thousand years groups of Malay peoples in large, double outrigger canoes spread out across the Pacific and Indian Oceans—half the circumference of the earth—to settle thousands of islands.

The inhabitants of Southeast Asia clustered along riverbanks or in fertile volcanic plains. Their fields and villages were never far from the rain forest, with its wild animals and numerous plant species. Forest trees provided fruit, wood, and spices. The shallow waters surrounding the islands teemed with fish. This region was also an early center of metallurgy. Metalsmiths heated copper and tin ore to the right temperature for producing and shaping bronze implements by using hollow bamboo tubes to funnel oxygen to the furnace.

External Influences

Northern Indochina, by its geographic proximity, was vulnerable to Chinese pressure and cultural influences, and it was under Chinese political control for a thousand years beginning in the second century B.C.E. Farther south, larger states emerged in the early centuries C.E. in response to two powerful forces: commerce and Hindu-Buddhist culture. Southeast Asia was situated along the trade routes that merchants used to carry Chinese silk westward to India and the Mediterranean. The movements of nomadic peoples had disrupted the old land route across Central Asia. But in India demand for silk was increasing—both for domestic use and for transshipment to satisfy the fast-growing luxury market in the Roman Empire. Gradually merchants extended this exchange network to include goods from Southeast Asia, such as aromatic woods, resins, and cinnamon, pepper, cloves, nutmeg, and other spices. By serving this trade network and controlling key points, Southeast Asian centers rose to prominence.

The other force leading to the rise of larger political entities was the influence of Hindu-Buddhist culture imported from India. Commerce brought Indian merchants and sailors into the ports of Southeast Asia. As Buddhism spread, Southeast Asia became a way station for Indian missionaries and East Asian pilgrims going to and coming from the birthplace of their faith. Shrewd Malay rulers looked to Indian traditions as a rich source of ideas and prestige. They borrowed Sanskrit terms such as *maharaja* (mah-huh-RAH-juh) (great king), utilized Indian models of bureaucracy, ceremonial practices, and forms of artistic representation, and employed priests, administrators, and scribes skilled in Sanskrit writing to expedite government business. Their special connection to powerful gods and higher knowledge raised them above their rivals.

The Southeast Asian kingdoms, however, were not just passive recipients of Indian culture. They took what was useful to them and synthesized it with indigenous beliefs, values, and institutions—for example, local concepts of chiefship, ancestor worship, and forms of oaths. Moreover, they trained their own people in the new ways, so that the bureaucracy contained both foreign experts and native disciples. The whole process amounted to a cultural dialogue between India and Southeast Asia, in which both were active participants.

Funan An early complex society in Southeast Asia between the first and sixth centuries C.E. It was centered in the rich rice-growing region of southern Vietnam, and it controlled the passage of trade across the Malaysian isthmus.

Funan

The first major Southeast Asian center, called "**Funan**" (FOO-nahn) by Chinese visitors, flourished between the first and sixth centuries C.E. (see Map 6.2). Its capital was at the modern site of Oc-Eo in southern Vietnam. Funan occupied the delta of the Mekong (MAY-kawng) River, a "rice bowl" capable of supporting a large population. The rulers mobilized large numbers of laborers to dig irrigation channels and prevent destructive floods. By extending its control over most of southern Indochina and the Malay Peninsula, Funan was able to dominate the trade route from India to China. The route began in the ports of northeast India, crossed the Bay of

Bengal, continued by land over the Isthmus of Kra on the Malay Peninsula, and then continued across the South China Sea (see Map 6.2). Indian merchants found that offloading their goods from ships and carrying them across the narrow strip of land was safer than making the 1,000-mile (1,600-kilometer) voyage around the Malay Peninsula—a dangerous trip marked by treacherous currents, rocky shoals, and pirates. Once the portage across the isthmus was finished, the merchants needed food and lodging while waiting for the monsoon winds to shift so they could make the last leg of the voyage to China by sea. Funan stockpiled food and provided security for those engaged in this trade—in return for customs duties and other fees.

Chinese observers have left reports of the prosperity and sophistication of Funan, emphasizing the presence of walled cities, palaces, archives, systems of taxation, and state-organized agriculture. Nevertheless, Funan declined in the sixth century. The most likely explanation is that international trade routes changed and Funan no longer held a strategic position.

SECTION REVIEW

- Climate and resources enabled Southeast Asia to support large human populations.
- Located on the trade and pilgrimage routes between China and India, Southeast Asia came under strong Hindu and Buddhist influence.
- Shrewd rulers used Indian knowledge and personnel to enhance their power and prestige.
- Funan rose to prominence between the first and sixth centuries C.E. by controlling the trade route across the Malay Peninsula.

CONCLUSION

This chapter traces the emergence of complex societies in India and Southeast Asia between the second millennium B.C.E. and the mid-first millennium C.E. Because of migrations, trade, and the spread of belief systems, an Indian style of civilization spread throughout the subcontinent and adjoining regions and eventually made its way to the mainland and island chains of Southeast Asia. In this period were laid cultural foundations that in large measure still endure.

The development and spread of belief systems—Vedism, Buddhism, Jainism, and Hinduism—have a central place in this chapter because nearly all the sources of information are religious. A museum visitor examining artifacts from ancient Mesopotamia, Egypt, the Greco-Roman Mediterranean, and China will find many objects of a religious nature. Only the Indian artifacts, however, will be almost exclusively from the religious sphere.

Writing came later to India than to other parts of the Eastern Hemisphere, for reasons particular to the Indian situation. Like Indian artifacts, most ancient Indian texts are of a religious nature. Ancient Indians did not develop a historical consciousness and generate historiographic texts like their Israelite, Greek, and Chinese contemporaries, primarily because they held a strikingly different view of time. The distinctive Indian conception—of vast epochs in which universes are created and destroyed again and again and the essential spirit of living creatures is reincarnated repeatedly—made the particulars of any brief moment seem relatively unilluminating.

The tension between divisive and unifying forces can be seen in many aspects of Indian life. Political and social division has been the norm throughout much of the history of India, a consequence of the topographical and environmental diversity of the subcontinent and the complex mix of ethnic and linguistic groups inhabiting it. The elaborate structure of classes and castes was a response to this diversity—an attempt to organize the population and position individuals within an accepted hierarchy, as well as to regulate group interactions. Strong central governments, such as those of the Mauryan and Gupta kings, gained ascendancy for a time and promoted prosperity and development. They rose to dominance by gaining control of metal resources and important trade routes, developing effective military and administrative institutions, and creating cultural forms that inspired admiration and emulation. However, as in Archaic Greece and Warring States China, the periods of fragmentation and multiple small centers of power seemed as economically and intellectually dynamic as the periods of unity.

Many distinctive social and intellectual features of Indian civilization—the class and caste system, models of kingship and statecraft, and Vedic, Jainist, and Buddhist belief systems—originated in the great river valleys of the north, where descendants of Indo-European immigrants predominated. Hinduism then embraced elements drawn from the Dravidian cultures of the south as well as from Buddhism. The capacity of the Hindu tradition to assimilate a wide range of popular beliefs facilitated the spread of a common Indian civilization across the subcontinent, although there was, and is, considerable variation from one region to another.

KEY TERMS

monsoon p. 174
Vedas p. 175
varna p. 176
jati p. 176
karma p. 176
moksha p. 178
Buddha p. 179
Mahayana Buddhism p. 180
Theravada Buddhism p. 180
Hinduism p. 180
Mauryan Empire p. 183
Ashoka p. 183
Mahabharata p. 184
Bhagavad-Gita p. 184
Tamil kingdoms p. 185
Gupta Empire p. 185
theater-state p. 185
Funan p. 192

EBOOK AND WEBSITE RESOURCES

Primary Sources

The *Rig Veda*

Setting in Motion the Wheel of Law

The *Laws of Manu*

Interactive Maps

Map 6.1 Ancient India

Map 6.2 Southeast Asia

Plus flashcards, practice quizzes, and more. Go to: www.cengage.com/history/bullietearthpeople5e

SUGGESTED READING

Avari, Burjor. *India: The Ancient Past: A History of the Indian Sub-Continent from c. 7000 BC to AD 1200*. 2007. A clear, concise introduction to ancient Indian history.

Brook, Peter, director. *The Mahabharata* (3 videos). 1989. This filmed version of a stage production generated much controversy because of its British director and multicultural cast, but it is a painless introduction to the plot and main characters of the great Indian epic.

Diskul, M. C. S. *The Art of Srivijaya*. 1980. Covers the art of early Southeast Asia.

Embree, Ainslee T. *Sources of Indian Tradition*, vol. 1, 2nd ed. 1988. Contains translations of primary texts, with the emphasis almost entirely on religion and few materials from southern India.

Huntington, Susan L., and John C. Huntington. *The Art of Ancient India*. 1985. Focuses on the art and architecture of antiquity.

Kinsley, David R. *Hinduism: A Cultural Perspective*. 1982. Presents fundamental Indian social and religious conceptions.

Lang, Karen. "Women in Ancient India," in *Women's Roles in Ancient Civilizations: A Reference Guide*, ed. Bella Vivante. 1999. An up-to-date overview of women in ancient India, with bibliography.

Miller, Barbara Stoler. *The Bhagavad-Gita: Krishna's Counsel in Time of War*. 1986. A readable translation of this ancient classic with a useful introduction and notes.

Ramaswamy, T. N. *Essentials of Indian Statecraft: Kautilya's Arthashastra for Contemporary Readers*. 1962. A fascinating treatise on state building supposedly composed by the adviser to the founder of the Mauryan Empire.

Schmidt, Karl J. *An Atlas and Survey of South Asian History*. 1995. Maps and facing text illustrating geographic, environmental, cultural, and historical features of South Asian civilization.

Sedlar, Jean W. *India and the Greek World: A Study in the Transmission of Culture*. 1980. Explores the interaction of Greek and Indian civilizations.

Shaffer, Lynda. *Maritime Southeast Asia to 1500*. 1996. Focuses on early Southeast Asian history in a world historical context.

Sharma, R. S. *India's Ancient Past*. 2005. An up-to-date account of the history of ancient India.

Thapar, Romila. *Asoka and the Decline of the Mauryas*, rev. ed. 1997. A detailed study of the most interesting and important Mauryan king.

Trainor, Kevin, ed. *Buddhism: The Illustrated Guide*. 2001. Devotes several chapters to Buddhism in ancient India.

NOTES

1. Barbara Stoler Miller, *The Bhagavad-Gita: Krishna's Counsel in Time of War* (New York: Bantam, 1986), 98–99.
2. B. G. Gokhale, *Asoka Maurya* (New York: Twayne, 1966), 152–153, 156–157, 160.
3. James Legge, *The Travels of Fa-hien: Fa-hien's Record of Buddhistic Kingdoms* (Delhi: Oriental Publishers, 1971), 77–79.

AP* REVIEW QUESTIONS FOR CHAPTER 6

1. Indian societies, like other societies, developed ways to regulate relations between different groups. One of these ways was through
   (A) the Vedas.
   (B) polytheism.
   (C) the varna system.
   (D) the use of dowries.

2. Which of the following was a pull factor for people to settle in the Ganges Plain?
   (A) A lack of monsoons
   (B) Easy access to the sea
   (C) Fertile, well-watered soil
   (D) The offer of free land by the local king

3. The most serious threats to the Vedic religion came from
   (A) Mongol invaders from the north.
   (B) nomadic invaders from Thailand.
   (C) Alexander the Great.
   (D) Jainism and Buddhism.

4. India's first centralized empire was formed by
   (A) Chandragupta Maurya.
   (B) Alexander the Great.
   (C) Devi the Great.
   (D) Ashoka.

5. Ashoka extended the boundaries of his empire and later converted to which religion?
   (A) Jainism
   (B) Islam
   (C) Hinduism
   (D) Buddhism

6. As in Mesopotamia, Greece, and China, the role of women in India
   (A) remained stable as the region developed into a more complex empire.
   (B) declined as the social structure became more complex.
   (C) was controlled by the leader.
   (D) was limited in religious observances only.

7. Among the early converts to the Buddhist way were
   (A) soldiers, who sought redemption.
   (B) the nobility, because they could read and write.
   (C) women, as a way to gain more freedom.
   (D) the priests, because they needed to make more money for temples.

8. In Southeast Asia, the first political units
   (A) were copies of those in India and based on caste.
   (B) took parts of Indian culture that were useful to them and synthesized them with indigenous beliefs, values, and institutions.
   (C) used a hereditary king based on clan systems.
   (D) tended to reflect the Chinese systems of the time due to trade with China.

9. The first major center in Southeast Asia was Funan, in modern-day
   (A) Myanmar.
   (B) Singapore.
   (C) Thailand.
   (D) Vietnam.

10. While the dominant population of Southeast Asia is Malay, culturally it is
    (A) a blend of Indian, Malay, and Chinese.
    (B) mainly Indian.
    (C) a blend of Cambodian and Indian.
    (D) mainly Chinese.

11. Most of India's earliest writings are
    (A) stories that tell the origin of the Indian people.
    (B) historiography of the early Indian empires.
    (C) religious in nature.
    (D) trade reports and tax collections.

ORAL SOCIETIES AND THE CONSEQUENCES OF LITERACY

The availability of written documents is a key factor used by historians to divide human prehistory from history. When we can read what people of the past thought and said about their lives, we begin to understand their cultures, institutions, values, and beliefs in ways that are not possible based only on the material remains unearthed by archaeologists.

Literacy and nonliteracy are not absolute alternatives. Personal literacy ranges from illiteracy through many shades of partial literacy (the ability to write one's name or to read simple texts with difficulty) to the fluent ability to read that is possessed by anyone reading this textbook. And there are degrees of societal literacy, ranging from nonliteracy through so-called craft literacy—in which a small specialized elite uses writing for limited purposes, such as administrative recordkeeping—up to the near-universal literacy and the use of writing for innumerable purposes that is the norm in the developed world in our times.

The vast majority of human beings of the last five to six thousand years, even those living in societies that possessed the technology of writing, were not themselves literate. If most people in a society rely on the spoken word and memory, that culture is essentially "oral" even if some members know how to write. The differences between oral and literate cultures are immense, affecting not only the kinds of knowledge that are valued and the forms in which information is preserved, but also the very use of language, the categories for conceptualizing the world, and ultimately the hard-wiring of the individual human brain (now recognized by neuroscientists to be strongly influenced by individual experience and mental activity).

Ancient Greece of the Archaic and Classical periods (ca. 800–323 B.C.E.) offers a particularly instructive case study because we can observe the process by which writing was introduced into an oral society as well as the far-reaching consequences. The Greeks of the Dark Age and early Archaic period lived in a purely oral society; all knowledge was preserved in human memory and passed on by telling it to others. The *Iliad* and the *Odyssey* (ca. 700 B.C.E.), Homer's epic poems, reflect this state of affairs. Scholars recognize that the creator of these poems was an oral poet, almost certainly not literate, who had heard and memorized the poems of predecessors and retold them his own way. The poems are treasuries of information that this society regarded as useful—events of the past; the conduct expected of warriors, kings, noblewomen, and servants; how to perform a sacrifice, build a raft, put on armor, and entertain guests; and much more.

Embedding this information in a story and using the colorful language, fixed phrases, and predictable rhythm of poetry made it easier for poet and audience to remember vast amounts of material. The early Greek poets, drawing on their strong memories, skill with words, and talent for dramatic performance, developed highly specialized techniques to assist them in memorizing and presenting their tales. They played a vital role in the preservation and transmission of information and thus enjoyed a relatively high social standing and comfortable standard of living. Analogous groups can be found in many other oral cultures of the past, including the bards of medieval Celtic lands, Norse *skalds*, west African *griots*, and the tribal historians of Native American peoples.

Nevertheless, human memory, however cleverly trained and well practiced, can only do so much. Oral societies must be extremely selective about what information to preserve in the limited storage medium of human memory, and they are slow to give up old information to make way for new.

Sometime in the eighth century B.C.E. the Greeks borrowed the system of writing used by the Phoenicians of Lebanon and, in adapting it to their language, created the first purely alphabetic writing, employing several dozen symbols to express the sounds of speech. The Greek alphabet, although relatively simple to learn as compared to the large and cumbersome sets of symbols in such craft literacy systems as cuneiform, hieroglyphics, or Linear B, was probably known at first only to a small number of people and used for restricted purposes. Scholars believe that it may have taken three or four centuries for knowledge of reading and writing to spread to large numbers of Greeks and for the written word to become the primary storage medium for the accumulated knowledge of Greek civilization. Throughout that time Greece was still primarily an oral society, even though some Greeks, mostly highly educated members of the upper classes, were beginning to write down poems, scientific speculations, stories about the past, philosophic musings, and the laws of their communities.

It is no accident that some of the most important intellectual and artistic achievements of the Greeks, including early science, history, drama, and rhetoric, developed in the period when oral and literate ways existed side by side. Scholars have persuasively argued that writing, by opening up a virtually limitless capacity to store information, released the human mind from the hard discipline of memorization and ended the need to be so painfully selective about what was preserved. This made previously unimaginable innovation and experimentation possible. The Greeks began to organize and categorize information in linear ways, perhaps inspired by the linear sequence of the alphabet; and they began to engage in abstract thinking now that it was no longer necessary to put everything in a story format. We can observe changes in the Greek language as it developed a vocabulary full of abstract nouns, accompanied by increasingly complex sentence structure now that the reader had time to go back over the text.

Nevertheless, all the developments associated with literacy were shaped by the deeply rooted oral habits of Greek culture. It is often said that Plato (ca. 429–347 B.C.E.) and his contemporaries of the later Classical period may have been the first generation of Greeks who learned much of what they knew from books. Even so, Plato was a disciple of the philosopher Socrates, who wrote nothing, and Plato employed the oral form of the dialogue, a dramatized sequence of questions and answers, to convey his ideas in written form.

The transition from orality to literacy met stiff resistance in some quarters. Groups whose position in the oral culture was based on the special knowledge only they possessed—members of the elite who judged disputes, priests who knew the time-honored formulas and rituals for appeasing the gods, oral poets who preserved and performed the stories of a heroic past—resented the consequences of literacy. They did what they could to inflame the common people's suspicions of the impiety of literate men who sought scientific explanations for phenomena, such as lightning and eclipses, that had traditionally been attributed to the will and action of the gods. The elite attacked the so-called Sophists, or "wise men," who charged fees to teach what they claimed were the skills necessary for success, accusing them of subverting traditional morals and corrupting the young.

Other societies, ancient and modern, offer parallel examples of these processes. Oral "specialists" in antiquity, including the Brahmin priests of India and the Celtic Druids, preserved in memory valuable religious information about how to win the favor of the gods. These groups jealously guarded their knowledge because it was the basis of their livelihood and social standing. In their determination to select and to maintain control over those who received this knowledge, they resisted committing it to writing, even after that technology was available. The ways in which oral authorities feel threatened by writing and resist it can be seen in the following quotation from a twentieth-century C.E. "griot," an oral rememberer and teller of the past in Mali in West Africa:

> *We griots are depositories of the knowledge of the past. . . . Other peoples use writing to record the past, but this invention has killed the faculty of memory among them. They do not feel the past anymore, for writing lacks the warmth of the human voice. With them everybody thinks he knows, whereas learning should be a secret. . . . What paltry learning is that which is congealed in dumb books! . . . For generations we have passed on the history of kings from father to son. The narrative was passed on to me without alteration, for I received it free from all untruth.*[1]

This point of view is hard for us to grasp, living as we do in an intensely literate society in which the written word is often felt to be more authoritative and objective than the spoken word. It is important, in striving to understand societies of the past, not to superimpose our assumptions on them and to appreciate the complex interplay of oral and literate patterns in many of them.

NOTE

1. D. T. Niane, *Sundiata: An Epic of Old Mali* (Harlow, UK: Longman, 1986), 41.

CHAPTER 7

CHAPTER OUTLINE

- The Silk Road
- The Indian Ocean Maritime System
- Routes Across the Sahara
- Sub-Saharan Africa
- The Spread of Ideas
- Conclusion

DIVERSITY + DOMINANCE *Travel Accounts of Africa and India*

ENVIRONMENT + TECHNOLOGY *Camel Saddles*

Allan Eaton/Ancient Art & Architecture

Indian Ocean Sailing Vessel Ships like this one, in a rock carving on the Buddhist temple of Borobodur in Java, probably carried colonists from Indonesia to Madagascar.

Visit the website and ebook for additional study materials and interactive tools: www.cengage.com/history/bullietearthpeople5e

Networks of Communication and Exchange, 300 B.C.E.–600 C.E.

- What factors contributed to the growth of trade along the Silk Road?
- How did geography affect Indian Ocean trade routes?
- Why did trade begin across the Sahara Desert?
- What accounts for the substantial degree of cultural unity in Africa south of the Sahara?
- Why do some goods and ideas travel more easily than others?

Inspired by the tradition of the Silk Road, a Chinese poet named Po Zhuyi (boh joo-yee) nostalgically wrote:

> Iranian whirling girl, Iranian whirling girl—
> Her heart answers to the strings,
> Her hands answer to the drums.
> At the sound of the strings and drums, she raises her arms,
> Like whirling snowflakes tossed about, she turns in her twirling dance.
> Iranian whirling girl,
> You came from Sogdiana (sog-dee-A-nuh).
> In vain did you labor to come east more than ten thousand tricents.
> For in the central plains there were already some who could do the Iranian whirl,
> And in a contest of wonderful abilities, you would not be their equal.[1]

The western part of Central Asia, the region around Samarkand (SAM-mar-kand) and Bukhara (boo-CAR-ruh) known in the eighth century C.E. as Sogdiana, was 2,500 miles (4,000 kilometers) from the Chinese capital of Chang'an (chahng-ahn). Caravans traveling the Silk Road took more than four months to trek across the mostly unsettled deserts, mountains, and grasslands of Inner Asia that stood between Sogdiana and China, carrying with them agricultural goods, manufactured products, and ideas. Musicians and dancing girls traveled, too—as did camel pullers, merchants, monks, and pilgrims. The Silk Road was not just a means of bringing peoples and parts of the world into contact; it was also a social system.

With every expansion of territory, the growing wealth of temples, kings, and emperors enticed traders to venture ever farther afield for precious goods. For the most part, the customers were wealthy elites. But the new products, agricultural and industrial processes, and foreign ideas and customs these long-distance traders brought with them sometimes affected an entire society.

Travelers and traders seldom owned much land or wielded political power. Socially isolated (sometimes by law) and secretive because any talk about markets, products, routes, and travel conditions could help their competitors, they nevertheless contributed more to drawing the world together than did all but a few kings and emperors.

This chapter examines the social systems and historical impact of exchange networks that developed between 300 B.C.E. and 600 C.E. in Europe, Asia, and Africa. The Silk Road and the Indian Ocean maritime system illustrate the nature of long-distance trade in this era.

---

[1]From *The Columbia Anthology of Traditional Chinese Literature*, edited and translated by Victor H. Mair. Copyright © 1994 Columbia University Press. Reprinted with permission of the publisher.

AP* Exam Tip Overland trade routes, including the Silk Road, are a common essay topic on the exam.

However, trading networks were not the only medium for the spread of new ideas, products, and customs. This chapter also compares developments along trade routes with folk migration by looking at the beginnings of contact across the Sahara and the simultaneous spread of Bantu-speaking peoples within sub-Saharan Africa. Chapter 5 discussed a third pattern of cultural contact and exchange, that taking place with the beginning of Christian missionary activity in the Roman Empire. This chapter further explores the process by examining the spread of Buddhism in Asia and Christianity in Africa and Asia.

THE SILK ROAD

Silk Road Caravan routes connecting China and the Middle East across Central Asia and Iran.

Archaeology and linguistic studies show that the peoples of Central Asia engaged in long-distance movement and exchange from at least 1500 B.C.E. In Roman times Europeans became captivated by the idea of a trade route linking the lands of the Mediterranean with China by way of Mesopotamia, Iran, and Central Asia. The **Silk Road**, as this route came to be called in modern times, experienced several periods of heavy use (see Map 7.1). The first began around 100 B.C.E.

Origins and Operations

Iranians and Chinese

Parthians Iranian ruling dynasty between ca. 250 B.C.E. and 226 C.E.

The Seleucid kings who succeeded to the eastern parts of Alexander the Great's empire in the third century B.C.E. focused their energies on Mesopotamia and Syria. This allowed an Iranian nomadic leader to establish an independent kingdom of a people called the **Parthians** in northeastern Iran. Originally from east of the Caspian Sea, the Parthians become a major force by 247 B.C.E. They left few written sources, and recurring wars with Greeks and Romans to the west prevented travelers from the Mediterranean region from gaining firm knowledge of their kingdom. It seems likely, however, that they helped foster the Silk Road by being located on the threshold of Central Asia and sharing customs with steppe nomads farther to the east.

In 128 B.C.E. a Chinese general named Zhang Jian (jahng jee-en) made his first exploratory journey across the deserts and mountains of Inner Asia on behalf of Emperor Wu of the Han dynasty. The objective of the expedition was to gain knowledge of the nomad-inhabited lands on China's northwest frontier. After crossing the broad and desolate Tarim Basin north of Tibet, he reached the fertile valley of Ferghana (fer-GAH-nuh) and for the first time encountered westward-flowing rivers. There he found horse breeders whose animals far outclassed any horses he had seen. Later Chinese historians looked on General Zhang, who ultimately led eighteen expeditions, as the originator of overland trade with the western lands and credited him, often wrongly, with personally introducing a whole garden of new plants and trees to China.

Long-distance travel suited the people of the steppes more than the Chinese. The populations of Ferghana and neighboring regions included many nomads who followed their herds. Their migrations had little to do with trade, but they provided pack animals and controlled transit across their lands. The trading demands that brought the Silk Road into being were Chinese eagerness for western products, especially horses, and, on the western end, the organized Parthian state, which had captured the flourishing markets of Mesopotamia from the Seleucids.

By 100 B.C.E., Greeks could buy Chinese silk from Parthian traders in Mesopotamian border entrepôts. Yet caravans also bought and sold goods along the way in prosperous Central Asian cities like Samarkand and Bukhara. These cities grew and flourished, often under the rule of local princes.

Iranian Musicians from Silk Road This three-color glazed pottery figurine, 23 inches (58.4 centimeters) high, comes from a northern Chinese tomb of the Tang era (sixth to ninth centuries C.E.). The musicians playing Iranian instruments confirm the migration of Iranian culture across the Silk Road. At the same time, dishes decorated by the Chinese three-color glaze technique were in vogue in northern Iran.

CHRONOLOGY

	Silk Road	Indian Ocean Trade	Saharan Trade
500 B.C.E.			500 B.C.E.–ca. 1000 C.E. Bantu migrations
	247 B.C.E. Parthian rule begins in Iran		ca. 200 B.C.E. Camel nomads in southern Sahara
	128 B.C.E. General Zhang Jian reaches Ferghana		
	100 B.C.E.–300 C.E. Kushans rule northern Afghanistan and Sogdiana		46 B.C.E. First mention of camels in northern Sahara
1 C.E.	1st cent. C.E. First evidence of the stirrup	1st cent. C.E. *Periplus of the Erythaean Sea*; Indonesian migration to Madagascar	
	224–651 Sasanid Empire		
300 C.E.			ca. 300 Beginning of camel nomadism in northern Sahara
	ca. 400 Buddhist pilgrim Faxian travels Silk Road		

New Crops

General Zhang definitely seems to have brought two plants to China: alfalfa and wine grapes. The former provided the best fodder for horses. In addition, Chinese farmers adopted pistachios, walnuts, pomegranates, sesame, coriander, spinach, and other new crops. Chinese artisans and physicians made good use of other trade products, such as jasmine oil, oak galls (used in tanning animal hides, dyeing, and making ink), sal ammoniac (for medicines), copper oxides, zinc, and precious stones.

Traders going west from China carried new fruits such as peaches and apricots, which the Romans mistakenly attributed to other eastern lands, calling them Persian plums and Armenia plums, respectively. They also carried cinnamon, ginger, and other spices that could not be grown in the West.

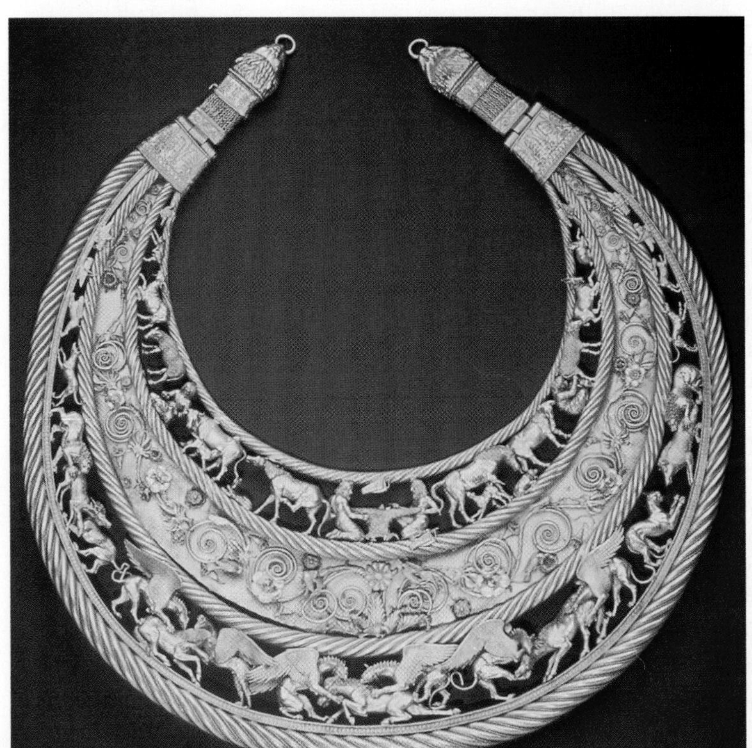

Lee Boltin/The Bridgeman Art Library

Scythian Breastplate This superbly crafted gold ornament from the fourth century B.C.E. features animal combat in the lower tier, flower motifs in the center, and scenes from Scythian pastoral life in the upper. Two men prepare a fleece garment in the middle of the upper tier while on either side young animals are suckling and a ewe is being milked. Note the contrast between the simplicity of nomadic life and the luxury represented by the gold ornament itself.

Nomadism in Central and Inner Asia

The Silk Road could not have functioned without pastoral nomads to provide animals, animal handlers, and protection. Descriptions of steppe nomads known as Scythians appear in the history of the Greek writer Herodotus in the sixth century B.C.E. He portrays them as superb riders, herdsmen, and hunters living in Central Asia, the

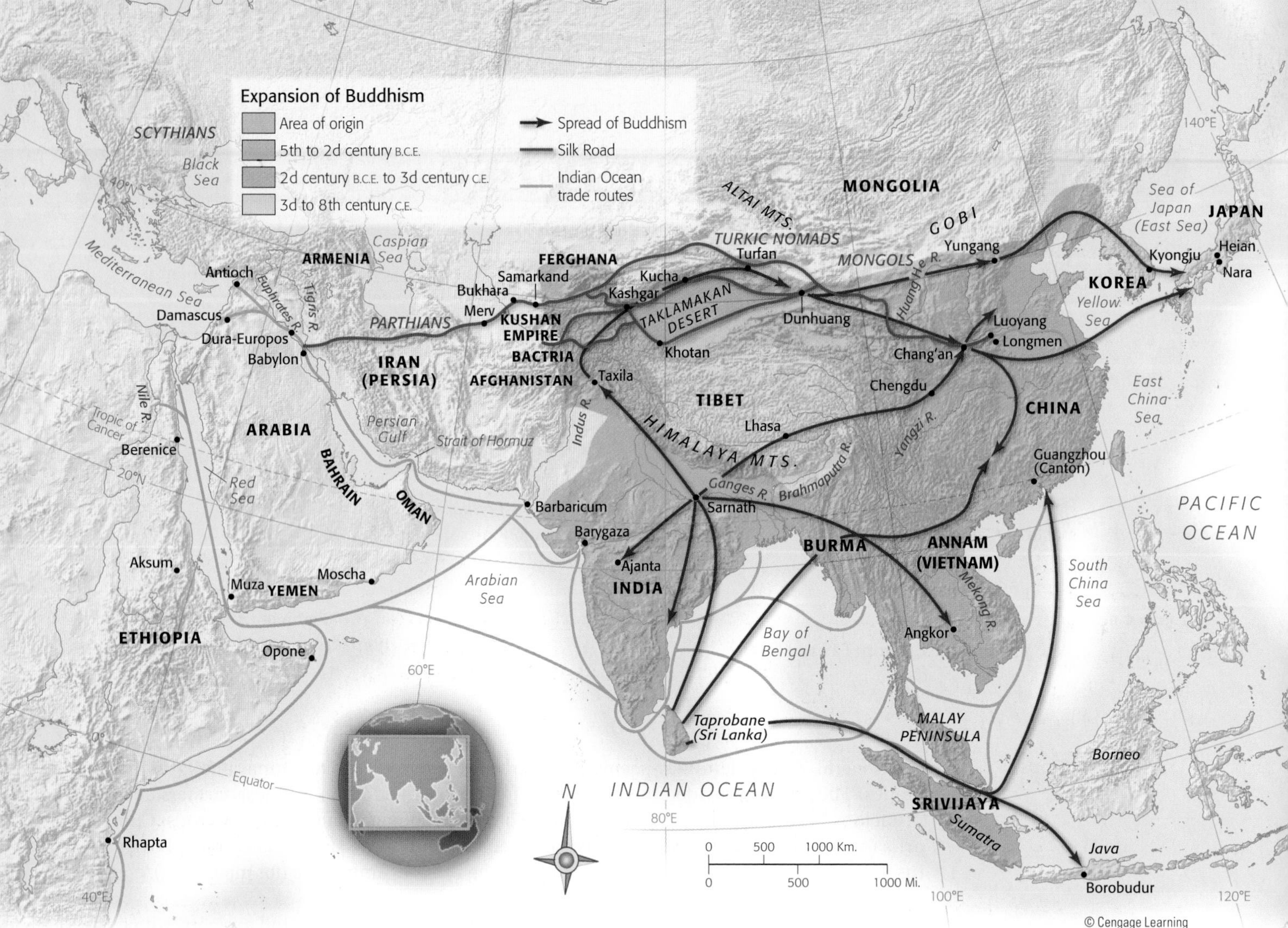

MAP 7.1 Asian Trade and Communication Routes The overland Silk Road was vulnerable to political disruption, but it was much shorter than the maritime route from the South China Sea to the Red Sea, and ships were more expensive than pack animals. Moreover, China's political centers were in the north.

Interactive Map

Scythians

lands to the north of the Black and Caspian Seas. Moving regularly and efficiently with flocks and herds of enormous size prevented overgrazing. Though the Scythians were fearsome horse archers, their homes, which were made of felt spread over a lightweight framework, were transported on four-wheeled wagons drawn by oxen. This custom continued in some parts of Inner Asia, the grasslands and deserts extending eastward from Central Asia to the borders of China, for another two thousand years.

The Nomadic Lifestyle

Nomads were not unfamiliar with agriculture or unwilling to use products grown by farmers, but their ideal was self-sufficiency. Since their wanderings with their herds normally took them far from any farming region, self-sufficiency dictated foods they could provide for themselves—primarily meat and milk—and clothing made from felt, leather, and furs. Women oversaw the breeding and birthing of livestock and the preparation of furs.

AP* Exam Tip Understand how specific ideas and knowledge, including religion, spread across the overland trade routes.

Nomads were most dependent on settled regions for the bronze or iron used in bridles, stirrups, cart fittings, and weapons. They acquired metal implements in trade and reworked them to suit their purposes. Scythians in the Ukraine worked extensively with iron as early as the fourth century B.C.E., and Turkish-speaking peoples had large ironworking stations south of the Altai Mountains in western Mongolia in the 600s C.E. Steppe nomads situated near settled areas also traded wool, leather, and horses for wood, silk, vegetables, and grain.

The Silk Road and the Spread of Religion

The Sasanid Empire

As the Silk Road grew in importance, a new Iranian dynasty centered in Iraq gave increased emphasis to the full extent of the route from China to Mesopotamia. The period of the

Sasanid Empire Iranian empire, established ca. 224, with a capital in Ctesiphon, Mesopotamia. The Sasanid emperors established Zoroastrianism as the state religion. Islamic Arab armies overthrew the empire ca. 640.

Sasanid Empire also saw the Silk Road becoming an avenue for the transfer of religious ideas. Ardashir, whose dynasty takes its name from an ancestor named Sasan, defeated the Parthians around 224 and established the Sasanid kingdom. To the west, the new rulers confronted the Romans, whom later historians frequently refer to as the Byzantines after about 330. The rival empires launched numerous attacks on each other across that frontier between the 340s and 628. In times of peace, however, exchange between the empires flourished, allowing goods transported over the Silk Road to enter the zone of Mediterranean trade.

The Arab pastoralists who inhabited the desert between Syria and Mesopotamia supplied camels and guides for the extension of the Silk Road from Euphrates River to the Mediterranean coast. During the Sasanid period, they also played a primary role in transforming the transportation economy of the Middle East. The militarily efficient North Arabian camel saddle (see Environment and Technology: Camel Saddles later in this chapter), developed around the third century B.C.E., provided the tool the Arabs needed to seize control of the caravan trade in their territories from the city merchants who had previously been dominant. As their military and economic influence increased, wheeled vehicles—mostly ox carts and horse-drawn chariots—all but disappeared by the sixth century C.E.

Warrior Nobles

The mountains and plateaus of Iran proper formed the Sasanids' political hinterland, often ruled by the cousins of the shah (king) or by powerful nobles. Cities there were small walled communities that served more as military strong points than as centers of population and production. Society revolved around a local aristocracy that lived on rural estates and cultivated the arts of hunting, feasting, and war just like the noble warriors described in the sagas of ancient kings and heroes sung at their banquets.

Despite the dominance of powerful aristocratic families, long-lasting political fragmentation of the medieval European variety did not develop (see Chapter 9). Also, although many nomads lived in the mountain and desert regions, no folk migration took place comparable to that of the Germanic peoples who defeated Roman armies and established kingdoms in formerly Roman territory from about the third century C.E. onward. The Sasanid and Byzantine Empires successfully maintained central control of imperial finances and military power and found effective ways of integrating frontier peoples as mercenaries or caravaneers.

Zoroastrians and Christians

The Sasanids established their Zoroastrian faith (see Chapter 4), which the Parthians had not particularly stressed, as a state religion similar to Christianity in the Byzantine Empire (see Chapter 9). The proclamation of Christianity and Zoroastrianism as official faiths marked the fresh emergence of religion as an instrument of politics both within and between the empires, setting a precedent for the subsequent rise of Islam as the focus of a political empire (see Chapter 8).

Religion permeated all aspects of community life. Most subjects of the Byzantine emperors and Sasanid shahs identified themselves first and foremost as members of a religious community. Their schools and law courts were religious, and they looked on priests, monks, rabbis, and the Zoroastrian mobads as moral guides in daily life. Most books discussed religious subjects. In some areas, religious leaders represented their flocks even in such secular matters as tax collection.

Both Zoroastrianism and Christianity practiced intolerance. A late-third-century inscription in Iran boasts of the persecutions of Christians, Jews, and Buddhists carried out by the Zoroastrian high priest. Yet sizable Christian and Jewish communities remained, especially in Mesopotamia. Similarly, from the fourth century onward, councils of Christian bishops declared many theological beliefs heretical—so unacceptable that they were un-Christian.

Christians then became pawns in the political rivalry with the Byzantines and were sometimes persecuted, sometimes patronized, by the Sasanid kings. In 431 a council of bishops called by the Byzantine emperor declared the Nestorian Christians heretics for overemphasizing the humanness of Christ. The Nestorians believed that human characteristics and divinity coexisted in Jesus and that Mary was not the mother of God, as many other Christians maintained, but the mother of the human Jesus. After the bishops' ruling, the Nestorians sought refuge under the Sasanid shah and eventually extended their missionary activities along the Central Asian trade routes.

Manichaeism

In the third century a preacher named Mani had founded a new religion in Mesopotamia: Manichaeism. He preached a dualist faith—a struggle between Good and Evil—theologically derived from Zoroastrianism. Although at first Mani enjoyed the favor of the shah, he and many of his followers were martyred in 276. However, his religion survived and spread widely.

Nestorian missionaries in Central Asia competed with Manichaean missionaries for converts. In later centuries, the term *Manichaean* was applied to all sorts of beliefs about a cosmic struggle between Good and Evil.

Religion and the Silk Road

Various forms of Christianity and Zoroastrianism were spread by missionaries and travelers along the Silk Road. Jews also made their way across Inner Asia to China. Everywhere, religion played an increasing role in defining community identity and political allignments. For example, the Arab nomads who protected the Byzantine borders adopted a Monophysite theology, which emphasized Christ's divine nature, while the allies of the Sasanids adopted the Nestorian faith, which also linked them to Nestorian communities across Inner Asia. Through these Arab groups, knowledge of Christianity penetrated deep into the Arabian peninsula during the fifth and sixth centuries, eventually influencing Islam (see Chapter 8).

Turkic-Speaking Nomads and Buddhism

Buddhism was another religion that moved along the Silk Road. As trade became a more important part of Central Asian life, the Iranian-speaking peoples increasingly settled in trading cities and surrounding farm villages. By the sixth century C.E., nomads originally from the Altai Mountains farther east had spread across the steppes and become the dominant pastoral group. These peoples spoke Turkic languages unrelated to the Iranian tongues. Since they did not move south of the deserts of Turkmenistan and Uzbekistan that separated the Sasanid Empire from Central Asia, their impact was felt mostly by Iranians who lived outside Sasanid control to the northest.

AP* Exam Tip Specific inventions and technology, such as the stirrup and camel saddle, may be tested on the exam.

The Turkic nomads continued to live in the round, portable felt huts called yurts that can still occasionally be seen in Central Asia, but prosperous individuals, both Turks and Iranians, built stately homes decorated with brightly colored wall paintings. The paintings show people wearing Chinese silks and Iranian brocades and riding on richly outfitted horses and camels. They also indicate an avid interest in Buddhism (see below), which competed with Nestorian Christianity, Manichaeism, and Zoroastrianism in a lively and inquiring intellectual milieu.

stirrup Device for securing a horseman's feet, enabling him to wield weapons more effectively. First evidence of the use of stirrups was among the Kushan people of northern Afghanistan in approximately the first century C.E.

The Impact of the Silk Road on Technology

Warriors and Missionaries

Whereas missionary influences exemplify the impact of foreign customs and beliefs on the peoples along the Silk Road, military technology affords an example of the opposite phenomenon: steppe customs radiating into foreign lands. Chariot warfare and the use of mounted bowmen originated in Central Asia and spread eastward and westward through military campaigns and folk migrations that began in the second millennium B.C.E. and recurred throughout the period of the Silk Road.

Invention of the Stirrup

Evidence of the **stirrup**, one of the most important inventions, comes first from the Kushan people who ruled northern Afghanistan between roughly 100 B.C.E. and 300 C.E. At first a solid bar, then a loop of leather to support the rider's big toe, and finally a device of leather and metal or wood supporting the instep, the stirrup gave riders far greater stability in the saddle—which itself was in all likelihood an earlier Central Asian invention.

Using stirrups, a mounted warrior could supplement his bow and arrow with a long lance and charge his enemy at a gallop without fear that the impact of his attack would push him off his mount. Far to the west, the stirrup made possible the armored knights who dominated the battlefields of Europe (see Chapter 9), while also contributing to the superiority of the Tang cavalry in China (see Chapter 10).

SECTION REVIEW

- The rise of the Parthian kingdom helped foster the Silk Road, a route by which Chinese products were exchanged with goods from the Mediterranean region.
- General Zhang led expeditions that established the route from China through Central Asia.
- As Central Asian nomads facilitated the movement of goods through their lands, Central Asian cities grew.
- Originating in southern Iran, the Sasanids overthrew the Parthians and continued their predecessors' rivalry with Rome.
- Sasanid kings made Zoroastrianism the state religion, and other religions, particularly Christianity, experienced both toleration and persecution; various forms of these religions also traveled along the Silk Road.
- Some important military technologies used in both the East and West originated in Central Asia: chariot warfare, mounted bowmen, and, most important, the stirrup.

THE INDIAN OCEAN MARITIME SYSTEM

Indian Ocean Maritime System In premodern times, a network of seaports, trade routes, and maritime culture linking countries on the rim of the Indian Ocean from Africa to Indonesia.

While the Silk Road provided movement over land, a multilingual, multiethnic society of seafarers established the **Indian Ocean Maritime System**, a trade network across the Indian Ocean and the South China Sea. These people left few records and seldom played a visible part in the rise and fall of kingdoms and empires, but they forged increasingly strong economic and social ties between the coastal lands of East Africa, southern Arabia, the Persian Gulf, India, Southeast Asia, and southern China.

This trade took place in three distinct regions: (1) In the South China Sea, Chinese and Malays (including Indonesians) dominated trade. (2) From the east coast of India to the islands of Southeast Asia, Indians and Malays were the main traders. (3) From the west coast of India to the Persian Gulf and the east coast of Africa, merchants and sailors were predominantly Persians and Arabs. However, Chinese and Malay sailors could and did voyage to East Africa, and Arab and Persian traders reached southern China.

Sailors' Tales

From the time of Herodotus in the fifth century B.C.E., Greek writers regaled their readers with stories of marvelous voyages down the Red Sea into the Indian Ocean and around Africa from the west. Most often, they attributed such trips to the Phoenicians, the most fearless of Mediterranean seafarers. Occasionally a Greek appears. One such was Hippalus, a Greek ship's pilot who was said to have discovered the seasonal monsoon winds that facilitate sailing across the Indian Ocean (see Diversity and Dominance: Travel Accounts of Africa and India).

AP* Exam Tip Ocean trade routes and overland trade routes are comparison topics for the essay portion of the AP exam.

Of course, the regular, seasonal alternation of steady winds could not have remained unnoticed for thousands of years, waiting for an alert Greek to happen along. The great voyages and discoveries made before written records became common should surely be attributed to the peoples who lived around the Indian Ocean rather than to interlopers from the Mediterranean Sea. The story of Hippalus resembles the Chinese story of General Zhang Jian, whose role in opening trade with Central Asia overshadows the anonymous contributions made by the indigenous peoples. The Chinese may indeed have learned from General Zhang and the Greeks from Hippalus, but other people played important roles anonymously.

Sailing and Ship Design

Mediterranean sailors of the time of Alexander used square sails and long banks of oars to maneuver among the sea's many islands and small harbors. In contrast, Indian Ocean vessels relied on roughly triangular lateen sails and normally did without oars in running before the wind on long ocean stretches. Whereas Mediterranean shipbuilders nailed their vessels together, the planks of Indian Ocean ships were pierced, tied together with palm fiber, and caulked with bitumen. Mediterranean sailors rarely ventured out of sight of land, but Indian Ocean sailors, thanks to the monsoon winds, could cover long reaches entirely at sea.

These technological differences prove that the world of the Indian Ocean developed differently than the world of the Mediterranean Sea, where the Phoenicians and Greeks established colonies that maintained contact with their home cities (see Chapters 3 and 4). The traders of the Indian Ocean, where distances were greater and contacts less frequent, seldom retained political ties with their homelands. The colonies they established were sometimes socially distinctive but rarely independent of the local political powers.

Origins of Contact and Trade

By 2000 B.C.E. Sumerian records indicate regular trade between Mesopotamia, the islands of the Persian Gulf, Oman, and the Indus Valley. However, this early trading contact broke off, and later Mesopotamian trade references mention East Africa more often than India.

Indonesians in Madagascar

A similarly early chapter in Indian Ocean history concerns migrations from Southeast Asia to Madagascar, the world's fourth largest island, situated off the southeastern coast of Africa. About two thousand years ago, people from one of the many Indonesian islands of Southeast Asia established themselves in that forested, mountainous land 6,000 miles (9,500 kilometers) from home. They could not possibly have carried enough supplies for a direct voyage across the Indian Ocean, so their route must have touched the coasts of India and southern Arabia. No physical remains of their journeys have been discovered, however.

Bananas and Yams

Apparently, the sailing canoes of these people plied the seas along the increasingly familiar route for several hundred years. Settlers farmed the new land and entered into relations with Africans who found their way across the 250-mile-wide (400-kilometer-wide) Mozambique

Travel Accounts of Africa and India

The most revealing description of ancient trade in the Indian Ocean and of the diversity and economic forces shaping the Indian Ocean trading system, "The Periplus of the Erythraean Sea," a sailing itinerary (periplus in Greek), was composed in the first century C.E. *by an unknown Greco-Egyptian merchant. It highlights the diversity of peoples and products from the Red Sea to the Bay of Bengal. Historians believe that the descriptions of market towns were based on firsthand experience. The following passages deal with East Africa and the coastal lands subcontinent (see Map 7.1).*

Of the designated ports on the Erythraean Sea [Indian Ocean], and the market-towns around it, the first is the Egyptian port of Mussel Harbor. To those sailing down from that place, on the right hand . . . there is Berenice. The harbors of both are at the boundary of Egypt. . . .

On the right-hand coast next below Berenice is the country of the Berbers. Along the shore are the Fish-Eaters, living in scattered caves in the narrow valleys. Further inland are the Berbers, and beyond them the Wild-flesh-Eaters and Calf-Eaters, each tribe governed by its chief; and behind them, further inland, in the country towards the west, there lies a city called Meroe.

Below the Calf-Eaters there is a little market-town on the shore . . . called Ptolemais of the Hunts, from which the hunters started for the interior under the dynasty of the Ptolemies. . . . But the place has no harbor and is reached only by small boats. . . .

Beyond this place, the coast trending toward the south, there is the Market and Cape of Spices, an abrupt promontory, at the very end of the Berber coast toward the east. . . . A sign of an approaching storm . . . is that the deep water becomes more turbid and changes its color. When this happens they all run to a large promontory called Tabae, which offers safe shelter. . . .

Beyond Tabae [lies] . . . another market-town called Opone. . . . [I]n it the greatest quantity of cinnamon is produced . . . and slaves of the better sort, which are brought to Egypt in increasing numbers. . . .

[Ships also come] from the places across this sea, from . . . Barygaza, bringing to these . . . market-towns the products of their own places; wheat, rice, clarified butter, sesame oil, cotton cloth . . . and honey from the reed called sacchari [sugar cane]. Some make the voyage especially to these market-towns, and others exchange their cargoes while sailing along the coast. This country is not subject to a King, but each market-town is ruled by its separate chief.

Beyond Opone, the shore trending more toward the south . . . this coast [the Somali region of Azania, or East Africa] is destitute of harbors . . . until the Pyralax islands [Zanzibar]. . . . [A] little to the south of south-west . . . is the island Menuthias [Madagascar], about three hundred stadia from the mainland, low and wooded, in which there are rivers and many kinds of birds and the mountain-tortoise. There are no wild beasts except the crocodiles; but there they do not attack men. In this place there are sewed boats, and canoes hollowed from single logs. . . .

Two days' sail beyond, there lies the very last market-town of the continent of Azania, which is called Rhapta [Dar es-Salaam]; which has its name from the sewed boats (*rhapton ploiarion*) . . . ; in which there is ivory in great quantity, and tortoise-shell. Along this coast live men of piratical habits, very great in stature, and under separate chiefs for each place. . . .

And these markets of Azania are the very last of the continent that stretches down on the right hand from Berenice; for beyond these places the unexplored ocean curves around toward the west, and running along by the regions to the south of Aethiopia and Libya and Africa, it mingles with the western sea. . . .

Now the whole country of India has very many rivers, and very great ebb and flow of the tides. . . . But about Barygaza [Broach] it is much greater, so that the bottom is suddenly seen, and now parts of the dry land are sea, and now it is dry where ships were sailing just before; and the rivers, under the inrush of the flood tide, when the whole force of the sea is directed against them, are driven upwards more strongly against their natural current. . . .

The country inland from Barygaza is inhabited by numerous tribes. . . . Above these is the very warlike nation of the Bactrians, who are under their own king. And Alexander, setting out from these parts, penetrated to the Ganges. . . . [T]o the present day ancient drachmae are current in Barygaza, coming from this country, bearing inscriptions in Greek letters, and the devices of those who reigned after Alexander. . . .

Inland from this place and to the east, is the city called Ozene [Ujjain]. . . . [F]rom this place are brought down all things needed for the welfare of the country about Barygaza, and many things for our trade: agate and carnelian, Indian muslins. . . .

There are imported into this market-town, wine, Italian preferred, also Laodicean and Arabian; copper, tin, and lead; coral and topaz; thin clothing and inferior sorts of all kinds . . . gold and silver coin, on which there is a profit when exchanged for the money of the country. . . . And for the King there are

(moe-zam-BEEK) Channel around the fifth century C.E. Descendants of the seafarers preserved the language of their homeland and some of its culture, such as the cultivation of bananas, yams, and other native Southeast Asian plants. These food crops spread to mainland Africa. But the memory of their distant origins gradually faded, not to be recovered until modern times, when scholars established the linguistic link between the two lands.

brought into those places very costly vessels of silver, singing boys, beautiful maidens for the harem, fine wines, thin clothing of the finest weaves, and the choicest ointments. There are exported from these places [spices], ivory, agate and carnelian . . . cotton cloth of all kinds, silk cloth. . . .

Beyond Barygaza the adjoining coast extends in a straight line from north to south. . . . The inland country back from the coast toward the east comprises many desert regions and great mountains; and all kinds of wild beasts—leopards, tigers, elephants, enormous serpents, hyenas, and baboons of many sorts; and many populous nations, as far as the Ganges. . . .

This whole voyage as above described . . . they used to make in small vessels, sailing close around the shores of the gulfs; and Hippalus was the pilot who by observing the location of the ports and the conditions of the sea, first discovered how to lay his course straight across the ocean. . . .

About the following region, the course trending toward the east, lying out at sea toward the west is the island Palaesimundu, called by the ancients Taprobane [Sri Lanka]. . . . It produces pearls, transparent stones, muslins, and tortoise-shell. . . .

Beyond this, the course trending toward the north, there are many barbarous tribes, among whom are the Cirrhadae, a race of men with flattened noses, very savage; another tribe, the Bargysi; and the Horse-faces and the Long-faces, who are said to be cannibals.

After these, the course turns toward the east again, and sailing with the ocean to the right and the shore remaining beyond to the left, Ganges comes into view. . . . And just opposite this river there is an island in the ocean, the last part of the inhabited world toward the east, under the rising sun itself; it is called Chryse; and it has the best tortoise-shell of all the places on the Erythraean Sea.

After this region under the very north, the sea outside ending in a land called This, there is a very great inland city called Thinae, from which raw silk and silk yarn and silk cloth are brought on foot. . . . But the land of This is not easy of access; few men come from there, and seldom.

The Chinese traveler Xuanzang (600–664) journeyed across Inner Asia to India, making pilgrimage to Buddhist holy places and searching for Sanskrit scriptures to take back to China with him. His descriptions of the places he visited reflect his interests. The following passages come from his description of India.

Towns and Buildings

The towns and villages have inner gates; the walls are wide and high; the streets and lanes are tortuous, and the roads winding. The thoroughfares are dirty and the stalls arranged on both sides of the road with appropriate signs. Butchers, fishers, dancers, executioners, and scavengers, and so on, have their abodes without the city. In coming and going these persons are bound to keep on the left side of the road till they arrive at their homes. Their houses are surrounded by low walls, and form the suburbs. The earth being soft and muddy, the walls of the town are mostly built of brick or tiles. The towers on the walls are constructed of wood or bamboo; the houses have balconies and belvederes, which are made of wood, with a coating of lime or mortar, and covered with tiles. The different buildings have the same form as those in China: rushes, or dry branches, or tiles, or boards are used for covering them. The walls are covered with lime and mud, mixed with cow's dung for purity. At different seasons they scatter flowers about. Such are some of their different customs.

Dress and Appearance

Their clothing is not cut or fashioned; they mostly affect fresh-white garments; they esteem little those of mixed color or ornamented. The men wind their garments round their middle, then gather them under the armpits, and let them fall down across the body, hanging to the right. The robes of the women fall down to the ground; they completely cover their shoulders. They wear a little knot of hair on their crowns, and let the rest of their hair fall loose. Some of the men cut off their moustaches, and have other odd customs. . . . In North India, where the air is cold, they wear short and close-fitting garments. . . . The dress and ornaments worn by the nonbelievers are varied and mixed. Some wear peacocks' feathers; some wear as ornaments necklaces made of skull bones; some have no clothing, but go naked; some wear leaf or bark garments; some pull out their hair and cut off their moustaches; others have bushy whiskers and their hair braided on the top of their heads. The costume is not uniform, and the color, whether red or white, not constant.

QUESTIONS FOR ANALYSIS

1. **How do the differing interests of a trader and a religious pilgrim show up in what they report?**
2. **How do these narratives show the influence of the countries the authors are coming from?**
3. **Given the different viewpoints of travelers, what is the value of travel accounts as sources for history?**

Source: Samuel Beal, *Buddhist Records of the Western World, Translated from the Chinese of Hiuen Tsiang (A.D. 629)* (London: Trubner and Company, 1884; reprint Delhi: Oriental Books Reprint Corporation, 1969), 73–76.

The Impact of Indian Ocean Trade

Incense and Pottery

The demand for products from the coastal lands inspired mariners to persist in their long ocean voyages. Africa produced exotic animals, wood, and ivory. Since ivory also came from India, Mesopotamia, and North Africa, the extent of African ivory exports cannot be determined. The

Courtesy, Bahrain National Museum

Asklepios, the Greek God of Medicine This representation, found in the sea off the coast of Bahrain in the Persian Gulf, reflects the extension of Greek culture along sea routes into distant lands. Greek medical knowledge and principles became known as far away as India. The crude craftsmanship of this effigy indicates that it was locally made and not imported from Greece.

highlands of northern Somalia and southern Arabia grew the scrubby trees whose aromatic resins were valued as frankincense and myrrh. Pearls abounded in the Persian Gulf, and evidence of ancient copper mines has been found in Oman in southeastern Arabia. India shipped spices and manufactured goods, and more spices came from Southeast Asia, along with manufactured items, particularly pottery, obtained in trade with China. In sum, the Indian Ocean trading region had a great variety of highly valued products. Given the long distances and the comparative lack of islands, however, the volume of trade there was undoubtedly much lower than in the Mediterranean Sea.

Eastern and Western Ocean Trade

Also unlike in the Mediterranean, the culture of the Indian Ocean ports was often isolated from the hinterlands, particularly in the western areas. The coasts of the Arabian peninsula, the African side of the Red Sea, southern Iran, and northern India (today's Pakistan) were mostly barren desert. Ports in all these areas tended to be small, and many suffered from meager supplies of fresh water. Farther south in India, the monsoon provided ample water, but steep mountains cut off the coastal plain from the interior of the country. Thus few ports between Zanzibar and Sri Lanka had substantial inland populations within easy reach. The head of the Persian Gulf was one exception: ship-borne trade was possible from the port of Apologus (later called Ubulla, the precursor of modern Basra) as far north as Babylon and, from the eighth century C.E., nearby Baghdad.

By contrast, eastern India, the Malay Peninsula, and Indonesia afforded more hospitable and densely populated shores with easier access to inland populations. Though the fishers, sailors, and traders of the western Indian Ocean system supplied a long series of kingdoms and empires, none of these consumer societies became primarily maritime in orientation, as the Greeks and Phoenicians did in the Mediterranean. In contrast, seaborne trade and influence seem to have been important even to the earliest states of Southeast Asia.

Women and Cultural Diversity

In coastal areas throughout the Indian Ocean system, small groups of seafarers sometimes had a significant social impact despite their usual lack of political power. Women seldom accompanied the men on long sea voyages, so sailors and merchants often married local women in port cities. The families thus established were bilingual and bicultural. As in many other situations in world history, women played a crucial though not well-documented role as mediators between cultures. Not only did they raise their children to be more cosmopolitan than children from inland regions, but they also introduced the men to customs and attitudes that they carried with them when they returned to sea. As a consequence, the designation of specific seafarers as Persian, Arab, Indian, or Malay often conceals mixed heritages and a rich cultural diversity.

SECTION REVIEW

- The Indian Ocean Maritime System grew from the voyages of diverse seafaring traders.
- Unlike the Mediterranean, the Indian Ocean developed no network of colonies with home ties.
- The system originated in early Mesopotamian trade routes and the migrations of Southeast Asian peoples to Madagascar.
- Trade in a broad range of goods flourished in ports where distinct cultures evolved.

ROUTES ACROSS THE SAHARA

The windswept Sahara, a desert stretching from the Red Sea to the Atlantic Ocean and broken only by the Nile River, isolates sub-Saharan Africa from the Mediterranean world (see Map 7.2). The current dryness of the Sahara dates only to about 2500 B.C.E. The period of drying out that preceded that date lasted twenty-five centuries and encompassed several cultural changes. During that time, travel between a slowly shrinking number of grassy areas was comparatively easy. However, by 300 B.C.E., scarcity of water was restricting travel to a few difficult routes initially known only to desert nomads. Trade over these **trans-Saharan caravan routes**, at first only a trickle, eventually expanded into a significant stream.

trans-Saharan caravan routes Trading network linking North Africa with sub-Saharan Africa across the Sahara.

Early Saharan Cultures

A Growing Desert

Sprawling sand dunes, sandy plains, and vast expanses of exposed rock make up most of the great desert. Stark and rugged mountain and highland areas separate its northern and southern portions. The cliffs and caves of these highlands, the last spots where water and grassland could be found as the climate changed, preserve rock paintings and engravings that constitute the primary evidence for early Saharan history.

Rock Paintings

Though dating is difficult, what appear to be the earliest images, left by hunters in much wetter times, include elephants, giraffes, rhinoceros, crocodiles, and other animals that have long been extinct in the region. Overlaps in the artwork indicate that the hunting societies were gradually joined by new cultures based on cattle breeding and well adapted to the sparse grazing that remained. Domestic cattle may have originated in western Asia or in North Africa. They certainly reached the Sahara before it became completely dry. The beautiful paintings of cattle and scenes of daily life seen in the Saharan rock art depict pastoral societies that bear little similarity to any in western Asia. The people seem physically akin to today's West Africans, and the customs depicted, such as dancing and wearing masks, as well as the breeds of cattle, particularly those with piebald coloring (splotches of black and white), strongly suggest later societies

Cattle Herders in Saharan Rock Art These paintings represent the most artistically accomplished type of Saharan art. Herding societies of modern times living in the Sahel region south of the Sahara strongly resemble the society depicted here.

Henri Lhote

to the south of the Sahara. These factors support the hypothesis that some southern cultural patterns originated in the Sahara.

Overlaps in artwork also show that horse herders succeeded the cattle herders. The rock art changes dramatically in style, from the superb realism of the cattle pictures to sketchier images that are often strongly geometric. Moreover, the horses are frequently shown drawing light chariots. According to the most common theory, intrepid charioteers from the Mediterranean shore drove their flimsy vehicles across the desert and established societies in the few remaining grassy areas of the central Saharan highlands. Some scholars suggest possible chariot routes that refugees from the collapse of the Mycenaean and Minoan civilizations of Greece and Crete (see Chapter 3) might have followed deep into the desert around the twelfth century B.C.E. However, no archaeological evidence of actual chariot use in the Sahara has been discovered, and it is difficult to imagine large numbers of refugees from the politically chaotic Mediterranean region driving chariots into a waterless, trackless desert in search of a new homeland somewhere to the south.

As with the cattle herders, therefore, the identity of the Saharan horse breeders and the source of their passion for drawing chariots remain a mystery. Only with the coming of the camel, which appear in the southern Sahara around 200 B.C.E. and in the northern desert some five hundred years later, is it possible to make firm connections with the Saharan nomads of today through the depiction of objects and geometric patterns still used by the veiled, blue-robed Tuareg (TWAH-reg) people of the highlands in southern Algeria, Niger, and Mali.

The Coming of the Camel

Some historians maintain that the Romans inaugurated an important trans-Saharan trade, but they lack firm archaeological evidence. More plausibly, Saharan trade relates to the spread of camel domestication. Supporting evidence comes from rock art, where overlaps of images imply that camel riders in desert costume constitute the latest Saharan population. The camel-oriented images are decidedly the crudest to be found in the region.

The first mention of camels in North Africa comes in a Latin text of 46 B.C.E. Since the native camels of Africa probably died out before the era of domestication, the domestic animals probably reached the Sahara from Arabia, probably by way of Egypt in the first millennium B.C.E. They could have been adopted by peoples farther and farther to the west, from one central Saharan highland to the next, only much later spreading northward and coming to the attention of the Romans. Camel herding made it easier for people to move away from the Saharan highlands and roam the deep desert (see Environment and Technology: Camel Saddles).

Trade Across the Sahara

Linkage between two different trading systems, one in the south, the other in the north, developed slowly. Southern traders concentrated on supplying salt from large deposits in the southern desert to the peoples of sub-Saharan Africa. Traders from the equatorial forest zone brought forest products, such as kola nuts (a condiment and source of caffeine) and edible palm oil, to trading centers near the desert's southern fringe. Each received the products they needed in their homelands from the other, or from the farming peoples of the **Sahel** (SAH-hel)—literally "the coast" in Arabic, the southern borderlands of the Sahara (see Map 7.2). Middlemen who were native to the Sahel played an important role in this trade, but precise historical details are lacking.

Sahel Belt south of the Sahara; literally "coastland" in Arabic.

Romans in the North

In the north, Roman colonists supplied Italy with agricultural products, primarily wheat and olives. Surviving mosaic pavements depicting scenes from daily life show that people living on the farms and in the towns of the interior consumed Roman manufactured goods and shared Roman styles. This northern pattern began to change only in the third century C.E. with the decline of the Roman Empire, the abandonment of many Roman farms, the growth of nomadism, and a lessening of trade across the Mediterranean.

SECTION REVIEW

- Early Saharan cultures included hunting societies and, in isolated areas, groups of cattle breeders.
- Later, horse and camel herders joined these groups.
- Camel-riding nomads most likely pioneered the trans-Saharan trade routes, linking North African and sub-Saharan trade networks.

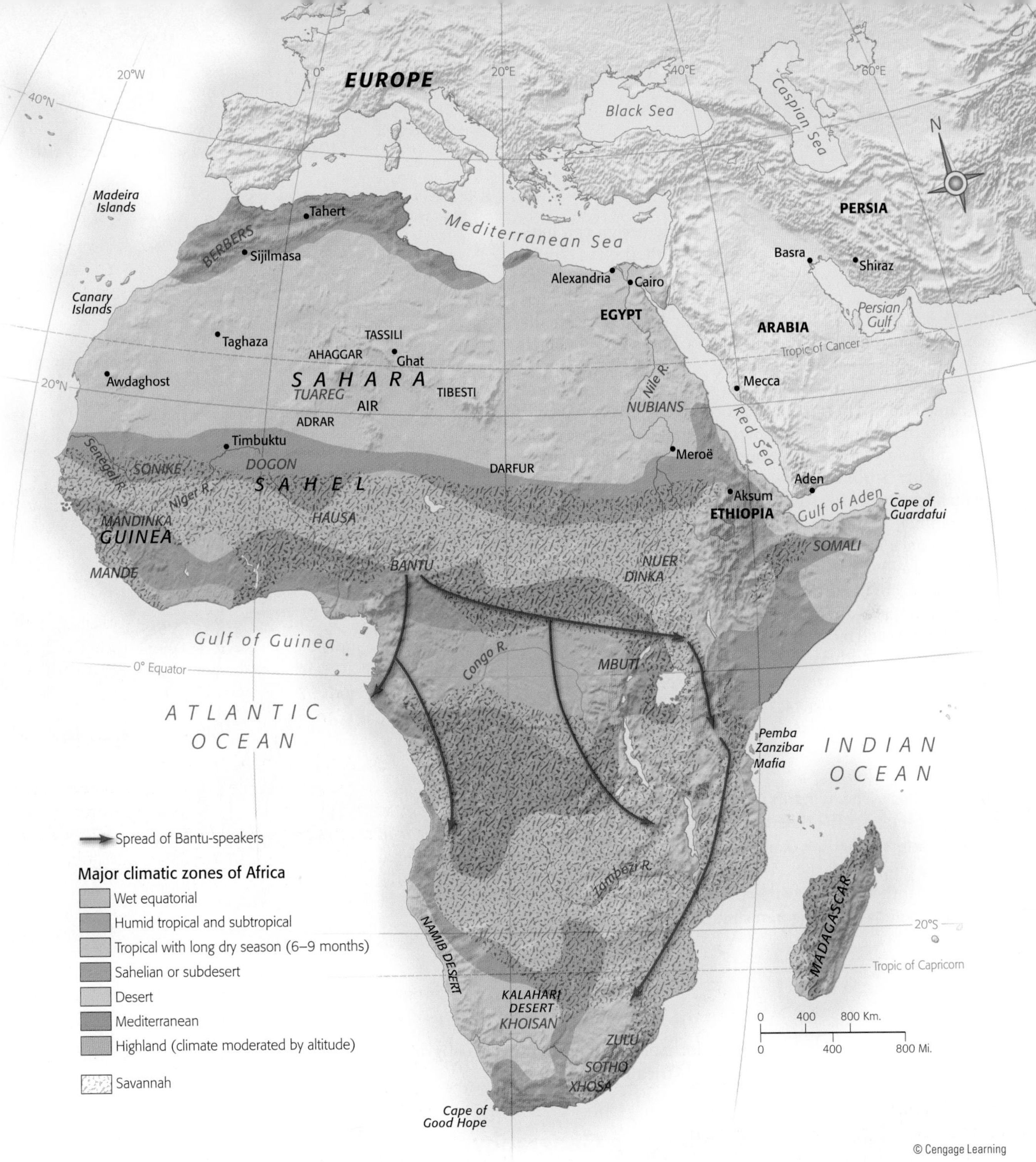

MAP 7.2 Africa and the Trans-Saharan Trade Routes The Sahara and the surrounding oceans isolated most of Africa from foreign contact before 1000 C.E. The Nile Valley, a few trading points on the east coast, and limited transdesert trade provided exceptions to this rule; but the dominant forms of sub-Saharan African culture originated far to the west, north of the Gulf of Guinea.

Interactive Map

SUB-SAHARAN AFRICA

sub-Saharan Africa Portion of the African continent lying south of the Sahara.

The Indian Ocean network and later trade across the Sahara provided **sub-Saharan Africa**, the portion of Africa south of the Sahara, with a few external contacts. The most important African network of cultural exchange from 300 B.C.E. to 1100 C.E., however, arose within the region and

ENVIRONMENT + TECHNOLOGY

Camel Saddles

As seemingly simple a technology as saddle design can indicate a society's economic structure. The south Arabian saddle, a Tunisian example of which is shown to the right, was good for riding, and baggage could easily be tied to the wooden arches at its front. It was militarily inefficient, however, because the rider knelt on the cushion behind the camel's hump, which made it difficult to use weapons.

The north Arabian saddle was a significant improvement that came into use in the first centuries B.C.E. The two arches anchoring the front end of the south Arabian saddle were separated and greatly enlarged, one arch going in front of the hump and the other behind. This formed a solid wooden framework to which loads could easily be attached, but the placement of the prominent front and back arches seated the rider on top of the camel's hump instead of behind it and thereby gave warriors a solid seat and the advantage of height over enemy horsemen. Arabs in northern Arabia used these saddles to take control of the caravan trade through their lands.

The lightest and most efficient riding saddles, shown below, come from the southern Sahara, where personal travel and warfare took priority over trade. These excellent war saddles could not be used for baggage because they did not offer a convenient place to tie bundles.

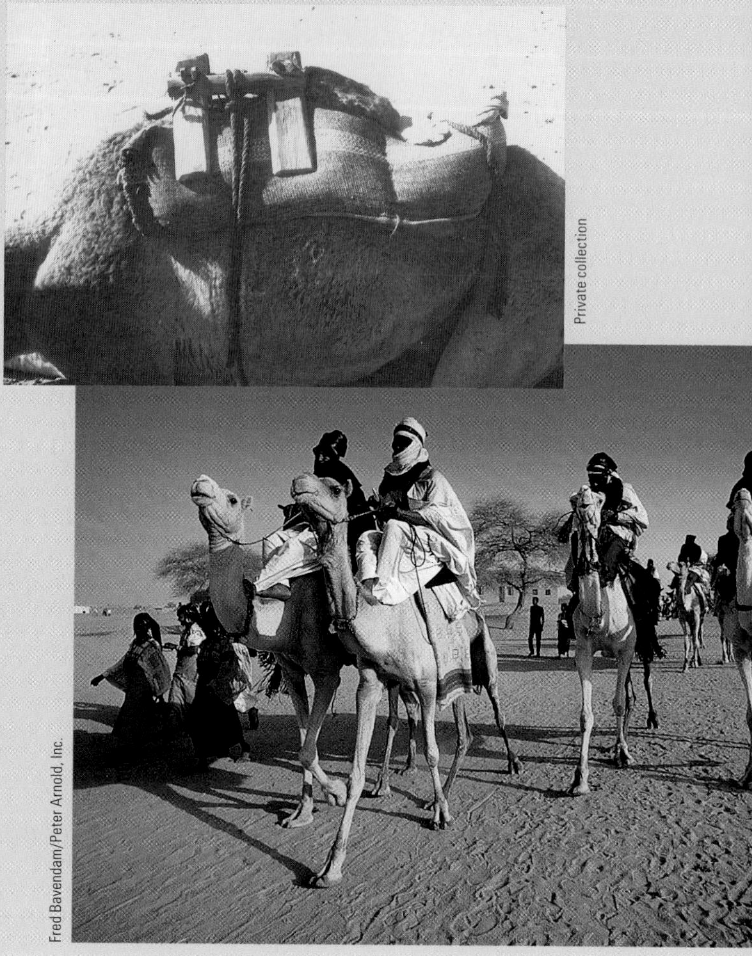

Private collection

Fred Bavendam/Peter Arnold, Inc.

Camel Saddles The militarily inefficient south Arabian saddle (above) seats the rider behind the animal's hump atop its hindquarters. The rider controls his mount by tapping its neck with a long camel stick. The Tuareg saddle (below) seats the rider over the animal's withers, leaving his hands free to wield a sword and letting him control his mount with his toes.

took the form of folk migration. These migrations and exchanges put in place enduring characteristics of African culture.

steppes Treeless plains, especially the high, flat expanses of northern Eurasia, which usually have little rain and are covered with coarse grass. They are good lands for nomads and their herds. Living on the steppes promoted the breeding of horses and the development of military skills that were essential to the rise of the Mongol Empire.

A Challenging Geography

Many geographic obstacles impede access to and movement within sub-Saharan Africa (see Map 7.2). The Sahara, the Atlantic and Indian Oceans, and the Red Sea form the boundaries of the region. With the exception of the Nile, a ribbon of green traversing the Sahara from south to north, the major river systems empty into oceans: the Senegal, Niger, and Zaire (zah-EER) Rivers empty into the Atlantic, and the Zambezi River empties into the Mozambique Channel of the Indian Ocean. Rapids limit the use of these rivers for navigation.

Varying Environments

Stretching over 50 degrees of latitude, sub-Saharan Africa encompasses dramatically different environments. A 4,000-mile (6,500-kilometer) trek from the southern edge of the Sahara to the Cape of Good Hope would take a traveler from the flat, semiarid **steppes** of the Sahel region to tropical **savanna** covered by long grasses and scattered forest, and then to **tropical rain forest** on the lower Niger and in the Zaire Basin. The rain forest gives way to another broad expanse of savanna, followed by more steppe and desert, and finally by a region of temperate highlands at the southern extremity, located as far south of the equator as Greece and Sicily are to its north.

savanna Tropical or subtropical grassland, either treeless or with occasional clumps of trees. Most extensive in sub-Saharan Africa but also present in South America.

tropical rain forest High-precipitation forest zones of the Americas, Africa, and Asia lying between the Tropic of Cancer and the Tropic of Capricorn.

"great traditions" Historians' term for a literate, well-institutionalized complex of religious and social beliefs and practices adhered to by diverse societies over a broad geographical area.

East-west travel is comparatively easy in the steppe and savanna regions—a caravan from Senegal to the Red Sea would have traversed a distance comparable to that of the Silk Road—but difficult in the equatorial rain-forest belt and across the mountains and deep rift valleys that abut the rain forest to the east and separate East from West Africa.

The Development of Cultural Unity

Cultural heritages shared by the educated elites within each region of the world—heritages that some anthropologists call **"great traditions"**—typically include a written language, common legal and belief systems, ethical codes, and other intellectual attitudes. They loom large in written records as traditions that rise above the diversity of local customs and beliefs commonly distinguished as **"small traditions."**

By the year 1 C.E. sub-Saharan Africa had become a distinct cultural region, though one not shaped by imperial conquest or characterized by a shared elite culture, a "great tradition." The cultural unity of sub-Saharan Africa rested on similar characteristics shared to varying degrees by many popular cultures, or "small traditions." These had developed during the region's long period of isolation from the rest of the world and had been refined, renewed, and interwoven by repeated episodes of migration and social interaction. Historians know little about this complex prehistory. Thus, to a greater degree than in other regions, they call on anthropological descriptions, oral history, and comparatively late records of various "small traditions" to reconstruct the broad outlines of cultural formation.

Sub-Saharan Small Traditions

"small traditions" Historians' term for a localized, usually nonliterate, set of customs and beliefs adhered to by a single society, often in conjunction with a "great tradition."

Sub-Saharan Africa's cultural unity is less immediately apparent than its diversity. By one estimate, Africa is home to two thousand distinct languages, many corresponding to social and belief systems endowed with distinctive rituals and cosmologies. There are likewise numerous food production systems, ranging from hunting and gathering—very differently carried out by the Mbuti (m-BOO-tee) Pygmies of the equatorial rain forest and the Khoisan (KOI-sahn) peoples of the southwestern deserts—to the cultivation of bananas, yams, and other root crops in forest clearings and of sorghum and other grains in the savanna lands. Pastoral societies, particularly those depending on cattle, display somewhat less diversity across the Sahel and savanna belt from Senegal to Kenya.

Sub-Saharan Africa covered a larger and more diverse area than any other cultural region in the first millennium C.E. and had a lower overall population density. Thus societies and polities had ample room to form and reform, and a substantial amount of space separated different groups. The contacts that did occur did not last long enough to produce rigid cultural uniformity.

An Isolated World

In addition, for centuries external conquerors could not penetrate the region's natural barriers and impose a uniform culture. The Egyptians occupied Nubia, and some traces of Egyptian influence appear in Saharan rock art farther west, but the Nile cataracts and the vast swampland in the Nile's upper reaches blocked movement farther south. The Romans sent expeditions against pastoral peoples living in the Libyan Sahara but could not incorporate them into the Roman world. Not until the nineteenth century did outsiders gain control of the continent and begin the process of establishing an elite culture—that of European imperialism.

African Cultural Characteristics

European travelers who got to know the sub-Saharan region well in the nineteenth and twentieth centuries observed broad commonalities underlying African life and culture. In agriculture, the common technique was cultivation by hoe and digging stick. Musically, different groups of Africans played many instruments, especially types of drums, but common features, particularly in rhythm, gave African music as a whole a distinctive character. Music played an important role in social rituals, as did dancing and wearing masks, which often showed great artistry in their design.

Kingship and Social Status

Although African kingdoms varied, kingship displayed common features, most notably the ritual isolation of the king himself. Fixed social categories—age groupings, kinship divisions, distinct gender roles and relations, and occupational groupings—also show resemblances from one region to another, even in societies too small to organize themselves into kingdoms. Though not hierarchical, these categories played a role similar to the divisions between noble, commoner, and slave prevalent where kings ruled.

Migration from an Expanding Desert

Some historians hypothesize that these common cultural features emanated from the peoples who once occupied the southern Sahara. In Paleolithic times, periods of dryness alternated with periods of wetness as the Ice Age that locked up much of the world's fresh water in glaciers and icecaps came and went. When European glaciers receded with the waning of the Ice Age, a storm belt brought increased wetness to the Saharan region. Rushing rivers scoured deep canyons. Now filled with fine sand, those canyons are easily visible on flights over the southern parts of the desert. As the glaciers receded farther, the storm belt moved northward to Europe, and dryness set in after 5000 B.C.E. As a consequence, runs the hypothesis, the region's population migrated southward, becoming increasingly concentrated in the Sahel, which may have been the initial incubation center for Pan-African cultural patterns.

Increasing dryness and the resulting difficulty in supporting the population would have driven some people out of this core into more sparsely settled lands to the east, west, and south. In a parallel development farther to the east, migration away from the growing aridity of the desert seems to have contributed to the settling of the Nile Valley and the emergence of the Old Kingdom of Egypt (see Chapter 1).

It seems likely, however, that models of migration and expansion of this sort oversimplify the complexity of contacts between human groups. The idea of migrants with supposedly superior skills asserting dominance over preexisting populations in other historical situations has often been refuted by deeper historical research.

The Advent of Iron and the Bantu Migrations

Archaeology confirms that agriculture had become common between the equator and the Sahara by the early second millennium B.C.E. It then spread southward, displacing hunting and gathering as a way of life. Moreover, botanical evidence indicates that banana trees, probably introduced to southeastern Africa from Southeast Asia, made their way north and west, retracing in the opposite direction the presumed migration routes of the first agriculturists.

Archaeology has also uncovered traces of copper mining in the Sahara from the early first millennium B.C.E. Copper appears in the Niger Valley somewhat later and in the Central African copper belt after 400 C.E. Most important of all, iron smelting began in northern sub-Saharan Africa in the early first millennium C.E. and spread southward from there.

Early Metalworking

Many historians believe that the secret of smelting iron, which requires very high temperatures, was discovered only once, by the Hittites of Anatolia (modern Turkey) around 1500 B.C.E. (see Chapter 3). If that is the case, it is hard to explain how iron smelting reached sub-Saharan Africa. The earliest evidence of ironworking from the kingdom of Meroë, situated on the upper Nile and in cultural contact with Egypt, is no earlier than the evidence from West Africa (northern Nigeria). Even less plausible than the Nile Valley as a route of technological diffusion is the idea of a spread southward from Phoenician settlements in North Africa, since archaeological evidence has failed to substantiate the vague Greek and Latin accounts of Phoenician excursions to the south.

A more plausible scenario focuses on Africans' discovering for themselves how to smelt iron. Some historians suggest that they might have done so while firing pottery in kilns. No firm evidence exists to prove or disprove this theory.

Linguistic Relations

Bantu Collective name of a large group of sub-Saharan African languages and of the peoples speaking these languages.

AP* Exam Tip The Bantu migrations is an important comparison topic.

Linguistic analysis provides the strongest evidence of extensive contacts among sub-Saharan Africans in the first millennium C.E.—and offers suggestions about the spread of iron. More than three hundred languages spoken south of the equator belong to the branch of the Niger-Congo family known as **Bantu**, after the word meaning "people" in most of the languages.

The distribution of the Bantu languages both north and south of the equator is consistent with a divergence beginning in the first millennium B.C.E. By comparing core words common to most of the languages, linguists have drawn some conclusions about the original Bantu-speakers, whom they call "proto-Bantu." These people engaged in fishing, using canoes, nets, lines, and hooks. They lived in permanent villages on the edge of the rain forest, where they grew yams and grains and harvested wild palm nuts from which they pressed oil. They possessed domesticated goats, dogs, and perhaps other animals. They also made pottery and cloth. Linguists surmise that the proto-Bantu homeland was near the modern boundary of Nigeria and Cameroon.

Because the presumed home of the proto-Bantu lies near the known sites of early iron smelting, migration by Bantu-speakers seems a likely mechanism for the southward spread of iron. The migrants probably used iron axes and hoes to hack out forest clearings and plant crops. According to this scenario, their actions would have established an economic basis for new societies capable of sustaining much denser populations than could earlier societies dependent on hunting and gathering alone. Thus the period from 500 B.C.E. to 1000 C.E. saw a massive transfer of Bantu traditions and practices southward, eastward, and westward and their transformation, through intermingling with preexisting societies, into Pan-African traditions and practices.

SECTION REVIEW

- An environmentally diverse region, sub-Saharan Africa includes many barriers to travel and communication.
- Sub-Saharan Africa achieved a cultural unity of similar "small traditions," including agricultural methods, approaches to music, forms of kingship, and fixed social categories.
- The likely mechanism of this unity was the Bantu migrations, which were also responsible for the spread of iron smelting throughout sub-Saharan Africa.

THE SPREAD OF IDEAS

Ideas, like social customs, religious attitudes, and artistic styles, can spread along trade routes and through folk migrations. In both cases, documenting the dissemination of ideas, particularly in preliterate societies, poses a difficult historical problem.

Ideas and Material Evidence

Domestic Pigs

Historians know about some ideas only through the survival of written sources. Other ideas do not depend on writing but are inherent in material objects studied by archaeologists and anthropologists. Customs surrounding the eating of pork are a case in point. Scholars disagree about whether pigs became domestic in only one place, from which the practice of pig keeping spread elsewhere, or whether several peoples hit on the same idea at different times and in different places.

Southeast Asia was an important early center of pig domestication. Anthropological studies tell us that the eating of pork became highly ritualized in this area and that it was sometimes allowed only on ceremonial occasions. On the other side of the Indian Ocean, wild swine were common in the Nile swamps of ancient Egypt. There, too, pigs took on a sacred role, being associated with the evil god Set, and eating them was prohibited. The biblical prohibition on the Israelites' eating pork, echoed later by the Muslims, probably came from Egypt in the second millennium B.C.E.

In a third locale in eastern Iran, an archaeological site dating from the third millennium B.C.E. provides evidence of another religious taboo relating to pork. Although the area around the site was swampy and home to many wild pigs, not a single pig bone has been found. Yet small pig figurines seem to have been used as symbolic religious offerings, and the later Iranian religion associates the boar with an important god.

What accounts for the apparent connection between domestic pigs and religion in these far-flung areas? There is no way of knowing. It has been hypothesized that pigs were first domesticated in Southeast Asia by people who had no herd animals—sheep, goats, cattle, or horses—and who relied on fish for most of their animal protein. The pig therefore became a special animal to them. The practice of pig herding, along with religious beliefs and rituals associated with the consumption of pork, could conceivably have spread from Southeast Asia along the maritime routes of the Indian Ocean, eventually reaching Iran and Egypt. But no evidence survives to support this hypothesis. In this case, therefore, material evidence can only hint at the spread of religious ideas, leaving the door open for other explanations.

The Beginning of Coinage

A more certain example of objects' indicating the spread of an idea is the practice of hammering a carved die onto a piece of precious metal and using the resulting coin as a medium of exchange. From its origin in the Lydian kingdom in Anatolia in the first millennium B.C.E. (see Chapter 4), the idea of trading by means of struck coinage spread rapidly to Europe, North Africa, and India. Was the low-value copper coinage of China, made by pouring molten metal

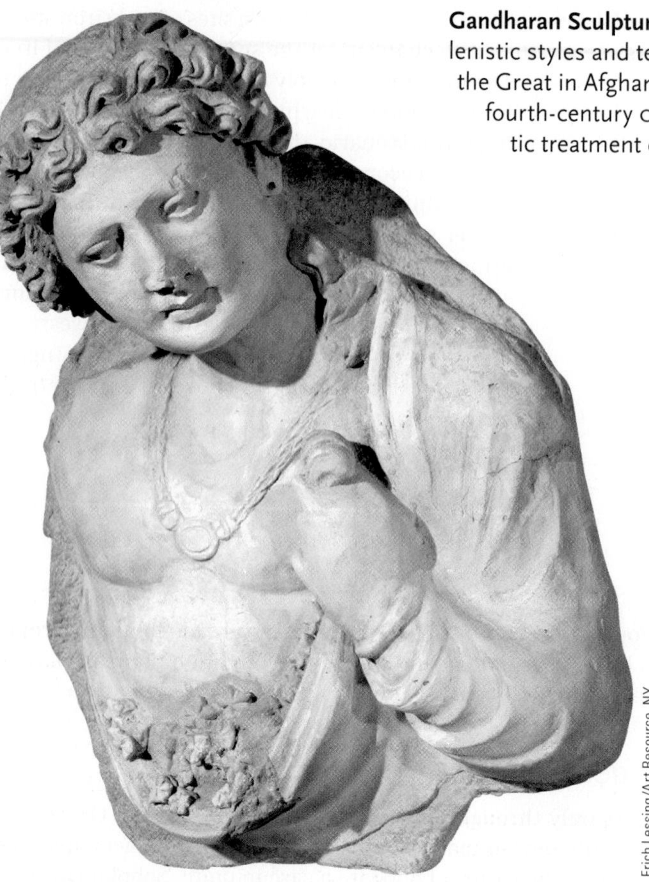

Gandharan Sculpture The art of Gandhara in northwest Pakistan featured Hellenistic styles and techniques borrowed from the cities founded by Alexander the Great in Afghanistan. Though much Gandharan art is Buddhist in spirit, this fourth-century C.E. image of a flower-bearer is strongly Greek in the naturalistic treatment of the head and left arm.

Erich Lessing/Art Resource, NY

into a mold, also inspired by this practice from far away? It may have been, but it might also derive from indigenous Chinese metalworking. There is no way to be sure.

The Spread of Buddhism

While material objects associated with religious beliefs and rituals are important indicators of the spread of spiritual ideas, written sources deal with the spread of today's major religions. Buddhism grew to become, with Christianity and Islam (see Chapter 8), one of the most popular and widespread religions in the world. In all three cases, the religious ideas spread without dependency on a single ethnic or kinship group.

Two Kings: Ashoka and Kanishka

King Ashoka, the Mauryan ruler of India, and Kanishka, the greatest king of the Kushans of northern Afghanistan, promoted Buddhism between the third century B.C.E. and the second century C.E. However, monks, missionaries, and pilgrims who crisscrossed India, followed the Silk Road, or took ships on the Indian Ocean brought the Buddha's teachings to Southeast Asia, China, Korea, and ultimately Japan (see Map 7.1).

e PRIMARY SOURCE: Memorial on Buddhism Read how Han Yu, upset at the growing influence of Buddhism, denigrated that religion as "un-Chinese" in a text addressed to the Tang emperor.

The Chinese pilgrim Faxian (fah-shee-en) (died between 418 and 423 C.E.) left a written account of his travels. Faxian began his trip in the company of a Chinese envoy to an unspecified ruler or people in Central Asia. After traveling from one Buddhist site to another across Afghanistan and India, he reached Sri Lanka, a Buddhist land, where he lived for two years. He then embarked for China on a merchant ship with two hundred men aboard. A storm drove the ship to Java, which he chose not to describe since it was Hindu rather than Buddhist. After five months ashore, Faxian finally reached China on another ship.

Less reliable accounts make reference to missionaries traveling to Syria, Egypt, and Macedonia, as well as to Southeast Asia. One of Ashoka's sons allegedly led a band of missionaries to Sri Lanka. Later, his sister brought a company of nuns there, along with a branch of the sacred Bo tree under which the Buddha had received enlightenment. At the same time, there are reports of other monks traveling to Burma, Thailand, and Sumatra. Ashoka's missionaries may also have reached Tibet by way of trade routes across the Himalayas.

Theravada and Mahayana Buddhism

The different lands that received the story and teachings of the Buddha preserved or adapted them in different ways. Theravada Buddhism, "Teachings of the Elder," was centered in Sri Lanka. Holding closely to the Buddha's earliest teachings, it maintained that the goal of religion, available only to monks, is *nirvana*, the total absence of suffering and the end of the cycle of rebirth (see Chapter 6). This teaching contrasted with Mahayana, or "Great Vehicle" Buddhism, which stressed the goal of becoming a *bodhisattva*, a person who attains nirvana but chooses to remain in human company to help and guide others.

The Spread of Christianity

The post-Roman development of Christianity in Europe is discussed in Chapter 9. The Christian faith enjoyed an earlier spread in Asia and Africa before its confrontation with Islam (described

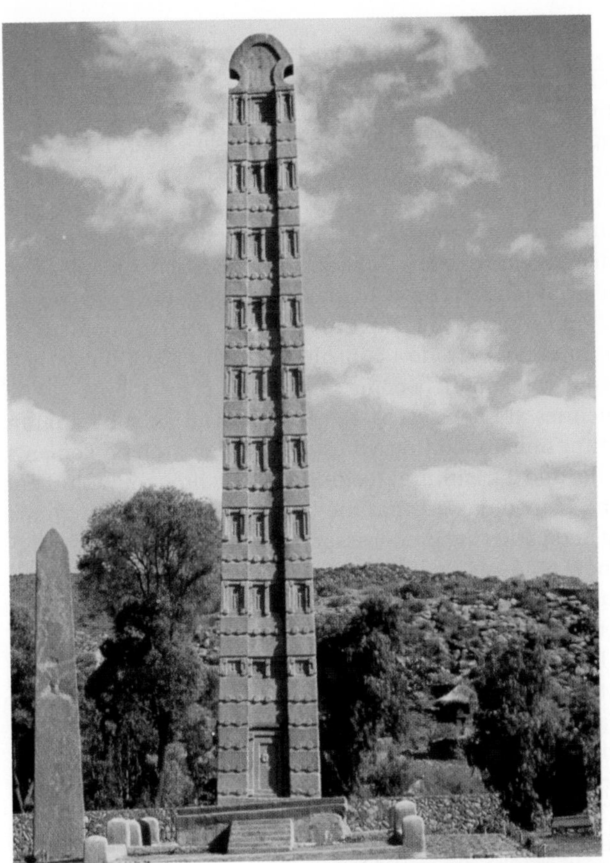

J. Allan Cash

Stele of Aksum This 70-foot (21-meter) stone is the tallest remnant of a field of stelae, or standing stones, marking the tombs of Aksumite kings. The carvings of doors, windows, and beam ends imitate common features of Aksumite architecture, suggesting that each stele symbolized a multistory royal palace. The largest stelae date from the fourth century C.E.

in Chapter 8). Jerusalem in Palestine, Antioch in Syria, and Alexandria in Egypt became centers of Christian authority soon after the crucifixion, but the spread of Christianity to Armenia and Ethiopia illustrates the connections between religion, trade, and imperial politics.

Situated in eastern Anatolia (modern Turkey), **Armenia** served recurrently as a battleground between Iranian states to the south and east and Mediterranean states to the west. Each imperial power wanted to control this region so close to the frontier where Silk Road traders met their Mediterranean counterparts. In Parthian times, Armenia's kings favored Zoroastrianism. The invention of an Armenian alphabet in the early fifth century opened the way to a wider spread of Christianity. The Iranians did not give up domination easily, but within a century the Armenian Apostolic Church had become the center of Armenian cultural life.

Armenia

Armenia One of the earliest Christian kingdoms, situated in eastern Anatolia and the western Caucasus and occupied by speakers of the Armenian language.

Ethiopia and Aksum

Ethiopia East African highland nation lying east of the Nile River.

Far to the south Christians similarly sought to outflank Iran. The Christian emperors in Constantinople (see Chapter 9) sent missionaries along the Red Sea trade route to seek converts in Yemen and **Ethiopia**. In the fourth century C.E. a Syrian philosopher traveling with two young relatives sailed to India. On the way back the ship docked at a Red Sea port occupied by Ethiopians from the prosperous kingdom of Aksum. Being then at odds with the Romans, the Ethiopians killed everyone on board except the two boys, Aedisius—who later narrated this story—and Frumentius. Impressed by their learning, the king made the former his cupbearer and the latter his treasurer and secretary.

When the king died, his wife urged Frumentius to govern Aksum on her behalf and that of her infant son, Ezana. As regent, Frumentius sought out Roman Christians among the merchants who visited the country and helped them establish Christian communities. When he became king, Ezana, who may have become a Christian, permitted Aedisius and Frumentius to return to Syria. The patriarch of Alexandria, on learning about the progress of Christianity in Aksum, elevated Frumentius to the rank of bishop, though he had not previously been a clergyman, and sent him back to Ethiopia as the first leader of its church.

The spread of Christianity into Nubia, the land south of Egypt along the Nile River, proceeded from Ethiopia rather than Egypt. Politically and economically, Ethiopia became a power at the western end of the Indian Ocean trading system, occasionally even extending its influence across the Red Sea and asserting itself in Yemen (see Map 7.2).

SECTION REVIEW

- Material evidence can only offer hints about the spread of ideas, such as the widespread veneration of pigs.
- Material and documentary evidence show the spread of Buddhism from India along the land and sea trade routes to elsewhere in Asia.
- Lands in which Buddhism took hold adapted its teachings in different ways, a process that resulted in the split between Mahayana and Theravada.
- Christianity spread through a combination of trade and imperial politics, with significant Christian societies emerging in Armenia and Ethiopia.

CONCLUSION

Exchange facilitated by the early long-distance trading systems differed in many ways from the ebb and flow of culture, language, and custom that folk migrations brought about. Transportable goods and livestock and ideas about new technologies and agricultural products sometimes worked great changes on the landscape and in people's lives. But nothing resembling the commonality of African cultural features observed south of the Sahara can be attributed to the societies involved in the Silk Road, Indian Ocean, or trans-Saharan exchanges. Few people were directly involved in these complex social systems of travel and trade compared with the populations with whom they were brought into contact, and their lifestyles as pastoral nomads or seafarers isolated them still more. Communities of traders contributed to this isolation by their reluctance to share knowledge with people who might become commercial competitors.

The Bantu, however, if current theories are correct, spread far and wide in sub-Saharan Africa with the deliberate intent of settling and implanting a lifestyle based on iron implements and agriculture. The metallurgical skills and agricultural techniques they brought with them permitted much denser habitation and helped ensure that the languages of the immigrants would supplant those of their hunting and gathering predecessors. Where the trading systems encouraged diversity by introducing new products and ideas, the Bantu migrations brought a degree of cultural dominance that strongly affected later African history.

An apparent exception to the generalization that trading systems have less impact than folk migrations on patterns of dominance lies in the intangible area of ideas. Christianity, Judaism, Zoroastrianism (the state religion of the Sasanid Empire), and Buddhism both spread along trade routes, at least to some degree. Each instance of spread, however, gave rise to new forms of cultural diversity even as overall doctrinal unity made these religions dominant. As "great traditions," the new faiths based on conversion linked priests, monks, nuns, and religious scholars across vast distances. However, these same religions merged with myriad "small traditions" to provide for the social and spiritual needs of peoples living in many lands under widely varying circumstances.

KEY TERMS

Silk Road p. 202
Parthians p. 202
Sasanid Empire p. 205
stirrup p. 206
Indian Ocean Maritime System p. 207
trans-Saharan caravan routes p. 211
Sahel p. 212
sub-Saharan Africa p. 213
steppes p. 214
savanna p. 215
tropical rain forest p. 215
"great traditions" p. 215
"small traditions" p. 215
Bantu p. 216
Armenia p. 219
Ethiopia p. 219

EBOOK AND WEBSITE RESOURCES

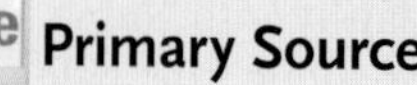

Primary Source

Memorial on Buddhism

Interactive Maps

Map 7.1 Asian Trade and Communication Routes

Map 7.2 Africa and the Trans-Saharan Trade Routes

Plus flashcards, practice quizzes, and more. Go to: www.cengage.com/history/bullietearthpeople5e

SUGGESTED READING

Ajayi, J. F. A., and Michael Crowder. *A History of West Africa*, vol. 1. 1976. A broad survey.

Bulliet, Richard W. *The Camel and the Wheel*. 1975. Deals with camel use in the Middle East, along the Silk Road, and in North Africa and the Sahara.

Chaudhuri, K. N. *Trade and Civilization in the Indian Ocean: An Economic History from the Rise of Islam to 1750*. 1985. First volume of a comprehensive history.

Curtin, Philip D. *Cross-Cultural Trade in World History*. 1985. A broad and suggestive overview on cross-cultural exchange.

Ehret, Christopher. *An African Classical Age: Eastern and Southern Africa in World History, 1000 B.C. to A.D. 400*. 2001. A historical survey.

Foltz, Richard. *Religions of the Silk Road*. 1999. An excellent brief introduction covering Buddhism, Zoroastrianism, and Islam.

Fowden, Garth. *Empire to Commonwealth: Consequences of Monotheism in Late Antiquity*. 1993. A history of early Christianity placing special stress on Africa and Asia.

Franck, Irene M., and David M. Brownstone. *The Silk Road: A History*. 1986. A readable overview.

Jettmar, Karl. *Art of the Steppes*, rev. ed. 1967. A well-illustrated introduction to early Central Asia.

Lattimore, Owen. *The Desert Road to Turkestan*. 1928. Gives a first-person account of traveling by camel caravan.

Lhote, Henri. *The Search for the Tassili Frescoes: The Story of the Prehistoric Rock-Paintings of the Sahara*. 1959. A well-illustrated account of discovering Saharan rock art.

Maquet, Jacques. *Africanity: The Cultural Unity of Black Africa*. 1972. An interpretation informed by anthropological insights.

Rolle, Renate. *The World of the Scythians*. 1989. Early evidence of the lifestyles of Central Asian nomads.

Toussaint, August. *History of the Indian Ocean*. 1966. A readable but sketchy historical overview.

Villiers, Alan. *Sons of Sinbad*. 1940. Recounts what it was like to sail dhows (Indian Ocean sailing vessels) between East Africa and the Persian Gulf.

NOTES

1. Victor H. Mair, ed., *The Columbia Anthology of Traditional Chinese Literature* (New York: Columbia University Press, 1994), 485; translated by Victor H. Mair.

AP* REVIEW QUESTIONS FOR CHAPTER 7

1. Samarkand, Bukhara, and Chang'an all have in common the fact that

   (A) they were all part of the Persian Empire.
   (B) they were all cities on the Silk Road.
   (C) they were all part of the Tang Empire.
   (D) they were major port cities along the Indian Ocean.

2. The Chinese emperor Wu commanded Zhang Jian to cross the western mountains into Central Asia to

   (A) explore the lands of the nomads who lived on China's northwest frontier.
   (B) find new markets for Chinese products.
   (C) defeat the Parthians.
   (D) obtain new silver deposits to expand the Chinese coinage system.

3. In comparison to the Parthians, the Sasanids

   (A) expanded into Egypt and Saudi Arabia.
   (B) encouraged the growth of Buddhism in Iran.
   (C) were centered primarily in Iraq.
   (D) expanded into Indian Ocean trading.

4. Which of the following is true of Zoroastrianism?

   (A) It was founded by Hindus fleeing Buddhist persecution.
   (B) Its emergence as a major religion is due entirely to the Silk Road trade.
   (C) It has its origins in the Malay Peninsula and entered Iran via sea trade.
   (D) It became the official faith of the Sasanid Empire.

5. One of the most important early cultural products to cross the Silk Road was

   (A) wheat.
   (B) lateen sails.
   (C) the hand loom.
   (D) the stirrup.

6. Which of the following is true of Indian Ocean trade before 600 C.E.?

   (A) It was likely established by multilingual, multiethnic seafarers.
   (B) It was limited to the Persian Gulf region of the Indian Ocean.
   (C) It was a one-way trade from India to China.
   (D) It included all Indian Ocean regions except Africa.

7. As the Indian Ocean trade began to develop in the time prior to 600 C.E.,

   (A) the volume of goods traded across the Indian Ocean is likely to have rivaled the trade on the Mediterranean Sea in that time period.
   (B) direct voyages across the Indian Ocean were unlikely, making southern Arabia and India probable stopping places.
   (C) Indian Ocean trade was always directly linked to trade in the hinterlands.
   (D) East African slaves became major trade goods across the Indian Ocean.

8. Which of the following is true of the trans-Saharan trade route prior to 600 C.E.?

   (A) It was established under the Roman Empire.
   (B) Its growth relates largely to the spread of camel domestication.
   (C) It dates to the time of the Egyptian Empire.
   (D) It was a major link to the Indian Ocean routes.

9. By 1 C.E. sub-Saharan Africa

   (A) was divided into six large empires.
   (B) had no major ethnic diversities.
   (C) was culturally similar in many characteristics.
   (D) was linguistically unified by Swahili.

10. Which of the following is the best example of ideas spreading across a trade route?

    (A) Coins as a medium of exchange
    (B) Religious rivalries
    (C) Social customs
    (D) Clothing styles

PART III

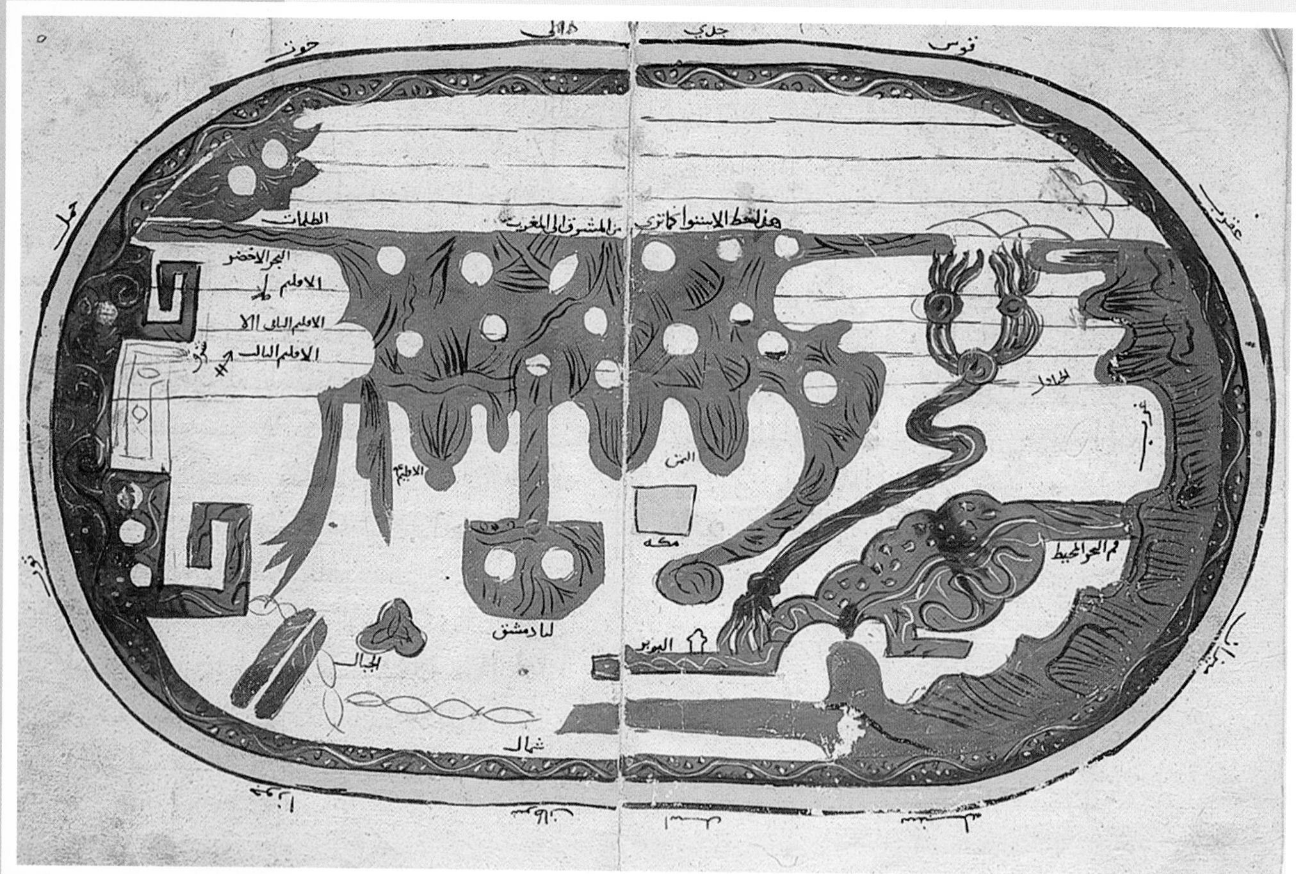

Courtesy, Suleymaniye Library, Istanbul

Islamic World Map The oldest surviving world maps come from medieval Islamic culture. This example, a fourteenth-century copy of a presumed tenth-century original, is unusual in being oblong instead of round. South is at the top. The Mediterranean Sea is in blue in the lower right quadrant, with the Nile River extending upward until it ends in two sets of smaller streams at the Mountains of the Moon. Other bodies of water are green, except for the Encircling Sea that surrounds the entire map. The yellow square is Mecca.

Growth and Interaction of Cultural Communities, 600–1200

In 300 B.C.E., societies had only limited contacts beyond their frontiers. By 1200 C.E., this situation had changed. Traders, migrating peoples, and missionaries brought peoples together. Products and technologies moved along long-distance trade networks: the Silk Road across Asia, Saharan caravan routes, and sea-lanes connecting the Indian Ocean coastlands.

Migrating Bantu peoples from West Africa spread iron and new farming techniques through much of sub-Saharan Africa and helped foster a distinctive African culture. Conquering Arabs from the Arabian peninsula, inspired by the Prophet Muhammad, established Muslim rule from Spain to India, laying the foundation of a new culture.

In Asia, missionaries and pilgrims helped Buddhism spread from India to Sri Lanka, Tibet, Southeast Asia, and East Asia. The new faith interacted with older philosophies and religions to produce distinctive cultural patterns. Simultaneously, the Tang Empire in China disseminated Chinese culture and technologies throughout Inner and East Asia.

In Europe, monks and missionaries spread Christian beliefs that became enmeshed with new political and social structures: a struggle between royal and church authority in western Europe; a union of religious and imperial authority in the Byzantine east; and a similar but distinctive society in Kievan Russia. The Crusades reconnected western Europe with the lands of the east.

In the Western Hemisphere, the development of urban, agricultural civilizations in the Andes, the Yucatán lowlands, and the central plateau of Mexico climaxed in the Maya, Aztec, and Inca cultures. The cultural exchanges and interactions that mark this era in Eurasia and Africa have counterparts in the Western Hemisphere.

CHAPTER

8

CHAPTER OUTLINE

- The Origins of Islam
- The Rise and Fall of the Caliphate, 632–1258
- Islamic Civilization
- Conclusion

DIVERSITY + DOMINANCE *Secretaries, Turks, and Beggars*

ENVIRONMENT + TECHNOLOGY *Chemistry*

MATERIAL CULTURE *Head Coverings*

Bibliotheque nationale de France

Baghdad Bookstore With the advent of papermaking, manufacturing books became increasingly common and inexpensive. As a result, bookstores also became more common. Notice how books are shelved on their sides in wall cubicles.

Visit the website and ebook for additional study materials and interactive tools: www.cengage.com/history/bullietearthpeople5e

The Rise of Islam, 600–1200

- How did the traditions and religious views of pre-Islamic peoples become integrated into the culture shaped by Islam?
- How did the Muslim community of the time of Muhammad differ from the society that developed after the Arab conquests?
- Was the Baghdad caliphate really the high point of Muslim civilization?
- How did regional diversity affect the development of Islamic civilization?

Knowledge of papermaking, which spread from China to the Middle East after Arab conquests in the seventh century C.E. established an Islamic caliphate stretching from Spain to Central Asia, provided a medium that was superior to papyrus and parchment and well suited to a variety of purposes. Maps, miniature paintings, and, of course, books became increasingly common and inexpensive. With cheaper books came bookstores, and one of the most informative manuscripts of the period of the Islamic caliphate is a *Fihrist*, or descriptive catalog, of the books sold at one bookstore in Baghdad.

Abu al-Faraj Muhammad al-Nadim, a man with good connections at the caliph's court, compiled the catalog, though his father probably founded the bookstore. Its latest entry dates to ca. 990, al-Nadim's death date. Superbly educated, al-Nadim wrote such well-informed comments on books and authors that his catalog presents a detailed survey of the intellectual world of Baghdad.

The first of the *Fihrist*'s ten books deals with Arabic language and sacred scriptures: the Quran, the Torah, and the Gospel. The second covers Arabic grammar, and the third writings from people connected with the caliph's court: historians, government officials, singers, jesters, and the ruler's boon companions. *Al-Nadim* means "book companion," so it is assumed that he knew this milieu well. After dealing with Arabic poetry, Muslim sects, and Islamic law in Books 3 through 6, he comes to Greek philosophy, science, and medicine in Book 7.

Most things we would find today in a bookstore are relegated to the final three chapters. Book 8 divides into three sections, the first being "Story Tellers and Stories." Here he lists a Persian book called *A Thousand Stories*, which in translation became *The Arabian Nights*. Al-Nadim's version no longer survives. The collection we have today comes from a manuscript written five hundred years later.

Then come sections about "Exorcists, Jugglers, and Magicians," followed by "Miscellaneous Subjects and Fables." These include sections on "Freckles, Twitching, Moles, and Shoulders," "Horsemanship, Bearing of Arms, the Implements of War," "Veterinary Surgery," "Birds of Prey, Sport with Them and Medical Care of Them," "Interpretation of Dreams," "Perfume," "Cooked Food," "Poisons," and "Amulets and Charms." Non-Muslim sects and foreign lands—India, Indochina, and China—fill Book 9, leaving Book 10 for a few final notes on philosophers not mentioned previously.

All together, the thousands of titles and authors commented on by al-Nadim provide both a panorama of what interested book buyers in tenth-century Baghdad and a saddening picture of how profound the loss of knowledge has been since that glorious era.

THE ORIGINS OF ISLAM

The Arabian Peninsula Before Muhammad

AP* Exam Tip The origin of Islam is an important topic on both the multiple choice and the essay section of the AP exam.

The Arabs of 600 C.E. lived exclusively in the Arabian peninsula and on the desert fringes of Syria, Jordan, and Iraq. Along their Euphrates frontier, the Sasanids (see Chapter 7) subsidized nomadic Arab chieftains to protect their empire from invasion. The Byzantines did the same with Arabs on their Jordanian frontier. Arab pastoralists farther to the south remained isolated and independent, seldom engaging the attention of the shahs and emperors. It was in these interior Arabian lands that the religion of Islam took form.

Throughout history more people living on the Arabian peninsula have subsisted as farmers than as pastoral nomads. Farming villages support the comparatively dense population of Yemen, where abundant rainfall waters the highlands during the spring monsoon. Small inlets along the southern coast favored fishing and trading communities. The enormous sea of sand known as the "Empty Quarter" isolated many southern regions from the Arabian interior. In the seventh century, most people in southern Arabia knew more about Africa, India, and the Persian Gulf than about the forbidding interior and the scattered camel- and sheep-herding nomads who lived there.

Caravan Trade

Caravan trading provided a rare link among peoples. Nomads derived income from providing camels, guides, and safe passage to merchants bringing the primary product of the south, the aromatic resins frankincense and myrrh, to northern customers. Return caravans brought manufactured products from Mesopotamia and Syria.

Nomad dominance of the caravan trade received a boost from the invention of militarily efficient camel saddles. This contributed to the rise of Arab-dominated caravan cities and to Arab pastoralists becoming the primary suppliers of animal power throughout the region. By 600 C.E., wheeled vehicles—mostly ox carts and horse-drawn chariots—had all but disappeared from the Middle East, replaced by pack camels and donkeys.

As explained in Chapter 7, Arabs who accompanied the caravans became familiar with the cultures and lifestyles of the Sasanid and Byzantine Empires, and many of those who pastured their herds on the imperial frontiers adopted one form or another of Christianity. Even in the interior deserts, Semitic polytheism, with its worship of natural forces and celestial bodies, began to encounter more sophisticated religions.

Mecca City in western Arabia; birthplace of the Prophet Muhammad and ritual center of the Islamic religion.

Mecca, a Caravan City

Mecca, a late-blooming caravan city, occupies a barren mountain valley halfway between Yemen and Syria and somewhat inland from the Red Sea coast (see Map 8.1). A nomadic kin group known as the Quraysh (koo-RYYSH) settled in Mecca in the fifth century and assumed control of trade. Mecca rapidly achieved a measure of prosperity, partly because it was too far from Byzantine Syria, Sasanid Iraq, and Ethiopian-controlled Yemen for them to attack it.

Pilgrimage Center

A cubical shrine with idols inside called the Ka'ba (KAH-buh), a holy well called Zamzam, and a sacred precinct surrounding the two wherein killing was prohibited contributed to the emergence of Mecca as a pilgrimage site. Some Meccans associated the shrine with stories known to Jews and Christians. They regarded Abraham (Ibrahim in Arabic) as the builder of the Ka'ba, and they identified a site outside Mecca as the location where God asked Abraham to sacrifice his son. The son was not Isaac (Ishaq in Arabic), the son of Sarah, but Ishmael (Isma'il in Arabic), the son of Hagar, cited in the Bible as the forefather of the Arabs.

Muhammad in Mecca

Muhammad Arab prophet; founder of religion of Islam.

Born in Mecca in 570, **Muhammad** grew up an orphan in the house of his uncle. He engaged in trade and married a Quraysh widow named Khadija (kah-DEE-juh), whose caravan inter-

CHRONOLOGY

	The Arab Lands	Iran and Central Asia
200		
	570–632 Life of the Prophet Muhammad	
600		
	634 Conquests of Iraq and Syria commence	
	639–42 Conquest of Egypt by Arabs	
	656–61 Ali caliph; first civil war	
	661–750 Umayyad Caliphate rules from Damascus	
700		
	711 Berbers and Arabs invade Spain from North Africa	711 Arabs capture Sind in India
		747 Abbasid revolt begins in Khurasan
	750 Beginning of Abbasid Caliphate	
	755 Umayyad state established in Spain	
	776–809 Caliphate of Harun al-Rashid	
800		
	835–92 Abbasid capital moved from Baghdad to Samarra	
		875 Independent Samanid state founded in Bukhara
900		
	909 Fatimids seize North Africa, found Shi'ite Caliphate	
	929 Abd al-Rahman III declares himself caliph in Cordoba	
	945 Shi'ite Buyids take control in Baghdad	945 Buyids from northern Iran take control of Abbasid Caliphate
	969 Fatimids conquer Egypt	
1000		
		1036 Beginning of Turkish Seljuk rule in Khurasan
	1055 Seljuk Turks take control in Baghdad	
	1099 First Crusade captures Jerusalem	
	1171 Fall of Fatimid Egypt	
	1187 Saladin recaptures Jerusalem	
	1250 Mamluks control Egypt	
	1258 Mongols sack Baghdad and end Abbasid Caliphate	
	1260 Mamluks defeat Mongols at Ain Jalut	

ests he superintended. Their son died in childhood, but several daughters survived. Around 610 Muhammad began meditating at night in the mountainous terrain around Mecca. During one night vigil, known to later tradition as the "Night of Power and Excellence," a being whom Muhammad later understood to be the angel Gabriel (Jibra'il in Arabic) spoke to him:

> *Proclaim! In the name of your Lord who created. Created man from a clot of congealed blood. Proclaim! And your Lord is the Most Bountiful. He who has taught by the pen. Taught man that which he knew not.*[1]

"Messenger of God"

For three years Muhammad shared this and subsequent revelations only with close friends and family members. This period culminated in his conviction that he was hearing the words of God (Allah [AH-luh] in Arabic). Khadija, his uncle's son Ali, his friend Abu Bakr (ah-boo BAK-uhr), and others close to him shared this conviction. The revelations continued until Muhammad's death in 632.

Like most people of the time, including Christians and Jews, the Arabs believed in unseen spirits: gods, demonic *shaitans*, and desert spirits called *jinns* who were thought to possess seers and poets. Therefore, when Muhammad recited his rhymed revelations in public, many people believed he was inspired by an unseen spirit, even if it was not, as Muhammad asserted, the one true god.

Muhammad's earliest revelations called on people to witness that one god had created the universe and everything in it, including themselves. At the end of time, their souls would be judged, their sins balanced against their good deeds. The blameless would go to paradise; the sinful would taste hellfire:

> *By the night as it conceals the light;*
> *By the day as it appears in glory;*
> *By the mystery of the creation of male and female;*
> *Verily, the ends ye strive for are diverse.*
> *So he who gives in charity and fears God,*
> *And in all sincerity testifies to the best,*
> *We will indeed make smooth for him the path to Bliss.*
> *But he who is a greedy miser and thinks himself self-sufficient,*
> *And gives the lie to the best,*
> *We will indeed make smooth for him the path to misery.*[2]

Muslim An adherent of the Islamic religion; a person who "submits" (in Arabic, *Islam* means "submission") to the will of God.

Islam Religion expounded by the Prophet Muhammad on the basis of his reception of divine revelations, which were collected after his death into the Quran. In the tradition of Judaism and Christianity, and sharing much of their lore, Islam calls on all people to recognize one creator god—Allah—who rewards or punishes believers after death according to how they led their lives.

The revelation called all people to submit to God and accept Muhammad as the last of his messengers. Doing so made one a **Muslim**, meaning one who makes "submission," **Islam**, to the will of God.

Because earlier messengers mentioned in the revelations included Noah, Moses, and Jesus, Muhammad's hearers connected his message with Judaism and Christianity, religions they were already familiar with. Yet his revelations charged the Jews and Christians with being negligent in preserving God's revealed word. Thus, even though they identified Abraham/Ibrahim, whom Muslims consider the first Muslim, as the builder of the Ka'ba, which superseded Jerusalem as the focus of Muslim prayer in 624, Muhammad's followers considered his revelation more perfect than the Bible because it had not gone through an editing process.

Some scholars maintain that Muhammad appealed especially to people distressed over wealth replacing kinship as the most important aspect of social relations and over neglect of orphans and other powerless people. Most Muslims, however, put less emphasis on a social message than on the power and beauty of Muhammad's recitations.

Formation of the Umma

The Hijra

Medina City in western Arabia to which the Prophet Muhammad and his followers emigrated in 622 to escape persecution in Mecca.

umma The community of all Muslims. A major innovation against the background of seventh-century Arabia, where traditionally kinship rather than faith had determined membership in a community.

Mecca's leaders, fearing that accepting Muhammad as the sole agent of the one true God would threaten their power and prosperity, pressured his kin to disavow him and persecuted the weakest of his followers. Stymied by this hostility, Muhammad and his followers fled Mecca in 622 to take up residence in the agricultural community of **Medina** 215 miles (346 kilometers) to the north. This hijra (HIJ-ruh) marks the beginning of the Muslim calendar.

Prior to the hijra, Medinan representatives had met with Muhammad and agreed to accept and protect him and his followers because they saw him as an inspired leader who could calm their perpetual feuding. Together, the Meccan migrants and major groups in Medina bound themselves into a single **umma** (UM-muh), a community defined by acceptance of Islam and of Muhammad as the "Messenger of God," his most common title. Partly because three Jewish kin groups chose to retain their own faith, the direction of prayer was changed from Jerusalem toward the Ka'ba in Mecca, now thought of as the "House of God."

Having left their Meccan kin groups, the immigrants in Medina felt vulnerable. During the last decade of his life, Muhammad took active responsibility for his umma. Fresh revelations provided a framework for regulating social and legal affairs and stirred the Muslims to fight against the still-unbelieving city of Mecca. At various points during the war, Muhammad charged the Jewish kin groups, whom he had initially hoped would recognize him as God's messenger, with disloyalty, and he finally expelled or eliminated them.

The Surrender of Mecca

The sporadic war, largely conducted by raiding and negotiating with desert nomads, sapped Mecca's strength and convinced many Meccans that God favored Muhammad. In 630 Mecca surrendered, and Muhammad and his followers made the pilgrimage to the Ka'ba unhindered.

MAP 8.1 Early Expansion of Muslim Rule Arab conquests of the first Islamic century brought vast territory under Muslim rule, but conversion to Islam proceeded slowly. In most areas outside the Arabian peninsula, the only region where Arabic was then spoken, conversion did not accelerate until the third century after the conquest.

Interactive Map

PRIMARY SOURCE: The Constitution of Medina: Muslims and Jews at the Dawn of Islam Learn how Muhammad, whose teaching was at first rejected in Mecca, met with success in Medina, in part by allying himself with the local Jewish community.

Muhammad stayed in Medina, which had grown into a bustling city-state. Delegations came to him from all over Arabia and returned home with believers who could teach them about Islam and collect their alms. Muhammad's mission to bring God's message to humanity had brought him unchallenged control of a state that was coming to dominate the Arabian peninsula.

In 632, after a brief illness, Muhammad died. Within twenty-four hours a group of Medinan leaders, along with three of Muhammad's close friends, determined that Abu Bakr, one of the earliest believers and the father of Muhammad's favorite wife A'isha (AH-ee-shah), should succeed him. They called him the *khalifa* (kah-LEE-fuh), or "successor," the English version of which is *caliph*. But calling Abu Bakr a successor did not clarify his powers. Everyone knew that neither Abu Bakr nor anyone else could receive revelations, and they likewise knew that Muhammad's revelations made no provision for succession or for any government purpose beyond maintaining the umma.

Abu Bakr continued and confirmed Muhammad's religious practices, notably the so-called Five Pillars of Islam: (1) avowal that there is only one god and Muhammad is his messenger, (2) prayer five times a day, (3) fasting during the lunar month of Ramadan, (4) paying alms, and (5) making the pilgrimage to Mecca at least once during one's lifetime. He also reestablished and expanded Muslim authority over Arabia's communities, some of which had abandoned their allegiance to Medina or followed various would-be prophets. Muslim armies fought hard to confirm the authority of the newborn **caliphate**. In the process, some fighting spilled over into non-Arab areas in Iraq.

caliphate Office established in succession to the Prophet Muhammad, to rule the Islamic empire; also the name of that empire.

Quran Book composed of divine revelations made to the Prophet Muhammad between ca. 610 and his death in 632; the sacred text of the religion of Islam.

Formation of the Quran

Reportedly, Abu Bakr ordered the men who had written down Muhammad's revelations to collect them in a book. Hitherto written haphazardly on pieces of leather or bone, these now became a single document gathered into chapters. Muslims believe the **Quran** (kuh-RAHN), or the Recitation, acquired its final form around the year 650. They see it not as the words of Muhammad but as the unalterable word of God. Theologically, it compares not so much to the Bible, a book written by many hands over many centuries, as to the person of Jesus Christ, whom Christians consider an earthly manifestation of God.

Muhammad's Cousin Ali

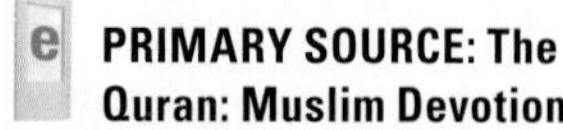

PRIMARY SOURCE: The Quran: Muslim Devotion to God These selections contain a number of the tenets of Islam and shed light on the connections between Islam, Judaism, and Christianity.

Shi'ites Muslims belonging to the branch of Islam believing that God vests leadership of the community in a descendant of Muhammad's son-in-law Ali. Shi'ism is the state religion of Iran.

Though united in accepting God's will, the umma soon disagreed over the succession to the caliphate. When rebels assassinated the third caliph, Uthman (ooth-MAHN), in 656 and nominated Ali, Muhammad's first cousin and the husband of his daughter Fatima, to succeed him, civil war broke out. Ali had been passed over three times previously, even though many people considered him to be the Prophet's natural heir. Those who believed Ali was the Prophet's heir came to be known as **Shi'ites**, after the Arabic term *Shi'at Ali* ("Party of Ali").

When Ali accepted the nomination to be caliph, two of Muhammad's close companions and his favorite wife A'isha challenged him. Ali defeated them in the Battle of the Camel (656), so called because the fighting raged around the camel on which A'isha was seated in an enclosed woman's saddle.

After the battle, the governor of Syria, Mu'awiya (moo-AH-we-yuh), a kinsman of the slain Uthman from the Umayya clan of the Quraysh, renewed the challenge. Inconclusive battle gave way to arbitration. The arbitrators decided that Uthman, whom his assassins considered corrupt, had not deserved death and that Ali had erred in accepting the caliphate. Ali rejected these findings, but before fighting could resume, one of his own supporters killed him for agreeing to the arbitration. Mu'awiya offered Ali's son Hasan a dignified retirement and thus emerged as caliph in 661.

Shi'ites and Sunnis

Umayyad Caliphate First hereditary dynasty of Muslim caliphs (661 to 750). From their capital at Damascus, the Umayyads ruled an empire that extended from Spain to India. Overthrown by the Abbasid Caliphate.

Sunnis Muslims belonging to branch of Islam believing that the community should select its own leadership. The majority religion in most Islamic countries.

Mu'awiya chose his own son, Yazid, to succeed him, thereby instituting the **Umayyad** (oo-MY-ad) **Caliphate**. When Hasan's brother Husayn revolted in 680 to reestablish the right of Ali's family to rule, Yazid ordered Husayn and his family killed. Sympathy for Husayn's martyrdom helped transform Shi'ism from a political movement into a religious sect.

Several variations in Shi'ite belief developed, but Shi'ites all agree that Ali was the rightful successor to Muhammad and that God's choice as Imam, leader of the Muslim community, has always been one or another of Ali's descendants. They see the caliphal office as more secular than religious. Because the Shi'ites seldom held power, their religious feelings came to focus on outpourings of sympathy for Husayn and other martyrs and on messianic dreams that one of their Imams would someday triumph.

Those Muslims who supported the first three caliphs gradually came to be called "People of Tradition and Community"—in Arabic, *Ahl al-Sunna wa'l-Jama'a*, **Sunnis** for short. Sunnis consider the caliphs to be Imams. As for Ali's followers who had abhorred his acceptance of arbitration, they evolved into small and rebellious Kharijite sects (from *kharaja*, meaning "to secede or rebel") claiming righteousness for themselves alone. These three divisions of Islam, the last now quite minor, still survive.

SECTION REVIEW

- Islam emerged among the nomadic pastoralists and caravan traders of the Arabian peninsula.
- Mecca grew as a caravan city and pilgrimage site identified with Jewish and Christian stories.
- Muhammad experienced revelations that called people to submit to God's will.
- Facing hostility in Mecca, Muhammad and his followers fled to Medina, where they formed the umma.
- As caliph succeeding Muhammad, Abu Bakr confirmed the Five Pillars of Islam and reportedly ordered the composition of the Quran.
- Civil war within the umma resulted in the Sunni/Shi'ite division and the foundation of the Umayyad Caliphate.

THE RISE AND FALL OF THE CALIPHATE, 632–1258

The Islamic caliphate built on the conquests the Arabs carried out after Muhammad's death gave birth to a dynamic and creative religious society. By the late 800s, however, one piece after another of this huge realm broke away. Yet the idea of a caliphate, however unrealistic, remains today a touchstone of Sunni belief in the unity of the umma.

Sunni Islam never gave a single person the power to define true belief, expel heretics, and discipline clergy. Thus, unlike Christian popes and patriarchs, the caliphs had little basis for reestablishing their universal authority once they lost political and military power.

The Islamic Conquests, 634–711

From Spain to Pakistan

Arab conquests outside Arabia began under the second caliph, Umar (r. 634–644). Arab armies wrenched Syria (636) and Egypt (639–642) away from the Byzantine Empire and defeated the last Sasanid shah, Yazdigird III (r. 632–651). After a decade-long lull, expansion began again. Tunisia fell and became the governing center from which was organized, in 711, the conquest of Spain by an Arab-led army mostly composed of Berbers from North Africa. In the same year, Sind—the southern Indus Valley in today's Pakistan—succumbed to invaders from Iraq. The Muslim dominion remained roughly stable in size for three centuries until conquest began anew in the eleventh century. India and Anatolia experienced invasions, and sub-Saharan Africa and other regions saw Islam expand peacefully by trade and conversion.

AP* Exam Tip The expansion of Islam to many parts of Afro-Eurasia is an important point on the AP exam.

Muhammad's close companions, men of political and economic sophistication inspired by his charisma, guided the conquests. The social structure and hardy nature of Arab society lent itself to flexible military operations; and the authority of Medina, reconfirmed during the caliphate of Abu Bakr, ensured obedience.

The decision made during Umar's caliphate to prohibit Arabs from assuming ownership of conquered territory proved important. Umar tied army service, with its regular pay and windfalls of booty, to residence in military camps—two in Iraq (Kufa and Basra), one in Egypt (Fustat), and one in Tunisia (Qairawan). East of Iraq, Arabs settled around small garrison towns at strategic locations and in one large garrison at Marv in present-day Turkmenistan. This policy kept the armies together and ready for action and preserved normal life in the countryside, where some three-fourths of the population lived. Only a tiny proportion of the Syrian, Egyptian, Iranian, and Iraqi populations understood the Arabic language.

The million or so Arabs who participated in the conquests over several generations constituted a small, self-isolated ruling minority living on the taxes paid by a vastly larger non-Arab, non-Muslim subject population. The Arabs had little material incentive to encourage conversion, and there is no evidence of coherent missionary efforts to spread Islam during the conquest period.

The Umayyad and Early Abbasid Caliphates, 661–850

The Umayyad caliphs presided over an Arab realm rather than a religious empire. Ruling from Damascus, their armies consisted almost entirely of Muslim Arabs. Sasanid and Byzantine administrative practices continued in force. Only gradually did the caliphs replace non-Muslim secretaries and tax officials with Muslims and introduce Arabic as the language of government. Distinctively Muslim silver and gold coins introduced early in the eighth century symbolized the new order. Henceforward, silver dirhams and gold dinars bearing Arabic religious phrases circulated in monetary exchanges from Morocco to the frontiers of China.

Non-Arab Converts to Islam

The Umayyad dynasty fell in 750 after a decade of growing unrest. Converts to Islam numbered no more than 10 percent of the indigenous population, but they were still important because of the comparatively small number of Arab warriors. These converts resented Arab social domination. In addition, non-Syrian Arabs envied the Syrian domination of caliphal affairs, and pious Muslims looked askance at the secular and even irreligious behavior of the caliphs. Finally, Shi'ites and Kharijites attacked the Umayyad family's legitimacy as rulers, launching a number of rebellions.

Abbasid Caliphate Descendants of the Prophet Muhammad's uncle, al-Abbas, the Abbasids overthrew the Umayyad Caliphate and ruled an Islamic empire from their capital in Baghdad (founded 762) from 750 to 1258.

The Abbasid Revolution

In 750 one rebellion, in the region of Khurasan (kor-uh-SAHN) in what is today northeastern Iran, overthrew the last Umayyad caliph, though one family member escaped to Spain to found an Umayyad principality there in 755. Many Shi'ites supported the rebellion, thinking they were fighting for the family of Ali. As it turned out, the family of Abbas, one of Muhammad's uncles, controlled the secret organization that coordinated the revolt. Upon victory they established the **Abbasid** (ah-BASS-id) **Caliphate**. Some of the Abbasid caliphs who ruled after 750 befriended their relatives in Ali's family, and one even flirted with transferring the caliphate to them. The Abbasid family, however, held on to the caliphate until 1258, when Mongol invaders killed the last of them in Baghdad (see Chapter 12).

Initially, the Abbasid dynasty made a fine show of leadership and piety. Theology and religious law became preoccupations at court and among a growing community of scholars devoted to interpreting the Quran, collecting the sayings of the Prophet, and compiling Arabic grammar. (In recent years, some Western scholars have maintained that the Quran, the sayings of the Prophet, and the biography of the Prophet were all composed around this time to provide a legendary base for the regime. This reinterpretation of Islamic origins has not been generally accepted either in the scholarly community or among Muslims.) Some caliphs sponsored ambitious projects to translate great works of Greek, Persian, and Indian thought into Arabic.

Persianization of the Caliphate

With its roots among the semi-Persianized Arabs of Khurasan, the new dynasty gradually adopted the ceremonies and customs of the Sasanid shahs. Government grew increasingly complex in Baghdad, the newly built capital city on the Tigris River. As more non-Arabs converted to Islam, the ruling elite became more cosmopolitan. Greek, Iranian, Central Asian, and African cultural currents met in the capital and gave rise to an abundance of literary works, a process facilitated by the introduction of papermaking from China. Arab poets neglected the traditional odes extolling life in the desert and wrote instead wine songs (despite Islam's prohibition of alcohol) or poems in praise of their patrons.

The translation of Aristotle into Arabic, the founding of the main currents of theology and law, and the splendor of the Abbasid court—reflected in stories of *The Arabian Nights* set in the time of the caliph Harun al-Rashid (hah-ROON al–rah-SHEED) (r. 776–809)—in some respects warrant calling the early Abbasid period a "golden age." Yet the refinement of Baghdad culture only slowly made its way into the provinces. Egypt remained predominantly Christian and Coptic-speaking in the early Abbasid period, and Iran never adopted Arabic as a spoken tongue. Most of Berber-speaking North Africa rebelled and freed itself of direct caliphal rule after 740.

Gradual conversion to Islam among the conquered population accelerated in the second quarter of the ninth century. Social discrimination against non-Arab converts gradually faded, and the Arabs themselves—at least those living in cosmopolitan urban settings—lost their previously strong attachment to kinship and ethnic identity.

Political Fragmentation, 850–1050

Abbasid decline became evident in the second half of the ninth century as conversion to Islam accelerated (see Map 8.2). No government ruling so vast an empire could hold power easily. Caravans traveled only 20 miles (32 kilometers) a day, and the couriers of the caliphal post system usually did not exceed 100 miles (160 kilometers) a day. News of frontier revolts took weeks to reach Baghdad. Military responses might take months.

During the first two Islamic centuries, revolts against Muslim rule had been a concern. The Muslim umma had therefore clung together, despite the long distances. But with the growing conversion of the population to Islam, fears that Islamic dominion might be overthrown faded. Once they became the overwhelming majority, Muslims realized that a highly centralized empire did not necessarily serve the interests of all the people.

By the middle of the ninth century, revolts targeting Arab or Muslim domination gave way to movements within the Islamic community concentrating on seizure of territory and formation of principalities. None of the states carved out of the Abbasid Caliphate after that time repudiated or even threatened Islam. They did, however, cut the flow of tax revenues to Baghdad, thereby increasing local prosperity.

Slave Soldiers

mamluks Under the Islamic system of military slavery, Turkic military slaves who formed an important part of the armed forces of the Abbasid Caliphate of the ninth and tenth centuries. Mamluks eventually founded their own state, ruling Egypt and Syria (1250–1517).

Increasingly starved for funds by breakaway provinces and by an unexplained fall in revenues from Iraq itself, the caliphate experienced a crisis in the late ninth century. Distrusting generals and troops from outlying areas, the caliphs purchased Turkic slaves, **mamluks** (MAM-luke), from Central Asia and established them as a standing army. Well trained and hardy, the Turks proved an effective but expensive military force. When the government could not pay them, the mamluks took it on themselves to seat and unseat caliphs, a process made easier by the construction of a new capital at Samarra, north of Baghdad on the Tigris River.

The Turks dominated Samarra without interference from an unruly Baghdad populace that regarded them as rude and highhanded. However, the money and effort that went into the huge city, which was occupied only from 835 to 892, further sapped the caliphs' financial strength and deflected labor from more productive pursuits.

MAP 8.2 **Rise and Fall of the Abbasid Caliphate** Though Abbasid rulers occupied the caliphal seat in Iraq from 750 to 1258, when Mongol armies destroyed Baghdad, real political power waned sharply and steadily after 850. The rival caliphates of the Fatimids (909–1171) and Spanish Umayyads (929–976) were comparatively short-lived.

Interactive Map

The Buyids

In 945, after several attempts to find a strongman to save it, the Abbasid Caliphate fell under the control of rude mountain warriors from Daylam in northern Iran. Led by the Shi'ite Buyid (BOO-yid) family, they conquered western Iran as well as Iraq. Each Buyid commander ruled his own principality. After two centuries of glory, the sun began to set on Baghdad. The Abbasid caliph remained, but the Buyid princes controlled him. Being Shi'ites, the Buyids had no special reverence for the Sunni caliph. The Shi'ite teachings they followed held that the twelfth and last Imam had disappeared around 873 and would return as a messiah only at the end of time. Thus they had no Shi'ite Imam to defer to and retained the caliph only to help control their predominantly Sunni subjects.

Iranian States

Dynamic growth in outlying provinces paralleled the caliphate's gradual loss of temporal power. In the east in 875, the dynasty of the Samanids (sah-MAN-id), one of several Iranian families to achieve independence, established a glittering court in Bukhara, a major city on the Silk Road (see Map 8.2). Samanid princes patronized literature and learning, but the language they favored was Persian written in Arabic letters. For the first time, a non-Arabic literature rose to challenge the eminence of Arabic within the Islamic world.

African States

In the west, the Berber revolts against Arab rule led to the appearance after 740 of the city-states of Sijilmasa (sih-jil-MAS-suh) and Tahert (TAH-hert) on the northern fringe of the Sahara. The Kharijite beliefs of these states' rulers interfered with their east-west overland trade and led them to develop the first regular trade across the Sahara desert. Once traders looked to the desert, they discovered that Berber speakers in the southern Sahara were already carrying salt from the desert into the Sahel region. The northern traders discovered that they could trade salt for gold by providing the southern nomads, who controlled the salt sources but had little use for gold, with more useful products, such as copper and manufactured goods. Sijilmasa and Tahert became wealthy cities, the former minting gold coins that circulated as far away as Egypt and Syria.

Ghana First known kingdom in sub-Saharan West Africa between the sixth and thirteenth centuries C.E. Also the modern West African country once known as the Gold Coast.

The earliest known sub-Saharan beneficiary of the new exchange system was the kingdom of **Ghana** (GAH-nuh), which first appears in an Arabic text of the late eighth century as the

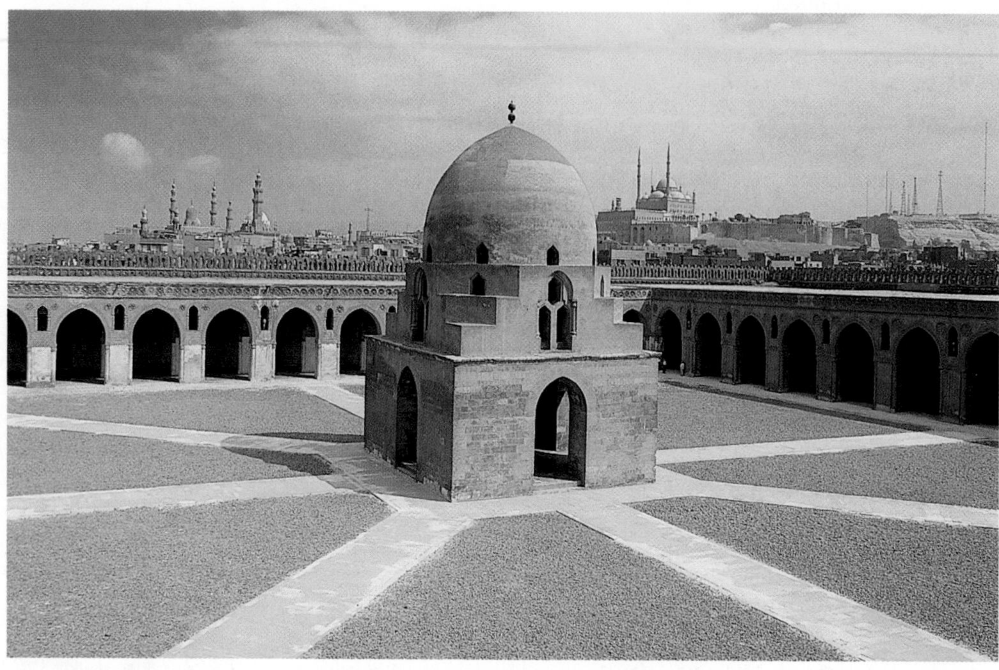

Ellen Rooney/Robert Harding World Imagery

Mosque of Ibn Tulun in Fustat Completed in 877, this mosque symbolized Egypt becoming for the first time a quasi-independent province under its governor. The kiosk in the center of the courtyard contains fountains for washing before prayer. Before its restoration in the thirteenth century, the mosque had a spiral minaret and a door to an adjoining governor's palace.

"land of gold." Few details survive about the early years of this realm, which was established by the Soninke (soh-NIN-kay) people and covered parts of Mali, Mauritania, and Senegal, but it prospered until 1076, when it was conquered by nomads from the desert. Ghana was one of the first lands outside the orbit of the caliphate to experience a gradual and peaceful conversion to Islam.

The Fatimid Caliphate

The North African city-states lost their independence after the Fatimid (FAT-uh-mid) dynasty, whose members claimed (perhaps falsely) to be Shi'ite Imams descended from Ali, established itself in Tunisia in 909. After consolidating their hold on northwest Africa, the Fatimids culminated their rise to power by conquering Egypt in 969. Claiming the title of caliph in a direct challenge to the Abbasids, the Fatimid rulers governed from a palace complex outside the old conquest-era garrison city of Fustat (fuss-THAT). They named the complex Cairo. For the first time Egypt became a major cultural, intellectual, and political center of Islam. The abundance of Fatimid gold coinage, now channeled to Egypt from West Africa, made the Fatimids an economic power in the Mediterranean.

Islamic Spain

Cut off from the rest of the Islamic world by the Strait of Gibraltar and, from 740 onward, by independent city-states in Morocco and Algeria, Umayyad Spain developed a distinctive Islamic culture blending Roman, Germanic, and Jewish traditions with those of the Arabs and Berbers. Historians disagree on how rapidly and completely the Spanish population converted to Islam. If we assume a process similar to that in the eastern regions, it seems likely that the most rapid surge in Islamization occurred in the middle of the tenth century.

AP* Exam Tip The Islamic political system in Spain is an important point for the AP exam.

As in the east, governing cities symbolized the Islamic presence in al-Andalus, as the Muslims called their Iberian territories. Cordoba, Seville, Toledo, and other cities grew substantially, becoming much larger and richer than contemporary cities in neighboring France. Converts to Islam and their descendants, unconverted Arabic-speaking Christians, and Jews joined with the comparatively few descendants of Arab settlers to create new architectural and literary styles. In the countryside, where the Berbers preferred to settle, a fusion of preexisting agricultural technologies with new crops, notably citrus fruits, and irrigation techniques from the east gave Spain the most diverse and sophisticated agricultural economy in Europe.

Religions Flourishing Together

The rulers of al-Andalus took the title *caliph* only in 929, when Abd al-Rahman (AHB-d al-ruh-MAHN) III (r. 912–961) did so in response to a similar declaration by the newly established (909) Fatimid ruler in Tunisia. By the century's end, however, this caliphate encountered challenges from breakaway movements that eventually splintered al-Andalus into a number of small states. Political decay did not impede cultural growth. Some of the greatest writers and think-

Tomb of the Samanids in Bukhara This early-tenth-century structure has the basic layout of a Zoroastrian fire temple: a dome on top of a cube. However, geometric ornamentation in baked brick marks it as an early masterpiece of Islamic architecture. The Samanid family achieved independence as rulers of northeastern Iran and western Central Asia in the tenth century.

Bridgeman-Giraudon/Art Resource, NY

ers in Jewish history worked in Muslim Spain in the eleventh and twelfth centuries, sometimes writing in Arabic, sometimes in Hebrew. Judah Halevi (1075–1141) composed exquisite poetry and explored questions of religious philosophy. Maimonides (1135–1204) made a major compilation of Judaic law and expounded on Aristotelian philosophy. At the same time, Islamic thought in Spain attained its loftiest peaks in Ibn Hazm's (994–1064) treatises on love and other subjects, the Aristotelian philosophical writings of Ibn Rushd (IB-uhn RUSHED) (1126–1198, known in Latin as Averroës [uh-VERR-oh-eez]) and Ibn Tufayl (IB-uhn too-FILE) (d. 1185), and the mystic speculations of Ibn al-Arabi (IB-uhn ahl–AH-rah-bee) (1165–1240). Christians, too, shared in the intellectual and cultural dynamism of al-Andalus. Translations from Arabic to Latin made during this period had a profound effect on the later intellectual development of western Europe (see Chapter 9).

The Samanids, Fatimids, and Spanish Umayyads, three of many regional principalities, represent the political diversity and awakening of local awareness that coincided with Abbasid decline. Yet drawing and redrawing political boundaries did not result in the rigid division of the Islamic world into kingdoms. Religious and cultural developments, particularly the rise in cities of a social group of religious scholars known as the **ulama** (oo-leh-MAH)—Arabic for "people with (religious) knowledge"—worked against any permanent division of the Islamic umma.

ulama Muslim religious scholars. From the ninth century onward, the primary interpreters of Islamic law and the social core of Muslim urban societies.

Assault from Within and Without, 1050–1258

Turks in the Middle East

The role played by Turkish mamluks in the decline of Abbasid power established an enduring stereotype of the Turk as a ferocious, unsophisticated warrior. This image gained strength in the 1030s when the Seljuk (sel-JOOK) family established a Turkish Muslim state based on nomadic power. Taking the Arabic title *Sultan*, meaning "power," and the revived Persian title *Shahan-shah*, or King of Kings, the Seljuk ruler Tughril (TUUG-ruhl) Beg created a kingdom that stretched from northern Afghanistan to Baghdad, which he occupied in 1055. After a century under the thumb of the Shi'ite Buyids, the Abbasid caliph breathed easier under the slightly

V&A Images/Victoria & Albert Museum

Spanish Muslim Textile of the Twelfth Century This fragment of woven silk, featuring peacocks and Arabic writing, is one of the finest examples of Islamic weaving. The cotton industry flourished in the early Islamic centuries, but silk remained a highly valued product. Some fabrics were treasured in Christian Europe.

lighter thumb of the Sunni Turks. The Seljuks pressed on into Syria and Anatolia, administering a lethal blow to Byzantine power at the Battle of Manzikert (MANZ-ih-kuhrt) in 1071. The Byzantine army fell back on Constantinople, leaving Anatolia open to Turkish occupation.

Under Turkish rule, cities shrank as pastoralists overran their agricultural hinterlands. Irrigation works suffered from lack of maintenance in the unsettled countryside. Tax revenues fell. Quarreling twelfth-century princes fought over cities, but few Turks participated in urban cultural and religious life. The gulf between a religiously based urban society and the culture and personnel of the government deepened. When factional riots broke out between Sunnis and Shi'ites, or between rival schools of Sunni law, rulers generally remained aloof, even as destruction and loss of life mounted.

Economic Decline

By the early twelfth century, unrepaired damage from floods, fires, and civil disorder had reduced old Baghdad on the west side of the Tigris to ruins. The withering of Baghdad reflected a broader environmental problem: the collapse of the canal system on which agriculture in the Tigris and Euphrates Valley depended. For millennia a center of world civilization, Mesopotamia underwent substantial population loss and never again regained its geographical importance.

The Turks alone cannot be blamed for the demographic and economic misfortunes of Iran and Iraq. Too-robust urbanization and an apparent chilling of the climate after 1000 had strained food resources. The growing practice of paying soldiers and courtiers with land grants led to absentee landlords using agents to collect taxes. These agents gouged villagers and took little interest in improving production, thus intensifying the agricultural crisis.

The Crusader Challenge

Internecine feuding was preoccupying the Seljuk family when the first Christian crusaders reached the Holy Land and captured Jerusalem in 1099 (see Chapter 9). Though charged with the stuff of romance, the Crusades had little lasting impact on the Islamic lands. The four crusader principalities of Edessa, Antioch, Tripoli, and Jerusalem simply became pawns in the shifting pattern of politics already in place. Newly arrived knights eagerly attacked the Muslim enemy, whom they called "Saracens (SAR-uh-suhn)"; but veteran crusaders recognized that practicing diplomacy and seeking partners of convenience among rival Muslim princes offered a sounder strategy.

The Muslims finally unified to face the European enemy in the mid-twelfth century. Nur al-Din ibn Zangi (NOOR al–DEEN ib-uhn ZAN-gee) established a strong state based in Damascus and sent an army to terminate the Fatimid Caliphate in Egypt. A nephew of the Kurdish commander of that expedition, Salah-al-Din, known in the West as Saladin, took advantage of Nur al-Din's timely death to seize power and unify Egypt and Syria. The Fatimid dynasty fell in 1171. In 1187 Saladin recaptured Jerusalem from the Europeans.

Saladin's descendants fought off subsequent Crusades. After one such battle, however, in 1250, Turkish mamluk troops seized control of the government in Cairo, ending Saladin's dynasty. In 1260 these mamluks rode east to confront a new invading force. At the Battle of Ain Jalut (ine jah-LOOT) (Spring of Goliath) in Syria, they met and defeated an army of Mongols from Central Asia (see Chapter 12), thus stemming an invasion that had begun several decades before and legitimizing their claim to dominion over Egypt and Syria.

Mamluk Sultans

During the ensuing Mamluk period a succession of slave-soldier sultans ruled Egypt and Syria until 1517. Fear of new Mongol attacks receded after 1300, but by then the new ruling system had become fixed. Young Turkish or Circassian slaves, the latter from the eastern end of the Black Sea, were imported from non-Muslim lands, raised in training barracks, and converted to Islam. Owing loyalty to the Mamluk officers who purchased them, they formed a military class that was socially disconnected from the Arabic-speaking native population.

The Mongol invasions, especially their destruction of the Abbasid Caliphate in Baghdad in 1258, shocked the world of Islam. The Mamluk sultan enthroned a relative of the last Baghdad caliph in Cairo, but the Egyptian Abbasids were mere puppets serving Mamluk interests. From Iraq eastward, non-Muslim rule lasted for much of the thirteenth century. Although the Mongols left few ethnic or linguistic traces in these lands, their initial destruction of cities and slaughter of civilian populations, their diversion of Silk Road trade from Baghdad to more northerly routes ending at Black Sea ports, and their casual disregard, even after conversion to Islam, for Muslim religious life and urban culture hastened currents of change already under way.

SECTION REVIEW

- By 711, Arab armies had conquered an empire stretching from Sind in the east to Spain in the west.
- The Umayyad caliphs ruled an ethnic empire; they governed from Damascus using Sasanid and Byzantine administrative methods.
- The Umayyads fell to rebels who established the Abbasid Caliphate at Baghdad, while surviving Umayyads fled to Spain.
- Influenced by Persian culture, the Abbasids presided over significant spiritual, intellectual, and artistic activity.
- Abbasid decline led to fragmentation of the caliphate into independent states, but the Islamic umma remained intact.
- Political divisions continued as successor states to the former caliphate fell, replaced by Seljuk Turk, Crusader, Mamluk, and Mongol states.

ISLAMIC CIVILIZATION

Though increasingly unsettled in its political dimension and subject to economic disruptions caused by war, the ever-expanding Islamic world underwent a fruitful evolution in law, social structure, and religious expression. Religious conversion and urbanization reinforced each other to create a distinct Islamic civilization. The immense geographical and human diversity of the Muslim lands allowed many "small traditions" to coexist with the developing "great tradition" of Islam.

Law and Dogma

The Shari'a, the law of Islam, provides the foundation of Islamic civilization. Yet aside from certain Quranic verses conveying specific divine ordinances—most pertaining to personal and family matters—Islam had no legal system in the time of Muhammad. Arab custom and the Prophet's own authority offered the only guidance. After Muhammad died, the umma tried to follow his example. This became harder and harder to do, however, as those who knew Muhammad best passed away and many Arabs found themselves living in far-off lands. Non-Arab converts to Islam, who at first tried to follow Arab customs they had little familiarity with, had an even harder time.

Sunna and Hadith

Islam slowly developed laws to govern social and religious life. The full sense of Islamic civilization, however, goes well beyond the basic Five Pillars mentioned earlier. Some Muslim thinkers felt that the reasoned consideration of a mature man offered the best resolution of issues not covered by Quranic revelation. Others argued for the sunna, or tradition, of the Prophet as the best guide. To understand that sunna they collected and studied thousands of reports, called **hadith** (hah-DEETH), purporting to convey the precise words or deeds of Muhammad. It became customary to precede each hadith with a chain of oral authorities leading back to the person who had direct acquaintance with the Prophet.

hadith A tradition relating the words or deeds of the Prophet Muhammad; next to the Quran, the most important basis for Islamic law.

Many hadith dealt with ritual matters, such as how to wash before prayer. Others provided answers to legal questions not covered by Quranic revelation or suggested principles for deciding such matters. By the eleventh century most legal thinkers had accepted the idea that

Muhammad's personal behavior provided the best role model and that the hadith constituted the most authoritative basis for law after the Quran itself.

Yet the hadith posed a problem because the tens of thousands of anecdotes included both genuine and invented reports, the latter sometimes politically motivated, as well as stories derived from non-Muslim religious traditions. Only a specialist could hope to separate a sound from a weak tradition. As the hadith grew in importance, so did the branch of learning devoted to their analysis. Scholars discarded thousands for having faulty chains of authority. The most reliable they collected into books that gradually achieved authoritative status. Sunnis placed six books in this category; Shi'ites, four.

As it gradually evolved, the Shari'a embodied a vision of an umma in which all subscribed to the same moral values and political and ethnic distinctions lost importance. Every Muslim ruler was expected to abide by and enforce the religious law. In practice, this expectation often lost out in the hurly-burly of political life. But the Shari'a proved an important basis for an urban lifestyle that varied surprisingly little from Morocco to India.

Converts and Cities

Conversion to Islam, more the outcome of people's learning about the new rulers' religion than an escape from the tax on non-Muslims, as some scholars have suggested, helped spur urbanization. Conversion did not require extensive knowledge of the faith. To become a Muslim, a person simply stated, in the presence of a Muslim: "There is no God but God, and Muhammad is the Messenger of God."

Impact of Conversion

Few converts spoke Arabic, and fewer could read the Quran. Many converts knew no more of the Quran than the verses they memorized for daily prayers. Muhammad had established no priesthood to define and spread the faith. Thus new converts, whether Arab or non-Arab, faced the problem of finding out for themselves what Islam was about and how they should act as Muslims. This meant spending time with Muslims, learning their language, and imitating their practices.

In many areas, conversion involved migrating to an Arab governing center. The alternative, converting to Islam but remaining in one's home community, was difficult because religion had become the main component of social identity in Byzantine and Sasanid times. Converts to Islam thus encountered discrimination if they stayed in their Christian, Jewish, or Zoroastrian communities. Migration both averted discrimination and took advantage of the economic opportunities opened up by tax revenues flowing into the Arab governing centers.

Urban Growth

The Arab military settlements of Kufa and Basra in Iraq blossomed into cities and became important centers for Muslim cultural activities. As conversion rapidly spread in the mid-ninth century, urbanization accelerated in other regions, most visibly in Iran, where most cities previously had been quite small. Nishapur in the northeast grew from fewer than 10,000 pre-Islamic inhabitants to between 100,000 and 200,000 by the year 1000. Other Iranian cities experienced similar growth. In Iraq, Baghdad and Mosul joined Kufa and Basra as major cities. In Syria, Aleppo and Damascus flourished under Muslim rule. Fustat in Egypt developed into Cairo, one of the largest and greatest Islamic cities. The primarily Christian patriarchal cities of Jerusalem, Antioch, and Alexandria, not being Muslim governing centers, shrank and stagnated.

Conversion-related migration meant that cities became heavily Muslim before the countryside did. This reinforced the urban orientation deriving from the fact that Muhammad and his first followers came from the commercial city of Mecca. Mosques in large cities served both as ritual centers and as places for learning and social activities.

Islam and Society

Islam colored all aspects of urban social life (see Diversity and Dominance: Secretaries, Turks, and Beggars). Initially the new Muslims imitated Arab dress and customs and emulated people they regarded as particularly pious. In the absence of a central religious authority, local variations developed in the way people practiced Islam and in the hadith they attributed to the Prophet. This gave the rapidly growing religion the flexibility to accommodate many different social situations.

By the tenth century, urban growth was affecting the countryside by expanding the consumer market. Citrus fruits, rice, and sugar cane, introduced by the Sasanids, increased in acreage and spread to new areas. Cotton became a major crop in Iran and elsewhere and stimulated textile production. Irrigation works expanded. Abundant coinage facilitated a flourishing

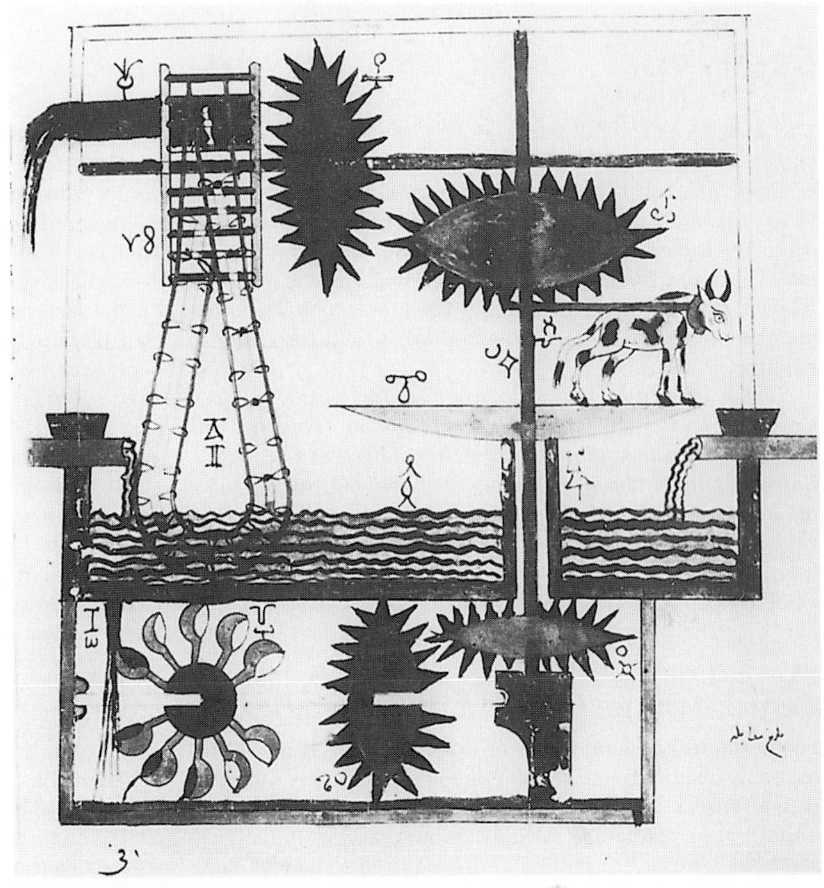

Visual Connection Archive

Model of a Water-Lifting Device The artist's effort to render a three-dimensional construction in two dimensions shows a talent for schematic drawing.

intercity and long-distance trade that provided regular links between isolated districts and integrated the pastoral nomads, who provided pack animals, into the region's economy. Trade encouraged the manufacture of cloth, metal goods, and pottery.

Technology and Science

Science and technology also flourished (see Environment and Technology: Chemistry). Building on Hellenistic traditions and their own observations and experience, Muslim doctors and astronomers developed skills and theories far in advance of their European counterparts. Working in Egypt in the eleventh century, the mathematician and physicist Ibn al-Haytham (IB-uhn al–HY-tham) wrote more than a hundred works. Among other things, he determined that the Milky Way lies far beyond earth's atmosphere, proved that light travels from a seen object to the eye and not the reverse, and explained why the sun and moon appear larger on the horizon than overhead.

Women and Slaves

Women seldom traveled. Those living in rural areas worked in the fields and tended animals. Urban women, particularly members of the elite, lived in seclusion and did not leave their homes without covering themselves (see Material Culture: Head Coverings). Seclusion of women and veiling in public already existed in Byzantine and Sasanid times. Through interpretation of specific verses from the Quran, these practices now became fixtures of Muslim social life. Although women sometimes became literate and studied with relatives, they did so away from the gaze of unrelated men, and while they played influential roles within the family, public roles were generally barred. Only slave women could perform before unrelated men as musicians and dancers. A man could have sexual relations with as many slave concubines as he pleased, in addition to marrying as many as four wives.

AP* Exam Tip The role of women in Islamic societies is an important comparison topic on the essay portion of the exam.

Women's Legal Status

Muslim women fared better legally under Islamic law than did Christian and Jewish women under their respective religious codes. Because Islamic law guaranteed daughters a share in

DIVERSITY + DOMINANCE

Secretaries, Turks, and Beggars

The passages below fall into the category of Arabic literature known as adab, or belles-lettres. The purpose of adab was to entertain and instruct through a succession of short anecdotes, verses, and expository discussions. It attracted the finest writers of the Abbasid era and affords one of the richest sources for looking at everyday life, always keeping in mind that the intended readers were a restricted class of educated men, including merchants, court and government officials, and even men of religion.

One of the greatest masters of Arabic prose, Jahiz (776–869), was a famously ugly man—his name means "Popeyed"—of Abyssinian family origin. Spending part of his life in his native Basra, in southern Iraq, and part in Baghdad, the Abbasid capital, he wrote voluminously on subjects ranging from theology to zoology to miserliness. These excerpts are from two of his short essays, "Censure of the Conduct of Secretaries" and "The Virtues of the Turks."

Censure of the Conduct of Secretaries

Furthermore, the foundation on which writing is based [is] that only a subordinate should take [it] up and only one who is in a sense a servant [can] master it. We have never seen an important person undertake it for its own sake or share in his secretary's work. Every secretary is required to be loyal and requested to bear hardship patiently. The most diverse conditions are imposed on him and he is sorely tried. The secretary has no right to set any of those conditions. On the contrary, he is thought slow at the first lapse even if exhausted and censured at the first error even if unintentional. A slave is entitled to many complaints against his master. He can request his sale to another if he wishes. The secretary has no way to lay claim to his late back wages or to leave his patron if he acts unfairly. He is governed by the rules for slaves. His status is that of a dolt.

It should be enough for you to know of this group that the noblest of them is at the bottom of the pay scale. The most wealthy of them are the least regarded by the ruler. The head of the secretariat who acts as spokesman to the nation earns a tenth of the income of the head of land tax. The scribe whose handwriting lends beauty to the communications of the caliph earns a fraction of the income of the head copyist in the land tax bureau. The correspondence secretary is not fetched for a disaster nor is his aid sought in a crisis. When the ministers have settled on a course of action and agreed in their appraisal, a note is tossed him with the gist of the order. He prepares the text. When he has finished his editing and straightened out the words, he brings in his copyist. He sits as near as anyone to the caliph, in a restricted location away from visitors. Once that task is completed, however, there is no difference between those two scribes and the common people.

The Virtues of the Turks

The Turk has with him at the moment of attack everything he needs for himself, his weapons, his mount, and equipment for it. His endurance is quite amazing for long riding, continuous travel, lengthy night trips, and crossing a land. . . . The Turk is more skilled than the veterinarian and better at teaching his mount what he wants than trainers. He bred it and raised it as a foal. It followed him if he called and galloped behind him when he galloped. . . . If you sum up the life of the Turk and reckon his days you will find he sits longer on the back of his mount than on the face of the earth.

inheritance equal to half that of a son, the majority of women inherited some amount of money or real estate. This remained their private property to keep or sell. Muslim law put the financial burden of supporting a family exclusively on the husband, who could not legally compel his wife to help out.

Women could also remarry if their husbands divorced them, and they received a cash payment upon divorce. Although a man could divorce his wife without stating a cause, a woman could initiate divorce under specified conditions. Women could also practice birth control. They could testify in court, although their testimony counted as half that of a man. They could also go on pilgrimage. Nevertheless, a misogynistic tone sometimes appears in Islamic writings. One saying attributed to the Prophet observed: "I was raised up to heaven and saw that most of its denizens were poor people; I was raised into the hellfire and saw that most of its denizens were women."[3]

Muhammad's Wife A'isha

In the absence of writings by women about women from this period, the status of women must be deduced from the writings of men. Two episodes involving the Prophet's wife A'isha, the daughter of Abu Bakr, provide examples of how Muslim men appraised women in society. Only eighteen when Muhammad died, A'isha lived for another fifty years. Early reports stress her status as Muhammad's favorite, the only virgin he married and the only wife to see the angel

If he is unable to hunt people, he hunts wild animals. If he is unsuccessful in that or needs nourishment, he bleeds one of his riding animals. If thirsty he milks one of his mares. If he wants to rest the one under him he mounts another without touching the ground. There is no one on earth besides him whose body would not reel against eating only meat. His mount is likewise satisfied with stubble, grass, and shrubs. He does not shade it from the sun or cover it against the cold. . . .

The Turk is a herdsman, groom, trainer, trader, veterinarian, and rider. A single Turk is a nation in himself.

Though rulers, warriors, and religious scholars dominate the traditional narratives, the society that developed over the early centuries of Islam was remarkably diverse. Beggars, tricksters, and street performers belonged to a single loose fraternity: the Banu Sasan, or Tribe of Sasan. Tales of their tricks and exploits amused staid, pious Muslims, who often encountered them in cities and on their scholarly travels. The tenth-century poet Abu Dulaf al-Khazraji, who lived in Iran, studied the jargon of the Banu Sasan and their way of life and composed a long poem in which he cast himself as one of the group. However, he added a commentary to each verse to explain the jargon words that his sophisticated court audience would have found unfamiliar.

We are the beggars' brotherhood, and no one can deny us our lofty pride. . . .
And of our number is the feigned madman and mad woman, with metal charms strung from their necks.
And the ones with ornaments drooping from their ears, and with collars of leather or brass round their necks. . . .
And the one who simulates a festering internal wound, and the people with false bandages round their heads and sickly, jaundiced faces.
And the one who slashes himself, alleging that he has been mutilated by assailants, or the one who darkens his skin artificially pretending that he has been beaten up and wounded. . . .
And the one who practices as a manipulator and quack dentist, or who escapes from chains wound round his body, or the one who uses almost invisible silk thread mysteriously to draw off rings. . . .
And of our number are those who claim to be refugees from the Byzantine frontier regions, those who go round begging on pretext of having left behind captive families. . . .
And the one who feigns an internal discharge, or who showers the passers-by with his urine, or who farts in the mosque and makes a nuisance of himself, thus wheedling money out of people. . . .
And of our number are the ones who purvey objects of veneration made from clay, and those who have their beards smeared with red dye.
And the one who brings up secret writing by immersing it in what looks like water, and the one who similarly brings up the writing by exposing it to burning embers.

QUESTIONS FOR ANALYSIS

1. **Why might the ruling elite have found the descriptions of diverse social groups entertaining?**
2. **What role does religion appear to play in the culture that patronized this type of literature?**
3. **How does the personality of the author show up in these passages?**

Sources: First selection excerpts from *Nine Essays of al-Jahiz*, trans. William M. Hutchins (New York: Peter Lang, 1989), 56, 64, 196. Reprinted by permission of Peter Lang Publishing. Second selection excerpts from Clifford Edmund Bosworth, *The Mediaeval Islamic Underworld: The Banu Sasan in Arabic Society and Literature* (Leiden: E. I. Brill, 1976), 191–199. Copyright © 1976. With kind permission of © Koninklijke Brill N.V. Leiden, the Netherlands.

Gabriel. These reports emanate from A'isha herself, who was an abundant source of hadith. As a fourteen-year-old she had become separated from a caravan and rejoined it only after traveling through the night with a man who found her alone in the desert. Gossips accused her of being untrue to the Prophet, but a revelation from God proved her innocence. The second event was her participation in the Battle of the Camel, fought to derail Ali's caliphate. These two episodes came to epitomize what Muslim men feared most about women: sexual infidelity and meddling in politics. Even though the earliest literature dealing with A'isha stresses her position as Muhammad's favorite, his first wife, Khadija, and his daughter, Ali's wife Fatima, eventually surpassed A'isha as ideal women. Both appear as model wives and mothers with no suspicion of sexual irregularity or political manipulation.

Homosexuality

As the seclusion of women became commonplace in urban Muslim society, some writers extolled homosexual relationships, partly because a male lover could appear in public or go on a journey. Although Islam deplored homosexuality, one ruler wrote a book advising his son to follow moderation in all things and thus share his affections equally between men and women. Another ruler and his slave-boy became models of perfect love in the verses of mystic poets.

Slavery

Islam allowed slavery but forbade Muslims from enslaving other Muslims or so-called People of the Book—Jews, Christians, and Zoroastrians, who revered holy books respected by the

ENVIRONMENT + TECHNOLOGY

Chemistry

Muslim scientists developed sophisticated chemical processes and used them to produce a broad range of goods, including glazes for pottery, rosewater (the distilled essence of roses), hard soap, gunpowder, and various types of glass. The words *chemistry* and *alchemy* are both related to the Arabic term for these activities, *al-kimiya*, and many chemical processes passed from the Muslim world to Europe.

Distillation was used at Baku in Azerbaijan to produce a light flammable liquid called "white *naft*," roughly equivalent to kerosene, from crude oil. Special military units wearing fire-resistant clothing were trained to use white *naft* as an incendiary weapon. Flaming liquids, whose exact composition is still uncertain, could be put into pots and thrown, placed in containers attached to arrows, or pumped from a tube.

The Corning Museum of Glass, 68.1.1

Islamic Glassware This glass bottle from Syria shows the skill of Muslim chemists and artisans in producing clear, transparent glass. The scratched decoration reflects the Muslim taste for geometric design.

Muslims. Being enslaved as a prisoner of war constituted an exception. Later centuries saw a constant flow of slaves into Islamic territory from Africa and Central Asia. A hereditary slave society, however, did not develop. Usually slaves converted to Islam, and many masters then freed them as an act of piety. The offspring of slave women and Muslim men were born free.

The Recentering of Islam

Early Islam centered on the caliphate, the political expression of the unity of the umma. No formal organization or hierarchy, however, directed the process of conversion. Thus there emerged a multitude of local Islamic communities so disconnected from each other that numerous competing interpretations of the developing religion arose. Inevitably, the centrality of the caliphate diminished (see Map 8.1). The appearance of rival caliphates in Tunisia and Cordoba accentuated the problem of decentralization.

The Ulama

The rise of the ulama as community leaders did not prevent growing fragmentation because the ulama themselves divided into contentious factions. During the twelfth century factionalism began to abate, and new socioreligious institutions emerged to provide the umma with a different sort of religious center. These new developments stemmed in part from an exodus of religious scholars from Iran in response to economic and political disintegration during the late eleventh and twelfth centuries. The flow of Iranians to the Arab lands and to newly conquered territories in India and Anatolia increased after the Mongol invasion.

Madrasas

Fully versed in Arabic as well as their native Persian, immigrant scholars were warmly received. They brought with them a view of religion developed in Iran's urban centers. A type of religious college, the *madrasa* (MAH-dras-uh), gained sudden popularity outside Iran, where madrasas had been known since the tenth century. Scores of madrasas, many founded by local rulers, appeared throughout the Islamic world.

Head Coverings

Covering the head is one of the most universal of human cultural characteristics. It is also one of the most common ways of signaling social status. Examples can be drawn from every part of the world, from earliest times down to the modern era. In premodern Chinese society, the color and design of a man's cap indicated his rank as clearly as the insignia on military head coverings does today. In most European societies in the seventeenth and eighteenth centuries, men and frequently women of the higher social orders wore wigs, a practice that still survives in the costume of British judges.

Head coverings were particularly important for royalty. From ancient Egypt, where the earliest Pharaonic crowns symbolized the union of the northern and southern parts of the Nile Valley, down to the twentieth century and the jewel-studded crown of the shah of Iran, each land developed its own distinctive royal headdress. This also held true for Native American societies in pre-Columbian times and for African and Polynesian societies. In some societies, such as Sasanid Iran and the Ottoman Empire in what is today Turkey, each ruler's crown or turban had a distinctive design that signaled his rule.

Bibliothèque nationale de France, Ms Arabe 5847 (Schefer Hariri) folio 26 recto

Muslim Headcoverings The man standing before a governor in this thirteenth century miniature painting wears a simple skullcap indicating his low social status. The two attendants wear turbans, but the governor's turban is built into a high, conical shape. The folds and tails of turbans signified not only rank, but also place of origin. To this day, men from western Afghanistan wear tightly wound white turbans with long tails while men from eastern Afghanistan wear loose colorful turbans.

Head coverings have also played significant roles in religion. In orthodox Judaism, for example, men wear hats or skullcaps, and married women wear wigs, as signs of acceptance of God's laws. In Islam, head coverings for women, borrowed from pre-Islamic practice in the Middle East, have become politically controversial in recent years; but prior to the twentieth century it was considered equally improper for a Muslim man to go bareheaded.

Wearing no hat at all was usually a characteristic of slaves or of the poorest elements in society. But it could also signify a deliberate desire to be regarded as humble. Sumerian priests, Buddhist monks and nuns, and certain Sufis in the Muslim world shaved their heads clean. In Europe, early Christian monks and priests shaved the crown of their heads in the Roman Catholic tradition. This form of tonsure competed with and eventually superseded an Irish Catholic practice of shaving the front of the head. Yet head shaving did not always signify humility. Japanese samurai, or warriors, also shaved the front of their heads.

Head coverings for women, as well as wigs and hairdressing styles, sometimes show greater diversity than those for men. This has been particularly true in societies where women of high status mix with men on public occasions. A magnificent wig, hat, or coiffure under these circumstances might speak as much for the social rank of the woman's husband as for her own.

Given this long history of distinctive head coverings, the abandonment of both men's and women's hats in the second half of the twentieth century marked a major turning point in the history of symbolism. Around the world, the hat-making industry has greatly contracted. Whether one visits China, Egypt, India, France, or Brazil, one finds it difficult to determine the rank or status of most people by looking at what they have on their heads. Heads of government typically pose for group photographs with no hats on at all. Aside from conservative religious groups, the head coverings that remain most often indicate occupations: military, police, construction, athletics, and so on.

The reasons for this change are unclear. The spread of democracy and decline of aristocracy may have contributed to it, but hats have become equally uncommon in dictatorships. A more likely cause is the worldwide role of news photographs, movies, and other pictorial media. The media developed in Europe and the United States tend to take Western customs as normal and exoticize non-Western styles as "native costumes." People everywhere have thus felt pressure to switch to Western styles, including bareheadedness, to fit into the image of the modern world.

Women Playing Chess in Muslim Spain As shown in this thirteenth-century miniature, women in their own quarters, without men present, wore whatever clothes and jewels they liked. Notice the henna decorating the hands of the woman in the middle. The woman on the left, probably a slave, plays an oud.

Sufi Brotherhoods

Iranians also contributed to the growth of mystic groups known as *Sufi* brotherhoods in the twelfth and thirteenth centuries. The doctrines and rituals of certain Sufis spread from city to city, giving rise to the first geographically extensive Islamic religious organizations. Sufi doctrines varied, but a quest for a sense of union with God through rituals and training was a common denominator. Sufism had begun in early Islamic times and had doubtless benefited from the ideas and beliefs of people from religions with mystic traditions who converted to Islam.

The early Sufis had been saintly individuals given to ecstatic and poetic utterances and wonder-working. They attracted disciples but did not try to organize them. The growth of brotherhoods, a less ecstatic form of Sufism, set a tone for society in general. It soon became common for most Muslim men, particularly in the cities, to belong to at least one brotherhood.

A sense of the social climate the Sufi brotherhoods fostered can be gained from a twelfth-century manual:

> *Every limb has its own special ethics.... The ethics of the tongue. The tongue should always be busy in reciting God's names (*dhikr*) and in saying good things of the brethren, praying for them, and giving them counsel.... The ethics of hearing. One should not listen to indecencies and slander.... The ethics of sight. One should lower one's eyes in order not to see forbidden things.*[4]

SECTION REVIEW

- The foundation of Islamic civilization is the Shari'a, which is derived from the Quran and hadith.
- Urbanization and religious conversion reinforced each other and prompted the expansion of agriculture, trade, science, and technology.
- Women in general enjoyed relatively high status under Islamic law, though urban women tended to live in seclusion.
- Islamic attitudes toward homosexuality were ambivalent, and slavery was an accepted and continuous practice.
- Migrations of Iranian scholars centered Islam on the madrasa and contributed to the rise of Sufism.

Cambridge University Library

Quran Page Printed from a Woodblock Printing from woodblocks or tin plates existed in Islamic lands between approximately 800 and 1400. Most prints were narrow amulets designed to be rolled and worn around the neck in cylindrical cases. Less valued than handwritten amulets, many prints came from Banu Sasan con men. Why block-printing had so little effect on society in general and eventually disappeared is unknown.

Special dispensations allowed people who merely wanted to emulate the Sufis and enjoy their company to follow less demanding rules:

> *It is allowed by way of dispensation to possess an estate or to rely on a regular income. The Sufis' rule in this matter is that one should not use all of it for himself, but should dedicate this to public charities and should take from it only enough for one year for himself and his family. . . .*
>
> *There is a dispensation allowing one to watch all kinds of amusement. This is, however, limited by the rule: What you are forbidden from doing, you are also forbidden from watching.*[5]

Some Sufi brotherhoods spread in the countryside. Local shrines and pilgrimages to the tombs of Muhammad's descendants and saintly Sufis became popular. The end of the Abbasid Caliphate enhanced the religious centrality of Mecca, which eventually became an important center of madrasa education, and gave renewed importance to the annual pilgrimage.

CONCLUSION

Islam arose in a religious atmosphere created by the Sasanid Empire, which favored Zoroastrianism, and Byzantium, which favored Christianity. These strong state religions led to conflict among religious sects and also raised the possibility of the founder of a new religion commanding both political and religious loyalty on an unprecedented scale. This possibility was realized in the career of the prophet Muhammad in the seventh century.

Islam culminated the trend toward identity based on religion. The concept of the umma united all Muslims in a universal community embracing enormous diversity of language, appearance, and social custom. Though Muslim communities adapted to local "small traditions," by the twelfth century a religious scholar could travel anywhere in the Islamic world and blend easily into the local Muslim community.

By the ninth century, the forces of conversion and urbanization fostered social and religious experimentation in urban settings. From the eleventh century onward, political disruption and the spread of pastoral nomadism slowed this early economic and technological dynamism. Muslim communities then turned to new religious institutions, such as the madrasas and Sufi brotherhoods, to create the flexible and durable community structures that carried Islam into new regions and protected ordinary believers from capricious political rule.

KEY TERMS

Mecca p. 228
Muhammad p. 228
Muslim p. 230
Islam p. 230
Medina p. 230
umma p. 230
caliphate p. 231
Quran p. 231
Shi'ites p. 232
Umayyad Caliphate p. 232
Sunnis p. 232
Abbasid Caliphate p. 233
mamluks p. 234
Ghana p. 235
ulama p. 237
hadith p. 239

EBOOK AND WEBSITE RESOURCES

Primary Sources

The Constitution of Medina: Muslims and Jews at the Dawn of Islam

The Quran: Muslim Devotion to God

Interactive Maps

Map 8.1 Early Expansion of Muslim Rule

Map 8.2 Rise and Fall of the Abbasid Caliphate

Plus flashcards, practice quizzes, and more. Go to: www.cengage.com/history/bullietearthpeople5e

SUGGESTED READING

al-Hassan, Ahmad Y., and Donald R. Hill. *Islamic Technology: An Illustrated History.* 1986. Introduces a little-studied field.

Armstrong, Karen. *Muhammad: A Biography of the Prophet.* 1993. A sympathetic work with an ecumenical tone.

Berkey, Jonathan. *The Formation of Islam: Religion and Society in the Near East, 600–1800.* 2003. A short and lively survey.

Bloom, Jonathan. *Paper Before Print.* 2001. A superb study of paper and papermaking in medieval Islamic culture.

Bulliet, Richard W. *Islam: The View from the Edge.* 1993. An approach that concentrates on the lives of converts to Islam and local religious notables.

Choksy, Jamsheed K. *Conflict and Cooperation: Zoroastrian Subalterns and Muslim Elites in Medieval Iranian Society.* 1997. Exploits Arabic and Middle Persian sources to detail the interaction of religious communities.

Donner, Fred. *Narratives of Islamic Origins.* 1998. Discusses the new school of thought that rejects the traditional accounts of Muhammad's life and of the origins of the Quran.

Gervers, Michael, and Ramzi Jibran Bikhazi, eds. *Conversion and Continuity: Indigenous Christian Communities in Islamic Lands, Eighth to Eighteenth Centuries.* 1990. Articles in this collection detail Christian responses to Islam.

Glick, Thomas F. *From Muslim Fortress to Christian Castle: Social and Cultural Change in Medieval Spain.* 1995. Questions standard ideas about Christians and Muslims from a geographical and technological standpoint.

Lapidus, Ira M. *A History of Islamic Societies,* 2nd ed. 2002. A lengthy work that focuses on social developments and includes Islam outside the Middle East.

Laroui, Abdallah. *The History of the Maghrib: An Interpretive Essay.* 1977. Challenges traditional French scholarship on North Africa.

Lassner, Jacob. *A Mediterranean Society: An Abridgement in One Volume.* 1999. Summary of S. D. Goitein's multivolume study of the Jews of medieval Egypt.

Sells, Michael. *Approaching the Qur'an: The Early Revelations.* 1999. An insightful reading of parts of the Quran, which Muslims regard as untranslatable. Most "interpretations" in English adhere reasonably closely to the Arabic text.

Spellberg, Denise. *Politics, Gender, and the Islamic Past: The Legacy of A'isha bint Abi Bakr.* 1994. A pathbreaking work on the methodology of women's history.

Waines, David. *An Introduction to Islam.* 1995. A reliable starting point for studying the religion of Islam.

Wiesehöfer, Josef. *Ancient Persia.* 2001. A solid survey that includes the Sasanid period.

NOTES

1. Quran. Sura 96, verses 1–5.
2. Quran. Sura 92, verses 1–10.
3. Richard W. Bulliet, *Islam: The View from the Edge* (New York: Columbia University Press, 1994), 87.
4. Abu Najib al-Suhrawardi, *A Sufi Rule for Novices*, trans. Menahem Milson (Cambridge, MA: Harvard University Press, 1975), 45–58.
5. Ibid., 73–82.

AP* REVIEW QUESTIONS FOR CHAPTER 8

1. Which of the following is true of southern Arabia by the 600s?
   (A) It was an isolated and remote region that had seen no development.
   (B) Most people in the region had some familiarity with Africa, India, and the Persian Gulf region.
   (C) It had been annexed to the Sasanid Empire.
   (D) The Byzantine Empire treated it as a tributary state.

2. As the caravan trade across Arabia developed, Arab pastoralists
   (A) raided caravans for their wealth.
   (B) became merchants and sold Arabian goods to caravan leaders.
   (C) became part-time farmers and produced food crops to sell to the caravans.
   (D) became the primary providers of animal power throughout the region.

3. Muhammad became a caravan merchant
   (A) because his father was one.
   (B) through his marriage to Khadija.
   (C) late in his life as a way to support spreading his message.
   (D) as a way to increase his political role in Arab society.

4. In Arabic, *Islam* means
   (A) holy warrior for God.
   (B) one who appears before God in glory.
   (C) one who makes submission to the will of God.
   (D) obedient servant of God.

5. In Medina, Muhammad and his followers formed the community of believers in Islam and in Muhammad as the "Messenger of God," called the
   (A) hijira.
   (B) caliphate.
   (C) fatwa.
   (D) hajj.

6. The schism in Islam was caused by
   (A) the fact that Muhammad had not clarified his successor.
   (B) Iranian followers who believed that the Quran was sacred.
   (C) the marriage of Khadija to Ishmael.
   (D) Meccans who reverted to Judaism.

7. Which of the following is true of the Quran?
   (A) It was written and published by Muhammad.
   (B) It is not published even today.
   (C) Only the priests of the faith can possess the text.
   (D) Abu Bakr reportedly ordered that it be written down.

8. The Muslims who supported the first four caliphs came to be called "People of tradition and Community," or
   (A) Shi'ites.
   (B) Israelites.
   (C) Kharijites.
   (D) Sunnis.

9. Between 636 and 639, the Muslims wrenched both Syria and Egypt from
   (A) the Byzantine Empire.
   (B) the Greeks.
   (C) the Egyptians.
   (D) the Sasanids.

10. By the early 700s, the Muslim empire stretched from
    (A) Mecca to Baghdad.
    (B) Spain to India.
    (C) Turkey to Iran.
    (D) Arabia to Syria and Egypt.

11. Which of the following is true of the regions conquered by the Muslims between 636 and the early 700s?

(A) The people were forced to convert to Islam or perish.
(B) The Muslim invaders displaced the wealthy and confiscated their homes and lands.
(C) The majority of the people lived their lives unchanged.
(D) Jews and Christians were openly persecuted by the Muslims.

12. Which of the following is true of the Umayyad caliphs?

(A) They were devout Muslims and forced all of their subjects to be Muslims.
(B) They moved the Muslim capital to Basra.
(C) Their armies lost major conflicts with the Byzantine Empire.
(D) They ruled over an ethnically defined Arab realm rather than a Muslim empire.

13. The Abbasid caliphs

(A) ruled over an increasingly Muslim empire.
(B) refused to allow the construction of any large mosques in Baghdad.
(C) refrained from allowing the reinterpretation of the Quran.
(D) banned Islamic education.

14. One of the major problems the Abbasid caliphs faced was

(A) frontier revolts that they were slow to reach.
(B) diminishing harvest due to overuse of the land.
(C) attacks from the ulama for being religiously tolerant.
(D) a shortage of gold and silver coins.

15. By the late eighth century, it is known that the Muslims had expanded their trade empire to

(A) England.
(B) Russia.
(C) Ghana.
(D) Zimbabwe.

16. Which of the following is true of the early rule of the Seljuk Turks?

(A) Their rule was accompanied by a general decline in both Iran and Iraq.
(B) They persecuted the most devout of the Muslims and tolerated only the moderate sects of Islam.
(C) They began the minting of gold coins and banned the use of copper coins.
(D) Under their rule only non-Muslims paid taxes.

17. Which of the following is an accurate statement?

(A) None of the Muslim leaders adopted Shari'a law because they believed they would lose control under it.
(B) High taxation led to a decline in the food supplies in the Muslim empires.
(C) Islamic law granted women greater status than did Jewish or Christian law.
(D) Arabic became the universal language of the Muslim empire under the Seljuk Turks.

CHAPTER

9

CHAPTER OUTLINE

- The Byzantine Empire, 600–1200
- Early Medieval Europe, 600–1000
- The Western Church
- Kievan Russia, 900–1200
- Western Europe Revives, 1000–1200
- The Crusades, 1095–1204
- Conclusion

ENVIRONMENT + TECHNOLOGY *Iron Production*

DIVERSITY + DOMINANCE *The Struggle for Christian Morality*

Musée de Bayeaux/Michael Holford

Boatbuilding Scene from the Bayeaux Tapestry Eleventh-century shipwrights prepare vessels for William of Normandy's invasion of England.

Visit the website and ebook for additional study materials and interactive tools: www.cengage.com/history/bullietearthpeople5e

Christian Societies Emerge in Europe, 600–1200

- How did the Byzantine Empire maintain Roman imperial traditions in the east?
- How did the culture of early medieval Europe develop in the absence of imperial rule?
- What role did the Western Church play in the politics and culture of Europe?
- What was the significance of the adoption of Orthodox Christianity by Kievan Russia?
- How did Mediterranean trade help revive western Europe?
- What were the origins and impact of the Crusades?

Christmas Day in 800 found Charles, king of the Franks, in Rome instead of at his palace at Aachen in northwestern Germany. At six-foot-three, Charles towered over the average man of his time, and his royal career had been equally gargantuan. Crowned king in his mid-twenties in 768, he had criss-crossed Europe for three decades, waging war on Muslim invaders from Spain, Avar (ah-vahr) invaders from Hungary, and a number of German princes.

Charles had subdued many enemies and had become protector of the papacy. So not all historians believe the eyewitness report of his secretary and biographer that Charles was surprised when, as the king rose from his prayers, Pope Leo III placed a new crown on his head. "Life and victory to Charles the August, crowned by God the great and pacific Emperor of the Romans," proclaimed the pope.[1] Then, amid the cheers of the crowd, he humbly knelt before the new emperor.

Charlemagne (SHAHR-leh-mane) (from Latin *Carolus magnus*, "Charles the Great") was the first in western Europe to bear the title *emperor* in over three hundred years. Rome's decline and Charlemagne's rise marked a shift of focus for Europe—away from the Mediterranean and toward the north and west. German custom and Christian piety transformed the Roman heritage to create a new civilization. Irish monks preaching in Latin became important intellectual influences in some parts of Europe, while the memory of Greek and Roman philosophy faded. Urban life continued the decline that had begun in the later days of the Roman Empire. Historians originally called this era "**medieval**," literally "middle age," because it comes between the era of Greco-Roman civilization and the intellectual, artistic, and economic changes of the Renaissance in the fourteenth century; but research has uncovered many aspects of medieval culture that are as rich and creative as those that came earlier and later.

Charlemagne was not the only ruler in Europe to claim the title emperor. Another emperor held sway in the Greek-speaking east, where Rome's political and legal heritage continued. The Eastern Roman Empire was often called the **Byzantine Empire** after the seventh century, and it was known to the Muslims as Rum. Western Europeans lived amid the ruins of empire, while the Byzantines maintained and reinterpreted Roman traditions. The authority of the Byzantine emperors blended with the influence of the Christian church to form a cultural synthesis that helped

Charlemagne King of the Franks (r. 768–814); emperor (r. 800–814). Through a series of military conquests he established the Carolingian Empire, which encompassed all of Gaul and parts of Germany and Italy. Though illiterate himself, he sponsored a brief intellectual revival.

medieval Literally "middle age," a term that historians of Europe use for the period ca. 500 to ca. 1500, signifying its intermediate point between Greco-Roman antiquity and the Renaissance.

Byzantine Empire Historians' name for the eastern portion of the Roman Empire from the fourth century onward, taken from "Byzantium," an early name for Constantinople, the Byzantine capital city. The empire fell to the Ottomans in 1453.

Kievan Russia State established at Kiev in Ukraine ca. 880 by Scandinavian adventurers asserting authority over a mostly Slavic farming population.

PRIMARY SOURCE: The Life of Charlemagne: The Emperor Himself Learn what Charles liked to eat, drink, and study—from his adviser and biographer, Einhard.

shape the emerging kingdom of **Kievan Russia**. Byzantium's centuries-long conflict with Islam helped spur the crusading passion that overtook western Europe in the eleventh century.

The comparison between western and eastern Europe appears paradoxical. Byzantium inherited a robust and self-confident late Roman society and economy, while western Europe could not achieve political unity and suffered severe economic decline. Yet by 1200 western Europe was showing renewed vitality and flexing its military muscles, while Byzantium was showing signs of decline and military weakness. As we explore the causes and consequences of these different historical paths, we must remember that the emergence of Christian Europe included both developments.

THE BYZANTINE EMPIRE, 600–1200

The Byzantine emperors established Christianity as their official religion (see Chapter 5). They also represented a continuation of Roman imperial rule and tradition that was largely absent in the kingdoms that succeeded Rome in the west. Byzantium inherited imperial law intact; only provincial forms of Roman law survived in the west. Combining the imperial role with political oversight over the Christian church, the emperors made a comfortable transition into the role of all-powerful Christian monarchs. The Byzantine drama, however, played on a steadily shrinking stage. Territorial losses and almost constant military pressure from north and south deprived the empire of long periods of peace.

An Empire Beleaguered

Arab Invasions

Having a single ruler endowed with supreme legal and religious authority prevented the breakup of the Eastern Empire into petty principalities, but a series of territorial losses sapped the empire's strength. Between 634 and 650, Arab armies destroyed the Sasanid Empire and captured Byzantine Egypt, Syria, and Tunisia (see Chapter 8). Islam posed a religious as well as a political challenge. By the end of the twelfth century, some two-thirds of the Christians in these former Byzantine territories had adopted the Muslim faith (see Map 9.1).

The loss of such populous and prosperous provinces shook the empire and reduced its power. Although it had largely recovered and reorganized militarily by the tenth century, it never regained the lost lands. Though Crusaders from western Europe established short-lived Christian principalities at the eastern end of the Mediterranean Sea in the eleventh century, the Byzantines found them almost as hostile as the Muslims (see the section below on the Crusades). Eventually the empire succumbed to Muslim conquest in 1453.

The later Byzantine emperors faced new enemies in the north and south. Following the wave of Germanic migrations (see Chapter 5), Slavic and Turkic peoples appeared on the northern frontiers as part of centuries-long and poorly understood population migrations in Eurasian steppe lands. Other Turks led by the Seljuk family became the primary foe in the south (see Chapter 8).

Religious Schism

schism A formal split within a religious community.

At the same time, relations with the popes and princes of western Europe steadily worsened. In the mid-ninth century the patriarchs of Constantinople (cahn-stan-tih-NO-pul) had challenged the territorial jurisdiction of the popes of Rome and some of the practices of the Latin Church. These arguments worsened over time and in 1054 culminated in a formal **schism** (SKIZ-uhm) between the Latin Church and the Orthodox Church—a break that has been only partially mended.

Society and Urban Life

Urban Decline

Imperial authority and urban prosperity in the eastern provinces of the Late Roman Empire initially sheltered Byzantium from many of the economic reverses and population losses suffered

CHRONOLOGY

	Western Europe	Eastern Europe
600		634–650 Muslims conquer Byzantine provinces of Syria, Egypt, and Tunisia
	711 Muslim conquest of Spain	
	732 Battle of Tours	
800	800 Coronation of Charlemagne	
	843 Treaty of Verdun divides Carolingian Empire among Charlemagne's grandsons	
		ca. 880 Varangians take control of Kiev
	910 Monastery of Cluny founded	
	962 Beginning of Holy Roman Empire	
		980 Vladimir becomes grand prince of Kievan Russia
1000		
	1054 Formal schism between Latin and Orthodox Churches	
	1066 Normans under William the Conqueror invade England	
	1076–1078 Climax of investiture controversy	
		1081–1118 Alexius Comnenus rules Byzantine Empire, calls for western military aid against Muslims
	1095 Pope Urban II preaches First Crusade	
1200		
		1204 Western knights sack Constantinople in Fourth Crusade

by western Europe. However, the two regions shared a common demographic crisis during a sixth-century epidemic of bubonic plague known as "the plague of Justinian," named after the emperor who ruled from 527 to 565. A similar though gradual and less pronounced social transformation set in around the seventh century, possibly sparked by further epidemics and the loss of Egypt and Syria to the Muslims. Narrative histories tell us little, but popular narratives of saints' lives show a transition from stories about educated saints hailing from cities to stories about saints who originated as peasants. In many areas, barter replaced money transactions; some cities declined in population and wealth; and the traditional class of local urban notables nearly disappeared.

As the urban elite class shrank, the importance of high-ranking aristocrats at the imperial court and of rural landowners increased. Power organized by family began to rival power from class-based officeholding. By the end of the eleventh century, a family-based military aristocracy had emerged. Of Byzantine emperor Alexius Comnenus (uh-LEX-see-uhs kom-NAY-nuhs) (r. 1081–1118) it was said: "He considered himself not a ruler, but a lord, conceiving and calling the empire his own house."[2] The situation of women changed, too. Although earlier Roman family life was centered on a legally all-powerful father, women had enjoyed comparative freedom in public. After the seventh century women increasingly found themselves confined to the home. Some sources indicate that when they went out, they concealed their faces behind veils. The only men they socialized with were family members. Paradoxically, however, from 1028 to 1056 women ruled the Byzantine Empire alongside their husbands. These social changes and the apparent increase in the seclusion of women resemble simultaneous developments in neighboring Islamic countries, but historians have not uncovered any firm linkage between them.

Economically, the Byzantine emperors continued the Late Roman inclination to set prices, organize grain shipments to the capital, and monopolize trade in luxury goods like Tyrian purple

Byzantine Church from a Twelfth-Century Manuscript The upper portion shows the church façade and domes. The lower portion shows the interior with a mosaic of Christ enthroned at the altar end.

Bibliothèque nationale de France

cloth. Such government intervention may have slowed technological development and economic innovation. So long as merchants and pilgrims hastened to Constantinople from all points of the compass, aristocrats could buy rare and costly goods. Just as the provisioning and physical improvement of Rome overshadowed the development of other cities at the height of the Roman Empire, so other Byzantine cities suffered from the intense focus on Constantinople. In the countryside, Byzantine farmers continued to use slow oxcarts and light scratch plows, which were efficient for many, but not all, soil types, long after farmers in western Europe had begun to adopt more efficient techniques (discussed later in this chapter).

Constantinople

Because Byzantium's Roman inheritance remained so much more intact than western Europe's, few people recognized the slow deterioration. Gradually, however, pilgrims and visitors from the west saw the reality beyond the awe-inspiring, incense-filled domes of cathedrals and beneath the glitter and silken garments of the royal court. An eleventh-century French visitor wrote:

> *The city itself [Constantinople] is squalid and fetid and in many places harmed by permanent darkness, for the wealthy overshadow the streets with buildings and leave these dirty, dark places to the poor and to travelers; there murders and robberies and other crimes which love the darkness are committed. Moreover, since people live lawlessly in this city, which has as many lords as rich men and almost as many thieves as poor men, a criminal knows neither fear nor shame, because crime is not punished by law and never entirely comes to light. In every respect she exceeds moderation; for, just as she surpasses other cities in wealth, so too, does she surpass them in vice.*[3]

A Byzantine contemporary, Anna Comnena, the brilliant daughter of Emperor Alexius Comnenus, expressed the view from the other side. She scornfully described a prominent churchman and philosopher who happened to be from Italy: "Italos . . . was unable with his barbaric, stupid temperament to grasp the profound truths of philosophy; even in the act of learning he utterly rejected the teacher's guiding hand, and full of temerity and barbaric folly, [believed] even before study that he excelled all others."[4]

Cultural Achievements

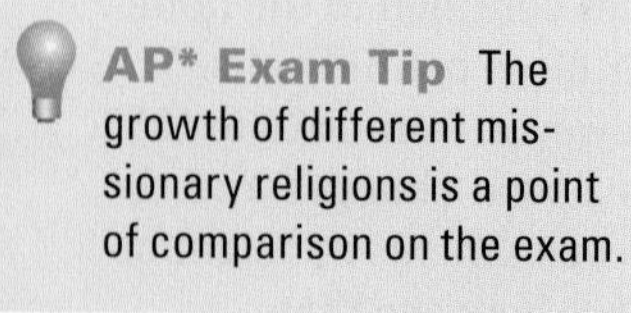

AP* Exam Tip The growth of different missionary religions is a point of comparison on the exam.

Though the greatest Byzantine architectural monument, Constantinople's Hagia Sophia (AH-yah SOH-fee-uh) ("Sacred Wisdom") cathedral, dates to the reign of Justinian, artistic creativity continually manifested itself in the design and ornamentation of other churches and monasteries. Byzantine religious art, featuring stiff but arresting images of holy figures against gold backgrounds, strongly influenced painting in western Europe down to the thirteenth century, and Byzantine musical traditions strongly affected the chanting employed in medieval Latin churches.

Cyrillic Alphabet

Another important Byzantine achievement dates to the empire's long period of political decline. In the ninth century brothers named Cyril and Methodius embarked on a highly successful mission to the Slavs of Moravia (part of the modern Czech Republic). They preached in the local language, and their followers perfected a writing system, called Cyrillic (sih-RIL-ik), that came to be used by Slavic Christians adhering to the Orthodox—that is, Byzantine—rite. Their careers also mark the beginning of a competition between the Greek and Latin forms of Christianity for the allegiance of the Slavs. The use today of the Cyrillic alphabet among the Russians and other Slavic peoples of Orthodox Christian faith, and of the Roman alphabet among the Poles, Czechs, and Croatians, testifies to this competition (see the section on Kievan Russia).

SECTION REVIEW

- Unlike the Western Roman Empire, the Eastern Roman Empire retained its unity and became the Byzantine Empire, headed by an emperor who held both political and religious power.
- A schism split the Orthodox Church from the Catholic Church in the west.
- The Byzantine Empire suffered territorial losses, and its urban centers gradually declined.
- The culture of the Byzantine Empire made many important aesthetic contributions to the art of Europe.
- Byzantine missionaries spread their faith and the Cyrillic alphabet into eastern Europe.

Interactive Map

MAP 9.1 The Spread of Christianity By the early eighth century, Christian areas around the southern Mediterranean from northern Syria to northern Spain, accounting for most of the Christian population, had fallen under Muslim rule; the slow process of conversion to Islam had begun. This accentuated the importance of the patriarchs of Constantinople, the popes in Rome, and the later converting regions of northern and eastern Europe.

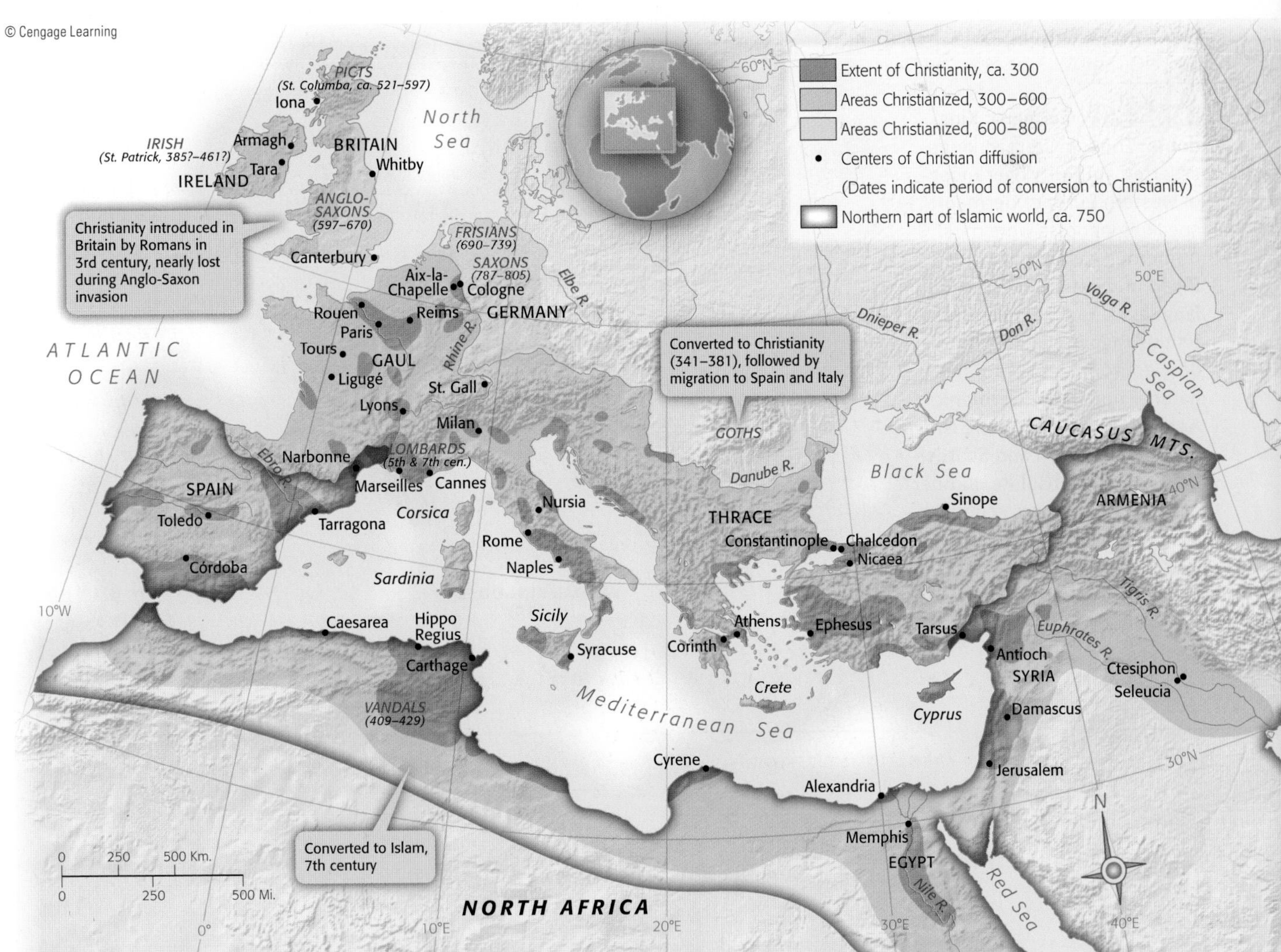

EARLY MEDIEVAL EUROPE, 600–1000

The disappearance of the imperial legal framework that had persisted to the final days of the Western Roman Empire (see Chapter 5) and the rise of various kings, nobles, and chieftains changed the legal and political landscape of western Europe. In region after region, the family-based traditions of the Germanic peoples, which often fit local conditions better than previous practices, supplanted the edicts of the Roman emperors (see Map 9.2).

Fear and physical insecurity led communities to seek the protection of local strongmen. In places where looters and pillagers might appear at any moment, a local lord with a castle at which peasants could take refuge counted for more than a distant king. Dependency of weak people on strong people became a hallmark of the post-Roman period in western Europe.

The Time of Insecurity

Muslim Invasions

In 711 a frontier raiding party of Arabs and Berbers, acting under the authority of the Umayyad caliph in Syria, crossed the Strait of Gibraltar and overturned the kingdom of the Visigoths in Spain (see Chapter 8). The disunited Europeans could not stop them from consolidating their hold on the Iberian Peninsula. After pushing the remaining Christian chieftains into the northern mountains, the Muslims moved on to France. They occupied much of the southern coast and penetrated as far north as Tours, less than 150 miles (240 kilometers) from the English Channel, before Charlemagne's grandfather, Charles Martel, stopped their most advanced raiding party in 732.

The Carolingian Empire

Military effectiveness was the key element in the rise of the Carolingian (kah-roe-LIN-gee-uhn) family (from Latin *Carolus*, "Charles"), first as protectors of the Frankish (French) kings, then as kings themselves under Charlemagne's father Pepin (r. 751–768), and finally, under Char-

MAP 9.2 Germanic Kingdoms Though German kings asserted authority over most of western Europe, German-speaking peoples were most numerous east of the Rhine River. In most other areas, Celtic languages, for example, Breton on this map, or languages derived from Latin predominated. Though the Germanic Anglo-Saxon tongue increasingly supplanted Welsh and Scottish in Britain, the absolute number of Germanic settlers seems to have been fairly limited.

 Interactive Map

Viking Runestone Pre-Christian symbols and myths from northern Europe appear on stones like this one from Sweden. An inscription containing names written in the runic alphabet had elaborately intertwined ornaments at the ends, a feature that reappears in the Christian Book of Kells (see page 267). The scene at the top is thought to depict Odin, the chief god of the Vikings.

Werner Forman/Art Resource, NY

lemagne, as emperors. At the peak of Charlemagne's power, the Carolingian Empire encompassed all of Gaul and parts of Germany and Italy, with the pope ruling part of the latter. When Charlemagne's son, Louis the Pious, died, the Germanic tradition of splitting property among sons led to the Treaty of Verdun (843), which split the empire into three parts. French-speaking in the west (France) and middle (Burgundy), and German-speaking in the east (Germany), the three regions never reunited. Nevertheless, the Carolingian economic system based on landed wealth and a brief intellectual revival sponsored personally by Charlemagne—though he himself was illiterate—provided a common heritage.

Viking Raids

A new threat to western Europe appeared in 793, when the Vikings, sea raiders from Scandinavia, attacked and plundered a monastery on the English coast, the first of hundreds of such raids. Local sources from France, the British Isles, and Muslim Spain attest to widespread dread of Viking warriors descending from multi-oared, dragon-prowed boats to pillage monasteries, villages, and towns. Viking shipbuilders made versatile vessels that could brave the stormy North Atlantic and also maneuver up rivers to attack inland towns. As we shall see, in the ninth century raiders from Denmark and Norway harried the British and French coasts while Varangians (va-RAN-gee-anz) (Swedes) pursued raiding and trading interests, and eventually the building of kingdoms, along the rivers of eastern Europe and Russia. Although many Viking raiders sought booty and slaves, in the 800s and 900s Viking captains organized the settlement of Iceland, Greenland, and, around the year 1000, Vinland on the northern tip of Newfoundland.

AP* Exam Tip It is more important to understand the impact of Viking explorations and expansion than the specific Viking leaders.

Vikings long settled on lands they had seized in Normandy (in northwestern France) organized the most important and ambitious expeditions in terms of numbers of men and horses and long-lasting impact. William the Conqueror, the duke of Normandy, invaded England in 1066 and brought Anglo-Saxon domination of the island to an end. Other Normans (from "north men") attacked Muslim Sicily in the 1060s and, after thirty years of fighting, permanently severed it from the Muslim world.

A Self-Sufficient Economy

Roman Decline

Archaeology and records kept by Christian monasteries and convents reveal a profound economic transformation that accompanied the new Germanic political order. The new rulers cared little for the urban-based civilization of the Romans, which accordingly shrank in importance. Though the pace of change differed from region to region, most cities lost population, in some cases becoming villages. Roman roads fell into disuse and disrepair. Small thatched houses sprang up beside abandoned villas, and public buildings made of marble became dilapidated in the absence of the laborers, money, and civic leadership needed to maintain them. Paying for purchases in coin largely gave way to bartering goods and services.

Trade across the Mediterranean did not entirely stop after the Muslim conquests; occasional shipments from Egypt and Syria continued to reach western ports. But most of western Europe came to rely on meager local resources. These resources, moreover, underwent redistribution.

Roman centralization had channeled the wealth and production of the empire to the capital, which in turn radiated Roman cultural styles and tastes to the provinces. As Roman governors were replaced by Germanic territorial lords, who found the riches of their own culture more appealing than those of Rome, local self-sufficiency became more important. The decline of literacy and other aspects of Roman life made room for the growth of Germanic cultural traditions.

Germanic Customs

The diet in the northern countries featured beer, lard or butter, and bread made of barley, rye, or wheat, all supplemented by pork from herds of swine fed on forest acorns and beechnuts, and by game from the same forests. Nobles ate better than peasants, but even the peasant diet was reasonably balanced. The Roman diet based on wheat, wine, and olive oil persisted in the south. The average western European of the ninth century was probably better nourished than his or her descendants three hundred years later, when population was increasing and the nobility monopolized the resources of the forests.

The Manorial System

manor In medieval Europe, a large, self-sufficient landholding consisting of the lord's residence (manor house), outbuildings, peasant village, and surrounding land.

In both north and south, self-sufficient farming estates known as **manors** became the primary centers of agricultural production. Fear of attack led many common farmers in the most vulnerable regions to give their lands to large landowners in return for political and physical protection. The warfare and instability of the post-Roman centuries made unprotected country houses especially vulnerable to pillaging. Isolated by poor communications and lack of organized government, landowners depended on their own resources for survival. Many became warriors or maintained a force of armed men. Others swore allegiance to landowners who had armed forces to protect them.

A well-appointed manor possessed fields, gardens, grazing lands, fishponds, a mill, a church, workshops for making farm and household implements, and a village where the farmers dependent on the lord of the manor lived. Depending on local conditions, protection ranged from a ditch and wooden stockade to a stone wall surrounding a fortified keep (a stone building). Fortification tended to increase until the twelfth century, when stronger monarchies made it less necessary.

serf In medieval Europe, an agricultural laborer legally bound to a lord's property and obligated to perform set services for the lord.

Manor life reflected personal status. Nobles and their families exercised almost unlimited power over the **serfs**—agricultural workers who belonged to the manor, tilled its fields, and owed other dues and obligations. Serfs could not leave the manor where they were born and attach themselves to another lord. Most peasants in England, France, and western Germany were unfree serfs in the tenth and eleventh centuries. In Bordeaux (bore-DOE), Saxony, and a few other regions, free peasantry survived based on the egalitarian social structure of the Germanic peoples during their period of migration. Outright slavery, the mainstay of the Roman economy (see Chapter 5), diminished as more and more peasants became serfs in return for a lord's protection. At the same time, the enslavement of prisoners to serve as laborers became less important as an object of warfare.

Early Medieval Society in the West

Europe's reversion to a self-sufficient economy limited the freedom and potential for personal achievement of most people, but an emerging class of nobles reaped great benefits. During the Germanic migrations and later among the Vikings of Scandinavia, men regularly answered the call to arms issued by war chiefs, to whom they swore allegiance. All warriors shared in the booty gained from raiding. As settlement enhanced the importance of agricultural tasks, laying down the plow and picking up the sword at the chieftain's call became harder.

Those who, out of loyalty or desire for adventure, continued to join the war parties included a growing number of horsemen. Mounted warriors became the central force of the Carolingian

Noblewoman Directing Construction of a Church This picture of Berthe, wife of Girat de Rouissillion, acting as mistress of the works comes from a tenth-century manuscript that shows a scene from the ninth century. Wheelbarrows rarely appear in medieval building scenes.

army. At first, fighting from horseback did not make a person either a nobleman or a landowner. By the tenth century, however, nearly constant warfare to protect land rights or support the claims of a lord brought about a gradual transformation in the status of the mounted warrior, which led, at different rates in different areas, to landholding becoming almost inseparable from military service.

"Feudalism"

In trying to understand long-standing traditions of landholding and obligation, lawyers in the sixteenth century and later simplified thousands of individual agreements into a neat system they called "feudalism," from Latin *feodum*, meaning a land awarded for military service. It became common to refer to medieval Europe as a "feudal society" in which kings and lords gave land to "vassals" in return for sworn military support. By analyzing original records, more recent historians have discovered this to be an oversimplification. Relations between landholders and serfs and between lords and vassals differed too much from one place to another, and from one time to another, to fit together in anything resembling a system.

AP* Exam Tip For the multiple choice section, understanding feudalism is important, but it is not essential to know specific feudal monarchs.

The German foes of the Roman legions had equipped themselves with helmets, shields, and swords, spears, or throwing axes. Some rode horses, but most fought on foot. Before the invention of the stirrup by Central Asian pastoralists in approximately the first century C.E., horsemen had gripped their mounts with their legs and fought with bows and arrows, throwing javelins, stabbing spears, and swords. Stirrups allowed a rider to stand in the saddle and absorb the impact when his lance struck an enemy at full gallop. This type of warfare required grain-fed horses that were larger and heavier than the small, grass-fed animals of the Central Asian nomads, though smaller and lighter than the draft horses bred in later times for hauling heavy loads. Thus agricultural Europe rather than the grassy steppes produced the charges of armored knights that came to dominate the battlefield.

Knights

By the eleventh century, the knight, called by different terms in different places, had emerged as the central figure in medieval warfare. He wore an open-faced helmet and a long linen shirt, or hauberk (HAW-berk), studded with small metal disks (see Environment and Technology:

ENVIRONMENT + TECHNOLOGY

Iron Production

Despite the collapse of the Roman economy, ironworking expanded throughout Europe. The iron swords of the Germans outperformed traditional Roman weapons, which became obsolete. The spreading use of armor also increased the demand for iron. Archaeologists have found extensive evidence of iron smelting well beyond the frontiers of the Roman Empire. Helg Island in a lake near Stockholm, Sweden, had a large walled settlement that relied entirely on iron trading. Discoveries of a Buddha from India and a christening spoon from Egypt, both datable to the sixth century C.E., indicate the range of these trade contacts. At Zelechovice in the Czech Republic remains of fifty "slag-pit" furnaces have been dated to the ninth century.

Most iron smelting was done on a small scale. Ore containing iron oxide was shoveled onto a charcoal fire in an open-air hearth pit. The carbon in the charcoal combined with the oxygen in the ore to form carbon dioxide gas. This left behind a soft glowing lump of iron called a "bloom." This bloom was then pounded on a stone to remove the remaining impurities, like sand and clay, before being turned over to the blacksmith for fabricating into swords or armor.

During the post-Roman centuries, smelters learned to build walls around the hearth pits and then to put domes and chimneys on them. The resulting "slag-pit" furnaces produced greater amounts of iron. They also consumed great amounts of wood. Twelve pounds of charcoal, made from about 25 pounds of wood, were needed to produce 1 pound of bloom iron, and about 3 pounds of useless slag. Though bellows were developed to force oxygen into the fire, temperatures in slag-pit furnaces never became high enough to produce molten metal.

Iron Smelting Two bellows blowing alternately provide a constant stream of air to the furnace. The man on the right pounds the bloom into bars or plates that a blacksmith will reheat and shape.

fief In medieval Europe, land granted in return for a sworn oath to provide specified military service.

vassal In medieval Europe, a sworn supporter of a king or lord committed to rendering specified military service to that king or lord.

Iron Production). A century later, knightly equipment commonly included a visored helmet that covered the head and neck and a hauberk of chain mail.

Fiefs, Nobles, and Vassals

Each increase in armor for knight and horse entailed a greater financial outlay. Since land was the basis of wealth, a knight needed financial support from land revenues. Accordingly, kings began to reward armed service with grants of land from their own property. Lesser nobles with extensive properties built their own military retinues the same way.

A grant of land in return for a pledge to provide military service was often called a **fief**. At first, kings granted fiefs to their noble followers, known as **vassals**, on a temporary basis. By the tenth century, most fiefs could be inherited as long as the specified military service continued to be provided. Though patterns varied greatly, the association of landholding with military service made the medieval society of western Europe quite different from the contemporary city-based societies of the Islamic world.

Kings and lords might be able to command the service of their vassals for only part of the year. Vassals could hold land from several different lords and owe loyalty to each one. Moreover, the allegiance that a vassal owed to one lord could entail military service to that lord's master in time of need.

A "typical" medieval realm—actual practices varied between and within realms—consisted of lands directly owned by a king or a count and administered by his royal officers. The king's or count's major vassals held and administered other lands, often the greater portion, in return for military service. These vassals, in turn, granted land to their own vassals.

The lord of a manor provided governance and justice, direct royal government being quite limited. The king had few financial resources and seldom exercised legal jurisdiction at a local level. Members of the clergy, as well as the extensive agricultural lands owned by monasteries and nunneries, fell under the jurisdiction of the church, which further limited the reach and authority of the monarch.

Noblewomen

Noblewomen became enmeshed in this tangle of obligations as heiresses and as candidates for marriage. A man who married the widow or daughter of a lord with no sons could gain control of that lord's property. Marriage alliances affected entire kingdoms. Noble daughters and sons had little say in marriage matters; issues of land, power, and military service took precedence. Noblemen guarded the women in their families as closely as their other valuables.

Nevertheless, women could own land. A noblewoman sometimes administered her husband's estates when he was away at war. Nonnoble women usually worked alongside their menfolk, performing agricultural tasks such as raking and stacking hay, shearing sheep, and picking vegetables. As artisans, women spun, wove, and sewed clothing. The Bayeux (bay-YUH) Tapestry, a piece of embroidery 230 feet (70 meters) long and 20 inches (51 centimeters) wide depicting William the Conqueror's invasion of England in 1066, was designed and executed entirely by women, though historians do not agree on who those women were.

SECTION REVIEW

- In the west, German kingdoms divided territory seized from Rome, and German lifestyles gradually replaced Roman ones.
- Raids by warrior peoples, including Muslims and Vikings, forced an emphasis on warfare.
- The Carolingians created an empire that was later split into three realms.
- Society focused on rural villages and estates–manors—rather than cities.
- Rulers and nobles granted land to vassals in return for military service, thus creating the armed knight.

THE WESTERN CHURCH

 **AP* Exam Tip** Understand the papacy as an institution, but don't stress about memorizing names of specific popes.

Just as the Christian populations in eastern Europe followed the religious guidance of the patriarch of Constantinople appointed by the Byzantine emperor, so the pope commanded similar authority over church affairs in western Europe. And just as missionaries in the east spread Christianity among the Slavs, so missionaries in the west added territory to Christendom with forays into the British Isles and the lands of the Germans. Throughout the period covered by this chapter, Christian society was emerging and changing in both areas.

The Papacy

papacy The central administration of the Roman Catholic Church, of which the pope is the head.

In the west Roman nobles lost control of the **papacy**—the office of the pope—and it became a more powerful international office after the tenth century. Councils of bishops—which normally set rules, called canons, to regulate the priests and laypeople (men and women who were not members of the clergy) under their jurisdiction—became increasingly responsive to papal direction.

Nevertheless, regional disagreements over church regulations, shortages of educated and trained clergy, difficult communications, political disorder, and the general insecurity of the period posed formidable obstacles to unifying church standards and practices (see Diversity and Dominance: The Struggle for Christian Morality). Clerics in some parts of western Europe were still issuing prohibitions against the worship of rivers, trees, and mountains as late as the

The Struggle for Christian Morality

Ireland

The medieval church believed that Christians could be absolved of their sins by performing public or private penalties, or acts of humiliation. Priests listened to the believers confess their sins and then set the nature and duration of the penance. Books called penitentials guided the priests by stipulating the appropriate penance for specific sins. These books varied over time and tended to reflect local conditions. One of the earliest is attributed to Saint Patrick, who began his missionary work in Ireland in 432. The selections below deal not just with penalties for sin but also with efforts to impose church discipline on priests.

§ There shall be no wandering cleric in a parish.

§ If any cleric, from sexton [church caretaker] to priest, is seen without a tunic, and does not cover the shame and nakedness of his body; and if his hair is not shaven according to the Roman custom, and if his wife goes about with her head unveiled, he shall be alike despised by laymen and separated from the Church.

§ A monk and a virgin, the one from one place, the other from another, shall not dwell together in the same inn, nor travel in the same carriage from village to village, nor continually hold conversation with each other.

§ It is not permitted to the Church to accept alms from pagans.

§ A Christian who believes that there is a vampire in the world, that is to say, a witch, is to be anathematized [condemned by the Church]; whoever lays that reputation upon a living being, shall not be received into the Church until he revokes with his own voice the crime that he has committed and accordingly does penance with all diligence.

§ A Christian who defrauds anyone with respect to a debt in the manner of the pagans, shall be excommunicated [barred from Christian society] until he pays the debt.

England and Southern Germany

Boniface (ca. 675–754), a widely esteemed bishop of the southern German city of Mainz, began life with the name Winfrid in Anglo-Saxon Britain. After working as a missionary in Frisia in the Netherlands, he devoted the bulk of his life to establishing Christianity and respect for Christian law and morality in southern Germany. His letters reflect his passion for reforming personal behavior along Christian lines.

Boniface to Pope Zacharias, 742

We must confess, our father and lord, that after we learned from messengers that your predecessor in the apostolate [i.e., papacy], Gregory of reverend memory . . . had been set free from the prison of the body and had passed on to God, nothing gave us greater joy or happiness than the knowledge that the Supreme Arbiter had appointed your fatherly clemency to administer the canon law and to govern the Apostolic See. . . .

Some of the ignorant common people, Alemanians, Bavarians, and Franks, hearing that many of the offenses prohibited by us are practiced in the city of Rome imagine that they are allowed by the priests there and reproach us for causing them to incur blame in their own lives. They say that on the first day of January year after year, in the city of Rome and in the neighborhood of St. Peter's church by day or night, they have seen bands of singers parading the streets in pagan fashion, shouting and chanting sacrilegious songs and loading tables with food day and night, while no one in his own house is willing to lend his neighbor fire or tools or any other convenience. They say also that they have seen there women with amulets and bracelets of heathen fashion on their arms and legs, offering them for sale to willing buyers. . . .

Boniface and Other Bishops to King Ethelbald of Mercia (a Saxon Kingdom in England), 746–747

We have heard that you are very liberal in almsgiving, and congratulate you thereon. . . . We have heard also that you repress robbery and wrongdoing, perjury, and rapine with a strong hand, and that you have established peace within your kingdom. . . .

But amidst all this, one evil report as to the manner of life of Your Grace has come to our hearing, which has greatly grieved us and which we would wish were not true. We have learned from many sources that you have never taken to yourself a lawful wife. . . . If you had willed to do this for the sake of chastity and abstinence . . . we should rejoice, for that is not worthy of blame but rather of praise. But if, as many say—but which God forbid!—you have neither taken a lawful spouse nor observed chastity for God's sake but, moved by desire, have defiled your

eleventh century. Church problems included lingering polytheism, lax enforcement of prohibitions against marriage of clergy, nepotism (giving preferment to one's close kin), and simony (selling ecclesiastical appointments, often to people who were not members of the clergy). The persistence of the papacy in asserting its legal jurisdiction over clergy, combating polytheism and heretical beliefs, and calling on secular rulers to recognize the pope's authority, including unpopular rulings like a ban on first-cousin marriage, constituted a rare force for unity and order in a time of disunity and chaos.

good name before God and man by the crime of adulterous lust, then we are greatly grieved because this is a sin in the sight of God and is the ruin of your fair fame among men.

And now, what is worse, our informants say that these atrocious crimes are committed in convents with holy nuns and virgins consecrated to God, and this, beyond all doubt, doubles the offense. . . .

This is held to be a shame and disgrace, not by Christians only but even by pagans. For the pagans themselves, although ignorant of the true God, keep in this matter the substance of the law and the ordinance of God from the beginning, inasmuch as they respect their wives with the bond of matrimony and punish fornicators and adulterers. In Old Saxony, if a virgin disgraces her father's house by adultery or if a married woman breaks the bond of wedlock and commits adultery, they sometimes compel her to hang herself with her own hand and then hang the seducer above the pyre on which she has been burned. Sometimes a troop of women get together and flog her through the towns, beating her with rods and stripping her to the waist, cutting her whole body with knives . . . until finally they leave her for dead or almost dead. . . .

Northern Germany and Scandinavia

Adam of Bremen's History of the Archbishops of Hamburg-Bremen *consists of four sections. The third is devoted to the Archbishop Adalbert, whose death in 1072 stirred Adam to write. References to classical poets, the lives of saints, and royal documents show that Adam, a churchman, had a solid education and access to many sources, including conversations with kings and nobles.*

This remarkable man [i.e., Archbishop Adalbert] may . . . be extolled with praise of every kind in that he was noble, handsome, wise, eloquent, chaste, temperate. All these qualities he comprised in himself and others besides, such as one is wont to attach to the outer man: that he was rich, that he was successful, that he was glorious, that he was influential. All these things were his in abundance. Moreover, in respect of the mission to the heathen, which is the first duty of the Church at Hamburg, no one so vigorous could ever be found. . . .

As soon as the metropolitan [i.e., Archbishop Adalbert] had entered upon his episcopate, he sent legates to the kings of the north in the interest of friendship. There were also dispersed throughout all Denmark and Norway and Sweden and to the ends of the earth admonitory letters in which he exhorted the bishops and priests living in those parts . . . fearlessly to forward the conversion of the pagans. . . . [One Danish king] forgot the heavenly King as things prospered with him and married a blood relative from Sweden. This mightily displeased the lord archbishop, who sent legates to the rash king, rebuking him severely for his sin, and who stated finally that if he did not come to his senses, he would have to be cut off with the sword of excommunication. Beside himself with rage, the king then threatened to ravage and destroy the whole diocese of Hamburg. Unperturbed by these threats, our archbishop, reproving and entreating, remained firm, until at length the Danish tyrant was prevailed upon by letters from the pope to give his cousin a bill of divorce. . . .

In Norway . . . King Harold surpassed all the madness of tyrants in his savage wildness. Many churches were destroyed by that man; many Christians were tortured to death by him. But he was a mighty man and renowned for the victories he had previously won in many wars with barbarians in Greece and in the Scythian regions [i.e. , while assisting the Byzantine empress Zoë fight the Seljuk Turks]. After he came into his fatherland, however, he never ceased from warfare; he was the thunderbolt of the north. . . . And so, as he ruled over many nations, he was odious to all on account of his greed and cruelty. He also gave himself up to the magic arts and, wretched man that he was, did not heed the fact that his most saintly brother [i.e., Saint Olaf, one of Harold's predecessors] had eradicated such illusions from the realm and striven even unto death for the adoption of the precepts of Christianity. . . .

Across the Elbe [i.e., east of the river Hamburg is on] and in Slavia our affairs were still meeting with great success. For Gottschalk . . . married a daughter of the Danish king and so thoroughly subdued the Slavs that they feared him like a king, offered to pay tribute, and asked for peace with subjection. Under these circumstances our Church at Hamburg enjoyed peace, and Slavia abounded in priests and churches. . . .

QUESTIONS FOR ANALYSIS

1. **How are the practices of non-Christians used as good and bad examples for Christians?**
2. **What limits, if any, do church officials recognize in their role as moral judges?**
3. **How does the church confront royal authority?**

Sources: Excerpts from John T. McNeill and Helena M. Gamer, *Medieval Handbooks of Penance* (New York: Columbia University Press, 1938), 77–78; *The Letters of Saint Boniface*, tr. Ephraim Emerton (New York: Columbia University Press, 2000), 56, 59–60, 103–105; and *History of the Archbishops of Hamburg-Bremen*, tr. Francis J. Tschan (New York: Columbia University Press, 1959 [new ed. 2002]), 114–133.

Politics and the Church

The Holy Roman Empire

In politically fragmented western Europe, the pope needed allies. Like his son, Charlemagne's father Pepin was a strong supporter of the papacy. The relationship between kings and popes was tense, however, since both thought of themselves as ultimate authorities. In 962 the pope crowned the first "Holy Roman Emperor" (Charlemagne never held this full title). This designation of a secular political authority as the guardian of general Christian interests proved more apparent

Holy Roman Empire Loose federation of mostly German states and principalities, headed by an emperor elected by the princes. It lasted from 962 to 1806.

then real. Essentially a loose confederation of German princes who named one of their own to the highest office, the **Holy Roman Empire** had little influence west of the Rhine River.

Although the pope crowned the early Holy Roman Emperors, this did not signify political superiority. The law of the church (known as canon law because each law was called a canon) gave the pope exclusive legal jurisdiction over all clergy and church property wherever located. But bishops who held land as vassals owed military support or other services and dues to kings and princes. The secular rulers argued that they should have the power to appoint those bishops because that was the only way to guarantee fulfillment of their duties as vassals. The popes disagreed.

In the eleventh century, this conflict over the control of ecclesiastical appointments came to a head. Hildebrand (HILL-de-brand), an Italian monk, capped a career of reorganizing church finances when the cardinals (a group of senior bishops) meeting in Rome selected him to be Pope Gregory VII in 1073. His personal notion of the papacy (preserved among his letters) represented an extreme position, stating among other claims, that

§ *The pope can be judged by no one;*
§ *The Roman church has never erred and never will err till the end of time;*
§ *The pope alone can depose and restore bishops;*
§ *He alone can call general councils and authorize canon law;*
§ *He can depose emperors;*
§ *He can absolve subjects from their allegiance;*
§ *All princes should kiss his feet.*[5]

The Investiture Controversy

investiture controversy Dispute between the popes and the Holy Roman Emperors over who held ultimate authority over bishops in imperial lands.

Such claims antagonized lords and monarchs, who had become accustomed to *investing*—that is, conferring a ring and a staff as symbols of authority on bishops and abbots in their domains. Historians apply the term **investiture controversy** to the medieval struggle between the church and the lay lords to control ecclesiastical appointments; the term also refers to the broader conflict of popes versus emperors and kings. When Holy Roman Emperor Henry IV defied Gregory's reforms, Gregory excommunicated him in 1076, thereby cutting him off from church rituals. Stung by the resulting decline in his influence, Henry stood barefoot in the snow for three days outside a castle in northern Italy waiting for Gregory, a guest there, to receive him. Henry's formal act of penance induced Gregory to forgive him and restore him to the church; but the reconciliation, an apparent victory for the pope, did not last. In 1078 Gregory declared Henry deposed. The emperor then forced Gregory to flee from Rome to Salerno, where he died two years later.

The struggle between the popes and the emperors continued until 1122, when a compromise was reached at Worms, a town in Germany. In the Concordat of Worms, Emperor Henry V renounced his right to choose bishops and abbots or bestow spiritual symbols upon them. In return, Pope Calixtus II permitted the emperor to invest papally appointed bishops and abbots with any lay rights or obligations before their spiritual consecration. Such compromises did not fully solve the problem, but they reduced tensions between the two sides.

Assertions of royal authority triggered other conflicts as well. Though barely twenty when he became king of England in 1154, Henry II, a great-grandson of William the Conqueror, instituted reforms designed to strengthen the power of the Crown and weaken the nobility. He appointed traveling justices to enforce his laws and made juries, a holdover from traditional Germanic law, into powerful legal instruments. He also established the principle that criminal acts violated the "king's peace" and should be tried and punished in accordance with charges brought by the Crown instead of in response to charges brought by victims.

Henry II of England and Thomas à Becket

Henry had a harder time controlling the church. His closest friend and chancellor, or chief administrator, Thomas à Becket (ca. 1118–1170), lived the grand and luxurious life of a courtier. In 1162 Henry persuaded Becket to become a priest and assume the position of archbishop of Canterbury, the highest church office in England. Becket agreed but cautioned that from then on he would act solely in the interest of the church if it came into conflict with the Crown. When Henry sought to try clerics accused of crimes in royal instead of ecclesiastical courts, Archbishop Thomas, now leading an austere and pious life, resisted.

In 1170 four of Henry's knights, knowing that the king desired Becket's death, murdered the archbishop in Canterbury Cathedral. Their crime backfired, and an outpouring of sympathy caused Canterbury to become a major pilgrimage center. In 1173 the pope declared the mar-

Illustrated Manuscript from Monastic Library This page from the Book of Kells, written around 800 in Ireland, combines an icon-like image of a gospel writer with complex interwoven patterns in the margin that derive from the pre-Christian art of northern Europe. Note the evangelist's blonde hair.

Trinity College Library Dublin/The Bridgeman Art Library

tyred Becket a saint. Henry allowed himself to be publicly whipped twice in penance for the crime, but his authority had been badly damaged.

Henry II's conflict with Thomas à Becket, like the Concordat of Worms, yielded no clear victor. The problem of competing legal traditions made political life in western Europe more complicated than in Byzantium or the lands of Islam (see Chapter 8). Feudal law, rooted in Germanic custom, gave supreme power to the king. Canon law, based on Roman precedent, visualized a single hierarchical legal institution with jurisdiction over all of Western Christendom. In the eleventh century Roman civil law, contained in the *Corpus Juris Civilis*, added a third tradition.

monasticism Living in a religious community apart from secular society and adhering to a rule stipulating chastity, obedience, and poverty. It was a prominent element of medieval Christianity and Buddhism. Monasteries were the primary centers of learning and literacy in medieval Europe.

Monasticism

Monasticism featured prominently in the religious life of almost all medieval Christian lands. The origins of group monasticism lay in the eastern lands of the Roman Empire. Pre-Christian practices such as celibacy, continual devotion to prayer, and living apart from society (alone or in small groups) came together in Christian form in Egypt.

The Benedictine Rule

The most important form of monasticism in western Europe, however, involved groups of monks or nuns living together in organized communities. The person most responsible for introducing this originally Egyptian practice in the Latin west was Benedict of Nursia (ca. 480–547)

PRIMARY SOURCE: The Rule of Saint Benedict: Work and Pray In this selection from his rules for monastic life, Benedict urged monks to avoid idleness by devoting themselves to physical labor, prayer, and reading.

in Italy. Benedict began his pious career as a hermit in a cave but eventually organized several monasteries, each headed by an abbot. In the seventh century monasteries based on his model spread far beyond Italy. The Rule Benedict wrote to govern the monks' behavior envisions a balanced life of devotion and work, along with obligations of celibacy, poverty, and obedience to the abbot. Those who lived by this or other monastic rules became *regular clergy,* in contrast to *secular clergy,* priests who lived in society instead of in seclusion and did not follow a formal code of regulations. The Rule of Benedict was the starting point for most forms of western European monastic life and remains in force today in Benedictine monasteries.

Though monks and nuns, women who lived by monastic rules in convents, made up a small percentage of the total population, their secluded way of life reinforced the separation of religious affairs from ordinary politics and economics. Monasteries followed Jesus' axiom to "render unto Caesar what is Caesar's and unto God what is God's" better than the many town-based bishops who behaved like lords.

Preservation of Knowledge

Monasteries preserved literacy and learning in the early medieval period, although some rulers, like Charlemagne, encouraged scholarship at court. Many illiterate lay nobles interested themselves only in warfare and hunting. Monks (but seldom nuns) saw copying manuscripts and even writing books as a religious calling. Monastic scribes preserved many ancient Latin works that would otherwise have disappeared. The survival of Greek works depended more on Byzantine and Muslim scribes in the east.

Monasteries and convents served other functions as well. A few planted Christianity in new lands, as Irish monks did in parts of Germany. Most serviced the needs of travelers, organized agricultural production on their lands, and took in infants abandoned by their parents. Convents provided refuge for widows and other women who lacked male protection in the harsh medieval world or who desired a spiritual life. These religious houses presented problems of oversight to the church, however. A bishop might have authority over an abbot or abbess (head of a convent), but he could not exercise constant vigilance over what went on behind monastery walls.

Cluny

The failure of some abbots to maintain monastic discipline led to the growth of a reform movement centered on the Benedictine abbey of Cluny (KLOO-nee) in eastern France. Founded in 910 by William the Pious, the first duke of Aquitaine, who completely freed it of lay authority, Cluny gained similar freedom from the local bishop a century later. Its abbots pursued a vigorous campaign, eventually in alliance with reforming popes like Gregory VII, to improve monastic discipline and administration. A magnificent new abbey church symbolized Cluny's claims to eminence. With later additions, it became the largest church in the world.

At the peak of Cluny's influence, nearly a thousand Benedictine abbeys and priories (lower-level monastic houses) in various countries accepted the authority of its abbot. The Benedictine Rule had presumed that each monastery would be independent; the Cluniac reformers stipulated that every abbot and every prior (head of a priory) be appointed by the abbot of Cluny and have personal experience of the religious life of Cluny. Monastic reform gained new impetus in the second half of the twelfth century with the rapid rise of the Cistercian order, which emphasized a life of asceticism and poverty. These movements set the pattern for the monasteries, cathedral clergy, and preaching friars that would dominate ecclesiastical life in the thirteenth century.

SECTION REVIEW

- Christianity in western Europe focused on the pope in Rome, but conflict with Holy Roman Emperors led to the investiture controversy.
- Likewise, conflict grew between Henry of England and the archbishop Thomas à Becket, leading to Becket's martyrdom.
- One religious constant was life in monasteries; Benedict of Nursia founded the Benedictine Rule, and later the need for greater discipline over monks and nuns led to the founding of Cluny, a center of monastic reform.
- Monasteries provided many charitable services and preserved learning.

KIEVAN RUSSIA, 900–1200

Though Latin and Orthodox Christendom followed different paths in later centuries, which had a more promising future was not apparent in 900. The Poles and other Slavic peoples living in the north eventually accepted the Christianity of Rome as taught by German priests and missionaries. The Serbs and other southern Slavs took their faith from Constantinople.

The conversion of Kievan Russia, farther to the east, shows how economics, politics, and religious life were closely intertwined. The choice of orthodoxy over Catholicism had important consequences for later European history.

The Rise of the Kievan Empire

The territory between the Black and Caspian Seas in the south and the Baltic and White Seas in the north divides into a series of east-west zones. Frozen tundra in the far north gives way to a cold forest zone, then to a more temperate forest, then to a mix of forest and steppe grasslands, and finally to grassland only. Several navigable rivers, including the Volga, the Dnieper (d-NYEP-er), and the Don, run from north to south across these zones.

The Culture of the Steppes

Early historical sources reflect repeated linguistic and territorial changes, seemingly under pressure from poorly understood population migrations. Most of the Germanic peoples, along with some Iranian and west Slavic peoples, migrated into eastern Europe from Ukraine and Russia in Roman times. The peoples who remained behind spoke eastern Slavic languages, except in the far north and south: Finns and related peoples lived in the former region, Turkic-speakers in the latter.

Forest dwellers, farmers, and steppe nomads complemented each other economically. Nomads traded animals for the farmers' grain; and honey, wax, and furs from the forest became important exchange items. Traders could travel east and west by steppe caravan (see Chapters 7 and 12), or they could use boats on the rivers to move north and south.

Varangian Traders

Hoards containing thousands of Byzantine and Islamic coins buried in Poland and on islands in the Baltic Sea where fairs were held attest to the trading activity of Varangians (Swedish Vikings) who sailed across the Baltic and down Russia's rivers. They exchanged forest products and slaves for manufactured goods and coins, which they may have used as jewelry rather than as money, at markets controlled by the Khazar Turks. The powerful Khazar kingdom centered around the mouth of the Volga River.

Historians debate the early meaning of the word *Rus* (from which *Russia* is derived), but at some point it came to refer to Slavic-speaking peoples ruled by Varangians. Unlike western European lords, the Varangian princes and their *druzhina* (military retainers) lived in cities, while the Slavs farmed. The princes occupied themselves with trade and fending off enemies. The Rus of the city of Kiev (KEE-yev), which was taken over by Varangians around 880, controlled trade on the Dnieper River and dealt more with Byzantium than with the Muslim world because the Dnieper flows into the Black Sea. The Rus of Novgorod (NOHV-goh-rod) played the same role on the Volga. The semilegendary account of the Kievan Rus conversion to Christianity must be seen against this background.

Vladimir I of Kiev

In 980 Vladimir (VLAD-ih-mir) I, a ruler of Novgorod who had fallen from power, returned from exile to Kiev with a band of Varangians and made himself the grand prince of Kievan Russia (see Map 9.3). Though his grandmother Olga had been a Christian, Vladimir built a temple on Kiev's heights and placed there the statues of the six gods his Slavic subjects worshiped. The earliest Russian chronicle reports that Vladimir and his advisers decided against Islam as the official religion because of its ban on alcohol, rejected Judaism (the religion to which the Khazars had converted) because they thought that a truly powerful god would not have let the ancient Jewish kingdom be destroyed, and even spoke with German emissaries advocating Latin Christianity. Why Vladimir chose Orthodox Christianity over the Latin version is not precisely known. The magnificence of Constantinople seems to have been a consideration. After visiting Byzantine churches, his agents reported: "We knew not whether we were in heaven or on earth, for on earth there is no such splendor of [sic] such beauty, and we are at a loss how to describe it. We know only that God dwells there among men, and their service is finer than the ceremonies of other nations."[6]

Christianity Spreads

After choosing a reluctant bride from the Byzantine imperial family, Vladimir converted to Orthodox Christianity, probably in 988, and opened his lands to Orthodox clerics and missionaries. The patriarch of Constantinople appointed a metropolitan (chief bishop) at Kiev to govern ecclesiastical affairs. Churches arose in Kiev, one of them on the ruins of Vladimir's earlier hilltop temple. Writing was introduced, using the Cyrillic alphabet devised earlier for the western Slavs. This extension of Orthodox Christendom northward provided a barrier against the eastward expansion of Latin Christianity. Kiev became firmly oriented toward trade with Byzantium and turned its back on the Muslim world, though the Volga trade continued through Novgorod.

MAP 9.3 Kievan Russia and the Byzantine Empire in the Eleventh Century By the mid-eleventh century, the princes of Kievan Russia had brought all the eastern Slavs under their rule. The loss of Egypt, Syria, and Tunisia to Arab invaders in the seventh to eighth century had turned Byzantium from a far-flung empire into a fairly compact state. From then on the Byzantine rulers looked to the Balkans and Kievan Russia as the primary arena for extending their political and religious influence.

 Interactive Map

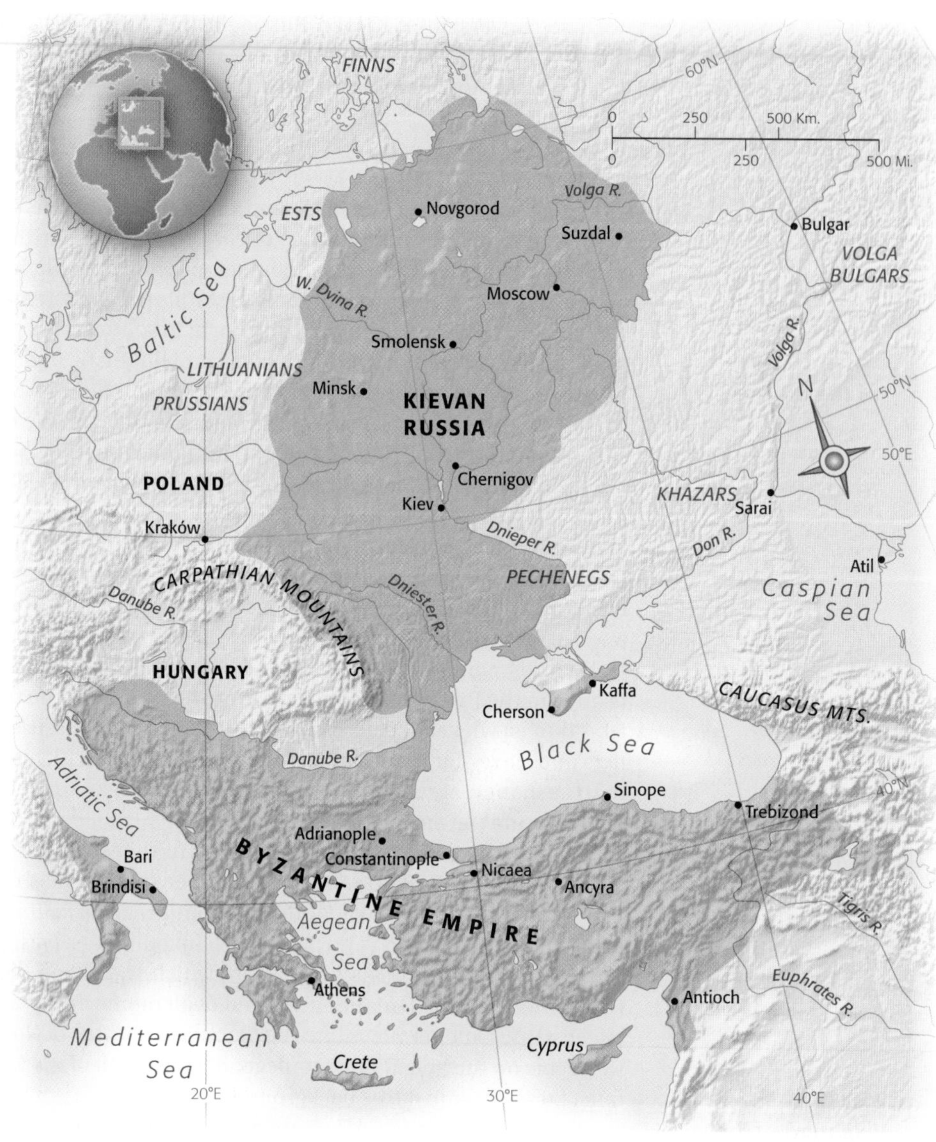

Struggles within the ruling family and with other enemies, most notably the steppe peoples of the south, marked the later political history of Kievan Russia. But down to the time of the Mongols in the thirteenth century (see Chapter 12), the state remained and served as an instrument for the Christianization of the eastern Slavs.

Society and Culture

In Kievan Russia political power derived from trade rather than from landholding, so the manorial agricultural system of western Europe never developed. Farmers practiced shifting cultivation of their own lands. They would burn a section of forest, then lightly scratch the ash-strewn surface with a plow. When fertility waned, they would move to another section of forest. Poor land and a short growing season in the most northerly latitudes made food scarce. Living on their own estates, the druzhina evolved from infantry into cavalry and focused their efforts more on horse breeding than on agriculture.

Urban Life

Large cities like Kiev and Novgorod may have reached thirty thousand or fifty thousand people—roughly the size of contemporary London or Paris, but far smaller than Constantinople

TASS/Sovfoto

Cathedral of Saint Dmitry in Vladimir Built between 1193 and 1197, this Russian Orthodox cathedral shows Byzantine influence. The three-arch façade, small dome, and symmetrical Greek Cross floor plan strongly resemble features of the Byzantine church shown on page 256.

SECTION REVIEW

- Power in Kievan Russia depended on trade rather than agriculture; thus there was no manorial system, and lords ruled from cities.
- Varangian traders established political dominion over Slavic peoples.
- The cities of Kiev and Novgorod provided the nucleus of Russian principalities.
- The Kievan ruler Vladimir I made Orthodox Christianity the official religion in Kievan Russia, though it penetrated the population slowly.
- Kievan cities reflected some aspects of Byzantine culture, especially in crafts such as glassmaking.

or major Muslim metropolises like Baghdad and Nishapur. Many cities amounted to little more than fortified trading posts. Yet they served as centers for the development of crafts, some, such as glassmaking, based on skills imported from Byzantium. Artisans enjoyed higher status in society than peasant farmers. Construction relied on wood from the forests, although Christianity brought the building of stone cathedrals and churches on the Byzantine model.

Christianity penetrated the general population slowly. Several polytheist uprisings occurred in the eleventh century, particularly in times of famine. Passive resistance led some groups to reject Christian burial and persist in cremating the dead and keeping the bones of the deceased in urns. Women continued to use polytheist designs on their clothing and bracelets, and as late as the twelfth century they were still turning to polytheist priests for charms to cure sick children. Traditional Slavic marriage practices involving casual and polygamous relations particularly scandalized the clergy.

Christianity eventually triumphed, and its success led to increasing church engagement in political and economic affairs. In the twelfth century, Christian clergy became involved in government administration, some of them collecting fees and taxes related to trade. Direct and indirect revenue from trade provided the rulers with the money they needed to pay their soldiers. The rule of law also spread as Kievan Russia experienced its peak of culture and prosperity in the century before the Mongol invasion of 1237.

WESTERN EUROPE REVIVES, 1000–1200

Between 1000 and 1200 western Europe slowly emerged from nearly seven centuries of subsistence economy—in which most people who worked on the land could meet only their basic needs for food, clothing, and shelter. Population and agricultural production climbed, and a growing food surplus found its way to town markets, speeding the return of a money-based economy and providing support for larger numbers of craftspeople, construction workers, and traders.

Historians have attributed western Europe's revival to population growth spurred by new technologies and to the appearance in Italy and Flanders, on the coast of the North Sea, of self-governing cities devoted primarily to seaborne trade. For monarchs, the changes facilitated improvements in central administration, greater control over vassals, and consolidation of realms on the way to becoming stronger kingdoms.

The Role of Technology

Population Growth

A lack of concrete evidence confirming the spread of technological innovations frustrates efforts to relate the exact course of Europe's revival to technological change. Nevertheless, most historians agree that technology played a significant role in the near doubling of the population of western Europe between 1000 and 1200. The population of England seems to have risen from 1.1 million in 1086 to 1.9 million in 1200, and the population of the territory of modern France seems to have risen from 5.2 million to 9.2 million over the same period.

Horses and Plows

Examples that illustrate the difficulty of drawing historical conclusions from scattered evidence of technological change were a new type of plow and the use of efficient draft harnesses for pulling wagons. The Roman plow, which farmers in southern Europe and Byzantium continued to use, scratched shallow grooves, as was appropriate for loose, dry Mediterranean soils. The new plow cut deep into the soil with a knifelike blade, while a curved board mounted behind the blade lifted the cut layer and turned it over. This made it possible to farm the heavy, wet clays of the northern river valleys. Pulling the new plow took more energy, which could mean harnessing several teams of oxen or horses.

Horses plowed faster than oxen but were more delicate. Iron horseshoes, which were widely adopted in this period, helped protect their feet, but like the plow itself, they added to the farmer's expenses. Roman horse harnesses, inefficiently modeled on the yoke used for oxen, put such pressure on the animal's neck that a horse pulling a heavy load risked strangulation. A mystery surrounds the adoption of more efficient designs. The **horse collar**, which moves the point of traction from the animal's throat to its shoulders, first appeared around 800 in a miniature painting, and it is shown clearly as a harness for plow horses in the Bayeux Tapestry, embroidered after 1066. The breast-strap harness, which is not as well adapted for the heaviest work but was preferred in southern Europe, seems to have appeared around 500. In both cases, linguists have tried to trace key technical terms to Chinese or Turko-Mongol words and have argued for technological diffusion across Eurasia. Yet third-century Roman farmers in Tunisia and Libya used both types of harness to hitch horses and camels to plows and carts. This technology, which is

horse collar Harnessing method that increased the efficiency of horses by shifting the point of traction from the animal's neck to the shoulders; its adoption favors the spread of horse-drawn plows and vehicles.

Vertical Two-Beam Loom These women weavers set up their loom out-of-doors. The vertical strands are the warp threads around which the weft is interwoven. The pole across the bottom of the loom holds the warp threads taut. The kneeling weaver holds a beater to compact the weft at the loom's bottom. In Europe, horizontal looms were more common and paved the way for the mechanization of weaving.

still employed in Tunisia, appears clearly on Roman bas-reliefs and lamps; but there is no more evidence of its movement northward into Europe than there is of similar harnessing moving across Asia. Thus the question of where efficient harnessing came from and whether it began in 500 or in 800, or was known even earlier but not extensively used, cannot be easily resolved.

Hinging on this problem is the question of when and why landowners in northern Europe began to use teams of horses to pull plows through moist, fertile river-valley soils that were too heavy for teams of oxen. Stronger and faster than oxen, horses increased productivity by reducing the time needed for plowing, but they cost more to feed and equip. Thus, it is difficult to say that one technology was always better: Although agricultural surpluses did grow and better plowing did play a role in this growth, areas that continued to use oxen and even old-style plows seem to have shared in the general population growth of the period.

Cities and the Rebirth of the Trade

Independent Cities in Italy

Independent cities governed and defended by communes appeared first in Italy and Flanders and then elsewhere. Communes were groups of leading citizens who banded together to defend their cities and demand the privilege of self-government from their lay or ecclesiastical lord. Lords who granted such privileges benefited from the commune's economic dynamism. Lacking extensive farmlands, these cities turned to manufacturing and trade, which they encouraged through the laws they enacted. Laws making serfs free once they came into the city, for example, attracted many workers from the countryside. Cities in Italy that had shrunk within walls built by the Romans now pressed against those walls, forcing the construction of new ones. Pisa built a new wall in 1000 and expanded it in 1156. Other twelfth-century cities that built new walls include Florence, Brescia (BREH-shee-uh), Pavia, and Siena (see-EN-uh).

Settlers on a group of islands at the northern end of the Adriatic Sea that had been largely uninhabited in Roman times organized themselves into the city of Venice. In the eleventh

AP* Exam Tip Understand the growth and the role of cities in early medieval Europe.

century it became the dominant sea power in the Adriatic. Venice competed with Pisa and Genoa, its rivals on the western side of Italy, for leadership in the trade with Muslim ports in North Africa and the eastern Mediterranean. A somewhat later merchant's list mentions trade in some three thousand "spices" (including dyestuffs, textile fibers, and raw materials), some of them products of Muslim lands and some coming via the Silk Road or the Indian Ocean trading system (see Chapter 7). Among them were eleven types of alum (for dyeing), eleven types of wax, eight types of cotton, four types of indigo, five types of ginger, four types of paper, and fifteen types of sugar, along with cloves, caraway, tamarind, and fresh oranges. By the time of the Crusades (see below), maritime commerce throughout the Mediterranean had come to depend heavily on ships from Genoa, Venice, and Pisa.

Flanders and Northern Europe

Ghent, Bruges (broozh), and Ypres (EEP-r) in Flanders rivaled the Italian cities in prosperity, trade, and industry. Enjoying comparable independence based on privileges granted by the counts of Flanders, these cities centralized the fishing and wool trades of the North Sea region. Around 1200 raw wool from England began to be woven into woolen cloth for a very large market.

More abundant coinage also signaled the upturn in economic activity. In the ninth and tenth centuries most gold coins had come from Muslim lands and the Byzantine Empire. Being worth too much for most trading purposes, they seldom reached Germany, France, and England. The widely imitated Carolingian silver penny sufficed. With the economic revival of the twelfth century, minting of silver coins began in Scandinavia, Poland, and other outlying regions. In the following century the reinvigoration of Mediterranean trade made possible a new and abundant gold coinage.

SECTION REVIEW

- Western Europe became more dynamic after 1000.
- Population grew, and cities expanded both in area and commercial activity, with some cities gaining independence from religious and lay authorities.
- New technologies, such as better plows and horse collars, probably contributed to the economic revival, though how they arrived is unclear.
- Northern Italy and Flanders took the lead as maritime trading centers.
- Gold coinage reappeared after centuries of disuse.

THE CRUSADES, 1095–1204

Crusades (1095–1204) Armed pilgrimages to the Holy Land by Christians determined to recover Jerusalem from Muslim rule. The Crusades brought an end to western Europe's centuries of intellectual and cultural isolation.

Western European revival coincided with and contributed to the **Crusades**, a series of religiously inspired Christian military campaigns against Muslims in the eastern Mediterranean that dominated the politics of Europe from 1095 to 1204 (see Chapter 8 and Map 9.4). Four great expeditions, the last redirected against the Byzantines and resulting in the Latin capture of Constantinople, constituted the region's largest military undertakings since the fall of Rome. As a result of the Crusades, noble courts and burgeoning cities in western Europe consumed more goods from the east. This set the stage for the later adoption of ideas, artistic styles, and industrial processes from Byzantium and the lands of Islam.

The Roots of the Crusades

The Truce of God

PRIMARY SOURCE: Annals Read a harrowing, firsthand account of the pillage of Constantinople by western crusaders on April 13, 1204.

Several social and economic currents of the eleventh century contributed to the Crusades. First, reforming leaders of the Latin Church, seeking to soften the warlike tone of society, popularized the Truce of God. This movement limited fighting between Christian lords by specifying times of truce, such as during Lent (the forty days before Easter) and on Sundays. Many knights welcomed a religiously approved alternative to fighting other Christians. Second, ambitious rulers, like the Norman chieftains who invaded England and Sicily, were looking for new lands to conquer. Nobles, particularly younger sons in areas where the oldest son inherited everything, were hungry for land and titles to maintain their status. Third, Italian merchants wanted to increase trade in the eastern Mediterranean and acquire trading posts in Muslim territory. However,

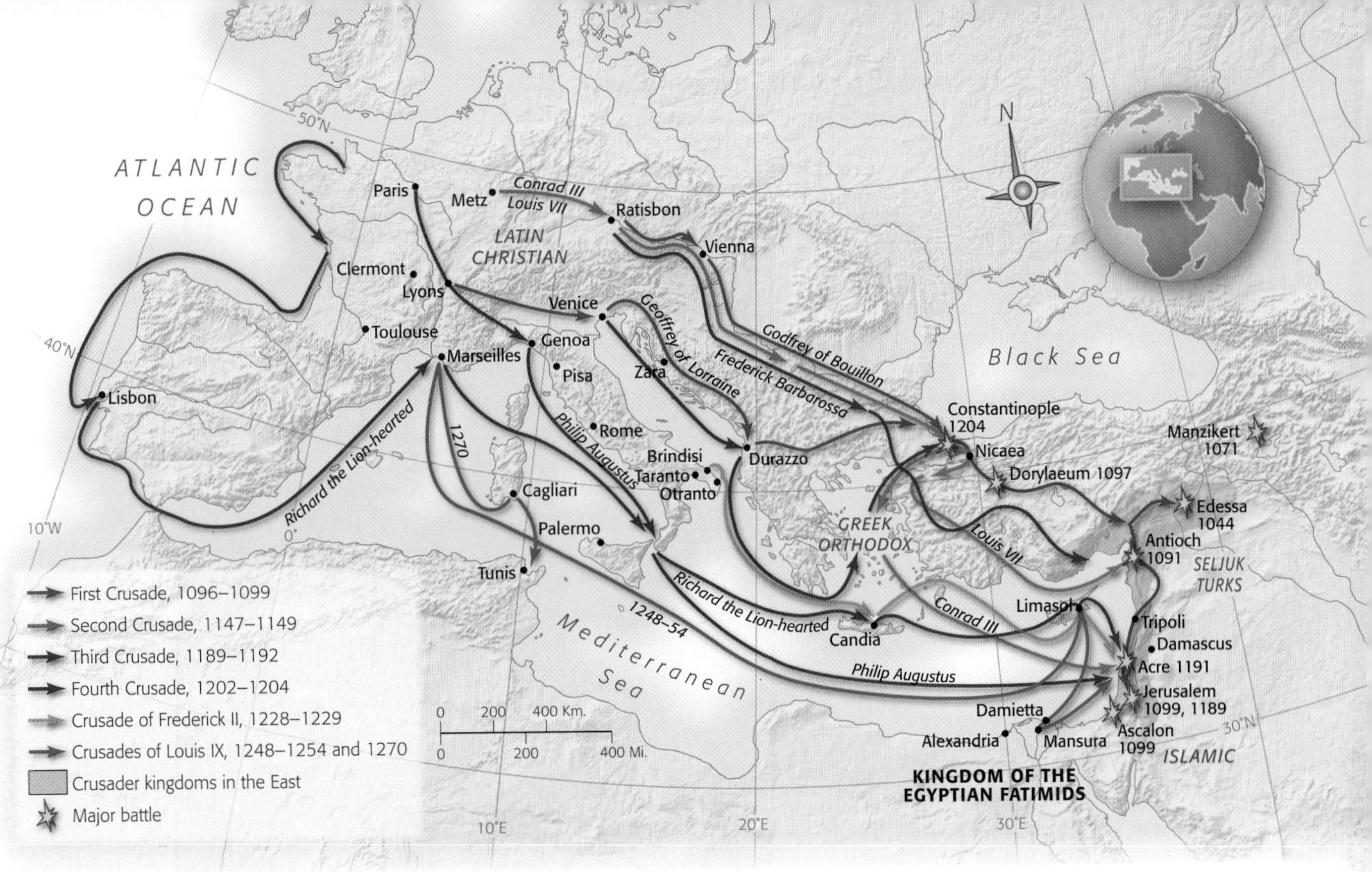

MAP 9.4 The Crusades The first two Crusades proceeded overland through Byzantine territory. The Third Crusade included contingents under the French and English kings, Philip Augustus and Richard Lion-Heart, that traveled by sea, and a contingent under the Holy Roman Emperor Frederick Barbarossa that took the overland route. Frederick died in southern Anatolia. Later Crusades were mostly seaborne, with Sicily, Crete, and Cyprus playing important roles.

Interactive Map

without the rivalry between popes and kings already discussed, and without the desire of the church to demonstrate political authority over western Christendom, the Crusades might never have occurred.

Pilgrimages

pilgrimage Journey to a sacred shrine by Christians seeking to show their piety, fulfill vows, or gain absolution for sins. Other religions also have pilgrimage traditions, such as the Muslim pilgrimage to Mecca and the pilgrimages made by early Chinese Buddhists to India in search of sacred Buddhist writings.

Several factors focused attention on the Holy Land, which had been under Muslim rule for four centuries. **Pilgrimages** played an important role in European religious life. In western Europe, pilgrims traveled under royal protection, with a few in their number actually being tramps, thieves, beggars, peddlers, and merchants for whom pilgrimage was a safe way of traveling. Genuinely pious pilgrims often journeyed to visit the old churches and sacred relics preserved in Rome or Constantinople. The most intrepid went to Jerusalem, Antioch, and other cities under Muslim control to fulfill a vow or to atone for a sin.

Knights who followed a popular pilgrimage route across northern Spain to pray at the shrine of Santiago de Compostela learned of the expanding efforts of Christian kings to dislodge the Muslims. The Umayyad Caliphate in al-Andalus had broken up in the eleventh century, leaving its smaller successor states prey to Christian attacks from the north (see Chapter 8). This was the beginning of a movement of reconquest that culminated in 1492 with the surrender of the last Muslim kingdom. The word *crusade*, taken from Latin *crux* for "cross," was first used in Spain. Stories also circulated of the war conducted by seafaring Normans against the Muslims in Sicily, whom they finally defeated in the 1090s after thirty years of fighting.

The tales of pilgrims returning from Palestine further induced both churchmen and nobles to consider the Muslims a proper target for Christian militancy. Muslim rulers, who had controlled Jerusalem, Antioch, and Alexandria since the seventh century, generally tolerated and protected Christian pilgrims. But after 1071, when a Seljuk army defeated the Byzantine emperor at the Battle of Manzikert (see Chapter 8), Turkish nomads spread throughout the region, and security

Armored Knights in Battle This painting from around 1135 shows the armament of knights at the time of the Crusades. Chain mail, a helmet, and a shield carried on the left side protect the rider. The lance carried underarm and the sword are the primary weapons. Notice that riders about to make contact with lances have their legs straight and braced in the stirrups, while riders with swords and in flight have bent legs.

along the pilgrimage route through Anatolia, already none too good, deteriorated further. The decline of Byzantine power threatened ancient centers of Christianity, such as Ephesus in Anatolia, previously under imperial control.

Pope Urban II

Despite the theological differences between the Orthodox and Roman churches, the Byzantine emperor Alexius Comnenus asked the pope and western European rulers to help him confront the Muslim threat and reconquer what the Christians termed the Holy Land, the early centers of Christianity in Palestine and Syria. Pope Urban II responded at the Council of Clermont in 1095. He addressed a huge crowd of people gathered in a field and called on them, as Christians, to stop fighting one another and go to the Holy Land to fight Muslims.

"God wills it!" exclaimed voices in the crowd. People cut cloth into crosses and sewed them on their shirts to symbolize their willingness to march on Jerusalem. Thus began the holy war now known as the "First Crusade." People at the time more often used the word *peregrinatio*, "pilgrimage." Urban promised to free crusaders who had committed sins from their normal penance, or acts of atonement, the usual reward for peaceful pilgrims to Jerusalem.

The First Crusade captured Jerusalem in 1099 and established four crusader principalities, the most important being the Latin Kingdom of Jerusalem. The next two expeditions strove with diminishing success to protect these gains. Muslim forces retook Jerusalem in 1187. By the time of the Fourth Crusade in 1204, the original religious ardor had so diminished that the commanders agreed, at the urging of the Venetians, to sack Constantinople first to help pay the cost of transporting the army by ship.

The Impact of the Crusades

Exposure to Muslim culture in Spain, Sicily, and the crusader principalities established in the Holy Land made many Europeans aware of things lacking in their own lives. Borrowings from Muslim society occurred gradually and are not always easy to date, but Europeans eventually learned how to manufacture pasta, paper, refined sugar, colored glass, and many other items that had formerly been imported. Arabic translations of and commentaries on Greek philosophical and scientific works, and equally important original works by Arabs and Iranians, provided a vital stimulus to European thought.

Translations from Arabic to Latin

Some works were brought directly into the Latin world through the conquests of Sicily, parts of Spain and the Holy Land, and Constantinople (for Greek texts). Others were rendered into Latin by translators who worked in parts of Spain that continued under Muslim rule. Generations passed before all these works were studied and understood, but they eventually transformed the intellectual world of the western Europeans, who previously had had little familiarity with Greek writings. The works of Aristotle and the Muslim commentaries on them were of particular importance to theologians, but Muslim writers like Avicenna (980–1037) were of parallel importance in medicine.

Eleanor of Aquitaine

Changes affecting the lifestyle of the nobles took place more quickly. Eleanor of Aquitaine (1122?–1204), one of the most influential women of the crusading era, accompanied her husband, King Louis VII of France, on the Second Crusade (1147–1149). The court life of her uncle Raymond, ruler of the crusader principality of Antioch, particularly appealed to her. After her return to France, a lack of male offspring led to an annulment of her marriage with Louis, and she married Henry of Anjou in 1151. He inherited the throne of England as Henry II three years later. Eleanor's sons Richard Lion-Heart, famed in romance as the chivalrous foe of Saladin during the Third Crusade (1189–1192), and John rebelled against their father but eventually succeeded him as kings of England.

In Aquitaine, a powerful duchy in southern France, Eleanor maintained her own court for a time. The poet-singers called troubadours who enjoyed her favor made her court a center for new music based on the idea of "courtly love," an idealization of feminine beauty and grace that influenced later European ideas of romance. Thousands of troubadour melodies survive in manuscripts, and some show the influence of the poetry styles then current in Muslim Spain. The favorite troubadour instrument, moreover, was the lute, a guitar-like instrument with a bulging shape whose design and name (Arabic *al-ud*) come from Muslim Spain. In centuries to come the lute would become the mainstay of Renaissance music in Italy.

SECTION REVIEW

- The Crusades began because of the Truce of God, which asked Christians to stop fighting one another, and hunger for land and trade.
- Pilgrimages to the Holy Land brought attention to that area, and Pope Urban's sermon initiated the crusader effort.
- The Crusaders captured Jerusalem and established four principalities.
- Muslim counterattacks provoked additional Crusades, and as energy flagged the crusaders sacked Constantinople.
- The cultural contact with Muslim lands brought to Europe Muslim interpretations of ancient Greek learning and stimulated other changes in European thought and society.
- Eleanor of Aquitane, the spouse and later the mother of crusading monarchs, promoted the culture of courtly love.

CONCLUSION

The legacy of Roman rule affected eastern and western Europe in different ways. Byzantium inherited the grandeur, pomp, and legal supremacy of the imperial office and merged it with leadership of the Christian church. Byzantium guarded its shrinking frontiers against foreign invasion but gradually contracted around Constantinople, its imperial capital, as more and more territory was lost. By contrast, no Roman core survived in the west. The Germanic peoples overwhelmed the legions guarding the frontiers and established kingdoms based on their own traditions. The law of the king and the law of the church did not echo each other. Yet memories of Roman grandeur and territorial unity resurfaced with the idea of a Holy Roman Empire, however unworkable that empire proved to be.

The competition between the Orthodox and Catholic forms of Christianity complicated the role of religion in the emergence of medieval European society and culture. The Byzantine Empire, constructed on a Roman political and legal heritage that had largely passed away in the west, was generally more prosperous than the Germanic kingdoms of western Europe, and its arts and culture were initially more sophisticated. Furthermore, Byzantine society became deeply Christian well before a comparable degree of Christianization had been reached in western Europe. Yet despite their success in transmitting their version of Christianity and imperial rule to Kievan Russia, and in the process erecting a barrier between the Orthodox Russians and the Catholic Slavs to their west, the Byzantines failed to demonstrate the dynamism and ferment that characterized both the Europeans to their west and the Muslims to their south. Byzantine armies played only a supporting role in the Crusades, and the emperors lost their capital and their power, at least temporarily, to western crusaders in 1204.

Technology and commerce deepened the political and religious gulf between the two Christian zones. Changes in military techniques in western Europe increased battlefield effectiveness, while new agricultural technologies led to population increases that revitalized urban life and contributed to the crusading movement by making the nobility hunger for new lands. At the same time, the need to import food for growing urban populations contributed to the growth of maritime commerce in the Mediterranean and North Seas. Culture and manufacturing benefited greatly from the increased pace of communication and exchange. Lacking parallel developments of a similar scale, the Byzantine Empire steadily lost the dynamism of its early centuries and by the end of the period had clearly fallen behind western Europe in prosperity and cultural innovation.

KEY TERMS

Charlemagne p. 253
medieval p. 253
Byzantine Empire p. 253
Kievan Russia p. 254
schism p. 254
manor p. 260
serf p. 260
fief p. 262
vassal p. 262
papacy p. 263
Holy Roman Empire p. 266
investiture controversy p. 266
monasticism p. 267
horse collar p. 272
Crusades p. 274
pilgrimage p. 275

EBOOK AND WEBSITE RESOURCES

Primary Sources

The Life of Charlemagne: The Emperor Himself

The Rule of St. Benedict: Work and Pray

Annals

Interactive Maps

Map 9.1 The Spread of Christianity

Map 9.2 Germanic Kingdoms

Map 9.3 Kievan Russia and the Byzantine Empire in the Eleventh Century

Map 9.4 The Crusades

Plus flashcards, practice quizzes, and more. Go to: www.cengage.com/history/bullietearthpeople5e

SUGGESTED READING

Bartlett, Robert Merrill. *The Making of Europe*. 1994. Emphasizes developments in frontier regions.

Bynum, Caroline. *Jesus as Mother: Studies in the Spirituality of the High Middle Ages*. 1982. Describes changing Christian views about women.

Collins, Roger. *Early Medieval Europe, 300–1000*. 1991. A lively survey that concentrates on religious and political developments.

Constable, Olivia Remie. *Housing the Stranger in the Mediterranean World: Lodging, Trade, and Travel in Late Antiquity and the Middle Ages*. 2004. A pioneering work in a new field.

Duby, Georges. *Rural Economy and Country Life in the Medieval West*. 1990. A detailed introduction to agricultural history.

Kazhdan, A. P., and Ann Wharton Epstein. *Change in Byzantine Culture in the Eleventh and Twelfth Centuries*. 1985. Concentrates on social and economic issues.

Keller, Amy. *Eleanor of Aquitaine and the Four Kings*. 1950. Lively biography of a major female figure.

Labarge, Margaret Wade. *A Small Sound of the Trumpet: Women in Medieval Life*. 1986. A look at the lives of women at all social levels.

Martin, Janet. *Medieval Russia, 980–1584*. 1995. An up-to-date survey work.

Reynolds, Susan. *Kingdoms and Communities in Western Europe, 900–1300*, 2nd ed. 1997. A survey that shows why *feudalism* is a questionable term.

Riley-Smith, Jonathan. *The Crusades: A Short History*. 1987. The current standard work in this field.

Runciman, Steven. *A History of the Crusades*, 3 vols. 1987. A masterful account with a Byzantine viewpoint.

Southern, Richard W. *Western Society and the Church in the Middle Ages*. 1970. One of many good books on medieval Christendom.

Treadgold, Warren. *A History of Byzantine State and Society*. 1997. A recent general survey.

White, Lynn, Jr. *Medieval Technology and Social Change*. 1962. Classic starting point for history of technology.

NOTES

1. Lewis G. M. Thorpe, *Two Lives of Charlemagne* (Harmondsworth, England: Penguin, 1969).
2. A. P. Kazhdan and Ann Wharton Epstein, *Change in Byzantine Culture in the Eleventh and Twelfth Centuries* (Berkeley: University of California Press, 1985), 71.
3. Ibid., 248.
4. Ibid., 255.
5. R. W. Southern, *Western Society and the Church in the Middle Ages* (Harmondsworth, England: Penguin, 1970), 102.
6. S. A. Zenkovsky, ed., *Medieval Russia's Epics, Chronicles, and Tales* (New York: New American Library, 1974), 67.

AP* REVIEW QUESTIONS FOR CHAPTER 9

1. While the Byzantine Empire flourished after the fall of Rome,
   (A) the western Europeans lived amidst the ruins of an empire.
   (B) the pope became the spiritual, as well as the political, leader of the Western Empire.
   (C) the Huns gained complete control over the Western Empire.
   (D) there was a resurgence of Greco-Roman civilization.

2. The Byzantine rulers set prices, controlled grain shipments to the cities, and monopolized trade in luxury goods. This government intervention
   (A) encouraged the development of new trading businesses and an increase in caravan merchants.
   (B) was the way the Byzantines kept control over tax payments and prevented corruption.
   (C) created a huge number of government jobs, which greatly decreased unemployment and caused a demographic shift to the cities.
   (D) may have slowed technological development and economic innovation.

3. Byzantine achievements in art and architecture include
   (A) graceful paintings of religious figures.
   (B) the Hagia Sophia cathedral.
   (C) the Praetorian Gate.
   (D) the Arch of Triumph.

4. The battle fought at Tours
   (A) prevented Alexius Comnenus from becoming the pope.
   (B) guaranteed the split between the Eastern Empire and the Western Empire.
   (C) was provoked by French merchants who were opposed to new taxes.
   (D) ensured that the Muslims would not encroach further into Europe.

5. Sicily, which was controlled by the Muslims, was conquered by
   (A) Charlemagne's armies who annexed the island.
   (B) Normans who attacked for three decades.
   (C) Christian armies from Italy.
   (D) Huns who raided the island for its wealth.

6. As the Muslims extended their control across North Africa and the Middle East, western Europe
   (A) maintained good trade relationships to ensure caravan routes would not be constricted.
   (B) resorted to sea trade to maintain the supplies of necessary goods.
   (C) encouraged raiding into Muslim North Africa.
   (D) came to rely on meager local resources.

7. The manor
   (A) was a self-sufficient farming estate and the primary center of agricultural production.
   (B) was often given as part of a dowry in marriage contracts.
   (C) channeled wealth and production from the countryside into the cities of Europe.
   (D) developed as a way to allow the best knights to train full time.

8. Which of the following was true of the medieval realm?
   (A) In many respects, the lord of the manor had more direct control than did a king.
   (B) The lack of written law made all justice arbitrary.
   (C) No woman could own land.
   (D) The church administered local law, and parish priests sat as judges in local courts.

9. By the tenth century, the office of the pope had
   (A) become more powerful and was, at last, freed from control of the Roman nobles.
   (B) diminished with the diminishing of the Roman Empire.
   (C) consolidated control over a vast territory that ran from England to Iran.
   (D) managed to abolish the issue of nepotism in the church.

10. One major controversy in the church concerned the question of who should appoint bishops and abbots. This conflict is known as
   (A) the Capet Controversy.
   (B) monasticism.
   (C) the investiture controversy.
   (D) primogeniture.

11. The Rus city of Kiev developed as
   (A) a military outpost to prevent Mongol incursions into Russia.
   (B) a trade city on the Dnieper River.
   (C) an important link to trade with the Byzantines.
   (D) a trade port on the Baltic Sea.

12. Kievan Russia became firmly oriented toward the Byzantine world and turned away from the Muslim world once
   (A) it viewed the Muslims as a threat following the Battle at Manzikert.
   (B) the Crusades began.
   (C) Vladimir I converted to Christianity.
   (D) the Holy Roman Empire was founded.

13. As western Europe began to experience a revival in the period from 1000 to 1200,
   (A) it also began a tremendous demographic shift toward the Byzantine Empire.
   (B) the Muslim world began to collapse.
   (C) western Europeans were finally able to drive the Mongols out of Poland.
   (D) the Byzantine Empire and Russia did not share in the same revival.

14. As the two different centers of Christianity developed differing theological viewpoints,
   (A) the church split into many different sects.
   (B) Rome wrote religious books in Latin while the Byzantines wrote them in Greek.
   (C) Spanish Christians converted to Islam.
   (D) the Christianization of Europe reached its peak.

CHAPTER 10

CHAPTER OUTLINE

- The Sui and Tang Empires, 581–755
- The Emergence of East Asia, to 1200
- New Kingdoms in East Asia and Southeast Asia
- Conclusion

DIVERSITY + DOMINANCE *Law and Society in China and Japan*

ENVIRONMENT + TECHNOLOGY *Writing in East Asia, 400–1200*

Fujita Art Museum

Buddhism at a Distance The Buddhist monk Xuanzang returns to the Tang capital Chang'an from Tibet in 645, his ponies laden with Sanskrit texts.

Visit the website and ebook for additional study materials and interactive tools: www.cengage.com/history/bullietearthpeople5e

Inner and East Asia, 600–1200

- What is the importance of Inner and Central Asia as a region of interchange during the Tang period?
- What were the effects of the fracturing of power in Central Asia and China?
- How did East Asia develop between the fall of the Tang and 1200?
- To what extent do shared philosophies, technologies, and commercial contacts justify thinking of East Asia as a unified cultural region in the post-Tang era?

The powerful and expansive Tang Empire (618–907) ended four centuries of rule by short-lived and competing states that had brought turmoil to China after the fall of the Han Empire in 220 C.E. (see Chapter 5). Tang rule also encouraged the spread of Buddhism, brought by missionaries from India and by Chinese pilgrims returning with sacred Sanskrit texts. The Tang left an indelible mark on the Chinese imagination long after it too fell.

According to surviving memoirs, people watched shadow plays and puppet shows, listened to music and scholarly lectures, or took in less edifying spectacles like wrestling and bear baiting in the urban entertainment quarters that flourished in southern China under the succeeding Song (soong) Empire. From the 1170s onward, singer-storytellers spun long romantic narratives that alternated prose passages with sung verse.

Master Tung's *Western Chamber Romance* stood out for its literary quality. In 184 prose passages and 5,263 lines of verse the narrator tells of a love affair between Chang, a young Confucian scholar, and Ying-ying, a ravishing damsel. Secondary characters include Ying-ying's shrewd and worldly mother, a general who practices just and efficient administration, and a fighting monk named Fa-ts'ung (fa-soong). The romance is based on *The Story of Ying-ying* by the Tang period author Yüan Chen (you-ahn shen) (779–831).

As the tale begins, the abbot of a Buddhist monastery responds to Chang's request to rent him a study, singing:

> Sir, you're wrong to offer me rent.
> We Buddhists and Confucians are of one family.
> As things stand, I can't give you
> A place in our dormitory,
> But you're welcome to stay
> In one of the guest apartments.

As soon as Chang spies Ying-ying, who lives there with her mother, thoughts of studying flee his mind. Romance takes a detour, however, when bandits attack the monastery. A prose passage explains:

> During the T'ang dynasty, troops were stationed in the P'u prefecture. The year of our story, the commander of the garrison, Marshal Hun, died. Because the second-in-command, Ting Wen-ya, did not have firm control of the troops, Flying Tiger Sun, a

> subordinate general, rebelled with five thousand soldiers. They pillaged and plundered the P'u area. How do I know this to be true? It is corroborated by *The Ballad of the True Story of Ying-ying.*

As the monks cower before the bandits, one of them lifts his robe to reveal his "three-foot consecrated sword."

> [Prose] Who was this monk? He was none other than Fa-ts'ung. Fa-ts'ung was a descendant of a tribesman from western Shensi. When he was young he took great pleasure in archery, fencing, hunting, and often sneaked into foreign states to steal. He was fierce and courageous. When his parents died, it suddenly became clear to him that the way of the world was frivolous and trivial, so he became a monk in the Temple of Universal Salvation. . . .
>
> [Song] He didn't know how to read sutras;
> He didn't know how to follow rituals;
> He was neither pure nor chaste
> But indomitably courageous. . . .[1]

Amidst the love story, the ribaldry, and the derring-do, the author implants historical vignettes that mingle fact and fiction. Sophisticates of the Song era, living a life of ease, enjoyed these romanticized portrayals of Tang society.

THE SUI AND TANG EMPIRES, 581–755

Grand Canal The 1,100-mile (1,771-kilometer) waterway linking the Yellow and the Yangzi Rivers. It was begun in the Han period and completed during the Sui Empire.

AP* Exam Tip Be prepared to discuss the major economic and technological advances of Tang and Song China, such as the Grand Canal.

After the fall of the Han dynasty, China was fragmented for several centuries. It was reunified under the Sui (sway) dynasty, father and son rulers who held power from 581 until Turks from Inner Asia (the part of the Eurasian steppe east of the Pamir Mountains) defeated the son in 615. He was assassinated three years later, and the Tang filled the political vacuum.

The small kingdoms of northern China and Inner Asia that had come and gone during the centuries following the fall of the Han Empire had structured themselves around a variety of political ideas and institutions. Some favored the Chinese tradition, with an emperor, a bureaucracy using the Chinese language exclusively, and a Confucian state philosophy (see Chapter 5). Others reflected Tibetan, Turkic, or other regional cultures and depended on Buddhism to legitimate their rule. Throughout the period the relationship between northern China and the deserts and steppe of Inner Asia remained a central focus of political life, a key commercial linkage, and a source of new ideas and practices.

Reunification of China Under Sui

The Sui rulers called their new capital Chang'an (chahng-ahn) in honor of the old Han capital nearby in the Wei (way) River Valley (modern Shaanxi province). Though northern China constituted the Sui heartland, population centers along the Yangzi (yahng-zeh) River in the south grew steadily and pointed to what would be the future direction of Chinese expansion. To facilitate communication and trade with the south, the Sui built the 1,100-mile (1,771-kilometer) **Grand Canal** linking the Yellow River with the Yangzi, and they also constructed irrigation systems in the Yangzi Valley. On their northern frontier, the Sui also improved the Great Wall, the barrier against nomadic incursions that had been gradually constructed by several earlier states.

Li Shimin One of the founders of the Tang Empire and its second emperor (r. 626–649). He led the expansion of the empire into Central Asia.

Tang Empire Empire unifying China and part of Central Asia, founded 618 and ended 907. The Tang emperors presided over a magnificent court at their capital, Chang'an.

Sui military ambition, which extended to Korea and Vietnam as well as Inner Asia, required high levels of organization and mustering of resources—manpower, livestock, wood, iron, and food supplies. The same was true of their massive public works projects. These burdens proved more than the Sui could sustain. Overextension compounded the political dilemma stemming from the military defeat and subsequent assassination of the second Sui emperor. These circumstances opened the way for another strong leader to establish a new state.

In 618 the powerful Li family took advantage of Sui disorder to carve out an empire of similar scale and ambition. They adopted the dynastic name Tang (Map 10.1). The brilliant emperor **Li Shimin** (lee shir-meen) (r. 626–649) extended his power primarily westward into Inner Asia. Though he and succeeding rulers of the **Tang Empire** retained many Sui governing practices,

CHRONOLOGY

	Inner Asia	China	Northeast Asia	Japan
		581–618 Sui unification		
600		618 Tang Empire founded		
		626–649 Li Shimin reign		645–655 Taika era
		690–705 Wu Zhao reign	668 Silla victory in Korea	
				710–784 Nara as capital
	751 Battle of Talas River	755–763 An Lushan rebellion		752 "Eye-Opening" ceremony
				794 Heian era
800				
		840 Suppression of Buddhism		866–1180 Fujiwara influence
		879–881 Huang Chao rebellion		
		907 End of Tang Empire	916 Liao Empire founded	
			918 Koryo founded	
		960 Song Empire founded		
1000				ca. 1000 *The Tale of Genji*
	1038–1227 Tanggut state on China's northwest frontier		1115 Jin Empire founded	
		1127–1279 Southern Song period		1185 Kamakura Shogunate founded
1200				

Li Shimin and Tang Empire

they avoided overcentralization by allowing local nobles, gentry, officials, and religious establishments to exercise significant power (see Diversity and Dominance: Law and Society in China and Japan).

The Tang emperors and nobility descended from the Turkic elites that built small states in northern China after the Han, as well as from Chinese officials and settlers who had moved there. They appreciated the pastoral nomadic culture of Inner Asia (see Chapter 7) as well as Chinese traditions. Some of the most impressive works of Tang art, for example, are large pottery figurines of the horses and two-humped camels used along the Silk Road, brilliantly colored with glazes devised by Chinese potters. In warfare, the Tang combined Chinese weapons—the crossbow and armored infantrymen—with Inner Asian expertise in horsemanship and the use of iron stirrups. At their peak, from about 650 to 751, when they were defeated in Central Asia (present-day Kyrgyzstan) by an Arab Muslim army at the Battle of Talas River, the Tang armies were a formidable force.

AP* Exam Tip Understand reasons for the spread of major religions such as Buddhism, but don't stress about memorizing the various sects of Buddhism.

Buddhism and the Tang Empire

The Tang rulers followed Inner Asian precedents in their political use of Buddhism. State cults based on Buddhism had flourished in Inner Asia and north China since the fall of the Han. Some interpretations of Buddhist doctrine accorded kings and emperors the spiritual function of welding humankind into a harmonious Buddhist society. Protecting spirits were to help the ruler govern and prevent harm from coming to his people.

Mahayana Sect

Mahayana (mah-HAH-YAH-nah), or "Great Vehicle," Buddhism predominated. Mahayana fostered faith in enlightened beings—bodhisattvas—who postpone nirvana (see Chapter 6) to help others achieve enlightenment. This permitted the absorption of local gods and goddesses into Mahayana sainthood and thereby made conversion more attractive to the common people. Mahayana also encouraged translating Buddhist scripture into local languages, and it accepted religious practices not based on written texts. The tremendous reach of Mahayana views, which proved adaptable to different societies and classes of people, invigorated travel, language learning, and cultural exchange.

Early Tang princes competing for political influence enlisted monastic leaders to pray for them, preach on their behalf, counsel aristocrats to support them, and—perhaps most important—contribute monastic wealth to their war chests. In return, the monasteries received tax exemptions, land privileges, and gifts.

Interregional Contacts

As the Tang Empire expanded westward, contacts with Central Asia and India increased, and so did the complexity of Buddhist influence throughout China. Chang'an, the Tang capital, became the center of a continent-wide system of communication. Central Asians, Tibetans, Vietnamese, Japanese, and Koreans regularly visited the capital and took away with them the most recent ideas and styles. Thus the Mahayana network connecting Inner Asia and China intersected a vigorous commercial world in which material goods and cultural influences mixed. Though Buddhism and Confucianism proved attractive to many different peoples, regional cultures and identities remained strong, just as regional commitments to Tibetan, Uighur (WEE-ger), and other languages and writing systems coexisted with the widespread use of written Chinese. Textiles reflected Persian, Korean, and Vietnamese styles, while influences from every

e Interactive Map

MAP 10.1 The Tang Empire in Inner and Eastern Asia, 750 For over a century the Tang Empire controlled China and a very large part of Inner Asia. The defeat of Tang armies in 751 by a force of Arabs, Turks, and Tibetans at the Talas River in present-day Kyrgyzstan ended Tang westward expansion. To the south the Tang dominated Annam, and Japan and the Silla kingdom in Korea were leading tributary states of the Tang.

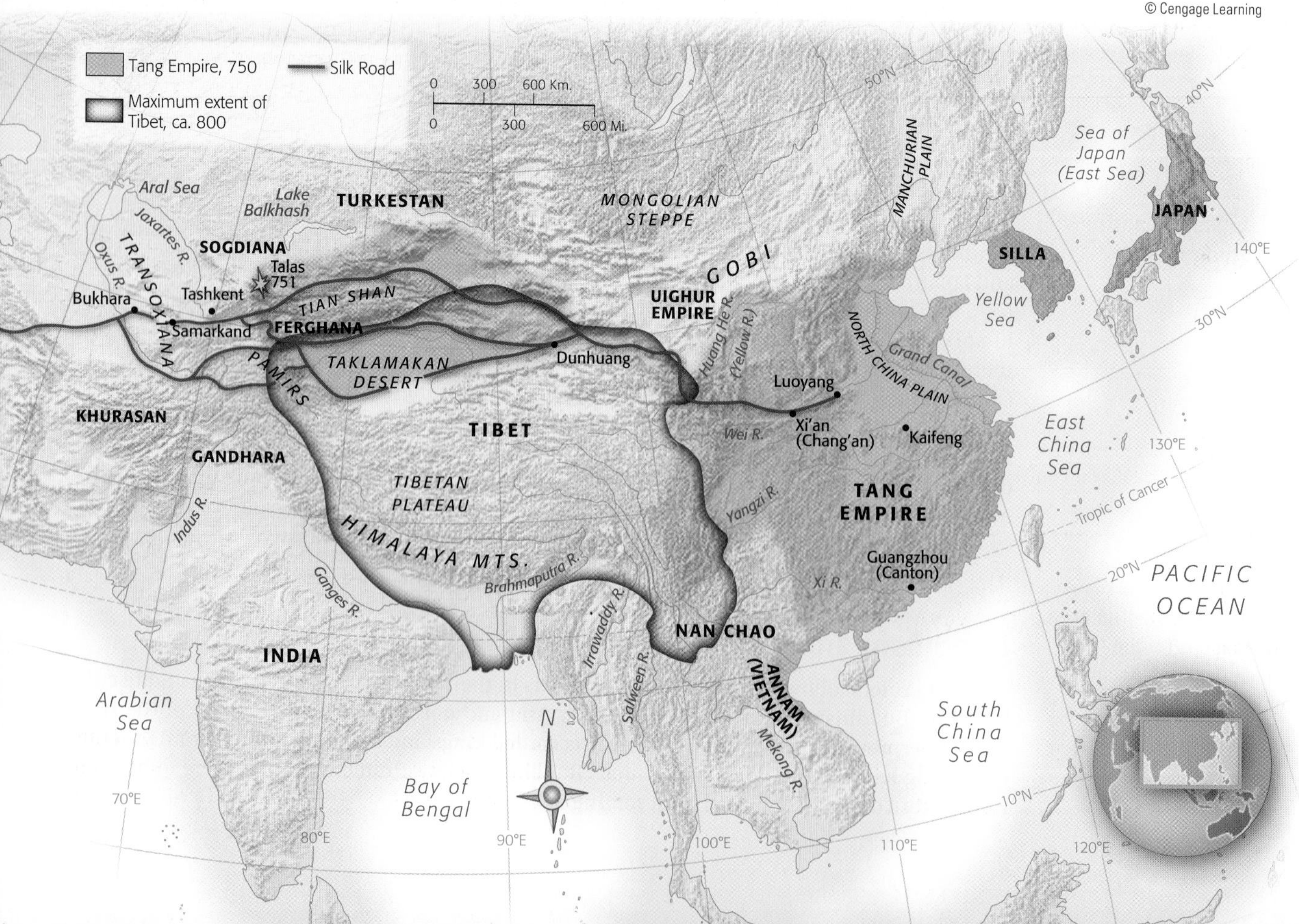

Iron Stirrups This bas-relief from the tomb of Li Shimin depicts the type of horse on which the Tang armies conquered China and Inner Asia. Saddles with high supports in front and back, breastplates, and cruppers (straps beneath the tail that help keep the saddle in place) point to the importance of high speeds and quick maneuvering. Central and Inner Asian horsemen had iron stirrups available from the time of the Huns (fifth century). Earlier stirrups were of leather or wood. Stirrups could support the weight of shielded and well-armed soldiers rising in the saddle to shoot arrows or use lances.

tributary system A system in which, from the time of the Han Empire, countries in East and Southeast Asia not under the direct control of empires based in China nevertheless enrolled as tributary states, acknowledging the superiority of the emperors in China in exchange for trading rights or strategic alliances.

part of Asia appeared in sports, music, and painting. Many historians characterize the Tang Empire as "cosmopolitan" because of its breadth and diversity.

To Chang'an by Land and Sea

Tribute

Well-maintained roads and water transport connected Chang'an, the capital and hub of Tang communications, to the coastal towns of south China, most importantly Canton (Guangzhou [gwahng-jo]). Though the Grand Canal did not reach Chang'an, it was the key component of this transportation network. Chang'an became the center of what is often called the **tributary system**, a type of political relationship dating from Han times by which independent countries acknowledged the Chinese emperor's supremacy. Each tributary state sent regular embassies to the capital to pay tribute. As symbols of China's political supremacy, these embassies sometimes meant more to the Chinese than to the tribute-payers, who might have seen them more as a means of accessing the Chinese trading system.

PRIMARY SOURCE: Memorial on Buddhism Find out what it is about the practice of Buddhism in China that causes Han Yu to report that he is "truly alarmed, truly afraid."

Upheavals and Repression, 750–879

Opposition to Buddhism

The later years of the Tang Empire saw increasing turmoil as a result of conflict with Tibetans and Turkic Uighurs. One result was a backlash against "foreigners," which to Confucians included Buddhists. The Tang elites came to see Buddhism as undermining the Confucian idea

Law and Society in China and Japan

The Tang law code, compiled in the early seventh century, served as the basis for the Tang legal system and as a model for later dynastic law codes. It combined the centralized authority of the imperial government, as visualized in the legalist tradition dating back to Han times, with Confucian concern for status distinctions and personal relationships. Like contemporary approaches to law in Christian Europe and the Islamic world, it did not fully distinguish between government as a structure of domination and law as an echo of religious and moral values.

Following a Preface, 502 articles, each with several parts, are divided into twelve books. Each article contains a basic ordinance with commentary, subcommentary, and sometimes additional questions. Excerpts from a single article from Book 1, General Principles, follow.

The Ten Abominations

Text: The first is called plotting rebellion.

Subcommentary: The *Gongyang* (GON-gwang) *Commentary* states: "The ruler or parent has no harborers [of plots]. If he does have such harborers, he must put them to death." This means that if there are those who harbor rebellious hearts that would harm the ruler or father, he must then put them to death.

The king occupies the most honorable position and receives Heaven's precious decrees. Like Heaven and Earth, he acts to shelter and support, thus serving as the father and mother of the masses. As his children, as his subjects, they must be loyal and filial. Should they dare to cherish wickedness and have rebellious hearts, however, they will run counter to Heaven's constancy and violate human principle. Therefore this is called plotting rebellion.

Text: The second is called plotting great sedition.

Subcommentary: This type of person breaks laws and destroys order, is against traditional norms, and goes contrary to virtue. . . .

Commentary: Plotting great sedition means to plot to destroy the ancestral temples, tombs, or palaces of the reigning house.

Text: The third is called plotting treason.

Subcommentary: The kindness of father and mother is like "great heaven, illimitable." . . . Let one's heart be like the *xiao* bird or the *jing* beast, and then love and respect both cease. Those whose relationship is within the five degrees of mourning are the closest of kin. For them to kill each other is the extreme abomination and the utmost in rebellion, destroying and casting aside human principles. Therefore this is called contumacy.

Commentary: Contumacy means to beat or plot to kill [without actually killing] one's paternal grandparents or parents; or to kill one's paternal uncles or their wives, or one's elder brothers or sisters, or one's maternal grandparents, or one's husband, or one's husband's paternal grandparents, or his parents. . . .

Text: The fifth is called depravity.

Subcommentary: This article describes those who are cruel and malicious and who turn their backs on morality. Therefore it is called depravity.

Commentary: Depravity means to kill three members of a single household who have not committed a capital crime, or to dismember someone. . . .

Commentary: The offense also includes the making or keeping of poison or sorcery.

Subcommentary: This means to prepare the poison oneself, or to keep it, or to give it to others in order to harm people. But if the preparation of the poison is not yet completed, this offense does not come under the ten abominations. As to sorcery, there are a great many methods, not all of which can be described.

Text: The tenth is called incest.

Subcommentary: The *Zuo Commentary* states: "The woman has her husband's house; the man has his wife's chamber; and

of the family as the model for the state. The Confucian scholar Han Yu (768–824) spoke powerfully for a return to traditional Confucian practices. In "Memorial on the Bone of Buddha" written to the emperor in 819 on the occasion of ceremonies to receive a bone of the Buddha in the imperial palace, he scornfully disparages the Buddha and his followers:

> *Now Buddha was a man of the barbarians who did not speak the language of China and wore clothes of a different fashion. His sayings did not concern the ways of our ancient kings, nor did his manner of dress conform to their laws. He understood neither the duties that bind sovereign and subject nor the affections of father and son. If he were still alive today and came to our court by order of his ruler, Your Majesty might condescend to receive him, but . . . he would then be escorted to the borders of the state, dismissed, and not allowed to delude the masses. How then, when he has long been dead, could his rotten bones, the*

there must be no defilement on either side." If this is changed, then there is incest. If one behaves like birds and beasts and introduces licentious associates into one's family, the rules of morality are confused. Therefore this is called incest.

Commentary: This section includes having illicit sexual intercourse with relatives who are of the fourth degree of mourning or closer. . . .

In Japan during the same period, Prince Shotoku (573–621), who governed on behalf of the empress Suiko, his aunt, set forth seventeen governing principles: "Prince Shotoku's Constitution." These principles, which continued to influence Japanese government for many centuries, reflect Confucian ideals even though the prince was himself a devout Buddhist. The complete text of five of these principles follows:

I

Harmony is to be valued, and contentiousness avoided. All men are inclined to partisanship and few are truly discerning. Hence there are some who disobey their lords and fathers and who maintain feuds with the neighboring villages. But when those above are harmonious and those below are conciliatory and there is concord in the discussion of all matters, the disposition of affairs comes about naturally. Then what is there that cannot be accomplished?

VIII

Let ministers and functionaries attend the courts early in the morning, and retire late. The business of the state does not admit of remissness, and the whole day is hardly enough for its accomplishment. If, therefore, the attendance at court is late, emergencies cannot be met; if officials retire soon, the work cannot be completed.

IX

Trustworthiness is the foundation of right. In everything let there be trustworthiness, for in this there surely consists the good and the bad, success and failure. If the lord and the vassal trust one another, what is there which cannot be accomplished? If the lord and the vassal do not trust one another, everything without exception ends in failure.

XIII

Let all persons entrusted with office attend equally to their functions. Owing to their illness or to their being sent on missions, their work may sometimes be neglected. But whenever they become able to attend to business, let them be as accommodating as if they had cognizance of it from before and not hinder public affairs on the score of their not having had to do with them.

XVII

Matters should not be decided by one person alone. They should be discussed with many others. In small matters, of less consequence, many others need not be consulted. It is only in considering weighty matters, where there is a suspicion that they might miscarry, that many others should be involved in debate and discussion so as to arrive at a reasonable conclusion.

QUESTIONS FOR ANALYSIS

1. **Why is one of these documents called a law code and the other a constitution?**
2. **How is the Confucian concern for family relations, duty, and social status differently manifested in the Chinese and Japanese documents?**
3. **Do these documents seem intended for government officials or for common people?**

Sources: First selection from William Theodore de Bary and Irene Bloom, eds., *Sources of Chinese Tradition*, vol. I, 2nd ed., (New York, Columbia University Press, 1999), pp. 549–552. Second selection from William Theodore de Bary et al., eds., *Sources of Japanese Tradition, vol. I, From Earliest Times to 1600*, 2nd ed. (New York: Columbia University Press, 2001), 50–54.

foul and unlucky remains of his body, be rightly admitted to the palace? Confucius said, "Respect spiritual beings, while keeping at a distance from them."[2]

Wu Zhao, a Female Emperor

Buddhism was also attacked for encouraging women in politics. Wu Zhao (woo jow), a woman who had married into the imperial family, seized control of the government in 690 and declared herself emperor. She based her legitimacy on claiming to be a bodhisattva, an enlightened soul who had chosen to remain on earth to lead others to salvation. She also favored Buddhists and Daoists over Confucianists in her court and government.

Later Confucian writers expressed contempt for Wu Zhao and other powerful women, such as the concubine Yang Guifei (yahng gway-fay). Bo Zhuyi (baw joo-ee), in his poem "Everlasting Remorse," lamented the influence of women at the Tang court, which had caused "the hearts of fathers and mothers everywhere not to value the birth of boys, but the birth of girls."[3]

Xinjiang Uighur Autonomous District Museum

Women of Turfan Grinding Flour Women throughout Inner and East Asia were critical to all facets of economic life. In the Turkic areas of Central and Inner Asia, women commonly headed households, owned property, and managed businesses. These small figurines, made to be placed in tombs, portray women of Turfan—an Inner Asian area crossed by the Silk Road—performing tasks in the preparation of wheat flour.

Confucian elites heaped every possible charge on prominent women who offended them, accusing Emperor Wu of grotesque tortures and murders, including tossing the dismembered but still living bodies of enemies into wine vats and cauldrons. They blamed Yang Guifei for the outbreak of the An Lushan rebellion in 755 (see below).

Serious historians dismiss the stories about Wu Zhao as stereotypical characterizations of "evil" rulers. Eunuchs (castrated palace servants) charged by historians with controlling Chang'an and the Tang court and publicly executing rival bureaucrats represent a similar stereotype. In fact Wu seems to have ruled effectively and was not deposed until 705, when extreme old age (eighty-plus) incapacitated her. Nevertheless, traditional Chinese historians commonly describe unorthodox rulers and all-powerful women as evil, and the truth about Wu will never be known.

Closing the Monasteries

Even Chinese gentry living in safe and prosperous localities associated Buddhism with social ills. People who worried about "barbarians" ruining their society pointed to Buddhism as evidence of the foreign evil, since it had such strong roots in Inner Asia and Tibet. Because Buddhism shunned earthly ties, monks and nuns severed relations with the secular world in search of enlightenment. They paid no taxes, served in no army. They deprived their families of advantageous marriage alliances and denied descendants to their ancestors. The Confucian elites saw all this as threatening to the family and to the family estates that underlay the Tang economic and political structure.

By the ninth century, hundreds of thousands of people had entered tax-exempt Buddhist institutions. In 840 the government moved to crush the monasteries whose tax exemption had allowed them to accumulate land, serfs, and precious objects, often as gifts. Within five years 4,600 temples had been destroyed. Now an enormous amount of land and 150,000 workers were returned to the tax rolls.

SECTION REVIEW

- After the period of disunity following the fall of the Han, China was united under the Sui, followed by the Tang with its founder Li Shimin.
- Tang culture was based on both Inner Asia nomadic culture and war expertise and Chinese tradition.
- The Tang Empire, along with the rival Uighur and Tibetan states, experienced political problems that steadily weakened it.
- In China, this turmoil resulted in a backlash against foreign and female cultural influences and especially Buddhism, as Tang elites led a neo-Confucian reaction.
- The Tang fell due to a combination of destabilizing forces.

Pierre Colombel/Corbis

Buddhist Cave Painting at Dunhuang Hundreds of caves dating to the period when Buddhism enjoyed popularity and government favor in China survive in Gansu province, which was beyond the reach of the Tang rulers when they turned against Buddhism. This cave, dated to the period 565–576, depicts the historical Buddha flanked by bodhisattvas. Scenes of the Buddha preaching appear on the wall to the left.

Buddhist centers like the cave monasteries at Dunhuang were protected by local warlords loyal to Buddhist rulers in Inner Asia. Nevertheless, China's cultural heritage suffered a great loss in the dissolution of the monasteries. Some sculptures and grottoes survived only in defaced form. Wooden temples and façades sheltering great stone carvings burned to the ground. Monasteries became legal again in later times, but Buddhism never recovered the influence of early Tang times.

The End of the Tang Empire, 879–907

An Lushan Rebellion

The campaigns of expansion in the seventh century had left the empire dependent on local military commanders and a complex tax collection system. Reverses like the Battle of the Talas River in 751, where Arabs halted Chinese expansion into Central Asia, led to military demoralization and underfunding. In 755 An Lushan, a Tang general on the northeast frontier, led about 200,000 soldiers in rebellion. The emperor fled Chang'an and executed his favorite concubine, Yang Guifei, who was rumored to be An Lushan's lover. The rebellion lasted for eight years and resulted in new powers for the provincial military governors who helped suppress it.

Further Unrest

A disgruntled member of the gentry, Huang Chao (wang show), led the most devastating uprising between 879 and 881. Despite his ruthless treatment of the villages he controlled, his rebellion attracted poor farmers and tenants who could not protect themselves from local bosses and oppressive landlords, or who simply did not know where else to turn in the deepening chaos. The new hatred of "barbarians" spurred the rebels to murder thousands of foreign residents in Canton and Beijing (bay-jeeng).

Local warlords finally wiped out the rebels, but Tang society did not find peace. Refugees, migrant workers, and homeless people became common sights. Residents of northern China fled to the southern frontiers as groups from Inner Asia moved into localities in the north. Though Tang emperors continued in Chang'an until a warlord terminated their line in 907, they never regained power after Huang Chao's rebellion.

THE EMERGENCE OF EAST ASIA, TO 1200

In the aftermath of the Tang, three new states emerged and competed to inherit its legacy (see Map 10.2). The Liao (lee-OW) Empire of the Khitan (kee-THAN) people, pastoral nomads related to the Mongols living on the northeastern frontier, established their rule in the north. They centered their government on several cities, but the emperors preferred life in nomad encampments. On the Inner Asian frontier in northwestern China, the Minyak people (cousins of the Tibetans) established a state they called "Tanggut" (1038–1227) (TAHNG-gut) to show their connection with the fallen empire. The third state, the Chinese-speaking **Song Empire**, came into being in 960 in central China.

Competing Traditions

Song Empire Empire in central and southern China (960–1126) while the Liao people controlled the north. Empire in southern China (1127–1279; the "Southern Song") while the Jin people controlled the north. Distinguished for its advances in technology, medicine, astronomy, and mathematics.

These states embodied the political ambitions of peoples with different religious and philosophical systems—Mahayana Buddhism among the Liao, Tibetan Buddhism among the Tanguts, and Confucianism among the Song. Cut off from Inner Asia, the Song used advanced seafaring and sailing technologies to forge maritime connections with other states in East, West, and Southeast Asia. The Song elite shared the late Tang dislike of "barbaric" or "foreign" influences as they tried to cope with multiple enemies that heavily taxed their military capacities. Meanwhile, Korea, Japan, and some Southeast Asian states strengthened political and cultural ties with China.

The Liao and Jin Challenge

Khitan People

The Liao Empire of the Khitan people extended from Siberia to Inner Asia. Variations on the Khitan name became the name for China in these distant regions: "Kitai" for the Mongols, "Khitai" for the Russians, and "Cathay" for Italian merchants like Marco Polo who reported on China in Europe (see Chapter 12).

The Liao rulers prided themselves on their pastoral traditions as horse and cattle breeders, the continuing source of their military might, and they made no attempt to create a single elite culture. They encouraged Chinese elites to use their own language, study their own classics, and see the emperor through Confucian eyes; and they encouraged other peoples to use their own languages and see the emperor as a champion of Buddhism or as a nomadic chieftain. On balance, Buddhism far outweighed Confucianism in this and other northern states, where rulers depended on their roles as bodhisattvas or as Buddhist kings to legitimate power. Liao rule lasted from 916 to 1125.

e Interactive Map

Superb horsemen and archers, the Khitans also challenged the Song with siege machines from China and Central Asia. A truce concluded in 1005 required the Song emperor to pay the Liao great quantities of cash and silk annually. A century later, the Song tired of paying tribute and secretly allied with the Jurchens of northeastern Asia, who also resented Liao rule. In 1115 the Jurchens first destroyed the Liao capital in Mongolia and proclaimed their own empire, the Jin (see Map 10.2), and then turned on the Song.

The Jurchens grew rice, millet, and wheat, but they also spent a good deal of time hunting, fishing, and tending livestock. Using Khitan military arts and political organization, they became formidable enemies in an all-out campaign against the Song in 1127. They laid siege to the Song capital, Kaifeng (kie-fuhng), and captured the Song emperor. Within a few years the Song withdrew south of the Yellow River and established a new capital at Hangzhou (hahng-jo), leaving central as well as northern China in Jurchen control (see Map 10.3). Annual payments to the Jin Empire staved off further warfare. Historians generally refer to this period as the "Southern Song" (1127–1279).

Song Industries

The Southern Song came closer to initiating an industrial revolution than any other premodern state. Many Song

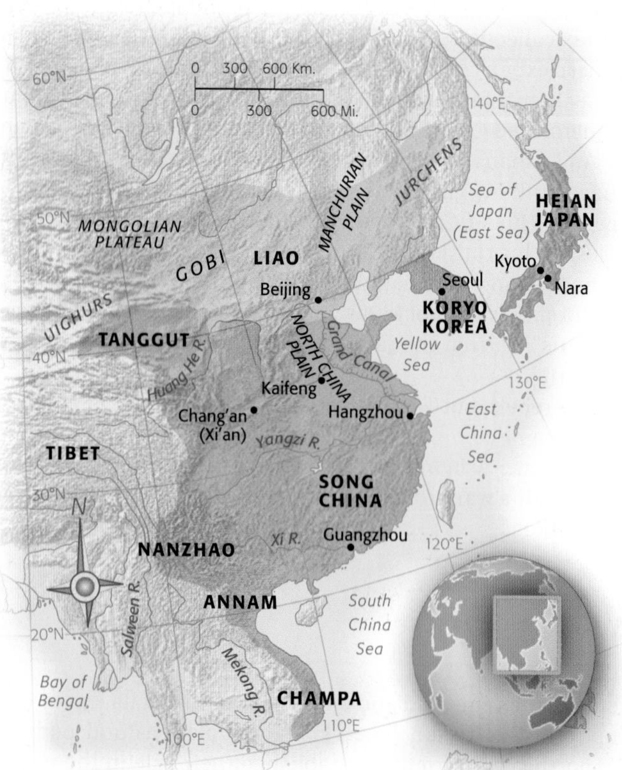

MAP 10.2 **Liao and Song Empires, ca. 1100** The states of Liao in the north and Song in the south generally ceased open hostilities after a treaty in 1005 stabilized the border and imposed an annual payment on Song China.

AP* Exam Tip Be aware of the intellectual and technological developments of major empires, including Tang and Song China.

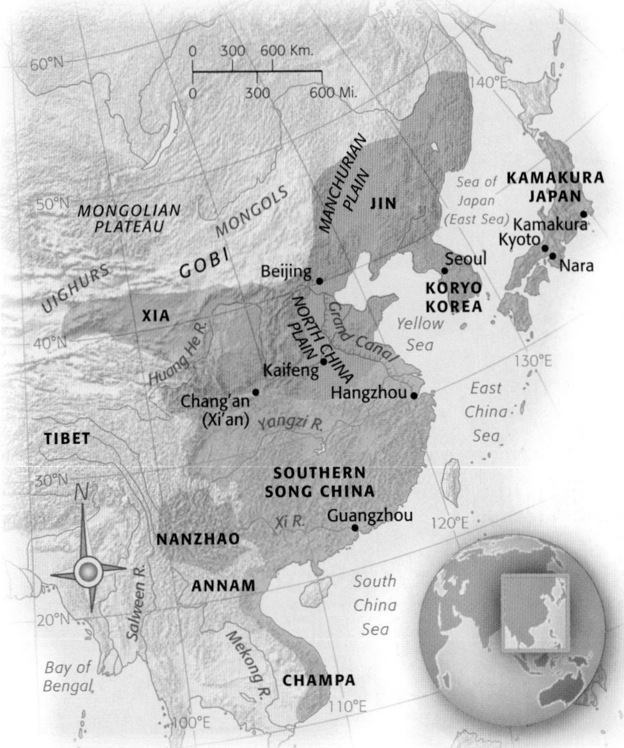

MAP 10.3 **Jin and Southern Song Empires, ca. 1200** After 1127 Song abandoned its northern territories to Jin. The Southern Song continued the policy of annual payments—to Jin rather than Liao—and maintained high military preparedness to prevent further invasions.

Interactive Map

advances in technology, medicine, astronomy, and mathematics had come to China in Tang times, sometimes from very distant places. Song officials, scholars, and businessmen had the motivation and resources to adapt this Tang lore to meet their military, agricultural, and administrative needs.

Song mathematicians introduced the use of fractions, first employing them to describe the phases of the moon. From lunar observations, Song astronomers constructed a very precise calendar and, alone among the world's astronomers, noted the explosion of the Crab Nebula in 1054. Song inventors drew on their knowledge of celestial coordinates, particularly the Pole Star, to refine compass design. The magnetic compass, an earlier Chinese invention, shrank in size in Song times and gained a fixed pivot point for the needle. With a protective glass cover, the compass now became suitable for seafaring, a use first attested in 1090.

Development of the seaworthy compass coincided with new techniques in building China's main oceangoing ship, the **junk**. A stern-mounted rudder improved the steering of the large ship in uneasy seas, and watertight bulkheads helped keep it afloat in emergencies. The shipwrights of the Persian Gulf soon copied these features in their ship designs.

Iron and Steel

junk A very large flatbottom sailing ship produced in the Tang, Song, and Ming Empires, specially designed for long-distance commercial travel.

gunpowder A mixture of saltpeter, sulfur, and charcoal, in various proportions. The formula, brought to China in the 400s or 500s, was first used to make fumigators to keep away insect pests and evil spirits. In later centuries it was used to make explosives and grenades and to propel cannonballs, shot, and bullets.

neo-Confucianism Term used to describe new approaches to understanding classic Confucian texts that became the basic ruling philosophy of China from the Song period to the twentieth century.

Because they needed iron and steel to make weapons for their army of 1.25 million men, the Song rulers fought their northern rivals for control of mines in north China. Production of coal and iron soared. By the end of the eleventh century cast iron production reached about 125,000 tons (113,700 metric tons) annually, putting it on a par with the output of eighteenth-century Britain. Engineers became skilled at high-temperature metallurgy using enormous bellows, often driven by water wheels, to superheat the molten ore. Military engineers used iron to buttress defensive works because it was impervious to fire or concussion. Armorers mass-produced body armor. Iron construction also appeared in bridges and small buildings. Mass-production techniques for bronze and ceramics in use in China for nearly two thousand years were adapted to iron casting and assembly.

To counter cavalry assaults, the Song experimented with **gunpowder**, which they initially used to propel clusters of flaming arrows. During the wars against the Jurchens in the 1100s the Song introduced a new and terrifying weapon. Shells launched from Song fortifications exploded in the midst of the enemy, blowing out iron shrapnel and dismembering men and horses. The short range of these shells limited them to defensive uses.

Economy and Society in Song China

In a warlike era, Song elite culture idealized civil pursuits. Socially, the civil man outranked the military man. Private academies, designed to train young men for the official examinations, became influential in culture and politics. New interpretations of Confucian teachings became so important and influential that the term **neo-Confucianism** is used for Song and later versions of Confucian thought.

Zhu Xi (jew she) (1130–1200), the most important early neo-Confucian thinker, wrote in reaction to the many centuries during which Buddhism and Daoism had overshadowed the precepts of Confucius. He and others worked out a systematic approach to cosmology that focused on the central conception that human nature is moral, rational, and essentially good. To combat the Buddhist dismissal of worldly affairs as a transitory distraction, they reemphasized

Su Song's Astronomical Clock This gigantic clock built at Kaifeng between 1088 and 1092 combined mathematics, astronomy, and calendar-making with skillful engineering. The team overseen by Su Song placed an armillary sphere on the observation platform and linked it with chains to the water-driven central mechanism shown in the cutaway view. The water wheel also rotated the Buddha statues in the multistory pagoda the spectators are looking at. Other devices displayed the time of the day, the month, and the year.

From Joseph Needham's *Science and Civilization in China*, Vol 4. After the original diagram in Su Song's treatise Xinyi Xiangfayao, 1092.

individual moral and social responsibility. Their human ideal was the sage, a person who could preserve mental stability and serenity while dealing conscientiously with troubling social problems. Whereas earlier Confucian thinkers had written about sage kings and political leaders, the neo-Confucians espoused the spiritual idea of universal sagehood, a state that could be achieved through proper study of the new Confucian principles and cosmology.

Meditative Buddhism

Popular Buddhist sects also persisted during the Song, as indicated by the song-story line quoted at the beginning of this chapter: "We Buddhists and Confucians are of one family." While historically suitable for the time before the Tang abolition of Buddhist monasteries when the original story of Ying-ying was written, it is unlikely that the line would have pleased a Song audience if anti-Buddhist feelings had remained so ferocious. Some Buddhists elaborated on Tang-era folk practices derived from India and Tibet. The best known, Chan Buddhism (known as **Zen** in Japan and as Son in Korea), asserted that mental discipline alone could win salvation.

Zen The Japanese word for a branch of Mahayana Buddhism based on highly disciplined meditation. It is known in Sanskrit as *dhyana*, in Chinese as *chan*, and in Korean as *son*.

Meditation, a key Chan practice, was employed by Confucians as well as Buddhists. It afforded prospective officials relief from studying for civil service examinations, which continued into the Song from the Tang period. Unlike the ancient Han policy of hiring and promoting on the basis of recommendations, Song-style examinations involved a large bureaucracy. Test questions, which changed each time the examinations were given, often related to economic management or foreign policy even though they were always based on Confucian classics.

Examination System

Hereditary class distinctions meant less than they had in Tang times, when noble lineages played a greater role in the structure of power. The new system recruited the most talented men, whatever their origin. Yet men from wealthy families enjoyed an advantage. Preparation for the tests consumed so much time that peasant boys could rarely compete.

Success in the examinations brought good marriage prospects, the chance for a high salary, and enormous prestige. Failure could bankrupt a family and ruin a man both socially and psychologically. This put great pressure on candidates, who spent days writing essays in tiny, dim, airless examination cells.

Printing

A technical change from woodblock to an early form of **movable type** made printing cheaper. To promote its ideological goals, the Song government authorized the mass production of test preparation books in the years before 1000. Although a man had to be literate to read the preparation books and basic education was still rare, a growing number of candidates entered the Song bureaucracy without noble, gentry, or elite backgrounds.

movable type Type in which each individual character is cast on a separate piece of metal. It replaced woodblock printing, allowing for the arrangement of individual letters and other characters on a page, rather than requiring the carving of entire pages at a time. It may have been invented in Korea in the thirteenth century.

The availability of printed books changed country life as well, since landlords gained access to expert advice on planting and irrigation techniques, harvesting, tree cultivation, threshing, and weaving. Landlords frequently gathered their tenants and workers to show them illustrated texts and explain their meaning. New agricultural land was developed south of the Yangtze River, and iron implements such as plows and rakes, first used in the Tang era, were adapted to southern wet-rice cultivation.

The growing profitability of agriculture interested ambitious members of the gentry. Still a frontier for Chinese settlers under the Tang, the south saw increasing concentration of land in the hands of a few wealthy families. In the process, the indigenous inhabitants of the region, related to the modern-day populations of Malaysia, Thailand, and Laos, retreated into the mountains or southward toward Vietnam.

Population Growth

During the 1100s the total population of the Chinese territories, spurred by prosperity, rose above 100 million. The leading Song cities had fewer than a million inhabitants but were still among the largest cities in the world. Health and crowding posed problems in the Song capitals. Multistory wooden apartment houses fronted on narrow streets—sometimes only 4 or 5 feet (1.2 to 1.5 meters) wide—that were clogged by peddlers or families spending time outdoors. The crush of people called for new techniques in waste management, water supply, and firefighting.

In Hangzhou engineers diverted the nearby river to flow through the city, flushing away waste and disease. Arab and European travelers who had firsthand experience with the Song capital, and who were sensitive to urban conditions in their own societies, expressed amazement at Hangzhou's amenities: restaurants, parks, bookstores, wine shops, tea houses, theaters, and the entertainments mentioned at the start of this chapter.

Going Up the River Song cities hummed with commercial and industrial activity, much of it concentrated on the rivers and canals linking the capital Kaifeng to the provinces. This detail from *Going Upriver at the Qingming [Spring] Festival* shows a tiny portion of the scroll painting's panorama. Painted by Zhang Zeduan sometime before 1125, its depiction of daily life makes it an important source of information on working people. Before open shop fronts and tea houses a camel caravan departs, donkey carts are unloaded, a scholar rides loftily (if gingerly) on horseback, and women of wealth go by in closed sedan-chairs.

The "Players" Women—often enslaved—entertained at Chinese courts from early times. Tang art often depicts women with slender figures, but Tang taste also admired more robust physiques. Song women, usually pale with willowy figures, appear as here with bound feet. The practice appeared in Tang times but was not widespread until the Song, when the image of weak, housebound women unable to work became a status symbol and pushed aside the earlier enthusiasm for healthy women who participated in family business.

The Palace Museum, Beijing

Trade and Credit

The idea of credit, originating in the robust long-distance trade of the Tang period, spread widely under the Song. Intercity or interregional credit—what the Song called "flying money"—depended on the acceptance of guarantees that the paper could be redeemed for coinage at another location. The public accepted the practice because credit networks tended to be managed by families, so that brothers and cousins were usually honoring each other's certificates.

"Flying money" certificates differed from government-issued paper money, which the Song pioneered. In some years, military expenditures consumed 80 percent of the government budget. The state responded to this financial pressure by distributing paper money. But this made inflation so severe that by the beginning of the 1100s paper money was trading for only 1 percent of its face value. Eventually the government withdrew paper money and instead imposed new taxes, sold monopolies, and offered financial incentives to merchants.

Tax Farming

Hard-pressed for the revenue needed to maintain the army, canals, roads, waterworks, and other state functions, the government finally resorted to tax farming, selling the rights to tax collection to private individuals. Tax farmers made their profit by collecting the maximum amount and sending an agreed-upon smaller sum to the government. This meant exorbitant rates for taxable services, such as tolls, and much heavier tax burdens on the common people.

New Class Structure

Rapid economic growth undermined the remaining government monopolies and the traditional strict regulation of business. Now merchants and artisans as well as gentry and officials could make fortunes. With land no longer the only source of wealth, the traditional social hierarchy common to an agricultural economy weakened, while cities, commerce, consumption, and the use of money and credit boomed. Urban life reflected the elite's growing taste for fine fabrics, porcelain, exotic foods, large houses, and exquisite paintings and books.

Status of Women

In conjunction with the backlash against Buddhism and revival of Confucianism that began under the Tang and intensified under the Song, women experienced subordination, legal disenfranchisement, and social restriction. Merchants spent long periods away from home, and many maintained several wives in different locations. Frequently they depended on wives to manage their homes and even their businesses in their absence. But though women took on responsibility for the management of their husbands' property, their own property rights suffered legal erosion. Under Song law, a woman's property automatically passed to her husband, and women could not remarry if their husbands divorced them or died.

The subordination of women proved compatible with Confucianism, and it became fashionable to educate girls just enough to read simplified versions of Confucian philosophy that emphasized the lowly role of women. Modest education made these young women more desirable as companions for the sons of gentry or noble families and as literate mothers in lower-ranking families aspiring to improve their status. The poet Li Qingzhao (lee CHING-jow) (1083–1141) acknowledged and made fun of her unusual status as a highly celebrated female writer:

AP* Exam Tip The reasons for footbinding and its relation to status in Song China are important to understand.

Although I've studied poetry for thirty years
I try to keep my mouth shut and avoid reputation.
Now who is this nosy gentleman talking about my poetry
Like Yang Ching-chih (yahng SHING-she)
Who spoke of Hsiang Ssu (sang sue) *everywhere he went.*[4]

Her reference is to a hermit poet of the ninth century who was continually and extravagantly praised by a court official, Yang Ching-chih.

Footbinding

Female footbinding first appeared among slave dancers at the Tang court, but it did not become widespread until the Song period. The bindings forced the toes under and toward the heel, so that the bones eventually broke and the woman could not walk on her own. In noble and gentry families, footbinding began between ages five and seven. In less wealthy families, girls worked until they were older, so footbinding began only in a girl's teens.

Many literate men condemned the maiming of innocent girls and the general uselessness of footbinding. Nevertheless, bound feet became a status symbol. By 1200 a woman with unbound feet had become undesirable in elite circles, and mothers of elite status, or aspiring to such status, almost without exception bound their daughters' feet. They knew that girls with unbound feet faced rejection. Working women and the indigenous peoples of the south, where northern practices took a longer time to penetrate, did not practice footbinding. Consequently they enjoyed considerably more mobility and economic independence than did elite Chinese women.

SECTION REVIEW

- Several rival states replaced the fallen Tang Empire, and the close relations between Central Asia and East Asia ended.
- The Liao and Jin Empires encouraged culturally diverse societies and confronted Song China with formidable military threats.
- The Song Empire of central and southern China built upon Tang achievements in technology and science and promoted civil ideals.
- Under the Song, print culture developed, urban populations rose, commercial activity grew through innovation, and women were subordinated to men.

NEW KINGDOMS IN EAST ASIA AND SOUTHEAST ASIA

Confucian Culture

The best possibilities for expanding the Confucian world-view of the Song lay with newly emerging kingdoms to the east and south. Korea, Japan, and Vietnam, like Song China, devoted great effort to the cultivation of rice. This fit well with Confucian social ideas. Tending the young rice plants, irrigating the rice paddies, and managing the harvest required coordination among many village and kin groups and rewarded hierarchy, obedience, and self-discipline.

Confucianism also justified using agricultural profits to support the education, safety, and comfort of the literate elite. In each of these new kingdoms Song civilization melded with indigenous cultural and historical traditions to create a distinctive synthesis. Farther to the south, the Buddhist kingdom of Srivijaya marked the boundary of Chinese influence. It maintained close maritime relations with merchants from the Indian Ocean.

Chinese Influences

Korea, Japan, and Vietnam had first centralized power under ruling houses in the early Tang period, and their state ideologies continued to resemble that of the early Tang, when Buddhism and Confucianism seemed compatible. Government offices went to noble families and did not

ENVIRONMENT + TECHNOLOGY

Writing in East Asia, 600–1200

An ideographic writing system that originated in China became a communications tool throughout East Asia. Variations on this system, based more on depictions of meanings than representations of sound, spread widely by the time of the Sui and Tang Empires. Many East Asian peoples adapted ideographic techniques to writing languages unrelated to Chinese in grammar or sound.

The Vietnamese, Koreans, and Japanese often simplified Chinese characters and associated them with the sounds of their own non-Chinese languages. For instance, the Chinese character *an*, meaning "peace" (Fig. 1), was pronounced "an" in Japanese and was familiar as a Chinese character to Confucian scholars in Japan's Heian (hay-ahn) period. However, nonscholars simplified the character and used it to write the Japanese sound "a" (Fig. 2). A set of more than thirty of these syllabic symbols adapted from Chinese characters could represent the inflected forms (forms with grammatical endings) of any Japanese word. Murasaki Shikibu used such a syllabic system when she wrote *The Tale of Genji*.

In Vietnam and later in northern Asia, phonetic and ideographic elements combined in new ways. The apparent circles in some *chu nom* writing from Vietnam (Fig. 3) derive from the Chinese character for "mouth" and indicate a primary sound association for the word. The Khitans, who spoke a language related to Mongolian, developed an ideographic system of their own, inspired by Chinese characters. The Chinese character *wang* (Fig. 4), meaning "king, prince, ruler," was changed to represent the Khitan word for "emperor" by adding an upward stroke representing a "superior" ruler (Fig. 5). Because the system was ideographic, we do not know the pronunciation of this Khitan word. The Khitan character for "God" or "Heaven" adds a top stroke representing the "supreme" ruler or power to the character meaning "ruler" (Fig. 6). Though inspired by Chinese characters, Khitan writings could not be read by anyone who was not specifically educated in them.

The Khitans developed another system to represent the sounds and grammar of their language. They used small, simplified elements arranged within an imaginary frame to indicate the sounds in any word. This idea might have come from the phonetic script used by the Uighurs. Here (Fig. 7) we see the word for horse in a Khitan inscription. Fitting sound elements within a frame also occurred later in *hangul*, the Korean phonetic system introduced in the 1400s. Here (Fig. 8) we see the two words making up the country name "Korea."

The Chinese writing system served the Chinese elite well. But peoples speaking unrelated languages continually experimented with the Chinese invention to produce new ways of expressing themselves. Some of the resulting sound-based writing systems remain in common use; others are still being deciphered.

Figure 1

Figure 2

Figure 3

Figure 4

Figure 5

Figure 6

Figure 7

Figure 8

depend on passing examinations on Confucian texts. Landowning and agriculture remained the major sources of income, and landowners faced no challenges from a merchant class or urban elite.

Nevertheless, learned men prized literacy in classical Chinese and a good knowledge of Confucian texts (see Environment and Technology: Writing in East Asia, 600–1200). Though formal education was available to only a small number of people, the ruling and landholding elites sought to instill Confucian ideals of hierarchy and harmony among the general population (see Diversity and Dominance: Law and Society in China and Japan).

Korea

shamanism The practice of identifying special individuals (shamans) who will interact with spirits for the benefit of the community. Characteristic of the Korean kingdoms of the early medieval period and of early societies of Central Asia.

Our first knowledge of Korea, Japan, and Vietnam comes from early Chinese officials and travelers. When the Qin Empire established its first colony in the Korean peninsula in the third century B.C.E., Chinese bureaucrats began documenting Korean history and customs. Han writers noted the horse breeding, strong hereditary elites, and **shamanism** (belief in the ability of certain individuals to contact ancestors and the invisible spirit world) of Korea's small kingdoms. But Korea quickly absorbed Confucianism and Buddhism.

Mountainous in the east and north, Korea was heavily forested until modern times. The land that can be cultivated (less than 20 percent) lies mostly in the south, where a warm climate and

Kim Wonyong, ed. *The Complete Collection of Korean Art*, Vol 4. Seoul: Tonghwa ch'ulp'an kongsa, 1974, plate 55, p. 76

Korean Wall Painting This depiction of women dancing before an audience comes from a sixth-century tomb near an early Korean capital north of the Yalu River.

monsoon rains support two crops per year. Population movements from Manchuria, Mongolia, and Siberia to the north and to Japan in the south promoted the spread of languages that were very different from Chinese but distantly related to the Turkic tongues of Inner Asia.

Aristocratic Families

In the sixth century the dominant landholding families made inherited status—the "bone ranks"—permanent in Silla (SILL-ah or SHILL-ah), a kingdom in the southeast of the peninsula. In 668 the northern Koguryo kingdom came to an end after prolonged conflict with the Sui and Tang. Supported by the Tang, Silla took control of much of the Korean peninsula. The Silla rulers imitated Tang government and examined officials on the Confucian classics. The fall of the Tang in the early 900s coincided with Silla's collapse and enabled the ruling house of **Koryo** (KAW-ree-oh), from which the modern name "Korea" derives, to rule a united peninsula for the next three centuries. Threatened constantly by the Liao and then the Jin in northern China, Koryo maintained amicable relations with Song China in the south. The Koryo kings supported Buddhism and made superb printed editions of Buddhist texts.

Koryo Korean kingdom founded in 918 and destroyed by a Mongol invasion in 1259.

Printing with Movable Type

The oldest surviving woodblock print in Chinese characters comes from Korea in the middle 700s. Commonly used during the Tang period, woodblock printing required great technical skill. A calligrapher would write the text on thin paper, which would then be pasted upside down on a block of wood. Once wetted, the characters showed through from the back, and an artisan would carve away the wooden surface surrounding each character. A fresh block had to be carved for each printed page. Korean artisans developed their own advances in printing, including experiments with movable type. By Song times, Korean experiments reached China, where further improvements led to metal or porcelain type from which texts could be cheaply printed.

Japan

Islands and Mountains

Japan consists of four main islands and many smaller ones stretching in an arc from as far south as Georgia to as far north as Maine. The nearest point of contact with the Asian mainland lies 100 miles away in southern Korea. In early times Japan was even more mountainous and heavily forested than Korea, with only 11 percent of its land area suitable for cultivation. Mild winters and monsoon rains supported the earliest population centers on the coastlands of the Inland Sea between Honshu and Shikoku Islands. The first rulers to extend their power broadly in the fourth and fifth centuries C.E. were based in the Yamato River Basin on the Kinai Plain at the eastern end of the sea.

The Yamato Regime

The first Chinese description of Japan, dating from the fourth century, tells of an island at the eastern edge of the world, divided into hundreds of small countries and ruled over by a shamaness named Himiko or Pimiko. How the unification of Japan occurred remains a question, but horse-riding warriors from Korea may have played a central role in uniting these small countries under the Yamato-based rulers.

In the mid-600s these rulers implemented the Taika (TIE-kah) and other reforms, giving the Yamato regime the key features of Tang government, which they knew of from Korean contacts and embassies to Chang'an sent by five different kings. A legal code, an official variety of Confucianism, and an official reverence for Buddhism blended with the local recognition of indigenous and immigrant chieftains as territorial administrators. Within a century, a centralized government with a complex system of law had emerged, as attested by a massive history in the Confucian style.

Women Rulers

Women from the aristocracy became royal consorts and thereby linked their kinsmen with the royal court. At the death of her husband in 592, Suiko, a woman from the immigrant aristocratic family of Soga, became empress. She occupied the throne until 628, enjoying a longer reign than any other ruler down to the nineteenth century. Asuka, her capital, saw a flowering of Buddhist art, and her nephew Shotoku opened relations with Sui China and promulgated in 604

Imperial Palace in Kyoto The first version of the palace was built in the eighth century two kilometers away from the current site. The Kyoto palace complex was the primary residence of the Japanese emperors until the middle of the nineteenth century, when the imperial capital moved to Tokyo. Being built of wood with cypress-bark roofing, the buildings have been repeatedly ravaged by fire, but each restoration has utilized traditional materials in an effort to preserve the historical forms. The latest rebuilding took place in 1855. The palace complex includes gardens and numerous buildings in a variety of styles particular to different periods in its history.

Christian Kober/Alamy

a "Constitution" that had lasting influence on Japan's governing philosophy (see Diversity and Dominance: Law and Society in China and Japan).

Chinese Influences

The Japanese mastered Chinese building techniques so well that Nara (NAH-rah) and Kyoto, Japan's early capitals, provide invaluable evidence of the wooden architecture long since vanished from China. During the eighth century Japan in some ways surpassed China in Buddhist studies. In 752 dignitaries from all over Mahayana Buddhist Asia gathered at the enormous Todaiji temple, near Nara, to celebrate the "eye-opening" of the "Great Buddha" statue.

Differences from China

AP* Exam Tip Be aware of the impact that China had on its neighbors during this period.

Though the Japanese adopted Chinese building styles and some street plans, Japanese cities were built without walls. Central Japan was not plagued by constant warfare. Also, the Confucian Mandate of Heaven, which justified dynastic changes, played no role in legitimating Japanese government. The *tenno*—often called "emperor" in English—belonged to a family believed to have ruled Japan since the beginning of history. The dynasty never changed. A prime minister and the leaders of the native religion, in later times called Shinto, the "way of the gods," exercised real control.

By 750 the government in Nara had reached its zenith, employing 7,000 men in its central bureaucracy. The rulers encouraged an extension of Japanese rice-growing culture into the territory of the Hayato people of southern Kyushu and into northeastern Honshu, where the Emishi, a non-Japanese indigenous population, practiced slash-and-burn agriculture.

Fujiwara Clan

Fujiwara Aristocratic family that dominated the Japanese imperial court between the ninth and twelfth centuries.

In 794 the central government moved to Kyoto, usually called by its ancient name, Heian (hay-ahn). Legally centralized government lasted there until 1185, though power became decentralized toward the end. Members of the **Fujiwara** (foo-jee-WAH-rah) clan—a family of priests, bureaucrats, and warriors who had succeeded the Soga clan in influence—controlled power and protected the emperor. Fujiwara dominance favored men of Confucian learning over the generally illiterate warriors. Noblemen of the Fujiwara period read the Chinese classics and appreciated painting and poetry.

Pursuit of an aesthetic way of life prompted the Fujiwara nobles to entrust responsibility for local government, policing, and tax collection to their warriors. Though often of humble origins, a small number of warriors had achieved wealth and power by the late 1000s. By the middle 1100s the nobility had lost control, and civil war between rival warrior clans engulfed the capital.

***The Tale of Genji* of Lady Murasaki**

Like other East Asian states influenced by Confucianism, the elite families of Fujiwara Japan did not encourage education for women. However, this did not prevent exceptional women from having a strong cultural impact. The hero of the celebrated Japanese novel about Fujiwara court culture, *The Tale of Genji*, written around the year 1000 by the noblewoman Murasaki Shikibu, remarks: "Women should have a general knowledge of several subjects, but it gives a bad impression if they show themselves to be attached to a particular branch of learning."[5]

Fujiwara noblewomen lived in near-total isolation, generally spending their time on cultural pursuits and the study of Buddhism. To communicate with their families or among themselves, they depended on writing. The simplified syllabic script that they used represented the Japanese language in its fully inflected form (the Chinese classical script used by Fujiwara men could not do so). Loneliness, free time, and a ready instrument for expression produced an outpouring of poetry, diaries, and storytelling by women of the Fujiwara era.

The *Pillow Book* of Sei Shonagon

Sei Shonagon (SAY SHOH-nah-gohn), a lady attending one of the royal consorts, composed her *Pillow Book* between 996 and 1021. Most likely named for being kept by the author's pillow so she could jot down occasional thoughts, this famous work begins:

> *Spring is best at dawn as gradually the hilltops lighten, while the light grows brighter until there are purple-tinged clouds trailing through the sky.*
>
> *Summer is best at night. That goes without saying when there is a full moon. But when fireflies flit here and there in a dark sky, that too is wonderful. It is even wonderful when it is raining.*[6]

The Shogunate

Kamakura Shogunate The first of Japan's decentralized military governments (1185–1333).

Military values acquired increasing importance during the period 1156–1185 when warfare between rival clans culminated in the establishment of the **Kamakura** (kah-mah-KOO-rah) **Shogunate** in eastern Honshu, far from the old religious and political center at Kyoto. The standing of the Fujiwara family fell as nobles and the emperor hurried to accommodate the new warlords. *The Tale of the Heike*, an anonymously composed thirteenth-century epic account of the clan war, reflects a Buddhist appreciation of the impermanence of worldly things, a view that became common among the new warrior class. This class, in later times called *samurai*, eventually absorbed some of the Fujiwara aristocratic values, but the ascendancy of the nonmilitary civil elite had come to an end.

Vietnam

Rice Agriculture

Not until Tang times did the relationship between Vietnam and China become close enough for economic and cultural interchange to play an important role. Occupying the coastal regions east of the mountainous spine of mainland Southeast Asia, Vietnam's economic and political life centered on two fertile river valleys, the Red River in the north and the Mekong (may-KONG) in the south. The rice-based agriculture of Vietnam made the region well suited for integration with southern China. In both regions the wet climate and hilly terrain demanded expertise in irrigation.

Relations with China

Early Vietnamese peoples may have preceded the Chinese in using draft animals in farming and working with metal. But in Tang and Song times the elites of "Annam" (ahn-nahm)—as the Chinese called early Vietnam—adopted Confucian bureaucratic training, Mahayana Buddhism, and other aspects of Chinese culture. Annamese elites continued to rule in the Tang style after that dynasty's fall. Annam assumed the name Dai Viet (die vee-yet) in 936 and maintained good relations with Song China as an independent country.

Champa rice Quick-maturing rice that can allow two harvests in one growing season. Originally introduced into Champa from India, it was later sent to China as a tribute gift by the Champa state.

Champa, located in what is now southern Vietnam, rivaled the Dai Viet state. The cultures of India and the Malay Peninsula strongly influenced Champa through maritime networks of trade and communication. During the Tang period, Champa fought with Dai Viet, but both kingdoms cooperated with the less threatening Song. Among the tribute gifts brought to the Song court by Champa emissaries was **Champa rice** (originally from India). Chinese farmers soon made use of this fast-maturing variety to improve their yields of the essential crop.

Women's Roles

Vietnam shared the general Confucian interest in hierarchy, but attitudes toward women, like those in Korea and Japan, differed from the Chinese model. None of the societies adopted footbinding. In Korea strong family alliances that functioned like political and economic organizations allowed women a role in negotiating and disposing of property. Before the adoption of Confucianism, Annamese women had enjoyed higher status than women in China, perhaps because both women and men participated in wet-rice cultivation. The Trung sisters of Vietnam, who lived in the second century C.E. and led local farmers in resistance against the Han Empire, still serve as national symbols in Vietnam and as local heroes in southern China.

Srivijaya A state based on the Indonesian island of Sumatra, between the seventh and eleventh centuries C.E. It amassed wealth and power by a combination of selective adaptation of Indian technologies and concepts, control of the lucrative trade routes between India and China, and skillful showmanship and diplomacy in holding together a disparate realm of inland and coastal territories.

Srivijaya

To the south of the zone of Confucian influence, an all-sea route between east and west had developed by the sixth century (see Chapter 6). Merchants from south India and Sri Lanka sailed through the Strait of Malacca (between the west side of the Malay Peninsula and the northeast coast of the island of Sumatra) and into the South China Sea. A new center of power, **Srivijaya** (sree-vih-JUH-yuh)—Sanskrit for "Great Conquest"— dominated this new route by 683 C.E. The kingdom gained ascendancy over its rivals and assumed control of the international trade route by bringing four distinct ecological zones under its control.

The core area was the agricultural plain along the Musi River in Sumatra. The king and his clerks, judges, and tax collectors controlled this zone directly from Palembang, the capital. Control was less direct over the second zone, the upland regions of Sumatra's interior, which yielded commercially valuable forest products. Local rulers there were bound to the center by oaths of loyalty, elaborate court ceremonies, and the sharing of profits from trade. The third zone consisted of river ports that had been Srivijaya's main rivals. Srivijaya allied with neighboring sea nomads, pirates who served as a Srivijayan navy in return for a steady income, to control these. The fourth zone was a fertile "rice bowl" on the central plain of the nearby island of

SECTION REVIEW

- Korea, Japan, and Vietnam adapted Chinese cultural and political models, including the Tang blend of Confucianism and Buddhism.
- In all three cultures, landowning and agriculture remained the principal source of wealth.
- The southern kingdom of Srivijaya was more influenced by India than by China.

Java—a region so productive, because of its volcanic soil, that it houses and feeds the majority of the population of present-day Indonesia.

The Srivijayan king, drawing upon Mahayana Buddhist conceptions, presented himself as a bodhisattva, one who had achieved enlightenment and utilized his precious insights for the betterment of his subjects. He was believed to have magical powers, controlling powerful forces of fertility associated with the rivers in flood and mediating between the spiritually potent realms of the mountains and the sea. The kings built and patronized Buddhist monasteries and schools. Though they encouraged Sanskrit learning, they had few contacts with the Mahayana Buddhist network that spread through China from the north under the Tang. After Srivijaya's decline in the eleventh century, Theravada Buddhism became the prevailing religious orientation.

CONCLUSION

The Tang Empire put into place a solid system of travel, trade, and communications that allowed cultural and economic influences to move quickly from Central Asia to Japan. Diversity within the empire produced great wealth and new ideas. But tensions among rival groups weakened the political structure and led to great violence and misery.

The post-Tang fragmentation permitted regional cultures to emerge. They experimented with and often improved on Tang military, architectural, and scientific technologies. In northern and Central Asia, these refinements included state ideologies based on Buddhism, bureaucratic practices based on Chinese traditions, and military techniques combining nomadic horsemanship and strategies with Chinese armaments and weapons. In Song China, the spread of Tang technological knowledge resulted in the privatization of commerce, major advances in technology and industry, increased productivity in agriculture, and deeper exploration of ideas relating to time, cosmology, and mathematics.

The brilliant achievements of the Song period came from mutually reinforcing developments in economy and technology. Avoiding the Tang's distortion of trade relations and inhibition of innovation and competition, the Song economy, though much smaller than its predecessor, showed great productivity, circulating goods and money throughout East Asia and stimulating the economies of neighbors.

Korea, Japan, and Vietnam developed distinct social, economic, and political systems. Buddhism became the preferred religion in all three regions, but Chinese influences, largely deriving from a universal esteem for Confucian thought and writings, put down deep roots. All of these societies made advances in agricultural technology and productivity and raised their literacy rates as printing spread. In terms of industrial specialization, Song China dominated military technology and engineering, Japan developed advanced techniques in steel making, and Korea excelled in textiles and agriculture.

In the absence of a land border with China, Japan retained greater political independence than Korea and Vietnam. The culture of its imperial center reached a high level of perfection, but the political system was ultimately based on a warrior aristocracy. Farther to the south, the maritime kingdom of Srivijaya remained largely immune to Chinese influence.

KEY TERMS

Grand Canal p. 284
Li Shimin p. 284
Tang Empire p. 284
tributary system p. 287
Song Empire p. 292
junk p. 293
gunpowder p. 293
neo-Confucianism p. 293
Zen p. 294
movable type p. 295
shamanism p. 298
Koryo p. 299
Fujiwara p. 301
Kamakura Shogunate p. 301
Champa rice p. 302
Srivijaya p. 302

EBOOK AND WEBSITE RESOURCES

Primary Source

Memorial on Buddhism

Interactive Maps

Map 10.1 The Tang Empire in Inner and Eastern Asia, 750

Map 10.2 Liao and Song Empires, ca. 1100

Map 10.3 Jin and Southern Song Empires, ca. 1200

Plus flashcards, practice quizzes, and more. Go to: www.cengage.com/history/bullietearthpeople5e

SUGGESTED READING

Barfield, Thomas. *The Perilous Frontier: Nomadic Empires and China*. 1992. An anthropologist's view of the relationship between pastoralists and agriculturists in the region.

Batten, B. L. *To the Ends of Japan: Premodern Frontiers, Boundaries, and Interactions*. 2003. Japan in the overall history of Northeast Asia.

Ch'oe, Yongho, et al., eds. *Sources of Korean Tradition*. 2000. Key texts and sound interpretations.

De Bary, W. T., W-T Chan, and B. Watson, compilers. *Sources of Chinese Tradition*, vol. 1, 2nd ed. 1999. Key texts and sound interpretations of neo-Confucianism and Buddhism.

Ebrey, Patricia. *The Inner Quarters: Marriage and the Lives of Chinese Women in the Sung Period*. 1993. Uncommon study of Chinese women's history.

Elvin, Mark. *The Pattern of the Chinese Past*. 1973. A classic thesis on Song advancement (and Ming backwardness); see particularly Part II.

Hymes, Robert P. *Way and Byway: Taoism, Local Religion, and Models of Divinity in Sung China*. 2002. A study of post-Tang religious matters.

Nahm, Andrew C. *Introduction to Korean History and Culture*. 1993. A general survey.

Rossabi, Morris, ed. *China Among Equals: The Middle Kingdom and Its Neighbors, 10th–14th Centuries*. 1983. General account of post-Tang political relationships.

Taylor, Keith Weller. *The Birth of Vietnam*. 1983. A general survey.

Tsunoda, R., W. T. de Bary, and D. Keene, compilers. *Sources of Japanese Tradition*, vol. 1, 2nd ed. 2002. Key texts and sound interpretations.

Varley, Paul H. *Japanese Culture*. 1984. A classic introduction.

Wright, Arthur F., and David Twitchett, eds. *Perspectives on the T'ang*. 1973. A variety of enduring essays.

NOTES

1. *Master Tung's Western Chamber Romance*, trans. Li-li Ch'en (New York: Columbia University Press, 1994), 22, 42–43, 45–46.
2. Theodore de Bary, ed., *Sources of Chinese Tradition*, vol. 1, 2nd ed. (New York: Columbia University Press, 1999), 584.
3. Quoted in David Lattimore, "Allusion in T'ang Poetry," in *Perspectives on the T'ang*, ed. Arthur F. Wright and David Twitchett (New Haven, CT: Yale University Press, 1973), 436.
4. Quoted at "Women's Early Music, Art, Poetry," http://music.acu.edu/www/iawm/pages/reference/tzusongs.html.
5. Quoted in Ivan Morris, *The World of the Shining Prince: Court Life in Ancient Japan* (New York: Penguin Books, 1979), 221–222.
6. Quoted in Ivan Morris, trans., *The Pillow Book of Sei Shonagon* (New York: Columbia University Press, 1991), section 1.

AP* REVIEW QUESTIONS FOR CHAPTER 10

1. Under the leadership of the Tang rulers,
   (A) the spread of Buddhism was encouraged.
   (B) China banned trade with all outsiders.
   (C) female footbinding began.
   (D) the practice of Confucian teachings was banned.

2. One reason the Tang rulers expanded their empire into Inner Asia was
   (A) to create a highly centralized state based on control of trade.
   (B) that the founders were of Turkic extraction and shared common traits with the people of the region.
   (C) to seek allies in a war against the Han Chinese for control of China.
   (D) that they needed to increase the amount of tribute received to pay for the public works they commissioned.

3. As Buddhism began to spread in Tang China,
   (A) the Tang rulers forbade Chinese men to become monks.
   (B) Legalist scholars began to convert to the new faith because they viewed it as being more ethical than Taoism.
   (C) Mahayana Buddhism became the predominant form of Buddhism in China because of its tolerance of local custom.
   (D) Buddhist monasteries were forced to pay larger amounts of tribute because of the wealth they received from their followers.

4. During the Tang
   (A) countries in East and Southeast Asia became tributary states in exchange for trading rights or strategic alliances.
   (B) corruption cost the government vast amounts of wealth that was derived from trade.
   (C) nomadic incursions stopped because the nomads were rewarded with jobs operating and supplying caravans.
   (D) Tibet became a major partner in developing improved trade with Central Asia.

5. Serious challenge to Tang rule in the western portion of China came from the
   (A) Persians.
   (B) Uighurs.
   (C) Kazaks.
   (D) Mughals.

6. Which of the following is true of the collapse of the Tang?
   (A) Military revolts and tax collection issues that they could not control brought down the Tang rulers.
   (B) The last of the Tang emperors was assassinated by a Tibetan monk and, with no successor, the Tang collapsed.
   (C) Tanggut leaders proclaimed that they held the "Mandate of Heaven" and called for an end to the dynasty.
   (D) The empire was plagued with drought and famine, which caused it to collapse.

7. The Song Empire was able to take control of China following the Tang, but
   (A) it needed the aid of the Annamese people to the south.
   (B) Theravada Buddhism had to be legalized.
   (C) it lost vast amounts of territory to the Liao and the Tanggut Empires.
   (D) it expanded west into Sogdiana.

8. The Song developed ________ as a weapon of war but not in the same way that the West would use it.
   (A) armored ships
   (B) gunpowder
   (C) the crossbow
   (D) cannon

9. Song and later versions of Confucian thought are known as
   (A) Zen.
   (B) ancestor veneration.
   (C) neo-Confucianism.
   (D) filial piety.

10. During the 1100s, spurred by prosperity, China's population rose above 100 million people. One consequence of the population growth was

    (A) urban crowding.
    (B) widespread famine.
    (C) rebellion over food price increases.
    (D) wide-ranging price controls on food and housing.

11. Traditionally, in Korea, Japan, and Vietnam,

    (A) the culture was based on Indian traits.
    (B) government offices went to the noble families.
    (C) Buddhism was the state religion.
    (D) written language developed independently from other parts of Asia.

12. Like Japan, Korea's earliest history

    (A) is based solely on creation myths.
    (B) is well documented in written court records.
    (C) comes from Chinese records.
    (D) is based on epic poetry.

13. During the Heian period of Japan, the capital city was

    (A) Tokyo.
    (B) Edo.
    (C) Kyoto.
    (D) Kamakura.

14. During the period of the Kamakura Shogunate, a new class appeared in Japan. This was the

    (A) slave class.
    (B) merchant class.
    (C) samurai, or warrior, class.
    (D) priestly class.

15. Vietnam, Korea, and Japan all adopted forms of Confucian government; however, none of them adopted ________ from China.

    (A) the practice of footbinding
    (B) rice farming as the principal form of agriculture
    (C) a written language
    (D) clothing styles

CHAPTER 11

CHAPTER OUTLINE

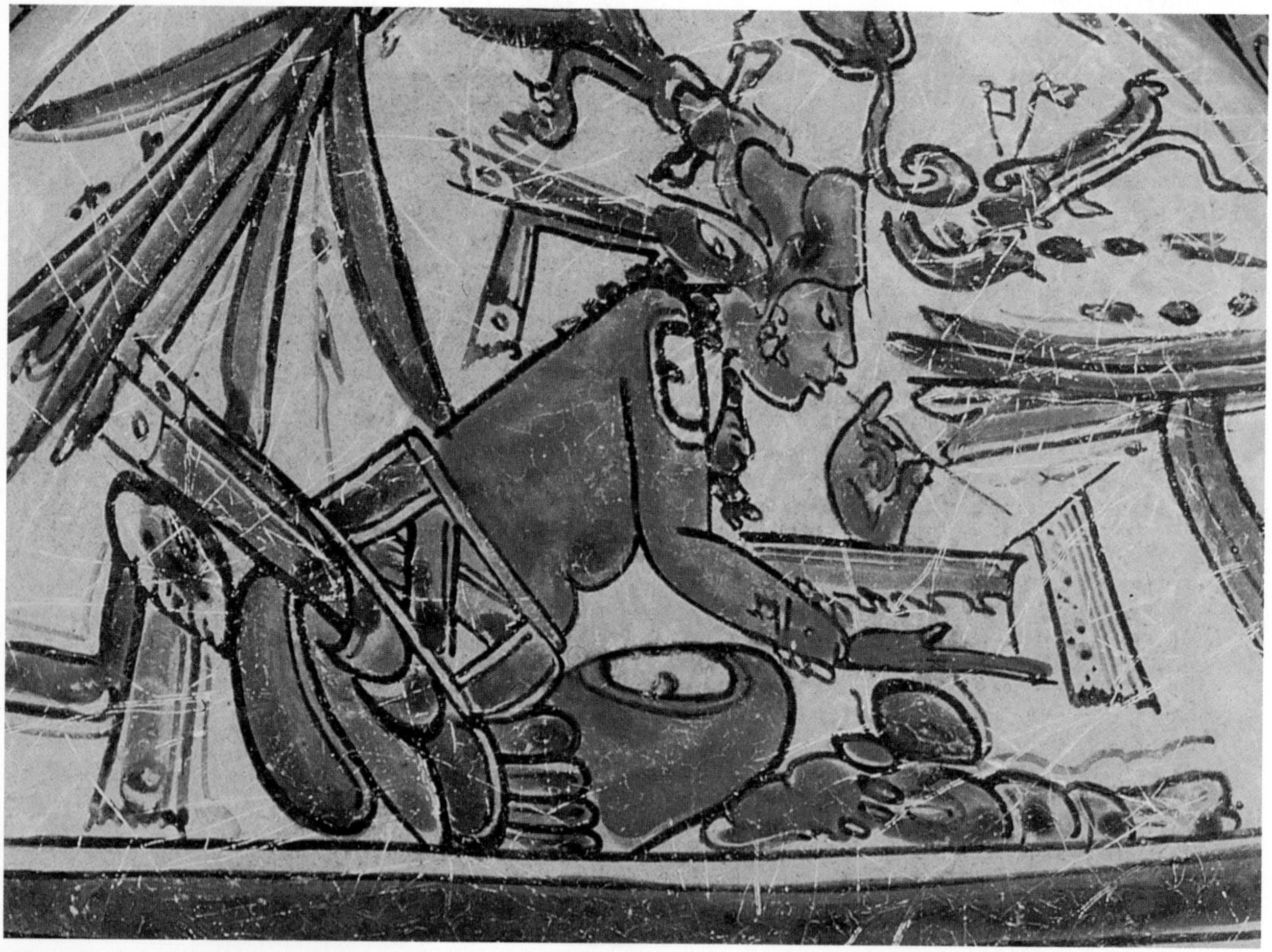

© Justin Kerr

Maya Scribe Maya scribes used a complex writing system to record religious concepts and memorialize the actions of their kings. An artisan painted this picture of a scribe on a ceramic plate.

Visit the website and ebook for additional study materials and interactive tools: www.cengage.com/history/bullietearthpeople5e

Peoples and Civilizations of the Americas, 600–1500

- What were the most important shared characteristics of Mesoamerican cultures in the classic period?
- What role did warfare play in the postclassic period of Mesoamerica?
- In what ways did Mesoamerica influence the cultural centers in North America?
- How did the Amerindian peoples of the Andean area adapt to their environment and produce socially complex and politically advanced societies?

The ancient Mesoamerican civilization of the Maya (MY-ah) developed a complex written language that enabled scribes like the one in this illustration to record the important actions of rulers and military events. Recent translations give us a glimpse into the life of a Maya princess. In late August 682 C.E. the Maya princess Lady Wac-Chanil-Ahau (wac-cha-NEEL-ah-HOW) walked down the steps from her family's residence and mounted a litter decorated with rich textiles and animal skins. As the procession exited from the urban center of Dos Pilas (dohs PEE-las), her military escort spread out through the fields and woods along its path to prevent ambush by enemies. Lady Wac-Chanil-Ahau's destination was the Maya city of Naranjo (na-RAHN-hoe), where she was to marry a powerful nobleman. Her father arranged this marriage to reestablish Naranjo's royal dynasty eliminated when Caracol, the region's major military power, conquered the city. Lady Wac-Chanil-Ahau's passage to Naranjo symbolized her father's desire to forge a military alliance that could resist Caracol. For us, the story of Lady Wac-Chanil-Ahau illustrates the importance of marriage and lineage in the politics of the classic-period Maya.

K'ak Tiliw Chan Chaak (kahk-tee-lew-CHAN-cha-ahk), the son of Lady Wac-Chanil-Ahau, ascended the throne of Naranjo as a five-year-old in 693 C.E. During his long reign he proved to be a careful diplomat and formidable warrior. He was also a prodigious builder, leaving behind an expanded and beautified capital as part of his legacy. Mindful of the importance of his mother and her lineage from Dos Pilas, he erected numerous steles (carved stone monuments) that celebrated her life.[1]

The world of Wac-Chanil-Ahau was challenged by warfare and dynastic crisis as population increased and competition for resources grew more violent. In this environment the rise of Caracol undermined long-standing commercial and political relations in much of southern Mesoamerica and led to more than a century of conflict. Eventually, the dynasty created at Dos Pilas by the heirs of Lady Wac-Chanil-Ahau challenged Caracol. Despite a shared culture and religion, the great Maya cities remained divided by the dynastic ambitions of their rulers and by the competition for resources.

As the story of Lady Wac-Chanil-Ahau's marriage and her role in the development of a Maya dynasty suggests, the peoples of the Americas were in constant competition for resources. Members of hereditary elites organized their societies to meet these challenges, even as their ambition for greater power predictably ignited new conflicts. No single set of political institutions or technologies worked in every environment, and enormous cultural diversity existed in the ancient Americas. In Mesoamerica (Mexico and northern Central America) and in the Andean region of South America, Amerindian peoples developed an extraordinarily productive and diversified agriculture. They also built great cities that rivaled the capitals of the Chinese and Roman Empires in size and beauty. The Olmec of Mesoamerica and Chavín (cha-VEEN) of the Andes were among the earliest civilizations of the Americas (see Chapter 2). In the rest of the hemisphere, indigenous peoples adapted combinations of hunting and agriculture to maintain a wide variety of settlement patterns, political forms, and cultural traditions. All the cultures and civilizations of the Americas experienced cycles of expansion and contraction as they struggled with the challenges of environmental change, population growth, and war.

CLASSIC-ERA CULTURE AND SOCIETY IN MESOAMERICA, 200–900

AP* Exam Tip The nature and causes of changes in the world history framework for this region are important to understand for the exam.

Between about 200 and 900 C.E. the peoples of Mesoamerica created a remarkable civilization. Despite enduring differences in language and the absence of regional political integration, Mesoamericans were unified by similarities in material culture, religious beliefs and practices, and social structures. Building on the earlier achievements of the Olmec and others, the peoples of the area that is now Central America and south and central Mexico developed new forms of political organization, made great strides in astronomy and mathematics, and improved the productivity of their agriculture. Archaeologists call this mix of achievements the classic period. During this period, a growing population traded a greater variety of products over longer distances, and social hierarchies became more complex. Great cities were constructed that served as centers of political life and as arenas of religious ritual and spiritual experience.

Classic-period civilizations built on the religious and political foundations established earlier in Olmec centers (see Chapter 2). Like these earlier centers, the cities of the classic period were built around raised platforms and pyramids devoted to religious functions, but they were more impressive and architecturally diversified. They also had large full-time populations divided into classes and dominated by hereditary political and religious elites who controlled nearby towns and villages and imposed their will on the rural peasantry.

The political and cultural innovations of this period did not depend on the introduction of new technologies. The agricultural foundations of Mesoamerican civilization were in place centuries earlier. Major innovations in agriculture such as irrigation, the draining of wetlands, and the terracing of hillsides had all been in place for more than a thousand years when great cities were first developed around 200 C.E. Instead, the achievements of the classic era depended on the ability of increasingly powerful elites to organize and command growing numbers of laborers and soldiers.

Teotihuacan

Teotihuacan A powerful city-state in central Mexico (100 B.C.E.–750 C.E.). Its population was about 150,000 at its peak in 600.

Located about 30 miles (48 kilometers) northeast of modern Mexico City, **Teotihuacan** (teh-o-tee-WAH-kahn) (100 C.E.–750 C.E.) was one of Mesoamerica's most important classic-period civilizations (see Map 11.2 on page 318). At the height of its power around 450 C.E., it was the largest city in the Americas. With between 125,000 and 150,000 inhabitants, it was larger than all but a small number of contemporary European and Asian cities.

The Role of Religion

Religious architecture rose above a city center aligned with nearby sacred mountains that reflected the movement of the stars. The people of Teotihuacan recognized and worshiped many gods and lesser spirits. Enormous pyramids dedicated to the Sun and Moon and more than twenty smaller temples devoted to other gods were arranged along a central avenue. They

CHRONOLOGY

	Mesoamerica	Northern Peoples	Andes
100	100 Teotihuacan temple complex built	100–400 Hopewell culture in Ohio River Valley	
	250 Maya early classic period begins		200–700 Moche culture
500			500–1000 Tiwanaku and Wari control Peruvian highlands
700	ca. 750 Teotihuacan destroyed	700–1300 Anasazi culture	
	800–900 Maya centers abandoned, end of classic period	ca. 800 beginnings of Mississippian culture	
	968 Toltec capital of Tula founded		
1000		1050–1250 Cahokia reaches peak power	
	1175 Tula destroyed	1150 Collapse of Anasazi centers begins	
1300	1325 Aztec capital Tenochtitlan founded		1430s Inca expansion begins
1500	1502 Moctezuma II crowned Aztec ruler	1500 Mississippian culture declines	1500–1525 Inca conquer Ecuador

dedicated the largest pyramids to the Sun and the Moon and to Quetzalcoatl (kate-zahl-CO-ah-tal), the feathered serpent, a culture-god believed to be the originator of agriculture and the arts. Murals suggest that another pair of powerful gods, the storm-god Tlaloc and a powerful female god associated with fertility, were also central figures in the city's religious life. Like the earlier

G.Dagli Orti/The Art Archive

The Temple of the Sun The temple of the sun is the largest pyramid in Tenochtitlan. The smaller temple of Quetzalcoatl displays the serpent images associated with this culture god common to most Mesoamerican civilizations.

Olmec, people living at Teotihuacan practiced human sacrifice, illustrated by the discovery of more than a hundred sacrificial victims during the excavation of the temple of Quetzalcoatl. Scholars believe that residents viewed sacrifice as a sacred duty to the gods and as essential to the well-being of society.

AP* Exam Tip Migration into and out of regions is important information to know for the exam.

The rapid growth in urban population initially resulted from a series of volcanic eruptions that disrupted agriculture. Later, as the city elite increased their power, they forced farm families from the smaller villages in the region to relocate to the urban core. As a result, more than two-thirds of the city's residents retained their dependence on agriculture, walking out from urban residences to their fields. The elite organized the city's growing labor resources to bring marginal lands into production, drain swamps, construct irrigation canals, and build terraces into hillsides. They also expanded the use of **chinampas** (chee-NAM-pahs), sometimes called "floating gardens." These were narrow artificial islands constructed along lakeshores or in marshes by farmers who heaped lake muck and waste material on beds of reeds and anchored them to the shore. Chinampas permitted year-round agriculture—because of subsurface irrigation and resistance to frost—and thus played a crucial role in sustaining the region's growing population.

chinampas Raised fields constructed along lakeshores in Mesoamerica to increase agricultural yields.

The city's role as a religious center and commercial power provided both divine approval of and a material basis for the elite's increased wealth and status. Members of the elite controlled the state bureaucracy, tax collection, and commerce. Their rich and ornate clothing, their abundant diet, and their large, well-made residences signaled the wealth and power of aristocratic families. Temple and palace murals make clear the central position and great prestige of the priestly class as well. Teotihuacan's economy and religious influence drew pilgrims from as far away as Oaxaca and Veracruz. Many became permanent residents.

Unlike the other classic-period civilizations, the people of Teotihuacan did not concentrate power in the hands of a single ruler. Although the ruins of their impressive housing compounds demonstrate the wealth and influence of the city's aristocracy, there is no clear evidence that individual rulers or a ruling dynasty gained overarching political power. In fact, some scholars suggest that alliances among elite families or weak kings who were the puppets of these powerful families ruled Teotihuacan.

Historians debate the role of the military in the development of Teotihuacan. The absence of walls or other defensive structures before 500 C.E. suggests that Teotihuacan enjoyed relative peace during its early development. Archaeological evidence, however, reveals that the city created a powerful military to protect long-distance trade and to compel peasant agriculturalists to transfer their surplus production to the city. Unlike later postclassic civilizations, however, Teotihuacan was not an imperial state controlled by a military elite.

Decline and Collapse

It is unclear what forces brought about the collapse of Teotihuacan about 750 C.E. By 500 C.E. the urban population had declined to about 40,000 and the city's residents had begun to build defensive walls. Pictorial evidence from murals indicates that the city's final decades were violent. Scholars have uncovered evidence that the elite had mismanaged resources. Resulting divisions among the ruling elite then led to class conflict and the breakdown of public order. As a result, the most important temples in the city center were destroyed and religious images defaced. Evidence also shows that elite palaces were systematically burned and many of their residents killed. Regardless of the causes, the eclipse of Teotihuacan was felt throughout Mexico and into Central America.

The Maya

Maya Mesoamerican civilization concentrated in Mexico's Yucatán Peninsula and in Guatemala and Honduras but never unified into a single empire. Major contributions were in mathematics, astronomy, and development of the calendar.

During Teotihuacan's ascendancy in the north, the **Maya** developed an impressive civilization in the region that today includes Guatemala, Honduras, Belize, and southern Mexico (see Map 11.1). Given the difficulties imposed by a tropical climate and fragile soils, the cultural and architectural achievements of the Maya were remarkable. Although they shared a single culture, the Maya never created a single, unified state. Instead, rival kingdoms led by hereditary rulers struggled with each other for regional dominance, much like the Mycenaean-era Greeks (see Chapter 3).

Agriculture and Urbanization

Today Maya farmers prepare their fields by cutting down small trees and brush and then burning the dead vegetation to fertilize the land. Such swidden agriculture (also called shifting agriculture or slash and burn agriculture) can produce high yields for a few years. However,

MAP 11.1 Maya Civilization, 250–1400 C.E. The Maya never created an integrated and unified state. Instead Maya civilization developed as a complex network of independent city states.

Interactive Map

it uses up the soil's nutrients, eventually forcing farmers to move to more fertile land. The high population levels of the Maya classic period (250–900 C.E.) required more intensive forms of agriculture. Maya living near the major urban centers achieved high agricultural yields by draining swamps and building elevated fields. They used irrigation in areas with long dry seasons, and they terraced hillsides in the cooler highlands. Maya agriculturists also managed nearby forests, favoring the growth of the trees and shrubs that were most useful to them, as well as promoting the conservation of deer and other animals hunted for food.

During the classic period, Maya city-states proliferated. The most powerful cities controlled groups of smaller dependent cities and a broad agricultural zone by building impressive religious temples and by creating rituals that linked the power of kings to the gods. Open plazas were surrounded by high pyramids and by elaborately decorated palaces often built on high ground or on constructed mounds. The effect was to awe the masses drawn to the centers for religious and political rituals.

The Great Plaza at Tikal The impressive architectural and artistic achievements of the classic-era Maya are still visible in the ruins of Tikal, in modern Guatemala. Maya centers provided a dramatic setting for the rituals that dominated public life. Construction of Tikal began before 150 B.C.E.; the city was abandoned about 900 C.E. A ball court and residences for the elite were part of the Great Plaza.

Martha Cooper/Peter Arnold, Inc.

Chrysler Museum of Art/Justin Kerr

The Mesoamerican Ball Game From Guatemala to Arizona, archaeologists have found evidence of an ancient ball game played with a solid rubber ball on slope-sided courts shaped like a capital T. Among the Maya the game was associated with a creation myth and thus had deep religious meaning. Evidence suggests that some players were sacrificed. In this scene from a ceramic jar, players wearing elaborate ritual clothing—which includes heavy, protective pads around the chest and waist—play with a ball much larger than the ball actually used in such games. Some representations show balls drawn to suggest a human head.

The Maya loved decoration. Carved decorations painted in bright colors covered nearly all public buildings. Religious allegories, the genealogies of rulers, and important historical events were the most common motifs. The Maya also erected beautifully carved altars and stone monoliths near major temples. This rich legacy of monumental architecture was constructed without the aid of wheels—no pulleys, wheelbarrows, or carts—or metal tools. Masses of men and women aided only by levers and stone tools cut and carried construction materials and lifted them into place.

Religion and Political Organization

The Maya divided the cosmos into three layers connected along a vertical axis that traced the course of the sun. The earthly arena of human existence held an intermediate position between the heavens, conceptualized by the Maya as a sky-monster, and a dark underworld. The Maya believed that a sacred tree rose through the three layers; its roots were in the underworld, and its branches reached into the heavens. The temple precincts of Maya cities physically represented essential elements of this religious cosmology. The pyramids were sacred mountains reaching to the heavens. The doorways of the pyramids were portals to the underworld.

Rulers and other members of the elite served both priestly and political functions. They decorated their bodies with paint and tattoos and wore elaborate costumes of textiles, animal skins, and feathers to project both secular power and divine sanction. These lords communicated directly with the supernatural residents of the other worlds and with deified royal ancestors through bloodletting rituals and hallucinogenic trances.

The Maya infused warfare with religious meaning and celebrated it in elaborate rituals. Battle scenes and the depiction of the torture and sacrifice of captives were frequent decorative themes. Typically, Maya military forces fought to secure captives rather than territory. The king, his kinsmen, and other ranking nobles actively participated in war. Elite captives were nearly always sacrificed; captured commoners were more likely to be forced to labor for their captors.

Maya Women

Few women directly ruled Maya kingdoms, but Maya women of the ruling lineages did play important political and religious roles. The consorts of male rulers participated in bloodletting rituals and in other important public ceremonies, and their noble blood helped legitimate the rule of their husbands. Although Maya society was patrilineal (tracing descent in the male line), there is clear evidence that some male rulers traced their lineages bilaterally (in both the male and female lines). Others, like Lady Wac-Chanil-Ahau's son discussed earlier, emphasized the female line if it held higher status. Little is known about the lives of poorer women, but scholars believe that women played a central role in the religious rituals of the home. They were also heal-ers and shamans. Women were essential to the household economy, maintaining essential garden plots and weaving, and in the management of family life.

The Maya made important contributions to the development of the Mesoamerican calendar and to mathematics and writing. Time was a central concern, and they developed an accurate calendar system. They identified each day by three separate dating systems. The Maya calendar tracked a ritual cycle (260 days divided into thirteen months of 20 days). A second calendar tracked the solar year (365 days divided into eighteen months of 20 days, plus 5 unfavorable days at the end of the year). The Maya believed that the very survival of humanity was threatened every fifty-two years when the two calendars coincided. Alone among Mesoamerican peoples, the Maya also maintained a continuous "long count" calendar, which began with creation in 3114 B.C.E.

Maya mathematics and writing provided the foundations for both the calendars and the astronomical observations on which they were based. Their system of mathematics incorporated the concept of the zero and place value but had limited notational signs. Maya writing was a form of hieroglyphic inscription that signified whole words or concepts as well as phonetic cues or syllables. Scribes recorded aspects of public life, religious belief, and the biographies of rulers and their ancestors in books, on pottery, and on the stone columns and monumental buildings of the urban centers. In this sense every Maya city was a sacred text.

SECTION REVIEW

- Teotihuacan, one of the largest Mesoamerican cities, was ruled by elites who used religious rituals and military power to legitimize their authority over the many laborers who worked the surrounding fields.
- Teotihuacan's impressive urban architecture, complex agriculture, and extensive trade made it a dominating cultural presence throughout Mesoamerica. Its collapse around 750 C.E. resulted from conflicts within the elite and resource mismanagement.
- The Maya shared a single culture but never created a single, unified state. Instead the Maya developed numerous powerful city-states. Each city, filled with highly decorated monumental architecture, was a religious and political center for the surrounding region.
- Religious architecture dominated the centers of Teotihuacan and Maya cities. Many gods were worshipped and religious ritual, including, human sacrifice, organized collective life.
- The Maya devised an elaborate calendar system, the concept of zero, and writing.
- After centuries of expansion, the power of the Maya cities declined due to an intensified struggle for resources, leading to class conflict and warfare.

The End of the Classic Era

Between 800 and 900 C.E. the Maya abandoned many of their major urban centers. Many cities were destroyed by violence, although a small number of classic-period centers survived for centuries. Decades of urban decline, social conflict, and increased levels of warfare preceded this collapse in some areas. The earlier collapse of Teotihuacan around 750 had disrupted long-distance trade in ritual goods and may have begun to undermine the legitimacy of Maya rulers tied to that distant center. Certainly, rising regional population, climatic change, and environmental degradation undermined the fragile agricultural system that sustained Maya cities long before the collapse. But it was the growing scale and destructiveness of warfare that finally undermined the political legitimacy of ruling lineages and disrupted the web of economic relationships that tied rural agriculturalists to Maya cities.

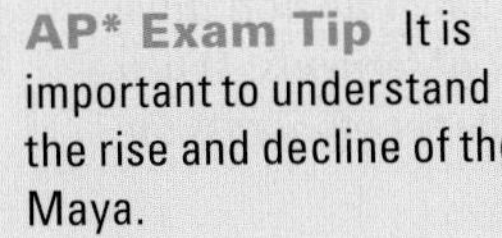

AP* Exam Tip It is important to understand the rise and decline of the Maya.

THE POSTCLASSIC PERIOD IN MESOAMERICA, 900–1500

The division between the classic and postclassic periods is somewhat arbitrary. Not only is there no single explanation for the collapse of Teotihuacan and many of the major Maya centers, but these events occurred over more than a century and a half. In fact, some important classic-period civilizations survived unscathed while elsewhere the essential cultural characteristics of the classic period survived in the postclassic era.

At the same time, there were some important differences between the periods. There is evidence that the population of Mesoamerica expanded during the postclassic period. Resulting pressures led to an intensification of agricultural practices and to increased warfare. The governing elites of the major postclassic states—the Toltecs and the Aztecs—responded to these harsh realities by increasing the size of their armies and by developing political institutions that facilitated their control of large and culturally diverse territories acquired through conquest.

The Toltecs

Toltecs Powerful postclassic empire in central Mexico (900–1175 C.E.). It influenced much of Mesoamerica. Aztecs claimed ties to this earlier civilization.

While modern archaeology has revealed the civilizations of the Maya and Teotihuacan in previously unimaginable detail, the history of the **Toltecs** (TOLL-tek) remains in dispute. The Aztecs regarded the Toltecs as powerful and influential predecessors, much as the Romans regarded the Greeks. Memories of Toltec military achievements and the violent imagery of their political and religious rituals dominated the Mesoamerican imagination throughout the late postclassic period. The Aztecs and their fifteenth-century contemporaries erroneously believed that the Toltecs were the source of nearly all the great cultural achievements of the Mesoamerican world. As one Aztec source later recalled:

> *In truth [the Toltecs] invented all the precious and marvelous things. . . . All that now exists was their discovery. . . . And these Toltecs were very wise; they were thinkers, for they originated the year count, the day count. All their discoveries formed the book for interpreting dreams. . . . And so wise were they [that] they understood the stars which were in the heavens.*[2]

Origins

In fact, all these contributions to Mesoamerican culture were in place long before Toltec power spread across central Mexico. Some scholars speculate that the Toltecs were originally a satellite population that Teotihuacan had placed on the northern frontier to protect against the incursions of nomads. Others suggest that the Toltecs were migrants from the north who later borrowed from the cultural legacies of Teotihuacan and other cultures. Regardless of their origins, it is clear that the Toltecs created a state based largely on military power, which they used to extend their influence from their political capital at Tula (TOO-la) (also called Tollan; founded in 968 C.E.) north of modern Mexico City to Central America.

The End of Toltec Power

Until recently historians relied primarily on sources from the era of European conquests. According to these sources, two chieftains or kings shared power, and this division of responsibility eventually weakened Toltec power. Sometime after 1150 C.E. a struggle between elite groups identified with rival religious cults undermined the Toltecs. Legends that survived among the Aztecs claimed that Topiltzin (tow-PEELT-zeen)—one of the two rulers and a priest of the cult of Quetzalcoatl—and his followers bitterly accepted exile in the east, "the land of the rising sun." One of the ancient texts relates these events in the following manner:

> *Thereupon he [Topiltzin] looked toward Tula, and then wept. . . . And when he had done these things . . . he went to reach the seacoast. Then he fashioned a raft of serpents. When he had arranged the raft, he placed himself as if it were his boat. Then he set off across the sea.*[3]

Similarities in architecture and urban planning in the Toltec heartland and in some Maya postclassic centers, like Chichen Itza (CHEECH-ehn EET-zah) in the Yucatán Peninsula, led some scholars to suggest a Toltec presence in the Maya region. Scholars now dispute this linkage.

We do know that the Toltec state entered a period of steep decline after 1150 C.E. that included internal power struggles and a military threat from the north. By 1175 disaster had befallen the once-great city of Tula. Scholars generally agree that a site north of Mexico City includes the ruins of this once powerful city (see Map 11.2). Its public architecture features colonnaded patios and numerous temples in the Toltec style. Representations of warriors and scenes suggesting human sacrifice decorate nearly all public buildings and temples. Even in ruins, the grandeur, creativity, and power of the Toltecs as celebrated by the Aztecs are visible at Tula.

The Aztecs

altepetl An ethnic state in ancient Mesoamerica, the common political building block of that region.

The Mexica (meh-SHE-ca) were among the northern peoples who pushed into central Mexico in the wake of the Toltec collapse. As their power grew through political alliances and military conquest, they created a Mexica-dominated regional power called the Aztec Empire (see Map 11.2). At the time of their arrival the Mexica were organized as an **altepetl** (al-TEH-peh-tel), an

The Bodleian Library, University of Oxford, Selder. A.I. fol. 64r

Costumes of Aztec Warriors
In Mesoamerican warfare individual warriors sought to gain prestige and improve their status by taking captives. An Amerindian artist employed by the Franciscans produced this illustration in the sixteenth-century Codex Mendoza. It shows the Aztecs' use of distinctive costumes to acknowledge the prowess of warriors. The individual on the bottom right shown without a weapon was a military leader. As was common in Mesoamerican illustrations of military conflict, the captives, held by their hair, are shown kneeling before the victors.

AP* Exam Tip The rise of the Inca is important to understand.

Aztec Origins

calpolli A group of up to a hundred families that served as a social building block of an altepetl in ancient Mesoamerica.

Tenochtitlan Capital of the Aztec Empire, located on an island in Lake Texcoco. Its population was about 150,000 on the eve of Spanish conquest. Mexico City was constructed on its ruins.

Aztecs Also known as Mexica, the Aztecs created a powerful empire in central Mexico (1325–1521 C.E.). They forced defeated peoples to provide goods and labor as a tax.

ethnic state led by a tlatoani (tlah-toh-AHN-ee) or ruler. The altepetl, the common political building block across the region, directed the collective religious, social, and political obligations of the ethnic group. A group of **calpolli** (cal-POH-yee), each with up to a hundred families, served as the foundation of the altepetl, controlling land allocation, tax collection, and local religious life.

In their new environment the Mexica began to adopt the political and social practices that they found among the urbanized agriculturalists of the valley. At first, they served their more powerful neighbors as serfs and mercenaries. As their strength grew, they relocated to small islands near the shore of Lake Texcoco, and around 1325 C.E. they began the construction of their twin capitals, **Tenochtitlan** (teh-noch-TIT-lan) and Tlatelolco (tla-teh-LOHL-coh) (together the foundation for modern Mexico City).

Military successes allowed the Mexica to seize control of additional agricultural land along the lakeshore and to forge military alliances with neighboring altepetl. Once these more complex political and economic arrangements were in place, the Mexica-dominated alliance became the Aztec Empire (see Map 11.2). With increased economic independence, greater political security, and territorial expansion, the **Aztecs** transformed their political organization by introducing a monarchical system similar to that found in more powerful neighboring states. A council of powerful aristocrats selected new rulers from among male members of the ruling lineage. Once selected, the ruler had to renegotiate the submission of tribute dependencies and then demonstrate his divine mandate by undertaking a new round of military conquests. For the Aztecs war was infused with religious meaning, providing the ruler with legitimacy and increasing the prestige of successful warriors.

The Aztecs succeeded in developing a remarkable urban landscape. The population of Tenochtitlan and Tlatelolco combined with that of the cities and towns of the surrounding lakeshore was approximately 500,000 by 1500 C.E. Three causeways connected this island capital to the lakeshore. Planners laid out the urban center as a grid where canals and streets intersected at right angles to facilitate the movement of people and goods.

MAP 11.2 Major Mesoamerican Civilizations, 1000 B.C.E.–1519 C.E. The Aztec Empire in 1518 was based on military conquest. The Aztec capital of Tenochtitlan was located near the classic era's largest city, Teotihuacan, and Tula, capital city of the postclassic Toltecs.

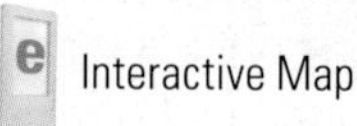
Interactive Map

Aztec Social Structure

Although warfare gave increased power and privilege to males, women held substantial power and exercised broad influence in Aztec society. The roles of women and men were clearly distinguished, but women were held in high esteem. Scholars call this "gender complementarity." Following the birth of a boy, his umbilical cord was buried on the battlefield and he was given implements to signal his occupation or his role as a warrior. In the case of a girl, her umbilical cord was buried near the hearth and she was given weaving implements and female clothing. Women dominated the household and the markets, and they also served as teachers and priestesses. They were also seen as the founders of lineages, including the royal line.

Aztec military successes and territorial expansion allowed the warrior elite to seize land and peasant labor as spoils of war. In time, the royal family and highest-ranking members of the aristocracy possessed extensive estates that were cultivated by slaves and landless commoners. The lower classes received some material rewards from imperial expansion but lost most of their ability to influence or control decisions. Some commoners were able to achieve some social mobility through success on the battlefield.

However, by 1500 C.E. great inequalities in wealth and privilege characterized Aztec society. One of the Spaniards who participated in the conquest of the Aztec Empire remembered his first meeting with the Aztec ruler Moctezuma (mock-teh-ZU-ma) II (r. 1502–1520): "Many great lords walked before the great Montezuma [Moctezuma II], sweeping the ground on which he was to tread and laying down cloaks so that his feet should not touch the earth. Not one of these chieftains dared look him in the face."[4] While commoners lived in small dwellings and ate a limited diet of staples, members of the nobility lived in large, well-constructed, two-story houses and consumed a diet rich in animal protein.

A specialized class of merchants controlled long-distance trade. Given the absence of draft animals and wheeled vehicles, lightweight and valuable products like gold, jewels, feathered garments, cacao, and animal skins dominated this commerce. Merchants also provided essential political and military intelligence for the Aztec elite. Although merchants became wealthy and powerful as the Aztecs expanded their empire, they were denied the privileges of the high nobility, which was jealous of its power.

The Aztec Economy

tribute system A system in which defeated peoples were forced to pay a tax in the form of goods and labor. This forced transfer of food, cloth, and other goods subsidized the development of large cities. An important component of the Aztec and Inca economies.

The Aztec state met the challenge of feeding an urban population of approximately 150,000 by efficiently organizing the labor of the calpolli and of additional laborers sent by defeated peoples to expand agricultural land. Aztec chinampas contributed maize, fruits, and vegetables to the markets of Tenochtitlan. The imposition of a **tribute system** on conquered peoples also helped relieve some of the pressure of Tenochtitlan's growing population. Unlike the tribute system of Tang China, where tribute had a more symbolic character (see Chapter 10), one-quarter of the Aztec capital's food requirement was satisfied by tribute payments of maize, beans, and other foods sent by nearby political dependencies.

Like commerce throughout the Mesoamerican world, Aztec commerce was carried on without money and credit. Barter was facilitated by the use of cacao, quills filled with gold, and cotton cloth as standard units of value to compensate for differences in the value of bartered goods. Aztec expansion facilitated the integration of producers and consumers in the central Mexican economy. Hernán Cortés (1485–1547), the Spanish adventurer who eventually conquered the Aztecs, expressed his admiration for the abundance of the Aztec marketplace:

> *One square in particular is twice as big as that of Salamanca and completely surrounded by arcades where there are daily more than sixty thousand folk buying and selling. Every kind of merchandise such as may be met with in every land is for sale. . . . There is nothing to be found in all the land which is not sold in these markets, for over and above what I have mentioned there are so many and such various things that on account of their very number . . . I cannot detail them.*[5]

Aztec Religion

Religious rituals dominated public life in Tenochtitlan. Like the other cultures of the Mesoamerican world, the Aztecs worshiped a large number of gods. Most of these gods had a dual nature—both male and female. The chief god of the Mexica was Huitzilopochtli (wheat-zeel-oh-POSHT-lee) or southern hummingbird. Originally associated with war, the Aztecs later identified this god with the Sun. Tenochtitlan was architecturally dominated by a great twin temple devoted to Huitzilopochtli and Tlaloc, the storm-god, symbolizing the two bases of the Aztec economy: war and agriculture.

The Aztecs believed that Huitzilopochtli required a diet of human hearts to sustain him in his daily struggle to bring the Sun's warmth to the world. Sacrifices were devoted to other gods as well. Although human sacrifice had been practiced since early times in Mesoamerica, the Aztecs and other societies of the late postclassic period transformed this religious ritual by dramatically increasing its scale. Military expansion and conquest had become the basis of empire and sacrifice its ritual center.

SECTION REVIEW

- In the postclassic era, large, professional militaries allowed Mesoamerican elites to create empires through conquest, resulting in increasingly hierarchical societies.
- The Toltecs used military conquest to create a powerful empire with its capital at Tula. Their influence spread across central Mexico.
- After the Toltecs, the Aztecs gradually built an empire from their island center of Tenochtitlan, which became powerful from forced transfers of labor and goods from defeated peoples.
- The Aztec religion, reflecting this permanent state of war, demanded increasing numbers of human sacrifices.
- Aztec merchants controlled long-distance trade, and Aztec women had substantial power.

NORTHERN PEOPLES

By the end of the classic period in Mesoamerica, around 900 C.E., important cultural centers had appeared in the southwestern desert region and along the Ohio and Mississippi River Valleys of what is now the United States (see Map 11.3). In both regions improved agricultural productivity and population growth led to increased urbanization and more complex social and political structures. In the Ohio Valley Amerindian peoples who depended on locally domesticated seed crops as well as traditional hunting and gathering developed large villages with monumental

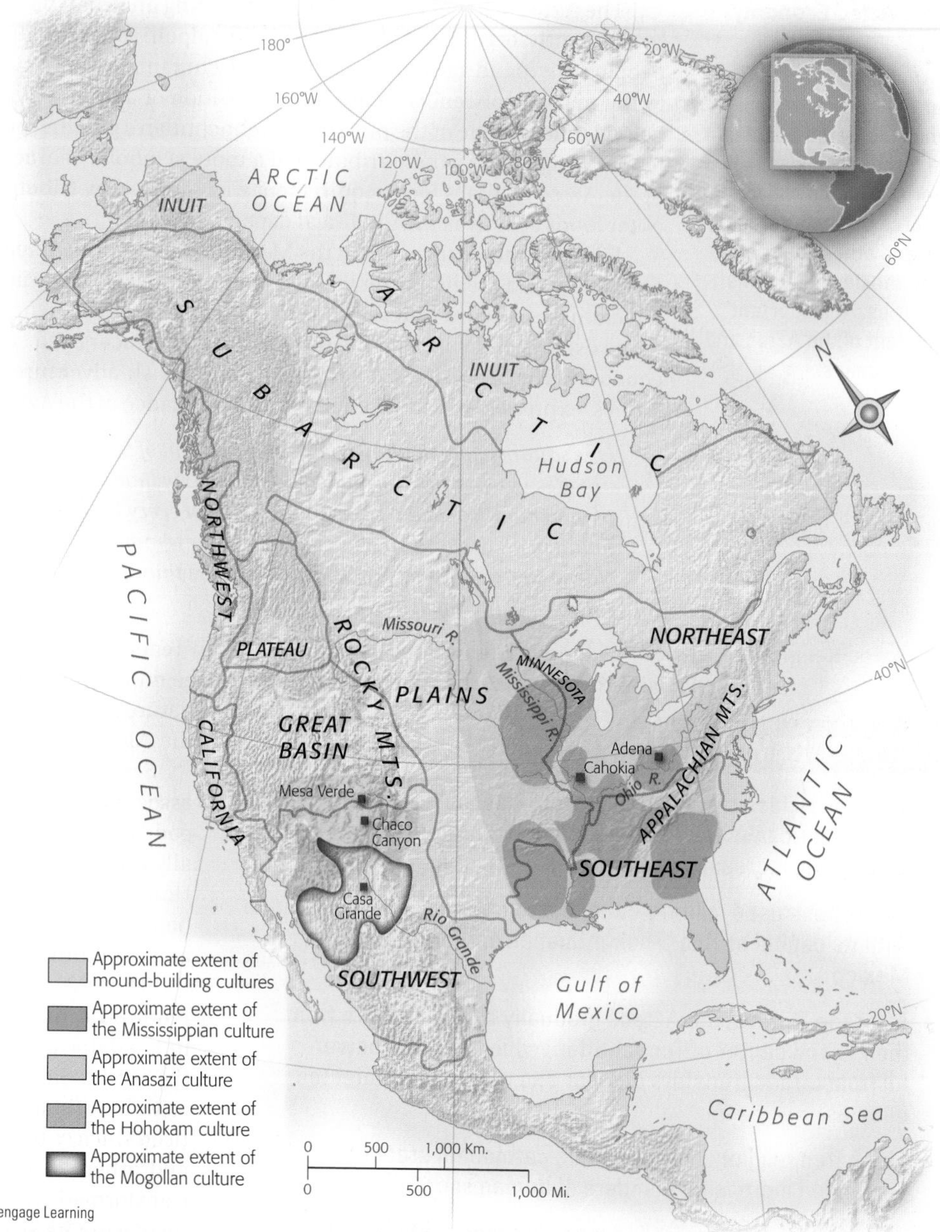

Interactive Map

MAP 11.3 Culture Areas of North America In each of the large ecological regions of North America, native peoples evolved distinctive cultures and technologies. Here the Anasazi of the arid southwest and the mound-building cultures of the Ohio and Mississippi River Valleys are highlighted.

earthworks. The introduction of maize, beans, and squash into this region from Mesoamerica after 1000 B.C.E. played an important role in the development of complex societies.

In both the southwestern desert and the eastern river valleys, growing populations built large-scale irrigation projects as they came to depend on maize as a dietary staple. This development is a sign of increasingly centralized political power and growing social stratification. The two regions, however, evolved different political traditions. The Anasazi (ah-nah-SAH-zee) and their neighbors in the southwest maintained a relatively egalitarian social structure and retained collective forms of political organization based on kinship and age. The mound builders of the eastern river valleys evolved more hierarchical political institutions: groups of small

Kenneth Murray/Photo Researchers, Inc.

Mesa Verde Cliff Dwelling Located in southern Colorado, the Anasazi cliff dwellings of the Mesa Verde region hosted a population of about 7,000 in 1250 C.E. The construction of housing complexes and religious buildings in the area's large caves was prompted by increased warfare in the region.

towns were subordinate to a political center ruled by a hereditary chief who wielded both secular and religious authority.

Anasazi Important culture of what is now the southwest United States (700–1300 C.E.). Centered on Chaco Canyon in New Mexico and Mesa Verde in Colorado, the Anasazi culture built multistory residences and worshiped in subterranean buildings called kivas.

Southwestern Desert Cultures

Around 300 B.C.E. in what is today Arizona, contacts with Mexico led to the introduction of agriculture based on irrigation. Because irrigation allowed the planting of two crops per year, the population grew and settled village life soon appeared. Of all the southwestern cultures, the Hohokam of the Salt and Gila River Valleys show the strongest Mexican influence. Hohokam sites have platform mounds and ball courts similar to those of Mesoamerica. Hohokam pottery, clay figurines, cast copper bells, and turquoise mosaics also reflect Mexican influence. By 1000 C.E. the Hohokam had constructed an elaborate irrigation system. Hohokam agricultural and ceramic technology spread over the centuries to neighboring peoples, but it was the Anasazi to the north who left the most vivid legacy of these desert cultures.

The Anasazi

Archaeologists use **Anasazi**, a Navajo word meaning "ancient ones," to identify a number of dispersed, though similar, desert cultures located in what is now the Four Corners region of Arizona, New Mexico, Colorado, and Utah (see Map 11.3). Between 450 and 750 C.E. the Anasazi developed an economy based on maize, beans, and squash. Their successful adaptation of these crops permitted the formation of larger villages and led to an enriched cultural life centered in underground buildings called kivas. They produced pottery decorated with geometric patterns, learned to weave cotton cloth, and, after 900 C.E., began to construct large multistory residential and ritual centers.

Chaco Canyon

One of the largest Anasazi communities was located in Chaco Canyon in what is now northwestern New Mexico. There were eight large towns in the canyon and four more on surrounding mesas, suggesting a regional population of 15,000. Pueblo Bonito (founded in 919 C.E.) had more than 650 rooms arranged in a four-story block of residences and storage rooms; it also had thirty-eight kivas, including a great kiva more than 65 feet (19 meters) in diameter. Hunting, trade, and the need to maintain irrigation works often drew men away from the village. Women shared in agricultural tasks, were specialists in many crafts, and were responsible for food preparation and childcare. If the practice of the modern Pueblos, cultural descendants of the Anasazi, is a guide, houses and furnishings may have belonged to the women, who formed extended families with their mothers and sisters.

At Chaco Canyon the high-quality construction, the size and number of kivas, and the system of roads linking the canyon to outlying towns all suggest that Pueblo Bonito and its nearest neighbors exerted some kind of political and religious dominance over a large region. Some archaeologists have suggested that the Chaco Canyon culture originated as a colonial appendage of Mesoamerica, but the archaeological record provides little evidence for this theory. Merchants from Chaco did provide Toltec-period peoples of northern Mexico with turquoise in exchange for shell jewelry, copper bells, macaws, and trumpets, but these exchanges occurred late in Chaco's development. More importantly, the signature elements of Mesoamerican influence, such as pyramid-shaped mounds and ball courts, are missing at Chaco.

Decline and Dispersal of Anasazi

The abandonment of the major sites in Chaco Canyon in the twelfth century most likely resulted from a long drought that undermined the culture's fragile agricultural economy. Nevertheless, the Anasazi continued in the Four Corners region for more than a century after the abandonment of Chaco Canyon. There were major centers at Mesa Verde in present-day Colorado and at Canyon de Chelly and Kiet Siel in Arizona. Anasazi constructed these settlements in large natural caves high above valley floors. These hard-to-reach locations suggest increased levels of warfare, probably provoked by population pressure on limited arable land.

Mound Builders: The Hopewell and Mississippian Cultures

From around 100 C.E. the Hopewell culture spread through the Ohio River Valley. Hopewell people constructed large villages and monumental earthworks. Once established, Hopewell influence spread west to Illinois, Michigan, and Wisconsin, east to New York and Ontario, and south to Alabama, Louisiana, Mississippi, and even Florida (see Map 11.3). For the necessities of daily life Hopewell depended on hunting and gathering and a limited agriculture. Hopewell is an early example of a North American **chiefdom**—populations as large as 10,000 and rule by a chief, a hereditary leader with both religious and secular responsibilities. Chiefs organized periodic rituals of feasting and gift giving to link diverse kinship groups and guarantee access to specialized crops and craft goods. They also managed long-distance trade for luxury goods and additional food supplies.

chiefdom Form of political organization with rule by a hereditary leader who held power over a collection of villages and towns. Less powerful than kingdoms and empires, chiefdoms were based on gift giving and commercial links.

The largest Hopewell towns in the Ohio River Valley had several thousand inhabitants and served as ceremonial and political centers. Large mounds built to house burials and serve as platforms for religious rituals dominated major Hopewell centers. Some mounds were oriented to reflect sunrise and moonrise patterns. They buried deceased leaders in vaults surrounded by valuable goods such as river pearls, copper jewelry, and, in some cases, women and retainers who may have been sacrificed to accompany a dead chief into the afterlife. The abandonment of major sites around 400 C.E. marked the decline of Hopewell culture.

Mississippian Culture

Hopewell culture influenced the later development of Mississippian culture (800–1500 C.E.). As in the case of the Anasazi, some experts have suggested that contacts with Mesoamerica influenced Mississippian culture, but there is no convincing evidence to support this theory. It is true that maize, beans, and squash, all first domesticated in Mesoamerica, were crucial to the urbanized Mississippian culture. But these plants and related technologies were most likely acquired via intervening cultures.

The development of urbanized Mississippian chiefdoms resulted instead from the accumulated effects of small increases in agricultural productivity, the adoption of the bow and arrow, and the expansion of trade networks. An improved economy led to population growth, the building of cities, and social stratification. The largest towns shared a common urban plan based on a central plaza surrounded by large platform mounds. Major towns were trade centers where people bartered essential commodities, such as the flint used for weapons and tools.

Cahokia

The Mississippian culture reached its highest stage of evolution at the great urban center of Cahokia, located near the modern city of East St. Louis, Illinois (see Map 11.3). At the center of this site was the largest mound constructed in North America, a terraced structure 100 feet (30 meters) high and 1,037 by 790 feet (316 by 241 meters) at the base. Areas where commoners lived ringed the center area of elite housing and temples. At its height in about 1200 C.E., Cahokia had a population of about 20,000—about the same as some of the postclassic Maya cities.

Cahokia controlled surrounding agricultural lands and a number of secondary towns ruled by subchiefs. Its political and economic influence depended on its location on the Missouri, Mississippi, and Illinois Rivers, a location that permitted commercial exchanges as far away as the coasts of the Atlantic and the Gulf of Mexico. Traders brought seashells, copper, mica, and flint to the city, where they were used as ritual goods and tools. Burial evidence suggests that the rulers of Cahokia were rich and powerful. In one burial more than fifty young women and retainers were sacrificed to accompany a ruler on his travels after death.

There is no evidence linking the decline and eventual abandonment of Cahokia after 1250 C.E. with the effects of military defeat or civil war. Instead it appears that climate changes and population pressures, exacerbated by environmental degradation caused by deforestation and more intensive farming practices, undermined the power of Cahokia. Smaller Mississippian centers continued to flourish in the southeast of the present-day United States until the arrival of Europeans.

SECTION REVIEW

- Transfer of irrigation and corn agriculture from Mesoamerica stimulated the development of Hohokam and Anasazi cultures.
- The Anasazi concentrated in the Four Corners region of the southwestern United States, especially in Chaco Canyon, where they built cities with underground kivas.
- Hopewell culture, organized around chiefdoms in the Ohio River Valley, developed based on long-distance trade and religious ritual life centered on large mounds.
- The political organization, trade practices, and mound building of Hopewell were continued by the Mississippian culture, with its largest city, Cahokia, at the site of East St. Louis.
- Environmental changes probably undermined both Anasazi and Mississippian cultures.

ANDEAN CIVILIZATIONS, 200–1500

The Andean region of South America was an unlikely environment for the development of rich and powerful civilizations (see Map 11.4). Much of the region's mountainous zone is at altitudes that seem too high for agriculture and human habitation. Along the Pacific coast an arid climate posed a difficult challenge to the development of agriculture. To the east of the Andes Mountains, the hot and humid tropical environment of the Amazon headwaters also offered formidable obstacles to the organization of complex societies. Yet the Amerindian peoples of the Andean area produced some of the most socially complex and politically advanced societies of the Western Hemisphere. The very harshness of the environment compelled the development of productive and reliable agricultural technologies and attached them to a complex fabric of administrative structures and social relationships that became the central features of Andean civilization.

Cultural Response to Environmental Challenge

From the time of Chavín (see Chapter 2) all of the great Andean civilizations succeeded in connecting the distinctive resources of the coastal region, with its abundant fisheries and irrigated maize fields, to the mountainous interior with its herds of llamas and rich mix of grains and tubers. Both regions faced significant environmental challenges. Droughts and shifting sands that clogged irrigation works periodically overwhelmed the coastal region's fields and the mountainous interior presented enormous environmental challenges, since it averaged between 250 and 300 frosts per year.

The development of compensating technologies required an accurate calendar to time planting and harvests and the domestication of frost-resistant varieties of potatoes and grains. Native peoples learned to practice dispersed farming at different altitudes to reduce risks from frosts,

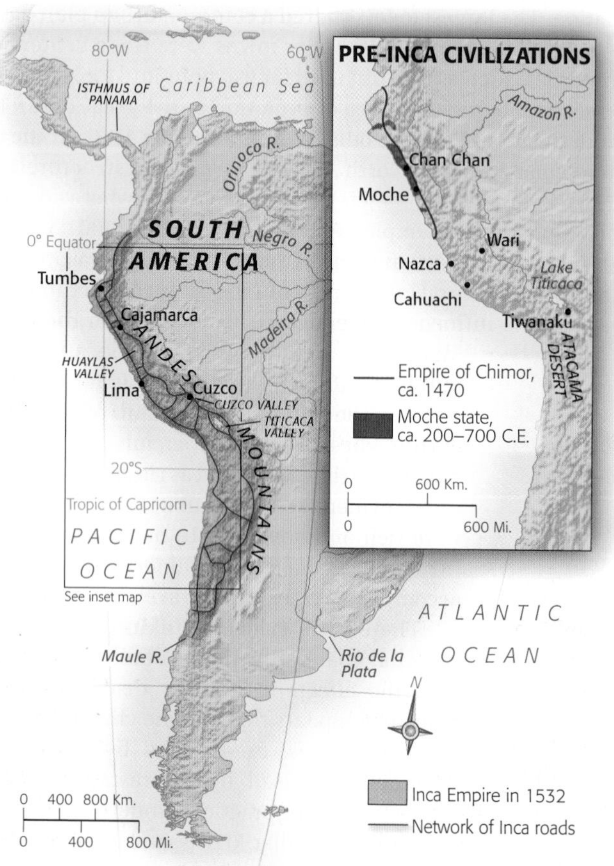

MAP 11.4 Andean Civilizations, 200 B.C.E.–1532 C.E. In response to environmental challenges posed by an arid coastal plain and high interior mountain ranges, Andean peoples made complex social and technological adaptations. Irrigation systems, the domestication of the llama, metallurgy, and shared labor obligations helped provide a firm economic foundation for powerful, centralized states. In 1532 the Inca Empire's vast territory stretched from modern Chile in the south to Colombia in the north.

Interactive Map

and they terraced hillsides to create micro environments within a single area. They also discovered how to use the cold, dry climate to produce freeze-dried vegetable and meat products that prevented famine when crops failed. The domestication of the llama and alpaca also proved crucial, providing meat, wool, and long-distance transportation that linked coastal and mountain economies.

It was the clan, or **ayllu** (aye-YOU), that provided the foundation for Andean achievement. Members of an ayllu held land communally. Ayllu members thought of each other as brothers and sisters and were obligated to aid each other in tasks that required more labor than a single household could provide. These reciprocal obligations provided the model for the organization of labor and the distribution of goods at every level of Andean society. Just as individuals and families were expected to provide labor to kinsmen, members of an ayllu were expected to provide labor and goods to their hereditary chief.

ayllu Andean lineage group or kin-based community.

mit'a Andean labor system based on shared obligations to help kinsmen and work on behalf of the ruler and religious organizations.

With the development of territorial states ruled by hereditary aristocracies and kings after 1000 B.C.E., these obligations were organized on a larger scale. The **mit'a** (MEET-ah) was a rotational labor draft that organized members of ayllus to work the fields and care for the llama and alpaca herds owned by religious establishments, the royal court, and the aristocracy. Each ayllu contributed a set number of workers for specific tasks each year. Mit'a laborers built and maintained roads, bridges, temples, palaces, and large irrigation and drainage projects. They produced textiles and goods essential to ritual life, such as beer made from maize and coca (dried leaves chewed as a stimulant and now also the source of cocaine).

Andeans divided work along gender lines, but the work of men and women was interdependent. Hunting, military service, and government were largely reserved for men. Women had numerous responsibilities in textile production, agriculture, and the home. One early Spanish commentator described the responsibilities of Andean women in terms that emphasize the importance of their labor power:

> *[T]hey did not just perform domestic tasks, but also [labored] in the fields, in the cultivation of their lands, in building houses, and carrying burdens. . . . [A]nd more than once I heard that while women were carrying these burdens, they would feel labor pains, and giving birth, they would go to a place where there was water and wash the baby and themselves. Putting the baby on top of the load they were carrying, they would then continue walking as before they gave birth. In sum, there was nothing their husbands did where their wives did not help.*[6]

The ayllu was intimately tied to a uniquely Andean system of production and exchange. Because the region's mountain ranges created a multitude of small ecological areas with specialized resources, each community sought to control a variety of environments so as to guarantee access to essential goods. Coastal regions produced maize, fish, and cotton. Mountain valleys contributed quinoa (the local grain) as well as potatoes and other tubers. Higher elevations contributed the wool and meat of llamas and alpacas, and the Amazonian region provided coca

Moche Warrior The Moche of ancient Peru were among the most accomplished ceramic artists of the Americas. Moche potters produced representations of gods and spirits, scenes of daily life, and portrait vases of important people. This warrior is armed with a mace, shield, and protective helmet.

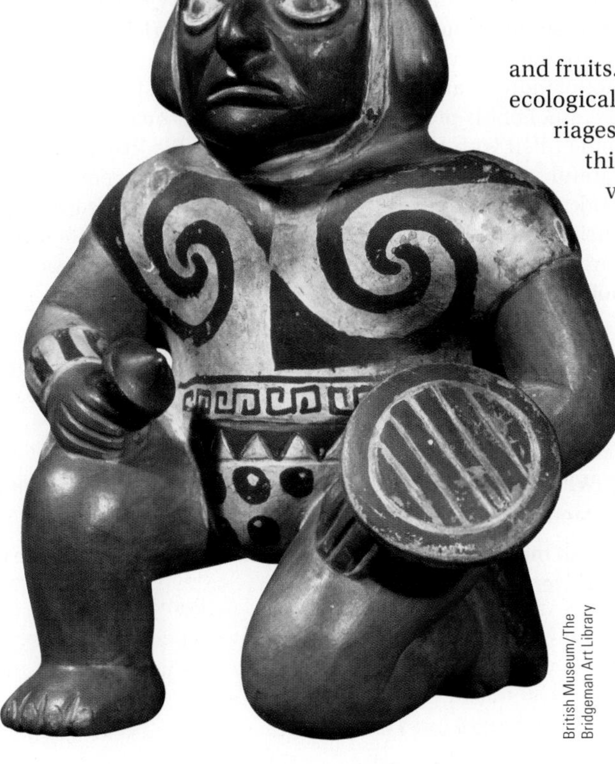

British Museum/The Bridgeman Art Library

and fruits. Ayllus sent out colonists to exploit the resources of these distinct ecological niches, retaining the loyalty of the colonists by arranging marriages and coming together for rituals. Historians commonly refer to this system of controlled exchange across ecological boundaries as vertical integration, or verticality.

Moche

Around 200 C.E., some four centuries after the collapse of Chavín (see Chapter 2), the **Moche** (MO-che) developed cultural and political tools that allowed them to dominate the north coastal region of Peru. Although they did not establish a formal empire or create unified political structures, they exercised authority over a broad region. The most powerful of the Moche urban centers, such as Cerro Blanco located near the modern Peruvian city of Trujillo (see Map 11.4), established hegemony over smaller towns and villages and then extended political and economic control over more distant neighbors militarily.

Archaeological evidence indicates that the Moche cultivated maize, quinoa, beans, manioc, and sweet potatoes with the aid of massive irrigation works, a complex network of canals and aqueducts that connected fields with water sources as far away as 75 miles (121 kilometers). Moche rulers forced commoners and subject peoples to build and maintain these hydraulic works. The Moche relied on large herds of alpacas and llamas to transport goods across the region's difficult terrain. Their wool, along with cotton provided by farmers, provided the raw material for the thriving Moche textile production. Their meat provided an important part of the diet.

Moche Social Order

Moche Civilization of north coast of Peru (200–700 C.E.). An important Andean civilization that built extensive irrigation networks as well as impressive urban centers dominated by brick temples.

Evidence from surviving murals and decorated ceramics suggests that Moche society was highly stratified and theocratic. Wealth and power was concentrated, along with political control, in the hands of priests and military leaders. The military conquest of neighboring regions reinforced hierarchy. Because the elite constructed their residences atop large platforms at Moche ceremonial centers, the powerful literally looked down on commoners. Their power was also apparent in their rich clothing and jewelry, which confirmed their divine status and set them farther apart from commoners. Moche rulers and other members of the elite wore tall headdresses and rich garments. The use of gold jewelry also marked high social position.

Moche burial practices reflected these deep social distinctions. A recent excavation in the Lambeyeque Valley discovered the tomb of a warrior-priest buried with a rich treasure of gold, silver, and copper jewelry, textiles, feather ornaments, and shells (see Diversity and Dominance: Burials as Historical Texts). A group of retainers and servants were executed and then buried with this powerful man in order to serve him in the afterlife.

Most commoners, on the other hand, devoted their time to subsistence farming and to the payment of labor dues owed to their ayllu and to the elite. Both men and women were involved in agriculture, care of llama herds, and the household economy. They lived with their families in one-room buildings clustered in the outlying areas of cities and in surrounding agricultural zones.

The high quality of Moche textiles, ceramics, and metallurgy indicates the presence of numerous skilled artisans. Women had a special role in the production of textiles, and even elite women devoted time to weaving. Moche culture developed a brilliant representational art. Craftsmen produced highly individualized portrait vases and decorated other ceramics with

DIVERSITY + DOMINANCE

Burials as Historical Texts

Efforts to reveal the history of the Americas before the arrival of Europeans depend on the work of archaeologists. The burials of rulers and other members of elites can be viewed as historical texts that describe how textiles, precious metals, beautifully decorated ceramics, and other commodities were used to reinforce the political and cultural power of ruling lineages. In public, members of the elite were always surrounded by the most desirable goods and rarest products as well as by elaborate rituals and ceremonies. The effect was to create an aura of godlike power. The material elements of political and cultural power were also integrated into the experience of death and burial as members of the elite were sent into the afterlife.

The first photograph is of an excavated Moche tomb in Sipán, Peru. The Moche (200–ca. 700 C.E.) were one of the most important of the pre-Inca civilizations of the Andean region. They were masters of metallurgy, ceramics, and textiles. The excavations at Sipán revealed a "warrior-priest" buried with an amazing array of gold ornaments, jewels, textiles, and ceramics. Also buried with him were five human sacrifices, two women, perhaps wives or concubines, two male servants, and a warrior. Three of these victims—the warrior, one woman, and a male servant—are each missing a foot, perhaps cut off to guarantee their continued faithfulness to the deceased ruler in the afterlife.

The second photograph shows the excavation of a classic-era (250–ca. 800 C.E.) Maya burial at Río Azul in Guatemala. After death this elite male was laid out on a carved wooden platform and cotton mattress and his body was painted with decorations. Mourners covered his body in rich textiles and surrounded him with valuable goods. These included a necklace of individual stones carved in the shape of heads, perhaps a symbol of his prowess in battle, and high-quality ceramics, some filled with foods consumed by the elite like cacao. The careful preparation of the burial chamber had required the work of numerous artisans and laborers, as was the case in the burial of the Moche warrior-priest. In death, as in life, these early American civilizations acknowledged the high status, political power, and religious authority of their elites.

QUESTIONS FOR ANALYSIS

1. **If these burials are texts, what are stories?**
2. **Are there any visible differences in the two burials?**
3. **What questions might historians ask of these burials that cannot be answered?**
4. **Can modern burials be read as texts in similar ways to these ancient burials?**

representations of myths and rituals. They were also accomplished metal-smiths, producing beautiful gold and silver religious objects and jewelry for elite adornment. Metallurgy served more practical ends as well: Artisans produced a range of tools made of heavy copper and copper alloy for agricultural and military purposes.

Environmental Crisis and Decline of the Moche

The archaeological record makes clear that the rapid decline of major Moche centers coincided with a succession of natural disasters in the sixth century and with the rise of a new military power in the Andean highlands. Long-term climate changes also threatened the Moche region. A thirty-year drought expanded the area of coastal sand dunes during the sixth century, and powerful winds pushed sand onto fragile agricultural lands, overwhelming the irrigation system. As the land dried, periodic heavy rains caused erosion that damaged fields and weakened the economy that had sustained ceremonial and residential centers. Despite massive efforts to keep the irrigation canals open and despite the construction of new urban centers in less vulnerable valleys to the north, Moche civilization never recovered. In the eighth century, the rise of a new military power, the **Wari** (WAH-ree), also contributed to the disappearance of the Moche by putting pressure on trade routes that linked the coastal region with the highlands.

Wari Andean civilization culturally linked to Tiwanaku, perhaps beginning as a colony of Tiwanaku.

Tiwanaku Name of capital city and empire centered on the region near Lake Titicaca in modern Bolivia (375–1000 C.E.).

Tiwanaku and Wari

After 500 C.E. two powerful civilizations developed in the Andean highlands. The ruins of **Tiwanaku** (tee-wah-NA-coo) (see Map 11.4) still stand at nearly 13,000 feet (3,962 meters) near Lake Titicaca in modern Bolivia. Tiwanaku's expansion after 200 C.E. depended on the adoption of technologies that increased agricultural productivity. Modern excavations provide the out-

© Heinze Plenge/NGS Image Collection

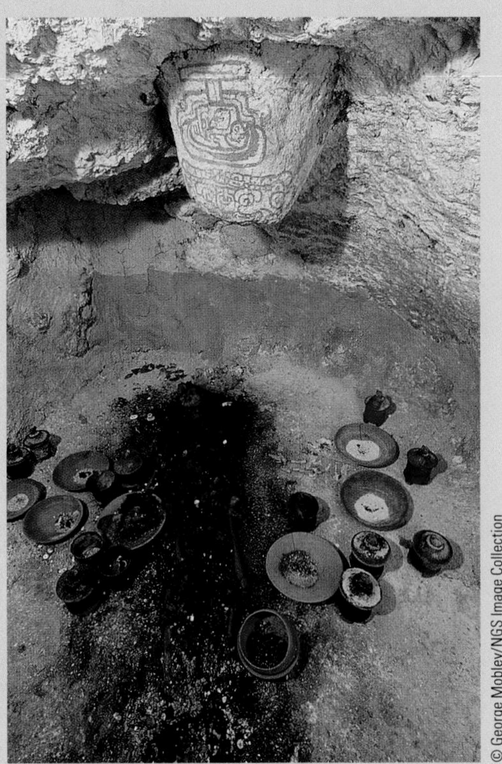

© George Mobley/NGS Image Collection

Burials Reveal Ancient Civilizations (Left) Buried around 300 C.E., this Moche warrior-priest was buried amid rich tribute at Sipán in Peru. Also buried were the bodies of retainers or kinsmen probably sacrificed to accompany this powerful man. The body lies with the head on the right and the feet on the left. (Right) Similarly, the burial of a member of the Maya elite at Río Azul in northern Guatemala indicates the care taken to surround the powerful with fine ceramics, jewelry, and other valuable goods.

line of vast drainage projects that reclaimed nearly 200,000 acres (80,000 hectares) of rich lakeside marshes for agriculture. This system of raised fields and ditches permitted intensive cultivation similar to that achieved by the use of chinampas in Mesoamerica. Fish from the nearby lake and llamas added protein to a diet largely dependent on potatoes and grains. Llamas were also crucial for the maintenance of long-distance trade relationships that brought in corn, coca, tropical fruits, and medicinal plants.

Tiwanaku was distinguished by the scale of its construction and by the high quality of its stone masonry. Thousands of laborers were mobilized to cut and move the large stones used to construct a large terraced pyramid, walled enclosures, and a reservoir. Despite a limited metallurgy that produced only tools of copper alloy, Tiwanaku's artisans built large structures of finely cut stone that required little mortar to fit the blocks. They also produced gigantic human statuary. The largest example, a stern figure with a military bearing, was cut from a single block of stone that measures 24 feet (7 meters) high.

Tiwanaku Social Structure

It is clear that Tiwanaku was a highly stratified society ruled by a hereditary elite. This elite controlled a large, disciplined labor force in the surrounding region. Military conquests and the establishment of colonial populations provided dependable supplies of products from ecologically distinct zones. Tiwanaku cultural influence extended eastward to the jungles and southward to the coastal regions and oases of the Atacama Desert in Chile. But archaeological evidence suggests that Tiwanaku, in comparison with contemporary Teotihuacan in central Mexico, had a relatively small full-time population of around 30,000. It was not a metropolis like the largest Mesoamerican cities; it was a ceremonial and political center for a large regional population.

Wari

The contemporary site of Wari was located about 450 miles (751 kilometers) to the northwest of Tiwanaku, near the modern Peruvian city of Ayacucho. Wari clearly shared elements of the culture and technology of Tiwanaku, but the exact nature of this relationship remains unclear. Some scholars argue that Wari began as a dependency of Tiwanaku, while others suggest that they were joint capitals of a single empire. Wari was larger than Tiwanaku, measuring nearly 4 square miles (10 square kilometers). A massive wall surrounded the city center, which was dominated by a large temple and multifamily housing for elites and artisans. Housing for commoners was located in a sprawling suburban zone. The small scale of its monumental architecture relative to Tiwanaku and the near absence of cut stone masonry in public and private buildings suggest either the weakness of the elite or the absence of specialized construction crafts compared with other Andean centers. A distinctive Wari ceramic style allows experts to trace Wari's influence to the coastal area and to the northern highlands. This expansion occurred at a time of increasing warfare throughout the Andes that led to the eclipse of both Tiwanaku and Wari by about 1000 C.E. The Inca inherited their political legacies.

The Inca

Inca Largest and most powerful Andean empire. Controlled the Pacific coast of South America from Ecuador to Chile from its capital of Cuzco.

In little more than a hundred years, the **Inca** developed a vast imperial state, which they called "Land of Four Corners." By 1525 the empire had a population of more than 6 million and stretched from the Maule River in Chile to northern Ecuador and from the Pacific coast across the Andes to the upper Amazon and, in the south, into Argentina (see Map 11.4). In the early fifteenth century the Inca were one of many competing military powers in the southern highlands, an area of limited political significance after the collapse of Wari. Centered in the valley of Cuzco, the Inca were initially organized as a chiefdom based on reciprocal gift giving and the redistribution of food and textiles. Strong and resourceful leaders consolidated political authority in the 1430s and undertook an ambitious campaign of military expansion.

The Foundations of Inca Rule

The Inca state, like earlier highland powers, utilized traditional Andean social customs and economic practices. Tiwanaku had relied in part on the use of colonists to provide supplies of resources from distant, ecologically distinct zones. The Inca built on this legacy by conquering additional distant territories and increasing the scale of forced exchanges. Crucial to this process was the development of a large military. Unlike the peoples of Mesoamerica, who distributed specialized goods through markets and tribute relationships, Andean peoples used state power to broaden and expand the vertical exchange system that had permitted ayllus to exploit a range of ecological niches. The Inca were pastoralists as earlier highland civilizations had been. Inca prosperity and military strength depended on vast herds of llamas and alpacas, which provided food and clothing as well as transport for goods, but they gained access to corn, cotton, and other goods from the coastal region via forced exchanges.

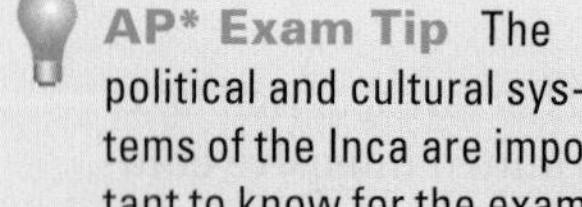

AP* Exam Tip The political and cultural systems of the Inca are important to know for the exam.

Collective efforts by mit'a laborers made the Inca Empire possible. Cuzco, the imperial capital, and the provincial cities, the royal court, the imperial armies, and the state's religious cults all rested on this foundation. The mit'a system also created the material surplus that provided the bare necessities for the old, weak, and ill of Inca society. Each ayllu contributed approximately one-seventh of its adult male population to meet these collective obligations. These draft laborers served as soldiers, construction workers, craftsmen, and runners to carry messages along post roads. They also drained swamps, terraced mountainsides, filled in valley floors, built and maintained irrigation works, and built storage facilities and roads. Inca laborers constructed 13,000 miles (20,930 kilometers) of road, facilitating military troop movements, administration, and trade (see Environment and Technology: Inca Roads).

The hereditary chiefs of ayllus, a group that included women, carried out local administrative and judicial functions. As the Inca expanded, they generally left local rulers in place. By doing so they risked rebellion, but they controlled these risks by means of a thinly veiled system of hostage taking and the use of military garrisons. The rulers of defeated regions were required to send their heirs to live at the Inca royal court in Cuzco. Inca leaders even required that defeated peoples send representations of important local gods to Cuzco to be included in the imperial pantheon. These measures promoted imperial integration while at the same time providing hostages to ensure the good behavior of subject peoples.

ENVIRONMENT + TECHNOLOGY

Inca Roads

From the time of Chavín (900–250 B.C.E.), Andean peoples have built roads to facilitate trade across ecological boundaries and to project political power over conquered peoples. In the fifteenth and sixteenth centuries, the Inca extended and improved the networks of roads constructed in earlier eras. Roads were crucially important to Inca efforts to collect and redistribute tribute paid in food, textiles, and *chicha* (corn liquor).

Inca Road The Inca built roads to connect distant parts of the empire to Cuzco, the Inca capital. These roads are still used in Peru.

Two roads connected Cuzco, the Inca capital in southern Peru, to Quito, Ecuador, in the north and to Chile farther south. One ran along the flat and arid coastal plain, the other through the mountainous interior. Shorter east-west roads connected important coastal and interior cities. The Inca placed regional administrative centers along these routes to expedite rapid communication with the capital. They built rest stops at convenient distances to provide shelter and food to traveling officials and runners who carried messages between Cuzco and the empire's cities and towns. Food and military supplies were also collected at large warehouses along the roads to provide food and military supplies for passing Inca armies or to supply local laborers who worked on construction projects or cultivated the ruler's fields.

Because communication with regional administrative centers and the movement of troops were the central objectives of the Inca leadership, they selected routes to avoid natural obstacles and to reduce travel time. Mit'a laborers recruited from nearby towns and villages built and maintained the roads, taking care to repair damage caused by rain runoff or other drainage problems. Roads were commonly paved with stone or packed earth and often were bordered by stone or adobe walls to keep soldiers or pack trains of llamas from straying into farmers' fields. Whenever possible, roadbeds were made level, but in mountainous terrain some roads were little more than improved paths. In flat country three or four people could walk abreast.

The achievement of Inca road builders is clearest in the mountainous terrain of the interior, where they built suspension bridges across high gorges and cut roadbeds into the face of cliffs. A Spanish priest living in Peru in the seventeenth century commented that the Inca roads "were magnificent constructions, which could be compared favorably with the most superb roads of the Romans."

Source: Quotation from Father Bernabe Cobo, *History of the Inca Empire. An account of the Indians' customs and origin together with a treatise on Inca legends, history, and social institutions* (Austin: University of Texas Press, 1983), 223.

Conquests magnified the authority of the Inca ruler and led to the creation of an imperial bureaucracy drawn from among his kinsmen. The royal family claimed descent from the Sun, the primary Inca god. Members of the royal family lived in palaces maintained by armies of servants. The lives of the ruler and members of the royal family were dominated by political and religious rituals that helped legitimize their authority. Among the many obligations associated with kingship was the requirement to extend imperial boundaries by warfare. Thus each new ruler began his reign with conquest.

Tenochtitlan, the Aztec capital, had a population of about 150,000 in 1520. At the height of Inca power in 1530, Cuzco had a population of less than 30,000. Nevertheless, Cuzco was a remarkable place. The Inca were highly skilled stone craftsmen and constructed their most impressive buildings of carefully cut stones fitted together without mortar. Planners laid the city out in the shape of a giant puma (a mountain lion). At the city center were the palaces of rulers as

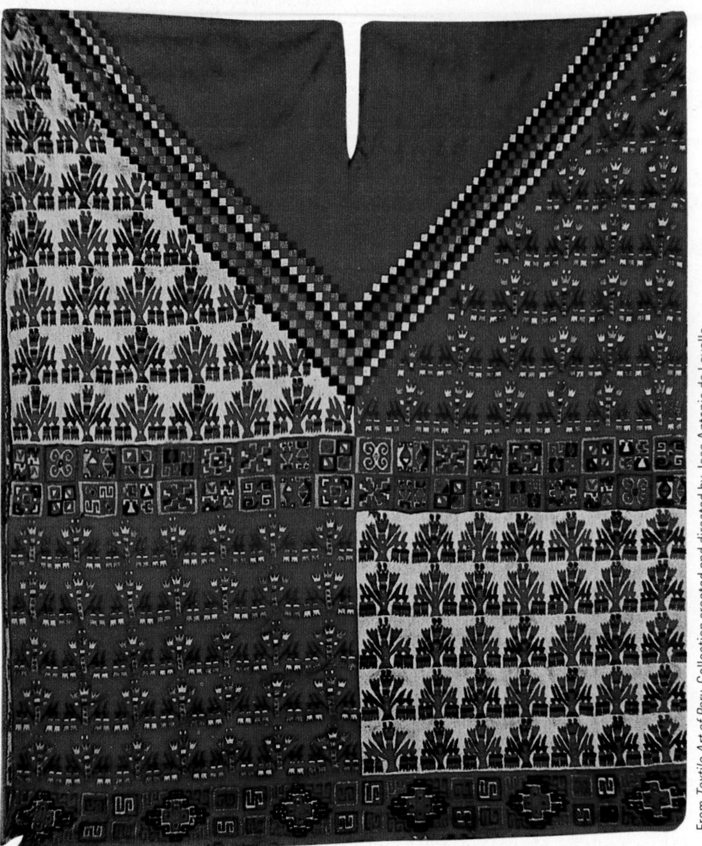

From *Textile Art of Peru*. Collection created and directed by Jose Antonio de Lavalle and Jose Alejandro Gonzalez Garcia [L. L. Editores, 1989]

Inca Tunic Andean weavers produced beautiful textiles from cotton and from the wool of llamas and alpacas. The Inca inherited this rich craft tradition and produced some of the world's most remarkable textiles. The quality and design of each garment indicated the weaver's rank and power in this society. This tunic was an outer garment for a powerful male.

well as the major temples. The richest was the Temple of the Sun, its interior lined with sheets of gold and its patio decorated with golden representations of llamas and corn. The ruler made every effort to awe and intimidate visitors and residents alike with a nearly continuous series of rituals, feasts, and sacrifices. Sacrifices of textiles, animals, and other goods sent as tribute dominated the city's calendar. The destruction of these valuable commodities, and a small number of human sacrifices, helped give the impression of splendor and sumptuous abundance that appeared to demonstrate the ruler's claimed descent from the Sun.

Inca cultural achievement rested on the strong foundation of earlier Andean civilizations. We know that astronomical observation was a central concern of the priestly class, as in Mesoamerica. The collective achievements of Andean peoples were accomplished with a limited recordkeeping system adapted from earlier Andean civilizations. Administrators used knotted colored cords, called **khipus** (KEY-pooz), for public administration, population counts, and tribute obligations. Inca weaving and metallurgy, also based on earlier regional development, was more advanced than in Mesoamerica. Inca craftsmen produced utilitarian tools and weapons of copper and bronze as well as decorative objects of gold and silver. Inca women produced textiles of extraordinary beauty from cotton and the wool of llamas and alpacas.

khipus System of knotted colored cords used by preliterate Andean peoples to transmit information.

Although the Inca did not introduce new technologies, they increased economic output and added to the region's prosperity. The conquest of large populations in environmentally distinct regions allowed the Inca to multiply the yields produced by the traditional exchanges between distinct ecological niches. This expansion of imperial economic and political power was purchased at the cost of reduced equality and diminished local autonomy. Members of the imperial elite, living in richly decorated palaces in Cuzco and other

SECTION REVIEW

- Andean societies developed by devising solutions to their complex environment of arid coastlands, cold highlands, and tropical forests.
- The ayllu and mit'a provided the social base for Andean social and political organization.
- The Moche developed a powerful state based on irrigated agriculture, exchange between ecological regions, and a powerful religious elite.
- Tiwanaku and Wari used their powerful militaries to extend their power over large regions and create long-distance networks of trade.
- The Inca developed from a chiefdom to a formal empire based on military conquest and the forced transfer of food and other products from defeated peoples through tribute.
- The Inca used roads, irrigation networks, terracing, and other technologies to provide material in a region with a difficult climate and topography.
- Civil war weakened the Inca on the eve of European arrival.

PRIMARY SOURCE: Chronicles Learn how the Incas used mysterious knotted ropes called khipus as recordkeeping devices to help them govern a vast empire.

urban centers, were increasingly distant from the masses of Inca society. Even members of the provincial nobility were held at arm's length from the royal court, while commoners could be executed if they dared to look directly at the ruler's face.

After only a century of regional dominance, the Inca Empire faced a crisis in 1525. The death of the ruler Huayna Capac at the conclusion of the conquest of Ecuador initiated a bloody struggle for the throne. The rivalry of two sons compelled both the professional military and the hereditary Inca elite to choose sides. Civil war was the result. Regionalism and ethnic diversity had always posed a threat to the empire. Now civil war weakened the imperial state and ignited the resentments of conquered peoples on the eve of the arrival of Europeans.

CONCLUSION

The Aztec and Inca Empires represent the culmination of long historical development in Mesoamerica and the Andes, respectively. Each empire was created militarily, its survival depending as much on the power of its armies as on the productivity of its economy or the wisdom of its rulers. Both depended on political institutions, economic forms and technologies, and religious practices inherited from their predecessors. Both Mesoamerica and the Andes were also ethnically and environmentally diverse regions. Rulers in both regions legitimized their authority religiously, serving as priestly intermediaries with the gods. Major cities operated as religious as well as political centers and were dominated by religious architecture. Both regions had long depended on the mobilization of ever-larger work forces to meet growing needs rather than on rapid technological innovation.

There were important differences as well. Mesoamerican cultures had developed elementary markets to distribute specialized regional production, although the forced payment of goods as tribute remained important to sustain cities like Tenochtitlan. In the Andes reciprocal labor obligations and managed exchange relationships were used to allocate goods. The Aztecs used their military to force defeated peoples to provide food, textiles, and even sacrificial captives as tribute, but they left local hereditary elites in place. The Inca, in contrast, created a more centralized imperial administrative structure managed by a trained bureaucracy and used reciprocal labor obligations to produce and distribute goods.

We can find similar patterns in North America. The transfer of agricultural technology from Mesoamerica, with its dependence on corn, beans, and squash, influenced the mound-building cultures of the Ohio and Mississippi River Valleys and the desert cultures of the southwest. In the desert region of what is now the southwest of the United States, the Anasazi and other peoples also utilized irrigated agriculture, a technology crucial to both Mesoamerican and Andean cultures. Both the desert and mound-building cultures of North America experienced cycles when powerful new political centers expanded the territories they controlled and consolidated their power until overwhelmed by environmental challenges or displaced by military rivals.

As the Western Hemisphere's long isolation drew to a close in the late fifteenth century, the Aztecs and Incas, the most powerful civilizations of Mesoamerica and the Andean region, respectively, were challenged by powerful neighbors and by internal revolts. In earlier periods similar threats had contributed to the decline of great civilizations in both Mesoamerica and the Andean region as well as in the less powerful cultures of the desert southwest and the Ohio and Mississippi River Valleys. In all these cases, a long period of cultural and political adjustment led eventually to the creation of new indigenous institutions, the adoption of new technologies, and the appearance of new centers of power in new locations. With the arrival of Europeans, this cycle of crisis and adjustment would be transformed, and the future of Amerindian peoples would become linked to the cultures of the Old World.

KEY TERMS

Teotihuacan p. 310
chinampas p. 312
Maya p. 312
Toltecs p. 316
altepetl p. 316
calpolli p. 317
Tenochtitlan p. 317
Aztecs p. 317
tribute system p. 319
Anasazi p. 321
chiefdom p. 322
ayllu p. 324
mit'a p. 324
Moche p. 325
Wari p. 326
Tiwanaku p. 326
Inca p. 328
khipus p. 330

EBOOK AND WEBSITE RESOURCES

Primary Source

Chronicles

Interactive Maps

Map 11.1 Maya Civilization, 250–1400 C.E.

Map 11.2 Major Mesoamerican Civilizations, 1000 B.C.E.–1519 C.E.

Map 11.3 Culture Areas of North America

Map 11.4 Andean Civilizations, 200 B.C.E.–1532 C.E.

Plus flashcards, practice quizzes, and more. Go to: www.cengage.com/history/bullietearthpeople5e

SUGGESTED READING

Bawden, Garth. *The Moche.* 1996. Among the best studies of this early culture in Peru.

Bruhns, Karen Olsen. *Ancient South America.* 1994. An introduction to current scholarship on early Andean societies.

Crown, Patricia L., and W. James Judge, eds. *Chaco and Hohokam.* 1991. A good summary of current research issues in the American southwest.

Davies, Nigel. *The Aztec Empire: The Toltec Resurgence.* 1987. The best summary of Aztec history.

Dickason, Olive Patricia. *Canada's First Nations.* 1992. A well-written survey that traces the history of Canada's Amerindian peoples to the modern era.

Fiedel, Stuart. *Prehistory of the Americas.* 1987. An excellent summary of the early history of the Western Hemisphere.

Kellogg, Susan. *Weaving the Past.* 2005. Early chapters provide an excellent synthesis of the place of women in early Mesoamerican and Andean societies.

Mastache, Alba Guadalupe, Robert H. Cobean, and Dan M. Healan. *Ancient Tollan, Tula and the Toltec Heartland.* 2002. Among the best studies of Toltec era and controversies over location of Tula.

Murra, John. *The Economic Organization of the Inca State.* 1956. Originator of the theory of the vertical interdependence of Andean peoples.

Pasztori, Esther. *Teotihuacan.* 1997. A good summary of recent research.

Rostworowski de Diez Canseco, María. *History of the Inca Realm,* trans. by Harry B. Iceland. 1999. The best modern synthesis of Incan history.

Schele, Linda, and David Freidel. *A Forest of Kings.* 1990. An excellent summary of recent research on the classic-period Maya.

Shutler, Richard, Jr. *Early Man in the New World.* 1983. A good brief introduction.

Silverberg, Robert. *Mound Builders of Ancient America.* 1968. A good introduction to this topic.

Silverblatt, Irene. *Moon, Sun, and Witches: Gender Ideologies and Class in Inca and Colonial Peru.* 1987. A challenging and readable account of how the Spanish conquest changed the position of women.

NOTES

1. This summary closely follows the historical narrative and translation of names offered by Linda Schele and David Freidel in *A Forest of Kings: The Untold Story of the Ancient Maya* (New York: Morrow, 1990), 182–186.
2. From the Florentine Codex, quoted in Inga Clendinnen, *Aztecs* (New York: Cambridge University Press, 1991), 213.
3. Quoted in Nigel Davies, *The Toltec Heritage: From the Fall of Tula to the Rise of Tenochtitlán* (Norman: University of Oklahoma Press, 1980), 3.
4. Bernal Díaz del Castillo, *The Conquest of New Spain*, trans. J. M. Cohen (London: Penguin Books, 1963), 217.
5. Hernando Cortés, *Five Letters, 1519–1526*, trans. J. Bayard Morris (New York: Norton, 1991), 87.
6. Quoted in Irene Silverblatt, *Moon, Sun, and Witches: Gender Ideologies and Class in Inca and Colonial Peru* (Princeton, NJ: Princeton University Press, 1987), 10.

AP* REVIEW QUESTIONS FOR CHAPTER 11

1. Ancient Mesoamerican and Andean cities
   (A) were scattered along the coastline and not of great importance to their society.
   (B) were very large and rivaled those of Han China and Rome.
   (C) were built on the style of the Aztecs.
   (D) appeared only about 100 years prior to contact with the Spanish and Portuguese.

2. In the city of Teotihuacan, in central Mexico,
   (A) rulers appeared in statues and public art celebrating their deeds.
   (B) people lived in egalitarian communities with no divisions based on rank.
   (C) more than two-thirds of the population made their living from agriculture.
   (D) there is no evidence of a strong military.

3. Teotihuacan's long-distance trade is evidenced by
   (A) archaeological evidence of a large military designed to protect trade.
   (B) Inca goods in trash pits.
   (C) pictorial evidence of trade with Indian tribes in what today is Texas.
   (D) similar food crops being grown throughout Central America.

4. While the Maya shared a single culture,
   (A) they had different religious beliefs.
   (B) women were treated in different ways by different tribes.
   (C) they were never united politically.
   (D) each city grew different crops and produced different finished goods.

5. The Maya "long count" calendar is most likely
   (A) one they adopted from the Inca.
   (B) associated with their understanding of their creation.
   (C) linked to their planting and harvesting cycles.
   (D) the calendar used to trace family lineage among Maya rulers.

6. Which was true of Maya writing?
   (A) It was derived from the system used by the Olmec.
   (B) It was used only for telling stories about creation.
   (C) The Maya used it to record only trade relations, tax collection, and government business transactions.
   (D) It was a form of hieroglyphic writing that included whole words, concepts, phonetic cues, and syllables.

7. The Toltec state was
   (A) built on military power and conquest.
   (B) a farming state that incorporated trade in Mesoamerica.
   (C) created by nomads who moved into Mexico from what today is California.
   (D) relatively weak due to a lack of central governmental control.

8. Aztec rule was based on
   (A) primogeniture.
   (B) a council of aristocrats selecting new rulers.
   (C) matrilineal heritage.
   (D) two nobles competing in combat with the winner becoming the leader.

9. Besides enslaving captives, the Aztecs also
   (A) allowed for the assimilation of conquered people.
   (B) developed a tribute system to increase food supplies and trade goods.
   (C) allowed captives to barter for their freedom.
   (D) encouraged intermarriage with conquered groups to expand the nobility.

10. In general, public life in Tenochtitlan was dominated by
    (A) agricultural pursuits.
    (B) bureaucratic duties.
    (C) religious rituals.
    (D) family concerns.

11. Cahokia is an example of

    (A) an urban settlement in the Ohio River Valley area.
    (B) a mound-building culture.
    (C) one of the most distant of the Aztec satellite kingdoms.
    (D) Chaco Canyon turquoise culture.

12. The Inca, unlike the native groups of Mesoamerica and Mexico,

    (A) practiced human sacrifice.
    (B) had no nobility or political hierarchy.
    (C) were pastoralists.
    (D) did not have an army.

13. Andean civilizations

    (A) undertook large-scale irrigation projects and built terraces to control erosion.
    (B) intermarried and developed a clan-based culture.
    (C) practiced polytheism, whereas the Aztecs did not.
    (D) never adopted the practice of any divine mandate of rule.

RELIGIOUS CONVERSION

Religious conversion has two meanings that often get confused. The term can refer to the inner transformation an individual may feel on joining a new religious community or becoming revitalized in his or her religious belief. Conversions of this sort are often sudden and deeply emotional. In historical terms, they may be important when they transform the lives of prominent individuals.

In its other meaning, *religious conversion* refers to a change in the religious identity of an entire population, or a large portion of a population. This generally occurs slowly and is hard to trace in historical documents. As a result, historians have sometimes used superficial indicators to trace the spread of a religion. Doing so can result in misleading conclusions, such as considering the spread of the Islamic faith to be the result of forced conversion by Arab conquerors, or taking the routes traveled by Christian or Buddhist missionaries as evidence that the people they encountered adopted their spiritual message, or assuming that a king or chieftain's adherence to a new religion immediately resulted in a religious change among subjects or followers.

In addition to being difficult to document, religious conversion in the broad societal sense has followed different patterns according to changing circumstances of time and place. Historians have devised several models to explain the different conversion patterns. According to one model, religious labels in a society change quickly, through mass baptism, for example, but devotional practices remain largely the same. Evidence for this can be found in the continuation of old religious customs among people who identify themselves as belonging to a new religion. Another model sees religious change as primarily a function of economic benefit or escape from persecution. Taking this approach makes it difficult to explain the endurance of certain religious communities in the face of hardship and discrimination. Nevertheless, most historians pay attention to economic advantage in their assessments of mass conversion. A third model associates a society's religious conversion with its desire to adopt a more sophisticated way of life, by shifting, for example, from a religion that does not use written texts to one that does.

One final conceptual approach to explaining the process of mass religious change draws on the quantitative models of innovation diffusion that were originally developed to analyze the spread of new technologies in the twentieth century. According to this approach, new ideas, whether in the material or religious realm, depend on the spread of information. A few early adopters—missionaries, pilgrims, or conquerors, perhaps—spread word of the new faith to the people they come in contact with, some of whom follow their example and convert. Those converts in turn spread the word to others, and a chain reaction picks up speed in what might be called a bandwagon effect. The period of bandwagon conversion tapers off when the number of people who have not yet been offered an opportunity to convert diminishes. The entire process can be graphed as a *logistic* or S-shaped curve. Figure 1, the graph of conversion to Islam in Iran based on changes from Persian (non-Islamic) to Arabic (Islamic) names in family genealogies, shows such a curve over a period of almost four centuries.

In societies that were largely illiterate, like those in which Buddhism, Christianity, and Islam slowly achieved spiritual dominance, information spread primarily by word of mouth. The proponents of the new religious views did not always speak the same language as the people they hoped to bring into the faith. Under these circumstances, significant conversion, that is, conversion that involved some understanding of the new religion, as opposed to forced baptism or imposed mouthing of a profession of faith, must surely have started with fairly small numbers.

Language was crucial. Chinese pilgrims undertook lengthy travels to visit early Buddhist sites in India. There they acquired Sanskrit texts, which they translated into Chinese. These translations became the core texts of Chinese Buddhism. In early Christendom, the presence of bilingual (Greek-Aramaic) Jewish communities in the eastern parts of the Roman Empire facilitated the early spread of the religion beyond its Aramaic-speaking homeland. By contrast, Arabic, the language of Islam, was spoken only in the Arabian peninsula and the desert borderlands that extended northwards from Arabia between Syria, Jordan, and Iraq. This initial impediment to the spread of knowledge about Islam dissolved only when intermarriage with non-Muslim, non-Arab women, many of them taken captive and distributed as booty during the conquests, produced bilingual offspring. Bilingual preachers of the Christian faith were similarly needed in the Celtic-, Germanic-, and Slavic-language areas of western and eastern Europe.

This slow process of information diffusion, which varied from region to region, made changing demands on religious leaders and institutions. When a faith was professed primarily by a ruler, his army, and his dependents, religious leaders gave the highest priority to servicing the needs of the ruling minority and perhaps discrediting, denigrating, or exterminating the practices of the majority. Once a few centuries had passed and the new faith had become the religion of the great majority of the population, religious leaders turned to establishing popular institutions and reaching out to the common people. Historical interpretation can benefit from knowing where a society is in a long-term process of conversion.

These various models reinforce the importance of distinguishing between emotional individual conversion experiences and broad changes in a society's religious identity. New converts are commonly thought of as especially zealous in their faith, and that description is often apt in instances of individual conversion experiences. It is less appropriate, however, to broader episodes of conversion. In a conversion wave that starts slowly, builds momentum in the bandwagon phase, and then tapers off, the first individuals to convert are likely to be more spiritually motivated than those who join the movement toward its end. Religious growth depends as much on making the faith attractive to late converts as to ecstatic early converts.

FIGURE 1 Conversion to Islam in Iran

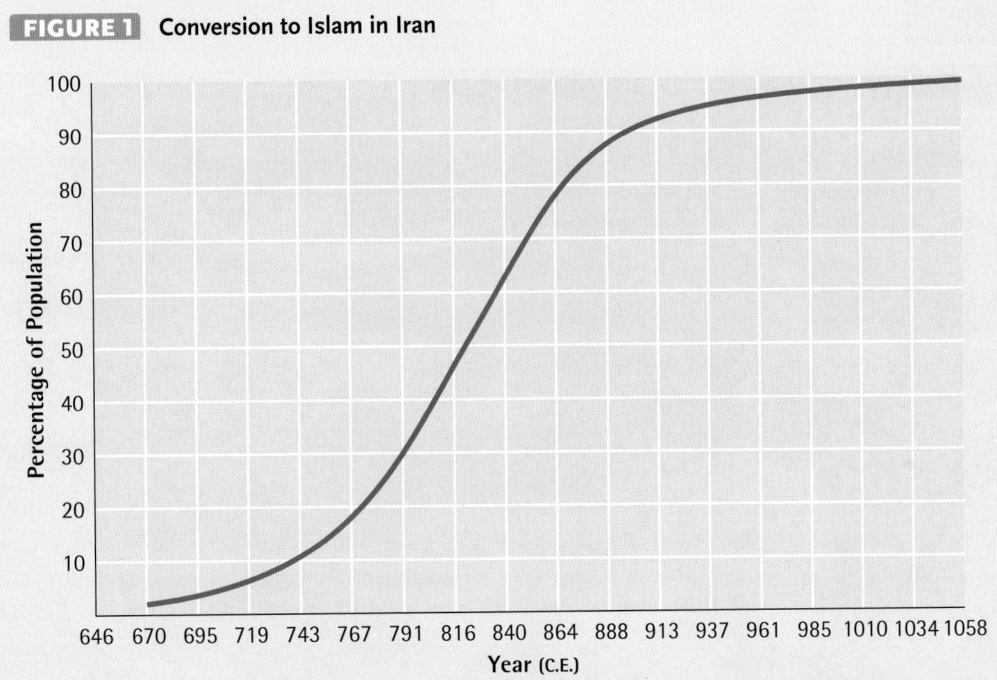

Source: Richard W. Bulliet, *Conversion to Islam in the Medieval Period*, Cambridge, MA: Harvard University Press, 1979, 23. Copyright © 1979 by the President and Fellows of Harvard College.

PART IV

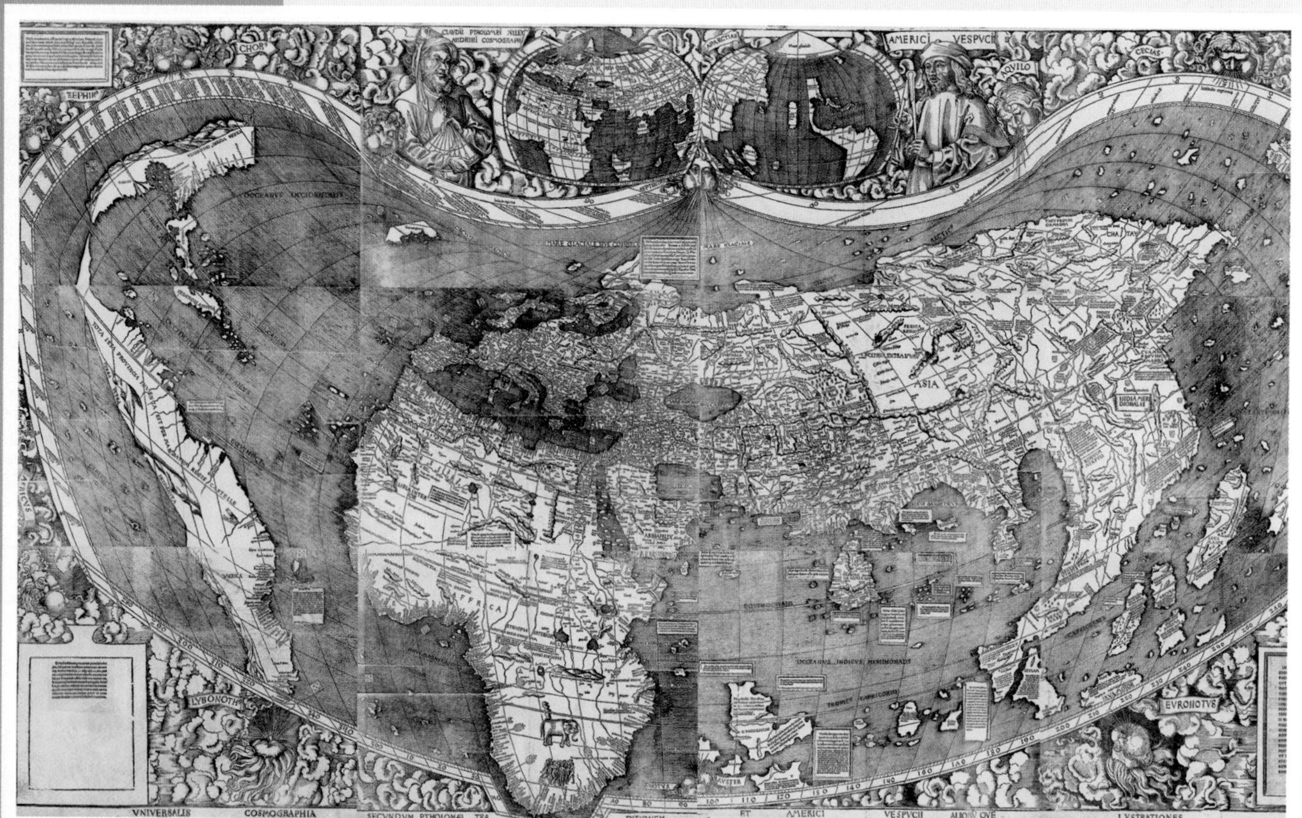

Library of Congress

Martin Waldseemüller's Map of the World This map, published in 1507 and included in a German geography book entitled Cosmographiae Introductio, marks the first usage of the name America, placed one-third of the way from the bottom of the New World's southern continent. Amerigho (original spelling) Vespucci sailed twice to the New World as a navigator in 1499 and 1501. Letters he wrote misled the author into thinking that Vespucci, and not Columbus, had been the first to land on the mainland. "I do not see what right any one would have to object to calling this part after Americus, who discovered it and who is a man of intelligence, [and so to name it] Amerige, that is, the Land of Americus, or America: since both Europa and Asia got their names from women."

Interregional Patterns of Culture and Contact, 1200–1550

Overland trade along the Silk Road peaked under the Mongols. The empire formed on Genghis Khan's conquests made Mongolia the center of an administrative and trading system linking Europe, the Middle East, Russia, and East Asia. Some lands flourished; others groaned under tax burdens and physical devastation.

Societies that escaped conquest also felt the Mongol impact. Around the eastern Mediterranean coast and in eastern Europe, Southeast Asia, and Japan, fear of Mongol attack stimulated defense planning and accelerated processes of urbanization, technological development, and political centralization.

By 1500, Mongol dominance had waned. A new Chinese empire, the Ming, was expanding its influence in Southeast Asia. The Ottomans had overthrown the Byzantine Empire, and Christian monarchs in Spain and Portugal, victorious over Muslim enemies, were laying the foundations of new overseas empires.

As Eurasia's overland trade faded, merchants, soldiers, and explorers took to the seas. State-sponsored long-distance voyages undertaken by the Chinese admiral Zheng He were spectacular but without long-term results. Africans explored the Atlantic, and Polynesians colonized the central and eastern Pacific in the 1300s and 1400s. By 1500 Christopher Columbus had reached the Americas; within twenty-five years a Portuguese ship would sail around the world.

The overland routes of Eurasia had generated massive wealth in East Asia and a growing hunger for commerce in Europe. These factors similarly spurred the development of maritime trade. Exposure to the achievements, wealth, and resources of the Americas, sub-Saharan Africa, and Asia guaranteed the further expansion of European exploration and maritime power.

CHAPTER 12

CHAPTER OUTLINE

- The Rise of the Mongols, 1200–1260
- The Mongols and Islam, 1260–1500
- Regional Responses in Western Eurasia
- Mongol Domination in China, 1271–1368
- The Early Ming Empire, 1368–1500
- Centralization and Militarism in East Asia, 1200–1500
- Conclusion

DIVERSITY + DOMINANCE *Observations of Mongol Life*

ENVIRONMENT + TECHNOLOGY *From Gunpowder to Guns*

Laurie Platt Winfrey/The Art Archive

Defending Japan Japanese warriors board Mongol warships with swords to prevent the landing of the invasion force in 1281.

Visit the website and ebook for additional study materials and interactive tools: www.cengage.com/history/bullietearthpeople5e

Mongol Eurasia and Its Aftermath, 1200–1500

- What accounts for the magnitude and speed of the Mongol conquests?
- How did Mongol expansion and Islam affect each other?
- What benefits resulted from the integration of Eurasia into the Mongol Empire?
- How did Mongol rule in China foster cultural and scientific exchange?
- In what ways did the Ming Empire continue or discontinue Mongol practices?
- What are some of the similarities and differences in how Korea and Japan responded to the Mongol threat?

When Temüjin (TEM-uh-jin) was a boy, a rival group murdered his father. Temüjin's mother tried to shelter him, but she could not find a safe haven. At fifteen Temüjin sought refuge with the leader of the Keraits (keh-rates), a warring confederation whose people spoke Turkic and respected both Christianity and Buddhism. Temüjin learned the importance of religious tolerance, the necessity of dealing harshly with enemies, and the variety of Inner Asia's cultural and economic traditions.

In 1206 the **Mongols** and their allies acknowledged Temüjin as **Genghis Khan** (GENG-iz KAHN), or supreme leader. His advisers spoke many languages and belonged to different religions. His deathbed speech, which cannot be literally true even though a contemporary recorded it, captures the strategy behind Mongol success: "If you want to retain your possessions and conquer your enemies, you must make your subjects submit willingly and unite your diverse energies to a single end."[1] By implementing this strategy, Genghis Khan became the most famous conqueror in history, initiating an expansion of Mongol dominion that by 1250 stretched from Poland to northern China.

Mongols A people of this name is mentioned as early as the records of the Tang Empire, living as nomads in northern Eurasia. After 1206 they established an enormous empire under Genghis Khan, linking western and eastern Eurasia.

Genghis Khan The title of Temüjin when he ruled the Mongols (1206–1227). It means the "oceanic" or "universal leader." Genghis Khan was the founder of the Mongol Empire.

Scholars today stress the positive developments that transpired under Mongol rule. European and Asian sources of the time, however, vilify the Mongols as agents of death, suffering, and conflagration, a still-common viewpoint based on reliable accounts of horrible massacres.

The tremendous extent of the Mongol Empire promoted the movement of people and ideas from one end of Eurasia to the other. Trade routes improved, markets expanded, and the demand for products grew. Trade on the Silk Road, which had declined with the fall of the Tang Empire (see Chapter 10), revived.

Between 1218 and about 1350 in western Eurasia and down to 1368 in China, the Mongols focused on specific economic and strategic interests, usually permitting local cultures to survive and develop. In some regions, local reactions to Mongol domination sowed seeds of regional and ethnic identity that blossomed in the period of Mongol decline. Regions as widely separated as Russia, Iran, China, Korea, and Japan benefited from the Mongol stimulation of economic and cultural exchange and also found in their opposition to the Mongols new bases for political consolidation and affirmation of cultural difference.

AP* Exam Tip Be prepared to discuss the development of the Mongol Empire.

THE RISE OF THE MONGOLS, 1200–1260

nomadism A way of life, forced by a scarcity of resources, in which groups of people continually migrate to find pastures and water.

The Mongol Empire owed much of its success to the cultural institutions and political traditions of the Eurasian steppes (prairies) and deserts. The pastoral way of life known as **nomadism** gives rise to imperial expansion only occasionally, and historians disagree about what triggers these episodes. In the case of the Mongols, a precise assessment of the personal contributions of Genghis Khan and his successors remains uncertain.

Nomadism in Central and Inner Asia

Mongol Society

The pastoral nomads of the Eurasian steppes played an on-again, off-again role in European, Middle Eastern, and Chinese history for hundreds of years before the rise of the Mongols (see Chapter 7). The Mongol way of life probably did not differ materially from that of those earlier peoples (see Diversity and Dominance: Observations of Mongol Life). Traditional accounts maintain that the Mongols put their infants on goats to accustom them to riding. Moving regularly and efficiently with flocks and herds required firm decision making, and the independence of individual Mongols and their families made this decision making public, with many voices being heard. A council with representatives from powerful families ratified the decisions of the leader, the *khan*. Yet people who disagreed with a decision could strike off on their own. Even during military campaigns, warriors moved with their families and possessions.

Menial work in camps fell to slaves—people who were either captured during warfare or who sought refuge in slavery to escape starvation. Weak groups secured land rights and protection from strong groups by providing them with slaves, livestock, weapons, silk, or cash. More powerful groups, such as Genghis Khan's extended family and descendants, lived almost entirely off tribute, so they spent less time and fewer resources on herding and more on warfare designed to secure greater tribute.

Mongol Women

 **AP* Exam Tip** The role of women in Mongol society is an important point to know for the exam.

Leading families combined resources and solidified intergroup alliances through arranged marriages and other acts, a process that helped generate political federations. Marriages were arranged in childhood—in Temüjin's case, at the age of eight—and children thus became pawns of diplomacy. Women from prestigious families could wield power in negotiation and management, though they ran the risk of assassination or execution just like men.

The wives and mothers of Mongol rulers traditionally managed state affairs during the interregnum between a ruler's death and the selection of a successor. Princes and heads of ministries treated such regents with great deference and obeyed their commands without question. Since a female regent could not herself succeed to the position of khan, her political machinations usually focused on gaining the succession for a son or other male relative.

The Khan

Families often included believers in two or more religions, most commonly Buddhism, Christianity, or Islam. Virtually all Mongols observed the practices of traditional shamanism, rituals in which special individuals visited and influenced the supernatural world. Whatever their faith, the Mongols believed in world rulership by a khan who, with the aid of his shamans, could speak to and for an ultimate god, represented as Sky or Heaven. This universal ruler transcended particular cultures and dominated them all.

The Mongol Conquests, 1215–1283

Shortly after his acclamation in 1206, Genghis initiated two decades of Mongol aggression. By 1209 he had cowed the Tanggut (TAHNG-gut) rulers of northwest China, and in 1215 he captured the Jin capital of Yanjing, today known as Beijing (bay-jeeng). He turned westward in 1219 with an invasion of Khwarezm (kaw-REZM), a state east of the Caspian Sea that included much of Iran. After 1221, when most of Iran had fallen, Genghis left the command of most campaigns to subordinate generals.

Genghis Khan's Successors

Ögödei (ERG-uh-day), Genghis's son, became the Great Khan in 1227 after his father's death (see Figure 12.1). He completed the destruction of the Tanggut and the Jin and put their terri-

CHRONOLOGY

	Mongolia and China	Central Asia and Middle East	Russia	Korea, Japan, and Southeast Asia
1200	1206 Temüjin chosen Genghis Khan of the Mongols	1219–1223 First Mongol attacks in Iran	1221–1223 First Mongol attacks on Russia	
	1227 Death of Genghis Khan			
	1227–1241 Reign of Great Khan Ögödei			
	1234 Mongols conquer northern China		1240 Mongols sack Kiev	
			1242 Alexander Nevskii defeats Teutonic Knights	
		1258 Mongols sack Baghdad and kill the caliph		1258 Mongols conquer Koryo rulers in Korea
		1260 Mamluks defeat Il-khans at Ain Jalut	1260 War between Il-khans and Golden Horde	
	1271 Founding of Yuan Empire			1274, 1281 Mongols attack Japan
	1279 Mongol conquest of Southern Song			1283 Yuan invades Champa
				1293 Yuan attacks Java
1300		1295 Il-khan Ghazan converts to Islam		1333–1338 End of Kamakura Shogunate in Japan, beginning of Ashikaga
		1349 End of Il-khan rule	1346 Plague outbreak at Kaffa	
		ca. 1350 Egypt infected by plague		
	1368 Ming Empire founded	1370–1405 Reign of Timur		1392 Founding of Yi kingdom in Korea
1400	1403–1424 Reign of Yongle	1402 Timur defeats Ottoman sultan		
	1405–1433 Voyages of Zheng He	1453 Ottomans capture Constantinople	1462–1505 Ivan III establishes authority as tsar. Moscow emerges as major political center.	1471–1500 Annam conquers Champa

tories under Mongol governors. By 1234 he controlled most of northern China and was threatening the Southern Song (see Chapter 10). Two years later Genghis's grandson Batu (BAH-too) (d. 1255) attacked Russian territories, took control of the towns along the Volga (VOHL-gah) River, and conquered Kievan Russia, Moscow, Poland, and Hungary in a five-year campaign. Only the death of Ögödei in 1241, which caused a suspension of campaigning, saved Europe from graver damage. With Genghis's grandson Güyük (gi-yik) installed as the new Great Khan, the conquests resumed. In the Middle East a Mongol army sacked Baghdad in 1258 and executed the last Abbasid caliph (see Chapter 8).

Genghis Khan's original objective had probably been collecting tribute, but the success of the Mongol conquests created a new situation. Ögödei unquestionably sought to rule a united empire based at his capital, Karakorum (kah-rah-KOR-um), and until his death he controlled the subordinate Mongol domains: the Golden Horde in Russia and the Jagadai (JAH-guh-die)

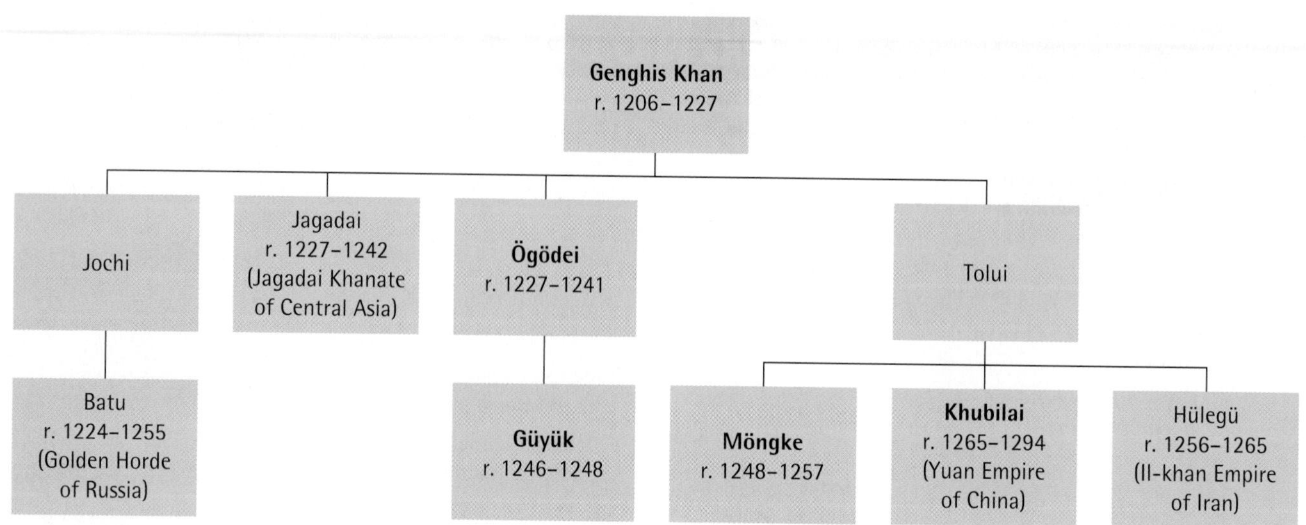

FIGURE 12.1 **Mongol Rulers, 1206–1260** The names of the Great Khans are shown in bold type. Those who founded the regional khanates are listed with their dates of rule.

domains in Central Asia (see Map 12.1). After Ögödei's death, however, family unity began to unravel; when Khubilai (KOO-bih-lie) declared himself Great Khan in 1265, the descendants of Genghis's son Jagadai (d. 1242) and other branches of the family refused to accept him. As Karakorum was destroyed in the ensuing fighting, Khubilai transferred his court to the old Jin capital now renamed Beijing. In 1271 he declared himself founder of the **Yuan Empire**.

Yuan Empire Empire created in China and Siberia by Khubilai Khan.

Jagadai's descendants continued to dominate Central Asia and enjoyed close relations with the region's Turkic-speaking nomads. This, plus a continuing hatred of Khubilai, contributed to Central Asia becoming an independent Mongol center and to the spread of Islam there.

After the Yuan destroyed the Southern Song (see Chapter 10) in 1279, Mongol troops attacked Annam—now northern Vietnam. They occupied Hanoi three times and then withdrew after arranging for tribute. In 1283 Khubilai's forces invaded Champa—now southern Vietnam—and made it a tribute nation as well. A plan to invade Java by sea failed, as did two invasions of Japan in 1274 and 1281.

Military Techniques

The Mongols seldom outnumbered their enemies, but they were extraordinary riders and utilized superior bows. The Central Asian bow, made by laminating layers of wood, leather, and bone, could shoot one-third farther (and was correspondingly more difficult to pull) than the bows used by sedentary enemies.

Rarely did an archer expend all of the five dozen arrows in his quiver. As the battle opened, arrows shot from a distance decimated enemy marksmen. Then the Mongols charged the enemy's infantry to fight with sword, lance, javelin, and mace. The Mongol cavalry met its match only at the Battle of Ain Jalut (ine jah-LOOT), where an under-strength force confronted Turkic-speaking Mamluks whose war techniques matched their own (see Chapter 8).

Siege and Terror

The Mongols also fired flaming arrows and hurled enormous projectiles—sometimes flaming—from catapults. The first Mongol catapults, built on Chinese models, transported easily but had short range and poor accuracy. During western campaigns in Central Asia, however, the Mongols encountered a design that was half again as powerful. They used it to hammer the cities of Iran and Iraq.

Cities that resisted faced siege and annihilation. Surrender was the only option. The slaughter the Mongols inflicted on Balkh (bahlk) (in present-day northern Afghanistan) and other cities spread terror and caused other cities to surrender. Each conquered area contributed men to the "Mongol" armies. In the Middle East, on the western fringe of their empire, a few Mongol officers commanded armies of recently recruited Turks and Iranians.

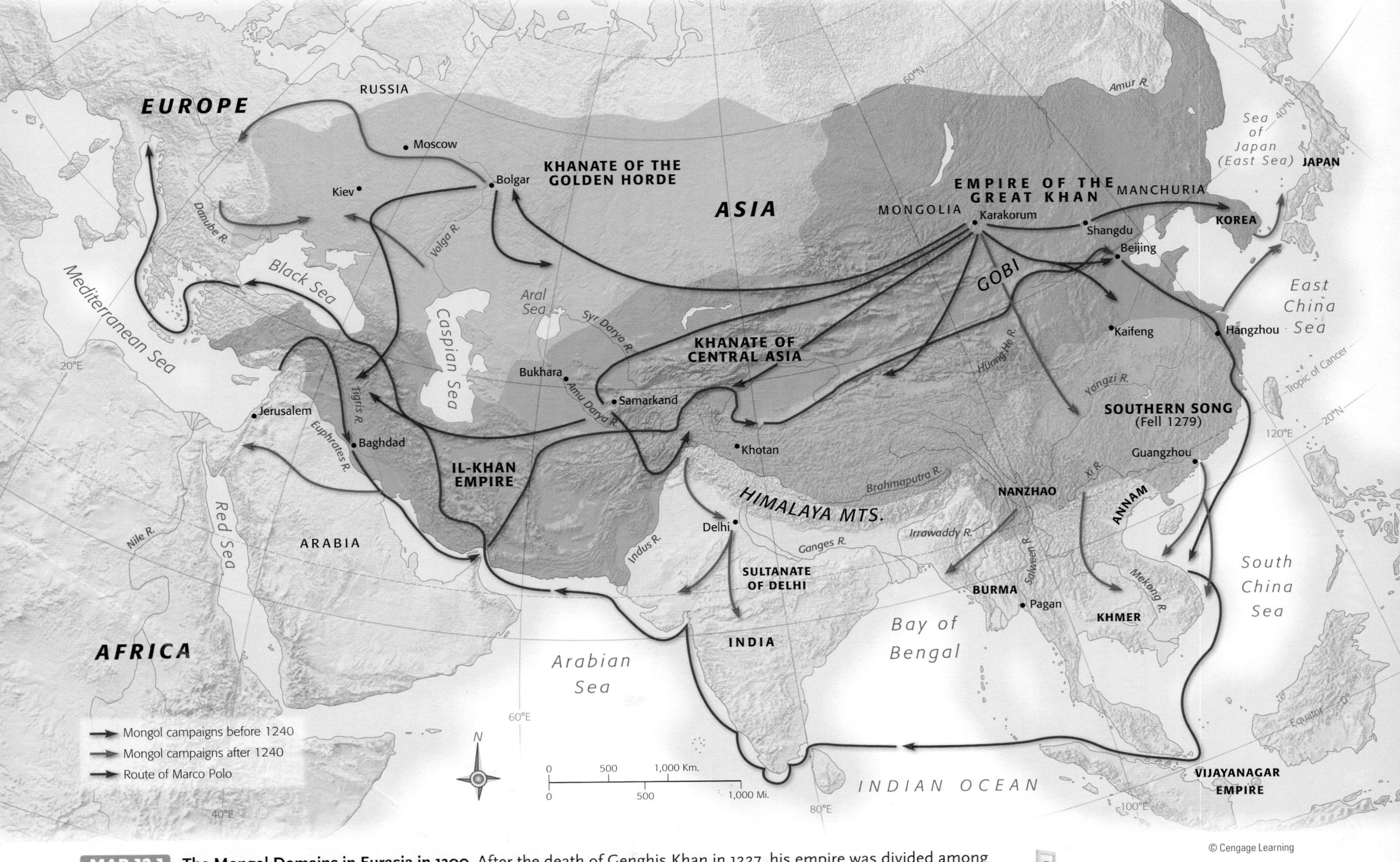

MAP 12.1 The Mongol Domains in Eurasia in 1300 After the death of Genghis Khan in 1227, his empire was divided among his sons and grandsons. Son Ögödei succeeded Genghis as Great Khan. Grandson Khubilai expanded the domain of the Great Khan into southern China by 1279. Grandson Hülegü was the first Il-khan in the Middle East. Grandson Batu founded the Khanate of the Golden Horde in southern Russia. Son Jagadai ruled the Jagadai Khanate in Central Asia.

Interactive Map

Observations of Mongol Life

The Mongols, despite the power, geographical extent, and durability of their empire, are known mainly from the observations made by non-Mongols who either traveled in their territory or worked for them. The following passages come from three such authors.

William of Rubruck, a Franciscan friar, journeyed to the court of the Great Khan Mönke in 1253–1255 after living for some period of time in crusader territory in the Middle East. He carried a letter from the French king, Louis IX (ruled 1226–1270), asking that the friar and a companion be allowed to stay with the Mongols, preach Christianity, and comfort German prisoners. William never made contact with the Germans, but his highly personal observations on Mongol life fascinated European readers.

The dwelling in which they sleep is based on a hoop of interlaced branches, and its supports are made of branches, converging at the top around a smaller hoop, from which projects a neck like a chimney. They cover it with white felt: quite often they also smear the felt with chalk or white clay and ground bones to make it gleam whiter, or sometimes they blacken it. . . . These dwellings are constructed to such a size as to be on occasion thirty feet across: I myself once measured a breadth of twenty feet between the wheeltracks of a wagon, and when the dwelling was on the wagon it protruded beyond the wheels by at least five feet on either side. I have counted twenty-two oxen to one wagon, hauling along a dwelling, eleven in a row, corresponding to the width of the wagon, and another eleven in front of them. The wagon's axle was as large as a ship's mast, and one man stood at the entrance of the dwelling on top of the wagon, driving the oxen. . . .

The married women make themselves very fine wagons. . . . One rich Mo'al [i.e., Mongol] or Tartar has easily a hundred or two hundred such wagons with chests. Baatu has twenty-six wives, each of whom has a large dwelling, not counting the other, smaller ones placed behind the large one, which are chambers, as it were, where the maids live: to each of these dwellings belong a good two hundred wagons. When they unload the dwellings, the chief wife pitches her residence at the westernmost end, and the others follow according to rank. . . . Hence the court of one wealthy Mo'al will have the appearance of a large town, though there will be very few males in it. . . . One woman will drive twenty or thirty wagons, since the terrain is level. The ox- or camel-wagons are lashed together in sequence, and the woman will sit at the front driving the ox, while all the rest follow at the same pace. If at some point the going happens to become difficult, they untie them and take them through one at a time. For they move slowly, at the pace at which a sheep or an ox can walk.

The History of the World-Conqueror *by the Iranian historian 'Ata-Malik Juvaini, who worked for the Mongols in Iran, was written in elegant Persian during the 1250s. It combines a glorification of the Mongol rulers with an unflinching picture of the cruelties and devastation inflicted by their conquests.*

He [i.e., Chingiz-Khan] paid great attention to the chase and used to say that the hunting of wild beasts was a proper occupation for the commanders of armies; and that instruction and training therein was incumbent on warriors and men-at-arms. . . . Whenever the Khan sets out on the great hunt (which takes place at the beginning of the winter season), he issues orders that the troops stationed around his headquarters and in the neighborhood . . . shall make preparation for the chase. . . .

The right wing, left wing and center of the army are drawn up and entrusted to the great emirs; and they set out together with the Royal Ladies and the concubines, as well as provisions of food and drink. For a month, or two, or three they form a hunting ring and drive the game slowly and gradually before them, taking care lest any escape from the ring. . . . Finally, when the ring has been contracted to a diameter of two or three parasangs [approximately 7 to 10 miles] they bind ropes together and cast felts over them; while the troops come to a halt all around the ring, standing shoulder to shoulder. The ring is now filled with the cries and commotion of every manner of game and the roaring and tumult of every kind of ferocious beast . . . lions becoming familiar with wild asses, hyaenas friendly with foxes, wolves intimate with hares.

When the ring has been so much contracted that the wild beasts are unable to stir, first the Khan rides in together with some of his retinue; then after he has wearied of the sport, they dismount upon high ground in the center . . . to watch the princes likewise entering the ring, and after them, in due order, the *noyans* [chiefs], the commanders and the troops. Several days pass in this manner; then, when nothing is left of the game but a few wounded and emaciated stragglers, old men and greybeards humbly approach the Khan, offer up prayers for his well-being and intercede for the lives of the remaining animals asking that they be suffered to depart to someplace nearer to grass and water. . . .

Now war—with its killing, counting of the slain and sparing of the survivors—is after the same fashion, and indeed analogous in every detail, because all that is left in the neighborhood of the battlefield are a few broken-down wretches.

Hu Szu-hui, a physician of Chinese-Turkic family background, presented the Yuan emperor with a manual entitled Proper and Essential Things for the Emperor's Food and Drink *in 1330. His work reflects both the meat-heavy diet of the steppes and traditional Chinese concern with good nutrition.*

Foods That Cure Various Illnesses [60 entries]

Donkey's Head Gruel

It cures apoplexy-vertigo, debility of hand and foot, annoying pain of extremities, and trouble in speaking:

> *Black donkey's head (one; remove hair and wash clean), black pepper (two measures), tsaoko cardamom (two measures). Cook ingredients until overcooked. Add the five spices in fermented black bean juice. Flavor with the spices. Flavor evenly. Eat on an empty stomach.*

Donkey's Meat Soup

It cures wind, mania and depression and pacifies the heart:

> *Meat of black donkey. (The quantity does not matter. Cut up.) Cook ingredient until overcooked in fermented black beans. When done add the five spices. Eat on an empty stomach.*

Fox Meat Gruel

It cures infantile convulsion, epilepsy, spiritual confusion, indistinct speech, and inappropriate singing and laughing:

> *Fox meat. (The quantity does not matter. Include organ meat.) [To] ingredient add the five spices according to the regular method. Cook until overcooked. When done eat on an empty stomach.*

Bear Meat Gruel

It cures the various winds, foot numbness-insensitivity, and five flaccidities, tendon and muscle spasms:

> *Bear meat (one measure). [To] ingredient add the five spices in fermented black beans. [Add] onions and sauce. Cook. When done eat on an empty stomach.*

Foodstuffs That Mutually Conflict [55 entries]

Horse meat cannot be eaten together with granary rice.

Horse meat cannot be eaten with cocklebur. It can be eaten with ginger.

Pork cannot be eaten together with beef.

Sheep's liver cannot be eaten together with pepper. It wounds the heart.

Hare meat cannot be eaten together with ginger.

Beef cannot be eaten together with chestnuts.

Mare's milk cannot be eaten together with fish hash. It produces obstruction of the bowels.

Venison cannot be eaten together with catfish.

Beef stomach cannot be eaten together with dog meat. Quail meat cannot be eaten together with pork. The face will turn black.

Pheasant eggs cannot be eaten together with onions. It produces vermin.

Meat of sparrows cannot be eaten together with plums. Eggs cannot be eaten together with turtle meat.

QUESTIONS FOR ANALYSIS

1. **Can you determine from the subject matter of these passages the different viewpoints of a European, an Iranian, and a Chinese?**
2. **Is there anything in these passages to indicate that the Mongols were Muslims, Christians, Buddhists, or Confucians?**
3. **Do you expect the observations of a traveler to be more or less valuable as historical sources than those of someone who served a Mongol ruler?**

Sources: From *The Mission of Friar William of Rubruck. His Journey to the Court of the Great Khan Mönke 1253–1255*, translated by Peter Jackson, pp. 73–74. Reprinted by permission of the publisher from Ata-Malik Juvani's *The History of the World Conqueror*, translated by Andrew Boyle, pp. 27–29, Cambridge, Mass.: Harvard University Press, Copyright © 1958 by Manchester University Press. Paul D. Buell and Eugene N. Anderson, *A Soup for the Qan*, 2000, pp. 428–429, 438–440. Reprinted by permission of the authors.

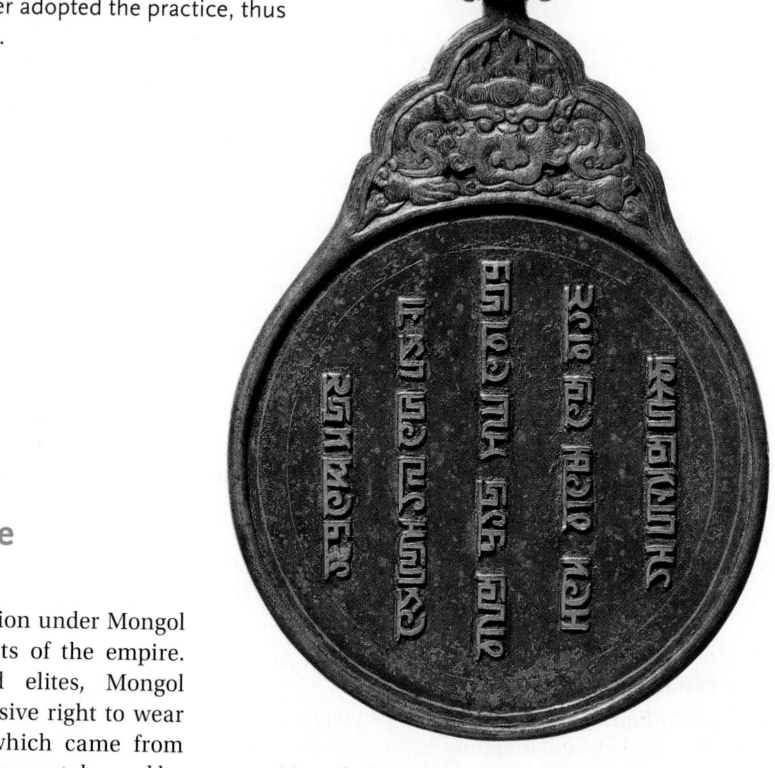

Passport The Mongol Empire facilitated the movement of products, merchants, and diplomats over long distances. Travelers frequently encountered new languages, laws, and customs. The *paisa* (from a Chinese word for "card" or "sign"), with its inscription in Mongolian, proclaimed that the traveler had the ruler's permission to travel through the region. Europeans later adopted the practice, thus making the *paisa* the ancestor of modern passports.

bubonic plague A bacterial disease of fleas that can be transmitted by flea bites to rodents and humans; humans in late stages of the illness can spread the bacteria by coughing. Because of its very high mortality rate and the difficulty of preventing its spread, major outbreaks have created crises in many parts of the world.

Overland Trade and Disease

Commercial integration under Mongol rule affected all parts of the empire. Like earlier nomad elites, Mongol nobles had the exclusive right to wear silk, almost all of which came from China. Trade brought new styles and huge quantities of silk westward to feed the luxury trade in the Middle East and Europe. Artistic motifs from Japan and Tibet reached as far as England and Morocco. Porcelain, another eastern luxury, became important in trade and strongly influenced later tastes in the Islamic world.

Traveler's Accounts: Marco Polo

Merchants encountered ambassadors, scholars, and missionaries over the long routes to the Mongol courts. Some of the resulting travel literature, like the account of the Venetian Marco Polo (mar-koe POE-loe) (1254–1324), freely mixed the fantastic with the factual. Stories of fantastic wealth stimulated a European ambition to find easier routes to Asia.

Rats and Fleas

Exchange also spread disease. In southwestern China **bubonic plague** had festered since the early Tang period. In the mid-thirteenth century, supply trains servicing the Mongol garrison in Yunnan (YOON-nahn) province facilitated the spread of rats carrying infected fleas. Marmots and other rodents along the caravan routes became infected and passed the disease to dogs and people. Plague incapacitated the Mongol army during its assault on the city of Kaffa (KAH-fah) in Crimea (cry-MEE-ah) in 1346. They withdrew, but the plague remained. From Kaffa flea-infested rats reached Europe and Egypt by ship (see Chapter 14).

Typhus, influenza, and smallpox traveled the same route. The combination of these and other diseases created what is called the "great pandemic" of 1347–1352 and spread devastation far in excess of what the Mongol armies inflicted. Peaceful trade, not conquest, ended up taking the greatest toll in lives.

SECTION REVIEW

- The society of the nomadic Mongols functioned through kinship and tribute ties, in which women often played important roles.
- Genghis Khan began the period of Mongol conquest to win tribute from Eurasian kingdoms.
- His successors turned to territorial rule, yet internal politics split the empire into smaller ones in China and Central Asia.
- The Mongols won territory through superior battle tactics and integrated it into a vast overland commercial network.
- That network allowed the bubonic plague and other diseases to spread across Asia into Europe.

THE MONGOLS AND ISLAM, 1260–1500

From the perspective of Mongol imperial history, the issue of which branches of the family adopted Islam and which did not mostly concerns political rivalries. From the standpoint of Islamic history, however, recovery from the devastation that culminated in the destruction of the Abbasid Caliphate in Baghdad in 1258 attests to the vitality of the faith and the ability of Muslims to overcome adversity. Within fifty years of its darkest hour, Islam reemerged as a potent ideological and political force.

Mongol Rivalry

Il-khans and Golden Horde

Il-khan A "secondary" or "peripheral" khan based in Persia. The Il-khans' khanate was founded by Hülegü, a grandson of Genghis Khan, and was based at Tabriz in the Iranian province of Azerbaijan. It controlled much of Iran and Iraq.

Golden Horde Mongol khanate founded by Genghis Khan's grandson Batu. It was based in southern Russia and quickly adopted both the Turkic language and Islam. Also known as the Kipchak Horde.

By 1260 the **Il-khan** (IL-con) state, established by Genghis's grandson Hülegü, controlled Iran, Azerbaijan, Mesopotamia, and parts of Armenia. North of the Caspian Sea the Mongols who had conquered southern Russia established the capital of their Khanate of the **Golden Horde** (also called the Kipchak [KIP-chahk] Khanate) at Sarai (sah-RYE) on the Volga River. Like the Il-khans, they ruled an indigenous Muslim population, mostly Turkic-speaking.

Some members of the Mongol imperial family professed Islam before the Mongol assault on the Middle East, and Turkic Muslims served the family in various capacities. Hülegü himself, though a Buddhist, had a trusted Shi'ite adviser and granted privileges to the Shi'ites. However, the Mongols under Hülegü's command came only slowly to Islam.

Islamic doctrines clashed with Mongol ways. Muslims abhorred the Mongols' worship of Buddhist and shamanist idols. Furthermore, Mongol law specified slaughtering animals without spilling blood, which involved opening the chest and stopping the heart. This horrified Muslims, who were forbidden to consume blood and slaughtered animals by slitting their throats and draining the blood.

Islam became a point of inter-Mongol tension when Batu's successor as leader of the Golden Horde declared himself a Muslim. He swore to avenge the murder of the Abbasid caliph and laid claim to the Caucasus—the mountains between the Black and Caspian Seas—which the Il-khans also claimed (see Map 12.2).

Some European leaders believed that if they helped the non-Muslim Il-khans repel the Golden Horde from the Caucasus, the Il-khans would help them relieve Muslim pressure on the crusader principalities in Syria, Lebanon, and Palestine (see Chapter 8). This resulted in a brief correspondence between the Il-khan court and Pope Nicholas IV (r. 1288–1292) and a diplomatic mission that sent two Christian Turks to western Europe as Il-khan ambassadors in the late 1200s. The Golden Horde responded by seeking an alliance with the Muslim Mamluks in Egypt (see Chapter 8) against both the crusaders and the Il-khans. These complicated efforts extended the life of the crusader principalities, but the Mamluks finally ended their existence in the fifteenth century.

AP* Exam Tip
Although it is important to understand Mongol expansion, knowledge of specific khanates is not required for the multiple choice section of the exam.

Ghazan Converts to Islam

Before the Europeans' diplomatic efforts could bear fruit, a new Il-khan ruler, Ghazan (haz-ZAHN) (1271–1304), declared himself a Muslim in 1295. Conflicting indications of Sunni and Shi'ite affiliation, such as coin inscriptions, indicate that Ghazan had a casual attitude toward theological matters. It is similarly unclear whether the Muslim Turkic nomads who served in the army were Shi'ite or Sunni.

Islam and the State

Taxes and Administration

The Il-khans gradually came to appreciate the traditional urban culture of the Muslim territories they ruled. Nevertheless, they used tax farming, a fiscal method developed earlier in the Middle East, to extract maximum wealth from their subjects. The government sold tax-collecting contracts to small partnerships, mostly consisting of merchants who might also finance caravans, small industries, or military expeditions. Whoever offered to collect the most revenue for the government won the contracts. They could use whatever methods they chose and could keep anything over the contracted amount.

Contracting tax collection initially lowered administrative costs; but over the long term, the extortions of the tax farmers drove many landowners into debt and servitude. Agricultural productivity declined, making it hard to supply the army. So the government resorted to taking land to grow its own grain. Like land held by religious trusts, this land paid no taxes. Thus the tax base shrank even as the demands of the army and the Mongol nobility continued to grow.

Paper Money

Ghazan faced many economic problems. Citing Islam's humane values, he promised to reduce taxes. But the need for revenue kept the decrease from becoming permanent. The Chinese practice of printing paper money had been tried unsuccessfully by a predecessor. Now it was tried again. The experiment, to which the Il-khan's subjects responded negatively, pushed the economy into a depression that lasted beyond the end of the Il-khan state in 1349. Mongol nobles competed among themselves for the decreasing revenues, and fighting among Mongol factions destabilized the government.

Timur Member of a prominent family of the Mongols' Jagadai Khanate, Timur through conquest gained control over much of Central Asia and Iran. He consolidated the status of Sunni Islam as orthodox, and his descendants, the Timurids, maintained his empire for nearly a century and founded the Mughal Empire in India.

While the Golden Horde and the Il-khan Empire quarreled, a new power was emerging in the Central Asian Khanate of Jagadai (see Map 12.1). The leader **Timur** (TEE-moor), known to Europeans as Tamerlane, maneuvered himself into command of the Jagadai forces and launched campaigns into western Eurasia, apparently seeing himself as a new Genghis Khan. By ethnic background he was a Turk with only an in-law relationship to the family of the Mongol conqueror. This prevented him from assuming the title *khan*, but not from sacking the Muslim sultanate of Delhi in northern India in 1398 or defeating the sultan of the rising Ottoman Empire

Interactive Map

MAP 12.2 Western Eurasia in the 1300s Ghazan's conversion to Islam in 1295 upset the delicate balance of power in Mongol domains. European leaders abandoned their hope of finding an Il-khan ally against the Muslim defenders in Palestine, while an alliance between the Mamluks and the Golden Horde kept the Il-khans from advancing west. This helped the Europeans retain their lands in Palestine and Syria.

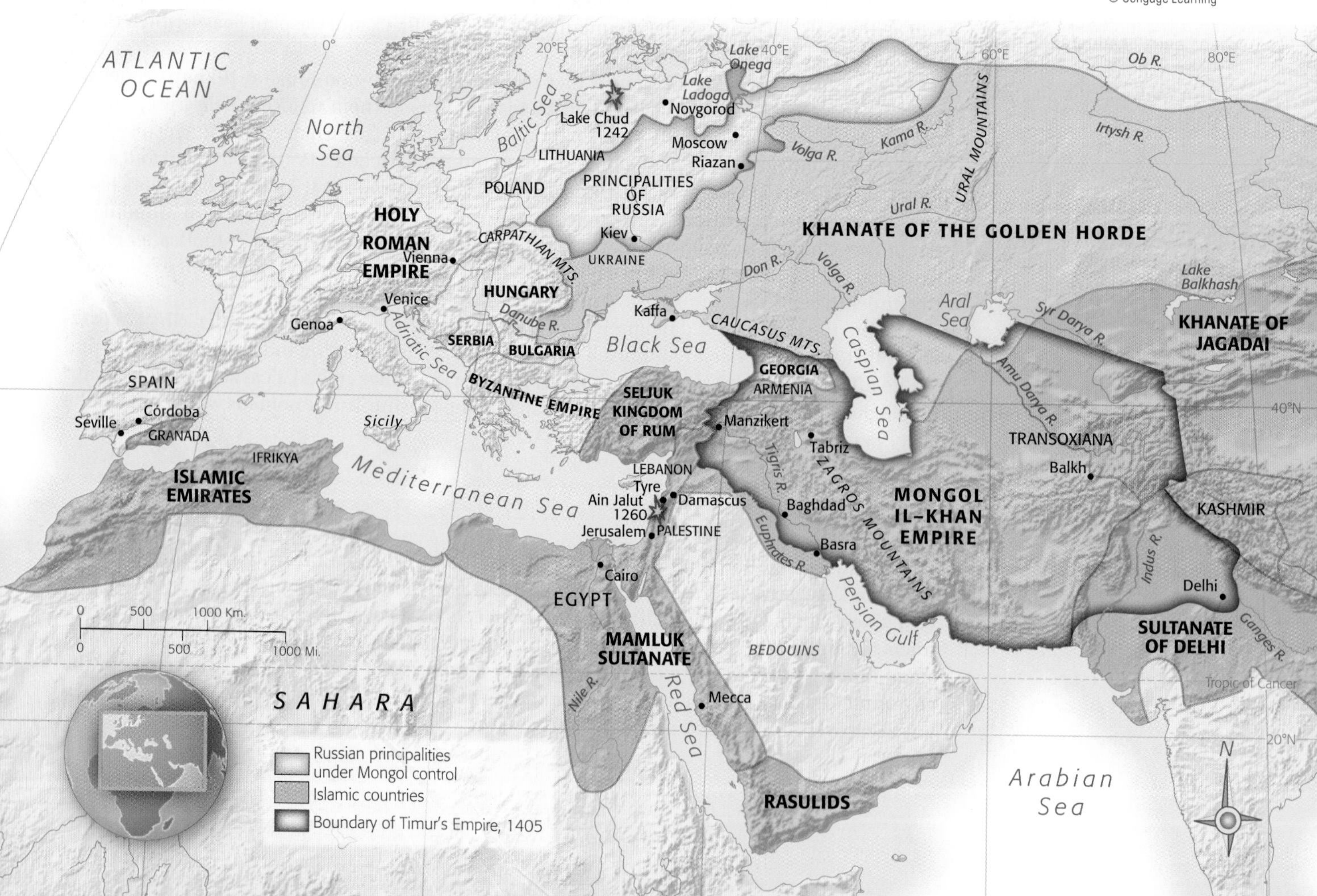

in Anatolia in 1402. He was reportedly preparing to march on China when he died in 1405. However, Timur's descendants could not hold the empire together.

Culture and Science in Islamic Eurasia

The Il-khans and Timurids (descendants of Timur) presided over a brilliant cultural flowering in Iran, Afghanistan, and Central Asia based on blending Iranian and Chinese artistic trends and cultural practices. The dominant cultural tendencies were Muslim, however. Timur died before he could reunite Iran and China, but by transplanting Middle Eastern scholars, artists, and craftsmen to his capital, Samarkand, he fostered the cultural achievements of his descendants.

Administrators and Historians

The historian Juvaini (joo-VINE-nee) (d. 1283), who recorded Genghis Khan's deathbed speech cited at the beginning of this chapter, came from the city of Balkh, which the Mongols had devastated in 1221. His family switched their allegiance to the Mongols, and both Juvaini and his older brother assumed high government posts. The Il-khan Hülegü, seeking to immortalize and justify his conquests, enthusiastically supported Juvaini's writing of the first comprehensive narrative of Genghis Khan's empire.

Rashid al-Din Adviser to the Il-khan ruler Ghazan, who converted to Islam on Rashid's advice.

Juvaini combined a florid style with historical objectivity, often criticizing the Mongols. This approach served as an inspiration to **Rashid al-Din** (ra-SHEED ad-DEEN), Ghazan's prime

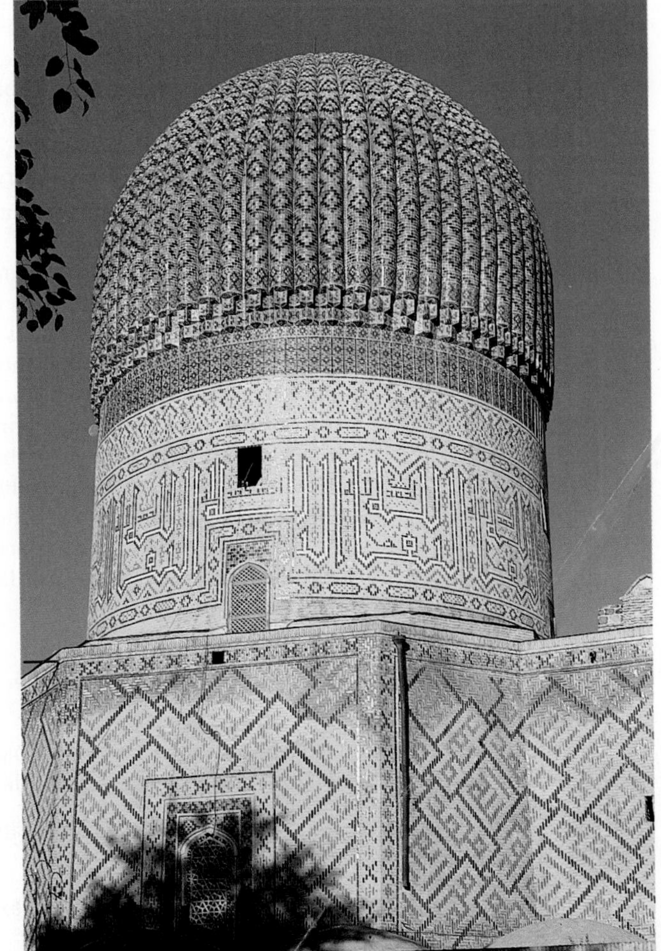

Sassoon/Robert Harding Picture Library

Tomb of Timur in Samarkand The turquoise tiles that cover the dome are typical of Timurid architectural decoration. Timur's family ornamented his capital with an enormous mosque, three large religious colleges facing one another on three sides of an open plaza, and a lane of brilliantly tiled Timurid family tombs in the midst of a cemetery. Timur brought craftsmen to Samarkand from the lands he conquered to build these magnificent structures.

minister, when he attempted the first history of the world. Rashid al-Din's work included the earliest known general history of Europe, derived from conversations with European monks, and a detailed description of China based on information from an important Chinese Muslim official stationed in Iran. The miniature paintings that accompanied some copies of Rashid al-Din's work included depictions of European and Chinese people and events and reflected the artistic traditions of both cultures. The Chinese techniques of composition helped inaugurate the greatest period of Islamic miniature painting under the Timurids.

Rashid al-Din traveled widely and collaborated with administrators from other parts of the far-flung Mongol dominions. His idea that government should be in accord with the moral principles of the majority of the population buttressed Ghazan's adherence to Islam. Administratively, however, Ghazan did not restrict himself to Muslim precedents but employed financial and monetary techniques that roughly resembled those used in Russia and China.

Under the Timurids, the tradition of the Il-khan historians continued. After conquering Damascus, Timur himself met there with the greatest historian of the age, Ibn Khaldun (ee-bin hal-DOON) (1332–1406), a Tunisian. In a scene reminiscent of Ghazan's answering Rashid al-Din's questions on the history of the Mongols, Timur and Ibn Khaldun exchanged historical, philosophical, and geographical viewpoints. Like Genghis, Timur saw himself as a world conqueror. At their capitals of Samarkand and Herat (in western Afghanistan), later Timurid rulers sponsored historical writing in both Persian and Turkish.

Islamic Science and Astronomy

Nasir al-Din Tusi Persian mathematician and cosmologist whose academy near Tabriz provided the model for the movement of the planets that helped to inspire the Copernican model of the solar system.

A Shi'ite scholar named **Nasir al-Din Tusi** (nah-SEER ad-DEEN TOO-si) represents the beginning of Mongol interest in the scientific traditions of the Muslim lands. Nasir al-Din may have joined the entourage of Hülegü during a campaign in 1256 against the Assassins, a Shi'ite religious sect derived from the Fatimid dynasty in Egypt and at odds with his more mainstream Shi'ite views (see Chapter 8). Nasir al-Din wrote on history, poetry, ethics, and religion, but he made his most outstanding contributions in mathematics and cosmology. Following Omar Khayyam (oh-mar kie-YAM) (1038?–1131), a poet and mathematician of the Seljuk (SEL-jook) period, he laid new foundations for algebra and trigonometry. Some followers working at an observatory built for Nasir al-Din at Maragheh (mah-RAH-gah), near the Il-khan capital of Tabriz, used the new mathematical techniques to reach a better understanding of celestial orbits.

The mathematical tables and geometric models of lunar motion devised by one of his students somehow became known to Nicholas Copernicus (1473–1543), a Polish monk and astronomer. Copernicus adopted this lunar model as his own, virtually without revision. He then proposed the model of lunar movement developed under the Il-khans as the proper model for planetary movement as well—but with the planets circling the sun.

Observational astronomy and calendar-making had engaged the interest of earlier Central Asian rulers, particularly the Uighurs (WEE-ger) and the Seljuks. Under the Il-khans, the astronomers of Maragheh excelled in predicting eclipses. Astrolabes, armillary spheres, three-dimensional quadrants, and other instruments acquired new precision.

The remarkably accurate eclipse predictions and tables prepared by Il-khan and Timurid astronomers reached the hostile Mamluk lands in Arabic translation. Byzantine monks took them to Constantinople and translated them into Greek, Christian scholars working in Muslim Spain translated them into Latin, and in India the sultan of Delhi ordered them translated into Sanskrit.

The Great Khan Khubilai (discussed later in this chapter) summoned a team of Iranians to Beijing to build an observatory for him. Timur's grandson Ulugh Beg (oo-loog bek) (1394–1449), whose avocation was astronomy, constructed a great observatory in Samarkand and actively participated in com-

SECTION REVIEW

- For the Mongols of the Il-khan and Golden Horde states, Islam became a matter of political rivalry.
- In the Il-khan state Islamic values struggled with economic needs, and the resulting unrest left it open to invasions by Golden Horde Mongols.
- At the same time, Timur took control of the Jagadai territory and began his own imperial conquests.
- Under the Il-khans and Timurids, Iran and Central Asia experienced a flowering of Islamic culture.
- These rulers fostered great achievements in historical writing, literature, art, mathematics, and astronomy.

Istanbul University Library

Astronomy and Engineering Observational astronomy went hand in hand not only with mathematics and calendrical science but also with engineering as the construction of platforms, instruments for celestial measurement, and armillary spheres became more sophisticated. This manual in Persian, completed in the 1500s but illustrating activities of the Il-khan period, illustrates the use of a plumb line with an enormous armillary sphere.

piling observational tables that were later translated into Latin and used by European astronomers.

Decimal Notation

A further advance made under Ulugh Beg came from the mathematician Ghiyas al-Din Jamshid al-Kashi (gee-YASS ad-DIN jam-SHEED al-KAH-shee), who noted that Chinese astronomers had long used one ten-thousandth of a day as a unit in calculating the occurrence of a new moon. This seems to have inspired him to employ decimal notation, by which quantities less than one could be represented by a marker to show place. Al-Kashi's proposed value for *pi* (π) was far more precise than any previously calculated. This innovation arrived in Europe by way of Constantinople, where a Greek translation of al-Kashi's work appeared in the fifteenth century.

REGIONAL RESPONSES IN WESTERN EURASIA

Safe, reliable overland trade benefited Mongol ruling centers and commercial cities along the Silk Road. But the countryside, ravaged by conquest, sporadic violence, and heavy taxes, suffered terribly. As Mongol control weakened, regional forces in Russia, eastern Europe, and Anatolia reasserted themselves. Sometimes this meant collaborating with the Mongols. At other times it meant using local ethnic or religious traditions to resist or roll back Mongol influence.

Russia and Rule from Afar

The Golden Horde, established after Genghis's grandson Batu defeated a combined Russian and Kipchak (a Turkic people) army in 1223, started as a unified state but gradually lost unity as some districts crystallized into smaller khanates. The White Horde, for instance, ruled much of southeastern Russia in the fifteenth century, and the Crimean khanate on the northern shore of the Black Sea succumbed to Russian power only in 1783.

(Old) Sarai

East-west routes across the steppe and north-south routes along the rivers of Russia and Ukraine (you-CRANE) conferred importance on certain trading entrepôts (places where goods are stored and from which they are distributed), as they had under Kievan Russia (see Chapter 9). The Golden Horde capital was (Old) Sarai, just north of where the Volga flows into the Caspian Sea (see Map 12.1). It ruled its Russian domains to the north and east from afar. To facilitate control, it granted privileges to the Orthodox Church, which then helped reconcile the Russian people to their distant masters.

Growth of Russian Language

The politics of language played a role in subsequent history. Old Church Slavonic, an ecclesiastical language, revived; but Russian steadily acquired greater importance and eventually became the dominant written language. Russian scholars shunned Byzantine Greek, previously the main written tongue, even after the Golden Horde permitted renewed contacts with Constantinople. The Golden Horde enlisted Russian princes to act as their agents, primarily as tax collectors and census takers.

Economic Problems

The flow of silver and gold into Mongol hands starved the local economy of precious metal. Like the Il-khans, the khans of the Golden Horde attempted to introduce paper money as a response to the currency shortage. The unsuccessful experiment left such a vivid memory that the Russian word for money (*denga* [DENG-ah]) comes from the Mongolian word for the stamp (*tamga* [TAHM-gah]) used to create paper currency. In fact, commerce depended more on direct exchange of goods than on currency transactions.

Alexander Nevskii

Alexander Nevskii Prince of Novgorod (r. 1236–1263). He submitted to the invading Mongols in 1240 and received recognition as the leader of the Russian princes under the Golden Horde.

Alexander Nevskii (nih-EFF-skee) (ca. 1220–1263), the prince of Novgorod, persuaded some fellow princes to submit to the Mongols. In return, the Mongols favored both Novgorod and the emerging town of Moscow, ruled by Alexander's son Daniel. As these towns eclipsed Kiev (earlier devastated by the Mongols) as political, cultural, and economic centers, they drew people northward to open new agricultural land far from the Mongol steppe lands. Decentralization continued in the 1300s, with Moscow only very gradually becoming Russia's dominant political center.

In appraising the Mongol era, some historians stress Mongol destructiveness and brutality in tax collecting. Ukraine, a fertile and well-populated region in the late Kievan period (1000–1230), suffered severe population loss from these sources. Isolated from developments to the west, Russia and parts of eastern Europe are portrayed as suffering under the "Mongol yoke."

The "Mongol Yoke"

AP* Exam Tip The impact of the Mongol Empire on the world is an important point for the course.

Other historians point out that even before the Mongols struck Kiev had declined economically and ceased to mint coins. Yet the Russian territories regularly paid the heavy Mongol taxes in silver, indicating both economic surpluses and an ability to convert goods into cash. The burdensome taxes stemmed less from the Mongols than from their tax collectors, Russian princes who often exempted their own lands and shifted the load to the peasants.

As for Russia's cultural isolation, skeptics observe that before the Mongol invasion, the powerful and constructive role played by the Orthodox Church oriented Russia primarily toward Byzantium (see Chapter 9). This situation discouraged but did not eliminate contacts with western Europe, which probably would have become stronger after the fall of Constantinople to the Ottomans in 1453 regardless of Mongol influence.

tsar (czar) From Latin *caesar*, this Russian title for a monarch was first used in reference to a Russian ruler by Ivan III (r. 1462–1505).

The traditional structure of local government survived Mongol rule, as did the Russian princely families, who continued to battle among themselves for dominance. The Mongols merely added a new player to those struggles.

Title of Tsar

Ivan (ee-VAHN) III, the prince of Moscow (r. 1462–1505), established himself as an autocratic ruler in the late 1400s. Before Ivan, the title **tsar** (from *caesar*), of Byzantine origin, applied

Transformation of the Kremlin Like other northern Europeans, the Russians preferred to build in wood, which was easy to handle and comfortable to live in. But they fortified important political centers with stone ramparts. In the 1300s, the city of Moscow emerged as a new capital, and its old wooden palace, the Kremlin, was gradually transformed into a stone structure.

RIA-Novosti

only to foreign rulers, whether the emperors of Byzantium or the Turkic khans of the steppe. Ivan's use of the title probably represents an effort to establish a basis for legitimate rule with the decline of the Golden Horde and the disappearance of the Byzantine Empire.

New States in Eastern Europe and Anatolia

Anatolia and parts of Europe responded dynamically to the Mongol challenges. Raised in Sicily, the Holy Roman Emperor Frederick II (r. 1212–1250) appreciated Muslim culture and did not recoil from negotiating with Muslims. When the pope threatened to excommunicate him unless he waged a crusade, Frederick nominally regained Jerusalem through a flimsy treaty with the Mamluk sultan in Egypt. Dissatisfied, the pope continued to quarrel with the emperor, leaving Hungary, Poland, and Lithuania to deal with the Mongol onslaught on their own. Many princes capitulated and went to (Old) Sarai to offer their submission to Batu.

Teutonic Knights

However, the Teutonic (two-TOHN-ik) Knights resisted. These German-speaking warriors were dedicated to Christianizing the Slavic and Kipchak populations of northern Europe and to colonizing their territories with German settlers. To protect Slav territory, Alexander Nevskii joined the Mongols in fighting the Teutonic Knights and their Finnish allies. The latter suffered a catastrophe in 1242, when many broke through an icy northern lake and drowned. This destroyed the power of the Knights, and the northern Crusades virtually ceased.

The "Mongol" armies encountered by the Europeans consisted mostly of Turks, Chinese, Iranians, a few Europeans, and at least one Englishman, who went to crusade in the Middle East but joined the Mongols and served in Hungary. But most commanders were Mongol.

Transfer of Knowledge

Initial wild theories describing the Mongols as coming from Hell or from caves where Alexander the Great confined the monsters of antiquity gradually yielded to a more sophisticated understanding as European embassies to Mongol courts returned with reliable intelligence. In some quarters terror gave way to appreciation. Europeans learned about diplomatic passports, coal mining, movable type, high-temperature metallurgy, higher mathematics, gunpowder, and, in the fourteenth century, the casting and use of bronze cannon. Yet with the outbreak of bubonic plague in the late 1340s (see Chapter 14), the memory of Mongol terror helped ignite religious speculation that God might again be punishing the Christians.

Lithuania

In the fourteenth century several regions, most notably Lithuania (lith-oo-WAY-nee-ah), escaped the Mongol grip. When Russia fell to the Mongols, Lithuania had experienced an unprecedented centralization and military strengthening. Like Alexander Nevskii, the Lithuanian leaders maintained their independence by cooperating with the Mongols. In the late 1300s Lithuania capitalized on its privileged position to dominate Poland and ended the Teutonic Knights' hope of regaining power.

Serbian Empire

Ottoman Empire Islamic state founded by Osman in northwestern Anatolia ca. 1300. After the fall of the Byzantine Empire, the Ottoman Empire was based at Istanbul (formerly Constantinople) from 1453 to 1922. It encompassed lands in the Middle East, North Africa, the Caucasus, and eastern Europe.

In the Balkans independent kingdoms separated themselves from the chaos of the Byzantine Empire and thrived amidst the political uncertainties of the Mongol period. The Serbian king Stephen Dushan (ca. 1308–1355) proved the most effective leader. Seizing power from his father in 1331, he took advantage of Byzantine weakness to turn the archbishop of Serbia into an independent patriarch. In 1346 the patriarch crowned him "tsar and autocrat of the Serbs, Greeks, Bulgarians, and Albanians," a title that fairly represents the wide extent of his rule. As in the case of Timur, however, his kingdom declined after his death in 1355 and disappeared entirely after a defeat by the Ottomans at the battle of Kosovo in 1389.

The Turkic nomads whose descendants established the **Ottoman Empire** came to Anatolia in the same wave of Turkic migrations as the Seljuks (see Chapter 8). Though Il-khan influence was strong in eastern Anatolia, a number of small Turkic principalities emerged in the west. The Ottoman principality was situated in the northwest, close to the Sea of Marmara. This not only put them in a position to cross into Europe and take part in the dynastic struggles of the declining Byzantine state, but it also attracted Muslim religious warriors who wished to do battle with Christians on the frontiers. The defeat of the Ottoman sultan by Timur in 1402 was only a temporary setback. In 1453 Sultan Mehmet II captured Constantinople and brought the Byzantine Empire to an end.

The Ottoman sultans, like the rulers of Russia, Lithuania, and Serbia, seized opportunities that arose with the decay of Mongol power. The powerful states they created put strong emphasis on religious and linguistic identity, factors that the Mongols themselves did not stress. As we shall see, Mongol rule stimulated similar reactions in the lands of East and Southeast Asia.

SECTION REVIEW

- Mongol conquest devastated Kievan Russia, but the Russian language achieved greater importance, and many Russian traditions survived.
- Mongol conquest prompted decentralization of Russian power away from Kiev, but the Golden Horde's decline set the stage for the rise of Russian autocracy.
- The decline of Mongol power and Byzantine weakness enabled the rise of Lithuania and Serbia in eastern Europe and of the Ottoman Empire in Anatolia.

MONGOL DOMINATION IN CHINA, 1271–1368

After conquering northern China in the 1230s, Great Khan Ögödei told a Confucian adviser that he planned to turn the heavily populated North China Plain into a pasture for livestock. The adviser reacted calmly but argued that taxing the cities and villages would bring greater wealth. The Great Khan agreed, but he imposed an oppressive tax-farming system instead of the fixed-rate method traditional to China.

The Chinese suffered under this system during the early years, but the Yuan Empire, established by Genghis Khan's grandson Khubilai in 1271, also brought benefits: secure trade routes; exchange of experts between eastern and western Eurasia; and transmission of information, ideas, and skills.

The Yuan Empire, 1271–1368

Khubilai Khan Last of the Mongol Great Khans (r. 1260–1294) and founder of the Yuan Empire.

lama In Tibetan Buddhism, a teacher.

The Yuan sought a fruitful synthesis of the Mongol and Chinese traditions. **Khubilai Khan** gave his oldest son a Chinese name and had Confucianists participate in the boy's education. In public announcements and the crafting of laws, he took Confucian conventions into consideration. Buddhist and Daoist leaders who visited the Great Khan came away believing that they had all but convinced him of their beliefs.

Buddhist priests from Tibet called **lamas** (LAH-mah) became popular with some Mongol rulers. Their idea of a militant universal ruler bringing the whole world under control of the Buddha and thus pushing it nearer to salvation mirrored an ancient Inner Asian idea of universal rulership.

Beijing as Yuan Capital

Beijing China's northern capital, first used as an imperial capital in 906 and now the capital of the People's Republic of China.

Beijing, the Yuan capital, became the center of cultural and economic life. Karakorum had been geographically remote, but Beijing served as the eastern terminus of caravan routes that began near Tabriz, the Il-khan capital, and (Old) Sarai, the Golden Horde capital. A horseback courier system utilizing hundreds of stations maintained communications along routes that were generally safe for travelers. Ambassadors and merchants arriving in Beijing found a city that was much more Chinese in character than Karakorum had been.

Called Great Capital (Dadu) or City of the Khan (khan-balikh [kahn-BAL-ik], Marco Polo's "Cambaluc"), Khubilai's capital included the Forbidden City, a closed imperial complex with wide streets and a network of linked lakes and artificial islands. In summer, Khubilai practiced riding and shooting at a palace and park in Inner Mongolia. This was Shangdu (shahng-DOO), the "Xanadu" (ZAH-nah-doo) with its "stately pleasure dome" celebrated by the English poet Samuel Taylor Coleridge.

Yuan Society

Before the arrival of the Mongols, three separate states competed in China (see Chapter 10). The Tanggut and Jin Empires controlled the north, and the Southern Song controlled most of the area south of the Yellow River. They had different languages, writing systems, forms of government, and elite cultures. The Great Khans destroyed all three and encouraged the restoration or preservation of many features of Chinese government and society.

By law, Mongols ranked highest. Below them came Central Asians and Middle Easterners, then northern Chinese, and finally southern Chinese. This ranking reflected a hierarchy of functions. The Mongols were the empire's warriors, the Central Asians and Middle Easterners its census takers and tax collectors. The northern Chinese outranked the southern Chinese because they came under Mongol control almost two generations earlier.

Though Khubilai included some "Confucians" (under the Yuan, a formal and hereditary status) in government, their position compared poorly with pre-Mongol times. The Confucians disparaged merchants, many of whom were from the Middle East or Central Asia, and physicians. They regarded doctors as mere technicians or Daoist mystics, but the Yuan encouraged them and began the process of integrating Chinese medical approaches with those contained in Muslim and Hellenistic sources.

Yuan Administration

Like the Il-khans, the Yuan rulers stressed census taking and tax collecting. Persian, Arab, and Uighur administrators staffed the offices of taxation and finance, and Muslim scholars worked at calendar-making and astronomy. The Mongols organized all of China into provinces. Central appointment of provincial governors, tax collectors, and garrison commanders marked a radical change by systematizing control in all parts of the country.

Many cities seem to have prospered: in north China by being on the caravan routes; in the interior by being on the Grand Canal; and along the coast by participation in maritime grain shipments from south China. The reintegration of East Asia (though not Japan) with the overland Eurasian trade, which had lapsed with the fall of the Tang (see Chapter 10), stimulated the urban economies.

Growth of Commerce

With merchants a privileged group, life in the cities changed. So few government posts were open to the old Chinese elite that families that had previously spent fortunes on educating sons for government service sought other opportunities. Many gentry families chose commerce. Corporations—investor groups that behaved as single commercial and legal units and shared the risk of doing business—handled most economic activities, starting with financing caravans and expanding into tax farming and lending money to the Mongol aristocracy. Central Asians and

Middle Easterners headed most corporations in the early Yuan period; but as Chinese bought shares, many acquired mixed membership, or even complete Chinese ownership.

The agricultural base, damaged by war, overtaxation, and the passage of armies, could not satisfy the financial needs of the Mongol aristocracy. Following earlier precedent, the imperial government made up the shortfall with paper money. But people doubted the value of the notes, which were unsecured. Copper coinage partially offset the failure of the paper currency. During the Song, exports of copper to Japan, where the metal was scarce, had caused a severe shortage in China, leading to a rise in the value of copper in relation to silver. By cutting off trade with Japan, the Mongols intentionally or unintentionally stabilized the value of copper coins.

Merchant Tastes

Many gentry families moved from their traditional homes in the countryside to engage in urban commerce as city life began to cater to the tastes of merchants instead of scholars. Specialized shops selling clothing, grape wine, furniture, and religiously butchered meats became common. Teahouses offered sing-song girls, drum singers, operas, and other entertainments previously considered coarse. Writers published works in the style of everyday speech. And the increasing influence of the northern, Mongolian-influenced Chinese language, often called Mandarin in the West, resulted in lasting linguistic change.

Agriculture

Cottage industries linked to the urban economies dotted the countryside, where 90 percent of the people lived. Some villages cultivated mulberry trees and cotton using dams, water wheels, and irrigation systems patterned in part on Middle Eastern models. Treatises on planting, harvesting, threshing, and butchering were published. One technological innovator, Huang Dao Po (hwahng DOW poh), brought knowledge of cotton growing, spinning, and weaving from her native Hainan Island to the fertile Yangzi Delta.

Yet on the whole, the countryside did poorly during the Yuan period. Initially, the Mongol princes evicted many farmers and subjected the rest to brutal tax collection. By the time the Yuan shifted to lighter taxes and encouragement of farming at the end of the 1200s, it was too late. Servitude or homelessness had overtaken many farmers. Neglect of dams and dikes caused disastrous flooding, particularly on the Yellow River.

Population Loss

According to Song records from before the Mongol conquest and the Ming census taken after their overthrow—each, of course, subject to inaccuracy or exaggeration—China's population may have shrunk by 40 percent during eighty years of Mongol rule, with many localities in northern China losing up to five-sixths of their inhabitants. Scholars have suggested several causes: prolonged warfare, rural distress causing people to resort to female infanticide, bubonic plague, a southward flight of refugees, and flooding on the Yellow River. The last helps explain why losses in the north exceeded those in the south and why the population along the Yangzi River markedly increased.

SECTION REVIEW

- The Great Khans reunified China and fostered a synthesis of ideas and cultural traditions.
- Khubilai Khan made Beijing the capital of the Yuan Empire and presided over a social hierarchy with Mongols at the top and southern Chinese at the bottom.
- Mongol rule systematized government, but cities benefited more from Mongol policies than did the countryside.
- China's population shrank as a result of Mongol conquest and rule.
- Mongol-protected trade routes encouraged a steady exchange of scientific and cultural ideas.
- Internal strife weakened the Yuan Empire, which fell to the Ming in 1368, but many Mongols remained in China.

The Fall of the Yuan Empire

In the 1340s strife broke out among the Mongol princes. Within twenty years farmer rebellions and inter-Mongol feuds engulfed the land. Amidst the chaos, a charismatic Chinese leader, Zhu Yuanzhang (JOO yuwen-JAHNG), mounted a campaign that destroyed the Yuan Empire and brought China under control of his new empire, the Ming, in 1368. Many Mongols—as well as the Muslims, Jews, and Christians who had come with them—remained in China. Most of their descendants took Chinese names and became part of the diverse cultural world of China.

Many other Mongols, however, had never moved out of their home territories in Mongolia. Now they welcomed back refugees from the Yuan collapse. Though Turkic peoples were becoming predominant in the steppe regions in the west, including territories still ruled by descendants of Genghis Khan, Mongols continued to predominate in Inner Asia, the steppe regions bordering on Mongolia. Some Mongol groups adopted Islam; others favored Tibetan Buddhism. But religious affiliation proved less important than Mongol identity in fostering a renewed sense of unity.

The Ming thus fell short of dominating all the Mongols. The Mongols of Inner Asia paid tribute to the extent that doing so facilitated their trade. Other Mongols, however, remained a continuing threat on the northern Ming frontier.

THE EARLY MING EMPIRE, 1368–1500

Ming Empire Empire based in China that Zhu Yuanzhang established after the overthrow of the Yuan Empire. The Ming emperor Yongle sponsored the building of the Forbidden City and the voyages of Zheng He. The later years of the Ming saw a slowdown in technological development and economic decline.

Historians of China, like historians of Russia and Iran, divide over the overall impact of the Mongol era. Since the **Ming Empire** reestablished many practices that are seen as purely Chinese, it receives praise from people who ascribe central importance to Chinese traditions. On the other hand, historians who look upon the Mongol era as a pivotal historical moment when communication across the vast interior of Eurasia served to bring east and west together sometimes see the inward-looking Ming as less productive than the Yuan.

Ming China on a Mongol Foundation

Zhu Yuanzhang, a former monk, soldier, and bandit, had watched his parents and other family members die of famine and disease, conditions he blamed on Mongol misrule. During the Yuan Empire's chaotic last decades, he vanquished rival rebels and assumed imperial power under the name Hongwu (r. 1368–1398).

Emperor Hongwu

AP* Exam Tip The rise of the Ming Empire is important information for the exam.

Hongwu moved the capital to Nanjing (nahn-JING) ("southern capital") on the Yangzi River, turning away from the Mongol's Beijing ("northern capital"; see Map 12.3). Though Zhu Yuanzhang the rebel had espoused a radical Buddhist belief in a coming age of salvation, once in power he used Confucianism to depict the emperor as the champion of civilization and virtue.

Hongwu choked off relations with Central Asia and the Middle East and imposed strict limits on imports and foreign visitors. Silver replaced paper money for tax payments and commerce. These practices, illustrative of an anti-Mongol ideology, proved as economically unhealthy as some of the Yuan economic policies and did not last. Eventually, the Ming government came to resemble the Yuan. Ming rulers retained the provincial structure and continued to observe the hereditary professional categories of the Yuan period. Muslims made calendars and astronomical calculations at a new observatory at Nanjing, a replica of Khubilai's at Beijing. The Mongol calendar continued in use.

Yongle The third emperor of the Ming Empire (r. 1403–1424). He sponsored the building of the Forbidden City, a huge encyclopedia project, the expeditions of Zheng He, and the reopening of China's borders to trade and travel.

Continuities with the Yuan became more evident after an imperial prince seized power through a coup d'état to rule as the emperor **Yongle** (yoong-LAW) (r. 1403–1424). He returned the capital to Beijing, enlarging and improving Khubilai's Forbidden City, which now acquired its present features: moats, orange-red outer walls, golden roofs, and marble bridges. Yongle intended this combination fortress, religious site, bureaucratic center, and imperial residential park to overshadow Nanjing, and it survives today as China's most imposing traditional architectural complex.

Emperor Yongle

Explorer Zheng He

Yongle also restored commercial links with the Middle East. Because hostile Mongols still controlled much of the caravan route, Yongle explored maritime connections. In Southeast Asia, Annam became a Ming province as the early emperors continued the Mongol program of aggression. This focus on the southern frontier helped inspire the naval expeditions of the trusted imperial eunuch **Zheng He** (JEHNG HUH) from 1405 to 1433.

Zheng He An imperial eunuch and Muslim, entrusted by the Ming emperor Yongle with a series of state voyages that took his gigantic ships through the Indian Ocean, from Southeast Asia to Africa.

A Muslim whose father and grandfather had made the pilgrimage to Mecca, Zheng He had a good knowledge of the Middle East; and his religion eased relations with the states of the Indian subcontinent, where he directed his first three voyages. Subsequent expeditions reached Hormuz on the Persian Gulf, sailed the southern coast of Arabia and the Horn of Africa (modern Somalia), and possibly reached as far south as the Strait of Madagascar.

End of Ming Sea Expeditions

On early voyages Zheng He visited long-established Chinese merchant communities in Southeast Asia in order to cement their allegiance to the Ming Empire and to collect taxes. When

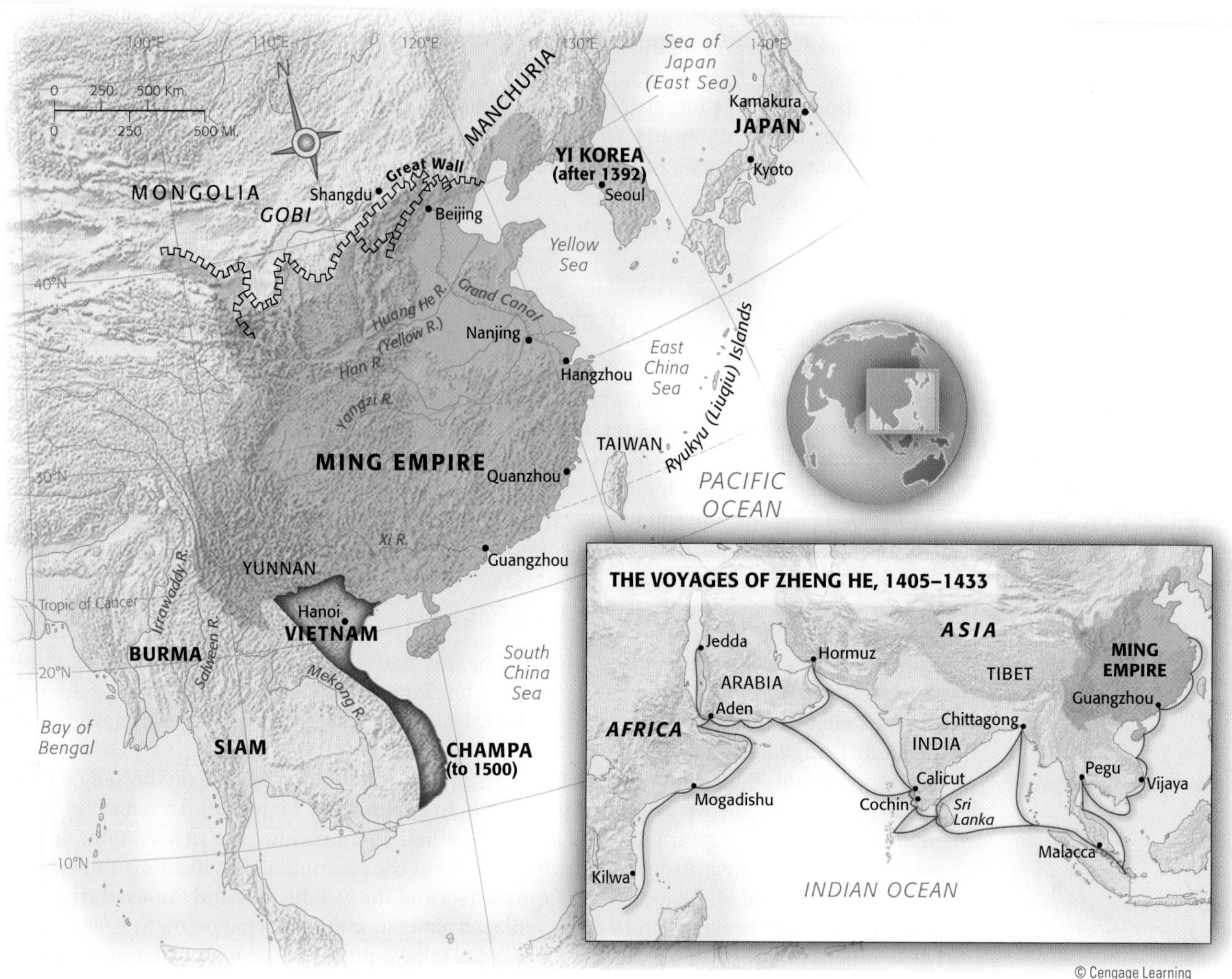

MAP 12.3 The Ming Empire and Its Allies, 1368–1500 The Ming Empire controlled China but had a hostile relationship with peoples in Mongolia and Inner Asia who had been under the rule of the Mongol Yuan emperors. Mongol attempts at conquest by sea were continued by the Ming mariner Zheng He. Between 1405 and 1433 he sailed to Southeast Asia and then beyond, to India, the Persian Gulf, and East Africa.

e Interactive Map

a community on the island of Sumatra resisted, he slaughtered the men to set an example. The expeditions added some fifty new tributary states to the Ming imperial universe, but trade did not increase as dramatically. Sporadic embassies reached Beijing from rulers in India, the Middle East, Africa, and Southeast Asia. During one visit the ruler of Brunei (broo-NIE) died and received a grand burial at the Chinese capital. The expeditions stopped in the 1430s after the deaths of Yongle and Zheng He.

Why did the Chinese not develop seafaring for commercial and military gain? Contemporaries considered the voyages a personal project of Yongle, an upstart ruler who had always sought to prove his worthiness. Building the Forbidden City in Beijing and sponsoring gigantic encyclopedia projects might be taken to reflect a similar character. Yongle may also have been emulating Khubilai Khan's sea expeditions against Japan and Southeast Asia. This would fit with the rumor spread by Yongle's political enemies that he was actually a Mongol.

A less speculative approach starts with the fact that the new commercial opportunities fell short of expectations, despite bringing foreign nations into the Ming orbit. In the meantime, Japanese coastal piracy intensified, and Mongol threats in the north and west grew. The human and financial demands of fortifying the north, redesigning and strengthening Beijing, and outfitting campaigns against the Mongols ultimately took priority over the quest for maritime empire.

Technology and Population

Technological Slowdown

The Ming government limited mining, partly to keep the value of metal coins and partly to tax the industry. As a consequence, metal implements became more expensive for farmers. Techniques for making the high-quality bronze and steel used for weapons also declined. Japan quickly surpassed China in the production of extremely high-quality swords.

After the death of Emperor Yongle in 1424, shipbuilding skills deteriorated, and few advances occurred in printing, timekeeping, and agricultural technology. Agricultural production peaked around the mid-1400s and remained level for more than a century. New weaving techniques did appear, but technological development in this field had peaked by 1500.

Population Growth and Agriculture

Reactivation of the examination system for recruiting government officials (see Chapter 10) drew large numbers of ambitious men into a renewed study of the Confucian classics. This reduced the vitality of commerce, where they had previously been employed, just as population growth was creating a labor surplus. Records indicating a growth from 60 million at the end of the Yuan period in 1368 to nearly 100 million by 1400 may not be entirely reliable, but rapid population growth encouraged the production of staples—wheat, millet, and barley in the north and rice in the south—at the expense of commercial crops such as cotton that had stimulated many technological innovations under the Song. Staple crops yielded lower profits, which further discouraged capital improvements. New foods, such as sweet potatoes, became available but were little adopted. Population growth in southern and central China caused deforestation and raised the price of wood.

Military Technology

Against the Mongol horsemen in the north the Ming used scattershot mortars and explosive canisters. They even used a few cannon, which they knew about from contacts with the Middle East and later with Europeans (see Environment and Technology: From Gunpowder to Guns). Fearing a loss of technological secrets, the government censored the chapters on gunpowder

Examination Cells Students taking examinations on the Confucian classics to gain admission to the class of officials occupied these cells for 24 to 72 hours, depending on the level they were attempting. In the city of Guangdong there were 7,500 cells in long rows. Candidates were identified only by number, and their essays were rewritten to prevent their handwriting being recognized. Approximately 5 percent of the candidates passed the examination.

Courtesy, Church Mission Society, London

ENVIRONMENT + TECHNOLOGY

From Gunpowder to Guns

Long before the invention of guns, gunpowder was used in China and Korea to excavate mines, build canals, and channel irrigation. Alchemists in China used related formulas to make noxious gas pellets to paralyze enemies and expel evil spirits. A more realistic benefit was eliminating disease-carrying insects, a critical aid to the colonization of malarial regions in China and Southeast Asia. The Mongol Empire staged fireworks displays on ceremonial occasions, delighting European visitors to Karakorum who saw them for the first time.

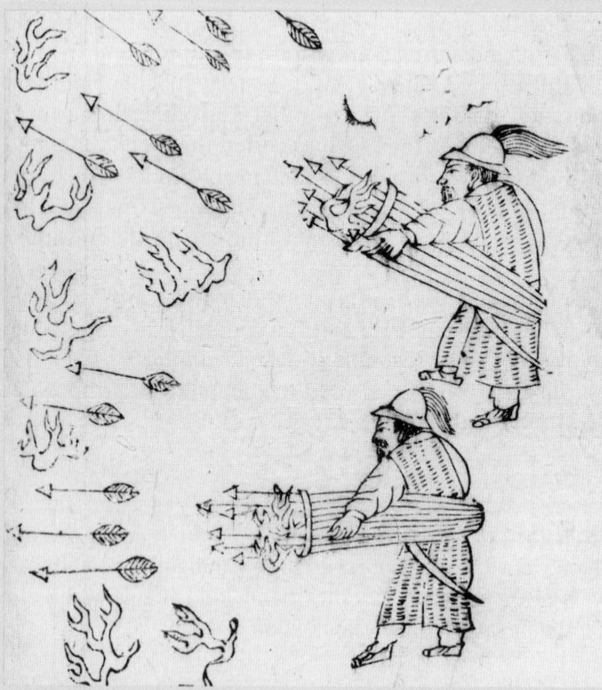

Launching Flaming Arrows Song soldiers used gunpowder to launch flaming arrows.

Anecdotal evidence in Chinese records gives credit for the introduction of gunpowder to a Sogdian Buddhist monk of the 500s. The monk described the wondrous alchemical transformation of elements produced by a combination of charcoal and saltpeter. In this connection he also mentioned sulfur. The distillation of naphtha, a light, flammable derivative of oil or coal, seems also to have been first developed in Central Asia, the earliest evidence coming from the Gandhara region (in modern Pakistan).

By the eleventh century, the Chinese had developed flamethrowers powered by burning naphtha, sulfur, or gunpowder in a long tube. These weapons intimidated and injured foot soldiers and horses and also set fire to thatched roofs in hostile villages and, occasionally, the rigging of enemy ships.

In their long struggle against the Mongols, the Song learned to enrich saltpeter to increase the amount of nitrate in gunpowder. This produced forceful explosions rather than jets of fire. Launched from catapults, gunpowder-filled canisters could rupture fortifications and inflict mass casualties. Explosives hurled from a distance could sink or burn ships.

The Song also experimented with firing projectiles from metal gun barrels. The earliest gun barrels were broad and squat and were transported on special wagons to their emplacements. The mouths of the barrels projected saltpeter mixed with scattershot minerals. The Chinese and then the Koreans adapted gunpowder to shooting masses of arrows—sometimes flaming—at enemy fortifications.

In 1280 weapons makers of the Yuan Empire produced the first device featuring a projectile that completely filled the mouth of the cannon and thus concentrated the explosive force. The Yuan used cast bronze for the barrel and iron for the cannonball. The new weapon shot farther and more accurately, and was much more destructive, than the earlier Song devices.

Knowledge of the cannon and cannonball moved westward across Eurasia. By the end of the thirteenth century cannon were being produced in the Middle East. By 1327 small, squat cannon called "bombards" were being used in Europe.

and guns in early Ming encyclopedias. Shipyards and ports shut down to avoid contact with Japanese pirates and to prevent Chinese from migrating to Southeast Asia.

A technology gap with Korea and Japan opened up nevertheless. When superior steel was needed, supplies came from Japan. Korea moved ahead of China in the design and production of firearms and ships, in printing techniques, and in the sciences of weather prediction and calendar-making. The desire to tap the wealthy Ming market spurred some of these advances.

The Ming Achievement

Chinese Novels

In the late 1300s and the 1400s the wealth and consumerism of the early Ming stimulated high achievement in literature, the decorative arts, and painting. The plain writing of the Yuan period had produced some of the world's earliest novels. This genre flourished under the Ming. *Water Margin*, which originated in the raucous drum-song performances loosely related to Chinese opera, features dashing Chinese bandits who struggle against Mongol rule. Many authors had a hand in the final print version.

Luo Guanzhong (law gwahn-joong), one of the authors of *Water Margin*, is also credited with *Romance of the Three Kingdoms*, based on a much older series of stories that in some ways resemble the Arthurian legends. It describes the attempts of an upright but doomed war leader and his followers to restore the Han Empire of ancient times and resist the power of the cynical but brilliant villain. *Romance of the Three Kingdoms* and *Water Margin* express the militant but joyous pro-China sentiment of the early Ming era and remain among the most appreciated Chinese fictional works.

Probably the best-known product of Ming technological advance was porcelain. The imperial ceramic works at Jingdezhen (JING-deh-JUHN) experimented with new production techniques and new ways of organizing and rationalizing workers. "Ming ware," a blue-on-white style developed in the 1400s from Indian, Central Asian, and Middle Eastern motifs, became especially prized. Other Ming goods in high demand included furniture, lacquered screens, and silk, all of which found ready markets in Southeast Asia and the Pacific, India, the Middle East, and East Africa.

SECTION REVIEW

- The first Ming emperor, Hongwu, based his policies on an anti-Mongol ideology, but the Ming government came to adopt Yuan practices.
- Yongle reestablished international commerce and sent Zheng He to explore maritime connections to the Middle East.
- Technological innovation continued, but with less frequent advances and reduced output, and some techniques became guarded secrets.
- The Ming reestablished the Confucian examination system, reducing the vitality of commerce.
- The greatest Ming achievements were in literature, the arts, and porcelain production.

CENTRALIZATION AND MILITARISM IN EAST ASIA, 1200–1500

Korea, Japan, and Annam, the other major states of East Asia, were all affected by confrontation with the Mongols, but with differing results. Japan and Annam escaped Mongol conquest but changed in response to the Mongol threat, becoming more effective and expansive regimes with enhanced commitments to independence.

AP* Exam Tip Make sure you understand the influence of China on surrounding areas.

As for Korea, just as the Ming stressed Chinese traditions and identity in the aftermath of Yuan rule, so Mongol domination contributed to revitalized interest in Korea's own language and history. The Mongols conquered Korea after a difficult war, and though Korea suffered socially and economically under Mongol rule, members of the elite associated closely with the Yuan Empire. After the fall of the Yuan, merchants continued the international connections established in the Mongol period, while Korean armies consolidated a new kingdom and fended off pirates.

Korea from the Mongols to the Yi, 1231–1500

Mongol Conquest

Korea was the answer to the Mongol search for coastal areas from which to launch naval expeditions and choke off the sea trade of their adversaries. When the Mongols attacked in 1231, the leader of a prominent Korean family assumed the role of military commander and protector of the king (not unlike the shoguns of Japan). Twenty years of defensive war left a ravaged countryside, exhausted armies, and burned treasures, including the renowned nine-story pagoda at Hwangnyong-sa (hwahng-NEEYAHNG-sah) and the wooden printing blocks of the Tripitaka (tri-PIH-tah-kah), a ninth-century masterpiece of printing art. The commander's underlings

Movable Type The improvement of cast bronze tiles, each showing a single character, eliminated the need to cast or carve whole pages. Individual tiles—the ones shown are Korean—could be moved from page frame to page frame and gave an even and pleasing appearance. All parts of East Asia eventually adopted this form of printing for cheap, popular books. In the mid-1400s Korea also experimented with a fully phonetic form of writing, which in combination with movable type allowed Koreans unprecedented levels of literacy and access to printed works.

Courtesy, Yushin Yoo

killed him in 1258. Soon afterward the Koryo (KAW-ree-oh) king surrendered to the Mongols and became a subject monarch by linking his family to the Great Khan by marriage.

By the mid-1300s the Koryo kings were of mostly Mongol descent and favored Mongol dress, customs, and language. The kings, their families, and their entourages often traveled between China and Korea, thus exposing Korea to the philosophical and artistic styles of Yuan China: neo-Confucianism, Chan Buddhism (called Seon in Korea), and celadon (light green) pottery.

Breakdown of Isolation

Mongol control broke down centuries of comparative isolation. Cotton was introduced in southern Korea; gunpowder came into use; and the art of calendar-making stimulated astronomical observation and mathematics. Avenues of advancement opened for Korean scholars willing to learn Mongolian, landowners willing to open their lands to falconry and grazing, and merchants servicing the new royal exchanges with Beijing. These developments contributed to the rise of a new landed and educated class.

Yi Dynasty

Yi The Yi dynasty ruled Korea from the fall of the Koryo kingdom to the colonization of Korea by Japan.

When the Yuan Empire fell in 1368, the Koryo ruling family remained loyal to the Mongols and had to be forced to recognize the new Ming Empire. In 1392 the **Yi** (YEE) established a new kingdom with a capital in Seoul and sought to reestablish a distinctive Korean identity. Like Russia and Ming China, the Yi regime publicly rejected the period of Mongol domination. Yet the Yi government continued to employ Mongol-style land surveys, taxation in kind, and military garrison techniques.

Like the Ming emperors, the Yi kings revived the study of the Confucian classics, an activity that required knowledge of Chinese and showed the dedication of the state to learning. This revival may have led to a key technological breakthrough in printing technology.

Korean Printing

Koreans had begun using Chinese woodblock printing in the 700s. This technology worked well in China, where a large number of buyers wanted copies of a comparatively small number of texts. But in Korea, the comparatively few literate men had interests in a wide range of texts. Movable wooden or ceramic type appeared in Korea in the early thirteenth century and may have been invented there. But the texts were frequently inaccurate and difficult to read. In the 1400s Yi printers, working directly with the king, developed a reliable device to anchor the pieces of type to the printing plate: they replaced the old beeswax adhesive with solid copper frames. This improved the legibility of the printed page, and high-volume, accurate production became possible. Combined with the phonetic han'gul (HAHN-goor) writing system, this printing technology laid the foundation for a high literacy rate in Korea.

Yi publications told readers how to produce and use fertilizer, tran engineer reservoirs. Building on Eurasian knowledge imported by th under the Koryo, Yi scholars developed a meteorological science of tl redesigned instruments to measure wind speed and rainfall and per minute comparisons of the Chinese and Islamic systems.

Cotton and Gunpowder

In agriculture, farmers expanded the cultivation of cash crops, t... pening in Ming China. Cotton, the primary crop, enjoyed such high value that the sta... it for tax payments. The Yi army used cotton uniforms, and cotton became the favored fabric of the Korean elite. With cotton gins and spinning wheels powered by water, Korea advanced more rapidly than China in mechanization and began to export considerable amounts of cotton to China and Japan.

Although both the Yuan and the Ming withheld the formula for gunpowder from the Korean government, Korean officials acquired the information by subterfuge. By the later 1300s they had mounted cannon on ships that patrolled against pirates and used gunpowder-driven arrow launchers against enemy personnel and the rigging of enemy ships. Combined with skills in armoring ships, these techniques made the small Yi navy a formidable defense force.

Political Transformation in Japan, 1274–1500

Mongol Attacks

Having secured Korea, the Mongols looked toward Japan, a target they could easily reach from Korea. Their first thirty-thousand-man invasion force in 1274 included Mongol cavalry and archers and sailors from Korea and northeastern Asia. Its weaponry included light catapults and incendiary and explosive projectiles of Chinese manufacture. The Mongol forces landed successfully and decimated the Japanese cavalry, but a great storm on Hakata (HAH-kah-tah) Bay on the north side of Kyushu (KYOO-shoo) Island (see Map 12.4) prevented the establishment of a beachhead and forced the Mongols to sail back to Korea.

Kamakura Shogunate

The invasion hastened social and political changes that were already under way. Under the Kamakura (kah-mah-KOO-rah) Shogunate established in 1185—another powerful family actually exercised control—the shogun, or military leader, distributed land and privileges to his followers. In return they paid him tribute and supplied him with soldiers. This stable, but decentralized, system depended on balancing the power of regional warlords. Lords in the north and east of Japan's main island were remote from those in the south and west. Beyond devotion to the emperor and the shogun, little united them until the terrifying Mongol threat materialized.

After the return of his fleet, Khubilai sent envoys to Japan demanding submission. Japanese leaders executed them and prepared for war. The shogun took steps to centralize his military government. The effect was to increase the influence of warlords from the south and west of Honshu (Japan's main island) and from the island of Kyushu, because this was where invasion seemed most likely, and they were the local commanders acting under the shogun's orders.

Military planners studied Mongol tactics and retrained and outfitted Japanese warriors for defense against advanced weaponry. Farm laborers drafted from all over the country constructed defensive fortifications. This effort demanded, for the first time, a national system to move resources toward western points rather than toward the imperial or shogunal centers to the east.

Kamikaze: "Divine Wind"

The Mongols attacked in 1281. They brought 140,000 warriors, including many non-Mongols, as well as thousands of horses, in hundreds of ships. However, the wall the Japanese had built to cut off Hakata Bay from the mainland deprived the Mongol forces of a reliable landing point. Japanese swordsmen rowed out and boarded the Mongol ships lingering offshore. Their superb steel swords shocked the invaders. After a prolonged standoff, a typhoon struck and sank perhaps half of the Mongol ships. The remainder sailed away, never again to harass Japan. The Japanese gave thanks to the "wind of the Gods"—***kamikaze*** (KUM-i-kuh-zee)—for driving away the Mongols.

kamikaze The "divine wind," which the Japanese credited with blowing Mongol invaders away from their shores in 1281.

Nevertheless, the Mongol threat continued to influence Japanese development. Prior to his death in 1294, Khubilai had in mind a third invasion. His successors did not carry through with it, but the shoguns did not know that the Mongols had given up the idea. They rebuilt coastal defenses well into the fourteenth century, helping to consolidate the social position of Japan's warrior elite and stimulating the development of a national infrastructure for trade and commu-

Interactive Map

MAP 12.4 Korea and Japan, 1200–1500 The proximity of Korea and northern China to Japan gave the Mongols the opportunity to launch enormous fleets against the Kamakura Shogunate, which controlled most of the three islands (Honshu, Shikoku, and Kyushu) of central Japan.

nication. But the Kamakura Shogunate, based on regionally collected and regionally dispersed revenues, suffered financial strain in trying to pay for centralized road and defense systems.

Ashikaga Shogunate

Ashikaga Shogunate The second of Japan's military governments headed by a shogun (a military ruler). Sometimes called the Muromachi Shogunate.

Between 1333 and 1338 the emperor Go-Daigo broke the centuries-old tradition of imperial seclusion and aloofness from government and tried to reclaim power from the shoguns. This ignited a civil war that destroyed the Kamakura system. In 1338, with the Mongol threat waning, the **Ashikaga** (ah-shee-KAH-gah) **Shogunate** took control at the imperial center of Kyoto.

Provincial warlords enjoyed renewed independence. Around their imposing castles, they sponsored the development of market towns, religious institutions, and schools. The application of technologies imported in earlier periods, including water wheels, improved plows, and Champa rice, increased agricultural productivity.

Zen Buddhism

Growing wealth and relative peace stimulated artistic creativity, mostly reflecting Zen Buddhist beliefs held by the warrior elite. In the simple elegance of architecture and gardens, in the contemplative landscapes of artists, and in the eerie, stylized performances of the Noh theater, the aesthetic code of Zen became established in the Ashikaga era.

Onin War

Despite the technological advancement, artistic productivity, and rapid urbanization of this period, competition among warlords and their followers led to regional wars. By the later 1400s these conflicts resulted in the near destruction of the warlords. The great Onin War in 1477 left Kyoto devastated and the Ashikaga Shogunate a central government in name only. Ambitious but low-ranking warriors, some with links to trade with the continent, began to scramble for control of the provinces.

After the fall of the Yuan in 1368 Japan resumed overseas trade, exporting raw materials and swords, as well as folding fans, invented in Japan during the period of isolation. Japan's primary imports from China were books and porcelain. The volatile political environment in Japan gave rise to partnerships between warlords and local merchants. All worked to strengthen their own towns and treasuries through overseas commerce or, sometimes, through piracy.

The Emergence of Vietnam, 1200–1500

Annam and Champa

Before the first Mongol attack in 1257, the states of Annam (northern Vietnam) and Champa (southern Vietnam) had clashed frequently. Annam (once called Dai Viet) looked toward China and had once been subject to the Tang. Chinese political ideas, social philosophies, dress, religion, and language heavily influenced its official culture. Champa related more closely to the trading networks of the Indian Ocean; its official culture was strongly influenced by Indian religion, language, architecture, and dress. Champa's relationship with China depended in part on how close its enemy Annam was to China at any particular time. During the Song period Annam was neither formally subject to China nor particularly threatening to Champa militarily, so Champa inaugurated a trade and tribute relationship with China that spread fast-ripening Champa rice throughout East Asia.

Annam's Victory

The Mongols exacted tribute from both Annam and Champa until the fall of the Yuan Empire in 1368. Mongol political and military ambitions were mostly focused elsewhere, however, which minimized their impact on politics and culture. The two Vietnamese kingdoms soon resumed their warfare. When Annam moved its army to reinforce its southern border, Ming troops occu-

Noh Drama Performance This slow, rhythmic, chanted form of drama appealed to the military elite with its stories of warriors, women, gods, and demons. The minimal stage is normally bare except for a painting at the rear of a pine tree, symbolizing the means by which deities descend to earth, and a narrow bridge to the left by which major actors enter the stage. The actors wear masks and lavish costumes. Four instrumentalists playing a flute and three types of drum punctuate the chanting.

pied the capital, Hanoi, and installed a puppet government. Almost thirty years elapsed before Annam regained independence and resumed a tributary status. By then the Ming were turning to meet Mongol challenges to their north. In a series of ruthless campaigns, Annam terminated Champa's independence, and by 1500 the ancestor of the modern state of Vietnam, still called Annam, had been born.

The new state still relied on Confucian bureaucratic government and an examination system, but some practices differed from those in China. The Vietnamese legal code, for example, preserved group landowning and decision making within the villages, as well as women's property rights. Both developments probably had roots in an early rural culture based on the growing of rice in wet paddies; by this time the Annamese considered them distinctive features of their own culture.

SECTION REVIEW

- Mongol conquest devastated Korea, but Mongol rule opened it to new ideas and technologies.
- The Yi dynasty succeeded the Koryo and fostered local identity while encouraging economic expansion and technological innovation.
- In Japan, the Mongol threat forced military and organizational innovations, but the expense of these defenses weakened the Kamakura Shogunate.
- Go-Daigo's failed attempt to reassert imperial power resulted in the rise of the Ashikaga Shogunate.
- The warring states of Vietnam avoided Mongol conquest but paid tribute to the Yuan Empire.
- After the Ming withdrawal, Annam conquered Champa, establishing a unified state on both Confucian and local practices.

CONCLUSION

Despite their brutality and devastation, the Mongol conquests brought a degree of unity to the lands between China and Europe that had never before been known. Nomadic mobility and expertise in military technology contributed to communication across vast spaces and initially, at least, an often-callous disregard for the welfare of farmers, as manifested in oppressive tax policies. By contrast, trade received active Mongol stimulation through the protection of routes and encouragement of industrial production.

The Mongols ruled with an unprecedented openness, employing talented people irrespective of their linguistic, ethnic, or religious affiliations. As a consequence, the period of comparative Mongol unity, which lasted less than a century, saw a remarkable exchange of ideas, techniques, and products across the breadth of Eurasia. Chinese gunpowder spurred the development of Ottoman and European cannon; Muslim astronomers introduced new instruments and mathematical techniques to Chinese observatories.

However, rule over dozens of restive peoples could not endure. Where Mongol military enterprise reached its limit of expansion, it stimulated local aspirations for independence. Division and hostility among branches of Genghis Khan's family—between the Yuan in China and the Jagadai in Central Asia or between the Golden Horde in Russia and the Il-khans in Iran—provided opportunities for achieving these aspirations. The Russians gained freedom from Mongol domination in western Eurasia, and the general political disruption and uncertainty of the Mongol era assisted the emergence of the Lithuanian, Serbian, and Ottoman states.

In the east, China, Korea, and Annam similarly found renewed political identity in the aftermath of Mongol rule, while Japan fought off two Mongol invasions and transformed its internal political and cultural identity in the process. In every case, the reality or threat of Mongol attack and domination encouraged centralization of government, improvement of military techniques, and renewed stress on local cultural identity. Thus, in retrospect, despite its traditional association with death and destruction, the Mongol period appears as a watershed, establishing new connections between widespread parts of Eurasia and leading to the development of strong, assertive, and culturally creative regional states.

KEY TERMS

Mongols p. 341
Genghis Khan p. 341
nomadism p. 342
Yuan Empire p. 344
bubonic plague p. 348
Il-khan p. 349
Golden Horde p. 349
Timur p. 350
Rashid al-Din p. 351
Nasir al-Din Tusi p. 352
Alexander Nevskii p. 354
tsar p. 354
Ottoman Empire p. 356
Khubilai Khan p. 357
lama p. 357
Beijing p. 357
Ming Empire p. 359
Yongle p. 359
Zheng He p. 359
Yi p. 364
kamikaze p. 365
Ashikaga Shogunate p. 366

EBOOK AND WEBSITE RESOURCES

Interactive Maps

Map 12.1 The Mongol Domains in Eurasia in 1300

Map 12.2 Western Eurasia in the 1300s

Map 12.3 The Ming Empire and Its Allies, 1368–1500

Map 12.4 Korea and Japan, 1200–1500

Plus flashcards, practice quizzes, and more. Go to: www.cengage.com/history/bullietearthpeople5e

SUGGESTED READING

Adshead, S. A. M. *Central Asia in World History.* 1993. Central Asia after the conquests.

Allsen, Thomas T. *Commodity and Exchange in the Mongol Empire: A Cultural History of Islamic Textiles.* 2002. A look at exchange on the Silk Road.

Allsen, Thomas T. *Culture and Conquest in Mongol Eurasia.* 2001. A careful study of comparative practices in Mongol China and Iran.

Christian, David. *A History of Russia, Central Asia, and Mongolia.* 1998. A one-volume account of the Mongols in Russia.

Frank, André Gunder. *ReORIENT: Global Economy in the Asian Age.* 1998. An important interpretation of Ming economic achievement.

Hall, John W., and Toyoda Takeshi, eds. *Japan in the Muromachi Age.* 1977. History of a period of civil war.

Henthorn, William E. *Korea: The Mongol Invasions.* 1963. A less emphasized aspect of Mongol history.

Jackson, Peter. *The Mongols and the West: 1221–1410.* 2005. Europe's encounter with the Mongols.

Keene, Donald. *Yoshimasa and the Silver Pavilion: The Creation of the Soul of Japan.* 2003. A delightful introduction to the cultural changes of the fourteenth century.

Levathes, Louise. *When China Ruled the Seas.* 1993. Popular account of the voyages of Zheng He.

Manz, Beatrice Forbes. *The Rise and Rule of Tamerlane.* 1989. The most recent scholarly study of Timur.

McNeill, William H. *Plagues and Peoples.* 1976. Discusses the demographic effects of the Mongol conquests.

Mokyr, Joel. *The Lever of Riches: Technological Creativity and Economic Progress.* 1990. Looks at comparative technological developments across Eurasia.

Morgan, David. *The Mongols.* 1986. An accessible introduction to the Mongol Empire.

Rossabi, Morris. *Khubilai Khan: His Life and Times.* 1988. China under Mongol rule.

NOTES

1. Quotation adapted from Desmond Martin, *Chingis Khan and His Conquest of North China* (Baltimore: The John Hopkins Press, 1950), 303.

AP* REVIEW QUESTIONS FOR CHAPTER 12

1. One benefit of the size of the Mongol Empire was that
   (A) it was easier to force all people to speak one language.
   (B) religious homogeneity was easier to establish.
   (C) it promoted the movement of people, ideas, and goods.
   (D) it promoted the development of ethnic identity.

2. Under Khubilai Khan
   (A) the Mongol Empire expanded to include Vietnam, Korea, and part of Japan.
   (B) the Mughal Empire was founded in India.
   (C) the Yuan dynasty was founded in China.
   (D) Islam became the dominant religion of the empire.

3. The Mongol leader Timur
   (A) gained control of much of the Middle East but never assumed the title of *khan.*
   (B) conquered the Delhi Sultanate and the Ottoman Empire but never conquered the Golden Horde.
   (C) became a Sunni scholar and retired to live in Mecca.
   (D) most likely was a fictional character because there is little evidence of his life.

4. The achievements of Nasir al-Din are evidence of
   (A) the Mongols encouraging the continuation of science and learning.
   (B) Muslim interference in the governing of Mongol lands.
   (C) expansion of Mongol conquests in North Africa.
   (D) Korean adaptation of Muslim culture.

5. Which of the following is true of the Golden Horde?
   (A) They refused to pay tribute to Batu.
   (B) They began as a unified state but soon fragmented.
   (C) Their low taxes encouraged the growth of business and trade.
   (D) They adopted Orthodox Christianity as their faith and assimilated with the Russians.

6. Overall, Mongol rule in Russia
   (A) was devastating because of warfare, raiding, tax collection, and the spread of disease.
   (B) encouraged the growth of long-distance trade and brought Russia wealth in the long run.
   (C) encouraged the Russians to seek alliances with the Ottomans to force the Mongols out of Russia.
   (D) was harmful to all places except the city of Kiev.

7. Understanding the history of the Yuan dynasty is difficult because
   (A) Mongol writing is difficult to translate accurately.
   (B) much of the recorded history was destroyed by Chinese scholars who despised the Mongols.
   (C) the best records come from European travelers, like Polo, who wrote with a European point of view.
   (D) the vast majority of what we have are commercial records and very few details of social history.

8. Hongwu, the founder of the Ming dynasty,
   (A) kept many of the Mongol practices in place.
   (B) established his power base in northern China by making an alliance with the Khitans.
   (C) used Confucianism to help solidify his power and control in China.
   (D) was the only emperor who was a eunuch.

9. Under Ming leadership, China
   (A) encouraged naval expeditions into the Indian Ocean.
   (B) destroyed the Korean army, conquering Korea and Japan.
   (C) began to develop its mining capabilities and improve its smelting of steel.
   (D) abolished the practice of footbinding.

10. During the Koryo period, Korean kings were

    (A) interested in new ways of governing and sought advice from Japan.
    (B) mainly Mongol in descent and favored Mongol dress and customs.
    (C) strong allies of the Ming Chinese.
    (D) descended from the Japanese emperors and strongly disliked the Ming Chinese.

11. With the establishment of the Ming dynasty in China, Japan

    (A) began to fear renewed attacks from China.
    (B) allied with Korea and the Taiwanese against China.
    (C) reopened trade with China.
    (D) adopted the Confucian examination system for its bureaucracy.

12. The culture of the southern portion of today's Vietnam has been strongly influenced by

    (A) China.
    (B) India.
    (C) Japan.
    (D) Indonesia.

CHAPTER

13

CHAPTER OUTLINE

- Tropical Lands and Peoples
- New Islamic Empires
- Indian Ocean Trade
- Social and Cultural Change
- Conclusion

DIVERSITY + DOMINANCE *Personal Styles of Rule in India and Mali*

ENVIRONMENT + TECHNOLOGY *The Indian Ocean Dhow*

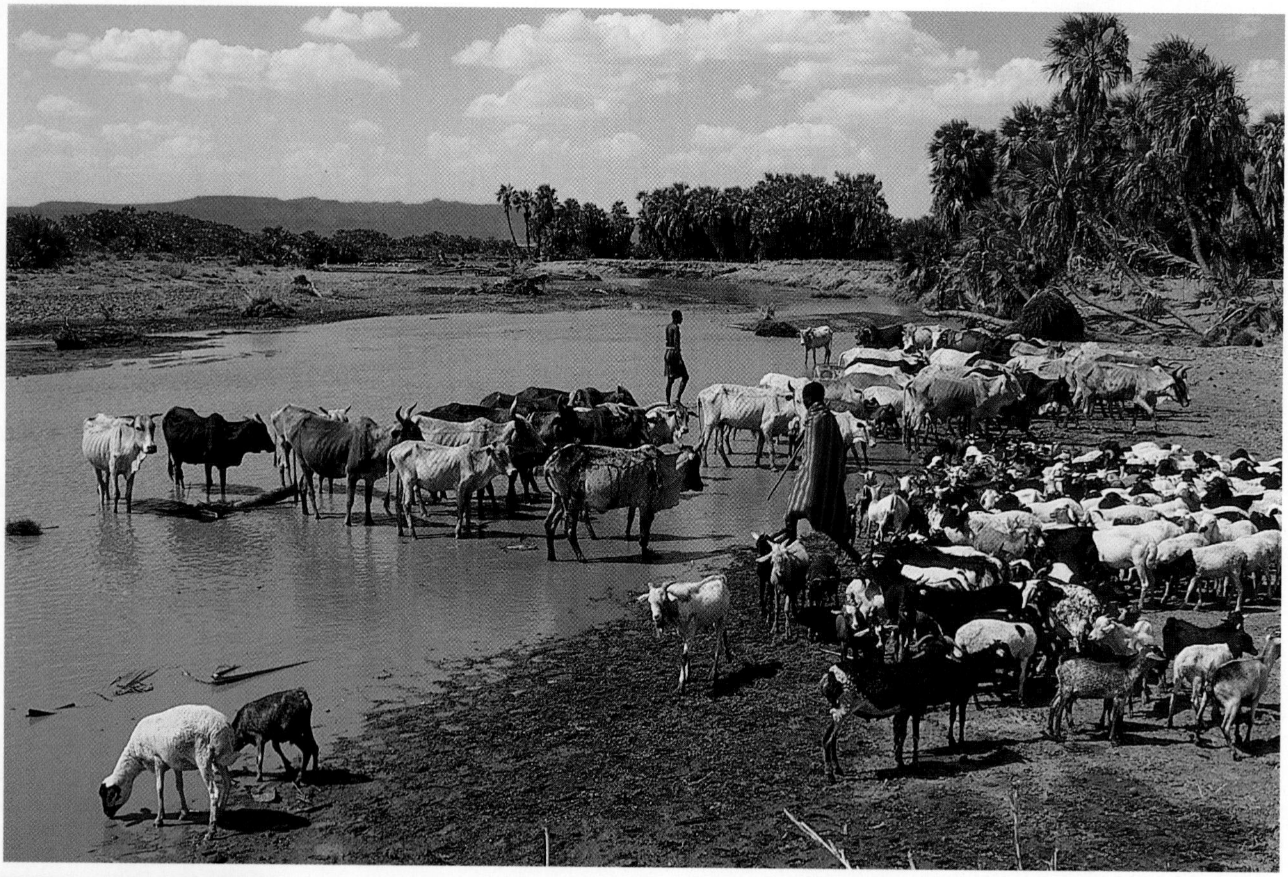

East African Pastoralists Herding large and small livestock has long been a way of life in drier parts of the tropics.

Visit the website and ebook for additional study materials and interactive tools: www.cengage.com/history/bullietearthpeople5e

Tropical Africa and Asia, 1200–1500

- How did environmental differences shape cultural differences in tropical Africa and Asia?
- Under what circumstances did the first Islamic empires arise in Africa and India?
- How did cultural and ecological differences promote trade, and in turn how did trade and other contacts promote state growth and the spread of Islam?
- What social and cultural changes are reflected in the history of peoples living in tropical Africa and Asia during this period?

Sultan Abu Bakr (a-BOO BAK-uhr) customarily offered hospitality to distinguished visitors to his city of Mogadishu, an Indian Ocean port on the northeast coast of Africa. In 1331, he provided food and lodging for Muhammad ibn Abdullah **Ibn Battuta** (IB-uhn ba-TOO-tuh) (1304–1369), a young Muslim scholar from Morocco who had set out to explore the Islamic world. With a pilgrimage to Mecca and travel throughout the Middle East behind him, Ibn Battuta was touring the trading cities of the Red Sea and East Africa. Subsequent travels took him to Central Asia and India, China and Southeast Asia, Muslim Spain, and sub-Saharan West Africa. Recounting some 75,000 miles (120,000 kilometers) of travel over twenty-nine years, Ibn Battuta's journal provides invaluable information on these lands.

Ibn Battuta Moroccan Muslim scholar, the most widely traveled individual of his time. He wrote a detailed account of his visits to Islamic lands from China to Spain and the western Sudan.

Hospitality being considered a noble virtue among Muslims, regardless of physical and cultural differences, the reception at Mogadishu mirrored that at other cities. Ibn Battuta noted that Sultan Abu Bakr had skin darker than his own and spoke a different native language (Somali), but as brothers in faith, they prayed together at Friday services, where the sultan greeted his foreign guest in Arabic, the common language of the Islamic world: "You are heartily welcome, and you have honored our land and given us pleasure." When Sultan Abu Bakr and his jurists heard and decided cases after the mosque service, they used the religious law familiar in all Muslim lands.

Islam aside, the most basic links among the diverse peoples of Africa and southern Asia derived from the tropical environment itself. A network of overland and maritime routes joined their lands (see Chapter 7), providing avenues for the spread of beliefs and technologies, as well as goods. Ibn Battuta sailed with merchants down the coast of East Africa and joined trading caravans across the Sahara to West Africa. His path to India followed overland trade routes, and a merchant ship carried him on to China.

TROPICAL LANDS AND PEOPLES

To obtain food, the people who inhabited the tropical regions of Africa and Asia used methods that generations of experimentation had proved successful, whether at the desert's edge, in grasslands, or in tropical rain forests. Much of their success lay in learning how to blend human activities with the natural order, but they also modified the environment to suit their needs with irrigation works and mining.

The Tropical Environment

tropics Equatorial region between the Tropic of Cancer and the Tropic of Capricorn. It is characterized by generally warm or hot temperatures year-round, though much variation exists due to altitude and other factors. Temperate zones north and south of the tropics generally have a winter season.

Because of the angle of earth's axis, the sun's rays warm the **tropics** year-round. The equator marks the center of the tropical zone, and the Tropic of Cancer and Tropic of Capricorn mark its outer limits. Africa lies almost entirely within the tropics, as do southern Arabia, most of India, and all of the Southeast Asian mainland and islands (see Map 13.1).

Lacking the hot and cold seasons of temperate lands, the rainy and dry seasons of the Afro-Asian tropics derive from wind patterns across the surrounding oceans. Winds from a permanent high-pressure air mass over the South Atlantic deliver heavy rainfall to the western coast of Africa during much of the year. However, in December and January, large high-pressure zones over northern Africa and Arabia produce a southward movement of dry air that limits the inland penetration of the moist ocean winds.

Monsoon System

monsoon Seasonal winds in the Indian Ocean caused by the differences in temperature between the rapidly heating and cooling landmasses of Africa and Asia and the slowly changing ocean waters. These strong and predictable winds have long been ridden across the open sea by sailors, and the large amounts of rainfall that they deposit on parts of India, Southeast Asia, and China allow for the cultivation of several crops a year.

In the lands around the Indian Ocean, the rainy and dry seasons reflect the influence of alternating winds known as **monsoons**. A gigantic high-pressure zone over the Himalaya (him-uh-LAY-uh) Mountains that peaks from December to March produces southern Asia's dry season through a strong southward air movement (the northeast monsoon) in the western Indian Ocean. Between April and August, a low-pressure zone over India creates a northward movement of air from across the ocean (the southwest monsoon) that brings southern Asia the heavy rains of its wet season.

Areas with the heaviest rainfall—the broad belt along the equator in coastal West Africa and West-Central Africa, parts of coastal India, and Southeast Asia—have dense rain forests. Lighter rains produce other forest patterns. The English word *jungle* comes from an Indian word for the tangled undergrowth in the forests that once covered most of India.

Some other parts of the tropics rarely see rain at all. The world's largest desert, the Sahara, stretches across northern Africa and continues eastward across Arabia, southern Iran and Pakistan, and northwest India. Another desert occupies southwestern Africa. Most of tropical India and Africa falls between the deserts and rain forests and experiences moderate rainy seasons. These lands range from fairly wet woodlands to the much drier grasslands characteristic of much of East Africa.

Altitude produces other climatic variations. Thin atmospheres at high altitudes hold less heat than atmospheres at lower elevations. Snow covers some of the volcanic mountains of eastern Africa all or part of the year. The snowcapped Himalayas that form India's northern frontier rise so high that they block cold air from moving south and thus give northern India a more tropical climate than its latitude would suggest. The plateaus of inland Africa and the Deccan (DEK-uhn) Plateau of central India also enjoy cooler temperatures than the coastal plains.

Human Ecosystems

Thinkers in temperate lands once imagined surviving in the tropics to be simply a matter of picking wild fruit off trees. A careful observer touring the tropics in 1200 would have noticed, however, many differences in societies deriving from their particular ecosystems—that is, from how human groups used the plants, animals, and other resources of their physical environments.

Hunters and Fishers

Domesticated plants and animals had become commonplace long before 1200, but people in some environments continued to rely primarily on hunting, fishing, and gathering. For Pygmy (PIG-mee) hunters in the dense forests of Central Africa, small size permitted pursuit of prey through dense undergrowth. Hunting also prevailed in the upper altitudes of the Himalayas and in some desert environments. A Portuguese expedition led by Vasco da Gama visited the arid coast of southwestern Africa in 1497 and saw there a healthy group of people feeding themselves on "the flesh of seals, whales, and gazelles, and the roots of wild plants." Fishing, which

CHRONOLOGY

	Tropical Africa	Tropical Asia
1200		1206 Delhi Sultanate founded in India
	1230s Mali Empire founded	
	1270 Solomonic dynasty in Ethiopia founded	
		1298 Delhi Sultanate annexes Gujarat
1300		
	1324–1325 Mansa Musa's pilgrimage to Mecca	
		1398 Timur sacks Delhi; Delhi Sultanate declines
1400	1400s Great Zimbabwe at its peak	
	1433 Tuareg retake Timbuktu; Mali declines	
1500		1500 Port of Malacca at its peak

was common along all the major lakes and rivers as well as in the oceans, might be combined with farming. The ocean fishermen of East Africa, Southeast Asia, and coastal India had boating skills that often led to engagement in ocean trade.

Herders

Herding provided sustenance in areas too arid for agriculture. Pastoralists consumed milk from their herds and traded hides and meat to farmers in return for grain and vegetables. The world's largest concentration of pastoralists inhabited the arid and semiarid lands of northeastern Africa and Arabia. Like Ibn Battuta's host at Mogadishu, some Somalis lived in towns, but most grazed goats, donkeys, and camels in the desert hinterland of the Horn of Africa. The western Sahara sustained herds of sheep and camels belonging to the Tuareg (TWAH-reg), whose intimate knowledge of the desert made them invaluable as guides to caravans. Along the Sahara's southern edge the cattle-herding Fulani (foo-LAH-nee) people gradually extended their range. By 1500, they had spread throughout the western and central Sudan. A few weeks after encountering the hunter-gatherers of Southwest Africa, Vasco da Gama's expedition bartered for meat with a pastoral people possessing cattle and sheep.

Farmers

The density of agricultural populations reflected the adequacy of rainfall and soils. South and Southeast Asia were generally wetter than tropical Africa, making intensive cultivation possible. High yields supported dense populations. In 1200, over 100 million people lived in South and Southeast Asia, more than four-fifths of them on the fertile Indian mainland. Though a little less than the population of China, this was triple the number of people living in all of Africa and nearly double the number in Europe.

India's lush vegetation led one Middle Eastern writer to call it "the most agreeable abode on earth. Its delightful plains resemble the garden of Paradise."[1] Rice cultivation dominated in the fertile Ganges plain of northeast India, mainland Southeast Asia, and southern China. In drier areas, farmers grew grains—wheat, sorghum, and millet—and legumes such as peas and beans whose ripening cycles matched the pattern of the rainy and dry seasons. Tubers and tree crops characterized farming in rain-forest clearings.

The spread of farming, including the movement to Africa of Asian crops like yams, cocoyams, and bananas, did not necessarily change the natural environment. In most of sub-Saharan Africa and much of Southeast Asia, extensive rather than intensive cultivation prevailed. Instead of enriching fields with manure and vegetable compost so they could be cultivated year after year, farmers abandoned fields when the natural fertility of the soil fell and cleared new fields. Ashes from the brush, grasses, and tree limbs they cut down and burned boosted the new fields' fertility. Shifting to new land every few years made efficient use of labor in areas with comparatively poor soils.

Water Systems and Irrigation

Irrigation Systems

Though the inland delta of the Niger River received naturally fertilizing annual floods and could grow rice for sale to the trading cities along the Niger bend, many tropical farmers had to move

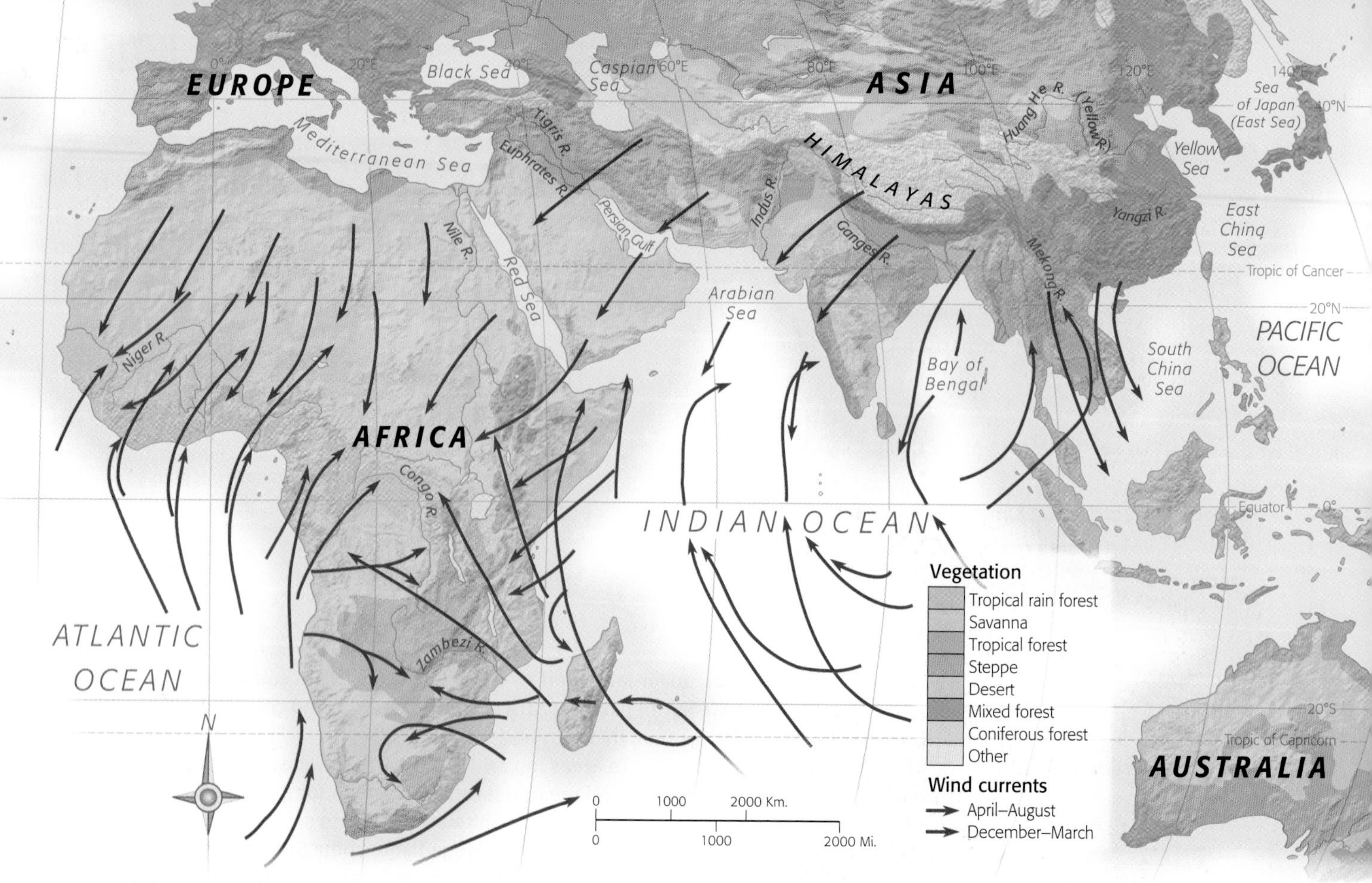

MAP 13.1 Africa and the Indian Ocean Basin: Physical Characteristics Seasonal wind patterns control rainfall in the tropics and produce the different tropical vegetation zones to which human societies have adapted over thousands of years. Wind patterns have also dominated sea travel in the Indian Ocean.

e Interactive Map

the water to their crops. Conserving some of the monsoon rainfall for use during the dry season helped in Vietnam, Java, Malaya, and Burma, which had terraced hillsides with special water-control systems for growing rice. North and south India also had water-storage dams and irrigation canals. In this time period, villagers in southeast India built stone and earthen dams across rivers to store water for gradual release through elaborate irrigation canals. Extended over many generations, these canals irrigated a wide area.

Delhi Sultanate Centralized Indian empire of varying extent, created by Muslim invaders.

As had been true since the days of the first river-valley civilizations (see Chapter 1), governments built and controlled the largest irrigation systems. The **Delhi** (DEL-ee) **Sultanate** (1206–1526) in northern India acquired extensive new water-control systems. Ibn Battuta admired a large reservoir constructed in the first quarter of the thirteenth century that supplied the city of Delhi with water. Farmers planted sugar cane, cucumbers, and melons along the reservoir's rim as the water level fell during the dry season. In the fourteenth century, the Delhi sultan built in the Ganges plain a network of irrigation canals that remained unsurpassed until the nineteenth century. Such systems made it possible to grow crops throughout the year.

Since the tenth century, the Indian Ocean island of Ceylon (modern Sri Lanka [sree LAHNG-kuh]) had been home to the world's greatest concentration of irrigation reservoirs and canals. These facilities supported the large population of the Sinhalese (sin-huh-LEEZ) kingdom in arid northern Ceylon. In Southeast Asia, another impressive system of reservoirs and canals served Cambodia's capital city, Angkor (ANG-kor).

Between 1250 and 1400, however, the irrigation complex in Ceylon fell into ruin when invaders from south India disrupted the Sinhalese government. As a result, malaria spread by mosquitoes breeding in the irrigation canals ravaged the population. In the fifteenth century, the great Cambodian system fell into ruin when the government that maintained it collapsed. Neither system was ever rebuilt.

Andre Held Collection, The Bridgeman Art Library

King and Queen of Ife This copper-alloy work shows the royal couple of the Yoruba kingdom of Ife, the oldest and most sacred of the Yoruba kingdoms of southwestern Nigeria. The casting dates to the period between 1100 and 1500, except for the reconstruction of the male's face, the original of which shattered in 1957 when the road builder who found it accidentally struck it with his pick.

The vulnerability of complex irrigation systems built by powerful governments contrasts with village-based irrigation systems. Invasion and natural calamity might damage the latter, but they usually bounced back because they depended on local initiative and simpler technologies.

Mineral Resources

The most productive metal trade in the tropics, ironworking, provided the hoes, axes, and knives farmers used to clear and cultivate their fields. Between 1200 and 1500, the rain forests of coastal West Africa and Southeast Asia opened up for farming. Iron also supplied spear and arrow points, needles, and nails. Indian metalsmiths became known for forging strong and beautiful swords. In Africa, many people attributed magical powers to iron smelters and blacksmiths.

African Copper and Gold

Copper and its alloys had special importance in the Copperbelt of southeastern Africa during the fourteenth and fifteenth centuries. Smelters cast the metal into large X-shaped ingots (metal castings). Local coppersmiths worked these into wire and decorative objects.

In the western Sudan, Ibn Battuta described a mining town that produced two sizes of copper bars that served as currency in place of coins. Some coppersmiths in West Africa cast copper and brass (an alloy of copper and zinc) statues and heads that now rank as masterpieces of world art. They utilized the "lost-wax" method, in which molten metal melts a thin layer of wax sandwiched between clay forms, replacing the "lost" wax with hard metal.

African gold moved in quantity across the Sahara and into the Indian Ocean and Red Sea trades. Some came from streambeds along the upper Niger River and farther south in modern Ghana (GAH-nuh). In the hills south of the Zambezi (zam-BEE-zee) River (in modern Zimbabwe [zim-BAHB-way]), archaeologists have discovered thousands of mineshafts, dating from 1200, that were sunk up to 100 feet (30 meters) into the ground to get at gold ores. Although panning for gold remained important in the streams descending from the mountains of northern India, the gold and silver mines in India seem to have been exhausted by this period. Thus, Indians imported from Southeast Asia and Africa considerable quantities of gold for jewelry and temple decoration.

SECTION REVIEW

- The environment of tropical Africa and Asia is governed by wind patterns across oceans and the resulting rainfall.
- Deserts and rain forests mark the extreme climate variations in these regions, while mountain ranges produce further variations.
- Depending on the regional environment, people fed themselves mainly through hunting and gathering, herding, or farming.
- In West Africa, India, and Southeast Asia, human societies depended on river and irrigation systems of varying complexity.
- Iron, copper, and gold were central to the local economies and long-distance trade systems of tropical Africa and Asia.

NEW ISLAMIC EMPIRES

Mali Empire created by indigenous Muslims in western Sudan of West Africa from the thirteenth to fifteenth century. It was famous for its role in the trans-Saharan gold trade.

The empires of Mali in West Africa and Delhi in northern India, the largest and richest tropical states of the period between 1200 and 1500, both utilized administrative and military systems introduced from the Islamic heartland. Yet **Mali**, an indigenous African dynasty that had earlier adopted Islam through the peaceful influence of Muslim merchants and scholars, differed in many ways from the Delhi Sultanate founded and ruled by invading Turkish and Afghan Muslims. The wealth of Mali depended on trans-Saharan trade, but long-distance trade played only a minor role in Delhi.

Mali in the Western Sudan

Muslim rule beginning in the seventh century (see Chapter 8) greatly stimulated increased trade along the routes that crossed the Sahara. In the centuries that followed, the faith of Muhammad gradually spread to the lands south of the desert, which the Arabs called the *bilad alsudan* (bih-LAD uhs-soo-DAN), "land of the blacks."

Muslim Advances

Muslim Berbers invading out of the desert in 1076 caused the collapse of Ghana, the empire that preceded Mali in the western Sudan (see Chapter 8), but their conquest did little to spread Islam. To the east, the Muslim attacks that destroyed the Christian Nubian kingdoms on the upper Nile in the late thirteenth century opened that area to Muslim influences, but Christian Ethiopia successfully withstood Muslim advances. Instead, Islam's spread south of the Sahara usually followed a pattern of gradual and peaceful conversion. The expansion of commercial contacts in the western Sudan and on the East African coast greatly promoted the conversion process. Most Africans found meaning and benefit in the teachings of Islam. Takrur (TAHK-roor) in the far western Sudan became the first sub-Saharan African state to adopt the new faith around 1030.

AP* Exam Tip The political systems of the Sudanic empires, such as Mali, are important to know.

Sundiata

Shortly after 1200, Takrur expanded under King Sumanguru (soo-muhn-GOO-roo), only to suffer a major defeat some thirty years later at the hands of Sundiata (soon-JAH-tuh), the upstart leader of the Malinke (muh-LING-kay) people. Though both leaders professed Islam, Malinke legends recall their battles as clashes between powerful magicians, suggesting how

Map of the Western Sudan (1375) A Jewish geographer on the Mediterranean island of Majorca drew this lavish map in 1375, incorporating all that was known in Europe about the rest of the world. This portion of the Catalan Atlas shows a North African trader approaching the king of Mali, who holds a gold nugget in one hand and a golden scepter in the other. A caption identifies the black ruler as Mansa Musa, "the richest and noblest king in all the land."

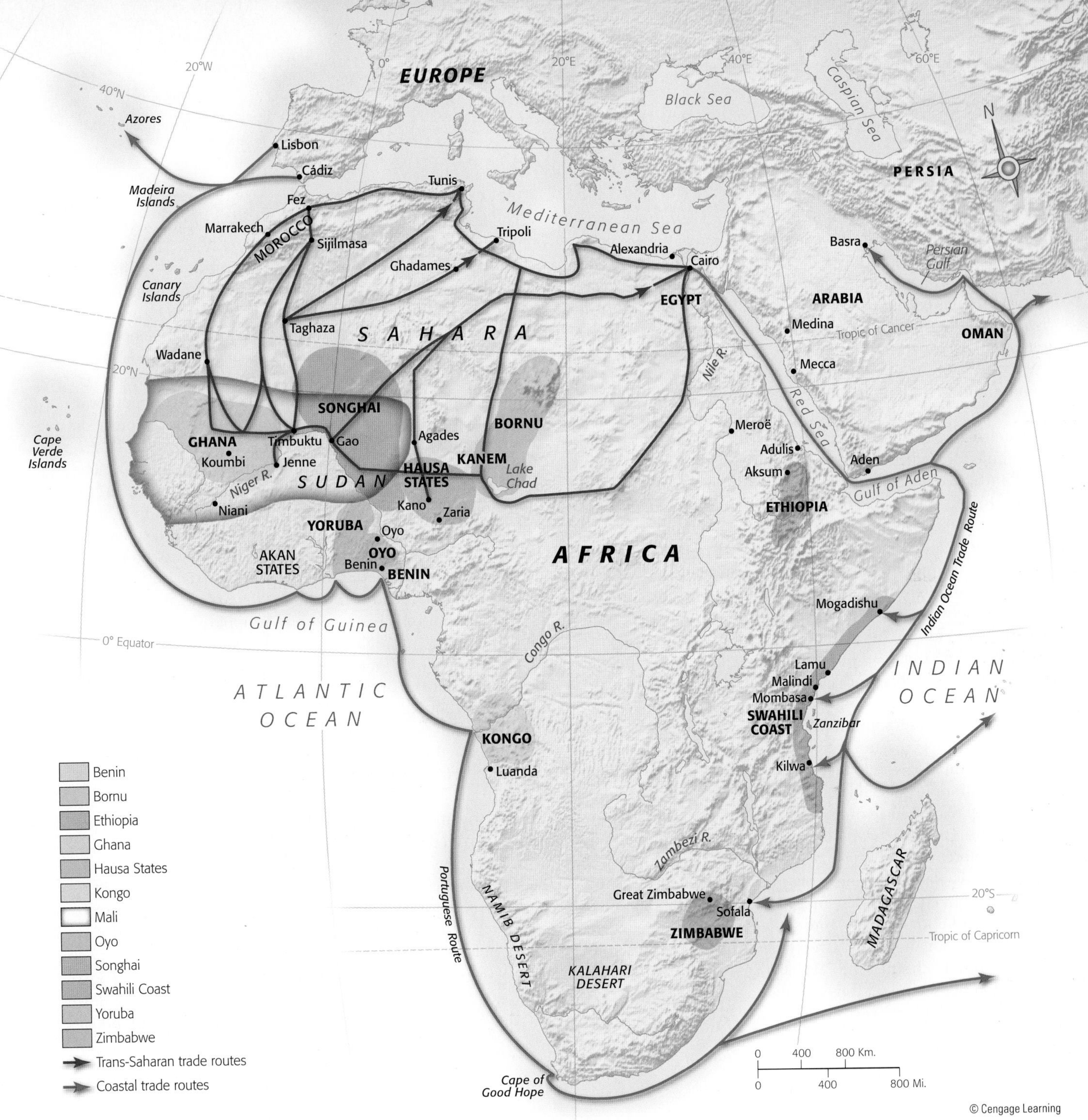

MAP 13.2 Africa, 1200–1500 Many African states had beneficial links to the trade that crossed the Sahara and the Indian Ocean. Before 1500, sub-Saharan Africa's external ties were primarily with the Islamic world.

Interactive Map

much old and new beliefs mingled. Sumanguru could reportedly appear and disappear at will, assume dozens of shapes, and catch arrows in midflight. Sundiata defeated Sumanguru's much larger forces through superior military maneuvers and by successfully wounding his adversary with a special arrow that robbed him of his magical powers. This victory was followed by others that created Sundiata's Mali Empire (see Map 13.2).

Sundiata's empire depended on a well-developed agricultural base and control of the regional and trans-Saharan trade routes, as had Ghana before it. Mali, however, controlled a

DIVERSITY + DOMINANCE

Personal Styles of Rule in India and Mali

Ibn Battuta wrote vivid descriptions of the powerful men who dominated the Muslim states he visited. Although his accounts are explicitly about the rulers, they also raise important issues about their relations with their subjects. The following account of Sultan Muhammad ibn Tughluq of Delhi may be read as a treatise on the rights and duties of rulers and ways in which individual personalities shaped diverse governing styles.

Muhammad is a man who, above all others, is fond of making presents and shedding blood. There may always be seen at his gate some poor person becoming rich, or some living one condemned to death. His generous and brave actions, and his cruel and violent deeds, have obtained notoriety among the people. In spite of this, he is the most humble of men, and the one who exhibits the greatest equity. The ceremonies of religion are dear to his ears, and he is very severe in respect of prayer and the punishment which follows its neglect. . . .

When drought prevailed throughout India and Sind, . . . the Sultan gave orders that provisions for six months should be supplied to all the inhabitants of Delhi from the royal granaries. . . . The officers of justice made registers of the people of the different streets, and these being sent up, each person received sufficient provisions to last him for six months.

The Sultan, notwithstanding all I have said about his humility, his justice, his kindness to the poor, and his boundless generosity, was much given to bloodshed. It rarely happened that the corpse of some one who had been killed was not seen at the gate of his palace. I have often seen men killed and their bodies left there. One day I went to his palace and my horse shied. I looked before me, and I saw a white heap on the ground, and when I asked what it was, one of my companions said it was the trunk of a man cut into three pieces. The sovereign punished little faults like great ones, and spared neither the learned, the religious, nor the noble. Every day hundreds of individuals were brought chained into his hall of audience; their hands tied to their necks and their feet bound together. Some of them were killed, and others were tortured, or well beaten. . . .

The Sultan has a brother named Masud Khan, [who] was one of the handsomest fellows I have ever seen. The king suspected him of intending to rebel, so he questioned him, and, under fear of the torture, Masud confessed the charge. Indeed, every one who denies charges of this nature, which the Sultan brings against him, is put to the torture, and most people prefer death to being tortured. The Sultan had his brother's head cut off in the palace, and the corpse, according to custom, was left neglected for three days in the same place. The mother of Masud had been stoned two years before in the same place on a charge of debauchery or adultery. . . .

One of the most serious charges against this Sultan is that he forced all the inhabitants of Delhi to leave their homes. [After] the people of Delhi wrote letters full of insults and invectives against [him,] the Sultan . . . decided to ruin Delhi, so he purchased all the houses and inns from the inhabitants, paid them the price, and then ordered them to remove to Daulatabad. . . .

The greater part of the inhabitants departed, but [h]is slaves found two men in the streets: one was paralyzed, the other blind. They were brought before the sovereign, who ordered the paralytic to be shot away from a *manjanik* [catapult], and the blind man to be dragged from Delhi to Daulatabad, a journey of forty days' distance. The poor wretch fell to pieces during the journey, and only one of his legs reached Daulatabad. All of the inhabitants of Delhi left; they abandoned their baggage and their merchandize, and the city remained a perfect desert.

A person in whom I felt confidence assured me that the Sultan mounted one evening upon the roof of his palace, and, casting his eyes over the city of Delhi, in which there was neither fire, smoke, nor light, he said, "Now my heart is satisfied, and my feelings are appeased." . . . When we entered this capital, we found it in the state which has been described. It was empty, abandoned, and had but a small population.

In his description of Mansa Suleiman of Mali in 1353, Ibn Battuta places less emphasis on personality, a difference that may

greater area than Ghana, including not only the core trading area of the upper Niger but also the gold fields of the Niger headwaters to the southwest. Moreover, its rulers fostered the spread of Islam among the empire's political and trading elites. Control of the gold and copper trades and contacts with North African Muslim traders gave Mali unprecedented prosperity.

Mansa Musa

Mansa Kankan Musa Ruler of Mali (r. 1312–1337). His pilgrimage through Egypt to Mecca in 1324–1325 established the empire's reputation for wealth in the Mediterranean world.

Under the ruler **Mansa Kankan Musa** (MAHN-suh KAHN-kahn MOO-suh) (r. 1312–1337), the empire's reputation for wealth spread far and wide. Mansa Musa's pilgrimage to Mecca in 1324–1325 fulfilled his personal duty as a Muslim and at the same time put on display his exceptional wealth. He traveled with a large entourage. Besides his senior wife and five hundred of her ladies in waiting and their slaves, one account says there were also sixty thousand porters and a vast caravan of camels carrying supplies and provisions. For purchases and gifts, he brought along eighty packages of gold, each weighing 122 ounces (3.8 kilograms). In addition, five hundred slaves each carried a golden staff. Mansa Musa dispersed so many gifts when he passed through Cairo that the value of gold was depressed for years.

only be due to the fact that he had little personal contact with him. He stresses the huge social distance between the ruler and the ruled, between the master and the slave, and goes on to tell more of the ways in which Islam had altered life in Mali's cities; he also complains about customs that the introduction of Islam had not changed.

It happened that Mansa Suleiman, the Sultan of Mali, a most avaricious and worthless man, made a feast by way of kindness. I was present at the entertainment with some of our theologians. When the assembly broke up, I saluted him, having been brought to his knowledge by the theologians. When I had left the place he sent me a meal, which he forwarded to the house of the Judge. Upon this occasion the Judge came walking hastily to me, and said: Up, for the Sultan has sent you a present. I hastened, expecting that a dress of honour, some horses, and other valuables, had been sent; but, behold! they were only three crusts of bread, with a piece of fried fish, and a dish of sour milk. I smiled at their simplicity, and the great value they set on such trifles as these. I stayed here, after this meal, two months; but saw nothing from him, although I had often met him in their friendly meetings. I one day, however, rose up in his presence, and said: I have travelled the world over, and have seen its kings; and now, I have been four months in thy territories, but no present, or even provision from thee, has yet reached me. Now, what shall I say of thee, when I shall be interrogated on the subject hereafter? Upon this, he gave me a house for my accommodation, with suitable provisions. After this, the theologians visited me in the month of Ramadan, and, out of their whole number, they gave me three and thirty methkals of gold. Of all people, the blacks debase themselves most in the presence of their king: for when any one of them is called upon to appear before him, he will immediately put off his usual clothing, and put on a worn-out dress, with a dirty cap; he will then enter the presence like a beggar, with his clothes lifted up to the middle of his legs; he will then beat the ground with both his elbows, and remain in the attitude of a person performing a prostration. When the Sultan addresses one of them, he will take up the garment off his back, and throw dust upon his head; and, as long as the Sultan speaks, every one present will remain with his turban taken off. One of the best things in these parts is, the regard they pay to justice; for, in this respect, the Sultan regards neither little nor much. The safety, too, is very great; so that a traveller may proceed alone among them, without the least fear of a thief or robber. Another of their good properties is, that when a merchant happens to die among them, they will make no effort to get possession of his property: but will allow the lawful successors to it to take it. Another is, their constant custom of attending prayers with the congregation; for unless one makes haste, he will find no place left to say his prayers in. Another is, their insisting on the Koran's being committed to memory: for if a man finds his son defective in this, he will confine him till he is quite perfect, nor will he allow him his liberty until he is so. As to their bad practices, they will exhibit their little daughters, as well as their male and female slaves, quite naked. In the same manner will the women enter into the presence of the King, which his own daughters will also do. Nor do the free women ever clothe themselves till after marriage.

QUESTIONS FOR ANALYSIS

1. **How would the actions of these rulers have enhanced their authority? To what extent do their actions reflect Islamic influences?**
2. **Although Ibn Battuta tells what the rulers did, can you imagine how one of their subjects would have described his or her perception of the same events and customs?**
3. **Which parts of Ibn Battuta's descriptions seem to be objective and believable? Which parts are more reflective of his personal values?**

Sources: First selection from Henry M. Elliot, *The History of India as Told by Its Own Historians* (London: Trübner and Co., 1869–1871) 3:611–614. Second selection as seen in *The Travels of Ibn Battuta in the Near East, Asia and Africa, 1325–1354*, translated and edited by Rev. Samuel Lee, 2004, pp. 239–240.

Ibn Battuta in Mali

On his return from this pilgrimage, Mansa Musa built new mosques and opened Quran schools in the cities along the Niger bend. Ibn Battuta, who visited Mali from 1352 to 1354 during the reign of Mansa Musa's successor, Mansa Suleiman (MAHN-suh SOO-lay-mahn) (r. 1341–1360), lauded the Malians for their faithful recitation of prayers and their zeal in teaching children the Quran. He also reported that "complete and general safety" prevailed in the vast territories ruled by Suleiman and that foreign travelers had no reason to fear being robbed or having their goods confiscated if they died. (For Ibn Battuta's account of the sultan's court and his subjects' respect, see Diversity and Dominance: Personal Styles of Rule in India and Mali.)

Fall of Mali

Two centuries after its founding, Mali began to disintegrate. Mansa Suleiman's successors could not prevent rebellions breaking out among the diverse peoples subjected to Malinke rule. Other groups attacked from without. The desert Tuareg retook their city of Timbuktu (tim-buk-TOO) in 1433. By 1500, the rulers of Mali had dominion over little more than the Malinke heartland.

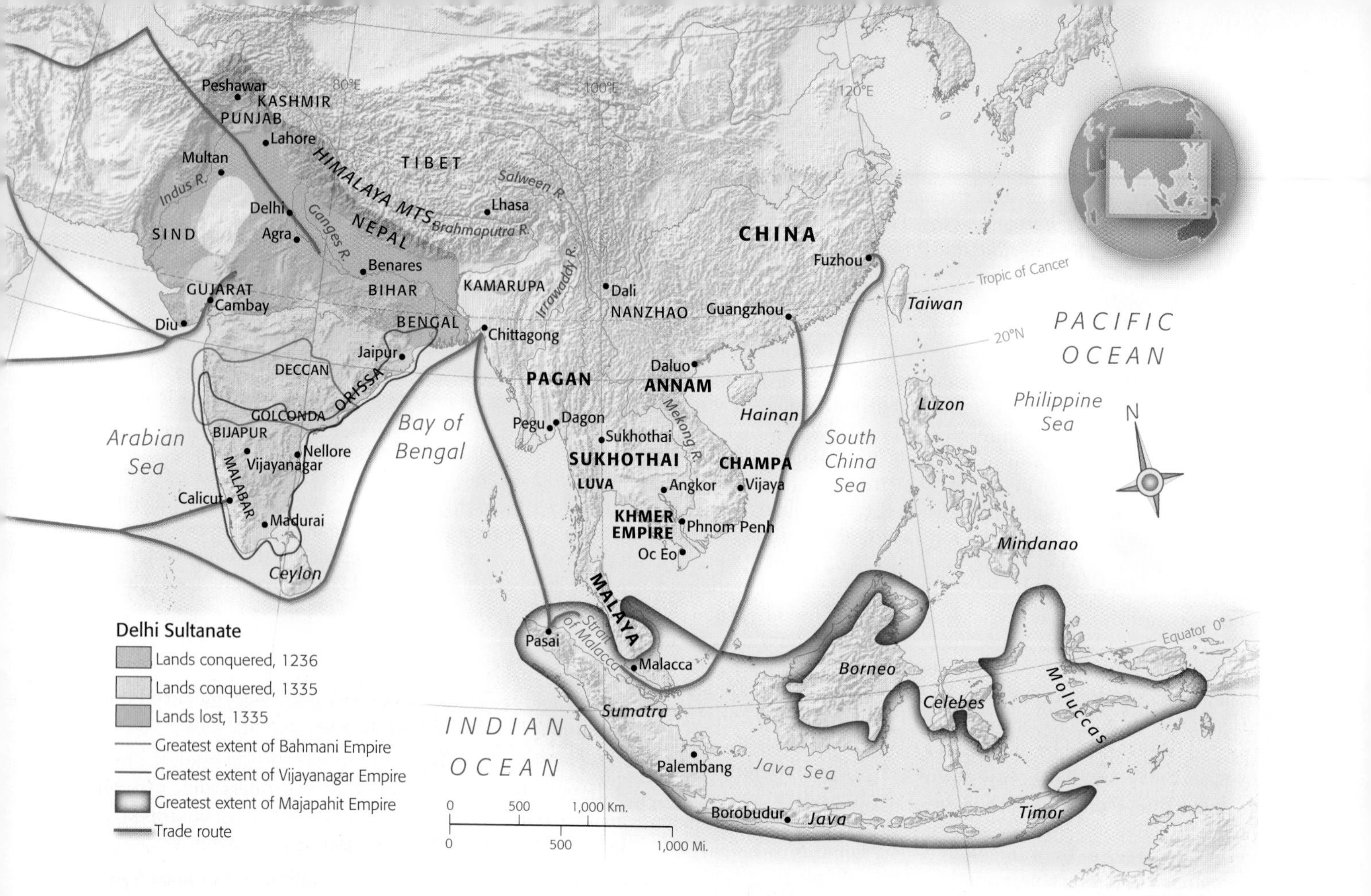

© Cengage Learning

MAP 13.3 **South and Southeast Asia, 1200–1500** The rise of new empires and the expansion of maritime trade reshaped the lives of many tropical Asians.

Interactive Map

The cities of the upper Niger survived Mali's collapse, but some trade and intellectual life moved east to the central Sudan. Shortly after 1450, the rulers of several Hausa city-states officially adopted Islam. These states took on importance as manufacturing and trading centers, becoming famous for cotton textiles and leatherworking. The central Sudanic state of Kanem-Bornu (KAH-nuhm–BOR-noo) also expanded in the late fifteenth century from the ancient kingdom of Kanem, whose rulers had accepted Islam in about 1085. At its peak around 1250, Kanem had absorbed the state of Bornu south and west of Lake Chad and gained control of routes crossing the central Sahara. As Kanem-Bornu's armies conquered new territories, they also spread the rule of Islam.

The Delhi Sultanate in India

AP* Exam Tip It is important to understand the rise of the Delhi Sultanate.

Having long ago lost the defensive unity of the Gupta Empire (see Chapter 6), the divided states of northwest India fell prey to raids by Afghan warlords beginning in the early eleventh century. In the last decades of the twelfth century, a Turkish dynasty armed with powerful crossbows captured the northern Indian cities of Lahore and Delhi. One partisan Muslim chronicler wrote: "The city [Delhi] and its vicinity was freed from idols and idol-worship, and in the sanctuaries of the images of the [Hindu] Gods, mosques were raised by the worshippers of one God."[2] Turkish adventurers from Central Asia flocked to join the invading armies, overwhelming the small Indian states, which were often at war with one another.

Sultan Iltutmish

Between 1206 and 1236, the Muslim invaders extended their rule over the Hindu princes and chiefs in much of northern India. Sultan Iltutmish (il-TOOT-mish) (r. 1211–1236) consolidated the conquest in a series of military expeditions that made his realm the largest in India (see Map 13.3). He also secured official recognition of the Delhi Sultanate as a Muslim state by the caliph of Baghdad. Although pillaging continued, especially on the frontiers, the incorporation of north India into the Islamic world marked the beginning of the invaders' transformation

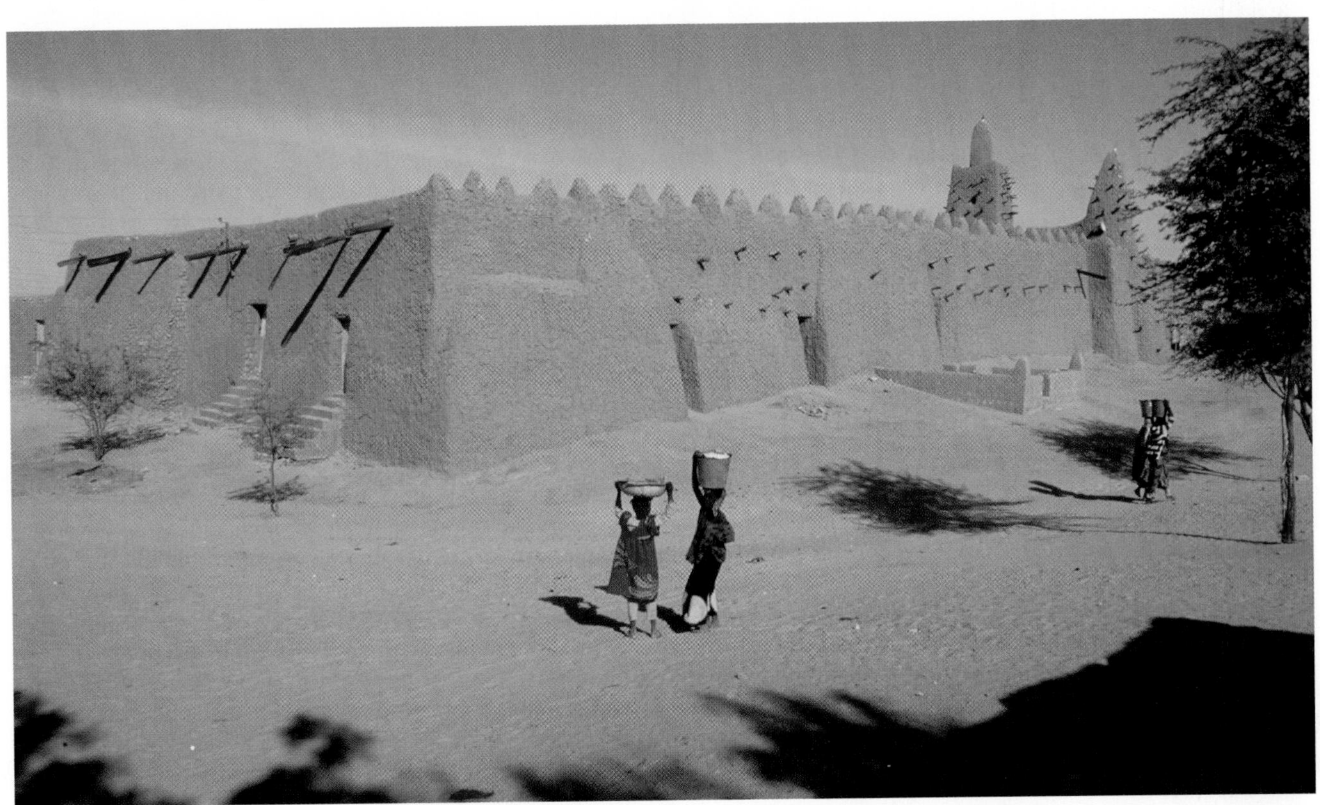
Nik Wheeler/Corbis

Dijinguere Ber Mosque in Timbuktu Built almost entirely of earth and organic materials, this fourteenth-century mosque can accommodate 2,000 worshippers. Mansa Kankan Musa, the most famous ruler of the Empire of Mali, is said to have paid Abu Ishaq al-Sahili, a native of Granada in Muslim Spain, 200 kilograms of gold for designing this masterful combination of Islamic and African traditions.

from brutal conquerors to somewhat more benign rulers. Muslim commanders extended protection to the conquered, freeing them from persecution in return for payment of a special tax. Yet Hindus never forgot the intolerance and destruction of their first contacts with the invaders.

Raziya, a Female Sultan

Iltutmish astonished his ministers by passing over his weak and pleasure-seeking sons and designating as his heir his beloved and talented daughter Raziya (RAH-zee-uh). When they questioned the unprecedented idea of a woman ruling a Muslim state, he said, "My sons are devoted to the pleasures of youth: no one of them is qualified to be king. . . . There is no one more competent to guide the State than my daughter." Her brother—who delighted in riding his elephant through the bazaar, showering the crowds with coins—ruled ineptly for seven months before the ministers relented and put Raziya on the throne.

A chronicler who knew her explained why this able ruler lasted less than four years (r. 1236–1240):

> *Sultan Raziya was a great monarch. She was wise, just, and generous, a benefactor to her kingdom, a dispenser of justice, the protector of her subjects, and the leader of her armies. She was endowed with all the qualities befitting a king, but she was not born of the right sex, and so in the estimation of men all these virtues were worthless. May God have mercy upon her!*[3]

Doing her best to prove herself a proper king, Raziya dressed like a man and led her troops atop an elephant. In the end, however, the Turkish chiefs imprisoned her; she escaped, but she was killed by a robber soon after.

Annexation of Gujarat

After a half-century of stagnation and rebellion, the ruthless but efficient policies of Sultan Ala-ud-din Khalji (uh-LAH-uh–DEEN KAL-jee) (r. 1296–1316) increased control over the empire's outlying provinces. Successful frontier raids and high taxes kept his treasury full, wage and price controls in Delhi kept down the cost of maintaining a large army, and a network of spies

Gujarat Region of western India famous for trade and manufacturing; the inhabitants are called Gujaratis.

stifled intrigue. When a Mongol threat from Central Asia eased, Ala-ud-din's forces extended the sultanate's southern flank, seizing the rich trading state of **Gujarat** (goo-juh-RAHT) in 1298, and then drove southward, briefly seizing the southern tip of the Indian peninsula.

Muslims and Hindus

When Ibn Battuta visited Delhi, Sultan Muhammad ibn Tughluq (TOOG-look) (r. 1325–1351) received him in his celebrated Hall of a Thousand Pillars. The world traveler praised the sultan's piety and generosity, but he also recounted his cruelties (see Diversity and Dominance: Personal Styles of Rule in India and Mali). The sultan enlarged the sultanate to its greatest extent at the expense of the independent Indian states but balanced his aggressive policy with religious toleration. He even attended Hindu religious festivals. However, his successor, Firuz Shah (fuh-ROOZ shah) (r. 1351–1388), alienated powerful Hindus by taxing the Brahmins, preferring to cultivate good relations with the Muslim elite. Muslim chroniclers praised him for constructing forty mosques, thirty colleges, and a hundred hospitals.

A small minority in a giant land, the Turkish rulers relied on terror to keep their subjects submissive, on harsh military reprisals to put down rebellion, and on pillage and high taxes to sustain the ruling elite in luxury and power. Though little different from most other large states of this time (including Mali) in being more a burden than a benefit to most of its subjects, the sultanate never lost the disadvantage of foreign origins and alien religious identity. Nevertheless, over time, the sultans did incorporate some Hindus into their administrations, and some members of the ruling elite also married women from prominent Hindu families, though the brides had to become Muslim.

South Indian Kingdoms

Personal and religious rivalries within the Muslim elite, along with Hindu discontent, threatened the Delhi Sultanate whenever it showed weakness and finally hastened its end. In the mid-fourteenth century, Muslim nobles challenged the sultan's dominion and established the independent Bahmani (bah-MAHN-ee) kingdom (1347–1482) on the Deccan Plateau. Defending against the southward push of Bahmani armies, the Hindu states of south India united to form

Meenakshi Temple, Madurai, India Some 15,000 pilgrims a day visit the large Hindu temple of Meenakshi (the fish-eyed goddess) in the ancient holy city of Madurai in India's southeastern province of Tamil Nadu. The temple complex dates from at least 1000 C.E., although the elaborately painted statues of these gopuram (gate towers) have been rebuilt and restored many times. The largest gopura rises 150 feet (46 meters) above the ground.

Jean Louis Nou/akg-images

the Vijayanagar (vee-juh-yah-NAH-gar) Empire (1336–1565), which at its height controlled the rich trading ports on both coasts of south India and held Ceylon as a tributary state.

The elites of Vijayanagar and the Bahmani state turned a blind eye to religious differences when doing so favored their interests. Bahmani rulers sought to balance Muslim domination with the practical policies of incorporating the Hindu leaders into the government, marrying Hindu wives, and appointing Brahmins to high offices. Vijayanagar rulers hired Muslim horsemen and archers to strengthen their military forces and formed an alliance with the Muslim-ruled state of Gujarat.

Timur Sacks Delhi

By 1351, when all of south India had cast off Delhi's rule, much of north India rose in rebellion. In the east, Bengal broke away from the sultanate in 1338, becoming a center of the mystical Sufi tradition of Islam (see Chapter 8). In the west, Gujarat regained its independence by 1390. The weakening of Delhi's central authority tempted fresh Mongol interest in the area. In 1398, the Turko-Mongol leader Timur (see Chapter 12) captured the city of Delhi. When his armies withdrew the next year with vast quantities of loot and tens of thousands of captives, the largest city in southern Asia lay empty and in ruins. The Delhi Sultanate never recovered.

For all its shortcomings, the Delhi Sultanate triggered the development of centralized political authority in India. Prime ministers and provincial governors serving under the sultans established a bureaucracy, improved food production, promoted trade, and put in circulation a common currency. Despite the many conflicts that Muslim conquest and rule provoked, Islam gradually acquired a permanent place in South Asia.

SECTION REVIEW

- Islam spread into western sub-Saharan Africa usually by peaceful conversion through trading contacts.
- Founded by Sundiata, Mali depended on agriculture and control of trade routes, and Islam spread among its elites.
- Mali reached its height under Mansa Kankan Musa but declined after the death of his successor, and power shifted eastward.
- Muslim Turkish invaders conquered much of Hindu northern India to establish the Delhi Sultanate.
- The sultanate grew to encompass most of India; the sultans ruled through terror, pillage, and heavy taxation.
- Though efficient, the sultanate suffered from internal struggles and fell under pressure from rival states and invaders.

INDIAN OCEAN TRADE

AP* Exam Tip Interregional networks and contacts, such as Indian Ocean trade, are major points to know.

When the collapse of the Mongol Empire in the fourteenth century disrupted overland routes across Central Asia, the Indian Ocean assumed greater strategic importance in tying together the peoples of Eurasia and Africa. Between 1200 and 1500, the volume of trade in the Indian Ocean increased. The Indian Ocean routes also facilitated the spread of Islam.

Monsoon Mariners

Trade Goods

The prosperity of Islamic and Mongol empires in Asia, cities in Europe, and new kingdoms in Africa and Southeast Asia stimulated and contributed to the vitality of the Indian Ocean network. The demand for luxuries—precious metals and jewels, rare spices, fine textiles, and other manufactures—rose. Larger ships made shipments of bulk cargoes of ordinary cotton textiles, pepper, food grains (rice, wheat, barley), timber, horses, and other goods profitable. Some goods were transported from one end of this trading network to the other, but few ships or crews made a complete circuit. Instead, the Indian Ocean trade divided into two legs: from the Middle East across the Arabian Sea to India and from India across the Bay of Bengal to Southeast Asia (see Map 13.4).

Dhows

dhows Characteristic cargo and passenger ships of the Arabian Sea.

Shipyards in ports on the Malabar Coast (southwestern India) built large numbers of **dhows** (dow), the characteristic cargo and passenger ships of the Arabian Sea. They grew from an average capacity of 100 tons in 1200 to 400 tons in 1500. On a typical expedition, a dhow might sail west from India to Arabia and Africa on the northeast monsoon winds (December to March) and return on the southwest monsoons (April to August). Small dhows kept the coast in sight. Relying on the stars to guide them, skilled pilots steered large vessels by the quicker route straight across the water. A large dhow could sail from the Red Sea to mainland Southeast Asia in two to

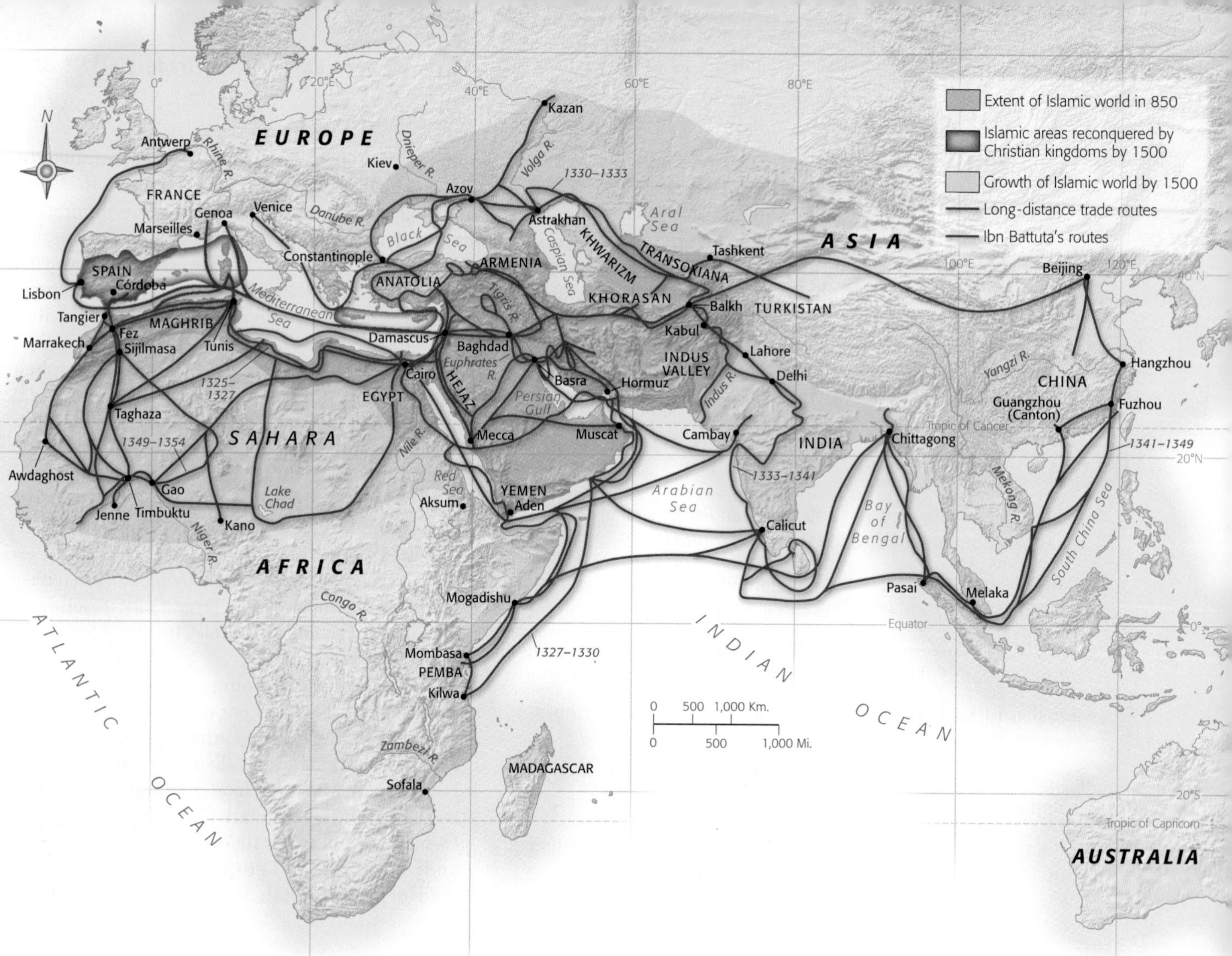

MAP 13.4 **Arteries of Trade and Travel in the Islamic World, to 1500** Ibn Battuta's journeys across Africa and Asia made use of land and sea routes along which Muslim traders and the Islamic faith had long traveled.

Interactive Map

four months, but few did so. Eastbound cargoes and passengers from dhows reaching India were likely to be transferred to junks, which dominated the eastern half of the Indian Ocean and the South China Sea (see Environment and Technology: The Indian Ocean Dhow).

Chinese Junks

The largest, most technologically advanced, and most seaworthy vessels of this time, junks first appeared in China and spread with Chinese influence. Enormous nails held together hulls of heavy spruce or fir planks, in contrast with dhows, whose planks were sewn together with palm fiber. Below the deck, watertight compartments minimized flooding in case of damage to the ship's hull. According to Ibn Battuta, the largest junks had twelve sails made of bamboo and carried a crew of a thousand men, including four hundred soldiers. A large junk might accommodate a hundred passenger cabins and a cargo of over 1,000 tons. Junks dominated China's foreign shipping to Southeast Asia and India, but the Chinese did not control all of the junks that plied these waters. During the fifteenth century, similar vessels came out of shipyards in Bengal and Southeast Asia to be sailed by local crews.

Swahili Coast East African shores of the Indian Ocean between the Horn of Africa and the Zambezi River; from the Arabic *sawahil*, meaning "shores."

From Africa to China

Decentralized and cooperative commercial interests, rather than political authorities, connected the several regions that participated in the Indian Ocean trade. The **Swahili** (swah-HEE-lee) **Coast** supplied gold from inland areas of eastern Africa. Ports around the Arabian peninsula supplied horses and goods from the northern parts of the Middle East, the Mediterranean, and eastern Europe. Merchants in the cities of coastal India received goods from east and west,

The Indian Ocean Dhow

The sailing vessels that crossed the Indian Ocean shared the diversity of that trading area. The name by which we know them, *dhow*, comes from the Swahili language of the East African coast. The planks of teak from which their hulls were constructed were hewn from the tropical forests of south India and Southeast Asia. Their pilots, who navigated by stars at night, used the ancient technique that Arabs had used to find their way across the desert. Some pilots used a magnetic compass, which originated in China.

Dhows came in various sizes and designs, but all had two distinctive features in common. The first was hull construction. The hulls of dhows consisted of planks that were sewn together, not nailed. Cord made of fiber from the husk of coconuts or other materials was passed through rows of holes drilled in the planks. Because cord is weaker than nails, outsiders considered this shipbuilding technique strange. Marco Polo fancifully suggested that it indicated sailors' fear that large ocean magnets would pull any nails out of their ships. More probable explanations are that pliant sewn hulls were cheaper to build than rigid nailed hulls and were less likely to be damaged if the ships ran aground on coral reefs.

The second distinctive feature of dhows was their triangular (lateen) sails made of palm leaves or cotton. The sails were suspended from tall masts and could be turned to catch the wind.

The sewn hull and lateen sails were technologies developed centuries earlier, but there were two innovations between 1200 and 1500. First, a rudder positioned at the stern (rear end) of the ship replaced the large side oar that formerly had controlled steering. Second, shipbuilders increased the size of dhows to accommodate bulkier cargoes.

National Maritime Museum, London

Dhow This modern model shows the vessel's main features.

sold some locally, passed others along, and added Indian goods to the trade. The Strait of Malacca (meh-LAK-eh), between the eastern end of the Indian Ocean and the South China Sea, provided a meeting point for trade from Southeast Asia, China, and the Indian Ocean. In each region, certain ports functioned as giant emporia, consolidating goods from smaller ports and inland areas for transport across the seas.

Africa: The Swahili Coast and Zimbabwe

Trade expanded steadily along the East African coast from about 1250, giving rise to between thirty and forty separate city-states by 1500. After 1200, masonry buildings as much as four stories high replaced mud and thatch dwellings, and archaeological findings include imported glass beads, Chinese porcelain, and other exotic goods. Coastal and island peoples shared a common culture and a language built on African grammar and vocabulary but enriched with many Arabic and Persian terms and written in Arabic script. In time, these people became known as "Swahili," from the Arabic name *sawahil* (suh-WAH-hil) *al-sudan*, meaning "shores of the blacks."

Ibn Battuta in Kilwa

Sometime after Ibn Battuta's visit to Mogadishu in 1331, the more southerly city of Kilwa surpassed it as the Swahili Coast's most important commercial center (see Map 13.2). Ibn Battuta

Embassy Photo/Visual Connection Archive

Royal Enclosure, Great Zimbabwe Inside these oval stone walls the rulers of the trading state of Great Zimbabwe lived. Forced to enter the enclosure through a narrow corridor between two high walls, visitors were meant to be awestruck.

declared Kilwa "one of the most beautiful and well-constructed towns in the world." He noted its inhabitants' dark skins and Muslim piety, and he praised their ruler for the traditional Muslim virtues of humility and generosity.

Great Zimbabwe

What attracted the Arab and Iranian merchants whom oral traditions associate with the Swahili Coast's commercial expansion? By the late fifteenth century, Kilwa was annually exporting a ton of gold mined by inland Africans much farther south. Much of it came from or passed through a powerful state on the plateau south of the Zambezi River. At its peak in about 1400, its capital city, now known as **Great Zimbabwe**, occupied 193 acres (78 hectares) and had some eighteen thousand inhabitants.

Great Zimbabwe City, now in ruins (in the modern African country of Zimbabwe), whose many stone structures were built between about 1250 and 1450, when it was a trading center and the capital of a large state.

Between about 1250 and 1450, local African craftsmen built stone structures for Great Zimbabwe's rulers, priests, and wealthy citizens. The largest structure, an enclosure the size and shape of a large football stadium with walls of unmortared stone 17 feet (5 meters) thick and 32 feet (10 meters) high, served as the king's court. A large conical stone tower was among the many buildings inside the walls.

As in Mali, mixed farming and cattle herding provided the economic basis of the Great Zimbabwe state, but long-distance trade brought added wealth. Trade began regionally with copper ingots from the upper Zambezi Valley, salt, and local manufactures. Gold exports to the coast expanded in the fourteenth and fifteenth centuries and brought Zimbabwe to its peak. However, historians suspect that the city's residents depleted nearby forests for firewood while their cattle overgrazed surrounding grasslands. The resulting ecological crisis hastened the empire's decline in the fifteenth century.

Arabia: Aden and the Red Sea

Aden Port city in the modern south Arabian country of Yemen. It has been a major trading center in the Indian Ocean since ancient times.

The city of **Aden** (AY-den) near the southwestern tip of the Arabian peninsula had a double advantage in the Indian Ocean trade. Monsoon winds brought enough rainfall to supply drinking water to a large population and grow grain for export, and its location made it a convenient stopover for trade with India, the Persian Gulf, East Africa, and Egypt. Aden's merchants dealt in cotton cloth and beads from India; spices from Southeast Asia; horses from Arabia and Ethiopia;

pearls from the Red Sea; manufactured luxuries from Cairo; slaves, gold, and ivory from Ethiopia; and grain, opium, and dyes from Aden's own hinterland.

Ibn Battuta in Aden

After visiting Mecca in 1331, Ibn Battuta sailed down the Red Sea to Aden, probably wedged in among bales of trade goods. His comments on the wealth of Aden's leading merchants include a story about the slave of one merchant who bought a ram for the fabulous sum of 400 dinars in order to keep the slave of another merchant from buying it. Instead of punishing the slave for extravagance, the master freed him as a reward for outdoing his rival. Ninety years later, a Chinese Muslim visitor, Ma Huan, found "the country . . . rich, and the people numerous," living in stone residences several stories high.

Yemen and Ethiopia

Common commercial interests generally promoted good relations among the different religions and cultures of this region. For example, in the mid-thirteenth century, a wealthy Jew from Aden named Yosef settled in Christian Ethiopia, where he acted as an adviser. South Arabia had been trading with neighboring parts of Africa since before the time of King Solomon of Israel. The dynasty that ruled Ethiopia after 1270 claimed descent from Solomon and from the South Arabian princess Sheba. Solomonic Ethiopia's consolidation accompanied a great increase in trade through the Red Sea port of Zeila (ZEYE-luh), including slaves, amber, and animal pelts, which went to Aden and on to other destinations.

Friction sometimes arose, however. In the fourteenth century, the Sunni Muslim king of Yemen sent materials for building a large mosque in Zeila, but the local Somalis (who were Shi'ite Muslims) threw the stones into the sea. This resulted in a yearlong embargo of Zeila ships in Aden. In the late fifteenth century, Ethiopia's territorial expansion and efforts to increase control over the trade provoked conflicts with Muslims who ruled the coastal states of the Red Sea.

India: Gujarat and the Malabar Coast

AP* Exam Tip For the multiple choice section of the exam, it is important to understand the nature of the Indian Ocean trade, but not specifically the Gujarati merchants.

The state of Gujarat in western India prospered from the expanding trade of the Arabian Sea and the rise of the Delhi Sultanate. Blessed with a rich agricultural hinterland and a long coastline, Gujarat attracted new trade after the Mongol destruction of Baghdad in 1258 disrupted the northern land routes. After the initial violence of its forced incorporation into the Delhi Sultanate in 1298, Gujarat prospered from increased trade with Delhi's ruling class, despite occasional military crackdowns. Independent again after 1390, the Muslim rulers of Gujarat extended their control over neighboring Hindu states and regained their preeminent position in the Indian Ocean trade.

Maritime Trade

Gujaratis exported cotton textiles and indigo to the Middle East and Europe, in return for gold and silver. They also shipped cotton cloth, carnelian beads, and foodstuffs to the Swahili Coast in exchange for ebony, slaves, ivory, and gold. During the fifteenth century, traders expanded eastward to the Strait of Malacca. These Gujarati merchants helped spread the Islamic faith among East Indian traders, some of whom even imported specially carved gravestones from Gujarat.

Unlike Kilwa and Aden, Gujarat manufactured goods for trade. According to the thirteenth-century Venetian traveler Marco Polo, Gujarat's leatherworkers dressed enough skins in a year to fill several ships to Arabia and other places. They made sleeping mats for export to the Middle East "in red and blue leather, exquisitely inlaid with figures of birds and beasts, and skillfully embroidered with gold and silver wire," as well as leather cushions embroidered in gold.

Cambay and Calicut

Later observers compared the Gujarati city of Cambay with cities in Flanders and northern Italy (see Chapter 14) in the scale, artisanry, and diversity of its textile industries. Cotton, linen, and silk cloth, along with carpets and quilts, found a large market in Europe, Africa, the Middle East, and Southeast Asia. Cambay also produced polished gemstones, gold jewelry, carved ivory, stone beads, and both natural and artificial pearls. At the height of its prosperity in the fifteenth century, its well-laid-out streets and open places boasted fine stone houses with tiled roofs. Although Muslim residents controlled most Gujarati overseas trade, its Hindu merchant caste profited so much from related commercial activities that their wealth and luxurious lives became the envy of other Indians.

More southerly cities on the Malabar Coast duplicated Gujarat's success. Calicut (KAL-ih-cut) and other coastal cities prospered from locally made cotton textiles and locally grown grains and spices, and they also served as clearing-houses for the long-distance trade of the Indian Ocean. The Zamorin (ZAH-much-ruhn) (ruler) of Calicut presided over a loose federation of its

Hindu rulers that united the coastal region. As in eastern Africa and Arabia, rulers generally tolerated religious and ethnic groups who contributed to commercial profits. Most trading activity lay in the hands of Muslims, many originally from Iran and Arabia, who intermarried with local Indian Muslims. Jewish merchants also operated from Malabar's trading cities.

Southeast Asia

At the eastern end of the Indian Ocean, the Strait of Malacca between the Malay Peninsula and the island of Sumatra provided the principal passage into the South China Sea (see Map 13.3). As trade increased in the fourteenth and fifteenth centuries, this commercial choke point became the site of political rivalry.

Kingdom of Majapahit

The mainland kingdom of Siam controlled most of the upper Malay Peninsula, while the Java-based kingdom of Majapahit (mah-jah-PAH-hit) extended its dominion over the lower Malay Peninsula and much of Sumatra. Majapahit, however, could not suppress a nest of Chinese pirates based at the Sumatran city of Palembang (pah-lem-BONG) who preyed on ships sailing through the strait. In 1407, a fleet sent from China smashed the pirates' power and took their chief back home for trial.

Malacca Port city in the modern Southeast Asian country of Malaysia, founded about 1400 as a trading center on the Strait of Malacca.

The Rise of Malacca

Majapahit, weakened by internal struggles, could not take advantage of China's intervention, making the chief beneficiary the newer port of **Malacca** (or Melaka), which dominated the narrowest part of the strait. Under a prince from Palembang, Malacca had grown from an obscure fishing village into an important port through a series of astute alliances. Nominally subject to the king of Siam, Malacca also secured an alliance with China that was sealed by the visit of the imperial fleet in 1407. The conversion of an early ruler from Hinduism to Islam helped promote trade with Muslim merchants from Gujarat and elsewhere. Merchants also appreciated Malacca's security and low taxes.

Malacca served not just as a meeting point but also as an emporium for Southeast Asian products: rubies and musk from Burma, tin from Malaya, gold from Sumatra, cloves and nutmeg from the Moluccas (or Spice Islands, as Europeans later dubbed them). Shortly after 1500, when Malacca was at its height, one resident counted eighty-four languages spoken among the merchants gathered there, who came from as far away as Turkey, Ethiopia, and the Swahili Coast. Four officials administered the foreign merchant communities: one for the Gujaratis, one for other Indians and Burmese, one for Southeast Asians, and one for the Chinese and Japanese. Malacca's wealth and its cosmopolitan residents set the standard for luxury in Malaya for centuries to come.

SECTION REVIEW

- Traversed by dhows and junks, the maritime trade network of the Indian Ocean tied together peoples of Asia, Africa, and Europe.
- Decentralized commercial interests rose throughout the network, including the Swahili city-states that exported African gold from Great Zimbabwe.
- Aden dealt in a variety of goods from Africa, Arabia, and Southeast Asia and traded with Zeila on the Red Sea.
- Despite political turmoil, the cities of Gujarat and the Malabar Coast prospered through agriculture, manufacture, and trade.
- Through astute alliances, Malacca grew into the predominant emporium of Southeast Asia.

SOCIAL AND CULTURAL CHANGE

State growth, commercial expansion, and the spread of Islam between 1200 and 1500 led to many changes in the social and cultural life of tropical peoples. The political and commercial elites grew in size and power, as did the number of slaves they owned. The spread of Muslim practices and beliefs affected social and cultural life—witness words of Arabic origin like *Sahara, Sudan, Swahili,* and *monsoon*—yet local traditions remained important.

Architecture, Learning, and Religion

Temples and Mosques

Social and cultural changes typically affected cities more than rural areas. As Ibn Battuta and other travelers observed, wealthy merchants and ruling elites spent lavishly on mansions, pal-

Church of Saint George, Ethiopia King Lalibela, who ruled the Christian kingdom of Ethiopia between about 1180 and 1220, had a series of churches carved out of solid volcanic rock to adorn his kingdom's new capital (also named Lalibela). The church of Saint George, excavated to a depth of 40 feet (13 meters) and hollowed out inside, has the shape of a Greek cross.

S. Sassoon/ Robert Harding World Imagery

aces, and places of worship. Most places of worship surviving from this period blend older traditions and new influences. African Muslims produced Middle Eastern mosque designs in local building materials: sun-baked clay and wood in the western Sudan and coral stone on the Swahili Coast. Hindu temple architecture influenced mosque designs in Gujarat, which sometimes incorporated pieces of older structures.

The congregational mosque at Cambay, built in 1325 with the traditional Islamic courtyard, cloisters, and porches, utilized pillars, porches, and arches taken from sacked Hindu and Jain (jine) temples. The congregational mosque erected at the Gujarati capital of Ahmadabad (AH-muhd-ah-bahd) in 1423 had the open courtyard typical of mosques everywhere, but the surrounding verandas incorporated many typical Gujarati details and architectural conventions.

In Africa, King Lalibela (LAH-lee-BEL-uh) of Ethiopia constructed his capital, Lalibela, during the first third of the thirteenth century and ordered eleven churches to be carved out of solid rock, each commemorating a sacred Christian site in Jerusalem. These structures carried on an old Ethiopian tradition of rock sculpture, though on a far grander scale.

Urdu A Persian-influenced literary form of Hindi written in Arabic characters and used as a literary language since the 1300s.

Spread of Literacy

Mosques, churches, and temples were centers of education as well as prayer. Muslims promoted literacy among their sons (and sometimes their daughters) so that they could read sacred texts. Ibn Battuta reported seeing several boys in Mali wearing chains until they completed memorizing passages of the Quran. Literacy and Islam spread together in sub-Saharan Africa, where Christian Ethiopia had previously been the only literate society. In time, scholars adapted the Arabic alphabet to write local languages.

Islam affected literacy less in India, which had a long literate heritage. Arabic served primarily for religious purposes, while Persian became the language of high culture used at court. Eventually **Urdu** (ER-doo) arose, a Persian-influenced literary form of Hindi written in Arabic characters. Muslims also introduced papermaking in India.

Timbuktu City on the Niger River in the modern country of Mali. It was founded by the Tuareg as a seasonal camp sometime after 1000. As part of the Mali Empire, Timbuktu became a major terminus of the trans-Saharan trade and a center of Islamic learning.

Timbuktu

Advanced Muslim scholars studied Islamic law, theology, and administration, as well as works on mathematics, medicine, science, and philosophy, partly derived from ancient Greek writings. In sixteenth-century **Timbuktu** (see Map 13.2), over 150 schools taught the Quran while leading clerics taught advanced classes in mosques or homes. Books imported from North Africa brought high prices. Al-Hajj Ahmed, a scholar who died in Timbuktu in 1536, possessed some seven hundred volumes, an unusually large library for that time. In Southeast Asia, Malacca became a center of Islamic learning from which scholars spread Islam throughout the region. Other important centers of learning developed in Muslim India, particularly in Delhi, the capital.

Spread of Islam

AP* Exam Tip It is important to understand the spread of religions.

Even in lands seized by conquest, Muslim rulers seldom required conversion. Example and persuasion by merchants and Sufis proved more effective. Many Muslims worked hard to persuade others of Islam's superiority. Muslim domination of long-distance trade assisted the adoption of Islam. Commercial transactions could take place across religious boundaries, but the common code of morality and law that Islam provided encouraged trust and drew many local merchants to Islam. From the major trading centers along the Swahili Coast, in the Sudan, in coastal India, and in Southeast Asia, Islam's influence spread along regional trade routes.

Islam also spread among rural peoples, such as the pastoral Fulani of West Africa and Somali of northeastern Africa and various pastoralists in northwest India. In Bengal, Muslim religious figures oversaw the conversion of jungle into farmland and thereby gained many converts.

Marriage also played a role. Single Muslim men traveling to and settling in tropical Africa and Asia often married local women. Their children grew up in the Islamic faith. Some wealthy men had dozens of children from up to four wives and additional slave concubines. Servants and slaves in such households normally professed Islam.

The spread of Islam did not mean simply the replacement of one set of beliefs by another. Islam adapted to the cultures of the regions it penetrated, developing African, Indian, and Indonesian varieties.

End of Indian Buddhism

In India, Muslim invasions eliminated the last strongholds of long-declining Buddhism, including, in 1196, the great Buddhist center of study at Nalanda (nuh-LAN-duh) in Bihar (bee-HAHR). Its manuscripts were burned and thousands of monks killed or driven into exile in Nepal and Tibet. With Buddhism reduced to a minor faith in the land of its birth, Islam emerged as India's second most important religion. Hinduism still prevailed in 1500, but Islam displaced Hinduism in most of maritime Southeast Asia.

Social and Gender Distinctions

A growth in slavery accompanied the rising prosperity of the elites. Military campaigns in India, according to Islamic sources, reduced hundreds of thousands of Hindu "infidels" to slavery. Delhi overflowed with slaves. Sultan Ala ud-Din owned 50,000 and Firuz Shah 180,000, including 12,000 skilled artisans. Sultan Tughluq sent 100 male slaves and 100 female slaves as a gift to the emperor of China in return for a similar gift.

Indian Woman Spinning, ca. 1500 This drawing of a Muslim woman by an Indian artist shows the influence of Persian styles. The spinning of cotton fiber into thread—women's work—was made much easier by the spinning wheel, which the Muslim invaders introduced. Men then wove the threads into the cotton textiles for which India was celebrated.

The Slave Trade

Mali and Bornu sent slaves across the Sahara to North Africa, including beautiful maidens and eunuchs (castrated males). The expanding Ethiopian Empire regularly sent captives for sale to Aden traders at Zeila. According to modern estimates, Saharan and Red Sea traders sold about 2.5 million enslaved Africans between 1200 and 1500. African slaves from the Swahili Coast played conspicuous roles in the navies, armies, and administrations of some Indian states, especially in the fifteenth century. A few African slaves even reached China, where a source from about 1225 says rich families preferred gatekeepers with bodies "black as lacquer."

With "free" labor abundant and cheap, few slaves worked as farmers. In some places, hereditary castes of slaves dominated certain trades and military units. Indeed, the earliest rulers of the Delhi Sultanate rose from military slavery. A slave general in the western Sudan named Askia Muhammad seized control of the Songhai Empire (Mali's successor) in 1493. Less fortunate slaves, like the men and women who mined copper in Mali, did hard menial work.

Wealthy households used many slave servants. Eunuchs guarded the harems of wealthy Muslims, but women predominated as household slaves, serving also as entertainers and concubines. Some rich men aspired to having a concubine from every part of the world. One of Firuz Shah's nobles reportedly had two thousand harem slaves, including women from Turkey and China.

Sultan Ala ud-Din's campaigns against Gujarat at the end of the thirteenth century yielded a booty of twenty thousand maidens in addition to innumerable younger children of both sexes. The supply of captives became so great that the lowest grade of horse sold for five times as much as an ordinary female slave, although beautiful young virgins commanded far higher prices.

Status of Women

Hindu legal digests and commentaries suggest that the position of Hindu women may have improved somewhat compared to earlier periods. The ancient practice of sati (suh-TEE)—that is, of an upper-caste widow throwing herself on her husband's funeral pyre—remained a meritorious act strongly approved by social custom. But Ibn Battuta makes it clear that sati was strictly optional. Since the Hindu commentaries devote considerable attention to the rights of widows without sons to inherit their husbands' estates, one may even conclude that sati was exceptional.

Indian parents still gave their daughters in marriage before the age of puberty, but consummation of the marriage took place only when the young woman was ready. Wives faced far stricter rules of fidelity and chastity than their husbands and could be abandoned for any serious breach. But other offenses against law and custom usually brought lighter penalties than for men. A woman's male master—father, husband, or owner—determined her status. Women seldom played active roles in commerce, administration, or religion.

Adopting Islam did not necessarily mean accepting the social customs of the Arab world. In Mali's capital, Ibn Battuta was appalled that Muslim women both free and slave did not completely cover their bodies and veil their faces when appearing in public. He considered their nakedness an offense to women's (and men's) modesty. In another part of Mali, he berated a Muslim merchant from Morocco for permitting his wife to sit on a couch and chat with her male friend. The husband replied, "The association of women with men is agreeable to us and part of good manners, to which no suspicion attaches." Ibn Battuta refused to visit the merchant again.

Women's Activities

Besides child rearing, women involved themselves with food preparation and, when not prohibited by religious restrictions, brewing. In many parts of Africa, women commonly made beer from grains or bananas. These mildly alcoholic beverages played an important part in male rituals of hospitality and relaxation.

Throughout tropical Africa and Asia, women did much of the farm work. They also toted home heavy loads of food, firewood, and water balanced on their heads. Other common female activities included making clay pots for cooking and storage and making clothing. In India, the spinning wheel, introduced by the Muslim invaders, greatly reduced the cost of making thread for weaving. Women typically spun at home, leaving weaving to men. In West Africa, women often sold agricultural products, pottery, and other craftwork in the markets.

SECTION REVIEW

- Social and cultural life changed as a result of state formation, commercial expansion, and the spread of Islam.
- These changes mostly affected cities, where elites financed building programs, fostering hybrid styles of religious architecture.
- Islam spread mainly through peaceful adaptation and promoted education and scholarship.
- With rising prosperity came the expansion of slavery, which was endorsed by Islam.
- The position of Indian women seems to have improved, and the spread of Islam did not mean adoption of Arab gender customs.

CONCLUSION

Tropical Africa and Asia contained 40 percent of the world's population and over a quarter of its habitable land. Between 1200 and 1500, commercial, political, and cultural currents drew the region's peoples closer together. The Indian Ocean became the world's most important and richest trading area. The Delhi Sultanate brought the greatest political unity to India since the decline of the Guptas. Mali extended the political and trading role pioneered by Ghana in the western Sudan. Trade and empire followed closely the enlargement of Islam's presence and the accompanying diversification of Islamic customs.

Yet many social and cultural practices remained stable. Most tropical Africans and Asians never ventured far outside the rural communities where their families had lived for generations. Their lives followed the pattern of the seasons, the cycle of religious rituals and festivals, and the stages from childhood to elder status. Most people engaged in farming, herding, and fishing. Village communities proved remarkably hardy. They might be ravaged by natural disaster or pillaged by advancing armies, but over time most recovered. Empires and kingdoms rose and fell, but the villages endured.

KEY TERMS

Ibn Battuta p. 373
tropics p. 374
monsoon p. 374
Delhi Sultanate p. 376
Mali p. 378
Mansa Kankan Musa p. 380
Gujarat p. 384
dhows p. 385
Swahili Coast p. 386
Great Zimbabwe p. 388
Aden p. 388
Malacca p. 390
Urdu p. 391
Timbuktu p. 391

EBOOK AND WEBSITE RESOURCES

e **Interactive Maps**

Map 13.1 Africa and the Indian Ocean Basin: Physical Characteristics

Map 13.2 Africa, 1200–1500

Map 13.3 South and Southeast Asia, 1200–1500

Map 13.4 Arteries of Trade and Travel in the Islamic World, to 1500

Plus flashcards, practice quizzes, and more. Go to: www.cengage.com/history/bullietearthpeople5e

SUGGESTED READING

Cady, John F. *Southeast Asia: Its Historical Development.* 1964. Useful reading on Southeast Asia.

Chaudhuri, K. N. *Asia Before Europe: Economy and Civilization of the Indian Ocean from the Rise of Islam to 1750.* 1991. A broad conceptual approach.

Coedes, G. *The Indianized States of Southeast Asia*, ed. Walter F. Vella. 1968. Remains a basic text in this field.

Connah, Graham. *African Civilizations: Precolonial Cities and States in Tropical Africa: An Archaeological Perspective.* 1987. See especially later chapters.

Dunn, Ross E. *The Adventures of Ibn Battuta: A Muslim of the 14th Century.* 1986. Provides a modern retelling of his travels with commentary.

Ehret, Christopher. *The Civilizations of Africa: A History to 1800.* 2002. Chapters 6 and 7 summarize a great deal of new scholarship on Africa in this period.

Hourani, George F. *Arab Seafaring*, expanded ed. 1995. The most accessible survey of Indian Ocean sea travel.

Lieberman, Victor. *Strange Parallels: Integration on the Mainland, Southeast Asia in Global Context*, c. 800–1830. 2003. Integrates several national histories over a long period.

Lovejoy, Paul E. *Transformations in Slavery: A History of Slavery in Africa*, 2nd ed. 2000. See the first two chapters.

Ludden, David. *A Peasant History of South India.* 1985. Presents an intriguing perspective.

Majumdar, R. C., ed. *The History and Culture of the Indian People*, vol. 4, *The Delhi Sultanate*, 2nd ed. 1967. A comprehensive coverage of India.

Risso, Patricia. *Merchants and Faith: Muslim Commerce and Culture in the Indian Ocean.* 1995. A fine place to begin.

Tarling, Nicholas, ed. *The Cambridge History of Southeast Asia*, vol. 1. 1992. Various authors cover the period from prehistory to 1500 C.E.

NOTES

1. Tarikh-i-Wassaf, in Henry M. Elliot, *The History of India as Told by Its Own Historians*, ed. John Dowson (London: Trübner and Co., 1869–1871), 2:28.
2. Hasan Nizami, Taju-l Ma-asir, in ibid., 2:219.
3. Minhaju-s Siraj, Tabakat-i Nasiri, in ibid., 2:332–333.

AP* REVIEW QUESTIONS FOR CHAPTER 13

1. Like other governments in the tropics, the Delhi Sultanate
   (A) claimed ownership of all resources and then taxed their use.
   (B) encouraged the development of privately owned farms and independent labor.
   (C) introduced extensive new water-control systems that were developed through public works projects.
   (D) fostered the development of alluvial fertilization through flooding of fields.

2. Whereas Mali was founded as an African dynasty that had adopted Islam earlier,
   (A) the Delhi Sultanate was founded by outsiders who brought Islam with them.
   (B) Zimbabwe adopted religious tolerance after its experience with Chinese trade.
   (C) Mansa Musa brought Islam back to Senegal with him.
   (D) the Berbers resisted conversion and remained polytheistic.

3. While Mali depended on agriculture and caravan trade for its economic base, it also
   (A) raided other African states for wealth.
   (B) employed thousands of skilled workers who produced finished goods for market.
   (C) controlled the gold fields of the Niger headwaters.
   (D) received extensive tribute payments that made up most of its wealth.

4. As sultan, Raziya is remembered for
   (A) expanding the Delhi Sultanate into Vietnam.
   (B) converting all of the people to Islam.
   (C) being a harsh ruler who showed no mercy to enemies.
   (D) being a female sultan.

5. At its height, the Delhi Sultanate controlled
   (A) all of South and Southeast Asia.
   (B) the Indian subcontinent, Tibet, and much of modern Iran.
   (C) only a small portion of northern India.
   (D) all of India and much of modern Pakistan and Bangladesh, but not Sri Lanka.

6. The fourteenth-century collapse of the Mongol Empire
   (A) encouraged nomadic herders to settle in modern Iran and form their own empire.
   (B) stimulated trade along the trade route from India to China.
   (C) caused prices of goods to fall in Europe due to lower taxation on the overland routes.
   (D) stimulated expansion of trade in the Indian Ocean.

7. The largest and most seaworthy ship in the Indian Ocean trade before 1500 was the
   (A) Arab dhow.
   (B) Vietnamese sampan.
   (C) Portuguese caravel.
   (D) Chinese junk.

8. Archaeology reveals that by 1200 Indian Ocean trade from China had reached
   (A) Kongo.
   (B) Senegal.
   (C) the southern Swahili Coast.
   (D) Ethiopia.

9. In southern Africa, the largest trade city of the fourteenth century was
   (A) Mogadishu.
   (B) Great Zimbabwe.
   (C) Johannesburg.
   (D) Kongo.

10. In the fourteenth century, the port of Aden on the southern Arabian peninsula found that
    (A) common commercial interests promoted good commercial relations among diverse people.
    (B) Islamic law controlled feuding interests in the port of Aden better than silk.
    (C) European goods were of poor quality in comparison with goods from Asia.
    (D) it needed imports more than exports.

11. In fourteenth-century India, the status of a woman was
    (A) very similar to that of a man in the same caste.
    (B) unchanged from earlier times.
    (C) largely determined by the status of her male master.
    (D) improving inasmuch as women could take part in commercial activities.

CHAPTER

14

CHAPTER OUTLINE

- Rural Growth and Crisis
- Urban Revival
- Learning, Literature, and the Renaissance
- Political and Military Transformations
- Conclusion

DIVERSITY + DOMINANCE *Persecution and Protection of Jews, 1272–1349*

ENVIRONMENT + TECHNOLOGY *The Clock*

Burying Victims of the Black Death This scene from Tournai, Flanders, captures the magnitude of the plague.

Visit the website and ebook for additional study materials and interactive tools: www.cengage.com/history/bullietearthpeople5e

The Latin West, 1200–1500

- How well did inhabitants of the Latin West, rich and poor, urban and rural, deal with their natural environment?
- What social and economic factors led to the growth of cities in late medieval Europe?
- What factors were responsible for the promotion of learning and the arts in the Latin West?
- What social, political, and military developments contributed to the rise of European nations in this period?

In the summer of 1454, a year after the Ottoman Turks captured the Greek Christian city of Constantinople, Aeneas Sylvius Piccolomini (uh-NEE-uhs SIL-vee-uhs pee-kuh-lo-MEE-nee), destined in four years to become pope, expressed doubts as to whether anyone could persuade the rulers of Christian Europe to take up arms together against the Muslims: "Christendom has no head whom all will obey—neither the pope nor the emperor receives his due." The Christian states thought more of fighting each other. French and English armies had been battling for over a century. The German emperor presided over dozens of states but did not really control them. The numerous kingdoms and principalities of Spain and Italy could not unite. With only slight exaggeration, Aeneas Sylvius moaned, "Every city has its own king, and there are as many princes as there are households." He attributed this lack of unity to European preoccupation with personal welfare and material gain. Both pessimism about human nature and materialism had increased during the previous century, after a devastating plague had carried off a third of western Europe's population.

Yet despite all these divisions, disasters, and wars, historians now see the period from 1200 to 1500 (Europe's Later Middle Ages) as a time of unusual progress. Prosperous cities adorned with splendid architecture, institutions of higher learning, and cultural achievements counterbalanced the avarice and greed that Aeneas Sylvius lamented. Frequent wars caused havoc and destruction, but they also promoted the development of military technology and more unified monarchies.

Although their Muslim and Byzantine neighbors commonly called western Europeans "Franks," they ordinarily referred to themselves as "Latins," underscoring their allegiance to Roman Catholicism and the Latin language used in its rituals. Some common elements promoted the **Latin West**'s vigorous revival: competition, the pursuit of success, and the effective use of borrowed technology and learning.

Latin West Historians' name for the territories of Europe that adhered to the Latin rite of Christianity and used the Latin language for intellectual exchange in the period ca. 500–1500.

RURAL GROWTH AND CRISIS

Between 1200 and 1500, the Latin West brought more land under cultivation using new farming techniques and made greater use of machinery and mechanical forms of energy. Yet for the nine out of ten people who lived in the countryside, hard labor brought meager returns, and famine, epidemics, and war struck often. After the devastation of the Black Death between 1347 and 1351, social changes speeded up by peasant revolts released many persons from serfdom and brought some improvements to rural life.

Peasants, Population, and Plague

Rural Life

In 1200, most western Europeans lived as serfs tilling the soil on large estates owned by the nobility and the church (see Chapter 9). They owed their lord both a share of their harvests and numerous labor services. As a consequence of the inefficiency of farming practices and their obligations to landowners, peasants received meager returns for their hard work. Even with numerous religious holidays, peasants labored some fifty-four hours a week in their fields, more than half the time in support of the local nobility. Each noble household typically lived from the labor of fifteen to thirty peasant families. The standard of life in the lord's stone castle or manor house contrasted sharply with the peasant's one-room thatched cottage containing little furniture and no luxuries.

Scenes of rural life show both men and women at work in the fields, but equality of labor did not mean equality in decision making at home. In the peasant's hut as elsewhere in medieval Europe, women were subordinate to men. The influential theologian Thomas Aquinas (uh-KWY-nuhs) (1225–1274) spoke for his age when he argued that although both men and women were created in God's image, there was a sense in which "the image of God is found in man, and not in woman: for man is the beginning and end of woman; as God is the beginning and end of every creature."[1]

Rural poverty resulted from rapid population growth as well as inefficient farming methods and social inequality. In 1200, China's population may have exceeded Europe's by two to one; by 1300, the population of each was about 80 million. China's population fell because of the Mongol conquest (see Chapter 12), while Europe's more than doubled between 1100 and 1445. Some historians believe the reviving economy stimulated the increase. Others argue that severe epidemics were few, and warmer-than-usual temperatures reduced mortality from starvation and exposure.

Musée Conde, Chantilly, France/Bridgeman-Giraudon/ Art Resource, NY

Rural French Peasants Many scenes of peasant life in winter are visible in this small painting by the Flemish Limbourg brothers from the 1410s. Above the snow-covered beehives one man chops firewood, while another drives a donkey loaded with firewood to a little village. At the lower right a woman, blowing on her frozen fingers, heads past the huddled sheep and hungry birds to join other women warming themselves in the cottage (whose outer wall the artists have cut away).

CHRONOLOGY

	Technology and Environment	Culture	Politics and Society
1200	1200s Widespread use of crossbows and windmills		1200s Champagne fairs flourish
			1204 Fourth Crusade
		1210s Teutonic Knights, Franciscans, Dominicans	
			1215 Magna Carta issued
		1225–1274 Philosopher-monk Thomas Aquinas	
1300		1300–1500 Rise of universities	
	1315–1317 Great Famine	1313–1375 Giovanni Boccaccio, humanist writer	1337 Start of Hundred Years War
	1347–1351 Black Death ca.		
	1350 Growing deforestation		1381 Wat Tyler's Rebellion
		ca. 1390–1441 Jan van Eyck, painter	
1400	1400s Cannon and hand-held firearms in use		1415 Portuguese take Ceuta
			1431 Joan of Arc burned
	1454 Gutenberg Bible	1452–1519 Leonardo da Vinci, artist	1453 End of Hundred Years War; Ottomans take Constantinople
		1492 Expulsion of Jews from Spain	1492 Fall of Muslim state of Granada

New Farming Technology

three-field system A rotational system for agriculture in which two fields grow food crops and one lies fallow. It gradually replaced the two-field system in medieval Europe.

More people required more productive farming and new agricultural settlements. One widespread new technique, the **three-field system**, replaced the custom of leaving half the land fallow (uncultivated) every year to regain its fertility. Farmers grew crops on two-thirds of their land each year, alternating wheat and rye with oats, barley, or legumes. The third field was left fallow. The oats restored nitrogen to the depleted soil and produced feed for plow horses. In much of Europe, however, farmers continued to let half of their land lie fallow and use oxen (less efficient but cheaper than horses) to pull their plows.

New Settlements

AP* Exam Tip General knowledge of land management systems, but not specific details of the three-field system, is required for the multiple choice portion of the exam.

Population growth also encouraged new agricultural settlements. In the twelfth and thirteenth centuries, large numbers of Germans migrated into the fertile lands east of the Elbe River and into the eastern Baltic states. Knights belonging to Latin Christian religious orders slaughtered or drove away native inhabitants who had not yet adopted Christianity. During the thirteenth century, the Order of Teutonic Knights conquered, resettled, and administered a vast area along the Baltic that later became Prussia (see Map 14.3 on page 418). Other Latin Christians founded new settlements on lands conquered from the Muslims and Byzantines in southern Europe and on Celtic lands in the British Isles.

Famines

Draining swamps and clearing forests also brought new land under cultivation. But as population continued to rise, some people had to farm lands that had poor soils or were vulnerable to flooding, frost, or drought. Average crop yields fell accordingly after 1250, and more people lived at the edge of starvation. According to one historian, "By 1300, almost every child born in western Europe faced the probability of extreme hunger at least once or twice during his expected 30 to 35 years of life."[2] One unusually cold spell produced the Great Famine of 1315–1317, which affected much of Europe.

Black Death An outbreak of bubonic plague that spread across Asia, North Africa, and Europe in the mid-fourteenth century, carrying off vast numbers of persons.

The **Black Death** reversed the population growth. This terrible plague originated in China and spread across Central Asia with the Mongol armies (see Chapter 12). In 1346, the Mongols attacked the city of Kaffa (KAH-fah) on the Black Sea; a year later, Genoese (JEN-oh-eez) traders in Kaffa carried the disease to Italy and southern France. For two years, the Black Death spread across Europe, in some places carrying off two-thirds of the population. Average losses in western Europe amounted to one in three.

AP* Exam Tip The impact of the plague pandemics on the world is specifically highlighted in the course outline.

Victims developed boils the size of eggs in their groins and armpits, black blotches on their skin, foul body odors, and severe pain. In most cases, death came within a few days. Town officials closed their gates to people from infected areas and burned the victims' possessions. Such measures helped to spare some communities but could not halt the advance of the disease (see Map 14.1). Bubonic plague, the primary form of the Black Death, spreads from person to person and through the bites of fleas infesting the fur of certain rats. Although medieval doctors did not associate the disease with rats, eliminating the rats that thrived on urban refuse would have been difficult.

The plague left a psychological mark, bringing home to people how sudden and unexpected death could be. Some people became more religious, giving money to the church or hitting themselves with iron-tipped whips to atone for their sins. Others chose reckless enjoyment, spending their money on fancy clothes, feasts, and drinking. Whatever their mood, most survivors soon resumed their daily routines.

Periodic returns of plague made recovery from population losses slow and uneven. Europe's population in 1400 equaled that in 1200. Not until after 1500 did it rise above its preplague level.

Social Rebellion

Wat Tyler

In addition to its demographic and psychological effects, the Black Death triggered social changes in western Europe. Skilled and manual laborers who survived demanded higher pay for their services. At first, authorities tried to freeze wages at the old levels. Seeing this as a plot by the rich, peasants rose up against wealthy nobles and churchmen. During a widespread revolt in France in 1358, known as the Jacquerie, peasants looted castles and killed dozens of persons. In a large revolt led by Wat Tyler in 1381, English peasants invaded London, calling for an end to serfdom and obligations to landowners. Demonstrators murdered the archbishop of Canterbury and many royal officials. Authorities put down these rebellions with even greater bloodshed and cruelty, but they could not stave off the higher wages and other social changes the rebels demanded.

Better Rural Conditions

Serfdom practically disappeared in western Europe as peasants bought their freedom or ran away. Many free persons earning higher wages saved their money and bought land. Some English landowners who could no longer afford to hire enough fieldworkers began pasturing sheep for their wool. Others grew crops that required less care or made greater use of draft animals and laborsaving tools. Because the plague had not killed wild and domesticated animals, survivors had abundant meat and leather for shoes. Thus, the welfare of the rural masses generally improved after the Black Death, though the gap between rich and poor remained wide.

In urban areas, employers raised wages to attract workers. Guilds (discussed later in this chapter) shortened the period of apprenticeship. Competition within crafts also became more common. Although the overall economy shrank with the decline in population, per capita production actually rose.

Mills and Mines

Mining, metalworking, and the use of mechanical energy expanded so greatly in the centuries before 1500 that some historians speak of an "industrial revolution" in medieval Europe. That may be too strong a term, but the landscape fairly bristled with mechanical devices. Mills powered by water or wind ground grain, sawed logs, crushed olives, tanned leather, and made paper.

Watermills

In 1086, 5,600 watermills flanked England's many rivers. After 1200, mills spread rapidly across the western European mainland. By the early fourteenth century, entrepreneurs had crammed 68 watermills into a 1-mile section of the Seine (sen) River in Paris. Less efficient **water wheels** depended on the flow of a river passing beneath them. Greater efficiency came from channeling water to fall over the top of the wheel so that gravity added force to the water's flow. Dams ensured a steady flow of water throughout the year. Some watermills in France and England even harnessed the power of ocean tides.

water wheel A mechanism that harnesses the energy in flowing water to grind grain or to power machinery. It was used in many parts of the world but was especially common in Europe from 1200 to 1900.

Windmills multiplied in comparatively dry lands like Spain and in northern Europe, where ice made water wheels useless in winter. Designs for watermills dated back to Roman times, and the Islamic world, which inherited Hellenistic technologies, knew both water wheels and windmills. But people in the medieval Latin West used these devices on a much larger scale than did people elsewhere.

Milling and Iron Making

Owners invested heavily in building mills, but since nature furnished the energy to run them for free, they returned great profits. While individuals or monasteries constructed some mills, most were built by groups of investors. Rich millers often aroused the jealousy of their neighbors. In his *Canterbury Tales*, the English poet Geoffrey Chaucer (ca. 1340–1400) captured their unsavory reputation by portraying a miller as "a master-hand at stealing grain" by pushing down on the balance scale with his thumb.[3]

Waterpower aided the great expansion of iron making. Water powered the stamping mills that broke up the iron, the trip hammers that pounded it, and the bellows (first documented in the West in 1323) that raised temperatures to the point where the iron was liquid enough to be poured into molds. Blast furnaces producing high-quality iron are documented from 1380. Finished products ranged from armor to nails, from horseshoes to hoes.

Growth of Industry

Demand stimulated iron mining in many parts of Europe. In addition, new silver, lead, and copper mines in Austria and Hungary supplied metal for coins, church bells, cannon, and statues. Techniques of deep mining developed in central Europe spread west in the latter part of the fifteenth century. A building boom stimulated stone quarrying in France during the eleventh, twelfth, and thirteenth centuries.

Industrial growth changed the landscape. Towns grew outward and new ones were founded, dams and canals changed the flow of rivers, and quarries and mines scarred the hillsides. Urban tanneries (factories that cured and processed leather), the runoff from slaughterhouses, and human waste polluted streams. England's Parliament enacted the first recorded antipollution law in 1388, but enforcement proved difficult.

e Interactive Map

MAP 14.1 The Black Death in Fourteenth-Century Europe Spreading out of southwestern China along the routes opened by Mongol expansion, the plague reached the Black Sea port of Kaffa in 1346. This map documents its deadly progress year by year from there into the Mediterranean and north and east across the face of Europe.

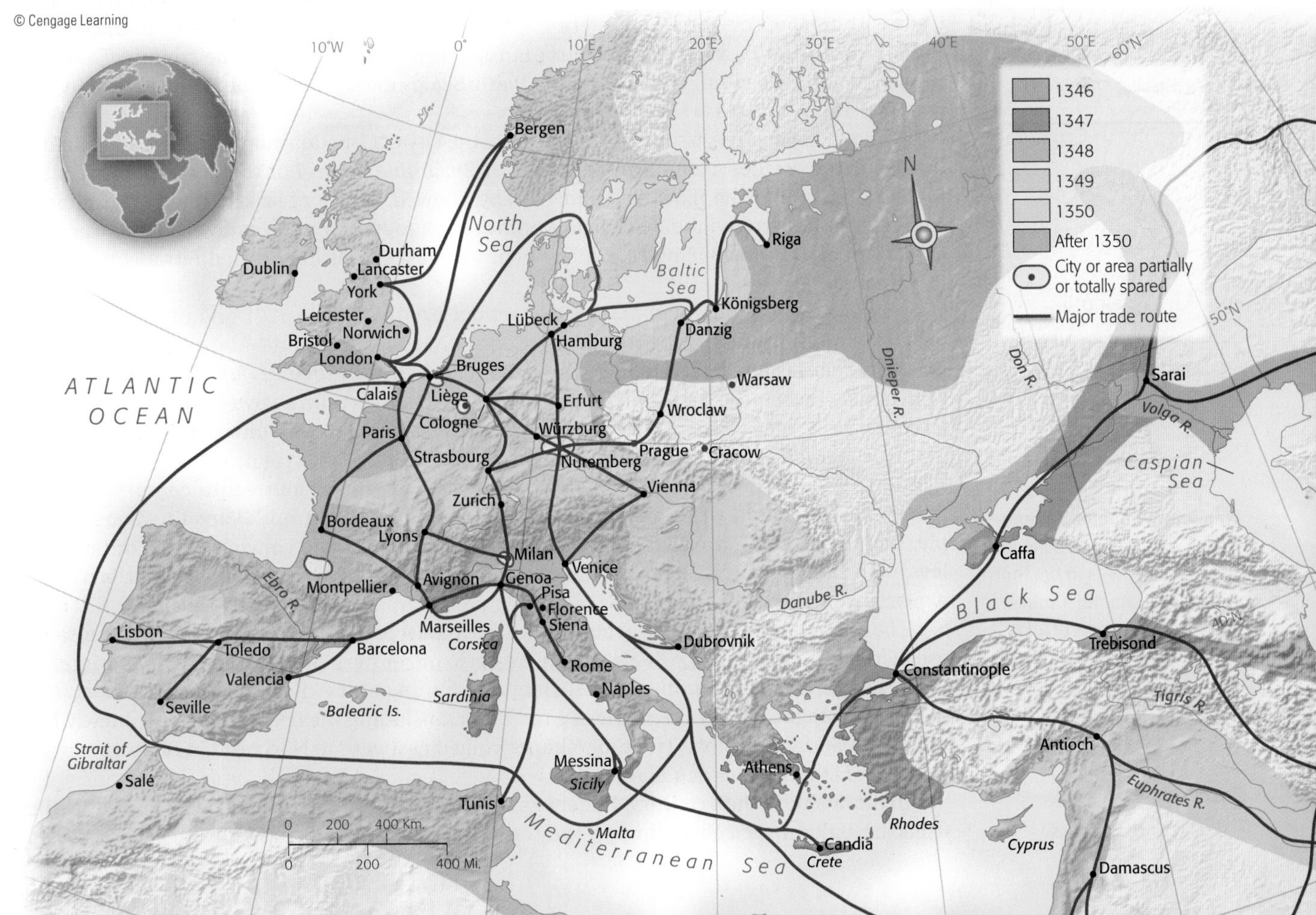

SECTION REVIEW

- Population growth stimulated improved farming methods and agricultural expansion, but peasant life did not significantly improve.
- Famine and the Black Death reversed the population growth and resulted in social change throughout western Europe.
- Improved mill designs and other technology stimulated further industrial growth, which, in turn, changed the landscape.

Deforestation accelerated. Trees provided timber for buildings and ships. Tanneries stripped bark to make acid for tanning leather. Many forests gave way to farmland. The glass and iron industries used great quantities of charcoal, made by controlled burning of oak or other hardwood, to produce the high temperatures required. A single iron furnace could consume all the trees within five-eighths of a mile (1 kilometer) in just forty days. Consequently, the later Middle Ages saw the end of many of western Europe's once-dense forests, except in places where powerful landowners established hunting preserves.

URBAN REVIVAL

AP* Exam Tip It is important to be able to compare the role of cities in various regions.

In the tenth century, no town in the Latin West could compete in size, wealth, or comfort with the cities of Byzantium and Islam. Yet by the later Middle Ages, the Mediterranean, Baltic, and Atlantic coasts boasted wealthy port cities, as did some major rivers draining into these seas (see Map 14.2). Some Byzantine and Muslim cities still exceeded those of the West in size, but not in commercial, cultural, and administrative dynamism, as marked by impressive new churches, guild halls, and residences.

PRIMARY SOURCE: Description of the World Follow Marco Polo, and hear him relate the natural, and sometimes supernatural, wonders he encountered on his journey to Khubilai Khan.

Trading Cities

Most urban growth after 1200 resulted from manufacturing and trade, both between cities and their hinterlands and over long distances. Northern Italy particularly benefited from maritime trade with the port cities of the eastern Mediterranean and, through them, the markets of the Indian Ocean and East Asia. In northern Europe, commercial cities in the county of Flanders (roughly today's Belgium) and around the Baltic Sea profited from regional networks and from overland and sea routes to the Mediterranean.

The Fourth Crusade

A Venetian-inspired assault in 1204 against the city of Constantinople, misleadingly named the "Fourth Crusade," temporarily eliminated Byzantine control of the passage between the Mediterranean and the Black Sea and thereby allowed Venice to seize Crete and expand its trading colonies around the Black Sea. Another boon to Italian trade came from the westward expansion of the Mongol Empire, which opened trade routes from the Mediterranean to China (see Chapter 12).

Marco Polo

A young merchant named Marco Polo set out from Venice in 1271 and reached the Mongol court in China after a long trek across Central Asia. He served the emperor Khubilai Khan for many years as an ambassador and governor of a Chinese province. Some scholars question Marco's later account of these adventures and a treacherous return voyage through the Indian Ocean that returned him to Venice in 1295, after an absence of twenty-four years. Similar reports of the riches of the East came from other European travelers.

When Mongol decline interrupted the caravan trade in the fourteenth century, Venetian merchants purchased eastern silks and spices brought by other middlemen to Constantinople, Damascus, and Cairo. Three times a year, Venice dispatched convoys of two or three galleys, with sixty oarsmen each, capable of bringing back 2,000 tons of goods. Other merchants explored new overland or sea routes.

Hanseatic League An economic and defensive alliance of the free towns in northern Germany, founded about 1241 and most powerful in the fourteenth century.

Genoa and Hanseatic League

The sea trade of Genoa on northern Italy's west coast probably equaled that of Venice. Genoese merchants established colonies in the western and eastern Mediterranean and around the Black Sea. In northern Europe, an association of trading cities known as the **Hanseatic** (han-see-AT-ik) **League** traded extensively in the Baltic, including the coasts of Prussia, newly conquered by German knights. Their merchants ranged eastward to Novgorod in Russia and westward across the North Sea to London.

Flemish Cities and Textiles

In the late thirteenth century, Genoese galleys from the Mediterranean and Hanseatic ships from the Baltic were converging on the trading and manufacturing cities in Flanders. Arti-

Stedelijke Openbare Bibliotheek, Ypres

Flemish Weavers, Ypres The spread of textile weaving gave employment to many people in the Netherlands. The city of Ypres in Flanders (now northern Belgium) was an important textile center in the thirteenth century. This drawing from a fourteenth-century manuscript shows a man and a woman weaving cloth on a horizontal loom, while a child makes thread on a spinning wheel.

sans in the Flemish towns of Bruges (broozh), Ghent (gent [hard g as in *get*]), and Ypres (EE-pruh) transformed raw wool from England into a fine cloth that was softer and smoother than the coarse "homespuns" from simple village looms. Dyed in vivid hues, these Flemish textiles appealed to wealthy Europeans, who also appreciated fine textiles from Asia.

Trade Fairs

Along the overland route connecting Flanders and northern Italy, important trading fairs developed in the Champagne (sham-PAIN) region of Burgundy. The Champagne fairs began as regional markets, exchanging manufactured goods, livestock, and farm produce once or twice a year. When the king of France gained control of Champagne at the end of the twelfth century, royal guarantees of safe conduct to merchants turned these markets into international fairs that were important for currency exchange and other financial transactions as well. A century later, fifteen Italian cities had permanent consulates in Champagne to represent the interests of their citizens. During the fourteenth century, the large volume of trade made it cheaper to ship Flemish woolens to Italy by sea than to pack them overland on animal backs. Champagne's fairs consequently lost some international trade, but they remained important as regional markets.

The Wool Trade

In the late thirteenth century, the English monarchy raised taxes on exports of raw wool, making cloth manufacture in England more profitable than in Flanders. Flemish specialists crossed the English Channel and introduced the spinning wheel and other devices to England. Annual raw wool exports fell from 35,000 sacks of wool at the beginning of the fourteenth century to 8,000 in the mid-fifteenth century, while English wool cloth production rose from 4,000 pieces just before 1350 to 54,000 a century later.

Florence also replaced Flemish imports with its own woolens industry financed by local banking families. In 1338, Florence manufactured 80,000 pieces of cloth, while importing only 10,000. These changes in the textile industry show how competition promoted the spread of manufacturing and encouraged new specialties.

The growing textile industries used the power of wind and water channeled through gears, pulleys, and belts to drive all sorts of machinery. Flemish mills cleaned and thickened woven

MAP 14.2 Trade and Manufacturing in Later Medieval Europe The economic revival of European cities was associated with great expansion of commerce. Notice the concentration of wool and linen textile manufacturing in northern Italy, the Netherlands, and England; the importance of trade in various kinds of foodstuffs; and the slave-exporting markets in Cairo, Kiev, and Rostov.

Interactive Map

cloth by beating it in water, a process known as fulling. Other mills produced paper, starting in southern Europe in the thirteenth century. Unlike the Chinese and Muslim papermakers, who had pursued the craft for centuries, the Europeans introduced machines to do the heavy work.

Venice

In the fifteenth century, Venice surpassed its European rivals in the volume of its trade in the Mediterranean as well as across the Alps into central Europe. Its craftspeople manufactured luxury goods once obtainable only from eastern sources, notably silk and cotton textiles, glassware and mirrors, jewelry, and paper. Exports of Italian and northern European woolens to the eastern Mediterranean also rose. In the space of a few centuries, western European cities had used the eastern trade to increase their prosperity and then reduce their dependence on eastern goods.

Civic Life

Most northern Italian and German cities were independent states, much like the port cities of the Indian Ocean Basin (see Chapter 13). Other European cities held royal charters exempting them from the authority of local nobles. Their autonomy enabled them to adapt to changing market conditions more quickly than cities controlled by imperial authorities, as in China and the Islamic world. Since anyone who lived in a chartered city for over a year could claim freedom, urban life promoted social mobility.

Jews in Europe

Europe's Jews mostly lived in cities. Spain had the largest communities because of the tolerance of earlier Muslim rulers. Commercial cities elsewhere welcomed Jews with manufacturing and business skills. Despite official protection by certain Christian princes and kings, Jews endured violent religious persecutions or expulsions in times of crisis, such as during the Black Death (see Diversity and Dominance: Persecution and Protection of Jews, 1272–1349). In 1492, the Spanish monarchs expelled all Jews in the name of religious and ethnic purity. Only the papal city of Rome left its Jews undisturbed throughout the centuries before 1500.

Artisan Guilds

guild In medieval Europe, an association of men (rarely women), such as merchants, artisans, or professors, who worked in a particular trade and banded together to promote their economic and political interests. Guilds were also important in other societies, such as the Ottoman and Safavid Empires.

Within most towns and cities, powerful associations known as guilds dominated civic life. **Guilds** brought together craft specialists, such as silversmiths, or merchants working in a particular trade, to regulate business practices and set prices. Guilds also trained apprentices and promoted members' interests with the city government. By denying membership to outsiders and Jews, guilds protected the interests of families that already belonged to them. Guilds also perpetuated male dominance of most skilled jobs.

Nevertheless, in a few places, women could join guilds either on their own or as the wives, widows, or daughters of male guild members. Large numbers of poor women also toiled in non-guild jobs in urban textile industries and in the food and beverage trades, generally receiving lower wages than men.

Women

Some women advanced socially through marriage to wealthy men. One of Chaucer's *Canterbury Tales* concerns a woman from Bath, a city in southern England, who became wealthy by marrying a succession of old men for their money (and then two other husbands for love), "aside from other company in youth." She was also a skilled weaver, Chaucer says: "In making cloth she showed so great a bent, / She bettered those of Ypres and of Ghent."

Banking

By the fifteenth century, a new class of wealthy merchant-bankers was operating on a vast scale and specializing in money changing and loans and making investments on behalf of other parties. Merchants great and small used their services. They also handled the financial transactions of ecclesiastical and secular officials and arranged for the transmission to the pope of funds known as Peter's pence, a collection taken up annually in every church in the Latin West. Princes and kings supported their wars and lavish courts with credit. Some merchant-bankers even developed their own news services, gathering information on any topic that could affect business.

The Fugger Bank

Florentine financiers invented checking accounts, organized private shareholding companies (the forerunners of modern corporations), and improved bookkeeping techniques. In the fifteenth century, the Medici (MED-ih-chee) family of Florence operated banks in Italy, Flanders, and London. Medicis also controlled the government of Florence and commissioned art works. The Fuggers (FOOG-uhrz) of Augsburg, who had ten times the Medici bank's lending capital, topped Europe's banking fraternity by 1500. Beginning as cloth merchants under Jacob "the Rich" (1459–1525), the family's many activities included the trade in Hungarian copper, essential for casting cannon.

Persecution and Protection of Jews, 1272–1349

Because they did not belong to the dominant Latin Christian faith, Jews suffered from periodic discrimination and persecution. For the most part, religious and secular authorities tried to curb such anti-Semitism. Jews, after all, were useful citizens who worshiped the same God as their Christian neighbors. Still, it was hard to know where to draw the line between justifiable and unjustifiable discrimination. The famous reviser of Catholic theology, St. Thomas Aquinas, made one such distinction in his Summa Theologica *with regard to attempts at forced conversion.*

Now, the practice of the Church never held that the children of Jews should be baptized against the will of their parents. . . . Therefore, it seems dangerous to bring forward this new view, that contrary to the previously established custom of the Church, the children of Jews should be baptized against the will of their parents.

There are two reasons for this position. One stems from danger to faith. For, if children without the use of reason were to receive baptism, then after reaching maturity they could easily be persuaded by their parents to relinquish what they had received in ignorance. This would tend to do harm to the faith.

The second reason is that it is opposed to natural justice . . . it [is] a matter of natural right that a son, before he has the use of reason, is under the care of his father. Hence, it would be against natural justice for the boy, before he has the use of reason, to be removed from the care of his parents, or for anything to be arranged for him against the will of his parents.

The "new view" Aquinas opposed was much in the air, for in 1272 Pope Gregory X issued a decree condemning forced baptism. The pope's decree reviews the history of papal protection given to the Jews, starting with a quotation from Pope Gregory I dating from 598, and decrees two new protections of Jews' legal rights.

Even as it is not allowed to the Jews in their assemblies presumptuously to undertake for themselves more than that which is permitted them by law, even so they ought not to suffer any disadvantage in those [privileges] which have been granted them.

Although they prefer to persist in their stubbornness rather than to recognize the words of their prophets and the mysteries of the Scriptures, and thus to arrive at a knowledge of Christian faith and salvation; nevertheless, inasmuch as they have made an appeal for our protection and help, we therefore admit their petition and offer them the shield of our protection through the clemency of Christian piety. In so doing we follow in the footsteps of our predecessors of happy memory, the popes of Rome—Calixtus, Eugene, Alexander, Clement, Celestine, Innocent, and Honorius.

We decree moreover that no Christian shall compel them or any one of their group to come to baptism unwillingly. But if any one of them shall take refuge of his own accord with Christians, because of conviction, then, after his intention will have been made manifest, he shall be made a Christian without any intrigue. For indeed that person who is known to come to Christian baptism not freely, but unwillingly, is not believed to possess the Christian faith.

Moreover, no Christian shall presume to seize, imprison, wound, torture, mutilate, kill, or inflict violence on them; furthermore no one shall presume, except by judicial action of the authorities of the country, to change the good customs in the land where they live for the purpose of taking their money or goods from them or from others.

In addition, no one shall disturb them in any way during the celebration of their festivals, whether by day or by night, with clubs or stones or anything else. Also no one shall exact any compulsory service of them unless it be that which they have been accustomed to render in previous times.

Inasmuch as the Jews are not able to bear witness against the Christians, we decree furthermore that the testimony of Christians against Jews shall not be valid unless there is among these Christians some Jew who is there for the purpose of offering testimony.

Since it occasionally happens that some Christians lose their Christian children, the Jews are accused by their enemies of secretly carrying off and killing these same Christian children, and of making sacrifices of the heart and blood of these very children. It happens, too, that the parents of these children, or some other Christian enemies of these Jews, secretly hide these very children in order that they may be able to injure these Jews, and in order that they may be able to extort from them a certain amount of money by redeeming them from their straits.

And most falsely do these Christians claim that the Jews have secretly and furtively carried away these children and killed them, and that the Jews offer sacrifice from the heart and the blood of these children, since their law in this matter precisely and expressly forbids Jews to sacrifice, eat, or drink the blood, or eat the flesh of animals having claws. This has been demonstrated many times at our court by Jews converted to the Christian faith: nevertheless very many Jews are often seized and detained unjustly because of this.

We decree, therefore, that Christians need not be obeyed against Jews in such a case or situation of this type, and we order that Jews seized under such a silly pretext be freed from imprisonment, and that they shall not be arrested henceforth on such a miserable pretext, unless—which we do not believe—they be caught in the commission of the crime. We decree that no Christian shall stir up anything against them, but that they should be maintained in that status and position in which they were from the time of our predecessors, from antiquity till now.

We decree, in order to stop the wickedness and avarice of bad men, that no one shall dare to devastate or to destroy a cemetery of the Jews or to dig up human bodies for the sake of getting money [by holding them for ransom]. Moreover, if anyone, after having known the content of this decree, should—which we hope will not happen—attempt audaciously to act contrary to it, then let him suffer punishment in his rank and position, or let him be punished by the penalty of excommunication, unless he makes amends for his boldness by proper recompense. Moreover, we wish that only those Jews who have not attempted to contrive anything toward the destruction of the Christian faith be fortified by the support of such protection. . . .

Despite such decrees, violence against Jews might burst out when fears and emotions were running high. This selection is from the official chronicles of the upper-Rhineland towns.

In the year 1349 there occurred the greatest epidemic that ever happened. Death went from one end of the earth to the other, on that side and this side of the [Mediterranean] sea, and it was greater among the Saracens [Muslims] than among the Christians. In some lands everyone died so that no one was left. Ships were also found on the sea laden with wares; the crew had all died and no one guided the ship. The Bishop of Marseilles and priests and monks and more than half of all the people there died with them. In other kingdoms and cities so many people perished that it would be horrible to describe. The pope at Avignon stopped all sessions of court, locked himself in a room, allowed no one to approach him and had a fire burning before him all the time. And from what this epidemic came, all wise teachers and physicians could only say that it was God's will. And the plague was now here, so it was in other places, and lasted more than a whole year. This epidemic also came to Strasbourg in the summer of the above mentioned year, and it is estimated about sixteen thousand people died.

In the matter of this plague the Jews throughout the world were reviled and accused in all lands of having caused it through the poison which they are said to have put into the water and the wells—that is what they were accused of—and for this reason the Jews were burnt all the way from the Mediterranean into Germany, but not in Avignon, for the pope protected them there.

Nevertheless they tortured a number of Jews in Berne and Zofingen who admitted they had put poison into many wells, and they found the poison in the wells. Thereupon they burnt the Jews in many towns and wrote of this affair to Strasbourg, Freibourg, and Basel in order that they too should burn their Jews. . . . The deputies of the city of Strasbourg were asked what they were going to do with their Jews. They answered and said that they knew no evil of them. Then . . . there was a great indignation and clamor against the deputies from Strasbourg. So finally the Bishop and the lords and the Imperial Cities agreed to do away with the Jews. The result was that they were burnt in many cities, and wherever they were expelled they were caught by the peasants and stabbed to death or drowned. . . .

On Saturday—that was St. Valentine's Day—they burnt the Jews on a wooden platform in their cemetery. There were about two thousand people of them. Those who wanted to baptize themselves were spared. Many small children were taken out of the fire and baptized against the will of their fathers and mothers. And everything that was owed to the Jews was cancelled, and the Jews had to surrender all pledges and notes that they had taken for debts. The council, however, took the cash that the Jews possessed and divided it among the working-men proportionately. The money was indeed the thing that killed the Jews. If they had been poor and if the feudal lords had not been in debt to them, they would not have been burnt.

QUESTIONS FOR ANALYSIS

1. **Why do Aquinas and Pope Gregory oppose prejudicial actions against Jews?**
2. **Why did prejudice increase at the time of the Black Death?**
3. **What factors account for the differences between the views of Christian leaders and the Christian masses?**

PRIMARY SOURCE: The Practice of Commerce Get advice from an experienced Florentine merchant before planning your next overland business trip to Cathay!

Since Latin Christians generally considered charging interest (usury) sinful, Jews predominated in money lending. Christian bankers devised ways to profit from loans indirectly in order to get around the condemnation of usury. Some borrowers repaid loans in a different currency at a rate of exchange favorable to the lender. Others added to their repayment a "gift" in thanks to the lender. For example, in 1501, church officials agreed to repay a Fugger loan of 6,000 gold ducats in five months along with a "gift" of 400 ducats, amounting to an effective interest rate of 16 percent a year. In fact, the return was less since the church failed to repay the loan on time.

Yet most residents of western European cities lived in poverty and squalor rather than wealth. European cities generally lacked civic amenities, such as public baths and water supply systems, that had existed in the cities of Western antiquity and still survived in cities of the Islamic Middle East.

Gothic cathedrals Large churches originating in twelfth-century France; built in an architectural style featuring pointed arches, tall vaults and spires, flying buttresses, and large stained-glass windows.

Gothic Cathedrals

Master builders and associated craftsmen counted among the skilled people in greatest demand. Though cities competed with one another in the magnificence of their guild halls, town halls, and other structures (see Environment and Technology: The Clock), **Gothic cathedrals**, first

Cathedral at Autun in Eastern France Begun around 1120 and sufficiently completed to receive the relics of St. Lazaire in 1146, this cathedral reflected Romanesque architectural design and artistic taste. In the fifteenth century a rebuilding program changed the cathedral's external appearance from Romanesque to Gothic, but the images above the west portal survive in their original form. Carved by a sculptor named Gislebertus between 1130 and 1135, they depict the Last Judgment, with Christ enthroned between the saved souls on his right and those condemned to Hell on his left. The sharply angular figures are typical of Romanesque style. Scenes like these taught important religious messages to illiterate worshipers.

ENVIRONMENT + TECHNOLOGY

The Clock

Clocks were a prominent feature of the Latin West in the late medieval period. The Song-era Chinese had built elaborate mechanical clocks centuries earlier (see Chapter 10), but the West was the first part of the world where clocks became a regular part of urban life. Whether mounted in a church steeple or placed on a bridge or tower, mechanical clocks proclaimed Western people's delight with mechanical objects, concern with precision, and display of civic wealth.

The word *clock* comes from a word for bell. The first mechanical clocks that appeared around 1300 in western Europe were simply bells with an automatic mechanical device to strike the correct number of hours. The most elaborate Chinese clock had been powered by falling water, but this was impractical in cold weather. The levers, pulleys, and gears of European clocks were powered by a weight hanging from a rope wound around a cylinder. An "escapement" lever regulated the slow, steady unwinding.

Early Clock This weight-driven clock dates from 1454.

Bodleian Library, University of Oxford, Ms. Laud Misc. 570, 25v.

Enthusiasm for building expensive clocks came from various parts of the community. For some time, monks had been using devices to mark the times for prayer. Employers welcomed chiming clocks to regulate the hours of their employees. Universities used them to mark the beginning and end of classes. Prosperous merchants readily donated money to build a splendid clock that would display their city's wealth. The city of Strasbourg, for example, built a clock in the 1350s that included statues of the Virgin, the Christ Child, and the three Magi; a mechanical rooster; the signs of the zodiac; a perpetual calendar; and an astrolabe—and it could play hymns, too!

By the 1370s and 1380s clocks were common enough for their measured hours to displace the older system that varied the length of the hour in proportion to the length of the day. Previously, for example, the London hour had varied from thirty-eight minutes in winter to eighty-two minutes in summer. By 1500 clocks had numbered faces with hour and minute hands. Small clocks for indoor use were also in vogue. Though not very accurate by today's standards, these clocks were still a great step forward. Some historians consider the clock the most important of the many technological advances of the later Middle Ages because it fostered so many changes during the following centuries.

appearing about 1140 in France, cost the most and brought the greatest prestige. The pointed, or Gothic, arch, replacing the older round, or Roman, arch, proved a hallmark of the new design. External (flying) buttresses stabilizing the high, thin, stone columns below the arches constituted another distinctive feature. This method of construction enabled master builders to push the Gothic cathedrals to great heights and fill the outside walls with giant windows depicting religious scenes in brilliantly colored stained glass. During the next four centuries, interior heights soared ever higher, towers and spires pierced the heavens, and walls became dazzling curtains of stained glass.

SECTION REVIEW

- After 1200, most cities grew through manufacture and trade, particularly those of northern Italy, Flanders, and the Baltic coast.
- Expanding trade and technological innovation ultimately reduced Europe's dependence on eastern goods.
- Cities fostered social mobility, but civic life was dominated by guilds, wealthy merchants, and bankers.
- Most urban residents lived in squalor without the amenities of Islamic Middle Eastern cities.
- Gothic cathedrals became signs of special civic pride and prestige in European cities.

The men who designed and built the cathedrals had little or no formal education and limited understanding of the mathematical principles of modern civil engineering. Master masons sometimes miscalculated, causing parts of some overly ambitious cathedrals to collapse. The record-high choir vault of Beauvais Cathedral, for instance—154 feet (47 meters) in height—came tumbling down in 1284. But as builders gained experience and invented novel solutions to their problems, success rose from the rubble of their mistakes. The cathedral spire in Strasbourg reached 466 feet (142 meters) into the air—as high as a forty-story building. Such heights were unsurpassed until the twentieth century.

LEARNING, LITERATURE, AND THE RENAISSANCE

The Roman Heritage

Throughout the Middle Ages, people in the Latin West lived amid reminders of the achievements of the Romans. They wrote and worshiped in a version of their language, traveled their roads, and obeyed some of their laws. The vestments and robes of popes, kings, and emperors followed the designs of Roman officials. Yet the learning of Greco-Roman antiquity virtually disappeared with the rise of the biblical world described in the Hebrew and Christian scriptures.

The Renaissance

Renaissance (European) A period of intense artistic and intellectual activity, said to be a "rebirth" of Greco-Roman culture. Usually divided into an Italian Renaissance, from roughly the mid-fourteenth to mid-fifteenth century, and a Northern (trans-Alpine) Renaissance, from roughly the early fifteenth to early seventeenth century.

A small revival of learning associated with the court of Charlemagne in the ninth century was followed by a larger renaissance (rebirth) in the twelfth century. Cities became centers of intellectual and artistic life. The universities established across the Latin West after 1200 contributed to this cultural revival. In the mid-fourteenth century, the pace of intellectual and artistic life quickened in what is often called the **Renaissance**, which began in northern Italy and later spread to northern Europe. Some Italian authors saw the Italian Renaissance as a sharp break with an age of darkness. Others see this era as the high noon of a day that had been dawning for several centuries.

Translations from Arabic

Before 1100, Byzantine and Islamic scholarship generally surpassed scholarship in Latin Europe. When Latin Christians wrested southern Italy from the Byzantines and Sicily and Toledo from the Muslims in the eleventh century, they acquired many manuscripts of Greek and Arabic works. These included works by Plato and Aristotle (AR-ih-stah-tahl) and Greek treatises on medicine, mathematics, and geography, as well as scientific and philosophical writings by Muslim writers. Latin translations of the Iranian philosopher Ibn Sina (IB-uhn SEE-nah) (980–1037), known in the West as Avicenna (av-uh-SEN-uh), had great influence because of their sophisticated blend of Aristotelian and Islamic philosophy. Jewish scholars contributed significantly to the translation and explication of Arabic and other manuscripts.

Universities

universities Degree-granting institutions of higher learning. Those that appeared in the Latin West from about 1200 onward became the model of all modern universities.

The thirteenth century saw the foundation of two new religious orders, the Dominicans and the Franciscans, some of whose most talented members taught in the independent colleges that arose after 1200. Some scholars believe that the colleges established in Paris and Oxford patterned themselves on similarly endowed places of study then spreading in the Islamic world—*madrasas*, which provided subsidized housing for poor students and paid the salaries of their teachers. The Latin West, however, innovated the idea of **universities**, degree-granting corporations specializing in multidisciplinary research and advanced teaching.

Between 1300 and 1500, sixty universities joined the twenty established before that time. Students banded together to start some of them; guilds of professors founded others. Teaching guilds, like the guilds overseeing manufacturing and commerce, set standards for the profession, trained apprentices and masters, and defended their professional interests.

Universities set the curriculum for each discipline and instituted final examinations for degrees. Students who passed the exams that ended their apprenticeship received a "license" to teach. Students who completed longer training and defended a masterwork of scholarship became "masters" and "doctors." The University of Paris gradually absorbed the city's various colleges, but the colleges of Oxford and Cambridge remained independent, self-governing organizations.

Specialized Training

Since all universities used Latin, students and masters could move freely across political and linguistic lines, seeking the courses they wanted and the most interesting professors. Some universities offered specialized training. Legal training centered on Bologna (buh-LOHN-yuh); Montpellier and Salerno focused on medicine; Paris and Oxford excelled in theology.

scholasticism A philosophical and theological system, associated with Thomas Aquinas, devised to reconcile Aristotelian philosophy and Roman Catholic theology in the thirteenth century.

The prominence of theology stemmed from many students aspiring to ecclesiastical careers, but scholars also saw theology as "queen of the sciences"—the central discipline encompassing all knowledge. Hence, thirteenth-century theologians sought to synthesize the rediscovered philosophical works of Aristotle and the commentaries of Avicenna with the Bible's revealed truth. These efforts to synthesize reason and faith were known as **scholasticism** (skoh-LAS-tih-sizm).

Thomas Aquinas

e **PRIMARY SOURCE: *Summa Theologica*: On Free Will** This selection from Thomas Aquinas, on the question of free will, shows a synthesis of Aristotelian logic and Christian theology.

Thomas Aquinas, a brilliant Dominican priest who taught theology at the University of Paris, wrote the most notable scholastic work, the *Summa Theologica* (SOOM-uh thee-uh-LOH-jih-kuh), between 1267 and 1273. Although his exposition of Christian belief organized on Aristotelian principles came to be accepted as a masterly demonstration of the reasonableness of Christianity, scholasticism upset many traditional thinkers. Some church authorities tried to ban Aristotle from the curriculum. In addition, rivalry between the leading Dominican and Franciscan theological scholars continued over the next two centuries. However, the considerable freedom of medieval universities from both secular and religious authorities enabled the new ideas to prevail over the fears of church administrators.

Humanists and Printers

Dante's *Divine Comedy*

This period also saw important literary contributions. The Italian Dante Alighieri (DAHN-tay ah-lee-GYEH-ree) (1265–1321) completed a long, elegant poem, the *Divine Comedy,* shortly before his death. This supreme expression of medieval preoccupations tells the allegorical story of Dante's journey through the nine circles of Hell and the seven terraces of Purgatory, followed by his entry into Paradise. The Roman poet Virgil guides him through Hell and Purgatory; Beatrice, a woman he had loved from afar since childhood and whose death inspired the poem, guides him to Paradise.

The *Divine Comedy* foreshadows the literary fashions of the later Italian Renaissance. Like Dante, later Italian writers made use of Greco-Roman classical themes and mythology and sometimes courted a broader audience by writing not in Latin but in their local language (Dante used the vernacular spoken in Tuscany [TUS-kuh-nee]).

Chaucer's *Canterbury Tales*

The poet Geoffrey Chaucer (c. 1343–1400), many of whose works show the influence of Dante, wrote in vernacular English. The *Canterbury Tales,* a lengthy poem written in the last dozen years of his life, contains often humorous and earthy tales told by fictional pilgrims on their way to the shrine of Thomas à Becket in Canterbury (see Chapter 9). They present a vivid cross-section of medieval people and attitudes.

Humanities

humanists (Renaissance) European scholars, writers, and teachers associated with the study of the humanities (grammar, rhetoric, poetry, history, languages, and moral philosophy), influential in the fifteenth century and later.

Dante influenced a literary movement of the **humanists** that began in his native Florence in the mid-fourteenth century. The term refers to their interest in grammar, rhetoric, poetry, history, and moral philosophy (ethics)—subjects known collectively as the humanities, an ancient discipline. With the brash exaggeration characteristic of new intellectual fashions, humanist writers like the poet Francesco Petrarch (fran-CHES-koh PAY-trahrk) (1304–1374) and the poet and storyteller Giovanni Boccaccio (jo-VAH-nee boh-KAH-chee-oh) (1313–1375) proclaimed a revival of the classical Greco-Roman tradition they felt had for centuries lain buried under the rubble of the Middle Ages.

This idea of a rebirth of learning dismisses too readily the monastic and university scholars who for centuries had been recovering all sorts of Greco-Roman learning, as well as writers like Dante (whom the humanists revered), who anticipated humanist interests by a generation. Yet the humanists had a great impact as educators, advisers, and reformers. Their greatest influence came in reforming secondary education. They introduced a curriculum centered on the languages and

akg-images

Dante's Divine Comedy This fifteenth-century painting by Domenico di Michelino shows Dante holding a copy of the *Divine Comedy*. Hell is depicted to the poet's right and the terraces of Purgatory behind him, surmounted by the earthly and heavenly Paradise. The city of Florence, with its recently completed cathedral, appears to Dante's left.

literature of Greco-Roman antiquity, which they felt provided intellectual discipline, moral lessons, and refined tastes. This curriculum dominated European secondary schools well into the twentieth century. The universities felt the humanist influence less, mostly after 1500. Theology, law, medicine, and branches of philosophy other than ethics remained prominent in university education during this period.

Boccaccio's *Decameron*

Many humanists tried to duplicate the elegance of classical Latin and (to a lesser extent) Greek, which they revered as the pinnacle of learning, beauty, and wisdom. Boccaccio gained fame with his vernacular writings, which resemble Dante's, and especially for the *Decameron*, an earthy work that has much in common with Chaucer's boisterous tales. Under Petrarch's influence, however, Boccaccio turned to writing in classical Latin.

Erasmus of Rotterdam

As humanist scholars mastered Latin and Greek, they turned their language skills to restoring the original texts of Greco-Roman writers and of the Bible. By comparing different manuscripts, they eliminated errors introduced by generations of copyists. To aid in this task, Pope Nicholas V (r. 1447–1455) created the Vatican Library, buying scrolls of Greco-Roman writings and paying to have accurate copies and translations made. Working independently, the Dutch scholar Erasmus (uh-RAZ-muhs) of Rotterdam (ca. 1466–1536) produced a critical edition of the New Testament in Greek. Erasmus corrected many errors and mistranslations in the Latin text that had been in general use throughout the Middle Ages. Later, this humanist priest and theologian wrote—in classical Latin—influential moral guides, including the *Enchiridion militis christiani* (*The Manual of the Christian Knight*, 1503) and *The Education of a Christian Prince* (1515).

printing press A mechanical device for transferring text or graphics from a woodblock or type to paper using ink. Presses using movable type first appeared in Europe in about 1450.

The influence of the humanists grew as the new technology of printing made their critical editions of ancient texts, literary works, and moral guides more available. The Chinese and the Arabs used carved woodblocks for printing, and block-printed playing cards circulated in Europe before 1450, but after that date three European improvements revolutionized printing: (1) movable pieces of type consisting of individual letters, (2) new ink suitable for printing on paper, and (3) the **printing press**, a mechanical device that pressed inked type onto sheets of paper.

Gutenberg's Printing Press

Johann Gutenberg (yoh-HAHN GOO-ten-burg) (ca. 1394–1468) of Mainz led the way. The Gutenberg Bible of 1454, the first book in the West printed from movable type, exhibited a

The Art Archive

A French Printshop, 1537 A workman operates the "press," quite literally a screw device that presses the paper to the inked type. Other employees examine the printed sheets, each of which holds four pages. When folded, the sheets make a book. The man on the right is selecting pieces of type from a compartmented box and placing them in a frame for printing.

beauty and craftsmanship that bore witness to the printer's years of experimentation. Humanists worked closely with the printers, who spread the new techniques to Italy and France. Erasmus did editing and proofreading for the Italian scholar-printer Aldo Manuzio (1449–1515) in Venice. Manuzio's press published many critical editions of classical Latin and Greek texts.

By 1500, at least 10 million printed volumes flowed from presses in 238 European towns, launching a revolution that affected students, scholars, and a growing literate population. These readers consumed unorthodox political and religious tracts along with ancient texts.

Renaissance Artists

Although the artists of the fourteenth and fifteenth centuries continued to depict biblical subjects, the Greco-Roman revival led some, especially in Italy, to portray ancient deities and myths. Another popular trend involved scenes of daily life.

Neither theme was entirely new, however. Renaissance art, like Renaissance scholarship, owed a debt to earlier generations. Italian painters of the fifteenth century credited the Florentine painter Giotto (JAW-toh) (ca. 1267–1337) with single-handedly reviving the "lost art of painting." In religious scenes, Giotto replaced the stiff, staring figures of the Byzantine style, which were intended to overawe viewers, with more natural and human portraits with whose

Michelangelo's Tomb Statue of Lorenzo de Medici The greatest of the Medici bankers, Lorenzo governed Florence during the height of the Renaissance. At the time of his death in 1492 he had fallen under the influence of Girolamo Savonarola, a stern, moralistic priest who felt that art and morals had departed too far from proper Christianity. Nevertheless, the Roman armor and pensive expression of this statue epitomize the antique revival and dedication to thought associated with the term Renaissance.

emotions of grief and love viewers could identify. Rather than floating on backgrounds of gold leaf, his saints inhabit earthly landscapes.

Flemish Art

North of the Alps, the Flemish painter Jan van Eyck (yahn vahn IKE) (ca. 1390–1441) mixed his pigments with linseed oil in place of the egg yolk of earlier centuries. Oil paints dried more slowly and gave pictures a superior luster. Italian painters quickly copied van Eyck's technique, though his own masterfully realistic paintings on religious and domestic themes remained distinctive.

Leonardo da Vinci (lay-own-AHR-doh dah-VIN-chee) (1452–1519) used oil paints for his *Mona Lisa*. Renaissance artists like Leonardo worked in many media, including bronze sculptures and frescos (painting on wet plaster) like *The Last Supper*. Leonardo's notebooks also contain imaginative designs for airplanes, submarines, and tanks. His younger contemporary Michelangelo (my-kuhl-AN-juh-low) (1472–1564) painted frescoes of biblical scenes on the ceiling of the Sistine Chapel in the Vatican, sculpted statues of David and Moses, and designed the dome for a new Saint Peter's Basilica in Rome.

Italian Art

The patronage of wealthy and educated merchants and prelates underlay the artistic blossoming in the cities of northern Italy and Flanders. The Florentine banker Cosimo de' Medici (1389–1464) and his grandson Lorenzo (1449–1492), known as "the Magnificent," spent immense

SECTION REVIEW

- Greco-Roman learning returned to the Latin West through a series of revivals that culminated with the Renaissance.
- An infusion of Greek and Islamic scholarship during the eleventh century helped to prompt the revival of the twelfth and thirteenth centuries.
- Colleges and universities grew, with theology as the preeminent discipline.
- Foreshadowed by Dante, humanism, with its focus on classical languages, literature, ethics, and education, emerged in Italy.
- The influence of the humanists spread through the new print technology.
- Renaissance artists enlarged the thematic and technical resources of painting, sculpture, and architecture.

sums on paintings, sculpture, and public buildings. In Rome, the papacy (PAY-puh-see) launched a building program that culminated in the construction of the new Saint Peter's Basilica and a residence for the pope.

These scholarly and artistic achievements exemplify the innovation and striving for excellence of the Late Middle Ages. The new literary themes and artistic styles of this period had lasting influence on Western culture. But the innovations in the organization of universities, in printing, and in oil painting had wider implications, for they were later adopted by cultures all over the world.

POLITICAL AND MILITARY TRANSFORMATIONS

AP* Exam Tip It is important to know the similarities and contrasts between feudalism in Europe and Japan.

Stronger and more unified states and armies developed in western Europe in parallel with the economic and cultural revivals (see Map 14.3). Through the prolonged struggle of the Hundred Years War, French and English monarchs forged closer ties with the nobility, the church, and the merchants. Crusades against Muslim states brought consolidation to Spain and Portugal. In Italy and Germany, however, political power remained in the hands of small states and loose alliances.

Monarchs, Nobles, and the Church

Thirteenth-century states continued early medieval state structures (see Chapter 9). Hereditary monarchs topped the political pyramid, but modest treasuries and the rights of nobles and the church limited their powers. Powerful noblemen who controlled vast estates had an important voice in matters of state. The church guarded closely its traditional rights and independence. Towns, too, had acquired rights and privileges. Towns in Flanders, the Hanseatic League, and Italy approached independence from royal interference. In theory the ruler's noble vassals owed military service in time of war. In practice, vassals sought to limit the monarch's power.

Crossbows and Firearms

In the year 1200, knights still formed the backbone of western European armies, but changes in weaponry brought this into question. Improved crossbows could shoot metal-tipped arrows with enough force to pierce helmets and light body armor. Professional crossbowmen, hired for wages, became increasingly common and much feared. Indeed, a church council in 1139 outlawed the crossbow—ineffectively—as being too deadly for use against Christians. The arrival in Europe of firearms based on the Chinese invention of gunpowder (see Chapter 12) further transformed the medieval army.

Rome Versus Avignon

The church also resisted royal control. In 1302, the outraged Pope Boniface VIII (r. 1294–1303) asserted that divine law made the papacy superior to "every human creature," including monarchs. Issuing his own claim of superiority, King Philip "the Fair" of France (r. 1285–1314) sent an army to arrest the pope, a chastisement that hastened Pope Boniface's death. Philip then engineered the election of a French pope, who established a new papal residence at Avignon (ah-vee-NYON) in southern France in 1309.

Great Western Schism A division in the Latin (Western) Christian Church between 1378 and 1415, when rival claimants to the papacy existed in Rome and Avignon.

A succession of French-dominated popes residing in Avignon improved church discipline but at the price of compromising their neutrality in the eyes of other rulers. The **Great Western Schism** between 1378 and 1415 saw rival papal claimants at Avignon and Rome vying for Christian loyalties. The papacy eventually regained its independence and returned to Rome, but the

MAP 14.3 Europe in 1453 This year marked the end of the Hundred Years War between France and England and the fall of the Byzantine capital city of Constantinople to the Ottoman Turks. Muslim advances into southeastern Europe were offset by the Latin Christian reconquests of Islamic holdings in southern Italy and the Iberian Peninsula and by the conversion of Lithuania.

Interactive Map

The Magna Carta One of four extant copies, this document shows the ravages of time, but the symbolic importance of the charter King John of England signed under duress in 1215 for English constitutional history has not been diminished. Originally a guarantee of the barons' feudal rights, it came to be seen as a limit on the monarch's authority over all subjects.

The National Archives, Public Record Office and Historical Manuscripts Commission

PRIMARY SOURCE: Magna Carta: The Great Charter of Liberties Learn what rights and liberties the English nobility, on behalf of all free Englishmen, forced King John to grant them in 1215.

Magna Carta

long crisis broke the pope's ability to challenge the rising power of monarchs like Philip, who had used the dispute to persuade his nobles to grant him a new tax.

The English monarchy wielded more centralized power as a result of consolidation that took place after the Norman conquest of 1066. The Anglo-Norman kings also extended their realm by assaults on their Celtic neighbors. Between 1200 and 1400, they incorporated Wales and reasserted control over most of Ireland. Nevertheless, under King John (r. 1199–1216), royal power suffered a severe setback. Forced to acknowledge the pope as his overlord in 1213, he lost his bid to reassert claims to Aquitaine in southern France the following year and then yielded to his nobles by signing the Magna Carta in 1215. This "Great Charter" affirmed that monarchs were subject to established law, confirmed the independence of the church and the city of London, and guaranteed the nobles' hereditary rights.

The Hundred Years War

Hundred Years War (1337–1453) Series of campaigns over control of the throne of France, involving English and French royal families and French noble families.

The conflict between the king of France and his vassals known as the **Hundred Years War** (1337–1453) affords a key example of the transformation in politics and war. These vassals included the kings of England (for lands that belonged to their Norman ancestors), the counts of prosperous and independent-minded Flanders, and the dukes of Brittany and Burgundy. In typical fashion, the conflict grew out of a marriage alliance.

Marriage between Princess Isabella of France and King Edward II of England (r. 1307–1327) should have ensured the king's loyalty, as a vassal, to the French monarchy. However, when the next generation of the French ruling house produced no other sons, Isabella's son, King Edward III of England (r. 1327–1377), laid claim to the French throne in 1337. French courts instead awarded the throne to a more distant (and more French) cousin. Edward decided to fight for his rights.

Military Technology

The new military technology shaped the conflict. Early in the war, hired Italian crossbowmen reinforced the French cavalry, but the English longbow proved superior. Adopted from the Welsh, the 6-foot (1.8-meter) longbow could shoot farther and more rapidly than the crossbow. Its arrows could not pierce armor, but concentrated volleys found gaps in the knights' defenses or struck their less-protected horses. Heavier and more encompassing armor provided a defense but limited a knight's movements. Once pulled off his steed by a foot soldier armed with a pike (hooked pole), he could not get up.

Later in the Hundred Years War, firearms gained prominence. The first cannon scared the horses with smoke and noise but did little damage. As they grew larger, however, they proved effective in battering the walls of castles and towns. The first artillery use against the French, at the Battle of Agincourt (1415), gave the English an important victory.

Joan of Arc

Faced with a young French peasant woman called Joan of Arc, subsequent English gains stalled. Acting, she believed, on God's instructions, she put on armAor and rallied the French troops to defeat the English in 1429. Shortly afterward, she fell into English hands; she was tried by English churchmen and burned at the stake as a witch in 1431.

In the final battles, French cannon demolished the walls of once-secure castles held by the English and their allies. The truce that ended the struggle in 1453 left the French monarchy in firm control.

New Monarchies in France and England

new monarchies Historians' term for the monarchies in France, England, and Spain from 1450 to 1600. The centralization of royal power was increasing within more or less fixed territorial limits.

The war proved a watershed in the rise of **new monarchies** in France and England, centralized states with fixed "national" boundaries and stronger representative institutions. English monarchs after 1453 consolidated control over territory within the British Isles, though the Scots defended their independence. The French monarchs also turned to consolidating control over powerful noble families, especially those headed by women. Mary of Burgundy (1457–1482) was forced to surrender most of her family's vast holdings to the king. Then in 1491, Anne of Brittany's forced marriage to the king led to the eventual incorporation of her duchy (DUTCH-ee) into France.

Military technology undermined the nobility. Smaller, more mobile cannon developed in the late fifteenth century pounded castle walls. Improvements in hand-held firearms, able by the late fifteenth century to pierce the heaviest armor, ended the domination of the armored knight. Armies now depended less on knights and more on bowmen, pikemen, musketeers, and artillerymen.

The Cost of War

The new monarchies needed a way to finance their full-time armies. Some nobles agreed to money payments in place of military service and to additional taxes in time of war. For example, in 1439 and 1445, Charles VII of France (r. 1422–1461) successfully levied a new tax on his vassals' land. This not only paid the costs of the war with England but also provided the monarchy a financial base for the next 350 years.

Merchants' taxes also provided revenues. Taxes on the English wool trade, begun by King Edward III, paid most of the costs of the Hundred Years War. Some rulers taxed Jewish merchants or extorted large contributions from wealthy towns. Individual merchants sometimes curried royal favor with loans. The fifteenth-century French merchant Jacques Coeur (cur) gained many social and financial benefits for himself and his family by lending money to French courtiers, but his debtors accused him of murder and had his fortune confiscated.

Church Versus State

The church provided a third source of revenue through voluntary contributions to support a war. English and French monarchs won the right to appoint important church officials in their realms in the fifteenth century. They subsequently used state power to enforce religious orthodoxy more vigorously than the popes had been able to do. But reformers complained that the church's spiritual mission became subordinate to political and economic concerns.

The shift in power to the monarchs and away from the nobility and the church did not deprive nobles of their social position and roles as government officials and military officers. Moreover, the kings of England and France in 1500 had to deal with representative institutions that had not existed in 1200. The English Parliament proved a permanent check on royal power: the House of Lords contained the great nobles and church officials; the House of Commons represented the towns and the leading citizens of the counties. In France, the Estates General, a similar but less effective representative body, represented the church, the nobles, and the towns.

reconquest of Iberia Beginning in the eleventh century, military campaigns by various Iberian Christian states to recapture territory taken by Muslims. In 1492 the last Muslim ruler was defeated, and Spain and Portugal emerged as united kingdoms.

Iberian Unification

Spain and Portugal's **reconquest of Iberia** from Muslim rule expanded the boundaries of Latin Christianity. The knights who pushed the borders of their kingdoms southward furthered both Christianity and their own interests. The spoils of victory included irrigated farmland, rich cities, and ports on the Mediterranean Sea and Atlantic Ocean. Serving God, growing rich, and living off the labor of others became a way of life for the Iberian nobility.

DeA Picture Library/Art Resource, NY

Conquest of Granada A Muslim state since 1238, Granada was conquered in 1492 by the armies of Ferdinand of Aragon and Isabella of Castile. This relief sculpture from the sixteenth century shows the sultan Mohammad XI surrendering the keys of the capital city.

Portugal and Africa

The reconquest proceeded over several centuries. Toledo fell and became a Christian outpost in 1085. English crusaders bound for the Holy Land helped take Lisbon in 1147. It displaced the older city of Oporto (meaning "the port"), from which Portugal took its name, as both capital and the kingdom's leading city. After a Christian victory in 1212 broke the back of Muslim power, the reconquest accelerated. Within decades, Portuguese and Castilian forces captured the prosperous cities of Cordova (1236) and Seville (1248) and drove the Muslims from the southwestern region known as Algarve (ahl-GAHRV) ("the west" in Arabic). Only the small kingdom of Granada hugging the Mediterranean coast remained in Muslim hands.

By incorporating Algarve in 1249, Portugal attained its modern territorial limits. After a pause to colonize, Christianize, and consolidate this land, Portugal took the crusade to North Africa. In 1415, Portuguese knights seized the port of Ceuta (say-OO-tuh) in Morocco, where they learned more about the Saharan caravan trade in gold and slaves. During the next few decades, Portuguese mariners sailed down the Atlantic coast of Africa seeking rumored African Christian allies and access to this trade (see Chapter 15).

Elsewhere in Iberia, the reconquest continued. Spain came into being when the marriage of Princess Isabella of Castile and Prince Ferdinand of Aragon in 1469 led to the union of their kingdoms when they inherited their respective thrones a decade later. Their conquest of Granada in 1492 secured the final piece of Muslim territory for the new kingdom.

King Ferdinand and Queen Isabella

Ferdinand and Isabella sponsored the first voyage of Christopher Columbus in 1492 (see Chapter 15). In a third momentous event of that year, the monarchs manifested their crusading mentality by ordering all Jews expelled from their kingdoms. Attempts to convert or expel the remaining Muslims led to a revolt at the end of 1499 that lasted until 1501. The Spanish rulers expelled the last Muslims in 1502. Portugal expelled the Jews in 1496, including 100,000 refugees from Spain.

SECTION REVIEW

- Between 1200 and 1500, monarchs, nobles, and the church struggled over political power.
- Tensions between the French monarchy and the papacy resulted in the Great Western Schism.
- In England, royal power was checked by the papacy and nobility, the latter imposing the Magna Carta on King John.
- The Hundred Years War between the French monarchy and its vassals introduced new military technologies.
- The war also stimulated the rise of the new centralized monarchies of England and France.
- Spain and Portugal continued the reconquest of Muslim Iberia, a process completed by Ferdinand and Isabella.

CONCLUSION

Ecologically, the peoples of Latin Europe harnessed the power of wind and water and mined and refined their mineral wealth at the cost of localized pollution and deforestation. However, inability to improve food production and distribution in response to population growth created a demographic crisis that climaxed with the Black Death that devastated Europe in the mid-fourteenth century.

Politically, basic features of the modern European state began to emerge. Frequent wars caused kingdoms of moderate size to develop exceptional military strength. The ruling class saw economic strength as the twin of political power and promoted the welfare of cities specializing in trade, manufacturing, and finance, the profits of which they taxed.

Culturally, autonomous universities and printing supported the advance of knowledge. Art and architecture reached unsurpassed peaks in the Renaissance. Late medieval society displayed a fundamental fascination with tools and techniques. New inventions and improved versions of old ones underlay the new dynamism in commerce, warfare, industry, and navigation.

Ironically, many of the tools that the Latin West would use to challenge Eastern supremacy—printing, firearms, and navigational devices—originally came from the East. However, western European success depended as much on strong motives for expansion. From the eleventh century onward, population pressure, religious zeal, economic enterprise, and intellectual curiosity drove an expansion of territory and resources that took the crusaders to the Holy Land, merchants to the eastern Mediterranean and Black Seas, the English into Wales and Ireland, German settlers across the Elbe River, and Iberian Christians into the Muslim south. The early voyages into the Atlantic, discussed in the next chapter, extended these activities.

KEY TERMS

Latin West p. 399
three-field system p. 401
Black Death p. 401
water wheel p. 402
Hanseatic League p. 404
guild p. 407
Gothic cathedrals p. 410
Renaissance (European) p. 412
universities p. 412
scholasticism p. 413
humanists (Renaissance) p. 413
printing press p. 414
Great Western Schism p. 417
Hundred Years War p. 420
new monarchies p. 420
reconquest of Iberia p. 421

EBOOK AND WEBSITE RESOURCES

Primary Sources

Description of the World

The Practice of Commerce

Summa Theologica: On Free Will

Magna Carta: The Great Charter of Liberties

Interactive Maps

Map 14.1 The Black Death in Fourteenth-Century Europe

Map 14.2 Trade and Manufacturing in Later Medieval Europe

Map 14.3 Europe in 1453

Plus flashcards, practice quizzes, and more. Go to: www.cengage.com/history/bullietearthpeople5e

SUGGESTED READING

Alland, Christopher. *The Hundred Years War: England and France at War, ca. 1300–ca. 1450*. 1988. Key events in the Anglo-French dynastic conflict.

Bartlett, Robert. *The Making of Europe: Conquest, Colonization, and Cultural Change*. 1993. Shows Europe as the product of conquest and colonization before it became a colonizer.

Bechmann, Roland. *Trees and Man: The Forest in the Middle Ages*. 1990. A pioneering work in environmental history.

Cantor, Norman F. *In the Wake of the Plague: The Black Death and the World It Made*. 2001. A thorough introduction.

Gies, Frances, and Joseph Gies. *Women in the Middle Ages*. 1978. A general introduction.

Gimpel, Jean. *The Medieval Machine: The Industrial Revolution of the Middle Ages*. 1977. A general introduction to the technological issues of the period.

Holmes, George. *Europe: Hierarchy and Revolt, 1320–1450*, 2nd ed. 2000. A comprehensive overview.

Huizinga, Johan. *The Waning of the Middle Ages*. 1924. A classic account of the "mind" of the fifteenth century.

Jardine, Lisa. *Worldly Goods: A New History of the Renaissance*. 1996. A well-illustrated and balanced survey.

Lopez, Robert S. *The Commercial Revolution of the Middle Ages, 950–1350*. 1976. Surveys the West's economic revival and growth.

McNeill, William H. *The Pursuit of Power: Technology, Armed Force, and Society Since* A.D. 1000. 1982. An influential interpretation by an eminent world historian.

O'Callaghan, Joseph F. *A History of Medieval Spain*. 1975. Provides the best one-volume coverage.

Oakley, Francis C. *The Western Church in the Later Middle Ages*. 1985. A reliable summary of modern scholarship.

Phillips, J. R. S. *The Medieval Expansion of Europe*, 2nd ed. 1998. European adventurism from Greenland to West Africa to China.

Stow, Kenneth R. *Alienated Minority: The Jews of Medieval Latin Europe*. 1992. A fine survey through the fourteenth century.

NOTES

1. Quoted in Marina Warner, *Alone of All Her Sex: The Myth and Cult of the Virgin Mary* (New York: Random House, 1983), 179.
2. Harry Miskimin, *The Economy of the Early Renaissance, 1300–1460* (Englewood Cliffs, NJ: Prentice Hall, 1969), 26–27.
3. Quotations here and later in the chapter are from Geoffrey Chaucer, *The Canterbury Tales*, trans. Nevill Coghill (New York: Penguin Books, 1952), 25, 29, 32.

AP* REVIEW QUESTIONS FOR CHAPTER 14

1. Western Europeans of the eleventh through the fourteenth centuries tended to refer to themselves as
   (A) Romans.
   (B) Latins.
   (C) Burgundians.
   (D) Germans.

2. Between 1100 and 1350, Europe's population more than doubled. Historians believe that this increase may have been due to
   (A) better hygiene practices.
   (B) cooler temperatures killing off germs.
   (C) a general decrease in warfare.
   (D) a revival in the economy of Europe.

3. In response to the increase in population, some farmers in Europe
   (A) tried new methods of increasing yields like the three-field system.
   (B) borrowed money from banks to rent land for planting crops.
   (C) gave up farming and began herding, which was more lucrative.
   (D) rented lands directly from the landowners.

4. The majority of the urban growth in Europe from 1200 to 1500 was due to
   (A) the growth in population.
   (B) land enclosures.
   (C) the growth in trade and manufacturing.
   (D) access to less expensive food.

5. The decline of the Mongol Empire disrupted the caravan trade into Europe. In response, European merchants
   (A) began to explore new overland routes and new sea routes.
   (B) became dependant on the Muslims for trade goods.
   (C) learned to become self-sufficient and do without goods from Asia.
   (D) launched Crusades to reestablish the trade routes to China.

6. In most towns and cities, merchants and skilled craftsmen regulated business practices, membership, and training and promoted the interests of their members in city government through
   (A) payment of feudal obligations.
   (B) guilds.
   (C) the church.
   (D) the encomienda.

7. The spread of the humanist movement benefited from
   (A) local kings who supported it.
   (B) support from the church.
   (C) common people wanting to learn more about their world.
   (D) the development of the printing press.

8. By the thirteenth century
   (A) wealthy nobles were seeking to limit the power of the king.
   (B) the church gave local control of parishes to local nobles.
   (C) overseas trade was supplanting overland trade.
   (D) England and France had established parliaments.

9. By the mid-thirteenth century, Portugal had
   (A) become one of the most advanced trading kingdoms in Europe.
   (B) merged with Spain to become a joint kingdom.
   (C) become warriors for the church.
   (D) challenged the Italian city-states on the Mediterranean Sea.

CHAPTER

15

CHAPTER OUTLINE

- Global Maritime Expansion Before 1450
- European Expansion, 1400–1550
- Encounters with Europe, 1450–1550
- Conclusion

ENVIRONMENT + TECHNOLOGY *Vasco da Gama's Fleet*

DIVERSITY + DOMINANCE *Kongo's Christian King*

The Granger Collection, New York

Ferdinand Magellan Navigating the Straits Connecting the Atlantic and Pacific Oceans This late-sixteenth-century print uses fanciful representations of native peoples and creatures to embellish Magellan's circumnavigation of the globe.

Visit the website and ebook for additional study materials and interactive tools: www.cengage.com/history/bullietearthpeople5e

The Maritime Revolution, to 1550

- What were the objectives and major accomplishments of the voyages of exploration undertaken by Chinese, Polynesians, and other non-Western peoples?
- In this era of long-distance exploration, did Europeans have any special advantages over other cultural regions?
- What explains the different nature of Europe's interactions with Africa, India, and the Americas?

In 1511 young Ferdinand Magellan sailed from Europe around the southern tip of Africa and eastward across the Indian Ocean as a member of the first Portuguese expedition to explore the East Indies (maritime Southeast Asia). Eight years later, this time in the service of Spain, he led an expedition that sought to reach the East Indies by sailing westward. By the middle of 1521 Magellan's expedition had achieved its goal by sailing across the Atlantic, rounding the southern tip of South America, and crossing the Pacific Ocean—but at a high price.

Of the five ships that had set out from Spain in 1519, only three made the long passage across the vast Pacific. Dozens of sailors died from starvation and disease during the voyage. In the Philippines, Magellan, having survived numerous mutinies during the voyage, died in battle on April 27, 1521, while aiding a local ruler who had promised to become a Christian.

To consolidate their dwindling resources, the expedition's survivors burned the least seaworthy of their remaining three ships and consolidated men and supplies. In the end only the *Victoria* made it home across the Indian Ocean and back to Europe. Nevertheless, the *Victoria*'s return to Spain on September 8, 1522, was a crowning example of Europeans' determination to make themselves masters of the oceans. A century of daring and dangerous voyages backed by the Portuguese crown had opened new routes through the South Atlantic to Africa, Brazil, and the rich trade of the Indian Ocean. Rival voyages sponsored by Spain since 1492 opened new contacts with the American continents. A maritime revolution was under way that would change the course of history.

This new maritime era marked the end of a long period when Asia had initiated most overland and maritime expansion. Asia had been the source of the most useful technologies and the most influential systems of belief. It was also home to the most powerful states and the richest trading networks. The success of Iberian voyages of exploration in the following century would redirect the world's center of power, wealth, and innovation to the West.

This maritime revolution broadened and deepened contacts, alliances, and conflicts across ancient cultural boundaries. Some of these contacts ended tragically for individuals like Magellan. Some proved disastrous for entire populations: Amerindians, for instance, suffered conquest, colonization, and a rapid decline in numbers. And sometimes the results were mixed: Asians and Africans found both risks and opportunities in their new relations with Europe.

GLOBAL MARITIME EXPANSION BEFORE 1450

Since ancient times travel across the world's seas and oceans had been one of the great challenges to technological ingenuity. Ships had to be sturdy enough to survive heavy winds and seas, and pilots had to learn how to cross featureless expanses of water to reach their destinations. In time ships, sails, and navigational techniques perfected in the more protected seas were adapted to open oceans.

AP* Exam Tip Interregional trade and exchange are important topics.

However complex the solutions and dangerous the voyages, the rewards of sea travel made them worthwhile. Ships could move goods and people more profitably than any form of overland travel then possible. Crossing unknown waters, finding new lands, developing new markets, and establishing new settlements attracted adventurers from every continent. By 1450 daring mariners had discovered and settled most of the islands of the Pacific, the Atlantic, and the Indian Ocean, but no one had yet crossed the Pacific in either direction. Even the smaller Atlantic remained a barrier to contact between the Americas, Europe, and Africa. The inhabitants of Australia were also cut off from contact with the rest of humanity. All this was about to change.

The Pacific Ocean

Polynesian Voyages

The ancestors of the Polynesians originated in Asia. After centuries of island-hopping migrations that led from Melanesia (mel-uh-NEE-zhuh) to Fiji and Tonga, Polynesians had developed larger, more sea-worthy canoes, some 120 feet long (37 meters), and improved navigational skills that allowed them to extend their voyages over ever-greater distances (see Map 15.1). Between 100 and 300 B.C.E. they colonized the Marquesas (mar-KAY-suhs). No later than 500 C.E. Polynesians had settled the Hawaiian Islands 2,200 miles (3,541 kilometers) away. Around the same time Polynesian voyagers established settlements on Easter Island and New Zealand, both more

Polynesian Canoes Pacific Ocean mariners sailing canoes such as these, shown in an eighteenth-century painting, made epic voyages of exploration and settlement. A large platform connects two canoes at the left, providing more room for the members of the expedition, and a sail supplements the paddlers.

"Tereoboo, King of Owyhee, bringing presents to Captain Cook," D. L. Ref. p. xx 2f. 35. Courtesy, The Dixon Library, State Library of New South Wales

CHRONOLOGY

	Pacific Ocean	Atlantic Ocean	Indian Ocean
	100 B.C.E.–800 C.E. Polynesian settlement of Pacific islands	770–1200 Viking voyages	
	1200–1300 Polynesian societies in Hawaii develop clear class structures with hereditary chiefs	1300s Settlement of Madeira, Azores, Canaries	
		Early 1300s Mali voyages	
1400			1405–1433 Voyages of Zheng He
		1418–1460 Voyages of Henry the Navigator	
		1440s First slaves from West Africa sent to Europe	
		1482 Portuguese at Gold Coast and Kongo	
		1486 Portuguese at Benin	
		1488 Bartolomeu Dias reaches Indian Ocean	
		1492 Columbus reaches Caribbean	
		1492–1500 Spanish conquer Hispaniola	
		1493 Columbus returns to Caribbean (second voyage)	
		1498 Columbus reaches mainland of South America (third voyage)	1497–1498 Vasco da Gama reaches India
1500		1500 Cabral reaches Brazil	1505 Portuguese bombard Swahili Coast cities
			1510 Portuguese take Goa
			1511 Portuguese take Malacca
			1515 Portuguese take Hormuz
	1519–1522 Magellan expedition	1519–1521 Cortés conquers Aztec Empire	
		1531–1533 Pizarro conquers Inca Empire	
		1536 Rebellion of Maco Inca in Peru	1535 Portuguese take Diu
			1538 Portuguese defeat Ottoman fleet
			1539 Portuguese aid Ethiopia

than 2,300 miles (3,702 kilometers) distant. These voyagers eventually reached the mainland of the Americas where they gained access to the sweet potato, domesticated first in South America. Long-distance voyages then spread this nutritious plant to Polynesian settlements as far away as New Zealand and beyond.

Both DNA evidence and linguistic similarities indicate that the Polynesian settlement of the islands of the eastern Pacific was planned and not the result of accident. Following voyages of reconnaissance, Polynesian mariners carried colonizing expeditions in fleets of large double-hulled canoes that relied on scores of paddlers as well as sails. A wide platform connected the two hulls of these crafts and permitted the transportation of passengers, domesticated animals, and plants crucial to the success of distant and isolated settlements. Success depended upon reliably navigating across thousands of miles of ocean using careful observation of the currents

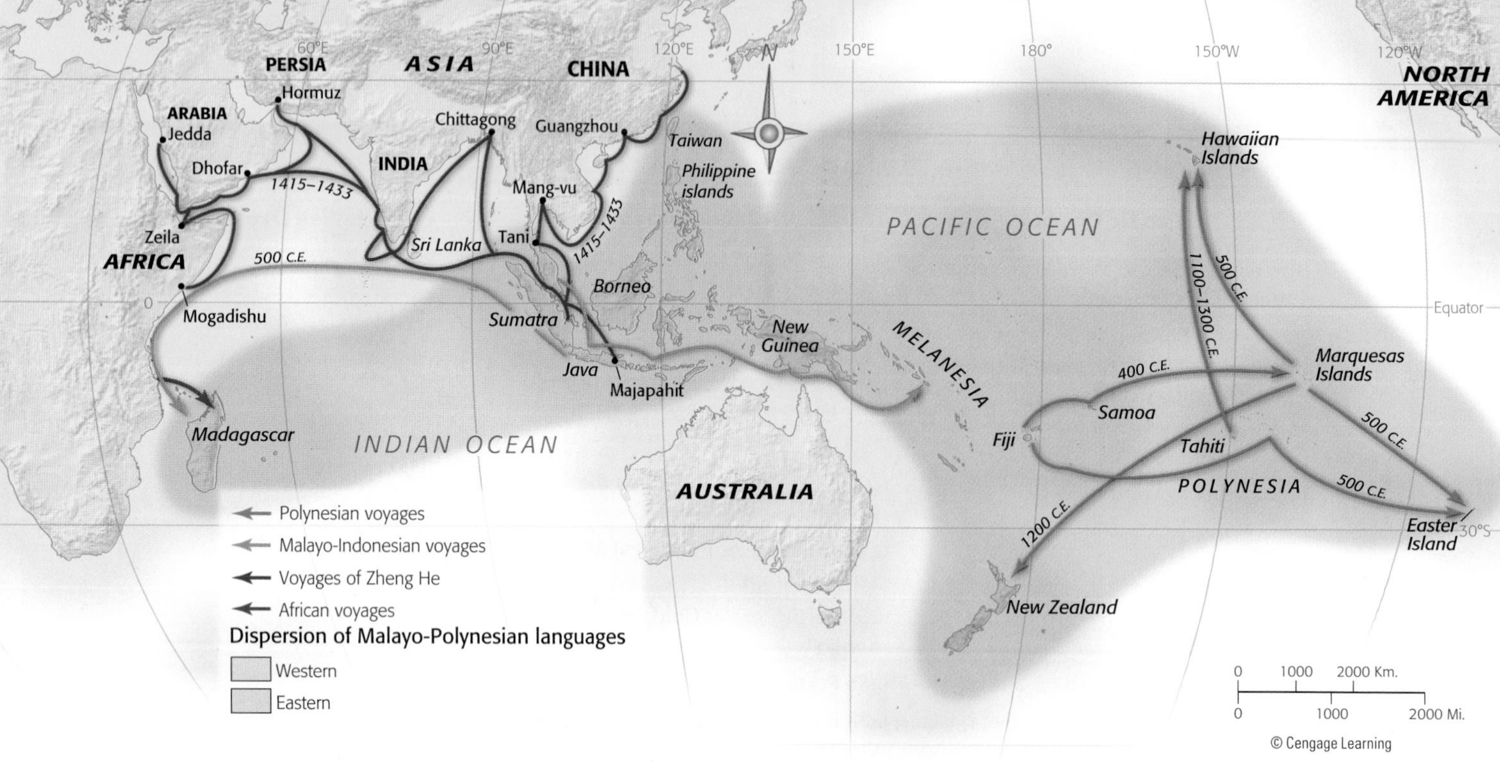

MAP 15.1 Exploration and Settlement in the Indian and Pacific Oceans Before 1500 Over many centuries, mariners originating in Southeast Asia gradually colonized the islands of the Pacific and Indian Oceans. The Chinese voyages led by Zheng He in the fifteenth century were lavish official expeditions.

Interactive Map

and stars as the crews searched for evidence of land. Once established, each satellite settlement developed distinctive cultural attributes, since ongoing contact was very difficult. With population growth after 1200 C.E. these societies became more hierarchical and violent.

The Indian Ocean

While Polynesian mariners were settling Pacific islands, other Malayo-Indonesians were sailing westward across the Indian Ocean and colonizing the large island of Madagascar off the southeastern coast of Africa. These voyages continued through the fifteenth century, and today the inhabitants of Madagascar still speak Malayo-Polynesian languages. However, part of the island's population is descended from Africans who had crossed the 300 miles (500 kilometers) from the mainland to Madagascar, most likely in the centuries before 1500.

Other peoples had been using the Indian Ocean for trade since ancient times. Southeast Asia and eastern Africa as well as the Indian subcontinent provided coasts that seafarers might safely follow and coves for protection. Moreover, seasonal winds known as monsoons are so predictable and steady that navigation in these waters using sailing vessels called dhows (dow) was less difficult and dangerous than elsewhere.

The rise of medieval Islam gave Indian Ocean trade an important boost. The great Muslim cities of the Middle East provided a demand for valuable commodities, and networks of Muslim traders were active across the region. These traders shared a common language, ethic, and law and actively spread their religion to distant trading cities. By 1400 there were Muslim trading communities all around the Indian Ocean.

Chinese Voyages

These Indian Ocean traders largely operated outside the control of the empires and states they served, but in East Asia imperial China's rulers were growing more and more interested in these wealthy ports of trade. In 1368 the Ming dynasty overthrew Mongol rule and began to reestablish China's predominance and prestige abroad.

Having restored Chinese dominance in East Asia, the Ming moved to establish direct contacts with the peoples around the Indian Ocean, sending out seven imperial fleets between 1405 and 1433 (see Chapter 12). The enormous size of these expeditions, far larger than needed for exploration or promoting trade, indicates that the Ming sought to inspire awe of their power and

Dugald Stermer

Chinese Junk This modern drawing shows how much larger one of Zheng He's ships was than one of Vasco da Gama's vessels. Watertight interior bulkheads made junks the most seaworthy large ships of the fifteenth century. Sails made of pleated bamboo matting hung from the junk's masts, and a stern rudder provided steering. European ships of exploration, though smaller, were faster and more maneuverable.

achievements. While curiosity about this prosperous region may have also been a motive, the fact that the ports visited by the fleets were major commercial centers suggests that expanding China's trade was an objective as well.

The scale of the Ming expeditions to the Indian Ocean Basin reflects imperial China's resources and importance. The first consisted of sixty-two specially built "treasure ships," large Chinese junks each about 300 feet long by 150 feet wide (90 by 45 meters). There were also at least a hundred smaller vessels. Each treasure ship had nine masts, twelve sails, many decks, and a carrying capacity of 3,000 tons (six times the capacity of Columbus's entire fleet). One expedition carried over 27,000 individuals, including infantry and cavalry troops. The ships were armed with small cannon, but in most Chinese sea battles arrows from highly accurate crossbows dominated the fighting.

Zheng He An imperial eunuch and Muslim, entrusted by the Ming emperor Yongle with a series of state voyages that took his gigantic ships through the Indian Ocean, from Southeast Asia to Africa.

Admiral **Zheng He** (jung huh) (1371–1435) commanded the expeditions. A Chinese Muslim with ancestral connections to the Persian Gulf, Zheng was a fitting emissary to the increasingly Muslim-dominated Indian Ocean Basin. The expeditions carried other Arabic-speaking Chinese as interpreters. One interpreter kept a journal that recorded local customs and beliefs. He observed new flora and fauna, noting exotic animals such as the black panther of Malaya and the tapir of Sumatra. In India he described the division of the coastal population into five classes, which correspond to the four Hindu varna and a separate Muslim class. He also recorded that traders in the rich Indian trading port of Calicut (KAL-ih-kut) could perform error-free calculations by counting on their fingers and toes rather than using the Chinese abacus. After his return, the interpreter went on tour in China, telling of these exotic places and "how far the majestic virtue of [China's] imperial dynasty extended."[1]

The Chinese "treasure ships" carried rich silks, precious metals, and other valuable goods intended as gifts for distant rulers. In return those rulers sent back gifts of equal or greater value to the Chinese emperor. Although the main purpose of these exchanges was diplomatic, they also stimulated trade between China and its southern neighbors. Interest in new contacts was not limited to the Chinese.

At least three trading cities on the Swahili (swah-HEE-lee) Coast of East Africa sent delegations to China between 1415 and 1416. The delegates from one of them, Malindi, presented the emperor of China with a giraffe, creating quite a stir among normally reserved imperial officials. These African delegations may have encouraged more contacts because the next three of Zheng's voyages reached the African coast. Unfortunately, no documents record how Africans and Chinese reacted to each other during these historic meetings between 1417 and 1433, but it appears that China's lavish gifts stimulated the Swahili market for silk and porcelain. An increase in Chinese imports of pepper from southern Asian lands also resulted from these expeditions.

Had the Ming court wished to promote trade for the profit of its merchants, Chinese fleets might have continued to play a dominant role in Indian Ocean trade. But some high Chinese officials opposed increased contact with peoples whom they regarded as barbarians incapable of making contributions to China. Such opposition caused a suspension in the voyages from 1424 to 1431. The final Chinese expedition sailed between 1432 and 1433. Later Ming emperors would focus their attention on internal matters, leaving a power vacuum in the Indian Ocean.

The Atlantic Ocean

Early European Maritime Expansion

The Vikings were the greatest mariners of the Atlantic in the early Middle Ages. These northern European raiders used their small, open ships to attack Europe's coastal settlements for several centuries. They also discovered and settled one island after another in the North Atlantic during these centuries of warmer temperatures. Like the Polynesians, the Vikings used their knowledge of the heavens and the seas rather than maps and other navigational devices to find their way over long distances.

The Vikings first settled Iceland in 770 and established a colony on Greenland in 982. By accident one group sighted North America in 986. Fifteen years later Leif Ericsson established a short-lived Viking settlement on the island of Newfoundland, which he called Vinland. When a colder climate returned after 1200, the northern settlements in Greenland went into decline and the Vikings abandoned Vinland.

Some southern Europeans applied maritime skills acquired in the Mediterranean and along the North Atlantic coast to explore to the south. Genoese and Portuguese expeditions pushed into the Atlantic in the fourteenth century, eventually exploring and settling the islands of Madeira (muh-DEER-uh), the Azores (A-zorz), and the Canaries.

African Voyages of Discovery

There is some evidence of African voyages of exploration in this period. The celebrated Syrian geographer al-Umari (1301–1349) relates that when Mansa Kankan Musa (MAHN-suh KAHN-kahn MOO-suh), the ruler of the West African empire of Mali, passed through Egypt on his lavish pilgrimage to Mecca in 1324, he told of voyages into the Atlantic undertaken by his predecessor, Mansa Muhammad. According to this source, Muhammad had sent out four hundred vessels with men and supplies, telling them, "Do not return until you have reached the other side of the ocean or if you have exhausted your food or water." After a long time one canoe returned, reporting that the others were lost in a "violent current in the middle of the sea." Muhammad himself then set out at the head of a second, even larger, expedition, from which no one returned.

Arawak Amerindian peoples who inhabited the Greater Antilles of the Caribbean at the time of Columbus.

Amerindian Voyages

In the Americas, early Amerindian voyagers from South America colonized the West Indies, and there were limited maritime contacts between Pacific coast populations in South America and Central America. By the year 1000 Amerindians known as the **Arawak** (AR-uh-wahk) (also called Taino) had followed the small islands of the Lesser Antilles (Barbados, Martinique, and Guadeloupe) to the Greater Antilles (Cuba, Hispaniola, Jamaica, and Puerto Rico) as well as to the Bahamas (see Map 15.2). The Carib followed the same route in later centuries, and by the late fifteenth century they had overrun most Arawak settlements in the Lesser Antilles and were raiding parts of the Greater Antilles. Both Arawak and Carib peoples also made contact with the North American mainland.

SECTION REVIEW

- Polynesians explored and settled the eastern Pacific from the Marquesas to Hawaii and Easter Island.
- The Indian Ocean became a center of commerce and cultural exchange. Between 1405 and 1433 Chinese Admiral Zheng He's seven expeditions established contacts with south Asian and African peoples.
- Vikings, Amerindians, and Africans also pursued long-distance explorations and settlements.

EUROPEAN EXPANSION, 1400–1550

The preceding survey shows that maritime expansion occurred in many parts of the world before 1450. Nevertheless, the epic sea voyages sponsored by the Iberian kingdoms of Portugal and Spain are of special interest because they began a maritime revolution that profoundly altered the course of world history. The Portuguese and Spanish expeditions ended the isolation of the Americas and increased the volume of global interaction.

Iberian overseas expansion was the product of two related phenomena. First, Iberian rulers had strong economic, religious, and political motives to expand their influence. And second, improvements in maritime and military technologies gave Iberians the means to master treacherous and unfamiliar ocean environments, seize control of existing maritime trade routes, and conquer new lands.

Motives for Exploration

The ambitions and adventurous personalities of the rulers of Portugal and Spain led them to sponsor voyages of exploration in the fifteenth century, but these voyages built upon four trends evident in the Latin West since about the year 1000: (1) the revival of urban life and trade, (2) the

e Interactive Map

MAP 15.2 Middle America to 1533 Early Amerindian voyages from South America brought new settlers to the West Indies and western Mexico. The arrival of Europeans in 1492 soon led to the conquest and depopulation of Amerindians.

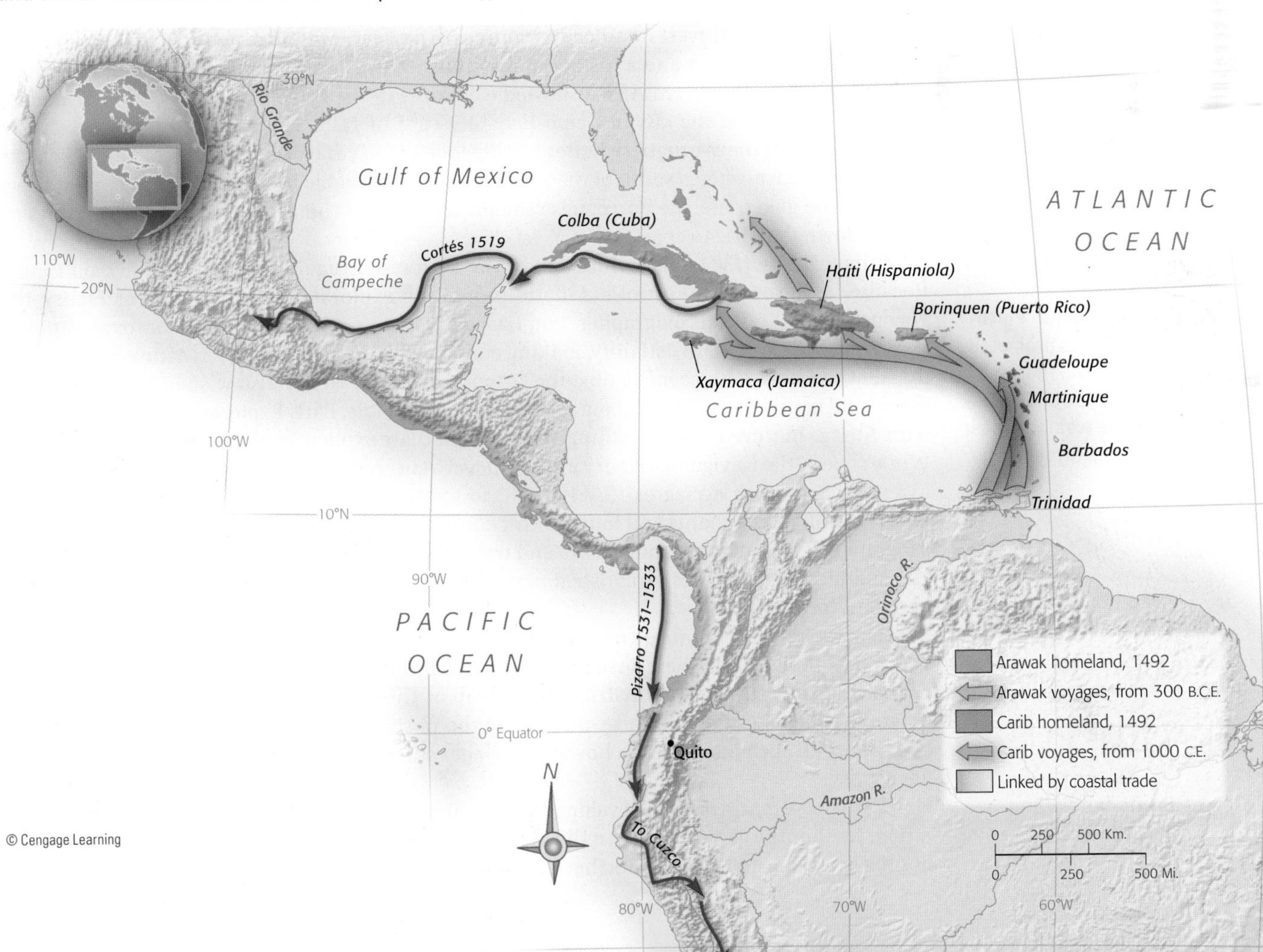

unique alliance between merchants and rulers in Europe, (3) a struggle with Islamic powers for dominance of the Mediterranean that mixed religious motives with the desire for trade, and (4) growing intellectual curiosity about the outside world.

By 1450 the city-states of northern Italy had well-established trade links to northern Europe, the Indian Ocean, and the Black Sea, and their merchant princes had also sponsored an intellectual and artistic Renaissance. The Italian trading states of Venice and Genoa also maintained profitable commercial ties in the Mediterranean that depended on alliances with Muslims and gave their merchants privileged access to lucrative trade from the East. Even after the expansion of the Ottoman Empire disrupted their trade to the East, these cities did not take the lead in exploring the Atlantic. However, many individual Italians played leading roles in the Atlantic explorations.

The Iberian Background

In contrast, the special history and geography of the Iberian kingdoms led them in a different direction. Muslim invaders from North Africa had conquered most of Iberia in the eighth century. Centuries of warfare between Christians and Muslims followed, and by 1250 the Iberian kingdoms of Portugal, Castile, and Aragon had reconquered all of Iberia except the southern Muslim kingdom of Granada (see Chapter 14). The dynastic marriage of Isabel of Castile and Ferdinand of Aragon in 1469 facilitated the conquest of Granada in 1492 and the creation of Spain, sixteenth-century Europe's most powerful state.

AP* Exam Tip Make sure you understand the impact of European exploration on the world, but individual explorers are not covered on the multiple choice section.

Christian militancy continued to be an important motive for both Portugal and Spain in their overseas ventures. But the Iberian rulers and their adventurous subjects also sought material returns. With only a modest share of the Mediterranean trade, they were much more willing than the Italians to seek new routes to the rich trade of Africa and Asia via the Atlantic. Both kingdoms participated in the shipbuilding and the gunpowder revolutions that were under way in Atlantic Europe. Though not centers of Renaissance learning, both were especially open to new geographical knowledge.

Portuguese Voyages

Portugal's decision to invest significant resources in new exploration rested on a well-established Atlantic fishing industry and a history of anti-Muslim warfare. When the Muslim government of Morocco in northwestern Africa showed weakness in the fifteenth century, the Portuguese attacked, conquering the city of Ceuta (say-OO-tuh) in 1415. The capture of this rich North African city gave the Portuguese better intelligence of the caravans bringing gold and slaves to Ceuta from African states south of the Sahara. Militarily unable to push inland and gain direct access to the gold trade, the Portuguese sought more direct contact with the gold producers by sailing down the African coast.

Prince Henry of Portugal

Henry the Navigator Portuguese prince who promoted the study of navigation and directed voyages of exploration down the western coast of Africa in the fifteenth century.

Prince Henry (1394–1460), third son of the king of Portugal, had led the attack on Ceuta. Because he devoted the rest of his life to promoting exploration, he is known as **Henry the Navigator**. His official biographer emphasized Henry's mixed motives for exploration—converting Africans to Christianity, making contact with Christian rulers in Africa, and launching joint crusades with them against the Ottomans. Prince Henry also wished to discover new places and hoped that such new contacts would be profitable. Early explorations were concerned with Africa, but eventually reaching India became an explicit goal of Portuguese explorers. While called "the Navigator," Henry himself never ventured far from home. Instead, he founded a center of research at Sagres (SAH-gresh) to study navigation that built on the pioneering efforts of Italian merchants and fourteenth-century Jewish cartographers. This center collected geographical information from sailors and travelers and sponsored new expeditions to explore the Atlantic. Henry's ships established permanent contact with the islands of Madeira in 1418 and the Azores in 1439.

Henry's staff also improved navigational instruments that had come into Europe from China and the Islamic world. These instruments included the magnetic compass, first developed in China, and the astrolabe, an instrument of Arab or Greek invention that enabled mariners to determine their location at sea by measuring the position of the sun or the stars in the night sky. Even with such instruments, however, voyages still depended on the skill and experience of navigators.

European Sailing Technologies

Portuguese mariners also developed vessels appropriate for voyages of long-distance exploration. Neither the galleys in use in the Mediterranean, powered by large numbers of oarsmen, nor the three-masted ships of northern Europe with their square sails proved adequate for the

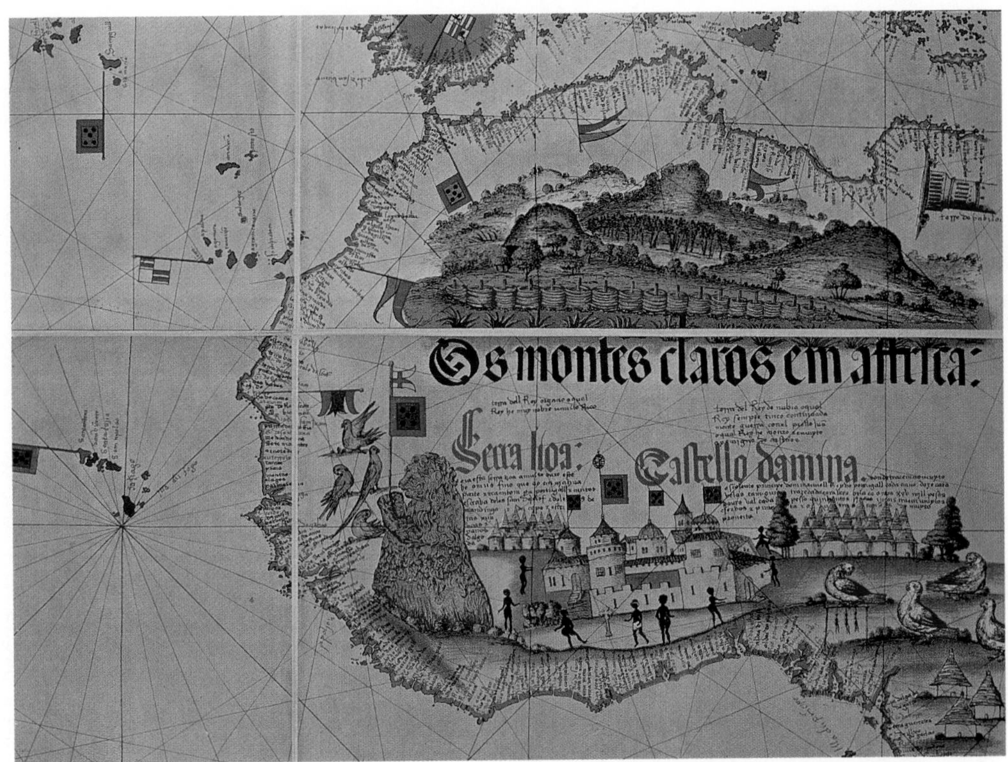

akg-images

Portuguese Map of Western Africa, 1502 This map shows in great detail a section of African coastline that Portuguese explorers charted and named in the fifteenth century. The cartographer illustrated the African interior, which was almost completely unknown to Europeans, with drawings of birds and views of coastal sights: Sierra Leone (Serra lioa), named for a mountain shaped like a lion, and the Portuguese Castle of the Mine (Castello damina) on the Gold Coast.

caravel A small, highly maneuverable three-masted ship used by the Portuguese and Spanish in the exploration of the Atlantic.

Atlantic. The large crews of the galleys could not carry enough supplies for long voyages and the square-rigged northern vessels had trouble sailing at an angle to the wind. Instead, the voyages of exploration made use of a new vessel, the **caravel** (KAR-uh-vel), that was much smaller than the largest European ships and the Chinese junks Zheng used to explore the Indian Ocean. Their size permitted them to enter shallow coastal waters and explore upriver, but they were strong enough to weather ocean storms. They could be equipped with triangular lateen sails that could take the wind on either side for enhanced maneuverability or fitted with square Atlantic sails for greater speed in a following wind. The addition of small cannon made them good fighting ships as well. The caravels' economy, speed, agility, and power justified a contemporary's claim that they were "the best ships that sailed the seas."[2]

Pioneering captains had to overcome the common fear that South Atlantic waters were boiling hot or contained ocean currents that would prevent any ship entering them from ever returning home. It took Prince Henry fourteen years—from 1420 to 1434—to coax an expedition to venture beyond southern Morocco (see Map 15.3). These fears proved unfounded, but the next stretch of coast, 800 miles (1,300 kilometers) of desert, offered little to induce explorers south. It would take the Portuguese four decades to cover the 1,500 miles (2,400 kilometers) from Lisbon to Sierra Leone (see-ER-uh lee-OWN); it then took only three decades to explore the remaining 4,000 miles (6,400 kilometers) to the southern tip of the African continent.

In the years that followed, Portuguese explorers learned how to return to home speedily. Instead of battling the prevailing northeast trade winds and currents back up the coast, they discovered that by sailing northwest into the Atlantic to the latitude of the Azores, ships could pick up prevailing westerly winds that would blow them back to Portugal. The knowledge that ocean winds tend to form large circular patterns helped explorers discover many other ocean routes.

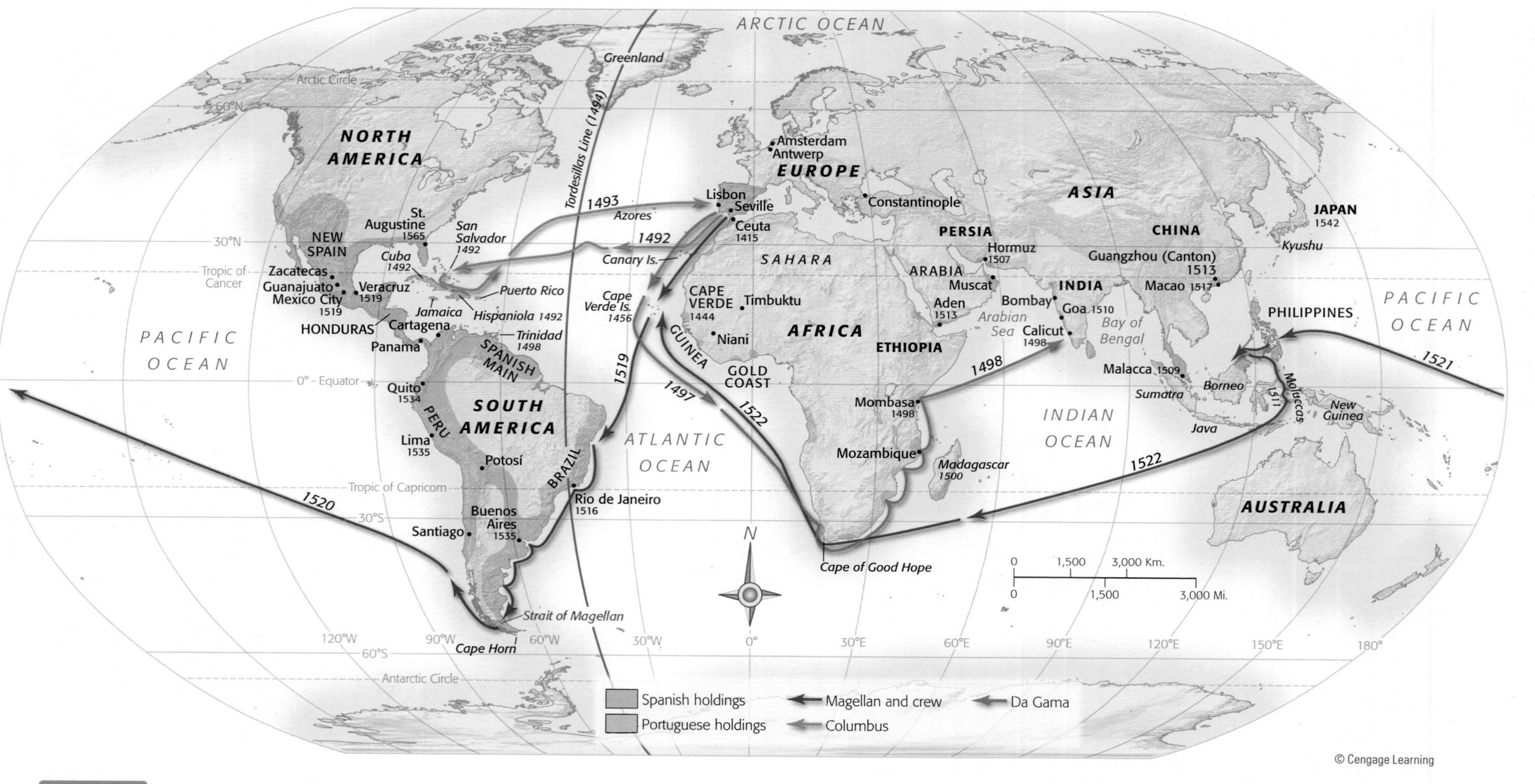

MAP 15.3 **European Exploration, 1420–1542** Portuguese and Spanish explorers showed the possibility and practicality of intercontinental maritime trade. Before 1540 European trade with Africa and Asia was much more important than that with the Americas, but after the Spanish conquest of the Aztec and Inca Empires transatlantic trade began to increase. Notice the Tordesillas line, which in theory separated the Spanish and Portuguese spheres of activity.

Interactive Map

The Portuguese in Africa and Asia

Gold Coast Region of the Atlantic coast of West Africa occupied by modern Ghana; named for its gold exports to Europe from the 1470s onward.

Bartolomeu Dias Portuguese explorer who in 1488 led the first expedition to sail around the southern tip of Africa from the Atlantic and sight the Indian Ocean.

Vasco da Gama Portuguese explorer. In 1497–1498 he led the first naval expedition from Europe to sail to India, opening an important commercial sea route.

Portuguese raids on the northwest coast of Africa and the Canary Islands during the 1440s initiated a profitable slave trade. The total number of Africans captured or purchased on voyages exceeded eighty thousand by the end of the century and rose steadily thereafter. However, the gold trade quickly became more important once the Portuguese contacted the trading networks that flourished in West Africa and reached across the Sahara. By 1457 enough African gold was coming back to Portugal for the kingdom to issue a new gold coin called the *cruzado* (crusader), another reminder of how deeply the Portuguese entwined religious and secular motives.

While the Portuguese crown continued to sponsor voyages of exploration, speedier progress resulted from the growing participation of private commercial interests. In 1469 a prominent Lisbon merchant named Fernão Gomes purchased from the Crown the privilege of exploring 350 miles (550 kilometers) of African coast in return for a trade monopoly. He discovered the uninhabited island of São Tomé (sow toh-MAY) located on the equator and converted it to a major producer of sugar dependent on slaves imported from the African mainland. In the next century the island served as a model for the sugar plantations of Brazil and the Caribbean. Gomes also explored the **Gold Coast**, which became the headquarters of Portugal's West African trade.

The expectation of finding a passage around Africa to the rich trade of the Indian Ocean spurred the final thrust down the African coast. In 1488 **Bartolomeu Dias** became the first Portuguese explorer to round the southern tip of Africa and enter the Indian Ocean. Then in 1497–1498 **Vasco da Gama** sailed around Africa and reached India (see Environment and Technology: Vasco da Gama's Fleet). In 1500 ships on the way to India under the command of Pedro Alvares Cabral (kah-BRAHL) sailed too far west and reached the South American mainland. This discovery established Portugal's claim to Brazil, which would become one of the Western Hemisphere's richest colonies. The gamble that Prince Henry had begun eight decades earlier was about to pay off handsomely.

Spanish Voyages

In contrast to the persistence and planning behind Portugal's century-long exploration of the South Atlantic, haste and blind luck lay behind Spain's early discoveries. Throughout most of the fifteenth century, the Spanish kingdoms were preoccupied with internal affairs: completion of the reconquest of southern Iberia from the Muslims; amalgamation of the various dynasties; and the conversion or expulsion of religious minorities. The Portuguese had already found a new route to the Indian Ocean by the time the Spanish monarchs were ready to turn to overseas exploration.

Columbus and Spanish Exploration

Christopher Columbus Genoese mariner who in the service of Spain led expeditions across the Atlantic, reestablishing contact between the peoples of the Americas and the Old World and opening the way to Spanish conquest and colonization.

The leader of the Spanish overseas mission was **Christopher Columbus** (1451–1506), a Genoese mariner. His four voyages between 1492 and 1504 established the existence of a vast new world across the Atlantic, whose existence few in "old world" Eurasia and Africa had ever suspected. But Columbus refused to accept that he had found unknown new continents and peoples, insisting that he had succeeded in finding a shorter route to the Indian Ocean.

As a young man Columbus gained considerable experience of the South Atlantic while participating in Portuguese explorations along the African coast, but he had become convinced there was a shorter way to reach the riches of the East than the route around Africa. By his reckoning (based on a serious misreading of a ninth-century Arab authority), the Canaries were a mere 2,400 nautical miles (4,450 kilometers) from Japan. The actual distance was five times as far.

It was not easy for Columbus to find a sponsor willing to underwrite the costs of testing his theory that one could reach Asia by sailing west. Portuguese authorities twice rejected his plan. Columbus received a more sympathetic hearing in 1486 from Castile's able ruler, Queen Isabel, but no commitment of support. After a four-year study a Castilian commission concluded that a westward sea route to the Indies rested on many questionable geographical assumptions, but Columbus's persistence finally won over the queen and her husband, King Ferdinand of Aragon. In 1492 they agreed to fund a modest expedition.

Columbus recorded in his log that he and his crew of ninety men "departed Friday the third day of August of the year 1492" toward "the regions of India." Their mission, the royal contract stated, was "to discover and acquire certain islands and mainland in the Ocean Sea." He carried letters of introduction from the Spanish sovereigns to Eastern rulers, including one to the "Grand Khan" (meaning the Chinese emperor), and brought an Arabic interpreter to facilitate

ENVIRONMENT + TECHNOLOGY

Vasco da Gama's Fleet

The four small ships that sailed for India from Lisbon in June 1497 may seem a puny fleet compared to the sixty-two Chinese vessels that Zheng He had led into the Indian Ocean ninety-five years earlier. But given the fact that China had a hundred times as many people as Portugal, Vasco da Gama's fleet represented at least as great a commitment of resources. In any event, the Portuguese expedition had a far greater impact on the course of history. Having achieved its aim of inspiring awe at China's greatness, the Chinese throne sent out no more expeditions after 1433. Although da Gama's ships seemed more odd than awesome to Indian Ocean observers, that modest fleet began a revolution in global relations.

Portugal spared no expense in ensuring that the fleet would make it to India and back. Craftsmen built extra strength into the hulls to withstand the powerful storms that Dias had encountered in 1488 at the tip of Africa. Small enough to be able to navigate any shallow harbors and rivers they might encounter, the ships were crammed with specially strengthened casks and barrels of water, wine, oil, flour, meat, and vegetables far in excess of what was required even on a voyage that would take the better part of a year. Arms and ammunition were also in abundance.

Three of da Gama's ships were rigged with square sails on two masts for speed and a lateen sail on the third mast. The fourth vessel was a caravel with lateen sails. Each ship carried three sets of sails and plenty of extra rigging so as to be able to repair any damages due to storms. The crusaders' red crosses on the sails signaled one of the expedition's motives.

The captains and crew—Portugal's most talented and experienced—received extra pay and other rewards for their service. Yet there was no expectation that the unprecedented sums spent on this expedition would bring any immediate return. According to a contemporary chronicle, the only immediate return the Portuguese monarch received was "the knowledge that some part of Ethiopia and the beginning of Lower India had been discovered." However, the scale and care of the preparations suggest that the Portuguese expected the expedition to open up profitable trade to the Indian Ocean. And so it did.

Vasco da Gama's Flagship This vessel carried the Portuguese captain on his second expedition to India in 1505.

The Pierpont Morgan Library/Art Resource, New York

PRIMARY SOURCE: The Agreement with Columbus on April 17 and April 30, 1492 Read the contract signed by Columbus and his royal patrons, and see what riches he hoped to gain from his expedition.

communication with the peoples of eastern Asia. The expedition traveled in three small ships, the *Santa María*, the *Niña*, and the *Pinta*. The *Niña* and the *Pinta* were caravels.

Unfavorable headwinds had impeded other attempts to explore the Atlantic west of the Azores, but Columbus chose a southern route because he had learned in his service with the Portuguese of west-blowing winds in the latitudes of the Canaries. In October 1492 the expedition reached the islands of the Caribbean. Columbus insisted on calling the inhabitants "Indians" because he believed that the islands were part of the East Indies. A second voyage to the Caribbean in 1493 did nothing to change his mind. Even when, two months after Vasco da Gama reached India in 1498, Columbus first sighted the mainland of South America on his third voyage, he stubbornly insisted it was part of Asia. But by then other Europeans were convinced that he had discovered islands and continents previously unknown to the Old World. Amerigo Vespucci's explorations, first on behalf of Spain and then for Portugal, led mapmakers to name the new continents "America" after him, rather than "Columbia" after Columbus.

To prevent disputes arising from their efforts to exploit their new discoveries and spread Christianity, Spain and Portugal agreed to split the world between them. The Treaty of Tordesillas (tor-duh-SEE-yuhs), negotiated by the pope in 1494, drew an imaginary line down the middle of the North Atlantic Ocean. The treaty allocated lands east of the line in Africa and southern Asia to Portugal; lands to the west in the Americas were reserved for Spain. Cabral's discovery of Brazil, however, gave Portugal a valid claim to the part of South America located east of the line.

Where would Spain's and Portugal's spheres of influence divide in the East? Given Europeans' ignorance of the earth's true size in 1494, it was not clear whether the Moluccas (muh-LOO-kuhz), whose valuable spices had been a goal of the Iberian voyages, were on Portugal's or Spain's side of the Tordesillas line. The size of the Pacific Ocean would determine the boundary. By chance, in 1513 a Spanish adventurer named Vasco Núñez de Balboa (bal-BOH-uh) crossed the Isthmus (a narrow neck of land) of Panama from the east and sighted the Pacific Ocean. Then in 1519 **Ferdinand Magellan** (ca. 1480–1521) began his expedition to complete Columbus's interrupted westward voyage by sailing around the Americas and across the Pacific. The Moluccas turned out to lie well within Portugal's sphere, as Spain formally acknowledged in 1529.

Ferdinand Magellan Portuguese navigator who led the Spanish expedition of 1519–1522 that was the first to sail around the world.

Despite Magellan's death during his voyage for the king of Spain, he was considered the first person to encircle the globe because a decade earlier he had sailed from Europe to the East Indies as part of an expedition sponsored by his native Portugal. His two voyages took him across the Tordesillas line, through the separate spheres claimed by Portugal and Spain, establishing the basis for Spanish colonization of the Philippines after 1564. Of course, in 1500 these European claims were largely theoretical.

Although Columbus failed to find a new route to the East, the consequences of his voyages for European expansion were momentous. Those who followed in his wake laid the basis for Spain's large colonial empire in the Americas and for the empires of other European nations. In turn, these empires promoted the growth of a major new trading network whose importance rivaled and eventually surpassed the Indian Ocean network. Both the eastward and the westward voyages of exploration marked a tremendous expansion of Europe's role in world history.

SECTION REVIEW

- Portugal and Spain initiated oversees explorations to expand Christianity and gain new markets.
- Portugal, aided by Prince Henry the Navigator, created a trading empire in Africa and the Indian Ocean.
- Columbus first revealed the Americas to Europe, and other Spanish explorers reached Asia by crossing the Pacific.

ENCOUNTERS WITH EUROPE, 1450–1550

European actions alone did not determine the global consequences of these new contacts. The ways in which Africans, Asians, and Amerindians perceived these visitors and interacted with them influenced developments as well. Everywhere indigenous peoples evaluated the Europeans as potential allies or enemies, and everywhere Europeans attempted to insert themselves into existing commercial and geopolitical arrangements. In general, Europeans made slow progress in establishing colonies and asserting political influence in Africa and Asia, even while profiting from new commercial ties. In the Americas, however, Spain, Portugal, and later other European powers moved rapidly to create colonial empires. In this case the long isolation of the Amerindians from the rest of the world made them more vulnerable to the diseases that these outsiders introduced, limiting their potential for resistance and facilitating European settlement.

Western Africa

The Portuguese in Africa

Many along the West African coast were eager for trade with the Portuguese, since it offered new markets for exports and access to imports cheaper than those transported overland from the Mediterranean. This was evident along the Gold Coast of West Africa, first visited by the Portuguese in 1471. Miners in the hinterland had long sold their gold to traders, who took it to trading cities along the southern edge of the Sahara, where it was sold to traders who had crossed the

Bronze Figure of Benin Ruler Both this prince and his horse are protected by chain mail introduced in the fifteenth century to Benin by Portuguese merchants.

desert from North Africa. Recognizing that they might get more favorable terms from the new visitors from the sea, coastal Africans were ready to negotiate with the royal representative of Portugal who arrived in 1482 to seek permission to erect a trading fort.

This Portuguese noble and his officers (likely including the young Christopher Columbus, who had entered Portuguese service in 1476) were eager to make a proper impression. They dressed in their best clothes, erected and decorated a reception platform, celebrated a Catholic Mass, and signaled the start of negotiations with trumpets, tambourines, and drums. The African king, Caramansa, staged his entrance with equal ceremony, arriving with a large retinue of attendants and musicians. Through an African interpreter, the two leaders exchanged flowery speeches pledging goodwill and mutual benefit. Caramansa then gave permission for a small trading fort, assured, he said, by the appearance of the Portuguese that they were honorable persons, unlike the "few, foul, and vile" Portuguese visitors of the previous decade.

Neither side made a show of force, but the Africans' upper hand was evident in Caramansa's warning that he and his people would move away, depriving their fort of food and trade, if the Portuguese acted aggressively. Trade at the post of Saint George of the Mine (later called Elmina) enriched both sides. The Portuguese crown had soon purchased gold equal to one-tenth of the world's production at the time. In return, Africans received large quantities of goods that Portuguese ships brought from Asia, Europe, and other parts of Africa.

After a century of aggressive expansion, the kingdom of Benin in the Niger Delta was near the peak of its power when it first encountered the Portuguese. Its oba (king) presided over an elaborate bureaucracy from a spacious palace in his large capital city, also known as Benin. In response to a Portuguese visit in 1486, the oba sent an ambassador to Portugal to learn more about these strangers. He then established a royal monopoly on trade with the Portuguese, selling pepper and ivory tusks (for export to Portugal) as well as stone beads, textiles, and prisoners of war (for resale at Elmina). In return, Portuguese merchants provided Benin with copper and brass, fine textiles, glass beads, and a horse for the king's royal procession. In the early sixteenth century, as the demand for slaves for the Portuguese sugar plantations on the nearby island of São Tomé grew, the oba first raised the price of slaves and then imposed restrictions that limited their sale.

Early contacts generally involved a mix of commercial, military, and religious exchanges. Some African rulers appreciated the advantage of European firearms over spears and arrows in conflicts with their enemies and actively sought them in trade. Because African religions were generally not exclusive, coastal rulers were also willing to test the value of the Christian practices promoted by the Portuguese. The rulers of Benin and Kongo, the two largest coastal kingdoms, accepted both Portuguese missionaries and soldiers as allies in battle to test the efficacy of the Christian religion and European weaponry.

However, Portuguese efforts to persuade the king and nobles of Benin to accept the Catholic faith ultimately failed. Early kings showed some interest, but after 1538 rulers declined to receive more missionaries. They also closed the market in male slaves for the rest of the sixteenth century. We do not know why Benin chose to limit its contacts with the Portuguese, but the result makes clear that these rulers had the power to control their contacts with Europeans.

The Kingdom of the Kongo

Farther south, on the lower Congo River, relations between the kingdom of Kongo and the Portuguese began similarly but had a very different outcome. Like the oba of Benin, the manikongo (mah-NEE-KONG-goh) (king of Kongo) sent delegates to Portugal, established a royal monopoly on trade with the Portuguese, and expressed interest in Christian teachings. Deeply impressed with the new religion, the royal family made Catholicism the kingdom's official faith. But Kongo, lacking ivory and pepper, had less to trade than Benin. To acquire the goods brought by Portugal and to pay the costs of the missionaries, it had to sell more and more slaves.

Soon the manikongo began to lose his royal monopoly over the slave trade. In 1526 the Christian manikongo, Afonso I (r. 1506–ca. 1540), wrote to his royal "brother," the king of Portugal, begging for his help in stopping the trade because unauthorized Kongolese were kidnapping and selling people, even members of good families (see Diversity and Dominance: Kongo's Christian King). Alfonso's appeals for help received no reply from Portugal, whose interests were now concentrated in the Indian Ocean. Soon rebellion and the relocation of the slave trade from his kingdom to the south weakened the manikongo's authority.

Eastern Africa

Different still were the reactions of the Muslim rulers of the coastal trading states of eastern Africa. As Vasco da Gama's fleet sailed up the coast in 1498, most rulers gave the Portuguese a cool reception, suspicious of the intentions of visitors who painted crusaders' crosses on their sails. But the ruler of one of the ports, Malindi, seeing the Portuguese as potential allies who could help him expand the city's trading position, provided da Gama with a pilot to guide him to India. The initial suspicions of the other rulers were proven correct seven years later when a Portuguese war fleet bombarded and looted most of the coastal cities of eastern Africa in the name of Christianity and commerce, while sparing Malindi.

The Portuguese and Ethiopia

Christian Ethiopia was another eastern African state that saw potential benefit in an alliance with the Portuguese. In the fourteenth and early fifteenth centuries, Ethiopia faced increasing conflict with Muslim states along the Red Sea. Emboldened by the rise of the Ottoman Turks, who had conquered Egypt in 1517 and launched a major fleet in the Indian Ocean to counter the Portuguese, the talented warlord of the Muslim state of Adal launched a furious assault on Ethiopia. Adal's decisive victory in 1529 reduced the Christian kingdom to a precarious state. At that point Ethiopia's contacts with the Portuguese became crucial.

For decades, delegations from Portugal and Ethiopia had explored a possible alliance based on their mutual adherence to Christianity. A key figure was Queen Helena of Ethiopia, who acted as regent for her young sons after her husband's death in 1478. In 1509 Helena sent a letter to "our very dear and well-beloved brother," the king of Portugal, along with a gift of two tiny crucifixes said to be made of wood from the cross on which Christ had died in Jerusalem. In her letter she proposed an alliance between her army and Portugal's fleet against the Turks; however, Helena's death in 1522 occurred before the alliance could be arranged. Ethiopia's situation then grew more desperate.

Finally, in 1539 when another woman ruler was holding what was left of the empire together, a small Portuguese force commanded by Vasco da Gama's son Christopher arrived to aid Ethiopia. With Portuguese help the Ethiopians renewed their struggle. While Muslim forces captured and tortured to death Christopher da Gama, their attack failed when their own leader was mortally wounded in battle. Portuguese aid helped the Ethiopian kingdom save itself from extinction, but a permanent alliance faltered because Ethiopian rulers refused to transfer their Christian affiliation from the patriarch of Alexandria to the Latin patriarch of Rome (the pope) as the Portuguese insisted.

As these examples illustrate, African encounters with the Portuguese before 1550 varied considerably, as much because of the strategies and leadership of particular African states as because of Portuguese policies. Africans and Portuguese might become royal brothers, bitter opponents, or partners in a mutually profitable trade, but Europeans remained a minor presence in most of Africa in 1550. By then the Portuguese had become far more interested in the Indian Ocean trade.

Kongo's Christian King

The new overseas voyages brought conquest to some and opportunities for fruitful borrowings and exchanges to others. The decision of the ruler of the kingdom of Kongo to adopt Christianity in 1491 added cultural diversity to Kongolese society and in some ways strengthened the hand of the king. From then on Kongolese rulers sought to introduce Christian beliefs and rituals while at the same time Africanizing Christianity to make it more intelligible to their subjects. In addition, the kings of Kongo sought a variety of more secular aid from Portugal, including schools and medicine. Trade with the Portuguese introduced new social and political tensions, especially in the case of the export trade in slaves for the Portuguese sugar plantations on the island of São Tomé to the north.

Two letters sent to King João (zhwao) III of Portugal in 1526 illustrate how King Afonso of Kongo saw his kingdom's new relationship with Portugal and the problems that resulted from it. (Afonso adopted that name when baptized as a young prince.) After the death of his father in 1506, Afonso successfully claimed the throne and ruled until 1542. His son Henrique became the first Catholic bishop of the Kongo in 1521.

These letters were written in Portuguese and penned by the king's secretary João Teixera (tay-SHER-uh), a Kongo Christian, who, like Afonso, had been educated by Portuguese missionaries.

6 July 1526

To the very powerful and excellent prince Dom João, our brother:

On the 20th of June just past, we received word that a trading ship from your highness had just come to our port of Sonyo. We were greatly pleased by that arrival for it had been many days since a ship had come to our kingdom, for by it we would get news of your highness, which many times we had desired to know, . . . and likewise as there was a great and dire need for wine and flour for the holy sacrament; and of this we had had no great hope for we have the same need frequently. And that, sir, arises from the great negligence of your highness's officials toward us and toward shipping us those things. . . .

Sir, your highness should know how our kingdom is being lost in so many ways that we will need to provide the needed cure, since this is caused by the excessive license given by your agents and officials to the men and merchants who come to this kingdom to set up shops with goods and many things which have been prohibited by us, and which they spread throughout our kingdoms and domains in such abundance that many of our vassals, whose submission we could once rely on, now act independently so as to get the things in greater abundance than we ourselves; whom we had formerly held content and submissive and under our vassalage and jurisdiction, so it is doing a great harm not only to the service of God, but also to the security and peace of our kingdoms and state.

And we cannot reckon how great the damage is, since every day the mentioned merchants are taking our people, sons of the land and the sons of our noblemen and vassals and our relatives, because the thieves and men of bad conscience grab them so as to have the things and wares of this kingdom that they crave; they grab them and bring them to be sold. In such a manner, sir, has been the corruption and deprivation that our land is becoming completely depopulated, and your highness should not deem this good nor in your service. And to avoid this we need from these kingdoms [of yours] no more than priests and a few people to teach in schools, and no other goods except wine and flour for the holy sacrament, which is why we beg of your highness to help and assist us in this matter. Order your agents to send here neither merchants nor wares, because it is our will that in these kingdoms there should not be any dealing in slaves nor outlet for them, for the reasons stated above. Again we beg your highness's agreement, since otherwise we cannot cure such manifest harm. May Our Lord in His mercy have your highness always under His protection and may you always do the things of His holy service. I kiss your hands many times.

From our city of Kongo. . . .

The King, Dom Afonso

Indian Ocean States

Vasco da Gama did not make a great impression on the citizens of Calicut when he arrived on the Malabar Coast of India in May 1498. Da Gama's four small ships were far less imposing than the Chinese fleets that had called at Calicut sixty-five years earlier and no larger than many of the dhows that filled the harbor of this rich and important trading city. The samorin (ruler) of Calicut and his Muslim officials showed only mild interest in the Portuguese as new trading partners, since the gifts brought by da Gama had provoked derisive laughter. Twelve pieces of fairly ordinary striped cloth, four scarlet hoods, six hats, and six wash basins seemed inferior goods to those accustomed to the luxuries of the Indian Ocean trade. When da Gama tried to defend his gifts as those of an explorer, not a rich merchant, the samorin cut him short, asking

18 October 1526

Very high and very powerful prince King of Portugal, our brother,

Sir, your highness has been so good as to promise us that anything we need we should ask for in our letters, and that everything will be provided. And so that there may be peace and health of our kingdoms, by God's will, in our lifetime. And as there are among us old folks and people who have lived for many days, many and different diseases happen so often that we are pushed to the ultimate extremes. And the same happens to our children, relatives, and people, because this country lacks physicians and surgeons who might know the proper cures for such diseases, as well as pharmacies and drugs to make them better. And for this reason many of those who had been already confirmed and instructed in the things of the holy faith of Our Lord Jesus Christ perish and die. And the rest of the people for the most part cure themselves with herbs and sticks and other ancient methods, so that they live putting all their faith in these herbs and ceremonies, and die believing that they are saved; and this serves God poorly.

And to avoid such a great error, I think, and inconvenience, since it is from God and from your highness that all the good and the drugs and medicines have come to us for our salvation, we ask your merciful highness to send us two physicians and two pharmacists and one surgeon, so that they may come with their pharmacies and necessary things to be in our kingdoms, for we have extreme need of each and every one of them. We will be very good and merciful to them, since sent by your highness, their work and coming should be for good. We ask your highness as a great favor to do this for us, because besides being good in itself it is in the service of God as we have said above.

Moreover, sir, in our kingdoms there is another great inconvenience which is of little service to God, and this is that many of our people, out of great desire for the wares and things of your kingdoms, which are brought here by your people, and in order to satisfy their disordered appetite, seize many of our people, freed and exempt men. And many times noblemen and the sons of noblemen, and our relatives are stolen, and they take them to be sold to the white men who are in our kingdoms and take them hidden or by night, so that they are not recognized. And as soon as they are taken by the white men, they are immediately ironed and branded with fire. And when they are carried off to be embarked, if they are caught by our guards, the whites allege that they have bought them and cannot say from whom, so that it is our duty to do justice and to restore to the free their freedom. And so they went away offended.

And to avoid such a great evil we passed a law so that every white man living in our kingdoms and wanting to purchase slaves by whatever means should first inform three of our noblemen and officials of our court on whom we rely in this matter, namely Dom Pedro Manipunzo and Dom Manuel Manissaba, our head bailiff, and Gonçalo Pires, our chief supplier, who should investigate if the said slaves are captives or free men, and, if cleared with them, there will be no further doubt nor embargo and they can be taken and embarked. And if they reach the opposite conclusion, they will lose the aforementioned slaves. Whatever favor and license we give them [the white men] for the sake of your highness in this case is because we know that it is in your service too that these slaves are taken from our kingdom; otherwise we should not consent to this for the reasons stated above that we make known completely to your highness so that no one could say the contrary, as they said in many other cases to your highness, so that the care and remembrance that we and this kingdom have should not be withdrawn. . . .

We kiss your hands of your highness many times.

From our city of Kongo, the 18th day of October,

The King, Dom Afonso

QUESTIONS FOR ANALYSIS

1. **What sorts of things does King Afonso desire from the Portuguese?**
2. **What is he willing and unwilling to do in return?**
3. **What problem with his own people has the slave trade created, and what has King Afonso done about it?**
4. **Does King Afonso see himself as an equal to King João or his subordinate? Do you agree with that analysis?**

Source: From António Brásio, ed., *Monumenta Missionaria Africana: Africa Ocidental (1471-1531)* (Lisbon: Agência Geral do Ultramar, 1952), I: 468, 470–471, 488–491. Translated by David Northrup.

whether he had come to discover men or stones: "If he had come to discover men, as he said, why had he brought nothing?"

Indian Ocean Trade and the Portuguese

Coastal rulers soon discovered that the Portuguese had no intention of remaining poor competitors in the rich trade of the Indian Ocean. Upon da Gama's return to Portugal in 1499, the jubilant King Manuel styled himself "Lord of the Conquest, Navigation, and Commerce of Ethiopia, Arabia, Persia, and India," setting forth the ambitious scope of his plans. Previously the Indian Ocean had been an open sea, used by merchants (and pirates) of all the surrounding coasts. Now the Portuguese crown intended to make it a Portuguese sea, the private property of Portugal alone.

The ability of little Portugal to assert control over the Indian Ocean stemmed from the superiority of its ships and weapons over those of the regional powers, especially the lightly armed

Ms. 1889, c. 97, Biblioteca Casanateunse Rome. Photo: Humberto Nicoletti Serra

Portuguese in India In the sixteenth century Portuguese men moved to the Indian Ocean Basin to work as administrators and traders. This Indo-Portuguese drawing from about 1540 shows a Portuguese man speaking to an Indian woman, perhaps making a proposal of marriage.

merchant dhows. In 1505 a Portuguese fleet of eighty-one ships and some seven thousand men bombarded Swahili Coast cities. Next on the list were Indian ports. Goa, on the west coast of India, fell to a well-armed fleet in 1510, becoming the base from which the Portuguese menaced the trading cities of Gujarat (goo-juh-RAHT) to the north and Calicut and other Malabar Coast cities to the south. The Portuguese took the port of Hormuz, controlling entry to the Persian Gulf, in 1515, but Aden, at the entrance to the Red Sea, successfully resisted. The addition of the Gujarati port of Diu in 1535 consolidated Portuguese dominance of the western Indian Ocean.

Meanwhile, Portuguese explorers had been reconnoitering the Bay of Bengal and the waters farther east. The city of Malacca (muh-LAH-kuh) on the strait between the Malay Peninsula and Sumatra became the focus of their attention. During the fifteenth century Malacca had become the main entrepôt (ON-truh-poh) (a place where goods are stored or deposited and from which they are distributed) for the trade from China, Japan, India, the Southeast Asian mainland, and the Moluccas. Among the city's more than 100,000 residents an early Portuguese visitor counted eighty-four different languages, including those of merchants from as far west as Cairo, Ethiopia, and the Swahili Coast of East Africa. Many non-Muslim residents of the city supported letting the Portuguese join its cosmopolitan trading community, perhaps hoping to offset the growing solidarity of Muslim traders. In 1511, however, the Portuguese seized this strategic trading center outright with a force of a thousand fighting men, including three hundred recruited in southern India.

Force was not always necessary. On the China coast, local officials and merchants interested in profitable new trade with the Portuguese persuaded the imperial government to allow the Portuguese to establish a trading post at Macao (muh-COW) in 1557. Operating from Macao, Portuguese ships came to nearly monopolize trade between China and Japan.

In the Indian Ocean, the Portuguese used their control of major port cities to enforce an even larger trading monopoly. As their power grew, they required all spices, as well as goods carried between major ports like Goa and Macao, to be carried in Portuguese ships. In addition, the Portuguese tried to control and tax other Indian Ocean trade by requiring all merchant ships entering and leaving one of their ports to carry a Portuguese passport and pay customs duties. Portuguese patrols seized vessels that attempted to avoid these monopolies, confiscated their cargoes, and either killed the captain and crew or sentenced them to forced labor.

Reactions to this power grab varied. Like the emperors of China, the Mughal (MOO-gahl) emperors of India largely ignored Portugal's maritime intrusions, seeing their interests as maintaining control over their vast land possessions. The Ottomans responded more aggressively, supporting Egypt against the Christian intruders with a large fleet and fifteen thousand men between 1501 and 1509. Then, having absorbed Egypt into their empire, the Ottomans sent another large expedition against the Portuguese in 1538. Both expeditions failed because Ottoman galleys were no match for the faster, better-armed Portuguese vessels in the open ocean. However, the Ottomans continued to exercise control over the Red Sea and Persian Gulf.

The smaller trading states of the region were less capable of challenging Portuguese domination head-on, since rivalries among them impeded the formation of a common front. Some chose to cooperate with the Portuguese to maintain their prosperity and security. Others engaged in evasion and resistance. Two examples illustrate the range of responses among Indian Ocean peoples.

The merchants of Calicut put up some of the most sustained resistance. In retaliation, the Portuguese embargoed all trade with Aden, Calicut's principal trading partner, and centered their trade on the port of Cochin, which had once been a dependency of Calicut. Some Calicut merchants became adept at evading Portuguese naval patrols, but the price of resistance was the shrinking of Calicut's commercial importance as Cochin gradually became the major pepper-exporting port on the Malabar Coast.

The traders and rulers of the state of Gujarat farther north had less success in keeping the Portuguese at bay. At first they resisted Portuguese attempts at monopoly and in 1509 joined Egypt's failed effort to sweep the Portuguese from the Arabian Sea. But in 1535, finding his state at a military disadvantage due to Mughal attacks, the ruler of Gujarat made the fateful decision to allow the Portuguese to build a fort at Diu in return for their support. Once established, the Portuguese gradually extended their control, so that by midcentury they were licensing and taxing all Gujarati ships. Even after the Mughals (who were Muslims) took control of Gujarat in 1572, the Mughal emperor Akbar permitted the Portuguese to continue their maritime monopoly in return for allowing one ship a year to carry pilgrims to Mecca without paying the Portuguese any fee.

The Portuguese never gained complete control of the Indian Ocean trade, but their naval supremacy allowed them to dominate key ports and trade routes during the sixteenth century. The resulting profits from spices and other luxury goods had a dramatic effect. The Portuguese were now able to break the pepper monopoly long held by Venice and Genoa, who both depended on Egyptian middlemen, by selling at much lower prices. They were also able to fund a more aggressive colonization of Brazil.

In both Asia and Africa the consequences flowing from these events were startling. Asian and East African traders were now at the mercy of Portuguese warships, but their individual responses affected their fates. Some were devastated. Others prospered by meeting Portuguese demands or evading their patrols. Because the Portuguese sought to control trade routes, not occupy large territories, Portugal had little impact on the Asian and African mainlands, in sharp contrast to what was occurring in the Americas.

The Americas

The Spanish established a vast territorial empire in the Americas in contrast to the trading empires the Portuguese created in Africa and Asia. This outcome had little to do with differences between the two kingdoms, even though Spain had a much larger population and greater resources. The Spanish and Portuguese monarchies had similar motives for expansion and used identical ships and weapons. Rather, the isolation of the Amerindian peoples made their responses to outside contacts different from those of African and Indian Ocean peoples. Isolation slowed the development of metallurgy and other militarily useful technologies in the Americas and also made these large populations more susceptible to new diseases. It was the spread of deadly new diseases, especially smallpox, among Amerindians after 1518 that weakened their ability to resist and facilitated Spanish and Portuguese occupation.

The Spanish in the Caribbean

The first Amerindians to encounter Columbus were the Arawak of Hispaniola (modern Haiti and the Dominican Republic) in the Greater Antilles and the Bahamas to the north (see Map 15.2). They cultivated maize (corn), cassava (a tuber), sweet potatoes, and hot peppers, as well as cotton and tobacco. Although the islands did not have large gold deposits, and, unlike West Africans, the Arawak did not trade gold over long distances, the natives were skilled at working gold. While the Arawak at first extended a cautious welcome to the Spanish, they learned to tell exaggerated stories about gold in other places to persuade them to move on.

e **PRIMARY SOURCE: A Dominican Voice in the Wilderness: Preaching Against Tyranny in Hispaniola** A Dominican friar, and former landholder, expresses his outrage at the injustices committed against the native people.

When Columbus made his second trip to Hispaniola in 1493, he brought several hundred settlers who hoped to make their fortune, as well as missionaries who were eager to persuade the Amerindians to accept Christianity. The settlers demanded indigenous labor to look for gold, stole gold ornaments, confiscated food, and sexually assaulted native women, provoking the Arawak to rebel in 1495. In this and later conflicts, steel swords, horses, and body armor led to Spanish victories and the slaughter of thousands. Thousands more were forced to labor for the Spanish. Meanwhile, cattle, pigs, and goats introduced by the settlers devoured the Arawak's food crops, causing deaths from famine and disease. A governor appointed by the Spanish crown in 1502 institutionalized these demands by dividing the surviving Arawak on Hispaniola among his allies as laborers.

conquistadors Early-sixteenth-century Spanish adventurers who conquered Mexico, Central America, and Peru.

The actions of the Spanish in the Antilles imitated Spanish actions and motives during the wars against the Muslims in Spain in the previous centuries: they sought to serve God by defeating nonbelievers and placing them under Christian control—and to become rich in the process. Individual **conquistadors** (kon-KEY-stuh-dor) (conquerors) extended that pattern around the Caribbean as gold and indigenous labor became scarce on Hispaniola. New expeditions searched for gold and Amerindian labor across the Caribbean region, capturing Amerindians and relocating them to Hispaniola as slaves. The island of Borinquen (Puerto Rico) was conquered in 1508 and Cuba between 1510 and 1511.

The Conquest of the Aztecs

Hernán Cortés Spanish explorer and conquistador who led the conquest of Aztec Mexico in 1519–1521 for Spain.

Following two failed expeditions to Mexico, Governor Velázquez of Cuba appointed an ambitious and ruthless nobleman, **Hernán Cortés** (kor-TEZ) (1485–1547) to undertake a new effort. Cortés left Cuba in 1519 with six hundred fighting men, including many who had sailed with the earlier expeditions, and most of the island's stock of weapons and horses. After demonstrating his military skills in a series of battles with the Maya, Cortés learned of the rich Aztec Empire in central Mexico.

AP* Exam Tip Make sure you understand the impact of the European arrival in the Americas.

The Aztecs had conquered their vast empire only during the previous century, and many subject peoples were ready to embrace the Spanish as allies. They resented the tribute payments, forced labor, and large-scale human sacrifices demanded by the Aztecs. The Aztecs also had powerful native enemies, including the Tlaxcalans (thlash-KAH-lans), who became crucial supporters of Cortés. Like the peoples of Africa and Asia when confronted by Europeans, Amerindian peoples, like the Tlaxcalans of Mexico, calculated as best they could the potential benefit or threat represented by these strange visitors. Individual Amerindians also made these calculations. Malintzin (mah-LEENT-zeen) (also called Malinche), a native woman given to Cortés shortly after his arrival in the Maya region, became his translator, key source of intelligence, and mistress. As peoples and as individuals, native allies were crucial to the Spanish campaign.

Moctezuma II Aztec emperor who died while in custody of the Spanish conquistador Hernán Cortés.

While the emperor **Moctezuma II** (mock-teh-ZOO-ma) (r. 1502–1520) hesitated to use force and attempted diplomacy instead, Cortés pushed toward the Aztec capital of Tenochtitlan (teh-noch-TIT-lan). Spanish forces used firearms, cavalry tactics, and steel swords to great advantage in battles along their route. In the end Moctezuma agreed to welcome the Spaniards. As they approached his island capital, the emperor went out in a great procession, dressed in his finery, to welcome Cortés.

Despite Cortés's initial pledge that he came in friendship, Moctezuma was quickly imprisoned. The Spanish looted his treasury, interfered with the city's religious rituals, and eventually massacred hundreds during a festival. These actions provoked a mass rebellion directed against both the Spanish and Moctezuma. During the Spaniards' desperate escape, the Aztecs killed

Coronation of Emperor Moctezuma This painting by an unnamed Aztec artist depicts the Aztec ruler's coronation. Moctezuma, his nose pierced by a bone, receives the crown from a prince in the palace at Tenochtitlan.

Oronoz

half the Spanish force and four thousand of Cortés's native allies. In the confusion Moctezuma also lost his life, either killed by the Spanish or in the Aztec attack.

AP* Exam Tip The Columbian Exchange, in positive and negative terms, is important information for the exam.

The survivors, strengthened by Spanish reinforcements and aided by the Tlaxcalans, renewed their attack and captured Tenochtitlan in 1521. Their victory was aided by a smallpox epidemic that killed more of the city's defenders than did the fighting. One source remembered that the disease "spread over the people as a great destruction." Many Amerindians as well as Europeans blamed the devastating spread of this disease on supernatural forces. Cortés and other Spanish leaders then led expeditions to the north and south accompanied by the Tlaxcalans and other indigenous allies. Everywhere epidemic disease, especially smallpox, helped crush indigenous resistance.

The Conquest of the Inca

Spanish settlers in Panama had heard tales of rich and powerful civilizations to the south even before the conquest of the Aztecs. During the previous century the Inca had built a vast empire along the Pacific coast of South America (see Chapter 11). As the empire expanded through conquest, the Inca enforced new labor demands and taxes and even exiled rebellious populations from their lands.

About 1525 the Inca ruler Huayna Capac (WHY-nah KAH-pak) died in Quito, where he had led a successful military campaign. Two of his sons then fought for the throne. In the end **Atahualpa** (ah-tuh-WAHL-puh) (r. 1531–1533), the candidate of the northern army, defeated Huascar, the candidate of the royal court at Cuzco. As a result, the Inca military was decimated and the empire's political leadership weakened by the violence; at this critical time **Francisco Pizarro** (pih-ZAHR-oh) (ca. 1478–1541) and his force of 180 men, 37 horses, and two cannon entered the region.

Atahualpa Last ruling Inca emperor of Peru. He was executed by the Spanish.

Francisco Pizarro Spanish explorer who led the conquest of the Inca Empire of Peru in 1531–1533.

Pizarro had come to the Americas in 1502 at the age of twenty-five to seek his fortune and had participated in the conquest of Hispaniola and in Balboa's expedition across the Isthmus of

The Execution of Inca Ruler Atahualpa Felipe Guaman Poma de Ayala, a native Andean from the area of Huamanga in Peru, drew this representation of the execution. While Pizarro sentenced Atahualpa to death by strangulation, not beheading, Guaman Poma's illustration forcefully made the point that Spain had imposed an arbitrary and violent government on the Andean people.

Musee du Quai Branley/Scala Picture Library

Panama. In the 1520s he gambled his fortune to finance the exploration of the Pacific south of the equator, where he learned of the riches of the Inca. With a license from the king of Spain, he set out from Panama in 1531 to conquer them.

Having seen signs of the civil war after landing, Pizarro arranged to meet the Inca emperor, Atahualpa, near the Andean city of Cajamarca (kah-hah-MAHR-kah) in November 1532. With supreme boldness and brutality, Pizarro's small band of armed men attacked Atahualpa and his followers as they entered an enclosed courtyard. Though surrounded by an Inca army of at least forty thousand, the Spaniards were able to use their cannon to create confusion while their swords brought down thousands of the emperor's lightly armed retainers and servants. Pizarro now replicated in Peru Cortés's strategy by capturing the Inca ruler.

Atahualpa, seeking to guard his authority, quickly ordered the execution of his imprisoned brother Huascar. He also attempted to purchase his freedom. Having noted the glee with which the

SECTION REVIEW

- African kingdoms reacted in various ways to the opportunities and threats created by the arrival of the Portuguese, but only Kongo embraced Christianity and accepted a large Portuguese military presence in the sixteenth century.
- However, the Portuguese used military force to consolidate a trade empire in the Indian Ocean.
- After the Spanish occupied the Caribbean, Cortés led an expedition that conquered the Aztecs, weakened by epidemic.
- The Spanish under Pizarro conquered the Inca Empire, already suffering from civil war, and then fell on each other, but surviving conquistadors continued to explore the Americas.

Spaniards seized gold and silver, Atahualpa offered a ransom he thought would satisfy even the greediest among them: rooms filled to shoulder height with gold and silver. The Inca paid the ransom of 13,400 pounds (6,000 kilograms) of gold and 26,000 pounds (12,000 kilograms) of silver, but the Spaniards still executed Atahualpa. With the unity of the Inca Empire already battered by the civil war and the deaths of Atahualpa and his brother Huascar, the Spanish occupied Cuzco, the capital city.

Nevertheless, Manco Inca, whom the Spanish had placed on the throne following the execution of his brother Atahualpa, led a massive native rebellion in 1536. Although defeated by the Spanish, Manco Inca and his followers retreated to the interior and created a much-reduced independent kingdom that survived until 1572. The victorious Spaniards, now determined to settle their own rivalries, initiated a bloody civil war fueled by greed and jealousy. Before peace was established, this struggle took the lives of Francisco Pizarro and most of the other prominent conquistadors. Incited by the fabulous wealth of the Aztecs and Inca, conquistadors now extended their exploration and conquest of South and North America, dreaming of new treasures to loot.

CONCLUSION

The voyages of exploration undertaken by the Chinese and Polynesians pursued diverse objectives. The great voyages of the Chinese in the early fifteenth century were motivated by an interest in trade, curiosity, and the desire to project imperial power. For the Polynesians, exploration opened the opportunity to both project power and demonstrate expertise while at the same time settling satellite populations that would relieve population pressures. The Vikings, Africans, and Amerindians all undertook long-distance explorations as well, although with fewer lasting consequences. The projection of European influence between 1450 and 1550 was in some ways similar to that of other cultural regions in that it expanded commercial linkages, increased cross-cultural contacts, and served the ambitions of political leaders. But the result of their voyages proved to be a major turning point in world history. During those years European explorers opened new long-distance trade routes across the world's three major oceans, for the first time establishing regular contact among all the continents. As a result, a new balance of power arose in parts of Atlantic Africa, the Indian Ocean, and the Americas.

The rapid expansion of European empires and the projection of European military power around the world would have seemed unlikely in 1492. No European power matched the military and economic strength of China, and few could rival the Ottomans. Spain lacked strong national institutions, and Portugal had a small population; both had limited economic resources. Because of these limitations, the monarchs of Spain and Portugal allowed their subjects greater initiative as they engaged distant cultures.

The pace and character of European expansion in Africa and Asia were different than in the Americas. In Africa local rulers were generally able to limit European military power to coastal outposts and to control European trade. Only in the Kongo were the Portuguese able to project their power inland. In the Indian Ocean there were mature markets and specialized production for distant consumers when Europeans arrived. Here Portuguese (and later Dutch and British) naval power allowed Europeans to harvest large profits and influence regional commercial patterns, but most native populations continued to enjoy effective autonomy for centuries.

In the Americas, however, the terrible effects of epidemic disease and the destructiveness of the conquest led to the rapid creation of European settlements and the subordination of the surviving indigenous population. The Spanish and Portuguese found few long-distance markets and little large-scale production of goods that they could export profitably to Europe. The Americas would eventually produce great amounts of wealth, but this production of gold, silver, and sugar resulted from the introduction of new technologies, the imposition of oppressive new forms of labor, such as slavery, and the development of new roads and ports.

KEY TERMS

Zheng He p. 431
Arawak p. 432
Henry the Navigator p. 434
caravel p. 435
Gold Coast p. 437
Bartolomeu Dias p. 437
Vasco da Gama p. 437
Christopher Columbus p. 437
Ferdinand Magellan p. 439
conquistadors p. 446
Hernán Cortés p. 446
Moctezuma II p. 446
Atahualpa p. 447
Francisco Pizarro p. 447

EBOOK AND WEBSITE RESOURCES

Primary Sources

The Agreement with Columbus on April 17 and April 30, 1492

A Dominican Voice in the Wilderness: Preaching Against Tyranny in Hispaniola

Interactive Maps

Map 15.1 Exploration and Settlement in the Indian and Pacific Oceans Before 1500

Map 15.2 Middle America to 1533

Map 15.3 European Exploration, 1420–1542

Plus flashcards, practice quizzes, and more. Go to: www.cengage.com/history/bullietearthpeople5e

SUGGESTED READING

Abu-Lughod, Janet. *Before European Hegemony: The World System,* A.D. *1250–1350.* 1989. A speculative reassessment of the Mongols and the Indian Ocean trade in the creation of an economic world system.

Cipolla, Carlo M. *Guns, Sails, and Empires: Technological Innovation and the Early Phases of European Expansion, 1400–1700.* 1965. A simple introduction to the technologies of European expansion.

Cuyvers, Luc. *Into the Rising Sun: The Journey of Vasco da Gama and the Discovery of the Modern World.* 1998. Examines the impact of finding a sea route to India.

Fernandez-Armesto, Felipe. *Before Columbus: Exploration and Colonization from the Mediterranean to the Atlantic, 1229–1492.* 1987. Examines the medieval background to European intercontinental voyages.

Jennings, Jesse D., ed. *The Prehistory of Polynesia.* 1979. A reliable guide to Polynesian expansion.

Kamen, Henry. *Spain, 1469–1714: A Society of Conflict,* 2nd ed. 1991. A reliable guide to Spain in the age of maritime empire.

Levenson, Joseph R., ed. *European Expansion and the Counter Example of Asia, 1300–1600.* 1967. A collection of essays on the different expansions covered by this chapter.

McNeil, William F. *Visitors to Ancient America: The Evidence for European and Asian Presence in America Prior to Columbus.* 2004. Examines evidence of early voyages and contacts across both the Atlantic and Pacific.

Northrup, David. *Africa's Discovery of Europe, 1450–1850.* 2002. Looks at the perceptions of the peoples European explorers encountered.

Parry, J. H. *The Age of Reconnaissance: Discovery, Exploration, and Settlement, 1450–1650.* 1963. A general history with an emphasis on maritime techniques.

Phillips, William D., and Carla Rhan Phillips. *The Worlds of Christopher Columbus.* 1992. Examines the mariner and his times in terms of modern concerns.

Reid, Anthony. *Southeast Asia in the Age of Commerce, 1450–1680,* 2 vols. 1988, 1993. Deals with what were known as the East Indies.

Restall, Matthew. *Seven Myths of the Spanish Conquest.* 2003. Concentrates on continuities of Amerindian life in the face of European onslaught.

Russell-Wood, A. J. R. *The Portuguese Empire: A World on the Move.* 1998. The earliest European maritime empire.

Scammell, G. V. *The World Encompassed: The First European Maritime Empires, c. 800–1650.* 1981. A good general introduction to European expansion.

Severin, Tim. *The Brendan Voyage.* 2000. Vividly recounts a modern retracing of pre-Columbian Irish voyages.

Thornton, John. *Africa and Africans in the Making of the Atlantic World, 1400–1800,* 2nd ed. 1998. Examines Africans' encounters with Europeans and their involvement in the Atlantic economy.

Todorov, Tzvetan. *The Conquest of America.* 1985. Focuses on the shortcomings of Columbus and his Spanish peers.

NOTES

1. Ma Huan, *Ying-yai Sheng-lan: "The Overall Survey of the Ocean's Shores,"* ed. Feng Ch'eng-Chün, trans. J. V. G. Mills (Cambridge, England: Cambridge University Press, 1970), 180.
2. Alvise da Cadamosto in *The Voyages of Cadamosto and Other Documents*, ed. and trans. G. R. Crone (London: Hakluyt Society, 1937), 2.

AP* REVIEW QUESTIONS FOR CHAPTER 15

1. Which of the following was true by 1600?
   (A) Asia no longer initiated the majority of overland and maritime trade.
   (B) All major European nations had begun to colonize in South Asia and Southeast Asia.
   (C) England had become the largest slaving nation in Europe.
   (D) Polynesians were just settling the Pacific islands.

2. Most historians agree that the fact that the sweet potato, domesticated in South America, became a staple in the Polynesian diet prior to the arrival of Europeans
   (A) is an example of independent development.
   (B) suggests that the Polynesians were able to sail to South America and back.
   (C) indicates that storm debris can float a long way and deposit seeds anywhere.
   (D) indicates that Thor Heyerdahl's thesis regarding settlement from South America is correct.

3. By 1400, the Indian Ocean trade had
   (A) dwindled to a fraction of the trade moved overland through China.
   (B) been completely taken over by the Swahili Coast states.
   (C) received a major boost due to the demand for goods in Muslim cities in the Middle East.
   (D) reached parity with the overland routes through China and the Middle East.

4. Chinese sea trade reached its peak during the
   (A) Warring States Period.
   (B) Yuan dynasty.
   (C) Song dynasty.
   (D) Ming dynasty.

5. Chinese ships reached as far as Africa under the command of
   (A) Wu Di.
   (B) Zheng He.
   (C) Shih Huangdi.
   (D) Pa Chen.

6. In the early Middle Ages, the greatest of the Atlantic mariners were the
   (A) Portuguese.
   (B) English.
   (C) French.
   (D) Vikings.

7. Viking settlements in the Atlantic region included Iceland, Greenland, and
   (A) Newfoundland.
   (B) New York.
   (C) Rhode Island.
   (D) Bermuda.

8. By the year 1000, the Arawak had settled
   (A) the Greater Antilles and the Bahamas.
   (B) the Lesser Antilles and Cuba.
   (C) the northern coast of Venezuela and the Lesser Antilles.
   (D) the Lesser Antilles and Brazil.

9. Portuguese and Spanish success in exploring the Atlantic Ocean and colonizing in the New World
   (A) led to immediate and prolonged warfare among the European nations.
   (B) made Portugal and Spain the wealthiest nations in Europe in the 1500s.
   (C) encouraged the Italian states to begin to explore the Atlantic Ocean.
   (D) encouraged the Muslim states to begin to explore the Atlantic Ocean.

10. Portuguese explorers of the Indian Ocean benefited from
    (A) the desire of the natives for European trade goods.
    (B) the development of the caravel.
    (C) the detailed maps they purchased from the Chinese.
    (D) African trade centers.

11. In an effort to head off conflict, the pope divided the world between Spain and Portugal in

(A) the Great Schism.
(B) a papal bull.
(C) a treatise of nonintervention.
(D) the Treaty of Tordesillas.

12. Which of the following is true?

(A) The Spanish and Portuguese brought African slaves with them on the first voyages to the New World.
(B) European nations made slow progress in establishing colonies in Africa and Asia in the early 1500s.
(C) Portugal opted to bring Indian slaves to the New World and not use slaves from Africa.
(D) The pope ordered all slaves to be converted to Christianity.

13. In the Indian Ocean during the 1500s, Portugal was able to control

(A) East Africa and the southern coast of Arabia.
(B) all trade with India.
(C) the spice trade.
(D) all Indian Ocean trade.

14. Despite the fact that disease greatly helped Cortes in conquering the Aztecs,

(A) the Aztecs nearly defeated him in battle.
(B) he also had reinforcement from other Amerindians hostile to the Aztecs.
(C) he was reinforced by Balboa and Pizarro.
(D) he used siege warfare and starved the Aztecs into surrender.

15. Both the Spanish and the Portuguese found that the Americas offered

(A) well-developed markets and an advanced system of trade.
(B) few long-distance markets and little production of goods that could be profitably exported to Europe.
(C) slave markets already in place for their plantations.
(D) well-developed farming methods that provided ample food supplies.

CLIMATE AND POPULATION TO 1500

During the millennia before 1500, human populations expanded in three momentous surges. The first occurred after 50,000 B.C.E. when humans emigrated from their African homeland to all of the inhabitable continents. After that, the global population remained steady for several millenniA. During the second expansion, between about 5000 and 500 B.C.E., population rose from about 5 million to 100 million as agricultural societies spread around the world (see Figure 1). Again population growth then slowed for several centuries before a third surge took world population to over 350 million by 1200 C.E. (Figure 2 shows population in China and Europe).

For a long time historians tended to attribute these population surges to cultural and technological advances. Indeed, a great many changes in culture and technology are associated with adaptation to different climates and food supplies in the first surge and with the domestication of plants and animals in the second. However, historians have not found a cultural or technological change to explain the third surge, nor can they explain why creativity would have stagnated for long periods between the surges. Something else must have been at work.

Recently historians have begun to pay more attention to the impact of long-term variations in global climate. By examining ice cores drilled out of glaciers, scientists have been able to compile records of thousands of years of climate change. The comparative width of tree rings from ancient forests has provided additional data on periods of favorable and unfavorable growth. Such evidence shows that cycles of population growth and stagnation followed changes in global climate.

Historians now believe that global temperatures were above normal for extended periods from the late 1100s to the late 1200s C.E. In the temperate lands where most of the

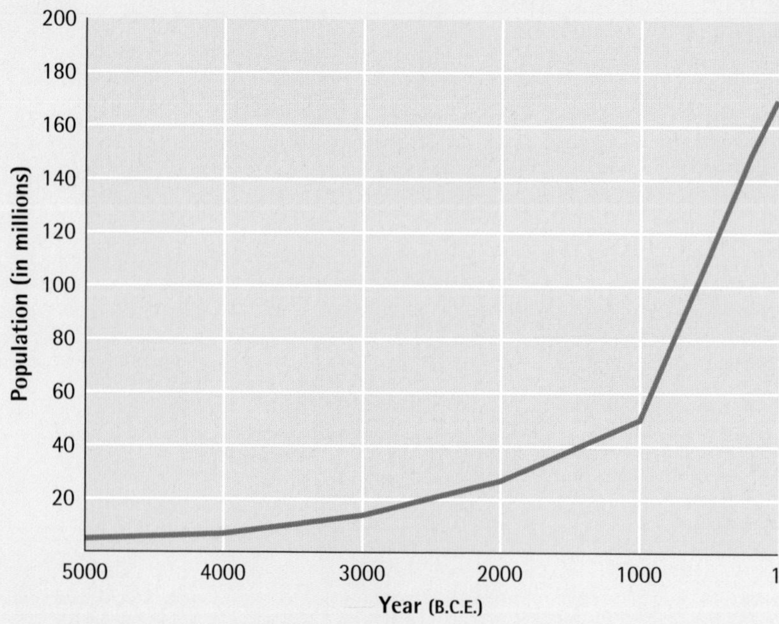

FIGURE 1 World Population, 5000–1 B.C.E.

world's people lived, above-normal temperatures meant a longer growing season, more bountiful harvests, and thus a more adequate and reliable food supply. The ways in which societies responded to the medieval warm period are as important as the climate change, but it is unlikely that human agency alone would have produced the medieval surge. One notable response was that of the Vikings, who increased the size and range of their settlements in the North Atlantic, although their raids also caused death and destruction.

Some of the complexities involved in the interaction of human agency, climate, and other natural factors are also evident in the demographic changes that followed the medieval warm period. During the 1200s the Mongol invasions caused death and disruption of agriculture across Eurasia. China's population, which had been over 100 million in 1200, declined by a third or more by 1300. The Mongol invasions did not cause harm west of Russia, but climate changes in the 1300s resulted in population losses in Europe. Unusually heavy rains caused crop failures and a prolonged famine in northern Europe from 1315 to 1319.

The freer movement of merchants within the Mongol Empire also facilitated the spread of disease across Eurasia, culminating in the great pandemic known as the Black Death in Europe. The demographic recovery under way in China was reversed. The even larger population losses in Europe may have been affected by the decrease in global temperatures to their lowest point in many millennia between 1350 and 1375. After 1400 improving economic conditions enabled population to recover more rapidly in Europe than in China, where the conditions of rural life remained harsh.

Because many other historical circumstances interact with changing weather patterns, historians have a long way to go in deciphering the role of climate in history. Nevertheless, it is a factor that can no longer be ignored.

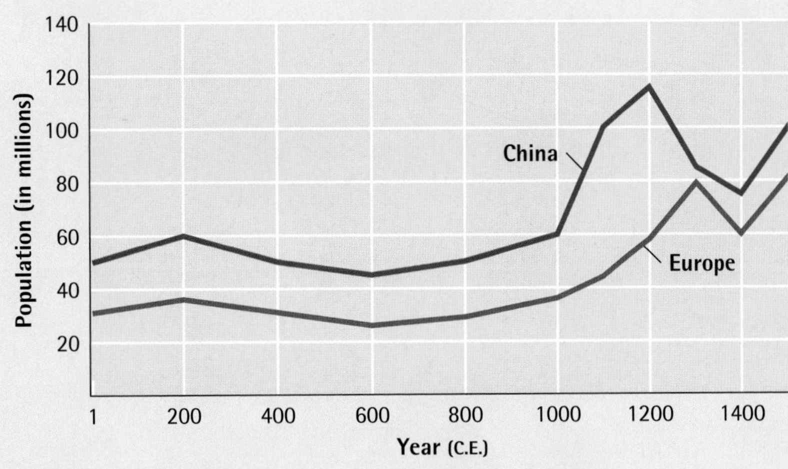

FIGURE 2 Population in China and Europe, 1–1500 C.E.

PART V

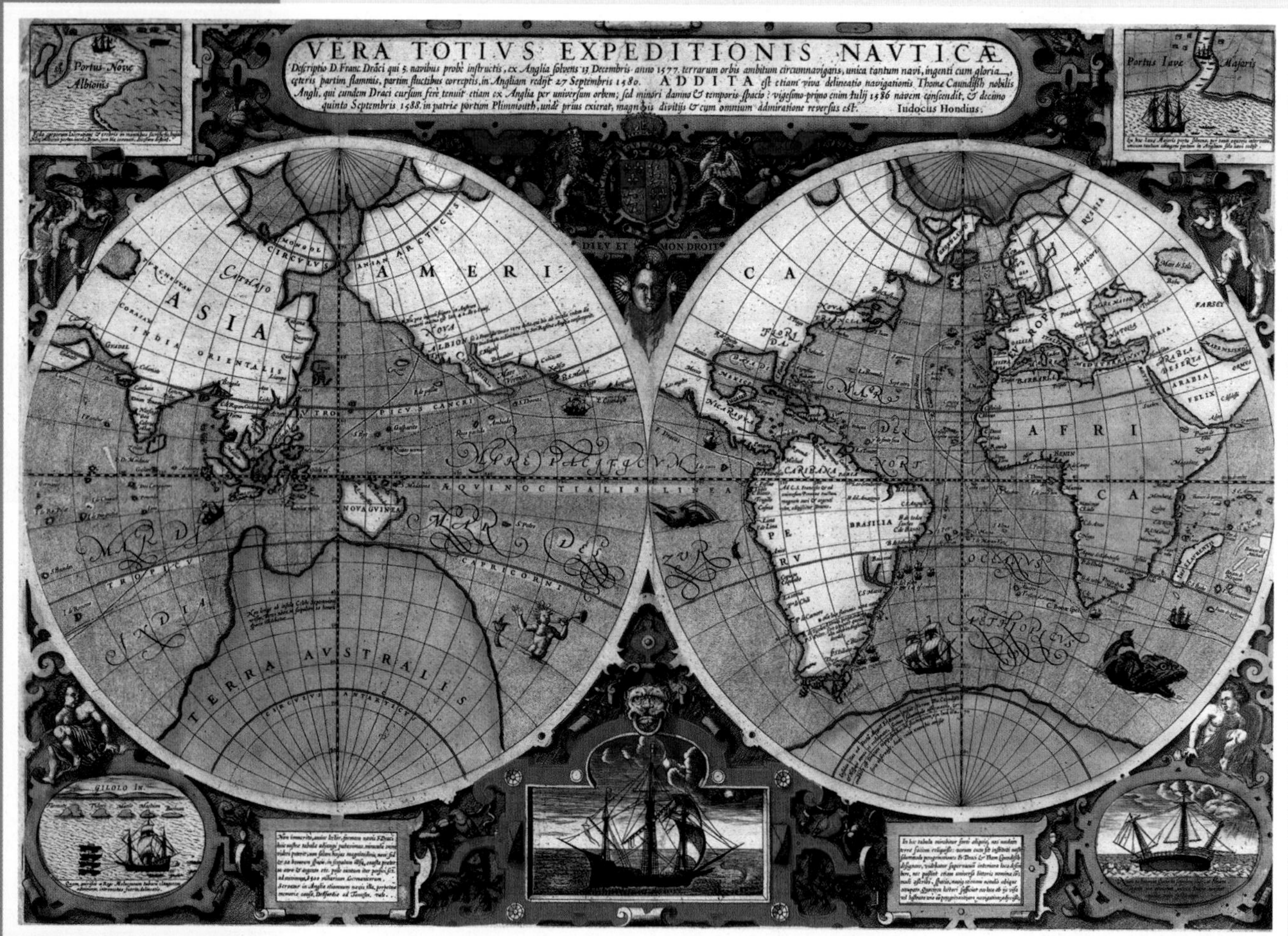

Library of Congress

Map of the World, ca. 1595 After Ferdinand Magellan, the next explorer to circumnavigate the world was Sir Francis Drake (ca. 1540–1596). Departing with five ships in 1577, Drake nonetheless completed the majority of his voyage in a single ship, the *Golden Hind*, returning to England in 1580. This hand-colored engraving by Jodocus Hondius shows his route. Supported by Queen Elizabeth and other investors, Drake raided Spanish ships and ports and returned with great riches. Unlike Magellan, he traveled far northward before crossing the Pacific, harboring for several weeks near San Francisco Bay and making friendly contact with the native peoples there. Drake played a decisive role in England's victory against the Spanish Armada in 1588.

The Globe Encompassed, 1500–1750

The decades between 1500 and 1750 witnessed a tremendous expansion of commercial, cultural, and biological exchanges around the world. New long-distance sea routes linked Europe with sub-Saharan Africa and the existing maritime networks of the Indian Ocean and East Asia. Spanish and Portuguese voyages ended the isolation of the Americas and created new webs of exchange in the Atlantic and Pacific. Overland expansion of Muslim, Russian, and Chinese empires also increased global interaction.

These expanding contacts had major demographic and cultural consequences. Domesticated animals and crops from the Old World transformed agriculture in the Americas, while Amerindian foods such as the potato became staples of the diet of the Old World. European diseases, meanwhile, devastated the Amerindian population, facilitating the establishment of large Spanish, Portuguese, French, and British empires. Europeans introduced enslaved Africans to relieve the labor shortage. Immigrant Africans and Europeans brought new languages, religious practices, music, and forms of personal adornment.

In Asia and Africa, by contrast, the most important changes owed more to internal forces than to European actions. The Portuguese seized control of some important trading ports and networks in the Indian Ocean and pioneered new contacts with China and Japan. In time, the Dutch, French, and English expanded these profitable connections, but in 1750 Europeans were still primarily a maritime force. Asians and Africans generally retained control of their lands and participated freely in overseas trade.

The Islamic world saw the dramatic expansion of the Ottoman Empire in the Middle East and the establishment of the Safavid Empire in Iran and the Mughal Empire in South Asia. In northern Eurasia, Russia and China acquired vast new territories and populations, while a new national government in Japan promoted economic development and stemmed foreign influence.

CHAPTER

16

CHAPTER OUTLINE

- Culture and Ideas
- Social and Economic Life
- Political Innovations
- Conclusion

ENVIRONMENT + TECHNOLOGY *Mapping the World*

DIVERSITY + DOMINANCE *Political Craft and Craftiness*

Kunsthistorisches Museum, Vienna/The Bridgeman Art Library

Hunters in the Snow, 1565 This January scene, by the Flemish artist Pieter Bruegel the Elder, shows many everyday activities.

Visit the website and ebook for additional study materials and interactive tools: www.cengage.com/history/bullietearthpeople5e

Transformations in Europe, 1500–1750

- How did the interplay of traditional beliefs and revolutionary ideas influence the cultural history of early modern Europe?
- What factors contributed to the wealth of some Europeans and the great poverty of others in this period?
- How did differing policies in the areas of religion, foreign relations, and economics determine the very different experiences of early modern European states?

Four years before his death, the Flemish artist Pieter Bruegel the Elder (ca. 1525–1569) painted *Hunters in the Snow*, a masterpiece of the cultural revival that later ages would call the European **Renaissance**. After a period of apprenticeship, in 1551 Bruegel became a master painter in the Antwerp Painters Guild. Though he also painted biblical and allegorical subjects, Bruegel is remembered best for his technical skill and powers of observation, which were demonstrated in his depictions of the everyday life that surrounded him. Other forms of culture flourished as well in early modern Europe, as exemplified by the musical compositions of Johann Sebastian Bach (1685–1750) in Germany and Antonio Vivaldi (ca. 1675–1741) in Italy, and by the literature of William Shakespeare (1564–1616) in England and Miguel de Cervantes (1547–1616) in Spain.

Renaissance (European) A period of intense artistic and intellectual activity, said to be a "rebirth" of Greco-Roman culture. Usually divided into an Italian Renaissance, from roughly the mid-fourteenth to mid-fifteenth century, and a Northern (trans-Alpine) Renaissance, from roughly the early fifteenth to early seventeenth century.

In this period Europe also developed powerful and efficient armies, economies, and governments, which larger states elsewhere in the world feared, envied, and sometimes imitated. The balance of power was shifting slowly in Europe's favor. At the beginning of this era, the Ottomans threatened Europe, but by 1750, as the remaining chapters of Part Five detail, Europeans had brought much of the world under their control. No single nation was responsible for this success. The Dutch eclipsed the pioneering Portuguese and Spanish; then the English and French bested the Dutch. This was also a period of dynamic cultural change. At the beginning of this era a single Christian tradition dominated western Europe. By its end secular political institutions and economic interests had grown stronger, while Catholic and Protestant churches were weakened by religious wars. Equally influential was the challenge to Christianity's long domination of European intellectual life posed by the Scientific Revolution and the Enlightenment.

The years from 1500 to 1750 were not simply an age of progress for Europe. For many, the ferocious competition of European armies, merchants, and ideas was a wrenching experience. The growth of powerful states extracted a terrible price in death and destruction. The Reformation brought widespread religious persecution and religious warfare as well as greater individual choice in religion. Women's fortunes remained closely tied to their social class, and few gained equality with men. The expanding economy benefited members of the emerging merchant elite and their political allies, but in an era of rising prices Europe's urban and rural poor struggled to survive.

CULTURE AND IDEAS

During the Reformation, theological controversies broke the religious unity of the Latin Church and contributed to long and violent wars. A huge witch scare demonstrated the endurance of traditional folklore and popular beliefs. While the influence of classical ideas from Greco-Roman antiquity increased among better-educated Europeans, some bold thinkers challenged the authority of the ancients. They introduced new ideas about the motion of the planets and encouraged others to challenge traditional social and political systems; these new ideas would help promote revolutionary changes in the period after 1750. Each of these events had its own causes, but the technology of the printing press broadened the impact of all.

AP* Exam Tip It is important to understand the papacy, but not individual popes, for the exam.

Early Reformation

papacy The central administration of the Roman Catholic Church, of which the pope is the head.

indulgence The forgiveness of the punishment due for past sins, granted by the Catholic Church authorities as a reward for a pious act. Martin Luther's protest against the sale of indulgences is often seen as touching off the Protestant Reformation.

In 1500 the **papacy**, the central government of Latin Christianity, simultaneously gained stature and suffered from corruption and dissent. Recovered from a period when competing popes supported by rival rulers disputed control of the church, popes now exercised greater power funded by larger donations and tax receipts. The construction of fifty-four new churches and other buildings in Rome served to demonstrate the church's power and showcase the artistic Renaissance then under way. The church leadership intended the size and splendor of the magnificent new Saint Peter's Basilica in Rome to glorify God, display the skill of Renaissance artists and builders, and enhance the standing of the papacy, but the vast expense of its construction and rich decoration also caused scandal.

The skillful overseer of the design and financing of the Saint Peter's Basilica was Pope Leo X (r. 1513–1521), a member of the wealthy Medici (MED-ih-chee) family of Florence, famous for its patronage of the arts. Pope Leo's artistic taste was superb and his personal life free from scandal, but he was more a man of action than a spiritual leader. During his papacy the church aggressively raised funds for the basilica and other ambitious projects. The sale of **indulgences**—a forgiveness of the punishment due for past sins, was seen by many as abusive and scandalous.

Private Collection/The Bridgeman Art Library

Luther and the Reformation This sixteenth-century woodcut of Martin Luther shows him writing his demands for religious reform with a symbolically oversized quill pen on the door of All Saints Church in Wittenberg, Germany.

CHRONOLOGY

	Politics and Culture	Environment and Technology	Warfare
1500	1500s Spain's golden century		
	1519 Protestant Reformation begins		1526–1571 Ottoman attack on Hapsburg Empire
	1540s Scientific Revolution begins		
	1545 Catholic Reformation begins		1546–1555 German Wars of Religion
			1562–1598 French Wars of Religion
			1566–1648 Netherlands Revolt
	Late 1500s Witch-hunts increase		
		1590s Dutch develop flyboats; Little Ice Age begins	
1600	1600s Holland's golden century	1600s Depletion of forests growing	
		1609 Galileo's astronomical telescope	
			1618–1648 Thirty Years War
			1642–1648 English Civil War
			1652–1678 Anglo-Dutch Wars
			1667–1697 Wars of Louis XIV
		1682 Canal du Midi completed	1683–1697 Ottoman wars
			1701–1714 War of the Spanish Succession
1700	1700s The Enlightenment begins		
		1750 English mine nearly 5 million tons of coal a year	
		1755 Lisbon earthquake	

Martin Luther

PRIMARY SOURCE: Table Talk Read Martin Luther in his own words, speaking out forcefully and candidly—and sometimes with humor—against Catholic institutions.

Protestant Reformation Religious reform movement within the Latin Christian Church beginning in 1519. It resulted in the "protesters" forming several new Christian denominations, including the Lutheran and Reformed Churches and the Church of England.

A young professor of sacred scripture, Martin Luther (1483–1546), objected to this practice and to other excesses. As the result of a powerful religious experience, Luther had forsaken money and marriage for a monastic life of prayer, self-denial, and study. In his religious quest, he found personal consolation in a passage in Saint Paul's Epistle stating that salvation resulted from religious faith, not from "doing certain things." That passage led Luther to object to the way preachers emphasized giving money to the church more than they emphasized faith. He wrote to Pope Leo to complain of this abuse and challenged the preachers to a debate on the theology of indulgences.

This theological dispute was also a contest between two strong-willed men. Largely ignoring the theological objections, Pope Leo regarded Luther's letter as a challenge to papal power and moved to silence him. During a debate in 1519, a papal representative led Luther into open disagreement with church doctrines, for which the papacy condemned him. Blocked in his effort to reform the church from within, Luther burned the papal bull (document) of condemnation, rejected the pope's authority, and began the movement known as the **Protestant Reformation**.

Accusing those whom he called "Romanists" (Roman Catholics) of relying on "good works," Luther insisted that the only way to salvation was through faith in Jesus Christ. He further declared that Christian belief should be based on the word of God in the Bible and on Christian tradition, not on the authority of the pope. Luther's use of the printing press to spread his ideas won him the support of powerful Germans, who responded to his nationalist portrayal of an Italian pope seeking to beautify Rome with German funds.

The Reformation Spreads

AP* Exam Tip Make sure you are able to discuss the creation of new religions.

Luther's denunciation of the ostentation and corruption of the church led others to call for a return to authentic Christian practices and beliefs. John Calvin (1509–1564), a well-educated Frenchman who left the study of law for theology after experiencing a religious conversion, became an influential Protestant leader. As a young man, Calvin published a synthesis of Christian teachings in 1535, *The Institutes of the Christian Religion*. Although Calvin agreed with Luther's emphasis on faith over works, he denied that human faith alone could merit salvation. Salvation, Calvin believed, was a gift God gave to those He "predestined." Calvin also went farther than Luther in curtailing the power of the clerical hierarchy and in simplifying religious rituals. Calvinist congregations elected their own governing committees and created regional and national synods (councils) to regulate doctrinal issues. Calvinists also displayed simplicity in dress, life, and worship, avoiding ostentatious living and stripping churches of statues, most musical instruments, stained-glass windows, incense, and vestments.

The Reformers appealed to genuine religious sentiments, but their successes and failures were also due to local political and economic conditions. It was no coincidence that German-born Luther had his greatest success among German speakers and linguistically related Scandinavians and not surprising that peasants and urban laborers sometimes defied their masters by adopting a different faith. Protestants were no more inclined than Roman Catholics to question male dominance in the church and the family, but most Protestants rejected the medieval tradition of celibate priests and nuns and advocated Christian marriage for all adults.

The Counter Reformation and the Politics of Religion

Catholic Reformation Religious reform movement within the Latin Christian Church, begun in response to the Protestant Reformation. It clarified Catholic theology and reformed clerical training and discipline.

Shaken by the intensity of the Protestant attack, the Catholic Church undertook its own reforms. A council that met at the city of Trent in northern Italy between 1545 and 1563 sought to distinguish Catholic doctrines from Protestant "errors" and reaffirmed the supremacy of the pope. The council also called for bishops to reside in their dioceses and dioceses to maintain a theological seminary to train priests. The creation in 1540 of a new religious order, the Society of Jesus, or "Jesuits," by a Spanish nobleman, Ignatius of Loyola (1491–1556), was among the most important events of the **Catholic Reformation**. Well-educated Jesuits helped stem the Protestant tide by their teaching and preaching (see Map 16.1), and they gained converts through overseas missions (see Chapters 17 and 20).

Religion and the Ambitions of Kings

Given the complexity and intensity stirred by the Protestant Reformation, it is not surprising that both sides persecuted and sometimes executed those of differing views. Bitter "wars of religion" would continue in parts of western Europe until 1648. The rulers of Spain and France actively defended the Catholic tradition against Protestant challenges. Following the pattern used by his predecessors to suppress Jewish and Muslim practices, King Philip II of Spain used the Inquisition to enforce religious orthodoxy. Suspected Protestants, as well as critics of the king, were accused of heresy, some were punished by death, and even those acquitted learned not to challenge the church or the king again.

In France the Calvinist opponents of the Valois dynasty gained the military advantage in the French Wars of Religion (1562–1598). In the interest of national unity, their leader Prince Henry of Navarre ultimately embraced the Catholic faith of the majority of his subjects when he ruled as Henry IV of France. In their embrace of a union of church and state, Henry IV, his son King Louis XIII, and his grandson King Louis XIV supported the Catholic Church. Ultimately, Louis XIV revoked the Edict of Nantes (nahnt) by which his grandfather had granted religious freedom to his Protestant supporters in 1598.

In England King Henry VIII had initially been a strong defender of the papacy against Lutheran criticism. But when Henry failed to obtain a papal annulment of his marriage to Catherine of Aragon, who had not furnished him with a male heir, he challenged the papacy's authority over the English church. First the English archbishop of Canterbury annulled Henry's marriage in 1533 and then Parliament made the king head of an autonomous Church of England.

Like many Protestant rulers, Henry used his authority to disband monasteries and convents and seize their lands. He gave some land to his powerful allies and sold other land to pay for his new navy. While the king's power had grown at the expense of the Catholic Church, religious belief and practice were changing also. The new Anglican Church distanced itself from Catholic ritual and theology, but English Puritans (Calvinists who wanted to "purify" the church of all

Catholic practices and beliefs) sought more. When Puritans petitioned to eliminate bishops in 1603, the first Stuart king, James I, reminded them of the traditional role of religion in supporting royal power: "No bishops, no king."

Local Religion, Traditional Culture, and Witch-Hunts

witch-hunt The pursuit of people suspected of witchcraft, especially in northern Europe in the late sixteenth and seventeenth centuries.

Both in the Protestant north and the Catholic south the institutions of religious orthodoxy were weakest in villages and small towns. In these settings, local religion commonly blended the rituals and beliefs of the established churches with local folk customs, pre-Christian beliefs, ancient curing practices, love magic, and the casting of spells. The vigor and power of these local religious traditions ebbed and flowed in response to the strength of national and regional religious institutions everywhere in Europe. The widespread **witch-hunts** that Protestants and Catholics undertook in early modern Europe were one manifestation of the ongoing contest between formal religious institutions and local beliefs and cultural heritage.

The World of Magic and Spirits

Prevailing European ideas about the natural world blended two distinct traditions. One was the folklore about magic and forest spirits passed down orally from pre-Christian times. The second was the biblical teachings of the Christian and Jewish scriptures, heard by all in church and read by growing numbers in vernacular translations. In the minds of most people, Christian teachings about miracles, saints, and devils mixed easily with folklore.

Zentralbibliothek Zurich, Ms. F. 23, p. 56

Death to Witches This woodcut from 1574 depicts three women convicted of witchcraft being burned alive in Baden, Switzerland. The well-dressed townsmen look on stolidly.

MAP 16.1 **Religious Reformation in Europe** The Reformation brought greater religious freedom but also led to religious conflict and persecution. In many places the Reformation accelerated the trend toward state control of religion and added religious differences to the motives for wars among Europeans.

Interactive Map

Like people in other parts of the world, most early modern Europeans believed that natural events could have supernatural causes. When crops failed or domestic animals died unexpectedly, many people blamed unseen spirits and sought the help of men and women seen to have special powers. Many believed these same intermediaries had the power to solve romantic problems, fix disputes with masters or employers, or satisfy a desire for revenge.

Europeans continued to attribute human triumphs and tragedies to supernatural causes as well. When an earthquake destroyed much of Lisbon, Portugal's capital city, in November 1755, for example, both educated and uneducated people saw the event as a punishment sent by God. A Jesuit charged it "scandalous to pretend that the earthquake was just a natural event." An English Protestant leader agreed, comparing Lisbon's fate with that of Sodom, the city that God destroyed because of the sinfulness of its citizens, according to the Hebrew Bible.

The Witch-Hunts

The extraordinary fear of the power of witches that swept across northern Europe in the late sixteenth and seventeenth centuries was powerful testimony to belief in the spiritual causes of natural events. Historians estimate that secular and church authorities tried over a hundred thousand people—some three-fourths of them women—for practicing witchcraft. Trial records make it clear that both the accusers and the accused believed that it was possible for angry and jealous individuals to use evil magic and the power of the Devil to cause people and domestic animals to sicken and die or to cause crops to wither in the fields. Researchers think that at least some of those accused in early modern Europe may really have tried to use witchcraft to harm their enemies. However, it was the Reformation's focus on the Devil—the enemy of God—as the source of evil and the Counter Reformation Catholic Church's enforcement of orthodoxy that promoted and justified these efforts to identify and punish witchcraft.

No single reason can explain the rise in witchcraft accusations and fears in early modern Europe, but, for both the accusers and the accused, there are plausible connections between the witch-hunts and rising social tensions, rural poverty, and environmental strains. Far from being a bizarre aberration, witch-hunts reflected the tension between popular beliefs and practices and the ambitions of aggressive new religious and political institutions.

The Scientific Revolution

Among the educated, the writings of Greco-Roman antiquity and the Bible were the most trusted guides to the natural world. The Renaissance had recovered many manuscripts of ancient writers, some of which were printed and widely circulated. The greatest authority on physics was Aristotle, a Greek philosopher who taught that everything on earth was reducible to four elements. The surface of the earth was composed of the two heavy elements, earth and water. The atmosphere was made up of two lighter elements, air and fire, which floated above the ground. Higher still were the sun, moon, planets, and stars, which, according to Aristotelian physics, were so light and pure that they floated in crystalline spheres. This division between the ponderous, heavy earth and the airy, celestial bodies accorded perfectly with the commonsense perception that all heavenly bodies revolved around the earth.

The prevailing conception of the universe was also influenced by the ancient Greek mathematician Pythagoras, who proved the famous theorem that still bears his name: in a right triangle, the square of the hypotenuse is equal to the sum of the squares of the other two sides ($a^2 + b^2 = c^2$). Pythagoreans attributed the ability of simple mathematical equations to describe physical objects to mystical properties. They attached special significance to the simplest (to them perfect) geometrical shapes: the circle (a point rotated around another point) and the sphere (a circle rotated on its axis). They believed that celestial objects were perfect spheres orbiting the earth in circular orbits.

Scientific Revolution The intellectual movement in Europe, initially associated with planetary motion and other aspects of physics, that by the seventeenth century had laid the groundwork for modern science.

New Questions and Methods

In the sixteenth century, however, the careful observations and mathematical calculations of some daring and imaginative European investigators began to challenge these prevailing conceptions of the physical world. These pioneers of the **Scientific Revolution** demonstrated that natural causes could explain the workings of the universe.

Over the centuries, observers of the nighttime skies had plotted the movements of the heavenly bodies, and mathematicians had worked to fit these observations into the prevailing theories of circular orbits. To make all the evidence fit, they had come up with eighty different spheres and some ingenious theories to explain the many seemingly irregular movements. Pondering these complications, a Polish monk and mathematician named Nicholas Copernicus

Maritime Museum Kronberg Castle Denmark/ G.Dagli Orti/The Art Archive

Tycho Brahe at Work Between 1576 and 1597, on the island of Ven between Denmark and Sweden, Tycho built the best observatory in Europe and set a new standard for accurate celestial observations before the invention of the telescope. This contemporary hand-colored engraving shows the Danish astronomer at work.

(1473–1543) came up with a simpler solution: switching the center of the different orbits from the earth to the sun.

Copernicus did not challenge the idea that the sun, moon, and planets were light, perfect spheres or that they moved in circular orbits. But his placement of the sun, not the earth, at the center began a revolution in understanding the structure of the heavens and the central place of humans in the universe. To escape anticipated controversies, Copernicus delayed the publication of his heliocentric (sun-centered) theory until the end of his life.

Other astronomers, including the Danish Tycho Brahe (1546–1601) and his German assistant Johannes Kepler (1571–1630), strengthened and improved on Copernicus's model, showing that planets actually move in elliptical, not circular, orbits. The most brilliant of the Copernicans was the Italian Galileo Galilei (gal-uh-LAY-oh gal-uh-LAY-ee) (1564–1642). In 1609 Galileo built a telescope through which he could look more closely at the heavens. Able to magnify distant objects thirty times beyond the power of the naked eye, Galileo saw that heavenly bodies were not the perfectly smooth spheres of the Aristotelians. The moon, he reported in *The Starry Messenger* (1610), had mountains and valleys; the sun had spots; other planets had their own moons. In other words, the earth was not alone in being heavy and changeable.

PRIMARY SOURCE: Letter to the Grand Duchess Christina Read Galileo's passionate defense of his scientific research against those who would condemn it as un-Christian.

AP* Exam Tip The Scientific Revolution is a major intellectual development.

At first, the Copernican universe found more critics than supporters because it so directly challenged not just popular ideas but also the intellectual synthesis of classical and biblical authorities. Is the Bible wrong, asked the theologians, when the Book of Joshua says that, by God's command, "the sun [not the earth] stood still . . . for about a whole day" to give the ancient Israelites victory in their conquest of Palestine? If Aristotle's physics was wrong, worried other traditionalists, would not the theological synthesis built on other parts of his philosophy be open to question?

Intellectual and religious leaders encouraged political authorities to suppress the new ideas. Most Protestant leaders, following the lead of Martin Luther, condemned the heliocentric universe as contrary to the Bible. Catholic authorities waited longer to act. After all, both Copernicus and Galileo were Roman Catholics. Copernicus had dedicated his book to the pope, and in 1582 another pope, Gregory XIII, had used the latest astronomical findings to issue a new and more accurate calendar (still used today). Galileo ingeniously argued that the conflict between scripture and science was only apparent because the word of God was expressed in the language of ordinary people, but in nature God's truth was revealed more perfectly in a language that could be learned by careful observation and scientific reasoning. Galileo also ridiculed those who were slow to accept his findings. Smarting under Galileo's stinging sarcasm, his enemies complained to the Inquisition, which prohibited him from publishing further on the subject.

Scientific Knowledge Expands

Despite official opposition, printed books spread the new scientific ideas among scholars across Europe. In England, Robert Boyle (1627–1691) demonstrated the usefulness of the experimental method and along with others became an enthusiastic missionary of mechanical science, using the Royal Society, chartered in London in 1662, to promote knowledge of the natural world. Another Englishman, the mathematician Isaac Newton (1642–1727), carried Galileo's demonstration that the heavens and earth share a common physics to its logical conclusion by formulating mathematical laws that governed all physical objects. His Law of Gravity and his role in developing calculus made him the most famous and influential man of his era, serving as president of the Royal Society from 1703 until his death.

As late as 1700 most religious and intellectual leaders viewed the new science with suspicion or outright hostility because of the unwanted challenge it posed to established ways of thought. Yet most of the principal pioneers of the Scientific Revolution were convinced that scientific discoveries and revealed religion were not in conflict. However, by showing that the Aristotelians and biblical writers held ideas about the natural world that were untrue, these pioneers opened the door to others who used reason to challenge a broader range of unquestioned traditions and superstitions. The world of ideas was forever changed.

The Early Enlightenment

Advances in scientific thought inspired some to question the reasonableness of everything from agricultural methods to laws, religion, and social hierarchies. They believed that they could apply the scientific method to analyze economics, politics, and social organization and devise the best policies. This enthusiasm for an open and critical examination of human society energized a movement known as the **Enlightenment**. Like the Scientific Revolution, this movement was the work of a few "enlightened" individuals, who often faced bitter opposition from the political and religious establishments. Leading Enlightenment thinkers became accustomed to having their books burned or banned, and many spent long periods in exile to escape persecution.

Enlightenment A philosophical movement in eighteenth-century Europe that fostered the belief that one could reform society by discovering rational laws that governed social behavior and were just as scientific as the laws of physics.

Influences besides the Scientific Revolution affected the Enlightenment. The religious warfare and intolerance associated with the struggle between Catholicism and Protestantism undermined the moral authority of religion for many, and the efforts of church authorities to impugn the breakthroughs of science pushed European intellectual life in a secular direction. The popular bigotry manifested in the brutal treatment of suspected witches also shocked many thoughtful people. The leading French thinker Voltaire (1694–1778) declared: "No opinion is worth burning your neighbor for."

The Enlightenment and Cultural Change

Although many circumstances shaped "enlightened" thinking, the new scientific methods and discoveries provided the clearest model for changing European society. Voltaire posed the issues in these terms: "It would be very peculiar that all nature, all the planets, should obey eternal laws" but a human being, "in contempt of these laws, could act as he pleased solely according to his caprice." The English poet Alexander Pope (1688–1774) made a similar point in verse: "Nature and Nature's laws lay hidden in night; / God said, 'Let Newton be' and all was light."

PRIMARY SOURCE: Treatise on Toleration Voltaire makes a powerful argument for cultural and religious tolerance.

The Enlightenment was more a frame of mind than a coherent movement. Individuals who embraced it drew inspiration from different sources and promoted different agendas. Its proponents were clearer about what they disliked than about what changes were necessary. Some thought an "enlightened" society could function with the mechanical orderliness of planets spinning in their orbits. Nearly all were optimistic that—at least in the long run—their discoveries would improve human beliefs and institutions. This faith in progress would help foster political and social revolutions after 1750, as Chapter 21 recounts.

While the Catholic Church and many Protestant clergymen opposed the Enlightenment, European monarchs selectively endorsed new ideas. Monarchs, ambitious to increase their power, found anticlerical intellectuals useful allies against church power and wealth. More predictably, monarchs and their reforming advisers discovered in the Enlightenment's demand for more rational and predictable policies justification for the expansion of royal authority and modern tax systems. Europe in 1750 was a place where political and religious divisions, growing literacy, and the printing press made it possible for these controversial and exciting new ideas to thrive in the face of opposition from ancient and powerful institutions.

SECTION REVIEW

- Outraged by corrupt church practices, reformers like Luther and Calvin challenged papal authority and traditional Catholic theology.
- In response to the Protestant reformers, the Catholic Church launched a Counter Reformation.
- Both Protestants and Catholics, seeking to enforce orthodoxy, sanctioned widespread witch-hunts.
- The thinkers of the Scientific Revolution challenged traditional biblical and Greco-Roman conceptions of the cosmos.
- The advances in science prompted Enlightenment thinkers to question many conventional ideas and practices.

SOCIAL AND ECONOMIC LIFE

European society was dominated by a small number of noble families who enjoyed privileged access to high offices in the church, government, and military and, in most cases, exemption from taxation. Below them was a much larger class of prosperous commoners that included many clergy, bureaucrats, professionals, and military officers as well as merchants, some artisans, and rural landowners. The vast majority of men and women were very poor. Laborers, journeymen, apprentices, and rural laborers struggled to earn their daily bread but often faced unemployment and privation. The poorest members of society lived truly desperate lives, surviving only through guile, begging, or crime. Women remained subordinated to men.

Some social mobility did occur, however, particularly in the middle. The principal engine of social change was the economy, and the locations where social change occurred most readily were the cities. A secondary means of change was education—for those who could get it.

The Bourgeoisie

Europe's cities grew in response to expanding trade. In 1500 Paris was the only northern European city with over 100,000 inhabitants. By 1700 both Paris and London had populations over 500,000, and twenty other European cities contained over 60,000 people.

Cities as Engines of Change

bourgeoisie In early modern Europe, the class of well-off town dwellers whose wealth came from manufacturing, finance, commerce, and allied professions.

Urban wealth came from manufacturing and finance, but especially from trade, both within Europe and overseas. The French called the urban class that dominated these activities the **bourgeoisie** (boor-zwah-ZEE) (burghers, town dwellers). Members of the bourgeoisie devoted long hours to their businesses and poured much of their profits back into them or into new ventures. Even so, most had enough money to live comfortably in large houses, and some had servants. In the seventeenth and eighteenth centuries wealthier consumers could buy exotic luxuries imported from the far corners of the earth—Caribbean and Brazilian sugar and rum, Mexican chocolate, Virginia tobacco, North American furs, East Indian cotton textiles and spices, and Chinese tea.

The Netherlands

The Netherlands provides a good example of bourgeois enterprise. Dutch manufacturers and craftsmen turned out a variety of goods in their factories and workshops. The highly successful textile industry concentrated on the profitable weaving, finishing, and printing of cloth, leaving the spinning to low-paid workers elsewhere. Along with fine woolens and linens, the Dutch made cheaper textiles for mass markets. Other factories in Holland refined West Indian sugar, brewed beer from Baltic grain, cut Virginia tobacco, and made imitations of Chinese ceramics (see Environment and Technology: East Asian Porcelain in Chapter 20). Free from the censorship imposed by political and religious authorities in neighboring countries, Holland's printers published books in many languages, including manuals with the latest advances in machinery, metallurgy, agriculture, and other technical areas. For a small nation that lacked timber and other natural resources, this was a remarkable achievement.

With a population of 200,000 in 1700, Amsterdam was Holland's largest city and Europe's major port. The Dutch developed huge commercial fleets that dominated sea trade in Europe and overseas. They introduced new ship designs, including the *fluit*, or "flyboat," a large-capacity cargo ship that was inexpensive to build and required only a small crew. Another successful type of merchant ship, the heavily armed "East Indiaman," helped the Dutch establish their supremacy in the Indian Ocean. By one estimate, the Dutch conducted more than half of all the oceangoing commercial shipping in the world in the seventeenth century (for details see Chapters 19 and 20). Dutch mapmaking supported these distant commercial connections (see Environment and Technology: Mapping the World). Amsterdam also served as Europe's financial center. Seventeenth-century Dutch banks had such a reputation for security that wealthy individuals and governments from all over western Europe entrusted them with their money. The banks in turn invested these funds in real estate, loaned money to factory owners and governments, and provided capital for big business operations overseas.

Like merchants in the Islamic world, Europe's merchants relied on family and ethnic networks. In addition to families of local origin, the most dynamic northern European cities were culturally diverse, hosting merchant colonies from Venice, Florence, Genoa, and other Italian cities as well

Rijksmuseum-Amsterdam

The Fishwife, 1572 Women were essential partners in most Dutch family businesses. This scene by the Dutch artist Adriaen van Ostade shows a woman preparing fish for retail sale.

as Jewish merchants who had fled religious persecution in Iberia. Other Jewish communities emigrated from eastern Europe to the German states, especially after the Thirty Years War.

The bourgeoisie sought mutually beneficial alliances with European monarchs, who welcomed economic growth as a means of increasing state revenues. The Dutch government pioneered chartering **joint-stock companies** like the Dutch East and West India Companies, which were granted monopolies for trade with the East and West Indies. France and England chartered companies of their own. These companies then sold shares to individuals to raise large sums for overseas enterprises while spreading the risks (and profits) among many investors (see Chapter 18). Investors could buy and sell shares in specialized financial markets called **stock exchanges**, an Italian innovation transferred to the cities of northwestern Europe in the sixteenth century. The greatest stock market in the seventeenth and eighteenth centuries was the Amsterdam Exchange, founded in 1530. Large insurance companies also emerged in this period, and insuring long voyages against loss became a standard practice after 1700.

joint-stock company A business, often backed by a government charter, that sold shares to individuals to raise money for its trading enterprises and to spread the risks (and profits) among many investors.

stock exchange A place where shares in a company or business enterprise are bought and sold.

Governments also sought to promote trade by investing in infrastructure. The Dutch built numerous canals to improve transport and drain the lowlands for agriculture. Other governments financed canals as well, including systems of locks to raise barges up over hills. One of the most important was the 150-mile (240-kilometer) Canal du Midi built by the French government between 1661 and 1682 to link the Atlantic and the Mediterranean.

England and France

After 1650 the Dutch faced growing competition from the English, who were developing their own close association between business and government. With government support, the English merchant fleet doubled between 1660 and 1700, and foreign trade rose by 50 percent. As a result, state revenue from customs duties tripled. In a series of wars (1652–1678) the English

ENVIRONMENT + TECHNOLOGY

Mapping the World

In 1602 in China the Jesuit missionary Matteo Ricci printed an elaborate map of the world. Working from maps produced in Europe and incorporating the latest knowledge gathered by European maritime explorers, Ricci introduced two changes to make the map more appealing to his Chinese hosts. He labeled it in Chinese characters, and he split his map down the middle of the Atlantic so that China lay in the center. This version pleased the Chinese elite, who considered China the "Middle Kingdom" surrounded by lesser states. A copy of Ricci's map in six large panels adorned the emperor's Beijing palace.

The stunningly beautiful maps and globes of sixteenth-century Europe were the most complete, detailed, and useful representations of the earth that any society had ever produced. The best mapmaker of the century was Gerhard Kremer, who is remembered as Mercator (the merchant) because his maps were so useful to European ocean traders. By incorporating the latest discoveries and scientific measurements, Mercator could depict the outlines of the major continents in painstaking detail, even if their interiors were still largely unknown to outsiders.

To represent the spherical globe on a flat map, Mercator drew the lines of longitude as parallel lines. Because such lines actually meet at the poles, Mercator's projection greatly exaggerated the size of every landmass and body of water distant from the equator. However, Mercator's rendering offered a very practical advantage: sailors could plot their course by drawing a straight line between their point of departure and their destination. Because of this useful feature, the Mercator projection of the world remained in common use until quite recently. To some extent, its popularity came from the exaggerated size this projection gave to Europe. Like the Chinese, Europeans liked to think of themselves as at the center of things. Europeans also understood their true geographical position better than people in any other part of the world.

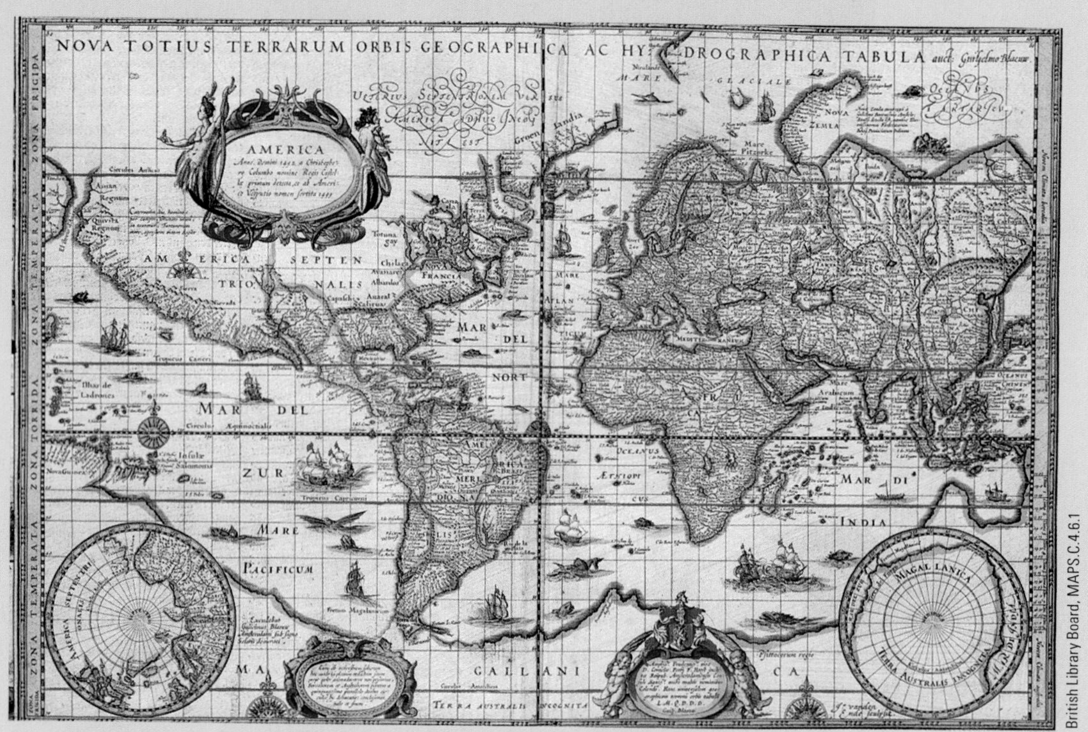

Dutch World Map, 1641 It is easy to see why the Chinese would not have liked to see their empire at the far right edge of this widely printed map. Besides the distortions caused by the Mercator projection, geographical ignorance exaggerates the size of North America and Antarctica.

government used its new naval might to break Dutch dominance in overseas trade and to extend England's colonial empire.

gentry The class of landholding families in England below the aristocracy.

Some successful members of the bourgeoisie in England and France chose to use their wealth to raise their social status. By retiring from their businesses and buying country estates, they could become members of the **gentry**. They loaned money to impoverished peasants and to

Mansell/TimeLife Pictures/Getty Images

Port of Amsterdam Ships, barges, and boats of all types are visible in this busy seventeenth-century scene. The large building in the center is the Admiralty House, the headquarters of the Dutch East India Company.

members of the nobility and in time increased their land ownership. Some sought aristocratic husbands for their daughters. The old nobility found such alliances attractive because of the large dowries that the bourgeoisie provided. In France a family could gain the exemption from taxation by living in gentility for three generations or, more quickly, by purchasing a title from the king.

Peasants and Laborers

Serfdom, which bound men and women to land owned by a local lord, had begun to decline after the great plague of the mid-fourteenth century. As population recovered in western Europe, the competition for work exerted a downward pressure on wages, reducing the usefulness of serfdom to landowners. In eastern Europe, on the other hand, large-scale landowners producing grain for cities found the bound labor of serfs crucial for profits. There had been a brief expansion of slavery in southern Europe with the introduction of African slaves around 1500, but after 1600 Europeans shipped nearly all African slaves to the Americas.

The Rural Poor

There is much truth in the argument that western Europe continued to depend on unfree labor but kept it at a distance in its colonies rather than at home. In any event, legal freedom did little to make a peasant's life safer and more secure. The efficiency of European agriculture had improved little since 1300. As a result, bad years brought famine; good ones provided only small surpluses. Indeed, the material conditions experienced by the poor in western Europe may have worsened between 1500 and 1750 as the result of warfare, environmental degradation, and economic contractions. Europeans also felt the adverse effects of a century of relatively cool climate that began in the 1590s. During this **Little Ice Age** average temperatures fell only a few degrees, but the effects were startling (see Issues in World History: The Little Ice Age on page 596).

Little Ice Age A century-long period of cool climate that began in the 1590s. Its ill effects on agriculture in northern Europe were notable.

By 1700 high-yielding new crops from the Americas were helping the rural poor avoid starvation. Once grown only as famine foods, potatoes and maize (corn) became staples for the rural poor in the eighteenth century. Potatoes sustained life in northeastern and central Europe and in Ireland, while poor peasants in Italy subsisted on maize. The irony is that all of these lands were major exporters of wheat, but most of those who planted and harvested it could not afford to eat it.

Deforestation

Other rural residents made their living as miners, lumber-jacks, and charcoal makers. The expanding iron industry in England provided work for all three, but the high consumption of

deforestation The removal of trees faster than forests can replace themselves.

wood fuel caused serious **deforestation**. One early-seventeenth-century observer lamented: "Within man's memory, it was held impossible to have any want of wood in England. But . . . at present, through the great consuming of wood . . . and the neglect of planting of woods, there is a great scarcity of wood throughout the whole kingdom."[1] Eventually, the high price of wood and charcoal encouraged smelters to use coal as an alternative fuel. England's coal mining increased twelvefold, from 210,000 tons in 1550 to 2,500,000 tons in 1700 and nearly 5 million tons by 1750.

France was more heavily forested than England, but increasing deforestation prompted Jean Baptiste Colbert, France's minister of finance, to predict that "France will perish for lack of wood." By the late eighteenth century deforestation had become an issue even in Sweden and Russia, where iron production had become a major industry.

Poverty and Violence

Even in the prosperous Dutch towns, half of the population lived in acute poverty. Authorities estimated that permanent city residents who were too poor to tax, the "deserving poor," made up 10 to 20 percent of the population. That calculation did not include the large numbers of "unworthy poor"—recent migrants from impoverished rural areas, peddlers traveling from place to place, and beggars (many with horrible deformities and sores) who tried to survive on charity. The pervasive poverty of rural and urban Europe shocked those who were not hardened to it. In about 1580 the mayor of the French city of Bordeaux (bor-DOH) asked a group of visiting Amerindian chiefs what impressed them most about European cities. The chiefs are said to have expressed astonishment at the disparity between the fat, well-fed people and the poor, half-starved men and women in rags. Why, the visitors wondered, did the poor not grab the rich by the throat or set fire to their homes?[2]

In fact, misery provoked many rebellions in early modern Europe. For example, in 1525 peasant rebels in the Alps attacked both nobles and the clergy as representatives of the privileged and landowning classes. They had no love for merchants either, whom they denounced for lending at interest and charging high prices. Rebellions multiplied as rural conditions worsened. In southwestern France alone some 450 uprisings occurred between 1590 and 1715, many of them set off by food shortages and tax increases. A rebellion in southern France in 1670 began when a mob of townswomen attacked the tax collector. It quickly spread to the country, where peasant leaders cried, "Death to the people's oppressors!" Authorities dealt severely with such revolts and executed or maimed their leaders.

Women and the Family

Women's social and economic status was closely tied to that of their husbands. In some nations a woman could inherit a throne (see Table 16.1 on page 478 for examples)—in the absence of a male heir. These rare exceptions do not negate the rule that women everywhere ranked below men, but one should also not forget that class and wealth defined a woman's position in life more than her sex. The wife or daughter of a rich man, for example, though often closely confined, had a materially better life than any poor man. Sometimes a single woman might secure a position of responsibility, as in the case of women from good families who headed convents in Catholic countries. But while unmarried women were routinely controlled by fathers and married women controlled by husbands, some widows independently controlled substantial properties and other assets.

Marriage and the Family

In contrast to the arranged marriages that prevailed in much of the rest of the world, young men and women in early modern Europe often chose their own spouses, but privileged families were much more likely to arrange marriages than poor ones. Royal and noble families carefully plotted the suitability of their children's marriages in furthering family interests. Bourgeois parents were less likely to force their children into arranged marriages, but the fact that nearly all found spouses within their own social class strongly suggests that the bourgeoisie promoted marriages that furthered their business alliances.

Europeans also married later than people in other cultural regions. Sons often put off marriage until they could live on their own. Many young women also had to work—helping their parents, as domestic servants, or in some other capacity—to save money for the dowry expected by potential husbands. A dowry was the money and household goods—the amount varied by social class—that enabled a young couple to begin marriage independent of their parents. The typical groom in western and central Europe could not hope to marry before his late twenties, and his bride would be a few years younger—in contrast to the rest of the world, where people usually married in their teens.

Besides enabling young people to be independent of their parents, the late age of marriage in early modern Europe also held down the birthrate and thus limited family size. Even so, about one-tenth of urban births were to unmarried women, often servants. Many mothers, unable to provide for these infants, left them on the doorsteps of churches, convents, or rich households. Many perished. Delayed marriage and poverty helped force unfortunate young women newly arrived from the countryside into brothels.

Education

Bourgeois parents were very concerned that their children have the education and training necessary for success. They promoted the establishment of municipal schools to provide a solid education, including Latin and perhaps Greek, for their sons, who were then sent abroad to learn modern languages or to a university to earn a law degree. Legal training was useful for conducting business and was a prerequisite for obtaining judicial or treasury positions. Daughters were less likely to be formally educated, but women with basic education often helped their husbands as bookkeepers, and some inherited businesses.

The fact that most schools barred female students, as did most guilds and professions, explains why women were not prominent in the cultural Renaissance, the Reformation, the Scientific Revolution, and the Enlightenment. Yet from a global perspective, women in early modern Europe were more prominent in the creation of culture than were women in most other parts of the world. Recent research has discovered numerous successful women who were painters, musicians, and writers. Indeed, the spread of learning, the stress on religious reading, and the growth of business likely meant that Europe led the world in female literacy. In the late 1600s some wealthy French women began organizing intellectual gatherings, and many were prominent letter writers. Galileo's daughter, Maria Celeste Galilei, carried on a detailed correspondence with her father from the confinement of the convent she had vowed never to leave. Nevertheless, in a period when most men were illiterate, the number of literate women was small, and only women in wealthier families might have a good education.

SECTION REVIEW

- Early modern European society was more fluid than it appeared, with an expanding economy and improved education promoting some mobility.
- The urban bourgeoisie created much of Europe's wealth through trade, manufacture, finance, and technological innovation.
- Monarchs sought alliances with the bourgeoisie, whose wealth afforded them political and social advancement as well as revenue.
- Oppressed by economic and environmental trends, peasants and laborers generally lived in poverty, and their misery often provoked rebellion.
- Although women remained subordinate to men, class and wealth were the main determinants of their positions in life.

POLITICAL INNOVATIONS

The monarchs of early modern Europe occupied the apex of the social order, were arbitrators of the intellectual and religious conflicts of their day, and exercised important influence on the economies of their realms. Many European monarchs introduced reforms in this era that achieved a higher degree of political centralization and order, but their ambitions and rivalries could also provoke destructive and costly conflicts. In some cases, civil and international conflicts forced monarchs to find common ground with potential enemies or introduce political innovations that strengthened their nations. During this period, political leadership in Europe passed from Spain to the Netherlands and then to England and France.

State Development

Holy Roman Empire Loose federation of mostly German states and principalities, headed by an emperor elected by the princes. It lasted from 962 to 1806.

There was a great deal of political diversity in early modern Europe. City-states and principalities abounded, either independently or bound together in federations, of which the **Holy Roman Empire** of the German heartland was the most notable example. There were also a small number

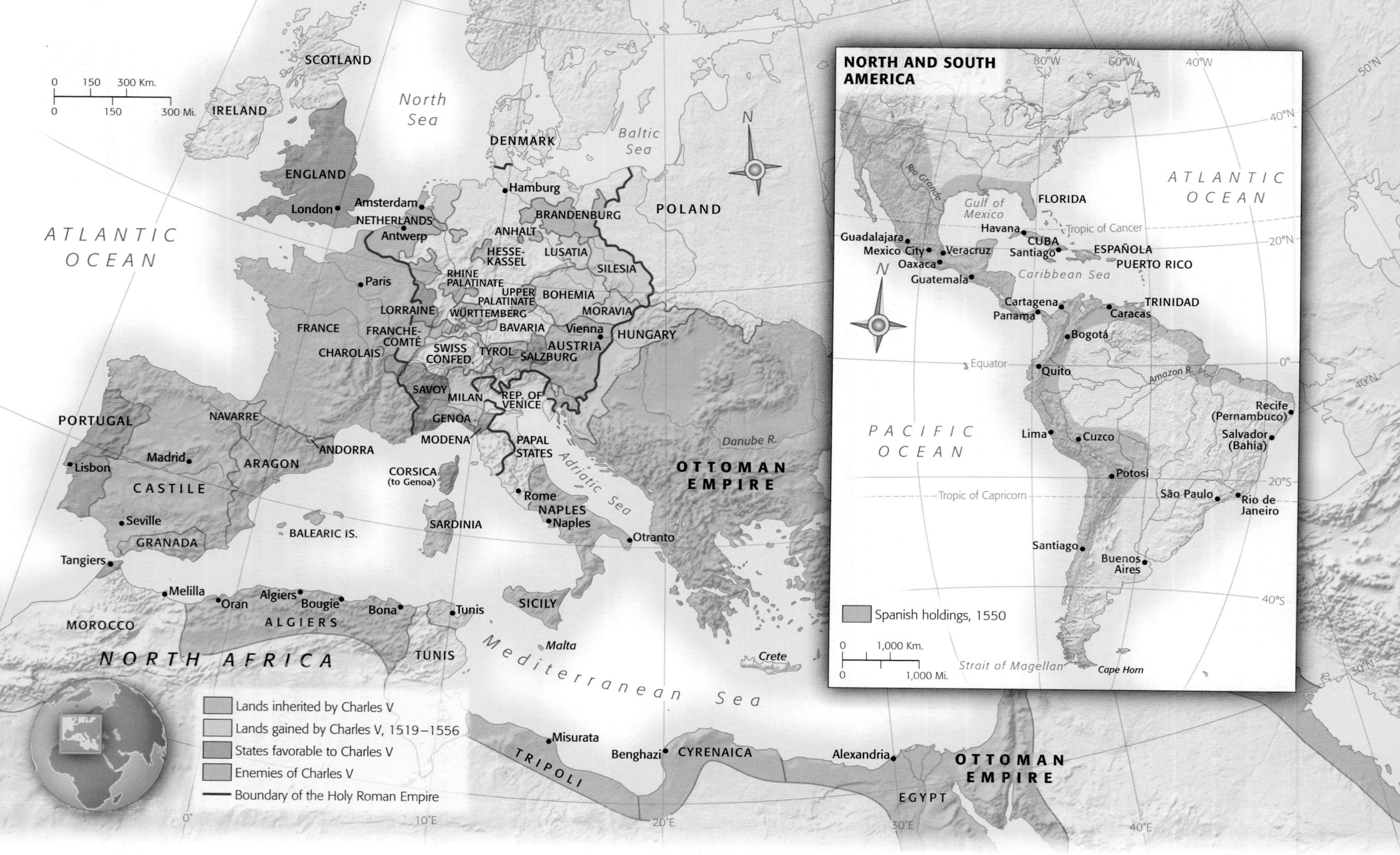

MAP 16.2 **The European Empire of Charles V** Charles was Europe's most powerful monarch, ruling Spain from 1516 and the Holy Roman Empire from 1519 to his abdication in 1556. The map does not show his extensive holdings in the Americas and Asia.

Interactive Map

of republics. At the same time a number of strong monarchies emerged and developed national identities.

Charles V

Dynastic ambitions and historical circumstances combined to favor and then block the creation of a single, integrated empire in the early sixteenth century. In 1519 electors of the Holy Roman Empire chose Charles V (r. 1519–1556) to be the new emperor. Like his predecessors for three generations, Charles belonged to the powerful **Habsburg** (HABZ-berg) family of Austria, but he had also inherited the Spanish thrones of Castile and Aragon in 1516. With these vast resources (see Map 16.2), Charles hoped lead a Christian coalition to halt the advance into southeastern Europe of the Ottoman Empire, whose Muslim rulers already controlled most of the Middle East and North Africa.

Habsburg A powerful European family that provided many Holy Roman Emperors, founded the Austrian (later Austro-Hungarian) Empire, and ruled sixteenth- and seventeenth-century Spain.

Charles and his Christian allies did stop the Ottomans at the gates of Vienna in 1529, although Ottoman attacks continued until 1697. But Charles's efforts to forge his several possessions into Europe's strongest state failed. Francis I of France, who had also sought election as Holy Roman Emperor, openly supported the Muslim Turks to weaken his rival. In addition, many German princes, swayed by Luther's appeals to German nationalism, opposed Charles's defense of Catholic doctrine in the imperial Diet (assembly).

AP* Exam Tip The multiple choice portion of the exam requires a general understanding of European absolutism but not knowledge of individual rulers.

After these disputes turned to open warfare in 1546 (the German Wars of Religion), Charles V gave up his efforts at unification, abdicated control of his various possessions to different heirs, and retired to a monastery in 1556. By the Peace of Augsburg (1555), he had already recognized the princes' right to choose whether Catholicism or Lutheranism would prevail in their particular states, and permitted them to keep the church lands they had seized. The triumph of religious diversity ended Charles's political ambitions and put off German political unification for three centuries.

The Growing Power of Kings

The rulers of Spain, France, and England were more successful in promoting national political unification and religious unity. The most successful rulers reduced the autonomy of the church and the nobility by making them part of a unified national structure with the monarch at its head (see Diversity and Dominance: Political Craft and Craftiness). The imposition of royal power over the church in the sixteenth century was stormy, but the outcome was clear. Bringing the nobles and other powerful interests into a centralized political system took longer and led to more diverse outcomes.

The Monarchies of England and France

Over the course of the seventeenth century, the monarchs of England and France faced intense conflict with powerful rivals. Religion was never absent as an issue in these struggles, but the different constitutional outcomes they produced were of more significance in the long run.

England

To evade any check on his power, King Charles I of England (see Table 16.1) ruled for eleven years without summoning Parliament, his kingdom's representative body. Lacking Parliament's consent to new taxes, he raised funds by coercing "loans" from wealthy subjects and applying existing tax laws more broadly. In 1640 a rebellion in Scotland forced him to summon Parliament to approve new taxes to pay for an army. Noblemen and churchmen sat in the House of Lords while representatives from towns and counties sat in the House of Commons. Before it would authorize new taxes, Parliament insisted on strict guarantees that the king would never again ignore the body's traditional rights. King Charles refused and attempted to arrest of his critics in the House of Commons in 1642, plunging the kingdom into the **English Civil War**.

English Civil War (1642–1649) A conflict over royal versus parliamentary rights, caused by King Charles I's arrest of his parliamentary critics and ending with his execution. Its outcome checked the growth of royal absolutism and, with the Glorious Revolution of 1688 and the English Bill of Rights of 1689, ensured that England would be a constitutional monarchy.

Militarily defeated in 1648, Charles refused to compromise. A year later a "Rump" Parliament purged of his supporters ordered his execution. Parliament then replaced the monarchy with a republic led by the Puritan general Oliver Cromwell who ruled until his death in 1658. Cromwell expanded England's presence overseas and imposed firm control over Ireland and Scotland, but was also unwilling to share power with Parliament. Parliament restored the Stuart line in the person of Charles II (r. 1660–1685). James II, his brother, inherited the throne, but provoked new conflict by refusing to respect Parliament's rights and by baptizing his heir as a Roman Catholic. The leaders of Parliament forced him into exile in the bloodless Glorious Revolution of 1688. The Bill of Rights of 1689 formalized this new constitutional order by requiring the king to call Parliament frequently to consent to changes in laws or to raise an army in peacetime. Another law reaffirmed the official status of the Church of England but extended religious toleration to dissenting Puritans.

Political Craft and Craftiness

Political power was becoming more highly concentrated in early modern Europe, but absolute dominance was more a goal than a reality. Whether subject to constitutional checks or not, rulers were very concerned with creating and maintaining good relations with their more powerful subjects. Their efforts to manipulate public opinion and perceptions have much in common with the efforts of modern politicians to manage their "image."

A diplomat and civil servant in the rich and powerful Italian city-state of Florence, Niccolò Machiavelli, is best known for his book The Prince (1532). This influential essay on the proper exercise of political power has been interpreted as cynical by some and as supremely practical and realistic by others. Because Machiavelli did not have a high opinion of the intelligence and character of most people, he urged rulers to achieve obedience by fear and deception. But he also suggested that genuine mercy, honesty, and piety may be superior to feigned virtue.

In What Manner Princes Should Keep Their Faith

It must be evident to every one that it is more praiseworthy for a prince always to maintain good faith, and practice integrity rather than craft and deceit. And yet the experience of our own times has shown those princes have achieved great things who made small account of good faith, and who understood by cunning to circumvent the intelligence of others; and that in the end they got the better of those whose actions were dictated by loyalty and good faith. You must know, therefore, that there are two ways of carrying on a struggle; one by law and the other by force. The first is practiced by men, and the other by animals; and as the first is often insufficient, it becomes necessary to resort to the second.

. . . If men were altogether good, this advice would be wrong; but since they are bad and will not keep faith with you, you need not keep faith with them. Nor will a prince ever be short of legitimate excuses to give color to his breaches of faith. Innumerable modern examples could be given of this; and it could easily be shown how many treaties of peace, and how many engagements, have been made null and void by the faithlessness of princes; and he who has best known how to play the fox has ever been the most successful.

But it is necessary that the prince should know how to color this nature well, and how to be a great hypocrite and dissembler. For men are so simple, and yield so much to immediate necessity, that the deceiver will never lack dupes. I will mention one of the most recent examples. [Pope] Alexander VI never did nor ever thought of anything but to deceive, and always found a reason for doing so . . . and yet he was always successful in his deceits, because he knew the weakness of men in that particular.

It is not necessary, however, for a prince to possess all the above-mentioned qualities; but it is essential that he should at least seem to have them. I will even venture to say, that to have and practice them constantly is pernicious, but to seem to have them is useful. For instance, a prince should seem to be merciful, faithful, humane, religious, and upright, and should even be so in reality; but he should have his mind so trained that, when occasion requires it, he may know how to change to the opposite. And it must be understood that a prince, and especially one who has but recently acquired his state, cannot perform all those things which cause men to be esteemed as good; he being obligated, for the sake of maintaining his state, to act contrary to humanity, charity, and religion. And therefore, it is necessary that he should have a versatile mind, capable of changing readily, according as the winds and changes of fortune bid him; and, as has been said above, not to swerve from the good if possible, but to know how to resort to evil if necessity demands it.

A prince then should be very careful never to allow anything to escape his lips that does not abound in the abovementioned five qualities, so that to see and to hear him he may seem all charity, integrity, and humanity, all uprightness and all piety. And more than all else is it necessary for a prince to seem to possess the last quality; for mankind in general judge more by what they see than by what they feel, every one being capable of the former, and few of the latter. Everybody sees what you seem to be, but few really feel what you are; and those few dare

France

Versailles The huge palace built for French king Louis XVI south of Paris. The palace symbolized both French power and the triumph of royal authority over the French nobility.

In France the Estates General, like the English Parliament, represented the traditional rights of the clergy, the nobility, and the towns (that is, the bourgeoisie). The Estates General was able to assert its rights during the sixteenth-century French Wars of Religion, when the monarchy was weak. Thereafter Bourbon monarchs generally ruled without calling it into session. They avoided financial crises by more efficient tax collection and by selling appointments to high government offices. In justification they claimed that the monarch had absolute authority to rule in God's name on earth.

Louis XIV moved his court to a gigantic new palace at **Versailles** (vuhr-SIGH) in 1682. The palace helped the French monarch triumph over the traditional rights of the nobility, clergy, and not oppose the opinion of the many, who are protected by the majority of the state; for the actions of all men, and especially those of princes, are judged by the result, where there is no other judge to whom to appeal.

A prince should look mainly to the successful maintenance of his state. For the means which he employs for this will always be counted honorable, and will be praised by everybody; for the common people are always taken in by appearances and by results, and it is the vulgar mass that constitutes the world.

Because, as Machiavelli argued, appearances count for as much in the public arena as realities, it is difficult to judge whether rulers' statements expressed their real feelings and beliefs or what may have been the most expedient to say at the moment. An example is this speech Queen Elizabeth of England made at the end of November 1601 to Parliament after a particularly difficult year. One senior noble had led a rebellion and was subsequently executed. Parliament was pressing for extended privileges. Having gained the throne in 1558 after many difficulties (including a time in prison), the sixty-eight-year-old queen had much experience in the language and wiles of politics and was well aware of the importance of public opinion. Reprinted many times, the speech became famous as "The Golden Speech of Queen Elizabeth."

I do assure you, there is no prince that loveth his subjects better, or whose love can countervail our love. There is no jewel, be it of never so rich a price, which I set before this jewel: I mean your love. For I do esteem it more than any treasure or riches; for that we know how to prize, but love and thanks I count invaluable.

And, though God has raised me high, yet this I count the glory of my crown, that I have reigned with your loves. This makes me that I do not so much rejoice that God hath made me to be a Queen, as to be Queen over so thankful a people.

Therefore, I have cause to wish nothing more than to content the subjects; and that is the duty I owe. Neither do I desire to live longer days than I may see your prosperity; and that is my only desire.

And as I am that person that still (yet under God) has delivered you, so I trust, by the almighty power of God, that I shall be His instrument to preserve you from every peril, dishonour, shame, tyranny, and oppression. . . .

Of myself I must say this: I was never any greedy scraping grasper, nor a straight, fast-holding prince, nor yet a waster. My heart was never set on worldly goods, but only for my subjects' good. What you bestow on me, I will not hoard it up, but receive it to bestow on you again. Yea, mine own properties I count yours, and to be expended for your good. . . .

To be a king and wear a crown is a thing more glorious to them that see it, than it is pleasing to them that bear it. For myself, I was never so much enticed with the glorious name of king, or royal authority of a queen, as delighted that God made me his instrument to maintain his truth and glory, and to defend this Kingdom (as I said) from peril, dishonour, tyranny and oppression.

There will never Queen sit in my seat with more zeal to my country, care for my subjects, and that sooner with willingness will venture her life for your good and safety than myself. For it is not my desire to live nor reign longer than my life and reign shall be for your good. And though you have had and may have many more princes more mighty and wise sitting in this state, yet you never had or shall have any that will be more careful and loving. Shall I ascribe anything to myself and my sexly weakness? I were not worthy to live then; and of all, most unworthy of the great mercies I have had from God, who has even yet given me a heart, which never feared foreign or home enemy. I speak to give God the praise . . . That I should speak for any glory, God forbid.

QUESTIONS FOR ANALYSIS

1. **Do you find Machiavelli's advice to be cynical or realistic?**
2. **Describe how a member of Parliament might have responded to Queen Elizabeth's declarations of her concern for the welfare of her people above all else.**
3. **Can a ruler be sincere and manipulative at the same time?**

Source: From *The Historical, Political, and Diplomatic Writings of Niccolo Machiavelli*, trans. Christian E. Detmold (Boston: Houghton Mifflin and Company, 1891), II: 54–59; and Heywood Townshend, *Historical Collections, or an Exact Account of the Proceedings of the Last Four Parliaments of Q. Elizabeth* (London: Basset, Crooke, and Cademan, 1680), 263–266.

towns, since the elaborate ceremonies and banquets at the royal court served to keep nobles away from their estates where they might plot rebellion. Capable of housing ten thousand people and surrounded by elaborately landscaped grounds and parks, the palace became an effective symbol of royal absolutism.

While the balance of powers in the English model would be widely admired in later times, most European rulers admired and imitated the centralized powers and absolutist claims of the French. The checks and balances of the English model gained a favorable press with the beginnings of the Enlightenment. In his influential *Second Treatise of Civil Government* (1690), the English political philosopher John Locke (1632–1704) disputed monarchial claims to absolute

TABLE 16.1 Rulers in Early Modern Western Europe

Spain	*France*	*England/Great Britain*
Habsburg Dynasty	**Valois Dynasty**	**Tudor Dynasty**
Charles I (King of Spain 1516–1556), also known as Charles V (Holy Roman Emperor 1519–1556)	Francis I (1515–1547)	Henry VIII (1509–1547)
	Henry II (1547–1559)	Edward VI (1547–1553)
	Francis II (1559–1560)	Mary I (1553–1558)
Philip II (1556–1598)	Charles IX (1560–1574)	Elizabeth I (1558–1603)
	Henry III (1574–1589)	
Philip III (1598–1621)	**Bourbon Dynasty**	**Stuart Dynasty**
Philip IV (1621–1665)	Henry IV (1589–1610)[a]	James I (1603–1625)
Charles II (1665–1700)	Louis XIII (1610–1643)	Charles I (1625–1649)[a,b]
	Louis XIV (1643–1715)	(Puritan Republic, 1649–1660)
		Charles II (1660–1685)
		James II (1685–1688)[b]
		William III (1689–1702) and Mary II (1689–1694)
		Anne (1702–1714)
Bourbon Dynasty		**Hanoverian Dynasty**
Philip V (1700–1746)		
Ferdinand VI (1746–1759)		George I (1714–1727)
	Louis XV (1715–1774)	George II (1727–1760)

[a]Died a violent death. [b]Was overthrown.

authority by divine right. He argued that rulers derived their authority from the consent of the governed and were subject to the law. If monarchs overstepped the law, Locke asserted, citizens had the right and the duty to rebel. The consequences of this idea are considered in Chapter 21.

Warfare and Diplomacy

In addition to the civil wars that afflicted the Holy Roman Empire, France, and England, European states fought numerous international conflicts. Warfare was almost constant in early modern Europe (see the Chronology at the beginning of the chapter). In their pursuit of power monarchs expended vast sums of money and caused widespread devastation and death. The worst of the international conflicts, the Thirty Years War (1618–1648), caused long-lasting depopulation and economic decline in much of the Holy Roman Empire.

European Militaries

These wars also led to dramatic improvements in the skill and weaponry of European armed forces, making them among the most powerful in the world. The numbers of men in arms increased steadily throughout the early modern period. French forces, for example, grew from about 150,000 in 1630 to 400,000 by the early eighteenth century. Even smaller European states built up impressive armies. Sweden, with under a million people, had one of the finest and best-armed military forces in the seventeenth century. Though the country had fewer than 2 million inhabitants in 1700, Prussia's army made it one of Europe's major powers.

Larger armies required more effective command structures. In the words of a modern historian, European armies "evolved . . . the equivalent of a central nervous system, capable of activating technologically differentiated claws and teeth."[3] New signaling techniques improved control of battlefield maneuvers. Frequent drills for professional troops and militias trained

Erich Lessing/Art Resource, NY

Versailles Constructed during the reign of Louis XVI of France, the palace of Versailles could house ten thousand people. Surrounded by elaborately landscaped grounds and parks, the palace became an effective symbol of royal absolutism.

AP* Exam Tip Be prepared to analyze empire building for the exam.

troops to obey orders instantly and improved morale. New fortifications able to withstand cannon bombardments were constructed to protect major urban centers. While each state tried to outdo its rivals by improvements in military hardware, battles between evenly matched armies often ended in stalemates that prolonged the wars. Victory increasingly depended on naval superiority.

England was the only major nation that did not maintain an army. Its power depended on its navy. England's rise as a sea power had begun under King Henry VIII, who spent heavily on ships and promoted a domestic iron industry to supply cannon. The crushing defeat of the Spanish Armada in 1588 by Henry's daughter, Elizabeth I, demonstrated the usefulness of these decisions. The Royal Navy also copied innovative ship designs from the Dutch in the second half of the seventeenth century. By the early eighteenth century, the Royal Navy had surpassed the rival French fleet in numbers. Now more secure, England merged with Scotland to become Great Britain. It then annexed Ireland and built a North American empire.

balance of power The policy in international relations by which, beginning in the eighteenth century, the major European states acted together to prevent any one of them from becoming too powerful.

Although France was Europe's most powerful state, coalitions of the other great powers frustrated Louis XIV's efforts to expand its borders. In a series of eighteenth-century wars beginning with the War of the Spanish Succession (1701–1714), the combination of Britain's naval strength and the land armies of Austria and Prussia blocked French expansionist efforts and prevented the Bourbons from uniting the thrones of France and Spain.

Balance of Power

This defeat of the French monarchy's empire-building efforts illustrated the principle of **balance of power** in international relations: the major European states formed temporary

MAP 16.3 **Europe in 1740** By the middle of the eighteenth century the great powers of Europe were France, the Austrian Empire, Great Britain, Prussia, and Russia. Spain, the Holy Roman Empire, and the Ottoman Empire were far weaker in 1740 than they had been two centuries earlier.

Interactive Map

University Library Geneva/Gianni Dagli Orti/The Art Archive

The Spanish Armada King Phillip II of Spain sent a massive fleet against England in 1588. England's defeat of the Spanish fleet weakened Spain and began England's rise to naval dominance.

alliances to prevent any one state from becoming too powerful. During the next two centuries, though adhering to four different branches of Christianity, the great powers of Europe—Catholic France, Anglican Britain, Catholic Austria, Lutheran Prussia, and Orthodox Russia (see Map 16.3)—maintained an effective balance of power in Europe by shifting their alliances for geopolitical rather than religious reasons. These pragmatic alliances were the first successful efforts at international peacekeeping.

Paying the Piper

To pay these extremely heavy military costs, European rulers had to increase their revenues. The most successful of them after 1600 promoted mutually beneficial, if often uneasy, alliances with commercial elites. Merchants and bankers sought to limit taxation and regulation and enhance the enforcement of contracts and the collection of debts without accepting insupportable tax burdens. Both sides believed that military power capable of protecting overseas expansion was crucial to economic growth, but they also knew that the cost of defending distant colonies could be overwhelming.

Spain and the Balance Sheet of Empire

Spain, sixteenth-century Europe's mightiest state, illustrates the costs of an aggressive military policy when coupled with a failure to promote economic development. Expensive wars against the Ottomans, northern European Protestants, and rebellious Dutch subjects led Spain to default and bankruptcy four times during the reign of King Philip II. The Spanish rulers' concerns for religious uniformity and traditional aristocratic privilege further undermined the country's economy. In the name of religious uniformity they expelled Jewish merchants, persecuted Protestant dissenters, and forced tens of thousands of Muslim farmers and artisans into exile. In the name of aristocratic privilege the 3 percent of the population that controlled 97 percent of the land in 1600 was exempt from taxation, while high sales taxes discouraged manufacturing.

For a time, vast imports of silver and gold from Spain's American colonies filled the treasury. These bullion shipments led to inflation (rising prices) across Europe, but prices rose fastest in Spain, making goods imported from France or other European nations cheaper than local goods. As a result, by 1700 most goods imported into Spain's colonies were of foreign origin. A Spanish saying captured the problem: American silver was like rain on the roof—it poured down and washed away.

Commerce and the Rise of the Netherlands

The rise of the Netherlands as an economic power stemmed from very different policies. The Spanish crown had acquired these resource-poor but commercially successful provinces as part of Charles V's inheritance. The decision of his son, King Philip II, to impose Spain's ruinous sales tax and to enforce Catholic orthodoxy drove the Dutch to revolt in 1566 and again in 1572. If successful, those measures would have discouraged business and driven away the Calvinists, Jews, and others who were essential to Dutch prosperity. The Dutch fought with skill and ingenuity, raising and training an army and a navy that were among the most effective in Europe. Unable to bear the military costs any longer, Spain accepted a truce that recognized autonomy in the northern Netherlands in 1609. Finally, in 1648, the independence of the seven United Provinces of the Free Netherlands (their full name) became final.

Rather than being ruined by the long war, the Netherlands emerged as the world's greatest trading nation. This economic success owed much to a decentralized government. During the long struggle against Spain, the provinces united around the prince of Orange, their sovereign, who served as commander-in-chief of the armed forces. But in economic matters each province was free to pursue its own interests. The maritime province of Holland grew rich by favoring commercial interests.

International Competition

After 1650 the Dutch faced growing competition from the English, who were developing their own close association of business and government. In a series of wars (1652–1678) England used its naval might to break Dutch dominance in overseas trade and extend its own colonial empire. With government support, the English merchant fleet doubled between 1660 and 1700, and foreign trade rose by 50 percent. As a result, state revenue from customs duties tripled. During the eighteenth century Britain's trading position strengthened still more.

The debts run up by the Anglo-Dutch Wars helped persuade the English monarchy to greatly enlarge the government's role in managing the economy. The government increased revenues by taxing the formerly exempt landed estates of the aristocrats and by collecting taxes directly. Previously, private individuals known as tax farmers had advanced the government a fixed sum of money; in return they could keep whatever money they were able to collect from taxpayers. To secure cash quickly for warfare and other emergencies and to reduce the burden of debts from earlier wars, England imitated the Dutch by creating a central bank that could issue long-term loans at low rates.

The French government also developed its national economy, especially under the royal advisor Jean Baptiste Colbert. He streamlined tax collection, promoted French manufacturing and shipping by imposing taxes on foreign goods, and improved transportation within France itself. Yet the power of the wealthy aristocrats kept the French government from following England's lead in taxing wealthy landowners, collecting taxes directly, and securing low-cost loans. Nor did France succeed in managing its debt as efficiently as England. (The role of governments in promoting overseas trade is also discussed in Chapter 18.)

SECTION REVIEW

- Greater political centralization enabled early modern monarchs to exert increased influence on economic, religious, and social life.
- While the Holy Roman Empire fragmented along religious and political lines, Spain, France, and England achieved greater centralization and religious unity.
- Spain enforced Catholic unity through the Inquisition and France through Bourbon policy, while in England the church became an arm of royal power.
- In both England and France, monarchs struggled with rivals over the limits of royal authority.
- Armies grew larger and more sophisticated while European powers strove to maintain a balance of power.
- High military costs drove the European powers to attempt a variety of tax and financial policies, the most successful being those of England and the Netherlands.

CONCLUSION

Early modern Europe witnessed the weakening of the Catholic Church and the Protestant Reformation. Rejecting the authority of the pope and criticizing the institution of indulgences, Luther insisted on the moral primacy of faith over deeds; Calvin went further, holding that salvation was predestined by God. The pioneers of the Scientific Revolution such as Copernicus and Newton showed that they could explain the workings of the physical universe in natural terms. These scientists did not see any conflict between science and religion, but they paved the way for more secular thinkers of the Enlightenment, who believed that human reason was capable of—and responsible for—discovering the laws that govern social behavior.

Thanks to foreign and domestic trade, European cities in this period experienced rapid growth and the rise of a wealthy commercial class. The Netherlands in particular prospered from expanded manufacturing and trade: with the formation of joint-stock companies and a powerful stock market, Amsterdam became Europe's major port and financial center. For peasants and laborers, however, life did not improve much: serfdom had all but ended in western Europe, only to rise in eastern Europe. Agricultural techniques had not improved substantially since medieval times, and environmental hardships such as the Little Ice Age and deforestation caused by mining and logging brought great difficulties to the poor. Rural poverty, coupled with the exemption from taxation enjoyed by wealthy landowners, sparked numerous armed rebellions. Women were dependent on their families' and husbands' wealth or lack of it, and were barred from attending schools or joining guilds and professions.

Differing policies in the areas of religion, foreign relations, and economics explain the different histories of Europe's early modern states. Charles V, unable to reconcile the diverse interests of his Catholic and Protestant territories and their powerful local rulers, failed to create a unified Holy Roman Empire. Henry VIII, having failed to win an annulment of his marriage to Catherine of Aragon, severed all ties with the pope and led Parliament to accept him as head of the Church of England. Power struggles in England during this period led to a stronger Parliament, while in France a stronger monarchy emerged, symbolized by Louis XIV's construction of the palace at Versailles. Spain was Europe's mightiest state in the sixteenth century, but its failure to suppress the Netherlands Revolt and the costs of other wars led to bankruptcy. In the seventeenth century the United Netherlands had become the dominant commercial power on the continent.

The growth of English naval power led to the defeat of the Dutch in the Anglo-Dutch Wars and of France in the early eighteenth century when it attempted to expand its own empire through a union with Spain. Unlike Spain and France, which maintained aristocrats' traditional exemption from taxation, England began to tax their estates, and this policy—together with the establishment of direct taxation and the creation of a central bank from which it could secure low-cost loans—gave England a stronger financial foundation than its rivals enjoyed.

KEY TERMS

Renaissance (European) p. 459
papacy p. 460
indulgence p. 460
Protestant Reformation p. 461
Catholic Reformation p. 462
witch-hunt p. 463
Scientific Revolution p. 465
Enlightenment p. 467
bourgeoisie p. 468
joint-stock company p. 469
stock exchange p. 469
gentry p. 470
Little Ice Age p. 471
deforestation p. 472
Holy Roman Empire p. 473
Habsburg p. 475
English Civil War p. 475
Versailles p. 476
balance of power p. 479

EBOOK AND WEBSITE RESOURCES

Primary Sources

Table Talk

Letter to the Grand Duchess Christina

Treatise on Toleration

Interactive Maps

Map 16.1 Religious Reformation in Europe

Map 16.2 The European Empire of Charles V

Map 16.3 Europe in 1740

Plus flashcards, practice quizzes, and more. Go to: www.cengage.com/history/bullietearthpeople5e

SUGGESTED READING

Bergin, Joseph. *The Short Oxford History of Europe: The Seventeenth Century.* 2001. A general overview.

Braudel, Fernand. *Civilization and Capitalism, 15th–18th Century.* Trans. Siân Reynolds. 3 vols. 1992. A sweeping interpretation by an eminent historian.

Casey, James. *Early Modern Spain: A Social History.* 1999. A general look at an important country.

Cipolla, Carlo M. *Before the Industrial Revolution: European Society and Economy, 1000–1700,* 3rd ed. 1993. An excellent introduction to social and economic life.

Fagan, Brian. *The Little Ice Age: How Climate Made History, 1300–1850.* 2000. An important episode in climate history.

Hall, A. R. *The Scientific Revolution, 1500–1800: The Formation of the Modern Scientific Attitude,* 2nd ed. 1962. A basic introduction to the intellectual ferment of the era.

Huppert, George. *After the Black Death: A Social History of Early Modern Europe,* 2nd ed. 1998. An excellent introduction to this period's social and economic history.

Israel, Jonathan. *The Dutch Republic: Its Rise, Greatness and Fall, 1477–1806.* 1995. Study of a key country.

Jütte, Robert. *Poverty and Deviance in Early Modern Europe.* 1994. Looks at non-elite perspectives.

Le Roy Ladurie, Emmanuel. *The Royal French State, 1460–1610.* Trans. Juliet Vale. 1994. *The Ancien Régime: A History of France, 1610–1774.* Trans. Mark Greengrass. 1996. A two-volume look at a key country by an eminent historian.

Levack, Brian P. *The Witch-Hunt in Early Modern Europe,* 2nd ed. 1995. A good starting point for studying Europe's obsession with witchcraft.

Outram, Dorinda. *The Enlightenment,* 2nd ed. 2005. Provides a recent summary of research.

Parker, Geoffrey. *Military Revolution: Military Innovation and the Rise of the West, 1500–1800,* 2nd ed. 1996. Technological development in a violent era.

Shapin, Steven. *The Scientific Revolution.* 1996. An accessible introduction.

Sharpe, J. A. *Early Modern England: A Social History, 1550–1760,* 2nd ed. 1997. A good single-country survey.

Wallerstein, Immanuel. *The Modern World-System,* vol. 2, *Mercantilism and the Consolidation of the European World-Economy, 1600–1750.* 1980. Presents an influential economic theory of Europe's relation to the world.

Wiesner, Merry E. *Women and Gender in Early Modern Europe,* 2nd ed. 2000. Examines topics in women's history.

NOTES

1. Quoted by Carlo M. Cipolla, "Introduction," *The Fontana Economic History of Europe*, vol. 2, *The Sixteenth and Seventeenth Centuries* (Glasgow: Collins/Fontana Books, 1976), 11–12.
2. Michel de Montaigne, *Essais* (1588), ch. 31, "Des Cannibales."
3. William H. McNeill, *The Pursuit of Power: Technology, Armed Force, and Society Since A.D. 1000* (Chicago: University of Chicago Press, 1982), 124.

AP* REVIEW QUESTIONS FOR CHAPTER 16

1. The Protestant Reformation is said to have begun with
   (A) the Treaty of Tordesillas.
   (B) the ascension of Ferdinand and Isabella to the Spanish throne.
   (C) Martin Luther's rejection of papal authority.
   (D) the French Wars of Religion.

2. Unlike the Roman Catholic Church and Martin Luther, John Calvin
   (A) believed that the world was flat.
   (B) taught that salvation was predestined.
   (C) opposed conversion of the Amerindians.
   (D) believed that women should preach.

3. Contemporaneous with the Scientific Revolution was the movement known as the Enlightenment. This movement
   (A) encouraged people to reject formal religion and to become deists.
   (B) was adopted only in Germanic kingdoms that had broken away from the Roman Catholic Church.
   (C) encouraged people to adopt Chinese discoveries in mathematics and science.
   (D) taught that human reason could discover the laws that governed social behavior.

4. The French class known as the bourgeoisie is best described as
   (A) the lesser nobles and the wealthy bureaucrats.
   (B) the city dwellers who owned businesses or were skilled workers.
   (C) artists, writers, musicians, and poets.
   (D) all the people below the nobility.

5. The Dutch government's method of funding businesses for overseas exploration was to grant companies monopolies over trade in an area. The companies then sold shares to spread the risk. This practice is known as
   (A) corporate financing.
   (B) government financing.
   (C) dealing in a stock exchange.
   (D) the use of a joint-stock company.

6. One impact of the growth of manufacturing in urban areas between 1500 and 1750 was that
   (A) many rural poor moved to the towns and cities in hopes of better jobs.
   (B) shortages of staple foods became acute.
   (C) many more people became migrants to the colonies.
   (D) wages dropped as skilled crafts became flooded with workers.

7. Unlike in other portions of the world, young men and women in early modern Europe
   (A) married young and had very large families.
   (B) based their marriages solely on improving their economic standing in society.
   (C) often chose their own spouses.
   (D) often had to migrate to a new city to marry.

8. For the most part, early modern Europe was made up of
   (A) kingdoms and principalities that had political ties to the church.
   (B) city-states, principalities, and loose federations of states.
   (C) kingdoms unified by a national language and a common heritage.
   (D) religiously unified lands under a central governing authority.

9. The rulers of Spain successfully defended Roman Catholicism against Protestant challenges. Following the patterns of his predecessors, Philip II of Spain
   (A) repented and permitted Jews, Muslims, and Protestants to live in peace in his lands.
   (B) ordered the expulsion of all non-Spaniards from Spanish lands.
   (C) forced non-Catholics to move to the Spanish colonies.
   (D) used ecclesiastical courts to bring into line those who resisted his authority.

10. The English Civil War

    (A) began when the Dutch monarch claimed the English throne.
    (B) was caused by Charles I ignoring limits on his powers and the rights of Parliament.
    (C) was caused by the proposed marriage of Elizabeth I to Philip II of Spain.
    (D) began when Roman Catholics in England attempted to restore Catholicism as a state religion.

11. Which of the following would be a good example of both a theme park for royal absolutism and Baroque architecture?

    (A) The palace of Louis XIV at Versailles
    (B) St. Peter's Square
    (C) The English Parliament
    (D) The Estates-General

12. As the cost of warfare, in both human and financial terms, increased in the early eighteenth century, European states

    (A) began to follow England's example of not keeping a standing army in peacetime.
    (B) began to depend on large naval forces rather than land armies.
    (C) began to form temporary alliances to prevent any one state from becoming too powerful.
    (D) increased taxes to fund new war technologies.

13. By the seventeenth century, Spain, which had been the most powerful European state in the sixteenth century,

    (A) became the moneylender to the rest of Europe as it exploited South American gold and silver mines.
    (B) was forced to join with the Netherlands in commercial ventures.
    (C) spent so heavily on wars and its growing empire that it ended up bankrupt.
    (D) had to enlarge the government's role in the economy to maintain economic growth.

14. Which of the following is true of the period from 1500 to 1750?

    (A) Rapid economic growth led to major improvements in life, particularly among the lower classes and the working classes in Russia.
    (B) Portugal, Spain, and France all succumbed to overspending and military action.
    (C) While there was broad economic growth in Europe, life for peasants and laborers did not improve much.
    (D) The Holy Roman Empire became the dominant power in central Europe, as well as in eastern Europe.

CHAPTER 17

CHAPTER OUTLINE

- The Columbian Exchange
- Spanish America and Brazil
- English and French Colonies in North America
- Colonial Expansion and Conflict
- Conclusion

ENVIRONMENT + TECHNOLOGY *A Silver Refinery at Potosí, Bolivia, 1700*

DIVERSITY + DOMINANCE *Race and Ethnicity in the Spanish Colonies: Negotiating Hierarchy*

Choctaw Village in Louisiana at Time of French Colonial Rule This scene of village life illustrates the integration of the Choctaw in the colonial economy. The painting places a young African slave and European trade goods in a scene where the Choctaw pursue traditional tasks.

Visit the website and ebook for additional study materials and interactive tools: www.cengage.com/history/bullietearthpeople5e

The Diversity of American Colonial Societies, 1530–1770

- How did the Columbian Exchange alter the natural environment of the Americas?
- What role did forced labor play in the main industries of Spanish America and Brazil?
- What were the main similarities and differences among colonies of Spain, Portugal, England, and France?
- What were the effects of the colonial reforms and wars among imperial powers that dominated the Americas during the eighteenth century?

Shulush Homa—an eighteenth-century Choctaw leader called "Red Shoes" by the English—faced a dilemma. For years he had befriended the French who had moved into the lower Mississippi Valley, protecting their outlying settlements from other indigenous groups and producing a steady flow of deerskins for trade. In return he received guns and gifts as well as honors previously given only to chiefs. Though born a commoner, he had parlayed his skillful politicking with the French—and the shrewd distribution of the gifts he received—to enhance his position in Choctaw society. Then his fortunes turned. In the course of yet another war between England and France, the English cut off French shipping. Faced with followers unhappy over his sudden inability to supply French guns, Red Shoes forged a dangerous new arrangement with the English that led his former allies, the French, to put a price on his head. His murder in 1747 launched a civil war among the Choctaw. By the end of this conflict both the French colonial population and the Choctaw people had suffered greatly.

The story of Red Shoes reveals a number of themes from the period of European colonization of the Americas. First, although the wars, epidemics, and territorial loss associated with European settlement threatened Amerindians, many adapted the new technologies and new political possibilities to their own purposes and thrived—at least for a time. In the end, though, the best that they could achieve was a holding action. The people of the Old World were coming to dominate the people of the New World.

Second, after centuries of isolation, the political and economic demands of European empires forced the Americas onto the global stage. The influx of Europeans and Africans resulted in a vast biological and cultural transformation, as new plants, animals, diseases, peoples, and technologies fundamentally altered the natural environment. This was not a one-way transfer, however. The technologies and resources of the New World also contributed to profound changes in the Old. Among them, American staple crops helped fuel a population spurt in Europe, Asia, and Africa while American riches altered European economic, social, and political relations.

Third, the story of Red Shoes and the Choctaw illustrates the complexity of colonial society, in which Amerindians, Europeans, and Africans all contributed to the creation of new cultures. Although similar processes took place throughout the Americas, the particulars varied from place to place, creating a diverse range of cultures. The society that arose in each colony reflected the colony's mix of native peoples, its connections to the slave trade, and the characteristics of the European society establishing the colony. As the colonies matured, new concepts of identity developed, and those living in the Americas began to see themselves as distinct.

THE COLUMBIAN EXCHANGE

Columbian Exchange The exchange of plants, animals, diseases, and technologies between the Americas and the rest of the world following Columbus's voyages.

The term **Columbian Exchange** refers to the transfer of peoples, animals, plants, and diseases between the New and Old Worlds. The European invasion and settlement of the Western Hemisphere opened a long era of biological and technological transfers that altered American environments. Within a century of first settlement, the domesticated livestock and major agricultural crops of the Old World (the known world before Columbus's voyage) had spread over much of the Americas, and the New World's useful staple crops had enriched the agricultures of Europe, Asia, and Africa. Old World diseases that entered the Americas with European immigrants and African slaves devastated indigenous populations. These dramatic population changes weakened native peoples' capacity for resistance and accelerated the transfer of plants, animals, and related technologies. As a result, the colonies of Spain, Portugal, England, and France became vast arenas of cultural and social experimentation.

Demographic Changes

AP* Exam Tip Be prepared to compare demographic changes across regions and across time.

Because of their long isolation from other continents (see Chapter 15), the peoples of the New World lacked immunity to diseases introduced from the Old World. As a result, death rates among Amerindian peoples during the epidemics of the early colonial period were very high. The lack of reliable estimates of the Amerindian population at the moment of contact has frustrated efforts to measure the deadly impact of these diseases, but scholars agree that Old World diseases had a terrible effect on native peoples. According to one estimate, the population of central Mexico fell from more than 13 million to approximately 700,000 in the century that followed 1521. In this same period the populations of the Maya and Inca regions declined by nearly 75 percent or more. Brazil's native population fell by more than 50 percent within a century of the arrival of the Portuguese.

Early Epidemics

Smallpox, which arrived in the Caribbean in 1518, was the most deadly of the early epidemics. In Mexico and Central America, 50 percent or more of the Amerindian population died during the first wave of smallpox epidemics. The disease then spread to South America with equally devastating effects. Measles arrived in the New World in the 1530s and was followed by diphtheria, typhus, influenza, and pulmonary plague. Mortality was often greatest when two or more diseases struck at the same time. Between 1520 and 1521 influenza and other ailments attacked the Cakchiquel of Guatemala. Their chronicle recalls:

> *Great was the stench of the dead. After our fathers and grandfathers succumbed, half the people fled to the fields. The dogs and vultures devoured the bodies. . . . So it was that we became orphans, oh my sons! . . . We were born to die!*[1]

By the mid-seventeenth century malaria and yellow fever were also present in tropical regions of the Americas. The deadliest form of malaria arrived with the African slave trade, ravaging the already reduced native populations and afflicting Europeans as well.

The development of English and French colonies in North America in the seventeenth century led to similar patterns of contagion and mortality. In 1616 and 1617 epidemics nearly exterminated New England's indigenous groups. Epidemics also followed French fur traders as far as Hudson Bay and the Great Lakes. Although there is very little evidence that Europeans con-

CHRONOLOGY

	Spanish America	Brazil	British America	French America
1500	1518 Smallpox arrives in Caribbean 1535 Creation of Viceroyalty of New Spain 1540s Creation of Viceroyalty of Peru 1542 New Laws attempt to improve treatment of Amerindians 1545 Silver discovered at Potosí, Bolivia	1520 Appointment of first Viceroy of Brazil 1540–1600 Era of Amerindian slavery After 1540 Sugar begins to dominate the economy		1534–1542 Jacques Cartier's voyages to explore Newfoundland and Gulf of St. Lawrence
1600	1625 Population of Potosí reaches 120,000	By 1620 African slave trade provides majority of plantation workers 1630s Quilombo of Palmares founded	1607 Jamestown founded 1620 Plymouth founded 1660 Slave population in Virginia begins period of rapid growth 1664 English take New York from Dutch	1608 Quebec founded 1699 Louisiana founded
1700	1700 Last Habsburg ruler of Spain dies 1713 First Bourbon ruler of Spain crowned 1770s and 1780s Amerindian revolts in Andean region	1750–1777 Reforms of marquis de Pombal	1754–1763 French and Indian War	1760 English take Canada

sciously used disease as a tool of empire, the deadly results of contact clearly undermined the ability of native peoples to resist settlement.

Transfer of Plants and Animals

Even as epidemics swept through the indigenous population, the New and the Old Worlds were participating in a vast exchange of plants and animals that radically altered diet and lifestyles in both regions. Settlers brought all the staples of southern European agriculture—such as wheat, olives, grapes, and garden vegetables—to the Americas soon after contact. Colonization also introduced African and Asian crops such as rice, bananas, coconuts, breadfruit, and sugar. While natives remained loyal to their traditional staples, they added many foods like citrus fruits, melons, figs, and sugar as well as onions, radishes, and salad greens to their cuisines.

Diffusion of Plants and Animals

In return the Americas offered the Old World an abundance of useful plants. Maize, potatoes, and manioc revolutionized agriculture and diet in parts of Europe, Africa, and Asia (see

Oronoz

The Columbian Exchange In this painting an Amerindian woman milks a cow, suggesting how the Columbian Exchange altered native culture and environment. While livestock sometimes destroyed the fields of native peoples, cattle, sheep, pigs, and goats also provided food, leather, and wool.

Environment and Technology: Amerindian Foods in Africa, in Chapter 18). Many experts assert that the growth of world population after 1700 resulted from the spread of these useful crops, which provided more calories per acre than did most Old World staples. Beans, squash, tomatoes, sweet potatoes, peanuts, chilies, and chocolate also gained widespread acceptance in the Old World. In addition, the New World provided the Old with plants that provided dyes, medicine, varieties of cotton, and tobacco.

The introduction of European livestock had a dramatic impact on New World environments and cultures. Faced with few natural predators, cattle, pigs, horses, and sheep, as well as pests like rats and rabbits, multiplied rapidly in the Americas. On the vast plains of southern Brazil, Uruguay, and Argentina, for example, herds of wild cattle and horses exceeded 50 million by 1700.

Where Old World livestock spread most rapidly, environmental changes were dramatic. Many priests and colonial officials noted the destructive impact of marauding livestock on Amerindian agriculturists. The first viceroy of Mexico, Antonio de Mendoza, wrote to the Spanish king: "May your Lordship realize that if cattle are allowed, the Indians will be destroyed." Sheep, which grazed grasses close to the ground, were also an environmental threat.

Yet the viceroy's stark choice misrepresented the complex response of indigenous peoples to these new animals. Wild cattle on the plains of South America, northern Mexico, and Texas provided indigenous peoples with abundant supplies of meat and hides, for example. In the present-day southwestern United States, the Navajo became sheepherders and expert weavers. Even in the centers of European settlement, Amerindians turned European animals to their own advantage by becoming muleteers, cowboys, and sheepherders.

No animal had a more striking effect on the cultures of native peoples than the horse, which increased the efficiency of hunters and the military capacity of warriors on the plains. The horse permitted the Apache, Sioux, Blackfoot, Comanche, Assiniboine, and others to more efficiently hunt the vast herds of buffalo in North America. The horse also revolutionized the cultures of the Mapuche and Pampas peoples in South America.

SECTION REVIEW

- The creation of Spanish and Portuguese empires in America accelerated global exchanges of peoples, plants, animals, diseases, and technologies.
- Old World diseases decimated New World peoples and made them vulnerable to European expansion, and Old World animals overran the landscape and changed New World practices.
- Both the Old and New Worlds also profited from the introduction of new plants and animals.

SPANISH AMERICA AND BRAZIL

The frontiers of conquest and settlement expanded rapidly. Within one hundred years of Columbus's first voyage to the Western Hemisphere, the Spanish Empire in America included most of the islands of the Caribbean and a vast area that stretched from northern Mexico to the plains of the Rio de la Plata region (a region that includes the modern nations of Argentina, Uruguay, and Paraguay). Portuguese settlement developed more slowly, but before the end of the sixteenth century, Portugal had occupied most of the Brazilian coast.

Forging Colonial Society

Early settlers from Spain and Portugal sought to create colonial societies based on the institutions and customs of their homelands. They viewed society as a vertical hierarchy of estates (classes of society), as uniformly Catholic, and as an arrangement of patriarchal extended-family networks. They quickly moved to establish the religious, social, and administrative institutions that were familiar to them.

Despite the imposition of foreign institutions and loss of life caused by epidemics, indigenous peoples exercised a powerful influence on the development of colonial societies. Aztec and Inca elite families sought to protect their traditional privileges and rights through marriage or less formal alliances with Spanish settlers. They also used colonial courts to defend their claims to land. In Spanish and Portuguese colonies, indigenous military allies and laborers proved crucial to the development of European settlements. Nearly everywhere, Amerindian religious beliefs and practices survived beneath the surface of an imposed Christianity. Amerindian languages, cuisines, medical practices, and agricultural techniques also survived the conquest and influenced the development of Latin American culture.

e **PRIMARY SOURCE: General History of the Things in New Spain** Read an account of the Spanish conquest of the Aztec Empire, compiled from eyewitness testimony by the Aztecs themselves.

The African slave trade added a third cultural stream to colonial Latin American society. At first, African slaves were concentrated in plantation regions of Brazil and the Caribbean (see Chapter 18), but by the end of the colonial era, Africans and their descendants were living throughout Spanish and Portuguese America, introducing elements of their agricultural practices, music, religious beliefs, cuisine, and social customs to colonial societies.

State and Church

The Spanish crown moved quickly to curb the independent power of the conquistadors and to establish royal authority over both defeated native populations and European settlers, but geography and technology thwarted this ambition. European officials could not control the distant colonies too closely because it took a ship more than two hundred days to make a roundtrip voyage from Spain to Veracruz, Mexico. Additional months of travel were required to reach Lima, Peru.

Spanish and Portuguese Colonial Governments

As a result, the highest-ranking Spanish officials in the colonies, the viceroys of New Spain and Peru, enjoyed broad power, but they also faced obstacles to their authority in the vast territories they sought to control. Created in 1535, the Viceroyalty of New Spain, with its capital in Mexico City, included Mexico, the southwest of what is now the United States, Central America, and the islands of the Caribbean. Created five years later, the Viceroyalty of Peru, with its capital in Lima, governed Spanish South America (see Map 17.1).

Until the seventeenth century, most colonial officials were born in Spain, but fiscal mismanagement eventually forced the Crown to sell appointments. As a result, local-born members of the colonial elite gained many offices.

In the sixteenth century Portugal concentrated its resources and energies on Asia and Africa. Because early settlers found neither mineral wealth nor rich native empires in Brazil, the Portuguese king was slow to create expensive mechanisms of colonial government in the New World, but mismanagement forced the king to appoint a governor-general in 1549 and make Salvador Brazil's capital. In 1720 the king named the first viceroy of Brazil.

The government institutions of the Spanish and Portuguese colonies had a more uniform character and were much more extensive and costly than those later established in North America by France and Great Britain. The enormous wealth produced in Spanish America by silver and gold mines and in Brazil by sugar plantations and, after 1690, gold mines financed these large and intrusive colonial bureaucracies. These institutions made the colonies more responsive to the initiatives of Spanish and Portuguese monarchs, but they also thwarted local

MAP 17.1 Colonial Latin America in the Eighteenth Century Spain and Portugal controlled most of the Western Hemisphere in the eighteenth century. In the sixteenth century they had created new administrative jurisdictions—viceroyalties—to defend their respective colonies against European rivals. Taxes assessed on colonial products helped pay for this extension of governmental authority.

Interactive Map

Saint Martín de Porres (1579–1639) Martín de Porres was the illegitimate son of a Spanish nobleman and a black servant. He entered the Dominican Order in Lima, Peru, where he was known for his generosity, his religious visions, and his ability to heal the sick. In this painting the artist celebrates Martín de Porres's spirituality while representing him doing the type of work presumed to be suitable for a person of mixed descent.

economic initiative and political experimentation. More importantly, the heavy tax burden imposed by these colonial states drained capital from the colonies, slowing investment and retarding economic growth.

The Catholic Church

In both Spanish America and Brazil, the Catholic Church became the primary agent for the introduction and transmission of Christian belief as well as European language and culture. The church undertook the conversion of Amerindians, ministered to the spiritual needs of European settlers, and promoted intellectual life through the introduction of the printing press and the founding of schools and universities.

Spain and Portugal justified their American conquests by assuming an obligation to convert native populations to Christianity. This effort to convert America's native peoples expanded Christianity on a scale similar to its earlier expansion in Europe at the time of Constantine in the fourth century. In New Spain alone hundreds of thousands of conversions and baptisms were achieved within a few years of the conquest. However, the small numbers of missionaries limited quality of indoctrination. One Dominican claimed to the king that the Franciscans "have taken and occupied three fourths of the country, though they do not have enough friars for it. . . . In most places they are content to say a mass once a year; consider what sort of indoctrination they give them!"[2]

The Catholic clergy sought to achieve their evangelical ends by first converting members of the Amerindian elites, in the hope that they could persuade others to follow their example. To pursue this objective, Franciscan missionaries in Mexico created a seminary to train members of the indigenous elite to become priests, but they curtailed these idealistic efforts when church authorities discovered that many converts were secretly observing old beliefs and rituals. The trial and punishment of two converted Aztec nobles for heresy in the 1530s and the torture of hundreds of Maya in the 1560s repelled the church hierarchy, ending both the violent repression of native religious practice and the effort to recruit an Amerindian clergy.

Bartolomé de Las Casas

Despite its failures, the Catholic clergy did provide native peoples with some protections against the abuse and exploitation of Spanish settlers. The priest **Bartolomé de Las Casas** (1474–1566) was the most influential defender of the Amerindians in the early colonial period. He arrived in Hispaniola in 1502 as a settler and initially lived off the forced labor of Amerindians. Deeply moved by the deaths of so many Amerindians and by the misdeeds of the Spanish, Las Casas entered the Dominican Order and later became the first bishop of Chiapas, in southern Mexico. For the remainder of his long life Las Casas served as the most important advocate for native peoples. His most important achievement was the enactment of the New Laws of 1542—reform legislation that outlawed the enslavement of Amerindians and limited other forms of forced labor.

Bartolomé de Las Casas First bishop of Chiapas, in southern Mexico. He devoted most of his life to protecting Amerindian peoples from exploitation. His major achievement was the New Laws of 1542, which limited the ability of Spanish settlers to compel Amerindians to labor for them.

European clergy had arrived in the Americas with the intention of transmitting Catholic Christian belief and ritual without alteration. The linguistic diversity of Amerindian populations and their geographic dispersal over a vast landscape defeated this ambition. The resulting slow progress and limited success of evangelization led to the appearance of a unique Amerindian Christianity that blended European Christian beliefs with important elements of traditional native cosmology and ritual. The Catholic clergy and most European settlers viewed this evolving mixture as the work of the Devil or as evidence of Amerindian inferiority. Instead, it was one component of the process of cultural borrowing and innovation that contributed to a distinct and original Latin American culture.

After 1600 the terrible loss of Amerindian population caused by epidemics and growing signs of resistance to conversion led the Catholic Church to redirect most of its resources from native regions in the countryside to growing colonial cities and towns with large European populations. One important outcome of this altered mission was the founding of universities and secondary schools and the stimulation of urban intellectual life. Over time, the church became the richest institution in the Spanish colonies, controlling ranches, plantations, and vineyards as well as serving as the society's banker.

Colonial Economies

AP* Exam Tip Be prepared to discuss colonial labor systems in detail.

The silver mines of Peru and Mexico and the sugar plantations of Brazil dominated the economic development of colonial Latin America. The mineral wealth of the New World fueled the early development of European capitalism and funded Europe's greatly expanded trade with Asia. Profits produced in these economic centers also promoted the growth of colonial cities, concentrated scarce investment capital and labor resources, and stimulated the development of livestock raising and agriculture in neighboring rural areas (see Map 17.1). Once established, this colonial dependence on mineral and agricultural exports left an enduring social and economic legacy in Latin America.

Colonial Mining

The Spanish and later the Portuguese produced gold worth millions of pesos, but silver mines in the Spanish colonies generated the most wealth and therefore exercised the greatest economic influence. The first important silver strikes occurred in Mexico in the 1530s and 1540s. In 1545 the Spanish discovered the single richest silver deposit in the Americas at **Potosí** (poh-toh-SEE) in Alto Peru (what is now Bolivia). The silver of Alto Peru and Peru dominated the Spanish colonial economy until 1680, when it was surpassed by Mexican silver production. At first, miners extracted silver ore by smelting: crushed ore, packed with charcoal, was fired in a furnace, but this wasteful use of forest resources destroyed forests near the mining centers. Faced with rising fuel costs, Mexican miners developed an efficient method of chemical extraction that relied on mixing mercury with the silver ore (see Environment and Technology:

Potosí Located in Bolivia, one of the richest silver mining centers and most populous cities in colonial Spanish America.

A Silver Refinery at Potosí, Bolivia, 1700

The silver refineries of Spanish America were among the largest and most heavily capitalized industrial enterprises in the Western Hemisphere during the colonial period. By the middle of the seventeenth century the mines of Potosí, Bolivia, had attracted a population of more than 120,000.

The accompanying illustration shows a typical refinery (*ingenio*). Aqueducts carried water from large reservoirs on nearby mountainsides to the refineries. The water wheel shown on the right drove two sets of vertical stamps that crushed ore. Each iron-shod stamp was about the size and weight of a telephone pole. Amerindian laborers then sorted, dried, and mixed the crushed ore with mercury and other catalysts to extract the silver. Miners then separated the amalgam using a combination of washing and heating. The end result was a nearly pure ingot of silver that was later assayed and taxed at the mint.

Silver production carried a high environmental cost. Forests were cut to provide fuel and the timbers needed to shore up mine shafts and construct stamping mills and other machinery. Unwanted base metals produced in the refining process poisoned the soil. In addition, the need for tens of thousands of horses, mules, and oxen to drive machinery and transport material led to overgrazing and widespread erosion.

A Bolivian Silver Refinery, 1700
The silver refineries of Spanish America were among the largest industrial establishments in the Western Hemisphere.

Legend
(A) Storage sheds for ore
(B) Two water-driven stamping mills to crush ore
(C) Additional stamping mill
(D) Screen to sort ore
(E) Ore packed in mixing box
(F) Mercury and catalysts added to ore
(G) Amalgamation occurs
(H) Ore dried in furnace
(I) Mercury removed
(J) Refined ore washed
(K) Ore assayed
(L) Poor-quality ore remixed with catalysts
(M) Housing
(N) Offices and sheds
(O) Aqueduct
(P) Chapel
(Q) Mill owner's house

A Silver Refinery at Potosí, Bolivia, 1700). Silver yields and profits increased with the use of mercury amalgamation, but this process, too, had severe environmental costs, since mercury is a poison that contaminated the environment and sickened the Amerindian work force.

Encomienda and Mita

encomienda A grant of authority over a population of Amerindians in the Spanish colonies. It provided the grant holder with a supply of cheap labor and periodic payments of goods by the Amerindians. It obliged the grant holder to Christianize the Amerindians.

AP* Exam Tip
Vocabulary words, such as *encomienda* and *mita*, are tested on the multiple choice section of the exam.

From the time of Columbus, indigenous populations had been compelled to provide labor for European settlers in the Americas. Until the 1540s in Spanish colonies, Spanish authorities divided Amerindians among settlers, who forced them to provide labor or goods. This form of forced labor was called **encomienda** (in-co-mee-EN-dah). As epidemics and mistreatment led to the decline in Amerindian population, reforms such as the New Laws sought to eliminate the encomienda. The discovery of silver, however, led to new forms of compulsory labor. In the mining region of Mexico, where epidemics had reduced Amerindian populations, silver miners came to rely on wage laborers. Peru's Amerindian population survived in larger numbers, allowing the Spanish to impose a form of labor called the mita (MEE-tah). Under this system, one-seventh of adult male Amerindians were compelled to work for two to four months each year in mines, farms, or textile factories.

As the Amerindian population declined with new epidemics, villages were forced to shorten the period between mita obligations. Instead of serving every seven years, many men returned to mines after only a year or two. Unwilling to accept mita service and the other tax burdens imposed on Amerindian villages, thousands abandoned traditional agriculture and moved permanently to Spanish mines and farms as laborers. The long-term result of these individual decisions weakened Amerindian village life and promoted the assimilation of Amerindians into Spanish-speaking Catholic colonial society.

Before the settlement of Brazil, the Portuguese had already developed sugar plantations using African slave labor on the Atlantic islands of Madeira, the Azores, the Cape Verdes, and São Tomé. Because of the success of these early experiences, they were able to quickly transfer this profitable form of agriculture to Brazil. After 1540 sugar production expanded rapidly, and by the seventeenth century it dominated the Brazilian economy.

Slavery and Slave Trade

At first the Portuguese sugar planters enslaved Amerindians captured in war or seized from their villages. Thousands of Amerindian slaves died during the epidemics that raged across Brazil in the sixteenth and seventeenth centuries. This led to the development of an internal slave

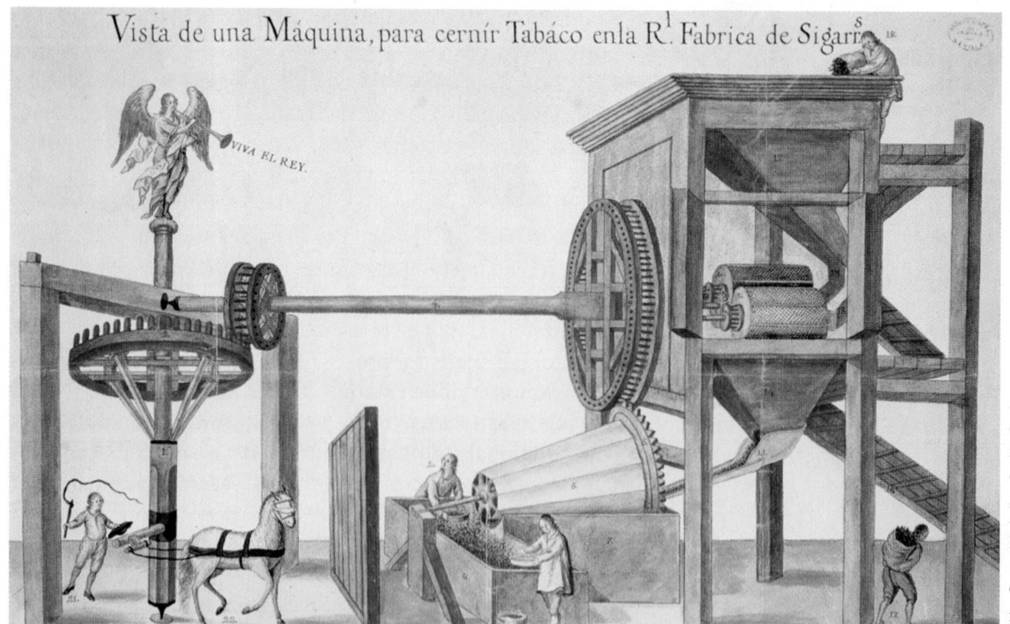

Archivo General de Indias, Seville, Spain

Tobacco Factory Machinery in Colonial Mexico City The tobacco factory in eighteenth-century Mexico City used a horse-driven mechanical shredder to produce snuff and cigarette tobacco.

trade by slave raiders who pushed into the interior, even attacking Amerindian populations in neighboring Spanish colonies.

Amerindian slaves remained an important source of labor and slave raiding a significant business in frontier regions into the eighteenth century. But sugar planters eventually came to rely more on African slaves. African slaves at first cost much more than Amerindian slaves, but planters found them more productive and more resistant to disease. As profits from the plantations increased, imports of African slaves rose from an average of two thousand per year in the late sixteenth century to approximately seven thousand per year a century later, outstripping the immigration of free Portuguese settlers. Between 1650 and 1750, for example, nearly five African slaves arrived in Brazil for every immigrant from Europe.

Colonial Networks of Trade

Within Spanish America, the mining centers of Mexico and Peru eventually exercised global economic influence. American silver increased the European money supply, promoting commercial expansion and, later, industrialization. Large amounts of silver also flowed across the Pacific to the Spanish colony of the Philippines, where it paid for Asian spices, silks, and pottery.

The rich mines of Peru, Bolivia, and Mexico stimulated urban population growth as well as commercial links with distant agricultural and textile producers. The population of the city of Potosí, high in the Andes, reached 120,000 inhabitants by 1625. This rich mining town became the center of a vast regional market that depended on Chilean wheat, Argentine livestock, and Ecuadorian textiles.

The sugar plantations of Brazil played a similar role in integrating the economy of the south Atlantic region. Brazil exchanged sugar, tobacco, and reexported slaves for yerba (Paraguayan tea), hides, livestock, and silver produced in neighboring Spanish colonies. Portugal's increasing openness to British trade also allowed Brazil to become a conduit for an illegal trade between Spanish colonies and Europe. At the end of the seventeenth century, the discovery of gold in Brazil promoted further regional and international economic integration.

Society in Colonial Latin America

creoles In colonial Spanish America, term used to describe someone of European descent born in the New World. Elsewhere in the Americas, the term is used to describe all nonnative peoples.

With the exception of some early viceroys, few members of Spain's nobility came to the New World. *Hidalgos* (ee-DAHL-goes)—lesser nobles—were well represented, as were Spanish merchants, artisans, miners, priests, and lawyers. Small numbers of criminals, beggars, and prostitutes also found their way to the colonies. This flow of immigrants from Spain was never large, and Spanish settlers were always a tiny minority in a colonial society numerically dominated by Amerindians and rapidly growing populations of Africans, **creoles** (whites born in America to European parents), and people of mixed ancestry (see Diversity and Dominance: Race and Ethnicity in the Spanish Colonies: Negotiating Hierarchy).

Colonial Elites

The most powerful conquistadors and early settlers sought to create a hereditary social and political class comparable to the European nobility. But their systematic abuse of Amerindian communities and the catastrophic effects of the epidemics of the sixteenth century undermined their economic position. Colonial officials, the clergy, and the richest merchants inherited their social position. Europeans dominated the highest levels of the church and government as well as commerce, while wealthy American-born creoles controlled colonial agriculture and mining. Although tensions between Spaniards and creoles were inevitable, most elite families included both groups.

Amerindian Adaptations

Before the Europeans arrived in the Americas, the native peoples were members of a large number of distinct cultural and linguistic groups. The effects of conquest and epidemics undermined this rich social and cultural complexity and the relocation of Amerindian peoples to promote conversion or provide labor further eroded ethnic boundaries among native peoples. Application of the racial label "Indian" by colonial administrators and settlers helped organize the tribute and labor demands imposed on native peoples, but it also registered the cultural costs of colonial rule.

Amerindian elites struggled to survive in the new political and economic environments created by military defeat and European settlement. Some sought to protect their positions by forging marriage or less formal relations with colonists. As a result, some indigenous and settler families were tied together by kinship in the decades after conquest, but these links weakened

Race and Ethnicity in the Spanish Colonies: Negotiating Hierarchy

Many European visitors to colonial Latin America were interested in the mixing of Europeans, Amerindians, and Africans in the colonies. Many also commented on the treatment of slaves. The passages that follow allow us to examine two colonial societies.

Two young Spanish naval officers and scientists, Jorge Juan and Antonio de Ulloa, arrived in the colonies in 1735 as members of a scientific expedition. They later wrote the first selection after visiting the major cities of the Pacific coast of South America and traveling across some of the most difficult terrain in the hemisphere. In addition to their scientific chores, they described architecture, local customs, and the social order. In this section they describe the ethnic mix in Quito, now the capital of Ecuador.

The second selection was published in Lima under the pseudonym Concolorcorvo around 1776. We now know that the author was Alonso Carrío de la Vandera. Born in Spain, he traveled to the colonies as a young man. He served in many minor bureaucratic positions, one of which was the inspection of the postal route between Buenos Aires and Lima. Carrío turned his long and often uncomfortable trip into an insightful, and sometimes highly critical, examination of colonial society. The selection that follows describes Córdoba, Argentina.

Juan and Ulloa and Carrío seem perplexed by colonial efforts to create and enforce a racial taxonomy that stipulated and named every possible mixture of European, Amerindian, and African, and they commented on the vanity and social presumptions of the dominant white population. We are fortunate to have these contemporary descriptions of the diversity of colonial society, but it is important to remember that these authors were clearly rooted in their time and confident in the superiority of Europe. Although they noted many of the abuses of Amerindian, mixed, and African populations and sometimes punctured the pretensions of colonial elites, they were also quick to assume the inferiority of the nonwhite population.

Quito

This city is very populous, and has, among its inhabitants, some families of high rank and distinction; though their number is but small considering its extent, the poorer class bearing here too great a proportion. The former are the descendants either of the original conquerors, or of presidents, auditors, or other persons of character [high rank], who at different times came over from Spain invested with some lucrative post, and have still preserved their luster, both of wealth and descent, by intermarriages, without intermixing with meaner families though famous for their riches. The commonalty may be divided into four classes; Spaniards or Whites, Mestizos, Indians or Natives, and Negroes, with their progeny. These last are not proportionally so numerous as in the other parts of the Indies; occasioned by it being something inconvenient to bring Negroes to Quito, and the different kinds of agriculture being generally performed by Indians.

The name of Spaniard here has a different meaning from that of Chapitone *[sic]* or European, as properly signifying a person descended from a Spaniard without a mixture of blood. Many Mestizos, from the advantage of a fresh complexion, appear to be Spaniards more than those who are so in reality; and from only this fortuitous advantage are accounted as such. The Whites, according to this construction of the word, may be considered as one sixth part of the inhabitants.

The Mestizos are the descendants of Spaniards and Indians, and are to be considered here in the same different degrees between the Negroes and Whites, as before at Carthagena *[sic]*; but with this difference, that at Quito the degrees of Mestizos are not carried so far back; for, even in the second or third generations, when they acquire the European color, they are considered as Spaniards. The complexion of the Mestizos is swarthy and reddish, but not of that red common in the fair Mulattos. This is the first degree, or the immediate issue of a Spaniard and Indian. Some are, however, equally tawny with the Indians themselves, though they are distinguished from them by their beards: while others, on the contrary, have so fine a complexion that they might pass for Whites, were it not for some signs which betray them, when viewed attentively. Among these, the most remarkable is the lowness of the forehead, which often leaves but a small space between their hair and eye-brows; at the same time the hair grows remarkably forward on the temples, extending to the lower part of the ear. Besides, the hair itself is harsh, lank, coarse, and very black; their nose very small, thin, and has a little rising on the middle, from whence it forms a small curve, terminating in a point, bending towards the upper lip. These marks, besides some dark spots on the body, are so constant and invariable, as to make it very difficult to conceal the fallacy of their complexion. The Mestizos may be reckoned a third part of the inhabitants.

The next class is the Indians, who form about another third; and the others, who are about one sixth, are the Castes [mixed]. These four classes, according to the most authentic accounts taken from the parish register, amount to between 50 and 60,000 persons, of all ages, sexes, and ranks. If among these classes the Spaniards, as is natural to think, are the most eminent for riches, rank, and power, it must at the same time be owned, however melancholy the truth may appear, they are in proportion the most poor, miserable and distressed; for they refuse to apply themselves to any mechanic business, considering it as a disgrace to that quality they so highly value themselves upon, which consists in not being black, brown, or of a copper color. The Mestizos, whose pride is regulated by prudence, readily apply themselves to arts and trades, but chose those of the greatest repute, as painting, sculpture, and the like, leaving the meaner sort to the Indians.

Córdoba

There was not a person who would give me even an estimate of the number of residents comprising this city, because neither the secular nor the ecclesiastical council has a register, and I know not how these colonists prove the ancient and distinguished nobility of which they boast; it may be that each family has its genealogical history in reserve. In my computation, there must be within the city and its limited common lands around 500 to 600 residents, but in the principal houses there are a very large number of slaves, most of them Creoles [native born] of all conceivable classes, because in this city and in all of Tucumán there is no leniency about granting freedom to any of them. They are easily supported since the principal aliment, meat, is of such moderate price, and there is a custom of dressing them only in ordinary cloth which is made at home by the slaves themselves, shoes being very rare. They aid their masters in many profitable ways and under this system do not think of freedom, thus exposing themselves to a sorrowful end, as is happening in Lima.

As I was passing through Córdoba, they were selling 2,000 Negroes, all Creoles from Temporalidades [property confiscated from the Jesuit order in 1767], from just the two farms of the [Jesuit] colleges of this city. I have seen the lists, for each one has its own, and they proceed by families numbering from two to eleven, all pure Negroes and Creoles back to the fourth generation, because the priests used to sell all of those born with a mixture of Spanish, mulatto, or Indian blood. Among this multitude of Negroes were many musicians and many of other crafts; they proceeded with the sale by families. I was assured that the nuns of Santa Teresa alone had a group of 300 slaves of both sexes, to whom they give their just ration of meat and dress in the coarse cloth which they make, while these good nuns content themselves with what is left from other ministrations. The number attached to other religious establishments is much smaller, but there is a private home which has 30 or 40, the majority of whom are engaged in various gainful activities. The result is a large number of excellent washerwomen whose accomplishments are valued so highly that they never mend their outer skirts in order that the whiteness of their undergarments may be seen. They do the laundry in the river, in water up to the waist, saying vaingloriously that she who is not soaked cannot wash well. They make ponchos [hand-woven capes], rugs, sashes, and sundries, and especially decorated leather cases which the men sell for 8 reales each, because the hides have no outlet due to the great distance to the port; the same thing happens on the banks of the Tercero and Cuarto rivers, where they are sold at 2 reales and frequently for less.

The principal men of the city wear very expensive clothes, but this is not true of the women, who are an exception in both Americas and even in the entire world, because they dress decorously in clothing of little cost. They are very tenacious in preserving the customs of their ancestors. They do not permit slaves, or even freedmen who have a mixture of Negro blood, to wear any cloth other than that made in this country, which is quite coarse. I was told recently that a certain bedecked mulatto [woman] who appeared in Córdoba was sent word by the ladies of the city that she should dress according to her station, but since she paid no attention to this reproach, they endured her negligence until one of the ladies, summoning her to her home under some other pretext, had the servants undress her, whip her, burn her finery before her eyes, and dress her in the clothes befitting her class; despite the fact that the [victim] was not lacking in persons to defend her, she disappeared lest the tragedy be repeated.

QUESTIONS FOR ANALYSIS

1. **What do the authors of these selections seem to think about the white elites of the colonies? Are there similarities in the ways that Juan and Ulloa and Carrío describe the mixed population of Quito and the slave population of Córdoba?**
2. **How do these depictions of mestizos and other mixtures compare with the image of the family represented in the painting of castas on page 502?**
3. **What does the humiliation of the mixed-race woman in Córdoba tell us about ideas of race and class in this Spanish colony?**

Sources: Jorge Juan and Antonio de Ulloa, *A Voyage to South America*, The John Adams translation (abridged), Introduction by Irving A. Leonard (New York: Alfred A. Knopf, 1964), 135–137, copyright © 1964 by Alfred A. Knopf, Inc. Used by permission of Alfred A. Knopf, a division of Random House, Inc.; Concolorcorvo, *El Lazarillo, A Guide for Inexperienced Travelers Between Buenos Aires and Lima, 1773*, translated by Walter D. Kline (Bloomington: Indiana University Press, 1965), 78–80. Used with permission of Indiana University Press.

with the passage of time. Indigenous leaders also established political alliances with members of the colonial administrative classes. Hereditary native elites gained some security by becoming essential intermediaries between the indigenous masses and colonial administrators, collecting Spanish taxes and organizing the labor of their dependents for colonial enterprises.

Indigenous commoners suffered the heaviest burdens. Tribute payments, forced labor obligations, and the loss of traditional land rights were common. European domination dramatically changed the indigenous world by breaking the connections between peoples and places and transforming religious life, marriage practices, diet, and material culture. The survivors of these terrible shocks learned to adapt to the new colonial environment by embracing some elements of the dominant colonial culture or entering the market economies of the cities. They also learned new forms of resistance, like using colonial courts to protect community lands or to resist the abuses of corrupt officials.

Afro Latin American Experience

Thousands of blacks, many born in Iberia or long resident there, participated in the conquest and settlement of Spanish America. Most of these were slaves; more than four hundred slaves participated in the conquests of Peru and Chile alone. In the fluid social environment of the conquest era, many were able to gain their freedom. Juan Valiente escaped from his master in Mexico and then participated in Francisco Pizarro's conquest of the Inca Empire. He later became one of the most prominent early settlers of Chile.

With the opening of a direct slave trade with Africa (for details, see Chapter 18), the cultural character of the black population of colonial Latin America was altered dramatically. While Afro-Iberians spoke Spanish or Portuguese and were Catholic, African slaves arrived in the colonies with different languages, religious beliefs, and cultural practices. European settlers viewed these differences as signs of inferiority that served as a justification for prejudice and discrimination.

A large percentage of slaves imported in the sixteenth century came from West Central Africa where they had had exposure to elements of Iberian culture including religion, language, and technology. The legacy of these common cultural elements facilitated African influence on the emerging colonial cultures of Latin America. But significant differences were present as

Painting of Castas This is an example of a common genre of colonial Spanish American painting. In the eighteenth century there was increased interest in ethnic mixing, and wealthy colonials as well as some Europeans commissioned sets of paintings that showed mixed families. The artist typically placed the couples in what he believed was an appropriate setting. In this example, the artist depicted the Amerindian husband with his mestiza (European and Amerindian mixture) wife in an outdoor market where they sold fowl. Colonial usage assigned their child the dismissive racial label "coyote."

Unknown Mexican artist, "De indio y mestiza sale coyote." Reproduced with the permission of the Collection of Jan and Frederick Mayer, Denver well and in regions with large slave majorities, especially the sugar-producing regions of Brazil, these cultural and linguistic barriers often divided slaves and made resistance more difficult. Over time, elements from many African traditions blended and mixed with European (and in some cases Amerindian) language and beliefs to forge distinct local cultures.

Slave resistance took many forms, including sabotage, malingering, running away, and rebellion. Although many slave rebellions occurred, colonial authorities were always able to reestablish control. Groups of runaway slaves, however, were sometimes able to defend themselves for years. In both Spanish America and Brazil, communities of runaways (called quilombos [key-LOM-bos] in Brazil and palenques [pah-LEN-kays] in Spanish colonies) were common. The largest quilombo was Palmares in Brazil.

AP* Exam Tip Be prepared to compare the social structures of colonial possessions over time and space.

Slaves served as skilled artisans, musicians, servants, artists, cowboys, and even soldiers. However, the vast majority worked in agriculture. Conditions for slaves were worst on the sugar plantations of Brazil and the Caribbean, where harsh discipline, brutal punishments, and backbreaking labor were common. Because planters preferred to buy male slaves, there was always a gender imbalance on plantations, proving a significant obstacle to the traditional marriage and family patterns of both Africa and Europe.

Brazil attracted smaller numbers of European immigrants than did Spanish America, and its native populations were smaller and less urbanized. It also came to depend on the African slave as a source of labor earlier than any other American colony. By the early seventeenth century, Africans and their American-born descendants were by far the largest racial group in Brazil. As a result, Brazilian colonial society (unlike Spanish Mexico and Peru) was more influenced by African culture than by Amerindian culture.

Both Spanish and Portuguese law provided for manumission, the granting of freedom to individual slaves, and colonial courts sometimes intervened to protect slaves from the worst physical abuse or to protect married couples from forced separation. The majority of those gaining their liberty had saved money and purchased their own freedom. This meant that manumission was more about the capacity of individual slaves and slave families to earn income and save than about the generosity of slave owners. Among the minority of slaves to be freed without compensation, household servants were the most likely beneficiaries. Slave women received the majority of manumissions, and because children born subsequently were considered free, the free black population grew rapidly.

mestizo The term used by Spanish authorities to describe someone of mixed Amerindian and European descent.

New Peoples and New Identities

mulatto The term used in Spanish and Portuguese colonies to describe someone of mixed African and European descent.

Within a century of settlement, groups of mixed descent were in the majority in many regions. There were few marriages between Amerindian women and European men, but less formal relationships were common. Few European fathers recognized their mixed offspring, who were called **mestizos** (mess-TEE-zoh). Nevertheless, this rapidly expanding group came to occupy a middle position in colonial society, dominating urban artisan trades and small-scale agriculture and ranching. In frontier regions many members of the elite were mestizos, some proudly asserting their descent from the Amerindian elite. The African slave trade also led to the appearance of new American ethnicities. Individuals of mixed European and African descent—called **mulattos**—came to occupy an intermediate position in the tropics similar to the social position of mestizos in Mesoamerica and the Andean region. In Spanish Mexico and Peru and in Brazil, mixtures of Amerindians and Africans were also common. These mixed-descent groups were called castas (CAZ-tahs) in Spanish America.

The American colonies of Spain and Portugal grew rich from the export of silver, gold, and sugar, but depended on the forced labor of Amerindians and African slaves. The Catholic Church provided for the spiritual needs of settlers but also converted Amerindians and Africans to Christianity. As time passed, new peoples—the mixed offspring of Amerindians, Europeans, and Africans—and new blended American cultures developed.

SECTION REVIEW

- Colonial governments were created to rule distant colonies.
- The Catholic Church led conversion of Amerindian peoples and spread European cultures and languages.
- Silver mining and sugar production dominated colonial Latin American economies.
- Spanish and Portuguese colonies relied on forced labor of Amerindians and African slaves.
- New peoples and new cultures resulted from colonial contacts among Amerindians, Europeans, and Africans.

ENGLISH AND FRENCH COLONIES IN NORTH AMERICA

The North American colonial empires of England and France and the colonies of Spain and Portugal had many characteristics in common (see Map 17.1). The governments of England and France hoped to find easily extracted forms of wealth or great indigenous empires like those of the Aztecs or Inca. Like the Spanish and Portuguese, English and French settlers responded to native peoples with a mixture of diplomacy and violence. African slaves proved crucial to the development of all four colonial economies.

Important differences, however, distinguished North American colonial development from the Latin American model. The English and French colonies were developed nearly a century after Cortés's conquest of Mexico and Portuguese settlement of Brazil. The intervening period witnessed significant economic and demographic growth in Europe. It also witnessed the Protestant Reformation, which helped propel English and French settlement in the Americas. By the time England and France secured a foothold in the Americas, increased trade had led to greater integration of world cultural regions. Distracted by ventures elsewhere and by increasing military confrontation in Europe, neither England nor France imitated the large and expensive colonial bureaucracies established by Spain and Portugal. As a result, private companies and individual proprietors played a much larger role in the development of English and French colonies.

Early English Experiments

England's effort to gain a foothold in the Americas in the late sixteenth century failed, but its effort to establish colonies in the seventeenth century proved more successful. The English relied on private capital to finance settlement and continued to hope that the colonies would become sources of high-value products such as silver, citrus, and wine. English experience in colonizing Ireland after 1566 also influenced these efforts. In Ireland land had been confiscated, cleared of its native population, and offered for sale to English investors. The city of London, English guilds, and wealthy private investors all purchased Irish "plantations" and then recruited "settlers." By 1650 investors had sent nearly 150,000 English and Scottish immigrants to Ireland. Indeed, Ireland attracted six times as many colonists in the early seventeenth century as did New England.

The South

In 1606 London investors organized as the Virginia Company took up the challenge of colonizing Virginia. A year later 144 settlers disembarked at Jamestown, an island 30 miles (48 kilometers) up the James River in the Chesapeake Bay region. Additional settlers arrived in 1609. The investors and settlers hoped for immediate profits, but the location was a swampy and unhealthy place where nearly 80 percent of the settlers died in the first fifteen years from disease or Amerindian attacks. There was no mineral wealth, no passage to Asia, and no docile and exploitable native population.

In 1624 the English crown dissolved the Virginia Company because of its mismanagement. Freed from the company's commitment to the original location, colonists pushed deeper into the interior and developed a sustainable economy based on furs, timber, and, increasingly, tobacco. The profits from tobacco soon attracted new immigrants. Along the shoreline of Chesapeake Bay and the rivers that fed it, settlers spread out, developing plantations and farms. Colonial Virginia's dispersed population contrasted with the greater urbanization of Spanish and Portuguese America, where large and powerful cities and networks of secondary towns flourished. No city of any significant size developed in colonial Virginia.

indentured servant
A migrant to British colonies in the Americas who paid for passage by agreeing to work for a set term ranging from four to seven years.

Indentured Servants and Slaves

From the beginning, colonists in Latin America had relied on forced labor of Amerindians to develop the region's resources. The African slave trade compelled the migration of millions of additional forced laborers to the colonies of Spain and Portugal. The English settlement of the Chesapeake Bay region added a new system of forced labor to the American landscape: indentured servitude. **Indentured servants** were racially and religiously indistinguishable from free settlers and eventually accounted for approximately 80 percent of all English immigrants to Virginia and the neighboring colony of Maryland. A young man or woman unable to pay for transportation to the New World accepted an indenture (contract) that bound him or her to a term ranging from four to seven years of labor in return for passage and, at the end of the contract, a small parcel of land, some tools, and clothes.

During the seventeenth century approximately fifteen hundred indentured servants, mostly male, arrived each year (see Chapter 18 for details on the indentured labor system). Planters were more likely to purchase the cheaper limited contracts of indentured servants rather than African slaves during the initial period of high mortality rates. As life expectancy improved, planters began to purchase more slaves because they believed they would earn greater profits from slaves owned for life than from indentured servants bound for short periods of time. As a result, Virginia's slave population grew rapidly from 950 in 1660 to 120,000 by 1756.

Virginia Government

House of Burgesses Elected assembly in colonial Virginia, created in 1618.

By the 1660s Virginia was administered by a Crown-appointed governor and by representatives of towns meeting together as the **House of Burgesses**. When elected representatives began to meet alone as a deliberative body, they initiated a form of democratic representation that distinguished the English colonies of North America from the colonies of other European powers. Ironically, this expansion in colonial liberties and political rights occurred along with the dramatic increase in the colony's slave population. The intertwined evolution of American freedom and American slavery gave England's southern colonies a unique and conflicted political character that endured after independence.

Carolina Fur Trade

English settlement of the Carolinas initially relied on profits from the fur trade. English fur traders pushed into the interior to compete with French trading networks based in New Orleans and Mobile. Native peoples eventually provided over 100,000 deerskins annually to this profitable commerce, but at a high environmental and cultural cost. As Amerindian peoples hunted more intensely, they disrupted the natural balance of animals and plants in southern forests. The profits of the fur trade altered Amerindian culture as well, leading villages to place less emphasis on subsistence hunting, fishing, and traditional agriculture. Amerindian life was profoundly altered by deepening dependencies on European products, including firearms, metal tools, textiles, and alcohol.

While being increasingly tied to the commerce and culture of the Carolina colony, indigenous peoples were simultaneously weakened by epidemics, alcoholism, and a rising tide of ethnic conflicts generated by competition for hunting grounds. Conflicts among indigenous peoples—who now had firearms—became more deadly, and many captured Amerindians were sold as slaves to local colonists, who used them as agricultural workers or exported to the sugar plantations of the Caribbean. Dissatisfied with the terms of trade imposed by fur traders and angered by this slave trade, Amerindians launched attacks on English settlements in the early 1700s. Their defeat by colonial military forces inevitably led to new seizures of Amerindian land by European settlers.

South Carolina, a Colony of Plantations and Slaves

The northern part of the Carolinas, settled from Virginia, followed that colony's mixed economy of tobacco and forest products. Slavery expanded slowly in this region. Charleston and the interior of South Carolina followed a different path. Settled first by planters from Barbados in 1670, this colony developed an economy based on plantations and slavery in imitation of the colonies of the Caribbean and Brazil. In 1729 North and South Carolina became separate colonies.

Despite an unhealthy climate, the prosperous rice and indigo plantations near Charleston attracted both free immigrants and increasing numbers of African slaves. African slaves were present from the founding of Charleston and were instrumental in introducing irrigated rice agriculture along the coastal lowlands. They were also crucial to developing plantations of indigo (a plant that produced a blue dye) at higher elevations away from the coast. Many slaves were given significant responsibilities. As one planter sending two slaves and their families to a frontier region put it: "[They] are likely young people, well acquainted with Rice & every kind of plantation business, and in short [are] capable of the management of a plantation themselves."[3]

As profits from rice and indigo rose, the importation of African slaves created a black majority in South Carolina. African languages, as well as African religious beliefs and diet, strongly influenced this unique colonial culture. Gullah, a dialect with African and English roots, evolved as the common idiom of the Carolina coast. Africans played a major role in South Carolina's largest slave uprising, the Stono Rebellion of 1739. After a group of about twenty slaves, many of them African Catholics who sought to flee south to Spanish Florida, seized firearms, about a hundred slaves from nearby plantations joined them. The colonial militia defeated the rebels and executed many of them, but the rebellion shocked slave owners throughout England's southern colonies and led to greater repression.

Colonial South Carolina was the most hierarchical society in British North America. Planters controlled the economy and political life. The richest families maintained impressive households in Charleston, the largest city in the southern colonies, as well as on their plantations in the countryside. Small farmers, cattlemen, artisans, merchants, and fur traders held an intermediate but clearly subordinate social position. Native peoples continued to participate in colonial society but lost ground from the effects of epidemic disease and warfare. As in colonial Latin America, a large mixed population blurred racial and cultural boundaries. On the frontier, the children of white men and Amerindian women held an important place in the fur trade. In the plantation regions and Charleston, the offspring of white men and black women often held preferred positions within the slave work force.

New England

Pilgrims Group of English Protestant dissenters who established Plymouth Colony in Massachusetts in 1620 to seek religious freedom after having lived briefly in the Netherlands.

Puritans English Protestant dissenters who believed that God predestined souls to heaven or hell before birth. They founded Massachusetts Bay Colony in 1629.

The colonization of New England by two separate groups of Protestant dissenters, Pilgrims and Puritans, put the settlement of this region on a different course. The **Pilgrims**, who came first, wished to break completely with the Church of England, which they believed was still essentially Catholic. As a result, in 1620 approximately one hundred settlers—men, women, and children—established the colony of Plymouth on the coast of present-day Massachusetts. Although nearly half of the settlers died during the first winter, the colony survived until 1691, when the larger Massachusetts Bay Colony of the Puritans absorbed Plymouth.

The **Puritans** wished to "purify" the Church of England, not break with it. They wanted to abolish its hierarchy of bishops and priests, free it from governmental interference, and limit membership to people who shared their beliefs. Subjected to increased discrimination in England for their efforts to transform the church, large numbers of Puritans began emigrating from England in 1630.

Dissenters and Merchants of Massachusetts

The Puritan leaders of the Massachusetts Bay Company—the joint-stock company that had received a royal charter to finance the Massachusetts Bay Colony—carried the company charter with them from England to Massachusetts. By bringing the charter, which spelled out company rights and obligations as well as the direction of company government, they limited Crown efforts to control them. By 1643 more than twenty thousand Puritans had settled in the Bay Colony.

Immigration to Massachusetts differed from immigration to the Chesapeake and to South Carolina. Most newcomers to Massachusetts arrived with their families. Whereas 84 percent of Virginia's white population in 1625 was male, Massachusetts had a normal gender balance in its population almost from the beginning. It was also the healthiest of England's colonies. The result was a rapid natural increase in population. The population of Massachusetts quickly became more "American" than the population of southern or Caribbean colonies, whose survival depended on a steady flow of English immigrants and slaves to counter high mortality rates. Massachusetts also was more homogeneous and less hierarchical than the southern colonies.

Political institutions evolved from the terms of the company charter. Settlers elected a governor and a council of magistrates drawn from the board of directors of the Massachusetts Bay Company. By 1650, disagreements between this council and elected representatives of the towns led to the creation of a lower legislative house that selected its own speaker and developed procedures and rules similar to those of the House of Commons in England. The result was much greater autonomy and greater local political involvement than in the colonies of Latin America.

Economically, Massachusetts differed dramatically from the southern colonies. Agriculture met basic needs, but poor soils and harsh climate offered no opportunity to develop cash crops like tobacco or rice. To pay for imported tools, textiles, and other essentials, the colonists needed to discover some profit-making niche in the growing Atlantic market. Fur, timber, and fish provided the initial economic foundation, but New England's economic well-being soon depended on providing commercial and shipping services in a dynamic and far-flung commercial arena that included the southern colonies, the Caribbean islands, Africa, and Europe.

In Spanish and Portuguese America, heavily capitalized monopolies (companies or individuals given exclusive economic privileges) dominated international trade. In New England, by

AP* Exam Tip Colonial trade systems are a possible comparison point on the exam.

contrast, individual merchants survived by discovering smaller but more sustainable profits in diversified trade across the Atlantic. The colony's commercial success rested on market intelligence, flexibility, and streamlined organization. Urban population growth suggests the success of this development strategy. With sixteen thousand inhabitants in 1740, Boston, the capital of Massachusetts Bay Colony, was the largest city in British North America.

Lacking a profitable agricultural export like tobacco, New England did not develop the extreme social stratification of the southern plantation colonies. Slaves and indentured servants were present, but in very small numbers. While New England was ruled by the richest colonists and shared the racial attitudes of the southern colonies, it also was the colonial society with fewest differences in wealth and status and with the most uniformly British and Protestant population in the Americas.

Iroquois Confederacy An alliance of five northeastern Amerindian peoples (six after 1722) that made decisions on military and diplomatic issues through a council of representatives. Allied first with the Dutch and later with the English, the Confederacy dominated the area from western New England to the Great Lakes.

The Middle Atlantic Region

Diversity and Dynamism of New York and Pennsylvania

Much of the future success of English-speaking America was rooted in the rapid economic development and remarkable cultural diversity that appeared in the Middle Atlantic colonies. In 1624 the Dutch West India Company established the colony of New Netherland and located its capital on Manhattan Island. Although poorly managed and underfinanced from the start, the colony commanded the potentially profitable and strategically important Hudson River. Dutch merchants established trading relationships with the **Iroquois Confederacy**—an alliance among the Mohawk, Oneida, Onondaga, Cayuga, and Seneca peoples—and with other native peoples that gave them access to the rich fur trade of Canada. When confronted by an English military expedition in 1664, the Dutch surrendered without a fight. James, duke of York and later King James II of England, became proprietor of the colony, which was renamed New York.

Tumultuous politics and corrupt public administration characterized New York, but the development of New York City as a commercial and shipping center guaranteed the colony's success. Located at the mouth of the Hudson River, the city played an essential role in connecting the region's grain farmers to the booming markets of the Caribbean and southern Europe.

"Johnson Hall," by E. L. Henry. Courtesy, Albany Institute of History and Art

The Home of Sir William Johnson, British Superintendent for Indian Affairs, Northern District As the colonial era drew to a close, the British attempted to limit the cost of colonial defense by negotiating land settlements with native peoples, but the growing tide of western migration doomed these agreements. William Johnson (1715–1774) maintained a fragile peace along the northern frontier by building strong personal relations with influential leaders of the Mohawk and other members of the Iroquois Confederacy. His home in present-day Johnstown, New York, shows the mixed nature of the frontier—the relative opulence of the main house offset by the two defensive blockhouses built for protection.

By the early eighteenth century, New York Colony had a diverse population that included English colonists; Dutch, German, and Swedish settlers; and a large slave community.

Pennsylvania began as a proprietary colony and as a refuge for Quakers, a persecuted religious minority. Because the English king Charles II was indebted to his father, William Penn secured an enormous grant of territory (nearly the size of England) in 1682. As proprietor (owner) of the land, Penn had sole right to establish a government, subject only to the requirement that he provide for an assembly of freemen.

Penn quickly lost control of the colony's political life, but the colony enjoyed remarkable success. By 1700 Pennsylvania had a population of more than 21,000, and Philadelphia, its capital, soon passed Boston to become the largest city in the British colonies. Healthy climate, excellent land, relatively peaceful relations with native peoples (prompted by Penn's emphasis on negotiation rather than warfare), and access through Philadelphia to good markets led to rapid economic and demographic growth in the colony.

Both Pennsylvania and South Carolina were grain-exporting colonies, but they were very different societies. South Carolina's rice plantations required large numbers of slaves. In Pennsylvania free workers produced the bulk of the colony's grain crops on family farms. As a result, Pennsylvania's economic expansion in the late seventeenth century occurred without reproducing South Carolina's hierarchical and repressive social order. By the early eighteenth century, however, the prosperous city of Philadelphia did have a large population of black slaves and freedmen. Many were servants in the homes of wealthy merchants, but the fast-growing economy offered many opportunities in skilled trades as well.

French America

Patterns of French settlement more closely resembled those of Spain and Portugal than of England. The French were committed to missionary activity among Amerindian peoples and emphasized the extraction of natural resources—furs rather than minerals. Between 1534 and 1542 the navigator and promoter Jacques Cartier explored the region of Newfoundland and the Gulf of St. Lawrence in three voyages. A contemporary of Cortés and Pizarro, Cartier hoped to find mineral wealth, but the stones he brought back to France turned out to be quartz and iron pyrite, "fool's gold."

New France French colony in North America, with a capital in Quebec, founded 1608. New France fell to the British in 1763.

The French waited more than fifty years before establishing settlements in North America. Coming to Canada after spending years in the West Indies, Samuel de Champlain founded the colony of **New France** at Quebec (kwuh-BEC), on the banks of the St. Lawrence River, in 1608. This location provided ready access to Amerindian trade routes, but it also compelled French settlers to take sides in the region's ongoing warfare. Champlain allied New France with the Huron and Algonquin peoples, traditional enemies of the powerful Iroquois Confederacy. Although French firearms and armor at first tipped the balance of power to France's native allies, the Iroquois Confederacy proved to be a resourceful and persistent enemy.

The Fur Trade

coureurs de bois French fur traders, many of mixed Amerindian heritage, who lived among and often married with Amerindian peoples of North America.

The European market for fur, especially beaver, fueled French settlement. Young Frenchmen were sent to live among native peoples to master their languages and customs. These **coureurs de bois** (koo-RUHR day BWA), or runners of the woods, often began families with indigenous women. Their mixed children, called métis (may-TEES), helped direct the fur trade. Amerindians actively participated in the trade because they came to depend on the goods they received in exchange for furs—firearms, metal tools, textiles, and alcohol. This change in the material culture of native peoples led to overhunting, which rapidly transformed the environment and led to the depletion of beaver and deer populations. It also increased competition among native peoples for hunting grounds, thus promoting warfare.

The proliferation of firearms made indigenous warfare more deadly. The Iroquois Confederacy responded to the increased military strength of France's Algonquin allies by forging commercial and military links with Dutch and later English settlements along the Hudson River. Now well armed, the Iroquois Confederacy nearly eradicated the Huron in 1649 and inflicted a series of humiliating defeats on the French. At the high point of their power in the early 1680s, Iroquois hunters and military forces gained control of much of the Great Lakes region and the Ohio River Valley. A large French military expedition and a relentless attack focused on Iroquois villages and agriculture finally checked Iroquois power in 1701.

Frances Anne Hopkins, "Shooting the Rapids," Library and Archives Canada, Ref. # C-2774

Canadian Fur Traders The fur trade provided the economic foundation of early Canadian settlement. Fur traders were cultural intermediaries. They brought European technologies and products like firearms and machine-made textiles to native peoples and native technologies and products like canoes and furs to European settlers. This canoe with sixteen paddlers was adapted from the native craft by fur traders to transport large cargoes.

The Catholic Church in Canada

In French Canada, the Jesuits led the effort to convert native peoples to Christianity as they had in Brazil and Paraguay. Missionaries mastered native languages, created boarding schools for young boys and girls, and set up model agricultural communities for converted Amerindians. The Jesuits' greatest successes coincided with a destructive wave of epidemics and renewed warfare among native peoples in the 1630s. Eventually, they established churches throughout Huron and Algonquin territories. Nevertheless, native culture persisted. In 1688 a French nun who had devoted her life to instructing Amerindian girls expressed her frustration with the resilience of indigenous culture:

> *We have observed that of a hundred that have passed through our hands we have scarcely civilized one. . . . When we are least expecting it, they clamber over our wall and go off to run with their kinsmen in the woods, finding more to please them there than in all the amenities of our French house.*[4]

Even though the fur trade flourished, population growth was slow. Founded at about the same time as French Canada, Virginia had twenty times more European residents by 1627. Canada's small settler population and the fur trade's dependence on the voluntary participation of Amerindians allowed indigenous peoples to retain greater independence and more control over their traditional lands than was possible in the colonies of Spain, Portugal, or England. Unlike these colonial regimes, which sought to transform ancient ways of life or force the transfer of native lands, the French were compelled to treat indigenous peoples as allies and trading partners.

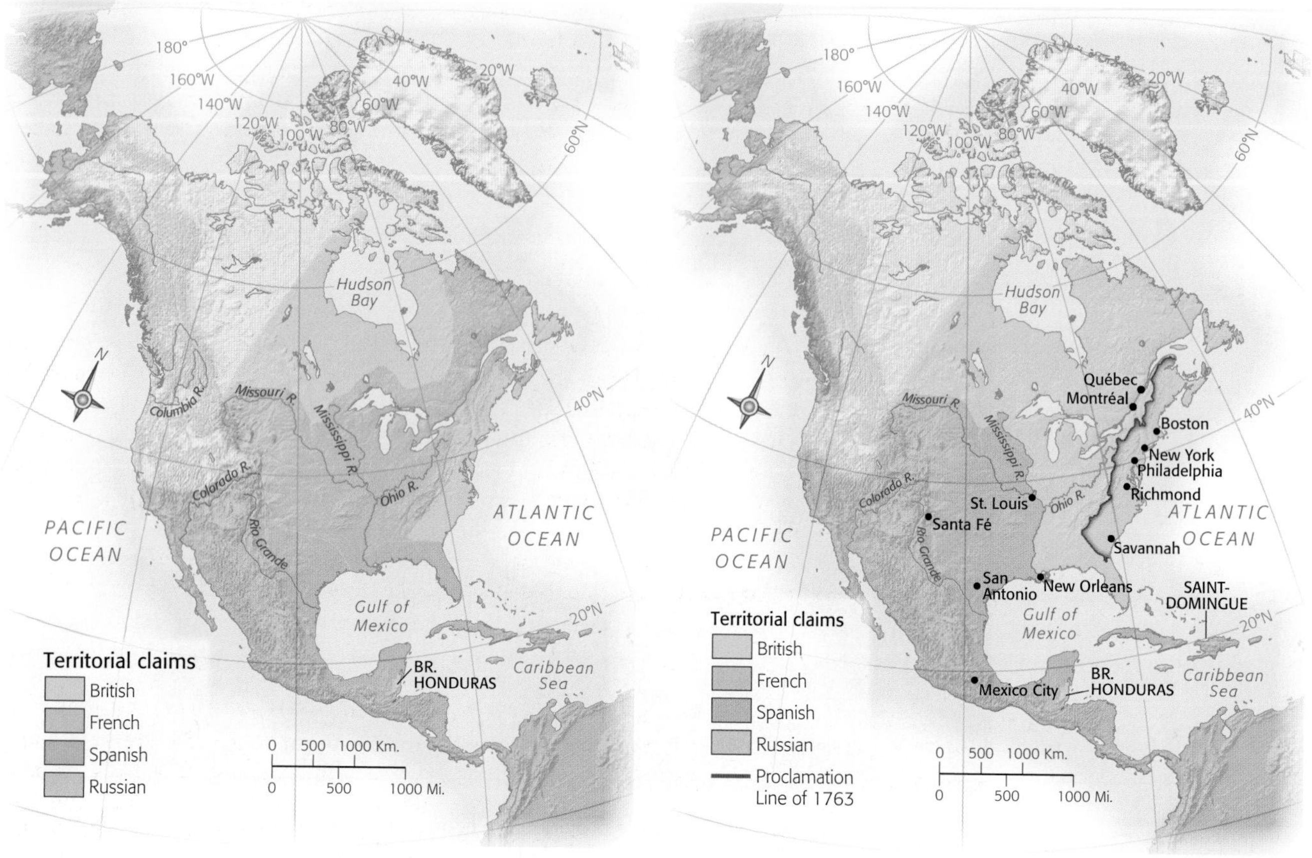

MAP 17.2 European Claims in North America, 1755–1763 The results of the French and Indian War dramatically altered the map of North America. France's losses precipitated conflicts between Amerindian peoples and the rapidly expanding population of the British colonies.

Interactive Map

French Colonial Expansion

Despite Canada's small population and limited resources, the French aggressively expanded to the west and south. They founded Louisiana in 1699, but by 1708 there were fewer than three hundred soldiers, settlers, and slaves in the territory. Like Canada, Louisiana depended on the fur trade and on alliances with Amerindian peoples who became dependent on European goods. In 1753 a French official reported a Choctaw leader as saying, "[The French] were the first . . . who made [us] subject to the different needs that [we] can no longer now do without."[5]

France's North American colonies were threatened by wars between France and England and by the population growth and increasing prosperity of neighboring English colonies. The "French and Indian War" that began in 1754 led to the wider conflict called the Seven Years War, 1756–1763, that determined the fate of French Canada (see Map 17.2). England committed a larger military force to the struggle and, despite early defeats, took the French capital of Quebec in 1759. The peace agreement forced France to yield Canada to the English and cede Louisiana to Spain. Amerindian populations soon recognized the difference between the

SECTION REVIEW

- Without Latin America's wealth in silver, gold, and sugar, British North American colonies developed strong regional characters and strong local political traditions.
- British colonies attracted large numbers of free immigrants, but indentured servitude and slavery were crucial to economic development.
- The southern colonies' dependence on forced labor and plantation agriculture led to a society that was more hierarchical and less democratic that those found in the colonies of New England and the Middle Atlantic region.
- With small population and limited resources, French colonies in North America depended on political and military alliances and commercial relations with native peoples.
- Eventually England defeated France and gained control of North America east of the Mississippi.

English and the French. One Canadian indigenous leader commented to a British officer after the French surrender: "We learn that our lands are to be given away not only to trade thereon but also . . . in full title to various [English] individuals. . . . We have always been a free nation, and now we will become slaves, which would be very difficult to accept after having enjoyed our liberty so long."[6] With the loss of Canada the French concentrated their efforts on their sugar-producing colonies in the Caribbean (see Chapter 18).

COLONIAL EXPANSION AND CONFLICT

Beginning in the last decades of the seventeenth century, nearly all the European colonies in the Americas experienced economic expansion and population growth. In the next century, the imperial powers responded by strengthening administrative and economic control of their colonies. They also sought to force colonial populations to pay a larger share of the costs of administration and defense. These efforts at reform and restructuring coincided with a series of imperial wars fought along Atlantic trade routes and in the Americas. France's loss of its North American colonies in 1763 was one of the most important results of these struggles. Equally significant, colonial populations throughout the Americas became more aware of separate national identities and more aggressive in asserting local interests against the will of distant monarchs.

Imperial Reform in Spanish America and Brazil

Spain's Habsburg dynasty ended when Charles II died without an heir in 1700 (see Table 16.1 on page 478). After thirteen years of conflict involving the major European powers, Philip of Bourbon, grandson of Louis XIV of France, gained the Spanish throne. Under Philip V and his heirs, Spain reorganized its administration and tax collection and liberalized colonial trade policies. Spain also created new commercial monopolies and strengthened its navy to protect colonial trade.

For most of the Spanish Empire, the eighteenth century was a period of remarkable economic expansion associated with population growth. Amerindian populations began to recover from the early epidemics; the flow of Spanish immigrants increased; and the slave trade to plantation colonies was expanded. Mining production increased, with silver production rising steadily into the 1780s. Agricultural exports also expanded, especially exports of tobacco, dyes, hides, chocolate, cotton, and sugar.

The Spanish and Portuguese kings also sought to reduce the power of the Catholic Church while at the same time transferring some church wealth to their treasuries. These efforts led to a succession of confrontations between colonial officials and the church hierarchy. To the kings of Portugal and Spain, the Jesuits symbolized the independent power of the church. This led the Portuguese king to expel this powerful order from his territories in 1759. The Spanish king followed this decision in 1767. In practice these actions forced many colonial-born Jesuits from their native lands and closed the schools that had educated many members of the colonial elite.

Colonial Grievances and Rebellion

Bourbon political and fiscal reforms also contributed to a growing sense of colonial grievance by limiting creoles' access to colonial offices and by imposing new taxes and monopolies that transferred more colonial wealth to Spain. Consumer and producer resentment in the colonies led to a series of violent confrontations with Spanish administrators. Colonial residents viewed the reforms as a more intrusive and expensive colonial government that overturned the informal constitution that had long governed the empire. However, the Spanish effort to recruit local elites as military officers to improve imperial defense offered some colonial residents a compensatory opportunity for higher social status and greater responsibility.

Tupac Amaru II Member of Inca aristocracy who led a rebellion against Spanish authorities in Peru in 1780–1781. He was captured and executed with his wife and other members of his family.

In addition to tax rebellions and urban riots, colonial reforms also provoked Amerindian uprisings. In 1780 the Peruvian Amerindian leader José Gabriel Condorcanqui began the largest rebellion. He assumed the name of his Inca ancestor Tupac Amaru (TOO-pack a-MAH-roo), whom the Spanish executed in 1572. Although a hereditary Quechua leader, **Tupac Amaru II** received his education from the Jesuits and had close ties to the local bishop and other powerful colonial authorities. He was also actively involved in colonial trade. Tupac Amaru II did not clearly state whether he sought to end local injustices or overthrow Spanish rule, but he clearly

Sir Henry Chamberlain, *Views and Costumes of the City and Neighborhoods of Rio de Janeiro*, London, 1822

Market in Rio de Janeiro In many of the cities of colonial Latin America, female slaves and black free women dominated retail markets. In this scene from late colonial Brazil, Afro-Brazilian women sell a variety of foods and crafts.

sought to redress the grievances of Amerindian communities who suffered from the mita and from taxes. As his rebellion spread, he attracted creoles, mestizos, and slaves as well as Amerindians to his cause. After his capture in 1781, the Spanish brutally executed Tupac Amaru II along with his wife and fifteen other family members and allies. By the time Spanish authority was firmly reestablished, more than 100,000 lives had been lost and enormous amounts of property destroyed.

Brazil also experienced a similar period of expansion and reform after 1700. Portugal created new administrative positions and gave monopoly companies exclusive rights to little-developed regions. As in Spanish America, a more intrusive colonial government that imposed new taxes led to rebellions and plots, including open warfare in 1707 between local-born "sons of the soil" and "outsiders" in São Paulo. The most aggressive period of reform occurred during the ministry of the marquis of Pombal (1750–1777). The discovery in Brazil of gold in the 1690s and diamonds after 1720 financed the reforms. Brazil's exports of minerals as well as coffee and cotton deepened dependence on the slave trade, and nearly 2 million African slaves were imported in the eighteenth century.

Reform and Reorganization in British America

England's efforts to reform and reorganize its North American colonies began earlier than the Bourbon initiative in Spanish America. After the period of Cromwell's Puritan Republic (see Chapter 16), the restored Stuart king, Charles II, undertook an ambitious campaign to establish greater control over the colonies. Between 1651 and 1673 a series of Navigation Acts sought to severely limit colonial trading and colonial production that competed directly with English manufacturers. England also attempted to increase royal control over colonial political life by replacing colonial charters and proprietorships. Because the king viewed the New England colonies as centers of smuggling, he temporarily suspended their elected assemblies while appointing colonial governors and granting them new fiscal and legislative powers.

Settler Resistance in British North America

James II's overthrow in the Glorious Revolution of 1688 ended this confrontation, but not before colonists were provoked to resist and, in some cases, rebel. Colonials overthrew the governors of New York and Massachusetts and removed the Catholic proprietor of Maryland. William and Mary restored relative peace, but these conflicts alerted colonials to the potential aggression of the English government. Colonial politics would remain confrontational until the American Revolution.

During the eighteenth century the English colonies experienced renewed economic growth and attracted a new wave of European immigration, but social divisions were increasingly evident. The colonial population in 1770 was more urban, more clearly divided by class and race, and more vulnerable to economic downturns. Crises were provoked when imperial wars with France and Spain disrupted trade in the Atlantic, increased tax burdens, forced military mobilizations, and provoked frontier conflicts with the Amerindians. On the eve of the American Revolution, England defeated France and weakened Spain. The cost, however, was great. Administrative, military, and tax policies imposed to gain this empire-wide victory alienated much of the American colonial population.

SECTION REVIEW

- In the eighteenth century all European imperial powers attempted to impose reforms on their American colonies.
- Colonial reforms disrupted colonial economic and political accommodations and led to rebellion and resistance.

CONCLUSION

The New World colonial empires of Spain, Portugal, France, and England had many characteristics in common. All subjugated Amerindian peoples and introduced large numbers of enslaved Africans. Within all four empires European settlement and the introduction of Old World animals and plants altered the natural environment. Europeans also introduced Old World diseases, such as smallpox, that had a devastating effect on the native populations. Colonists in all four applied the technologies of the Old World to the resources of the New, producing mineral and agricultural wealth and exploiting the commercial possibilities of the emerging Atlantic market in ways that accelerated the integration of Europe, Asia, and America.

Each of the New World empires also reflected the distinctive cultural and institutional heritages of its colonizing power. Mineral wealth allowed Spain to develop the most centralized empire, with political and economic power concentrated in great cities like Mexico City and Lima. Portugal and France pursued objectives similar to Spain's, but neither Brazil's agricultural economy, based on sugar, nor France's Canadian fur trade produced the financial resources and levels of centralized control achieved by Spain. Nevertheless, unlike Britain, all three of these Catholic powers were able to impose and enforce significant levels of religious and cultural uniformity.

Greater cultural and religious diversity characterized British North America. Immigrants came to the colonies from the British Isles, including all of Britain's religious traditions, as well as from Germany, Sweden, the Netherlands, and France. British colonial government varied somewhat from colony to colony and was more responsive to local interests. Thus colonists in British North America were better able than those in the areas controlled by Spain, Portugal, and France to respond to changing economic and political circumstances and to influence government policies. Most importantly, the British colonies attracted many more European immigrants than did the other New World colonies. Between 1580 and 1760 French colonies received 60,000 European immigrants, Brazil 523,000, and the Spanish colonies 678,000. Within a shorter period—between 1600 and 1760—the British settlements welcomed 746,000. Population in British North America—free and slave combined—had reached an extraordinary 2.5 million by 1775.

KEY TERMS

Columbian Exchange p. 490
Bartolomé de Las Casas p. 496
Potosí p. 496
encomienda p. 498
creoles p. 499
mestizo p. 503
mulatto p. 503
indentured servant p. 504
House of Burgesses p. 505
Pilgrims p. 506
Puritans p. 506
Iroquois Confederacy p. 507
New France p. 508
coureurs de bois p. 508
Tupac Amaru II p. 511

EBOOK AND WEBSITE RESOURCES

Primary Source

General History of the Things in New Spain

Interactive Maps

Map 17.1 Colonial Latin America in the Eighteenth Century

Map 17.2 European Claims in North America, 1755–1763

Plus flashcards, practice quizzes, and more. Go to: www.cengage.com/history/bullietearthpeople5e

SUGGESTED READING

Bailyn, Bernard. *The Origins of American Politics*. 1986. A helpful introduction to early American politics.

Blackburn, Carole. *Harvest of Souls: The Jesuit Missions and Colonialism in North America, 1632–1650*. 2000. An essential examination of the conversion efforts in French Canada.

Burkholder, Mark A., and Lyman L. Johnson. *Colonial Latin America*, 5th ed. 2005. Provides a good introduction to early Latin America.

Bushman, Richard. *King and People in Provincial Massachusetts*. 1985. A strong discussion of politics in late colonial New England.

Crosby, Alfred W., Jr. *The Columbian Exchange: Biological and Cultural Consequences of 1492*. 1972. *Ecological Imperialism*. 1986. Pioneering works in the study of cross-Atlantic history.

Curtin, Philip D. *The Rise and Fall of the Plantation Complex*. 1990. Excellent introduction to the Atlantic system.

Davis, David Brion. *The Problem of Slavery in Western Culture*. 1966. A classic study of this topic from a broad perspective.

Eccles, William J. *France in America*, rev. ed. 1990. An excellent overview of French colonialism in North America.

Elliott, J. H. *Empires of the Atlantic World*. 2006. A masterful comparative study of European New World empires.

Eltis, David. *The Rise of African Slavery in the Americas*. 2000.

Fischer, David Hackett. *Albion's Seed: Four British Folkways in America*. 1989. A general study of the British colonies.

Gallay, Alan. *The Indian Slave Trade: The Rise of the English Empire in the American South, 1670–1717*. 2002. An important examination of the Indian slave trade and its consequences.

Klein, Herbert S. *The Atlantic Slave Trade*. 1999.

McAlister, Lyle N. *Spain and Portugal in the New World, 1492–1700*. 1984. A useful introduction to the era of Iberian rule.

Melville, Elinor G. K. *A Plague of Sheep: Environmental Consequences of the Spanish Conquest of Mexico*. 1994. Looks at what happens when a new domestic species is introduced.

Miller, Shawn William. *An Environmental History of Latin America*. 2007. The first three chapters provide an excellent introduction to environmental change in the colonial period.

Nash, Gary B. *Red, White, and Black: The Peoples of Early America*, 5th ed. 2005. Studies the complexity of colonial society in North America.

Schwartz, Stuart B. *Sugar Plantations in the Formation of Brazilian Society: Bahia, 1550–1835*. 1985. This book remains the best analysis of the Brazilian sugar sector.

Serulnikov, Sergio. *Subverting Colonial Authority*. 2003. An excellent study of native rebellions in late colonial Spanish America.

Taylor, William. *Magistrates of the Sacred: Priests and Parishioners in Eighteenth-Century Mexico*. 1996. An essential study of the colonial church in Mexico.

Usner, Daniel H., Jr. *Indians, Settlers, and Slaves in a Frontier Exchange Economy: The Lower Mississippi Valley Before 1783*. 1992. One of the most useful examinations of the intersection of indigenous peoples and European empires.

NOTES

1. Quoted in Alfred W. Crosby, Jr., *The Columbian Exchange: Biological and Cultural Consequences of 1492* (Westport, CT: Greenwood, 1972), 58.
2. Fray Andés de Moguer, 1554, quoted in James Lockhart and Enrique Otte, eds., *Letters and People of the Spanish Indies Sixteenth Century* (1976), 216.
3. Crosby, *The Columbian Exchange*, 58.
4. Quoted in R. Douglas Francis, Richard Jones, and Donald B. Smith, *Origins: Canadian History to Confederation* (Toronto: Holt, Rinehart, and Winston of Canada, 1992), 52.
5. Quoted in Daniel H. Usner, Jr., *Indians, Settlers and Slaves in a Frontier Exchange Economy: The Lower Mississippi Valley Before 1783*, Institute of Early American History and Culture Series (Chapel Hill: University of North Carolina Press, 1992), 96.
6. Quoted in Cornelius J. Jaenen, "French and Native Peoples in New France," in *Interpreting Canada's Past*, ed. J. M. Bumsted, vol. 1, 2nd ed. (Toronto: Oxford University Press, 1993), 73.

AP* REVIEW QUESTIONS FOR CHAPTER 17

1. In Mexico, the most devastating effect of the Columbian Exchange was
   (A) the introduction of African slavery.
   (B) the increase in famine and water shortages.
   (C) smallpox, which may have killed 50 percent or more of the Amerindian population in Mexico and Central America.
   (D) the introduction of large-scale cash crop farming.

2. In contrast to Spanish settlement in the New World, Portuguese settlement in Brazil
   (A) depended on how much money Portugal received from the Asian spice trade and allocated to spending in Brazil.
   (B) was able to develop without any government interference from Portugal.
   (C) failed because of diseases and native attacks on the settlements.
   (D) was limited mainly to coastal regions.

3. In both Spanish colonies and in Portuguese Brazil,
   (A) the Catholic Church was the primary agent for the transmission of Christian belief as well as European language and culture.
   (B) joint-stock companies sold land to settlers.
   (C) other than the viceroy, officials were elected by the wealthy landowners.
   (D) baptism of the Amerindians was forbidden.

4. The most influential defender of the Amerindians in the Spanish colonies was
   (A) the Council of the Indies.
   (B) Bartolomé de Las Casas.
   (C) Vasco Núñez de Balboa.
   (D) Hernán Cortés.

5. In the 1500s, the majority of the wealth in the American colonies came from
   (A) growing cash crops such as tobacco.
   (B) the importation of African slaves.
   (C) the sale of finished goods to the Amerindians.
   (D) silver from the mines in Potosí.

6. In the Spanish colonies, the colonizers adopted
   (A) the native language of the Amerindians as the official language.
   (B) forced labor of the Amerindians.
   (C) the diet of the Amerindians, which was superior in nutrients.
   (D) laws and trade regulations devised by the Amerindians.

7. Unlike the Portuguese and Spanish settlements, the English settlements in North America
   (A) encouraged the use of indentured servants as their initial forced labor system.
   (B) brought slaves from Africa but did not use them in their colonies.
   (C) encouraged all settlers to enslave Amerindians as a labor force.
   (D) never adopted a forced labor system.

8. The first representative assembly in the New World was
   (A) Mexico's Governor's Council.
   (B) Brazil's Congress.
   (C) the House of Burgesses in Virginia.
   (D) the French government's council in Quebec.

9. Unlike the settlements in the Chesapeake Bay region and the Carolinas, settlements in Massachusetts, Connecticut, and Rhode Island
   (A) were made up mainly of males for the first two decades.
   (B) encouraged intermarriage with the natives.
   (C) had a normal gender balance.
   (D) had low mortality rates from the start.

10. Unlike in the Spanish and Portuguese colonies, in the English colonies
    (A) women had political and civil rights.
    (B) taxation was local, and no taxes were assessed on exports.
    (C) trade with the Amerindians was not lucrative.
    (D) merchants engaged in more trade across the Atlantic.

11. Unlike the English colonies, the French colonies in the Americas

(A) resembled the settlement patterns of the Spanish and Portuguese colonies.
(B) existed without much direct aid from the French government.
(C) had few French soldiers due to the decimation of the Amerindian population.
(D) avoided the use of slavery, which they viewed as a sin.

12. By the late 1700s, the wealthiest and most influential of Spain's colonial societies had come to view the Spanish government as

(A) the homeland and savior of the economy.
(B) the protector on foreign affairs and trade.
(C) an impediment to growth and prosperity.
(D) a drain on natural resources.

13. Besides the occasional tax revolts and urban riots in the Spanish New World, the most dangerous internal threat to Spanish rule in the 1700s was

(A) the slave rebellion in Bolivia.
(B) the attempted secession of Argentina.
(C) the world economic downturn at the end of the century.
(D) pirates who raided in the Caribbean and looted Spanish shipping.

14. In comparison to the Spanish and Portuguese colonies of the Americas, the English colonies

(A) were unified by religion.
(B) were generally more diverse.
(C) were not sustainable over the long run.
(D) contained far more gold and silver deposits.

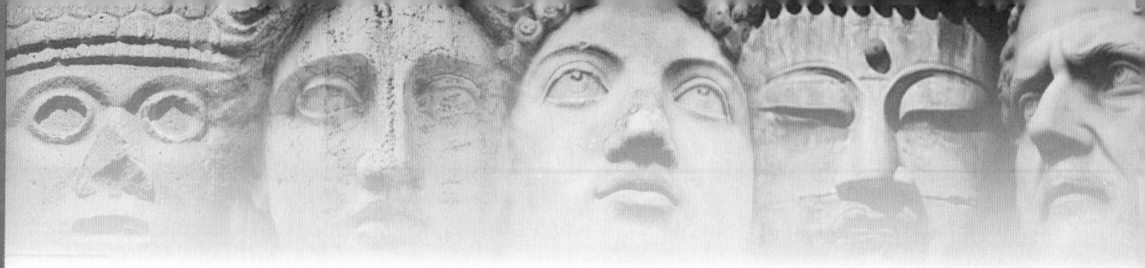

CHAPTER

18

CHAPTER OUTLINE

- Plantations in the West Indies
- Plantation Life in the Eighteenth Century
- Creating the Atlantic Economy
- Africa, the Atlantic, and Islam
- Conclusion

ENVIRONMENT + TECHNOLOGY *Amerindian Foods in Africa*

DIVERSITY + DOMINANCE *Slavery in West Africa and the Americas*

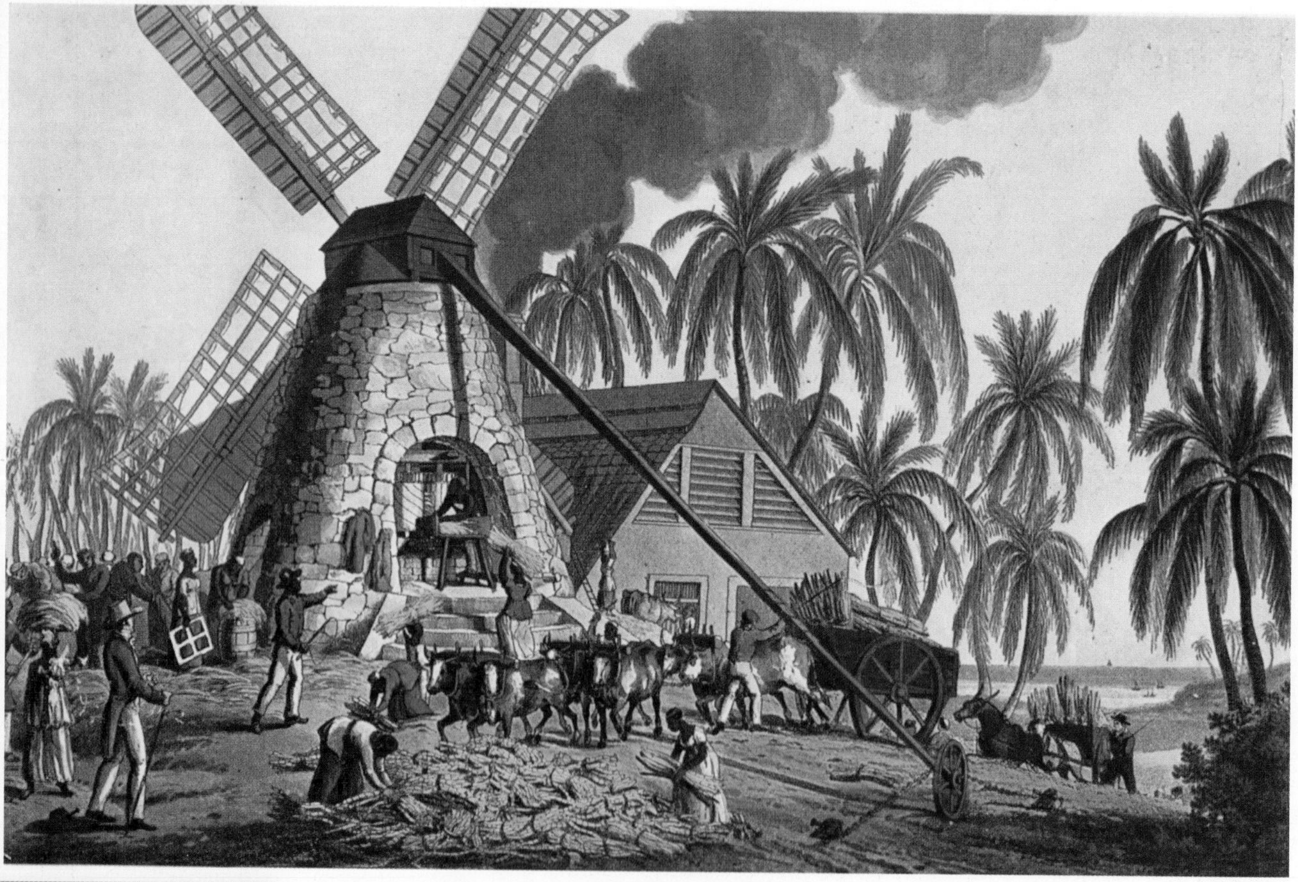

Caribbean Sugar Mill The windmill crushes sugar cane, whose juice is boiled down in the smoking building next door.

Visit the website and ebook for additional study materials and interactive tools: www.cengage.com/history/bullietearthpeople5e

The Atlantic System and Africa, 1550–1800

- How important was sugar production to the European colonies of the West Indies and to the expansion of the African slave trade?
- What effect did sugar plantations have on the natural environment and on living conditions?
- What was the relationship between private investors and European governments in the development of the Atlantic economy?
- How did sub-Saharan Africa's expanding contacts in the Atlantic compare with its contacts with the Islamic world?

By the eighteenth century, Caribbean colonies had become the largest producers of sugar in the world. Slaves represented about 90 percent of the islands' population and provided nearly all the labor for harvesting and processing sugar cane. The profitable expansion of sugar agriculture in the seventeenth century opened a new era in the African slave trade. As larger and faster ships carried growing numbers of slaves from Africa, the human cost escalated, as the following example demonstrates.

In 1694 the English ship *Hannibal* called at the West African port of Whydah (WEE-duh) to purchase slaves. The king of Whydah invited the ship's captain and officers to his residence, where they negotiated an agreement on the prices for slaves. In all, the *Hannibal* purchased 692 slaves, of whom about a third were women and girls. The ship's doctor then carefully inspected the naked captives to be sure they were of sound body, young, and free of disease. After their purchase, the slaves were branded with an H (for *Hannibal*) to establish ownership. Once they were loaded on the ship, the crew put shackles on the men to prevent their escape.

To keep the slaves healthy, the captain had the crew feed them twice a day on boiled corn meal and beans brought from Europe and flavored with hot peppers and palm oil purchased in Africa. Each slave received a pint (half a liter) of water with every meal. In addition, the slaves were made to "jump and dance for an hour or two to our bagpipe, harp, and fiddle" every evening to keep them fit. Despite the incentives and precautions for keeping the cargo alive, deaths were common among the hundreds of people crammed into every corner of a slave ship. The *Hannibal*'s experience was worse than most; it lost 320 slaves and 14 crew members to smallpox and dysentery during the seven-week voyage to Barbados.

As the *Hannibal*'s experience suggests, the Atlantic slave trade took a devastating toll in African lives and was far from a sure-fire money maker for European investors, who in this case lost more than £3,000 on the voyage. Nevertheless, the slave trade and plantation slavery were crucial pieces of a booming new **Atlantic system** that moved goods and wealth, as well as peoples and cultures, around the Atlantic.

Atlantic system The network of trading links after 1500 that moved goods, wealth, people, and cultures around the Atlantic Basin.

PLANTATIONS IN THE WEST INDIES

The West Indies was the first place in the Americas reached by Columbus, and it was also the first region in the Americas where native populations collapsed from epidemics. It took a long time to repopulate these islands and forge economic links with other parts of the Atlantic. But after 1650 sugar plantations, African slaves, and European capital made these islands a major center of the Atlantic economy.

Colonization Before 1650

Spanish settlers introduced sugar-cane cultivation into the West Indies shortly after 1500, but these colonies soon fell into neglect as attention shifted to colonizing the American mainland. After 1600 the West Indies revived as a focus of colonization, this time by northern Europeans interested in growing tobacco and other crops. In the 1620s and 1630s, English and French colonists settled many islands of the Antilles. With greater government support, the English colonies prospered first, largely by producing tobacco.

The Tobacco Era

Tobacco, a New World leaf long used by Amerindians for recreation and medicine, was finding a new market among seventeenth-century Europeans. Despite the opposition of individuals like King James I of England, who condemned tobacco smoke as "dangerous to the eye, hateful to the nose, harmful to the brain, and dangerous to the lungs," the habit spread. By 1614 seven thousand shops in and around London sold tobacco.

The first tobacco colonies suffered from diseases, hurricanes, and attacks by native Caribs and the Spanish. They also suffered from shortages of supplies from Europe and shortages of labor sufficient to clear land and plant tobacco. The governments of France and England controlled costs by allowing private investors organized as **chartered companies** to develop the colonies in exchange for monopoly control and annual fees. These companies provided passage to the colonies for poor Europeans who were obligated to work three or four years as indentured servants (see Chapter 17). As a result the French and English populations grew rapidly in the 1630s and 1640s. By the middle of the century, however, these Caribbean colonies were in crisis due to stiff competition from Virginia tobacco, also cultivated by indentured servants. Profits grew when the English, French, and Dutch colonies of the Caribbean switched from tobacco to sugar cane and from European indentured laborers to the labor of African slaves.

chartered companies Groups of private investors who paid an annual fee to France and England in exchange for a monopoly over trade to the West Indies colonies.

The Portuguese and the Dutch and Sugar

The Portuguese first developed sugar plantations that relied on African slaves on islands along the African coast. They later introduced this complex in Brazil (see Chapter 17). By 1600 Brazil was the Atlantic world's greatest sugar producer. The Dutch were early participants in the Brazilian sugar business as investors, merchants, and processors. Dutch independence from Spain early in the seventeenth century threatened this profitable commerce because the Spanish crown ruled Portugal and Brazil. As part of its struggle with Spain, the Dutch government chartered the **Dutch West India Company** in 1621. This powerful private trading company captured a Spanish treasure fleet in 1628 and used some of the windfall to finance an assault on Brazil's valuable sugar-producing areas. By 1635 the Dutch company controlled much of Brazil's sugar region. Over the next fifteen years the Dutch improved the efficiency of the Brazilian sugar industry and also profited from supplying African slaves and European goods.

Dutch West India Company Trading company chartered by the Dutch government to conduct its merchants' trade in the Americas and Africa.

Like its assault on Brazil, the Dutch West India Company's entry into the African slave trade combined economic and political motives. It seized the important West African trading station of Elmina from the Portuguese in 1638 and took their port of Luanda (loo-AHN-duh) on the Angolan coast in 1641. From these coasts the Dutch shipped slaves to Brazil and the West Indies. Although the Portuguese were able to drive the Dutch out of Angola after a few years, Elmina remained the Dutch West India Company's headquarters in West Africa.

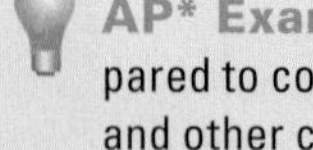

AP* Exam Tip Be prepared to compare slavery and other coercive labor systems for the exam.

Once free of Spanish rule in 1640, the Portuguese crown turned its attention to reconquering Brazil and by 1654 had driven the last of the Dutch from that country. Some of the expelled planters transplanted their capital and knowledge of sugar production to Dutch Caribbean colonies as well as to the English and French islands.

CHRONOLOGY

	West Indies	Atlantic	Africa
1500	ca. 1500 Spanish settlers introduce sugar-cane cultivation	1530 Amsterdam Exchange opens	1500–1700 Gold trade predominates
			1591 Morocco conquers Songhai
1600	1620s and 1630s English and French colonies in Caribbean	1621 Dutch West India Company chartered	1638 Dutch take Elmina
	1640s Dutch bring sugar plantation system from Brazil		
	1655 English take Jamaica	1654 Dutch expelled from Brazil	
		1660s English Navigation Acts	
	1670s French occupy western half of Hispaniola (modern Haiti)	1672 Royal African Company chartered	1680s Rise of Asante
		1698 French *Exclusif*	
1700	1700 West Indies surpass Brazil in sugar production	1700 to present Atlantic system flourishing	1700–1830 Slave trade predominates
		1713 English receive slave trade monopoly from Spanish Empire	1720s Rise of Dahomey
			1730 Oyo makes Dahomey pay tribute
	1760 Tacky's rebellion in Jamaica		

Sugar and Slaves

The infusion of Dutch expertise and money revived the French colonies of Guadeloupe and Martinique, but the English colony of Barbados best illustrates the dramatic transformation that sugar brought to the seventeenth-century Caribbean. In 1640 Barbados's economy depended largely on tobacco, mostly grown by European settlers, both free and indentured. By the 1680s sugar had become the principal crop and enslaved Africans were three times as numerous as Europeans. Exporting up to 15,000 tons of sugar a year, Barbados had become the wealthiest and most populous of England's American colonies. By 1700 Barbados and other West Indian colonies had collectively surpassed Brazil as the world's principal source of sugar.

The Slave Trade

The expansion of sugar plantations in the West Indies required a sharp increase in the volume of the slave trade from Africa (see Figure 18.1). During the first half of the seventeenth century about ten thousand slaves a year had arrived from Africa. Most were destined for Brazil and the mainland Spanish colonies. In the second half of the century the trade averaged twenty thousand slaves, and more than half landed in the English, French, and Dutch West Indies. A century later, as sugar production increased and the Spanish colony of Cuba became a major importer of slaves, the volume of the Atlantic slave trade tripled.

Indentured Servants

Cash-short tobacco planters in the seventeenth century preferred indentured Europeans to African slaves because they cost half as much. Poor European men and women were willing to work for little in order to get to the Americas, where they could acquire their own land cheaply at the end of their term of service. However, as the cultivation of sugar spread after 1750, speculators drove land prices in the West Indies so high that former indentured servants could no longer afford to buy land. As a result, poor Europeans chose to indenture themselves in Britain's North American colonies, where cheap land was still available. Rather than raise wages to attract European laborers, Caribbean sugar planters switched to slaves.

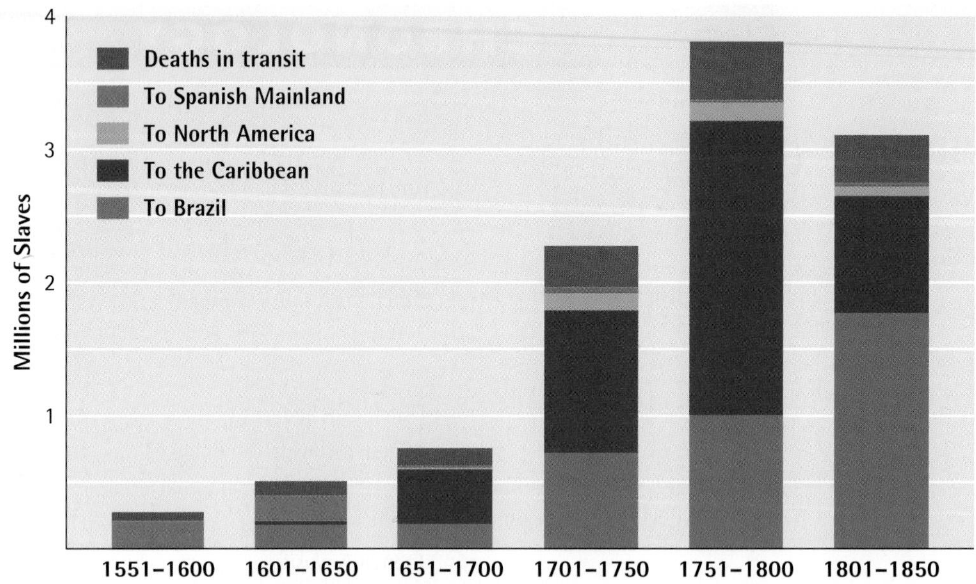

FIGURE 18.1 **Transatlantic Slave Trade from Africa, 1551–1850** *Source:* Data from David Eltis, "The Volume and Structure of the Transatlantic Slave Trade: A Reassessment," *William and Mary Quarterly*, 3rd Series, 58 (2001), tables II and III.

SECTION REVIEW

- England and France relied on private investors organized as chartered companies to develop their Caribbean colonies.
- European colonies in the Caribbean at first depended on tobacco exports but then concentrated on producing sugar, which was more profitable.
- The Dutch helped develop the sugar industry as investors, refiners, slave traders, and disseminators of technology.
- European indentured servants provided crucial labor for Caribbean plantations in the early years, but planters switched to African slaves when the flow of indentured laborers was redirected to North America.

Rising sugar prices helped the West Indian sugar planters afford the higher cost of African slaves. The fact that slaves lived seven years on average after their arrival, while the typical indentured labor contract was for only three or four years, also made slaves a better investment. Dutch and other traders responded to rising demand by increasing the flow of slaves to meet the needs of the expanding plantations (see Figure 18.1), but slave prices rose throughout the eighteenth century. These high labor costs were one more factor favoring large plantations over smaller operations.

PLANTATION LIFE IN THE EIGHTEENTH CENTURY

To find more land for sugar plantations, France and England expanded their Caribbean holdings by attacking older Spanish colonies. In 1655 the English seized Jamaica from the Spanish (see Map 17.1 on page 494). They also took Havana, Cuba, in 1762 and held the city for a year. By the time the occupation ended, English merchants had imported large numbers of slaves and Cuba had begun to switch from tobacco to sugar production. The French seized the western half of the Spanish island of Hispaniola in the 1670s. During the eighteenth century this new French colony of Saint Domingue (san doh-MANGH) (present-day Haiti) became the greatest producer of sugar in the Atlantic world, while Jamaica surpassed Barbados as England's most important sugar colony. The technological, environmental, and social transformation of these island colonies illustrates the power of the new Atlantic system.

Plantation Scene, Antigua, British West Indies The sugar made at the mill in the background was sealed in barrels and loaded on carts that oxen and horses drew to the beach. By means of a succession of vessels the barrels were taken to the ship that hauled the cargo to Europe. The importance of African labor is evident from the fact that only one white person appears in the painting.

Technology and Environment

AP* Exam Tip Be aware of human impact on the environment, such as the introduction of new plants and animals into a region.

Sugar production had both an agricultural and an industrial character. On both small farms and large plantations, growing and harvesting sugar cane required only simple tools like spades, hoes, and machetes. Once the cane was cut, however, a more complex and expensive process was needed to produce sugar. Slaves rushed the cane to mills, where it was crushed and the juice extracted. Lead-lined wooden troughs carried cane juice to a series of large copper kettles where excess water was boiled off, leaving thick syrup. Placed in conical clay molds, the syrup turned to crystallized sugar as it dried. The small refiners used crushing mills driven by animals or even laborers, while the large plantations used larger and more efficient mills that relied on wind or water power. These economies of scale meant that over time large producers had lower costs and greater profits.

Large Plantations

To make the operation more efficient and profitable, investors sought to utilize the costly crushing and refining machinery intensively. As a result, West Indian plantations expanded from an average of around 100 acres (40 hectares) in the seventeenth century to at least twice that size in the eighteenth century. Some plantations were even larger. In 1774 Jamaica's 680 sugar plantations averaged 441 acres (178 hectares), with the largest over 2,000 acres (800 hectares). Jamaica specialized so heavily in sugar production that the island had to import most of its food. Saint Domingue had a comparable number of plantations of smaller average size but generally higher productivity. The French colony was also more diverse in its economy. Although sugar production was paramount, some planters raised provisions for local consumption and crops such as coffee and cacao for export.

Plantations and the Environment

Sugar agriculture had a mixed environmental record. Some practices were not destructive. Planters powered their mills by water, wind, or animals and fueled their boilers by burning crushed cane. They fertilized their fields using manure from their cattle. Yet high profits led planters to exploit nature ruthlessly in other ways. Repeated cultivation of a single crop removes more nutrients from the soil than animal fertilizer and fallow periods can restore. Instead of rotating sugar with other crops to restore the nutrients naturally, planters found it more profitable to clear new lands when yields declined in the old fields. When land was exhausted, planters often moved on to new islands. Many of the English who settled Jamaica had been planters on Barbados. Similarly, the pioneer planters on Saint Domingue came from older French sugar colonies. In the second half of the eighteenth century, Jamaican sugar production began to fall behind Saint Domingue, which still had virgin land.

In addition to soil exhaustion and deforestation, the introduction of nonnative animals and cultivated plants transformed the Caribbean region. The Spanish brought cattle, pigs, and horses, which multiplied rapidly. They also introduced new plants. Bananas and plantains from the Canary Islands were a valuable addition to the food supply, and sugar and rice formed the basis of plantation agriculture, along with native tobacco. Other food crops arrived with the slaves from Africa, including okra, black-eyed peas, yams, grains such as millet and sorghum, and mangoes. Many of these new animals and plants were useful additions to the islands, but they crowded out indigenous species. New World foods also found their way to Africa (see Environment and Technology: Amerindian Foods in Africa).

The most tragic and dramatic transformation of the West Indies was demographic. Chapter 15 detailed how disease and abuse nearly eliminated the indigenous peoples of the large islands within fifty years of Columbus's first voyage. Far earlier and more completely than in any mainland colony, the West Indies were repeopled from across the Atlantic—first from Europe and then from Africa.

Slaves' Lives

plantocracy In the West Indian colonies, the rich men who owned most of the slaves and most of the land, especially in the eighteenth century.

During the eighteenth century West Indian plantation colonies were the world's most polarized societies. On most islands 90 percent or more of the inhabitants were slaves. Power resided in the hands of a **plantocracy**, a small number of very rich men who owned most of the slaves and most of the land. Between the slaves and the masters was a small middle group of estate managers, government officials, artisans, and small farmers, nearly all white. Some free blacks owned property or entered commerce. It is only a slight simplification to describe eighteenth-century Caribbean society as being made up of a large, abject class of slaves and a small, powerful class of masters.

The Organization of Slave Labor

The profitability of a Caribbean plantation depended on extracting as much work as possible from the slaves, and plantations achieved exceptional productivity through the threat and use of force. The slaves' long workday might stretch to eighteen hours or more when the cane harvest and milling were in full swing. As Table 18.1 shows, on a typical Jamaican plantation about 80 percent of the slaves were actively engaged in productive tasks; the only exceptions were infants, the seriously ill, and the very old.

Table 18.1 also illustrates how planters organized slaves by age, sex, and ability. Only 2 or 3 percent of the slaves were house servants. About 70 percent of the able-bodied slaves worked in the fields, generally in one of three labor gangs. A "great gang," made up of the strongest slaves in the prime of life, did the heaviest work, such as breaking up the soil at the beginning of the planting season. A second gang of youths, elders, and less fit slaves did somewhat lighter work. A "grass gang," composed of children under the supervision of an elderly slave, was responsible for weeding and other simple work, such as collecting grass for the animals. Women often formed the majority of the field laborers, even in the great gang. Nursing mothers took their babies with them to the fields. Slaves too old for field labor tended the toddlers.

Because the slave trade imported twice as many males as females, men outnumbered women on Caribbean plantations. As Table 18.1 shows, a little over half of adult males did non-gang work. Some tended livestock, and others were skilled craftsmen, such as blacksmiths and carpenters. The most important artisan slave was the head boiler, who oversaw the delicate process of reducing the cane sap to crystallized sugar and molasses.

The Treatment of Slaves

driver A privileged male slave whose job was to ensure that a slave gang did its work on a plantation.

Planters often rewarded skilled slaves with better-quality food and clothing or time off, but most slaves were compelled to work hard by fear of the lash. Slave gangs were led by a privileged male slave, appropriately called the "**driver**," whose job was to ensure that the gang completed its work. Since production quotas were high, slaves toiled in the fields from sunup to sunset, except for meal breaks. Those who fell behind due to fatigue or illness soon felt the sting of the whip. Planters punished openly rebellious slaves who refused to work, disobeyed orders, or tried to

ENVIRONMENT + TECHNOLOGY

Amerindian Foods in Africa

The migration of European plants and animals across the Atlantic to the New World was one side of the Columbian Exchange (see Chapter 17). The Andean potato, for example, became a staple crop of the poor in Europe, and cassava (a Brazilian plant cultivated for its edible roots) and maize (corn) moved across the Atlantic to Africa.

Maize was a high-yielding grain that could produce much more food per acre than many grains indigenous to Africa. The varieties of maize that spread to Africa were not modern highbred "sweet corn" but starchier types found in white and yellow corn meal. Cassava—not well known to modern North Americans except perhaps in the form of tapioca—became the most important New World food in Africa. Truly a marvel, cassava had the highest yield of calories per acre of any staple food and thrived even in poor soils and during droughts. Both the leaves and the root could be eaten. Ground into meal, the root could be made into a bread that would keep for up to six months, or it could be fermented into a beverage.

Cassava and maize were probably accidentally introduced into Africa by Portuguese ships from Brazil that discarded leftover supplies after reaching Angola. It did not take long for local Africans to recognize the food value of these new crops, especially in drought-prone areas. As the principal farmers in Central Africa, women must have played an important role in learning how to cultivate, harvest, and prepare these foods. By the eighteenth century Lunda rulers hundreds of miles from the Angolan coast were actively promoting the cultivation of maize and cassava on their royal estates in order to provide a more secure food supply.

Some historians of Africa believe that in the inland areas these Amerindian food crops provided the nutritional base for a population increase that partially offset losses due to the Atlantic slave trade. By supplementing the range of food crops available and by enabling populations to increase in lightly settled or famine-prone areas, cassava and maize, along with peanuts and other New World legumes, permanently altered Africans' environmental prospects.

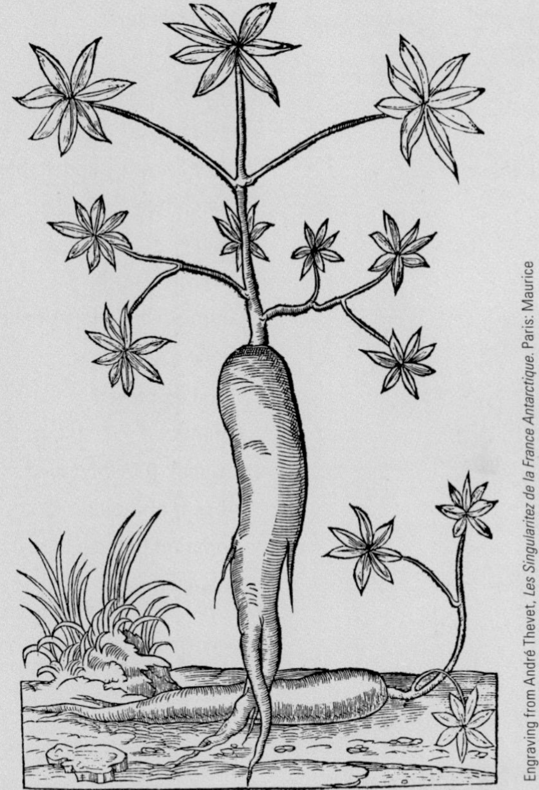

Engraving from André Thevet, *Les Singularitez de la France Antarctique*. Paris: Maurice de la Porte, 1557. Courtesy of the James Bell Library, University of Minnesota

Cassava Plant Both the leaves and the starchy root of the cassava plant could be eaten.

AP* Exam Tip It is important to understand slave systems in general, but not necessarily the details of a slave system in any specific nation.

escape with floggings, confinement in irons, or mutilation. While slaves usually did not work in the fields on Sunday, they could not rest, but had to use this time to farm their own provisioning grounds to supplement meager rations, maintain their dwellings, and do other chores, such as washing and mending their rough clothes.

Except for occasional holidays—including the Christmas-week revels in the British West Indies—there was little time for recreation and relaxation. Slaves might sing in the fields, but singing was simply a way to distract themselves from fatigue and the monotony of the work. There was certainly no time for schooling, nor were masters willing to educate slaves beyond skills useful to the plantation.

Slave Health

Time for family life was also inadequate. Although the large proportion of young adults in plantation colonies ought to have led to a high rate of natural increase, despite the sex imbalance that resulted from the slave trade, the opposite occurred. Poor nutrition and overwork lowered fertility. The continuation of heavy fieldwork made it difficult for a pregnant woman to carry a child to term or a mother to ensure an infant's survival. As a result of these conditions, along with disease and accidents from dangerous mill equipment, deaths heavily outnumbered births on West Indian plantations (see Table 18.2). Life expectancy for slaves in nineteenth-century

TABLE 18.1 Slave Occupations on a Jamaican Sugar Plantation, 1788

Occupations and Conditions	*Men*	*Women*	*Boys and Girls*	*Total*
Field laborers	62	78		140
Tradesmen	29			29
Field drivers	4			4
Field cooks		4		4
Mule-, cattle-, and stablemen	12			12
Watchmen	18			18
Nurse		1		1
Midwife		1		1
Domestics and gardeners		5	3	8
Grass-gang			20	20
Total employed	**125**	**89**	**23**	**237**
Infants			23	23
Invalids (18 with yaws)				32
Absent on roads				5
Superannuated [elderly]				7
Overall total				**304**

Source: From Michael Craton, James Walvin, and David Wright, eds., *Slavery, Abolition and Emancipation*, p. 103. Copyright © 1976. Reprinted by permission of Pearson Education Limited.

TABLE 18.2 Birth and Death on a Jamaican Sugar Plantation, 1779–1785

	Born			*Died*		
Year	*Males*	*Females*	*Purchased*	*Males*	*Females*	*Proportion of Deaths*
1779	5	2	6	7	5	1 in 26
1780	4	3	—	3	2	1 in 62
1781	2	3	—	4	2	1 in 52
1782	1	3	9	4	5	1 in 35
1783	3	3	—	8	10	1 in 17
1784	2	1	12	9	10	1 in 17
1785	2	3	—	0	3	1 in 99
Total	19	18	27	35	37	
	Born 37				Died 72	

Source: From Michael Craton, James Walvin, and David Wright, eds., *Slavery, Abolition and Emancipation*, p. 105. Copyright © 1976. Reprinted by permission of Pearson Education Limited.

seasoning An often difficult period of adjustment to new climates, disease environments, and work routines, such as that experienced by slaves newly arrived in the Americas.

Brazil was only 23 years of age for males and 25.5 years for females. The figures were probably similar for the eighteenth-century Caribbean. A callous opinion, common among slave owners in the Caribbean and in parts of Brazil, held that it was cheaper to import a youthful new slave from Africa than to raise one to the same age on a plantation.

The harsh conditions of plantation life played a major role in shortening slaves' lives, but the greatest killer was disease. Dysentery caused by contaminated food and water was common. Slaves newly arrived from Africa went through the period of adjustment to a new environment known as **seasoning**, during which one-third, on average, died of unfamiliar diseases. Slaves

Fotomas/Topham/The Image Works

Punishment for Slaves In addition to whipping and other cruel punishments, slave owners devised other ways to shame and intimidate slaves into obedience. This metal face mask prevented the wearer from eating or drinking.

also suffered from diseases brought with them, including malaria. On the plantation profiled in Table 18.1, for example, more than half of the slaves incapacitated by illness had yaws, a painful and debilitating skin disease common in Africa. As a consequence, only slave populations in the healthier temperate zones of North America experienced natural increase.

Such high mortality greatly added to the volume of the Atlantic slave trade, since plantations had to continually purchase new slaves to replace those who died (see Table 18.2). The high mortality and low fertility of this cruel labor system meant that increased sugar production depended on an ever-expanding slave trade. As a result, the majority of slaves on most West Indian plantations were African-born, and African religious beliefs, patterns of speech, styles of dress and adornment, and music were prominent parts of West Indian life.

Slave Resistance

PRIMARY SOURCE: The Interesting Narrative of Olaudah Equiano and Written by Himself Read selections from an ex-slave's autobiography, one of the most influential abolitionist books published in England.

Given the harsh conditions of their lives, it is not surprising that slaves in the West Indies often sought to gain their freedom. Individual slaves often ran away. Sometimes large groups of plantation slaves rose in rebellion against their bondage and abuse. For example, a slave named Tacky, who had been a chief on the Gold Coast of Africa, led a large rebellion in Jamaica in 1760. After his followers broke into a fort and armed themselves, slaves from nearby plantations joined them. This force attacked several plantations, setting them on fire and killing the planter families. Tacky died in the fighting, and three of his lieutenants stoically endured cruel deaths by torture meant to deter others from rebellion.

Because European planters believed that slaves with the strongest African heritage led rebellions, they tried to curtail African cultural traditions. They required slaves to learn the colonial language and discouraged the use of African languages by deliberately mixing slaves from different parts of Africa. In French and Portuguese colonies, slaves were encouraged to adopt Catholic religious practices, though African deities, beliefs, and practices survived, serving as the foundation for modern African-derived religions like candomblé. In the British West Indies, where only Quaker slave owners encouraged Christianity among their slaves before 1800, African herbal medicine remained strong, as did African beliefs concerning nature spirits and witchcraft.

Free Whites and Free Blacks

The lives of the free population were very different from the lives of slaves. In the French colony of Saint Domingue, which had nearly half of all slaves in the Caribbean in the eighteenth century, there were three categories of free people. At the top were wealthy owners of large sugar plantations (the *grands blancs* [grawn blawnk], or "great whites"), who dominated the economy and society of the island. Second came less-well-off Europeans (*petits blancs* [pay-TEE blawnk], or "little whites"). Most served as colonial officials, retail merchants, or small-scale agriculturalists. Most members of both groups owned slaves. Third came the free blacks. There were almost as many free blacks as free whites. While they ranked below whites socially, many free blacks owned property, and a surprising number also owned slaves.

The Planter Elite

The plantation elite was even more powerful in British colonies. Whereas sugar constituted about half of Saint Domingue's exports, in Jamaica the figure was over 80 percent. Such concentration on sugar crowded out small cultivators, white or black, and confined most landholding to

Courtesy of National Library, Institute of Jamaica

Cudjoe, Leader of the Jamaican Maroons, Negotiates a Peace Treaty In 1738, after decades of successful resistance to the British, the maroon Cudjoe negotiated a peace treaty that recognized the freedom of his runaway followers. Unable to defeat the maroons, the British also granted land and effective self-government to the maroons in exchange for an end to raids on plantations and the promise to return future slave runaways.

a few larger owners. At midcentury three-quarters of the farmland in Jamaica belonged to individuals who owned 1,000 acres (400 hectares) or more.

One source estimated that a planter had to invest nearly £20,000 ($100,000) to acquire a medium-size Jamaican plantation of 600 acres (240 hectares) in 1774. A third of this money went for land on which to grow sugar and food crops, pasture animals, and cut timber and firewood. A quarter of the expense was for the mill and refinery. The largest expense was the purchase of 200 slaves at £40 ($200) each. In comparison, the wage of an English rural laborer at this time was about £10 ($50) a year (one-fourth the price of a slave), and the annual incomes in 1760 of the ten wealthiest noble families in Britain averaged only £20,000 each.

manumission A grant of legal freedom to an individual slave.

Reputedly the richest Englishmen of this time, West Indian planters often translated their wealth into political power and social prestige. The richest planters put their plantations under the direction of managers and lived in Britain. Between 1730 and 1775 seventy absentee planters secured election to the British Parliament, where they formed an influential voting bloc. Those who resided in the West Indies exercised political power through the control of colonial assemblies.

In most European plantation colonies it was possible to grant freedom to an individual slave or group of slaves. **Manumission** (the legal grant of freedom by an owner) was more common in Brazil and the Spanish and French colonies than in English colonies. Among English colonies, manumissions were more common in the Caribbean than in North America. While some plantation owners in the Caribbean freed slave women with whom they had had sexual relationships or freed the children of their mistresses, the largest group of freed slaves across the Americas had purchased their freedom. Manumissions led to the development of a large free black population in many colonies. Since the legal condition of children followed that of the mother, slave families often struggled to free women in childbearing years first so that their children would be born free. By the late eighteenth

SECTION REVIEW

- Sugar production required larger investments in land, slaves, and machinery than other forms of colonial agriculture.
- Large-scale sugar plantations were more efficient and profitable than smaller plantations.
- Sugar plantations had high environmental costs due to deforestation and soil exhaustion.
- Slaves were closely organized and forced to be productive through the use of harsh punishments.
- Slave populations of the Caribbean experienced high mortality rates and low fertility rates.
- Slaves sought freedom through manumission or flight or rebellion; some groups of runaways, maroons, forced authorities to recognize their freedom.

century free blacks made up a large portion of the black populations of Brazil and the French colonies.

Runaway Communities

maroon A slave who ran away from his or her master. Often a member of a community of runaway slaves in the West Indies and South America.

As in Brazil and Spanish colonies (see Chapter 17), escaped slaves constituted another part of the free black population. Communities of runaways, called **maroons**, were numerous in Jamaica and Hispaniola as well as in the Guianas (guy-AHN-uhs). Jamaican maroons, after withstanding several attacks by the colony's militia, signed a treaty in 1738 that recognized their independence in return for their cooperation in stopping new runaways and suppressing slave revolts. Unable to win decisive victories, colonial authorities in Spanish, Dutch, and Portuguese colonies signed similar treaties with runaway leaders as well.

CREATING THE ATLANTIC ECONOMY

At once archaic in their cruel system of slavery and oddly modern in their specialization in a single product for export, the West Indian plantation colonies were the bittersweet fruits of a new Atlantic trading system. Changes in the character of Atlantic commerce illustrate the rise of this new system. In the sixteenth century Spanish treasure fleets laden with silver and gold bullion had dominated Atlantic trade. In the late seventeenth and eighteenth centuries the Atlantic trade was dominated by sugar ships returning to Europe from the West Indies and Brazil and by slave ships transporting an average of 250 African captives each to the Americas.

In addition to the plantation system, new economic institutions, new partnerships between private investors and governments in Europe, and new working relationships between European and African merchants created the Atlantic economy. This new trading system is a prime example of how European capitalist relationships were reshaping the world.

Capitalism and Mercantilism

Many of the Spanish and Portuguese voyages of exploration in the fifteenth and sixteenth centuries were government ventures, and both Spain and Portugal tried to restrict the overseas trade of their colonies using royal monopolies (see Chapters 15 and 17). Monopoly control, however, proved both expensive and inefficient. The success of the Atlantic economy in the seventeenth and eighteenth centuries depended much more on private enterprise, which made trade more efficient and profitable. European private investors were attracted to colonial trade by the rich profits generated by New World agriculture and mining, but their success depended on new institutions and the continuation of government protection to reduce the possibility of catastrophic loss.

Capitalism and the Atlantic World

capitalism The economic system of large financial institutions—banks, stock exchanges, investment companies—that first developed in early modern Europe. *Commercial capitalism*, the trading system of the early modern economy, is often distinguished from *industrial capitalism*, the system based on machine production.

The growth of the Atlantic economy was one part of the development of modern **capitalism**. The essence of this economic system was the expansion of credit and the development of large financial institutions—banks, stock exchanges, and chartered trading companies—that enabled merchants and investors to conduct business at great distances from their homes while reducing risks and increasing profits. Originally developed for business dealings within Europe, the capitalist system expanded overseas in the seventeenth century, when slow economic growth in Europe led many investors to seek profits in the production and export of colonial products like sugar and tobacco and in satisfying the colonial demand for European products.

Banks were crucial to this process. By the early seventeenth century Dutch banks had developed such a reputation for security that individuals and governments from all over western Europe entrusted them with large sums of money. To make a profit, Dutch and other European banks invested these funds in real estate, industries, loans to governments, and overseas trade.

Individuals seeking higher returns than those provided by banks could purchase shares in a joint-stock company, a sixteenth-century forerunner of the modern corporation. Individuals bought and sold shares in specialized financial markets called stock exchanges. The Amsterdam Exchange, founded in 1530, became the greatest stock market in the seventeenth and eighteenth centuries. To reduce risks in overseas trading, merchants and trading companies bought insurance on their ships and cargoes to cover potential losses. Banks and stock markets appeared much later in the Iberian world, slowing the rate of economic growth.

Mercantilism

mercantilism European government policies of the sixteenth, seventeenth, and eighteenth centuries designed to promote overseas trade between a country and its colonies and accumulate precious metals by requiring colonies to trade only with their motherland country. The British system was defined by the Navigation Acts, the French system by laws known as the *Exclusif.*

Royal African Company A trading company chartered by the English government in 1672 to conduct its merchants' trade on the Atlantic coast of Africa.

European states sought to monopolize the profits produced in their colonial empires by controlling trade and accumulating capital in the form of gold and silver. This system was called **mercantilism**. Mercantilist policies strongly discouraged citizens from trading with foreign merchants and used armed force when necessary to secure exclusive relations.

Chartered companies were an important part of mercantilist capitalism. In 1602 the Netherlands gave the Dutch East India Company a monopoly over trade in the Indian Ocean. Private investors who bought shares in the company were amply rewarded when the Dutch East India Company captured control of long-distance trade in the Indian Ocean from the Portuguese (see Chapter 19). As we have seen, the Dutch West India Company, chartered in 1621, sought similar benefits in the Atlantic trade by seizing sugar-producing areas in Brazil and African slaving ports from the Portuguese.

These successes inspired other governments to set up their own chartered companies. In 1672 a royal charter placed all English trade with West Africa in the hands of the **Royal African Company (RAC)**, which established its headquarters at Cape Coast Castle, just east of Elmina on the Gold Coast. The French government also chartered companies and promoted overseas trade and colonization. Jean Baptiste Colbert (kohl-BEAR), King Louis XIV's minister of finance from 1661 to 1683, chartered the French East India and French West India Companies to expel Dutch and English traders from French colonies.

French and English governments also used military force to gain trade advantages in the Americas. Restrictions on Dutch access to French and English colonies provoked a series of wars with the Netherlands between 1652 and 1678 (see Chapter 16). The larger English and French navies defeated the Dutch and drove the Dutch West India Company into bankruptcy. Military and diplomatic pressure also forced Spain after 1713 to grant England and later France monopoly rights to supply slaves to its colonies.

With Dutch competition in the Atlantic reduced, the French and English limited the privileges of their chartered companies. Such new mercantilist policies fostered competition among a nation's own citizens, while using high tariffs and restrictions to exclude foreigners. In the 1660s England passed a series of Navigation Acts that confined trade with its colonies to English ships and cargoes; it later opened trade in Africa to any English subject, claiming that competition would cut the cost of slaves to West Indian planters. The French called their mercantilist legislation, codified in 1698, the *Exclusif* (ek-skloo-SEEF), highlighting its exclusionary intentions. Other mercantilist laws sought to protect national manufacturing and agricultural interests from the competition of colonies, imposing prohibitively high taxes on their manufactured goods and products like refined sugar.

As a result of these mercantilist measures, the Atlantic became Britain, France, and Portugal's most important overseas trading area. The value of imports from West Indian colonies alone accounted for over one-fifth the value of total British imports, while French West Indian colonies played an even larger role in France's overseas trade. Only the Dutch, closed out of much of the American trade, depended more heavily on Asian trade (see Chapter 19). Profits from the Atlantic economy, in turn, promoted further economic expansion and increased the revenues of European governments.

The Atlantic Circuit

Atlantic Circuit The network of trade routes connecting Europe, Africa, and the Americas that underlay the Atlantic system.

Middle Passage The part of the Atlantic Circuit involving the transportation of enslaved Africans across the Atlantic to the Americas.

At the heart of this trading system was a clockwise network of sea routes known as the **Atlantic Circuit** (see Map 18.1). The first leg, from Europe to Africa, carried European manufactures—notably metals, hardware, and guns—as well as great quantities of cotton textiles brought from India. While some of these goods were exchanged for West African gold, ivory, timber, and other products, most goods went to purchase slaves, who were transported across the Atlantic to the plantation colonies in what was known as the **Middle Passage**. On the third leg, plantation goods from the colonies returned to Europe. Each leg carried goods from where they were abundant and relatively cheap to where they were scarce and therefore valuable. Thus, in theory, each leg of the Atlantic Circuit could earn profits. In practice, shipwrecks, deaths, piracy, and other risks could turn profit into loss.

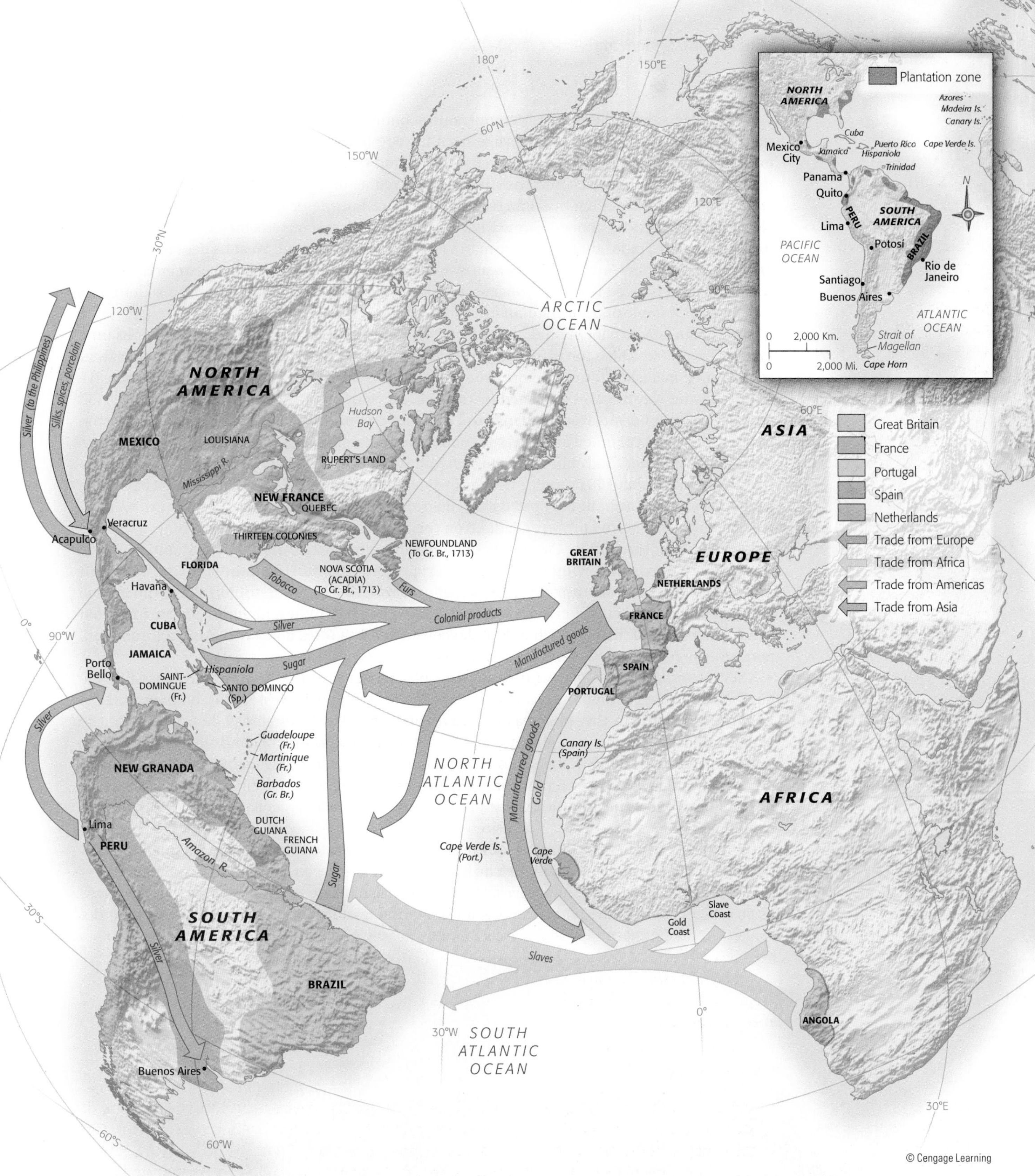

MAP 18.1 **The Atlantic Economy** By 1700 the volume of maritime exchanges among the Atlantic continents had begun to rival the trade of the Indian Ocean Basin. Notice the trade in consumer products, slave labor, precious metals, and other goods. Silver trade to East Asia laid the basis for a Pacific Ocean economy.

e Interactive Map

The three-sided Atlantic Circuit is only one of many commercial routes that serviced Atlantic trade. Ships making the long voyage from Europe to the Indian Ocean and Asia typically exchanged African gold and American silver for cotton textiles and spices. Merchants then sold these Asian goods in Africa and the Americas as well as in Europe. Many commercial routes were more direct, carrying manufactured goods from Europe or foodstuffs and lumber from New England to the Caribbean. Some Rhode Island and Massachusetts merchants participated in a "Triangular Trade" that carried rum to West Africa, slaves to the West Indies, and molasses and rum back to New England. There was also a considerable two-way trade between Brazil and Angola that exchanged Brazilian tobacco and liquor for slaves. Brazilian tobacco also found its way north as a staple of the Canadian fur trade.

European investment capital, manufactured goods, and shipping dominated the Atlantic system. Europe was also the principal market for American plantation products, products that transformed material culture. Before the seventeenth century, sugar was scarce and expensive in Europe and was mostly consumed by the rich. As colonial production increased, prices fell and consumption of sugar in England rose to about 4 pounds (nearly 2 kilograms) per person in 1700. Europeans of modest means spooned sugar into popular new beverages imported from overseas—tea, coffee, and chocolate—to overcome the beverages' natural bitterness. Consumption increased to about 18 pounds (8 kilograms) by the early nineteenth century (well below the American average of about 100 pounds [45 kilograms] a year in 1960).

The African Slave Trade

The flow of sugar to Europe depended on the flow of slaves from Africa (see Map 18.2). The rising volume of the Middle Passage is one measure of the expansion of the Atlantic system. During the 150 years following the arrival of Europeans in the Americas, the slave trade brought some 800,000 Africans across the Atlantic. Volume rose to nearly 7.5 million slaves during the boom in sugar production between 1650 and 1800. The West Indies, including Cuba, imported nearly 50 percent of this total, while Brazil received nearly a third and North America another 5 percent. The rest went to Spain's mainland colonies (see Figure 18.1).

Seventeenth-century mercantilist policies placed much of the Atlantic slave trade in the hands of chartered companies. During their existence the Dutch West India Company and the English Royal African Company each carried about 100,000 slaves across the Atlantic. In the eighteenth century private English traders from Liverpool and Bristol controlled about 40 percent of the slave trade. The French, operating out of Nantes and Bordeaux, handled about 20 percent and the Dutch only 6 percent. The Portuguese supplying Brazil and other places had nearly 30 percent of the Atlantic slave trade, in contrast to the 3 percent carried in North American ships.

Conditions in the Middle Passage

While the volume and duration of the slave trade indicate that it was profitable, the relative value of European goods and African slaves as well as slave prices in American ports determined the profit of individual voyages. Slave traders also had to deliver as many healthy slaves as possible for sale in the plantation colonies, but the terrible conditions on slave ships and a

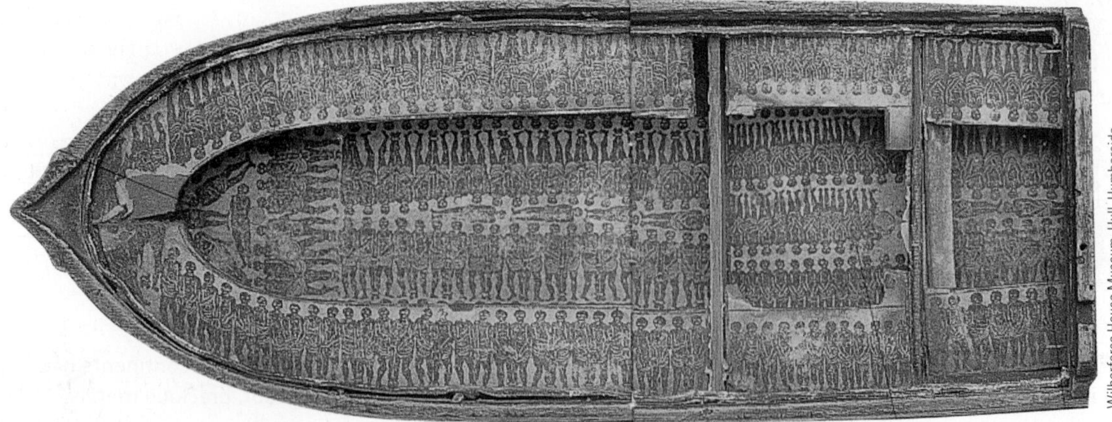

Wilberforce House Museum, Hull, Humberside, UK/ The Bridgeman Art Library

Slave Ship This model of the English vessel *Brookes* shows the specially built section of the hold where enslaved Africans were packed together during the Middle Passage. Girls, boys, and women were confined separately.

MAP 18.2 **The African Slave Trade, 1500–1800** After 1500 a vast new trade in slaves from sub-Saharan Africa to the Americas joined the ongoing slave trade to the Islamic states of North Africa, the Middle East, and India. The West Indies were the major destination of the Atlantic slave trade, followed by Brazil.

e Interactive Map

long and treacherous voyage lasting from six to ten weeks led to high mortalities. Some ships arrived with all of their slaves alive, but large, even catastrophic, losses of life were common (see Figure 18.1). On average, however, slave traders succeeded in lowering mortality during the Middle Passage from about 23 percent on voyages before 1700 to half that in the last half of the eighteenth century.

Failed escapes and mutinies contributed to mortality. When opportunities presented themselves (nearness to land, illness among the crew), some enslaved Africans tried to overpower their captors and escape. Male slaves were routinely shackled together to prevent escapes while they were still in sight of land or when mutiny was feared while at sea. As a precaution, slave traders also commonly confined male slaves below deck during most of the voyage, except at mealtimes, when the crew brought them up in small groups under close supervision. In any event, "mutinies" were rarely successful and defeated mutineers were treated with brutality.

Mistreatment also contributed to the high mortality of the Middle Passage. Although it was in the interests of the captain and crew to deliver their slave cargo in good condition, slavers used whippings, beatings, and even executions to maintain order. Some slaves developed deep psychological depression, known to contemporaries as "fixed melancholy," and refused to eat. Crews attempted to force-feed these slaves, but some successfully

SECTION REVIEW

- Banks, stock markets, and insurance companies helped European nations to develop their colonial empires.
- European nations used mercantilism, a mix of fiscal and trade policies, to monopolize the economic benefits from colonial possessions.
- The Atlantic Circuit was a network of trade networks that connected Europe with Africa and the Western Hemisphere.
- Between 1650 and 1800, 7.5 million African slaves were brought to Europe's American colonies, nine times the number imported in the previous 150 years.
- Conditions on the slave ships were unhealthy and harsh, and mortality rates were high.

willed themselves to death. The dangers and brutalities of the slave trade were so notorious that many ordinary seamen shunned such work. As a consequence, cruel and brutal officers and crews abounded on slave ships.

Although examples of unspeakable cruelties are common in the records, most deaths in the Middle Passage were the result of disease. Dysentery spread by contaminated food and water caused many deaths. Others died of contagious diseases such as smallpox carried on board by infected slaves or crew members. These maladies spread quickly in the crowded and unsanitary confines of the ships, claiming the lives of slaves already physically weakened and mentally traumatized by their ordeals. Crew members were exposed to the same epidemics. It is a measure of the callousness of the age, as well as the cheapness of European labor, that over the course of a round-trip voyage from Europe the proportion of crew deaths could be as high as the slave deaths.

AFRICA, THE ATLANTIC, AND ISLAM

The Atlantic system took a terrible toll in African lives both during the Middle Passage and under the harsh conditions of plantation slavery. Many other Africans died while being marched to African ports for sale. The overall effects on Africa of these losses and of other aspects of the slave trade have been the subject of considerable historical debate. It is clear that the trade's impact depended on the intensity and terms of different African regions' involvement.

Any assessment of the Atlantic system's effects in Africa must also take into consideration the fact that some Africans profited from the trade by capturing and selling slaves. They chained the slaves together or bound them to forked sticks for the march to the coast, then bartered them to the European slavers for trade goods. The effects on the enslaver were different from the effects on the enslaved. Finally, a broader understanding of the Atlantic system's effects in sub-Saharan Africa comes from comparisons with the effects of Islamic contacts.

The Gold Coast and the Slave Coast

As Chapter 15 showed, early European visitors to Africa's Atlantic coast were interested more in trading than in colonizing the continent. As the Africa trade mushroomed after 1650, this pattern continued. African kings and merchants sold slaves and goods at many coastal sites, but the growing slave trade did not lead to substantial European colonization.

The transition to slave trading was not sudden. Even as slaves were becoming Atlantic Africa's most valuable export, goods such as gold, ivory, and timber remained important. For example, during its eight decades of operation from 1672 to 1752, the Royal African Company made 40 percent of its profits from gold, ivory, and forest products. In some parts of West Africa, such nonslave exports remained predominant even at the peak of the trade.

African Participation in the Slave Trade

African merchants were very discriminating about merchandise they took in exchange for slaves or goods. A ship that arrived with goods of low quality or not suited to local tastes found it hard to purchase a cargo at a profitable price. European guidebooks to the African trade carefully noted the color and shape of beads, the pattern of textiles, the type of guns, and the sort of metals that were in demand on each section of the coast (see Map 18.3). Although African preferences for merchandise varied, textiles, hardware, and guns were in high demand. Of the goods the Royal African Company traded in West Africa in the 1680s, over 60 percent were Indian and European textiles and 30 percent were hardware and weaponry. In the eighteenth century, tobacco and rum from the Americas became welcome imports.

e PRIMARY SOURCE: A Voyage to New Calabar River in the Year 1699 Learn about the slave trade in West Africa, from a Frenchman on an English slave-trading expedition.

Both Europeans and Africans attempted to drive the best bargain for themselves and sometimes engaged in deceitful practices. The strength of the African bargaining position, however, may be inferred from the fact that as the demand for slaves rose, so too did their price in Africa. In the course of the eighteenth century the value of goods needed to purchase a slave on the Gold Coast doubled and in some places tripled or quadrupled.

African governments on the Gold and Slave Coasts forced Europeans to observe African trading customs and prevented them from taking control of African territory. Rivalry among

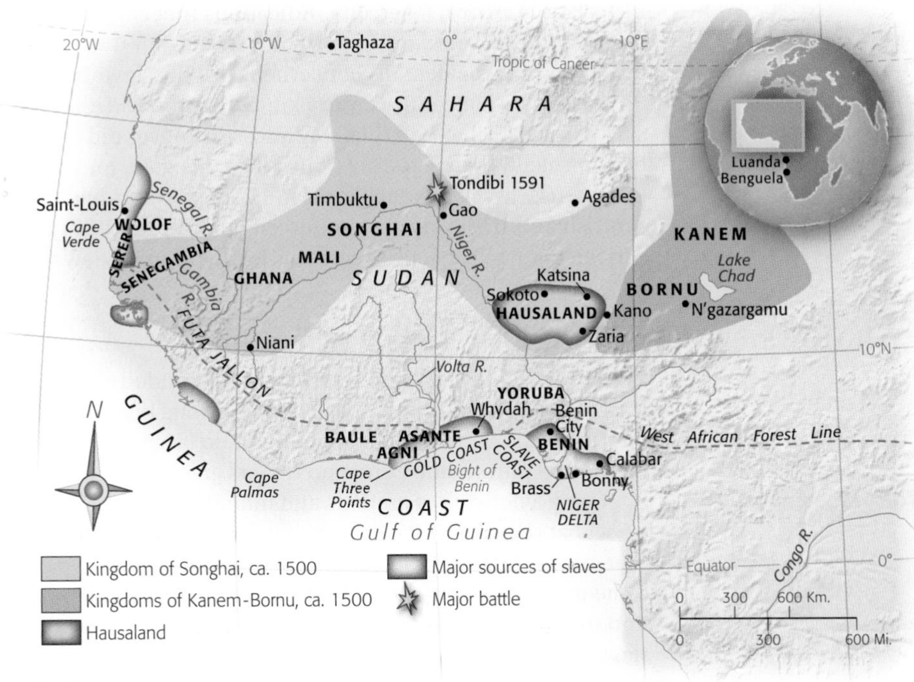

Interactive Map

MAP 18.3 West African States and Trade, 1500–1800 The Atlantic and the trans-Saharan trade brought West Africans new goods and promoted the rise of powerful states and trading communities. The Moroccan invasion of Songhai and Portuguese colonization of the Angolan ports of Luanda and Benguela showed the political dangers of such relations.

European nations, each of which established its own trading "castles" along the Gold Coast, also reduced bargaining strength because Africans could shop for better deals among these competitors. In 1700 the head of the Dutch East India Company in West Africa, Willem Bosman (VIL-uhm boos-MAHN), bemoaned the fact that, to stay competitive against other European traders, his company had to include large quantities of muskets and gunpowder in the goods it exchanged, thereby adding to Africans' military power.

Bosman also related that his agents had to first pay the local king a substantial customs duty before buying slaves at Whydah and then had to pay a premium price for the slaves. By African standards, Whydah was a rather small kingdom controlling only the port and its immediate hinterland. In 1727, Dahomey (dah-HOH-mee), strengthened militarily by firearms acquired in the slave trade, annexed Whydah.

Two other regional powers, the kingdoms of Oyo (aw-YOH) and Asante (uh-SHAN-tee), also participated in the Atlantic trade, but neither kingdom was as dependent on it as Dahomey. Overseas trade formed a relatively modest part of the economies of these large and populous states, which maintained extensive overland trade with their northern neighbors and with states across the Sahara. Like the great medieval empires of the western Sudan, Oyo and Asante grew more powerful from external trade but were not dependent on it. In 1730, the Oyo kingdom overran Dahomey, forcing it to pay an annual tribute to keep its independence.

How did African kings and merchants obtain slaves for sale? Bosman dismissed misconceptions prevailing in Europe in his day. "Not a few in our country," he wrote to a friend in 1700, "fondly imagine that parents here sell their children, men their wives, and one brother the other. But those who think so, do deceive themselves; for this never happens on any other account but that of necessity, or some great crime; but most of the slaves that are offered to us are prisoners of war, which are sold by the victors as their booty."[1] His statement confirms other accounts claiming that prisoners of war were the most common source of slaves, but it is harder to prove that capturing slaves for export was a main cause of wars. "Here and there," conclude two respected historians of Africa, "there are indications that captives taken in the later and more peripheral stages of these wars were exported overseas, but it would seem that the main impetus of conquest was only incidentally concerned with the slave-trade."[2]

An early-nineteenth-century king of Asante had a similar view: "I cannot make war to catch slaves in the bush, like a thief. My ancestors never did so. But if I fight a king, and kill him when he is insolent, then certainly I must have his gold, and his slaves, and his people are mine too. Do not the white kings act like this?"[3] English rulers had indeed sentenced seventeenth-century Scottish and Irish prisoners to forced labor in the West Indies. One may imagine that neither African nor European prisoners shared their kings' view that such actions were legitimate.

The Bight of Biafra and Angola

In the eighteenth century the slave trade expanded eastward to the Bight (bite) of Biafra. In contrast to the Gold and Slave Coasts, where strong kingdoms predominated, the densely populated interior of the Bight of Biafra contained no large states. Even so, powerful merchant princes of the coastal ports made European traders give them rich presents.

The Trade Expands

Using a network of markets and inland routes, regional merchants supplied European slave traders at the coast with debtors, victims of kidnapping, and convicted criminals. As the volume of the Atlantic trade along the Bight of Biafra expanded in the late eighteenth century, some inland markets evolved into giant fairs with different sections specializing in slaves and imported goods. In the 1780s an English ship's doctor reported that African merchants collected slaves at fairs in the interior and that groups of twelve hundred to fifteen hundred enslaved men and women were then sent to the coast from a single fair.[4]

The local context of the Atlantic trade was different south of the Congo estuary at Angola, the greatest source of slaves for the Atlantic trade (see Map 18.2). This was also the one place along

Luanda, Angola Luanda was founded by the Portuguese in 1575 and became the center of the slave trade to Brazil. In this eighteenth-century print the city's warehouses and commercial buildings line the city streets. In the foreground captives are dragged to the port for shipment to the Western Hemisphere.

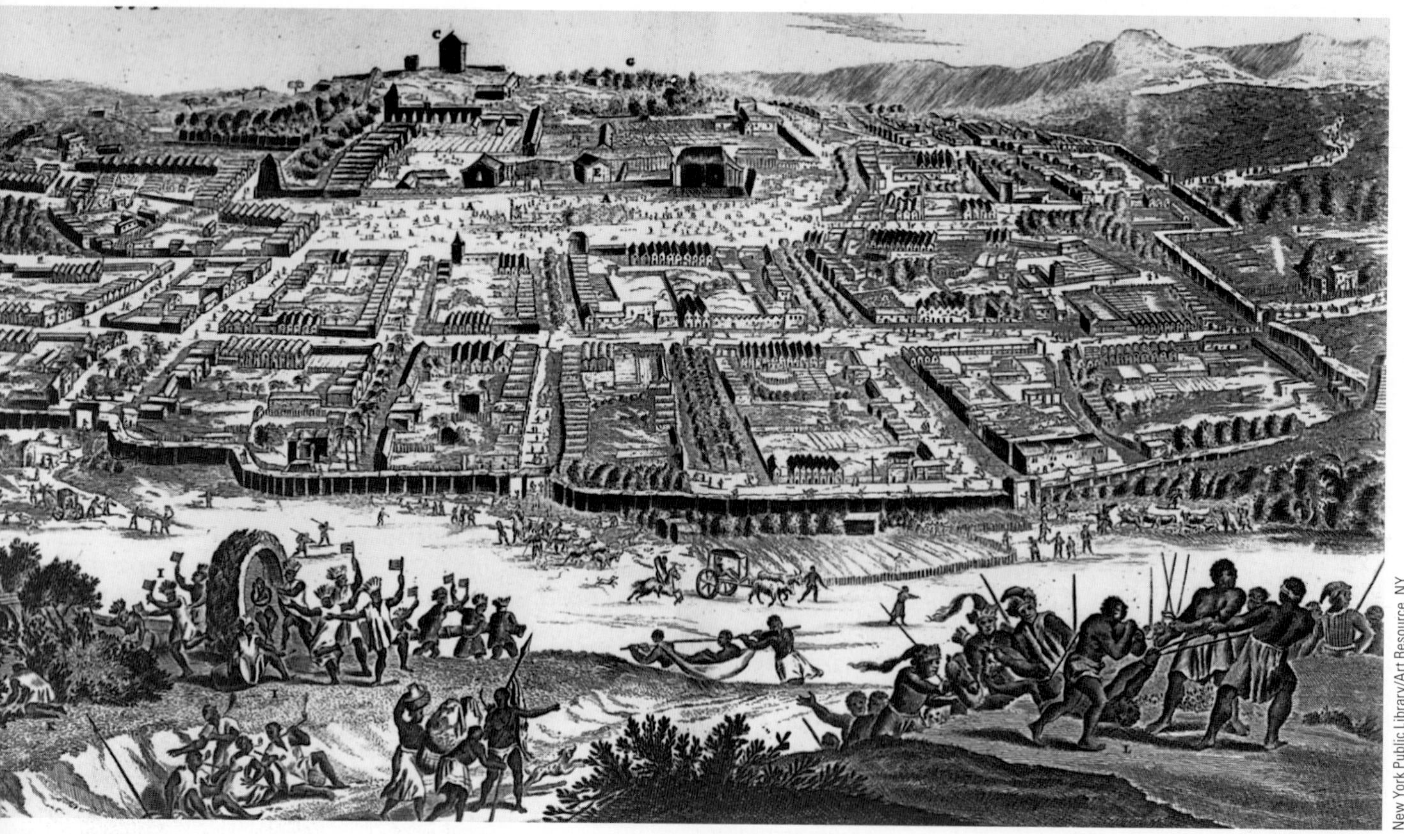

New York Public Library/Art Resource, NY

the Atlantic coast where a single European nation, Portugal, controlled a significant amount of territory. Except for a brief period when the Dutch exercised control in the seventeenth century, Portuguese residents of the main ports of Luanda and Benguela (ben-GWAY-luh) served as middlemen between the caravans that arrived from the interior and the ships that crossed from Brazil. From these coastal cities Afro-Portuguese traders guided large caravans of trade goods inland to exchange for slaves at special markets.

Many of the slaves sold at these markets were prisoners of war captured by expanding African states. By the late eighteenth century prisoners captured in wars fought as far away as 600 to 800 miles (1,000 to 1,300 kilometers) were carried to the ports for transportation. Many were victims of wars of expansion fought by the giant federation of Lunda kingdoms. As elsewhere in Africa, prisoners sold as slaves seem to have been a byproduct of African wars, rather than the objective of the warring parties.

Research has identified a link between severe eighteenth-century droughts and the development of the Angolan slave trade. The environmental crisis in the hinterland drove famished refugees to better-watered areas.[5] Powerful African leaders gained control of these refugees in return for supplying them with food and water. These leaders valued refugee children, who would quickly assimilate, and adult women, who were valued as food producers and for reproduction. They often sold adult male refugees as slaves because they were more likely than women and children to escape or challenge the ruler's authority. They used the textiles, weapons, and alcohol they received in return for slaves as gifts to attract new followers and to cement the loyalty of their established allies. The most successful became heads of powerful new states, stabilizing areas devastated by war and drought and repopulating them with the refugees and prisoners.

Although the organization of Atlantic trade varied from African region to region, it expanded and prospered because both European merchants and African elites benefited. African rulers and merchants exported slaves and other products to obtain foreign goods that made them wealthier and more powerful. Most of the exported slaves were prisoners taken in wars associated with African state growth. But strong African states or powerful merchant communities also proved better able to defend African territory and limit European economic advantages. The Africans who gained from this trade were the rich and powerful few. Many more Africans were losers in the exchanges.

Africa's European and Islamic Contacts

The ways in which sub-Saharan Africans established new contacts with Europe paralleled their much older pattern of relations with the Islamic world. But there were striking similarities and differences in Africans' political, commercial, and cultural interactions with these two external influences between 1500 and 1800.

During the three and a half centuries of contact up to 1800, Africans ceded very little territory to Europeans. Local African rulers kept close tabs on the European trading posts they permitted along the Gold and Slave Coasts and collected lucrative rents and fees. Aside from some uninhabited islands off the Atlantic coast, Europeans established colonial beachheads in only two places, the Portuguese colony of Angola and the Dutch East India Company's Cape Colony at the southern tip of the continent. The Dutch colony was tied to Indian Ocean trade, not to the Atlantic trade, and, unlike Angola, did not export slaves. Most the Cape Colony's 25,750 slaves in 1793 were from Madagascar, South Asia, and the East Indies, not Africa.

West Africa and Islam

Songhai A people, language, kingdom, and empire in western Sudan in West Africa. At its height in the sixteenth century, the Muslim Songhai Empire stretched from the Atlantic to the land of the Hausa and was a major player in the trans-Saharan trade.

North Africa had become a part of the Islamic world in the first century of Islamic expansion. Sub-Saharan Africans gradually learned of Muslim beliefs and practices from traders who crossed the Sahara from North Africa or who sailed from the Middle East to the Swahili trading cities of East Africa. In the sixteenth century the new Islamic Ottoman Empire annexed all of North Africa except Morocco, while Ethiopia lost extensive territory to other Muslim conquerors.

Until 1590 the Sahara remained an effective buttress against invasion from powerful northern states. The **Songhai** (song-GAH-ee) Empire of West Africa challenged the status quo when it pushed its frontier into the Sahara from the south. Ruled by an indigenous Muslim dynasty, Songhai drew its wealth from the trans-Saharan trade (see Map 18.3). This expansion led the kingdom of Morocco to challenge Songhai by sending a military expedition of four thousand

Hausa An agricultural and trading people of central Sudan in West Africa. Aside from their brief incorporation into the Songhai Empire, the Hausa city-states remained autonomous until the Sokoto Caliphate conquered them in the early nineteenth century.

men south across the desert. Although half the invading force perished, the survivors armed with firearms defeated Songhai's army of forty thousand in 1591. While Morocco was never able to annex the western Sudan, its forces extracted a massive tribute in slaves and goods from the local population and imposed tolls on trade for the next two centuries.

With Morocco's destruction of Songhai, the **Hausa** trading cities in the central Sudan attracted most of the caravans bringing textiles, hardware, and weapons across the Sahara. The goods the Hausa imported and distributed through their trading networks were similar to those that coastal African traders commanded from the Atlantic trade, except for the absence of alcohol, prohibited to Muslims. The goods they sent back in return also resembled the major African exports into the Atlantic: gold, textiles and leather goods, and slaves.

The Islamic Slave Trade

Few statistics of the slave trade to the Islamic north exist, but the size of the trade seems to have been substantial, if smaller than the transatlantic trade at its peak. Between 1600 and 1800 slave traders sent about 850,000 slaves to Muslim North Africa (see Map 18.2). A nearly equal number of slaves from sub-Saharan Africa entered the Islamic Middle East and India by way of the Red Sea and the Indian Ocean.

In contrast to the plantation slavery of the Americas, most African slaves in the Islamic world were soldiers and servants. In the late seventeenth and eighteenth centuries Morocco's rulers employed an army of 150,000 African slaves, trusting their loyalty more than that of recruits from their own lands. Moroccans also used slaves on sugar plantations, as servants, and as artisans. Unlike in the Americas, the majority of African slaves in the Islamic world were women who served wealthy households as concubines, servants, and entertainers. The trans-Saharan slave trade also included a much higher proportion of children than the Atlantic trade.

Bornu A powerful West African kingdom at the southern edge of the Sahara in the Central Sudan, which was important in trans-Saharan trade and in the spread of Islam. Also known as Kanem-Bornu, it endured from the ninth century to the end of the nineteenth.

The central Sudanese kingdom of **Bornu** illustrates several aspects of trans-Saharan contacts. Ruled by the same dynasty since the ninth century, this Muslim state had grown and expanded in the sixteenth century as the result of guns imported from the Ottoman Empire. Bornu retained many captives from its wars or sold them as slaves to the north in return for the firearms and horses that underpinned the kingdom's military power. One Bornu king, Mai Ali, conspicuously displayed his kingdom's new power and wealth while on four pilgrimages to

Traders Approaching Timbuktu As they had done for centuries, traders brought their wares to this ancient desert-edge city. Timbuktu's mosques tower above the ordinary dwellings of the fabled city.

Mecca between 1642 and 1667. On the last, an enormous entourage of slaves—said to number fifteen thousand—accompanied him.

Like Christians of this period, Muslims saw no moral impediment to owning or trading in slaves. Indeed, Islam considered enslaving "pagans" to be a meritorious act because it brought them into the faith. Although Islam forbade the enslavement of Muslims, Muslim rulers in Bornu, Hausaland, and elsewhere were not strict observers of that rule (see Diversity and Dominance: Slavery in West Africa and the Americas).

Sub-Saharan Africans had much longer exposure to Islamic cultural influences than to European cultural influences. Scholars and merchants learned to use the Arabic language to communicate with visiting North Africans and to read the Quran. Islamic beliefs and practices as well as Islamic legal and administrative systems were influential in African trading cities on the southern edge of the Sahara and on the Swahili coast. In some places Islam had extended its influence among rural people, but in 1750 it was still very much an urban religion.

European cultural influence in Africa was more limited. Some coastal Africans had shown an interest in Western Christianity after contacts with the Portuguese, but in the 1700s only Angola had a significant number of Christians. Coastal African traders found it useful to learn European languages, but African languages continued to dominate inland trade routes. A few African merchants sent their sons to Europe to learn European ways. One of these young men, Philip Quaque (KWAH-kay), who was educated in England, was ordained as a priest in the Church of England and became the official chaplain of the Cape Coast Castle from 1766 until his death in 1816.

Atlantic and Muslim Slave Trades Compared

AP* Exam Tip The AP* course highlights comparisons of slave systems.

Overall, how different and similar were the material effects of Islam and Europe in sub-Saharan Africa by 1800? While Muslims and Europeans obtained slaves from sub-Saharan Africa, the European trade was larger. The Atlantic trade carried about 8 million Africans to the Americas between 1550 and 1800. During this period the Islamic trade to North Africa and the Middle East transported perhaps 2 million African captives. What were the effects on Africa's population? Scholars generally agree on three points: (1) even at the peak of the trade in the 1700s, sub-Saharan Africa's overall population remained very large; (2) localities that contributed heavily to the slave trade, such as lands near the Slave Coast, suffered acute losses; (3) the ability of a population to recover from losses was related to the proportion of fertile women who were shipped away. The fact that Africans sold fewer women than men into the larger Atlantic trade somewhat reduced the long-term demographic effects of this larger trade.

The slave trade had a mixed impact on sub-Saharan economies. Africans were very particular about what they received in exchange for slaves, and their imports reflected their tastes and needs. The limited volume of manufactured imports could not overwhelm established African weavers, metalworkers, and other producers, and some imported products like textiles and metal bars stimulated the local production of tools and clothing. However, while African as well as European states benefited by taxing this trade, most of the economic benefits went to European nations and to their American colonies.

Profits from transporting and selling slaves mostly went to European merchants and ship owners. European manufacturers, like the producers of textiles and metal goods, profited as well. But Europe's American colonies were the major beneficiaries of the African slave trade. With Amerindian population diminished by epidemics and European immigration inadequate to develop American resources, it was the forced labor of African slaves that made possible the enormous wealth produced in a vast region that spread from the Chesapeake to the Río de la Plata. This wealth accelerated the rapid expansion of Western capitalism in the seventeenth and eighteenth centuries, a period that witnessed the political and economic decline of the Ottoman Empire, the dominant state of the Middle East, and other Muslim kingdoms (see Chapter 19).

SECTION REVIEW

- Powerful rulers and merchants protected African territory from Europeans and imposed control over trade terms.
- Most slaves exported to the Western Hemisphere were prisoners of war.
- African trade and cultural relations with European nations paralleled already-established relations with Muslim regions.
- The African slave trade with the Muslim world was smaller than the Atlantic slave trade but lasted longer.
- Most African slaves sent to the Islamic world served as soldiers or servants.

Slavery in West Africa and the Americas

Social diversity was common in Africa, and the domination of masters over slaves was a feature of many societies. Ahmad Baba (1556–1627) was an outstanding Islamic scholar in the city of Timbuktu. He came from an old Muslim family of the city. In about 1615 he replied to some questions that had been sent to him. His answers reveal a great deal about the official and unofficial condition of slavery in the Sudan of West Africa, especially in the Hausa states of Kano and Katsina (see Map 18.3).

You asked: What have you to say concerning the slaves imported from the lands of the Sudan whose people are acknowledged to be Muslims, such as Bornu, . . . Kano, Goa, Songhay, Katsina and others among whom Islam is widespread? Is it permissible to possess them [as slaves] or not?

Know—may God grant us and you success—that these lands, as you have stated are Muslim. . . . But close to each of them are lands in which are unbelievers whom the Muslim inhabitants of these lands raid. Some of these unbelievers are under the Muslims' protection and pay them [taxes]. . . . Sometimes there is war between the Muslim sultans of some of these lands and one attacks the other, taking as many prisoners as he can and selling the captive though he is a free-born Muslim. . . . This is a common practice among them in Hausaland; Katsina raids Kano, as do others, though their language is one and their situations parallel; the only difference they recognize among themselves is that so-and-so is a born Muslim and so-and-so is a born unbeliever. . . .

Whoever is taken prisoner in a state of unbelief may become someone's property, whoever he is, as opposed to those who have become Muslims of their own free will . . . and may not be possessed at all.

A little over a century later another African provided information about enslavement practices in the Western Sudan. Ayuba Suleiman Diallo (ah-YOO-bah SOO-lay-mahn JAH-loh) (1701–?) of the state of Bondu some 200 miles from the Gambia River was enslaved and transported to Maryland, where he was a slave from 1731 to 1733. When an Englishman learned of Ayuba's literacy in Arabic, he recorded his life story, anglicizing his name to Job Solomon. According to the account, slaves in Bondu did much of the hard work, while men of Ayuba's class were free to devote themselves to the study of Islamic texts.

In February, 1730, Job's father hearing of an English ship at Gambia River, sent him, with two servants to attend him, to sell two Negroes, and to buy paper, and some other necessaries; but desired him not to venture over the river, because the country of the Mandingoes, who are enemies to the people of Futa, lies on the other side. Job not agreeing with Captain Pike (who commanded the ship, lying then at Gambia, in the service of Captain Henry Hunt, brother to Mr. William Hunt, merchant, in Little Tower-street, London) sent back the two servants to acquaint his father with it, and to let him know that he intended to go no farther. Accordingly . . . he crossed the River Gambia, and disposed of his Negroes for some cows. As he was returning home, he stopped for some refreshment at the house of an old acquaintance; and the weather being hot, he hung up his arms in the house, while he refreshed himself. . . . It happened that a company of the Mandingoes, . . . passing by at that time, and observing him unarmed, rushed in, to the number of seven or eight at once, at a back door, and pinioned Job, before he could get his arms, together with his interpreter, who is a slave in Maryland still. They then shaved their heads and beards, which Job and his man resented as the highest indignity; tho' the Mandingoes meant no more by it, than to make them appear like slaves taken in war. On the 27th of February, 1730, they carried them to Captain Pike at Gambia, who purchased them; and on the first of March they were put on board. Soon after Job found means to acquaint Captain Pike that he was the same person that came to trade with him a few days before, and after what manner he had been taken. Upon this Captain Pike gave him free leave to redeem himself and his man; and Job sent to an acquaintance of his father's, near Gambia, who promised to send to Job's father, to inform him of what had happened, that he might take some course to have him set at liberty. But it being a fortnight's [two weeks'] journey between that friend's house and his father's, and the ship sailing in about a week after, Job was brought with the rest of the slaves to Annapolis in Maryland, and delivered to Mr. Vachell Denton. . . .

Mr. Vachell Denton sold Job to one Mr. Tolsey in Kent Island in Maryland, who put him to work in making tobacco; but he was soon convinced that Job had never been used to such labour. He every day showed more and more uneasiness under this exercise, and at last grew sick, being no way able to bear it; so his master was obliged to find easier work for him, and therefore put him to tend the cattle. Job would often leave the cattle, and withdraw into the woods to pray; but a white boy frequently watched him, and whilst he was at his devotion would mock him and throw dirt in his face. This very much disturbed Job, and added considerably to his other misfor-

CONCLUSION

European merchants and investors played a central role in the creation of the Atlantic system. European merchants had expanded trade in the century before Columbus, trading over longer distances and using new credit mechanisms to facilitate transactions. They had engaged the

Ayuba Suleiman Diallo (1701–??)

British Library Board

tunes; all which were increased by his ignorance of the English language, which prevented his complaining, or telling his case to any person about him. Grown in some measure desperate, by reason of his present hardships, he resolved to travel at a venture; thinking he might possibly be taken up by some master, who would use him better, or otherwise meet with some lucky accident, to divert or abate his grief. Accordingly, he travelled thro' the woods, till he came to the County of Kent, upon Delaware Bay. . . . There is a law in force, throughout the [mid-Atlantic] colonies . . . as far as Boston in New England, viz. that any Negroe, or white servant who is not known in the county, or has no pass, may be secured by any person, and kept in the common [jail], till the master of such servant shall fetch him. Therefore Job being able to give no account of himself, was put in prison there.

This happened about the beginning of June 1731, when I, who was attending the courts there, and heard of Job, went with several gentlemen to the [jailer's] house, being a tavern, and desired to see him. He was brought into the tavern to us, but could not speak one word of English. Upon our talking and making signs to him, he wrote a line to two before us, and when he read it, pronounced the words Allah and Mahommed; by which, and his refusing a glass of wine we offered him, we perceived he was a Mahometan [Muslim], but could not imagine of what country he was, or how he got thither; for by his affable carriage, and the easy composure of his countenance, we could perceive he was no common slave.

When Job had been some time confined, an old Negroe man, who lived in that neighborhood, and could speak the Jalloff [Wolof] language, which Job also understood, went to him, and conversed with him. By this Negroe the keeper was informed to whom Job belonged, and what was the cause of his leaving his master. The keeper thereupon wrote to his master, who soon after fetched him home, and was much kinder to him than before; allowing him place to pray in, and in some other conveniences, in order to make his slavery as easy as possible. Yet slavery and confinement was by no means agreeable to Job, who had never been used to it; he therefore wrote a letter in Arabick to his father, acquainting him with his misfortunes, hoping he might yet find means to redeem him. . . . It happened that this letter was seen by James Oglethorpe, Esq. [founder of the colony of Georgia and director of the Royal African Company]; who, according to his usual goodness and generosity, took compassion on Job, and [bought him from his master]; his master being very willing to part with him, as finding him no ways fit for his business.

In spring 1733 Job's benefactors took him to England, teaching him passable English during the voyage, and introduced him to the English gentry. Job attracted such attention that local men took up a collection to buy his freedom and pay his debts, and they also introduced him at the royal court. In 1735 Job returned to Gambia in a Royal African Company ship, richly clothed and accompanied by many gifts.

QUESTIONS FOR ANALYSIS

1. **Since Ahmad Baba points out that Islamic law permitted a Muslim to raid and enslave non-Muslims, do you think that the non-Muslim Mandinka (Mandingoes) would have considered it justifiable to enslave Ayuba, since he was a Muslim?**
2. **Which aspects of Ayuba Suleiman's experiences of enslavement were normal, and which unusual?**
3. **How different might Ayuba's experiences of slavery have been had he been sold in Jamaica rather than Maryland?**
4. **How strictly was the ban against enslaving Muslims observed in Hausaland?**

Source: Thomas Hodgkin, ed., *Nigerian Perspectives: An Historical Anthology*, 2nd ed. (London: Oxford University Press, 1975), 154–156; Thomas Bluett, *Some Memoirs of the Life of Job, the Son of Solomon the High Priest of Boonda in Africa* (London: Richard Ford, 1734), 16–24.

markets of Asia through Muslim middlemen and initiated the first tentative contacts with African markets. By the seventeenth century a more confident and adventurous European investor class was ready to promote colonial production and long-distance trade in a much more aggressive way. The development of banks, stock exchanges, and chartered companies supported these new ambitions.

The new Atlantic trading system had great importance in world history. In the first phase of their expansion Europeans conquered and colonized the Americas and captured major Indian Ocean trade routes. The development of the Atlantic system showed their ability to move beyond capturing the benefits of existing systems to create a major new trading network. Beginning in the seventeenth century, the English, Dutch, and French created new colonies in the Caribbean to compete with earlier colonies created by the Spanish and Portuguese (see Chapter 17). While these colonies remained fragile for decades, settlers found ways to profitably produce goods sought by European consumers. Tobacco was the first, but sugar soon supplanted it.

The establishment of plantation societies was not just a matter of replacing native vegetation with alien plants and native peoples with Europeans and Africans. More fundamentally, it made these once-isolated islands part of a dynamic trading system controlled from Europe. The West Indies was not the only place affected. Brazil, large parts of Spanish Central and South America, and the southern region of British North America developed similar linkages, producing sugar, cacao, cotton, coffee, and indigo and using slave labor.

Despite the central importance of their shared dependence on export markets and African slaves, there were important differences among Europe's American tropical colonies. Only the English experimented with indentured labor on a large scale. But like the colonies of the Portuguese, Dutch, and French, they soon depended on African slave labor. Joint-stock companies and individual investors were crucial to the English colonies. The French entered the process late, but the French state and French monopoly companies quickly produced a massive flow of slaves while securing a profitable home market for the sugar of Saint Domingue and other colonies. After the Dutch attacked but failed to hold Portugal's sugar-producing colony of Brazil and the slave-exporting colony of Angola, they became influential in the transfer of sugar technology and the expansion of the slave trade. While Spain had introduced sugar to the Caribbean and imported African slaves in the early sixteenth century, its most important Caribbean colony, Cuba, joined the sugar revolution late, becoming the major destination for the slave trade and the major producer of sugar by 1820.

While Africa played an essential role in the Atlantic system, importing trade goods and exporting slaves to the Americas, the Atlantic system dominated Europe's American colonies much more comprehensively. Africans remained in control of their continent and interacted culturally and politically more with the Islamic world than with the Atlantic.

Sub-Saharan Africa had long-established trade connections with the Islamic world that included the sale of slaves. These trade relationships facilitated the spread of Islam to sub-Saharan Africa and the creation of Islamic states like Mali and Songhai (see Chapter 13). The volume of the Atlantic trade was much larger than the Islamic slave trade, but the Islamic trade persisted after reformers ended the Atlantic trade (see Chapter 23). Between 1550 and 1800 four slaves crossed the Atlantic to European colonies for every slave carried across the Sahara. While more males were carried across the Atlantic, the Islamic trade took more women and children, and few slaves in the Islamic region were subjected to the brutal labor conditions of the West Indian plantations.

KEY TERMS

Atlantic system p. 519
chartered companies p. 520
Dutch West India Company p. 520
plantocracy p. 524
driver p. 524
seasoning p. 526
manumission p. 526
maroon p. 529
capitalism p. 529
mercantilism p. 530
Royal African Company p. 530
Atlantic Circuit p. 530
Middle Passage p. 530
Songhai p. 537
Hausa p. 538
Bornu p. 538

EBOOK AND WEBSITE RESOURCES

Primary Sources

The Interesting Narrative of Olaudah Equiano and Written by Himself

A Voyage to New Calabar River in the Year 1699

Interactive Maps

Map 18.1 The Atlantic Economy

Map 18.2 The African Slave Trade, 1500–1800

Map 18.3 West African States and Trade, 1500–1800

Plus flashcards, practice quizzes, and more. Go to: www.cengage.com/history/bullietearthpeople5e

SUGGESTED READING

Blackburn, Robin. *The Making of New World Slavery*. 1997. A reliable introduction to the topic.

Curtin, Philip D. *The Rise and Fall of the Plantation Complex*. 1990. Excellent introduction to the Atlantic system.

Davis, David Brion. *Inhuman Bondage. The Rise and Fall of Slavery in the New World*. 2006. While centered on the American South, Davis provides a challenging summary of the larger implications of slavery in the Americas.

Davis, David Brion. *The Problem of Slavery in Western Culture*. 1966. A classic study from a broad perspective.

Eltis, David. *The Rise of African Slavery in the Americas*. 2000.

Heywood, Linda M., and John K. Thornton. *Central Africans, Atlantic Creoles, and the Foundation of the Americas, 1585–1660*. Examines the cultural influences of Central Africans in the development of the Americas.

Klein, Herbert S. *African Slavery in Latin America and the Caribbean*. 1986. A fine synthesis of research on New World slavery, including North American slave systems.

Lovejoy, Paul. *Transformations in Slavery: A History of Slavery in Africa*, 2nd ed. 2000. Contains recent research on slavery and the African, Atlantic, and Muslim slave trades.

Manning, Patrick. *Slavery and African Life: Occidental, Oriental, and African Slave Trades*. 1990. A reliable comparison of the Atlantic and Muslim slave trades.

Northrup, David. *Africa's Discovery of Europe, 1450–1850*. 2002. An exploration of connections of African communities to the Atlantic world.

Northrup, David, ed. *The Atlantic Slave Trade*, 2nd ed. 2002. A collection of debates on the slave trade.

Ogot, B. A., ed. *UNESCO General History of Africa*, vol. 5. 1992. A good place for students to begin research on African topics.

Oliver, Roland, and Anthony Atmore. *The African Middle Ages, 1400–1800*, 2nd ed. 2003. A useful summary of African history in this period.

Price, Richard, ed. *Maroon Societies: Rebel Slave Communities in the Americas*, 2nd ed. 1979. The classic study of slave runaway communities in the Caribbean.

Thomas, Hugh. *The Slave Trade: The Story of the Atlantic Slave Trade, 1440–1870*. 1999. This is one of the best comprehensive treatments of the slave trade.

Thornton, John. *Africa and Africans in the Making of the Atlantic World, 1400–1800*, 2nd ed. 1998. Examines cultural connections among African communities on both sides of the Atlantic.

Trimingham, J. Spencer. *The Influence of Islam upon Africa*. 1968.

Wallerstein, Immanuel. *The Modern World-System*, 3 vols. (1974–1989). An examination of the global context of early modern capitalism.

Webb, James L. A., Jr. *Desert Frontier: Ecological and Economic Change Along the Western Sahel, 1600–1850*. 1995. A useful introduction to Islam's cultural and commercial contacts with sub-Saharan Africa.

NOTES

1. Willem Bosman, *A New and Accurate Description of Guinea, etc.* (London, 1705), quoted in David Northrup, ed., *The Atlantic Slave Trade* (Lexington, MA: D. C. Heath, 1994), 72.
2. Roland Oliver and Anthony Atmore, *The African Middle Ages, 1400–1800* (Cambridge, England: Cambridge University Press, 1981), 100.
3. King Osei Bonsu, quoted in Northrup, ed., *The Atlantic Slave Trade*, 93.
4. Alexander Falconbridge, *Account of the Slave Trade on the Coast of Africa* (London: J. Phillips, 1788), 12.
5. Joseph C. Miller, "The Significance of Drought, Disease, and Famine in the Agriculturally Marginal Zones of West-Central Africa," *Journal of African History*, 23 (1982): 17–61.

AP* REVIEW QUESTIONS FOR CHAPTER 18

1. A main impetus for the introduction of African slavery in the Americas was the
   (A) introduction of cash crops such as sugar cane.
   (B) need to lower the population in African colonies.
   (C) desire to Christianize the entire region.
   (D) Amerindians' refusal to work for the Europeans.

2. The establishment of plantation agriculture in the Americas was based on the belief that these plantations would
   (A) be completely self-sufficient and develop products in an efficient manner.
   (B) encourage improved use of the land.
   (C) help to decrease the need for labor.
   (D) benefit everyone who worked on one of them.

3. Particularly in the West Indies, the power resided
   (A) with the home government in Europe.
   (B) with the merchants who purchased crops from the islands.
   (C) in the hands of the plantocracy on each island.
   (D) with the small farmers who produced the food for the islands.

4. One reason for the high volume of slaves transported from Africa to the New World was that
   (A) French colonial laws allowed for the execution of slaves for minor offenses.
   (B) slaves had a high mortality rate during the first year in the New World.
   (C) thousands of slaves ran away and joined forces with the Indians.
   (D) slaves were inexpensive, and even small farmers owned slaves.

5. The practice of accumulating capital in your own state and limiting trade with other nations is
   (A) capitalism.
   (B) mercantilism.
   (C) democracy.
   (D) triangular trade.

6. One reason that many African tribes did not initially fight the Europeans over capturing slaves was that
   (A) African rulers and merchants exported slaves to obtain foreign goods.
   (B) the Europeans took non-Muslims as slaves.
   (C) they had no weapons that could oppose the Europeans.
   (D) African tribes were overpopulated, and slavery was a way to lower their population.

7. The majority of the slaves in the Islamic world were
   (A) converts to Islam.
   (B) not permanent slaves.
   (C) soldiers or house servants.
   (D) mistresses kept in harems.

8. In the seventeenth century,
   (A) most European monarchs were funding colonies in Africa and Asia.
   (B) the importation of slaves from Africa began to decline.
   (C) the demand for profits drove new European investors to sink money in long-distance trade and colonial ventures.
   (D) colonial wars forced most monarchs to take direct control of their colonies.

9. Unlike European slave trading, Islamic slave trading
   (A) was not profitable.
   (B) took more women and children from Africa than men.
   (C) was focused mainly on the sale of slaves to Mughal India.
   (D) was directly linked to the caravan trade.

10. In the English colonies, slavery became more common as
   (A) the use of indentured servants became more costly.
   (B) the Crown banned the use of indentured servants.
   (C) the price of slaves decreased with the increase in supply.
   (D) mercantilist policies in Europe began to increase.

CHAPTER 19

CHAPTER OUTLINE

- The Ottoman Empire, to 1750
- The Safavid Empire, 1502–1722
- The Mughal Empire, 1526–1761
- The Maritime Worlds of Islam, 1500–1750
- Conclusion

DIVERSITY + DOMINANCE *Islamic Law and Ottoman Rule*

ENVIRONMENT + TECHNOLOGY *Tobacco and Waterpipes*

Funeral Procession of Suleiman the Magnificent Each Ottoman sultan wore a distinctive turban, hence the visible turban representing the body in the hearse.

Visit the website and ebook for additional study materials and interactive tools: www.cengage.com/history/bullietearthpeople5e

Southwest Asia and the Indian Ocean, 1500–1750

- How did the Ottoman Empire rise to power, and what factors contributed to its transformation?
- How did the Safavid Empire both resemble and differ from its neighbors?
- How did the Mughal Empire combine Muslim and Hindu elements into an effective state?
- What role does maritime history play in the political and economic life of this period?

In 1541 a woman named Sabah appeared before an Ottoman judge in the town of Aintab in southern Turkey to answer several charges: that she had brought men and women together illegally and that she had fostered heresy. In her court testimony, she stated the following:

> I gather girls and brides and women in my home. I negotiated with Ibrahim b. Nazih and the two youths who are his apprentices, and in exchange for paying them a month's fee, I had them come every day to the girls and brides in my house and I had them preach and give instruction. There are no males at those sessions besides the said Ibrahim and his apprentices; there are only women and girls and young brides. This kind of thing is what I have always done for a living.[1]

Two male neighbors testified differently:

> She holds gatherings of girls and brides and women in her home. . . . While she says that she has [Ibrahim] preach, she actually has him speak evil things. She has him conduct spiritual conversations with these girls and brides. . . . [I]n the ceremonies, the girls and brides and women spin around waving their hands, and they bring themselves into a trancelike state by swaying and dancing. They perform the ceremonies according to Kizilbash teachings. We too have wives and families, and we are opposed to illegal activities like this.[2]

The judge made no finding on the charge of heresy, but he ordered Sabah to be publicly humiliated and banished from town for unlawfully mixing the sexes. Ibrahim was also banished.

This uncommon story taken from Ottoman religious court records sheds light on several aspects of daily life in a provincial town. It provides an example of a woman making her living by arranging religious instruction for other women. It also demonstrates the willingness of neighbors, in this case males, to complain in court about activities they considered immoral. And its suggestion that Sabah was promoting the qizilbash heresy, which at that time was considered a state threat because it was the ideology of the enemy Safavid Empire next door, shows that townspeople thought it plausible that women could act to promote religious doctrines.

Studies of everyday life through court records and other state and nonstate documents are a recent development in Ottoman and Safavid history. They produce an image of these societies that differs greatly from the pomp and formality conveyed by European travelers and official histories. As a consequence, accounts of capricious and despotic actions taken by shahs and sultans are increasingly being balanced by stories of common people, who were much more concerned with the maintenance of a sound legal and moral order than were some of the denizens of the imperial palaces. The doings of rulers remain an important historical focus, of course, but stories about ordinary folk perhaps give a better picture of the habits and mores of the majority of the population.

THE OTTOMAN EMPIRE, TO 1750

Ottoman Empire Islamic state founded by Osman in northwestern Anatolia ca. 1300. After the fall of the Byzantine Empire, the Ottoman Empire was based at Istanbul (formerly Constantinople) from 1453 to 1922. It encompassed lands in the Middle East, North Africa, the Caucasus, and eastern Europe.

The most long-lived of the post-Mongol Muslim empires was the **Ottoman Empire**, founded around 1300 (see Map 19.1). By extending Islamic conquests into eastern Europe, starting in the late fourteenth century, and by taking Syria and Egypt from the Mamluk rulers in the early sixteenth, the Ottomans seemed to recreate the might of the original Islamic caliphate, the empire established by the Muslim Arab conquests in the seventh century. However, the empire was actually more like the new centralized monarchies of France and Spain (see Chapter 16) than any medieval model.

Enduring more than five centuries, until 1922, the Ottoman Empire survived several periods of wrenching change, some caused by internal problems, others by the growing power of European adversaries. These periods of change reveal the problems faced by huge land-based empires around the world.

Expansion and Frontiers

Established around 1300, the Ottoman Empire grew from a tiny state in northwestern Anatolia because of three factors: (1) the shrewdness of its founder, Osman (from which the name *Ottoman* comes), and his descendants, (2) control of a strategic link between Europe and Asia on the Dardanelles strait, and (3) the creation of an army that took advantage of the traditional skills of the Turkish cavalryman and the new military possibilities presented by gunpowder.

The Battle of Kosovo

At first, Ottoman armies concentrated on Christian enemies in Greece and the Balkans, in 1389 conquering a strong Serbian kingdom at the Battle of Kosovo (KO-so-vo). Much of southeastern Europe and Anatolia was under the control of the sultans by 1402. In 1453, Sultan Mehmed II, "the Conqueror," laid siege to Constantinople. His forces used enormous cannon to bash in the city's walls, dragged warships over a high hill from the Bosporus strait to the city's inner harbor to get around its sea defenses, and finally penetrated the city's land walls through a series of direct infantry assaults. The fall of Constantinople—henceforth commonly known as Istanbul—brought to an end over eleven hundred years of Byzantine rule and made the Ottomans seem invincible.

Suleiman the Magnificent

Suleiman the Magnificent The most illustrious sultan of the Ottoman Empire (r. 1520–1566); also known as Suleiman Kanuni, "The Lawgiver." He significantly expanded the empire in the Balkans and eastern Mediterranean.

Selim (seh-LEEM) I, "the Grim," conquered Egypt and Syria in 1516 and 1517, making the Red Sea the Ottomans' southern frontier. His son, **Suleiman** (SOO-lay-man) **the Magnificent** (r. 1520–1566), presided over the greatest Ottoman assault on Christian Europe. Suleiman seemed unstoppable: he conquered Belgrade in 1521, expelled the Knights of the Hospital of St. John from the island of Rhodes the following year, and laid siege to Vienna in 1529. Vienna was saved by the need to retreat before the onset of winter more than by military action. In later centuries, Ottoman historians looked back on the reign of Suleiman as the period when the imperial system worked to perfection, and they spoke of it as the golden age of Ottoman greatness.

While Ottoman armies pressed deeper and deeper into eastern Europe, the sultans also sought to control the Mediterranean. Between 1453 and 1502, the Ottomans fought the opening rounds of a two-century war with Venice, the most powerful of Italy's commercial city-states. The initial fighting left Venice in control of its lucrative islands for another century. But it also left Venice a reduced military power compelled to pay tribute to the Ottomans.

The Portuguese Threat

In the early sixteenth century, merchants from southern India and Sumatra sent emissaries to Istanbul requesting naval support against the Portuguese. The Ottomans responded vigorously to Portuguese threats close to their territories, such as at Aden at the southern entrance

CHRONOLOGY

	Ottoman Empire	Safavid Empire	Mughal Empire
1500		1502–1524 Shah Ismail establishes Safavid rule in Iran	
	1516–1517 Selim I conquers Egypt and Syria		
	1520–1566 Reign of Suleiman the Magnificent; peak of Ottoman Empire		1526 Babur defeats last sultan of Delhi
	1529 First Ottoman siege of Vienna		
			1556–1605 Akbar rules in Agra; peak of Mughal Empire
	1571 Ottoman naval defeat at Lepanto		
		1587–1629 Reign of Shah Abbas the Great; peak of Safavid Empire	
1600			
	1610 End of Anatolian revolts		
			1658–1707 Aurangzeb imposes conservative Islamic regime
1700			
		1722 Afghan invaders topple last Safavid shah	
	1730 Janissary revolt begins period of Ottoman conservatism	1736–1747 Nadir Shah temporarily reunites Iran; invades India (1739)	1739 Iranians under Nadir Shah sack Delhi

Robert Frerck/Woodfin Camp & Associates

Aya Sofya Mosque in Istanbul Originally a Byzantine cathedral, Aya Sofya (in Greek, Hagia Sophia) was transformed into a mosque after 1453, and four minarets were added. It then became a model for subsequent Ottoman mosques. To the right behind it is the Bosporus strait dividing Europe and Asia, to the left the Golden Horn inlet separating the old city of Istanbul from the newer parts. The gate to the Ottoman sultan's palace is to the right of the mosque. The pointed tower to the left of the dome is part of the palace.

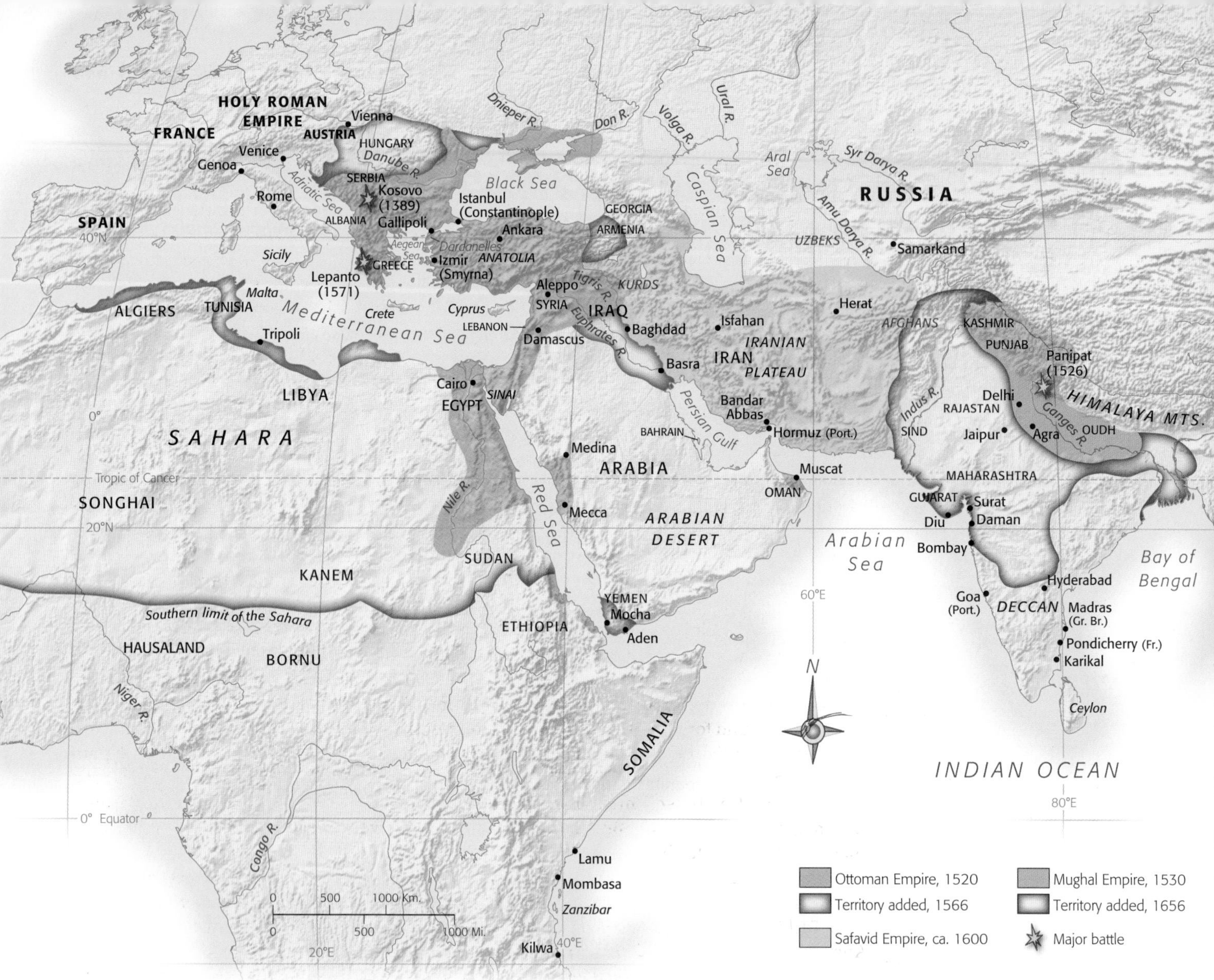

MAP 19.1 Muslim Empires in the Sixteenth and Seventeenth Centuries Iran, a Shi'ite state flanked by Sunni Ottomans on the west and Sunni Mughals on the east, had the least exposure to European influences. Ottoman expansion across the southern Mediterranean Sea intensified European fears of Islam. The areas of strongest Mughal control dictated that Islam's spread into Southeast Asia would be heavily influenced by merchants and religious figures from Gujarat instead of from eastern India.

e Interactive Map

to the Red Sea, but their efforts farther afield were insufficient to stifle growing Portuguese domination.

Eastern luxury products still flowed to Ottoman markets. Portuguese power was territorially limited to fortified coastal points, such as Hormuz at the entrance to the Persian Gulf, Goa in western India, and Malacca in Malaya. It never occurred to the Ottomans that a sea empire held together by flimsy ships could truly rival a great land empire fielding an army of a hundred thousand men. Why commit major resources to subduing an enemy whose main threat was a demand that merchant vessels, mostly belonging to non-Ottoman Muslims, buy protection from Portuguese attack? The Ottomans did send a small naval force to Indonesia, but they never formulated a consistent or aggressive policy with regard to political and economic developments in the Indian Ocean.

Central Institutions

The Janissary Corps

By the 1520s, the Ottoman Empire was the most powerful and best-organized state in either Europe or the Islamic world. Its military was balanced between cavalry archers, primarily

Janissaries Infantry, originally of slave origin, armed with firearms and constituting the elite of the Ottoman army from the fifteenth century until the corps was abolished in 1826.

Turks, and **Janissaries** (JAN-nih-say-rees), Christian prisoners of war induced to serve as military slaves.

Slave soldiery had a long history in Islamic lands, but the conquest of Christian territories in the Balkans in the late fourteenth century gave the Ottomans access to a new military resource. Converted to Islam, these "new troops," called *yeni cheri* in Turkish and *Janissaries* in English, gave the Ottomans unusual military flexibility. Since horseback riding and bowmanship were not part of their cultural backgrounds, they readily accepted the idea of fighting on foot and learning to use guns, which at that time were still too heavy and awkward for a horseman to load and fire. The Janissaries lived in barracks and trained all year round.

Child Levy

AP* Exam Tip Ottoman social and political institutions are topics that are tested on the exam.

The process of selection for Janissary training changed early in the fifteenth century. The new system, called the *devshirme*, imposed a regular levy of male children on Christian villages in the Balkans and occasionally elsewhere. Recruited children were placed with Turkish families to learn their language and then were sent to the sultan's palace in Istanbul for an education that included instruction in Islam, military training, and, for the most talented, what we might call liberal arts. This regime, sophisticated for its time, produced not only the Janissary soldiers but also, from among the chosen few who received special training, senior military commanders and heads of government departments up to the rank of grand vizier.

The cavalrymen were supported by land grants and administered most rural areas in Anatolia and the Balkans. They maintained order, collected taxes, and reported for each summer's campaign with their horses, retainers, and supplies, all paid for from the taxes they collected. When not campaigning, they stayed at home.

Naval Warfare

A galley-equipped navy was manned by Greek, Turkish, Algerian, and Tunisian sailors, usually under the command of an admiral from one of the North African ports. The balance of the Ottoman land forces brought success to Ottoman arms in recurrent wars with the Safavids, who were much slower to adopt firearms, and in the inexorable conquest of the Balkans. Expansion by sea was less dramatic. A major expedition against Malta in the western Mediterranean failed in 1565. Combined Christian forces also achieved a massive naval victory at the Battle of Lepanto, off Greece, in 1571. But the Ottomans' resources were so extensive that in a year's time they had replaced all of the galleys sunk in that battle.

The Military Class

The Ottoman Empire became cosmopolitan in character. The sophisticated court language, Osmanli (os-MAHN-lih) (the Turkish form of *Ottoman*), shared basic grammar and vocabulary with Turkish, but Arabic and Persian elements made it distinct from the language spoken by Anatolia's nomads and villagers. Everyone who served in the military or the bureaucracy and conversed in Osmanli was considered to belong to the *askeri* (AS-keh-ree), or "military," class. Members of this class were exempt from taxes and owed their well-being to the sultan.

The Ottomans saw the sultan as providing justice for his "flock of sheep" (*raya* [RAH-yah]) and the military protecting them. In return, the raya paid the taxes that supported both the sultan and the military. In reality, the sultan's government remained comparatively isolated from the lives of most subjects. As Islam gradually became the majority religion in Balkan regions, Islamic law (the Shari'a [sha-REE-ah]) conditioned urban institutions and social life (see Diversity and Dominance: Islamic Law and Ottoman Rule). Local customs prevailed among non-Muslims and in many rural areas, and non-Muslims looked to their own religious leaders for guidance in family and spiritual matters.

Crisis of the Military State, 1585–1650

As military technology evolved, cannon and lighter-weight firearms played an ever-larger role on the battlefield. Accordingly, the size of the Janissary corps—and its cost to the government—grew steadily, and the role of the Turkish cavalry diminished. To pay the Janissaries, the sultan started reducing the number of landholding cavalrymen. Revenues previously spent on their living expenses and military equipment went directly into the imperial treasury. Inflation caused by a flood of cheap silver from the New World bankrupted many of the remaining landholders, who were restricted by law to collecting a fixed amount of taxes. Their land was returned to the state. Displaced cavalrymen, armed and unhappy, became a restive element in rural Anatolia.

Crisis and Revolt

This complicated situation resulted in revolts that devastated Anatolia between 1590 and 1610. Former landholding cavalrymen, short-term soldiers released at the end of the campaign season, peasants overburdened by emergency taxes, and even impoverished students of reli-

Islamic Law and Ottoman Rule

Ebu's-Su'ud was the Mufti of Istanbul from 1545 to 1574, serving under the sultans Suleiman the Magnificent (1520–1566) and his son Selim II (1566–1574). Originally one of many city-based religious scholars giving opinions on matters of law, the mufti of Istanbul by Ebu's-Su'ud's time had become the top religious official in the empire and the personal adviser to the sultan on religious and legal matters. The position would later acquire the title Shaikh al-Islam.

Historians debate the degree of independence these muftis had. Since the ruler, as a Muslim, was subject to the Shari'a, the mufti could theoretically veto his policies. On important matters, however, the mufti more often seemed to come up with the answer that best suited the sultan who appointed him. This bias is not apparent in more mundane areas of the law.

The collection of Ebu's-Su'ud's fatwas, or legal opinions, from which the examples below are drawn shows the range of matters that came to his attention. They are also an excellent source for understanding the problems of his time, the relationship between Islamic law and imperial governance, and the means by which the state asserted its dominance over the common people. Some opinions respond directly to questions posed by the sultan. Others are hypothetical, using the names Zeyd, 'Amr, and Hind the way police today use John Doe and Jane Doe. While qadis, or Islamic judges, made findings of fact in specific cases on trial, muftis issued only opinions on matters of law. A qadi as well as a plaintiff or defendant might ask a question of a mufti. Later jurists consulted collections of fatwas for precedents, but the fatwas had no permanent binding power.

On the plan of Selim II to attack the Venetians in Crete in 1570

A land was previously in the realm of Islam. After a while, the abject infidels overran it, destroyed the colleges and mosques, and left them vacant. They filled the pulpits and the galleries with the tokens of infidelity and error, intending to insult the religion of Islam with all kinds of vile deeds, and by spreading their ugly acts to all corners of the earth.

His Excellency the Sultan, the Refuge of Religion, has, as zeal for Islam requires, determined to take the aforementioned land from the possession of the shameful infidels and to annex it to the realm of Islam.

When peace was previously concluded with the other lands in the possession of the said infidels, the aforenamed land was included. An explanation is sought as to whether, in accordance with the pure shari'a, this is an impediment to the Sultan's determining to break the treaty.

Answer: There is no possibility that it could ever be an impediment. For the Sultan of the People of Islam (may God glorify his victories) to make peace with the infidels is legal only when there is a benefit to all Muslims. When there is no benefit, peace is never legal. When a benefit has been seen, and it is then observed to be more beneficial to break it, then to break it becomes absolutely obligatory and binding.

His Excellency [Muhammad] the Apostle of God (may God bless him and give him peace) made a ten-year truce with the Meccan infidels in the sixth year of the Hegira. His Excellency 'Ali (may God ennoble his face) wrote a document that was corroborated and confirmed. Then, in the following year, it was considered more beneficial to break it and, in the eighth year of the Hegira, [the Prophet] attacked [the Meccans], and conquered Mecca the Mighty.

On war against the Shi'ite Muslim Safavids of Iran

Is it licit according to the shari'a to fight the followers of the Safavids? Is the person who kills them a holy warrior, and the person who dies at their hands a martyr?

Answer: Yes, it is a great holy war and a glorious martyrdom.

Assuming that it is licit to fight them, is this simply because of their rebellion and enmity against the [Ottoman] Sultan of the People of Islam, because they drew the sword against the troops of Islam, or what?

Answer: They are both rebels and, from many points of view, infidels.

Can the children of Safavid subjects captured in the Nakhichevan campaign be enslaved?

Answer: No.

The followers of the Safavids are killed by order of the Sultan. If it turns out that some of the prisoners, young and old, are [Christian] Armenian[s], are they set free?

Answer: Yes. So long as the Armenians have not joined the Safavid troops in attacking and fighting against the troops of Islam, it is illegal to take them prisoner.

On the Holy Land

Are all the Arab realms Holy Land, or does it have specific boundaries, and what is the difference between the Holy Land and other lands?

Answer: Syria is certainly called the Holy Land. Jerusalem, Aleppo and its surroundings, and Damascus belong to it.

On land-grants

What lands are private property, and what lands are held by feudal tenure [i.e., assignment in exchange for military service]?

Answer: Plots of land within towns are private property. Their owners may sell them, donate them or convert them to trust. When [the owner] dies, [the land] passes to all the heirs. Lands held by feudal tenure are cultivated lands around villages, whose occupants bear the burden of their services and pay a portion of their [produce in tax]. They cannot sell the land, donate it or convert it to trust. When they die, if they have sons, these have the use [of the land]. Otherwise, the cavalryman gives [it to someone else] by *tapu* [title deed].

On the consumption of coffee

Zeyd drinks coffee to aid concentration or digestion. Is this licit?

Answer: How can anyone consume this reprehensible [substance], which dissolute men drink when engaged in games and debauchery?

The Sultan, the Refuge of Religion, has on many occasions banned coffee-houses. However, a group of ruffians take no notice, but keep coffee-houses for a living. In order to draw the crowds, they take on unbearded apprentices, and have ready instruments of entertainment and play, such as chess and backgammon. The city's rakes, rogues and vagabond boys gather there to consume opium and hashish. On top of this, they drink coffee and, when they are high, engage in games and false sciences, and neglect the prescribed prayers. In law, what should happen to a judge who is able to prevent the said coffee-sellers and drinkers, but does not do so?

Answer: Those who perpetrate these ugly deeds should be prevented and deterred by severe chastisement and long imprisonment. Judges who neglect to deter them should be dismissed.

On matters of theft

How are thieves to be "carefully examined"?

Answer: His Excellency 'Ali (may God ennoble his face) appointed Imam Shuraih as judge. It so happened that, at that time, several people took a Muslim's son to another district. The boy disappeared and, when the people came back, the missing boy's father brought them before Judge Shuraih. [When he brought] a claim [against them on account of the loss of his son], they denied it, saying: "No harm came to him from us." Judge Shuraih thought deeply and was perplexed.

When the man told his tale to His Excellency 'Ali, [the latter] summoned Judge Shuraih and questioned him. When Shuraih said; "Nothing came to light by the shari'a," ['Ali] summoned all the people who had taken the man's son, separated them from one another, and questioned them separately. For each of their stopping places, he asked: "What was the boy wearing in that place? What did you eat? And where did he disappear?" In short, he made each of them give a detailed account, and when their words contradicted each other, each of their statements was written down separately. Then he brought them all together, and when the contradictions became apparent, they were no longer able to deny [their guilt] and confessed to what had happened.

This kind of ingenuity is a requirement of the case. [This fatwa appears to justify investigation of crimes by the state instead of by the qadi. Judging from court records, which contain very few criminal cases, it seems likely that in practice, many criminal cases were dealt with outside the jurisdiction of the qadi's court.]

Zeyd takes 'Amr's donkey without his knowledge and sells it. Is he a thief?

Answer: His hand is not cut off.

Zeyd mounts 'Amr's horse as a courier and loses it. Is compensation necessary?

Answer: Yes.

In which case: What if Zeyd has a Sultanic decree [authorizing him] to take horses for courier service?

Answer: Compensation is required in any case. He was not commanded to lose [the horse]. Even if he were commanded, it is the person who loses it who is liable.

On homicides

Zeyd enters Hind's house and tries to have intercourse forcibly. Since Hind can repel him by no other means, she strikes and wounds him with an axe. If Zeyd dies of the wound, is Hind liable for anything?

Answer: She has performed an act of Holy War [*jihad*].

QUESTIONS FOR ANALYSIS

1. **What do these fatwas indicate with regard to the balance between practical legal reasoning and religious dictates?**
2. **How much was the Ottoman government constrained by the Shari'a?**
3. **What can be learned about day-to-day life from materials of this sort?**

Source: Excerpts from Colin Imber, *Ebu's-Su'ud: The Islamic Legal Tradition*.

Ottoman Glassmakers on Parade Celebrations of the circumcisions of the sultan's sons featured parades organized by the craft guilds of Istanbul. This float features glassmaking, a common craft in Islamic realms. The most elaborate glasswork included oil lamps for mosques and colored glass for the small stained-glass windows below mosque domes.

Topkapi Palace Museum

gion formed bands of marauders. Anatolia experienced the worst of the rebellions and suffered greatly from emigration and the loss of agricultural production. But an increase in banditry, made worse by the government's inability to stem the spread of muskets among the general public, beset other parts of the empire as well.

Janissary Privileges

In the meantime, the Janissaries took advantage of their growing influence to gain relief from prohibitions on their marrying and engaging in business. Janissaries who involved themselves in commerce lessened the burden on the state budget, and married Janissaries who enrolled sons or relatives in the corps made it possible in the seventeenth century for the government to save state funds by abolishing forced recruitment. These savings, however, were more than offset by the increase in the total number of Janissaries and in their steady deterioration as a military force, which necessitated the hiring of more and more supplemental troops.

Economic Change and Growing Weakness

A very different Ottoman Empire emerged from this crisis. The sultan once had led armies. Now he mostly resided in his palace and had little experience of the real world, and the affairs of government were overseen more and more by the chief administrators—the grand viziers.

Tax Farming

The Janissaries took advantage of their increased power to make membership in their corps hereditary. Their involvement in crafts and trading took a toll on their military skills, but they continued to be a powerful faction in urban politics. Land grants in return for military service also disappeared, and tax farming arose in their place. Tax farmers paid specific taxes, such as customs duties, in advance in return for the privilege of collecting a greater amount from the actual taxpayers.

Rural administration, already disrupted by the rebellions, suffered from the transition to tax farms. The former military landholders had kept order on their lands in order to maintain their incomes. Tax farmers were less likely to live on the land. The imperial government therefore faced greater administrative burdens and came to rely heavily on powerful provincial governors or on wealthy men who purchased lifelong tax collection rights and behaved more or less like private landowners.

The Port of Izmir

Rural disorder and decline in administrative control sometimes opened the way for new economic opportunities. The port of Izmir (IZ-meer), known to Europeans by the ancient name "Smyrna," had a population in 1580 of around two thousand, many of them Greek-speaking Christians. By 1650 the population had increased to between thirty thousand and forty thousand. Along with refugees from the Anatolian uprisings and from European pirate attacks along the coast came European merchants and large colonies of Armenians and Jews. A French traveler in 1621 wrote: "At present, Izmir has a great traffic in wool, beeswax, cotton, and silk, which the Armenians bring there instead of going to Aleppo . . . because they do not pay as many dues."[3]

Izmir transformed itself between 1580 and 1650 from a small town into a multiethnic, multireligious, multilinguistic entrepôt because of the Ottoman government's inability to control trade and the slowly growing dominance of European traders in the Indian Ocean. Spices from the East, though still traded in Aleppo and other long-established Ottoman centers, were not to be found in Izmir. Aside from Iranian silk brought in by caravan, European traders at Izmir purchased local agricultural products—dried fruits, sesame seeds, nuts, and olive oil. As a consequence, local farmers who previously had grown grain for subsistence shifted their plantings more and more to cotton and other cash crops, including, after its introduction in the 1590s, tobacco, which quickly became popular in the Ottoman Empire despite government prohibitions (see Environment and Technology: Tobacco and Waterpipes). In this way, the agricultural economy of western Anatolia, the Balkans, and the Mediterranean coast—the Ottoman lands most accessible to Europe (see Map 19.1)—became enmeshed in a growing European commercial network.

Second Siege of Vienna

At the same time, military power slowly ebbed. The ill-trained Janissaries sometimes resorted to hiring substitutes to go on campaign, and the sultans relied on partially trained seasonal recruits and on armies raised by the governors of frontier provinces. A second mighty siege on Vienna failed in 1683, and by the middle of the eighteenth century it was obvious to the Austrians and Russians that the Ottoman Empire was weakening. On the eastern front, however, Ottoman exhaustion after many wars was matched by the demise in 1722 of their perennial adversary, the Safavid state of Iran.

Trade Agreements

The Ottoman Empire lacked both the wealth and the inclination to match European economic advances. Overland trade from the East dwindled as political disorder in Safavid Iran cut deeply into Iranian silk production. Coffee, an Arabian product that rose from obscurity in the fifteenth century to become the rage first in the Ottoman Empire and then in Europe, was grown in the highlands of Yemen and exported by way of Egypt. By 1770, however, Muslim merchants trading in the Yemeni port of Mocha (MOH-kuh) (literally "the coffee place") were charged 15 percent in duties and fees. But European traders, benefiting from long-standing trade agreements with the Ottoman Empire, paid little more than 3 percent.

Such trade agreements, called capitulations, from Latin *capitula*, or chapter, were first granted as favors by powerful sultans, but they eventually led to European domination of Ottoman seaborne trade. Nevertheless, the Europeans did not control strategic ports in the Mediterranean comparable to Malacca in the Indian Ocean and Hormuz on the Persian Gulf, so their economic power stopped short of colonial settlement or direct control in Ottoman territories.

The Tulip Period

Tulip Period (1718–1730) Last years of the reign of Ottoman sultan Ahmed III, during which European styles and attitudes became briefly popular in Istanbul.

A few astute Ottoman statesmen observed the growing disarray of the empire and advised the sultans to reestablish the land-grant and devshirme systems of Suleiman's reign. Most people, however, could not perceive the downward course of imperial power, much less the reasons behind it. Far from seeing Europe as the enemy that would eventually dismantle the empire, the Istanbul elite experimented with European clothing and furniture styles and purchased printed books from the empire's first (and short-lived) press. Ottoman historians named the period between 1718 and 1730 when European fashions were in favor the **"Tulip Period"** because of the craze for high-priced tulip bulbs that swept Ottoman ruling circles. The craze echoed a Dutch tulip mania that had begun in the mid-sixteenth century, when the flower was introduced into Holland from Istanbul. The mania peaked in 1636 with particularly rare bulbs going for 2,500 florins apiece—the value of twenty-two oxen.

Patrona Halil Rebellion

In 1730, however, gala soirees at which guests watched turtles with candles on their backs wander in the dark through massive tulip beds gave way to a conservative Janissary revolt with strong religious overtones. Sultan Ahmed III abdicated, and the leader of the revolt, Patrona Halil (pa-TROH-nuh ha-LEEL), an Albanian former seaman and stoker of the public baths, swaggered around the capital for several months dictating government policies before he was seized and executed.

ENVIRONMENT + TECHNOLOGY

Tobacco and Waterpipes

Tobacco, a plant native to the Western Hemisphere, may have been introduced into Ottoman Syria as early as 1570 and was certainly known in Istanbul by 1600. In Iran, one historian noted that when an Uzbek ruler entered the northeast province of Khurasan in 1612 and called for tobacco, it was quickly provided for him, while a Spanish diplomat remarked just a few years later that Shah Abbas, who had banned smoking as a sinful practice, nevertheless permitted an envoy from the Mughal sultan to indulge. European traders initially brought tobacco by sea, but it quickly became a cultivated crop in Mughal India, whence it was exported to Iran. By the middle of the seventeenth century, however, it had also become a significant crop in Ottoman and Safavid territories.

The waterpipe became a distinctive means of smoking in the Islamic world, but when the device came into use is disputed. Iranian historians assert that it was invented in Iran, where one reference in poetry goes back to before 1550. This early date suggests that waterpipes may have been used for smoking some other substance before tobacco became known. Straight pipes of clay or wood were also used, especially in Turkish areas and among poorer people.

The Persian word for a waterpipe, *qalyan*, comes from an Arabic verb meaning "to boil, or bubble." Arabic has two common words: *nargila*, which derives ultimately from the Sanskrit word for "coconut," and *shisha*, which means "glass" in Persian. In India, where coconuts were often used to contain the water, the usual term was *hookah*, meaning "jar." The absence of a clear linguistic indication of the country of origin enhances the possibility that waterpipes evolved and spread before the introduction of tobacco.

All levels of society took to smoking, with women enjoying it as much as men. The leisurely ceremony of preparing and lighting the waterpipe made it an ideal pastime in coffeehouses, which became popular in both the Ottoman and Safavid Empires. In other settings, the size and fragility of the waterpipe could cause inconvenience. When traveling, wealthy Iranian men sometimes had a pipe carrier in their entourage who carried the *qalyan* in his hand and had a small pot containing hot coals dangling from his saddle in case his master should wish to light up on the road.

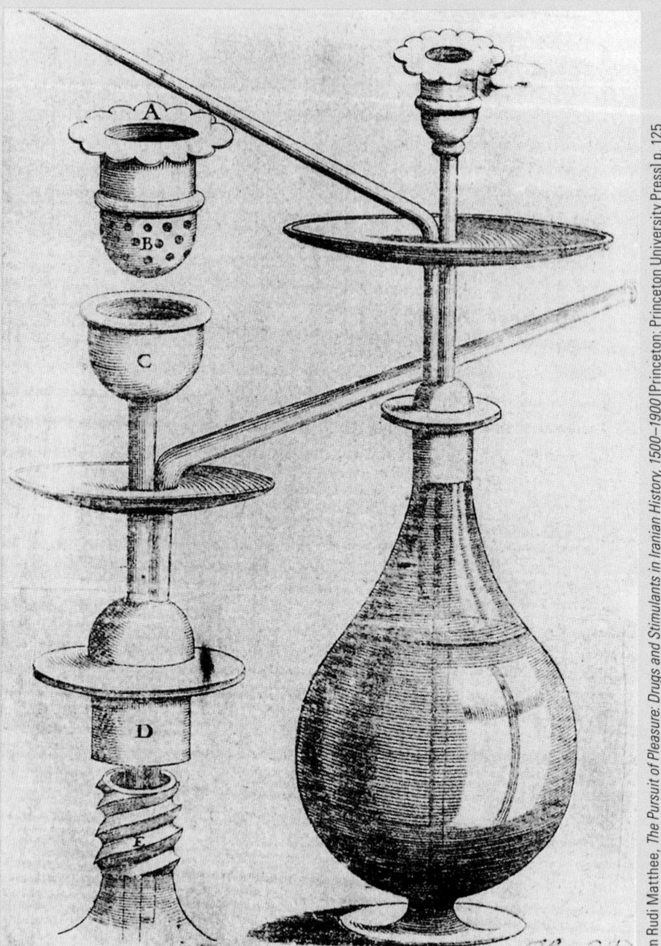

From Rudi Matthee, *The Pursuit of Pleasure: Drugs and Stimulants in Iranian History, 1500–1900* (Princeton: Princeton University Press) p. 125

Iranian Waterpipe Moistened tobacco is placed in cup A, and a glowing coal is put on top of it to make it smolder. When the smoker draws on the stem sticking out to the side, the smoke bubbles up from beneath the water, which cools and filters it. The sophisticated manufacture shown in this drawing, which was rendered in 1622, supports the theory that the waterpipe went through a lengthy period of development before the seventeenth century.

The Patrona Halil rebellion confirmed the perceptions of a few that the Ottoman Empire was facing severe difficulties. Yet decay at the center spelled benefit elsewhere. In the provinces, ambitious and competent governors, wealthy landholders, urban notables, and nomad chieftains took advantage of the central government's weakness. By the middle of the eighteenth century groups of Mamluks had regained a dominant position in Egypt. Though Selim I had defeated the Mamluk sultanate in the early sixteenth century, the practice of buying slaves in the Caucasus and training them as soldiers reappeared by the end of the century in several Arab cities. In Baghdad, Janissary commanders and Georgian mamluks competed for power, with the latter emerging triumphant by the mid-eighteenth century.

Muhammad ibn Abd al-Wahhab

In Aleppo and Damascus, however, the Janissaries came out on top. Meanwhile, in central Arabia, a puritanical Sunni movement inspired by Muhammad ibn Abd al-Wahhab began a remarkable rise beyond the reach of Ottoman power. Although no region declared full independence, the sultan's power was slipping away to the advantage of a broad array of lower officials and upstart chieftains in all parts of the empire while the Ottoman economy was reorienting itself toward Europe.

SECTION REVIEW

- The Ottoman Empire grew through the skill of its founding rulers, control of strategic territory, and military power.
- The empire expanded into southern and eastern Europe, the Middle East, and Africa, reaching its height under Suleiman the Magnificent.
- Unwilling to build a strong navy, the Ottomans never adapted to developments in the Indian Ocean.
- The empire rested on the military led by the sultan, and changes in military structure ultimately weakened the state.
- As the imperial economy reoriented toward Europe, the central government weakened, permitting the rise of local powers.

THE SAFAVID EMPIRE, 1502–1722

Safavid Empire Iranian kingdom (1502–1722) established by Ismail Safavi, who declared Iran a Shi'ite state.

The **Safavid Empire** of Iran (see Map 19.1) resembled its long-time Ottoman foe in many ways: it initially relied militarily on cavalry paid through land grants; its population spoke several different languages; and it was oriented inward away from the sea. It also had distinct qualities that to this day set Iran off from its neighbors: it derived part of its legitimacy from the pre-Islamic dynasties of ancient Iran, and it adopted the Shi'ite form of Islam.

Safavid Society and Religion

Iranian Shi'ism

Shi'ites Muslims belonging to the branch of Islam believing that God vests leadership of the community in a descendant of Muhammad's son-in-law Ali. Shi'ism is the state religion of Iran.

The ultimate victor in a complicated struggle for power among Turkish chieftains west of the Ottoman Empire was Ismail (IS-ma-eel), a boy of Kurdish, Iranian, and Greek ancestry. In 1502, at the age of sixteen, Ismail proclaimed himself shah of Iran and declared that from that time forward his realm would be devoted to **Shi'ite** Islam, which revered the family of Muhammad's son-in-law Ali. Although Ismail's reasons for compelling Iran's conversion to Shi'ism are unknown, the effect of this radical act was to create a deep chasm between Iran and its neighbors, all of which were Sunni. Iran became a truly separate country for the first time since its incorporation into the Islamic caliphate in the seventh century.

Persian Culture

The imposition of Shi'ite belief made the split permanent, but differences between Iran and its neighbors had long been in the making. Persian, written in the Arabic script from the tenth century onward, had emerged as the second language of Islam. Iranian scholars and writers normally read Arabic as well as Persian and sprinkled their writings with Arabic phrases, but their Arab counterparts were much less inclined to learn Persian. After the Mongols destroyed Baghdad, the capital of the Islamic caliphate, in 1258, Iran developed largely on its own, having more extensive contacts with India—where Muslim rulers favored the Persian language—than with the Arabs.

In the post-Mongol period, artistic styles in Iran, Afghanistan, and Central Asia also went their own way. Painted and molded tiles and tile mosaics, often in vivid turquoise blue, became the standard exterior decoration of mosques in Iran but never were used in Syria and Egypt. Persian poets raised verse to peaks of perfection that had no reflection in Arabic poetry, generally considered to be in a state of decline.

Freer Gallery of Art, Smithsonian Institution, Washington, D.C.: Purchase, F1945.9a

Mughal Emperor Jahangir Embracing the Safavid Shah Abbas Painted by the Mughal artist Abu al-Hasan around 1620, this miniature shows the artist's patron, Jahangir, on the right standing on a lion, dominating the diminutive Shah Abbas, standing on a sheep. Though this may accurately reflect Jahangir's view of their relationship, in fact Shah Abbas was a powerful rival for control of Afghanistan, the gateway to India and the meeting point of the lion and the sheep. The globe the monarchs stand on reflects the spread of accurate geographical ideas into the Muslim world.

To be sure, Islam itself provided a tradition of belief, learning, and law that crossed ethnic and linguistic borders, but Shah Ismail's imposition of Shi'ism set Iran significantly apart. Shi'ite doctrine says that all temporal rulers, regardless of title, are temporary stand-ins for the **"Hidden Imam"**: the twelfth descendant of Ali, the prophet Muhammad's cousin and son-in-law, who disappeared as a child in the ninth century. Some Shi'ite scholars concluded that the faithful should calmly accept the world as it was and wait quietly for the Hidden Imam's return. Others maintained that they themselves should play a stronger role in political affairs because they were best qualified to know the Hidden Imam's wishes. These two positions, which still play a role in Iranian Shi'ism, tended to enhance the self-image of religious scholars as independent of imperial authority and stood in the way of their becoming subordinate government functionaries, as happened in the Ottoman Empire.

Hidden Imam Last in a series of twelve descendants of Muhammad's son-in-law Ali, whom Shi'ites consider divinely appointed leaders of the Muslim community. In occlusion since ca. 873, he is expected to return as a messiah at the end of time.

Shi'ism also affected the psychological life of the people. Annual commemoration of the martyrdom of Imam Husayn (d. 680), Ali's son and the third Imam, regularized an emotional outpouring with no parallel in Sunni lands. Day after day for two weeks, preachers recited the woeful tale to crowds of weeping believers, and elaborate street processions, often organized by craft guilds, paraded chanting and self-flagellating men past crowds of reverent onlookers. Of course, Shi'ites elsewhere observed rites of mourning for Imam Husayn, but the impact of these rites was especially great in Iran, where 90 percent of the population was Shi'ite. Over time, the subjects of the Safavid shahs came to feel more than ever a people apart.

A Tale of Two Cities: Isfahan and Istanbul

Shah Abbas

Shah Abbas I The fifth and most renowned ruler of the Safavid dynasty in Iran (r. 1587–1629). Abbas moved the royal capital to Isfahan in 1598.

Outwardly, the Ottoman capital of Istanbul looked quite different from Isfahan (is-fah-HAHN), which became Iran's capital in 1598 by decree of **Shah Abbas I** (r. 1587–1629). Built on seven hills on the south side of the narrow Golden Horn inlet, Istanbul boasted a skyline punctuated by the gray stone domes and thin, pointed minarets of the great imperial mosques. The mosques surrounding the royal plaza in Isfahan, in contrast, had unobtrusive minarets and brightly tiled domes that rose to gentle peaks. High walls surrounded the sultan's palace in Istanbul. Shah Abbas in Isfahan focused his capital on the giant royal plaza, which was large enough for his army to play polo, and he used an airy palace overlooking the plaza to receive dignitaries and review his troops.

Differences and Similarities

The harbor of Istanbul, the primary Ottoman seaport, teemed with sailing ships and smaller craft, many of them belonging to a colony of European merchants perched on a hilltop on the north side of the Golden Horn. Isfahan, far from the sea, was only occasionally visited by Europeans. Most of its trade was in the hands of Jews, Hindus, and especially a colony of Armenian Christians brought in by Shah Abbas.

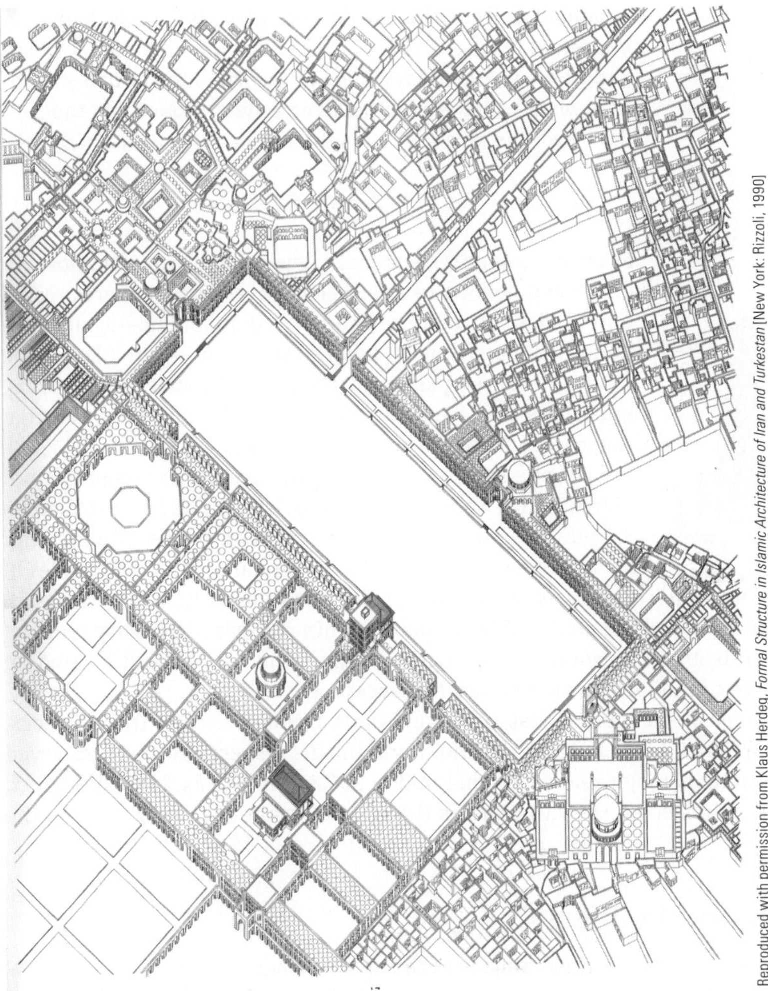

Royal Square in Isfahan Built by the order of Shah Abbas over a period of twenty years starting in 1598, the open space is as long as five football fields (555 by 172 yards). At the upper left end of the square in this drawing is the entrance to the covered bazaar, at the bottom the immense Royal Mosque. The left-hand side adjoins the shah's palace and state administrative office. A multistory pavilion for reviewing troops and receiving guests overlooks the square across from the smaller domed personal mosque of the shah.

Beneath these superficial differences, the two capitals had much in common. Wheeled vehicles were scarce in hilly Istanbul and nonexistent in Isfahan. Both cities were built for walking and, aside from the royal plaza in Isfahan, lacked the open spaces common in contemporary European cities. Streets were narrow and irregular. Houses crowded against each other in dead-end lanes. Residents enjoyed their privacy in interior courtyards. Artisans and merchants organized themselves into guilds that had strong social and religious as well as economic bonds. The shops of each guild adjoined each other in the markets.

Concealment of Women

Women were seldom seen in public, even in Istanbul's mazelike covered market or in Isfahan's long, serpentine bazaar. At home, the women's quarters—called *anderun* (an-deh-ROON), or "interior," in Iran and *harem*, or "forbidden area," in Istanbul—were separate from the public rooms where the men of the family received visitors. In both areas, low cushions, charcoal braziers for warmth, carpets, and small tables constituted most of the furnishings.

The private side of family life has left few traces, but it is apparent that women's society—consisting of wives, children, female servants, and sometimes one or more eunuchs—was not entirely cut off from the outside world. Ottoman court records reveal that women, using male agents, were very active in the urban real estate market. Often they were selling inherited shares of their father's estate, but some both bought and sold real estate on a regular basis and even established religious endowments for pious purposes.

Women and Islamic Law

The fact that Islamic law, unlike some European codes, permitted a wife to retain her property after marriage gave some women a stake in the general economy and a degree of independence from their spouses. Women also appeared in other types of court cases, where they often testified for themselves, for Islamic courts did not recognize the role of attorney. Although comparable Safavid court records do not survive, historians assume that a parallel situation prevailed in Iran.

Styles of Dress

European travelers commented on the veiling of women outside the home, but the norm for both sexes was complete coverage of arms, legs, and hair. Miniature paintings indicate that ordinary female garb consisted of a long, ample dress with a scarf or long shawl pulled tight over the forehead to conceal the hair. Lightweight trousers, either close-fitting or baggy, were often worn under the dress. This mode of dress was not far different from that of men. Poor men wore light trousers, a long shirt, a jacket, and a hat or turban. Wealthier men wore over their trousers ankle-length caftans, often closely fitted around the chest.

Public life was almost entirely the domain of men. Poetry and art, both somewhat more elegantly developed in Isfahan than in Istanbul, were as likely to extol the charms of beardless boys

Austrian National Library, picture archive

Istanbul Family on the Way to a Bath House Public baths, an important feature of Islamic cities, set different hours for men and women. Young boys, such as the lad in the turban shown here, went with their mothers and sisters. Notice that the children wear the same styles as the adults.

as pretty women. Despite religious disapproval of homosexuality, attachments to adolescent boys were neither unusual nor hidden. Women who appeared in public—aside from non-Muslims, the aged, and the very poor—were likely to be slaves. Miniature paintings frequently depict female dancers, musicians, and even acrobats in attitudes and costumes that range from decorous to decidedly erotic.

Cosmopolitan Istanbul

Despite social similarities, the overall flavors of Isfahan and Istanbul were not the same. Isfahan had its prosperous Armenian quarter across the river from the city's center, but it was not a truly cosmopolitan capital, just as the peoples of the Safavid realm were not remarkably diverse. Like other rulers of extensive land empires, Shah Abbas located his capital toward the center of his domain within comparatively easy reach of any threatened frontier. Istanbul, in contrast, was a great seaport and a crossroads located on the straits separating the sultan's European and Asian possessions.

People of all sorts lived or spent time in Istanbul: Venetians, Genoese, Arabs, Turks, Greeks, Armenians, Albanians, Serbs, Jews, Bulgarians, and more. In this respect, Istanbul conveyed the cosmopolitan character of major seaports from London to Canton (Guangzhou) and belied the fact that its prosperity rested on the vast reach of the sultan's territories rather than on the voyages of its merchants.

Economic Crisis and Political Collapse

The silk fabrics of northern Iran were the mainstay of the Safavid Empire's foreign trade. However, the manufacture that eventually became most powerfully associated with Iran was the deep-pile carpet made by knotting colored yarns around stretched warp threads. Different cities produced distinctive carpet designs. Women and girls did much of the actual knotting work. Overall, Iran's manufacturing sector was neither large nor notably productive. Most of the shah's subjects, whether Iranians, Turks, Kurds, or Arabs, lived by subsistence farming or herding. Neither area of activity recorded significant technological advances during the Safavid period.

Military Costs

The Safavids, like the Ottomans, had difficulty finding the money to pay troops armed with firearms. This crisis occurred somewhat later in Iran because of its greater distance from Europe. By the end of the sixteenth century, it was evident that a more systematic adoption of cannon and firearms in the Safavid Empire would be needed to hold off the Ottomans and the Uzbeks (UHZ-bex) (Turkish rulers who had succeeded the Timurids on Iran's Central Asian frontier; see Map 19.1). Like the Ottoman cavalry a century earlier, the warriors furnished by the nomad leaders were not inclined to trade in their bows for firearms. Shah Abbas responded by establishing a slave corps of year-round soldiers and arming them with guns. The Christian converts to Islam who initially provided the manpower for the new corps were mostly captives taken in raids on Georgia in the Caucasus (CAW-kuh-suhs).

In the late sixteenth century, the inflation caused by cheap silver spread into Iran; then overland trade through Safavid territory declined because of mismanagement of the silk monopoly after Shah Abbas's death in 1629. As a result, the country faced the unsolvable problem of finding money to pay the army and bureaucracy. Trying to

SECTION REVIEW

- The rise of the Shi'ite Safavid Empire completed the long-growing split between Iran and its neighbors.
- Despite significant differences, Istanbul and Isfahan showed some cultural similarities between the Ottoman and Safavid Empires.
- Silks and carpets were important manufactures, but most Safavid subjects made a living by farming or herding.
- High military costs, inflation, and decline of overland trade weakened the state, which fell to Afghan invaders in 1722.

Nomads and Inflation

unseat the nomads from their lands to regain control of taxes was more difficult and more disruptive militarily than the piecemeal dismantlement of the land-grant system in the Ottoman Empire. The nomads were still a cohesive military force, and pressure from the center simply caused them to withdraw to their mountain pastures until the pressure subsided. By 1722, the government had become so weak and commanded so little support from the nomadic groups that an army of marauding Afghans was able to capture Isfahan and effectively end Safavid rule.

THE MUGHAL EMPIRE, 1526–1761

What distinguished the Indian empire of the Mughal (MOH-guhl) sultans from the empires of the Ottomans and Safavids was the fact that India was a land of Hindus ruled by a Muslim minority. Muslim dominion in India was the result of repeated military campaigns from the early eleventh century onward, and the Mughals had to contend with the Hindus' long-standing resentment of the destruction of their culture by Muslims. Thus, the challenge facing the Mughals was not just conquering and organizing a large territorial state but also finding a formula for Hindu-Muslim coexistence.

Mughal Empire Muslim state (1526–1857) exercising dominion over most of India in the sixteenth and seventeenth centuries.

Political Foundations

Babur and Akbar

Babur (BAH-bur) (1483–1530), the founder of the **Mughal Empire**, was a Muslim descendant of both Timur and Genghis Khan (*Mughal* is Persian for "Mongol"). Invading from Central Asia, Babur defeated the last Muslim sultan of Delhi (DEL-ee) in 1526. Babur's grandson **Akbar** (r. 1556–1605), a brilliant but mercurial man, established the central administration of the expanding state. Under him and his three successors—the last of whom died in 1707—all but the southern tip of India fell under Mughal rule, administered first from Agra and then from Delhi.

Akbar Most illustrious sultan of the Mughal Empire in India (r. 1556–1605). He expanded the empire and pursued a policy of conciliation with Hindus.

Akbar granted land revenues to military officers and government officials in return for their service. Ranks, called ***mansabs*** (MAN-sabz), some high and some low, entitled their holders to revenue assignments. As in the other Islamic empires, revenue grants were not considered hereditary, and the central government kept careful track of their issuance.

mansabs In India, grants of land given in return for service by rulers of the Mughal Empire.

Akbar's Reign

With a population of 100 million, a thriving trading economy based on cotton cloth, and a generally efficient administration, India under Akbar was probably the most prosperous empire of the sixteenth century. He and his successors faced few external threats and experienced generally peaceful conditions in their northern Indian heartland.

Foreign trade boomed at the port of Surat in the northwest, which also served as an embarkation point for pilgrims on their way to Mecca. Like the Safavids, the Mughals had no navy or merchant ships. The government saw the Europeans—after Akbar's time, primarily Dutch and English, the Portuguese having lost most of their Indian ports—less as enemies than as shipmasters whose naval support could be procured as needed in return for trading privileges.

Hindus and Muslims

Rajputs

The Mughal state inherited traditions of unified imperial rule from both the Islamic caliphate and the more recent examples of Genghis Khan and Timur. Those traditions did not necessarily mean religious intolerance. Seventy percent of the *mansabdars* (man-sab-DAHRZ) (officials holding land revenues) appointed under Akbar were Muslim soldiers born outside India, but 15 percent were Hindus. Most of the Hindu appointees were warriors from the north called **Rajputs** (RAHJ-putz), one of whom rose to be a powerful revenue minister.

Rajputs Members of a mainly Hindu warrior caste from northwest India. The Mughal emperors drew most of their Hindu officials from this caste, and Akbar married a Rajput princess.

Akbar, the most illustrious ruler of his dynasty, differed from his Ottoman and Safavid counterparts—Suleiman the Magnificent and Shah Abbas the Great—in his striving for social harmony and not just for more territory and revenue. His marriage to a Rajput princess signaled his desire for reconciliation and even intermarriage between Muslims and Hindus. The birth of a son in 1569 ensured that future rulers would have both Muslim and Hindu ancestry.

Akbar ruled that in legal disputes between two Hindus, decisions would be made according to village custom or Hindu law as interpreted by local Hindu scholars. Shari'a law was in force for Muslims. Akbar made himself the legal court of last resort, creating an appeals process not usually present in Islamic jurisprudence.

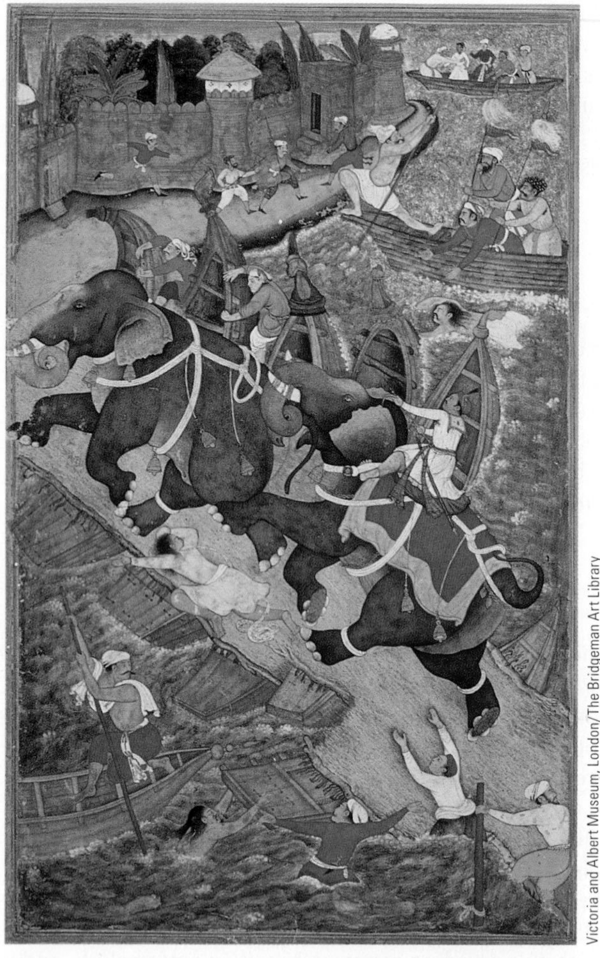

Victoria and Albert Museum, London/The Bridgeman Art Library

Elephants Breaking Bridge of Boats This illustration of an incident in the life of Akbar illustrates the ability of Mughal miniature painters to depict unconventional action scenes. Because the flow of rivers in India and the Middle East varied greatly from dry season to wet season, boat bridges were much more common than permanent constructions.

Akbar also made himself the center of a new "Divine Faith" incorporating Muslim, Hindu, Zoroastrian, Sikh (sick), and Christian beliefs. He was strongly attracted by Sufi ideas, which permeated the religious rituals he instituted at his court. To promote serious consideration of his religious principles, he oversaw, from a catwalk high above the audience, debates among scholars of all religions assembled in his octagonal private audience chamber. When courtiers uttered the Muslim exclamation "Allahu Akbar"—"God is great"—they also understood it in its second grammatical meaning: "God is Akbar."

Akbar's religious views did not survive him, but the court culture he fostered, reflecting a mixture of Muslim and Hindu traditions, flourished until his zealous great-grandson Aurangzeb (ow-rang-ZEB) (r. 1658–1707) reinstituted many restrictions on Hindus. Mughal and Rajput miniature paintings reveled in precise portraits of political figures and depictions of scantily clad women, even though they brought frowns to the faces of pious Muslims, who deplored the representation of human beings. Most of the leading painters were Hindus. In addition to the florid style of Persian verse favored at court, a new taste developed for poetry and prose in the popular language of the Delhi region. The modern descendant of this language is called *Urdu* in Pakistan and *Hindi* in India.

Central Decay and Regional Challenges

Nadir Shah's Sack of Delhi

Mughal power did not long survive Aurangzeb's death in 1707. Some historians consider the land-grant system a central element in the rapid decline of imperial authority, but other factors were at play as well. Aurangzeb's additions to Mughal territory in southern India were not all well integrated into the imperial structure, and strong regional powers arose to challenge Mughal military supremacy. A climax came in 1739 when Nadir Shah, a warlord who had seized power in Iran after the fall of the Safavids, invaded the Mughal capital and carried off to Iran the "peacock throne," the priceless jewel-encrusted symbol of Mughal grandeur. Another throne was found for the later Mughals to sit on; but their empire, which survived in name to 1857, was finished.

Increasing Fragmentation

In 1723, Nizam al-Mulk (nee-ZAHM al-MULK), the powerful vizier of the Mughal sultan, gave up on the central government and established his own nearly independent state at Hyderabad in the eastern Deccan. Other officials bearing the title *nawab* (nah-WAHB) became similarly independent in Bengal and Oudh (OW-ad) in the northeast, as did the Marathas in the center. In the northwest, simultaneous Iranian and Mughal weakness allowed the Afghans to establish an independent kingdom.

Some of these regional powers, and the smaller princely states that arose on former Mughal territory, were prosperous and benefited from the removal of the sultan's heavy hand. Linguistic and religious communities, freed from the religious intolerance instituted during the reign of Aurangzeb, similarly enjoyed greater opportunity for political expression. However, this disintegration of central power favored the intrusion of European adventurers.

French Traders

In 1741 Joseph François Dupleix (doo-PLAY) took over the presidency of the French stronghold of Pondicherry (pon-dih-CHER-ree) and began a new phase of European involvement in India. He captured the English trading center of Madras and used his small contingent of European and European-trained Indian troops to become a power broker in southern India. Though offered the title *nawab,* Dupleix preferred to operate behind the scenes, using Indian princes as puppets. His career ended in 1754 when he was called home. Deeply involved in wars in Europe, the French government was unwilling to pursue further adventures in India. Dupleix's departure opened the way for the British, whose ventures in India are described in Chapter 25.

SECTION REVIEW

- Founded by Babur, the Mughal Empire grew under Akbar and his successors to encompass most of India.
- The empire prospered through trade and granted trade privileges to Europeans in exchange for naval support.
- Akbar included both Muslims and Hindus in his government, respected Hindu customs, and strove for religious harmony.
- A hybrid culture flourished, but Aurangzeb practiced Muslim intolerance.
- After Aurangzeb's death, the empire declined through foreign invasion, the rise of regional powers, and European encroachment.

THE MARITIME WORLDS OF ISLAM, 1500–1750

As land powers, the Mughal, Safavid, and Ottoman Empires faced similar problems in the seventeenth and eighteenth centuries. Complex changes in military technology and in the world economy, along with the increasing difficulty of basing an extensive land empire on military forces paid through land grants, affected them all adversely. These difficulties contributed to the often dynamic development of power centers away from the imperial capital.

Joint-Stock Companies

The new pressures faced by land powers were less important to seafaring countries intent on turning trade networks into maritime empires. Improvements in ship design, navigation accuracy, and the use of cannon gave an ever-increasing edge to European powers competing with local seafaring peoples. Moreover, the development of joint-stock companies, in which many merchants pooled their capital, provided a flexible and efficient financial instrument for exploiting new possibilities. The English East India Company was founded in 1600, the Dutch East India Company in 1602.

AP* Exam Tip
Changes and continuities in interregional trading patterns are covered on the multiple choice and essay sections of the exam.

Although the Ottomans, Safavids, and Mughals did not effectively contest the growth of Portuguese and then Dutch, English, and French maritime power, the majority of non-European shipbuilders, captains, sailors, and traders were Muslim. Groups of Armenian, Jewish, and Hindu traders were also active, but they remained almost as aloof from the Europeans as the Muslims did. The presence in every port of Muslims following the same legal traditions and practicing their faith in similar ways cemented the Muslims' trading network. Islam, from its very outset in the life and preaching of Muhammad (570–632), had favored trade and traders. Unlike Hinduism, it was a proselytizing religion, a factor that encouraged the growth of coastal Muslim communities as local non-Muslims associated with Muslim commercial activities converted and intermarried with Muslims from abroad.

Jesuit Missionaries

Although European missionaries, particularly the Jesuits, tried to extend Christianity into Asia and Africa (see Chapters 15 and 20), most Europeans, the Portuguese excepted, did not treat local converts or the offspring of mixed marriages as full members of their communities. Islam was generally more welcoming. As a consequence, Islam spread extensively into East Africa and Southeast Asia during precisely the same time as rapid European commercial expansion. Even without the support of the Muslim land empires, Islam became a source of resistance to growing European domination.

Muslims in Southeast Asia

Indians in the East Indies

Historians disagree about the chronology and manner of Islam's spread in Southeast Asia. Arab traders appeared in southern China as early as the eighth century, so Muslims probably reached the East Indies (the island portions of Southeast Asia) at a similarly early date. Nevertheless, the dominance of Indian cultural influences in the area for several centuries thereafter indicates that early Muslim visitors had little impact on local beliefs. Clearer indications of conversion and the formation of Muslim communities date from roughly the fourteenth century, with the strongest overseas linkage being to the port of Cambay in India (see Map 19.2) rather than to the Arab world. Islam first took root in port cities and in some royal courts and spread inland only slowly, possibly transmitted by itinerant Sufis.

Although appeals to the Ottoman sultan for support against the Europeans ultimately proved futile, Islam strengthened resistance to Portuguese, Spanish, and Dutch intruders. When the Spaniards conquered the Philippines during the decades following the establishment of their first fort in 1565, they encountered Muslims on the southern island of Mindanao (min-duh-NOW) and the nearby Sulu archipelago. They called them "Moros," the Spanish term for their old enemies, the Muslims of North Africa. In the ensuing Moro wars, the Spaniards portrayed the Moros as greedy pirates who raided non-Muslim territories for slaves. In fact, they were political, religious, and commercial competitors whose perseverance enabled them to establish the Sulu Empire based in the southern Philippines, one of the strongest states in Southeast Asia from 1768 to 1848.

Acheh Sultanate Muslim kingdom in northern Sumatra. Main center of Islamic expansion in Southeast Asia in the early seventeenth century, it declined after the Dutch seized Malacca from Portugal in 1641.

Other local kingdoms that looked on Islam as a force to counter the aggressive Christianity of the Europeans included the actively proselytizing Brunei (BROO-neye) Sultanate in northern Borneo and the **Acheh** (AH-cheh) **Sultanate** in northern Sumatra. At its peak in the early seventeenth century, Acheh succeeded Malacca as the main center of Islamic expansion in Southeast Asia. It prospered by trading pepper for cotton cloth from Gujarat in India. Acheh declined after the Dutch seized Malacca from Portugal in 1641.

The Dutch Capture Malacca

How well Islam was understood in these Muslim kingdoms is open to question. In Acheh, for example, a series of women ruled between 1641 and 1699. This practice ended when local Muslim scholars obtained a ruling from scholars in Mecca and Medina that Islam did not approve of female rulers. After this ruling, scholarly understandings of Islam gained greater prominence in the East Indies.

Islam and Literacy

Historians have looked at merchants, Sufi preachers, or both as the first propagators of Islam in Southeast Asia. The scholarly vision of Islam, however, took root in the sixteenth century by way of pilgrims returning from years of study in Mecca and Medina. Islam promoted the dissemination of writing in the region. Some of the returning pilgrims wrote in Arabic, others in Malay or Javanese. As Islam continued to spread, *adat* ("custom"), a form of Islam rooted in pre-Muslim religious and social practices, retained its preeminence in rural areas over practices centered on the Shari'a, the religious law. But the royal courts in the port cities began to heed the views of the pilgrim teachers. Though different in many ways, both varieties of Islam provided believers with a firm basis of identification in the face of the growing European presence. Christian missionaries gained most of their converts in regions that had not yet converted to Islam, such as the northern Philippines.

Muslims in Coastal Africa

Muslim rulers also governed the East African ports that the Portuguese began to visit in the fifteenth century, though they were not allied politically (see Map 19.2). People living in the millet and rice lands of the Swahili Coast—from the Arabic *sawahil* (suh-WAH-hil) meaning "coasts"—had little contact with those in the dry hinterlands. Throughout this period, the East African lakes region and the highlands of Kenya witnessed unprecedented migration and relocation of peoples because of drought conditions that persisted from the late sixteenth through most of the seventeenth century.

Trading Ports

Cooperation among the trading ports of Kilwa, Mombasa, and Malindi was hindered by the thick bush country that separated the cultivated tracts of coastal land and by the fact that the ports competed with one another in the export of ivory; ambergris (AM-ber-grees) (a whale byproduct used in perfumes); and forest products such as beeswax, copal tree resin, and wood. Kilwa also exported gold. In the eighteenth century slave trading, primarily to Arabian ports but also to India, increased in importance. Because Europeans—the only peoples who kept consistent records of slave-trading activities—played a minor role in this slave trade, few records have survived to indicate its extent. Perhaps the best estimate is that 2.1 million slaves were exported between 1500 and 1890, a little over 12.5 percent of the total traffic in African slaves during that period (see Chapter 18).

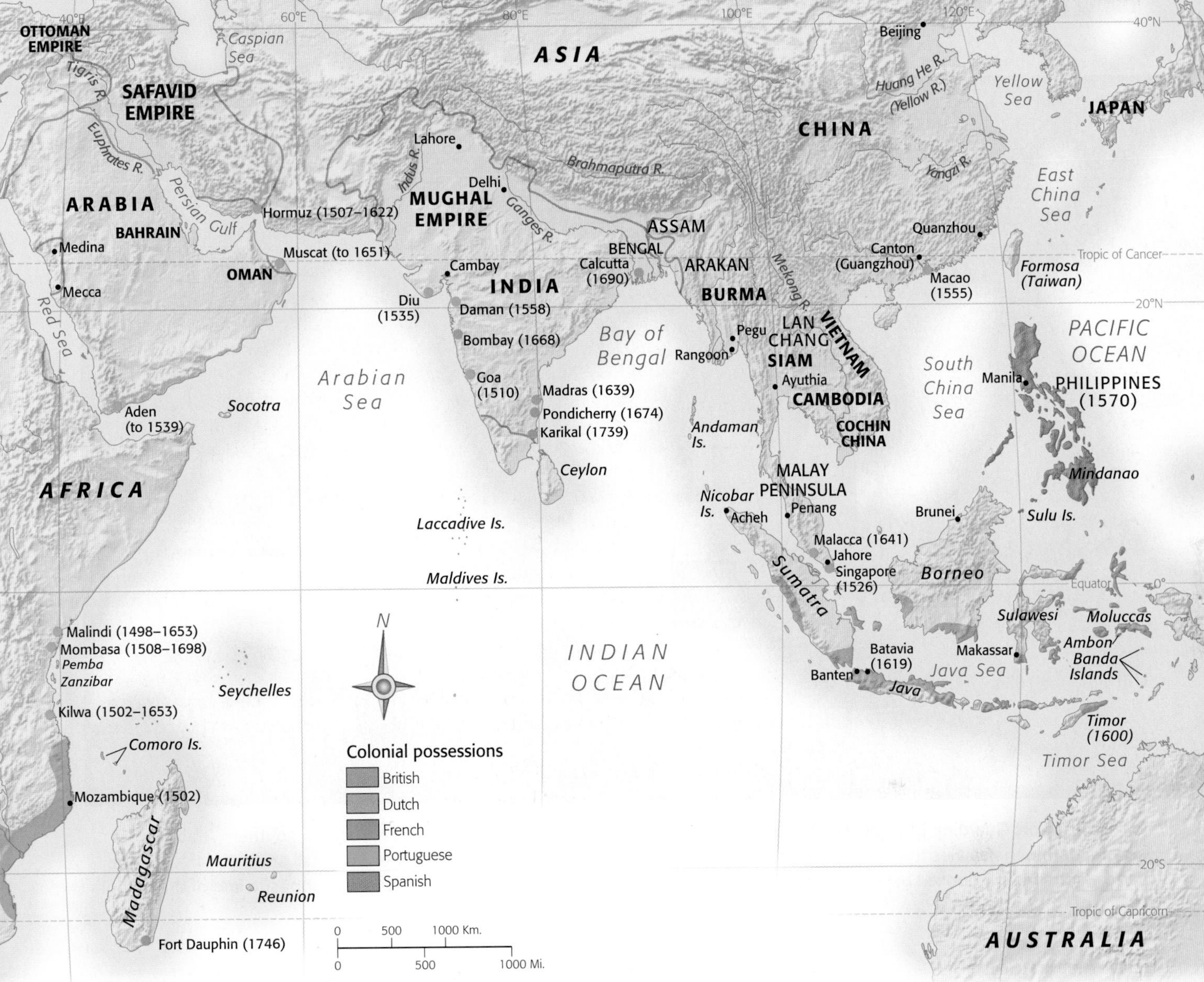

MAP 19.2 European Colonization in the Indian Ocean, to 1750 Since Portuguese explorers were the first Europeans to reach India by rounding Africa, Portugal gained a strong foothold in both areas. Rival Spain was barred from colonizing the region by the Treaty of Tordesillas in 1494, which limited Spanish efforts to lands west of a line drawn through the mid-Atlantic Ocean. The line carried around the globe provided justification of Spanish colonization in the Philippines. French, British, and Dutch colonies date from after 1600, when joint-stock companies provided a new stimulus for overseas commerce.

e Interactive Map

Malindi

The Portuguese conquered all the coastal ports from Mozambique northward except Malindi, with whose ruler Portugal cooperated. A Portuguese description of the ruler names some of the cloth and metal goods that Malindi imported, as well as some local manufactures:

> *The King wore a robe of damask trimmed with green satin and a rich [cap]. He was seated on two cushioned chairs of bronze, beneath a rough sunshade of crimson satin attached to a pole. An old man, who attended him as a page, carried a short sword in a silver sheath. There were many players on [horns], and two trumpets of ivory richly carved and of the size of a man, which were blown through a hole in the side, and made sweet harmony with the [horns].*[4]

Robert Harding World Imagery

Portuguese Fort Guarding Musqat Harbor Musqat in Oman and Aden in Yemen, the best harbors in southern Arabia, were targets for imperial navies trying to establish dominance in the Indian Ocean. Musqat's harbor is small and circular, with one narrow entrance overlooked by this fortress. The palace of the sultan of Oman is still located at the opposite end of the harbor.

Oman Arab state based in Musqat, the main port in the southeast region of the Arabian peninsula. Oman succeeded Portugal as a power in the western Indian Ocean in the eighteenth century.

Initially, the Portuguese favored the port of Malindi, which caused the decline of Kilwa and Mombasa. Repeatedly plagued by local rebellion, Portuguese power suffered severe blows when the Arabs of **Oman** in southeastern Arabia captured their south Arabian stronghold at Musqat (1650) and then went on to seize Mombasa (1698), which had become the Portuguese capital in East Africa. The Portuguese briefly retook Mombasa but lost control permanently in 1729. From then on, the Portuguese had to content themselves with Mozambique in East Africa and a few remaining ports in India (Goa) and farther east (Macao and Timor).

Oman Builds an Empire

Swahili Bantu language with Arabic loanwords spoken in coastal regions of East Africa.

The Omanis created a maritime empire of their own, one that worked in greater cooperation with the African populations. The Bantu language of the coast, broadened by the absorption of Arabic, Persian, and Portuguese loanwords, developed into **Swahili** (swah-HEE-lee), which was spoken throughout the region. Arabs and other Muslims who settled in the region intermarried with local families, giving rise to a mixed population that played an important role in developing a distinctive Swahili culture.

Islam also spread in the southern Sudan in this period, particularly in the dry areas away from the Nile River. This growth coincided with a waning of Ethiopian power as a result of Portugal's stifling of trade in the Red Sea. Yet no significant contact developed between the emerging Muslim Swahili culture and that of the Muslims in the Sudan to the north.

Muslim Revival in Morocco

In Northwest Africa the seizure by Portugal and Spain of coastal strongholds in Morocco provoked a militant response. The Sa'adi family, which claimed descent from the Prophet Muhammad, led a resistance to Portuguese aggression that climaxed in victory at the battle of al-Qasr al-Kabir (Ksar el Kebir) in 1578. The triumphant Moroccan sultan, Ahmad al-Mansur, restored his country's strength and independence. By the early seventeenth century naval expeditions from the port of Salé, referred to in British records as "the Sally Rovers," raided European shipping as far as Britain itself.

Corsairs, or sea raiders, working out of Algerian, Tunisian, and Libyan ports brought the same sort of warfare to the Mediterranean. European governments called these Muslim raiders pirates and slave-takers, and they leveled the same charges against other Muslim mariners in the Persian Gulf and the Sulu Sea. But there was little distinction between the actions of the Muslims and of their European adversaries.

European Powers in Southern Seas

The Dutch in the East Indies

Through their well-organized Dutch East India Company, the Dutch played a major role in driving the Portuguese from their possessions in the East Indies. Just as the Portuguese had tried to dominate the trade in spices, so the Dutch concentrated at first on the spice-producing islands of Southeast Asia. The Portuguese had seized Malacca, a strategic town on the narrow strait at the end of the Malay Peninsula, from a local Malay ruler in 1511 (see Chapter 15). The Dutch took it away from them in 1641, leaving Portugal little foothold in the East Indies except the islands of Ambon (am-BOHN) and Timor (see Map 19.2).

Batavia, the Center of Dutch Trade

Batavia Fort established ca. 1619 as headquarters of Dutch East India Company operations in Indonesia; today the city of Jakarta.

Although the United Netherlands was one of the least autocratic countries of Europe, the governors-general appointed by the Dutch East India Company deployed almost unlimited powers in their efforts to maintain their trade monopoly. They could even order the execution of their own employees for "smuggling"—that is, trading on their own. Under strong governors-general, the Dutch fought a series of wars against Acheh and other local kingdoms on Sumatra and Java. In 1628 and 1629 their new capital at **Batavia**, now the city of Jakarta on Java, was besieged by a fleet of fifty ships belonging to the sultan of Mataram (MAH-tah-ram), a Javanese kingdom. The Dutch held out with difficulty and eventually prevailed when the sultan was unable to get effective help from the English.

Suppressing local rulers, however, was not enough to control the spice trade once other European countries adopted Dutch methods, learned more about where goods might be acquired, and started to send more ships to Southeast Asia. In the course of the eighteenth century, therefore, the Dutch gradually turned from being middlemen between Southeast Asian producers and European buyers to producing crops in areas they controlled, notably in Java. Javanese teak forests yielded high-quality lumber, and coffee, transplanted from Yemen, grew well in the western hilly regions. In this new phase of colonial export production, Batavia developed from being the headquarters town of a far-flung enterprise to being the administrative capital of a conquered land.

Beyond the East Indies, the Dutch utilized their discovery of a band of powerful eastward-blowing winds (called the "Roaring Forties" because they blow throughout the year between 40 and 50 degrees south latitude) to reach Australia in 1606. In 1642 and 1643 Abel Tasman became the first European to set foot on Tasmania and New Zealand and to sail around Australia, signaling European involvement in that region (see Chapter 25).

SECTION REVIEW

- From its inception in the time of Muhammad, Islam flowered in places of trade, and beginning around 1500, the majority of non-European shipbuilders, captains, sailors, and traders were Muslim.
- A number of local kingdoms in Southeast Asia took on Islam as a force to resist the aggressive Christianity of the Europeans.
- Many Muslims in coastal Africa intermarried with locals, creating a mixed population that played a key part in the development of a distinctive Swahili culture.
- Over time the successes of European trading companies changed the balance of power in the southern seas, but local merchants never completely disappeared from the commercial scene.

CONCLUSION

It is no coincidence that the Mughal, Safavid, and Ottoman Empires declined simultaneously in the seventeenth and eighteenth centuries. The complex changes in military technology and in the world economy that were under way in smaller European countries either passed them by or affected them adversely. Despite their efforts on conquering more and more land, these land-based empires faced increasing difficulty in maintaining traditional military forces paid through land grants.

The opposite was true for seafaring countries intent on turning trade networks into maritime empires. Improvements in ship design, navigation accuracy, and the use of cannon gave an ever-increasing edge to European powers competing with local seafaring peoples. In contrast to the age-old Asian tradition that imperial wealth came from control of broad expanses of agricultural land, European countries promoted joint-stock companies and luxuriated in the prosperity gained from their ever-increasing control of Indian Ocean commerce.

That a major shift in world economic and political alignments was well under way by the late seventeenth century was scarcely perceivable in those parts of Asia and Africa ruled by the Ottoman and Mughal sultans and the Safavid shahs. They relied mostly on land taxes, usually indirectly collected via holders of land grants or tax farmers, rather than on customs duties or control of markets to fill the government coffers. With ever-increasing military expenditures, these taxes fell short of the rulers' needs. Oblivious to the fundamental problem of the entire economic system, imperial courtiers pursued their luxurious ways, poetry and the arts continued to flourish, and the quality of manufacturing and craft production remained generally high. Eighteenth-century European observers marveled no less at the riches and industry of these eastern lands than at the fundamental weakness of their political and military systems.

KEY TERMS

Ottoman Empire p. 548
Suleiman the Magnificent p. 548
Janissaries p. 551
Tulip Period p. 555
Safavid Empire p. 557
Shi'ites p. 557
Hidden Imam p. 558
Shah Abbas I p. 558
Mughal Empire p. 561
Akbar p. 561
mansabs p. 561
Rajputs p. 561
Acheh Sultanate p. 564
Oman p. 566
Swahili p. 566
Batavia p. 567

EBOOK AND WEBSITE RESOURCES

e Interactive Maps

Map 19.1 Muslim Empires in the Sixteenth and Seventeenth Centuries

Map 19.2 European Colonization in the Indian Ocean, to 1750

Plus flashcards, practice quizzes, and more. Go to: www.cengage.com/history/bullietearthpeople5e

SUGGESTED READING

Arjomand, Said Amir. *The Shadow of God and the Hidden Imam: Religion, Political Order, and Societal Change in Shi-ite Iran from the Beginning to 1890.* 1984. Contains the best analysis of the complicated relationship between Shi'ism and monarchy.

Braude, Benjamin, and Bernard Lewis, eds. *Christians and Jews in the Ottoman Empire: The Functioning of a Plural Society.* 1982. Diverse studies dealing with religious minorities.

Goffman, Daniel. *The Ottoman Empire and Early Modern Europe.* 2002. Compares the Ottomans with contemporary European kingdoms.

Hattox, Ralph S. *Coffee and Coffeehouses: The Origins of a Social Beverage in the Medieval Near East.* 1988. An excellent contribution to Ottoman social history.

Ikram, S. M. *History of Muslim Civilization in India and Pakistan.* 1989. A broad treatment of the entire development of Islamic society in India with emphasis on the Mughal period.

Imber, Colin. *The Ottoman Empire, 1300–1650: The Structure of Power.* 2002. On the Ottoman Empire in its prime.

Inalcik, Halil, and Donald Quataert, eds. *An Economic and Social History of the Ottoman Empire, 1300–1914.* 1994. A valuable collection of articles on nonpolitical matters.

Lapidus, Ira. *A History of Islamic Societies*, 2nd ed. 2002. Offers the best comprehensive and comparative account of the post-Mongol Islamic land empires.

Marcus, Abraham. *The Middle East on the Eve of Modernity: Aleppo in the Eighteenth Century.* 1989. An outstanding study of an Arab city under Ottoman rule.

Martin, Esmond Bradley, and Chryssee Perry Martin. *Cargoes of the East: The Ports, Trade and Culture of the Arabian Seas and Western Indian Ocean.* 1978. A popular and well-illustrated work on the western Indian Ocean.

Matthee, Rudi. *The Pursuit of Pleasure: Drugs and Stimulants in Iranian History, 1500–1900.* 2005. Studies court life and popular culture through wine, tobacco, opium, coffee, and tea.

Newman, Andrew. *Safavid Iran: Rebirth of a Persian Empire.* 2006. A provocative reinterpretation of Safavid rule.

Ogot, B. A., ed. *UNESCO General History of Africa*, vol. 5, *Africa from the Sixteenth to the Eighteenth Century.* 1992. A useful collection of articles on an understudied field.

Peirce, Leslie. *The Imperial Harem: Women and Sovereignty in the Ottoman Empire.* 1993. Skillfully treats the role of women in the governance of the empire.

Richards, John F. *The Mughal Empire.* 1993. A comprehensive history.

NOTES

1. Leslie Peirce, *Morality Tales: Law and Gender in the Ottoman Court of Aintab* (Berkeley: University of California Press, 2003), 258.
2. Ibid., 262.
3. Daniel Goffman, *Izmir and the Levantine World, 1550–1650* (Seattle: University of Washington Press, 1990), 52.
4. Edmund Bradley Martin and Chryssee Perry Martin, *Cargoes of the East: The Ports, Trade and Culture of the Arabian Seas and Western Indian Ocean* (1978), 17.

AP* REVIEW QUESTIONS FOR CHAPTER 19

1. One of the major reasons for the early success of the Ottoman armies was
   (A) their use of the saddle.
   (B) the fact that they used Mongol war tactics.
   (C) their use of gunpowder.
   (D) their superior generals.

2. The Ottoman armies conquered
   (A) Mamluk Egypt.
   (B) Songhai.
   (C) Kiev.
   (D) Sicily.

3. Enslaved Christian prisoners were often converted to Islam. The males who converted were often
   (A) made to farm for the Ottomans.
   (B) encouraged to marry Muslim women.
   (C) enlisted into the Ottoman armies as "Janissaries."
   (D) given positions in the Ottoman government because they were not biased.

4. In the middle 1600s, the Ottoman government had to stop providing land grants in return for military service. This system
   (A) was stopped because the imams indicated that it was a violation of Muslim law.
   (B) caused tax revenues to decrease to the point of bankruptcy.
   (C) was replaced with tax farming.
   (D) was replaced with a new system of internal duties on crops.

5. The Ottoman government did not react quickly to changes in trade and taxes in its empire. One example of this problem was
   (A) the shift in trade to India and away from the Ottoman lands.
   (B) the use of capitulations to benefit European over Ottoman merchants in places like Mocha coffee markets.
   (C) the diversion of caravans into southern Russia as a way to avoid having to pay taxes in Ottoman cities.
   (D) the loss of the spice trade to Malacca and ports in areas controlled by the Portuguese.

6. Under the Safavid founder, Ismail, Iran became
   (A) a Turkish kingdom.
   (B) the major trade center of the Ottoman Empire.
   (C) Shi'ite.
   (D) a provider of caravan goods.

7. Which of the following is true of the Safavid Empire?
   (A) Nomadic groups made up the bulk of its population.
   (B) Its manufacturing sector was neither large nor overly productive.
   (C) Under Ismail, it developed the largest army in the region.
   (D) Isfahan was a very cosmopolitan city and brought people from all over the region.

8. One major weakness of the Safavid Empire is that it
   (A) never developed a naval force.
   (B) used only gold as a medium of exchange.
   (C) encouraged Hindus and Buddhists to settle in its territories.
   (D) severed all relations with the Mongols to its north.

9. Mughal India was

   (A) never a power on the Indian subcontinent.
   (B) linked by marriage with the Ottoman Empire and the Byzantine Empire.
   (C) a land of Hindus ruled by a Muslim minority.
   (D) the most inclusive of the governments of the region.

10. Under the Mughal ruler Akbar

   (A) the empire was threatened by nomadic invaders from the north.
   (B) the empire built a very strong naval force.
   (C) foreign trade dwindled.
   (D) the economy, based on cotton cloth, thrived.

11. One reason for the failure of the European explorers to extend Christianity into the region around the Indian Ocean was that

   (A) Europeans did not welcome converts as full members of their communities.
   (B) Islamic leaders killed all converts to Christianity.
   (C) Buddhism was more appealing to any person who wanted to leave the Muslim faith.
   (D) the Mughal Empire and the Safavid Empire banned Christian missionaries.

12. The Bantu language of the East African ports of Kilwa, Mombasa, and Malindi

   (A) dominated the region and spread into Oman and the southern regions of the Arabian peninsula.
   (B) absorbed Arabic, Persian, and Portuguese loanwords and developed into Swahili.
   (C) is not related to the Bantu spoken in West Africa or in southern Africa.
   (D) was the language spoken by the majority of the slaves brought into the region.

13. Over time, the economic gains made by European trading companies changed the balance of power in the Indian Ocean

   (A) and led to the domination of the region by strong, unified European colonies.
   (B) and led to the development of powerful Muslim naval forces.
   (C) but local traders never disappeared from the scene.
   (D) and the Hindu majority in India controlled trade there.

CHAPTER

20

CHAPTER OUTLINE

RIA-Novosti

Russian Ambassadors to Holland Display Their Furs, 1576 Representatives from Muscovy impressed the court of King Maximilian II of Bohemia with their sable coats and caps.

Visit the website and ebook for additional study materials and interactive tools: www.cengage.com/history/bullietearthpeople5e

Northern Eurasia, 1500–1800

- How did Japan respond to domestic social changes and the challenges posed by contact with foreign cultures?
- How did China deal with military and political challenges both inside and outside its borders?
- To what extent was Russia's expanding empire influenced by relations with western Europe in this period?

In the seventeenth century, the Ming dynasty in China was threatened by **Manchu** armies from Manchuria in the northeast. To pay the army defending Beijing (bay-JING), the emperor slashed the government payroll. Among those thrown out of his job as an apprentice ironworker was one Li Zicheng (lee ZUH-cheng). By 1630 Li Zicheng had found work as a soldier, but he and his fellow soldiers mutinied when the government failed to provide needed supplies. A natural leader, Li soon headed several thousand Chinese rebels. In 1635 he and other rebel leaders gained control over much of north central China.

Manchu Federation of Northeast Asian peoples who founded the Qing Empire.

Wedged between the Manchu armies to the north and the rebels to the southwest, the Ming government tottered. Li Zicheng's forces began to move toward Beijing, along the way conscripting young men from captured towns into their army. The rebels promised to end the abuses of the Ming and restore peace and prosperity. In April 1644 Li's forces took over Beijing without a fight. The last Ming emperor hanged himself in the palace garden, bringing to an end the dynasty that had ruled China since 1368.

Victory was short-lived, however. Fearful of uneducated, violent men like Li ruling the land, the Ming general Wu Sangui joined forces with the Manchus. Li had incidentally captured one of the general's favorite concubines and taken her for himself. Together Wu and the Manchus retook Beijing in June. Li's forces scattered, and a year later he was dead, either a suicide or beaten to death by peasants whose food he tried to steal.[1]

Meanwhile, the Manchus made it clear that they were the new masters of China. They installed their young sovereign as emperor and over the next two decades hunted down the last of the Ming loyalists and heirs to the throne.

China was not the only state in northern Eurasia facing foreign threats and uprisings from within. Between 1500 and 1800 Japan and Russia experienced similar turbulence as they underwent massive political and economic change. Besides challenges from nearby neighbors, the three also faced new contacts and challenges from the commercially and militarily powerful European states.

JAPANESE REUNIFICATION

Japan experienced three major changes between 1500 and 1800: internal and external military conflicts, political growth and strengthening, and expanded commercial and cultural contacts. Along with its culturally homogenous population and natural boundaries, Japan's smaller size made the process of political unification shorter than in the great empires of China and Russia. Japan also differed in its responses to new contacts with western Europeans.

Civil War and the Invasion of Korea, 1500–1603

Daimyo and Samurai

In the twelfth century different parts of Japan had fallen under the rule of warlords known as ***daimyo*** (DIE-mee-oh) (see Chapter 10). Each daimyo had a castle town, a small bureaucracy, and a band of warriors, the ***samurai*** (SAH-moo-rye). Daimyo pledged a loose allegiance to the Japanese emperor residing in the capital city of Kyoto (KYOH-toh) and to the shogun, the hereditary chief of the emperor's government and armies. But neither figure held significant political power.

Hideyoshi

Warfare among the different daimyo was common, and in the late 1500s it culminated in a prolonged civil war. The warlord to emerge from the war was Hideyoshi (HEE-duh-YOH-shee). In 1592, buoyed with his success in Japan, the supremely confident Hideyoshi invaded the Asian mainland with 160,000 men. He apparently intended to first conquer Korea and then make himself emperor of China.

daimyo Literally, great name(s). Japanese warlords and great landowners, whose armed samurai gave them control of the Japanese islands from the eighth to the later nineteenth century. Under the Tokugawa Shogunate they were subordinated to the imperial government.

samurai Literally "those who serve," the hereditary military elite of the Tokugawa Shogunate.

The Korean and Japanese languages are closely related, but the dominant influence on Korean culture had long been China, to which Korean rulers generally paid tribute. In many ways the Yi dynasty that ruled Korea from 1392 to 1910 was a model Confucian state. Although Korea had developed its own system of writing in 1443 and made extensive use of printing with movable type from the fifteenth century on, most printing continued to use Chinese characters.

Against Hideyoshi's invaders the Koreans employed all the technological and military skill for which the Yi period was renowned. Ingenious covered warships, or "turtle boats," intercepted a portion of the Japanese fleet. The mentally unstable Hideyoshi countered with brutal punitive measures as his armies advanced through the Korean peninsula and into the Chinese province of Manchuria. However, after Hideyoshi's death in 1598, the other Japanese military leaders withdrew their forces, and the Japanese government made peace in 1606.

The invasion devastated Korea. In the turmoil after the Japanese withdrawal, the Korean *yangban* (nobility) laid claim to so much taxpaying land that royal revenues may have fallen by two-thirds. China suffered even more dire consequences. The battles in Manchuria weakened Chinese garrisons there, permitting Manchu opposition to consolidate. Manchu forces invaded Korea in the 1620s and eventually compelled the Yi to become a tributary state. As already related, the Manchus would be in possession of Beijing, China's capital, by 1644.

AP* Exam Tip
Tokugawa foreign policy is a highlighted point in the AP* course.

The Tokugawa Shogunate, to 1800

Tokugawa Ieyasu

After Hideyoshi's demise, Tokugawa Ieyasu (TOH-koo-GAH-wah ee-ay-YAH-soo) (1543–1616) asserted his domination over other daimyo and in 1603 established a new military government known as the **Tokugawa Shogunate**. The shoguns created a new administrative capital at Edo (ED-oh) (now Tokyo). Trade along the well-maintained road between Edo and the imperial capital of Kyoto promoted the development of the Japanese economy and the formation of other trading centers (see Map 20.1 on page 580).

Tokugawa Shogunate The last of the three shogunates of Japan.

Economic Growth

Although the Tokugawa Shogunate gave Japan more political unity than the islands had seen in centuries, the regionally based daimyo retained a great deal of power and autonomy. Ieyasu and his successors struggled for political centralization, but economic integration proved to be a more important feature of Tokugawa Japan. Because shoguns required the daimyo to visit Edo frequently, good roads and maritime transport linked the city to the castle towns on three of Japan's four main islands. Commercial traffic developed along these routes. The shogun paid the lords in rice, and the lords paid their followers in rice. Recipients converted much of this rice into cash, a practice that led to the development of rice exchanges at Edo and at Osaka (OH-sah-kah), where merchants speculated in rice prices. By the late seventeenth century Edo was one of the largest cities in the world, with nearly a million inhabitants.

The domestic peace of the Tokugawa era forced the warrior class to adapt to the growing bureaucratic needs of the state. As the samurai became better educated and more attuned to

CHRONOLOGY

	Korea and Japan	China and Central Asia	Russia
1500			
		1517 Portuguese embassy to China	
	1543 First Portuguese contacts		1547 Ivan IV adopts title of tsar
			1582 Russians conquer Khanate of Sibir
	1592 Japanese invasion of Korea		
1600		1601 Matteo Ricci allowed to reside in Beijing	
	1603 Tokugawa Shogunate formed		1613–1645 Rule of Mikhail, the first Romanov tsar
	1633–1639 Edicts close down trade with Europe		
		1644 Qing conquest of Beijing	1649 Subordination of serfs complete
		1662–1722 Rule of Emperor Kangxi	
		1689 Treaty of Nerchinsk with Russia	1689–1725 Rule of Peter the Great
		1691 Qing control of Inner Mongolia	
1700	1702 Trial of the Forty-Seven Ronin		1712 St. Petersburg becomes Russia's capital
		1736–1796 Rule of Emperor Qianlong	
			1762–1796 Rule of Catherine the Great
	1792 Russian ships first spotted off the coast of Japan		1799 Alaska becomes a Russian colony

the tastes of the civil elite, they became important customers for merchants dealing in silks, *sake* (SAH-kay) (rice wine), fans, porcelain, lacquer ware, books, and moneylending. The state attempted—unsuccessfully—to curb the independence of the merchants when the economic well-being of the samurai was threatened by low rice prices or high interest rates.

The 1600s and 1700s were centuries of high achievement in artisanship. Japanese skills in steel making, pottery, and lacquer ware were joined by excellence in the production of porcelain (see Environment and Technology: East Asian Porcelain), thanks in no small part to Korean experts brought back to Japan after the invasion of 1592. In the early 1600s manufacturers and merchants amassed enormous family fortunes. Several of the most important industrial and financial enterprises—for instance, the Mitsui (MIT-soo-ee) companies—had their origins

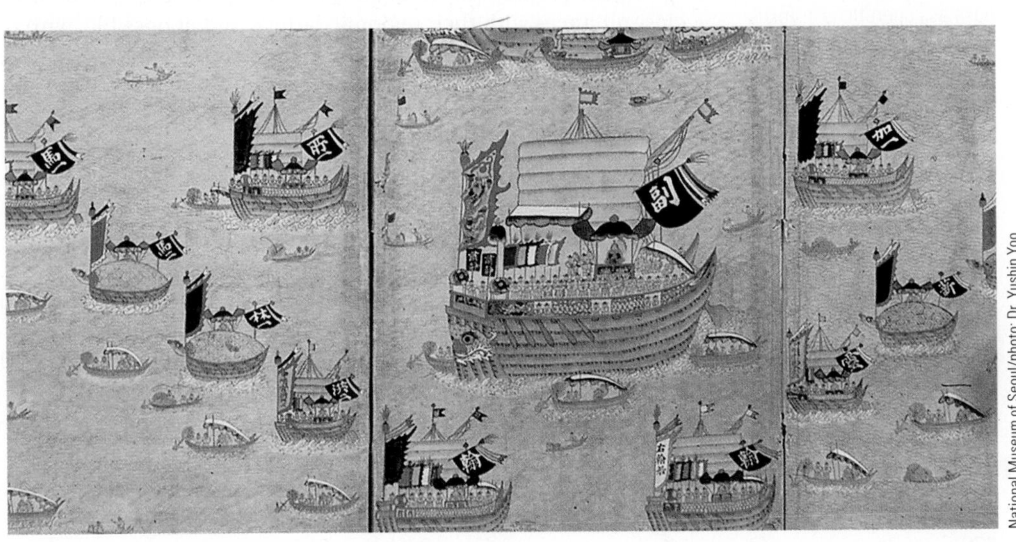

Korean Turtle Boats This painting shows a fleet of Korean warships under the command of Admiral Yi SunShin, who repelled numerous attacks by the Japanese in the last decade of the sixteenth century. Yi SunShin is celebrated for his invention of the "turtle boat," the world's first ironclad warship.

National Museum of Seoul/photo: Dr. Yushin Yoo

ENVIRONMENT + TECHNOLOGY

East Asian Porcelain

By the 1400s artisans in China, Korea, and Japan were all producing high-quality pottery with lustrous surface glazes. The best quality, intended for the homes of the wealthy and powerful, was made of pure white clay and covered with a hard translucent glaze. Artisans often added intricate decorations in cobalt blue and other colors. Cheaper pottery found a huge market in East Asia.

Such pottery was also exported to Southeast Asia, the Indian Ocean, and the Middle East. Little found its way to Europe before 1600, but imports soared once the Dutch established trading bases in East Asia. Europeans called the high-quality ware "porcelain." Blue and white designs were especially popular.

One of the great centers of Chinese production was at the large artisan factory at Jingdezhen (JING-deh-JUHN). No sooner had the Dutch tapped into this source than the civil wars and Manchu conquests disrupted production in the middle 1600s. Desperate for a substitute source, the Dutch turned to porcelain from Japanese producers at Arita and Imari, near Nagasaki. Despite Japan's restriction of European trade, the Dutch East India Company transported some 190,000 pieces of Japanese ceramic ware to the Netherlands between 1653 and 1682.

In addition to a wide range of Asian designs, Chinese and Japanese artisans made all sorts of porcelain for the European market. These included purely decorative pottery birds, vases, and pots as well as utilitarian vessels and dishes intended for table use. The serving dish illustrated here came from dinnerware sets the Japanese made especially for the Dutch East India Company. The VOC logo at the center represents the first letters of the company's name in Dutch. It is surrounded by Asian design motifs.

After the return of peace in China, the VOC imported tens of thousands of Chinese porcelain pieces a year. The Chinese artisans sometimes produced imitations of Japanese designs that had become popular in Europe. Meanwhile, the Dutch were experimenting with making their own imitations of East Asian porcelain, right down to the Asian motifs and colors that had become so fashionable in Europe.

Photograph courtesy Peabody Essex Museum, #83830

Japanese Export Porcelain Part of a larger set made for the Dutch East India Company.

PRIMARY SOURCE: Some Observations on Merchants Read more about business operations in Tokugawa Japan and learn the recipe for merchant success put forward by business owner Mitsui Takafusa.

in sake breweries of the early Tokugawa period and then branched out into manufacturing, finance, and transport.

Wealthy merchants weakened the Tokugawa policy of controlling commerce by cultivating close alliances with their regional daimyo and, if possible, with the shogun himself. By the end of the 1700s the merchant families of Tokugawa Japan held the key to future modernization and the development of heavy industry.

Japan and the Europeans

Direct contacts with Europeans presented Japan with new opportunities and problems. Within thirty years of the arrival of the first Portuguese in 1543, the daimyo were fighting with Western-style firearms, copied and improved upon by Japanese armorers.

The Japanese welcomed but closely regulated traders from Portugal, Spain, the Netherlands, and England. Aside from the brief boom in porcelain exports in the seventeenth century, few Japanese goods went to Europe, and not much from Europe found a market in Japan. The Japanese sold the Dutch copper and silver, which the Dutch exchanged in China for silks that they then resold in Japan. The Japanese, of course, had their own trade with China.

Jesuit Missionaries

Portuguese and Spanish merchant ships also brought Catholic missionaries. One of the first, Francis Xavier, went to India in the mid-sixteenth century looking for converts and later

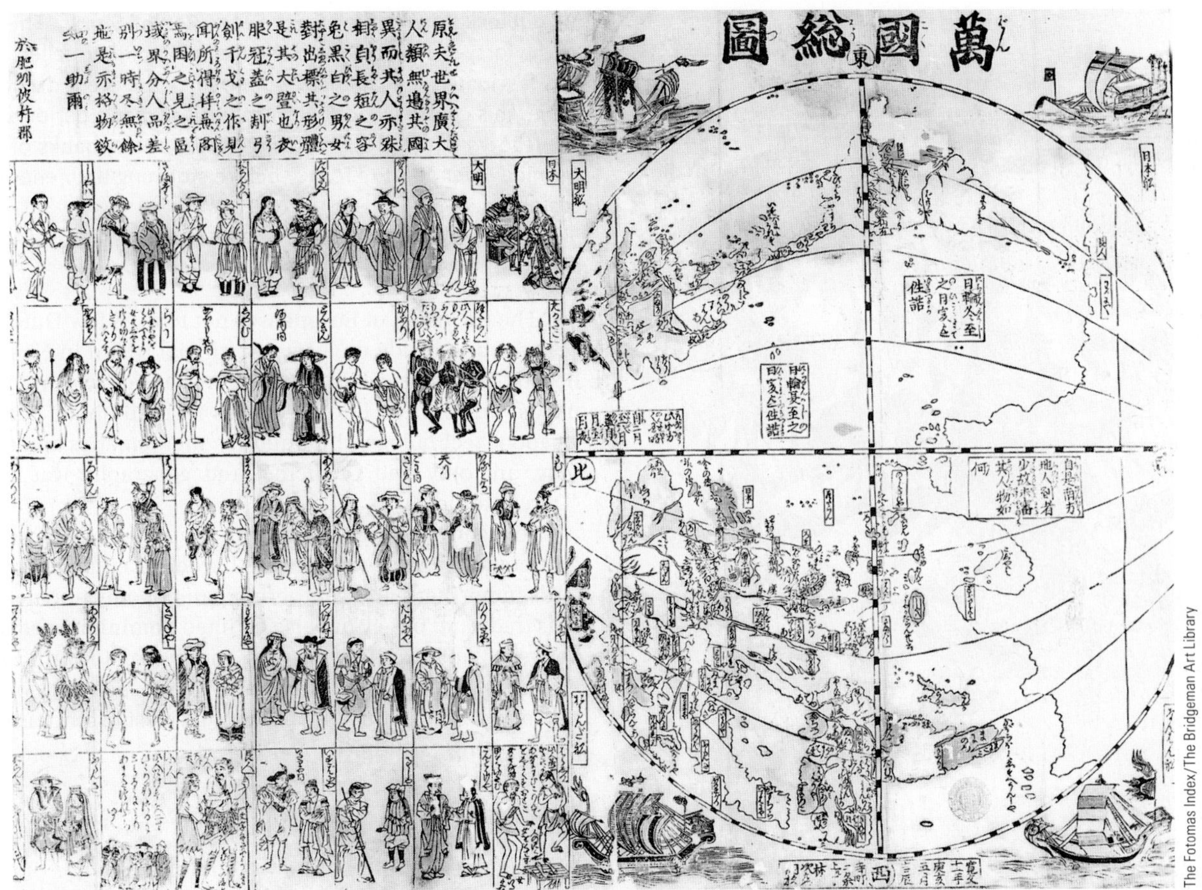

Comprehensive Map of the Myriad Nations Thanks to the "Dutch studies" scholars and to overseas contacts, many Japanese were well informed about the cultures, technologies, and political systems of various parts of the world. This combination map and ethnographic text of 1671 enthusiastically explores the differences among the many peoples living or traveling in Asia. The map of the Pacific hemisphere has the north pole on the left and the south pole on the extreme right of the drawing.

traveled throughout Southeast and East Asia. He spent two years in Japan and died in 1552, hoping to gain entry to China.

Japanese responses to Xavier and other Jesuits (members of the Catholic religious order the Society of Jesus) were mixed. Many ordinary Japanese found the new faith deeply meaningful, but the Japanese elite more often opposed it as disruptive and foreign. By 1580 more than 100,000 Japanese had become Christians, and one daimyo gave Jesuit missionaries the port city of Nagasaki (NAH-guh-SAHK-kee). In 1613 Date Masamune (DAH-tay mah-suh-MOO-nay), the fierce and independent daimyo of northern Honshu (HOHN-shoo), sent his own embassy to the Vatican, by way of the Philippines (where there were significant communities of Japanese merchants and pirates) and Mexico City. Some daimyo converts ordered their subjects to become Christians as well.

Japanese Christianity

By the early seventeenth century there were some 300,000 Japanese Christians and even some Japanese priests. However, suspicions about the intentions of the Europeans turned the new shogunate in Edo into a center of hostility toward Christianity. A decree issued in 1614 banned Christianity and charged its adherents with seeking to overthrow true doctrine, change the government, and seize the country. Some missionaries left Japan; others worked underground. The government began persecutions in earnest in 1617, and the beheadings, crucifixions, and forced recantations over the next several decades destroyed almost the entire Christian community.

To keep Christianity from resurfacing, a series of decrees issued between 1633 and 1639 sharply curtailed trade with Europe. Europeans who entered illegally faced the death penalty. Japanese subjects were required to produce certificates from Buddhist temples attesting to their religious orthodoxy and loyalty to the regime.

Archives Charmet/The Bridgeman Art Library

Woodblock Print of the "Forty-Seven Ronin" Story The saga of the forty-seven ronin and the avenging of their fallen leader has fascinated the Japanese public since the event occurred in 1702. This colored woodcut from the Tokugawa period shows the leaders of the group pausing on the snowy banks of the Sumida River in Edo (Tokyo) before storming their enemy's residence.

The exclusion of Europe was not total. A few Dutch were permitted to reside on a small artificial island in Nagasaki's harbor, and a few Japanese were licensed to supply their needs. What these intermediaries learned about European weapons technology, shipbuilding, mathematics and astronomy, anatomy and medicine, and geography was termed "Dutch studies."

Tokugawa restrictions on the number of Chinese ships that could trade in Japan were harder to enforce. Regional lords in northern and southern Japan not only pursued overseas trade and piracy but also claimed dominion over islands between Japan and Korea and southward toward Taiwan, including present-day Okinawa. Despite such evasions, the new shogunate unquestionably achieved substantial success in exercising its authority.

Elite Decline and Social Crisis

During the 1700s population growth put a great strain on the well-developed lands of central Japan. In more remote provinces, where the lords promoted new settlements and agricultural expansion, the rate of economic growth was significantly greater.

A Rice Economy

Also troubling the Tokugawa government in the 1700s was the shogunate's inability to stabilize rice prices and halt the economic decline of the samurai. The Tokugawa government realized that the rice brokers could manipulate prices and interest rates to enrich themselves at the expense of the samurai, who had to convert their rice allotments into cash. Early Tokugawa laws designed to regulate interest and prices were later supplemented by laws requiring moneylenders to forgive samurai debts. But these laws were not always enforced. By the early 1700s many lords and samurai were dependent on the willingness of merchants to provide credit.

The legitimacy of the Tokugawa shoguns rested on their ability to reward and protect the interests of the lords and samurai who had supported their rise to power. Moreover, the Tokugawa government, like the governments of China, Korea, and Vietnam, accepted the Confucian idea that agriculture should be the basis of state wealth and that merchants, who were considered morally weak, should occupy lowly positions in society. Tokugawa decentralization, however, not only failed to hinder but actually stimulated the growth of commercial activities.

From the founding of the Tokugawa Shogunate in 1603 until 1800, the economy grew faster than the population. Household amenities and cultural resources that in China appeared only in the cities were common in the Japanese countryside. Despite official disapproval, merchants enjoyed relative freedom and influence in eighteenth-century Japan. They produced a vivid culture of their own, fostering the development of *kabuki* theater, colorful woodblock prints and silk-screened fabrics, and restaurants.

SECTION REVIEW

- From the civil war among the daimyo emerged Hideyoshi, who, as supreme warlord, invaded Korea and China.
- After Hideyoshi's death, Tokugawa Ieyasu established the Tokugawa Shogunate, with its capital at Edo.
- The Tokugawa provided political unity and fostered economic expansion but failed to control commerce.
- The Japanese engaged in regulated trade with Europeans, but rising suspicions caused the Tokugawa to restrict foreign contacts.
- Economic growth nourished a new merchant-class culture, but the position of the samurai deteriorated under economic and social pressures.

Ronin

The "Forty-Seven Ronin" (ROH-neen) incident of 1701–1703 exemplified the ideological and social crisis of Japan's transformation from a military to a civil society. A senior minister provoked a young daimyo into drawing his sword at the shogun's court. For this offense the young lord was sentenced to commit *seppuku* (SEP-poo-koo), the ritual suicide of the samurai. His own followers then became *ronin,* "masterless samurai," obliged by the traditional code of the warrior to avenge their deceased master. They broke into the house of the senior minister and killed him and others in his household. Then they withdrew to a temple in Edo and notified the shogun of what they had done out of loyalty to their lord and to avenge his death.

A legal debate ensued. To deny the righteousness of the ronin would be to deny samurai values. But to approve their actions would create social chaos, undermine laws against murder, and deny the shogunal government the right to try cases of samurai violence. The shogun ruled that the ronin had to die but would be permitted to die honorably by committing seppuku. Traditional samurai values had to surrender to the supremacy of law. The purity of purpose of the ronin is still celebrated in Japan, but since then Japanese writers, historians, and teachers have recognized that the self-sacrifice of the ronin for the sake of upholding civil law was necessary.

THE LATER MING AND EARLY QING EMPIRES

Like Japan, China after 1500 experienced civil and foreign wars, an important change in government, and new trading and cultural relations with Europe and its neighbors. The internal and external forces at work in China were different and operated on a much larger scale, but they led in similar directions. By 1800 China had a greatly enhanced empire, an expanding economy, and growing doubts about the importance of European trade and Christianity.

Ming Empire Empire based in China that Zhu Yuanzhang established after the overthrow of the Yuan Empire. The Ming emperor Yongle sponsored the building of the Forbidden City and the voyages of Zheng He. The later years of the Ming saw a slowdown in technological development and economic decline.

The Ming Empire, 1500–1644

The economic and cultural achievements of the early **Ming Empire** (see Chapter 12) continued during the 1500s. But this productive period was followed by many decades of political weakness, warfare, and rural woes until a new dynasty, the Qing (ching) from Manchuria, guided China back to peace and prosperity.

The Europeans whose ships began to seek out new contacts with China in the early sixteenth century left many accounts of their impressions. They were astonished at Ming China's imperial power, exquisite manufactures, and vast population. European merchants bought such large quantities of the high-grade blue-on-white porcelain commonly used by China's upper classes that in English all fine dishes became known simply as "china."

Economic Growth

AP* Exam Tip Understand the developments caused by changes in interregional trade.

The growing integration of China into the world economy stimulated rapid growth in the silk, cotton, and porcelain industries. Agricultural regions that supplied raw materials to these industries and food for the expanding urban populations also prospered. In exchange for Chinese exports, tens of thousands of tons of silver from Japan and Latin America flooded into China in the century before 1640. The influx of silver led many Chinese to substitute payments in silver for land taxes, labor obligations, and other kinds of dues.

Ming cities had long been culturally and commercially vibrant. Many large landowners and absentee landlords lived in town, as did officials, artists, and rich merchants who had purchased ranks or prepared their sons for the examinations. The elite classes had created a brilliant culture in which novels, operas, poetry, porcelain, and painting were all closely interwoven. Small businesses catering to the urban elites prospered through printing, tailoring, running restaurants, or selling paper, ink, ink-stones, and writing brushes. The imperial government operated factories for the production of ceramics and silks. Enormous government complexes at Jingdezhen and elsewhere invented assembly-line techniques and produced large quantities of high-quality ceramics for sale in China and abroad.

Despite these achievements, serious problems developed that left the Ming Empire economically and politically exhausted. There is evidence that the climate changes known as the Little Ice Age in seventeenth-century Europe affected the climate in China as well (see Issues in World History: The Little Ice Age on page 596). Annual temperatures dropped, reached a low point about 1645, and remained low until the early 1700s. The resulting agricultural distress and famine fueled large uprisings that speeded the end of the Ming Empire. The devastation caused by these uprisings and the spread of epidemic disease resulted in steep declines in local populations.

Problems of Adjustment

The rapid urban growth and business speculation that were part of the burgeoning of the trading economy also produced problems. Some provinces suffered from price inflation caused by the flood of silver. In contrast to the growing involvement of European governments in promoting economic growth, the Ming government pursued some policies that hindered growth. Despite the fact that earlier experiments with paper currency had failed, Ming governments persisted in issuing new paper money and copper coinage, even after abundant supplies of silver had won the approval of the markets. Corruption was also a serious government problem. By the end of the Ming period disorder and inefficiency plagued the imperial factories, touching off strikes in the late sixteenth and seventeenth centuries. During a labor protest at Jingdezhen in 1601, workers threw themselves into the kilns to protest working conditions.

Yet the urban and industrial sectors of later Ming society fared much better than the agricultural sector, which failed to maintain the strong growth of early Ming times. Despite knowledge of new African and American crops gained from European traders, farmers were slow to change their ways. Neither the rice-growing regions in southern China nor the wheat-growing regions in northern China experienced a meaningful increase in productivity under the later Ming. After 1500 economic depression in the countryside, combined with recurring epidemics in central and southern China, kept rural population growth in check.

Ming Collapse and the Rise of the Qing

e Interactive Map

Although these environmental, economic, and administrative problems existed, the primary reasons for the fall of the Ming Empire were internal rebellion and rising Manchu power. Inse-

MAP 20.1 The Qing Empire, 1644–1783 The Qing Empire began in Manchuria and captured north China in 1644. Between 1644 and 1783 the Qing conquered all the former Ming territories and added Taiwan, the lower Amur River basin, Inner Mongolia, eastern Turkestan, and Tibet. The resulting state was more than twice the size of the Ming Empire.

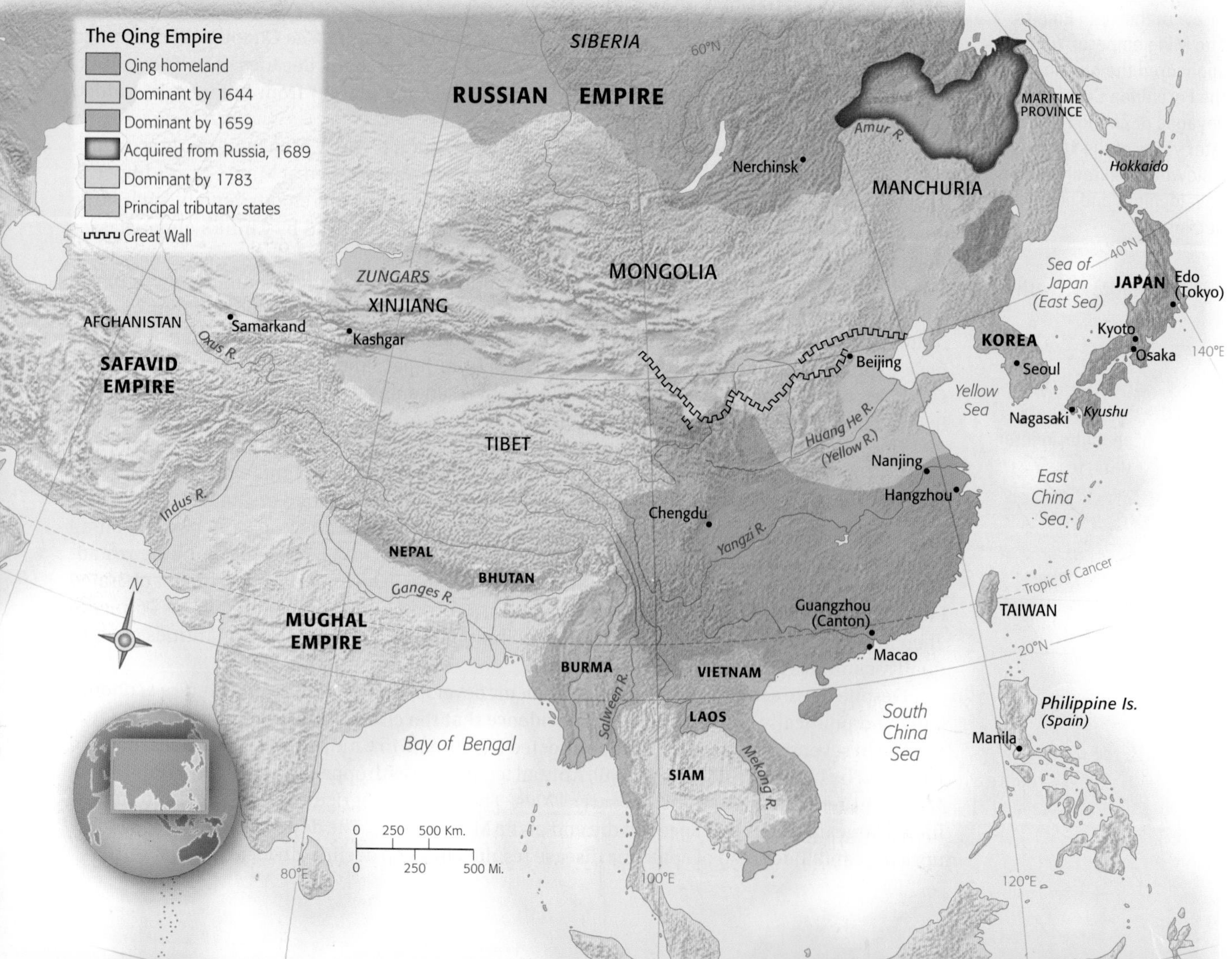

Mongols and Manchus

cure boundaries had been a recurrent peril. The Ming had long been under pressure from the powerful Mongol federations of the north and west. In the late 1500s large numbers of Mongols were unified by their devotion to the Dalai Lama (DAH-lie LAH-mah), or universal teacher of Tibetan Buddhism. Building on this spiritual unity, a brilliant leader named Galdan restored Mongolia as a regional military power around 1600. The Manchus, an agricultural people who controlled the region north of Korea, grew stronger in the northeast.

In the southwest, native peoples repeatedly resisted the immigration of Chinese farmers. Pirates based in Okinawa and Taiwan, many of them Japanese, frequently looted the southeast coast. Ming military resources, concentrated against the Mongols and the Manchus in the north, could not be deployed to defend the coasts. As a result, many southern Chinese migrated to Southeast Asia to profit from the sea-trading networks of the Indian Ocean.

The Japanese invasion of 1592 to 1598 (see section on Japan) prompted the Ming to seek the assistance of Manchu troops that they were then unable to restrain. With the rebel leader Li Zicheng in possession of Beijing (see the beginning of this chapter) and the emperor dead by his own hand, a Ming general joined forces with the Manchu leaders in the summer of 1644. Instead of restoring the Ming, however, the Manchus claimed China for their own and began a forty-year conquest of the rest of the Ming territories, as well as Taiwan and parts of Mongolia and Central Asia (see Map 20.1 and Diversity and Dominance: Gendered Violence: The Yangzhou Massacre).

Qing Empire Empire established in China by Manchus who overthrew the Ming Empire in 1644. At various times the Qing also controlled Manchuria, Mongolia, Turkestan, and Tibet. The last Qing emperor was overthrown in 1911.

A Manchu family headed the new **Qing Empire**, and Manchu generals commanded the military forces. But Manchus made up a very small portion of the population. The overwhelming majority of Qing officials, soldiers, merchants, and farmers were ethnic Chinese. Like other successful invaders of China, the Qing soon adopted Chinese institutions and policies.

Trading Companies and Missionaries

For European merchants, the China trade was second in importance only to the spice trade of southern Asia. China's vast population and manufacturing skills drew a steady stream of ships from western Europe, but enthusiasm for the trade developed only slowly at the imperial court.

A Portuguese ship reached China at the end of 1513 but was not permitted to trade. A formal Portuguese embassy in 1517 got bogged down in Chinese protocol and procrastination, and China expelled the Portuguese in 1522. Finally, in 1557 the Portuguese gained the right to trade from a base in Macao (muh-KOW) on the southern coast. Spain's Asian trade was conducted from Manila in the Philippines, which also linked with South America across the Pacific. For a time, the Spanish and the Dutch both maintained trading outposts on the island of Taiwan, but in 1662 they were forced to concede control to the Qing, who for the first time incorporated Taiwan into China.

The Dutch East India Company

By then, the Dutch East India Company (VOC) had displaced the Portuguese as the major European trader in the Indian Ocean and was establishing itself as the main European trader in East Asia. VOC representatives courted official favor in China by acknowledging the moral superiority of the emperor. They performed the ritual kowtow (in which the visitor knocked his head on the floor while crawling toward the throne) to the Ming emperor.

Jesuits in China

Catholic missionaries accompanied the Portuguese and Spanish merchants to China, just as they did to Japan. While the Franciscans and Dominicans pursued the conversion efforts at the bottom of society that had worked so well in Japan, the Jesuits focused on China's intellectual and political elite. In this they were far more successful than they had been in Japan—at least until the eighteenth century.

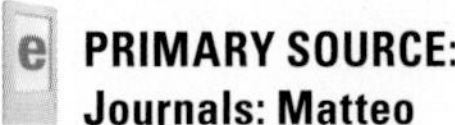
PRIMARY SOURCE: Journals: Matteo Ricci This story about Jesuit missionaries in China provides an interesting look at the nexus of religion and politics in the early seventeenth century.

The outstanding Jesuit of late Ming China, Matteo Ricci (mah-TAY-oh REE-chee) (1552–1610), became expert in the Chinese language and an accomplished scholar of the Confucian classics. Under Ricci's leadership, the Jesuits adapted Catholicism to Chinese cultural traditions while introducing the Chinese to the latest science and technology from Europe. From 1601 Ricci resided in Beijing on an imperial stipend as a Western scholar. Later Jesuits headed the office of astronomy that issued the official calendar.

Emperor Kangxi

Kangxi Qing emperor (r. 1662–1722). He oversaw the greatest expansion of the Qing Empire.

The seventeenth and eighteenth centuries—particularly the reigns of the **Kangxi** (KAHNG-shee) (r. 1662–1722) and Qianlong (chee-YEN-loong) (r. 1736–1796) emperors—were a period of economic, military, and cultural achievement in China. The early Qing emperors repaired the roads and waterworks, lowered transit taxes, cut rents and interest rates, and established incentives for resettling areas devastated by peasant rebellions. Foreign trade was encouraged.

DIVERSITY + DOMINANCE

Gendered Violence: The Yangzhou Massacre

The Qing were not eager for reminders of their brutal takeover to circulate. This rare eyewitness account smuggled out of China reveals not just the violence of the conquest but also the diversity of its impact on men and women.

The account begins in 1645 as rumors of approaching Manchu soldiers spread through Yangzhou, an important city near the juncture of the Yangzi River and the Grand Canal, and the soldiers charged with its defense begin to flee.

Crowds of barefoot and disheveled refugees were flocking into the city. When questioned, they were too distraught to reply. At that point dozens of mounted soldiers in confused waves came surging south looking as though they had given up all hope. Among them appeared a man who turned out to be the commandant himself. It seems he had intended to leave by the east gate but could not because the enemy soldiers outside the wall were drawing too near; he was therefore forced to cut across this part of town to reach the south gate. This is how we first learned for sure that the enemy troops would enter the city. . . .

My house backed against the city wall, and peeping through the chinks in my window, I saw the soldiers on the wall marching south then west, solemn and in step. Although the rain was beating down, it did not seem to disturb them. This reassured me because I gathered that they were well-disciplined units.

. . . For a long time no one came. I retreated again to the back window and found that the regiment on the wall had broken ranks; some soldiers were walking about, others standing still.

All of a sudden I saw some soldiers escorting a group of women dressed in Yangzhou fashion. This was my first real shock. Back in the house, I said to my wife, "Should things go badly when the soldiers enter the city, you may need to end your life."

"Yes," she replied, "Whatever silver we have you should keep. I think we women can stop thinking about life in this world." She gave me all the silver, unable to control her crying. . . .

Soon my younger brother arrived, then my two older brothers. We discussed the situation and I said, "The people who live in our neighborhood are all rich merchants. It will be disastrous if they think we are rich too." I then urged my brothers to brave the rain and quickly take the women by the back route to my older brother's house. His home was situated behind Mr. He's graveyard and was surrounded by the huts of poor families. . . .

The cunning soldiers, suspecting that many people were still hidden, tried to entice them out by posting a placard promising clemency. About fifty to sixty people, half of them women, emerged. My elder brother said, "We four by ourselves will never survive if we run into these vicious soldiers, so we had better join the crowd. Since there are so many of them, escape will be easier. . . ."

The leaders were three Manchu soldiers. They searched my brothers and found all the silver they were carrying, but left me untouched. At that point some women appeared, two of whom called out to me. I recognized them as the concubines of my friend Mr. Zhu Shu and stopped them anxiously. They were disheveled and partly naked, their feet bare and covered with mud up to the ankles. One was holding a girl whom the soldiers hit with a whip and threw into the mud. Then we were immediately driven on. One soldier, sword in hand, took the lead; another drove us from behind with a long spear; and a third walked along on our right and left flanks alternately, making sure no one escaped. In groups of twenty or thirty we were herded along like sheep and cattle. If we faltered we were struck, and some people were even killed on the spot. The women were tied together with long chains around their necks, like a clumsy string of pearls. Stumbling at every step, they were soon covered with mud. Here and there on the ground lay babies, trampled by people or horses.

. . . We then entered the house of [a] merchant, . . . which had been taken over by the three soldiers. Another soldier was already there. He had seized several attractive women and was rifling their trunks for fancy silks, which he piled in a heap. Seeing the three soldiers arrive, he laughed and pushed several dozen of us into the back hall. The women he led into a side chamber. . . .

The three soldiers stripped the women of their wet clothing all the way to their underwear, then ordered the seamstress to measure them and give them new garments. The women, thus coerced, had to expose themselves and stand naked. What shame they endured! Once they had changed, the soldiers grabbed them and forced them to join them in eating and

Vietnam, Burma, and Nepal sent embassies to the Qing tribute court and carried the latest Chinese fashions back home. Overland routes from Korea to Central Asia revived.

The Manchu aristocrats who led the conquest of Beijing and north China dominated the first Qing emperor and served as regents for his young son, who was declared emperor in 1662. This child-emperor, Kangxi, sparred politically with the regents until 1669, when at age sixteen he executed the chief regent and thereby gained real control of the government. An intellectual prodigy who had mastered classical Chinese, Manchu, and Mongolian and memorized the Chinese classics, Kangxi guided imperial expansion and maintained stability until his death in 1722.

Amur River This river valley was a contested frontier between northern China and eastern Russia until the settlement arranged in the Treaty of Nerchinsk (1689).

In the north, the Qing rulers feared an alliance between Galdan's Mongol state and the expanding Russian presence along the **Amur** (AH-moor) **River**. In the 1680s Qing forces attacked drinking, then did whatever they pleased with them, without any regard for decency.

[The narrator escapes and hides atop a wooden canopy over a bed.] Later on a soldier brought a woman in and wanted her to sleep with him in the bed below me. Despite her refusal he forced her to yield. "This is too near the street. It is not a good place to stay," the woman said. I was almost discovered, but after a time the soldier departed with the woman. . . . [The narrator flees again and is reunited with his wife and relatives.]

At length, however, there came a soldier of the "Wolf Men" tribe, a vicious-looking man with a head like a mouse and eyes like a hawk. He attempted to abduct my wife. She was obliged to creep forward on all fours, pleading as she had with the others, but to no avail. When he insisted that she stand up, she rolled on the ground and refused. He then beat her so savagely with the flat of his sword that the blood flowed out in streams, totally soaking her clothes. Because my wife had once admonished me, "If I am unlucky I will die no matter what; do not plead for me as a husband or you will get caught too," I acted as if I did not know she was being beaten and hid far away in the grass, convinced she was about to die. Yet the depraved soldier did not stop there; he grabbed her by the hair, cursed her, struck her cruelly, and then dragged her away by the leg. . . . Just then they ran into a body of mounted soldiers. One of them said a few words to the soldier in Manchu. At this he dropped my wife and departed with them. Barely able to crawl back, she let out a loud sob, every part of her body injured. . . .

Unexpectedly there appeared a handsome looking man of less than thirty, a double-edged sword hung by his side, dressed in Manchu-style hat, red coat, and a pair of black boots. His follower, in a yellow jacket, was also very gallant in appearance. Immediately behind them were several residents of Yangzhou. The young man in red, inspecting me closely, said, "I would judge from your appearance that you are not one of these people. Tell me honestly, what class of person are you?"

I remembered that some people had obtained pardons and others had lost their lives the moment they said that they were poor scholars. So I did not dare come out at once with the truth and instead concocted a story. He pointed to my wife and son and asked who they were, and I told him the truth. "Tomorrow the prince will order that all swords be sheathed and all of you will be spared," he said and then commanded his followers to give us some clothes and an ingot of silver. He also asked me, "How many days have you been without food?"

"Five days," I replied.

"Then come with me," he commanded. Although we only half trusted him, we were afraid to disobey. He led us to a well-stocked house, full of rice, fish, and other provisions. "Treat these four people well," he said to a woman in the house and then left. . . .

The next day was [April 30]. Killing and pillaging continued, although not on the previous scale. Still the mansions of the rich were thoroughly looted, and almost all the teenage girls were abducted. . . . every grain of rice, every inch of silk now entered these tigers' mouths. The resulting devastation is beyond description.

[May 2]. Civil administration was established in all the prefectures and counties; proclamations were issued aimed at calming the people, and monks from each temple were ordered to burn corpses. The temples themselves were clogged with women who had taken refuge, many of whom had died of fright or starvation. The "List of Corpses Burned" records more than eight hundred thousand, and this list does not include those who jumped into wells, threw themselves into the river, hanged themselves, were burned to death inside houses, or were carried away by the soldiers. . . .

When this calamity began there had been eight of us: my two elder brothers, my younger brother, my elder brother's wife, their son, my wife, my son, and myself. Now only three of us survived for sure, though the fate of my wife's brother and sister-in-law was not yet known. . . .

From the 25th of the fourth month to the 5th of the fifth month was a period of ten days. I have described here only what I actually experienced or saw with my own eyes; I have not recorded anything I picked up from rumor or hearsay.

QUESTIONS FOR ANALYSIS

1. **What accounts for the soldiers' brutal treatment of the women?**
2. **What did different women do to protect themselves?**
3. **Having conquered, what did the Manchu do to restore order?**

Source: Reprinted with permission of the Free Press, a division of Simon and Schuster Adult Publishing Group from *Chinese Civilization: A Sourcebook*, Second Edition, edited by Patricia Buckley Ebrey, pp. 272–279. Copyright © 1993 by Patricia Buckley Ebrey.

Contact with Russia

the wooden forts built by hardy Russian scouts on the river's northern bank. Neither empire sent large forces into the Amur territories, so the contest was partly a struggle for the goodwill of the local peoples. The Qing emperor emphasized the importance of treading lightly in the struggle:

> *Upon reaching the lands of the Evenks and the Dagurs you will send to announce that you have come to hunt deer. Meanwhile, keep a careful record of the distance and go, while hunting, along the northern bank of the Amur until you come by the shortest route to the town of Russian settlement at Albazin. Thoroughly reconnoiter its location and situation. I don't think the Russians will take a chance on attacking you. If they offer you food, accept it and show your gratitude. If they do attack you, don't fight back. In that case, lead your people and withdraw into our own territories.*[2]

The Palace Museum, Beijing

Emperor Kangxi In a portrait from about 1690, the young Manchu ruler is portrayed as a refined scholar in the Confucian tradition. He was a scholar and had great intellectual curiosity, but this portrait would not suggest that he was also capable of leading troops in battle.

Qing forces twice attacked Albazin. The Qing were worried about Russian alliances with other frontier peoples, while Russia wished to protect its access to the furs, timber, and metals concentrated in Siberia, Manchuria, and Yakutsk. The Qing and Russians were also rivals for control of northern Asia's Pacific coast. Seeing little benefit in continued conflict, in 1689 the two empires negotiated the Treaty of Nerchinsk, using Jesuit missionaries as interpreters. The treaty fixed the border along the Amur River and regulated trade across it. Although this was a thinly settled area, the treaty proved important, and the frontier it demarcated has long endured.

The next step was to settle the Mongolian frontier. Kangxi personally led troops in the great campaigns that defeated Galdan and brought Inner Mongolia under Qing control by 1691.

Unlike the rulers of Japan, who drove Christian missionaries out, Kangxi welcomed Jesuit advisers, discussed scientific and philosophical issues with them, and put them in important offices. Jesuits helped create maps in the European style as practical guides to newly conquered regions and as symbols of Qing dominance. Kangxi considered introducing the European calendar, but protests from the Confucian elite caused him to drop the plan. When he fell ill with malaria in the 1690s, Jesuit medical treatment (in this case, South American quinine) aided his recovery. Kangxi also ordered the creation of illustrated books in Manchu detailing European anatomical and pharmaceutical knowledge.

Christian Compromises

To gain converts, the Jesuits made important compromises in their religious teaching. Most importantly, they tolerated Confucian ancestor worship. This aroused controversy between the Jesuits and their Catholic rivals in China, the Franciscans and Dominicans, and also between the Jesuits and the pope. In 1690 the disagreement reached a high pitch. Kangxi wrote to Rome supporting the Jesuit position and after further dispute ordered the expulsion of all missionaries who refused to sign a certificate accepting his position. The Jesuit presence in China declined in the eighteenth century, and later Qing emperors persecuted Christians rather than naming them to high offices.

Chinese Influences on Europe

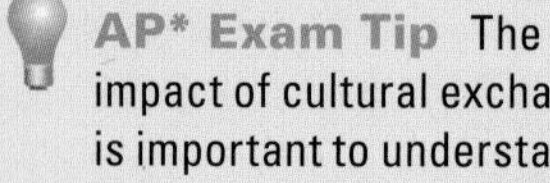

AP* Exam Tip The impact of cultural exchange is important to understand.

The exchange of information that Kangxi had fostered was never one-way. While the Jesuits brought forward new knowledge of anatomy, for example, the Qing demonstrated an early form of inoculation, called "variolation," that had helped curtail smallpox after the conquest of Beijing. The technique inspired Europeans to develop other vaccines.

Similarly, Jesuit writings about China excited admiration in Europe. The wealthy and the aspiring middle classes demanded Chinese things—or things that looked to Europeans as if they could be Chinese. Silk, porcelain, and tea were avidly sought, along with cloisonné jewelry, jade, lacquered and jeweled room dividers, painted fans, and carved ivory (which originated in Africa and was finished in China). Wallpaper began as an adaptation of the Chinese practice of covering walls with enormous loose-hanging watercolors or calligraphy scrolls. By the mid-1700s special workshops throughout China were producing wallpaper and other consumer items according to the specifications of European merchants. The items were exported to Europe via Canton.

Qing Political Philosophy

Qing political philosophy impressed Europeans, too. In the late 1770s poems supposedly written by Emperor Qianlong were translated into French and disseminated in intellectual circles. In them the Qing emperors rule as benevolent despots campaigning against superstition

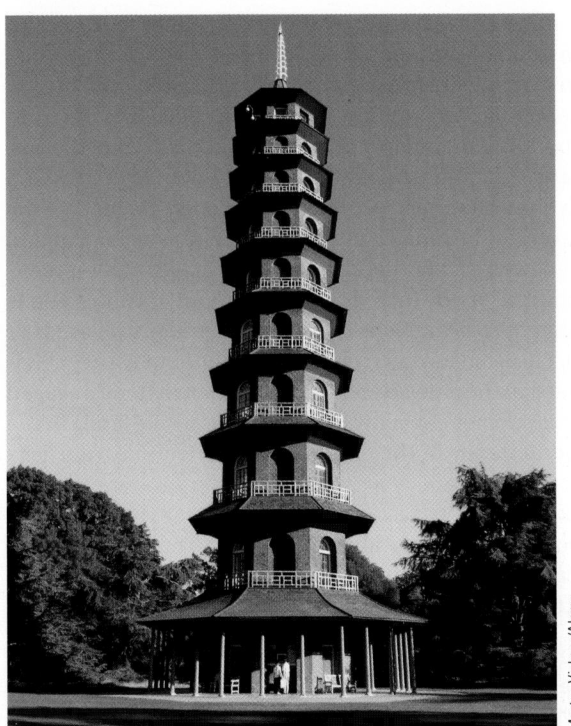

Great Pagoda at Kew Gardens A testament to Europeans' fascination with Chinese culture is the towering Pagoda at the Royal Botanic Gardens in London. Completed in 1762, it was designed by Sir William Chambers as the principal ornament in the pleasure grounds of the White House at Kew, residence of Augusta, the mother of King George III.

and ignorance, curbing aristocratic excesses, and patronizing science and the arts. This image of a practical, secular, compassionate ruler impressed the French thinker Voltaire, who proclaimed that Qing emperors were model philosopher-kings and advocated such rulership as a protection against the growth of aristocratic privilege.

Tea and Diplomacy

To maintain control over trade, facilitate tax collection, and suppress piracy, the Qing permitted only one market point for each foreign sector. Thus Europeans could trade only at Canton.

Britain and the Trade Deficit

This system worked well enough until the late 1700s, when Britain became worried about its massive trade deficit with China. From bases in India and Singapore, British traders moved eastward and by the early 1700s dominated European trading in Canton, displacing the Dutch. The directors of the East India Company (EIC) anticipated limitless profits from China's gigantic markets and advanced technologies.

Tea from China had spread overland to Russia, Central Asia, and the Middle East in medieval and early modern times to become a prized import. Consumers knew it by its northern Chinese name, *cha*—as did the Portuguese. Other western Europeans acquired tea from the sea routes and with it the name used in the Fujian province of coastal China and Taiwan: *te*. In much of Europe, tea competed with chocolate and coffee as a fashionable drink by the mid-1600s.

The Macartney Mission

British tea importers accumulated great fortunes. However, the Qing Empire took payment in silver and rarely bought anything from Britain. With domestic revenues declining in the later 1700s, the Qing government needed the silver and was disinclined to loosen import restrictions. To make matters worse, the East India Company had managed its worldwide holdings badly. As it teetered on bankruptcy, its attempts to manipulate Parliament became increasingly intrusive. In 1792 the British government dispatched Lord George Macartney, a well-connected peer with practical experience in Russia and India, to China. Staffed by scientists, artists, and translators as well as guards and diplomats, the **Macartney mission** showed Britain's great interest in the Qing Empire as well as the EIC's desire to revise the trade system.

Macartney mission The unsuccessful attempt by the British Empire to establish diplomatic relations with the Qing Empire.

To fit Chinese traditions, Macartney portrayed himself as a "tribute emissary" come to salute the Qianlong emperor's eightieth birthday. However, he refused to perform the kowtow, though he did agree to bow on one knee as he would to King George III. The Qianlong emperor received Macartney courteously in September 1793 but refused to alter the Canton trading system, open new ports of trade, or allow the British to establish a permanent mission in Beijing. The emperor sent a letter to King George explaining that China had no need to increase its foreign trade, had no use for Britain's ingenious devices and manufacturers, and set no value on closer diplomatic ties.

Dutch, French, and Russian missions to achieve what Macartney could not do also failed. European frustration mounted while admiration for China faded. The Qing court would not communicate with foreign envoys or observe the simplest rules of the European diplomatic system. In Macartney's view, China was like a venerable old warship, well maintained and splendid to look at, but obsolete and no longer up to the task.

Population and Social Stress

The Chinese who escorted Macartney and his entourage in 1792–1793 took them through China's prosperous cities and productive farmland. They did not see, however, the economic and environmental decline that had set in during the last decades of the 1700s.

Environmental Deterioration

e PRIMARY SOURCE: Edict on Trade with Great Britain Learn why elaborate gifts brought by a British delegation and bestowed personally by Lord Macartney on Emperor Qianlong failed to convince him to accept Britain's trade proposals.

Population growth—a tripling in size since 1500—had intensified demand for food and for more intensive agriculture. With an estimated 350 million people in the late 1700s, China had twice the population of all of Europe. Despite efficient farming and the gradual adoption of New World crops like corn and sweet potatoes, population pressure touched off social and environmental problems. Increased demand for building materials and firewood reduced woodlands. Deforestation, in turn, accelerated wind and water erosion and increased flooding. Dams and dikes were not maintained, and silted-up river channels were not dredged. By the end of the eighteenth century parts of the thousand-year-old Grand Canal linking the rivers of north and south China were nearly unusable, and the towns that bordered it were starved for commerce.

Some interior districts responded to this misery by increasing their output of export goods like tea, cotton, and silk. Some peasants sought seasonal jobs in better-off agricultural areas or worked in low-status jobs as barge pullers, charcoal burners, or night soil (human waste) carriers. Begging, prostitution, and theft increased in the cities. Rebellions broke out in flood-ravaged central and southwestern China. Indigenous peoples concentrated in the less fertile lands in the south and in the northern and western borderlands of the empire often joined in revolts (see Map 20.2).

The Qing government was not up to controlling its vast empire. It was twice the size of the Ming geographically, but it employed about the same number of officials. The government's dependence on working alliances with local elites had led to widespread corruption and shrinking government revenues. The Qing's spectacular rise had ended, and decline had set in.

 Interactive Map

MAP 20.2 Climate and Diversity in the Qing Empire The Qing Empire encompassed different environmental zones, and the climate differences corresponded to population density and cultural divisions. Wetter regions to the east of the 15-inch rainfall line also contained the most densely populated 20 percent of Qing land. The drier, less densely populated 80 percent of the empire was home to the greatest portion of peoples who spoke languages other than Chinese. Many were nomads, fishermen, hunters, and farmers who raised crops other than rice.

SECTION REVIEW

- After the year 1500, financial, environmental, and administrative problems weakened the Ming empire, and it fell to the Manchus.
- European merchants pursued trade contacts with China despite official resistance, and missionaries worked successfully until the eighteenth century.
- Kangxi expanded the Qing Empire's borders, subdued or contained rival powers, and presided over a flourishing economy and culture.
- The Qing and Europeans engaged in productive exchanges of ideas, and Chinese producers supplied growing European consumer markets.
- The one-sided Qing trade system prompted the Macartney mission and other European embassies to the Qing court, but the Qing refused all requests for more equitable trading conditions.
- By the late eighteenth century, population growth had created social and environmental problems that the Qing could not control.

THE RUSSIAN EMPIRE

From modest beginnings in 1500, Russia expanded rapidly during the next three centuries to create an empire that stretched from eastern Europe across northern Asia and into North America. Russia also became one of the major powers of Europe by 1750.

Muscovy Russian principality that emerged gradually during the era of Mongol domination. The Muscovite dynasty ruled without interruption from 1276 to 1598.

The Drive Across Northern Asia

During the centuries just before 1500, the history of the Russians had been dominated by steppe nomads (see Chapter 12). The Mongol Khanate of the Golden Horde ruled the Russians and their neighbors from the 1240s until 1480.

The Rise of Muscovy

Under the Golden Horde Moscow became the most important Russian city and the center of political power. Moscow lay in the forest zone that stretched across Eurasia north of the treeless steppe (grasslands) favored by Mongol horsemen. The princes of **Muscovy** (MUSS-koe-vee), the territory surrounding the city of Moscow, led the movement against the Golden Horde and ruthlessly annexed the territories of the neighboring Russian state of Novgorod in 1478.

Ural Mountains This north-south range separates Siberia from the rest of Russia. It is commonly considered the boundary between the continents of Europe and Asia.

Once free from Mongol domination, the princes of Moscovy set out on conquests that in time made them masters of all the Golden Horde territories and then of a far greater empire. Prince Ivan IV (r. 1533–1584) pushed the conquests south and east at the expense of the Khanates of Kazan and Astrakhan (see Map 20.3).

tsar (czar) From Latin caesar, this Russian title for a monarch was first used in the sixteenth century.

At the end of the sixteenth century, Russians ruled the largest state in Europe and large territories on the Asian side of the **Ural Mountains** as well. After 1547 the Russian ruler used the title **tsar** (zahr) (from the Roman imperial title *caesar*), the term Russians had used for the rulers of the Mongol Empire. The Russian church promoted the idea of Moscow as the "third Rome," successor to the Roman Empire's second capital, Constantinople, which had fallen to the Ottoman Turks in 1453.

The Problem of Seaports

Yet Russian claims to greatness were also exaggerated: in 1600 the empire was poor, backward, and landlocked. Only one seaport—often frozen Arkhangelsk in the north—connected to the world's oceans. The Crimean Turks to the south were powerful enough to sack Moscow in 1571. Beyond them, the Ottoman Empire controlled access to the Black Sea, while the Safavid rulers of Iran dominated the trade of southern Central Asia. The powerful kingdoms of Sweden and Poland-Lithuania to the west similarly blocked Russian access to the Baltic Sea.

Siberia The extreme northeastern sector of Asia, including the Kamchatka Peninsula and the present Russian coast of the Arctic Ocean, the Bering Strait, and the Sea of Okhotsk.

The one route open to expansion, **Siberia**, had much to recommend it. Many Russians preferred the forested north to the open steppes; and the thinly inhabited region abounded in valuable resources, most notably the soft, dense fur that forest animals grew to survive the long winters. Like their counterparts in Canada (see Chapter 17), Russian pioneers in Siberia made a living from animal pelts. The foreign merchants who came to buy these furs in Moscow provided the tsars with revenue and European contacts.

Strogonov Fur Traders

The Strogonovs, a wealthy Russian trading family, led the early Russian exploration of Siberia. The small indigenous bands of foragers had no way of resisting the armed adventurers the Strogonovs hired. Using rifles, their troops attacked and destroyed the only political power in the region, the Khanate of Sibir, in 1582. Moving through the dense forests by river, Russian fur trappers were able to reach the Pacific during the seventeenth century and soon crossed over into Alaska. Russian political control followed more slowly into what was more a frontier zone with widely scattered forts than a province under full control. Beginning in the early seventeenth century the tsar also used Siberia as a penal colony for criminals and political prisoners.

In the 1640s Russian settlers began to grow grain in the Amur River Valley east of Mongolia. As seen already, by the time the Qing reacted to the Russian presence, the worrisome threat of Galdan's Mongol military power had arisen. Equally concerned about the Mongols, the Russians were pleased to work out a frontier agreement. The 1689 Treaty of Nerchinsk recognized Russian claims west of Mongolia but required the Russians to withdraw their settlements farther east.

Russian Society and Politics to 1725

Russian expansion involved demographic changes as well as new relations between the tsar and the elite classes. A third transformation affected the freedom and mobility of the Russian peasantry.

As the empire expanded, it incorporated people with different languages, religious beliefs, and ethnic identities. Orthodox missionaries made great efforts to Christianize the peoples of Siberia in much the same way that Catholic missionaries did in Canada. But among the relatively more populous steppe peoples, Islam prevailed over Christianity as the dominant religion. Differences in how people made their living were equally fundamental. Russians tended to live as farmers, hunters, builders, scribes, or merchants, while those newly incorporated into the empire were mostly herders, caravan workers, and soldiers.

Cossacks

Cossacks Peoples of the Russian Empire who lived outside the farming villages, often as herders, mercenaries, or outlaws. Cossacks led the conquest of Siberia in the sixteenth and seventeenth centuries.

As people mixed, individual and group identities became complex. There was diversity even among Russian speakers who were Russian Orthodox in faith. The name ***Cossack***, which applied to bands of people living on the steppes between Moscovy and the Caspian and Black Seas, probably comes from a Turkic word for a warrior or mercenary soldier. Actually, Cossacks had diverse origins and beliefs, but they all belonged to close-knit bands, fought superbly from the saddle, and terrified both villagers and legal authorities. Cossack allegiances with rulers were temporary; loyalty to the chiefs of their bands was paramount.

Cossacks provided most of the soldiers and settlers employed by the Strogonovs, and they founded every major town in Russian Siberia. They also manned the Russian camps on the Amur River. West of the Urals the Cossacks defended Russia against Swedish and Ottoman incursions, but they also preserved their political autonomy. Those in the rich and populous lands of the Ukraine, for example, rebelled when the tsar agreed to a division of their lands with Poland-Lithuania in 1667.

The Romanovs

In the early seventeenth century Swedish and Polish forces briefly occupied Moscow on separate occasions. This "Time of Troubles" marked the end of the old line of Muscovite rulers. The Russian aristocracy—the boyars (BOY-ar)—allowed one of their own, Mikhail Romanov (ROH-man-off or roh-MAN-off) (r. 1613–1645), to inaugurate a dynasty that would soon consolidate its own authority while successfully competing with neighboring powers. The Romanovs often represented conflicts between Slavic Russians and Turkic steppe peoples as being between Christians and "infidels" or between the civilized and the "barbaric." Despite this rhetoric, it is important to understand that these cultural groups were defined less by blood ties than by the ways in which they lived.

Serfs

As centralized tsarist power rose, the freedom of the peasants who tilled the land in European Russia fell. The Moscovy rulers and early tsars rewarded their loyal nobles with grants of land that obliged the local peasants to work for the lords. Law and custom permitted peasants to change masters during a two-week period each year, which encouraged lords to treat their peasants well; but the rising commercialization of agriculture also raised the value of these labor obligations.

MAP 20.3 The Expansion of Russia, 1500–1800 Sweden and Poland initially blocked Russian expansion in Europe, while the Ottoman Empire blocked the southwest. In the sixteenth century, Russia began to expand east, toward Siberia and the Pacific Ocean. By the end of the rule of Catherine the Great in 1796, Russia encompassed all of northern and northeastern Eurasia.

e Interactive Map

Long periods of warfare in the late sixteenth and early seventeenth centuries disrupted peasant life and caused many to flee to the Cossacks or across the Urals. Some who couldn't flee sold themselves into slavery to keep from starving. When peace returned, landlords sought to recover the runaways and bind them more tightly to their land. A law change in 1649 finally transformed the peasants into **serfs** by eliminating the period when they could change masters and ordering runaways to return to their masters.

serf In medieval Europe, an agricultural laborer legally bound to a lord's property and obligated to perform set services for the lord. In Russia some serfs worked as artisans and in factories; serfdom was not abolished there until 1861.

Like slavery, serfdom was hereditary. In theory the serf was tied to a piece of land, not owned by a master. In practice, strict laws narrowed the difference between serf and slave. In the Russian census of 1795, serfs made up over half the population. Landowners made up only 2 percent, or roughly the same as they did in the Caribbean.

Peter the Great

Peter the Great Russian tsar (r. 1689–1725). He enthusiastically introduced Western languages and technologies to the Russian elite, moving the capital from Moscow to the new city of St. Petersburg.

The greatest of the Romanovs, Tsar **Peter the Great** (r. 1689–1725), reduced Russia's isolation and increased the empire's size and power. He turned Russia away from its Asian cultural connections and toward what he deemed the advanced civilization of the West. In fact, he accelerated trends under way for some time. When he ascended the throne, there were already hundreds of foreign merchants in Moscow. Military officers from western Europe had already trained a major part of the army in new weapons and techniques, and Italian builders were already influencing church and palace architecture. Peter accelerated these tendencies.

Peter matured quickly both physically and mentally. In his youth the government was in the hands of his half-sister Sophia, who was regent for him and her sickly brother Ivan. Living on an estate near the foreigners' quarter outside Moscow, Peter learned what he could of life outside Russia and busied himself gaining practical skills in blacksmithing, carpentry, shipbuilding, and the arts of war. He organized his own military drill unit among other young men. When Princess Sophia tried to take complete control of the government in 1689, Peter rallied enough support to send her to a monastery, secure the abdication of Ivan, and take charge of Russia. He was still in his teens.

Peter concerned himself with Russia's expansion and modernization. To secure a port on the Black Sea, he constructed a small but formidable navy. Describing his wars with the Ottoman Empire as a new crusade to liberate Constantinople from the Muslim sultans, Peter also fancied himself the legal protector of Orthodox Christians living under Ottoman rule. Peter's forces seized the port of Azov in 1696 but lost it again in 1713, thus calling a halt to southward expansion.

In the winter of 1697–1698, after his Black Sea campaign, Peter traveled in disguise across Europe to discover how western European societies were becoming so powerful and wealthy. He paid special attention to ships and weapons, even working for a time as a ship's carpenter in the Netherlands. With great insight, he perceived that western European success owed as much to trade and toleration as to technology. Trade generated the money to spend on weapons, while toleration attracted talented persons fleeing persecution. Upon his return to Russia, Peter resolved to expand and reform his vast and backward empire.

In the long and costly Great Northern War (1700–1721), his modernized armies broke Swedish control of the Baltic Sea, making possible more direct contacts between Russia and Europe. Peter's victory forced the European powers to recognize Russia as a major power for the first time.

On land captured from Sweden at the eastern end of the Baltic, Peter built St. Petersburg, his window on the West. In 1712 the city became Russia's capital. To demonstrate Russia's new sophis-

Peter the Great This portrait from his time as a student in Holland in 1697 shows Peter as ruggedly masculine and practical, quite unlike most royal portraits of the day that posed rulers in foppish elegance and haughty majesty. Peter was a popular military leader as well as an autocratic ruler.

Engraving, after M. I. Makhaiev, from the official series of 1753. Courtesy of the Trustees of the British Museum

The Fontanka Canal in St. Petersburg in 1753 The Russian capital continued to grow as a commercial and administrative center. As in Amsterdam, canals were the city's major arteries. On the right is a new summer palace built by Peter's successor.

tication, Peter ordered architects to build St. Petersburg's houses and public buildings in the baroque style then fashionable in France.

Peter also pushed the Russian elite to imitate European fashions. He personally shaved off his noblemen's long beards to conform to Western styles. To end the traditional seclusion of upper-class Russian women, Peter required officials, military officers, and merchants to bring their wives to the social gatherings he organized in the capital. He also directed the nobles to educate their children.

e PRIMARY SOURCE: Edicts and Decrees Read a selection of Peter the Great's decrees, and find out how he wished to modernize, and westernize, Russia.

Another strategy was to reorganize Russian government along the lines of the powerful German state of Prussia. He sharply reduced the traditional roles of the boyars in government and the army, replacing the old boyar council with a group of appointed advisers in St. Petersburg. Members of the traditional nobility continued to serve as generals and admirals, but officers in Peter's modern, professional army and navy were promoted according to merit, not birth.

A decree of 1716 proclaimed that the tsar "is not obliged to answer to anyone in the world for his doings, but possesses power and authority over his kingdom and land, to rule them at his will and pleasure as a Christian ruler." Under this expansive definition of his role, Peter brought the Russian Orthodox Church more firmly under state control, built factories and iron and copper foundries to provide munitions and supplies for the military, and increased the burdens of taxes and forced labor on the serfs. Peter was an absolutist ruler of the sort then common in western Europe, and he had no more intention of improving the conditions of the serfs than did the European slave owners of the Americas.

SECTION REVIEW

- Muscovy became the center of Russian political power and led the movement against Mongol domination.
- Ivan IV expanded Muscovy, and the Strogonovs sponsored exploration of fur-rich Siberia.
- Russian society blended diverse ethnicities, religions, and cultural practices, a mixture embodied in the Cossacks.
- Emerging from the Time of Troubles, the Romanov tsars worked to centralize royal authority and to institutionalize serfdom.
- Peter the Great accelerated Russia's westernization, fought wars of expansion, and enlarged the power of the tsar.
- Expansion continued eastward and westward, and Catherine the Great continued Peter's westernizing policies.

Consolidation of the Empire

Russia's eastward expansion continued under Peter the Great and his successors. The frontier settlement with China and Kangxi's quashing of Inner Mongolia in 1689 freed Russians to concentrate on the northern Pacific. The Pacific northeast was colonized, and in 1741 an expedition led by Captain Vitus Bering crossed the strait (later named for him) into North America. In 1799 a Russian company of merchants received a monopoly over the Alaskan fur trade, and its agents were soon active along the entire northwestern coast of North America.

Far more important than these immense territories in the cold and thinly populated north were the populous agricultural lands to the west acquired during the reign of Catherine the Great (r. 1762–1796). A successful war with the Ottoman Empire gave Russia control of the north shore of the Black Sea by 1783, though not of the straits leading to the Mediterranean. Three successive partitions of the once powerful kingdom of Poland between 1772 and 1795 advanced Russia's frontiers 600 miles (nearly 1,000 kilometers) to the west (see Map 20.3). When Catherine died, the Russian Empire extended from Poland in the west to Alaska in the east, from the Barents Sea in the north to the Black Sea in the south.

Catherine also made important additions to Peter's policies of promoting industry and building a canal system to improve trade. Besides furs, the Russians had also become major exporters of gold, iron, and timber. Catherine implemented administrative reforms and showed a special talent for diplomacy. Through her promotion of the ideas of the Enlightenment, she expanded Peter's policies of westernizing the Russian elite.

CONCLUSION

China and Russia are examples of the phenomenal flourishing of empires in Eurasia between 1500 and 1800. Already a vast empire under the Ming, China doubled in size under the Qing, mostly through westward expansion into less densely populated areas. In expanding from a modestly sized principality into the world's largest land empire, Russia added rich and well-populated lands to the west and south and far larger but less populous lands to the east. Russia and China were land based, just like the Ottoman and Mughal Empires, with the strengths and problems of administrative control and tax collection that size entailed.

Japan was different. Though nominally headed by an emperor, Japan's size and ethnic homogeneity do not support calling it an empire in the same breath with China and Russia. Tokugawa Japan was similar in size and population to France, the most powerful state of western Europe, but its political system was much more decentralized. Japan's efforts to add colonies on the East Asian mainland had failed.

China had once led the world in military innovation (including the first uses of gunpowder), but the modern "gunpowder revolution" of the fifteenth and sixteenth centuries was centered in the Ottoman Empire and western European states. Although the centuries after 1500 were full of successful military operations, Chinese armies continued to depend on superior numbers and tactics for their success, rather than on new technology. As in the past, infantrymen armed with guns served alongside others armed with bows and arrows, swords, and spears.

The military forces of Japan and Russia underwent more innovative changes than those of China, in part through Western contacts. In the course of its sixteenth-century wars of unification, Japan produced its own gunpowder revolution but thereafter lacked the motivation and the means to stay abreast of the world's most advanced military technology. By the eighteenth century Russia had made greater progress in catching up with its European neighbors, but its armies still relied more on their size than on the sophistication of their weapons.

Naval power provides the greatest military contrast among China, Russia, and Japan. Eighteenth-century Russia constructed modern fleets of warships in the Baltic and Black Seas, but neither China nor Japan developed navies commensurate with their size and coastlines. China's defenses against pirates and other sea invaders were left to its maritime provinces, whose small war junks were armed with only a half-dozen cannon. Japan's naval capacity was similarly decentralized. In 1792, when Russian ships exploring the North Pacific turned toward the Japanese coast, the local daimyo used his own forces to chase them away. All Japanese daimyo understood that they would be on their own if foreign incursions increased.

The expansion of China and Russia incorporated not just new lands but also diverse new peoples. Chinese society had long been diverse, and its geographical, occupational, linguistic, and religious differences grew as the Qing expanded (see Map 20.1). China had also long used Confucian models, imperial customs, and a common system of writing to transcend such differences and to assimilate elites. Russia likewise approached its new peoples with a mixture of pragmatic tolerance and a propensity for seeing Russian ways and beliefs as superior. The Russian language was strongly promoted. Religion was a particular sore point, as Russian Orthodox missionaries, with the support of the tsars, encouraged conversion of Siberian peoples. Russia absorbed new ideas and styles from western Europe, although even among the elite these influences often overlay Russian traditions in a very superficial way. In contrast, Japan remained more culturally homogeneous, and the government reacted with great intolerance to the growing influence of converts to western Christianity.

Forced labor remained common in the Russian and Chinese Empires. Serfdom grew more brutal and widespread in Russia in the seventeenth and eighteenth centuries, although the expansion of the frontier eastward across Siberia also opened an escape route for many peasants and serfs. Some Chinese peasants also improved their lot by moving to new territories, but population growth increased overall misery in the eighteenth century. China was also notable for the size of its popular insurrections, especially the one that toppled the Ming.

KEY TERMS

Manchu p. 573
daimyo p. 574
samurai p. 574
Tokugawa Shogunate p. 574
Ming Empire p. 579
Qing Empire p. 581
Kangxi p. 581
Amur River p. 582
Macartney mission p. 585
Muscovy p. 587
Ural Mountains p. 587
tsar (czar) p. 587
Siberia p. 587
Cossacks p. 588
serf p. 590
Peter the Great p. 590

EBOOK AND WEBSITE RESOURCES

Primary Sources

Some Observation on Merchants

Journals: Matteo Ricci

Edict on Trade with Great Britain

Edicts and Decrees

Interactive Maps

Map 20.1 The Qing Empire, 1644–1783

Map 20.2 Climate and Diversity in the Qing Empire

Map 20.3 The Expansion of Russia, 1500–1800

Plus flashcards, practice quizzes, and more. Go to: www.cengage.com/history/bullietearthpeople5e

SUGGESTED READING

Berry, Mary Elizabeth. *Hideyoshi*. 1982. An account of the reunification of Japan at the end of the sixteenth century.

Chie Nakane and Shinzaburo Oishi. *Tokugawa Japan: The Social and Economic Antecedents of Modern Japan*. Trans. Conrad Totman. 1990. Early modern Japan from a contemporary perspective.

Cooper, Michael, and Jonathan D. Spence. *The Memory Palace of Matteo Ricci*. 1984. An engrossing account of Jesuits in East Asia in the sixteenth and seventeenth centuries.

Crossley, Pamela Kyle. *The Manchus*. 2002. A history of the people who ruled China during the Qing dynasty.

Crummey, Robert O. *Aristocrats and Servitors: The Boyar Elite in Russia, 1613–1689*. 1983. Russia before Peter the Great.

Kappeler, Andreas. *The Russian Empire: A Multiethnic History*. 2001. Deals with all of the empire's peoples, not just the Russians.

Keay, John. *The Honourable Company: A History of the English East India Company*. 1994. A study of Indian Ocean trade and colonization.

Massie, Robert K. *Peter the Great: His Life and World*. 1980. A highly readable biography for a general audience.

Morris-Suzuki, Tessa. *The Technological Transformation of Japan from the Seventeenth to the Twenty-first Century*. 1994. Analyzes the roots of modern Japanese technological development.

Rawski, Evelyn Sakakida. *The Last Emperors: A Social History of Qing Imperial Institutions*. 1998. A reinterpretation of the success of the Manchus' Qing Empire.

Spence, Jonathan D. *The Search for Modern China*. 1990. China during the transition from the Ming to Qing periods.

Wills, John E. *Pepper, Guns, and Parleys: The Dutch East India Company and China, 1662–1681*. 2005. Describes China's relations with European traders.

Wills, John E., Jr. *1688: A Global History*. 2001. Part III, "Three Worlds Apart: Russia, China, and Japan," provides stimulating comparisons.

NOTES

1. Adapted from Jonathan D. Spence, *The Search for Modern China* (New York: W. W. Norton, 1990), 21–25.
2. Adapted from G. V. Melikhov, "Manzhou Penetration into the Basin of the Upper Amur in the 1680s," in *Manzhou Rule in China*, ed. S. L. Tikhvinshii (Moscow: Progress Publishers, 1983).

AP* REVIEW QUESTIONS FOR CHAPTER 20

1. In 1603, after a long civil war, Japan was united
   (A) under Korean conquerors.
   (B) under Tokugawa Ieyasu.
   (C) by the threat of a Portuguese invasion.
   (D) by the arrival of a Qing naval force.

2. In the twelfth century Japan's imperial unity collapsed, allowing the warlords to take over. These warlords were called
   (A) samurai.
   (B) daimyo.
   (C) shogun.
   (D) Edo.

3. Under the Tokugawa shoguns, the capital was moved from Kyoto to
   (A) Hiroshima.
   (B) Hokkaido.
   (C) Tokyo.
   (D) Nara.

4. Under the Tokugawa shoguns, Japan attempted to become politically centralized, but it was actually more
   (A) Confucian.
   (B) of a limited monarchy.
   (C) economically centralized.
   (D) of a confederacy.

5. By the end of the 1700s Japan had developed
   (A) a powerful and modern naval force.
   (B) a strong army supported by gunpowder weapons instead of traditional weapons.
   (C) a parliament built around the samurai families.
   (D) a powerful merchant class that controlled the keys to modernization.

6. By the early seventeenth century there were over 300,000 Japanese Christians. Fearing their power, the shogun
   (A) ordered all Christian missionaries out of Japan and began to persecute the Japanese Christians.
   (B) ordered all Japanese to convert to Zen.
   (C) declared war on the Portuguese, whom he blamed for Christianity in Japan.
   (D) pronounced the legal toleration of all religions in Japan.

7. One reason for the collapse of the Ming was
   (A) the death of the emperor and the fact that he left no heir.
   (B) the loss in the war against Korea.
   (C) economic inefficiency and a government that was not interested in developing its economy.
   (D) the power of the eunuchs to control the government and the emperor.

8. Like other successful invaders of China, the Manchu rulers
   (A) ordered the adoption of the Manchu language as the official language of the empire.
   (B) soon adopted Chinese institutions and policies.
   (C) created a new government bureaucracy.
   (D) abolished the use of court eunuchs.

9. Unlike the rulers of Japan, the Qing emperor Kangxi
   (A) never built a naval force to protect the shores of China.
   (B) welcomed Christian missionaries into the empire.
   (C) saw Korea as unimportant to China's economy.
   (D) converted to Buddhism.

10. Under the Qing, foreign sea trade was

    (A) encouraged and heavily taxed as a way to increase the royal treasury.
    (B) limited to the port of Canton.
    (C) limited to tea and silk.
    (D) always run at a deficit for the Chinese.

11. One result of the long peace under the Qing was

    (A) plentiful supplies of food for the population.
    (B) good relations with Vietnam, Korea, and Japan.
    (C) a population explosion.
    (D) the growth of the size of the imperial family.

12. By the end of the sixteenth century, the largest state in Europe was

    (A) Austria-Hungary.
    (B) France.
    (C) Russia.
    (D) England.

13. The early exploration of Siberia was undertaken not by the Russian state but by

    (A) its generals and the army.
    (B) wealthy trading families looking for furs and forest products.
    (C) lesser nobles looking for fame and fortune.
    (D) gold miners who located gold east of the Ural Mountains.

14. Whether or not Peter I actually initiated it, he is often credited with

    (A) defeating the Austro-Hungarian forces and gaining control of the Bosporus and the Dardanelles.
    (B) westernizing Russia.
    (C) bringing Roman Catholicism to Russia.
    (D) creating a limited monarchy in Russia.

THE LITTLE ICE AGE

A giant volcanic eruption in the Peruvian Andes in 1600 affected the weather in many parts of the world for several years. When volcanic ash from the eruption of Mount Huanyaputina (hoo-AHN-yah-poo-TEE-nuh) shot into the upper atmosphere and spread around the world, it screened out sunlight. As a result, the summer of 1601 was the coldest in two hundred years in the Northern Hemisphere.

Archaeologist Brian Fagan has pointed out that Mount Huanyaputina's chilling effects were a spectacular event in a much longer pattern of climate change that has been called the Little Ice Age.[1] Although global climate had been cooling since the late 1200s, in the northern temperate regions the 1590s had been exceptionally cold. Temperatures remained cooler than normal throughout the seventeenth century.

The most detailed information on the Little Ice Age comes from Europe. Glaciers in the Alps grew much larger. Trade became difficult when rivers and canals that had once been navigable in winter froze solid from bank to bank. In the coldest years, the growing season in some places was as much as two months shorter than normal. Unexpectedly late frosts withered the tender shoots of newly planted crops in spring. Wheat and barley ripened more slowly during cooler summers and were often damaged by early fall frosts.

People could survive a smaller-than-average harvest in one year by drawing on food reserves, but when cold weather damaged crops in two or more successive years, the consequences were devastating. Deaths due to malnutrition and cold increased sharply when summer temperatures in northern Europe registered 2.7°F (1.5°C) lower than average in 1674 and 1675 and again in 1694 and 1695. The cold spell of 1694 and 1695 caused a famine in Finland that carried off a quarter to a third of the population.

At the time people had no idea what was causing the unusual cold of the Little Ice Age. Advances in climate history make it clear that the cause was not a single terrestrial event such as the eruption of Mount Huanyaputina. Nor was the Little Ice Age the product of human actions, unlike some climate changes such as today's global warming.

Ultimately, the earth's weather is governed by the sun. In the seventeenth century astronomers in Europe reported seeing fewer sunspots, dark spots on the sun's surface that are indicative of solar activity and thus the sun's warming power. Diminished activity in the sun was primarily responsible for the Little Ice Age.

If the sun was the root cause, the effects of global cooling should not have been confined to northern Europe. Although contemporary accounts are much scarcer in other parts of the world, there is evidence of climate changes around the world in this period. Observations of sunspots in China, Korea, and Japan drop to zero between 1639 and 1700. China experienced unusually cool weather in the seventeenth century, but the warfare and disruption accompanying the fall of the Ming and the rise of the Qing probably were much more to blame for the famines and rural distress of that period.

By itself, a relatively slight decrease in average annual temperature would not have a significant effect on human life outside the northern temperate areas. However, evidence suggests that there was also a significant rise in humidity in this period in other parts of the world. Ice cores drilled into ancient glaciers in the Arctic and Antarctic show increased snowfall. Information compiled by historian James L. A. Webb, Jr., shows that lands south of the Sahara received more rainfall between 1550 and 1750 than they had during the previous era.[2] Increased rainfall would have been favorable for pastoral people, whose herds found new pasture in what had once been desert, and for the farmers farther south whose crops got more rain.

In the eighteenth century the sun's activity began to return to normal. Rising temperatures led to milder winters and better harvests in northern Eurasia. Falling rainfall allowed the Sahara to advance southward, forcing the agricultural frontier to retreat.

NOTES

1. Brian Fagan, *The Littlest Ice Age: How Climate Made History, 1300–1850* (New York: Basic Books, 2000).
2. James L. A. Webb, Jr., *Desert Frontier: Ecological Change Along the Western Sahel, 1600–1850* (Madison: University of Wisconsin Press, 1995).

PART VI

CHAPTER 21 **Revolutionary Changes in the Atlantic World, 1750–1850**

CHAPTER 22 **The Early Industrial Revolution, 1760–1851**

CHAPTER 23 **Nation Building and Economic Transformation in the Americas, 1800–1890**

CHAPTER 24 **Land Empires in the Age of Imperialism, 1800–1870**

CHAPTER 25 **Africa, India, and the New British Empire, 1750–1870**

Library of Congress

South America 1820s This map of South America from the 1820s records the comprehensive success of the independence movements. With the exception of the Guyanas, no colonial governments remain. As we examine this map, we are also reminded of the failure of two political experiments designed to hold together geographically and ethnically diverse regions in a single national government. In the northwest is Colombia (also called Gran Colombia) created by the era's greatest revolutionary leader, Simón Bolívar. It quickly broke apart to form the modern nations of Venezuela, Colombia, and Ecuador. The United Provinces of Río de la Plata, located in the southeast, also soon collapsed, giving birth to the nations of Argentina, Paraguay, and Uruguay.

Revolutions Reshape the World, 1750–1870

Between 1750 and 1870, nearly every part of the world experienced dramatic political, economic, and social change. The beginnings of industrialization, the American, French, and Haitian revolutions, as well as the revolutions for independence in Latin America, transformed political and economic life. European nations expanded into Africa, Asia, and the Middle East while Russia and the United States acquired vast new territories.

The Industrial Revolution introduced new technologies and patterns of work that made these societies wealthier and militarily more powerful. Western intellectual life became more secular. The Atlantic slave trade and later slavery itself were abolished, and the first efforts to improve the status of women were initiated.

The Industrial Revolution led to a new wave of imperialism. France conquered Algeria, and Great Britain expanded its colonial rule in India and established colonies in Australia and New Zealand. European political and economic influence also expanded in Africa and Asia. The Ottoman Empire and the Qing Empire met this challenge by implementing reform programs that preserved traditional structures while adopting elements of Western technology and organization. Though lagging behind western Europe in transforming its economy and political institutions, Russia attempted modernization efforts, including the abolition of serfdom.

The economic, political, and social revolutions that began in the mid-eighteenth century shook the foundations of European culture and led to the expansion of Western power around the globe. Some of the nations of Asia, Africa, and Latin America reformed and strengthened their own institutions and economies, while others pushed for more radical change. After 1870 Western imperialism became more aggressive, and few parts of the world were able to resist it.

CHAPTER 21

CHAPTER OUTLINE

- Prelude to Revolution: The Eighteenth-Century Crisis
- The American Revolution, 1775–1800
- The French Revolution, 1789–1815
- Revolution Spreads, Conservatives Respond, 1789–1850
- Conclusion

ENVIRONMENT + TECHNOLOGY *The Guillotine*

DIVERSITY + DOMINANCE *Robespierre and Wollstonecraft Defend and Explain the Terror*

Archives Charmet/The Bridgeman Art Library

Burning of Cap Français, Saint Domingue, in 1793 In 1791, the slaves of Saint Domingue, France's richest colony, began a rebellion that, after years of struggle, ended slavery and created the Western Hemisphere's second independent nation, Haiti.

Visit the website and ebook for additional study materials and interactive tools: www.cengage.com/history/bullietearthpeople5e

Revolutionary Changes in the Atlantic World, 1750–1850

- How did the costs of imperial wars and the Enlightenment challenge the established political structures and forms of governance and religion in Europe and the American colonies?
- What were the direct causes of the American Revolution?
- What were the origins and accomplishments of the French Revolution?
- How did revolution in one country help incite revolution elsewhere?

In August 1791 slaves and free blacks began an insurrection in the plantation district of northern Saint Domingue (san doe-MANG) (present-day Haiti). During the following decade and a half, Haitian revolutionaries abolished slavery; defeated military forces from Britain and France; and achieved independence.

News and rumors about revolutionary events in France had helped move the island's slave community to rebel. These same events had divided the island's white population into royalists (supporters of France's King Louis XVI) and republicans (who sought an end to monarchy). The large free mixed-race population secured some political rights from the French Assembly but then rose in rebellion when the slave-owning elite reacted violently.

A black freedman, François Dominique Toussaint, led the insurrection. Taking the name Toussaint L'Ouverture (too-SAN loo-ver-CHORE), he became one of the most remarkable representatives of the revolutionary era. He organized the rebels militarily, negotiated with the island's competing factions and with representatives of Britain and France, and wrote his nation's first constitution. Commonly portrayed as a fiend by slave owners, Toussaint became a towering symbol of resistance to oppression to slaves everywhere.

The Haitian slave rebellion was an important event in the political and cultural transformation of the Western world. Profound changes to the economy, politics, and intellectual life occurred as well. The Industrial Revolution (see Chapter 22) increased manufacturing productivity and led to greater global interdependence, new patterns of consumerism, and altered social structures. At the same time, intellectuals questioned the traditional place of monarchy and religion in society. Merchants, professionals, and manufacturers enriched by economic dynamism provided an audience for the new intellectual currents as they pressed for a larger political role.

This revolutionary era turned the Western world "upside down." The *ancien régime* (ahn-see-EN ray-ZHEEM), the French term for Europe's old order, rested on medieval principles: politics dominated by powerful monarchs, intellectual and cultural life dominated by religion, and economics dominated by hereditary agricultural elites. In the West's new order, commoners entered political life; science took the place of religion in intellectual life; and economies opened to competition.

This radical transformation did not take place without false starts or setbacks. Imperial powers resisted the loss of colonies; monarchs and nobles struggled to retain their ancient privileges; and the church fought against the claims of science. While the liberal and nationalist ideals of the eighteenth-century revolutionary movements were sometimes thwarted in Europe and the Americas, belief in national self-determination and universal suffrage and a passion for social justice continued to animate reformers into the twentieth century.

PRELUDE TO REVOLUTION: THE EIGHTEENTH-CENTURY CRISIS

The cost of wars fought among Europe's major powers over colonies and trade helped precipitate the revolutionary era that began in 1775 with the American Revolution. Britain, France, and Spain were the central actors in these global struggles, but other imperial powers participated as well. While these nations had previously fought unpopular and costly wars and paid for them with new taxes, changes in Western intellectual and political environments now produced a much more critical response. Any effort to extend monarchical power or impose new taxes now raised questions about the rights of individuals and the authority of political institutions.

Colonial Wars and Fiscal Crises

AP* Exam Tip Be able to compare colonial wars and fiscal crises in different empires as part of the analysis of empire development.

In the seventeenth century competition among European powers became global in character. The newly independent Netherlands attacked the American and Asian colonies of Spain and Portugal, even seizing parts of Portugal's colonial empire in Brazil and Angola. Europe's other emerging sea power, Great Britain, attacked Spanish fleets and seaports in the Americas. These rivalries made the defense of trade routes and distant colonies more expensive and difficult.

The eighteenth century further tested the ability of European powers to pay for their imperial ambitions. As Dutch power ebbed, Britain and France began a long struggle for political preeminence in western Europe and for territory and trade outlets in the Americas and Asia as the older empires of Spain and Portugal struggled to hang on. Nearly all of Europe's great powers participated in the War of the Spanish Succession (1701–1714). A war between Britain and Spain over smuggling broadened into a generalized European conflict, the War of Austrian Succession (1740–1748). A frontier conflict between French and British forces and their Amerindian allies then led to a wider struggle, the Seven Years War (1756–1763). With peace Britain emerged with undisputed control of North America east of the Mississippi River and France had surrendered Canada and its holdings in India.

The Cost of War

The enormous cost of these conflicts distinguished them from earlier wars. Traditional taxes collected in traditional ways no longer covered the obligations of governments. While Britain's total budget before the Seven Years War had averaged only £8 million, in 1763 war debt had reached £137 million and interest payments alone exceeded £5 million. Even as European economies expanded, fiscal crises overtook one European government after another. In an intellectual environment transformed by the Enlightenment, the need for new revenues provoked debate and confrontation within a vastly expanded and more critical public.

The Enlightenment and the Old Order

Enlightenment A philosophical belief system in eighteenth-century Europe that claimed that one could reform society by discovering rational laws that governed social behavior and were just as scientific as the laws of physics.

The complex and diverse intellectual movement called the **Enlightenment** applied the methods and questions of the Scientific Revolution of the seventeenth century to the study of human society as well as to the natural world. But some European intellectuals sought to systematize knowledge and organize reference materials. For example, the Swedish botanist Carolus Linnaeus (kar-ROLL-uhs lin-NEE-uhs) sought to categorize all living organisms, and Samuel Johnson published a comprehensive English dictionary. In France Denis Diderot (duh-nee DEE-duh-roe) worked with other thinkers to create a compendium of human knowledge, the thirty-five-volume *Encyclopédie*.

CHRONOLOGY

	The Americas	Europe
1750	1754–1763 French and Indian War	1756–1763 Seven Years War
	1770 Boston Massacre	
1775	1776 American Declaration of Independence	
	1778 United States alliance with France	1778 Death of Voltaire and Rousseau
	1781 British surrender at Yorktown	
	1783 Treaty of Paris ends American Revolution	
	1791 Slaves revolt in Saint Domingue (Haiti)	1789 Storming of Bastille begins French Revolution; Declaration of Rights of Man and Citizen in France
		1793–1794 Reign of Terror in France
		1795–1799 The Directory rules France
	1798 Toussaint L'Ouverture defeats British in Haiti	1799 Napoleon overthrows the Directory
1800	1804 Haitians defeat French invasion and declare independence	1804 Napoleon crowns himself emperor
		1814 Napoleon abdicates; Congress of Vienna opens
		1815 Napoleon defeated at Waterloo
		1830 Greece gains independence; revolution in France overthrows Charles X
		1848 Revolutions in France, Austria, Germany, Hungary, and Italy

The Intellectual Challenge to Old Order

AP* Exam Tip Be sure to study how changes in social structure led to revolution in the eighteenth and nineteenth centuries.

Other thinkers pursued lines of inquiry that challenged long-established religious and political institutions (see Chapter 17). Some argued that if scientists could understand the laws of nature, then surely similar forms of disciplined investigation might reveal laws of human nature. Others wondered whether society and government could be better regulated and more productive if guided by science rather than by hereditary rulers and the church. These new perspectives and the intellectual optimism that fed them helped guide the revolutionary movements of the late eighteenth century.

The English political philosopher John Locke (1632–1704) argued in 1690 that governments were created to protect life, liberty, and property and that the people had a right to rebel when a monarch violated these natural rights. Locke's closely reasoned theory began with the assumption that individual rights were the foundation of civil government. In *The Social Contract*, published in 1762, the French-Swiss intellectual Jean-Jacques Rousseau (zhan-zhock roo-SOE) (1712–1778) asserted that the will of the people was sacred and that the legitimacy of monarchs depended on the consent of the people. Although both men believed that government rested on the will of the people, Locke emphasized the importance of individual rights secured institutionally while Rousseau, much more distrustful of society and government, envisioned the people acting collectively as a result of shared historical experience.

e PRIMARY SOURCE: Rousseau Espouses Popular Sovereignty and the General Will Modern democracies owe much to the political ideas of this French philosopher.

All Enlightenment thinkers were not radicals like Rousseau. There was never a uniform program for political and social reform, and the era's intellectuals often disagreed about principles and objectives. While the Enlightenment is commonly associated with hostility toward religion and monarchy, few intellectuals openly expressed republican or atheist sentiments. Even Voltaire, one of the Enlightenment's most critical intellects and great celebrities, believed that Europe's monarchs were likely agents of political and economic reform.

Monarchs and the Enlightenment

Indeed, sympathetic members of the nobility and reforming European monarchs such as Charles III of Spain (r. 1759–1788), Catherine the Great of Russia (r. 1762–1796), and Frederick the Great of Prussia (r. 1740–1786) actively sponsored and promoted the dissemination of new ideas, providing patronage for many intellectuals. They recognized that elements of the Enlightenment buttressed their own efforts to expand royal authority at the expense of religious institutions, the nobility, and regional autonomy. Goals such as the development of national bureaucracies staffed by civil servants selected on merit, the creation of national legal systems, and the modernization of tax systems united many of Europe's monarchs and intellectuals. Monarchs also understood that the era's passion for science and technology held the potential of fattening national treasuries and improving economic performance.

Though willing to embrace reform proposals when they served royal interests, Europe's monarchs moved quickly to suppress or ban radical ideas that promoted republicanism or directly attacked religion. However, too many channels of communication were open to permit a thoroughgoing suppression of ideas. In fact, censorship tended to enhance intellectual reputations, and persecuted intellectuals generally found patronage in the courts of foreign rivals.

The Community of Belief Systems

Many of the major intellectuals of the Enlightenment corresponded with each other as well as with political leaders. This communication led to numerous firsthand contacts among the intellectuals of different nations and helped create a more coherent assault on what they saw as ignorance—beliefs and values associated with the ancien régime. Rousseau met the Scottish philosopher David Hume in Paris. Later, when Rousseau feared arrest, Hume helped him seek refuge in Britain. Similarly, Voltaire sought patronage and protection in England and later in Prussia.

Women were instrumental in the dissemination of the new ideas. In England educated middle-class women purchased and discussed books and pamphlets. Some were important contributors to intellectual life as writers and commentators, raising by example and in argument the issue of the rights of women. In Paris wealthy women made their homes centers of debate, intellectual speculation, and free inquiry. Their salons brought together philosophers, social critics, artists, members of the aristocracy, and the commercial elite.

The intellectual ferment of the era deeply influenced the expanding middle class in Europe and the Western Hemisphere. Members of this class were eager consumers of books and inexpensive newspapers and journals that were widely available. This broadening of the intellectual audience overwhelmed traditional institutions of censorship. New public venues like the thousands of coffee-houses and teashops of cities and market towns also became locations to discuss scientific discoveries, new technologies, and controversial works on human nature and politics.

The Enlightenment and the New World

Many European intellectuals were interested in the Americas. Some Europeans continued to dismiss the region as barbaric and inferior, but others used idealized accounts of the New World to support their critiques of European society. Many looked to Britain's North American colonies for confirmation of their belief that human nature unconstrained by the corrupted practices of Europe's old order would quickly produce material abundance and social justice. More than any other American, the writer and inventor **Benjamin Franklin** came to symbolize the vast potential of America.

Benjamin Franklin American intellectual, inventor, and politician who helped negotiate French support for the American Revolution.

Born in Boston in 1706, the young Franklin trained as a printer. In Philadelphia he succeeded in business and became famous for his *Poor Richard's Almanac*. He retired at forty-two to pursue writing, science, and public affairs. Franklin was instrumental in the creation of the Philadelphia Free Library, the American Philosophical Society, and the University of Pennsylvania. His contributions were both practical and theoretical. He was the inventor of bifocal glasses, the lightning rod, and an efficient wood-burning stove. In 1751 he published the scientific paper, *Experiments and Observations on Electricity*, which won him acclaim from European intellectuals.

Franklin was also an important political figure. He served in many capacities in the colonies and was selected as a delegate to the Continental Congress that issued the Declaration of Independence in 1776. He later became ambassador to Paris, where his achievements, witty conversation, and careful self-promotion made him the symbol of the era. His life seemed to confirm the Enlightenment's most radical objective, the freeing of human potential from the effects of inherited privilege.

e **PRIMARY SOURCE: The United States Declaration of Independence** Read a selection from Jefferson's famous text, which lays out the Enlightenment principles on which the United States was founded.

As Franklin demonstrates, the Western Hemisphere shared in Europe's intellectual ferment. As the Enlightenment penetrated the New World, intellectuals actively debated the legitimacy of colonialism itself. European efforts to reform colonial policies by unilaterally altering colonial institutions and overturning long-established political practices further radicalized colonial intellectuals. Among peoples compelled to accept the dependence and inferiority explicit in colonial rule, the idea that government authority rested on the consent of the governed proved explosive.

The Counter Enlightenment

Many intellectuals resisted the Enlightenment, seeing it as a dangerous assault on the authority of the church and monarchy. This Counter Enlightenment was most influential in

Beer Street (1751) William Hogarth's engraving shows an idealized London street scene where beer drinking is associated with manly strength, good humor, and prosperity. The self-satisfied corpulent figure in the left foreground reads a copy of the king's speech to Parliament. We can imagine him offering a running commentary to his drinking companions as he reads.

France and other Catholic nations. Its adherents emphasized the importance of faith to human happiness and social well-being. They also emphasized duty and obligation to the community of believers in opposition to the concern for individual rights and individual fulfillment common in the works of the Enlightenment. Most importantly for the politics of the era, they rejected their enemies' enthusiasm for change and utopianism, reminding their readers of human fallibility and the importance of history. While the central ideas of the Enlightenment gained strength across the nineteenth century, the Counter Enlightenment provided ideological support for the era's conservatism and later popular antidemocratic movements.

Folk Cultures and Popular Protest

While intellectuals and the reforming royal courts of Europe debated the rational and secular enthusiasms of the Enlightenment, most people in Western society remained loyal to competing cultural values grounded in the preindustrial past. Regional folk cultures were rooted in the memory of shared experience and nourished by religious practices that encouraged emotional release. These cultural traditions included coherent expressions of the rights and obligations that connected people with their rulers. Authorities who violated these understandings were likely to face violent opposition.

Reform and Popular Culture

In the eighteenth century, European monarchs sought to increase their authority and to centralize power by reforming tax collection, judicial practice, and public administration. Although monarchs viewed these changes as reforms, common people often saw them as violations of sacred customs and responded with bread riots, tax protests, and attacks on royal officials. These violent actions sought to preserve custom and precedent rather than overturn traditional authority. In Spain and the Spanish colonies protesting mobs often expressed love for the monarch while at the same time assaulting his officials and preventing the implementation of reforms, shouting "Long Live the King! Death to Bad Government!"

Enlightenment-era reformers sought to bring order and discipline to the citizenry by banning or altering numerous popular traditions—such as harvest festivals, religious holidays, and country fairs—that enlivened the drudgery of everyday life. These events were popular celebrations of sexuality and individuality as well as opportunities for masked and costumed celebrants to mock the greed, pretension, and foolishness of government officials, the wealthy, and the clergy. Hard drinking, gambling, and blood sports like cockfighting and bearbaiting were popular in preindustrial mass culture, but reformers viewed them as corrupt and decadent. Reforming governments undertook to substitute civic rituals, patriotic anniversaries, and institutions of self-improvement for older customs, often provoking protests and riots.

The efforts of ordinary men and women to resist the growth of government power and the imposition of new cultural forms provide an important political undercurrent to much of the revolutionary agitation and conflict between 1750 and 1850. Spontaneous popular uprisings and protests punctuated nearly every effort at reform in the eighteenth century. But popular protest gained revolutionary potential only when it coincided with ideological division and conflict within the governing class.

SECTION REVIEW

- Wars fought to protect colonies and trade routes overwhelmed the fiscal resources of European powers.
- European intellectuals applied the methods of scientific inquiry to political structures and forms of governance in the Enlightenment.
- In the Counter Enlightenment some intellectuals rejected attacks on tradition and religion.
- The effort to create uniform and rational administration provoked defense of folk culture and tradition.

THE AMERICAN REVOLUTION, 1775–1800

In British North America, clumsy efforts to increase colonial taxes to cover rising defense expenditures and to diminish the power of elected colonial legislatures outraged a populace accustomed to local autonomy. Once begun, the American Revolution ushered in a century-long process of political and cultural transformation in Europe and the Americas. By the end of this revolutionary century constitutions had limited or overturned the authority of monarchs, and religion had lost its dominance of Western intellectual life. At the same time revolutionary changes in manufacturing and commerce replaced the long-established social order determined by birth with a new social ideal emphasizing competition and social mobility.

Frontiers and Taxes

After defeating the French in 1763, the British government faced two related problems in its North American colonies. As settlers pushed west into Amerindian lands, Britain feared the likelihood of renewed conflict and rising military expenses. Already burdened with heavy debts, Britain tried to limit settler pressure on Amerindian lands and get colonists to shoulder more of the costs of colonial defense and administration.

British Frontier Policy

In the Great Lakes region the British tried to contain costs by reducing fur prices and by refusing to continue the French practice of giving gifts and paying rent for frontier forts to Amerindian peoples. But lower fur prices forced native peoples to hunt more aggressively, putting pressure on the environment and endangering some species. The situation got worse as settlers and white trappers pushed across the Appalachians to compete with indigenous hunters. The predictable result was renewed violence along the frontier led by Pontiac, an Ottawa chief. His broad alliance of native peoples drove the British military from some western outposts but was defeated within a year.

The British government's panicked reaction was the Proclamation of 1763, which established a western limit for settlement, undermining the claims of thousands of established farmers without effectively protecting Amerindian land. No one was satisfied. In 1774 Britain tried again to slow the movement of settlers onto Amerindian lands by annexing western territories to the province of Quebec. This provoked bitter resentment in the colonies.

New Colonial Tax and Commercial Policies

While frontier issues increased colonial hostility and suspicion, they did not lead to a breach. But British efforts to transfer the cost of imperial wars to the colonists through a campaign of fiscal reforms and new taxes sparked a political confrontation that ultimately led to rebellion. New British commercial regulations endangered New England's profitable trade with Spanish and French Caribbean sugar colonies. More disruptive still was Britain's outlawing of colonial issues of paper money, a custom made necessary by the colonies' chronic balance-of-payments deficits. Colonial legislatures responded by protesting these measures while angry colonists organized boycotts of British goods.

Colonial Protests

Colonists deeply resented the Stamp Act of 1765, a tax on all legal documents, newspapers, pamphlets, and nearly all printed material. Now propertied colonists, including holders of high office and members of the colonial elite, assumed leading roles in protests. Critics of these measures used fiery political language, identifying Britain's rulers as "parricides" and "tyrants," while women from prominent colonial families organized boycotts of British goods. Colonial women now viewed the production of homespun textiles as a patriotic obligation. Organizations such as the Sons of Liberty were more confrontational, holding public meetings, intimidating royal officials, and organizing committees to enforce the boycotts. Although this combination of protest and boycott forced the repeal of the Stamp Act, Britain soon imposed new taxes and duties. Parliament also sent British troops to quell colonial riots. One indignant woman expressed her anger to a British officer:

> *[T]he most ignorant peasant knows . . . that no man has the right to take their money without their consent. The supposition is ridiculous and absurd, as none but highwaymen and robbers attempt it. Can you, my friend, reconcile it with your own good sense, that a body of men in Great Britain, who have little intercourse with America . . . shall invest themselves with a power to command our lives and properties [?]*[1]

British authorities reacted to boycotts and attacks on royal officials by threatening colonial liberties. They dissolved the colonial legislature of Massachusetts and sent two regiments of soldiers to reestablish control of Boston's streets. Popular support for a complete break with Britain grew after March 5, 1770, when British soldiers fired at an angry Boston crowd, killing five civilians. The "Boston Massacre" exposed the naked force on which colonial rule rested and radicalized public opinion throughout the colonies.

Parliament attempted to calm colonial opinion by repealing some taxes and duties, but it stumbled into another crisis when it granted the East India Company a monopoly to import tea to the colonies. This decision raised again the constitutional issue of Parliament's right to tax the colonies. The crisis came to a head when protesters dumped tea worth £10,000 into Boston harbor. Britain responded by appointing a military man, Thomas Gage, as governor of Massachusetts and by closing the port of Boston. British troops now enforced public order in Boston, and public administration was in the hands of a general. This militarization of colonial government undermined Britain's constitutional authority and made rebellion inevitable.

The Granger Collection, New York

The Tarring and Feathering of a British Official, 1774 British periodicals responded to the rising tide of colonial protest by focusing on mob violence and the breakdown of public order. This illustration portrayed the brutal treatment given John Malcomb, commissioner of customs at Boston. For many in Britain, colonial demands for liberty were little more than an excuse for mob violence.

The Course of Revolution, 1775–1783

When representatives elected to the Continental Congress met in Philadelphia in 1775, patriot militia had already fought British troops at Lexington and Concord, Massachusetts (see Map 21.1). Events were propelling the colonies toward revolution. Congress assumed the powers of government. They created a currency and organized an army led by **George Washington** (1732–1799), a Virginia planter who had served in the French and Indian War.

George Washington Military commander of the American Revolution. He was the first elected president of the United States (1789–1799).

The angry rhetoric of thousands of street-corner speakers and the inflammatory pamphlet *Common Sense*, written by Thomas Paine, a recent immigrant from England, propelled popular support for independence. On July 4, 1776, Congress approved the Declaration of Independence, the document that proved to be the most enduring statement of the revolutionary era's ideology:

> *We hold these truths to be self evident: That all men are created equal; that they are endowed by their creator with certain unalienable rights; that among these are life, liberty and the pursuit of happiness; that, to secure these rights, governments are instituted among men, deriving their just powers from the consent of the governed.*

The Declaration's affirmation of popular sovereignty and individual rights would influence the language of revolution and popular protest around the world.

Great Britain reacted by sending additional military forces to pacify the colonies. By 1778 Britain had 50,000 British troops and 30,000 German mercenaries in the colonies. Despite the existence of a large loyalist community, the British army found it difficult to control the countryside. Although British forces won most of the battles, Washington slowly built a competent Continental army as well as civilian support networks that provided supplies and financial resources.

The British government also tried to find a political compromise that would satisfy colonial grievances. Half-hearted efforts to resolve the conflict over taxes failed, and an offer to roll back the clock and reestablish the administrative arrangements of 1763 made little headway. Overconfidence in its military and poor leadership kept the British from finding a political solution before revolutionary institutions were in place and the armies engaged. By allowing confrontation to occur, the British government lost the opportunity to mobilize and give direction to the large numbers of loyalists and pacifists in the colonies.

Along the Canadian border, both sides solicited Amerindians as allies and feared them as potential enemies. For over a hundred years, members of the powerful Iroquois Confederacy—Mohawk, Oneida, Onondaga, Cayuga, Seneca, and (after 1722) Tuscarora—had protected their traditional lands with a combination of diplomacy and warfare. Just as the American Revolution forced settler families to join the rebels or remain loyal, it divided the Iroquois, who fought on both sides.

Joseph Brant Mohawk leader who supported the British during the American Revolution.

The Mohawk proved to be valuable British allies. Their loyalist leader **Joseph Brant** (Thayendanegea [ta-YEHN-dah-NEY-geh-ah]) organized Britain's most potent fighting force along the Canadian border. His raids along the northern frontier earned him the title "Monster" Brant, but he was actually a man who moved easily between European and Amerindian cultures. Educated by missionaries, he was fluent in English and helped translate Protestant religious tracts into Mohawk. He was friendly with many loyalist families and British officials and had traveled to London for an audience with George III (r. 1760–1820).

The defeat in late 1777 of Britain's general John Burgoyne by General Horatio Gates at Saratoga, New York, put the future of the Mohawk at risk. American forces followed this victory with destructive attacks on Iroquois villages that reduced their political and military power. After Britain's defeat, Brant and the Mohawk joined the loyalist exodus to Canada.

The British defeat at Saratoga also convinced France to enter the war as an ally of the United States in 1778. French military help proved crucial, supplying American forces and forcing the British to defend their colonies in the Caribbean. The French contribution was most clear in the final battle, fought at Yorktown, Virginia, in 1781 (see Map 21.1). With the American army supported by French soldiers and a French fleet, General Charles Cornwallis surrendered to Washington as the British military band played "The World Turned Upside-Down."

This victory effectively ended the war, and the Continental Congress sent representatives to the peace conference with instructions to work in tandem with the French. Believing that France was more concerned with containing British power than with guaranteeing a strong

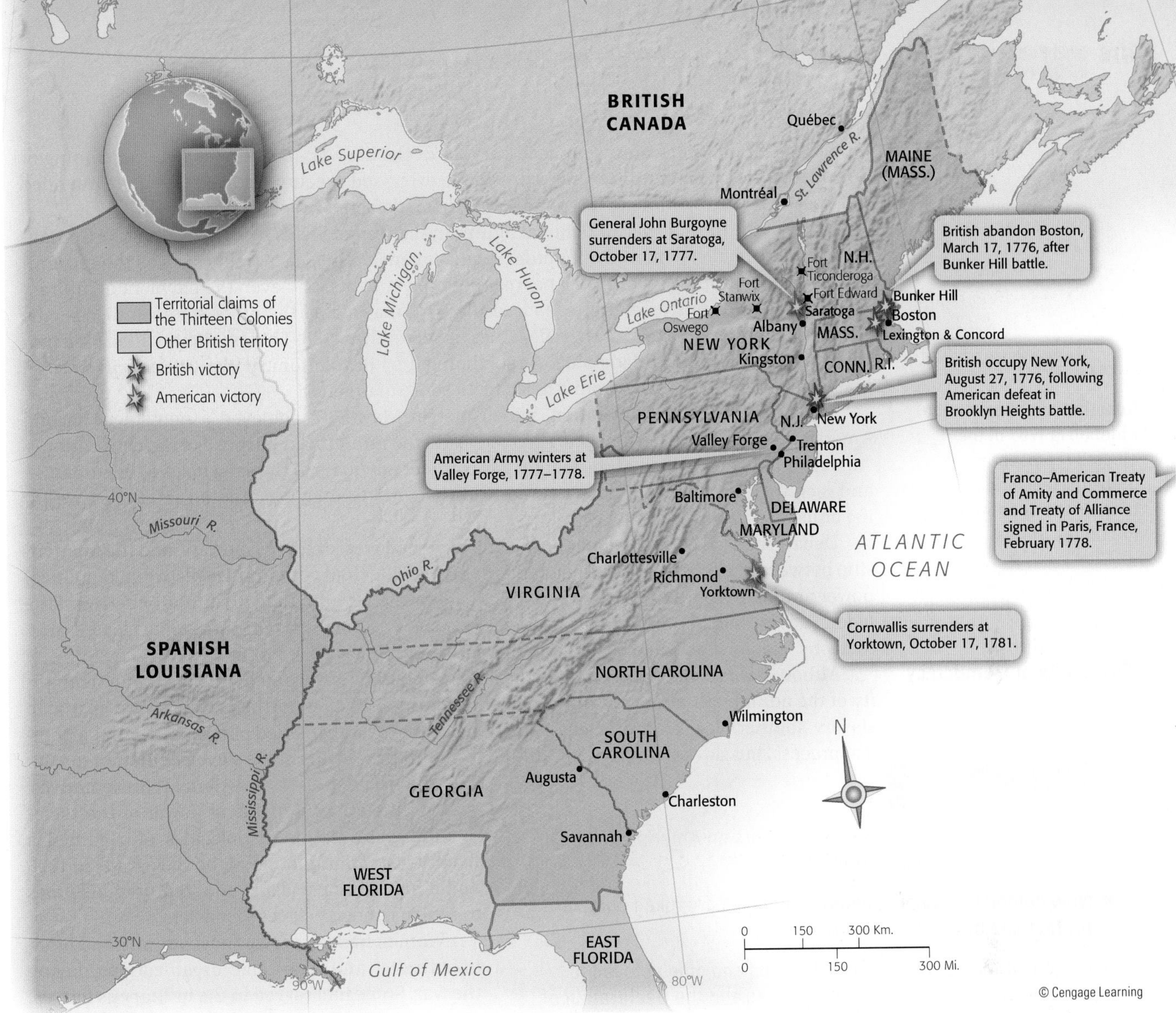

MAP 21.1 **The American Revolutionary War** The British army won most of the major battles, and British troops held most of the major cities. Even so, the American revolutionaries eventually won a comprehensive military and political victory.

e Interactive Map

United States, America's peace delegation chose to negotiate directly with Britain and gained a generous settlement. The Treaty of Paris (1783) granted unconditional independence and established generous boundaries for the former colonies. In return the United States promised to repay prewar debts due to British merchants and to allow loyalists to recover property confiscated by patriot forces. In the end, loyalists were badly treated, and thousands left for Canada.

The Construction of Republican Political Structures, to 1800

Even before the Declaration of Independence, many colonies had created new governments. Leaders in the new states summoned constitutional conventions to draft formal charters. Europeans were fascinated by the drafting of written constitutions and by their ratification by popular vote. Many early state constitutions were translated and published in Europe. Remembering colonial conflicts with royal governors, state constitutions placed severe limits on executive authority and granted broad powers to legislatures. Many state constitutions included bills of rights to provide further protection against tyranny.

Creating a New Government

It proved more difficult to frame a national constitution. The Second Continental Congress sent the Articles of Confederation—the first constitution of the United States—to the states for approval in 1777, but it was not accepted until 1781. It created a one-house legislature in which each state had a single vote. While a simple majority of the thirteen states was sufficient to pass minor legislation, nine votes were necessary for declaring war, imposing taxes, and coining or borrowing money. A committee, not a president, exercised executive power. Given the intended weakness of this government, it is remarkable that it defeated Great Britain.

Many of the most powerful political figures in the United States recognized that the Confederation was unable to enforce unpopular requirements of the peace treaty such as the recognition of loyalist property claims, the payment of prewar debts, and even the payment of military salaries and pensions to veterans. As a result, Virginia invited the other states to discuss the government's failure to deal with trade issues in September 1786. This assembly called for a new convention to meet in Philadelphia. A rebellion led by Revolutionary War veterans in western Massachusetts gave the assembling delegates a sense of urgency.

Constitutional Convention Meeting in 1787 of the elected representatives of the thirteen original states to write the Constitution of the United States.

The **Constitutional Convention**, which met in May 1787, achieved a nonviolent second American Revolution. The delegates pushed aside the announced purpose of the convention—"to render the constitution of the federal government adequate to the exigencies of the union"—and secretly undertook to write a new constitution with George Washington serving as presiding officer.

Debate focused on representation, electoral procedures, executive powers, and the relationship between the federal government and the states. The final compromise distributed political power among executive, legislative, and judicial branches and divided authority between the federal government and the states. The chief executive—the president—was to be elected indirectly by "electors" selected by ballot in the states.

The Limits of Democracy

Although this constitution created the most democratic government of the era, only a minority of the adult population had full political rights. While some northern states were hostile to slavery, southern leaders protected the institution. Slaves were denied participation in the political process, but slave states were permitted to count three-fifths of the slave population to allocate the number of congressional representatives, thus multiplying the political power of the slave-owning class. Southern delegates also gained a twenty-year continuation of the slave trade to 1808 and a fugitive slave clause that required all states to return runaway slaves to masters.

Women had led prewar boycotts and had organized relief and charitable organizations during the war. Some had served in the military as nurses, and a smaller number had joined the ranks disguised as men. Nevertheless, women were denied political rights in the new republic. Only New Jersey granted the vote to women and African Americans who met property requirements, and in 1807 state lawmakers eliminated this right.

SECTION REVIEW

- Britain tried to prevent new settlements on Amerindian lands and limit the expense of frontier defense.
- New colonial tax and commercial policies provoked colonial protest and boycotts in North America.
- Armed conflict between British troops and colonists led to the calling of the Continental Congress and the Declaration of Independence.
- French support for the American Revolution proved crucial.
- The American states supported the creation of a new constitution that divided the powers of government.

THE FRENCH REVOLUTION, 1789–1815

The French Revolution undermined traditional monarchy and hereditary aristocracy as well as the power of the Catholic Church but, unlike the American Revolution, did not create enduring representative institutions. The colonial revolution in North America, however, did not confront so directly the entrenched privileges of an established church, monarchy, and aristocracy. Among its achievements, the French Revolution expanded mass participation in political life and radicalized the democratic tradition inherited from the English and American experiences. The political passions unleashed by revolutionary events in France also ultimately led to rule by popular demagogues and the dictatorship of Napoleon.

French Society and Fiscal Crisis

French society was divided in three estates. The clergy, called the First Estate, numbered about 130,000 in a nation of 28 million. The Catholic clergy was organized hierarchically, and members of the hereditary nobility held almost all top positions in the church. The church owned about

10 percent of the nation's land and extracted substantial amounts of wealth from the economy in the form of tithes and ecclesiastical fees, but it paid few taxes.

The 300,000 members of the nobility, the Second Estate, controlled about 30 percent of the land and retained ancient rights on much of the rest. Nobles held most high administrative, judicial, military, and church positions. Though barred from some types of commercial activity, nobles were important participants in wholesale trade, banking, manufacturing, and mining. Like the clergy, this estate was hierarchical: important differences in wealth, power, and outlook separated the higher from the lower nobility. In the eighteenth century many wealthy commoners who purchased administrative and judicial offices claimed noble status.

The Third Estate

The Third Estate included everyone else, from wealthy financiers to beggars. The number of propertied and successful commoners grew rapidly in the eighteenth century. Commerce, finance, and manufacturing accounted for much of the wealth of the Third Estate. Wealthy commoners also owned nearly a third of the nation's land. This literate and socially ambitious group supported an expanding publishing industry, subsidized the fine arts, and purchased many of the extravagant new homes built in Paris and other cities.

Artisans, shopkeepers, and small landowners owned property and lived decently when crops were good and prices stable, but by 1780 poor harvests had increased their cost of living and led to a decline in consumer demand for their products. They were rich enough to fear the loss of their property and status and well educated enough to be aware of the growing criticism of the king, but they lacked the means to influence policy.

The Poor

Poverty was common. Peasants accounted for 80 percent of the French population. The poverty and vulnerability of peasant families forced young children to seek seasonal work and led many to crime and beggary. In Paris and other French cities the vile living conditions and unhealthy diet of the urban poor were startling to visitors from other European nations. City streets swarmed with beggars and prostitutes. The problem of child abandonment suggests the wretchedness of the French poor. On the eve of the French Revolution parents gave up at least 40,000 children per year. Their belief that these children would be adopted was no more than a convenient fiction; in reality the majority died of neglect.

Unable to afford decent housing, obtain steady employment, or protect their children, the poor periodically erupted in violent protest and rage. In the countryside the decisions of the nobility or clergy to increase taxes and other burdens often led to violence. In towns and cities any increase in the price of bread could spark a riot, since bread prices determined the quality of life of the poor. These explosive episodes, however, were not revolutionary in character; rioters sought immediate relief rather than structural change. That was to change when the Crown tried to solve its fiscal crisis.

The cost of the War of the Austrian Succession began the crisis. Louis XV (r. 1715–1774) tried to impose new taxes on the nobility and other privileged groups, but this led to widespread protests. New debt from the Seven Years War deepened the crisis and compelled the king to impose emergency fiscal measures. The Parlement of Paris, an appeal

Private Collection

Parisian Stocking Mender The poor lived very difficult lives. This woman uses a discarded wine barrel as a shop where she mends socks.

The Politics of Debts and Taxes

court, resisted these measures. Frustrated by these actions, French authorities exiled members of the Parlement and pushed through a series of unpopular fiscal measures.

When the twenty-two-year-old Louis XVI assumed the throne in 1774, he faced a desperate fiscal situation compounded by the growing opposition of French courts. In 1774 his chief financial adviser warned that the government could barely afford to operate; as he put it, "the first gunshot [act of war] will drive the state to bankruptcy." Despite this warning, the king decided to support the American Revolution, delaying collapse by borrowing enormous sums and disguising the growing debt in misleading fiscal accounts. By the end of the war, more than half of France's national budget was required to pay the interest on its debt.

In 1787 the desperate king called an Assembly of Notables to approve a radical and comprehensive reform of the economy and fiscal policy. Despite the fact that the king's advisers selected this assembly from the high nobility, the judiciary, and the clergy, these representatives of privilege proved unwilling to support the proposed reforms and new taxes.

Estates General France's traditional national assembly with representatives of the three estates, or classes, in French society: the clergy, nobility, and commoners. The calling of the Estates General in 1789 led to the French Revolution.

Protest Turns to Revolution, 1789–1792

In frustration, the king dismissed the Notables and attempted to implement reforms on his own, but his effort was met by an increasingly hostile judiciary and by popular demonstrations. The refusal of the elite to grant needed tax concessions forced the king to call the **Estates General**, a customary consultative body representing the three estates that had not met since 1614. The narrow self-interest and greed of the rich—who would not tolerate an increase in their own taxes—rather than the grinding poverty of the common people had created the conditions for revolution.

The Third Estate Acts

In late 1788 and early 1789 members of the three estates came together throughout the nation to discuss grievances and elect representatives to meet at Versailles (vuhr-SIGH). The Third Estate's representatives were mostly men of substantial property, but some were angry with the king's ministers and inclined to move France toward constitutional monarchy with an elected legislature. Many nobles and members of the clergy sympathized with the reform agenda of the Third Estate, but deep internal divisions over procedural and policy issues limited the power of the First and the Second Estates. Nevertheless, some clergy, and eventually nobles, joined with the Third Estate.

After six weeks of deadlock, the Third Estate, with allies from the other estates, signaled its ambitions by calling itself the National Assembly. Fearful of the growing assertiveness of these representatives, the king locked them out of their meeting place. They moved to an indoor tennis court and pledged to write a constitution. The ascendant ideas of the era, that the people are sovereign and the legitimacy of rulers depends on their fulfilling the people's will, now swept away the king's narrow desire to solve the nation's fiscal crisis. Louis prepared for a confrontation with the National Assembly by moving military forces to Versailles. Before he could act, the people of Paris intervened.

A succession of bad harvests beginning in 1785 had propelled bread prices upward throughout France and provoked an economic depression as demand for nonessential goods collapsed. By the time the Estates General met, nearly a third of the Parisian work force was unemployed. Hunger and anger marched hand in hand through working-class neighborhoods.

The Bastille Falls

When the people of Paris heard that the king was massing troops in Versailles to arrest the representatives, crowds of common people began to seize arms and mobilize. On July 14, 1789, a crowd attacked the Bastille (bass-TEEL), a medieval fortress used as a prison. The futile defense of the Bastille cost ninety-eight lives before its garrison surrendered. Enraged, the attackers hacked the commander to death and then paraded through the city with his head and that of Paris's chief magistrate stuck on pikes.

Declaration of the Rights of Man and the Citizen Statement of fundamental political rights adopted by the French National Assembly at the beginning of the French Revolution.

These events coincided with uprisings by peasants in the country. Peasants sacked manor houses and destroyed documents that recorded their traditional obligations. They refused to pay taxes and dues to landowners and seized common lands. Forced to recognize the fury raging through rural areas, the National Assembly voted to end traditional obligations and the privileges of the nobility and church, essentially ending the feudal system. Having won this victory, peasants ceased their revolt.

Declaration of the Rights of Man and the Citizen

These popular uprisings strengthened the hand of the National Assembly in its dealings with the king and led to passage of the **Declaration of the Rights of Man and the Citizen**, which stated the principles for a future constitution. There were similarities between the language

Photos12.com-ARJ

Parisians Storm the Bastille An eyewitness to the storming of the Bastille on July 14, 1789, painted this representation of this epochal event, still celebrated by the French as a national holiday.

PRIMARY SOURCE: The Declaration of the Rights of Man and the Citizen This document, drafted by the National Assembly of France, is an Enlightenment cousin of Jefferson's Declaration.

of this declaration and the U.S. Declaration of Independence. Thomas Jefferson, author of the American document, was U.S. ambassador to Paris and offered his opinion to those drafting the French statement. The French declaration, however, was more sweeping in its language. Among the enumerated natural rights were "liberty, property, security, and resistance to oppression." The Declaration of the Rights of Man and the Citizen also guaranteed free expression of ideas, equality before the law, and representative government.

The Women of Paris Act

While delegates debated political issues in Versailles, the economic crisis worsened in Paris. Women employed in the garment industry and small shopkeepers were particularly hard hit. Because the working women of Paris faced high food prices every day as they struggled to feed their families, their anger had a hard edge. Public markets became political arenas where the urban poor met daily in angry assembly. Here the revolutionary link between the material deprivation of the French poor and the political aspirations of the French bourgeoisie was forged.

On October 5, thousands of market women marched the 12 miles (19 kilometers) to Versailles. They forced their way into the National Assembly to demand action: "the point is that we want bread," they shouted. The crowd then entered the royal apartments, killed some of the king's guards, and searched for Queen Marie Antoinette (ann-twah-NET), whom they hated as a symbol of extravagance. They then forced the royal family to relocate to Paris.

Revolutionary Changes Begin

With the king's ability to resist democratic change overcome by the Paris crowd, the National Assembly achieved a radically restructured French society in the next two years. It passed a new constitution that dramatically limited monarchial power and abolished the nobility as a hereditary class. Economic reforms swept away monopolies and trade barriers within France. Renamed the Legislative Assembly, legislators took on the church, seizing its lands to use as collateral for a new paper currency, mandating the election of priests, and placing them on the public payroll. When the Assembly forced priests to take a loyalty oath, however, many Catholics joined a growing counterrevolutionary movement.

At first, many European monarchs welcomed the weakening of the French king, but by 1791 Austria and Prussia threatened to intervene in support of the monarchy. The Legislative Assembly responded by declaring war. Although the war went badly at first for French forces, people across France responded patriotically to foreign invasions, forming huge new volunteer armies and mobilizing national resources to meet the challenge.

The Terror, 1793–1794

In this period of national crisis and foreign threat, the French Revolution entered its most radical phase. A failed effort by the king and queen to escape from Paris cost the king his remaining popular support. On August 10, 1792, a crowd invaded his palace in Paris, forcing the king to seek protection in the Legislative Assembly, which suspended his authority and ordered his imprisonment. These actions helped lead to the creation of a new legislative and executive body, the National Convention.

Rumors of counterrevolutionary plots kept working-class neighborhoods in an uproar, and in September a mob surged through the city's prisons, killing nearly half the prisoners. Swept along by popular passion, the newly elected National Convention convicted Louis XVI of treason, sentenced him to death, and proclaimed France a republic. The guillotine ended the king's life in January 1793 (see Environment and Technology: The Guillotine). These events precipitated a wider war with nearly all of Europe's powers allied against France.

The Jacobins

Jacobins Radical republicans during the French Revolution. They were led by Maximilien Robespierre from 1793 to 1794.

Maximilien Robespierre Young provincial lawyer who led the most radical phases of the French Revolution. His execution ended the Reign of Terror.

The National Convention—the new legislature of the French Republic—convened in September. Almost all its members were from the middle class, and nearly all were **Jacobins** (JAK-uh-bin)—the most uncompromising democrats. Deep political differences, however, separated moderate Jacobins—called "Girondists (juh-RON-dist)," after a region in southern France—and radicals known as "the Mountain." Members of the Mountain—so named because their seats were on the highest level in the assembly hall—were more sympathetic than the Girondists to the demands of the Parisian working class and less patient with parliamentary procedure. **Maximilien Robespierre** (ROBES-pee-air), a young, little-known lawyer influenced by Rousseau's ideas, dominated the Mountain.

With the French economy in crisis and Paris suffering from inflation, high unemployment, and scarcity, Robespierre used the popular press and political clubs to forge an alliance with the volatile Parisian working class. His growing strength in the streets allowed him to purge and execute many of his enemies in the National Convention and to restructure the government. He placed executive power in the hands of the newly formed Committee of Public Safety, which created special courts to seek out and punish enemies of the Revolution.

Women and the Revolution

Among the groups that lost influence were the active feminists of the Parisian middle class and the working-class women who had sought the right to bear arms in defense of the Revolution. These women had provided decisive leadership at crucial times, helping propel the Revolution toward widened suffrage and a more democratic structure. Armed women had actively participated in every confrontation with conservative forces. It is ironic that the National Convention—the revolutionary era's most radical legislative body—chose to repress the militant feminist forces that had prepared the ground for its creation.

Faced with rebellion in the provinces and foreign invasion, Robespierre and his allies unleashed a period of repression called the Reign of Terror (1793–1794) (see Diversity and Dominance: Robespierre and Wollstonecraft Defend and Explain the Terror). During the Terror, executions and deaths in prison claimed 40,000 lives while another 300,000 suffered imprisonment. The revolutionary government took new actions against the clergy as well, including the provocative measure of forcing priests to marry. Even time was subject to revolutionary change. A new republican calendar created twelve 30-day months divided into 10-day weeks. Sunday, with its Christian meanings, disappeared from the calendar.

The End of Robespierre

By spring 1794 the Revolution was secure from foreign and domestic enemies, but repression continued. Among the victims were some of Robespierre's closest political collaborators during the Terror. The execution of these former allies prepared the way for Robespierre's own fall by undermining the sense of invulnerability that had secured the loyalty of his remaining

Playing Cards from the French Revolution Even playing cards could be used to attack the aristocracy and Catholic Church. In this pack of cards, "Equality" and "Liberty" replaced kings and queens.

Archives Charmet/ The Bridgeman Art Library

ENVIRONMENT + TECHNOLOGY

The Guillotine

No machine more powerfully symbolizes the revolutionary era than the guillotine. The machine immortalizes Joseph Ignace Guillotin (1738–1814), a physician and member of the French Constituent Assembly. In 1789 Guillotin recommended that executions be made more humane by use of a beheading device. He sought to replace hangings, used for commoners, and beheadings by axe, used for the nobility. Both forms of execution were often conducted with little skill, leading to gruesome and painful deaths. Guillotin believed that a properly designed machine would produce predictable, nearly painless deaths and remove the social distinction between commoners and nobles, embarrassing in a more egalitarian age.

After 1791 execution by beheading became the common sentence for all capital crimes. Another physician, Antoine Louis, secretary of the College of Surgeons, designed the actual machine. Once directed to produce a suitable device, Louis, in many ways a typical technician of his time, systematically examined devices used elsewhere and experimented until satisfied with his results. Praised by contemporaries because it seemed to remove human agency, and therefore revenge, from the death penalty, the guillotine became the physical symbol of the Terror.

The Guillotine The guillotine, introduced as a more humane and democratic alternative to traditional executions, came to symbolize the arbitrary violence of the French Revolution. In this contemporary cartoon Robespierre, the architect of the Terror, serves as executioner while surrounded by guillotines.

The Art Archive

partisans. After French victories eliminated the immediate foreign threat in 1794, conservatives in the Convention voted to arrest Robespierre and then ordered his execution along with that of nearly a hundred of his allies in July 1794.

Reaction and the Rise of Napoleon, 1795–1815

Napoleon Bonaparte General who overthrew the French Directory in 1799 and became emperor of the French in 1804. Failed to defeat Great Britain and abdicated in 1814. Returned to power briefly in 1815 but was defeated and died in exile.

Purged of Robespierre's collaborators, the Convention began to undo the radical reforms. It removed emergency economic controls that held down prices and protected the working class. Gone also was toleration for violent popular demonstrations. When the Paris working class rose in protest in 1795, the Convention reacted with overwhelming military force. It allowed the Catholic Church to regain much of its former influence, but it did not return the church's confiscated wealth. It also put in place a more conservative constitution that protected property, established a voting process that reduced the power of the masses, and created a new executive authority, the Directory.

After losing the election of 1797, the Directory refused to give up power, effectively ending the republican phase of the Revolution. Political authority now depended on coercive force rather than elections. Two years later, a brilliant young general in the French army, **Napoleon Bonaparte** (1769–1821), seized power. Just as the American and French Revolutions had been the start of the modern democratic tradition, the military intervention that brought Napoleon to power in 1799 marked the advent of another modern form of government: popular authoritarianism.

Napoleon

and Wollstonecraft Defend and Explain the Terror

*who had been sympathetic to the French Revo-
elled by the Terror. In 1793 and 1794, while France
with Austria, Prussia, Great Britain, Holland, and
volutionaries in Paris executed about 2,600 people,
ng the king and queen, members of the nobility, and
olic clergy. Critics of the Revolution asked if these excesses
re not worse than those committed by the French monarchy. Others defended the violence as necessary, arguing that enemies of the Revolution provoked the Terror.*

The following two opinions date from 1794. Maximilien Robespierre was the head of the Committee of Public Safety, the effective head of the revolutionary government. He was a provincial lawyer who rose to power in Paris as the Revolution radicalized. In the statement that follows he argues that violence is necessary in the defense of liberty, making this statement on the eve of his own political demise. In 1794 the revolutionary movement he had helped create removed him from power and ordered his execution.

Mary Wollstonecraft, an English intellectual and advocate for women's rights who was living in Paris at the time of the execution of Louis XVI, was troubled by the violence, and her discussion of these events is more an apology than a defense. She had published her famous A Vindication of the Rights of Woman *in 1792, after which she left for Paris. Wollstonecraft left Paris after war broke out between France and Britain. She remained an important force in European intellectual life until her death from complications of childbirth in 1797.*

Maximilien Robespierre, "On the Moral and Political Principles of Domestic Policy"

[L]et us deduce a great truth: the characteristic of popular government is confidence in the people and severity towards itself.

The whole development of our theory would end here if you had only to pilot the vessel of the Republic through calm waters; but the tempest roars, and the revolution imposes on you another task.

This great purity of the French revolution's basis, the very sublimity of its objective, is precisely what causes both our strength and our weakness. Our strength, because it gives to us truth's ascendancy over imposture, and the rights of the public interest over private interests; our weakness, because it rallies all vicious men against us, all those who in their hearts contemplated despoiling the people and all those who intend to let it be despoiled with impunity, both those who have rejected freedom as a personal calamity and those who have embraced the revolution as a career and the Republic as prey. Hence the defection of so many ambitious or greedy men who since the point of departure have abandoned us along the way because they did not begin the journey with the same destination in view. The two opposing spirits that have been represented in a struggle to rule nature might be said to be fighting in this great period of human history to fix irrevocably the world's destinies, and France is the scene of this fearful combat. Without, all the tyrants encircle you; within, all tyranny's friends conspire; they will conspire until hope is wrested from crime. We must smother the internal and external enemies of the Republic or perish with it; now in this situation, the first maxim of your policy ought to be to lead the people by reason and the people's enemies by terror.

If the spring of popular government in time of peace is virtue, the springs of popular government in revolution are at once virtue and terror: virtue, without which terror is fatal; terror, without which virtue is powerless. Terror is nothing other than justice, prompt, severe, inflexible; it is therefore an emanation of virtue; it is not so much a special principle as it is a consequence of the general principle of democracy applied to our country's most urgent needs.

It has been said that terror is the principle of despotic government. Does your government therefore resemble despotism? Yes, as the sword that gleams in the hands of the heroes of liberty resembles that with which the henchmen of tyranny are armed. Let the despot govern by terror his brutalized subjects; he is right, as a despot. Subdue by terror the enemies of liberty, and you will be right, as founders of the Republic. The government of the revolution is liberty's despotism against tyranny. Is force made only to protect crime? And is the thunderbolt not destined to strike the heads of the proud?

. . . Society owes protection only to peaceable citizens; the only citizens in the Republic are the republicans. For it, the royalists, the conspirators are only strangers or, rather, enemies. This terrible war waged by liberty against tyranny is it not indivisible? Are the enemies within not the allies of the enemies without? The assassins who tear our country apart, the intriguers who buy the consciences that hold the people's

The American and French Revolutions resulted in part from conflicts over representation. If the people were sovereign, what institutions best expressed popular will? In the United States the answer was the expansion of the right to vote and creation of representative institutions. The French Revolution took a different direction with the Reign of Terror. Interventions on the floor of the National Convention by market women and soldiers, the presence of common people at revolutionary tribunals and at public executions, and the expansion of military service were all mandate; the traitors who sell them; the mercenary pamphleteers hired to dishonor the people's cause, to kill public virtue, to stir up the fire of civil discord, and to prepare political counterrevolution by moral counterrevolution—are all those men less guilty or less dangerous than the tyrants whom they serve?

Mary Wollstonecraft, "An Historical and Moral View of the Origin and Progress of the French Revolution"

Weeping scarcely conscious that I weep, O France! Over the vestiges of thy former oppression, which, separating man from man with a fence of iron, sophisticated [complicated] all, and made many completely wretched; I tremble, lest I should meet some unfortunate being, fleeing from the despotism of licentious freedom, hearing the snap of the guillotine at his heels, merely because he was once noble, or has afforded an asylum to those whose only crime is their name—and, if my pen almost bound with eagerness to record the day that leveled the Bastille [an abbey used as a prison before the Revolution] with the dust, making the towers of despair tremble to their base, the recollection that still the abbey is appropriated to hold the victims of revenge and suspicion [she means that the Bastille remained a prison for those awaiting revolutionary justice]. . . .

Excuse for the Ferocity of the Parisians

The deprivation of natural, equal, civil, and political rights reduced the most cunning of the lower orders to practice fraud, and the rest to habits of stealing, audacious robberies, and murders. And why? Because the rich and poor were separated into bands of tyrants and slaves, and the retaliation of slaves is always terrible. In short, every sacred feeling, moral and divine, has been obliterated, and the dignity of man sullied, by a system of policy and jurisprudence as repugnant to reason as at variance with humanity.

The only excuse that can be made for the ferocity of the Parisians is then simply to observe that they had not any confidence in the laws, which they had always found to be merely cobwebs to catch small flies [the poor]. Accustomed to be punished themselves for every trifle, and often for only being in the way of the rich, or their parasites, when, in fact, had the Parisians seen the execution of a noble, or priest, though convicted of crimes beyond the daring of vulgar minds? When justice, or the law, is so partial, the day of retribution will come with the red sky of vengeance, to confound the innocent with the guilty. The mob were barbarous beyond the tiger's cruelty. . . .

Let us cast our eyes over the history of man, and we shall scarcely find a page that is not tarnished by some foul deed or bloody transaction. Let us examine the catalogue of the vices of men in a savage state, and contrast them with those of men civilized; we shall find that a barbarian, considered as a moral being, is an angel, compared with the refined villain of artificial life. Let us investigate the causes which have produced this degeneracy, and we shall discover that they are those unjust plans of government which have been formed by peculiar circumstances in every part of the globe.

Then let us coolly and impartially contemplate the improvements which are gaining ground in the formation of principles of policy; and I flatter myself it will be allowed by every humane and considerate being that a political system more simple than has hitherto existed would effectually check those aspiring follies, which, by imitation, leading to vice, have banished from governments the very shadow of justice and magnanimity.

Thus had France grown up and sickened on the corruption of a state diseased. . . . it is only the philosophical eye, which looks into the nature and weighs the consequences of human actions, that will be able to discern the cause, which has produced so many dreadful effects.

QUESTIONS FOR ANALYSIS

1. **Why does Robespierre believe that revolution cannot tolerate diversity of opinion? Are his reasons convincing?**
2. **How does Robespierre distinguish the terror of despots from the terror of liberty?**
3. **How does Wollstonecraft explain the "ferocity" of the Parisians?**
4. **What does Wollstonecraft believe will come from this period of violence?**

Sources: Maximilien Robespierre, "On the Moral and Political Principles of Domestic Policy," February 5, 1794, *Modern History Sourcebook: Robespierre: Terror and Virtue, 1794, http://www.fordham.edu/halsall/mod/robespierre-terror.html*; Mary Wollstonecraft, "An Historical and Moral View of the Origin and Progress of the French Revolution," *A Mary Wollstonecraft Reader*, ed. Barbara H. Solomon and Paula S. Berggren (New York: New American Library, 1983), 374–375, 382–383.

forms of political communication that temporarily satisfied the French people's desire to influence their government. Napoleon tamed these forms of political expression to organize Europe's first popular dictatorship. He succeeded because his military reputation promised order to a society exhausted by a decade of crisis, turmoil, and bloodshed.

France Under Napoleon

Napoleon sought to realize France's dream of dominating Europe while providing effective protection for persons and property at home. Negotiations with the Catholic Church led to the

Concordat of 1801. This agreement gave French Catholics the right to freely practice their religion, but it also recognized the French government's authority to nominate bishops and retain priests on the state payroll. In his comprehensive rewriting of French law, the Civil Code of 1804, Napoleon won the support of the peasantry and the middle class by asserting two basic principles inherited from the moderate first stage of the French Revolution: equality in law and protection of property. Some members of the nobility were won over when Napoleon declared himself emperor and France an empire in 1804. Despite his willingness to make dramatic changes, he continued the denial of political rights for women begun during the Terror. The Civil Code denied women basic political rights and only allowed them to participate in the economy with the guidance and supervision of fathers and husbands.

While it reestablished order, the Napoleonic system denied or restricted many individual rights. Free speech was limited. Criticism of the government, viewed as subversive, was proscribed, and most opposition newspapers disappeared. Spies and informers directed by the minister of police enforced these draconian policies.

French Expansion and Defeat

Ultimately, the Napoleonic system depended on the success of French arms (see Map 21.2). From Napoleon's assumption of power until his fall, no single European state could defeat the French military. Austria and Prussia suffered humiliating defeats and became allies of France. Only Britain, protected by its powerful navy, remained able to thwart Napoleon's plans to dominate Europe.

Desiring to again extend French power to the Americas, Napoleon invaded Portugal in 1807 and Spain in 1808. Spanish and Portuguese patriots supported by Great Britain eventually tied French armies down in a costly conflict. Frustrated by events on the Iberian Peninsula and faced with a faltering economy, Napoleon made the fateful decision to invade Russia. In June 1812 he began his campaign with the largest army ever assembled in Europe, approximately 600,000 men. His army took Moscow but after five weeks abandoned the city. During the retreat, the brutal Russian winter and attacks by Russian forces destroyed Napoleon's army. A broken and battered remnant of 30,000 made it back to France.

After the debacle in Russia, Austria and Prussia deserted Napoleon and entered an alliance with England and Russia against France. Unable to defend Paris, Napoleon abdicated the throne in April 1814 and was exiled to the island of Elba off the coast of Italy. The victorious allies then restored the French monarchy. The following year Napoleon escaped from Elba and returned to France, but an allied army defeated his forces in 1815 at Waterloo, in Belgium. His final exile was on the distant island of St. Helena in the South Atlantic, where he died in 1821.

SECTION REVIEW

- The heavy burden of debt, caused in part by support of the American Revolution, forced Louis XVI to call the Estates General.
- When some members of the nobility and clergy joined the rebellious Third Estate they formed the National Assembly.
- The hungry Parisian masses radicalized the movement for reform by storming the Bastille and forcing the king to move to Paris.
- The Legislative Assembly, led by Robespierre, executed the king and initiated the Terror.
- Exhausted by the violence of the Terror and threatened by foreign enemies, France turned to Napoleon Bonaparte, who dominated Europe until he was defeated in 1814.

REVOLUTION SPREADS, CONSERVATIVES RESPOND, 1789–1850

Even as the dictatorship of Napoleon tamed the democratic legacy of the French Revolution, revolutionary ideology was spreading and taking hold in Europe and the Americas. In Europe the French Revolution promoted nationalism and republicanism. In the Americas the legacies of the American and French Revolutions led to a new round of struggles for independence. News of revolutionary events in France destabilized the colonial regime in Saint Domingue (present-day Haiti), a small French colony on the western half of the island of Hispaniola, and helped initiate the first successful slave rebellion. In Europe, however, the spread of revolutionary fervor was met by the concerted reaction of an alliance of conservative monarchs committed to extinguishing further revolutionary outbreaks.

The Haitian Revolution, 1789–1804

AP* Exam Tip Be able to compare the Haitian Revolution with the French Revolution.

In 1789 the French colony of Saint Domingue was among the richest colonies in the Americas. Its production of sugar, cotton, indigo, and coffee accounted for two-thirds of France's tropical imports and generated nearly one-third of all French foreign trade. This wealth depended on a brutal slave regime. The harsh punishments and poor living conditions experienced by Saint Domingue's slaves were notorious throughout the Caribbean. The resulting high mortality and low fertility rates created an insatiable demand for African slaves. As a result, in 1790 the majority of the colony's 500,000 slaves were African-born.

gens de couleur Free men and women of color in Haiti. They sought greater political rights and later supported the Haitian Revolution.

The Haitian Revolution Begins

When news of the meeting of the Estates General arrived on the island in 1789, wealthy planters sent a delegation to Paris to seek more home rule and greater economic freedom for Saint Domingue. The free mixed-race population, the ***gens de couleur*** (zhahn deh koo-LUHR), also sent representatives. Representing a large class of free black planters and urban merchants who owned slaves, they sought to limit race discrimination, not to end slavery. As the French Revolution became more radical, the gens de couleur forged an alliance with sympathetic French radicals, who saw the colony's wealthy planters as royalists and aristocrats.

The political turmoil in France weakened the authority of colonial administrators in Saint Domingue. In the vacuum that resulted, rich planters, poor whites, and the gens de couleur all pursued their narrow interests, engendering an increasingly bitter and confrontational struggle. Given the slaves' hatred of the brutal regime that oppressed them and the accumulated grievances of the free people of color, there was no way to limit the violence once the control of the slave owners slipped. When Vincent Ogé (oh-ZHAY), leader of the gens de couleur mission to France, returned to Saint Domingue in 1790, the planters captured him and ordered his torture and execution. The free black and slave populations soon repaid this cruelty in kind.

François Dominique Toussaint L'Ouverture Leader of the Haitian Revolution. He freed the slaves and gained effective independence for Haiti despite military interventions by the British and French.

By 1791 whites, led by the planter elite, and the gens de couleur were engaged in open warfare. A slave rebellion begun on the plantations of the north transformed this conflict (see Map 21.3). Rebelling slaves destroyed plantations, killed masters and overseers, and burned crops. Their emerging leadership relied on elements of African political practice and revolutionary ideology from France to mobilize and direct the rebelling slaves.

Toussaint L'Ouverture

The rebellious slaves gained the upper hand under the command of **François Dominique Toussaint L'Ouverture**, a former domestic slave, who created a disciplined military force. The 1794 decision of the radical National Convention in Paris to abolish slavery in all French possessions strengthened Toussaint politically. As leader he swept aside his local rivals, defeated a British expeditionary force in 1798, and then led an invasion of the neighboring Spanish colony

Bettmann/Corbis

Haiti's Former Slaves Defend Their Freedom In this representation, a veteran army sent by Napoleon to reassert French control in Haiti battles with Haitian forces in a tropical forest. The combination of Haitian resistance and yellow fever defeated the French invasion.

MAP 21.2 **Napoleon's Europe, 1810** By 1810 Great Britain was the only remaining European power at war with Napoleon. Because of the loss of the French fleet at the Battle of Trafalgar in 1805, Napoleon was unable to threaten Britain with invasion, and Britain was able to actively assist the resistance movements in Spain and Portugal, thereby helping weaken French power.

Interactive Map

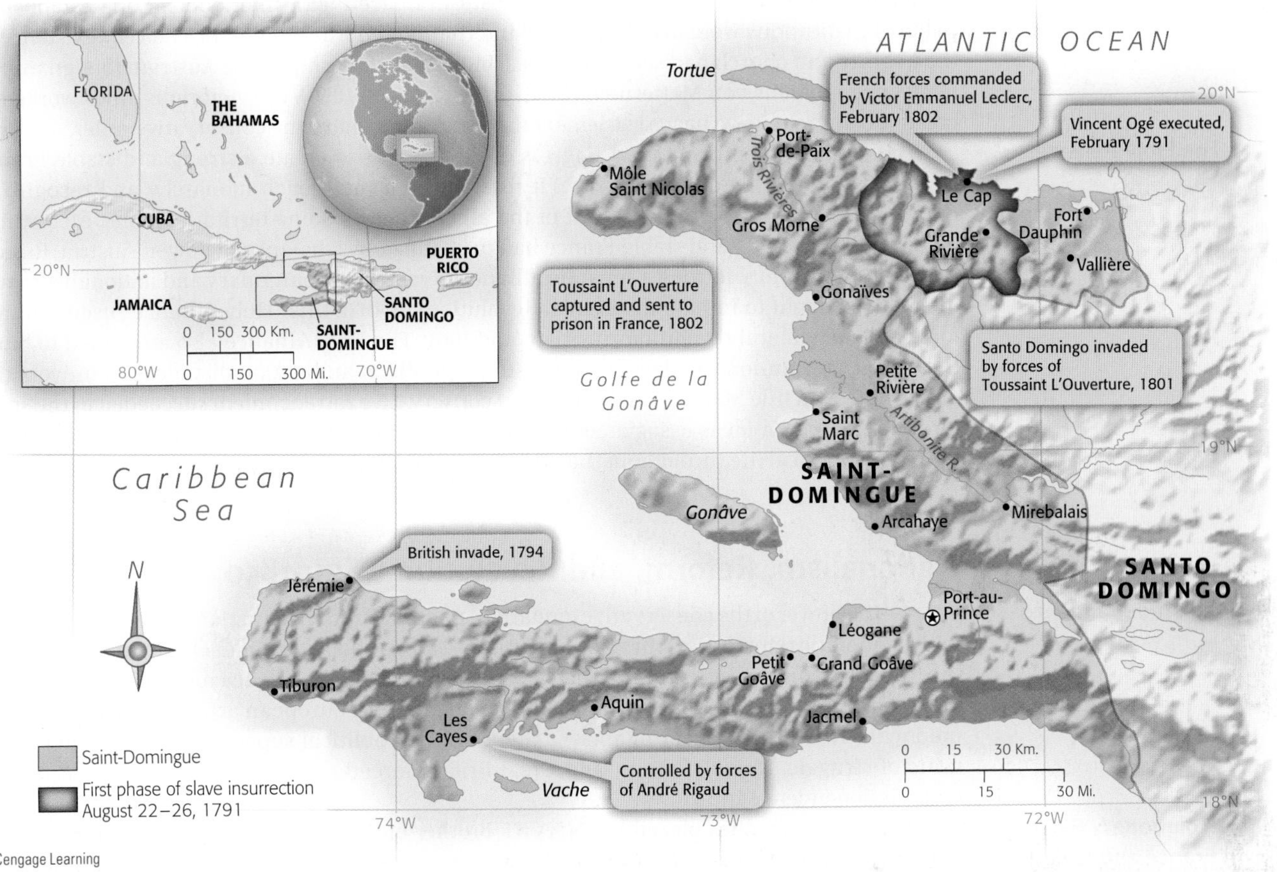

ATLANTIC OCEAN

French forces commanded by Victor Emmanuel Leclerc, February 1802

Vincent Ogé executed, February 1791

Toussaint L'Ouverture captured and sent to prison in France, 1802

Santo Domingo invaded by forces of Toussaint L'Ouverture, 1801

British invade, 1794

Controlled by forces of André Rigaud

Caribbean Sea

Golfe de la Gonâve

SAINT-DOMINGUE

SANTO DOMINGO

Saint-Domingue

First phase of slave insurrection August 22–26, 1791

MAP 21.3 The Haitian Revolution On their way to achieving an end to slavery and gaining national independence, the Haitian revolutionaries were forced to defeat British and French military interventions as well as the local authority of the slave masters.

Interactive Map

of Santo Domingo, freeing slaves there. While Toussaint asserted his loyalty to France, he gave the French government no effective role in local affairs.

As reaction overtook revolution in France, both the abolition of slavery and Toussaint's political position were threatened. When the Directory contemplated the reestablishment of slavery, Toussaint protested:

> *Do they think that men who have been able to enjoy the blessing of liberty will calmly see it snatched away? They supported their chains only so long as they did not know any condition of life more happy than slavery. But today when they have left it, if they had a thousand lives they would sacrifice them all rather than be forced into slavery again.*[2]

In 1802 Napoleon sent a large military force to reestablish both French colonial authority and slavery in Saint Domingue (see Map 21.3). At first French forces were successful, capturing Toussaint and sending him to France, where he died in prison. Eventually, however, the loss of thousands of lives to yellow fever and the resistance of the revolutionaries turned the tide. In 1804 Toussaint's successors declared independence, and the free republic of Haiti joined the United States as the second independent nation in the Western Hemisphere.

The Congress of Vienna and Conservative Retrenchment, 1815–1820

Congress of Vienna Meeting of representatives of European monarchs called to reestablish the old order after the defeat of Napoleon I.

In 1814–1815 representatives of Britain, Russia, Austria, Prussia, and other European nations met as the **Congress of Vienna** to reestablish political order in Europe. The French Revolution and Napoleon's imperial ambitions had threatened the survival of Europe's old order. Ancient monarchies had been overturned and dynasties replaced with interlopers. Long-established political institutions were overturned and international borders ignored. The very existence of the nobility and church had seemed at risk. Under the leadership of the Austrian foreign minister, Prince Klemens von Metternich (MET-uhr-nik) (1773–1859), the victorious allies worked to create a comprehensive peace settlement that would safeguard the conservative order.

The Holy Alliance

The central objective of the Congress of Vienna was to create a strong and stable France as the best guarantee of future peace. It reestablished the French monarchy and recognized France's 1792 borders, although most of the allies received some territorial gains. Metternich believed that a strong and stable France had to be offset by a balance of power. Austria, Russia, and Prussia therefore formed a separate alliance to repress revolutionary and nationalist movements that sought to imitate the French Revolution. In 1820 this "Holy Alliance" used military force to defeat liberal revolutions in Spain and Italy. The Holy Alliance also attempted to blunt the force of revolutionary ideas by repressing republican and nationalist ideas in universities and the press. While Metternich's program of conservative retrenchment succeeded in the short term, the powerful ideas associated with liberalism and nationalism remained a vital part of European political life throughout the nineteenth century.

Nationalism, Reform, and Revolution, 1821–1850

Greek Independence

Despite the power of the conservative monarchs, popular support for national self-determination and democratic reform grew throughout Europe. Greece had been under Ottoman control since the fifteenth century. In 1821 Greek patriots launched an independence movement. Metternich and other conservatives opposed Greek independence, but European artists and writers enamored with the cultural legacy of ancient Greece rallied political support for intervention. After years of struggle, Russia, France, and Great Britain forced the Ottoman Empire to recognize Greek independence in 1830.

Revolutionary Fears in France and Britain

The victorious allies placed Louis XVIII, brother of the executed Louis XVI, on the throne of France in 1814. Unlike his ancestors, he ruled as a constitutional monarch until his death in 1824. His brother, the conservative Charles X, inherited the throne. His decision to repudiate the constitution in 1830 provoked a mass uprising in Paris that forced him to abdicate. The crown then went to the king's cousin, Louis Philippe (loo-EE fee-LEEP) (r. 1830–1848), who agreed to accept the constitution and extended voting privileges.

AP* Exam Tip Be familiar with the rise of nationalism.

Revolutionary violence in France made the British aristocracy and the conservative Tory Party fearful of democracy and mass movements of any kind. In 1815 the British government passed the Corn Laws, which limited the importation of foreign grains. The laws favored the profits of wealthy landowners who produced grain, rather than the poor who would now be forced to pay more for their bread. When poor consumers organized to overturn these laws, the government outlawed public meetings and used troops to crush protest in Manchester. Reacting against these policies, English reformers increased the power of the House of Commons, redistributed votes from agricultural to industrial districts, and increased the number of voters by nearly 50 percent. Although the most radical demands of reformers, called Chartists, were defeated, new labor and economic reforms addressing the grievances of workers were put in place (see Chapter 22).

The Revolutions of 1848

Revolutions of 1848 Democratic and nationalist revolutions that swept across Europe. The monarchy in France was overthrown. In Germany, Austria, Italy, and Hungary the revolutions failed.

Despite the achievement of Greek independence and limited political reform in France and Great Britain, conservatives continued to hold the upper hand. In 1848 the desire for democratic reform and national self-determination led to upheavals across Europe. The **Revolutions of 1848** began in Paris, where members of the middle class and workers united to overthrow the regime of Louis Philippe and create the Second French Republic. Reformers gave adult men voting rights, abolished slavery in French colonies, ended the death penalty, and legislated the ten-hour workday. But Parisian workers' demands for programs to reduce unemployment and prices provoked conflicts with the middle class, which wanted to protect property rights. When workers rose up against the government, French troops crushed them. Desiring the reestablishment of order, the French elected Louis Napoleon, nephew of the former emperor, president in December 1848. Three years later, he overturned the constitution and, after ruling briefly as dictator, proclaimed himself Emperor Napoleon III.

The Revolution of 1830 in Belgium After the 1830 uprising that overturned the restored monarchy in France, Belgians rose up to declare their independence from Holland. In Poland and Italy, similar uprisings combining nationalism and a desire for self-governance failed. This painting by Baron Gustaf Wappers romantically illustrates the popular nature of the Belgian uprising by bringing to the barricades men, women, and children drawn from both the middle and the working classes.

In 1848 reformers in Hungary, Italy, Bohemia, and elsewhere pressed for greater national self-determination from the Austro-Hungarian Empire. When the monarchy did not meet their demands, students and workers in Vienna took to the streets to force political reforms similar to those sought in Paris. With revolution spreading throughout the Empire, Metternich, the symbol of reaction, fled Vienna in disguise. Little lasting change occurred, however, because the new Austrian emperor, Franz Joseph (r. 1848–1916), used Russian military assistance and loyal Austrian troops to reestablish his authority.

Similarly, middle-class reformers and workers in Berlin joined forces to force the Prussian king to accept a liberal constitution and seek German unification. But the Constituent Assembly called to write a constitution and negotiate national integration was diverted to deal with diplomatic conflicts with Austria and Denmark. As a result, Frederick William IV (r. 1840–1861) reasserted his authority and thwarted constitutional reform and unification.

Despite their heroism on the barricades of Paris, Vienna, Rome, and Berlin, the revolutionaries of 1848 failed to gain their nationalist and republican objectives. Monarchs retained the support not only of aristocrats but also of professional militaries, largely recruited from among peasants who had little sympathy for urban workers. Revolutionary coalitions, in contrast, proved fragile, as when workers' demands for higher wages and labor reform drove their middle-class allies into the arms of the reactionaries.

SECTION REVIEW

- The slaves of Saint Domingue, led by Toussaint L'Ouverture, overthrew slavery and gained independence.
- The Congress of Vienna and the Holy Alliance attempted to prevent new revolutionary outbreaks in Europe.
- Nationalism and the desire for democracy led to revolutions in 1830 and 1848, but most failed.

CONCLUSION

The last decades of the eighteenth century began a long period of revolutionary upheaval in the Atlantic world. Costly wars in Europe and along Europe's colonial frontiers in the Americas and Asia helped to provoke change, forcing European monarchs to impose new and unpopular taxes. The American Revolution initiated these transformations. Having defeated Britain, the citizens of this new American republic created the most democratic government of the time. While full rights were limited and slavery persisted, many Europeans saw this experiment as demonstrating the efficacy of the Enlightenment's most revolutionary political ideas. In the end, however, the compromises over slavery that had made the Constitution possible in 1787 failed, and, as discussed in Chapter 23, the new nation nearly disintegrated after 1860.

The French Revolution led temporarily to a more radical formulation of representative democracy, but it also led to the Terror, which cost thousands of lives, the militarization of western Europe, and a destructive cycle of wars. Yet, despite these terrible costs, the French Revolution propelled the idea of democracy and the ideal of equality far beyond the boundaries established by the American Revolution. The Haitian Revolution, set in motion by events in France, not only created the second independent nation of the Western Hemisphere but also delivered a powerful blow to the institution of slavery. In Europe the excesses of the French Revolution and the wars that followed in its wake promoted the political ascent of Napoleon Bonaparte and democracy's modern nemesis, popular authoritarianism.

Each revolution had its own character. The revolutions in France and Haiti proved to be more violent and destructive than the American Revolution. American revolutionaries defeated Great Britain and established independence without overturning a colonial social order that depended on slavery in most of the southern colonies. Revolutionaries in France and Haiti faced more strongly entrenched and more powerful oppositions as well as greater social inequalities than American revolutionaries. The resistance of entrenched and privileged elites led inexorably to greater violence. Both French and Haitian revolutionaries also faced powerful foreign interventions that intensified the bloodshed and destructiveness of these revolutions.

The conservative retrenchment that followed the defeat of Napoleon succeeded in the short term. Monarchy, multinational empires, and the established church retained the loyalty of millions of Europeans and could count on the support of many of Europe's wealthiest and most powerful individuals. But liberalism and nationalism continued to stir revolutionary sentiment. The contest between adherents of the old order and partisans of change was to continue well into the nineteenth century. In the end, the nation-state, the Enlightenment legacy of rational inquiry, broadened political participation, and secular intellectual culture prevailed. This outcome was determined in large measure by the old order's inability to satisfy the demands of new social classes tied to an emerging industrial economy. The narrow confines of a hereditary social system could not contain the material transformations generated by industrial capitalism, and the doctrines of traditional religion could not contain the rapid expansion of scientific learning.

These revolutions began the transformation of Western society, but they did not complete it. Only a minority gained full political rights. Women did not achieve full political rights until the twentieth century. Democratic institutions, as in revolutionary France, often failed. Moreover, as Chapter 23 discusses, slavery endured in the Americas past the mid-1800s, despite the revolutionary era's enthusiasm for individual liberty.

KEY TERMS

Enlightenment p. 602
Benjamin Franklin p. 604
George Washington p. 608
Joseph Brant p. 608
Constitutional Convention p. 610
Estates General p. 612
Declaration of the Rights of Man and the Citizen p. 612
Jacobins p. 614
Maximilien Robespierre p. 614
Napoleon Bonaparte p. 615
gens de couleur p. 619
François Dominique Toussaint L'Ouverture p. 619
Congress of Vienna p. 621
Revolutions of 1848 p. 622

EBOOK AND WEBSITE RESOURCES

Primary Sources

Rousseau Espouses Popular Sovereignty and the General Will

The United States Declaration of Independence

The Declaration of the Rights of Man and the Citizen

Interactive Maps

Map 21.1 The American Revolutionary War

Map 21.2 Napoleon's Europe, 1810

Map 21.3 The Haitian Revolution

Plus flashcards, practice quizzes, and more. Go to: www.cengage.com/history/bullietearthpeople5e

SUGGESTED READING

Andress, David. *The Terror: The Merciless War for Freedom in Revolutionary France.* 2006. A recent summary of this era.

Bell, David A. *The First Total War: Napoleon's Europe and the Birth of Warfare as We Know It.* 2008.

Craveri, Benedetta. *The Age of Conversation.* 2005. Illuminates the culture of the French aristocracy prior to the French Revolution.

Damrosch, Leo. *Jean-Jacques Rousseau.* 2005. The best biography of Rousseau.

Dubois, Laurent. *A Colony of Citizens.* 2004. Connects the revolutions in France and Haiti to create a single struggle for liberty and citizenship.

Fenton, William N. *The Great Law and the Long-house: A Political History of the Iroquois Confederacy.* 1998. An essential study of this powerful indigenous alliance.

Fick, Carolyn E. *The Making of Haiti: The Saint Domingue Revolution from Below.* 1990. The best recent synthesis of the Haitian Revolution.

Fitzsimmons, Michael. *The Night the Old Regime Ended: August 14, 1789, and the French Revolution.* 1998.

Godineau, Dominique. *The Women of Paris and Their French Revolution.* 1998. Essential introduction to topic.

Goldstone, Lawrence. *Dark Bargain: Slavery, Profits and the Struggle for the Constitution.* 2005.

Goodman, Dena. *The Republic of Letters: A Cultural History of the Enlightenment.* 1994. Studies male and female intellectuals in the era of revolutions.

Hobsbawm, Eric. *The Age of Revolution.* 1962. Provides a clear analysis of the class issues that appeared during this era.

Holtman, Robert B. *The Napoleonic Revolution.* 1967. Provides a reliable summary of the period.

Hunt, Lynn. *The Family Romance of the French Revolution.* 1992. Examines the gender content of revolutionary politics.

James, C. L. R. *The Black Jacobins*, 2nd ed. 1963. Classic study of the Haitian Revolution.

Lefebvre, Georges. *The Coming of the French Revolution.* Trans. R. R. Palmer. 1947. A classic class-based analysis.

Lindemann, Albert. *History of European Socialism.* 1983. Surveys the development of European social reform movements.

McMahon, Darrin M. *Enemies of the Enlightenment, The French Counter-Enlightenment and the Making of Modernity.* 2001. A helpful discussion of the Counter Enlightenment.

Norton, Mary Beth. *Liberty's Daughters: The Revolutionary Experience of American Women, 1750–1800.* 1980. Studies the role of women in the revolutionary era.

Rudé, George. *The Crowd in History: Popular Disturbances in France and England.* 1981. The best introduction to the role of mass protest in the revolutionary period.

Stearns, Peter, and Herrick Chapman. *European Society in Upheaval.* 1991. Valuable summary of events.

Taylor, Alan. *The Divided Ground. Indians, Settlers, and the Northern Borderland of the American Revolution.* 2006. The best analysis of the topic.

Taylor, Barbara. *Eve and the New Jerusalem: Socialism and Feminism in the Nineteenth Century.* 1983. Analyzes connections between workers' and women's rights issues in England.

Te Brake, Wayne. *Shaping History: Ordinary People in European Politics, 1500–1700.* 1998. Discusses the "underside" of this era and the importance of "folk culture."

Will, Gary. *Inventing America, Jefferson's Declaration of Independence.* 1978. An essential inquiry into this pivotal moment.

Wood, Gordon S. *Revolutionary Characters. What Made the Founders Different.* 2006. A convincing exploration of this crucial generation.

NOTES

1. Quoted in Ray Raphael, *A People's History of the American Revolution* (New York: Perennial, 2001), 141.
2. Quoted in C. L. R. James, *The Black Jacobins*, 2nd ed. (New York: Vintage Books, 1963), 196.

AP* REVIEW QUESTIONS FOR CHAPTER 21

1. In the early 1600s, the rivalry among the European powers intensified when
   (A) Russia joined the balance of power.
   (B) the Dutch began an assault on the American and Asian colonies of Spain and Portugal.
   (C) England and Portugal became allies against France.
   (D) English settlers in North America attacked the French colony in Canada.

2. Which of the following is true of seventeenth- and eighteenth-century warfare in Europe?
   (A) Increased trade and wealth from the colonies more than made up for the cost of the wars.
   (B) The majority of the wars were fought at sea and required large navies.
   (C) The balance of power tipped in favor of the Catholic nations.
   (D) The cost of the wars led nation after nation into fiscal crises.

3. John Locke, an English political philosopher, argued that
   (A) monarchs ruled with God's grace.
   (B) no government should have an executive.
   (C) the government should own the means of production.
   (D) the people had a right to revolt when the monarch violated their natural rights.

4. Though willing to embrace Enlightenment ideals when they served royal interests, the monarchs of Europe
   (A) suppressed or banned radical ideas that promoted republicanism or directly attacked religion.
   (B) really supported any Enlightenment ideal that undermined their enemies.
   (C) only supported the ideas that helped develop more trade.
   (D) generally viewed the Enlightenment as a new way to create wealth.

5. Besides being an inventor and a writer, Benjamin Franklin was also
   (A) an important advocate of socialism.
   (B) an important actor in the political debate that would lead to the American Revolution.
   (C) a major landholder in Pennsylvania and Georgia.
   (D) a leading member of the House of Lords.

6. One reason for the passage of the Proclamation of 1763 was to
   (A) increase the cost of lands west of the Appalachian Mountains.
   (B) prevent the French from moving into the New England colonies.
   (C) prevent costly wars among the colonists and the Indians as the colonists moved west.
   (D) increase tax revenues from taxes on lumber and furs.

7. One common way that the English colonists protested increased taxation was to
   (A) only pay the lower price for goods.
   (B) substitute barter for the use of coin and currency.
   (C) write letters of protest to their representatives in Parliament.
   (D) boycott the goods being taxed.

8. Prior to 1789, French society was divided into Estates. The largest of these was the
   (A) Second Estate.
   (B) Third Estate.
   (C) First Estate.
   (D) Estates General.

9. Besides undergoing a financial crisis, in the period from 1785 to 1789, France
   (A) was stricken with a plague.
   (B) experienced poor harvests and famine.
   (C) lost one war each year.
   (D) suffered the loss of fifteen colonies that provided resources.

10. The most uncompromising democrats in the French Revolution were the
    (A) Louisettes.
    (B) Republicans.
    (C) Girondists.
    (D) Jacobins.

11. One result of the beginning of revolution in France was
    (A) war with Austria and Prussia in support of the French monarchy.
    (B) the United States directly aiding the revolution.
    (C) Belgium declaring its independence from France.
    (D) Great Britain supporting the revolution.

12. Which group lost social, economic, and political standing with the rise of Napoleon?
    (A) French citizens born in the French colonies
    (B) Women
    (C) Soldiers who served in the French army
    (D) Common laborers

13. One reason that Napoleon needed to suppress the revolution in Haiti was that
    (A) he could not afford to send a large naval and military force to Haiti while he was at war in Europe.
    (B) Haiti was the richest colony that France possessed.
    (C) it would have been an international embarrassment for him to lose it.
    (D) the revolution in Haiti was a slave rebellion and needed to be stopped to prevent other slave rebellions in other French colonies.

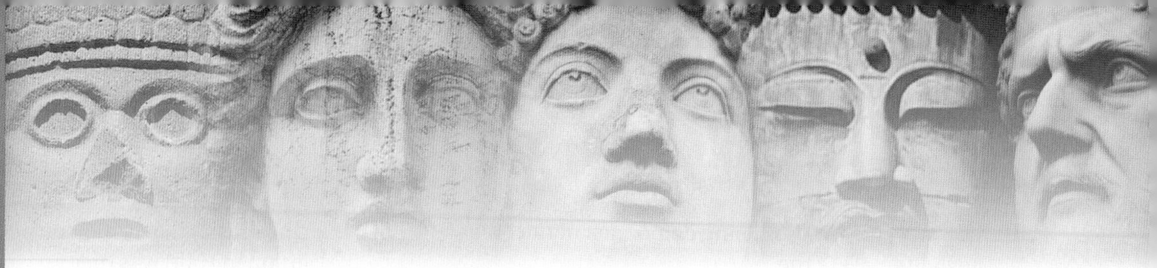

CHAPTER

22

CHAPTER OUTLINE

Manchester, the First Industrial City The first cotton mills, built on the banks of the River Irwell in northern England, transformed Manchester from a country town into a booming industrial city. The use of chemicals to bleach and dye the cloth and the introduction of steam engines in the early nineteenth century to power the spinning and weaving machines made Manchester, for a time, the most polluted city on earth.

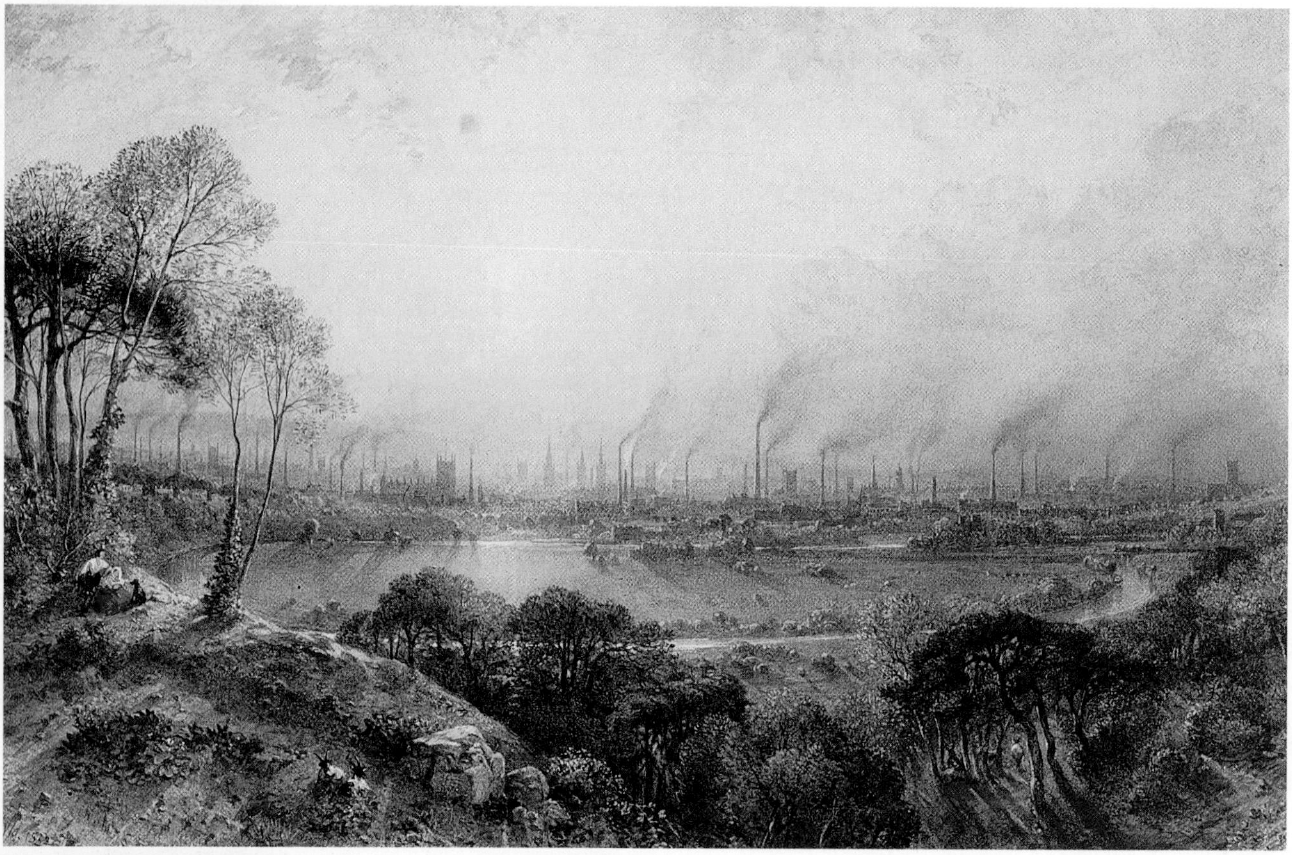

Visit the website and ebook for additional study materials and interactive tools: www.cengage.com/history/bullietearthpeople5e

The Early Industrial Revolution, 1760–1851

- What caused the Industrial Revolution?
- What were the key technological innovations that increased productivity and drove industrialization?
- What was the impact of these changes on the social structures and environment of the industrializing countries?
- How did the Industrial Revolution influence the rise of new economic and political ideologies and belief systems?
- How did the Industrial Revolution affect the relations between the industrialized and the nonindustrialized parts of the world?

Manchester was just a small town in northern England in the early eighteenth century. A hundred years later, it had turned into the fastest-growing city in history. To contemporaries, it was both a marvel and a horror. Cotton mills were interspersed with workers' housing, built as cheaply as possible. The economist Nassau Senior described these workers' quarters:

> But when I went through their habitations . . . my only wonder was that tolerable health could be maintained by the inmates of such houses. These towns . . . have been erected by small speculators with an utter disregard to everything except immediate profit. . . . In one place we saw a whole street following the course of a ditch, in order to have deeper cellars (cellars for people, not for lumber) without the expense of excavation. Not a house in this street escaped cholera. . . . the streets are unpaved, with a dunghill or a pond in the middle; the houses built back to back, without ventilation or drainage, and whole families occupy each a corner of a cellar or of a garret.[1]

Not everyone deplored the living conditions in the new industrial city. Friedrich Engels recounts a meeting with a well-to-do citizen:

> One day I walked with one of these middle-class gentlemen into Manchester. I spoke to him about the disgraceful unhealthy slums and drew his attention to the disgusting condition of that part of the town in which the factory workers lived. I declared that I had never seen so badly built a town in my life. He listened patiently and at the corner of the street at which we parted company, he remarked: "And yet there is a great deal of money made here. Good morning, Sir!"[2]

Manchester's rise as a large, industrial city was a result of what historians call the **Industrial Revolution**, the most profound transformation in human life since the beginnings of agriculture. This revolution involved dramatic innovations in manufacturing, mining, transportation, and communications and equally rapid changes in society and commerce. New relationships between social groups created an environment that was conducive to technical innovation and economic growth. New technologies and new social and economic arrangements allowed the industrializing countries—first Britain, then western Europe and the United States—to unleash massive increases in production and productivity, exploit the world's natural resources as never before, and transform the environment and human life in unprecedented ways.

Industrial Revolution The transformation of the economy, the environment, and living conditions, occurring first in England in the eighteenth century, that resulted from the use of steam engines, the mechanization of manufacturing in factories, and innovations in transportation and communication.

Industrialization widened the gap between rich and poor. The people who owned and controlled the innovations amassed wealth and power over nature and over other people. While some lived in spectacular luxury, workers, including children, worked long hours in dangerous factories and lived crowded together in unsanitary tenements.

The effect of the Industrial Revolution around the world was also very uneven. The first countries to industrialize grew rich and powerful. In Egypt and India, the economic and military power of the European countries stifled the tentative beginnings of industrialization. Regions that had little or no industry were easily taken advantage of. The disparity between the industrial and the developing countries that exists today has its origins in the early nineteenth century.

CAUSES OF THE INDUSTRIAL REVOLUTION

What caused the Industrial Revolution, and why did it begin in England in the late eighteenth century? These are two of the great questions of history. The basic preconditions of this momentous event seem to have been economic development propelled by population growth, an agricultural revolution, the expansion of trade, and an openness to innovation.

Population Growth

The population of Europe rose in the eighteenth century—slowly at first, faster after 1780, even faster in the early nineteenth century. The population of England and Wales rose from 5.5 million in 1688 to 9 million in 1801 and 18 million by 1851—increases never before experienced in European history.

The growth of population resulted from more widespread resistance to disease and more reliable food supplies, thanks to the new crops that originated in the Americas (see Chapter 17). More job opportunities led people to marry at earlier ages and have more children. In the early nineteenth century some 40 percent of the population of Britain was under fifteen years of age. This high proportion of youths explains both the vitality of the British people in that period and the widespread use of child labor. People also migrated at an unprecedented rate—from the countryside to the cities, from Ireland to England, and, more generally, from Europe to the Americas. Thanks to immigration, the population of the United States rose from 4 million in 1791 to 9.6 million in 1820 and 31.5 million in 1860—faster than in any other part of the world at the time.

agricultural revolution The transformation of farming that resulted in the eighteenth century from the spread of new crops, improvements in cultivation techniques and livestock breeding, and the consolidation of small holdings into large farms from which tenants and sharecroppers were forcibly expelled.

The Agricultural Revolution

Potatoes and Corn

A revolution in farming provided food for city dwellers and forced poorer peasants off the land. This **agricultural revolution** had begun long before the eighteenth century. One important aspect was the acceptance of the potato, introduced from South America in the sixteenth century. In the cool and humid regions of Europe, potatoes yielded two or three times more food per acre than did the wheat, rye, and oats they replaced. Maize (American corn) was grown across Europe from northern Iberia to the Balkans. Turnips, legumes, and clover did not deplete the soil and could be fed to cattle, sources of milk and meat. Manure from cattle in turn fertilized the soil for other crops.

Enclosure Movement

Prosperous landowners with secure titles to their land could afford to bear the risk of trying new methods and new crops. Rich landowners therefore "enclosed" the land—that is, consolidated their holdings—and got Parliament to give them title to the commons that in the past had been open to all. Once in control of the land, they could drain and improve the soil, breed better livestock, and introduce crop rotation. This "enclosure movement" turned tenants and sharecroppers into landless farm laborers. Many moved to the cities to seek work; others became vagrants; still others emigrated to Canada, Australia, and the United States.

CHRONOLOGY

	Technology	Economy, Society, and Politics
	1702–1712 Thomas Newcomen builds first steam engine	
1750	1759 Josiah Wedgwood opens pottery factory	
	1764 Spinning jenny	
	1769 Richard Arkwright's water frame; James Watt patents steam engine	1776 Adam Smith's *Wealth of Nations*
		1776–1783 American Revolution
	1779 First iron bridge	
	1785 Samuel Crompton's mule	1789–1799 French Revolution
	1793 Eli Whitney's cotton gin	1792 Mary Wollstonecraft's *A Vindication of the Rights of Woman*
1800	1800 Alessandro Volta's battery	1804–1815 Napoleonic Wars
	1807 Robert Fulton's *North River*	
	1820s Construction of Erie Canal	1820s U.S. cotton industry begins
	1829 *Rocket*, first prize-winning locomotive	1833 Factory Act in Britain
	1837 Wheatstone and Cooke's telegraph; Morse's code	1834 German Zollverein; Robert Owen's Grand National Consolidated Trade Union
	1838 First ships steam across the Atlantic	
	1840 *Nemesis* sails to China	
	1843 Samuel Morse's Baltimore-to-Washington telegraph	1846 Repeal of British Corn Laws
		1847–1848 Irish famine
		1848 Collapse of Chartist movement; revolutions in Europe
1850	1851 Crystal Palace opens in London	1854 First cotton mill in India

Trade and Inventiveness

In most of Europe the increasing demand that accompanied the growth of population was met by increasing production in traditional ways. Roads were improved so stagecoaches could travel faster. Royal manufacturers trained craftsmen to produce fine china, silks, and carpets by hand. In rural areas much production was carried out through cottage industries. Merchants delivered raw materials to craftspeople (often farmers in the off-season) and picked up the finished products. The growth of the population and food supply was accompanied by the growth of trade. Most of it was local trade in traditional goods and services, but a growing share came from far away.

During the eighteenth century, sugar from Caribbean slave plantations was the most profitable item in international trade. Even people of modest means began drinking tea, coffee, and cocoa at home and eating pastries and candies. These habits in turn stimulated the demand for porcelain cups and other dinnerware. More and more people wore clothes of silk or cotton imported from Asia.

Technology

Technology and innovation fascinated educated people throughout Europe and eastern North America. The French *Encyclopédie* contained articles and illustrations of crafts and manufacturing (see Diversity and Dominance: Adam Smith and the Division of Labor). The French and British governments sent expeditions around the world to collect plants that could profitably be grown in their colonies. They also offered prizes to anyone who could find a method of determining the longitude of a ship at sea to avoid the shipwrecks that had cost the lives of thousands of sailors. Benjamin Franklin, like many others, experimented with electricity. In France, the Montgolfier brothers invented a hot-air balloon. Claude Chappe (SHAPP) created the first semaphore telegraph. The American Eli Whitney and his associate John Hall invented machine tools, that is, machines capable of making other machines. These machines greatly increased the productivity of manufacturing.

Britain and Continental Europe

Rise of Industrialization in Britain

Industrialization did not take place everywhere at once. To understand why, we must look at the peculiar role of Great Britain. Britain enjoyed a rising standard of living during the eighteenth century, thanks to good harvests and a booming overseas trade. Britain was the world's leading exporter of tools, guns, hardware, clocks, and other craft goods (see Map 22.1). Its mining and metal industries employed engineers willing to experiment with new ideas. It had the largest

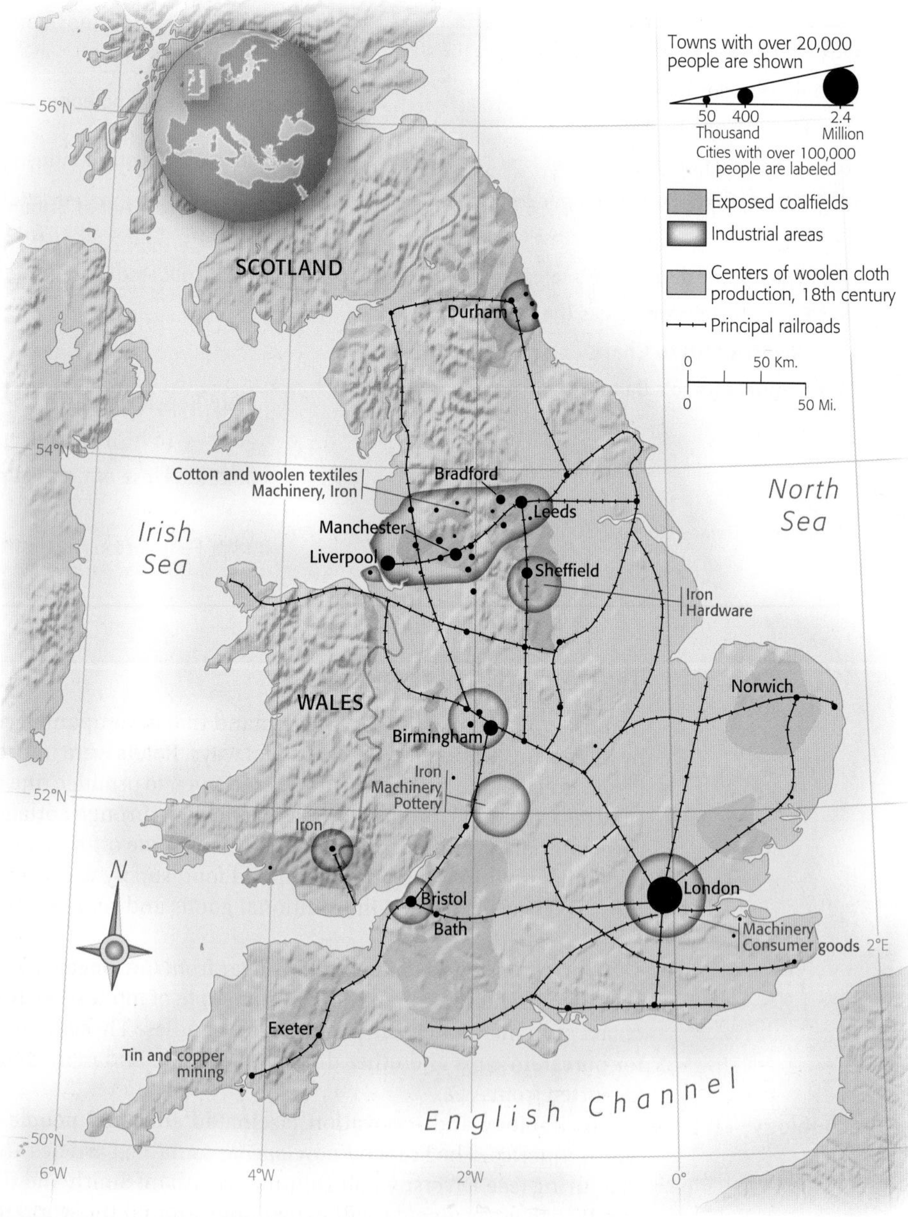

MAP 22.1 The Industrial Revolution in Britain, ca. 1850 The first industries arose in northern and western England. These regions had abundant coal and iron-ore deposits for the iron industry, as well as moist climate and fast-flowing rivers, factors important for the cotton textile industry.

e Interactive Map

merchant marine and produced more ships, naval supplies, and navigation instruments than other countries.

Until the mid-eighteenth century the British were known for their cheap imitations, but they put inventions into practice more quickly than other people, as the engineer John Farey told a parliamentary committee in 1829: "The prevailing talent of English and Scotch people is to apply new ideas to use and to bring such applications to perfection, but they do not imagine as much as foreigners."[3]

British Advantages over Europe

Before 1790 Britain also had a more fluid society than the rest of Europe. The court was less ostentatious, its aristocracy was less powerful, and the lines separating the social classes were not as sharply drawn as elsewhere. Political power was not as centralized as on the European continent, and the government employed fewer bureaucrats and officials. Members of the gentry married into merchant families. Intermarriage among the families of petty merchants, yeoman farmers, and town craftsmen was common. Ancestry remained important, but wealth also commanded respect. A businessman with enough money could buy a landed estate, a seat in Parliament, and the social status that accompanied them.

At a time when transportation by land was very costly, Great Britain had good water transportation thanks to its indented coastline, navigable rivers, and growing network of canals. It had a unified internal market with none of the duties and tolls that goods had to pay every few miles in France. This encouraged regional specialization, such as tin mining in Cornwall and cotton manufacturing in Lancashire, and a growing trade between regions.

Britain was also highly commercial; more people were involved in production for export and in trade and finance than in any other major country. It was especially active in overseas trade. It had financial and insurance institutions able to support growing business enterprises and a patent system that offered inventors the hope of rich rewards. The example of men who became wealthy and respected for their inventions stimulated others.

In the eighteenth century, the economies of continental Europe were hampered by high transportation costs, misguided government regulations, and rigid social structures. The Low Countries were laced with canals, but the terrain elsewhere in Europe made canal building costly and difficult. Attempts to import British techniques and organize factory production foundered for lack of markets or management skills. In addition, from 1789 to 1815 Europe was scarred by revolutions and wars. Although war created opportunities for suppliers of weapons, uniforms, and horses, the interruption of trade between Britain and continental Europe slowed the diffusion of new techniques, and the insecurity of countries at war discouraged businessmen from investing in factories and machinery.

Rise of Industrialization in Europe

The political revolutions swept away the restrictions of the old regimes. After 1815 the economies of western Europe were ready to begin industrializing. Industrialization took hold in Belgium and northern France, as businessmen visited Britain to observe the changes and spy out industrial secrets. By the 1820s several thousand Britons were at work on the continent of Europe setting up machines, training workers in the new methods, and even starting their own businesses.

Acutely aware of Britain's head start and the need to stimulate their own industries, European governments took action. They created technical schools. They eliminated internal tariff barriers, tolls, and other hindrances to trade. They encouraged the formation of joint-stock companies and banks to channel private savings into industrial investments. By 1830 the political climate in western Europe was as favorable to business as Britain's had been a half-century earlier.

Abundant coal and iron-ore deposits determined the concentration of industries in a swath of territories running from northern France through Belgium and the Ruhr district of western Germany to Silesia in Prussia (now part of Poland). By the 1850s France, Belgium, and the German states were in the midst of an industrial boom like that of Britain, based on iron, cotton, steam engines, and railroads.

SECTION REVIEW

- The Industrial Revolution arose from population growth, an agricultural revolution, increased trade, and an interest in technological innovation.
- Britain industrialized first, thanks to its fluid political and social structures, transportation infrastructure, inventiveness, and society open to talented and enterprising people.
- Among educated Europeans, practical subjects like business, science, and technology became fashionable.
- On the European continent, the revolutions of 1789–1815 swept away the restrictions of the old aristocratic regimes and allowed for more industrial growth.

DIVERSITY + DOMINANCE

Adam Smith and the Division of Labor

Adam Smith (1723–1790), a Scottish philosopher, is famous for his book An Inquiry into the Nature and Causes of the Wealth of Nations, *first published in 1776. It was the first work to explain the economy of a nation as a system. Smith criticized the notion, common in the eighteenth century, that a nation's wealth was synonymous with the amount of gold and silver in the government's coffers. Instead, he defined wealth as the amount of goods and services produced by a nation's people. By this definition, labor and its products are an essential element in a nation's prosperity.*

In the passage that follows, Smith contrasts two methods of making pins. In one a team of workers divided up the job of making pins and produced a great many every day; in the other pin workers "wrought separately and independently" and produced very few pins per day. It is clear that the division of labor produces more pins per worker per day. But who benefits? Left unsaid is that a pin factory had to be owned and operated by a manufacturer who hired workers and assigned a task to each one.

The illustration shows a pin-maker's workshop in late-eighteenth-century France. Each worker is performing a specific task on a few pins at once, and all the energy comes from human muscles. These are the characteristics of a proto-industrial workshop.

To take an example, therefore, from a very trifling manufacture—but one in which the division of labour has been very often taken notice of—the trade of the pin-maker: a workman not educated to this business (which the division of labour has rendered a distinct trade), nor acquainted with the use of machinery employed in it (to the invention of which the same division of labour has probably given occasion), could scarce, perhaps, with his utmost industry, make one pin in a day, and certainly could not make twenty. But in the way in which this business is now carried on, not only the whole work is a peculiar trade, but it is divided into a number of branches, of which the greater part are likewise peculiar trades. One man draws out the wire, another straights it, a third cuts it, a fourth points it, a fifth grinds it at the top for receiving the head; to make the head requires two or three distinct operations, to put it on, is a peculiar business, to whiten the pins is another; it is even a trade by itself to put them into the paper; and the important business of making a pin is, in this manner, divided into about eighteen distinct operations, which, in some manufactories, are all performed by distinct hands, though in others the same man will sometimes perform two or three of them. I have seen a small manufactory of this kind where ten men only were employed, and where some of them, consequently, performed two or three distinct operations. But though they were very poor, and therefore but indifferently accommodated with the necessary machinery, they could, when they exerted themselves, make among them about twelve pounds of pins in a day.

There are in a pound upwards of four thousand pins of a middling size. Those ten persons, therefore, could make among them upwards of forty-eight thousand pins in a day. Each person, therefore, making a tenth part of forty-eight thousand pins, might be considered as making four thousand eight hundred pins a day. But if they had all wrought separately and independently, and without any of them having been educated to this peculiar business, they certainly could not each of them have made twenty, perhaps not one pin in a day; that

THE TECHNOLOGICAL REVOLUTION

Five innovations spurred industrialization: (1) mass production through the division of labor, (2) new machines and mechanization, (3) a great increase in the manufacture of iron, (4) the steam engine, and (5) the electric telegraph. China had achieved the first three of these during the Song dynasty (960–1279), but it had not developed the steam engine or electricity. The continued success of Western industrialization depended heavily on these new forms of energy.

mass production The manufacture of many identical products by the division of labor into many small repetitive tasks. This method was introduced into the manufacture of pottery by Josiah Wedgwood and into the spinning of cotton thread by Richard Arkwright.

Mass Production: Pottery

The pottery industry offers a good example of **mass production**, the making of many identical items by breaking the process into simple repetitive tasks. Before the mid-eighteenth century only the wealthy could afford Chinese porcelain. Middle-class people used pewter tableware, and the poor ate from wooden or earthenware bowls. Royal manufactures produced exquisite handmade products for the courts and aristocracy, but their products were much too expensive for mass consumption. As more and more Europeans acquired a taste for tea, cocoa, and coffee, they wanted porcelain that would not spoil the flavor of hot beverages. This demand created opportunities for inventive entrepreneurs.

Division of Rare and Manuscript Collections, Cornell University Library

A Pin-Maker's Workshop The man in the middle (Fig. 2) is pulling wire off a spindle (G) and through a series of posts. This ensures that the wire will be perfectly straight. The worker seated on the lower right (Fig. 3) takes the long pieces of straightened wire and cuts them into shorter lengths. The man in the lower left-hand corner (Fig. 5) sharpens twelve to fifteen wires at a time by holding them against a grindstone turned by the worker in Fig. 6. The men in Figs. 4 and 7 put the finishing touches on the points. Other operations—such as forming the wire to the proper thickness, cleaning and coating it with tin, and attaching the heads—are depicted in other engravings in the same encyclopedia.

is, certainly, not the two hundred and fortieth, perhaps not the four thousand eight hundredth part of what they are at present capable of performing, in consequence of a proper division and combination of their different operations.

QUESTIONS FOR ANALYSIS

1. **Why does dividing the job of pin-making into ten or more operations result in the production of more pins per worker? How much more productive are these workers than if each one made complete pins from start to finish?**
2. **How closely does the picture of a pin-maker's workshop illustrate Smith's verbal description?**
3. **What disadvantage would there be to working in a pin factory where the job was divided as in Smith's example, compared to making entire pins from start to finish?**
4. **What other examples can you think of, from Adam Smith's day or from more recent times, of the advantages of the division of labor?**

Source: Adam Smith, *An Inquiry into the Nature and Causes of the Wealth of Nations*, ed. Edward Gibbon Wakefield (London: Charles Knight and Co., 1843), 7–9.

Josiah Wedgwood English industrialist whose pottery works were the first to produce fine-quality pottery by industrial methods.

Wedgwood Pottery

division of labor A manufacturing technique that breaks down a craft into many simple and repetitive tasks that can be performed by unskilled workers. Pioneered in the pottery works of Josiah Wedgwood and in other eighteenth-century factories, it greatly increased the productivity of labor and lowered the cost of manufactured goods.

Britain had many small pottery workshops where craftsmen made a few plates and cups at a time. Much of this activity took place in a part of the Midlands that possessed good clay, coal for firing, and lead for glazing. In 1759, **Josiah Wedgwood**, the son of a potter, started his own pottery business. He had a scientific bent and invented a device to measure the extremely high temperatures that are found in kilns during the firing of pottery. Today the name Wedgwood is associated with expensive, highly decorated china. But Wedgwood's most important contribution lay in producing ordinary porcelain cheaply by means of the **division of labor** (see Diversity and Dominance: Adam Smith and the Division of Labor).

Wedgwood subdivided the work into simple repetitive tasks, such as unloading the clay, mixing it, pressing flat pieces, dipping the pieces in glaze, putting handles on cups, packing kilns, and carrying things from one part of his plant to another. To prevent interruptions, he instituted strict discipline among his workers. He substituted molds for the potter's wheel wherever possible, a change that not only saved labor but also created plates and bowls that could be stacked.

Wedgwood's interest in applying technology to manufacturing was sparked by his membership in the Lunar Society, a group of businessmen, scientists, and craftsmen that met each month when the moon was full to discuss the practical application of knowledge. In 1782 the naturalist Erasmus Darwin encouraged him to purchase a steam engine from Boulton and Watt, the firm founded by two other members of the society. The engine that Wedgwood bought to mix clay

Mary Evans Picture Library

Wedgwood's Potteries In Staffordshire, England, Josiah Wedgwood established a factory to mass-produce beautiful and inexpensive china. The bottle-shaped buildings are kilns in which thousands of pieces of china could be fired at one time. Kilns, factories, and housing were all mixed together in pottery towns, and smoke from burning coal filled the air.

and grind flint was one of the first to be installed in a factory. The division of labor and new machinery allowed Wedgwood to lower the cost of his products while improving their quality, and to offer his wares for sale at lower prices. His factory grew far larger than his competitors' factories and employed several hundred workers. His salesmen traveled throughout England touting his goods, and his products were sold on the European continent as well.

Mechanization: The Cotton Industry

The cotton industry, the largest in this period, illustrates the role of **mechanization**, the use of machines to do work previously done by hand. Cotton had long been grown in China, India, and the Middle East, where it was spun and woven by hand. The cloth was so much cooler, softer, and cleaner than wool that wealthy Europeans developed a liking for the costly import. When the powerful English woolen industry persuaded Parliament to forbid the import of cotton cloth, that prohibition stimulated attempts to import cotton fiber and make the cloth locally. Here was an opportunity for enterprising inventors to reduce costs with laborsaving machinery.

mechanization The application of machinery to manufacturing and other activities. Among the first processes to be mechanized were the spinning of cotton thread and the weaving of cloth in late-eighteenth- and early-nineteenth-century England.

Beginning in the 1760s a series of inventions revolutionized the spinning of cotton thread. The first was the jenny, invented in 1764, which mechanically drew out the cotton fibers and twisted them into thread. The jenny was simple, cheap to build, and easy for one person to operate. Early models spun six or seven threads at once, later ones up to eighty. The thread, however, was soft and irregular and could be used only in combination with linen, a strong yarn derived from the flax plant.

Innovations in Cotton Manufacturing

In 1769 **Richard Arkwright** invented another spinning machine, the water frame, which produced thread strong enough to be used without linen. Arkwright was both a gifted inventor and a successful businessman. His machine was larger and more complex than the jenny and required a source of power such as a water wheel, hence the name "water frame." To obtain the necessary energy he installed dozens of machines in a building next to a fast-flowing river. The resemblance to a flour mill gave such enterprises the name *cotton mill*.

Richard Arkwright English inventor and entrepreneur who became the wealthiest and most successful textile manufacturer of the early Industrial Revolution. He invented the water frame, a machine that, with minimal human supervision, could spin many strong cotton threads at once.

In 1785 Samuel Crompton patented a machine that combined the best features of the jenny and the water frame. This device, called a mule, produced a strong thread that was thin enough to be used to make a better type of cotton cloth called muslin. The mule could make a finer, more even thread than could any human being, and at a lower cost. At last British industry could undersell high-quality handmade cotton cloth from India. British cotton output increased tenfold between 1770 and 1790.

The boom in thread production and the soaring demand for cloth encouraged inventors to mechanize the rest of textile manufacturing. Power looms were perfected after 1815. Other inventions of the period included carding machines, chlorine bleach, and cylindrical presses to print designs on fabric. By the 1830s large textile mills powered by steam engines were performing all the steps necessary to turn raw cotton into printed cloth.

Mechanization offered two advantages: increased productivity for the manufacturer and lower prices for the consumer. Whereas in India it took five hundred hours to spin a pound of cotton, the mule of 1790 could do so in three person-hours, and the self-acting mule—an improved version introduced in 1830—required only eighty minutes. Cotton mills needed very few skilled workers, and managers often hired children to tend the spinning machines. The same was true of power looms, which gradually replaced handloom weaving: the number of power looms rose from 2,400 in 1813 to 500,000 by 1850. Meanwhile, the price of cloth fell by 90 percent between 1782 and 1812 and kept on dropping.

The industrialization of Britain made cotton America's most valuable crop. In the 1790s most of Britain's cotton came from India. In 1793 the American Eli Whitney patented his cotton gin, a simple device that separated the bolls or seedpods from the fiber and made cotton growing economical. This invention permitted the spread of cotton farming into Georgia, then into Alabama, Mississippi, and Louisiana, and finally as far west as Texas. By the late 1850s the southern states were producing a million tons of cotton a year, five-sixths of the world's total.

With the help of British craftsmen who introduced jennies, mules, and power looms, Americans developed their own cotton industry in the 1820s. By 1840 the United States had twelve hundred cotton mills, two-thirds of them in New England, that served the booming domestic market.

The Iron Industry

Iron making also was transformed during the Industrial Revolution. Throughout Eurasia and Africa, iron had long been used for tools, weapons, and household items. During the Song period, Chinese forges had produced cast iron in large quantities. Production declined after the Song, but iron continued to be common and inexpensive in China. Wherever iron was produced, however, deforestation eventually drove up the cost of charcoal (used for smelting) and restricted output. Furthermore, iron had to be repeatedly heated and hammered to drive out impurities, a difficult and costly process. Because of limited wood supplies and the high cost of skilled labor, iron was a rare and valuable metal outside China before the eighteenth century.

Innovations in Iron Making

A first breakthrough occurred in 1709 when Abraham Darby discovered that coke (coal from which the impurities have been cooked out) could be used in place of charcoal. The resulting metal was of lower quality than charcoal-smelted iron but much cheaper to produce, for coal was plentiful. In 1784 Henry Cort found a way to remove some of the impurities in coke-iron by puddling—stirring the molten iron with long rods. Cort's process made it possible to turn coal into coke to produce wrought iron (a soft and malleable form of iron) very cheaply. By 1790 four-fifths of Britain's iron was made with coke, while other countries still used charcoal. Coke-iron allowed a great expansion in the size of individual blast furnaces. Britain's iron production rose fast, from 17,000 tons in 1740 to 3 million tons in 1844, as much as in the rest of the world put together.

In turn, there seemed no limit to the novel applications for this cheap and useful material. In 1779 Abraham Darby III (grandson of the first Abraham Darby) built a bridge of iron across

Pit Head of a Coal Mine This is a small coal mine. In the center of this picture stands a Newcomen engine used to pump water. The work of hauling coal out of the mine was still done by horses and mules. The smoke coming out of the smokestack is a trademark of the early industrial era.

Walker Art Gallery, National Museums Liverpool/The Bridgeman Art Library

Crystal Palace Building erected in Hyde Park, London, for the Great Exhibition of 1851. Made of iron and glass, like a gigantic greenhouse, it was a symbol of the industrial age.

the Severn River. In 1851 Londoners marveled at the **Crystal Palace**, a huge greenhouse made entirely of iron and glass and large enough to enclose the tallest trees.

The availability of cheap iron made the mass production of objects such as guns, hardware, and tools appealing. However, fitting together the parts of these products required a great deal of labor. To reduce labor costs, manufacturers turned to the idea of interchangeable parts. By the mid-nineteenth century, interchangeable-parts manufacturing had been adopted in the manufacture of firearms, farm equipment, and sewing machines. At the Crystal Palace exhibition of 1851, Europeans called it the "American system of manufactures." In the next hundred years the use of machinery to mass-produce consumer items was to become the hallmark of American industry.

steam engine A machine that turns the energy released by burning fuel into motion. Thomas Newcomen built the first crude but workable steam engine in 1712. James Watt vastly improved his device in the 1760s and 1770s. Steam power was later applied to moving machinery in factories and to powering ships and locomotives.

The Steam Engine

In the history of the world, there had been a number of periods of great technological inventiveness and economic growth. But in all previous cases, the dynamism eventually faltered. The Industrial Revolution, in contrast, has only accelerated. One reason has been increased interactions between scientists, technicians, and businesspeople. Another has been access to a source of cheap energy, namely fossil fuels. The first machine to transform fossil fuel into mechanical energy was the **steam engine**, a device that set the Industrial Revolution apart from all previous periods of growth and innovation.

The Newcomen and Watt Engines

James Watt Scot who invented the condenser and other improvements that made the steam engine a practical source of power for industry and transportation. The watt, an electrical measurement, is named after him.

Before the eighteenth century, deep mines filled with water faster than horses could pump it out. Then, between 1702 and 1712 Thomas Newcomen developed the first practical steam engine, a crude but effective device that could pump water out of mines as fast as four horses and could run day and night without getting tired. The Newcomen engine's voracious appetite for fuel mattered little in coal mines, where fuel was cheap, but it made the engine too costly for other uses. In 1764 **James Watt**, a maker of scientific instruments at Glasgow University in Scotland, was asked to repair the university's model Newcomen engine. Watt realized that the engine wasted fuel because the cylinder had to be alternately heated and cooled. He developed a separate condenser—a vessel into which the steam was allowed to escape after it had done its work, leaving the cylinder always hot and the condenser always cold. Watt patented his idea in 1769. He enlisted the help of the iron manufacturer Matthew Boulton to turn his invention into a commercial product. Their first engines were sold to pump water out of copper and tin mines, where fuel was too costly for Newcomen engines. In 1781 Watt invented the sun-and-planet gear, which turned the back-and-forth action of the piston into rotary motion. This allowed steam engines to power machinery in flour and cotton mills, pottery manufactures, and other industries. Because there seemed almost no limit to the amount of coal in the ground, steam-

Transatlantic Steamship Race In 1838, two ships equipped with steam engines, the *Sirius* and the *Great Western*, steamed from England to New York. Although the *Sirius* left a few days earlier, the *Great Western*—shown here arriving in New York harbor—almost caught up with it, arriving just four hours after the *Sirius*. This race inaugurated regular transatlantic steamship service.

Courtesy of the Mariners' Museum, Newport News, VA

generated energy appeared to be an inexhaustible source of power, and steam engines could be used where animal, wind, and water power were lacking.

Steamboats and Ships

Inspired by the success of Watt's engine, several inventors put steam engines on boats. The first commercially successful steamboat was Robert Fulton's *North River*, which steamed up and down the Hudson River between New York City and Albany, New York, in 1807. Soon steamboats were launched on the Ohio and the Mississippi, gateways to the Midwest. In the 1820s the Erie Canal linked the Atlantic seaboard with the Great Lakes and opened Ohio, Indiana, and Illinois to European settlement. By 1830 some three hundred steamboats plied the Mississippi and its tributaries. The United States was fast becoming a nation that moved by water.

Oceangoing steam-powered ships were much more difficult to build than river boats, for the first steam engines used so much coal that no ship could carry more than a few days' supply. The *Savannah*, which crossed the Atlantic in 1819, was a sailing ship with an auxiliary steam engine that was used for only ninety hours of its twenty-nine-day trip. Engineers soon developed more efficient engines, and in 1838 two steamers, the *Great Western* and the *Sirius*, crossed the Atlantic on steam power alone.

Railroads

After Watt's patent expired in 1800, inventors experimented with lighter, more powerful high-pressure engines—an idea Watt had rejected as too dangerous. In 1804 Richard Trevithick built an engine that consumed twelve times less coal than Newcomen's and three times less than Watt's; with it, he built several steam-powered vehicles able to travel on roads or rails.

By the 1820s England had many railways on which horses pulled heavy wagons. In 1829, the owners of the Liverpool and Manchester Railway organized a contest between steam-powered locomotives and horse-drawn wagons. George Stephenson and his son Robert won the contest with their locomotive *Rocket*, which pulled a 20-ton train at up to 30 miles (48 kilometers) per hour. After that triumph, a railroad-building mania swept Britain. In the late 1830s, as passenger traffic soared, entrepreneurs built lines between the major cities and even to small towns. Railroads were far cheaper, faster, and more comfortable than stagecoaches, and millions of people got in the habit of traveling.

Railroads in America

In the United States entrepreneurs built railroads as quickly and cheaply as possible. By the 1840s, 6,000 miles (10,000 kilometers) of track radiated from Boston, New York, Philadelphia, and Baltimore. In the 1850s, 21,000 miles (34,000 kilometers) of new track were laid, much of it westward across the Appalachians to Memphis, St. Louis, and Chicago. After 1856 the trip from

Bettmann/Corbis

The *De Witt Clinton* Locomotive, 1835–1840 The *De Witt Clinton* was the first steam locomotive built in the United States. The high smokestack let the hot cinders cool so they would not set fire to nearby trees, an important consideration at a time when eastern North America was still covered with forest. The three passenger cars are clearly horse carriages fitted with railroad wheels.

New York to Chicago, which had once taken three weeks by boat and on horseback, could be made in forty-eight hours. It was the railroads that opened up the Midwest, turning the vast prairie into farms to feed the industrial cities of the eastern United States.

Railroads in Europe

Railways also triggered the industrialization of Europe (see Map 22.2). Belgium, independent since 1830, quickly copied the British railways. In France and Prussia, construction was delayed until the mid-1840s. When it began, however, it not only satisfied the long-standing need for transportation but also stimulated the iron, machinery, and construction industries.

electric telegraph A device for rapid, long-distance transmission of information over an electric wire. It was introduced in England and North America in the 1830s and 1840s and replaced telegraph systems that utilized visual signals such as semaphores.

Communication over Wires

After the Italian scientist Alessandro Volta invented the battery in 1800, making it possible to produce an electric current, many inventors tried to apply electricity to communication. The first practical **electric telegraph** systems were developed almost simultaneously in England and America. In 1837 in England Charles Wheatstone and William Cooke introduced a five-wire telegraph, while the American Samuel Morse introduced a code of dots and dashes that could be transmitted with a single wire.

The railroad companies allowed telegraph companies to string wires along the tracks in exchange for the right to send telegrams from station to station announcing the departure and arrival of trains. Such messages made railroads much safer as well as more efficient. By the late 1840s telegraph wires crisscrossed the eastern United States and western Europe. In 1851 the first submarine telegraph cable was laid across the English Channel from England to France; it was the beginning of a network that eventually connected the entire globe. No longer were communications limited to the speed of a sailing ship, a galloping horse, or a fast-moving train.

SECTION REVIEW

- A series of technological and organizational innovations transformed manufacturing, transportation, and communication.
- Mechanization, pioneered by Wedgwood, meant that work formerly done by skilled craftsmen was divided into many simple tasks assigned to workers in factories.
- New machines allowed the mass-production of cotton yarn and cloth.
- The use of coke and new machines made iron cheap and abundant.
- Steam engines provided power for mines, factories, ships, and railroads.
- Electricity found its first practical application in telegraphy.

THE IMPACT OF THE EARLY INDUSTRIAL REVOLUTION

 **AP* Exam Tip** The transformative effects of the Industrial Revolution are an important topic for the AP* course.

The Industrial Revolution led to profound changes in society, politics, and the economy. At first, the changes were local. Some people became wealthy and built mansions, while others lived in slums with polluted water and air. By the mid-nineteenth century, the worst local effects were being alleviated and cities became cleaner and healthier. Replacing them were more complex problems: business cycles, labor conflicts, and the transformation of entire regions into industrial landscapes. At the global level, industrialization empowered the nations of western Europe and North America at the expense of the rest of the world.

The New Industrial Cities

The most dramatic environmental changes brought about by industrialization occurred in the towns. Never before had towns grown so fast. London, one of the largest cities in Europe in 1700 with 500,000 inhabitants, grew to 959,000 by 1800 and to 2,363,000 by 1850; it was then the largest city the world had ever known. Manchester, a small town of 20,000 in 1758, reached 400,000 a century later, a twentyfold increase. New York City, already 100,000 strong in 1815, reached 600,000 (including Brooklyn) in 1850. In some areas, towns merged and formed megalopolises, such as Greater London, the English Midlands, central Belgium, and the Ruhr district of Germany.

A great deal of money went into the building of fine homes, churches, museums, and theaters in wealthy neighborhoods. Much of the beauty of London dates from the time of the Industrial

Revolution. Yet, by all accounts, the industrial cities grew much too fast, and much of the growth occurred in the poorest neighborhoods. As poor migrants streamed in from the countryside, developers built the cheap, shoddy row houses for them to rent that Nassau Senior described.

Urban Environments

Sudden population growth caused serious urban environmental problems. Town dwellers recently arrived from the country brought country ways with them. People threw their sewage and trash out the windows to be washed down the gutters in the streets. The poor kept pigs and chickens; the rich kept horses; and pedestrians stepped into the street at their own risk. Air pollution from burning coal, a problem since the sixteenth century, got steadily worse. People drank water drawn from wells and rivers contaminated by sewage and industrial runoff. The River Irwell, which ran through Manchester, was, in the words of one visitor, "considerably less a river than a flood of liquid manure."[4]

"Every day that I live," wrote an American visitor to Manchester, "I thank Heaven that I am not a poor man with a family in England."[5] In his poem "Milton," William Blake (1757–1827) expressed the revulsion of sensitive people at the spoliation of England's "mountains green" and "pleasant pastures":

And did the Countenance Divine
Shine forth upon our clouded hills?
And was Jerusalem builded here
Among these dark Satanic Mills?

Railroads invaded the towns, bringing noise and smoke into densely populated neighborhoods. Railroad companies built their stations as close to the heart of cities as they could. On

Interactive Map

MAP 22.2 Industrialization in Europe, ca. 1850 In 1850 industrialization was in its early stages on the European continent. The first industrial regions were comparatively close to England and possessed rich coal deposits: Belgium and the Ruhr district of Germany. Politics determined the location of railroads. Notice the star-shaped French network of rail lines emanating from Paris and the lines linking the different parts of the German Confederation.

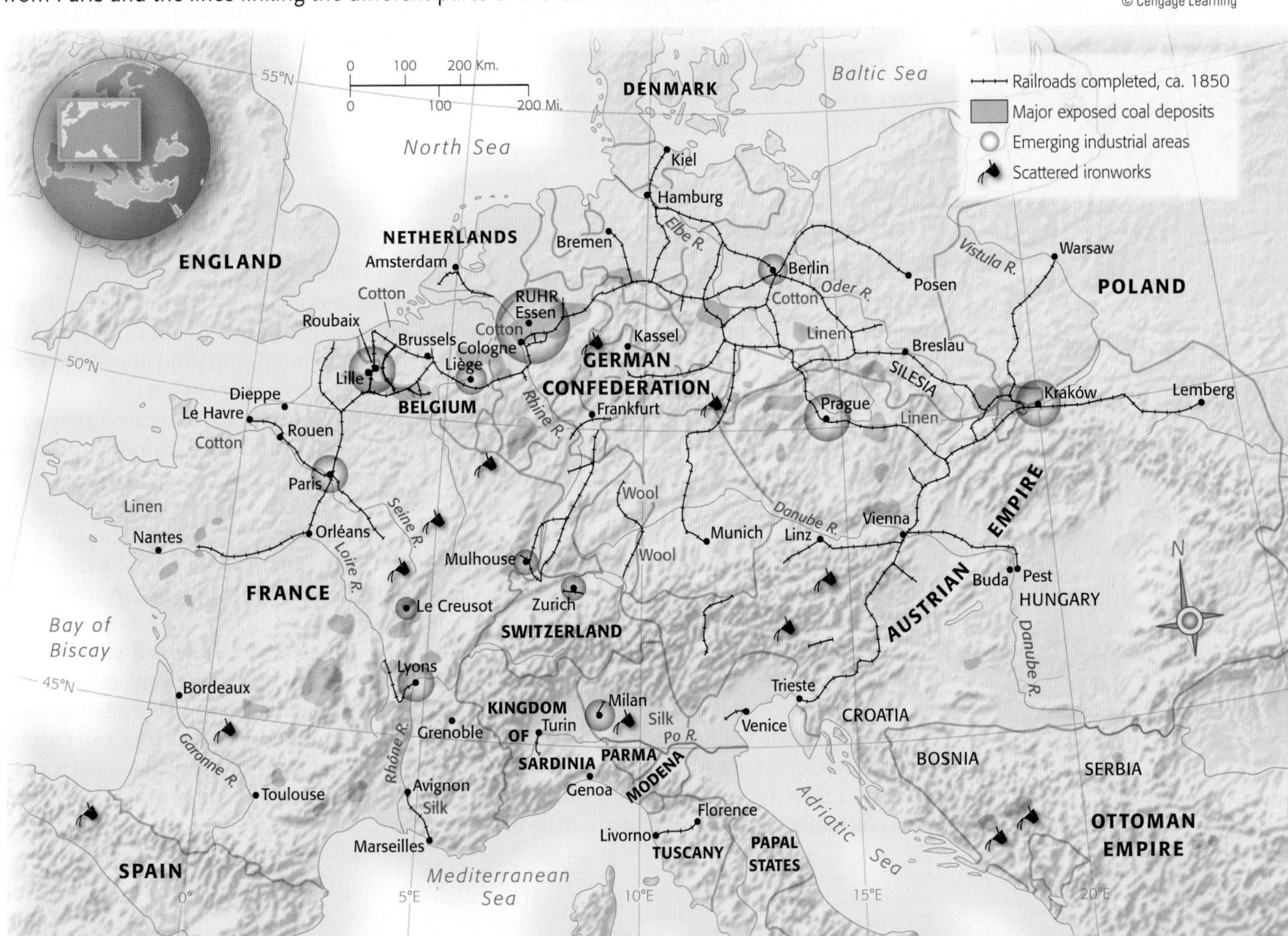

Bibliothèque nationale de France

Paris Apartment at Night This cutaway drawing in a French magazine shows the vertical segregation by social class that prevailed in the 1840s. The lower level is occupied by the concierge and her family. The first floor belongs to a wealthy family throwing a party for high-society friends. Middle-class people living on the next floor seem annoyed by the noise coming from below. Above them, a thief has entered an artist's studio. A poor seamstress and her child live in the garret under the roof. When elevators were introduced in the late nineteenth century, people of different income levels became segregated by neighborhoods instead of by floors.

the outskirts of cities, railroad yards, sidings, and repair shops covered acres of land, surrounded by miles of warehouses and workers' housing.

Under these conditions, diseases proliferated. To the long list of preindustrial diseases, industrialization added new ailments. Rickets, a bone disease caused by lack of sunshine, became endemic in dark and smoky industrial cities. Steamships brought cholera from India, causing great epidemics that struck poor neighborhoods especially hard. Observers documented the horrors of slum life in vivid detail. Their shocking reports led to municipal reforms, such as garbage removal, water and sewage systems, and parks and schools. These measures began to alleviate the ills of urban life after the mid-nineteenth century.

Rural Environments

Long before the Industrial Revolution began, practically no wilderness areas were left in Britain and very few in western Europe. Almost every piece of land was covered with fields, forests, or pastures shaped by human activity, or by towns; yet humans continued to alter the environment. As they had been doing for centuries, people cut timber to build ships and houses, to heat homes, and to manufacture bricks, iron, glass, beer, bread, and many other items.

North American Environments

North Americans transformed their environment faster than Europeans because they saw nature as an obstacle to be overcome and dominated. The Canadian and American governments seized land from the Indians and made it available at low cost to white farmers and logging companies. Settlers viewed forests not as a valuable resource but as a hindrance to development. In their haste to "open up the wilderness," pioneers felled trees and burned them, built houses and abandoned them, and moved on. The cultivation of cotton in the South was especially harmful. Planters cut down forests, grew cotton for a few years until it depleted the soil, then moved west, abandoning the land to scrub pines.

Environments in Europe

In Europe, raw materials once grown on the land—such as wood, hay, and wool—were replaced by materials found underground, like iron ore and coal, or obtained overseas, like cotton. While forested countries continued to smelt iron with charcoal, western Europeans substituted coke made from coal. As the population increased and land grew scarcer, the cost of growing feed for horses rose, creating incentives to find new, less land-hungry means of transportation. Likewise, as iron became cheaper and wood more expensive, ships and many other objects formerly made of wood began to be made of iron.

Bibliotheque des Arts Decoratifs, Paris/Gianni Dagli Ordi/The Art Archive

An Industrial Canal In the late eighteenth and early nineteenth centuries, before railroads were introduced, many canals were constructed in England so that barges could transport heavy materials cheaply, such as coal for industrial works and steam engines, stone and bricks for buildings, clay for pottery works, and ores for metal foundries. Canals such as this one, which ran alongside a copper foundry, contributed greatly to Britain's industrial development.

To contemporaries, the most obvious changes in rural life were brought about by the new transportation systems. In the eighteenth century France had a network of quality roads, which Napoleon extended into Italy and Germany. In Britain local governments' neglect of the roads that served long-distance traffic led to the formation of private "turnpike trusts" that built numerous toll roads. The growing volume of heavy freight triggered canal-building booms in Britain, France, and the Low Countries in the late eighteenth century. Some canals, like the duke of Bridgewater's canal in England, connected coal mines to towns or navigable rivers. Others linked navigable rivers and created national transportation networks.

Canals were where engineers learned skills they were able to apply to the next great transportation system: the railroads. They laid track across rolling country by cutting deeply into hillsides and erecting daringly long bridges across valleys. Soon, trains pulled by puffing, smoke-belching locomotives were invading long-isolated districts.

Working Conditions

Industrialization offered new opportunities to the enterprising. Carpenters, metalworkers, and machinists were in great demand. Some workers became engineers or went into business for themselves. The boldest Britons moved to the European continent, the Americas, or India, using their skills to establish new industries.

The successful, however, were a minority. Most industrial jobs were unskilled, repetitive, and boring. Factory work did not vary with the seasons or the time of day but began and ended by the clock. Gas lighting expanded the working day past sunset (see Environment and Technology: Gas Lighting). Workdays were long, there were few breaks, and foremen watched constantly. Workers who performed one simple task over and over had little sense of achievement or connection to the final product. Industrial accidents were common and could ruin a family. Factory workers had no control over their tools, jobs, or working hours.

Gas Lighting

Before the nineteenth century, the night was a dangerous time to be out. Oil lanterns and candles made of tallow or beeswax were expensive. Almost everyone went to bed at sundown and got up at dawn.

There was a big demand for better lighting. For the managers of industrial establishments, daylight hours were too short, especially in the winter months; they knew that they could keep running after sunset if they had light, but lanterns and candles were costly and dangerous. Wealthy people wanted to light up their homes. Businesses and government offices also needed light. The demand inspired inventors to look for new ways to produce light.

The French engineer Philippe Lebon knew that heating wood to make charcoal produced a flammable gas. In the 1790s he channeled this gas through pipes to illuminate a home and garden. In Britain, the engineer William Murdock used the gas released in the process of making coke to light up a house. Moving from these experiments to commercial applications was a long and complicated process, however. Coal gas was smelly and explosive and full of impurities that gave off toxic fumes when it burned. Engineers had to learn ways to extract the gas efficiently, make strong pipes that did not leak, and market the product. In 1806 Frederick Albert Winsor founded the National Light and Heat Company to produce and distribute gas in London. By 1816, London had 26 miles of gas mains bringing gas to several neighborhoods. That same year, Baltimore became the first American city to install gas mains and streetlamps. In the following decades, engineers developed ways of making gas safer and cleaner. They also invented meters to measure the amount of gas consumed and burners that produced a brighter light. As a result of these improvements, the cost of gas dropped to less than a third that of oil lamps of equivalent lighting power. From the 1840s until the early twentieth century, gaslights were installed in homes, businesses, and factories and along streets in the major cities of Europe and America.

The results were astonishing and delighted city dwellers. Mills and factories could operate on two eight- to ten-hour shifts instead of one long dawn-to-dusk shift. Businesses stayed open late. Theaters gave evening performances. And people could now walk the streets safely. Evening illumination also contributed to the tremendous increase in adult education, as working people attended classes after work. Sales of books soared as increasing numbers of people stayed up late reading. Brightly lit cities attracted migrants from the still-dark countryside. Gas lighting had banished the terrors of the night.

Mary Evans Picture Library/The Image Works

Gas Lighting For city dwellers, one of the most dramatic improvements brought by industrialization was the introduction of gas lighting. The gas used was a byproduct of heating coal to make coke for the iron industry, and the gas was distributed in iron pipes throughout the wealthier neighborhoods of big cities. Every evening at dusk, lamplighters went around lighting the street lamps.

Women and Industry

Industrial work had a major impact on women and family life. Women who could not afford servants had always worked, but mostly within the family: spinning and weaving, sewing hats and clothes, preparing food, washing, and doing a myriad other household chores. In rural areas, women also did farmwork, especially caring for gardens and small animals.

In the early years of industrialization, even where factory work was available, it was never the main occupation of working women. Most young women who sought paid employment became domestic servants in spite of the low pay, drudgery, and risk of sexual abuse by male employers. Women with small children tried hard to find work they could do at home, such as laundry, sewing, embroidery, millinery, or taking in lodgers. Those who worked in factories were concentrated in textile mills, because textile work required less strength than metalworking, construction, or hauling. On average, women earned one-third to one-half as much as men. The

From William Playfair, The Commercial and Political Atlas, 1801. Visual Connection Archive

"Love Conquers Fear" This is a sentimental Victorian drawing of children in a textile mill. Child labor was common in the first half of the nineteenth century, and workers were exposed to dangerous machines and moving belts, as well as to dust and dirt.

economist Andrew Ure wrote in 1835: "It is in fact the constant aim and tendency of every improvement in machinery to supersede human labour altogether or to diminish its cost, by substituting the industry of women and children for that of men."[6] Young unmarried women worked to support themselves or to save for marriage. Married women took factory jobs when their husbands were unable to support the family. Mothers of infants faced a hard choice: whether to leave their babies with wet nurses at great expense or bring them to the factory and keep them drugged. Husbands and wives increasingly worked in different places.

As in preindustrial societies, parents thought children should contribute to their upkeep as soon as they were able to. The first generation of workers brought children as young as five or six with them to the factories and mines; there were no public schools or day-care centers. Employers preferred child workers because they were cheaper and more docile than adults and were better able to tie broken threads or crawl under machines to sweep the dust. In Arkwright's cotton mills two-thirds of the workers were children. Children worked fourteen to sixteen hours a day and were beaten if they made mistakes or fell asleep. Mine operators used children to pull coal carts along the low passageways from the coal face to the mine shaft.

In the early nineteenth century Americans still remembered their revolutionary ideals. When Francis Cabot Lowell built a cotton mill in Massachusetts, he hired the unmarried daughters of New England farmers, promising them decent wages and housing in dormitories under careful moral supervision. Other manufacturers eager to combine profits with morality followed his example. But soon the profit motive won out, and manufacturers imposed longer hours, harsher working conditions, and lower wages. When the young women went on strike, the mill owners replaced them with Irish immigrants willing to accept lower pay and worse conditions.

Industry and Slavery

AP* Exam Tip Be sure to understand how the Industrial Revolution influenced changes in social structure.

While the cotton boom enriched planters, merchants, and manufacturers, African Americans paid for it with their freedom. In the 1790s, 700,000 slaves of African descent lived in the United States. As the "Cotton Kingdom" expanded, the number of slaves rose, and by 1850 there were 3.2 million slaves in the United States, 60 percent of whom grew cotton. Similarly, demand for sugar prolonged slavery in the plantations of the West Indies and caused it to spread to the coffee-growing regions of southern Brazil. Slavery was not, as white American southerners maintained, a "peculiar institution," a consequence of biological differences or biblical injunctions, but part of the Industrial Revolution.

Changes in Society

In his novel *Sybil*; or, *The Two Nations*, the British politician Benjamin Disraeli (diz-RAY-lee) (1804–1881) spoke of "two nations between whom there is no intercourse and no sympathy, who are as ignorant of each other's habits, thoughts, and feelings as if they were dwellers in different zones, or inhabitants of different planets . . . the rich and the poor."[7]

Handloom Weavers and Factory Workers

In Britain the worst-off were those who clung to an obsolete skill or craft. The high wages and low productivity of handloom weavers in the 1790s induced inventors to develop power looms. As a result, by 1811 handloom weavers' wages had fallen by a third; by 1832, by two-thirds. Even by working longer hours, they could not escape destitution. The standard of living of factory workers did not decline steadily like those of handloom weavers but fluctuated wildly.

Improvements and Setbacks

During the war years of 1792 to 1815, the price of food, on which the poor spent most of their income, rose faster than wages, causing widespread hardship. Then, in the 1820s real wages and public health began to improve. Prices fell and wages rose. Even the poor could afford comfortable, washable cotton clothes and underwear. Hard times returned in the "hungry forties." In 1847–1848 the potato crop failed in Ireland. One-quarter of the Irish population died in the resulting famine, and another quarter emigrated to England and North America.

The New Middle Class

The real beneficiaries of the early Industrial Revolution were the middle class. In Britain landowning gentry and merchants had long shared wealth and influence. In the late eighteenth century a new group arose: entrepreneurs whose money came from manufacturing. Most, like Arkwright and Wedgwood, were the sons of middling shopkeepers, craftsmen, or farmers. Their enterprises were usually self-financed, for little capital was needed to start a cotton-spinning or machine-building business. A generation later, in the nineteenth century, some newly rich industrialists bought their way into high society. The same happened in western Europe after 1815.

 **AP* Exam Tip** Understand the changes in gender roles that developed as part of the Industrial Revolution.

Middle-Class Women and Middle-Class Attitudes

Before the Industrial Revolution, wives of merchants had often participated in the family business; widows occasionally managed sizable businesses on their own. With industrialization came a "cult of domesticity" to justify removing middle-class women from contact with the business world. Instead, they became responsible for the home, the servants, the education of children, and the family's social life (see Chapter 26). Not all women accepted the change; Mary Wollstonecraft (1759–1797) wrote the first feminist manifesto, *Vindication of the Rights of Woman*, in 1792.

Middle-class people who attributed their success to their own efforts and virtues believed that if some people could succeed through hard work, thrift, and temperance, then those who did not succeed had no one but themselves to blame. Many workers, however, were newly arrived from rural districts and earned too little to save for the long stretches of unemployment they experienced. The squalor and misery of life in factory towns led to a noticeable increase in drunkenness on paydays. The moral position of the middle class mingled condemnation with concern, coupled with feelings of helplessness in the face of terrible social problems, such as drunkenness, prostitution, and child abandonment.

SECTION REVIEW

- The Industrial Revolution changed people's lives and the environments in which they lived.
- Mass migrations made cities grow huge and, for most of their inhabitants, unsightly and unhealthy.
- Roads, canals, and railroads crisscrossed open land, changing rural environments.
- Middle-class women were consigned to caring for the home and children, while many working-class women had to earn their living in mines and factories.
- Serious social problems arose, such as unemployment, alcoholism, and the abandonment of children.

NEW ECONOMIC AND POLITICAL BELIEF SYSTEMS

Changes as profound as the Industrial Revolution triggered political ferment and ideological conflict. So many wars and revolutions took place during those years that we cannot neatly separate out the consequences of industrialization from the rest. But it is clear that by undermining social traditions and causing a growing gap between rich and poor, the Industrial Revolution strengthened the ideas of laissez faire (LAY-say fair) and socialism and sparked workers' protests.

laissez faire The idea that government should refrain from interfering in economic affairs. The classic exposition of laissez-faire principles is Adam Smith's *Wealth of Nations* (1776).

Laissez Faire and Its Critics

Adam Smith and Laizzez Faire

The most celebrated exponent of **laissez faire** ("let them do") was Adam Smith (1723–1790), a Scottish economist. In *The Wealth of Nations* (1776) Smith argued that if individuals were allowed to seek personal gain, the effect, as though guided by an "invisible hand," would be to increase the general welfare. The government should refrain from interfering in business, except to protect private property; it should even allow duty-free trade with foreign countries. By advocating free-market capitalism, Smith was challenging the prevailing economic doctrine,

mercantilism European government policies of the sixteenth, seventeenth, and eighteenth centuries designed to promote overseas trade between a country and its colonies and accumulate precious metals by requiring colonies to trade only with their motherland country. The British system was defined by the Navigation Acts, the French system by laws known as the *Exclusif*.

mercantilism, which argued that governments should regulate trade in order to maximize their hoard of precious metals (Chapter 18).

Persuaded by Adam Smith's arguments, governments after 1815 dismantled many of their regulations. Britain even lowered its import duties. Nonetheless, it was obvious that industrialization was causing widespread misery. Two other thinkers, Thomas Malthus (1766–1834) and David Ricardo (1772–1832), attempted to explain the poverty they saw without challenging the basic premises of laissez faire. The cause of the workers' plight, they said, was the population boom, which outstripped the food supply and led to falling wages. The workers' poverty, they claimed, was as much a result of "natural law" as the wealth of successful businessmen, and the only way the working class could avoid mass famine was to delay marriage and practice self-restraint and sexual abstinence.

Businesspeople in Britain eagerly adopted laissez-faire ideas that justified their activities and kept the government at bay. But not everyone accepted the grim conclusions of the "dismal science," as economics was then known. The British philosopher Jeremy Bentham (1748–1832) believed that it was possible to maximize "the greatest happiness of the greatest number," if only Parliament would study the social problems of the day and pass appropriate legislation. The German economist Friedrich List (1789–1846) rejected laissez faire and free trade as a British trick "to make the rest of the world, like the Hindus, its serfs in all industrial and commercial relations." To protect their "infant industries" from British competition, he argued, the German states had to erect high tariff barriers against imports from Britain. On the European continent, List's ideas were as influential as those of Smith and Ricardo and led in 1834 to the formation of the Zollverein (TSOLL-feh-rine), a customs union of most of the German states.

Positivism

positivism A philosophy developed by the French count of Saint-Simon. Positivists believed that social and economic problems could be solved by the application of the scientific method, leading to continuous progress. Their ideas became popular in France and Latin America in the nineteenth century.

French social thinkers, moved by sincere concern for the poor, offered a radically new vision of a just civilization. Espousing a philosophy called **positivism**, the count of Saint-Simon (1760–1825) and his disciple Auguste Comte (COMB-tuh) (1798–1857) argued that the scientific method could solve social as well as technical problems. They recommended that the poor, guided by scientists and artists, form workers' communities under the protection of benevolent business leaders. These ideas attracted the enthusiastic support of bankers and entrepreneurs, for whom positivism provided a rationale for investing in railroads, canals, and other symbols of modernity.

Protests and Reforms

Workers benefited little from the ideas of these middle-class philosophers. Instead, they resisted the harsh working conditions in their own ways. Periodically, they rioted or went on strike, especially when food prices were high or when downturns in the business cycle left many unemployed. In some places, craftsmen broke into factories and destroyed the machines that threatened their livelihoods. Such acts of resistance did nothing to change the nature of industrial work.

Workers' Organizations

Gradually, workers organized to demand universal male suffrage and shorter workdays. In 1834 Robert Owen founded the Grand National Consolidated Trade Union to lobby for an eight-hour workday; it quickly gained half a million members but collapsed a few months later in the face of government prosecution. A new movement called Chartism arose soon thereafter, led by William Lovett and Fergus O'Connor, that appealed to miners and industrial workers. It demanded universal male suffrage, the secret ballot, salaries for members of Parliament, and annual elections. It gathered 1.3 million signatures on a petition, but Parliament rejected it. Chartism collapsed in 1848, but it left a legacy of labor organizing.

Eventually, mass movements persuaded the British Parliament to investigate conditions in factories and mines. The Factory Act of 1833 prohibited the employment of children younger than nine in textile mills. It also limited the working hours of children between the ages of nine and thirteen to eight hours a day and of fourteen- to

SECTION REVIEW

- Many people sought explanations and proposed solutions for the changes in social structures and economic systems.
- Some economists defended the growing disparities between rich and poor in the name of laissez faire, the free-market idea proposed by Adam Smith that appealed to businesspeople.
- Positivists deplored the hardships caused by industrialization but asserted that they could be ameliorated by technological advances and wise policies.
- Agitation by workers led politicians to investigate the working conditions in mines and factories, especially the work of women and children.

Reforms

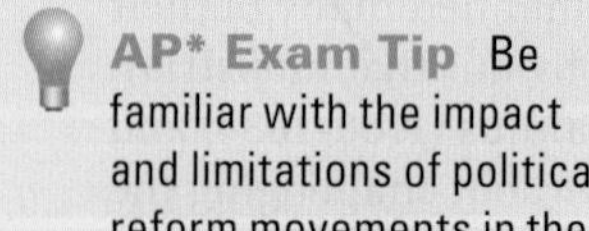
AP* Exam Tip Be familiar with the impact and limitations of political reform movements in the nineteenth century.

eighteen-year-olds to twelve hours. The Mines Act of 1842 prohibited the employment of women and boys under age ten underground.

Most important was the struggle over the Corn Laws—tariffs on imported grain. Their repeal in 1846, in the name of "free trade," was designed to lower the cost of food for workers and allow employers to pay lower wages. The repeal represented a victory for the rising class of manufacturers over the conservative landowners who had long dominated politics and whose harvests faced competition from cheaper imported food.

The British learned to seek reform through accommodation. On the European continent, in contrast, the revolutions of 1848 revealed widespread discontent with repressive governments but failed to soften the hardships of industrialization (see Chapter 26).

THE LIMITS OF INDUSTRIALIZATION OUTSIDE THE WEST

Egypt

The spread of the Industrial Revolution in the early nineteenth century transformed the relations of western Europe and North America with the rest of the world. Egypt, strongly influenced by European ideas since the French invasion of 1798, began to industrialize in the early nineteenth century. The driving force was its ruler, Muhammad Ali (1769–1849), a man who was to play a major role in the history of the Middle East and East Africa (see Chapters 24 and 25). Muhammad Ali wanted to build up the Egyptian economy and military in order to become less dependent on the Ottoman sultan, his nominal overlord. To do so, he imported advisers and technicians from Europe and built cotton mills, foundries, shipyards, weapons factories, and other industrial enterprises. To pay for all this, he made the peasants grow wheat and cotton, which the government bought at a low price and exported at a profit. He also imposed high tariffs on imported goods to force the pace of industrialization.

Muhammad Ali's efforts fell afoul of the British, who did not want a powerful country threatening to interrupt the flow of travelers and mail across Egypt, the shortest route between Europe and India. When Egypt went to war against the Ottoman Empire in 1839, Britain intervened and forced Muhammad Ali to eliminate all import duties in the name of free trade. Unprotected, Egypt's fledgling industries could not compete with the flood of cheap British products. Thereafter, Egypt exported raw cotton, imported manufactured goods, and became an economic dependency of Britain.

India

Until the late eighteenth century, India had been the world's largest producer and exporter of cotton textiles, handmade by skilled spinners and weavers. The British East India Company took over large parts of India just as the Industrial Revolution was beginning in Britain (see Chapter 25 and Map 25.2). It allowed cheap British factory-made yarn and cloth to flood the Indian market duty-free, putting spinners and handloom weavers out of work. Unlike Britain, India had no factories to which displaced handicraft workers could turn for work. Most of them became landless peasants, eking out a precarious living.

Like other tropical regions, India became an exporter of raw materials and an importer of British industrial goods. To hasten the process, British entrepreneurs and colonial officials introduced railroads into the subcontinent. The construction of India's railroad network began in the mid-1850s, along with coal mining to fuel the locomotives and the installation of telegraph lines to connect the major cities.

Some Indian entrepreneurs saw opportunities in the atmosphere of change that the British created. In 1854 the Bombay merchant Cowasjee Nanabhoy Davar imported an engineer, four skilled workers, and several textile machines from Britain and started India's first textile mill. This was the beginning of India's mechanized cotton industry. Despite many gifted entrepreneurs, however, India's industrialization proceeded at a snail's pace, for the government was in British hands and the British did nothing to encourage Indian industry.

A Railroad Bridge Across the Nile In the second half of the nineteenth century, industrialized nations, especially Great Britain, sent engineers and equipment to build railroads in less-industrialized parts of the world, such as India, South Africa, Latin America, and the Middle East. One such railway connected Cairo and Alexandria in Egypt. Here a railroad bridge crosses the Nile at Benha near the Pyramids. (Corbis)

China

China stagnated at the very time when first Britain and then western Europe and North America were becoming industrialized. It had the resources, both human and natural, to advance technologically and economically, but a conservative elite stood in the way of change (see Chapter 20). When faced with Western industrial technology, China became weaker rather than stronger.

In January 1840 a shipyard in Britain launched a radically new ship. The *Nemesis* had an iron hull, a flat bottom that allowed it to navigate in shallow waters, and a steam engine to power it upriver and against the wind. In November it arrived off the coast of China, heavily armed. Though ships from Europe had been sailing to China for three hundred years, the *Nemesis* was the first steam-powered iron gunboat in Asian waters. A Chinese observer noted: "Iron is employed to make it strong. The hull is painted black, weaver's shuttle fashion. On each side is a wheel, which by the use of coal fire is made to revolve as fast as a running horse. . . . At the vessel's head is a Marine God, and at the head, stern, and sides are cannon, which give it a terrific appearance. Steam vessels are a wonderful invention of foreigners, and are calculated to offer delight to many."[8]

Instead of offering delight, the *Nemesis* and other steam-powered warships that soon joined it steamed up the Chinese rivers, bombarded forts and cities, and transported troops and supplies from place to place along the coast and up rivers far more quickly than Chinese soldiers could move on foot. With this new weapon, Britain, a small island nation half a world away, was able to defeat the largest and most populated country in the world (see Chapter 24).

The cases of Egypt, India, and China show how the demands of Western nations and the military advantage that industrialization gave them led them to interfere in the internal affairs of nonindustrial societies. As we shall see in Chapter 27, this was the start of a new age of Western dominance.

SECTION REVIEW

- Industrialization gave the newly industrialized nations of the West the power to coerce non-Western societies.
- Britain snuffed out the incipient industrialization in Egypt and India and turned these countries intro producers of raw materials.
- China stagnated and was defeated by Britain and its steam-powered gunboats.

CONCLUSION

The Industrial Revolution was the most momentous transformation in history since the beginning of agriculture. The steam engine and other new machines greatly lowered the cost and increased the production of goods like cotton and iron and the speed of transportation and communication.

The process caused social upheavals and environmental problems, however. Many entrepreneurs and businesspeople became very wealthy, while industrial workers—many of them children—worked under appalling conditions and lived in overcrowded tenements in badly polluted cities. Economists and philosophers proposed many theories and offered many solutions to the radical problems of industrial societies.

Industrialization had political consequences on a global scale. A small number of industrializing nations—first Great Britain, then those of western Europe and North America—grew more powerful. Other parts of the world were left behind to become political or economic dependencies of the powerful nations.

Eventually the industrial nations learned to alleviate their social problems, but the disparity between the rich and poor nations persisted for two centuries or more, and the environmental effects of industrialization changed from local to global.

KEY TERMS

Industrial Revolution p. 629
agricultural revolution p. 630
mass production p. 634
Josiah Wedgwood p. 635
division of labor p. 635
mechanization p. 636
Richard Arkwright p. 636
Crystal Palace p. 638
steam engine p. 638
James Watt p. 638
electric telegraph p. 640
laissez faire p. 646
mercantilism p. 647
positivism p. 647

EBOOK AND WEBSITE RESOURCES

Interactive Maps

Map 22.1 The Industrial Revolution in Britain, ca. 1850

Map 22.2 Industrialization in Europe, ca. 1850

Plus flashcards, practice quizzes, and more. Go to: www.cengage.com/history/bullietearthpeople5e

SUGGESTED READING

Ashton, T. S. *The Industrial Revolution, 1760–1830*. 1948. A classic account the British industrial revolution.

Goodman, J., and K. Honeyman. *Gainful Pursuits: The Making of Industrial Europe: 1600–1914*. 1988. Discusses industrialization outside of Britain.

Inkster, Ian. *Technology and Industrialization: Historical Case Studies and International Perspectives*. 1998. A global view of the Industrial Revolution.

Jeremy, David. *Artisans, Entrepreneurs, and Machines: Essays on the Early Anglo-American Textile Industry, 1770–1840*. 1998. Describes how American industry got started.

Landes, David. *The Unbound Prometheus: Technological Change and Industrial Development in Western Europe from 1750 to the Present*, 2nd ed. 2003. A broad synthesis of modern industrial development.

McClellan, James, III, and Harold Dorn. *Science and Technology in World History*. 1999. Emphasizes the intersection of technology and science.

Mokyr, Joel. *The Gifts of Athena: Historical Origins of the Knowledge Economy*. 2002. Examines the role and institutional bases of knowledge in the growth of the modern industrial world.

Mokyr, Joel. *The Lever of Riches: Technological Creativity and Economic Progress*. 1990. An optimistic overview of technological change.

Pomeranz, Kenneth. *The Great Divergence: Europe, China, and the Making of the Modern World Economy*. 2000. An important work comparing China and Europe in the eighteenth century.

Stearns, Peter. *The Industrial Revolution in World History.* 1993. The first book to treat industrialization as a global phenomenon.

Thompson, E. P. *The Making of the English Working Class.* 1963. Classic work on the impact on workers of industrialization.

Tilly, Louise, and Joan Scott. *Women, Work, and Family.* 1978. The impact of industrialization on women.

Tucker, Richard, and John Richards. *Global Deforestation in the Nineteenth-Century World Economy.* 1983. Looks at the negative consequences of industrialization.

Wilkinson, Richard. *Poverty and Progress: An Ecological Perspective on Economic Development.* 1973. Explores the environmental impact of industrialization.

NOTES

1. Nassau W. Senior, *Letters on the Factory Act, as it affects the cotton manufacture, addressed to the Right Honourable, the President of the Board of Trade*, 2nd ed. (London: Fellows, 1844), 20.
2. Friedrich Engels, *Condition of the Working Class in England*, trans. and ed. by W. O. Henderson and W. H. Chaloner (Oxford: Blackwell, 1958), 312.
3. Quoted in Joel Mokyr, *The Lever of Riches: Technological Creativity and Economic Progress* (New York and Oxford: Oxford University Press, 1990), 240.
4. Quoted in Lewis Mumford, *The City in History* (New York: Harcourt Brace, 1961), 460.
5. Quoted in F. Roy Willis, *Western Civilization: An Urban Perspective*, vol. II (Lexington, MA: D.C. Heath, 1973), 675.
6. Quoted in Joan W. Scott, "The Mechanization of Women's Work," *Scientific American* 247, no. 3 (September 1982): 171.
7. J. P. T. Bury, *The New Cambridge Modern History*, vol. X (Cambridge: Cambridge University Press, 1967), 10.
8. *Nautical Magazine* 12 (1843): 346.

AP* REVIEW QUESTIONS FOR CHAPTER 22

1. Which of the following was true of the Industrial Revolution?
   (A) The distribution of wealth and power generated by the Industrial Revolution was uneven.
   (B) The Industrial Revolution began with the Chinese and spread to western Europe.
   (C) Spain and Portugal became the only colonial powers that did not industrialize their colonial possessions in the New World.
   (D) The Industrial Revolution benefited only western Europe.

2. The rapid population growth experienced by Great Britain was due mainly to
   (A) having fewer colonial wars.
   (B) widespread resistance to disease and increased food supplies.
   (C) second-generation colonials returning for education.
   (D) girls being married at a younger age than they had in the Middle Ages.

3. The planting of new crops led to a second agricultural revolution in the early 1800s in western Europe. In Great Britain, in particular, this led landowners to
   (A) employ many more farmers and sharecroppers than before as a way to increase their agricultural output.
   (B) bring Irish immigrants to Great Britain because of a farm labor shortage.
   (C) enclose their lands and force tenant farmers and sharecroppers off the land.
   (D) plant American cotton to increase the amount of profit they made at market.

4. By the early eighteenth century, which of the following was a result of the Industrial Revolution?
   (A) Most European states had experienced bankruptcy due to inefficient monetary practices.
   (B) Nearly all of the food had to be imported from the colonies.
   (C) It began to create an emerging consumer economy in all of western Europe.
   (D) It generated common monetary practices, such as standardized exchange rates.

5. In comparison to other European nations in the 1790s, the aristocracy in Great Britain
   (A) was powerful and controlled all of the major economic activities in the empire.
   (B) made up the bulk of the British bureaucracy.
   (C) prohibited intermarriage among social classes to preserve its lineage.
   (D) was generally less powerful and not as centralized as in other European nations.

6. Which of the following is an accurate statement of Great Britain in the eighteenth and early nineteenth centuries?
   (A) Great Britain's true wealth came from its farmers, who produced profits with food exports.
   (B) Government intervention in the economy had launched Great Britain into becoming a true world power.
   (C) Great Britain's wealth came from African colonies and slave trading.
   (D) In Great Britain more people were involved in production for export, trade, and finance than in any other major country.

7. As in Great Britain, most nations on the continent focused their first industrial enterprises on
   (A) cotton cloth.
   (B) supplying cities with more meat and grain products.
   (C) the manufacturing of steel.
   (D) the development of a large merchant fleet.

8. Some early industrialists, such as Josiah Wedgwood, mastered the mass production of goods through
   (A) using government funds to pay the workers a decent wage.
   (B) the use of division of labor in their factories.
   (C) using only children as labor because they were fast and efficient.
   (D) hiring only young, unmarried women who needed to work.

9. One important byproduct of Watt's perfection of Newcomen's steam engine was that
   (A) beasts of burden were no longer needed for transportation.
   (B) it freed up men and women to work on farms instead of in factories.
   (C) it allowed factories to be built anywhere, not just near an energy source.
   (D) it led to an increase in the need for coal miners in Great Britain.

10. The most dramatic environmental changes brought about by the Industrial Revolution
   (A) were deforestation and famine in the New World.
   (B) were declining crop yields and crop blights.
   (C) occurred in towns.
   (D) were unemployment and homelessness.

11. In the first half of the nineteenth century in Canada and the United States, the most serious environmental impact of the Industrial Revolution was
   (A) a lack of good farmland.
   (B) strip mining for mineral resources.
   (C) deforestation.
   (D) the damming of the rivers.

12. Which of the following was true of industrial work in the first half of the nineteenth century?
   (A) It required a great deal of technical skill and led to the need for a complete education.
   (B) Most industrial jobs were unskilled, boring, and repetitive.
   (C) Only Great Britain and the United States used women and children in industrial work.
   (D) Better lighting for factories led to the majority of the work being done over two shifts, one at night.

13. The idea that government should refrain from interference in business, except to protect private property, is known as
   (A) mercantilism.
   (B) neo-Confucianism.
   (C) laissez faire.
   (D) utopian socialism.

14. The British government repealed the Corn Laws in 1846 in the name of "free trade"; however, the real intent was to
   (A) increase the numbers of workers who could be employed in factories rather than on farms.
   (B) lower the cost of food for industrial workers, which would allow employers to offer lower wages.
   (C) send cheap grain to colonies that did not have enough food.
   (D) manipulate the price of grain on the grain market and make big profits for the British government.

15. One major impediment to Chinese industrialization in the early nineteenth century was
   (A) having a foreign emperor.
   (B) a conservative elite.
   (C) a lack of capital to begin industrial enterprises.
   (D) having only one major export crop, silk.

CHAPTER

23

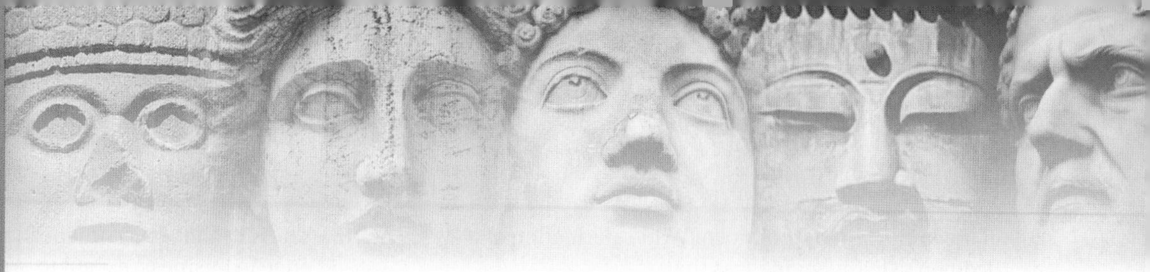

CHAPTER OUTLINE

- Independence in Latin America, 1800–1830
- The Problem of Order, 1825–1890
- The Challenge of Social and Economic Change
- Conclusion

DIVERSITY + DOMINANCE *The Afro-Brazilian Experience, 1828*

ENVIRONMENT + TECHNOLOGY *Constructing the Port of Buenos Aires, Argentina*

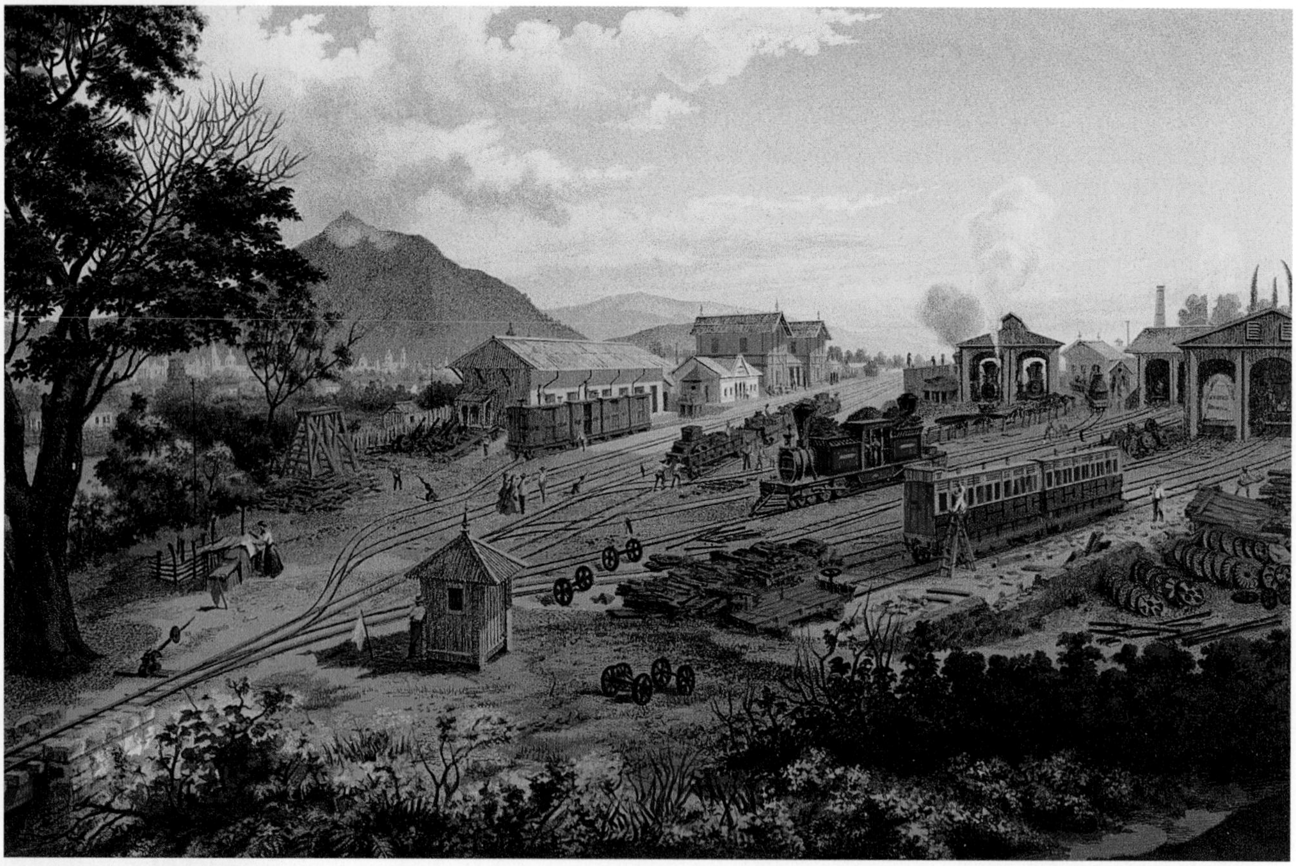

The Train Station in Orizaba, Mexico, 1877 In the last decades of the nineteenth century Mexico's political leaders actively promoted economic development. The railroad became the symbol of this ideal.

Visit the website and ebook for additional study materials and interactive tools: www.cengage.com/history/bullietearthpeople5e

State Building and Economic Transformation in the Americas, 1800–1890

- What were the causes of the revolutions for independence in Latin America?
- What major political challenges did Western Hemisphere nations face in the nineteenth century?
- How did economic modernization and the effects of abolition, immigration, and women's rights change the nations of the Western Hemisphere?

During the nineteenth century the newly independent nations of the Western Hemisphere sought to emulate the rapid economic progress of Europe under the influence of the Industrial Revolution. No technology seemed to represent that progress better than railroads. Everywhere from Argentina to Canada, governments sponsored railroad development. By 1850 there were 9,000 miles (14,480 kilometers) of track in the United States, as much as in the rest of the world. Latin American nations committed to this technology later than the United States, but railroads there also soon proved important to exports, to new industries, and to political and cultural integration.

Mexico granted the first concession for railroad construction in 1837, but the first significant rail line was completed in 1873. Few new projects were begun until the presidency of Porfirio Díaz (1876–1880 and 1884–1911), who promoted railroad construction. By the time revolutionaries forced him from office in 1910, Mexico had 12,000 miles (19,300 kilometers) of track. Railroads proved crucial to Mexican economic growth, but there was a downside. Foreign investment helped pay for new railroads, but this dependence on foreign capital led to political protests and economic nationalism. Railroad development also had a powerful effect on native peoples, who still controlled large areas of rural Mexico. Railroads made their lands more valuable, and, as a result, powerful landed families used their political influence to strip this land from indigenous subsistence farmers and use it to produce export crops. As Amerindian villagers lost their traditional lands, the number of rural uprisings increased.

In the nineteenth century the Western Hemisphere witnessed radical political and social changes in addition to technological innovations and economic expansion. Brazil and nearly all of Spain's colonies achieved independence by 1825. As was true in the earlier American and French Revolutions (see Chapter 21), rising nationalism and the ideal of political freedom promoted these changes. Despite the achievement of independence, Mexico and other nations in the hemisphere faced foreign interventions and other threats to sovereignty, including regionalism and civil war.

The new nations of the Western Hemisphere faced difficult questions. If colonies could reject submission to imperial powers, could not regions with distinct cultures, social structures, and economies refuse to accept the political authority of newly formed national governments? How could nations born in revolution accept the political strictures of written constitutions—even those they wrote themselves? How could the ideals of liberty and freedom expressed in those constitutions be reconciled with the denial of rights to Amerindians, slaves, recent immigrants, and women?

While trying to resolve these political questions, the new nations also attempted to promote economic growth. They imported new technologies like railroads, opened new areas to settlement, and promoted immigration. But the legacy of colonial economic development, with its emphasis on agricultural and mining exports, inhibited efforts to promote diversification and industrialization, just as the legacy of class and racial division thwarted the realization of political ideals.

INDEPENDENCE IN LATIN AMERICA, 1800–1830

As the eighteenth century drew to a close, Spain and Portugal held vast colonial possessions in the Western Hemisphere, although their power had declined relative to that of their British and French rivals. Both Iberian empires had reformed their colonial administration and strengthened their military forces in the eighteenth century (see Chapter 17). Despite these efforts, the same economic and political forces that had undermined British rule in its colonies were present in Spanish America and Brazil.

Roots of Revolution, to 1810

The great works of the Enlightenment as well as revolutionary documents like the American Declaration of Independence and the French Declaration of the Rights of Man and the Citizen circulated widely in Latin America, but few colonial residents wanted revolutionary change. While colonial elites and middle classes were frustrated by imperial policies, it was events in Europe that propelled the colonies toward independence. Napoleon's decision to invade Portugal (1807) and Spain (1808), not revolutionary ideas, created a crisis of legitimacy that undermined the authority of colonial officials and ignited Latin America's struggle for independence.

Napoleon Invades Portugal and Spain

As a French army neared Lisbon in 1808, the Portuguese royal family fled to Brazil. King John VI maintained his court there for over a decade. Soon Napoleon forced King Ferdinand VII of Spain to abdicate and placed his own brother, Joseph Bonaparte, on the throne. Spanish patriots fighting against the French created a new political body, the Junta (HUN-tah) Central, to administer the areas they controlled. The junta claimed authority over Spain's colonies, inviting the election of colonial deputies to help write a constitution.

Most residents of colonial Spanish America favored obedience to the Junta Central and many colonies elected deputies, but a vocal minority, including some members of the elite, objected. These dissenters argued that they were subjects of the king, not dependents of the Spanish nation. They wanted to create local juntas and govern their own affairs until Ferdinand regained the throne. Spanish loyalists resisted this assertion of local autonomy, provoking armed uprisings. In late 1808 and 1809 popular movements overthrew Spanish colonial officials in Venezuela, Mexico, and Alto Peru (modern Bolivia) and created local juntas. In each case, Spanish officials quickly reasserted control and punished the leaders. This harsh repression, however, further polarized public opinion in the colonies and gave rise to a greater sense of a separate American nationality. By 1810 Spanish colonial authorities were facing a new round of revolutions now focused on independence.

Spanish South America, 1810–1825

Revolutions Begin

In Caracas (the capital city of modern Venezuela) a revolutionary junta led by creoles (colonial-born whites) declared independence in 1811. Although this group espoused representative

CHRONOLOGY

	United States and Canada	Mexico and Central America	South America
1800	1789 U.S. Constitution ratified		
	1803 Louisiana Purchase		
			1808 Portuguese royal family arrives in Brazil
			1808–1809 Revolutions for independence begin in Spanish South America
	1812–1815 War of 1812	1810–1821 Mexican movement for independence	
1825			1822 Brazil gains independence
	1836 Texas gains independence from Mexico		1831 Brazil signs treaty with Great Britain to end slave trade. Illegal trade continues.
	1845 Texas admitted as a state	1846–1848 War between Mexico and the United States	
	1848 Women's Rights Convention in Seneca Falls, New York	1847–1870 Caste War	
1850			1850 Brazilian illegal slave trade suppressed
		1857 Mexico's new constitution limits power of Catholic Church and military	
	1861–1865 Civil War	1862–1867 French invade Mexico	1865–1870 Argentina, Uruguay, and Brazil wage war against Paraguay
	1867 Creation of Dominion of Canada	1867 Emperor Maximilian executed	
1875	1876 Sioux and allies defeat U.S. Army in Battle of Little Bighorn		1870s Governments of Argentina and Chile begin final campaigns against indigenous peoples
			1879–1881 Chile wages war against Peru and Bolivia; telegraph, refrigeration, and barbed wire introduced in Argentina
			1888 Abolition of slavery in Brazil
	1890 "Jim Crow" laws enforce segregation in South		
	1890s United States becomes world's leading steel producer		

democracy, its leaders were landowners who defended slavery and opposed full citizenship for the black and mixed-race majority. Their aim was to expand their own privileges by eliminating Spaniards from the upper levels of government and the church. The junta's narrow agenda spurred Spanish loyalists to rally thousands of free blacks and slaves to defend the Spanish Empire. Faced with this determined resistance, the revolutionary movement placed overwhelming political authority in the hands of its military leader **Simón Bolívar** (see-MOAN bow-LEE-varh) (1783–1830), who would become the preeminent leader of the independence movement.

Simón Bolívar The most important military leader in the struggle for independence in South America. Born in Venezuela, he led military forces there and in Colombia, Ecuador, Peru, and Bolivia.

Simón Bolívar

The son of wealthy Venezuelan planters, Bolívar had traveled in Europe and studied the works of the Enlightenment. He was a charismatic personality who effectively mobilized political support and held the loyalty of his troops. Defeated on many occasions, Bolívar successfully adapted his objectives and policies to attract new allies and build coalitions. Although initially opposed to the abolition of slavery, for example, he agreed to support emancipation in order to draw slaves and freemen to his cause and to gain supplies from Haiti. Bolívar was also capable of using harsh methods to ensure victory, proclaiming in 1813 that, "any Spaniard who does not . . .

AP* Exam Tip Latin American independence movements are important to understand.

work against tyranny in behalf of this just cause will be considered an enemy and punished; as a traitor to the nation, he will inevitably be shot by a firing squad."[1]

Military advantage shifted back and forth between the patriots and loyalists until Bolívar enlisted demobilized English veterans of the Napoleonic Wars and a military revolt in Spain in 1820 weakened Spanish resolve. The English veterans, hardened by combat, improved the battlefield performance of Bolívar's army, while the revolt in Spain in 1820 forced Ferdinand VII—restored to power in 1814—to accept a constitution that limited the powers of both the monarch and the church. Colonial loyalists who for a decade had fought to maintain the authority of monarch and church viewed these reforms as unacceptably liberal.

PRIMARY SOURCE: The Jamaica Letter Simón Bolívar shares his thoughts in 1815 on the present and future of the Latin American independence movement.

With the king's supporters divided, momentum swung to the patriots. After liberating present-day Venezuela, Colombia, and Ecuador, Bolívar's army entered Peru and Bolivia (colonial Alto Peru) and defeated the last Spanish armies in 1824. Bolívar and his supporters then attempted to create a confederation of the former Spanish colonies. The first steps were the creation of Gran Colombia (now Venezuela, Colombia, and Ecuador) and the unification of Peru and Bolivia, but these initiatives had failed by 1830 (see Map 23.1).

Independence of Argentina

Buenos Aires (the capital city of modern Argentina) was the second important center of revolutionary activity in Spanish South America. In Buenos Aires news of French victories in Spain led to the creation of a junta organized by militia commanders, merchants, and ranchers, which overthrew the viceroy in 1810. To deflect the opposition of Spanish loyalists, the junta claimed loyalty to the imprisoned king. Two years after Ferdinand regained the Spanish throne in 1814, junta leaders declared independence as the United Provinces of the Río de la Plata.

Patriot leaders in Buenos Aires at first sought to retain control over the territory of the Viceroyalty of Río de la Plata, but Spanish loyalists in Uruguay and Bolivia and a separatist movement in Paraguay defeated these ambitions. Even within the territory of Argentina, the government in Buenos Aires was unable to control regional rivalries and political differences. As a result, the region rapidly descended into political chaos.

San Martín and Chile

A weak succession of juntas, collective presidencies, and dictators lost control over much of the interior of Argentina. But the government in Buenos Aires did manage to support a mixed force of Chileans and Argentines led by José de San Martín (hoe-SAY deh san mar-TEEN) (1778–1850), who crossed the Andes Mountains to attack Spanish forces in Chile and Peru. During this campaign San Martín's most effective troops were former slaves, who had gained their freedom by enlisting in the army. After gaining victory in Chile, San Martín pushed on to Peru in 1820, but he failed to gain a clear victory there. Unable to make progress, San Martín surrendered command of patriot forces in Peru to Simón Bolívar, who overcame final Spanish resistance in 1824.

Mexico, 1810–1823

In 1810 Mexico was Spain's wealthiest and most populous colony. Its silver mines were the richest in the world, and the colony's capital, Mexico City, was larger than any city in Spain. Mexico also had the largest population of Spanish immigrants among the colonies. When news of Napoleon's invasion of Spain reached Mexico, conservative Spaniards in Mexico City overthrew the local viceroy because he was too sympathetic to the creoles. This action by Spanish loyalists underlined the new reality: with the king removed from his throne by the French, colonial authority now rested on brute force.

The first stage of the revolution against Spain occurred in central Mexico, where ranchers and farmers had aggressively forced Amerindian communities from their traditional agricultural lands. Crop failures and epidemics afflicted the region's rural poor, while miners and the urban poor faced higher food prices and rising unemployment as well. With the power of colonial authorities weakened by events in Spain, anger and fear spread through towns and villages in central Mexico.

Miguel Hidalgo y Costilla Mexican priest who led the first stage of the Mexican independence war in 1810. He was captured and executed in 1811.

Hidalgo and Morelos

On September 16, 1810, the parish priest of the small town of Dolores, **Miguel Hidalgo y Costilla** (mee-GEHL ee-DAHL-go ee cos-TEA-ah), rang the church bells and attracted a crowd. In a fiery speech he urged the crowd to rise up against the oppression of Spanish officials. Tens of thousands of the rural and urban poor soon joined his movement. While they lacked military discipline and weapons, they knew who their oppressors were, the Spanish and colonial-born whites who owned the ranches and mines. Recognizing the threat posed by the angry masses

MAP 23.1 **Latin America by 1830** By 1830 patriot forces had overturned the Spanish and Portuguese Empires of the Western Hemisphere. Regional conflicts, local wars, and foreign interventions challenged the survival of many of these new nations following independence.

Interactive Map

Schaalkwijk/Art Resource, NY

Padre Hidalgo Padre Miguel Hidalgo y Costilla led the first stage of Mexico's revolution for independence by rallying the rural masses. His defeat, trial, and execution made him one of Mexico's most important political martyrs.

following Hidalgo, most wealthy Mexicans supported Spanish authorities. The military tide quickly turned, and Spanish forces captured and executed Hidalgo in 1811.

The revolution continued under the leadership of another priest, **José María Morelos** (hoe-SAY mah-REE-ah moh-RAY-los), a former student of Hidalgo's. A more adept military and political leader than his mentor, Morelos created a formidable fighting force and, in 1813, convened a congress that declared independence and drafted a constitution. Despite these achievements, loyalist forces defeated and executed Morelos in 1815. Although small numbers of insurgents continued to fight Spanish forces, colonial rule seemed secure in 1820, but news of the military revolt in Spain unsettled the conservative groups who had opposed Hidalgo and Morelos. In 1821 Colonel Agustín de Iturbide (ah-goos-TEEN deh ee-tur-BEE-deh) and other loyalist commanders forged an alliance with insurgents to declare Mexico's independence. The conservative origins of Mexico's independence were made clear by the decision to create a monarchial government and crown Iturbide emperor. In early 1823, however, the army overthrew Iturbide and Mexico became a republic. When Iturbide returned to Mexico from exile in 1824, he was captured and, like Hidalgo and Morelos, was executed by a firing squad.

José María Morelos Mexican priest and former student of Miguel Hidalgo y Costilla, he led the forces fighting for Mexican independence until he was captured and executed in 1815.

Brazil, to 1831

The arrival of the Portuguese royal family in Brazil in 1808 helped maintain the loyalty of the colonial elite. With Napoleon's defeat, the Portuguese government called for King John VI to return to Portugal. At first he resisted, but a liberal revolt in Portugal forced the king to return to Portugal in 1821 to protect his throne. He left his son Pedro in Brazil as regent.

By 1820 the Spanish colonies along Brazil's borders had experienced ten years of revolution and civil war, and some, like Argentina and Paraguay, had gained independence. Unable to ignore these struggles, some Brazilians began to reevaluate Brazil's relationship with Portugal. Many Brazilians resented their homeland's economic subordination to Portugal, while the arrogance of Portuguese soldiers and bureaucrats led others to talk openly of independence.

Pedro I and Brazilian Independence

Unwilling to return to Portugal and committed to maintaining his family's hold on Brazil, Pedro aligned himself with the rising tide of sentiment, and in 1822 he declared Brazilian independence. Pedro's decision launched Brazil on a unique political trajectory. Unlike its neighbors, which became constitutional republics, Brazil gained independence as a constitutional monarchy with Pedro I, son of the king of Portugal, as emperor.

Pedro I was committed to both monarchy and to liberal principles. The constitution of 1824 provided for an elected assembly and granted rights to the political opposition, but Pedro made enemies by protecting the Portuguese who remained in Brazil from arrest and seizure of property. Pedro I also opposed slavery, even though the slave-owning class dominated Brazil. In 1823 he anonymously published an article that characterized slavery as a "cancer eating away at Brazil" (see Diversity and Dominance: The Afro-Brazilian Experience, 1828). His decision in 1831 to ratify a treaty with Great Britain ending Brazilian participation in the slave trade provoked opposition, as did his use of military force to control neighboring Uruguay. As military losses and costs rose, the Brazilian public grew impatient. A vocal minority that sought the creation of a democracy used these issues to rally public opinion against the emperor. Confronted by street demonstrations, Pedro I abdicated the throne in 1831 in favor of his five-year-old son Pedro II. After a nine-year regency, Pedro II assumed full powers as emperor of Brazil and reigned until overthrown by republicans in 1889.

SECTION REVIEW

- The French invasion of Portugal and Spain created a political crisis in their American colonies that in turn led to independence movements.
- Under the leadership of Simón Bolívar, several South American countries gained independence.
- Mexico gained independence after a long and destructive war.
- Led by the son of the Portuguese king, Brazil gained independence as a monarchy.

THE PROBLEM OF ORDER, 1825–1890

All the newly independent nations of the Western Hemisphere encountered difficulties establishing stable political institutions. Popular sovereignty found broad support across the hemisphere as all the new nations sought to establish constitutions and elected assemblies. However, this widespread support for constitutional order and for representative government failed to prevent bitter factional conflict, regionalism, and the threats posed by charismatic political leaders and military uprisings.

Constitutional Experiments

In reaction to what they saw as arbitrary and tyrannical rule by colonial authorities, revolutionary leaders in the United States and Latin America espoused constitutionalism. They believed that the careful description of political powers in written constitutions offered the best protection for individual rights and liberties. In practice, however, many new constitutions proved unworkable. In the United States, George Washington and other leaders became dissatisfied with the first constitution, the Articles of Confederation, and helped write a new constitution. In Latin America few constitutions survived the rough-and-tumble of national politics. For example, Venezuela and Chile ratified and then rejected a combined total of nine constitutions between 1811 and 1833.

Important differences in colonial political experience influenced later political developments in the Americas. The ratification of a new constitution in the United States was the culmination of a long historical process that had begun with the development of English constitutional law and continued under colonial charters. The British colonies provided many opportunities for holding elective offices, and, by the time of independence, citizens had grown accustomed to elections, political parties, and factions. In contrast, neither Brazil nor Spanish America had significant experience with elections and representative institutions.

Canadian Government

Democratic passions and the desire for effective self-rule led to significant political reform in the Americas, even in regions that remained colonies. British Canada included a number of separate colonies and territories, each with a separate government. A provincial governor and appointed advisory council drawn from the local elite dominated political life in each colony, while elected assemblies exercised limited power. The desire to make government responsive to

DIVERSITY + DOMINANCE

The Afro-Brazilian Experience, 1828

Brazil was the most important destination for the Atlantic slave trade. From the sixteenth century to the 1850s it imported more than 2 million African slaves. Beginning in the 1820s, Great Britain, Brazil's main trading partner, began to press for an end to the slave trade. British visitors to Brazil became an important source of critical information for those who sought to end the trade.

A British clergyman, Robert Walsh, who traveled widely in Brazil in 1828 and 1829 left an account of the complex and unexpected ways that slaves and black freedmen were integrated into Brazilian society.

[At the Alfandega, or custom house,] ... for the first time I saw the Negro population under circumstances so striking to a stranger. The whole labour of bearing and moving burdens is performed by these people, and the state in which they appear is revolting to humanity. Here were a number of beings entirely naked, with the exception of a covering of dirty rags tied about their waists. Their skins, from constant exposure to the weather, had become hard, crusty, and seamed, resembling the coarse black covering of some beast, or like that of an elephant, a wrinkled hide scattered with scanty hairs. On contemplating their persons, you saw them with a physical organization resembling beings of a grade below the rank of man. . . . Some of these beings were yoked to drays, on which they dragged heavy burdens. Some were chained by the necks and legs, and moved with loads thus encumbered. Some followed each other in ranks, with heavy weights on their heads, chattering the most inarticulate and dismal cadence as they moved along. Some were munching young sugar-canes, like beasts of burden eating green provender [animal feed], and some were seen near water, lying on the bare ground among filth and offal, coiled up like dogs, and seeming to expect or require no more comfort or accommodation, exhibiting a state and conformation so un-human, that they not only seemed, but actually were, far below the inferior animals around them. Horses and mules were not employed in this way; they were used only for pleasure, and not for labour. They were seen in the same streets, pampered, spirited, and richly caparisoned, enjoying a state far superior to the negroes, and appearing to look down on the fettered and burdened wretches they were passing, as on beings of an inferior rank in the creation to themselves. . . .

The first impression of all this on my mind, was to shake the conviction I had always felt, of the wrong and hardship inflicted on our black fellow creatures, and that they were only in that state which God and nature had assigned them; that they were the lowest grade of human existence, and the link that connected it with the brute, and that the gradation was so insensible, and their natures so intermingled, that it was impossible to tell where one had terminated and the other commenced; and that it was not surprising that people who contemplated them every day, so formed, so employed, and so degraded, should forget their claims to that rank in the scale of beings in which modern philanthropists are so anxious to place them. I did not at the moment myself recollect, that the white man, made a slave on the coast of Africa, suffers not only a similar mental but physical deterioration from hardships and emaciation, and becomes in time the dull and deformed beast I now saw yoked to a burden.

A few hours only were necessary to correct my first impressions of the negro population, by seeing them under a different aspect. We were attracted by the sound of military music, and found it proceeded from a regiment drawn up in one of the streets. Their colonel had just died, and they attended to form a procession to celebrate his obsequies. They were all of different shades of black, but the majority were negroes. Their equipment was excellent; they wore dark jackets, white pantaloons, and black leather caps and belts, all which, with their arms, were in high order. Their band produced sweet and agreeable music, of the leader's own composition, and the men went through some evolutions with regularity and dexterity. They were only a militia regiment, yet were as well appointed and disciplined as one of our regiments of the line. Here then was the first step in that gradation by which the black population of this country ascend in the scale of humanity; he advances from the state below that of a beast of burden into a military rank, and he shows himself as capable of discipline and improvement as a human being of any other colour.

Our attention was next attracted by negro men and women bearing about a variety of articles for sale; some in baskets, some on boards and cases carried on their heads. They

Confederation of 1867 Negotiated union of the formerly separate colonial governments of Ontario, Quebec, New Brunswick, and Nova Scotia. This new Dominion of Canada with a central government in Ottawa is seen as the beginning of the Canadian nation.

the will of the assemblies led to armed rebellion in 1837. Britain responded by establishing limited self-rule in each of the Canadian provinces. By the 1860s regional political leaders realized that economic development required a government with a "national" character. Negotiations among Canadian leaders and with the British crown led to a union of Canadian provinces, the **Confederation of 1867**, and to the creation of the Dominion of Canada with a central government in Ottawa (see Map 23.2).

The path to effective constitutional government was rockier to the south. Because neither Spain nor Portugal had permitted anything like the elected legislatures and municipal governments of colonial British America, the drafters of Latin American constitutions were less con-

belonged to a class of small shopkeepers, many of whom vend their wares at home, but the greater number send them about in this way, as in itinerant shops. A few of these people were still in a state of bondage, and brought a certain sum every evening to their owners, as the produce of their daily labour. But a large proportion, I was informed, were free, and exercised this little calling on their own account. They were all very neat and clean in their persons, and had a decorum and sense of respectability about them, superior to whites of the same class and calling. All their articles were good in their kind, and neatly kept, and they sold them with simplicity and confidence, neither wishing to take advantage of others, nor suspecting that it would be taken of themselves. I bought some confectionary from one of the females, and I was struck with the modesty and propriety of her manner; she was a young mother, and had with her a neatly dressed child, of which she seemed very fond. I gave it a little comfit [candy covered nut], and it turned up its dusky countenance to her and then to me, taking my sweetmeat, and at the same time kissing my hand. As yet unacquainted with the coin of the country, I had none that was current about me, and was leaving the articles; but the poor young woman pressed them on me with a ready confidence, repeating in broken Portuguese, out of tempo, I am sorry to say, the "other time" never came, for I could not recognize her person afterwards to discharge her little debt, though I went to the same place for the purpose.

It soon began to grow dark, and I was attracted by a number of persons bearing large lighted wax tapers, like torches, gathering before a house. As I passed by, one was put into my hand by a man who seemed in some authority, and I was requested to fall into a procession that was forming. It was the preparation for a funeral, and on such occasions, I learned that they always request the attendance of a passing stranger, and feel hurt if they are refused. I joined the party, and proceeded with them to a neighbouring church. When we entered we arranged ourselves on each side of a platform which stood near the choir, on which was laid an open coffin, covered with pink silk and gold borders. The funeral service was chanted by a choir of priests, one of whom was a negro, a large comely man, whose jet black visage formed a strong and striking contrast to his white vestments. He seemed to perform his part with a decorum and sense of solemnity, which I did not observe in his brethren. After scattering flowers on the coffin, and fumigating it with incense, they retired, the procession dispersed, and we returned on board. I had been but a few hours on shore, for the first time, and I saw an African negro under four aspects of society; and it appeared to me, that in every one his character depended on the state in which he was placed, and the estimation in which he was held. As a despised slave, he was far lower than other animals of burthen that surrounded him; more miserable in his look, more revolting in his nakedness, more distorted in his person, and apparently more deficient in intellect than the horses and mules that passed him by. Advanced to the grade of a soldier, he was clean and neat in his person, amenable to discipline, expert at his exercises, and showed the port [sic.] and being of a white man similarly placed. As a citizen, he was remarkable for the respectability of his appearance, and the decorum of his manners in the rank assigned him; and as a priest, standing in the house of God, appointed to instruct society on their most important interests, and in a grade in which moral and intellectual fitness is required, and a certain degree of superiority is expected, he seemed even more devout in his impressions, and more correct in his manners, than his white associates. I came, therefore, to the irresistible conclusion in my mind, that colour was an accident affecting the surface of a man, and having no more to do with his qualities than his clothes—that God had equally created an African in the image of his person, and equally given him an immortal soul; and that an European had no pretext but his own cupidity, for impiously thrusting his fellow man from that rank in the creation which the Almighty had assigned him, and degrading him below the lot of the brute beasts that perish.

QUESTIONS FOR ANALYSIS

1. What is the author's first impression of the Brazilian slave population?
2. What does the author later observe that changes this opinion?
3. How did slavery dehumanize slaves?
4. What circumstances or opportunities permitted Brazil's free blacks to improve their lives?

Source: Robert Edgar Conrad, *Children of God's Fire: A Documentary History of Black Slavery in Brazil* (Princeton, N.J.: Princeton University Press, 1983), 216–220. Reprinted by permission of the author.

Creating Latin American Nations

strained by practical political experience. As a result, many of the new Latin American nations experimented with untested political institutions.

Latin American nations found it particularly difficult to define the role of the Catholic Church after independence. In the colonial period the Catholic Church was a religious monopoly that controlled all levels of education and dominated intellectual life. Many early constitutions aimed to reduce this power by making education secular and by permitting other religions. The church reacted by organizing and financing conservative movements. Conflicts between liberals who sought the separation of church and state and conservatives who supported the church dominated political life in the nineteenth century.

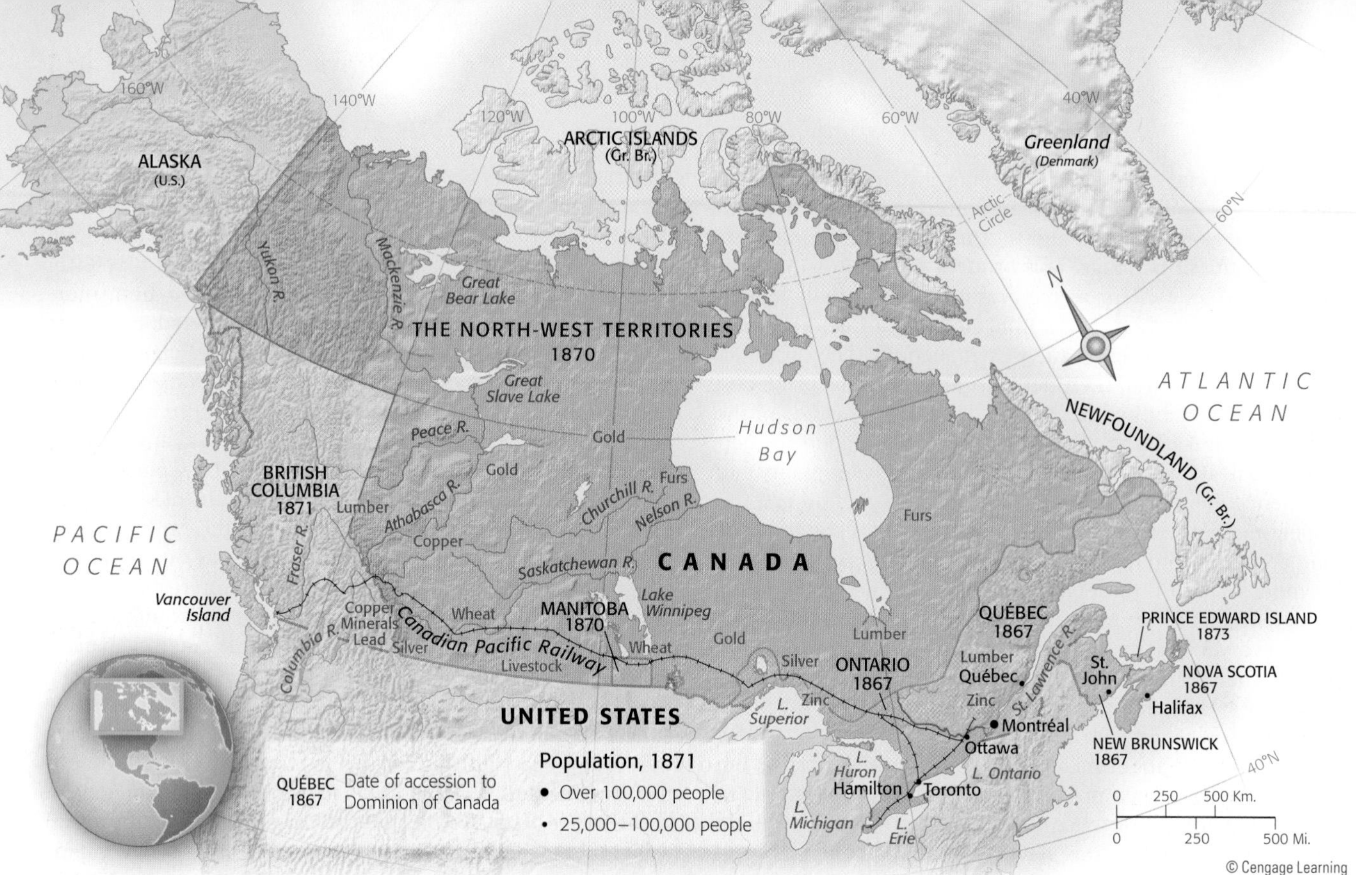

MAP 23.2 **Dominion of Canada, 1873** Although independence was not yet achieved and settlement remained concentrated along the U.S. border, Canada had established effective political and economic control over its western territories by 1873.

e Interactive Map

Limiting the power of the military was another obstacle to the creation of constitutional governments in Latin America. The wars for independence elevated the prestige of military leaders, and, when the wars were over, military commanders seldom proved willing to subordinate themselves to civilian authorities. Frustrated by the chaotic workings of democracy, many citizens saw dictatorship as a better protection for their lives and property.

Personalist Leaders

personalist leaders Political leaders who rely on charisma and their ability to mobilize and direct the masses of citizens outside the authority of constitutions and laws. Nineteenth-century examples include José Antonio Páez of Venezuela and Andrew Jackson of the United States. Twentieth-century examples include Getulio Vargas of Brazil and Juan Perón of Argentina.

Patriot leaders in both the United States and Latin America gained mass followings during the wars for independence, and some used these followings to gain political power. George Washington's ability to dominate early republican politics in the United States anticipated the later political ascendancy of revolutionary heroes such as Iturbide in Mexico and Bolívar in Gran Colombia. In each case, military reputation provided the foundation for personal political power. Washington was distinguished from these leaders by his willingness to surrender power. More commonly, **personalist leaders** relied on their mass followings rather than on constitutions and laws to govern. In Latin America, a personalist leader who gained and held political power without constitutional sanction was called a *caudillo* (kouh-DEE-yoh).

Two Personalist Leaders: Jackson and Páez

Powerful personal followings allowed **Andrew Jackson** of the United States and **José Antonio Páez** (hoe-SAY an-TOE-nee-oh PAH-ays) of Venezuela to challenge constitutional limits to their authority. During the independence wars in Venezuela and Colombia, Páez (1790–1873) was one of Bolívar's most successful generals. Like most of his followers, Páez was uneducated and poor, but his physical strength, courage, and guile made him a natural guerrilla leader and helped him build a powerful political base. Páez described his authority in the following manner: "[The soldiers] resolved to confer on me the supreme command and blindly to obey my will, confident . . . that I was the only one who could save them."[2] Able to count on the personal loyalty of his followers, Páez was seldom willing to accept the constitutional authority of a distant president.

Andrew Jackson First president of the United States to be born in humble circumstances. He was popular among frontier residents, urban workers, and small farmers. He had a successful political career as judge, general, congressman, senator, and president. After being denied the presidency in 1824 in a controversial election, he won in 1828 and was reelected in 1832.

José Antonio Páez Venezuelan soldier who led Simón Bolívar's cavalry force. He became a successful general in the war and built a powerful political base. Unwilling to accept the constitutional authority of Bolívar's government in distant Bogotá, he declared Venezuela's independence from Gran Colombia in 1829.

After defeating the Spanish, Bolívar pursued his dream of forging a union of former Spanish colonies modeled on the United States. But he underestimated the strength of nationalist sentiment unleashed by the independence wars. Páez and other Venezuelan leaders resisted the surrender of their hard-won power to Bolívar's Gran Colombian government in distant Bogotá. When political opponents challenged Bolívar in 1829, Páez declared Venezuela's independence. Merciless to his enemies and indulgent with his followers, Páez ruled the country as president or dictator for the next eighteen years. Despite implementing an economic program favorable to the elite, Páez remained popular with the masses. Even as his personal wealth grew, Páez took care to present himself as a common man.

Andrew Jackson (1767–1845) was the first U.S. president born in humble circumstances. A self-made man who eventually acquired substantial property and owned over a hundred slaves, Jackson was extremely popular among frontier residents, urban workers, and small farmers. Although he was notorious for his untidy personal life as well as for dueling, his courage, individualism, and willingness to challenge authority helped him attain political success as judge, general, congressman, senator, and president.

During his military career, Jackson proved to be impatient with civilian authorities. Widely known because of his victories over the Creek and Seminole peoples, he was elevated to the pinnacle of American politics by his celebrated defeat of the British at the Battle of New Orleans in 1815 and by his seizure of Florida from the Spanish in 1818. In 1824 he received a plurality of the popular votes for president but failed to win a majority of electoral votes. His followers were embittered when the House of Representatives chose John Quincy Adams as president.

Jackson's followers viewed his landslide election victory in 1828 and reelection in 1832 as the triumph of democracy over entrenched aristocracy. In office Jackson challenged constitutional limits on his authority, increasing presidential power at the expense of Congress and the Supreme Court. Like Páez, Jackson was able to dominate national politics by blending a populist political style that celebrated the virtues and cultural enthusiasms of common people with support for policies that promoted the economic interests of powerful propertied groups.

Personalist leaders were common in both Latin America and the United States, but Latin America's weaker constitutional tradition, more limited protection of property rights, lower literacy levels, and less-developed communications systems facilitated the ambitions of popular politicians. Latin America's personalist leaders often ignored constitutional restraints on their authority, and election results seldom determined access to presidential power. As a result, by 1900 every Latin American nation had experienced periods of dictatorship.

The Threat of Regionalism

After independence, national governments were generally weaker than the colonial governments they replaced. Debates over tariffs, tax and monetary policies, and, in many nations, slavery and the slave trade led regional elites to attempt secession. Some of the hemisphere's newly independent nations did not survive these struggles, while others lost territories to aggressive neighbors.

In Spanish America all postindependence efforts to forge large multistate federations failed. The Viceroyalty of New Spain included Central America and Mexico, but after independence this union failed when in 1823 local elites broke with Mexico to form the Republic of Central America. A new round of regional disputes and civil wars led to the creation of five separate nations during the 1820s and 1830s. In South America, Bolívar attempted to maintain the colonial unity of Venezuela, Colombia, and Ecuador by creating Gran Colombia with its capital in Bogotá. But even before his death in 1830, Venezuela and Ecuador had become independent states. In the colonial era Argentina, Uruguay, Paraguay, and Bolivia were organized as a single viceroyalty with its capital in Buenos Aires. After the defeat of Spain the leaders in Paraguay, Uruguay, and Bolivia declared their independence from Argentina.

Regionalism threatened the United States as well. The defense of state and regional interests played an important role in the framing of the U.S. Constitution. Many important constitutional provisions represented compromises forged among competing state and regional leaders. Yet, despite these constitutional compromises, regional rivalries still threatened the nation.

Slavery divided the nation into two separate and competitive societies. A rising tide of immigration to the northern states in the 1830s and 1840s began to move the center of political power away from the south. Southern leaders sought to protect slavery by expanding into new territories. They supported the Louisiana Purchase in 1803 (see Map 23.3), which transferred to the United States a vast French territory extending from the Gulf of Mexico to Canada, and the Mexican-American War in 1846. However, this territorial expansion forced a national debate about slavery that led to the election of Abraham Lincoln as president in 1860.

Lincoln was committed to checking the spread of slavery, and his election provoked the southern planter elite to choose the dangerous course of secession from the Union. The seceding states formed a new government, the Confederate States of America, known as the Confederacy. Lincoln preserved the Union but at an enormous cost. The U.S. Civil War (1861–1865) was the most destructive conflict in the history of the Western Hemisphere. More than 600,000 lives were lost before the Confederacy surrendered in 1865. The Union victory led to the abolition of slavery and also transferred national political power to a northern elite committed to industrial expansion and federal support for the construction of railroads and other internal improvements.

e Interactive Map

MAP 23.3 Territorial Growth of the United States, 1783–1853 The rapid western expansion of the United States resulted from aggressive diplomacy and warfare against Mexico and Amerindian peoples. Railroad development helped integrate the trans-Mississippi west and promote economic expansion.

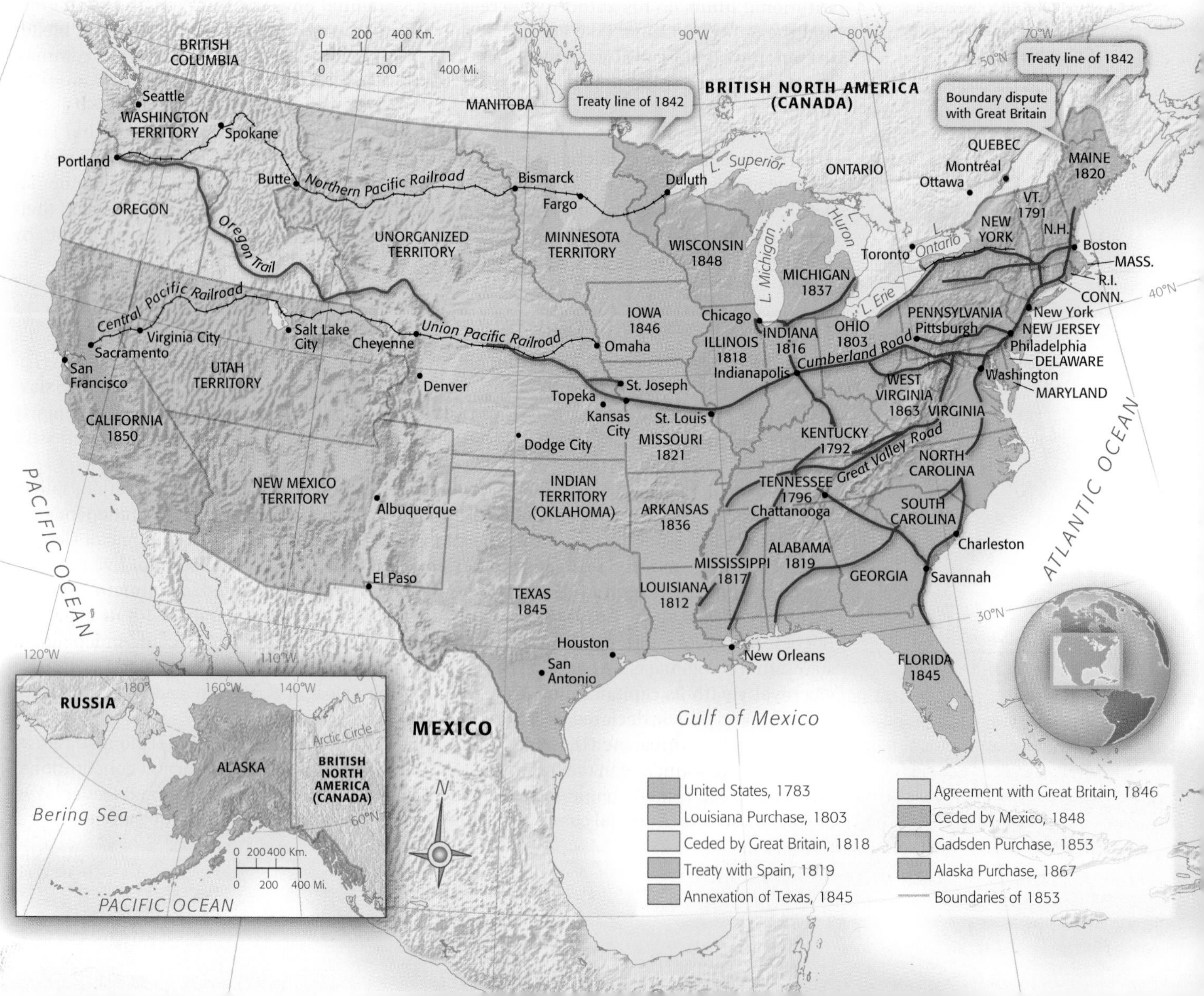

The Confederate States of America was better prepared politically and economically for independence than were the successful secessionist movements that broke up Gran Colombia and other Spanish American federations. Nevertheless, the Confederacy failed, in part because of poor timing. The new nations of the Western Hemisphere were most vulnerable to secessionist movements in the early years of their existence; indeed, all the successful secessions occurred shortly after independence. In the case of the United States, an experienced national government legitimated and strengthened by more than seven decades of relative stability and reinforced by dramatic economic and population growth defeated secession only with enormous effort.

Foreign Interventions and Regional Wars

Wars often determined national borders, access to natural resources, and control of markets in the Western Hemisphere. Even after the achievement of independence, Mexico and other Western Hemisphere nations had to defend themselves against Europe's great powers. Contested national borders and regional rivalries also led to wars between Western Hemisphere nations. By the end of the nineteenth century the United States, Brazil, Argentina, and Chile had all successfully waged wars against their neighbors and established themselves as regional powers.

Wars with European Powers

Within thirty years of independence, the United States fought a second war with England—the War of 1812. The burning of the White House and Capitol by British troops in 1814 symbolized the weakness of the new republic. By the end of the nineteenth century, however, the United States was the hemisphere's greatest military power. Its war against Spain in 1898–1899 created an American empire that reached from the Philippines in the Pacific Ocean to Puerto Rico in the Caribbean Sea (see Chapter 27).

European powers also challenged the sovereignty of Latin American nations. Following independence Argentina faced British and French naval blockades, and British naval forces systematically violated Brazil's territorial waters to stop the importation of slaves. Mexico faced the most serious threats to sovereignty, defeating a weak Spanish invasion in 1829, a French assault on the city of Veracruz in 1838, and a French invasion in 1862.

Threats to Mexican Sovereignty

Mexico also faced a grave threat from the United States. In the 1820s Mexico had encouraged Americans to immigrate to its northern province of Texas. By the early 1830s Americans outnumbered Mexican nationals in Texas and were aggressively challenging Mexican laws such as

Execution of Emperor Maximilian of Mexico This painting by Edouard Manet shows the 1867 execution by firing squad of Maximilian and two of his Mexican generals. The defeat of the French intervention was a great triumph for Mexican patriots led by Benito Juárez.

Erich Lessing/Art Resource, NY

the prohibition of slavery. An alliance of Mexican liberals and American settlers rebelled in 1835 and gained its independence in 1836. In 1845 the United States made Texas a state, provoking war with Mexico a year later. The surrender of Mexico City in 1848 to American forces compelled Mexico to accept a harsh treaty that forced it to cede vast territories to the United States, including present-day New Mexico, Arizona, and California. In return Mexico received $15 million. When gold was discovered in California in 1848, the magnitude of Mexico's loss became clear.

Benito Juárez President of Mexico (1858–1872). Born in poverty in Mexico, he was educated as a lawyer and rose to become chief justice of the Mexican supreme court and then president. He led Mexico's resistance to a French invasion in 1862 and the installation of Maximilian as emperor.

With the very survival of the nation at stake, Mexico's liberals took power and imposed sweeping reforms, including a new constitution in 1857 that limited the power of the Catholic Church and military. This provoked a civil war with conservatives (1858–1861). **Benito Juárez** (beh-NEE-toh WAH-rez) assumed the presidency and defeated the conservatives, who then turned to Napoleon III of France for assistance. In 1862, French forces invaded Mexico, forced Juárez to flee Mexico City, and installed the Austrian Habsburg Maximilian as emperor of Mexico. After years of warfare, Juárez drove the French army out of Mexico in 1867, aided by U.S. diplomatic pressure. After capturing Maximilian, Juárez ordered his execution.

This victory over a powerful foreign enemy redeemed a nation earlier humiliated by the United States. But the creation of democracy proved more elusive than the protection of Mexican sovereignty. Despite the Mexican constitution's prohibition of presidential reelection, Juárez would serve as president until his death in 1872.

Wars Among American Nations

As was clear in the Mexican-American War, wars between Western Hemisphere nations could lead to dramatic territorial changes. Chile established itself as the leading military and economic power on the west coast of South America when it fought two successful wars against an alliance of Peru and Bolivia (1836–1839 and 1879–1883). The second contest, the War of the Pacific, forced Bolivia to cede its only outlet to the sea and Peru to yield rich mining districts.

Argentina and Brazil fought for control of Uruguay in the 1820s, but a military stalemate eventually forced them to recognize Uruguayan independence. Then, in 1865, Argentina and Uruguay joined Brazil to wage war against Paraguay (War of the Triple Alliance). After five years of warfare, the Paraguayan dictator Francisco Solano López (fran-CEES-co so-LAN-oh LOH-pehz) and more than 20 percent of the nation's population had died. Paraguay then experienced military occupation, loss of territory, and economic penalties.

Native Peoples and the Nation-State

Both diplomacy and war shaped relations between the Western Hemisphere's new nation-states and indigenous peoples. During late colonial times, Spanish, Portuguese, and British colonial governments attempted to restrict the expansion of settlements into territories occupied by Amerindians. With independence, the colonial powers' role as mediator and protector ended.

Still-independent Amerindian peoples posed a significant military challenge to many Western Hemisphere republics. Weakened by civil wars and constitutional crises, new nations were less able to maintain frontier peace than the colonial governments they replaced. After independence Amerindian peoples in Argentina, the United States, Chile, and Mexico succeeded in pushing back frontier settlements. Despite early victories, native military resistance was overcome by 1890.

The United States and Native Peoples

Tecumseh Shawnee leader who attempted to organize an Amerindian confederacy to prevent the loss of additional territory to American settlers. He became an ally of the British in War of 1812 and died in battle.

After the American Revolution, tens of thousands of settlers entered territories previously guaranteed to Amerindians by treaties with Britain. Indigenous leaders responded by forging military alliances with British officials in Canada and with other native peoples. In the Ohio River Valley two Shawnee brothers, **Tecumseh** (teh-CUM-sah) and Prophet (Tenskwatawa), created a broad, well-organized alliance among Amerindian peoples that gained British support. During the War of 1812, American military forces defeated the alliance. Tecumseh died in battle fighting alongside his British allies.

Throughout the 1820s native peoples lost lands to settlers across the Midwest and Southeast. The 1828 presidential election of Andrew Jackson, a veteran of earlier wars against native peoples, brought matters to a head. The Indian Removal Act of 1830 forced the resettlement of Cherokee, Creek, Choctaw, and other eastern peoples to land west of the Mississippi River. Nearly half these forced migrants died on this journey, known as the Trail of Tears.

The native peoples of the Great Plains offered formidable resistance to the expansion of white settlement. By the time substantial numbers of white buffalo hunters, cattlemen, and

National Anthropological Archives, Smithsonian Institution, SPC BAE 4420 Vol 6 01007800

Navajo Leaders Gathered in Washington to Negotiate As settlers pushed west in the nineteenth century, Amerindian peoples were forced to negotiate territorial concessions with the U.S. government. This photo shows Navajo leaders and their Anglo translators in Washington, D.C., in 1874.

settlers reached the American west, indigenous peoples were skilled in the use of horses and firearms. These technologies allowed the Sioux, Comanche, Pawnee, Kiowa, and other plains peoples to hunt more efficiently and develop potent military capacities.

After the Civil War a new wave of settlers pushed onto the plains. Buffalo herds were hunted to near extinction and native lands lost to farmers and ranchers. Amerindian resistance led to four decades of armed conflict with the United States Army. The U.S. government forced the Comanche, who had long dominated the southern plains, to cede their traditional lands in Texas in 1865. The Sioux and their allies held out longer, overwhelming General George Armstrong Custer and the Seventh Cavalry in the Battle of Little Bighorn in 1876, but they were also soon forced to accept reservation life. Military campaigns in the 1870s and 1880s then broke the resistance of the Apache.

Defeat of the Amerindians of Argentina and Chile

The indigenous peoples of Argentina and Chile experienced a similar trajectory of adaptation, resistance, and defeat. Herds of wild cattle provided these peoples with a limitless food supply, and their mastery of the horse increased their military capacities. For a while the natives of Argentina and Chile were able to check the southern expansion of agriculture and ranching. Unable to defeat these resourceful enemies, the governments of Argentina and Chile relied on an elaborate system of gift giving and prisoner exchanges to maintain peace on the frontier.

By the 1860s, however, population increase, political stability, and military modernization allowed Argentina and Chile to take the offensive. In the 1870s the government of Argentina used a large military force armed with modern weapons to crush native resistance on the pampas. In the 1850s, civil war and an economic depression weakened the Chilean government, and the Mapuches (mah-POO-chez) (also called "Araucanians") pushed back frontier settlements, but by the 1870s Chilean forces had overwhelmed Amerindian resistance.

In Chile, Argentina, and the United States, national governments justified military campaigns by demonizing native peoples. Newspaper editorials and the speeches of politicians

Caste War A rebellion of the Maya people against the government of Mexico in 1847 that nearly returned the Yucatán to Maya rule. Some Maya rebels retreated to unoccupied territories, where they held out until 1901.

portrayed Amerindians as brutal and cruel, and as obstacles to progress. In April 1859 a Chilean newspaper commented:

> *The necessity, not only to punish the Araucanian [Mapuche] race, but also to make it impotent to harm us, is well recognized . . . as the only way to rid the country of a million evils. It is well understood that they are odious and prejudicial guests in Chile . . . conciliatory measures have accomplished nothing with this stupid race—the infamy and disgrace of the Chilean nation.*[3]

Political divisions and civil wars within the new nations also provided opportunities for some long-pacified native peoples to rebel. In the Yucatán region of Mexico, large landowners forced many Maya (MY-ah) communities from traditional agricultural lands, reducing thousands to peonage. Weakened by internal rebellions and by the American invasion, the Mexican government faced a mass rebellion by the Maya in 1847. This well-organized and popular uprising, known as the **Caste War**, nearly returned the Yucatán to native control. Grievances accumulated over more than three hundred years led to great violence and property destruction. The end of the war with the United States allowed the government of Mexico to regain control of major towns. Even then, some Maya rebels retreated to unoccupied territories and created an independent state, which they called the "Empire of the Cross." Organized around a mix of traditional beliefs and Christian symbols, this indigenous state resisted Mexican forces until 1870. A few Maya strongholds survived until 1901.

SECTION REVIEW

- The new states of the Western Hemisphere, including the United States, found it difficult to establish constitutional governments.
- Charismatic military leaders with large followings, like Andrew Jackson and José Antonio Páez, often took power and challenged constitutional limits on presidential power.
- Secessionist movements and civil wars threatened the survival of many Latin American nations and the United States.
- Wars with foreign powers and neighboring states endangered the independence and national borders of many Western Hemisphere nations.
- Native peoples throughout the hemisphere tried to defend their territories, but by the end of the nineteenth century, national governments had overcome native resistance.

THE CHALLENGE OF SOCIAL AND ECONOMIC CHANGE

During the nineteenth century the newly independent nations of the Western Hemisphere struggled to realize the Enlightenment ideals of freedom and individual liberty that had helped ignite the revolutions for independence. The persistence of slavery and other oppressive colonial-era institutions slowed this process. Nevertheless, by century's end reform movements had ended the slave trade, abolished slavery, expanded voting rights, and assimilated immigrants from Asia and Europe.

Industrialization and integration in the world economy sometimes challenged political stability and social arrangements. While a small number of Western Hemisphere nations embraced industrialization, most were dependent on the export of agricultural and mining production. By the end of the century it was clear that the industrializing nations had grown richer than the nations that remained exporters of raw materials. All the region's economies, regardless of development path, had become more vulnerable and volatile as a result of greater dependence on foreign markets. Like contemporary movements for social reform, efforts to assert economic sovereignty produced powerful new political forces.

The Abolition of Slavery

Leaders of the independence movements of the United States and Latin America asserted ideals of universal freedom and citizenship that contrasted sharply with the reality of slavery. Those

abolitionists Men and women who agitated for a complete end to slavery. Abolitionist pressure ended the British transatlantic slave trade in 1808 and slavery in British colonies in 1834. In the United States the activities of abolitionists were one factor leading to the Civil War (1861–1865).

who sought to end the institution were called **abolitionists**. Despite their efforts, slavery survived in most of the hemisphere until the 1850s. It proved most difficult to achieve the abolition of slavery in regions where the export of plantation products was most important—such as the United States, Brazil, and Cuba.

Slavery in the United States was weakened first by the abolition of slavery in some northern states and by the end of the African slave trade in 1808. But the profitable expansion of cotton agriculture after the War of 1812 stalled progress. In Spanish America tens of thousands of slaves gained freedom by joining revolutionary armies during the wars for independence. After independence, most Spanish American republics prohibited the slave trade, but growing international demand for sugar and coffee slowed the achievement of abolition. As prices rose for plantation products, Brazil and Cuba increased their imports of slaves.

Abolition in the United States

During the long struggle to end slavery in the United States, American abolitionists argued that slavery offended Christian morality and the universal rights asserted in the Declaration of Independence. Abolitionist Theodore Weld articulated the religious objection to slavery in 1834:

> *No condition of birth, no shade of color, no mere misfortune of circumstance, can annul the birth-right charter, which God has bequeathed to every being upon whom he has stamped his own image, by making him a free* moral agent *[emphasis in original], and that he who robs his fellow man of this tramples upon right, subverts justice, outrages humanity . . . and sacrilegiously assumes the prerogative of God.*[4]

AP* Exam Tip
Changes in social structure, such as the abolition of slavery, are important concepts to understand.

Two groups denied full rights under the Constitution, women and free African Americans, played important roles in the abolition of slavery. Women were among the leaders of the American Anti-Slavery Society and produced effective propaganda against slavery. Eventually, thousands of women joined the abolitionist cause. Social conservatives attacked their highly visible public role, leading many women to become public advocates of female suffrage as well. Frederick Douglass, a former slave, was one of the most visible and effective leaders of the abolitionist movement. Some black leaders, believing that peaceful means would fail, pushed the abolitionist movement to accept the inevitability of violence. In 1843 Henry Highland Garnet stirred the National Colored Convention when he demanded, "Brethren, arise, arise, arise! . . . Let every slave in the land do this and the days of slavery are numbered."[5]

In the 1850s the electoral strength of the newly formed Republican Party forced a confrontation between slave and free states. Following the election of Abraham Lincoln in 1860, eleven southern states seceded from the Union. During the Civil War pressure for emancipation rose as tens of thousands of black freemen and escaped slaves joined the Union army. In 1863, in the midst of the Civil War and two years after the abolition of serfdom in Russia (see Chapter 25), Lincoln issued the Emancipation Proclamation, ending slavery in rebel states not occupied by the Union army. In 1865 the Thirteenth Amendment to the Constitution abolished slavery completely, but most African Americans continued to live in harsh conditions. By the end of the century southern states had instituted "Jim Crow" laws that segregated blacks in public transportation, jobs, and schools. The implementation of these laws coincided with increased racial violence that saw an average of fifty African Americans lynched each year.

Abolition in Brazil

In Brazil slavery survived for more than two decades after abolition in the United States. Britain, Brazil's major trading partner, pressed for an end to the slave trade. Despite an 1830 agreement to end the trade, Brazil imported another half-million African slaves before the British navy forced compliance in the 1850s. The Brazilian emperor, Pedro II, and many liberals worked to abolish slavery, but their effort to find a form of gradual emancipation acceptable to slave owners failed.

During Brazil's war with Paraguay (1865–1870), large numbers of slaves joined the Brazilian army in exchange for freedom. Their patriotism and heroism convinced many Brazilians of the injustice of slavery. Educated Brazilians had also come to view slavery as an obstacle to economic development and an impediment to democratic reform. When political support for slavery weakened in the 1880s, growing numbers of slaves fled their masters and army officers resisted demands to capture and return the runaways. Brazil finally abolished slavery in 1888. A year later a rebellion ended the Brazilian monarchy.

Courtesy, Fundacao Biblioteca Nacional, Brazil

A Former Brazilian Slave Returns from Military Service The heroic actions of black freemen and slaves in the Paraguayan War (1865–1870) led many Brazilians to condemn slavery. The original caption for this drawing reads: "On his return from the war in Paraguay: Full of glory, covered with laurels, after having spilled his blood in defense of the fatherland and to free a people from slavery, the volunteer sees his own mother bound and whipped! Awful reality!"

The Caribbean region received almost 40 percent of all African slaves shipped to the New World. Throughout the region, tiny white minorities lived surrounded by slave and free colored majorities. In the eighteenth century the slave rebellion in Saint Domingue (see Chapter 21) spread terror among slave owners across the Caribbean, convincing slave owners that any effort to overthrow colonial rule would unleash new insurrection. As a result, there was little local support for abolition in the Caribbean. In these colonies abolition would result from decisions made in Europe by imperial governments.

Abolition in the Caribbean

In the Caribbean, as in Brazil and other plantation economies, slaves helped to force abolition by rebelling, running away, and resisting in more subtle ways. Although slave rebellions in Jamaica and Cuba and other Caribbean colonies failed to imitate the success of the Haitian Revolution (1791–1804), they made clear that slaves would never accept their condition.

After 1800, when the profitability of sugar plantations in the British West Indian colonies declined, a coalition of British labor unions, Protestant ministers, and free traders pushed for the abolition of slavery. Britain, the major participant in the eighteenth-century expansion of slavery in the Americas, ended its participation in the slave trade in 1807. It then negotiated treaties with Spain, Brazil, and other importers of slaves to eliminate the slave trade and used its naval forces to force compliance.

Abolition in British colonies occurred in 1834, but "freed" slaves were compelled to remain with former masters as "apprentices." Abuses by planters and resistance to apprenticeship by former slaves led to complete abolition in 1838. A decade later, France abolished slavery in its Caribbean colonies. Abolition of slavery in the Dutch Empire in 1863 freed 33,000 slaves in Surinam and 12,000 in the Antilles.

In the Caribbean, slavery lasted longest in Spain's remaining colonies of Cuba and Puerto Rico. Britain used diplomatic pressure and naval force to undermine the slave trade after 1820, but local support for abolition appeared as well. Both Cuba and Puerto Rico had larger white and free colored populations than did the Caribbean colonies of Britain and France, and there was little fear that abolition would lead to the political ascendancy of former slaves. In Puerto Rico, where slaves numbered approximately 30,000, local reformers secured the abolition of slavery in 1873. In Cuba, where slavery was much more important, forces supporting independence propelled the Spanish colonial government toward abolition. Beginning in the 1870s, Spain passed a series of laws promoting gradual abolition but requiring long periods of service to former masters. Spain finally abolished slavery in 1886.

Immigration

During the colonial period free Europeans were a minority among immigrants to the Western Hemisphere. From 1500 to 1760 African slaves entering the Western Hemisphere outnumbered European immigrants by nearly two to one. Another 4 million African slaves were imported before the end of the slave trade in the 1850s. After the African slave trade came to an end, millions of Europeans and Asians arrived in the Western Hemisphere as immigrants. These

Vancouver Public Library, Special Collections, VPL #17064

Chinese Funeral in Vancouver, Canada In the 1890s Vancouver was an important destination for Chinese immigrants. This photo shows how an important element of traditional Chinese culture thrived among the storefronts and streetcar lines of the late-Victorian Canadian city.

nineteenth-century immigrants helped foster the rapid economic growth and territorial occupation of frontier regions in the United States, Canada, Argentina, Chile, and Brazil. By century's end nearly all of the hemisphere's fastest-growing cities (Buenos Aires, Chicago, New York, and São Paulo, for example) had large immigrant populations. In general, European immigrants avoided regions that had depended on slavery with their tradition of repression and low wages. Tens of thousands of immigrants from China and India arrived with indenture contracts that directed them to plantation zones in the Caribbean.

European Immigration

Europe provided the majority of immigrants to the Western Hemisphere in the nineteenth century. Initially, most came from western Europe, but after 1870 most immigrants were southern or eastern Europeans. The United States received approximately 600,000 European immigrants in the 1830s, 1.5 million in the 1840s, and then 2.5 million per decade until 1880. In the 1890s an astonishing total of 5.2 million immigrants arrived. Immigration helped push national population from 39 million in 1871 to 63 million in 1891. Most of the immigrants settled in cities. Chicago, for example, grew from 444,000 in 1870 to 1.7 million in 1900.

European immigration to Latin America also increased dramatically. Combined immigration to Argentina and Brazil rose from under 130,000 in the 1860s to 1.7 million in the 1890s. By 1910, 30 percent of the Argentine population was foreign-born, more than twice the proportion in the U.S. population. Argentina was an extremely attractive destination for European immigrants, receiving more than twice as many immigrants as Canada between 1870 and 1930. Even so, immigration to Canada increased tenfold during this period.

Asian Immigration

Asian immigration to the Western Hemisphere also increased after 1850. Between 1849 and 1875, approximately 100,000 Chinese immigrants arrived in Peru and another 120,000 entered Cuba. Canada attracted about 50,000 Chinese immigrants in the second half of the century, and the United States received 300,000 immigrants between 1854 and 1882. India also contributed to the social transformation of the Western Hemisphere, sending more than a half-million immigrants to the Caribbean region. British Guiana alone received 238,000 immigrants, mostly indentured laborers, from the Asian subcontinent.

Anti-Immigrant Movements

Despite the obvious economic benefits that accompanied this inflow of people, hostility to immigration mounted in many nations. Nativist political movements argued that it was impossible to integrate large numbers of foreigners into national political cultures. By the end of the century, fear and prejudice led many governments in the Western Hemisphere to limit immigration or to distinguish between "desirable" and "undesirable" immigrants, commonly favoring Europeans over Asians.

AP* Exam Tip Be able to discuss the causes and the effects of demographic changes in various regions.

Asians faced more obstacles than did Europeans and were more often victims of violence and discrimination. In the 1870s and 1880s anti-Chinese riots erupted in many western cities in the United States. Congress responded to this wave of racism by passing the Chinese Exclusion Act in 1882, which eliminated most Chinese immigration. In 1886 popular fears that "inferior races" threatened Canada led that government to impose a head tax, making immigration more difficult for Chinese families. During this same period strong anti-Chinese prejudice surfaced in Peru, Mexico, and Cuba. Japanese immigrants in Brazil and East Indians in the English-speaking Caribbean faced similar prejudice.

European immigrants faced prejudice and discrimination as well. Popular opinion portrayed Italians as criminals or anarchists. In Argentina and the United States, some social scientists argued that Italian immigrants were more violent and less honest than the native-born population. Immigrants from Spain were widely stereotyped in Argentina as miserly and dishonest. Eastern European Jews seeking to escape pogroms and discrimination at home found themselves barred from many educational institutions and professional careers in both the United States and Latin America. Irish, German, Swedish, Polish, and Middle Eastern immigrants received negative stereotypes as well. The justifications for these prejudices were remarkably similar from Canada to Argentina. Immigrants, critics claimed, threatened the well-being of native-born workers by accepting low wages and threatened national culture by resisting assimilation.

Many intellectuals and political leaders wondered if the evolving mix of culturally diverse populations could sustain a common citizenship. This concern led to efforts to compel immigrants to assimilate. Schools became cultural battlegrounds where language, cultural values, and patriotic attitudes were transmitted to the children of immigrants. Ignoring Canada's large French-speaking population, an English-speaking Canadian reformer commented on recent immigration: "If Canada is to become in a real sense a nation, if our people are to become one people, we must have one language."[6] These fears and prejudices promoted the singing of patriotic songs, the veneration of national flags and other symbols, and the writing of national histories that emphasized patriotism and civic virtue.

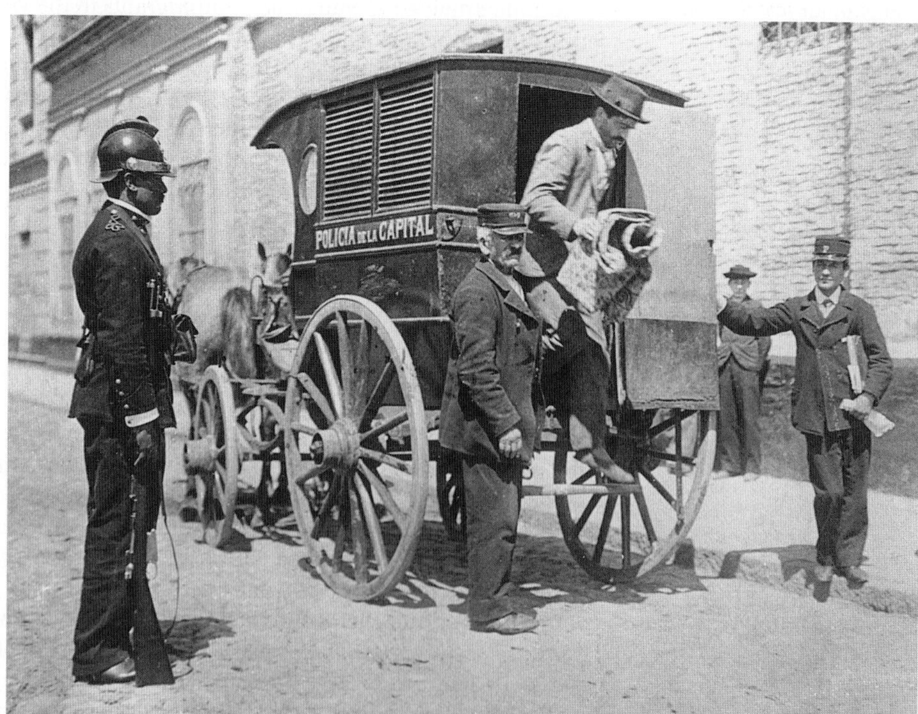

Arrest of Labor Activist in Buenos Aires The labor movement in Buenos Aires grew in numbers and became more radical with the arrival of tens of thousands of Italian and Spanish immigrants. Fearful of socialist and anarchist unions, the government of Argentina used an expanded police force to break strikes.

Archivo General de la Nación, Buenos Aires

American Cultures

Despite discrimination, immigrants continued to stream into the Western Hemisphere, where they introduced new languages, living arrangements, technologies, and customs. Immigrants also altered politics in many of the hemisphere's nations as they sought to influence government policies and gain access to power. To compensate for their isolation from home, language, and culture, most immigrant groups created ethnically based mutual aid societies, sports and leisure clubs, and neighborhoods. These organizations provided valuable social and economic support for recent arrivals while sometimes worsening the fears of the native-born that immigration posed a threat to national culture. At the same time, shared experiences in their adopted nations as workers, neighbors, or soldiers changed immigrants individually and collectively as well. The modification of language, customs, values, and behaviors as a result of contact with people from another culture is called **acculturation**.

acculturation The adoption of the language, customs, values, and behaviors of host nations by immigrants.

The Immigrant Legacy

Immigrants and their children, in turn, made their mark on the cultures of their adopted nations. They learned the language spoken in their adopted countries as fast as possible in order to improve their earning capacity, while words and phrases from their languages entered the vocabularies of the host nations. Languages as diverse as Yiddish and Italian strongly influenced American English, Argentine Spanish, and Brazilian Portuguese. Dietary practices introduced from Europe and Asia altered the cuisine of nearly every American nation. In popular music, the Argentine tango, based on African rhythms, was transformed by new instrumentation and orchestral arrangements brought by Italian immigrants. Mexican ballads blended with English folk music in the U.S. Southwest, and Italian operas played to packed houses in Buenos Aires.

Union movements and electoral politics in the hemisphere also felt the influence of new arrivals who aggressively sought to influence politics and improve working conditions. The anarchist and socialist beliefs of European immigrants influenced the labor movements of Mexico, Argentina, and the United States. Immigrants also helped form new political movements. Their mutual benevolent societies and less-formal ethnic associations pooled resources to help immigrants open businesses, aid the immigration of relatives, or bury family members.

Women's Rights and the Struggle for Social Justice

Women's Rights Convention An 1848 gathering of women angered by their exclusion from an international antislavery meeting. They met at Seneca Falls, New York, to discuss women's rights.

In 1848 a group of women angered by their exclusion from an international antislavery meeting issued a call for a conference to discuss women's rights. The resulting **Women's Rights Convention** at Seneca Falls, New York, issued a statement that said, in part, "We hold these truths to be self-evident: that all men and women are equal." While moderates focused on the issues of economic independence and legal rights, increasing numbers of women demanded the right to vote. Others lobbied to provide better conditions for women working outside the home, especially in textile factories. Sarah Grimké responded to criticism of women's activism:

> *This has been the language of man since he laid aside the whip as a means to keep woman in subjection. He spares her body, but the war he has waged against her mind, her heart, and her soul, has been no less destructive to her as a moral being. How monstrous is the doctrine that woman is to be dependent on man!*[7]

Access to Education and the Professions

Progress toward equality between men and women was equally slow in Canada and in Latin America. Canada's first women doctors received their training in the United States because women could not receive medical degrees until 1895. Argentina and Uruguay were among the first Latin American nations to provide public education for women, introducing coeducation in the 1870s. Chilean women gained access to some careers in medicine and law in the 1870s, while in Brazil the first women graduated in medicine in 1882. In Argentina the first woman doctor graduated from medical school in 1899.

Throughout the hemisphere more rapid progress occurred in lower-status careers that threatened male economic power less directly, and, by the end of the century, women dominated elementary school teaching. From Canada to Argentina and Chile, the majority of working-class women, although having no direct involvement in reform movements, succeeded in transforming gender relations in their daily lives. By the end of the nineteenth century, large numbers of poor women worked outside the home on farms, in markets, and, increasingly, in factories.

Many bore full responsibility for providing for their children. Whether men thought women should remain in the home or not, by the end of the century women were unambiguously present in the economy (see also Chapter 26).

The Search for Racial Justice

There was little progress toward eliminating racial discrimination in the nineteenth century. Blacks were denied the vote throughout the southern United States and were subjected to the indignity of segregation—consigned to separate schools, hotels, restaurants, seats in public transportation, and even water fountains. Racial discrimination against men and women of African descent was also common in Latin America. Unlike the southern states of the United States, however, Latin American nations did not insist on formal racial segregation or permit lynching. Nor did they enforce a strict color line. Many men and women of mixed background were able to enter the skilled working class or middle class. Latin Americans tended to view racial identity across a continuum of physical characteristics rather than in the narrow terms of black and white that defined race relations in the United States.

The abolition of slavery in Latin America did not end discrimination. Some leaders of the abolition struggles later organized to promote racial integration. They demanded access to education, the right to vote, and greater economic opportunity, pointing out the economic and political costs of denying full rights to all citizens. Their success depended on effective political organization and on forging alliances with sympathetic white politicians. Black intellectuals also struggled to overturn racist stereotypes. In Brazil, Argentina, and Cuba, as in the United States, political and literary magazines celebrating black cultural achievement became powerful weapons in the struggle against racial discrimination. While men and women of African descent continued to experience prejudice and discrimination everywhere in the Americas, successful men and women of mixed descent in Latin America confronted fewer obstacles to advancement than did similar groups in the United States.

Development and Underdevelopment

 **AP* Exam Tip** Be prepared to discuss the impact of new technology on the development of nations.

While the Atlantic economy experienced three periods of severe economic contraction during the nineteenth century, nearly all the nations of the Western Hemisphere were richer in 1900 than in 1800. The Industrial Revolution, worldwide population growth, and an increasingly integrated world market stimulated economic expansion (see Environment and Technology: Constructing the Port of Buenos Aires, Argentina). Wheat, corn, wool, meats, and nonprecious minerals joined the region's earlier exports of silver, sugar, dyes, coffee, and cotton. The United States was the only Western Hemisphere nation to industrialize, but nearly every government promoted new industries and technologies. Governments invested in roads, railroads, canals, and telegraph systems to better serve distant markets, while adopting tariff and monetary policies to foster economic diversification and growth. Despite these efforts, by 1900 only three Western Hemisphere nations—the United States, Canada, and Argentina—achieved individual income levels similar to those of western Europe. All three nations had open land, temperate climates, diverse resources, and large inflows of immigrants.

New demands for copper, zinc, lead, coal, and tin unleashed by the Industrial Revolution led to mining booms in the western United States, Mexico, and Chile. The mining companies of the late nineteenth century were heavily capitalized international corporations that could bully governments and buy political favors. European and North American corporations owned nearly all the largest mining enterprises in Latin America. Petroleum development, which occurred at the end of the century in Mexico and elsewhere, followed this pattern as well (see the discussion of the Mexican economy during the Díaz dictatorship in Chapter 30).

The Role of Technology

New technology accelerated economic integration, but the high cost of this technology often increased dependence on foreign capital. Many governments promoted railroads by granting tax benefits, free land, and monopoly rights to both domestic and foreign investors. As a result, by 1890 vast areas of the Great Plains in the United States, the Canadian prairie, the Argentine pampas, and parts of northern Mexico were producing grain and livestock for foreign markets opened by the development of railroads. Steamships also lowered the cost of transportation to

ENVIRONMENT + TECHNOLOGY

Constructing the Port of Buenos Aires, Argentina

Located on the banks of the Río de la Plata, Buenos Aires had been a major commercial center and port since the late eighteenth century. But Buenos Aires was not a natural harbor. Because of the shallowness of the river, the largest oceangoing ships were forced to anchor hundreds of yards offshore while goods and passengers were unloaded by small boats or by specially built ox carts with huge wheels. Smaller vessels docked at a river port to the city's south.

By the 1880s the Argentine economy was transformed by the growing demands of European consumers for meat and grain. As exports surged and land values exploded, the wages of Argentines rose, and the nation became a favored destination for European immigrants. Argentina was becoming the wealthiest nation in Latin America.

The nation's political and economic elites decided that future growth required the modernization and expansion of port facilities. They debated two competing plans. The first emphasized the incremental expansion and dredging of the river port and was supported by local engineers and political groups suspicious of foreign economic interests. The second, and ultimately successful, plan involved dredging a port and deepwater channel from the low mud flats near the city center. Argentine economic interests closely tied to the European export trade and national political leaders who believed progress and prosperity required the imitation of European models supported this more expensive plan, which relied on British engineering firms, British banks, and British technology. The British were also Argentina's primary creditors, as well as developers of the nation's railroads, streetcar lines, and gas works.

The photograph shows the construction of Puerto Madero, the new port of Buenos Aires, in the 1890s. Recent immigrants provided most of the labor, and British experts dominated the engineering staff. The local elite found their profits in real estate deals and commissions associated with construction. Puerto Madero opened in stages beginning in 1890. However, cost overruns and corruption stretched out completion to 1898. By 1910 arrivals and departures reached thirty thousand ships and 18 million tons, but design problems forced "improvements" into the 1920s.

Why had the government of Argentina chosen the costliest and most difficult design? Argentine politicians sought to demonstrate their nation's modernity and so chose the most complex and technologically sophisticated solution to the port problem. They also believed that British engineering and British capital were guarantees of modernity. While the new port facilities facilitated a boom in exports and imports and the huge public works budget did provide incomes for thousands of laborers, debts, design flaws, and the increased influence of foreign capital in Argentina left a legacy of problems. (See the discussion of Juan Perón in Chapter 30.)

Courtesy, Hack Hoffenburg

Excavation of Port of Buenos Aires, Argentina Relying on foreign capital and engineering, the government of Argentina improved the port to facilitate the nation's rapidly expanding export economy.

distant markets, and the telegraph stimulated expansion by speeding information about the demand for and availability of products.

The simultaneous acquisition of several new technologies could have a dramatic effect. In Argentina the railroad, the telegraph, barbed wire, and refrigeration all appeared in the 1870s and 1880s. Although Argentina had had abundant livestock herds since the colonial period,

New Technologies Change the Mining Industry Powerful hydraulic technologies were introduced in western mining sites in the United States. This early photo shows how high-power water jets could transform the natural environment.

the distance from Europe's markets prevented Argentine cattle raisers from exporting fresh meat or live animals. Technology overcame these obstacles. The combination of railroads and the telegraph lowered freight costs and improved information about markets. Steamships shortened trans-Atlantic crossings, and refrigerated ships made it possible to sell meat in distant markets. As land values rose and livestock breeding improved, ranchers protected new investments with barbed wire, the first inexpensive fencing available on the nearly treeless plains.

development In the nineteenth and twentieth centuries, the economic process that led to industrialization, urbanization, the rise of a large and prosperous middle class, and heavy investment in education.

Rich and Poor Nations

underdevelopment The condition experienced by economies that depend on colonial forms of production such as the export of raw materials and plantation crops with low wages and low investment in education.

Growing interdependence and increased competition produced deep structural differences among Western Hemisphere economies by 1900. Two distinct economic tracks became visible. One led to industrialization and prosperity: **development**. The other continued colonial dependence on exporting raw materials and on low-wage industries: **underdevelopment**. By 1900 prosperity was greater and economic development more diversified in English-speaking North America than in the nations of Latin America. With a temperate climate, vast fertile prairies, and an influx of European immigrants, Argentina was the only Latin American nation to approach the prosperity of the United States and Canada.

Changes in the performance of international markets helped determine the trajectory of Western Hemisphere economies as new nations promoted economic development. When the United States gained independence, the world economy enjoyed rapid growth. With a large merchant fleet, a diversified economy that included some manufacturing, and adequate banking and insurance services, the United States benefited from this expansion. Rapid population growth due in large measure to immigration, high levels of individual wealth, widespread landownership, and relatively high literacy rates also fostered rapid economic development. In 1865 the United States had the world's largest railroad network, but by 1915, it had multiplied elevenfold (see Map 23.4). Steel production grew rapidly as well, with the United States overtaking Britain and Germany in the 1890s.

Canada's achievement of greater political autonomy, the Confederation of 1867, coincided with a second period of global economic expansion. Canada also benefited from a special trading relationship with Britain, the world's preeminent industrial nation, and from a rising tide

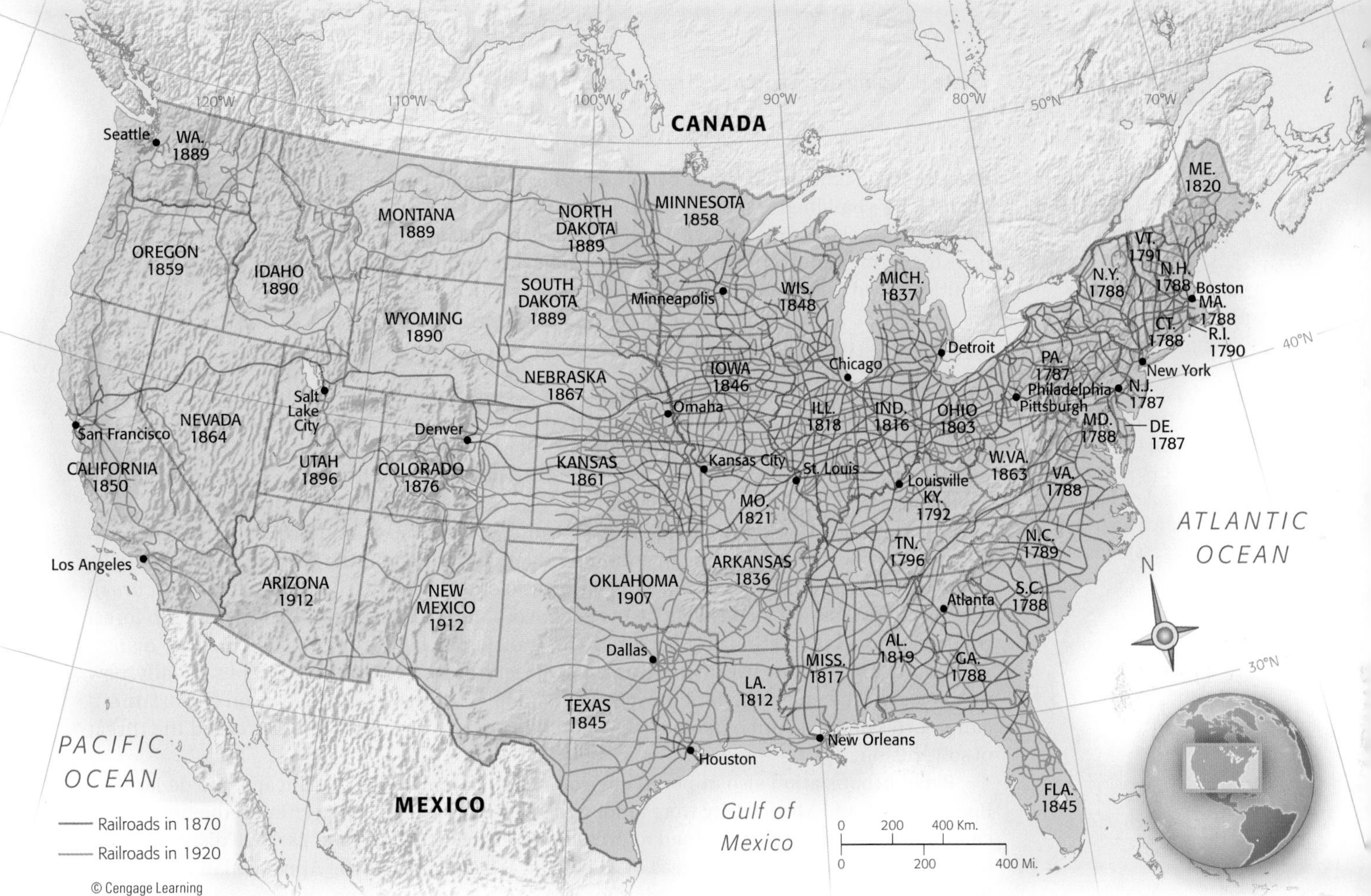

MAP 23.4 The Expansion of the United States, 1850–1920 The settlement of western territories and their admission as states depended on migration, the exploitation of natural resources, and important new technologies like railroads and telegraphs that facilitated economic and political integration.

e Interactive Map

of immigrants after 1850. Nevertheless, some regions within each of these prosperous North American nations—Canada's Maritime Provinces and the southern part of the United States—demonstrated the same patterns of underdevelopment found in Latin America.

Most Latin American nations gained independence in the 1820s when the global economy contracted. In the colonial period, Spain and Portugal had promoted the production of agricultural and mining exports in their colonies. After independence these exports faced increased competition. Although these sectors experienced periods of great prosperity in the nineteenth century, they also faced stiff competition and falling prices as new regions began production or competing products captured markets.

The history of the Latin American economies, subject to periodic problems of oversupply and low prices, was one of boom and bust. Many Latin American governments sought to promote exports in the face of increased competition and falling prices by resisting union activity and demands for higher wages and by opening domestic markets to foreign manufactures. The resulting low wages and an abundance of foreign manufactured goods, in turn, undermined efforts to promote industrialization in Latin America.

Weak governments, political instability, and, in some cases, civil war also slowed Latin American economic development. Because Latin America was also dependent on importing foreign capital and technology, Great Britain and, by the end of the century, the United States often imposed unfavorable trade conditions or even intervened militarily to protect their investments. The combined impact of these domestic and international impediments to development became clear when Mexico, Chile, and Argentina failed to achieve high levels of domestic investment in manufacturing late in the nineteenth century, despite a rapid accumulation of wealth derived from traditional exports.

Altered Environments

AP* Exam Tip The environmental changes brought about by migrations and the development of industry are important topics to understand.

Population growth, economic expansion, new technologies, and the introduction of foreign plants and animals had dramatically altered American environments. Cuba's planters cut down the island's forests in the early nineteenth century to expand sugar production. Growing demand for meat led ranchers to expand livestock-raising into fragile environments in Argentina, Uruguay, southern Brazil, and the southwestern United States. Other forms of commercial agriculture also threatened the environment. Farmers in South Carolina and Georgia gained a short-term increase in cotton production by abandoning crop rotation after 1870, but this practice quickly led to soil exhaustion and erosion. Similarly, coffee planters in Brazil exhausted fertility with a destructive cycle of overplanting followed by expansion onto forest reserves cleared by cutting and burning. The transfers of land from public to private ownership in order to promote livestock-raising and agriculture also altered landscapes. Finally, new technologies had environmental effects. For example, the use of steel plows on North American prairies and Argentine pampas eliminated many native grasses and increased the threat of soil erosion.

Rapid urbanization also imposed environmental costs. New York, Chicago, Rio de Janeiro, Buenos Aires, and Mexico City were among the world's fastest-growing cities in the nineteenth century, and governments strained to provide sewers, clean water, and garbage disposal. Timber companies clear-cut large areas of Michigan, Wisconsin, and the Appalachian Mountains in the United States to provide lumber for railroad ties and housing, pulp for paper, and fuel for locomotives and foundries. At the same time, the forest industries of British Honduras (now Belize), Nicaragua, and Guatemala grew rapidly in response to demand in Europe and North America for tropical hardwoods like mahogany. As forests throughout the hemisphere were cleared, animal habitats and native plant species disappeared.

The scale of mining in Nevada, Montana, and California accelerated erosion and pollution. Similar results occurred in other mining areas as well. Nitrate mining and open-pit copper mining in Chile scarred and polluted the environment. The state of Minas Gerais (ME-nas JER-aize) in Brazil experienced a series of mining booms that began with gold in the late seventeenth century and continued with iron ore in the nineteenth. By the end of the nineteenth century, its red soil had been ripped open, its forests depleted, and erosion uncontrolled. Similar devastation afflicted parts of Bolivia and Mexico.

By the end of the nineteenth century, small-scale conservation efforts were under way in many nations, and the first national parks and nature reserves were created. In the United States large areas remained undeveloped. In 1872 Yellowstone in Wyoming became the first national park. President Theodore Roosevelt (1901–1909) and the naturalist John Muir played major roles in preserving large areas of the western states. Canada created its first national park in Banff in 1885 and expanded it from 10 to 260 square miles (26 to 673 square kilometers) two years later. When confronted with a choice between economic growth and environmental protection, however, the hemisphere's nations embraced growth.

SECTION REVIEW

- Following independence, American nations eventually abolished the slave trade and slavery.
- After the abolition of slavery, a rush of immigrants from Europe and Asia diversified American nations, though most immigrants faced prejudice.
- The long struggle to achieve women's rights and end racial and ethnic discrimination altered the Western Hemisphere's political structures and belief systems.
- Although most Western Hemisphere nations were richer in 1900 than in 1800, only Argentina could match the levels of average wealth found in the United States and Canada; nations and regions dependent on exporting raw materials remained underdeveloped.
- Increased logging, grazing, and mining ruined vast areas of the hemisphere, but minor conservation efforts were under way by the end of the nineteenth century.

CONCLUSION

While the new nations of the Western Hemisphere faced similar challenges in the nineteenth century, they had developed from different colonial traditions. The effort to establish stable constitutional systems proved difficult nearly everywhere. While the constitution of the United States endured, conflict over slavery led to a civil war that threatened the nation's survival. Elsewhere most new constitutions failed within a generation. In Argentina, for example, fifty years passed before a stable national government was in place. Personalist political leaders with large followings, like José Antonio Páez and Andrew Jackson, resisted the constraints of constitutions. Regionalism, ideological confrontations, racial divisions, and conflict with native peoples all threatened stability as well.

New nations also faced foreign interventions and local wars with regional powers. By 1850 Mexico had lost 50 percent of its territory to the United States and then faced a French invasion in 1862. Bolivia and Peru lost territory to an expansive Chile, while Paraguay lost a disastrous war to an alliance of Argentina, Brazil, and Uruguay. The nations of the Americas also fought numerous wars with indigenous peoples, crushing resistance by the 1890s.

The nations of the hemisphere also experienced a series of dramatic social and economic changes in this period. The slave trade and slavery persisted long after independence (see Chapter 18) but after a century of protest and political mobilization, the hemisphere's last slave state, Brazil, freed its slaves in 1888. Slavery left a legacy of racism and discrimination across the Americas. In places where the institution was most important, the plantation regions of Brazil, the Caribbean, and the American South, racial prejudice, discrimination, and persistent low levels of investment in education and internal improvements slowed economic growth and weakened democracy. By 1890 many of the hemisphere's poorest nations or poorest regions within nations were those that had depended on slavery.

Amerindian populations experienced centuries of exploitation, forced integration in market economies, and compulsory removal to marginal lands. In most of Latin America, Amerindians had been subjected to exploitation for centuries when the Spanish and Portuguese empires finally fell. Once in place, forced labor and other abuses persisted in nations like Guatemala and Bolivia. With independence, new national governments undertook the pacification of the hemisphere's remaining independent native peoples. By the 1890s nearly all were reduced to reservations or forced onto marginal lands. As a result, Amerindians were among the poorest peoples in the hemisphere, suffering oppression, poverty, and disenfranchisement.

Immigration transformed many Western Hemisphere nations. As a general rule, the millions of European immigrants that entered the Western Hemisphere in the nineteenth century avoided regions where slavery dominated or where indigenous populations were compelled to labor. Argentina, Brazil, Canada, and the United States were the most popular destinations, and immigrants to Brazil and the United States avoided the former plantation zones. Instead, hundreds of thousands of Chinese and East Indians, migrating as indentured laborers, were directed to plantation regions, where they faced racism and discrimination.

Industrialization had a transforming effect on the hemisphere. Wealth, political power, and population were increasingly concentrated in urban areas, and bankers and manufacturers, rather than farmers and plantation owners, increasingly directed national destinies. Industrialization altered the natural environment in dramatic ways. Modern factories consumed huge amounts of raw materials and energy. Copper mines in Chile and Mexico, Cuban sugar plantations, Brazilian coffee plantations, and Canadian lumber companies all left their mark on the natural environment, and all had ties to markets in the United States.

In 1900 nearly every American nation was wealthier, better educated, more democratic, and more populous than at independence. But these nations were also more vulnerable to distant economic forces, more profoundly split between haves and have-nots, and more clearly divided into a rich north and a poorer south. A small number of nations located in the temperate regions—Canada, the United States, Argentina, and Chile—had become prosperous regional powers relative to their neighbors. While most of the hemisphere's growth continued to depend on the export of agricultural goods and raw materials—sugar, cotton, grains, minerals, and livestock products—the United States had become a major industrial nation by 1890.

KEY TERMS

Simón Bolívar p. 657
Miguel Hidalgo y Costilla p. 658
José María Morelos p. 660
Confederation of 1867 p. 662
personalist leaders p. 664
Andrew Jackson p. 665
José Antonio Páez p. 665
Benito Juárez p. 668
Tecumseh p. 668
Caste War p. 670
abolitionists p. 671
acculturation p. 675
Women's Rights Convention p. 675
development p. 678
underdevelopment p. 678

EBOOK AND WEBSITE RESOURCES

Primary Source

The Jamaica Letter

Interactive Maps

Map 23.1 Latin America by 1830
Map 23.2 Dominion of Canada, 1873
Map 23.3 Territorial Growth of the United States, 1783–1853
Map 23.4 The Expansion of the United States, 1850–1920

Plus flashcards, practice quizzes, and more. Go to: www.cengage.com/history/bullietearthpeople5e

SUGGESTED READING

Andrews, George Reid. *Afro-Latin America, 1800–2000.* 2004. An excellent synthesis of the Latin American experience.

Barth, Gunther. *Bitter Strength: A History of Chinese in the United States, 1850–1870.* 1964. A reliable introduction to this topic.

Brands, H. W. *Andrew Jackson, His Life and Times.* 2005.

Burns, E. Bradford. *The Poverty of Progress: Latin America in the Nineteenth Century.* 1980. A useful examination of the politics of development.

Bushnell, David, and Neil Macaulay. *The Emergence of Latin America in the Nineteenth Century.* 1988.

Careless, J. M. S. *The Union of the Canadas: The Growth of Canadian Institutions, 1841–1857.* 1967.

Cronon, William. *Nature's Metropolis: Chicago and the Great West.* 1991. An excellent discussion of the environment during nineteenth-century development.

Crosby, Alfred. *Ecological Imperialism: The Biological Expansion of Europe, 900–1900.* 1986. A seminal study of environment.

Dean, Warren. *With Broadax and Firebrand: The Destruction of the Brazilian Atlantic Forest.* 1995.

Dickason, Olive Patricia. *Canada's First Nations.* 1993.

Du Bois, Ellen C. *Feminism and Suffrage: The Emergence of an Independent Woman's Movement in the Nineteenth Century.* 1984.

Ginzberg, Lori D. *Women and the Work of Benevolence: Morality, Politics, and Class in the Nineteenth-Century United States.* 1990.

Graden, Dale T. *From Slavery to Freedom in Brazil: Bahia, 1835–1900.* 2006.

Green, William A. *British Slave Emancipation: The Sugar Colonies and the Great Experiment, 1830–1865.* 1973.

Halperin-Donghi, Tulio. *The Contemporary History of Latin America.* 1993.

Kinsbruner, Jay. *Independence in Spanish America,* 2nd ed. 2000. The best short analysis of the independence period.

Kohl, Lawrence Frederick. *The Politics of Individualism: Parties and the American Character in the Jacksonian Era.* 1989.

Krech III, Shepard. *The Ecological Indian.* 1999.

Larson, John Lauritz. *Internal Improvement: National Public Works and the Promise of Popular Government in the Early United States.* 2001.

Martin, Ged, ed. *The Causes of Canadian Confederation.* 1990.

Miller, Francesca. *Latin American Women and the Search for Social Justice.* 1991.

Nugent, Walter. *Crossing: The Great Transatlantic Migrations, 1870–1914.* 1992.

Petulla, Joseph M. *American Environmental History.* 1973.

Quarles, Benjamin. *Black Abolitionists.* 1969.

Remini, Robert V. *Andrew Jackson and His Indian Wars.* 2001.

Rodriguez O., Jaime. *The Origins of Mexican National Politics.* 1997.

Scott, Rebecca. *Slave Emancipation in Cuba: The Transition to Free Labor, 1860–1899.* 1985.

Thomas, Victor Bulmer. *The Economic History of Latin America Since Independence.* 2003.

Worster, Donald. *Rivers of Empire: Water, Aridity, and the Growth of the American West.* 1985.

NOTES

1. Quoted in Lyman L. Johnson, "Spanish American Independence and Its Consequences," in *Problems in Modern Latin American History: A Reader*, ed. John Charles Chasteen and Joseph S. Tulchin (Wilmington, DE: Scholarly Resources, 1994), 21.
2. José Antonio Páez, *Autobiografía del General José Antonio Páez*, vol. 1 (New York: Hallety Breen, 1869), 83.
3. Quoted in Brian Loveman, *Chile: The Legacy of Hispanic Capitalism* (New York: Oxford University Press, 1979), 170.
4. Quoted in Bernard Bailyn, David Brion Davis, David Herbert Donald, John L. Thomas, Robert H. Wiebe, and Gordon S. Wood, *The Great Republic: A History of the American People* (Lexington, MA: D. C. Heath, 1981), 398.
5. Quoted in Mary Beth Norton et al., *A People and a Nation: A History of the United States*, 6th ed. (Boston: Houghton Mifflin, 2001), 284.
6. J. S. Woodsworth in 1909, quoted in R. Douglas Francis, Richard Jones, and Donald B. Smith, *Destinies: Canadian History Since Confederation*, 2nd ed. (Toronto: Holt, Rinehart and Winston, 1992), 141.
7. Sarah Grimké, "Reply to the Massachusetts Clergy," in *Early American Women: A Documentary History, 1600–1900*, ed. Nancy Woloch (Belmont, CA: Wadsworth, 1992), 343.

AP* REVIEW QUESTIONS FOR CHAPTER 23

1. One of the issues that led to revolution in Latin America in the early nineteenth century was
   (A) frustration over the political and economic power of colonial administrators.
   (B) dissatisfaction with the availability of finished goods being imported from Europe.
   (C) the legal change that allowed mestizos the right to vote in local elections.
   (D) the dissatisfaction with the availability of inexpensive labor in the region.

2. In Venezuela, in 1811, a junta of creoles declared independence from Spain. Their main goal was
   (A) to create a democratic government and equal rights for all the people in Venezuela.
   (B) to expand their own rights and privileges by eliminating Spaniards from the upper levels of the government.
   (C) the redistribution of wealth according to utopian socialist ideals.
   (D) to create a confederacy with Mexico and other newly independent nations in the region.

3. Simón Bolívar realized that an effective revolution in northern Latin America would require
   (A) direct economic aid from a large nation such as the United States or Great Britain.
   (B) maintaining African slaves as a labor force so as to attract the landowners.
   (C) building coalitions of people in the region.
   (D) him becoming the dictator as a way to unify disparate regions.

4. After several attempts at achieving independence, Mexico finally became free from Spain in 1821. The new government, under Augustín de Iturbide, was
   (A) reactionary in that it granted freedom and voting rights to all Mexicans.
   (B) conservative and monarchical.
   (C) initially led by a confederacy of church leaders and landowners.
   (D) supported by direct military aid from the United States.

5. Unlike its neighbors, Brazil gained independence in 1822
   (A) through direct U.S. intervention and the issuance of the Monroe Doctrine.
   (B) through the assassination of the king.
   (C) when the Congress of Vienna reapportioned land in Europe and the colonies.
   (D) as a monarchy under Pedro I, the heir to the Portuguese throne.

6. Which of the following was a stumbling block to the creation of constitutional government in Latin America?
   (A) Providing financial support for the government
   (B) Limiting the power of the military
   (C) Providing arable land
   (D) Providing economic opportunities for the large landowners

7. Which of the following was true of British North America in comparison to Spanish Latin America regarding independent government?
   (A) North America's mineral resources led to the quick development of democratic government as a way to quickly exploit wealth.
   (B) Latin America was linguistically unified, whereas the former British colonies were not.
   (C) Residents of British North America had more experience with voting and holding office than did the residents of Spanish colonies.
   (D) In Latin America wealth was not a determinant in government, whereas it was in the British colonies.

8. The U.S. president Andrew Jackson and José Antonio Páez of Venezuela
   (A) had both worked their way up in the government to become the leader.
   (B) came from exceptionally wealthy backgrounds and used their personal wealth to secure their positions.
   (C) both supported the abolition of slaveholding in their nations.
   (D) were personalist leaders.

9. After independence, one of the biggest threats to the new nations of the Americas was
   (A) regionalism.
   (B) demands for equal rights by the poor.
   (C) slave rebellions.
   (D) famine.

10. In the latter half of the nineteenth century, the indigenous people of Argentina and Chile
    (A) received complete civil and political rights in those nations.
    (B) remained independent of the governments of the new nations.
    (C) welcomed the new independent governments and aided outside settlement on their lands.
    (D) faced problems very similar to those experienced by the indigenous people of the United States.

11. In the Caribbean, slavery
    (A) lasted the longest in Cuba and Puerto Rico.
    (B) existed only in former French colonies, such as Haiti.
    (C) declined as income from export crops increased and allowed a switch to free labor.
    (D) was driven by the U.S. demand for slaves for plantations in the southern United States.

12. Like the United States in the late nineteenth century, Latin America
    (A) experienced a tremendous industrial and urban "boom."
    (B) faced financial ruin due to wars and poor harvests.
    (C) experienced a large increase in immigration from Europe.
    (D) established racial segregation.

13. In the late nineteenth and early twentieth centuries, the progress toward equality between men and women
    (A) moved faster in Canada than in the United States or in Latin America.
    (B) was equally slow in the United States, Canada, and Latin America.
    (C) tended to be an economic issue in Latin America and a cultural issue in the United States and Canada.
    (D) never enjoyed real support in the United States, Canada, or Latin America.

CHAPTER

24

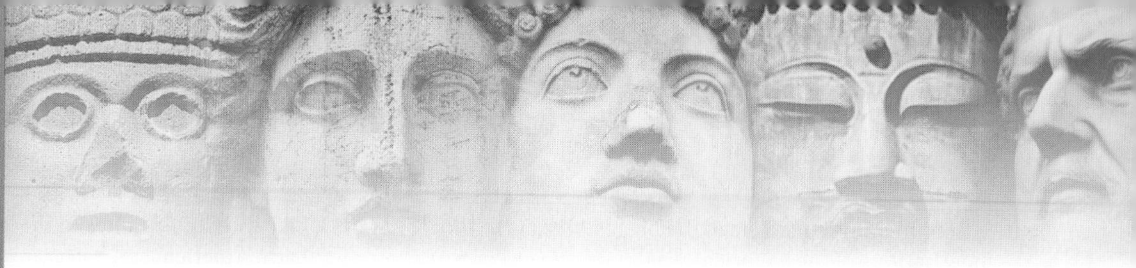

CHAPTER OUTLINE

Trade Warehouse in Guangzhou A European merchant enters in the background while Chinese workers pack tea and porcelain.

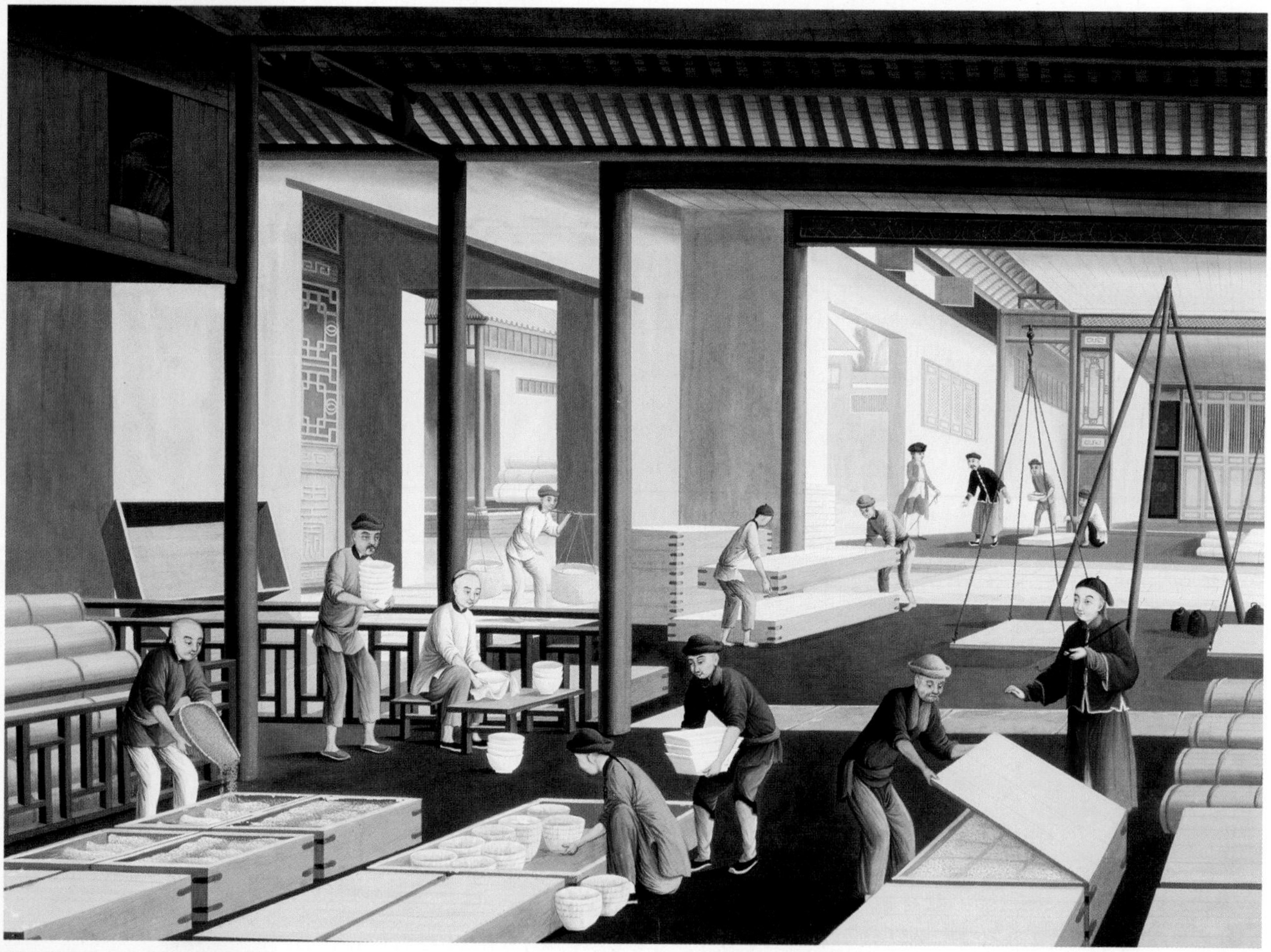

Visit the website and ebook for additional study materials and interactive tools: www.cengage.com/history/bullietearthpeople5e

Land Empires in the Age of Imperialism, 1800–1870

- What were the benefits and the drawbacks to the Ottoman Empire of the reforms adopted during the Tanzimat period?
- How did the Russian Empire maintain its status as both a European power and a great Asian land empire?
- How did the impact of European imperialism on China differ from its impact on Russia and the Ottoman Empire?

When the emperor of the Qing (ching) (the last empire to rule China) died in 1799, the imperial court received a shock. For decades officials had known that the emperor was indulging his handsome young favorite, Heshen (huh-shun), allowing him extraordinary privileges and power. Senior bureaucrats hated Heshen, suspecting him of overseeing a widespread network of corruption. They believed he had been scheming to prolong the inconclusive wars against the native Miao (mee-ow) peoples of southwest China in the late 1700s. Glowing reports of successes against the rebels had poured into the capital, and enormous sums of government money had flowed to the battlefields. But there was no adequate accounting for the funds, and the war persisted.

After the emperor's death, Heshen's enemies ordered his arrest. When they searched his mansion, they discovered a magnificent hoard of silk, furs, porcelain, furniture, and gold and silver. His personal cash alone exceeded what remained in the imperial treasury. The new emperor ordered Heshen to commit suicide with a rope of gold silk. The government seized Heshen's fortune, but the financial damage could not be undone. The declining agricultural base could not replenish the state coffers, and much of the income that did flow in was squandered by an increasingly corrupt bureaucracy. In the 1800s the Qing Empire faced increasing challenges from Europe and the United States with an empty treasury, a stagnant economy, and a troubled society.

The Qing Empire's problems were not unique. They were common to all the land-based empires of Eurasia, where old and inefficient ways of governing put states at risk. The international climate was increasingly dominated by industrializing European economies drawing on the wealth of their overseas colonies. During the early 1800s rapid population growth and slow agricultural growth affected much of Eurasia. In addition, earlier military expansion had stretched the resources of imperial treasuries (see Chapter 20), leaving the land-based empires vulnerable to European military pressure. Responses to this pressure varied, with reform and adaptation gaining headway in some lands and tradition being reasserted in others. In the long run, attempts to meet western Europe's economic and political demands produced financial indebtedness to France, Britain, and other Western powers.

This chapter contrasts the experiences of the Qing Empire with those of the Russian and Ottoman Empires. Whereas the Qing opted for resistance, the others made varying attempts to adapt and reform. Russia eventually became part of Europe and shared in many aspects of European culture, while the Ottomans and the Qing became subject to ever-greater imperialist pressure. These different responses raise the question of the role of culture in shaping western Europe's relations with the rest of the world in the nineteenth century.

THE OTTOMAN EMPIRE

Fragmentation of Power

During the eighteenth century the central government of the Ottoman Empire lost much of its power to provincial governors, military commanders, ethnic leaders, and bandit chiefs. In several parts of the empire local officials and large landholders tried to increase their independence and divert imperial funds into their own coffers.

A kingdom in Arabia led by the Saud family, following the puritanical and fundamentalist religious views of an eighteenth-century leader named Muhammad ibn Abd al-Wahhab (moo-HAH-muhd ib-uhn ab-dahl-wa-HAHB), took control of the holy cities of Mecca and Medina and deprived the sultan of the honor of organizing the annual pilgrimage. In Egypt factions of mamluk slave-soldiers purchased as boys in Georgia and nearby parts of the Caucasus and educated for war reasserted their influence. Such soldiers had ruled Egypt between 1260 and 1517, when they were defeated by the Ottomans. Now Ottoman weakness allowed mamluk factions based on a revival of the slave-soldier tradition to reemerge as local military forces.

For the sultans, the outlook was bleak. At the end of the eighteenth century, the inefficient Janissary corps used the political power it enjoyed in Istanbul to force Sultan Selim III to abandon efforts to train a modern, European-style army. This situation unexpectedly changed when France invaded Egypt.

Egypt and the Napoleonic Example

Napoleon Bonaparte and an invasion force of 36,000 men and four hundred ships invaded Egypt in May 1798. The French quickly defeated the mamluk forces that for several decades had dominated the country under the loose jurisdiction of the Ottoman sultan in Istanbul. Fifteen months later, after being stopped by Ottoman land and British naval forces in an attempted invasion of Syria, Napoleon secretly left Cairo and returned to France. Three months later he seized power and made himself emperor.

Muhammad Ali

Muhammad Ali Leader of Egyptian modernization in the early nineteenth century. He ruled Egypt as an Ottoman governor but had imperial ambitions. His descendants ruled Egypt until overthrown in 1952.

Back in Egypt, his generals tried to administer a country that they only poorly understood. Cut off from France by British ships in the Mediterranean, they had little hope of remaining in power and agreed to withdraw in 1801. For the second time in three years, a collapse of military power produced a power vacuum in Egypt. The winner of the ensuing contest was **Muhammad Ali** (moo-HAM-mad AH-lee), the commander of a contingent of Albanian soldiers sent by the sultan to restore imperial control. By 1805 he had taken the place of the official Ottoman governor, and by 1811 he had dispossessed the mamluks of their lands and privileges.

Reforms on European Models

Muhammad Ali's rise to power coincided with the meteoric career of Emperor Napoleon I. It is not surprising, therefore, that he adopted many French practices in rebuilding the Egyptian state. Militarily, he established special schools for training artillery and cavalry officers, army surgeons, military bandmasters, and others. The curricula of these schools featured European skills and sciences, and Muhammad Ali began to send promising officer trainees to France for education. In 1824 he started a gazette devoted to official affairs, the first newspaper in the Islamic world.

As discussed in Chapter 22, Muhammad Ali built all sorts of factories to outfit his new army. These did not prove efficient enough to survive, but they showed a determination to achieve independence and parity with the European powers.

Egypt in Syria and Greece

In the 1830s Muhammad Ali's son Ibrahim invaded Syria and instituted some of the changes already under way in Egypt. The improved quality of the new Egyptian army had been proven during the Greek war of independence (see below), when Ibrahim had commanded an expeditionary force to help the sultan. In response, the sultan embarked on building his own new

CHRONOLOGY

	Ottoman Empire	Russian Empire	Qing Empire
			1794–1804 White Lotus Rebellion
1800	1805–1849 Muhammad Ali governs Egypt	1801–1825 Reign of Alexander I	
	1808–1839 Rule of Mahmud II	1812 Napoleon's retreat from Moscow	
		1825 Decembrist revolt	
		1825–1855 Reign of Nicholas I	
	1826 Janissary corps dissolved		
	1829 Greek independence		
	1839 Abdul Mejid begins Tanzimat reforms		1839–1842 Opium War
1850	1853–1856 Crimean War	1853–1856 Crimean War	1850–1864 Taiping Rebellion
		1855–1881 Reign of Alexander II	1856–1860 Arrow War
		1861 Emancipation of the serfs	
	1876 First constitution by an Islamic government		

army in 1826. The two armies met when Ibrahim attacked northward into Anatolia in 1839 and defeated the army of his suzerain, the Ottoman sultan. The road to Istanbul seemed open until the European powers intervened and forced a withdrawal to the present-day border between Egypt and Israel.

Muhammad Ali remained Egypt's ruler, under the suzerainty of the sultan, until his death in 1849; and his family continued to rule the country until 1952. But his dream of making Egypt a mighty country capable of standing up to Europe faded. What survived was the example he had set for the sultans in Istanbul.

Janissaries Infantry, originally of slave origin, armed with firearms and constituting the elite of the Ottoman army from the fifteenth century until the corps was abolished in 1826.

Ottoman Reform and the European Model, 1807–1853

At the end of the eighteenth century Sultan Selim (seh-LEEM) III (r. 1789–1807), a forward-looking ruler who stayed abreast of events in Europe, introduced reforms to create European-style military units, bring provincial governors under central government control, and standardize taxation. The rise in government expenditures to implement the reforms was supposed to be offset by taxes on selected items, primarily tobacco and coffee.

Janissary Problems

The reforms failed for political more than economic reasons. The most violent and persistent opposition came from the **Janissary** (JAN-nih-say-ree) military corps (see Chapter 19). Originally Christian boys taken from their homes in the Balkans, converted to Islam, and required to serve for life in the Ottoman army, in the eighteenth century the Janissaries became a significant political force in Istanbul and in provincial capitals like Damascus and Aleppo. Their interest in preserving special economic privileges made them resist the creation of new military units.

Serbia The Ottoman province in the Balkans that rose up against Janissary control in the early 1800s.

At times, Janissary power produced military uprisings. In the Ottoman territory of **Serbia**, local residents intensely resented the control exercised by Janissary governors. The Orthodox Christians claimed that the Janissaries abused them. In response, Selim threatened to reassign the Janissaries to Istanbul. Suspecting that the sultan wanted to curb their political power, in 1805 the Janissaries revolted and massacred Christians in Serbia. Unable to reestablish central Ottoman rule over Serbia, the sultan had to rely on the ruler of Bosnia, another Balkan province, who joined his troops with the peasants of Serbia to suppress the Janissary uprising. The threat

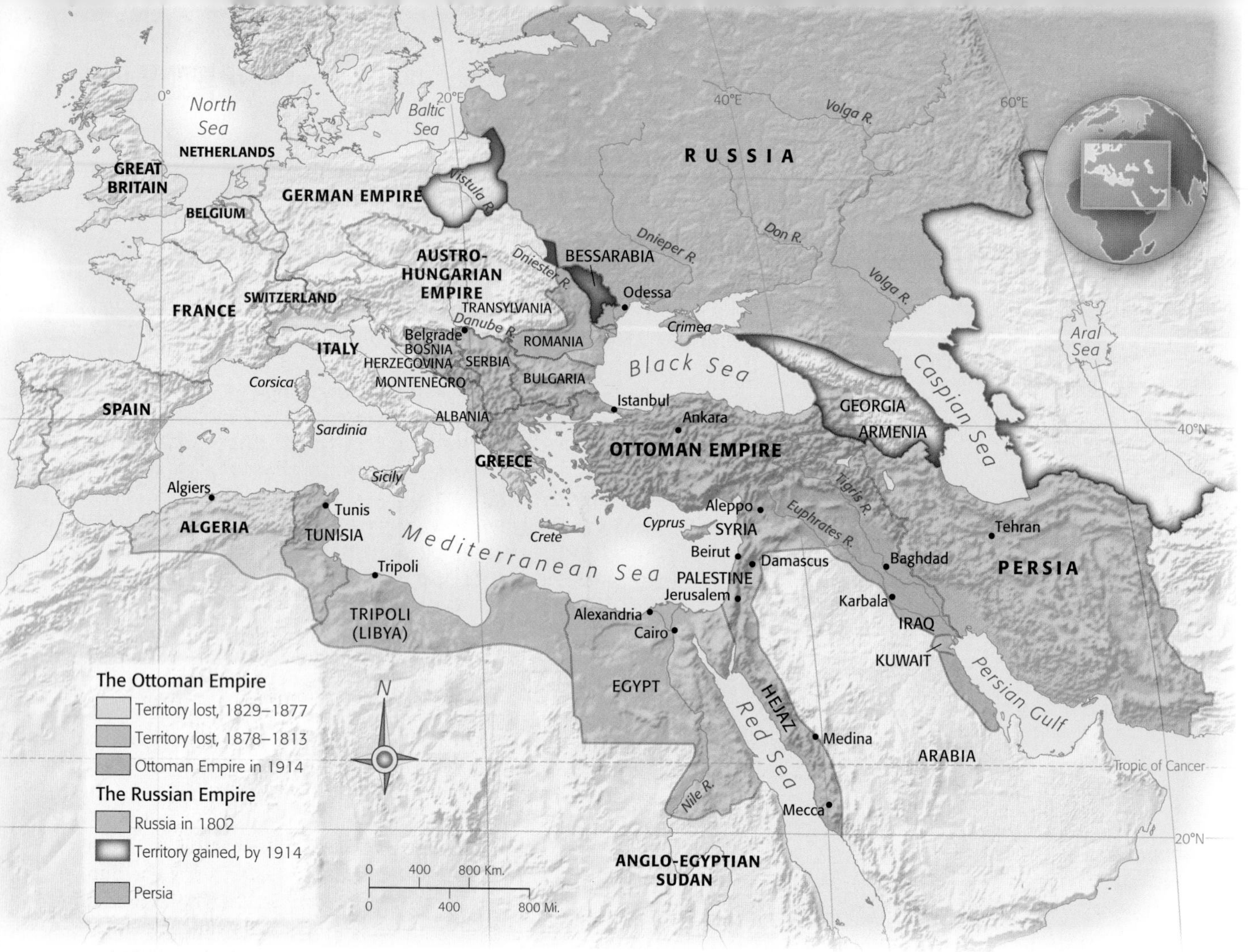

MAP 24.1 The Ottoman and Russian Empires, 1829–1914 At its height the Ottoman Empire controlled most of the perimeter of the Mediterranean Sea. But in the 1800s Ottoman territory shrank as many countries gained their independence. The Black Sea, where the Turkish coast was vulnerable to assault, became a weak spot as Russian naval power grew. Russian challenges to the Ottomans at the eastern end of the Black Sea and to the Persians east and west of the Caspian aroused fears in Europe that Russia was trying to reach the Indian Ocean.

e Interactive Map

of Russian intervention prevented the Ottomans from disarming the victorious Serbians, so Serbia became effectively independent.

Sultan Mahmud II

Other opponents of reform included ulama, or Muslim religious scholars, who distrusted the secularization of law and taxation that Selim proposed. In the face of widespread rejection of his reforms, Selim suspended his program in 1806. Nevertheless, a massive military uprising occurred at Istanbul, and the sultan was deposed and imprisoned. Reform forces recaptured the capital, but not before Selim had been executed. Selim's cousin, Sultan Mahmud (mah-MOOD) II (r. 1808–1839), cautiously revived Selim's program, but he realized that reforms needed to be more systematic and imposed more forcefully. The effectiveness of radical reform in Muhammad Ali's Egypt drove this lesson home, as did the insurrection in Greece, during which the Egyptian military performed much better than the main Ottoman army.

Greek independence in 1829 had dramatic international significance. A combination of Greek nationalist organizations and interlopers from Albania formed the independence movement. Europe's interest in the classical age of Greece and Rome led many Europeans to consider the Greeks' struggle for independence a campaign to recapture their classical glory from Muslim oppression. Some—including the "mad, bad and dangerous to know" English poet Lord Byron, who lost his life in the war—went to Greece to fight as volunteers. When the combined squadrons of the British, French, and Russian fleets, under orders to observe but not intervene in the war, made an unauthorized attack that sank the Ottoman fleet at the Battle of Navarino, Greek victory was assured (see Map 24.1).

Destruction of the Janissaries

Mahmud II concurred with the pro-Greek Europeans in viewing Ottoman military reversals in Greece as a sign of profound weakness. With popular outrage over the military setbacks strong, the sultan made his move in 1826. First he announced the creation of a new artillery unit, which he had secretly been training. When the Janissaries rose in revolt, he ordered the new unit to bombard the Janissary barracks. The Janissary corps was officially dissolved.

Like Muhammad Ali, Mahmud felt he could not implement major changes without reducing the political power of the religious elite. He visualized restructuring the bureaucracy and the educational and legal systems, where ulama power was strongest. Before such strong measures could be undertaken, however, Ibrahim attacked from Syria in 1839. Battlefield defeat, the decision of the rebuilt Ottoman navy to switch sides and support Egypt, and the death of Mahmud, all in the same year, left the empire completely dependent on the European powers for survival.

The Tanzimat

Tanzimat Restructuring reforms by the nineteenth-century Ottoman rulers, intended to move civil law away from the control of religious elites and make the military and the bureaucracy more efficient.

Mahmud's reforming ideas received their widest expression in the **Tanzimat** (TAHNZ-ee-MAT) ("reorganization"), a series of reforms announced by his sixteen-year-old son and successor, Abdul Mejid (ab-dul meh-JEED), in 1839 and strongly endorsed by the European ambassadors. One proclamation called for public trials and equal protection under the law for all, whether Muslim, Christian, or Jew. It also guaranteed some rights of privacy, equalized the eligibility of men for conscription into the army (a practice copied from Egypt), and provided for a new, formalized method of tax collection that legally ended tax farming in the Ottoman Empire. It took many years and strenuous efforts by reforming bureaucrats, known as the "men of the Tanzimat," to give substance to these reforms.

Over time, one legal code after another—commercial, criminal, civil procedure—was introduced to take the place of the corresponding areas of religious legal jurisdiction. All the codes were modeled closely on those of Europe. The Shari'a, or Islamic law, gradually became restricted to matters of family law such as marriage and inheritance. As the Shari'a was displaced, job opportunities for the ulama shrank.

e **PRIMARY SOURCE: Tanzimat Decree** This document marks the beginning of the Tanzimat.

European observers praised the reforms for their noble principles and rejection of religious influence. Ottoman citizens were more divided; the Christians and Jews, for whom the Europeans showed the greatest concern, were generally more enthusiastic than the Muslims. Many historians see the Tanzimat as the dawn of modern thought and enlightened government in the Middle East. Others point out that removing the religious elite from influence in government also removed the one remaining check on authoritarian rule.

Military Reforms

AP* Exam Tip Be familiar with the reforms of the Ottoman Empire, but don't spend time memorizing the names of military and political leaders.

Like Muhammad Ali, Sultan Mahmud sent military cadets to France and the German states for training. In the 1830s an Ottoman imperial school of military sciences, later to become Istanbul University, was established. Instructors from western Europe taught chemistry, engineering, mathematics, and physics in addition to military history. Military education became the model for more general educational reforms. In 1838 the first medical school was established to train army doctors and surgeons. Later, a national system of preparatory schools was created to feed graduates into the military schools. The subjects that were taught and many of the teachers were foreign, raising the issue of whether Turkish should be a language of instruction. Because it was easier to import and use foreign textbooks than to write new ones in Turkish, French became the preferred language in all advanced professional and scientific training. In numerical terms, however, the great majority of students still learned to read and write in Quran schools down to the twentieth century.

In the capital city of Istanbul, the reforms stimulated the growth of a small but cosmopolitan milieu embracing European language and culture. The first Turkish newspaper, a government gazette modeled on that of Muhammad Ali, appeared in 1831. Other newspapers followed, many written in French. Travel to Europe—particularly to England and France—became popular among wealthy Turks. Interest in importing European military, industrial, and communications technology remained strong through the 1800s.

Introduction of the Fez

Changes in military practice had unforeseen cultural and social effects. Accepting the European notion that modern weapons and drill required modern military dress, beards were deemed unhygienic and, in artillery units, a fire hazard. Military headgear also became controversial. European military caps, which had leather bills on the front to protect against the glare of the sun, were not acceptable because they interfered with Muslim soldiers' touching their foreheads to the ground in prayer. The compromise was the brimless cap now called the *fez*, which was adopted by the military and then by Ottoman civil officials in the early years of Mahmud II's reign.

Modernized Ottoman Troops This photograph of a contingent of Imperial Guards in the late nineteenth century shows them equipped and uniformed much like any other European army of the time. The only distinctive feature is the fez, a brimless hat adopted earlier in the century as a symbol of reform. Comparison with the soldiers in the funeral procession of Suleiman the Magnificent (page 546) shows the degree of change from the traditional military uniforms that were still being worn in the eighteenth century.

The empire's new orientation spread beyond the military. Government ministries that normally recruited from traditional bureaucratic families and relied on on-the-job training were gradually transformed into formal civil services hiring men educated in the new schools. Among self-consciously progressive men, particularly those in government service, European dress became the fashion in the Ottoman cities of the later 1800s, while traditional dress became a symbol of the religious, the rural, and the parochial.

Legal Reforms

Secularization of the legal code particularly affected non-Muslim Ottoman subjects. Islamic law had required non-Muslims to pay a special head tax that was sometimes explained as a substitute for military service. Under the Tanzimat, the tax was abolished and non-Muslims became liable for military service—unless they bought their way out by paying a new military exemption tax. The new law codes gave all male subjects equal access to the civil courts, while the operations of the Islamic law courts shrank. What enhanced the status of non-Muslims most, however, was the strong concern for their welfare consistently expressed by the European powers. The Ottoman Empire became a rich field of operation for Christian missionaries and European supporters of Jewish community life in the Muslim world.

Status of Women

The public rights and political participation granted during the Tanzimat applied specifically to men. Private life, including everything connected to marriage and divorce, remained within the sphere of religious law, and at no time was there a question of political participation or reformed education for women. Indeed, the reforms may have decreased the influence of women. The political changes ran parallel to economic changes that also narrowed women's opportunities.

After silver from the Americas began to flood the empire in the 1600s, workers were increasingly paid in cash rather than in goods, and businesses associated with banking and finance developed. But women were barred from the early industrial labor and the professions, and traditional "woman's work" such as weaving was increasingly mechanized and done by men.

Nevertheless, in the early 1800s women retained considerable power in the management and disposal of their own property, gained mostly through fixed shares of inheritance. After marriage a woman was often pressured to convert her landholdings to cash in order to transfer her personal wealth to her husband's family, with whom she and her husband would reside. However, this was not a requirement, since men were legally obligated to support their families single-handedly. Until the 1820s many wealthy women retained their say in the distribution of property through the creation of charitable trusts for their sons. Because these trusts were set up in the religious courts, they could be designed to conform to the wishes of family members. Then, in the 1820s and 1830s the secularizing reforms of Mahmud II, which did not always pro-

From Ignatius Mouradgea d'Ohsson, *Tableau General de l'Empire Ottoman*, large folio edition, Paris, 1787–1820, pl. 178, following p. 340

Interior of the Ottoman Financial Bureau This engraving from the eighteenth century depicts the governing style of the Ottoman Empire before the era of westernizing reforms. By the end of the Tanzimat period in 1876, government offices and the costumes of officials looked much more like those in contemporary European capitals.

duce happy results, transferred jurisdiction over the charitable trusts from religious courts to the state and ended women's control over this form of property.

The Crimean War and Its Aftermath

Since the reign of Peter the Great (r. 1689–1725), the Russian Empire had been attempting to expand southward at the Ottomans' expense (see the section on Russia and Asia). By 1815 Russia had pried the Georgian region of the Caucasus away from the Ottomans, and the threat of Russian intervention had prevented the Ottomans from crushing Serbian independence. When Muhammad Ali's Egyptian army invaded Syria in 1833, Russia signed a treaty in support of the Ottomans. In return, the sultan recognized Russia's claim to being the protector of all of the empire's Orthodox subjects. This set the stage for an obscure dispute that resulted in war.

The Eastern Question

Bowing to British and French pressure, the sultan named France Protector of the Holy Sepulchre in Jerusalem in 1852. Russia protested, but the sultan held firm. So Russia invaded Ottoman territories in what is today Romania, and Britain and France went to war as allies of the sultan. The real causes of the war went beyond church quarrels in Jerusalem and involved diplomatic maneuvering among European powers over whether the Ottoman Empire should continue to exist and, if not, who should take over its territory. The Eastern Question was the simple name given to this complex issue. Though the powers, including Russia, had agreed to save the empire in 1839, Britain subsequently became suspicious of Russian ambitions. Prominent anti-Russian politicians in Britain feared that Russia would threaten the British hold on India.

Siege of Sevastopol

Crimean War Conflict between the Russian and Ottoman Empires fought primarily in the Crimean Peninsula. To prevent Russian expansion, Britain and France sent troops to support the Ottomans.

Between 1853 and 1856 the **Crimean** (cry-ME-uhn) **War** raged in Romania, on the Black Sea, and on the Crimean peninsula. Britain, France, and the Italian kingdom of Sardinia-Piedmont sided with the Ottomans. Austria mediated the outcome. Britain and France trapped the Russian fleet in the Black Sea, where its commanders decided to sink the ships to protect the approaches to Sevastopol, their main base in Crimea. However, an army largely made up of British and French troops landed and laid siege to the city. Official corruption and lack of railways hampered the Russians' attempts to supply their forces. On the Romanian front, the Ottomans resisted effectively. At Sevastopol, the Russians were outmatched militarily and suffered badly from disease. Tsar Nicholas died as defeat loomed, leaving his successor, Alexander II (r. 1855–1881), to sue for peace when Sevastopol finally fell three months later.

The Crimean War brought significant changes to all the combatants. The tsar and his government, already beset by demands for the reform of serfdom, education, and the military (discussed later), were further discredited. In Britain and France, the conflict was accompanied by massive propaganda campaigns. For the first time newspapers effectively mobilized public support for a war. British press accounts so glamorized British participation that the false impression has lingered that Ottoman troops played a negligible role in the conflict. At the time, however,

From Edward William Lane, *The Manners and Customs of the Modern Egyptians* (London: J. M. D & Co. 1860)

Street Scene in Cairo This engraving from Edward William Lane's influential travel book, *Account of the Manners and Customs of the Modern Egyptians Written in Egypt During the Years 1833–1835* conveys the image of narrow lanes and small stores that became stock features of European thinking about Middle Eastern cities.

British and French commanders noted the massive losses among Turkish troops in particular. The French press, dominant in Istanbul, promoted a sense of unity between Turkish and French society that continued to influence many aspects of Turkish urban culture.

The larger significance of the Crimean War was that it marked the transition from traditional to modern warfare (see Environment and Technology: The Web of War). All the combatants had previously prided themselves on the use of highly trained cavalry to smash through the front lines of infantry. Cavalry coexisted with firearms until the early 1800s, primarily because early rifles were awkward to load and not very accurate. Cavalry could attack during the intervals between volleys. Then in the 1830s and 1840s percussion caps that did away with pouring gunpowder into the barrel of a musket came into use. In Crimean War battles many cavalry units were destroyed by the rapid fire of rifles that loaded at the breech rather than down the barrel. That was the fate of the famed British Light Brigade, which was sent to relieve an Ottoman unit surrounded by Russian troops.

Commercial Expansion

After the Crimean War, the Ottoman Empire increased its involvement with European commerce. The Ottoman imperial bank was founded in 1840, and a few years later currency reform pegged the value of Ottoman gold coins to the British pound. Sweeping changes in the 1850s expedited the creation of banks, insurance companies, and legal firms throughout the empire. Bustling trade also encouraged a migration from country to city between about 1850 and 1880. Many of the major cities of the empire—Istanbul, Damascus, Beirut, Alexandria, Cairo—expanded. A small but influential urban professional class emerged, as did a considerable class of wage laborers. Other demographic shifts involved refugees from Poland and Hungary, where rivalry between the European powers and the Russian Empire caused political tension and sporadic warfare, and from Georgia and other parts of the Caucasus, where Russian expansion forced many Muslims to emigrate (discussed later).

extraterritoriality The right of foreign residents in a country to live under the laws of their native country and disregard the laws of the host country. In the nineteenth and early twentieth centuries, European and American nationals living in certain areas of Chinese and Ottoman cities were granted this right.

However, commercial vigor and urbanization could not make up for declining revenues and the chronic insolvency and corruption of the imperial government. From the conclusion of the Crimean War in 1856 on, the Ottoman government became heavily dependent on foreign loans. In return it lowered tariffs to favor European imports and allowed European banks to open in Ottoman cities. Europeans living in Istanbul and other commercial centers enjoyed **extraterritoriality**, the right to be subject to their own laws and exempt from Ottoman jurisdiction.

Foreign Debt

As the result of these measures, imported goods multiplied, but—apart from tobacco and the Turkish opium that American traders took to China to compete against British opium from India—Anatolia produced few exports. As foreign debt grew, so did inflationary trends that left urban populations in a precarious position. By contrast, Egyptian cotton exports soared during the American Civil War, when American cotton exports plummeted; but the profits benefited Muhammad Ali's descendants, who had become the hereditary governors of Egypt, rather than the Ottoman government. The Suez Canal, which was partly financed by cotton profits, opened in 1869, and Cairo was redesigned and beautified. Eventually overexpenditure on such projects plunged Egypt into the same debt crisis that plagued the empire as a whole.

The decline of Ottoman power and prosperity had a strong impact on a group of well-educated young urban men who aspired to wealth and influence. They doubted that the empire's

ENVIRONMENT + TECHNOLOGY

The Web of War

The lethal military technologies of the mid-nineteenth century that were used on battlefields in the United States, Russia, India, and China were rapidly transmitted from one conflict to the next. This dissemination was due not only to the rapid development of communications but also to the existence of a new international network of soldiers who moved from one trouble spot to another, bringing expertise in the use of new techniques.

General Charles Gordon (1833–1885), for instance, was commissioned in the British army in 1852, then served in the Crimean War after Britain entered on the side of the Ottomans. In 1860 he was dispatched to China. He served with British forces during the Arrow War and took part in the sack of Beijing. Afterward, he stayed in China and was assigned to the Qing imperial government until the suppression of the Taipings in 1864, earning himself the nickname "Chinese" Gordon. Gordon later served the Ottoman rulers of Egypt as governor of territory along the Nile. He was killed in Egypt in 1885 while leading his Egyptian troops in defense of the city of Khartoum against an uprising by the Sudanese religious leader, the Mahdi.

Journalism played an important part in the developing web of telegraph communications that sped orders to and from the battlefields. Readers in London could learn details of the drama occurring in the Crimea or in China within a week—or in some cases days—after they occurred. Print and, later, photographic journalism created new "stars" from these war experiences. Charles Gordon was one. Florence Nightingale was another.

In the great wars of the 1800s, the vast majority of deaths resulted from infection or excessive bleeding, not from the wounds themselves. Florence Nightingale (1820–1910), while still a young woman, became interested in hospital management and nursing. She went to Prussia and France to study advanced techniques. Before the outbreak of the Crimean War she was credited with bringing about marked improvement in British health care. When the public reacted to news reports of the suffering in the Crimea, the British government sent Nightingale to the region. Within a year of her arrival the death rate in the military hospitals there dropped from 45 percent to under 5 percent. Her techniques for preventing septicemia and dysentery, essentially sanitary measures like washing bed linens after a death and emptying toilet buckets outside, were quickly adopted by those working for and with her. On her return to London, Nightingale established institutes for nursing that soon were recognized as leaders around the world. She herself was lionized by the British public and received the Order of Merit in 1907, three years before her death.

The importance of Nightingale's innovations in public hygiene is underscored by the life of her contemporary, Mary Seacole (1805–1881). A Jamaican woman who volunteered to nurse British troops in the Crimean War, Seacole was repeatedly excluded from nursing service by British authorities. She eventually went to Crimea and used her own funds to run a hospital there, bankrupting herself in the process. The drama of the Crimean War moved the British public to support Seacole after her sacrifices were publicized. She was awarded medals by the British, French, and Turkish governments and today is recognized with her contemporary Florence Nightingale as an innovative field nurse and a champion of public hygiene in peacetime.

Florence Nightingale During Crimean War This 1856 lithograph shows Florence Nightingale supervising nursing care in a hospital in Scutari (Uskudar) across the Bosphorus strait from Istanbul. Though the artist may have exaggerated the neatness and cleanliness of the ward, sanitary measures proved the key to Nightingale's raising of the survival rate of sick and wounded soldiers.

rulers and the Tanzimat officials who worked for them would ever stand up to European domination. Though lacking a sophisticated organization, these Young Ottomans (sometimes called Young Turks, though that term properly applies to a later movement) promoted a mixture of liberal ideas derived from Europe, national pride in Ottoman independence, and modernist views of Islam. Prominent Young Ottomans helped draft a constitution that was promulgated in 1876 by a new and as yet untried sultan, Abdul Hamid II. This apparent triumph of liberal reform was short-lived. With war against Russia again threatening in the Balkans in 1877, Abdul Hamid suspended the constitution and the parliament that had been elected that year. Though he ruthlessly opposed further political reforms, the Tanzimat programs of extending modern schooling, utilizing European military practices and advisers, and making the government bureaucracy more orderly continued during his reign.

SECTION REVIEW

- After French withdrawal from Egypt, Muhammad Ali seized control and began a French-influenced modernization program.
- His successors continued the program and attacked the Ottoman Empire, but they were thwarted by the European powers.
- The Greek insurrection, European intervention, and Egyptian attack drove the westernizing reform efforts of Mahmud II and his successors.
- The most comprehensive reform initiative was Abdul Mejid's Tanzimat program.
- The Crimean War marked the transition from traditional to modern warfare and drew the Ottoman Empire into greater involvement with European commerce.
- Declining power and prosperity led to the rise of the Young Ottomans.

THE RUSSIAN EMPIRE

In 1812, when Napoleon's march on Moscow ended in a disastrous retreat brought on more by what a later tsar called "Generals January and February" than by Russian military action, the European image of Russia changed. Just as Napoleon's withdrawal from Egypt led to Muhammad Ali briefly becoming a political power, so his withdrawal from Russia conferred status on Tsar Alexander I (r. 1801–1825). Conservative Europeans still saw Russia as alien, backward, and oppressive, but they acknowledged its immensity and potential and included the tsar in efforts to suppress revolutionary tendencies throughout Europe.

Russia Compared with Ottomans

In several important respects Russia resembled the Ottoman Empire more than the conservative kingdoms of Europe whose autocratic practices it so staunchly supported. Socially dominated by nobles whose country estates were worked by unfree serfs, Russia had almost no middle class. Industry was still at the threshold of development by the standards of the rapidly industrializing European powers, though it was somewhat more dynamic than Ottoman industry. Like Egypt and the Ottoman Empire, Russia engaged in reforms from the top down under Alexander I, but when his conservative brother Nicholas I (r. 1825–1855) succeeded to the throne, iron discipline and suspicion of modern ideas took priority over reform.

AP* Exam Tip Be prepared to compare empires such as the Ottoman Empire and the Russia Empire.

Russia and Europe

In 1700 only three Russians out of a hundred lived in cities, two-thirds of them in Moscow alone. By the mid-1800s the town population had grown tenfold, though it still accounted for only 6 percent of the total because the territories of the tsars had grown greatly through wars and colonization (see Chapter 20). These figures demonstrate that, like the Ottoman Empire, Russia was an overwhelmingly agricultural land. However, it had poorer transportation than the Ottoman Empire, since many Ottoman cities were seaports. Both empires encompassed peoples speaking many different languages.

Slow Pace of Reform

Well-engineered roads did not begin to appear until 1817, and steam navigation commenced on the Volga in 1843. Tsar Nicholas I built the first railroad from St. Petersburg, the Russian capital, to his summer palace in 1837. A few years later his commitment to strict discipline led him to insist that the trunk line from St. Petersburg to Moscow run in a perfectly straight line. American engineers, among them the father of the painter James McNeill Whistler, who learned to paint in St. Petersburg, oversaw the laying of track and built locomotive workshops. Industrialization projects depended heavily on foreign expertise. British engineers set up the textile mills that gave woolens and cottons a prominent place among Russia's industries.

Tsar Nicholas I

Until the late nineteenth century the Russian government's interest in industry was limited. An industrial revolution required educated and independent-minded artisans and entrepreneurs, but Nicholas feared the spread of literacy and modern education—especially anything smacking of liberalism, socialism, or revolution—beyond the minimum needed to train the officer corps and the bureaucracy. He preferred serfs to factory workers, and he paid for imported industrial goods with exports of grain and timber.

Like Egypt and the Ottoman Empire, Russia aspired to Western-style economic development. But when France and Britain entered the Crimean War, they faced a Russian army equipped with obsolete weapons and bogged down by lack of transportation. At a time when European engineers were making major breakthroughs in loading cannon through an opening at the breech end, muzzle-loading artillery remained the Russian standard.

Russia and Europe

Yet in some ways Russia bore a closer resemblance to other European countries than the Ottoman Empire did. From the point of view of the French and the British, the Cyrillic alphabet and the Russian Orthodox form of Christianity seemed foreign, but they were not nearly as foreign as the Arabic alphabet and the Muslim faith. Britain and France feared Russia as a rival for power in the east, but they increasingly accepted Tsar Nicholas's view of the Ottoman Empire as "the sick man of Europe," capable of surviving only so long as the European powers permitted.

Slavophiles Russian intellectuals in the early nineteenth century who favored resisting western European influences and taking pride in the traditional peasant values and institutions of the Slavic people.

From the Russian point of view, kinship with western Europe was of questionable value. Westernizers, like the men of the Tanzimat in the Ottoman Empire, put their trust in technical advances and governmental reform. Opposing them were intellectuals known as **Slavophiles**, who considered the Orthodox faith, the solidity of peasant life, and the tsar's absolute rule to be the proper bases of Russian civilization. After Russia's humiliation in the Crimea, the Slavophile tendency gave rise to **Pan-Slavism**, a militant political doctrine advocating unity of all the Slavic peoples, including those living under Austrian and Ottoman rule.

Pan-Slavism

Pan-Slavism Movement among Russian intellectuals in the second half of the nineteenth century to identify culturally and politically with the Slavic peoples of eastern Europe.

On the diplomatic front, the tsar's inclusion as a major European ruler contrasted sharply with the sultan's exclusion. However, this did not prevent a powerful sense of Russophobia from developing in the West. Britain in particular saw Russia as a threat to India and despised the subjection of the serfs, who gained their freedom from Tsar Alexander II only in 1861, twenty-seven years after the British had abolished slavery. In addition, the passions generated by the Crimean War and its outcome affected the relations of Russia, Europe, and the Ottoman Empire for the remainder of the nineteenth century.

Russia and Asia

Southward Expansion

The Russian drive to the east in the eighteenth century brought the tsar's empire to the Pacific Ocean and the frontiers of China (see Map 20.1) by century's end. In the nineteenth century Russian expansionism focused on the south. There the backwardness of the Russian military did not matter since the peoples they faced were even less industrialized and technologically advanced. In 1860 Russia established a military outpost on the Pacific coast that would eventually grow into the great naval port of Vladivostok, today Russia's most southerly city. In Central Asia the steppe lands of the Kazakh nomads came under Russian control early in the century, setting the stage for a confrontation with three Uzbek states farther south. They succumbed one by one, beginning in 1865, giving rise to the new province of Turkestan, with its capital at Tashkent in present-day Uzbekistan.

In the region of the Caucasus Mountains, the third area of southward expansion, Russia first took over Christian Georgia (1786), Muslim Azerbaijan (ah-zer-by-JAHN) (1801), and Christian Armenia (1813) before gobbling up the many small principalities in the heart of the mountains. Between 1829 and 1864 Dagestan, Chechnya (CHECH-nee-yah), Abkhazia (ab-KAH-zee-yah), and other regions became parts of the Russian Empire.

The drive to the south intensified political friction with Russia's new neighbors: Qing China and Japan in the east, Iran on the Central Asian and Caucasus frontiers, and the Ottoman Empire at the eastern end of the Black Sea. In the latter two instances, Muslim refugees from the territories newly absorbed by Russia spread anti-Russian feelings, though some of them brought with them modern skills and ideas gained from exposure to Russian administration and education.

Russia Confronts British India

The Russian drive to the south added a new element to the Eastern Question. Many British statesmen and strategists reckoned that a warlike Russia would press on until it had conquered all the lands separating it from British India, a prospect that made them shudder, given India's enormous contribution to Britain's prosperity. The competition that ensued over which power would control southern Central Asia resulted in a standoff in Afghanistan, which became a buffer zone under the control of neither. In Iran, the standoff between the powers helped preserve the weak Qajar dynasty of shahs.

Cultural Trends

Tsar Alexander I

Unlike Egypt and the Ottoman Empire, which began to send students to Europe for training only in the nineteenth century, Russia had been in cultural contact with western Europe since the time of Peter the Great (r. 1689–1725). Members of the Russian court knew Western languages, and the tsars employed officials and advisers from Western countries. Peter had also enlisted the well-educated Ukrainian clerics who headed the Russian Orthodox Church to help spread a Western spirit of education. As a result, Alexander I's reforms met a more positive reception than those of Muhammad Ali and Mahmud II. However, his reforms promised more on paper than they brought about in practice. It took many years to develop a sufficient pool of trained bureaucrats to make the reforms effective.

Ironically, much of the opposition to Alexander's reforms came from well-established families that were not at all unfriendly to Western ideas. Their fear was that the new government bureaucrats, who often came from humbler social origins, would act as agents of imperial tyranny. This fear was realized during the conservative reign of Nicholas I in the same way that the Tanzimat-inspired bureaucracy of the Ottoman Empire served the despotic purposes of Sultan Abdul Hamid II after 1877. Individuals favoring more liberal reforms, including military officers who had served in western Europe, intellectuals who read Western political tracts, and members of Masonic lodges who exchanged views with Freemasons in the West, formed secret societies of opposition. Some placed their highest priority on freeing the serfs; others advocated a constitution and a republican form of government. When Alexander I died in December 1825, confusion over who was to succeed him encouraged a group of reform-minded army officers to try to take over the government and provoke an uprising. This so-called **Decembrist revolt** failed, and many of the participants were severely punished. These events ensured that the new tsar, Nicholas I, would pay little heed to calls for reform over the next thirty years.

Decembrist revolt Abortive attempt by army officers to take control of the Russian government upon the death of Tsar Alexander I in 1825.

Tsar Alexander II

The great powers meeting in Paris to settle the Crimean War in 1856 forced Russia to return land to the Ottomans in both Europe and Asia. This humiliation spurred Nicholas's son and successor, Alexander II (r. 1855–1881), to institute major new reforms to reinvigorate the country. The greatest of his reforms was the emancipation of the serfs in 1861. He also authorized new joint-stock companies, projected a railroad network to tie the country together, and modernized the legal and administrative arms of government.

Raising of the Alexander Monument in St. Petersburg The death of Alexander I in 1825 brought to power his conservative brother Nicholas I. Yet Alexander remained a heroic figure for his resistance to Napoleon. This monument in Winter Palace Square was erected in 1829.

Visual Connection Archive

Intellectual Awakening

Earlier intellectual and cultural trends flourished under Alexander II. More and more people became involved in intellectual, artistic, and professional life. Most prominent intellectuals received some amount of instruction at Moscow University or some German university. Universities also appeared in provincial cities like Kharkov in Ukraine and Kazan on the Volga River. Student clubs, along with Masonic lodges, became places for discussing new ideas. As Russian scholars and scientists began to achieve recognition for their contributions to European thought, scholarly careers attracted young men from clerical families, who in turn helped stimulate reforms in religious education.

Just as the Tanzimat reforms of the Ottoman Empire preceded the emergence of the Young Ottomans as a new and assertive political and intellectual force in the second half of the nineteenth century, so the initially ineffective reforms of Alexander I set in motion cultural currents that would make Russia a dynamic center of intellectual, artistic, and political life under his nephew Alexander II. Thus Russia belonged to two different spheres of development. It entered the nineteenth century a recognized force in European politics, but in other ways it resembled the Ottoman Empire. Rulers in both empires instituted reforms, overcame opposition, and increased the power of their governments. These activities stimulated intellectual and political trends that would ultimately work against the absolute rule of tsar and sultan. Yet Russia would eventually develop much closer relations with western Europe and become an arena for every sort of European intellectual, artistic, and political tendency, while the Ottoman Empire would ultimately succumb to European imperialism.

SECTION REVIEW

- Russian society resembled Ottoman society, but Alexander I undertook top-down westernizing reforms.
- Nicholas I's suspicion of Western ideas stalled reform and slowed industrial development.
- Slavophiles opposed westernizers and, after the Crimean War, embraced Pan-Slavism, contributing to Russophobia in the West.
- Russian expansion southward and eastward added vast territories to the empire and caused friction with China, Japan, Iran, and the Ottoman Empire.
- Resistance to Alexander I's bureaucratic reforms sparked the Decembrist revolt, which stiffened Nicholas I's hostility to Western ideas.
- The humiliation of the Crimean War drove Alexander II's reforms, including emancipation of the serfs.

THE QING EMPIRE

In 1800 the Qing Empire faced many problems, but no reform movement of the kind initiated by Sultan Selim III emerged in China. The reasons are not difficult to understand. The Qing emperors had skillfully countered Russian strategic and diplomatic moves in the 1600s. Instead of having a Napoleon threatening them with invasion, they enjoyed the admiration of Jesuit priests, who likened them to enlightened philosopher-kings. In 1793, however, a British attempt to establish diplomatic and trade relations—the Macartney mission—turned European opinion against China (see Chapter 20).

"Canton System"

China's most serious crises were domestic, not foreign: rebellions by displaced indigenous peoples and the poor, and protests against the injustice of the local magistrates. The Qing dealt with these problems in the usual way, by suppressing rebels and dismissing incompetent or untrustworthy officials. They paid little attention to the far-off Europeans and brushed aside the complaints from European merchants who chafed against the restrictions of the "Canton system" by which the Qing limited and controlled foreign trade.

Economic and Social Disorder

Population Pressure

Early Qing successes and territorial expansion sowed the seeds of the domestic and political chaos of the later period. The early emperors encouraged the recovery of farmland, the opening of previously uncultivated areas, and the restoration and expansion of the road and canal systems. These measures expanded the agricultural base and supported a doubling of the population between about 1650 and 1800. Enormous numbers of farmers, merchants, and day laborers migrated in search of less crowded conditions, and a permanent floating population of the unemployed and homeless emerged. By 1800 population strain had caused serious environmental damage in some parts of central and western China.

While farmers tried to cope with agricultural deterioration, other groups vented grievances against the government: minority peoples in central and southwestern China complained about being driven off their lands during the boom of the 1700s; Mongols resented appropriation of their grazing lands and the displacement of their traditional elites. In some regions, village vigilante organizations took over policing and governing functions from Qing officials who had lost control. Growing numbers of people mistrusted the government, suspecting that all officials were corrupt. The increasing presence of foreign merchants and missionaries in Canton and in the Portuguese colony of Macao aggravated discontent in neighboring districts.

White Lotus Rebellion

In some parts of China the Qing were hated as foreign conquerors and were suspected of sympathy with the Europeans. In 1794 the White Lotus Rebellion—partly inspired by a messianic ideology that predicted the restoration of the Chinese Ming dynasty and the coming of the Buddha—raged across central China and was not suppressed until 1804. It initiated a series of internal conflicts that continued through the 1800s. Ignited by deepening social instabilities, these movements were sometimes intensified by local ethnic conflicts and by unapproved religions. The ability of some village militias to defend themselves and attack others intensified the conflicts, though the same techniques proved useful to southern coastal populations attempting to fend off British invasion.

The Opium War and Its Aftermath, 1839–1850

Imports from India

AP* Exam Tip Be prepared to discuss the impact of outside forces on China in the nineteenth century.

Unlike the Ottomans, the Qing knew little about the enormous fortunes being made in the early 1800s by European and American merchants smuggling opium into China. They did not know that silver gained in this illegal trade was helping finance the industrial transformation of England and the United States. Only slowly did Qing officials become aware of British colonies in India that grew and exported opium, and of the major naval base at Singapore through which British opium reached East Asia.

In 1729 the first Qing law banning opium imports was promulgated. By 1800, however, opium smuggling had swelled the annual import level to as many as four thousand chests. Though British merchants had pioneered this profitable trade, Chinese merchants likewise profited from distributing the drugs. A price war in the early 1820s stemming from competition between British and American importers raised demand so sharply that as many as thirty thousand chests were being imported by the 1830s. Addiction spread to people at all levels of Qing society, including high-ranking officials. The Qing emperor and his officials debated whether to legalize and tax opium or to enforce the existing ban more strictly. Having decided to root out the use and importation of opium, in 1839 they sent a high official to Canton to deal with the matter.

Military Weakness

Opium War War between Britain and the Qing Empire that was, in the British view, occasioned by the Qing government's refusal to permit the importation of opium into its territories. The victorious British imposed the one-sided Treaty of Nanking on China.

Britain considered the ban on opium importation an intolerable limitation on trade, a direct threat to Britain's economic health, and a cause for war. British naval and marine forces arrived on the south China coast in late 1839. The **Opium War** (1839–1842) broke out when negotiations between the Qing official and British representatives reached a stalemate. The war exposed the fact that the traditional, hereditary soldiers of the Qing Empire—the **Bannermen**—were, like the Janissaries of the Ottoman Empire, hopelessly obsolete. As in the Crimean War, the British excelled at sea, where they deployed superior technology. British ships landed marines who pillaged coastal cities and then sailed to new destinations (see Map 24.2). The Qing had no imperial navy. Thus until they were able to engage the British in prolonged fighting on land, they were unable to defend themselves against British attacks. Even in the land engagements, Qing resources proved woefully inadequate. The British could quickly transport their forces by sea along the coast, whereas Qing troops moved primarily on foot. Moving Qing reinforcements from central to eastern China took more than three months; and when the defense forces arrived, they were exhausted and basically without weapons.

Bannermen Hereditary military servants of the Qing Empire, in large part descendants of peoples of various origins who had fought for the founders of the empire.

The Bannermen used the few muskets the Qing had imported during the 1700s. The weapons were matchlocks, which required the soldiers to ignite the load of gunpowder in them by hand. Firing the weapons was dangerous, and the canisters of gunpowder that each musketeer carried on his belt were likely to explode if a fire broke out nearby—a frequent occurrence in encounters with British artillery. Most of the Bannermen, however, had no guns at all and fought with swords, knives, spears, and clubs. Soldiers under British command—many of them Indians—carried percussion-cap rifles, which were far quicker, safer, and more accurate than the matchlocks. In addition, the long-range British artillery could be moved from place to place and proved deadly in the cities and villages of eastern China.

British Gunboats

Qing commanders thought that British gunboats rode so low in the water that they could not sail up the Chinese rivers. So they evacuated the coastal areas to counter the British threat. But the British deployed new gunboats for shallow waters and moved without difficulty up the Yangzi River (see Chapter 22).

Most Favored Nation

When the invaders approached Nanjing, the former Ming capital, the Qing decided to negotiate. In 1842 the terms of the **Treaty of Nanking** (the British name for Nanjing) dismantled the old Canton system. The number of **treaty ports**—cities opened to foreign residents—increased from one (Canton) to five (Canton, Xiamen, Fuzhou, Ningbo, and Shanghai [shahng-hie]). The island of Hong Kong became a British colony, and British residents in China gained extraterritorial rights. The Qing government agreed to set a low tariff of 5 percent on imports and to pay Britain an indemnity of 21 million ounces of silver as a penalty for having started the war. A supplementary treaty the following year guaranteed **most-favored-nation status** to Britain: any privileges that China granted to another country would be automatically extended to Britain as well. This provision effectively prevented the colonization of China, because giving land to one country would have necessitated giving it to all.

Treaty of Nanking The treaty that concluded the Opium War. It awarded Britain a large indemnity from the Qing Empire, denied the Qing government tariff control over some of its own borders, opened additional ports of residence to Britons, and ceded the island of Hong Kong to Britain.

treaty ports Cities opened to foreign residents as a result of the forced treaties between the Qing Empire and foreign signatories. In the treaty ports, foreigners enjoyed extraterritoriality.

most-favored-nation status A clause in a commercial treaty that awards to any later signatories all the privileges previously granted to the original signatories.

With each round of treaties came a new round of privileges for foreigners. In 1860 a new treaty legalized their right to import opium. Later, French treaties established the rights of foreign missionaries to travel in the Chinese countryside and preach their religion. The number of treaty ports grew, too; by 1900 they numbered more than ninety.

The treaty system and the principle of extraterritoriality resulted in the colonization of small pockets of Qing territory, where foreign merchants lived at ease. Greater territorial losses resulted when outlying regions gained independence or were ceded to neighboring countries. Districts north and south of the Amur River in the northeast fell to Russia by treaty in 1858 and 1860; parts of modern Kazakhstan and Kyrgyzstan in the northwest met the same fate in 1864. From 1865 onward the British gradually gained control of territories on China's Indian frontier. In the late 1800s France forced the court of Vietnam to end its tribute relationship to the Qing, while Britain encouraged Tibetan independence.

European Zones

In Canton, Shanghai, and other coastal cities, Europeans and Americans maintained offices and factories that employed local Chinese as menial laborers. The foreigners built comfortable housing in zones where Chinese were not permitted to live, and they entertained themselves in exclusive restaurants and bars. Around the foreign establishments, gambling and prostitution offered employment to part of the local urban population.

Whether in town or in the countryside, Christian missionaries whose congregations sponsored hospitals, shelters, and soup kitchens or gave stipends to Chinese who attended church enjoyed a good reputation. But just as often the missionaries themselves were regarded as another evil. They seemed to subvert Confucian beliefs by condemning ancestor worship, pressuring poor families to put their children into orphanages, or fulminating against footbinding. The growing numbers of foreigners, and their growing privileges, became targets of resentment for a deeply dissatisfied, daily more impoverished, and increasingly militarized society.

The Taiping Rebellion, 1850–1864

Taiping Rebellion A Christian-inspired rural rebellion that threatened to topple the Qing Empire.

The inflammatory mixture of social unhappiness and foreign intrusion exploded in the great civil war usually called the **Taiping** (tie-PING) **Rebellion**. In Guangxi, where the Taiping movement originated, entrenched social problems had been generating disorders for half a century. Agriculture in the region was unstable, and many people made their living from arduous and despised trades such as disposing of human waste, making charcoal, and mining. Ethnic divisions complicated economic distress. The lowliest trades frequently involved a minority group, the Hakkas, and tensions between them and the majority were rising. Problems may have been intensified by sharp fluctuations in the opium trade and reactions to the cultural and economic impact of the Europeans and Americans in Canton.

"Younger Brother of Jesus"

Hong Xiuquan (hoong shee-OH-chew-an), the founder of the Taiping movement, experienced all of these influences. Hong came from a humble Hakka background. After years of study, he competed in the provincial Confucian examinations, hoping for a post in government. He failed the examinations repeatedly, and it appears that he suffered a nervous breakdown in his late thirties. Afterward he spent some time in Canton, where he met both Chinese and American

Protestant missionaries, who inspired him with their teachings. Hong had his own interpretation of the Christian message. He saw himself as the younger brother of Jesus, commissioned by God to found a new kingdom on earth and drive the Manchu conquerors, the Qing, out of China. The result would be universal peace. Hong called his new religious movement the "Heavenly Kingdom of Great Peace."

Hong quickly attracted a community of believers, primarily Hakkas like himself. They believed in the prophecy of dreams and claimed they could walk on air. Hong and his rivals for leadership in the movement went in and out of ecstatic trances. They denounced the Manchus as creatures of Satan. News of the sect reached the government, and Qing troops arrived to arrest the Taiping leaders. But the Taipings soundly repelled the imperial troops. Local loyalty to the Taipings spread quickly; their numbers multiplied; and they began to enlarge their domain.

e Interactive Map

MAP 24.2 Conflicts in the Qing Empire, 1839–1870 In both the Opium War of 1839–1842 and the Arrow War of 1856–1860, the seacoasts saw most of the action. Since the Qing had no imperial navy, the well-armed British ships encountered little resistance as they shelled the southern coasts. In inland conflicts, such as the Taiping Rebellion, the opposing armies were massive and slow moving. Battles on land were often prolonged attempts by one side to starve out the other side before making a major assault.

Areas of Taiping rebellion
1853–1857
1857–1863
Areas of Nian rebellion, 1853–1868
Areas of Muslim revolts, 1855–1873
British attacks during the Opium War, 1839–1842
British and French attacks during the Arrow War, 1858–1860
Conflict with Romanovs, 1850s
Treaty port
0 250 500 Km.
0 250 500 Mi.
N
RUSSIA
Amur R.
USSURI (to Russia, 1860)
MANCHURIA
Sea of Japan (East Sea)
Yalu R.
MONGOLIAN STEPPE
MONGOLIA
GOBI
KOREA
JAPAN
XINJIANG
Urumqi
Beijing
TIAN SHAN
Turfan
QING CHINA
Yellow Sea
Kashgar
Huang He R. (Yellow R.)
Suzhou
TAKLAMAKAN DESERT
Nanjing
Shanghai
Ningbo
Xi'an
Wei R.
East China Sea
Ryukyu Is.
TIBETAN PLATEAU
Fuzhou
TIBET
Yangzi R.
Amoy (Xiamen)
Tropic of Cancer
HIMALAYA MTS.
Lhasa
GUANGXI
Brahmaputra R.
Canton (Guangzhou)
Ganges R.
Irrawaddy R.
Kunming
Xi R.
Jintian/ Thistle Mt.
Macao
Hong Kong (Gr. Br., 1842)
PACIFIC OCEAN
INDIA
ANNAM (VIETNAM)
BURMA
LAOS
Mekong R.
Salween R.
South China Sea
Philippine Is.
Bay of Bengal
90°E
100°E
110°E
120°E
130°E
10°N
20°N
30°N
40°N

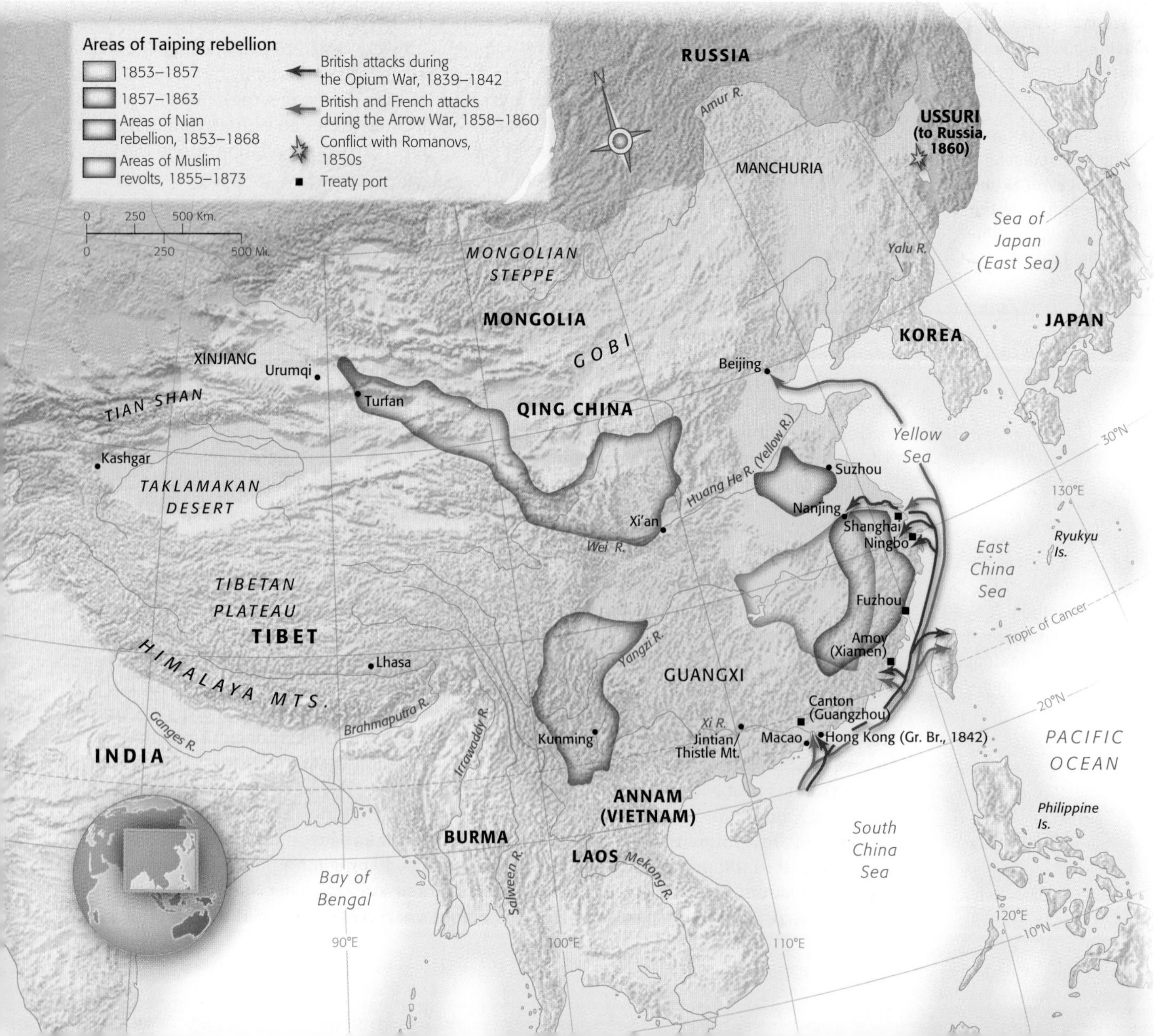

Roger-Viollet/Getty Images

Nanjing Encircled For a decade the Taipings held the city of Nanjing as their capital. For years Qing and international troops attempted to break the Taiping hold. By the summer of 1864, Qing forces had built tunnels leading to the foundations of Nanjing's city walls and had planted explosives. The detonation of the explosives signaled the final Qing assault on the rebel capital. As shown here, the common people of the city, along with their starving livestock, were caught in the crossfire. Many of the Taiping leaders escaped the debacle at Nanjing, but nearly all were hunted down and executed.

Hakkas versus Manchus

The Taipings relied at first on Hakka sympathy and the charismatic appeal of their religious doctrine to attract followers. But as their numbers and power grew, they altered their methods of preaching and governing. They replaced the anti-Chinese appeals used to enlist Hakkas with anti-Manchu rhetoric designed to enlist Chinese. They forced captured villages to join their movement. Once people were absorbed, the Taipings strictly monitored their activities. They segregated men and women and organized them into work and military teams. Women were forbidden to bind their feet (the Hakkas had never practiced footbinding) and participated fully in farming and labor. Brigades of women soldiers took to the field against Qing forces.

Capture of Nanjing

As the movement grew, it began to move toward eastern and northern China (see Map 24.2). Panic preceded the Taipings. Villagers feared being forced into Taiping units, and Confucian elites recoiled in horror from the bizarre ideology of foreign gods, totalitarian rule, and walking, working, warring women. But the huge numbers the Taipings were able to muster overwhelmed attempts at local defense. The tremendous growth in the number of Taiping followers required the movement to establish a permanent base. When the rebel army conquered Nanjing in 1853, the Taiping leaders decided to settle there and make it the capital of the new "Heavenly Kingdom of Great Peace."

Military Reforms

Qing forces attempting to defend north China became more successful as problems of organization and growing numbers slowed Taiping momentum. Increasing Qing military success resulted mainly from the flexibility of the imperial military commanders in the face of an unprecedented challenge. In addition, the military commanders received strong backing from a group of civilian provincial governors who had studied the techniques developed by local militia forces for self-defense. Certain provincial governors combined their knowledge of civilian

Photo by John Thomson/George Eastman House/Getty Images

Street Scene in Guangzhou This photograph taken in the 1860s by an Englishman shows a comparatively wide market street with signs advertising drugs, cushions, seals, ink, etc. The engraving of a Cairo street scene (page 694) shows a much more exotic stereotype of the orient, complete with young girl displaying her body while covering her face.

self-defense and local terrain with more efficient organization and the use of modern weaponry. The result was the formation of new military units, in which many of the Bannermen voluntarily served under civilian governors. The Qing court agreed to special taxes to fund the new armies and acknowledged the new combined leadership.

When the Taipings settled into Nanjing, the new Qing armies surrounded the city, hoping to starve out the rebels. The Taipings, however, had provisioned and fortified themselves well. They also had the services of several brilliant young military commanders, who mobilized enormous campaigns in nearby parts of eastern China, scavenging supplies and attempting to break the encirclement of Nanjing. For more than a decade the Taiping leadership remained ensconced at Nanjing, and the "Heavenly Kingdom" endured.

European Intervention

In 1856 Britain and France, freed from their preoccupation with the Crimean War, turned their attention to China. European and American missionaries had visited Nanjing, curious to see what their fellow Christians were up to. Their reports were discouraging. Hong Xiuquan and the other leaders appeared to lead lives of indulgence and abandon, and more than one missionary accused them of homosexual practices. Relieved of the possible accusation of quashing a pious Christian movement, the British and French surveyed the situation. Though the Taipings were not going to topple the Qing, rebellious Nian ("Bands") in northern China added a new threat in the 1850s. A series of simultaneous large insurrections might indeed destroy the empire. Moreover, since the Qing had not observed all the provisions of the treaties signed after the Opium War, Britain and France were now considering renewing war on the Qing themselves.

In 1856 the British and French launched a series of swift, brutal coastal attacks—a second opium war, called the Arrow War (1856–1860)—which culminated in a British and French invasion of Beijing and the sacking of the Summer Palace in 1860. A new round of treaties punished the Qing for not enacting all the provisions of the Treaty of Nanking. Having secured their principal objective, the British and French forces then joined the Qing campaign against the Taipings. Attempts to coordinate the international forces were sometimes riotous and sometimes tragic, but the injection of European weaponry and money helped quell both the Taiping and the Nian rebellions during the 1860s.

The Taiping Rebellion ranks as the world's bloodiest civil war and the greatest armed conflict before the twentieth century. Estimates of deaths range from 20 million to 30 million. The loss of life came primarily from starvation and disease, for most engagements consisted of surrounding fortified cities and waiting until the enemy forces died, surrendered, or were so weakened that they could be easily defeated. Many sieges continued for months. Reports of people eating grass, leather, hemp, and human flesh were widespread. The dead were rarely buried properly, and epidemic disease was common.

Death and Disease

The area of early Taiping fighting was close to the regions of southwest China in which bubonic plague had been lingering for centuries. When the rebellion was suppressed, many Taiping followers sought safety in the highlands of Laos and Vietnam, which soon showed infestation by plague. Within a few years the disease reached Hong Kong. From there it spread to Singapore, San Francisco, Calcutta, and London. In the late 1800s there was intense apprehension over the possibility of a worldwide outbreak, and Chinese immigrants were regarded as likely carriers. This fear became a contributing factor in the passage of discriminatory immigration bans on Chinese in the United States in 1882.

Lasting Devastation

The Taiping Rebellion devastated the agricultural centers of China. Many of the most intensely cultivated regions of central and eastern China were depopulated. Some were still uninhabited decades later, and major portions of the country did not recover until the twentieth century.

Cities, too, were hard hit. Shanghai, a treaty port of modest size before the rebellion, saw its population multiplied many times by the arrival of refugees from war-blasted neighboring provinces. The city then endured months of siege by the Taipings. Major cultural centers in eastern China lost masterpieces of art and architecture; imperial libraries were burned or their collections exposed to the weather; and the printing blocks used to make books were destroyed. While the empire faced the mountainous challenge of dealing with the material and cultural destruction of the war, it also was burdened by a major ecological disaster in the north. The Yellow River changed course in 1855, destroying the southern part of impoverished Shandong province with flood and initiating decades of drought along the former riverbed in northern Shandong.

Decentralization at the End of the Qing Empire, 1864–1875

The Qing government emerged from the 1850s with no hope of achieving solvency. The corruption of the 1700s, attempts in the very early 1800s to restore waterworks and roads, and declining yields from land taxes had bankrupted the treasury. By 1850, before the Taiping Rebellion, Qing government expenditures were ten times revenues. The indemnities demanded by Europeans

Cixi's Allies In the 1860s and 1870s, Cixi was a supporter of reform (see page 708). In later years she was widely regarded as corrupt and self-centered and as an obstacle to reform. Her greatest allies were the court eunuchs. Introduced to palace life in early China as managers of the imperial harems, eunuchs became powerful political parties at court. The first Qing emperors refused to allow the eunuchs any political influence, but by Cixi's time the eunuchs once again were a political factor.

DIVERSITY + DOMINANCE

Chinese Responses to Imperialism

The Opium War, followed by the Taiping Rebellion, revealed China's weakness for all to see, but there was no agreement on what should be done to restore its strength. A few provincial officials were able to take effective action, but the competing ideas that were heard at the imperial court tended to cancel each other out.

Feng Guifen, an official and a scholar, came into contact with Westerners defending Shanghai when he took refuge there from the Taipings. The following is from a book of essays he published in 1861.

According to a general geography compiled by an Englishman, the territory of China is eight times that of Russia, ten times that of the United States, one hundred times that of France, and two hundred times that of Great Britain. . . . Yet we are shamefully humiliated by the four nations, not because our climate, soil, or resources are inferior to theirs, but because our people are inferior. . . . Now, our inferiority is not due to our allotment from Heaven [i.e., our inherent nature], but is rather due to ourselves. . . .

Why are the Western nations small and yet strong? Why are we large and yet weak? We must search for the means to become their equal, and that depends solely upon human effort. . . .

We have only one thing to learn from the barbarians, and that is strong ships and effective guns. . . . Funds should be allotted to establish a shipyard and arsenal in each trading port. A few barbarians should be employed, and Chinese who are good in using their minds should be selected to receive instruction so that in turn they may teach many craftsmen. When a piece of work is finished and is as good as that made by the barbarians, the makers should be rewarded with an official *juren* degree and be permitted to participate in the metropolitan examinations on the same basis as other scholars. Those whose products are of superior quality should be rewarded with the *jinshi* degree [ordinarily conferred in the metropolitan examinations] and be permitted to participate in the palace examinations like others. The workers should be paid double so that they will not quit their jobs.

Our nation's emphasis on civil service examinations has sunk deep into people's minds for a long time. Intelligent and brilliant scholars have exhausted their time and energy in such useless things as the stereotyped examination essays, examination papers, and formal calligraphy. . . . We should now order one-half of them to apply themselves to the manufacturing of instruments and weapons and to the promotion of physical studies. . . . The intelligence and ingenuity of the Chinese are certainly superior to those of the various barbarians; it is only that hitherto we have not made use of them. When the government above takes delight in something, the people below will pursue it further: their response will be like an echo carried by the wind. There ought to be some people of extraordinary intelligence who can have new ideas and improve on Western methods. At first they may take the foreigners as their teachers and models; then they may come to the same level and be their equals; finally they may move ahead and surpass them. Herein lies the way to self-strengthening.

In 1867 the debate over how to resist foreign military pressure surged through the imperial court. Woren, a Mongol who held the rank of grand secretary, spoke for the conservatives.

Mathematics, one of the six arts, should indeed be learned by scholars as indicated in the imperial decree, and it should not be considered an unworthy subject. But according to the viewpoint of your servant, astronomy and mathematics are of very little use. If these subjects are going to be taught by Westerners as regular studies, the damage will be great. . . . Your servant

after the Opium and Arrow Wars compounded the problem. Vast stretches of formerly productive rice land were devastated, and the population was dispersed. Refugees pleaded for relief, and the imperial, volunteer, foreign, and mercenary troops that had suppressed the Taipings demanded unpaid wages.

Foreign Debt

Britain and France became active participants in the period of recovery that followed the rebellion (see Diversity and Dominance: Chinese Responses to Imperialism). To ensure repayment of the debt to Britain, Robert Hart was installed as inspector-general of a newly created Imperial Maritime Customs Service. Britain and the Qing split the revenues he collected. Britons and Americans worked for the Qing government as advisers and ambassadors, attempting to smooth communications between the Qing, Europe, and the United States.

Strength in the Provinces

The real work of the recovery, however, was managed by provincial governors who had come to the forefront in the struggle against the Taipings. To prosecute the war, they had won the right to levy their own taxes, raise their own troops, and run their own bureaucracies. These special powers were not entirely canceled when the war ended. Chief among these governors was Zeng Guofan (zung gwoh-FAN), who oversaw programs to restore agriculture, communications, has learned that the way to establish a nation is to lay emphasis on rites and rightness, not on power and plotting. The fundamental effort lies in the minds of people, not in techniques. Now, if we seek trifling arts and respect barbarians as teachers . . . all that can be accomplished is the training of mathematicians. From ancient down to modern times, your servant has never heard of anyone who could use mathematics to raise the nation from a state of decline or to strengthen it in time of weakness. . . .

Since the conclusion of the peace, Christianity has been prevalent, and half of our ignorant people have been fooled by it. The only thing we can rely on is that our scholars should clearly explain to the people the Confucian tenets, which may be able to sustain the minds of the ignorant populace. Now if these brilliant and talented scholars, who have been trained by the nation and reserved for great future usefulness, have to change from their regular course of study to follow the barbarians, then the correct spirit will not be developed, and accordingly the evil spirit will become stronger. After several years it will end in nothing less than driving the multitudes of the Chinese people into allegiance to the barbarians.

The opposing group of ministers who backed the idea of "self-strengthening" responded.

Your ministers have examined the memorial of Woren: the principles he presents are very lofty and the opinion he maintains is very orthodox. Your ministers' point of view was also like that before they began to manage foreign affairs; and yet today they do not presume to insist on such ideas, because of actual difficulties that they cannot help. . . .

From the beginning of foreign relations to the present there have been twenty or thirty years. At first the officials inside and outside the capital did not grasp the crux of the matter, and whether they negotiated peace or discussed war, generally these were empty words without effect. . . . Therefore your ministers have pondered a long-term policy and discussed the situation thoroughly with all the provincial officials. Proposals to learn the written and spoken languages of foreign countries, the various methods of making machines, the training of troops with foreign guns, the dispatching of officials to travel in all countries, the investigation of their local customs and social conditions . . . all these painstaking and special decisions represent nothing other than a struggle for self-strengthening. . . .

We too are afraid that the people who are learning these things will have no power of discrimination and are likely to be led astray by foreigners, as Woren fears. Therefore we have deliberated and decided that those who participate in these examinations must be persons from regular scholastic channels. It is indeed those students who have read widely and who understand right principles and have their minds set upon upright and grand purposes—and the present situation is just what causes the scholars and officials to feel pain in heart and head—who would certainly be able to lie on faggots and taste gall [i.e., nurse vengeance] in order to encourage each other vigorously to seek the actual achievement of self-strengthening. They are different from those who have vague, easygoing, or indifferent ideas.

QUESTIONS FOR ANALYSIS

1. **How do the views of the writers reflect their own backgrounds as officials who achieved their offices through the traditional examination system?**
2. **In what ways do these passages indicate a deep or a shallow understanding of the West?**
3. **How do the ideas expressed here compare with the attitudes toward reform in the Ottoman and Russian Empires as discussed elsewhere in this chapter?**

Source: Wm. Theodore de Bary and Richard Lafrano, *Sources of Chinese Tradition*, vol. 2, 2nd ed. (New York: Columbia University Press, 2000), 235–236, 238–239.

education, and publishing, as well as efforts to reform the military and industrialize armaments manufacture.

Like many provincial governors, Zeng preferred to look to the United States rather than to Britain for models and aid. He therefore hired American advisers to run his weapons factories, shipyards, and military academies. He also sponsored a daring program in which promising Chinese boys were sent to Hartford, Connecticut, a center of missionary activity, to learn English, science, mathematics, engineering, and history. They returned to China to assume some of the positions previously held by foreign advisers. Though Zeng was never an advocate of participation in public life by women, his Confucian convictions taught him that educated mothers were more than ever a necessity. He not only encouraged but also partly oversaw the advanced classical education of his own daughters. Zeng's death in 1872 deprived the empire of a major force for reform.

Dowager Empress Cixi

The period of recovery marked a fundamental structural change in the Qing Empire. Although the emperors after 1850 were ineffective rulers, a coalition of aristocrats supported the reform and recovery programs. Without their legitimization of the new powers of provincial governors like Zeng Guofan, the empire might have evaporated within a generation. A crucial member of this alliance was Cixi (TSUH-shee), who was known as the "Empress Dowager" after the 1880s. Later observers, both Chinese and foreign, reviled her as a monster of corruption and arrogance. But in the 1860s and 1870s Cixi supported the provincial governors, some of whom became so powerful that they were managing Qing foreign policy as well as domestic affairs.

No longer a conquest regime dominated by a Manchu military caste and its Chinese civilian appointees, the empire came under the control of a group of reformist aristocrats and military men, independently powerful civilian governors, and a small number of foreign advisers. The Qing lacked strong, central, unified leadership and could not recover their powers of taxation, legislation, and military command once these had been granted to the provincial governors. From the 1860s forward, the Qing Empire disintegrated into a number of large power zones in which provincial governors handed over leadership to their protégés in a pattern that the Qing court eventually could only ritually legitimate.

SECTION REVIEW

- Social unrest grew in Qing China through a combination of discontent among the poor and displaced indigenous peoples and resentment of growing European influence.
- Qing attempts to ban opium imports provoked the Opium War with Britain, which exposed Qing military inferiority.
- The Treaty of Nanking gave extraterritoriality and other privileges to Britain and led to further losses to other Western powers.
- Social resentment and foreign intrusion ignited the Taiping Rebellion, which, after the Arrow War, the Qing quelled with British and French aid.
- The rebellion encouraged epidemics, devastated agriculture, produced overcrowded cities filled with refugees, and coincided with environmental disasters.
- The rebellion and China's recovery afterward resulted in a process of decentralization led by reformist aristocrats.

CONCLUSION

Most of the subjects of the Ottoman, Russian, and Qing rulers did not think of European pressure or competition as determining factors in their lives during the first half of the nineteenth century. They continued to live according to the social and economic institutions they inherited from previous generations. By the 1870s, however, the challenge of Europe had become widely realized. The Crimean War, where European allies achieved a hollow victory for the Ottomans and then pressured the sultan for more reforms, confirmed both Ottoman and Russian military weakness. The Opium War did the same for China. But China, unlike the other empires, was also stricken by rampaging civil war and regional uprisings.

Though all three empires faced similar problems of reform, military rebuilding, and financial disarray, China was geographically remote from Europe and thus removed from the geostrategic tug-of-war between Britain and Russia. Despite British fears about Russian threats to India, the tsars enjoyed the advantage of being included in high-level deliberations among European powers. The Ottoman Empire, which had once dominated eastern Europe, was largely excluded from these deliberations. To many European diplomats and overseas investors, its final demise seemed only a matter of time, leaving up in the air the question of who would reap the benefits.

In analyzing the crises of the three empires, historians today stress European economic pressures and observe that all three empires ultimately became insolvent and saw the overthrow of their ruling dynasties. However, at the time what most impressed the Ottomans, Russians, and Chinese was European military superiority, as demonstrated in the Greek war of independence, the Crimean War, and the Opium War. Thus for all three empires, dealing with military emergency took priority over deeper reforms throughout most of the time period of this chapter.

KEY TERMS

Muhammad Ali p. 688
Janissaries p. 689
Serbia p. 689
Tanzimat p. 691
Crimean War p. 693
extraterritoriality p. 694
Slavophiles p. 697
Pan-Slavism p. 697
Decembrist revolt p. 698
Opium War p. 700
Bannermen p. 700
Treaty of Nanking p. 701
treaty ports p. 701
most-favored-nation status p. 701
Taiping Rebellion p. 701

EBOOK AND WEBSITE RESOURCES

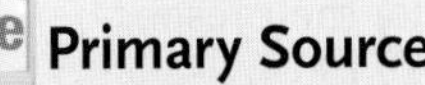

Primary Source

Tanzimat Decree

Interactive Maps

Map 24.1 The Ottoman and Russian Empires, 1829–1914
Map 24.2 Conflicts in the Qing Empire, 1839–1870

Plus flashcards, practice quizzes, and more. Go to: www.cengage.com/history/bullietearthpeople5e

SUGGESTED READING

Bassin, Mark. *Imperial Visions: Nationalist Imagination and Geographical Expansion in the Russian Far East, 1840–1865.* 1999. Addresses Russia's little-studied eastward expansion.

Blackwell, W. L. *The Beginnings of Russian Industrialization, 1800–1860.* 1968. A standard introduction.

Crossley, Pamela Kyle. *Orphan Warriors: Three Manchu Generations and the End of the Qing World.* 1990. Presents a Manchu perspective on the late Qing.

Deringil, Selim. *The Well-Protected Domains: Ideology and the Legitimation of Power in the Ottoman Empire, 1876–1909.* 1998. A revisionist view of the reign of Abdul Hamid II.

Field, Daniel. *The End of Serfdom: Nobility and Bureaucracy in Russia, 1855–1861.* 1976. Studies the primary problem besetting Russian society during this period.

Kappeler, Andreas. *The Russian Multi-Ethnic Empire.* 2001. Puts an emphasis on ethnic diversity.

Lewis, Bernard. *The Emergence of Modern Turkey,* 3rd ed. 2001. A treatment of late Ottoman history based on Europeanization as a sign of progress.

Mardin, Serif. *The Genesis of Young Ottoman Thought: A Study in the Modernization of Turkish Political Ideas.* Reprint, 2000. Classic study of intellectual developments.

Pamuk, Sevket. *The Ottoman Empire and European Capitalism, 1820–1913: Trade, Investment, and Production.* 1987. An economic analysis of the Ottoman Empire.

Polachek, James M. *The Inner Opium War.* 1992. Details a major event in Chinese-Western confrontation.

Quataert, Donald. *The Ottoman Empire, 1700–1922,* 2nd ed. 2005. A survey of late Ottoman history.

Raeff, Marc. *Understanding Imperial Russia.* 1984. Sets nineteenth-century Russian developments in a broad context and challenges many standard ideas.

Spence, Jonathan D. *God's Chinese Son: The Taiping Heavenly Kingdom of Hong Xiuquan.* 1996. A highly readable account of the Taiping movement that focuses on religious leadership.

Walicki, Andrzej. *The Slavophile Controversy.* 1975. A study in intellectual history.

Zelin, Madeleine. *The Merchants of Zigong: Industrial Entrepreneurship in Early Modern China.* 2005. A revealing study of indigenous economic development.

AP* REVIEW QUESTIONS FOR CHAPTER 24

1. One way that Muhammad Ali solidified his power in Egypt was
   (A) by limiting the power and wealth of the mamluks.
   (B) through heavy taxation on the peasant farmers.
   (C) by placing promising young Egyptians in the army as officer candidates.
   (D) through his marriage to an Egyptian woman who came from a wealthy family.

2. In the first half of the nineteenth century, the most opposition to reform in the Ottoman Empire came from
   (A) the nobility.
   (B) the merchant class.
   (C) Muslim clerics.
   (D) the Janissaries.

3. The Tanzimat reforms
   (A) were rejected by the Muslim majority in the Ottoman Empire.
   (B) were attempts at westernizing the Ottoman Empire.
   (C) increased taxes on non-Muslims.
   (D) unified civil and religious courts.

4. One reason that Great Britain and France aided the Ottoman Empire against Russia in the Crimean War was that
   (A) the British and French controlled the oil in Iraq and wanted to make sure Russia did not get it.
   (B) they feared Russia would challenge them in India.
   (C) Russian industrial output would outpace that of Great Britain and France if Russia gained access to resources in eastern Europe.
   (D) they feared the power of the Russian navy in the Mediterranean Sea.

5. One similarity between the Civil War in the United States and the Crimean War is that they both
   (A) led to the use of gold coins as the medium of exchange.
   (B) were times when huge numbers of young men refused to serve in the army.
   (C) were part of the transition from traditional warfare to modern warfare.
   (D) were great nationalistic victories for their respective nations.

6. Which of the following was true of Russia in the nineteenth century?
   (A) Like the rest of Europe, Russia was beginning to become more democratic.
   (B) Russia's government had little interest in industrialization until late in the nineteenth century.
   (C) Russia had followed Great Britain's lead and abolished slavery in the 1830s.
   (D) Land reform put into place in the 1700s had dramatically increased food supplies, which allowed an urban laboring class to develop.

7. The greatest of the reforms of Tsar Alexander II was
   (A) granting civil rights to women.
   (B) modernizing the bureaucracy.
   (C) freeing the serfs.
   (D) abolishing the military draft.

8. Unlike the Ottoman Empire, which had faced the threat of Napoleon and his army, the Qing rulers of China
   (A) signed treaties of friendship with neighboring states.
   (B) was viewed by the West as a modern, Western-style nation.
   (C) faced rebellions led by displaced indigenous persons and the poor.
   (D) avoided Western interference because of the silk trade.

9. The treaty system that was established in China at the end of the Opium War

   (A) kept other European nations from taking advantage of China.
   (B) gave Great Britain the sole right to trade in China.
   (C) was never ratified by the Qing government.
   (D) resulted in the eventual colonization of small pockets of Qing territory.

10. Which of the following was true of the Taiping Rebellion?

   (A) It was supported by the British and the French.
   (B) The Qing government easily defeated the Taipings and executed their leader.
   (C) It was a rebellion led by Tibetans who had been displaced from their traditional lands.
   (D) It was both anti-Manchu and antiforeigner.

11. In comparison with the Ottoman Empire and Russia, China in the nineteenth century was

   (A) more developed economically because of trade along the Silk Road.
   (B) wealthier because it relied on receiving silver coins and bars in return for goods.
   (C) internally more peaceful and not wracked by religious conflicts.
   (D) relatively isolated from the geostrategic tug-of-war between European powers.

CHAPTER 25

CHAPTER OUTLINE

- Changes and Exchanges in Africa
- India Under British Rule
- Britain's Eastern Empire
- Conclusion

DIVERSITY + DOMINANCE *Ceremonials of Imperial Domination*

ENVIRONMENT + TECHNOLOGY *Whaling*

Private Collection

Indian Railroad Station, 1866 British India built the largest network of railroads in Asia. People of every social class traveled by train.

Visit the website and ebook for additional study materials and interactive tools: www.cengage.com/history/bullietearthpeople5e

Africa, India, and the New British Empire, 1750–1870

- How did different African leaders and peoples interact with each other, and how did European nations' relationship to African peoples change during this period?
- How did Britain secure its hold on India, and what colonial policies led to the beginnings of Indian nationalism?
- What role did the abolition of slavery and the continued growth of British overseas trade play in the immigration to the Caribbean and elsewhere of peoples from Africa, India, and Asia?

In 1782 Tipu Sultan inherited the throne of the state of Mysore (my-SORE), which his father had made the most powerful state in south India. The ambitious and talented new ruler distrusted the territorial ambitions of Great Britain's East India Company. In 1785, before the company could invade Mysore, Tipu Sultan launched his own attack. He then sent an embassy to France in 1788, seeking an alliance against Britain. Tipu's struggle with the East India Company went badly. A military defeat in 1792 forced him to surrender most of his coastal lands. Despite the loose alliance with France, he was unable to stop further British advances. Tipu lost his life in 1799 while defending his capital against a British assault. Mysore was divided between the British and their Indian allies.

As these events illustrate, local leaders and European powers all tried to expand their influence in South Asia and Africa between 1750 and 1870. Midway through that period, it was by no means clear who would gain the upper hand. Britain and France were as likely to fight each other as they were to fight an Asian or African state. In 1800 the two nations were engaged in their third major war for overseas supremacy since 1750.

By 1870, Britain had gained a decisive advantage. The new British Empire included the subcontinent of India, settler colonies in Australia and New Zealand, and a growing network of trading outposts. By 1870 Britain had completed the campaign to replace the overseas slave trade from Africa with "legitimate" trade and had spearheaded new Asian and South Pacific labor migrations into a new string of tropical colonies.

CHANGES AND EXCHANGES IN AFRICA

In the century before 1870 Africa underwent dynamic political changes and a great expansion of foreign trade. Indigenous African leaders and Middle Eastern and European imperialists built powerful new states and expanded old ones. As the slave trade died under British pressure, trade in other goods grew sharply. In return Africans imported large quantities of machine-made textiles and firearms. These complex changes are best understood by looking at African regions separately.

New African States

Internal forces produced clusters of new states in two parts of sub-Saharan Africa between 1750 and 1870. In southern Africa a powerful Zulu kingdom arose. In inland West Africa Islamic reformers created the Sokoto (SOH-kuh-toh) Caliphate and companion states (see Map 25.1).

Shaka Zulu

For many centuries the Nguni (ng-GOO-nee) peoples had farmed and raised cattle in the fertile coast-lands of southeastern Africa. When a serious drought hit the region at the beginning of the nineteenth century, an upstart military genius named Shaka (r. 1818–1828) created the **Zulu** kingdom in 1818. Strict military drill and close-combat tactics featuring ox-hide shields and lethal stabbing spears made the Zulu the most powerful and most feared fighters in southern Africa.

Zulu A people of modern South Africa whom King Shaka united in 1818.

Shaka expanded his kingdom by raiding his African neighbors, seizing their cattle, and capturing their women and children. Breakaway military bands spread this system of warfare and state building inland to the high plateau country as far north as Lake Victoria. As the power and population of these new kingdoms increased, so too did the number of displaced and demoralized refugees around them.

AP* Exam Tip Nationalism in Africa is an important point for the course.

To protect themselves from the Zulu, some neighboring Africans created their own states. The Swazi kingdom consolidated north of the Zulu, and the kingdom of Lesotho (luh-SOO-too) grew by attracting refugees to strongholds in southern Africa's highest mountains. Both Lesotho and Swaziland survive as independent states to this day.

Although Shaka ruled for little more than a decade, he succeeded in creating a new national identity as well as a new kingdom. He grouped all the young people in his domains by age into regiments. Regiment members lived together and immersed themselves in Zulu lore and customs, including fighting methods. A British trader named Henry Francis Fynn expressed his "astonishment at the order and discipline" he found everywhere in the Zulu kingdom. He witnessed public festivals of loyalty to Shaka at which regiments of young men and women numbering in the tens of thousands danced around the king for hours. Parades showed off the king's enormous herds of cattle, a Zulu measure of wealth.

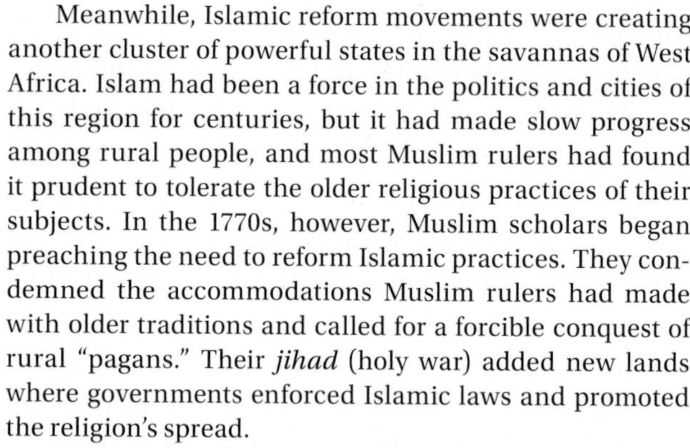

Meanwhile, Islamic reform movements were creating another cluster of powerful states in the savannas of West Africa. Islam had been a force in the politics and cities of this region for centuries, but it had made slow progress among rural people, and most Muslim rulers had found it prudent to tolerate the older religious practices of their subjects. In the 1770s, however, Muslim scholars began preaching the need to reform Islamic practices. They condemned the accommodations Muslim rulers had made with older traditions and called for a forcible conquest of rural "pagans." Their *jihad* (holy war) added new lands where governments enforced Islamic laws and promoted the religion's spread.

The largest of the new Muslim reform movements occurred in the Hausa (HOW-suh) states (in northern Nigeria) under the leadership of Usuman dan Fodio (OO-soo-mahn dahn FOH-dee-oh) (1745–1817). He charged that the Hausa kings, despite their official profession of Islam, were "undoubtedly unbelievers ... because they practice polytheistic rituals and turn people away from the path of God." Distressed by the lapses of the king of Gobir, Usuman issued a call in 1804 for a jihad to overthrow him.

Killie Campbell Africana Library. Photo: Jane Taylor/Sonia Halliday Photographs

Zulu in Battle Dress, 1838 Elaborate costumes helped impress opponents with the Zulus' strength. Shown here are long-handled spears and thick leather shields.

CHRONOLOGY

	Empire	Africa	India
1750			
	1763 End of Seven Years War		1756 Black Hole of Calcutta
	1769–1778 Captain James Cook explores New Zealand and eastern Australia		1765 East India Company (EIC) rule of Bengal begins
	1795 End of Dutch East India Company	1795 Britain takes Cape Colony	1796 Britain annexes Ceylon
		1798 Napoleon invades Egypt	1799 EIC defeats Mysore
1800			
	1807 Britain outlaws slave trade	1805 Muhammad Ali seizes Egypt	
		1808 Britain takes over Sierra Leone	
		1809 Sokoto Caliphate founded	
		1818 Shaka founds Zulu kingdom	1818 EIC creates Bombay Presidency
		1821 Foundation of Liberia	1826 EIC annexes Assam and northern Burma
			1828 Brahmo Samaj founded
	1834 Britain frees slaves in its colonies	1831–1847 Algerians resist French takeover	1834 Indentured labor migrations begin
		1836–1839 Afrikaners' Great Trek	
		1840 Omani sultan moves capital to Zanzibar	
1850			
	1867 End of Atlantic slave trade		1857–1858 Sepoy Rebellion leads to end of EIC rule and Mughal rule
	1877 Queen Victoria becomes Empress of India	1869 Jaja founds Opobo	

Sokoto Caliphate

Sokoto Caliphate A large Muslim state founded in 1809 in what is now northern Nigeria.

modernization The process of reforming political, military, economic, social, and cultural traditions in imitation of the early success of Western societies, often with regard for accommodating local traditions in non-Western societies.

Muslims unhappy with their social or religious position spread the movement to other Hausa states. The successful armies united the conquered Hausa states and neighboring areas under a caliph (sultan) who ruled from the city of Sokoto. The **Sokoto Caliphate** (1809–1906) was the largest state in West Africa since the sixteenth century.

These new Muslim states became centers of Islamic learning and reform. Schools for training boys in Quranic subjects spread rapidly, and the great library at Sokoto attracted many scholars. Officials permitted non-Muslims within the empire to follow their religions in exchange for paying a special tax, but they suppressed dances and ceremonies associated with traditional religions. During the jihads, many who resisted the expansion of Muslim rule were killed, enslaved, or forced to convert.

Sokoto's leaders sold many captives into the trans-Saharan slave trade, which carried ten thousand slaves a year, mostly women and children, across the desert to North Africa and the Middle East. Slavery also increased greatly within the Sokoto Caliphate and other new Muslim states. It is estimated that by 1865 there were more slaves in the Sokoto Caliphate than in any remaining slave-holding state in the Americas.[1] Most of the slaves raised food, making possible the seclusion of free women in their homes in accordance with reformed Muslim practice.

Modernization in Egypt and Ethiopia

Muhammad Ali

While new states were arising elsewhere, in northeastern Africa the ancient states of Egypt and Ethiopia were undergoing growth and **modernization**. Napoleon's invading army had withdrawn from Egypt by 1801, but the shock of this display of European strength and Egyptian weakness

Muhammad Ali Leader of Egyptian modernization in the early nineteenth century. He ruled Egypt as an Ottoman governor but had imperial ambitions. His descendants ruled Egypt until overthrown in 1952.

was long-lasting. The successor to Napoleon's rule was **Muhammad Ali** (see Chapter 24), who ruled Egypt from 1805 to 1849 and who began the reforms that created modern Egypt. In the 1830s Muhammad Ali headed the strongest state in the Islamic world and the first to employ Western methods and technology. The technical expertise of the West was combined with Islamic religious and cultural traditions. For example, the Egyptian printing industry, begun to provide Arabic translations of technical manuals, turned out critical editions of Islamic classics and promoted a revival of Arabic writing and literature.

By the end of Muhammad Ali's reign in 1849, the population had nearly doubled; trade with Europe had expanded by almost 600 percent; and a new class of educated Egyptians had begun to replace the old ruling aristocracy. Egyptians were replacing many of the foreign experts, and the fledgling program of industrialization was providing the country with its own textiles, paper, weapons, and military uniforms. The demands on peasant families for labor and military service, however, were acutely disruptive.

Ismail

Ali's grandson Ismail (is-MAH-eel) (r. 1863–1879) placed even more emphasis on westernizing Egypt. "My country is no longer in Africa," Ismail declared, "it is in Europe."[2] His efforts increased the number of European advisers in Egypt, as well as Egypt's debts to French and British banks. In the first decade of his reign, revenues increased thirtyfold and exports doubled (largely because of a huge increase in cotton exports during the American Civil War). By 1870 Egypt had a network of new irrigation canals, 800 miles (1,300 kilometers) of railroads, a modern postal service, and the dazzling new capital city of Cairo. When the market for Egyptian cotton collapsed after the American Civil War, however, Egypt's debts to British and French investors led to the country's partial occupation.

Ethiopia

State building and reform were also under way in Ethiopia, whose rulers had been Christian for fifteen hundred years. Beginning in the 1840s, Ethiopian rulers purchased modern weapons from European sources and created strong armies loyal to the ruler. Emperor Téwodros (tay-WOH-druhs) II (r. 1833–1868) also encouraged the manufacture of weapons locally. With the aid of Protestant missionaries his craftsmen even constructed a giant cannon capable of firing a half-ton shell. However, his efforts to coerce more technical aid by holding some British officials captive backfired when the British invaded instead. As the British forces advanced, Téwodros

Téwodros's Mighty Cannon Like other modernizers in the nineteenth century, Emperor Téwodros of Ethiopia sought to reform his military forces. In 1861 he forced resident European missionaries and craftsmen to build guns and cannon, including this 7-ton behemoth. It took five hundred men to haul it across Ethiopia's hilly terrain.

From Hormuzd Rassam, *Narrative of the British Mission to Theodore, King of Abyssinia, II*, London 1869, John Murray

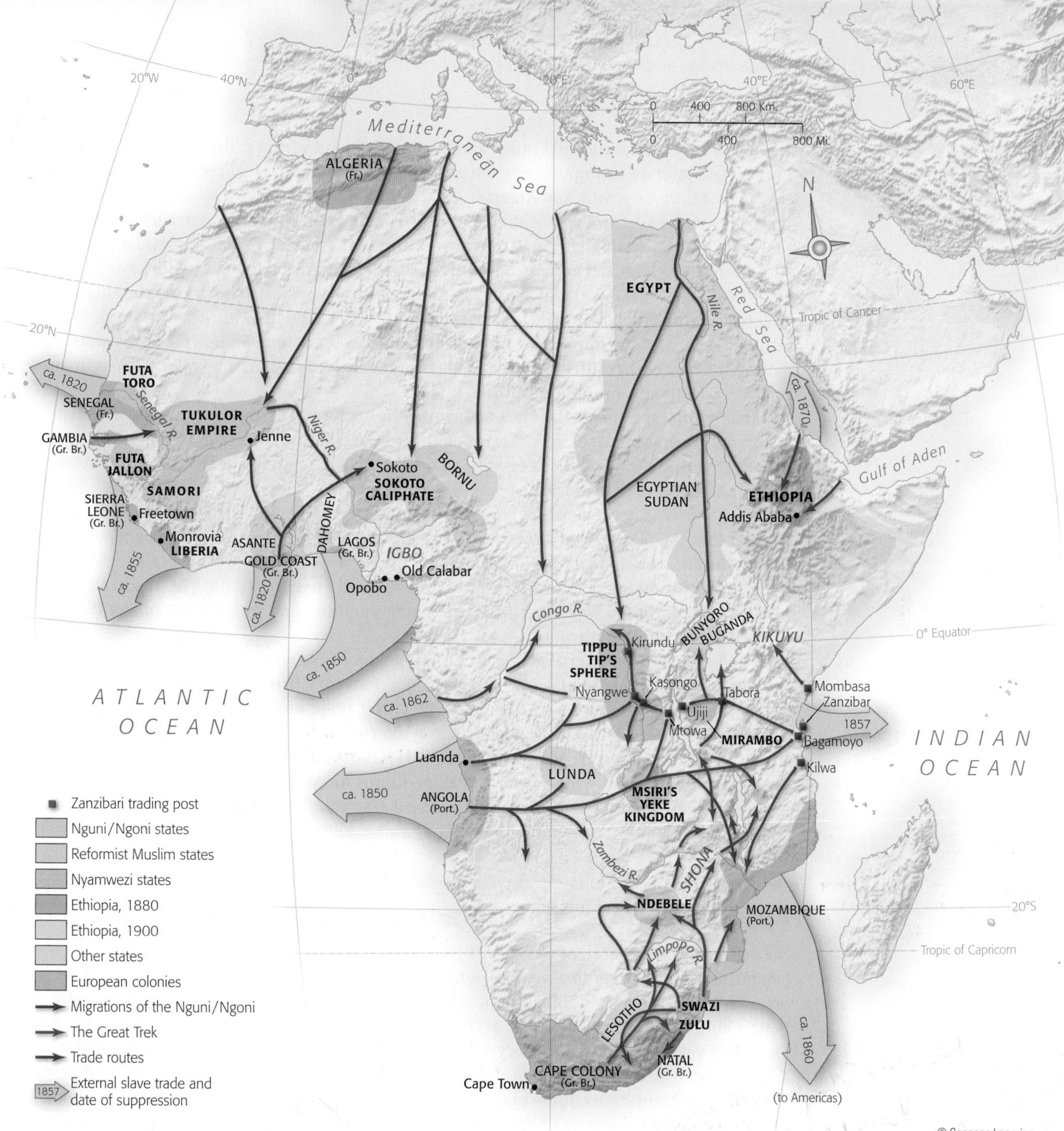

MAP 25.1 Africa in the Nineteenth Century Expanding trade drew much of Africa into global networks, but foreign colonies in 1870 were largely confined to Algeria and southern Africa. Growing trade, Islamic reform movements, and other internal forces created important new states throughout the continent.

e Interactive Map

committed suicide to avoid being taken prisoner. Satisfied that their honor was avenged, the British withdrew. Under Téwodros and his successor Yohannes (yoh-HAHN-nehs) IV (r. 1872–1889), most highland regions were brought back under imperial rule. The only large part of ancient Ethiopia that remained outside Emperor Yohannes's rule was the Shoa kingdom, ruled by King Menelik (MEN-uh-lik) from 1865.

European Penetration

Algeria

France's conquest of Algeria anticipated the general European "scramble" for Africa after 1870. Long an exporter of grain and olive oil to France, Algeria had even supplied Napoleon with grain for his 1798 invasion of Egypt. The failure of French governments to repay this debt led to many disputes between Algeria and France and eventually to a severing of diplomatic relations in 1827. Three years later an unpopular French government, hoping to stir French nationalism with an easy overseas victory, attacked Algeria.

The French government was soon overthrown, but the war in Algeria dragged on for eighteen years. The attack by an alien Christian power united the Algerians behind 'Abd al-Qadir (AHB-dahl-KAH-deer), a gifted and resourceful Muslim holy man. To achieve victory, the French built up an army of over 100,000 that broke Algerian resistance by destroying farm animals and crops and massacring villagers by the tens of thousands. After 'Abd al-Qadir was captured and exiled in 1847, the resistance movement fragmented, but the French occupiers faced resistance in the mountains for another thirty years. European settlers, who rushed in to take possession of Algeria's rich coastlands, numbered 130,000 by 1871.

Explorers

Meanwhile, small expeditions of adventurous explorers, using their own funds or financed by private geographical societies, were seeking to uncover the mysteries of inner Africa. Besides discovering the course of Africa's rivers, they wished to assess the continent's mineral wealth or convert Africans to Christianity.

Many of them were concerned with tracing the course of Africa's great rivers. Explorers learned that the Niger River flowed from west to east and that the small streams entering the Gulf of Guinea were in fact the Niger Delta.

The north-flowing Nile similarly attracted explorers bent on finding its headwaters. In 1770 Lake Tana in Ethiopia was established as a major source, and in 1861–1862 Lake Victoria was found to be the other main source.

The Scottish missionary doctor David Livingstone (1813–1873) explored southern and central Africa. His primary goal was to scout out locations for Christian missions, but he also traced the course of the Zambezi River between 1853 and 1856, naming its greatest waterfall for the British Queen Victoria. In 1871, while tracing the course of the upper Congo River, he encountered the journalist Henry Morton Stanley (1841–1904) on a publicity-motivated search for the "lost" missionary doctor. Stanley's large expeditions fought their way across the continent, but Livingstone's modest expeditions, which posed no threat to anyone, regularly received warm hospitality.

Abolition and Legitimate Trade

No sooner was the mouth of the Niger River discovered than eager entrepreneurs began to send expeditions up the river to assess its potential for trade. The value of trade between West Africa and the West more than doubled between the 1730s and the 1780s, then doubled again by 1870.[3] Before about 1825 the slave trade accounted for most of that increase, but thereafter African exports of vegetable oils, gold, ivory, and other goods drove overseas trade to new heights.

Slave Trade

AP* Exam Tip Understand the effects of slavery in various parts of the world and be prepared to discuss the end of the slave trade in Africa.

The successful slave revolt in Saint Domingue in the 1790s (see Chapter 21) ended slavery in the largest plantation colony in the West Indies. Elsewhere in the Americas slave revolts were brutally repressed. As news of the slave revolts and their repression spread, humanitarians and religious reformers called for an end to the trade. Support for abolition of the trade was found even among Americans wanting to preserve slavery. In 1807 both Great Britain and the United States made importing slaves from Africa illegal for their citizens. Most other Western countries followed suit by 1850, but few enforced abolition with the vigor of the British.

Once the world's greatest slave traders, the British became the most aggressive abolitionists. Britain sent a naval patrol to enforce the ban along the African coast and negotiated treaties allowing the patrol to search other nations' vessels suspected of carrying slaves. Although British patrols captured 1,635 slave ships and liberated over 160,000 enslaved Africans, the trade proved difficult to stop. Cuba and Brazil continued to import huge numbers of slaves, which drove prices up and persuaded some African rulers and merchants to continue to sell slaves and to help foreign slavers evade the British patrols. Because the slave trade moved to other parts of Africa, the transatlantic slave trade did not end until 1867.

"legitimate" trade Exports from Africa in the nineteenth century that did not include the newly outlawed slave trade.

In exchange for slaves, Africans purchased cloth, metals, and other goods. To continue those imports, Africans expanded their **"legitimate" trade** (exports other than slaves). They revived old exports or developed new ones as the Atlantic slave trade was shut down. The most successful of the new exports from West Africa was palm oil, used by British manufacturers for soap,

Palm Oil

King Jaja of Opobo This talented man rose from slavery in the Niger Delta port of Bonny to head one of the town's major palm-oil trading firms, the Anna Pepple House, in 1863. Six years later, Jaja founded and ruled his own trading port of Opobo.

candles, and lubricants. Though still a major source of slaves until the mid-1830s, the trading states of the Niger Delta emerged as the premier exporters of palm oil. Coastal African traders bought the palm oil at inland markets and delivered it to European ships at the coast.

The dramatic increase in palm-oil exports—from a few hundred tons at the beginning of the century to tens of thousands of tons by midcentury—altered the social structure of the coastal trading communities. Coastal traders used their wealth to buy slaves to paddle the giant dugout canoes that transported palm oil from inland markets along the narrow delta creeks to the trading ports. Niger Delta slavery could be as harsh and brutal as slavery on New World plantations, but it offered some slaves a chance to gain wealth and power. Male slaves who supervised canoe fleets were well compensated, and a few even became wealthy enough to take over the leadership of coastal "canoe houses" (companies). The most famous, known as "Jaja" (ca. 1821–1891), rose from canoe slave to become the head of a major canoe house. In 1869, to escape discrimination by free-born Africans, he founded the new port of Opobo, which he ruled as king. In the 1870s Jaja of Opobo was the greatest palm-oil trader in the Niger Delta.

Another effect of the suppression of the slave trade was the spread of Western cultural influences in West Africa. To serve as a base for their anti-slave-trade naval squadron, the British had taken over the small colony of Sierra Leone (see-AIR-uh lee-OWN) in 1808. Over the next several years, 130,000 men, women, and children taken from "captured" vessels were liberated in Sierra Leone. Christian missionaries helped settle these **recaptives** in and around Freetown, the capital. Mission churches and schools made many converts among such men and women.

Recaptives

recaptives Africans rescued by Britain's Royal Navy from the illegal slave trade of the nineteenth century and restored to free status.

Sierra Leone's schools also produced a number of distinguished graduates. Samuel Adjai Crowther (1808–1891), freed from a slave ship in 1821, became the first Anglican bishop in West Africa in 1864, administering a pioneering diocese along the lower Niger River. James Africanus Horton (1835–1882), the son of slaves liberated in Sierra Leone, became a doctor and the author of many studies of West Africa.

Other Western cultural influences came from people of African birth or descent returning to their ancestral homeland. In 1821, free black Americans founded a settlement that grew into the Republic of Liberia, a place of liberty at a time when slavery was legal and flourishing in the United States. After their emancipation in 1865 other African Americans moved to Liberia. Emma White, a literate black woman from Kentucky, moved from Liberia to Opobo in 1875, where King Jaja employed her to write his commercial correspondence and run a school for his children. Edward Wilmot Blyden (1832–1912), born in the West Indies and proud of his West African parentage, emigrated to Liberia in 1851 and became a professor of Greek, Latin, and Arabic at the fledgling Liberia College. Free blacks from Brazil and Cuba chartered ships to return to their West African homelands, bringing Roman Catholicism, architectural motifs, and clothing fashions from the New World. Although the number of Africans exposed to Western culture in 1870 was still small, their influence grew rapidly.

Secondary Empires in Eastern Africa

When British patrols hampered the slave trade in West Africa, slavers moved to eastern Africa. There the Atlantic slave trade joined an existing trade in slaves to the Islamic world that also was expanding. Two-thirds of the 1.2 million slaves exported from eastern Africa in the nineteenth century went to markets in North Africa and the Middle East; the other third went to plantations in the Americas and to European-controlled Indian Ocean islands.

Zanzibar

Slavery also became more prominent within eastern Africa itself. Between 1800 and 1873 Arab and Swahili (swah-HEE-lee) owners of clove plantations along the coast purchased some 700,000 slaves to do the hard work of harvesting this spice. The plantations were on Zanzibar Island and in neighboring territories belonging to the Sultanate of Oman, an Arabian kingdom on the Persian Gulf that had been expanding its control over the East African coast since 1698. The sultan had even moved his court to Zanzibar in 1840 to take advantage of the burgeoning trade in cloves. Zanzibar also was an important center of slaves and ivory. Most of the ivory was shipped to India, where much of it was carved into decorative objects for European markets.

Tippu Tip

Ivory caravans came to the coast from hundreds of miles inland under the direction of African and Arab merchants. Some of these merchants brought large personal empires under their control by using capital they borrowed from Indian bankers and modern firearms they bought from Europeans and Americans. The largest of these personal empires, along the upper Congo River, was created by Tippu Tip (ca. 1830–1905), a trader from Zanzibar. Livingstone, Stanley, and other explorers who received Tippu Tip's gracious hospitality in the remote center of the continent praised their host's intelligence and refinement. On an 1876 visit, Stanley recorded in his journal that Tippu Tip was "a remarkable man," a "picture of energy and strength" with "a fine intelligent face: almost courtier-like in his manner."

Tippu Tip also composed a detailed memoir of his adventures in the heart of Africa, written in the Swahili language of the coast. In it he mocked innocent African villagers for believing that his gunshots were thunder. Modern rifles not only felled countless elephants for their ivory tusks but also inflicted widespread devastation and misery on the people of this isolated area.

Europeans supplied the weapons and were major consumers of ivory and cloves. For this reason histories refer to the states carved out of eastern Africa by the sultans of Oman, Tippu Tip, and others as "secondary empires," in contrast to the empire that Britain was establishing directly. At the same time, British officials pressured the sultan of Oman into halting the Indian Ocean slave trade from Zanzibar in 1857 and ending the import of slaves into Zanzibar in 1873.

SECTION REVIEW

- Shaka established a powerful Zulu kingdom in the south.
- Usuman dan Fodio conquered the former Hausa states in the west and formed the Sokoto Caliphate.
- In Egypt Muhammad Ali combined Western expertise with Islamic traditions; his grandson Ismail developed the country's infrastructure.
- Under Emperor Téwodros and his successor, Ethiopia grew stronger by purchasing and manufacturing modern weapons.
- When France invaded Algeria in 1830, Algerians united behind the Muslim cleric 'Abd al-Qadir, but were defeated.
- Commercial ties between Europe and Africa grew enormously.
- No country enforced the abolition of slavery more effectively than Britain. British antislavery naval operations settled freed captives in Sierra Leone.
- The slave trade exploited the market for slaves in North Africa and the Middle East.

INDIA UNDER BRITISH RULE

The people of South Asia felt the impact of European commercial, cultural, and colonial expansion more immediately and profoundly than did the people of Africa. While Europeans were laying claim to only small parts of Africa between 1750 and 1870, nearly all of India (with three times the population of all of Africa) came under British rule. During the 250 years after the founding of the East India Company in 1600, British interests commandeered the colonies and trade of the Dutch, fought off French and Indian challenges, and picked up the pieces of the decaying Mughal (MOO-guhl) Empire. By 1763 the French were stymied; in 1795 the Dutch East India Company was dissolved; and in 1858 the last Mughal emperor was dethroned, leaving the vast subcontinent in British hands.

Company Men

nawab A Muslim prince allied to British India; technically, a semi-autonomous deputy of the Mughal emperor.

sepoy A soldier in South Asia, especially in the service of the British.

East India Company

As Mughal power weakened, Iranian armies defeated the Mughal forces in 1739, sacked Delhi, and returned home with vast amounts of booty. Indian states also took advantage of Mughal weakness to assert their independence. By midcentury, the Maratha (muh-RAH-tuh) Confederation, a coalition of states in central India, controlled more land than the Mughals did (see Map 25.2). Also ruling their own powerful states were the **nawabs** (NAH-wab), a term used for Muslim princes who were deputies of the Mughal emperor, though in name only.

British, Dutch, and French companies were also eager to expand their profitable trade into India in the eighteenth century. Such far-flung European trading companies were speculative and risky ventures in 1750. Their success depended on ambitious young "company men," who used hard bargaining, and hard fighting when necessary, to persuade Indian rulers to allow them to establish trading posts at strategic points along the coast. To protect their fortified warehouses from attack, they trained Indian troops known as **sepoys** (SEE-poy). In divided India these private armies came to hold the balance of power.

In 1691 Great Britain's East India Company (EIC) had convinced the nawab of the large state of Bengal in northeast India to let the company establish a fortified outpost at the fishing port of Calcutta. A new nawab, pressing claims for additional tribute from the prospering port, overran the fort in 1756 and imprisoned a group of EIC men in a cell so small that many died of suffocation. To avenge their deaths in this "Black Hole of Calcutta," a large EIC force from Madras, led by Robert Clive, overthrew the nawab. The weak Mughal emperor was persuaded to acknowledge

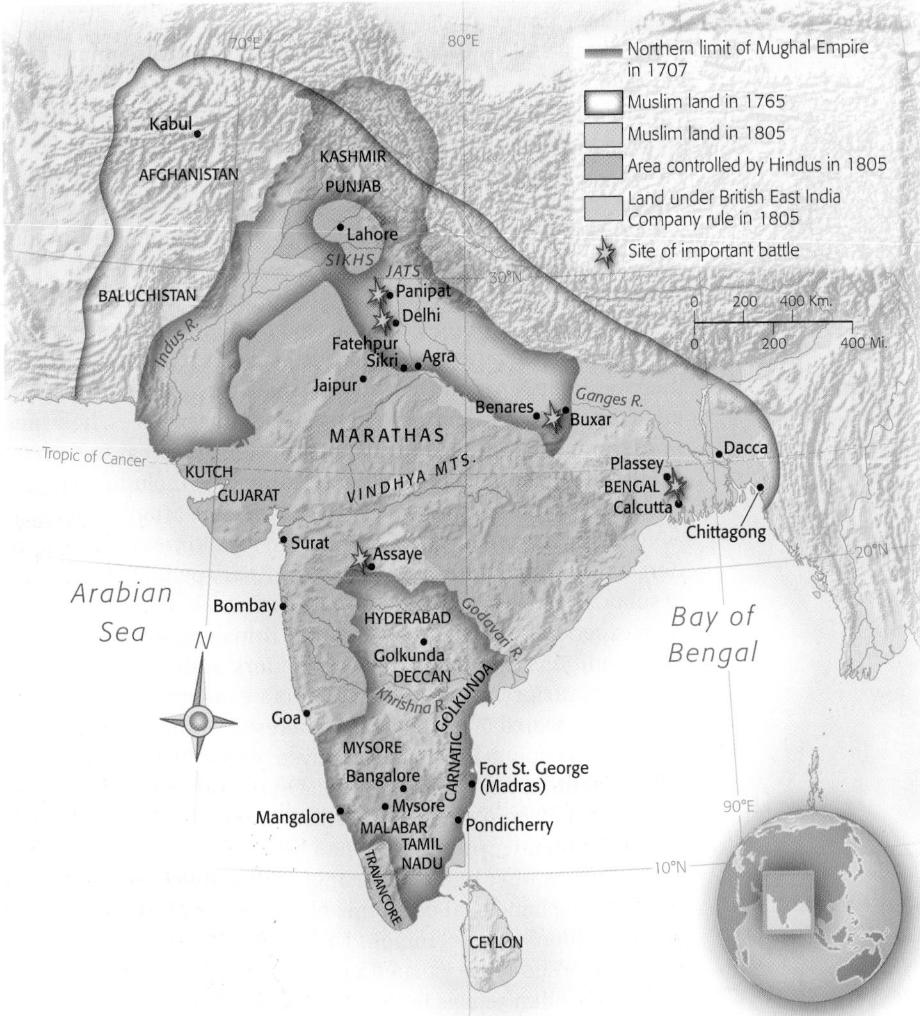

MAP 25.2 India, 1707–1805 As Mughal power weakened during the eighteenth century, other Indian states and the East India Company expanded their territories.

Interactive Map

AP* Exam Tip Be sure to understand the expansion of European colonialism and imperialism into all regions of the world.

the East India Company's right to rule Bengal in 1765. The EIC profited from the tax revenues of Bengal as well as from trade. Calcutta grew into a city of 250,000 by 1788.

In southern India, Clive had used EIC forces from Madras to secure victory for the British Indian candidate for nawab of Arcot during the Seven Years War (1756–1763), thereby gaining an advantage over French traders who had supported the loser. The defeat of Tipu Sultan of Mysore at the end of the century secured south India for the company and prevented a French resurgence.

Along with Calcutta and Madras, the third major center of British power in India was Bombay. There, in 1818, the East India Company annexed large territories to form the core of what was called the "Bombay Presidency." Some states were taken over completely, as Bengal had been, but very many others remained in the hands of local princes who accepted the political control of the company.

Raj and Rebellion, 1818–1857

British raj The rule over much of South Asia between 1765 and 1947 by the East India Company and then by a British government.

In 1818 the East India Company controlled an empire with more people than in all of western Europe and with fifty times the population of the colonies the British had lost in North America. One goal of the **British raj** (reign) was to remake India on a British model through administrative and social reform, economic development, and the introduction of new technology. Yet the company men—like the Mughals before them—had to temper their interference with Indian social and religious customs lest they provoke rebellion or lose the support of their Indian princely allies.

British Rule

The EIC's main goal was to create a powerful and efficient system of government, backed by military power. It also gave free rein to Christian missionaries eager to convert and uplift India's masses. Few converts were made, but the missionaries kept up steady pressure for social reforms.

Another key British policy was to substitute private property for India's complex and overlapping patterns of landholding. In Bengal this reform worked to the advantage of large landowners, but in Mysore the peasantry gained. Private ownership made it easier for the state to collect the taxes that were needed to pay for administration, the army, and economic reform.

Such policies of "westernization, Anglicization, and modernization," as they have been called, were only one side of British rule. The other side was the bolstering of "traditions"—both real and newly invented. In the name of tradition the Indian princes who ruled nearly half of British India were frequently endowed by their British overlords with greater power and splendor and longer tenure than their predecessors had ever had. Likewise, Hindu and Muslim holy men were able to expand their "traditional" power over property and people far beyond what had been the case in earlier times. At the same time, princes, holy men, and other Indians frequently used claims of tradition to resist British rule as well as to turn it to their advantage. The British rulers themselves invented many "traditions"—including elaborate parades and displays—half borrowed from European royal pomp, half from Mughal ceremonies.

The British and Indian elites worked sometimes in close partnership, sometimes in opposition, but always at the expense of the ordinary people of India. Women of every status, members of subordinate Hindu castes, the "untouchables" and "tribals" outside the caste system, and the poor experienced few benefits from the British reforms and much new oppression from the taxes and "traditions" that exalted their superiors' status.

The transformation of British India's economy was also doubled-edged. On the one hand, British raj created many new jobs as a result of the growth of trade and expanded crop production, such as opium in Bengal, largely for export to China (see Chapter 24); coffee in Ceylon; and tea in Assam in northeastern India. On the other hand, competition from cheap cotton goods produced in Britain's industrial mills drove many Indians out of the handicraft textile industry. In the eighteenth century India had been the world's greatest exporter of cotton textiles; in the nineteenth century India increasingly shipped raw cotton fiber to Britain.

Sepoy Rebellion

Even the beneficial economic changes introduced under British rule were disruptive, and local rebellions were common. During the first half of the nineteenth century, British rulers readily handled these isolated uprisings, but they were more concerned about the continuing loyalty of Indian sepoys in the East India Company's army. The EIC employed 200,000 sepoys in 1857, along with 38,000 British troops. Armed with modern rifles and disciplined in fighting methods, the sepoys had a potential for successful rebellion that other groups lacked.

In fact, discontent was growing among Indian soldiers. In the early decades of EIC rule, most sepoys came from Bengal, one of the first states the company had annexed. The Bengali sepoys resented the active recruitment of other ethnic groups into the army after 1848, such as Sikhs (seek) from Punjab and Gurkhas from Nepal. In addition, many high-caste Hindus objected to a new law in 1856 requiring new recruits to be available for service overseas in the growing Indian Ocean empire, for their religion prohibited ocean travel. Finally, the replacement of the standard military musket by the far more accurate Enfield rifle in 1857 also caused problems. Soldiers were ordered to use their teeth to tear open the ammunition cartridges, which were greased with animal fat. Hindus were offended by this order if the fat came from cattle, which they considered sacred. Muslims were offended if the fat came from pigs, which they considered unclean.

Although the cartridge-opening procedure was quickly changed, the initial discontent grew into rebellion by Hindu sepoys in May 1857. British troubles mushroomed when Muslim sepoys, peasants, and discontented elites joined in. The rebels asserted old traditions to challenge British authority: sepoy officers in Delhi proclaimed their loyalty to the Mughal emperor; others rallied behind the Maratha leader Nana Sahib. The rebellion was put down by March 1858, but it shook this empire to its core.

Sepoy Rebellion The revolt of Indian soldiers in 1857 against certain practices that violated religious customs; also known as the Sepoy Mutiny.

Historians have attached different names and meanings to the events of 1857 and 1858. Concentrating on the fact that the uprising was an unlawful action by soldiers, nineteenth-century British historians labeled it the "**Sepoy Rebellion**" or "Mutiny." Seeing in these events the beginnings of the later movement for independence, some modern Indian historians have termed it the "Revolution of 1857." In reality, it was much more than a simple mutiny, because it involved more than soldiers, but it was not yet a nationalist revolution, for the rebels had little sense of a common Indian national identity.

Political Reform and Industrial Impact

The events of 1857–1858 marked a turning point in the history of modern India. In their wake Indians gained a new centralized government, entered a period of rapid economic growth, and began to develop a new national consciousness.

In 1858 Britain eliminated the last traces of Mughal and Company rule. In their place, a new secretary of state for India in London oversaw Indian policy, and a new governor-general in Delhi acted as the British monarch's viceroy. In November 1858 Queen Victoria guaranteed all Indians equal protection of the law and the freedom to practice their religions and social customs, but she also assured Indian princes that so long as they were loyal to the queen British India would respect their control of territories and "their rights, dignity and honour."[4]

Durbars

durbar An elaborate display of political power and wealth in British India in the nineteenth century, ostensibly in imitation of the pageantry of the Mughal Empire.

British rule continued to emphasize both tradition and reform after 1857. At the top, the British viceroys lived in enormous palaces amid hundreds of servants and gaudy displays of luxury meant to convince Indians that the British viceroys were legitimate successors to the Mughal emperors. They treated the quasi-independent Indian princes with elaborate ceremonial courtesy and maintained them in splendor. When Queen Victoria was proclaimed "Empress of India" in 1877 and periodically thereafter, the viceroys put on great pageants known as **durbars**. At the durbar in Delhi in 1902–1903 to celebrate the coronation of King Edward VII, Viceroy Lord Curzon honored himself with a 101-gun salute and a parade of 34,000 troops in front of 50 princes and 173,000 visitors (see Diversity and Dominance: Ceremonials of Imperial Domination).

Indian Civil Service

Indian Civil Service The elite professional class of officials who administered the government of British India. Originally composed exclusively of well-educated British men, it gradually added qualified Indians.

Meanwhile, a powerful and efficient bureaucracy controlled India. Members of the elite **Indian Civil Service** (ICS) held the senior administrative and judicial posts. Numbering only a thousand at the end of the nineteenth century, these men visited the villages in their districts, heard lawsuits and complaints, and passed judgments.

Recruitment into the ICS was by open examinations. In theory any British subject could take these exams; since they were given in England, however, in practice the system worked to exclude Indians. In 1870 only one Indian was a member of the ICS. Subsequent reforms led to fifty-seven Indian appointments by 1887, but there the process stalled. Working under the ICS were thousands of lesser Indian officials.

DIVERSITY + DOMINANCE

Ceremonials of Imperial Domination

This letter to Queen Victoria from Edward Robert Bulwer-Lytton, Earl of Lytton and viceroy of India, describes the elaborate durbar that the government of India staged in 1876 in anticipation of her being named "Empress of India." It highlights the effects these ceremonies had on the Indian princes who governed many parts of India as agents ("feudatories") of the British or as independent rulers.

British India's power rested on the threat of military force, but the letter points up how much it also depended on cultivating the allegiance of powerful Indian rulers. For their part, as the letter suggests, such rulers were impressed with such displays of majesty and organization and found much to be gained from granting the British their support.

The day before yesterday (December 23), I arrived, with Lady Lytton and all my staff at Delhi. . . . I was received at the [railroad] station by all the native chiefs and princes, and, . . . after shaking hands . . . , I immediately mounted my elephant, accompanied by Lady Lytton, our two little girls following us on another elephant. The procession through Delhi to the camp . . . lasted upwards of three hours. . . . The streets were lined for many miles with troops; those of the native princes being brigaded with those of your Majesty. The crowd along the way, behind the troops, was dense, and apparently enthusiastic; the windows, walls, and housetops being thronged with natives, who salaamed, and Europeans, who cheered as we passed along. . . .

My reception by the native princes at the station was most cordial. The Maharaja of Jeypore informed Sir John Strachey that India had never seen such a gathering as this, in which not only all the great native princes (many of whom have never met before), but also chiefs and envoys from Khelat, Burmah, Siam, and the remotest parts of the East, are assembled to do homage to your Majesty. . . .

On Tuesday (December 26) from 10 A.M. till past 7 P.M., I was, without a moment's intermission, occupied in receiving visits from native chiefs, and bestowing on those entitled to them the banners, medals, and other honours given by your Majesty. The durbar, which lasted all day and long after dark, was most successful. . . . Your Majesty's portrait, which was placed over the Viceregal throne in the great durbar tent, was thought by all to be an excellent likeness of your Majesty. The native chiefs examined it with special interest.

On Wednesday, the 27th, I received visits from native chiefs, as before, from 10 A.M. til 1 P.M., and from 1:30 P.M. to 7:30 P.M., was passed in returning visits. I forgot to mention that on Tuesday and Wednesday evenings I gave great State dinners to the Governors of Bombay and Madras. Every subsequent evening of my stay at Delhi was similarly occupied by state banquets and receptions [for officials, foreign dignitaries, and] many distinguished natives. After dinner on Thursday, I held a levee [reception], which lasted till one o'clock at night, and is said to have been attended by 2,500 persons—the largest, I believe, ever held by any Viceroy or Governor-General in India. . . .

The satisfactory and cordial assurances received from [the ruler of] Kashmir are, perhaps, less important, because his loyalty was previously assumed. But your Majesty will, perhaps, allow me to mention, in connection with the name of this prince, one little circumstance which appears to me very illustrative of the effect which the assemblage has had on him and others. In the first interviews which took place months ago between myself and Kashmir, which resulted in my securing his assent to the appointment of a British officer at Gilgit, I noticed that, though perfectly courteous, he was extremely mistrustful of the British Government and myself. He seemed to think that every word I had said to him must have a hidden meaning against which he was bound to be on his guard. During our negotiations he carefully kept all his councillors round him, and he referred to them before answering any question I put to him, and, although he finally agreed to my proposals, he did so with obvious reluctance and suspicion, after taking a night to think them over. On the day following the Imperial assemblage, I had another private interview with Kashmir for the settlement of some further details. His whole manner and language on this last occasion were strikingly different. [He said:] "I am now convinced that you mean nothing that is not

The reason qualified Indians were denied entry into the upper administration of their country was the racist contempt most British officials felt for the people they ruled. When he became commander-in-chief of the Indian army in 1892, Lord Kitchener declared:

> *It is this consciousness of the inherent superiority of the European which had won for us India. However well educated and clever a native may be, and however brave he may have proved himself, I believe that no rank we can bestow on him would cause him to be considered an equal of the British officer.*[5]

After 1857 the government invested millions of pounds sterling in harbors, cities, irrigation canals, and other public works. Forests were felled to make way for tea plantations. Indian farmers were persuaded to grow cotton and jute for export. Engineers built great irrigation systems to alleviate the famines that periodically decimated whole provinces. As a result, India's trade expanded rapidly.

for the good of me and mine. Our interests are identical with those of the empire. Give me your orders and they shall be obeyed."

I have already mentioned to your Majesty that one of the sons of Kashmir acted as my page at the assemblage. I can truly affirm that all the native princes, great and small, with whom I was previously acquainted vied with each other in doing honor to the occasion, and I sincerely believe that this great gathering has also enabled me to establish the most cordial and confidential personal relations with a great many others whom I then met for the first time.

. . . If the vast number of persons collected together at Delhi, and all almost entirely under canvas, be fairly taken into consideration—a number alluding the highest executive officers of your Majesty's administration from every part of India, each with his own personal staff; all the members of my own Council, with their wives and families, who were entertained as the Viceroy's personal guests; all the representatives of the Press, native and European; upwards of 15,000 British troops, besides about 450 native princes and nobles, each with a following of from 2 to 500 attendants; the foreign ambassadors with their suites; the foreign consuls; a large number of the rudest and most unmanageable transfrontier chieftains with their horses and camels, Etc.; and then an incalculably large concourse of private persons attracted by curiosity from every corner of the country—I say if all this be fairly remembered, no candid person will, I think, deny that to bring together, lodge, and feed so vast a crowd without a single case of sickness, or a single accident due to defective arrangements, without a moment's confusion or an hour's failure in the provision of supplies, and then to have sent them all away satisfied and loud in their expressions of gratitude for the munificent hospitality with which they had been entertained (at an expenditure of public money scrupulously moderate), was an achievement highly creditable to all concerned in carrying it out. Sir Dinkur Rao (Sindiah's great Minister) said to one of my colleagues: "If any man would understand why it is that the English are, and must necessarily remain, the masters of India, he need only go up to the Flagstaff Tower, and look down upon this marvellous camp. Let him notice the method, the order, the cleanliness, the discipline, the perfection of its whole organisation, and he will recognise in it at once the epitome of every title to command and govern which one race can possess over others." This anecdote reminds me of another which may perhaps please your Majesty. [The ruler of] Holkar said to me when I took leave of him: "India has been till now a vast heap of stones, some of them big, some of them small. Now the house is built, and from roof to basement each stone of it is in the right place."

The Khan of Khelat and his wild Sirdars were, I think, the chief objects of curiosity and interest to our Europeans. . . . On the Khan himself and all his Sirdars, the assemblage seems to have made an impression more profound even than I had anticipated. Less than a year ago they were all at war with each other, but they have left Delhi with mutual embraces, and a very salutary conviction that the Power they witnessed there is resolved that they shall henceforth keep the peace and not disturb its frontiers with their squabbles. The Khan asked to have a banner given to him. It was explained to His Highness that banners were only given to your Majesty's feudatories, and that he, being an independent prince, could not receive one without compromising his independence. He replied: "But I am a feudatory of the Empress, a feudatory quite as loyal and obedient as any other. I don't want to be an independent prince, and I do want to have my banner like all the rest. Pray let me have it."

QUESTIONS FOR ANALYSIS

1. **What is significant about the fact that Lord Lytton and his family arrived in Delhi by train and then chose to move through the city on elephants?**
2. **What impression did the viceroy intend to create in the minds of the Indian dignitaries by assembling so many of them together and bestowing banners, medals, and honors on them?**
3. **What might account for some Indians' remarkable changes of attitude toward the viceroy and the empire? How differently might a member of the Indian middle class or an unemployed weaver have reacted?**

Source: Lady Betty Balfour, *The History of Lord Lytton's Indian Administration, 1876 to 1880* (London: Longmans, Green, and Co., 1899), 116–125.

Most of the exports were agricultural commodities: cotton fiber, opium, tea, silk, and sugar. In return India imported manufactured goods from Britain, including machine-made cotton textiles that undercut Indian hand-loom weavers. Some women found jobs at very low pay on plantations or in the growing cities, where prostitution flourished. Others struggled to hold families together or ran away from abusive husbands. Everywhere in India poverty remained the norm.

Railroads

The Indian government also promoted the introduction of new technologies into India. Earlier in the century there were steamboats on the rivers and a massive program of canal building for irrigation. Beginning in the 1840s a railroad boom gave India its first national transportation network, followed by telegraph lines, and by 1870 India had the fifth largest rail network in the world. Originally designed to serve British commerce, the railroads were owned by British companies, constructed with British rails and equipment, and paid dividends to British investors. Ninety-nine percent of the railroad employees were Indians, but Europeans occupied all the top

Topham/The Image Works

Delhi Durbar, January 1, 1903 The parade of Indian princes on ornately decorated elephants and accompanied by retainers fostered their sense of belonging to the vast empire of India that British rule had created.

positions—"like a thin film of oil on top of a glass of water, resting upon but hardly mixing with [those] below," as one official report put it.

Although some Indians opposed the railroads at first because the trains mixed people of different castes, faiths, and sexes, the Indian people took to rail travel with great enthusiasm. Indians rode trains on business, on pilgrimage, and in search of work. In 1870 over 18 million passengers traveled along the network's 4,775 miles (7,685 kilometers) of track, and more than half a million messages were sent up and down the 14,000 miles (22,500 kilometers) of telegraph wires.

But the freer movement of Indian pilgrims and the flood of poor Indians into the cities also promoted the spread of cholera (KAHL-uhr-uh), a disease transmitted through water contaminated by human feces. Cholera deaths rose rapidly during the nineteenth century, and eventually the disease spread to Europe. In many Indian minds *kala mari* ("the black death") was a divine punishment for failing to prevent the British takeover. This chastisement also fell heavily on British residents, who died in large numbers. In 1867 officials demonstrated the close connection between cholera and pilgrims who bathed in and drank from sacred pools and rivers. The installation of a new sewerage system (1865) and a filtered water supply (1869) in Calcutta dramatically reduced cholera deaths there. Similar measures in Bombay and Madras also led to great reductions, but most Indians lived in small villages where famine and lack of sanitation kept cholera deaths high.

Indian National Congress A movement and political party founded in 1885 to demand greater Indian participation in government. Its membership was middle class, and its demands were modest until World War I. Led after 1920 by Mohandas K. Gandhi, it appealed increasingly to the poor, and it organized mass protests demanding self-government and independence.

Indian Nationalism

Both the successes and the failures of British India stimulated the development of Indian nationalism. After the failure of the rebellion of 1857 to overthrow British rule, some Indians argued that the only way for Indians to regain control of their destiny was to reduce their country's social and ethnic divisions and promote Pan-Indian nationalism.

Rammohun Roy

Individuals such as Rammohun Roy (1772–1833) had promoted development along these lines a generation earlier. A Western-educated Bengali from a Brahmin family, Roy was a suc-

Bristol City Museum and Art Gallery, UK/The Bridgeman Art Library

Rammohun Roy This portrait of the Indian reformer emphasizes his scholarly accomplishments and India's traditional architecture and natural beauty.

cessful administrator for the East India Company and a student of comparative religion. His Brahmo Samaj (BRAH-moh suh-MAHJ) (Divine Society), founded in 1828, attracted Indians who sought to reconcile the values of the West with the religious traditions of India. They advocated reforming some Hindu customs, such as the caste system and child marriage, and urged a return to the founding principles of the *Upanishads*, ancient sacred writings of Hinduism. They also backed British efforts to ban practices they found repugnant. Widow burning (*sati* [suh-TEE]) was outlawed in 1829 and slavery in 1843. Reformers sought to correct other abuses of women: prohibitions against widows remarrying were revoked in 1856, and female infanticide was made a crime in 1870.

Although Brahmo Samaj remained influential after the rebellion of 1857, many Indian intellectuals turned to Western secular values and nationalism as the way to reclaim India. In this process the spread of Western education played an important role, a process aided by European and American missionaries. Roy had studied both Indian and Western subjects and helped found the Hindu College in Calcutta in 1816. Other Western-curriculum schools quickly followed, including Bethune College in Calcutta, the first secular school for Indian women, in 1849. India's three universities were established in 1857. In 1870 there were over 24,000 elementary and secondary schools, whose graduates articulated a new Pan-Indian nationalism that transcended regional and religious differences.

Indian National Congress

Many of the new nationalists came from the Indian middle class, which had prospered from the increase of trade and manufacturing. Educated people were angered by the obstacles that British rules and prejudices put in the way of their advancement. Hoping to increase their influence and improve their employment opportunities in the Indian government, they convened the first **Indian National Congress** in 1885. The members sought a larger role for Indians in the Civil Service. They also called for reductions in military expenditures, which consumed 40 percent of the government's budget, so that more could be spent on alleviating the poverty of the Indian masses. But although the Indian National Congress promoted unity among the country's many religions and social groups, most early members were upper-caste Western-educated Hindus and Parsis. Until it attracted the support of the masses, it could not hope to challenge British rule.

AP* Exam Tip It is important to be able to compare Pan-Africanism and the Indian National Congress.

SECTION REVIEW

- Between 1757 and 1857, Britain gained nearly complete control of India.
- With its armies of sepoys, the British East India Company was able to secure control of Calcutta, Madras, and Bombay.
- The British instituted a powerful colonial government and skillfully exploited native traditions and local rulers. The power given to Indians who governed on their behalf increased, while the life of the masses deteriorated.
- The Sepoy Rebellion of 1857–1858 prompted a wave of reforms. Great sums of money were invested in harbors, canals, trains, and telegraph lines, but profits remained in colonial hands.
- In response to modernization, Indian nationalism arose in the increasingly educated middle class.

BRITAIN'S EASTERN EMPIRE

In 1750 Britain's empire was centered on slave-based plantation and settler colonies in the Americas. A century later its main focus was on commerce and colonies in the East. Several distinct changes facilitated the expansion and transformation of Britain's overseas empire. A string of military victories pushed aside rivals for overseas trade and colonies; new policies favored free trade over mercantilism; and changes in shipbuilding techniques increased the speed and volume of maritime commerce. Linked to these changes were new European settlements in southern Africa, Australia, and New Zealand and the growth of a new long-distance trade in indentured labor.

Colonies and Commerce

At the end of the eighteenth century, France was still a serious rival for dominion in the Indian Ocean. However, defeats in the wars of the French Revolution (see Chapter 21) ended Napoleon's dream of restoring French dominance overseas. The wars also dismantled much of the Netherlands' Indian Ocean empire. When French armies occupied the Netherlands, the Dutch ruler, who had fled to Britain in January 1795, authorized the British to take over Dutch possessions overseas in order to keep them out of French hands. During 1795 and 1796 British forces quickly occupied the Cape Colony at the southern tip of Africa, the strategic Dutch port of Malacca on the strait between the Indian Ocean and the South China Sea, and the island of Ceylon (see Map 25.3).

Then the British occupied Dutch Guiana (ghee-AH-nuh) and Trinidad in the southern Caribbean. In 1811 they even seized the island of Java, the center of the Netherlands' East Indian empire. British forces also seized the French islands of Mauritius (moh-RIHS-uhs) and Réunion in the Indian Ocean. At the end of the Napoleonic Wars in 1814, Britain returned Java to the Dutch and Réunion to the French but kept the Cape Colony, British Guiana (once part of Dutch Guiana), Trinidad, Ceylon, Malacca, and Mauritius.

Afrikaners

The Cape Colony was valuable because of Cape Town's strategic importance as a supply station for ships making the long voyages between Britain and India. With the port city came some twenty thousand descendants of Dutch and French settlers who occupied farms and ranches in its hinterland. Despite their European origins, these people thought of themselves as permanent residents of Africa and were beginning to refer to themselves as "Afrikaners" (af-rih-KAHN-uhr). British governors prohibited any expansion of the white settler frontier because such expansion invariably led to wars with indigenous Africans. This decision, along with the imposition of laws protecting African rights within Cape Colony (including the emancipation of slaves in 1834), alienated many Afrikaners.

Between 1836 and 1839 parties of Afrikaners embarked on a "Great Trek," leaving British-ruled Cape Colony for the fertile high *veld* (plateau) to the north that two decades of Zulu wars had depopulated. The Great Trek laid the foundation of three new settler colonies in southern Africa: the Afrikaners' Orange Free State and Transvaal on the high veld and the British colony of Natal on the Indian Ocean coast. Although firearms enabled the settlers to win some important battles against the Zulu and other Africans, they were still a tiny minority surrounded by the populous and powerful independent African kingdoms that had grown up at the beginning of the century.

Singapore

Meanwhile, another strategic British outpost was being established in Southeast Asia. One prong of the advance was led by Thomas Stamford Raffles, who had governed Java from 1811 to 1814. After Java's return to the Dutch, Raffles helped establish a new free port at Singapore in 1824, on the site of a small Malay fishing village with a superb harbor. By attracting British merchants and Chinese businessmen and laborers, Singapore soon became the center of trade and shipping between the Indian Ocean and China. Along with Malacca and other possessions on the strait, Singapore formed the "Straits Settlements," which British India administered until 1867.

Burma

Further British expansion came more quickly in neighboring Burma. Burma had emerged as a powerful kingdom by 1750. In 1785 Burma tried to annex neighboring territories of Siam (now Thailand) to the east, but a coalition of Thai leaders thwarted Burmese advances by 1802. Burma next attacked Assam to the west, but this provoked a war with British India. After a two-year war, India annexed Assam in 1826 and occupied two coastal provinces of northern Burma. As the rice and timber trade from these provinces grew important, the occupation became permanent, and in 1852 British India annexed the rest of coastal Burma.

Great Trek Aided by African servants, the ox-drawn wagons of the Afrikaners struggled over the Drakensberg Mountains to the high plains in an effort to escape British control.

Hulton Archive/Getty Images

Imperial Policies and Shipping

Free Trade

Through such piecemeal acquisitions, by 1870 Britain had added several dozen colonies to the twenty-six colonies it had in 1792. The underlying goal of most British imperial expansion during these decades was trade rather than territory. Most of the new colonies were meant to serve as ports in the growing network of shipping that encircled the globe or as centers of production and distribution for those networks.

This new commercial expansion was closely tied to the needs of Britain's growing industrial economy and reflected a new philosophy of overseas trade. Rather than rebuilding the closed mercantilist network of trade with its colonies, Britain sought to trade freely with all parts of the world. Free trade was also a wise policy in light of the independence of so many former colonies in the Americas (see Chapter 23).

Whether colonized or not, more and more lands were being drawn into the commercial networks created by British expansion and industrialization. Uncolonized parts of West Africa became major exporters to Britain of vegetable oils and forest products, while areas of eastern Africa free of European control exported ivory that ended up as piano keys and decorations in the homes of the middle and upper classes. From the far corners of the world came coffee, cocoa, tea, and sugar for the tables of Western consumers, and indigo dyes and cotton fibers for the expanding textile factories.

In return, the factories of the industrialized nations supplied manufactured goods at very attractive prices. By the mid-nineteenth century a major part of their textile production was destined for overseas markets. Sales of cotton cloth to Africa increased 950 percent from the 1820s to the 1860s. British trade to India grew 350 percent between 1841 and 1870, while India's exports increased 400 percent. Trade with other regions also expanded rapidly. In most cases

MAP 25.3 **European Possessions in the Indian Ocean and South Pacific, 1870** By 1870 the British controlled much of India, were settling Australia and New Zealand, and possessed important trading enclaves throughout the region.

Interactive Map

such trade benefited both sides, but there is no question that the industrial nations were the dominant partners.

Clipper Ships

A second impetus to global commercial expansion was the technological revolution in the construction of oceangoing ships under way in the nineteenth century. The middle decades of the century were the golden age of the sailing ship. Using iron to fasten timbers together permitted shipbuilders to construct much larger vessels. Merchant ships in the eighteenth century rarely exceeded 300 tons, but after 1850 **clipper ships** of 2,000 tons were commonplace in the British merchant fleet. Huge canvas sails made the streamlined clippers faster than earlier vessels. Ships from the East Indies or India had taken six months to reach Europe in the seventeenth century; after 1850 the new ships could complete the voyage in half that time.

clipper ship Large, fast, streamlined sailing vessel, often American built, of the mid-to-late nineteenth century rigged with vast canvas sails hung from tall masts.

This increase in size and speed lowered shipping costs and further stimulated maritime trade. The tonnage of British merchant shipping quadrupled between 1778 and 1860. Clippers intended for eastern service generally were built of teak and other tropical hardwoods from new British colonies in South and Southeast Asia.

Colonization of Australia and New Zealand

Australia

In the once-remote South Pacific, British settlers displaced the indigenous populations of Australia and New Zealand, just as they had done in North America. Portuguese mariners had sighted Australia in the early seventeenth century, but it was too remote to be of much interest to Europeans. However, after the English captain James Cook explored New Zealand and the eastern coast of Australia between 1769 and 1778, expanding shipping networks brought in growing numbers of visitors and settlers.

At the time of Cook's visits, Australia was the home of about 650,000 hunting-and-gathering people, whose Melanesian (mel-uh-NEE-zhuhn) ancestors had settled there some forty thousand years earlier. New Zealand was inhabited by about 250,000 Maori (MOW-ree [ow as in cow]), who practiced hunting, fishing, and simple forms of agriculture, which their Polynesian ancestors had introduced around 1200. Because of their long isolation from the rest of humanity, the populations of Australia and New Zealand were as vulnerable as the Amerindians had been to unfamiliar diseases introduced by new overseas contacts. By the 1890s, only 93,000 aboriginal Australians and 42,000 Maori survived, and British settler populations outnumbered and dominated the indigenous peoples.

The first permanent British settlers in Australia were 736 convicts, of whom 188 were women, sent into exile in 1788. Over the next few decades, Australian penal colonies grew slowly and had only slight contact with the indigenous population, whom the British called "Aborigines." However, the discovery of gold in 1851 brought a flood of free European settlers (and some Chinese) and hastened the end of the penal colonies. When the gold rush subsided, government subsidies enabled tens of thousands of British settlers to settle "down under." Though it still took more than three months to reach Australia from Britain, by 1860 Australia had a million immigrants, and the settler population doubled during the next fifteen years.

New Zealand

British settlers were drawn more slowly to New Zealand. Some of the first were temporary residents along the coast who slaughtered seals and exported pelts to Western countries to be made into men's felt hats. A single ship in 1806 took away sixty thousand sealskins. By the early 1820s overhunting had nearly exterminated the seal population. Special ships also hunted sperm whales extensively near New Zealand for their oil, used for lubrication, soap, and lamps; ambergris (AM-ber-grees), an ingredient in perfume; and bone, used in women's corsets (see Environment and Technology: Whaling). A brief gold rush and faster ships and subsidized passages attracted more British immigrants after 1860. The colony especially courted women immigrants to offset the preponderance of single men. By the early 1880s this most distant frontier of the British Empire had a settler population of 500,000. Britain encouraged the settlers in Australia and New Zealand to become self-governing, following the 1867 model that had formed the Dominion of Canada out of the diverse and thinly settled colonies of British North America. Britain's policies toward its settler colonies in Canada and the South Pacific reflected a desire to avoid the conflicts that had led to the American Revolution. By gradually turning over governing power to the colonies' inhabitants, Britain accomplished three things. It satisfied the settlers' desire for greater control over their own territories; it muted demands for independence; and it made the colonial governments responsible for most of their own expenses. Indigenous peoples were outvoted by the settlers or excluded from voting.

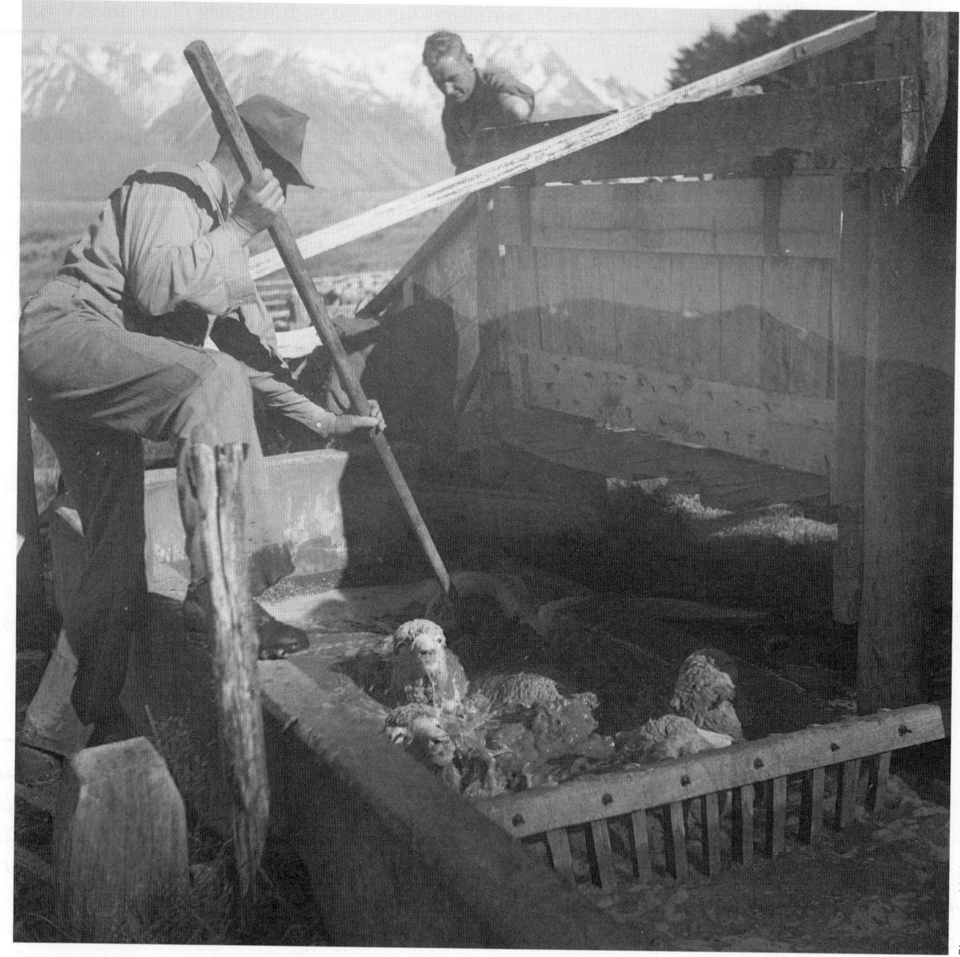

New Zealand Sheep Farming In New Zealand, populist government policies made land available at low cost to European settlers. Here, two sheep farmers are immersing their animals in sheep dip, an insecticide solution that kills parasites.

Photographic Archive, Alexander Turnbull Library, National Library of New Zealand. Photographer: John Dobree Pascoe

North American patterns also shaped the indigenous peoples' fate. Aborigines lacked the rights of Australian citizens. The requirement that voters had to be able to read and write English kept Maori from voting in early New Zealand elections, but four seats in the lower house of the legislature were reserved for Maori from 1867 on.

New Labor Migrations

Between 1834 and 1870 many thousands of Indians, Chinese, and Africans went overseas to work, especially on sugar plantations. In the half-century after 1870, tens of thousands of Asians and Pacific islanders made similar voyages.

In part these migrations were linked to the end of slavery. After their emancipation in British colonies in 1834, many slaves left the plantations. To compete with sugar plantations in Cuba, Brazil, and the French Caribbean that were still using slave labor, British colonies had to recruit new laborers.

India's impoverished people seemed one obvious alternative. After planters on Mauritius successfully introduced Indian laborers, the Indian labor trade moved to the British Caribbean in 1838. In 1841 the British government also allowed Caribbean planters to recruit Africans whom British patrols had rescued from slave ships and liberated in Sierra Leone and elsewhere. By 1870 nearly 40,000 Africans had settled in British colonies, along with over a half-million Indians and over 18,000 Chinese. After the French and Dutch abolished slavery in 1848, their colonies also recruited new laborers from Asia and Africa.

Slavery was not abolished in Cuba until 1886, but the rising cost of slaves led the burgeoning sugar plantations to recruit 138,000 new laborers from China between 1847 and 1873. Inden-

ENVIRONMENT + TECHNOLOGY

Whaling

The rapid expansion of whaling aptly illustrates the growing power of technology over nature in this period. Many contemporaries, like many people today, were sickened by the killing of the planet's largest living mammals. American novelist Herman Melville captured the conflicting sentiments in his epic whaling story, *Moby Dick* (1851). One of his characters enthusiastically explains why the grisly and dangerous business existed:

> *But, though the world scorns us as whale hunters, yet does it unwittingly pay us the profoundest homage; yea, an all abounding adoration! for almost all the tapers, lamps, and candles that burn around the globe, burn, as before so many shrines, to our glory!*

Melville's character overstates the degree to which whale oil dominated illumination and does not mention its many other industrial uses. Neither does he describe the commercial importance of whalebone (baleen). For a time its use in corsets allowed fashionable women to achieve the hourglass shape that fashion dictated. Whalebone's use for umbrella stays, carriage springs, fishing rods, suitcase frames, combs, brushes, and many other items made it the plastic of its day.

New manufacturing technologies went hand in hand with new hunting technologies. The revolution in ship design enabled whalers from Europe and North America to extend the hunt into the southern oceans off New Zealand. By the nineteenth century whaling ships were armed with guns that shot a steel harpoon armed with vicious barbs deep into the whale. In the 1840s explosive charges on harpoon heads ensured the whale's immediate death. Yet, as this engraving of an expedition off New Zealand shows, flinging small harpoons from rowboats in the open sea continued to be part of the dangerous work.

Another century of extensive hunting devastated many whale species before international agreements finally limited the killing of these giant sea creatures.

The Granger Collection, New York

South Pacific Whaling One boat was swamped, but the hunters killed the huge whale.

contract of indenture A voluntary agreement binding a person to work for a specified period of years in return for free passage to an overseas destination. Before 1800 most indentured servants were Europeans; after 1800 most indentured laborers were Asians.

Indenture

tured labor recruits also became the mainstay of new sugar plantations in places that had never known slave labor. After 1850 American planters in Hawaii recruited labor from China and Japan; British planters in Natal recruited from India; and those in Queensland (in northeastern Australia) relied on laborers from neighboring South Pacific islands.

Larger, faster ships made transporting laborers halfway around the world affordable, though voyages from Asia to the Caribbean still took an average of three months. Despite close regulation and supervision of shipboard conditions, the crowded accommodations encouraged the spread of cholera and other contagious diseases that took many migrants' lives.

All of these laborers served under **contracts of indenture**, which bound them to work for a specified period (usually from five to seven years) in return for free passage to their overseas destination. They were paid a small salary and were provided with housing, clothing, and medical care. Indian indentured laborers also received the right to a free passage home if they worked a second five-year contract. British Caribbean colonies required forty women to be recruited for every hundred men as a way to promote family life. So many Indians chose to stay in Mauritius, Trinidad, British Guiana, and Fiji that they constituted a third or more of the total population of these colonies by the early twentieth century.

The indentured labor trade reflected the unequal commercial and industrial power of the West, but it was not an entirely one-sided creation. The men and women who signed indentured contracts were trying to improve their lives by emigrating, and many succeeded. Whether for good or ill, more and more of the world's peoples saw their lives being influenced by the existence of Western colonies, Western ships, and Western markets.

SECTION REVIEW

- By 1850 the British Empire was no longer focused on slave-based colonies in the Americas but on commercial networks and colonies in the East.
- Fast and large clipper ships facilitated the expansion of the British merchant fleet.
- The British took control of the Cape Colony in southern Africa, Ceylon, and the port of Malacca. Singapore soon became the center of trade between the Indian Ocean and China.
- After 1778, growing numbers of settlers to Australia and New Zealand displaced the native Australian and Maori peoples. New and devastating diseases killed over 80 percent of native New Zealanders and Australians.
- After Britain, France, and the Netherlands abolished slavery, thousands of Indians, Chinese, Africans, and Pacific islanders immigrated to British colonies under contracts of indenture.

CONCLUSION

What is the global significance of these complex political and economic changes in southern Asia, Africa, and the South Pacific? One perspective stresses the continuing exploitation of African, Asian, and Pacific peoples by more powerful Europeans. In this view, the emergence of Britain as a dominant power continues the European expansion that the Portuguese, the Spanish, and the Dutch pioneered. Likewise, Britain's control over South and Southeast Asia and over Australia and New Zealand can be seen as a continuation of the conquest and colonization of the Americas.

From another perspective what was most important about this period was not the political and military strength of the Europeans but their growing domination of the world's commerce, especially long-distance ocean shipping. Like other Europeans, the British were drawn to Africa and southern Asia by a desire to obtain new materials. However, Britain's commercial expansion in the nineteenth century was also the product of Easterners' demand for industrial manufactures. The growing exchanges could be mutually beneficial. African and Asian consumers found industrially produced goods far cheaper and sometimes better than the handicrafts they replaced. Industrialization also created new markets for African and Asian goods, as in the case of the vegetable-oil trade in West Africa or cotton in Egypt and India. There were also negative impacts, as in the case of the weavers of India and the damage to species of seals and whales.

Europeans' military and commercial strength did not reduce Africa, Asia, and the Pacific to mere appendages of Europe. While the balance of power shifted in the Europeans' favor between 1750 and 1870, other cultures were still vibrant and local initiatives often dominant. Islamic reform movements and the rise of the Zulu nation had greater significance for their respective regions of Africa than did Western forces. Despite European power, Southeast Asians were still largely in control of their own destinies. Even in India, most people's lives and beliefs showed continuity with the past.

Asians and Africans were not powerless in dealing with European expansion. The Indian princes who extracted concessions from the British in return for their cooperation and the Indians who rebelled against the raj both forced the system to accommodate their needs. Some Asians and Africans were also beginning to use European education, technology, and methods to transform their own societies. Leaders in Egypt, India, and other lands were learning to challenge the power of the West on its own terms. In 1870 no one could say how long and how difficult that learning process would be, but Africans and Asians would continue to shape their own futures.

KEY TERMS

Zulu p. 714
Sokoto Caliphate p. 715
modernization p. 715
Muhammad Ali p. 716
"legitimate" trade p. 718
recaptives p. 719
nawab p. 721
sepoy p. 721
British raj p. 722
Sepoy Rebellion p. 723
durbar p. 723
Indian Civil Service p. 723
Indian National Congress p. 726
clipper ship p. 731
contract of indenture p. 733

EBOOK AND WEBSITE RESOURCES

e Interactive Maps

Map 25.1 Africa in the Nineteenth Century

Map 25.2 India, 1707–1805

Map 25.3 European Possessions in the Indian Ocean and South Pacific, 1870

Plus flashcards, practice quizzes, and more. Go to: www.cengage.com/history/bullietearthpeople5e

SUGGESTED READING

Bayly, C. A. *Indian Society and the Making of the British Empire*. 1987. How Indians adapted to, and resisted, British rule.

Bennett, Norman R. *Arab Versus European: Diplomacy and War in Nineteenth Century East Central Africa*. 1986. Describes the wars and rivalries over northeastern Africa.

Bose, Sugata. *A Hundred Horizons: The Indian Ocean in the Age of Global Empire*. 2006. Discusses British dominance in South Asia and the Indian Ocean.

Bose, Sugata, and Ayeshia Jalal. *Modern South Asia: History, Culture, Political Economy*, 2nd ed. 2003. A readable introduction to India in the age of the British raj.

Eltis, David. *Economic Growth and the Ending of the Transatlantic Slave Trade*. 1987. Discusses the British naval patrols against slavers and their effects.

Gadgil, Madhav, and Ramachandra Guha. *This Fissured Land: An Ecological History of India*. 1993. Describes the environmental changes in India that resulted from modernization.

Headrick, Daniel. *The Tentacles of Progress: Technology Transfer in the Age of Imperialism, 1850–1940*. 1988. Describes the impact of Western technology on India.

Jackson, Gordon. *The British Whaling Trade*. 2005. An outstanding analysis of British whaling.

Keith Sinclair, ed. *The Oxford Illustrated History of New Zealand*. 1996. A wide-ranging introduction to that nation.

Morris, Donald R. *The Washing of the Spears*. 1965. A very readable account of the rise and fall of Shaka's Zulu kingdom.

Northrup, David. *Indentured Labor in the Age of Imperialism, 1834–1922*. 1995. Summarizes recent scholarship on the indentured labor trade.

Rotberg, Robert I., ed., *Africa and Its Explorers: Motives, Methods, and Impact*. 1970. A classic account of the "opening" of Africa to Europeans.

SarDesai, D. R. *Southeast Asia: Past and Present*, 5th ed. 2004. A good introduction to the complexities of Southeast Asian history.

Whitlock, Gillian, and David Carter, eds. *Images of Australia: An Introductory Reader in Australian Studies*. 1992. Presents a multicultural and gendered perspective.

Woodruff, William. *Impact of Western Man: A Study of Europe's Role in the World Economy, 1750–1960*. 1982. A general overview of the period covered in this chapter.

NOTES

1. Paul E. Lovejoy and Jan S. Hogendorn, *Slow Death for Slavery: The Course of Abolition in Northern Nigeria, 1897–1936* (New York: Cambridge University Press, 1993).
2. Quoted in P. J. Vatikiotis, *The History of Modern Egypt: From Muhammad Ali to Mubarak*, 4th ed. (Baltimore: Johns Hopkins University Press, 1991), 74.
3. David Eltis, "Precolonial Western Africa and the Atlantic Economy," in *Slavery and the Rise of the Atlantic Economy*, ed. Barbara Solow (New York: Cambridge University Press, 1991), table 1.
4. Quoted by Bernard S. Cohn, "Representing Authority in Victorian India," in *The Invention of Tradition*, ed. Eric Hobsbawm and Terence Ranger (Cambridge, England: Cambridge University Press, 1983), 165.
5. James Truslow, *Empire of the Seven Seas: The British Empire 1784–1939* (New York: Charles Scribners Sons, 2007), 268.

AP* REVIEW QUESTIONS FOR CHAPTER 25

1. Which of the following was true of sub-Saharan Africa in the early nineteenth century?
   (A) Only areas already under European control experienced any real industrial development.
   (B) Competition among African tribes had led to the beginning of national identity among some African groups.
   (C) European colonial powers still practiced slavery in Africa and sold slaves to the Ottoman Empire.
   (D) Famine and drought had forced most Africans to move into coastal cities.

2. In West Africa, cultural influences from the Americas were added to traditional African cultures by
   (A) slavers who were smuggling slaves into the United States.
   (B) Catholic priests from Brazil and former Spanish colonies.
   (C) free blacks who returned to their West African homelands.
   (D) mercenary soldiers brought in by colonial powers.

3. To protect their warehouses from attack from Europeans or native states, trading companies in India
   (A) paid local rulers to protect them from harm.
   (B) never kept large amounts of trade goods in the warehouses.
   (C) employed retired soldiers from their own countries.
   (D) used Indian sepoy soldiers..

4. The main policy of British rule in India was to
   (A) use India as a base from which to expand into Asia and the Pacific region.
   (B) create a powerful and efficient system of government.
   (C) develop a large tax base to lower taxes on the British citizens at home.
   (D) convert India to a Christian land.

5. Though the participants in the Sepoy Rebellion lacked a common identity, some modern Indian historians say that the rebellion
   (A) was a nascent nationalist rebellion against British rule.
   (B) began when the durbar was banned by the British.
   (C) began when the British began to limit Hindu practices such as sati.
   (D) began when the British banned Indians from serving in the Indian Civil Service.

6. Which of the following was true of the Indian National Congress?
   (A) It was controlled by the Muslim minority in India.
   (B) It was made up mainly of upper-caste Western-educated Hindus and Parsis.
   (C) It was funded by the British as a way to control Indian nationalism.
   (D) It was composed mainly of Indian civil servants.

7. The Cape Colony in South Africa was important to the British because
   (A) it was their only major trade port in sub-Saharan Africa.
   (B) it was a strategic supply station for ships traveling between Great Britain and India.
   (C) Great Britain gained control of the slave trade in this part of Africa.
   (D) it had already developed basic industry under the Dutch.

8. By the mid-nineteenth century, Great Britain sought free trade instead of mercantilist practices because
   (A) it feared competition with other nations such as the United States and France.
   (B) it already held plentiful supplies of gold and silver.
   (C) its naval forces could protect British merchant ships on the seas.
   (D) of the commercial needs of Great Britain's growing industrial economy at home.

9. Great Britain's colony in Australia grew slowly until 1851, when
   (A) the government in London exiled large numbers of Irish to the colony as prisoners.
   (B) the demand for meat in Great Britain made cattle ranching in Australia profitable.
   (C) the settlers discovered large aquifers that would provide ample quantities of water for farming.
   (D) the discovery of gold brought thousands of Europeans to the colony as free settlers.

10. Like the United States, by the end of the nineteenth century Australia had
   (A) settled nearly all of the continent.
   (B) begun to develop heavy industry.
   (C) segregated the majority of its indigenous people onto reservations.
   (D) abolished slavery, but not indentured servitude.

STATE POWER, THE CENSUS, AND THE QUESTION OF IDENTITY

Between the American Revolution and the last decades of the nineteenth century, Europe and the Americas were transformed. The ancient power of kings and the authority of religion were eclipsed by muscular new ways of organizing political, economic, and intellectual life. The Western world was vastly different in 1870 than it had been a century earlier. One of the less heralded but enduringly significant changes was the huge expansion of government statistical services.

The rise of the nation-state was associated with the development of modern bureaucratic departments that depended on reliable statistics to measure the nation's achievements and discover its failures. The nation-state, whether democratic or not, mobilized resources on a previously unimaginable scale. Modern states were more powerful and wealthier, and they were also more ambitious and more intrusive. The growth of their power can be seen in the modernization of militaries, the commitment to internal improvements such as railroads, and the growth in state revenues. In recent years historians have begun to examine a less visible but equally important manifestation of growing state power: census taking.

Governments and religious authorities have counted people since early times. Our best estimates of the Amerindian population of the Western Hemisphere in 1500 rest almost entirely on what were little more than missionaries' guesses about the numbers of people they baptized. Spanish and Portuguese kings were eager to count native populations, since "indios" (adult male Amerindians) were subject to special labor obligations and tribute payments. So, from the mid-sixteenth century onward, imperial officials conducted regular censuses of Amerindians, adapting practices already in place in Europe.

The effort to measure and categorize populations was transformed in the last decades of the eighteenth century when the nature of European governments began to change. The Enlightenment belief that the scientific method could be applied to human society proved to be attractive both to political radicals, like the French Revolutionaries, and to reforming monarchs like Maria Theresa of Austria. Enlightenment philosophers had argued that a science of government could remove the inefficiencies and irrationalities that had long subverted the human potential for prosperity and happiness. The French intellectual Condorcet wrote in 1782:

> *Those sciences, created almost in our own days, the object of which is man himself, the direct goal of which is the happiness of man, will enjoy a progress no less sure than that of the physical sciences. . . . In meditating on the nature of the moral sciences [what we now call the social sciences], one cannot help seeing that, as they are based like the physical sciences on the observation of fact, they must follow the method, acquire a language equally exact and precise, attaining the same degree of certainty.*[1]

As confidence in this new "science" grew, the term previously used to describe the collection of numbers about society, *political arithmetic*, was abandoned by governments and practitioners in favor of *statistics*, a term that clearly suggests its close ties to the "state." In the nineteenth century the new objectives set out by Condorcet and others led to both the formal university training of statisticians and the creation of government statistical services.

The ambitions of governments in this new era were great. Nation-states self-consciously sought to transform society, sponsoring economic development, education, and improvements in health and welfare. They depended on statistics to measure the effectiveness of their policies and, as a result, were interested in nearly everything. They counted taverns, urban buildings, births and deaths, and arrests and convictions. They also counted their populations with a thoroughness never before seen. As statistical reporting became more uniform across Europe and the Americas, governments could measure not only their own progress but also that of their neighbors and rivals.

The revolutionary governments of France modernized the census practices of the overthrown monarchy. They spent much more money, hired many more census takers, and devoted much more energy to training the staff that designed censuses and analyzed results. Great Britain set up an official census in 1801, but it established a special administrative structure only in the 1830s. In the Western Hemisphere nearly every independent nation provided for "scientific" censuses. In the United States the federal constitution required that a census be taken every ten years. Latin American nations, often torn by civil war in the nineteenth century, took censuses less regularly, but even the poorest nations took censuses when they could. It was as if the census itself confirmed the existence of the government, demonstrating its modernity and seriousness.

Until recently, historians who relied on these documents in their research on economic performance, issues of race and ethnicity, family life, and fertility and mortality asked few questions about the politics of census design. What could be more objective than rows of numbers? But the advocates of statistics who managed census taking were uninhibited in advertising the usefulness of reliable numbers to the governments that employed them. At the 1860 International Statistical Congress held in London one speaker said, "I think the true meaning to be attached to 'statistics' is not every collection of figures, but figures collected with the sole purpose of applying the principles deduced from them to questions of importance to the state."[2] The desire to be useful meant that statistics could not be fully objective.

Subjectivity was an unavoidable problem with censuses. Censuses identified citizens and foreign residents by place of residence, sex, age, and family relationships within households as well as profession and literacy. These determinations were sometimes subjective. Modern scholars have demonstrated that census takers also often undercounted the poor and those living in rural areas.

Because census takers, as agents of nation-states, were determined to be useful, they were necessarily concerned with issues of nationality and, in the Americas, with race because these characteristics commonly determined political rights and citizenship. The assessment and recording of nationality and race would prove to be among the most politically problematic objectives of the new social sciences.

Nationality had not been a central question for traditional monarchies. For the emerging nation-state, however, nationality was central. A nation's strength was assumed to depend in large measure on the growth of its population, a standard that, once articulated, suggested that the growth of minority populations was dangerous. Who was French? Who was Austrian or Hungarian? European statisticians relied on both *language of use* and *mother tongue* as proxies for *nationality*, the first term being flexible enough to recognize the assimilation of minorities, the second suggesting a more permanent identity based on a person's original language. Both terms forced bilingual populations to simplify their more complex identities. Ethnic minorities, once identified, were sometimes subject to discrimination such as exclusion from military careers or from universities. In parts of Spanish America language was used as a proxy for *race*. Those who spoke Spanish were citizens in the full sense, even if they were indistinguishable from Amerindians in appearance. Those who spoke indigenous languages were "indios" and therefore subject to special taxes and labor obligations and effectively denied the right to vote.

Beyond providing a justification for continuing discrimination, census categories compressed and distorted the complexity and variety of human society to fit the preconceptions of bureaucrats and politicians. Large percentages of the residents of Mexico, Peru, and Bolivia, among other parts of the Americas, were descended from both Europeans and Amerindians and, in the Caribbean region, from Europeans and Africans. Census categories never adequately captured the complexities of these biological and cultural mixtures. We now know that the poor were often identified as "indios" or "blacks" and the better-off were often called something else, "Americanos," "criollos" (creoles), or even whites. Since this process flattened and streamlined the complexities of identity, censuses on their own are not reliable guides to the distribution of ethnicity and race in a population.

In Europe the issue of nationality proved similarly perplexing for census takers and similarly dangerous to those identified as minorities. Linguistic and ethnic minorities had always lived among the politically dominant majorities: Jewish and Polish minorities in areas controlled by German speakers, German speakers among the French, and Serbo-Croatian speakers among Hungarians, for example. The frontiers between these minority populations and their neighbors were always porous. Sexual unions and marriages were common, and two or more generations of a family often lived together in the same household, with the elder members speaking one language and the younger members another. Who was what? In a very real sense, nationality, like race in the Americas, was ultimately fixed by the census process, where the nation-state forced a limited array of politically utilitarian categories onto the rich diversity of ethnicity and culture.

NOTES

1. Quoted in James C. Scott, *Seeing like a State. How Certain Schemes to Improve the Human Condition Have Failed* (New Haven: Yale University Press, 1998), 91.
2. This discussion relies heavily on Eliza Johnson (now Ablovatski), "Counting and Categorizing: The Hungarian Gypsy Census of 1893" (M.A. Thesis, Columbia University, 1996), especially Chapter III. She quotes from the *Proceedings of the Sixth International Statistical Congress Held in London, 1860,* 379.

PART VII

Victoria & Albert Museum, London/Art Resource, NY

Highways of the Empire In the late nineteenth century, Europeans believed the world revolved around their subcontinent. World maps printed in Great Britain showed the British Empire in red, with informal dependencies and protectorates in pink. This map, a polar projection with Britain in the exact center, shows the major shipping routes and submarine telegraph cable lines that made London the center of global commerce and finance and ensured the supremacy of the Royal Navy around the world.

Global Diversity and Dominance, 1850–1945

In 1850, the world embraced a huge diversity of societies and cultures. During the century that followed, Europe, the United States, and Japan dominated much of the world and tried to convert other peoples to their own belief systems and ways of life.

In Europe, mounting tensions led to the Great War of 1914–1918. Russia and China erupted in revolution. Soon after, the heartland of the Ottoman Empire became modern Turkey, while its Arab provinces were taken over by France and Britain.

The political structures and economic system the European powers crafted after the war fell apart in the 1930s. While the capitalist nations fell into a depression, the Soviet Union industrialized at breakneck speed. In Germany and Japan, extremists sought to solve their countries' grievances by military conquest.

World War II caused the death of millions of people and the destruction of countless cities. The war also weakened Europe's overseas empires. Nationalists in Asia, Latin America, and Africa yearned for independence and the benefits of industrialization. India gained its independence in 1947. Two years later, Mao Zedong led the Chinese communists to victory. Latin American leaders embraced nationalist economic and social policies. Of all the once great powers, only the United States and the Soviet Union remained to compete for global dominance.

CHAPTER 26

CHAPTER OUTLINE

- New Technologies and the World Economy
- Social Changes
- Socialism and Labor Movements
- Nationalism and the Rise of Italy, Germany, and Japan
- The Great Powers of Europe, 1871–1900
- China, Japan, and the Western Powers
- Conclusion

ENVIRONMENT + TECHNOLOGY *Railroads and Immigration*

DIVERSITY + DOMINANCE *Marx and Engels on Global Trade and the Bourgeoisie*

MATERIAL CULTURE *Cotton Clothing*

Courtesy of the Trustees of the British Museum/The Art Archive

Arrivals from the East In 1853, Commodore Matthew Perry's fleet sailed into Edo (now Tokyo) Bay. The first steam-powered warships to appear in Japanese waters caused a sensation among the Japanese. In this print done after the Meiji Restoration, the traditionally dressed local samurai go out to confront the mysterious "black ships."

Visit the website and ebook for additional study materials and interactive tools: www.cengage.com/history/bullietearthpeople5e

The New Power Balance, 1850–1900

- What new technologies and industries appeared between 1850 and 1900, and how did they affect the world economy?
- How did the social structures of the industrial countries change during this period?
- How did industrialization contribute to the socialist and labor movements?
- How was nationalism transformed from a revolutionary to a conservative ideology?
- How did the forces of nationalism affect the major powers of Europe?

On July 8, 1853, four American warships, two of them steam-powered, appeared in Edo Bay, close to the capital of Japan. The commander of the fleet, **Commodore Matthew Perry**, delivered a letter from the president of the United States, demanding that Japan open its ports to foreign trade. Perry's "black ships" were the first to break through the barriers that had kept Japan isolated from the rest of the world for two and a half centuries. It was not the foreign interlopers who created such a sensation among the Japanese, but the machines they came in.

A year later, Perry returned to receive the answer from the Japanese government. The Americans also brought a miniature railroad, a short telegraph line, and other marvels of Western technology. For the next twenty years, Japanese society was torn between those who wanted to retreat into isolation and those who wished to embrace the foreign ways and acquire their machines. For it was clear that only by industrializing could Japan escape the fate of weaker nations then being taken over by Europe and the United States.

Commodore Matthew Perry A navy commander who, on July 8, 1853, became the first foreigner to break through the barriers that had kept Japan isolated from the rest of the world for 250 years.

In the late nineteenth century a very small number of states, known as "great powers," dominated the world. Great Britain, France, and Russia had been recognized as great powers long before the industrial age. Russia began industrializing in the late nineteenth century, as did Germany, the United States, and Japan. The rise of the United States was covered in Chapter 23; here we will turn to the other great powers of the age. In the next chapter, which deals with the "New Imperialism" (1870–1914), we will see how these nations used their power to establish colonial empires in Asia and Africa and to control Latin America. Together, Chapters 26 and 27 describe an era in which a handful of wealthy industrialized nations imposed on the other peoples of the world a domination more powerful than any experienced before or since.

NEW TECHNOLOGIES AND THE WORLD ECONOMY

The Industrial Revolution marked the beginning of a massive transformation of the world. In the nineteenth century the technologies discussed in Chapter 22—textile mills, railroads, steamships, the telegraph, and others—spread from Britain to other parts of the world. By 1890 Germany and the United States had surpassed Great Britain as the world's leading industrial powers. Industrialization also introduced entirely new technologies that revolutionized everyday life and transformed the world economy. The motive force behind this second phase of industrialization consisted of potent combinations of business, engineering, and science. By the mid-nineteenth century this combination was institutionalized in engineering schools and research laboratories, first in Germany and then in the United States. Electricity and the steel and chemical industries were the first results of this new force.

Railroads

railroads Networks of iron (later steel) rails on which steam (later electric or diesel) locomotives pulled long trains at high speeds. The first railroads were built in England in the 1830s. Their success caused a railroad-building boom throughout the world that lasted well into the twentieth century.

By the mid-nineteenth century, steam engines had become the prime mover of industry and commerce. Nowhere was this more evident than in the spread of **railroads**. By 1850 the first railroads had proved so successful that every industrializing country, and many that aspired to become industrial, began to build lines. The next fifty years saw a tremendous expansion of the world's rail networks. After a rapid spurt of building new lines, British railroad mileage leveled off in the 1870s at around 20,000 miles (over 32,000 kilometers). France and Germany built networks longer than Britain's, as did Canada and Russia. When Japan began building its railway network in the 1870s, it imported several hundred engineers from the United States and Britain, then replaced them with newly trained Japanese engineers in the 1880s.

Railroads were not confined to the industrialized nations; they could be constructed almost anywhere they would be of value to business or government. That included regions with abundant raw materials or agricultural products, like South Africa, Mexico, and Argentina, and densely populated countries like Egypt. The British built the fourth largest rail network in the world in India in order to reinforce their presence and develop trade with their largest colony.

AP* Exam Tip The transformative effects of new technology on societies are an important topic.

With one exception, European or American engineers built these railroads with equipment imported from the West. In 1855, barely a year after Commodore Perry's visit, the Japanese instrument maker Tanaka Hisashige built a model steam train that he demonstrated to an admiring audience. In the 1870s the Japanese government hired British engineers to build the first line from Tokyo to Yokohama, then sent them home again as soon as they had trained Japanese engineers. Within a few years, Japan began manufacturing its own equipment.

Railroads consumed huge amounts of land. Many old cities doubled in size to accommodate railroad stations, sidings, tracks, warehouses, and repair shops. In the countryside, railroads required bridges, tunnels, and embankments. Railroads also consumed vast quantities of timber for ties to hold the rails and for bridges, often consuming trees for miles on either side of the tracks. Throughout the world, they opened new land to agriculture, mining, and other human exploitation of natural resources.

Steamships and Telegraph Cables

In the mid-nineteenth century, a series of developments radically transformed ocean shipping. First iron, then steel, replaced the wood that had been used for hulls since shipbuilding began. Propellers replaced paddle wheels, and engineers built more powerful and fuel-efficient engines. The average size of freighters increased from 200 tons in 1850 to 7,500 tons in 1900. Coaling stations and ports able to handle large ships were built around the world. The Suez Canal, constructed in 1869, shortened the distance between Europe and Asia and triggered a massive switch from sail power to steam (see Chapter 27).

submarine telegraph cables Insulated copper cables laid along the bottom of a sea or ocean for telegraphic communication. The first short cable was laid across the English Channel in 1851; the first successful transatlantic cable was laid in 1866.

The world's fleet of merchant ships grew from 9 million tons in 1850 to 35 million tons in 1910. Shipping lines offered fast, punctual, and reliable service on a fixed schedule for passengers, mail, and perishable freight. Meanwhile, tramp freighters sailed from one port to another under orders from their company headquarters in Europe or North America.

To control their ships, shipping companies used a new medium of communications: **submarine telegraph cables**. By the turn of the century cables connected every country and almost every inhabited island. As cables became the indispensable tools of modern shipping and business, the public and the press extolled the "annihilation of time and space."

CHRONOLOGY

	Political Events	Social, Cultural, and Technological Events
1850		1851 Majority of British population living in cities
	1853–1854 Commodore Matthew Perry visits Japan	1856 Bessemer converter; first synthetic dye
		1859 Charles Darwin, *On the Origin of Species*
1860	1860–1870 Unification of Italy	
	1861–1865 American Civil War	1861 Emancipation of serfs (Russia)
	1862–1908 Rule of Empress Dowager Cixi (China)	1866 Alfred Nobel develops dynamite
		1867 Karl Marx, *Das Kapital*
	1868 Meiji Restoration begins modernization drive in Japan	1868–1894 Japan undergoes Western-style industrialization and societal changes
1870	1870–1871 Franco-Prussian War	
	1871 Unification of Germany	1879 Thomas Edison develops incandescent lamp
1880		
1890	1894 Sino-Japanese War	
1900	1900 Boxer Uprising (China)	
	1904–1905 Russo-Japanese War	
	1905 Revolution in Russia	
	1910 Japan annexes Korea	

The Steel and Chemical Industries

steel A form of iron that is both durable and flexible. It was first mass-produced in the 1860s and quickly became the most widely used metal in construction, machinery, and railroad equipment.

Until the nineteenth century **steel** could be made only by skilled blacksmiths in very small quantities and was reserved for swords, knives, axes, and watch springs. Then came a series of inventions that made it the cheapest and most versatile metal ever known. In the 1850s the American William Kelly and the Englishman Henry Bessemer discovered that air forced through molten pig iron by powerful pumps turned it into steel without additional fuel. Other new processes permitted steel to be made from scrap iron, an increasingly important raw material, and from the phosphoric iron ores common in western Europe. Steel became cheap and abundant enough to make rails, bridges, ships, and even "tin" cans meant to be used once and thrown away.

The chemical industry followed a similar pattern. In 1856 the Englishman William Perkin created the first synthetic dye, aniline purple, from coal tar; the next few years were known in Europe as the "mauve decade" from the color of fashionable women's clothes. Industry began mass-producing other organic chemicals—compounds containing carbon atoms. Toward the end of the century German chemists synthesized red, violet, blue, brown, and black dyes as well. These bright, long-lasting colors were cheaper to manufacture and could be produced in much greater quantities than natural dyes. They delighted consumers but ruined the indigo plantations of India. Chemistry also made important advances in the manufacture of explosives. The first of these, nitroglycerin, was so dangerous that it exploded when shaken. In 1866 the Swedish scientist Alfred Nobel found a way to turn nitroglycerin into a stable solid—dynamite. This and other new explosives were useful in mining and were critical in the construction of railroads and canals. They also enabled the armies and navies of the great powers to arm themselves with increasingly accurate and powerful rifles and cannon.

The growing complexity of industrial chemistry made it one of the first fields where science and technology interacted on a daily basis. This development gave a great advantage to Germany, which had the most advanced engineering schools and scientific institutes of the time and whose government funded research and encouraged cooperation between universities and industries. By the end of the nineteenth century, Germany was the world's leading producer of dyes, drugs, synthetic fertilizers, ammonia, and nitrates used in making explosives.

Environmental Problems

Industrialization affected entire regions such as the English Midlands, the German Ruhr, parts of Pennsylvania in the United States, and the regions around Tokyo and Osaka in Japan.

The new steel mills took up as much space as whole towns, belched smoke and particulates, and left behind huge hills of slag and other waste products. Railroad locomotives and other steam engines polluted the air with coal smoke. The dyestuff and other chemicals produced toxic effluents that were dumped into nearby rivers. Industrialization unrestrained by environmental regulations caused considerable damage to nature and to the health of nearby inhabitants.

Electricity

Thomas Edison

electricity A form of energy used in telegraphy from the 1840s on and for lighting, industrial motors, and railroads beginning in the 1880s.

Thomas Edison American inventor best known for inventing the electric light bulb, acoustic recording on wax cylinders, and motion pictures.

No innovation of the late nineteenth century changed people's lives as radically as **electricity**. As an energy source, electricity was more flexible and much easier to use than water power or stationary steam engines. At first, producing electric current was so costly that it was used only for electroplating and telegraphy. Then in 1831 the Englishman Michael Faraday showed that the motion of a copper wire through a magnetic field induced an electric current in the wire. Based on his discovery, inventors in the 1870s devised generators that turned mechanical energy into electric current.

Electricity now had a host of new applications. Arc lamps lit up public squares, theaters, and stores. For a while, homes continued to rely on gas lamps, which produced a softer light. Then in 1879 in the United States **Thomas Edison** developed an incandescent lamp well suited to lighting small rooms. In 1882 Edison created the world's first electrical distribution network in New York City. By the turn of the century electric lighting was rapidly replacing gas lamps in the cities of Europe and North America.

Other uses of electricity quickly appeared. Electric streetcars and subways transported people throughout the cities of Europe and North America. Electric motors replaced steam engines and power belts, increasing productivity and improving workers' safety. As demand for electricity grew, engineers built hydroelectric plants. The plant at Niagara Falls, on the border between Ontario, Canada, and New York State, produced an incredible 11,000 horsepower when it opened in 1895. At the newly created Imperial College of Engineering in Japan, an Englishman, William Ayrton, became the first professor of electrical engineering anywhere in the world; his students later went on to found major corporations and government research institutes.

Paris Lit Up by Electricity, 1900 The electric light bulb was invented in the United States and Britain, but Paris made such extensive use of the new technology that it was nicknamed "City of Lights." To mark the Paris Exposition of 1900, the Eiffel Tower and all the surrounding buildings were illuminated with strings of light bulbs while powerful spotlights swept the sky.

World Trade and Finance

World trade expanded tenfold between 1850 and 1913. Europe imported wheat from the United States and India, wool from Australia, and beef from Argentina, while it exported coal, railroad equipment, textiles, and machinery to Asia and the Americas. Because steamships were much more efficient than sailing ships, the cost of freight dropped between 50 and 95 percent, making it worthwhile to ship even cheap and heavy products over very long distances.

The growth of world trade transformed different parts of the world in different ways. The economies of western Europe and North America, the first to industrialize, grew more diversified and prosperous. Industries mass-produced consumer goods for a growing number of middle-class and even working-class customers: soap, canned and packaged foods, ready-made clothes, household items, and small luxuries like cosmetics and engravings.

Business Cycles and Globalization

Capitalist economies, however, were prey to sudden swings in the business cycle—booms followed by deep depressions in which workers lost their jobs and investors their fortunes. Because of the close connections among the industrial economies, the collapse of a bank in Austria in 1873 triggered a depression that spread to the United States, causing mass unemployment. Worldwide recessions occurred in the mid-1880s and mid-1890s as well.

Tariffs could not insulate countries from the business cycle, for money continued to flow almost unhindered around the world. One of the main causes of the growing interdependence of the global economy was the financial power of Great Britain, which dominated the flow of trade, finance, and information. In 1900 two-thirds of the world's submarine cables were British or passed through Britain, and over half of the world's shipping was British owned. Britain invested one-fourth of its national wealth overseas, much of it in the United States and Argentina. British money financed many of the railroads, harbors, mines, and other big projects outside Europe. While other currencies fluctuated, the pound sterling was as good as gold, and nine-tenths of international transactions used sterling.

Nonindustrial areas also were tied to the world economy as never before. They were more vulnerable to changes in price and demand than were the industrialized nations, for many of them produced raw materials that could be replaced by synthetic substitutes (like dyestuffs) or alternative sources of supply. Nevertheless, until 1913 the value of exports from the tropical countries generally kept up with the growth of their populations.

SECTION REVIEW

- Industrialization spread throughout the world through trade and new technologies.
- Railroads, almost always financed by Western nations, spread to all continents, changing and enlarging cities.
- Steamships and telegraph cables connected continents and encouraged trade.
- In three new industries—steel, chemicals, and electricity—the United States and Germany surpassed Great Britain.
- World trade boomed in an age of globalization.

SOCIAL CHANGES

As fast-growing population swelled cities to unprecedented size, millions of Europeans emigrated to the Americas. Strained relations between industrial employers and workers spawned labor movements and new forms of radical politics. Women found their lives dramatically altered, both in the home and in the public sphere.

Population and Migrations

European Migrations

The population of Europe grew faster from 1850 to 1914 than ever before or since, almost doubling from 265 million to 468 million. In non-European countries with predominantly white populations—the United States, Canada, Australia, New Zealand, and Argentina—the increase was even greater because of the inflow of Europeans. There were many reasons for the mass migrations of this period: the Irish famine of 1847–1848; the persecution of Jews in Russia; poverty and population growth in Italy, Spain, Poland, and Scandinavia; and the cultural ties between Great Britain and English-speaking countries overseas. Equally important was the availability of cheap and rapid steamships and railroads serving travelers at both ends (see Environment and Technology: Railroads and Immigration). Between 1850 and 1900, on average,

400,000 Europeans migrated overseas every year; between 1900 and 1914 the flood rose to over 1 million a year. From 1850 to 1910 the population of the United States and Canada rose from 25 million to 98 million, and the proportion of people of European ancestry in the world's population rose from one-fifth to one-third.

Why did the number of Europeans and their descendants overseas jump so dramatically? Much of the increase came from a drop in the death rate, as epidemics and starvation became less common. The Irish famine was the last peacetime famine in European history. As farmers plowed up the plains of North America and planted wheat, much of which was shipped to Europe, food supplies increased faster than the population. Canning and refrigeration made food abundant year-round. The diet of Europeans and North Americans improved as meat, fruit, vegetables, and oils became part of the daily fare of city dwellers in winter as well as in summer.

Asian Migrations

During this period Asians also migrated in large numbers as indentured laborers recruited to work on plantations, in mines, and on railroads. Indians went to Africa, Southeast Asia, and other tropical colonies of Great Britain. Chinese and Indians emigrated to Southeast Asia, the East Indies, and the Caribbean to work on sugar plantations. Japanese migrated to Brazil and other parts of Latin America. Many Japanese, as well as Chinese and Filipinos, went to work in agriculture and menial trade in Hawaii and California, where they encountered growing hostility from European-Americans.

Urbanization and Urban Environments

AP* Exam Tip Students should be able to discuss the environmental impact of nineteenth-century migrations and urban development.

In 1851 Britain became the first nation with a majority of its population living in towns and cities. By 1914, 80 percent of its population was urban, as were 60 percent of Germans and 45 percent of the French. Cities grew to unprecedented size. London grew from 2.7 million in 1850 to 6.6 million in 1900. New York, a small town of 64,000 people in 1800, reached 3.4 million by 1900, a fiftyfold increase. In 1800 New York had covered only the southernmost quarter of Manhattan Island, some 3 square miles (nearly 8 square kilometers); by 1900 it covered 150 square miles (390 square kilometers). In the English Midlands, in the German Ruhr, and around Tokyo Bay, towns fused into one another, filling in the fields and woods that once had separated them.

As cities grew, they changed in character. Newly built railroads not only brought goods into the cities on a predictable schedule but also allowed people to live farther apart. At first, only the well-to-do could afford to commute by train; by the end of the century, electric streetcars and subways allowed working-class people to live miles from their workplaces.

Sanitation

In preindustrial and early industrial cities, the poor crowded together in tenements; sanitation was bad; water often was contaminated with sewage; and darkness made life dangerous. New urban technologies and the growing powers and responsibilities of governments transformed city life for all but the poorest residents. The most important change was the installation of pipes to bring in clean water and to carry away sewage. First gas lighting and then electric lighting made cities safer at night. By the turn of the twentieth century municipal governments provided police and fire protection, sanitation and garbage removal, building and health inspection, schools, parks, and other amenities unheard of a century earlier.

As sanitation improved, epidemics became rare. For the first time, urban death rates fell below birthrates. The decline in infant mortality was especially significant. Confident that their children would survive infancy, couples began to limit the number of children they had, and ancient scourges like infanticide and child abandonment became less frequent.

Housing

To accommodate the growing population, builders created new neighborhoods, from crowded tenements for the poor to opulent mansions for the newly rich. In the United States planners laid out new cities, such as Chicago, on rectangular grids, and middle-class families moved to new developments on the edges of cities. In Paris older neighborhoods with narrow crooked streets and rickety tenements were torn down to make room for broad boulevards and modern apartment buildings. Brilliantly lit by gas and electricity, Paris became the "city of lights," a model for city planners from New Delhi to Buenos Aires. The rich continued to live in inner cities that contained the monuments, churches, and palaces of preindustrial times, while workers moved to the outskirts.

Lower population densities and better transportation divided cities into industrial, commercial, and residential zones occupied by different social classes. Improvements such as water and sewerage, electricity, and streetcars always benefited the wealthy first, then the middle

Railroads and Immigration

Why did so many Europeans emigrate to North America in the late nineteenth and early twentieth centuries? The quick answer is that millions of people longed to escape the poverty or tyranny of their home countries and start new lives in a land of freedom and opportunity. Personal desire alone, however, does not account for the migrations. After all, poverty and tyranny existed long before the late nineteenth century. Two other factors helped determine when and where people migrated: whether they were allowed to migrate, and whether they were able to.

In the nineteenth century Asians were recruited to build railroads and work on farms. But from the 1890s on, the United States and Canada closed their doors to non-Europeans, so regardless of what they wanted, they could not move to North America. In contrast, emigrants from Europe were admitted until after the First World War.

The ability to travel was a result of improvements in transportation. Until the 1890s most immigrants came from Ireland, England, or Germany—countries with good rail transportation to their own harbors and low steamship fares to North America. As rail lines were extended into eastern and southern Europe, more and more immigrants came from Italy, Austria-Hungary, and Russia.

Similarly, until the 1870s most European immigrants to North America settled on the east coast. Then, as the railroads pushed west, more of them settled on farms in the central and western parts of the continent. The power of railroads moved people as much as their desires did.

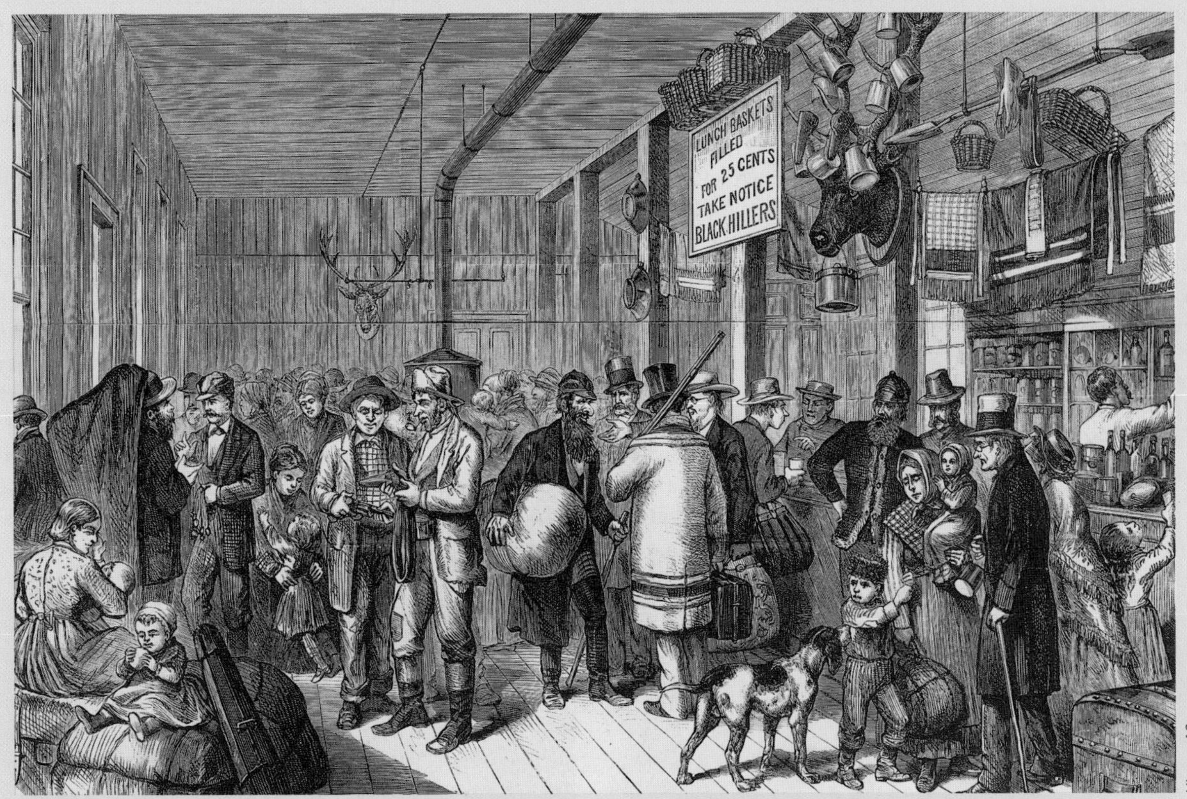

Emigrant Waiting Room The opening of the western region of the United States attracted settlers from the east coast and from Europe. These migrants are waiting for a train to take them to the Black Hills of Dakota during one of the gold rushes of the late nineteenth century.

class, and finally the working class. In the complex of urban life, businesses of all kinds arose, and the professions—engineering, accounting, research, journalism, and the law, among others—took on increased importance. The new middle class exhibited its wealth in fine houses with servants and in elegant entertainment.

Air Pollution

While urban environments improved in many ways, air quality worsened. Coal, burned to power steam engines and heat buildings, polluted the air, creating unpleasant and sometimes dangerous "pea-soup" fog and coating everything with a film of grimy dust. The thousands of horses that pulled the carts and carriages covered the streets with their wastes, causing a terrible stench. The introduction of electricity helped alleviate some of these environmental problems. Electric motors and lamps did not pollute the air. Power plants were built at a distance from cities. As electric trains and streetcars began replacing horse-drawn trolleys and coal-burning locomotives, cities became cleaner and healthier. However, most of the environmental benefits of electricity were to come in the twentieth century.

Middle-Class Women's "Separate Sphere"

Victorian Age The reign of Queen Victoria of Great Britain (r. 1837–1901). The term is also used to describe late-nineteenth-century society, with its rigid moral standards and sharply differentiated roles for men and women and for middle-class and working-class people.

In English-speaking countries the period from about 1850 to 1901 is known as the "**Victorian Age**." The expression refers not only to the reign of Queen Victoria of England (r. 1837–1901) but also to rules of behavior and to an ideology surrounding the family and the relations between men and women. The Victorians contrasted the masculine ideals of strength and courage with the feminine virtues of beauty and kindness, and they idealized the home as a peaceful and loving refuge from the dog-eat-dog world of competitive capitalism.

Victorian morality claimed to be universal, yet it best fit upper- and middle-class European families. Men and women were thought to belong in **"separate spheres."** Successful businessmen spent their time at work or relaxing in men's clubs. They put their wives in charge of rearing the children, running the household, and spending the family money to enhance the family's social status.

Middle-Class Homes

"separate spheres" Nineteenth-century idea in Western societies that men and women, especially of the middle class, should have clearly differentiated roles in society: women as wives, mothers, and homemakers; men as breadwinners and participants in business and politics.

Before electric appliances, maintaining a middle-class home involved enormous amounts of work. Not only were families larger, but middle-class couples entertained often and lavishly. Carrying out these tasks required servants. A family's status and the activities and lifestyle of the "mistress of the house" depended on the availability of servants to help with household tasks. Only families that employed at least one full-time servant were considered middle class.

Toward the turn of the century modern technology began to transform middle-class homes. Plumbing eliminated the pump and the outhouse. Central heating replaced fireplaces, stoves, trips to the basement for coal, and endless dusting. Gas and electricity lit houses and cooked food without soot, smoke, and ashes. In the early twentieth century wealthy families acquired the first vacuum cleaners and washing machines. These technological advances did not mean less housework for women. As families acquired new household technologies, they raised their standards of cleanliness, thus demanding just as much labor as before.

The most important duty of middle-class women was raising children. Victorian mothers nursed their own babies and showered their children with love and attention. Even those who could afford governesses remained personally involved in their children's education. Girls' edu-

Mary Evans Picture Library

Visual Connection

Separate Spheres in Great Britain In the Victorian Age, men and women of the middle and upper classes led largely separate lives. In *Aunt Emily's Visit* (1845), we see women and children at home, tended by a servant. *The Royal Exchange*, meanwhile, was a place for men to transact business.

cation was very different from that of boys. While boys were being prepared for the business world or the professions, girls were taught embroidery, drawing, and music, skills that enhanced their social graces and marriage prospects.

Jobs and Careers

Young middle-class women could work until they got married, but only in genteel places like stores and offices, never in factories. When the typewriter and telephone were introduced into the business world in the 1880s, businessmen found that they could get better work at lower wages from educated young women than from men, and operating these machines was typecast as women's work.

AP* Exam Tip Ideas about gender and changes in gender structure, such as work patterns, are possible topics on the essay portion of the exam.

Most professional careers were closed to women, and few universities granted women degrees. In the United States higher education was available to women only at elite colleges in the East and teachers' colleges in the Midwest. European women had fewer opportunities. Before 1914 very few women became doctors, lawyers, or professional musicians. Instead, women were considered well suited to teaching young children and girls—an extension of the duties of Victorian mothers—but only until marriage. A married woman was expected to become pregnant right away and to stay home taking care of her own children rather than other people's.

Suffragists

A home life, no matter how busy, did not satisfy all middle-class women. Some became volunteer nurses or social workers, receiving little or no pay. Others organized to fight prostitution, alcohol, and child labor. By the turn of the century a few challenged male domination of politics and the law. Suffragists, led in Britain by Emmeline Pankhurst and in the United States by Elizabeth Cady Stanton and Susan B. Anthony, demanded the right to vote. By 1914 U.S. women had won the right to vote in twelve states. British women did not vote until 1918.

Working-Class Women

Domestic Servants

In the new industrial cities, men and women no longer worked together at home or in the fields. The separation of work and home affected women even more than men. While working-class women formed a majority of the workers in the textile industries and in domestic service, they also needed to keep homes and raise children. As a result, they led lives of toil and pain. Parents expected girls as young as ten to contribute to the household. In Japan, as in Ireland and New England, tenant farmers, squeezed by rising taxes and rents, were forced to send their daughters to work in textile mills. Others became domestic servants, commonly working sixteen or more hours a day, six and a half days a week, for little more than room and board, usually in attics or basements. Without appliances, much of their work was physically hard: hauling coal and water up stairs, washing laundry by hand.

Young women often preferred factory work to domestic service. Men worked in construction, iron and steel, heavy machinery, or on railroads; women worked in textiles and the clothing trades, extensions of traditional women's household work (see Material Culture: Cotton Clothing). Appalled by the abuses of women and children in the early years of industrialization, most industrial countries passed protective legislation limiting the

Mary Evans Picture Library

Emmeline Pankhurst Under Arrest The leader of the British women's suffrage movement frequently called attention to her cause by breaking the law to protest discrimination against women. Here she is being arrested and carried off to jail by the police.

Cotton Clothing

Of all the things that bring us comfort, nothing compares to cotton. For clothes, sheets, and towels, it is the world's favorite textile. And no wonder: cotton is cool next to the skin, can be dyed in bright colors, absorbs moisture, and, unlike other fabrics such as wool, can be washed easily.

The use of cotton for clothing has a long history dating back to 3000 B.C.E., when it was grown in the Indus River Valley. Originally, the cotton plant was grown and the cloth woven only in India, Mexico, Peru, and a few other places in the tropics. The Maya wove fine textiles from cotton and traded them with other parts of Mesoamerica. Indian cottons were particularly fine and exported as luxury items to China and Rome. Cotton replaced hemp clothing in China and was used extensively by the Mongols for turbans, pants, and other items of clothing. The Arabs spread cotton growing and weaving to the Middle East and Spain. By the tenth century, it was a major crop in Iran and elsewhere in the region. Many of our names for particular kinds of cotton fabric come from cities in India, like *calico* (from Calicut) or *madras*, or in the Middle East, like *damask* (from Damascus) or *muslin* (from Mosul in Iraq).

Around 800 C.E., Arab merchants brought cotton cloth to Europe, where it became as precious as silk. With the invention of machines like the spinning jenny and the water frame in the eighteenth century (see Chapter 22), cotton became less precious and more available. Cotton yarn and cloth were the first items to be mass-produced in the Industrial Revolution, with important consequences for India, the American South, and other countries.

Mass production means mass consumption. In the nineteenth century, for the first time, the poor could afford to wear bright, colorful clothes and—even more important—to wash them. These clothes were made almost exclusively by women. Wealthy European families hired seamstresses who came to the house, took measurements, and returned a few days later with finished clothes. Other women sewed clothes for themselves and their families.

Sewing by hand was very time-consuming and increasingly costly compared to the declining price of cloth. By the mid-nineteenth century, prosperity and a faster pace of life in Europe and America provided an incentive for inventors to devise a machine that could sew. In 1850, Isaac Singer manufactured the first practical machine for commercial use. A few years later, he designed the "Singer Family Sewing Machine" with an iron stand and a foot-treadle for home use. By 1891 Singer alone had manufactured 10 million machines in the United States and Europe. Some were industrial machines sold to makers of ready-to-wear clothes in the new garment districts. Others were home models, some inexpensive enough for the working class. There were even portable models that seamstresses could take with them to their clients' homes.

Private Collection

The Sewing Machine The Japanese imported many innovations from the West after the Meiji Restoration of 1868. Among the most popular were Western-style clothing and sewing machines. Sewing was a gendered activity in Japan as in the West, with the woman sewing and the man looking on.

The combination of cotton cloth and sewing machines revolutionized clothing. A shirt that took fourteen and a half hours to sew by hand could be made in an hour and a quarter on a machine; an apron could be made in nine minutes instead of an hour and a half. Now the poor could afford to own several shirts, skirts, or pants, even underwear. Better-off homemakers subscribed to fashion magazines, bought patterns, and made blouses and dresses, even complicated items like crinolines and hoopskirts, which would once have been too tedious to sew by hand.

Today, the world uses more cotton than any other fiber. China is the largest producer (and consumer) of cotton, followed by the United States, India, and Pakistan. Almost all of the cotton clothing sold is produced on powerful computerized machines in the developing countries of Asia and Latin America.

Factory Workers

hours or forbidding the employment of women in the hardest and most dangerous occupations, such as mining and foundry work. Such legislation reinforced gender divisions in industry, keeping women in low-paid, subordinate positions. Female factory workers earned between one-third and two-thirds of men's wages.

Workers' Homes

Married women with children were expected to stay home, even if their husbands did not make enough to support the family. Yet they had to contribute to the family's income. Families who had room to spare, even a bed or a corner in the kitchen, took in boarders. Many women did piecework such as sewing dresses, making hats or gloves, or weaving baskets. The hardest and worst-paid work was washing other people's clothes. Many women worked at home ten to twelve hours a day and enlisted the help of their small children, perpetuating practices long outlawed in factories. Without electric lighting and indoor plumbing, even ordinary household duties like cooking and washing remained heavy burdens.

SECTION REVIEW

- As European population grew, millions migrated to other continents.
- Cities grew to enormous size, changing in character and posing difficult housing, sanitation, and environmental problems.
- Middle-class women inhabited a "separate sphere" from men and devoted their lives to their homes and families, but a few fought for equal rights.
- Working-class women, who had to keep a home while earning a living, led hard lives.

AP* Exam Tip Political dissent and alternative political views are covered on the exam.

SOCIALISM AND LABOR MOVEMENTS

socialism A political ideology that originated in Europe in the 1830s. Socialists advocated government protection of workers from exploitation by property owners and government ownership of industries. This ideology led to the founding of socialist or labor parties throughout Europe in the second half of the nineteenth century.

labor union An organization of workers in a particular industry or trade, created to defend the interests of members through strikes or negotiations with employers.

Industrialization combined with the revolutionary ideas of the late eighteenth century to produce two kinds of movements calling for further changes: socialism and labor unions. **Socialism** was an ideology developed by radical thinkers who questioned the sanctity of private property and argued in support of industrial workers against their employers. **Labor unions** were organizations formed by industrial workers to defend their interests in negotiations with employers. The socialist and labor movements were never identical. Most of the time they were allies; occasionally they were rivals.

Marx and Socialism

By far the best-known socialist was **Karl Marx** (1818–1883), a German journalist and writer who spent most of his life in England and collaborated with another socialist, Friedrich Engels (1820–1895), author of *The Condition of the Working Class in England in 1844* (1845). Together, they combined German philosophy, French revolutionary ideas, and knowledge of British industrial conditions.

The Communist Manifesto

Karl Marx German journalist and philosopher, founder of the Marxist branch of socialism. He is known for two books: *Manifesto of the Communist Party* (1848) and *Das Kapital* (Vols. I–III, 1867–1894).

Marx expressed his ideas succinctly in the *Manifesto of the Communist Party* (1848) (see Diversity and Dominance: Marx and Engels on Global Trade and the Bourgeoisie) and in great detail in *Das Kapital* (DUSS cop-ee-TAHL) (1867). He saw history as a long series of conflicts between social classes, the latest being between property owners (the bourgeoisie) and workers (the proletariat). He argued that the capitalist system allowed the bourgeoisie to extract the "surplus value" of workers' labor—that is, the difference between their wages and the value of the goods they manufactured. He saw business enterprises becoming larger and more monopolistic and workers growing more numerous and impoverished with every downturn in the business cycle. He concluded that this conflict would inevitably lead to a revolution and the overthrow of the bourgeoisie, after which the workers would establish a communist society without classes.

What Marx called "scientific socialism" provided an intellectual framework for the growing dissatisfaction with raw industrial capitalism. In the late nineteenth century business tycoons spent money lavishly on displays of wealth that contrasted sharply with the poverty of the workers. Even though industrial workers were not becoming poorer as Marx believed, the class struggle between workers and employers was brutally real. Marx offered a persuasive explanation of the causes of this contrast and the antagonisms it bred.

DIVERSITY + DOMINANCE

Marx and Engels on Global Trade and the Bourgeoisie

In 1848 Karl Marx (1818–1883) and Friedrich Engels (1820–1895) published the Manifesto of the Communist Party. *In it, they tried to explain why business owners—the "bourgeoisie"—had become the wealthiest and most powerful class of people in industrializing countries like Britain, and why industrial workers—the "proletariat"—lived in poverty. In their view, the dominance of the bourgeoisie was destroying the diversity of human cultures, reducing all classes in Europe and all cultures to the status of proletarians selling their labor.*

In the Manifesto, *Marx and Engels called for a revolution in which the workers would overthrow the bourgeoisie and establish a new society without private property or government. Their* Manifesto *was soon translated into many languages and became the best-known expression of radical communist ideology.*

Marx and Engels's ideas are especially interesting from the perspective of global history because of the way in which they connect the rise of the bourgeoisie with world trade and industrial technology. The following paragraphs explain these connections.

The history of all hitherto existing society is the history of class struggles. . . .

In the earlier epochs of history, we find almost everywhere a complicated arrangement of society into various orders, a manifold gradation of social rank. In ancient Rome we have patricians, knights, plebeians, slaves; in the middle ages, feudal lords, vassals, guild-masters, journeymen, apprentices, serfs; in almost all of these classes, again, subordinate gradations.

The modern bourgeois society that has sprouted from the ruins of feudal society, has not done away with class antagonisms. It has but established new classes, new conditions of oppression, new forms of struggle in place of the old ones.

Our epoch, the epoch of the bourgeoisie, possesses, however, this distinctive feature; it has simplified the class antagonisms. Society as a whole is more and more splitting up into two great hostile camps, into two great classes directly facing each other: Bourgeoisie and Proletariat. . . .

The discovery of America, the rounding of the Cape, opened up fresh ground for the rising bourgeoisie. The East-Indian and Chinese markets, the colonization of America, trade with the colonies, the increase in the means of exchange and in commodities generally, gave to commerce, to navigation, to industry, an impulse never before known, and thereby, to the revolutionary element in the tottering feudal society, a rapid development. . . .

Modern industry has established the world-market, for which the discovery of America paved the way. This market has given an immense importance to commerce, to navigation, to communication by land. This development has, in its turn, reacted on the extension of industry; and in proportion as industry, commerce, navigation, railways extended, in the same proportion the bourgeoisie developed, increased its capital, and pushed into the background every class handed down from the Middle Ages. . . .

The bourgeoisie, historically, has played a most revolutionary part. . . .

It has been the first to show what man's activity can bring about. It has accomplished wonders far surpassing Egyptian pyramids, Roman aqueducts, and Gothic cathedrals; it has conducted expeditions that put in the shade all former Exoduses of nations and crusades. . . .

The need of a constantly expanding market for its products chases the bourgeoisie over the whole surface of the globe. It must nestle everywhere, settle everywhere, establish connexions everywhere.

e PRIMARY SOURCE: Working Men of All Countries, Unite! Read these excerpts from the *Manifesto of the Communist Party* and find out why "the proletarians have nothing to lose but their chains."

Labor Unions and Movements

Since the beginning of the nineteenth century, workers had united to create "friendly societies" for mutual assistance in times of illness, unemployment, or disability. Laws that forbade workers to strike were abolished in Britain in the 1850s and in the rest of Europe soon thereafter. Labor unions sought not only better wages but also improved working conditions and insurance against illness, accidents, disability, and old age. They grew slowly because they required a permanent staff and a great deal of money to sustain their members during strikes. Still, by the end of the century British labor unions counted 2 million members, and German and American unions had 1 million members each.

Universal Male Suffrage

Just as labor unions strove to share in the benefits of a capitalist economy, so did electoral politics persuade workers to become part of the existing political system. The nineteenth century saw a gradual extension of the right to vote throughout Europe and North America. Universal male suffrage became law in the United States in 1870, in France and Germany in 1871, in Britain in 1885, and in the rest of Europe soon thereafter. With so many newly enfranchised workers, socialist politicians hoped to capture many seats in their nations' parliaments. Rather than seize power through revolution, the socialists expected to obtain concessions from government and eventually even to form a government.

The bourgeoisie has through its exploitation of the world-market given a cosmopolitan character to production and consumption in every country. To the great chagrin of Reactionists, it has drawn from under the feet of industry the national ground on which it stood. All old-fashioned national industries have been destroyed or are daily being destroyed. They are dislodged by new industries, whose introduction becomes a life or death question for all civilised nations, by industries that no longer work up indigenous raw material, but raw material drawn from the remotest zones; industries whose products are consumed, not only at home, but in every quarter of the globe. In place of the old wants, satisfied by the productions of the country, we find new wants, requiring for their satisfaction the products of distant lands and climes. In place of the old local and national seclusion and self-sufficiency, we have intercourse in every direction, universal inter-dependence of nations. And as in material, so also in intellectual production. The intellectual creations of individual nations become common property. National one-sidedness and narrow-mindedness become more and more impossible, and from the numerous national and local literatures there arises a world-literature.

The bourgeoisie, by the rapid improvement of all instruments of production, by the immensely facilitated means of communication, draws all, even the most barbarian, nations into civilisation. The cheap prices of its commodities are the heavy artillery with which it batters down all Chinese walls, with which it forces the barbarians' intensely obstinate hatred of foreigners to capitulate. It compels all nations, on pain of extinction, to adopt the bourgeois mode of production; it compels them to introduce what it calls civilisation into their midst, i.e., to become bourgeois themselves. In a word, it creates a world after its own image.

The bourgeoisie has subjected the country to the rule of the towns. It has created enormous cities, has greatly increased the urban population as compared with the rural, and has thus rescued a considerable part of the population from the idiocy of rural life. Just as it has made the country dependent on the towns, so it has made barbarian and semi-barbarian countries dependent on the civilised ones, nations of peasants on nations of bourgeois, the East on the West. . . .

The bourgeoisie, during its rule of scarce one hundred years, has created more massive and more colossal productive forces than have all preceding generations together. Subjection of Nature's forces to man, machinery, application of chemistry to industry and agriculture, steam-navigation, railways, electric telegraphs, clearing of whole continents for cultivation, canalization of rivers, whole populations conjured out of the ground—what earlier century had even a presentiment that such productive forces slumbered in the lap of social labour?

QUESTIONS FOR ANALYSIS

1. **How did the growth of world trade since the European discovery of America affect relations between social classes in Europe?**
2. **Compare Marx and Engels's views on industrial production with those of Adam Smith that you read in Chapter 22. Do they contradict each other? Or does Smith's description of pin-making explain the rise of what Marx and Engels call "the giant, Modern Industry"?**
3. **What effect did the growth of trade and industry have on products, intellectual creations, and consumer tastes around the world?**

Source: Karl Marx and Frederick Engels, *Manifesto of the Communist Party,* Authorized English Translation: Edited and Annotated by Frederick Engels (Chicago: Charles H. Kerr & Company, 1906), pp. 12–20.

Women Revolutionaries

anarchists Revolutionaries who wanted to abolish all private property and governments, usually by violence, and replace them with free associations of groups.

Working-class women, burdened with both job and family responsibilities, found little time for politics and were not welcome in the male-dominated trade unions or radical political parties. A few radicals such as the German socialist Rosa Luxemburg and the American **anarchist** Emma Goldman in the United States became famous but did not have a large following. It was never easy to reconcile the demands of workers and those of women. In 1889 the German socialist Clara Zetkin wrote: "Just as the male worker is subjected by the capitalist, so is the woman by the man, and she will always remain in subjugation until she is economically independent. Work is the indispensable condition for economic independence." Six years later, she recognized that the liberation of women would have to await a change in the position of the working class as a whole: "The proletarian woman cannot attain her highest ideal through a movement for the equality of the female sex, she attains salvation only through the fight for the emancipation of labor."[1]

SECTION REVIEW

- Karl Marx expected a workers' revolution, but later socialists hoped to gain influence through elections.
- Labor movements and unions worked to improve workers' pay and working conditions.

NATIONALISM AND THE RISE OF ITALY, GERMANY, AND JAPAN

nationalism A political ideology that stresses people's membership in a nation—a community defined by a common culture and history as well as by territory. In the late eighteenth and early nineteenth centuries, nationalism was a force for unity in western Europe. In the late nineteenth century it hastened the disintegration of the Austro-Hungarian and Ottoman Empires. In the twentieth century it provided the ideological foundation for scores of independent countries emerging from colonialism.

The most influential idea of the nineteenth century was **nationalism**. Whereas people had previously been considered the subjects of a sovereign, the French revolutionaries defined people as the citizens of a *nation*—a concept identified with a territory, the state that ruled it, and the culture of its people.

Language and National Identity in Europe Before 1871

Language was usually the crucial element in creating a feeling of national unity. It was important both as a way to unite the people of a nation and as the means of persuasion by which political leaders could inspire their followers. Language was the tool of the new generation of political activists, most of them lawyers, teachers, students, and journalists. Yet language and citizenship seldom coincided.

The fit between France and the French language was closer than in most large countries, though some French-speakers lived outside of France and some French people spoke other languages. Italian- and German-speaking people, however, were divided among many small states. Living in the Austrian Empire were peoples who spoke German, Czech, Slovak, Hungarian, Polish, and other languages. Even where people spoke a common language, they could be divided by religion or institutions. The Irish, though English-speaking, were mostly Catholic, whereas the English were primarily Protestant.

The idea of redrawing the boundaries of states to accommodate linguistic, religious, or cultural differences was revolutionary. In Italy and Germany it led to the forging of large new states out of many small ones in 1871. In central and eastern Europe, nationalism threatened to break up large states into smaller ones.

Liberalism

liberalism A political ideology that emphasizes the civil rights of citizens, representative government, and the protection of private property. This ideology, derived from the Enlightenment, was especially popular among the property-owning middle classes of Europe and North America.

Until the 1860s nationalism was associated with **liberalism**, the revolutionary middle-class ideology that emerged from the French Revolution, asserted the sovereignty of the people, and demanded constitutional government, a national parliament, and freedom of expression. The most famous nationalist of the early nineteenth century was the Italian liberal Giuseppe Mazzini (jew-SEP-pay mots-EE-nee) (1805–1872), the leader of the failed revolution of 1848 in Italy. Mazzini sought to unify the Italian peninsula into one nation and associated with revolutionaries elsewhere to bring nationhood and liberty to all peoples oppressed by tyrants and foreigners. The governments of Russia, Prussia, and Austria censored the new ideas but could not quash them.

The revolutions of 1848 convinced conservatives that governments could not forever keep their citizens out of politics and that mass politics, if properly managed, could strengthen rather than weaken the state. A new generation of conservative political leaders learned how to preserve the status quo through public education, universal military service, and colonial conquests, all of which built a sense of national unity.

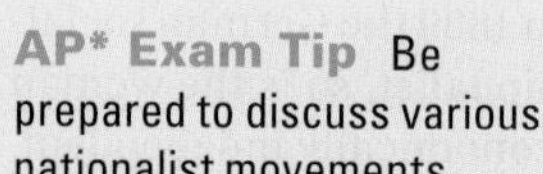

AP* Exam Tip Be prepared to discuss various nationalist movements.

The Unification of Italy, 1860–1870

By midcentury, popular sentiment was building throughout Italy for unification. Opposing it were Pope Pius IX, who abhorred everything modern, and Austria, which controlled two Italian provinces, Lombardy and Venetia (see Map 26.1). The prime minister of Piedmont-Sardinia, Count Camillo Benso di Cavour, saw the rivalry between France and Austria as an opportunity to unify Italy. He secretly formed an alliance with France, then instigated a war with Austria in 1858. The war was followed by uprisings throughout northern and central Italy in favor of joining Piedmont-Sardinia, a moderate constitutional monarchy under King Victor Emmanuel.

Giuseppe Garibaldi Italian nationalist and revolutionary who conquered Sicily and Naples and added them to a unified Italy in 1860.

Cavour and Garibaldi

If the conservative, top-down approach to unification prevailed in the north, a more radical approach was still possible in the south. In 1860 the fiery revolutionary **Giuseppe Garibaldi** (jew-SEP-pay gary-BAHL-dee) and a small band of followers landed in Sicily and then in southern Italy, overthrew the Kingdom of the Two Sicilies, and prepared to found a democratic republic. The royalist Cavour, however, took advantage of the unsettled situation to sideline Garibaldi

MAP 26.1 Unification of Italy, 1859–1870 The unification of Italy was achieved by the expansion of the kingdom of Piedmont-Sardinia, with the help of France.

Interactive Map

and expand Piedmont-Sardinia into a new Kingdom of Italy. Unification was completed with the addition of Venetia in 1866 and the Papal States in 1870.

The process of unification illustrates the shift of nationalism from a radical democratic idea to a conservative method of building popular support for a strong centralized government, even an aristocratic and monarchical one.

The Unification of Germany, 1866–1871

The unification of most German-speaking people into a single state in 1871 had momentous consequences for the world. Until the 1860s the region of central Europe where people spoke German consisted of Prussia, the western half of the Austrian Empire, and numerous smaller states (see Map 26.2). Some German nationalists wanted to unite all Germans under the Austrian throne. Others wanted to exclude Austria with its many non-Germanic peoples and unite all other German-speaking areas under Prussia. The divisions were also religious: Austria and southwestern Germany were Catholic; Prussia and the northeast were Lutheran. The Prussian state had two advantages: (1) the newly developed industries of the Rhineland, and (2) the first European army to make use of railroads, telegraphs, breechloading rifles, steel artillery, and other products of modern industry.

Bismarck Attacks Austria and France

Otto von Bismarck Chancellor (prime minister) of Prussia from 1862 until 1871, when he became chancellor of Germany. A conservative nationalist, he led Prussia to victory against Austria (1866) and France (1870) and was responsible for the creation of the German Empire in 1871.

During the reign of King Wilhelm I (r. 1861–1888), Prussia was ruled by a brilliant and authoritarian aristocrat, Chancellor **Otto von Bismarck** (UTT-oh von BIS-mark) (1815–1898). Bismarck was determined to use Prussian industry and German nationalism to make his state the dominant power in Germany. In 1866 Prussia attacked and defeated Austria. To everyone's surprise, Prussia took no Austrian territory. Instead, Prussia and some smaller states formed the North German Confederation, the nucleus of a future Germany. Then in 1870 Bismarck attacked France. Prussian armies, joined by troops from other German states, used their superior firepower and tactics to achieve a quick victory. "Blood and iron" were the foundation of the new German Empire.

The spoils of victory included a large indemnity and two provinces of France bordering on Germany: Alsace and Lorraine. The French paid the indemnity easily enough but resented the loss of their provinces. To the Germans, this region was German because a majority of its inhabitants spoke German. To the French, it was French because most of its inhabitants considered themselves French. These two conflicting definitions of nationalism kept enmity between France and Germany smoldering for decades. In this case, nationalism turned out to be a divisive rather than a unifying force.

The West Challenges Japan

The Shogunate

In Japan the emperor was revered but had no power. Instead, Japan was governed by the Tokugawa Shogunate—a secular government under a military leader, or *shogun,* that had come to power in 1600 (see Chapter 20). Local lords, called *daimyos,* were permitted to control their lands and populations with very little interference from the shogunate.

When threatened from outside, this system showed many weaknesses. For one thing, it did not permit the coordination of resources necessary to resist a major invasion. Attempting to minimize exposure to foreign powers, in the early 1600s the shoguns prohibited foreigners from entering Japan and Japanese from going abroad. The penalty for breaking these laws was death, but many Japanese ignored them. The most flagrant violators were powerful lords in southern Japan who ran large and very successful pirate or black-market operations. In their entrepreneurial activities they benefited from the decentralization of the shogunal political system. But when a genuine foreign threat was suggested—as when, in 1792, Russian and British ships were spotted off the Japanese coast—the local lords realized that Japan was too weak and decentralized to resist a foreign invasion. As a result, a few of the regional lords began to develop their own reformed armies, arsenals, and shipyards.

By the 1800s Satsuma (SAT-soo-mah) and Choshu (CHOE-shoo), two large domains in southern Japan, had become wealthy and ambitious, enjoying high rates of revenue and population growth. Their remoteness from the capital Edo (now Tokyo) and their economic vigor also fostered a strong sense of local self-reliance.

Commodore Perry's Fleet

In 1853 the American commodore Matthew C. Perry arrived off the coast of Japan and demanded that Japan open its ports to trade and allow American ships to refuel and take on supplies during their voyages between China and California. He promised to return a year later to receive the Japanese answer. Perry's demands sparked a crisis in the shogunate. After consultation with the provincial daimyos, the shogun's advisers advocated capitulation to Perry, pointing to China's humiliating defeats in the Opium and Arrow Wars. In 1854, when Perry returned, representatives of the shogun indicated their willingness to sign the Treaty of Kanagawa (KAH-nah-GAH-wah), modeled on the unequal treaties between China and the Western powers. Angry and disappointed, some provincial governors began to encourage an underground movement calling for the destruction of the Tokugawa regime and the banning of foreigners from Japan.

Tensions between the shogunate and some provincial leaders, particularly in Choshu and Satsuma, increased in the early 1860s. Young, ambitious, educated men who faced mediocre prospects under the rigid Tokugawa class system emerged as provincial leaders. When British and French ships shelled the southwestern coasts in 1864 to protest the treatment of foreigners, the action enraged the provincial samurai who rejected the Treaty of Kanagawa and resented the shogunate's inability to protect the country. In 1867 the Choshu leaders Yamagata Aritomo and Ito Hirobumi finally realized that they should stop warring with their rival province, Satsuma, and join forces to lead a rebellion against the shogunate.

MAP 26.2 Unification of Germany, 1866–1871 Germany was united after a series of short, successful wars by the kingdom of Prussia against Austria in 1866 and against France in 1871.

Interactive Map

The Meiji Restoration and the Modernization of Japan, 1868–1894

Meiji Restoration The political program that followed the destruction of the Tokugawa Shogunate in 1868, in which a collection of young leaders set Japan on the path of centralization, industrialization, and imperialism.

The civil war was intense but brief. In 1868 provincial rebels overthrew the Tokugawa Shogunate and declared young emperor Mutsuhito (moo-tsoo-HE-toe) (r. 1868–1912) "restored." The new leaders called their regime the "**Meiji** (MAY-gee) **Restoration**" after Mutsuhito's reign name (*Meiji* means "enlightened rule"). The "Meiji oligarchs," as the new rulers were known, were extraordinarily talented and far-sighted. Determined to protect their country from Western imperialism, they encouraged its transformation into "a rich country with a strong army" with world-class industries. Though imposed from above, the Meiji Restoration marked as profound a change as the French Revolution (see Map 26.3).

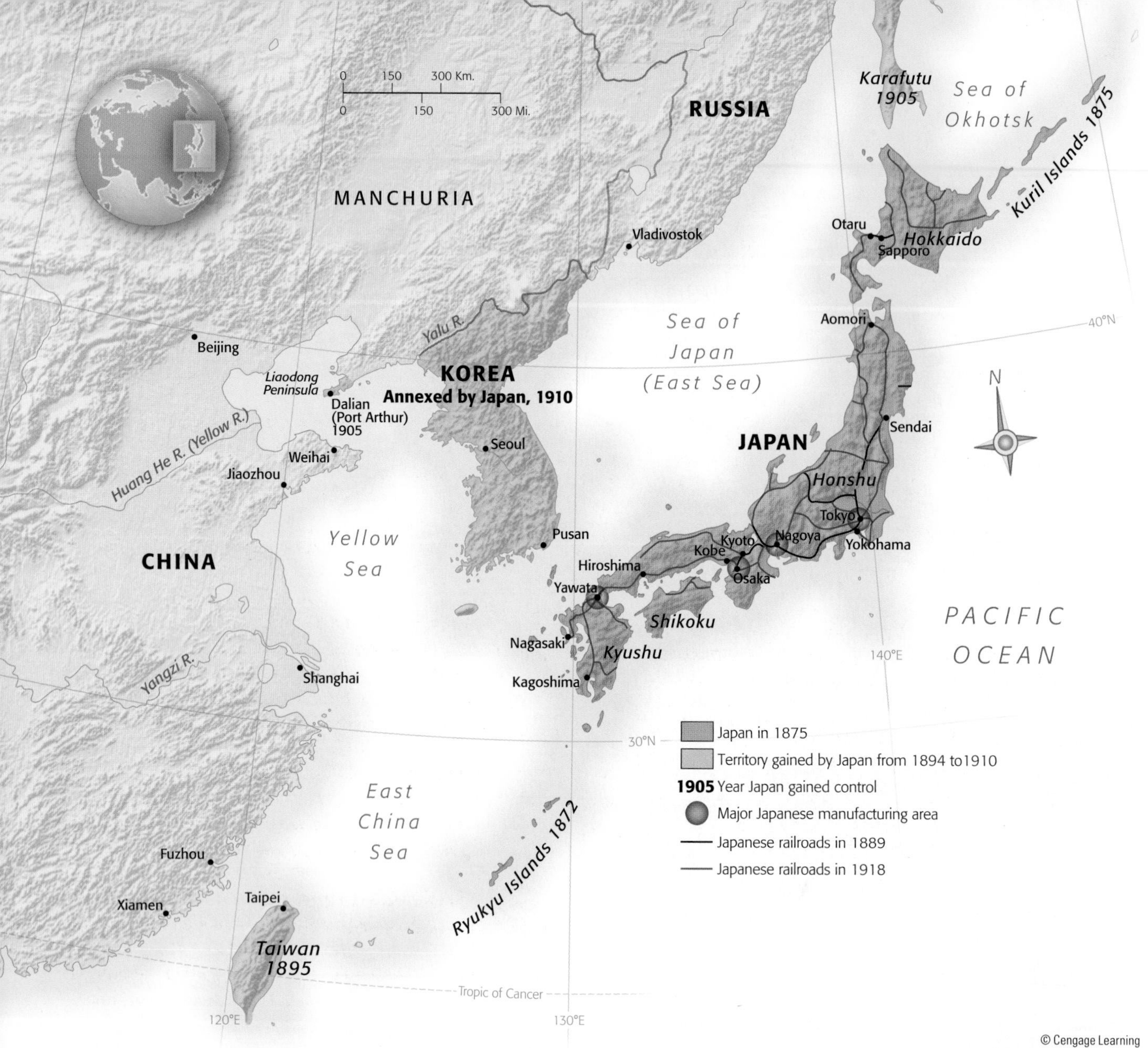

MAP 26.3 **Expansion and Modernization of Japan, 1868–1918** As Japan acquired modern industry, it followed the example of the European powers in seeking overseas colonies. Its colonial empire grew at the expense of its neighbors: Taiwan was taken from China in 1895; Karafutu (Sakhalin) from Russia in 1905; and all of Korea became a colony in 1910.

e Interactive Map

The oligarchs were under no illusion that they could fend off the Westerners without changing their institutions and their society. In the Charter Oath issued in 1868, the young emperor included a prophetic phrase: "Knowledge shall be sought throughout the world and thus shall be strengthened the foundation of the imperial polity." It was to be the motto of a new Japan, which embraced all foreign ideas, institutions, and techniques that could strengthen the nation. The literacy rate in Japan was the highest in Asia at the time, and the oligarchs shrewdly exploited it in their introduction of new educational systems, a conscript army, and new communications. The government was able to establish heavy industry, thanks to decades of industrial development and financing in the provinces in the earlier 1800s. With a conscript army and a revamped educational system, the oligarchs attempted to create a new citizenry that was literate and competent but also loyal and obedient.

The Meiji leaders copied the government structure of imperial Germany and modeled the new Japanese navy on the British and the army on the Prussian. They also introduced Western-style postal and telegraph services, railroads and harbors, banking, clocks, and calendars. To

Japan's New Army After the Meiji Restoration in 1868, the leaders of the new government set out to make Japan "a rich country with a strong army." They modeled the new army on the European armies of the time, with Western-style uniforms, rifles, cannon, and musical instruments.

Laurie Platt Winfrey/The Granger Collection, New York

learn the secrets of Western strength, they sent hundreds of students to Britain, Germany, and the United States. Western-style clothing and hairstyles and garden parties and formal dances became popular.

The government was especially interested in Western technology. It opened vocational, technical, and agricultural schools, founded four imperial universities, and brought in foreign experts to advise on medicine, science, and engineering. To encourage industrialization, the government set up state-owned enterprises to manufacture cloth and inexpensive consumer goods for sale abroad. The first Japanese industries exploited their workers ruthlessly, just as the first industries in Europe and America had done. In 1881 the government sold these enterprises to private investors, mainly large *zaibatsu* (zye-BOT-soo), or conglomerates, and also encouraged individual technological innovation. Thus the carpenter Toyoda Sakichi founded the Toyoda Loom Works (now Toyota Motor Company) in 1906; ten years later he patented the world's most advanced automatic loom.

PRIMARY SOURCE: Letter to Mitsubishi Employees Iwasaki Yaturo announces government aid in the effort to defeat foreign competition for control of Japanese coastal trade.

AP* Exam Tip Be familiar with Social Darwinism for the multiple choice section of the exam, but don't worry about characteristics of individual philosophers such as Herbert Spencer.

Charles Darwin

Nationalism and Social Darwinism

The Franco-Prussian War of 1870–1871 changed the political climate of Europe, making France more liberal. The kingdom of Italy completed the unification of the peninsula. Germany, Austria-Hungary (as the Austrian Empire had renamed itself in 1867), and Russia remained conservative and used nationalism to maintain the status quo.

Nationalism and parliamentary elections made politicians of all parties appeal to public opinion. They were greatly aided by the press, especially cheap daily newspapers that sought to increase circulation by publishing sensational articles about overseas conquests and foreign threats. As governments increasingly came to recognize the advantages of an educated population in the competition between states, they opened public schools in every town and admitted women into public-service jobs for the first time. Politicians and journalists appealed to the emotions of the poor, diverting their anger from their employers to foreigners and their votes from socialist to nationalist parties.

In many countries the dominant group used nationalism to impose its language, religion, or customs on minority populations. The Russian Empire attempted to "Russify" its diverse ethnic populations. The Spanish government made Spanish compulsory in the schools, newspapers, and courts of its Basque- and Catalan-speaking provinces. Immigrants to the United States were expected to learn English.

Western culture in the late nineteenth century exalted the powerful over the weak, men over women, rich over poor, Europeans over other races, and humans over nature. Some people looked to science for support of political dominance. One of the most influential scientists of the century, and the one whose ideas were most widely cited and misinterpreted, was the English biologist Charles Darwin (1809–1882).

In his 1859 book *On the Origin of the Species,* Darwin argued that the earth was much older than previously believed. He proposed that over the course of hundreds of thousands of years living beings had either evolved in the struggle for survival or become extinct.

The philosopher Herbert Spencer (1820–1903) and others took up Darwin's ideas of "natural selection" and "survival of the fittest" and applied them to human society. Social Darwinists developed elaborate pseudo-scientific theories of racial differences, claiming that they were the result not of history but of biology. They saw social and racial differences as resulting from natural processes and opposed state intervention to alleviate inequities. Although not based on any research, these ideas gave a scientific-sounding justification for the power of the privileged.

SECTION REVIEW

- Nationalism, the most powerful new ideology of the nineteenth century, defined nations primarily on the basis of language.
- Garibaldi helped unify Italy between 1860 and 1870, and Bismarck unified Germany from 1866 to 1871.
- In response to Western intrusion, provincial Japanese lords launched the Meiji Restoration and quickly transformed Japan into a modern industrial nation.
- During this era, Charles Darwin's theory of evolution was often misinterpreted to justify the power of the privileged few.

THE GREAT POWERS OF EUROPE, 1871–1900

After the middle of the century, politicians and journalists discovered that minor events involving foreigners could be used to stir up popular indignation against neighboring countries. Military officers, impressed by the awesome power of the weapons that industry provided, began to think that the weapons were invincible. Rivalries over colonial territories, ideological differences, even minor border incidents or trade disagreements contributed to a growing international tension.

PRIMARY SOURCE: Extracts from History of Germany in the Nineteenth Century and Historical and Political Writings A nineteenth-century German historian proclaims a racist and militarist ideology.

Germany at the Center of Europe

International relations revolved around Germany because it was located in the center of Europe and had the most powerful army on the European continent. After creating a unified Germany in 1871, Bismarck declared that his country had no further territorial ambitions, and he put his effort into maintaining the peace in Europe. To isolate France, he forged a loose coalition with Austria-Hungary and Russia, the other two conservative powers. Despite their competing ambitions in the Balkans, he was able to keep his coalition together for twenty years.

German Social Policies

Bismarck proved equally adept at strengthening German unity at home. To weaken the influence of middle-class liberals, he extended the vote to all adult men, thereby allowing Socialists to win seats in the *Reichstag* or parliament. By imposing high tariffs on manufactured goods and wheat, he gained the support of both the wealthy industrialists of the Rhineland and the great landowners of eastern Germany, traditional rivals for power. He also introduced social legislation—medical, unemployment, and disability insurance and old-age pensions—long before other industrial countries. His government supported public and technical education. Under his leadership, the German people developed a strong sense of national unity and pride in their industrial and military power.

Wilhelm II

In 1888 Wilhelm I was succeeded by his grandson Wilhelm II (r. 1888–1918), an insecure and arrogant man who tried to gain respect by making belligerent speeches. Within two years he had dismissed Chancellor Bismarck and surrounded himself with yes men. He talked about his "global policy" and demanded a colonial empire. Ruler of the nation with the mightiest army and the largest industrial economy in Europe, he felt that Germany deserved "a place in the sun."

The Liberal Powers: France and Great Britain

France

France, once the dominant nation in Europe, had difficulty reconciling itself to being in second place. Though a prosperous country with flourishing agriculture and a large colonial empire, the French republic had some serious weaknesses. For example, its population was scarcely growing; in 1911 France had only 39 million people compared to Germany's 64 million. In an age when the power of nations was roughly proportional to the size of their armies, France could field an army only two-thirds the size of Germany's.

The French people were also deeply divided over the very nature of the state: some were monarchists and Catholic, but a growing number held republican and anticlerical views. Yet if French political life seemed fragile and frequently in crisis, a long tradition of popular participation in politics and a strong sense of nationhood, reinforced by a fine system of public education, gave the French people a deeper cohesion than appeared on the surface.

Britain and the Irish

Great Britain had a long experience with parliamentary elections and competing parties. The British government alternated smoothly between the Liberal and Conservative Parties, and the income gap between rich and poor gradually narrowed. Nevertheless, Britain had problems that grew more apparent as time went on. One was Irish resentment of English rule. Nationalism had strengthened the allegiance of the English, Scots, and Welsh to the British state. But the Irish, excluded because they were Catholic and predominantly poor, saw the British as a foreign occupying force.

Another problem was the British economy. Great Britain had fallen behind the United States and Germany in such important industries as steel, chemicals, electricity, and textiles. Even in shipbuilding and shipping, Britain's traditional specialty, Germany was catching up.

Britain's Empire

Britain was preoccupied with its enormous and fast-growing empire. A source of wealth for investors and the envy of other imperialist nations, the empire was a constant drain on Britain's finances, for it required Britain to maintain costly fleets of warships throughout the world.

For most of the nineteenth century Britain pursued a policy of "splendid isolation." Britain's preoccupation with India led British statesmen to exaggerate the Russian threat to the Ottoman Empire and to the Central Asian approaches to India. Periodic "Russian scares" and Britain's age-old rivalry with France for overseas colonies diverted the attention of British politicians from the rise of Germany.

The Conservative Powers: Russia and Austria-Hungary

The forces of nationalism weakened rather than strengthened Russia and Austria-Hungary. Their populations were far more divided, socially and ethnically, than were the German, French, or British peoples.

Balkan Rivalries

Nationalism was most divisive in south-central Europe, where many different language groups lived in close proximity. In 1867 the Austrian Empire renamed itself the Austro-Hungarian Empire to appease its Hungarian critics. Its attempts to promote the cultures of its Slavic-speaking minorities failed to gain their political allegiance. However, it still thought of itself as a great power and attempted to dominate the Balkans. This strategy irritated Russia, which thought of itself as the protector of Slavic peoples everywhere.

Minorities in Russia

Ethnic diversity also contributed to the instability of imperial Russia. The Polish people rebelled in 1830 and 1863–1864. The tsarist empire also included Finland, Estonia, Latvia, Lithuania, and Ukraine; the Caucasus; and the Muslim population of Central Asia conquered between 1865 and 1881. Furthermore, Russia had the largest Jewish population in Europe, and the harshness of its anti-Semitic laws and periodic *pogroms* (massacres) prompted many Jews to flee to America. The state's attempts to impose the Russian language on its subjects were divisive instead of unifying forces.

Emancipation of the Serfs

In 1861 the moderate conservative Tsar Alexander II (r. 1855–1881) emancipated the peasants from serfdom. He did so partly out of a genuine desire to strengthen the bonds between the monarchy and the Russian people, and partly to promote industrialization by enlarging the labor pool. That half-hearted measure, however, only turned serfs into farm workers with few skills and little capital. Though "emancipated," the great majority of Russians had little education, few legal rights, and no say in the government. After Alexander's assassination in 1881, his successors Alexander III (r. 1881–1894) and Nicholas II (r. 1894–1917) reluctantly permitted half-hearted attempts at social change. The Russian commercial middle class was small and had little influence. Industrialization consisted largely of state-sponsored projects, such as railroads, iron foundries, and armament factories, and led to social unrest among urban workers. Wealthy landowning aristocrats dominated the Russian court and administration and blocked most reforms.

The Doss House Late-nineteenth-century cities showed more physical than social improvements. This painting by Makovsky of a street in St. Petersburg contrasts the broad avenue and impressive new buildings with the poverty of the crowd.

The Russo-Japanese War and Revolution

The weaknesses in Russia's society and government became glaringly obvious during a war with Japan in 1904 and 1905. The fighting took place in Manchuria, a province in northern China far from European Russia. The Russian army, which received all its supplies by means of the inefficient Trans-Siberian Railway, was defeated by the better-trained and better-equipped Japanese. After a long journey around Eurasia and Africa, the Russian navy was sunk by the Japanese fleet at Tsushima Strait in 1905.

The shock of defeat caused a revolution in 1905 that forced Tsar Nicholas II to grant a constitution and an elected Duma (parliament). But as soon as he was able to rebuild the army and the police, he reverted to the traditional despotism of his forefathers. Small groups of radical intellectuals, angered by the contrast between the wealth of the elite and the poverty of the common people, began plotting the violent overthrow of the tsarist autocracy.

SECTION REVIEW

- A united Germany, the most powerful state in Europe, became a threat to peace under Wilhelm II.
- France and Great Britain, though liberal democracies, faced difficulties at home and overseas.
- Russia and Austria-Hungary, two conservative empires, failed to adapt their politics to the modernization of their societies.

CHINA, JAPAN, AND THE WESTERN POWERS

After 1850 China and Japan—the two largest countries in East Asia—felt the influence of the Western powers as never before, but their responses were completely opposite. China resisted Western influence and became weaker, while Japan transformed itself into a major industrial and military power. One reason for this difference was the Western powers' heavy involvement in China and the distance to Japan, the nation most remote from Europe by ship. More important was the difference between the Chinese and Japanese elites' attitudes toward foreign cultures.

China in Turmoil

China had been devastated by the Taiping (tie-PING) Rebellion that raged from 1850 to 1864 (see Chapter 24). The French and British took advantage of China's weakness to demand treaty

Douzième année.— N° 597. Huit pages : CINQ centimes Dimanche 15 Juillet 1900

Le Petit Parisien

TOUS LES JOURS
Le Petit Parisien
5 CENTIMES.

SUPPLÉMENT LITTÉRAIRE ILLUSTRÉ
DIRECTION: 18, rue d'Enghien, PARIS

TOUS LES JEUDIS
SUPPLÉMENT LITTÉRAIRE
5 CENTIMES.

Les Événements de Chine
MORT AUX ÉTRANGERS!

The Boxer Uprising In 1900 a Chinese secret society, the Righteous Fists, rose up with the encouragement of the Empress Dowager Cixi and attacked foreigners and their establishments. In the Western press they were known as "Boxers." These men are putting up a poster that reads "Death to Foreigners!"

ports where they could trade at will. The British took over China's customs and allowed the free import of opium until 1917. A Chinese "self-strengthening movement" tried in vain to bring about significant reforms by reducing government expenditures and eliminating corruption. The **Empress Dowager Cixi** (TSUH-shee) (r. 1862–1908) opposed railways and other foreign technologies that could carry foreign influences to the interior. Government officials, who did not dare resist the Westerners outright, secretly encouraged crowds to attack and destroy the intrusive devices. They were able to slow the foreign intrusion, but in doing so, they denied themselves the best means of defense against foreign pressure.

Empress Dowager Cixi Empress of China and mother of Emperor Guangxi. She put her son under house arrest, supported antiforeign movements, and resisted reforms of the Chinese government and armed forces.

Japan Confronts China

The late nineteenth century marked the high point of European power and arrogance, as the nations of Europe, in a frenzy known as the "New Imperialism," rushed to gobble up the last remaining unclaimed pieces of the world. Yet at that very moment two nations outside Europe were becoming great powers. One of them, the United States, was inhabited mainly by people of European origin. Its rise to great-power status had been predicted early in the nineteenth century by astute observers like the French statesman Alexis de Tocqueville. The other one, Japan, seemed so distant and exotic in 1850 that no European guessed that it would join the ranks of the great powers.

Japanese Imperialism

The motive for the transformation of Japan was to protect the nation from the Western powers, but the methods that strengthened Japan against the imperial ambitions of others could also be used to carry out its own conquests. Japan's path to imperialism was laid out by **Yamagata Aritomo**, a leader of the Meiji oligarchs. He believed that to be independent Japan had to define a "sphere of influence" that included Korea, Manchuria, and part of China (see Map 26.3). If other countries controlled this sphere, Japan would be at risk. To protect this sphere of influence, Yamagata insisted, Japan must sustain a vigorous program of military industrialization, culminating in the building of battleships.

Yamagata Aritomo One of the leaders of the Meiji Restoration.

As Japan grew stronger, China was growing weaker. In 1894 the two nations went to war over Korea. The Sino-Japanese War lasted less than six months, and it forced China to evacuate Korea, cede Taiwan and the Liaodong (li-AH-oh-dong) Peninsula, and pay a heavy indemnity. France, Germany, Britain, Russia, and the United States, upset at seeing a newcomer join the ranks of the imperialists, made Japan give up Liaodong in the name of the "territorial integrity" of China. In exchange for their "protection," the Western powers then made China grant them territorial and trade concessions, including ninety treaty ports.

The Boxer Rebellion

In 1900 Chinese officials around the Empress Dowager Cixi encouraged a series of antiforeign riots known as the Boxer Uprising. Military forces from the European powers, Japan, and the United States put down the riots and occupied Beijing. Emboldened by China's obvious weakness, Japan and Russia competed for possession of the mineral-rich Chinese province of Manchuria.

SECTION REVIEW

- China was weakened by the Taiping Rebellion, a reactionary government under Empress Dowager Cixi, and the demands of the West.
- Japan, in contrast, built up its military and industrial strength and became another imperial power, taking advantage of China's weakness to seize Korea, Taiwan, and southern Manchuria.

Japan's participation in the suppression of the Boxer Uprising demonstrated its military power in East Asia. Then in 1905 Japan surprised the world by defeating Russia in the Russo-Japanese War. By the Treaty of Portsmouth that ended the war, Japan established a protectorate over Korea. In spite of Western attempts to restrict it to the role of junior partner, Japan continued to increase its influence. It gained control of southern Manchuria, with its industries and railroads, and in 1910 it finally annexed Korea, joining the ranks of the world's colonial powers.

CONCLUSION

After World War I broke out in 1914, many people, especially in Europe, looked back on the period from 1850 to 1914 as a golden age. For some, and in certain ways, it was. Industrialization was a powerful torrent changing Europe, North America, and East Asia. While shipping and railroads increased their global reach, new technologies—electricity, the steel and chemical industries, and the global telegraph network—contributed to the enrichment and empowerment of the industrial nations.

With these new technologies, memories of the great scourges—famines, wars, and epidemics—faded. Clean water, electric lights, and railways began to improve the lives of city dwellers, even the poor. Municipal services made city life less dangerous and chaotic. Goods from distant lands, even travel to other continents, came within the reach of millions. Middle-class women continued to focus on domestic pursuits and lived in a "separate sphere" from men. Many working-class women took jobs in the textile industry, yet their work outside the home did not lessen their domestic and child-rearing responsibilities.

Though Karl Marx predicted a class struggle between workers and employers, socialism became more of an intellectual movement. Through labor unions, workers achieved some measure of recognition and security. By the turn of the century, liberal political reforms had taken hold in western Europe. Universal male suffrage became law in the United States in 1870 and in various parts of Europe by the 1880s.

The framework for all these changes was the nation-state. Until the 1860s nationalism was associated with liberalism, but later generations of conservatives used public education, military service, and colonial conquests to build a sense of national unity. By 1871 both Italy and Germany had become unified states. In Japan, the Meiji Restoration restored power to the emperor and ushered in a period of Western influences.

The world economy, international politics, and even cultural and social issues revolved around a handful of countries—the great powers—that believed they controlled the destiny of the world. These included the most powerful European nations of the previous century, as well as three newcomers—Germany, the United States, and Japan.

KEY TERMS

Commodore Matthew Perry p. 743
railroads p. 744
submarine telegraph cables p. 744
steel p. 745
electricity p. 746
Thomas Edison p. 746
Victorian Age p. 750
"separate spheres" p. 750
socialism p. 753
labor union p. 753
Karl Marx p. 753
anarchists p. 755
nationalism p. 756
liberalism p. 756
Giuseppe Garibaldi p. 756
Otto von Bismarck p. 758
Meiji Restoration p. 759
Empress Dowager Cixi p. 765
Yamagata Aritomo p. 765

EBOOK AND WEBSITE RESOURCES

Primary Sources

Working Men of All Countries, Unite!

Letter to Mitsubishi Employees

Extracts from History of Germany in the Nineteenth Century and Historical Political Writings

Interactive Maps

Map 26.1 Unification of Italy, 1859–1870

Map 26.2 Unification of Germany, 1866–1871

Map 26.3 Expansion and Modernization of Japan, 1868–1918

Plus flashcards, practice quizzes, and more. Go to: www.cengage.com/history/bullietearthpeople5e

SUGGESTED READING

Anderson, Benedict. *Imagined Communities: Reflections on the Origin and Spread of Nationalism.* 1991. Describes how nationalism spread beyond Europe.

Branca, Patricia. *Silent Sisterhood: Middle-Class Women in the Victorian Home.* 1975. Discusses how "Victorian morality" affected women.

Craig, Gordon A. *Germany, 1866–1945.* 1980. The classic overview.

Duus, Peter. *The Rise of Modern Japan,* 2nd ed. 1998. A clear explanation of the Meiji Restoration.

Fairbank, John King. *The Great Chinese Revolution, 1800–1985.* 1987. The classic synthesis of China's decline and recovery.

Hobsbawm, E. J. *Nation and Nationalism Since 1780.* 1990. Deals mainly with Europe.

Landes, David. *The Unbound Prometheus: Technological Change and Industrial Development in Western Europe from 1750 to the Present.* 1969. A classic narrative history.

Lindemann, Albert. *A History of European Socialism.* 1983. Covers the labor movements as well.

Moore, Barrington. *The Social Origins of Dictatorship and Democracy.* 1966. A classic essay on European society.

Pflanze, Otto. *Bismarck and the Development of Germany.* 1990. The best biography of Bismarck.

Read, Donald. *The Age of Urban Democracy: England, 1868–1914.* 1994. An excellent social history.

Rogger, Hans. *Russia in the Age of Modernization and Revolution, 1881–1917.* 1983. Discusses how Western influences corroded the tsarist empire.

Sked, Alan. *The Decline and Fall of the Habsburg Empire, 1815–1918.* 1989. Discusses how nationalism destroyed the Austrian state.

Spence, Jonathan D. *The Search for Modern China.* 1990. A monumental account of a complex society.

Stearns, Peter. *The Industrial Revolution in World History.* 1993. The first truly global history of industrialization.

Tilly, Louise, and Joan Scott. *Women, Work, and Family.* 1987. A wide-ranging history of Western women.

Weber, Eugen. *Peasants into Frenchmen.* 1976. Describes the creation of French nationhood.

NOTES

1. Quoted in Bonnie S. Anderson and Judith P. Zinsser, *A History of Their Own: Women in Europe from Prehistory to the Present,* vol. 2 (New York: Harper & Row, 1988), 372, 387.

AP* REVIEW QUESTIONS FOR CHAPTER 26

1. Railroads were important to colonial powers because
   (A) they could be constructed almost anywhere in the world.
   (B) only the developed nations had them.
   (C) they provided jobs for the lower classes in the colonies.
   (D) they were relatively inexpensive to build and maintain.

2. Which of the following nations led the world in engineering schools and scientific institutes by 1900?
   (A) The United States
   (B) Germany
   (C) France
   (D) Russia

3. Which of the following had the most radical impact on the quality of people's lives by the end of the nineteenth century?
   (A) Steel
   (B) Telegraph
   (C) Steam engine
   (D) Electricity

4. The expansion of world trade between 1850 and 1913
   (A) led directly to economic collapses around the world.
   (B) encouraged militarism to develop as a way to protect colonial possessions.
   (C) strained the relationships between the developed nations.
   (D) tied nonindustrial areas to the world economy as never before.

5. The first nation to have the majority of its citizens living in cities was
   (A) Germany.
   (B) Russia.
   (C) the United States.
   (D) Great Britain.

6. In the "Victorian Age," middle-class status meant that a family
   (A) employed at least one servant.
   (B) had only one wage earner.
   (C) had electricity in their home.
   (D) owned an automobile.

7. Socialism is an ideology developed by radical thinkers who
   (A) questioned the sanctity of private property and argued in support of industrial workers against their employers.
   (B) organized industrial laborers to defend their interests in the workplace through negotiations with their employers.
   (C) wanted to see all property owned by the government and to place the government in charge of the distribution of wealth.
   (D) formed the first political party to successfully challenge the established government in Great Britain and Germany.

8. Unlike the revolutions in the United States and France, the revolution in Italy was
   (A) a conservative revolution.
   (B) more of a process than an actual revolution.
   (C) a rebellion against the Vatican.
   (D) a dismal failure because it did not establish any type of democratic rule.

9. In Japan, the Meiji Restoration ended the Tokugawa Shogunate, but it was also
   (A) an attempt to restore the power of the daimyo.
   (B) a way for Japan to gain control of Korea.
   (C) a time when Japan modernized itself as a way to avoid Western imperialism.
   (D) a time when socialism rose in Japan.

10. Social Darwinism fit neatly into Western imperialism because it gave imperialistic nations a way to

    (A) profit from their colonies.
    (B) use scientific knowledge to improve industrial growth.
    (C) try to justify having their colonies around the world.
    (D) settle imperial struggles without having wars.

11. France was losing power in Europe at the end of the nineteenth century partly because

    (A) it had regressive taxation policies.
    (B) its low birthrates had led to smaller population growth.
    (C) it lacked rich colonies around the world.
    (D) its industrial base had been dormant since the Franco-Prussian War.

12. In both Russia and Austria-Hungary, nationalism

    (A) increased the power of the ruling family and strengthened the government.
    (B) weakened both governments as ethnic minorities began to demand self-rule.
    (C) encouraged the government of each nation to grant political rights to all citizens.
    (D) led to the formation of strong parties advocating democratic government.

13. In Qing dynasty China, one of the major impediments to industrialization was that

    (A) China had no labor force for new industries.
    (B) China had few natural resources.
    (C) China had few markets for its goods.
    (D) the government was corrupt and inefficient.

CHAPTER

27

CHAPTER OUTLINE

- The New Imperialism: Motives and Methods
- The Scramble for Africa
- Imperialism in Asia and the Pacific
- Imperialism in Latin America
- The World Economy and the Global Environment
- Conclusion

DIVERSITY + DOMINANCE *Two Africans Recall the Arrival of the Europeans*

ENVIRONMENT + TECHNOLOGY *Imperialism and Tropical Ecology*

Bildarchiv Preussischer Kulturbesitz/Art Resource, NY

Opening the Suez Canal When the canal opened in 1869, thousands of dignitaries and ordinary people gathered to watch the ships go by.

Visit the website and ebook for additional study materials and interactive tools: www.cengage.com/history/bullietearthpeople5e

The New Imperialism, 1869–1914

- What motivated the industrial nations to conquer new territories, and what means did they use?
- Why were imperialists drawn to the natural resources of Africa, and how did their presence on that continent change the environment?
- What were the social and cultural effects of imperialism in Asia?
- What were the economic motives behind imperialism in Latin America?
- How did imperialism contribute to the growth and globalization of the world economy?

In 1869 Ismail (is-mah-EEL), the khedive (kuh-DEEV) (ruler) of Egypt, invited all the Christian princes of Europe and all the Muslim princes of Asia and Africa—except the Ottoman sultan, his nominal overlord—to celebrate the inauguration of the greatest construction project of the century: the **Suez Canal**. Sixteen hundred dignitaries from the Middle East and Europe assembled at Port Said (port sah-EED). A French journalist wrote:

> This multitude, coming from all parts of the world, presented the most varied and singular spectacle. All races were represented. . . . We saw, coming to attend this festival of civilization, men of the Orient wearing clothes of dazzling colors, chiefs of African tribes wrapped in their great coats, Circassians in war costumes, officers of the British army of India with their shakos [hats] wrapped in muslin, Hungarian magnates wearing their national costumes.[1]

Suez Canal Ship canal dug across the isthmus of Suez in Egypt, designed by Ferdinand de Lesseps. It opened to shipping in 1869 and shortened the sea voyage between Europe and Asia. Its strategic importance led to the British conquest of Egypt in 1882.

Ismail used the occasion to emphasize the harmony and cooperation between the peoples of Africa, Asia, and Europe and to show that Egypt was not only independent but was also an equal of the great powers. To bless the inauguration, Ismail had invited clergy of the Muslim, Orthodox, and Catholic faiths. A reporter noted: "The Khedive . . . wished to symbolize thereby the unity of men and their brotherhood before God, without distinction of religion; it was the first time that the Orient had seen such a meeting of faiths to celebrate and bless together a great event and a great work."[2]

The canal was a great success, but not in the way Ismail intended. Ships using it could travel between Europe and India in less than two weeks—much less time than the month or longer consumed by sailing around Africa and across the Indian Ocean. By lowering freight costs, the canal stimulated shipping and the construction of steamships, giving an advantage to nations that had heavy industry and a large maritime trade over land-based empires and countries with few merchant ships. Great Britain benefited more than any other nation. France, which provided half the capital and most of the engineers, came in a distant second, for it had less trade with Asia than Britain did. Egypt, which contributed the other half of the money and most of the labor, was the loser. Instead of making Egypt powerful and independent, the Suez Canal provided the excuse for a British invasion and occupation of that country.

e **PRIMARY SOURCE: Convention on Free Navigation of the Suez Canal Between the European Powers and the Ottoman Empire, October 29, 1888** Read about the laws governing the Suez Canal and the code of conduct for parties sharing this passage.

Far from inaugurating an era of harmony among the peoples of three continents and three faiths, the canal triggered a wave of European domination over Africa and Asia. Between 1869 and 1914 Germany, France, Britain, Russia, Japan, and the United States used industrial technology to impose their will on the nonindustrial parts of the world. Historians call this exercise of power the **New Imperialism**.

THE NEW IMPERIALISM: MOTIVES AND METHODS

New Imperialism Historians' term for the late-nineteenth- and early-twentieth-century wave of conquests by European powers, the United States, and Japan, which were followed by the development and exploitation of the newly conquered territories for the benefit of the colonial powers.

AP* Exam Tip The rise of Western imperialism is an important topic on both the multiple choice section and the essay section of the exam.

Europe had a long tradition of imperialism reaching back to the twelfth century. During the first two-thirds of the nineteenth century the European powers continued to increase their influence overseas (see Chapter 25). The New Imperialism was characterized by an explosion of territorial conquests even more rapid than the Spanish conquests of the sixteenth century. Between 1869 and 1914, in a land grab of unprecedented speed, Europeans seized territories in Africa and Central Asia, and both Europeans and Americans took territories in Southeast Asia and the Pacific. Approximately 10 million square miles (26 million square kilometers) and 150 million people fell under the rule of Europe and the United States in this period.

The New Imperialism was more than a land grab. The imperial powers used economic and technological means to reorganize dependent regions and bring them into the world economy as suppliers of foodstuffs and raw materials and as consumers of industrial products. In Africa and other parts of the world, this was done by conquest and colonial administration. The Latin American republics, though remaining politically independent, became economic dependencies of the United States and Europe.

What inspired Europeans and Americans to venture overseas and impose their will on other societies? Economic, cultural, and political motives were involved in all cases.

Political Motives

The great powers of the late nineteenth century, as well as less powerful countries like Italy, Portugal, and Belgium, were competitive and hypersensitive about their status. French leaders, humiliated by their defeat by Prussia in 1871 (see Chapter 26), sought to reestablish their nation's prestige through territorial acquisitions overseas. Great Britain, already in possession of the world's largest empire, felt the need to protect India by acquiring colonies in East Africa and Southeast Asia. German Chancellor Otto von Bismarck had little interest in acquiring colonies, but many Germans believed that a country as important as theirs required an impressive empire overseas.

Political motives were not limited to statesmen in the capital cities. Colonial governors, even officers posted to the farthest colonial outposts, practiced their own diplomacy. They often decided on their own to claim a piece of land before some rival got it. Armies fighting frontier wars found it easier to defeat their neighbors than to make peace with them. In response to border skirmishes with neighboring states, colonial agents were likely to send in troops, take over their neighbors' territories, and then inform their home governments. Governments felt obligated to back up their men-on-the-spot. The great powers of Europe acquired much of West Africa, Southeast Asia, and the Pacific islands in this manner.

Cultural Motives

The late nineteenth century saw a Christian revival in Europe and North America, as both Catholics and Protestants founded new missionary societies. Their purpose was not only religious—to convert nonbelievers, whom they regarded as "heathen"—but also cultural. They were determined to abolish slavery in Africa and bring Western education, medicine, hygiene, and monogamous marriage to all the world's peoples.

Among those attracted by religious work overseas were many women who joined missionary societies to become teachers and nurses. Although they did not challenge colonialism directly, their influence often helped soften the harshness of colonial rule—for example, by calling attention to issues of maternity and women's health. Mary Slessor, a British missionary who lived for

CHRONOLOGY

	Africa	Asia and the Pacific	Latin America
		1862–1895 French conquer Indochina	
		1865–1876 Russian forces advance into Central Asia	
1870	1869 Opening of the Suez Canal		1870–1910 Railroad building boom in Argentina, Brazil, and Mexico
	1874 Warfare between Britain and Asante (Gold Coast)		
	1877–1879 Warfare between Britain and the Xhosa and the Zulu (South Africa)	1878 United States obtains Pago Pago Harbor (Samoa)	
	1882 British forces occupy Egypt		
	1884–1885 Berlin Conference; Leopold II obtains Congo Free State	1885 Britain completes conquest of Burma	
		1887 United States obtains Pearl Harbor (Hawaii)	
1890			
	1896 Ethiopians defeat Italian army at Adowa	1894–1895 China defeated in Sino-Japanese War	1895–1898 Cubans revolt against Spanish rule
	1898 Battle of Omdurman	1898 United States annexes Hawaii and Guam and purchases Philippines from Spain	1898 Spanish-American War; United States annexes Puerto Rico and Hawaii
1900	1899–1902 South African War between Afrikaners and British	1899–1902 U.S. forces conquer and occupy Philippines	1901 United States imposes Platt Amendment on Cuba
	1902 First Aswan Dam completed (Egypt)	1903 Russia completes Trans-Siberian Railway	1903 United States backs secession of Panama from Colombia
		1904–1905 Russia defeated in Russo-Japanese War	1904–1907, 1916 U.S. troops occupy Dominican Republic
1910	1908 Belgium annexes Congo		1904–1914 United States builds Panama Canal
			1912 U.S. troops occupy Nicaragua and Honduras

forty years among the people of southeastern Nigeria, campaigned against slavery, human sacrifice, and the killing of twins and, generally, for women's rights. In India missionaries denounced the customs of child marriages and *sati* (the burning of widows on their husbands' funeral pyres). Such views often clashed with the customs of the people among whom they settled.

Racism

The sense of moral duty and cultural superiority was not limited to missionaries. Many Europeans and Americans equated technological innovations with progress. They believed that Western technology proved the superiority of Western ideas, customs, and culture. More harmful were racist ideas that relegated non-Europeans to a status of permanent inferiority. Racists assigned different stages of biological development to peoples of different races and cultures (see Chapter 26). They divided humankind into several races based on physical appearance and ranked these races in a hierarchy that ranged from "civilized" down through "semibarbarous," "barbarian," and finally, at the bottom, "savage." Whites were always at the top of this ranking. Such ideas were often presented as an excuse for permanent rule over Africans and Asians.

Young men, finding few opportunities for adventure and glory at home in an era of peace, sought them overseas. At first, European people and parliaments were indifferent or hostile to overseas adventures, but a few easy victories in the 1880s helped to overcome their reluctance. The United States was fully preoccupied with its westward expansion until the 1880s, but in the 1890s popular attention shifted to lands outside U.S. borders. Newspapers, which achieved wide readership in the second half of the nineteenth century, discovered that they could boost circulation with reports of wars and conquests. By the 1890s imperialism was a popular cause, the overseas extension of the nationalism of the time.

Economic Motives

The industrialization of Europe and North America stimulated the demand for minerals—copper for electrical wiring, tin for canning, chrome and manganese for the steel industry, coal for steam engines, and, most of all, gold and diamonds. The demand for such industrial crops as cotton and rubber and for stimulants such as sugar, coffee, tea, and tobacco also grew. These products were found in the tropics, but never in sufficient quantities.

An economic depression lasting from the mid-1870s to the mid-1890s caused European businessmen to seek protection against foreign competition (see below). They argued that their respective countries needed secure sources of tropical raw materials and protected markets for their industries. Declining business opportunities at home prompted entrepreneurs and investors to look for profits in Asia, Africa, and Latin America. Since investment in countries so different from their own was extremely risky, businessmen sought the backing of their governments, preferably with soldiers.

These reasons explain why Europeans and Americans wished to expand their influence over other societies. Yet motives do not adequately explain the events of that time. What made it possible to conquer a piece of Africa, convert the "heathen," and start plantations was the sudden increase in the power that industrial peoples could wield over nonindustrial peoples and over the forces of nature. Technological advances explain both the motives and the outcome of the New Imperialism.

The Tools of the Imperialists

To succeed, empire builders needed the means to achieve their objectives at a reasonable cost. These means were provided by the Industrial Revolution (see Chapter 22). In the early nineteenth century technological innovations began to tip the balance of power in favor of Europe.

Shipping

Europeans had dominated the oceans since about 1500, and their naval power increased still more with the introduction of steamships. The first steamer reached India in 1825 and was soon followed by regular mail service in the 1830s. The building of the Suez Canal and the development of increasingly efficient engines led to a boom in shipping to the Indian Ocean and East Asia. Submarine telegraph cables connected Europe with North America in the 1860s, with Latin America and Asia in the 1870s, with Africa in the 1880s, and finally across the Pacific in 1904.

Gunboats

Europeans used gunboats with considerable success in China, Burma, Indochina, and the Congo Basin. Although gunboats opened the major river basins to European penetration, the invaders often found themselves hampered by other natural obstacles. *Falciparum* malaria, found only in Africa, was so deadly to Europeans that few explorers survived before the 1850s. In 1854 a British doctor discovered that the drug quinine, taken regularly during one's stay in Africa, could prevent the disease. This and a few sanitary precautions reduced the annual death rate among whites in West Africa from between 250 and 750 per thousand in the early nineteenth century to between 50 and 100 per thousand after 1850. This reduction was sufficient to open the continent to merchants, officials, and missionaries.

Firearms

The development of new and much deadlier firearms in the 1860s and 1870s shifted the balance of power on land between Westerners and other peoples. One of these was the breechloader, which could be fired accurately ten times as fast as, and five or six times farther than, a musket. By the 1870s all armies in Europe and the United States had switched to these new rifles. Repeating rifles could shoot fifteen rounds in fifteen seconds. In the 1890s European and American armies began using machine guns, which could fire eleven bullets per second. As European firearms improved, the firepower gap widened, making colonial conquests easier than ever before. By the 1880s and 1890s European-led forces of a few hundred could defeat non-European armies of thousands. Against the latest weapons, African and Asian soldiers armed with muskets or spears did not stand a chance, no matter how numerous and courageous they were.

Battle of Omdurman British victory over the Mahdi in the Sudan in 1898. General Kitchener led a mixed force of British and Egyptian troops armed with rapid-firing rifles and machine guns.

A classic example is the **Battle of Omdurman** in Sudan. On September 2, 1898, forty thousand Sudanese attacked an Anglo-Egyptian expedition that had come up the Nile on six steamers and four other boats to avenge the defeat of General Charles Gordon in 1885 (see Chapter 24). General Horatio Kitchener's troops had twenty machine guns and four artillery pieces; the

The Art Archive

The Battle of Omdurman In the late nineteenth century, most battles between European-led troops and African forces were one-sided encounters because of the disparity in the opponents' firearms and tactics. The Battle of Omdurman in Sudan in 1898 is a dramatic example. The forces of the Mahdi, some on horseback, were armed with spears and single-shot muskets. The British troops and their Egyptian allies, lined up in the foreground, used repeating rifles and machine guns able to shoot much farther than the Sudanese weapons. As a result, there were many Sudanese casualties but very few British and Egyptian casualties.

Sudanese were equipped with muskets and spears. Within a few hours eleven thousand Sudanese and forty-eight British lay dead.

Colonial Agents and Administration

colonialism Policy by which a nation administers a foreign territory and develops its resources for the benefit of the colonial power.

Once colonial agents took over a territory, their home government expected them to cover their own costs and, if possible, return some profit to the home country. The system of administering and exploiting colonies for the benefit of the home country is known as **colonialism**. In some cases, such as along the West African coast or in Indochina, there was already a considerable trade that could be taxed. In other places profits could come only from investments and a thorough reorganization of the indigenous societies. In applying modern scientific and industrial methods to their colonies, colonialists started the transformation of Asian and African societies and landscapes that has continued to our day.

White Settlers

One important factor was the presence or absence of European settlers. In Canada, Australia, and New Zealand, whites were already in the majority by 1869, and Britain encouraged them to elect parliaments and rule themselves. Where European settlers were numerous but still a minority of the population, as in Algeria and South Africa, settlers and the home country struggled for control over the indigenous population. In colonies with few white settlers, the European governors ruled autocratically.

In the early years of the New Imperialism, colonial administrations consisted of a governor and his staff, a few troops to keep order, and a small number of tax collectors and magistrates. Nowhere could colonialism operate without the cooperation of indigenous elites, because no colony was wealthy enough to pay the salaries of more than a handful of European officials. In most cases the colonial governors exercised power through traditional rulers willing to cooperate.

A Colonial Lady In many tropical colonies in the nineteenth century, there were few good roads, but labor was abundant. European colonial officials and their wives often traveled in a tonjon, or sedan chair carried by porters. This image of a lady in India dates from 1828.

Eileen Tweedy/The Art Archive

Colonial governments also educated a few local youths for "modern" jobs as clerks, nurses, policemen, customs inspectors, and the like. Thus colonialism relied on two rival indigenous elites.

White Women

European and American women seldom took part in the early stages of colonial expansion. As conquest gave way to peaceful colonialism and as steamships and railroads made travel less difficult, colonial officials and settlers began bringing their wives to the colonies. The arrival of white women in Asia and Africa led to increasing racial segregation. Sylvia Leith-Ross, wife of a colonial officer in Nigeria, explained: "When you are alone, among thousands of unknown, unpredictable people, dazed by unaccustomed sights and sounds, bemused by strange ways of life and thought, you need to remember who you are, where you come from, what your standards are."[3] Many colonial wives found themselves in command of numerous servants and expected to follow the complex etiquette of colonial entertainment in support of their husbands' official positions. Some found opportunities to exercise personal initiative, usually charitable work involving indigenous women and children. However well meaning, their efforts were always subordinate to the work of men.

SECTION REVIEW

- From 1864 to 1914 Europeans and Americans conquered 10 million square miles and 150 million people.
- The European powers were motivated by political rivalries.
- Missionaries and the press supported the conquests. So did businessmen eager to invest capital, sell their products, and obtain raw materials.
- New industrial technologies—gunboats, rifles, and quinine—made it possible for Europeans to conquer other lands.
- Colonial agents transformed the societies and peoples they ruled; white women participated in the enterprise.

THE SCRAMBLE FOR AFRICA

Until the 1870s African history was largely shaped by internal forces and the spread of Islam (see Chapter 25). Outside Algeria and southern Africa, only a handful of Europeans had ever visited the interior of Africa, and European countries possessed only small enclaves on the coasts. As late as 1879 Africans ruled more than 90 percent of the continent. Then, within a decade, Africa was invaded and divided among the European powers in a movement often referred to as the **"scramble" for Africa** (see Map 27.1). Let us look at the most significant cases, beginning with Egypt, the wealthiest and most populated part of the continent.

"scramble" for Africa Sudden wave of conquests in Africa by European powers in the 1880s and 1890s. Britain obtained most of eastern Africa, France most of northwestern Africa. Other countries (Germany, Belgium, Portugal, Italy, and Spain) acquired lesser amounts.

Egypt

Ironically, European involvement in Egypt resulted from Egypt's attempt to free itself from Ottoman rule. Throughout the mid-nineteenth century the khedives of Egypt had tried to modernize their armed forces; build canals, harbors, railroads, and other public works; and reorient

MAP 27.1 Africa in 1878 and 1914 In 1878 the European colonial presence was limited to a few coastal enclaves, plus portions of Algeria and South Africa. By 1914, Europeans had taken over all of Africa except Ethiopia and Liberia.

Interactive Map

agriculture toward export crops, especially cotton (see Chapters 22 and 25). Their interest in the Suez Canal was also part of this policy. Khedive Ismail even tried to make Egypt the center of an empire reaching south into Sudan and Ethiopia.

These ambitions cost vast sums of money, which the khedives borrowed from European creditors at high interest rates. By 1876 Egypt's foreign debt had risen to £100 million sterling, and the interest payments alone consumed one-third of its foreign export earnings. To avoid bankruptcy the Egyptian government sold its shares in the Suez Canal to Great Britain and accepted four foreign "commissioners of the debt" to oversee its finances. French and British bankers, still not satisfied, lobbied their governments to secure the loans by stronger measures. In 1878 the two governments obliged Ismail to appoint a Frenchman as minister of public works and a Briton as minister of finance. When high taxes caused hardship and popular discontent, the French and British persuaded the Ottoman sultan to depose Ismail. This foreign intervention provoked a military uprising under Egyptian army colonel Arabi Pasha, which threatened the Suez Canal.

Britain Occupies Egypt

Fearing for their investments, the British sent an army into Egypt in 1882. So important was the Suez Canal to Britain's maritime supremacy that they stayed for seventy years. During those years the British ruled Egypt "indirectly"—that is, they maintained the Egyptian government and the fiction of Egyptian sovereignty but retained real power in their own hands.

Eager to develop Egyptian cotton production, the British brought in engineers and contractors to build the first dam across the Nile, at Aswan in upper Egypt. When completed in 1902, it captured the annual Nile flood and released its waters throughout the year, allowing farmers to grow two, sometimes three, crops a year. The economic development of Egypt by the British enriched a small elite of landowners and merchants, many of them foreigners. Egyptian peasants got little relief from the heavy taxes collected to pay for their country's crushing foreign debt and the expenses of the British army of occupation. Western ways that conflicted with the teachings of Islam—such as the drinking of alcohol and the relative freedom of women—offended Muslim religious leaders. Most Egyptians found British rule more onerous than that of the Ottomans. By the 1890s Egyptian politicians and intellectuals were demanding that the British leave.

Henry Morton Stanley British-American explorer of Africa, famous for his expeditions in search of Dr. David Livingstone. Stanley helped King Leopold II establish the Congo Free State.

King Leopold II King of Belgium (r. 1865–1909). He was active in encouraging the exploration of Central Africa and became the ruler of the Congo Free State (to 1908).

Savorgnan de Brazza Franco-Italian explorer sent by the French government to claim part of equatorial Africa for France. Founded Brazzaville, capital of the French Congo, in 1880.

Western and Equatorial Africa

While the British were taking over Egypt, the French were planning to extend their empire into the interior of West Africa. Starting from the coast of Senegal, which had been in French hands for centuries, they hoped to build a railroad from the upper Senegal River to the upper Niger in order to open the interior to French merchants. This in turn led the French military to undertake the conquest of western Sudan.

Meanwhile, the actions of three individuals, rather than a government, brought about the occupation of the Congo Basin, an enormous forested region in the heart of equatorial Africa (see Map 27.1). In 1879 the American journalist **Henry Morton Stanley**, who had explored the area (see Chapter 25), persuaded **King Leopold II** of Belgium to invest his personal fortune in "opening up" equatorial Africa. With Leopold's money, Stanley returned to Africa from 1879 to 1884 to establish trading posts along the southern bank of the Congo River. At the same time, **Savorgnan de Brazza**, an Italian officer serving in the French army, obtained from an African ruler living on the opposite bank a treaty that placed the area under the "protection" of France.

The Berlin Conference

Berlin Conference Conference that German chancellor Otto von Bismarck called to set rules for the partition of Africa. It led to the creation of the Congo Free State under King Leopold II of Belgium.

These events sparked a flurry of diplomatic activity. German chancellor Bismarck called the **Berlin Conference** on Africa of 1884 and 1885. There the major powers agreed that henceforth "effective occupation" would replace the former trading relations between Africans and Europeans. Every country with colonial ambitions had to send troops into Africa and participate in the division of the spoils. As a reward for triggering the "scramble" for Africa, Leopold II acquired a personal domain under the name "Congo Free State," while France and Portugal took most of the rest of equatorial Africa. In this manner, the European powers and King Leopold managed to divide Africa among themselves, at least on paper.

"Effective occupation" required many years of effort. In the interior of West Africa, Muslim rulers resisted the French invasion for up to thirty years. The French advance encouraged the Germans to stake claims to parts of the region and the British to move north from their coastal enclaves, until the entire region was occupied by Britain, France, and Germany.

AP* Exam Tip Be able to compare the colonial administration of African colonies with the colonial administration of Indian and Asian colonies.

Because West Africa had long had a flourishing trade, the new rulers took advantage of existing trade networks, taxing merchants and farmers, investing the profits in railroads and harbors, and paying dividends to European stockholders. In the Gold Coast (now Ghana) British trading companies bought the cocoa grown by African farmers at low prices and resold it for large profits. The interior of French West Africa lagged behind. Although the region could produce cotton, peanuts, and other crops, the difficulties of transportation limited its development before 1914.

Compared to West Africa, equatorial Africa had few inhabitants and little trade. Rather than try to govern these vast territories directly, authorities in the Congo Free State, the French Congo, and the Portuguese colonies of Angola and Mozambique farmed out huge pieces of land to private concession companies, offering them monopolies on the natural resources and trade of their territories and the right to employ soldiers and tax the inhabitants. Freed from outside supervision, the companies forced the African inhabitants at gunpoint to produce cash crops

From H. M. Stanley, *The Congo*, vol. 2, London, 1885

A Steamboat for the Congo River Soon after the Congo Basin was occupied by Europeans, the new colonial rulers realized they needed to improve transportation. Since access from the sea was blocked by rapids on the lower Congo River, steamboats had to be brought in sections, hauled from the coast by thousands of Congolese over very difficult terrain. This picture shows the pieces arriving at Stanley Pool, ready to be reassembled.

and carry them, on their heads or backs, to the nearest railroad or navigable river. The worst abuses took place in the Congo Free State, where a rubber boom made it profitable for private companies to coerce Africans to collect latex from vines that grew in the forests. One Congolese refugee told the British consul Roger Casement who investigated the atrocities:

> *We begged the white men to leave us alone, saying we could get no more rubber, but the white men and their soldiers said: "Go. You are only beasts yourselves, you are only* nyama *(meat)." We tried, always going further into the forest, and when we failed and our rubber was short, the soldiers came to our towns and killed us. Many were shot, some had their ears cut off; others were tied up with ropes around their necks and bodies and taken away.*[4]

After 1906 the British press began publicizing the horrors. The public outcry that followed, coinciding with the end of the rubber boom, convinced the Belgian government to take over Leopold's private empire in 1908.

Afrikaners South Africans descended from Dutch and French settlers of the seventeenth century. Their Great Trek founded new settler colonies in the nineteenth century. Though a minority among South Africans, they held political power after 1910, imposing a system of racial segregation called apartheid after 1949.

Southern Africa

The history of southern Africa between 1869 and 1914 differs from that of the rest of the continent in several important respects. One was that the land had long attracted settlers. African pastoralists and farmers had inhabited the region for centuries. **Afrikaners**, descendants of Dutch settlers on the Cape of Good Hope, moved inland throughout the nineteenth century; British prospectors and settlers arrived later in the century; and, finally, Indians were brought over by the British and stayed.

Southern Africa attracted European settlers because of its good pastures and farmland and its phenomenal deposits of diamonds, gold, and copper, as well as coal and iron ore. This was the new El Dorado that imperialists had dreamed of since the heyday of the Spanish Empire.

Diamonds

The discovery of diamonds at Kimberley in 1868 lured thousands of European prospectors as well as Africans looking for work. Great Britain, colonial ruler of the Cape Colony, annexed the diamond area in 1871, angering the Afrikaners. Once in the interior, the British defeated the

Xhosa (KOH-sah) people in 1877 and 1878. Then in 1879 they confronted the Zulu, militarily the most powerful of the African peoples in the region.

The Zulu, led by their king Cetshwayo (set-SHWAH-yo), resented their encirclement by Afrikaners and British. Their proud military tradition led them into a war with the British in 1879. They defeated the British at Isandhlwana (ee-sawn-dull-WAH-nuh), but a few months later they were in turn defeated. Cetshwayo was captured and sent into exile, and the Zulu lands were given to white ranchers. Yet throughout those bitter times, the Zulu's sense of nationhood remained strong.

Cecil Rhodes British entrepreneur and politician involved in the expansion of the British Empire from South Africa into Central Africa. The colonies of Southern Rhodesia (now Zimbabwe) and Northern Rhodesia (now Zambia) were named after him.

Relations between the British and the Afrikaners, already tense as a result of British encroachment, took a turn for the worse when gold was discovered in the Afrikaner republic of Transvaal (trans-VAHL) in 1886. In the gold rush that ensued, the British soon outnumbered the Afrikaners.

Britain's invasion of southern Africa was driven in part by the ambition of **Cecil Rhodes** (1853–1902), who once declared that he would "annex the stars" if he could. Rhodes made his fortune in the Kimberley diamond fields, founding De Beers Consolidated, a company that has dominated the world's diamond trade ever since. He then turned to politics. He encouraged a concession company, the British South Africa Company, to push north into Central Africa, where he named two new colonies after himself: Southern Rhodesia (now Zimbabwe) and Northern Rhodesia (now Zambia). The Ndebele (en-duh-BELL-ay) and Shona peoples, who inhabited the region, resisted this invasion, but the machine guns of the British finally defeated them.

Britain Versus Afrikaners

British attempts to annex the two Afrikaner republics, Transvaal and Orange Free State, and the inflow of English-speaking whites into the gold- and diamond-mining areas led to the South African War, which lasted from 1899 to 1902. At first the Afrikaners had the upper hand, for they were highly motivated, possessed modern rifles, and knew the land. In 1901, however, Great Britain brought in 450,000 troops and crushed the Afrikaner armies. Ironically, the Afrikaners' defeat in 1902 led to their ultimate victory. Wary of costly commitments overseas, the British government expected European settlers in Africa to manage their own affairs, as they were doing in Canada, Australia, and New Zealand. Thus, in 1910 the European settlers created the Union of South Africa, in which the Afrikaners eventually emerged as the ruling element.

Unlike Canada, Australia, and New Zealand, South Africa had a majority of indigenous inhabitants and substantial numbers of Indians and "Cape Coloureds" (people of mixed ancestry). Yet the Europeans were both numerous enough to demand self-rule and powerful enough to deny the vote and other civil rights to the majority. In 1913 the South African parliament passed the Natives Land Act, assigning Africans to reservations and forbidding them to own land elsewhere. This and other racial policies turned South Africa into a land of segregation and oppression.

Political and Social Consequences

At the time of the European invasion, Africa contained a wide variety of societies. Some parts of the continent had long-established kingdoms with aristocracies or commercial towns dominated by a merchant class. In other places agricultural peoples lived in villages without any outside government. Elsewhere pastoral nomads were organized along military lines. In some remote areas people lived from hunting and gathering. Not surprisingly, these societies responded in very different ways to the European invasion.

Collaborators and Resisters

Asante African kingdom on the Gold Coast that expanded rapidly after 1680. Asante participated in the Atlantic economy, trading gold, slaves, and ivory. It resisted British imperial ambitions for a quarter century before being absorbed into Britain's Gold Coast colony in 1902.

Some peoples welcomed the invaders as allies against local enemies. Once colonial rule was established, they sought work in government service or in European firms and sent their children to mission schools. In exchange, they were often the first to receive benefits such as clinics and roads. Peoples with a pastoral or a warrior tradition, however, fought tenaciously. Examples abound, from the Zulu and Ndebele of southern Africa to the pastoral Herero (hair-AIR-oh) people of Southwest Africa (now Namibia), who rose up against German invaders in 1904; in repressing their uprising, the Germans exterminated two-thirds of them. In the Sahel, a belt of grasslands south of the Sahara, charismatic leaders rose up in the name of a purified Islam, gathered a following of warriors, and led them on part religious, part empire-building campaigns called *jihads*. All of them eventually came into conflict with European-led military expeditions and were defeated.

Some commercial states with long histories of contact with Europeans also fought back. The kingdom of **Asante** (uh-SHAWN-tee) in Gold Coast rose up in 1874, 1896, and 1900 before it was

Victorious Ethiopians Among the states of Africa, Ethiopia alone was able to defend itself against European imperialism. In the 1880s, Ethiopia purchased modern weapons and trained its army to use them. Thus prepared, the Ethiopians defeated an Italian invasion at Adowa in 1896. These Ethiopian army officers wore their most elaborate finery to pose for a photograph after their victory.

National Archives

AP* Exam Tip Be able to discuss examples of successful rejection of imperialism, such as Ethiopia.

finally overwhelmed. In the Niger Delta, the ancient city of Benin, rich with artistic treasures, resisted colonial control until 1897, when a British "punitive expedition" set it on fire and carted its works of art off to Europe.

Ethiopian Success

Menelik Emperor of Ethiopia (r. 1889–1911). He enlarged Ethiopia to its present dimensions and defeated an Italian invasion at Adowa (1896).

One resistance movement succeeded, to the astonishment of Europeans and Africans alike. When **Menelik** became emperor of Ethiopia in 1889 (see Chapter 25), his country was threatened by Sudanese Muslims to the west and by France and Italy, which controlled the coast of the Red Sea to the east. For many years, Ethiopia had been purchasing European and American weapons. When Italians attempted to establish a protectorate over Ethiopia, they found the Ethiopians armed with thousands of rifles and even machine guns and artillery pieces. Although Italy sent twenty thousand troops to attack Ethiopia, in 1896 they were defeated at Adowa (AH-do-ah) by a larger and better-trained Ethiopian army.

Most Africans neither joined nor fought the European invaders but tried to continue living as before. They found this increasingly difficult because colonial rule disrupted every traditional society. The presence of colonial officials meant that rights to land, commercial transactions, and legal disputes were handled very differently and that traditional rulers lost all authority, except where Europeans used them as local administrators.

African Land and Labor

Changes in landholding were especially disruptive, for most Africans were farmers or herders for whom access to land was a necessity. In areas with a high population density, such as Egypt and West Africa, colonial rulers left peasants in place, encouraged them to grow cash crops, and collected taxes on the harvest. Elsewhere, the new rulers declared any land that was not farmed to be "vacant" and gave it to private concession companies or to European planters and ranchers. In Kenya, Northern Rhodesia, and South Africa, Europeans found the land and climate to their liking. White settlers forced Africans to become squatters, sharecroppers, or ranch hands on land they had farmed for generations. In South Africa they forced many Africans off their lands and onto "reserves."

Although the colonial rulers harbored designs on the land, they were even more interested in African labor. They did not want to pay wages high enough to attract workers voluntarily. Instead, they imposed various taxes, such as the hut tax and the head tax, which Africans had to pay regardless of their income. To find the money, Africans had little choice but to accept whatever work the Europeans offered. In this way Africans were recruited to work on plantations, railroads, and other modern enterprises. In the South African mines Africans were paid, on average, one-tenth as much as Europeans.

DIVERSITY + DOMINANCE

Two Africans Recall the Arrival of the Europeans

We know a great deal about the arrival of the Europeans into the interior of Africa from the perspective of the conquerors, but very little about how the events were experienced by Africans. Here are two accounts by African women, one from northern Nigeria whose land was occupied by the British, the other from the Congo Free State, a colony of King Leopold II of Belgium. They show not only how Africans experienced European colonial dominance but also how diverse these African experiences were.

Baba of Karo, a Nigerian Woman, Remembers Her Childhood

When I was a maiden the Europeans first arrived. Ever since we were quite small the *malams* had been saying that the Europeans would come with a thing called a train, they would come with a thing called a motor-car, in them you would go and come back in a trice. They would stop wars, they would repair the world, they would stop oppression and lawlessness, we should live at peace with them. We used to go and sit quietly and listen to the prophecies.

I remember when a European came to Karo on a horse, and some of his foot soldiers went into the town. Everyone came out to look at them, but in Zerewa they didn't see the European. Everyone at Karo ran away—"There's a European, there's a European!"

At that time Yusufu was the king of Karo. He did not like the Europeans, he did not wish them, he would not sign their treaty. Then he say that perforce he would have to agree, so he did. We Habe wanted them to come, it was the Fulani who did not like it. When the Europeans came the Habe saw that if you worked for them they paid you for it, they didn't say, like the Fulani, "Commoner, give me this! Commoner, bring me that!" Yes, the Habe wanted them; they saw no harm in them.

The Europeans said that there were to be no more slaves; if someone said "Slave!" you could complain to the *alkali* who would punish the master who said it, the judge said, "That is what the Europeans have decreed." The first order said that any slave, if he was younger than you, was your younger brother, if he was older than you was your elder brother—they were all brothers of their master's family. No one used the word "slave" any more. When slavery was stopped, nothing much happened at our *rinji* except that some slaves whom we had bought in the market ran away. Our own father went to his farm and worked, he and his son took up their large hoes; they loaned out their spare farms. Tsoho our father and Kadiri my brother with whom I live now and Babambo worked, they farmed guinea-corn and millet and groundnuts and everything; before this they had supervised the slaves' work—now they did their own.

In the old days if the chief liked the look of your daughter he would take her and put her in his house; you could do nothing about it. Now they don't do that.

Ilanga, a Congolese Woman, Recounts Her Capture by Agents of the Congo Free State

. . . we were all busy in the fields hoeing our plantations, for it was the rainy season, and the weeds sprang quickly up, when a runner came to the village saying that a large band of men was coming, that they all wore red caps and blue cloth, and carried guns and long knives, and that many white men were with them, the chief of whom was *Kibalanga* (Michaux). Niendo at once called all the chief men to his house, while the drums were beaten to summon the people to the village. A long consultation was held, and finally we were all told to go quietly to the fields and bring in ground-nuts, plantains, and cassava for the warriors who were coming, and goats and fowl for the white men. The women all went with baskets and filled them, and put them in the road, which was blocked up, so many were there. Niendo then commanded everyone to go and sit quietly

Some Africans came to the cities and mining camps seeking a better life than they had on the land. Many migrated great distances and stayed away for years at a time. Most migrant workers were men who left their wives and children behind in villages and on reserves. In some cases the authorities did not allow them to bring their families and settle permanently in the towns. This caused great hardship for African women, who had to grow food for their families during the men's absences and care for sick and aged workers. Long separations between spouses also led to an increase in prostitution and to the spread of sexually transmitted diseases.

African Women

Some African women welcomed colonial rule, for it brought an end to fighting and slave raiding, but others were led into captivity (see Diversity and Dominance: Two Africans Recall the Arrival of the Europeans). A few succeeded in becoming wealthy traders or owners of livestock. On the whole, however, African women benefited less than men from the economic changes that colonialism introduced. In areas where the colonial rulers replaced communal property with private property, property rights were assigned to the head of the household—that is, to the man. Almost all the jobs open to Africans, even those considered "women's work" in Europe, such as nursing and domestic service, were reserved for men.

in the houses until he gave other orders. This we did, everyone remaining quietly seated while Niendo went up the road with the head men to meet the white chief. We did not know what to think, for most of us feared that so many armed men coming boded evil; but Niendo thought that, by giving presents of much food, he would induce the strangers to pass on without harming us. And so it proved, for the soldiers took the baskets, and were then ordered by the white men to move off through the village. Many of the soldiers looked into the houses and shouted at us words we did not understand. We were glad when they were all gone, for we were much in fear of the white men and the strange warriors, who are known to all the people as being great fighters, bringing war wherever they go. . . .

When the white men and their warriors had gone, we went again to our work, and were hoping that they would not return; but this they did in a very short time. As before, we brought in great heaps of food; but this time *Kibalanga* did not move away directly, but camped near our village, and his soldiers came and stole all our fowl and goats and tore up our cassava; but we did not mind as long as they did not harm us. The next morning it was reported that the white men were going away; but soon after the sun rose over the hill, a large band of soldiers came into the village, and we all went into the houses and sat down. We were not long seated when the soldiers came rushing in shouting, and threatening Niendo with their guns. They rushed into the houses and dragged the people out. Three or four came to our house and caught hold of me, also my husband Oleka and my sister Katinga. We were dragged into the road, and were tied together with cords about our necks, so that we could not escape. We were all crying, for now we knew that we were to be taken away to be slaves. The soldiers beat us with the iron sticks from their guns, and compelled us to march to the camp of *Kibalanga,* who ordered the women to be tied up separately, ten to each cord, and the men in the same way. When we were all collected—and there were many from other villages whom we now saw, and many from Waniendo—the soldiers brought baskets of food for us to carry, in some of which was smoked human flesh (*niama na nitu*).

We then set off marching very quickly. My sister Katinga had her baby in her arms, and was not compelled to carry a basket; but my husband Oleka was made to carry a goat. We marched until the afternoon, when we camped near a stream, where we were glad to drink, for we were much athirst. We had nothing to eat, for the soldiers would give us nothing, so we lay upon the ground, and at night went to sleep. The next day we continued the march, and when we camped at noon were given some maize and plantains, which were gathered near a village from which the people had run away. So it continued each day until the fifth day, when the soldiers took my sister's baby and threw it in the grass, leaving it to die, and made her carry some cooking pots which they found in the deserted village. On the sixth day we became very weak from lack of food and from constant marching and sleeping in the damp grass, and my husband, who marched behind us with the goat, could not stand up longer, and so he sat down beside the path and refused to walk more. The soldiers beat him, but still he refused to move. Then one of them struck him on the head with the end of his gun, and he fell upon the ground. One of the soldiers caught the goat, while two or three others stuck the long knives they put on the ends of their guns into my husband. I saw the blood spurt out, and then saw him no more, for we passed over the brow of a hill and he was out of sight. Many of the young men were killed the same way, and many babies thrown into the grass to die. A few escaped; but we were so well guarded that it was almost impossible.

QUESTIONS FOR ANALYSIS

1. **How do Baba and Ilanga recall their existence before the Europeans came?**
2. **What did they expect when they first heard of the arrival of Europeans? Instead, what happened to them, their relatives, and their towns?**
3. **How do you explain the difference between these two accounts?**

Source: From M. F. Smith, ed., *Baba of Karo: A Woman of the Muslim Hausa* (New York: Philosophical Library, 1955), 66–68. Edgar Canisius, *A Campaign Amongst Cannibals* (London: R. A. Everett & Co., 1903), 250–256. Used by permission of the Philosophical Library.

Cultural Responses

Africans had more contact with missionaries than with any other Europeans. Missionaries, both men and women, opened schools to teach reading, writing, and arithmetic to village children. Boys were taught crafts such as carpentry and blacksmithing, while girls learned domestic skills such as cooking, laundry, and childcare.

Mission Schools

Along with basic skills, the first generation of Africans educated in mission schools acquired Western ideas of justice and progress. Samuel Ajayi Crowther, a Yoruba rescued from slavery as a boy and educated in mission schools in Sierra Leone, went on to become an Anglican minister and, in 1864, the first African bishop. Crowther thought that Africa needed European assistance in achieving both spiritual and economic development:

> *Africa has neither knowledge nor skill . . . to bring out her vast resources for her own improvement. . . . Therefore to claim Africa for the Africans alone, is to claim for her the right of a continued ignorance. . . . For it is certain, unless help [comes] from without, a nation can never rise above its present state.*[5]

After the first generation, many of the teachers in mission schools were African, themselves the products of a mission education. They discovered that Christian ideals clashed with the reality of colonial exploitation. One convert wrote in 1911:

> *There is too much failure among all Europeans in Nyasaland. The three combined bodies—Missionaries, Government and Companies or gainers of money—do form the same rule to look upon the native with mockery eyes. . . . If we had enough power to communicate ourselves to Europe, we would advise them not to call themselves Christendom, but Europeandom. Therefore the life of the three combined bodies is altogether too cheaty, too thefty, too mockery. Instead of "Give," they say "Take away from." There is too much breakage of God's pure law.*[6]

Christian missionaries from Europe and America were not the only ones to bring religious change to Africa. In southern and Central Africa indigenous preachers adapted Christianity to African values and customs and founded new denominations known as "Ethiopian" churches.

Christianity proved successful in converting followers of traditional religions but made no inroads among Muslims. Instead, Islam, long predominant in northern and eastern Africa, spread southward as Muslim teachers established Quranic schools in the villages and founded Muslim brotherhoods. European colonialism unwittingly helped the diffusion of Islam. By building cities and increasing trade, colonial rule permitted Muslims to settle in new areas. As Islam—a universal religion without the taint of colonialism—became increasingly relevant to Africans, the number of Muslims in sub-Saharan Africa probably doubled between 1869 and 1914.

SECTION REVIEW

- In the late nineteenth century, the European powers divided Africa among themselves.
- Britain took over Egypt when it could not repay its debts.
- King Leopold II of Belgium initiated the partition of Africa by claiming the Congo.
- The discovery of gold and diamonds in southern Africa triggered clashes between British and Afrikaners, with the British emerging victorious.
- African reactions to the invasion varied widely; some collaborated, others resisted, but few benefited.
- Only Ethiopia, because it had adequate firearms, was able to defend its independence.
- Many African men lost their lands and migrated to cities and mines, leaving families behind.
- Many Africans turned to Christianity or Islam.

IMPERIALISM IN ASIA AND THE PACIFIC

Europeans had traded along the coasts of Asia and the East Indies since the early sixteenth century. By 1869 Britain already controlled most of India and Burma; Spain occupied the Philippines; and the Netherlands held large parts of the East Indies (now Indonesia). Between 1862 and 1895 France conquered Indochina (now Vietnam, Kampuchea, and Laos). Let us look at the impact of the New Imperialism on Central and Southeast Asia, Indonesia, the Philippines, and Hawaii (see Map 27.2).

Central Asia

For over seven centuries Russians had been at the mercy of the nomads of the Eurasian steppe extending from the Black Sea to Manchuria. When the nomadic tribesmen were united, as they were under the Mongol ruler Genghis Khan (r. 1206–1227), they could defeat the Russians; when they were not, the Russians moved into the steppe. This age-old ebb and flow ended when Russia acquired modern rifles and artillery.

Russian Imperialism

Between 1865 and 1876 Russian forces advanced into Central Asia. The Kazakhs, who lived east of the Caspian Sea, fought bravely but in vain. The fertile agricultural land of Kazakhstan attracted 200,000 Russian settlers. Although the governments of Tsars Alexander II (r. 1855–1881) and Alexander III (r. 1881–1894) claimed not to interfere in indigenous customs, they declared communally owned grazing lands "vacant" and turned them over to farmers from Russia. By the end of the nineteenth century the nomads were reduced to starvation. Echoing the beliefs of other European imperialists, an eminent Russian jurist declared: "International rights cannot be taken into account when dealing with semibarbarous peoples."

South of the Kazakh steppe land were deserts dotted with oases where the fabled cities of Tashkent, Bukhara, and Samarkand served the caravan trade between China and the Middle East. By the 1860s and 1870s it was fairly easy for Russian expeditions to conquer the indigenous peoples in these areas. Russia thereby acquired land suitable for cotton, along with a large and growing Muslim population. The Russians abolished slavery, built railroads to link the region with Europe, and planted hundreds of thousands of acres of cotton. Unlike the British in India, however, they did not attempt to change the customs, languages, or religious beliefs of their subjects.

Southeast Asia and Indonesia

The peoples of the Southeast Asian peninsula and the Indonesian archipelago had been in contact with outsiders—Chinese, Indians, Arabs, Europeans—for centuries. Java and the Spice Islands had long been subject to Portuguese and later Dutch domination. Until the mid-nineteenth century, however, most of the region was made up of independent kingdoms.

As in Africa, there is considerable variation in the history of different parts of the region, yet all came under intense imperialist pressure during the nineteenth century. Burma (now Myanmar), nearest India, was gradually taken over by the British in the course of the century, until the last piece was annexed in 1885. Indochina fell under French control piece by piece until it was finally subdued in 1895. Similarly, Malaya (now Malaysia) came under British rule in stages during the 1870s and 1880s. By the early 1900s the Dutch had subdued northern Sumatra. Only Siam (now Thailand) remained independent, although it lost several border provinces.

Tropical Agriculture

Despite their varied political histories, all these regions had features in common. They all had fertile soil, constant warmth, and heavy rains. Furthermore, the peoples of the region had a long tradition of intensive gardening, irrigation, and terracing. In parts of the region where the population was not very dense, Europeans found it easy to import landless laborers from China and India. Another reason for the region's wealth was the transfer of commercially valuable plants from other parts of the world. Tobacco, cinchona (sin-CHO-nah) (an antimalarial drug), manioc (an edible root crop), maize (corn), and natural rubber were brought from the Americas; sugar from India; tea from China; and coffee and oil palms from Africa. By 1914 much of the world's supply of these valuable products—in the case of rubber, almost all—came from Southeast Asia and Indonesia (see Environment and Technology: Imperialism and Tropical Ecology).

Most of the wealth of Southeast Asia and Indonesia was exported to Europe and North America. In exchange, the inhabitants of the region received two benefits from colonial rule: peace and a reliable food supply. As a result, their numbers increased at an unprecedented rate. For

Mary Evans Picture Library/The Image Works

A Rubber Plantation As bicycles and automobiles proliferated in the early twentieth century, the demand for rubber outstripped the supply available from wild rubber trees in the Amazon forest. Rubber grown on plantations in Southeast Asia came on the market from 1910 on. The rubber trees had to be tapped very carefully and on a regular schedule to obtain the latex or sap from which rubber was extracted. In this picture a woman and a boy perform this operation on a plantation in British Malaya.

MAP 27.2 **Asia in 1914** By 1914, much of Asia was claimed by colonial powers. The southern rim, from the Persian Gulf to the Pacific, was occupied by Great Britain, France, the Netherlands, and the United States. Central Asia had been incorporated into the Russian Empire. Japan, now industrialized, had joined the Western imperialist powers in expanding its territory and influence at the expense of China.

e Interactive Map

ENVIRONMENT + TECHNOLOGY

Imperialism and Tropical Ecology

Like all conquerors before them, the European imperialists of the nineteenth century exacted taxes and rents from the peoples they conquered. But they also sent botanists and agricultural experts to their tropical colonies to increase the production of commercial crops, radically changing the landscapes.

The most dramatic effects were brought about by the deliberate introduction of new crops. In the early nineteenth century tea was transferred from China to India and Ceylon. In the 1850s British and Dutch botanists smuggled seeds of the cinchona tree from the Andes to India and Java. With the seeds, the Europeans established cinchona plantations to produce quinine, used as an antimalarial drug and a flavoring for tonic water. In the 1870s British agents stole seeds of rubber trees from the Amazon rain forest and transferred them to Malaya and Sumatra.

Before these transfers, vast forests covered the highlands of India, Southeast Asia, and Indonesia, the lands where the new plants grew best. So European planters had the forests cut down and replaced with thousands of acres of commercially profitable trees and bushes, all lined up in perfect rows and tended by indigenous laborers to satisfy the demands of customers in faraway lands. The crops that poured forth from the transformed environments brought great wealth to the European planters and the imperial powers. In 1909 the British botanist John Willis justified the transformation in these terms:

> *Whether planting in the tropics will always continue to be under European management is another question, but the northern powers will not permit that the rich and as yet comparatively undeveloped countries of the tropics should be entirely wasted by being devoted merely to the supply of the food and clothing wants of their own people, when they can also supply the wants of the colder zones in so many indispensable products.*

This quotation raises important questions about trade versus self-sufficiency. If a region's economy supplies the food and clothing wants of its own people, is its output "entirely wasted"? What is the advantage of trading the products of one region (such as the tropics) for those of another (such as the colder zones)? Is this trade an obligation? Should one part of the world (such as the "northern powers") let another refuse to develop and sell its "indispensable products"? Can you think of a case where a powerful country forced a weaker one to trade?

Branch of a Cinchona Tree The bark of the cinchona tree was the source of quinine, the only antimalarial drug known before the 1940s. Quinine made it much safer for Europeans to live in the tropics.

Source: The quotation is from John Christopher Willis, *Agriculture in the Tropics: An Elementary Treatise* (Cambridge: Cambridge University Press, 1909), 38–39.

instance, the population of Java (an island the size of Pennsylvania) doubled from 16 million in 1870 to over 30 million in 1914.

Social Changes

Colonialism and the growth of population brought many social changes. Agricultural and commercial peoples gradually moved into mountainous and forested areas, displacing the earlier inhabitants who practiced hunting and gathering or shifting agriculture. The migrations of the Javanese to Borneo and Sumatra are but one example. Immigrants from China and India (see Chapter 25) changed the ethnic composition and culture of every country in the region. Thus the population of the Malay Peninsula became part Malay, part Chinese, and part Indian.

As in Africa, European missionaries attempted to spread Christianity under the colonial umbrella. Islam, however, was much more successful in gaining new converts, for it had been established in the region for centuries and people did not consider it a religion imposed on them by foreigners.

Nationalism

Education and European ideas had an impact on the political perceptions of the peoples of Southeast Asia and Indonesia. Just as important was their awareness of events in neighboring Asian countries: India, where a nationalist movement arose in the 1880s; China, where modernizers were undermining the authority of the Qing; and especially Japan, whose rapid industrialization culminated in its brilliant victory over Russia in the Russo-Japanese War (1904–1905; see Chapter 26). The spirit of a rising generation was expressed by a young Vietnamese writing soon after the Russo-Japanese War:

> *I, . . . an obscure student, having had occasion to study new books and new doctrines, have discovered in a recent history of Japan how they have been able to conquer the impotent Europeans. This is the reason why we have formed an organization. . . . We have selected from young Annamites [Vietnamese] the most energetic, with great capacities for courage, and are sending them to Japan for study. . . . Several years have passed without the French being aware of the movement. . . . Our only aim is to prepare the population for the future.*[7]

Hawaii and the Philippines, 1878–1902

By the 1890s the United States had a fast-growing population and industries that produced more manufactured goods than they could sell at home. Merchants and bankers began to look for export markets. The political mood was also expansionist, and many echoed the feelings of the naval strategist Alfred T. Mahan (mah-HAHN): "Whether they will or no, Americans must now begin to look outward. The growing production of the country requires it."

Annexation of Hawaii

Some Americans had been looking outward for quite some time, especially across the Pacific to China and Japan. In 1878 the United States obtained the harbor of Pago Pago in Samoa as a coaling and naval station, and in 1887 it secured the use of Pearl Harbor in Hawaii for the same purpose. By 1898 the United States under President William McKinley (1897–1901) had become openly imperialistic and annexed Hawaii as a steppingstone to Asia. As the United States became ever more involved in Asian affairs, Hawaii's strategic location brought an inflow of U.S. military personnel, and its fertile land caused planters to import laborers from Japan, China, and the Philippines. These immigrants soon outnumbered the native Hawaiians.

The United States Conquers the Philippines

Emilio Aguinaldo Leader of the Filipino independence movement against Spain (1895–1898). He proclaimed the independence of the Philippines in 1899, but his movement was crushed and he was captured by the United States Army in 1901.

While large parts of Asia were falling under colonial domination, the people of the Philippines were chafing under their Spanish rulers. **Emilio Aguinaldo**, leader of a secret society, rose in revolt and proclaimed a republic in 1899. The revolutionaries had a good chance of winning independence, for Spain had its hands full with a revolution in Cuba. Unfortunately for Aguinaldo and his followers, the United States declared war against Spain in April 1898 and quickly overcame Spanish forces in the Philippines and Cuba. After the Spanish defeat, President McKinley realized that a weakened Spain might lose the islands to another imperialist power. Japan, having recently defeated China in the Sino-Japanese War (1894–1895) and annexed Taiwan (see Chapter 26), was eager to expand its empire. So was Germany, which had taken over parts of New Guinea and Samoa and several Pacific archipelagoes during the 1880s. To forestall them, McKinley purchased the Philippines from Spain for $20 million.

The Filipinos were not eager to trade one master for another. For a while, Aguinaldo cooperated with the Americans in the hope of achieving full independence. When his plan was rejected, he rose up again in 1899 and proclaimed the independence of his country. In spite of protests by anti-imperialists in the United States, the U.S. government decided that its global interests outweighed the interests of the Filipino people. In rebel areas, a U.S. army of occupation tortured prisoners, burned villages and crops, and forced the inhabitants into "reconcentration camps." By the end of the insurrection in 1902, the war had cost the lives of 5,000 Americans and 200,000 Filipinos.

SECTION REVIEW

- Once it had modern firearms, Russia easily conquered and settled the countries of Central Asia.
- Britain, France, and the Netherlands turned their colonies in Southeast Asia and Indonesia into producers of tropical crops.
- The United States took over Hawaii in 1898; after four years of war, it secured the Philippines from Spain and crushed a Filipino rebellion.

Corbis

Emilio Aguinaldo In 1896, a revolt led by Emilio Aguinaldo attempted to expel Spaniards from the Philippines. When the United States purchased the Philippines from Spain two years later, the Filipino people were not consulted. Aguinaldo continued his campaign, this time against the American occupation forces, until his capture in 1901. In this picture, he appears on horseback, surrounded by some of his troops.

After the insurrection ended, the United States attempted to soften its rule with public works and economic development projects. New buildings went up in the city of Manila; roads, harbors, and railroads were built; and the Philippine economy was tied ever more closely to that of the United States. In 1907 Filipinos were allowed to elect representatives to a legislative assembly, but ultimate authority remained in the hands of a governor appointed by the president of the United States. In 1916 the Philippines were the first U.S. colony to be promised independence, a promise fulfilled thirty years later.

IMPERIALISM IN LATIN AMERICA

Nations in the Americas followed two divergent paths (see Chapter 23). In Canada and the United States manufacturing industries, powerful corporations, and wealthy financial institutions arose. Latin America and the Caribbean exported raw materials and foodstuffs and imported manufactured goods. The poverty of their people, the preferences of their elites, and the pressures of the world economy made them increasingly dependent on the industrialized countries. Their political systems saved them from outright annexation, but their natural resources made them attractive targets for manipulation by the industrial powers, including the United States, in a form of economic dependence called **free-trade imperialism**. In the larger republics of South America, the pressure was mostly financial and economic. In Central America and the Caribbean, it also included military intervention by the United States.

free-trade imperialism Economic dominance of a weaker country by a more powerful one, while maintaining the legal independence of the weaker state. In the late nineteenth century, free-trade imperialism characterized the relations between the Latin American republics, on the one hand, and Great Britain and the United States, on the other.

Railroads and the Imperialism of Free Trade

Latin America's economic potential was huge, for the region could produce many agricultural and mineral products in demand in the industrial countries. What was needed was a means of opening the interior to development. Railroads seemed the perfect answer.

Foreign merchants and bankers and Latin American landowners and politicians embraced the new technology. Starting in the 1870s, almost every country in Latin America acquired railroads, usually connecting mines or agricultural regions with the nearest port rather than linking up the different parts of the interior. All the equipment and building material came from Britain or the United States. So did the money to build the networks, the engineers who designed and maintained them, and the managers who ran them.

Argentina, a land of rich soil that produced wheat, beef, and hides, gained the longest and best-developed rail network south of the United States. By 1914, 86 percent of the railroads in Argentina were owned by British firms; 40 percent of the employees were British; and the official language of the railroads was not Spanish but English. The same was true of mining and industrial enterprises and public utilities throughout Latin America.

In many ways, the situation resembled those of India and Ireland, which also obtained rail networks in exchange for raw materials and agricultural products. The Argentine nationalist Juan Justo saw the parallel:

> *English capital has done what English armies could not do. Today our country is tributary to England . . . the gold that the English capitalists take out of Argentina or carry off in the form of products does us no more good than the Irish get from the revenues that the English lords take out of Ireland.*[8]

The difference was that the Indians and Irish had little say in the matter because they were under British rule. But in Latin America the political elites encouraged foreign companies with generous concessions as the most rapid way to modernize their countries and enrich the property owners. The majority were neither consulted nor allowed to benefit from the railroad boom.

American Expansionism and the Spanish-American War, 1898

The United States had long had interests in Cuba, the closest and richest of the Caribbean islands and a Spanish colony. American businesses had invested great sums of money in Cuba's sugar and tobacco industries, and thousands of Cubans had migrated to the United States. In 1895 the Cuban nationalist José Martí started a revolution against Spanish rule. American newspapers thrilled readers with lurid stories of Spanish atrocities; businessmen worried about their investments; and politicians demanded that the U.S. government help liberate Cuba.

On February 15, 1898, the U.S. battleship *Maine* accidentally blew up in Havana harbor, killing 266 American sailors. The U.S. government immediately blamed Spain and issued an ultimatum that the Spanish evacuate Cuba. Spain agreed to the ultimatum, but the American press and Congress were eager for war, and President McKinley did not restrain them.

The Spanish-American War was over quickly. On May 1, 1898, U.S. warships destroyed the Spanish fleet at Manila in the Philippines. Two months later the United States Navy sank the Spanish Atlantic fleet off Santiago, Cuba. By mid-August Spain was suing for peace. U.S. Secretary of State John Hay called it "a splendid little war." The United States purchased the Philippines from Spain but took over Puerto Rico and Guam as war booty. The two islands remain American possessions to this day. Cuba became an independent republic, subject to interference by the United States.

American Intervention in the Caribbean and Central America, 1901–1914

The nations of the Caribbean and Central America were small and poor, and their governments were corrupt, unstable, and often bankrupt. They seemed to offer an open invitation to foreign interference. A government would borrow money to pay for railroads, harbors, electric power, and other symbols of modernity. When it could not repay the loan, the lending banks in Europe or the United States would ask for assistance from their home governments, which sometimes threatened to intervene. To ward off European intervention, the United States sent in the marines on more than one occasion.

Presidents Theodore Roosevelt (1901–1909), William Taft (1909–1913), and Woodrow Wilson (1913–1921) felt impelled to intervene in the region, though they differed sharply on the proper policy the United States should follow toward the small nations to the south. Roosevelt

Panama Canal Ship canal cut across the isthmus of Panama by United States Army engineers; it opened in 1915. The canal greatly shortened the sea voyage between the east and west coasts of North America. The United States turned the canal over to Panama on January 1, 2000.

encouraged regimes friendly to the United States; Taft sought to influence them through loans from American banks; and the moralist Wilson tried to impose clean governments by military means.

Having "liberated" Cuba from Spain, in 1901 the United States forced the Cuban government to accept the Platt Amendment, which gave the United States the "right to intervene" to maintain order on the island. The United States used this excuse to occupy Cuba militarily from 1906 to 1909, in 1912, and again from 1917 to 1922. In all but name Cuba became an American protectorate. U.S. troops also occupied the Dominican Republic from 1904 to 1907 and again in 1916, Nicaragua and Honduras in 1912, and Haiti in 1915. They brought sanitation and material progress but no political improvements.

The United States was especially forceful in Panama, which was a province of Colombia. Here the issue was not corruption or debts but a more vital interest. When the United States acquired Hawaii and the Philippines, it recognized the need for a canal that would allow warships to move quickly between the Atlantic and Pacific Oceans. The main obstacle was Colombia, which refused to give the United States a piece of its territory. In 1903 the U.S. government supported a Panamanian rebellion against Colombia and quickly recognized the independence of Panama. In exchange, it obtained the right to build a canal and to occupy a zone 5 miles (8 kilometers) wide on either side of it. Work began in 1904, and the **Panama Canal** opened on August 15, 1914.

SECTION REVIEW

- Britain and the United States collaborated with Latin American elites to exploit the Latin American republics economically; a key factor was the expansion of railroads.
- After defeating Spain in 1898, the United States sent troops to Cuba and other Caribbean and Central American republics; through the Platt Amendment, it also claimed the right to interfere in Cuban affairs.
- The United States helped Panama secede from Colombia so that it could build the Panama Canal.

THE WORLD ECONOMY AND THE GLOBAL ENVIRONMENT

The New Imperialists were not traditional conquerors or empire builders like the Spanish conquistadors. Although their conquests were much larger (see Map 27.3), their aim was not only to extend their power over new territories and peoples but also to control both the natural world and indigenous societies and put them to work more efficiently than had ever been done before. They expressed their belief in progress and their good intentions in the clichés of the time: "the conquest of nature," "the annihilation of time and space," "the taming of the wilderness," and "our civilizing mission."

Expansion of the World Economy

AP* Exam Tip Patterns of world trade and the impact of changes in world trade are recurring topics on the AP* exam.

For centuries Europe had been a ready market for spices, sugar, silk, and other exotic or tropical products. The Industrial Revolution vastly expanded this demand. Imports of foods and stimulants such as tea, coffee, and cocoa increased substantially during the nineteenth century. The trade in industrial raw materials grew even faster. Some were the products of agriculture, such as cotton, jute for bags, and palm oil for soap and lubricants. Others were minerals such as diamonds, gold, and copper. There also were wild forest products that only later came to be cultivated: timber for buildings and railroad ties, cinchona bark, rubber for rainwear and tires, and gutta-percha (gut-tah-PER-cha) (the sap of a Southeast Asian tree) to insulate electric cables.

The growing needs of the industrial world could not be met by the traditional methods of production and transportation of the nonindustrial world. When the U.S. Civil War interrupted the export of cotton to England in the 1860s, the British turned to India and Egypt, but they found that Indian cotton was ruined by exposure to rain and dust during the long trip from the interior of the country to the harbors. To prevent the expansion of their industry from being stifled by the technological backwardness of their newly conquered territories, the imperialists made every effort to bring those territories into the mainstream of the world market.

The Transportation Revolution

One great change was in transportation. The Suez and Panama Canals cut travel time and lowered freight costs dramatically. Steamships became more numerous, and as their size increased, new, deeper harbors were needed. The Europeans also built railroads throughout the

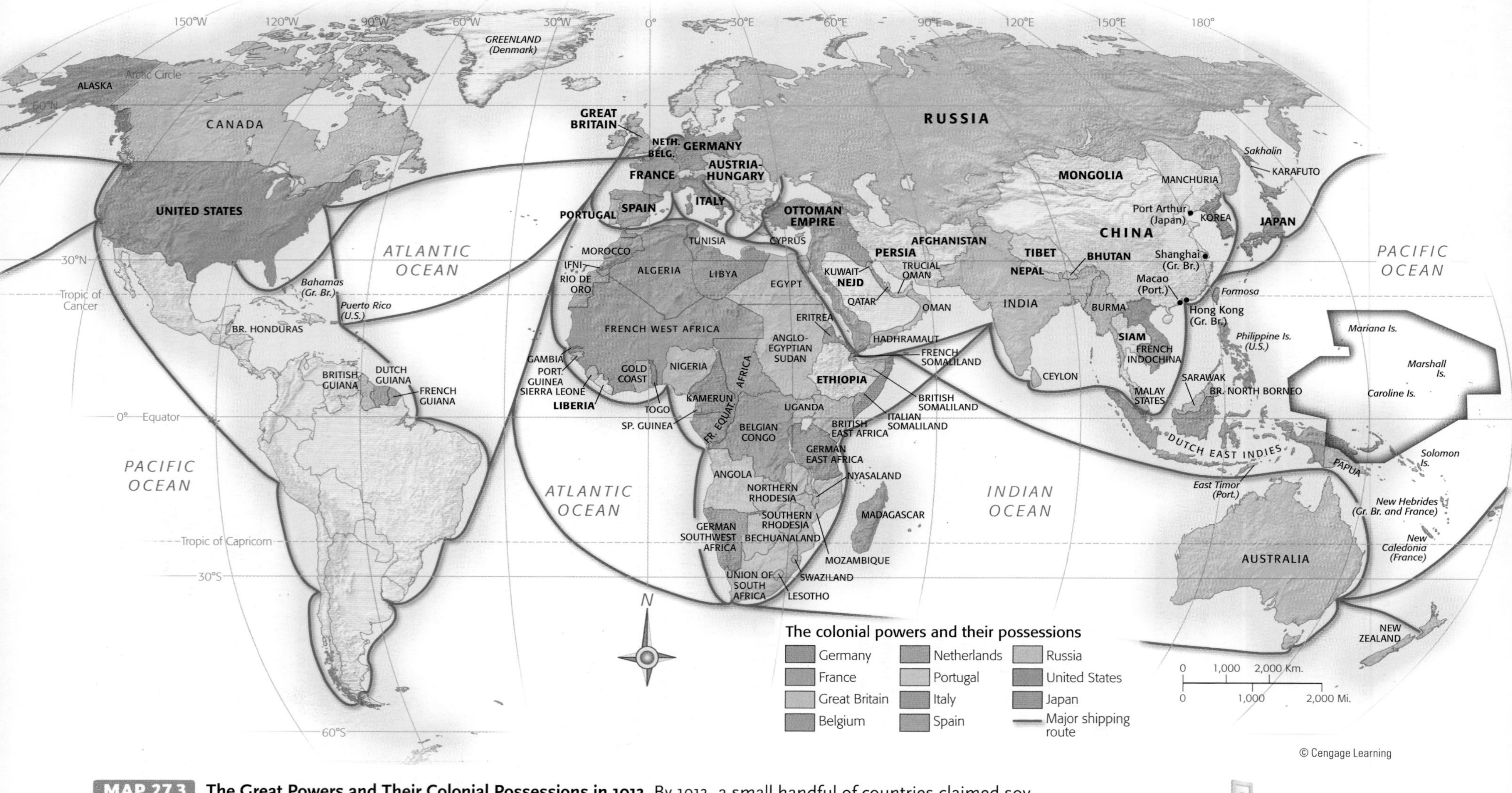

MAP 27.3 **The Great Powers and Their Colonial Possessions in 1913** By 1913, a small handful of countries claimed sovereignty over more than half the land area of the earth. Global power was closely connected with industries and a merchant marine, rather than with a large territory. This explains why Great Britain, the smallest of the great powers, possessed the largest empire.

world; India alone had 37,000 miles (nearly 60,000 kilometers) of track by 1915, almost as much as Germany or Russia. Railroads reached into the interior of Latin America, Canada, China, and Australia. In 1903 the Russians completed the Trans-Siberian Railway from Moscow to Vladivostok on the Pacific. Visionaries even made plans for railroads from Europe to India and from Egypt to South Africa.

Transformation of the Global Environment

The economic changes brought by Europeans and Americans also altered environments around the world. The British, whose craving for tea could not be satisfied with the limited exports available from China, introduced tea into Ceylon and northeastern India. In those areas and in Java, thousands of square miles of tropical rain forests were felled to make way for tea plantations.

Economic Botany

Economic botany and agricultural science were applied to every promising plant species. European botanists had long collected and classified exotic plants from around the world. In the nineteenth century they founded botanical gardens in Java, India, Mauritius (maw-REE-shuss), Ceylon, Jamaica, and other tropical colonies. These gardens not only collected local plants but also transferred commercially valuable plant species from one tropical region to another. Cinchona, tobacco, sugar, and other crops were introduced, improved, and vastly expanded in the colonies of Southeast Asia and Indonesia (see Environment and Technology: Imperialism and Tropical Ecology). Cocoa and coffee growing spread over large areas of Brazil and Africa; oil-palm plantations were established in Nigeria and the Congo Basin. After 1910, rubber, used to make waterproof garments and bicycle tires, came from plantations in Southeast Asia.

Throughout the tropics, land once covered with forests or devoted to shifting slash-and-burn agriculture was transformed into permanent farms and plantations. Even in areas not developed to export crops, growing populations put pressure on the land. In Java and India farmers felled trees to obtain arable land and firewood. They terraced hillsides, drained swamps, and dug wells.

Irrigation

Irrigation and water control transformed the dry parts of the tropics as well. British engineers in India built new irrigation canals, turning thousands of previously barren acres into well-watered, densely populated farmland. The migration of European experts spread the newest techniques of irrigation engineering around the world. By the turn of the century irrigation projects were under way wherever rivers flowed through dry lands. In Egypt and Central Asia irrigation brought more acres under cultivation in one forty-year span than in all previous history.

Railroads had voracious appetites for land and resources. They cut into mountains, spanned rivers and canyons, and covered as much land with their freight yards as whole cities had needed in previous centuries. They also consumed vast quantities of iron, timber for ties, and coal or wood for fuel. Most important of all, railroads brought people and their cities, farms, and industries to areas previously occupied by small, scattered populations.

Gardiner F. Williams/NGS Image Collection

South African Diamond Mine When diamonds were found in Kimberley, South Africa, in 1868, the discovery precipitated a rush of prospectors from Europe and America. As soon as surface deposits were exhausted, their claims were bought by large companies that could afford the heavy equipment needed to mine deep underground. By the early twentieth century, diamonds came from major industrial mines like the Premier Mine shown here.

SECTION REVIEW

- The world economy, fueled by European ideas of "progress," expanded quickly between 1860 and 1914, thanks to cheaper and faster transportation made possible with canals and railroads.
- Europeans made Latin America, Africa, and Asia into producers of raw materials and crops and into markets for industrial goods.
- Europeans studied botany and brought huge areas of land into cultivation through irrigation.
- Railroads transformed the land, and mining often polluted it.

Prospectors looking for valuable minerals opened the earth to reveal its riches. Where mines were dug deep inside the earth, the dirt and rocks brought up with the ores formed huge mounds near mine entrances. Open mines dug to obtain ores lying close to the surface created a landscape of lunar craters, and runoff from the minerals poisoned the water for miles around. Refineries that processed the ores fouled the environment with slag heaps and more toxic runoff.

The transformation of the land by human beings, a constant throughout history, accelerated sharply. Only the changes occurring since 1914 can compare with the transformation of the global environment that took place between 1869 and 1914.

CONCLUSION

The imperial powers were driven by many motives. Governments used colonies to enhance their prestige and power. Missionaries sought not only to convert native peoples but also to "civilize" their behavior. Colonizers were led by the growing demand for natural resources. The imperialists used steamships, gunboats, and improved firearms to build their empires.

The "scramble" for Africa began in the 1870s. Britain secured the Suez Canal and constructed a dam across the Nile. Elsewhere, European companies exploited rubber plantations, diamond mines, and other resources. Local reaction to colonial rule varied greatly, as traditional land use patterns were disrupted. All Africans were affected by changes in social and cultural customs.

The effects of colonialism varied throughout Asia, although in all regions the economic changes benefited the Europeans rather than the indigenous peoples. Southeast Asia's fertile soil and heavy rains made various crops, especially rubber, very profitable. In Hawaii, Americans and foreign laborers eventually outnumbered the native Hawaiians. Europeans differed in their approach to indigenous cultures and religions. Russians did not attempt to impose their customs, language, or religious beliefs on Central Asians, whereas Christian missionaries in Southeast Asia worked to spread their beliefs. Their efforts gained only limited success in lands in which Islam or Hinduism had been dominant for centuries.

Latin America had great economic potential. The construction of railroads, using equipment and funding from Britain and the United States, helped to connect the interior regions with the ports. Americans invested heavily in the sugar and tobacco industries of Cuba. The United States also supported a Panamanian rebellion against Colombia in order to build the Panama Canal.

Imperialism, both formal and informal, opened up the world to increased trade and communication. Shipping, canals, and railroads were the most visible means of globalization. Farming, mining, labor migrations, and urbanization were profoundly affected as well. In the process, natural environments were transformed as never before. Forests were replaced by plantations. Irrigation schemes opened dry lands to agriculture. And railroads and mines cut into the landscape, leaving scars and pollution.

KEY TERMS

Suez Canal p. 771
New Imperialism p. 772
Battle of Omdurman p. 774
colonialism p. 775
"scramble" for Africa p. 776
Henry Morton Stanley p. 778
King Leopold II p. 778
Savorgnan de Brazza p. 778
Berlin Conference p. 778
Afrikaners p. 779
Cecil Rhodes p. 780
Asante p. 780
Menelik p. 781
Emilio Aguinaldo p. 788
free-trade imperialism p. 789
Panama Canal p. 791

EBOOK AND WEBSITE RESOURCES

Primary Source

Convention on Free Navigation of the Suez Canal Between the European Powers and the Ottoman Empire, October 29, 1888

Interactive Maps

Map 27.1 Africa in 1878 and 1914

Map 27.2 Asia in 1914

Map 27.3 The Great Powers and Their Colonial Possessions in 1913

Plus flashcards, practice quizzes, and more. Go to: www.cengage.com/history/bullietearthpeople5e

SUGGESTED READING

Achebe, Chinua. *Things Fall Apart.* 1958. A classic novel describing the impact of colonialism in Nigerian society.

Cook, Scott B. *Colonial Encounters in the Age of High Imperialism.* 1996. A brief, well-written account of the New Imperialism.

Headrick, Daniel R. *The Tools of Empire: Technology and European Imperialism in the Nineteenth Century,* 1981; and *The Tentacles of Progress: Technology Transfer in the Age of Imperialism, 1850–1940.* 1988. Two books emphasizing the importance of technology in the conquests and the colonial era.

Healy, David. *Drive to Hegemony: The United States in the Caribbean, 1898–1917.* 1989. The best summary of "dollar diplomacy."

Hochschild, Adam. *King Leopold's Ghost: A Story of Greed, Terror, and Heroism in Colonial Africa.* 1998. A dramatic account of the conquest and exploitation of the Belgian Congo.

Hopkirk, Peter. *The Great Game: The Struggle for Empire in Central Asia.* 1994. Describes the rivalry between Russia and Great Britain.

Huttenback, Robert. *Racism and Empire: White Settlers and Colored Immigrants in the British Self-Governing Colonies, 1830–1910.* 1976. Analyzes racism and race relations in Australia, Canada, New Zealand, and South Africa.

Iriye, Akira. *Across the Pacific: An Inner History of American-East Asian Relations.* 1992. Describes American policy toward Japan and China.

Karnow, Stanley. *In Our Image: America's Empire in the Philippines.* 1989. How the United States conquered and rule the Philippines.

MacKenzie, John. *Imperialism and the Natural World.* 1990. The impact of economic development and agriculture on colonial environments.

McCracken, Donal. *Gardens of Empire: Botanical Institutions of the Victorian British Empire.* 1997. How British botanists contributed to plant transfers and commercial agriculture in the tropics.

Northrup, David. *Indentured Labor in the Age of Imperialism, 1834–1922.* 1995. How colonial enterprises imported workers from China and India to work in mines and plantations in Southeast Asia, Oceania, the Caribbean, and Africa.

Oliver, Caroline. *Western Women in Colonial Africa.* 1982. On the role of wives of colonial officials and women missionaries in the colonies.

Oliver, Roland, and Anthony Atmore. *Africa Since 1800,* new ed. 1994. A classic account of modern African history.

Vandervort, Bruce. *Wars of Imperial Conquest in Africa, 1830–1914.* 1998. A brief account of the conflicts between Europeans and Africans during the New Imperialism.

NOTES

1. *Journal Officiel* (November 29, 1869), quoted in Georges Douin, *Histoire du Règne du Khédive Ismaïl* (Rome: Reale Societá di Geografia d'Egitto, 1933), 453.
2. E. Desplaces in *Journal de l'Union des Deux Mers* (December 15, 1869), quoted ibid., 453.
3. Michael Adas, *Islamic and European Expansion* (Philadelphia: Temple University Press, 1993), 365.
4. "Correspondence and Report from His Majesty's Consul at Boma respecting the Administration of the Independent State of the Congo," *British Parliamentary Papers, Accounts and Papers, 1904* (Cd. 1933), lxii, 357.
5. Robert W. July, *A History of the African People,* 3d ed. (New York: Charles Scribner's Sons, 1980), 323.
6. George Shepperson and Thomas Price, *Independent African* (Edinburgh: University Press, 1958), 163–164, quoted in Roland Oliver and Anthony Atmore, *Africa Since 1800,* 4th ed. (Cambridge: Cambridge University Press, 1994), 150.
7. Thomas Edson Ennis, *French Policy and Development in Indochina* (Chicago: University of Chicago Press, 1936), 178, quoted in K. M. Panikkar, *Asia and Western Dominance* (New York: Collier, 1969), 167.
8. Quoted in Stanley J. Stein and Barbara H. Stein, *The Colonial Heritage of Latin America* (New York: Oxford University Press, 1970), 151.

AP* REVIEW QUESTIONS FOR CHAPTER 27

1. Which of the following would have been a motive of nineteenth-century European imperialism?
   (A) The desire to develop the industrial base of former colonies
   (B) The desire to gain control of foreign companies
   (C) The belief in the superiority of Western technology and Western culture
   (D) The desire to hem in Islam and prevent its growth in other parts of the world

2. A colony that retained its traditional government, even a monarch, but had a European "resident" or "consul-general" to "advise" it was a
   (A) province.
   (B) enclave.
   (C) crown colony.
   (D) protectorate.

3. In the early stages of European and American colonial expansion,
   (A) European and American women were seldom part of the settlement.
   (B) westerners had to teach people how to trade.
   (C) taxes were always kept low to avoid rebellion.
   (D) missionaries were always the first ones to arrive.

4. Unlike West Africa, equatorial Africa in the nineteenth century
   (A) readily accepted the Europeans as colonizers.
   (B) had not developed any sort of trade network and had little to trade.
   (C) was governed directly by the European nations that colonized the region.
   (D) was of little interest to the European colonial powers.

5. In South Africa, the British attempt to take control of Transvaal and the Orange Free State
   (A) succeeded only when malaria wiped out the resident population.
   (B) met with support from the native tribes.
   (C) led to the South African War.
   (D) encouraged farmers to settle in the region.

6. One of the only African kingdoms to defeat a European attempt to colonize it was
   (A) Liberia.
   (B) Senegal.
   (C) Congo.
   (D) Ethiopia.

7. One common way of recruiting workers in African colonies was through
   (A) the use of slaves.
   (B) the use of a variety of taxes, which forced the Africans to work for wages.
   (C) emigration from European nations with too many people.
   (D) the confiscation of land from those who refused to work on government projects.

8. Particularly in Southeast Asia, areas were coveted as colonies because
   (A) they were close to China.
   (B) they had good mineral deposits.
   (C) commercially valuable plants could be grown there.
   (D) indigenous populations had been weakened by disease.

9. One reason for American expansion in the Pacific was
   (A) the desire to prevent the British from controlling the Pacific Ocean trade routes.
   (B) the U.S. demand for high-phosphate fertilizers derived for guano.
   (C) a European depression that had caused a decline in the demand for American goods in Europe.
   (D) the fact that U.S. industries were producing more goods than they could sell at home.

10. In the late nineteenth and early twentieth centuries, European nations invested in Latin America, but they refrained from territorial acquisitions because
    (A) they had exhausted their funds for building new colonies.
    (B) as former colonial powers, they had good relations with Latin America.
    (C) Latin America was not politically stable.
    (D) they feared the United States would invoke the Monroe Doctrine.

11. One good example of U.S. imperialism in Latin America would be
    (A) U.S. intervention in Panama.
    (B) the United States loaning money to Haiti.
    (C) U.S. protection of Mexico against a French invasion.
    (D) U.S. government loans to Latin American nations wishing to build a modern military force.

12. One result of imperialism is that it
    (A) increased population in remote and unpopulated regions of the world.
    (B) opened the world to increased trade and communication.
    (C) led to decreased warfare.
    (D) gave non-Europeans more wealth.

CHAPTER 28

CHAPTER OUTLINE

Imperial War Museum/The Art Archive

The Western Front in World War I In a landscape ravaged by artillery fire, two soldiers dash for cover amid shell holes and the charred remains of a forest.

Visit the website and ebook for additional study materials and interactive tools: www.cengage.com/history/bullietearthpeople5e

The Crisis of the Imperial Order, 1900–1929

- What led to the outbreak of the First World War?
- How did the war lead to revolution in Russia?
- What role did the war play in eroding European dominance in the world?
- Why did China and Japan follow such divergent paths in this period?
- How did the Middle East change as a result of the war?
- How did European and North American society and technology change in the aftermath of the war?

On June 28, 1914, Archduke Franz Ferdinand, heir to the throne of Austria-Hungary, was riding in an open carriage through Sarajevo, a city Austria had annexed six years earlier. When the carriage stopped momentarily, Gavrilo Princip, member of a pro-Serbian conspiracy, fired his pistol twice, killing the archduke and his wife.

Those shots ignited a global conflict. All previous wars had caused death and destruction, but they were also marked by heroism and glory. In this new war, four years of bitter fighting produced no victories, no gains, and no glory, only death for millions of soldiers. The war became global as the Ottoman Empire fought against Britain and Japan attacked German positions in China. France and Britain involved their empires in the war and brought Africans, Indians, Australians, and Canadians to Europe to fight and labor on the front lines. Finally, in 1917, the United States entered the fray.

The next three chapters tell a story of violence and hope. In this chapter, we will look at the causes of war between the great powers, the consequences of that conflict in Europe, the Middle East, and Russia, and the upheavals in China and Japan. At the same time, we will review the technological changes that made war more dangerous, yet also allowed far more people to live healthier, more comfortable, and more interesting lives than ever before.

ORIGINS OF THE CRISIS IN EUROPE AND THE MIDDLE EAST

When the twentieth century opened, the world seemed firmly under the control of the great powers (see Chapter 26). The first decade of the twentieth century was a period of relative peace and economic growth in most of the world. Several new technologies—airplanes, automobiles, radio, and cinema—aroused much excitement. The great powers consolidated their colonial conquests of the previous decades, and their alliances were evenly matched. The only international war of the period, the Russo-Japanese War (1904–1905), ended quickly with a decisive Japanese victory.

However, two major changes undermined the apparent stability of the world. In Europe, tensions mounted as Germany, with its growing industrial and military might, challenged

Britain at sea and France in Morocco. The Ottoman Empire grew weaker, leaving a dangerous power vacuum. The resulting chaos in the Balkans gradually drew the European powers into a web of hostilities.

The Ottoman Empire and Balkans

From the fifteenth to the nineteenth centuries the Ottoman Empire was one of the most powerful states. By the late nineteenth century, however, it had fallen behind economically, technologically, and militarily. Europeans referred to it as the "sick man of Europe."

As the Ottoman Empire weakened, it began losing provinces closest to Europe: Macedonia in 1902–1903, Bosnia in 1908, Crete in 1909, Albania in 1910. In 1912 Italy conquered Libya, the Ottomans' last foothold in Africa. In 1912–1913 Serbia, Bulgaria, Romania, and Greece chased the Turks out of Europe, except for a small enclave around Constantinople.

The Young Turks

In reaction, the Turks began to assert themselves against rebellious minorities and meddling foreigners. Many officers in the army, the most Europeanized segment of Turkish society, blamed Sultan Abdul Hamid II (r. 1876–1909) for the decline of the empire. A group known as "Young Turks" plotted to force a constitution on the sultan. They alienated other anti-Ottoman groups by advocating centralized rule and the Turkification of ethnic minorities.

In 1909 the parliament, dominated by Young Turks, overthrew Abdul Hamid. The new regime began to reform the police, the bureaucracy, and the educational system. At the same time, it cracked down on Greek and Armenian minorities. Galvanized by their defeat in the Balkan Wars, the Turks hired a German general to modernize their armed forces. The dangerous mixture of modern armies and nationalism was not limited to the Ottoman Empire, however.

Nationalism, Alliances, and Military Strategy

The assassination of Franz Ferdinand triggered a chain of events over which military and political leaders lost control. The escalation from assassination to global war had causes that went back many years. One was nationalism, which bound citizens to their ethnic group and led them, when called upon, to kill people they viewed as enemies. Another was the system of alliances and military plans that the great powers had devised to protect themselves from their rivals. A third was Germany's yearning to dominate Europe.

Nationalism

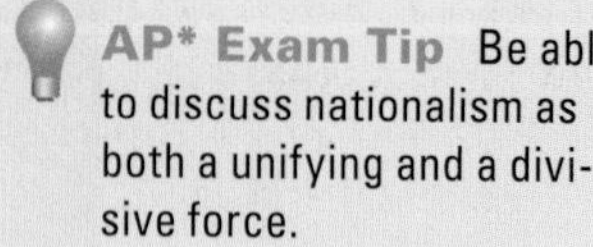
AP* Exam Tip Be able to discuss nationalism as both a unifying and a divisive force.

Nationalism united the citizens of France, Britain, and Germany behind their respective governments and gave them tremendous cohesion and strength of purpose. Only the most powerful feelings could inspire millions of men to march into battle and could sustain civilian populations through years of hardship.

Nationalism could also be a dividing force. The large but fragile multinational Russian, Austro-Hungarian, and Ottoman Empires contained numerous ethnic and religious minorities. Having repressed the other minorities for centuries, the governments could never count on their full support. The very existence of an independent Serbia threatened Austria-Hungary by stirring up the hopes and resentments of its Slavic populations.

Imbued with nationalism, most people viewed war as a crusade for liberty or as long-overdue revenge for past injustices. During the nineteenth century, as memories of the misery and carnage caused by the Napoleonic Wars faded, revulsion against war gradually weakened. The Crimean War of 1853–1856 and the Franco-Prussian War of 1871 had caused few casualties or long-term consequences. And in the wars of the New Imperialism (see Chapter 27), Europeans almost always had been victorious at a small cost in money and manpower.

What turned an incident in the Balkans into a conflict involving all the great powers was the system of alliances. At the center of Europe stood Germany, the most heavily industrialized country in Europe. Its army was the best trained and equipped, and it challenged Great Britain's naval supremacy by building "dreadnoughts"—heavily armed battleships. In 1882 it joined Austria-Hungary and Italy in the Triple Alliance, while France allied itself with Russia. In 1904 Britain and France reached an Entente (on-TONT) ("understanding"), joined by Russia in 1907. Europe was thus divided into two blocs of roughly equal power (see Map 28.1).

The alliance system was cursed by inflexible military planning. In 1914 western and central Europe had highly developed railroad networks but very few motor vehicles, and European

CHRONOLOGY

	Europe and North America	Middle East	East Asia
1900			1900 Boxer uprising in China
	1904 British-French Entente		1904–1905 Russo-Japanese War
	1907 British-Russian Entente	1909 Young Turks overthrow Sultan Abdul Hamid	
1910	1912–1913 Balkan Wars	1912 Italy conquers Libya, last Ottoman territory in Africa	1911 Chinese revolutionaries led by Sun Yat-sen overthrow Qing dynasty
	1914 Assassination of Archduke Franz Ferdinand sparks World War I	1915 British defeat at Gallipoli	1915 Japan presents Twenty-One Demands to China
	1916 Battles of Verdun and the Somme	1916 Arab Revolt in Arabia	
	1917 Russian Revolutions; United States enters the war	1917 Balfour Declaration	
	1918 Armistice ends World War I		
	1918–1921 Civil war in Russia		
	1919 Treaty of Versailles	1919–1922 War between Turkey and Greece	1919 May Fourth Movement in China
1920	1920 First commercial radio broadcast (United States)	1922 Egypt nominally independent	
	1923–1928 New Economic Policy in Russia	1923 Mustafa Kemal proclaims Turkey a republic	
	1927 Charles Lindbergh flies alone across the Atlantic		1927 Guomindang forces occupy Shanghai and expel Communists

armies had grown to include millions of soldiers and reservists. To mobilize these forces and transport them to battle would require thousands of trains running on precise schedules. Once under way, a country's mobilization could not be canceled or postponed without causing chaos.

In the years before World War I, military planners in France and Germany had worked out elaborate railroad timetables to mobilize their respective armies in a few days. Russia, a large country with an underdeveloped rail system, needed several weeks to mobilize its forces. Britain, with a tiny volunteer army, had no mobilization plans, and German planners believed that the British would stay out of a war on the European continent. So that Germany could avoid having to fight France and Russia at the same time, German war planners expected to defeat France in a matter of days, then transport the entire army across Germany to the Russian border by train before Russia could fully mobilize.

The War Begins

On July 28, Austria-Hungary declared war on Serbia. The declaration of war triggered the general mobilization plans of Russia, France, and Germany. On July 29 the Russian government ordered general mobilization to force Austria to back down. On August 1 France ordered general mobilization. Minutes later Germany did likewise. Because of the rigid railroad timetables, war was now automatic.

The German plan was to wheel around through neutral Belgium and into northwestern France. The German General Staff expected France to capitulate before the British could get involved. But on August 3, when German troops entered Belgium, Britain demanded their withdrawal. When Germany refused, Britain declared war on Germany.

SECTION REVIEW

- As the Ottoman Empire declined, nationalists calling themselves Young Turks tried to create a new Turkish nation.
- Nationalism, competing alliances, and inflexible military plans based on railroads turned an assassination into a cause for war.

MAP 28.1 Europe in 1913 On the eve of World War I, Europe was divided between two great alliance systems—the Triple Alliance (Germany, Austria-Hungary, and Italy) and the Entente (France, Great Britain, and Russia)—and their respective colonial empires. These alliances were not stable. When war broke out, the Triple Alliance lost Italy but gained the Ottoman Empire.

e Interactive Map

THE "GREAT WAR" AND THE RUSSIAN REVOLUTIONS, 1914–1918

Throughout Europe, people greeted the outbreak of war with parades and flags, expecting a quick victory. German troops marched off to the front shouting "To Paris!" Spectators in France encouraged marching French troops with shouts of "Send me the Kaiser's moustache!" The German sociologist Max Weber wrote: "This war, with all its ghastliness, is nevertheless grand and wonderful. It is worth experiencing."[1] When the war began, very few imagined that their side might not win. No one foresaw that everyone would lose.

Stalemate, 1914–1917

The war that erupted in 1914 was known as the "Great War" until the 1940s, when a far greater one overshadowed it. Its form came as a surprise to all belligerents, from the generals on down. In the classic battles that every officer studied, the advantage always went to the fastest-moving army led by the boldest general. In 1914 the generals' carefully drawn plans went awry from the start. Believing that a spirited attack would always prevail, French generals hurled their troops, dressed in bright blue-and-red uniforms, against the well-defended German border and suffered a crushing defeat. In battle after battle the much larger German armies defeated the French and the British. By early September the Germans held Belgium and northern France and were fast approaching Paris.

German victory seemed assured. But German troops, who had marched and fought for a month, were exhausted, and their generals wavered. A gap opened between two German armies along the Marne River, into which General Joseph Joffre moved France's last reserves. At the Battle of the Marne (September 5–12, 1914), the Germans were thrown back several miles.

Trench Warfare

Western Front A line of trenches and fortifications in World War I that stretched without a break from Switzerland to the North Sea. Scene of most of the fighting between Germany, on the one hand, and France and Britain, on the other.

During the next month, both sides spread out until they formed an unbroken line extending over 300 miles (some 500 kilometers) from the North Sea to the border of Switzerland. All along this **Western Front**, the opposing troops prepared their defenses. Their most potent weapons were machine guns, which provided an almost impenetrable defense against advancing infantry but were useless for the offensive because they were too heavy for one man to carry and took too much time to set up.

To escape the deadly streams of bullets, soldiers dug holes in the ground, connected the holes to form shallow trenches, then dug communications trenches to the rear. Within weeks, the battlefields were scarred by lines of trenches several feet deep, their tops protected by sandbags and their floors covered with planks. Trenches were nothing new. What was extraordinary was that the trenches along the entire Western Front were connected, leaving no gaps through which armies could advance (see Map 28.2). How, then, could either side ever hope to win?

For four years, generals on each side again and again ordered their troops to attack. In battle after battle, thousands of young men on one side climbed out of their trenches, raced across the open fields, and were mowed down by enemy machine-gun fire. Hoping to destroy the machine guns, the attacking force would saturate the entrenched enemy lines with artillery barrages. But this tactic alerted the defenders to an impending attack and allowed them to rush in reinforcements and set up new machine guns.

The year 1916 saw the bloodiest and most futile battles of the war. The Germans attacked French forts at Verdun, losing 281,000 men and causing 315,000 French casualties. In retaliation, the British attacked the Germans at the Somme River and suffered 420,000 casualties—60,000 on the first day alone—while the Germans lost 450,000 and the French 200,000.

Warfare had never been waged this way before. It was mass slaughter in a moonscape of mud, steel, and flesh. Both sides attacked and defended, but neither side could win, for the armies were stalemated by trenches and machine guns. During four years of the bloodiest fighting the world had ever seen, the Western Front moved no more than a few miles one way or another.

The War at Sea

At sea, the war was just as inconclusive. As soon as war broke out, the British cut the German overseas telegraph cables, blockaded the coasts of Germany and Austria-Hungary, and set out to capture or sink all enemy ships still at sea. The German High Seas Fleet, built at enormous cost, seldom left port. Only once, in May 1916, did it confront the British Grand Fleet. At the Battle of Jutland, off the coast of Denmark, the two fleets lost roughly equal numbers of ships, and the Germans escaped back to their harbors.

In early 1915, in retaliation for the British naval blockade, Germany announced a blockade of Britain by submarines. German submarines attacked every vessel they could. One of their victims was the British ocean liner *Lusitania*. The death toll from that attack was 1,198 people, 139 of them Americans. When the United States protested, Germany ceased its submarine campaign, hoping to keep America neutral.

Airplanes were used for reconnaissance and engaged in spectacular but inconsequential dogfights above the trenches. Poison gas, introduced on the Western Front in 1915, killed and wounded attacking soldiers as well as their intended victims, adding to the horror of battle. Primitive tanks aided, but did not cause, the collapse of the German army in the last weeks of the war. Although these weapons were of limited effectiveness in World War I, they offered an insight into the future of warfare.

MAP 28.2 **The First World War in Europe** After an initial surge through Belgium into northern France, the German offensive bogged down for four years along the Western Front. To the East, the German armies conquered a large part of Russia during 1917 and early 1918. Despite spectacular victories in the east, Germany lost the war because its armies collapsed along the strategically important Western Front.

e Interactive Map

Imperial War Museum/The Art Archive

Women in World War I Women played a more important role in World War I than in previous wars. As the armies drafted millions of men, employers hired women for essential war work. This poster extolls the importance of women workers in supplying munitions.

The Home Front and the War Economy

Trench-bound armies demanded ever more weapons, ammunition, and food, so civilians had to work harder, eat less, and pay higher taxes. Textiles, coal, meat, fats, and imported products such as tea and sugar were strictly rationed. Governments gradually imposed stringent controls over all aspects of their economies.

The war economy transformed civilian life. In France and Britain food rations were allocated according to need, improving nutrition among the poor. Unemployment vanished. Thousands of Africans, Indians, and Chinese were recruited for heavy labor in Europe. Employers hired women to fill jobs vacated by men off to war. Some women became streetcar drivers, mail carriers, and police officers. Others found work in the burgeoning government bureaucracies. Many joined auxiliary military services as doctors, nurses, mechanics, and ambulance drivers; after 1917, as the war took its toll of young men, the British government established women's auxiliary units for the army, navy, and air force. These positions gave thousands of women a sense of participation in the war effort and a taste of personal and financial independence.

German civilians paid an especially high price for the war, for the British naval blockade severed their overseas trade. Wheat flour disappeared, replaced first by rye, then by potatoes and turnips, then by acorns and chestnuts, and finally by sawdust. After the failure of the potato crop in 1916 came the "turnip winter," when people had to survive on 1,000 calories per day, half the normal amount that an active adult needed. Women, children, and the elderly were especially hard hit. Soldiers at the front raided enemy lines to scavenge food.

Africa in the War

AP* Exam Tip Be prepared to explain the globalization of war in the twentieth century.

The war also brought hardships to Europe's African colonies. When the war began, the British and French overran German Togo on the West African coast. The much larger German colonies of Southwest Africa and German Cameroon were conquered in 1915. In German East Africa, the Germans remained undefeated until the end of the war. The Europeans requisitioned foodstuffs, imposed heavy taxes, and forced Africans to grow export crops and sell them at low prices. As Europeans stationed in Africa joined the war, the combination of increased demands on Africans and fewer European officials led to uprisings that lasted for several years. Over a million Africans served in the various armies, and perhaps three times that number were drafted as porters to carry army equipment. Faced with a shortage of young Frenchmen, France drafted Africans into its army, where many fought side by side with Europeans.

The United States

One country grew rich during the war: the United States. For two and a half years the United States stayed technically neutral but did a roaring business supplying France and Britain. When the United States entered the war in 1917, businesses engaging in war production made spectacular profits. Civilians were exhorted to help the war effort by investing their savings in war bonds and growing food in backyard "victory gardens." Employment opportunities created by the war played a major role in the migration of African Americans from the rural south to the cities of the north.

PRIMARY SOURCE: Letter from Turkey, Summer 1915 Read an eyewitness account of the Armenian genocide, by an American missionary from Massachusetts.

The Ottoman Empire at War

On August 2, 1914, the Turks signed a secret alliance with Germany. In November they joined the fighting, hoping to gain land at Russia's expense. During the campaign in the Caucasus the Turks expelled the Armenians, whom they suspected of being pro-Russian, from their homelands in eastern Anatolia. During the forced march across the mountains in the winter, hundreds of thousands died of hunger and exposure.

Gallipoli and the Arab Revolt

Faisal Arab prince, leader of the Arab Revolt in World War I. The British made him king of Iraq in 1921, and he reigned under British protection until 1933.

The Turks also closed the Dardanelles, the strait between the Mediterranean and Black Seas (see Map 28.2). Seeing little hope of victory on the Western Front, Britain tried to open the Dardanelles by landing troops on the nearby Gallipoli Peninsula in 1915. Turkish troops pushed the invaders back into the sea. The British then promised the emir (prince) of Mecca, Hussein ibn Ali, a kingdom of his own if he would lead an Arab revolt against the Turks. In 1916 Hussein rose up and was proclaimed king of Hejaz (hee-JAHZ) (western Arabia). His son **Faisal** (FIE-sahl) then led an Arab army in support of the British advance from Egypt into Palestine and Syria. The Arab Revolt of 1916 did not affect the struggle in Europe, but it did contribute to the defeat of the Ottoman Empire.

Britain and the Jewish National Homeland

Theodore Herzl Austrian journalist and founder of the Zionist movement urging the creation of a Jewish national homeland in Palestine.

The British made promises to Jews as well as Arabs. For centuries, Jewish minorities in eastern and central Europe had developed a thriving culture despite frequent persecutions. By the early twentieth century a nationalist movement called Zionism, led by **Theodore Herzl**, arose among those who wanted to return to their ancestral homeland in Palestine. The concept of a Jewish homeland appealed to many Europeans as a humanitarian solution to the problem of anti-Semitism.

e **PRIMARY SOURCE: The Balfour Declaration** Learn which questions were considered—and which were ignored—as Britain prepared to support the Zionist movement.

By 1917 Chaim Weizmann (hi-um VITES-mun), leader of the British Zionists, had persuaded several British politicians that a Jewish homeland in Palestine should be carved out of the Ottoman Empire and placed under British protection, thereby strengthening the Allied cause. In November, as British armies were advancing on Jerusalem, Foreign Secretary Sir Arthur Balfour wrote:

> *His Majesty's Government view with favor the establishment in Palestine of a national home for the Jewish people and will use their best endeavours to facilitate the achievement of that object, it being clearly understood that nothing shall be done which may prejudice the civil and religious rights of existing non-Jewish communities in Palestine.*[2]

Balfour Declaration Statement issued by Britain's Foreign Secretary Arthur Balfour in 1917 favoring the establishment of a Jewish national homeland in Palestine.

The British did not foresee that this statement, known as the **Balfour Declaration**, would lead to conflicts between Palestinians and Jewish settlers.

Double Revolution in Russia

At the beginning of the war Russia had the largest army in the world, but its generals were incompetent, supplies were lacking, and soldiers were poorly trained and equipped. In August 1914 two Russian armies invaded eastern Germany but were thrown back.

In 1916, after a string of defeats, the Russian army ran out of ammunition and other essential supplies. Soldiers were ordered into battle unarmed and told to pick up the rifles of fallen comrades. Railroads broke down for lack of fuel and parts, and crops rotted in the fields. Civilians faced shortages and widespread hunger. In the cities food and fuel became scarce. During the bitterly cold winter of 1916–1917 factory workers and housewives had to line up in front of grocery stores before dawn to get food. The court of Tsar Nicholas II, however, remained as extravagant and corrupt as ever.

Bolsheviks Radical Marxist political party founded by Vladimir Lenin in 1903. Under Lenin's leadership, the Bolsheviks seized power in November 1917 during the Russian Revolution.

In early March 1917 (February by the old Russian calendar), food ran out in Petrograd (St. Petersburg), the capital. Women staged mass demonstrations, and soldiers mutinied and joined striking workers to form soviets (councils) to take over factories and barracks. A few days later the tsar abdicated, and leaders of the parliamentary parties, led by Alexander Kerensky, formed a Provisional Government. Thus began what Russians called the "February Revolution."

Lenin and the Bolsheviks

Vladimir Lenin Leader of the Bolshevik (later Communist) Party. He lived in exile in Switzerland until 1917, then returned to Russia to lead the Bolsheviks to victory during the Russian Revolution and the civil war that followed.

Revolutionaries formerly hunted by the tsar's police came out of hiding. Most numerous were the Social Revolutionaries, who advocated the redistribution of land to the peasants. The Mensheviks advocated electoral politics and reform in the tradition of European socialists and had a large following among intellectuals and factory workers. The **Bolsheviks**, their rivals, were a small but tightly disciplined group of radicals obedient to the will of their leader, **Vladimir Lenin** (1870–1924).

Lenin, the son of a government official, became a revolutionary in his teens when his older brother was executed for plotting to kill the tsar. He spent years in exile, first in Siberia and later in Switzerland, where he devoted his full attention to organizing his followers. His goal was to create a party that would lead the revolution rather than wait for it. He explained: "The will of a class is sometimes fulfilled by a dictator. . . . Soviet socialist democracy is not in the least incompatible with individual rule and dictatorship."[3]

Woodrow Wilson President of the United States (1913–1921) and the leading figure at the Paris Peace Conference of 1919. He was unable to persuade the U.S. Congress to ratify the Treaty of Versailles or join the League of Nations.

In early April 1917 the German government, hoping to destabilize Russia, allowed Lenin to travel from Switzerland to Russia in a sealed railway car. As soon as he arrived in Petrograd, he announced his program: immediate peace, all power to the soviets, and transfers of land to the peasants and factories to the workers. This plan proved immensely popular among soldiers and workers exhausted by the war.

The next few months witnessed a tug-of-war between the Provisional Government and the various revolutionary factions in Petrograd. When Kerensky ordered another offensive against the Germans, Russian soldiers began to desert by the hundreds of thousands, throwing away their rifles and walking back to their villages. As the Germans advanced, the government lost the little support it had.

The October Revolution

Meanwhile, the Bolsheviks were gaining support among the workers of Petrograd and the soldiers and sailors stationed there. On November 6, 1917 (October 24 in the Russian calendar), they rose up and took over the city, calling their action the "October Revolution." Their sudden move surprised rival revolutionary groups that believed that a "socialist" revolution could happen only after many years of "bourgeois" rule. Lenin, more interested in power than in the fine points of Marxist doctrine, overthrew the Provisional Government and arrested Mensheviks, Social Revolutionaries, and other rivals.

Fourteen Points A peace program presented to the U.S. Congress by President Woodrow Wilson in January 1918. It called for the evacuation of German-occupied lands, the drawing of borders and the settling of territorial disputes by the self-determination of the affected populations, and the founding of an association of nations to preserve the peace and guarantee their territorial integrity. It was rejected by Germany, but it made Wilson the moral leader of the Allies in the last year of World War I.

Seizing Petrograd was only the first step, for the rest of Russia was in chaos. The Bolsheviks nationalized all private land and ordered the peasants to hand over their crops without compensation. The peasants, having seized their landlords' estates, resisted. In the cities the Bolsheviks took over the factories and drafted the workers into compulsory labor brigades. To enforce his rule Lenin created the Cheka, a secret police force with powers to arrest and execute opponents.

The Bolsheviks also sued for peace with Germany and Austria-Hungary. By the Treaty of Brest-Litovsk, signed on March 3, 1918, Russia lost territories containing a third of its population and wealth. Poland, Finland, and the Baltic states (Estonia, Latvia, and Lithuania) became independent republics. Russian colonies in Central Asia and the Caucasus broke away temporarily.

The End of the War in Western Europe, 1917–1918

Like many Americans, President **Woodrow Wilson** wanted to stay out of the European conflict. For nearly three years he kept the United States neutral and tried to persuade the belligerents to compromise. But in late 1916 German leaders decided to starve the British into submission by using submarines to sink ships carrying food supplies to Great Britain. The Germans knew that unrestricted submarine warfare was likely to bring the United States into the war, but they were willing to gamble that Britain and France would collapse before the United States could send enough troops to help them.

The submarine campaign resumed on February 1, 1917, and the German gamble failed. The British organized their merchant ships into convoys protected by destroyers, and on April 6 President Wilson asked the United States Congress to declare war on Germany.

In January 1918, President Wilson presented his **Fourteen Points**, a peace plan that called for the German evacuation of occupied lands, the settling of territorial disputes by the decisions of the local populations, and the formation of an association of nations to guarantee the independence and territorial integrity of all states. In response, General Erich von Ludendorff launched a series of surprise attacks that pushed to within 40 miles (64 kilometers)

SECTION REVIEW

- Europeans greeted the outbreak of war with joy.
- After a month-long German advance into Belgium and France, armies got bogged down in a line of trenches along the Western Front.
- Huge battles cost tens of thousands of casualties but did not bring victory.
- On the home fronts, civilians suffered shortages and women entered the work force, while the United States grew richer.
- The entry of the Ottoman Empire into the war did not tip the balance.
- Great Britain promised Jews a "national homeland" in Palestine.
- As Russia weakened, Lenin's Bolsheviks seized power in November 1917.
- In 1917 the United States entered the war on the Allied side, and Germany began to retreat.
- The war ended on November 11, 1918, with the defeat of Germany.

of Paris, but victory eluded him. Meanwhile, every month brought another 250,000 American troops to the front. In August the Allies counterattacked, and the Germans began a retreat that could not be halted.

In late October Ludendorff resigned, and sailors in the German fleet mutinied. Two weeks later, a new German government signed an armistice. At 11 A.M. on November 11, the guns on the Western Front went silent.

PEACE AND DISLOCATION IN EUROPE, 1919–1929

The Great War lasted four years. Millions of people had died or been disabled; political tensions and resentments lingered; and national economies remained depressed until the mid-1920s. In the late 1920s peace and prosperity finally seemed assured, but this hope proved to be illusory.

The Impact of the War

Between 8 million and 10 million people died in the war, almost all of them young men. Among the dead were about 2 million Germans, 1.7 million Russians, and 1.7 million Frenchmen. Austria-Hungary lost 1.5 million, the British Empire a million, Italy 460,000, and the United States 115,000. Perhaps twice that many returned home wounded, gassed, or shell-shocked, many of them injured for life.

Refugees and Immigrants

War and revolution forced almost 2 million Russians, 750,000 Germans, and 400,000 Hungarians to flee their homes. War also led to the expulsion of hundreds of thousands of Greeks from Anatolia and Turks from Greece. Many refugees found shelter in France, which welcomed 1.5 million people to bolster its declining population. About 800,000 immigrants reached the United States before immigration laws passed in 1921 and 1924 closed the door to eastern and southern Europeans. Canada, Australia, and New Zealand adopted similar restrictions on immigration. The Latin American republics welcomed European refugees, but their poverty discouraged potential immigrants.

The Flu Epidemic

One unexpected byproduct of the war was the great influenza epidemic of 1918–1919, which started among soldiers heading for the Western Front. This virulent strain infected almost everyone on earth and killed one person in every forty. Half a million Americans perished in the epidemic—five times as many as died in the war. Worldwide, some 20 million people died.

Environmental Damage

The war also caused serious damage to the environment. No place was ever so completely devastated as the scar across France and Belgium known as the Western Front. The fighting ravaged forests and demolished towns. The earth was gouged by trenches, pitted with craters, and littered with ammunition, broken weapons, chunks of concrete, and the bones of countless soldiers. After the war, it took a decade to clear away the debris, rebuild the towns, and create dozens of military cemeteries with neat rows of crosses stretching for miles.

The Peace Treaties

In early 1919 delegates of the victorious powers met in Paris. The defeated powers were kept out until the treaties were ready for signing. Russia was not invited.

From the start, three men dominated the Paris Peace Conference: U.S. president Wilson, British prime minister David Lloyd George, and French premier Georges Clemenceau (zhorzh cluh-mon-SO). They ignored the Italians, who had joined the Allies in 1915. They paid even less attention to the delegates of smaller European nations. They rejected the Japanese proposal that all races be treated equally. They ignored the Pan-African Congress organized by the African American W. E. B. Du Bois to call attention to the concerns of African peoples around the world. They also ignored the ten thousand other delegates of various nationalities that did not represent sovereign states—the Arab leader Faisal, the Zionist Chaim Weizmann, and several Armenian delegations—who came to Paris to lobby for their causes. They were, in the words of Britain's Foreign Secretary Balfour, "three all-powerful, all-ignorant men, sitting there and carving up continents"[4] (see Map 28.3).

The League of Nations

Wilson, a high-minded idealist, wanted to apply the principle of self-determination to European affairs, by which he meant creating nations that reflected ethnic or linguistic divisions. He

League of Nations International organization founded in 1919 to promote world peace and cooperation but greatly weakened by the refusal of the United States to join. It proved ineffectual in stopping aggression by Italy, Japan, and Germany in the 1930s, and it was superseded by the United Nations in 1945.

proposed a **League of Nations**, a world organization to safeguard the peace and foster international cooperation. His idealism clashed with the more hardheaded and self-serving nationalism of the Europeans. Lloyd George insisted that Germany pay a heavy indemnity. Clemenceau wanted Germany to return Alsace and Lorraine, provinces of France before 1871.

The result was a series of compromises that satisfied no one. The European powers formed a League of Nations, but the United States Congress refused to let the United States join. France recovered Alsace and Lorraine but had to content itself with vague promises of British and American protection if Germany ever rebuilt its army. Britain acquired new territories in Africa and the Middle East but was greatly weakened by human losses and the disruption of its trade.

The Treaty of Versailles

PRIMARY SOURCE: Comments of the German Delegation to the Paris Peace Conference on the Conditions of Peace, October 1919 Read Germany's response to the Treaty of Versailles, which deprived it of its colonies, 13 percent of its land, and 10 percent of its population.

Treaty of Versailles The treaty imposed on Germany by France, Great Britain, the United States, and other Allied Powers after World War I. It demanded that Germany dismantle its military and give up some lands to Poland. It was resented by many Germans.

PRIMARY SOURCE: An Economist Analyzes the Versailles Treaty and Finds It Lacking Read how an American economist condemned the Allies for ignoring, in the provisions of the Versailles Treaty, "the economic rehabilitation of Europe."

On June 28, 1919, the German delegates reluctantly signed the **Treaty of Versailles** (vuhr-SIGH). Germany was forbidden to have an air force and was permitted only a token army and navy. It also gave up large parts of its eastern territory to a newly reconstituted Poland. The Allies made Germany promise to pay reparations to compensate the victors for their losses, but they did not set a figure or a period of time for payment. A "guilt clause," which was to rankle for years to come, obliged the Germans to accept "responsibility for causing all the loss and damage" of the war. The treaty left Germany humiliated but largely intact. Establishing a peace neither of punishment nor of reconciliation, it was one of the great failures in history.

Meanwhile, the Austro-Hungarian Empire fell apart. New countries appeared in the lands lost by Russia, Germany, and Austria-Hungary: Poland, resurrected after over a century; Czechoslovakia, created from the northern third of Austria-Hungary; and Yugoslavia, combining Serbia and the former south Slav provinces of Austria-Hungary. The new boundaries coincided with the major linguistic groups of eastern Europe, but they all contained disaffected minorities. These small nations were safe only as long as Germany and Russia lay defeated and prostrate.

Russian Civil War and the New Economic Policy

In December 1918, civil war broke out in Russia. The Communists—as the Bolsheviks called themselves after March 1918—held central Russia, but all the surrounding provinces rose up against them. Counter-revolutionary armies led by former tsarist officers obtained weapons and supplies from the Allies. For three years the two sides burned farms and confiscated crops, causing a famine that claimed 3 million victims, more than had died in Russia in seven years of fighting. By 1921 the Communists had defeated most of their enemies.

Finland, the Baltic states, and Poland remained independent, but the Red Army reconquered other parts of the tsar's empire one by one. In 1922, Ukraine merged with Russia to create the Union of Soviet Socialist Republics (USSR), or Soviet Union. In 1920–1921 the Red Army reconquered the Caucasus and replaced the indigenous leaders with Russians. In 1922 the new Soviet republics of Georgia, Armenia, and Azerbaijan joined the USSR. In this way the Bolsheviks retained control over lands and peoples that had been part of the tsar's empire.

New Economic Policy Policy proclaimed by Vladimir Lenin in 1923 to encourage the revival of the Soviet economy by allowing small private enterprises. Joseph Stalin ended the NEP in 1928 and replaced it with a series of Five-Year Plans.

Years of warfare, revolution, and mismanagement had ruined the Russian economy. Factories and railroads had shut down for lack of fuel, raw materials, and parts. Farmland had been devastated and livestock killed, causing hunger in the cities. Finding himself master of a country in ruin, Lenin announced the **New Economic Policy** (NEP) in 1923. It allowed peasants to own land and sell their crops, private merchants to trade, and private workshops to produce goods and sell them on the free market. Only the biggest businesses, such as banks, railroads, and factories, remained under government ownership.

The relaxation of controls had an immediate effect. Production began to climb, and food and other goods became available. But the NEP reflected no change in the ultimate goals of the Communist Party. It merely provided breathing space, what Lenin called "two steps back to advance one step forward." The Communists had every intention of creating a modern industrial economy without private property. This meant investing in heavy industry and electrification and moving farmers to the cities to work in the new industries. It also meant providing food for the urban workers without spending scarce resources to purchase it from the peasants. In other words, it meant making the peasants, the great majority of the Soviet people, pay for the industrialization of Russia. This policy turned them into bitter enemies of the Communists.

AP* Exam Tip Be able to identify and discuss the social reforms that developed with revolutions such as the Russian Revolution.

When Lenin died in January 1924, his associates jockeyed for power. The leading contenders were Leon Trotsky, commander of the Red Army, and Joseph Stalin, general secretary of the Communist Party. Trotsky had the support of many "Old Bolsheviks" who had joined the party before the revolution. Having spent years in exile, he saw the revolution as a spark that would

© Cengage Learning

MAP 28.3 Territorial Changes in Europe After World War I Although the heaviest fighting took place in western Europe, the territorial changes there were relatively minor. In eastern Europe, in contrast, the changes were enormous. The disintegration of the Austro-Hungary Empire and the defeat of Russia allowed a belt of new countries to arise, stretching from Finland in the north to Yugoslavia in the south.

Interactive Map

Stalin and Trotsky

ignite a world revolution of the working class. Stalin, the only leading Communist who had never lived abroad, insisted that socialism could survive "in one country."

Stalin filled the party bureaucracy with individuals loyal to himself. In 1926–1927 he had Trotsky expelled for "deviation from the party line," and in January 1929 he forced Trotsky to flee the country. Then, as absolute master of the party, he prepared to industrialize the Soviet Union at breakneck speed.

An Ephemeral Peace

After the enormous sacrifices made during the war, the survivors developed hugely unrealistic expectations and were soon disillusioned. Conservatives in Britain and France longed for a return to the stability of the prewar era—the hierarchy of social classes, prosperous world trade, and European dominance over the rest of the world. All over the rest of the world, people's hopes had been raised by the rhetoric of the war, then dashed by its outcome. In Europe, Germans felt

David King Collection

Lenin the Orator The leader of the Bolshevik revolutionaries was a spellbinding orator. Here Lenin is addressing Red Army soldiers in Sverdlov Square, Moscow, in 1920.

cheated out of a victory that had seemed within their grasp, and Italians were disappointed that their sacrifices had not been rewarded with large territorial gains. Arabs and Indians longed for independence; the Chinese looked for social justice and a lessening of foreign intrusion; and the Japanese hoped to expand their influence in China. In Russia, the Communists were eager to consolidate their power and export their revolution to the rest of the world.

German Hyperinflation

In 1923 Germany suspended reparations payments. In retaliation for the French occupation of the Ruhr, the German government began printing money recklessly, causing the most severe inflation the world had ever seen. Soon German money was worth so little that it took a wheel-barrow full of it to buy a loaf of bread. As Germany teetered on the brink of civil war, radical nationalists tried to overthrow the government. Finally, the German government issued a new currency and promised to resume reparations payments, and the French agreed to withdraw their troops from the Ruhr.

Beginning in 1924 the world enjoyed a few years of calm and prosperity. After the end of the German crisis of 1923, the western European nations became less confrontational, and Germany joined the League of Nations. The vexed issue of reparations also seemed to vanish, as Germany borrowed money from New York banks to make its payments to France and Britain,

SECTION REVIEW

- The war caused millions of deaths and injuries and millions of refugees.
- France, Britain, and the United States dominated the Paris Peace Conference, refusing to listen to other voices.
- The United States refused to join the League of Nations, thereby weakening it.
- The Treaty of Versailles humiliated Germany but did not weaken it, thus becoming one of the big mistakes in history.
- When Austria-Hungary and Russia fell apart, several smaller nations arose in Europe, creating another source of potential conflict.
- After the Bolshevik victory in the Civil War, the Russian economy was in ruins, and Stalin took power.
- After the German hyperinflation of 1923 was resolved, the world economy began to prosper in 1924.

Mid-Twenties Prosperity

which used the money to repay their wartime loans from the United States. This triangular flow of money, based on credit, stimulated the rapid recovery of the European economies. France began rebuilding its war-torn northern zone; Germany recovered from its hyperinflation; and a boom began in the United States that was to last for five years.

While their economies flourished, governments grew more cautious and businesslike. Even the Communists, after Lenin's death, seemed to give up their attempts to spread revolution abroad. Yet neither Germany nor the Soviet Union accepted its borders with the small nations that had arisen between them. In 1922 they signed a secret pact allowing the German army to conduct maneuvers in Russia (in violation of the Versailles treaty) in exchange for German help in building up Russian industry and military potential.

The League of Nations proved adept at resolving numerous technical issues pertaining to health, labor relations, and postal and telegraph communications. Without U.S. participation, however, sanctions against states that violated League rules carried little weight.

CHINA AND JAPAN: CONTRASTING DESTINIES

AP* Exam Tip The rise of nationalism in China and Japan is an important comparison point.

China and Japan were both subject to Western pressures, but their modern histories have been completely opposite. China clung much longer than Japan to a traditional social structure and economy, then collapsed into chaos and revolution. Japan experienced reform from above (see Chapter 26), acquiring industry and a powerful military, which it used to take advantage of China's weakness. Their different reactions to the pressures of the West put these two great nations on a collision course.

The Bund in Shanghai On the Bund, the most important street in Shanghai, banks, corporate headquarters, and luxury hotels faced the waterfront where ships from around the world docked. Although Shanghai was China's industrial and commercial center, many of its workers loaded and unloaded ships by hand or pulled wealthy customers in rickshaws.

Bettmann/Corbis

Social and Economic Change

China's population—about 400 million in 1900—was the largest of any country in the world and growing fast. In 1900 peasant plots averaged between 1 and 4 acres (less than 2 hectares) apiece, half as large as they had been two generations earlier. Farming methods had not changed in centuries, and landlords and tax collectors took more than half of the harvest. Most Chinese worked incessantly, survived on a diet of grain and vegetables, and spent their lives in fear of floods, bandits, and tax collectors.

Above the peasantry, Chinese society was divided into many groups and strata. Landowners lived off the rents of their tenants. Officials, chosen through an elaborate examination system, enriched themselves from taxes and the government's monopolies on salt, iron, and other products. Shanghai, China's financial and commercial center, was famous for its wealthy foreigners and its opium addicts, prostitutes, and gangsters.

Although foreign trade represented only a small part of China's economy, contact with the outside world had a tremendous impact on Chinese politics. Young men living in the treaty ports saw no chance for advancement in the old system of examinations and official positions. Some learned foreign ideas in Christian mission schools or abroad. The contrast between the squalor in which most urban residents lived and the luxury of the foreigners' enclaves in the treaty ports sharpened the resentment of educated Chinese.

Japan had few natural resources and very little arable land on which to grow food for its rising population. Typhoons regularly hit its southern regions, and earthquakes periodically shook the country, which lies on the great ring of tectonic fault lines that surround the Pacific Ocean. The Kanto earthquake of 1923 destroyed all of Yokohama and half of Tokyo and killed some 200,000 people.

Japan's population reached 60 million in 1925 and was increasing by a million a year. The crash program of industrialization begun in 1868 by the Meiji oligarchs (see Chapter 26) accelerated during the First World War, when Japan's economy grew four times as fast as western Europe's and eight times faster than China's.

The "New Rich"

Economic growth aggravated social tensions. The *narikin* ("new rich") affected Western ways and lifestyles that clashed with the austerity of earlier times. In the big cities *mobos* (modern boys) and *mogas* (modern girls) shocked traditionalists with their foreign ways: dancing together, wearing short skirts and tight pants, and behaving like Americans. Students who flirted with dangerous thoughts were called "Marx boys."

The main beneficiaries of prosperity were the *zaibatsu* (zie-BOT-soo), or conglomerates, four of which—Mitsubishi, Sumitomo, Yasuda, and Mitsui—controlled most of Japan's industry and commerce. Farmers, who constituted half of the population, remained poor; in desperation some sold their daughters to textile mills or into domestic service. Labor unions were weak and repressed by the police.

Japanese prosperity depended on foreign trade. The country exported silk and light manufactures and imported almost all its fuel, raw materials, and machine tools, and even some of its food. Though less at the mercy of the weather than China, Japan was much more vulnerable to swings in the world economy.

e **PRIMARY SOURCE: Two Proclamations of the Boxer Rebellion** The secret society known as "The Righteous and Harmonious Fists" announces its intention to kill the "foreign devils" plaguing China.

Revolution and War, 1900–1918

In 1900 China's Empress Dowager Cixi (TSUH-shee), who had seized power in a palace coup two years earlier, encouraged a secret society, the Righteous Fists, or Boxers, to rise up and expel all the foreigners from China. When the Boxers threatened the foreign legation in Beijing, an international force from the Western powers and Japan captured the city and forced China to pay a huge indemnity. Shocked by these events, many Chinese students became convinced that China needed a revolution to get rid of the Qing dynasty and modernize their country.

Sun Yat-sen Chinese nationalist revolutionary, founder and leader of the Guomindang until his death. He attempted to create a liberal democratic political movement in China but was thwarted by military leaders.

Sun Yat-sen and Yuan Shikai

When Cixi died in 1908, the Revolutionary Alliance led by **Sun Yat-sen** (soon yot-SEN) (1867–1925) prepared to take over. Sun had spent much of his life in Japan, England, and the United States, plotting the overthrow of the Qing dynasty. His ideas were a mixture of nationalism, socialism, and Confucian philosophy. His patriotism, his powerful ambition, and his tenacious spirit attracted a large following.

Yuan Shikai Chinese general and first president of the Chinese Republic (1912–1916). He stood in the way of the democratic movement led by Sun Yat-sen.

Guomindang Nationalist political party founded on democratic principles by Sun Yat-sen in 1912. After 1925, the party was headed by Chiang Kai-shek, who turned it into an increasingly authoritarian movement.

PRIMARY SOURCE: The Three People's Principles and the Future of the Chinese People Decrying the gulf between rich and poor in Europe and America, Sun Yat-sen calls for a revolution in China that will ensure prosperity and social justice.

The military thwarted Sun's plans. After China's defeat in the war with Japan in 1895, the government had agreed to equip the army with modern rifles and machine guns. This, combined with the fact that local armies were beholden to warlords rather than to the central government, created a threatening situation for the Qing. When a regional army mutinied in October 1911, **Yuan Shikai** (you-AHN she-KIE), the most powerful of the regional generals, refused to defend the Qing. A revolutionary assembly at Nanjing elected Sun Yat-sen president of China in December 1911, but he had no military forces at his command. To avoid a clash with the army, he resigned after a few weeks, and a new national assembly elected Yuan president of the new Chinese republic.

Yuan was an able military leader, but he had no political program. When Sun reorganized his followers into a political party called **Guomindang** (gwo-min-dong) (National People's Party), Yuan quashed every attempt at creating a Western-style government and harassed Sun's followers. Victory in the first round of the struggle to create a new China went to the military.

Meanwhile, the Japanese were quick to join the Allied side in World War I, since they saw the war as an opportunity to advance their interests while the Europeans were occupied elsewhere. They quickly conquered the German colonies in the northern Pacific and on the coast of China, then turned their attention to the rest of China. In 1915 Japan presented China with Twenty-One Demands, which would have turned it into a virtual protectorate. Britain and the United States persuaded Japan to soften the demands but could not prevent it from keeping the German coastal enclaves and extracting railroad and mining concessions at China's expense. In protest, anti-Japanese riots and boycotts broke out throughout China. Thus began a bitter struggle between the two countries that was to last for thirty years.

Chinese Warlords and the Guomindang, 1919–1929

Chiang Kai-shek Chinese military and political leader. Succeeded Sun Yat-sen as head of the Guomindang in 1925; headed the Chinese government from 1928 to 1949; fought against the Chinese Communists and Japanese invaders. After 1949 he headed the Chinese Nationalist government in Taiwan.

Chiang Kai-shek

At the Paris Peace Conference, the great powers accepted Japan's seizure of the German enclaves in China. To many Chinese, this decision was a cruel insult. On May 4, 1919, students demonstrated in front of the Forbidden City of Beijing. Despite a government ban, the May Fourth Movement spread to other parts of China. A new generation was growing up to challenge the old officials, the regional generals, and the foreigners.

Sun Yat-sen tried to make a comeback in Guangzhou (Canton) in the early 1920s. Though not a Communist, he was impressed with the efficiency of Lenin's revolutionary tactics and let a Soviet adviser reorganize the Guomindang along Leninist lines. He also welcomed members of the newly created Chinese Communist Party into the Guomindang.

When Sun died in 1925, the leadership of his party passed to Jiang Jieshi, known in the West as **Chiang Kai-shek** (chang kie-shek) (1887–1975). An officer and director of the military academy, Chiang trained several hundred young officers who remained loyal to him thereafter. In 1927 he determined to defeat the regional warlords. As his army moved north from its base in Canton, he briefly formed an alliance with the Communists. Once his troops occupied Shanghai, however, he crushed the labor unions and decimated the Communists, whom he considered a threat. He then defeated or co-opted most of the other warlords and established a dictatorship.

Chiang's government issued ambitious plans to build railroads, develop agriculture and industry, and modernize China from the top down. However, his followers were neither competent administrators nor ruthless modernizers. Instead, his government attracted thousands of opportunists whose goals were to "become officials and get rich" by taxing and plundering businesses. In the countryside tax collectors and landowners squeezed the peasants ever harder, even in times of natural disasters. What little money reached the government's coffers went to the military. Thus for twenty years after the fall of the Qing, China remained mired in poverty, subject to corrupt officials and the whims of nature.

SECTION REVIEW

- Japan prospered during the war and quickly modernized; it also began preying on China.
- When the Qing dynasty ended in 1911, the regional general Yuan Shikai took over China and repressed Sun Yat-sen's party, the Guomindang.
- After Sun Yat-sen's death, Chiang Kai-shek established a corrupt military dictatorship.

THE NEW MIDDLE EAST

After the war, the Arab peoples expected to have a say in the outcome of the Great War. But the victorious French and British planned to treat the Middle East like a territory open to colonial rule. The result was a legacy of instability that has persisted to this day.

The Mandate System

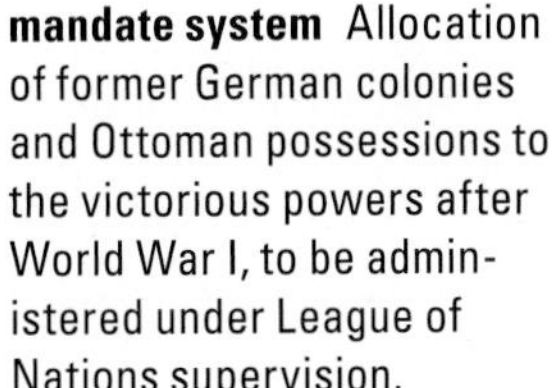
mandate system Allocation of former German colonies and Ottoman possessions to the victorious powers after World War I, to be administered under League of Nations supervision.

At the Paris Peace Conference, France, Britain, Italy, and Japan proposed to divide the former German colonies and the territories of the Ottoman Empire among themselves, but their ambitions clashed with President Wilson's ideal of national self-determination. Eventually, the victors arrived at a compromise solution called the **mandate system**: colonial rulers would administer the territories but would be accountable to the League of Nations for "the material and moral well-being and the social progress of the inhabitants."

Class C Mandates—those with the smallest populations—were treated as colonies by their conquerors. South Africa replaced Germany in Southwest Africa (now Namibia); Britain, Australia, New Zealand, and Japan took over the German islands in the Pacific. Class B Mandates, larger than Class C but still underdeveloped, were to be ruled for the benefit of their inhabitants under League of Nations supervision. Most of Germany's African colonies fell into this category.

The Arab-speaking territories of the old Ottoman Empire were Class A Mandates. The League of Nations declared that they had "reached a state of development where their existence as independent nations can be provisionally recognized subject to the rendering of administrative advice and assistance by a Mandatory, until such time as they are able to stand alone." While Arabs interpreted this ambiguous wording as a promise of independence, Britain and France sent troops into the region "for the benefit of its inhabitants." Palestine (now Israel), Transjordan (now Jordan), and Iraq (formerly Mesopotamia) became British mandates; France claimed Syria and Lebanon (see Map 28.4). (See Diversity and Dominance: The Middle East After World War I.)

The Rise of Modern Turkey

At the end of the war, as the Ottoman Empire teetered on the brink of collapse, France, Britain, and Italy saw an opportunity to expand their empires, and Greece eyed those parts of Anatolia inhabited by Greeks. In 1919 French, British, Italian, and Greek forces occupied Constantinople and parts of Anatolia. By the Treaty of Sèvres (1920) the Allies made the sultan give up most of his lands.

In 1919 Mustafa Kemal had formed a nationalist government in central Anatolia with the backing of fellow army officers. In 1922, after a short but fierce war against invading Greeks, his armies reconquered Anatolia and the area around Constantinople. The victorious Turks forced hundreds of thousands of Greeks from their ancestral homes in Anatolia. In response the Greek government expelled all Muslims from Greece.

Stock Montage

Mustafa Kemal Atatürk After World War I, Mustafa Kemal was determined to modernize Turkey on the Western model. Here he is shown wearing a European-style suit and teaching the Latin alphabet.

DIVERSITY + DOMINANCE

The Middle East After World War I

During the First World War, Entente forces invaded and occupied Palestine, Mesopotamia, and Syria. This raised the question of what to do with these territories after the war. Would they be returned to the Ottoman Empire? Would they simply be added to the colonial empires of Britain and France? Or would they become independent Arab states?

The following documents illustrate the diversity of opinions among various groups planning the postwar settlement: Great Britain, concerned with defeating Germany and maintaining its empire; the United States, basing its policies on lofty principles; and Arab delegates from the Middle East, seeking self-determination.

In the early twentieth century, in response to the rise of anti-Semitism in Europe, a movement called Zionism had arisen among European Jews. Zionists, led by Theodore Herzl, hoped for a return to Israel, the ancestral homeland of the Jewish people. For two thousand years this land had been a province of various empires—the Roman, Byzantine, Arab, and Ottoman—and was inhabited by Arabic-speaking people, most of whom practiced the Islamic religion.

During the war the British government was receptive to the idea of establishing a Jewish homeland in Palestine. It was motivated by the need to win the war, but it also considered the more distant future. The result was a policy statement, sent by Foreign Secretary Arthur James Balfour to Baron Rothschild, a prominent supporter of the Zionist movement in England. This statement, called the "Balfour Declaration," has haunted the Middle East ever since.

The Balfour Declaration of 1917

Foreign Office
November 2nd, 1917

Dear Lord Rothschild:

I have much pleasure in conveying to you, on behalf of His Majesty's Government, the following declaration of sympathy with Jewish Zionist aspirations which have been submitted to, and approved by, the Cabinet:

> His Majesty's Government view with favor the establishment in Palestine of a national home for the Jewish people, and will use their best endeavors to facilitate the achievement of this object, it being clearly understood that nothing shall be done which may prejudice the civil and religious rights of existing non-Jewish communities in Palestine, or the rights and political status enjoyed by Jews in any other country.

I should be grateful if you would bring this declaration to the knowledge of the Zionist Federation.

Yours,
Arthur James Balfour

On January 8, 1918, the American president Woodrow Wilson issued his famous Fourteen Points proposal to end the war. Much of his speech was devoted to European affairs or to international relations in general, but two of his fourteen points referred to the Arab world.

Woodrow Wilson's Fourteen Points

What we demand in this war . . . is that the world be made fit and safe to live in; and particularly that it be made safe for every peace-loving nation which, like our own, wishes to live its own life, determine its own institutions, be assured of justice and fair dealing by the other peoples of the world as against force and selfish aggression. All the peoples of the world are in effect partners in this interest, and for our own part we see very clearly that unless justice be done to others it will not be done to us. The programme of the world's peace, therefore, is our programme; and that programme, the only possible programme, as we see it, is this:

XII. The Turkish portions of the present Ottoman Empire should be assured a secure sovereignty, but the other nationalities which are now under Turkish rule should be assured an undoubted security of life and an

Atatürk The founder of modern Turkey. He distinguished himself in the defense of Gallipoli in World War I and expelled a Greek expeditionary army from Anatolia in 1921–1922. He replaced the Ottoman Empire with the Turkish Republic in 1923. As president, he pushed through a radical Westernization and reform of Turkish society.

As a war hero and proclaimed savior of his country, Kemal was able to impose wrenching changes on his people. An outspoken modernizer, he was eager to bring Turkey closer to Europe as quickly as possible. He abolished the sultanate, declared Turkey a secular republic, and introduced European laws. In a radical break with Islamic tradition, he suppressed Muslim courts, schools, and religious orders and replaced the Arabic alphabet with the Latin alphabet.

Kemal attempted to westernize the traditional Turkish family. Women received civil equality, including the right to vote and to be elected to the national assembly. Kemal forbade polygamy and instituted civil marriage and divorce. He even changed people's clothing, strongly discouraging women from veiling their faces, and replaced the fez, until then the traditional Turkish men's hat, with the European brimmed hat. He ordered everyone to take a family name, choosing the name **Atatürk** ("father of the Turks") for himself. His reforms spread quickly in the cities; but in rural areas, where Islamic traditions remained strong, people resisted them for a long time.

absolutely unmolested opportunity of autonomous development. . . .

When the war ended, the victorious Allies assembled in Paris to determine, among other things, the fate of the former Arab provinces of the Ottoman Empire. Arab leaders had reason to doubt the intentions of the great powers, especially Britain and France. When the Allies decided to create mandates in the Arab territories on the grounds that the Arab peoples were not ready for independence, Arab leaders expressed their misgivings, as in the following statement:

Memorandum of the General Syrian Congress, July 2, 1919

We the undersigned members of the General Syrian Congress, meeting in Damascus on Wednesday, July 2nd, 1919, made up of representatives from the three Zones, viz., The Southern, Eastern, and Western, provided with credentials and authorizations by the inhabitants of our various districts, Moslems, Christians, and Jews, have agreed upon the following statement of the desires of the people of the country who have elected us. . . .

1. We ask absolutely complete political independence for Syria. . . .
3. Considering the fact that the Arabs inhabiting the Syrian area are not naturally less gifted than other more advanced races and that they are by no means less developed than the Bulgarians, Serbians, Greeks, and Roumanians at the beginning of their independence, we protest against Article 22 of the Covenant of the League of Nations, placing us among the nations in their middle stage of development which stand in need of a mandatory power.
4. . . . . relying on the declarations of President Wilson that his object in waging war was to put an end to the ambition of conquest and colonization, . . . and believing that the American Nation is furthest from any thought of colonization and has no political ambition in our country, we will seek the technical and economic assistance from the United States of America, provided that such assistance does not exceed 20 years.
5. In the event of America not finding herself in a position to accept our desire for assistance, we will seek this assistance from Great Britain, also provided that such does not prejudice our complete independence and unity of our country and that the duration of such assistance does not exceed that mentioned in the previous article.
6. We do not acknowledge any right claimed by the French Government in any part whatever of our Syrian country and refuse that she should assist us or have a hand in our country under any circumstances and in any place.
7. We opposed the pretensions of the Zionists to create a Jewish commonwealth in the southern part of Syria, known as Palestine, and oppose Zionist migration to any part of our country; for we do not acknowledge their title but consider them a grave peril to our people from the national, economical, and political points of view. Our Jewish compatriots shall enjoy our common rights and assume our common responsibilities.

QUESTIONS FOR ANALYSIS

1. **Was there a contradiction between Balfour's proposal to establish "a national home for the Jewish people" and the promise "that nothing shall be done which may prejudice the civil and religious rights of existing non-Jewish communities in Palestine"? If so, why did he make two contradictory promises?**
2. **How would Woodrow Wilson's statements about "an absolutely unmolested opportunity of autonomous development" apply to Palestine?**
3. **Why did the delegates to the Syrian General Congress object to the plan to create mandates in the former Ottoman provinces? What alternatives did they offer?**
4. **Why did the delegates object to the creation of a Jewish commonwealth?**

Source: The Balfour Declaration, *The Times* (London), November 9, 1917. Memorandum of the General Syrian Congress, *Foreign Relations of the United States: Paris Peace Conference*, vol. 12 (Washington, DC: Government Printing Office, 1919), 780–781.

Arab Lands and the Question of Palestine

Among the Arab people, the thinly disguised colonialism of the mandate system set off protests and rebellions. Arabs viewed the European presence not as liberation from Ottoman oppression, but as foreign occupation.

After World War I Middle Eastern society underwent dramatic changes. Trucks replaced camel caravans. Landless peasants migrated to the swelling cities. The population of the region is estimated to have increased by 50 percent between 1914 and 1939, while that of large cities such as Constantinople, Baghdad, and Cairo doubled.

The urban and mercantile middle class, encouraged by the transformation of Turkey, adopted Western ideas, customs, and styles of housing and clothing. Some families sent their sons to European secular or mission schools, then to Western colleges in Cairo and Beirut or universities abroad, to prepare for jobs in government and business. A few women became

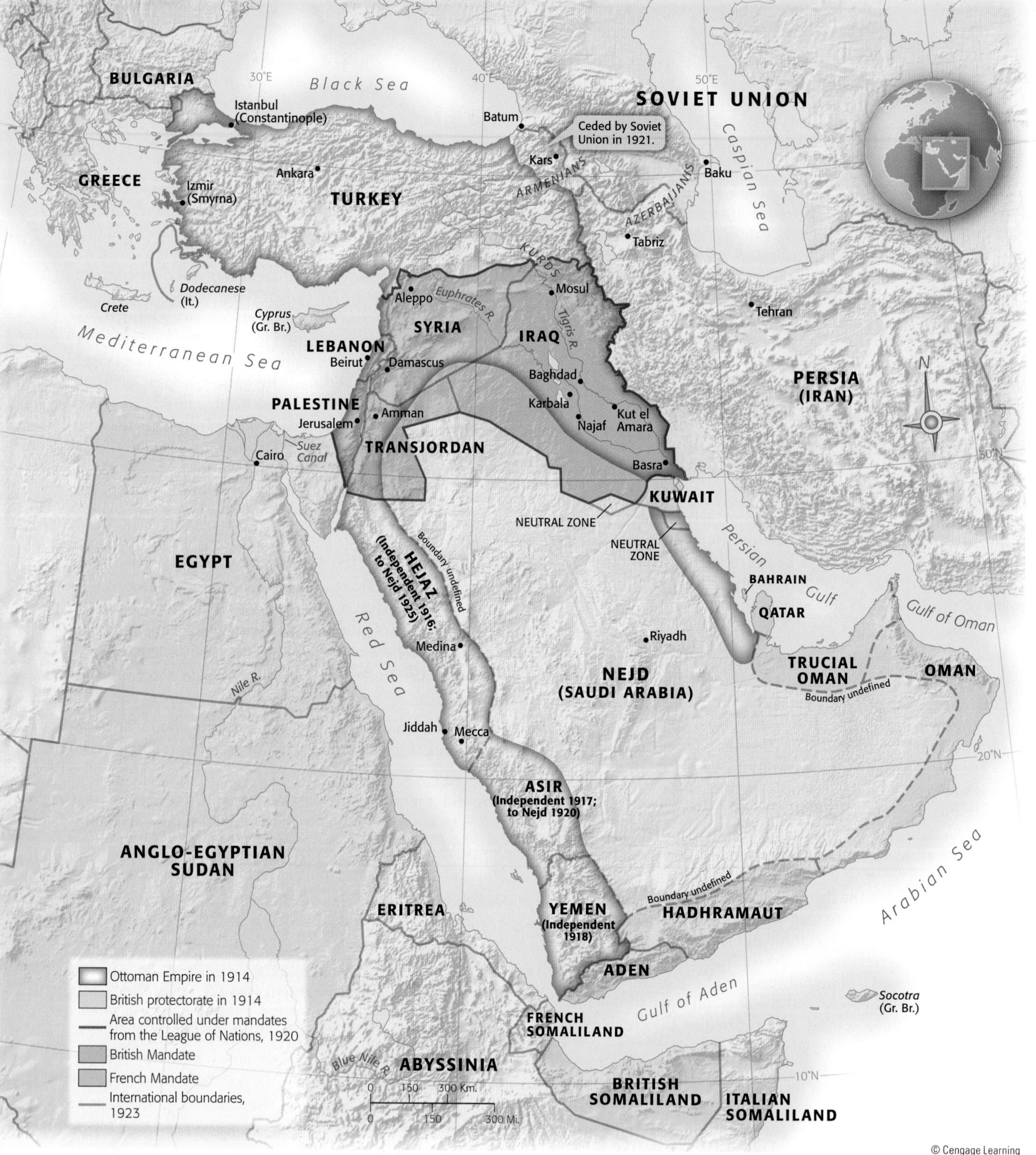

MAP 28.4 Territorial Changes in the Middle East After World War I The defeat and dismemberment of the Ottoman Empire at the end of World War I resulted in an entirely new political map of the region. The Turkish Republic inherited Anatolia and a small piece of the Balkans, while the Ottoman Empire's Arab provinces were divided between France and Great Britain. Only Iran and Egypt did not change.

Interactive Map

schoolteachers or nurses. There were great variations, ranging from Lebanon, with its strong French influence, to Arabia and Iran, which retained their cultural traditions.

The region in closest contact with Europe was the Maghrib—Algeria, Tunisia, and Morocco—which the French army considered its private domain. Alongside the old native quarters, the French built modern neighborhoods inhabited mainly by Europeans. France had occu-

Hulton Archive/Getty Images

The Jewish Settlement of Palestine Thousands of Jews fleeing persecution and discrimination in Europe settled on the land and founded *kibbutzim*, or collective farms. In this picture taken in 1912, an eighty-four-year-old immigrant from Russia learns to plow the land.

pied Algeria since 1830 and had encouraged European immigration. The settlers owned the best lands and monopolized government jobs and businesses, while Arabs and Berbers remained poor and suffered intense discrimination.

Britain in the Middle East

The British attempted to control the Middle East with a mixture of bribery and intimidation. They made Faisal, leader of the Arab Revolt, king of Iraq and used bombers to quell rural insurrections. In 1931 they reached an agreement with King Faisal's government: official independence for Iraq in exchange for the right to keep two air bases, a military alliance, and an assured flow of petroleum. France, meanwhile, sent thousands of troops to Syria and Lebanon to crush nationalist uprisings.

In Egypt, as in Iraq, the British substituted a phony independence for official colonialism. They declared Egypt independent in 1922 but reserved the right to station troops along the Suez Canal to secure their link with India in the event of war. Most galling to the Wafd (Nationalist) Party was the British attempt to remove Egyptian troops from Sudan, a land many Egyptians considered a colony of Egypt. Britain was successful in keeping Egypt in limbo—neither independent nor a colony—thanks to an alliance with King Fouad and conservative Egyptian politicians who feared both secular and religious radicalism.

Before the war, a Jewish minority lived in Palestine, as in other Arab countries. Small numbers of Jews had been immigrating to Palestine since the nineteenth century, but as soon as Palestine became a British mandate in 1920, many more came from Europe, encouraged by the Balfour Declaration of 1917. Most settled in the cities, but

SECTION REVIEW

- Former Arab provinces of the Ottoman Empire became "mandates" under French or British control.
- Mustafa Kemal Atatürk expelled the Greek minority from Anatolia and founded the Turkish Republic, then pushed it toward secular reform.
- As Middle Eastern society modernized, the Arabs became more politically active but had to endure the mandate system.
- Jewish immigration to Palestine caused growing tensions between Jews, Arabs, and the British.

some established *kibbutzim,* or communal farms. Their goals were to become self-sufficient and to reestablish their ties to the land of their ancestors. The purchases of land by Jewish agencies angered the indigenous Palestinians, especially tenant farmers who had been evicted to make room for settlers. In 1920–1921 riots erupted between Jews and Arabs. When far more Jewish immigrants arrived than they had anticipated, the British tried to limit immigration, thereby alienating the Jews without mollifying the Arabs. Increasingly, Jews arrived without papers, smuggled in by militant Zionist organizations. In the 1930s the country was torn by strikes and guerrilla warfare that the British could not control. In the process, Britain earned the hatred of both sides and of many other people in the Arab world.

Jewish Migration to Palestine

SOCIETY, CULTURE, AND TECHNOLOGY IN THE INDUSTRIALIZED WORLD

With the signing of the peace treaties, the countries that had fought for four years turned their efforts toward building a new future. Advances in science offered astonishing new insights into the mysteries of nature and the universe. New technologies, many of them pioneered in the United States, promised to change the daily lives of millions of people.

Class and Gender

The war had left a deep imprint on European society and culture. After the war, class distinctions began to fade. Many European aristocrats had died on the battlefields, and with them went their class's long domination of the army, the diplomatic corps, and other elite sectors of society. The United States and Canada had never had as rigidly defined a class structure as European societies or as elaborate a set of traditions and manners. On both sides of the Atlantic, engineers, businessmen, lawyers, and other professionals rose to prominence, increasing the relative importance of the middle class.

The activities of governments had expanded during the war and continued to grow, creating a need for thousands more bureaucrats. Governments provided housing, highways, schools, public health facilities, broadcasting, and other services. Department stores, banks, insurance companies, and other businesses also increased the white-collar work force. The working class did not expand, however. The introduction of new machines and new ways of organizing work, such as the automobile assembly line that Henry Ford devised, increased workers' productivity so that greater outputs could be achieved without a larger labor force.

Women's Lives

AP* Exam Tip Women's rights are an important issue for the exam.

Women's lives changed more rapidly in the 1920s than ever before. Although the end of the war marked a retreat from wartime job opportunities, some women remained in the work force. The young and wealthy enjoyed more personal freedoms than their mothers had before the war; they drove cars, played sports, traveled alone, and smoked in public. For others, the upheavals of war brought more suffering than liberation. Millions of women had lost their fathers, brothers, sons, husbands, and fiancés in the war or in the great influenza epidemic. After the war many single women led lives of loneliness and destitution.

In Europe and North America advocates of women's rights had been demanding the vote for women since the 1890s. New Zealand was the only nation to grant women the vote before the twentieth century. Women in Norway were the first to obtain it in Europe, in 1915. Russian women followed in 1917, and Canadians and Germans in 1918. Britain gave women over age thirty the vote in 1918 and later extended it to younger women. The Nineteenth Amendment to the U.S. Constitution granted suffrage to American women in 1920. Women in Turkey began voting in 1934. Most other countries did not allow women to vote until after 1945. Everywhere, their influence on politics was less radical than feminists had hoped and conservatives had feared. Even when it did not alter politics and government, however, the right to vote was a potent symbol.

Women were active in many other areas besides the suffrage movement. On both sides of the Atlantic women participated in social reform movements to prevent mistreatment of women and children and of industrial workers. In the United States such reforms were championed by Progressives such as Jane Addams (1860–1935), who founded a settlement house in a poor neighborhood and received the Nobel Peace Prize in 1931. In Europe reformers were generally aligned with Socialist or Labour Parties.

Margaret Sanger American nurse and author; pioneer in the movement for family planning; organized conferences and established birth control clinics.

Among the most controversial, and eventually most effective, of the reformers were those who advocated contraception, such as the American **Margaret Sanger** (1883–1966). Her campaign brought her into conflict with the authorities, who equated birth control with pornography. Finally, in 1923 she was able to found a birth control clinic in New York. In France, the government prohibited contraception and abortion in 1920 in an effort to increase the birthrate and make up for the loss of so many young men in the war. Russian communists allowed abortion for ideological reasons.

Revolution in the Sciences

The New Physics

Max Planck German physicist who developed quantum theory and was awarded the Nobel Prize for physics in 1918.

Albert Einstein German physicist who developed the theory of relativity, which states that time, space, and mass are relative to each other and not fixed.

At the end of the nineteenth century, a revolution in physics undermined all the old certainties about nature. Physicists discovered that atoms, the building blocks of matter, are not indivisible, but consist of far smaller subatomic particles. In 1900 the German physicist **Max Planck** (1858–1947) found that atoms emit or absorb energy in discrete amounts called *quanta*. These findings seemed strange enough, but what really undermined Newtonian physics was the general theory of relativity developed by **Albert Einstein** (1879–1955). In 1916 Einstein announced that not only is matter made of insubstantial particles, but that time, space, energy, and mass are not fixed but are relative to one another. Other physicists said that light is made up of either waves or particles, depending on the observer, and that an experiment could determine either the speed or the position of a particle of light, but never both.

To nonscientists it seemed as though theories expressed in arcane mathematical formulas were replacing truth and common sense. Far from being mere speculation, however, the new physics promised to unlock the secrets of matter and provide humans with plentiful—and potentially dangerous—sources of energy.

The New Social Sciences

Sigmund Freud Austrian psychiatrist, founder of psychoanalysis. He argued that psychological problems were caused by traumas, especially sexual experiences in early childhood, that were repressed in later life. His ideas caused considerable controversy among psychologists and in the general public. Although his views on repressed sexuality are no longer widely accepted, his psychoanalytic methods are still very influential.

The new social sciences were even more unsettling than the new physics, for they challenged Victorian morality, middle-class values, and notions of Western superiority. **Sigmund Freud** (1856–1939), a Viennese physician, developed the technique of psychoanalysis to probe the minds of his patients. He found not only rationality but also hidden layers of emotion and desire repressed by social restraints. "The primitive, savage and evil impulses have not vanished from any individual, but continue their existence, although in a repressed state,"[5] he warned. Meanwhile, sociologists and anthropologists had begun the empirical study of societies, both Western and non-Western. Before the war the French sociologist Emile Durkheim (1858–1917) had come to the then-shocking conclusion that "there are no religions that are false. All are true after their own fashion."[6]

If the words *primitive* and *savage* applied to Europeans as well as to other peoples, and if religions were all equally "true," then what remained of the superiority of Western civilization? Cultural relativism, as the new approach to human societies was called, was as unnerving as relativity in physics.

Although these ideas had been expressed before 1914, wartime experiences called into question the West's faith in reason and progress. Some people accepted the new ideas with enthusiasm. Others condemned and rejected them, clinging to the sense of order and faith in progress that had energized European and American culture before the war. Yet others were overcome with feelings of uncertainty and despair in a world in which human existence seemed to have lost its meaning and purpose.

New Technologies of Modernity

AP* Exam Tip Be prepared to discuss the globalization of science and technology.

Some people viewed the sciences with mixed feelings, but the new technologies aroused almost universal excitement. In North America even working-class people could afford some of the new products of scientific research, inventors' ingenuity, and industrial production. Mass consumption lagged in Europe, but science and technology were just as advanced, and public fascination with the latest inventions—the cult of the modern—was just as strong.

Aviation

Wilbur and Orville Wright American bicycle mechanics; the first to build and fly an airplane, at Kitty Hawk, North Carolina, December 7, 1903.

Of all the innovations of the time, none attracted public interest as much as airplanes. In 1903 two young American mechanics, **Wilbur and Orville Wright**, built the first aircraft that was heavier than air and could be maneuvered in flight. From that moment on, airplanes fascinated people. During the war the exploits of air aces relieved the tedium of news from the front. In the 1920s aviation became a sport and a form of entertainment, and flying daredevils achieved extraordinary fame. Among the most celebrated pilots were three Americans. Amelia Earhart was the first woman to fly across the Atlantic Ocean, and her example encouraged other women to fly. Richard Byrd flew over the North Pole in 1926. The most admired of all was Charles Lindbergh, the first person to fly alone across the Atlantic in 1927 (see Environment and Technology: The Birth of Civil Aviation).

Electricity and Radio

Electricity, produced in industrial quantities since the 1890s (see Chapter 26), began to transform home life. The first home use of electricity was for lighting, thanks to the economical and long-lasting tungsten bulb. Then, having persuaded people to wire their homes, electrical utilities joined manufacturers in advertising electric irons, fans, washing machines, hot plates, and other appliances.

Radio had served ships and the military during the war as a means of point-to-point telecommunication. After the war, amateurs used surplus radio equipment to talk to one another. The first commercial station began broadcasting in Pittsburgh in 1920. By the end of 1923 six hundred stations were broadcasting news, sports, soap operas, and advertising to homes throughout North America. By 1930, 12 million families owned radio receivers. In Europe radio spread more slowly because governments reserved the airwaves for cultural and official programs and taxed radio owners to pay for the service.

Cinema

Another medium that spread explosively in the 1920s was film. Motion pictures had begun in France in 1895 and flourished there and elsewhere in Europe, where the dominant concern was to reproduce stage plays. American filmmakers, however, aimed to entertain audiences rather than preserve outstanding theatrical performances. In competing for audiences they looked to cinematic innovation, broad humor, and exciting spectacles.

Diversity was a hallmark of the early film industry. After World War I filmmaking took root and flourished in Japan, India, Turkey, Egypt, and Hollywood, California. American and European movie studios were successful in exporting films, since silent movies presented no language problems. Then in 1927 the United States introduced the first "talking" motion picture, *The Jazz Singer,* which changed all the rules.

The number of Americans who went to see their favorite stars in thrilling adventures and heart-breaking romances rose from 40 million in 1922 to 100 million in 1930, at a time when the population of the country was about 120 million. Europeans had the technology and the art but neither the wealth nor the huge market of the United States. Hollywood studios began the diffusion of American culture that has continued to this day.

Health

Health and hygiene were also part of the cult of modernity. Advances in medicine—some learned in the war—saved many lives. Wounds were regularly disinfected, and x-ray machines helped diagnose fractures. Cities built costly water supply and sewage treatment systems. By the 1920s indoor plumbing and flush toilets were becoming common even in working-class neighborhoods.

Interest in cleanliness altered private life. Doctors and home economists bombarded women with warnings and advice on how to banish germs. Soap and appliance manufacturers filled women's magazines with advertisements for products to help housewives keep their family's homes and clothing spotless and their meals fresh and wholesome. The decline in infant mortality and improvements in general health and life expectancy in this period owe as much to the cult of cleanliness as to advances in medicine.

Technology and the Environment

The New Architecture

Two new technologies—the skyscraper and the automobile—transformed the urban environment even more radically than the railroad had done in the nineteenth century. At the end of the nineteenth century architects had begun to design ever-higher buildings using load-bearing

The Birth of Civil Aviation

Antoine de Saint-Exupéry, best known for his children's book *The Little Prince,* was a pilot for Aéropostale, a French airline that served South America. In his book *Vol de Nuit* (Night Flight), he tells a harrowing tale of a pilot blown out to sea in a storm over Argentina:

> *One of the radio operators at the Comodoro Rivadavia station in Patagonia made a sudden gesture and all those who were keeping a helpless vigil there crowded around him. . . .*
>
> *"Storm?"*
>
> *He nodded yes; static prevented him from hearing the message. Then he scrawled some illegible signs, then words. Then the text came out:*
>
> *"Cut off at 12,000 feet above the storm. Proceeding due west toward interior; we were carried out to sea. No visibility below. Do not know if still flying over sea. Report if storm extends interior." . . .*
>
> *Buenos Aires transmitted a reply.*
>
> *"Storm covers all interior. How much gasoline left?"*
>
> *"Half an hour."*
>
> *These words sped from post to post back to Buenos Aires. The plane was doomed to plunge in less than half an hour into a hurricane that would smash it to earth. . . .*

Today, airplanes are safer than cars, but in the 1920s, when regular airline service began, air travel was dangerous. Airplanes, many of them converted World War I bombers, were made of wood and cloth, with open cockpits for the pilot and navigator and wicker chairs for passengers. Pilots located their position by looking for towns and railroad tracks. At night and in cloudy weather, they often got lost. And yet, with these machines they conquered the skies.

Source: Antoine de Saint-Exupéry, *Vol de nuit* (Paris: Gallimard, 1939), 147–149.

An Early Passenger Plane After World War I, aviators and aircraft manufacturers turned their attention to civil aviation, using planes to distribute mail, dust crops, and carry passengers. This British-made De Havilland-34 biplane, photographed before 1924, was designed to carry up to ten passengers.

Mary Evans Picture Library/The Image Works

steel frames and passenger elevators. Major corporations in Chicago and New York competed to build the most daring buildings in the world, such as New York's fifty-five-story Woolworth Building (1912). A building boom in the late 1920s produced dozens of skyscrapers, culminating with the eighty-six-story Empire State Building in New York in 1932.

Herald Examiner Collection/Los Angeles Public Library

The Archetypal Automobile City As Los Angeles grew from a modest town into a sprawling metropolis, broad avenues, parking lots, and garages were built to accommodate automobiles. By 1929, most families owned a car and streetcar lines had closed for lack of passengers.

European cities restricted the height of buildings to protect their architectural heritage; Paris forbade buildings over 56 feet (17 meters) high. In the 1920s the Swiss architect Charles Edouard Jeanneret (1887–1965), known as Le Corbusier (luh cor-booz-YEH), outlined a new approach to architecture that featured simplicity of form, absence of surface ornamentation, easy manufacture, and inexpensive materials. Other architects—including the Finn Eero Saarinen, the Germans Ludwig Mies van der Rohe (LOOD-vig MEES fon der ROW-uh) and Walter Gropius, and the American Frank Lloyd Wright—also contributed to what became known as the International Style.

Automobiles and Suburbs

Meanwhile, outlying areas were spreading far into the countryside, thanks to the automobile. The assembly line pioneered by Henry Ford mass-produced vehicles in ever-greater volume and at falling prices. By 1929 the United States had one car for every five people, five-sixths of the world's automobiles. Automobiles were praised as the solution to urban pollution; as they replaced carts and carriages, horses disappeared from city streets, as did tons of manure.

The most important environmental effect of automobiles was suburban sprawl. Middle-class families could now live in single-family homes too far apart to be served by public transportation. As middle- and working-class families bought cars, cities acquired rings of automobile suburbs. Los Angeles, the first true automobile city, consisted of suburbs spread over hundreds of square miles and linked together by broad avenues. Many Americans saw Los Angeles as the portent of a glorious future in which everyone would have a car.

Technological advances also transformed rural environments. Automobile owners drove out to the country on weekends or holidays. Farmers bought cars and light trucks to transport

SECTION REVIEW

- Government bureaucracies and the middle class grew after the war, but not the working class.
- In many countries, women gained the right to vote and led reform movements.
- Max Planck and Albert Einstein led a revolution in physics.
- Social scientists like Sigmund Freud undermined the old certainties of European culture by revealing a dark side to human nature.
- After the Wright brothers' first flight, other aviation pioneers set flying records.
- Electricity, radio, and cinema changed lifestyles and cultures, and the cult of cleanliness improved health.
- American cities were transformed by skyscrapers, and the automobile led to the creation of suburbs.

produce as well as passengers. Governments obliged by building new roads and paving old ones to make automobile travel smoother and safer.

In 1915 Ford introduced a gasoline-powered tractor, and by the mid-1920s these versatile machines began replacing horses. Larger farms profited most from this innovation, while small farmers sold their land and moved to the cities. Tractors and other expensive equipment hastened the transformation of agriculture from family enterprises to large agribusinesses.

In India, Australia, and the western United States, where there was little virgin rain-watered land left to cultivate, engineers built dams and canals to irrigate dry lands. Dams offered the added advantage of producing electricity, for which there was a booming demand. The immediate benefits of irrigation—land, food, and electricity—far outweighed such distant consequences as salt deposits on irrigated lands and harm to wildlife.

CONCLUSION

In the late 1920s it seemed as though the victors in the Great War might reestablish the prewar prosperity and European dominance of the globe. But the spirit of the 1920s was not real peace; instead it was the eye of a hurricane.

The Great War caused a major realignment among the nations of the world. France and Britain, the two leading colonial powers, emerged economically weakened despite their victory. The war brought defeat and humiliation to Germany but did not reduce its military or industrial potential. It destroyed the old regime of Russia, leading to civil war and revolution from which the victorious powers sought to isolate themselves. Two other old empires—the Austro-Hungarian and the Ottoman—were divided into many smaller and weaker nations.

Japan took advantage of the European conflict to develop its industries and press its demands on a China weakened by domestic turmoil and social unrest. The United States emerged as the most prosperous and potentially most powerful nation, restrained only by the isolationist sentiments of many Americans.

In the Middle East, the fall of the Ottoman Empire awakened aspirations of nationhood among the Turkish and Arab inhabitants and Jewish immigrants. These aspirations were thwarted when France and Great Britain tried to impose their rule upon the former Ottoman lands, causing conflicts and bitter enmities.

The war challenged social traditions in many ways. Many women who had participated in the war effort remained in the work force and demanded voting and other rights. Governments took on new responsibilities for education, public health, and social welfare. Automobiles, movies, and radio broadcasts were eagerly adopted by western Europeans and North Americans, and aviation aroused tremendous enthusiasm. Advances in the sciences, especially in physics and psychology, undermined the old cultural certainties, while birth control and family planning provoked considerable opposition from traditionalists.

KEY TERMS

Western Front p. 803
Faisal p. 806
Theodore Herzl p. 806
Balfour Declaration p. 806
Bolsheviks p. 806
Vladimir Lenin p. 806
Woodrow Wilson p. 807
Fourteen Points p. 807
League of Nations p. 809
Treaty of Versailles p. 809
New Economic Policy p. 809
Sun Yat-sen p. 813
Yuan Shikai p. 814
Guomindang p. 814
Chiang Kai-shek p. 814
mandate system p. 815
Atatürk p. 816
Margaret Sanger p. 821
Max Planck p. 821
Albert Einstein p. 821
Sigmund Freud p. 821
Wilbur and Orville Wright p. 822

EBOOK AND WEBSITE RESOURCES

Primary Sources

Letter from Turkey, Summer 1915

The Balfour Declaration

Comments of the German Delegation to the Paris Peace Conference on the Conditions of Peace, October 1919

An Economist Analyzes the Versailles Treaty and Finds It Lacking

Two Proclamations of the Boxer Rebellion

The Three People's Principles and the Future of the Chinese People

Interactive Maps

Map 28.1 Europe in 1913

Map 28.2 The First World War in Europe

Map 28.3 Territorial Changes in Europe After World War I

Map 28.4 Territorial Changes in the Middle East After World War I

Plus flashcards, practice quizzes, and more. Go to: www.cengage.com/history/bullietearthpeople5e

SUGGESTED READING

Bianco, Lucien. *Origins of the Chinese Revolution, 1915–1949.* 1971. A succinct account of the rise of communism in China.

DuBois, Ellen. *Woman Suffrage and Women's Rights.* 1998. The best description of the women's movement at the beginning of the twentieth century.

Figes, Orlando. *A People's Tragedy: The Russian Revolution, 1891–1924.* 1996. A well-written overview of the Russian Revolution.

Fritzsche, Peter. *A Nation of Fliers: German Aviation and the Popular Imagination.* 1992. On the rise of aviation in Germany.

Fromkin, David. *A Peace to End All Peace.* 1989. An excellent introduction of twentieth-century Middle Eastern history.

Higonnet, Margaret, et al., eds. *Behind the Lines: Gender and the Two World Wars.* 1987. Describes the contributions of women during wartime.

Hughes, H. Stuart. *Consciousness and Society: The Reorientation of European Social Thought, 1890–1930.* 1958. An intellectual and cultural history of early twentieth-century Europe.

Keegan, John. *The First World War.* 1999. A short account of the war by an eminent military historian.

Nye, David E. *Electrifying America: Social Meanings of a New Technology.* 1990. The cultural history of American electrification and modernization.

Remarque, Erich Maria. *All Quiet on the Western Front.* 1928. The classic novel about war from the soldiers' viewpoint.

Roberts, A. D., ed. *Cambridge History of Africa,* vol. 7, *1905–1940.* 1986. A complete but readable analysis of early twentieth-century African history.

Sontag, Raymond. *A Broken World, 1919–1939.* 1971. Describes how the problems left by the First World War led to the Second World War.

Tuchman, Barbara. *The Guns of August.* 1962. A classic and very readable account of the first month of the Great War.

NOTES

1. Frank B. Tipton, *A History of Modern Germany since 1815* (Berkeley: University of California Press, 2003), 295.
2. Walter Z. Laqueur and Barry Rubin, eds., *The Arab-Israeli Reader: A Documentary History of the Middle East Conflict*, 4th ed. (New York: Penguin Books, 1984), 18.
3. David Shub, *Lenin: A Biography* (Garden City, N.Y.: Doubleday, 1948), 257.
4. David Vital, *A People Apart: The Jews of Europe*, 1789–1939 (Oxford: Oxford University Press, 1999), 756.
5. Ragnhild Fiebig von Hase and Ursula Lehmkuhl, *Enemy Images in American History* (Oxford: Berghahn Books, 1997), 5.
6. Emile Durkheim, *The Elementary Forms of Religious Life*, trans. by Karen Elise Fields (New York: Free Press, 1995), 2.

AP* REVIEW QUESTIONS FOR CHAPTER 28

1. In the early twentieth century, the rapid industrial growth of Germany and the declining power of the Ottoman Empire
   (A) led to the rise of Japan as a major power in Asia.
   (B) increased African and Asian nationalism.
   (C) created a dangerous power vacuum in the European balance of power.
   (D) led to the Ottoman Empire beginning its industrialization.

2. Mainly army officers, this group attempted to force a constitution on the Ottoman sultan, along with the Turkification of ethnic minorities and the establishment of a strong central government.
   (A) The Dervishes
   (B) The Young Turks
   (C) The Pan-Slavic Movement
   (D) The Young Democrats

3. Because of the spread of nationalism, most people in Europe viewed war as
   (A) dangerous to the growth of the new nations in the world.
   (B) a way that large imperialistic nations gained control over smaller nations.
   (C) a crusade for liberty or revenge for past injustices.
   (D) dangerous because of the new modern weapons that had been developed.

4. For Russia the effect of World War I was especially devastating because
   (A) Russian troops did not fight well and embarrassed the government.
   (B) it led Russia into an alliance with Japan.
   (C) it opened the door to revolution and civil war and introduced a radical new political system.
   (D) it led to the tsar and the nobles cracking down harshly on anyone in Russia who was not an ethnic Russian.

5. In 1915 Germany announced a submarine blockade of Great Britain because
   (A) it needed to end the war quickly, since it did not have large amounts of wealth to support the war.
   (B) it hoped to lure the British navy into a decisive sea battle and end the war.
   (C) the British had blockaded Germany.
   (D) it hoped to seize raw materials coming from the British colonies in Africa and Asia.

6. One way that the war transformed the lives of everyone in Europe was that
   (A) the nations at war needed to draft women and old men to send more troops to the front.
   (B) wages were reduced and hours were cut as cost-saving measures.
   (C) food was strictly rationed in all European nations.
   (D) schools were closed, and everyone over the age of ten had to work in the war effort.

7. Which of the following is true of the Arab Revolt of 1916?
   (A) It helped to turn the tide of the war in Europe.
   (B) It was mercilessly crushed by the Ottoman government.
   (C) It led to the Balfour Declaration.
   (D) It ultimately contributed to the defeat of the Ottoman Empire.

8. Under the Treaty of Brest-Litovsk, the Bolshevik government of Russia
   (A) joined the side of Germany against Great Britain and France.
   (B) gained control of the Bosporus and Dardanelles.
   (C) ended its participation in World War I and gave up huge areas of land and wealth.
   (D) passed land reform measures that gave land to the peasants in Russia.

9. As a way to safeguard peace and to foster international cooperation, President Wilson proposed
   (A) that a League of Nations be created.
   (B) that war be outlawed as a method of diplomacy.
   (C) an end to colonial practices and immediate independence for all remaining colonies.
   (D) that Germany and Austria-Hungary be punished economically for having caused the war.

10. One byproduct of the end of the war and peace was the creation of new nations in Europe, including Finland, Czechoslovakia, Yugoslavia, Romania, and
    (A) Switzerland.
    (B) Poland.
    (C) Denmark.
    (D) Belgium.

11. In 1921 Lenin announced the New Economic Policy, which
    (A) gave the Bolshevik government complete control over all the means of production as well as ownership of all mineral wealth in the nation.
    (B) called for the issuance of a new form of currency and limited international trade to those nations that respected the new government of the USSR.
    (C) allowed peasants to own their own land and sell their crops, merchants to trade, and private workshops to produce goods and sell them on the free market.
    (D) granted land ownership to the peasants and ownership of industries to the workers.

12. Sun Yat-sen, the leader of China's Revolutionary Alliance and later the Guomindang, envisioned a China
    (A) built on American ideals of democratic government.
    (B) that was nationalistic and socialistic yet still maintained a Confucian philosophy.
    (C) created around a modern constitutional monarchy.
    (D) that was an absolute dictatorship under a strong military leader.

13. One reason that Japan joined the side of the Allies in World War I was
    (A) to gain access to British, French, and U.S. industrial goods and military supplies.
    (B) to test out its new ships and new guns on a weak nation.
    (C) to advance its own opportunities in Asia while the Europeans were occupied elsewhere.
    (D) that the emperor had promised the nation that it would be like the European nations.

14. The mandate system was designed to
    (A) ensure that the people in the remaining colonies in Asia and Africa were given civil and political rights.
    (B) force nations to not use war as a primary means of achieving international objectives.
    (C) separate religion from government in nations that had not already done so.
    (D) provide some oversight in former German and Ottoman lands that were taken over by Great Britain and France after World War I.

15. As the new leader of Turkey after World War I, Mustafa Kemal's main goal was
    (A) the modernization and westernization of Turkey.
    (B) regaining Turkey's lost empire as soon as possible.
    (C) reforming Turkey into an Islamic republic.
    (D) reinstating the Ottoman nobility to a position of power.

16. Which of the following is true of the women's rights movements around the world?
    (A) Most of them were successful in gaining suffrage rights prior to World War I.
    (B) The only movements that had any real success in gaining suffrage rights prior to 1945 were those in Western nations.
    (C) Since Europe and the United States had already granted women full political rights, they pushed African and Asian nations to follow suit.
    (D) Generally, these movements were led by religious leaders, which made it difficult for them to spread around the world.

CHAPTER

29

CHAPTER OUTLINE

- The Stalin Revolution
- The Depression
- The Rise of Fascism
- East Asia, 1931–1945
- The Second World War
- The Character of Warfare
- Conclusion

DIVERSITY + DOMINANCE *Women, Family Values, and the Russian Revolution*

ENVIRONMENT + TECHNOLOGY *The Enigma Machine*

akg-images

German Dive-Bomber over Eastern Europe A German Messerschmidt Bf-110 fighter plane attacks a Soviet troop convoy on the Eastern Front.

Visit the website and ebook for additional study materials and interactive tools: www.cengage.com/history/bullietearthpeople5e

The Collapse of the Old Order, 1929–1949

- How did the Soviet Union change under Stalin, and at what cost?
- What caused the Depression, and what effects did it have on the world?
- How did fascism in Italy and Germany lead to the Second World War?
- What were the economic reasons behind Japan's invasion of Manchuria?
- How was the war fought, and why did Japan and Germany lose?
- How did science and technology change the nature of warfare?

Before the First World War the Italian poet Filippo Marinetti exalted violence as noble and manly: "We want to glorify war, the world's only hygiene—militarism, deed, destroyer of anarchisms, the beautiful ideas that are death-bringing, and the subordination of women."[1] His friend Gabriele d'Annunzio added: "If it is a crime to incite citizens to violence, I shall boast of this crime."[2] Poets are sometimes more prescient than they imagine.

In the nineteenth century the governments of the great powers were manipulated by politicians through appeals to popular nationalism. Internationally, the world order relied on the maintenance of empires by military or economic means. And the global economy was based on free-market capitalism in which the industrial countries exchanged manufactured goods for the agricultural and mineral products of the nonindustrial world.

After the trauma of World War I the world seemed to return to what U.S. president Warren Harding called "normalcy": prosperity in Europe and America, European colonialism in Asia and Africa, American domination of Latin America, and peace almost everywhere. But in 1929 normalcy vanished. As the Great Depression spread around the world, governments turned against one another in desperate attempts to protect their people's livelihood.

Most survivors of the war had learned to abhor violence. For a few, however, war and domination became a creed, a goal, and a solution to their problems. The Japanese military tried to save their country from the Depression by conquering China, which erupted in revolution. In Germany many blamed their troubles on Communists and Jews and turned to the Nazis, who promised to save German society by crushing others. In the Soviet Union, Stalin used energetic and murderous means to force his country into a Communist version of the Industrial Revolution.

As the old order collapsed, the world was engulfed by a second Great War, one far more global and destructive than the first. Unlike World War I, this was a war of movement in which entire countries were conquered in a matter of weeks. It was also a war of machines: fighter planes and bombers that targeted civilians, tanks, aircraft carriers, and, finally, atomic bombs that obliterated entire cities.

At the end of World War II much of Europe and East Asia lay in ruins, and millions of destitute refugees sought safety in other lands. The colonial powers were either defeated or so weakened that they could no longer prevent their Asian and African subjects from demanding independence.

THE STALIN REVOLUTION

During the 1920s the Soviet Union recovered from the Revolutions of 1917 and the civil war that followed (see Chapter 28). After Stalin achieved total mastery over this huge nation in 1929, he led it through an economic and social transformation that turned it into a great industrial and military power and intensified both admiration for and fear of communism throughout the world.

Joseph Stalin Bolshevik revolutionary, head of the Soviet Communist Party after 1924, and dictator of the Soviet Union from 1928 to 1953. He led the Soviet Union with an iron fist, using Five-Year Plans to increase industrial production and terror to crush all opposition.

Five-Year Plans Plans that Joseph Stalin introduced to industrialize the Soviet Union rapidly, beginning in 1928. They set goals for the output of steel, electricity, machinery, and most other products and were enforced by the police powers of the state. They succeeded in making the Soviet Union a major industrial power before World War II.

Five-Year Plans

Joseph Stalin (1879–1953) was the son of a poor shoemaker. Before becoming a revolutionary, he studied for the priesthood. Under the name *Stalin* (Russian for "man of steel"), he played a small part in the Revolutions of 1917. He was a hard-working and skillful administrator who rose within the party bureaucracy and filled its upper ranks with men loyal to himself. He then proceeded to make himself absolute dictator and transform Soviet society.

Stalin's ambition was to turn the USSR into an industrial nation. However, industrialization was to serve a different purpose than in other countries. It was not expected to produce consumer goods for a mass market or to enrich individuals. Instead, its aim was to increase the power of the Communist Party domestically and that of the Soviet Union in relation to other countries.

Stalin was determined to prevent a repetition of the humiliating defeat Russia had suffered at the hands of Germany in 1917. His goal was to quintuple the output of electricity and double that of heavy industry—iron, steel, coal, and machinery—in five years. To do so, he devised the first of a series of **Five-Year Plans**. Beginning in October 1928, the Communist Party and government created whole industries and cities from scratch, then trained millions of peasants to work in the new factories, mines, and offices. In every way except actual fighting, Stalin's Russia resembled a nation at war.

Rapid industrialization hastened environmental changes. Hydroelectric dams turned rivers into strings of reservoirs. Roads, canals, and railroad tracks cut the landscape. Forests and grassland were turned into farmland. From an environmental perspective, the Five-Year Plans resembled the transformation that had occurred in the United States and Canada a few decades earlier.

Collectivization of Agriculture

Since the Soviet Union was still a predominantly agrarian country, the only way to pay for these massive investments, provide the labor, and feed the millions of new industrial workers was to squeeze the peasantry. Stalin therefore proceeded with the most radical social experiment conceived up to that time: the collectivization of agriculture.

David King Collection

The Collectivization of Soviet Agriculture One of the goals of collectivization was to introduce modern farm machinery. This poster shows delighted farmers operating new tractors and threshers.

CHRONOLOGY

	United States, Europe, and North Africa	Asia and the Pacific
1920		
	1928 Stalin introduces Five-Year Plans and the collectivization of agriculture	
	1929 Great Depression begins in U.S.	
1930	1931 Great Depression reaches Europe	1931 Japanese forces occupy Manchuria
	1933 Hitler comes to power in Germany	1934–1935 Mao leads Communists on Long March
1935	1936 Hitler invades the Rhineland	1937 Japanese troops invade China, conquer coastal provinces; Chiang Kai-shek flees to Sichuan
		1937–1938 Japanese troops take Nanjing
	1939 (Sept. 1) German forces invade Poland	
1940	1940 (March–April) German forces conquer Denmark, Norway, the Netherlands, and Belgium	
	1940 (May–June) German forces conquer France	
	1940 (June–Sept.) Battle of Britain	
	1941 (June 21) German forces invade USSR	1941 (Dec. 7) Japanese aircraft bomb Pearl Harbor
	1942–1943 Allies and Germany battle for control of North Africa	1942 (Jan.–March) Japanese conquer Thailand, Philippines, Malaya
		1942 (June) United States Navy defeats Japan at Battle of Midway
	1943 Soviet victory in Battle of Stalingrad	
	1943–1944 Red Army slowly pushes Wehrmacht back to Germany	
	1944 (June 6) D-day: U.S., British, and Canadian troops land in Normandy	
1945	1945 (May 7) Germany surrenders	1945 (Aug. 6) United States drops atomic bomb on Hiroshima
		1945 (Aug. 14) Japan surrenders
		1945–1949 Civil war in China
		1949 (Oct. 1) Communists defeat Guomindang; Mao proclaims People's Republic of China

Collectivization meant consolidating small private farms into vast collectives and making the farmers work together in commonly owned fields. Each collective was expected to supply the government with a fixed amount of food and distribute what was left among its members. Collectives were to become outdoor factories where food was manufactured through the techniques of mass production and the application of machinery. The purpose of this collectivization was to bring the peasants under government control so they never again could withhold food supplies, as they had done during the Russian civil war of 1918–1921.

Kulaks

When collectivization was announced, the government mounted a massive propaganda campaign and sent party members into the countryside to enlist the farmers' support. At first all seemed to go well, but soon *kulaks* (COO-lox) ("fists"), the better-off peasants, began to resist giving up all their property. When soldiers came to force them into collectives at gunpoint, they burned their crops, smashed their equipment, and slaughtered their livestock. Within a few months they slaughtered half of the Soviet Union's horses and cattle and two-thirds of the sheep and goats. In retaliation, Stalin ruthlessly ordered the "liquidation of kulaks as a class" and incited the poor peasants to attack their wealthier neighbors. Over 8 million kulaks were arrested. Many were executed, and the rest were sent to slave labor camps, where most starved to death.

Famine

The peasants who were left had been the least successful before collectivization and proved to be the least competent after. Many were sent to work in factories. The rest were forbidden to leave their farms. With half of their draft animals gone, they could not plant or harvest enough to meet the swelling demands of the cities. Yet government agents took whatever they could find, leaving little or nothing for the farmers themselves. After bad harvests in 1933 and 1934, a famine swept through the countryside, killing some 5 million people, about one in every twenty farmers.

Stalin's second Five-Year Plan, designed to run from 1933 to 1937, was originally intended to produce consumer goods. But when the Nazis took over Germany in 1933 (see below), Stalin changed the plan to emphasize heavy industries that could produce armaments. Between 1927 and 1937 the Soviet output of metals and machines increased fourteen-fold while consumer goods became scarce and food was rationed. After a decade of Stalinism, the Soviet people were more poorly clothed, fed, and housed than they had been before the war.

Terror and Opportunities

AP* Exam Tip New political innovations and economic developments are especially important.

The 1930s brought both terror and opportunities to the Soviet people. The forced pace of industrialization, the collectivization of agriculture, and the uprooting of millions of people could be accomplished only under duress. To prevent any possible resistance or rebellion, the NKVD, Stalin's secret police force, created a climate of suspicion and fear.

As early as 1930 Stalin had hundreds of engineers and technicians arrested on trumped-up charges of counterrevolutionary ideas and sabotage. Three years later, he expelled a million members of the Communist Party—one-third of the membership—on similar charges. He then turned on his most trusted associates.

The Purge Trials

In December 1934 Sergei Kirov, the party boss of Leningrad (now St. Petersburg), was assassinated, perhaps on Stalin's orders. Stalin made a public display of mourning Kirov while blaming others for the crime. He then ordered a series of spectacular purge trials in which he accused most of Lenin's associates of treason. In 1937 he had his eight top generals and many lower officers executed, leaving the Red Army dangerously weakened. Under torture or psychological pressure, almost all the accused confessed to the "crimes" they were charged with.

Gulags

While "Old Bolsheviks" and high officials were being put on trial, terror spread steadily downward. The government regularly made demands that people could not meet, so everyone was guilty of breaking some regulation or other. People from all walks of life were arrested, some on mere suspicion or because of a false accusation by a jealous coworker or neighbor, some for expressing a doubt or working too hard or not hard enough, some for being related to someone previously arrested, some for no reason at all. Millions of people were sentenced without trials. At the height of the terror, some 8 million were sent to *gulags* (GOO-log) (labor camps), where perhaps a million died each year of exposure or malnutrition. To its victims the terror seemed capricious and random. Yet it turned a sullen and resentful people into docile hard-working subjects of the party.

In spite of the fear and hardships, many Soviet citizens supported Stalin's regime. Suddenly, with so many people gone and new industries and cities being built everywhere, there were opportunities for those who remained, especially the poor and the young. Women entered careers and jobs previously closed to them, becoming steelworkers, physicians, and office managers; but they retained their household and child-rearing duties, receiving little help from men (see Diversity and Dominance: Women, Family Values, and the Russian Revolution). People who moved to the cities, worked enthusiastically, and asked no questions could hope to rise into the upper ranks of the Communist Party, the military, the government, or the professions—where the privileges and rewards were many.

Stalin's brutal methods helped the Soviet Union industrialize faster than any country had ever done. By the late 1930s the USSR was the

SECTION REVIEW

- Once in power, Stalin issued Five-Year Plans to accelerate Soviet industrialization.
- When farms were merged into collectives, millions of farmers who resisted were deported and killed; those who were left suffered famine.
- Under the terror, Stalin executed many generals and government officials and sent millions of people to slave labor camps.
- Stalin's measures subjugated the Russian people and made the Soviet Union the world's third largest industrial power.

world's third largest industrial power, after the United States and Germany. To foreign observers it seemed to be booming with construction projects and labor shortages. Even anti-Communist observers admitted that government planning worked. To millions of Soviet citizens who took pride in the new strength of their country and to many foreigners who contrasted conditions in the Soviet Union with the unemployment and despair in the West, Stalin's achievement seemed worth any price.

THE DEPRESSION

AP* Exam Tip Be sure to understand major economic developments, such as the Great Depression.

On October 24, 1929—"Black Thursday"—the New York stock market went into a dive. Within days stocks had lost half their value. The fall continued for three years, ruining millions of investors. People with bank accounts rushed to make withdrawals, causing thousands of banks to collapse.

Economic Crisis

What began as a stock market crash soon turned into the deepest depression in history. As consumers reduced their purchases, businesses cut production, laying off thousands of workers. Female employees were the first laid off on the grounds that men had to support families while women worked only for "pin money." Jobless men deserted their families. Small farmers went bankrupt and lost their land. By mid-1932 the American economy had shrunk by half, and unemployment had risen to an unprecedented 25 percent of the work force. Many observers thought that free-enterprise capitalism was doomed.

In 1930 the U.S. government, hoping to protect American industries from foreign competition, imposed the Smoot-Hawley tariff, the highest in American history. In retaliation, other countries raised their tariffs in a wave of "beggar thy neighbor" protectionism. The result was crippled export industries and shrinking world trade. While global industrial production declined by 36 percent between 1929 and 1932, world trade dropped by a breathtaking 62 percent.

Time Life Pictures/Getty Images

Two Views of the American Way In this classic photograph, *Life* magazine photographer Margaret Bourke-White captured the contrast between advertisers' view of the ideal American family and the reality of bread lines for the poor.

DIVERSITY + DOMINANCE

Women, Family Values, and the Russian Revolution

The Bolsheviks were of two minds on the subject of women. They were opposed to bourgeois morality and to the oppression of women, especially working-class women, under capitalism. But what to put in its place?

Alexandra Kollontai was the most outspoken of the Bolsheviks on the subject of women's rights. She advocated the liberation of women, the replacement of housework by communal kitchens and laundries, and divorce on demand. Under socialism, love, sex, and marriage would be entirely equal, reciprocal, and free of economic obligations. Childbearing would be encouraged, but children would be raised communally: "The worker mother . . . must remember that there are henceforth only our children, those of the communist state, the common possession of all workers."

In a lecture she gave at Sverdlov University in 1921, Kollontai declared:

. . . it is important to preserve not only the interests of the woman but also the life of the child, and this is to be done by giving the woman the opportunity to combine labour and maternity. Soviet power tries to create a situation where a woman does not have to cling to a man she has learned to loathe only because she has nowhere else to go with her children, and where a woman alone does not have to fear for her life and the life of her child. In the labour republic it is not the philanthropists with their humiliating charity but the workers and peasants, fellow-creators of the new society, who hasten to help the working woman and strive to lighten the burden of motherhood. . . . I would like to say a few words about a question which is closely connected with the problem of maternity—the question of abortion, and Soviet Russia's attitude toward it. On 20 November 1920 the labour republic issued a law abolishing the penalties that had been attached to abortion. What is the reason behind this new attitude? Russia after all suffers not from an overproduction of living labour but rather from a lack of it. Russia is thinly, not densely populated. Every unit of labour power is precious. Why then have we declared abortion to be no longer a criminal offence? . . .

Abortion exists and flourishes everywhere, and no laws or punitive measures have succeeded in rooting it out. A way round the law is always found. But "secret help" only cripples women; they become a burden on the labour government, and the size of the labour force is reduced. Abortion, when carried out under proper medical conditions, is less harmful and dangerous, and the woman can get back to work quicker. Soviet power realizes that the need for abortion will only disappear on the one hand when Russia has a broad and developed network of institutions protecting motherhood and providing social education, and on the other hand when women understand that *childbirth is a social obligation*; Soviet power has therefore allowed abortion to be performed openly and in clinical conditions.

Besides the large-scale development of motherhood protection, the task of labour Russia is to strengthen in women the healthy instinct of motherhood, to make motherhood and labour for the collective compatible and thus do away with the need for abortion. This is the approach of the labour republic to the question of abortion, which still faces women in the bourgeois countries in all its magnitude. In these countries women are exhausted by the dual burden of hired labour for capital and motherhood. In Soviet Russia the working woman and peasant woman are helping the Communist Party to build a new society and to undermine the old way of life that has enslaved women. As soon as woman is viewed as being essentially a labour unit, the key to the solution of the complex question of maternity can be found. . . . The emancipation of women can only be completed when a fundamental transformation of living is effected; and life-styles will change only

Depression in Industrial Nations

By 1931 the Depression had spread to Europe. Governments canceled reparations payments and war loans, but it was too late to save the world economy. Though their economies stagnated, France and Britain weathered the Depression by making their colonial empires purchase their products rather than the products of other countries. Nations that relied on exports to pay for imported food and fuel suffered much more. In Germany unemployment reached 6 million by 1932, twice as high as in Britain. Half the German population lived in poverty, while those who kept their jobs saw their salaries cut and their living standards fall. In Japan the burden of the Depression fell hardest on the farmers and fishermen.

This massive economic upheaval had profound political repercussions. Nationalists everywhere called for autarchy, or independence from the world economy. In the United States Franklin D. Roosevelt was elected president in 1932 on a "New Deal" platform of government programs to stimulate and revitalize the economy. Although the American, British, and French governments intervened in their economies, they remained democratic. In Germany and Japan, with the fundamental transformation of all production and the establishment of a communist economy. The revolution in everyday life is unfolding before our very eyes, and in this process the liberation of women is being introduced in practice.

Fifteen years later Joseph Stalin reversed the Soviet policy on abortion.

The published draft of the law prohibiting abortion and providing material assistance to mothers has provoked a lively reaction throughout the country. It is being heatedly discussed by tens of millions of people and there is no doubt that it will serve as a further strengthening of the Soviet family. . . .

When we speak of strengthening the Soviet family, we are speaking precisely of the struggle against the survivals of a bourgeois attitude towards marriage, women, and children. So-called "free love" and all disorderly sex life are bourgeois through and through, and have nothing to do with either socialist principles or the ethics and standards of conduct of the Soviet citizens. Socialist doctrine shows this, and it is proved by life itself.

The elite of our country, the best of the Soviet youth, are as a rule also excellent family men who dearly love their children. And vice versa: the man who does not take marriage seriously, and abandons his children to the whims of fate, is usually also a bad worker and a poor member of society. . . .

It is impossible even to compare the present state of the family with that which obtained before the Soviet regime—so great has been the improvement towards greater stability and, above all, greater humanity and goodness. The single fact that millions of women have become economically independent and are no longer at the mercy of men's whims, speaks volumes. Compare, for instance, the modern woman collective farmer who sometimes earns more than her husband, with the pre-revolutionary peasant woman who completely depended on her husband and was a slave in the household. Has not this fundamentally changed family relations, has it not rationalized and strengthened the family? The very motives for setting up a family, for getting married, have changed for the better, have been cleansed of atavistic and barbaric elements. Marriage has ceased to be a matter of sell-and-buy. Nowadays a girl from a collective farm is not given away (or should we say "sold away"?) by her father, for now she is her own mistress, and no one can give her away. She will marry the man she loves. . . .

We alone have all the conditions under which a working woman can fulfill her duties as a citizen and as a mother responsible for the birth and early upbringing of her children.

A woman without children merits our pity, for she does not know the full joy of life. Our Soviet women, full-blooded citizens of the freest country in the world, have been given the bliss of motherhood. We must safeguard the family and raise and rear healthy Soviet heroes!

QUESTIONS FOR ANALYSIS

1. **How does Kollontai expect women to be both workers and mothers without depending on a man? How would Soviet society make this possible?**
2. **Why does Alexandra Kollontai advocate the legalization of abortion in Soviet Russia? Does she view abortion as a permanent right or as a temporary necessity?**
3. **Why does Stalin characterize a "lighthearted, negligent attitude toward marriage" and "all disorderly sex life" as "bourgeois through and through"?**
4. **How does Stalin's image of the Soviet family differ from Kollontai's? Are his views a variation of her views, or the opposite?**

Source: First selection from Alexandra Kollontai, "The Labour of Women in the Revolution of the Economy," in *Selected Writings of Alexandra Kollontai*, translated by Alix Holt (Lawrence Hill & Company, 1978), pp. 148–149. Used with permission of Lawrence Hill Books. Second selection from Joseph Stalin, *Law on the Abolition of Legal Abortion* (1936).

as economic grievances worsened long-festering political resentments, radical leaders came to power and turned their nations into military machines, hoping to acquire, by war if necessary, empires large enough to support self-sufficient economies.

Depression in Nonindustrial Regions

The Depression also spread to Asia, Africa, and Latin America, but very unevenly. In 1930 India erected a wall of import duties to protect its infant industries from foreign competition; its living standards stagnated but did not drop. China was little affected by trade with other countries; its problems were more political than economic.

Asia

Countries that depended on exports were hard hit by the Depression. Malaya, Indochina, and the Dutch East Indies produced most of the world's natural rubber; when automobile production in the United States and Europe dropped by half, so did imports of rubber, devastating their economies. Egypt, dependent on cotton exports, was also affected, and in the resulting political strife, the government became autocratic and unpopular.

Latin America

Throughout Latin America unemployment and homelessness increased markedly. The industrialization of Argentina and Brazil was set back a decade or more. Disenchanted with liberal politics, military officers seized power in several Latin American countries. Consciously imitating dictatorships emerging in Europe, they imposed authoritarian control over their economies, hoping to stimulate local industries and curb imports.

Africa

Other than the USSR, only southern Africa boomed during the 1930s. As other prices dropped, gold became relatively more valuable. Copper deposits, found in Northern Rhodesia (now Zambia) and the Belgian Congo, proved to be cheaper to mine than Chilean copper. But this mining boom benefited only a small number of European and white South African mine owners. For Africans it was a mixed blessing; mining provided jobs and cash wages to men while women stayed behind in the villages, farming, herding, and raising children without their husbands' help.

SECTION REVIEW

- The New York stock market crash of 1929 caused business and bank failures and massive unemployment.
- The Depression soon spread to all industrial nations, especially Germany and Japan.
- Nonindustrial countries, especially those that depended on exports to industrial countries, were also hard hit; only southern Africa was spared.
- In the face of this threat, some countries turned to dictatorship to save their economies.

THE RISE OF FASCISM

AP* Exam Tip Be sure to understand new forces of nationalism, such as fascism.

The Russian Revolution and its Stalinist aftermath frightened property owners in Europe and North America. In western Europe and North America, middle- and upper-income voters took refuge in conservative politics. In southern and central Europe, the war had turned people's hopes of victory to bitter disappointment. Many blamed ethnic minorities, especially Jews, for their troubles. In their yearning for a mythical past of family farms and small shops, increasing numbers rejected representative government and sought more dramatic solutions.

Radical politicians quickly learned to apply wartime propaganda techniques to appeal to a confused citizenry. They promised to use any means necessary to bring back full employment, stop the spread of communism, and achieve the territorial conquests that World War I had denied them. While defending private property from communism, they borrowed the communist model of politics: a single party and a secret police that ruled by terror and intimidation.

Benito Mussolini Fascist dictator of Italy (1922–1943). He led Italy to conquer Ethiopia (1935), joined Germany in the Axis pact (1936), and allied Italy with Germany in World War II. He was overthrown in 1943 when the Allies invaded Italy.

Fascist Party Italian political party created by Benito Mussolini during World War I. It emphasized aggressive nationalism and was Mussolini's instrument for the creation of a dictatorship in Italy from 1922 to 1943.

Mussolini's Italy

The first country to seek radical answers was Italy. World War I, which had never been popular, left thousands of veterans who found neither pride in their victory nor jobs in the postwar economy. Unemployed veterans and violent youths banded together into *fasci di combattimento* (fighting units) to demand action and intimidate politicians. When workers threatened to strike, factory and property owners hired gangs of these *fascisti* to defend them.

Benito Mussolini (1883–1945) had supported Italy's entry into the war. A spellbinding orator, he quickly became the leader of the **Fascist Party**, which glorified warfare and the Italian nation. By 1921 the party had 300,000 members, many of whom used violent methods to repress strikes, intimidate voters, and seize municipal governments. A year later Mussolini threatened to march on Rome if he was not appointed prime minister. The government, composed of timid parliamentarians, gave in.

Fascism

Mussolini proceeded to install Fascist Party members in all government jobs, crush all opposition parties, and jail anyone who criticized him. The party took over the press, public education, and youth activities and gave employers control over their workers. The Fascists lowered living standards but reduced unemployment and provided social security and public services. They proved to be neither ruthless radicals nor competent administrators.

What Mussolini and the Fascist movement really excelled at was bombastic speeches, spectacular parades, and signs everywhere proclaiming "Il Duce (eel DOO-chay) [the Leader] is always right!" Mussolini's genius was to apply the techniques of modern mass communica-

Adolf Hitler Born in Austria, Hitler became a radical German nationalist during World War I. He led the National Socialist German Workers' Party—the Nazis—in the 1920s and became dictator of Germany in 1933. He led Europe into World War II.

Nazis German political party led by Adolf Hitler, emphasizing nationalism, racism, and war. When Hitler became chancellor of Germany in 1933, the Nazis became the only legal party and an instrument of Hitler's absolute rule. The party's formal name was National Socialist German Workers' Party.

tions and advertisement to political life. Movie footage and radio news bulletins galvanized the masses in ways never before done in peacetime. His techniques of whipping up public enthusiasm were not lost on other radicals. By the 1930s fascist movements had appeared in most European countries, as well as in Latin America, China, and Japan. Fascism appealed to many people who were frightened by rapid changes and placed their hopes in charismatic leaders. Of all of Mussolini's imitators, none was as sinister as Adolf Hitler.

Hitler's Germany

Germany had lost the First World War after coming very close to winning. The hyperinflation of 1923 wiped out the savings of middle-class families. Less than ten years later the Depression caused more unemployment and misery than in any other country. Millions of Germans blamed Socialists, Jews, and foreigners for their troubles.

Adolf Hitler (1889–1945) joined the German army in 1914 and was wounded at the front. He later looked back fondly on the clear lines of authority and the camaraderie he had experienced in battle. After the war he used his gifts as an orator to lead a political splinter group called the National Socialist German Workers' Party—**Nazis** for short. While serving a brief jail sentence he wrote *Mein Kampf* (mine compf) (*My Struggle*), in which he outlined his goals and beliefs.

Nazi Racism

When it was published in 1925, *Mein Kampf* attracted little notice. Its ideas seemed so insane that almost no one took it, or its author, seriously. Hitler's ideas went far beyond ordinary nationalism. He believed that Germany should incorporate all German-speaking areas, even those in neighboring countries. He distinguished among a "master race" of Aryans (he meant Germans, Scandinavians, and Britons), a degenerate "Alpine" race of French and Italians, and an inferior race of Russian and eastern European Slavs, fit only to be slaves of the master race. He reserved his most intense hatred for Jews, on whom he blamed every disaster that had befallen Germany, especially the defeat of 1918. He glorified violence and looked forward to a future war in which the "master race" would defeat and subjugate all others.

Hitler's first goal was to repeal the humiliation and military restrictions of the Treaty of Versailles. Then he planned to annex all German-speaking territories to a greater Germany, then gain *Lebensraum* (LAY-bens-rowm) (room to live) at the expense of Poland and the USSR. Finally, he planned to eliminate all Jews from Europe.

From 1924 to 1930 Hitler's followers remained a tiny minority, for most Germans found his ideas too extreme. But when the Depression hit, the Nazis gained supporters among the unemployed, who believed their promises of jobs for all, and among property owners frightened by the growing popularity of Communists.

The Third Reich

In March 1933 Hitler became chancellor of Germany. Once in office, he quickly assumed dictatorial powers. He put Nazis in charge of all government agencies, educational institutions, and professional organizations; banned all other political parties; and threw their leaders into concentration camps. The Nazis deprived Jews of their citizenship and civil rights, prohibited them from marrying "Aryans," ousted them from the professions, and confiscated their property. In August 1934 Hitler proclaimed himself *Führer* (FEW-rer) ("leader") and called Germany the "Third Reich," the third German empire after the Holy Roman Empire of medieval times and the German Empire of 1871 to 1918.

The Nazis' economic and social policies were spectacularly effective. The government undertook massive public works projects. Businesses got contracts to manufacture weapons. Women who had entered the work force were urged to release their jobs to men. By 1936 business was booming; unemployment was at its lowest level since the 1920s; and living standards were rising. Most Germans believed that their economic well-being outweighed the loss of liberty.

The Road to War, 1933–1939

However, Hitler's goal was not prosperity or popularity, but conquest. As soon as he came to office, he began to build up the armed forces. Meanwhile, he tested the reactions of the other powers through a series of surprise moves followed by protestations of peace.

In 1933 Hitler withdrew Germany from the League of Nations. Two years later he announced that Germany was going to introduce conscription, build up its army, and create an air force—in violation of the Versailles treaty. Neither Britain nor France was willing to risk war by standing up to Germany.

A Nazi Rally Hitler organized mass rallies at Nuremberg to whip up popular support for his regime and to indoctrinate young Germans with a martial spirit. Thousands of men in uniform marched in torch-lit parades before Hitler and his top officials.

AP Images

Fascist Aggression

In 1935, emboldened by the weakness of the democracies, Italy invaded Ethiopia, the last independent state in Africa and a member of the League of Nations. The League and the democracies protested but refused to close the Suez Canal to Italian ships or impose an oil embargo. The following year, when Hitler sent troops into the Rhineland on the borders of France and Belgium, the other powers merely protested.

By 1938 Hitler decided that his rearmament plans were far enough advanced that he could afford to escalate his demands. In March Germany invaded Austria. Most Austrians were German-speakers and accepted the annexation of their country without protest. Then came Czechoslovakia, where a German-speaking minority lived along the German border. Hitler first demanded their autonomy from Czech rule, then their annexation to Germany. Throughout the summer he threatened to go to war. At the Munich Conference of September 1938, the leaders of France, Britain, and Italy gave him everything he wanted without consulting Czechoslovakia. Once again, Hitler learned that aggression paid off.

Appeasement

The weakness of the democracies—now called "appeasement"—had three causes. The first was the deep-seated fear of war among people who had lived through World War I. Unlike the dictators, politicians in the democracies could not ignore their constituents' yearnings for peace. Most people believed that the threat of war might go away if they wished for peace fervently enough. The second cause of appeasement was fear of communism among conservatives, who feared Stalin more than Hitler because Hitler claimed to respect Christianity and private property. The third cause was the very novelty of fascist tactics. Britain's prime minister Neville Chamberlain assumed that political leaders (other than the Bolsheviks) were honorable men and that an agreement was as valid as a business contract. Thus, when Hitler promised to incorporate only German-speaking people into Germany and said he had "no further territorial demands," Chamberlain believed him.

After Munich it was too late to stop Hitler, short of war. Germany and Italy signed an alliance called the Axis, and in March 1939 Germany invaded what was left of Czechoslovakia. Belatedly realizing that Hitler could not be trusted, France and Britain sought Soviet help. Stalin, however, distrusted the

SECTION REVIEW

- The Depression gave opportunities to ultranationalist politicians who promised prosperity and order.
- Mussolini, head of the Fascist Party, became dictator of Italy in 1922 and proceeded to quell all opposition.
- After gaining power in 1933, Hitler began to transform the German economy and society and to build up the German armed forces.
- Germany and Italy made aggressive moves that the democracies, fearing another war, did not oppose, but when Germany invaded Poland, Hitler's aggressive objectives were clear.

Alliances

"capitalists" as much as they distrusted him. When Hitler offered to divide Poland between Germany and the Soviet Union, Stalin accepted. The Nazi-Soviet Pact of August 23, 1939, freed Hitler from the fear of a two-front war and gave Stalin time to build up his armies. One week later, on September 1, German forces swept into Poland, and the war was on.

EAST ASIA, 1931–1945

When the Depression hit, the collapse of demand for silk and rice ruined thousands of Japanese farmers; to survive, many sold their daughters into prostitution while their sons flocked to the military. Ultranationalists resented their country's dependence on foreign trade. If only Japan had a colonial empire, they thought, it would not be beholden to the rest of the world. But Europeans and Americans had already taken most potential colonies in Asia. Japanese nationalists saw the conquest of China, with its vast population and resources, as the solution to their country's problems.

The Manchurian Incident of 1931

Meanwhile, in China the Guomindang (gwo-min-dong) was becoming stronger and preparing to challenge the Japanese presence in Manchuria, a province rich in coal and iron ore. Junior officers in the Japanese army, frustrated by the caution of their superiors, took action. In September 1931 an explosion on a railroad track, probably staged, gave them an excuse to conquer the entire province. In Tokyo weak civilian ministers acquiesced to the attack to avoid losing face. Japan thereupon recognized the "independence" of Manchuria under the name *Manchukuo* (man-CHEW-coo-oh).

The U.S. government condemned the Japanese conquest, and the League of Nations refused to recognize Manchukuo and urged the Japanese to remove their troops from China. Persuaded that the Western powers would not fight, Japan resigned from the League.

During the next few years the Japanese built railways and heavy industries in Manchuria and northeastern China and sped up their rearmament. At home, production was diverted to the military, especially to building warships. The government grew more authoritarian, jailing thousands of dissidents. On several occasions, superpatriotic junior officers mutinied or assassinated leading political figures. The mutineers received mild punishments, and generals and admirals sympathetic to their views replaced more moderate civilian politicians.

Chiang Kai-shek Chinese military and political leader. Succeeded Sun Yat-sen as head of the Guomindang in 1925; headed the Chinese government from 1928 to 1948; fought against the Chinese Communists and Japanese invaders. After 1949 he headed the Chinese Nationalist government in Taiwan.

Mao Zedong Leader of the Chinese Communist Party (1927–1976). He led the Communists on the Long March (1934–1935) and rebuilt the Communist Party and Red Army during the Japanese occupation of China (1937–1945). After World War II, he led the Communists to victory over the Guomindang. He ordered the Cultural Revolution in 1966.

The Long March

Until the Japanese seized Manchuria, the Chinese government seemed to be creating conditions for a national recovery. The main challenge to the government of **Chiang Kai-shek** (chang kie-shek) came from the Communists. The Chinese Communist Party had been founded in 1921 by a handful of intellectuals, and for several years it lived in the shadow of the Guomindang. Its efforts to recruit members among industrial workers came to naught in 1927, when Chiang Kai-shek arrested and executed Communists and labor leaders alike. The few Communists who escaped the mass arrests fled to the remote mountains of Jiangxi (jang-she), in southeastern China.

Mao Zedong and Maoism

Among them was **Mao Zedong** (ma-oh zay-dong) (1893–1976), a farmer's son who had left home to study philosophy. Mao was a man of action whose first impulse was to call for violent effort: "To be able to leap on horseback and to shoot at the same time; to go from battle to battle; to shake the mountains by one's cries, and the colors of the sky by one's roars of anger." In the early 1920s Mao discovered the works of Karl Marx, joined the Communist Party, and soon became one of its leaders.

In Jiangxi Mao began studying conditions among the peasants, in whom Communists had previously shown no interest. He planned to redistribute land from the wealthier to the poorer peasants, thereby gaining adherents for the coming struggle with the Guomindang army. His goal was a complete social revolution from the bottom up. Mao's reliance on the peasantry was a radical departure from Marxist-Leninist ideology, which stressed the backwardness of the peasants and pinned its hopes on industrial workers. Mao therefore had to be careful to cloak his pragmatic tactics in Communist rhetoric to allay the suspicions of Stalin and his agents.

Mao was an advocate of women's equality. Before 1927 the Communists had organized the women who worked in Shanghai's textile mills, the most exploited of all Chinese workers. Later, in their mountain stronghold in Jiangxi, they organized women farmers, allowed divorce, and banned arranged marriages and footbinding. But the party was still run by men whose primary task was warfare.

The Guomindang army pursued the Communists into the mountains, building small forts throughout the countryside. Rather than risk direct confrontations, Mao responded with guerrilla warfare. He harassed the army at its weak points with hit-and-run tactics, relying on the terrain and the support of the peasantry. Whereas government troops often mistreated civilians, Mao insisted that his soldiers help the peasants, pay a fair price for food and supplies, and treat women with respect.

The Long March

Long March The 6,000-mile flight of Chinese Communists from southeastern to northwestern China. The Communists, led by Mao Zedong, were pursued by the Chinese army under orders from Chiang Kai-shek. The four thousand survivors of the march formed the nucleus of a revived Communist movement that defeated the Guomindang after World War II.

In spite of their good relations with the peasants of Jiangxi, the Communists gradually found themselves encircled by government forces. In 1934 Mao and his followers decided to break out of the southern mountains and trek to Shaanxi (SHAWN-she), an even more remote province in northwestern China. The so-called **Long March** took them 6,000 miles (nearly 9,700 kilometers) in one year over desolate mountains and through swamps and deserts, pursued by the army and bombed by Chiang's aircraft. Of the 100,000 Communists who left Jiangxi in October 1934, only 4,000 reached Shaanxi a year later (see Map 29.1). Chiang's government thought it was finally rid of the Communists.

The Sino-Japanese War, 1937–1945

In Japan politicians, senior officers, and business leaders disagreed on how to solve their country's economic problems. Some proposed a quick conquest of China; others advocated war with the Soviet Union. While their superiors hesitated, junior officers decided to take matters into their own hands.

On July 7, 1937, Japanese troops attacked Chinese forces near Beijing. The junior officers who ordered the attack quickly obtained the support of their commanders and then, reluctantly, of the government. Within weeks Japanese troops seized Beijing, Tianjin, Shanghai, and other coastal cities, and the Japanese navy blockaded the entire coast of China.

Once again, the United States and the League of Nations denounced the Japanese aggression. Yet the Western powers were too preoccupied with events in Europe and with their own economic problems to risk a military confrontation in Asia. When the Japanese sank a U.S. gunboat and shelled a British ship on the Yangzi River, the U.S. and British governments responded only with righteous indignation and pious resolutions.

The Chinese armies were large and fought bravely, but they were poorly led and armed and lost every battle. Japanese planes bombed cities while soldiers broke dikes and burned villages, killing thousands of civilians. Within a year Japan controlled the coastal provinces of China and the lower Yangzi and Yellow River Valleys, China's richest and most populated regions (see Map 29.1).

In spite of Japanese organizational and fighting skills, the attack on China did not bring the victory Japan had hoped for. The Chinese people continued to resist, either in the army or with the Communist guerrilla forces. As Japan sank deeper into the Chinese quagmire, life became harsher and more repressive for the Japanese people, as taxes rose, food and fuel became scarce, and more and more young men were drafted.

Warfare between the Chinese and Japanese was incredibly violent. In the winter of 1937–1938 Japanese troops took Nanjing, raped 20,000 women, killed 200,000 prisoners and civilians, and looted and burned the city. To slow them down, Chiang ordered the Yellow River dikes blasted open, causing a flood that destroyed four thousand villages, killed 890,000 people, and made 12.5 mil-

SECTION REVIEW

- Seeing conquest as a solution to its economic problems, in 1931 Japan conquered Manchuria.
- The Chinese government under Chiang Kai-shek fought both the Japanese and the Communists led by Mao Zedong, who fled into the mountains of northern China.
- In 1937, Japanese forces conquered the coastal provinces of China; in the ensuing violent war, however, Japan gained few real advantages.
- Chiang Kai-shek fled to the interior and prepared to fight the Communists.

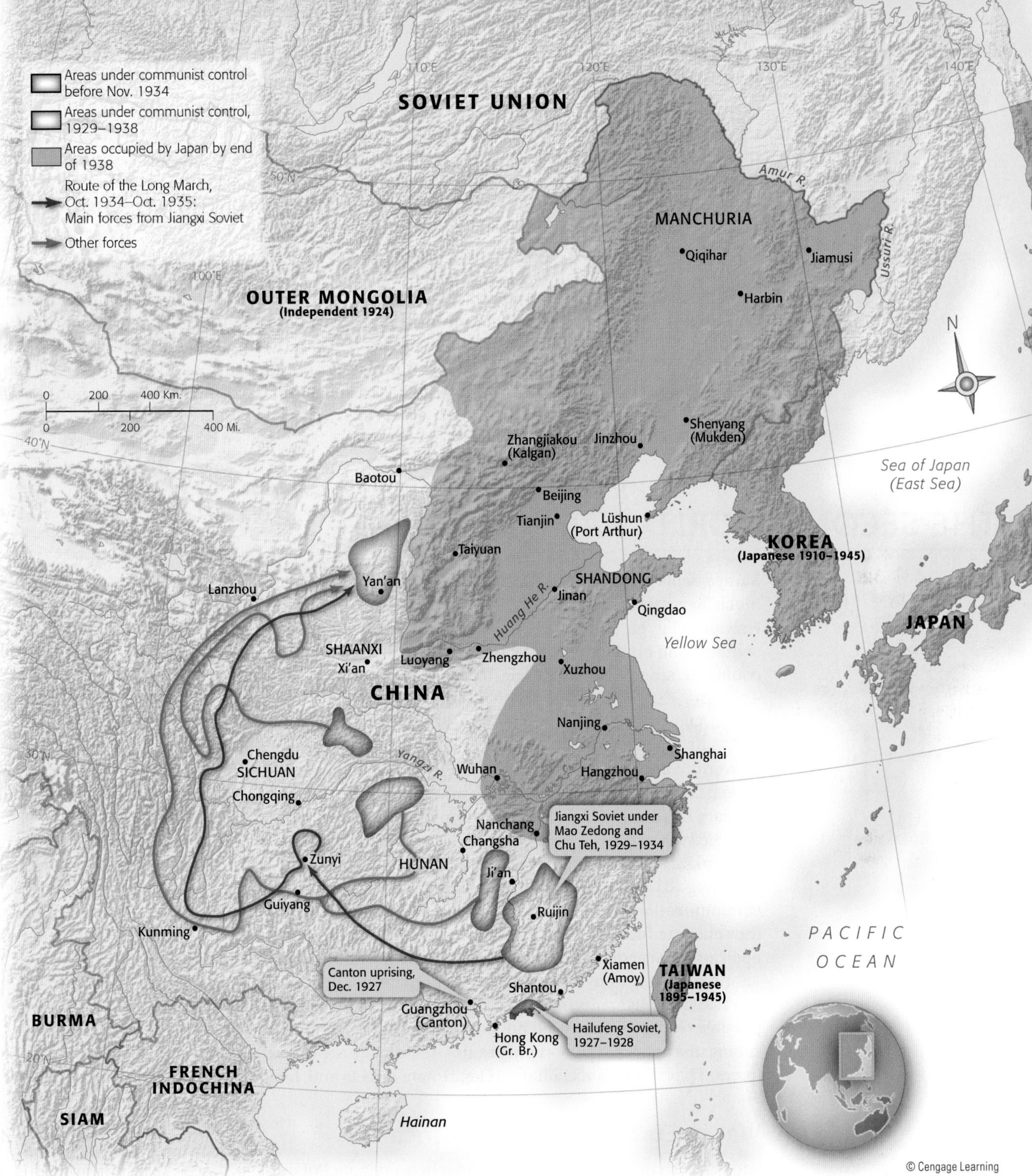

MAP 29.1 Chinese Communist Movement and the Sino-Japanese War, to 1938 During the 1930s, China was the scene of a three-way war. The Nationalist government attacked and pursued the Communists, who escaped into the mountains of Shaanxi. Meanwhile, Japanese forces, having seized Manchuria in 1931, attacked China in 1937 and quickly conquered its eastern provinces.

Interactive Map

lion homeless. Two years later, when the Communists ordered a massive offensive, the Japanese retaliated with a "kill all, burn all, loot all" campaign, destroying hundreds of villages down to the last person, building, and farm animal.

The Guomindang

The Chinese government, led by Chiang Kai-shek, escaped to the mountains of Sichuan in the center of the country. There Chiang built up a huge army, not to fight Japan but to prepare for a future confrontation with the Communists. The army drafted over 3 million men, even though it had only a million rifles and could not provide food or clothing for all its soldiers. The Guomindang raised farmers' taxes, even when famine forced farmers to eat the bark of trees. Such taxes were not enough to support both a large army and the thousands of government officials and hangers-on who had fled to Sichuan. To avoid taxing its wealthy supporters the government printed money, causing inflation, hoarding, and corruption.

The Communists

From his capital of Yan'an in Shaanxi province, Mao also built up his army and formed a government. Unlike the Guomindang, the Communists listened to the grievances of the peasants, especially the poor, to whom they distributed land confiscated from wealthy landowners. They imposed rigid discipline on their officials and soldiers and tolerated no dissent or criticism from intellectuals. Though they had few weapons, the Communists obtained support and intelligence from farmers in Japanese-occupied territory. They turned military reversals into propaganda victories, presenting themselves as the only group in China that was serious about fighting the Japanese.

THE SECOND WORLD WAR

Many people feared that the Second World War would be a repetition of the First. Instead, it was much bigger in every way. It was fought around the world, from Norway to New Guinea and from Hawaii to Egypt, and on every ocean. It killed far more people than World War I, involved all civilians and productive forces, and showed how effectively industry, science, and nationalism could be channeled into mass destruction.

The War of Movement

In World War II motorized weapons gave back the advantage to the offensive. Opposing forces moved fast, their victories hinging as much on the aggressive spirit of their commanders and the military intelligence they obtained as on numbers of troops and firepower.

Blitzkrieg

The Wehrmacht (VAIR-mokt), or German army, was the first to learn this lesson. It not only had tanks, trucks, and fighter planes but had also perfected their combined use in a tactic called *Blitzkrieg* (BLITS-creeg) (lightning war): fighter planes scattered enemy troops and disrupted communications, tanks punctured the enemy's defenses, and then, with the help of the infantry, they encircled and captured enemy troops. At sea, both Japan and the United States had developed aircraft carriers that could launch planes against targets hundreds of miles away.

Armies ranged over vast theaters of operation, and countries were conquered in days or weeks. The belligerents mobilized the economies of entire continents, squeezing them for every possible resource. They tried not only to defeat their enemies' armed forces but—by blockades, submarine attacks, and bombing raids—to damage the economies that supported those armed forces. They thought of civilians as legitimate targets and, later, as vermin to be exterminated.

War in Europe and North Africa

It took less than a month for the Wehrmacht to conquer Poland (see Map 29.2). Britain and France declared war on Germany but took no military action. Meanwhile, the Soviet Union invaded eastern Poland and the Baltic republics. Although the Poles fought bravely, their infantry and cavalry were no match for German and Russian tanks. During the winter of 1939–1940 Germany and the Western democracies faced each other in what soldiers called a "phony war."

In March 1940 Hitler went on the offensive again, conquering Denmark, Norway, the Netherlands, and Belgium in less than two months. In May he attacked France. Although the French army had as many soldiers, tanks, and aircraft as the Wehrmacht, its morale was low and it quickly collapsed. By the end of June Hitler was master of all of Europe between Russia and Spain.

The Battle of Britain

Germany still had to face Britain. The British had no army to speak of, but they had other assets: the English Channel, the Royal Navy and Air Force, and a tough new prime minister, Winston Churchill. The Germans knew they could invade Britain only by gaining control of the airspace over the Channel, so they launched a massive air attack—the Battle of Britain—lasting from June through September. The attack failed because the Royal Air Force used radar and code-breaking to detect approaching German planes.

The Nazi-Soviet War

Frustrated in the west, Hitler turned his attention eastward, even though it meant fighting a two-front war. So far he had gotten the utmost cooperation from Stalin, who supplied Germany with grain, oil, and strategic raw materials. Yet he had always wanted to conquer Lebensraum in the east and enslave the Slavic peoples who lived there, and he feared that if he waited, Stalin would build a dangerously strong army. In June 1941 Hitler launched the largest attack in history, with 3 million soldiers and thousands of planes and tanks. Within five months the Wehrmacht conquered the Baltic states, Ukraine, and half of European Russia, captured a million prisoners of war, and reached the very gates of Moscow and Leningrad. The USSR seemed on the

Interactive Map

MAP 29.2 World War II in Europe and North Africa In a series of quick and decisive campaigns from September 1939 to December 1941, German forces overran much of Europe and North Africa. There followed three years of bitter fighting as the Allies slowly pushed the Germans back.

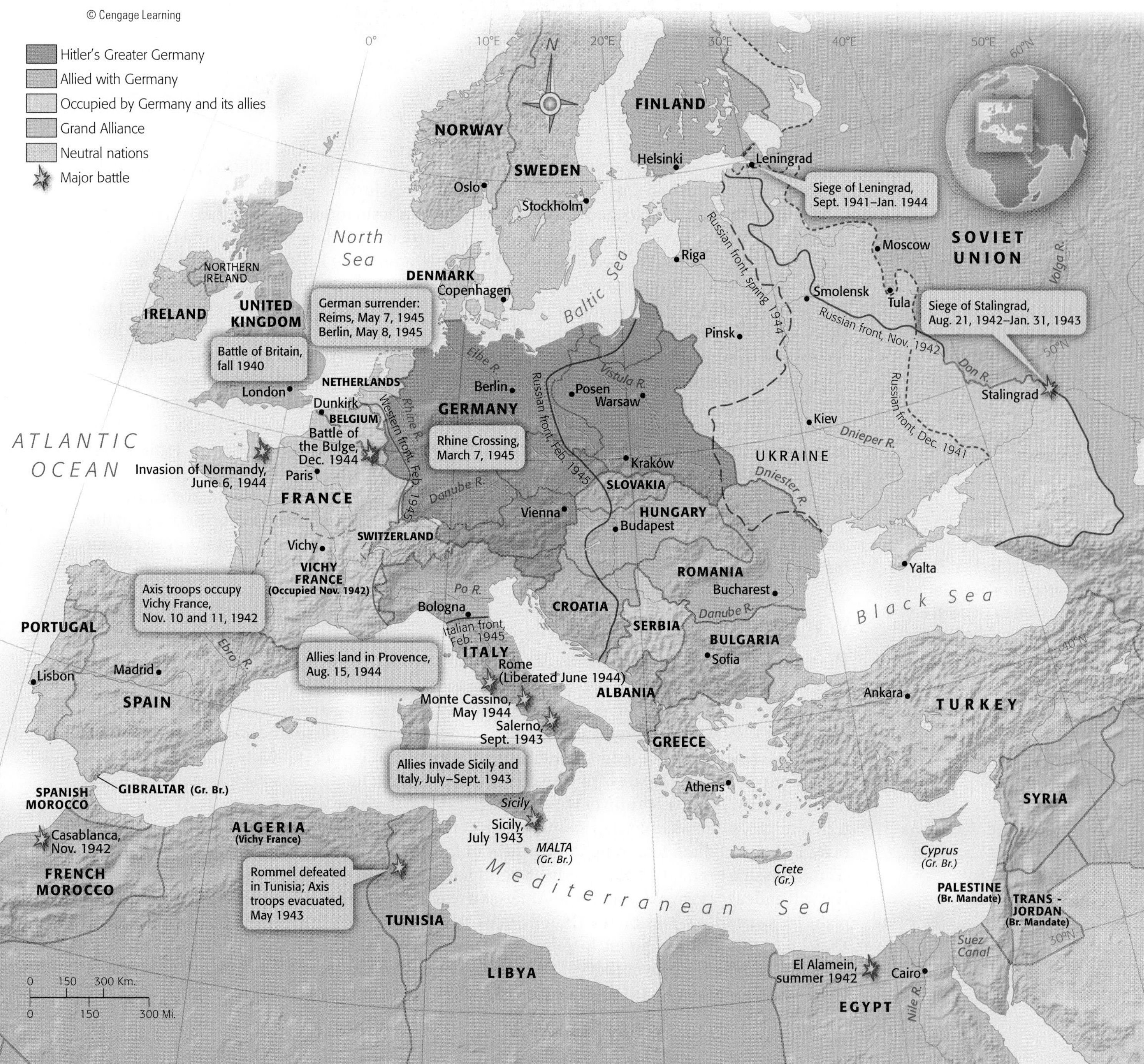

Soviet Tanks at Stalingrad In the winter of 1942–1943, the Red Army encircled a German army at Stalingrad, a strategic city in southern Russia that marked the furthest eastward advance of the Wehrmacht. The Soviets deployed their new T-34s, the best tanks in the world at the time. Unlike the Germans, Soviet soldiers were equipped with warm winter uniforms with a white outer layer for camouflage in the snow.

TASS-Sovfoto

Stalingrad City in Russia, site of a Red Army victory over the German army in 1942–1943. The Battle of Stalingrad was the turning point in the war between Germany and the Soviet Union. Today Volgograd.

verge of collapse. Then the weather turned cold, machines froze, and the fighting came to a halt. Like Napoleon, Hitler had ignored the environment of Russia to his peril.

Stalingrad

The next spring the Wehrmacht renewed its offensive. It surrounded Leningrad in a siege that was to cost a million lives. Leaving Moscow aside, it turned toward the Caucasus and its oil wells. In August the Germans attacked **Stalingrad** (now Volgograd), the key to the Volga River and the supply of oil. For months German and Soviet soldiers fought over every street and every house. When winter came, the Red Army counterattacked and encircled the city. In February 1943 the remnants of the German army in Stalingrad surrendered. Hitler had lost an army of 200,000 men and his last chance of defeating the Soviet Union and of winning the war (see Map 29.2).

North Africa

From Europe the war spread to Africa. When France fell in 1940, Mussolini decided that the time had come to realize his imperial ambitions. Italian forces quickly overran British Somaliland, then invaded Egypt. Their victories were ephemeral, however, for when the British counterattacked, Italian resistance crumbled. During 1941 British forces conquered Italian East Africa and invaded Libya as well. The Italian rout in North Africa brought the Germans to their rescue, and during 1942 the German army and the forces of the British Commonwealth seesawed back and forth across the deserts of Libya and Egypt. At **El Alamein** in northern Egypt the British prevailed because they had more weapons and supplies and were better informed about their enemies' plans. The Germans were finally expelled from Africa in May 1943.

El Alamein Town in Egypt, site of the victory by Britain's Field Marshal Bernard Montgomery over German forces led by General Erwin Rommel (the "Desert Fox") in 1942–1943.

War in Asia and the Pacific

The fall of France and the involvement of Britain and the USSR against Germany presented Japan with the opportunity it had been looking for. Suddenly the European colonies in Southeast Asia, with their abundant oil, rubber, and other strategic materials, seemed ripe for the taking. In July 1941, when the French government allowed Japanese forces to occupy Indochina, the United States stopped shipments of steel, scrap iron, oil, and other products that Japan desperately needed. This left Japan with three alternatives: giving up its conquests, as the Americans insisted; facing economic ruin; or widening the war. Japan chose war.

Japanese War Plans

Admiral Isoroku Yamamoto, commander of the Japanese fleet, told Prime Minister Fumimaro Konoye: "If I am told to fight regardless of the consequences, I shall run wild for the first six months or a year, but I have utterly no confidence for the second or third year. . . . I hope that you will endeavor to avoid a Japanese-American war." Ignoring his advice, the war cabinet made plans for a surprise attack on the United States Navy, followed by an invasion of Southeast Asia. They knew they could not hope to defeat the United States, but they calculated that the shock of the attack would be so great that isolationist Americans would accept the Japanese conquest of Southeast Asia as readily as they had acquiesced to Hitler's conquests in Europe.

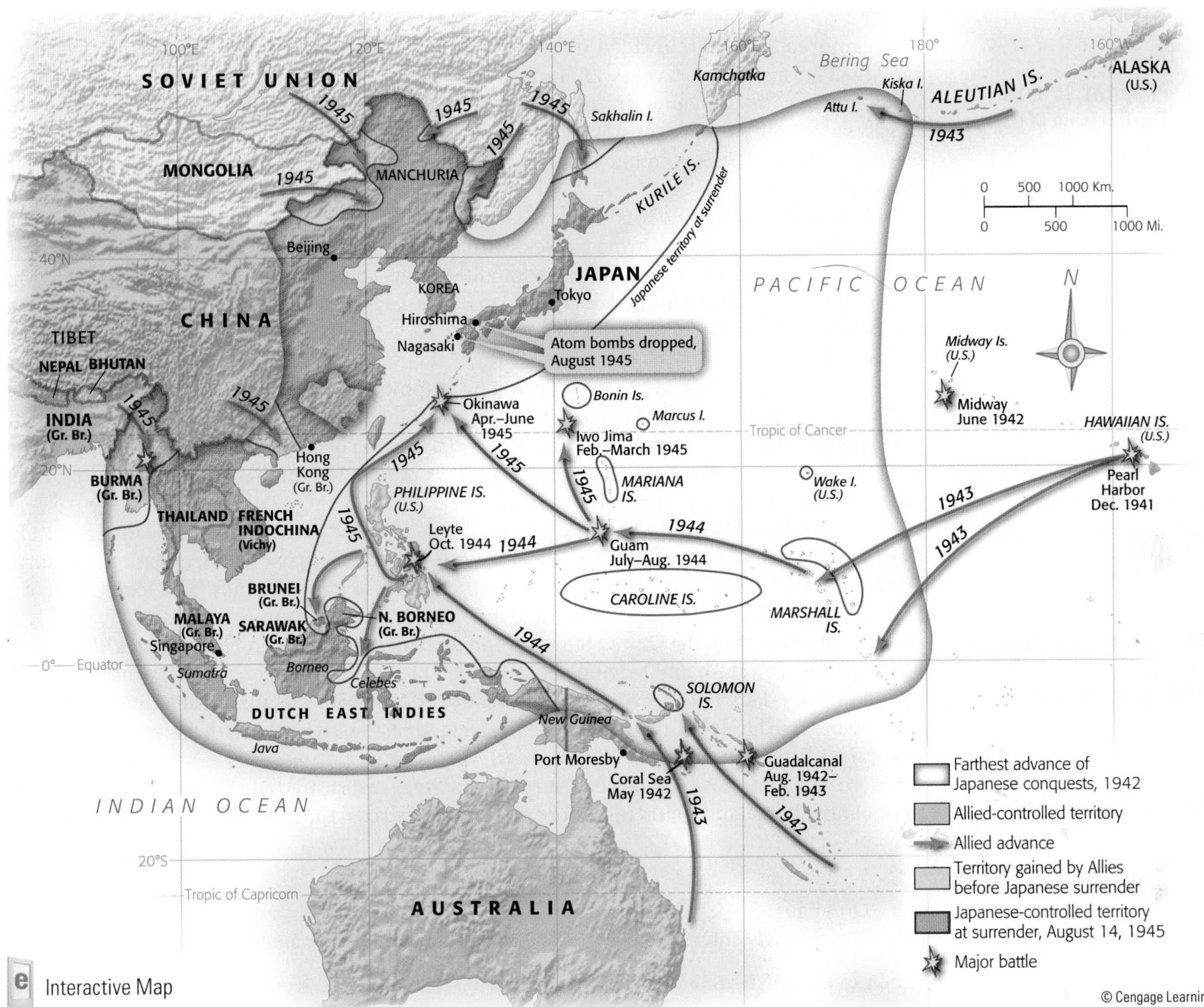

MAP 29.3 **World War II in Asia and the Pacific** Having conquered much of China between 1937 and 1941, Japanese forces launched a sudden attack on Southeast Asia and the Pacific in late 1941 and early 1942. American forces slowly reconquered the Pacific islands and the Philippines. In August 1945, the atomic bombing of Hiroshima and Nagasaki forced Japan's surrender.

Pearl Harbor

Pearl Harbor Naval base in Hawaii attacked by Japanese aircraft on December 7, 1941. The sinking of much of the U.S. Pacific Fleet brought the United States into World War II.

Battle of Midway U.S. naval victory over the Japanese fleet in June 1942, in which the Japanese lost four of their best aircraft carriers. It marked a turning point in World War II.

On December 7, 1941, Japanese planes bombed the U.S. naval base at **Pearl Harbor,** sinking or damaging scores of warships but missing the aircraft carriers, which were at sea. Then, in early 1942, the Japanese conquered all of Southeast Asia and the Dutch East Indies. They soon began to confiscate food and raw materials and demand heavy labor from the inhabitants.

Japan's dream of an East Asian empire seemed within reach, for its victories surpassed even Hitler's in Europe. The United States, however, quickly began preparing for war. In April 1942 American planes bombed Tokyo. In May the United States Navy defeated a Japanese fleet in the Coral Sea, ending Japanese plans to conquer Australia. A month later, at the **Battle of Midway,** Japan lost four of its six largest aircraft carriers. Without them, Japan faced a long and hopeless war (see Map 29.3).

The End of War

After the Battle of Stalingrad the advantage on the Eastern Front shifted to the Soviet Union. By 1943 the Red Army was receiving a growing stream of supplies from factories in Russia and the United States. Slowly at first and then with increasing vigor, it pushed the Wehrmacht back toward Germany.

D-day

The Western powers, meanwhile, staged two invasions of Europe. Beginning in July 1943 they captured Sicily and invaded Italy. Italy signed an armistice, but German troops held off the Allied advance for two years. On June 6, 1944—forever after known as D-day—156,000 British, American, and Canadian troops landed on the coast of Normandy in western France—the largest shipborne assault ever staged. Within a week the Allies had more troops in France than Germany did, and by September Germany faced an Allied army of over 2 million men and half a million vehicles.

e PRIMARY SOURCE: The Decision to Use the Atomic Bomb Learn why President Truman was advised to drop atomic bombs on Japan—from the chairman of the committee that gave him that advice.

Although the Red Army was on the eastern border of Germany, ready for the final push, Hitler transferred part of the Wehrmacht westward. Despite overwhelming odds, Germany held out for almost a year, a result of the fighting qualities of its soldiers and the terror inspired by the Nazi regime, which commanded obedience to the end. On May 7, 1945, a week after Hitler committed suicide, German military leaders surrendered.

The Pacific War

Japan fought on a while longer because the United States had aimed most of its war effort at Germany. Pacific islands had to be captured by amphibious landings, with high casualty rates on both sides. In June 1944 U.S. bombers began attacking Japan and American submarines sank Japanese merchant ships, cutting Japan off from its sources of oil and other raw materials. After May 1945, with Japanese fighters grounded for lack of fuel, U.S. planes began destroying Japanese shipping, industries, and cities at will.

Even as their homeland was being pounded, the Japanese still held strong positions in Asia. Despite its name, "Greater East Asian Co-Prosperity Sphere," the Japanese occupation was harsh and brutal. By 1945 Asians were eager to see the Japanese leave, but not to welcome back the Europeans. Instead, they looked forward to independence (see Chapters 30 and 31).

Hiroshima and Nagasaki

Hiroshima City in Japan, the first to be destroyed by an atomic bomb, on August 6, 1945. The bombing hastened the end of World War II.

On August 6, 1945, the United States dropped an atomic bomb on **Hiroshima**, killing some 80,000 people in a flash and leaving about 120,000 more to die in agony from burns and radiation. Three days later another atomic bomb destroyed Nagasaki. On August 14 Emperor Hirohito gave the order to lay down arms. Two weeks later Japanese leaders signed the terms of surrender. The war was officially over.

Were these atomic weapons necessary? At the time, Americans believed that the conquest of the Japanese homeland would take more than a year and cost the lives of hundreds of thousands

Hiroshima After the Atomic Bomb On August 6, 1945, an atomic bomb destroyed the city, killing some eighty thousand people. This photo shows the devastation of the city center, where only a few concrete buildings remained standing.

Corbis

Sale of Gold in the Last Days of the Guomindang This picture was taken by famed French photojournalist Henri Cartier-Bresson in Shanghai just before the arrival of the Communist-led People's Liberation Army in 1949. It shows people desperate to buy gold before their Guomindang currency becomes worthless.

Henri Cartier-Bresson/Magnum Photos

of American soldiers. Although some believed the Japanese were determined to fight to the bitter end, others thought they would surrender if they could retain their emperor. Winston Churchill wrote: "It would be a mistake to suppose that the fate of Japan was settled by the atomic bomb. Her defeat was certain before the first bomb fell."[3]

Collapse of the Guomindang and Communist Victory

The formal Japanese surrender in September 1945 surprised the Guomindang. The United States gave millions of dollars of aid and weapons to the Guomindang, all the while urging "national unity" and a "coalition government" with the Communists. But Chiang used all means available to prepare for a civil war. By late 1945 he had U.S. support, control of China's cities, and an army of 2.7 million, more than twice the size of the Communist forces. But the Guomindang's behavior eroded whatever popular support they had. As they moved into formerly Japanese-held territory, they acted like an occupation force. They taxed the people they "liberated" more heavily than the Japanese had, confiscated supplies, and enriched themselves at the expense of the population. Chiang's government printed money so fast that it soon lost all its value. In the countryside the Guomindang's brutality alienated the peasants.

Meanwhile, the Communists obtained Japanese equipment seized by the Soviets in the last weeks of the war and American weapons brought over by deserting Guomindang soldiers. In Manchuria, where they were strongest, they pushed through a radical land reform program, distributing the properties of wealthy landowners among the poorest peasants. In battles against government forces, the higher morale and popular support they enjoyed outweighed the heavy equipment of the Guomindang, whose soldiers began deserting by the thousands.

By 1949 the Guomindang armies were collapsing everywhere, defeated more by their own greed

SECTION REVIEW

- World War II was a war of machines and movement covering entire continents and oceans.
- Hitler's armies quickly overran western Europe, but Hitler failed to defeat Britain by air.
- In 1941 Germany attacked the USSR, but its defeat at Stalingrad in the winter of 1942–1943 sealed its fate.
- After the United States stopped shipments of vital supplies to Japan, in December 1941 Japanese planes bombed Pearl Harbor; a few months later Japan conquered Southeast Asia and Indonesia.
- After mid-1942, however, American forces pushed the Japanese back across the Pacific and began bombing Japan.
- In 1944, on D-day, the Allies landed troops on Norway and then fought their way into Germany; meanwhile, two atomic bombs forced Japan to surrender.
- After Japan's defeat, Chiang Kai-shek's army failed from its own ineptness and Mao's Communists took over China.

and ineptness than by the Communists. As the Communists advanced, high-ranking members of the Guomindang fled to Taiwan, protected from the mainland by the U.S. Navy. On October 1, 1949, Mao Zedong announced the founding of the People's Republic of China.

THE CHARACTER OF WARFARE

The war left an enormous death toll. Recent estimates place the figure at close to 60 million deaths, six to eight times more than in World War I. Over half of the dead were civilian victims of massacres, famines, and bombs. The Soviet Union lost between 20 million and 25 million people, more than any other country. China suffered 15 million deaths; Poland lost some 6 million, of whom half were Jewish; the Jewish people lost another 3 million outside Poland. Over 4 million Germans and over 2 million Japanese died. Great Britain lost 400,000 people, and the United States 300,000. In much of the world, families mourned one or more of their members.

Many parts of the world were flooded with refugees. Some 90 million Chinese fled the Japanese advance. In Europe millions fled from the Nazis or the Red Army or were herded back and forth on government orders. Many refugees never returned to their homes.

Belligerents identified not just soldiers but entire peoples as enemies. Some even labeled their own ethnic minorities as "enemies." Another reason for the devastation was the appearance of new technologies that carried destruction deep into enemy territory, far beyond the traditional battlefields. New technologies of warfare and changes in morality formed a lethal combination.

AP* Exam Tip The exam requires a broad understanding of the globalization of science and technology that developed during and after World War II.

The Science and Technology of War

As fighting spread around the world, the mobilization of manpower and economies and the mobility of the armed forces grew increasingly important, while new aspects of war took on a growing importance. Chemists found ways to make synthetic rubber from coal or oil. Physicists perfected radar, which warned of approaching enemy aircraft and submarines. Cryptanalysts broke enemy codes and were able to penetrate secret military communications (see Environment and Technology: The Enigma Machine). Pharmacologists developed antibiotics that saved the lives of wounded soldiers, who in any earlier war would have died of infections.

Warplanes

Aircraft development was especially striking. As war approached, German, British, and Japanese aircraft manufacturers developed fast, maneuverable fighter planes. U.S. industry was especially noted for heavy bombers designed to fly in huge formations and drop tons of bombs on enemy cities. Germany responded with radically new designs, including the first jet fighters, low-flying buzz bombs, and, finally, V-2 missiles against which there was no warning or defense.

Atom Bombs

Military planners expected scientists to furnish secret weapons that could doom the enemy. In October 1939 President Roosevelt received a letter from physicist Albert Einstein, a Jewish refugee from Nazism, warning of the dangers of nuclear power: "There is no doubt that subatomic energy is available all around us, and that one day man will release and control its almost infinite power. We cannot prevent him from doing so and can only hope that he will not use it exclusively in blowing up his next door neighbor." Roosevelt placed the vast resources of the U.S. government at the disposal of physicists and engineers. By 1945 they had built two atomic bombs, each one powerful enough to annihilate an entire city.

Bombing Raids

Since it was very hard to pinpoint individual buildings, especially at night, British air chief marshal Arthur "Bomber" Harris decided that "operations should now be focused on the morale of the enemy civilian population and in particular the industrial workers."

In May 1942, 1,000 British planes dropped incendiary bombs on Cologne, setting fire to the old city. Between July 24 and August 2, 1943, 3,330 British and American planes fire-bombed Hamburg, killing 50,000 people, mostly women and children. Later raids destroyed Berlin, Dresden, and other German cities. The bombing raids against Germany killed 600,000 people—more than half of them women and children—and injured 800,000, but they failed to break the morale of the German people. German armament production continued to increase until late 1944, and

The Enigma Machine

Since ancient times, governments and armies have used various methods of encrypting messages, that is, making them unreadable to people who do not possess the proper code (words replaced by other words using a codebook) or cipher (letters replaced by numbers). The introduction of radio, which could be easily monitored by agents of foreign powers, turned cryptography (secret writing) into a necessity of diplomacy and war. Yet encrypting and decrypting messages required expert code clerks and took time. Furthermore, since each nation used several codes and ciphers and changed them periodically, a breakthrough in one code or cipher did not necessarily make other messages easier to decrypt.

After World War I, inventors in several countries set out to create machines that could encrypt and decrypt messages automatically while also making them harder to crack than manual codes and ciphers. The invention that was most successful was the Enigma, first produced by a German company in 1923. It consisted of a typewriter keyboard, a set of rotors containing electrical wires and contacts, and a series of lights marked with letters. When the operator entered a letter on the keyboard, an electrical current went through the rotors and lit up a letter different from the one entered. With each keystroke, the rotors also turned, so that the next time the same key was pushed, a different light went on. At the receiving end, if the operator had set his rotors in the same pattern as the sender, entering the encrypted letters on the keyboard lit up the letters of the original plaintext. Anyone who had an Enigma but was not privy to the rotor settings and attempted to read an encrypted message would have to try an almost infinite number of settings. This might take months or years, by which time the information would no longer have any value.

As war approached, the German armed forces purchased thousands of Enigma machines, each the size of a portable typewriter. They accompanied ships at sea, frontline troops, and squadrons of airplanes. The Germans considered their cipher unbreakable and their secrets safe from enemy eyes. They were wrong. Before the war began, Polish cryptanalysts had figured out how the Enigma worked and built some replicas. They also devised an electromechanical device they called "bomba" that went through rotor settings at blazing speed until it encountered an expression, such as "Heil Hitler," that often appeared in German messages. When the war broke out, these cryptanalysts fled to France. From there, the secret of the bomba passed to British cryptanalysts at a secret installation at Bletchley Park, north of London.

With this breakthrough, the British were able to read many Luftwaffe signals during the Battle of Britain in 1940. Cracking the German navy and army Enigmas proved to be much more difficult, for the other services used more rotors, changed the settings more frequently, and, most importantly, learned to avoid stock phrases. Nonetheless, by the spring of 1942, Bletchley Park had a staff of 1,500 handling some 40,000 German military messages a month. Their ability to read German messages was instrumental in the Allied victories against General Rommel in North Africa in 1942 and against the German U-boats in the Battle of the Atlantic in 1943.

Courtesy, Brian Johnson

The Enigma Machine During World War II, German armed forces used Enigma machines like the one seen here in the vehicle of a German tank commander. With Enigmas, they could encrypt and decrypt radio messages, keeping them secret (they believed) from enemy code-breakers.

the population remained obedient and hard working. However, bombing raids against oil depots and synthetic fuel plants almost brought the German war effort to a standstill by early 1945.

Japanese cities were also the targets of American bombing raids. As early as April 1942 sixteen planes launched from an aircraft carrier bombed Tokyo. Later, as American forces captured islands close to Japan, the raids intensified. Their effect was even more devastating than the fire-bombing of German cities, for Japanese cities were made of wood. In March 1945 bombs set Tokyo ablaze, killing 80,000 people and leaving a million homeless.

Hulton Deutsch Collection/Corbis

U.S. Army Medics and Holocaust Victims When Allied troops entered the Nazi concentration camps, they found the bodies of thousands of victims of the Holocaust. In Dachau in southern Germany, two U.S. Army medics are overseeing a truckload of corpses to be taken to a burial site.

The Holocaust

In World War II, for the first time, more civilians than soldiers were deliberately put to death. The champions in the art of killing defenseless civilians were the Nazis. Their murders were not the accidental byproducts of some military goal but a calculated policy of exterminating whole races of people.

Their first targets were Jews. Soon after Hitler came to power, he deprived German Jews of their citizenship and legal rights. When eastern Europe fell under Nazi rule, the Nazis herded its large Jewish population into ghettos in the major cities, where many died of starvation and disease. Then, in early 1942, the Nazis decided to carry out Hitler's "final solution to the Jewish problem" by applying modern industrial methods to the slaughter of human beings. Thousands of ordinary German citizens supported and aided the genocide. Every day trainloads of cattle cars arrived at the extermination camps in eastern Europe and disgorged thousands of captives and the corpses of those who had died along the way. The strongest survivors were put to work and fed almost nothing until they died. Women, children, the elderly, and the sick were shoved into gas chambers and asphyxiated with poison gas. **Auschwitz**, the biggest camp, was a giant industrial complex designed to kill up to twelve thousand people a day. This mass extermination, now called the **Holocaust** ("burning"), claimed some 6 million Jewish lives.

Auschwitz Nazi extermination camp in Poland, the largest center of mass murder during the Holocaust. Close to a million Jews, Gypsies, Communists, and others were killed there.

Holocaust Nazis' program during World War II to kill people they considered undesirable. Some 6 million Jews perished during the Holocaust, along with millions of Poles, Gypsies, Communists, Socialists, and others.

Besides the Jews, the Nazis also killed 3 million Polish Catholics—especially professionals, army officers, and the educated—in an effort to reduce the Polish people to slavery. They also exterminated homosexuals, Jehovah's Witnesses, Gypsies, the disabled, and the mentally ill—all in the interests of "racial purity." Whenever a German was killed in an occupied country, the Nazis retaliated by burning a village and all its inhabitants. After the invasion of Russia the Wehrmacht was given orders to execute all captured communists, government employees, and officers. They also worked millions of prisoners of war to death or let them die of starvation.

The Home Front in Europe and Asia

In the First World War there had been a clear distinction between the "front" and the "home front." Not so in World War II, where rapid military movements and air power carried the war into people's homes. For the civilian populations of China, Japan, Southeast Asia, and Europe, the war was far more terrifying than their worst nightmares. Armies swept through the land, confiscating food, fuel, and anything else of value. Bombers and heavy artillery pounded cities into rubble, leaving only the skeletons of buildings, while survivors cowered in cellars. Even when a city was not targeted, air-raid sirens awakened people throughout the night. In countries occupied by the Germans, the police arrested civilians, deporting many to die in concentration camps or to work as slave laborers in armaments factories. Millions fled their homes in terror, losing their families and friends. Even in Britain, children and the elderly were sent to live in the countryside.

e **PRIMARY SOURCE: Memoirs** Read what the man responsible for administering and overseeing the Holocaust thought and felt about his "work."

Civilian Contributions

The war demanded an enormous and sustained effort from all civilians, but more so in some countries than in others. In 1941, the Soviets dismantled over fifteen hundred factories and rebuilt them in the Ural Mountains and Siberia, where they soon turned out more tanks and artillery than the Axis.

Half of the ships afloat in 1939 were sunk during the war, but the Allied losses were more than made up for by American shipyards, while Axis shipping was reduced to nothing by 1945. The production of aircraft, trucks, tanks, and other materiel showed a similar imbalance. Although the Axis powers made strenuous efforts to increase their production, they could not compete with the vast outpouring of Soviet tanks and American materiel.

Women at War

The Red Army eventually mobilized 22 million men; Soviet women took over half of all industrial and three-quarters of all agricultural jobs. In the other Allied countries, women also played major roles in the war effort, replacing men in fields, factories, and offices. The Nazis, in contrast, believed that German women should stay home and bear children, and they imported 7 million "guest workers"—a euphemism for captured foreigners.

The Home Front in the United States

The United States flourished during the war. Safe behind their oceans, Americans felt no bombs, saw no enemy soldiers, had almost no civilian casualties, and suffered fewer military casualties than other countries. The economy went into a prolonged boom after 1940. By 1944 the United States was producing twice as much as all the Axis powers combined. Thanks to huge military orders, jobs were plentiful, bread lines disappeared, and nutrition and health improved. Most Americans saved part of their paychecks, laying the basis for a phenomenal postwar consumer boom. Many Americans later looked back on the conflict as the "good war."

American Women

World War II also did much to weaken the hold of traditional ideas, as employers recruited women and members of racial minorities to work in jobs once reserved for white men. Six million women entered the labor force during the war, 2.5 million of them in manufacturing jobs previously considered "men's work." In a book entitled *Shipyard Diary of a Woman Welder* (1944), Augusta Clawson recalled her experiences in a shipyard in Oregon:

> *The job confirmed my strong conviction—I have stated it before—what exhausts the woman welder is not the work, not the heat, nor the demands upon physical strength. It is the apprehension that arises from inadequate skill and consequent lack of confidence; and this* can *be overcome by the right kind of training. . . . And so, in spite of the discomforts of climbing, heavy equipment, and heat, I enjoyed the work today because* I could do it.[4]

Many men opposed women doing work that would take them away from their families. As the labor shortage got worse, however, employers and politicians grudgingly admitted that the government ought to help provide day care for the children of working mothers. The entry of women into the labor force proved to be one of the most significant consequences of the war.

Racial Minorities

The war loosened racial bonds as well. Seeking work in war industries, 1.2 million African Americans migrated to the north and west. In the southwest Mexican immigrants took jobs in agriculture and war industries. But no new housing was built to accommodate the influx of migrants to the industrial cities, and many suffered from overcrowding and discrimination. In addition, 112,000 Japanese-Americans living on the west coast of the United States were arrested and herded into internment camps in the desert until the war was over, ostensibly for fear of spying and sabotage, but actually because of their race.

SECTION REVIEW

- World War II caused 60 million deaths, most of them civilians, as well as many refugees.
- Scientific technology, especially aircraft design, contributed to the mobility and violence of warfare.
- Allied bombing raids set fire to entire cities in both Europe and Japan.
- In the Holocaust, the Nazis murdered millions of Jews, Poles, Gypsies, and other minorities.
- Industrial economies, especially in the United States and Russia, mobilized civilians to manufacture war materiel.
- A booming American economy provided jobs for women and African Americans.
- Environments in war zones were badly damaged, and construction for the war transformed the environments of many countries.

War and the Environment

During the Depression, construction and industry had slowed to a crawl, reducing environmental stress. The war reversed this trend, sharply accelerating pressures on the environment.

One reason for the change was the fighting itself. Battles scarred the landscape, leaving behind spent ammunition and damaged equipment. Retreating armies flooded large areas of China and the Netherlands. The bombing of cities left ruins that remained visible for a generation or more.

Construction

The main cause of environmental stress, however, was not the fighting but the economic development that sustained it. The war's half-million aircraft required thousands of air bases, many of them in the Pacific, China, Africa, and other parts of the world that had seldom seen an airplane before. Barracks, shipyards, docks, warehouses, and other military construction sprouted on every continent.

As war industries boomed, so did the demand for raw materials. Mining companies opened new mines and towns in Africa to supply strategic minerals. Latin American countries deprived of manufactured imports began building their own steel mills, factories, and shipyards. In India, China, and Europe, timber felling accelerated far beyond the reproduction rate of trees, replacing forests with denuded land. In a few instances, however, the war was good for the environment. For example, submarine warfare made fishing and whaling so dangerous that fish and whale populations had a few years in which to increase.

CONCLUSION

After the Great War ended, the world seemed to return to its prewar state, but it was an illusion. In the Soviet Union, Joseph Stalin was determined to turn his country into a modern industrial state at breakneck speed, regardless of the human cost. Several million people—most of them peasants—died, and millions more were enslaved during the Five-Year Plans and the collectivization of agriculture. By 1941 the USSR was much better prepared for a war with Germany than Russia had been in 1914–1917.

In 1929, after a few years of prosperity, the New York stock market collapsed. Within a few months, the world economy fell into the Great Depression, throwing millions out of work throughout the world. France and Britain survived the Depression by making their colonial empires purchase their products. Countries that were dependent on exports, such as Germany and Japan, suffered more. Only the USSR and southern Africa boomed during the 1930s.

In Italy, Mussolini installed Fascist Party members in all government jobs and jailed anyone who criticized him. In Germany, economic collapse led people to entrust their government to Adolf Hitler and his Nazi followers, who quickly set to work establishing a totalitarian government. Nazi Germany's rebuilding of its military and its invasion of Austria and Czechoslovakia were greeted with a policy of appeasement by Western democracies, until finally they could no longer overlook Germany's intentions.

Hard hit by the Depression, Japan saw China as a potential colony with resources to help solve its economic problems. In 1931, Japan conquered Manchuria. The United States and the League of Nations protested but did little else. Starting in 1937, a long and brutal war with China became a drain on the Japanese economy and resources. Meanwhile, the Communists, led by Mao Zedong, were slowly gaining support in the Chinese countryside.

The war spread to Europe in 1939 when Germany conquered Poland, then Denmark, Norway, the Low Countries, and France in 1940. The war turned global in 1941 when Germany invaded the Soviet Union and Japan attacked the United States. In 1943, the Red Army began to push the Germans back. Beginning in June 1944, Anglo-American forces, backed by the overwhelming industrial resources of the United States, drove German forces back from the west. U.S. naval victories in the Pacific and atomic weapons defeated Japan and ended the war in 1945.

The Second World War was by far the deadliest in history. Modern mechanized forces swept across entire nations and oceans. Their targets were not only each other's armed forces, but their civilian populations as well. Though Germany had considerable scientific and technical talent, the war favored the nations with the most heavy industries, namely, the United States and the Soviet Union. The Allies destroyed German and Japanese cities with fire-bombs, and the United States dropped atomic bombs on Hiroshima and Nagasaki. Of the roughly 60 million people who died in the war, most were civilians.

KEY TERMS

Joseph Stalin p. 832
Five-Year Plans p. 832
Benito Mussolini p. 838
Fascist Party p. 838
Adolf Hitler p. 839
Nazis p. 839
Chiang Kai-shek p. 841
Mao Zedong p. 841
Long March p. 842
Stalingrad p. 846
El Alamein p. 846
Pearl Harbor p. 847
Battle of Midway p. 847
Hiroshima p. 848
Auschwitz p. 852
Holocaust p. 852

EBOOK AND WEBSITE RESOURCES

Primary Sources

The Decision to Use the Atomic Bomb

Memoirs

Interactive Maps

Map 29.1 Chinese Communist Movement and the Sino-Japanese War, to 1938

Map 29.2 World War II in Europe and North Africa

Map 29.3 World War II in Asia and the Pacific

Plus flashcards, practice quizzes, and more. Go to: www.cengage.com/history/bullietearthpeople5e

SUGGESTED READING

Burleigh, Michael. *Third Reich: A New History.* 2000. A thorough and up-to-date analysis of the history of Nazi Germany.

Chang, Iris. *The Rape of Nanking: The Forgotten Holocaust of World War II.* 1997. A best-selling account of one of the most sordid events of the Sino-Japanese War.

Chang, Jung. *Wild Swans: Three Daughters of China.* 1991. A biography of three generations of Chinese women who lived through the wars and revolutions of twentieth-century China.

Conquest, Robert. *The Great Terror: A Reassessment.* 1990. The definitive account of Stalin's purges and terror during the 1930s.

Dower, John. *War Without Mercy: Race and Power in the Pacific War.* 1987. An analysis of the role of racism—on both sides—that made the Pacific War especially brutal.

Frank, Anne. *The Diary of a Young Girl.* 1952. A classic account of the life of a Jewish family in hiding during the Nazi occupation of the Netherlands.

Hsiung, James, and Steven Levine, eds. *China's Bitter Victory: The War with Japan, 1937–1945.* 1992. Documents and accounts of the war in China.

Keegan, John. *The Second World War.* 1990. The best short history of the war by an eminent military historian.

McElvaine, Robert. *The Great Depression: America, 1929–1941.* 1993. A brief but well written account of the hardships of the 1930s.

Rhodes, Richard. *The Making of the Atomic Bomb.* 1986. A fascinating account of the Manhattan Project and its consequences.

Solzhenitsyn, Alexander. *One Day in the Life of Ivan Denisovich.* 1978. The novel that first revealed the existence of Stalin's concentration camps.

Spector, Ronald. *Eagle Against the Sun.* 1988. A popular history of the Pacific War.

Terkel, Studs. *"The Good War": An Oral History of World War Two.* 1984. Interviews with Americans about their experiences during World War II.

Volkogonov, Dmitrii. *Stalin: Triumph and Tragedy.* 1991. A classic biography of the great tyrant.

Wiesel, Eli. *Night.* 1960. The classic work recounting the horrors of the Holocaust.

NOTES

1. Apollonio Umbro, ed., *Documents of Twentieth Century Art: Futurist Manifestos* (New York: Viking Press, 1973), 23.
2. Richard F. Hamilton and Holger H. Herwig, *Decisions for War, 1914–1917* (Cambridge: Cambridge University Press, 2004), 199.
3. Gar Alperowitz, *Atomic Diplomacy: Hiroshima and Potsdam* (New York: Simon & Schuster, 1965), 176–181 and 236–242.
4. Rosalyn Fraad Baxandall, Linda Gordon, and Susan Reverby, eds., *America's Working Women* (New York: Random House, 1976), 253.

AP* REVIEW QUESTIONS FOR CHAPTER 29

1. Stalin instituted the USSR's Five-Year Plans as a way to
   (A) increase foreign trade for the USSR.
   (B) quintuple the output of electricity and double the output of heavy industry.
   (C) regain territories given up at the end of World War I.
   (D) rid the Soviet Union of anyone who opposed its government.

2. The Great Depression in the United States
   (A) had a ripple effect across the world and impacted many nations in Europe, Africa, and Asia.
   (B) was limited to the United States, and then only a small segment of the U.S. population.
   (C) was caused by the expenses of World War I and the inability of the U.S. government to pay for the war.
   (D) was caused by weaknesses in the economies of the European nations that had borrowed money from the United States during World War I.

3. The first fascist leader to gain control of a nation in the twentieth century was
   (A) Adolf Hitler.
   (B) Francisco Franco.
   (C) Benito Mussolini.
   (D) Juan Perón.

4. Hitler's goal was not prosperity or popularity but
   (A) conquest and revenge for World War I.
   (B) wealth and power for himself and his party leaders.
   (C) peace and security for Germany and the rest of Europe.
   (D) regaining Germany's African and Asian colonies.

5. One of the founders and eventual leader of China's Communist Party was
   (A) Chiang Kai-shek.
   (B) Yuan Shikai.
   (C) Mao Zedong.
   (D) Cixi.

6. The so-called Long March
   (A) is the name given to the escape of the Chinese Communist Party from the Guomindang attempt to eradicate them.
   (B) is the name used for the way the Chinese army walked to Korea to fight against Japan in World War II.
   (C) commemorates the escape of Chiang Kai-shek to the island of Taiwan.
   (D) is the name used to describe the process of China becoming a modern nation.

7. When Japan attacked China in 1937,
   (A) the Soviet Union encouraged Japan to attack.
   (B) Japan's leaders hoped for a quick victory and an end to Japan's economic problems.
   (C) Great Britain and France declared war on Japan for having violated the Treaty of Versailles.
   (D) Hitler decided to model his new army on the Japanese model because of their lightning-quick victory.

8. By the end of June 1940, Hitler
   (A) had conquered almost all of Europe except Spain, Great Britain, and the USSR.
   (B) had ordered his armies to attack Switzerland because he needed the Swiss banks and their financial resources.
   (C) had launched his campaign against the Catholic Church and was calling for the destruction of all Catholic property in Germany.
   (D) had already killed the majority of the Jews and gypsies in Europe.

9. By the middle of 1943, it was becoming apparent that neither Germany nor Japan could win the war. In part this was due to
   (A) the decisive battles in North Africa and New Guinea.
   (B) the fact that neither could keep up with the war production rate of the United States.
   (C) the superiority of U.S. soldiers, sailors, and marines to the German or Japanese soldiers.
   (D) the fact that Japan and Germany were diplomatically isolated by the Allies.

10. Following the end of World War II in 1945, the Guomindang and the Chinese Communist Party

 (A) came to a diplomatic understanding and created two separate Chinas.
 (B) renewed their war against each other and for control of China's government.
 (C) appealed to the United States for economic and military aid for having helped defeat Japan in the war.
 (D) healed their wounds and joined together to rebuild China into a modern industrial power.

11. Unlike in World War I, in World War II

 (A) there was no clear picture of who was winning until late in the war.
 (B) nations were slow to join the Allied cause against Germany and Japan.
 (C) there was less of a distinction between the "front" and the "home front."
 (D) civilian effort in the war was significantly less.

CHAPTER

30

CHAPTER OUTLINE

- The Indian Independence Movement, 1905–1947
- Sub-Saharan Africa, 1900–1945
- Mexico, Argentina, and Brazil, 1900–1949
- Conclusion

ENVIRONMENT + TECHNOLOGY *Gandhi and Technology*

DIVERSITY + DOMINANCE *A Vietnamese Nationalist Denounces French Colonialism*

Genevieve Naylor, photographer/Reznikoff Artistic Partnership, NY

Rush Hour in Brazil In Latin American countries, modern conveniences, when first introduced, were often insufficient to meet the demand from eager customers. This streetcar in Rio de Janeiro carries twice as many passengers as it was designed for.

Visit the website and ebook for additional study materials and interactive tools: www.cengage.com/history/bullietearthpeople5e

Striving for Independence: India, Africa, and Latin America, 1900–1949

- Why did the educated elites of India want independence? What were ordinary Indians hoping for?
- What changes did foreign rule bring to Africa, and how did Africans respond?
- What could Latin Americans do to achieve social justice and economic development? Were these two goals compatible?

Modern technologies first appeared in the wealthier countries of Europe and North America. When they were transferred to Asia, Africa, and Latin America, they reinforced those countries' dependence on the industrialized countries and widened the gap between their social classes. The tensions of modernization contributed to popular movements for independence and social justice.

The previous two chapters focused on a world convulsed by war and revolution. The world wars involved Europe, East Asia, the Middle East, and the United States and sparked violent revolutions in Russia and China. Parts of the world that were little touched by war also underwent profound changes in this period, partly for internal reasons and partly because of the warfare and revolution in other parts of the world.

In this chapter we examine the changes that took place in India, in sub-Saharan Africa, and in Mexico, Brazil, and Argentina. These three regions represent three very distinct cultures, yet they had much in common. India and Africa were colonies of Europe, both politically and economically. Though politically independent, the Latin American republics were dependent on Europe and the United States for the sale of commodities and for imports of manufactured goods, technology, and capital. In all three regions independence movements tried to wrest control from distant foreigners and improve the livelihood of their peoples. Their success was partial at best.

THE INDIAN INDEPENDENCE MOVEMENT, 1905–1947

Under British rule India acquired railroads, harbors, modern cities, and cotton and steel mills, as well as an active and worldly middle class. The economic transformation of the region awakened in this educated middle class a sense of national dignity that demanded political fulfillment. In response, the British gradually granted India a limited amount of political autonomy while maintaining overall control. Religious and communal tensions among the Indian peoples were carefully papered over, and when the British withdrew in 1947, violent conflicts tore India apart (see Map 30.1).

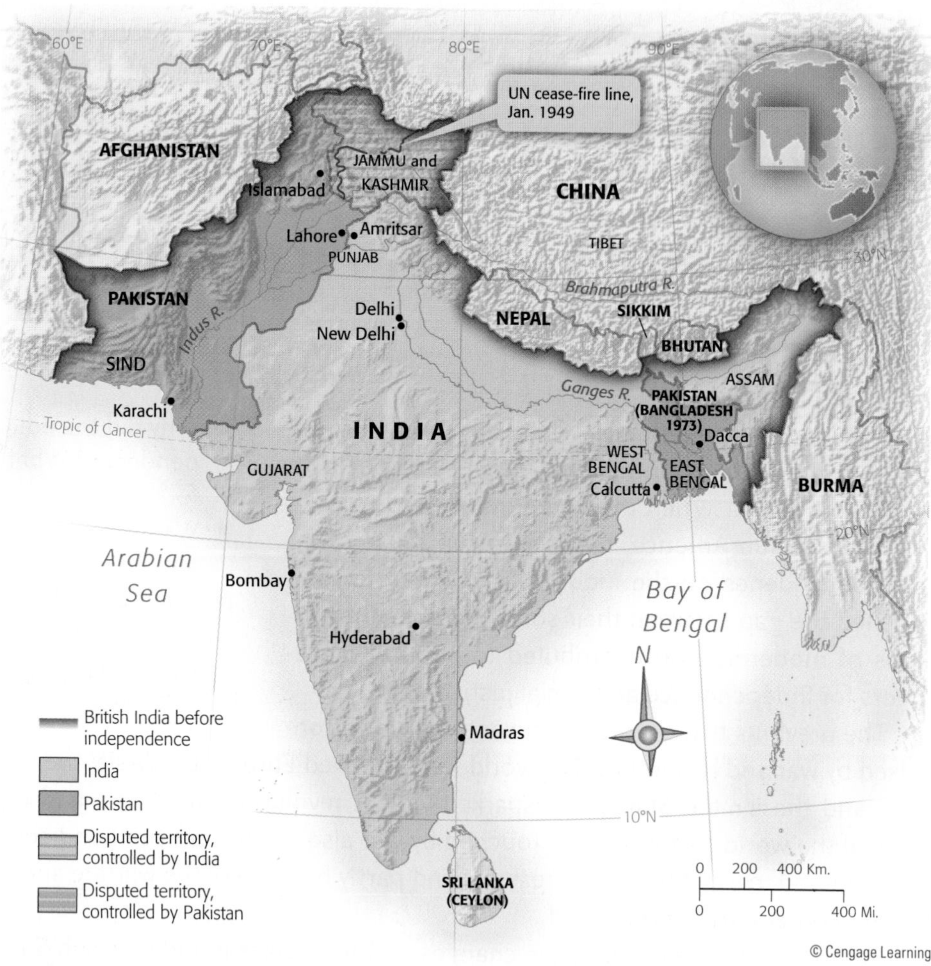

Interactive Map

MAP 30.1 The Partition of India, 1947 Before the British, India was divided among many states, ethnic groups, and religions. When the British left in 1947, the subcontinent split along religious lines. The predominantly Muslim regions in the northwest and East Bengal in the east formed the new nation of Pakistan. The predominantly Hindu center became the Republic of India. Jammu and Kashmir remained disputed territories and poisoned relations between the two new countries.

The Land and the People

AP* Exam Tip Be prepared to compare and contrast the colonial legacy created by the European powers.

Much of India is fertile land, but it is vulnerable to droughts caused by the periodic failure of the monsoons. When the rains failed from 1896 to 1900, 2 million people died of starvation.

Despite periodic famines, the Indian population grew from 250 million in 1900 to 319 million in 1921 and 389 million in 1941. This growth created pressures in many areas. Landless young men converged on the cities, exceeding the number of jobs available in the slowly expanding industries. To produce timber for construction and railroad ties and to clear land for tea and rubber plantations, foresters cut down most of the tropical hardwood forests that had covered the subcontinent in the nineteenth century. But in spite of deforestation and extensive irrigation, the amount of land available to peasant families shrank with each successive generation. Economic development hardly benefited the average Indian.

Classes and Languages

Indians were divided into many classes. Peasants, always the great majority, paid rents to landowners, interest to village moneylenders, and taxes to the government and had little left to improve their land or raise their standard of living. The government protected property owners, from village moneylenders all the way up to the maharajahs (mah-huh-RAH-juh) or ruling princes, who owned huge tracts of land. The cities were crowded with craftsmen, traders, and

CHRONOLOGY

	India	Africa	Latin America
			1876–1910 Porfirio Díaz, dictator of Mexico
1900		1900s Railroads connect ports to the interior	
	1905 Viceroy Curzon splits Bengal; mass demonstrations		
	1906 Muslims found All-India Muslim League		
	1911 British transfer capital from Calcutta to Delhi	1912 African National Congress founded	1911–1919 Mexican Revolution
			1917 New constitution proclaimed in Mexico
	1919 Amritsar Massacre		
1920		1920s J. E. Casely Hayford organizes political movement in British West Africa	1928 Plutarco Elías Calles founds Mexico's National Revolutionary Party
	1929 Gandhi leads Walk to the Sea		
1930	1930s Gandhi calls for independence; he is repeatedly arrested		1930–1945 Getulio Vargas, dictator of Brazil
			1934–1940 Lázaro Cárdenas, president of Mexico
	1939 British bring India into World War II	1939–1945 A million Africans serve in World War II	1938 Cárdenas nationalizes Mexican oil industry; Vargas proclaims Estado Novo in Brazil
1940	1940 Muhammad Ali Jinnah demands a separate nation for Muslims		
			1943 Juan Perón leads military coup in Argentina
	1947 Partition and independence of India and Pakistan		1946 Perón elected president of Argentina

workers of all sorts, most very poor. Although the British had banned the burning of widows on their husbands' funeral pyres, in other respects women's lives changed little under British rule.

Indians also spoke many different languages. As a result of British rule and increasing trade and travel, English became the common medium of communication of the Western-educated middle class. This new class of English-speaking bureaucrats, professionals, and merchants was to play a leading role in the independence movement.

Religions

The majority of Indians who practiced Hinduism were subdivided into hundreds of castes, each affiliated with a particular occupation. Hinduism discouraged intermarriage and other social interactions among the castes and with non-Hindus. Until they were displaced by the British in the eighteenth century, Muslim rulers had dominated northern and central India, and Muslims now constituted one-quarter of the people of India but formed a majority in the northwest and in eastern Bengal. They felt discriminated against by both British and Hindus.

British Rule and Indian Nationalism

Colonial India was ruled by a viceroy appointed by the British government and administered by a few thousand members of the Indian Civil Service. These men, drawn mostly from the English gentry, believed it was their duty to protect the Indian people from the dangers of industrialization and to defend their own positions from Indian nationalists.

As Europeans they admired modern technology. They encouraged railroads, harbors, telegraphs, and other communications technologies, as well as irrigation and plantations, because these increased India's foreign trade and strengthened British control. Yet, they discouraged the cotton and steel industries and limited the training of Indian engineers, to spare India the social upheavals that had accompanied the Industrial Revolution in Europe while protecting British industry from Indian competition.

Construction Site in Colonial India British civil engineers were active throughout India building roads, railroads, and canals. Here, a British official supervises Indian workers building a bridge.

The Billie Love Collection

Indian National Congress A movement and political party founded in 1885 to demand greater Indian participation in government. Its membership was middle class, and its demands were modest until World War I. Led after 1920 by Mohandas K. Gandhi, it appealed increasingly to the poor, and it organized mass protests demanding self-government and independence.

Bengal Region of northeastern India. It was the first part of India to be conquered by the British in the eighteenth century and remained the political and economic center of British India throughout the nineteenth century. The 1905 split of the province into predominantly Hindu West Bengal and predominantly Muslim East Bengal (now Bangladesh) sparked anti-British riots.

All-India Muslim League Political organization founded in India in 1906 to defend the interests of India's Muslim minority. Led by Muhammad Ali Jinnah, it attempted to negotiate with the Indian National Congress. In 1940, the League began demanding a separate state for Muslims, to be called Pakistan.

AP* Exam Tip On the multiple choice portion of the exam, the Indian independence movement may be tested.

At the turn of the century most Indians—especially peasants, landowners, and princes—accepted British rule. But the Europeans' racist attitude toward dark-skinned people increasingly offended Indians who had learned English and absorbed English ideas of freedom and representative government, only to discover that racial quotas excluded them from the Indian Civil Service, the officer corps, and prestigious country clubs.

In 1885 a small group of English-speaking Hindu professionals founded a political organization called the **Indian National Congress**. For twenty years its members respectfully petitioned the government for access to higher administrative positions and for a voice in official decisions, but they had little influence. Then, in 1905, Viceroy Lord Curzon divided the province of **Bengal** in two to improve the efficiency of its administration. This decision, made without consulting anyone, angered not only educated Indians, who saw it as a way to lessen their influence, but also millions of uneducated Hindu Bengalis, who found themselves outnumbered by Muslims in East Bengal. Soon Bengal was the scene of demonstrations, boycotts of British goods, and even incidents of violence against the British.

In 1906, while the Hindus of Bengal were protesting the partition of their province, Muslims, fearful of Hindu dominance elsewhere in India, founded the **All-India Muslim League**. The government responded by granting Indians a limited franchise based on wealth. Muslims, however, were on average poorer than Hindus, for many poor and low-caste Hindus had converted to Islam to escape caste discrimination. Taking advantage of these religious divisions, the British instituted separate representation and different voting qualifications for Hindus and Muslims. Then, in 1911, the British transferred the capital of India from Calcutta to Delhi (DEL-ee), the former capital of the Mughal (MOO-guhl) emperors. These changes disturbed Indians of all classes and religions and raised their political consciousness. Politics, once primarily the concern of westernized intellectuals, turned into two mass movements: one by Hindus and one by Muslims.

British geologists looked for minerals, such as coal or manganese, that British industry required. However, when the only Indian member of the Indian Geological Service, Pramatha Nath Bose, wanted to prospect for iron ore, he had to resign because the government wanted no part of an Indian steel industry that could compete with that of Britain. Bose joined forces with Jamsetji Tata, a Bombay textile magnate who decided to produce steel in spite of British opposition. With the help of German and American engineers and equipment, Tata's son Dorabji opened the first steel mill in India in 1911, in a town called Jamshedpur in honor of his father. Although it produced only a fraction of the steel that India required, Jamshedpur became a pow-

The Indian Steel Industry

erful symbol of Indian national pride. It also prompted Indian nationalists to ask why a country that could produce its own steel needed foreigners to run its government.

During World War I Indians supported Britain enthusiastically; 1.2 million men volunteered for the army, and millions more voluntarily contributed money to the government. Many expected the British to reward their loyalty with political concessions. Others organized to demand a voice in the government. In 1917, in response to the agitation, the British government announced "the gradual development of self-governing institutions with a view to the progressive realization of responsible government in India as an integral part of the British Empire." This sounded like a promise of self-government, but the timetable was so vague that nationalists denounced it as a devious maneuver to postpone India's independence.

e **PRIMARY SOURCE: An Indian Nationalist Condemns the British Empire** In this excerpt from a speech, an Indian nationalist and feminist accuses the British Empire of betraying its ideals and losing its soul.

The Amritsar Massacre

On April 13, 1919, in the city of Amritsar, General Reginald Dyer ordered his troops to fire into a peaceful crowd of some 10,000 demonstrators, killing at least 379 and wounding 1,200. While waves of angry demonstrations swept over India, the British House of Lords voted to approve Dyer's actions, and a fund was raised in appreciation of his services. Indians interpreted these gestures as showing British contempt for their colonial subjects. In the charged atmosphere of the time, the period of gradual accommodation between the British and the Indians came to a close.

Mahatma Gandhi and Militant Nonviolence

Mohandas K. Gandhi Leader of the Indian independence movement and advocate of nonviolent resistance. After being educated as a lawyer in England, he returned to India and became leader of the Indian National Congress in 1920. He appealed to the poor, led nonviolent demonstrations against British colonial rule, and was jailed many times. Soon after independence he was assassinated for attempting to stop Hindu-Muslim rioting.

For the next twenty years India teetered on the edge of violent uprisings and harsh repression, possibly even war. That it did not succumb was due to **Mohandas K. Gandhi** (GAHN-dee) (1869–1948), a man known to his followers as "Mahatma," the "great soul."

Gandhi began life with every advantage. His family was wealthy enough to send him to England for his education. After his studies he lived in South Africa and practiced law for the small Indian community there. During World War I he returned to India and was one of many Western-educated Hindu intellectuals who joined the Indian National Congress.

Unlike many radical political thinkers of his time, Gandhi denounced the popular ideals of power, struggle, and combat. Instead, inspired by both Hindu and Christian ideals, he preached the saintly virtues of *ahimsa* (uh-HIM-sah) (nonviolence) and *satyagraha* (suh-TYAH-gruh-huh) (the search for truth). He refused to countenance violence among his followers and called off several demonstrations when they turned violent.

In 1921 Gandhi gave up the Western-style suits worn by lawyers and the fine raiment of wealthy Indians and henceforth wore simple peasant garb: a length of homespun cloth below his waist and a shawl to cover his torso (see Environment and Technology: Gandhi and Technology). He spoke for the farmers and the outcasts, whom he called *harijan* (HAH-ree-jahn), "children of God." He attracted ever-larger numbers of followers among the poor and the illiterate, who soon began to revere him; and he transformed the cause of Indian independence from an elite movement of the educated into a mass movement with a quasi-religious aura.

Gandhi was a brilliant political tactician and a master of public relations gestures. In 1929, for instance, he led a few followers on an 80-mile (129-kilometer) walk, camped on a beach, and gathered salt from the sea in a blatant and well-publicized act of civil disregard for the government's monopoly on salt. But he discovered that unleashing the power of popular participation was one thing and controlling its direction was quite another. Within days of his "Walk to the Sea," demonstrations of support broke out all over India, in which the police killed a hundred demonstrators and arrested over sixty thousand.

Many times during the 1930s Gandhi threatened to fast "unto death," and several times he came close to death, to protest the violence of both the police and his followers and to demand independence. He was repeatedly arrested and spent a total of six years in jail. But every arrest made him more popular. He became a cult figure not only in his own country but also in the Western media. In the words of historian Percival Spear, he made the British "uncomfortable in their cherished field of moral rectitude," and he gave Indians the feeling that theirs was the ethically superior cause.

India Moves Toward Independence

In the 1920s, slowly and reluctantly, the British handed over control of "national" areas such as education, the economy, and public works to Indians. They also gradually admitted more Indians into the Civil Service and the officer corps.

ENVIRONMENT + TECHNOLOGY

Gandhi and Technology

In the twentieth century all political leaders but one embraced modern industrial technology. That one exception is Gandhi.

After deciding to wear only handmade cloth, Gandhi made a bonfire of imported factory-made cloth and began spending half an hour every day spinning yarn on a simple spinning wheel, a task he called a "sacrament." The spinning wheel became the symbol of his movement and was later incorporated into the Indian flag. Any Indian who wished to come before him had to dress in handwoven cloth.

Gandhi had several reasons for reviving this ancient craft. One was his revulsion against "the incessant search for material comforts," an evil to which Europeans were "becoming slaves." He blamed the impoverishment of the Indian people on the cotton industries of England and Japan, which had ruined the traditional cotton manufacturing by which India had once supplied all her own needs. Gandhi looked back to a time before India became a colony of Britain, when "our women spun fine yarns in their own cottages, and supplemented the earnings of their husbands." The spinning wheel, he believed, was "presented to the nation for giving occupation to the millions who had, at least four months of the year, nothing to do." A return to the spinning wheel would provide employment to millions of Indians and would also become a symbol of "national consciousness and a contribution by every individual to a definite constructive national work."

Nevertheless, Gandhi was a shrewd politician who understood the usefulness of modern devices for mobilizing the masses and organizing his followers. He wore a watch and used the telephone and the printing press to keep in touch with his followers. When he traveled by train, he rode third class—but in a third-class railroad car of his own. His goal was the independence of his country, and he pursued it with every nonviolent means he could find.

Time Life Pictures/Getty Images

Gandhi at the Spinning Wheel Mahatma Gandhi chose the spinning wheel as his symbol because it represented the traditional activity of millions of rural Indians whose livelihoods were threatened by industrialization.

Gandhi's ideas challenge us to rethink the purpose of technology. Was he opposed on principle to all modern devices? Was he an opportunist who used those devices that served his political ends and rejected those that did not? Or did he have a higher principle that accounts for his willingness to use the telephone and the railroad but not factory-made cloth?

Jawaharlal Nehru Indian statesman who succeeded Mohandas K. Gandhi as leader of the Indian National Congress. He negotiated the end of British colonial rule in India and became India's first prime minister (1947–1964).

In the years before the Second World War, Indian politicians obtained the right to erect high tariff barriers against imports to protect India's infant industries from foreign competition. Behind these barriers, Indian entrepreneurs built plants to manufacture iron and steel, cement, paper, textiles, sugar, and other products. This early industrialization did not provide enough jobs to improve the lives of the Indian peasants or urban poor, but it created a class of wealthy Indian businessmen who supported the Indian National Congress and its demands for independence. Though paying homage to Gandhi, they preferred his designated successor as leader of the Indian National Congress, **Jawaharlal Nehru** (NAY-roo) (1889–1964). Unlike Gandhi, Nehru looked forward to creating a modern industrial India.

India in World War II

Congress politicians won regional elections but continued to be excluded from the viceroy's cabinet, the true center of power. When World War II began, Viceroy Lord Linlithgow declared war without consulting a single Indian. The Congress-dominated provincial governments resigned in protest and found that boycotting government office increased their popular support. When the British offered to give India its independence once the war ended, Gandhi demanded full independence immediately. His "Quit India" campaign aroused popular demonstrations against the British and provoked a wave of arrests, including his own. The Second World War divided the Indian people. Most Indian soldiers felt they were fighting to defend their country rather than to support the British Empire. As in World War I, Indians contributed heav-

Margaret Bourke-White, Time Life Pictures/Getty Images

The Partition of India When India became independent, Muslims fled from Hindu regions, and Hindus fled from Muslims. Margaret Bourke-White photographed a long line of refugees, with their cows, carts, and belongings, trudging down a country road toward safety.

ily to the Allied war effort, supplying 2 million soldiers and enormous amounts of resources, especially the timber needed for emergency construction. A small number of Indians, however, were so anti-British that they joined the Japanese side.

Muhammad Ali Jinnah Indian Muslim politician who founded the state of Pakistan. A lawyer by training, he joined the All-India Muslim League in 1913. As leader of the League from the 1920s on, he negotiated with the British and the Indian National Congress for Muslim participation in Indian politics. From 1940 on, he led the movement for the independence of India's Muslims in a separate state of Pakistan, founded in 1947.

Partition and Independence

When the war ended, Britain's new Labour Party government prepared for Indian independence, but deep suspicions between Hindus and Muslims complicated the process. The break between the two communities had started in 1937, when the Indian National Congress won provincial elections and refused to share power with the Muslim League. In 1940 the leader of the League, **Muhammad Ali Jinnah** (JEE-nah) (1876–1948), demanded what many Muslims had been dreaming of for years: a country of their own, to be called Pakistan.

As independence approached, talks between Jinnah and Nehru broke down and battle lines were drawn. Violent rioting between Hindus and Muslims broke out. Gandhi's appeals for tolerance and cooperation fell on deaf ears. The British made frantic proposals to keep India united, but their authority was waning fast.

In early 1947 the Indian National Congress accepted the partition of India into two states, one secular but dominated by Hindus, the other Muslim. On August 15 British India gave way to a new India and Pakistan. The Indian National Congress, led by Nehru, formed the first government of India; Jinnah and the Muslim League established a government for the provinces that made up Pakistan.

Violence

The rejoicing over independence was marred by violent outbreaks between Muslims and Hindus. In protest against the mounting chaos, Gandhi refused to attend the independence day celebration. Throughout the land, Muslim and Hindu neighbors turned on one another, and armed members of one faith hunted down people of the other faith. Leaving most of their possessions behind, Hindus fled from predominantly Muslim areas, and Muslims fled from Hindu areas. Trainloads of desperate refugees of one faith were attacked and massacred by members of the other or were left stranded in the middle of deserts. Within a few months some 12 million people had abandoned their ancestral homes and a half-million lay dead. In January 1948 Gandhi died too, gunned down by an angry Hindu refugee.

After the sectarian massacres and flights of refugees, Muslims were a minority in all but one state of India. That state was Kashmir, a strategically important region in the foothills of the Himalayas. India annexed Kashmir because the local maharajah was Hindu and because the state held the headwaters of the rivers that irrigated millions of acres of farmland. Most inhabitants would have joined Pakistan if they had been allowed to vote on the matter. The annexation of Kashmir turned India and Pakistan into bitter enemies that have fought several wars in the past half-century.

SECTION REVIEW

- Under British rule, India's population grew but remained divided by religion and caste.
- The British introduced certain modern technologies but discouraged Indian industry that might compete with British industry.
- British racial policies, brutality, and arrogance awakened a sense of nationhood among educated Indians.
- The Indian National Congress and the All-India Muslim League demanded independence.
- Mahatma Gandhi led the independence movement using nonviolent tactics and turned an upper-class rebellion into one involving all of India.
- Nehru, Gandhi's successor, wanted to modernize India, and the Indian National Congress resisted British rule during World War II.
- When the British left India in 1947, it split into two nations amidst widespread riots and massacres between Hindus and Muslims.

SUB-SAHARAN AFRICA, 1900–1945

Of all the continents, Africa was the last to come under European rule (see Chapter 27). The first half of the twentieth century, the time when nationalist movements threatened European rule in Asia (see Diversity and Dominance: A Vietnamese Nationalist Denounces French Colonialism), was Africa's period of classic colonialism. After World War I Britain, France, Belgium, and South Africa divided Germany's African colonies among themselves. Then in the 1930s Italy invaded Ethiopia. The colonial empires reached their peak shortly before World War II.

Colonial Africa: Economic and Social Changes

Outside of Algeria, Kenya, and South Africa, few Europeans lived in Africa. In 1930 Nigeria, with a population of 20 million, was ruled by 386 British officials and by 8,000 policemen and military, of whom 150 were European. Yet even such a small presence stimulated deep social and economic changes.

The colonial powers had built railroads from coastal cities to mines and plantations in the interior to transport raw materials to the industrial world, but few Africans benefited from these changes. Colonial governments took lands from Africans and sold or leased them to European companies or to white settlers. Large European companies dominated wholesale commerce, while Indians, Greeks, and Syrians handled much of the retail trade.

African Farmers

Where land was divided into small farms, some Africans benefited from the boom. Farmers in the Gold Coast (now Ghana [GAH-nuh]) profited from the high price of cocoa, as did palm-oil producers in Nigeria and coffee growers in East Africa. In most of Africa women played a major role in the retail trades, selling cloth, food, pots and pans, and other items in the markets. Many maintained their economic independence and kept their household finances separate from those of their husbands, following a custom that predated the colonial period.

For many Africans, however, economic development meant working in European-owned mines and plantations, often under compulsion. Colonial governments were eager to develop the resources of the territories under their control but would not pay wages high enough to attract

Making Palm Oil Palm oil is one of the most important crops of West Africa. Here two farm women are extracting the oil from palm kernels with a simple press.

Embassy of Nigeria/Visual Connection Archive

workers. Instead, they used their police powers to force Africans to work under harsh conditions for little or no pay. In the 1920s, when the government of French Equatorial Africa decided to build a railroad from Brazzaville to the Atlantic coast, a distance of 312 miles (502 kilometers), it drafted 127,000 men to carve a roadbed across mountains and through rain forests. For lack of food, clothing, and medical care, 20,000 of them died, an average of 64 deaths per mile of track.

African Health

Europeans prided themselves on bringing modern health care to Africa; yet before the 1930s other aspects of colonialism actually worsened public health. Migrants and soldiers spread syphilis, gonorrhea, tuberculosis, and malaria. Sleeping sickness and smallpox epidemics raged throughout Central Africa. In recruiting men to work, colonial governments also depleted rural areas of farmers needed to plant and harvest crops. Forced requisitions of food to feed the workers left the remaining populations undernourished and vulnerable to diseases. Not until the 1930s did colonial governments realize the negative consequences of their labor policies and begin to invest in agricultural development and health care for Africans.

In 1900 Ibadan (ee-BAH-dahn) in Nigeria was the only city in sub-Saharan Africa with more than 100,000 inhabitants; fifty years later, dozens of cities had reached that size. Africans migrated to cities because they offered hope of jobs and excitement and, for a few, the chance to become wealthy.

However, migrations damaged the family life of those involved, for almost all the migrants were men leaving women in the countryside to farm and raise children. Reflecting the colonialists' attitudes, cities built during the colonial period had racially segregated housing, clubs, restaurants, hospitals, and other institutions. Patterns of racial discrimination were most rigid in the white-settler colonies of eastern and southern Africa.

Religious and Political Changes

Traditional religious belief could not explain the dislocations that foreign rule, migrations, and sudden economic changes brought to the lives of Africans. Many therefore turned to Christianity or Islam.

DIVERSITY + DOMINANCE

A Vietnamese Nationalist Denounces French Colonialism

Movements for independence were a worldwide phenomenon. The tactics that different peoples used to achieve their goals differed widely. Among countries that were formal colonies, the case of India is unique in that its nationalist movement was led by Mahatma Gandhi, a man committed to nonviolent passive resistance. Elsewhere, revolutionary movements were often associated with violent uprisings. French Indochina is a case in point.

Indochina was conquered by the French from 1862 to 1895, after overcoming fierce resistance. Thereafter, France modernized the cities and irrigation systems and transformed the country into a leading producer of tea, rice, and natural rubber. This meant transferring large numbers of landless peasants to new plantations and destroying the traditional social structure. To govern Indochina, the French brought in more soldiers and civil administrators than the British had in all of India, a far larger colony. While they succeeded in crushing the resistance of the peasants and the old elites, the French were educating a new elite in the French language. These youths, inspired by French ideas of liberty and nationhood and by the example of neighboring China, formed the core of two new revolutionary movements.

One movement was the Vietnamese Revolutionary Youth League founded by Ho Chi Minh (1890–1969) in 1925, which later became the Indochinese Communist Party. The other was the Vietnamese Nationalist Party, founded in 1927 by a schoolteacher named Nguyen Thai Hoc (1904–1930). This party attracted government employees, soldiers, and small businessmen. At first Nguyen Thai Hoc lobbied the colonial government for reforms, but in vain. Two years later he turned to revolutionary action. In February 1930 he led an uprising at Yen Bay that the French quickly crushed. He and many of his followers were executed four months later, leaving Ho Chi Minh's Communists as the standard-bearers of nationalist revolution in Vietnam.

While awaiting his execution, Nguyen Thai Hoc wrote the following letter to the French Chamber of Deputies to justify his actions.

Gentlemen:

I, the undersigned, Nguyen Thai Hoc, a Vietnamese citizen, twenty-six years old, chairman and founder of the Vietnamese Nationalist Party, at present arrested and imprisoned at the jail of Yen Bay, Tongking, Indochina, have the great honor to inform you of the following facts:

According to the tenets of justice, everyone has the right to defend his own country when it is invaded by foreigners, and according to the principles of humanity, everyone has the duty to save his compatriots when they are in difficulty or in danger. As for myself, I have assessed the fact that my country has been annexed by you French for more than sixty years. I realize that under your dictatorial yoke, my compatriots have experienced a very hard life, and my people will without doubt be completely annihilated, by the naked principle of natural selection. Therefore, my right and my duty have compelled me to seek every way to defend my country which has been invaded and occupied, and to save my people who are in great danger.

At the beginning, I had thought to cooperate with the French in Indochina in order to serve my compatriots, my country and my people, particularly in the areas of cultural and economic development. As regards economic development, in 1925 I sent a memorandum to Governor General Varenne, describing to him all our aspirations concerning the protection of local industry and commerce in Indochina. I urged strongly in the same letter the creation of a Superior School of Industrial Development in Tongking. In 1926 I again addressed another letter to the then Governor General of Indochina in which I included some explicit suggestions to relieve the hardships of our poor people. In 1927, for a third time, I sent a letter to the Résident Supérieur [provincial administrator] in Tongking, requesting permission to publish a weekly magazine with the aim of safeguarding and encouraging local industry and com-

Christianity and Islam

Christianity was introduced into Africa by Western missionaries, except in Ethiopia, where it was indigenous. It was most successful in West and South Africa, where the European influence was strongest. A major attraction of the Christian denominations was their mission schools, which taught both craft skills and basic literacy, providing access to employment as minor functionaries, teachers, and shopkeepers. These schools educated a new elite, many of whom learned not only skills and literacy but Western political ideas as well. Many Africans accepted Christianity enthusiastically, reading the suffering of their own peoples into the biblical stories of Moses and the parables of Jesus. The churches trained some of the brighter pupils to become catechists, teachers, and clergymen. Independent Christian churches associated Christian beliefs with radical ideas of racial equality and participation in politics.

Islam spread inland from the East African coast and southward from the Sahel (SAH-hel) through the influence and example of Arab and African merchants. Islam also emphasized merce. With regard to the cultural domain, I sent a letter to the Governor General in 1927, requesting (1) the privilege of opening tuition-free schools for the children of the lower classes, particularly children of workers and peasants; (2) freedom to open popular publishing houses and libraries in industrial centers.

It is absolutely ridiculous that every suggestion has been rejected. My letters were without answer; my plans have not been considered; my requests have been ignored; even the articles that I sent to newspapers have been censored and rejected. From the experience of these rejections, I have come to the conclusion that the French have no sincere intention of helping my country or my people. I also concluded that we have to expel France. For this reason, in 1927, I began to organize a revolutionary party, which I named the Vietnamese Nationalist Party, with the aim of overthrowing the dictatorial and oppressive administration of our country. We aspire to create a Republic of Vietnam, composed of persons sincerely concerned with the happiness of the people. My party is a clandestine organization, and in February 1929, it was uncovered by the security police. Among the members of my party, a great number have been arrested. Fifty-two persons have been condemned to forced labor ranging from two to twenty years. Although many have been detained and many others unjustly condemned, my party has not ceased its activity. Under my guidance, the Party continues to operate and progress towards its aim.

During the Yen Bay uprising someone succeeded in killing some French officers. The authorities accused my party of having organized and perpetrated this revolt. They have accused me of having given the orders for the massacre. In truth, I have never given such orders, and I have presented before the Penal Court of Yen Bay all the evidence showing the inanity of this accusation. Even so, some of the members of my party completely ignorant of that event have been accused of participating in it. The French Indochinese government burned and destroyed their houses. They sent French troops to occupy their villages and stole their rice to divide it among the soldiers. Not just members of my party have been suffering from this injustice—we should rather call this cruelty rather than injustice—but also many simple peasants, interested only in their daily work in the rice fields, living miserable lives like buffaloes and horses, have been compromised in this reprisal. At the present time, in various areas there are tens of thousands of men, women, and children, persons of all ages, who have been massacred. They died either of hunger or exposure because the French Indochinese government burned their homes. I therefore beseech you in tears to redress this injustice which otherwise will annihilate my people, which will stain French honor, and which will belittle all human values. . . .

If France wants to stay in peace in Indochina, if France does not want to have increasing troubles with revolutionary movements, she should immediately modify the cruel and inhuman policy now practiced in Indochina. The French should behave like friends to the Vietnamese, instead of being cruel and oppressive masters. They should be attentive to the intellectual and material sufferings of the Vietnamese people, instead of being harsh and tough. Please, Gentlemen, receive my gratitude.

QUESTIONS FOR ANALYSIS

1. **When he first became involved in politics, what were Nguyen Thai Hoc's views of French colonialism?**
2. **What were his first initiatives, and what response did he get from the French colonial administration?**
3. **What motivated Nguyen Thai Hoc to organize an uprising, and what was the response of the French?**
4. **Compare Nguyen Thai Hoc's views and methods and the French response with the situation in India.**

Source: Harry Benda and John Larkin, *The World of Southeast Asia* (New York: Harper & Row, 1967), 182–185. Reprinted by permission of the author.

A Quranic School In Muslim countries, religious education is centered on learning to read, write, and recite the Quran, the sacred book of the Islamic religion, in the original Arabic. This picture shows boys in a Libyan madrasa (Quranic school) studying writing and religion.

Olivier Martel/Corbis

literacy—in Arabic rather than in a European language—and was less disruptive of traditional African customs such as polygamy.

Early Political Movements

In Dakar in Senegal and Cape Town in South Africa, small numbers of Africans could obtain secondary education. Even smaller numbers went on to college in Europe or America. Though few in number, they became the leaders of political movements. The contrast between the liberal ideas imparted by Western education and the realities of racial discrimination under colonial rule contributed to the rise of nationalism among educated Africans. In Senegal **Blaise Diagne** (dee-AHN-yuh) agitated for African participation in politics and fair treatment in the French army during World War I, and in the 1920s J. E. Casely Hayford began organizing a movement for greater autonomy in British West Africa. These nationalist movements were inspired by the ideas of Pan-Africanists from America such as W. E. B. Du Bois and Marcus Garvey, who advocated the unity of African peoples around the world, as well as by European ideas of liberty and nationhood. To defend the interests of Africans, Western-educated lawyers and journalists in South Africa founded the **African National Congress** in 1912. Before World War II, however, these nationalist movements were small and had little influence.

Blaise Diagne Senegalese political leader. He was the first African elected to the French National Assembly. During World War I, in exchange for promises to give French citizenship to Senegalese, he helped recruit Africans to serve in the French army. After the war, he led a movement to abolish forced labor in Africa.

Africa in World War II

The Second World War had a profound effect on the peoples of Africa, even those far removed from the theaters of war. The war brought hardships, such as increased forced labor, inflation, and requisitions of raw materials. Yet it also brought hope. During the campaign to oust the Italians from Ethiopia, Emperor **Haile Selassie** (HI-lee seh-LASS-ee) (r. 1930–1974) led his own troops into Addis Ababa, his capital, and reclaimed his title. A million Africans served as soldiers and carriers in Burma, North Africa, and Europe, where many became aware of Africa's role in helping the Allied war effort. They listened to Allied propaganda in favor of European liberation movements and against Nazi racism and returned to their countries with new and radical ideas.

SECTION REVIEW

- Colonial rule developed Africa's economies at the expense of its peoples' livelihoods and health.
- Many Africans turned to Christianity or Islam; some, especially those who participated in World War II, began to demand independence.

MEXICO, ARGENTINA, AND BRAZIL, 1900–1949

Latin America achieved independence from Spain and Portugal in the nineteenth century but did not industrialize. Most Latin American republics, suffering from ideological divisions, unstable governments, and violent upheavals, traded their commodities for foreign manufactured goods and investments and became economically dependent on the United States and Great Britain. Their societies remained deeply split between wealthy landowners and desperately poor peasants.

Mexico, Brazil, and Argentina contained well over half of Latin America's land, population, and wealth, and their relations with other countries and their economies were quite similar. Mexico, however, underwent a traumatic social revolution, while Argentina and Brazil evolved more peaceably.

African National Congress An organization dedicated to obtaining equal voting and civil rights for black inhabitants of South Africa. Founded in 1912 as the South African Native National Congress, it changed its name in 1923. Though it was banned and its leaders were jailed for many years, it eventually helped bring majority rule to South Africa.

Haile Selassie Emperor of Ethiopia (r. 1930–1974) and symbol of African independence. He fought the Italian invasion of his country in 1935 and regained his throne during World War II, when British forces expelled the Italians. He ruled Ethiopia as a traditional autocracy until he was overthrown in 1974.

Background to Revolution: Mexico in 1910

At the beginning of the twentieth century Mexican society was divided into rich and poor and into persons of Spanish, Indian, and mixed ancestry. A few very wealthy families of Spanish origin, less than 1 percent of the population, owned 85 percent of Mexico's land, mostly in huge *haciendas* (estates). A handful of American and British companies controlled most of Mexico's railroads, silver mines, plantations, and other productive enterprises. At the other end of the social scale were Indians, many of whom did not speak Spanish. *Mestizos* (mess-TEE-so), people of mixed Indian and European ancestry, were only slightly better off; most of them were peasants who worked on the haciendas or farmed small communal plots near their ancestral villages.

After independence in 1821 wealthy Mexican families and American companies used bribery and force to acquire millions of acres of good agricultural land from villages in southern

Mexico. Peasants lost not only their fields but also their access to firewood and pasture for their animals and had little choice but to work on haciendas. To survive, they had to buy food and other necessities on credit from the landowner's store; eventually, they fell permanently into debt.

The Díaz Regime

For thirty-four years General Porfirio Díaz (DEE-as) (1830–1915) had ruled Mexico under the motto "Liberty, Order, Progress." To Díaz "liberty" meant freedom for rich hacienda owners and foreign investors to acquire more land. The government imposed "order" through rigged elections, bribes to Díaz's supporters, and summary justice for those who opposed him. "Progress" meant mainly the importing of foreign capital, machinery, and technicians to take advantage of Mexico's labor, soil, and natural resources.

During the Díaz years (1876–1910) Mexico City became a showplace with paved streets, streetcar lines, electric street lighting, and public parks. New telegraph and railroad lines connected cities and towns throughout Mexico. But this material progress benefited only a handful of well-connected businessmen and lowered the average Mexican's standard of living.

Emiliano Zapata Revolutionary and leader of peasants in the Mexican Revolution. He mobilized landless peasants in south-central Mexico in an attempt to seize and divide the lands of the wealthy landowners. Though successful for a time, he was ultimately defeated and assassinated.

Though a mestizo himself, Díaz discriminated against the nonwhite majority of Mexicans. He and his supporters tried to eradicate what they saw as Mexico's rustic traditions. On many middle- and upper-class tables French cuisine replaced traditional Mexican dishes, and the wealthy replaced sombreros and ponchos with European garments. To the educated middle class—the only group with a strong sense of Mexican nationhood—this devaluation of Mexican culture became a symbol of the Díaz regime's failure to defend national interests against foreign influences.

Revolution and Civil War in Mexico

The Mexican Revolution was a social revolution that developed haphazardly under ambitious but limited leaders, each representing a different segment of Mexican society. The first was Francisco I. Madero (1873–1913), the son of a wealthy landowning and mining family, educated in the United States. When minor uprisings broke out in 1911, the government collapsed and Díaz fled into exile. The Madero presidency was welcomed by some, but it aroused opposition from peasant leaders like **Emiliano Zapata** (sah-PAH-tah) (1879–1919). In 1913, after two years as president, Madero was overthrown and murdered by one of his former supporters, General Victoriano Huerta. Woodrow Wilson (1856–1924), president of the United States, showed his displeasure by sending the United States Marines to occupy Veracruz.

The inequities of Mexican society and foreign intervention angered Mexico's middle class and industrial workers. They found leaders in Venustiano Carranza, a landowner, and in Alvaro Obregón (oh-bray-GAWN), a schoolteacher. Calling themselves Constitutionalists, Carranza and Obregón organized private armies and overthrew Huerta in 1914. By then, the revolution had spread to the countryside.

Brown Brothers

Emiliano Zapata Zapata, the leader of a peasant rebellion in southern Mexico during the Mexican Revolution, stands in full revolutionary regalia: sword, rifles, bandoleers, boots, and sombrero.

The Granger Collection, New York

Francisco "Pancho" Villa Francisco "Pancho" Villa led an army of cowboys and ranch hands in northern Mexico during the revolution. He became very popular by confiscating large haciendas and dividing them among the poor. In March 1916 he entered the United States with 500 soldiers and attacked the town of Columbus, New Mexico, provoking an American invasion of Mexico. He was assassinated in 1923.

Zapata and Villa

Zapata, an Indian farmer, had led a revolt against the haciendas in the mountains of Morelos, south of Mexico City (see Map 30.2). His soldiers were peasants mounted on horseback and armed with pistols and rifles. For several years they periodically came down from the mountains, burned hacienda buildings, and returned land to the Indian villages to which it had once belonged.

Francisco "Pancho" Villa A popular leader during the Mexican Revolution. An outlaw in his youth, when the revolution started, he formed a cavalry army in the north of Mexico and fought for the rights of the landless in collaboration with Emiliano Zapata. He was assassinated in 1923.

Another leader appeared in Chihuahua, a northern state where seventeen individuals owned two-fifths of the land and 95 percent of the people had no land at all. Starting in 1913, **Francisco "Pancho" Villa** (1877–1923), a former ranch hand, mule driver, and bandit, organized an army of three thousand men, most of them cowboys, and divided large haciendas into family ranches.

Zapata and Villa enjoyed tremendous popular support but could never rise above their regional and peasant origins and lead a national revolution. The Constitutionalists had fewer soldiers than Zapata and Villa, but they held the major cities and used the proceeds of oil sales to buy modern weapons. Gradually the Constitutionalists took over most of Mexico. In 1919 they defeated and killed Zapata; Villa was assassinated four years later. An estimated 2 million people lost their lives in the civil war, and much of Mexico lay in ruins.

The Constitution of 1917

During their struggle to win support against Zapata and Villa, the Constitutionalists adopted many of their rivals' agrarian reforms, such as restoring communal lands to the Indians of Morelos. The Constitutionalists also proposed social programs designed to appeal to workers and the middle class. The Constitution of 1917 promised universal suffrage and a one-term presidency; state-run education to free the poor from the hold of the Catholic Church; the end of debt peonage; restrictions on foreign ownership of property; and laws specifying minimum wages and maximum hours to protect laborers. Although these reforms were too costly to implement right away, they had important symbolic significance, for they enshrined the dignity of Mexicans and the equality of Indians, mestizos, and whites, as well as of peasants and city people.

Lázaro Cárdenas President of Mexico (1934–1940). He brought major changes to Mexican life by distributing millions of acres of land to the peasants, bringing representatives of workers and farmers into the inner circles of politics, and nationalizing the oil industry.

In the early 1920s, after a decade of violence that exhausted all classes, the Mexican Revolution lost momentum, and President Obregón and his closest associates made all the important decisions. His successor, Plutarco Elías Calles (KAH-yace), founded the National Revolutionary Party, or PNR (the abbreviation of its name in Spanish). The PNR was a forum where all the pressure groups and vested interests—labor, peasants, businessmen, landowners, the military, and others—worked out compromises. The establishment of the PNR gave the Mexican Revolution a second wind.

The Cárdenas Reforms

Lázaro Cárdenas (LAH-sah-roe KAHR-dih-nahs), chosen by Calles to be president in 1934, brought peasants' and workers' organizations into the party and removed the generals from government positions. Then he set to work implementing the reforms promised in the Constitution of 1917. Cárdenas redistributed 44 million acres (17.6 million hectares) to peasant communes, replaced church-run schools with government schools, and nationalized the railroads and numerous other businesses.

In 1938 Cárdenas seized the foreign-owned oil industry. The American and British oil companies expected their governments to come to their rescue, perhaps with military force. But Mexico and the United States chose to resolve the issue through negotiation, and Mexico retained control of its oil industry.

When Cárdenas's term ended in 1940, Mexico was still a land of poor farmers with a small industrial base. The Revolution had brought great changes, however. The political system was free of both chaos and dictatorships. A few wealthy people no longer monopolized land and other resources. The military was tamed; the Catholic Church no longer controlled education; and the nationalization of oil had demonstrated Mexico's independence from foreign corporations and military intervention.

The Mexican Revolution did not fulfill the democratic promise of Madero's campaign, for it brought to power a party that monopolized the government for eighty years. However, it allowed far more sectors of the population to participate in politics and made sure no president stayed in office more than six years. The Revolution also promised far-reaching social reforms, such as free education, higher wages for workers, and the redistribution of land to the peasants. These long-delayed reforms began to be implemented during the Cárdenas administration. They fell short of the ideals expressed by the revolutionaries, but they laid the foundation for the later industrialization of Mexico.

Interactive Map

MAP 30.2 The Mexican Revolution The Mexican Revolution began in two distinct regions of the country. One was the mountainous and densely populated area south of Mexico City, particularly Morelos, homeland of Emiliano Zapata. The other was the dry and thinly populated ranch country of the north, home of Pancho Villa. The fighting that ensued crisscrossed the country along the main railroad lines, shown on the map.

Revolutionary Art

In the arts the Mexican Revolution sparked a surge of creativity. The political murals of José Clemente Orozco and Diego Rivera and the paintings of Frida Kahlo focused on social themes, showing scenes from the Revolution. These works of art gave Mexicans a sense of national unity and pride in the achievements of the Revolution that lasted long after the revolutionary fervor had dissipated.

The Transformation of Argentina

Most of Argentina consists of *pampas* (POM-pus), flat, fertile land that is easy to till, much like the prairies of the midwestern United States and Canada. At the end of the nineteenth century railroads and refrigerator ships, which allowed the safe transportation of meat, changed not only the composition of Argentina's exports but even the land itself. European consumers preferred the soft flesh of Lincoln sheep and Hereford cattle, but these valuable animals were carefully bred and fed alfalfa and oats. To safeguard them, the pampas had to be divided, plowed, cultivated, and fenced with barbed wire. Once fenced, the land could be used to produce wheat as well as beef and mutton. Within a few years grasslands that had stretched to the horizon were transformed into farmland. Like the North American Midwest, the pampas became one of the world's great producers of wheat and meat.

The *Oligarquía*

Argentina's government represented the interests of the *oligarquía* (oh-lee-gar-KEE-ah), a small group of wealthy landowners who raised cattle and sheep and grew wheat for export. They owned fine homes in Buenos Aires (BWAY-nos EYE-res), a city that was built to resemble Paris, traveled frequently to Europe, and spent lavishly. However, they showed little interest in any business other than farming and were content to let British companies build Argentina's railroads, processing plants, and public utilities. In exchange for its agricultural exports, Argentina imported almost all its manufactured goods from Europe and the United States. So important were British interests in the Argentinean economy that English, not Spanish, was used on the railroads, and the biggest department store in Buenos Aires was a branch of Harrods of London.

Brazil and Argentina, to 1929

Before the First World War, Brazil produced most of the world's coffee and cacao, grown on vast estates, and natural rubber, gathered by Indians from rubber trees growing wild in the Amazon rain forest. Thus Brazil's elite was made up of coffee and cacao planters and rubber exporters. Like their Argentinean counterparts, they spent their money lavishly, building palaces in Rio de Janeiro (REE-oh day zhuh-NAIR-oh) and an opera house deep in the Amazon. Also as in Argentina, they let British companies build railroads, harbors, and other infrastructure and imported most manufactured goods. At the time this seemed to allow each country to do what it did best. If Britain did not grow coffee, why should Brazil build locomotives?

Both Argentina and Brazil had small but outspoken middle classes that demanded a share in government and looked to Europe as a model. Beneath each middle class were the poor. In Argentina these were mainly Spanish and Italian immigrants who had ended up as landless farm laborers or workers in urban packing plants. In Brazil there was a large class of sharecroppers and plantation workers, many of them descendants of slaves.

Hipólito Irigoyen Argentine politician, president of Argentina from 1916 to 1922 and 1928 to 1930. The first president elected by universal male suffrage, he began his presidency as a reformer but later became conservative.

Rubber exports collapsed after 1912, replaced by cheaper plantation rubber from Southeast Asia. Then the outbreak of war in 1914 put an end to imports from Europe as Britain and France focused all their industries on war production and Germany was cut off entirely. The disruption of the old trade patterns weakened the landowning class. In Argentina the urban middle class obtained the secret ballot and universal male suffrage in 1916 and elected a liberal politician, **Hipólito Irigoyen** (ee-POH-lee-toe ee-ree-GO-yen), as president. To a certain extent, the United States replaced the European countries as suppliers of machinery and consumers of coffee. European immigrants built factories to manufacture textiles and household goods.

Postwar Prosperity

The postwar years were a period of prosperity in South America. Trade with Europe resumed; prices for agricultural exports remained high; and both Argentina and Brazil used profits accumulated during the war to industrialize and improve their transportation systems and public utilities. Yet it was also a time of social turmoil, as workers and middle-class professionals demanded social reforms and a larger voice in politics. In Argentina students' and workers' demonstrations were brutally crushed. In Brazil junior officers rose up several times against the government. Though they accomplished little, they laid the groundwork for later reformist movements. In neither country did the urban middle class take power away from the wealthy landowners. Instead, the two classes shared power at the expense of both the landless peasants and the urban workers.

Yet as Argentina and Brazil were moving forward, new technologies again left them dependent on the advanced industrial countries. Aviation reached Latin America after World War I, when European and American companies such as Aéropostale and Pan American Airways introduced airmail service between cities and linked Latin America with the United States and Europe.

Before and during World War I, radio was used only for point-to-point communications. Transmitters powerful enough to send messages across oceans or continents were extraordinarily complex and expensive: their antennas covered many acres, and they used as much electricity as a small town. Right after the war, the major powers scrambled to build powerful transmitters on every continent to take advantage of the boom in international business and news reporting. At the time, no Latin American country possessed the knowledge or funds to build its own transmitters. Four powerful radio companies—one British, one French, one German, and one American—formed a cartel to control all radio communications in Latin America. Thus, even as Brazil and Argentina were taking over their railroads and older industries, the major industrial countries controlled the diffusion of the newer aviation and radio technologies.

The Depression and the Vargas Regime in Brazil

The Depression hit Latin America as hard as it hit Europe and the United States; in many ways, it marks a more important turning point for the region than either of the world wars. As long-term customers cut back their orders, the value of agricultural and mineral exports fell by two-thirds between 1929 and 1932. Argentina and Brazil could no longer afford to import manufactured goods. An imploding economy also undermined their shaky political systems. Like European countries, Argentina and Brazil veered toward authoritarian regimes that promised to solve their economic problems.

Getulio Vargas Dictator of Brazil from 1930 to 1945 and from 1951 to 1954. Defeated in the presidential election of 1930, he overthrew the government and created Estado Novo ("New State"), a dictatorship that emphasized industrialization and helped the urban poor but did little to alleviate the problems of the peasants.

In 1930 **Getulio Vargas** (jay-TOO-lee-oh VAR-gus) (1883–1954), a state governor, staged a coup and proclaimed himself president of Brazil. He proved to be a masterful politician. He wrote a new constitution that broadened the franchise and limited the president to one term. He also raised import duties and promoted national firms and state-owned enterprises. By 1936 industrial production had doubled, especially in textiles and small manufactures. Under his guidance, Brazil was on its way to becoming an industrial country. Vargas's policy became a model for other Latin American countries as they attempted to break away from neocolonial dependency.

The Environment

The industrialization of Brazil brought all the familiar environmental consequences. Powerful new machines allowed the reopening of old mines and the digging of new ones. Cities grew as poor peasants looking for work arrived from the countryside. In Rio de Janeiro and São Paulo (sow PAL-oh), the poor turned steep hillsides and vacant lands into immense *favelas* (feh-VEL-luhs) (slums) of makeshift shacks.

The countryside also was transformed. Scrubland was turned into pasture or planted in wheat, corn, and sugar cane. Even the Amazon rain forest—half of the land area of Brazil—was affected. In 1930 American industrialist Henry Ford invested $8 million to clear land along the Tapajós River and prepare it to become the site of the world's largest rubber plantation. Ford encountered opposition from Brazilian workers and politicians; the rubber trees proved vulnerable to diseases; and he had to abandon the project—but not before leaving 3 million acres (1.2 million hectares) denuded of trees.

Vargas's Legacy

Although Vargas instituted many reforms favorable to urban workers, he refused to take any measures that might help the millions of landless peasants or harm the interests of the great landowners. In 1938, prohibited by his own constitution from being reelected, Vargas staged another coup, abolished the constitution, and instituted the Estado Novo (esh-TAH-doe NO-vo), or "New State," with himself as supreme leader. He abolished political parties, jailed

Juan and Eva Perón Juan Perón's presidency of Argentina (1946–1955) relied on his, and especially on his wife Eva's, popularity with the working class. To sustain their popularity, they often organized parades and demonstrations in imitation of the fascist dictators of Europe. This picture shows them riding in a procession in Buenos Aires in 1952.

Bettmann/Corbis

opposition leaders, and turned Brazil into a fascist state. When the Second World War broke out, Vargas contributed troops and ships to the Allied war effort.

Despite his economic achievements, Vargas harmed Brazil. By running roughshod over laws, constitutions, and rights, he infected not only Brazil but also all of South America with the temptations of political violence.

Juan Perón President of Argentina (1946–1955, 1973–1974). As a military officer, he championed the rights of labor. Aided by his wife Eva Duarte Perón, he was elected president in 1946. He built up Argentinean industry, became very popular among the urban poor, but harmed the economy.

Juan Perón

Argentina After 1930

Economically, the Depression hurt Argentina almost as badly as it hurt Brazil. Politically, however, the consequences were delayed for many years. In 1930 General José Uriburu (hoe-SAY oo-ree-BOO-roo) overthrew the popularly elected President Irigoyen. For thirteen years the generals and the oligarchy ruled, doing nothing to lessen the poverty of the workers or the frustrations of the middle class. When World War II broke out, Argentina remained officially neutral.

In 1943 another military revolt flared, this one among junior officers led by Colonel **Juan Perón** (hoo-AHN pair-OWN) (1895–1974). The intentions of the rebels were clear:

> *Civilians will never understand the greatness of our ideal; we shall therefore have to eliminate them from the government and give them the only mission which corresponds to them: work and obedience.*[1]

Once in power the officers took over the highest positions in government and business and began to lavish money on military equipment and their own salaries. Their goal, inspired by Nazi victories, was nothing less than the conquest of South America.

Eva Duarte Perón Wife of Juan Perón and champion of the poor in Argentina. She was a gifted speaker and popular political leader who campaigned to improve the life of the urban poor by founding schools and hospitals and providing other social benefits.

As the war turned against the Nazis, the officers saw their popularity collapse. Perón, however, had other plans. Inspired by his charismatic wife **Eva Duarte Perón** (AY-vuy doo-AR-tay pair-OWN) (1919–1952), he appealed to the urban workers. Eva Perón became the champion of the *descamisados* (des-cah-mee-SAH-dohs), or "shirtless ones," and campaigned tirelessly for social benefits and for the cause of women and children. With his wife's help, Perón won the presidency in 1946 and created a populist dictatorship in imitation of the Vargas regime in Brazil.

Like Brazil, Argentina industrialized rapidly under state sponsorship. Perón spent lavishly on social welfare projects as well as on the military, depleting the capital that Argentina had earned during the war. Though a skillful demagogue who played off the army against the navy and both against the labor unions, Perón could not create a stable government. When Eva died in 1952, he lost his political skills (or perhaps they were hers), and soon thereafter was overthrown in yet another military coup.

SECTION REVIEW

- Mexican society was deeply split between rich landowners and the poor.
- The Díaz regime introduced modern technologies while also lowering the living standards of the poor still further.
- Revolution broke out in Mexico in 1910, as different leaders vied for power.
- In the 1920s a single party, the Constitutionalists, emerged to rule Mexico.
- Lázaro Cárdenas fulfilled some of the promises of the revolution and nationalized the oil industry.
- Under its landowning oligarchy, Argentina became a major exporter of beef and wheat and depended on Europeans for its industrial products.
- After World War I, Argentina and Brazil prospered but were still dependent on the United States and Europe for advanced technology.
- Brazil and Argentina suffered greatly from the Depression; in the 1930s Vargas's dictatorship modernized Brazil but left the majority in poverty.
- Argentina, under Juan Perón, also industrialized, but his unstable government came to an end in the 1950s.

CONCLUSION

The wars and revolutions that engulfed the Northern Hemisphere between 1900 and 1949 affected India, sub-Saharan Africa, and Latin America by placing heavy demands on their peoples and raising their hopes for a better life. Sub-Saharan Africa and India were still under colonial rule, and their political life revolved around the desire of their elites for political independence while ordinary people yearned for social justice. Mexico, Argentina, and Brazil were politically independent, but their economies, like those of Africa and India, were closely tied to the economies of the industrial nations with which they traded. When the Depression hit, all three turned to state intervention. Like all industrializing countries, they did so at the expense of the natural environment. Their deeply polarized societies and the stresses caused by their dependence on the industrial countries clashed with the expectations of their peoples.

In Mexico these stresses brought about a long and violent social revolution, out of which Mexicans forged a lasting sense of national identity. Argentina and Brazil moved toward greater economic independence, but the price was social unrest, militarism, and dictatorship. They languished under conservative regimes devoted to the interests of wealthy landowners, sporadically interrupted by military coups and populist demagogues. In India the conflict between growing expectations and the reality of colonial rule produced both a movement for independence and an ethnic split that tore the nation apart. In sub-Saharan Africa demands for national self-determination and economic development were only beginning to be voiced by 1949.

Nationalism and the yearning for social justice were the two most powerful forces for change in the early twentieth century. These ideas originated in the industrialized countries but resonated in the independent countries of Latin America as well as in colonial regions such as India and sub-Saharan Africa. However, they did not always unite people against their colonial rulers or foreign oppressors; instead, they often divided them along social, ethnic, or religious lines. Western-educated elites looked to industrialization as a means of modernizing their country and ensuring their position in it, while peasants and urban workers supported nationalist and revolutionary movements in the hope of improving their lives. Often these goals were not compatible.

KEY TERMS

Indian National Congress p. 862
Bengal p. 862
All-India Muslim League p. 862
Mohandas K. Gandhi p. 863
Jawaharlal Nehru p. 864
Muhammad Ali Jinnah p. 865
Blaise Diagne p. 870
African National Congress p. 870
Haile Selassie p. 870
Emiliano Zapata p. 871
Francisco "Pancho" Villa p. 872
Lázaro Cárdenas p. 872
Hipólito Irigoyen p. 874
Getulio Vargas p. 875
Juan Perón p. 876
Eva Duarte Perón p. 877

EBOOK AND WEBSITE RESOURCES

Primary Source

An Indian Nationalist Condemns the British Empire

Interactive Maps

Map 30.1 The Partition of India, 1947

Map 30.2 The Mexican Revolution

Plus flashcards, practice quizzes, and more. Go to: www.cengage.com/history/bullietearthpeople5e

SUGGESTED READING

Achebe, Chinua. *Arrow of God*. 1964. A classic novel about the conflict between traditional beliefs and Christianity in a Nigerian village.

Adelman, Jeremy. *Frontier Development: Land, Labour and Capital on the Wheatlands of Argentina and Canada, 1890–1914*. 1994. An analysis of the contrasting development of two major American nations.

Boahen, Adu. *African Perspectives on Colonialism*. 1987. A work recounting the African reactions to colonial rule.

Brown, Judith M. *Gandhi: Prisoner of Hope*. 1989. The classic biography of the Indian leader.

Burns, E. Bradford. *A History of Brazil*, 3rd ed. 1993. The definitive history of a great nation.

Collins, Larry, and Dominique Lapierre. *Freedom at Midnight*. 1975. A popular account of the coming of independence and the partition of India.

Dean, Warren. *Brazil and the Struggle for Rubber: A Study in Environmental History*. 1987. Describes the destruction of the rainforest and of its inhabitants who were coerced to produce rubber for the automobile boom.

Gadgil, M., and R. Guha, *This Fissured Land: An Ecological History of India*. 1993. The classic work on the history of the Indian environment.

Jefferson, Mark. *Peopling the Argentine Pampas*. 1971. How immigrants from Spain and Italy made the Argentine nation.

Knight, Alan. *The Mexican Revolution*, 2 vols. 1986. The definitive history of the revolution.

Krauze, Enrique. *Mexico: Biography of Power: A History of Modern Mexico, 1810–1996*. 1997. The political history of a nation in turmoil.

Machado, Manuel. *Centaur of the North: Francisco Villa, the Mexican Revolution, and Northern Mexico*. 1988. A biography of the famous bandit-revolutionary.

Meyer, Michael, and William Beezley, *Oxford History of Mexico*. 2000. The definitive account.

Oliver, Roland, and Anthony Atmore, *Africa Since 1800*, 4th ed. 1994. The best-known history of modern Africa.

Sarkar, Sumit. *Modern India, 1885–1947.* 1983. The classic history of the independence movement.

NOTES

1. George Blankstein, *Perón's Argentina* (Chicago: University of Chicago Press, 1953), 37.

AP* REVIEW QUESTIONS FOR CHAPTER 30

1. Which of the following was true of the Indian Civil Service?
   (A) Its members believed it was their duty to protect the Indian people from the dangers of industrialization and to defend their own positions from Indian nationalists.
   (B) Most of its members had served in the British army prior to coming to India.
   (C) It supported industrializing India and encouraged the introduction of modern technology.
   (D) Its staff was composed of 50 percent Hindus and 50 percent Muslims to reflect Indian society.

2. In the interwar period (1919–1939), India never experienced a violent revolution because
   (A) the Muslims and Hindus in India generally got along with each other.
   (B) Mohandas Gandhi and others like him provided able leadership.
   (C) the Indians were more concerned with food than revolution, so revolutionary leaders found it hard to develop a following.
   (D) India had already established craft unions as part of the caste system.

3. Muhammad Ali Jinnah, the leader of the Muslim League, became the first of the Muslim Indian leaders to
   (A) become a member of the Indian parliament.
   (B) call for supporting the British in World War II.
   (C) call for an independent Muslim state to be called Pakistan.
   (D) call for an end to the sectarian fighting in India.

4. In 1912 Western-educated lawyers and journalists founded the African National Congress
   (A) as a way to develop African industrialization.
   (B) to prevent the formation of socialist and communist political parties.
   (C) to encourage education of the brightest Africans.
   (D) as a Pan-African nationalist organization like the Indian National Congress.

5. The Mexican Revolution of 1910 began as
   (A) a revolt against high taxation on food production.
   (B) a simple demand for suffrage rights for adult males.
   (C) a demand for the government to end the raiding by Emiliano Zapata.
   (D) a revolt of the poor against the wealthy.

6. In the early twentieth century both Brazil and Argentina
   (A) had small but outspoken middle classes that were demanding a share in government and looked to Europe as a model.
   (B) moved closer to an American-style democracy and granted suffrage rights to all citizens over the age of eighteen.
   (C) emerged as industrial giants in South and Central America.
   (D) encouraged social reforms that made both nations attractive to European immigration.

7. Although the Mexican Revolution of 1910 allowed more sectors of the population to participate in government,
   (A) it encouraged the formation of parties that preached socialism and communism.
   (B) it brought to power a party that would monopolize the Mexican government for eighty years.
   (C) it also ensured that the indigenous population could not vote.
   (D) it never altered the constitution, which allowed for dictatorial government.

8. Although Mexico, Argentina, and Brazil were all independent nations,
   (A) they never achieved any real democratic reforms before the twentieth century.
   (B) they were closely tied to the industrial nations with which they traded.
   (C) Europe treated them as if they were still colonies.
   (D) the Allies refused their participation in the world wars.

9. In the early twentieth century, the two most powerful forces of change in Latin America and Africa were
   (A) fascism and industrialization.
   (B) nationalism and the yearning for social justice.
   (C) women's rights and suffrage rights.
   (D) ethnic equality and nationalism.

FAMINES AND POLITICS

Human history is filled with tales of famines—times when crops failed, food supplies ran out, and people starved.

Natural Famines

India, dependent on the monsoon rains, has been particularly prone to such calamities, with famines striking two to four times a century, whenever the rains fail for several years in succession. Three times in the eighteenth century famines killed several million people. The nineteenth century was worse, with famines in 1803–1804, 1837–1838, 1868–1870, and 1876–1878. The famine of 1876–1878 also afflicted northern China, causing between 9 and 13 million deaths from hunger and from the diseases of malnutrition. There were even incidents of cannibalism, as starving adults ate starving children.

When drought hit a region, it decimated not only the human population but also the animals they relied on to transport crops or plow the land. When water levels dropped in rivers and canals, food could not be transported by boat to areas where people were starving.

Commercial Famines

That all changed in the nineteenth century. Railroads and steamships could transport foodstuffs quickly across great distances, regardless of the weather. Great Britain became dependent on imports of wheat and beef. Yet the global death toll from starvation has been far higher since the mid-nineteenth century than ever before. Why?

Consider Ireland. By the early nineteenth century the potato had become the main source of nutrition for the Irish people. Potatoes grew abundantly and produced more calories per acre than any other crop, allowing the population to increase dramatically.

In 1845 a blight turned the potatoes in the fields black, mushy, and inedible. The harvest was ruined the following year as well. It recovered slightly in 1847 but was bad again in 1848. Tens of thousands died of starvation, while hundreds of thousands died from dysentery, typhus, or cholera. Travelers saw corpses rotting in their hovels or on the sides of roads. Altogether, a million or more people died, while another million emigrated, reducing the population of Ireland by half.

Throughout those years, Ireland exported wheat to England, where people had money to pay for it. Food cost money, and the Irish, poor even before the famines, were destitute and could not afford to buy wheat or bread. The British government was convinced that interfering with the free market would only make things worse. Relief efforts were half-hearted at best; the official responsible for Irish affairs preferred to leave the situation to "the operation of natural causes."

The same held true in India, like Ireland a colony of Great Britain. The drought of 1876–1878 killed over 5 million Indians in the Deccan region, while British officials stood by helpless or indifferent. Part of the problem was transportation. In the 1870s most goods were still transported in bullock carts, but the bullocks starved during the drought. Another obstacle was political. The idea that a government should be responsible for feeding the population was unthinkable at the time. And so, while millions were starving in the Deccan, the Punjab was exporting wheat to Britain.

Over the next twenty years, so-called famine railways were built in the regions historically most affected by the failures of the monsoon. When drought struck again at the end of the century, the railways were ready to transport food to areas that had previously been accessible only by bullock carts. However, the inhabitants of the affected regions had no money with which to buy what little food there was, and the government was still reluctant to interfere with free enterprise. Grain merchants bought all the stocks, hoarded them until the price rose, then used the railways to transport them out of the famine regions to regions where the harvests were better and people had more money.

In the twentieth century, commercial famines became rare as governments realized that they had a responsibility to provide food not only for their own people but also for people in other countries. Yet commercial famines have not entirely disappeared. In 1974, when a catastrophic flood covered half of Bangladesh, the government was too disorganized to distribute its stocks of rice, while merchants bought what they could and exported it to India. Thousands died, and thousands more survived only because of belated shipments of food from donor countries.

Political Famines

To say that governments are responsible for food supplies does not mean that they exercise that responsibility for the good of the people. Some do, but in many instances food is used as a weapon. In the twentieth century global food supplies were always adequate for the population of the world, and transportation was seldom a problem. Yet the century witnessed the most murderous famines ever recorded.

As commercial famines declined, war famines became common. The destruction or requisitioning of crops caused famines in the Russian civil war of 1921–1922, the Japanese occupation of Indochina in 1942–1945, and the Biafran war in Nigeria in 1967–1969.

In 1942 the Japanese army had conquered Burma, a rich rice-producing colony. Food supplies in Bengal, which imported rice from Burma, dropped by 5 percent. As prices began to rise, merchants bought stocks of rice and held them in the hope that prices would continue to increase. Sharecroppers sold their stocks to pay off their debts to landlords and village moneylenders. Meanwhile, the railroads that in peacetime would have carried food from other parts of India were fully occupied with military traffic. By the time Viceroy Lord Wavell ordered the army to transport food to Bengal in October 1943, between 1.5 and 2 million Bengalis had died.

Worst of all were the famines caused by deliberate government policies. The most famous was the famine of 1932–1933 caused by Stalin's collectivization of agriculture. The Communists tried to force the peasants to give up their land and livestock and join collectives, where they could be made to work harder and provide food for the growing cities and industries. When the peasants resisted, their crops were seized. Millions were sent to prison camps, and millions of others died of starvation.

An even worse famine took place in China from 1958 to 1961 during the "Great Leap Forward" (see Chapter 31). Communist Party Chairman Mao Zedong decided to hasten the transformation of China into a communist state by relying not on the expertise of economists and technocrats but on the enthusiasm of the masses. Farms were consolidated into huge communes. Peasants were told to make steel out of household utensils in backyard furnaces. The harvest of 1959 was poor, and later ones were even worse. The amount of grain per person declined from 452 pounds (205 kilograms) in 1957 to 340 pounds (154 kilograms) in 1961. Since the Central Statistical Bureau had been shut down, the central government was unaware of the shortages and demanded ever higher requisitions of food to feed the army and urban and industrial workers and to export to the Soviet Union to pay off China's debts. The amount of food left to the farmers was between one-fifth and one-half of their usual subsistence diet. From 1958 to 1961 between 20 and 30 million Chinese are estimated to have starved or died of the diseases of malnutrition. It was the worst famine in the history of the world. Mao denied its existence.

Nothing quite as horrible has happened since the Great Leap Forward. During the droughts in Africa in the 1970s and 1980s, most people in the affected regions received international food aid. However, to crush rebellions, the governments of Ethiopia and Sudan denied that their people were hungry and prevented food shipments from reaching drought victims.

In the world today, natural disasters are as frequent as ever, and many countries are vulnerable to food shortages. No one now claims that governments have no business providing food to the starving. Though food is not equitably distributed, there is enough for all human beings now, and there will be enough for the foreseeable future. However, humanitarian feelings compete with other political agendas, and the specter of politically motivated famines still stalks the world.

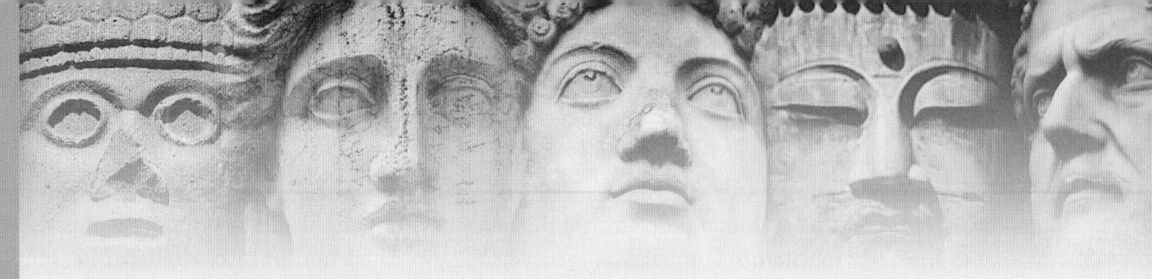

PART VIII

- **CHAPTER 31** The Cold War and Decolonization, 1945–1975
- **CHAPTER 32** The End of the Cold War and the Challenge of Economic Development and Immigration, 1975–2000
- **CHAPTER 33** New Challenges in a New Millennium

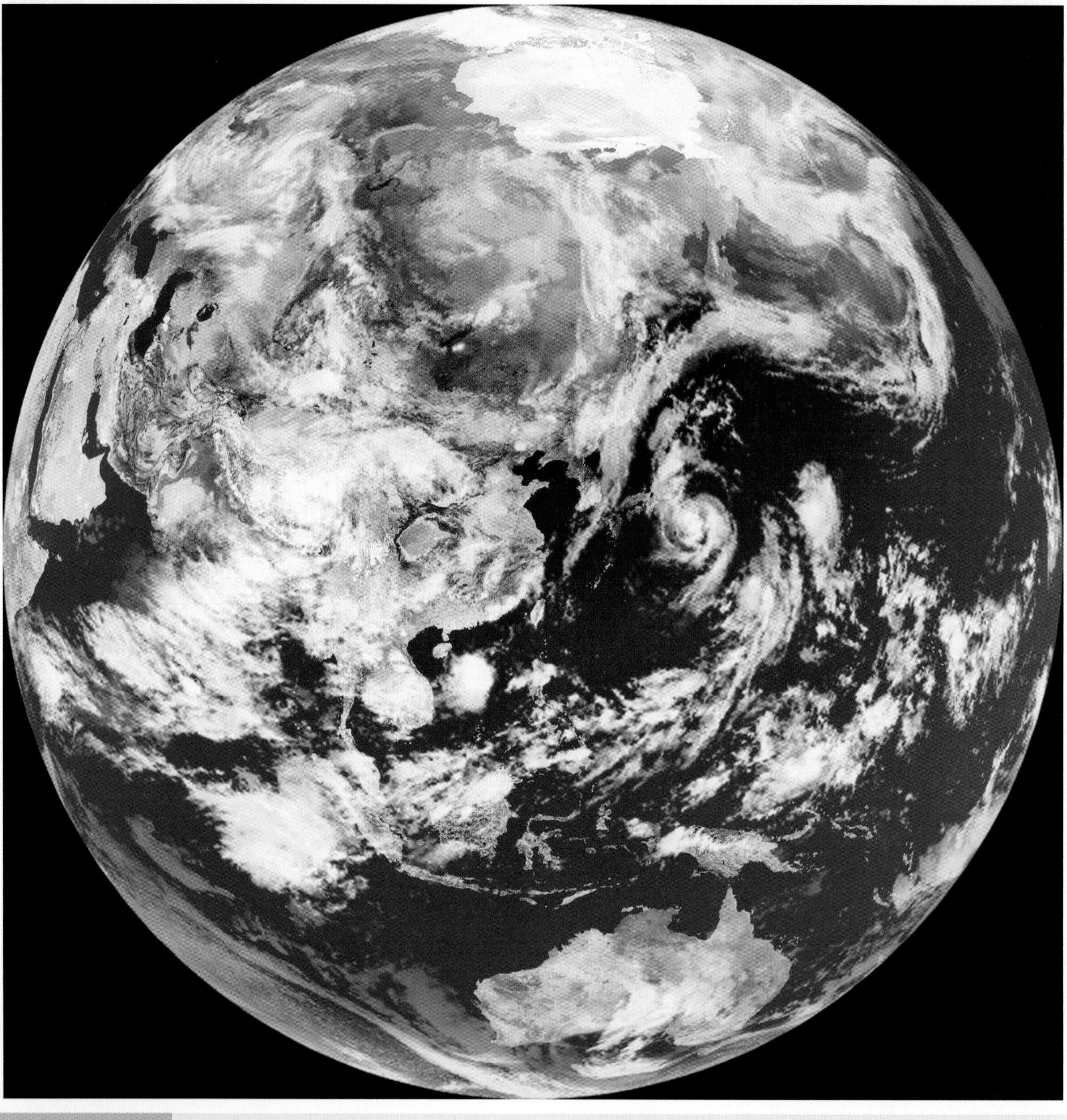

NASA/Getty Images

Satellite Photograph of the Globe Photography from space revolutionized mapping, making physical features more important than political boundaries and clearly displaying transient features, such as cloud coverage and storm patterns. In this photograph the distinctive whorl of a tropical storm is visible off the east coast of Japan. More specialized photographic techniques are used to appraise natural resources and environmental problems.

Perils and Promises of a Global Community, 1945 to the Present

An increasingly interconnected world faced new hopes and fears after World War II. The United Nations promoted peace, international cooperation, and human rights. Colonized peoples gained independence, and global trade expanded.

However, Cold War rhetoric and nuclear stalemate dispelled dreams of world peace. Wars in Korea and Vietnam, as well as proxy conflicts from Nicaragua to Afghanistan, pitted the United States against communist regimes. Following the Cold War nuclear proliferation and terrorism became top concerns. The 9/11 attacks by Muslim extremists on the World Trade Center and the Pentagon triggered an American "global war on terrorism." The ensuing invasions of Afghanistan and Iraq made the Middle East a top danger spot.

The industrialized nations, including Germany and Japan, recovered well from World War II. Elsewhere economic development came slowly, except in a handful of countries: South Korea, Taiwan, Brazil, Argentina, and, after 2000, China and India. In Africa and other poor regions, population growth usually offset economic gains.

Although the Green Revolution of the 1960s and genetic engineering thirty years later alleviated much world hunger, industrial growth and automobile use increased pollution and competition for petroleum supplies. Global warming became an international concern, along with overfishing, deforestation, and endangerment of wild species.

Globalization affected culture as well. Transnational corporations selling uniform products threatened localized economic enterprises, and Western popular culture aroused fears of cultural imperialism. The Internet and the emergence of English as the global language improved international communication but also stimulated fears that cultural diversity would be lost.

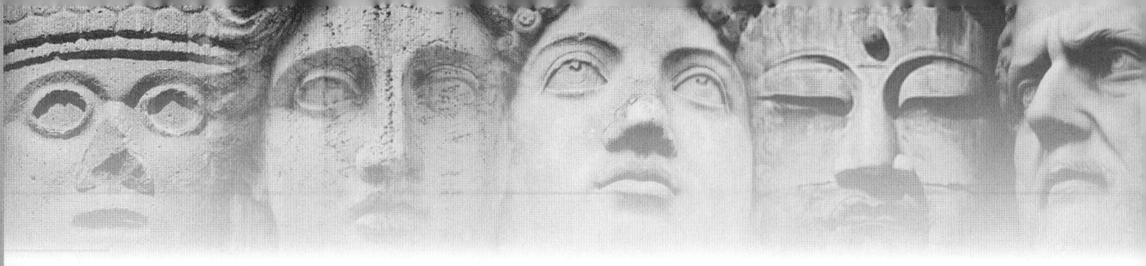

CHAPTER

31

CHAPTER OUTLINE

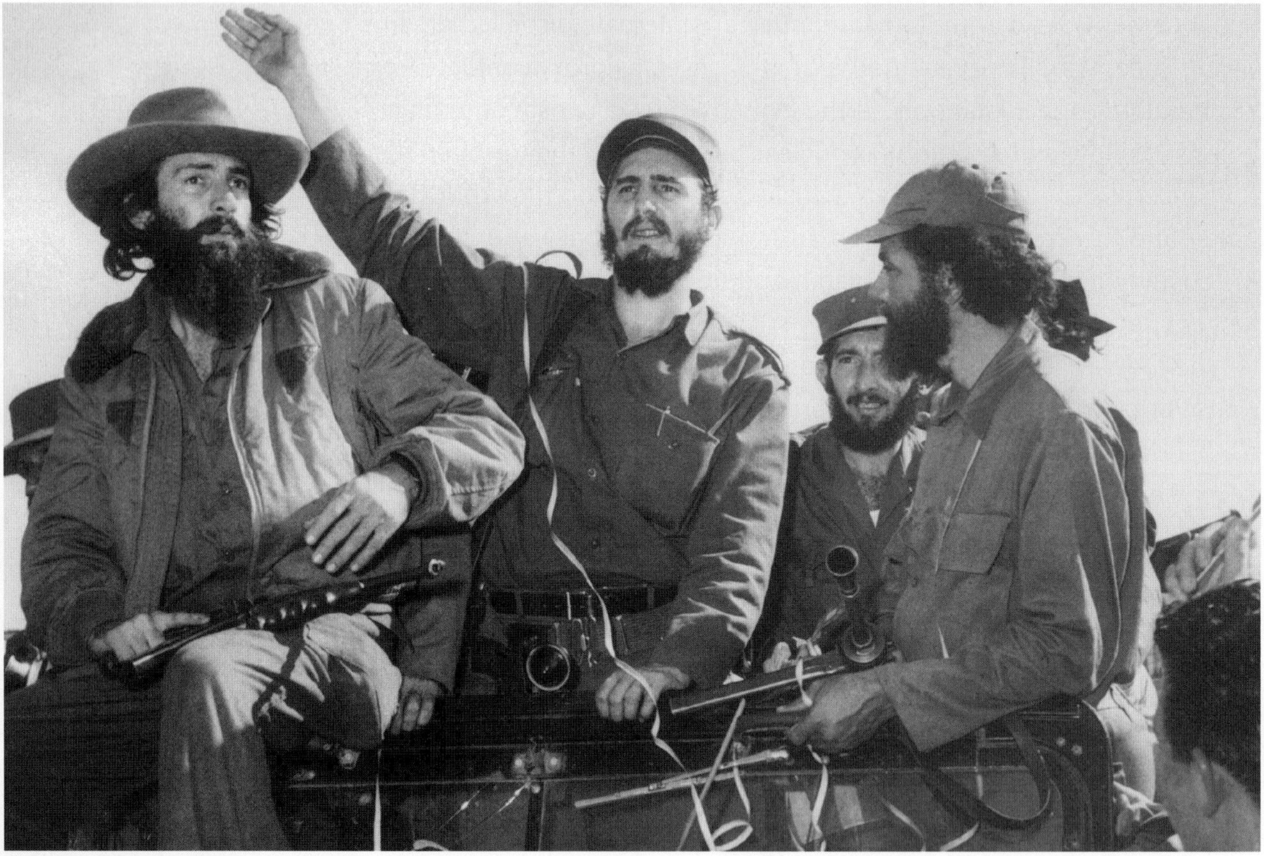

Bettmann/Corbis

Fidel Castro Arrives in Havana Castro and his supporters overthrew a brutal dictatorship and began the revolutionary transformation of Cuba that led to a confrontation with the United States.

Visit the website and ebook for additional study materials and interactive tools: www.cengage.com/history/bullietearthpeople5e

The Cold War and Decolonization, 1945–1975

- What were the major threats to world peace during the Cold War?
- How were the experiences of Asia, Africa, and Latin America similar in this period?
- How did the rivalry between the Cold War superpowers affect the rest of the world?

On January 1, 1959, Fidel Castro entered Havana, Cuba, after having successfully defeated the dictatorship of Fulgencio Batista (ful-HEHN-see-oh bah-TEES-tah). Castro had initiated his revolution in 1953 with an attack on a military barracks, but the attack failed. At his trial, Castro put on a spirited defense that he later published as *History Will Absolve Me*. He proclaimed his objectives as the restoration of Cuban democracy and an ambitious program of social and economic reforms designed to ameliorate the effects of underdevelopment.

On September 26, 1960, Castro addressed the United Nations General Assembly. Relations between the Castro government and the United States were already heading toward confrontation as a result of Castro's policies. In his speech, Castro offered a broad internationalist and anti-imperialist criticism of the world's developed nations and of the United Nations. He criticized the role of the United Nations in the Congo, suggesting that it had supported Colonel Mobutu Sese Seko, a client of imperialism, rather than Patrice Lumumba, identified by the United States as a dangerous radical. He also strongly supported the independence struggle of the Algerians against the French.

In this speech, Castro outlined an ambitious program of new revolutionary reforms in Cuba, claiming that the United States had supported the Batista dictatorship to protect American investors. Once back in Cuba, Castro pressed ahead with economic reforms that included nationalizing most American investments. Cuba became a flash point in the Cold War when the United States tried and failed to overthrow Castro in 1961. Castro declared himself to be a socialist and forged an economic and military alliance with the Soviet Union that led in 1962 to the Cuban missile crisis.

The intensity of the Cold War, with its accompanying threat of nuclear destruction, obscured a postwar phenomenon of more enduring importance. The colonial empires of the New Imperialism disappeared, and Western power and influence declined in Asia, Africa, and Latin America. The leaders who headed these new nations were sometimes able to use Cold War antagonism to their own advantage when they sought economic or military assistance. Some, like Castro, became front-line participants in this struggle, but most focused on state building.

Each former colony had its own history and followed its own route to independence. Thus these new nations had difficulty finding a collective voice in a world increasingly oriented toward two superpowers, the United States and the Soviet Union. Some former colonies sided openly with one or the other, while others banded together in a posture of neutrality. All spoke with one voice about their need for economic and technical assistance and the obligation of the wealthy nations to satisfy those needs.

The Cold War military rivalry led to extraordinary advances in weaponry and associated technologies, but many new nations faced basic problems of educating their citizens, nurturing industry, and escaping the economic constraints imposed by their former imperialist masters. The environment suffered severe pressures from oil exploration and transport to support the growing economies of the wealthy nations and from deforestation and urbanization in poor regions. Neither rich nor poor nations fully understood the costs associated with these environmental changes.

AP* Exam Tip Make sure to understand the growth of global institutions following World War II.

THE COLD WAR

iron curtain Winston Churchill's term for the Cold War division between the Soviet-dominated East and the U.S.-dominated West.

Cold War The ideological struggle between communism (Soviet Union) and capitalism (United States) for world influence. The Cold War came to an end when the Soviet Union dissolved in 1991.

North Atlantic Treaty Organization (NATO) Organization formed in 1949 as a military alliance of western European and North American states against the Soviet Union and its east European allies.

Warsaw Pact The 1955 treaty binding the Soviet Union and countries of eastern Europe in an alliance against the North Atlantic Treaty Organization.

United Nations International organization founded in 1945 to promote world peace and cooperation. It replaced the League of Nations.

For more than a century, political and economic leaders in the industrialized West had viewed socialism as a threat to free markets and untrammeled capital investment. The wartime alliance between the United States, Great Britain, and the Soviet Union had succeeded despite these deep structural differences. With the defeat of Germany, however, growing Soviet assertiveness in Europe and communist insurgencies in China and elsewhere confirmed to Western leaders the threat of worldwide revolution.

Western leaders saw the Soviet Union as the sponsor of world revolution and as a military power capable of launching a war as destructive and terrible as the one recently ended. As early as 1946 Great Britain's wartime leader, Winston Churchill, said in a speech in Missouri, "From Stettin in the Baltic to Trieste in the Adriatic, an iron curtain has descended across the Continent. . . . I am convinced there is nothing they [the communists] so much admire as strength, and there is nothing for which they have less respect than weakness, especially military weakness." The phrase "**iron curtain**" became a watchword of the **Cold War**, the state of political tension and military rivalry then beginning between the United States and its allies and the Soviet Union and its allies.

Once the United States and the nations of western Europe established the **North Atlantic Treaty Organization (NATO)** military alliance in 1949, Soviet leaders felt surrounded by hostile forces as they struggled to recover from the terrible losses sustained in the war against the Axis. In response, the Soviet Union created its own military alliance, the **Warsaw Pact**, in 1955. The distrust and suspicion between the two sides played out on a worldwide stage, and the United Nations was often the location of confrontational debate.

The United Nations

In 1944 representatives from the United States, Great Britain, the Soviet Union, and China drafted proposals that led to a treaty called the United Nations Charter, ratified on October 24, 1945. Like the earlier League of Nations, the **United Nations** had two main bodies: the General Assembly, with representatives from all member states; and the Security Council, with five permanent members—China, France, Great Britain, the United States, and the Soviet Union—and seven rotating members. A full-time bureaucracy headed by a Secretary General carried out the organization's day-to-day business and directed agencies focused on specialized international problems—for example, UNICEF (United Nations Children's Emergency Fund), FAO (Food and Agriculture Organization), and UNESCO (United Nations Educational, Scientific and Cultural Organization) (see Environment and Technology: The Green Revolution). Unlike the League of Nations, which required unanimous agreement in both deliberative bodies, the United Nations operated by majority vote, except that the five permanent members of the Security Council had veto power in that chamber.

Political Divisions and the United Nations

All signatories to the United Nations Charter renounced war and territorial conquest. Nevertheless, peacekeeping, the sole preserve of the Security Council, became a vexing problem as

CHRONOLOGY

	Cold War	Decolonization
1945	1947–1948 Soviet blockade of Berlin	1947 Partition of India
	1949 NATO formed	1949 Dutch withdraw from Indonesia
1950	1950–1953 Korean War	
	1952 United States detonates first hydrogen bomb	
	1954 Jacobo Arbenz overthrown in Guatemala, supported by CIA	1954 CIA intervention in Guatemala; defeat at Dienbienphu ends French hold on Vietnam
1955	1955 Warsaw Pact created	1955 Bandung Conference
	1956 Soviet Union suppresses Hungarian revolt	
	1957 Soviet Union launches first artificial satellite into earth orbit	1957 Ghana becomes first British colony in Africa to gain independence
		1959 Triumph of Fidel Castro's revolution in Cuba
1960		1960 Shootings in Sharpeville intensify South African struggle against apartheid; Nigeria becomes independent
	1961 East Germany builds Berlin Wall	
	1961 Bay of Pigs (Cuba)	
	1962 Cuban missile crisis	1962 Algeria wins independence
	1968 Nuclear Non-Proliferation Treaty	
1970		1971 Bangladesh secedes from Pakistan
	1975 Helsinki Accords; end of Vietnam War	

permanent members exercised their vetoes to protect their allies and interests. Throughout the Cold War the United Nations was seldom able to forestall or quell international conflicts, though from time to time it sent observers or peacekeeping forces to monitor truces or other international agreements.

The decolonization of Africa and Asia greatly swelled the size of the General Assembly but not the Security Council. Many newly independent nations looked to the United Nations for material assistance and access to a wider political world. While the rivalry of the Security Council's permanent members stymied actions that even indirectly touched on Cold War concerns, the General Assembly became an arena for debates over issues like decolonization and development.

In the early years of the United Nations, General Assembly resolutions carried great weight. An example is a 1947 resolution that sought to divide Palestine into sovereign Jewish and Arab states. Gradually, though, the flood of new members produced a voting majority concerned more with poverty, racial discrimination, and the struggle against imperialism than with the Cold War. As a result, Western powers increasingly disregarded the General Assembly, in effect allowing new nations to have their say but effectively preventing any collective action contrary to their interests.

World Bank A specialized agency of the United Nations that makes loans to countries for economic development, trade promotion, and debt consolidation. Its formal name is the International Bank for Reconstruction and Development.

Capitalism and Communism

In July 1944, with Allied victory inevitable, economic specialists representing over forty countries met at Bretton Woods, a New Hampshire resort, to devise a new international monetary system. The signatories eventually agreed to fix exchange rates and to create the International Monetary Fund (IMF) and World Bank. The IMF used currency reserves from member nations to finance temporary trade deficits, while the **World Bank** provided funds for reconstructing Europe and helping needy countries after the war.

Two Distinct Economic Systems

The Soviet Union attended the Bretton Woods Conference and signed the agreements that went into effect in 1946. But growing hostility between the Soviet Union and the United States and Britain undermined cooperation. While the United States held reserves of gold and the rest of the world held reserves of dollars to maintain the stability of the monetary system, the Soviet

ENVIRONMENT + TECHNOLOGY

The Green Revolution

Concern about world food supplies grew from the serious shortages caused by the devastation and trade disruptions of World War II. The Food and Agriculture Organization of the United Nations, the Rockefeller Foundation, and the Ford Foundation took leading roles in fostering crop research and agricultural education. In 1966 the International Rice Research Institute (established in 1960–1962) began distributing seeds for an improved rice variety known as IR-8. Crop yields from this and other new varieties, along with improved farming techniques, were initially so impressive that a hoped-for new era in agriculture was called the *Green Revolution*.

After the successful introduction of new rice strains, scientists developed new varieties of corn and wheat. Building on twenty years of Rockefeller-funded research in Mexico, the Centro Internacional de Mejoramiento de Maiz y Trigo (International Center for the Improvement of Maize and Wheat) was established in 1966 under Norman Borlaug, who was awarded the Nobel Peace Prize four years later. This organization distributed new varieties of wheat that were resistant to disease and responsive to fertilizer.

By 1970 other centers for research on tropical agriculture were established, but experts believed that the success of the Green Revolution required a more comprehensive effort. The Consultative Group on International Agricultural Research brought together World Bank expertise, private foundations, international organizations, and national foreign aid agencies to undertake worldwide support of efforts to increase food productivity and improve natural resource management.

Early optimism about these innovations is now muted. Although crop yields often improved as a result of new seeds, improved fertilizers, and irrigation, these improvements were too expensive for poor farmers to employ. This meant in practice that, as agricultural production rose, land was increasingly concentrated in the hands of the rich and the rural poor were forced to become laborers or migrate to cities.

Victor Englebert

Miracle Rice New strains of so-called miracle rice made many nations in South and Southeast Asia self-sufficient in food production after decades of worry that population growth would outstrip agricultural productivity.

Union established a closed monetary system for itself and allied communist regimes in eastern Europe. In Western countries, supply and demand determined production priorities and prices; in the Soviet command economy, government agencies allocated goods and set prices according to governmental priorities, irrespective of market forces.

Many leaders of newly independent states, having won their nation's independence from European colonial powers, preferred the Soviet Union's socialist example to the capitalism of their former masters. Thus, the relative success of economies patterned on Eastern or Western

Cold War Confrontation in 1959 U.S. vice president Richard M. Nixon and Soviet premier Nikita Khrushchev had a heated exchange of views during Nixon's visit to a Moscow trade fair. Two years earlier, the Soviet Union launched the world's first space satellite.

Seymour Raskin/Magnum Photos, Inc.

models became part of the Cold War argument. Each side trumpeted economic successes measured by industrial output, changes in per capita income, and productivity gains.

Recovery in the United States and Western Europe

During World War II the U.S. economy escaped the lingering effects of the Great Depression (see Chapter 29) as increased military spending and the military draft raised employment and wages. During the war, U.S. factories were converted from the production of consumer goods to weapons. With peace, the pent-up demand for consumer goods led to a period of rapid economic growth and prosperity. Europe, still rebuilding from the destruction of the war, at first lagged behind.

Marshall Plan U.S. program to support the reconstruction of western Europe after World War II. By 1961 more than $20 billion in economic aid had been dispersed.

World War II had heavily damaged the economy of western Europe. Bombs had flattened cities and destroyed railroads, port facilities, and communication networks. Populations had lost their savings and struggled to find employment. Seeking to forestall the radicalization of European politics, the United States decided to support the reconstruction of Europe. The **Marshall Plan** and other aid programs provided more than $20 billion to Europe by 1961. European determination backed by American aid spurred recovery, and by 1963 the resurgent European economies had doubled their total 1940 output.

Recovering western European governments sought a greater role in economic management than did the United States during this period. In Great Britain, for example, the Labour Party government of the early 1950s nationalized coal, steel, railroads, and health care. Similarly, the French government nationalized public utilities; the auto, banking, and insurance industries; and parts of the mining industry. These steps provided large infusions of capital for rebuilding and acquiring new technologies.

European Economic Integration

European Economic Community (Common Market) An organization promoting economic unity in Europe, formed in 1957 by consolidation of earlier, more limited, agreements. With the addition of many new nations it became the European Union (EU) in 1993.

In 1948 European nations initiated a process of economic cooperation and integration with the creation of the Organization of European Economic Cooperation (OEEC). They began by cooperating on coal and steel. Located in disputed border areas, these industries had previously been flash points that led to war. With success in these areas, some OEEC countries lowered tariffs to encourage trade. Then in 1957 France, West Germany, Italy, the Netherlands, Belgium, and Luxembourg signed a treaty creating the **European Economic Community**, also known as the **Common Market**. By the 1970s this economic alliance had nearly overtaken the United States in industrial production. Then between 1973 and 1995, Great Britain, Denmark, Greece, Ireland, Spain, Portugal, Finland, Sweden, and Austria joined the alliance, renamed the European Union (EU) in 1993 to reflect growing political integration.

The resulting prosperity brought dramatic changes to the societies of western Europe. Wages increased and social welfare benefits grew. Governments increased spending on health care, unemployment benefits, old-age pensions, public housing, and grants to poor families. The combination of economic growth and income redistribution raised living standards and fueled demand for consumer goods, leading to the development of a mass consumer society.

The Soviet Model

The Soviet experience was dramatically different. The rapid growth of the Soviet state after 1917 had challenged traditional Western assumptions about economic development and social policy. From the 1920s the Soviet state relied on bureaucratic agencies and political processes to determine the production, distribution, and price of goods. The government regulated and administered nearly every area of the society, including housing, medical services, retail shops, factories, and the land. Despite many problems, the Soviet state achieved a dramatic expansion in basic industrial production.

As in western Europe, the economies of the Soviet Union and its eastern European allies were devastated at the end of the Second World War, but they took a different path to reconstruction. The Soviet command economy had enormous natural resources, a large population, and abundant energy at its disposal. It also benefited from the state's large investments in technical and scientific education and heavy industries during the 1930s and war years.

As a result, recovery was rapid at first, creating the structural basis for modernization and growth. However, as industrial production throughout the world refocused on consumer goods such as television sets and automobiles rather than coal and steel, the inefficiencies of bureaucratic control became obvious. By the 1970s the gap with the West had widened. Soviet industry failed to meet domestic demand for clothing, housing, automobiles, and consumer electronics, while Soviet agricultural output lagged behind domestic needs.

West Versus East in Europe and Korea

In Germany, Austria, and Japan, the end of the war meant foreign military occupation and governments controlled by the victors. The Soviet Union initially seemed willing to accept governments in neighboring states that included a mix of parties as long as they were not hostile to local communist groups or to the Soviets. In the nations of central and eastern Europe, many remembered the Soviets as enemies of the fascists and were eager to support local communist parties. As relations between the Soviets and the West worsened in the late 1940s, communists gained a series of political victories across eastern Europe. Western leaders saw the emergence of communist regimes in Poland, Czechoslovakia, Hungary, Bulgaria, Romania, Yugoslavia, and Albania as a sign of growing Soviet aggressiveness.

The Cold War

By 1948 the United States viewed the Soviet Union as an adversary and threat. While the United States had seemed amenable to the Soviet desire for access to the Mediterranean through the Bosporus and Dardanelles straits at war's end, by 1947 it acted to strengthen Turkey and Greece to resist Soviet military pressure and local communist subversion. This decision to hold the line against further Soviet expansion led to the admission of Turkey and Greece to NATO and to the decision to allow West Germany to rearm (see Map 31.1). The Soviets created the Warsaw Pact in 1955 as a strategic counterweight.

Increased hostility did not lead to a direct military confrontation between the two great alliances. But the Soviet Union did test Western resolve, first by blockading the British, French, and American zones of Berlin (located in Soviet-controlled East Germany) in 1947–1948 and then in 1961 by building the Berlin Wall to prevent East Germans from fleeing to West Berlin.

In turn, the West tested the East by encouraging divisions within the Warsaw Pact. This policy contributed to an armed anti-Soviet revolt in Hungary that Soviet troops crushed in 1956. In 1968 Soviet troops repressed a peaceful reform effort in Czechoslovakia, making clear that, like the West, it would defend its sphere of influence. By failing to support either of these challenges to Soviet control, the West effectively accepted the political and ideological boundaries established by the Cold War.

Korean War Conflict that began with North Korea's invasion of South Korea and that came to involve the United Nations (primarily the United States) allying with South Korea and the People's Republic of China allying with North Korea.

The Korean War

By the end of the Second World War, Soviet troops controlled the Korean peninsula north of the thirty-eighth parallel, while American troops controlled the south. When these two powers could not reach an agreement to hold countrywide elections, a communist North Korea and a noncommunist South Korea emerged as independent states in 1948. Two years later North Korea invaded South Korea. The United Nations Security Council, in the absence of the Soviet delegation, condemned the invasion and called on its members to come to the defense of South Korea. In the ensuing **Korean War**, which lasted until 1953, the United States was the primary ally of South Korea, while the People's Republic of China supported North Korea.

Because the United States feared that launching attacks into China might prompt China's ally, the Soviet Union, to retaliate, the conflict remained limited to the Korean peninsula. Victories by American and South Korean forces forced North Korean forces north until China entered the war. The contending armies eventually reached a stalemate along the thirty-eighth parallel. The two sides formally agreed to a truce but never signed a peace treaty. As a result, fear of renewed warfare between the two Koreas continued well past the end of the Cold War.

United States Defeat in Vietnam

AP* Exam Tip Be able to compare major forms of twentieth-century warfare.

The most important postwar communist movement arose in French Indochina in Southeast Asia. The Vietnamese leader Ho Chi Minh (hoe chee min) (1890–1969) had spent several years in France during World War I and helped form the French Communist Party. In 1930, after training in Moscow, he returned to Vietnam to found the Indochina Communist Party. Forced to take refuge in China during World War II, Ho cooperated with the United States while Japan controlled Vietnam.

Vietnam War Conflict pitting North Vietnam and South Vietnamese communist guerrillas against the South Vietnamese government, aided after 1961 by the United States.

At war's end the French government was determined to keep its colonial possessions. Ho Chi Minh's nationalist coalition, called the Viet Minh, fought the French with help from the People's Republic of China. After a brutal struggle, the French stronghold of Dienbienphu (dee-yen-bee-yen-FOO) fell in 1954, marking the end of France's colonial enterprise. Ho's Viet Minh government took over in the north, and a noncommunist nationalist government ruled in the south.

America in Vietnam

Under President Dwight D. Eisenhower (1953–1961), the United States provided limited support to the French but ultimately decided not to prop up French colonial rule in Vietnam, perceiving that the European colonial empires were doomed. After winning independence, communist North Vietnam supported a communist guerrilla movement—the Viet Cong—against the noncommunist government of South Vietnam. At issue was the ideological and economic orientation of an independent Vietnam.

President John F. Kennedy (served 1961–1963) changed American policy to support the South Vietnamese government of President Ngo Dinh Diem (dee-YEM). Although he knew that the Diem government was corrupt and unpopular, he feared that a communist victory would encourage communist movements throughout Southeast Asia and alter the Cold War balance of power. Kennedy increased the number of American military advisers while encouraging the overthrow of the Diem government, an event that led to Diem's execution.

Following the assassination of Kennedy, President Lyndon Johnson (served 1963–1969) gained congressional support for an unlimited U.S. military deployment that eventually reached 500,000 troops. Because South Vietnam's new rulers were as corrupt and unpopular as the earlier Diem government, many South Vietnamese supported the Viet Cong. Despite battlefield success in the **Vietnam War**, the United States failed to achieve a comprehensive victory. In the massive 1968 Tet Offensive, the Viet Cong guerrillas and their North Vietnamese allies gained significant military credibility while suffering significant losses. With a clear victory unlikely, the antiwar movement in the United States grew in strength (see below).

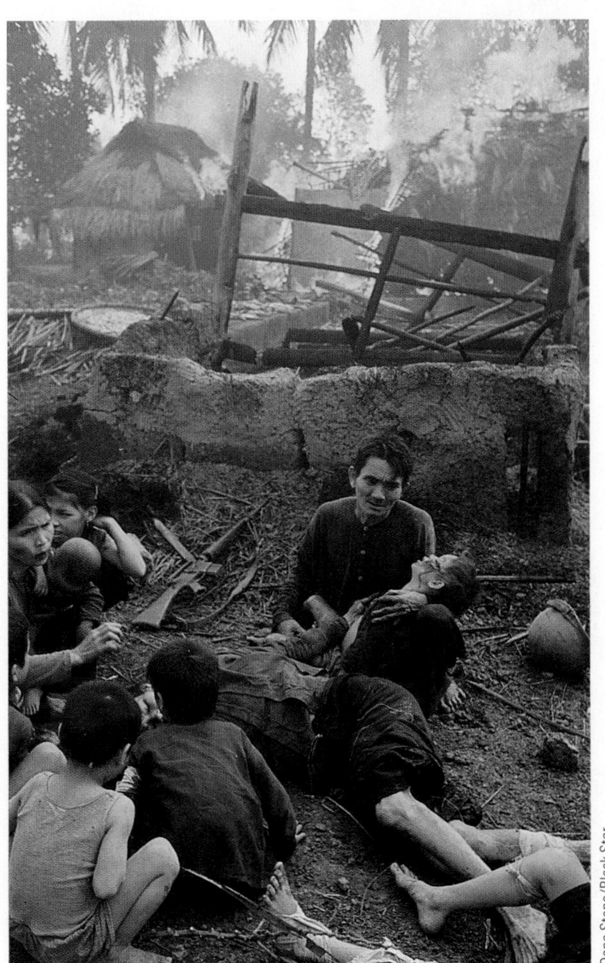

Dana Stone/Black Star

The Vietnamese People at War American and South Vietnamese troops burned many villages to deprive the enemy of civilian refuges. This policy undermined support for the South Vietnamese government in the countryside.

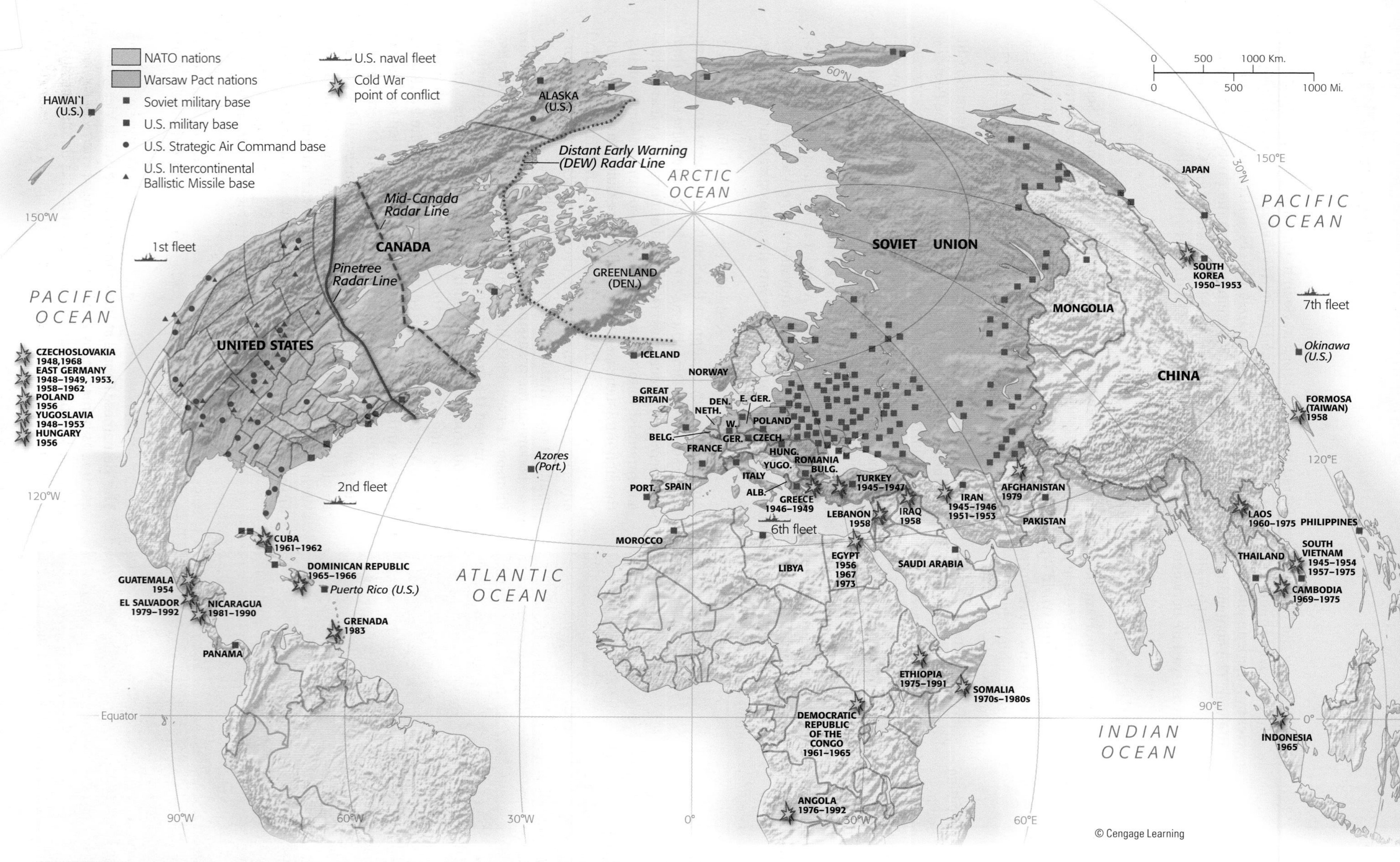

MAP 31.1 Cold War Confrontation A polar projection is shown on this map because Soviet and U.S. strategists planned to attack one another by missile in the polar region; hence the Canadian-American radar lines.

Interactive Map

In 1973 a treaty between North Vietnam and the United States ended U.S. involvement in the war and promised future elections. Two years later, in violation of the treaty, Viet Cong and North Vietnamese troops overran the South Vietnamese army and captured the southern capital of Saigon, renaming it Ho Chi Minh City. They then united the two Vietnams in a single state ruled from the north. Over a million Vietnamese and 58,000 Americans had died during the war.

Protests in the United States

President Johnson began his administration committed to a broad program of social reforms and civil rights initiatives, called the Great Society, and was instrumental in passing major civil rights legislation that responded to the heroic campaign for voting rights and integration led by Martin Luther King, Jr. As the commitment of U.S. troops in Vietnam grew, a massive antiwar movement applied the tactics of the civil rights movement to end the war. Growing economic problems and a rising tide of antiwar rallies, now international in character, undermined support for Johnson, who declined to seek reelection.

The Race for Nuclear Supremacy

AP* Exam Tip Be able to discuss the global balance of power in the post–World War II era.

The terrible devastation of Hiroshima and Nagasaki by atomic weapons (see Chapter 29) framed the strategic decisions in the Korean and Vietnamese wars. In both cases the United States took care not to expand the wars and challenge the Soviet Union or China (nuclear power from 1964). The Soviet Union had exploded its first nuclear device in 1949. The United States claimed a new advantage when it exploded a more powerful hydrogen bomb in 1952, but the Soviet Union followed suit less than a year later. In a world deeply scared by two world wars, the threat of nuclear war spread despair around the world.

In 1954 President Eisenhower warned Soviet leaders against attacking western Europe. In response to such an attack, he said, the United States would reduce the Soviet Union to "a smoking, radiating ruin at the end of two hours." A few years later the Soviet leader Nikita Khrushchev (KROOSH-chef) made an equally stark promise: "We will bury you." He was referring to economic competition, but Americans interpreted the statement to mean literal burial. Rhetoric aside, both men—and their successors—had the capacity to deliver on their threats, and everyone in the world knew that all-out war with nuclear weapons would produce the greatest global devastation in human history.

The Soviet Union's deployment of nuclear missiles to Cuba in 1962 pushed the two sides to the brink of war. Reacting to U.S. efforts to overthrow the Cuban government, Khrushchev and Fidel Castro decided that the deployment of nuclear weapons in Cuba would force the United States to accept the status quo. When the missiles were discovered, the United States declared a naval blockade and prepared to invade Cuba, forcing Khrushchev to remove the missiles. As frightening as the **Cuban missile crisis** was, the fact that the superpowers chose diplomacy over war gave reason to hope that nuclear weapons might be contained.

Cuban missile crisis Brink-of-war confrontation between the United States and the Soviet Union over the latter's placement of nuclear-armed missiles in Cuba.

Nuclear Nonproliferation

Fear of a nuclear holocaust produced an international effort to limit proliferation. In 1963 Great Britain, the United States, and the Soviet Union agreed to ban the testing of nuclear weapons in the atmosphere, in space, and under water, reducing the danger of radioactive fallout. In 1968 the United States and the Soviet Union together proposed a world treaty against further proliferation, leading ultimately to the Nuclear Non-Proliferation Treaty (NPT) signed by 137 countries. Not until 1972, however, did the two superpowers begin the arduous and extremely slow process of negotiating weapons limits.

The atomic powers France and Britain were economically unable to keep up with the Soviet-American arms race. Instead, they led the European states in an effort to relax tensions. Between 1972 and 1975 the Conference on Security and Cooperation in Europe (CSCE) brought delegates from thirty-seven European states, the United States, and Canada to Helsinki. The Soviet Union sought European acceptance of the political boundaries of the Warsaw Pact nations as a condition for broad cooperation. In the end, the **Helsinki Accords** affirmed these boundaries and also called for economic, social, and governmental contacts and for cooperation in humanitarian fields between the two alliances.

Helsinki Accords Political and human rights agreement signed in Helsinki, Finland, by the Soviet Union and western European countries.

Space exploration was another offshoot of the nuclear arms race. The contest to build larger and more accurate missiles prompted the superpowers to prove their skills in rocketry by launching space satellites. The Soviet Union placed a small *Sputnik* satellite into orbit around the earth in October 1957, and the United States responded with its own satellite three months later. The space race was on, a contest in which accomplishments in space were understood to signify equivalent achievements in the military sphere. In 1969, when Neil A. Armstrong and Edwin E. ("Buzz") Aldrin became the first humans to walk on the moon, America had demonstrated its technological superiority.

SECTION REVIEW

- The United Nations was created to manage international disputes and facilitate decolonization and development.
- The United States developed the Marshall Plan to aid European recovery from the devastation of World War II.
- The Cold War was a confrontation between two military alliances, NATO and the Warsaw Pact, and two distinct economic systems, capitalism and communism.
- The United States and the Soviet Union avoid a direct conflict, but the Cold War led to wars in Korea and Vietnam.
- The development of nuclear weapons made the Cold War a threat to the survival of the human race and led to nonproliferation treaties.

DECOLONIZATION AND STATE BUILDING

After World War I Germany, Austria-Hungary, and the Ottoman Empire lost their empires, and many colonies and dependencies were transferred to the victors, especially to Great Britain and France. In the two decades following World War II, nearly all remaining colonies gained independence (see Map 31.2). Circumstances differed profoundly from place to place. In some Asian countries, where colonial rule was of long standing, new states possessed viable industries, communications networks, and education systems. In other countries, notably in Africa, decolonized nations faced dire economic problems and disunity resulting from language and ethnic differences.

Most Latin American nations had achieved political independence in the nineteenth century (see Chapter 21). Following World War II, mass political movements in this region focused on the related issue of economic sovereignty—freedom from growing American economic domination. Great Britain and other European nations still retained colonies in the Caribbean after World War II. In the 1960s Barbados, Guyana, Jamaica, and Trinidad Tobago gained independence from Britain, and the smaller British colonies followed in the 1970s and 1980s, as did Surinam, which gained independence from the Netherlands.

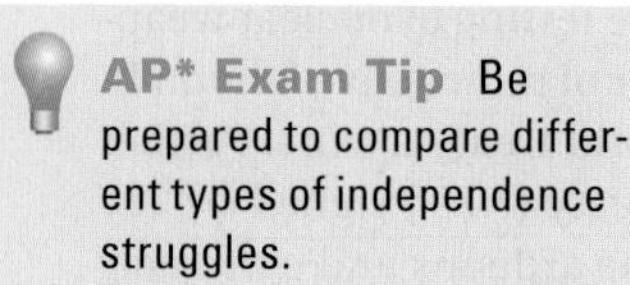
AP* Exam Tip Be prepared to compare different types of independence struggles.

Despite their differences, a sense of kinship arose among the nations of Latin America, Africa, and Asia. All shared feelings of excitement and rebirth. As North Americans, Europeans, and the Chinese settled into the exhausting deadlock of the Cold War, visions of independence and national development captivated the rest of the world.

New Nations in South and Southeast Asia

After partition in 1947 the independent states of India and Pakistan were strikingly dissimilar. Muslim Pakistan defined itself according to religion and quickly fell under the control of military leaders. India, a secular republic led by Prime Minister Jawaharlal Nehru, was much larger and inherited the considerable industrial and educational resources developed by the British, along with a large share of trained civil servants and military officers. Ninety percent of its population was Hindu and most of the rest Muslim.

India and Pakistan

Adding to the tensions of independence (see Chapter 30) was the decision by the Hindu ruler of the northwestern state Jammu and Kashmir, now commonly called Kashmir, without consulting his overwhelmingly Muslim subjects, to join India. War between India and Pakistan over Kashmir broke out in 1947 and ended with an uneasy truce. In 1965 war broke out again, this time involving large military forces and the use of air power by both sides. Kashmir has remained a flash point, with new clashes in 1999 and 2000.

Despite recurrent predictions that multilingual India might break up into a number of linguistically homogeneous states, most Indians recognized that unity benefited everyone; and the country pursued a generally democratic and socialist line of development. Pakistan, in contrast, did break up. In 1971 the Bengali-speaking eastern section seceded to become the independent country of Bangladesh. During the fighting Indian military forces again struck against Pakistan. Despite their shared political heritage, India, Pakistan, and Bangladesh have found cooperation difficult and have pursued markedly different economic, political, religious, and social paths.

Independence in Southeast Asia

During the war the Japanese supported anti-British Indian nationalists as a way to weaken their enemy; they also encouraged the aspirations of nationalists in the countries they occupied in Southeast Asia. Many Asian nationalists saw Japanese victories over British, French, and Dutch colonial armies as a demonstration of the political and military capacities of Asian peoples. In the Dutch East Indies, Achmad Sukarno (1901–1970) cooperated with the Japanese in the hope that the Dutch, who had dominated the region economically since the seventeenth century, could be expelled. The Dutch finally negotiated withdrawal in 1949, and Sukarno became the dictator of the resource-rich but underdeveloped nation of Indonesia. He ruled until 1965, when a military coup ousted him and brutally eliminated the nation's once powerful communist party.

Britain granted independence to Burma (now Myanmar [my-ahn-MAR]) in 1948 and established the Malay Federation the same year. Singapore, once a member of the federation, became an independent city-state in 1965. In 1946 the United States kept its promise of postwar independence for the Philippine Islands but retained close economic ties and leases on military bases.

The Struggle for Independence in Africa

Algerian Independence

Between 1952 and 1956 France granted independence to Tunisia and Morocco, but it sought to retain Algeria. France had controlled this colony for nearly 150 years and had encouraged settlement; in 1950, 10 percent of the Algerian population was of French or other European origin. France also granted political rights to the settler population and asserted the fiction of Algeria's political and economic integration in the French nation. In reality few Algerians benefited from this arrangement, and most resented their continued colonial status.

The Vietnamese military victory over France in 1954 helped provoke a nationalist uprising in Algeria, during which both sides acted brutally. The Algerian revolutionary organization, the Front de Libération National (FLN), was supported by Egypt and other Arab countries who sought the emancipation of all Arab peoples. French colonists considered the country theirs and fought to the bitter end. When Algeria finally won independence in 1962, a flood of angry colonists returned to France. Since few Arabs had received technical training, this departure undermined the economy. Despite harsh feelings left by the war, Algeria retained close and seemingly indissoluble economic ties to France, and Algerians in large numbers emigrated to France to take low-level jobs.

Independence in Africa

Independence was achieved in most of sub-Saharan Africa through negotiation, not revolution. In colonies with significant white settler minorities, however, the path to independence followed the violent experience of Algeria. African nationalists were forced to overcome many obstacles, but they were also able to take advantage of many consequential changes put in place during colonial rule. In the 1950s and 1960s world economic expansion and growing support for liberation overcame African worries about potential economic and political problems that might follow independence. Moreover, improvements in medical care and public health had led to rapid population growth in Africa, and the continent's young population embraced the idea of independence.

Western nationalist and egalitarian ideals also helped fuel resistance to colonialism. Most of the leaders of African independence movements were among the most westernized members of these societies. African veterans of Allied armies during World War II had exposure to Allied propaganda that emphasized ideas of popular sovereignty and self-determination. In addition, many leaders were recent graduates of educational institutions created by colonial governments, and a minority had obtained advanced education in Europe and the United States.

African nationalists were able to take advantage of other legacies of colonial rule as well. Schools, labor associations, and the colonial bureaucracy itself proved to be fertile nationalist recruiting centers. Languages introduced by colonial governments were useful in building multiethnic coalitions, while networks of roads and railroads built to promote colonial exports forged new national identities and a new political consciousness.

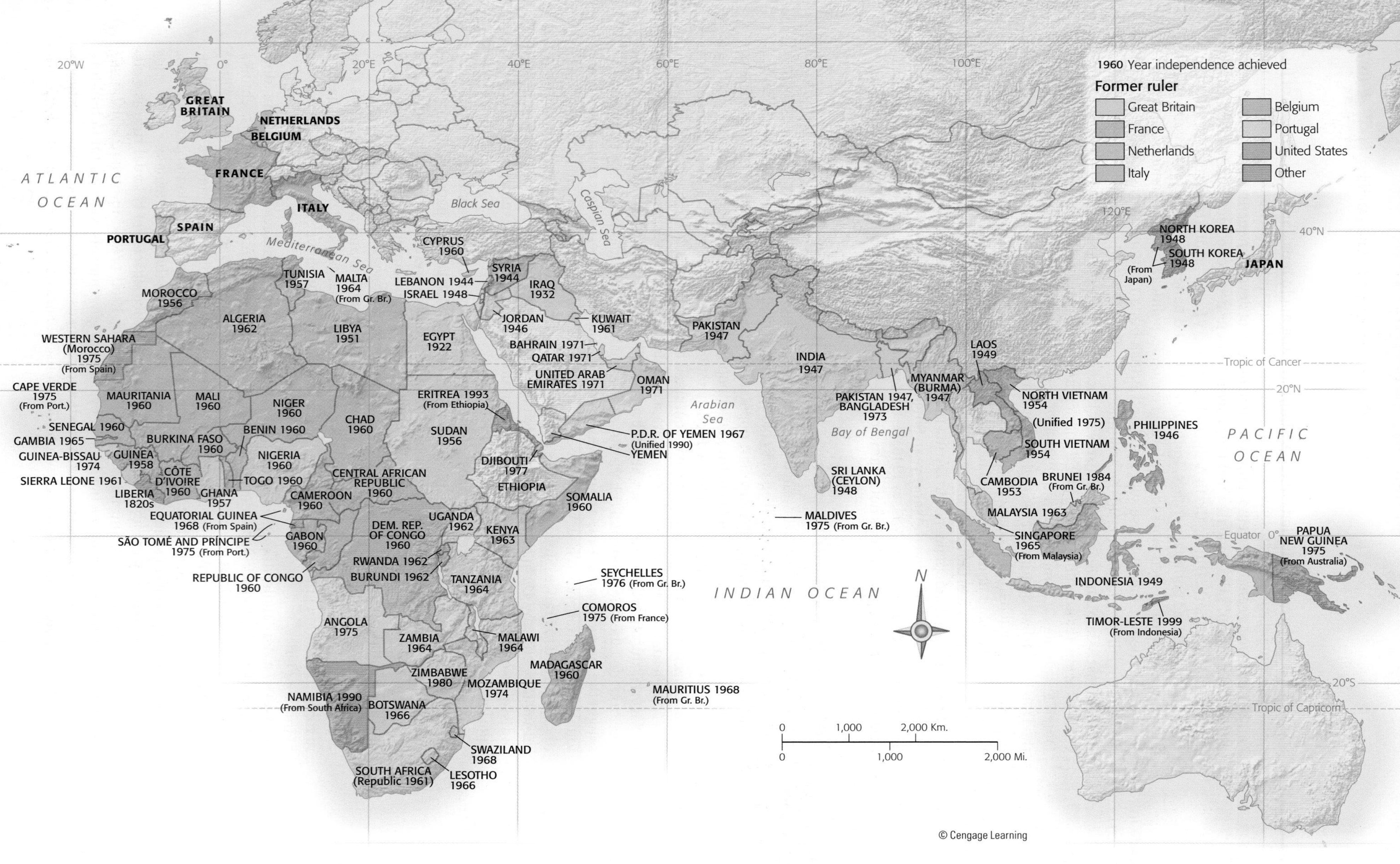

MAP 31.2 **Decolonization, 1947–1990** Independence was achieved a decade or so earlier in South and Southeast Asia than in Africa.

Interactive Map

Corbis

Jomo Kenyatta Kenya's newly elected premier, Jomo Kenyatta, cheered by crowds in Nairobi in 1963. Kenyatta (waving ceremonial "wisk") had led the struggle to end British colonial rule in Kenya.

The young politicians who led the nationalist movements devoted their lives to ridding their homelands of foreign occupation. An example is Kwame Nkrumah (KWAH-mee nn-KROO-muh) (1909–1972), who in 1957 became prime minister of Ghana (formerly the Gold Coast), the first British colony in West Africa to achieve independence. After graduating from a Catholic mission school and a government teacher-training college, Nkrumah spent a decade studying philosophy and theology in the United States, where he absorbed ideas about black pride and independence propounded by W. E. B. Du Bois and Marcus Garvey.

During a brief stay in Britain, Nkrumah joined Kenyan nationalist Jomo Kenyatta, a Ph.D. in anthropology, to found an organization devoted to African freedom. In 1947 Nkrumah returned to the Gold Coast to work for independence. The time was right. There was no longer strong public support in Britain for colonialism, and Britain's political leadership was not enthusiastic about investing resources to hold restive colonies. When Nkrumah's party won a decisive election victory in 1951, the British Gold Coast governor appointed him prime minister. Full independence came in 1957. Although Nkrumah remained an effective international spokesman for colonized peoples, he was overthrown in 1966 by a group of army officers.

Britain soon granted independence to its other West African colonies, including large and populous Nigeria in 1960. In some British colonies in eastern and southern Africa, however, white settler opposition resisted independence. In Kenya a small but influential group of wealthy coffee planters claimed that a protest movement among the Kikuyu (kih-KOO-you) people was proof that Africans were not ready for self-government. The settlers called the movement "Mau Mau," a made-up name meant to evoke primitive savagery. When violence between settlers and anticolonial fighters escalated after 1952, British troops hunted down movement leaders and resettled the Kikuyu in fortified villages. They also declared a state of emergency, banned all African political protest, and imprisoned Kenyatta and other nationalists. Released in 1961, Kenyatta negotiated with the British to write a constitution for an independent Kenya, and in 1964 he was elected the first president. Kenyatta proved to be an effective, though autocratic, ruler, and Kenya benefited from greater stability and prosperity than Ghana and many other former colonies.

Independence in French Africa

African leaders in the sub-Saharan French colonies were more reluctant than their counterparts in British colonies to call for full independence. Promises made in 1944 by the Free French movement of General Charles de Gaulle at a conference in Brazzaville, in French Equatorial Africa, seemed to offer dramatic changes without independence. Dependent on the troops and supplies of French African colonies, de Gaulle had promised Africans a more democratic government, broader suffrage, and greater access to employment in the colonial government. He had also promised better education and health services and an end to many abuses in the colonial system. He had not promised independence, but the politics of postwar colonial self-government led in that direction.

Most Africans elected to office following the reforms were trained civil servants. Because of the French policy of job rotation, they had typically served in a number of different colonies and

PRIMARY SOURCE: Comments on Algeria, April 11, 1961 Read excerpts of a press conference held by Charles de Gaulle, in which he declares France's willingness to accept Algerian independence.

thus had a broad regional outlook. They realized that some colonies—such as Ivory Coast, with coffee and cacao exports, fishing, and hardwood forests—had good economic prospects, while others, such as landlocked, desert Niger, did not. Furthermore, they recognized the importance of French public investment in the region—a billion dollars between 1947 and 1956—and their own dependence on civil service salaries. As a result, they generally looked to achieve greater self-government incrementally.

When Charles de Gaulle returned to power in France in 1958, at the height of the Algerian war, he warned that a rush to independence would have costs, saying: "One cannot conceive of both an independent territory and a France which continues to aid it." Ultimately, however, African patriotism prevailed in all of France's West African and Equatorial African colonies. Guinea, under the dynamic leadership of Sékou Touré (SAY-koo too-RAY), gained full independence in 1958 and the others in 1960.

The Belgian Congo

Independence in the Belgian Congo was chaotic and violent. Contending political and ethnic groups found external allies; some were supported by Cuba and the Soviet Union, while others were supported by the West or by business groups tied to the rich mines. Civil war, the introduction of foreign mercenaries, and the rhetoric of Cold War confrontation roiled the waters and led to a heavy loss of life and great property destruction. In 1965 Mobuto Sese Seko seized power in a military coup that included the assassination of Patrice Lumumba, the first prime minister. Mobuto controlled one of the region's most corrupt governments until driven from power in 1997.

South Africa

The opposition of European settlers delayed decolonization in southern Africa. While the settler minority tried to defend white supremacy, African-led liberation movements were committed to the creation of nonracial societies and majority rule. In the 1960s African guerrilla movements successfully fought to end Portuguese rule in Angola and Mozambique. Their efforts led to the overthrow of the antidemocratic government of Portugal in 1974 and independence the following year. After a ten-year fight, European settlers in the British colony of Southern Rhodesia accepted African majority rule in 1980. The new government changed the country's name to Zimbabwe, the name of a great stone city built by Africans long before the arrival of European settlers.

South Africa and neighboring Namibia remained in the hands of European minorities. The large white settler population of South Africa achieved effective independence in 1961 but kept the black and mixed-race majority in colonial-era subjection, separating the races in a system they called *apartheid* (a-PART-hite). Descendents of Dutch and English settlers made up 13 percent of the population but controlled the productive land, the industrial, mining, and commercial enterprises, and the government. Meanwhile, discrimination and segregation in housing, education, and employment confined the lives of people of mixed parentage (10 percent of the population) and South Asians (less than 3 percent).

Indigenous Africans, 74 percent of the population, were subjected to even stricter limitations on housing, freedom of movement, and access to jobs and public facilities. The government created fictional African "homelands" as a way of denying the African majority citizenship and political rights. Not unlike Amerindian reservations, these "homelands" were located in poor regions far from the more dynamic and prosperous urban and industrial areas. Overcrowded and lacking investment, they were impoverished and lacking in services and opportunities.

PRIMARY SOURCE: The Rivonia Trial Speech to the Court Read how Nelson Mandela defended himself against charges of treason before an all-white South African court in 1964.

The African National Congress (ANC), formed in 1912, led opposition to apartheid (see Diversity and Dominance: Race and the Struggle for Justice in South Africa). After police fired on demonstrators in the African town of Sharpeville in 1960 and banned all peaceful political protest by Africans, a lawyer named Nelson Mandela (b. 1918) organized guerrilla resistance by the ANC. The government sentenced Mandela to life in prison in 1964 and persecuted the ANC, but it was unable to defeat the movement. Facing growing opposition internationally, South Africa freed Mandela from prison in 1990 and began the transition to majority rule (see Chapter 33).

The Quest for Economic Freedom in Latin America

Although Latin America had achieved independence from colonial rule more than a hundred years earlier, European and American economic domination of the region created a semicolonial order (see Chapters 27 and 30). Foreigners controlled Chile's copper, Cuba's sugar, Colombia's coffee, and Guatemala's bananas, leading by the 1930s to growing support for economic nationalism. During the 1930s and 1940s populist political leaders experimented with programs that would constrain foreign investors or, alternatively, promote local efforts to industrialize (see discussion of Getulio Vargas and Juan Perón in Chapter 30).

The Struggle for Economic Justice in Latin America

In Mexico the revolutionary constitution of 1917 began an era of economic nationalism that culminated in the expropriation of foreign oil interests in 1938. The Institutional Revolutionary Party, or PRI (the abbreviation of its name in Spanish), controlled Mexico until the 1990s and had overseen a period of economic expansion during the war years. But a yawning gulf between rich and poor persisted. Although the government dominated important industries like petroleum and restricted foreign investment, rapid population growth, uncontrolled migration to Mexico City and other urban areas, and political corruption undermined efforts to lift the nation's poor. Economic power was concentrated at the top of society, with two thousand elite families controlling much of the nation's wealth. At the other end of the economic scale were the millions of poor Mexicans struggling to survive.

Guatemala and the CIA

Guatemala's situation was more representative of Latin America in 1950. An American corporation, the United Fruit Company, was Guatemala's largest landowner; it also controlled much of the nation's infrastructure, including port facilities and railroads. To limit banana production and keep prices high, United Fruit kept much of its Guatemalan lands fallow. Jacobo Arbenz Guzmán, elected in 1951, advocated positions broadly similar to those of leaders like Perón of Argentina and Vargas of Brazil (see Chapter 30), who confronted powerful foreign interests. He advocated land reform, which would have transferred these fallow lands to the nation's rural poor. The threatened expropriation angered the United Fruit Company. Simultaneously, Arbenz tried to reduce U.S. political influence, raising fears in Washington that he sought closer ties to the Soviet Union. Reacting to the land reform efforts and to reports that Arbenz was becoming friendly to communism, the U.S. Central Intelligence Agency (CIA), in one of its first major overseas operations, sponsored a takeover by the Guatemalan military in 1954. CIA intervention removed Arbenz, but it also condemned Guatemala to decades of governmental instability and violence.

The Cuban Revolution

In the 1950s American companies dominated the Cuban economy. They controlled sugar production, the nation's most important industry, as well as banking, transportation, tourism, and public utilities. The United States was also the most important market for Cuba's exports and the most important source of Cuba's imports. Thus the needs of the U.S. economy largely determined the ebb and flow of Cuban foreign trade. By 1956 sugar accounted for 80 percent of Cuba's exports and 25 percent of Cuba's national income. But demand in the United States dictated keeping only 39 percent of the land owned by the sugar companies in production, while Cuba experienced chronic underemployment. Similarly, immense deposits of nickel in Cuba went untapped because the U.S. government, which owned them, considered them to be a reserve.

While high unemployment and slow growth afflicted the nation, profits went north to the United States or to a small class of wealthy Cubans. Cuba's government was also notoriously corrupt and subservient to the wishes of American interests. As reform-minded young Cubans organized for a national election, Fulgencio Batista, a former military leader and president, illegally seized power in a coup in 1953. Hostility to Batista and anger with the corruption, repression, and foreign economic domination of his government gave rise to the revolution led by Fidel Castro.

Fidel Castro (b. 1927) was a young lawyer who led a failed uprising in 1953. He returned to Cuba after his conviction and exile to establish a successful revolutionary movement in the countryside that included student groups, labor unions, and supporters of Cuba's traditional parties. When he and his youthful followers took power in 1959, they vowed not to suffer the fate of Arbenz and the Guatemalan reformers. Ernesto ("Che") Guevara (CHAY-guh-VAHR-uh), Castro's chief lieutenant who

Christopher Morris/Black Star

Cuban Poster of Ernesto ("Che") Guevara Che became a leading theorist of communist revolution in Latin America. He died in 1967 while leading an insurgency in Bolivia.

DIVERSITY + DOMINANCE

Race and the Struggle for Justice in South Africa

One of South Africa's martyrs in the struggle against apartheid was the thinker and activist Steve Biko (1946–1977). Biko was one of the founders of the Black Consciousness Movement, which focused on the ways in which white settlers had stripped Africans of their freedom. Between 1975 and 1977 police arrested and interrogated him four times. After his arrest in August 1977, the police severely beat him and denied him medical care. His death in police custody caused worldwide outrage.

[T]hese are not the people we are concerned with [those who support apartheid]. We are concerned with that curious bunch of nonconformists who explain their participation in negative terms: that bunch of do-gooders that goes under all sorts of names—liberals, leftists etc. These are the people who argue that they are not responsible for white racism and the country's "inhumanity to the black man." These are the people who claim that they too feel the oppression just as acutely as the blacks and therefore should be jointly involved in the black man's struggle for a place under the sun. In short, these are the people who say that they have black souls wrapped up in white skins.

The role of the white liberal in the black man's history in South Africa is a curious one. Very few black organisations were not under white direction. True to their image, the white liberals always knew what was good for the blacks and told them so. The wonder of it all is that the black people have believed in them for so long. It was only at the end of the 50s that the blacks started demanding to be their own guardians.

Nowhere is the arrogance of the liberal ideology demonstrated so well as in their insistence that the problems of the country can only be solved by a bilateral approach involving both black and white. This has, by and large, come to be taken in all seriousness as the modus operandi in South Africa by all those who claim they would like a change in the status quo. Hence the multiracial political organisations and parties and the "nonracial" student organisations, all of which insist on integration not only as an end goal but also as a means.

The integration they talk about is first of all artificial in that it is a response to conscious manoeuvre rather than to the dictates of the inner soul. In other words the people forming the integrated complex have been extracted from various segregated societies with their in built [sic] complexes of superiority and inferiority and these continue to manifest themselves even in the "nonracial" setup of the integrated complex. As a result the integration so achieved is a one-way course, with the whites doing all the talking and the blacks the listening. Let me hasten to say that I am not claiming that segregation is necessarily the natural order; however, given the facts of the situation where a group experiences privilege at the expense of others, then it becomes obvious that a hastily arranged integration cannot be the solution to the problem. It is rather like expecting the slave to work together with the slave-master's son to remove all the conditions leading to [his] enslavement.

. . .

It will not sound anachronistic to anybody genuinely interested in real integration to learn that blacks are asserting themselves in a society where they are being treated as perpetual under-16s. One does not need to plan for or actively encourage real integration. Once the various groups within a given community have asserted themselves to the point that mutual respect has to be shown then you have the ingredients for a true and meaningful integration. At the heart of true integration is the provision for each man, each group to rise and attain the envisioned self. Each group must be able to attain its style of existence without encroaching on or being thwarted by another. Out of this mutual respect for each other and complete freedom of self-determination there will obviously arise a genuine fusion of the life-styles of the various groups. This is true integration.

From this it becomes clear that as long as blacks are suffering from [an] inferiority complex—a result of 300 years of deliberate oppression, denigration and derision—they will be useless as co-architects of a normal society where man is nothing else but man for his own sake. Hence what is necessary as a prelude to anything else that may come is a very strong grassroots build-up of black consciousness such that blacks can learn to assert themselves and stake their rightful claim.

Thus in adopting the line of a nonracial approach, the liberals are playing their old game. They are claiming a "monopoly on intelligence and moral judgement" and setting the pattern and pace for the realisation of the black man's aspirations. They want to remain in good books with both the black and white worlds. They want to shy away from all forms of "extremisms," condemning "white supremacy" as being just as bad as "Black Power!" They vacillate between the two worlds, verbalising all the complaints of the blacks beautifully while

became the main theorist of communist revolution in Latin America, had witnessed the CIA coup in Guatemala firsthand. He and Castro believed that confrontation with the United States was inevitable and moved quickly to remove the existing military leadership and begin revolutionary changes in the economy.

Within a year Castro's government seized and redistributed land, lowered urban rents, and raised wages, effectively transferring 15 percent of the national income from the rich to the poor.

skillfully extracting what suits them from the exclusive pool of white privileges. But ask them for a moment to give a concrete meaningful programme that they intend adopting, then you will see on whose side they really are. Their protests are directed at and appeal to white conscience, everything they do is directed at finally convincing the white electorate that the black man is also a man and that at some future date he should be given a place at the white man's table.

In the following selection Anglican bishop Desmond Tutu (b. 1931) expressed his personal anguish at the death of Steve Biko, summarizing Biko's contributions to the struggle for justice in South Africa. Tutu won the Noble Peace Prize in 1984 and was named archbishop in 1988. From 1995 to 1998 he chaired the Truth and Reconciliation Commission, which investigated atrocities in South Africa during the years of apartheid. He stated that his objective was to create "a democratic and just society without racial divisions."

When we heard the news "Steve Biko is dead" we were struck numb with disbelief. No, it can't be true! No, it must be a horrible nightmare, and we will awake and find that really it is different—that Steve is alive even if it be in detention. But no, dear friends, he is dead and we are still numb with grief, and groan with anguish "Oh God, where are you? Oh God, do you really care—how can you let this happen to us?"

It all seems such a senseless waste of a wonderfully gifted person, struck down in the bloom of youth, a youthful bloom that some wanted to see blighted. What can be the purpose of such wanton destruction? God, do you really love us? What must we do which we have not done, what must we say which we have not said a thousand times over, oh, for so many years—that all we want is what belongs to all God's children, what belongs as an inalienable right—a place in the sun in our own beloved mother country. Oh God, how long can we go on? How long can we go on appealing for a more just ordering of society where we all, black and white together, count not because of some accident of birth or a biological irrelevance—where all of us black and white count because we are human persons, human persons created in your own image.

God called Steve Biko to be his servant in South Africa—to speak up on behalf of God, declaring what the will of this God must be in a situation such as ours, a situation of evil, injustice, oppression and exploitation. God called him to be the founder father of the Black Consciousness Movement against which we have had tirades and fulminations. It is a movement by which God, through Steve, sought to awaken in the Black person a sense of his intrinsic value and worth as a child of God, not needing to apologise for his existential condition as a black person, calling on blacks to glorify and praise God that he had created them black. Steve, with his brilliant mind that always saw to the heart of things, realised that until blacks asserted their humanity and their personhood, there was not the remotest chance for reconciliation in South Africa. For true reconciliation is a deeply personal matter. It can happen only between persons who assert their own personhood, and who acknowledge and respect that of others. You don't get reconciled to your dog, do you? Steve knew and believed fervently that being pro-black was not the same thing as being anti-white. The Black Consciousness Movement is not a "hate white movement," despite all you may have heard to the contrary. He had a far too profound respect for persons as persons, to want to deal with them under readymade, shopsoiled [sic] categories.

All who met him had this tremendous sense of a warm-hearted man, and as a notable acquaintance of his told me, a man who was utterly indestructible, of massive intellect and yet reticent; quite unshakeable in his commitment to principle and to radical change in South Africa by peaceful means; a man of real reconciliation, truly an instrument of God's peace, unshakeable in his commitment to the liberation of all South Africans, black and white, striving for a more just and more open South Africa.

QUESTIONS FOR ANALYSIS

1. **What are Steve Biko's charges against white liberals in South Africa?**
2. **What was the proper role for whites in the antiapartheid movement according to Biko?**
3. **How does Bishop Tutu's eulogy differ from the political spirit and point of view expressed in Biko's 1970 essay?**
4. **According to Bishop Tutu, what were Biko's strongest characteristics? Were these characteristics demonstrated in Biko's essay?**

Source: First selection from Steve Biko, *I Write What I Like*, ed. by Aelred Stubbs C.R. Reprinted with the permission of Bowerdean Publishing Co., Ltd.; second selection from Bishop Desmond Tutu, *Crying in the Wilderness: The Struggle for Justice in South Africa*, ed. John Webster (William B. Eerdmans Publishing Co., 1982), pp. 61–63. Reprinted by permission of the Continuum International Publishing Group.

Within two years the Castro government had nationalized the property of almost all U.S. corporations in Cuba as well as the wealth of Cuba's elite. To achieve his revolutionary objectives, Castro sought economic support from the Soviet Union.

The United States responded by seeking to destabilize the Cuban economy and undermine the Castro government. U.S. punitive measures, the nationalization of so much of the economy, and the punishment of Batista supporters caused tens of thousands of Cubans to leave. Initially, most emigrants were from wealthy families and the middle class, but when the economic failures of the regime became clear, many poor Cubans fled to the United States or to other Latin American nations.

There is little evidence that Castro was committed to communism before the revolution, but his commitment to break the economic and political power of the United States in Cuba and undertake dramatic social reforms led inevitably to conflict with the United States and reliance on the Soviet Union. In April 1961, in an attempt to apply the strategy that had removed Arbenz from power in Guatemala, an army of Cuban exiles trained and armed by the CIA landed at the Bay of Pigs in an effort to overthrow Castro. The Cuban army defeated the attempted invasion in a matter of days. The Eisenhower administration had planned the invasion, but the new U.S. president, John F. Kennedy, agreed to carry it out and lived with the embarrassment. This failure helped precipitate the Cuban missile crisis. Fearful of a new invasion, Castro and Khrushchev placed nuclear weapons as well as missiles and bombers in Cuba to forestall the anticipated attack.

The failure of the Bay of Pigs tarnished the reputation of the United States and the CIA and gave heart to revolutionaries all over Latin America. But the armed revolutionary movements that imitated the tactics and objectives of Cuba's bearded revolutionaries experienced little success. Among the thousands to lose their lives was Che Guevara, captured and executed in 1967 by Bolivian troops trained by the United States. Nevertheless, Castro had demonstrated that revolutionaries could successfully challenge American power and put in place a radical program of economic and social reform in the Western Hemisphere.

SECTION REVIEW

- Independence in India and Pakistan led to war over Kashmir, which has continued to cause conflict.
- Algeria gained independence from France after a long and violent revolution.
- West African colonies eventually gained independence from Great Britain and France through negotiation, but the Belgian Congo fell under the power of a dictator.
- In southern African colonies large white settler populations resisted independence, and whites in South Africa instituted the system of segregation called apartheid.
- In Latin American nations economic nationalists sought to reduce or eliminate the economic influence of the United States.
- The CIA interfered forcefully in Guatemala, and its attempt to do the same in Cuba led to the Cuban missile crisis; meanwhile, Castro created a socialist economy.

BEYOND A BIPOLAR WORLD

Although no one doubted the dominating role of the East-West superpower rivalry in world affairs, newly independent nations had concerns that were primarily domestic and regional. Their challenge was to pursue their ends within the bipolar structure of the Cold War—and possibly to take advantage of the East-West rivalry. Where nationalist forces sought to assert political or economic independence, Cold War antagonists provided arms and political support even when the nationalist goals were quite different from those of the supporting superpower. For other nations, the ruinously expensive superpower arms race opened opportunities to expand industries and exports. In short, the superpowers dominated the world but did not control it.

The Third World

nonaligned nations Developing countries that announced their neutrality in the Cold War.

Third World Term applied to a group of developing countries who professed nonalignment during the Cold War.

As a leader of the decolonization movement, Indonesia's President Sukarno was an appropriate figure to host a 1955 meeting of twenty-nine African and Asian countries at Bandung, Indonesia, that proclaimed solidarity among those fighting against colonial rule. This conference marked the beginning of an effort by the many new, poor, mostly non-European nations emerging from colonialism to gain more influence in world affairs. The terms **nonaligned nations** and **Third World**, which became commonplace in the following years, signaled these countries' collective stance toward the rival sides in the Cold War. If the West, led by the United States, and the East, led by the Soviet Union, represented two worlds locked in mortal struggle, the Third World consisted of everyone else.

Leaders of so-called Third World countries preferred the label *nonaligned*, which signaled their independence from Soviet or U.S. control. Leaders in the West noted that the Soviet Union

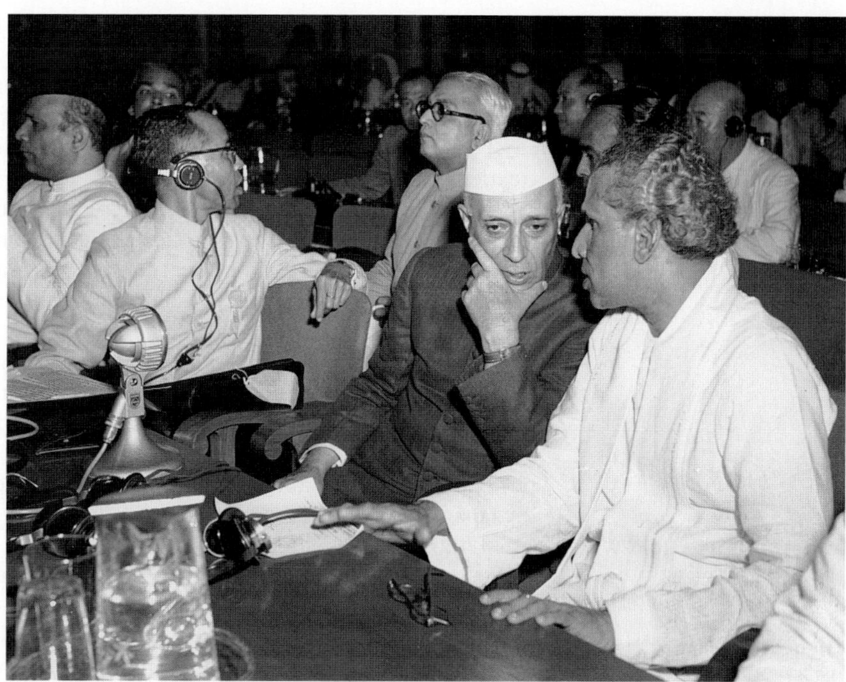
Bandung Conference, 1955 India's Jawaharlal Nehru (in white hat) was a central figure at the conference held in Indonesia to promote solidarity among nonaligned developing nations.

AP Images

The Nonaligned Movement

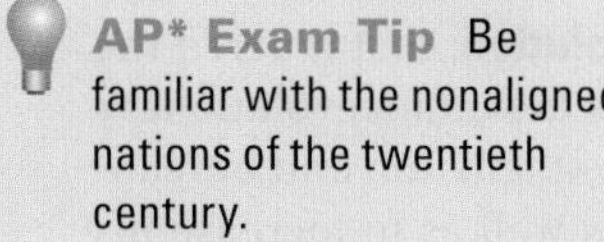
AP* Exam Tip Be familiar with the nonaligned nations of the twentieth century.

supported many national liberation movements and that the nonaligned movement included communist countries such as China and Yugoslavia. As a result, they refused to take the term *nonaligned* seriously. In a polarized world, they saw Sukarno, Nehru, Nkrumah, and Egypt's Gamal Abd al-Nasir (gah-MAHL AHB-d al–NAH-suhr) as stalking horses for a communist takeover of the world. This may have been the view of some Soviet leaders as well, since they were quick to offer military and financial aid to many nonaligned countries.

For the movement's leaders, however, nonalignment was primarily a way to extract money and support from one or both superpowers. By flirting with the Soviet Union or its ally, the People's Republic of China, a country could get weapons, training, and barter agreements that offered an alternative to selling agricultural or mineral products on Western-dominated world markets. The same flirtation might also prompt the United States and its allies to proffer grants and loans, cheap or free surplus grain, and investment for new industry or for infrastructure.

Nonaligned countries could sometimes play the Cold War rivals against each other. Nasir, who had led a military coup against the Egyptian monarchy in 1952, and his successor Anwar al-Sadat (al-seh-DAT) played this game skillfully. The United States offered to build a dam at Aswan (AS-wahn), on the Nile River, to increase Egypt's electrical generating and irrigation capacity, but it withdrew the offer when Egypt turned to the Warsaw Pact for arms in 1956. Worsened relations with the West then led Nasir to nationalize the Suez Canal and the Soviet Union to commit to building the dam. Later that same year Israel, Great Britain, and France allied to invade Egypt, aiming to overthrow Nasir, regain the Suez Canal, and secure Israel from any Egyptian threat. The invasion succeeded militarily, but the United States and the Soviet Union both pressured the invaders to withdraw, thus saving Nasir's government. In 1972 Sadat evicted Soviet military advisers, but a year later he used his Soviet weapons to attack Israel. After he lost that war, he improved relations with and sought increased aid from the United States.

Other nations adopted similar balancing strategies. In each case, local leaders sought to develop their nations' economies and assert or preserve their nations' interests. Manipulating the superpowers was a means toward those ends and implied very little about true ideological orientation.

Japan and China

No countries took more effective advantage of opportunities presented by the superpowers' preoccupations than Japan and China. Japan signed a peace treaty with most of its former enemies in 1951 and regained independence from American occupation the following year. Renouncing militarism and its imperialist past (see Chapter 26), Japan remained on the sidelines throughout the Korean War. Its new constitution, written under American supervision in 1946, allowed only a limited self-defense force, banned the deployment of Japanese troops abroad, and gave the vote to women.

Japanese Economic Development

The Japanese focused their resources on rebuilding industries and expanding trade. Peace treaties with countries in Southeast Asia specified reparations payable in the form of goods and services, thus reintroducing Japan to that region as a force for economic development rather than as a military occupier. Japan was closely tied to the West by trade and able to benefit from the postwar recovery. At the same time, controls placed on Japan by peace conditions kept its military expenditures low during the Cold War, providing an exceptional environment to develop its economy.

Three industries that took advantage of government aid and new technologies were key to Japan's emergence as an economic superpower after 1975. Electricity was in short supply in 1950, and Tokyo suffered from chronic power outages. Japan responded by building projects that produced 60 million kilowatts of electricity between 1951 and 1970, most relying on hydroelectric power. Between 1960 and 1970 steel production and shipbuilding also developed rapidly, placing Japan among world leaders in both industries.

China and the Cold War

While Japan benefited from avoiding the heavy defense costs associated with the Cold War, China was at the center of Cold War politics. When Mao Zedong (maow dzuh-dong) and the communists defeated the nationalists in 1949 and established the People's Republic of China (PRC), their main ally and source of arms was the Soviet Union. By 1956, however, the PRC and the Soviet Union were beginning to diverge politically, partly in reaction to the Soviet rejection of Stalinism and partly because of China's reluctance to accept the role of subordinate. Mao had his own notions of communism that focused strongly on the peasantry, which the Soviets had ignored in favor of the industrial working class.

Cultural Revolution (China) Campaign in China ordered by Mao Zedong to purge the Communist Party of his opponents and instill revolutionary values in the younger generation.

Mao's Great Leap Forward in 1958 was intended to propel China into the ranks of world industrial powers by maximizing the output of small-scale, village-level industries and by instituting mass collectivization in agriculture. These untested policies demonstrated Mao's willingness to carry out massive economic and social projects of his own devising in the face of criticism by the Soviets and by traditional economists. By 1962 the revolutionary reforms had failed comprehensively, leading to an estimated 20 to 30 million deaths.

In 1966 Mao instituted another radical program, the **Cultural Revolution**, that ordered the mass mobilization of Chinese youth into Red Guard units. His goal was to kindle revolutionary fervor in a new generation to ward off the stagnation and bureaucratization he saw in the Soviet Union, as well as to increase his own power within the Communist Party. Red Guard units criticized and purged teachers, party officials, and intellectuals for "bourgeois values." Executions, beatings, and incarcerations were widespread, leading to a half-million deaths and 3 million purged by 1971. Finally, Mao admitted that attacks on individuals had gotten out of hand and intervened to reestablish order. Mao's wife Jiang Qing (jyahn ching) and radical allies dominated the last years of the Cultural Revolution, harshly restricting artistic and intellectual activity.

The rift between the PRC and the Soviet Union allowed U.S. President Richard Nixon (served 1969–1974) to revive relations with China. In 1971 the United States agreed to allow the PRC to join the United Nations and occupy China's permanent seat on the

AP Images

Chinese Red Guards During the Cultural Revolution, the Red Guards, young Chinese militants, sought to identify enemies of the Communist Party and Chairman Mao, sometimes labeling their own teachers, parents, and neighbors as enemies of the people. In this photo a victim wears a dunce cap on which his crimes are written.

PRIMARY SOURCE: One Hundred Items for Destroying the Old and Establishing the New Read this document of support for Mao's socialist ideology and commitment to destroy the old ways of Chinese thinking by a student group of Red Guards.

Security Council. This decision necessitated the expulsion of the Chinese nationalist government based on the island of Taiwan, which had previously claimed to be the only legal Chinese authority. The following year, Nixon visited Beijing, initiating a new era of enhanced cooperation between the People's Republic of China and the United States.

The Middle East

Independence came gradually to the Arab countries of the Middle East. Britain granted Syria and Lebanon independence after World War II. Iraq, Egypt, and Jordan enjoyed nominal independence between the two world wars but remained under indirect British control until the 1950s. Military coups overthrew King Faruq (fuh-ROOK) of Egypt in 1952 and King Faisal (FIE-suhl) II of Iraq in 1958. King Husayn (hoo-SANE) of Jordan dismissed his British military commander in 1956 in response to the Suez crisis, but his poor desert country remained dependent on British and later American financial aid.

The Beginnings of the Israeli and Palestinian Conflict

Overshadowing all Arab politics, however, was the struggle with Israel, a clear illustration that the superpowers could not control all dangerous international disputes. British policy on Palestine between the wars oscillated between favoring Zionist Jews—who emigrated to Palestine, encouraged by the Balfour Declaration—and support for the indigenous Palestinian Arabs, who suspected that the Zionists were aiming at an independent state. As more and more Jews sought a safe haven from persecution by the Nazis, Arabs felt more and more threatened. The Arabs unleashed a guerrilla uprising against the British in 1936, and Jewish groups turned to militant tactics a few years later. Occasionally, Arabs and Jews confronted each other in riots or killings, making it clear that peaceful coexistence in Palestine would be difficult or impossible to achieve.

PRIMARY SOURCE: The Palestinian National Charter Read how attendees of the Fourth Palestine National Council defined their homeland and pledged to liberate it from Israel.

After the war, under intense pressure to resettle European Jewish refugees, Britain turned the Palestine problem over to the United Nations. In November 1947 the General Assembly voted in favor of partitioning Palestine into two states, one Jewish and one Arab. The Jewish community made plans to declare independence, while the Palestinians, who felt that the proposed land division was unfair, took up arms. When Israel declared its independence in May 1948, neighboring Arab countries sent armies to help the Palestinians crush the newborn state.

Israel prevailed and some 700,000 Palestinians became refugees, finding shelter in United Nations refugee camps in Jordan, Syria, Lebanon, and the Gaza Strip (a bit of coastal land on the Egyptian-Israeli border). The right of these refugees to return home remains a focal point of Arab politics. In 1967 Israel responded to threatening military moves by Egypt's Nasir by preemptively attacking Egyptian and Syrian air bases. In six days Israel won a smashing victory. When Jordan entered the war, Israel took control of Jerusalem, which it had previously split with Jordan, and the West Bank. Acquiring all of Jerusalem satisfied Jews' deep longing to return to their holiest city, but Palestinians continued to regard Jerusalem as their destined capital, and Muslims in many countries protested Israeli control of the Dome of the Rock, a revered Islamic shrine located in the city. Israel also occupied the Gaza Strip, the strategic Golan Heights in southern Syria, and the entire Sinai Peninsula (see Map 31.3). These acquisitions resulted in a new wave of Palestinian refugees.

The rival claims to Palestine continued to plague Middle Eastern politics. The Palestine Liberation Organization (PLO), headed by Yasir Arafat (AR-uh-fat), waged guerrilla war against Israel, frequently engaging in acts of terrorism. The Israelis were able to blunt or absorb these attacks and launch counterstrikes that likewise involved assassinations and bombings. Though the United States was a firm friend to Israel and the Soviet Union armed the Arab states, neither superpower saw the struggle between Zionism and Palestinian nationalism as a vital concern—until oil became a political issue.

OPEC

The phenomenal concentration of oil wealth in the Middle East—Saudi Arabia, Iran, Iraq, Kuwait, Libya, Qatar, Bahrain, and the United Arab Emirates—was not fully realized until after World War II, when demand for oil rose sharply as civilian economies recovered. In 1960, as world demand rose, oil-producing states formed the **Organization of Petroleum Exporting Countries (OPEC)** to promote their collective interest in higher revenues.

Organization of Petroleum Exporting Countries (OPEC) Organization formed in 1960 by oil-producing states to promote their collective interest in generating revenue from oil.

Oil politics and the Arab-Israeli conflict intersected in October 1973 during the Yom Kippur War. Surprise attacks by Syria and Egypt threw the Israelis into temporary disarray, but Israel won a clear military victory in the end. Supported by military supplies from the United States, it drove back Syrian forces and trapped an Egyptian army at the Suez Canal's southern end. The

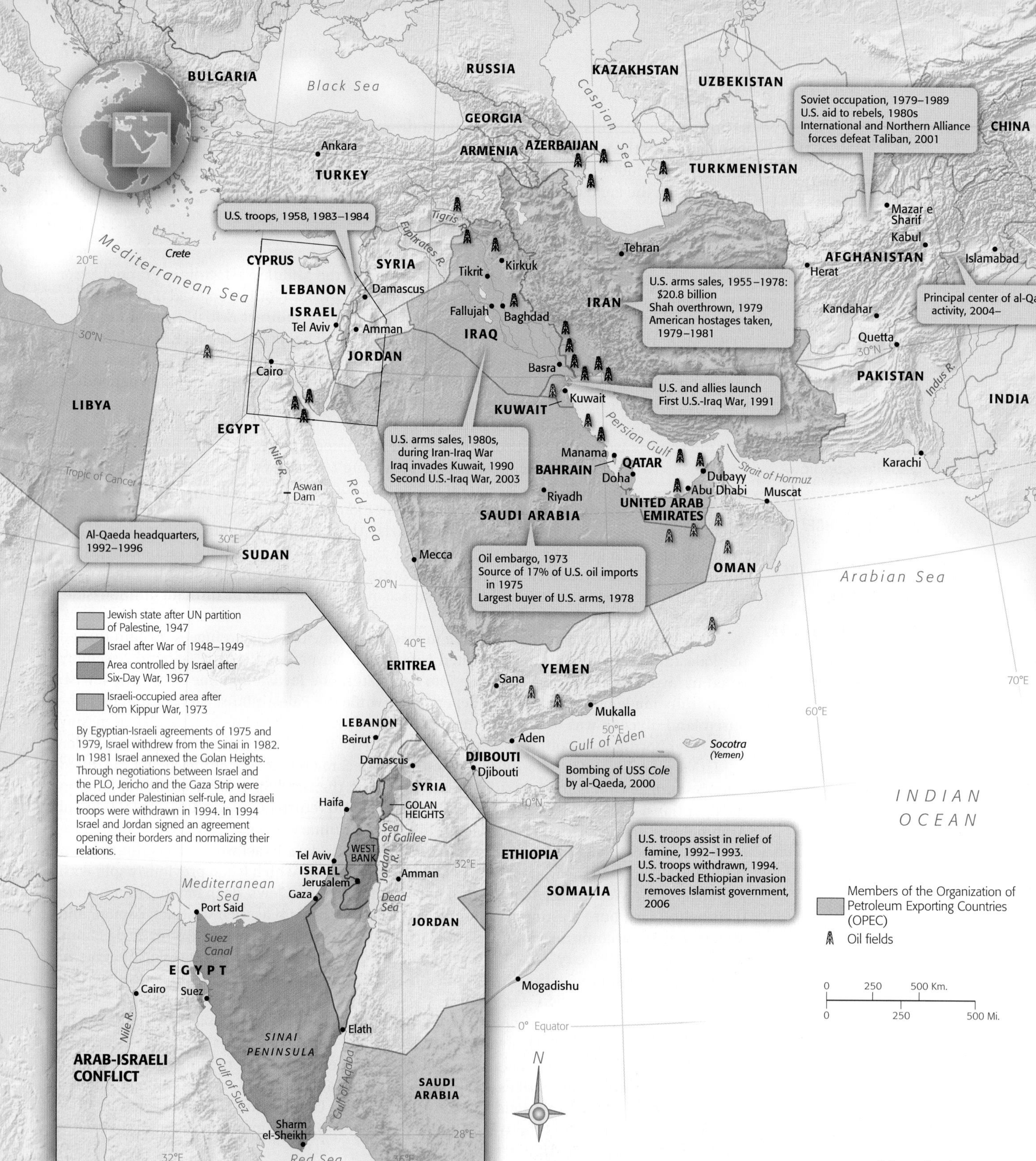

MAP 31.3 Middle East Oil and the Arab-Israeli Conflict, 1947–1973 Private European and American companies had long controlled oil resources. In the 1960s OPEC negotiated agreements for sharing control and eventually establishing national ownership. This set the stage for the use of oil as a weapon in the 1973 Arab-Israeli war as well as for subsequent price increases.

Interactive Map

Shortage at the Pumps As prices rose in the late 1970s, consumers tried to hoard supplies by filling gas cans at neighborhood stations. For the first time gas prices exceeded $1 a gallon.

James Pozarik/Getty Images

United States then arranged a ceasefire and the disengagement of forces. But before that could happen, the Arab oil-producing countries voted to embargo oil shipments to the United States and the Netherlands as punishment for their support of Israel.

The implications of using oil as an economic weapon profoundly disturbed the worldwide oil industry. Prices rose—along with feelings of insecurity. In 1974 OPEC responded to the turmoil in the oil market by quadrupling prices, setting the stage for massive transfers of wealth to the producing countries and provoking a feeling of crisis throughout the consuming countries.

The Emergence of Environmental Concerns

The Cold War and the massive investments made in postwar economic recovery focused public and governmental attention on technological innovations and enormous projects such as hydroelectric dams and nuclear power stations. Only a few people warned that untested technologies and industrial expansion were degrading the environment. The superpowers were particularly negligent of the environmental impact of pesticide and herbicide use, automobile exhaust, industrial waste disposal, and radiation.

The wave of student unrest that swept many parts of the world in 1968 and the early 1970s created a new awareness of environmental issues and a new constituency for environmental action. As youth activism grew, governments in the West began to pass new environmental regulations. Among them was the Clean Air Act of 1970. Earth Day, a benchmark of the new awareness, was also first celebrated in 1970, the year in which the United States also established its Environmental Protection Agency.

When oil prices skyrocketed, the problem of finite natural resources became more broadly recognized. Making gasoline engines and home

SECTION REVIEW

- After decolonization new nations organized the "Nonaligned Movement" to assert a middle ground between the Cold War rivals.
- After World War II Japan followed the capitalist industrial model while China under Mao tried and failed to industrialize using mass mobilizations and central planning.
- Israel's military victories over its Arab neighbors in 1967 and 1973 expanded the nation's borders, but initiated an enduring cycle of regional tensions and violence between Israelis and Palestinians.
- OPEC's 1973 embargo of oil shipments to nations that supported Israel soon led to steep price increases and a massive redistribution of wealth to oil-producing nations.
- During the 1970s young people provided crucial leadership to a worldwide movement to conserve natural resources and protect the environment.

heating systems more efficient and lowering highway speed limits to conserve fuel became matters of national debate in the United States, while poorer countries struggled to find the money to import oil. A widely read 1972 study called *The Limits of Growth* forecast a need to cut back on consumption of natural resources in the twenty-first century. Ecological and environmental problems now vied for public attention with superpower rivalry and Third World nation building.

CONCLUSION

The alliance between the Soviet Union and the Western democracies led by the United States did not survive into the post–World War II era. Shortly after the war, both sides began to prepare for a new round of hostilities, establishing competing military alliances and attempting to influence the new governments of nations formerly occupied by the Axis. In the end this confrontation was projected into space, as each side sought to advertise its technological capacity through satellite launches and finally a moon landing.

Each side portrayed this tension as a struggle between irreconcilably different social and economic systems, and each side emphasized the corruption, injustice, and unfairness of its opponent. When Winston Churchill spoke in 1946 of Soviet control in eastern Europe as an iron curtain, he suggested that the Soviet system was, in effect, a prison.

Massive armies armed with increasingly sophisticated weapons, including nuclear weapons far more destructive than those dropped on Japan, defended the boundary that separated the United States and its allies and the Soviet Union and its allies. This Cold War quickly became global in character as distant civil wars, regional conflicts, and nationalist revolutions were transformed by support provided by these rivals for global ascendancy.

The desire of colonized peoples to throw off imperial controls and establish independent nations provided many of the era's flash points. The Western nations had defined World War II as a war for freedom and self-determination. The Free French had promised greater autonomy to African colonies, the United States had used nationalist forces to fight against the Japanese in the Philippines and in Vietnam, and the British also had used forces recruited throughout its empire to fight the war. Once organized and set in motion, these nationalist energies eventually overwhelmed colonial rule. The most powerful force in the postwar era was nationalism, the desire of peoples to control their own destinies.

In Africa, the Middle East, South Asia, and Latin America, this desire to throw off foreign controls led to the creation of scores of new nations by the 1970s. Each nation's struggle had its own character. While in India these passions led to independence, similar sentiments led in China to the overthrow of a government seen as weak and subordinate to foreign powers and the creation of a communist dictatorship. In much of Africa, the Middle East, and the Caribbean, nationalism overturned colonial rule. In the Middle East the desire for self-government was complicated by the creation of the state of Israel. In Latin America, where most nations had been independent for well over a century, nationalist passions focused on a desire for economic independence and an end to foreign interventions.

The end of Japanese control in Korea and Vietnam led to territorial partitions that separated Soviet-leaning and Western-allied polities. Civil war and foreign interventions soon followed. In both cases the Soviet Union and China supported communist forces. The United States committed large military forces to protect the anticommunist governments, gaining a stalemate in Korea and eventually losing in Vietnam. While these outcomes were mixed for the superpowers, the wars were contained and managed so as to prevent direct engagement and nuclear conflict.

This period also witnessed the beginning of the international environmental movement. Public attention increasingly focused on resource management, pollution, and the preservation of endangered species. In response, the United States and governments in western Europe put in place the first generation of environmental laws.The Clean Air Act in the United States and other measures had an immediate impact, but both policymakers and the public grew aware of ever more serious challenges. The gas crisis of the 1970s gave these efforts a sense of urgency.

KEY TERMS

iron curtain p. 888
Cold War p. 888
North Atlantic Treaty Organization (NATO) p. 888
Warsaw Pact p. 888
United Nations p. 888
World Bank p. 889
Marshall Plan p. 891
European Economic Community (Common Market) p. 891
Korean War p. 892
Vietnam War p. 893
Cuban missile crisis p. 895
Helsinki Accords p. 895
nonaligned nations p. 904
Third World p. 904
Cultural Revolution (China) p. 906
Organization of Petroleum Exporting Countries (OPEC) p. 907

EBOOK AND WEBSITE RESOURCES

Primary Sources

Comments on Algeria, April 11, 1961

The Rivonia Trial Speech to the Court

One Hundred Items for Destroying the Old and Establishing the New

The Palestinian National Charter

Interactive Maps

Map 31.1 Cold War Confrontation

Map 31.2 Decolonization, 1947–1990

Map 31.3 Middle East Oil and the Arab-Israeli Conflict, 1947–1973

Plus flashcards, practice quizzes, and more. Go to: www.cengage.com/history/bullietearthpeople5e

SUGGESTED READING

Allison, Graham. *Essence of Decision: Explaining the Cuban Missile Crisis.* 1971. An influential study of decision making in a time of crisis.

Barraclough, Geoffrey. *An Introduction to Contemporary History.* 1964. A remarkable early effort at understanding the broad sweep of history.

Becker, Jasper. *Hungry Ghosts.* 1998. Explores the Great Leap Forward in China.

Chamberlain, M. E. *Decolonization: The Fall of the European Empires,* 2nd ed. 1999. A comprehensive overview.

De Witte, Ludo, trans. Ann Wright. *The Assassination of Lumumba.* 2003.

Dower, John. *Embracing Defeat: Japan in the Wake of World War II.* 1999. An excellent history of the American occupation of Japan.

Gelvin, James. *The Modern Middle East: A History.* 2007. A reliable introduction to the region.

Hitchcock, William. *The Struggle for Europe: The Turbulent History of a Divided Continent 1945–2002.* 2003. An excellent recent study of Cold War era Europe.

Karnow, Stanley. *Vietnam: A History,* 2nd ed. 1997. A detailed and balanced history.

Kyle, Keith. *Suez 1956.* 1991. Examines the international complications of a brief war.

Lapping, Brian. *End of Empire.* 1985. Covers the dissolution of the British Empire.

Leffler, Melvyn P., and David S. Painter, eds. *Origins of the Cold War: An International History.* 1994. Offers reconsiderations of earlier historical viewpoints.

Low, D. A. *The Egalitarian Moment: Asia and Africa, 1950–1980.* 1996. Explores the end of the colonial period.

MacDougall, Walter. *The Heavens and the Earth: A Political History of the Space Age.* 1985. Looks at the intersection of politics, technology, and international competition.

Mazower, Mark. *Dark Continent.* 1999. An outstanding reappraisal of Europe's twentieth-century history.

Meisner, Maurice. *Mao's China and After: A History of the People's Republic,* 3rd ed. 1999. A highly regarded survey.

Merrill, John. *Korea: The Peninsular Origins of the War.* 1989. Presents the Korean War as a civil and revolutionary conflict as well as part of the Cold War.

Nakamura, Takafusa. *A History of Showa Japan, 1926–1989.* 1998. A solid Japanese study of the reign of Emperor Hirohito.

Rabe, Stephen. *The Most Dangerous Area in the World: John F. Kennedy Confronts Communist Revolution in Latin America.* 1999. A useful exploration of the era.

Reynolds, David. *One World Divisible: A Global History Since 1945.* 2000. A very useful discussion of recent events.

Smith, Charles D. *Palestine and the Arab-Israeli Conflict,* 6th rev. ed. 2007. Comprehensive coverage of an ongoing crisis.

Walker, Martin. *The Cold War: A History.* 1993. A good general history.

Zubok, Vladislav, and Constantine Pleshakov. *Inside the Kremlin's Cold War: From Stalin to Khrushchev.* 1997. Among the best treatments of Cold War Soviet Union.

AP* REVIEW QUESTIONS FOR CHAPTER 31

1. In response to the Allies creating NATO, the USSR created
   (A) the Maginot Line.
   (B) SEATO.
   (C) the Warsaw Pact.
   (D) the Rio Treaty.

2. During the Cold War years, the United Nations
   (A) supported any conflict that pitted the democratic states of the world against communism.
   (B) was controlled by the United States and did not take military action.
   (C) supported insurgent groups against established dictatorships.
   (D) was seldom able to forestall or quell international conflicts.

3. Between 1948 and 1952, the Marshall Plan
   (A) aided the rearmament of all noncommunist nations in Europe.
   (B) was refused funding by the U.S. Congress because it would force the United States to become involved in world affairs.
   (C) helped to rebuild the economic infrastructure of western Europe.
   (D) assisted thousands of Jewish survivors of the Holocaust to resettle in Israel.

4. By the early 1970s, it was apparent that the USSR's command economy
   (A) was being built on the agricultural production of satellite states.
   (B) was based on slave laborers who had been captured in World War II.
   (C) was unable to meet the demand for consumer goods at home.
   (D) depended on gold coming from its trading partners in Africa.

5. The U.S. policy of lending direct military support to any nation that was fighting a communist subversion
   (A) was declared to be a violation of the UN charter.
   (B) was designed to rearm Germany.
   (C) led to the Chinese invasion of South Korea.
   (D) was designed to help Greece and Turkey resist Soviet military pressure.

6. In the Korean War, the United States limited its military action to the Korean peninsula because
   (A) it was afraid that the United Nations would sanction it.
   (B) it feared that in attacking China it would encourage the Soviet Union to enter the war as China's ally.
   (C) it did not have enough troops, and the U.S. people were tired of war.
   (D) it was able to quickly beat the North Korean and Chinese armies.

7. One reason that President Kennedy decided to become involved in the war in Vietnam was
   (A) to improve his popularity in the United States before reelection.
   (B) that he feared that a communist success in Vietnam would alter the balance of power in Southeast Asia.
   (C) to prevent the USSR from aiding South Vietnam.
   (D) to gain control of Vietnam's valuable rubber resources.

8. The "space race" began with
   (A) the USSR placing nuclear missiles in Cuba.
   (B) the 1969 U.S. moon landing.
   (C) the launching of *Sputnik* in 1957.
   (D) the signing of the Helsinki Accords.

9. One reason Bangladesh separated from Pakistan in 1971 was that
   (A) the two nations had different religions.
   (B) Pakistan was poorer and was draining wealth from Bangladesh.
   (C) it wanted to pursue an experiment with socialism.
   (D) the two nations were linguistically different.

10. One major reason that France opposed Algerian independence was that
    (A) the Algerians had no experience with self-government.
    (B) the United Nations had opposed Algeria's application for independence.
    (C) Algeria is strategically located in North Africa.
    (D) the economy of Algeria contributed greatly to France's economy.

11. Unlike Kwame Nkrumah, Jomo Kenyatta
    (A) was overthrown in 1966 by a group of army officers, but remained an effective international spokesman for colonized peoples.
    (B) was jailed because the British feared he would cause a revolt.
    (C) never encouraged his people to elect him to office.
    (D) came from the educated colonial elite.

12. The policy of racial separation in South Africa
    (A) was supported by the United Nations because it kept peace in the nation.
    (B) was called apartheid.
    (C) encouraged Europeans to invest in South Africa.
    (D) ended just prior to World War II.

13. Which of the following is indicative of the dependency of Latin American nations on the U.S. economy in the twentieth century?
    (A) The admission of the Latin American nations to the United Nations
    (B) The United Fruit Company
    (C) The death of Ernesto "Che" Guevara in Bolivia
    (D) The rise of Eva Perón in Argentina

14. Those nations that openly stated they did not want to be on either side in the Cold War were called
    (A) neutral states.
    (B) failed states.
    (C) nonaligned nations.
    (D) satellite nations.

15. In 1958, under Mao Zedong, China launched the Great Leap Forward, which was designed to
    (A) provide a high-quality education for all Chinese children.
    (B) develop the Chinese military.
    (C) make China a nuclear power.
    (D) vault China into the ranks of the world's industrial powers.

CHAPTER

32

CHAPTER OUTLINE

- Postcolonial Crises and Asian Economic Expansion
- The End of the Bipolar World
- The Challenge of Population Growth
- Unequal Development and the Movement of Peoples
- Technological and Environmental Change
- Conclusion

DIVERSITY + DOMINANCE *The Struggle for Women's Rights in an Era of Global Political and Economic Change*

ENVIRONMENT + TECHNOLOGY *The Computer Gets Personal*

MATERIAL CULTURE *Fast Food*

Dennis Cox/China Stock

Shanghai—Old Meets New The city of Shanghai is one of the great success stories in a rapidly growing Chinese economy, but its prosperity has left many behind. In this photo a poor woman walks past Shanghai's modern skyline carrying goods to market in baskets and a neck yoke, a technology thousands of years old.

Visit the website and ebook for additional study materials and interactive tools: www.cengage.com/history/bullietearthpeople5e

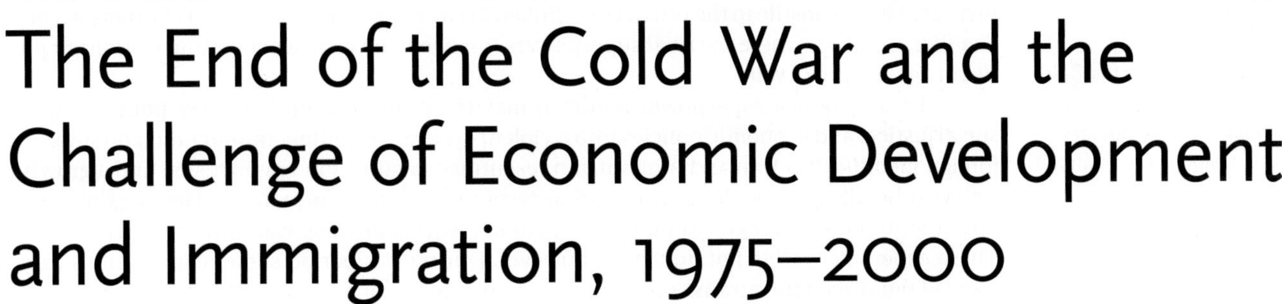

The End of the Cold War and the Challenge of Economic Development and Immigration, 1975–2000

- How did the Cold War affect politics in Latin America and the Middle East in the 1970s and 1980s?
- What forces led to the collapse of the Soviet Union?
- What explains differences in the rate of population growth among the world's cultural regions?
- How does wealth inequality among nations impact international migration patterns?
- How has technological change affected the global environment in the recent past?

At the end of the 1970s China began an ambitious program of economic reforms. Until then China, with the world's largest population, lagged far behind the mature industrialized nations of Europe and North America in economic performance, as well as behind neighboring nations like Japan and South Korea. Since the reforms, China has experienced rapid economic growth, becoming one of the few socialist nations to successfully make the transition to a market economy. Despite this remarkable expansion, over 100 million Chinese still lived in poverty in 2000. As is indicated in the opening illustration, ancient technology and poverty can exist in close proximity with modernity and affluence in China. These same problems of poverty and inequality exist across the globe. In an era of astounding technological change and, until 2008, spreading prosperity, 1.2 billion of the world's population lived on less than a dollar per day.

At the end of the twentieth century population growth continued to outstrip economic resources in many of the nations of the developing world. In wealthy industrialized nations as well, politicians and social reformers still worry about the effects of unemployment, family breakdown, substance abuse, and homelessness. In the last decades of the twentieth century, as in the Industrial Revolution (see Chapter 22), dramatic economic expansion, increased global economic integration, and rapid technological progress coincided with problems of social dislocation and inequality. Among the most important events of the period were the emergence of new industrial powers in Asia and the precipitous demise of the Soviet Union and its socialist allies.

POSTCOLONIAL CRISES AND ASIAN ECONOMIC EXPANSION

Between 1975 and the end of the century, wars and revolutions spread death and destruction through many of the world's least-developed regions. In most cases the origins of conflict were found in the experience of colonialism and foreign intervention, but each conflict also had a unique historical character. Throughout these decades of conflict the two superpowers sought to avoid direct military confrontation while working to gain strategic advantages. The United States and the Soviet Union each supplied arms and financial assistance to nations or insurgent forces hostile to the other. Once linked to superpower rivalries, local conflicts became deadlier. Conflicts where the rival superpowers financed and armed competing factions or parties are called **proxy wars**.

proxy wars During the Cold War, local or regional wars in which the superpowers armed, trained, and financed the combatants.

In Latin America superpower rivalry transformed limited conflicts over political rights, social justice, and economic policies into a violent cycle of revolution, military dictatorship, and foreign meddling. In Iran and Afghanistan resentment against foreign intrusion and a growing religious hostility to secular culture led to revolutionary transformations. Here again, superpower ambitions and regional political instability helped provoke war and economic decline. These experiences were not universal, however. During this period some Asian nations experienced rapid economic transformation. Japan emerged as one of the world's leading industrial powers, and a small number of other Asian economies entered the ranks of industrial and commercial powers, including socialist China, which initiated market-based economic reforms.

At the end of the 1980s the Cold War ended with the collapse of the Soviet system in eastern Europe, but the transition to democracy and market economy proved difficult. As both developing and former socialist nations opened their markets to foreign investment and competition, they experienced wrenching social change. Increased globalization coincided with increased inequality in many nations, but some developing nations also reaped substantial benefits from rapid technological change and world economic integration.

This period also witnessed a great increase in world population and international immigration. Population growth and increased levels of industrialization had a dramatic impact on the global environment, with every continent feeling the destructive effects of forest depletion, soil erosion, and pollution. Wealthy nations with slow population growth found it easier to respond to these environmental challenges than did poor nations experiencing rapid population growth.

Revolutions, Repression, and Democratic Reform in Latin America

In the 1970s Latin America entered a dark era of political violence. When revolutionary movements challenged the established order, militaries in many nations overturned democratic governments and instituted repressive measures. A region of weak democracy in 1960 became a region of military dictatorships with little patience for civil liberties and human rights fifteen years later.

The ongoing confrontation between Fidel Castro and the government of the United States (see Chapter 31) helped propel the region toward crisis. The fact that the Cuban communist government survived efforts by the United States to overthrow it energized the revolutionary left throughout Latin America. Fearful that revolution would spread across Latin America, the United States increased support for its political and military allies in that region, training many of the military leaders who led coups during this period.

The Brazilian Solution

Brazil was the first nation to experience the conservative reaction to the Cuban Revolution. Claiming that Brazil's civilian political leaders could not protect the nation from communist subversion, the army overthrew the constitutional government of President João Goulart (ju-wow go-LARHT) in 1964. The military suspended the constitution, outlawed all existing political parties, and exiled former presidents and opposition leaders. Death squads—illegal paramilitary organizations sanctioned by the government—detained, tortured, and executed thousands of citizens. The dictatorship also undertook an ambitious economic program that promoted industrialization through import substitution, using tax and tariff policies to compel foreign-owned companies to increase investment in manufacturing.

This combination of dictatorship, violent repression, and government promotion of industrialization came to be called the "Brazilian Solution." Elements of this "solution" were imposed across much of the region. In 1970 Chile's new president, **Salvador Allende** (sal-VAH-dor ah-YEHN-day), undertook an ambitious program of socialist reforms and nationalized Chile's heavy industry and mines, including the American-owned copper companies that dominated the economy. From the beginning of Allende's presidency the administration of President Richard Nixon (served 1969–1973) tried to subvert the Chilean government. Afflicted by inflation,

Salvador Allende Socialist politician elected president of Chile in 1970 and overthrown by the military in 1973. He died during the military attack.

CHRONOLOGY

	The Americas	Middle East/Africa	Asia	Eastern Europe
1970	1970 Salvador Allende elected president of Chile			
	1973 Allende overthrown		1975 Vietnam War ends	
	1976 Military takeover in Argentina			1978 USSR sends troops to Afghanistan
	1979 Sandinistas overthrow Anastasio Somoza in Nicaragua	1979 Shah of Iran overthrown in Islamic Revolution	1979 China begins economic reforms	
1980	1983–1990 Democracy returns in Argentina, Brazil, and Chile	1980–1988 Iran-Iraq War	1986 Average Japanese income overtakes income in United States	1985 Mikhail Gorbachev becomes Soviet head of state
	1989 United States invades Panama	1989 USSR withdraws from Afghanistan	1989 Tiananmen Square confrontation	1989 Berlin Wall falls 1989–1991 Communism ends in eastern Europe
1990	1990 Sandinistas defeated in elections in Nicaragua	1990 Iraq invades Kuwait 1991 Persian Gulf War	1990s Japanese recession	1990 Reunification of Germany 1992 Yugoslavia disintegrates; Croatia and Slovenia become independent nations 1992–1995 Bosnia crisis
	1998 Election of Hugo Chávez in Venezuela	1994 Nelson Mandela elected president of South Africa; Tutsi massacred in Rwanda	1997 Asian financial crisis begins	

Dirty War War waged by the Argentine military (1976–1983) against leftist groups. Characterized by the use of illegal imprisonment, torture, and executions by the military.

Sandinistas Members of a leftist coalition that overthrew the Nicaraguan dictatorship of Anastasia Somoza in 1979 and attempted to install a socialist economy. The United States financed armed opposition by the Contras. The Sandinistas lost national elections in 1990.

mass consumer protests, and declining foreign trade, a military uprising led by General Augusto Pinochet (ah-GOOS-toh pin-oh-CHET) and supported by the United States overthrew Allende in 1973. President Allende and thousands of Chileans died in the uprising, and thousands more were jailed, tortured, and imprisoned without trial. Once in power Pinochet rolled back Allende's reforms, dramatically reducing state participation in the economy and encouraging foreign investment.

In 1976 Argentina followed Brazil and Chile into dictatorship. Isabel Martínez de Perón (EES-ah-bell mar-TEEN-ehz deh pair-OWN) became president after the death of her husband Juan Perón in 1974 (see Chapter 30). Perón had been exiled in 1955, but returned and was elected president in 1973. Her administration faced a guerrilla insurgency, inflation, and labor protests. Impatient with the policies of the president, the military seized power and suspended the constitution. During the next seven years it fought what it called the **Dirty War** against terrorism. More than nine thousand Argentines lost their lives, and thousands of others endured arrest and torture.

Revolution and Counterrevolution in Central America

While the left suffered these reverses in South America, a revolutionary movement came to power in Nicaragua in 1979, overthrowing the corrupt dictatorship of Anastasio Somoza. This broad alliance of revolutionaries and reformers called themselves **Sandinistas** (sahn-din-EES-tahs). They took their name from Augusto César Sandino, who had led Nicaraguan opposition to U.S. military intervention between 1927 and 1932. Once in power, the Sandinistas sought to imitate the command economies of Cuba and the Soviet Union, nationalizing properties owned by members of the Nicaraguan elite and U.S. companies.

Susan Meiselas/Magnum Photos, Inc.

The Nicaraguan Revolution Overturns Somoza A revolutionary coalition that included Marxists drove the dictator Anastasio Somoza from power in 1979. The Somoza family had ruled Nicaragua since the 1930s and maintained a close relationship with the United States.

U.S. president Jimmy Carter (served 1977–1980) championed human rights in the hemisphere and stopped the flow of U.S. arms to regimes with the worst records. Carter also agreed to the reestablishment of Panamanian sovereignty in the Canal Zone at the end of 1999, but his effort to find common ground with the Sandinistas failed.

He was defeated in the next election by Ronald Reagan, who was committed to reversing the results of the Nicaraguan Revolution and defeating a revolutionary movement in neighboring El Salvador. Because the U.S. Congress resisted any use of U.S. combat forces in Nicaragua and El Salvador and put strict limits on military aid, the Reagan administration tried to roll back the Nicaraguan Revolution through punitive economic measures and the recruitment and arming of a proxy force of anti-Sandinista Nicaraguans, called Contras (counterrevolutionaries).

Confident that they were supported by the majority of Nicaraguans and assured that the U.S. Congress was close to cutting off aid to the Contras, the Sandinistas called for free elections in 1990. But they had miscalculated politically. Exhausted by more than a decade of violence, a majority of Nicaraguan voters rejected the Sandinistas and elected a middle-of-the-road coalition led by Violeta Chamorro (vee-oh-LET-ah cha-MOR-roe).

In neighboring El Salvador another guerrilla movement, the FMLN (Farabundo Martí [fah-rah-BOON-doh mar-TEE] National Liberation Front), seemed on the verge of taking power. The Reagan administration responded by providing hundreds of millions of dollars in military assistance and by training units of the El Salvadoran army. The assassination of Archbishop Oscar Romero and other members of the Catholic clergy by death squads tied to the Salvadoran government as well as the murder of thousands of noncombatants by military units trained by the United States undermined this effort. However, the electoral defeat of the Sandinistas in Nicaragua and the collapse of the Soviet Union (see below) finally forced the FMLN rebels to negotiate peace, transforming themselves into a civilian political party.

During this same period, the violent political confrontation of right and left abated in South America as well. The right-wing military dictatorships established in Brazil, Chile, and Argentina all came to an end between 1983 and 1990, brought down by their own excesses and by popular desires for a return to constitutional government. By 2000, with the Cold War ended, 95 percent of Latin America's population lived under civilian rule.

U.S. Influence in Latin America

At the same time, the influence of the United States grew substantially. The United States had thwarted the left in Nicaragua and El Salvador by funding military proxies. It used its own military in a 1983 invasion of the tiny Caribbean nation of Grenada and again in 1989 to overthrow and arrest dictator General Manuel Noriega (MAN-wel no-ree-EGG-ah) of Panama. These actions were powerful reminders to Latin Americans of prior interventions (see Chapter 23), but they also served as reminders of American power at a time when socialism was discredited by the collapse of the Soviet bloc.

From this position of strength the United States pushed Latin American nations to reform their economies by removing limitations on foreign investment, eliminating many social welfare programs, and reducing public-sector employment. Latin American governments responded by selling public-sector industries, like national airlines, manufacturing facilities, and public utilities, to foreign corporations. But popular support for these policies, what Latin Americans called neo-liberalism, eroded quickly due to political scandals and a slowing world economy. A catastrophic economic and political meltdown in Argentina between 2001 and 2002 contributed to the appearance of a reinvigorated nationalist left in Latin America that sought to roll back neo-liberal reforms (see Diversity and Dominance: The Struggle for Women's Rights in an Era of Global Political and Economic Change). Among the most vocal critic of neo-liberalism and American influence was Hugo Chávez (HUGH-go SHAH-vez), elected president of Venezuela in 1998.

Islamic Revolutions in Iran and Afghanistan

Ayatollah Ruhollah Khomeini Shi'ite philosopher and cleric who led the overthrow of the shah of Iran in 1979 and created an Islamic republic.

Although the Arab-Israel conflict and the oil crisis (see Chapter 31) concerned both superpowers, the prospect of direct military involvement remained remote. When unexpected crises developed in Iran and Afghanistan, however, significant strategic issues came to the foreground. Both countries adjoined Soviet territory, making Soviet military intervention more likely. Exercising post–Vietnam War caution, the United States reacted with restraint. The Soviet Union chose a bolder and ultimately disastrous course.

Muhammad Reza Pahlavi (REH-zah PAH-lah-vee) succeeded his father as shah of Iran in 1941. In 1953 covert intervention by the U.S. Central Intelligence Agency (CIA) helped the shah retain his throne in the face of a movement to overturn royal power. Even when he finally nationalized the foreign-owned oil industry, the shah continued to enjoy American support. As oil revenues increased following the price increases of the 1970s, the United States encouraged the shah to spend his nation's growing wealth on equipping the Iranian army with American weaponry. By the 1970s popular resentment against the ballooning wealth of the elite families that supported the shah and the brutality, inefficiency, malfeasance, and corruption of his government led to mass opposition.

Ayatollah Ruhollah Khomeini (A-yat-ol-LAH ROOH-ol-LAH ko-MAY-nee), a Shi'ite (SHE-ite) philosopher-cleric who had spent most of his eighty-plus years in religious and academic pursuits, became the leader of the opposition. Massive protests forced the shah to flee Iran and ended the monarchy in 1979. In the Islamic Republic of Iran, which replaced the monarchy, Ayatollah Khomeini was supreme

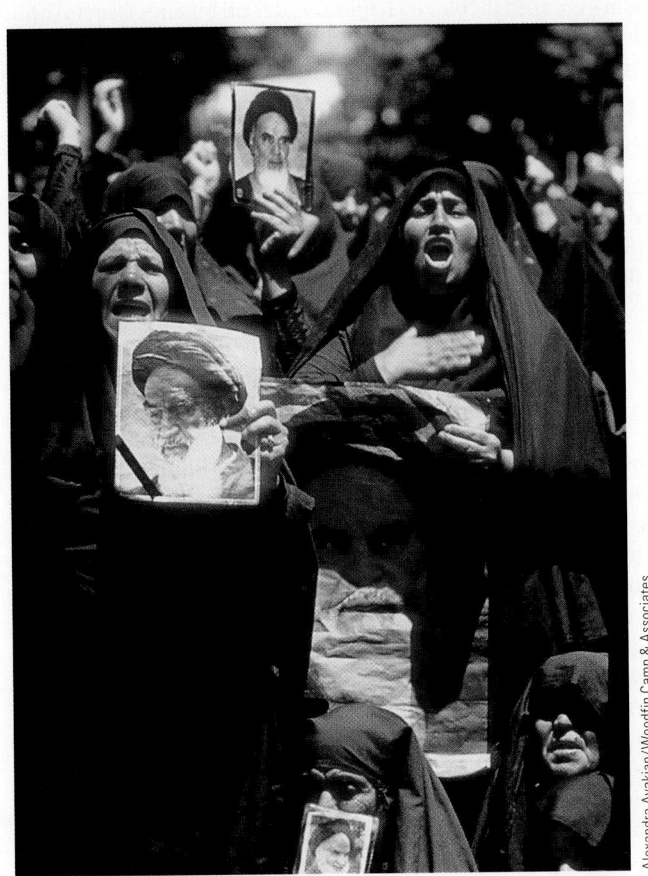

Alexandra Avakian/Woodfin Camp & Associates

Muslim Women Mourning the Death of Ayatollah Khomeini in 1989 An Islamic revolution overthrew the shah of Iran in 1979. Ayatollah Khomeini sought to lead Iran away from the influences of Western culture and challenged the power of the United States in the Persian Gulf.

DIVERSITY + DOMINANCE

The Struggle for Women's Rights in an Era of Global Political and Economic Change

The struggle for women's rights has been one of the most important social movements of the twentieth and twenty-first centuries. Although we can identify fundamental similarities in objectives across cultural and political boundaries, women in less developed nations are forced to recognize that their objectives and strategies must take into account international inequalities in power and wealth. In this section Gladys Acosta, a militant Peruvian feminist, discusses the appropriate agenda for this struggle in the era after the fall of the Soviet Union and the rise of neo-liberalism.

Neo-liberalism *is the term used in Latin America to identify the free-market economic policies advocated by the United States. Among its chief characteristics are an end to the protection of local industries, a reduction in government social welfare policies, a reduction in public-sector employment, a commitment to paying debts to international creditors, and the removal of impediments to foreign investment. Many Latin Americans believe that neo-liberalism is a new form of imperialism.*

No one can abstain from the debate about the great historical systems of our time. Not even those of us who are trying to change the complex web of human relationships from a feminist perspective. Everywhere people are talking about the end of ideologies. But before we can grasp the significance of current events and their consequences, we need to pinpoint our various doubts and blank spots. Capitalism is the main pivot of our lives because we were born under its influence. It [has] hegemony. . . .

Gender, the main distinction between all people, is ignored in most philosophical, political or economic discussions. The reason for this lies partly in the low level of women's participation, but not entirely, because women are not always aware of the system of submission and repression to which we are subjected against our will. We need to find something which unites women in a gender-specific manner. That doesn't mean sweeping under the carpet all the differences between us, like social position, culture or age. . . .

Neo-Liberalism in Action

For those of us who live under the influence of the capitalist system, the situation is different. When I talk of neo-liberalism, I mean austerity measures, foreign debts, and increased liberties for all those who have the power of money at their disposal and the power of repression over those who make demands. We have now reached a new form of capitalist accumulation. The world's economic system is in a state of change and capital has become more concentrated and centralised. I would not go as far as to say countries don't exist anymore but national identities do certainly play a different role now. It is important to understand the dynamics because otherwise historical responsibilities are obscured and we no longer know whom we're fighting against. If we look at the bare face of neo-liberalism from a woman's point of view, we cannot fail to notice its murderous consequences. To create a more humane society we must continue to reject neo-liberalism here and now in the hope of being able to change the dead present into a living future. Under neo-liberalism there is a breathtaking circulation of commodities, but also an exchange of ideas, illusions and dreams. At the moment we're experiencing capitalism's greatest ideological offensive. It's all business: everything is bought and sold and everything has its price.

The Consequences of Neo-Liberal Politics

We women play an important role in this ever-more internationalized economy because we represent, as ever, a particularly exploitable workforce. A number of studies have revealed the existence of subcontractor chains who work for transna-

neo-liberalism The term used in Latin America and other developing regions to describe free-market policies that include reducing tariff protection for local industries; the sale of public-sector industries, like national airlines and public utilities, to private investors or foreign corporations; and the reduction of social welfare policies and public-sector employment.

arbiter of disputes and guarantor of religious legitimacy. He oversaw a parliamentary regime based on European models, but he imposed religious control over legislation and public behavior. The electoral process was not open to monarchists, communists, and other opposition groups. Shi'ite clerics with little training for government service held many of the highest posts, and stringent measures were taken to combat Western styles and culture. Universities were temporarily closed, and their faculties were purged of secularists and monarchists. Women were compelled to wear modest Islamic garments outside the house, and semiofficial vigilante committees policed public morals and cast a pall over entertainment and social life.

President Carter had criticized the shah's repressive regime, but the overthrow of a long-standing ally and the creation of the Islamic Republic were blows to American prestige. The new Iranian regime was anti-Israeli and anti-American. Seeing the United States as a "Great Satan" opposed to Islam, Khomeini fostered Islamic revolutionary movements that threatened the United States and Israel. In November 1979 Iranian radicals seized the U.S. embassy in Tehran tional companies "informally" and mainly employ women. Basically we are dealing with a kind of integration into the world market which often uses our own homes as its outlet. Obviously, this work is badly paid and completely unprotected and has to be done without any of those social rights which were formerly achieved by trade union struggles. The most important thing for us is to keep hold of just one thread of the enterprise so we can show how the commodities make their way to their final destination. As it advances worldwide, this capitalism also encourages the expansion of certain kinds of tourism. A visible increase in prostitution is part of this, whereby women from poor countries are smuggled into large, internationally operated rings which exploit them. The reports of Filipina women traded on the West German market send shivers down our spines. . . . What kind of freedom are you talking about there?

How the Adoption of Austerity Measures Affects Women's Lives

It is obvious that foreign debt is one of the most inhuman forms of exploitation in our countries when one considers the ratio between work necessary for workers' needs and work producing profit for employers. The experts have already explained how the prevailing exchange and investment structures have created international finance systems which keep whole populations in inhuman conditions. Although many people might think it crazy, the development model of the global economy has a marked relation to gender. As long as prices were slapped on some luxury consumer items there weren't any serious problems; but now the snares have been set around basic commodities. Women in every household are suffering every day as a result of impoverished economies and those who are most exposed to the effects of foreign debt are women.

When it comes to shopping, caring for sick children or the impossibility of meeting their schooling costs, the illusion of "leaving poverty behind" evaporates. Yet the problem is not only of an economic nature because under such circumstances the constant tension leads to grave, often lasting exhaustion. The psychosocial damage is alarming. The situation is ready to explode, so to speak. . . . The adoption of austerity measures means a curtailment of the state's commitment to social services with a direct effect on women. Daily life becomes hell for them. The lack of even minimal state welfare presents women (and obviously children too) with crushing working days. There is a constant expenditure of human energy without any hope of rest! No relaxation, no breaks. . . . And if we consider what happens within the family, we notice that women keep the smallest portion of the meagre family income. They give everything to their children or those adults who bring home a pay packet. As a result malnutrition among women is increasing at an alarming rate and their frequent pregnancies represent a superhuman physical achievement.

We should not ignore the fact that violence of every form . . . goes hand-in-hand with the difficult situation I have described.[1] It's nothing new for women because the open wounds of sexual violence, abuse at home and the contempt of this *machista* culture, have always featured in our lives and our mothers' lives. The challenge is to prevent these from also affecting our future generations.

QUESTIONS FOR ANALYSIS

1. **What is neo-liberalism?**
2. **According to Acosta, how does global economic integration fostered by neo-liberalism affect the lives of women as workers?**
3. **Acosta claims that indebtedness to foreign lenders leads to austerity measures. How does this impact families in poor countries?**

Source: From Gladys Acosta, "The View of a Peruvian Militant," in *Compañeras. Voices from the Latin American Women's Movement*, edited by Gaby Küppers (London: Latin American Bureau, 1994). Reprinted with permission of the publisher.

1. In the last report of the Comisaria de mujeres in Lima (the only one in the country at present) 4,800 rapes were filed for 1990, of which 4,200 went to trial. The police commissioner, in reading the document, personally acknowledged the alarming social problem which is posed by the violence of men who are connected to their victims in some way and. which, indeed, persists throughout all levels of society.

Saddam Husain President of Iraq from 1979 until overthrown by an American-led invasion in 2003. Waged war on Iran from 1980 to 1988. His invasion of Kuwait in 1990 was repulsed in the Persian Gulf War in 1991.

and held fifty-two diplomats hostage for 444 days. Americans felt humiliated by their inability to rescue the hostages or negotiate their release.

In the fall of 1980, shortly after negotiations for the release of the hostages began, **Saddam Husain** (sah-DAHM hoo-SANE), the ruler of neighboring Iraq, invaded Iran to topple the Islamic Republic. His own dictatorial rule rested on a secular, Arab-nationalist philosophy and long-standing friendship with the Soviet Union, which had provided him with advanced weaponry. He feared that the fervor of Iran's revolutionary Shi'ite leaders would infect his own country's Shi'ite majority and threaten his power. The war pitted American weapons in the hands of the Iranians against Soviet weapons in the hands of the Iraqis, but the superpowers avoided overt involvement during eight years of bloodshed. Covertly, however, the United States used Israel to transfer arms to Iran, hoping to gain the release of other American hostages held by radical Islamic groups in Lebanon and to help finance the Contra war against the Sandinista government of Nicaragua. When this deal came to light in 1986, the resulting political scandal intensified American hostility to Iran. Openly tilting toward Iraq, President Reagan sent the United States Navy to the Persian Gulf, ostensibly to protect nonbelligerent shipping. The move helped force Iran to accept a cease-fire in 1988.

Soviet Invasion of Afghanistan

While the United States dealt with Iran, the Soviet Union faced even more serious problems in neighboring Afghanistan. In 1978 a Marxist party with a secular agenda had seized power. Offended by these efforts to reform education and grant rights to women, traditional ethnic and religious leaders led a successful rebellion. The Soviet Union responded by sending its army into Afghanistan to install a communist regime. With the United States, Saudi Arabia, and Pakistan paying, equipping, and training Afghan rebels, the Soviet Union found itself in an unwinnable war like the one the United States had stumbled into in Vietnam. Facing growing economic problems and widespread domestic discontent over the war, Soviet leaders withdrew their troops in 1989. Three years later rebel groups took control of the entire country and then began to fight among themselves over who should rule.

 **PRIMARY SOURCE: Islamic Government** Learn why the future leader of Iran called for the establishment of new governments along conservative religious lines.

Asian Transformation

Although Japan has few mineral resources and is dependent on oil imports, the Japanese economy weathered the oil price shocks of the 1970s much better than did the economies of Europe and the United States. In fact, Japan experienced a faster rate of economic growth in the 1970s and 1980s than did any other major developed economy, growing at about 10 percent a year. Average income also increased rapidly, overtaking that of the United States in 1986. But during the 1990s Japan entered a decade-long crisis that slowed GDP (gross domestic product) and average income growth dramatically.

Japanese Economic Expansion and Crisis

There are some major differences between the Japanese and U.S. industrial models. During the American occupation, Japanese industrial conglomerates known as *zaibatsu* (see Chapter 28) were broken up. Although ownership of major industries became less concentrated as a result, new industrial alliances appeared. During the period of dramatic growth there were six major **keiretsu** (kay-REHT-soo), each of which included a major bank and firms in industry, commerce, and construction tied together in an interlocking ownership structure. There were also minor keiretsu dominated by a major corporation, like Toyota.

keiretsu Alliances of corporations and banks that dominate the Japanese economy.

Tariffs and import regulations inhibiting foreign competition were crucial to the early stages of development of Japan's major industries. These restrictions and Japanese success at exporting manufactured goods through the 1970s and 1980s produced huge trade surpluses with other nations. Although the United States and the European Community engaged in tough negotiations to try to force open the Japanese market, these efforts had only limited success. In 1990 Japan's trade surplus with the rest of the world was double that of 1985. Many experts assumed that Japan's competitive advantages would propel it past the United States as the world's preeminent industrial economy, but its economy entered a deep recession in the 1990s and has not yet recovered. Before the crisis, housing and stock markets had become highly overvalued because large profits from trade fueled real estate and stock market speculation. The close relationship of government, banks, and industries also contributed to speculation and corruption. As the crisis deepened and prices collapsed, the close relationships between industry, government, and banks proved to be a liability, propping up inefficient companies. By the end of the 1990s Japan's GDP had suffered a loss greater than that suffered by the United States in the Great Depression and left the nation with a crushing debt burden.

 **AP* Exam Tip** Be familiar with the economic development of Asian nations in the post–World War II era.

The Asian Tigers

Other Asian states imitated the Japanese model of development in the 1970s. These nations protected new industries from foreign competition while encouraging close alliances among industries and banks. The Republic of Korea, commonly called South Korea, was the most successful, using a combination of inexpensive labor, strong technical education, and substantial domestic capital reserves to support industrialization. It became a major global force in heavy industries such as steel and shipbuilding as well as in consumer industries such as automobiles and consumer electronics.

The small nations of Taiwan, Hong Kong, and Singapore also became industrial powerhouses. As a result of their rapid growth, these three nations and South Korea were called the **Asian Tigers**. While Taiwan suffered a number of political reverses, including the loss of its United Nations seat to the People's Republic of China in 1971 and the withdrawal of diplomatic recognition by the United States, it achieved remarkable economic progress, based in large part

Asian Tigers Collective name for South Korea, Taiwan, Hong Kong, and Singapore nations that became economic powers in the 1970s and 1980s.

on investment in the economy of the People's Republic of China. Hong Kong and Singapore—both former British colonies with extremely limited resources—also enjoyed rapid economic development. Both were historically important Asian ports and commercial centers that then developed manufacturing, banking, and commercial sectors.

newly industrialized economies (NIEs) Rapidly growing, new industrial nations of the late twentieth century, including the Asian Tigers.

These **newly industrialized economies (NIEs)** shared many characteristics that helped explain their rapid industrialization. All had disciplined and hardworking labor forces, and all invested heavily in education. For example, as early as 1980 Korea had as many engineering graduates as Germany, Britain, and Sweden combined. All had very high rates of personal saving, about 35 percent of GDP, that funded new technologies, and all emphasized outward-looking export strategies. And, like Japan, all benefited from government sponsorship and protection. Despite this momentum, the region was deeply shaken by a financial crisis that began in 1997. Like the recession that afflicted Japan, a combination of bad loans, weak banks, and the international effects of currency speculation led to a deep regional crisis that was stabilized only by the efforts of the United States, Japan, and international institutions like the International Monetary Fund.

China Rejoins the World Economy

Deng Xiaoping Communist Party leader who forced Chinese economic reforms after the death of Mao Zedong.

Tiananmen Square Site in Beijing where Chinese students and workers gathered to demand greater political openness in 1989. The demonstration was crushed by Chinese military with great loss of life.

After Mao Zedong's death in 1976, the Chinese communist leadership began economic reforms that relaxed state control, allowing more initiative and permitting individuals to accumulate wealth. The results were remarkable. Under China's leader **Deng Xiaoping** (dung shee-yao-ping) China permitted foreign investment for the first time since the communists came to power in 1949. Between 1979 and 2005 foreign direct investment in China grew to $618 billion as McDonald's, General Motors, Coca-Cola, Airbus, and many other foreign companies began doing business. As a result, China became a major industrial exporter and the world's sixth most important trading nation. Despite these changes, state-owned enterprises still employed more than 100 million workers, and most foreign-owned companies were limited to special economic zones. The result was a dual industrial sector—one modern, efficient, and connected to international markets, the other directed by political decisions. While the Chinese did not privatize land, they did permit farmers to sell what they produced. By 1984, 93 percent of China's agricultural land was in effect in private hands.

By 2009 China had become the world's third largest economy, passing Germany, but, despite great improvements, the Chinese people remained poor on average. Although per capita GDP in China reached $2,360 in 2009, it remained lower than that of Mexico. The combination of economic reforms, massive investments, and technology transfers from developed nations made China one of the world's major industrial powers in the early twenty-first century. The worldwide economic crisis that began in 2008 has affected Japan more powerfully than China. As a result, China is now poised to become the word's second largest economy.

Deng Xiaoping's strategy of balancing change and continuity avoided some of the social and political costs experienced by Russia and other socialist countries that abruptly embraced capitalism and democracy, but he faced a major challenge in 1989. Responding to inflation and to worldwide mass movements in favor of democracy, Chinese students and intellectuals led a series of protests demanding more democracy and an end to corruption. This movement culminated in **Tiananmen** (tee-yehn-ahn-men) **Square**, in the heart of Beijing, where hundreds of thousands of protesters gathered and refused to leave. After weeks of standoff, tanks pushed into the square, killing hundreds and arresting thousands.

SECTION REVIEW

- During the 1970s and 1980s, political violence grew in Latin America, sponsored in part by U.S. fears of communist subversion.
- The United States opposed revolutionary movements in Nicaragua and El Salvador.
- In the 1990s the United States pushed Latin American nations to introduce neo-liberal reforms that opened economies to greater foreign investment.
- A radical anti-American Islamic revolution led by Ayatollah Khomeini triumphed in Iran in 1979, and led to a ten-year war with Iraq.
- The Soviets intervened in Afghanistan in 1979 but failed to defeat local opponents backed by the United States and Pakistan.
- After three decades of rapid economic growth, Japan entered a deep recession in the 1990s.
- The four Asian Tigers experienced rapid economic growth as did China after Deng Xiaoping reformed and modernized its economy.

THE END OF THE BIPOLAR WORLD

After the end of World War II, competition between the alliances led by the United States and the Soviet Union created a bipolar world. Every conflict, no matter how local its origins, had the potential of engaging the attention of one or both of the superpowers. The Korean War, decolonization in Africa, the Vietnam War, the Cuban Revolution, and hostilities between Israel and its neighbors increased tension between the nuclear-armed superpowers. Given this succession of provocations, politics everywhere was dominated by arguments over the relative merits of the competing systems.

Few in 1980 predicted the startling collapse of the Soviet Union. Western observers tended to see communist nations as both more uniform in character and more subservient to the Soviet Union than was true. Long before the 1980s, deep divisions had appeared among communist states. Among the once-independent nations and ethnic groups brought within the Soviet Union, nationalism reappeared in the late 1980s and overwhelmed communism.

Crisis in the Soviet Union

PRIMARY SOURCE: The Last Heir of Lenin Explains His Reform Plans: Perestroika and Glasnost Read President Gorbachev's analysis of the Soviet Union's decline and his prescriptions for reform.

Mikhail Gorbachev Head of the Soviet Union from 1985 to 1991. His liberalization effort improved relations with the West, but he lost power after his reforms led to the collapse of communist governments in eastern Europe.

perestroika Policy of "restructuring" that was the centerpiece of Mikhail Gorbachev's efforts to liberalize communism in the Soviet Union.

Under U.S. president Ronald Reagan and the Soviet Union's general secretary Leonid Brezhnev (leh-oh-NEED BREZ-nef), Cold War rhetoric remained intense. Massive new U.S. investments in armaments placed heavy burdens on a Soviet economy already suffering from shortages that had become a part of Soviet life. Obsolete industrial plants and centralized planning that stifled initiative led to a declining standard of living relative to the West, while the arbitrariness of the bureaucracy, the manipulation of information, and deprivations created a crisis in morale.

Despite the unpopularity of the war in Afghanistan and growing discontent, Brezhnev refused to modify his unsuccessful policies, but he could not escape criticism. Self-published underground writings (*samizdat* [sah-meez-DAHT]) by critics of the regime circulated widely despite government efforts to suppress them. In a series of powerful books, the writer Alexander Solzhenitzyn (sol-zhuh-NEET-sin) castigated the Soviet system. Although he won a Nobel Prize in literature, authorities charged him with treason and expelled him in 1974.

By the time **Mikhail Gorbachev** (GORE-beh-CHOF) came to power in 1985, weariness with war in Afghanistan, economic decay, and vocal protest had reached critical levels. Casting aside Brezhnev's hard line, Gorbachev authorized major reforms in an attempt to stave off total collapse. His policy of political openness (*glasnost*) permitted criticism of the government and the Communist Party. His policy of **perestroika** (per-ih-STROY-kuh) ("restructuring") was an attempt to address long-suppressed economic problems by moving away from central state planning. In 1989 he ended the unpopular war in Afghanistan.

The Collapse of the Socialist Bloc

Solidarity Polish trade union created in 1980 to protest working conditions and political repression. It began the nationalist opposition to communist rule that led in 1989 to the fall of communism in eastern Europe.

In 1980 protests by Polish shipyard workers in the city of Gdansk led to the formation of **Solidarity**, a labor union that grew to 9 million members. The Roman Catholic Church in Poland, strengthened by the elevation of a Pole, Karol Wojtyla (KAH-rol voy-TIL-ah), to the papacy as John Paul II in 1978, gave strong moral support to the protest movement.

The Polish government imposed martial law in 1981 in response to the growing power of Solidarity and its allies, giving the army effective political control. Seeing Solidarity under tight controls and many of its leaders in prison, the Soviet Union decided not to intervene. But Solidarity remained a potent force with a strong institutional structure and nationally recognized leaders. As Gorbachev loosened political controls in the Soviet Union after 1985, communist leaders elsewhere lost confidence in Soviet resolve, and critics and reformers in Poland and throughout eastern Europe were emboldened.

Communism Overthrown in Eastern Europe

Beleaguered Warsaw Pact governments vacillated between relaxation of control and suppression of dissent. Just as the Catholic clergy in Poland had supported Solidarity, Protestant and Orthodox religious leaders aided the rise of opposition groups elsewhere. This combination of nationalism and religion provided a powerful base for opponents of the communist regimes. Communist governments sought to quiet the opposition by turning to the West for trade and financial assistance. They also opened their nations to travelers, ideas, styles, and money from Western countries, all of which accelerated the demand for change.

The Fall of the Berlin Wall The Berlin Wall was the most important symbol of the Cold War. Constructed to keep residents of East Germany from fleeing to the West and defended by armed guards and barbed wire, it was the public face of communism. As the Soviet system fell apart, the residents of East and West Berlin broke down sections of the wall.

Bossu Regis/Corbis Sygma

By the end of 1989 communist governments across eastern Europe had fallen. The dismantling of the Berlin Wall vividly represented this transformation. While communist leaders in Poland, Hungary, Czechoslovakia, and Bulgaria decided that change was inevitable, the dictator Nicolae Ceausescu (nehk-oh-LIE chow-SHES-koo) of Romania refused to surrender power and was overthrown and executed. The comprehensiveness of these changes became clear in 1990, when the Polish people elected Solidarity leader Lech Walesa (leck wah-LEN-sah) as president and the people of Czechoslovakia elected dissident playwright Vaclav Havel (vah-SLAV hah-VEL) as president.

Following the fall of the Berlin Wall, a tidal wave of patriotic enthusiasm swept aside the once-formidable communist government of East Germany. In the chaotic months that followed, East Germans crossed to West Germany in large numbers, and government services in the eastern sector nearly disappeared. The collapse of the East German government led quickly in 1990 to reunification.

The End of the Soviet Union

Soviet leaders knew that similarly powerful nationalist sentiments existed within the Soviet Union as well. The year 1990 brought declarations of independence by Lithuania, Estonia, and Latvia, three small states on the Baltic Sea that the Soviet Union had annexed in 1939. The end of the Soviet Union then came suddenly in 1991 (see Map 32.1). After communist hardliners botched a coup against Gorbachev, disgust with communism boiled over. Boris Yeltsin, the president of the Russian Republic, emerged as the most powerful leader in the country. Russia, the largest republic in the Soviet Union, was effectively taking the place of the disintegrating USSR. In September 1991 the Congress of People's Deputies—the central legislature of the USSR—voted to dissolve the union. In December a weak successor state with little central control, the Commonwealth of Independent States (CIS), was created and Gorbachev resigned.

The End of Yugoslavia

ethnic cleansing Effort to eradicate a people and its culture by means of mass killing and the destruction of historical buildings and cultural materials. Ethnic cleansing was used by both sides in the conflicts that accompanied the disintegration of Yugoslavia in the 1990s.

The ethnic and religious passions that fueled the breakup of the Soviet Union overwhelmed the Balkan nation of Yugoslavia. In 1991 it dissolved into a morass of separatism and warring ethnic and religious groups. Slovenia and Croatia, the most westerly provinces, both heavily Roman Catholic, became independent states in 1992. The population of Bosnia and Herzegovina was more mixed: 40 percent were Muslims, 30 percent Serbian Orthodox, and 18 percent Catholics. Following the declaration of Bosnian national independence in 1992, the Orthodox Serbs attempted to rid the state of Muslims in a process called **ethnic cleansing**. After extensive television coverage of atrocities and wanton destruction, the United States intervened and eventually brokered a settlement in 1995.

In 1999 new fighting and a new round of ethnic cleansing occurred in the southernmost Yugoslavian province of Kosovo. Seen by Serbs as their homeland, Kosovo had a predominantly Muslim and Albanian population. When Serbia refused to stop military action, the United

States, Britain, and France acted on behalf of NATO by launching an aerial war that forced the withdrawal of Serbian forces from Kosovo.

Progress and Conflict in Africa

Sub-Saharan Africa has experienced political instability, military coups, civil wars, and conflicts over resources since independence. It has also remained among the poorest regions in the world. Southern Africa, however, has seen democratic progress and a steady decline in armed conflicts since 1991. A key change came in South Africa in 1994, when long-time political prisoner Nelson Mandela and his African National Congress (ANC) won the first national elections in which the African majority could participate equally. Also hopeful has been the return to democracy of Nigeria, Africa's most populous state, after decades of military rulers. In 1999, after a succession of military governments, Nigerians elected President Olusegun Obasanjo (oh-LOO-she-gun oh-BAH-san-jo) (a former coup leader), and a 2003 vote renewed his term, despite serious voting irregularities. Similarly, in 2002 Kenyans voted out the party that had held power for thirty-nine years.

Genocide in Rwanda

Africa was also a scene of ethnic cleansing. In 1994 the political leaders of the Central African nation of Rwanda incited Hutu people to massacre their Tutsi neighbors. Since the major powers had promised to intervene in genocides, they avoided using the word *genocide* to describe the slaughter. Without foreign intervention, the carnage claimed 750,000 lives with millions more refugees. Finally, the United States and other powers intervened and the United Nations set up a tribunal to try those responsible for the genocide. In 1998 violence spread from Rwanda to neighboring Congo, where growing opposition and ill health had forced President Joseph Mobutu from office after over three decades of dictatorial misrule. Various peacemaking attempts failed to restore order and by mid-2003 more than 3 million Congolese had died from disease, malnutrition, and injuries related to the fighting.

The Persian Gulf War

The Persian Gulf War was the first significant conflict to occur after the breakup of the Soviet Union and the end of the Cold War. Iraq's ruler, Saddam Husain, had borrowed a great deal of money from neighboring Kuwait and failed to get Kuwait's royal family to reduce this debt. He was also eager to control Kuwait's oil fields. Husain believed that the smaller and militarily weaker nation could be quickly defeated, and he suspected that the United States would not react. The invasion occurred in August 1990.

The United States decided to react. Saudi Arabia, an important ally of the United States and a major oil producer, also supported intervention. With his intention to use force endorsed by the United Nations and with many Islamic nations supporting military action, President George H. W. Bush ordered an attack in early 1991. Iraq's military defeat was comprehensive, but Husain remained in power, crushing an uprising just months following his defeat. The United States imposed various conditions on Iraq that kept tensions high, helping create the conditions for a new war in 2003.

SECTION REVIEW

- The Cold War ended when growing unrest and criticism led to the collapse of the Soviet Union and allied socialist nations. Mikhail Gorbachev's reform policies accelerated this process.
- The rise of ethnic nationalism led to war and genocide in Yugoslavia.
- South Africa, Nigeria, and Kenya escaped from oppressive conditions, but hundreds of thousands lost their lives in ethnic violence in Rwanda and Congo.
- After Saddam Husain invaded Kuwait, the United States and its allies defeated Iraq in the first Gulf War of 1990.

THE CHALLENGE OF POPULATION GROWTH

For most of human history governments viewed population growth as beneficial, a source of national wealth and power. Since the late eighteenth century, however, growing numbers of experts and politicians have viewed population increases with alarm, fearing that food supplies could not keep up with population growth. Late in the nineteenth century some social critics expressed concern that growing populations would lead to class and ethnic struggle. By

MAP 32.1 The End of the Soviet Union When communist hardliners failed to overthrow Gorbachev in 1991, popular anti-communist sentiment swept the Soviet Union. Following Boris Yeltsin's lead in Russia, the republics that constituted the Soviet Union declared their independence.

Interactive Map

the second half of the twentieth century, fears of population growth were primarily attached to environmental concerns. Are urban sprawl, pollution, and soil erosion the inevitable results of population growth? The questions and debates continue today, but clearly population growth is both a cause and a result of increased global interdependency.

Demographic Transition

AP* Exam Tip It is important to understand demographic shifts in all regions of the world.

The population of Europe almost doubled between 1850 and 1914, putting enormous pressure on rural land and urban housing and overwhelming fragile public institutions that provided crisis assistance (see Chapter 26). This dramatic growth forced a large wave of immigration across the Atlantic, helping to develop the Western Hemisphere and invigorating the Atlantic economy (see Chapter 23). Population growth also contributed to Europe's Industrial Revolution by lowering labor costs and increasing consumer demand.

Thomas Malthus

Thomas Malthus Eighteenth-century English intellectual who warned that population growth threatened future generations because, in his view, population growth would always outstrip increases in agricultural production.

While some Europeans of the nineteenth century saw the rapid increase in human population as a blessing, others warned of disaster. The best-known pessimist was the English cleric **Thomas Malthus**, who in 1798 argued that unchecked population growth would outstrip food production. When Malthus looked at Europe's future, he used a prejudiced image of China to terrify his readers. A visitor to China, he claimed, "will not be surprised that mothers destroy or expose many of their children; that parents sell their daughters for a trifle; . . . and that there should be such a number of robbers. The surprise is that nothing still more dreadful should happen."[1]

The generation that came of age in the years after World War II lived in a world where Malthus seemed to have little relevance. Industrial and agricultural productivity had multiplied supplies of food and other necessities. At the same time, cultural changes associated with expanded female employment, older age at marriage, and more effective family planning had slowed the rate of population increase. By the 1960s Europe and other industrial societies had

Chinese Family-Planning Campaign To slow population growth, the Chinese government have sought to limit parents to a single child. Billboards and other forms of mass advertising have been an essential part of the campaign.

Picard/Sipa Press

made the **demographic transition** to lower fertility rates (average number of births per woman) and reduced mortality. In fact, the number of births in developed nations was barely adequate to maintain population levels.

demographic transition A change in the rates of population growth. Before the transition, both birthrates and death rates are high, resulting in a slowly growing population; then the death rate drops but the birthrate remains high, causing a population explosion; finally the birthrate drops and the population growth slows down.

The Politics of Population

By the late 1970s, the Third World had still not made the demographic transition and population growth became politicized. Leaders in some developing nations actively promoted large families, arguing that larger populations increased national power. When industrialized nations, mostly white, raised concerns about rapid population growth in Asia, Africa, and Latin America, populist political leaders in these regions responded by asking whether these concerns were racist.

This question exposed the influence of racism in the population debate and temporarily disarmed Western advocates of birth control. However, once the economic shocks of the 1970s and 1980s revealed the vulnerability of poor nations, governments in the developing world jettisoned policies that promoted population growth. Mexico is a good example. In the 1970s the government had encouraged high fertility, and population grew by 3 percent per year. In the 1980s Mexico rejected these policies and began to promote birth control, leading by the 1990s to an annual population growth of 1.7.

Rhythms of World Population Change

World population exploded in the twentieth century, more than doubling between 1950 and 1995 (see Table 32.1). Although the rate of growth has slowed since the 1980s, world population still increases by a number equal to the total population of the United States every three years. If fertility were to remain constant from today, with a world average of 2.5 children per woman, world population would reach nearly 30 billion in 2150, more than three times the 2050 projection found in Table 32.1. This is not likely because fertility is declining in many developing nations. As a result, most experts estimate a world population in 2150 of less than 10 billion.

Mortality rates have also increased in some areas as immigration, commercial expansion, and improved transportation have facilitated the transmission of disease. The rapid spread of HIV/AIDS is an example of this phenomenon. Less developed regions with poorly funded public health institutions and with few resources to invest in prevention and treatment experience the highest rates of infection and the greatest mortality. In Russia, for example, new HIV infections rose from under five thousand in 1997 to over ninety thousand in 2001. AIDS has spread most quickly and with the most devastating results in Africa, the home of 28 million of the world's 40 million infected people.

The Industrialized Nations

In the developed industrial nations of western Europe and in Japan, fertility levels are so low that population would fall without immigration. Japanese women have an average of 1.4 chil-

TABLE 32.1 Population for World and Major Areas, 1750–2050

Population Size (Millions) Major Area	1750	1800	1850	1900	1950	1995	2050*
World	791	978	1,262	1,650	2,521	5,666	8,909
Africa	106	107	111	133	221	697	1,766
Asia	502	635	809	947	1,402	3,437	5,268
Europe	163	203	276	408	547	728	628
Latin America and the Caribbean	16	24	38	74	167	480	809
North America	2	7	26	82	172	297	398
Oceania	2	2	2	6	13	28	46
***Percentage Distribution* Major Area**	**1750**	**1800**	**1850**	**1900**	**1950**	**1995**	**2050***
World	100	100	100	100	100	100	100
Africa	13.4	10.9	8.8	8.1	8.8	12	23.7
Asia	63.5	64.9	64.1	57.4	55.6	61	57.1
Europe	20.6	20.8	21.9	24.7	21.7	13	5.3
Latin America and the Caribbean	2.0	2.5	3.0	4.5	6.6	8	9.4
North America	0.3	0.7	2.1	5.0	6.8	5	4.1
Oceania	0.3	0.2	0.2	0.4	0.5	1	0.5

* Estimated

Source: J. D. Durand, "Historical Estimates of World Population: An Evaluation" (Philadelphia: University of Pennsylvania, Population Studies Center, 1974, mimeographed); United Nations, *The Determinants and Consequences of Population Trends*, vol. 1 (New York: United Nations, 1973); United Nations, *World Population Prospects as Assessed in 1963* (New York: United Nations, 1966); United Nations, *World Population Prospects: The 1998 Revision* (New York: United Nations, forthcoming); United Nations Population Division, Department of Economic and Social Affairs, http://www.un.org/esa/population/publications/WPP2004/ 2004Highlights-finalrevised.pdf. The medium fertility estimate is used for the 2050 population projection.

dren and Italian women 1.2. Although Sweden tries to promote fertility with cash payments, tax incentives, and job leaves to families with children, the average number of births per woman is 1.4. By comparison, the average African woman has 5.1 children. Higher levels of female education and employment, the material values of consumer culture, and access to contraception and abortion explain the low fertility of mature industrial nations. An Italian woman in Bologna, the city with the lowest fertility in the world, put it this way: "I'm an only child and if I could, I'd have more than one child. But most couples I know wait until their 30's to have children. People want to have their own life, they want to have a successful career. When you see life in these terms, children are an impediment."[2]

The Aging Population of the Industrial World

In industrialized nations life expectancy improved as fertility declined. The combination of abundant food, improved hygiene, and more effective medicines and medical care has lengthened human lives. In 2000 about 20 percent of the population in developed nations was sixty-five or over. By 2050 this proportion should rise to one-third. Italy soon will have more than twenty adults fifty years old or over for each five-year-old child. Because of higher fertility and greater levels of immigration, the United States is moving in this direction more slowly than western Europe; by 2050 the median age in Europe will be fifty-two, while it will be thirty-five in the United States.

The combination of falling fertility and rising life expectancy in the industrialized nations presents a challenge very different from the one foreseen by Malthus. These nations generally offer a broad array of social services, including retirement income, medical services, and housing supplements for the elderly. As the number of retirees increases relative to the number of employed people, costs may become unsustainable. Economists track this problem by using the PSR (potential support ratio): the ratio of persons fifteen to sixty-four years old (likely workers) to persons sixty-five or older (likely retirees). Between 1950 and 2000 the world's PSR fell from twelve to nine. By 2050 it will fall to four.

In Russia and other former socialist nations, current birthrates are now actually lower than death rates. Birthrates were already low before the collapse of the socialist system and have contracted further with recent economic problems. Since 1975 fertility rates have fallen between 20 and 40 percent across the former Soviet bloc, and by the early 1980s abortions were as common as births in much of eastern Europe. Life expectancy has also fallen. Life expectancy for Russian men is now only fifty-seven years, down almost ten years since 1980. Much of the rest of eastern Europe has also experienced declining life expectancy caused by high unemployment, low incomes, food shortages, and the dismantling of the social welfare system of the communist era.

The Developing Nations

At current rates, 95 percent of all future population growth will be in developing nations (see Map 32.2 and Table 32.1). A comparison between Europe and Africa illustrates these changes. In 1950 Europe had twice the population of Africa. By 1985 Africa's population had drawn even with Europe, and, according to projections, its population will be three times larger than Europe's by 2050.

As the 1990s ended, other developing regions had rapid population growth as well. While all developing nations had an average birthrate of 33.6 per thousand inhabitants, Muslim countries had a rate of 42.1. This rate is more than 300 percent higher than the 13.1 births per thousand in the developed nations of the West. The populations of Latin America and Asia were also expanding, but at rates slower than sub-Saharan Africa and the Muslim nations. Latin America's population increased from 165 million in 1950 to 511 million in 1999 and is projected to reach 809 million in 2050, despite declining birthrates.

Despite efforts to reduce family size, the populations of India and China continue to grow. Today these two nations account for roughly one-third of the world's population. In China efforts to enforce a limit of one child per family led initially to female infanticide as rural families sought to produce male heirs. This is no longer the case. India's policies of forced sterilization created widespread outrage and led to the electoral defeat of the ruling Congress Party. Yet both countries achieved some successes. Between 1960 and 1982 India's birthrate fell from 48 to 34 per thousand, while China's rate declined even more sharply—from 39 to 19 per thousand. Still, by 2025 both China and India will each likely reach 1.5 billion.

Old and Young Populations

Population pyramids generated by demographers clearly illustrate the profound transformation in human reproductive patterns and life expectancy since World War II. Figure 32.1 shows

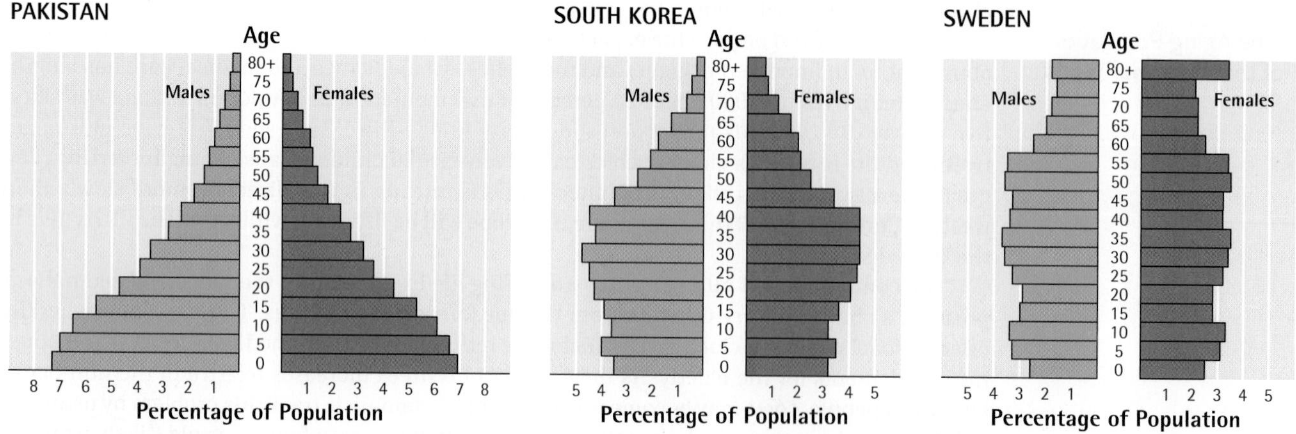

FIGURE 32.1 **Age Structure Comparison** Islamic Nation (Pakistan), Non-Islamic Developing Nation (South Korea), and Developed Nation (Sweden), 2001. *Source:* U.S. Bureau of the Census, *International Database*, 2001.

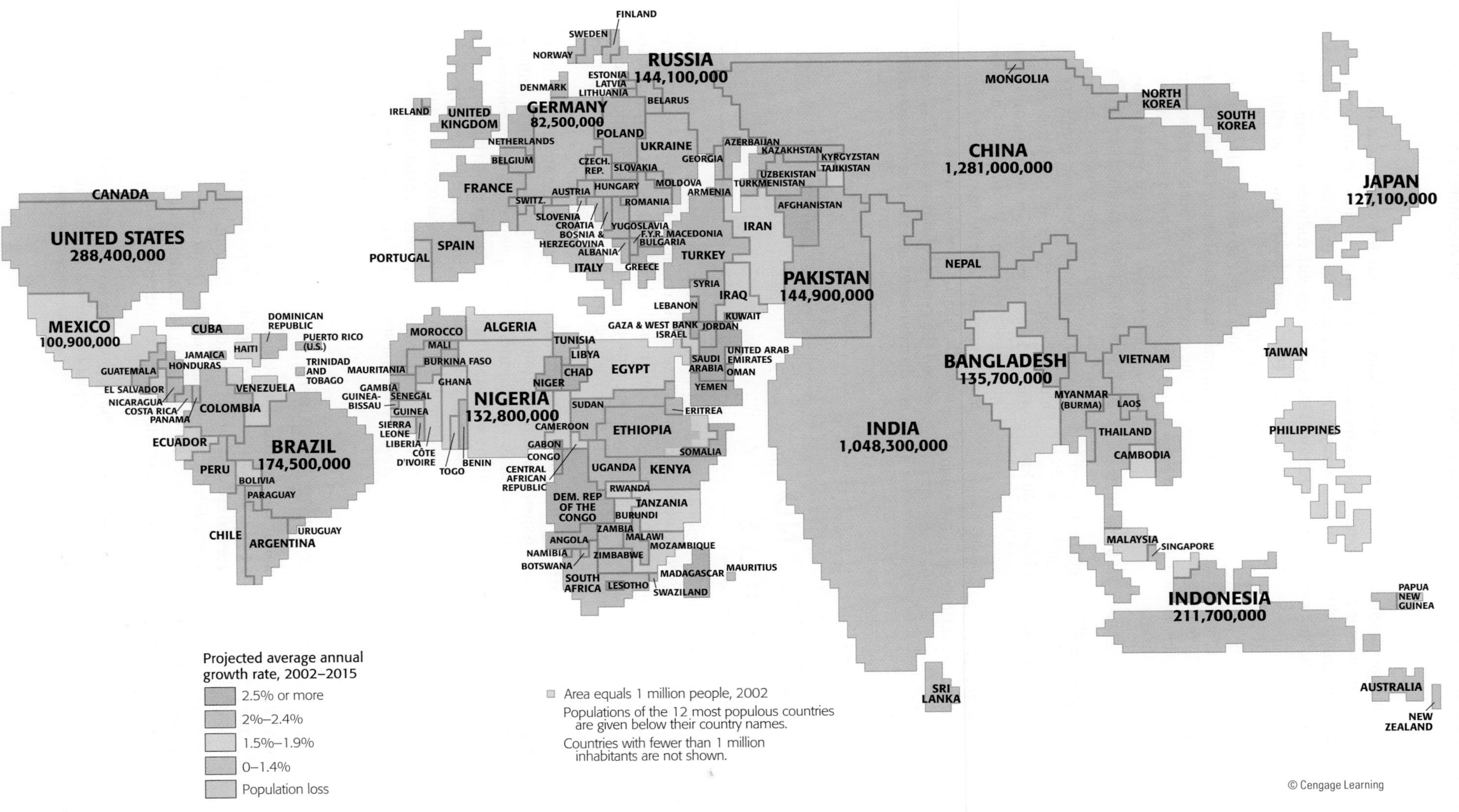

MAP 32.2 **World Population Growth** Every three years the world's population increases by the equivalent of a nation the size of the United States. Most of this population increase will be in some of the world's poorest nations. By 2050, for example, Pakistan, a nation of only 40 million in 1950, will have the world's third largest population. *Source:* Data from www.worldbank.org.

Interactive Map

the 2001 age distributions in Pakistan, South Korea, and Sweden—nations at three different stages of economic development. Sweden is a mature industrial nation. South Korea is rapidly industrializing and has surpassed many European nations in both industrial output and per capita wealth. Pakistan is a poor, traditional Muslim nation with rudimentary industrialization, low educational levels, and little effective family planning.

In 2001 nearly 50 percent of Pakistan's population was under age sixteen. The resulting pressures on the economy have been extraordinary. Every year approximately 150,000 men reach age sixty-five—and another 1.2 million turn sixteen. Pakistan, therefore, has to create more than a million new jobs a year or face growing unemployment and declining wages. Sweden confronts a different problem. Sweden's aging population, growing demand for social welfare benefits, and declining labor pool means that its industries may become less competitive and living standards may decline. In South Korea, a decline in fertility dramatically altered the ratio of children to adults, creating an age distribution similar to that of western Europe.

SECTION REVIEW

- In the twentieth century the developed nations made the demographic transition to low birthrates, while the developing nations began by stressing higher birthrates.
- World population more than doubled between 1950 and 1995.
- In rich nations birth rates fell but longer life expectancy led to slow population growth; in the former Soviet Union the combination of low birth rates and declining life expectancy led to contracting population.
- Developing nations will contribute most of the world's future population growth, despite birth control efforts as in India and China.

UNEQUAL DEVELOPMENT AND THE MOVEMENT OF PEOPLES

The Economics of World Population Flows

Two characteristics of the postwar world should now be clear. First, despite decades of experimentation with state-directed economic development, most nations that were poor in 1960 were still poor in 2000. The only exceptions were a few rapidly developing Asian industrial nations and an equally small number of oil-exporting nations. Second, world population increased to startlingly high levels, and most of the increase was, and will continue to be, in the poorest nations.

The combination of intractable poverty and growing population generated a surge in international immigration. Few issues stirred more controversy. Even moderate voices sometimes framed the discussion of immigration as a competition among peoples. Large numbers of legal and illegal immigrants from poor nations with growing populations are entering the developed industrial nations, with the exception of Japan. Large-scale migrations within developing countries are a related phenomenon. The movement of impoverished rural residents to the cities of Asia, Africa, and Latin America (see Map 32.2 and Table 32.2) has increased steadily since the 1970s. This internal migration often serves as the first step toward migration abroad.

The Problem of Growing Inequality

Since 1945 the global economy has expanded more rapidly than at any time in the past. Faster, cheaper communications and transportation have combined with improvements in industrial and agricultural technologies to create material abundance that would have amazed those who experienced the first Industrial Revolution (see Chapter 22). Despite this remarkable economic expansion, the industrialized nations of the Northern Hemisphere enjoy an even larger share of the world's wealth than they did a century ago, accounting for a startling 74 percent of the world's economy in 1998.

Rich and Poor Nations

The gap between rich and poor nations has grown much wider since 1945. In 2001 Luxembourg and Switzerland had the highest per capita GNI (gross national income)—$39,840 and

TABLE 32.2 The World's Largest Cities (Population of 10 Million or More)

City	1950	City	1975	City	2000	City	2015
1 New York	12.3	1 Tokyo	19.8	1 Tokyo	26.4	1 Tokyo	35.5
		2 New York	15.9	2 Mexico City	18.1	2 Mumbai	21.9
		3 Shanghai	11.4	3 Bombay	18.1	3 Mexico City	21.6
		4 Mexico City	11.2	4 São Paulo	17.8	4 São Paulo	20.5
		5 São Paulo2	10.0	5 New York	16.6	5 New York	19.9
				6 Lagos	13.4	6 Delhi	18.6
				7 Los Angeles	13.1	7 Shanghai	17.2
				8 Calcutta	12.9	8 Calcutta (Kolkata)	17.0
				9 Shanghai	12.9	9 Dhaka	16.8
				10 Buenos Aires	12.6	10 Jakarta	16.8
				11 Dhaka	12.3	11 Lagos	16.1
				12 Karachi	11.8	12 Karachi	15.2
				13 Delhi	11.7	13 Buenos Aires	13.4
				14 Jakarta	11.0	14 Cairo	13.1
				15 Osaka	11.0	15 Los Angeles	13.1
				16 Metro Manila	10.9	16 Manila	12.9
				17 Beijing	10.8	17 Beijing	12.8
				18 Rio de Janeiro	10.6	18 Rio de Janeiro	12.7
				19 Cairo	10.6	19 Osaka-Kobe	11.3
						20 Istanbul	11.2
						21 Moscow	11.0

Source: From the International Migration Report 2002, United Nations, Department of Economic and Social Affairs, Population Division. © United Nations, 2003; the 2015 projection is from United Nations World Urbanization Prospects: The 2007 Revision. © United Nations, 2008. Reproduced with permission.

$35,630, respectively; the U.S. figure was $34,280; and Greece, the poorest nation in the European Union, had a per capita GNI of $11,430. The nations of the former Soviet Union and eastern Europe had per capita GNIs lower than some developing nations in the Third World. Russia's per capita GNI was $1,750 in 2001, less than Mexico's $5,530 or South Africa's $2,820, but higher than the Philippines' $1,030. Among other developing economies, Nigeria, India, and China had GNIs below $1,000.

Even in the industrialized world, there are haves and have-nots. Wealth inequality in the United States is now as great as on the eve of the 1929 stock market crash. Scholars estimate that the wealthiest 1 percent of households in the United States now control more than 30 percent of the nation's total wealth, while the poorest households have average incomes of under $5,000. Even in Europe, where tax and inheritance laws redistributed wealth, unemployment, homelessness, and substandard housing have become increasingly common.

Internal Migration: The Growth of Cities

In developing nations migration from rural areas to urban centers increased threefold between 1925 and 1950; the pace of migration then accelerated (see Table 32.2). While slums around the major cities of developing nations are seen as signs of social breakdown and economic failure, life in these urban slums was generally better than life in the countryside. A World Bank study

Geoff Tompkinson/Aspect Picture Library Ltd.

Garbage Dump in Manila, Philippines In Third World nations thousands of poor families live by sorting and selling bottles, aluminum cans, plastic, and newspapers in urban landfills.

estimated that three out of four migrants to cities made economic gains. Residents of cities in sub-Saharan Africa, for example, were six times more likely than rural residents to have safe water. An unskilled migrant from the depressed northeast of Brazil could triple his or her income by moving to Rio de Janeiro.

As the scale of rural-to-urban migration grew, these benefits became more elusive. In the cities of the developing world basic services have been crumbling under the pressure of rapid population growth. In cities like Mexico City and Manila, which are among the world's largest cities, tens of thousands live in garbage dumps, scavenging for food. In Rio de Janeiro alone an estimated 350,000 abandoned children live in the streets and parks, begging, selling drugs, stealing, and engaging in prostitution to survive. Some nations have tried to relocate migrants back to the countryside. Indonesia, for example, has relocated more than a half-million urban residents since 1969.

Global Migration

Each year hundreds of thousands of men and women leave developing nations to go to industrialized nations. Dramatically rising numbers after 1960 led to increased ethnic and racial tensions. Political refugees and immigrants faced murderous violence in Germany; growing anti-immigrant sentiment strengthened right-wing political movements and led to riots in cities with large immigrant populations in France; and in the United States the government expanded its effort to control its southern border.

The Politics of Immigration

Immigrants from developing nations brought host nations many of the same benefits that the great migration of Europeans to the Americas provided a century earlier (see Chapter 23). The United States actively recruited Mexican workers during World War II and many European nations promoted guest worker programs and other inducements to immigration in the 1960s, when an expanding European economy experienced labor shortages. However, attitudes toward immigrants have changed as the size of immigrant populations grew, particularly during periods of economic contraction. Under pressure, native-born workers saw immigrants as competitors willing to work for lower wages and less likely to support labor unions. They demanded an end to immigration as a result.

High fertility among immigrants contributes to these tensions. Most immigrants are young adults who retain the positive attitudes toward early marriage and large families of their native cultures and have higher fertility rates than do host populations. In Germany in 1975, for example, immigrants made up only 7 percent of the population but accounted for nearly 15 percent of all births. Therefore, even without additional immigration, immigrant groups grow faster than longer-established populations. As immigrant populations increase in Europe and the United States in the twenty-first century, the resulting cultural conflicts will test definitions of citizenship and nationality.

SECTION REVIEW

- As the world economy expanded after World War II, the gap between rich and poor nations grew.
- In the fast-growing nations of the developing world urban populations have grown as a result of rural to urban migration.
- Most of the world's migration is the movement of young men and women from poor nations to rich nations.

TECHNOLOGICAL AND ENVIRONMENTAL CHANGE

AP* Exam Tip It is important to understand the impact of inventions and technology on all parts of the world.

Technological innovation powered the economic expansion that began after World War II. New technologies increased productivity and disseminated human creativity. They also altered the way people lived, worked, and played. Because most of the economic benefits were concentrated in the advanced industrialized nations, technology increased the power of those nations relative to the developing world. Even within developed nations, postwar technological innovations did not benefit all classes, industries, and regions equally. There were losers as well as winners.

Population growth and increased levels of migration and urbanization multiplied the numbers of acres farmed and factories, intensifying environmental threats. At the end of the twentieth century loss of rain forest, soil erosion, global warming, air and water pollution, and extinction of species threatened the quality of life and the survival of human societies. Environmental protection, like the acquisition of new technology, had progressed most in societies with the greatest economic resources.

New Technologies and the World Economy

Nuclear energy, jet engines, radar, and tape recording were among the many World War II developments that later had an impact on consumers' lives. New technology increased industrial productivity, reduced labor requirements, and improved the flow of information that made markets more efficient. The consumer electronics industry rapidly developed new products, changes seen in the music industry's movement from vinyl records to 8-track tapes, CDs, and then MP3 technologies.

Technology and Economic Growth

Improvements in existing technologies accounted for much of the developed world's productivity increases during the 1950s and 1960s, as faster, more efficient transportation and communication cut costs and expanded markets. But new technologies were important as well. Governments bore much of the cost of developing and constructing nuclear power plants and sponsored research into new technologies. None has proved more influential in the last three decades than the computer, which transformed both work and leisure (see Environment and Technology: The Computer Gets Personal). The first computers were expensive, large, and slow and only corporations, governments, and universities could afford them. Each new generation of computer was smaller, faster and less expensive. As a result, the serial utilization of desktops, laptops, and now hand-held devices transformed commerce, education, and government.

Computers also altered manufacturing. Small dedicated computers now control and monitor machinery in most industries. In the developed world factories forced by competition to

ENVIRONMENT + TECHNOLOGY

The Computer Gets Personal

The period since World War II witnessed wave after wave of technological innovations. None has had greater impact on the way people work, learn, and live than the computer. Until the 1970s most computing was done on large and expensive mainframe computers. These massive computers were primarily used for data storage and analysis, and the government agencies, universities, and large corporations that owned them controlled access.

Today most computers are in private hands, and most are devoted to communication and information searches, a transformation symbolized when the market value of the search engine Google surpassed that of IBM, developer of mainframe and PC computing. Few had anticipated the technological innovations that revolutionized the computer industry through miniaturization during the last three decades. The key development leading to smaller and cheaper computers was the microprocessor, a silicon chip that contained the computer's brains.

Initially developed to facilitate American defense research in the 1960s, the Internet was the second key to the communication revolution. It allowed smaller, faster computers and related devices to become research portals that could access a vast international database of research, opinion, entertainment, and commerce. Small personal computers and the Web have had a revolutionary impact on modern culture, allowing individuals and groups—without the support of governments, corporations, or other powerful institutions—to collect and disseminate information more freely than at any time in the past (see Chapter 33).

In the last decade new technologies have permitted the integration of previously distinct devices. As a result, software and hardware providers now routinely blend the functions and uses of small laptop computers, cellular phones, and MP3 players to provide new business and professional applications and entertainment. Hand-held "convergence devices" evolving from the cellular telephone allow users to make phone calls, send e-mail, search the Internet, store and play music and videos, and store electronic texts. One result of this technological revolution is the appearance of plugged-in, self-identifying communities in venues like blogs, Facebook, and chat rooms that transcend or supplement older forms of community based on ethnic, regional, or economic identities.

Anthony West/Corbis

James Leynse/Corbis

From Mainframe to Laptops and PDAs During the last forty years the computer revolution has changed the way we work.

improve efficiency and product quality depend on robots. Europe and the United States quickly followed Japan's lead in robotics, especially in automobile production and mining.

Globalization

The transnational corporation became the primary agent for these technological changes. By the twentieth century the growing economic power of corporations in industrialized nations allowed them to invest directly in the mines, plantations, and public utilities of less developed

AP* Exam Tip Be able to analyze the effects of the Western consumer society on the rest of the world.

regions. In the post–World War II years many of these companies became truly transnational, having multinational ownership and management. International trade agreements and open markets furthered the process. Ford, Nissan, and other car companies not only produced and sold cars internationally, but their shareholders, workers, and managers also came from numerous nations.

The location of manufacturing plants overseas and the acquisition of corporate operations by foreign buyers rendered such global firms as transnational as the products they sold. In the 1970s and 1980s American brand names like Levi's, Coca-Cola, Marlboro, Gillette, McDonald's, and Kentucky Fried Chicken were global phenomena (see Material Culture: Fast Food). But in time Asian names—Hitachi, Sony, Sanyo, and Mitsubishi—were blazoned in neon and on giant video screens on the sides of skyscrapers, along with European brands such as Nestlé, Mercedes, Pirelli, and Benetton.

As transnational manufacturers, agricultural conglomerates, and financial giants became wealthier and more powerful, they increasingly escaped the controls imposed by national governments. If labor costs were too high in Japan, antipollution measures too intrusive in the United States, or taxes too high in Great Britain, transnational companies relocated—or threatened to do so. In 1945, for example, the U.S. textile industry was located in low-wage southern states, dominating the American market and exporting to the world. As wages in the South rose and global competition increased, producers began relocating plants to Puerto Rico in the 1980s and to Mexico after NAFTA went into effect in 1994 (see Chapter 33). Now China is the primary manufacturer of textiles.

Loss of Brazilian Rain Forest The destruction of large portions of Brazil's virgin rain forest has come to symbolize the growing threat to the environment caused by population growth and economic development. In this photograph we see a tragic moonscape of tree stumps and fragile topsoil ripped open by settlers. The name given to this place is "Bom Futuro" ("Good Future" in English).

Claus Meyer/Peter Arnold, Inc.

Fast Food

Since early times empires and commercial enterprises have moved foods and beverages across national borders and cultural boundaries. The list of examples is very long. Sugar, coffee, tea, chocolate, corn, manioc, potatoes, wheat, wine, beer, distilled alcohols, tomatoes, and bananas are a small number of the foods and beverages carried from their origins to new continents and new peoples. In each case, host cultures accepted these additions to their cuisines while at the same time changing their preparation and altering their cultural meanings. Europeans sweetened chocolate, a bitter beverage consumed ritually by the Aztec elite, with sugar and it quickly became a beverage of mass consumption.

In modern industrialized nations fast food has come to cater to changing needs. Women and men in modern industrial societies marry later or not at all, and families have fewer meals together because of intense school and work schedules. As a result, fast food outlets have appeared everywhere to meet the needs of this busy, mobile population. In 2006 alone the world market for fast food grew by just under 7 percent, reaching sales of $155 billion.

Increased immigration and travel, as well as greater cultural connectivity promoted by films, television, and the Web, have combined to globalize ideas about food preparation and delivery. McDonald's now operates more than 31,000 restaurants in 119 countries. When a new franchise opened in Kuwait City, the drive-through line was over 10 kilometers long. Generally fast food meals cost the same in every cultural setting. In the United States, one of the richest countries in the world, McDonald's provides low-cost food to the masses, while in Pakistan, one of the poorest, these meals are luxuries. For many in the developing world, the fast food cuisines, restaurant designs, and styles of preparation represent the world of modernity and sophistication, not unlike the enthusiasm in the developed world for Mexican, Thai, or Ethiopian restaurants and cuisines.

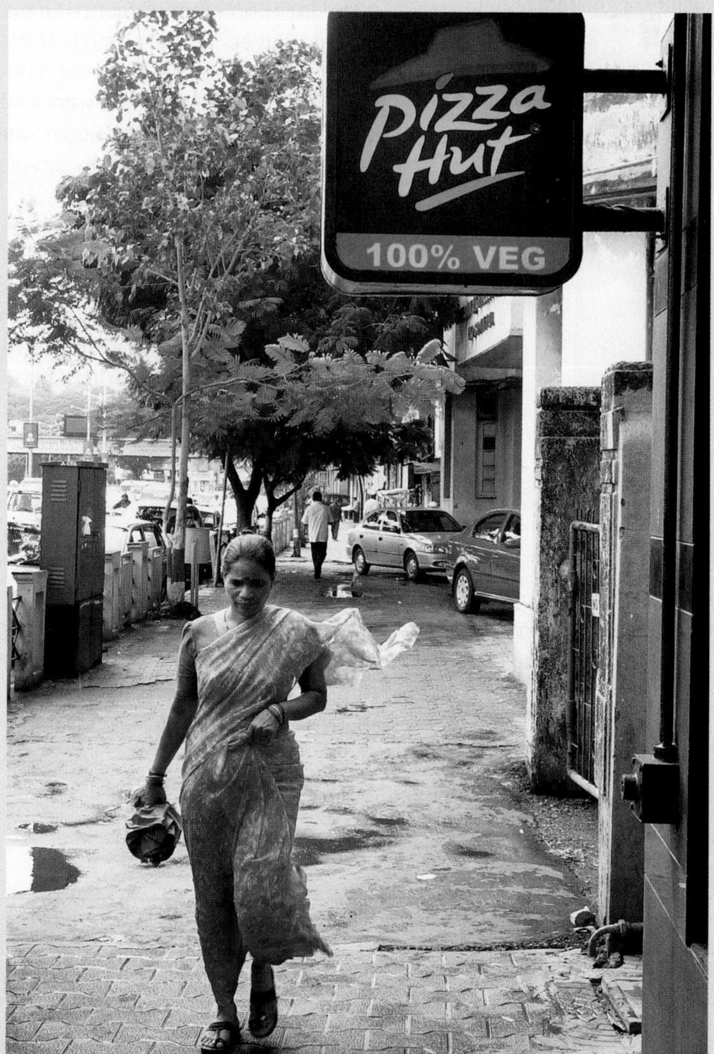

Ajaz Rahi/AP Images

Pizza Hut in India The booming, cosmopolitan city of Mumbai hosts India's most modern industries and many of the country's strictest vegetarians, as seen by the vegetarian menu advertised by this Pizza Hut restaurant.

Indeed, McDonald's is merely one of numerous examples of fast food globalization. KFC opened 1,500 outlets in China by the end of 2005, surpassing the McDonald's presence in this dynamic economy. Papa John's opened its fortieth outlet in Seoul and its twentieth outlet in Shanghai. Wendy's, Dominos, Cinnabon, and Subway have followed.

Many condemn this process as Yankee imperialism or as the unwanted homogenization of global culture. Tens of thousands have demonstrated, and some have gone to jail as a result of attacks on these symbols of foreign cultural penetration. Yet, as in earlier examples of unequal cultural exchange, local cultures have found ways to impose their tastes and values on these powerful international businesses. In Singapore McDonald's serves its signature hamburger on rice cakes instead of buns, and in Israel McDonald's established Kosher outlets. KFC, the most successful American chain in China, serves a Beijing Duck Wrap with spring onions and rice gruel for breakfast. In India, with its large vegetarian population, McDonald's, Pizza Hut, and other successful franchises devote as much as 75 percent of their menu to vegetarian foods.

Every society produces a range of products that serve as class and culture markers and as forms of self-expression. In the modern world food helps mark consumers as "traditional" or "sophisticated" and as "rich" or "poor." Both the global success of fast food companies and the popular protests against them suggest the complexity of this form of cultural transmission.

Conserving and Sharing Resources

In the 1960s environmental activists and political leaders began warning about the devastating environmental consequences of population growth, industrialization, and the expansion of agriculture onto marginal lands. Assaults on rain forests, the disappearance of species, and the poisoning of streams and rivers raised public consciousness, as did the depletion and pollution of the world's oceans. Environmental damage occurred both in the advanced industrial economies and in developing nations. The former Soviet Union, where industrial and nuclear wastes were routinely dumped with little concern for environmental consequences, had the worst environmental record.

In the developed world industrial activity increased much more rapidly than population grew, and the consumption of energy (coal, electricity, and petroleum) rose proportionally. Indeed, the consumer-driven economic expansion of the post–World War II years became an obstacle to addressing environmental problems, since modern economies depend on a profligate consumption of goods and resources (see Map 32.3). When consumption slows, industrial nations enter a recession. How could the United States, Germany, or Japan change consumption patterns to protect the environment without endangering corporate profits, wages, and employment levels?

Since 1945 population growth has been most dramatic in the developing countries, where environmental pressures have also been extreme. In Brazil, India, and China, for example, the need to expand food production led to rapid deforestation and the extension of farming and grazing onto marginal lands. The results were predictable: erosion and water pollution. These and many other poor nations sought to stimulate industrialization because they believed that the transition from agriculture to manufacturing was the only way to provide for their rapidly growing populations. The argument was compelling: Why should Indians or Brazilians remain poor while Americans, Europeans, and Japanese grew rich?

Responding to Environmental Threats

Despite the gravity of environmental threats, there were many successful efforts to preserve and protect the environment. The Clean Air Act, the Clean Water Act, and the Endangered Species Act were passed in the United States in the 1970s as part of an environmental effort that included the nations of the European Community and Japan. Grassroots political movements and the media encouraged environmental awareness, and most nations in the developed world enforced strict antipollution laws and sponsored massive recycling efforts. Many also encouraged resource conservation by rewarding energy-efficient factories and manufacturers of fuel-efficient cars and by promoting the use of alternative energy sources such as solar and wind power.

Environmental Reforms in the Developed World

Environmental efforts produced significant results. In western Europe and the United States, air quality improved dramatically. Smog levels in the United States fell nearly a third from 1970 to 2000, even though the number of automobiles increased more than 80 percent. Emissions of lead and sulfur dioxide were down as well. The Great Lakes, Long Island Sound, and Chesapeake Bay were all much cleaner at the end of the century than they had been in 1970.

New technologies made much of the improvement possible; for example, pollution controls on automobiles, planes, and factory smokestacks reduced harmful emissions. At the same time, the desire to preserve the natural environment was growing around the world. In developed nations continued political organization and enhanced awareness of environmental issues seemed likely to lead to step-by-step improvements in environmental policy. In the developing world and most of the former Soviet bloc, however, population

SECTION REVIEW

- Improvements in existing technology and new technologies such as the computer have improved manufacturing efficiency and transformed leisure.
- Globalization created a more integrated world economy, connecting producers and consumers from different regions and nations and reducing the ability of a single nation to escape the effects of distant events.
- The environmental movement achieved some successes in developed nations, reducing pollution and improving resource management, but global progress was hindered by a lack of cooperation between developed and developing nations.

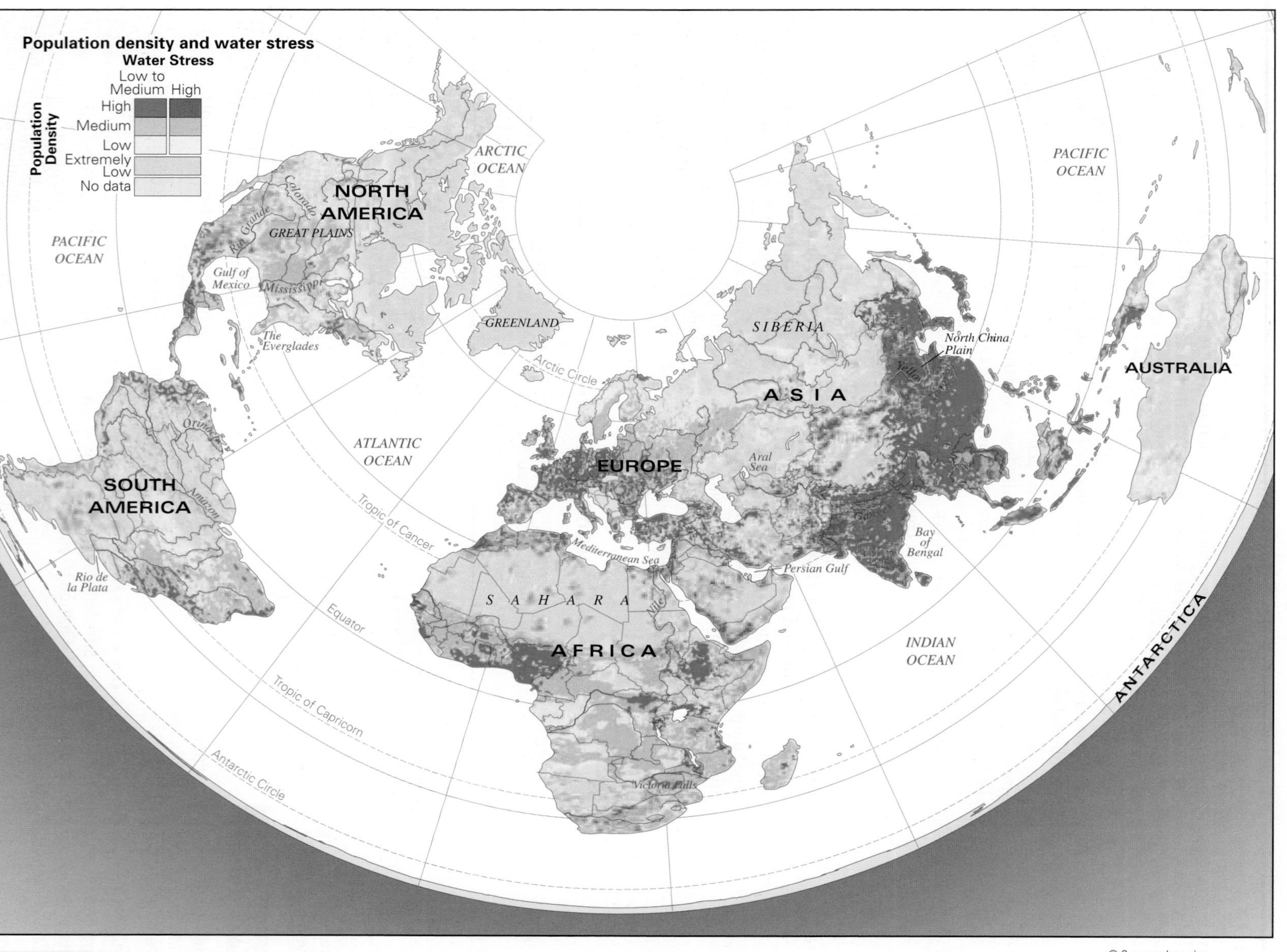

MAP 32.3 Fresh Water Resources This map links population density and the availability of water. Red areas are highly stressed environments where populations use at least 40 percent or more of available water. Less stressed environments are blue. The deeper the shade of red or blue the greater the environmental stress. *Source:* From "Global Water Stress," *National Geographic*, September 2002, pp. 14–16. Reprinted by permission of the National Geographic Society.

pressures and weak governments were major obstacles to effective environmental policies. Since the 1990s the rapid expansion of China's industrial sector has put additional pressure on the environment.

It now seems likely that industrialized nations will have to fund global improvements and that the cost will be high. Nevertheless, growing evidence of environmental degradation has continued to propel popular reform efforts, as when the media drew attention to the precipitous shrinkage of Peru's Andean glaciers and to loss of rain forest in Brazil. Yet, without broad agreement among the rich nations, the economic and political power necessary for environmental protections on a global scale will be very difficult to institute. When representatives from around the world negotiated a far-reaching treaty to reduce greenhouse gases in Kyoto, Japan, in 1997, President George W. Bush refused American participation even though the treaty was affirmed by nearly all other industrial nations.

CONCLUSION

The world was profoundly altered between 1975 and 2000. Both the United States and the Soviet Union feared that every conflict and every regime change represented a potential threat to their strategic interests, and every conflict threatened to provoke confrontation between them. As a result, the superpowers inserted themselves into a succession of civil wars and revolutions. The costs in lives and property were terrible, the gains small. As defense costs escalated, the Soviet system crumbled. By 1991 the Soviet Union and the socialist Warsaw Pact had disappeared, transforming the international stage.

The world was also altered by economic growth and integration, by population growth and movement, and by technological and environmental change. Led by the postwar recovery of the industrial powers and the remarkable economic expansion of Japan, the Asian Tigers, and more recently China, the world economy grew dramatically. The development and application of new technology contributed significantly to this process. International markets were more open and integrated than at any other time. However, not all the nations of the world benefited from the new wealth and exciting technologies of the postwar era. The capitalist West and a handful of Asian nations grew richer and more powerful, while most of the world's nations remained poor.

Population growth in the developing world was one reason for this divided experience. Most of the world's population growth in recent decades is in developing nations with limited economic growth. Unable to find adequate employment or, in many cases, bare subsistence, people in developing nations have migrated across borders, hoping to improve their lives. These movements have often provided valuable labor in the factories and farms of the developed world, but they have also provoked cultural, racial, and ethnic tension. Problems of inequality, population growth, and international migration will continue to challenge the global community in the coming decades.

Growing population and the development process have forced marginal lands into production and stimulated the exploitation of new resources. The need to feed a rapidly growing world population has also pressured ocean resources. As the world's population reached 6 billion and the largest cities reached 20 million, the need to produce and deliver raw materials and finished goods has put tremendous stress on the environment. In the 1990s the rapid development of the Chinese and Indian economies compounded these pressures.

At the same time, new technologies and the wealth produced by economic expansion have allowed the world's richest nations to implement ambitious programs of environmental protection. As a result, pollution produced by automobiles and factories has actually declined in the richest nations. The question that remains is whether rapidly developing nations, such as China and India, will move more quickly than the mature industrial nations did to introduce these new technologies.

KEY TERMS

proxy wars p. 916
Salvador Allende p. 916
Dirty War p. 917
Sandinistas p. 917
Ayatollah Ruhollah Khomeini p. 919
neo-liberalism p. 920
Saddam Husain p. 921
keiretsu p. 922
Asian Tigers p. 922
newly industrialized economies (NIEs) p. 923
Deng Xiaoping p. 923
Tiananmen Square p. 923
Mikhail Gorbachev p. 924
perestroika p. 924
Solidarity p. 924
ethnic cleansing p. 925
Thomas Malthus p. 927
demographic transition p. 928

EBOOK AND WEBSITE RESOURCES

Primary Sources

Islamic Government

The Last Heir of Lenin Explains His Reform Plans: Perestroika and Glasnost

Interactive Maps

Map 32.1 The End of the Soviet Union

Map 32.2 World Population Growth

Plus flashcards, practice quizzes, and more. Go to: www.cengage.com/history/bullietearthpeople5e

SUGGESTED READING

Adriaasen, W. L. M., and J. G. Waardensburg, eds. *A Dual World Economy: Forty Years of Development Experience*. 1989. A useful introduction to the complexity of development.

Bakhash, Shaul. *The Reign of the Ayatollahs: Iran and the Iranian Revolution*. 1990. An account of the Iranian Revolution and the early days of the Islamic Republic of Iran.

Berry, John A., and Carol Pott Berry, eds. *Genocide in Rwanda: A Collective Memory*. 1999. Covers a major calamity too readily forgotten.

Dyson, Tim, et al., eds. *Twenty-first Century India: Population, Economy, Human Development, and the Environment*. 2005. The culmination of a large research project.

Edgerton, Robert. *The Troubled Heart of Africa: A History of the Congo*. 2002. A convincing examination of this nation's history.

Foster, John Bellamy. *Economic History of the Environment*. 1994. An important synthesis.

Gaddis, John Lewis. *The Cold War: A New History*. 2005. A solid overview.

Kenez, Peter. *A History of the Soviet Union from the Beginning to the End*. 2006. Explains the demise of the USSR.

Kennedy, Paul M. *Preparing for the Twenty-first Century*. 1993. Asks whether world resources can cope with future population growth.

Krugman, Paul. *The Age of Diminished Expectations: U.S. Economic Policy in the 1990s*. 1997. An interesting criticism of American economic policy.

Lardy, Nicholas R. *China's Unfinished Economic Revolution*. 1998. A well-researched study of economic changes.

Maier, Charles. *Dissolution: The Crisis of Communism and the End of East Germany*. 1997. Covers the collapse of the Soviet empire in Europe.

McNeill, John R. *Something New Under the Sun: An Environmental History of the Twentieth Century World*. 2000. A survey coverage of a rising field of historical study.

Meredith, Martin. *The Fate of Africa: From the Hopes of Freedom to the Heart of Despair*. 2005. An overview of recent African history.

Rostow, W. W. *The Great Population Spike and After: Reflections on the 21st Century*. 1998. A challenging work that examines consequences of falling fertility in developed nations.

Rubin, Barnett. *The Fragmentation of Afghanistan*. 1995. Provides excellent coverage of the struggle between Soviet forces and the Muslim resistance.

Sampson, Anthony. *Mandela: The Authorized Biography*. 2000. A valuable introduction to the life and politics of the man.

Shenkar, Oded. *The Chinese Century: The Rising Chinese Economy and Its Impact on the Global Economy, the Balance of Power, and Your Job*. 2004. A business-oriented appraisal of the surging Chinese economy.

Skidmore, Thomas E., and Peter H. Smith. *Modern Latin America*, 6th ed. 2005. Provides an excellent general introduction to the period 1975 to 1991.

Stiglitz, Joseph E. *Globalization and Its Discontents*. 2003. An overview by a major economic thinker.

Thompson, Leonard. *A History of South Africa*, 3rd ed. 2005. Looks at a key African country.

Westad, Odd Arne. *The Global Cold War: Third World Interventions and the Making of Our Times*. 2005. A very useful discussion of the effects of Cold War rivalry on the developing world.

Wolf, M. *Revolution Postponed: Women in Contemporary China*. 1985.

NOTES

1. Quoted in Antony Flew, "Introduction," in Thomas Robert Malthus, *An Essay on the Principle of Population and a Summary View of the Principle of Population* (New York: Penguin Books, 1970), 30.
2. "Population Implosion Worries a Graying Europe," *New York Times*, July 10, 1998.

AP* REVIEW QUESTIONS FOR CHAPTER 32

1. Conflicts in which rival powers finance and arm competing factions or parties are called

   (A) civil wars.
   (B) police actions.
   (C) proxy wars.
   (D) democratic revolutions.

2. In Latin America, the combination of dictatorship, violent repression, and government promotion of industrialization was called

   (A) communist subversion.
   (B) nationalistic development.
   (C) the "Brazilian Solution."
   (D) internal intervention.

3. In Latin America President Jimmy Carter

   (A) agreed to reestablish Panamanian sovereignty in the Canal Zone at the end of 1999.
   (B) committed U.S. troops to Colombia to assist in fighting a dictatorial government.
   (C) established a joint military force with Costa Rica.
   (D) attempted to force the Sandinistas out of power in Nicaragua.

4. President Carter's attempts to deal with the formation of the Islamic Republic of Iran

   (A) were hailed by the United Nations as a great success.
   (B) encouraged Israel to sign a peace agreement with Egypt.
   (C) were designed to quell the rising power of Saddam Husain.
   (D) were a complete failure.

5. The four modern industrial and commercial economies of Taiwan, Hong Kong, Singapore, and South Korea are referred to as the

   (A) Bamboo Curtain.
   (B) Iron Triangle.
   (C) Asian Tigers.
   (D) Technology Titans.

6. In 1989 Chinese students began to protest for democracy in China. This led to what is known as the

   (A) October Reforms.
   (B) Tiananmen Square incident.
   (C) Manchurian incident.
   (D) Great Cultural Revolution.

7. Under the Soviet leader Mikhail Gorbachev, the USSR

   (A) entered a period of strict industrial isolation.
   (B) began perestroika.
   (C) encouraged its satellite nations to become noncommunist.
   (D) recognized the Roman Catholic Church as a legitimate religion in the Soviet Union.

8. The most visible event ending the Cold War was the

   (A) lowering of the Soviet flag over its embassy in Washington, D.C.
   (B) removal of all Soviet forces from eastern Europe.
   (C) toppling of the Berlin Wall.
   (D) U.S. government suspending the mission of the Strategic Air Command.

9. Following the declaration of the independence of Bosnia in 1992, Orthodox Serbs attempted to

   (A) join the Commonwealth of Independent States.
   (B) seek UN peacekeepers to assist in the move toward statehood.
   (C) rid the state of ethnic Muslims through ethnic cleansing.
   (D) promote foreign direct investment in the new nation.

10. In the post–World War II era, the capitalist West and a handful of Asian nations have grown richer and more powerful, while most of the world's nations have remained poor. In part this is due to

    (A) population growth in developing nations.
    (B) a lack of natural resources.
    (C) the poor nations not joining the United Nations.
    (D) the emergence of forced industrialization.

CHAPTER

33

CHAPTER OUTLINE

- Globalization and Economic Crisis
- The Question of Values
- Global Culture

ENVIRONMENT + TECHNOLOGY *Global Warming*

DIVERSITY + DOMINANCE *Conflict and Civilization*

Justin Lane/epa/Corbis

Watching Financial Markets Fall After years of economic boom, much of it fueled by inflated housing prices in the United States and ingenious new financial instruments that concealed risk, the world's stock markets fell drastically in 2008–2009. American stocks lost approximately one-third of their value. The banking crisis and resulting unemployment reminded economists of the Great Depression of the 1930s. People in all walks of life, from heads of state, to retirees, to ordinary workers, were forced to reappraise their financial situations.

Visit the website and ebook for additional study materials and interactive tools: www.cengage.com/history/bullietearthpeople5e

New Challenges in a New Millennium

- What are the main benefits and dangers of growing political, economic, and cultural integration?
- What roles do religious beliefs and secular ideologies play in the contemporary world?
- How has technology contributed to the process of global interaction?

The workday began normally at the World Trade Center in lower Manhattan on the morning of September 11, 2001. The 50,000 people who worked there were making their way to the two 110-story towers. Suddenly, at 8:46 A.M., an American Airlines Boeing 767 with 92 people on board, traveling at a speed of 470 miles per hour (756 kilometers per hour), crashed into floors 94 to 98 of the north tower, igniting the 10,000 gallons (38,000 liters) of fuel in its tanks. Just before 9:03 A.M. a United Airlines flight with 65 people on board and a similar fuel load hit floors 78 to 84 of the south tower.

As the burning jet fuel engulfed the collision areas, the buildings' occupants struggled through smoke-filled corridors and down dozens of flights of stairs. Many of those trapped above the crash sites used cell phones to say good-bye to loved ones. Rather than endure the flames and fumes, a few jumped to their deaths.

Just before 10 o'clock, temperatures that had risen to 2,300° Fahrenheit (1,260° Celsius) caused the steel girders in the impacted area of the south tower to give way. The collapsing upper floors crushed the floors underneath one by one, engulfing lower Manhattan in a dense cloud of dust. Twenty-eight minutes later the north tower pancaked in a similar manner. Miraculously, most of the buildings' occupants had escaped before the towers collapsed. Besides the people on the planes, nearly 2,600 lost their lives, including some 400 police officers and firefighters helping in the evacuation.

That same morning another American Airlines jet crashed into the Pentagon, killing all 64 people on board and 125 others inside the military complex near Washington, D.C. Passengers on a fourth plane managed to overpower their hijackers, and the plane crashed in rural Pennsylvania, killing all 45 on board.

The four planes had been hijacked by teams of Middle Eastern men who slit the throats of service and flight personnel and seized control. Of the nineteen hijackers, fifteen were from Saudi Arabia. All had links to an extremist Islamic organization, al-Qaeda (ahl–KAW-eh-duh) (the base or foundation), commanded by a rich Saudi named Usama bin Laden (oo-SAH-mah bin LAH-din), who was incensed with American political, military, and cultural influence in the Middle East. The men were educated and well traveled, had lived in the United States, and spoke English. Some had trained as pilots so that they could fly the hijacked aircraft.

PRIMARY SOURCE: The Last Night Read a list of instructions meant to be reviewed on September 10, 2001, by the terrorists who attacked the United States the next morning.

The hijackers left few records of their motives, but the acts spoke for themselves. The World Trade Center was a focal point of international business, the Pentagon the headquarters of the American military. The fourth plane was probably meant to hit the Capitol or the White House, the legislative and executive centers of the world's only superpower.

The events of September 11, which became commonly referred to as 9/11, can be understood on many levels. The hijackers and those who sympathized with them saw themselves as engaged in a holy struggle against economic, political, and military institutions they believed to be evil. People directly affected, political leaders around the world, and most television watchers described the attacks as evil deeds against innocent victims.

To understand why the nineteen attackers were heroes to some and terrorists to others, one needs to explore the historical context of global changes at the turn of the millennium and the ideological tensions they have generated. The unique prominence of the United States in every major aspect of global integration, as well as its support for pro-American governments overseas, also elicits sharply divergent views.

GLOBALIZATION AND ECONOMIC CRISIS

globalization The economic, political, and cultural integration and interaction of all parts of the world brought about by increasing trade, travel, and technology.

The turn of the millennium saw the intensification of **globalization** trends that had been building since the 1970s. Growing trade and travel and new technologies were bringing all parts of the world into closer economic, political, and cultural integration and interaction (see Maps 33.1 and 33.2). The collapse of the Soviet Union had completed the dissolution of territorial empires that had been under way throughout the twentieth century. Autonomous national states (numbering about two hundred) became an almost universal norm, and a growing number of them had embraced democratic institutions. However, increasing interdependency would also facilitate a global economic crisis that exploded in 2008 when the massive accumulation of debt in American financial institutions became unsustainable.

An Interconnected Economy

Trade and 9/11

The expansion of trade, global interconnections, and privatization of government enterprises that gained momentum with the dismantling of Soviet-style socialist economies in the 1990s cooled abruptly in the wake of 9/11. The rate of growth in world trade fell from 13 percent in 2000 to only 1 percent in 2001.

Petroleum Prices

Growth in China and India resumed quickly, however, and the large populations of these two countries marked them as future world economic powers. Their growth increased pressure on world energy supplies, though the United States continued to consume a quarter of the world's petroleum production. OPEC's manipulation of world oil prices, combined with political instability in the Middle East, had caused crude oil prices to soar between 1973 and 1985. But aside from those years, the average price of oil remained consistently below $20 per barrel (adjusted for inflation) throughout the second half of the twentieth century. In the year 2000, however, oil prices began a new period of increase caused not by OPEC but by rising demand and confidence in the fevered pace of world economic expansion. By the middle of 2006, the price of a barrel of crude had crept past $70, and in 2008 it spiked to $145 a barrel. This increase fueled ambitious economic programs in producing countries like Russia, Saudi Arabia, and the small sheikhdoms of the Persian Gulf. Then, with the economic crisis of 2008, prices fell abruptly, causing disruption in those same countries.

Regional Trade Organizations

Regional trade associations came into being to promote growth, reduce the economic vulnerability of member states, and, less explicitly, balance American economic dominance. The twenty-seven member European Union (EU) was the most successful (see Map 33.2). The euro, a common currency inaugurated in 2002 and used in twelve member states, competed with the U.S. dollar for investment and banking. However, unequal levels of development among mem-

CHRONOLOGY

	Politics	Economics and Society
2000	2000 Al-Qaeda attacks American destroyer USS *Cole* in Yemen	
2001	2001 George W. Bush becomes president of the United States 2001 Terrorists destroy the World Trade Center and damage the Pentagon on September 11 2001 United States armed forces overthrow Taliban regime in Afghanistan	2001–2003 Terrorist attacks trigger global recession 2001 Shanghai Cooperation Organization formed
2002		2002 Euro currency adopted in twelve European countries
2003	2003 Unfounded fears of weapons of mass destruction lead United States and Britain to invade and occupy Iraq	
2004	2004 Terrorists bomb Spanish trains 2004–2009 Genocidal conflict ongoing in Darfur region of Sudan	2004 Ten new members admitted to European Union
2005	2005 Terrorists bomb London transit system 2005 Mahmoud Ahmedinejad elected president of Iran	
2006	2006 Iraqis elect a government under a new constitution 2006 Hamas movement defeats PLO in Palestinian election 2006 Israel attacks Hezbollah in Lebanon in response to its seizure of Israeli soldiers	
2007	2007 Assassination of Benazir Bhutto deepens political crisis in Pakistan	
2008	2008 Barack Obama elected president of the United States	2008 Collapse of mortgage debt bubble in United States triggers global recession

bers became a source of friction in 2009 as the world economic downturn devastated stock markets and increased rates of unemployment.

Despite the EU's expansion, the North American Free Trade Agreement (NAFTA), which eliminated tariffs among the United States, Canada, and Mexico in 1994, governed the world's largest free-trade zone. Yet heated debate in the United States over illegal immigration across

Palm Island, Dubai The seemingly unlimited wealth of the oil-producing states of the Persian Gulf spurred ambitious development plans like this one in Dubai, one of the United Arab Emirates. Its publicists proclaimed that "'Palm Island' would include 2,000 villas, up to 40 luxury hotels, shopping complexes, cinemas, and the Middle East's "first marine park" and would be "visible from the moon."

Jorge Ferrari/epa/Corbis Sygma

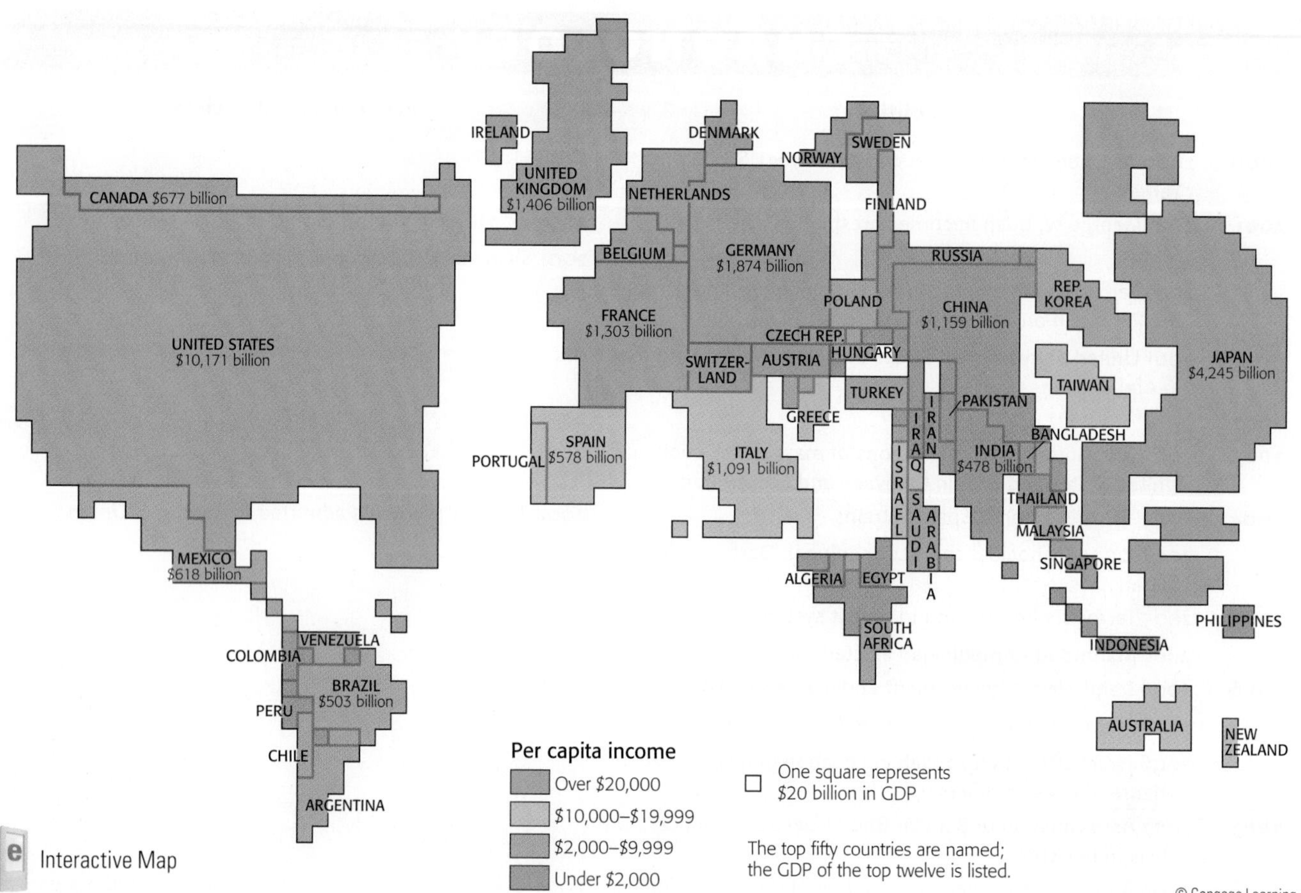

MAP 33.1 Global Distribution of Wealth Early industrialization and efficient investment contributed to individual prosperity for the citizens of Japan and Western countries by the 1990s. However, economic dynamism in late-industrializing countries like China and India began to change the world balance of economic power in the early twenty-first century. In nearly all countries the distribution of wealth among individuals varies tremendously, with the gap between rich and poor generally increasing.

the Mexican border, as well anti-Hispanic prejudice, limited popular enthusiasm for the agreement. The third largest free-trade zone, Mercosur, created by Argentina, Brazil, Paraguay, and Uruguay in 1991 and subsequently expanded to include five associate members, planned to elect a parliament in 2010. Other free-trade associations operated in West Africa, southern Africa, Southeast Asia, Central America, the Pacific Basin, and the Caribbean.

The Shanghai Cooperation Organization (SCO), formed in 2001 with China, Russia, and four former Soviet Central Asian republics as members, originally pursued common security interests, such as combating separatist movements and terrorism. But its announced twenty-year plan for reducing barriers to trade and population movement took a step forward when Mahmoud Ahmedinejad, the president of Iran, one of five countries with observer status, formally applied for full membership in 2008. Bringing Iran's oil-rich economy into alignment with a rapidly developing China and a similarly oil-rich Russia promised to complicate the world economic and political picture even before the onset of the global fiscal crisis later that year.

AP* Exam Tip Be able to discuss the global development of multinational corporations.

World Trade Organization

In 1995 the world's major traders established the **World Trade Organization (WTO)** dedicated to reducing barriers and enforcing international agreements. Despite a membership of 153 nations, the WTO had many critics and regularly encountered street protests during its ministerial meetings. Some protesters feared that low-cost foreign manufacturers would shrink the job opportunities in richer states; others demanded continuing tariff protection for local farmers.

World Trade Organization (WTO) An international body established in 1995 to foster and bring order to international trade.

Efforts to rescue countries in economic trouble became a concern of the International Monetary Fund (IMF) and World Bank (see Chapter 31) and of wealthy countries that could afford to extend foreign aid. But few suspected that the globalized economy would turn into a source of anxiety for everyone.

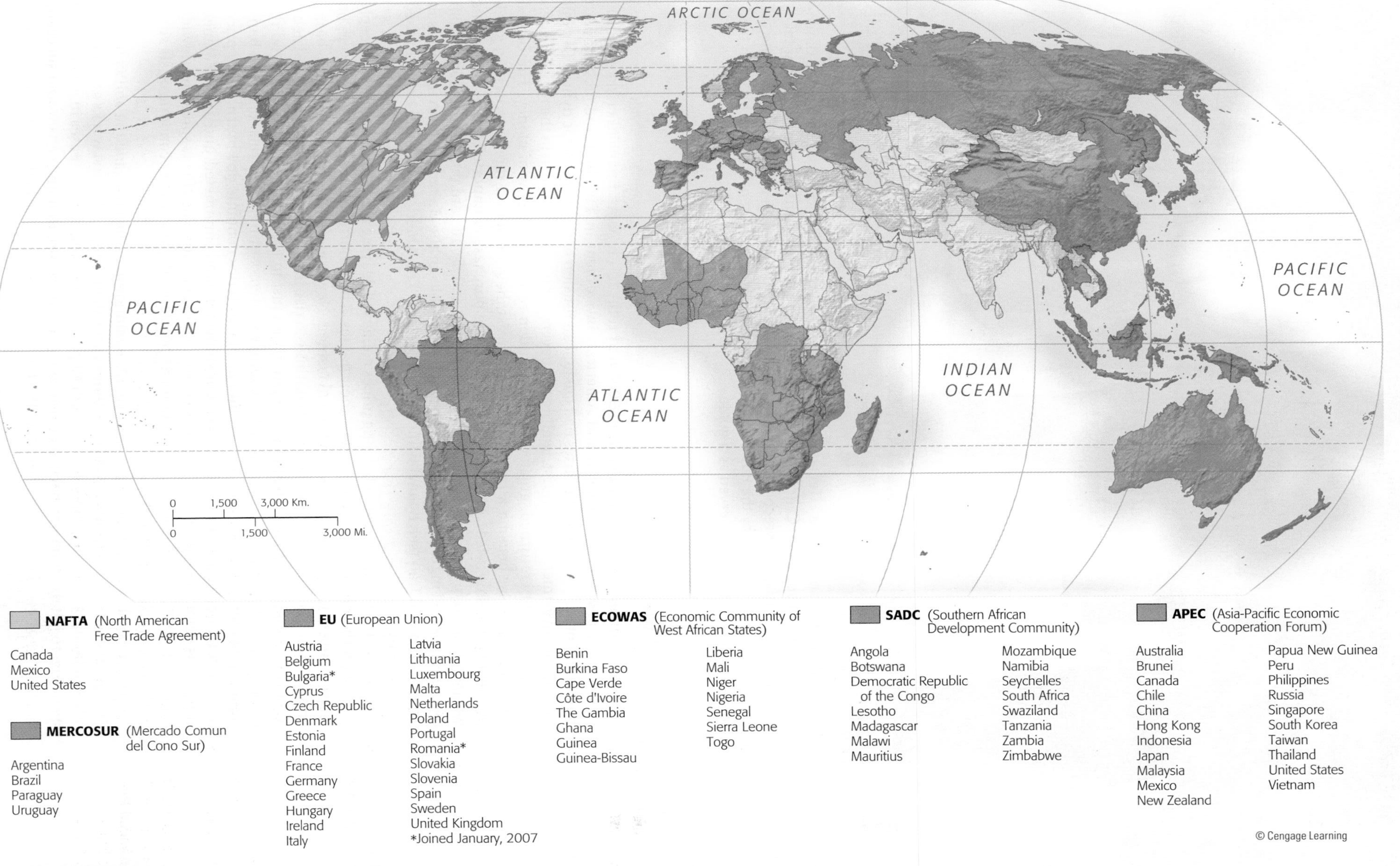

MAP 33.2 Regional Trade Associations, 2004 International trade and development are major concerns of governments in developed and developing countries. NAFTA, Mercosur, and the EU are free-trade areas. The other associations promote trade and development.

e Interactive Map

President Barack Obama at Cairo's Sultan Hassan Mosque Tensions between the United States and the Muslim world diminished somewhat after President Obama gave a speech in Cairo directed at Muslims. Speaking less than five months after taking office, he praised the positive elements of Islam and recognized the negative impact of American policies related to the Iraq War and the stringent anti-terrorist measures taken by the Bush administration. Iman Abdel Fateh, standing between the president and Secretary of State Hillary Rodham Clinton, served as a guide.

Global Financial Crisis

The global financial crisis that began in 2008 had roots in an Asian financial crisis a decade earlier. Vast amounts of European and American investment in Thailand, Indonesia, South Korea, and other East Asian countries had created an illusion of great economic dynamism; but in 1997 the investment boom burst, leading to a severe economic downturn in the region. When economic stability returned, greater investor caution reversed the flow of money. The United States in particular became a favorite place to invest, helping spur a rapid increase in stock market and housing prices and massive growth in the purchase of imported goods. Americans became wedded to borrowing money for houses, cars, and credit card purchases. Money from overseas invested in the U.S. treasury also made it possible for the United States to fight wars in Afghanistan and Iraq (see below) while lowering taxes. The American national debt climbed dramatically.

Collapse of the Housing Market

In 2008 the fevered boom in housing prices collapsed, leaving many homeowners so deeply in debt on their mortgages that they lost their homes. Their mortgage debts, however, were no longer being held by a bank in the traditional fashion. New and risky lending techniques based on an assumption that home prices would continue to rise indefinitely had caused the bad debts to be distributed throughout the banking system, not just in the United States but around the world. When Lehman Brothers, one of the country's foremost financial firms, declared bankruptcy in September, a recession turned into a catastrophic economic downturn. Stock prices fell, banks teetered on the brink of collapse, consumer demand plummeted, and unemployment climbed as employers laid off workers they could no longer afford. The effects spread worldwide. Knowledgeable political leaders and economists proclaimed it the worst economic crisis since the Great Depression of the 1930s.

Obama Financial Plans

The sense that Barack Obama had a firm understanding of the crisis and the ability to lead the country out of it contributed to his election as president. During the first weeks after he took office in January 2009, he proposed a series of steps, including massive increases in government spending, to jolt the economy back to health. Yet no one was sure that his plans would succeed, and no one expected the recovery to be swift. The trade expansion that had signaled the promise of globalization at the beginning of the century faded from memory, and the interdependence that had bound the world's economies in a cycle of growth became a dead weight that dragged many countries down.

Globalization and Democracy

The last decades of the twentieth century saw expansions of democratic institutions and personal freedom. People in many countries recognized that elections offered a peaceful way to settle differences among a country's social classes, cultural groups, and regions. Although majority votes could swing from one part of the political spectrum to another, democracies tended to encourage political moderation. Moreover, wars between fully democratic states were extremely rare.

Eastern Europe

The nations of eastern Europe embraced democracy after the fall of the Soviet Union, though some newly democratic states became subject to great mood swings among the electorate. The shift to private ownership of businesses after decades of rigid state control brought riches to a select few, and the removal of trade barriers characteristic of Cold War rivalry opened up new markets and fostered investment from the West.

By 2008, however, rising unemployment and falling export levels and stock prices threatened these experiments in free elections and free markets. Small countries like Iceland in the West and Latvia in the post-Soviet East saw governments fall, and fear of political instability spread widely. In Russia, the popular but somewhat authoritarian leader Vladimir Putin followed his country's constitution by stepping down in 2008 after two terms as president. However, he engineered the election of his protégé Dimitri Medvedev as his successor and assumed the office of prime minister himself. This move led some political thinkers to fear a possible return to Soviet era Russian domination.

Democracy in Asia

Asian democracies proved somewhat more stable. Beginning with free parliamentary elections in 1999, the populous state of Indonesia moved from years of authoritarian and corrupt rule toward more open political institutions. The following years saw a violent independence movement of the Acheh (ah-CHEH) district of northern Sumatra, the secession in 2002 of East Timor after years of brutal Indonesian military occupation, terrorist bombings on the island of Bali in 2004, and a devastating earthquake and tsunami in the same year. But democratic elections were regularly held. The losing candidates left office peacefully, and the populace at large accepted the results.

In India a major political shift seemed to be at hand in 1998 when the Bharatiya Janata Party (BJP) secured an electoral victory that interrupted four decades of Congress Party rule. The BJP success came through blatant appeals to Hindu nationalism, the condoning of violence against India's Muslims, and opposition to the social and economic progress of the Untouchables (those

Douglas E. Curran/Getty Images/Corbis

Sectarian Strife in India Hours after these Hindu youths clambered atop the sixteenth-century Babri Mosque in December 1992, hundreds of angry Hindu nationalists completely demolished the structure. The Hindus claimed that the Muslim place of worship in the northern Indian province of Uttar Pradesh had been erected upon the site of a temple commemorating the birthplace of Lord Ram, the incarnation of the Hindu god Vishnu. Thousands died in the riots that followed the razing of the temple. An Indian government archaeological team uncovered the foundation of an earlier temple-like structure.

traditionally confined to the dirtiest jobs). In 2004, however, the Congress Party returned to power and governmental stability proved strong even in the face of sensational terrorist attacks in Mumbai by Pakistani gunmen in 2008.

Instability in Pakistan

Democracy in Pakistan itself proved more uncertain. President and former military commander Pervez Musharraf's (pair-VEZ moo-SHAH-ef) abrupt firing of the country's chief justice, combined with his unpopular support of the Bush administration's war policies, sparked protests and calls for impeachment. He resigned the presidency in 2008. Asif Ali Zardari (AH-sef AH-lee zar-DAH-ree), who succeeded him, had inherited the leadership of the majority Pakistan People's Party after the assassination the year before of his charismatic wife Benazir Bhutto, the daughter of a popular earlier prime minister. Zardari faced difficulties forming a strong government because of the growing movement of the Pakistani Taliban to impose their own governance and a rigid Muslim behavioral code in outlying districts, as well as popular opposition to American antiterrorist attacks launched from Afghanistan.

African Regimes

In sub-Saharan Africa, democracy had mixed results. Nelson Mandela, the leader of the African National Congress (ANC) who had become the first postapartheid president of South Africa in 1994 (see Chapter 32), left office in 1999 and was succeeded by the deputy president and ANC leader Thabo Mbeki (TAA-boh um-BEH-kee). Mbeki stepped down in 2008 amidst turmoil in the leadership of the ANC. But the democratic system did not seem threatened. Elsewhere some elected leaders, such as Robert Mugabe (moo-GAH-bay) in Zimbabwe, used violence and intimidation to hold on to power, and other states, such as Congo, were plagued with internal revolts and civil wars. Liberians emerged from fourteen years of civil war in 2003 and two years later chose Ellen Johnson-Sirleaf (SUHR-leef) to be Africa's first elected female head of state. In Sudan, the general who had led a military coup in 1989, Omar al-Bashir, became the first sitting head of state to be charged with genocide and crimes against humanity by the International Criminal Court in 2009. A festering conflict in Darfur in western Sudan, which had then cost hundreds of thousands of lives and displaced over 2 million people, was at the heart of the charges.

Regime Change in Iraq and Afghanistan

Weapons of Mass Destruction

The most closely watched experiments in democratization took place in Iraq and Afghanistan, countries that the United States invaded after the terrorist attacks of 9/11. Afghanistan's provision of a safe haven for Usama bin Laden and his al-Qaeda organization gave clear justification for the overthrow in December 2001 of the militantly religious Taliban regime. However, the rationale for invading Iraq was less clear. Leading up to the war the American government contended that Iraq was a clear and present danger to the United States because it possessed **weapons of mass destruction** (WMDs): nuclear, chemical, and biological weapons that it might supply to terrorists like bin Laden.

weapons of mass destruction Nuclear, chemical, and biological devices that are capable of injuring and killing large numbers of people.

When United Nations inspectors failed to find any banned weapons, a split widened between those nations wanting to continue inspections and those, led by the United States, wanting to intervene militarily. Deciding to go it alone, an American-led "coalition of the willing" opened the invasion of Iraq with a spectacular aerial bombardment of Baghdad on March 20, 2003. Twenty-five days later the United States declared that "major fighting" had ended, little realizing that guerrilla insurgency, sectarian violence, and economic devastation would continue for years.

e PRIMARY SOURCE: Declaration of Jihad Against Americans Occupying the Land of the Two Holy Mosques Read a speech given by Osama bin Laden to his followers in Afghanistan, and soon published worldwide.

Though Iraq fell into a state of turmoil because the coalition army was too small or otherwise unprepared to prevent the looting and destruction of government facilities and other lawlessness, a thorough search was launched for WMDs. The search came up empty, and intelligence analyses failed to uncover any evidence that Saddam Husain, Iraq's fallen dictator, had played a role in the 9/11 attacks.

North Korea and Iran

However, American concern for WMDs was not eliminated. North Korea had an open program to build nuclear weapons, and Iran was suspected of having a covert plan based in part on technological aid secretly given by the head of Pakistan's successful nuclear program. Iran's outspokenly anti-American and anti-Israeli president, Mahmoud Ahmedinejad, elected in 2005, and North Korea's dictator Kim Jong-il (kim jong-ill) presented the United States with difficult challenges. But the military invasion option chosen for Iraq, though favored by some Bush advisers, was held in abeyance in favor of diplomatic initiatives.

IRNA/Reuters/Corbis

Iranian President Mahmoud Ahmedinejad After two terms under the comparatively liberal, but ineffective, government of President Mohammad Khatami, voters in the Islamic Republic of Iran elected a relatively unknown conservative in 2005. President Ahmedinejad has taken confrontational positions on international affairs, notably his denial of Israel's legitimacy as a state and his assertion of Iran's right to develop nuclear technology. This has enhanced his domestic popularity, while convincing many analysts that with the American defeat of Saddam Husain, Iran had become a major power in the Middle East and the Islamic world.

The failure to find Iraqi WMDs having undermined his war scenario, President George W. Bush declared that the United States had actually invaded Iraq to liberate the Iraqi people and substitute democracy for oppression. An intense debate followed within the United States about whether the Bush administration had used deception in leading the nation into war. However, the question of whether the war would ultimately be deemed successful came to hinge on the establishment of democratic institutions in both Afghanistan and Iraq.

Return of the Taliban

Unfortunately, the power of a new Afghan government elected in 2004 did not extend over the entire country. By 2008 the Taliban were again a serious threat, and opium production, the key to the country's unrest, was higher than ever. Though the United States was able to enlist the participation of NATO forces in helping to police Afghanistan, the prospects for the country were so dim that President Barack Obama, succeeding George Bush in 2009, made intensification of efforts to bring peace and stability and suppress terrorism a key part of his foreign policy.

The "Surge" in Iraq

In Iraq, the United States time and again declared that the country was finally emerging from chaos and proceeding on the path to democratic rule. In actuality, despite the adoption of a constitution in 2006, lethal resistance to coalition troops and the newly organized Iraqi security forces remained strong until 2008, when the United States, under a policy called "the surge," began to organize and pay segments of the resistance movement to join the coalition side.

Before "the surge" the question had frequently been asked whether Iraq was on the verge of, or already engaged in, a civil war. But as the level of violence plummeted, it became possible to envision an orderly withdrawal of American forces that would give the country a reasonable chance for stability, reconstruction, and the soothing of still potent political and sectarian divisions. Soon after being elected, President Obama announced that American combat brigades would be withdrawn from Iraq by August 2010, though a sizable residual force would remain to train the Iraqi army and suppress terrorist activities.

Looking at the level of destruction visited on Afghanistan and Iraq in the name of democratization, other Middle Eastern countries hesitated to follow American urgings to liberalize their political systems. Though some small oil-producing countries in the Persian Gulf took cautious steps toward democratization and Kuwait for the first time allowed women to vote in 2006, large countries like Egypt and Syria continued to suppress most critics. Their governments feared that free elections would lead to Islamic political parties gaining a share of power as the religious Shi'ite parties had done in Iraq's first elections.

Hezbollah

The capture of 23 out of 128 seats in the Lebanese parliament by the Lebanese Shi'ite movement Hezbollah in 2005 and the absolute majority of seats won by the militantly anti-Israeli

Hamas movement in elections for the Palestine Governing Authority in 2006 seemed to confirm this fear, since both movements were strongly religious in their policies. Attacks launched by Israel against both Hamas and Hezbollah in response to kidnappings of Israeli soldiers in 2006 suggested that fear of domination by Islamic movements might in the future become more important than democratization in the Middle East, regardless of American preferences.

Hamas

In 2007 the elected Hamas government succeeded in driving its Palestinian rivals out of the Gaza Strip. During the following months, largely inaccurate rocket barrages launched from there against Israel became a major factor in Israeli politics. A security barrier built on the West Bank had almost eliminated attacks by Palestinian suicide bombers, but the rockets provoked public outrage even though the number of casualties was very small. During the final month of the manifestly pro-Israeli Bush administration, the Israel Defense Force undertook to deal once and for all with Hamas in the Gaza Strip. Aerial bombardments and ground force incursions left well over a thousand Palestinians dead. Israeli casualties were negligible. However, there was no sign that Hamas had been seriously harmed as a political organization. Worldwide reactions to the closely watched Gaza campaign engendered great criticism of Israel but no relaxation of the American determination to shun Hamas until it abandoned its opposition to Israel's existence. In democratic terms, neither the Israeli nor the Palestinian political systems seemed likely to produce governments capable of meaningful peace negotiations.

SECTION REVIEW

- Since the Cold War, global political relations have been defined largely by economic interconnections.
- To manage economic change, many nations have joined a variety of trade organizations, and free-trade policies have caused widespread controversy.
- Global interdependence and rapid economic expansion and speculation led to a global financial crisis in 2008 that plunged the world into the worst economic slowdown since the Great Depression of the 1930s.
- There has been a general worldwide trend toward democracy, especially in Asian countries.
- However, U.S. intervention in Iraq and Afghanistan has shown that the promotion of democracy by military force is very difficult, and in the Middle East the Israeli-Palestinian deadlock stands in the way of fundamental political change.

THE QUESTION OF VALUES

As people around the world first faced the opportunities of globalization and then the fear of global recession, they tried to make sense of these changes in terms of their own value systems. With 6 billion people, the world was big enough to include many different approaches, whether religious or secular, local or international, traditional or visionary. In some cases, however, conflicting visions fed violence.

Faith and Politics

Religious beliefs increasingly inspired political actions during the second half of the twentieth century, and the trend intensified as the new century began (see Map 33.3). Though for Americans this change reversed two centuries of growing secularism, Western analysts did not agree on the cause of the religious revival.

Fundamentalism

Evangelical Protestants became a powerful conservative political force in the United States, particularly during the Bush presidency. Around the world, Catholic conservatives led by Pope John Paul II, and Pope Benedict XVI, who succeeded him in 2005, forcefully reiterated politically sensitive teachings: opposition to abortion, homosexuality, marriage of priests, and admission of women to the priesthood. In Israel, hyperorthodox Jews known as *haredim* played a leading role in settling the Palestinian territories captured by Israel in 1967 and vehemently resisted both Israel's unilateral withdrawal from Gaza in 2005 and subsequent plans for withdrawal from the West Bank. And in India, Hindu zealots made the BJP party a powerful political force (see above).

AP* Exam Tip Be able to discuss religious fundamentalism as it applies to the post–World War II period.

Yet most discussions of faith and politics focused on Islam (see Diversity and Dominance: Conflict and Civilization). The birth of the Islamic Republic of Iran in the revolution of 1979

Patrick Robert/Corbis

Darfur Refugees In 2003 a conflict broke out in the Darfur region of western Sudan. Marauding bands, largely from nomadic backgrounds, struck farming villages, killing ten of thousands. More than 100,000 people crossed the border into Chad as refugees. With both sides being of more or less the same ethnicity and religion, and with few great power interests at stake, the international community proved unable to take effective action.

made visible a current of Muslim political assertiveness that had been building for twenty years in several Muslim countries. But by the year 2000 acts of **terrorism** perpetrated by non-Iranian Muslim groups claiming to be acting for religious reasons were capturing the headlines.

Terrorism

terrorism Political belief that extreme and seemingly random violence will destabilize a government and permit the terrorists to gain political advantage. Though an old technique, terrorism gained prominence in the late twentieth century with the growth of worldwide mass media that, through their news coverage, amplified public fears of terrorist acts.

Terrorism is a political tactic by which comparatively weak militants use grotesquely inhumane and lethal acts to convince a frightened public that danger is everywhere and their government is incapable of protecting them. Although terrorism has a long history, the instantaneous media links made possible by satellite communications, and the tradition in the news business of publicizing violence, increased its effectiveness from the 1980s onward.

Bombings, kidnappings, and assassinations made political sense to all sorts of political groups: secular Palestinians confronting Israel; national separatists like the Tamils in Sri Lanka, Basques in Spain, and Chechens in Russia; and Catholic and Protestant extremists in Northern Ireland, to name a few. But Muslim groups gained the lion's share of attention when they targeted the United States and Europe, recruited from Muslim populations all over the world, and made effective use of news coverage and audiovisual communications.

Usama bin Laden

Usama bin Laden Saudi-born Muslim extremist who funded the al-Qaeda organization that was responsible for several terrorist attacks, including those on the World Trade Center and the Pentagon in 2001.

Their media star and ideological spokesman was **Usama bin Laden**. Born into a wealthy Saudi family and educated as an engineer, bin Laden fought against the Soviet Union in Afghanistan and there recruited and trained a core group of fighters called al-Qaeda. Though his family disowned him and Saudi Arabia stripped him of his citizenship, his calls for holy war (*jihad*) and his portrayal of the United States as a puppet-master manipulating both non-Muslim (e.g., Israel, India, Russia) and Muslim (e.g., Egypt, Algeria, Saudi Arabia) governments to murder and oppress innocent Muslims made sense to millions of Muslims, even if only a very few committed themselves to follow him into battle.

Al-Qaeda blew up American embassies in Kenya and Tanzania in 1998, crippled the U.S. Navy destroyer *Cole* during a port call in Yemen in 2000, and then capped everything by attacking the World Trade Center and the Pentagon on 9/11. When the "global war on terrorism" declared by President Bush failed to eliminate bin Laden, his mystique grew. Further terrorist attacks—by Indonesians on tourists on the island of Bali in 2002, by North Africans on commuter trains servicing Madrid in 2004, by English-born Muslims on the London transit system in 2005, and by Pakistanis on luxury hotels in Mumbai, India, in 2008—made it clear that the current of violence unleashed by al-Qaeda had become decentralized and that recruits and cells might no longer be taking orders from bin Laden. In the meantime, the primary center of terrorist activity had shifted to Iraq, where suicide bombings became commonplace. Most bombings there resulted in Muslim casualties as Sunni and Shi'ite groups squared off against one other, thus diminishing the image of the suicide bomber as a fanatic hater of the West.

Conflict and Civilization

In 1993 Samuel P. Huntington, a professor of government at Harvard University, published "The Clash of Civilizations?" in the journal Foreign Affairs. *This article provoked extraordinary debate, particularly after the 9/11 attacks on the World Trade Center and the Pentagon. Some readers deemed it an accurate description of a post–Cold War world in which Islamic countries were destined to conflict violently with the countries of Europe and North America. Others saw it as imprecise in its failure to clarify what a "civilization" is, imperialistic in its unquestioning assumption of Western superiority, and encouraging of anti-Muslim prejudice.*

Civilizational identity will be increasingly important in the future, and the world will be shaped in large measure by the interactions among seven or eight major civilizations. These include Western, Confucian, Japanese, Islamic, Hindu, Slavic-Orthodox, Latin American and possibly African civilization. The most important conflicts of the future will occur along the cultural fault lines separating these civilizations from one another.

Why will this be the case?

First, differences among civilizations are not only real; they are basic. Civilizations are differentiated from each other by history, language, culture, tradition and, most important, religion. The people of different civilizations have different views on the relations between God and man, the individual and the group, the citizen and the state, parents and children, husband and wife, as well as differing views of the relative importance of rights and responsibilities, liberty and authority, equality and hierarchy. These differences are the product of centuries. They will not soon disappear. They are far more fundamental than differences among political ideologies and political regimes. Differences do not necessarily mean conflict, and conflict does not necessarily mean violence. Over the centuries, however, differences among civilizations have generated the most prolonged and the most violent conflicts.

Second, the world is becoming a smaller place. The interactions between peoples of different civilizations are increasing; these increasing interactions intensify civilization consciousness and awareness of differences between civilizations and commonalities within civilizations. North African immigration to France generates hostility among Frenchmen and at the same time increased receptivity to immigration by "good" European Catholic Poles. Americans react far more negatively to Japanese investment than to larger investments from Canada and European countries. . . .

Third, the processes of economic modernization and social change throughout the world are separating people from long-standing local identities. They also weaken the nation state as a source of identity. In much of the world religion has moved in to fill this gap, often in the form of movements that are labeled "fundamentalist." Such movements are found in Western Christianity, Judaism, Buddhism and Hinduism, as well as in Islam. In most countries and most religions the people active in fundamentalist movements are young, college-educated, middle-class technicians, professionals and business persons. . . .

As people define their identity in ethnic and religious terms, they are likely to see an "us" versus "them" relation existing between themselves and people of different ethnicity or religion. The end of ideologically defined states in Eastern Europe and the former Soviet Union permits traditional ethnic identities and animosities to come to the fore. Differences in culture and religion create differences over policy issues, ranging from human rights to immigration to trade and commerce to the environment. . . . Most important, the efforts of the West to promote its values of democracy and liberalism to universal values, to maintain its military predominance and to advance its economic interests engender countering responses from other civilizations. . . .

The interactions between civilizations vary greatly in the extent to which they are likely to be characterized by violence. Economic competition clearly predominates between the American and European subcivilizations of the West and between both of them and Japan. On the Eurasian continent, however, the proliferation of ethnic conflict, epitomized at the extreme in "ethnic cleansing," has not been totally random. It has been most frequent and most violent between groups belonging to different civilizations. In Eurasia the great historic fault lines between civilizations are once more aflame. This is particularly true along the boundaries of the crescent-shaped Islamic bloc of nations from the bulge of Africa to central Asia. Violence also occurs between Muslims, on the one hand, and Orthodox Serbs in the Balkans, Jews in Israel, Hindus in India, Buddhists in Burma and Catholics in the Philippines. Islam has bloody borders.

Rejoinders to Huntington's thesis saw it as a cornerstone of the aggressive policies adopted by the Bush administration after 9/11. As an alternative, they stressed the common values held by peaceful societies and the need for intercultural understanding. Mohammed Khatami, the president of the Islamic Republic of Iran, found support for a more positive framing of the matter when the United Nations, following his proposal, declared 2001 the year of "Dialogue Among Civilizations." Almost simultaneously, the Organization of the Islamic Conference, a 57-member international body headquartered in Saudi Arabia and composed of states with large Muslim populations, elaborated upon this concept in the "Tehran Declaration on Dialogue Among Civilizations."

Tehran Declaration on Dialogue Among Civilizations

Praise be to Allah and peace and blessing be upon His prophet and kin and companion.

The representatives of Heads of State and Government of OIC member states . . . [recognizing] the United Nations General Assembly resolution 53/22, designating the year 2001 as the United Nations year of Dialogue among Civilizations;

Guided by the noble Islamic teachings and values [*each of the following principles is accompanied by reference to a verse in the Quran*] on human dignity and equality, tolerance, peace and justice for humankind, and promotion of virtues and proscription of vice and evil;

Drawing upon the Islamic principles of celebration of human diversity, recognition of diversified sources of knowledge, promotion of dialogue and mutual understanding, genuine mutual respect in human interchanges, and encouragement of courteous and civilized discourse based on reason and logic;

Reaffirming the commitment of their Governments to promote dialogue and understanding among various cultures and civilizations, aimed at reaching a global consensus to build a new order for the next millennium founded in faith as well as common moral and ethical values of contemporary civilizations;

Requests the Secretary-General of the OIC to submit this declaration for endorsement to the Chairman of the Eighth Islamic Summit and the 26th Islamic Conference of Foreign Ministers for appropriate action:

A) General principles of dialogue among civilizations

1. Respect for the dignity and equality of all human beings without distinctions of any kind and of nations large and small;
2. Genuine acceptance of cultural diversity as a permanent of human society and a cherished asset for the advancement and welfare of humanity at large;
3. Mutual respect and tolerance for the views and values of various cultures and civilizations, as well as the right of members of all civilizations to preserve their cultural heritage and values, and rejection of desecration of moral, religious or cultural values, sanctities and sanctuaries;
4. Recognition of diversified sources of knowledge throughout time and space, and the imperative of drawing upon the areas of strengths, richness and wisdom of each civilization in a genuine process of mutual enrichment;
5. Rejection of attempts for cultural domination and imposition as well as doctrines and practices promoting confrontation and clash between civilizations;
6. Search for common grounds between and within various civilizations in order to face common global challenges;

   Acceptance of cooperation and search for understanding as the appropriate mechanism for the promotion of common universal values as well as for the suppression of global threats;
7. Commitment to participation of all peoples and nations, without any discrimination, in their own domestic as well as global decision-making and value distribution processes;
8. Compliance with principles of justice, equity, peace and solidarity as well as fundamental principles of international law and the United Nations Charter. . . .

A few years later, a joint proposal by the governments of Spain and Turkey received a similar endorsement by the United Nations. This led to the creation of the Alliance of Civilizations. The underlying principles of this organization were expressed in the 2006 report of its "High-Level Group," a body of eminent political, intellectual, and spiritual figures from around the world.

Alliance of CivilizationsReport of the High-Level Group

I. Bridging the World's Divides

1.1 Our world is alarmingly out of balance. For many, the last century brought unprecedented progress, prosperity, and freedom. For others, it marked an era of subjugation, humiliation and dispossession. Ours is a world of great inequalities and paradoxes: a world where the income of the planet's three richest people is greater than the combined income of the world's least developed countries; where modern medicine performs daily miracles and yet 3 million people die every year of preventable diseases; where we know more about distant universes than ever before, yet 130 million children have no access to education; where despite the existence of multilateral covenants and institutions, the international community often seems helpless in the face of conflict and genocide. For most of humanity, freedom from want and freedom from fear appear as elusive as ever.

1.2 We also live in an increasingly complex world, where polarized perceptions, fueled by injustice and inequality, often lead to violence and conflict, threatening international stability. Over the past few years, wars, occupation and acts of terror have exacerbated mutual suspicion and fear within and among societies. Some political leaders and sectors of the media, as well as radical groups have exploited this environment, painting mirror images of a world made up of mutually exclusive cultures, religions, or civilizations, historically distinct and destined for confrontation.

1.3 The anxiety and confusion caused by the "clash of civilizations" theory regrettably has distorted the terms of the discourse on the real nature of the predicament the world is facing. The history of relations between cultures is not only one of wars and confrontation. It is also based on centuries of constructive exchanges, cross-fertilization, and peaceful co-existence. Moreover, classifying internally fluid and diverse societies along hard-and-fast lines of civilizations interferes with more illuminating ways of understanding questions of identity, motivation and behavior. Rifts between the powerful and the powerless or the rich and the poor or between different political groups, classes, occupations and nationalities have greater explanatory power than such cultural categories. Indeed, the latter stereotypes only serve to entrench already polarized opinions. Worse, by promoting the misguided view that cultures are set on an unavoidable collision course, they help turn negotiable disputes into seemingly intractable identity-based conflicts that take hold of the popular imagination. It is essential, therefore, to counter the stereotypes and misconceptions that deepen patterns of hostility and mistrust among societies.

QUESTIONS FOR ANALYSIS

1. **How important are culture and religion, as opposed to governing ideology or economic inequality, in explaining current world conflicts?**
2. **Do statements like these reflect the realities of international and intercommunal relations? Or do they merely serve the political interests of the authors?**
3. **Should general statements about culture play a role at the level of personal relations in the neighborhood, the workplace, or the classroom?**

Sources: Samuel P. Huntington, "The Clash of Civilizations?," Reprinted by permission of *Foreign Affairs* 72, no. 3 (Summer 1993). Copyright 1993 by the Council on Foreign Relations, Inc. www.ForeignAffairs.com; "The Tehran Declaration on Dialogue Among Civilizations," Organization of the Islamic Conference, www.isesco.org.ma/english/publications/dig/CH11.php; "High-Level Group Report," Alliance of Civilizations, available online at www.unaoc.org/content/view/64/94/lang,english/.

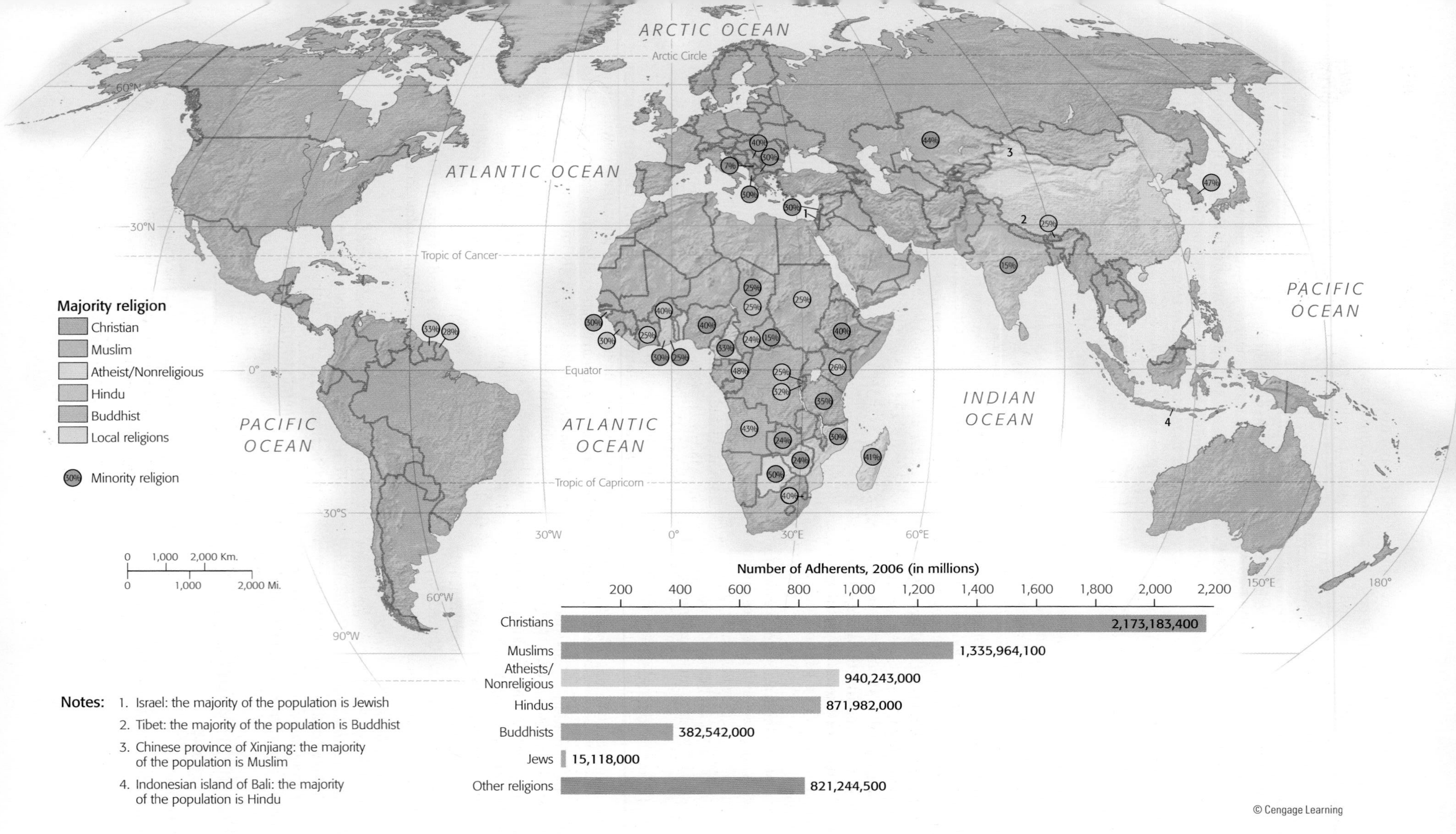

MAP 33.3 World Religions The distribution of Buddhism, Christianity, and Islam reflects centuries of missionary efforts. Hinduism and Judaism have expanded primarily through trade and migration. Chinese governments have actively curtailed religious practice. As religion revives as a source of social identity or a rationale for political assertion or mass mobilization, the possibility of religious activism across broad geographic regions becomes greater, as does the likelihood of domestic discord in multireligious states. (Data from *The New York Times 2003 Almanac*, ed. John W. Wright [New York: Penguin Books, 2002], 484–488. Copyright © The New York Times Company, 2002)

Interactive Map

Islam and Violence

In trying to explain a current of violence that could strike anywhere in the world but seemed to be centered on Muslims, some analysts argued that Islam itself encouraged violence against non-Muslims. The counterargument pointed out that terrorists came from many backgrounds and that the vast majority of Muslims saw their religion as one of peace. Others maintained that rigidly conservative Muslims like Usama bin Laden were blindly opposed to freedom and modernity. The counterargument pointed out that al-Qaeda used modern military and propaganda techniques and that many of its operatives, like bin Laden himself, graduated from modern technical programs. A third school of thought felt that the United States instigated al-Qaeda's wrath by supporting Israel and stationing troops in Saudi Arabia. The counterargument pointed out that the United States had also championed the Muslim cause in Bosnia and driven the secular dictator Saddam Husain out of Kuwait, an act that most Arab governments supported.

Universal Rights and Values

Universal Declaration of Human Rights A 1948 United Nations covenant binding signatory nations to the observance of specified rights.

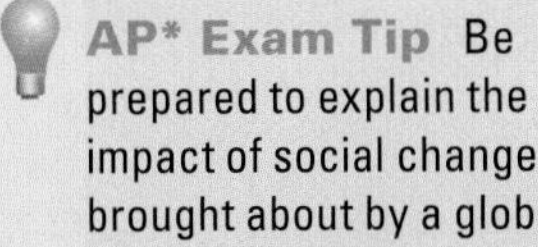

AP* Exam Tip Be prepared to explain the impact of social changes brought about by a globalizing world.

Alongside the growing influence of religion on politics, efforts to promote adherence to universal human rights also expanded. The modern human rights movement grew out of secular statements like the French Declaration of the Rights of Man (1789) and the U.S. Constitution (1788) and Bill of Rights (1791). The **Universal Declaration of Human Rights**, passed by the United Nations General Assembly in 1948, culminated this movement by proclaiming itself "a common standard of achievement for all peoples and nations." Its thirty articles condemned slavery, torture, cruel and inhuman punishment, and arbitrary arrest, detention, and exile. The Declaration called for freedom of movement, assembly, and thought. It asserted rights to life, liberty, and security of person; to impartial public trials; and to education, employment, and leisure. The principle of equality was most fully articulated in Article 2:

> *Everyone is entitled to all the rights and freedoms set forth in this Declaration, without distinction of any kind, such as race, color, sex, language, religion, or political or other opinion, national or social origin, property, birth or other status.*[1]

This passage reflected an international consensus against racism and imperialism and a growing acceptance of the importance of social and economic equality. Most newly independent countries joining the United Nations willingly signed the Declaration because it implicitly condemned European colonial regimes.

NGOs

nongovernmental organizations (NGOs) Nonprofit international organizations devoted to investigating human rights abuses and providing humanitarian relief. Two NGOs won the Nobel Peace Prize in the 1990s: International Campaign to Ban Landmines (1997) and Doctors Without Borders (1999).

Besides the official actions of the United Nations and various national governments, individual human rights activists, often working through philanthropic bodies known as **nongovernmental organizations (NGOs)**, have been important forces promoting human rights. Amnesty International, founded in 1961, concentrates on gaining the freedom of people who have been tortured or imprisoned without trial and campaigns against summary execution by government death squads or other gross violations of rights. Arguing that no right is more fundamental than the right to life, other NGOs have devoted themselves to famine relief, refugee assistance, and health care around the world. Médecins Sans Frontières (Doctors Without Borders), founded in 1971, was awarded the Nobel Peace Prize in 1999 for offering medical assistance in scores of crises.

While NGOs often worked in specific countries, other universal goals became enshrined in international agreements. Such agreements made genocide a crime and promoted environmental protection of the seas, of Antarctica, and of the atmosphere (see Environment and Technology: Global Warming). The United States and a few other nations were greatly concerned that such treaties would limit their sovereignty or threaten their national interests. For this reason the U.S. Congress delayed ratifying the 1949 convention on genocide until 1986. More recently the United States drew widespread criticism for demanding exemption for Americans from the jurisdiction of the International Criminal Court, created in 2002 to try international criminals, and for declaring that "enemy combatants" taken prisoner during the "global war on terrorism" should not be treated in accordance with the Third Geneva Convention (1950) on humane treatment of prisoners of war.

Obama and Human Rights

The 2008 election of Barack Obama as the first African-American to hold the office of president of the United States was widely thought to signal a change in American attitudes on international rights issues. Not only was he the living embodiment of the ability of the Americans to see past skin color in selecting a leader, but on taking office he immediately announced the

ENVIRONMENT + TECHNOLOGY

Global Warming

Until the 1980s environmental alarms focused mainly on localized episodes of air and water pollution, exposure to toxic substances, waste management, and the disappearance of wilderness. The development of increasingly powerful computers and complex models of ecological interactions in the 1990s, however, made people aware of the global scope of certain environmental problems.

Many scientists and policymakers came to perceive global warming, the slow increase of the temperature of the earth's lower atmosphere, as an environmental threat requiring preventive action on an international scale. The warming is caused by a layer of atmospheric gases (carbon dioxide, methane, nitrous oxide, and ozone) that allow solar radiation to reach earth and warm it but that keep infrared energy (heat) from radiating from earth's surface back into space. Called the *greenhouse effect*, this process normally keeps the earth's temperature at a level suitable for life. However, increases in greenhouse-gas emissions—particularly from the burning of fossil fuels in industry and transportation—have added to this insulating atmospheric layer.

Recent events have confirmed predictions of global temperature increases and melting glaciers and icecaps. Greenland glaciers and Arctic Ocean sea ice are melting at record rates, and huge sections of the Antarctic ice shelf are breaking off and floating away. Andean glaciers are shrinking so fast they could disappear in a decade, imperiling water supplies for drinking, irrigation, and hydroelectric production. Drought has affected much of the United States in recent years, and Australia has experienced the "Big Dry," its worst drought in a century.

Despite this evidence, governments of the industrialized countries that produce the most greenhouse gasses have been slow to adopt measures stringent enough to reduce emissions. They cite the negative effects they believe this could have on their economies. Because of these fears, many nations hesitated to sign the 1997 Kyoto Protocol, the first international agreement to impose penalties on countries that failed to cut greenhouse-gas emissions. It was a major environmental victory when Japan added its signature in March 2001, but to the consternation of many world leaders President George W. Bush rejected the agreement.

The American election of 2008 may have set the stage for changes that would finally make the climate control an area of action and not just worry. Shortly after being elected, Barack Obama announced to an audience of scientists and citizens concerned with climate matters: "You can be sure that the United States will once again engage vigorously in these negotiations, and help lead the world toward a new era of global cooperation on climate change."

D. Aubert/Corbis Sygma

Flooding in Bangladesh Typhoon-driven floods submerge the low-lying farmlands of Bangladesh with tragic regularity. Any significant rise in the sea level will make parts of the country nearly uninhabitable.

closing of the widely condemned prison for "enemy combatants" at Guantanamo Bay, an American naval base in Cuba, and chose for his cabinet men and women strongly associated with the protection of rights and of the country's natural heritage.

Women's Rights

Women's Rights Conferences

The women's rights movement, which began on both sides of the North Atlantic in the nineteenth century, became an important human rights issue in the twentieth century. Rights for women

Boulat/Sipa Press

Beijing Women's Conference in 1995 This gathering of women from every part of the world, under United Nations auspices, illustrated the challenges posed by women's search for equality. The Chinese government, consistent with its policies of suppressing dissent and closely regulating social life, tried to limit press access to the conference. As in many other instances, these efforts to silence or control women's voices on issues like abortion and family planning proved ineffective.

became accepted in Western countries and were enshrined in the constitutions of many nations newly freed from colonial rule. In 1979 the United Nations General Assembly adopted the Convention on the Elimination of All Forms of Discrimination Against Women, and in 1985 the first international conference on the status of women, sponsored by the United Nations Division for the Advancement of Women, was held in Nairobi, Kenya. A second conference in Beijing ten years later added momentum to the movement. By 2007, 183 countries had endorsed the 1979 convention.

Besides highlighting the problems women face around the world, international conferences have also revealed great variety in the views and concerns of women. Feminists from the West, who had been accustomed to dictating the agenda and who had pushed for the liberation of women in other parts of the world, sometimes found themselves accused of having narrow concerns and condescending attitudes. Some non-Western women complained about Western feminists' endorsement of sexual liberation and about the deterioration of family life in the West. They found Western feminists' concern with matters such as comfortable clothing misplaced and trivial compared to the issues of poverty and disease.

Other cultures came in for their share of criticism. Western women and many secular leaders in Muslim countries protested Islam's requirement that a woman cover her head and wear loose-fitting garments to conceal the shape of her body, practices enforced by law in countries such as Iran and Saudi Arabia. Nevertheless, many outspoken Muslim women voluntarily donned concealing garments as expressions of personal belief, statements of resistance to secular dictatorship, or defense against coarse male behavior.

The conferences were more important for the attention they focused on women's issues than for the solutions they generated. Such efforts raised the prominence of human rights as a global concern and put pressure on governments to consider human rights when making foreign policy decisions. Skeptics observed, however, that a Western country might successfully prod a non-Western country to improve its human rights performance—for example, by granting

SECTION REVIEW

- The second half of the twentieth century has seen an increase in political action inspired by religious belief.
- Militant Islam has risen in response to authoritarian oppression in many Muslim countries and to the claim that the United States supports such authoritarianism.
- Universal standards of human rights have gained wider acceptance and underlie the work of the United Nations, individual states, and NGOs.
- Concepts of human rights have expanded to address genocide and environmental protection.
- Global debates on women's rights have addressed a variety of economic, political, and social problems but have also involved clashes over cultural values.

Debates over Rights

women better access to education and careers—but that reverse criticism of a Western country often fell on deaf ears—for example, condemnation of the death penalty in the United States. For such critics the human rights movement was seen not as an effort to make the world more humane but as another form of Western cultural imperialism.

GLOBAL CULTURE

Because of changes in electronic technology, today political and economic events have almost instantaneous impact in all parts of the world. A global language, a global educational system, and global forms of artistic expression have all come into being. Trade, travel, and migration have made a common popular culture unavoidable. These changes have delighted and enriched some but angered others.

The Media and the Message

Cultural Imperialism

cultural imperialism Domination of one culture over another by a deliberate policy or by economic or technological superiority.

The fact that the most pervasive elements of global culture have their origins in the West raised concerns in many quarters about **cultural imperialism**. Critics complained that entertainment conglomerates were flooding the world's movie theaters and television screens with Western images and that goods catering to Western tastes but manufactured in countries with low production costs, like China and Indonesia, were flooding world markets. In this view, global marketing was especially insidious in trying to shape a world with a single Western outlook based on capitalist ideology, and at the same time suppressing or devaluing traditional cultures and alternative ideologies. As the leader of the capitalist world, the United States was seen as the primary culprit.

The pace of cultural globalization began to quicken during the economic recovery after World War II. The Hollywood films and American jazz recordings that had become popular in Europe and parts of Asia continued to spread. But the birth of electronic technology opened contacts with large numbers of people who could never have afforded to go to a movie or buy a record.

Electronic Media

The first step was the development of cheap transistor radios that could run on a couple of small batteries. Perfected by American scientists at Bell Telephone Laboratories in 1948, solid-state electronic transistors replaced power-hungry and less reliable electron tubes in radios and other devices. Just as tube radios had spread in Europe and America in the decades before the war, small portable transistor radios spread rapidly in parts of the world where homes lacked electricity.

Television, made possible by the electron-scanning gun invented in 1928, became widely available to Western consumers in the 1950s. In poorer parts of the world TVs were not common until the 1980s and 1990s, after mass production and cheap transistors made sets more affordable. Outside the United States, television broadcasting was usually a government monopoly at first, following the pattern of telegraph and postal service and radio broadcasting. Governments expected news reports and other programming to disseminate a unified national viewpoint.

However, government monopolies eroded as the high cost of television production opened up global markets for rebroadcasts of American soap operas, adventure series, and situation comedies. By the 1990s a global network of satellites brought privately owned television broadcasting to even remote areas of the world, and the VCR (videocassette recorder) provided an even greater variety of programs. In the following decade DVD players continued the trend. As a result of wider circulation of programming, people often became familiar with different dialects of English and other languages. People in Portugal who in the 1960s had found it difficult to understand Brazilian Portuguese became avid fans of Brazilian soap operas. And immigrants from Albania and North Africa often arrived in Italy with a command of Italian learned from Italian stations whose signals they could pick up at home.

Global Communication

CNN (Cable News Network) expanded its international market after becoming the most-viewed and informative news source during the 1991 Persian Gulf War, when it broadcast live from Baghdad. Other 24-hour news broadcasters followed this lead. Like CNN, they offered fundamentally American viewpoints. In response, Al-Jazeera, based in the Persian Gulf emirate of

Qatar, broadcast statements by Usama bin Laden from 2001 onward and offered video footage and interpretation that differed greatly from American coverage of the war in Iraq in 2003.

The Internet

The Internet, a linkage of academic, government, and business computers developed by the American Department of Defense in the 1960s, began to transform world culture in the early years of the twenty-first century. Personal computers proliferated in the 1980s, and with the establishment of the easy-to-use graphic interface of the World Wide Web in 1994, the number of Internet users skyrocketed. Myriad new companies formed to exploit "e-commerce," the commercial dimension of the Internet, and students were soon spending less time studying conventional books and more exploring the Web for information and entertainment. Blogs, or weblogs, offered a vehicle for anyone in the world to place his or her opinions, experiences, and creative efforts before anyone with access to a computer.

AP* Exam Tip A broad understanding of the globalization of pop culture is important.

As had happened so often throughout history, technological developments had unanticipated consequences. Although the new telecommunications and entertainment technologies derived disproportionately from American invention, industry, and cultural creativity, Japan and other East Asian nations took the lead in manufacturing and refining electronic devices. Cellular mobile phones became increasingly used for taking and transmitting pictures and connecting to the Internet. Non-Western countries that had adopted telephones late and had limited networks of copper wire benefited most from the improved communication. In 2007 the United States ranked seventy-second in per capita cellular phone use.

global pop culture Popular cultural practices and institutions that have been adopted internationally, such as music, the Internet, television, food, and fashion.

The Spread of Pop Culture

For most of history, popular culture consisted of folk tales and highly localized styles of dress, cooking, music, and visual expression. Only the literate few had full access to the riches of a broader "great tradition," such as Confucianism, Islam, or Buddhism. In modern times, government school systems increased literacy rates but also promoted specifically national values and cultural tastes. Prescribed languages of instruction eroded the use and memory of local languages and traditions. In their place there arose **global pop culture**.

Initially, the content was heavily American. Singer Michael Jackson was almost as well known to the youth of Dar-es-Salaam (Tanzania) and Bangkok (Thailand) as to American fans. Businesses sought out worldwide celebrities like basketball star Michael Jordan and championship golfer Tiger Woods to endorse their products. American television programs, following in the path of American movies, acquired immense followings and inspired local imitations.

But the United States had no monopoly on global pop culture. Latin American soap operas, *telenovelas*, had a vast following in the Americas, eastern Europe, and elsewhere. Mumbai, India, long the world's largest producer of films, made or inspired more films for international

Private Collection

Japanese Adult Male Comic Book After World War II comic magazines emerged as a major form of publication and a distinctive product of culture in Japan. Different series are directed to different age and gender groups. Issued weekly and running to some three hundred pages in black and white, the most popular magazines sell as many copies as do major newsmagazines in the United States.

audiences, like the 2009 Academy Award–winning *Slumdog Millionaire*. And the martial arts filmmakers of Hong Kong saw their style flourish in high-budget international spectaculars like director Ang Lee's *Crouching Tiger, Hidden Dragon* (2000) and the *Matrix* trilogy (1999–2003), which relied heavily on Hong Kong fight choreographers.

Emerging Global Elite Culture

global elite culture At the beginning of the twenty-first century, the attitudes and outlook of well-educated, prosperous, Western-oriented people around the world, largely expressed in European languages, especially English.

While the globalization of popular culture has been criticized, cultural links across national and ethnic boundaries at a more elite level have generated little controversy. The end of the Cold War reopened intellectual and cultural contacts between former adversaries, making possible such things as Russian-American collaboration on space missions and extensive business contacts among former rivals. The English language, modern science, and higher education became the key elements of this **global elite culture**.

Decolonization and Language

The emergence of English as the first global language began with the British Empire's introduction of the language to far-flung colonies. After achieving independence in the wake of World War II, most former colonies chose to continue using English as an official language because it provided national unity and a link to the outside world that local languages could not. Countries that chose instead to make a local language official often found the decision counterproductive. Indian nationalists had pushed for Hindi to be India's official language, but they found that students taught in Hindi were unable to compete internationally because of poor knowledge of English. Sri Lanka, which had made Sinhala its official language in 1956, reversed itself after local reporters revealed in 1989 that prominent officials were sending their children to English-medium private schools.

English as a Global Language

While similar postcolonial language developments extended the reach of French, Spanish, and other European tongues, the use of English as a second language was greatly stimulated by the importance of the United States in postwar world affairs. After the collapse of Soviet domination, students in eastern Europe flocked to study English instead of Russian. Ninety percent of students in Cambodia (a former French colony) chose to study English, even though a Canadian agency offered a sizable cash bonus if they would study French. In the 1990s China made the study of English as a second language nearly universal from junior high school onwards.

English has become the language of choice for most international academic conferences, business meetings, and diplomatic gatherings. International organizations that provide equal status to many languages, such as the United Nations and the European Union, often conduct informal committee meetings in English. In cities throughout the world, signs and notices are commonly posted in the local language and in English. Writers from Africa and India have received high honors for novels written in English, as have Arab and Caribbean authors for works written in French. Nevertheless, world literature remains highly diverse in form and language.

Global Science

By contrast, science and technology have become standardized components of global culture. Though imperialism helped spread the Western disciplines of biology, chemistry, and physics around the world, their importance expanded even further after decolonization as students from newly independent nations sought to compete at an international level. Standardization of scientific terms, weights and measures, and computer codes underlay the worldwide expansion of commerce.

Global University Education

The third pillar of global elite culture, along with science and globalized languages, is the university. The structure and curricula of modern universities are nearly indistinguishable around the world, making student experiences similar across national boundaries. Instruction in the pure sciences varies little from place to place. Some doctoral science programs in American universities now enroll mostly students from non-Western countries. Standardization is nearly as common in applied sciences such as engineering and medicine and only slightly less so in the social sciences. Although the humanities preserve greater diversity in subject matter and approach, professors and students around the world pay attention to the latest literary theories and topics of historical interest.

While university subjects are taught in many languages, instruction in English is spreading rapidly. Because discoveries are often first published in English, advanced students in science, business, and international relations need to know that language to keep up with the latest developments. Many courses in northern European countries have long been offered in English, and elsewhere in Europe courses taught in English have facilitated the EU's efforts to encourage students to study outside their home countries. The small Arab sheikhdoms of the Persian Gulf have led the way in persuading American universities to open up local branches and graduate programs.

Enduring Cultural Diversity

Although protesters regularly denounce the "Americanization" of the world, a closer look suggests that cultural globalization is more complex. Just as English has spread widely as a second language, so global culture is primarily a second culture that dominates some contexts but does not displace other traditions. From this perspective, American music, fast food, and fashions are more likely to add to a society's options than to displace local culture.

Japan and Cultural Diversity

Japan first demonstrated that a country with a non-Western culture could industrialize effectively. Individuality was less valued in Japan than the ability of each person to fit into a group, whether as an employee, a member of an athletic team, or a student in a class. Moreover, the Japanese considered it unmannerly to directly contradict, correct, or refuse the request of another person. From a Western point of view, these Japanese customs seemed to discourage individual initiative and personality development and to preserve traditional hierarchies. Japanese women, for example, even though they often worked outside the home, responded only slowly to the American and European feminist advocacy of equality in economic and social relations. However, the Japanese approach to social relations was well suited to an industrial economy. The efficiency, pride in workmanship, and group solidarity of Japanese workers played a major role in transforming Japan from a defeated nation with a demolished industrial base in 1945 to an economic power by the 1980s.

As awareness of the economic impact of Japanese culture and society began to spread, it became apparent that Taiwan and South Korea, along with Singapore and Hong Kong (a British colony before being reunited with China in 1997), were developing dynamic industrial economies of their own. Today India and the People's Republic of China are following the same path without forsaking their national tastes and heritages.

The Future of Diversity and Dominance

This does not mean that the world's cultural diversity is secure. Every decade a number of minority languages cease to be spoken. Televised national ceremonies or performances for tourists may prevent folk customs and costumes from dying out, but they also tend to devitalize rituals that once had many local variations. While a century ago it was possible to recognize the nationality of people from their clothing and grooming, today most urban men dress the same the world over, although women's clothing shows greater variety. As much as one may regret the disappearance or commercialization of some folkways, most anthropologists would agree that change is characteristic of all healthy cultures. What doesn't change risks extinction.

SECTION REVIEW

- The global pervasiveness of Western culture has provoked charges of U.S. cultural imperialism.
- Technology such as radio, television, and the Internet has played a major role in the spread of Western culture since World War II.
- Technology has also contributed to the emergence of a global pop culture that blends a variety of cultural elements from different countries.
- A global elite culture has also developed combining the English language, science, and higher education.
- Despite globalizing forces, cultural diversity remains strong, if not completely secure.

KEY TERMS

globalization p. 948
World Trade Organization (WTO) p. 950
weapons of mass destruction p. 954
terrorism p. 957
Usama bin Laden p. 957
Universal Declaration of Human Rights p. 961
nongovernmental organizations (NGOs) p. 961
cultural imperialism p. 964
global pop culture p. 965
global elite culture p. 966

EBOOK AND WEBSITE RESOURCES

Primary Sources

The Last Night

Declaration of Jihad Against Americans Occupying the Land of the Two Holy Mosques

Interactive Maps

Map 33.1 Global Distribution of Wealth

Map 33.2 Regional Trade Associations, 2004

Map 33.3 World Religions

Plus flashcards, practice quizzes, and more. Go to: www.cengage.com/history/bullietearthpeople5e

SUGGESTED READING

Appadurai, Arjun. *Modernity at Large: Cultural Dimensions of Globalization.* 1996. Treats the interrelationships between high culture and popular culture.

Barber, Benjamin R. *Jihad vs. McWorld: How Globalism and Tribalism Are Reshaping the World.* 1995. A widely read attempt to describe the world at the turn of the millennium.

Bulliet, Richard W. *The Case for Islamo-Christian Civilization.* 2004. Takes issue with Samuel Huntington's "clash of civilizations" theory.

Chua, Amy. *World on Fire: How Exporting Free Market Democracy Breeds Ethnic Hatred and Global Instability.* 2003. A pessimistic perspective on globalization and world trade.

Devine, Carol, and Carol Rae Hansen. *Human Rights: The Essential Reference.* 1999. A standard work on the subject.

Friedman, Thomas L. *The Lexus and the Olive Tree.* 1999. A readable and influential analysis of alternative pathways to the future.

Hoffman, Bruce. *Inside Terrorism*, 2nd ed. 2006. A well-regarded work on a complex topic.

Huntington, Samuel P. *The Clash of Civilizations and the Remaking of the World Order.* 1996. A controversial thesis that Islam and the West are destined for irresolvable conflict.

Kaplan, Robert. *Of Paradise and Power: America and Europe in the New World Order.* 2002. Examines the growing gulf between the United States and Europe.

Kupchan, Charles A. *The End of the American Era: U.S. Foreign Policy and the Geopolitics of the Twenty-first Century.* 2002. A realist perspective on the world balance of power.

Mamdani, Mahmood. *Good Muslim, Bad Muslim: America, the Cold War, and the Roots of Terror.* 2004. Explores the origins of Muslim militancy in opposition to the West.

Moore, Mike. *A World Without Walls: Freedom, Development, Free Trade and Global Governance.* 2003. A view of the global economy from a former director-general of the World Trade Organization.

Norris, Pippa. *Rising Tide: Gender Equality and Cultural Change Around the World.* 2003. Surveys the condition of women.

Pennycock, Alistaire. *The Cultural Politics of English as an International Language.* 1994. The rise of English as a global means of communication.

Priest, Dana. *Mission: Waging War and Keeping Peace with America's Military.* 2003. A critique of American military policies in the twenty-first century.

NOTES

1. "Universal Declaration of Human Rights," in *Twenty-five Human Rights Documents* (New York: Center for the Study of Human Rights, Columbia University, 1994), 6.

AP* REVIEW QUESTIONS FOR CHAPTER 33

1. The European Union is an attempt to
   (A) establish socialism in all of Europe.
   (B) balance American economic power in the world.
   (C) prevent Africa, Asia, and Latin America from growing into major trade regions.
   (D) buy oil from OPEC in bulk and at lower rates.

2. The trade agreement that eliminated tariffs among the United States, Canada, and Mexico is
   (A) OAS.
   (B) the Rio Treaty.
   (C) NAFTA.
   (D) the NPT.

3. The WTO encourages
   (A) nations not to trade with the United States.
   (B) lower wages for industrial workers to create more jobs.
   (C) loans from the World Bank to help increase industrial output and create more jobs.
   (D) reduced trading barriers and the enforcement of international trade agreements.

4. In March of 2003, the United States invaded Iraq on the grounds that Saddam Husain
   (A) owed Kuwait money and need to pay it in oil.
   (B) possessed weapons of mass destruction.
   (C) was pursing ethnic cleansing against the Turks.
   (D) was persecuting Christians in Iraq.

5. In the second half of the twentieth century,
   (A) the world entered a period of peaceful coexistence following the end of the Cold War.
   (B) the creation of a unipolar world ended all threats of nuclear holocaust.
   (C) religious beliefs increasingly inspired political actions.
   (D) totalitarianism began to reemerge in small, undeveloped nations.

6. Although all member states of the United Nations have signed the Universal Declaration of Human Rights,
   (A) most newly independent countries joining the United Nations willingly signed the Declaration because it implicitly condemned European colonial regimes.
   (B) it is vigorously enforced by the UN Security Council.
   (C) any nation that does not agree with it can simply void its signature.
   (D) it does not include religion or religious freedom.

7. One important force in promoting human rights has been
   (A) the U.S. military in places like Vietnam.
   (B) the Cuban government in Angola.
   (C) nongovernmental organizations such as Doctors Without Borders.
   (D) the passage of the Kyoto Protocol.

8. In the early twenty-first century, world culture was being transformed with the spread of
   (A) AIDS.
   (B) television.
   (C) pop music.
   (D) the Internet.

GLOSSARY

Abbasid Caliphate Descendants of the Prophet **Muhammad**'s uncle, al-Abbas, the Abbasids overthrew the **Umayyad Caliphate** and ruled an Islamic empire from their capital in Baghdad (founded 762) from 750 to 1258. *(p. 233)*

abolitionists Men and women who agitated for a complete end to slavery. Abolitionist pressure ended the British transatlantic slave trade in 1808 and slavery in British colonies in 1834. In the United States the activities of abolitionists were one factor leading to the Civil War (1861–1865). *(p. 671)*

acculturation The adoption of the language, customs, values, and behaviors of host nations by immigrants. *(p. 675)*

Acheh Sultanate Muslim kingdom in northern Sumatra. Main center of Islamic expansion in Southeast Asia in the early seventeenth century, it declined after the Dutch seized **Malacca** from Portugal in 1641. *(p. 564)*

Aden Port city in the modern south Arabian country of Yemen. It has been a major trading center in the Indian Ocean since ancient times. *(p. 388)*

African National Congress An organization dedicated to obtaining equal voting and civil rights for black inhabitants of South Africa. Founded in 1912 as the South African Native National Congress, it changed its name in 1923. Though it was banned and its leaders were jailed for many years, it eventually helped bring majority rule to South Africa. *(p. 870)*

Afrikaners South Africans descended from Dutch and French settlers of the seventeenth century. Their Great Trek founded new settler colonies in the nineteenth century. Though a minority among South Africans, they held political power after 1910, imposing a system of racial segregation called apartheid after 1949. *(p. 779)*

Agricultural Revolutions (ancient) The change from food gathering to food production that occurred between ca. 8000 and 2000 B.C.E. Also known as the Neolithic Revolution. *(p. 9)*

agricultural revolution (eighteenth century) The transformation of farming that resulted in the eighteenth century from the spread of new crops, improvements in cultivation techniques and livestock breeding, and the consolidation of small holdings into large farms from which tenants and sharecroppers were forcibly expelled. *(p. 630)*

Aguinaldo, Emilio (1869–1964) Leader of the Filipino independence movement against Spain (1895–1898). He proclaimed the independence of the Philippines in 1899, but his movement was crushed and he was captured by the United States Army in 1901. *(p. 788)*

Akbar (1542–1605) Most illustrious sultan of the Mughal Empire in India (r. 1556–1605). He expanded the empire and pursued a policy of conciliation with Hindus. *(p. 561)*

Akhenaten Egyptian pharaoh (r. 1353–1335 B.C.E.). He built a new capital at Amarna, fostered a new style of naturalistic art, and created a religious revolution by imposing worship of the sun-disk. The Amarna letters, largely from his reign, preserve official correspondence with subjects and neighbors. *(p. 73)*

Alexander (356–323 B.C.E.) King of Macedonia in northern Greece. Between 334 and 323 B.C.E. he conquered the Persian Empire, reached the Indus Valley, founded many Greek-style cities, and spread Greek culture across the Middle East. Later known as Alexander the Great. *(p. 130)*

Alexandria City on the Mediterranean coast of Egypt founded by **Alexander**. It became the capital of the Hellenistic kingdom of the **Ptolemies**. It contained the famous Library and the Museum, a center for leading scientific and literary figures. Its merchants engaged in trade with areas bordering the Mediterranean and the Indian Ocean. *(p. 131)*

Allende, Salvador (1908–1973) Socialist politician elected president of Chile in 1970 and overthrown by the military in 1973. He died during the military attack. *(p. 916)*

All-India Muslim League Political organization founded in India in 1906 to defend the interests of India's Muslim minority. Led by Muhammad Ali Jinnah, it attempted to negotiate with the **Indian National Congress**. In 1940, the League began demanding a separate state for Muslims, to be called Pakistan. (See also **Jinnah, Muhammad Ali**.) *(p. 862)*

altepetl An ethnic state in ancient Mesoamerica, the common political building block of that region. *(p. 316)*

amulet Small charm meant to protect the bearer from evil. Found frequently in archaeological excavations in Mesopotamia and Egypt, amulets reflect the religious practices of the common people. *(p. 21)*

Amur River This river valley was a contested frontier between northern China and eastern Russia until the settlement arranged in the Treaty of Nerchinsk (1689). *(p. 582)*

anarchists Revolutionaries who wanted to abolish all private property and governments, usually by violence, and replace them with free associations of groups. *(p. 755)*

Anasazi Important culture of what is now the southwest United States (700–1300 C.E.). Centered on Chaco Canyon in New Mexico and Mesa Verde in Colorado, the Anasazi culture built multistory residences and worshiped in subterranean buildings called kivas. *(p. 321)*

aqueduct A conduit, either elevated or underground, that used gravity to carry water from a source to a location—usually a city—that needed it. The Romans built many aqueducts in a period of substantial urbanization. *(p. 153)*

Arawak Amerindian peoples who inhabited the Greater Antilles of the Caribbean at the time of Columbus. *(p. 432)*

Arkwright, Richard (1732–1792) English inventor and entrepreneur who became the wealthiest and most successful textile manufacturer of the early **Industrial Revolution**. He invented the water frame, a machine that, with minimal human supervision, could spin many strong cotton threads at once. *(p. 636)*

Armenia One of the earliest Christian kingdoms, situated in eastern Anatolia and the western Caucasus and occupied by speakers of the Armenian language. *(p. 219)*

Asante African kingdom on the **Gold Coast** that expanded rapidly after 1680. Asante participated in the Atlantic economy, trading gold, slaves, and ivory. It resisted British imperial ambitions for a quarter century before being absorbed into Britain's Gold Coast colony in 1902. *(p. 780)*

Ashikaga Shogunate (1336–1573) The second of Japan's military governments headed by a shogun (a military ruler). Sometimes called the Muromachi Shogunate. *(p. 366)*

Ashoka Third ruler of the **Mauryan Empire** in India (r. 273–232 B.C.E.). He converted to Buddhism and broadcast his precepts on inscribed stones and pillars, the earliest surviving Indian writing. (*p. 183*)

Asian Tigers Collective name for South Korea, Taiwan, Hong Kong, and Singapore—nations that became economic powers in the 1970s and 1980s. (*p. 922*)

Atahualpa (1502?–1533) Last ruling **Inca** emperor of Peru. He was executed by the Spanish. (*p. 447*)

Atatürk, Kemal (1880–1938) The founder of modern Turkey. An army officer, he distinguished himself in the defense of Gallipoli in World War I and expelled a Greek expeditionary army from Anatolia in 1921–1922. He abolished the sultanate and replaced the Ottoman Empire with the Turkish Republic in 1923. As president until his death in 1938, he pushed through a radical Westernization and reform of Turkish society. *(p. 816)*

Atlantic Circuit The network of trade routes connecting Europe, Africa, and the Americas that underlay the Atlantic system. (*p. 530*)

Atlantic system The network of trading links after 1500 that moved goods, wealth, people, and cultures around the Atlantic Ocean Basin. (*p. 519*)

Augustus (63 B.C.E.–14 C.E.) Honorific name of Octavian, founder of the **Roman Principate**, the military dictatorship that replaced the failing rule of the **Roman Senate**. After defeating all rivals, between 31 B.C.E. and 14 C.E. he laid the groundwork for several centuries of stability and prosperity in the Roman Empire. (*p. 147*)

Auschwitz Nazi extermination camp in Poland, the largest center of mass murder during the **Holocaust**. Close to a million Jews, Gypsies, Communists, and others were killed there. (*p. 852*)

ayllu Andean lineage group or kin-based community. (*p. 324*)

Aztecs Also known as Mexica, the Aztecs created a powerful empire in central Mexico (1325–1521 C.E.). They forced defeated peoples to provide goods and labor as a tax. (*p. 317)*

Babylon The largest and most important city in Mesopotamia. It achieved particular eminence as the capital of the Amorite king **Hammurabi** in the eighteenth century B.C.E. and the Neo-Babylonian king Nebuchadnezzar in the sixth century B.C.E. (*p. 18*)

balance of power The policy in international relations by which, beginning in the eighteenth century, the major European states acted together to prevent any one of them from becoming too powerful. (*p. 479*)

Balfour Declaration Statement issued by Britain's Foreign Secretary Arthur Balfour in 1917 favoring the establishment of a Jewish national homeland in Palestine. (*p. 806*)

Bannermen Hereditary military servants of the **Qing Empire**, in large part descendants of peoples of various origins who had fought for the founders of the empire. (*p. 700*)

Bantu Collective name of a large group of sub-Saharan African languages and of the peoples speaking these languages. (*p. 216*)

Batavia Fort established ca. 1619 as headquarters of Dutch East India Company operations in Indonesia; today the city of Jakarta. (*p. 567*)

Battle of Midway U.S. naval victory over the Japanese fleet in June 1942, in which the Japanese lost four of their best aircraft carriers. It marked a turning point in World War II. (*p. 847*)

Battle of Omdurman British victory over the Mahdi in the Sudan in 1898. General Kitchener led a mixed force of British and Egyptian troops armed with rapid-firing rifles and machine guns. (*p. 774*)

Beijing China's northern capital, first used as an imperial capital in 906 and now the capital of the People's Republic of China. (*p. 357*)

Bengal Region of northeastern India. It was the first part of India to be conquered by the British in the eighteenth century and remained the political and economic center of British India throughout the nineteenth century. The 1905 split of the province into predominantly Hindu West Bengal and predominantly Muslim East Bengal (now Bangladesh) sparked anti-British riots. (*p. 862*)

Berlin Conference (1884–1885) Conference that German chancellor Otto von Bismarck called to set rules for the partition of Africa. It led to the creation of the Congo Free State under King **Leopold II** of Belgium. (See also **Bismarck, Otto von**.) (*p. 778*)

Bhagavad-Gita The most important work of Indian sacred literature, a dialogue between the great warrior Arjuna and the god Krishna on duty and the fate of the spirit. (*p. 184*)

bin Laden, Usama Saudi-born **Muslim** extremist who funded the al-Qaeda organization that was responsible for several terrorist attacks, including those on the World Trade Center and the Pentagon in 2001. (*p. 957*)

Bismarck, Otto von (1815–1898) Chancellor (prime minister) of Prussia from 1862 until 1871, when he became chancellor of Germany. A conservative nationalist, he led Prussia to victory against Austria (1866) and France (1870) and was responsible for the creation of the German Empire in 1871. (*p. 758*)

Black Death An outbreak of **bubonic plague** that spread across Asia, North Africa, and Europe in the mid-fourteenth century, carrying off vast numbers of persons. (*p. 401*)

Bolívar, Simón (1783–1830) The most important military leader in the struggle for independence in South America. Born in Venezuela, he led military forces there and in Colombia, Ecuador, Peru, and Bolivia. (*p. 657*)

Bolsheviks Radical Marxist political party founded by Vladimir Lenin in 1903. Under Lenin's leadership, the Bolsheviks seized power in November 1917 during the Russian Revolution. (See also **Lenin, Vladimir**.) (*p. 806*)

Bonaparte, Napoleon (1769–1821) General who overthrew the French Directory in 1799 and became emperor of the French in 1804. Failed to defeat Great Britain and abdicated in 1814. Returned to power briefly in 1815 but was defeated and died in exile. (*p. 615*)

Bornu A powerful West African kingdom at the southern edge of the Sahara in the Central Sudan, which was important in trans-Saharan trade and in the spread of **Islam**. Also known as Kanem-Bornu, it endured from the ninth century to the end of the nineteenth. (*p. 538*)

bourgeoisie In early modern Europe, the class of well-off town dwellers whose wealth came from manufacturing, finance, commerce, and allied professions. (*p. 468*)

Brant, Joseph (1742–1807) Mohawk leader who supported the British during the American Revolution. (*p. 608*)

Brazza, Savorgnan de (1852–1905) Franco-Italian explorer sent by the French government to claim part of equatorial Africa for France. Founded Brazzaville, capital of the French Congo, in 1880. (*p. 778*)

British raj The rule over much of South Asia between 1765 and 1947 by the East India Company and then by a British government. (*p. 722*)

bronze An alloy of copper with a small amount of tin (or sometimes arsenic), it is harder and more durable than copper alone. The term *Bronze Age* is applied to the era—the dates of which vary in different parts of the world—when bronze was the primary metal for tools and weapons. The demand for bronze helped create long-distance networks of trade. (*p. 23*)

bubonic plague A bacterial disease of fleas that can be transmitted by flea bites to rodents and humans; humans in late stages of the illness can spread the bacteria by coughing. Because of its very high mortality rate and the difficulty of preventing its spread, major outbreaks have created crises in many parts of the world. (See also **Black Death**.) (*p. 348*)

Buddha (563–483 B.C.E.) An Indian prince named Siddhartha Gautama, who renounced his wealth and social position. After becoming "enlightened" (the meaning of *Buddha*) he enunciated the principles of Buddhism. This doctrine evolved and spread throughout India and to Southeast, East, and Central Asia. (See also **Mahayana Buddhism**, **Theravada Buddhism**.) (*p. 179*)

Byzantine Empire Historians' name for the eastern portion of the Roman Empire from the fourth century onward, taken from "Byzantium," an early name for Constantinople, the Byzantine capital city. The empire fell to the Ottomans in 1453. (See also **Ottoman Empire**.) (*p. 253*)

caliphate Office established in succession to the Prophet **Muhammad**, to rule the Islamic empire; also the name of that empire. (See also **Abbasid Caliphate; Sokoto Caliphate; Umayyad Caliphate**.) (*p. 231*)

calpolli A group of up to a hundred families that served as a social building block of an **altepetl** in ancient Mesoamerica. (*p. 317*)

capitalism The economic system of large financial institutions—banks, stock exchanges, investment companies—that first developed in early modern Europe. *Commercial capitalism,* the trading system of the early modern economy, is often distinguished from *industrial capitalism,* the system based on machine production. (*p. 529*)

caravel A small, highly maneuverable three-masted ship used by the Portuguese and Spanish in the exploration of the Atlantic. (*p. 435*)

Cárdenas, Lázaro (1895–1970) President of Mexico (1934–1940). He brought major changes to Mexican life by distributing millions of acres of land to the peasants, bringing representatives of workers and farmers into the inner circles of politics, and nationalizing the oil industry. (*p. 872*)

Carthage City located in present-day Tunisia, founded by **Phoenicians** ca. 800 B.C.E. It became a major commercial center and naval power in the western Mediterranean until defeated by Rome in the third century B.C.E. (*p. 94*)

Caste War A rebellion of the Maya people against the government of Mexico in 1847 that nearly returned the Yucatán to Maya rule. Some Maya rebels retreated to unoccupied territories, where they held out until 1901. (*p. 670*)

Catholic Reformation Religious reform movement within the Latin Christian Church, begun in response to the **Protestant Reformation**. It clarified Catholic theology and reformed clerical training and discipline. (*p. 462*)

Celts Peoples sharing a common language and culture that originated in central Europe in the first half of the first millennium B.C.E. After 500 B.C.E. they spread as far as Anatolia in the east, Spain and the British Isles in the west, and later were overtaken by Roman conquest and Germanic invasions. Their descendants survive on the western fringe of Europe (Brittany, Wales, Scotland, Ireland). (*p. 55*)

Champa rice Quick-maturing rice that can allow two harvests in one growing season. Originally introduced into Champa from India, it was later sent to China as a tribute gift by the Champa state. (See also **tributary system**.) (*p. 302*)

Chang'an City in the Wei Valley in eastern China. It became the capital of the **Qin** and early **Han** Empires. Its main features were imitated in the cities and towns that sprang up throughout the Han Empire. (*p. 163*)

Charlemagne (742–814) King of the Franks (r. 768–814); emperor (r. 800–814). Through a series of military conquests he established the Carolingian Empire, which encompassed all of Gaul and parts of Germany and Italy. Though illiterate himself, he sponsored a brief intellectual revival. (*p. 253*)

chartered companies Groups of private investors who paid an annual fee to France and England in exchange for a monopoly over trade to the West Indies colonies. (*p. 520*)

Chavín The first major urban civilization in South America (900–250 B.C.E.). Its capital, Chavín de Huántar, was located high in the Andes Mountains of Peru. Chavín became politically and economically dominant in a densely populated region that included two distinct ecological zones, the Peruvian coastal plain and the Andean foothills. (*p. 61*)

Chiang Kai-shek (1887–1975) Chinese military and political leader. Succeeded Sun Yat-sen as head of the **Guomindang** in 1925; headed the Chinese government from 1928 to 1949; fought against the Chinese Communists and Japanese invaders. After 1949 he headed the Chinese Nationalist government in Taiwan. (*pp. 814, 841*)

chiefdom Form of political organization with rule by a hereditary leader who held power over a collection of villages and towns. Less powerful than kingdoms and empires, chiefdoms were based on gift giving and commercial links. (*p. 322*)

chinampas Raised fields constructed along lake shores in Mesoamerica to increase agricultural yields. (*p. 312*)

city-state A small independent state consisting of an urban center and the surrounding agricultural territory. A characteristic political form in early Mesopotamia, Archaic and Classical Greece, Phoenicia, and early Italy. (See also **polis**.) (*p. 17*)

civilization An ambiguous term often used to denote more complex societies but sometimes used by anthropologists to describe any group of people sharing a set of cultural traits. (*p. 5*)

Cixi, Empress Dowager (1835–1908) Empress of China and mother of Emperor Guangxi. She put her son under house arrest, supported antiforeign movements, and resisted reforms of the Chinese government and armed forces. (*p. 765*)

clipper ship Large, fast, streamlined sailing vessel, often American built, of the mid-to-late nineteenth century rigged with vast canvas sails hung from tall masts. (*p. 731*)

Cold War (1945–1991) The ideological struggle between communism (Soviet Union) and capitalism (United States) for world influence. The Soviet Union and the United States came to the brink of actual war during the **Cuban missile crisis** but never attacked one another. The Cold War came to an end when the Soviet Union dissolved in 1991. (See also **North Atlantic Treaty Organization; Warsaw Pact**.) (*p. 888*)

colonialism Policy by which a nation administers a foreign territory and develops its resources for the benefit of the colonial power. (*p. 775*)

Columbian Exchange The exchange of plants, animals, diseases, and technologies between the Americas and the rest of the world following Columbus's voyages. (*p. 490*)

Columbus, Christopher (1451–1506) Genoese mariner who in the service of Spain led expeditions across the Atlantic, establishing contact between the peoples of the Americas and the Old World and opening the way to Spanish conquest and colonization. (*p. 437*)

Confederation of 1867 Negotiated union of the formerly separate colonial governments of Ontario, Quebec, New Brunswick, and Nova Scotia. This new Dominion of Canada with a central government in Ottawa is seen as the beginning of the Canadian nation. (*p. 662*)

Confucius Western name for the Chinese philosopher Kongzi (551–479 B.C.E.). His doctrine of duty and public service had a great influence on subsequent Chinese thought and served as a code of conduct for government officials. (*p. 47*)

Congress of Vienna (1814–1815) Meeting of representatives of European monarchs called to reestablish the old order after the defeat of **Napoleon Bonaparte**. (*p. 621*)

conquistadors Early-sixteenth-century Spanish adventurers who conquered Mexico, Central America, and Peru. (See **Cortés, Hernán; Pizarro, Francisco**.) (*p. 446*)

Constantine (306–337 C.E.) Roman emperor (r. 312–337). After reuniting the Roman Empire, he moved the capital to Constantinople and made Christianity a favored religion. (*p. 156*)

Constitutional Convention Meeting in 1787 of the elected representatives of the thirteen original states to write the Constitution of the United States. (*p. 610*)

contract of indenture A voluntary agreement binding a person to work for a specified period of years in return for free passage to an overseas destination. Before 1800 most **indentured servants** were Europeans; after 1800 most indentured laborers were Asians. (*p. 733*)

Cortés, Hernán (1485–1547) Spanish explorer and **conquistador** who led the conquest of Aztec Mexico in 1519–1521 for Spain. (*p. 446*)

Cossacks Peoples of the Russian Empire who lived outside the farming villages, often as herders, mercenaries, or outlaws. Cossacks led the conquest of Siberia in the sixteenth and seventeenth centuries. (*p. 588*)

***coureurs des bois* (runners of the woods)** French fur traders, many of mixed Amerindian heritage, who lived among and often married with Amerindian peoples of North America. (*p. 508*)

creoles In colonial Spanish America, term used to describe someone of European descent born in the New World. Elsewhere in the Americas, the term is used to describe all non-native peoples. (*p. 499*)

Crimean War (1853–1856) Conflict between the Russian and Ottoman Empires fought primarily in the Crimean Peninsula. To prevent Russian expansion, Britain and France sent troops to support the Ottomans. (*p. 693*)

Crusades (1095–1204) Armed pilgrimages to the Holy Land by Christians determined to recover Jerusalem from Muslim rule. The Crusades brought an end to western Europe's centuries of intellectual and cultural isolation. (*p. 274*)

Crystal Palace Building erected in Hyde Park, London, for the Great Exhibition of 1851. Made of iron and glass, like a gigantic greenhouse, it was a symbol of the industrial age. (*p. 638*)

Cuban missile crisis (1962) Brink-of-war confrontation between the United States and the Soviet Union over the latter's placement of nuclear-armed missiles in Cuba. (*p. 895*)

cultural imperialism Domination of one culture over another by a deliberate policy or by economic or technological superiority. (*p. 964*)

Cultural Revolution (China) (1966–1976) Campaign in China ordered by **Mao Zedong** to purge the Communist Party of his opponents and instill revolutionary values in the younger generation. (*p. 906*)

culture Socially transmitted patterns of action and expression. *Material culture* refers to physical objects, such as dwellings, clothing, tools, and crafts. Culture also includes arts, beliefs, knowledge, and technology. (*p. 6*)

cuneiform A system of writing in which wedge-shaped symbols represented words or syllables. It originated in Mesopotamia and was used initially for Sumerian and Akkadian but later was adapted to represent other languages of western Asia. Because so many symbols had to be learned, literacy was confined to a relatively small group of administrators and scribes. (*p. 21*)

Cyrus (600–530 B.C.E.) Founder of the Achaemenid Persian Empire. Between 550 and 530 B.C.E. he conquered Media, Lydia, and **Babylon**. Revered in the traditions of both Iran and the subject peoples, he employed Persians and Medes in his administration and respected the institutions and beliefs of subject peoples. (*p. 110*)

czar See **tsar**.

daimyo Literally, great name(s). Japanese warlords and great landowners, whose armed ***samurai*** gave them control of the Japanese islands from the eighth to the later nineteenth century. Under the **Tokugawa Shogunate** they were subordinated to the imperial government. (*p. 574*)

Daoism Chinese school of thought, originating in the Warring States Period with Laozi. Daoism offered an alternative to the Confucian emphasis on hierarchy and duty. Daoists believe that the world is always changing and is devoid of absolute morality or meaning. They accept the world as they find it, avoid futile struggles, and deviate as little as possible from the *Dao,* or "path" of nature. (See also **Confucius**.) (*p. 47*)

Darius I (ca. 558–486 B.C.E.) Third ruler of the Persian Empire (r. 521–486 B.C.E.). He crushed the widespread initial resistance to his rule and gave all major government posts to Persians rather than to Medes. He established a system of provinces and tribute, began construction of **Persepolis**, and expanded Persian control in the east (Pakistan) and west (northern Greece). (*p. 111*)

Decembrist revolt Abortive attempt by army officers to take control of the Russian government upon the death of Tsar Alexander I in 1825. (*p. 698*)

Declaration of the Rights of Man and the Citizen (1789) Statement of fundamental political rights adopted by the French National Assembly at the beginning of the French Revolution. (*p. 612*)

deforestation The removal of trees faster than forests can replace themselves. (*p. 472*)

Delhi Sultanate (1206–1526) Centralized Indian empire of varying extent, created by Muslim invaders. (*p. 376*)

democracy A system of government in which all "citizens" (however defined) have equal political and legal rights, privileges, and protections, as in the Greek **city-state** of Athens in the fifth and fourth centuries B.C.E. (*p. 120*)

demographic transition A change in the rates of population growth. Before the transition, both birthrates and death rates are high, resulting in a slowly growing population; then the death rate drops but the birthrate remains high, causing a population explosion; finally the birthrate drops and the population growth slows down. This transition took place in Europe in the late nineteenth and early twentieth centuries, in North America and East Asia in the mid-twentieth, and, most recently, in Latin America and South Asia. (*p. 928*)

Deng Xiaoping (1904–1997) Communist Party leader who forced Chinese economic reforms after the death of **Mao Zedong**. (*p. 923*)

development In the nineteenth and twentieth centuries, the economic process that led to industrialization, urbanization, the rise of a large and prosperous middle class, and heavy investment in education. (*p. 678*)

dhows Characteristic cargo and passenger ships of the Arabian Sea. (*p. 385*)

Diagne, Blaise (1872–1934) Senegalese political leader. He was the first African elected to the French National Assembly. During World War I, in exchange for promises to give French citizenship to Senegalese, he helped recruit Africans to serve in the French army. After the war, he led a movement to abolish forced labor in Africa. (*p. 870*)

Dias, Bartolomeu (1450?–1500) Portuguese explorer who in 1488 led the first expedition to sail around the southern tip of Africa from the Atlantic and sight the Indian Ocean. (*p. 437*)

Diaspora A Greek word meaning "dispersal," used to describe the communities of a given ethnic group living outside their homeland. Jews, for example, spread from Israel to western Asia and Mediterranean lands in antiquity and today can be found throughout the world. (*p. 90*)

Dirty War War waged by the Argentine military (1976–1983) against leftist groups. Characterized by the use of illegal imprisonment, torture, and executions by the military. (*p. 917*)

division of labor A manufacturing technique that breaks down a craft into many simple and repetitive tasks that can be performed by unskilled workers. Pioneered in the pottery works of Josiah Wedgwood and in other eighteenth-century factories, it greatly increased the productivity of labor and lowered the cost of manufactured goods. (See also **Wedgwood, Josiah**.) (*p. 635*)

driver A privileged male slave whose job was to ensure that a slave gang did its work on a plantation. (*p. 524*)

Druids The class of religious experts who conducted rituals and preserved sacred lore among some ancient Celtic peoples. They provided education, mediated disputes between kinship groups, and were suppressed by the Romans as a potential focus of opposition to Roman rule. (See also **Celts**.) (*p. 56*)

durbar An elaborate display of political power and wealth in British India in the nineteenth century, ostensibly in imitation of the pageantry of the **Mughal Empire**. (*p. 723*)

Dutch West India Company (1621–1794) Trading company chartered by the Dutch government to conduct its merchants' trade in the Americas and Africa. (*p. 520*)

Edison, Thomas (1847–1931) American inventor best known for inventing the electric light bulb, acoustic recording on wax cylinders, and motion pictures. (*p. 746*)

Einstein, Albert (1879–1955) German physicist who developed the theory of relativity, which states that time, space, and mass are relative to each other and not fixed. (*p. 821*)

El Alamein Town in Egypt, site of the victory by Britain's Field Marshal Bernard Montgomery over German forces led by General Erwin Rommel (the "Desert Fox") in 1942–1943. (*p. 846*)

electricity A form of energy used in telegraphy from the 1840s on and for lighting, industrial motors, and railroads beginning in the 1880s. (*p. 746*)

electric telegraph A device for rapid, long-distance transmission of information over an electric wire. It was introduced in England and North America in the 1830s and 1840s and replaced telegraph systems that utilized visual signals such as semaphores. (See also **submarine telegraph cables**.) (*p. 640*)

encomienda A grant of authority over a population of Amerindians in the Spanish colonies. It provided the grant holder with a supply of cheap labor and periodic payments of goods by the Amerindians. It obliged the grant holder to Christianize the Amerindians. (*p. 498*)

English Civil War (1642–1649) A conflict over royal versus parliamentary rights, caused by King Charles I's arrest of his parliamentary critics and ending with his execution. Its outcome checked the growth of royal absolutism and, with the Glorious Revolution of 1688 and the English Bill of Rights of 1689, ensured that England would be a constitutional monarchy. (*p. 475*)

Enlightenment A philosophical belief system in eighteenth-century Europe that claimed that one could reform society by discovering rational laws that governed social behavior and were just as scientific as the laws of physics. (*pp. 467, 602*)

equites In ancient Italy, prosperous landowners second in wealth and status to the senatorial aristocracy. The Roman emperors allied with this group to counterbalance the influence of the old aristocracy and used the *equites* to staff the imperial civil service. (*p. 147*)

Estates General France's traditional national assembly with representatives of the three estates, or classes, in French society: the clergy, nobility, and commoners. The calling of the Estates General in 1789 led to the French Revolution. (*p. 612*)

Ethiopia East African highland nation lying east of the Nile River. (See also **Menelik**; **Selassie, Haile**.) (*p. 219*)

ethnic cleansing Effort to eradicate a people and its culture by means of mass killing and the destruction of historical buildings and cultural materials. Ethnic cleansing was used by both sides in the conflicts that accompanied the disintegration of Yugoslavia in the 1990s. (*p. 925*)

European Economic Community (Common Market) An organization promoting economic unity in Europe, formed in 1957 by consolidation of earlier, more limited, agreements. With the addition of many new nations it became the European Union (EU) in 1993. (*p. 891*)

extraterritoriality The right of foreign residents in a country to live under the laws of their native country and disregard the laws of the host country. In the nineteenth and early twentieth centuries, European and American nationals living in certain areas of Chinese and Ottoman cities were granted this right. (*p. 694*)

Faisal (1885–1933) Arab prince, leader of the Arab Revolt in World War I. The British made him king of Iraq in 1921, and he reigned under British protection until 1933. (*p. 806*)

Fascist Party Italian political party created by Benito Mussolini during World War I. It emphasized aggressive nationalism and was Mussolini's instrument for the creation of a dictatorship in Italy from 1922 to 1943. (See also **Mussolini, Benito**.) (*p. 838*)

fief In **medieval** Europe, land granted in return for a sworn oath to provide specified military service. (*p. 262*)

First Temple A monumental sanctuary built in Jerusalem by King Solomon in the tenth century B.C.E. to be the religious center for the Israelite god Yahweh. The Temple priesthood conducted sacrifices, received a tithe or percentage of agricultural revenues, and became economically and politically powerful. The First Temple was destroyed by the Babylonians in 587 B.C.E., rebuilt on a modest scale in the late sixth century B.C.E., and replaced by King Herod's Second Temple in the late first century B.C.E. (destroyed by the Romans in 70 C.E.) (*p. 86*)

Five-Year Plans Plans that Joseph Stalin introduced to industrialize the Soviet Union rapidly, beginning in 1928. They set goals for the output of steel, electricity, machinery, and most other products and were enforced by the police powers of the state. They succeeded in making the Soviet Union a major industrial power before World War II. (See also **Stalin, Joseph**.) (*p. 832*)

foragers People who support themselves by hunting wild animals and gathering wild edible plants and insects. (*p. 6*)

Fourteen Points A peace program presented to the U.S. Congress by President **Woodrow Wilson** in January 1918. It called for the evacuation of German-occupied lands, the drawing of borders and the settling of territorial disputes by the self-determination of the affected populations, and the founding of an association of nations to preserve the peace and guarantee their territorial integrity. It was rejected by Germany, but it made Wilson the moral leader of the Allies in the last year of World War I. (*p. 807*)

Franklin, Benjamin (1706–1790) American intellectual, inventor, and politician. He helped negotiate French support for the American Revolution. (*p. 604*)

free-trade imperialism Economic dominance of a weaker country by a more powerful one, while maintaining the legal independence of the weaker state. In the late nineteenth century, free-trade imperialism characterized the relations between the Latin American republics, on the one hand, and Great Britain and the United States, on the other. (*p. 789*)

Freud, Sigmund (1856–1939) Austrian psychiatrist, founder of psychoanalysis. He argued that psychological problems were caused by traumas, especially sexual experiences in early childhood, that were repressed in later life. His ideas caused considerable controversy among psychologists and in the general public. Although his views on repressed sexuality are no longer widely accepted, his psychoanalytic methods are still very influential. (*p. 821*)

Fujiwara Aristocratic family that dominated the Japanese imperial court between the ninth and twelfth centuries. (*p. 301*)

Funan An early complex society in Southeast Asia between the first and sixth centuries C.E. It was centered in the rich rice-growing region of southern Vietnam, and it controlled the passage of trade across the Malaysian isthmus. (*p. 192*)

Gama, Vasco da (1460–1524) Portuguese explorer. In 1497–1498 he led the first naval expedition from Europe to sail to India, opening an important commercial sea route. (*p. 437*)

Gandhi, Mohandas K. (Mahatma) (1869–1948) Leader of the Indian independence movement and advocate of nonviolent resistance. After being educated as a lawyer in England, he returned to India and became leader of the **Indian National Congress** in 1920. He appealed to the poor, led nonviolent demonstrations against British colonial rule, and was jailed many times. Soon after independence he was assassinated for attempting to stop Hindu-Muslim rioting. (*p. 863*)

Gaozu The throne name of Liu Bang, one of the rebel leaders who brought down the **Qin** and founded the **Han** dynasty in 202 B.C.E. (*p. 159*)

Garibaldi, Giuseppe (1807–1882) Italian nationalist and revolutionary who conquered Sicily and Naples and added them to a unified Italy in 1860. (*p. 756*)

Genghis Khan (ca. 1167–1227) The title of Temüjin when he ruled the Mongols (1206–1227). It means the "oceanic" or "universal" leader. Genghis Khan was the founder of the Mongol Empire. (*p. 341*)

gens de couleur Free men and women of color in Haiti. They sought greater political rights and later supported the Haitian Revolution. (See also **L'Ouverture, François Dominique Toussaint**.) (*p. 619*)

gentry In China, the class of prosperous families, next in wealth below the rural aristocrats, from which the emperors drew their administrative personnel. Respected for their education and expertise, these officials became a privileged group and made the government more efficient and responsive than in the past. The term *gentry* also denotes the class of landholding families in England below the aristocracy. (*pp. 163, 470*)

Ghana First known kingdom in sub-Saharan West Africa between the sixth and thirteenth centuries C.E. Also the modern West African country once known as the Gold Coast. (*p. 235*)

global elite culture At the beginning of the twenty-first century, the attitudes and outlook of well-educated, prosperous, Western-oriented people around the world, largely expressed in European languages, especially English. (*p. 966*)

global pop culture Popular cultural practices and institutions that have been adopted internationally, such as music, the Internet, television, food, and fashion. (*p. 965*)

globalization The economic, political, and cultural integration and interaction of all parts of the world brought about by increasing trade, travel, and technology. (*p. 948*)

Gold Coast Region of the Atlantic coast of West Africa occupied by modern Ghana; named for its gold exports to Europe from the 1470s onward. (*p. 437*)

Golden Horde Mongol khanate founded by Genghis Khan's grandson Batu. It was based in southern Russia and quickly adopted both the Turkic language and Islam. Also known as the Kipchak Horde. (*p. 349*)

Gorbachev, Mikhail (b. 1931) Head of the Soviet Union from 1985 to 1991. His liberalization effort improved relations with the West, but he lost power after his reforms led to the collapse of communist governments in eastern Europe. (*p. 924*)

Gothic cathedrals Large churches originating in twelfth-century France; built in an architectural style featuring pointed arches, tall vaults and spires, flying buttresses, and large stained-glass windows. (*p. 410*)

Grand Canal The 1,100-mile (1,771-kilometer) waterway linking the Yellow and the Yangzi Rivers. It was begun in the **Han** period and completed during the Sui Empire. (*p. 284*)

"great traditions" Historians' term for a literate, well-institutionalized complex of religious and social beliefs and practices adhered to by diverse societies over a broad geographical area. (See also "**small traditions**.") (*p. 215*)

Great Western Schism A division in the Latin (Western) Christian Church between 1378 and 1417, when rival claimants to the papacy existed in Rome and Avignon. (*p. 417*)

Great Zimbabwe City, now in ruins (in the modern African country of Zimbabwe), whose many stone structures were built between about 1250 and 1450, when it was a trading center and the capital of a large state. (*p. 388*)

guild In medieval Europe, an association of men (rarely women), such as merchants, artisans, or professors, who worked in a particular trade and banded together to promote their economic and political interests. Guilds were also important in other societies, such as the Ottoman and Safavid Empires. (*p. 407*)

Gujarat Region of western India famous for trade and manufacturing; the inhabitants are called Gujaratis. (*p. 384*)

gunpowder A mixture of saltpeter, sulfur, and charcoal, in various proportions. The formula, brought to China in the 400s or 500s, was first used to make fumigators to keep away insect pests and evil spirits. In later centuries it was used to make explosives and grenades and to propel cannonballs, shot, and bullets. (*p. 293*)

Guomindang Nationalist political party founded on democratic principles by **Sun Yat-sen** in 1912. After 1925, the party was headed by **Chiang Kai-shek**, who turned it into an increasingly authoritarian movement. (*p. 814*)

Gupta Empire (320–550 C.E.) A powerful Indian state based, like its Mauryan predecessor, on a capital at Pataliputra in the Ganges Valley. It controlled most of the Indian subcontinent through a combination of military force and its prestige as a center of sophisticated culture. (See also **theater-state**.) (*p. 185*)

Habsburg A powerful European family that provided many Holy Roman Emperors, founded the Austrian (later Austro-Hungarian) Empire, and ruled sixteenth- and seventeenth-century Spain. (*p. 475*)

hadith A tradition relating the words or deeds of the Prophet **Muhammad**; next to the Quran, the most important basis for Islamic law. (*p. 239*)

Hammurabi Amorite ruler of **Babylon** (r. 1792–1750 B.C.E.). He conquered many city-states in southern and northern Mesopotamia and is best known for a code of laws, inscribed on a black stone pillar, illustrating the principles to be used in legal cases. (*p. 18*)

Han A term used to designate (1) the ethnic Chinese people who originated in the Yellow River Valley and spread throughout regions of China suitable for agriculture and (2) the dynasty of emperors who ruled from 202 B.C.E. to 220 C.E. (*p. 157*)

Hanseatic League An economic and defensive alliance of the free towns in northern Germany, founded about 1241 and most powerful in the fourteenth century. (*p. 404*)

Harappa Site of one of the great cities of the Indus Valley civilization of the third millennium B.C.E. It was located on the northwest frontier of the zone of cultivation (in modern Pakistan), and it may have been a center for the acquisition of raw materials, such as metals and precious stones, from Afghanistan and Iran. (*p. 31*)

Hatshepsut Queen of Egypt (r. 1473–1458 B.C.E.). She dispatched a naval expedition down the Red Sea to Punt (possibly northeast Sudan or Eretria), the faraway source of myrrh. There is evidence of opposition to a woman as ruler, and after her death her name and image were frequently defaced. (*p. 73*)

Hausa An agricultural and trading people of central Sudan in West Africa. Aside from their brief incorporation into the Songhai Empire, the Hausa city-states remained autonomous until the **Sokoto Caliphate** conquered them in the early nineteenth century. (*p. 538*)

Hebrew Bible A collection of sacred books containing diverse materials concerning the origins, experiences, beliefs, and practices of the Israelites. Most of the extant text was compiled by members of the priestly class in the fifth century B.C.E. and reflects the concerns and views of this group. (*p. 84*)

Hellenistic Age Historians' term for the era, usually dated 323–30 B.C.E., in which Greek culture spread across western Asia and northeastern Africa after the conquests of **Alexander** the Great. The period ended with the fall of the last major Hellenistic kingdom to Rome, but Greek cultural influence persisted until the spread of Islam in the seventh century C.E. (*p. 130*)

Helsinki Accords (1975) Political and human rights agreement signed in Helsinki, Finland, by the Soviet Union and western European countries. (*p. 895*)

Henry the Navigator (1394–1460) Portuguese prince who promoted the study of navigation and directed voyages of exploration down the western coast of Africa in the fifteenth century. (*p. 434*)

Herodotus (ca. 485–425 B.C.E.) Heir to the technique of *historia* ("investigation") developed by Greeks in the late Archaic period. He came from a Greek community in Anatolia and traveled extensively, collecting information in western Asia and the Mediterranean lands. He traced the antecedents and chronicled the wars between the Greek city-states and the Persian Empire, thus originating the Western tradition of historical writing. (*p. 122*)

Herzl, Theodore (1860–1904) Austrian journalist and founder of the Zionist movement urging the creation of a Jewish national homeland in Palestine. (*p. 806*)

Hidalgo y Costilla, Miguel (1753–1811) Mexican priest who led the first stage of the Mexican independence war in 1810. He was captured and executed in 1811. (*p. 658*)

Hidden Imam Last in a series of twelve descendants of Muhammad's son-in-law Ali, whom **Shi'ites** consider divinely appointed leaders of the Muslim community. In occlusion since ca. 873, he is expected to return as a messiah at the end of time. (*p. 558*)

hieroglyphics A system of writing in which pictorial symbols represented sounds, syllables, or concepts. It was used for official and monumental inscriptions in ancient Egypt. Because of the long period of study required to master this system, literacy in hieroglyphics was confined to a relatively small group of **scribes** and administrators. Cursive symbol-forms were developed for rapid composition on other media, such as **papyrus**. (*p. 27*)

Hinduism A general term for a wide variety of beliefs and ritual practices that have developed in the Indian subcontinent since antiquity. Hinduism has roots in ancient Vedic, Buddhist, and south Indian religious concepts and practices. It spread along the trade routes to Southeast Asia. (*p. 180*)

Hiroshima City in Japan, the first to be destroyed by an atomic bomb, on August 6, 1945. The bombing hastened the end of World War II. (*p. 848*)

history The study of past events and changes in the development, transmission, and transformation of cultural practices. (*p. 6*)

Hitler, Adolf (1889–1945) Born in Austria, Hitler became a radical German nationalist during World War I. He led the National Socialist German Workers' Party—the **Nazis**—in the 1920s and became dictator of Germany in 1933. He led Europe into World War II. (*p. 839*)

Hittites A people from central Anatolia who established an empire in Anatolia and Syria in the Late Bronze Age. With wealth from the trade in metals and military power based on chariot forces, the Hittites vied with New Kingdom Egypt for control of Syria-Palestine before falling to unidentified attackers ca. 1200 B.C.E. (See also **Ramesses II**.) (*p. 72*)

Holocaust Nazis' program during World War II to kill people they considered undesirable. Some 6 million Jews perished during the Holocaust, along with millions of Poles, Gypsies, Communists, Socialists, and others. (*p. 852*)

Holy Roman Empire Loose federation of mostly German states and principalities, headed by an emperor elected by the princes. It lasted from 962 to 1806. (*pp. 266, 473*)

hoplite A heavily armored Greek infantryman of the Archaic and Classical periods who fought in the close-packed phalanx formation. Hoplite armies—militias composed of middle- and upper-class citizens supplying their own equipment—were for centuries superior to all other military forces. (*p. 119*)

horse collar Harnessing method that increased the efficiency of horses by shifting the point of traction from the animal's neck to the shoulders; its adoption favors the spread of horse-drawn plows and vehicles. (*p. 272*)

House of Burgesses Elected assembly in colonial Virginia, created in 1618. (*p. 505*)

humanists (Renaissance) European scholars, writers, and teachers associated with the study of the humanities (grammar, rhetoric, poetry, history, languages, and moral philosophy), influential in the fifteenth century and later. (*p. 413*)

Hundred Years War (1337–1453) Series of campaigns over control of the throne of France, involving English and French royal families and French noble families. (*p. 420*)

Husain, Saddam (b. 1937) President of Iraq from 1979 until overthrown by an American-led invasion in 2003. Waged war on Iran from 1980 to 1988. His invasion of Kuwait in 1990 was repulsed in the Persian Gulf War in 1991. (*p. 921*)

Ibn Battuta (1304–1369) Moroccan **Muslim** scholar, the most widely traveled individual of his time. He wrote a detailed account of his visits to Islamic lands from China to Spain and the western Sudan. (*p. 373*)

Il-khan A "secondary" or "peripheral" khan based in Persia. The Il-khans' khanate was founded by Hülegü, a grandson of **Genghis Khan**, and was based at Tabriz in modern Azerbaijan. It controlled much of Iran and Iraq. (*p. 349*)

Inca Largest and most powerful Andean empire. Controlled the Pacific coast of South America from Ecuador to Chile from its capital of Cuzco. (*p. 328*)

indentured servant A migrant to British colonies in the Americas who paid for passage by agreeing to work for a set term ranging from four to seven years. (*p. 504*)

Indian Civil Service The elite professional class of officials who administered the government of British India. Originally composed exclusively of well-educated British men, it gradually added qualified Indians. (*p. 723*)

Indian National Congress A movement and political party founded in 1885 to demand greater Indian participation in government. Its membership was middle class, and its demands were modest until World War I. Led after 1920 by Mohandas K. Gandhi, it appealed increasingly to the poor, and it organized mass protests demanding self-government and independence. (See also **Gandhi, Mohandas K.**) (*p. 726, 862*)

Indian Ocean Maritime System In premodern times, a network of seaports, trade routes, and maritime culture linking countries on the rim of the Indian Ocean from Africa to Indonesia. (*p. 207*)

indulgence The forgiveness of the punishment due for past sins, granted by the Catholic Church authorities as a reward for a pious act. Martin Luther's protest against the sale of indulgences is often seen as touching off the **Protestant Reformation**. (*p. 460*)

Industrial Revolution The transformation of the economy, the environment, and living conditions, occurring first in England in the eighteenth century, that resulted from the use of steam engines, the mechanization of manufacturing in factories, and innovations in transportation and communication. (*p. 629*)

investiture controversy Dispute between the popes and the Holy Roman Emperors over who held ultimate authority over bishops in imperial lands. (*p. 266*)

Irigoyen, Hipólito (1850–1933) Argentine politician, president of Argentina from 1916 to 1922 and 1928 to 1930. The first president elected by universal male suffrage, he began his presidency as a reformer, but later became conservative. (*p. 874*)

Iron Age Historians' term for the period during which iron was the primary metal for tools and weapons. The advent of iron technology began at different times in different parts of the world. (*p. 69*)

iron curtain Winston Churchill's term for the Cold War division between the Soviet-dominated East and the U.S.-dominated West. (*p. 888*)

Iroquois Confederacy An alliance of five northeastern Amerindian peoples (six after 1722) that made decisions on military and diplomatic issues through a council of representatives. Allied first with the Dutch and later with the English, the Confederacy dominated the area from western New England to the Great Lakes. (*p. 507*)

Islam Religion expounded by the Prophet **Muhammad** on the basis of his reception of divine revelations, which were collected after his death into the B. In the tradition of Judaism and Christianity, and sharing much of their lore, Islam calls on all people to recognize one creator god—Allah—who rewards or punishes believers after death according to how they led their lives. (See also **hadith.**) *(p. 230)*

Israel In antiquity, the land between the eastern shore of the Mediterranean and the Jordan River, occupied by the Israelites from the early second millennium B.C.E. The modern state of Israel was founded in 1948. *(p. 84)*

Jackson, Andrew (1767–1845) First president of the United States to be born in humble circumstances. He was popular among frontier residents, urban workers, and small farmers. He had a successful political career as judge, general, congressman, senator, and president. After being denied the presidency in 1824 in a controversial election, he won in 1828 and was reelected in 1832. *(p. 665)*

Jacobins Radical republicans during the French Revolution. They were led by Maximilien Robespierre from 1793 to 1794. (See also **Robespierre, Maximilien.**) *(p. 614)*

Janissaries Infantry, originally of slave origin, armed with fire-arms and constituting the elite of the Ottoman army from the fifteenth century until the corps was abolished in 1826. *(pp. 551, 689)*

jati. See ***varna.***

Jesus (ca. 5 B.C.E.–34 C.E.) A Jew from Galilee in northern Israel who sought to reform Jewish beliefs and practices. He was executed as a revolutionary by the Romans. Hailed as the Messiah and son of God by his followers, he became the central figure in Christianity, a belief system that developed in the centuries after his death. *(p. 152)*

Jinnah, Muhammad Ali (1876–1948) Indian Muslim politician who founded the state of Pakistan. A lawyer by training, he joined the **All-India Muslim League** in 1913. As leader of the League from the 1920s on, he negotiated with the British and the **Indian National Congress** for Muslim participation in Indian politics. From 1940 on, he led the movement for the independence of India's Muslims in a separate state of Pakistan, founded in 1947. *(p. 865)*

joint-stock company A business, often backed by a government charter, that sold shares to individuals to raise money for its trading enterprises and to spread the risks (and profits) among many investors. *(p. 469)*

Juárez, Benito (1806–1872) President of Mexico (1858–1872). Born in poverty in Mexico, he was educated as a lawyer and rose to become chief justice of the Mexican supreme court and then president. He led Mexico's resistance to a French invasion in 1862 and the installation of Maximilian as emperor. *(p. 668)*

junk A very large flat-bottom sailing ship produced in the **Tang**, **Ming**, and **Song** Empires, specially designed for long-distance commercial travel. *(p. 293)*

Kamakura Shogunate The first of Japan's decentralized military governments (1185–1333). *(p. 301)*

kamikaze The "divine wind," which the Japanese credited with blowing Mongol invaders away from their shores in 1281. *(p. 365)*

Kangxi (1654–1722) Qing emperor (r. 1662–1722). He oversaw the greatest expansion of the **Qing Empire**. *(p. 581)*

karma In Indian tradition, the residue of deeds performed in past and present lives that adheres to a "spirit" and determines what form it will assume in its next life cycle. The doctrines of karma and reincarnation were used by the elite in ancient India to encourage people to accept their social position and do their duty. *(p. 176)*

keiretsu Alliances of corporations and banks that dominate the Japanese economy. *(p. 922)*

khipus System of knotted colored cords used by preliterate Andean peoples to transmit information. *(p. 330)*

Khomeini, Ayatollah Ruhollah (1900?–1989) Shi'ite philosopher and cleric who led the overthrow of the shah of Iran in 1979 and created an Islamic republic. *(p. 919)*

Khubilai Khan (1215–1294) Last of the Mongol Great Khans (r. 1260–1294) and founder of the **Yuan Empire**. *(p. 357)*

Kievan Russia State established at Kiev in Ukraine ca. 882 by Scandinavian adventurers asserting authority over a mostly Slavic farming population. *(p. 254)*

King Leopold II (1835–1909) King of Belgium (r. 1865–1909). He was active in encouraging the exploration of Central Africa and became the ruler of the Congo Free State (to 1908). *(p. 778)*

Korean War (1950–1953) Conflict that began with North Korea's invasion of South Korea and that came to involve the United Nations (primarily the United States) allying with South Korea and the People's Republic of China allying with North Korea. *(p. 892)*

Koryo Korean kingdom founded in 918 and destroyed by a Mongol invasion in 1259. *(p. 299)*

Kush An Egyptian name for Nubia, the region alongside the Nile River south of Egypt, where an indigenous kingdom with its own distinctive institutions and cultural traditions arose beginning in the early second millennium B.C.E. It was deeply influenced by Egyptian culture and at times under the control of Egypt, which coveted its rich deposits of gold and luxury products from sub-Saharan Africa carried up the Nile corridor. *(p. 52)*

labor union An organization of workers in a particular industry or trade, created to defend the interests of members through strikes or negotiations with employers. *(p. 753)*

laissez faire The idea that government should refrain from interfering in economic affairs. The classic exposition of laissez-faire principles is Adam Smith's *Wealth of Nations* (1776). *(p. 646)*

lama In Tibetan Buddhism, a teacher. *(p. 357)*

Las Casas, Bartolomé de (1474–1566) First bishop of Chiapas, in southern Mexico. He devoted most of his life to protecting Amerindian peoples from exploitation. His major achievement was the New Laws of 1542, which limited the ability of Spanish settlers to compel Amerindians to labor for them. (See also **encomienda.**) *(p. 496)*

Latin West Historians' name for the territories of Europe that adhered to the Latin rite of Christianity and used the Latin language for intellectual exchange in the period ca. 1000–1500. *(p. 399)*

League of Nations International organization founded in 1919 to promote world peace and cooperation but greatly weakened by the refusal of the United States to join. It proved ineffectual in stopping aggression by Italy, Japan, and Germany in the 1930s, and it was superseded by the **United Nations** in 1945. *(p. 809)*

"legitimate" trade Exports from Africa in the nineteenth century that did not include the newly outlawed slave trade. *(p. 718)*

Lenin, Vladimir (1870–1924) Leader of the **Bolshevik** (later Communist) Party. He lived in exile in Switzerland until 1917, then returned to Russia to lead the Bolsheviks to victory during the Russian Revolution and the civil war that followed. *(p. 806)*

liberalism A political ideology that emphasizes the civil rights of citizens, representative government, and the protection of private property. This ideology, derived from the **Enlightenment**, was especially popular among the property-owning middle classes of Europe and North America. *(p. 756)*

Library of Ashurbanipal A large collection of writings drawn from the ancient literary, religious, and scientific traditions of Mesopotamia. It was assembled by the seventh-century B.C.E. Assyrian ruler Ashurbanipal. The many tablets unearthed by archaeologists constitute one of the most important sources of present-day knowledge of the long literary tradition of Mesopotamia. *(p. 83)*

Linear B A set of syllabic symbols, derived from the writing system of **Minoan** Crete, used in the Mycenaean palaces of the Late Bronze Age to write an early form of Greek. It was used primarily for palace records, and the surviving Linear B tablets provide substantial information about the economic organization of Mycenaean society and tantalizing clues about political, social, and religious institutions. (*p. 78*)

Li Shimin (599–649) One of the founders of the **Tang Empire** and its second emperor (r. 626–649). He led the expansion of the empire into Central Asia. (*p. 284*)

Little Ice Age A century-long period of cool climate that began in the 1590s. Its ill effects on agriculture in northern Europe were notable. (*p. 471*)

llama A hoofed animal indigenous to the Andes Mountains in South America. It was the only domesticated beast of burden in the Americas before the arrival of Europeans. It provided meat and wool. The use of llamas to transport goods made possible specialized production and trade among people living in different ecological zones and fostered the integration of these zones by **Chavín** and later Andean states. (*p.62*)

loess A fine, light silt deposited by wind and water. It constitutes the fertile soil of the Yellow River Valley in northern China. Because loess soil is not compacted, it can be worked with a simple digging stick, but it leaves the region vulnerable to devastating earthquakes. (*p. 40*)

Long March (1934–1935) The 6,000-mile (9,600-kilometer) flight of Chinese Communists from southeastern to northwestern China. The Communists, led by **Mao Zedong**, were pursued by the Chinese army under orders from **Chiang Kai-shek**. The four thousand survivors of the march formed the nucleus of a revived Communist movement that defeated the **Guomindang** after World War II. (*p. 842*)

L'Ouverture, François Dominique Toussaint (1743–1803) Leader of the Haitian Revolution. He freed the slaves and gained effective independence for Haiti despite military interventions by the British and French. (*p. 619*)

ma'at Egyptian term for the concept of divinely created and maintained order in the universe. Reflecting the ancient Egyptians' belief in an essentially beneficent world, the divine ruler was the earthly guarantor of this order. (See also **pyramid**.) (*p. 26*)

Macartney mission (1792–1793) The unsuccessful attempt by the British Empire to establish diplomatic relations with the **Qing Empire**. (*p. 585*)

Magellan, Ferdinand (1480?–1521) Portuguese navigator who led the Spanish expedition of 1519–1522 that was the first to sail around the world. (*p. 439*)

Mahabharata A vast epic chronicling the events leading up to a cataclysmic battle between related kinship groups in early India. It includes the **Bhagavad-Gita**, the most important work of Indian sacred literature. (*p. 184*)

Mahayana Buddhism "Great Vehicle" branch of Buddhism followed in China, Japan, and Central Asia. The focus is on reverence for **Buddha** and for bodhisattvas, enlightened persons who have postponed nirvana to help others attain enlightenment. (*p. 180*)

Malacca Port city in the modern Southeast Asian country of Malaysia, founded about 1400 as a trading center on the Strait of Malacca. Also spelled Melaka. (*p. 390*)

Mali Empire created by indigenous **Muslims** in western Sudan of West Africa from the thirteenth to fifteenth century. It was famous for its role in the trans-Saharan gold trade. (See also Mansa Kankan Musa and Timbuktu.) (*p. 378*)

Malthus, Thomas (1766–1834) Eighteenth-century English intellectual who warned that population growth threatened future generations because, in his view, population growth would always outstrip increases in agricultural production. (*p. 927*)

mamluks Under the Islamic system of military slavery, Turkic military slaves who formed an important part of the armed forces of the **Abbasid Caliphate** of the ninth and tenth centuries. Mamluks eventually founded their own state, ruling Egypt and Syria (1250–1517). (*p. 234*)

Manchu Federation of Northeast Asian peoples who founded the **Qing Empire**. (*p. 573*)

Mandate of Heaven Chinese religious and political ideology developed by the **Zhou**, according to which it was the prerogative of Heaven, the chief deity, to grant power to the ruler of China and to take away that power if the ruler failed to conduct himself justly and in the best interests of his subjects. (*p. 45*)

mandate system Allocation of former German colonies and Ottoman possessions to the victorious powers after World War I, to be administered under League of Nations supervision. (*p. 815*)

manor In medieval Europe, a large, self-sufficient landholding consisting of the lord's residence (manor house), outbuildings, peasant village, and surrounding land. (*p. 260*)

mansabs In India, grants of land given in return for service by rulers of the **Mughal Empire**. (*p. 561*)

Mansa Kankan Musa Ruler of Mali (r. 1312–1337). His pilgrimage through Egypt to **Mecca** in 1324–1325 established the empire's reputation for wealth in the Mediterranean world. (*p. 380*)

manumission A grant of legal freedom to an individual slave. (*p. 526*)

Mao Zedong (1893–1976) Leader of the Chinese Communist Party (1927–1976). He led the Communists on the **Long March** (1934–1935) and rebuilt the Communist Party and Red Army during the Japanese occupation of China (1937–1945). After World War II, he led the Communists to victory over the **Guomindang**. He ordered the **Cultural Revolution** in 1966. (*p. 841*)

maroon A slave who ran away from his or her master. Often a member of a community of runaway slaves in the West Indies and South America. (*p. 529*)

Marshall Plan U.S. program to support the reconstruction of western Europe after World War II. By 1961 more than $20 billion in economic aid had been dispersed. (*p. 891*)

Marx, Karl (1818–1883) German journalist and philosopher, founder of the Marxist branch of **socialism**. He is known for two books: *The Communist Manifesto* (1848) and *Das Kapital* (Vols. I–III, 1867–1894). (*p. 753*)

mass deportation The forcible removal and relocation of large numbers of people or entire populations. The mass deportations practiced by the Assyrian and Persian Empires were meant as a terrifying warning of the consequences of rebellion. They also brought skilled and unskilled labor to the imperial center. (*p. 82*)

mass production The manufacture of many identical products by the division of labor into many small repetitive tasks. This method was introduced into the manufacture of pottery by Josiah Wedgwood and into the spinning of cotton thread by Richard Arkwright. (See also **Arkwright, Richard**; **Industrial Revolution**; **Wedgwood, Josiah**.) (*p. 634*)

Mauryan Empire The first state to unify most of the Indian subcontinent. It was founded by Chandragupta Maurya in 324 B.C.E. and survived until 184 B.C.E. From its capital at Pataliputra in the Ganges Valley it grew wealthy from taxes on agriculture, iron mining, and control of trade routes. (See also **Ashoka**.) (*p. 183*)

Maya Mesoamerican civilization concentrated in Mexico's Yucatán Peninsula and in Guatemala and Honduras but never unified into a single empire. Major contributions were in mathematics, astronomy, and development of the calendar. (*p. 312*)

Mecca City in western Arabia; birthplace of the Prophet **Muhammad** and ritual center of the Islamic religion. (*p. 228*)

mechanization The application of machinery to manufacturing and other activities. Among the first processes to be mechanized were the spinning of cotton thread and the weaving of cloth in late-eighteenth- and early-nineteenth-century England. (*p. 636*)

medieval Literally "middle age," a term that historians of Europe use for the period ca. 500 to ca. 1500, signifying its intermediate point between Greco-Roman antiquity and the Renaissance. (*p. 253*)

Medina City in western Arabia to which the Prophet **Muhammad** and his followers emigrated in 622 to escape persecution in **Mecca**. (*p. 230*)

megaliths Structures and complexes of very large stones constructed for ceremonial and religious purposes in **Neolithic** times. (*p. 12*)

Meiji Restoration The political program that followed the destruction of the **Tokugawa Shogunate** in 1868, in which a collection of young leaders set Japan on the path of centralization, industrialization, and imperialism. (See also **Yamagata Aritomo**.) (*p. 759*)

Memphis The capital of Old Kingdom Egypt, near the head of the Nile Delta. Early rulers were interred in the nearby **pyramids**. (*p. 27*)

Menelik (1844–1911) Emperor of Ethiopia (r. 1889–1911). He enlarged Ethiopia to its present dimensions and defeated an Italian invasion at Adowa (1896). (*p. 781*)

mercantilism European government policies of the sixteenth, seventeenth, and eighteenth centuries designed to promote overseas trade between a country and its colonies and accumulate precious metals by requiring colonies to trade only with their motherland country. The British system was defined by the Navigation Acts, the French system by laws known as the *Exclusif.* (*pp. 530, 647*)

Meroë Capital of a flourishing kingdom in southern Nubia from the fourth century B.C.E. to the fourth century C.E. In this period Nubian culture shows more independence from Egypt and the influence of sub-Saharan Africa. (*p. 53*)

mestizo The term used by Spanish authorities to describe someone of mixed Amerindian and European descent. (*p. 503*)

Middle Passage The part of the **Atlantic Circuit** involving the transportation of enslaved Africans across the Atlantic to the Americas. (*p. 530*)

Ming Empire (1368–1644) Empire based in China that Zhu Yuanzhang established after the overthrow of the **Yuan Empire**. The Ming emperor **Yongle** sponsored the building of the Forbidden City and the voyages of **Zheng He**. The later years of the Ming saw a slowdown in technological development and economic decline. (*pp. 359, 579*)

Minoan Prosperous civilization on the Aegean island of Crete in the second millennium B.C.E. The Minoans engaged in far-flung commerce around the Mediterranean and exerted powerful cultural influences on the early Greeks. (*p. 76*)

mit'a Andean labor system based on shared obligations to help kinsmen and work on behalf of the ruler and religious organizations. (*p. 324*)

Moche Civilization of north coast of Peru (200–700 C.E.). An important Andean civilization that built extensive irrigation networks as well as impressive urban centers dominated by brick temples. (*p. 325*)

Moctezuma II (1466?–1520) Last Aztec emperor, overthrown by the Spanish conquistador Hernán Cortés. (*p. 446*)

modernization The process of reforming political, military, economic, social, and cultural traditions in imitation of the early success of Western societies, often with regard for accommodating local traditions in non-Western societies. (*p. 715*)

Mohenjo-Daro Largest of the cities of the Indus Valley civilization. It was centrally located in the extensive floodplain of the Indus River in contemporary Pakistan. Little is known about the political institutions of Indus Valley communities, but the large scale of construction at Mohenjo-Daro, the orderly grid of streets, and the standardization of building materials are evidence of central planning. (*p. 31*)

moksha The Hindu concept of the spirit's "liberation" from the endless cycle of rebirths. There are various avenues—such as physical discipline, meditation, and acts of devotion to the gods—by which the spirit can distance itself from desire for the things of this world and be merged with the divine force that animates the universe. (*p. 178*)

monasticism Living in a religious community apart from secular society and adhering to a rule stipulating chastity, obedience, and poverty. It was a prominent element of medieval Christianity and Buddhism. Monasteries were the primary centers of learning and literacy in medieval Europe. (*p. 267*)

Mongols A people of this name is mentioned as early as the records of the **Tang Empire**, living as nomads in northern Eurasia. After 1206 they established an enormous empire under **Genghis Khan**, linking western and eastern Eurasia. (*p. 341*)

monotheism Belief in the existence of a single divine entity. Some scholars cite the devotion of the Egyptian pharaoh **Akhenaten** to Aten (sun-disk) and his suppression of traditional gods as the earliest instance. The Israelite worship of Yahweh developed into an exclusive belief in one god, and this concept passed into Christianity and Islam. (*p. 87*)

monsoon Seasonal winds in the Indian Ocean caused by the differences in temperature between the rapidly heating and cooling landmasses of Africa and Asia and the slowly changing ocean waters. These strong and predictable winds have long been ridden across the open sea by sailors, and the large amounts of rainfall that they deposit on parts of India, Southeast Asia, and China allow for the cultivation of several crops a year. (*pp. 174, 374*)

Morelos, José María (1765–1815) Mexican priest and former student of Miguel Hidalgo y Costilla, he led the forces fighting for Mexican independence until he was captured and executed in 1815. (See also **Hidalgo y Costilla, Miguel**.) (*p. 660*)

most-favored-nation status A clause in a commercial treaty that awards to any later signatories all the privileges previously granted to the original signatories. (*p. 701*)

movable type Type in which each individual character is cast on a separate piece of metal. It replaced woodblock printing, allowing for the arrangement of individual letters and other characters on a page, rather than requiring the carving of entire pages at a time. It may have been invented in Korea in the thirteenth century. (See also **printing press**.) (*p. 295*)

Mughal Empire Muslim state (1526–1857) exercising dominion over most of India in the sixteenth and seventeenth centuries. (*p. 561*)

Muhammad (570–632 C.E.) Arab prophet; founder of religion of **Islam**. (*p. 228*)

Muhammad Ali (1769–1849) Leader of Egyptian modernization in the early nineteenth century. He ruled Egypt as an Ottoman governor but had imperial ambitions. His descendants ruled Egypt until overthrown in 1952. (*pp. 688, 716*)

mulatto The term used in Spanish and Portuguese colonies to describe someone of mixed African and European descent. (*p. 503*)

mummy A body preserved by chemical processes or special natural circumstances, often in the belief that the deceased will need it again in the afterlife. In ancient Egypt the bodies of people who could afford mummification underwent a complex process of removing organs, filling body cavities, dehydrating the corpse with natron, and then wrapping the body with linen bandages and enclosing it in a wooden sarcophagus. (*p. 30*)

Muscovy Russian principality that emerged gradually during the era of Mongol domination. The Muscovite dynasty ruled without interruption from 1276 to 1598. (*p. 587*)

Muslim An adherent of the Islamic religion; a person who "submits" (in Arabic, *Islam* means "submission") to the will of God. (*p. 230*)

Mussolini, Benito (1883–1945) Fascist dictator of Italy (1922–1943). He led Italy to conquer Ethiopia (1935), joined Germany in the Axis pact (1936), and allied Italy with Germany in World War II. He was overthrown in 1943 when the Allies invaded Italy. (*p. 838*)

Mycenae Site of a fortified palace complex in southern Greece that controlled a Late Bronze Age kingdom. In Homer's epic poems

Mycenae was the base of King Agamemnon, who commanded the Greeks besieging Troy. Contemporary archaeologists call the complex Greek society of the second millennium B.C.E. "Mycenaean." (*p. 78*)

Nasir al-Din Tusi (1201–1274) Persian mathematician and cosmologist whose academy near Tabriz provided the model for the movement of the planets that helped to inspire the Copernican model of the solar system. (*p. 352*)

nationalism A political ideology that stresses people's membership in a nation—a community defined by a common culture and history as well as by territory. In the late eighteenth and early nineteenth centuries, nationalism was a force for unity in western Europe. In the late nineteenth century it hastened the disintegration of the Austro-Hungarian and Ottoman Empires. In the twentieth century it provided the ideological foundation for scores of independent countries emerging from **colonialism**. (*p. 756*)

nawab A Muslim prince allied to British India; technically, a semi-autonomous deputy of the Mughal emperor. (*p. 721*)

Nazis German political party led by Adolf Hitler, emphasizing nationalism, racism, and war. When Hitler became chancellor of Germany in 1933, the Nazis became the only legal party and an instrument of Hitler's absolute rule. The party's formal name was National Socialist German Workers' Party. (See also **Hitler, Adolf**.) (*p. 839*)

Nehru, Jawaharlal (1889–1964) Indian statesman who succeeded Mohandas K. Gandhi as leader of the **Indian National Congress**. He negotiated the end of British colonial rule in India and became India's first prime minister (1947–1964). (*p. 864*)

Neo-Assyrian Empire An empire extending from western Iran to Syria-Palestine, conquered by the Assyrians of northern Mesopotamia between the tenth and seventh centuries B.C.E. They used force and terror and exploited the wealth and labor of their subjects. They also preserved and continued the cultural and scientific developments of Mesopotamian civilization. (*p. 80*)

Neo-Babylonian kingdom Under the Chaldaeans (nomadic kinship groups that settled in southern Mesopotamia in the early first millennium B.C.E.), **Babylon** again became a major political and cultural center in the seventh and sixth centuries B.C.E. After participating in the destruction of Assyrian power, the monarchs Nabopolassar and Nebuchadnezzar took over the southern portion of the Assyrian domains. By destroying the First Temple in Jerusalem and deporting part of the population, they initiated the Diaspora of the Jews. (*p. 97*)

neo-Confucianism Term used to describe new approaches to understanding classic Confucian texts that became the basic ruling philosophy of China from the **Song** period to the twentieth century. (*p. 293*)

neo-liberalism The term used in Latin America and other developing regions to describe free-market policies that include reducing tariff protection for local industries; the sale of public-sector industries, like national airlines and public utilities, to private investors or foreign corporations; and the reduction of social welfare policies and public-sector employment. (*p. 920*)

Neolithic The period of the **Stone Age** associated with the ancient **Agricultural Revolution(s)**. It follows the **Paleolithic** period. (*p. 6*)

Nevskii, Alexander (1220–1263) Prince of Novgorod (r. 1236–1263). He submitted to the invading Mongols in 1240 and received recognition as the leader of the Russian princes under the **Golden Horde**. (*p. 352*)

New Economic Policy Policy proclaimed by Vladimir Lenin in 1923 to encourage the revival of the Soviet economy by allowing small private enterprises. Joseph Stalin ended the NEP in 1928 and replaced it with a series of **Five-Year Plans**. (See also Lenin, Vladimir.) (*p. 809*)

New France French colony in North America, with a capital in Quebec, founded 1608. New France fell to the British in 1760. (*p. 508*)

New Imperialism Historians' term for the late-nineteenth and early-twentieth-century wave of conquests by European powers, the United States, and Japan, which were followed by the development and exploitation of the newly conquered territories for the benefit of the colonial powers. (*p. 772*)

newly industrialized economies (NIEs) Rapidly growing, new industrial nations of the late twentieth century, including the **Asian Tigers**. (*p. 923*)

new monarchies Historians' term for the monarchies in France, England, and Spain from 1450 to 1600. The centralization of royal power was increasing within more or less fixed territorial limits. (*p. 420*)

nomadism A way of life, forced by a scarcity of resources, in which groups of people continually migrate to find pastures and water. (*p. 342*)

nonaligned nations Developing countries that announced their neutrality in the **Cold War**. (*p. 904*)

nongovernmental organizations (NGOs) Nonprofit international organizations devoted to investigating human rights abuses and providing humanitarian relief. Two NGOs won the Nobel Peace Prize in the 1990s: International Campaign to Ban Landmines (1997) and Doctors Without Borders (1999). (*p. 961*)

North Atlantic Treaty Organization (NATO) Organization formed in 1949 as a military alliance of western European and North American states against the Soviet Union and its east European allies. (See also **Warsaw Pact**.) (*p. 888*)

Olmec The first Mesoamerican civilization. Between ca. 1200 and 400 B.C.E., the Olmec people of central Mexico created a vibrant civilization that included intensive agriculture, wide-ranging trade, ceremonial centers, and monumental construction. The Olmec had great cultural influence on later Mesoamerican societies, passing on artistic styles, religious imagery, sophisticated astronomical observation for the construction of calendars, and a ritual ball game. (*p. 59*)

Oman Arab state based in Musqat, the main port in the southwest region of the Arabian peninsula. Oman succeeded Portugal as a power in the western Indian Ocean in the eighteenth century. (*p. 566*)

Opium War (1839–1842) War between Britain and the **Qing Empire** that was, in the British view, occasioned by the Qing government's refusal to permit the importation of opium into its territories. The victorious British imposed the one-sided **Treaty of Nanking** on China. (*p. 700*)

Organization of Petroleum Exporting Countries (OPEC) Organization formed in 1960 by oil-producing states to promote their collective interest in generating revenue from oil. (*p. 907*)

Ottoman Empire Islamic state founded by Osman in northwestern Anatolia ca. 1300. After the fall of the **Byzantine Empire**, the Ottoman Empire was based at Istanbul (formerly Constantinople) from 1453 to 1922. It encompassed lands in the Middle East, North Africa, the Caucasus, and eastern Europe. (*pp. 356, 548*)

Páez, José Antonio (1790–1873) Venezuelan soldier who led Simón Bolívar's cavalry force. He became a successful general in the war and built a powerful political base. Unwilling to accept the constitutional authority of Bolívar's government in distant Bogotá, he declared Venezuela's independence from Gran Colombia in 1829. (*p. 665*)

Paleolithic The period of the **Stone Age** associated with the **evolution** of humans. It predates the **Neolithic** period. (*p. 6*)

Pan-Slavism Movement among Russian intellectuals in the second half of the nineteenth century to identify culturally and politically with the Slavic peoples of eastern Europe. (*p. 697*)

Panama Canal Ship canal cut across the isthmus of Panama by United States Army engineers; it opened in 1914. The canal greatly shortened the sea voyage between the east and west coasts of

North America. The United States turned the canal over to Panama on January 1, 2000. (*p. 791*)

papacy The central administration of the Roman Catholic Church, of which the pope is the head. (*pp. 263, 460*)

papyrus A reed that grows along the banks of the Nile River in Egypt. From it was produced a coarse, paperlike writing medium used by the Egyptians and many other peoples in the ancient Mediterranean and Middle East. (*p. 27*)

Parthians Iranian ruling dynasty between ca. 250 B.C.E. and 226 C.E. (*p. 202*)

patron/client relationship In ancient Rome, a fundamental social relationship in which the patron—a wealthy and powerful individual—provided legal and economic protection and assistance to clients, men of lesser status and means, and in return the clients supported the political careers and economic interests of their patron. (*p. 143*)

Paul (ca. 5–65 C.E.) A Jew from the Greek city of Tarsus in Anatolia, he initially persecuted the followers of Jesus but, after receiving a revelation on the road to Syrian Damascus, became a Christian. Taking advantage of his Hellenized background and Roman citizenship, he traveled throughout Syria-Palestine, Anatolia, and Greece, preaching the new religion and establishing churches. Finding his greatest success among pagans ("gentiles"), he began the process by which Christianity separated from Judaism. (*p. 152*)

pax romana Literally, "Roman peace," it connoted the stability and prosperity that Roman rule brought to the lands of the Roman Empire in the first two centuries C.E. The movement of people and trade goods along Roman roads and safe seas allowed for the spread of cultural practices, technologies, and religious ideas. (*p. 151*)

Pearl Harbor Naval base in Hawaii attacked by Japanese aircraft on December 7, 1941. The sinking of much of the U.S. Pacific Fleet brought the United States into World War II. (*p. 847*)

Peloponnesian War A protracted (431–404 B.C.E.) and costly conflict between the Athenian and Spartan alliance systems that convulsed most of the Greek world. The war was largely a consequence of Athenian imperialism. Possession of a naval empire allowed Athens to fight a war of attrition. Ultimately, Sparta prevailed because of Athenian errors and Persian financial support. (*p. 127*)

perestroika Policy of "openness" that was the centerpiece of Mikhail Gorbachev's efforts to liberalize communism in the Soviet Union. (See also **Gorbachev, Mikhail**.) (*p. 924*)

Pericles (ca. 495–429 B.C.E.) Aristocratic leader who guided the Athenian state through the transformation to full participatory democracy for all male citizens, supervised construction of the Acropolis, and pursued a policy of imperial expansion that led to the **Peloponnesian War**. He formulated a strategy of attrition but died from the plague early in the war. (*p. 123*)

Perón, Eva Duarte (1919–1952) Wife of **Juan Perón** and champion of the poor in Argentina. She was a gifted speaker and popular political leader who campaigned to improve the life of the urban poor by founding schools and hospitals and providing other social benefits. (*p. 877*)

Perón, Juan (1895–1974) President of Argentina (1946–1955, 1973–1974). As a military officer, he championed the rights of labor. Aided by his wife **Eva Duarte Perón**, he was elected president in 1946. He built up Argentinean industry, became very popular among the urban poor, but harmed the economy. (*p. 876*)

Perry, Commodore Matthew A navy commander who, on July 8, 1853, became the first foreigner to break through the barriers that had kept Japan isolated from the rest of the world for 250 years. (*p. 743*)

Persepolis A complex of palaces, reception halls, and treasury buildings erected by the Persian kings **Darius I** and Xerxes in the Persian homeland. It is believed that the New Year's festival was celebrated here, as well as the coronations, weddings, and funerals of the Persian kings, who were buried in cliff-tombs nearby. (*p. 112*)

Persian Wars Conflicts between Greek city-states and the Persian Empire, ranging from the Ionian Revolt (499–494 B.C.E.) through Darius's punitive expedition that failed at Marathon (490 B.C.E.) and the defeat of Xerxes' massive invasion of Greece by the Spartan-led Hellenic League (480–479 B.C.E.). This first major setback for Persian arms launched the Greeks into their period of greatest cultural productivity. **Herodotus** chronicled these events in the first "history" in the Western tradition. (*p. 124*)

personalist leaders Political leaders who rely on charisma and their ability to mobilize and direct the masses of citizens outside the authority of constitutions and laws. Nineteenth-century examples include José Antonio Páez of Venezuela and Andrew Jackson of the United States. Twentieth-century examples include Getulio Vargas of Brazil and Juan Perón of Argentina. (See also **Jackson, Andrew**; **Páez, José Antonio**; **Perón, Juan**; **Vargas, Getulio**.) (*p. 664*)

Peter the Great (1672–1725) Russian **tsar** (r. 1689–1725). He enthusiastically introduced Western languages and technologies to the Russian elite, moving the capital from Moscow to the new city of St. Petersburg. (*p. 590*)

pharaoh The central figure in the ancient Egyptian state. Believed to be an earthly manifestation of the gods, he used his absolute power to maintain the safety and prosperity of Egypt. (*p. 26*)

Phoenicians Semitic-speaking Canaanites living on the coast of modern Lebanon and Syria in the first millennium B.C.E. From major cities such as Tyre and Sidon, Phoenician merchants and sailors explored the Mediterranean, engaged in widespread commerce, and founded **Carthage** and other colonies in the western Mediterranean. (*p. 90*)

pilgrimage Journey to a sacred shrine by Christians seeking to show their piety, fulfill vows, or gain absolution for sins. Other religions also have pilgrimage traditions, such as the Muslim pilgrimage to **Mecca** and the pilgrimages made by early Chinese Buddhists to India in search of sacred Buddhist writings. (*p. 275*)

Pilgrims Group of English Protestant dissenters who established Plymouth Colony in Massachusetts in 1620 to seek religious freedom after having lived briefly in the Netherlands. (*p. 506*)

Pizarro, Francisco (ca. 1478–1541) Spanish explorer who led the conquest of the **Inca** Empire of Peru in 1531–1533. (*p. 447*)

Planck, Max (1858–1947) German physicist who developed quantum theory and was awarded the Nobel Prize for physics in 1918. (*p. 821*)

plantocracy In the West Indian colonies, the rich men who owned most of the slaves and most of the land, especially in the eighteenth century. (*p. 424*)

polis The Greek term for a **city-state**, an urban center and the agricultural territory under its control. It was the characteristic form of political organization in southern and central Greece in the Archaic and Classical periods. Of the hundreds of city-states in the Mediterranean and Black Sea regions settled by Greeks, some were oligarchic, others democratic, depending on the powers delegated to the Council and the Assembly. (*p. 118*)

positivism A philosophy developed by the French count of Saint-Simon. Positivists believed that social and economic problems could be solved by the application of the scientific method, leading to continuous progress. Their ideas became popular in France and Latin America in the nineteenth century. (*p. 647*)

Potosí Located in Bolivia, one of the richest silver mining centers and most populous cities in colonial Spanish America. (*p. 496*)

Principate A term used to characterize Roman government in the first three centuries C.E., based on the ambiguous title *princeps* ("first citizen") adopted by Augustus to conceal his military dictatorship. (*p. 147*)

printing press A mechanical device for transferring text or graphics from a woodblock or type to paper using ink. Presses using movable type first appeared in Europe in about 1450. (See also **movable type**.) *(p. 414)*

Protestant Reformation Religious reform movement within the Latin Christian Church beginning in 1519. It resulted in the "protesters" forming several new Christian denominations, including the Lutheran and Reformed Churches and the Church of England. *(p. 461)*

proxy wars During the Cold War, local or regional wars in which the superpowers armed, trained, and financed the combatants. *(p. 916)*

Ptolemies The Macedonian dynasty, descended from one of Alexander the Great's officers, that ruled Egypt for three centuries (323–30 B.C.E.). From their magnificent capital at Alexandria on the Mediterranean coast, the Ptolemies largely took over the system created by Egyptian pharaohs to extract the wealth of the land, rewarding Greeks and Hellenized non-Greeks serving in the military and administration. *(p. 131)*

Puritans English Protestant dissenters who believed that God predestined souls to heaven or hell before birth. They founded Massachusetts Bay Colony in 1629. *(p. 506)*

pyramid A large, triangular stone monument, used in Egypt and Nubia as a burial place for the king. The largest pyramids, erected during the Old Kingdom near Memphis with stone tools and compulsory labor, reflect the Egyptian belief that the proper and spectacular burial of the divine ruler would guarantee the continued prosperity of the land. (See also **ma'at**.) *(p. 26)*

Qin A people and state in the Wei Valley of eastern China that conquered rival states and created the first Chinese empire (221–206 B.C.E.). The Qin ruler, **Shi Huangdi**, standardized many features of Chinese society and ruthlessly marshaled subjects for military and construction projects, engendering hostility that led to the fall of his dynasty shortly after his death. The Qin framework was largely taken over by the succeeding **Han** Empire. *(p. 157)*

Qing Empire Empire established in China by Manchus who overthrew the **Ming Empire** in 1644. At various times the Qing also controlled Manchuria, Mongolia, Turkestan, and Tibet. The last Qing emperor was overthrown in 1911. *(p. 581)*

Quran Book composed of divine revelations made to the Prophet **Muhammad** between ca. 610 and his death in 632; the sacred text of the religion of **Islam**. *(p. 231)*

railroads Networks of iron (later steel) rails on which steam (later electric or diesel) locomotives pulled long trains at high speeds. The first railroads were built in England in the 1830s. Their success caused a railroad-building boom throughout the world that lasted well into the twentieth century. *(p. 744)*

Rajputs Members of a mainly Hindu warrior caste from northwest India. The Mughal emperors drew most of their Hindu officials from this caste, and **Akbar** married a Rajput princess. *(p. 561)*

Ramesses II A long-lived ruler of New Kingdom Egypt (r. 1290–1224 B.C.E.). He reached an accommodation with the **Hittites** of Anatolia after a standoff in battle at Kadesh in Syria. He built on a grand scale throughout Egypt. *(p. 74)*

Rashid al-Din (d. 1318) Adviser to the **Il-khan** ruler Ghazan, who converted to Islam on Rashid's advice. *(p. 351)*

recaptives Africans rescued by Britain's Royal Navy from the illegal slave trade of the nineteenth century and restored to free status. *(p. 719)*

reconquest of Iberia Beginning in the eleventh century, military campaigns by various Iberian Christian states to recapture territory taken by **Muslims**. In 1492 the last Muslim ruler was defeated, and Spain and Portugal emerged as united kingdoms. *(p. 421)*

Renaissance (European) A period of intense artistic and intellectual activity, said to be a "rebirth" of Greco-Roman culture. Usually divided into an Italian Renaissance, from roughly the mid-fourteenth to mid-fifteenth century, and a Northern (trans-Alpine) Renaissance, from roughly the early fifteenth to early seventeenth century. *(pp. 412, 459)*

Republic The period from 507 to 31 B.C.E., during which Rome was largely governed by the aristocratic Roman **Senate**. *(p. 142)*

Revolutions of 1848 Democratic and nationalist revolutions that swept across Europe. The monarchy in France was overthrown. In Germany, Austria, Italy, and Hungary the revolutions failed. *(p. 622)*

Rhodes, Cecil (1853–1902) British entrepreneur and politician involved in the expansion of the British Empire from South Africa into Central Africa. The colonies of Southern Rhodesia (now Zimbabwe) and Northern Rhodesia (now Zambia) were named after him. *(p. 780)*

Robespierre, Maximilien (1758–1794) Young provincial lawyer who led the most radical phases of the French Revolution. His execution ended the Reign of Terror. See **Jacobins**. *(p. 614)*

Romanization The process by which the Latin language and Roman culture became dominant in the western provinces of the Roman Empire. The Roman government did not actively seek to Romanize the subject peoples, but indigenous peoples in the provinces often chose to Romanize because of the political and economic advantages that it brought, as well as the allure of Roman success. *(p. 151)*

Royal African Company A trading company chartered by the English government in 1672 to conduct its merchants' trade on the Atlantic coast of Africa. *(p. 530)*

sacrifice A gift given to a deity, often with the aim of creating a relationship, gaining favor, and obligating the god to provide some benefit to the sacrificer, sometimes in order to sustain the deity and thereby guarantee the continuing vitality of the natural world. The object devoted to the deity could be as simple as a cup of wine poured on the ground, a live animal slain on the altar, or, in the most extreme case, the ritual killing of a human being. *(p. 120)*

Safavid Empire Iranian kingdom (1502–1722) established by Ismail Safavi, who declared Iran a Shi'ite state. *(p. 557)*

Sahel Belt south of the Sahara; literally "coastland" in Arabic. *(p. 212)*

samurai Literally "those who serve," the hereditary military elite of the Tokugawa Shogunate. *(p. 574)*

Sandinistas Members of a leftist coalition that overthrew the Nicaraguan dictatorship of Anastasia Somoza in 1979 and attempted to install a socialist economy. The United States financed armed opposition by the Contras. The Sandinistas lost national elections in 1990. *(p. 917)*

Sanger, Margaret (1883–1966) American nurse and author; pioneer in the movement for family planning; organized conferences and established birth control clinics. *(p. 821)*

Sasanid Empire Iranian empire, established ca. 224, with a capital in Ctesiphon, Mesopotamia. The Sasanid emperors established **Zoroastrianism** as the state religion. Islamic Arab armies overthrew the empire ca. 651. *(p. 205)*

satrap The governor of a province in the Achaemenid Persian Empire, often a relative of the king. He was responsible for protection of the province and for forwarding tribute to the central administration. Satraps in outlying provinces enjoyed considerable autonomy. *(p. 111)*

savanna Tropical or subtropical grassland, either treeless or with occasional clumps of trees. Most extensive in **sub-Saharan Africa** but also present in South America. *(p. 215)*

schism A formal split within a religious community. See **Great Western Schism**. *(p. 254)*

scholasticism A philosophical and theological system, associated with Thomas Aquinas, devised to reconcile Aristotelian philosophy and Roman Catholic theology in the thirteenth century. *(p. 413)*

Scientific Revolution The intellectual movement in Europe, initially associated with planetary motion and other aspects of physics, that by the seventeenth century had laid the groundwork for modern science. (*p. 465*)

"scramble" for Africa Sudden wave of conquests in Africa by European powers in the 1880s and 1890s. Britain obtained most of eastern Africa, France most of northwestern Africa. Other countries (Germany, Belgium, Portugal, Italy, and Spain) acquired lesser amounts. (*p. 776*)

scribe In the governments of many ancient societies, a professional position reserved for men who had undergone the lengthy training required to be able to read and write using **cuneiforms, hieroglyphics**, or other early, cumbersome writing systems. (*p. 20*)

seasoning An often difficult period of adjustment to new climates, disease environments, and work routines, such as that experienced by slaves newly arrived in the Americas. (*p. 526*)

Selassie, Haile (1892–1975) Emperor of Ethiopia (r. 1930–1974) and symbol of African independence. He fought the Italian invasion of his country in 1935 and regained his throne during World War II, when British forces expelled the Italians. He ruled **Ethiopia** as a traditional autocracy until he was overthrown in 1974. (*p. 870*)

Semitic Family of related languages long spoken across parts of western Asia and northern Africa. In antiquity these languages included Hebrew, Aramaic, and Phoenician. The most widespread modern member of the Semitic family is Arabic. (*p. 16*)

Senate A council whose members were the heads of wealthy, landowning families. Originally an advisory body to the early kings, in the era of the Roman **Republic** the Senate effectively governed the Roman state and the growing empire. Under Senate leadership, Rome conquered an empire of unprecedented extent in the lands surrounding the Mediterranean Sea. In the first century B.C.E. quarrels among powerful and ambitious senators and failure to address social and economic problems led to civil wars and the emergence of the rule of the emperors. (*p. 142*)

"separate spheres" Nineteenth-century idea in Western societies that men and women, especially of the middle class, should have clearly differentiated roles in society: women as wives, mothers, and homemakers; men as breadwinners and participants in business and politics. (*p. 750*)

sepoy A soldier in South Asia, especially in the service of the British. (*p. 721*)

Sepoy Rebellion The revolt of Indian soldiers in 1857 against certain practices that violated religious customs; also known as the Sepoy Mutiny. (*p. 723*)

Serbia The Ottoman province in the Balkans that rose up against **Janissary** control in the early 1800s. (*p. 689*)

serf In **medieval** Europe, an agricultural laborer legally bound to a lord's property and obligated to perform set services for the lord. In Russia some serfs worked as artisans and in factories; serfdom was not abolished there until 1861. (*pp. 260, 590*)

shaft graves A term used for the burial sites of elite members of Mycenaean Greek society in the mid-second millennium B.C.E. At the bottom of deep shafts lined with stone slabs, the bodies were laid out along with gold and bronze jewelry, implements, weapons, and masks. (*p. 78*)

Shah Abbas I The fifth and most renowned ruler of the **Safavid** dynasty in Iran (r. 1587–1629). Abbas moved the royal capital to Isfahan in 1598. (*p. 558*)

shamanism The practice of identifying special individuals (shamans) who will interact with spirits for the benefit of the community. Characteristic of the Korean kingdoms of the early medieval period and of early societies of Central Asia. (*p. 298*)

Shang The dominant people in the earliest Chinese dynasty for which we have written records (ca. 1750–1045 B.C.E.). Ancestor worship, **divination** by means of oracle bones, and the use of bronze vessels for ritual purposes were major elements of Shang culture. (*p. 42*)

Shi Huangdi Founder of the short-lived **Qin** dynasty and creator of the Chinese Empire (r. 221–210 B.C.E.). He is remembered for his ruthless conquests of rival states, standardization of practices, and forcible organization of labor for military and engineering tasks. His tomb, with its army of life-size terracotta soldiers, has been partially excavated. (*p. 157*)

Shi'ites Muslims belonging to the branch of **Islam** believing that God vests leadership of the community in a descendant of **Muhammad's** son-in-law Ali. Shi'ism is the state religion of Iran. (See also **Sunnis**.) (*pp. 232, 557*)

Siberia The extreme northeastern sector of Asia, including the Kamchatka Peninsula and the present Russian coast of the Arctic Ocean, the Bering Strait, and the Sea of Okhotsk. (*p. 587*)

Silk Road Caravan routes connecting China and the Middle East across Central Asia and Iran. (*p. 202*)

Sima Qian Chief astrologer for the **Han** dynasty emperor Wu. He composed a monumental history of China from its legendary origins to his own time and is regarded as the Chinese "father of history." (*p. 161*)

Slavophiles Russian intellectuals in the early nineteenth century who favored resisting western European influences and taking pride in the traditional peasant values and institutions of the Slavic people. (*p. 697*)

"small traditions" Historians' term for a localized, usually nonliterate, set of customs and beliefs adhered to by a single society, often in conjunction with a **"great tradition."** (*p. 215*)

socialism A political ideology that originated in Europe in the 1830s. Socialists advocated government protection of workers from exploitation by property owners and government ownership of industries. This ideology led to the founding of socialist or labor parties throughout Europe in the second half of the nineteenth century. (See also **Marx, Karl**.) (*p. 753*)

Socrates Athenian philosopher (ca. 470–399 B.C.E.) who shifted the emphasis of philosophical investigation from questions of natural science to ethics and human behavior. He attracted young disciples from elite families but made enemies by revealing the ignorance and pretensions of others, culminating in his trial and execution by the Athenian state. (*p. 126*)

Sokoto Caliphate A large Muslim state founded in 1809 in what is now northern Nigeria. (*p. 715*)

Solidarity Polish trade union created in 1980 to protest working conditions and political repression. It began the nationalist opposition to communist rule that led in 1989 to the fall of communism in eastern Europe. (*p. 924*)

Song Empire Empire in central and southern China (960–1126) while the Liao people controlled the north. Empire in southern China (1127–1279; the "Southern Song") while the Jin people controlled the north. Distinguished for its advances in technology, medicine, astronomy, and mathematics. (*p. 292*)

Songhai A people, language, kingdom, and empire in western Sudan in West Africa. At its height in the sixteenth century, the Muslim Songhai Empire stretched from the Atlantic to the land of the Hausa and was a major player in the trans-Saharan trade. (*p. 537*)

Srivijaya A state based on the Indonesian island of Sumatra, between the seventh and eleventh centuries C.E. It amassed wealth and power by a combination of selective adaptation of Indian technologies and concepts, control of the lucrative trade routes between India and China, and skillful showmanship and diplomacy in holding together a disparate realm of inland and coastal territories. (See also theater-state.) (*p. 302*)

Stalin, Joseph (1879–1953) Bolshevik revolutionary, head of the Soviet Communist Party after 1924, and dictator of the Soviet Union from 1928 to 1953. He led the Soviet Union with an iron fist, using **Five-Year Plans** to increase industrial production and terror to crush all opposition. (*p. 832*)

Stalingrad City in Russia, site of a Red Army victory over the German army in 1942–1943. The Battle of Stalingrad was the turning point in the war between Germany and the Soviet Union. Today Volgograd. (*p. 846*)

Stanley, Henry Morton (1841–1904) British-American explorer of Africa, famous for his expeditions in search of Dr. David Livingstone. Stanley helped King **Leopold II** establish the Congo Free State. (*p. 778*)

steam engine A machine that turns the energy released by burning fuel into motion. Thomas Newcomen built the first crude but workable steam engine in 1712. **James Watt** vastly improved his device in the 1760s and 1770s. Steam power was later applied to moving machinery in factories and to powering ships and locomotives. (*p. 638*)

steel A form of iron that is both durable and flexible. It was first mass-produced in the 1860s and quickly became the most widely used metal in construction, machinery, and railroad equipment. (*p. 745*)

steppes Treeless plains, especially the high, flat expanses of northern Eurasia, which usually have little rain and are covered with coarse grass. They are good lands for nomads and their herds. Living on the steppes promoted the breeding of horses and the development of military skills that were essential to the rise of the Mongol Empire. (*p. 214*)

stirrup Device for securing a horseman's feet, enabling him to wield weapons more effectively. First evidence of the use of stirrups was among the Kushan people of northern Afghanistan in approximately the first century C.E. (*p. 206*)

stock exchange A place where shares in a company or business enterprise are bought and sold. (*p. 469*)

Stone Age The historical period characterized by the production of tools from stone and other nonmetallic substances. It was followed in some places by the Bronze Age and more generally by the **Iron Age**. (*p. 6*)

submarine telegraph cables Insulated copper cables laid along the bottom of a sea or ocean for telegraphic communication. The first short cable was laid across the English Channel in 1851; the first successful transatlantic cable was laid in 1866. (See also **electric telegraph**.) (*p. 744*)

sub-Saharan Africa Portion of the African continent lying south of the Sahara. (*p. 213*)

Suez Canal Ship canal dug across the isthmus of Suez in Egypt, designed by Ferdinand de Lesseps. It opened to shipping in 1869 and shortened the sea voyage between Europe and Asia. Its strategic importance led to the British conquest of Egypt in 1882. (*p. 771*)

Suleiman the Magnificent (1494–1566) The most illustrious sultan of the **Ottoman Empire** (r. 1520–1566); also known as Suleiman Kanuni, "The Lawgiver." He significantly expanded the empire in the Balkans and eastern Mediterranean. (*p. 548*)

Sumerians The people who dominated southern Mesopotamia through the end of the third millennium B.C.E. They were responsible for the creation of many fundamental elements of Mesopotamian culture—such as irrigation technology, **cuneiform**, and religious conceptions—taken over by their **Semitic** successors. (*p. 16*)

Sunnis Muslims belonging to branch of Islam believing that the community should select its own leadership. The majority religion in most Islamic countries. (See also **Shi'ites**.) (*p. 232*)

Sun Yat-sen (1867–1925) Chinese nationalist revolutionary, founder and leader of the **Guomindang** until his death. He attempted to create a liberal democratic political movement in China but was thwarted by military leaders. (*p. 813*)

Swahili Bantu language with Arabic loanwords spoken in coastal regions of East Africa. (*p. 566*)

Swahili Coast East African shores of the Indian Ocean between the Horn of Africa and the Zambezi River; from the Arabic *sawahil*, meaning "shores." (*p. 386*)

Taiping Rebellion (1851–1864) The most destructive civil war before the twentieth century. A Christian-inspired rural rebellion that threatened to topple the **Qing Empire**. (*p. 701*)

Tamil kingdoms The kingdoms of southern India, inhabited primarily by speakers of Dravidian languages, which developed in partial isolation, and somewhat differently, from the Aryan north. They produced epics, poetry, and performance arts. Elements of Tamil religious beliefs were merged into the Hindu synthesis. (*p. 185*)

Tang Empire Empire unifying China and part of Central Asia, founded 618 and ended 907. The Tang emperors presided over a magnificent court at their capital, **Chang'an**. (*p. 284*)

Tanzimat "Restructuring" reforms by the nineteenth-century Ottoman rulers, intended to move civil law away from the control of religious elites and make the military and the bureaucracy more efficient. (*p. 691*)

Tecumseh (1768–1813) Shawnee leader who attempted to organize an Amerindian confederacy to prevent the loss of additional territory to American settlers. He became an ally of the British in War of 1812 and died in battle. (*p. 668*)

Tenochtitlan Capital of the Aztec Empire, located on an island in Lake Texcoco. Its population was about 125,000 on the eve of Spanish conquest. Mexico City was constructed on its ruins. (*p. 317*)

Teotihuacan A powerful **city-state** in central Mexico (100 B.C.E.–750 C.E.). Its population was about 150,000 at its peak in 600. (*p. 332*)

terrorism Political belief that extreme and seemingly random violence will destabilize a government and permit the terrorists to gain political advantage. Though an old technique, terrorism gained prominence in the late twentieth century with the growth of worldwide mass media that, through their news coverage, amplified public fears of terrorist acts. (*p. 957*)

theater-state Historians' term for a state that acquires prestige and power by developing attractive cultural forms and staging elaborate public ceremonies (as well as redistributing valuable resources) to attract and bind subjects to the center. Examples include the **Gupta Empire** in India and **Srivijaya** in Southeast Asia. (*p. 185*)

Thebes Capital city of Egypt and home of the ruling dynasties during the Middle and New Kingdoms. Amon, patron deity of Thebes, became one of the chief gods of Egypt. Monarchs were buried across the river in the Valley of the Kings. (*p. 27*)

Theravada Buddhism "Way of the Elders" branch of Buddhism followed in Sri Lanka and much of Southeast Asia. Therevada remains close to the original principles set forth by the **Buddha**; it downplays the importance of gods and emphasizes austerity and the individual's search for enlightenment. (*p. 180*)

Third-Century Crisis Historians' term for the political, military, and economic turmoil that beset the Roman Empire during much of the third century C.E.: frequent changes of ruler, civil wars, barbarian invasions, decline of urban centers, and near-destruction of long-distance commerce and the monetary economy. After 284 C.E. Diocletian restored order by making fundamental changes. (*p. 155*)

Third World Term applied to a group of developing countries who professed nonalignment during the **Cold War**. (*p. 904*)

three-field system A rotational system for agriculture in which one field grows grain, one grows legumes, and one lies fallow. It gradually replaced the two-field system in medieval Europe. (*p. 401*)

Tiananmen Square Site in Beijing where Chinese students and workers gathered to demand greater political openness in 1989.

The demonstration was crushed by Chinese military with great loss of life. (*p. 923*)

Timbuktu City on the Niger River in the modern country of Mali. It was founded by the Tuareg as a seasonal camp sometime after 1000. As part of the **Mali** Empire, Timbuktu became a major terminus of the trans-Saharan trade and a center of Islamic learning. (*p. 391*)

Timur (1336–1405) Member of a prominent family of the Mongols' Jagadai Khanate, Timur through conquest gained control over much of Central Asia and Iran. He consolidated the status of Sunni Islam as orthodox, and his descendants, the Timurids, maintained his empire for nearly a century and founded the **Mughal Empire** in India. (*p. 350*)

Tiwanaku Name of capital city and empire centered on the region near Lake Titicaca in modern Bolivia (375–1000 C.E.). (*p. 326*)

Tokugawa Shogunate (1603–1868) The last of the three shogunates of Japan. (*p. 574*)

Toltecs Powerful postclassic empire in central Mexico (900–1175 C.E.). It influenced much of Mesoamerica. Aztecs claimed ties to this earlier civilization. (*p. 316*)

trans-Saharan caravan routes Trading network linking North Africa with **sub-Saharan Africa** across the Sahara. (*p. 211*)

Treaty of Nanking (1842) The treaty that concluded the **Opium War**. It awarded Britain a large indemnity from the **Qing Empire**, denied the Qing government tariff control over some of its own borders, opened additional ports of residence to Britons, and ceded the island of Hong Kong to Britain. (*p. 701*)

Treaty of Versailles (1919) The treaty imposed on Germany by France, Great Britain, the United States, and other Allied Powers after World War I. It demanded that Germany dismantle its military and give up some lands to Poland. It was resented by many Germans. (*p. 809*)

treaty ports Cities opened to foreign residents as a result of the forced treaties between the **Qing Empire** and foreign signatories. In the treaty ports, foreigners enjoyed **extraterritoriality**. (*p. 701*)

tributary system A system in which, from the time of the Han Empire, countries in East and Southeast Asia not under the direct control of empires based in China nevertheless enrolled as tributary states, acknowledging the superiority of the emperors in China in exchange for trading rights or strategic alliances. (*p. 287*)

tribute system A system in which defeated peoples were forced to pay a tax in the form of goods and labor. This forced transfer of food, cloth, and other goods subsidized the development of large cities. An important component of the **Aztec** and **Inca** economies. (*p. 319*)

trireme Greek and Phoenician warship of the fifth and fourth centuries B.C.E. It was sleek and light, powered by 170 oars arranged in three vertical tiers. Manned by skilled sailors, it was capable of short bursts of speed and complex maneuvers. (*p. 125*)

tropical rain forest High-precipitation forest zones of the Americas, Africa, and Asia lying between the Tropic of Cancer and the Tropic of Capricorn. (*p. 215*)

tropics Equatorial region between the Tropic of Cancer and the Tropic of Capricorn. It is characterized by generally warm or hot temperatures year-round, though much variation exists due to altitude and other factors. Temperate zones north and south of the tropics generally have a winter season. (*p. 374*)

tsar (czar) From Latin *caesar,* this Russian title for a monarch was first used in reference to a Russian ruler by Ivan III (r. 1462–1505). (*pp. 354, 587*)

Tulip Period (1718–1730) Last years of the reign of Ottoman sultan Ahmed III, during which European styles and attitudes became briefly popular in Istanbul. (*p. 555*)

Tupac Amaru II Member of **Inca** aristocracy who led a rebellion against Spanish authorities in Peru in 1780–1781. He was captured and executed with his wife and other members of his family. (*p. 511*)

tyrant The term the Greeks used to describe someone who seized and held power in violation of the normal procedures and traditions of the community. Tyrants appeared in many Greek **city-states** in the seventh and sixth centuries B.C.E., often taking advantage of the disaffection of the emerging middle class and, by weakening the old elite, unwittingly contributing to the evolution of **democracy**. (*p. 120*)

ulama Muslim religious scholars. From the ninth century onward, the primary interpreters of Islamic law and the social core of Muslim urban societies. (*p. 237*)

Umayyad Caliphate First hereditary dynasty of Muslim caliphs (661 to 750). From their capital at Damascus, the Umayyads ruled an empire that extended from Spain to India. Overthrown by the **Abbasid Caliphate**. (*p. 232*)

umma The community of all **Muslims**. A major innovation against the background of seventh-century Arabia, where traditionally kinship rather than faith had determined membership in a community. (*p. 230*)

underdevelopment The condition experienced by economies that depend on colonial forms of production such as the export of raw materials and plantation crops with low wages and low investment in education. (*p. 678*)

United Nations International organization founded in 1945 to promote world peace and cooperation. It replaced the **League of Nations**. (*p. 888*)

Universal Declaration of Human Rights A 1948 United Nations covenant binding signatory nations to the observance of specified rights. (*p. 961*)

universities Degree-granting institutions of higher learning. Those that appeared in the **Latin West** from about 1200 onward became the model of all modern universities. (*p. 412*)

Ural Mountains This north-south range separates Siberia from the rest of Russia. It is commonly considered the boundary between the continents of Europe and Asia. (*p. 587*)

Urdu A Persian-influenced literary form of Hindi written in Arabic characters and used as a literary language since the 1300s. (*p. 391*)

Vargas, Getulio (1883–1954) Dictator of Brazil from 1930 to 1945 and from 1951 to 1954. Defeated in the presidential election of 1930, he overthrew the government and created Estado Novo ("New State"), a dictatorship that emphasized industrialization and helped the urban poor but did little to alleviate the problems of the peasants. (*p. 875*)

varna/jati Two categories of social identity of great importance in Indian history. *Varna* are the four major social divisions: the Brahmin priest class, the Kshatriya warrior/administrator class, the Vaishya merchant/farmer class, and the Shudra laborer class. Within the system of varna are many *jati,* regional groups of people who have a common occupational sphere and who marry, eat, and generally interact with other members of their group. (*p. 176*)

vassal In **medieval** Europe, a sworn supporter of a king or lord committed to rendering specified military service to that king or lord. (*p. 262*)

Vedas Early Indian sacred "knowledge"—the literal meaning of the term—long preserved and communicated orally by Brahmin priests and eventually written down. These religious texts, including the thousand poetic hymns to various deities contained in the Rig Veda, are our main source of information about the Vedic period (ca. 1500–500 B.C.E.). (*p. 175*)

Versailles The huge palace built for French king Louis XIV south of Paris in the town of the same name. The palace symbolized the preeminence of French power and architecture in Europe and the triumph of royal authority over the French nobility. (*p. 476*)

Victorian Age The reign of Queen Victoria of Great Britain (r. 1837–1901). The term is also used to describe late-nineteenth-century society, with its rigid moral standards and sharply differentiated roles for men and women and for middle-class and working-class people. (See also **"separate spheres."**) (*p. 750*)

Vietnam War (1954–1975) Conflict pitting North Vietnam and South Vietnamese communist guerrillas against the South Vietnamese government, aided after 1961 by the United States. (*p. 893*)

Villa, Francisco "Pancho" (1877–1923) A popular leader during the Mexican Revolution. An outlaw in his youth, when the revolution started, he formed a cavalry army in the north of Mexico and fought for the rights of the landless in collaboration with **Emiliano Zapata**. He was assassinated in 1923. (*p. 872*)

Wari Andean civilization culturally linked to **Tiwanaku**, perhaps beginning as a colony of Tiwanaku. (*p. 326*)

Warsaw Pact The 1955 treaty binding the Soviet Union and countries of eastern Europe in an alliance against the **North Atlantic Treaty Organization**. (*p. 888*)

Washington, George (1732–1799) Military commander of the American Revolution. He was the first elected president of the United States (1789–1799). (*p. 608*)

water wheel A mechanism that harnesses the energy in flowing water to grind grain or to power machinery. It was used in many parts of the world but was especially common in Europe from 1200 to 1900. (*p. 402*)

Watt, James (1736–1819) Scot who invented the condenser and other improvements that made the **steam engine** a practical source of power for industry and transportation. The watt, an electrical measurement, is named after him. (*p. 638*)

weapons of mass destruction Nuclear, chemical, and biological devices that are capable of injuring and killing large numbers of people. (*p. 954*)

Wedgwood, Josiah (1730–1795) English industrialist whose pottery works were the first to produce fine-quality pottery by industrial methods. (*p. 635*)

Western Front A line of trenches and fortifications in World War I that stretched without a break from Switzerland to the North Sea. Scene of most of the fighting between Germany, on the one hand, and France and Britain, on the other. (*p. 803*)

Wilson, Woodrow (1856–1924) President of the United States (1913–1921) and the leading figure at the Paris Peace Conference of 1919. He was unable to persuade the U.S. Congress to ratify the **Treaty of Versailles** or join the **League of Nations**. (*p. 807*)

witch-hunt The pursuit of people suspected of witchcraft, especially in northern Europe in the late sixteenth and seventeenth centuries. (*p. 463*)

Women's Rights Convention An 1848 gathering of women angered by their exclusion from an international antislavery meeting. They met at Seneca Falls, New York, to discuss women's rights. (*p. 675*)

World Bank A specialized agency of the United Nations that makes loans to countries for economic development, trade promotion, and debt consolidation. Its formal name is the International Bank for Reconstruction and Development. (*p. 889*)

World Trade Organization (WTO) An international body established in 1995 to foster and bring order to international trade. (*p. 950*)

Wright, Wilbur (1867–1912), and Orville (1871–1948) American bicycle mechanics; the first to build and fly an airplane, at Kitty Hawk, North Carolina, December 7, 1903. (*p. 822*)

Xiongnu A confederation of nomadic peoples living beyond the northwest frontier of ancient China. Chinese rulers tried a variety of defenses and stratagems to ward off these "barbarians," as they called them, and finally succeeded in dispersing the Xiongnu in the first century C.E. (*p. 158*)

Yamagata Aritomo (1838–1922) One of the leaders of the **Meiji Restoration**. (*pp. 765*)

Yi (1392–1910) The Yi dynasty ruled Korea from the fall of the **Koryo** kingdom to the colonization of Korea by Japan. (*p. 364*)

yin/yang In Chinese belief, complementary factors that help to maintain the equilibrium of the world. Yang is associated with masculine, light, and active qualities; yin with feminine, dark, and passive qualities. (*p. 50*)

Yongle The third emperor of the **Ming Empire** (r. 1403–1424). He sponsored the building of the Forbidden City, a huge encyclopedia project, the expeditions of **Zheng He**, and the reopening of China's borders to trade and travel. (*p. 359*)

Yuan Empire (1271–1368) Empire created in China and Siberia by **Khubilai Khan**. (*p. 344*)

Yuan Shikai (1859–1916) Chinese general and first president of the Chinese Republic (1912–1916). He stood in the way of the democratic movement led by **Sun Yat-sen**. (*p. 814*)

Zapata, Emiliano (1879–1919) Revolutionary and leader of peasants in the Mexican Revolution. He mobilized landless peasants in south-central Mexico in an attempt to seize and divide the lands of the wealthy landowners. Though successful for a time, he was ultimately defeated and assassinated. (*p. 871*)

Zen The Japanese word for a branch of **Mahayana Buddhism** based on highly disciplined meditation. It is known in Sanskrit as *dhyana,* in Chinese as *chan,* and in Korean as *son.* (*p. 294*)

Zheng He (1371–1435) An imperial eunuch and Muslim, entrusted by the Ming emperor **Yongle** with a series of state voyages that took his gigantic ships through the Indian Ocean, from Southeast Asia to Africa. (*pp. 359, 431*)

Zhou The people and dynasty that took over the dominant position in north China from the Shang and created the concept of the **Mandate of Heaven** to justify their rule. The Zhou era, particularly the vigorous early period (1045–771 B.C.E.), was remembered in Chinese tradition as a time of prosperity and benevolent rule. In the later Zhou period (771–221 B.C.E.), centralized control broke down, and warfare among many small states became frequent. (*p. 44*)

ziggurat A massive pyramidal stepped tower made of mud bricks. It is associated with religious complexes in ancient Mesopotamian cities, but its function is unknown. (*p. 20*)

Zoroastrianism A religion originating in ancient Iran with the prophet Zoroaster. It centered on a single benevolent deity, Ahuramazda, who engaged in a twelve-thousand-year struggle with demonic forces before prevailing and restoring a pristine world. Emphasizing truth-telling, purity, and reverence for nature, the religion demanded that humans choose sides in the struggle between good and evil. Those whose good conduct indicated their support for Ahuramazda would be rewarded in the afterlife. Others would be punished. The religion of the Achaemenid and Sasanid Persians, Zoroastrianism may have spread within their realms and influenced Judaism, Christianity, and other faiths. (*p. 114*)

Zulu A people of modern South Africa whom King Shaka united in 1818. (*p. 714*)

INDEX

Document-Based Questions (DBQs)

INTRODUCTION

Think of a Document-Based Question (DBQ) as a mini-research paper, or a mini-investigation. It is a chance to show that you, like a professional historian or detective, can read the documents, question your sources, understand the backgrounds and motivations, and produce a good case or interpretation. In the words of the AP World History course description book, a DBQ tests your ability "to formulate and support an answer from documentary evidence."* It *does not* test your historical recall: the multiple-choice questions and the free-response essays do that. The DBQ is a test of your document-reading and analytical skills.

That last point is worth repeating: the DBQ is a test of your skills. It is scored or graded with a list of skills: when the AP reader sees a skill demonstrated, the reader gives you a point. Your essay can receive a maximum of 9 points when it is scored by an AP reader. Your classroom teacher may use a different system of grading, but she or he will be looking to see if you demonstrate the same skills.

This section is designed to be used in conjunction with chapters in *The Earth and Its Peoples* and to give you practice on three of the most crucial and difficult skills: figuring out what exactly the question is asking you to do; writing an acceptable thesis statement; and analyzing a document for its content and point of view. The DBQs in this section mirror the format of the AP World History exam and feature 4 to 10 documents each. Each question is designed to be completed in 50 minutes or less; this time includes a 10-minute reading period. In addition to completing the three tasks just mentioned, in your answer you need to reference all the documents and suggest an additional type of document that would support your thesis.

When working with documents, try the following three-step process:

---

1. "Plot Summary": What is this document's basic subject matter and content? What is its date? Does it relate to some other important events in the same time period?

---

2. "Point of View" (POV):

a. The first question is, "Who produced it?" What are his or her gender, age, ethnicity, social status, religion, or intellectual beliefs? (Almost all the documents here are "primary sources"; that is, they were produced during the time in question. A few are "secondary sources," produced by historians after the fact. You will need to take that into account.)

b. The second question is, "Who was the intended audience?" Was it written privately, written to be read or heard by others (who?), an official document for a ruler to read, a commissioned painting, or some other type of document?

c. The third question, as any good detective knows, would be "Why?" What is the *motivation* of the writer or producer of the document, based on what you can surmise about him or her?

d. When you put these together, you get the POV: why *this* person would be producing *this* piece of information at *this* time. Then you can evaluate how much you "trust" the information in the document, or what you think was *really* going on. It is useful to consider the tone or vocabulary of the document, just as you would in analyzing a piece of literature. It will sometimes convey the intent or the point of view of the author (anger, disdain, admiration, etc.).

---

3. "Analysis": Now that you know the basic information and the POV of the author, how does this document help you to *answer the question that is being asked?*

---

* *2006, 2007 Course Description for AP World History* (College Entrance Examination Board, NY, 2005), p. 33. Available online at www.apcentral.collegeboard.com.

DBQ 1: Geography, Politics, and Religion (Chapters 1 and 2)

Question: Evaluate how geography influenced the roles that religion and politics played in ancient societies in Afro-Eurasia. What additional kind(s) of documents would help you analyze the complex relationship between ancient humans and the environment?

Document 1

Source: Early civilizations, 3500–1500 B.C.E.

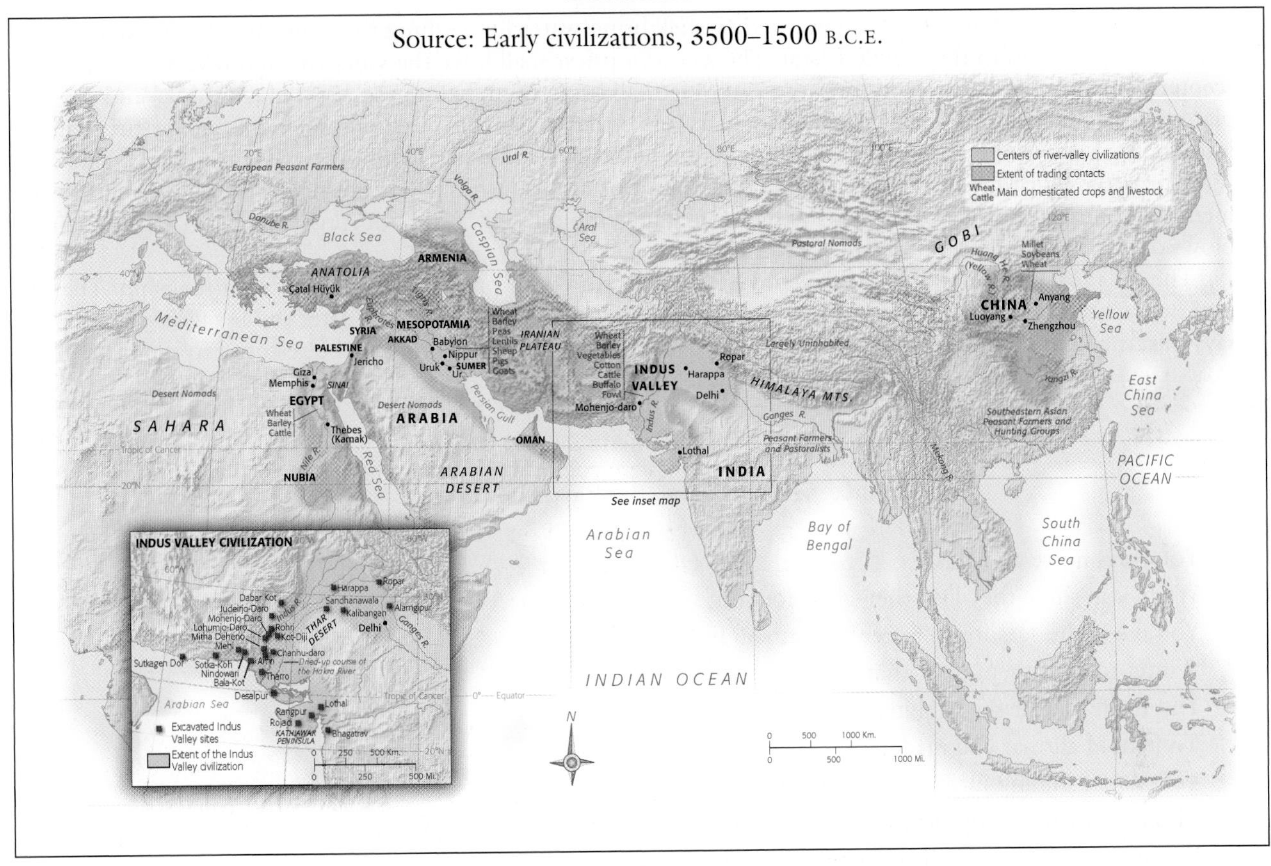

Document 2

Source: Description of Babylonian New Year's festival, 3rd century B.C.E., but representative of earlier Babylonian beliefs and practices.

On the fifth day of the month Nisannu . . . they shall bring water for washing the king's hands and then shall accompany him to the temple Esagil. The *urigallu*-priest shall leave the sanctuary and take away the scepter, the circle, and the sword from the king. He shall bring them before the god Bel [Marduk] and place them on a chair. He shall leave the sanctuary and strike the king's cheek. He shall accompany the king into the presence of the god Bel. He shall drag him by the ears and make him bow to the ground. The king shall speak the following only once: "I did not sin, lord of the countries. I was not neglectful of the requirements of your godship. I did not destroy Babylon. The temple Esagil, I did not forget its rites. I did not rain blows on the cheek of a subordinate." . . .

[The *urigallu*-priest responds:] "The god Bel will listen to your prayer. He will exalt your kingship. The god Bel will bless you forever. He will destroy your enemy, fell your adversary." After the *urigallu*-priest says this, the king shall regain his composure. The scepter, circle, and sword shall be restored to the king.

Document 3

Source: *Hymn to Aten*, the Egyptian sun-god.

Your rays nurse all fields,
When you shine they live, they grow for you;
You made the seasons to foster all that you made,
Winter to cool them, heat that they taste you.
You made the far sky to shine therein,
To behold all that you made;
You alone, shining in your form of living Aten,
Risen, radiant, distant, near.
You made millions of forms from yourself alone,
Towns, villages, fields, the river's course;
All eyes observe you upon them,
For you are the Aten of daytime on high.

Document 4

Source: Ancient Egypt, 2575–1070 B.C.E.

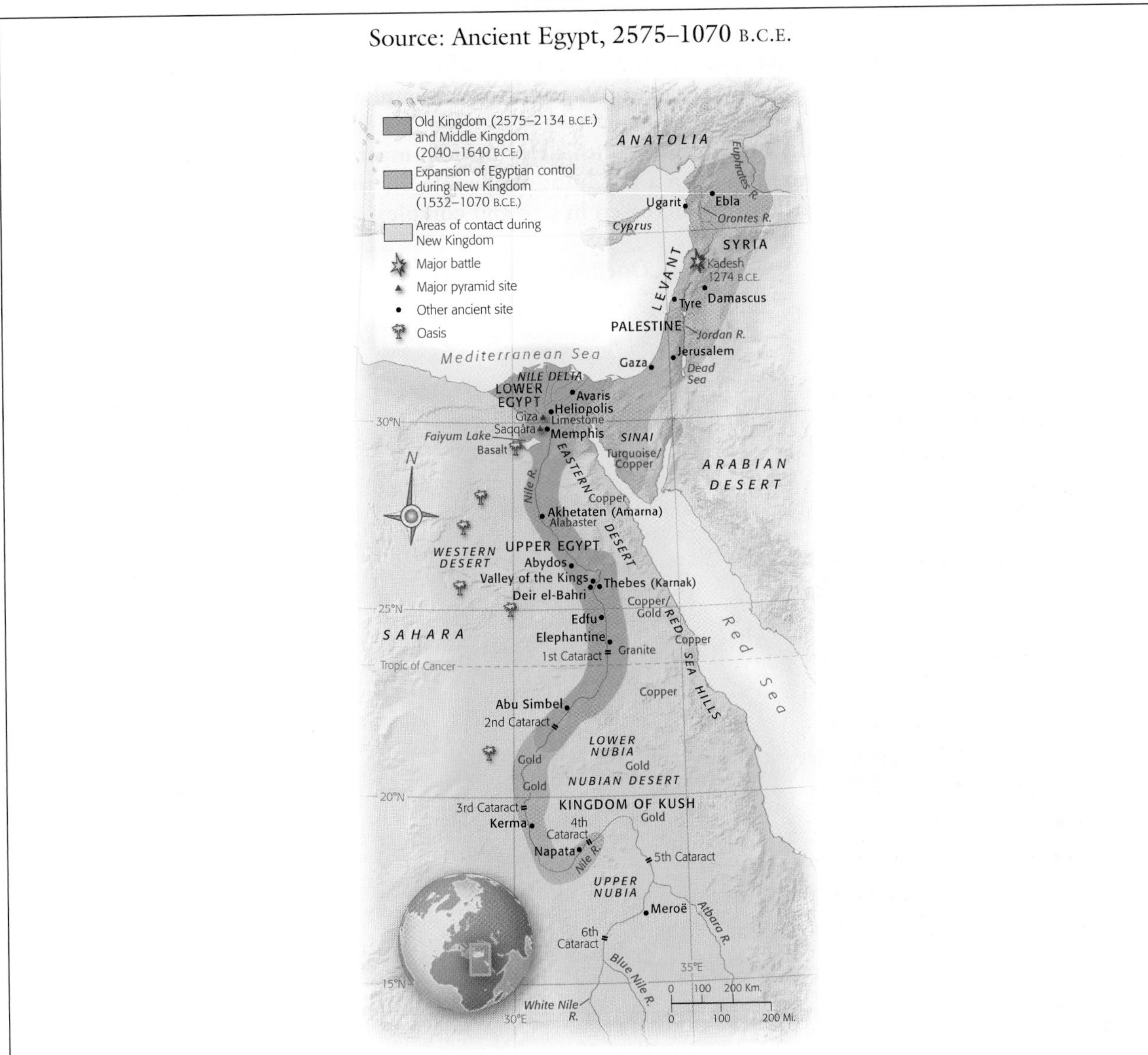

Document 5

Source: Mandate of Heaven, 6th century B.C.E.

Oh! do you, who now succeed to the throne, revere these warnings in your person. Think of them!—sacred counsels of vast importance, admirable words forcibly set forth! The ways of Heaven are not invariable: on the good-doer it sends down all blessings, and on the evil-doer it sends down all miseries. Do you but be virtuous, be it in small things or in large, and the myriad regions will have cause for rejoicing. If you not be virtuous, be it in large things or in small, it will bring the ruin of your ancestral temple.

DBQ 2: Socioeconomic Points of View (Chapters 3, 4, and 5)

Question: Analyze the causes of, and responses to, social inequality during the Classical Age (ca. 1000 B.C.E.–500 C.E.). How did one's status within society influence one's perspective of events in that society? What kinds of additional document(s) would help analyze the effects of increased social complexity?

Historical Background: During the Neolithic Revolution, most humans lived in small communities, usually no more than a few hundred people. As time progressed, human settlements increased in size and complexity.

Document 1

Source: Wall relief from the palace of Sannacherib at Nineveh, ca. 704–681 B.C.E.

Courtesy of the Trustees of the British Museum.

Document 2

Source: Excerpts from Hebrew Bible, book of Amos, ca. 750 B.C.E.

4:1 Listen to this message, you "cows of Bashan" who live on Mount Samaria! You oppress the poor; you crush the needy. You say to your husbands, "Bring us more to drink so we can party!" . . .

5:11 "Therefore, because you make the poor pay taxes on their crops and exact a grain tax from them, you will not live in the houses you built with chiseled stone, nor will you drink the wine from the fine vineyards you planted.

5:12 Certainly I am aware of your many rebellious acts and your numerous sins. You torment the innocent, you take bribes, and you deny justice to the needy at the city gate. . . ."

Document 3

Source: Unnamed Babylonian document, ca. 1000 B.C.E.

Narru, king of the gods, who created mankind.
And majestic Zulummar, who pinched of the clay for them,
And goddess Mami, the queen who fashioned them.
Gave twisted speech to the human race.
With lies, and not truth, they endowed them forever.
Solemnly they speak favorably of a rich man.
"He is kind," they say. "Riches should be his."
But they treat a poor man like a thief.
They have only bad to say of him and plot his murder.
Making him suffer every evil like a criminal, because he has no . . . [text uncertain]
Terrifyingly they bring him to his end, and extinguish him like glowing coals.

Document 4

Source: Inscription at Behistun, modern-day Iran, by Persian king Darius, ca. 500 B.C.E.

King Darius says: On this account [the god] Ahuramazda brought me help, and all the other gods, all that there are, because I was not wicked, nor was I a liar, nor was I a tyrant, neither I nor any of my family. I have ruled according to righteousness. Neither to the weak nor to the powerful did I do wrong. Whosoever helped my house, him I favored; he who was hostile, him I destroyed. . . .

Document 5

Source: Vase painting depicting women at an Athenian fountain house, ca. 520 B.C.E.

Scala/Art Resource, NY.

Document 6

Source: Greek historian Herodotus describing Persian king Xerxes (r. 486–465 B.C.E.) ordering a bridge to be built to transport his troops over the Hellespont strait.

The men who had been given this assignment made bridges starting from Abydos across to that headland; the Phoenicians one of flaxen cables, and the Egyptians a papyrus one. From Abydos to the opposite shore it is a distance of seven stadia.* But no sooner had the Hellespont strait been bridged than a great storm swept down, breaking and scattering everything. When Xerxes heard of this, he was very angry and commanded that the Hellespont be whipped with 300 lashes. I have even heard that he sent branders with them to brand the Hellespont. . . . He commanded that the sea receive these punishments and that the overseers of the bridge over the Hellespont be beheaded.

*7 stadia equals approximately 4⁄5 of a mile.

DBQ 3: Empire and Technology (Chapters 5, 6, and 7)

Question: Analyze the relationship between technology and the development of large Eurasian empires up to the year 600 C.E.

Document 1

Source: Economic aspect of the Roman Empire.

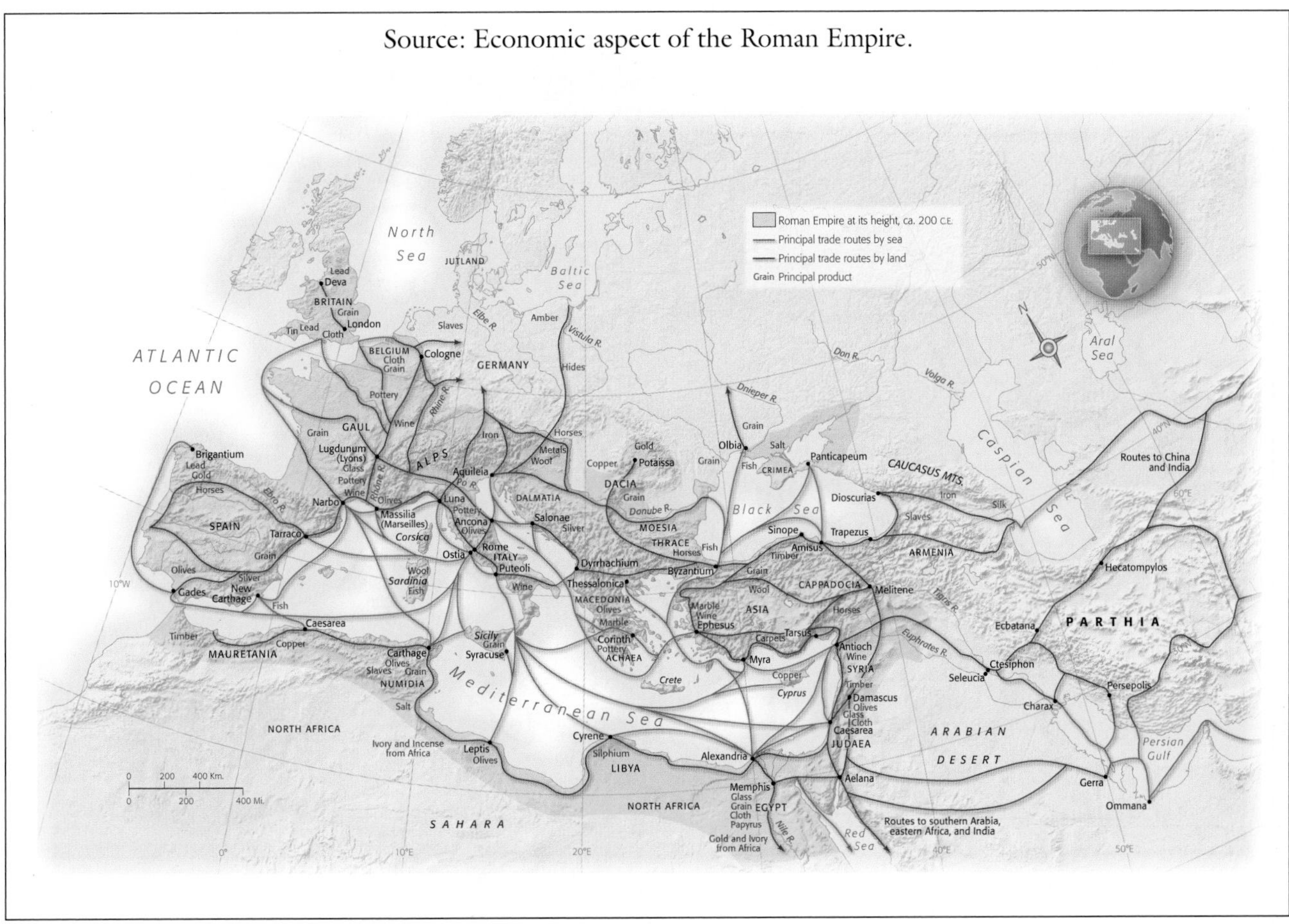

Document 2

Source: Han China, 206 B.C.E.–220 C.E.

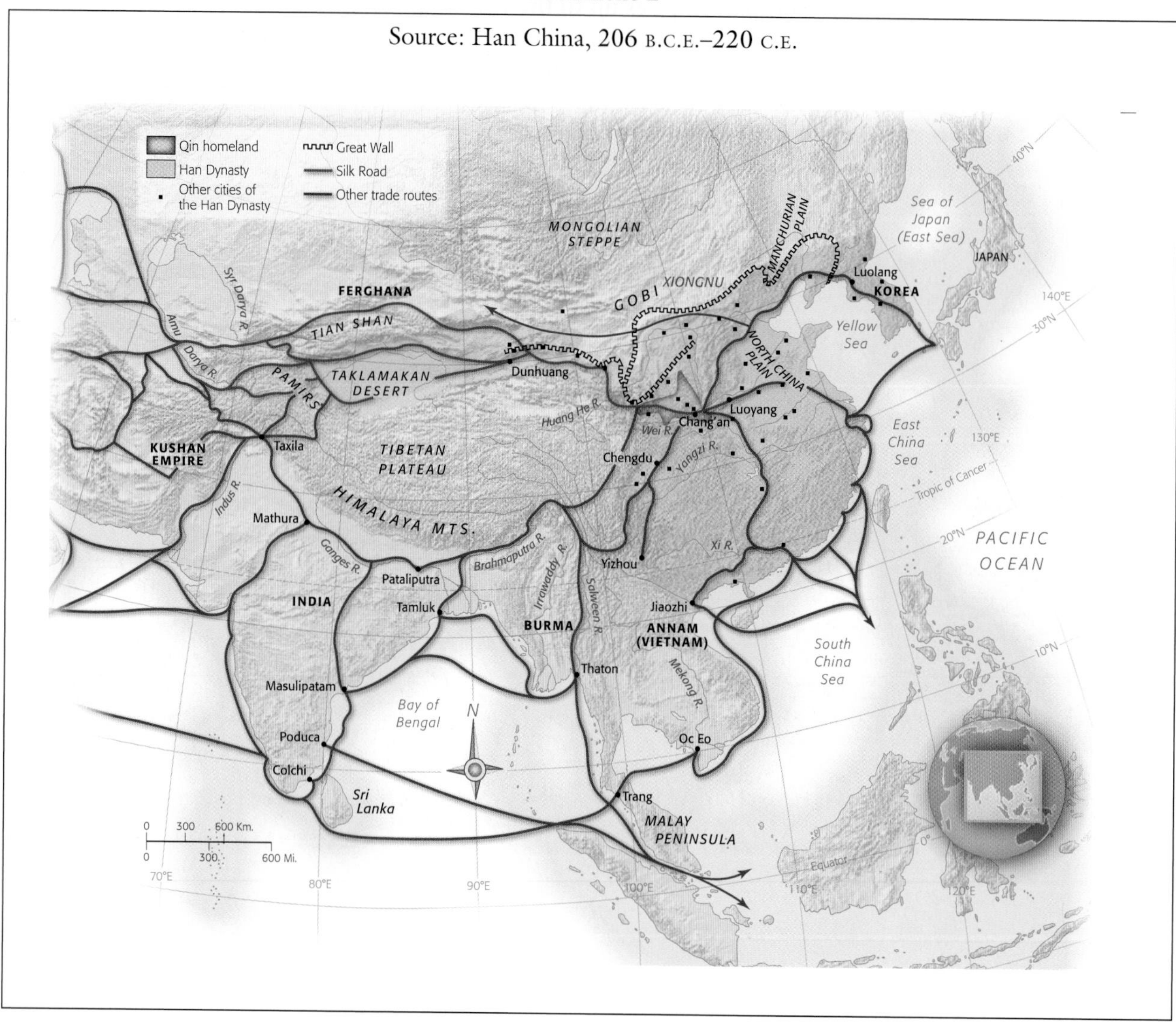

Document 3

Source: Roman aqueduct near Tarragona, Spain, constructed 98–117.

Robert Frerck/Woodfin Camp & Associates.

Document 4

Source: Asian trade and communication routes.

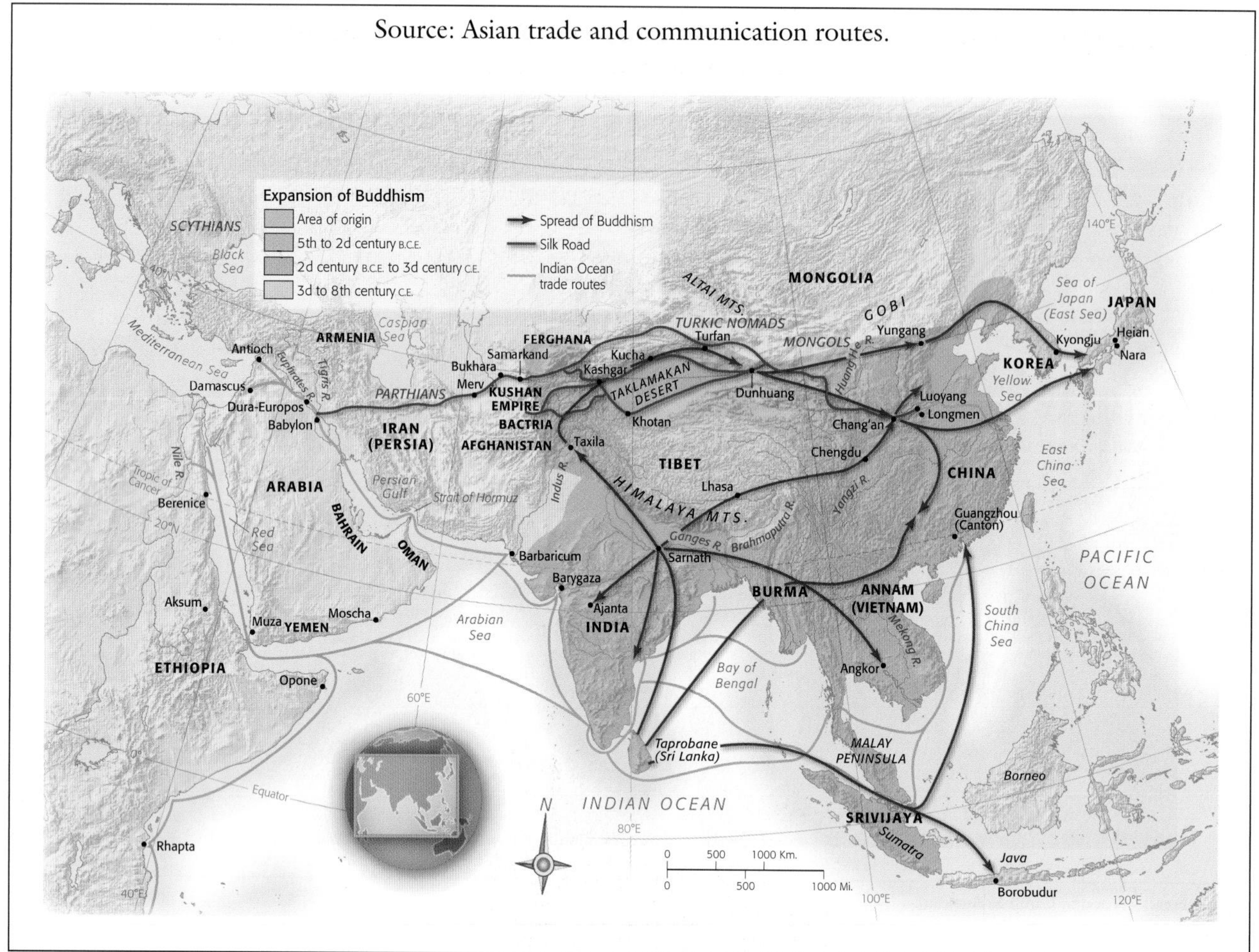

Document 5

Source: Indian Ocean sailing itinerary of unknown Greco-Egyptian merchant, 1st century C.E.

Inland from the place and to the east, is the city called Ozene [modern Ujjain in India]. . . . [F]rom this place are brought down all things needed for the welfare of the country about Barygaza, and many things for our trade; agate and carnelian, Indian muslins. . . .

There are imported into this market-town, wine, Italian preferred, also Laodicean [modern southwestern Turkey] and Arabian; copper, tin, and lead; coral and topaz; thin clothing and inferior sorts of all kinds . . . gold and silver coin, on which there is a profit when exchanged for the money of the country. . . . And for the King there are brought into those places very costly vessels of silver, singing boys, beautiful maidens for the harem, fine wines, thin clothing of the finest weaves, and the choicest ointments. There are exported from these places [spices], ivory, agate and carnelian . . . cotton cloth of all kinds, silk cloth. . . .

Document 6

Source: Chinese traveler Xuanzang (600–664), description of Indians he encountered while searching for Sanskrit scriptures to take back to China.

The towns and villages have inner gates; the walls are wide and high; the streets and lanes are tortuous, and the roads winding. The thoroughfares are dirty and the stalls arranged on both sides of the road with appropriate signs. Butchers, fishers, dancers, executioners, and scavengers, and so on, have their abodes [outside] the city. In coming and going these persons are bound to keep on the left side of the road till they arrive at their homes. Their houses are surrounded by low walls, and form the suburbs. The earth being soft and muddy, the walls of the town are mostly built of brick or tiles. The towers on the walls are constructed of wood or bamboo; the houses have balconies and belvederes, which are made of wood, with a coating of lime or mortar, and covered with tiles. The different buildings have the same form as those in China: rushes, or dry branches, or tiles, or boards are used for covering them. The walls are covered with lime and mud, mixed with cow's dung for purity. At different seasons they scatter flowers about. Such are some of their different customs.

Document 7

Source: Iranian musicians from the Silk Road.

DBQ 4: Post-Classical Science and Technology (Chapters 8, 9, and 10)

Question: Evaluate the degree that scientific discovery and technological invention developed in Muslim, Christian, and Chinese societies during the post-Classical Age (600–1450).

Historical Background: New political and religious movements characterized the centuries following the end of the Roman and Han Empires. Islam spread from Southwest Asia, Christianity spread throughout Europe, and Confucianism and Buddhism both influenced China under the Sui, Tang, and Song dynasties.

Document 1

Source: Muslim Quran, Book 28, Number 3865, ca. 650.

The Prophet (peace be upon him) said: Allah has sent down both the disease and the cure, and He has appointed a cure for every disease, so treat yourselves medically, but use nothing unlawful.

Document 2

Source: Autobiography of Avicenna (980–1037), Muslim scholar later known in Europe as the "prince of physicians."

By the time I was ten I had mastered the Koran and a great deal of literature, so that I was marveled at for my aptitude. . . . I now occupied myself with mastering the various texts and commentaries on natural science and metaphysics, until all the gates of knowledge were open to me. Next I desired to study medicine, and proceeded to read all the books that have been written on the subject. Medicine is not a difficult science, and naturally I excelled in it in a very short time, so that qualified physicians began to read medicine with me. I also undertook to treat the sick, and methods of treatment . . . revealed themselves to me such as baffle description. At the same time I continued between whiles to study and dispute on law, being now sixteen years of age.

Document 3

Source: Vertical two-beam loom, ca. 1100.

Courtesy, Master and Fellows of Trinity College, Cambridge, Ms. R17.l.f.260 [detail].

Document 4

Source: Spanish Muslim woven silk textile fragment, 12th century.

Document 5

Source: Page from the Book of Kells, ca. 800.

Trinity College Library Dublin/The Bridgeman Art Library.

Document 6

Source: Roger Bacon: despair over 13th-century learning, from *Compendium Studii Philosophiae*, 1271.

. . . comparing our state with that of the ancient Philosophers; who, though they were without that quickening grace which makes man worthy of eternal life, and where into we enter at baptism, yet lived beyond all comparison better than we, both in all decency and in contempt of the world, with all its delights and riches and honors; as all men may read in the works of Aristotle, Seneca, Tully [Cicero], Avicenna, Plato, Socrates, and others; and so it was that they attained to the secrets of wisdom and found out all knowledge. But we Christians have discovered nothing worthy of those philosophers, nor can we even understand their wisdom; which ignorance of ours springs from this cause, that our morals are worse than theirs.

Document 7

Source: Su Song's astronomical clock, 1088–1092.

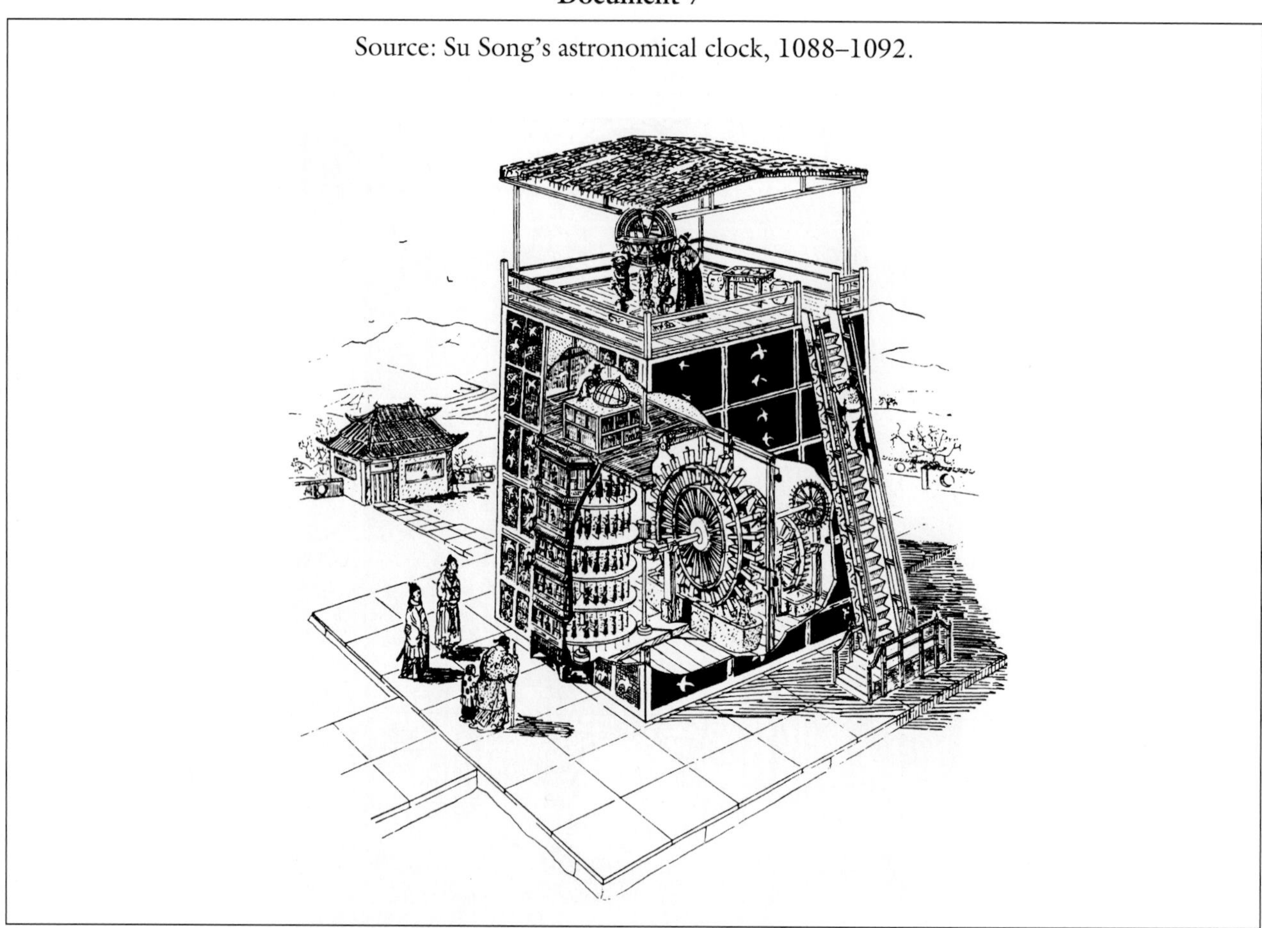

Courtesy, Joseph Needham, *Science and Civilization in China.*

DBQ 5: 1492 Turning Point (Chapters 11, 15, 17, and 18)

Question: Analyze the social and political changes in the Americas and Africa from 1492 to 1750.

Document 1

Source: The Americas and early European exploration.

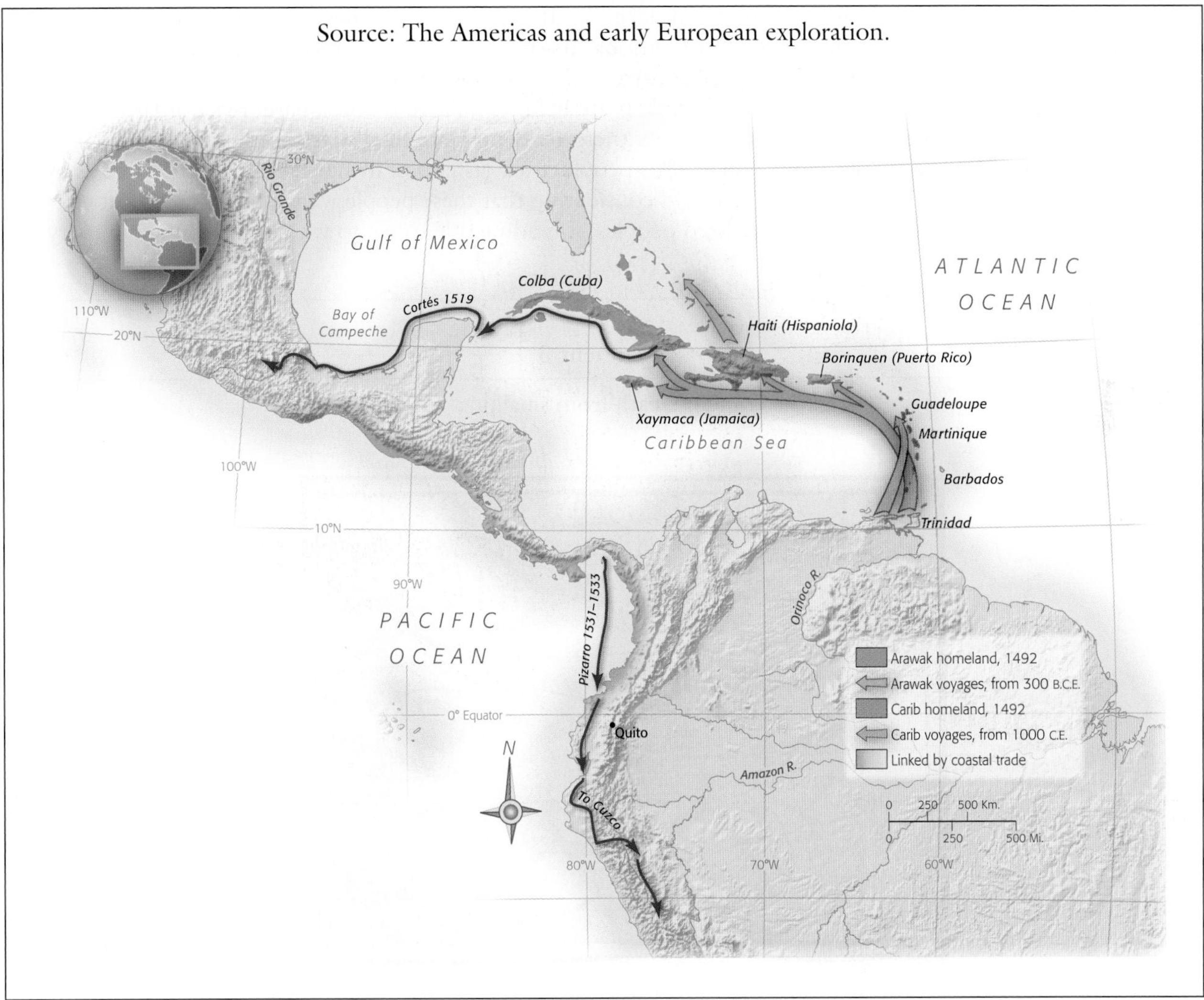

Document 2

Source: Hernan Cortés, letter to King Charles V, 1521.

This great city of Tenochtitlán is built on the salt lake. . . . It has four approaches by means of artificial causeways. . . . The city is as large as Seville or Cordoba. Its streets . . . are very broad and straight. . . . There are bridges, very large, strong, and well constructed, so that, over many, ten horsemen can ride abreast. . . . The city has many squares where markets are held. . . . There is one square, twice as large as that of Salamanca, all surrounded by arcades, where there are daily more than sixty thousand souls, buying and selling . . . in the service and manners of its people, their fashion of living was almost the same as in Spain, with just as much harmony and order; and considering that these people were barbarous, so cut off from the knowledge of God and other civilized peoples, it is admirable to see to what they attained in every respect.

Document 3

Source: Death from smallpox.

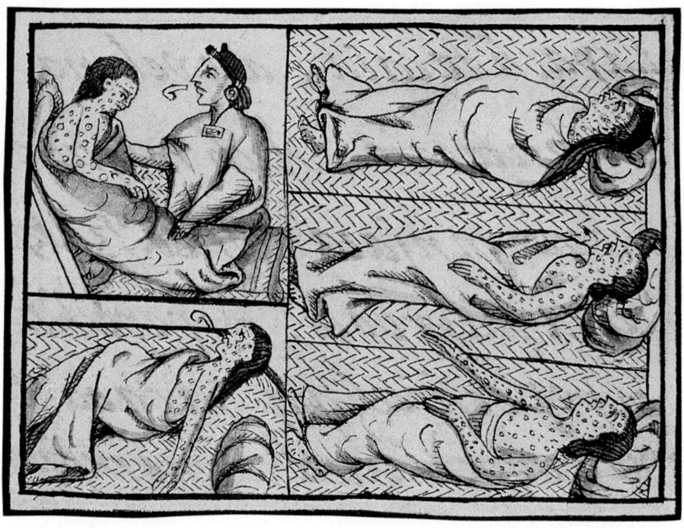

Document 4

Source: Letter from King Afonso of Kongo to King João III of Portugal, 1526.

. . . in our kingdoms there is another great inconvenience which is of little service to God.* and this is that many of our people, out of great desire for the wares and things of your kingdoms, which are brought here by your people and in order to satisfy their disordered appetite, seize many of our people, freed and exempt men. And many times noblemen and the sons of noblemen, and our relatives are stolen, and they take them to be sold to the white men who are in our kingdoms and take them hidden or by night, so that they are not recognized. And as soon as they are taken by the white men, they are immediately ironed and branded with fire. And when they are carried off to be embarked, if they are caught by our guards, the whites allege that they have bought them and cannot say from whom, so that it is our duty to do justice and to restore to the free their freedom.

*King Afonso converted to Christianity in 1491 C.E.

Document 5

Source: Antonio Vázquez de Espinosa, a Spanish priest, *Compendium and Description of the West Indies*, ca. 1625.

The ore at Potosí silver mine is very rich black flint, and the excavation so extensive that more than 3,000 Indians worked away hard with picks and hammers, breaking up that flint ore; and when they have filled their little sacks, the poor fellows, loaded down with ore, climb up those ladders or rigging, some like masts and others like cables, and so trying and distressing that even an empty-handed man can hardly get up them.

So huge is the wealth that has been taken out of this range since the year 1545, when it was discovered, up to the present year of 1628, that merely from the registered mines, according to most of the accounts in the Spanish royal records, 326,000,000 silver coins have been taken out.

Document 6

Source: Colonial Latin America in the 18th century.

Document 7

Source: Transatlantic slave trade from Africa, 1551–1850.

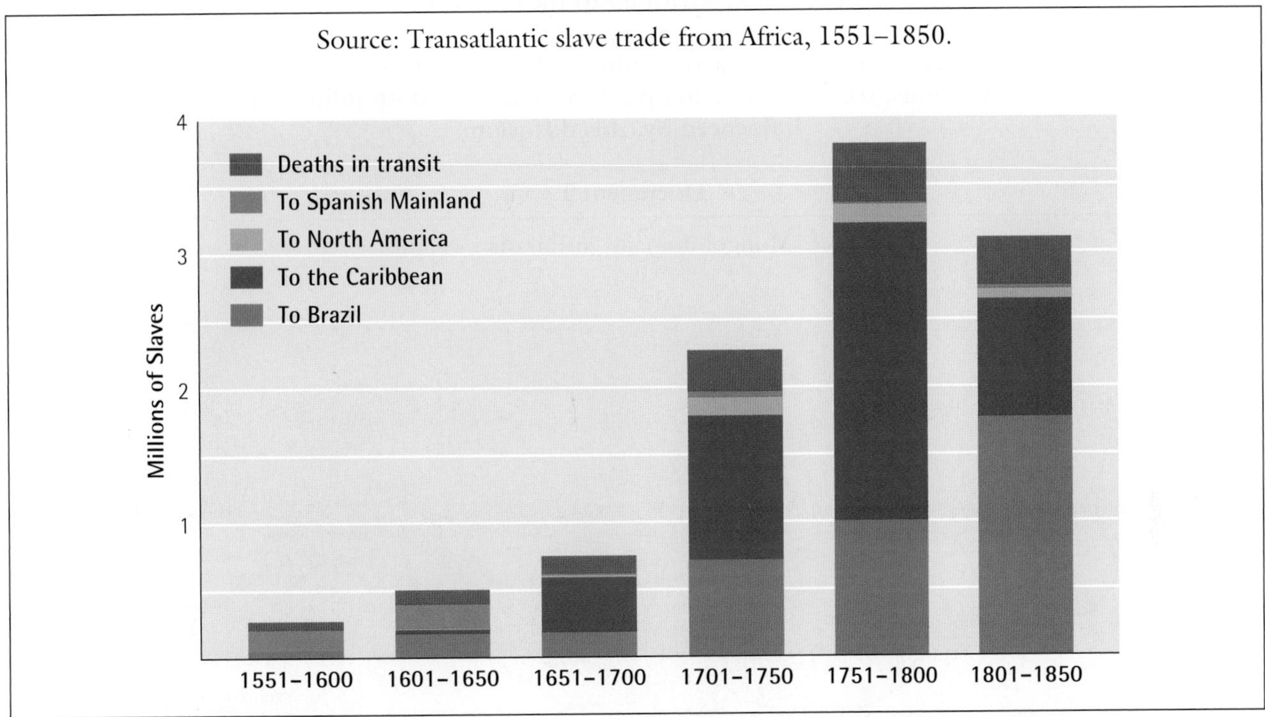

Data from David Eltis, "The Volume and Structure of the Transatlantic Slave Trade: A Reassessment," *William and Mary Quarterly*, 3rd Series, 58 (2001), tables II and III.

Document 8

Source: Jorge Juan and Antonio de Ulloa, *A Voyage to South America*, ca. 1735.

[The society in Quito, Ecuador] . . . is divided into four classes: Spaniards or Whites, Mestizos, Indians or Natives, and Negroes. . . .

. . . among these classes the Spaniards, as is natural to think, are the most eminent for riches, rank, and power, [but] it must at the same time be owned, however melancholy the truth may appear, they are in proportion the most poor, miserable and distressed; for they refuse to apply themselves to any mechanic business, considering it as a disgrace to that quality they so highly value themselves upon, which consists in not being black, brown, or of a copper color. The Mestizos, whose pride is regulated by prudence, readily apply themselves to arts and trades, but cho[o]se those of the greatest repute, as painting, sculpture, and the like, leaving the meaner sort to the Indians.

DBQ 6: Diffusion to 1500 (Chapters 12, 13, and 14)

Question: Evaluate the factors that influenced cultural and technological diffusion in Eurasia and Africa up to the year 1500.

Historical Background: Large empires dominated the post-Classical Age in Eurasia and Africa. Religious, technological, and political structures both influenced, and were influenced by, this diffusion.

Document 1

Source: Mongol domains in Eurasia in 1300.

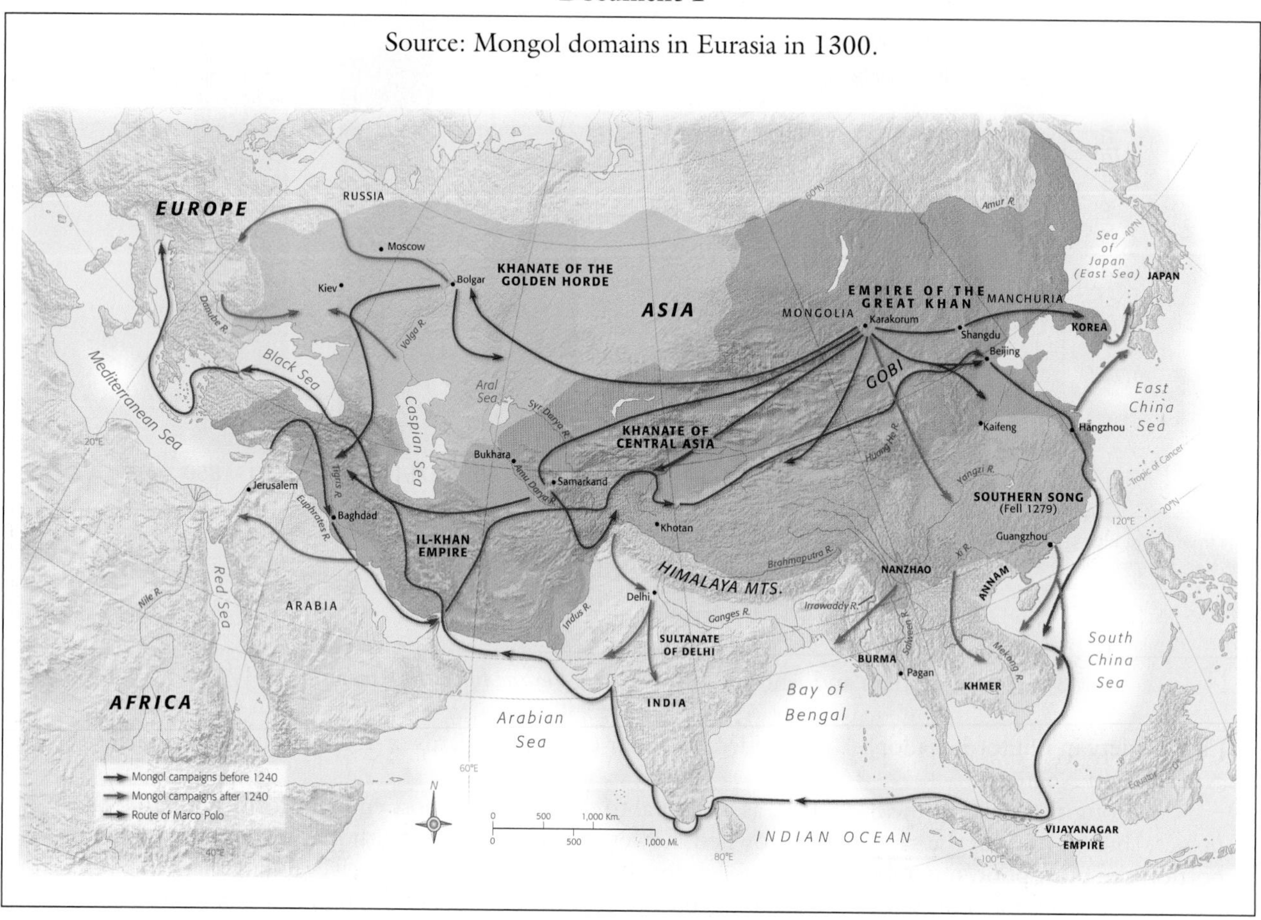

Document 2

Source: Moveable type: individual tiles—the ones shown are Korean—made printing easier and cheaper and contributed to increased levels of literacy.

Courtesy, Yushin Yoo.

Document 3

Source: Confucian examination cells, Ming dynasty (1368–1644) but common in China since the 12th century.

Courtesy, Church Mission, London.

Document 4

Source: Africa and Indian Ocean Basin, physical characteristics.

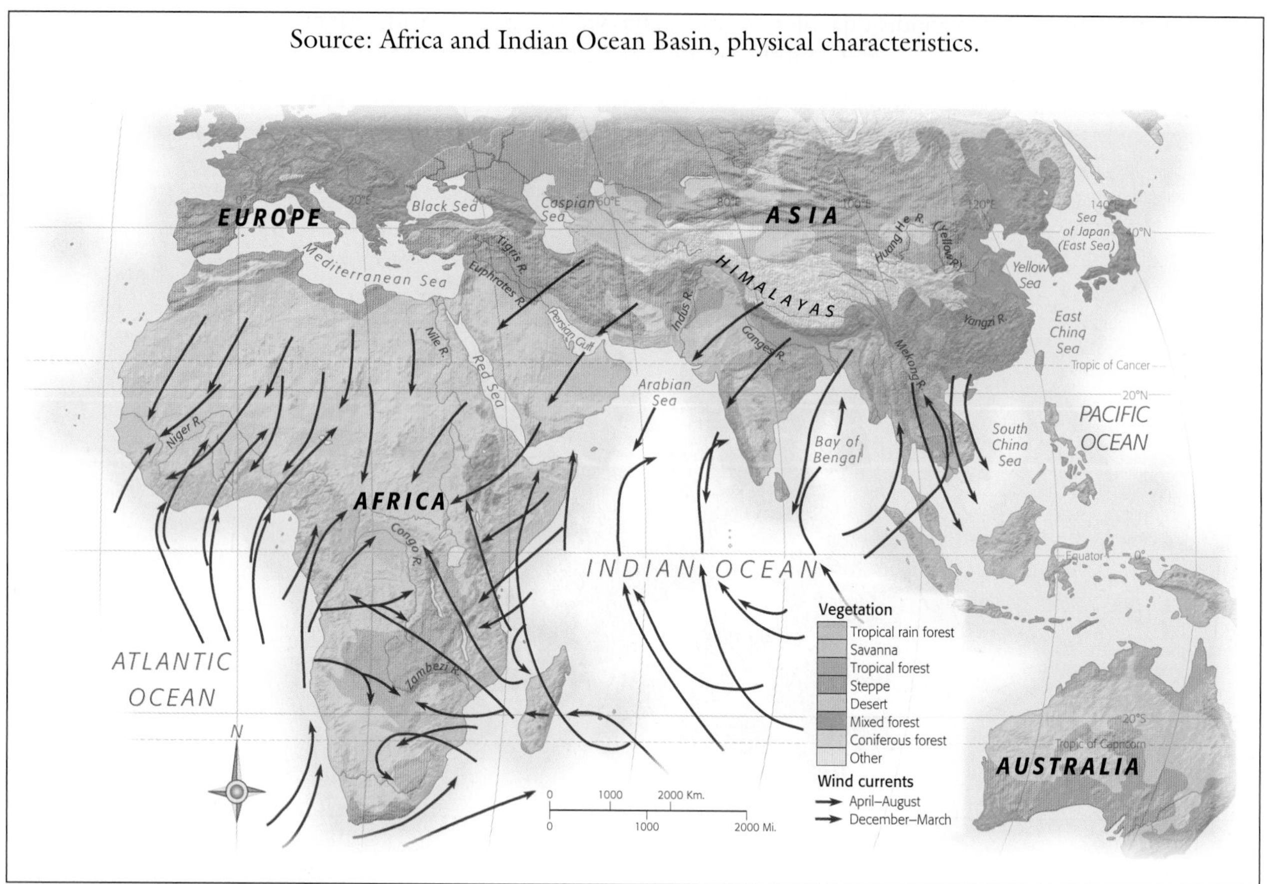

Document 5

Source: *Travels of Ibn Battuta in the Near East, Asia, and Africa, 1325–1354*, describing Battuta's visit in Mali during the reign of Mansa Suleiman in 1353.

One of the best things in these parts is, the regard they pay to justice; . . . in this respect the Sultan regards neither little nor much. The safety, too, is very great; so that a traveler may proceed along among them, without the least fear of a thief or robber. Another of their good properties is, that when a merchant happens to die among them, they will make no effort to get possession of his property; but will allow the lawful successors to . . . take it. Another is, their constant custom of attending prayers with the congregation. . . .

As to their bad practices, they will exhibit their little daughters, as well as their male and female slaves, quite naked. In the same manner will the women enter into the presence of the King, which his own daughters will also do. Nor do the free women ever clothe themselves till after marriage.

Document 6

Source: Black Death in 14th-century Europe.

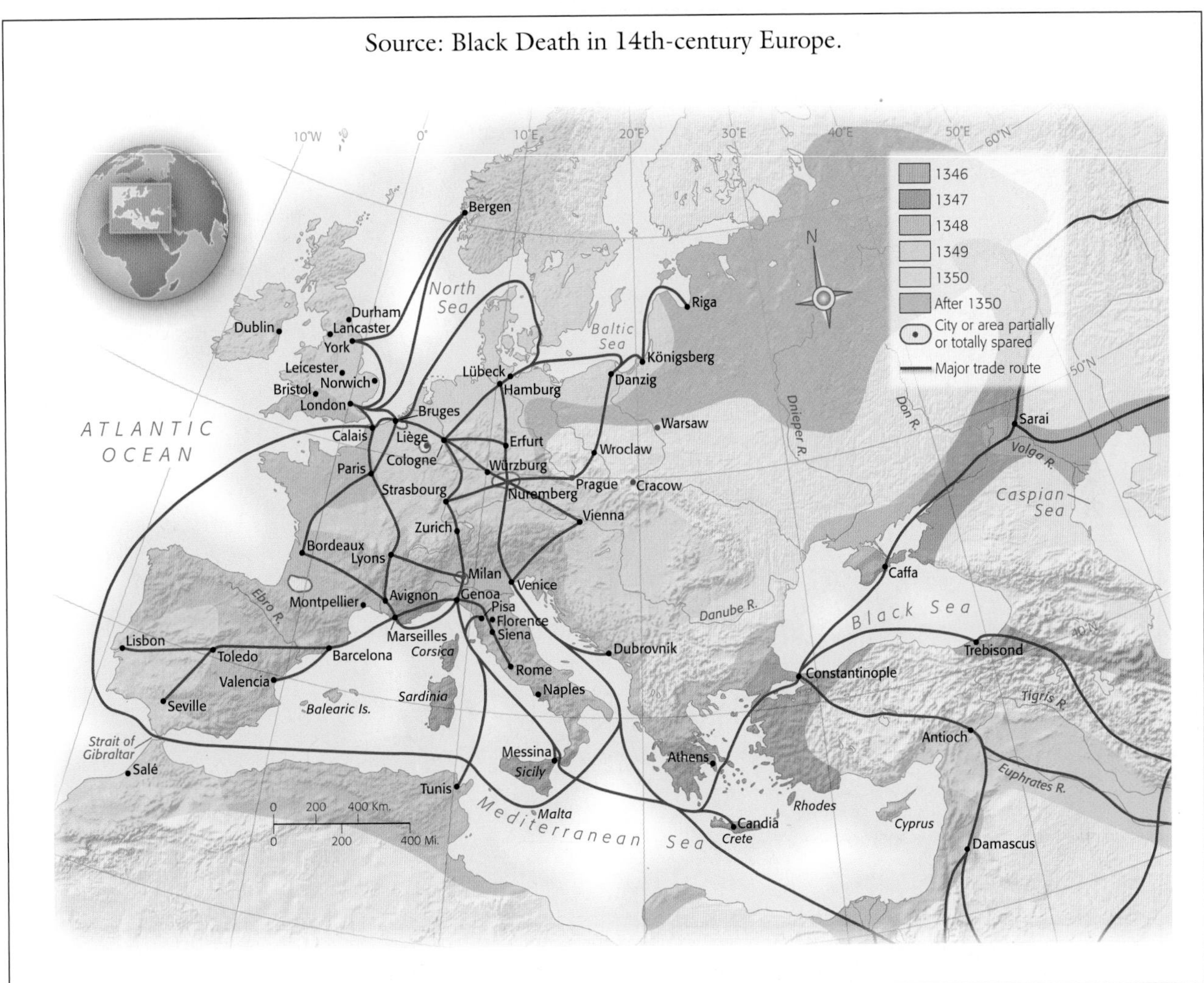

Document 7

Source: *Official chronicles of the upper-Rhineland towns* (modern-day Switzerland), ca. 1350.

In the year 1349 there occurred the greatest epidemic that ever happened. Death went from one end of the earth to the other, on [both sides] of the [Mediterranean] sea, and it was greater among the Saracens [Muslims] than among the Christians. . . .

In the matter of this plague the Jews throughout the world were reviled and accused in all lands of having caused it through the poison which they are said to have put into the waters and the wells . . . and for this reason the Jews were burnt all the way from the Mediterranean into Germany, but not in Avignon, for the pope protected them there.

Nevertheless they tortured a number of Jews in Berne and Zofingen.* . . . The deputies of the city of Strasbourg were asked what they were going to do with their Jews. They answered and said that they knew no evil of them. Then . . . there was a great indignation and clamor against the deputies from Strasbourg. So finally the Bishop and the lords and the Imperial Cities agreed to do away with the Jews.

*Cities in Switzerland.

Document 8

Source: The growth of printing in Europe.

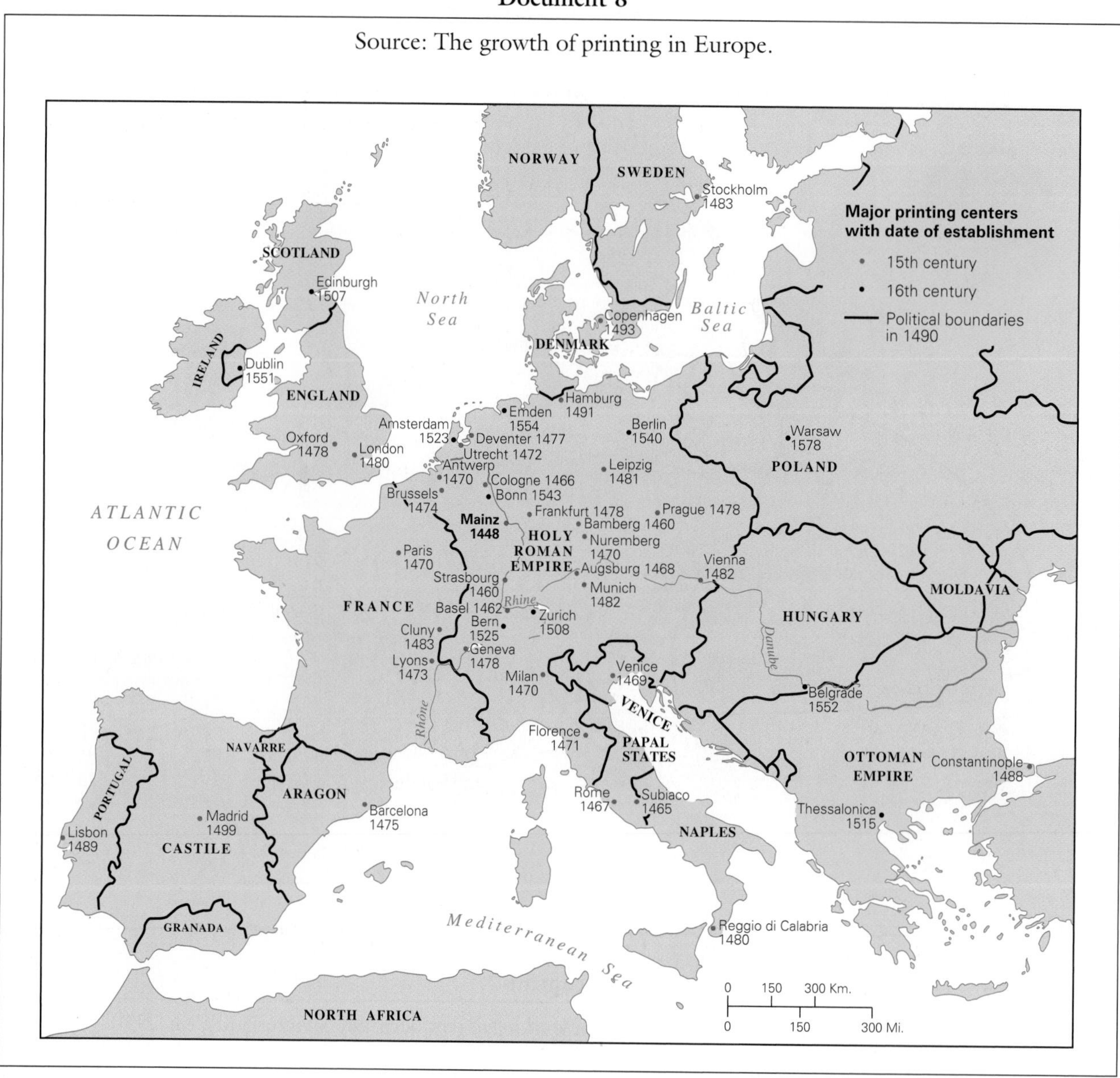

DBQ 7: Foreign Openness (Chapters 12, 16, 19, and 20)

Question: Using the following documents, assess the validity of this statement: "The period from 1350 to 1750 was marked by increasing openness to foreign ideas, culture, and peoples."

Historical Background: The centuries leading up to 1750 were marked by increasing contact among peoples around the world. The nature of these contacts varied widely.

Document 1

Source: Ming Empire and allies, 1368–1500 (including Zheng He voyages).

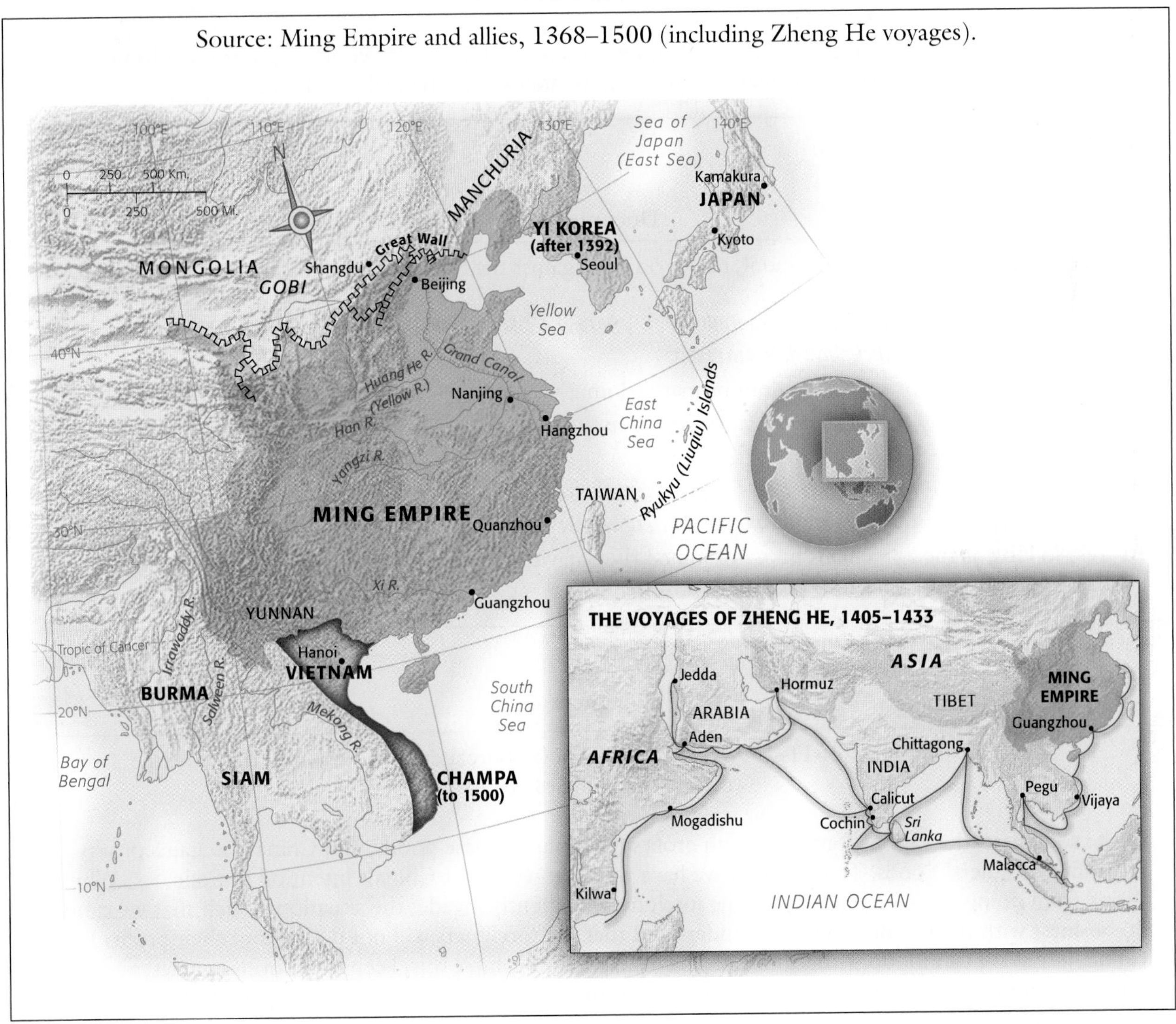

Document 2

Source: Ebu's-Su'ud, mufti* of Istanbul, ruling on Ottoman emperor Selim II's plan to attack the Venetians in Crete, 1570.

[This] land was previously in the realm of Islam. After a while, the abject infidels overran it, destroyed the colleges and mosques, and left them vacant. They filled the pulpits and the galleries with the tokens of infidelity and error, intending to insult the religion of Islam with all kinds of vile deeds, and by spreading their ugly acts to all corners of the earth.

His Excellency the Sultan, the Refuge of Religion, has, as zeal for Islam requires, determined to take [this land] from the possession of the shameful infidels and to annex it to the realm of Islam.

*Chief religious and legal adviser to the sultan.

Document 3

Source: Ebu's-Su'ud, mufti of Istanbul, ruling on war against the Shi'ite Muslim Safavids of Iran, ca. 1570.

Q: *Is it licit according to the shari'a* to fight the . . . Safavids? Is the person who kills them a holy warrior, and the person who dies at their hands a martyr?*

A: Yes, it is a great holy war and a glorious martyrdom.

Q: *Can the children of Safavid subject captured . . . be enslaved?*

A: No.

Q: *The followers of the Safavids are killed by order of the Sultan. If it turns out that some of the prisoners, young and old, are [Christian] Armenians, are they [to be] set free?*

A: Yes, so long as the Armenians have not joined the Safavid troops in attacking and fighting against the troops of Islam, it is illegal to take them prisoner.

*Islamic law.

Document 4

Source: Zhang Han (1511–1593 C.E.), Ming scholar-bureaucrat who was raised in a textile merchant family, ca. 1590.

In the southeast, the various foreigners gain profits from our Chinese goods, and China also gains profits from the foreigners' goods. Trading what we have for what we lack is China's intention in trade. . . . Why shrink from doing so? You might say, "The foreigners frequently invade; the situation is such that we cannot do business with them." But you don't understand that the foreigners will not do without their profits from China, just as we cannot do without our profits from them. Prohibit this, keep them from contact, and how can you avoid their turning to piracy? I maintain that once the maritime markets are opened, the aggressors will cease of their own accord.

Document 5

Source: Journal of Matteo Ricci, Jesuit priest, describing a Chinese court scene where Jesuit missionaries were accused of high treason against the Chinese throne, ca. 1607.

The Mayor, who was somewhat friendly with the [Jesuit] Fathers, . . . the Mayor examined the charges of the plaintiffs and the reply of the [Jesuit] defendants, he . . . took it upon himself to refute the accusers. He said he was fully convinced that these strangers were honest men, and that he knew that there were only two of them in their local residence and not twenty, as had been [charged]. To this [the accusers] replied that the Chinese were becoming [Christian] disciples. To which the Judge replied, "What of it? Why should we be afraid of our own people? Perhaps you are unaware of the fact that Matteo Ricci's company is cultivated by everyone in [Beijing] and that he is being subsidized by the royal treasury? How dare [you] who are living outside of the royal city expel men who have permission to live at the royal court! These men have lived here peacefully for twelve years. I command that the [Jesuits] buy no more large houses, and that the people are not to follow their law."

Document 6

Source: Tokugawa Iemitsu, Japanese shogun who ruled from 1623 to 1651, Closed Country Edict, Japan, 1635.

1. Japanese ships are strictly forbidden to leave for foreign countries.
2. No Japanese is permitted to go abroad. If there is anyone who attempts to do so secretly, he must be executed. The ship so involved must be impounded and its owner arrested, and the matter must be reported to the higher authority.
3. If any Japanese returns from overseas after residing there, he must be put to death.
4. If there is any place where the teachings of the [Catholic] priests are practiced, the two of you must order a thorough investigation.
5. Any informer revealing the whereabouts of the followers of the priests must be rewarded accordingly. If anyone reveals the whereabouts of a high ranking priest, he must be given one hundred pieces of silver. For those of lower ranks, depending on the deed, the reward must be set accordingly. . . .

8. All incoming ships must be carefully searched for the followers of the priests.

Document 7

Source: Iranian waterpipe, ca. 1600.

From Rudi Matthee, *The Pursuit of Pleasure: Drugs and Stimulants in Iranian History, 1500–1900* [Princeton: Princeton University Press] p. 125.

Document 8

Source: Peter the Great, tsar of Russia (r. 1689–1725), Decree on the Invitation of Foreigners, 1702.

We have always tried to maintain internal order, to defend the state against invasion, and in every possible way to improve and to extend trade. With this purpose we have been compelled to make some necessary . . . changes . . . in order that our subjects might more easily gain a knowledge of matters of which they were before ignorant, and become more skillful in their commercial relations. We have therefore given orders . . . for increasing trade with foreigners.

. . . the free exercise of religion of all other sects, although not agreeing with our church, is allowed [throughout Russia]. . . . We, by the power granted us by the Almighty, shall exercise no compulsion over the consciences of men, and shall gladly allow every Christian to care for his own salvation at his own risk.

Document 9

Source: Edict on Trade with Great Britain, letter from Chinese emperor Qianlong (r. 1736–1796) to King George III of Britain, 1792. (but representative of Chinese thought throughout the 18th century).

Yesterday your Ambassador petitioned . . . me regarding your trade with China, but his proposal is not consistent with our dynastic usage and cannot be entertained. [Up until now] all European nations, including your country's barbarian merchants, have carried on their trade with our Celestial Empire at Guangzhou*. Such has been the procedure for many years, although our Celestial Empire possesses all things in prolific abundance and lacks no product within its own borders. There was therefore no need to import the manufactures of outside barbarians in exchange for our own produce. But as the tea, silk, and porcelain that our Celestial Empire produces are absolute necessities to European nations and to yourselves, we have permitted, . . . so that your wants may be supplied and your country thus participate in our beneficence.

*Canton, a coastal city in southern China.

DBQ 8: Political, Economic, and Social Revolutions (Chapters 18, 21, 22, 23, and 26)

Question: How did the political and economic changes from 1750 to 1914 influence the social order in Europe and the Americas? What additional kind(s) of document(s) would help historians analyze the cause-effect relationship among these developments?

Document 1

Source: Transatlantic slave trade from Africa, 1551–1850.

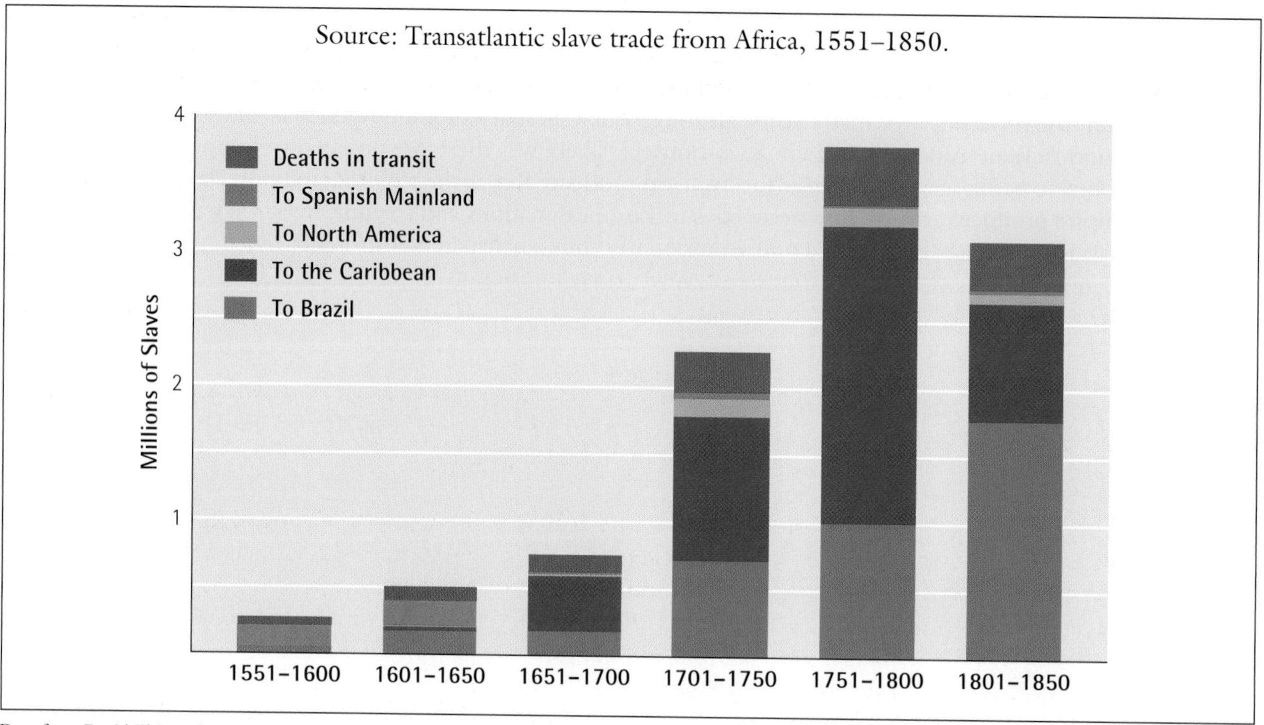

Data from David Eltis, "The Volume and Structure of the Transatlantic Slave Trade: A Reassessment," *William and Mary Quarterly,* 3rd Series, 58 (2001), tables I and III.

Document 2

Source: Rousseau, *The Social Contract,* 1762.

It follows from what precedes, that the general will is always right and always tends to the public advantage; but it does not follow that the resolutions of the people have always the same [virtue]. Men always desire their own good, but they do not always discern it; the people are never corrupted, though often deceived, and it is only then that they seem to will what is evil. . . .

The public . . . then, requires a suitable agent to concentrate it and put it in action according to the directions of the general will. . . . This is . . . the function of government.

Document 3

Source: *United States Constitution,* Article 1, Section 2, 1787.

Representatives and direct Taxes shall be apportioned among the several States which may be included within this Union, according to their respective Numbers, which shall be determined by adding to the whole Number of free Persons, including those bound to Service for a Term of Years, and excluding Indians not taxed, three fifths of all other Persons.

Document 4

Source: *Declaration of the Rights of Woman and the Female Citizen*, by Olympe De Gouges, 1791.

Man, are you capable of being just? It is a woman who poses the question; you will not deprive her of that right at least. Tell me, what gives you sovereign empire to oppress my sex? Your strength? Your talents? Observe the Creator in his wisdom; survey in all her grandeur that nature with whom you seem to want to be in harmony, and give me, if you dare, an example of this tyrannical empire. Go back to animals, consult the elements, study plants. . . . Everywhere you will find the [sexes] mingled; everywhere they cooperate in harmonious togetherness in this immortal masterpiece.

Man alone has raised his exceptional circumstances to a principle. Bizarre, blind, bloated with science and degenerated—in a century of enlightenment and wisdom—into the crassest ignorance, he wants to command as a despot a sex which is in full possession of its intellectual faculties; he pretends to enjoy the Revolution and to claim his rights to equality in order to say nothing more about it.

Document 5

Source: Simón Bolivar, leader of South American independence movement in the 1820s, The Jamaica Letter, 1815.

I look upon the present state of America as similar to that of Rome after its fall. . . . [W]e scarcely retain a vestige of what once was; we are, moreover, neither Indian nor European, but a species midway between the legitimate proprietors of this country and the Spanish usurpers. In short, though Americans by birth we derive our rights from Europe, and we have to assert these rights against the rights of the natives, and at the same time we must defend ourselves against the [European] invaders.

Americans today, and perhaps to a greater extent than ever before, who live within the Spanish system occupy a position in society no better than that of serfs destined for labor. . . . So negative [is] our existence that I can find nothing comparable in any other civilized society. . . .

Document 6

Source: Paris apartment at night, ca. 1845.

Bibliothèque nationale de France.

Document 7

Source: Karl Marx and Friedrich Engels, *The Communist Manifesto*, 1848.

The history of all hitherto existing society is the history of class struggles. . . .

In the earlier epochs of history, we find almost everywhere a complicated arrangement of society into various orders, a manifold gradation of social rank. In ancient Rome we have patricians, knights, plebeians, slaves; in the middle ages feudal lords, vassals, guild-masters, journeymen, apprentices, serfs. . . . The modern bourgeois society that has sprouted from the ruins of feudal society, has not done away with class antagonisms. It has but established new classes, new conditions of oppression, new forms of struggle in place of the old ones.

Document 8

Source: Former Brazilian slave returns from military service, ca. 1870.

Courtesy, Fundacao Biblioteca Nacional, Brazil.

Document 9

Source: Arrest of a labor activist in Buenos Aires, 1895.

Archivo General de la Nación, Buenos Aires.

Document 10

Source: Emmeline Pankhurst, British women's suffragist, being arrested, 1914.

Mary Evans Picture Library.

DBQ 9: Large Empires (Chapters 24, 25, and 27)

Question: Analyze the factors that encouraged and/or limited the rule of large empires in Africa and Eurasia from 1800 to 1914.

Document 1

Source: India, 1707–1805.

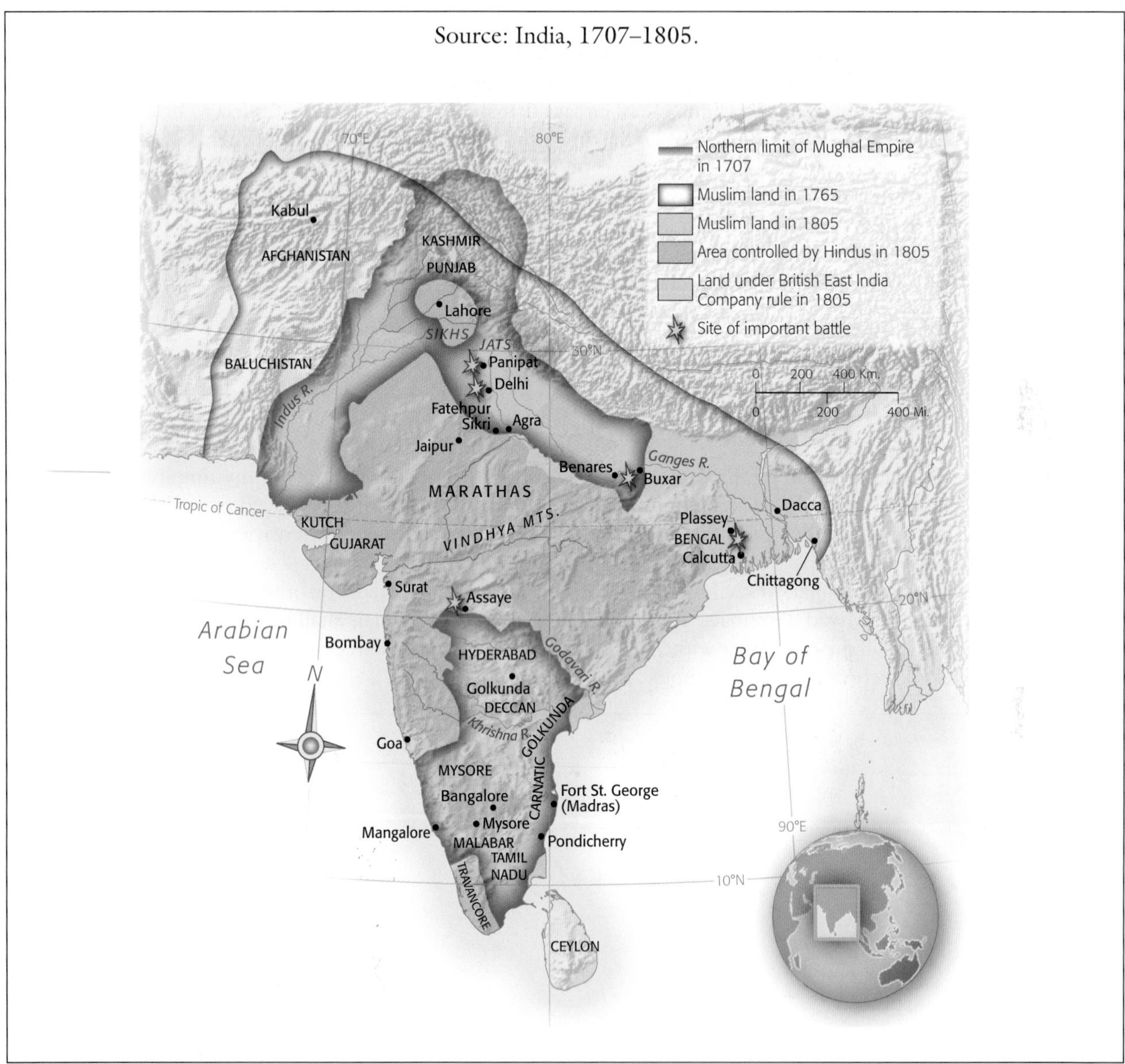

Document 2

Source: Lin Zexu, Chinese official in charge of stopping the opium trade in the city of Guangzhou [Canton], *Letter to Queen Victoria*, 1839.

I have heard that you are a kind, compassionate monarch. I am sure that you will not do to others what you yourself do not desire. I have also heard that you have instructed every British ship that sails for Guangzhou [Canton] not to bring any goods to China. . . . The fact that British ships have continued to bring opium to China results perhaps from the impossibility of making a thorough inspection of all of them owing to their large numbers. . . .

I have also heard that the areas under your direct jurisdiction such as London, Scotland, and Ireland do not produce opium; it is produced instead in your Indian possessions such as Bengal, Madras, Patna, and Malwa. In these possessions the English people not only plant opium poppies that grow from one mountain to another but also open factories to manufacture this terrible drug.

Document 3

Source: *Imperial Rescript*, 1856. Ottoman sultan Abdul Mejid (r. 1839–1861).

Every distinction or designation tending to make any class whatever of the subjects of my Empire inferior to another class, on account of their religions, language, or race, shall be forever effaced from Administrative Protocol. The laws shall be put in force against the use of any injurious or offensive term, either among private individuals or on the part of the authorities. . . .

All commercial, correctional, or civil suits between Muslims and Christians or other non-Muslin subjects . . . shall be referred to Mixed Tribunals. The proceedings of these Tribunals shall be public; the parties shall be confronted, and shall produce their witnesses, whose testimony shall be received, without distinction, upon an oath taken according to the religious law of each sect. . . .

Document 4

Source: Opening the Suez Canal, 1869.

Bildarchiv Preussischer Kulturbesitz.

Document 5

Source: Lord Edward Bulwer-Lytton, viceroy of India, letter to Queen Victoria, 1876.

After dinner . . . I held a reception, which lasted till one o'clock at night, and is said to have been attended by 2,500 persons—the largest, I believe, ever held by any Viceroy . . . in India.

. . . allow me to mention . . . one little circumstance which appears to me very illustrative of the effect which [this event] had on [the prince of Kashmir]. . . . In the first interviews which took place with him months ago . . . I noticed that, though perfectly courteous, he was extremely mistrustful of the British Government and myself. He seemed to think that every word I had said to him must have a hidden meaning against which he was bound to be on his guard . . . and although he finally agreed to my proposals, he did so with obvious reluctance and suspicion, after taking a night to think them over. On the day following the imperial assemblage . . . [h]is whole manner and language . . . were strikingly different. [He said:] "I am now convinced that you mean nothing that is not for the good of me and mine. Our interests are identical with those of the empire. Give me your orders and they shall be obeyed."

Document 6

Source: Excerpt from a proclamation during the Boxer Rebellion, 1900.

When all the military accomplishments or tactics
Are fully learned,
It will not be difficult to exterminate the "Foreign Devils" then.

Push aside the railway tracks,
Pull out the telephone poles,
Immediately after this destroy the steam[ships].

The great France
Will grow cold and downhearted.
The English and the Russians will certainly disperse.

Let the various "Foreign Devils" all be killed.
May the whole Elegant Empire of the great Qing Dynasty be ever prosperous!

Document 7

Source: South African diamond mine, early 20th century.

Gardiner F. Williams/NGS Image Collection.

Document 8

Source: Expansion and modernization of Japan, 1868–1918.

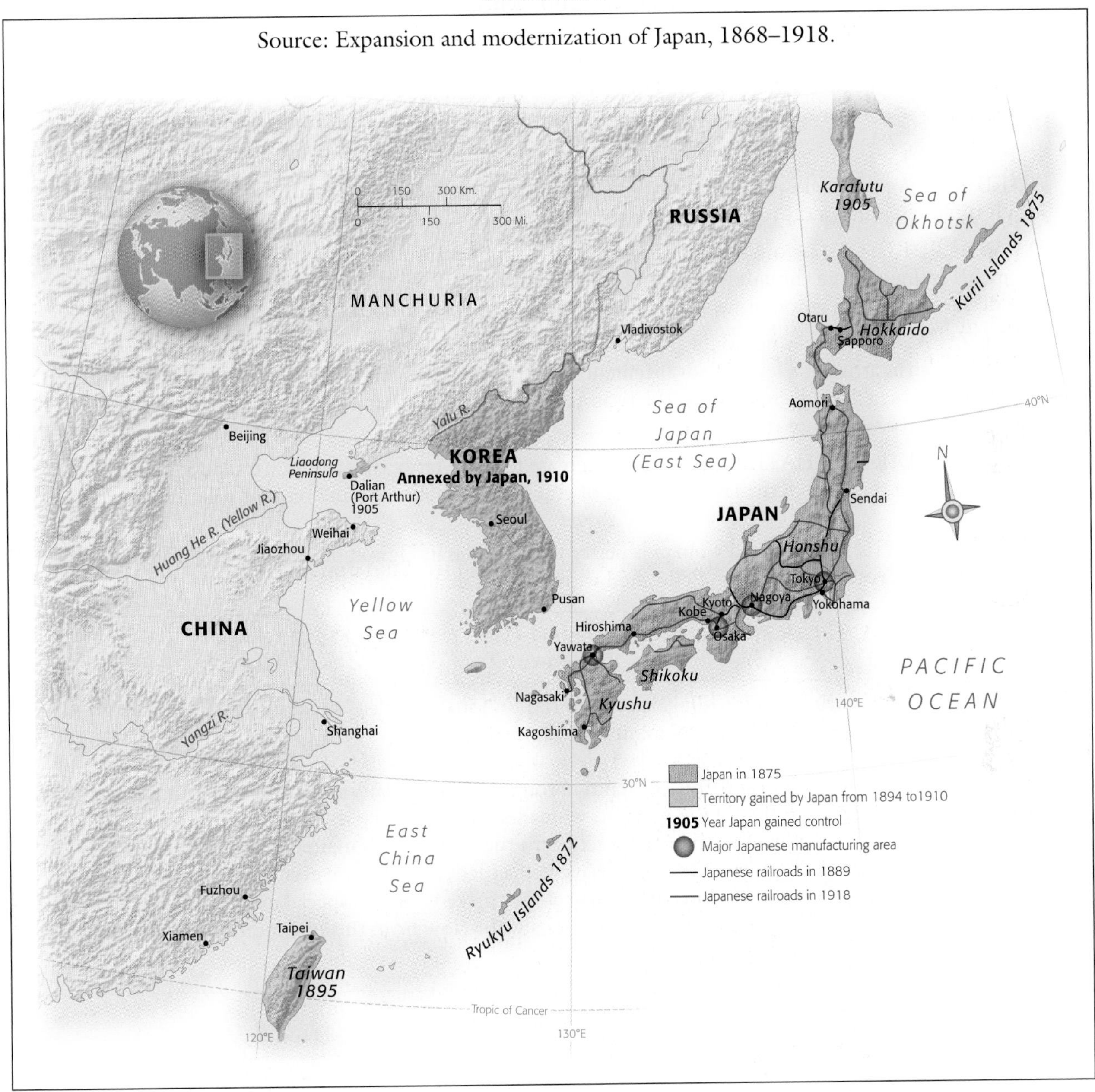

DBQ 10: Women's Challenges (Chapters 29–34)

Question: Analyze the social, economic, and political challenges that women faced in the 20th century.

Document 1

Source: Syrian Parliament debate about the relationship between gender and citizenship, April 25, 1920.

AL-KILANI: We are afraid this [question of women's suffrage] will cause social and political unrest. This idea is too premature, and I request that we reject it.

DA'AS AL JURJIS: . . . I would like to thank Mr. Al-Kilani because I understood from him that he supports [women's suffrage] even though he does not think it appropriate for this moment in time! It is true that 98% of our women are ignorant, which is why Al-Kilani [supports making] education a requirement.

'ADEL ZU'AYER: There is no doubt that each and every one of us want[s], desires, and must work to make the woman arrive at a level of advancement where she can take her right. And despite what has been said about the benefit of giving women the right to vote, I still see its approval at this moment does not coincide with the welfare of the nation.

'ABD AL-QADIR AL-KHATIB: Educated women are few and far between, and we cannot take the exceptions to be the basis of the law, and I beg of you not to undertake a matter that will do greater harm than good.

SUBHI AL TAWIL: An educated woman is better than a thousand ignorant men, so why would we give men the right to vote and yet deprive educated women from that same right?

Document 2

Source: Gertrud Scholtz-Klink, speech to the National Socialist Women's Association, Nuremburg, Germany, 1935.

I must deal briefly with a question that is constantly brought to our attention, that is, how our present attitude toward life differs from that of the previous women's movement. First, in principle we permit only Germans to be leaders of German women and to concern themselves with matters of importance to Germans. Second, as a matter of principle, we never have demanded, nor shall we ever demand, equal rights for women with the men of our nation. Instead we shall always make women's special interests dependent upon the needs of our entire nation. All further considerations will follow from this unconditional intertwining of the collective fate of the nation.

Document 3

Source: *Education, Civilization, and "Foreignization"* in Buganda [Uganda], by Kabaka Daudi Chwa (1897–1939), 1935.

In this connection I should like to point out that although polygamy was universally recognized among the Baganda* and was never considered as immoral yet prostitution was absolutely unheard of. Civilization, education, and freedom are the direct causes of the appalling state of affairs as regards prostitution and promiscuous relationships between the Baganda men and women. . . .

*People of Uganda.

Document 4

Source: Letter to Russian newspaper *Izvestia* regarding proposed law banning abortion, 1936.

Letter from a Student [K.B.]: "I have read in the press the draft law on the prohibition of abortion, aid to expectant mothers, etc. and cannot remain silent on this matter.

I love children and shall probably have some in four or five years' time. But can I have a child now? Having a child now would mean leaving the Institute [medical school], lagging behind my husband, forgetting everything I have learnt and probably leaving Moscow because there is nowhere to live."

Izvestia's reply: "[K.B.] completely ignored the fact that the government, by widening the network of child-welfare institutions, is easing the mother's task in looking after the child. The main mistake K.B. makes is . . . that she approaches the question as if it were a private matter."

Document 5

Source: "No More Miss America," ten-point manifesto by a radical New York women's group.

1. *The Degrading Mindless-Girlie Symbol.* The Pageant contestants epitomize the roles we are all forced to play as women. The parade down the runway blares the metaphor of the . . . county fair, where animals are judged for teeth, fleece, etc. and where the best "specimen" gets the blue ribbon. So are women in our society forced to daily compete for male approval, enslaved by ludicrous "beauty" standards we ourselves are conditioned to take seriously. . . .
9. *Miss America as Dream Equivalent To—?* In this reputed democratic society, where every little boy can grow up to be President, what can every little girl hope to grow up to be? Miss America. That's where it's at. Real power to control our own lives is restricted to men, while women get patronizing pseudo-power, an ermine cloak and a bunch of flowers; men are judged by their actions, women by their appearance.

Document 6

Source: Gladys Acosta, militant Peruvian feminist, 1994.

Gender, the main distinction between all people, is ignored in most philosophical, political, or economic discussions. The reason for this lies partly in the low level of women's participation, but not entirely, because women are not always aware of the system of submission and repression to which we are subjected against our will.

We women play an important role in this ever-more internationalized economy because we represent . . . a particularly exploitable workforce. A number of studies have revealed the existence of subcontractor chains who work for transnational companies "informally" and mainly employ women. . . . Obviously, this work is badly paid and completely unprotected and has to be done without any of those social rights which were formerly achieved by trade union struggles.

Document 7

Source: Chinese family planning campaign, encouraging the public to limit families to one child in the 1980s.

Picard/Sipa Press.

Document 8

Source: Darfur refugees, 2004.

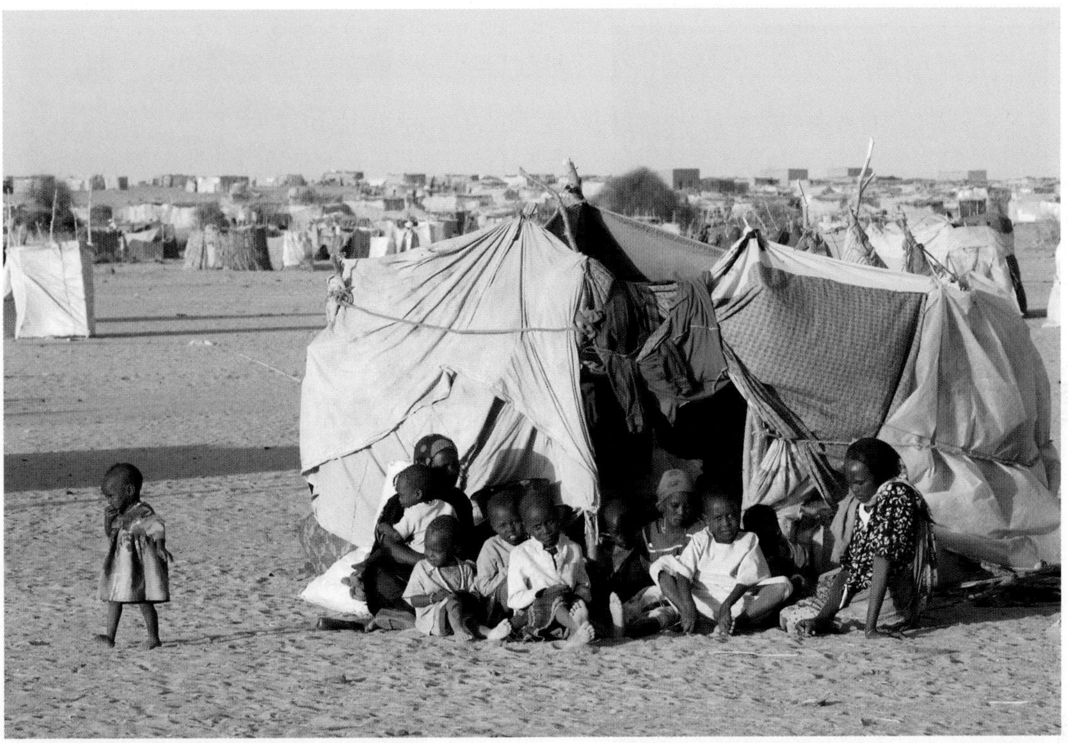

Patrick Robert/Corbis.

Document 9

Source: Women political leaders.

AFP/Getty Images

Cristina Fernandez de Kirchner, president of Argentina (2007–)

Joe Corrigan/Getty Images

Ellen Johnson Sirleaf, president of Liberia (2006–)

Sean Gallup/Getty Images

Angela Merkel, chancellor of Germany (2005–)

Luis Liwanag/Getty Images

Gloria Macapagul-Arroyo, president of the Philippines (2001–)